RANDOM HOUSE WEBSTER'S

Crossword Puzzle Dictionary

Third Edition

RANDOM HOUSE WEBSTER'S

Crossword Puzzle Dictionary

Third Edition

Random House
New York

Library of Congress Catalog Card Number: 98-67266

Visit the Random House Reference Web site at www.randomwords.com

Typeset and printed in the United States of America.

Third Edition
0 9 8 7
May 2002

ISBN 0-679-45856-5

New York Toronto London Sydney Auckland

Preface

Although various word games and puzzles have existed almost since the beginnings of language, the modern crossword puzzle is a 20th-century innovation. The first newspaper crossword appeared on December 21, 1913, in the *New York World,* and this new type of word puzzle quickly captured the public's fancy. Within a decade, crossword puzzles were featured in most American newspapers, and they soon became the rage in England as well. Since the 1920s, crossword puzzles have been a standard feature of daily newspapers and have proved enormously popular when collected in book form.

Now found in almost every language and in variations ranging from theme puzzles to diagramless puzzles, crosswords are available for almost any age and vocabulary level. Those who solve crossword puzzles invariably relish the challenge of completing a puzzle, of "getting it right." When faced with a clue they cannot answer, they resist "cheating"—looking at the puzzle's solution. One way out of this difficulty is to consult a reference work— just as the puzzle's creator may have done in finding words or crafting clues. Yet neither a dictionary nor an encyclopedia nor an almanac contains the necessary information in a useful, quick-reference format. A standard dictionary might give a few synonyms for a word, an encyclopedia would give information about countries or historical figures, and an almanac usually has information about sports figures or the Academy Awards, but only a crossword puzzle dictionary combines in one handy volume the information that might be found in all three. Equally important, it does so without extraneous information and with the convenience of an arrangement by the number of letters in each word, and it includes the many words that are common in crossword puzzles but too obscure to be in other references.

Random House Webster's Crossword Puzzle Dictionary, drawing on the resources of the Random House dictionaries and thesauruses, with research into a host of other topics, answers the need of crossword puzzlers for one single-purpose reference work. In addition to general vocabulary and synonyms, there are entries covering history; the natural and physical sciences; literature; music, painting, and other arts; religion; mythology; sports; popular culture; and current affairs, among others. Longer items provide easy-to-find detailed information on the continents and countries of the world, states of the United States, U.S. presidents, the months of the year, and other facts of special interest. This Third Edition has been fully updated, with special emphasis placed on the pop cultural questions that are now such an important part of puzzledom—sports teams, TV characters, even sneaker manufacturers.

While *Random House Webster's Crossword Puzzle Dictionary*'s primary purpose is to meet the needs of the growing numbers of people who find crosswords both relaxing and challenging, even a cursory glance will demonstrate the book's usefulness as a reference for trivia buffs. From who won the Academy Award for best actress in 1970 (Glenda Jackson) to the name of a coffee grown in Jamaica (Blue Mountain), it's all here.

Staff

Editor of Third Edition: Nancy Schuster
Project Editor: Jesse Sheidlower
Editor of First and Second Editions: Stephen P. Elliott/Sachem Publishing
   Associates
Editorial Staff: Jessica Erace, Michael Lewis
Contributors to Previous Editions: Julianne Arbo, Suzanne Stone Burke,
   Francine Esposito, Gretchen Ferrante, Jan Jamilkowski, Elizabeth Jewell,
   Rebecca Lyon, Julie E. Marsh, Blaine Merritt, Laurie Romanik, Christine
   Lindberg Stevens, and Diane Bell Surprenant
Database Manager: Constance A. Baboukis
Database Associate: Diane M. João
Managing Editor: Andrew Ambraziejus
Director of Production: Patricia W. Ehresmann
Editorial Director: Wendalyn Nichols
Associate Publisher: Page Edmunds
Publisher: Charles M. Levine

How To Use This Book

The main entries in *Random House Webster's Crossword Puzzle Dictionary* are words or phrases likely to appear as crossword puzzle clues. Each entry consists of a clue word or phrase and a list of answer words, arranged first by the number of letters in each word and then alphabetically. For example, if the main entry—**banal**—is the clue for a five-letter answer, the answer—"trite"—will be found alphabetically listed under the five-letter answer words. For phrases, such as **contracted form,** the answer could be "digest," "summary," or "synopsis." Entries may also contain indented subheads and secondary subheads. If, for instance, the clue is a phrase, like **cotton fabric,** the word **cotton** will be found as a main entry in the dictionary, and **fabric** will be found as a subhead under it, with such possible answer words as "terry," "poplin," and "gingham." In some cases, the answer can be found in more than one place. For example, if the clue is **Mexican coin,** the answer could be found by looking under the main entry **Mexico** and the subhead **monetary unit,** or by looking under the main entry **coin/currency** and the subhead **of Mexico.**

There are also cross references for alternate spellings and very closely related items. Many terms that do not have explicit cross references may still have valuable additional answers at related entries. The reader is encouraged to look up synonyms even when there is no explicit cross reference. To take one example, the clue **canine** has a short entry in this book, but **dog** has a much longer list that could be examined as well.

The main entries, subheads, secondary subheads, and numbers all appear in boldface type; the answer words are in regular roman type. Most punctuation and accent marks have been omitted, since they are not used in puzzle answers; occasionally, apostrophes and other marks have been included in answers to make them more readable.

RANDOM HOUSE WEBSTER'S

Crossword Puzzle Dictionary

Third Edition

aardvark
  also: 7 ant bear **8** anteater
  native to: 6 Africa
  food: 4 ants **8** termites
  name comes from: 9 Africaans
    meaning: 8 earth hog, earth pig

Aaron
  brother: 5 Moses
  father: 5 Amram
  mother: 8 Jochebed
  sister: 6 Miriam
  son: 5 Abihu, Nadab **7** Eleazar, Ithamar
  wife: 8 Elisheba
  successor: 7 Eleazar
  Aaron's Rod 21 miraculously blossomed
    yielded: 7 almonds
  deathplace: 3 Hor **8** Mount Hor
  priestly descendant of: 8 Aaronite
  set up: 10 golden calf

Aaron, Henry (Hank)
  sport: 8 baseball
  position: 10 outfielder
  record: 8 homeruns
  team: 13 Atlanta Braves **15** Milwaukee Braves **16** Milwaukee Brewers

Aaron's Rod 21 miraculously blossomed
  yielded: 7 almonds

Aatam *see* **4** Pima

Ab 16 fifth Hebrew month

Abaddon 4 hell **8** Appolyon

abaft 6 behind **11** to the rear of **12** to
the stern of

Abagtha 6 eunuch
  served: 9 Ahasuerus

abandon 4 dash, drop, elan, jilt, junk,
quit, stop **5** ardor, cease, forgo, gusto,
leave, let go, scrap, verve, waive **6**
desert, give up, spirit **7** discard, forfeit, forsake, freedom **8** abdicate,
evacuate, forswear, get rid of, renounce, run out on **9** animation, cast
aside, repudiate, surrender **10** depart
from, enthusiasm, exuberance, relinquish, wantonness **11** discontinue,
impetuosity, leave behind, spontaneity, unrestraint **12** immoderation, intemperance, recklessness, withdraw
from **13** impulsiveness

abandoned 4 lewd, wild **5** loose **6** impure, jilted, sinful, vacant, wanton,
wicked **7** debased, immoral **8** cast
away, degraded, deserted, desolate,
forsaken, marooned, rejected, un-

chaste **9** cast aside, debauched, discarded, dissolute, neglected, reprobate, shameless **10** dissipated, left
behind, licentious, profligate, unoccupied **11** unrepentant **12** disreputable,
incorrigible, irreformable, relinquished, unprincipled **13** irreclaimable

abandon oneself to 7 yield to **8** give
in to, give up to **9** indulge in

Abaris
  origin: 5 Greek
  form: 4 sage

Abas
  mentioned in: 5 Iliad
  king of: 7 Argolis
  father: 6 Celeus **7** Lynceus **9** Eurydamas
  mother: 8 Metanira **12** Hypermnestra
  wife: 6 Aglaia
  son: 7 Proetus **8** Acrisius
  daughter: 7 Idomene
  changed into: 4 bird **6** lizard
  mocked: 7 Demeter
  protected by: 11 magic shield
  companion: 8 Diomedes
  killed by: 8 Diomedes

a bas 8 down with **11** to the bottom

abase 4 mock **5** shame **6** debase, defame, demean, humble, malign, vilify
7 cheapen, degrade, mortify, put
down, vitiate **8** badmouth, belittle, besmirch, bring low, cast down, disgrace, dishonor **9** denigrate, devaluate, discredit, downgrade, humiliate
13 bring down a peg, cut down to
size

abash 3 awe, cow **4** dash, faze **5**
daunt **6** deject, dismay **7** depress **8**
dispirit **9** discomfit, embarrass **10** discompose, disconcert, discourage, dishearten

abashed 3 shy **5** cowed, fazed **7**
ashamed, bashful, crushed, daunted,
humbled, subdued **8** confused, dismayed, overawed **9** chagrined, mortified **10** bewildered, confounded, humiliated, nonplussed, taken aback **11**
dumbfounded, embarrassed, intimidated **12** disconcerted, disheartened
13 self-conscious

abate 3 ebb **4** cool, dull, ease, fade,
slow, wane **5** allay, blunt, lower,
quell, quiet, slack **6** dampen, go
down, lessen, pacify, recede, reduce,
soften, soothe, temper, weaken **7** assuage, curtail, decline, dwindle, fall

off, lighten, mollify, relieve, slacken,
subside **8** decrease, diminish, fade
away, fall away, mitigate, moderate,
palliate, restrain, restrict, slack off,
slow down, taper off **9** alleviate

Abba
  means: 6 father
  statesman: 4 Eban

abbey 6 cenoby, chapel, church, friary,
priory **7** convent, nunnery **8** cloister,
seminary **9** cathedral, hermitage,
monastery

Abbott, Bud
  real name: 14 William A Abbott
  partner: 11 Lou Costello
  born: 12 Asbury Park NJ
  roles: 11 Who's on First **12** Buck
  Privates **13** Hold that Ghost **33** Abbott and Costello Meet Frankenstein

abbreviate 3 cut **4** clip, trim **6** reduce
7 abridge, curtail, cut down, shorten
8 boil down, compress, condense,
contract, cut short, diminish, truncate
9 summarize, synopsize

abbreviated 5 brief, short **7** limited,
summary **8** abridged **9** condensed,
curtailed, shortened **10** compressed,
summarized

abbreviation 5 brief **6** digest **7** cutting, pruning, summary **8** abstract,
clipping, synopsis, trimming **9** lessening, reduction, short form **10** abridgment, diminution, shortening **11** abstraction, compression, contraction,
curtailment, cut-down form, reduced
form **12** condensation **13** condensed
form, shortened form **14** compressed
form, contracted form

abdicate 4 cede, quit **5** forgo, waive,
yield **6** abjure, give up, resign **7** abandon **8** abnegate, renounce **9** surrender
10 relinquish **15** vacate the throne

abdomen 3 gut, pot **5** belly, tummy **6**
paunch, venter **7** stomach **8** pot belly
9 bay window **11** breadbasket

abduct 5 seize, steal **6** kidnap **7** bear
off **8** carry off, take away **10** run off
with **11** make off with

Abduction from the Seraglio, The
  also: 25 Die Entführung aus dem Serail
  opera by: 6 Mozart
  character: 5 Osmin **6** Blonde **8** Bel-
  monte, Pedrillo **9** Constanze **10** Pasha Selim

Abdul-Jabbar, Kareem
  formerly: **11** Lew Alcindor
  sport: **10** basketball
  position: **6** center
  team: **8** LA Lakers **10** UCLA Bruins **14** Milwaukee Bucks **16** Los Angeles Lakers
  shot: **7** sky hook

Abednego
  companion: **6** Daniel
  friend: **8** Meschach, Shadrach
  former name: **7** Azariah

Abel
  father: **4** Adam
  mother: **3** Eve
  brother: **4** Cain, Seth
  killer: **4** Cain

Abel, Walter
  field: **9** film actor

Abe Lincoln in Illinois
  author: **14** Robert Sherwood
  director: **12** John Cromwell
  cast: **10** Alan Baxter, Mary Howard, Ruth Gordon (Mary Todd Lincoln) **11** Dorothy Tree, Minor Watson **12** Gene Lockhart **13** Howard da Silva, Raymond Massey (Abraham Lincoln)

aberrant 3 odd **7** unusual **8** abnormal, atypical, peculiar, uncommon **9** anomalous, eccentric, irregular

aberration 5 lapse, quirk **6** lunacy, oddity **7** anomaly, madness **8** delusion, illusion, insanity, mutation, rambling, straying **9** aberrance, aberrancy, curiosity, departure, deviation, exception, wandering **10** digression, distortion, divergence **11** abnormality, derangement, incongruity, mental lapse, peculiarity, singularity, strangeness

abet 3 aid **4** back, goad, help, spur, urge **5** egg on **6** assist, incite, lead on, second, uphold, urge on **7** advance, endorse, promote, support, sustain **8** advocate, join with, sanction **9** encourage, instigate

abettor 4 ally **6** cohort **7** partner **9** accessory, associate, colleague **10** accomplice **11** confederate **12** collaborator

abeyance 5 delay, on ice, pause **6** hiatus, recess **7** latency **8** deferral, dormancy, inaction **9** cessation, remission **10** quiescence, suspension **11** adjournment **12** intermission, postponement **13** in cold storage, on a back burner, waiting period **14** discontinuance

abhor 4 hate, shun **5** scorn **6** detest, eschew, loathe **7** despise, disdain, dislike **8** execrate, recoil at **9** abominate, can't stand, shudder at **10** shrink from **11** can't stomach **12** be revolted by **13** be nauseated by, find repulsive

abhorrence 4 hate **5** odium, scorn **6** hatred **7** disdain, disgust, dislike **8** aversion, contempt, distaste, loathing **9** antipathy, revulsion **10** repugnance **11** abomination

abhorrent 4 foul, vile **6** odious **7** hateful **8** accursed **9** execrable, loathsome, repellent, repugnant, repulsive, revolting **10** abominable, despicable, disgusting, nauseating

abide 3 sit **4** bear, last, live, stay, stop **5** brook, dwell, stand, tarry, visit **6** accept, endure, linger, remain, reside, suffer **7** sojourn, stomach **8** stand for, submit to, tolerate

abide by 4 obey **6** follow **8** accede to, adhere to, submit to **9** conform to **10** comply with **11** go along with

abiding 4 fast, firm **6** steady **7** durable, eternal, lasting **8** constant, enduring, unending **9** immutable, permanent, steadfast **10** changeless, continuing, unchanging, unshakable **11** everlasting **12** indissoluble, wholehearted **13** unquestioning

Abidjan
  capital of: **10** Ivory Coast

Abigail
  husband: **5** David, Nabal
  brother: **5** David

Abihu
  father: **5** Aaron
  mother: **8** Elisheba
  brother: **5** Nadab **7** Eleazar, Ithamar
  killed with: **5** Nadab
  accompanied to Mt Sinai: **5** Moses

Abijah
  father: **8** Rehoboam
  grandfather: **7** Solomon
  grandmother: **6** Naamah

ability 4 bent, gift **5** flair, knack, power, skill **6** acumen, genius, talent **7** faculty, knowhow, mind for **8** aptitude, capacity, facility **9** adeptness, expertise, potential **10** adroitness, capability, competence **11** proficiency **12** potentiality **13** qualification

Abimelech
  king of: **5** Gerar
  means: **15** the father is king
  father: **6** Gideon **8** Abiathar
  brother: **6** Jotham
  army commander: **7** Phichol

Abinoam
  father: **4** Saul
  son: **5** Barak

abject 3 low **4** base, mean, vile **6** sordid **7** ignoble **8** complete, cringing, hopeless, horrible, terrible, thorough, wretched **9** groveling, miserable **10** deplorable, despicable, spiritless **11** inescapable **12** contemptible

abjure 6 desert, give up, recant, reject **7** abandon, disavow, disallow, disclaim, forswear, renounce **9** repudiate **10** relinquish

ablaze 5 afire, eager, fiery **6** aflame, alight, ardent, fervid, on fire, red-hot **7** blazing, burning, excited, fervent, flaming, flushed, glowing, ignited, zealous **8** feverish, hopped-up, in flames, turned-on **10** passionate, switched-on **11** conflagrant, impassioned, intoxicated

able 3 apt, fit **4** good **5** adept **6** adroit, expert, fitted **7** capable, equal to, learned **8** adequate, skillful, talented **9** competent, effective, efficient, masterful, practiced, qualified **10** proficient **11** experienced **12** accomplished

able-bodied 5 beefy, hardy, husky, lusty, thewy **6** brawny, hearty, robust, rugged, strong, sturdy **8** athletic, muscular, powerful, stalwart, vigorous **9** herculean, strapping, well-built **15** broad-shouldered

ablution 4 bath, wash **7** bathing, washing **8** cleaning, lavation **9** cleansing **12** purification **13** ritual washing

Abnaki (Wabanaki)
  language family: **9** Algonkian **10** Algonquian
  tribe: **6** Micmac **8** Malecite **9** Penobscot **13** Norridegewock, Passamaquoddy
  location: **5** Maine **6** Canada, Quebec **7** Old Town **9** Norumbega **10** New England **12** New Brunswick

abnegate 5 forgo, waive **6** abjure, eschew, give up, refuse **7** abstain, forbear **8** renounce **9** repudiate **10** relinquish **11** deny oneself

abnegation 7 refusal **8** eschewal, giving up **9** rejection, sacrifice, surrender **10** abstinence, continence, forbearing, self-denial, temperance **11** forbearance, resignation **12** renunciation **14** relinquishment

Abner
  commanded: **9** Saul's army
  father: **3** Ner
  cousin: **4** Saul

abnormal 3 odd **4** rare **5** queer, weird **7** bizarre, curious, deviant, strange, unusual **8** aberrant, atypical, deformed, freakish, peculiar, uncommon **9** anomalous, eccentric, grotesque, irregular, monstrous, unheard of, unnatural **10** inordinate, outlandish, unexpected **11** exceptional **12** unaccustomed **13** extraordinary **14** unconventional

abnormality 6 oddity **7** anomaly **9** aberrance, curiosity, deformity, deviation **10** aberration, perversion **11** peculiarity **12** eccentricity, idiosyncrasy, irregularity, malformation, unconformity

abode 3 pad **4** home, nest **5** house **7** address, habitat, lodging **8** domicile, dwelling **9** residence **10** habitation **13** dwelling place **14** living quarters

abolish 3 end **5** annul, erase, quash **6** cancel, repeal, revoke **7** blot out, nullify, rescind, squelch, vitiate, wipe out **8** abrogate, set aside, stamp out **9** eliminate, eradicate, extirpate, repudiate, terminate **10** annihilate, do away with, extinguish, invalidate, obliterate, put an end to **11** exterminate **18** declare null and void

abolition 6 ending, repeal **9** annulment, vitiation **10** abrogation, extinction, rescinding, retraction, revocation **11** abolishment, dissolution, elimination, eradication, recantation, repudiation, termination **12** cancellation, invalidation **13** nullification

abominable 4 base, evil, foul, vile **5** awful, lousy **6** cursed, horrid, odious **7** hateful, heinous, hellish **8** accursed, damnable, horrible, infamous, terrible, wretched **9** abhorrent, atrocious, execrable, loathsome, miserable, repellent, repugnant, repulsive, revolting **10** deplorable, despicable, detestable, disgusting, unsuitable, villainous **11** ignominious **12** contemptible, disagreeable **13** reprehensible

abominate 4 hate **5** abhor, scorn **6** detest, loathe **7** despise **8** execrate **9** can't stand **10** recoil from, shrink from **11** can't stomach **12** be revolted by **13** find repugnant, find repulsive

abomination 4 evil, hate **6** hatred, horror, plague **7** bugbear, disgust, torment **8** anathema, aversion, disgrace, loathing **9** annoyance, antipathy, bete noire, obscenity, revulsion **10** abhorrence, affliction, defilement, repugnance **11** detestation

aboriginal 5 first, prime **6** native **7** ancient, endemic, primary **8** earliest, original, primeval **9** primitive **10** indigenous, primordial **13** autochthonous

aborigine 6 native **16** indigenous person **18** original inhabitant **19** primitive inhabitant

abort 3 end **4** fail, halt, stop **7** call off **8** miscarry **9** terminate

abortion 6 ending, fiasco **7** failure, halting **8** disaster **10** calling off **11** miscarriage, termination **16** fruitless attempt **19** unsuccessful attempt

abortive 4 vain **6** futile **7** sterile, useless **8** bootless **9** fruitless, nonviable, worthless **10** profitless, unavailing, unfruitful **11** ineffective, ineffectual, unrewarding **12** unproductive, unprofitable, unsuccessful **13** inefficacious

abound 4 gush, teem **5** swarm **6** thrive **7** run wild **8** be filled, be rich in, flourish, overflow **9** be flooded, luxuriate, spill over **10** be numerous **11** be plentiful, superabound, proliferate

abounding 4 rich, rife **5** ample **6** lavish, plenty **7** profuse, replete, teeming **8** abundant, brimming, swarming **9** bounteous, bountiful **11** overflowing, running over **14** more than enough

about 2 in, of, on **4** inre, near **5** astir, circa **6** abroad, almost, around, cir-

cum, nearby, nearly **7** close to **9** proximate, regarding **10** concerning, in regard to **13** approximately

about-face 5 shift **6** switch **7** reverse **8** reversal **9** disavowal, turnabout, volte-face **10** retraction, rightabout, turnaround **11** recantation **13** change of heart **14** tergiversation

above 4 atop, over **5** aloft, north, supra **6** before, beyond, dorsal, excess, heaven, higher **7** earlier **8** in heaven, overhead, superior, upstairs **9** exceeding **10** surpassing

aboveboard 4 just, open **5** blunt, frank, legal, legit, licit, moral, overt, plain **6** candid, direct, honest, public, square **7** artless, ethical, sincere, upright **8** revealed, straight, truthful, virtuous **9** disclosed, guileless, ingenuous, righteous **10** forthright, foursquare **11** unconcealed **12** on the up and up, plain-dealing, out in the open **13** square-dealing, undissembling **15** straightforward **16** straight-shooting

ab ovo 10 from the egg **16** from the beginning

abracadabra 5 charm, magic, spell **6** voodoo **7** sorcery **8** exorcism **10** hocus-pocus, invocation, magic spell, mumbo-jumbo, open sesame, witchcraft **11** incantation

abrade 3 rub **4** file, fray, sand **5** chafe, erode, grate, scour, scuff **6** scrape **7** scratch

Abraham
　　former name: 5 Abram
　　founded: 12 Hebrew nation
　　father: 5 Terah
　　wife: 5 Sarah, Sarai **7** Keturah
　　brother: 5 Haran, Nahor
　　son: 5 Isaac **6** Midian **7** Ishmael
　　nephew: 3 Lot
　　birthplace: 15 Ur of the Chaldees
　　received: 17 law of circumcision
　　sacrificed Isaac at: 6 Moriah
　　burial place: 6 Hebron
　　tomb in: 9 Machpelah

Abraham Lincoln
　　author: 12 Carl Sandburg

Abraham's bosom 6 heaven

Abram *see* **7** Abraham

Abrams, Creighton
　　served in: 4 WWII **10** Vietnam War
　　rank: 16 army chief of staff

abrasive 5 harsh, nasty, rough, sharp **6** biting, coarse **7** caustic, chafing, cutting, galling, grating, hurtful, rasping **8** annoying **10** irritating **11** excoriating **16** grinding material, scouring material, scraping material

abreast 6 in rank **7** aligned **8** arm in arm **10** side by side **11** in alignment

abridge 3 cut **4** trim **5** limit **6** digest, lessen, reduce **7** curtail, cut down, shorten **8** compress, condense, decrease, diminish, pare down, restrict,

take away, truncate **9** scale down, telescope **10** abbreviate

abridgment 6 digest **8** decrease **9** lessening, reduction, restraint **10** diminution, limitation, truncation **11** curtailment, diminishing, restriction **12** abbreviation, condensation

abroad 3 out **4** rife **5** astir, forth **7** at large, outside **8** overseas **9** all around **10** out of doors **13** in circulation, out of the house, round and about **15** making the rounds, out in the open air, out of the country

abrogate 3 end **4** junk, undo, void **5** annul, quash **6** abjure, cancel, negate, recall, repeal, revoke **7** abolish, nullify, rescind, retract, reverse, vitiate **8** dissolve, override, renounce, set aside, throw out, withdraw **9** repudiate, terminate **10** do away with, invalidate, put an end to **11** countermand

abrupt 4 curt, rude **5** blunt, brisk, crisp, gruff, hasty, quick, rapid, rough, sharp, sheer, short, steep, swift **6** sudden **7** brusque, uncivil **8** impolite **9** impulsive **10** unexpected, unforeseen, ungracious **11** precipitate, precipitous, unannounced, unlooked for **12** discourteous **13** instantaneous, unanticipated, unceremonious

Absalom
　　father: 5 David
　　mother: 6 Maacah
　　half-sister: 5 Tamar
　　brother: 7 Solomon **8** Adonijah
　　half-brother: 5 Amnon
　　defeated at: 6 Gilead
　　killed by: 4 Joab

Absalom, Absalom!
　　author: 15 William Faulkner
　　character: 5 Henry **6** Judith **10** Charles Bon **13** Rosa Coldfield **14** Quentin Compson, Shreve McCannon **16** Goodhue Coldfield **19** Colonel Thomas Sutpen **20** Ellen Coldfield Sutpen

Absalom and Achitophel
　　author: 10 John Dryden

abscond 3 fly **4** flee, skip **5** split **6** escape, run off, vanish **7** make off, run away, take off **8** steal off **9** disappear, steal away **10** take flight

absence 3 cut **4** lack, want **6** dearth **7** truancy **8** scarcity **10** deficiency, scantiness **11** absenteeism, nonpresence

absent 3 cut, out **4** away, AWOL, gone **5** blank, empty, vague **6** dreamy, musing, truant, vacant **7** faraway, missing, out of it, removed, unaware **8** heedless, keep away, stay away, tuned out **9** not appear, not show up, oblivious **10** distracted, nonpresent, not present, out to lunch, play truant, unthinking **11** inattentive, preoccupied, unconscious **12** nonattendant

absentee 6 no show, truant **10** nonpresent **11** nonattendee, nonpresence **12** nonattendant **13** nonattendance

absenteeism 5 hooky **7** truancy **11** nonpresence **13** nonappearance **19** absence without cause

absent-minded 5 blank, vague **6** dreamy **9** oblivious **10** abstracted, distracted **11** preoccupied **14** out in left field **17** out of it

Absent Without Leave
  author: **12** Heinrich Boll

absinthe
  ingredient: **8** licorice, wormwood **9** aromatics, star anise
  color: **11** yellow green
  substitute: **4** Ouzo **6** Pastis, Pernod **8** Anisette

absolute 4 full, pure, real, sure **5** sheer, total, utter **7** certain, genuine, perfect, supreme **8** complete, decisive, definite, outright, positive, reliable, thorough **9** confirmed, out-and-out, unbounded, unlimited **10** conclusive, consummate, infallible, undeniable

Absolute, Sir Anthony
  character in: **9** The Rivals
  author: **8** Sheridan

absolutely 3 yes **4** sure **5** truly **6** indeed, really, wholly **7** utterly **8** entirely **9** certainly, decidedly **10** completely, definitely, positively, thoroughly **11** indubitably, undoubtedly

absolution 5 mercy **6** pardon **7** amnesty, release **9** acquittal, clearance, quittance, remission **10** indulgence, liberation **11** deliverance, exculpation, exoneration, forgiveness, vindication **12** dispensation

absolve 4 free **5** clear, loose **6** acquit, exempt, pardon, shrive **7** deliver, forgive, release, set free **9** discharge, exculpate, exonerate, vindicate **10** excuse from **13** find not guilty, judge innocent

absolved 5 freed **6** exempt, spared **7** cleared, excused **8** forgiven, innocent, not guilty, pardoned, released, relieved **9** acquitted **10** discharged, exonerated, vindicated **13** found innocent

absorb 3 fix, get **5** grasp, rivet, sop up **6** arrest, digest, engage, enwrap, ingest, occupy, soak up, suck up, take up **7** consume, drink in, engross, immerse **8** sponge up **9** fascinate, preoccupy, swallow up **10** assimilate, understand **11** incorporate

absorbed 4 deep, rapt **8** immersed, involved, soaked up, sucked up **9** blotted up, engrossed

absorbent 6 porous, spongy **7** osmotic, thirsty **8** bibulous, pervious **9** permeable **10** absorptive, penetrable **12** assimilative

absorbing 8 engaging, exciting **9**

thrilling **10** engrossing, intriguing **11** captivating, fascinating, interesting

abstain 5 avoid, forgo **6** desist, eschew, refuse, resist **7** decline, forbear, refrain

abstainer 3 dry **7** ascetic **10** nondrinker, self-denier, teetotaler

abstemious 3 dry **5** sober **7** ascetic, austere, sparing, spartan **8** teetotal **9** abstinent, continent, temperate **10** forbearing **11** abstentious, self-denying, straitlaced, teetotaling **12** nonindulgent **15** self-disciplined

abstention 7 refusal **8** eschewal **9** avoidance, desisting, eschewing **10** abstaining, refraining, resistance **11** forbearance, holding back **13** nonindulgence **14** denying oneself **16** nonparticipation

abstinence 8 chastity, sobriety **10** abstention, continence, discipline, self-denial, temperance **11** forbearance, self-control **13** nonindulgence, self-restraint

abstinent 3 dry **5** sober **6** chaste **8** celibate, virginal **9** continent **10** abstemious, forbearing

abstract 4 take **5** brief **6** arcane, digest, precis, remote, remove, resume, subtle **7** abridge, extract, general, isolate, obscure, outline, summary, take out **8** abstruse, compress, condense, esoteric, profound, separate, synopsis, withdraw **9** imaginary, recondite, summarize, synopsize, theoretic, unapplied, visionary **10** abridgment, conceptual, dissociate, indefinite, intangible **11** generalized, impractical, nonspecific, theoretical **12** condensation, hypothetical, intellectual **14** recapitulation

abstruse 4 deep **6** arcane, remote, subtle **7** complex, obscure **8** abstract, esoteric, profound, puzzling **9** enigmatic, recondite **10** perplexing **11** complicated **12** unfathomable **16** incomprehensible

absurd 4 wild **5** crazy, funny, inane, kooky, silly **6** screwy, stupid **7** asinine, comical, foolish, idiotic **8** farcical **9** illogical, laughable, ludicrous, senseless **10** irrational, ridiculous **11** nonsensical **12** preposterous, unreasonable

absurdity 6 drivel, idiocy **7** fallacy, inanity **8** delusion, nonsense **9** asininity, falsehood, silliness **10** buffoonery **11** comicalness, foolishness **13** irrationality **14** ridiculousness **15** unbelievability **16** unreasonableness

Absyrtus see **8** Apsyrtus

Abu Dhabi
  capital of: **18** United Arab Emirates

Abuja
  capital of: **7** Nigeria

abundance 4 glut, heap **5** flood **6** bounty, excess, plenty, wealth **7** sur-

feit, surplus **8** plethora, richness **9** plenitude, profusion, repletion **10** cornucopia **11** copiousness, full measure, sufficiency

abundant 4 rich, rife **5** ample **6** enough, galore, lavish, plenty **7** copious, profuse, replete, teeming **8** brimming, prolific **9** abounding, bounteous, bountiful, luxuriant **10** sufficient

ab urbe condita 24 from the founding of the city

abuse 4 harm, hurt, slur **5** curse, scold **6** berate, carp at, defame, deride, illuse, injure, injury, insult, malign, misuse, rail at, revile, tirade, vilify **7** assault, bawl out, beating, carping, censure, cruelty, cursing, exploit, harming, insults, railing, slander, torment, upbraid **8** badmouth, belittle, berating, denounce, derision, diatribe, ill-treat, maltreat, mistreat, reproach, ridicule, scolding, sneering, torments **9** castigate, criticism, criticize, denigrate, disparage, excoriate, invective **10** belittling, defamation, impose upon, imposition, oppression, speak ill of, upbraiding **11** castigation **12** exploitation, maltreatment, mistreatment, vilification **13** disparagement, misemployment, tongue-lashing **14** inveigh against, misapplication **15** take advantage of

abusive 4 rude, vile **5** cruel, gross, harsh **7** harmful, hurtful, obscene **8** critical, improper, reviling, scornful **9** injurious, insulting, maligning, offensive, vilifying **10** censorious, defamatory, derogatory, scurrilous, slanderous **11** acrimonious, castigating, deprecatory, disparaging, foulmouthed **12** vituperative

abusive word 5 curse **6** insult **7** epithet **9** blasphemy, expletive, invective, obscenity

abut 4 join, meet **5** touch **6** adjoin, border

abutment 4 prop, stay **5** brace, union **7** contact, meeting, support **8** buttress, junction, shoulder, touching **9** adjacency

abutting 6 next to **7** joining, meeting **8** adjacent, touching **9** bordering **10** contiguous, juxtaposed **12** conterminous

abysmal 4 deep, vast **7** endless, extreme, immense **8** complete, enormous, profound, thorough, unending **9** boundless **10** bottomless, incredible, stupendous **12** unfathomable, unbelievable, unimaginable

abyss 4 gulf, void **5** depth, gorge, gully, nadir **7** fissure **8** crevasse **9** vast chasm **13** bottomless pit

Abyssinia see **8** Ethiopia

Acacallis
  father: **5** Minos

mother: **8** Pasiphae
   son: **11** Amphithemis
acacia 9 gum arabic
   also called: **5** thorn **6** mimosa, wattle
academic 4 moot **6** remote, school **7**
   bookish, erudite, general, learned **8**
   abstract, educated, pedantic, studious
   9 scholarly **10** collegiate, scholastic,
   university **11** conjectural, educational,
   liberal-arts, presumptive, speculative,
   theoretical **12** hypothetical, ivory-
   towered, nontechnical, not practical
   13 nonvocational, suppositional **14**
   nonspecialized **18** college-preparatory
Academus
   origin: **8** Arcadian
   owned: **6** estate
      located in: **6** Athens
      served as meeting place for: **12**
         philosophers
Academy Award
   also called: **5** Oscar
   1927-28:
      actor: **12** Emil Jannings
      actress: **11** Janet Gaynor
      director: **12** Frank Borzage **14**
         Lewis Milestone
      picture: **5** Wings
   1928-29:
      actor: **12** Warner Baxter
      actress: **12** Mary Pickford
      director: **10** Frank Lloyd
      picture: **14** Broadway Melody
   1929-30:
      actor: **12** George Arliss
      actress: **12** Norma Shearer
      director: **14** Lewis Milestone
      picture: **25** All Quiet on the West-
         ern Front
   1930-31:
      actor: **15** Lionel Barrymore
      actress: **13** Marie Dressler
      director: **12** Norman Taurog
      picture: **8** Cimarron
   1931-32:
      actor: **12** Fredric March
      actress: **10** Helen Hayes
      director: **12** Frank Borzage
      picture: **10** Grand Hotel
   1932-33:
      actor: **15** Charles Laughton
      actress: **16** Katharine Hepburn
      director: **10** Frank Lloyd
      picture: **9** Cavalcade
   1934:
      actor: **10** Clark Gable
      actress: **16** Claudette Colbert
      director: **10** Frank Capra
      picture: **18** It Happened One Night
   1935:
      actor: **14** Victor McLaglen
      actress: **10** Bette Davis
      director: **8** John Ford
      picture: **17** Mutiny on the Bounty
   1936:
      actor: **8** Paul Muni
      actress: **11** Luise Rainer
      director: **10** Frank Capra

picture: **16** The Great Ziegfeld
1937:
   actor: **12** Spencer Tracy
   actress: **11** Luise Rainer
   director: **10** Leo McCarey
   picture: **15** Life of Emile Zola
1938:
   actor: **12** Spencer Tracy
   actress: **10** Bette Davis
   director: **10** Frank Capra
   picture: **20** You Can't Take It with
      You
1939:
   actor: **11** Robert Donat
   actress: **11** Vivien Leigh
   director: **13** Victor Fleming
   picture: **15** Gone with the Wind
1940:
   actor: **12** James Stewart
   actress: **12** Ginger Rogers
   director: **8** John Ford
   picture: **7** Rebecca
1941:
   actor: **10** Gary Cooper
   actress: **12** Joan Fontaine
   director: **8** John Ford
   picture: **19** How Green Was My
      Valley
1942:
   actor: **11** James Cagney
   actress: **11** Greer Garson
   director: **12** William Wyler
   picture: **10** Mrs Miniver
1943:
   actor: **9** Paul Lukas
   actress: **13** Jennifer Jones
   director: **13** Michael Curtiz
   picture: **10** Casablanca
1944:
   actor: **10** Bing Crosby
   actress: **13** Ingrid Bergman
   director: **10** Leo McCarey
   picture: **10** Going My Way
1945:
   actor: **10** Ray Milland
   actress: **12** Joan Crawford
   director: **11** Billy Wilder
   picture: **14** The Lost Weekend
1946:
   actor: **12** Fredric March
   actress: **17** Olivia de Havilland
   director: **12** William Wyler
   picture: **22** The Best Years of Our
      Lives
1947:
   actor: **12** Ronald Colman
   actress: **12** Loretta Young
   director: **9** Elia Kazan
   picture: **19** Gentleman's Agreement
1948:
   actor: **15** Laurence Olivier
   actress: **9** Jane Wyman
   director: **10** John Huston
   picture: **6** Hamlet
1949:
   actor: **17** Broderick Crawford
   actress: **17** Olivia de Havilland
   director: **17** Joseph L Mankiewicz

picture: **14** All the King's Men
1950:
   actor: **10** Jose Ferrer
   actress: **12** Judy Holliday
   director: **17** Joseph L Mankiewicz
   picture: **11** All About Eve
1951:
   actor: **14** Humphrey Bogart
   actress: **11** Vivien Leigh
   director: **13** George Stevens
   picture: **17** An American in Paris
1952:
   actor: **10** Gary Cooper
   actress: **12** Shirley Booth
   director: **8** John Ford
   picture: **19** Greatest Show on Earth
1953:
   actor: **13** William Holden
   actress: **13** Audrey Hepburn
   director: **13** Fred Zinnemann
   picture: **18** From Here to Eternity
1954:
   actor: **12** Marlon Brando
   actress: **10** Grace Kelly
   director: **9** Elia Kazan
   picture: **15** On the Waterfront
1955:
   actor: **14** Ernest Borgnine
   actress: **11** Anna Magnani
   director: **11** Delbert Mann
   picture: **5** Marty
1956:
   actor: **10** Yul Brynner
   actress: **13** Ingrid Bergman
   director: **13** George Stevens
   picture: **26** Around the World in
      Eighty Days
1957:
   actor: **12** Alec Guinness
   actress: **14** Joanne Woodward
   director: **9** David Lean
   picture: **23** The Bridge on the River
      Kwai
1958:
   actor: **10** David Niven
   actress: **12** Susan Hayward
   director: **16** Vincente Minnelli
   picture: **4** Gigi
1959:
   actor: **14** Charlton Heston
   actress: **14** Simone Signoret
   director: **12** William Wyler
   picture: **6** Ben-Hur
1960:
   actor: **13** Burt Lancaster
   actress: **15** Elizabeth Taylor
   director: **11** Billy Wilder
   picture: **12** The Apartment
1961:
   actor: **16** Maximilian Schell
   actress: **11** Sophia Loren
   director: **10** Robert Wise **13** Jerome
      Robbins
   picture: **13** West Side Story
1962:
   actor: **11** Gregory Peck
   actress: **12** Anne Bancroft
   director: **9** David Lean

picture: **16** Lawrence of Arabia
1963:
actor: **13** Sidney Poitier
actress: **12** Patricia Neal
director: **14** Tony Richardson
picture: **8** Tom Jones
1964:
actor: **11** Rex Harrison
actress: **12** Julie Andrews
director: **11** George Cukor
picture: **10** My Fair Lady
1965:
actor: **9** Lee Marvin
actress: **13** Julie Christie
director: **10** Robert Wise
picture: **15** The Sound of Music
1966:
actor: **12** Paul Scofield
actress: **15** Elizabeth Taylor
director: **13** Fred Zinnemann
picture: **17** A Man for All Seasons
1967:
actor: **10** Rod Steiger
actress: **16** Katharine Hepburn
director: **11** Mike Nichols
picture: **19** In the Heat of the Night
1968:
actor: **14** Cliff Robertson
actress: **15** Barbra Streisand **16**
  Katharine Hepburn
director: **12** Sir Carol Reed
picture: **6** Oliver!
1969:
actor: **9** John Wayne
actress: **11** Maggie Smith
director: **15** John Schlesinger
picture: **14** Midnight Cowboy
1970:
actor: **12** George C Scott
actress: **13** Glenda Jackson
director: **17** Franklin Schaffner
picture: **6** Patton
1971:
actor: **11** Gene Hackman
actress: **9** Jane Fonda
director: **15** William Friedkin
picture: **19** The French Connection
1972:
actor: **12** Marlon Brando
actress: **11** Liza Minnelli
director: **8** Bob Fosse
picture: **12** The Godfather
1973:
actor: **10** Jack Lemmon
actress: **13** Glenda Jackson
director: **13** George Roy Hill
picture: **8** The Sting
1974:
actor: **9** Art Carney
actress: **12** Ellen Burstyn
director: **18** Francis Ford Coppola
picture: **12** The Godfather (Part II)
1975:
actor: **13** Jack Nicholson
actress: **14** Louise Fletcher
director: **11** Milos Forman
picture: **25** One Flew Over the
  Cuckoo's Nest

1976:
actor: **10** Peter Finch
actress: **11** Faye Dunaway
director: **13** John G Avildsen
picture: **5** Rocky
1977:
actor: **15** Richard Dreyfuss
actress: **11** Diane Keaton
director: **10** Woody Allen
picture: **9** Annie Hall
1978:
actor: **9** Jon Voight
actress: **9** Jane Fonda
director: **13** Michael Cimino
picture: **13** The Deer Hunter
1979:
actor: **13** Dustin Hoffman
actress: **10** Sally Field
director: **12** Robert Benton
picture: **14** Kramer vs Kramer
1980:
actor: **12** Robert De Niro
actress: **11** Sissy Spacek
director: **13** Robert Redford
picture: **14** Ordinary People
1981:
actor: **10** Henry Fonda
actress: **16** Katharine Hepburn
director: **12** Warren Beatty
picture: **14** Chariots of Fire
1982:
actor: **11** Ben Kingsley
actress: **11** Meryl Streep
director: **19** Richard Attenborough
picture: **6** Gandhi
1983:
actor: **12** Robert Duvall
actress: **15** Shirley MacLaine
director: **12** James L Brooks
picture: **17** Terms of Endearment
1984:
actor: **14** F Murray Abraham
actress: **10** Sally Field
director: **11** Milos Forman
picture: **7** Amadeus
1985:
actor: **11** William Hurt
actress: **13** Geraldine Page
director: **13** Sydney Pollack
picture: **11** Out of Africa
1986:
actor: **10** Paul Newman
actress: **12** Marlee Matlin
director: **11** Oliver Stone
picture: **7** Platoon
1987:
actor: **14** Michael Douglas
actress: **4** Cher
director: **18** Bernardo Bertolucci
picture: **14** The Last Emperor
1988:
actor: **13** Dustin Hoffman
actress: **11** Jodie Foster
director: **13** Barry Levinson
picture: **7** Rain Man
1989:
actor: **14** Daniel Day-Lewis
actress: **12** Jessica Tandy

director: **11** Oliver Stone
picture: **16** Driving Miss Daisy
1990:
actor: **11** Jeremy Irons
actress: **10** Kathy Bates
director: **12** Kevin Costner
picture: **16** Dances With Wolves
1991:
actor: **14** Anthony Hopkins
actress: **11** Jodie Foster
director: **13** Jonathan Demme
picture: **20** The Silence of the
  Lambs
1992:
actor: **8** Al Pacino
actress: **12** Emma Thompson
director: **13** Clint Eastwood
picture: **10** Unforgiven
1993:
actor: **8** Tom Hanks
actress: **11** Holly Hunter
director: **15** Steven Spielberg
picture: **14** Schindler's List
1994:
actor: **8** Tom Hanks
actress: **12** Jessica Lange
director: **14** Robert Zemeckis
picture: **11** Forrest Gump
1995:
actor: **11** Nicolas Cage
actress: **13** Susan Sarandon
director: **9** Mel Gibson
picture: **10** Braveheart
1996:
actor: **12** Geoffrey Rush
actress: **16** Frances McDormand
director: **16** Anthony Minghella
picture: **17** The English Patient
1997:
actor: **12** Jack Nicholson
actress: **9** Helen Hunt
director: James Cameron
picture: **7** Titanic
Accad
kingdom of: **6** Nimrod
location: **13** Plain of Shinar
captured by: **6** Sargon (I)
Acca Larentia
form: **7** goddess
corresponds to: **6** Dea Dia
accede 5 admit, grant **6** accept, permit
7 abide by, agree to, approve, concede, defer to, endorse, inherit, yield
to **8** assent to, submit to **9** acquiesce,
conform to, consent to, succeed to **10**
comply with, concur with **11** acknowledge, subscribe to, surrender to
accede to the throne 4 keep **5**
claim, usurp **6** ascend **7** possess, succeed **8** take over **9** be crowned **15** ascend the throne
accelerando
music: **15** becoming quicker
accelerate 4 rush, spur **5** hurry, impel
6 hasten, step up **7** advance, augment, further, promote, quicken,
speed up **8** expedite **9** intensify **10** fa-

cilitate, to go faster **11** pick up speed, precipitate

accelerator 3 gas **4** goad, prod, spur **8** gas pedal **13** encouragement

accent 4 hint, tone **5** drawl, touch, twang **6** detail, stress **7** feature **8** emphasis, ornament, tonality, trimming **9** adornment, emphasize, highlight, punctuate, spotlight, underline **10** accentuate, inflection, intonation, modulation, underscore **11** enunciation **12** articulation **13** embellishment, primary stress, pronunciation

accentuate 6 accent, stress **7** feature, point up **9** emphasize, punctuate, underline **10** underscore

accentuation 6 accent, stress **8** emphasis

accept 3 buy **4** avow, bear **5** admit **6** assume **7** agree to, fall for, swallow **8** accede to, assent to **9** consent to, undertake **11** acknowledge, go along with

acceptable 4 fair, good, so-so **6** proper, worthy **8** adequate, passable, suitable **9** agreeable, allowable, tolerable **10** admissible **12** satisfactory

acceptable person
Latin: **12** persona grata

acceptance 6 belief, taking **7** consent, receipt **8** approval, sanction **9** accepting, agreement, receiving, reception **10** concession, permission **11** affirmation, approbation, endorsement, recognition **12** acquiescence, confirmation **14** acknowledgment **15** stamp of approval

accepted 5 usual **6** common, normal **7** regular **8** approved, standard **9** confirmed, customary, universal **10** acceptable, agreed upon **11** established, time-honored **12** acknowledged, conventional

access 3 way **4** door, gate, path, road **5** entry **6** avenue, course, entree **7** gateway, passage **8** entrance **10** admittance

accessible 5 handy, on tap, ready **6** at hand, nearby, on hand **8** possible **9** available, reachable **10** attainable, obtainable **11** within reach **12** approachable

accession 7 seizure **9** induction **10** arrogation, assumption, investment, taking over, usurpation **11** inheritance **12** inauguration, installation

accessory 4 plus **6** accent, cohort, detail **7** adjunct, partner **8** addition **9** adornment, assistant, associate, auxiliary, colleague, component, extension **10** accomplice, attachment, complement, decoration, supplement **11** confederate, contributor **13** accompaniment

accident 4 fate, luck **5** crash, fluke, wreck **6** chance, mishap **7** smashup **8** fortuity **9** collision, mischance **10** mis-

fortune **11** good fortune, serendipity **12** happenstance, misadventure

accidental 6 chance, random **9** haphazard, unplanned, unwitting **10** fortuitous, incidental, unexpected, unforeseen

acclaim 4 hail, laud **5** cheer, exalt, extol, honor, kudos **6** bravos, praise, salute **7** applaud, commend, ovation **8** applause, cheering, eulogize, plaudits **9** celebrate, rejoicing **10** compliment, enthusiasm **11** acclamation, endorsement

acclamation 6 cheers, homage **7** acclaim, hurrahs, ovation, tribute **8** cheering, hosannas, plaudits **9** adulation **10** salutation **11** approbation

acclimate 5 adapt, enure, inure **6** adjust, orient **8** accustom **9** get used to, habituate, reconcile **11** accommodate **16** become seasoned to

acclimation 9 seasoning **10** adaptation, adjustment **11** habituation

acclivity 4 hill, ramp, rise **5** slope **6** ascent **9** elevation **11** upward slope

accolade 5 award, honor, prize **6** praise, trophy **7** acclaim, tribute **8** applause, citation **10** admiration, compliment, decoration **11** recognition, testimonial **12** commendation

accommodate 3 aid, fit **4** help, hold **5** adapt, board, house, lodge, put up **6** adjust, assist, billet, modify, oblige, supply **7** bed down, conform, contain, furnish, provide, quarter, shelter **8** accustom **9** acclimate, entertain, get used to, harmonize, lend a hand, reconcile

accommodating 4 kind **6** polite **7** helpful **8** friendly, gracious, obliging, yielding **9** courteous **10** hospitable, neighborly **11** considerate **12** conciliatory

accommodation 5 rooms **7** concord, housing **8** lodgings, quarters **9** agreement **10** adjustment, compromise, settlement **12** arrangements **14** reconciliation

accompaniment 6 escort **7** support **8** ornament **9** accessory, adornment **10** incidental

accompany 5 guard, usher **6** attend, back up, convoy, escort, follow **7** conduct, support **8** chaperon

accomplice 4 aide, ally **5** crony **6** cohort, helper, stooge **7** abettor, comrade, partner **8** henchman, sidekick **9** accessory, assistant, associate, colleague, supporter **11** confederate, participant, subordinate **12** collaborator **13** co-conspirator **14** partner-in-crime

accomplish 2 do **6** attain, finish **7** achieve, execute, fulfill, get done, perform, produce, realize **8** carry out, complete, expedite, knock off **9** succeed at **10** bring about

accomplished 3 apt **4** able, deft, fine **6** adroit, expert, gifted, proved, proven **7** capable, eminent, skilled **8** accepted, effected, existing, finished, masterly, polished, realized, seasoned, skillful, talented **9** brilliant, completed, concluded, practiced, qualified **10** cultivated, proficient **11** consummated, established, experienced, welltrained

accomplishment 3 act **4** deed, feat, gest, gift **5** skill, geste **6** talent **7** exploit, success, triumph, victory **9** execution **10** attainment, capability **11** achievement, carrying out, culmination, fulfillment, proficiency, realization, tour de force **12** consummation

accord 4 cede, give, jibe **5** agree, allow, award, grant, match, tally **6** bestow, concur, render, square, tender, unison **7** concede, concert, conform, entente, harmony, present, rapport **8** be in tune, bequeath, sympathy **9** agreement, harmonize, unanimity, vouchsafe **10** accordance, be in unison, comply with, conformity, consonance, correspond, uniformity **11** concurrence, go along with **19** mutual understanding

accordant 4 like **7** similar **8** parallel **10** consistent **11** homogeneous

accordingly 2 so **4** ergo, then, thus **5** hence **6** thence, whence **8** suitably **9** as a result, therefore, wherefore, whereupon **11** conformably, in due course, in which case **12** consequently **15** correspondingly

accost 3 nab **4** hail, halt, stop **5** greet **6** call to, salute, waylay **7** address, solicit **8** approach, confront **10** buttonhole **11** proposition

accouchement 10 childbirth **11** confinement

accoucheur 12 obstetrician **25** assistant during childbirth

accoucheuse 7 midwife **25** assistant during childbirth

account 3 IRA, use **4** deem, hold, note, rank, rate, sake, tale **5** basis, books, cause, count, gauge, honor, judge, merit, score, story, think, value, weigh, worth **6** esteem, import, reason, reckon, record, regard, report, repute, view as **7** believe, clarify, dignity, explain, grounds, history, justify, recital, version **8** appraise, consider, estimate, megillah, standing **9** calculate, chronicle, narration, narrative, statement **10** accounting, commentary, illuminate, importance

accountable 6 guilty, liable **7** at fault, to blame **8** beholden, culpable **9** obligated **10** answerable, chargeable **11** blameworthy, responsible

accountant 3 CPA **7** actuary, auditor **10** bookkeeper **25** certified public accountant

account for 6 excuse 7 explain, justify 9 answer for

accounting 5 cause 6 answer, motive, reason 7 warrant 10 motivation 11 explanation

account rendered
French: 11 compte rendu

accoutrements 4 gear 7 apparel 8 supplies 9 equipment, trappings 11 accessories, furnishings 13 paraphernalia

Accra, Akkra
capital of: 5 Ghana

accredit 6 assign, credit 7 ascribe, certify, empower, endorse, license 8 sanction 9 attribute, authorize, guarantee 10 commission 19 officially recognize 22 furnish with credentials

accredited 8 ascribed, assigned, endorsed, licensed 9 authentic, certified, empowered 10 attributed, authorized, recognized, sanctioned 12 commissioned 20 officially recognized

accretion 4 rise 6 growth 7 accrual 8 addition, increase 9 expansion, extension, increment 10 supplement 11 enlargement 12 accumulation, augmentation 13 amplification

accrue 4 grow 5 add up, amass 6 pile up 7 build up, collect 8 increase 10 accumulate

accumulate 4 grow 5 amass, hoard 6 accrue, garner, gather, heap up, pile up, save up 7 collect, store up 8 assemble, cumulate 9 aggregate 10 congregate 14 gather together

accumulation 4 heap, mass, pile 5 hoard, stack, stock, store 6 pile-up, supply 7 accrual 8 amassing, hoarding 9 acquiring, gathering, stockpile 10 assemblage, collecting, collection 11 aggregation 13 agglomerating 14 conglomeration

accuracy 5 truth 6 verity 8 fidelity 9 exactness, precision 10 exactitude 11 correctness 12 accurateness, faithfulness

accurate 4 true 5 exact, right 7 careful, correct, perfect, precise 8 faithful, truthful, unerring 9 authentic, faultless 10 meticulous, scrupulous 11 punctilious 12 without error

accursed 4 base, foul, vile 6 cussed, horrid, odious 7 hellish 8 damnable, horrible, infamous 9 abhorrent, atrocious, execrable, loathsome, revolting 10 abominable, despicable, detestable, disgusting 12 contemptible

accusation 6 charge 8 citation 9 complaint 10 allegation, imputation, indictment 11 insinuation 13 incrimination

accuse 4 cite 5 blame 6 charge, indict 7 arraign, upbraid 8 reproach 10 take to task 13 call to account 22 lodge a complaint against

accuser 8 attacker 11 complainant 13 finger pointer

accustomed 3 set 5 fixed, prone, trite, usual 6 cliche, common, inured, normal, used to, wonted 7 general, given to, regular, routine 8 everyday, expected, familiar, habitual, hardened, ordinary, seasoned 9 customary, hackneyed, ingrained, prevalent, well-known 10 acclimated, habituated, prevailing 11 commonplace, established 12 conventional, familiarized

ace 2 A-1 4 one, top, star, tops 5 crack, pilot, super 6 expert, master, tip-top, victor, winner 7 one-spot 8 champion, medalist, terrific, top-notch, top-rated, 9 excellent, first-rate, headliner 10 first-class 11 crackerjack, outstanding 12 front-ranking

Aceldama
means: 12 field of blood
purchased by: 5 Judas

Acerbas see 8 Sychaeus

acerbity 7 acidity, sarcasm 8 acridity, acrimony, pungency, sourness, tartness 9 nastiness, sharpness 10 bitterness 11 astringency, brusqueness 12 irascibility

aces 2 A-1 4 fine, tops 5 great, prime, super 6 grade-A, superb, tip-top 8 peerless, superior, terrific, top-notch 9 excellent, first-rate, marvelous, matchless, superfine, wonderful 10 first-class, tremendous 11 outstanding, superlative 13 extraordinary

Acesius
epithet of: 6 Apollo
means: 6 healer

Achaeus
founder of: 6 Achaea
father: 6 Xuthus
mother: 6 Creusa
brother: 3 Ion

Achan
punishment: 13 stoned to death

ache 4 hurt, need, pain, pang, want 5 covet, crave, mourn, smart, throb, yearn 6 be sore, desire, grieve, hanker, hunger, lament, sorrow, suffer, twinge 7 agonize, long for 8 soreness 10 discomfort

Achech
origin: 8 Egyptian
form: 8 creature
body of: 4 lion
wings of: 4 bird

Achelous
form: 3 god
habitat: 5 river
father: 7 Oceanus
mother: 6 Tethys
daughter: 6 Sirens 8 Castalia 10 Callirrhoe
defeated by: 8 Hercules
struggled over: 8 Deianira

Acheron
river in: 5 Hades

ferryman: 6 Charon
carries: 4 dead

Acheson, Dean
Secy. of State 6 Truman
author of: 20 Present at the Creation

a cheval 7 by horse 11 on horseback

achieve 2 do 3 get, win 4 earn, gain 5 reach 6 attain, effect, finish, obtain 7 acquire, fulfill, procure, realize 8 arrive at, carry out, complete, dispatch 9 succeed in 10 accomplish, bring about, effectuate 11 bring to pass

achievement 3 act 4 coup, deed, fear 5 skill 6 effort 7 command, exploit, mastery 9 expertise 10 attainment 11 acquirement, fulfillment, realization, tour de force 14 accomplishment

achieve recognition 6 arrive, make it 7 succeed 8 make good 10 be somebody 11 reach the top

Achilles
mentioned in: 5 Iliad
father: 6 Peleus
mother: 6 Thetis
foster father: 7 Phoenix
grandfather: 6 Aeacus
teacher: 6 Chiron
charioteer: 9 Automedon
friend: 9 Patroclus
warrior in: 9 Trojan War
vulnerability: 4 heel
killed: 6 Hector
killed by: 5 Paris

acid 4 sour, tart 5 acrid, harsh, nasty, sharp 6 biting, bitter, ironic 7 acerbic, caustic, crabbed, cutting, pungent 8 scalding, scathing, stinging, vinegary 9 acidulous, irascible, sarcastic, satirical, vitriolic 10 astringent, vinegarish 11 acrimonious

acidity 8 acerbity, pungency, sourness, tartness 9 sharpness 10 bitterness 11 astringency 13 nonalkalinity

Acis
lover: 7 Galatea
killed by: 10 Polyphemus

Acis and Galatea
opera by: 6 Handel

Acis et Galatee
opera by: 5 Lully

acknowledge 3 own 5 admit, allow, grant, yield 6 accede, accept, answer, assent, concur 7 concede, confess, own up to, reply to 8 call upon, thank for 9 recognize, respond to

acknowledgment 5 reply 6 answer, credit, thanks 8 response 9 admission, gratitude 10 concession, confession 11 affirmation, recognition 12 appreciation, recognizance

acme 3 top 4 apex, peak 5 crest, crown 6 apogee, climax, height, heyday, summit, zenith 8 pinnacle 9 flowering, high point 11 culmination 12 highest point
Latin: 11 ne plus ultra

Acmon
 companion: 8 Diomedes
 changed into: 4 bird
 defied: 9 Aphrodite

acolyte 3 fan **6** helper, novice **7** admirer, devotee, groupie **8** adherent, altar boy, follower **9** assistant, attendant

Acoma
 language family: 6 Pueblo
 location: 3 Ako **4** Acus **8** Valencia **9** New Mexico
 noted for: 7 pottery

acorn
 from: 3 oak
 shape: 8 balanoid

a couvert 9 sheltered **10** under cover

acquaint 4 meet, tell **6** advise, inform, notify, reveal **7** apprise **8** disclose **9** divulge to, enlighten, introduce, make aware **11** familiarize

acquaintance 8 dealings **9** awareness, knowledge **10** cognizance, friendship **11** association, conversance, familiarity **12** relationship

acquiesce 5 admit, agree, allow, bow to, grant, yield **6** accede, assent, comply, concur, give in, submit **7** concede, conform, consent **10** capitulate, fall in with **13** resign oneself **16** reconcile oneself

acquiescence 5 leave **7** consent **8** approval, giving in, sanction **10** permission, submission **11** concurrence

acquiescent 7 willing **8** amenable, yielding **9** agreeable **10** submissive

acquire 3 get, win **4** earn, gain **6** attain, obtain, pick up, secure **7** achieve, capture, procure, realize **9** cultivate

acquisition 4 gain **5** prize **8** property, purchase **10** attainment, obtainment, possession **11** achievement, acquirement, procurement

acquisitive 6 greedy **7** selfish **8** covetous, grasping **10** avaricious, possessive **13** materialistic

acquit 3 act **5** clear **6** behave, excuse, exempt, let off, pardon **7** absolve, comport, conduct, deliver, release, relieve, set free **8** liberate, reprieve **9** discharge, exculpate, exonerate, vindicate

Acraea
 epithet of: 9 Aphrodite
 means: 6 height

acre
 one-fourth: 4 rood
 one-half: 3 erf **5** erven
 two-thirds: 5 cover
 ten: 6 decare **7** furlong
 one hundred: 7 hectare
 one hundred twenty: 4 hide

Acres, Bob
 character in: 9 The Rivals
 author: 8 Sheridan

acrid 4 acid **5** harsh, nasty, sharp **6** biting, bitter, ironic, smelly **7** burning, caustic, pungent **8** stinging **9** sarcastic, satirical, vitriolic **10** irritating, malodorous **11** acrimonious **12** foul-smelling

acrimonious 4 sour **5** nasty, testy **6** biting, bitter **7** caustic, cutting, peevish **8** venomous, spiteful **9** corrosive, irascible, rancorous, sarcastic, splenetic, vitriolic **10** ill-natured

acrimony 5 anger, scorn, spite **6** animus, malice, rancor, spleen **7** ill will **8** asperity, derision **9** animosity, hostility, malignity **10** antagonism, bitterness, malignancy **12** hard feelings, spitefulness

Acrisius
 king of: 5 Argos
 father: 4 Abas
 mother: 6 Aglaia
 twin brother: 7 Proetus
 daughter: 5 Danae
 grandson: 7 Perseus
 killed by: 7 Perseus

acrophobia
 fear of: 7 heights

acrostic 6 cipher, puzzle **7** acronym

act 2 do **3** bit, gig, law **4** bill, deed, do it, fake, feat, move, play, pose, show, skit, step, work **5** edict, enact, feign, front, order, put-on **6** action, affect, behave, decree, stance **7** execute, exploit, go about, mandate, measure, operate, perform, portray, posture, press on, routine, statute **8** carry out, function, pretense, put forth, simulate **9** enactment, ordinance, represent **10** pretension, resolution **11** achievement, affectation, counterfeit, impersonate, legislation, performance, pretend to be **14** accomplishment

Actaeon
 form: 6 hunter
 father: 9 Aristaeus
 mother: 7 Autonoe
 changed into: 4 stag
 transformed by: 5 Diana
 killed by: 6 hounds
 killed at: 9 Gargaphia

acting 5 drama **6** deputy, ersatz, pro tem **7** interim, theater **8** the stage **9** dramatics, simulated, surrogate, temporary **10** dramaturgy, stagecraft, substitute, the theater **11** dramatic art, officiating, provisional, thespianism **12** stage playing

actinium *see* **8** elements

action 3 act **4** deed, feat, move, step, suit, work **5** force, power **6** battle, combat, effect, effort, motion **7** exploit, process, warfare **8** activity, conflict, endeavor, exertion, fighting, movement, progress **9** adventure, execution, influence, operation **10** enterprise, excitement, performing, production **11** achievement, functioning,

performance, prosecution **14** accomplishment

Actis
 father: 6 Helius
 mother: 5 Rhoda
 crime: 10 fratricide
 taught: 9 astrology
 fled to: 5 Egypt
 memorial: 16 Colossus of Rhodes

activate 4 stir **5** drive, impel, start **6** prompt, propel, turn on **7** actuate **8** energize, mobilize, motivate, vitalize **9** stimulate

activated 5 began **7** started **8** impelled, in action, in effect, turned on **9** effective, energized, mobilized, operative, vitalized **10** stimulated **11** in operation

active 4 busy, spry **5** agile, alert, alive, peppy, quick **6** acting, at work, frisky, lively, nimble **7** engaged, in force, on the go, working, zealous **8** animated, diligent, forceful, occupied, spirited, vigorous **9** ambitious, assertive, effectual, energetic, go-getting, operative, sprightly, strenuous **10** aggressive, productive **11** functioning, imaginative, industrious **12** enterprising **13** indefatigable

active person 4 doer **6** beaver, dynamo **7** hustler **8** activist, go-getter

activist 4 doer **6** zealot **7** apostle **8** advocate, exponent **9** proponent, supporter

activity 4 fuss, stir, to-do **6** action, bustle, flurry, hustle, tumult **7** project, pursuit, venture **8** endeavor, exercise, exertion, function, goings on, movement, vivacity **9** agitation, animation, avocation, commotion **10** assignment, enterprise, hurly-burly, liveliness, occupation **11** undertaking **13** sprightliness

act of the faith
 Spanish: 8 auto da fe, auto de fe

act of war 4 raid **6** attack, strike **7** assault, offense **8** invasion **10** aggression, hostile act

actor 3 ham **4** doer, star **6** player, walk on **7** starlet, trouper **8** thespian **9** bit player, performer **11** functionary, participant, perpetrator **14** dramatic artist **15** supporting actor
 type: 4 hero **5** cameo **7** feature, leading **9** character **10** supporting
 hint: 3 cue

Actor
 king of: 6 Phthia
 father: 8 Myrmidon
 mother: 8 Pasidice
 brother: 6 Augeas
 son: 7 Cteatus, Eurytus

actual 4 real, sure, true **7** certain, current, factual, genuine, present **8** bona fide, concrete, existent, existing, physical, tangible **9** authentic, confirmed, corporeal **10** legitimate, prevailing, true-to-life, verifiable

actual being 4 esse

actuality 4 fact, life **5** being, truth **6** effect, living, verity **7** reality **8** existing **9** existence, plain fact, substance **10** brutal fact **11** point of fact

actually 5 truly **6** indeed, in fact, really, verily **9** genuinely, literally
Latin: **7** ex facto

actually existing
Latin: **6** in esse **7** de facto

actuary 5 clerk **9** tabulator **12** statistician

actuate 4 move, stir **5** cause, drive, impel, rouse **6** arouse, excite, incite, induce, prompt **7** animate, inspire, trigger **8** activate, motivate **9** influence, instigate, stimulate **10** bring about

acumen 6 wisdom **7** insight **8** keenness, sagacity **9** acuteness, ingenuity, smartness **10** astuteness, cleverness, perception, shrewdness **11** discernment **12** intelligence, perspicacity **13** sound judgment **15** clearheadedness

acute 4 keen **5** sharp **6** clever, fierce, peaked, severe **7** intense, very bad **8** critical, piercing, powerful **9** agonizing, ingenious, intuitive, sensitive, very great **10** discerning, perceptive **11** distressing, penetrating **12** excruciating, needle-shaped **14** discriminating

acute suffering 5 agony **7** anguish, torment, torture **8** distress

A.D. see **10** anno Domini

adage 3 saw **4** quip, wise **5** axiom, maxim, motto **6** cliche, dictum, old saw, saying, truism **7** epigram, precept, proverb **8** aphorism **9** platitude **11** observation

adagio
music: **4** slow

Adah
also: **9** Bashemath
husband: **4** Esau **6** Lamech
son: **5** Jabal, Jubal **7** Eliphaz

Adam
wife: **3** Eve
son: **4** Abel, Cain, Seth
home: **4** Eden
grandson: **4** Enas **5** Enoch

adamant 3 set **4** firm **5** fixed, rigid, tough **7** uptight **8** obdurate, resolute, stubborn **9** immovable, insistent, unbending **10** determined, hard as rock, inexorable, inflexible, unyielding **12** intransigent **14** uncompromising

Adam Bede
author: **11** George Eliot
character: **8** Seth Bede **11** Dinah Morris, Hetty Sorrel **12** Martin Poyser **17** Arthur Donnithorne

Adams, Henry
author of: **6** Esther **9** Democracy **14** Chapters of Erie **24** History of the

United States (Under the Jefferson and Adams Administration), The Education of Henry Adams **26** Mont-Saint Michel and Chartres **34** The Degradation of the Democratic Dogma

Adams, John
nickname: **19** Atlas of Independence
presidential rank: **6** second
party: **10** Federalist
state represented: **2** MA
defeated: **9** Jefferson
vice president: **9** Jefferson
cabinet:
state: **8** (John) Marshall **9** (Timothy) Pickering
treasury: **6** (Samuel) Dexter **7** (Oliver) Wolcott
war: **6** (Samuel) Dexter **7** (James) McHenry
attorney general: **3** (Charles) Lee
navy: **8** (Benjamin) Stoddert
born: **2** MA **9** Braintree
town now called: **6** Quincy
died/buried: **6** Quincy
education: **7** Harvard
religion: **9** Unitarian
author: **18** Discourses on Davila **20** Thoughts on Government
political career: **13** vice president **24** First Continental Congress **25** Second Continental Congress
minister: **11** Netherlands **12** Great Britain
civilian career: **6** lawyer
notable events of lifetime/term: **9** XYZ Affair
act: **9** Judiciary **16** Alien and Sedition
father: **4** John
mother: **7** Susanna (Boylston)
siblings: **5** Elihu **13** Peter Boylston
wife: **7** Abigail (Smith)
children: **7** Charles, Susanna **10** John Quincy (6th president) **13** Abigail Amelia **14** Thomas Boylston

Adams, John Quincy
nickname: **14** Old Man Eloquent
presidential rank: **5** sixth
party: **4** Whig **10** Federalist **20** Democratic-Republican
state represented: **2** MA
defeated: **4** (Henry) Clay **7** (Andrew) Jackson **8** (William H) Crawford
vice president: **7** (John C) Calhoun
cabinet:
state: **4** (Henry) Clay
treasury: **4** (Richard) Rush
war: **6** (Peter Buell) Porter **7** (James) Barbour
attorney general: **4** (William) Wirt
navy: **8** (Samuel Lewis) Southard
born: **2** MA **9** Braintree
town now called: **6** Quincy
died: **2** DC **10** Washington
buried: **2** MA **6** Quincy
education:
studied in: **5** Paris **9** Amsterdam

11 Latin School
University of: **6** Leyden
College: **7** Harvard
religion: **9** Unitarian
author: **7** Memoirs **14** Eulogy to Monroe, The Adams Papers **17** Eulogy to Lafayette **18** Letters from Silesia
political career: **8** US Senate **19** Massachusetts Senate **24** US House of Representatives
secretary of: **5** state
minister: **6** Russia **7** Prussia **8** Portugal **11** Netherlands **12** Great Britain
civilian career: **6** lawyer
notable events of lifetime/term: **19** Pan-American Congress **20** Tariff of Abominations
father: **4** John
mother: **7** Abigail (Smith)
siblings: **7** Abigail, Charles, Susanna **14** Thomas Boylston
wife: **6** Louisa (Catherine Johnson)
children: **4** John **14** Charles Francis **15** Louisa Catherine **16** George Washington

Adams, Parson
character in: **13** Joseph Andrews
author: **8** Fielding

Adams, Richard
author of: **4** Maia **7** Shardik **12** Girl in a Swing **13** The Plague Dogs, Watership Down

Adam's Rib
director: **11** George Cukor
script by: **10** Ruth Gordon **11** Garson Kanin
cast: **8** Tom Ewell **9** Jean Hagen **10** David Wayne **12** Judy Holliday, Spencer Tracy **16** Katharine Hepburn

adapt 3 fit **4** suit **5** alter, frame, shape **6** adjust, change, modify, rework **7** conform, convert, fashion, make fit, remodel, reshape **8** attune to **9** acclimate, harmonize, recompose, reconcile, transform **10** assimilate, coordinate **11** accommodate, acculturate **12** make suitable

adaptable 6 pliant, usable **7** unrigid **8** amenable, flexible, obliging **9** alterable, compliant, easygoing, malleable, tractable **10** adjustable, applicable, changeable, open- minded **11** conformable, serviceable **13** accommodating, accommodative

adaptation 5 shift **6** change **8** revision **9** refitting, reshaping, reworking **10** adjustment, alteration, conversion, remodeling **12** modification **13** metamorphosis

Adar 18 twelfth Hebrew month

add 4 join **5** affix, sum up, total **6** append, attach, join on, reckon, tack on **7** combine, compute, count up, enlarge, include **8** figure up, increase **9**

calculate, enlarge by **10** increase by, supplement

Addams, Frankie
 character in: **19** A Member of the Wedding
 author: **15** Carson McCullers

Addams Family, The
 character: **5** Gomez, Lurch **7** Pugsley **8** Morticia **9** Cousin Itt, Grandmama, Wednesday **11** Uncle Fester
 cast: **9** John Astin **10** Lisa Loring, Ted Cassidy **11** Blossom Rock **12** Carolyn Jones, Jackie Coogan **13** Ken Weatherwax

add details 6 expand **7** clarify **9** elaborate, embellish **13** particularize

added 5 bonus, extra **6** joined **7** totaled **8** appended, attached, computed, included, joined on, reckoned, summed up, tacked on **9** counted up **10** additional, enlarged by, enumerated **11** increased by **13** supplementary

addendum 7 codicil **8** addition **9** appendage **10** attachment, postscript, supplement **12** afterthought

addict 3 fan, nut **4** buff, head, hook, user **5** freak, hound **6** junkie, submit, turn on, votary **7** acolyte, devotee, druggie, habitue **8** adherent **9** dope fiend, indulge in, surrender

addiction 5 craze, mania, quirk **6** fetish, hangup **8** fixation **9** cocainism, obsession **10** alcoholism, compulsion, dipsomania, morphinism **11** barbiturism, enslavement **12** addictedness, enthrallment **13** preoccupation

adding machine
 invented by: **6** Pascal **9** Burroughs

Addis Ababa
 capital of: **8** Ethiopia

Addison, Joseph
 author of: **4** Cato **9** The Tatler **12** The Spectator **13** The Freeholder
 co-author: **13** Richard Steele

addition 4 wing **5** annex, extra **6** adding **7** adjunct, joining **8** addendum, additive, annexing, increase, totaling **9** adjoining, appendage, appending, attaching, embracing, expansion, extending, extension, including, increment, reckoning, summation, summing up **10** counting up, increasing **11** enlargement, enumeration **12** appurtenance, augmentation, encompassing

additional 5 added, extra, spare **7** added on **8** appended **12** over-and-above **13** supplementary

additional feature 5 extra **7** adjunct **10** attachment, complement, supplement **12** appurtenance **13** accompaniment

additive 5 extra **8** addition **10** adulterant, supplement **12** augmentation, preservative

addle 5 mix up **6** muddle **7** confuse, nonplus, stupefy **8** befuddle

addled 5 silly **6** foolish, mixed-up, muddled **8** confused **9** befuddled, nonplused **10** nonplussed

add on 5 affix **6** append, attach, tack on **7** include **10** increase by

address 4 talk **5** greet, orate **6** salute, speech, talk to **7** lecture, oration, speak to, write to **8** dwelling, locality, location **9** discourse, statement

Address to the Deil
 author: **11** Robert Burns

add to 6 expand, extend, pad out **7** amplify, augment, bolster, enlarge **8** compound, increase, lengthen **10** strengthen, stretch out, supplement

Ade, George
 author of: **13** Fables in Slang **15** The College Widow **17** The County Chairman

Aden
 seaport of: **5** Yemen
 Gulf in: Arabian Sea

adept 3 apt **4** able, good **6** adroit, expert, gifted, master **7** skilled **8** skillful **9** dexterous, ingenious, masterful, practiced **10** proficient **12** accomplished

adequacy 7 fitness **11** sufficiency **16** satisfactoriness

adequate 3 fit **4** so-so **5** ample **6** enough **7** fitting **8** passable, suitable **9** tolerable **10** sufficient **12** satisfactory

a deux 6 for two **10** two at a time

ad extremum 6 at last **7** finally **12** to the extreme

ad fin 8 at the end **12** toward the end

adhere 3 fix **4** glue, hold, keep **5** cling, paste, stick **6** be true, cement, cleave, fasten, glue on, keep to **7** abide by, be loyal, stand by **8** maintain **9** stick fast **10** be constant, be faithful

adherence 7 fealty **8** loyalty **9** adhesion, devotion, fidelity **9** constancy, keeping to, obedience **10** allegiance, attachment, observance, stickiness **12** adhesiveness, faithfulness

adherent 3 fan **4** ally **5** gummy, pupil **6** sticky, viscid **7** acolyte, devotee, viscous **8** adhering, adhesive, advocate, champion, clinging, disciple, follower, partisan, sticking, upholder **9** supporter

adhesion 9 adherence **10** attachment, sticking to

adhesive 4 glue **5** epoxy, gummy, paste **6** cement, gummed, mortar, solder, sticky **7** stickum **8** adherent, adhering, clinging, sticking **12** mucilaginous, rubber cement

ad hoc 17 with respect to this **18** for this purpose only

ad hominem 8 to the man **17** against an opponent **20** appealing to prejudice

adieu 4 by-by, ciao, ta-ta **5** adios,

aloha **6** bye-bye, goodby, so long **7** a demain, cheerio, goodbye, good day **8** a bientot, au revoir, farewell, godspeed, toodle-oo **10** take it easy **11** leavetaking, see you later, valediction **14** Auf Wiedersehen

ad infinitum 9 endlessly **10** infinitely, to infinity, unendingly **11** boundlessly, ceaselessly, limitlessly, unceasingly **12** continuously, interminably, without limit

ad initium 14 at the beginning

ad interim 13 in the meantime

adios 4 by-by, ciao, ta-ta **5** adieu, aloha **6** bye-bye, goodby, so long **7** a demain, cheerio, goodbye, good day **8** a bientot, au revoir, farewell, godspeed, toodle-oo **10** take it easy **11** leavetaking, see you later, valediction **14** Auf Wiedersehen

adjacent 6 beside, next to **7** abutting, touching **9** bordering, proximate **10** contiguous, juxtaposed, next door to, tangential **12** conterminous

adjoining 6 joined **7** joining **8** nextdoor, touching **9** connected **10** contiguous **14** interconnected

adjourn 3 end **4** move **5** close **6** put off, recess, remove, repair **7** dismiss, suspend **8** break off, dissolve, postpone, withdraw **9** depart for, interrupt **11** discontinue

adjournment 6 recess **7** removal **8** abeyance **9** dismissal **10** suspension **12** postponement

adjudge 4 deem, rule **5** judge **6** decide, decree, ordain, rule on, settle, umpire **7** referee **8** consider **9** arbitrate, determine, pronounce **10** adjudicate

adjudicate 4 rule **5** judge **6** settle **7** adjudge **9** arbitrate

adjunct 9 accessory, auxiliary, secondary **10** complement, incidental, subsidiary, supplement **12** appurtenance

adjuration 4 oath, plea, suit **6** appeal **8** advising, entreaty **12** supplication

adjure 3 beg **5** plead **6** charge, enjoin, exhort **7** beseech, command, entreat, implore, solicit **8** appeal to, petition **9** importune **10** supplicate

adjust 3 fix, set **4** move **5** adapt, alter, order, reset **6** attune, change, modify **7** conform **8** accustom, regulate **9** acclimate, reconcile **11** accommodate

adjustable 7 movable **9** adaptable, alterable **11** rectifiable, regulatable **12** controllable

adjusting 8 adapting, altering **9** modifying **10** regulating **11** acclimating, controlling

adjusting device 5 lever, tuner, valve **6** handle **7** adapter **8** governor **9** modulator, regulator **11** control knob

adjustment 6 fixing **7** control, setting **8** adapting, focusing **9** adjusting, alignment, regulator **10** alteration, regulating, regulation, settlement, settling in **11** acclimation, orientation **12** modification **13** justification, rectification, straightening **14** reconciliation

adjutant 3 ADC **4** aide **9** assistant, right hand **10** aide-de-camp **12** righthand man

ad-lib 6 make up **9** improvise **11** extemporize **13** improvisation **14** speak impromptu **15** speak off the cuff **21** speak extemporaneously **23** extemporaneous wisecrack

ad loc, ad locum 10 at the place, to the place

ad majorem Dei gloriam 23 for the greater glory of God

Admete
  father: 10 Eurystheus
  received: 12 golden girdle
    belonged to: 4 Ares
    received from: 8 Hercules
    stolen from: 9 Hippolyte

Admeto, Re di Tessaglia
  also: 21 Admetus King of Thessaly
  opera by: 6 Handel

Admetus
  king of: 8 Thessaly
  member of: 9 Argonauts
  father: 6 Pheres
  wife: 8 Alcestis

administer 3 run **4** boss, give **5** apply **6** direct, govern, manage, tender **7** oversee **8** dispense **9** supervise **11** preside over, superintend **12** administrate

administering 7 bossing, running, tending **8** managing **9** directing, executing **10** dispensing, governance, overseeing **11** carrying out, supervising, supervision **14** administration, superintending

administration 5 brass **8** officers **9** execution, governing, tendering **10** executives, government, leadership, management, overseeing **11** application **12** dispensation, distribution **13** administering, governing body **15** superintendence

administrative 9 executive **10** management, managerial **11** supervisory **14** organizational

administrative head 3 CEO **7** manager **8** chairman, director **9** executive, president **10** supervisor **13** administrator **14** superintendent

admirable 6 worthy **8** laudable **9** estimable, venerable **11** commendable **12** praiseworthy

Admirable Crichton, The
  author: 12 James M Barrie

admiration 5 honor **6** esteem, praise **7** respect **8** approval **10** high regard, veneration **11** high opinion **12** commendation

admire 5 prize, value **6** esteem, praise **7** respect

admirer 3 fan **5** swain **6** suitor, votary **7** acolyte, devotee, groupie **8** adherent, advocate, champion, disciple, follower, partisan **9** attendant **10** aficionado

admissible 7 allowed **8** passable **9** allowable, permitted, tolerable, tolerated **10** acceptable, admittable, legitimate **11** permissible

admission 3 fee **5** entry **6** access, assent, charge, entree, tariff, ticket **8** entrance **10** admittance, concession, confession, profession **11** affirmation, declaration, entrance fee **14** acknowledgment

admit 3 let **5** allow, grant, let in, own up **6** induct, invest, permit **7** appoint, concede, confess, declare, profess, receive, welcome **8** let enter **11** acknowledge

admittable 7 allowed **9** allowable, permitted, tolerable, tolerated **10** acceptable, admissible **11** permissible

admittance 5 entry **6** access, entree **7** ingress **8** entrance **9** admission

admixture 4 mess, olio **5** blend **6** jumble, medley **7** amalgam, melange, mixture **8** compound, mishmash **9** composite, confusion, potpourri **10** commixture, hodgepodge, salmagundi **11** combination, commingling, gallimaufry **12** amalgamation, intermixture **13** intermingling **14** conglomeration

admonish 4 warn **5** chide, scold **6** advise, enjoin, rebuke, tip off **7** caution, censure, chasten, counsel, reprove, upbraid **8** reproach **9** criticize, reprimand **10** put on guard, take to task **11** remonstrate **13** call to account **16** rap on the knuckles

admonition 6 advice, rebuke **7** chiding, warning **8** reproach, scolding **9** reprimand **11** mild reproof **12** remonstrance **16** rap on the knuckles

Adnah
  deserted from: 4 Saul
  deserted to: 5 David
  fought against: 10 Amalekites
  commander for: 10 Jehosaphat

ado 4 fuss, stir, to-do **5** furor **6** bother, bustle, flurry, fracas, furore, hubbub, pother, racket, tumult, uproar **7** flutter, trouble, turmoil **9** agitation, commotion, confusion **10** hurlyburly

adobe 3 mud **4** clay, silt, tile **5** brick, marly **6** earthy **7** clayish **13** sun-dried brick

adolescence 5 teens, youth **7** puberty **10** pubescence

adolescent 3 lad **4** lass, teen **5** minor, youth **6** boyish, callow, lassie **7** babyish, girlish, puerile **8** childish, immature, juvenile, teenager, young man, youthful **9** fledgling, pubescent, schoolboy, stripling, young teen **10**

schoolgirl, sophomoric, young woman **11** undeveloped

Adolf Hitler 9 der Fuhrer **10** der Fuehrer

Adonai 3 God **6** my Lord

Adonijah
  father: 5 David
  mother: 7 Haggith
  brother: 5 Amnon **7** Absalom, Chileab
  executed by: 7 Solomon
  conspired to overthrow: 5 David

Adonis
  represents: 15 vegetation cycle
  father: 7 Cinyras
  mother: 6 Myrrha, Smyrna
  favorite of: 9 Aphrodite
  killed by: 4 boar
  festival in honor of: 6 Adonia

adopt 3 use **4** take **6** accept, affect, assume, choose, employ, follow, take up **7** approve, embrace, espouse, utilize **9** conform to **11** acknowledge, appropriate

adorable 4 cute **6** divine **7** darling, likable, lovable, winsome **8** charming, engaging, fetching, pleasing, precious **9** appealing **10** delightful **11** captivating **12** irresistible

adoration 5 honor **7** worship **8** devotion **9** adulation, reverence **10** exaltation, veneration, worshiping **11** idolization **13** glorification, magnification

adore 4 like, love **5** exalt, fancy, prize **6** admire, dote on, revere **7** cherish, glorify, idolize, worship **8** hold dear, venerate

adorer 3 fan **5** lover **7** admirer **8** follower **9** worshiper

adorn 5 array **6** bedeck **7** bejewel, deck out, furbish **8** beautify, decorate, ornament **9** embellish

adornment 6 attire, finery **7** jewelry **8** ornament **10** decoration **13** embellishment, ornamentation

ad patres 4 dead

Adrammelech 13 Sepharvite god
  father: 11 Sennacherib
  killed: 11 Sennacherib

Adrastea
  also: 7 Nemesis
  origin: 5 Greek
  goddess of: 17 divine retribution
  father: 9 Melisseus
  reared: 4 Zeus
  entrusted by: 4 Rhea

Adrastus
  also: 8 Adrastos
  king of: 5 Argos
  son: 8 Aegialus
  leader of: 18 Seven against Thebes
  companions: 6 Tydeus **8** Capaneus **9** Polynices **10** Amphiaraus, Hippomedon **13** Parthenopaeus
  horse: 5 Arion

ad rem 9 pertinent 15 straightforward 17 without digression

Adrian, Edgar Douglas
field: 8 medicine 10 physiology
nationality: 7 British
discovered function of: 10 nerve cells
awarded: 10 Nobel Prize

Adriana
character in: 17 The Comedy of Errors
author: 11 Shakespeare

adrift 4 lost 5 at sea 6 afloat, aweigh 8 confused, drifting, unmoored, unstable 9 perplexed, uncertain, unsettled 10 bewildered, irresolute, unanchored

adroit 3 apt 4 deft 5 slick 6 artful, clever, expert, facile, nimble 7 cunning, skilled 8 skillful 9 dexterous, masterful 10 proficient

adroitness 7 aptness 8 deftness, facility 9 dexterity, handiness 10 cleverness 11 proficiency 12 skillfulness
French: 11 savoir-faire

adulation 7 fawning 8 flattery 9 adoration 11 fulsomeness 13 fulsome praise

adulatory 7 fulsome 8 admiring 10 flattering 13 complimentary

adult 3 big, man 5 elder, of age, woman 6 father, granny, mature, mother, parent, senior, x-rated 7 grandma, grandpa, grownup, oldster 8 seasoned 9 developed, full-grown 11 experienced, grandfather, grandmother 13 senior citizen

adulterate 3 cut 4 thin 5 water 6 dilute 9 water down 10 depreciate 11 contaminate

adulterated 3 cut 6 impure, watery 7 debased, diluted, thinned, watered 8 doctored, weakened 11 watered down

adultery 3 sin 9 carnality, cuckoldry 10 unchastity 11 fornication, promiscuity 14 unfaithfulness 17 marital infidelity 18 illicit intercourse 21 extramarital relations

adulthood 8 maturity, ripeness 10 full growth 11 age of reason

adumbrate 3 dim 6 darken, sketch 7 obscure, outline 8 intimate 9 prefigure 10 foreshadow, overshadow

adumbrated 3 dim 5 murky 7 shadowy 8 darkened 9 intimated 10 indistinct, prefigured 12 foreshadowed, overshadowed

advance 3 pre 4 gain, lend, loan, pass, step 5 add to, offer, prior 6 assign, binder, growth, move up, pay now, propel, send up 7 bring up, forward, further, improve, in front, lay down, press on, proffer, promote, upgrade, up front 8 foremost, increase, multiply, overture, previous, progress 9 go forward, promotion 10 furthering, move onward, prepayment, put up

front 11 advancement, down payment, improvement, preliminary, proposition 12 breakthrough, bring forward, pay on account

advanced·7 extreme, far gone, radical 10 avant-garde 12 farther along, further along 14 industrialized

advanced in years 3 old 4 aged 5 hoary, older 7 ancient, antique, elderly 8 outmoded 9 senescent, venerable 10 antiquated, gray-haired

advancement 4 rise 5 boost 9 bettering, elevation, promotion 10 betterment, forwarding 11 improvement, progression

Advancement of Learning
author: 12 Francis Bacon

advance slowly 4 inch 5 crawl, creep

advantage 3 aid 4 boon, edge, help 5 asset, clout 6 profit 7 benefit, comfort, service, success, support 8 blessing 9 dominance, upper hand 10 precedence 11 convenience, superiority

advantageous 6 useful 7 helpful 8 enviable, superior, valuable 9 favorable, fortunate 10 auspicious, beneficial, dominating, profitable

advent 5 onset, start 6 coming 7 arrival 9 appearing, beginning, emergence, opening up 10 appearance, occurrence 12 commencement

adventitious 5 alien 6 exotic 7 foreign, strange 9 adventive, extrinsic 10 accidental

adventure 5 geste, quest 7 emprise, venture 8 escapade 10 enterprise 11 undertaking

adventurer 4 hero 7 heroine, upstart 8 romantic, vagabond 9 buccaneer, daredevil 11 giant-killer 12 dragon-slayer, swashbuckler 16 soldier of fortune

Adventures of Robin Hood, The
director: 13 Michael Curtiz 15 William Keighley
cast: 8 Alan Hale (Little John) 10 Errol Flynn (Robin Hood) 11 Claude Rains (Prince John) 13 Basil Rathbone 17 Olivia de Havilland (Lady Marion)
Oscar for: 5 score (Erich Wolfgang Korngold)

Adventures of Sherlock Holmes
author: 16 (Sir) Arthur Conan Doyle
character: 9 Mrs Hudson 10 Irene Adler 12 Dr John Watson 13 Mycroft Holmes 14 Sherlock Holmes 17 Inspector Lestrade, Professor Moriarty 21 Baker Street Irregulars

adventuresome 4 bold 6 daring 9 audacious, daredevil 11 adventurous

adventurous 4 bold 5 brave, risky 6 daring 7 valiant 8 intrepid, perilous 9 audacious, dangerous, hazardous 10

courageous 11 challenging, venturesome

ad verbum 8 verbatim 9 to the word

adversary 3 foe 5 enemy, rival 8 opponent 10 antagonist, competitor

adverse 3 ill 4 evil 7 harmful, hostile 8 contrary, inimical, negative, opposing 9 difficult, injurious 10 pernicious, unfriendly 11 detrimental, unfavorable 12 antagonistic, unpropitious

adversity 3 woe 4 ills 5 trial 6 mishap 7 bad luck, trouble 8 calamity, disaster, distress, hardship 9 suffering 10 affliction, ill-fortune, misfortune 11 catastrophe, tribulation

advertise 4 show, tout 5 vaunt 6 reveal 7 display 8 proclaim 9 broadcast, publicize 11 noise abroad

advertisement 4 spot 5 blurb, flier, pitch, promo 6 notice, poster, want ad 7 leaflet, placard, trailer 8 circular, handbill 9 billboard, broadside, throwaway 10 commercial 12 announcement, classified ad, public notice

advice 4 news, view, word 6 report 7 account, counsel, message, opinion, tidings 8 guidance 10 advisement, suggestion 11 information 12 intelligence, notification 13 communication 14 recommendation

advisable 3 fit 4 best, wise 5 smart, sound 6 proper, seemly 7 fitting, prudent 8 a good bet, suitable 9 expedient, judicious 13 recommendable

advise 4 tell, urge, warn 6 enjoin, exhort, inform, notify, report 7 apprise, caution, commend, counsel, suggest 8 admonish 9 encourage, make known, recommend, suggest to 10 give notice 11 communicate

advise against 5 deter 8 dissuade 10 discourage, disincline

advisement 5 study 7 thought 12 deliberation 13 consideration

adviser, advisor 4 aide 5 coach, guide, tutor 6 egeria, mentor, nestor 7 monitor, teacher 8 Dear Abby, director 9 admonitor, assistant, counselor, preceptor, surrogate 10 Ann Landers, consultant, idea person, instructor

advisory 7 caution, guiding, warning 10 admonitory, cautionary, counseling 11 informative, instructive 12 consultative, consultatory 13 informational

advisory board 7 cabinet, council 8 ministry

advocaat
type: 7 liqueur
origin: 7 Holland

advocacy 4 egis 5 aegis 7 backing, defense, support 8 auspices, espousal 9 patronage, promotion 10 furthering, supporting 11 advancement, endorsement, pressing for, propagation, sponsorship **12** championship **14** campaigning for, recommendation

advocate 4 back, urge **5** favor **6** advise, backer, lawyer, patron **7** advance, apostle, counsel, endorse, espouse, further, pleader, promote, propose, push for, support **8** argue for, attorney, believer, champion, defender, press for, promoter, upholder **9** apologist, barrister, counselor, encourage, prescribe, propagate, proponent, recommend, solicitor, spokesman, supporter **10** mouthpiece, stand up for **11** campaign for, speak out for **12** legal adviser, propagandist, spokesperson **13** attorney-at-law

advocatus diaboli 14 devil's advocate

adz or **adze 2** ax **3** axe **5** addis **7** hatchet

Aeacus
  descendants of: 8 Aeacides
  form: 5 judge
  habitat: 5 Hades
  father: 4 Zeus
  mother: 6 Aegina
  brother: 12 Rhadamanthys
  wife: 6 Endeis
  son: 6 Peleus, Phocus **7** Telamon
  grandson: 8 Achilles

Aeetes
  king of: 7 Colchis
  custodian of: 12 Golden Fleece
  father: 6 Helios
  mother: 5 Perse
  sister: 5 Circe **8** Pasiphae
  wife: 5 Idyia **9** Asterodea
  son: 8 Absyrtus, Apsyrtus
  daughter: 5 Medea **9** Chalciope

Aegaeon see **8** Briareus

Aegean Sea
  branch of: 13 Mediterranean
  islands: 5 Chios, Crete, Samos **6** Euboea, Lesbos, Rhodes **8** Cyclades **10** Dodecanese **16** Northern Sporades
  rivers into: 6 Struma, Vardar **7** Maritsa **8** Menderes
  surrounding countries: 6 Greece, Turkey

Aegeon
  character in: 17 The Comedy of Errors
  author: 11 Shakespeare

Aegeria see **6** Egeria

Aegesta see **6** Egesta

Aegeus
  king of: 6 Athens
  son: 6 Medeus **7** Theseus

Aegimius
  king of: 5 Doris **7** Dorians
  father: 5 Dorus
  son: 5 Dymas **9** Pamphylus

Aeginaea
  epithet of: 7 Artemis
  means: 11 goat goddess

Aegir
  origin: 6 Nordic

form: 5 giant
  god of: 3 sea
  wife: 3 Ran

aegis 4 wing **5** favor, guard **6** surety **7** backing, shelter, support **8** advocacy, auspices, guaranty **9** patronage **10** protection **11** sponsorship **12** championship, guardianship

Aegis
  form: 6 shield
  shield of: 4 Zeus **6** Athena

Aegisthus
  father: 8 Thyestes
  mother: 7 Pelopia
  cousin: 9 Agamemnon
  daughter: 7 Erigone
  seduced: 12 Clytemnestra
  killed by: 7 Orestes

Aegle
  member of: 8 Heliades **10** Hesperides
  mother of: 6 Graces

Aegyptus
  king of: 5 Egypt
  father: 5 Belus
  twin brother: 6 Danaus
  number of sons: 5 fifty

Aella
  form: 6 Amazon
  gift: 9 swiftness
  killed by: 8 Hercules

Aello
  member of: 7 Harpies

aelurophobia
  fear of: 4 cats

Aemilia
  character in: 17 The Comedy of Errors
  author: 11 Shakespeare

Aeneas
  hero of: 4 Troy
  father: 8 Anchises
  mother: 5 Venus
  grandfather: 5 Capys
  son: 5 Iulus **7** Silvius **8** Ascanius
  ancestor of: 6 Romans

Aeneas Silvius
  king of: 9 Alba Longa

Aeneid
  author: 6 Virgil
  character: 4 Gyas **5** Amata, Dares, Nisus **6** Arruns, Iarbas, Lausus, Pallas, Salius, Turnus **7** Acestes, Allecto, Camilla, Celaeno, Drances, Evander, Harpies, Helenus, Juturna, Latinus, Lavinia, Tarchon, Trojans, Venulus, Virbius **8** Ascanius, Entellus, Euryalus, Messapus **9** Cloanthus, Mezentius, Mnestheus, Palinurus, Sergestus **10** Andromache **12** Cumaean Sibyl
    gods: 4 Juno **5** Diana, Venus **6** Vulcan **7** Jupiter, Neptune
    Queen of Carthage: 4 Dido
    Aeneas' father: 8 Anchises
    Aeneas' mother: 9 Aphrodite
    Aeneas' wife: 6 Creusa
    Aeneas' son: 5 Iulus

Aeneas meets in underworld: 6 Charon **8** Cerberus **9** Palinurus
  parts of the underworld: 7 Elysium **8** Tartarus **9** Ivory Gate
    river: 4 Styx **5** Lethe
  Aeneas plucks: 11 Golden Bough
  Aeneas visits: 5 Crete, Delos **6** Latium, Sicily, Thrace **8** Carthage

Aeolus
  other name: 5 Eolis
  ruler of: 5 winds
  founder of: 8 Aeolians
  father: 6 Hellen
  mother: 6 Orseis
  brother: 5 Dorus **6** Xuthus
  wife: 7 Enarete
  son: 5 Deion **6** Magnes **7** Athamas, Misenus **8** Cretheus, Macareus, Perieres, Sisyphus **9** Salmoneus
  daughter: 6 Calyce, Canace **7** Alcyone **8** Cleobule, Perimede, Pisidice

aerate 3 air **9** ventilate **10** mix with air **11** expose to air

aerial 3 air **4** airy **5** by air, lofty **6** dreamy, flying, unreal **7** antenna, elusive, soaring, tenuous **8** airborne, ethereal, fanciful, in the air **9** ephemeral, imaginary, visionary **10** by aircraft, from the air, of aircraft **11** atmospheric, impractical, wind-created **13** unsubstantial **15** capable of flight

aerobatic group 10 Blue Angels

aeronautics 6 flight, flying **8** aviation

Aerope
  father: 7 Catreus, Cerheus
  husband: 6 Atreus **10** Plisthenes
  sister: 9 Clymene
  son: 8 Menelaus **9** Agamemnon

aerophobia
  fear of: 6 flying

aeroplane 5 plane **8** aircraft, airplane

Aeschylus
  author of: 8 Oresteia **9** Agamemnon, Choephori (The Libation-bearers), Eumenides **11** The Persians **13** The Suppliants **15** Prometheus Bound **16** The House of Atreus **18** Seven Against Thebes

Aesculapius
  origin: 5 Roman
  god of: 7 healing **8** medicine
  corresponds to: 9 Asclepius

Aesir
  also: 4 Asar
  means: 9 chief gods
  origin: 12 Scandinavian
  leader: 4 Odin **5** Othin
  home: 6 Asgard
  conflicting with: 5 Vanir

aesthetic see **8** Esthetic

Aethalides
  member of: 9 Argonauts
  father: 6 Hermes
  trait: 6 memory

Aether
  origin: 5 Greek
  personifies: 3 air, sky

Aethra
  father: 8 Pittheus
  son: 7 Theseus
Aethylla
  brother: 5 Priam
Afars and the Issas *see* **8** Djibouti
affability 9 geniality **10** amiability,
  cordiality **11** sociability **12** friendliness, pleasantness **13** compatibility
affable 4 open, warm **5** civil **6** genial
  7 amiable, cordial **8** friendly, gracious, mannerly, pleasant, sociable **9**
  agreeable, congenial, courteous, easygoing **10** compatible **11** good-
  humored, good-natured
affair 5 amour, event, party **6** effort,
  matter **7** concern, episode, liaison,
  pursuit, romance, shindig **8** activity,
  business, function, incident, interest,
  intrigue, occasion **9** adventure, festivity, happening, operation **10** love affair, occurrence, proceeding **11** celebration, transaction, undertaking **12**
  circumstance, relationship **14** social
  function **15** social gathering
affaire d'honneur 4 duel **13** affair of
  honor
affect 4 fake, move, stir **5** act on,
  adopt, alter, fancy, feign, put on,
  touch **6** assume, change, modify, regard **7** embrace, concern, imitate, impress **8** interest, relate to, simulate **9**
  impinge on, influence, pertain to, pretend to **10** tend toward **11** counterfeit
affectation 4 airs, sham **5** put-on **6**
  facade **8** false air, pretense **10** pretension **11** insincerity **13** artificiality,
  false mannerism
affected 4 vain **5** moved, phony,
  sorry, upset **6** harmed, la-di-da, unreal **7** assumed, changed, grieved, injured, pompous, stirred, studied,
  touched **8** impaired, mannered, troubled **9** acted upon, afflicted, concerned, conceited, contrived, impressed, pertinent, sorrowful,
  unnatural **10** artificial, distressed, influenced, interested, not genuine **11**
  pretentious **12** vainglorious
affectedness 4 airs **7** hauteur, tension
  9 formality **10** constraint **11** haughtiness, pretensions **12** affectations **15**
  pretentiousness
affection 4 love **6** liking, malady,
  warmth **7** ailment, disease, illness **8**
  disorder, fondness, sickness **10** proclivity, tenderness
affectionate 4 fond, warm **6** ardent,
  caring, doting, loving, tender **10**
  lovey-dovey **11** warmhearted **13** demonstrative, tenderhearted
affectionate term 3 hon **4** dear
  5 cheri, honey, sugar **7** pet name,
  sweetie, darling, dearest **8** nickname
  9 sobriquet **10** endearment
Affery

character in: 12 Little Dorrit
  author: 7 Dickens
affettuoso
  music: 8 tenderly
affiance 6 engage, pledge **7** betroth **13**
  engage to marry **15** solemnly promise
affiancing 5 troth **8** pledging **9** betrothal **10** engagement
affiche 6 poster **12** public notice
affidavit 4 oath **8** document **11** affirmation **14** sworn statement
affiliate 3 arm **4** ally, join, part **5**
  merge, unite **6** branch **7** chapter, connect, consort **8** division **9** associate,
  colleague **10** amalgamate, fraternize
  11 incorporate, subdivision **12** band
  together
affiliated 6 allied, joined, united **9**
  connected **10** associated **12** incorporated
affiliation 5 union **8** alliance **10** connection **11** association **12** relationship
affinity 4 bent **5** fancy **6** liking **7** leaning, rapport **8** fondness, homology,
  likeness, penchant, relation, sympathy, tendency **10** connection, partiality, proclivity, propensity, similarity
  11 inclination, parallelism **13** compatibility
affirm 4 aver, avow, hold **5** claim **6** allege, assert, ratify, uphold **7** approve,
  confirm, contend, declare, endorse,
  profess, support, sustain, warrant **8**
  maintain, proclaim, validate
affirmation 6 avowal **7** consent **8** approval **11** declaration, endorsement
  12 confirmation, ratification **13** certification
affirmative 3 yes **8** emphatic, positive
  9 affirming, approving, assenting, rati-
  fying **10** conclusive, concurring, confirming **11** affirmatory, categorical **12**
  confirmatory **13** corroborative
affix 3 fix, tag **4** glue, seal **5** add on,
  paste, put on, set to, stick **6** attach,
  fasten, tack on
afflict 5 beset **6** plague **7** oppress, torment **8** distress
afflicted 6 cursed **7** plagued **8** affected, troubled **9** tormented **10** distressed
affliction 4 pain **5** curse, trial **6** misery, ordeal **7** anguish, torment, trouble **8** calamity, distress, hardship **9**
  adversity **10** misfortune, oppression
  11 tribulation **12** wretchedness
affluence 5 money **6** plenty, riches,
  wealth **7** success **10** prosperity **14**
  prosperousness, successfulness
affluent 4 rich **6** loaded **7** moneyed,
  wealthy, well-off **8** well-to-do **9** well-
  fixed **10** prosperous, well-heeled
afford 4 bear, give, lend, risk **5** grant,
  offer, yield **6** chance, impart, manage,
  supply **7** command, furnish, provide,
  support, sustain

affray 4 fray **5** brawl, melee **6** fracas **7**
  contest, scuffle **8** conflict **9** encounter
  11 altercation
affright 4 fear **5** alarm, dread, panic,
  scare **6** dismay, fright, horror, terror **8**
  frighten
affront 4 slur **5** abuse, wrong **6** injury,
  insult, offend, slight **7** offense, outrage, provoke, put-down **8** disgrace,
  dishonor, ignominy, rudeness **9** indignity, insolence **11** discourtesy, humiliation **12** ill-treatment, impertinence
  13 mortification **16** contemptuousness
afghan 5 shawl, throw **7** blanket **8**
  covering, coverlet
Afghanistan
  other name: 6 Ariana, Aryana
  capital/largest city: 5 Kabul
  others: 3 Rui **4** Jurm, Nani, Wama **5**
  Asmar, Balkh, Doshi, Farah, Herat,
  Kunar, Makur, Maruf, Matun, Pahra,
  Tagab, Tulak, Urgan **6** Chaman,
  Gardez, Ghazni, Haibak, Kunduz,
  Nauzad, Panjao, Rustak, Sangan,
  Sarobi, Tukzar, Washir **7** Andkhui,
  Baghlan, Bamiyan, Dilaram, Ghurian,
  Girishk **8** Charikar, Faizabad, Kanda-
  har **9** Jalalabad **10** Daulatabad, Pul-i-
  Khumri, Shibarghan **12** Mazar-i-
  Sharif
  government:
    parliament: 10 Loya-Jirgah
    radical group: 7 Taliban
  leader: 4 amir, emir **5** ameer, emeer
    6 sharif, sherif
  measure: 3 paw, sir **5** jerib, karoh **6**
    khurds **7** kharwar
  monetary unit: 3 pul **5** abaze, riyal,
    rupee **6** abbasi, amania **7** afghani
  weight: 3 pau, paw, ser, sir
  lake: 13 Hamud-i-Helmand
  mountain: 3 Koh **5** Safeo **6** Chagai,
    Pamirs **7** Nowshak **8** Koh-i-Baba,
    Safed Koh, Sulaiman **9** Himalayas,
    Hindu Kush **11** Khwaja Amran,
    Paropamisus
  highest point: 9 Istoro Nal
  river: 4 Lora, Oxus **5** Cabul, Indus,
    Kabul, Kunar **6** Kokcha, Kunduz **7**
    Hari Rud, Helmand, Murghab, Mur-
    ghab, Taleqan **8** Amu Darya, Farah
    Rud, Harut Rud, Khash Rud **9** Arg-
    handab
  sea: 5 Darya
  physical feature:
    desert: 8 Registan
    panhandle: 6 Wakhan
    pass: 6 Khyber
    wind: 9 Afghanets
  people: 5 Aimak, Aymak, Kafir, Nuris
    6 Baloch, Baluch, Chahar, Durani,
    Hasara, Hazara, Kaffir, Kirgiz, Pa-
    than, Tajiks, Uzbeks **7** Beluchi,
    Belucki, Ghilzai, Pakhton, Pakhtun,
    Pashtun, Pukhtun, Pushtun, Sistani,
    Taimani, Taimuri **8** Jamshidi, Siah
    Push **9** Firuzkuhi, Safed Push, Safid
    Push

dynasty: 8 Barakzai
leader: 5 Najib 7 Mohmand 10 Najibullah 12 Babrak Karmal 14 Hafizullah Amin 17 Mohammad Zahir Shah, Mohammed Daoud Khan 18 Burhanuddin Rabbani Noor Mohammed Taraki
language: 4 Dari 5 Farsi 6 Afghan, Pashto, Pushtu 7 Balochi, Baluchi, Persian
religion: 5 Islam
place:
  dam: 6 Boghra 7 Kajakai 9 Arghandab
feature:
  clothing: 7 chaderi
  coat: 6 chapan
  dance: 5 attan
  game: 8 buz-kashi
  guest room: 5 hujra
  hat: 7 karakul
  head-cloth: 7 chawdar
  house with tower: 4 qala
  medicinal plant: 9 asafetida
  wrestling: 6 ghosai
food:
  potluck meal: 6 sohbat

aficionado 3 fan, nut 5 freak, pupil 7 devotee, pursuer, student 8 disciple

afield 5 amiss 6 abroad, astray 10 off the mark 11 out of the way 16 off the right track

afire 5 fiery 6 ablaze, aflame, alight, ardent, fervid, fuming, on fire 7 blazing, burning, fervent, flaming, flaring, glowing, ignited, smoking, zealous 8 aflicker, in flames, inspired 10 flickering, smoldering

afloat 5 at sea 6 adrift, wafted 7 sailing, wafting 8 drifting, floating

afoot 5 astir 8 underway 10 in the works

a fortiori 10 all the more

afraid 5 sorry 6 scared 7 alarmed, anxious, chicken, fearful, panicky, unhappy 8 cowardly, timorous 9 regretful, terrified 10 apologetic, frightened 11 lily-livered 12 apprehensive, disappointed, fainthearted 13 anxiety-ridden, panic-stricken 14 chickenhearted, chicken-livered, terror-stricken

Afreet
  also: 5 Afrit
  origin: 7 Arabian
  form: 5 demon

afresh 4 anew 5 again 11 from scratch 16 from the beginning
  Latin: 6 de novo

Africa
  country: 4 Chad, Mali, Togo 5 Benin, Congo, Egypt, Gabon, Ghana, Kenya, Libya, Niger, Sudan, Zaire 6 Angola, Gambia, Guinea, Malawi, Rwanda, Uganda, Zambia 7 Algeria, Burundi, Comoros, Eritrea, Lesotho, Liberia, Morocco, Namibia, Nigeria, Reunion, Senegal, Somalia, Tunisia 8 Botswana, Cameroon, Djibouti, Ethiopia, Tanzania, Zimbabwe 9 Cape Verde, The Gambia, Mauritius, Swaziland 10 Ivory Coast, Madagascar, Mauritania, Mozambique, Seychelles 11 Burkina Faso, Sierra Leone, South Africa 12 Guinea-Bissau 13 Canary Islands, Western Sahara 15 South-West Africa 16 Equatorial Guinea 18 Sao Tome and Principe 22 Central African Republic
  people: 2 Ga 3 Ibo, Kru, Luo, San, Tiv, Yao 4 Arab, Beja, Bobo, Boer, Fang, Hutu, Kota, Kuba, Luba, Nuba, Nuer, Nupe, Teda, Tibu, Zulu 5 Bemba, Dinka, Galla, Hausa, Kamba, Makua, Masai, Mende, Mongo, Negro, Pygmy, Rundi, Serer, Shona, Sotho, Swazi, Temne, Tigre, Tutsi, Wolof, Xhosa 6 Bateke, Berber, Fulani, Herero, Ibibjo, Kikuyu, Mau Mau, Nubian, Ovambo, Rwanda, Senufo, Sidamo, Somali, Tswana, Tuareg, Yoruba, Watusi 7 Ashanti, Baganda, Bambara, Bushmen, Chaamba, Makonde, Mashoma, Ndebele, Nilotic, Oshogbo, Songhai, Turkana 8 Khoikhoi, Mangbetu, Matabele 9 Africaner, Afrikaner, Hottentot
  desert: 5 Namib 6 Sahara 8 Kalahari
  island: 5 Bioko, Pemba 6 Canary 7 Comoros, Madeira, Mayotte, Reunion 8 St Helena, Zanzibar 9 Ascension, Cape Verde, Mauritius 10 Madagascar, Seychelles
  ancient people/empire: 3 Oyo 4 Kush, Mali, Toro 5 Aksum, Benin, Ghana, Kongo, Mossi, Nubia, Wadai 6 Ankole, Tekrur 7 Ashanti, Buganda, Bunyoro, Dahomey, Songhai 8 Baguirmi, Carthage 10 Kanem-Bornu, Monomotapa 11 Ife and Benin
  ancient city: 5 Kilwa, Meroe 8 Timbuktu
  language: 4 Afar, Peul, Teda 5 Bantu, Bemba, Click, Hausa, Masai, Wolof 6 Arabic, Berber, French, Kanuri, Tsonga 7 Amharic, Khoisan, Lingala, Nilotic, Songhai, Swahili, Turkana 8 Cushitic, Mandingo 9 Afrikaans
  river: 4 Juba, Nile, Sudd 5 Congo, Kasai, Niger 6 Kwango, Orange, Ubangi 7 Senegal, Zambezi 8 Blue Nile 9 White Nile
  lake: 4 Chad, Kivu, Tana 5 Assal, Nyasa 6 Albert, Edward, Kariba, Malawi, Nassar, Red Sea, Rudolf 8 Victoria 10 Tanganyika 12 Chott Melrhir
  falls: 8 Victoria
  mountain/mountain range: 3 Air 4 Bihu, Meru 5 Atlas, Elgon, Kenya 6 Hoggar 7 Ahaggar, Crystal, Tibesti, Toubkal 8 Cameroon 9 Emi Koussi, Munchinga, Ruwenzori 10 Futa Jallon 11 Drakensberg, Kilimanjaro 13 Tibesti Massif
  lowest point: 17 Qattari Depression
  mineral/natural resource: 3 oil, tin 4 gold 5 ivory 6 cloves, copper, rubber 7 diamond, palm oil, uranium
  disease: 4 AIDS 5 Ebola 7 malaria 9 bilharzia 11 yellow fever 16 sleeping sickness
  homeland: 5 Venda 6 Ciskei 8 Transkei 14 Bophuthatswana
  game reserve: 5 Tsavo 6 Kruger 8 Amboseli 9 Serengeti
  tree: 4 cork, teak 5 cedar, ebony, olive 6 acacia, baobab, okoume, rubber 7 juniper, oil palm 8 date palm, mahogany, tamarisk 10 silk-cotton
  animal: 4 lion 5 bongo, hippo, hyena, zebra 6 jackal, monkey 7 buffalo, cheetah, giraffe, gorilla, leopard, wild pig 8 aardvark, antelope, elephant 9 crocodile 10 chimpanzee, rhinoceros 11 wildebeeste 12 hippopotamus
  bird: 5 heron, stork 6 falcon 7 bustard, ostrich, pelican 8 flamingo, hornbill 10 kingfisher
  fly: 6 tsetse
  snake: 5 cobra, mamba 6 python

Africaine, L'
  also: 14 The African Girl
  opera by: 9 Meyerbeer

African Queen, The
  director: 10 John Huston
  cast: 12 Robert Morley 14 Humphrey Bogart 16 Katharine Hepburn
  setting: 5 Congo
  Oscar for: 5 actor (Bogart)

Afrit see 6 Afreet

after 4 next, post 5 later 6 behind 9 afterward, following 10 conclusion, subsequent, succeeding

aftereffect 6 result 11 consequence

After Hours
  director: 14 Martin Scorsese
  cast: 12 Griffin Dunne 15 Rosanna Arquette

Afterlife
  god of: 4 Gwyn

aftermath 6 payoff, result, sequel, upshot 7 outcome 8 follow-up, offshoot 9 byproduct 11 consequence

afterpart 4 back, tail 5 stern 6 far end 7 back end, rear end, tail end 8 backside, hind part 9 posterior

after the fact 4 late 5 tardy 7 belated, delayed, too late 10 behindhand, behind time

After the Fall
  author: 12 Arthur Miller

after this, therefore because of it
  Latin: 21 post hoc ergo propter hoc
  describes: 14 logical fallacy

afterword 4 coda 8 addendum, epilogue 10 conclusion

Agacles
  king of: 9 Myrmidons

Agag
  king of: **10** Amalekites
  captured by: **4** Saul
  killed by: **6** Samuel

again 3 bis **4** also, anew, more **6** encore **7** besides **8** moreover, once more **10** in addition, repetition **11** another time, duplication, furthermore **12** additionally
  Latin: **6** de novo

against 7 adverse, opposed **8** conflict, contrary, opposite **10** opposition **11** unfavorable

against an opponent
  Latin: **9** ad hominem

Against Our Will
  author: **16** Susan Brownmiller

against the property
  Latin: **5** in rem
  describes: **15** legal proceeding

against the thing
  Latin: **5** in rem

Agamemnon
  author: **9** Aeschylus
  mentioned in: **5** Iliad
  king of: **7** Mycenae
  leader of: **6** Greeks
  fought in: **9** Trojan War
  father: **6** Atreus
  brother: **8** Menelaus
  sister: **8** Anaxibia
  wife: **12** Clytemnestra
  daughter: **7** Electra **9** Iphigenia **12** Chrysothemis
  son: **7** Orestes
  cousin: **9** Aegisthus
  captive: **9** Cassandra
  Clytemnestra's lover: **9** Aegisthus
  killed by: **12** Clytemnestra

Aganippe 8 fountain
  location: **6** Greece **7** Helicon
  sacred to: **5** Muses

Aganus
  father: **5** Paris
  mother: **5** Helen

agape 4 agog **6** amazed, gaping **8** wide open **9** awestruck, stupefied **10** astonished, dumbstruck, spellbound **11** dumbfounded **12** wonderstruck **13** flabbergasted

Agassiz, Jean Louis Rodolphe
  field: **7** zoology
  worked on: **7** fossils **8** glaciers **14** classification

agate
  species: **6** quartz
  variety of: **10** chalcedony
  type: **3** eye **4** moss, onyx, ring **9** landscape **13** fortification
  source: **4** Ider **6** Brazil **7** Uruguay **9** Oberstein **14** Rio Grande de Sul

Agathon
  father: **5** Priam

Agathyrsus
  father: **8** Hercules

Agave

father: 6 Cadmus
  mother: **8** Harmonia
  sister: **3** Ino **6** Semele **7** Autonoe
  husband: **6** Echion
  son: **8** Pentheus

age 3 eon, era **4** date **5** epoch, phase, ripen **6** mature, mellow, period, season **7** develop, forever, make old **8** life span, lifetime **9** adulthood, a long time, grow older, seniority **10** generation, millennium **11** stage of life, stage of time
  French: **6** siecle

aged 3 old **4** ripe **6** mature, mellow **7** ancient, as old as, elderly, ripened **8** enduring, grown old **9** developed, full- grown, long-lived

Agee, James
  author of: **10** Agee on Film **17** A Death in the Family **23** Let Us Now Praise Famous Men
  screenwriter for: **15** The African Queen **19** The Night of the Hunter

Agelaus
  mentioned in: **5** Iliad **7** Odyssey
  occupation: **8** herdsman
  father: **8** Hercules, Phradmon
  mother: **7** Omphale
  courted: **8** Penelope
  raised: **5** Paris
  employer: **5** Priam

ageless 7 classic, eternal **8** enduring, timeless

agency 5 force, means, power **6** action, bureau, charge **8** activity **9** influence, mediation, operation **10** department, instrument **12** intervention **15** instrumentality

agenda 6 docket **7** program **8** schedule **9** timetable

agent 4 doer **5** cause, envoy, force, means, mover, power **6** agency, author, deputy, worker **7** vehicle **8** advocate, emissary, executor, operator **9** go-between, performer **10** instrument, negotiator **11** perpetrator **12** intermediary, practitioner **14** representative

Age of Innocence, The
  author: **12** Edith Wharton
  character: **10** May Welland **12** Ellen Olenska **13** Newland Archer

age-old 4 aged **7** ancient, antique, very old **9** venerable

agglomerate 4 clot, mass **5** amass, bunch, clump, rally **6** gather, heap up, muster, pile up **7** cluster, collect **8** assemble, condense, mobilize **10** accumulate, collection **12** accumulation, conglomerate, heap together, lump together **14** conglomeration **15** gather into a mass

agglomeration 4 heap, mass, pile **5** bunch, clump **7** cluster **10** collection **12** accumulation **14** conglomeration

aggrandize 5 bloat, exalt, widen **6** beef up, blow up, dilate, expand, extend, puff up, step up **7** amplify,

broaden, build up, distend, enhance, enlarge, inflate, magnify, stretch **8** escalate, increase **9** intensify **10** strengthen

aggrandizement 8 increase, widening **9** expansion, extension **10** broadening, escalation, exaltation, stepping up **11** enhancement, enlargement **13** amplification, magnification **15** intensification

aggravate 3 vex **4** rile **5** anger, annoy **6** nettle, worsen **7** affront, inflame **8** heighten, increase, irritate **9** intensify, make worse **10** exacerbate, exasperate

aggravating 7 irksome **9** inflaming, vexatious, worsening **10** irritating **11** heightening **12** exacerbating, exasperating, intensifying

aggregate 3 mix **4** mass **5** blend, union **7** mixture **8** amassing, compound **9** composite, gathering, summation **10** collection **11** combination **12** accumulation, conglomerate **14** conglomeration

aggregation 3 mob **4** army, band, bevy, crew, gang, host, mass, pack **5** crowd, horde, swarm **6** throng **7** cluster **9** multitude **10** collection

aggression 4 raid **7** assault, offense **8** act of war, invasion **9** hostility, pugnacity **11** viciousness **12** belligerence **13** combativeness

aggressive 4 bold **5** harsh, pushy **7** dynamic, hostile, intense, vicious, warlike, warring, zealous **8** forceful, militant **9** ambitious, assailant, assertive, attacking, combative, energetic **10** pugnacious **11** belligerent, competitive, contentious, quarrelsome **12** antagonistic, enterprising **15** selfassertive **15** tending to attack

aggressiveness 9 hostility, pugnacity **10** antagonism **12** belligerence **13** combativeness

aggressor 7 invader **8** attacker **9** assailant **11** belligerent **12** antagonistic

aggrieved 3 sad **4** hurt **5** stung **6** abused, pained **7** injured, put upon, tearful, wounded, wronged **8** grieving, mournful, offended, saddened, troubled **9** affronted, disturbed, sorrowful **10** distressed, ill-treated, maltreated, persecuted **11** imposed upon **13** griefstricken

aghast 6 amazed **7** shocked, stunned **8** appalled **9** astounded, horrified, terrified **10** astonished, fear-struck, frightened **12** horror-struck **13** thunderstruck

agile 4 keen, spry **5** alert, fleet, lithe, quick, swift **6** active, clever, limber, nimble, supple **8** athletic, graceful **9** dexterous

agility 8 alacrity, spryness **9** dexterity, quickness, swiftness **10** limberness, nimbleness **12** gracefulness

agitate 3 jar, mix **4** beat, goad, rock,**

stir **5** alarm, churn, shake, upset **6** excite, foment, stir up, work up **7** disturb, provoke, shake up, trouble **8** disquiet

agitated 5 tense **6** uneasy **7** anxious, frantic, nervous, uptight **8** confused, seething **9** disturbed, perturbed, unsettled **10** disquieted, distracted, distraught **11** discomfited, discomposed **12** disconcerted

agitation 7 anxiety **9** confusion **10** discomfort, uneasiness **11** disquietude, distraction, nervousness **12** discomfiture, discomposure, perturbation

agitato
music: **8** agitated

agitator 7 inciter **8** fomentor, inflamer, provoker **9** firebrand **10** incendiary, instigator **11** provocateur **12** rabblerouser, troublemaker **13** mischiefmaker, revolutionary **16** agent provocateur

Aglaia
member of: **6** Graces
father: **7** Jupiter
mother: **8** Eurynome
sister: **6** Thalia **10** Euphrosyne
husband: **4** Abas
son: **7** Proteus **8** Acrisius
daughter: **7** Idomene

aglow 4 warm **5** fiery **6** ablaze, redhot **7** blazing, glowing, radiant, shining

Agnes Grey
author: **10** Anne Bronte
character: **8** Mr Weston **13** Rosalie Murray

agnostic 5 pagan **7** atheist, doubter, heathen, heretic, infidel, skeptic **10** empiricist, free spirit, secularist, unbeliever **11** disbeliever, freethinker, nonbeliever **14** doubting Thomas

ago 4 gone, over, past **5** since **6** gone by **7** earlier **8** backward **15** retrospectively

agog 5 astir **7** excited **8** thrilled, worked up **9** awestruck **10** enthralled **11** openmouthed

Agon
ballet by: **10** Stravinsky

agonize 5 labor, sweat, worry **6** strain, suffer **7** anguish, wrestle **8** struggle

agonizing 6 severe **7** painful, racking **8** grievous, worrying **9** suffering, torturous **10** tormenting, unbearable **11** distressing, intolerable, unendurable **12** excruciating, insufferable

agony 3 woe **4** pain **5** trial **6** effort, misery, sorrow, strain, throes **7** anguish, anxiety, torment, torture **8** distress, striving, struggle **9** suffering **10** affliction **11** tribulation

Agony and the Ecstasy, The
author: **11** Irving Stone
about: **12** Michelangelo

Agoraea

epithet of: 6 Athena
means: **16** of the marketplace

agoraphobia
fear of: **10** open spaces

Agraeus
epithet of: **6** Apollo
means: **6** hunter

agrarian 5 rural **7** farming **8** pastoral **11** agronomical, crop-raising **12** agricultural

agree 4 jibe **5** admit, allow, chime, grant, match, tally **6** accede, accept, accord, assent, concur, settle, square **7** concede, conform, consent, support **8** coincide, side with **9** harmonize, subscribe **10** correspond, think alike

agreeable 4 nice **7** fitting **8** amenable, amicable, in accord, pleasant, pleasing, suitable **9** approving, complying, congenial **10** acceptable, concurring, consenting, gratifying **11** appropriate
German: **9** gemutlich

agreeableness 7 amenity **9** geniality **10** amiability **11** sociability **12** pleasantness

agreed
French: **7** d'accord

agreed upon 6 common, normal **8** accepted, approved **9** confirmed, customary **10** acceptable **11** established **12** acknowledged

agreement 4 deal, pact **6** accord **7** analogy, bargain, compact, concert, concord, harmony, promise **8** affinity, alliance, contract, covenant **10** accordance, compliance, conformity, settlement, similarity **11** arrangement, concordance, conformance **13** compatibility **14** correspondence

agricultural 4 farm **5** rural **7** farming **8** agrarian **9** gardening **11** agronomical, crop-raising **13** nonindustrial

agriculture 7 farming, tillage **8** agronomy **9** geoponics, husbandry **10** agronomics **11** crop-raising, cultivation **15** market gardening

Agriculture
god of: **4** Dago **5** Dagan, Dagon, Picus **6** Saturn **12** Bonus Eventus
goddess of: **5** Ceres **6** Brigit, Dea Dia, Vacuna **7** Demeter

Agriope see **8** Eurydice

Agrius
member of: **8** Gigantes
form: **7** centaur
mother: **5** Circe
father: **8** Odysseus
son: **9** Thersites
attacked: **8** Hercules

agronomics 7 farming, tillage **8** agronomy **9** geoponics **11** agriculture, cropraising

agronomy 7 farming **9** gardening, husbandry **11** agriculture, cultivation

aground 5 stuck **6** ashore **7** beached **8** grounded, stranded **9** foundered

ague 5 chill, fever **7** malaria, shivers **12** sweating fits

Aguecheek, Sir Andrew
character in: **12** Twelfth Night
author: **11** Shakespeare

Agyius
epithet of: **6** Apollo
means: **15** god of the streets

Ah, But Your Land Is Beautiful
author: **9** Alan Paton

Ah! Wilderness
author: **12** Eugene O'Neill

Ahab
character in: **8** Moby Dick
author: **8** Melville
rank: **7** captain
feature: **6** pegleg

Ahab
father: **4** Omri
wife: **7** Jezebel
son: **7** Ahaziah
daughter: **8** Athaliah
opposed: **6** Elijah
killed by: **4** Aram

Ahasuerus
known as: **6** Xerxes **8** Cyaxares
wife: **6** Esther
divorced: **6** Vashti
son: **6** Darius
eunuchs: **6** Biztha, Carcas, Zethar **7** Abagtha, Harbona, Mehuman
servant: **7** Abagtha
courtier: **5** Haman
conqueror of: **7** Nineveh

ahead of time 5 early **6** before, in time, sooner **7** betimes, earlier **9** before now, in advance **10** beforehand, in good time **13** before the fact

Ahib 16 first Hebrew month

Ahithophel
counseled: **5** David
rebelled with: **7** Absalom
granddaughter: **9** Bathsheba

aid 4 abet, alms, dole, help **5** serve **6** assist, foster, relief **7** advance, charity, further, promote, subsidy, support, sustain **8** donation, minister **9** allowance **10** assistance, contribute, facilitate **11** accommodate, helping hand **12** contribution

Aida 17 Ethiopian princess
opera by: **5** Verdi
character: **4** Aida **6** Ramfis **7** Amneris, Radames **8** Amonasro, Rhadames
set in: **5** Egypt

aide 5 gofer **6** deputy, helper **7** abettor, acolyte **8** adherent, adjutant, follower, retainer, sidekick **9** assistant, associate, auxiliary, man Friday **10** aide-decamp, apprentice, girl Friday, lieutenant **11** helping hand, subordinate **12** right-hand man

aide-de-camp 3 ADC **4** aide **6** helper **8** adjutant **9** assistant, man Friday, right hand **12** right-hand man

aide memoire 4 memo, note 10 memorandum

aider 4 aide 6 helper 7 abettor 9 assistant 11 helping hand

Aiken, Conrad Potter
author of: 6 Ushant 10 Blue Voyage 12 Reviewer's ABC 14 The Charnel Rose 15 Earth Triumphant

Aiken, Howard H
field: 11 mathematics
designed: 15 digital computer

ail 4 pain 5 annoy, be ill, upset, worry 6 be sick, bother, sicken 7 afflict, make ill, trouble 8 be infirm, be unwell, distress 12 be indisposed, fail in health

ailing 3 ill 4 sick 6 infirm, sickly, unwell 8 delicate

ailment 6 malady 7 disease, illness 8 disorder, sickness, weakness 9 complaint, infection, infirmity 10 affliction, disability, discomfort 13 indisposition

ailurophobia
fear of: 4 cats

aim 3 end, try 4 beam, goal, mean, plan, seek, want, wish 5 essay, focus, level, point, sight, slant 6 aiming, design, desire, direct, intend, intent, object, scheme, strive, target 7 attempt, be after, purpose, take aim, train on 8 ambition, aspire to, endeavor 9 intention 10 aspiration, have in mind, have in view, work toward 11 have an eye to, line of sight 12 marksmanship

aim at 4 seek 6 pursue, target 8 aspire to, shoot for

aimless 6 chance, random 7 erratic, wayward 8 unguided 9 frivolous, haphazard, hit-or-miss, pointless, unfocus(s)ed 10 accidental, rudderless, undirected 11 purposeless, unorganized 12 inconsistent, unsystematic 13 directionless, unpredictable 14 indiscriminate

aine 5 elder 6 eldest

Ainsworth, William Harrison
author of: 8 Boscobel, Crichton, Rookwood 9 Guy Fawkes 10 Old St Paul's 12 Jack Sheppard 13 Windsor Castle 16 The Flitch of Bacon, The Tower of London 17 The Miser's Daughter, The South Sea Bubble 20 The Lancashire Witches

Ainu
language spoken in: 8 Hokkaido, Sakhalin
native of: 5 Japan

air, airs 3 lay, sky 4 aura, look, mood, puff, song, tell, tone, tune, vent, waft, wind 5 blast, carol, ditty, draft, ozone, style, swank, utter, voice, whiff 6 aerate, ballad, breath, breeze, expose, manner, melody, reveal, spirit, strain, zephyr 7 declare, display, divulge, exhibit, express, feeling, hauteur, quality 8 ambience, disclose,

pretense, proclaim 9 arrogance, publicize, ventilate 10 appearance, atmosphere, make public 11 haughtiness, pretensions 12 affectations, affectedness, stratosphere 16 superciliousness

god of: 5 Enlil
goddess of: 6 Ninlil

airborne 5 aloft 6 aerial, Eolian 8 in flight 12 off the ground

aircraft 3 jet, SST 4 bird 5 blimp, crate, plane 6 copter, glider 7 balloon, chopper, prop-jet 8 airplane, jumbo jet, zeppelin 10 helicopter, whirlybird

air current 4 puff, wind 5 blast, draft, whiff 6 breeze, zephyr 11 breath of air

airdrome, aerodrome 7 airbase, airport, jet base 8 airfield 11 flying field 12 landing field

airfield 7 air base, airport, jet base 8 airstrip 11 flying field 12 landing field, landing strip

airfoil
insect: 4 wing

airless 8 stifling 10 overheated, sweltering 16 poorly ventilated

airlines, American 3 TWA 4 Reno, Mesa 5 Aloha, Delta, Pan Am, USAir 6 United, Alaska 7 Eastern, Simmons, ValuJet 8 American, Hawaiian, Carnival, TowerAir 9 Southwest, Northwest 10 Transworld, Horizon Air 11 Continental, America West, Trans States 12 Air Wisconsin 14 Western Pacific 16 American Trans Air 17 Atlantic Southeast 18 Continental Express 21 Continental Micronesia

airplane 3 jet 4 bird 5 crate, plane 7 airship, prop-jet 8 aircraft 9 aeroplane 11 flying jenny 19 heavier-than-air craft 20 propeller-driven plane
invented by:
automatic pilot: 6 Sperry
jet engine: 5 Ohain
with motor: 12 Wilbur Wright 13 Orville Wright 14 Wright Brothers
hydro: 7 Curtiss
first: 5 Flyer
part: 3 fin 4 flap, nose, tail, wing 5 cabin, cargo, pylon 6 rudder 7 aileron, cockpit, turbine 8 elevator, fuel tank, fuselage, throttle, turbofan, turbojet 9 empennage, propeller, turboprop 10 flight deck, power plant, stabilizer 11 landing gear 13 undercarriage
kind: 3 MIG 4 Zero 5 Eagle, Gotha, Piper, Sabre 6 Boeing, Cessna, Fokker, Mirage 7 Concorde, Piper Cub 10 Beechcraft, Dornier Do-X 11 Piper Navajo 12 Lockheed Vega, Sopwith Camel 13 Boeing Clipper, Messerschmitt, Piper Cherokee, Super Fortress 14 Cessna Citation, Flying Fortress, Grumman Hellcat, Stratofortress 15 Hawker Hurrican 16 De Havilland Comet

variation: 3 SST 4 STOL, VTOL 5 blimp, drone, VSTOL 6 glider 7 airship, fighter 8 zeppelin 10 hang glider, helicopter, supersonic
battle: 8 dog fight

airport 5 field 7 air base, jet base 8 airdrome, airfield, airstrip 9 aerodrome 11 flying field 12 landing field, landing strip
Paris: 4 Orly
Chicago: 5 O'Hare
New York: 3 JFK
London: 8 Heathrow
Boston: 5 Logan
Airport Abbreviations:
  Atlanta: 3 ATL (Hartsfield International)
  Boston: 3 BOS (Logan International)
  Chicago: 3 ORD (O'Hare)
  Dallas/Ft. Worth: 3 DFW
  Denver: 3 DEN
  Detroit: 3 DTW
  Honolulu: 3 HNL
  Houston: 3 IAH
  Las Vegas: 3 LAS (McCarren International)
  Los Angeles: 3 LAX
  Miami: 3 MIA
  Minneapolis/St. Paul: 3 MSP
  Newark: 3 EWR
  New York: 3 JFK, LGA (John F. Kennedy International, LaGuardia)
  Orlando: 3 MCO
  Phoenix: 3 PHX (Sky Harbor International)
  St. Louis: 3 STL (Lambert St. Louis International)
  San Francisco: 3 SFO
  Seattle/Tacoma 3 SEA

airship 5 blimp 7 balloon 9 dirigible 19 lighter-than-air craft

airship, rigid dirigible
invented by: 8 Zeppelin

airstrip 6 runway 12 landing field, landing strip

air weapon
German: 9 Luftwaffe

airy 5 light, merry, sunny, windy 6 breezy, cheery, drafty, dreamy, jaunty, lively 8 cheerful, ethereal, fanciful, gossamer, illusory, spacious 9 idealized, imaginary, sprightly 10 frolicsome, immaterial 11 unrealistic 12 lighthearted, light-of-heart 13 unsubstantial 14 well-ventilated

aisle 3 way 4 lane, path, walk 5 alley 6 avenue 7 passage, walkway 8 cloister, corridor 10 ambulatory, passageway

Aius Locutius
form: 5 voice
warned: 6 Romans
warned of: 14 Gallic invasion

ajar 4 open 5 agape 6 gaping 8 unclosed 10 partly open

Ajax

also: 4 Aias
called: 9 Great Ajax 10 Oilean Ajax 11 Locrian Ajax 13 Ajax the Lesser 14 Telamonian Ajax
king of: 7 Locrius
father: 6 Oileus 7 Telamon
mother: 8 Periboea
brother: 6 Teucer
author: 9 Sophocles
character: 8 Achilles, Odysseus 9 Agamemnon
  son: 9 Eurysaces
  slave: 8 Tecmessa
  seer: 7 Calchas
rescued body of: 8 Achilles
violated shrine of: 6 Athena
killed in: 9 shipwreck

Akela

character in: 14 The Jungle Books
author: 7 Kipling

Akh

origin: 8 Egyptian
transfiguration of: 4 dead

Akihito

position: 7 emperor 11 crown prince
reign name: 6 Heisei 17 Establishing Peace
family:
  father: 5 Showa 8 Hirohito
  mother: 6 Nagako
  wife: 7 Michiko
  children: 4 Hito 8 Narahito
schools: 6 Oxford 9 Gakushuin

akin 3 kin 4 like 5 alike 6 allied 7 kindred, related, similar, uniform 8 agreeing, parallel 9 analogous, congenial, connected, identical 10 affiliated, comparable, resembling 11 correlative 13 corresponding 14 consanguineous

Akkad see 5 Accad

Akutagawa, Ryunosuke

author of: 5 Kappa 8 Rashomon 13 The Hell Screen

a la 9 in honor of 13 in the manner of

Alabama

abbreviation: 2 AL 3 Ala
nickname: 6 Cotton 12 Heart of Dixie, Yellowhammer
capital: 10 Montgomery
largest city: 10 Birmingham
others: 5 Selma 6 Athens, Dothan, Marion, Mobile 7 Decatur, Gadsden 8 Anniston 10 Huntsville, Tuscaloosa
colleges: 5 Miles 6 Auburn 7 Alabama 8 Tuskegee 9 Talladega 10 Huntingdon
explorer: 12 Herman DeSoto
feature:
  festival: 11 Azalea Trail
  statue: 6 Vulcan
tribe: 5 Creek 6 Tohome 7 Alabamu, Alibamu, Koasati 8 Tuskegee
people: 8 Joe Louis 9 Hank Aaron, Hugo Black 10 Willie Mays 11 Helen Keller, Nat King Cole 13 George Wallace, William C Handy, William Gorgas
lake: 12 Guntersville
land rank: 11 twenty-ninth
physical feature:
  gulf: 6 Mexico
  highest point: 6 Cheaha
  highlands: 11 Appalachian
  river: 3 Pea 5 Coosa 6 Mobile 7 Alabama 9 Tombigbee, Tennessee 10 Tallapoosa 13 Chattahoochee
state admission: 12 twenty-second
state bird: 7 flicker 12 yellowhammer
state fish: 6 tarpon
state flower: 8 camellia 9 goldenrod
state motto: 21 We Dare Defend Our Rights
state song: 7 Alabama
state tree: 20 southern longleaf pine

Alabama, Alibamu

language family: 9 Muskogean
location: 5 Texas 9 Louisiana 10 Polk County 12 Alabama River
related to: 7 Koasati

alacrity 4 zeal 5 speed 6 fervor 7 agility, avidity 8 dispatch 9 alertness, briskness, eagerness, readiness 10 enthusiasm, liveliness, nimbleness, promptness 11 willingness 13 sprightliness

Aladdin

character in: 27 Arabian Nights' Entertainments
character: 13 Chinese sailor

Al Aiun, El Aaiun

capital of: 13 Western Sahara

a la mode 12 in the fashion, in the style of 13 in the manner of

Alarcon, Pedro Antonio de

author: 10 The Scandal 12 Captain Venom 14 El Nino de la Bola 19 The Three-Cornered Hat

alarm 4 fear 5 alert, panic, scare 6 appall, dismay, fright, terror, war cry 7 agitate, disturb, terrify, trouble, unnerve, warning 8 affright, distress, frighten 9 agitation, hue and cry, misgiving 11 trepidation 12 apprehension, perturbation 13 consternation

alarmed 6 afraid, scared 7 anxious, fearful, panicky, worried 8 dismayed 9 concerned, terrified 10 frightened 12 apprehensive 13 panic-stricken 14 terror-stricken

alarming 5 awful, dread, scary 7 fearful 8 dreadful 10 horrifying, terrifying 11 frightening, hair-raising

alas
expresses: 4 pity 5 grief 6 sorrow 7 concern 9 weariness 11 unhappiness 12 wretchedness
phrase: 7 woe is me

Alaska

abbreviation: 2 AK 4 Alas
nickname: 9 Great Land, Sourdough 12 Last Frontier 20 Land of the Midnight Sun
capital: 6 Juneau
largest city: 9 Anchorage
others: 4 Nome 5 Sitka 6 Barrow, Kodiak 7 Cordova, Douglas, Skagway 9 Fairbanks, Ketchikan
feature: 5 Alcan 13 Alaska Highway
  national park: 13 Mount McKinley
tribe: 3 Han 5 Aleut, Haida, Inuit 6 Ahtena, Akkhas, Eskimo, Karluk, Tetlin 7 Amerind, Ingalik, Kayukon, Khotana, Kutchin, Tanaina, Tlingit, Tlinkit, Venetie 9 Tsimshian, Unakalett
island: 4 Adak, Atka 5 Aleut 6 Kodiak, Unimak 7 Diomede, Nunivak 8 Aleutian, Pribilof 9 Alexander
lake: 6 Naknek 7 Iliamna 8 Becharof 9 Teshekpuk
land rank: 5 first
mountain: 3 Ada 4 Muir 5 Coast 6 Alaska, Brooks 7 Foraker, St Elias 8 Aleutian, Wrangell 9 Blackburn
  highest point: 8 McKinley
physical feature:
  bay: 7 Glacier, Prudhoe
  channel: 9 Gastineau
  glacier: 9 Malaspina
  pass: 8 Chilkoot
  peninsula: 5 Kenai 6 Alaska, Seward
  rapids: 10 Whitehorse
  sea: 6 Arctic 8 Beaufort
  strait: 6 Bering
river: 5 Kobuk, Yukon 6 Copper, Noatak, Tanana 7 Koyukuk, Susitna 8 Colville 9 Kuskokwim, Matanuska, Porcupine
sled race: 8 Iditarod
state admission: 10 forty-ninth
state bird: 15 willow ptarmigan
state fish: 10 king salmon
state flower: 11 forget-me-not
state motto: 16 North to the Future
state song: 11 Alaska's Flag
state symbol: 9 bald eagle
state tree: 11 sitka spruce

Alaskan Adventures

author: 8 Rex Beach

Albania

other name: 8 Shqiperi 9 Shqiprija, Shqyptare
capital/largest city: 6 Tirana, Tirane
others: 3 Opp 4 Fier, Klos, Puka, Puke 5 Berat, Dukat, Korce, Kruje, Pecin, Peqin, Qukes, Rubic, Spash, Vlore 6 Avlona, Bitsan, Dardhe, Durres, Karaje, Preshe, Valona 7 Chimara, Coritza, Durazzo, Elbasan, Koritsa, Preyesa, Scutari, Shkoder 8 Tepeleni 11 Gjirokaster
monetary unit: 3 lek 5 franc 6 qintar 7 quintar
island: 6 Saseno
lake: 4 Ulze 5 Matia, Ohrid 6 Prespa 7 Ochrida, Scutari, Shkoder 8 Ohridsko
mountain: 5 Shala 6 Pindus 8 Koritnjk 12 Albanian Alps

highest point: 10 Mount Korab
river: 3 Mat **4** Arta, Drin **5** Byene, Erzen, Seman **6** Bojana, Bojane, Vijosa, Vijosa, Vijose **7** Drin-i-ci, Shkumbi
sea: 6 Ionian **8** Adriatic
physical feature:
  bay: 5 Vlore
  cape: 6 Glossa
  gulf: 4 Drin
  lagoon: 10 Kara Vastas
  peninsula: 6 Balkan
  promontory: 13 acroceraunium
  strait: 7 Otranto
  wind: 4 bora
people: 3 Geg **4** Cham, Gheg, Gueg, Tosk **6** Arnaut, Arnout **8** Illyrian, Skipetar
  king: 3 Zog **9** Ahmet Zogu
  leader: 4 Alia **5** Hoxha **7** Berisha **10** Scanderbeg, Skenderbeg **13** Bishop Fan Noli
language: 3 Geg **4** Cham, Gheg, Hish, Tosk **5** Greek **8** Albanian
religion: 5 Islam **7** Bektash **13** Roman Catholic **15** Eastern Orthodox
place:
  square: 10 Skenderbeg
feature:
  lute: 6 luhata
  soldier: 7 palikar
  stone house: 4 kula
food:
  cheese: 8 kackaval
Albanian
  language family: 12 Indo-European
  spoken in: 7 Balkans
Albee, Edward
  author of: 3 Box **7** All Over **8** Seascape, Zoo Story **9** Tiny Alice **10** The Sandbox **16** A Delicate Balance, The American Dream **18** The Lady from Dubuque **21** The Ballad of the Sad Cafe, The Death of Bessie Smith **25** Who's Afraid of Virginia Woolf?
  identified with: 18 theater of the absurd
Albeniz, Isaac
  born: 5 Spain **9** Camprodon
  composer of: 6 Iberia **12** The Magic Opal **13** Henry Clifford
Alberich
  origin: 8 Teutonic
  king of: 6 dwarfs
  possessed treasure of: 8 Niblungs **9** Nibelungs
  also possessed: 9 Tarnkappe
Albert, Eddie
  real name: 21 Eddie Albert Heimberger
  wife: 5 Margo
  born: 12 Rock Island IL
  roles: 8 Oklahoma **10** Brother Rat, Green Acres **11** Room Service **12** Roman Holiday **13** The Longest Day **16** The Heartbreak Kid **19** The Boys from Syracuse
Alberta
  abbreviation: 4 Alta

capital/largest city: 8 Edmonton
  others: 7 Calgary, Reddeer **10** Lethbridge **11** Medicine Hat
  lakes: 5 Banff, Claire **6** Jasper **8** Waterton **9** Athabasca **11** Lesser Slave
  rivers: 3 Bow **4** Milk **6** Oldman, Wapiti **9** Athabasca **12** Saskatchewan
  religion: 13 Roman Catholic **20** United Church of Canada **22** Anglican Church of Canada
  people: 5 Dutch **6** French, German **7** British, English **9** Ukrainian **12** Scandinavia
Albert Herring
  opera by: 7 Britten
Alberti, Leon Battista
  architect of: 15 Palazzo Rucellai **18** Church of Sant' Andrea, Temple Malatestiano **20** Church of San Sebastian **25** Church of Santa Maria Novello
Albertson, Jack
  born: 8 Malden MA
  roles: 14 Chico and the Man **15** The Sunshine Boys **18** Days of Wine and Roses, The Subject Was Roses
album 2 LP **4** book **6** record **8** register **9** portfolio, scrapbook
Alceste
  opera by: 5 Gluck
Alcestis
  author: 9 Euripides
  character: 6 Apollo **7** Admetus **8** Heracles, Thanatos
Alcestis
  father: 6 Pelias
  mother: 8 Anaxibia **10** Phylomache
  husband: 7 Admetus
  son: 7 Eumelus **8** Hippasus
  returned from: 5 Hades
  returned by: 8 Hercules
Alchemist, The
  author: 9 Ben Jonson
  character: 4 Face **5** Surly **6** Dapper, Subtle **7** Ananias, Drugger, Kastril, Love-wit **9** Dol Common **10** Dame Pliant **16** Sir Epicure Mammon **20** Tribulation Wholesome
alchemy 5 magic **7** sorcery **8** wizardry **10** conversion, witchcraft **11** magic appeal **13** transmutation **17** medieval chemistry
  god of: 6 Hermes
  purpose: 12 lead into gold
Alcimede
  father: 8 Phylacus
  mother: 7 Clymene
  husband: 5 Aeson
  son: 5 Jason
Alcimedon
  origin: 8 Arkadian
  mentioned in: 5 Iliad
  father: 7 Laerces
  daughter: 6 Philao
  captain of: 9 Myrmidons
Alcina

opera by: 6 Handel
  character: 6 Alcina **8** Ruggiero
Alcindor, Lew
  former name of: 17 Kareem Abdul-Jabbar
Alcmaeon
  father: 10 Amphiaraus
  mother: 8 Eriphyle
  brother: 11 Amphilochus
  wife: 10 Callirrhoe
  son: 7 Acarnan **10** Amphoterus
  daughter: 9 Tisiphone
  commanded: 7 Thebans
Alcmene
  father: 9 Electryon
  mother: 5 Anaxo
  husband: 10 Amphitryon **12** Rhadamanthys
  twin sons: 8 Hercules, Iphicles
alcohol 3 ale **4** beer, wine **5** drink **6** liquor **7** whiskey **9** the bottle
  Latin: 9 aqua vitae
alcoholic 3 sot **4** hard, lush, soak **5** drunk, rummy, souse, toper **6** barfly, boozer, strong **7** guzzler, imbiber, tippler **8** drunkard **9** distilled, fermented, inebriate **10** spirituous **11** dipsomaniac, hard drinker, inebriating, inebriatic, whiskey head **12** intoxicating
alcoholism 3 DT's **9** oenomania **10** dipsomania **12** intemperance **15** delirium tremens
Alcon
  form: 6 archer, Trojan **7** warrior
  aided: 8 Hercules
  wounded: 8 Odysseus
  abducted: 13 Geryons cattle
  killed by: 8 Odysseus
Alcott, Louisa May
  author of: 7 Jo's Boys **9** Little Men **11** Little Women **12** Eight Cousins, Flower Fables **15** Aunt Jo's Scrap-Bag **18** An Old-Fashioned Girl
alcove 3 bay **4** nook **5** niche **6** corner, recess **7** cubicle, opening **11** compartment
Alcyoneus
  form: 5 giant
  hurled: 5 stone
  killed by: 8 Hercules
Alda, Alan
  born: 9 New York NY
  father: 10 Robert Alda
    real name: 15 Alfonso D'Abruzzo
  roles: 4 MASH **8** A New Life **9** Paper Lion, Playmates, White Nile **12** Sweet Liberty **13** Betsy's Wedding, Hawkeye Pierce, The Glass House **14** The Four Seasons **16** Same Time Next Year, The Mephisto Waltz
Alden, Roberta
  character in: 17 An American Tragedy
  author: 7 Dreiser
al dente 10 to the tooth
alder 5 Alnus
  varieties: 3 Red **5** Black, Hazel,

White, Witch **6** Oregon, Smooth, Yellow **7** Italian, Seaside **8** Japanese, Mountain, Speckled **9** Caucasian **10** Manchurian **13** American green, European green

Aldiss, Brian W
author of: **7** Non-Stop **9** Greybeard **13** The Saliva Tree **19** Frankenstein Unbound, The Billion Year Spree, The Eighty Minute Hour **20** The Trillion Year Spree

ale 4 beer, brew **5** stout **12** malt beverage **15** English festival

Alea
epithet of: **6** Athena
means: **9** sanctuary

Alecto
member of: **6** Furies

alehouse 3 pub **6** saloon, tavern **7** taproom **11** public house

Aleichem, Sholom
author of: **12** The Great Fair **14** Tevye's Daughter

Alembert, Jean le Rond d'
field: **11** mathematics
nationality: **6** French
studied: **13** fluid dynamics **18** celestial mechanics **28** partial differential equations

Aleph and Other Stories
author: **15** Jorge Luis Borges

alert 4 warn, wary **5** alarm, aware, quick, siren **6** active, inform, lively, nimble, notify, signal **7** careful, heedful, on guard, warning **8** diligent, forewarn, keen-eyed, vigilant, watchful **9** attentive, observant, sprightly, wideawake **10** perceptive **11** intelligent

alertness 8 alacrity, dispatch **9** awareness, readiness, vigilance **10** liveliness **12** watchfulness

Aleut
language family: **6** Eskimo
tribe: **4** Atka **8** Unalaska
location: **6** Alaska **15** Shumagin Islands **17** Aleutian Peninsula
noted for: **7** hunting

Aleutians
islands: **3** Fox, Rat **4** Attu, Near **5** Kiska **9** Andreanof **25** Islands of the Four Mountains
state: **6** Alaska
people: **6** Aleuts
language: **5** Atkan **9** Unalaskan

Alexander, Jane
real name: **11** Jane Quigley
born: **8** Boston MA
roles: **9** Testament **17** The Great White Hope **18** Eleanor and Franklin **19** All the President's Men

Alexander's Feast
author: **10** John Dryden

Alexander the Great
battle: **5** Issus **9** Gaugamela
birthplace: **5** Pella

conquered: **6** Darius, Persia
father: **8** Philip II
founded: **10** Alexandria
friend: **11** Hephaestion
general: **7** Cleitus **8** Philotas **9** Parmenion
horse: **10** Bucephalus
mother: **8** Olympias
nationality: **10** Macedonian
tutor: **9** Aristotle
wife: **6** Roxana

alexandrite
species: **11** chrysoberyl
source: **8** Sri Lanka
color: **3** red **5** green

Alfheim
origin: **12** Scandinavian
dwelling place of: **5** elves
location: **11** above ground

Alfie
director: **12** Lewis Gilbert
based on play by: **12** Bill Naughton
cast: **12** Michael Caine **14** Shelley Winters

alga, algae 6 fungus **8** pond scum
contains: **4** agar **5** algin **11** carrageenan, chlorophyll
type: **3** red **5** brown, green **9** blue-green, euglenids **11** golden-brown, yellow-green **15** dinoflagellates
forms: **4** kelp **5** dulse **7** diatoms, seaweed **8** plankton, rockweed **9** Irish moss, stonewort

Alger, Horatio
author of: **10** Ragged Dick **11** Tattered Tom **12** Luck and Pluck

Algeria
other name: **7** Algerie, Numidia, Pomaria **9** al-Djazair
capital/largest city: **7** Algiers
others: **4** Bona, Bone, Oran **5** Aflou, Arzew, Batna, Blida, Medea, Saida, Setif, Tenes **6** Abadla, Annaba, Aumale, Barika, Bechar, Bejaia, Benoud, Biskra, Bougie, Dellys, Djanet, Djelfa, Dzioua, Eloued, Frenda, Guelma, Skikda **7** Boghari, Mascara, Miliana, Negrine, Nemours, Ouargla, Tebessa, Tlemcen **8** Ghardaia, Laghouat **9** Touggourt **11** Constantine **12** Sidi-bel-abbes
division: **4** Oran **6** Annaba **7** Algiers **11** Constantine
leader: **3** bey, dey **6** disawa **9** beylerbey
measure: **3** pik **5** rebis, tarri **6** termin
monetary unit: **5** dinar **7** centime
weight: **4** rotl
lake: **5** Hodna **6** Sabkha **7** Cherqui, Fedjadj, Meirhir **10** Azzel Matti, Mekerrhane
mountain: **5** Aissa, Atlas, Aures, Dahra **6** Chelia **7** Ahaggar, Kabylia, Mouydir **8** Djurjura **9** Djurdjura, Tell Atlas **12** Saharan Atlas
highest point: **5** Tahat
river: **6** Shelif **7** Cheliff **8** Medjerda **15** Cheliffmedjerda

sea: **13** Mediterranean
physical feature: **14** Tropic of Cancer
desert: **6** Sahara
giant sand dune: **3** erg
grass: **4** diss **7** esparto
hill: **4** tell
oasis: **4** Mzab
oil field: **7** Edjeleh, El Gassi **10** Zarzaitine **13** Hassi Messaoud (happy spring), Tiguentourine
plain: **7** Cheliff, Mitidja
rocky plateau: **7** hammada
salt basin: **5** chott, shatt
wind: **7** sirocco
people: **4** Arab **6** Berber, Kabyle, Shawia, Tuareg **7** Haratin
author: **3** Dib **5** Camus, Fanon **6** Yacine
leader: **9** Bendjedid **10** Abd al-Qadir, Abd-al-Kader, Abd- el-Kader **11** Boumedienne **13** Ahmed Ben Bella
ruler: **8** Jugurtha **9** Masinissa
language: **6** Arabic, Berber, French, Zenata **7** Senhaja
religion: **5** Islam
place:
monastery: **5** Ribat
ruins: **7** Djemila
feature:
camel: **6** mehari
cavalry man: **5** spahi **6** spahee
commune: **5** setif
dwelling: **6** gourbi
French settler/landowner: **5** colon **8** piednoir
holy man: **8** marabout
kingdom: **7** Numidia
native quarter: **6** casbah, kasbah
pirate: **7** corsair
ship: **5** xebec, zebec
slum: **10** bidonville
food:
dish: **8** couscous
fruit drink: **5** syrop
seasoning: **4** mint **5** anise, cumin **6** cloves, fennel, ginger, pepper **7** parsley, pimento **8** cinnamon **9** coriander

Algiers
Arabic: **8** al-Jazair
building: **11** Great Mosque
capital of: **7** Algeria
center of city: **6** Casbah
French: **5** Alger
hills: **5** Sahel
Roman: **7** Icosium
ruled by: **5** Turks **6** French **7** Berbers **10** Free French **14** Barbary Pirates
sea: **13** Mediterranean

Algonkian-Ritwan
language family: **14** Algonkian-Mosan
subgroup: **3** Fox **4** Cree, Sauk **5** Wiyot, Yurok **6** Ojibwa **7** Abenaki, Arapaho, Mohican **8** Cheyenne, Delaware, Menomini **9** Blackfoot

Algonkin, Algonquin

language family: 9 Algonkian **10** Algonquian

tribe: 7 Abitibi **8** Algonkin **9** Nipissing **11** Temiscaming

location: 6 Canada **11** Ottawa River

spirit of nature: 7 Manitou

Algonquian, Algonkian

tribe: 3 Fox, Sac **4** Cree, Innu, Sauk **5** Miami **6** Abnaki, Atsina, Micmac, Ojibwa, Ottawa, Pequot **7** Arapaho, Mahican, Mohegan, Mohican, Ojibway, Shawnee **8** Algonkin, Cheyenne, Chippawa, Delaware, Haaninin, Iliniwek, Illinois, Kickapoo, Menomini, Merrimac, Powhatan, Puyallop **9** Algonquin, Blackfeet, Blackfoot, Massasoit, Menominee, Menomonie, Mesquakie, Pennacook, Penobscot, Twightwee, Wampanoag **10** Leni-Lenape, Potawatomi **11** Gros Ventres **12** Narragansett **17** Montagnais-Naskapi

algophobia

fear of: 4 pain

Algum 13 red sandalwood

Ali, Muhammad

formerly: 11 Cassius Clay

sport: 6 boxing

class: 11 heavyweight

won: 8 Olympics **16** heavyweight title

alias 9 pseudonym **11** assumed name, nom de guerre

Ali Baba

character in: 27 Arabian Nights' Entertainments

alibi 3 out **6** excuse **7** pretext **11** explanation **13** justification

Alice Adams

author: 15 Booth Tarkington

character: 6 Mr Lamb **11** Virgil Adams, Walter Adams **13** Arthur Russell, Mildred Palmer

Alice's Adventures in Wonderland

author: 12 Lewis Carroll **22** Charles Lutwidge Dodgson

character: 5 Alice **7** Duchess **9** Mad Hatter, March Hare **10** Mock Turtle **11** Cheshire Cat, White Rabbit **13** Knave of Hearts, Queen of Hearts

Alice Sit-by-the-Fire

author: 12 James M Barrie

alien 6 exotic, remote, unlike **7** distant, foreign, opposed, strange **8** contrary, newcomer, outsider, stranger **9** different, estranged, foreigner, immigrant, not native, outlander, separated, unrelated **10** dissimilar, outlandish **11** conflicting, incongruous, unconnected **12** incompatible, inconsistent **13** contradictory

German: 9 Auslander

alienate 7 divorce **8** estrange, separate, turn away

alienation 5 exile **7** divorce **9** isolation **10** separation, withdrawal **13** repulsiveness

alight 4 land **6** get off **7** deplane, descend, detrain, get down **8** come down, dismount **9** climb down, disembark, thump down, touch down

align 4 ally, even, join, side **6** even up, line up **9** affiliate, associate **10** straighten

alignment 7 allying, evening **9** evening up **13** straightening

alike 4 akin, even, same **5** equal **6** evenly **7** equally, kindred, uniform **8** of a piece, parallel **9** analogous, identical, similarly, uniformly **10** equivalent, synonymous **11** homogeneous, identically **13** corresponding

Alisande (Sandy)

character in: 36 A Connecticut Yankee in King Arthur's Court

author: 5 Twain

alive 4 spry **5** alert, aware, eager, quick, vital **6** active, extant, lively, living, viable **7** animate, in force, not dead **8** animated, possible, spirited, vigorous **9** breathing, energetic, operative, vivacious **10** subsisting, unquenched **11** above ground, in existence, in operation **14** unextinguished

alive to 5 alert, awake, aware **7** heedful, mindful **8** watchful **9** attentive, conscious, wide-awake

alkaline 3 lye **5** salty **7** antacid **9** nonacidic

alkaloid 7 alkaline, codeine, guinine **8** morphine, nicotine **16** colorless complex

all 4 each, full, very **5** any of, every, fully, total, utter, whole **6** each of, entire, to a man, utmost, wholly **7** highest, perfect, totally, utterly **8** any one of, complete, entirely, everyone, greatest, the sum of, the total, the whole **9** every item **10** altogether, completely, every one of, everything, the total of, the whole of **11** every member, every part of, exceedingly, the entirety

All About Eve

director: 17 Joseph L Mankiewicz

cast: 10 Anne Baxter, Bette Davis **11** Celeste Holm, Gary Merrill **12** Thelma Ritter **13** George Sanders, Marilyn Monroe

Oscar for: 7 picture **8** director **10** screenplay **15** supporting actor (George Sanders)

Allan-a-Dale, Alan-a-Dale

character in: 9 Robin Hood

allargando

music: 13 getting slower

all around 6 abroad **7** all over **10** everywhere, far and wide **15** making the rounds

all-around 5 broad **6** adroit, gifted **8** flexible **9** adaptable, many-sided, versatile **11** well-rounded **12** ambidextrous, multifaceted **13** comprehensive

allay 4 calm, dull, ease, hush **5** blunt, check, quell, quiet, slake **6** lessen, pacify, quench, reduce, smooth, soften, soothe, subdue **7** appease, assuage, lighten, mollify, relieve, slacken **8** diminish, mitigate, moderate **9** alleviate, put to rest **14** cause to subside

all but 6 almost, nearly **7** close to **8** not quite **10** not far from, very nearly **14** except everyone, within an inch of **16** everything except

all by oneself 5 alone **7** unaided **9** on one's own **10** unassisted **13** unaccompanied

all-consuming 3 hot **5** fiery **6** ardent, fervid, raging, red- hot **7** burning, fanatic, fervent, frantic, glowing, intense, zealous **8** frenzied **10** passionate **11** impassioned

allegation 5 claim **6** avowal, charge **9** assertion, statement **10** accusation, contention, indictment, profession **11** declaration

allege 3 say **4** aver, avow **5** claim, state **6** accuse, affirm, assert, charge, impugn, impute **7** contend, declare, profess **8** maintain

allegiance 6 fealty, homage **7** loyalty **8** devotion, fidelity **9** adherence, constancy, deference, obedience **12** faithfulness

allegory 5 fable **7** parable

allegro

music: 4 fast

all-embracing 5 broad **6** all-out **7** general, overall **8** complete, sweeping, thorough **9** expansive, extensive, universal, unlimited **10** exhaustive, widespread **11** far-reaching, wide-ranging **12** all-inclusive, encyclopedic **13** comprehensive

Allen, Arabella

character in: 14 Pickwick Papers

author: 7 Dickens

Allen, Ethan

served in: 16 Revolutionary War

commander of: 17 Green Mountain Boys

captured: 15 Fort Ticonderoga

state: 7 Vermont

Allen, Fred

real name: 20 John Florence Sullivan

born: 11 Cambridge MA

roles: 11 What's My Line **16** The Fred Allen Show

Allen, Steve

real name: 12 Stephen Allen

wife: 12 Jayne Meadows

nickname: 10 Mr Midnight

born: 9 New York NY

roles: 13 I've Got a Secret **14** The Tonight Show

Allen, William Hervey

author of: 7 Israfel **14** Anthony Adverse

Allen, Woody

author of: 11 Getting Even, Side Ef-

fects **15** Without Feathers
real name: 22 Allen Stewart Konigsberg
wife: 12 Louise Lasser, Soon-Yi Previn
born: 10 Brooklyn NY
films: 5 Alice, Zelig **7** Bananas, Sleeper **9** Annie Hall, Interiors, Manhattan, Radio Days **12** Casino Royale, Love and Death **14** New York Stories **15** Mighty Aphrodite, Scenes from a Mall **16** Husbands and Wives, Stardust Memories **17** Broadway Danny Rose **19** Bullets over Broadway, Hannah and Her Sisters **20** The Purple Rose of Cairo **21** Crimes and Misdemeanors **22** Manhattan Murder Mystery

alleviate 4 dull, ease, quit **5** abate, allay, blunt, check, slake **6** lessen, quench, reduce, soften, subdue, temper **7** assuage, lighten, mollify, relieve, slacken **8** diminish, mitigate, moderate

alleviation 6 easing, relief **9** lessening **10** palliation

alley 4 lane **5** byway **7** passage, pathway **10** passageway **16** narrow back street

Alley Oop
   creator: 14 Vincent T Hamlin
   character:
      girlfriend: 5 Ooola
      dinosaur: 5 Dinny
      king: 6 Guzzle
      scientist: 8 Dr Wonmug
   place:
      kingdom of: 3 Moo

All for Love
   author: 10 John Dryden
   character: 6 Antony, Caesar **7** Octavia **9** Cleopatra, Dolabella, Ventidius

All God's Chillun Got Wings
   author: 12 Eugene O'Neill
   character: 6 Mickey **9** Jim Harris **10** Ella Downey

alliance 4 pact **5** union **6** league, treaty **7** compact, company **9** agreement, coalition, concordat **10** federation **11** affiliation, association, confederacy, partnership **13** confederation **15** entente cordiale

allied 4 akin, like **5** alike, joint **6** united **7** cognate, kindred, related, similar **8** combined **9** corporate, federated **10** affiliated, associated, resembling **11** amalgamated **12** incorporated

all in 4 beat **5** spent, tired, weary **6** bushed, done in, pooped **7** drained, wearied, worn out **8** dog tired, fatigued, tired out **9** bone weary, dead tired, exhausted, played out

all in all 5 in sum **10** on the whole **20** when all is said and done

all-inclusive 5 broad **6** all-out, entire **7** general, overall **8** absolute, complete, sweeping, thorough **9** expansive, extensive, universal, unlimited **10** altogether, exhaustive, widespread **11** far-reaching, wide-ranging **12** all-embracing **13** comprehensive

All in the Family
   character: 10 Joey Stivic, Mike Stivic (Meathead) **11** Edith Bunker (Dingbat) **12** Archie Bunker **18** Gloria Bunker Stivic
   cast: 9 Rob Reiner **13** Jean Stapleton **14** Carroll O'Connor, Sally Struthers
   spinoffs: 5 Maude **12** Archie's Place **13** The Jeffersons

allocate 5 allot, allow **6** assign, budget **7** earmark **8** set aside **9** apportion, designate **11** appropriate

allocation 5 quota, share **7** measure, portion **8** division **9** allotment, meting out **10** dealing out **11** consignment, designation **12** apportioning, dispensation, distribution **13** apportionment

allot 4 dole, mete **5** allow, grant **6** assign **7** appoint, consign, dole out, earmark, give out, mete out, provide **8** allocate, dispense, divide up **9** apportion, parcel out **10** distribute, portion out

allotment 5 grant, quota, share **6** ration **7** measure, portion **9** allowance **10** allocation **11** consignment **12** dispensation **13** apportionment, appropriation

all-out 5 broad, total **7** full-out, maximum **8** complete, sweeping, thorough **9** extensive, full-scale **11** unqualified, unremitting **12** all-embracing, all-inclusive **13** comprehensive, thoroughgoing

all over 4 done **5** ended, kaput **8** finished **9** concluded **10** everywhere **11** universally

All Over
   author: 11 Edward Albee

allow 3 let **4** give **5** allot, grant **6** assign, permit **7** agree to, approve, concede, provide **8** allocate, sanction **9** authorize

allowable 7 allowed **8** accepted **9** permitted, tolerable, tolerated **10** acceptable, admissible, admittable, authorized, sanctioned **11** permissible

allowance 5 grant **6** bounty, income, ration **7** annuity, payment, pension, stipend, subsidy **8** discount **9** allotment, deduction, reduction **10** concession **11** subtraction

allow to go 4 free **5** let go **6** excuse, parole **7** dismiss, release, set free **8** liberate **9** discharge

allow to pass
   French: 13 laissez passer

alloy 3 mix **5** admix, blend **6** commix, dilute, fusion, impair **7** amalgam, combine, mixture **8** compound, intermix **9** admixture, composite, synthesis **10** adulterate, commixture, interblend **12** conglomerate

alloyed 5 mixed **6** impure **7** debased

All Quiet on the Western Front
   author: 18 Erich Maria Remarque
   character: 6 Muller, Tjaden **10** Paul Baumer **11** Albert Kropp, Haie Westhus **20** Stanislaus Katczinsky (Kat)
   director: 14 Lewis Milestone
   cast: 8 Lew Ayres **12** Louis Wolheim **14** Russell Gleason
   setting: 3 WWI
   Oscar for: 7 picture

all right 2 OK **3** yes **4** fair, hale, safe, sure, well **6** hearty **7** healthy **8** properly, unharmed **9** certainly, correctly, uninjured **10** absolutely, acceptably, unimpaired **14** satisfactorily
   Spanish: 5 bueno

All Said and Done
   author: 16 Simone de Beauvoir

allspice
   botanical name: 7 pimenta, p dioica **12** p officinalis
   also called: 7 pimento
   origin: 7 Jamaica **16** Caribbean Islands
   flavor: 5 clove **6** nutmeg **8** cinnamon
   use: 6 baking

Allston, Washington
   born: 10 Waccamaw SC
   artwork: 9 The Deluge **13** Uriel in the Sun **16** Belshazzar's Feast, Moonlit Landscape **20** Spanish Girl in Reverie

All's Well That Ends Well
   author: 18 William Shakespeare
   character: 5 Diana **6** Helena **7** Bertram **8** Parolles **12** King of France **14** Duke of Florence **19** Countess of Rousillon

All That Jazz
   director: 8 Bob Fosse
   cast: 9 Ben Vereen **11** Ann Reinking, Cliff Gorman, Roy Scheider **12** Jessica Lange, Leland Palmer

All the King's Men
   author: 16 Robert Penn Warren
   character: 10 Jack Burden, Judge Irwin, Sadie Burke **11** Adam Stanton, Willie Stark **12** Annie Stanton
   director: 12 Robert Rossen
   cast: 9 Joanne Dru, John Derek **11** John Ireland **17** Broderick Crawford **19** Mercedes McCambridge
   Oscar for: 5 actor (Crawford) **7** picture **17** supporting actress (McCambridge)

all the more
   Latin: 9 a fortiori

All the President's Men
   author: 11 Bob Woodward **13** Carl Bernstein
   subject: 16 Watergate scandal
   newspaper: 14 Washington Post
   director: 11 Alan J Pakula

cast: 10 Jack Warden **11** Hal Holbrook **12** Jason Robards, Martin Balsam **13** Dustin Hoffman (Carl Bernstein), Jane Alexander, Robert Redford (Bob Woodward)
Oscar for: 12 screenwriter **15** supporting actor (Robards)

all the same 5 alike **7** however, uniform **8** unvaried **9** identical **11** homogeneous

all together 7 en masse, in a body **8** as a group, in a group, in unison
French: 12 tout ensemble

all told 5 in sum, total **6** in toto **7** totally **8** as a whole **10** altogether

allude 4 hint **5** refer **7** mention, speak of, suggest **8** intimate **9** touch upon

allure 4 bait, lure **5** charm, tempt **6** entice, lead on, seduce **7** attract, beguile, enchant, glamour **8** intrigue **9** captivate, fascinate **10** attraction, enticement, temptation **11** enchantment, fascination

allurement 4 draw, lure **5** charm **9** magnetism **10** attraction **11** fascination

alluring 4 sexy **8** charming, enticing, magnetic **10** attractive **11** fascinating

allusion 4 hint **7** mention **9** reference **10** suggestion

Allworthy, Squire
character in: 8 Tom Jones
author: 8 Fielding

ally 5 unite **6** league **7** combine, partner **8** confrere **9** accessory, affiliate, associate, colleague **10** accomplice, join forces **11** confederate **12** band together, bind together, collaborator, join together

Ally McBeal
creator/writer: 11 David E Kelly
actor (role): 16 Calista Flockhart (**10** Ally McBeal) **19** Courtney Thorne-Smith (**7** Georgia) **11** Greg Germann (**11** Richard Fish) **16** Lisa Nicole Carson (**11** Renee Radick) **13** Jane Krakowski (**12** Elaine Vassal) Peter MacNicol (**8** John Cage) **10** Gil Bellows (**15** Billy Alan Thomas)
music: 13 Vonda Sheppard
setting: 6 Boston

Allyson, June
real name: 11 Ella Geisman
husband: 10 Dick Powell
born: 9 New York NY
roles: 8 Good News **9** Interlude, The Shrike **11** Little Women **12** My Man Godfrey **16** The Stratton Story **19** The Glenn Miller Story

Almagest
author: 7 Ptolemy
title means: 11 the greatest
subject: 9 astronomy

Al Maghrib *see* **7** Morocco

almandite

species: 6 garnet
color: 3 red

Almaviva, Count and Countess
author: 12 Beaumarchais
characters in: 18 The Barber of Seville **19** The Marriage of Figaro

Almayer's Folly
author: 12 Joseph Conrad

almighty 7 supreme **8** absolute, infinite **9** sovereign, unlimited **10** invincible, omnipotent **11** all-powerful **12** transcendent

Almira
opera by: 6 Handel

almond 12 Prunus dulcis
varieties: 4 Wild **5** Earth, Green, Sweet **6** Bitter, Desert, Indian **8** Tropical **9** Flowering **12** Dwarf Russian
candy: 8 marzipan
liqueur: 6 orgeat **7** ratafia

almost 5 about **6** all but, nearly **7** close to **8** not quite, well-nigh **9** just about **10** not far from, very nearly **11** practically, on the verge of **13** approximately **14** within an inch of

almost alike 5 close **7** similar **10** resembling **11** approaching, much the same **15** nearly identical

alms 3 aid **4** dole, gift **5** mercy **6** relief **7** charity, handout, largess, present, subsidy, tribute **8** donation, gratuity, offering, pittance **9** baksheesh **10** assistance **11** benefaction, beneficence **12** contribution

almshouse 6 asylum **9** poorhouse, workhouse

almsman 5 tramp **6** beggar **9** mendicant **10** panhandler

Almug 13 red sandalwood

aloe 4 balm **9** succulent
full name: 8: aloe vera
in: 6 lotion **7** shampoo

aloft 2 up **5** above, way up **6** high up, on high **7** skyward **8** in the air, in the sky, overhead **10** heavenward

Aloha State
nickname of: 6 Hawaii

alone 4 only, sole **6** lonely, single, singly, solely, unique **7** forlorn, unaided **8** deserted, desolate, forsaken, isolated, lonesome, peerless, singular, solitary, uniquely **9** abandoned, matchless, nonpareil, separated, unmatched, unrivaled **10** friendless, separately, singularly, solitarily, unassisted, unattended, unequalled, unescorted **11** unsurpassed, without help **12** incomparable, unchaperoned, unparalleled, without peers **13** unaccompanied, without others **14** single-handedly
Latin: 4 sola **5** solus
French: 4 seul

along 2 on **4** over **6** beside, during, onward **7** abreast, forward, through

alongside 2 at, by **6** beside, next to **7** abreast, close by **9** at the side **10** parallel to **12** collaterally, parallelwise **13** equidistantly

aloof 3 icy **4** cold, cool **5** above, apart **6** chilly, formal, remote **7** distant, haughty, high-hat **8** detached, reserved **10** unsociable **11** at a distance, indifferent, standoffish, unconcerned **12** uninterested, unresponsive **13** unsympathetic **14** unapproachable

aloofness 7 reserve **8** coldness, coolness **9** formality **10** detachment, remoteness **11** haughtiness **12** indifference **13** unsociability **15** standoffishness

aloud 7 audibly

alphabet 4 ABCs **6** schema **7** grammar, letters **8** elements **9** rudiments, tablature **10** characters, principles **13** writing system

Alphesiboea
also: 7 Arsinoe
form: 5 nymph
father: 4 Bias **7** Phegeus **9** Leucippus
mother: 9 Philodice
husband: 8 Alcmaeon
son: 6 Adonis
rejected: 8 Dionysus
nurse for: 7 Orestes

Alpheus
father: 7 Oceanus
mother: 6 Tethys
loved: 8 Arethusa
changed into: 5 river

Alphonse and Gaston
creator: 14 Frederick Opper
saying: 22 After you my dear Alphonse, No after you my dear Gaston

alpine 5 alpen, lofty **6** aerial **8** elevated, snow-clad, towering **9** subalpine **10** alpestrine, sky-kissing, snow-capped **11** cloud-capped, mountainous **13** cloud- piercing, cloud-touching **14** heaven-touching

Alps, Alpine
country: 5 Italy **6** France **7** Austria, Germany **10** Yugoslavia **11** Switzerland **13** Liechtenstein
range: 6 Carnic, Graian, Julian, Otztal **7** Bernese, Cottian, Pennine **8** Bavarian, Ligurian, Maritime, Rhaetian **9** Dolomites, Lepontine **10** Hohe Tauern
peak: 4 Rosa **5** Eiger, Monch **8** Jungfrau **10** Karawanken, Matterhorn, Piz Bernina **13** Grossglockner
highest point: 5 Blanc
pass: 7 Brenner, Simplon, Splugen, Stelvio **9** Semmering **10** St Gotthard **14** Great St Bernard
lake: 4 Como **6** Alpine, Geneva **7** Lucerne **8** Maggiore **9** Constance
phenomenon: 4 echo
resort: 7 Zermatt **8** Chamonix, Salzburg, St Moritz **9** Innsbruck **13**

Berchtesgaden
singing: 5 yodel
wind: 5 foehn

already 5 early, so far **6** before **8** formerly, hitherto, until now **10** heretofore, previously

already seen
French: 6 deja vu

also 3 and, too **4** more, plus **5** extra **6** as well **7** besides **8** moreover **9** including **10** in addition **12** additionally

Altaic
language branches: 6 Turkic **8** Tungusic **9** Mongolian

altar 5 bomos **6** hestia, scribis **7** eschara **8** credence **9** holy table, prothesis **10** Lord's table

Altar
constellation of: 3 Ara

Altdorfer, Albrecht
born: 7 Germany **10** Regensburg
artwork: 16 Susanna at the Bath **20** St George and the Dragon, Susannah and the Elders **24** Landscape with a Footbridge **39** The Battle of Alexander and Darius on the Issus

alter 4 vary **5** amend **6** change, modify, recast, revise **7** convert, remodel **9** transform **13** make different

alterable 7 unfixed **8** variable **9** adaptable **10** adjustable, changeable, modifiable **11** convertible

alteration 6 change **10** adjustment, conversion, remodeling **12** modification **13** transmutation **14** transformation

altercation 3 row **4** spat, tiff **5** brawl, broil, fight, melee, scene **6** affray, fracas, rumpus, scrape **7** discord, dispute, quarrel, scuffle **8** argument **9** bickering, wrangling **10** falling-out **11** controversy **12** disagreement

alter ego 4 twin **5** match **6** double **9** duplicate, other self, semblable **10** complement, other image, second self, simulacrum **11** counterpart **12** Doppelganger

alternate 3 sub **4** vary **5** alter, proxy **6** backup, change, deputy, rotate, second **7** another, standby, stand-in **9** surrogate, take turns **10** every other, reciprocal, substitute, successive, understudy **11** alternating, consecutive, every second, interchange, intersperse, pinch hitter

alternative 6 choice, option, way out **8** recourse **9** selection **10** substitute **11** other choice

although 3 but, yet **4** even **5** still **7** however **11** nonetheless **12** nevertheless **15** notwithstanding

altitude 4 apex **6** height, vertex, zenith **8** eminence, tallness **9** elevation, loftiness, sublimity **10** prominence

Altman, Robert
director of: 4 Aria, MASH **6** Popeye

8 A Wedding **9** Short Cuts, The Player, Streamers, Nashville **10** Kansas City **11** Ready to Wear **14** The Long Goodbye **17** The James Dean Story

altogether 5 fully, in all, in sum, quite **6** in toto, wholly **7** all told, totally, utterly **8** all in all, as a whole, entirely **9** in general, out and out, perfectly **10** absolutely, completely, in sum total, on the whole, thoroughly **12** all inclusive, collectively

altruism 7 charity **10** generosity **11** benevolence **12** philanthropy, public spirit **13** unselfishness **14** bigheartedness, charitableness **15** humanitarianism

altruistic 8 generous **9** unselfish **10** benevolent, charitable **12** humanitarian, largehearted **13** philanthropic **14** public-spirited

aluminum
chemical symbol: 2 Al

alumni 5 grads

alumnus, alumna 4 grad **8** graduate **13** former student

Alverio, Rosita Dolores
real name of: 10 Rita Moreno

always 7 forever **8** evermore **9** eternally, every time, regularly **10** for all time, invariably **11** continually, incessantly, perpetually, unceasingly **12** consistently **13** everlastingly, unremittingly **14** forever and ever

Amadan
origin: 5 Irish
form: 5 fairy

Amadeus
director: 11 Milos Forman
cast: 8 Tom Hulce (Wolfgang Amadeus Mozart) **14** F Murray Abraham (Antonio Salieri)
choreography: 10 Twyla Tharp
Oscar for: 5 actor (Abraham) **7** picture **8** director

Amadis of Gaul
author: 16 Garcia de Montalvo
character: 6 Oriana, Perion **7** Elisena **8** Garinter, Lisuarte

Amado, Jorge
author of: 14 Tent of Miracles **15** Home Is the Sailor **19** Shepherds of the Night **24** Gabriela Clove and Cinnamon **25** Dona Flor and Her Two Husbands **30** The Two Deaths of Quincas Wateryell

Amahl and the Night Visitors
opera by: 7 Menotti

Amalek
father: 7 Eliphaz
mother: 6 Timnah
grandfather: 4 Esau
descendant of: 9 Amalekite

amalgam 5 alloy, blend, combo, union **6** fusion, league, merger **7** joining, mixture **8** alliance, compound, mish-

mash **9** admixture, composite **10** assemblage, commixture **11** combination **12** amalgamation, intermixture

amalgamate 3 mix **4** fuse **5** blend, merge, unify, unite **7** combine **8** coalesce, federate **9** commingle, integrate **10** synthesize **11** consolidate, incorporate **12** join together

Amarcord
director: 15 Federico Fellini
cast: 10 Bruno Zanin, Magali Noel **13** Pupella Maggio

amaretto
type: 7 liqueur
origin: 5 Italy
flavor: 6 almond
with vodka: 9 Godmother

Amaryllis
character in: 9 Ecologues
author: 6 Virgil
represented: 11 shepherdess

amass 6 gather, heap up, pile up **7** acquire, collect, compile, round up **8** assemble **10** accumulate

amateur 4 tyro **6** novice, non-pro **7** dabbler **8** beginner, hobbyist, inexpert, neophyte **9** greenhorn, unskilled **10** dilettante, unpolished **13** inexperienced **14** unprofessional **15** nonprofessional

amateurish 5 inept **6** clumsy **7** awkward **8** inexpert, mediocre **9** unskilled, untrained **10** unskillful **11** incompetent, ineffective, unpracticed **13** inexperienced **14** unaccomplished, unprofessional

amatory 3 hot **4** fond, sexy **6** ardent, doting, erotic, loving, sexual, steamy, tender **7** adoring, amorous, devoted, fervent, sensual, sexed-up **8** lovesick, romantic, yearning **9** libidinal, loverlike, rapturous **10** infatuated, lascivious, passionate **11** impassioned, languishing

amaxophobia
fear of: 7 driving **8** vehicles

amaze 3 awe **4** daze, stun **5** shock **7** astound, stagger, stupefy **8** astonish, surprise **9** dumbfound **11** flabbergast

amazement 3 awe **5** shock **6** wonder **8** surprise **9** disbelief **11** incredulity **12** astonishment, bewilderment, stupefaction

Amazon
occupation: 7 warrior
sex: 6 female
queen: 9 Hippolyta
river: 6 Brazil

amazonite
species: 8 feldspar

Amazonomachia
battle between: 6 Greeks **7** Amazons

ambassador 5 agent, envoy **6** consul, deputy, legate, nuncio **7** attache, courier **8** diplomat, emissary, minister **9** go-between **11** diplomatist **12** intermediary **13** consul general **14** representative

Ambassadors, The
author: **10** Henry James
character: **8** Strether, Waymarsh **10** Mrs Newsome **11** Mamie Pocock, Sarah Pocock **12** Maria Gostrey **15** Chadwick Newsome **17** Comtesse de Vionnet

amber
formed from: **5** resin
color: **6** yellow
Greek: **8** elektron

ambiance 3 air **4** aura, mood, tone **5** tenor **6** spirit, flavor, milieu, temper **7** climate, setting **9** character **10** atmosphere **11** environment **12** surroundings

ambiguity 9 vagueness **11** uncertainty **12** abstruseness, doubtfulness, equivocation **14** indefiniteness
French: **13** double entente

ambiguous 5 vague **7** cryptic, unclear **8** doubtful, puzzling **9** enigmatic, equivocal, uncertain **10** indefinite, misleading

ambition 3 aim **4** goal, hope, plan, push, zeal **5** dream, drive **6** design, desire, intent **7** longing, purpose **8** striving, yearning **9** objective **10** aspiration

ambitious 4 avid **5** eager **6** ardent, intent **7** arduous, zealous **8** aspiring, desirous **9** difficult, energetic, grandiose, strenuous **10** determined **11** industrious **12** enterprising

ambivalent 5 mixed **7** warring **8** clashing, confused, opposing, wavering **9** equivocal, undecided, unfocused **10** wishy-washy **11** conflicting, fluctuating, vacillating **13** contradictory

amble 6 ramble, stroll **7** meander, saunter **15** wander aimlessly

Ambler, Eric
author of: **11** The Levanter **12** A Kind of Auger **13** The Care of Time **14** The Night-Comers, Uncommon Danger **15** Journey Into Fear, The Dark Frontier **16** The Light of the Day **19** A Coffin for Dimitrios **22** The Siege of the Villa Lipp

Ambling Alp, The
nickname of: **12** Primo Carnera

ambrosial 5 balmy **8** fragrant, luscious, perfumed **9** delicious **13** sweet-smelling

ambrosia of the gods 4 food **5** drink **6** nectar **7** perfume

ambulance chaser 4 beak **6** lawyer **8** attorney **9** counselor **10** mouthpiece **12** legal advisor

ambulatory 6 mobile, moving **7** walking **10** up and about **11** peripatetic

ambush 4 trap **5** blind, cover **6** attack, entrap, hiding, lay for, waylay **7** assault **8** hideaway, surprise **9** ambus-

cade **11** concealment, hiding place **13** stalking-horse

Ameche, Don
real name: **17** Dominic Felix Amici
born: **9** Kenosha WI
roles: **4** Pais **5** Folks (Oscar) **6** Cocoon (Oscar) **12** Things Change **13** Heaven Can Wait, Moon Over Miami, Silk Stockings, Trading Places **14** That Night in Rio **16** Down Argentine Way **18** The Three Musketeers **21** Harry and the Hendersons **29** The Story of Alexander Graham Bell

Amelia
author: **13** Henry Fielding
character: **10** Dr Harrison **11** Mrs Atkinson **12** Miss Matthews **19** Captain William Booth

ameliorate 4 heal, help, mend **5** amend, fix up **6** better, perk up, pick up, reform, remedy, revise **7** advance, correct, improve, patch up, promote, rectify **8** palliate, progress **9** come along, get better **10** grow better **11** improve upon

ameliorative 8 remedial **9** improving **10** corrective, palliative **11** therapeutic **12** compensatory

amen 5 truly **6** it is so, so be it, verily **8** hear hear **9** let it be so, yes indeed **11** so shall it be **17** would that it were so

Amen
also: **4** Amon **5** Ammon
origin: **8** Egyptian
king of: **4** gods
worshiped at: **6** Thebes
personifies: **3** air **6** breath
represented by: **3** ram **5** goose
patron of: **6** Thebes
corresponds to: **4** Jove, Zeus **6** Amen Ra, Amon Ra **7** Jupiter

amenable 4 open **7** cordial, willing **8** obliging, yielding **9** agreeable, tractable **10** open-minded, responsive, submissive **11** acquiescent, complaisant, cooperative, persuadable, sympathetic **17** favorably disposed

amend 3 fix **4** mend **5** alter, emend **6** better, change, modify, polish, reform, remedy, revise **7** correct, develop, enhance, improve, perfect, rectify

amendment 6 change, reform **7** adjunct **8** addition, revision **10** alteration, correction, emendation **11** improvement **12** modification **13** rectification

amends 7 apology, defense, payment, redress **8** requital **9** atonement, expiation **10** recompense, reparation **11** explanation, restitution, restoration, retribution, vindication **12** compensation, satisfaction **13** justification, peace offering **14** acknowledgment **15** indemnification

amenity, amenities 8 civility, mild-

ness, niceties **9** geniality, gentility **10** affability, amiability, courtesies, gentleness, politeness, refinement **11** gallantries, good manners **12** friendliness, graciousness, pleasantness **13** agreeableness

Amen Ra
also: **6** Amon Ra, Amen Re
origin: **8** Egyptian
god of: **8** universe
corresponds to: **4** Amen, Amon, Jove, Zeus **5** Ammon **7** Jupiter

America
author: **19** Stephen Vincent Benet

America, North
country: **4** Cuba **5** Haiti **6** Belize, Canada, Mexico, Panama **8** Honduras **9** Costa Rica, Guatemala, Nicaragua **10** El Salvador **12** United States **17** Dominican Republic
island: **5** Banks **6** Baffin, Kodiak **7** Bahamas, Bermuda **8** Victoria **9** Alexander, Anticosti, Ellesmere, Greenland, Vancouver **10** Aleutians, Cape Breton, Long Island, West Indies **11** Southampton **12** Newfoundland, Prince Edward **13** Prince of Wales **14** Queen Charlotte
mountain: **5** Coast, Rocky **6** Brooks **7** Cascade **9** Mackenzie **10** Bitterroot **11** Appalachian **12** Sierra Nevada
highest point: **8** McKinley
lowest point: **11** Death Valley
river: **3** Red **4** Ohio **5** Yukon **6** Copper, Fraser, Hudson, Nelson **8** Arkansas, Colorado, Columbia, Delaware, Missouri **9** Mackenzie **10** Coppermine, Sacramento, San Joaquin, St Lawrence **11** Connecticut, Mississippi
lake: **4** Erie **5** Huron **6** Carson, Walker **7** Nipigon, Ontario **8** Manitoba, Michigan, Reindeer, Superior, Winnipeg **9** Athabasca, Champlain, Great Bear, Great Salt **10** Great Slave **11** Yellowstone
animal: **3** bat, rat **4** bear, lynx, puma, wolf **5** bison, moose, skunk **6** beaver, musk ox **7** bighorn, caribou **8** sewellel **9** pronghorn, white goat
bird: **4** hawk **5** eagle, snipe **8** bobwhite, woodcock, wood ibis **9** blue heron, ptarmigan
sea: **6** Bering **7** Chukchi, Lincoln **8** Beaufort **9** Caribbean
religion: **7** Judaism **10** Protestant **13** Roman Catholic **27** Eastern Orthodox Christianity
people: **6** Eskimo **8** European **12** African Negro **14** American Indian
language: **6** French **7** English, Spanish

America, South
country: **4** Peru **5** Chile **6** Brazil, Guyana **7** Bolivia, Ecuador, Uruguay **8** Colombia, Paraguay, Suriname **9** Argentina, Venezuela
city: **4** Lima **5** Quito **6** Bogota, Recife

7 Caracas **8** Salvador, Santiago, Sao Paulo **10** Montevideo **11** Buenos Aires, Porto Alegre **12** Rio de Janeiro **13** Belo Horizonte
island: 6 Chiloe, Chonos, Marajo **9** Galapagos **10** Wellington **11** Madre de Dios **13** Juan Fernandez, Reina Adelaida **14** Tierra del Fuego
sea: 9 Caribbean
lake: 5 Patos, Poopo, Mirim **6** Viedma **8** Titicaca **9** Maracaibo, San Martin **10** Concepcion
mountain: 6 Andes **9** Pakaraima **12** Monte Fitz Roy **14** Cerro Aconcagua, Monte Sarmiento **15** Serra dos Parecis **16** Monte San Valentin, Serra do Espinhaco
highest point: 9 Aconcagua
lowest point: 15 Peninsula Valdes
river: 3 Ica **4** Beni, Iaco, Jari, Meta, Napo **5** Abuna, Cauca, Chico, Iriri, Ituxi, Jurua, Jutai, Negro, Palma, Pardo, Purus, Tiete, Tigre, Xingu **6** Amazon, Arauca, Branco, Chubut, Cumina, Curaco, Cuyuni, Grande, Gurupi, Iguacu, Japura, Javari, Mamore, Maroni, Mortes, Parana, Salado, Vaupes **7** Bermejo, Caqueta, Deseado, Guapore, Jamunda, Juruena, Madeira, Mapuera, Maranon, Orinoco, Oyapock, Ucayali, Vichada **8** Amazonas, Araguaia, Colorado, Guaviare, Jamachim, Paraguay, Parnaiba, Putumayo, Tapajoz, Urubamba, Uruguay **9** Essequibo, Jaguaribe, Paranaiba, Saladillo, Sao Manuel, Tocantins **10** Courantyne **12** Sao Francisco
animal: 3 bat **4** bear, deer **5** llama, sloth, tapir **6** alpaca, monkey, ocelot, weasel **7** opossum, peccary, raccoon **8** capybara, javelina **9** armadillo
bird: 3 owl **4** hawk, rhea **5** eagle **6** condor, falcon, jabiru **7** hoatzin **8** flamingo **11** hummingbird
people: 6 Indian **7** African, Chibcha, Mestizo, Mulatto, Spanish **10** Araucanian, Portuguese
religion: 7 Judaism **10** Protestant **13** Roman Catholic
language: 5 Dutch **7** English, Spanish **10** Portuguese

American, The
author: 10 Henry James
character: 8 Mrs Bread **10** Mr Tristram **11** Mrs Tristram **12** Noemie Nioche **13** Count Valentin **14** Claire de Cintre **17** Christopher Newman **25** Marquis Urbain de Bellegarde
setting: 5 Paris

American Caesar
author: 17 William Manchester

American Claimant, The
author: 9 Mark Twain

American Dreams
author: 11 Studs Terkel

American Graffiti
director: 11 George Lucas
cast: 9 Paul Le Mat, Ron Howard **10** Candy Clark **11** Wolfman Jack **12** Harrison Ford **13** Cindy Williams **15** Richard Dreyfuss **17** MacKenzie Phillips

American Indian see under **14** Native American

American in Paris, An
director: 16 Vincente Minnelli
cast: 8 Nina Foch **9** Gene Kelly **11** Leslie Caron, Oscar Levant **14** Georges Guetary
score: 14 George Gershwin
Oscar for: 7 picture

Americanization of Emily
director: 12 Arthur Hiller
script by: 14 Paddy Chayefsky
cast: 11 James Coburn, James Garner **12** Julie Andrews **13** Melvyn Douglas

American Tragedy, An
author: 15 Theodore Dreiser
character: 12 Roberta Alden **14** Clyde Griffiths, Sondra Finchley **15** Samuel Griffiths
movie: 14 A Place in the Sun

America's Sweetheart
nickname of: 12 Mary Pickford

amethyst
species: 6 quartz
color: 6 purple
month: 8 February

Amfortas
leader of: 7 knights
in search of: 9 holy grail

ami, amie 6 friend

amiability 10 good nature, kindliness **12** agreeability, friendliness, pleasantness

amiable 6 genial, kindly, polite **7** affable, cordial, winning **8** amicable, charming, engaging, friendly, gracious, obliging, pleasant, pleasing, sociable **9** agreeable, congenial **10** attractive **11** good-natured

amicability 5 amity **7** concord **8** good will **9** affection **10** cordiality, friendship **12** friendliness **14** neighborliness

amicable 4 kind **5** civil **6** kindly, polite **7** amiable, cordial **8** amenable, friendly, sociable **9** agreeable, courteous, peaceable **10** benevolent, harmonious, neighborly **11** kindhearted

Amici, Dominic Felix
real name of: 9 Don Ameche

amicus curiae 17 a friend of the court

amigo, amiga 6 friend

Amis, Kingsley
author of: 8 Ending Up, Lucky Jim **10** Colonel Sun, Jake's Thing **11** I Like It Here, The Green Man **16** One Fat Englishman, Take A Girl Like You **18** Russian Hide-and-Seek, The Anti-Death League **20** That Uncertain Feeling
father of: 10 Martin Amis

amiss 4 awry **5** askew, false, wrong **6** astray, faulty **7** falsely, mixed-up, off base, wrongly **8** faultily, improper, mistaken, untoward **9** erroneous, incorrect, out of line **10** fallacious, improperly, mistakenly, out of order, unsuitable, unsuitably, untowardly **11** erroneously, incorrectly **12** inaccurately **13** inappropriate **15** inappropriately

Amittai
son: 5 Jonah

amity 6 accord **7** concord, harmony **8** good will, sympathy **9** agreement **10** cordiality, fellowship, fraternity, friendship **11** brotherhood, cooperation **13** understanding

Ammishaddai
son: 7 Ahiezer

Ammon
father: 3 Lot
descendants: 9 Ammonites

Ammonite god 6 Molech, Moloch

ammunition 4 ammo, arms **5** shell **6** bullet, rocket **7** missile, torpedo **9** artillery, cartridge, small arms **11** iron rations **13** powder and shot

ammunition dump 7 arsenal **8** magazine **18** military storehouse, munitions warehouse

amnesia 4 daze **5** fugue **6** stupor **7** agnosia **8** blackout **9** memory gap **11** anterograde, trance state

amnesty 6 pardon **8** immunity, reprieve **10** absolution **11** forgiveness **14** reconciliation

amoeba, ameba 4 dyad, germ, mold **5** spore, virus **6** fungus **7** ciliate, microbe **8** bacteria, reovirus **9** bacterium, echovirus **13** microorganism
part: 7 nucleus **8** membrane **9** pseudopod **10** protoplasm **11** food vacuole **18** contractile vacuole
reproduction by: 7 fission

amok see **5** amuck

Amon see **5** Amen

among 2 at **3** mid **4** amid, with **6** amidst **7** amongst, between, betwixt **12** in the midst of

among other persons
Latin: 10 inter alios

among others 8 attended, escorted, in a crowd, in a group, together **11** accompanied

among other things
Latin: 9 inter alia

among themselves
Latin: 7 inter se

Amon Ra see **6** Amen Ra

Amor see **5** Cupid

Amore dei Tre Re, L'
opera by: 10 Montemezzi

Amoretti
author: 13 Edmund Spenser

amoretto
art figure: 5 Cupid

amorous 4 fond **6** ardent, doting, loving, tender **8** enamored, lovesick **10** passionate **11** impassioned **12** affectionate

amorousness 4 love **5** ardor **6** warmth **7** passion

amor patriae 10 patriotism **13** love of country

amorphous 5 vague **8** formless, unshapen **9** anomalous, shapeless, undefined **11** nondescript **12** undelineated **13** characterless, indeterminate

Amos
    father: **4** Naum

Amos 'n' Andy
    character: **8** Lightnin' **9** Amos Jones, Andy Brown **13** George (the King Fish) Stevens **15** Sapphire Stevens
    cast: **8** Tim Moore **13** Ernestine Wade, Horace Stewart **14** Alvin Childress **15** Spencer Williams

amount 3 sum **4** bulk, mass **5** total **6** extent, volume **7** measure **8** quantity, sum total **9** aggregate, magnitude

amour 6 affair **7** liaison, romance **8** intrigue **10** love affair

amour propre 8 self-love **10** self-esteem **11** self-respect

Ampelos
    form: **5** satyr

Ampere, Andre-Marie
    field: **7** physics **11** mathematics
    nationality: **6** French
    founded: **15** electrodynamics **16** electromagnetism

amphibian 8 seaplane **10** hydroplane, vertebrate **14** aerohydroplane
    kind: **4** frog, newt, toad **9** caecilian **10** salamander
    young: **6** larvae **7** tadpole **8** polliwog

Amphisbaena
    form: **7** serpent
    number of heads: **3** two

amphitheater 4 bowl **5** arena **7** gallery, stadium **8** coliseum **10** auditorium
    Roman: **9** Colosseum

Amphitrite
    origin: **5** Greek
    goddess of: **3** sea
    father: **6** Nereus
    mother: **5** Doris
    husband: **8** Poseidon

Amphitruo (Amphitryon)
    author: **7** Plautus
    character: **4** Zeus **7** Alcmena, Jupiter, Mercury **10** Amphitryon

Amphitryon
    father: **7** Alcaeus
    grandfather: **7** Perseus
    uncle: **9** Electryon, Sthenelus
    wife: **7** Alcmene
    son: **8** Iphicles
    daughter: **8** Perimede

Amphitryon 38
    author: **13** Jean Giraudoux

amphora 3 jar, jug, urn **4** vase

ample 3 big **4** huge, vast, wide **5** broad, large, roomy **6** enough, plenty **7** copious, immense, liberal, profuse **8** abundant, adequate, extended, generous, spacious **9** bountiful, capacious, expansive, extensive, outspread, plentiful **10** commodious, sufficient, voluminous **11** substantial **12** satisfactory **14** more than enough

amplification 7 raising **8** increase, widening **9** expansion, extension **10** developing, filling out, increasing **11** added detail, development, elaboration, enlargement, expatiation, fleshing out, heightening, lengthening, rounding out **12** augmentation **13** magnification **14** aggrandizement **15** supplementation

amplify 5 add to, raise, widen **6** deepen, expand, extend **7** augment, broaden, develop, enlarge, fill out **8** complete, heighten, increase, lengthen **9** elaborate (on), expatiate, intensify **10** illustrate, strengthen, supplement

amplitude 4 bulk, mass, size **5** range, reach, scope, sweep, width **6** extent, volume **7** bigness, breadth, compass, expanse **8** fullness, plethora, richness, vastness **9** abundance, dimension, largeness, magnitude, plenitude, profusion **11** copiousness **12** completeness, spaciousness **13** capaciousness

amply 5 fully **6** richly **8** lavishly **9** copiously, liberally, profusely **10** abundantly, adequately, completely, generously, thoroughly **11** bountifully, plentifully **12** sufficiently, unstintingly **14** satisfactorily

amputate 5 sever **6** cut off, excise, lop off, remove **9** dismember

Amram
    father: **4** Bani **6** Dishon
    son: **5** Aaron, Moses
    daughter: **6** Miriam

Amsterdam
    airport: **8** Schiphol
    canal: **11** Herengracht **13** Keizersgracht, Prinsengracht
    capital of: **7** Holland **11** Netherlands
    landmark: **8** Oude Kerk **10** Nieuwe Kerk
    museum: **7** Van Gogh **9** Stedelijk **11** Rijksmuseum
    nickname: **16** Venice of the North
    waters: **6** Amstel **7** Ij River **9** Zuiderzee **10** Ijsselmeer **13** North Sea

amuck 4 amok, nuts **6** wildly **7** berserk, bonkers **8** crackers, insanely **9** in a frenzy **10** frenziedly, maniacally **11** ferociously, murderously **14** uncontrollably

amulet 5 charm **6** fetish **8** talisman **10** lucky piece

amuse 5 cheer **6** absorb, divert, oc-cupy, please **7** beguile, engross, enliven, gladden **8** interest **9** entertain

amusement 3 fun **4** game, play **5** hobby, revel **7** delight, pastime **8** pleasure **9** avocation, diversion, enjoyment, merriment **10** recreation **11** distraction **13** entertainment

amusing 5 droll, funny, witty **7** comical, waggish **8** cheering, farcical, humorous, pleasant, pleasing **9** absorbing, beguiling, diverting **10** delightful, engrossing **11** interesting, pleasurable **12** entertaining

Amy, Gilbert
    composer of: **9** Alpha-Beth **10** Epigrammes, Mouvements **11** Antiphonies **12** Trajectories

anagram 4 code **6** cipher

Anakim 11 giant people

analects 8 extracts **9** gleanings **10** miscellany, selections **11** collectanea, miscellanea

Analects of Confucius, The
    author: **9** Confucius

analeptic 9 stimulant **11** restorative

analgesic 4 drug **6** opiate **7** anodyne **8** narcotic **10** anesthetic, painkiller

analogous 4 akin, like **7** similar **8** parallel **10** comparable, equivalent **11** correlative **13** corresponding

analogy 6 simile **8** likeness, metaphor **10** comparison, similarity, similitude **11** correlation, equivalence, parallelism, resemblance **14** correspondence

analysis 4 test **5** assay, brief, study **6** digest, precis, review, search **7** breakup, inquiry, outline, summary, therapy **8** abstract, judgment, synopsis, thinking **9** appraisal, breakdown, diagnosis, partition, reasoning, reduction **10** dissection, estimation, evaluation, resolution, separation **11** examination, observation, speculation **12** dissociation **13** investigation, psychotherapy **14** interpretation, psychoanalysis

analyst 5 judge **6** shrink, tester **8** examiner, observer **9** appraiser, estimator, evaluator **12** headshrinker, investigator **13** psychoanalyst

analytic, analytical 7 logical, testing **8** rational, studious **9** inquiring, organized, searching **10** diagnostic, systematic **14** problem-solving

analyze 5 assay, judge, study **6** search **7** examine **8** appraise, consider, diagnose, evaluate, question **9** reason out **11** investigate **12** think through

Ananais
    father: **8** Nebedeus
    wife: **8** Sapphira
    sent to: **4** Paul, Saul
    lied to: **5** Peter
    same as: **4** liar

anarchist 5 rebel **8** mutineer, nihilist **9**

insurgent, terrorist **11** syndicalist **13** revolutionary

anarchy 5 chaos **6** utopia **8** disorder **11** lawlessness **13** the millennium **19** absence of government

Anastasia
director: **13** Anatole Litvak
cast: **10** Helen Hayes, Yul Brynner **12** Akim Tamiroff **13** Ingrid Bergman (Oscar)

anathema 3 ban **5** curse, taboo **7** censure **11** abomination, malediction **12** condemnation, denunciation, proscription **13** unmentionable **15** excommunication

Anathema
author: **14** Leonid Andreyev

anathematize 4 damn **7** accurse, condemn **8** execrate, maledict **9** abominate **13** excommunicate **17** hold in abomination

Anatolia *see* **7** Armenia

Anatolian
language family: **12** Indo-European
includes: **6** Luwian Lycian Lydian **7** Hittite
spoken in: **9** Asia Minor
spoken by: **8** Hittites

anatomist 12 morphologist
American: **5** Allen, Evans **7** Herrick **8** Stockard
Arabian: **8** Avicenna
British: **4** Owen **5** Hooke **6** Harvey
Dutch: **10** Swammerdam
French: **6** Buffon, Cuvier
German: **5** Wolff **7** Schwann
Greek: **5** Galen **9** Aristotle **10** Herophilus **12** Erasistratus
Italian: **8** Malpighi
Scottish: **5** Brown

anatomize 7 analyze, dissect **18** separate into pieces

anatomy 4 body **8** analysis **9** structure **10** dissection **11** examination

Anatomy Lesson, The
author: **10** Philip Roth

Anatomy of a Murder
director: **13** Otto Preminger
cast: **8** Eve Arden **9** Lee Remick **10** Ben Gazzara **12** George C Scott, James Stewart, Kathryn Grant **14** Arthur O'Connell
score: **13** Duke Ellington

Anatomy of Melancholy, The
author: **12** Robert Burton

Anatosaurus
type: **8** dinosaur **10** ornithopod
period: **10** Cretaceous
characteristic: **10** duck-billed
location: **12** North America

Anaxibia
father: **6** Atreus
mother: **6** Aerope
brother: **8** Menelaus **9** Agamemnon
husband: **6** Nestor **9** Strophius
son: **7** Pylades

Anaximander
field: **11** mathematics
nationality: **5** Greek
doctrine: **11** single-world
first: **22** geometric universe model

ancestor 8 begetter, forebear **9** precursor, prototype **10** antecedent, forefather, forerunner, procreator, progenitor **11** predecessor

ancestry 4 line, race **5** house, stock **6** family, origin **7** descent, lineage **8** heredity, pedigree **9** ancestors, blood line, genealogy, parentage **10** derivation, extraction, family tree **11** progenitors

Anchisaurus
type: **8** dinosaur
location: **17** Connecticut Valley

Anchises
prince of: **4** Troy
father: **5** Capys
mother: **8** Themiste
grandfather: **9** Assaracus
uncle: **8** Laomedon
brother: **7** Laocoon
son: **5** Lyrus **6** Aeneas

anchor 3 fix **4** hook, moor **5** affix, basis **6** fasten, secure **7** bulwark, defense, mooring, support **8** mainstay, security **9** safeguard **10** foundation **12** ground tackle

anchorage 3 key **4** bund, dock, pier, port, quay, slip **5** berth, haven, jetty, wharf **6** harbor, marina **7** dockage, mooring, seaport **9** harborage, roadstead

ancient 3 old **4** aged **5** early, hoary, Greek, olden, passe, Roman **6** age-old, bygone, old hat, remote **7** antique, archaic, classic, very old **8** long past, obsolete, outmoded, primeval, timeworn **9** classical, out-of-date, primitive **10** antiquated, fossilized, Greco-Roman **11** obsolescent, prehistoric **12** old-fashioned, out-of-fashion

ancientness 8 great age **9** antiquity **11** advanced age

ancient times 9 antiquity **10** days of yore **12** the Golden Age

ancillary 5 minor **7** adjunct **8** inferior **9** accessory, auxiliary, dependent, secondary **10** additional, subsidiary **11** subordinate, subservient **12** contributory **13** supplementary

Ancius
form: **7** centaur

Ancus Marcius
king of: **4** Rome

and 3 too **4** also, more, plus **8** as well as **10** in addition **11** furthermore

andante
music: **4** even **14** moderately slow

Andean
language family: **16** Andean-Equatorial

group: **3** Ona **6** Aymara, Yahgan, Zaparo **7** Quechua **10** Araucanian

Andean-Equatorial
language branch: **6** Andean **10** Equatorial

and elsewhere 4 et al **7** et alibi

Andersen, Hans Christian
known for: **10** fairy tales
born: **7** Denmark
author of: **10** Thumbelina **11** The Red Shoes **12** The Snow Queen, The Swineherd, The Tinder Box **14** The Nightingale **15** The Ugly Duckling **16** The Little Mermaid **18** The Little Match Girl **20** The Princess and the Pea **21** The Emperor's New Clothes **22** The Steadfast Tin Soldier **25** The Shepherdess and the Sweep
played by: **9** Danny Kaye

Anderson, Frances Margaret
real name of: **14** Judith Anderson

Anderson, Judith
real name: **23** Frances Margaret Anderson
born: **8** Adelaide **9** Australia
roles: **5** Medea **6** Hamlet, Salome **7** Macbeth, Rebecca **8** Kings Row **16** Cat on a Hot Tin Roof

Anderson, Maxwell
author of: **7** High Tor **8** Key Largo **9** Winterset **11** Valley Forge **14** Both Your Houses, Lost in the Stars, Mary of Scotland, What Price Glory? **17** Elizabeth the Queen **20** Knickerbocker Holiday

Anderson, Sherwood
author of: **9** Poor White **12** Beyond Desire, Dark Laughter, Horses and Men **13** Many Marriages, Winesburg Ohio **15** Death in the Woods **18** The Triumph of the Egg

Anderson, Sparky (George Lee)
sport: **8** baseball
position: **7** manager
team: **9** Minnesota **14** Cincinnati Reds

Andersonville
author: **15** MacKinlay Kantor

Andersson, Bibi
born: **6** Sweden **9** Stockholm
roles: **14** The Seventh Seal **16** Wild Strawberries **19** Scenes from a Marriage **20** Smiles of a Summer Night

Andes
Spanish: **20** Cordillera de los Andes
peak: **6** Pissis, Sajama, Sorata **7** Illampu **8** Cotopaxi, Illimani **9** Huascaran **10** Chimborazo **14** Cristobal Colon
highest point: **9** Aconcagua
volcano: **6** Sangay, Tolima **8** Cotopaxi **10** Tungurahua
country: **4** Peru **5** Chile **6** Panama **7** Bolivia, Ecuador **8** Colombia **9** Argentina, Venezuela
river: **5** Cauca **6** Amazon, Parana **7** Orinoco, Ucayali **9** Magdalena

lake: 5 Poopo **8** Titicaca
animal: 5 llama **6** alpaca, condor, huemul **10** chinchilla

And I Worked at the Writer's Trade
  author: 13 Malcolm Cowley

Andorra
  other name: 13 Valls d'Andorra **16** Valleys of Andorra
  capital/largest city: 14 Andorra-la-Vella
  others: 3 Pal **5** Ramio **6** Ordino, Soldeu **7** Canillo, Certers **9** La Massana **11** Les Escaldes **16** San Julian de Loria
  division: 6 Encamp, Ordino **7** Andorra, Camillo **9** La Massana, Sant Julia
  heads of state: 13 Bishop of Urgel (Spain) **17** President of France
  head of government: 11 First Syndic
  monetary unit: 5 franc **6** peseta
  lake: 11 Engolasters
  location: 8 Pyrenees
  mountain: 6 d'Etats **8** l'Estanyo, Pyrenees **10** Cataperdis
  highest point: 11 Como Pedrosa
  neighbors: 5 Spain **6** France
  river: 6 Ariege, Valira
  people: 7 Catalan **8** Andosian
  language: 6 French **7** Catalan, Spanish
  religion: 13 Roman Catholic
  place: 12 Casa de la Vall
    Moorish ruin: 4 Ceca, Meka
  feature:
    co-princes' representative: 7 vigueer, viguier
    fiesta: 13 Bal de Morratxa
    food payment to bishop: 9 la quistia

Andorra-la-Vella
  capital of: 7 Andorra

and others 3 etc **4** et al **6** et alii **7** and so on **8** et cetera **10** and so forth, and the rest

And Quiet Flows the Don
  author: 15 Mikhail Sholokov
  character: 6 Piotra **7** Bunchuk, Natalia **14** Gregor Melekhov **16** Aksinia Astakhova

Andrea del Sarto
  real name: 32 Andrea Domenico d'Agnolo di Francesco
  born: 5 Italy **8** Florence
  artwork: 7 Caritas **9** A Young Man **16** Birth of the Virgin, Journey of the Magi **19** Madonna of the Harpies, Portrait of a Sculptor

Andrea del Sarto
  author: 14 Robert Browning

Andress, Ursula
  husband: 9 John Derek
  born: 5 Bern **11** Switzerland
  roles: 3 She **4** Dr No **12** Casino Royale, Four for Texas

Andrew 7 apostle
  brother: 5 Peter, Simon

Andrews, Dana
  real name: 17 Carver Dana Andrews
  brother: 12 Steve Forrest
  born: 9 Collins MS
  roles: 5 Laura **9** State Fair **12** Elephant Walk **13** A Walk in the Sun, Ox-Bow Incident **15** Two for the Seesaw **22** The Best Years of Our Lives

Andrews, Julie
  real name: 19 Julia Elizabeth Wells
  husband: 12 Blake Edwards
  born: 7 England **14** Walton-on-Thames
  roles: 10 My Fair Lady **11** Mary Poppins (Oscar) **14** Victor Victoria **15** The Sound of Music

Andreyev, Leonid Nikolaevich
  author of: 3 S O S **5** Savva **7** Lazarus, Silence **8** Anathema **10** To the Stars **11** The Red Laugh **12** The Life of Man **16** He Who Gets Slapped **18** Love of One's Neighbor **19** Seven That Were Hanged

Andria
  author: 7 Terence

Androcles
  origin: 5 Roman
  position: 5 slave

Androcles and the Lion
  author: 17 George Bernard Shaw
  removed: 5 thorn

androgenous 8 bisexual **14** hermaphroditic

Andromache
  father: 6 Eetion
  husband: 6 Hector
  son: 6 Pielus **8** Astyanax, Molossus, Pergamus **9** Cestrinus
  author: 9 Euripides
  character: 6 Peleus, Thetis **7** Orestes **8** Menelaus
    mistress of: 11 Neoptolemus
    rival: 8 Hermione
    son: 8 Molossus
  setting: 8 Thessaly

Andromaque
  author: 18 Jean Baptiste Racine
  character:
    son: 8 Astyanax
    king: 7 Pyrrhus
  setting: 6 Epirus

Andromeda
  astronomy: 13 constellation
  father: 7 Cepheus
  mother: 10 Cassiopeia
  husband: 7 Perseus
  son: 6 Mestor, Perses **7** Alcaeus, Heleius **9** Electryon, Sthenelus
  daughter: 10 Gorgophone
  rescued from: 10 sea monster
  rescued by: 7 Perseus

Andromeda Strain, The
  author: 15 Michael Crichton

androphobia
  fear of: 3 men

Androsphinx
  form: 6 sphinx
  head of: 3 man

and so forth 3 etc **7** and so on **8** et cetera **9** and others **10** and the rest

and so on 3 etc **8** et cetera **9** and others **10** and so forth, and the rest

And Then There Were None
  director: 9 Rene Clair
  based on novel by: 14 Agatha Christie
  cast: 11 Roland Young **12** Louis Hayward, Walter Huston **15** Barry Fitzgerald
  remade as: 16 Ten Little Indians

and thou, Brutus
  Latin: 9 et tu Brute
  spoken by: 12 Julius Caesar

Andvari
  origin: 6 Nordic
  form: 5 dwarf

Andy Capp
  creator: 14 Reginald Smythe
  character: 5 Vicar
    wife: 3 Flo
  plays: 7 snooker

Andy Griffith Show, The
  character: 10 Andy Taylor, Barney Fife, Goober Pyle, Helen Crump, Opie Taylor **11** Floyd Lawson **12** Otis Campbell **13** Aunt Bee Taylor, Howard Sprague
  cast: 8 Hal Smith **9** Don Knotts, Ron (Ronny) Howard **10** Jack Dodson **12** Andy Griffith, Anita Corsaut, Howard McNear **13** Frances Bavier, George Lindsey
  setting: 8 Mayberry
  Andy's job: 7 sheriff

anecdote 4 tale, yarn **5** story **6** sketch **12** brief account, reminiscence
  collection: 3 ana

anemic, anaemic 3 wan **4** dull, pale, weak **5** quiet **6** feeble, pallid **7** subdued **9** colorless **11** thin-blooded **13** characterless

anemone 4 lily **5** plant **6** flower

anesthesia, anaesthesia, anesthesis 6 stupor **8** numbness **11** insentience **13** loss of feeling **15** unconsciousness

anesthetic, anaesthetic 4 drug **5** ether, local **6** caudal, opiate, spinal **7** general **8** narcotic, procaine **9** analgesic, enflurane, halothane, lidocaine, peridural **10** chloroform, isoflurane, painkiller, tetracaine, thiopental **11** acupuncture, laughing gas **12** nitrous oxide **15** sodium pentothal

anesthetize 4 dope, drug, numb **6** deaden, sedate

anew 5 again, newly **6** afresh **8** once more **9** over again **11** from scratch
  Latin: 6 de novo

a new order of the ages is born
  Latin: 17 novus ordo seclorum

author: 6 Virgil
   work: 8 Eclogues
motto of: 11 US great seal
angel 3 gem **4** doll **5** jewel, power, saint **6** cherub, patron, seraph, throne, virtue **7** sponsor **8** cherabim, seraphim, treasure **9** archangel **10** benefactor, domination **11** underwriter **12** principality **14** celestial being, heavenly spirit, messenger of God **15** financial backer
Angel, fallen 5 Satan **6** Azazel **7** Lucifer
angelic 4 good, pure **5** ideal **6** divine, lovely **7** saintly **8** adorable, beatific, cherubic, ethereal, heavenly, innocent, seraphic **9** angel-like, beautiful, celestial, rapturous, spiritual **10** entrancing **11** enrapturing
Angelic Doctor
   nickname of: 15 St Thomas Aquinas
Angelico, Fra
   real name: 13 Guido di Pietro
   born: 7 Vicchio **14** Castell Vecchio
   artwork: 12 Annunciation **15** Madonna Annalena **19** Descent from the Cross **21** Coronation of the Virgin **29** Madonna of the Linen Drapers' Guild
Angelo
   character in: 17 Measure for Measure
   author: 11 Shakespeare
Angel of Fire, The
   also: 13 The Fiery Angel
   opera by: 9 Prokofiev
anger 3 ire, vex **4** bile, fury, gall, rage, rile **5** annoy, chafe, pique, wrath **6** choler, dander, enmity, enrage, hatred, madden, nettle, rankle, ruffle, spleen, temper **7** incense, inflame, outrage, provoke, umbrage **8** acrimony, embitter, irritate, vexation **9** animosity, annoyance, displease, hostility, hot temper, ill temper, infuriate, petulance **10** antagonism, antagonize, exacerbate, exasperate, irritation, resentment **11** displeasure, indignation **12** exasperation, make bad blood **14** disapprobation **15** get one's dander up **16** cause ill feelings **18** ruffle one's feathers
Anger
   author: 9 May Sarton
Angerboda
   also: 9 Angrbodha, Angurboda
   origin: 12 Scandinavian
   form: 8 giantess
   children: 3 Hel **6** Fenrir, Fenris **11** Iormungandr, Jormungandr **14** Midgard Serpent
angle 4 bend, cusp, edge, side, turn **5** focus, slant **6** aspect, corner **7** outlook **8** position **9** viewpoint **10** divergence, standpoint **11** perspective, point of view
   kind: 5 acute, right **6** obtuse **8** straight

point: 6 vertex
   measure: 7 degrees
angled 4 bent **6** fished **7** crooked, slanted **8** diverged
Anglo-Frisian
   language family: 12 Indo-European
   branch: 8 Germanic
   group: 15 Western Germanic
   language: 7 English, Frisian
Angola
   other name: 7 Bakongo **20** Portuguese West Africa
   capital/largest city: 6 Luanda
   others: 5 Dundo **6** Ambriz, Huambo, Lobito **7** Cabinda, Kampala, Malange, Malanje, Salazar **8** Benguela, Cassinga, Vila Luso **9** Ambrizete, Mocamedes **10** Mossamedes, Nova Lisboa, Silva Porto
   division: 3 Bie **4** Uige **5** Huila, Lunda, Zaire **6** Cunene, Huambo, Luanda, Moxico **7** Cabinda, Malanje **8** Benguela **9** Cuanza Sul, Mocamedes **11** Cuanza Norte **13** Cuando Cubango
   monetary unit: 6 escudo, macuta, macute **7** angolar, centavo
   mountain: 5 Chela **6** Loviti **16** Humpata Highlands
   highest point: 4 Moco
   river: 4 Cuvo **5** Congo, Cuito, Longa **6** Cassai, Coanza, Cuando, Cuanza, Cunene, Kunene, Kwango, Kwanza, Luando **7** Chiumbe, Cubango, Zambezi **11** Lungue- Bungo
   sea: 6 Indian **8** Atlantic
   physical feature:
     basin: 8 Okavango
     desert: 9 Mocamedes
     falls: 15 Catarata Ruacana, Duque de Braganca
     plain: 8 Planalto
     plateau: 4 Rand **5** Huila **11** Benguela Bie, Lunda Divide
   people: 5 Bantu, Kongo, Lundu **6** Chokwe, Herero, Mbundu, Ovambo **7** Bakongo, Kangela, Kikongo **8** Kimbundu, Kwangare **9** Ovinbundu **12** Nyaneka-Humbi
     leader: 13 Agostinho Neto **20** Jose Eduardo dos Santos
   language: 5 Bantu **8** Kimbundu, Oumbundu **9** Ovimbundu **10** Portuguese
   religion: 7 animism **10** Protestant **13** Roman Catholic
   place:
     fortress: 9 Sao Miguel
   feature:
     mahogany: 5 khaya
     weed: 6 archil
angry 3 mad **5** huffy, irate, riled, vexed **6** fuming, galled, piqued, raging **7** annoyed, boiling, burnt up, enraged, furious, hateful, hostile, nettled **8** incensed, inflamed, offended, outraged, petulant, provoked **9** affronted, indignant, irascible, irritated, resent-

ful, splenetic, turbulent **10** displeased, embittered, infuriated **11** acrimonious, exasperated, ill-tempered **12** antagonistic
angst 5 dread **6** unease **7** anxiety **10** foreboding, uneasiness **12** apprehension
angstrom
   abbreviation: 1 A
Angstrom, Anders Jon
   field: 7 physics **9** astronomy
   founded: 12 spectroscopy
   mapped: 11 solar system
   angstrom unit: 17 wavelength of light
Angstrom, Harry see **6** Updike
anguish 3 woe **4** pain **5** agony, grief **6** misery, sorrow **7** anxiety, despair, remorse, torment **8** distress **9** heartache, suffering
Anguish
   goddess of: 8 Angerona
anguished 6 pained **7** anxious, fearful **9** tormented **10** distressed **11** heartbroken
angular 4 bent, bony, lank, lean **5** gaunt, lanky, spare **6** jagged **7** crooked, scrawny **8** rawboned **13** sharp- cornered
Angus Og
   origin: 5 Irish
   god of: 4 love **5** youth **6** beauty
animadversion 4 flak **7** nagging, quibble **9** aspersion, criticism, pestering **12** faultfinding **14** censoriousness
animal 3 pet **5** beast, brute **6** mammal **8** creature, nonhuman, organism **9** quadruped
   group: 4 bird, fish, worm **6** insect, mammal, sponge **7** primate, reptile, rotifer **8** ruminant **9** amphibian **10** vertebrate **12** invertebrate
Animal Crackers
   director: 13 Victor Heerman
   cast: 5 Chico, Harpo, Zeppo **7** Groucho **11** Lillian Roth **12** Marx Brothers **14** Margaret Dumont
   song: 25 Hooray for Captain Spaulding
Animal Farm
   author: 12 George Orwell
   character: 5 Boxer **7** Mr Jones **8** Napoleon, Snowball
Animals in That Country, The
   author: 14 Margaret Atwood
animate 4 fire, goad, move, stir, urge, warm **5** alive, impel, liven, set on **6** arouse, excite, fire up, incite, moving, prompt, spur on, vivify, work up **7** actuate, enliven, inspire, provoke, quicken **8** activate, energize, vitalize **9** instigate, make alive, stimulate **10** invigorate, make lively **11** add spirit to **12** give energy to
animated 3 gay, hot **4** airy **5** brisk, quick, vivid **6** active, ardent, blithe,

breezy, bright, elated, lively **7** buoyant, dynamic, fervent, glowing, vibrant, zealous, zestful **8** exciting, spirited, sportive, vigorous **9** ebullient, energetic, sprightly, vivacious **10** passionate **12** invigorating

animation 3 vim **4** fire, glow, life, zest **5** ardor, verve, vigor **6** action, gaiety, spirit **7** elation **8** activity, alacrity, buoyancy, vibrancy, vitality, vivacity **9** alertness, briskness, eagerness, good cheer **10** brightness, ebullience, enthusiasm, excitement, liveliness **12** exhilaration, sportiveness **13** sprightliness

animosity 4 hate **5** anger **6** enmity, hatred, malice, rancor, strife **7** dislike, ill will **8** acrimony **9** antipathy, hostility, malignity **10** antagonism, bitterness, resentment **11** malevolence **14** unfriendliness

animus 5 anger, spite, venom **6** enmity, hatred, malice, rancor **7** disdain, dislike, ill will **8** acrimony, bad blood **9** animosity, antipathy, hostility **10** antagonism, bitterness, ill feeling, resentment **12** hard feelings

anise
botanical name: **16** Pimpinella Anisum
origin: **5** Egypt, India **13** Mediterranean
flavor: **8** licorice
use: **5** cakes, fruit, rolls **7** cookies
plant with similar flavor: **9** star anise
legend:
    safeguards against: **7** evil eye **10** nightmares **11** indigestion
    antidote to: **12** scorpion bite

anisette
type: **7** liqueur
origin: **6** France
flavor: **5** anise
drink: **17** Suissesse cocktail
with gin: **8** Snowball **11** Bachio Punch
substitute for: **8** Absinthe

Ankylosaurus
type: **8** dinosaur **10** ornithopod
location: **12** North America
period: **10** Cretaceous
characteristic: **7** armored

Anna
husband: **5** Tobit
daughter: **4** Mary
sister: **4** Dido
corresponds to: **11** Anna Perenna
died by: **8** drowning

Annabel Lee
author: **13** Edgar Allan Poe

Anna Christie
author: **12** Eugene O'Neill
character: **6** Marthy **8** Mat Burke **19** Chris Christopherson
ship: **14** Simeon Winthrop

Anna Karenina
author: **10** Leo Tolstoy
character: **12** Count Vronsky **13** Alexei Karenin **15** Konstantin Levin **19** Kitty Shcherbatskaya **20** Prince Stepan Oblonsky
setting: **6** Moscow, Russia **12** St Petersburg
director: **13** Clarence Brown
cast: **9** May Robson **10** Greta Garbo (Anna Karenina) **13** Basil Rathbone (Karenin), Frederic March (Vronsky) **16** Maureen O'Sullivan **18** Freddie Bartholomew
earlier film version: **4** Love

annals 7 history, minutes, records **8** archives **9** registers **10** chronicles, chronology **13** yearly records **15** historical rolls **20** chronological records

Annam see **7** Vietnam

Anna Marie
character in: **16** Giants of the Earth
author: **7** Rolvaag

Anna of the Five Towns
author: **13** Arnold Bennett

anneal 6 harden, temper **7** toughen

Anne of Geierstein (or, The Maiden of the Mist)
author: **14** Sir Walter Scott

annex 3 add **4** grab, join **5** affix, merge, seize **6** adjoin, append, attach, tack on **7** acquire, connect, subjoin **8** addition **9** appendage **10** attachment **11** appropriate, expropriate, incorporate

Annfwn
also: **5** Annwn
origin: **5** Welsh
means: **8** paradise

Annie Hall
director: **10** Woody Allen
cast: **9** Carol Kane, Paul Simon **10** Woody Allen **11** Diane Keaton, Tony Roberts **13** Shelley Duvall **15** Colleen Dewhurst
Oscar for: **7** actress (Keaton), picture **8** director (Allen) **10** screenplay

annihilate 3 end **5** erase, waste **7** abolish, destroy, wipe out **8** decimate, demolish, lay waste **9** eradicate, extirpate, liquidate **10** extinguish, obliterate **11** exterminate

annihilation 9 abolition, wiping out **11** destruction, extirpation, laying waste, liquidation **12** obliteration **13** extermination

anniversary 4 fete **7** holiday, name day **8** birthday, feast day **9** centenary **10** centennial **11** bicentenary, celebration **12** bicentennial **13** commemoration, golden jubilee **16** sesquicentennial

Ann-Margret
real name: **16** Ann-Margret Olsson
husband: **10** Roger Smith
born: **6** Sweden **9** Valsjobyn
roles: **5** Tommy **8** Scarlett **12** Bye-Bye Birdie **15** Carnal Knowledge, Grumpy Old Men **21** A Streetcar Named Desire

anno Domini 18 in the year of our Lord
abbreviation: **2** AD
alternative: **2** CE Common Era

anno mundi 19 in the year of the world

anno regni 19 in the year of the reign

annotate 5 gloss **6** remark **7** comment, explain, expound **8** construe, footnote **9** elucidate, explicate, interpret **10** commentate

annotation 4 note **5** gloss **6** remark **7** comment **8** exegesis, footnote **10** commentary, marginalia **11** elucidation, explication, observation

announce 5 herald, reveal, signal **7** betoken, declare, divulge, give out, portend, presage, publish, signify, trumpet **8** disclose, foretell, proclaim **9** advertise, broadcast, harbinger **10** promulgate **11** disseminate

announcement 9 broadcast, statement **11** declaration **12** proclamation

annoy 3 irk, nag, tax, vex **4** gall, rile **5** harry, tease, worry **6** badger, bother, harass, heckle, hector, nettle, pester, plague, ruffle **7** disturb, provoke, torment, trouble **8** distract, irritate **10** exasperate **13** inconvenience

annoyance 6 bother **8** irritant, nuisance, vexation **10** irritation **11** distraction, disturbance

annoyed 5 irked, upset, vexed **9** disturbed, irritated, perturbed **11** discomposed **12** disconcerted

annual 4 weed **5** plant **6** flower, serial **7** gazette, journal, reports **8** bulletin, magazine, notebook, periodic **9** vegetable **10** periodical, record book

annuity 6 income **7** pension, stipend **9** allowance

annul 4 undo, void **6** cancel, negate, recall, repeal, revoke **7** abolish, nullify, rescind, retract, reverse **8** abrogate, dissolve **10** invalidate

annulment 6 recall, repeal **7** undoing, voiding **8** reversal **9** abolition **10** abrogation, retraction, revocation **11** dissolution, repudiation **12** cancellation, invalidation **13** nullification

annus mirabilis 13 year of wonders

anodyne 4 balm **6** solace **7** comfort **9** comforter **10** palliative

anoint 3 oil **5** crown **6** ordain **8** put oil on **9** pour oil on

Anointed One 5 Jesus **7** Messiah

anomalous 3 odd **7** bizarre, strange **8** abnormal, atypical, peculiar **9** irregular, monstrous **11** incongruous **12** out of keeping

anomaly 6 oddity, rarity **9** deviation **10** aberration **11** abnormality, incongruity, peculiarity **12** eccentricity, irregularity **18** exception to the rule

anon 4 soon, then **5** again, later **7** by and by, shortly **8** tomorrow **9** afterward, presently **10** before long **11** immediately, in the future

anonymous 7 unnamed **8** nameless, unsigned **12** unidentified **13** bearing no name **14** unacknowledged **19** of unknown authorship

another 4 else, more **5** extra, other **7** further, renewed **9** accessory, otherwise **10** additional **12** supplemental **13** something else, supplementary **14** different thing

Anouilh, Jean
   author of: 6 Becket **8** Antigone, Eurydice, Leocadia, L'hermine **11** Dear Antoine **14** Time Remembered **15** Le Bal des Voleurs, Thieves' Carnival **16** Point of Departure, Ring Round the Moon **19** Waltz of the Toreadors **20** L'Invitation au Chateau **23** Traveller Without Luggage

ansate 7 handled

anser 5 goose **6** stupid **7** foolish **8** anserine

answer 3 say **4** fill, meet, suit **5** reply, serve, solve, write **6** be like, rejoin, retort **7** conform, fulfill, react to, resolve, respond **8** be enough, response, solution **9** be similar, rejoinder **10** be adequate, correspond, pass muster, resolution **11** acknowledge, explanation **12** be correlated, be equivalent, be sufficient, do well enough **14** acknowledgment, be satisfactory

answerable 6 liable **8** beholden **10** chargeable **11** accountable, responsible

Answer as a Man
   author: 14 Taylor Caldwell

ant
   caste: 4 male **5** queen **6** worker **7** soldier
   kind: 3 red **4** army, fire **5** dairy, thief **6** beggar, farmer, velvet, weaver **7** formica, janitor, pharaoh **8** honeypot, mushroom **9** Argentine, carpenter, cornfield, harvester, legionary **10** leaf cutter **11** little black **12** fungus grower, odorous house, southern fire **13** mound building **14** Texas harvester
   group of: 6 colony

antagonism 5 spite **6** animus, enmity, hatred, rancor, strife **7** discord, dislike, rivalry **8** aversion, clashing, conflict, friction **9** animosity, antipathy, hostility **10** bitterness, dissension, opposition, resentment **11** detestation

antagonist 3 foe **5** enemy, rival **7** opposer **8** attacker, opponent **9** adversary, assailant, disputant **10** competitor, contestant

antagonistic 7 hostile **8** contrary, inimical **9** rancorous **10** antisocial, unfriendly **11** belligerent **12** antipathetic, disputatious

antagonize 5 repel **6** offend **8** alienate, estrange

Antananarivo, Tananarive
   capital of: 10 Madagascar

Antarctica
   division: 10 Wilkes Land **13** Marie Byrd Land, Queen Maud Land **14** Edith Ronne Land **17** Ellsworth Highland
   island: 4 Ross **5** Peter, Scott **6** Biscoe, Hearst **7** Ballery, Charcot **8** Adelaide, Elephant **9** Alexander, Joinville, Roosevelt **10** Coronation, King George **11** South Orkney **13** South Shetland
   mountain: 8 Sentinel **9** Pensacola **14** Transantarctic **23** Executive Committee Range
   valley: 6 Wright
   river: 4 Onyx
   natural resource/mineral: 4 coal
   plant life: 4 moss **5** algae, fungi **6** lichen, pollen **8** bacteria
   animal: 4 lice, mite, tick **5** whale **7** fur seal **8** ross seal **9** crabeater **11** weddell seal, wingless fly
   bird: 4 skua **6** fulmar, petrel **7** penguin **10** cape pigeon
   sea: 4 Ross **5** Davis **6** Scotia **7** Weddell **8** Amundsen **14** Bellingshausen

ante 3 bet, pot **5** stake, wager **12** beginning bet

anteater 5 sloth **7** echidna **8** aardvark **9** armadillo

antecede 7 precede, predate **8** go before, preexist **10** anticipate

ante Christum 12 before Christ
   abbreviation: 2 AC

antedate 7 precede, predate **8** antecede, go before **9** come first **10** anticipate **12** happen before

Antediluvian 14 before the flood

antediluvian 7 antique, archaic **8** obsolete **10** antiquated

antelope 8 ruminant
   family: 7 Bovidae
   kind: 3 doe, gnu **4** buck, deer, fawn, kudu, oryx, roan **5** bongo, eland, moose, sable **6** dik-dik, duiker, impala, lechwe, nilgai **7** gazelle, gemsbok, gerenuk **8** bluebuck, bontebok, steinbok **9** blackbuck, sitatunga, springbok, waterbuck **10** four-horned **12** Klipspringer
   habitat: 4 Asia **6** Africa

Antelope State
   nickname of: 8 Nebraska

antenna 6 aerial, feeler

anterior 5 front, prior **7** forward, in front **8** previous **9** precedent **10** antecedent **12** placed before

Anteros
   brother: 4 Eros
   avenger of: 14 unrequited love

Anthea
   epithet of: 4 Hera
   means: 7 flowery

Antheil, George
   born: 9 Trenton NJ
   autobiography: 13 Bad Boy of Music
   composer of: 7 Volpone **12** Helen Retires, Jazz Symphony **13** Sonata Sauvage, Transatlantic **14** Airplane Sonata **15** Ballet Mecanique

anthem 4 hymn, song **5** carol, ditty, music, paean, psalm **6** ballad, sacred **7** cantata **8** doxology **11** church music

Anthesteria
   origin: 5 Greek
   festival of: 4 wine **6** spring **7** flowers

anthology 6 choice, digest **7** garland **8** analects, chapbook, extracts, treasury **9** gleanings, scrapbook **10** collection, compendium, miscellany, selections **11** collectanea, compilation, florilegium, miscellanea **15** commonplace book

Anthony, Susan B.
   leader in: 14 women's suffrage

Anthony Adverse
   author: 18 William Hervey Allen

anthophobia
   fear of: 7 flowers

anthropologist
   American: 4 Boas, Mead **5** Lowie, Sapir **6** Geertz, Linton, Morgan **7** Kroeber **8** Benedict
   British: 5 Leach, Tylor **6** Fortes, Leakey, Rivers **14** Evans-Pritchard, Radcliffe-Brown
   French: 5 Mauss **8** Durkheim **11** Levi-Strauss
   Polish: 10 Malinowski

anthropology
   term: 4 myth **6** custom, ritual **7** culture, kinship **8** artifact **9** ethnology, evolution, field work **11** ethnography **16** natural selection
   type/related study: 5 legal, urban **6** social **7** applied, medical **8** cultural, economic, physical **9** political **11** linguistics **12** human ecology **13** psychological **19** structural-symbolist
   famous study: 3 San **4** Kung **7** Eskimos, Samoans, Tasaday **10** Aborigines **16** Pacific Islanders

anthropophobia
   fear of: 6 people

antibiotic 4 drug **5** venom **6** poison **8** curative **9** antidotal, antitoxic, pesticide **10** wonder drug **11** insecticide, miracle drug
   kind: 8 neomycin, subtilin **9** mycomycin **10** ampicillin, penicillin **12** erythromycin

antic, antics 5 larks, sport **6** pranks, tricks **9** escapades **10** buffoonery, skylarking, tomfoolery **11** shenanigans **12** clownishness, monkeyshines **14** practical jokes

anticipate 5 await **6** expect **7** count on, foresee, long for, look for, predict **8** envision, forecast, foretell **9** pin hope on **10** look toward **13** look forward to

anticipation 4 hope **10** expectancy **11** expectation, preparation

anticlimax 7 letdown **8** comedown **14** disappointment

antidote 4 cure **6** remedy **9** antitoxin **10** antipoison, corrective **12** counteragent, countervenom **13** counterpoison **14** countermeasure

Antigone
  author: **9** Sophocles **11** Jean Anouilh
  character: **6** Ismene **8** Tiresias
    father: **7** Oedipus
    mother: **7** Jocasta
    brother: **8** Eteocles **9** Polynices
    sister: **6** Ismene
    uncle: **5** Creon
    cousin/lover: **6** Haemon
    defied: **5** Creon

Antigua and Barbuda
  capital/largest city: **7** St John's
  government:
    member of: **26** West Indies Associated States
    head of state: **14** British monarch **15** governor-general
  island: **4** Long **5** Guana **7** Antigua, Barbuda, Redonda
  highest point: **9** Boggy Peak
  sea: **9** Caribbean
  physical feature:
    cove: **5** Royal
    harbor/harbour: **7** English
  people: **7** African, British **8** Lebanese **10** Portuguese
  language: **7** English
  religion: **8** Anglican, Moravian **13** Roman Catholic
  feature: **15** Nelson's Dockyard

anti-intellectual 5 yahoo **7** lowbrow **9** ignoramus, vulgarian **10** illiterate, philistine

antimony
  chemical symbol: **2** Sb

Antinous
  suitor of: **8** Penelope
  killed by: **8** Odysseus

antipathetic 6 averse **7** hostile **8** inimical **9** rancorous **11** ill-disposed

antipathy 6 enmity, rancor **7** disgust, dislike, ill will **8** aversion, distaste, loathing **9** animosity, hostility, repulsion **10** abhorrence, antagonism, repugnance **14** unfriendliness

Antiphas
  father: **7** Laocoon

Antipholus
  character in: **17** The Comedy of Errors
  author: **11** Shakespeare

antiphony 6 chorus **7** refrain **8** response

antipode 8 contrary, opposite **10** antithesis

Antiquary, The
  author: **14** Sir Walter Scott

antiquated 5 dated, passe **7** antique, archaic **8** obsolete, outdated, outmoded **9** out-of-date **11** obsolescent **12** old-fashioned

antique 3 old **5** curio, relic **6** rarity **7** bibelot, trinket **9** objet d'art **10** antiquated, memorabile **11** memorabilia

antiquities 6 relics **8** artifact **9** monuments

antiquity 7 oldness **8** great age **11** ancientness **12** ancient times

antiseptic 6 iodine **7** aseptic, sterile **8** germ-free **9** germicide **10** germ killer **11** bactericide **12** disinfectant, prophylactic

antisocial 7 asocial, hostile **8** menacing, retiring, unsocial **9** alienated **10** disruptive, rebellious, unfriendly, unsociable **11** belligerent, sociopathic **12** antagonistic, misanthropic

antithesis 7 inverse, reverse **8** antipode, contrary, contrast, converse, opposite

antithetical 8 contrary, opposing, opposite **10** discrepant, refutatory **11** conflicting, disagreeing **13** contradictory **14** countervailing, irreconcilable

antitoxin 5 serum **8** antidote **9** antivenom **12** counteragent **13** counterpoison

antler 4 horn, knob, rack **5** spike **6** shovel **8** deerhorn, troching
  part: **3** bay **4** brow **5** crown, royal

ant lion
  also: **8** lacewing **9** doodlebug
  kind: **6** owlfly **9** dusty wing, mantidfly **12** spongillafly **13** brown lacewing, giant lacewing, green lacewing **14** beaded lacewing **15** ithonid lacewing **16** pleasing lacewing

Antonello da Messina
  born: **5** Italy **7** Messina
  artwork: **8** Ecce Homo **11** Three Angels **13** Il Condottiere (Portrait of a Man), Salvador Mundi **21** Saint Jerome in his Study

Antonio
  character in: **12** Twelfth Night **19** The Merchant of Venice
  author: **11** Shakespeare

Antonioni, Michelangelo
  director of: **6** Blowup **8** The Night **10** The Eclipse **12** The Adventure, The Passenger **14** Zabriskie Point

Antony, Mark
  also: **14** Marcus Antonius
  member of: **11** triumvirate
  other triumvirs: **7** Lepidus **8** Octavian (Caesar Augustus)
  lover: **9** Cleopatra
  cousin: **12** Julius Caesar
  wife: **7** Octavia
  battle: **6** Actium **8** Philippi **9** Pharsalus

invaded: **7** Parthia
  died by: **7** suicide

Antony and Cleopatra
  author: **18** William Shakespeare
  character: **7** Octavia **9** Cleopatra **10** Mark Antony **14** Octavius Caesar
  setting: **5** Egypt
  Cleopatra bitten by: **3** asp

antonym 8 opposite **10** antithesis
  abbreviation: **3** ant

Antrodemus
  type: **8** dinosaur, therapod
  also called: **10** Allosaurus
  period: **8** Jurassic **10** Cretaceous

Anu
  origin: **8** Akkadian
  god of: **6** heaven
  corresponds to: **2** An

Anubis
  origin: **8** Egyptian
  god of: **5** tombs **9** embalming
  weigher of: **15** hearts of the dead
  represented by head of: **6** jackal

anvil 5 block, incus **9** converter **11** transformer

anxiety 4 fear **5** alarm, angst, dread, worry **6** unease **7** anguish, concern, tension **8** disquiet, distress, suspense **9** misgiving **10** foreboding, solicitude, uneasiness **11** disquietude, fretfulness **12** apprehension

anxiety-ridden 7 anxious, fearful, nervous **10** distraught **11** worried sick **12** apprehensive

anxious 4 avid, keen **5** eager, tense **6** ardent, intent, uneasy **7** alarmed, earnest, fearful, fervent, fretful, itching, uptight, wanting, worried, zealous **8** desirous, troubled, yearning **9** anguished, concerned, disturbed, expectant, impatient **10** disquieted, distressed **11** overwrought **12** apprehensive

any 3 all, one **4** each, lone, sole, some **5** every **6** single, unique **8** anything, singular, solitary **9** something **10** individual, quantifier

anybody 3 any **6** anyone **8** anything

anyhow see **6** anyway

anything 3 any **4** some **5** aught **6** anyone **7** anybody

anyway 6 anyhow **8** sloppily **9** at any rate, in any case **10** carelessly, in any event, regardless **11** haphazardly, just the same, nonetheless **12** nevertheless **13** indifferently **14** without concern

anywhere 8 anyplace, wherever **11** wheresoever

A-1 3 ace **4** aces, fine, tops **5** great, prime, super **6** choice, grade-A, superb, tip-top **7** capital **8** sterling, superior, top-notch **9** excellent, first-rate, superfine **10** first-class, tremendous **11** crackerjack, outstanding, superlative

Aornis
tributary of: 4 Styx
Aornum
entrance to: 5 Hades
used by: 7 Orpheus
apace 4 fast 7 flat-out, hastily, quickly, rapidly, swiftly 8 speedily 9 posthaste 10 at top speed 11 double-quick, on the double 12 lickety-split 13 expeditiously, precipitately 18 hell bent for leather
Apache
language family: 10 Athabascan, Athapaskan
band: 9 Jacarilla, Mescalero, San Carlos 13 White Mountain
location: 7 Arizona 8 Oklahoma 9 New Mexico
leader: 7 Cochise 8 Geronimo
noted for: 8 basketry
apart 4 afar 5 alone, aloof, aside 6 cut off 7 asunder, distant 8 by itself, divorced, isolated, separate 9 by oneself, into parts, to one side 10 into pieces, separately
apartment 3 pad 4 flat 5 rooms, suite
Apartment, The
director: 11 Billy Wilder
cast: 10 Jack Lemmon, Ray Walston 13 Fred MacMurray 15 Shirley MacLaine
Oscar for: 7 picture
apathetic 4 cold 7 unmoved 9 impassive, unfeeling 10 disengaged, impossible, phlegmatic, spiritless 11 emotionless, indifferent, passionless, uncommitted, unconcerned, unemotional 12 uninterested, unresponsive
apathy 8 coolness, lethargy, numbness 9 lassitude, unconcern 11 impassivity, inattention, passiveness 12 indifference 13 impassibility, lack of feeling 14 lack of interest 15 emotionlessness 16 unresponsiveness
apatite
source: 5 Burma, Mogok
Apatosaurus see 12 Brontosaurus
ape 4 copy, echo, mock 5 mimic 6 follow, mirror, monkey, parody, parrot 7 emulate, imitate, primate 8 travesty 9 burlesque 10 caricature
family: 8 Pongidae
combining form: 8 pithecus
study of: 11 pithecology
kind: 6 gibbon 7 gorilla, siamang 9 orangutan 10 chimpanzee
famous: 8 Godzilla, King Kong
apercu 6 glance 7 glimpse, insight, outline, summary
aperture 3 gap 4 hole, rent, rift, slit, slot 5 chink, cleft, space 6 breach 7 fissure, opening, orifice 10 interstice
apex 3 cap, tip 4 acme, peak 5 crest, crown 6 apogee, climax, height, summit, vertex, zenith 8 pinnacle 11 culmination 12 consummation, highest point 13 crowning point

aphasic 4 dumb, mute 12 inarticulate 17 incapable of speech
aphid
variety: 3 pea 4 pine, rose 5 apple, grape, peach, tulip 6 cereal, cotton, potato, spruce 7 adelgid, cabbage 8 pear root 9 elm woolly, plant lice, water lily 10 gall-making, phylloxera
aphorism 3 saw 5 adage, axiom, maxim 6 dictum, old saw, saying, slogan, truism 7 epigram, proverb 8 apothegm
aphrodisiac 4 sexy 6 carnal, erotic, turn-on 7 fleshly, philter, raunchy 8 prurient 9 cantharis 10 love potion 11 cantharides, magic potion, stimulating
Aphrodite
also: 6 Urania 7 Cyprian, Paphian 8 Cytherea 10 Anadyomene
origin: 5 Greek
goddess of: 4 love 6 beauty
husband: 10 Hephaestus
lover: 4 Ares
son: 5 Lyrus 6 Deimos, Phobus, Rhodus 7 Priapus
daughter: 8 Harmonia
corresponds to: 5 Venus
epithet: 6 Acraea, Scotia 7 Doritis, Erycina, Limenia 8 Melaenis, Nymphaea, Pandemos 9 Migonitis 11 Aphrogeneia, Apostrophia
Apia
capital of: 12 Western Samoa
apiary 4 hive 7 beehive
apiece 4 each 9 severally 12 individually, respectively
a pied 6 on foot 7 walking
Apis
origin: 8 Egyptian
also: 3 Hap 4 Hapi
form: 4 bull
from: 7 Memphis
father: 6 Apollo 9 Phoroneus
mother: 8 Teledice
sister: 5 Niobe
nephew: 5 Argus
rid Argos of: 8 serpents
killed by: 7 Aetolus
worshipped at: 7 Memphis
aplomb 5 poise 7 balance 8 calmness, coolness 9 composure, sang-froid, stability 10 confidence, equanimity 11 intrepidity, savoir faire 13 self-assurance, self- composure 14 self-confidence, self-possession 15 level-headedness 16 imperturbability
Apocalypse Now
director: 18 Francis Ford Coppola
based on: 15 Heart of Darkness
novel by: 12 Joseph Conrad
cast: 11 Martin Sheen 12 Marlon Brando, Robert Duvall 16 Frederick Forrest
setting: 7 Vietnam
apocalyptic 4 dire 7 ominous 8 oracular 9 far-seeing, ill- boding, ill-omened, prescient, prophetic, reveal-

ing 10 disclosing, eye-opening, foreboding, portentous, predictive, revelatory 11 prophetical 12 inauspicious, revelational 15 prognosticative
apocryphal 7 dubious 8 disputed, doubtful, mythical, spurious 10 fabricated, fictitious, unofficial, unverified 11 unauthentic, uncanonical 12 questionable, unauthorized 14 probably untrue 15 unauthenticated, unsubstantiated
apogee 3 top 4 acme, apex, peak 5 crest, crown 6 climax, summit, vertex, zenith 8 meridian, pinnacle 9 high point 11 culmination 12 highest point
Apollo
also: 7 Phoebus, Pythius 9 Musagetes
origin: 5 Greek, Roman
god of: 5 light, music 6 beauty, poetry 7 healing 8 prophecy
father: 4 Zeus
mother: 4 Leto
twin sister: 7 Artemis
sons: 3 Ion 5 Iamus 8 Laodocus 9 Aristaeus, Asclepius, Philammon 10 Polypoetes
corresponds to: 5 Paeon 8 Hyperion
epithet: 6 Loxias 7 Acesius, Agraeus, Agyieus, Carneus, Phyteus, Spodius 8 Grynaeus 9 Parnopius, Smintheus 10 Alexicacus, Archegetes, Boedromius, Delphinius 11 Argyrotoxus, Epibaterius 12 Platanistius
Apollyon 4 hell 7 Abaddon
apologetic 5 sorry 8 contrite, penitent 9 defensive, regretful 10 excusatory, mitigatory, remorseful 11 exonerative, extenuatory, vindicatory 12 apologetical 13 justificatory, making excuses 15 self-reproachful
Apologia pro Vita Sua
author: 15 John Henry Newman (Cardinal)
Apologie for Poetrie (Defense for Poetry)
author: 15 Sir Philip Sidney
apologist 7 pleader 8 advocate, defender 9 supporter
apologize 9 beg pardon 11 make apology 13 express regret
apology 6 excuse 7 defense 11 explanation, vindication 13 begging pardon, justification
Apophis
also: 5 Apepi
form: 7 serpent
habitat: 8 darkness
destroyed daily by: 4 Dawn
Apophthegms New and Old
author: 12 Francis Bacon
apostasy 7 atheism, perfidy 8 unbelief 9 defection, disbelief, recreancy 10 disloyalty, infidelity, irreligion 11 godlessness 13 double-dealing
apostate 6 bolter 7 heretic, seceder, traitor 8 defector, deserter, recanter,

recusant, renegade, turncoat **9** dissenter, dissident, turnabout **10** backslider **13** nonconformist, tergiversator

apostle 5 envoy **6** zealot **7** pioneer, witness **8** activist, advocate, disciple, emissary, exponent, preacher **9** messenger, proponent, supporter **10** evangelist, missionary, propagator **12** propagandist, proselytizer, spokesperson

Apostle, The
   author: 10 Sholem Asch
   film by: 12 Robert Duvall

Apostles 4 John, Jude, Levi, Paul **5** Jacob, James, Peter, Simon **6** Andrew, Philip, Thomas **7** Matthew **8** Barnabas, Matthais **9** Nathanael, Thaddaeus **11** Bartholomew **12** James the Less **13** Judas Iscariot
   apostle to the Gentiles: 4 Paul
   apostle to the English: 9 Augustine
   apostle to the Irish: 7 Patrick
   apostle to the Goths: 7 Ulfilas
   apostle to the Germans: 8 Boniface
   apostle to the French: 5 Denis
   apostle to the American Indians: 9 John Eliot

apothegm 3 saw **5** adage, axiom, maxim, motto **6** dictum, slogan **7** epigram, proverb **8** aphorism **9** catchword, watchword

apotheosis 7 epitome, essence **9** elevation **10** embodiment, exaltation **11** deification **12** canonization, consecration, enshrinement, idealization, quintessence **13** dignification, glorification, magnification **15** immortalization

Appalachian Spring
   ballet by: 7 Copland

appall 4 stun **5** abash, alarm, repel, shock **6** dismay, offend, revolt, sicken **7** disgust, horrify, outrage, terrify, unnerve **8** frighten, nauseate **10** dishearten

appalled 6 aghast **7** alarmed, shocked **8** dismayed, outraged, repelled, revolted **9** disgusted, horrified, nauseated

appalling 4 dire, grim **5** awful **6** horrid **7** fearful, ghastly **8** alarming, dreadful, horrible, horrific, shocking, terrible **9** dismaying, frightful, repellent, repulsive, revolting, sickening **10** abominable, disgusting, horrifying, nauseating, outrageous, terrifying **11** frightening, intolerable **12** insufferable **13** disheartening

apparatus 4 gear **5** gismo, setup, tools **6** device, gadget, outfit, system, tackle **7** machine **8** material, utensils **9** appliance, equipment, machinery, materials, mechanism **10** implements **11** contraption, contrivance, instruments **12** organization **13** paraphernalia

apparel 4 duds, garb, gear, togs **5** array, dress, habit, robes **6** attire **7** clothes, costume, raiment, threads, vesture **8** clothing, garments **9** equipment, trappings, vestments **13** accoutrements

appareled 4 clad **5** robed **6** garbed, suited **7** attired, clothed, covered, dressed

apparent 4 open **5** clear, overt, plain **6** likely, marked, patent **7** blatant, evident, obvious, seeming, visible **8** clear-cut, distinct, manifest, probable **10** clear as day, ostensible, presumable **11** conspicuous, discernible, perceivable, perceptible, self-evident, unequivocal **12** unmistakable **14** understandable

apparently
   Latin: 7 ex facie

apparition 5 ghost, shade, spook **6** spirit, wraith **7** phantom, specter **8** phantasm, presence, revenant **10** phenomenon **13** manifestation **15** materialization

appeal 3 beg, SOS **4** plea, pull, suit **5** apply, charm, plead, sue to, tempt **6** adjure, allure, engage, entice, excite, invite, invoke **7** attract, beseech, entreat, implore, request, solicit **8** call upon, charisma, entreaty, interest, petition **9** fascinate **10** adjuration, attraction, supplicate **11** fascination **12** solicitation, supplication

appealing 7 likable, lovable **8** adjuring, charming, engaging, enticing, fetching, inviting, pleading, pleasing, tempting **10** attractive, entreating, requesting, soliciting **11** charismatic, petitioning **12** irresistible, supplicating

appear 4 look, seem, show **5** arise **6** crop up, emerge, loom up, show up, turn up **7** be clear, be plain, come out, perform, surface **8** be patent **9** be evident, be obvious **10** be apparent, be manifest **11** be published, come to light, materialize

appearance 4 look **5** guise, image **6** advent, aspect, coming **7** arrival, pretext **8** pretense **9** appearing, emergence, showing up, turning up **10** impression **11** outward show **13** manifestation **15** materialization

appear at 6 attend, show up **9** perform at

appease 4 calm, dull, ease, lull **5** abate, allay, blunt, quell, quiet, slake, still **6** pacify, quench, solace, soothe, temper **7** assuage, compose, mollify, placate, relieve, satisfy **8** mitigate **9** alleviate **10** conciliate, propitiate **11** accommodate

appeasement 6 easing **7** abating, dulling **8** allaying, blunting, giving in **9** abatement, assuasion, quenching **10** mitigation, submission **11** alleviation, assuagement **12** conciliation, pacification, propitiation, satisfaction **13** accommodation, gratification, mollification

appellation 3 tag **4** name **5** title **6** handle **7** epithet, moniker **8** cognomen **9** sobriquet **11** designation, nom de guerre

append 3 add **4** join **5** affix **6** attach, hang on, tack on **7** subjoin, suspend **10** supplement

appendage 3 arm, leg **4** limb, tail **6** branch, feeler, member **7** adjunct **8** addition, offshoot, tentacle **9** accessory, auxiliary, extension, extremity **10** attachment, supplement

appendix 7 codicil **8** addendum, addition **10** back matter, postscript, supplement

appertain 7 apply to, concern, refer to **8** bear upon, be part of, belong to, inhere in, relate to **9** touch upon

appetite 4 zest **5** gusto **6** desire, hunger, liking, relish, thirst **7** craving, passion, stomach **8** fondness, penchant, yearning **10** proclivity **11** inclination

appetizer 6 canape, dainty, savory, tidbit **8** aperitif, cocktail, delicacy **9** antipasto **11** bonne bouche, hors d'oeuvre

appetizing 6 savory **8** alluring, enticing, inviting, tempting **9** appealing, palatable, succulent **10** attractive **11** tantalizing **13** mouth-watering

applaud 4 clap, hail, laud **5** extol **6** praise **7** acclaim, commend **8** eulogize **10** compliment **12** congratulate

applaudable 8 laudable **9** admirable, desirable, excellent **11** commendable, meritorious, outstanding **12** praiseworthy

applause 5 kudos **6** praise **7** acclaim, ovation **8** approval, clapping, plaudits **9** accolades **11** compliments

apple 5 Malus **15** Malus Sylvestris
   varieties/fruit: 4 Crab, Lodi **6** Pippin **7** Baldwin, Stayman, Winesap **8** Ben Davis, Cortland, Jonathan, McIntosh **9** Delicious **10** Rome Beauty **11** Granny Smith, Gravenstein, Northern Spy, Summer Rambo **12** Grimes Golden, York Imperial **13** Yellow Newtown **14** Stayman Winesap **15** Yellow Delicious **17** Esopus Spitzenberg, Yellow Transparent **19** Rhode Island Greening
   varieties/tree: 2 Wi **3** Kai, Kau, Sea, Wax **4** Cane, Java, Jew's, Pond, Rose, Star **5** Adam's, Baked, Belle, Blade, Chess, Conch, Malay, Melon, Thorn **6** Balsam, Indian, Mammee, Possum **7** Chinese, Custard, Dead Sea, Mexican **8** Elephant, Kangaroo, Otaheite, Paradise, Peruvian **11** Soulard crab, Toringo crab **12** Siberian crab
   beverage: 5 cider **8** Calvados **9** Applejack

apple brandy
    drink: **8** Jack Rose **12** Jack-in-the-Box
    with rum: **6** Bolero **8** Apple Pie
applejack
    type: **6** brandy
    origin: **6** Canada **10** New England
    flavor: **10** apple cider
    drink: **11** Frozen Apple **13** Harvard
        Cooler
Apple of discord
    color: **6** golden
    thrown by: **4** Eris
    awarded to: **9** Aphrodite
    awarded by: **5** Paris
    inscription: **13** for the fairest
apple of one's eye 11 pride and joy
    15 light of one's life
applesauce 3 rot **4** bull, bunk **5** ho-
    kum, hooey **6** bunkum **7** baloney,
    hogwash, spinach **8** tommyrot **9** pop-
    pycock **12** fiddlesticks **13** horsefeath-
    ers **16** stuff and nonsense
Apples of the Hesperides
    color: **6** golden
    given to: **4** Hera
    kept by: **5** Ladon **10** Hesperides
appliance 4 gear **6** device **7** fixture,
    machine **9** apparatus, equipment, im-
    plement, mechanism **11** contraption,
    contrivance
applicable 3 apt, fit **6** useful **7** apro-
    pos, fitting, germane **8** relevant, suita-
    ble **9** adaptable, befitting, pertinent
applicant 7 hopeful **8** aspirant, claim-
    ant **9** candidate, job seeker, suppliant
    10 petitioner
application 4 balm, form, suit, wash
    5 claim, salve **6** appeal, lotion **7** re-
    quest, unguent **8** dressing, entreaty,
    industry, ointment, petition, poultice,
    solution **9** assiduity, attention, dili-
    gence, emollient, putting on, rele-
    vance **10** commitment, dedication,
    pertinence **11** germaneness, persist-
    ence, requisition, suitability **12** appo-
    siteness, perseverance, solicitation **13**
    attentiveness
Appling, Luke (Lucius Benjamin)
    nickname: **16** Old Aches and Pains
    sport: **8** baseball
    position: **9** shortstop
    team: **15** Chicago White Sox
apply 3 fit, use **4** suit **5** adapt, lay on,
    put on, refer **6** devote, direct, employ,
    relate **7** address, pertain, request, uti-
    lize **8** dedicate, exercise, petition,
    practice, spread on **9** implement
apply oneself 6 attend **10** buckle
    down **13** give oneself to **15** give it all
    one has **16** put one's heart into
appoint 3 fix, set **4** name **5** equip **6**
    assign, choose, engage, fit out, select,
    settle, supply **7** arrange, furnish, pro-
    vide **8** decide on, delegate, deputize,
    nominate **9** designate, determine, es-
    tablish, prescribe **10** commission
appointment 3 job **4** date, post, spot

5 berth, place **6** naming, office **7**
    meeting, station **8** choosing, position
    9 placement, selection, situation **10**
    assignment, engagement, nomination,
    rendezvous **11** designation, meeting
    time **13** commissioning
Appointment in Samarra
    author: **9** John O'Hara
    character: **8** Al Grecco, Caroline **11**
        Harry Reilly **13** Julian English
appointments 4 gear **6** outfit **8** equi-
    page **9** equipment, furniture **11**
    furnishings **13** accoutrements
apportion 5 allot, share **6** divide, ra-
    tion **7** consign, deal out, dole out,
    mete out, prorate **8** allocate, disperse
    9 parcel out, partition **10** measure out
apportioning 8 alloting, dividing **9**
    doling out, meting out **10** allocating,
    consigning, dealing out, dispensing **12**
    distributing
apportionment 5 quota **6** ration **7**
    measure, portion **8** division **9** allot-
    ment **10** allocation **11** consignment
    12 distribution, pro rata share
apposite 3 apt **7** apropos, fitting, ger-
    mane **8** material, relevant, suitable **9**
    pertinent **10** applicable **11** appropriate
appositeness 9 relevance **10** perti-
    nence **11** germaneness **15** appropri-
    ateness
appraisal 8 estimate, judgment **9** valu-
    ation **10** assessment, evaluation **14**
    estimated value
appraise 5 assay, judge, value **6** as-
    sess, review, size up **7** examine, in-
    spect **8** evaluate
appreciable 7 evident, obvious **8**
    clear-cut, definite **10** detectable, no-
    ticeable, pronounced **11** discernible,
    perceivable, perceptible, significant,
    substantial **12** recognizable **13** ascer-
    tainable
appreciate 4 like **5** prize, savor, value
    6 admire, esteem, relish **7** cherish, en-
    hance, improve, inflate, realize, re-
    spect **8** perceive, treasure **9** recognize
    10 comprehend, sympathize, under-
    stand **11** acknowledge
appreciation 4 rise **6** growth, liking,
    regard, relish, thanks **7** advance **8**
    sympathy **9** awareness, elevation,
    gratitude **10** admiration, cognizance
    12 gratefulness, thankfulness **13** com-
    prehension, understanding
apprehend 3 bag, nab, see **4** know **5**
    catch, grasp, seize, sense **6** arrest, col-
    lar **7** capture, discern, realize **8** per-
    ceive **9** recognize **10** comprehend, un-
    derstand **12** take prisoner **15** take into
    custody
apprehension 4 fear **5** alarm, dread,
    worry **6** arrest, dismay **7** anxiety, cap-
    ture, concern, seizure **8** disquiet, dis-
    tress, mistrust **9** misgiving, suspicion
    10 foreboding, perception, uneasiness
    11 premonition **12** presentiment **13**

comprehension, understanding **16** ap-
    prehensiveness
apprehensive 6 afraid, scared, uneasy
    7 alarmed, anxious, fearful, jittery,
    nervous, worried **9** concerned, misgiv-
    ing **10** disquieted, distressed, suspi-
    cious **11** distrustful
apprehensiveness 5 dread, worry **6**
    dismay **7** anxiety **9** misgiving **10** fore-
    boding, uneasiness **12** apprehension
apprentice 4 tyro **5** pupil **6** novice **7**
    learner, student **8** beginner, neophyte
    19 indentured assistant
apprise 4 tell **6** advise, inform, notify
    8 disclose **9** enlighten, make aware
approach 3 way **4** come, near, road **5**
    begin, equal, match **6** access, avenue,
    be like, method, system **7** advance,
    compare, passage, solicit **8** attitude,
    come near, draw near, embark on,
    gain upon, initiate, resemble, set
    about, sound out **9** come close, enter
    upon, procedure, technique, under-
    take **10** move toward, passageway **11**
    approximate
approachable 9 available, reachable
    10 accessible
approbation 6 praise **7** acclaim, sup-
    port **8** applause, approval, sanction **9**
    laudation **10** acceptance, compliment
    11 endorsement **12** commendation,
    ratification **14** congratulation
appropriate 3 apt **4** take **5** allot, seize
    6 assign, proper, seemly **7** apropos,
    correct, earmark, fitting, germane **8**
    allocate, relevant, set apart, suitable **9**
    apportion, befitting, belonging, con-
    gruous, opportune, pertinent **10** con-
    fiscate, to the point, well-chosen,
    well-suited **11** expropriate **12** to the
    purpose **14** characteristic
appropriateness 7 aptness, fitness **9**
    congruity, propriety, relevance **10** per-
    tinence **11** correctness, suitability
appropriation 6 taking **9** allotment
    10 allocation, arrogation, usurpation
    12 confiscation **13** expropriation,
    money set aside **16** misappropriation
approval 5 favor, leave **6** esteem, lik-
    ing, regard **7** acclaim, consent, li-
    cense, mandate, respect **8** sanction **9**
    agreement **10** acceptance, admiration,
    compliance, permission **11** approba-
    tion, concurrence, countenance, en-
    dorsement, good opinion **12** acquies-
    cence, appreciation, confirmation **13**
    authorization **14** acknowledgment
approve 4 like, pass **5** allow **6** accept,
    affirm, defend, esteem, permit, praise,
    ratify, second, uphold **7** condone,
    confirm, endorse, respect, sustain **8**
    accede to, advocate, assent to, concur
    in, sanction **9** authorize, consent to
    10 appreciate **11** countenance, go
    along with, rubber-stamp, subscribe to
approved 8 official **9** canonical **10** au-
    thorized, sanctioned

approving 9 endorsing, favorable 10 concurring 11 affirmative, sanctioning 12 appreciative

approximate 5 guess, rough 6 reckon 7 inexact, verge on 8 approach, border on, estimate, look like, relative, very near 9 estimated

approximately 5 circa 6 almost, around 7 close to 9 generally, just about 10 more or less, not far from, very nearly

appurtenance 4 wing 5 annex, extra 7 adjunct 8 addendum, addition 9 accessory, appendage, extension 10 attachment

APR
    abbreviation for: 14 above prime rate 20 annual percentage rate

Apres-midi d'un Faune, L' (The Afternoon of a Faun)
    author: 16 Stephane Mallarme
    (prelude) ballet music: 7 Debussy

April
    event: 11 Black Monday (13)
    flower: 5 daisy 8 sweet pea
    French: 5 Avril
    gem: 7 diamond
    German: 5 April
    holiday: 6 Easter 11 All Fool's Day (1) 13 April Fool's Day (1)
    Italian: 6 Aprile
    Latin: 7 Aprilis
    number of days: 6 thirty
    origin of name: 4 aper (wild boar) 6 aparas (following) 7 aperire (to open) 9 Aphrodite
    place in year:
      Gregorian: 6 fourth
      Roman: 6 second
    saying: 24 April is the cruellest month 27 April showers bring May flowers
    Spanish: 5 Abril
    zodiac signs: 5 Aries 6 Taurus

April Fool's Day
    French: 9 April Fish

a priori 6 theory 7 opinion 11 of reasoning

apron 3 bib 5 smock 8 covering 10 stagefront

apropos 3 apt 6 seemly 7 correct, fitting, germane, related 8 relevant, suitable 9 befitting, congruous, opportune, pertinent 10 applicable, to the point, well-suited 11 appropriate 12 just the thing

apry
    type: 7 liqueur
    origin: 6 France
    flavor: 7 apricot

Apsyrtus
    also: 8 Absyrtus
    father: 6 Aeetes
    sister: 5 Medea
    killed by: 5 Medea

apt 5 prone 6 bright, clever, gifted, liable, likely, proper, seemly 7 apropos, fitting, germane, given to 8 inclined, relevant, suitable 9 befitting, congruous, opportune, pertinent 10 disposed to, well-suited 11 appropriate, intelligent, predisposed

aptitude 4 bent, gift, turn 5 flair, knack, skill 6 genius, talent 7 ability, faculty, leaning 8 capacity, facility, penchant, tendency 9 endowment, proneness, quickness 10 capability, cleverness, proclivity, propensity 11 inclination, proficiency 12 predilection 14 predisposition

aptness 4 bent, gift 5 flair, knack 6 talent 7 ability, faculty 8 aptitude, facility 11 suitability 15 appropriateness

Apuleius
    author of: 12 The Golden Ass 13 Metamorphoses

aqua 4 blue 5 water 6 bluish 9 turquoise 10 aquamarine 12 greenish-blue

aquamarine 4 aqua, blue 5 beryl 9 turquoise 12 greenish-blue
    color: 9 blue-green

aquaphobia
    fear of: 5 water

aquarelle 10 watercolor

Aquarius
    symbol: 11 water bearer 12 water-carrier
    planet: 6 Saturn, Uranus
    rules: 5 hopes 7 friends
    born: 7 January 8 February

aquatic 6 marine 7 abyssal, fluvial, neritic, oceanic, pelagic 8 littoral 9 thalassic 10 fluviatile, lacustrine

aquavit
    type: 6 spirit
    origin: 11 Scandinavia
    flavor: 4 dill 7 caraway 9 coriander
    drink: 5 Glogg

aqua vitae 7 alcohol 11 water of life

aqueduct 4 duct, race 7 channel, conduit 11 watercourse 18 artificial waterway

aqueous 4 damp 5 moist 6 liquid, serous, watery 7 hydrous 8 waterish 9 lymphatic

Aquinas, St Thomas
    nickname: 13 Angelic Doctor
    followers: 8 Thomists
    author of: 15 Summa Theologica 21 Summa Totius Theologiae 34 Summa Catholicae Fidei contra Gentiles

Arab
    clothing: 3 fez 4 veil
    country: 4 Iraq, Oman 5 Egypt, Libya, Qatar, Sudan, Syria, Yemen 6 Jordan, Kuwait 7 Algeria, Bahrain, Lebanon, Morocco, Tunisia 11 Saudi Arabia 18 United Arab Emirates
    demon: 5 afrit 6 afreet
    habitat: 6 desert
    Holy City: 5 Mecca 6 Medina

    language: 6 Arabic
    people: 7 Semitic
    religion: 6 Muslim 7 Islamic
    tribe: 4 Kurd 6 Berber, Nubian, Tuareg

Arabella
    opera by: 7 (Richard) Strauss

Arabia
    ancient name: 14 Jazirat al-Arab
    ancient people: 6 Sabean 8 Egyptian 10 Babylonian
    bounded by: 5 Syria 6 Jordan, Red Sea 10 Gulf of Aden, Gulf of Oman 11 Indian Ocean, Persian Gulf
    country: 4 Oman 5 Qatar, Yemen 6 Kuwait 11 Saudi Arabia 18 United Arab Emirates
    highest peak: 11 Jabal Shayib
    holy book: 5 Koran
    Holy City: 5 Mecca 6 Medina
    island: 7 Bahrain, Socotra 9 Laccadive
    language: 6 Arabic
    mineral/natural resource: 3 oil 4 goat 5 sheep, wheat 6 barley, millet 7 iron ore, granite 8 porphyry 9 manganese, petroleum
    nomadic tribe: 5 Maaza 6 Ababda
    prophet: 8 Muhammad
    religion: 6 Muslim 7 Islamic
    river: 4 Nile, Oxus 5 Indus 6 Tigris 9 Euphrates
    sea: 3 Red 7 Arabian 11 Persian Gulf 13 Mediterranean

Arabian Nights
    director: 17 Pier Paolo Pasolini
    based on: 20 Thousand and One Nights
    cast: 11 Franco Citti 13 Ninetto Davoli 14 Ines Pellegrina

Arabian Nights' Entertainments, The (The Thousand and One Nights)
    author: 7 unknown
    storyteller: 12 Scheherazade
    character: 3 Roc 5 Ahmed 6 Fatima, Sinbad 7 Aladdin, Ali Baba, Sindbad 9 Abu Hassan

Arabic
    national language in: 4 Iraq 5 Syria 6 Jordan 7 Lebanon 11 North Africa 16 Arabian Peninsula
    also spoken in: 6 Israel 12 North America, South America 17 Soviet Central Asia, Sub-Saharan Africa
    language of: 5 Koran

arable 6 fecund 7 fertile 8 farmable, fruitful, plowable, tillable 10 cultivable, productive

Arachne
    origin: 6 Lydian
    challenged: 6 Athena
    contest: 7 weaving
    changed into: 6 spider

arachnid
    class: 4 mite, tick 6 spider 8 scorpion 13 daddy-long-legs

phylum: 9 Arthropod
pairs of legs: 4 four
respiratory organ: 12 pulmonary sac, tracheal tube
dwelling: 4 land **5** water
body part: 15 anterior prosoma **20** posterior opisthosoma
way of feeding: 8 parasite, predator **9** scavenger

arachnophobia
fear of: 7 spiders

Aram *see* **5** Syria

Aramis
character in: 18 The Three Musketeers
author: 5 Dumas (pere)

Arapaho
language family: 9 Algonkian **10** Algonquian
tribe: 6 Atsine **11** Gros Ventres **15** Northern Arapaho, Southern Arapaho
location: 6 Plains **8** Colorado, Red River
related to: 8 Cheyenne
ceremony: 8 sun dance

Arawak
language family: 8 Arawakan
tribe: 5 Taino **6** Igneri, Lucayo
location: 4 Cuba **5** Haiti **6** Guyana **8** Antilles, Colombia **9** Venezuela **12** South America

Arawakan
tribe: 6 Arawak **8** Boriquen **9** Borinquen

arbiter 5 judge **6** pundit, umpire **7** referee **9** authority **10** arbitrator **11** connoisseur

arbitrary 6 chance, random **7** summary, willful **8** absolute, despotic, fanciful, personal **9** frivolous, imperious, unlimited, whimsical **10** autocratic, capricious, peremptory, subjective **12** inconsistent, uncontrolled, unrestrained

arbitrate 5 judge **6** decide, settle, umpire **7** adjudge, mediate, referee **9** reconcile **10** adjudicate **12** bring to terms **13** sit in judgment

Arbitration, The
author: 8 Menander

arbitrator 5 judge **6** umpire **7** arbiter, referee **8** mediator **9** go-between, moderator **10** negotiator **11** adjudicator **12** intermediary

arbor 5 bower, folly, kiosk **6** gazebo, grotto **7** pergola **8** pavilion **9** belvedere **10** shaded walk **11** summerhouse

arc 3 bow **4** arch **5** curve **8** crescent, half-moon **10** semicircle

arcade 6 loggia, piazza **7** archway, areaway, gallery, skywalk **8** cloister, overpass **9** breezeway, colonnade, peristyle, underpass

Arcadia, The

author: 15 Sir Philip Sidney
character: 5 Mopsa **6** Pamela **7** Dametas, Gynecia, Zelmane **8** Basilius, Cecropia, Pyrocles **9** Amphialus, Musidorus, Philoclea, Plexistus

Arcadian stag *see* **8** Ceryneam

Arcanan
father: 8 Alcmaeon
mother: 10 Callirrhoe
brother: 10 Amphoterus

arcane 6 mystic, occult **7** obscure **8** abstruse, esoteric, hermetic, mystical **9** enigmatic, recondite **10** mysterious

arch 3 arc, bow, sly **4** bend, dome, main, span, wily **5** chief, curve, major, saucy, vault **7** cunning, primary, roguish **8** bow shape **9** curvature, designing, principal **10** curved span **11** mischievous

archaeologist
American: 7 Bingham **8** Douglass, Stephens
British: 5 Evans **6** Carter, Childe, Layard, Leakey, Petrie, Wooley **7** Lubbock, Ventris, Wheeler **9** Rawlinson **10** Pitt-Rivers **13** Caton-Thompson
Danish: 7 Thomsen, Worsaae
French: 5 Botta **8** Cousteau **11** Champollion
German: 5 Conze **7** Curtius **8** Dorpfeld, Koldewey **9** Grotefend **10** Schliemann **11** Winckelmann
Italian: 8 Fiorelli
Swedish: 4 Geer **9** Montelius

archaic 5 passe **6** bygone **7** ancient, antique **8** obsolete **9** out-of-date **10** antiquated **11** obsolescent **12** old-fashioned

archangel 5 Satan, Uriel **7** Gabriel, Michael, Raphael

arched 4 bent **5** bowed **6** curved

archenemy 3 foe **7** archfoe, bugbear, nemesis, scourge **8** opponent **9** adversary, assailant, bete noire, combatant, disputant **10** antagonist

archeology
term: 3 dig **6** midden **9** earthwork **11** burial mound **17** aerial photography
type: 7 salvage **8** American, medieval **9** classical, text- aided **10** Egyptology, industrial, underwater **11** Assyriology, prehistoric **12** Mesopotamian
ages: 4 Iron **6** Bronze
Old Stone Age: 11 Paleolithic
Middle Stone Age: 10 Mesolithic
New Stone Age: 9 Neolithic
dating method: 5 cross **8** absolute, carbon-14 **13** geochronology **16** dendrochronology **18** thermoluminescence **28** potassium-argon varved deposits
site/artifact: 2 Ur **4** Giza, Troy **5** Copan, Crete, Delos, Minos **6** Amarna, Carnac, Nimrud, Nippur, Tiryns **7** Alalakh, Babylon, Ephesus, Knossos, Mycenae, Nineveh, Olympia, Pom-

peii, Rio Azul **8** Behistun, Kuyunjik, Pergamum, pyramids **9** Arikamedu, Hissarlik, Khorsabad, New Grange, Tarquinia, Woodhenge **10** Carchemish, Persepolis, Samothrace, Stonehenge **11** Herculaneum, Machu Picchu, Mohenjodaro **12** Easter Island, Hadrian's Wall, Olduvai Gorge, Rosetta Stone **13** Avebury Circle, Zimbabwe Ruins **14** Dead Sea Scrolls, Laocoon statues **15** temple of Artemis **16** Valley of the Kings **18** Ostrava-Petrokovice, Royal Palace of Minos
tomb: 11 Tutankhamen **15** Ch'in Shih Huang Ti

archer 6 bowman **8** spearman
famous: 5 Cupid **9** Robin Hood **11** William Tell

Archer
constellation of: 11 Sagittarius

Archer, Isabel
character in: 18 The Portrait of a Lady
author: 5 James

Archer, Lew
created by: 13 Ross Macdonald
role: 10 private eye
played by: 10 Paul Newman (as Harper)
on TV: 10 Brian Keith

Archer, Miles
character in: 16 The Maltese Falcon
author: 7 Hammett

Archer, Newland
character in: 17 The Age of Innocence
author: 7 Wharton

Archer in Jeopardy
author: 13 Ross MacDonald

archery
athlete: 10 Linda Myers, Luanne Ryon **11** Darrell Pace

archetypal 5 model **7** classic **8** original **9** classical, exemplary **10** definitive, prototypal, protypical

archetype 5 model **7** classic **8** exemplar, original **9** prototype **12** prime example

Archias
founder of: 8 Syracuse
location: 6 Sicily
descendant of: 8 Hercules

Archie
creator: 10 Bob Montana **13** John Goldwater
character: 5 Betty, Moose **6** Reggie **7** Sabrina **8** Big Ethel, Veronica **11** Mr Weatherby **12** Jughead Jones
place: 9 Riverdale

Archimago
character in: 15 The Faerie Queene
author: 7 Spenser

Archipenko, Alexsandr
born: 4 Kiev **6** Russia
artwork: 8 Medranos **9** Gondolier, Medrano II, Pregnancy, The Bather

11 Boxing Match 12 Archipentura, Walking Woman 15 Geometric Statue 18 Wilhelm Furtwangler 19 Woman Combing Her Hair

architect 6 author, shaper 7 creator, deviser, founder, planner 8 designer, engineer 9 artificer, contriver, draftsman, innovator 10 instigator, originator, prime mover 13 master builder 16 building designer

name 3 Pei 4 Hunt, Mead, Pope, Root, Wren 5 Hoban, IM Pei, Jones, Le Vau, McKim, Mills, Roche, Stone, Tange, White, Wyatt 6 Breuer, Fuller, Owings, Smirke, Wright 7 Bernini, Burnham, Gilbert, Gropius, Johnson, Latrobe, Mansart, Merrill, Renwick 8 Bramante, Harrison, Palladio, Saarinen, Skidmore, Sullivan, Yamasaki 9 Jefferson 10 Richardson 11 Le Corbusier 12 Brunelleschi, Michelangelo 14 Mies van der Rohe 15 Hardouin-Mansart

legendary first: 8 Daedalus
designed: 18 Minotaur's Labyrinth
Roman: 9 Vitruvius

architecture 5 style 6 design 11 structuring 12 construction 14 architectonics 16 structural design

archives 6 annals, museum, papers 7 library, records 9 documents 10 chronicles, depository 11 memorabilia

arctic 3 icy 5 gelid, polar 6 bitter, frigid, frozen 7 glacial, ice-cold 8 freezing, icebound 9 North Pole 10 frostbound 11 far-northern, hyperborean 13 septentrional

Arden, Eve
real name: 13 Eunice Quedens
born: 12 Mill Valley CA
roles: 13 Mildred Pierce, Our Miss Brooks

ardent 4 keen 5 eager, fiery, lusty 6 fierce 7 earnest, fervent, intense, zealous 8 feverish, spirited, vehement 10 passionate 11 impassioned, tempestuous 12 enthusiastic

ardor 4 love, zeal 5 gusto, verve, vigor 6 fervor, spirit 7 feeling, passion, rapture 8 devotion 9 eagerness, intensity, vehemence 10 enthusiasm, excitement, fierceness 11 amorousness 12 feverishness

Ardrey, Robert
author of: 17 The Social Contract

arduous 4 hard 5 heavy, tough 6 severe, tiring, trying 7 onerous 8 toilsome, vigorous 9 difficult, energetic, fatiguing, Herculean, laborious, strenuous, wearisome 10 burdensome, exhausting, formidable 11 troublesome

arduousness 5 trial 8 tough job 10 difficulty, rough going, uphill work 12 hard sledding, toilsomeness 13 laboriousness, wearisomeness

area 4 turf, zone 5 arena, field, range, realm, scope, space, tract 6 domain, extent, region, sphere 7 expanse, portion, section, stretch, terrain 8 district, locality, precinct, province 9 territory

Areithous
origin: 5 Greek
mentioned in: 5 Iliad
king of: 7 Arcadia
son: 10 Menesthius
nickname: 7 maceman
weapon: 8 iron mace
killed by: 8 Lycurgus

Areius see 5 Areus

arena 4 area, bowl, ring 5 field, lists, realm, scene, stage 6 circus, domain, sector, sphere 7 stadium, theater 8 coliseum, platform, province 9 gymnasium, territory 10 hippodrome 11 battlefield, marketplace 12 amphitheater, battleground, playing field

Arendt, Hannah
author of: 10 On Violence 12 On Revolution 13 Life of the Mind 17 The Human Condition 19 Crises of the Republic, Eichmann in Jerusalem 27 The Origins of Totalitarianism

Arene
son: 4 Idas 7 Lynceus

Arensky, Anton Stepanovich (Antony)
born: 6 Russia 8 Novgorod
composer of: 7 Tempest 13 Egyptian Night 18 Variations on Legend

Areopagitica
author: 10 John Milton

Ares
also: 8 Theritas
origin: 5 Greek
god of: 3 war
father: 4 Zeus
mother: 4 Hera
sister: 4 Hebe
son: 5 Molus 6 Cycnus, Deimos, Phobos, Tereus 8 Diomedes, Eurytion, Meleager, Oenomaus, Phlegyas, Thestius 10 Ascalaphus
daughter: 7 Alcippe 8 Harmonia 9 Melanippe 11 Penthesilea
nurse: 5 Thero
corresponds to: 4 Mars
epithet: 8 Enyalius 14 Gynaecothoenas

Arete
father: 8 Rhexenor
husband: 8 Alcinous
daughter: 8 Nausicaa
personifies: 7 courage

Arethusa
form: 5 nymph
changed into: 6 spring
saved from: 7 Alpheus

Aretus
father: 5 Priam
killed by: 9 Automedon

Areus
also: 6 Areius
father: 4 Bias
mother: 4 Pero

brother: 6 Talaus 8 Leodocus
member of: 9 Argonauts
epithet of: 4 Zeus
means: 7 warlike

Are You There, God? It's Me, Margaret
author: 9 Judy Blume

Argades
father: 3 Ion

Argeiphontes
also: 11 Argiphontes
epithet of: 6 Hermes
means: 13 slayer of Argus

argent 5 white 6 silver 7 shining, silvery

Argentina
name means: 6 silver
capital/largest city: 11 Buenos Aires
others: 4 Acha, Azul, Goya, Oran, Puan, Rosa 5 Jujuy, Junin, Lanus, Lujan, Metan, Monte, Salta, Tigre 6 Parana, Rufino, Zarate 7 Bolivar, Caseros, Cordoba, Dolores, Formosa, LaBanda, LaPlata, LaRioja, Mendoza, Neuquen, Posadas, Quilmes, Rafaela, Rosario, San Juan, Santa Fe, Tucuman 9 Catamarca, Rio Cuerto 10 Avellaneda, Corrientes 11 Bahai Blanca, Mar del Plata, Resistencia 17 Santiago del Estero 20 San Carlos de Bariloche
division: 5 Andes, Chaco, Pampa 9 Patagonia 11 Mesopotamia 14 Tierra del Fuego
measure: 4 sino 5 legua 6 cuadra, lastre 7 manzana
monetary unit: 4 peso 7 centavo 9 argentino
weight: 4 last 5 libra 7 quintal 8 tonelada
island: 14 Tierra del Fuego
lake: 6 Viedma 7 Cardiel, Fagnano, Musters 11 Buenos Aires, Mar Chiquita, Nahuel Huapi
mountain: 4 Toro 5 Andes, Chato, Laudo, Potro 6 Bonete, Conico, Pissis, Rincon 8 Famatina, Murallon, Olivares, Tronador, Zapaleri 9 Aconcagua, Tupungato 10 Cordillera 13 Ojos del Salado 15 Cerro Mercedario, Sierra de Cordoba
highest point: 9 Aconcagua
river: 4 Sali 5 Atuel, Chico, Coyle, Dulce, Limay, Negro, Plata, Teuco 6 Blanco, Chubut, Cuarto, Flores, Grande, Iguazu, Parana, Quinto, Salado 7 Bermejo, Deseado, Iguassu, Mendoza, Tercero, Tunuyan, Uruguay 8 Colorado, Paraguay, Picomayo, Senguerr 9 Pilcomayo
sea: 8 Atlantic
physical feature:
falls: 6 Grande, Iguazu 7 Iguassu
lowland: 5 chaco
plains: 6 pampas
plateau: 4 Puna 6 Parana
salt flat: 14 Salinas Grandes
volcano: 5 Lanin, Maipo 6 Domuyo

7 Peteroa
wind: 5 Zonda **7** Pampero
people: 3 Api **4** Lule **5** Vejoz **6** Abipon, Vilela **7** Guarani, Puelche, Ranquel, Taluhet **8** Querandi, Querendy
  artist: 6 Borges
  author: 4 Wast **6** Banchs, Borges **7** Lugones **9** Guiraldes, Hernandez **10** Echeverria
  leader: 4 Roca **5** Illia, Menem, Mitre, Peron, Rosas **6** Videla **7** Urquiza **8** Aramburu, Belgrano, Eva Peron (Evita), Frondici, Galtieri **9** San Martin, Sarmiento **11** Isabel Peron
language: 7 Spanish
religion: 13 Roman Catholic
place:
  opera house: 11 Teatro Colon
  world's southernmost town: 7 Ushuaia
feature:
  bird: 6 chunga
  cowboy: 6 gaucho **7** vaquero
  dance: 5 samba, tango, zamba **6** cuando, gaucho **7** milonga **9** chacarera
  farm: 6 quinta
  knife: 5 facon
  metal straw: 8 bombilla
  ranch: 8 estancia
  school smock: 9 delantale
  shawl: 6 poncho
  trousers: 9 bombachas
  weapon: 4 bola
food:
  cocktail: 7 clarito
  dish: 4 luna **7** criollo, puchero **8** chivitos, empanada **10** parrillada

Arges
member of: 8 Cyclopes
Argia
  also: 5 Aegia
  father: 7 Oceanus
  mother: 6 Tethys
  husband: 7 Polybus
  son: 5 Argus
Argiope
  form: 5 nymph
  father: 8 Teuthras
  husband: 6 Agenor **8** Telephus
  son: 6 Cadmus
  daughter: 6 Europa
Argiphontes *see* **12** Argeiphontes
Argive
  pertaining to: 5 Argos
Argo
  built by: 5 Argus
  ship of: 4 Argo
argon
  chemical symbol: 2 Ar
Argonauts
  crew: 6 Castor, Mopsus, Peleus, Pollux **7** Acastus, Orpheus, Telamon **8** Atalanta, Heracles, Hercules, Melampus, Meleager **10** Polydeuces

searchers for: 12 Golden Fleece
leader: 5 Jason
ship: 4 Argo
sailed to: 7 Colchis
pilot: 6 Tiphys
argot 4 cant **5** idiom, lingo, slang **6** jargon, patois **10** vernacular
arguable 7 at issue **9** debatable **10** disputable **12** questionable **13** controversial, problematical
argue 4 hold, show **5** claim, imply, plead **6** assert, bicker, debate, denote, evince, reason **7** contend, display, dispute, exhibit, express, point to, quarrel, quibble, wrangle **8** indicate, maintain, manifest **11** demonstrate, expostulate, remonstrate
argument 3 row **4** case, gist, plot, spat, tiff **5** clash, fight, story **6** debate, reason **7** dispute, outline, quarrel, summary **8** abstract, contents, squabble, synopsis **9** bickering, imbroglio **10** war of words **11** altercation, central idea, controversy, embroilment **12** disagreement
argumentation 6 debate **7** dispute **8** argument **10** discussion
argumentative 5 testy **7** peevish, scrappy **8** contrary, petulant, snappish **9** combative, fractious, litigious, querulous **11** belligerent, contentious, quarrelsome **12** cantankerous, disputatious
aria 3 air **4** solo, song, tune **6** melody, number **7** arietta, excerpt, section **9** selection **10** canzonetta **13** aria cantabile
Ariadne
  also: 7 Ariadna
  father: 5 Minos
  mother: 8 Pasiphae
  husband: 8 Dionysus
  son: 8 Oenopion
  gave thread to: 7 Theseus
  deserted by: 7 Theseus
Ariadne auf Naxos
  also: 14 Ariadne on Naxos
  opera by: 7 (Richard) Strauss
  character: 7 Bacchus, Theseus **8** Composer **10** Zerbinetta
Ariana *see* **11** Afghanistan
Ariane et Barbe-Bleu
  also: 19 Ariadne and Bluebeard
  opera by: 5 Dukas
  character: 7 Ariadne **9** Bluebeard
Arianrhod
  origin: 5 Welsh
  form: 7 goddess
  brother: 7 Gwydion
  mistress of: 7 Gwydion
  son: 14 Llew Llew Gyffes
  cursed: 14 Llew Llew Gyffes
arid 3 dry **4** dull **5** vapid **6** barren, dreary, jejune **7** dried-up, parched, tedious **8** lifeless, pedantic **9** colorless, dry as dust, waterless **10** desertlike,

uninspired **13** unimaginative, uninteresting **15** drought-scourged
aridity 6 dearth **7** drought, dryness **8** aridness, dullness **10** barrenness **12** lifelessness, rainlessness **17** unimaginativeness
aridness 6 dearth **7** aridity, drought, dryness **8** dullness **10** barrenness **12** lifelessness, rainlessness **17** unimaginativeness
arid region 6 desert **9** wasteland **16** barren wilderness
Ariel
  author: 11 Shakespeare, Sylvia Plath
  character in: 10 The Tempest
Aries
  symbol: 3 ram
  planet: 4 Mars
  rules: 11 personality
  born: 5 April, March
Arimaspians
  member of: 9 Scythians
  number of eyes: 3 one
Arion
  form: 11 winged horse
  father: 8 Poseidon
  mother: 7 Demeter
Ariosto, Ludovico
  author of: 14 Orlando Furioso
arise 4 dawn, go up, rise, wake **5** awake, begin, climb, ensue, get up, mount, occur, set in, start **6** appear, ascend, crop up, emerge, result, wake up **7** emanate, stand up **8** commence, spring up, stem from **9** originate **11** come to light
arista 3 awn **7** bristle
aristocracy 5 elite **6** gentry **7** peerage, society **8** nobility **9** beau monde **10** patricians, upper class, upper crust **11** high society
aristocrat 4 duke, earl, lady, lord, peer **5** noble **7** Brahmin, duchess, grandee, marquis **8** countess, marquess, nobleman **9** blue blood, gentleman, patrician **10** noblewoman **11** gentlewoman **12** silk stocking
aristocratic 5 noble, regal, royal **6** lordly, titled **7** courtly, genteel, refined **8** highborn, highbred, wellborn **9** dignified, patrician **10** of high rank, upper-class **11** blue- blooded, gentlemanly **12** silk-stocking **13** of gentle blood
Aristophanes
  author of: 6 Plutus **8** The Birds, The Frogs, The Peace, The Wasps **9** The Clouds **10** Lysistrata, The Knights **13** Ecclesiazusae, The Acharnians
Aristotle
  author of: 7 Physics, Poetics **8** On Plants, Politics, Rhetoric, Sophisms **9** On the Soul **10** Generation **11** Metaphysics **12** On the Heavens **14** Parts of Animals, Prior Analytics **17** Ni-

comachean Ethics **18** Posterior Analytics **23** On Beginning and Perishing

Arizona
  abbreviation: 2 AZ **4** Ariz
  nickname: 11 Grand Canyon
  capital/largest city: 7 Phoenix
  others: 3 Ajo **4** Eloy, Mesa, Naco, Yuma **5** Globe, Leupp, Tempe **6** Bisbee, McNary, Salome, Toltec, Tucson **7** Cortaro **8** Chandler, Glendale, Prescott **9** Flagstaff **10** Scottsdale
  college: 11 Grand Canyon **12** Southwestern
  explorer: 8 Coronado **12** Marcos de Niza
  feature:
    dam: 6 Hoover **8** Coolidge **9** Roosevelt
    national park: 11 Grand Canyon **15** Petrified Forest
  tribe: 4 Hano, Hopi, Pima **6** Apache, Navaho, Navajo, Papago
  people: 7 Cochise **8** Geronimo **14** Barry Goldwater
  lake: 4 Mead **6** Havasu, Mohave, Mormon, Powell **9** Roosevelt
  land rank: 5 sixth
  mountain: 5 White **6** Lemmon **7** Hualpai **8** Mazatzal **9** Baldy Peak **13** Santa Catalina
    highest point: 13 Humphreys Peak
  physical feature:
    canyon: 5 Grand
    desert: 6 Sonora **7** Painted
    forest: 9 Petrified
  river: 4 Gila, Salt, Zuni **5** Verde **6** Puerco **8** Colorado **12** Bill Williams **14** Little Colorado
  state admission: 11 forty-eighth
  state bird: 10 cactus wren
  state flower: 13 saguaro cactus
  state motto: 11 God Enriches
  state song: 7 Arizona
  state tree: 9 palo verde

ark 3 box **4** ship **5** barge, chest **8** flatboat **9** houseboat **10** Noah's boat

Ark
  built by: 4 Noah
  landing place: 6 Ararat
  groups: 5 pairs

Arkansas
  abbreviation: 2 AR **3** Ark
  nickname: 4 Bear **9** Bowie Land **17** Land of Opportunity
  capital/largest city: 10 Little Rock
  others: 3 Coy, Cuy, Keo, Ola, Roe, Ulm **4** Alma, Bono, Casa, Dell, Diaz, Moro **5** Enola, Perla, Rondo **6** Alicia, Camden **8** El Dorado **9** Fort Smith, Jonesboro, Pine Bluff, Texarkana **10** Hot Springs **11** Blytheville **12** Fayetteville
  feature:
    national park: 10 Hot Springs
  tribe: 5 Caddo, Osage **6** Quapaw **7** Choctaw, Wichita **8** Cherokee
  people: 8 Alan Ladd **10** Dick Powell **11** Bill Clinton **16** Douglas Mac-

Arthur
  lake: 6 Beaver, Chicot, Conway, Nimrod **7** Greeson, Norfork **8** Maumelle, Ouachita **10** Bull Shoals **11** Greers Ferry **12** Blue Mountain
  land rank: 13 twenty-seventh
  mountain: 4 Blue **5** Ozark **6** Boston, Gaylor **7** Fourche **8** Magazine, Ouachita
    highest point: 8 Magazine
  river: 3 Red **5** Black, White **6** Saline **7** Buffalo, Current **8** Arkansas, Cossatot, Ouachita **9** St Francis **11** Mississippi
  state admission: 11 twenty-fifth
  state bird: 11 mockingbird
  state flower: 12 apple blossom
  state motto: 13 (Let) The People Rule
  state song: 8 Arkansas
  state tree: 13 shortleaf pine

Arkin, Alan
  born: 9 New York NY
  roles: 5 Simon **6** Havana **7** Catch-22 **9** The In-Laws, Rocketeer **12** Indian Summer, The **13** Wait Until Dark **16** Grosse Point Blank **17** Glengarry Glen Ross **21** Last of the Red-Hot Lovers **23** The Heart Is a Lonely Hunter **40** The Russians Are Coming The Russians Are Coming

Ark of the Covenant
  gold covering: 9 mercy seat **12** propitiatory

arm, arms 4 guns **5** brace, crest, equip, prime **6** branch, outfit, sector **7** forearm, fortify, prepare, protect, section, weapons **8** armament, blazonry, division, firearms, insignia, materiel, offshoot, ordnance, weaponry **9** appendage, make ready, upper limb **10** coat of arms, department, detachment, obtain arms, projection, strengthen, take up arms **12** anterior limb **13** prepare for war **14** heraldic emblem **18** furnish with weapons

armada 4 navy **5** fleet **8** flotilla, squadron **10** escadrille

armadillo 4 a par
  family: 11 Dasypodidae
  order: 9 Edentata
  body: 5 armor **6** plates
  habitat: 12 South America, United States **14** Central America
  habit: 9 nocturnal

Armageddon 8 doomsday **11** final battle **13** great conflict
  author: 8 Leon Uris

armagnac
  type: 6 brandy **7** liqueur
  origin: 6 France **7** Gascony

armament 4 arms, guns **7** weapons **8** ordnance, weaponry **9** equipment, munitions **10** outfitting **13** military might **16** war-making machine

Armenia
  other name: 5 Minni **6** Urartu **8** Ana-

tolia
  former name: 31 Armenian Soviet Socialist Republic
  capital/largest city: 6 Erivan **7** Yerevan
  ancient capital: 3 Ani **8** Artashat, Artaxata
  others: 3 Van **5** Sivas **7** Trabzon **9** Kirovakan, Leninakan, Trabizond **13** Bitlisarzurum
  head of state: 9 President
  monetary unit: 5 ruble
  lake: 3 Van **5** Sevan, Urmia **8** Urumiyah
  mountain: 6 Ararat, Taurus **7** Aladagh **8** Karabakh
  highest peak: 12 Mount Aragats
  river: 3 Ara **4** Aras, Kura **5** Araks, Cyrus, Halys, Zanga **6** Araxes, Razdan, Tigris **9** Euphrates **10** Kizil-Irmak
  physical feature:
    volcano: 7 Aragats
  people: 5 Armen, Ermyn, Gomer, Hadji
    apostle: 7 Gregory
    gypsy: 5 bosha
    hero: 4 haik **6** vartan
    leader: 26 Levon Akopovich Ter Petrosyan
    me: 3 ara
    saint: 5 Sahak **6** Mesrop
  language: 7 Russian **8** Armenian
  religion: 16 Armenian Orthodox
  feature:
    cap: 6 calpac
    fortress: 7 erebuni
    game: 7 barbout
    kingdom: 6 Urartu, Vannic **7** Cilicia, Sophene **8** Ardsruni
  food:
    bread: 4 peda
    cucumber: 4 guta
    dish: 7 lahvosh **9** paraghatz, soubeoreg

Armenian
  language family: 12 Indo-European
  spoken in: 4 USSR **6** Russia **7** Armenia

Armida
  opera by: 5 Gluck, Haydn, Lully **6** Dvorak **7** Rossini **10** Eszterhazy

Armies 7 Sabaoth

Armies of the Night
  author: 12 Norman Mailer

armistice 5 peace, truce **9** cease-fire **23** suspension of hostilities

armlet 6 bangle **8** bracelet, ornament

arm of the sea 5 bight, firth, fjord (fiord), inlet **6** strait **7** channel, estuary, narrows

armoire 8 cupboard, wardrobe **12** clothespress

armor 4 mail **5** chain **6** shield **7** bulwark **10** coat of mail, protection **11** suit of armor **18** protective covering

armorial bearings 4 arms **5** crest **10** coat of arms, escutcheon

armory 7 arsenal **9** arms depot **13** ordnance depot

Arms and the Man
author: **17** George Bernard Shaw

arms depot 6 armory **7** arsenal **13** ordnance depot **18** military storehouse

Armstrong, Henry
sport: **6** boxing
class: **11** lightweight **12** welterweight

army 3 mob **4** band, bevy, crew, gang, host, mass, pack **5** crowd, force, horde, swarm **6** legion, throng, troops **7** legions, militia **8** military, soldiers, soldiery **9** land force, multitude **10** land forces **11** aggregation, fighting men **12** congregation **13** military force **15** military machine

Arnaeus
also: **4** Irus
origin: **5** Greek
mentioned in: **7** Odyssey
form: **6** beggar **9** errandboy
errandboy for: **16** Penelopes suitors

Arne
author: **20** Bjornstjerne Bjornson

Arne
son: **6** Aeolus **7** Boeotus
foster father: **9** Desmontes

Arne, Thomas Augustine
born: **6** London **7** England
composer of: **6** Alfred, Judith **8** Rosamond, Tom Thumb **10** Artaxerxes **13** Rule, Britannia **14** Love in a Village, Thomas and Sally

Arness, James
real name: **12** James Aurness
brother: **11** Peter Graves
born: **13** Minneapolis MN
roles: **8** Gunsmoke **10** Matt Dillon

Arnold, Matthew
author of: **7** Thyrsis **10** Dover Beach **15** Sohrab and Rustum, The Scholar-Gypsy **16** Empedocles on Etna **17** Culture and Anarchy, Essays in Criticism **18** On Translating Homer

aroma 4 odor **5** savor, scent, smell **7** bouquet **9** fragrance, redolence

aromatic 5 spicy **7** odorous, piquant, pungent, scented **8** fragrant, perfumed, redolent **11** odoriferous

around 4 near **5** about, circa **10** encircling, on all sides, roundabout **11** surrounding

Around the World in Eighty Days
author: **10** Jules Verne
director: **15** Michael Anderson
character: **11** Phileas Fogg **12** Passepartout
cast: **10** Cantinflas, David Niven **12** Robert Newton **15** Marlene Dietrich, Shirley MacLaine
score: **11** Victor Young
Oscar for: **5** score **7** picture

arouse 3 fan **4** goad, move, spur,

warm, whet **5** pique, rouse, waken **6** awaken, bestir, excite, foment, foster, heat up, incite, kindle, stir up, wake up **7** provoke, quicken, sharpen **8** summon up **9** stimulate

Arowhena
character in: **7** Erewhon
author: **6** Butler

arpeggio 5 chord, scale **8** flourish **13** musical device

arraign 6 accuse, charge, impute, indict **7** censure **8** denounce **9** criticize

arrange 4 file, plan, plot, pose, rank, sort **5** adapt, array, fix up, group, order, range, score **6** assort, design, devise, lay out, line up, map out, set out, settle **7** agree to, marshal, prepare, provide **8** classify, contrive, organize, schedule **9** methodize **11** orchestrate, systematize

arrangement 5 order **8** arraying, disposal, grouping, ordering **10** assortment **12** distribution, organization **13** methodization **14** categorization, classification **15** systematization
German: **9** Ausgleich
flower: **7** ikebana

arrangements 5 plans, score, terms **7** compact **8** measures **9** agreement **10** adaptation, provisions, settlement **12** preparations **13** orchestration

arrant 4 rank **5** utter **7** extreme **8** flagrant, outright, thorough **9** confirmed, downright, egregious, notorious, out-and-out **11** undisguised, unmitigated **13** thoroughgoing

array 4 deck, garb, pose, rank, robe, show, wrap **5** adorn, align, dress, group, order, place, range **6** attire, bedeck, clothe, deploy, finery, fit out, outfit, parade, set out, supply **7** apparel, arrange, display, marshal, raiment **8** clothing, garments, organize **9** pageantry **10** assortment, collection, exhibition, marshaling **11** arrangement, disposition

arrears 5 debit **9** liability **10** balance due, obligation, unpaid debt **11** overdue debt **12** indebtedness **15** outstanding debt

arrest 3 end, fix, nab **4** bust, halt, hold, slow, stay, stop **5** block, catch, check, delay, pinch, rivet, roust, seize, stall **6** absorb, collar, detain, engage, hinder, occupy, retard, secure **7** attract, capture, engross, inhibit, seizure, slowing, staying **8** blocking, checking, hold back, restrain, stoppage, stopping, suppress **9** apprehend, interrupt, retention **10** inhibiting **11** holding back **12** apprehension, take prisoner

Arrhenius, Svante August
field: **7** physics **9** chemistry
nationality: **7** Swedish
theory of: **24** electrolytic dissociation

arriere pensee 12 hidden motive **17** mental reservation

arrival 5 comer **6** advent, coming **7** entrant, visitor **8** approach, arriving, entrance, newcomer, visitant **10** appearance

arrive 4 come, near **5** get to, occur, reach **6** appear, befall, happen, show up, turn up **7** succeed **8** approach, make good

arrivederci, a rivederci 7 goodbye **8** farewell **16** until we meet again

arrogance 5 scorn **6** egoism, vanity **7** bluster, conceit, disdain, swagger **8** contempt **9** assurance, insolence, loftiness, vainglory **10** lordliness, pretension **11** braggadocio, haughtiness, presumption **13** imperiousness **14** self-importance

arrogant 4 vain **6** lordly **7** haughty, pompous **8** insolent, scornful **9** conceited, imperious **10** disdainful, egoistical, swaggering **11** egotistical, overbearing, overweening, pretentious **12** contemptuous, presumptuous, self-assuming, supercilious, vainglorious **13** high-and-mighty, self-important

arrogate 5 adopt, claim, seize, usurp **6** assume **7** preempt **8** take over **10** commandeer **11** appropriate

arrogation 6 taking **7** seizure **10** assumption, usurpation **12** confiscation **13** appropriation, expropriation

arrow 3 bow **4** bolt, dart, nock **5** shaft **7** pointer **9** direction **12** pointed shaft

Arrow
constellation of: **7** Sagitta

Arrowsmith
author: **13** Sinclair Lewis
character: **10** Leora Tozer **11** Max Gottlieb **12** Terry Wickett **14** Capitola McGurk **15** Gustaf Sondelius **16** Martin Arrowsmith **18** Dr Almus Pickerbaugh

arroyo 4 wadi **5** gorge, gully **6** ravine, trench

arsenal 6 armory **7** weapons **8** magazine **9** arms depot **11** arms factory **13** ordnance depot **14** ammunition dump

arsenic
chemical symbol: **2** As

Arsenic and Old Lace
director: **10** Frank Capra
cast: **9** Cary Grant **10** Jack Carson, Peter Lorre **13** Josephine Hull, Priscilla Lane, Raymond Massey

Arsinoe see **11** Alphesiboea

Arsinous
son: **8** Aecamede

Arsippe
father: **6** Minyas
mocked: **8** Dionysus

ars longa, vita brevis 18 art is long, life short

Ars Poetica
author: **5** Homer

art, arts 5 craft, knack, skill **6** genius **7** finesse, mastery, methods **8** artistry, facility, strategy **9** dexterity, expertise, technique **10** fine points, humanities, principles, subtleties, virtuosity
goddess of: 6 Athena, Athene, Pallas, Saitis **7** Minerva **11** Tritogeneia **12** Pallas Athena **18** Alalcomenean Athena

Artegall
character in: 15 The Faerie Queene
author: 7 Spenser

Artemis
also: 7 Cynthia **9** Astrateia
origin: 5 Greek
form: 6 virgin **7** goddess **8** huntress
habitat: 4 moon
mother: 4 Leto
twin brother: 6 Apollo
companion: 4 Opis **5** Oread
corresponds to: 5 Diana **6** Phoebe, Selene **11** Britomartis
epithet: 6 Orthia **7** Eurippa, Laphria, Limnaea, Pyronia **8** Aeginaea, Agrotera, Calliste, Caryatis, Daphnaea **9** Hemerasia, Lygodesma **10** Polymastus **11** Leucophryne

artery 3 way **4** path, road, vein **5** aorta **6** street **7** channel, highway **11** blood vessel

artful 3 apt, sly **4** able, deft, foxy, wily **5** adept, quick, sharp, smart **6** adroit, astute, clever, crafty, gifted, shifty, shrewd, subtle, tricky **7** cunning, knowing, politic **8** masterly, scheming, skillful, talented **9** deceitful, deceptive, designing, dexterous, ingenious, inventive, strategic, underhand **10** contriving, diplomatic, proficient **11** imaginative, machinating, maneuvering, resourceful **12** disingenuous

artfulness 5 guile **6** deceit **7** cunning, slyness **8** artifice, foxiness, scheming, subtlety, trickery, wiliness **10** craftiness **11** machination

Arthur
director: 11 Steve Gordon
cast: 11 Dudley Moore, John Gielgud **12** Liza Minnelli **19** Geraldine Fitzgerald
Oscar for: 15 supporting actor (Gielgud)

Arthur
began: 10 Round Table
buried: 6 Avalon
chronicler: 4 Wace **6** Malory **8** Chretien
father: 14 Uther Pendragon
half-sister: 11 Morgan le Fay
home: 7 Camelot
island: 6 Avalon
knights: 3 Kay **6** Gareth, Gawain **7** Geraint **8** Bedivere, Lancelot, Percival, Tristram **9** Launcelot
knights sought: 9 Holy Grail
mother: 7 Igraine, Ygaerne
nephew: 6 Modred **7** Mordred

sword: 9 Excalibur
given by: 13 Lady of the Lake
wife: 9 Guinevere
wizard: 6 Merlin
women, Arthurian: 4 Anna, Enid **5** Nimue **6** Elaine, Gyneth, Iseult, Isolde **7** Igraine, Ygaerne **9** Bellicent, Guinivere **11** Morgan le Fay

Arthur, Chester Alan
nickname: 4 Chet **16** The Gentleman Boss
presidential rank: 11 twenty-first
party: 10 Republican
state represented: 2 NY
defeated: 5 no-one
succeeded upon death of: 8 Garfield
vice president: 4 none
cabinet:
state: 6 (James Gillespie) Blaine **13** (Frederick Theodore) Frelinghuysen
treasury: 6 (Charles James) Folger, (William) Windom **7** (Walter Quintin) Gresham **9** (Hugh) McCulloch
war: 7 (Robert Todd) Lincoln
attorney general: 8 (Benjamin Harris) Brewster, (Isaac Wayne) MacVeagh
navy: 4 (William Henry) Hunt **8** (William Eaton) Chandler
postmaster general: 4 (Timothy Otis) Howe **5** (Thomas Lemuel) James **6** (Frank) Hatton **7** (Walter Quinton) Gresham
interior: 6 (Henry Moore) Teller **8** (Samuel Jordan) Kirkwood
born: 2 VT (or Canada) **9** Fairfield
died: 2 NY **11** New York City
buried: 2 NY **6** Albany
education:
college: 5 Union
studied: 3 law
religion: 12 Episcopalian
interests: 8 good food (an epicure) **13** salmon fishing
political career: 13 vice president **26** customs collector for New York
civilian career: 6 lawyer **7** teacher
military service: 8 Civil War
quartermaster general of: 12 state militia (New York)
notable events of lifetime/term: 5 Panic (of 1883)
Act: 9 Pendleton **16** Chinese Exclusion **19** Edmunds Anti-Polygamy
father: 7 William
mother: 7 Malvina (Stone)
siblings: 4 Jane, Mary **6** Almeda, George, Regina **7** Malvina, William **8** Ann Eliza
wife: 5 Ellen (Lewis Herndon)
nickname: 4 Nell
children: 11 Chester Alan **12** Ellen Herndon **19** William Lewis Herndon

artichoke 14 Cynara Scolymus
varieties: 5 Globe **7** Chinese **8** Japa-

nese **9** Jerusalem **14** White Jerusalem

article 4 item, part, term **5** count, essay, paper, piece, point, story, theme, thing **6** clause, detail, matter, object, review, sketch **7** portion, product, proviso, write-up **8** division **9** commodity, condition, paragraph, provision, substance **10** commentary, particular **11** proposition, stipulation

articulate 4 join **5** hinge, state, utter, voice **6** convey, facile, fluent, hook up **7** connect, enounce, express **8** eloquent, organize **9** enunciate, formulate, pronounce **10** enunciated, expressive, meaningful, speechlike **12** intelligible

articulation 5 hinge, joint **7** diction **8** juncture **9** elocution, utterance **10** connection **11** enunciation **13** pronunciation

artifact 4 tool **7** manmade **9** arrowhead

artifice 4 hoax, ruse, trap, wile **5** blind, dodge, feint, guile, trick **6** deceit, device, tactic **7** cunning, slyness **8** foxiness, intrigue, maneuver, scheming, trickery, wiliness **9** deception, duplicity, falsehood, imposture, ingenuity, invention, stratagem **10** artfulness, cleverness, craftiness, subterfuge **11** contrivance, machination **13** inventiveness

artificer 7 artisan, deviser **9** contriver, craftsman

artificial 4 fake, mock, sham **5** bogus, false, phony, stagy **6** ersatz, forced **7** feigned, labored, manmade, stilted **8** affected, mannered, specious, spurious **9** imitation, insincere, pretended, simulated, synthetic, unnatural **10** factitious, non-natural, theatrical **11** counterfeit **12** manufactured

artillery 6 cannon **7** big guns **8** ordnance **11** mounted guns

artisan 6 master **9** craftsman **10** technician **14** handicraftsman

art is long, life short
Latin: 18 ars longa vita brevis

artist 6 expert, master **8** virtuoso

artistic 7 elegant, stylish **8** graceful, handsome, tasteful **9** aesthetic, exquisite **10** attractive

artistic ability 6 talent **7** mastery **8** artistry **10** virtuosity

artistry 5 taste, touch **6** talent **7** mastery **10** virtuosity **11** proficiency, sensibility **14** accomplishment

artless 4 naif, open, pure, true **5** crude, frank, naive, plain **6** candid, honest, humble, simple **7** natural, sincere **8** innocent, trusting **9** guileless, ingenuous, primitive, unadorned **10** inartistic, lacking art, unaffected, untalented **11** open-hearted, undesigning

13 unpretentious 15 straightforward, unselfconscious, unsophisticated

artlessness 6 candor 7 honesty, naivete 8 openness 9 frankness, sincerity 10 simplicity 11 naturalness 13 guilelessness, ingenuousness 14 unaffectedness

art object
   French: 9 objet d'art

Art of Living, The
   author: 11 John Gardner

Art of Love, The (Ars Amatoria)
   author: 4 Ovid

arty 6 dainty 7 foppish 8 affected, high- brow, overnice, precious 9 dandified, overblown 10 effeminate 11 overrefined, pretentious 12 artsycraftsy, bluestocking, high-sounding

Aryan
   modern name: 13 Indo-European
   origin: 10 North India 11 Central Asia
   family of languages: 5 Hindi 7 Bengali, Panjabi 9 Sinhalese
   religion: 8 Hinduism
   originated: 11 caste system

Aryana *see* 11 Afghanistan

as 4 that, when 5 while 7 because, equally

Asa
   father: 6 Abijah
   grandfather: 8 Rehoboam
   grandmother: 6 Maacah
   deposed: 6 Maacah
   defeated: 6 Baasha

as above
   Latin: 7 ut supra

as a group 7 en masse, in a body 8 as a whole, together 11 all together

as a matter of form
   Latin: 8 pro forma

Asar *see* 5 Aesir

as a result 2 so 5 due to 7 because 9 therefore, wherefore, whereupon 11 accordingly 12 consequently 13 in consequence

as a whole 6 in toto 8 all in all 10 altogether 19 all things considered
   French: 6 en bloc

as below
   Latin: 7 ut infra

Ascalaphus
   occupation: 6 sentry 8 gardener
   location: 10 underworld
   father: 4 Ares
   brother: 8 Ialmenus
   member of: 9 Argonauts
   killed by: 9 Deiphobus
   changed into: 3 owl
   changed by: 7 Demeter

Ascanius
   also: 5 Iulus
   father: 6 Aeneas
   mother: 6 Creusa
   founder of: 9 Alba Longa

ascend 4 rise 5 climb, mount, scale 7 inherit 9 succeed to

ascendancy, ascendance 4 edge, rule, sway 5 power, reign 7 command, control, mastery 8 whip hand 9 advantage, authority, dominance, influence, supremacy, upper hand 10 domination, leadership 11 preeminence, sovereignty, superiority 12 predominance

ascension 6 ascent, rising 7 scaling 8 climbing, mounting 10 ascendancy

ascent 4 rise 5 climb, grade, slope 6 rising 7 advance, incline, scaling, upgrade 8 climbing, gradient, mounting, progress 9 ascension 11 advancement, progression

ascertain 5 learn 6 detect, verify 7 certify, find out, unearth 8 discover 9 determine, establish, ferret out

ascertainable 10 detectable 11 discernible, perceivable, perceptible

ascetic 3 nun 4 monk, yogi 5 fakir, stern 6 essene, hermit, strict 7 austere, dervish, eremite, recluse, Spartan 8 celibate, cenobite, rigorous, solitary 9 abstainer, anchorite, religious 10 abstemious, flagellant, self-denier 11 self- denying 13 self-mortifier 14 self-mortifying

Asch, Sholem
   author of: 4 Mary 5 Moses 8 A Village 10 The Apostle, The Prophet 11 The Nazarene, Three Cities 15 Song of the Valley 17 The God of Vengeance

Asclepius
   origin: 5 Greek
   god of: 7 healing 8 medicine
   father: 6 Apollo
   mother: 7 Coronis
   wife: 6 Epione
   son: 7 Machaon 10 Podalirius
   daughter: 4 Iaso 6 Hygeia
   nurse: 6 Trygon
   corresponds to: 11 Aesculapius
   epithet: 8 Cotyleus

ascribe 6 assign, credit, impute, relate 7 trace to 8 accredit, charge to 9 attribute

asea 4 lost 6 addled, adrift 7 puzzled 8 confused 10 bewildered

Asgard
   home of: 4 Asar 5 Aesir
   origin: 12 Scandinavian
   connected to earth by: 7 bifrost 13 rainbow bridge
   location of: 8 Valhalla

ash 4 dust 6 cinder 7 residue 12 powdered lava
   family: 5 olive
   genus: 8 Fraxinus
   climatic zone: 17 northern temperate
   varieties: 3 Pop, Red, Sea 4 Blue 5 Black, Green, Manna, Texas, Wafer, Water, White 6 Alpine, Ground, Shamel, Syrian, Velvet 7 Arizona,

Modesto, Prickly 8 Carolina, Stinking 9 Evergreen, Flowering 10 Manchurian, Montebello 18 Yellow-topped mallee
   use: 4 fuel 6 timber 7 barrels 8 landscape 9 furniture 10 motor parts, sport goods
   most common species: 8 white ash

ashamed 3 shy 7 abashed, bashful, prudish 9 chagrined, mortified, squeamish 10 chapfallen, distressed, humiliated, shamefaced 11 crestfallen, discomfited, embarrassed 12 disconcerted 13 guilt-stricken 18 conscience-stricken

Ashby, Hal
   director of: 10 Being There, Coming Home

ashen 3 wan 4 gray, pale 5 livid, pasty 6 anemic, leaden, pallid 8 blanched

Asher
   father: 5 Jacob
   mother: 6 Zilpah
   brother: 3 Dan, Gad 4 Levi 5 Judah 6 Joseph, Reuben, Simeon 7 Zebulun 8 Benjamin, Issachar, Nephtali
   sister: 5 Dinah
   city in: 8 Manasseh
   descendant of: 8 Asherite

Ashkenaz
   father: 6 Japhet
   mother: 5 Gomer

Ashley, Lady Brett
   character in: 15 The Sun Also Rises
   author: 9 Hemingway

ashore 6 on land 7 aground 9 on dry land

Ashton-Warner, Sylvia
   author of: 5 Three 6 Myself 7 Teacher 8 Spinster 10 Greenstone

Ashtoreth
   origin: 7 Semitic
   corresponds to: 6 Inanna, Ishtar 7 Astarte, Mylitta

Ash Wednesday
   author: 7 T S Eliot

ashy 3 wan 4 pale 5 ashen, pasty, white 6 pallid, sallow 7 ghastly, ghostly 8 blanched 9 colorless

Asia
   country: 4 Iran, Iraq, Laos, Oman 5 Burma, China, India, Japan, Macao, Nepal, Qatar, Syria, Tibet, Yemen 6 Bhutan, Brunei, Cyprus, Israel, Jordan, Russia, Sikkim, Taiwan, Turkey 7 Armenia, Bahrain, Georgia, Kashmir, Lebanon, Myanmar, Vietnam 8 Cambodia, Hong Kong, Malaysia, Maldives, Mongolia, Pakistan, Sri Lanka, Thailand 9 East Timor, Indonesia, Kirghizia, Singapore 10 Azerbaijan, Bangladesh, Kazakhstan, Kyrgyzstan, North Korea, South Korea, Tajikistan, Uzbekistan 11 Afghanistan, Saudi Arabia 12 North Vietnam, South Vietnam, Turkmenistan 13 Inner Mongolia 14 Papua New

Guinea **15** Sinkiang-Uighur **18** United Arab Emirates

desert: 4 Gobi, Thar **6** Syrian **7** Arabian, Karakum **8** Kyzylkum **10** Takla Makan

island: 5 Kuril, Japan **6** Taiwan **7** Hai-nan **8** Sri Lanka **9** Indonesia: **3** Aru **4** Java, Sulu **5** Ceram, Sumba, Timor **6** Borneo, Flores **7** Celebes, Sumatra **8** Moluccas, Tanimbar **9** Halmahera, New Guinea **11** Philippines

ancient people/empire: 4 Elam, Thai **5** Akkad, Aryan, Indus, Khmer, Media, Shang **6** Mongol, Ohoman, Semite **7** Amorite, Assyria, Hwang Ho, Parthia, Persian **8** Sumerian **9** Babylonia, Dravidian, Sassanian **11** Hephthalite, Mesopotamia

ancient city: 2 Ur **5** Pagan, Sumer **6** Anyang **7** Ayuthia, Harappa **8** Mandalay **12** Mohenjo-daro

ancient leader: 5 Asoka, Kassi **6** Darius **9** Anawratha, Zoroaster **13** Cyrus the Great **17** Alexander the Great

religion: 5 Islam **6** Muslim, Shinto, Taoism **7** Jainism, Judaism **8** Buddhism, Hinduism **12** Christianity, Confucianism **13** Protestantism **16** Roman Catholicism

language: 5 Hindi, Malay **6** Arabic, French, Korean **7** Chinese, English, Russian, Spanish **8** Japanese **10** Indonesian, Portuguese

   Chinese dialects: 2 Wu **3** Min **5** Hakka **8** Mandarin **9** Cantonese

river: 2 Ob **3** Amu, Hsi, Syr **4** Amur, Lena **5** Indus **6** Ganges, Mekong, Tigris **7** Hwang Ho, Salween, Yangtze, Yenisei **9** Euphrates, Irrawaddy **11** Brahmaputra **16** Tigris-Euphrates

lake: 6 Baikal **7** Aral Sea **8** Balkhash **10** Caspian Sea

mountain/mountain range: 5 Altai, Urals **6** Kunlon, Pamirs, Taurus, Zagros **8** Caucasus, Sulaiman, Tien Shan **9** Himalayas, Hindu Kush, Karakoram **10** Arakan Yoma

highest point: 12 Mount Everest

lowest point: 7 Dead Sea

mineral/natural resources: 3 oil, tin **4** coal, mica, talc, zinc **7** bauxite, iron ore, mercury **8** chromium, graphite, selenium, tungsten **9** manganese **10** natural gas

largest city: 8 Shanghai

vegetation: 3 fir, sal **4** moss, pine, teak **5** larch **6** bamboo, lichen, spruce **8** ironwood

animal: 3 elk, yak **4** bear, wolf **5** camel, panda, sable, takin, tiger **6** ermine, kuland **7** markhor **8** antelope, elephant, reindeer **9** arctic fox, polar bear

people: 4 Huis, Kurd, Thai, Turk **5** Aryan, Khmer, Malay, Tungu **6** Buryat, Chuang, Kalmyk, Mongol, Semite, Vighor **7** Baluchi, Burmese, Chi-

nese, Chukchi, Persian, Russian, Tadzhik, Tibetan **8** Armenian, Filipino, Japanese **9** Dravidian **10** Han Chinese, Indonesian, Vietnamese

aside 4 away **5** apart **6** aslant, beside **7** whisper

As I Lay Dying
  author: 15 William Faulkner
  character:
    Bundren family: 4 Anse, Cash, Darl **5** Addie, Jewel **9** Dewey Dell

Asimov, Isaac
  author of: 6 I Robot **10** Foundation (trilogy) **12** Caves of Steel, Robots of Dawn **17** The Gods Themselves
  character: 12 Elijah Bailey **13** R Daneel Olivaw

asinine 5 silly **6** absurd, insane, stupid **7** foolish, idiotic, moronic, witless **9** brainless, imbecilic, senseless **10** halfwitted, irrational, muddlehead, ridiculous **11** lamebrained, thickheaded, thick-witted **12** dunderheaded, feebleminded, simpleminded, thick-skulled

asininity 5 folly **8** dumbness **9** silliness, stupidity **10** imbecility **11** doltishness, foolishness **16** simplemindedness

as it should be
  French: 11 comme il faut

Asius
  origin: 5 Greek
  mentioned in: 5 Iliad
  king of: 7 Percote
  father: 8 Hyrtacus
  killed by: 9 Idomeneus

ask 3 beg, bid, sue **4** call, pump, quiz, seek, urge **5** apply, claim, grill, plead, press, query **6** appeal, charge, demand, desire, expect, invite, summon **7** beseech, entreat, implore, inquire, request, solicit **8** petition, question, sound out **10** supplicate **11** interrogate

askance 11 skeptically **12** disdainfully, suspiciously **13** distrustfully, mistrustfully **14** disapprovingly

askew 4 awry **6** aslant **7** crooked **8** cockeyed, lopsided, sleeping **9** crookedly

Askkimey see **6** Eskimo

aslant 4 awry **5** askew **7** crooked **8** cockeyed, lopsided **9** crookedly, obliquely, slantwise

asleep 6 dozing **7** napping **10** slumbering **13** taking a siesta **14** dead to the world

as much as this
  Latin: 8 quoad hoc

Asner, Ed
  born: 12 Kansas City KS
  roles: 5 Roots **6** Daniel **8** El Dorado, Lou Grant **12** A Case of Libel, The Gathering, Silent Motive **14** Rich Man Poor Man **18** Mary Tyler Moore Show

asocial 8 unsocial **9** nonsocial, reclusive **10** antisocial **12** misanthropic

Asopus
  form: 3 god
  habitat: 5 river
  father: 7 Oceanus
  mother: 6 Tethys
  wife: 6 Metope
  son: 7 Ismenus, Pelagon
  number of daughters: 6 twenty

asparagus
  varieties: 4 Cape **6** Common, Garden, Smilax **7** Cossack **8** Prussian, Sprenger

aspect 3 air **4** look, side **5** angle, facet, point **7** feature **10** appearance **13** consideration

aspen 7 Populus
  varieties: 7 Chinese, Quaking **8** European, Japanese **9** Trembling **12** Large-toothed

asperity 5 rigor **6** rancor **8** acrimony, hardship, severity **9** harshness, hostility, roughness **10** difficulty

Aspern Papers, The
  author: 10 Henry James

aspersion 4 slur **5** abuse, smear **7** calumny, censure, obloquy, railing, slander **8** reproach, reviling **10** defamation, detraction **11** deprecation **12** vilification **13** disparagement

Asphodel Fields
  meadow of: 10 dead heroes

asphyxiate 5 choke **6** stifle **7** smother **9** suffocate **11** strangulate

aspirant 7 hopeful, nominee **9** applicant, candidate **10** competitor, contestant

aspiration 3 end **4** hope, mark, wish **6** design, desire, intent, object **7** craving, longing, purpose **8** ambition, daydream, endeavor, yearning **9** hankering, intention, objective

aspire 4 seek **5** aim at, covet, crave **6** desire, pursue **7** hope for, long for, pine for, wish for **8** yearn for **9** pant after **10** hunger over **11** hanker after, thirst after

ass 3 oaf **4** dolt, fool, jerk **5** booby, burro, dunce, idiot, moron, ninny **6** donkey, dum-dum, nitwit **7** half-wit, jackass **8** bonehead, imbecile, lunkhead, numskull **9** blockhead, lamebrain **10** dunderhead, nincompoop

assail 5 fly at **6** attack **7** assault, lunge at, set upon **9** pitch into **11** descend upon

assailant 6 mugger **8** assailer, attacker, molester **9** aggressor, assaulter

assailer 8 attacker **9** aggressor, assailant, assaulter

Assamese
  language family: 12 Indo-European
  branch: 11 Indo-Iranian
  group: 5 Indic
  spoken in: 5 (northern) India

Assaracus
origin: **5** Greek
mentioned in: **5** Iliad
father: **4** Tros
son: **5** Capys
founder of: **10** royal house

assassin 6 hit man, killer, slayer **8** murderer **11** executioner

assassinate 4 kill, slay **6** murder, rub out **7** bump off **9** do to death, liquidate **10** put to death **11** exterminate

assault 4 push, raid **5** drive, fly at, foray, lunge, sally, siege, storm **6** assail, attack, charge, invade, strike, thrust **7** besiege, bombard, lunge at, offense, set upon **8** fall upon, invasion, storming, strike at, thrust at **9** assailing, lash out at, onslaught **10** aggression **11** bombardment

assaulter 6 mugger **8** assailer, attacker **9** aggressor, assailant

assay 3 try **4** rate, test **5** essay, prove **6** assess **7** analyze, attempt **8** appraise, endeavor, estimate, evaluate **9** undertake

assemblage 4 body, heap, herd, mass, pack, pile **5** batch, bunch, clump, flock, group, stock, store **6** throng **7** cluster, company **8** assembly, conclave **9** aggregate, amassment, gathering **10** collection **11** aggregation **12** accumulation, congregation

assemble 4 join, meet **5** amass, flock, rally **6** gather, heap up, muster, pile up, summon **7** collect, compile, connect, convene, convoke, marshal, round up **9** construct, fabricate **10** accumulate, congregate **11** fit together, put together **12** call together, come together **13** bring together, group together

assembly 4 body, herd, mass, pack **5** crowd, flock, group, troop **6** throng **7** cluster, company, council **8** conclave, congress **9** aggregate, gathering **10** assemblage, collection **11** aggregation, convocation, legislature **12** congregation

assembly hall 8 auditory **10** auditorium **11** concert hall, lecture hall, meeting hall

assent 5 agree, allow, grant, yield **6** accept, accord, comply, concur, permit **7** approve, concede, consent, defer to **8** approval, sanction **9** acquiesce, admission, agreement **10** acceptance, compliance, concession, fall in with **11** affirmation, approbation, concurrence, endorsement, recognition, subscribe to **12** acquiescence, confirmation, ratification, verification **13** corroboration **14** acknowledgment

assent to 4 okay **5** allow **6** accept, permit **7** approve **8** sanction, say yes to **9** agree with, authorize **11** acquiesce to, go along with

assert 4 aver, avow **5** argue, claim, state, swear **6** accent, affirm, avouch, insist, stress, uphold **7** advance, contend, declare, profess **8** advocate, maintain, propound, set forth **9** emphasize **10** put forward

assertion 5 claim **6** avowal, dictum **8** argument, averment **9** statement, upholding **10** allegation, contention **11** declaration, maintaining **12** protestation

assertive 5 pushy **8** cocksure, decisive, emphatic, forceful, positive **9** confident, insistent, outspoken **10** aggressive **11** domineering, self-assured **12** strong-willed

assertiveness 10 insistence **11** forwardness **12** cocksureness, forcefulness, positiveness **13** agressiveness, outspokenness **14** self-confidence

assess 3 tax **4** levy **5** judge, value **6** charge **8** appraise, consider, estimate, evaluate, look over

assessment 3 fee, tax **4** dues, fine, rate, toll **6** charge, impost, tariff **8** judgment **9** appraisal **10** estimation, evaluation

asset 3 aid **4** boon, help, plus **7** benefit, service **9** advantage

assets 4 cash **5** goods, means, money **6** wealth **7** capital, effects **8** property, reserves **9** resources **10** belongings **11** possessions

asseverate 4 aver, avow **5** state, swear **6** affirm, assert, attest, avouch, insist **7** certify, contend, declare, protect **8** maintain, proclaim **9** emphasize, pronounce

as shown below
Latin: **7** ut infra

assiduity 8 industry, tenacity **9** diligence **10** dedication, doggedness **11** application, persistence **13** determination

assiduous 6 dogged **7** earnest **8** constant, diligent, sedulous, tireless, untiring **9** laborious, steadfast, tenacious **10** determined, persistent, unflagging **11** hardworking, industrious, persevering, unremitting **13** indefatigable

assign 3 fix, set **4** give, name **5** allot, grant **6** charge, choose, invest **7** appoint, consign, entrust, mete out, specify **8** allocate, delegate, dispense, set apart **9** apportion, designate, determine, prescribe, stipulate **10** commission, distribute

assignation 4 date **5** tryst **7** meeting **10** rendezvous **11** appointment

assignment 3 job **4** duty, post, task **5** chore **6** lesson **8** exercise, homework **9** allotment **10** allocation, commission **11** appointment, designation **12** distribution **13** apportionment

assimilate 6 absorb, digest, imbibe, in-

gest, take in **9** integrate **10** metabolize **11** incorporate

Assiniboine, Assiniboin
language family: **6** Siouan
location: **9** Minnesota **12** Lake Winnipeg, Saskatchewan
related to: **7** Dakotas

assist 3 aid **4** abet, hand, help **5** boost, serve **6** back up, uphold, wait on **7** benefit, support, sustain **9** cooperate, lend a hand, reinforce **11** accommodate, collaborate, helping hand

assistance 3 aid **4** alms, help **6** relief **7** charity, service, stipend, subsidy, support **10** sustenance **11** cooperation, helping hand **12** contribution **13** collaboration, reinforcement **16** financial support

assistant 3 aid **4** aide, ally **5** aider **6** helper **7** partner **8** adjutant, coworker, sidekick **9** accessory, associate, auxiliary, colleague, subaltern, supporter **10** accomplice, apprentice, cooperator, lieutenant **11** confederate, helping hand, subordinate **12** collaborator **15** second-in-command

associate 3 mix, pal, tie **4** ally, bind, chum, club, join, link, mate, pair, peer, yoke **5** buddy, crony, merge, unite **6** allied, couple, fellow, friend, hobnob, league, mingle, relate **7** combine, comrade, connect, consort, hang out, partner, related **8** confrere, coworker, identify, intimate, sidekick **9** affiliate, colleague, companion, confidant, correlate, pal around, rub elbows, run around **10** accomplice, affiliated, fraternize **11** confederate, subordinate **12** collaborator

associated 6 allied, joined, united **9** connected **10** affiliated **11** amalgamated

association 3 tie **4** body, bond, club, meld **5** blend, group, union **6** clique, league **7** combine, company, linkage, mixture, society **8** alliance, intimacy, mingling, relation **9** coalition, community, relations, syndicate **10** assemblage, connection, federation, fellowship, fraternity, friendship, membership **11** affiliation, camaraderie, combination, confederacy, corporation, correlation, familiarity, partnership **12** acquaintance, friendliness, organization, relationship **13** collaboration, companionship, confederation, participation **14** fraternization, identification

assorted 5 mixed **6** motley, sundry, varied **7** diverse, various **9** different **11** diversified **13** heterogeneous, miscellaneous

assortment 5 array, stock, store **6** medley, motley **7** melange, mixture, sorting, variety **8** grouping, quantity **9** arranging, assorting, diversity, potpourri, selection **10** collection, hodgepodge, miscellany **11** arrangement, classifying, disposition **14** classification, conglomeration

assuage 4 calm, ease **5** allay, quiet, still **6** lessen, pacify, soften, soothe, temper **7** appease, lighten, mollify, relieve **8** mitigate, tone down **9** alleviate **14** take the edge off

assuagement 6 easing, relief, solace **7** comfort **8** blunting, easement **9** abatement, lessening, tempering **10** mitigation **11** appeasement **13** mollification

assume 4 take **5** fancy, guess, infer, judge, seize, think, usurp **6** accept, deduce, gather, take on, take up **7** believe, imagine, presume, suppose, surmise, suspect **8** arrogate, shoulder, take over, theorize **9** postulate, speculate, undertake **10** commandeer, conjecture, understand **11** appropriate, expropriate, hypothesize **14** take for granted

assumed 4 fake **5** bogus, false, phony **6** made-up **8** presumed, supposed **9** falsified **10** fictitious **11** make-believe, presupposed, pseudonymic **12** pseudonymous

assumed name 5 alias **7** pen name **9** pseudonym **13** false identity
French: 10 nom de plume **11** nom de guerre

assuming 4 bold **5** nervy, pushy **6** brazen, cheeky **7** forward, haughty **8** arrogant, insolent **9** audacious, presuming **11** overbearing **12** presumptuous **13** self-assertive

assumption 6 belief, taking, theory **7** premise, seizure **8** assuming, taking on, taking up **9** accepting, postulate **10** acceptance, arrogation, hypothesis, usurpation **11** postulation, presumption, shouldering, supposition, undertaking **13** appropriating **14** presupposition

assurance 3 vow **4** oath **5** poise **6** binder, pledge **7** promise **8** averment, boldness, coolness, sureness, warranty **9** certainty, certitude, guarantee **10** confidence, profession **11** affirmation, assuredness, word of honor **12** self-reliance **14** aggressiveness, self-confidence, self-possession

assure 5 vow to **6** clinch, ensure, secure **7** confirm, promise **8** pledge to **9** guarantee **11** make certain **14** give one's word to

assured 4 sure **5** fixed **6** poised, secure **7** certain, settled **8** positive **9** confident, undoubted **10** dependable, guaranteed **11** indubitable, irrefutable **12** indisputable **13** self-confident, self-possessed **14** unquestionable

Astaire, Fred
real name: 19 Frederick Austerlitz
partner: 12 Ginger Rogers
born: 7 Omaha NE
roles: 6 Top Hat **9** Funny Face, Let's Dance, Swing Time **10** Holiday Inn **12** Easter Parade, Royal Wedding, Shall We Dance **14** The Gay Divorcee

Astarte
origin: 7 Semitic
goddess of: 9 fertility **12** reproduction
habitat: 4 moon
corresponds to: 6 Inanna, Ishtar **7** Mylitta **9** Ashtoreth

aster 12 Callistephus
varieties: 4 Tree **5** Black, China, Heath **6** Annual, Golden, Mojave, Stoke's **7** Italian **8** Blue-wood **9** Tartarian, White wood **10** New England **11** White upland

Asteria
form: 8 Titaness
father: 5 Coeus
mother: 6 Phoebe
sister: 4 Leto
husband: 6 Perses
son: 8 Paropeus
daughter: 6 Hecate
changed into: 5 Delos **6** island

Asterius
also: 8 Asterion
form: 5 giant **8** minotaur
king of: 5 Crete
father: 4 Anax **8** Tectamus **10** Cretan Bull, Hyperasius
mother: 8 Pasiphae
wife: 6 Europa
adopted sons: 5 Minos **8** Sarpedon **12** Rhadamanthys
daughter: 5 Crete
member of: 9 Argonauts

astern 3 aft **5** abaft **6** behind

asteroid 6 debris **9** planetoid

Asteropaeus
origin: 5 Greek
mentioned in: 5 Iliad
father: 7 Pelegon
ally of: 4 Troy
killed by: 8 Achilles

Asterope *see* **7** Sterope

astir 2 up **5** afoot, awake **6** active, roused **8** in motion, out of bed **10** up and about

astonish 4 daze, stun **5** amaze, shock **6** dazzle **7** astound, confuse, perplex, stagger, startle, stupefy **8** bewilder, confound, dumfound, surprise **9** electrify, overwhelm, take aback **10** strike dumb **11** flabbergast **15** make one's eyes pop **18** take one's breath away

astonishing 7 amazing **8** dazzling, shocking, striking **9** confusing, startling **10** astounding, impressive, perplexing, staggering, stupefying, surprising **11** bewildering, confounding **12** breathtaking, electrifying, overpowering, overwhelming

astonishment 3 awe **5** shock **6** wonder **8** surprise **9** amazement, confusion **10** perplexity, wonderment **12** bewilderment, stupefaction

Astor, Mary
real name: 28 Lucille Vasconcellos Langhanke
born: 8 Quincy IL
roles: 6 Marmee **11** Little Women, The Great Lie **15** Meet Me in St Louis **16** The Maltese Falcon **17** The Palm Beach Story **18** The Prisoner of Zenda

astound 4 daze, stun **5** amaze, shock **6** dazzle **7** stagger, startle, stupefy **8** astonish, dumfound, surprise, take back **9** electrify, overwhelm **10** strike dumb **11** flabbergast **15** make one's eyes pop **18** take one's breath away

Astrabacus
origin: 5 Greek **7** Spartan
form: 6 prince
found: 11 wooden image
hidden by: 7 Orestes
co-finder: 8 Alopecus

Astraea
also: 6 Astrea
goddess of: 7 justice
father: 4 Zeus
mother: 6 Themis

Astraeus
form: 5 Titan
consort of: 3 Eos
father of: 4 wind **5** stars

astral 6 starry **9** celestial **12** astronomical

Astrateia *see* **7** Artemis

astray 3 off **5** amiss **6** afield **10** off the mark **12** off the course **16** off the right track

Astrea *see* **7** Astraea

astringent 4 acid, keen, sour, tart **5** brisk, sharp, stern, tonic **6** biting, severe **7** acerbic, austere, bracing, puckery, styptic **8** curative, incisive, piercing, salutary, stabbing, vinegary **10** antiseptic, salubrious **11** contracting, penetrating, restorative **12** invigorating

astrology 6 Zodiac **9** horoscopy, starcraft **10** astromancy, astrometry, stargazing **11** genethliacs **13** mathematicals **14** astrodiagnosis
belief in: 8 siderism
term: 4 sign **5** house, trine **6** alnath, apheta, aspect **7** almuten, anareta, mansion, mundane, sextile **8** alkahest, nativity, quartile, synastry **9** planetary **10** opposition **11** conjunction

astronomer 4 Bode, Bopp, Gold, Hale **5** Adams, Baade, Bayer, Bethe, Gould, Hoyle, Royer **6** Bessel, Halley, Hubble, Jansky, Kepler, Newton, Piazzi **7** Bradley, Celcius, Galileo, Huggins, Huygens, Kapteyn, Laplace, Ptolemy, Russell, Shapley, Slipher **8** Angstrom, Einstein, Herschel, Hevelius, Lacaille, Lemaitre, Mercator **9** Eddington, Leverrier **10** Copernicus, Hipparchus, Tycho Brahe **11** Aristarchus, Hertzsprung **13** Petrus Apianus

astronomy
term: 5 comet, orbit **6** apogee, meteor, nebula, parsec, quasar **7** azimuth, eclipse, equinox, perigee, transit **8** aphelion, asteroid, ecliptic, meridian, solstice **9** meteorite, satellite **10** perihelion, precession **11** declination, occultation **12** perturbation, spectroscopy **16** celestial equator
type/related study: 9 cosmogony, cosmology **10** astrometry, photometry **12** astrophysics **18** celestial mechanics
see also **4** star

Astrophel and Stella
author: 15 Sir Philip Sidney

astute 3 sly **4** able, foxy, keen, wily **5** acute, sharp, smart **6** adroit, artful, bright, clever, crafty, shrewd, subtle **7** cunning, knowing, politic **9** designing, sagacious **10** discerning, keen-minded, perceptive **11** calculating, intelligent, penetrating **13** Machiavellian, perspicacious

astuteness 6 acumen **8** keenness **9** acuteness, smartness **10** cleverness, shrewdness **12** perspicacity

Astyanax
also: 11 Scamandrius
father: 6 Hector **9** Strophius
mother: 10 Andromache
thrown from: 11 Trojan walls
thrown by: 6 Greeks
slain by: 8 Menelaus

Asuncion
capital of: 8 Paraguay

asunder 4 rent **5** apart **8** in pieces, to shreds **9** torn apart **11** broken apart

asylum 4 home **5** haven **6** harbor, refuge **7** retreat, shelter **8** madhouse, preserve **9** almshouse, orphanage, poorhouse, sanctuary **10** sanatorium, sanitarium **11** institution **13** children's home, state hospital **14** mental hospital **15** place of immunity **17** mental institution **23** eleemosynary institution

Asynjur
origin: 12 Scandinavian
goddesses of: 4 Asar **5** Aesir
leader: 3 Fri **5** Frigg, Frija **6** Frigga

As You Like It
author: 18 William Shakespeare
character: 5 Celia (Aliena) **6** Audrey, Jaques, Oliver **7** Orlando **8** Rosalind (Ganymede) **9** Frederick **10** Touchstone

Atabyrian *see* **4** Zeus

at a distance 4 afar, away **5** above, aloof, apart **6** far off **9** separated

Atala
author: 21 Francois Chateaubriand

Atalanta
also: 8 Atalante
form: 6 virgin **8** huntress

father: 5 Iasus
mother: 7 Clymene
son: 9 Parthenopaeus
wounded: 14 Calydonian boar
lost race to: 10 Hippomenes

Atalanta in Calydon
author: 24 Algernon Charles Swinburne

at any rate 6 anyhow, anyway **9** in any case **10** in any event

at cross purposes 7 counter, opposed **8** contrary, converse, inimical, opposite **9** disparate **10** at variance, discordant **11** conflicting **12** antithetical, incompatible **13** contradictory

Ate
origin: 5 Greek
form: 7 goddess
personifies: 12 recklessness **16** divine punishment

at ease 4 calm, cool **6** at rest, serene **7** content, relaxed, unmoved **8** composed **9** at leisure, confident, unruffled **10** complacent, nonchalant, unbothered, untroubled **11** comfortable, unconcerned

a tergo 9 at the back **10** from behind

at fault 6 guilty **8** culpable **10** implicated **11** blameworthy, responsible

at full length
Latin: 9 in extenso

Athabascan, Athapascan (Slave Indians)
language family: 10 Athabascan, Athapaskan
location: 6 Canada **14** Great Slave Lake
dominated by: 4 Cree
related to: 9 Chipewyan
tribe: 4 Dine **5** Slave **6** Apache, Navaho, Navajo **9** Mescalero **10** Athabascan

Athalie
author: 18 Jean Baptiste Racine

Athamas
king of: 6 Thebes
father: 6 Aeolus
wife: 3 Ino **7** Nephele
son: 5 Ptous **6** Leucon **7** Phrixus **8** Learchus **10** Melicertes
daughter: 5 Helle

at hand 4 near, nigh **5** close, handy, on tap, ready **6** nearby **7** close by **8** imminent **9** available, impending **10** accessible, convenient **11** at one's elbow, forthcoming **14** at one's disposal **15** within arm's reach

atheism 8 apostasy, unbelief **9** disbelief **10** irreligion **11** godlessness

atheist 7 infidel **10** unbeliever **11** disbeliever, nonbeliever

Athena
also: 6 Athene, Pallas, Saitis **11** Tritogeneia **12** Pallas Athena **18** Alalcomenean Athena
origin: 5 Greek

goddess of: 4 arts **6** wisdom **7** warfare **9** fertility
father: 4 Zeus **6** Triton
mother: 5 Metis
sprang from head of: 4 Zeus
raised by: 12 Alalcomeneus
symbol: 3 owl
corresponds to: 7 Minerva
epithet: 4 Alea **5** Meter, Xenia **6** Ergane, Itonia, Polias **7** Agoraea, Cissaea, Paeonia, Pronaus, Pronoea **8** Anemotis, Poliates, Zosteria **9** Oxyderces, Parthenia, Poliuchus, Promachus **10** Axiopoenus, Chalinitis, Cyparissia **11** Promachorma

Athens
capital of: 6 Greece
Greek: 7 Athinai
hills: 9 Acropolis **14** Hagios Georgios
landmark: 4 Stoa **9** Areopagus, Parthenon **10** Erechtheum, Propylaeum **17** Theater of Dionysus
marketplace: 5 Agora
mountain: 6 Parnes **8** Aigaleos, Hymettus **10** Pentelikon
named for: 6 Athena
port: 7 Piraeus
river: 7 Ilissus
sea: 6 Aegean **11** Saronic Gulf
square: 8 Syntagma (Constitution)

Athens Graces 4 Auxe **8** Hegemone

athirst 4 avid, keen **5** eager **6** raring **7** longing, panting **8** yearning

athlete 4 jock **8** champion **9** contender, sportsman **10** contestant, game player

athletic 5 burly, hardy, husky, manly **6** brawny, robust, strong, sturdy, virile **8** muscular, powerful, stalwart, vigorous **9** masculine, strapping **10** able-bodied

athletics 5 games **6** sports **8** exercise **9** exercises **10** gymnastics

at home 6 at ease, inside, shut in **7** indoors **8** confined **10** in the house **11** comfortable
French: 4 chez

Athos
character in: 18 The Three Musketeers
author: 5 Dumas (pere)

athwart 6 across **7** astride **8** sideways, sidewise **9** crossways, crosswise **12** transversely

Atlanta
baseball team: 6 Braves
basketball team: 5 Hawks
football team: 7 Falcons
hockey team: 9 Thrashers

Atlantean
pertaining to: 5 Atlas

Atlantic City
director: 10 Louis Malle
cast: 8 Kate Reid **13** Burt Lancaster, Michel Piccoli, Susan Sarandon

at large 5 astir, loose **6** abroad **8** as a whole, at length **9** at liberty, in general **10** on the loose, unconfined **11** out and about **13** in circulation **14** around and about **15** making the rounds

Atlas
  form: 5 Titan
  father: 7 Iapetus
  mother: 7 Clymene
  brother: 9 Menoetius **10** Epimetheus, Prometheus
  wife: 7 Pleione
  daughters: 6 Hyades **7** Calypso **8** Pleiades **10** Hesperides
  supported: 3 sky
  identified with: 14 Atlas Mountains

Atlas Shrugged
  author: 7 Ayn Rand
  character: 8 John Galt **11** Hank Reardon **12** Dagny Taggart, James Taggart

at last
  Latin: 10 ad extremum

at leisure 4 idle **7** off duty **8** inactive **9** at liberty **10** unemployed, unoccupied

Atli
  origin: 12 Scandinavian
  sister: 8 Brynhild
  wife: 6 Gudrun, Kudrun **7** Guthrun
  killed by: 6 Gudrun, Kudrun **7** Guthrun
  represents: 6 Atilla

atmosphere 3 air **4** aura, feel, mood, tone **5** color **6** spirit **7** feeling, quality **8** ambience **11** environment **12** surroundings

atmospheric 3 air **4** airy **8** ethereal

at odds 6 unlike **8** contrary **9** different **10** at variance, discordant, discrepant, dissimilar **11** contrasting

at odds with 9 counter to **10** contrary to **14** at variance with

atoll 6 island
  made of: 5 coral
  pool: 6 lagoon
  famous: 6 Bikini **8** Eniwetok

atom 3 bit, dot, jot **4** iota, mite, mote, whit **5** crumb, grain, scrap, shred, speck, trace **6** morsel, tittle **7** smidgen **8** fragment, particle **9** scintilla **10** smithereen

atomic 6 cobalt **7** fission, neutron, nuclear, uranium **8** hydrogen **9** molecular, plutonium, subatomic, unseeable **10** impalpable **11** fissionable, microcosmic, microscopic, superatomic **13** imperceptible, indiscernible, infinitesimal, thermonuclear

atom part 6 proton **7** neutron **8** electron

at once
  French: 11 tout de suite

atone 6 pay for, redeem, repent, shrive **7** expiate **9** make up for **10** compensate, recompense, remunerate **12** do

penance for **13** make amends for **17** make reparation for

atonement 6 amends, shrift **7** penance, redress **9** expiation **10** recompense, redemption, reparation, repentance **12** compensation, satisfaction **14** penitential act

at one's disposal 5 handy **6** at hand, on hand **9** available **10** accessible, convenient **11** at one's elbow, ready for use **13** at one's service

at one's elbow 5 handy **6** at hand, nearby **9** available **10** accessible, convenient

at rest 5 quiet, still **6** asleep, at ease, serene **7** at peace, content **8** in repose **9** quiescent **10** motionless

Atreus
  father: 6 Pelops
  mother: 10 Hippodamia
  sister: 7 Nicippe
  wife: 6 Aerope
  son: 8 Menelaus **9** Agamemnon **10** Plisthenes
  daughter: 8 Anaxibia
  killed: 6 Aglaus

Atridae
  descendants of: 6 Atreus
  family name of: 8 Anaxibia, Menelaus **9** Agamemnon **10** Plisthenes

atrium 4 hall **6** cavity **7** auricle **8** entrance **13** Roman entrance

atrocious 3 bad, low **4** dark, evil, rude, vile **5** black, cruel **6** brutal, savage, tawdry, vulgar **7** heinous, hellish, inhuman, uncouth, vicious **8** dreadful, enormous, fiendish, flagrant, grievous, horrible, infamous, infernal, pitiless, ruthless, terrible **9** barbarous, execrable, merciless, monstrous, nefarious, tasteless **10** diabolical, outrageous, villainous

atrociousness 6 infamy **7** cruelty **8** enormity, vileness **9** barbarity, brutality, depravity **11** heinousness, viciousness **13** monstrousness, offensiveness **14** outrageousness

atrocity 6 horror **7** outrage **8** enormity, savagery, villainy **9** barbarism, barbarity, brutality **10** inhumanity **11** heinousness

atrophy 7 decline **8** decaying, drying up **9** lack of use, withering **10** emaciation, shriveling **11** wasting away **12** degeneration **13** deterioration

Atropos
  member of: 5 Fates
  cuts thread of: 4 life

Atsina (Gros Ventres, Haaninin)
  language family: 9 Algonkian **10** Algonquian
  location: 6 Canada **7** Montana **9** Milk River **12** Saskatchewan **13** Missouri River
  related to: 7 Arapaho

attach 3 fix **4** join **5** affix, allot, annex **6** append, assign, couple, detail, se-

cure **7** connect, destine, earmark **8** allocate, be fond of, fasten to, make fast **9** affiliate, associate, designate

attache 4 aide **5** envoy **6** consul **8** adjutant, diplomat, emissary, minister **9** assistant **10** ambassador, vice consul **11** diplomatist, subordinate **12** ambassadress **13** consul general

attachment 4 bond, love **6** fixing, liking, regard **7** adjunct, fixture, respect **8** addendum, addition, affinity, affixing, appendix, coupling, devotion, fondness, securing **9** accessory, affection, appendage, attaching, fastening **10** connection, friendship, supplement, tenderness **12** predilection

attack 3 fit **4** damn, go at **5** abuse, blame, effort, fault, fly at, onset, spasm, spell **6** assail, charge, impugn, strike, stroke, tackle **7** assault, censure, lunge at, offense, seizure **8** denounce, fall upon, invasion, paroxysm **9** criticism, criticize, denigrate, disparage, incursion, offensive, onslaught, pitch into, undertake **10** aggression, impugnment **11** denigration **13** disparagement

attacker 6 mugger **7** accuser **8** assailer, opponent **9** adversary, aggressor, assailant **10** antagonist **11** belligerent

attain 3 win **4** earn, gain, reap **5** reach **6** effect, obtain, secure **7** achieve, acquire, procure, realize **10** accomplish

attainable 6 at hand **9** available, reachable **10** accessible, achievable, realizable **11** within reach

attainment 5 skill **6** talent **7** earning, gaining, getting, mastery, success, winning **8** securing **9** acquiring, attaining, obtaining, procuring **10** competence **11** achievement, acquirement, acquisition, fulfillment, procurement, proficiency, realization **14** accomplishment

attempt 3 aim, try **4** seek **5** essay **6** attack, effort, hazard, strive, tackle, work at **7** assault, venture **8** endeavor **9** have a go at, onslaught, undertake **11** undertaking **12** make an effort, take a crack at, take a whack at

Attenborough, Richard
  director of: 6 Gandhi (Oscar) **7** Chaplin **10** Cry Freedom **11** A Chorus Line, Shadowlands **12** In Love and War, Young Winston **13** A Bridge Too Far
  roles: 10 Wavelength **12** Jurassic Park **14** The Great Escape **15** Doctor Doolittle **16** Ten Little Indians

attend 4 go to, heed, mark, mind, note **5** serve, usher, visit **6** convoy, escort, follow, show up, squire, tend to **7** care for, conduct, observe, oversee, service **8** appear at, consider, frequent, harken to, listen to, wait upon **9** accompany **11** superintend

French: 4 oyez
cry used by: 10 court crier
preceded: 12 proclamation

attendance 4 gate **5** crowd, house **8** audience, presence **10** appearance, assemblage, being there

attendant 3 aid **6** escort, flunky, helper, lackey, menial **7** related, servant **8** adherent, chaperon, follower **9** accessory, assistant, companion, underling **10** associated, consequent **12** accompanying

attention 4 care, heed, mind, note, suit **5** court **6** homage, notice, regard, wooing **7** concern, respect, service, thought **8** civility, courtesy, devotion, wariness **9** alertness, deference, diligence, vigilance **10** observance, politeness **11** assiduities, compliments, gallantries **12** deliberation **13** concentration, consideration, contemplation **14** thoughtfulness

attentive 5 alert, awake **6** intent, polite **7** devoted, heedful, mindful, zealous **8** diligent, obliging **9** courteous, dedicated, listening, observant, wide awake **10** respectful, thoughtful **11** considerate, deferential, painstaking **13** accommodating

attentiveness 7 concern **8** devotion, industry **9** alertness, attention, diligence **10** commitment, dedication **11** application, devotedness, heedfulness, mindfulness **14** thoughtfulness

attenuate 6 dilute, impair, lessen, reduce, weaken **7** draw out, spin out **8** decrease, diminish, enervate, enfeeble **9** water down **10** adulterate

attest 4 show **5** prove **6** affirm, assert, assure, evince, verify **7** bear out, certify, confirm, declare, display, exhibit, support, swear to, testify, warrant **8** vouch for **11** bear witness, corroborate, demonstrate **12** substantiate

attestation 9 testimony **10** deposition **11** declaration

at the back
Latin: 6 a tergo
at the beginning
Latin: 9 ad initium
at the bottom
French: 6 au fond
at the end
Latin: 5 ad fin
at the place
Latin: 5 ad loc **7** ad locum
At the Sign of the Reine Pedauque
author: 13 Anatole France
attic 4 loft **6** garret **7** mansard **8** cockloft **10** clerestory
French: 7 grenier
German: 9 Dachboden
Spanish: 9 guardilla

attire 3 don **4** duds, garb, gown, robe, togs **5** array, dress **6** bedeck, clothe,

finery, fit out, invest, outfit, rig out **7** apparel, clothes, costume, deck out, raiment, turn out **8** clothing, garments, glad rags, wardrobe **9** vestments **11** habiliments

Attis
also: 4 Atys
form: 5 youth
home: 7 Phrygia
loved: 6 Cybele
driven mad by: 6 Cybele

attitude 3 air **4** pose **6** manner, stance **7** outlook, posture **8** demeanor, position **11** disposition, frame of mind, perspective, point of view

attorney 4 beak **6** lawyer **7** counsel **8** advocate **9** barrister, counselor, solicitor **10** mouthpiece **12** legal adviser **14** member of the bar **15** ambulance chaser

attract 4 draw, lure, pull **5** cause, charm, evoke **6** allure, beckon, entice, induce, invite **7** bewitch, enchant, provoke **8** appeal to, interest **9** captivate, fascinate **11** precipitate

attraction 4 lure, pull **5** charm **6** allure, appeal **7** glamour **8** affinity, charisma, tendency **9** magnetism **10** enticement, inducement, temptation **11** captivation, enchantment, fascination **12** drawing power

attractive 4 chic, fair, foxy, sexy **6** lovely, pretty **7** elegant, likable, sightly, winning **8** alluring, becoming, charming, engaging, enticing, fetching, handsome, inviting, pleasant, pleasing, tasteful, tempting **9** agreeable, appealing, beautiful, seductive **10** bewitching, delightful, enchanting **11** captivating, charismatic, fascinating

attractiveness 5 charm **6** beauty **9** good looks **11** pulchritude **12** handsomeness

attribute 4 gift **5** facet, grace, lay to, trait **6** aspect, assign, credit, impute, talent, virtue **7** ability, ascribe, blame on, cause by, faculty, feature, quality, trace to **8** charge to, property **9** character, endowment, set down to **10** account for, attainment, derive from, saddle with **11** acquirement, bring home to, distinction **14** accomplishment, characteristic

attrition 4 loss **7** erosion **8** abrasion, decrease, friction, grinding, scraping **9** reduction **10** decimation **11** wearing away, wearing down **14** disintegration

attune 5 adapt **6** adjust, tailor **8** accustom **9** acclimate **11** acclimatize

attune to 3 fit **5** adapt **6** adjust **7** conform **9** harmonize **11** accommodate

at variance 7 counter, opposed **8** contrary, converse, inimical, opposite **9** disparate **10** discordant **11** conflicting **12** antithetical, incompatible **13** contradictory **15** at cross purposes

Atwood, Margaret

author of: 7 Cat's Eye **8** Survival **9** Surfacing **10** Alias Grace, Bodily Harm, Lady Oracle **11** Second Words **13** Bluebeard's Egg, Life Before Man, Power Politics, The Circle Game **14** The Robber Bride **16** The Handmaid's Tale

at work 4 busy **5** in use **6** active **7** engaged, working **8** occupied
Atymnius
mentioned in: 5 Iliad
companion of: 8 Sarpedon
killed by: 10 Antilochus

atypical 7 unusual **8** abnormal, contrary, uncommon **9** anomalous, irregular, unnatural, untypical **10** nontypical **11** uncustomary, unlooked for **12** out of keeping **16** unrepresentative

Atys *see* **5** Attis

Auber, Daniel Francois Esprit
born: 4 Caen **6** France
composer of: 6 Haydee **7** La Macon **10** Fra Diavolo **12** Le Domino Noir **14** The Bronze Horse **16** Le Cheval de Bronze, The Crown Diamonds **17** La Muette de Portici **19** La Bergere Chatelaine **20** The Dumb Girl of Portici **22** Le Premier Jour de Bonheur

auberge 3 inn **6** tavern

auburn 5 henna, tawny **6** russet **8** cinnamon, nutbrown **11** golden-brown, rust-colored **12** reddish-brown **13** copper-colored **15** chestnut-colored

Aucassin and Nicolette
author: 7 unknown
Auchincloss, Louis
author of: 10 Watchfires **11** The Dark Lady, The Partners **12** Second Chance, The Embezzler **14** A World of Profit **16** Powers of Attorney, Tales of Manhattan, The Country Cousin **17** The Rector of Justin **19** The Winthrop Covenant **20** Portrait in Brownstone

au contraire 13 on the contrary
au courant 8 up-to-date
auction 3 sale **7** bidding **8** offering
Auction Block, The
author: 8 Rex Beach

audacious 4 bold, pert, rash, rude, wild **5** bossy, brave, fresh, gutsy, risky, saucy **6** brazen, cheeky, daring, plucky **7** defiant, forward, valiant **8** assuming, fearless, heedless, impudent, insolent, intrepid, reckless, stalwart, unafraid, valorous **9** breakneck, daredevil, dauntless, desperate, foolhardy, hotheaded, imprudent, shameless, unabashed **10** courageous, outrageous, self-willed **11** adventurous, impertinent, injudicious, lionhearted, venturesome **12** death-defying, devil-may-care, discourteous, enterprising, presumptuous, stouthearted **13** disrespectful

audaciousness 6 daring **8** audacity,

boldness **11** forwardness **13** assertiveness **14** aggressiveness **15** adventurousness

audacity 4 gall, grit, guts **5** brass, cheek, nerve, pluck, spunk, valor **6** daring, mettle **7** bravery, courage **8** backbone, boldness, chutzpah, rashness, temerity **9** brashness, derring-do, impudence, insolence **10** brazenness, effrontery **11** forwardness, presumption **12** fearlessness, impertinence, recklessness **13** bumptiousness, foolhardiness, shamelessness **15** venturesomeness

Auden, W H
author of: **11** Another Time, Thank You Fog **12** Homage to Clio, The Dyer's Hand **13** About the House, Journey to a War **15** For the Time Being, The Age of Anxiety **16** City Without Walls, Epistle to a Godson **17** In Memory of W B Yeats, Musee des Beaux Arts **20** The Dog Beneath the Skin **22** Forewords and Afterwords

Audhumbla
also: **8** Audhumla
origin: **12** Scandinavian
form: **3** cow
owner: **4** Ymir
birth from: **3** ice
uncovered: **4** Buri

audible 5 clear, heard **8** distinct **11** discernible, perceptible

audience 4 talk **5** house **6** market, parley, public **7** hearing, meeting **8** assembly, audition **9** following, interview, listeners, onlookers, reception **10** conference, discussion, readership, spectators **12** congregation, constituency, consultation

audit 5 check **6** go over, review, verify **7** balance, examine, inspect **10** inspection, scrutinize **11** examination, investigate, take stock of **12** scrutinizing, verification **13** investigation

audition 6 tryout **7** hearing **15** test performance

auditor 8 listener **10** accountant, bookkeeper **11** comptroller **17** financial examiner

auditorium 4 hall **5** arena **7** theater **8** auditory, coliseum **11** concert hall, lecture hall, meeting hall **12** assembly hall

Audrey
character in: **11** As You Like It
author: **11** Shakespeare

Audubon, John James
born: **8** Les Cayes **12** Santo Domingo
artwork: **14** Birds of America **34** Viviparous Quadrupeds of North America

Auel, Jean M
author of: **15** Plains of Passage **17** The Mammoth Hunters, The Valley

of Horses **20** The Clan of the Cave Bear

Auerbach, Arnold (Red)
sport: **10** basketball
position: **5** coach
team: **13** Boston Celtics

au fait 6 expert, versed **11** experienced **13** knowledgeable

Aufklarung 13 enlightenment **16** the Enlightenment

au fond 9 basically, in reality **11** at the bottom

auf Wiedersehen 7 goodbye **8** farewell **16** until we meet again

Auge
priestess of: **6** Athena
father: **9** King Aleus
mother: **6** Neaera
son: **8** Telephus
assaulted by: **8** Hercules

Augean stables
owned by: **10** King Augeas
number of oxen: **13** three thousand
cleaned by: **8** Hercules
river running through: **7** Alpheus

auger 4 bore **5** drill **6** pierce **10** boring tool

aught 3 all, zip **4** love, nada, null, zero **6** naught **7** a cipher, nothing **8** goose egg **11** horse collar

augment 5 add to, boost, raise, swell, widen **6** deepen, expand, extend **7** amplify, build up, enlarge, inflate, magnify **8** flesh out, heighten, increase, lengthen **9** intensify

augmentation 5 boost, extra, raise **8** addition, increase, swelling, widening **9** deepening, expansion, extension, inflation **10** supplement **11** elaboration, enlargement, heightening, lengthening **13** amplification, magnification **15** intensification

augur 4 bode, seer **6** herald, oracle **7** diviner, portend, predict, presage, promise, prophet, signify **8** forecast, foretell, forewarn, intimate, prophesy **9** be a sign of **10** be an omen of, foreshadow, soothsayer **13** prognosticate **14** prognosticator

augury 4 omen, sign **5** token **6** herald **7** auspice, portent, promise, warning **8** prophecy **9** harbinger, precursor, sortilege **10** divination, forerunner, indication **11** forewarning, soothsaying **14** fortunetelling **15** prognostication

august 5 grand, lofty, noble, regal **6** solemn, superb **7** eminent, exalted, stately, sublime, supreme **8** glorious, imposing, majestic **9** dignified, estimable, grandiose, venerable **10** impressive, monumental **11** high-ranking, illustrious, magnificent **12** awe-inspiring **13** distinguished

August
Anglo-Saxon: **10** Weod-Monath
characteristic: **7** dog days

flower: **5** poppy
French: **4** Aout
gem: **7** peridot **8** sardonyx **9** carnelian
German: **6** August
holiday:
England/Scotland: **11** Harvest Home (1)
Italian: **6** Agosto
number of days: **9** thirty-one
original name: **8** Sextilis **12** Metageitnion
origin of name: **6** Augere (Latin to open) **8** Augustus (Roman emperor)
place in year:
Roman: **5** sixth
Gregorian: **6** eighth
Spanish: **6** Agosto
zodiac sign: **3** Leo **5** Virgo

Augustine, St (of Hippo)
author of: **10** Civitas Dei **11** Confessions, Enchiridion **12** The City of God

augustness 7 dignity, majesty **8** eminence, nobility **9** loftiness **11** distinction **13** monumentality **15** illustriousness

August 1914
author: **23** Aleksandr Solzhenitsyn Jr

au naturel 4 nude **8** uncooked **15** in a natural state

Auntie Mame
author: **13** Patrick Dennis

Aunt Jo's Scrap-Bag
author: **15** Louisa May Alcott

Aunt Julia and the Scriptwriter
author: **16** Mario Vargas Llosa

au pair 4 maid **5** nanny **9** governess **13** mother's helper

aura 3 air **4** feel, mood **5** aroma **7** essence, feeling, quality **8** ambience **9** character, emanation **10** atmosphere, suggestion

Aura
companion of: **7** Artemis
bore: **5** twins
fathered by: **9** Dionysius
changed into: **6** spring
changed by: **4** Zeus

au revoir 7 goodbye **8** farewell **16** until we meet again

Aurora
origin: **5** Roman
goddess of: **4** dawn
corresponds to: **3** Eos

Aurora Leigh
author: **24** Elizabeth Barrett Browning

Ausgleich 10 compromise **11** arrangement **12** equalization

Auslander 5 alien **9** foreigner, outlander

auspice 4 omen, sign **6** augury **7** portent, warning **10** indication **15** prognostication

auspices 4 care, egis **5** aegis **6** charge **7** control, support **8** advocacy, guidance **9** authority, influence, patronage **10** protection **11** countenance, sponsorship **12** championship

auspicious 4 good **5** happy, lucky **6** benign, timely **7** hopeful **9** favorable, fortunate, opportune, promising, red-letter **10** felicitous, heartening, propitious, reassuring, successful **11** encouraging

Austen, Jane
  author of: 4 Emma **10** Persuasion **13** Mansfield Park **15** Northanger Abbey **17** Pride and Prejudice **19** Sense and Sensibility

austere 5 rigid, spare, stark, stern **6** chaste, severe, simple, strict **7** ascetic, Spartan **8** rigorous **10** abstemious, forbidding **11** self-denying, strait-laced

Austerlitz, Frederick
  real name of: 11 Fred Astaire

Australia
  other name: 9 Down Under
  name means: 19 unknown southern land
  capital: 8 Canberra
  largest city: 6 Sydney
  others: 3 Ayr **4** Yass **5** Dubbo, Perth **6** Albury, Cairns, Casino, Coburg, Darwin, Hobart **7** Bendigo, Geelong, Kogarah, Mildura, Mitcham, Whyalla **8** Adelaide, Ballarat, Bathurst, Brighton, Brisbane, Essendon, Randwick, Ringwood **9** Melbourne, Newcastle, Port Pirie, Toowoomba **10** Broken Hill, Kalgoorlie, Waggawagga, Wollongong **11** Collingwood, Rockhampton **12** Alice Springs
  division: 8 Tasmania, Victoria **10** Queensland **13** New South Wales **14** South Australia **16** Western Australia **17** Northern Territory **26** Australian Capital Territory
  head of state: 14 British monarch **15** governor general
  measure: 4 arna, naut, saum
  monetary unit: 4 dump, tray, zack **5** pound **6** dollar **8** shilling
  island: 4 Cato, King **5** Cocos, Green, Timor **6** Barrow, Koolan **7** Coringa, Keeling, Neptune, Norfolk **8** Flinders, Kangaroo, Lacepede, Melville, Rottnest, Tasmania, Thursday **9** Admiralty
  lake: 4 Eyre **5** Carey, Cowan, Frome, Moore, Wells **6** Austin, Barlee, Bulloo, Dundas, Harris, Mackay **7** Amadeus, Blanche, Everard, Torrens **8** Carnegie, Gairdner **9** MacDonald **10** Yammayamma **14** Disappointment
  mountain: 3 Ise **4** Blue, Olga, Ossa, Zeil **5** Bruce, Snowy **6** Cradle, Doreen, Garnet, Gawler, Magnet, Morgan **7** Bongong, Gregory, Herbert **8** Augustus, Brockman, Cuthbert, Jusgrave, Mulligan, Surprise **9** Murchison, Woodroffe **14** Australian Alps

15 New England Range **18** Great Dividing Range
  highest point: 9 Kosciusko
  river: 3 Hay **4** Avon, Daly, Swan, Yule **5** Bullo, Comet, Drava, Naomi, Paroo, Roper, Yarra **6** Barcoo, Barwon, Bulloo, Culgoa, Degrey, Hunter, Isaacs, Murray, Norman **7** Darling, Derwent, Fitzroy, Georges, Gilbert, Lachlan, Staaten, Warrego **8** Belyando, Brisbane, Burdekin, Clarence, Drysdale, Flinders, Gascoyne, Georgina, Mitchell, Thompson, Victoria, Weeribee, Wooramel **9** Ashburton, Fortescue, Hawksbury, MacKenzie, Macquarie, Murchison, Saltwater **10** Diamantina, Shoalhaven **12** Murrambidgee
  sea: 5 Coral, Timor **6** Indian, Tasman **7** Arafura, Pacific
  physical feature:
    bay: 5 Bight, Shark **6** Botany **7** Moreton **11** Port Phillip
    cape: 4 Howe, York **5** Byron **9** Southeast
    channel: 5 Cowal **9** Anabranch, Billabong
    desert: 6 Arunta, Gibson, Stuart, Tanami **7** Simpson **10** Great Sandy **13** Great Victoria
    gulf: 8 Spencers **9** Van Dieman **11** Carpentaria **15** Joseph Bonaparte **20** Great Australian Bight
    peninsula: 4 Eyre
    reef: 12 Great Barrier
    strait: 4 Bass
  people: 3 Abo **4** Koko, Mara, Wong **5** Anzac, Binge, Dieri, Maori, Myall **6** Aranda, Arunta, Aussie, Binghi, Digger, Kipper, Papuan **7** Arawong, Ilpirra **8** Antipode, Barkinji, Billijim, Euahlayi, Warragal, Warrigal **9** Aborigine **10** Australoid, Melanesian, Sandgroper
    actor: 9 Judy Davis, Mel Gibson, Paul Hogan **10** Bryan Brown
    author: 4 West **5** White **7** Russell **10** Richardson
    explorer: 4 Bass, Cook **6** Mawson, Tasman **7** Wilkins
    leader: 4 Holt **5** Hawke **7** Keating, Menzies, Whitlam
    nurse: 11 Sister Kenny
  language: 7 English
  religion: 7 Judaism **8** Anglican **10** Protestant **13** Roman Catholic
  place: 7 outback **9** billabong **11** back country
    aborigine area: 9 Arhemland
    beach: 5 Manly
    dam: 4 Hume
  possession: 12 Cocos Islands **13** Norfolk Island **16** Christmas Islands
  feature:
    animal: 5 dingo **6** kelpie **7** wallaby **8** anteater, kangaroo **9** koala bear **18** duckbilled platypus
    bird: 3 emu **10** kookaburra

    cowboy: 6 waddie **8** jackaroo
    dance: 6 dreher
    flower: 7 boronia, fuchsia, waratah **9** coachwood **12** kangaroo paws
    game: 3 sye **10** tambaroora
    tree: 3 gum **10** eucalyptus
    weapon: 5 kiley, kyley **7** wommera **9** boomerang
  food: 3 kai **6** tucker
    cake: 6 damper **7** brownie
    dish: 8 coolamon
    drink: 9 arkaloola
    fruit: 5 nonda **7** kumquat **11** desert-lemon

Austria
  other name: 10 Osterreich
  name means: 12 eastern state
  capital/largest city: 6 Vienna
  others: 4 Enns, Graz, Lech, Linz, Ried, Wels **5** Krems, Steyr, Traun **6** Leoben **7** Bregenz, Modling, Spittal, Villach **8** Bad Ischl, Dornbirn, Salzburg **9** Innsbruck, Semmering **10** Kapfenberg, Klagenfurt **11** Sankt Polten **14** Wiener Neustadt
  division: 5 Tirol, Tyrol **6** Istria, Styria, Triest **7** Bohemia, Galicia, Moravia, Silesia **8** Bukowina, Dalmatia, Earniola, Gradisca **9** Earinthia **10** Burgenland, Vorarlberg **12** Lower Austria, Upper Austria
    Roman province: 6 Raetia **7** Noricum **8** Pannonia
  government:
    legislature: 9 Bundesrat, Reichsrat **10** Herrenhaus, Reichsrath
  head of government: 10 Chancellor
  other leader: 7 emperor **12** burgomeister
  measure: 4 fass, fuss, joch, mass, muth, yoke **5** halbe, linie, meile, metze, pfiff, punkt **6** achtel, becher, leipoa, seidel **7** dlafter, viertel **8** dreiling **12** futtermassel
  monetary unit: 4 lira **5** crown, ducat, krone **6** florin, gulden, heller, zehner **8** albertin, groschen, kreutzer **9** schilling
  weight: 4 marc, unze **5** denat, karch, stein **7** centner, pfennig **8** vierling **9** quantchen
  lake: 6 Almsee **7** Fertoto, Mondsee **8** Bodensee, Traunsee **9** Constance **10** Neusiedler
  mountain: 4 Alps **6** Stubai, Tirols, Tyrols **8** Eisenerz, Rhatikon **9** Dolomites, Kitzbuhel **10** Hohe Tauern **14** Silvretta Group
  highest point: 13 Grossglockner
  river: 3 Inn, Mur **4** Drau, Elbe, Enns, Iser, Kamp, Lech, Murz, Raab **5** Donau, Drava, Drave, March, Salza, Thaya, Traun **6** Danube, Moldau
  physical feature:
    basin: 7 Styrian
    canal: 6 Danube
    mountain pass: 7 Brenner
    wind: 6 Foehen

woods: 6 Vienna
people: 5 Poles **6** Croats, Czechs **7** Germans, Gypsies **8** Slovenes **10** Hungarians
botanist: 6 Mendel
composer: 5 Haydn **6** Czerny, Mahler, Mozart, Webern **7** Amadeus, Strauss **8** Bruckner, Schubert **9** Beethoven **10** Schoenberg
emperor: 7 Charles, Francis **9** Ferdinand, Habsburgs, Hapsburgs **10** Franz Josef
philosopher: 12 Wittgenstein
psychiatrist: 5 Adler, Freud, Reich
statesman: 10 Metternich **12** Kurt Waldheim
language: 5 Czech **6** German, Magyar **8** Croatian **9** Slovenian
religion: 7 Judaism **10** Protestant **13** Roman Catholic
place:
boulevard: 3 Kai **11** Ringstrasse
cathedral: 9 St Stephen
city hall: 7 Rathaus
fortress: 13 Hochosterwitz, Hohensalzburg
imperial palace: 7 Hofburg
monastery: 4 Melk **8** Gottweig **14** Klosterneuburg
museum: 6 Mozart **9** Johanneum
people's garden: 11 Volksgarten
resort: 5 Baden **7** Bregenz **8** Bad Ischl **9** Innsbruck, Semmering
feature: 8 yodelers **11** ice grottoes
clothing: 5 loden **10** lederhosen
dance: 5 waltz **6** dreher **7** landler **13** schuhplattler **14** grand polonaise
festival: 8 Salzburg
horse: 10 Lippizaner
pastry shop: 12 konditoreien
food:
breaded veal cutlet: 15 Wiener schnitzel
cake: 11 linzer torte, sacher torte
cookie: 7 kipferl
roll: 10 golatschen
Austroasiatic
language subfamily: 5 Khasi, Munda **8** Annamite, Mon-Khmer **9** Palaung-Wa **10** Nicobarese **11** Semang-Sakai **13** Annamite-Muong
spoken in: 5 Burma, India **7** Nicobar, Vietnam **8** Cambodia, Malaysia **9** Kampuchea
authentic 4 pure, real, true **5** valid **6** actual **7** factual, genuine **8** accurate, attested, bona fide, faithful, original, reliable, verified **9** veritable **10** accredited, dependable, legitimate **11** trustworthy **12** unquestioned **13** authoritative, unadulterated
authenticate 6 attest, avouch, verify **7** certify, confirm, endorse, warrant **8** document, validate, vouch for **9** guarantee **11** corroborate **12** substantiate
authenticated 7 genuine **8** attested,

verified **9** validated **10** accredited, vouched for **13** substantiated
authentication 7 voucher **10** validation **11** certificate **12** verification **13** authorization, certification
author 4 poet **5** maker **6** father, framer, writer **7** creator, founder, planner **8** essayist, inventor, novelist, producer **9** initiator, innovator, organizer **10** originator, playwright, prime mover **16** short-story writer
see author under each country
authoritarian 5 harsh **6** severe, strict, tyrant **7** austere, fascist **8** autocrat, dogmatic, martinet **9** by the book, by the rule **10** inflexible, tyrannical, unyielding **11** dictatorial, doctrinaire **12** disciplinary, rule follower **14** disciplinarian, little dictator, uncompromising
authoritative 5 sound, valid **6** lordly, ruling **7** factual, learned **8** arrogant, decisive, dogmatic, imposing, official, reliable **9** authentic, masterful, scholarly, sovereign **10** autocratic, commanding, definitive, dependable, imperative, impressive, peremptory, sanctioned, tyrannical **11** dictatorial, trustworthy **14** administrative
authoritativeness 6 belief **9** authority **10** conviction **11** credibility **14** conclusiveness
authorities 6 expert, police, pundit **7** scholar **10** mastermind, specialist **11** connoisseur, officialdom **12** powers that be
authority 4 rule, sway **5** clout, force, might, power **6** esteem, weight **7** command, control, respect **8** dominion, prestige, strength **9** influence, supremacy **10** domination, importance **12** jurisdiction **14** administration
authorization 7 license **8** approval, sanction **10** commission, imprimatur, permission **11** entitlement **12** confirmation, legalization **13** accreditation, certification
authorize 5 allow **6** enable, invest, permit **7** approve, certify, charter, confirm, empower, entitle, license, warrant **8** accredit, sanction, vouch for **9** give leave **10** commission
authorized 8 approved, official **9** canonical **10** sanctioned
Autobiography of Alice B Toklas
author: 13 Gertrude Stein
Autobiography of Miss Jane Pittman, The
author: 13 Ernest J Gaines
autochthonous 5 first **6** native, primal **7** ancient **8** earliest, original, primeval **10** aboriginal, indigenous, primordial
autocracy 7 czarism, tyranny **8** autarchy, monarchy **9** Caesarism, despotism, Hitlerism, kaiserism, monocracy, Stalinism **10** absolutism **11** Bonapart-

ism **12** dictatorship **14** tyrannical rule **15** totalitarianism
autocrat 5 ruler **6** despot, tyrant **7** monarch **8** dictator, overlord **13** absolute ruler
autocratic 8 despotic **9** czaristic, imperious, tyrannous **10** iron-handed, oppressive, repressive, tyrannical **11** dictatorial, monarchical **13** authoritarian
auto da fe, auto de fe 13 act of the faith **17** burning of heretics
from: 18 Spanish Inquisition
autograph 4 mark, sign **5** x-mark **9** John Henry, signature **11** endorsement, handwriting, inscription, John Hancock **16** countersignature
Autolycus
character in: 14 The Winter's Tale
author: 11 Shakespeare
Autolycus
form: 5 thief
father: 6 Hermes
mother: 6 Chione
half-brother: 9 Philammon
wife: 9 Amphithea
daughter: 8 Anticlea
grandson: 8 Odysseus
gift: 12 invisibility **13** shape changing
automated 9 automatic **10** mechanical, mechanized **15** machine-operated
automatic 6 reflex **7** natural, routine **8** electric, habitual, inherent, unwilled **9** automated **10** mechanical, push-button, self-acting, self-moving **11** instinctive, involuntary, spontaneous, unconscious **12** uncontrolled **13** nonvolitional, self-operating **14** self-propelling
automaton 4 pawn, tool **5** golem, patsy, robot **6** puppet, stooge **7** android, cat's-paw, fall guy, machine **10** fantoccino, marionette
automobile
invented by:
differential gear: 4 Benz
electric: 8 Morrison
gasoline: 6 Duryea **7** Daimler
muffler: 5 Maxim
self-starter: 9 Kettering
see also **3** car
automobiles
Buick: 7 LeSabre
Chevrolet: 6 Lumina **7** Beretta, Corsica
Chrysler-Plymouth: 7 LeBaron
Dodge: 4 Neon **8** Intrepid
Ford: 5 Tempo **6** Escort, Taurus **7** Mustang
Honda: 5 Civic **6** Accord
Lexus
Mercury: 5 Sable
Nissan: 6 Altima, Maxima, Sentra
Oldsmobile: 5 Ciera **7** Achieva **11** Ninety-Eight
Pontiac: 7 Grand Am, Trans Am **8** Firebird

Saturn
 Toyota: 5 Camry **7** Corolla
Autonoe
 father: 6 Cadmus
 mother: 8 Harmonia
 sister: 3 Ino **5** Agave **6** Semele
 husband: 9 Aristaeus
 son: 7 Actaeon
 daughter: 6 Macris
autonomous 4 free **9** sovereign **11** independent, self-reliant **13** self-governing **14** self-determined, self-sufficient
autonomy 7 freedom **8** home rule, self-rule **10** liberation **11** sovereignty **12** independence **14** self-government **17** self-determination
auto racing
 driver: 6 A J Foyt **7** Al Unser **8** Tom Sneva **9** Niki Lauda **10** Bobby Unser, Jeff Gordon, Juan Fangio **11** Jack Brabham **12** Bobby Allison, Janet Guthrie, Richard Petty **13** Jackie Stewart, Mario Andretti **14** Barney Oldfield, Cale Yarborough, Craig Breedlove **16** Johnny Rutherford
Autry, Gene
 horse: 8 Champion
 born: 7 Tioga TX
 roles: 11 Melody Ranch **16** The Singing Cowboy **19** Tumbling Tumbleweeds **22** Springtime in the Rockies
autumn 4 fall **11** harvest time **12** Indian summer **15** autumnal equinox
auxiliary 6 backup, helper **7** partner, reserve **9** accessory, ancillary, assistant, associate, companion, emergency, secondary **10** accomplice, subsidiary, supplement **11** subordinate **13** supplementary
avail 3 aid, use **4** help **5** serve **6** assist, profit **7** benefit, purpose, service, success, utilize **9** advantage
available 4 free, open **5** handy, on tap **6** at hand, on hand **9** in reserve **10** accessible, convenient, obtainable
avalanche 4 heap, mass, pile **5** flood **6** deluge **7** barrage, cascade, torrent **8** blizzard **9** cataclysm, rockslide, snowslide **10** earthslide, inundation **11** bombardment
Avalon
 island of: 8 Paradise
 burial place for: 6 heroes **10** King Arthur
avant-garde 7 leaders **8** pioneers, vanguard **10** innovators **11** forerunners, originators, tastemakers **12** advance guard, trailblazers, trendsetters
avarice 5 greed **6** penury **8** rapacity, venality **9** parsimony **10** greediness, stinginess **11** miserliness **12** covetousness, graspingness **13** moneygrubbing, niggardliness, pennypinching **15** close-fistedness
Ave Maria 8 Hail Mary

avenge 5 repay **6** injure, punish **7** revenge **9** retaliate
Avengers, The
 character: 8 Emma Peel, Tara King **9** John (Jonathan) Steed
 cast: 9 Diana Rigg **12** Linda Thorson **13** Patrick Macnee
 movie cast: 10 Uma Thurman **12** Ralph Fiennes
avenue 3 way **4** gate, path, road **5** means, route **6** access, chance, course, outlet **7** gateway, parkway, passage, pathway **8** approach **9** boulevard, concourse, direction, esplanade **10** passageway **11** opportunity **12** thoroughfare
aver 4 avow **5** state, swear **6** affirm, assert, avouch, insist, verify **7** certify, contend, declare, profess, protest **8** maintain, proclaim **9** emphasize, guarantee, pronounce, represent **10** asseverate
average 3 par **4** fair, mean, norm, so-so **5** ratio, usual **6** common, medial, median, medium, normal, not bad **7** the rule, typical **8** mediocre, midpoint, moderate, ordinary, passable, standard, standing, the usual **9** tolerable **10** mean amount **11** indifferent, rank and file **12** run-of-the-mill
averment 5 claim **6** avowal **8** argument **9** assertion, assurance **10** allegation, contention, profession **11** affirmation
averse 5 loath **7** opposed **8** inimical **9** reluctant, unwilling **10** indisposed, unamenable **11** disinclined, ill-disposed, unfavorable **12** antipathetic, recalcitrant
aversion 6 hatred, horror **7** disgust, dislike **8** distaste, loathing **9** animosity, antipathy, hostility, prejudice, repulsion, revulsion **10** abhorrence, opposition, reluctance, repugnance **11** detestation **13** unwillingness **14** disinclination
avert 4 turn **5** avoid, deter, shift **7** beat off, deflect, fend off, keep off, prevent, ward off **8** preclude, stave off, turn away **9** forestall, frustrate, keep at bay, sidetrack **11** nip in the bud
aviary 4 cage **9** birdhouse, enclosure
aviation 6 flight, flying **11** aeronautics **12** aerodynamics
aviator, aviatrix 4 bird **5** flyer, pilot **6** airman, fly-boy **7** birdman
avid 4 keen **5** eager, rabid **6** ardent, greedy, hungry **7** anxious, devoted, fanatic, intense, zealous **8** covetous, desirous, grasping **9** rapacious, voracious **10** avaricious, insatiable **11** acquisitive **12** enthusiastic
avidity 4 zeal **5** greed **6** fervor, hunger **8** rapacity, voracity **9** eagerness **10** enthusiasm, fanaticism, greediness **12** covetousness **15** acquisitiveness

Avignon Papacy 15 Babylonian Exile **19** Babylonian Captivity
avocado 9 dark green **13** alligator pear, tropical fruit
 origin: 6 Mexico **12** South America **14** Central America
 family: 9 Lauraceae
 used to make: 9 guacamole
avocation 5 hobby **7** pastime **8** sideline **9** diversion **10** recreation **11** distraction **13** entertainment
Avogadro, Amedeo
 field: 7 physics **9** chemistry
 nationality: 7 Italian
 formulated: 19 molecular hypothesis
avoid 4 shun **5** avert, dodge, elude, evade, skirt **6** escape, eschew **7** boycott, forbear, forsake **8** sidestep **10** fight shy of **11** refrain from **12** steer clear of
avoidance 7 eluding, evasion **8** shirking, shunning, skirting
avoid the issue 4 duck **5** dodge, evade, hedge, stall **10** equivocate **17** beat around the bush
a votre sante 5 toast **12** to your health
avouch 5 argue, swear **6** affirm **7** declare **8** advocate, maintain
avow 3 own **4** aver **5** admit, state, swear **6** affirm, assert, reveal **7** confess, declare, profess **8** announce, disclose, proclaim **11** acknowledge
avowal 4 word **8** averment **9** admission, assertion, assurance, statement **10** confession, profession **11** affirmation, declaration **12** proclamation, protestation **14** acknowledgment
avowed 5 sworn **8** admitted, declared **9** confessed, professed **12** acknowledged, self-declared **14** self-proclaimed
await 6 attend, expect **7** look for **10** anticipate
awake 5 alert, aware, spark **6** arouse, awaken, bestir, excite, incite **7** alive to, heedful, inspire, mindful, provoke **8** open-eyed, vigilant, watchful **9** attentive, conscious, stimulate
Awake and Sing!
 author: 13 Clifford Odets
awaken 3 fan **4** fire **6** arouse, excite, kindle, revive, stir up **9** stimulate
awakening 7 arising, arousal **8** sparking, stirring **11** stimulation
award 4 give **5** allot, allow, grant, honor, medal, prize **6** accord, assign, bestow, decree, trophy **7** appoint, concede, laurels, tribute **8** citation, confer on **10** decoration
aware 6 with it **7** alert to, alive to, awake to, mindful **8** apprised, informed, sensible, sentient **9** cognizant, conscious, tuned in to **10** conversant **11** enlightened **12** familiar with **13** knowledgeable

awareness 9 acuteness, alertness, appraisal, knowledge **10** cognizance, perception **11** familiarity, information, mindfulness, realization, recognition, sensibility **12** acquaintance **13** consciousness, understanding

away 3 far **4** gone **6** absent, at once, way off **8** distance **9** elsewhere

awe 3 cow **4** fear **5** abash, alarm, amaze, dread, panic, shock **6** dismay, fright, horror, terror, wonder **7** perturb, quaking, respect, terrify **8** astonish, disquiet, frighten **9** abashment, adoration, amazement, quivering, reverence, solemnity, trembling **10** exaltation, intimidate, veneration **11** disquietude, trepidation **12** apprehension, astonishment, perturbation **13** consternation

awe-inspiring 5 giant, grand, great, noble **6** august, mighty **7** eminent, exalted, mammoth, sublime, supreme, titanic **8** colossal, enormous, gigantic, glorious, imposing, majestic, wondrous **9** excessive **10** impressive, incredible, monumental, prodigious, stupendous, tremendous **11** astonishing, extravagant, illustrious, magnificent, spectacular **12** breathtaking, overwhelming

awesome 6 solemn **7** amazing, fearful **8** alarming, dreadful, fearsome, majestic, wondrous **9** inspiring **10** formidable, perturbing, stupefying, terrifying **11** astonishing, disquieting, frightening, magnificent **12** breathtaking, intimidating, overwhelming

awestruck 6 humble **8** overcome **11** reverential

awful 3 bad, low **4** base, dire, mean, ugly **5** lousy **6** solemn **7** amazing, awesome, fearful, ghastly, heinous, hideous **8** alarming, dreadful, fearsome, gruesome, horrible, majestic, shocking, terrible, wondrous **9** appalling, frightful, monstrous, revolting **10** deplorable, despicable, formidable, horrendous, horrifying, stupefying, terrifying, unpleasant **11** displeasing, disquieting, distressing, redoubtable **12** awe-inspiring, contemptible, disagreeable **13** reprehensible

awfully 4 very **5** quite **8** horribly, terribly **9** extremely, immensely **10** dreadfully **11** excessively **13** exceptionally

awkward 5 inept **6** clumsy, touchy, trying **7** unhandy **8** bungling, delicate, inexpert, ticklish, ungainly, unwieldy **9** difficult, graceless, maladroit **10** blundering, cumbersome, unpleasant, unskillful **11** troublesome **12** embarrassing, inconvenient, unmanageable **13** disconcerting, uncomfortable, uncoordinated
French: 6 gauche

Awkward Age, The
  author: 10 Henry James

awkwardness 9 gaucherie **10** clumsiness, difficulty, ineptitude **12** ungainliness, unwieldiness **13** embarrassment, inconvenience

awl 4 nail **6** gimlet **11** leather tool, sharp device

awning 4 hood **6** canopy **7** marquee **8** covering, sunshade

awry 5 amiss, askew, wrong **6** astray, uneven **7** crooked, twisted **8** unevenly **9** crookedly, obliquely **11** out of kilter

axe, ax 3 can **4** chop, fire, oust, sack **5** let go, split **6** bounce, cut out, delete, remove **7** cut down, dismiss **8** get rid of, tomahawk **9** discharge, terminate **11** send packing
  type: 4 pick **6** poleax **7** hatchet **8** tomahawk

Axelrod, Julius
  field: 9 chemistry
  studied: 24 nerve-impulse transmission
  awarded: 10 Nobel Prize

axiom 3 law **5** basic **7** precept **9** postulate, principle **10** assumption **14** fundamental law

axiomatic 5 banal, given **6** cliche **7** assumed **8** accepted, manifest **9** apodictic **10** aphoristic **11** self-evident **12** demonstrable, epigrammatic, indisputable, unquestioned **13** incontestable, platitudinous

axis 4 stem **5** pivot, shaft **7** compact, entente, spindle **8** alliance **9** alignment, coalition **10** center line **11** affiliation **12** pivotal point **13** confederation **14** line of rotation, line of symmetry

axle 3 bar, pin **5** shaft, wheel **7** spindle **8** crossbar **10** turning bar

ayah 4 maid **5** nurse

aye 3 yea, yes **11** affirmative

Aykroyd, Dan
  born: 6 Canada, Ottawa **7** Ontario
  roles: 6 My Girl **7** Dragnet **8** Sgt. Bilko **9** Coneheads **11** Spies Like Us **12** Ghostbusters **13** Doctor Detroit, Trading Places **16** The Blues Brothers, Driving Miss Daisy, The Great Outdoors, Grosse Point Blank **17** Saturday Night Live

Aymara
  location: 4 Peru **7** Bolivia **12** South America

Ayres, Lew
  wife: 8 Lola Lane **12** Ginger Rogers
  born: 13 Minneapolis MN
  roles: 7 Holiday, The Kiss **9** Dr Kildare **25** All Quiet on the Western Front

azalea 12 Rhododendron
  varieties: 4 Cork, Mock, Snow **5** Coast, Dwarf, Early, Flame, Hiryu, Hoary, Luchu, Royal, Sims's, Swamp, Sweet, Torch **6** Alpine, Balsam, Clammy, Indian, Korean, Kurume, Kyushu, Oconee, Pontic, Smooth, Spider, Summer, Yellow **7** Alabama, Chinese, Maries's, Mt Amagi, Oldham's, Western **8** Fiveleaf, Japanese, Piedmont, Rusticum, Yodogawa **9** Kirishima, Mayflower, Pink-shell, Rose-shell, Wild-thyme **10** Cumberland, Macranthum, Plum-leaved, White swamp **11** Gable hybrid, Ghent hybrid, Molle hybrid **12** Arnold hybrid, Florida flame, Sander hybrid **13** Indicum hybrid **15** Glenn Dale hybrid, Kaempferi hybrid, Knapp Hill hybrid **16** Rutherford hybrid **24** Rusticum Flore Pleno hybrid

Azan
  father: 5 Arcas
  mother: 5 Erato

Azariah
  also: 6 Uzziah
  father: 4 Jehu **5** Ethan **6** Nathan **7** Hilkiah, Jehoram, Johanan **11** Jehoshaphat
  son: 4 Joel
  known as: 8 Abednego
  companion: 6 Daniel
  friend: 7 Meshach **8** Shadrach
  succeeded: 5 Zadok

Azazel 9 scapegoat **11** fallen angel

Azerbaijan
  capital/largest city: 4 Baku
  others 9 Kirovabad
  division 24 Nagorno-Karabakh Territory **29** Nakhichevan Autonomous Republic
  head of state: 9 president
  government: 8 republic
  monetary unit: 5 manat
  mountain: 8 Caucasus
  sea: 7 Caspian
  people: 5 Azeri **11** Azerbaijani
  language: 6 Turkic
  religion: 6 Muslim

Aziz, Dr
  character in: 15 A Passage to India
  author: 7 Forster

Aztec (Nahua, Mexica)
  language family: 7 Nahuatl **10** Uto-Aztecan
  location: 6 Mexico, Puebla **8** Guerrero, Veracruz **9** Guatemala, Michoacan **11** Lake Texcoco **14** Central America
  leader: 9 Montezuma
  worshipped: 12 Quetzalcoatl
  capital: 12 Tenochtitlan
  conquerer: 6 Cortes, Cortez

Azuela, Mariano
  author of: 8 The Flies **9** The Bosses **12** The Underdogs **26** Trials of a Respectable Family

azure 4 blue **5** lapis **6** cobalt **7** sky blue **8** cerulean **9** clear blue, cloudless **11** lapis lazuli

Baade, Walter
field: **9** astronomy
discovered: **15** Hidalgo asteroid
Baal 3 god **5** deity
Baal Merodach *see* **6** Marduk
Babbage, Charles
field: **11** mathematics
nationality: **7** British, English
first: **15** actuarial tables
inventor of: **13** adding machine **18** calculating machine
invented forerunner of: **15** digital computer
planned: **10** calculator
Babbitt 9 bourgeois **10** conformist, middlebrow, philistine
Babbitt
author: **13** Sinclair Lewis
character: **11** Myra Babbitt, Seneca Deane **12** Paul Riesling **15** Mrs Tanis Judique **22** George Folansbee Babbitt
babble 3 coo, din, gab, hum **4** blab, talk **5** prate **6** burble, clamor, drivel, gabble, gibber, gurgle, hubbub, jabber, murmur **7** blabber, blather, chatter, prattle, twaddle **8** chitchat, rattle on **9** jabbering, murmuring **14** chitterchatter
babbling 6 drivel, hubbub **7** blabber, twaddle **8** burbling, gabbling, gurgling, nonsense **9** clamoring, gibberish, jabbering, murmuring
babe 3 tot **4** baby **5** child **6** infant
babe in arms 4 baby **6** infant **7** neonate, newborn
babe in the woods 8 innocent **9** fledgling, greenhorn **10** tenderfoot
babel, Babel 3 din **6** bedlam, clamor, hubbub, tumult, uproar **7** turmoil **9** confusion **10** hullabaloo **11** pandemonium
Babel, Isaac
author of: **9** Benia Krik **11** Odessa Tales **13** The Red Cavalry
Babe Ruth
nickname of: **16** George Herman Ruth
Babe the Blue Ox
character in: **10** Paul Bunyan
baboon 6 monkey
breeding: **9** year round
characteristic: **4** mane, pads **6** muzzle
diet: **6** plants **8** scorpion **12** small animals

dwelling: **5** Egypt, Sudan **6** Africa, Arabia **7** Somalia **8** Ethiopia
family: **15** cercopithecidae
habitat: **5** hills **6** plains
largest genus: **6** Chacma
most sacred: **6** Anobis
smallest genus: **7** Western
babushka 4 baba, veil **5** scarf, stole **8** kerchief **11** grandmother
baby 3 wee **4** babe, tiny **5** dwarf, humor, pygmy, small, spoil, young **6** bantam, coddle, coward, infant, little, midget, minute, pamper, petite **7** crybaby, indulge, neonate **8** dwarfish, sniveler **9** miniature, youngster **10** babe in arms, diminutive **11** mollycoddle, overindulge, pocket-sized
Baby
nickname of: **12** Lauren Bacall
baby carriage 4 cart, pram **6** cradle **12** perambulator
babyish 7 puerile **8** childish, immature, juvenile **9** infantile
babylike 4 wee **5** small **9** infantile **10** diminutive
Babylonian Captivity 13 Avignon Papacy **15** Babylonian Exile
Babylonian god 3 Bel **6** Marduk
Babylonian Mythology
chief of gods: **6** Marduk **8** Merodach **12** Baal Merodach
demon: **6** Namtar
goddess of air: **6** Ninlil
goddess of death: **10** Ereshkigal
goddess of love/war/ fertility: **6** Ananna, Inanna, Ishtar **7** Astarte, Mylitta **9** Ashtoreth
god of air: **5** Enlil
god of dead: **6** Nergal
god of fire: **5** Ishum
god of heaven: **2** An **3** Anu
god of moon: **3** Sin
god of pastures/vegetation: **6** Dumuzi
god of pestilence: **4** Irra
god of shepherds: **6** Tammuz
god of sun: **3** Utu **7** Shamash
god of wisdom: **4** Enki
hero: **5** Ninib **7** Ninurta
king: **9** Gilgamesh
king of gods: **5** Enlil
mother of gods: **5** Nammu
queen of heaven: **6** Ishtar
world of dead: **3** Kur
Baby Roo
character in: **13** Winnie-the-Pooh

author: **5** Milne
mother: **5** Kanga
Baby Snooks 10 Fanny Brice
Baby Snookums
character in: **12** The Newlyweds
Bacall, Lauren
real name: **15** Betty Joan Perske
husband: **12** Jason Robards **14** Humphrey Bogart
nickname: **4** Baby
born: **9** New York NY
roles: **8** Applause, Key Largo **11** Dark Passage, The Big Sleep **12** Cactus Flower **16** To Have and Have Not **22** How to Marry a Millionaire
Bacchae
form: **11** priestesses
attendants of: **7** Bacchus
participants in: **11** Bacchanalia
Bacchae, The
author: **9** Euripides
character: **4** Zeus **5** Agave **6** Cadmus, Semele **8** Dionysus, Pentheus, Tiresias
bacchanal 4 orgy **5** feast, revel, spree **6** frolic **7** carouse, debauch, revelry, wassail **8** carnival, carousal, festival **10** debauchery, Saturnalia **11** merrymaking
Bacchanalia
festival honoring: **7** Bacchus
Bacchant
priest who worships: **7** Bacchus
Bacchante
also: **6** Thyiad
priestess who worships: **7** Bacchus
Bacchus
also: **5** Evius **8** Dionysus
god of: **4** wine **5** drama **9** fertility
father: **4** Zeus
mother: **6** Semele
son: **6** Phlias **7** Narcaus, Priapus **8** Oenopion
epithet: **6** Lyaeus **7** Bromius, Cresius **8** Thyoneus, Triambus **9** Pyrigenes **11** Dithyrambus, Mitrephorus
Bach, Carl (Karl) Philipp Emanuel
born: **6** Weimar **7** Germany
father: **19** Johann Sebastian Bach
composer of: **14** Prussian Sonata **19** Wurtembergian Sonata
Bach, Johann Sebastian
born: **7** Germany **8** Eisenach
composer of: **8** Chaconne **10** Giant Fugue, Inventions, Magnificat,

Wedge Fugue **11** Dorian Fugue, Fiddle Fugue, Little Fugue **12** Corelli Fugue, French Suites, Fuga alla Giga, German Suites, St Anne's Fugue **13** Coffee Cantata, English Suites, St John Passion **14** Alla Breve Fugue, Easter Oratorio, Peasant Cantata, Wedding Cantata **15** Jesu Meine Freude, Musical Offering **16** St Matthew Passion, The Art of the Fugue **17** Christmas Oratorio **18** Goldberg Variations **20** Brandenburg Concertos **22** The Well-Tempered Clavier **24** The Wise and Foolish Virgins **30** The Dispute Between Phoebus and Pan

Bach, Richard
author of: **25** Jonathan Livingston Seagull

bachelor 6 single **9** single man, unmarried **12** unmarried man

Bachelor Father
character: **9** Peter Tong **10** Kelly Gregg **12** Bentley Gregg **13** Ginger Farrell
cast: **10** Sammee Tong **12** John Forsythe **14** Noreen Corcoran **17** Bernadette Withers

bachelorhood 8 celibacy **13** baccalaureate **14** unmarried state

bacillus 3 bug **4** germ **7** microbe **8** pathogen **9** bacterium **13** microorganism

back 3 aid, ebb **4** abet, gone, help, hind, late, past, rear, tail **5** after, guard, minor, rural, spine, tardy **6** affirm, assist, attest, behind, bygone, caudal, dorsal, dorsum, far end, former, hinder, hold up, praise, recede, recoil, remote, retire, return, revert, second, succor, tergal, uphold, verify **7** belated, bolster, certify, confirm, delayed, distant, earlier, elapsed, endorse, expired, far side, finance, not paid, overdue, promote, protect, rear end, rebound, retract, retreat, reverse, sponsor, support, sustain, tail end, warrant **8** advocate, backbone, hind part, hindmost, maintain, move away, obsolete, previous, sanction, secluded, turn tail, validate, vouch for, withdraw **9** afterpart, encourage, in arrears, out-of-date, patronize, posterior, reinforce, subsidize **10** retrogress, testify for, underwrite, untraveled **11** bear witness, corroborate, countenance, countrified, countryside, farthermost, furthermost, reverse side, undeveloped, unimportant, unpopulated **12** beat a retreat, hindquarters, spinal column, substantiate **13** take sides with

back away from 7 back off **11** retreat from **12** draw back from, withdraw from

backbiter 5 scold **6** carper, critic **7** reviler **8** vilifier **9** slanderer

backbiting 5 abuse, catty **6** gossip,

malice **7** abusive, calumny, gossipy, hurtful, obloquy, slander **8** libeling, reviling **9** aspersion, cattiness, censuring, contumely, injurious, invective, malicious, maligning, vilifying **10** belittling, bitchiness, calumnious, defamation, defamatory, derogating, detracting, detraction, scandalous, scurrility, slanderous, traduction **11** badmouthing, denigrating, deprecating, disparaging, traducement **12** backstabbing, calumniation, vilification, vituperation **13** disparagement, maliciousness **16** scandal-mongering

backbone 4 grit, guts, sand **5** basis, chine, nerve, pluck, spine, spunk **6** dorsum, mettle, spirit **7** bravery, courage, resolve **8** firmness, mainstay, strength, tenacity **9** character, fortitude, manliness, vertebrae **10** foundation, resolution **11** intrepidity **12** resoluteness, spinal column **13** dauntlessness, steadfastness **15** vertebral column **19** strength of character

back-country 4 farm **5** rural **6** rustic **7** farming **10** provincial

back down 7 back off **8** draw back, move away **9** withdrawn

backdrop 4 flat **7** curtain, scenery **10** background

backer 4 ally **5** angel **6** patron **7** sponsor **8** adherent, advocate, champion, follower, investor, promoter **9** financier, guarantor, supporter **10** wellwisher **11** underwriter

backfire 4 flop, miss **5** crash **6** fizzle, go awry **8** backlash, lay an egg, miscarry, ricochet **9** boomerang **10** bounce back, disappoint **11** come to grief, fall through **12** come to naught **13** come to nothing

background 3 set **4** past, rear **5** flats **6** milieu **7** context, history, rearing, setting **8** backdrop, breeding, distance, heritage, training **9** education, grounding, landscape, life story **10** experience, upbringing **11** antecedents, credentials, environment, mise-enscene, preparation **13** circumstances

backhanded 7 awkward **8** reversed **9** insincere

backing 3 aid **4** core, help **5** aegis **6** succor **7** support **8** advocacy, interior, sanction **9** patronage, prompting **10** assistance, inner layer, sustenance **11** championing, cooperation, endorsement, helping hand, sponsorship **13** encouragement

backlash 4 flop, snag **5** crash, ravel **6** fizzle, go away, recoil **7** rebound **8** backfire, kick back, miscarry, ricochet, snap back **9** animosity, boomerang, hostility, reversion **10** antagonism, bounce back, opposition, resistance **11** come to grief, fall through **12** come to naught **13** come to nothing, counteraction, recalcitrance

backlog 5 hoard, stock, store **6** assets, excess, supply **7** nest egg, reserve, savings **9** abundance, amassment, inventory, reservoir, stockpile **12** accumulation **13** reserve supply **14** superabundance

back matter 5 index **8** addendum, appendix **10** supplement **12** bibliography

back off 7 retreat **8** back down, pull back, withdraw

backpack 4 hike, load **5** pouch **6** bundle **8** knapsack

backside 3 can **4** buns, butt, duff, prat, rear, rump, seat, tail **5** fanny **6** behind, bottom, settee, setter, sitter **7** keister, rear end **8** buttocks, derriere **9** fundament, posterior

backslide 5 lapse **6** revert **7** relapse **10** recurrence, regression **11** deteriorate **14** slip from virtue

back street 5 alley, byway **8** alleyway **13** secondary road

Back Street
director:
1941 version: **15** Robert Stevenson
1961 version: **11** David Miller
based on story by: **11** Fannie Hurst
cast:
1932 version: **9** John Boles **10** Irene Dunne
1941 version: **12** Charles Boyer **16** Margaret Sullavan
1961 version: **9** John Gavin, Vera Miles **12** Susan Hayward

back talk 3 jaw, lip **4** gall, guff, rude, sass **5** cheek **8** pertness, rudeness **9** impudence, insolence, sassiness, sauciness **12** impertinence

Back to the Future
director: **14** Robert Zemeckis
cast: **11** Lea Thompson, Michael J Fox **16** Christopher Lloyd

backup 6 second **7** reserve, standby, stand-in **9** alternate, auxiliary, emergency, secondary **10** substitute, understudy **11** pinch-hitter **13** supplementary

back up 4 abet **6** assist, uphold **9** reinforce **11** corroborate

backward, backwards 3 shy **4** dull, slow **5** dense, tardy, timid, wrong **6** behind, ebbing, remiss, toward **7** bashful, impeded, laggard, messily, reverse, the rear **8** inverted, rearward, receding, reserved, retarded, reticent, reversed, sluggish **9** in retreat, in reverse, inside out, returning, slow-paced, to the past, to the rear, withdrawn **10** disorderly, improperly, regressive, retreating, retrograde, slow-witted, topsy-turvy, upside down **11** chaotically, undeveloped, withdrawing **12** wrong side out **13** retrogressive **15** uncommunicative
French: **9** en arriere

backwash 4 burg, wake **6** result,

sticks, upshot **7** boonies, outcome **8** frontier, tank town **9** aftermath, backwater, boondocks, provinces, upcountry **10** hinterland **11** aftereffect, backcountry, consequence

backwater 3 ebb **5** slack **7** retreat, reverse **8** holdback, stagnant, withdraw

backwoods 5 rural, wilds **6** rustic, simple, sticks **7** boonies, country **8** woodland **9** boondocks, rural area **10** hinterland, provincial **11** backcountry, countryside, hinterlands **15** unsophisticated

bacon 3 pig **4** pork **6** gammon **8** porkslab **10** smoked pork **11** porkbellies
measure: 6 rasher

Bacon, Francis
author of: 6 Essays **11** New Atlantis **12** Novum Organum **14** Maxims of the Law **16** Instauratio Magna **17** History of Henry VII **18** De Sapientia Veterum **20** Apophthegms New and Old **21** Advancement of Learning **25** Reading on the Statute of Uses

Bacon, Francis
born: 6 Dublin **7** Ireland
artwork: 15 Henrietta Moraes **35** Three Studies at the Base of a Crucifixion **44** Studies After Velazquez' Portrait of Pope Innocent X

Bacon, Henry
architect of: 15 Lincoln Memorial

bactericide 9 germicide **10** antiseptic, germ killer **12** disinfectant

bacteriologist
American: 4 Reed
British: 7 Fleming
German: 4 Koch **7** Behring, Ehrlich **10** Wassermann
Japanese: 7 Noguchi **8** Kitasato

bacterium 3 bug **4** germ **5** virus **7** microbe **8** bacillus, pathogen **13** microorganism

bad 3 ill, sad, sin **4** base, dire, evil, foul, glum, grim, mean, poor, rank, sick, sour, vile **5** acrid, acute, angry, awful, cross, false, fetid, grave, harsh, lousy, moldy, nasty, risky, sorry, unfit, wrong **6** ailing, bitter, crimes, faulty, gloomy, guilty, infirm, odious, putrid, rancid, rotten, severe, sickly, sinful, touchy, tragic, turned, unwell, wicked, wrongs **7** baneful, beastly, corrupt, decayed, harmful, hurtful, immoral, joyless, lacking, naughty, not good, noxious, painful, searing, serious, spoiled, tainted, unsound, useless **8** below par, contrite, criminal, dreadful, grievous, inferior, menacing, mildewed, offenses, polluted, terrible, troubled, villainy, wretched **9** agonizing, dangerous, defective, deficient, erroneous, frightful, hazardous, imperfect, incorrect, injurious, irascible, irritable, loathsome, miserable, nefarious, obnoxious, offensive, regretful, repugnant, repulsive, revolting, sad events,

sickening, troubling, unethical, unhealthy, unnerving, unwelcome, valueless **10** calamitous, decomposed, deplorable, detestable, disastrous, disgusting, distressed, disturbing, fallacious, immorality, inadequate, indisposed, melancholy, misfortune, nauseating, not correct, perfidious, putrescent, remorseful, second-rate, unpleasant, villainous, wickedness **11** detrimental, discouraged, distasteful, distractive, distressing, ineffective, inefficient, opprobrious, regrettable, substandard, troublesome, unpalatable **12** contaminated, disagreeable, discouraging, disreputable, excruciating, questionable, unprincipled, unproductive **13** below standard, disappointing, disheartening, harmful things, nonproductive, reprehensible, short-tempered **14** disappointment **15** disadvantageous, under the weather **18** conscience-stricken

bad faith 7 perfidy, treason **8** betrayal **9** falseness, treachery, two timing **10** disloyalty **11** double-cross **13** breach of faith, double-dealing **14** unfaithfulness

badge 4 mark, seal, sign, star **5** brand, stamp, token **6** device, emblem, ensign, shield, symbol **7** earmark **8** hallmark, insignia **9** medallion

badger 3 nag, vex **4** bait, goad **5** annoy, beset, bully, chafe, harry, hound, tease **6** coerce, harass, hector, nettle, pester, plague **7** provoke, torment, trouble **8** irritate **9** persecute
group of: 4 cete

Badger State
nickname of: 9 Wisconsin

badinage 5 chaff **6** banter, joking **7** jesting, joshing, kidding, ragging, ribbing, waggery **8** chaffing, raillery, repartee, word play

bad judgment 5 folly **10** imprudence **11** foolishness **12** carelessness **13** senselessness **15** thoughtlessness **16** shortsightedness, unperceptiveness

bad luck 6 mishap **7** ill wind **8** bad break **9** adversity, mischance **10** ill fortune, misfortune

badly 3 ill **5** wrong **6** basely, poorly, sorely, vilely **7** acutely, greatly, ineptly, not well, wrongly **8** faultily, horribly, severely, shoddily, sinfully, sloppily, terribly, very much, wickedly **9** corruptly, extremely, immorally, intensely, unsoundly **10** carelessly, criminally, dreadfully, improperly, wretchedly **11** defectively, deficiently, desperately, erroneously, exceedingly, frightfully, imperfectly, incorrectly, nefariously, offensively, unethically **12** disreputably, inadequately, villainously **13** incompetently, in the worst way **16** unsatisfactorily

bad manners 8 rudeness **9** surliness

10 incivility **11** boorishness, discourtesy **12** impoliteness

bad mark 4 blot **7** demerit **9** poor grade

badminton
racket: 10 battledore
racket used to hit: 4 bird **7** shuttle **11** shuttlecock
Indian version: 5 poona
stroke: 4 drop **5** clear, smash **7** service **13** backhand drive, forehand drive

badmouthing 5 barbs **7** dissing, insults, slander **9** criticism, insulting **10** slandering **11** criticizing

bad taste 9 crudeness, vulgarity **10** coarseness, garishness, tawdryness

bad tasting 4 sour **5** nasty **6** bitter **7** spoiled **9** medicinal, revolting **10** disgusting **11** unpalatable

bad-tempered 5 cross, testy **6** grumpy **7** grouchy **8** choleric, churlish **9** difficult, irascible, irritable **10** illnatured **11** acrimonious **12** disagreeable

bad times 4 bust **5** slump **9** hard times, recession **10** depression

bad turn 4 harm, hurt **5** wrong **6** injury **7** ill turn **8** disfavor **9** injustice **10** disservice **11** discourtesy

Baekleland, Leo Hendrik
field: 9 chemistry
invented: 8 Bakelite **32** artificial light photographic paper

Baer, Max (Maximillian Adalbert)
nickname: 17 Livermore Larruper
sport: 6 boxing
class: 11 heavyweight

Baeyer, Johann Friedrich Wilhelm Adolph von
field: 9 chemistry
nationality: 6 German
synthesized: 6 indigo
discovered: 13 phthalein dyes
awarded: 10 Nobel Prize

baffle 3 bar **4** daze, dull, foil, stop **5** amaze, check, stump **6** deaden, muddle, puz- zle, reduce, thwart **7** astound, confuse, inhibit, mystify, nonplus, perplex **8** astonish, befuddle, bewilder, confound, dumfound, minimize, restrain, surprise **10** disconcert

baffling 7 elusive **8** puzzling **9** confusing, enigmatic **10** mysterious, mystifying, perplexing **11** confounding **16** incomprehensible

bag 3 get, sag **4** hunt, kill, sack, take, trap **5** bulge, catch, droop, pouch, purse, shoot, snare **6** bundle, entrap, obtain, packet **7** acquire, capture, collect, ensnare **8** paper bag, protrude, suitcase **10** receptacle

bagatelle 6 trifle **7** nothing, trinket **10** knickknack, light music **11** unimportant

baggage 4 bags, gear **5** grips **6** trunks

7 bundles, effects, luggage, valises **8** movables, packages **9** apparatus, equipment, suitcases, trappings **10** belongings **11** impedimenta **13** accoutrements, paraphernalia

baggy 4 limp **5** loose, slack **6** droopy, flabby, puffed **7** bloated, bulbous, flac- cid, paunchy, sagging, swollen **9** unpressed, unshapely **12** loose-fitting

Baghdad
  capital of: 4 Iraq
  founder: 8 (Caliph) al-Mansur
  landmark:
    minaret: 10 Suq al-Ghazi
    mosque: 8 Madrasah **14** al-Mustansiriya
  means: 8 God-given
  river: 6 Tigris

Bagheera
  character in: 14 The Jungle Books
  author: 7 Kipling

bagnio 4 bath, stew **5** house **6** bordel, prison **7** brothel **8** bordello, cathouse **10** bawdy house, fancy house, whorehouse **13** sporting house **14** house of ill fame **16** house of ill repute **19** house of prostitution

Bagnold, Enid
  author of: 14 National Velvet, The Chalk Garden **23** The Chinese Prime Minister

Bagstock, Joe
  character in: 12 Dombey and Son
  author: 7 Dickens

Bahamas
  capital/largest city: 6 Nassau
  others: 8 Freeport **9** Rock Sound **10** George Town **11** Mastic Point **12** Spanish Wells
  head of state: 14 British monarch **15** governor general
  island: 3 Cat **4** Long **5** Berry, Exuma **6** Andros, Bimini, Caicos, Rum Cay **7** Crooked, Harbour, Watling **9** Eleuthera, Mayaguana **10** Great Abaco **11** Grand Bahama, Great Inagua, Great Ragged, San Salvador **13** New Providence
  sea: 8 Atlantic **9** Caribbean
  physical feature:
    strait: 7 Florida
    swamp: 8 mangrove
  people: 5 black **7** Haitian
  language: 6 Creole **7** English
  religion: 12 Christianity
  place:
    harbor: 9 Governors
    naval base: 9 Mayaguana
  feature:
    key: 3 cay
    native: 5 conch

Bahrain
  capital/largest city: 6 Manama
  others: 5 Rifaa **7** Jidhafs **8** Muharraq
  head of state/government: 4 emir
  monetary unit: 4 fils **5** dinar
  island: 5 Hawar, Jidda **6** Sitrah **7**

Bahrain **9** Umm Nassan **10** al-Muharraq **11** An Nabi Salih
  physical feature:
    gulf: 7 Bahrain, Persian
  people: 4 Arab **6** Indian **7** Persian **8** American, European **9** Pakistani
    ruling family: 9 al-Khalifa
  language: 4 Urdu **5** Farsi **6** Arabic **7** English, Persian
  religion: 5 Islam

bail 3 dip **4** bond, lade **5** ladle, scoop, spoon **6** surety **9** guarantee **11** post bond for

bailiff 6 deputy **8** marshall, overseer **9** assistant, constable **12** court officer

bailiwick 4 area, beat, turf **5** arena, orbit, place, realm **6** domain, sphere **7** compass **8** dominion, province **9** territory **10** department **12** neighborhood

Baird, Spencer Fullerton
  field: 7 zoology
  authority on: 5 birds **7** mammals
  established: 30 US Commission of Fish and Fisheries
  laboratory at: 11 Woods Hole MA

bait 3 vex **4** lure, ride, worm **5** annoy, bribe, harry, hound, tease, worry **6** allure, bad- ger, come-on, harass, heckle, hector, magnet, needle **7** provoke, torment **9** put bait on, tantalize **10** allurement, antagonize, attraction, enticement, inducement, temptation

bake 3 fry **4** boil, burn, cook, sear, stew **5** grill, roast, saute, toast **6** braise, pan-fry, scorch, simmer **7** parboil, swelter

Baked Bean State
  nickname of: 13 Massachusetts

Baker, Norma Jean Mortenson
  real name of: 13 Marilyn Monroe

Balaam
  father: 4 Beor
  brother: 4 Bela
  lived at: 4 Aram **6** Pethor
  commanded by: 5 Balak
  killed by: 6 Israel
  rebuked by: 3 ass

Balak
  father: 6 Zippor
  commanded: 6 Balaam

Balakiref, Mily
  born: 6 Russia **13** Nijni-Novgorod
  member of: 7 Kutchka, The Five
  composer of: 6 Russia, Tamara, Thamar **7** Islamey **8** King Lear (overture)

balance, balances 3 pay **4** cool, mean, rest **5** poise, ratio, scale, sum up, tally, total, tot up, weigh **6** aplomb, equate, offset, parity, ponder, reckon, scales, set off, square, steady, weight **7** compare, compute, harmony, opinion, reflect, remnant, residue **8** cogitate, consider, contrast, coolness, equality, estimate, evaluate, judgment, leftover, level off, parallel, presence, symmetry **9** appraisal,

calculate, composure, equipoise, juxtapose, make level, remainder, stability, stabilize **10** amount owed, comparison, counteract, deliberate, equanimity, evaluation, keep steady, neutralize, proportion, steadiness **11** equilibrium **12** counterpoise, equalization, middle ground **13** compensate for, consideration, judiciousness **14** amount credited, self-possession, unflappability **15** level-headedness **16** imperturbability
  constellation of: 5 Libra

balanced 4 fair, just **9** equitable, impartial **12** unprejudiced **13** disinterested

balance out 6 cancel, offset **9** make up for **10** neutralize **13** compensate for **14** counterbalance

Balanchine, George
  choreographer of: 4 Agon **6** Jewels **8** Episodes, Ivesiana, Serenade **15** Concerto Barocco **16** Allegro Brillante

balcony 4 deck **5** boxes, foyer, loges **6** loggia **7** portico, terrace, veranda **9** mezzanine

bald 4 bare, flat, open **5** blunt, naked, plain, stark, utter **6** barren, simple, smooth **7** denuded, obvious **8** flagrant, glabrous, hairless, outright, treeless **9** depilated, out- and-out, unadorned **11** categorical, undisguised, unqualified, unvarnished **12** without cover **13** unembellished, unequivocable **15** straightforward

Balder
  also: 5 Baldr **6** Baldur
  origin: 6 Nordic
  god of: 6 beauty **8** radiance
  father: 4 Odin **5** Othin
  mother: 3 Fri **5** Frigg, Frija **6** Frigga
  twin brother: 5 Hoder, Hodur
  killed by: 5 Hoder, Hodur

balderdash 3 rot **4** bosh, bull, bunk **5** crock, trash **6** bunkum, drivel, hot air **7** twaddle **8** buncombe, claptrap, flummery, nonsense, tommyrot **9** gibberish, poppycock **10** double-talk, tomfoolery **11** obfuscation **16** stuff and nonsense

baldheaded 8 hairless **9** baldpated, depilated **10** skin- headed **11** chrome-domed

Baldr
  see: 6 Balder

Baldung Grien, Hans
  born: 6 Alsace **10** Weyersheim
  artwork: 9 Todentanz **17** Death and the Maiden **19** Death Kissing a Maiden **21** The Bewitched Stable Boy **24** Rest on the Flight into Egypt

Baldur
  see: 6 Balder

Baldwin, James
  author of: 13 Giovanni's Room, The Amen Corner **14** Another Country **15**

Just Above My Head, The Fire Next Time **17** Going to Meet the Man, Nobody Knows My Name, No Name in the Street **21** Blues for Mister Charlie, Go Tell It on the Mountain

bale 4 case, load, pack **6** bundle, packet, parcel **7** package **11** bound bundle

balefire 6 beacon **9** watchfire **10** signal fire

baleful 3 icy **4** cold, dire, evil **6** deadly, malign **7** baneful, furious, harmful, hurtful, ominous **8** sinister, spiteful, venomous **9** malicious, malignant **10** malevolent **11** coldhearted, threatening

Balfe, Michael William
born: 6 Dublin **7** Ireland
composer of: 15 The Bohemian Girl, The Maid of Artois **17** I rivali di se stessi **18** The Siege of Rochelle

Balfour, David
character in: 9 Kidnapped
author: 9 Stevenson

Bali
province of: 9 Indonesia
capital: 8 Denpasar
city: 10 Singaraja
island: 11 Lesser Sunda
highest peak: 6 Agoeng
climate: 3 dry **7** monsoon
tree: 8 waringin
animal: 4 deer **5** tiger
people: 7 Malayan
religion: 8 Hinduism
agriculture: 3 pig **4** corn, rice **6** cattle, coffee **7** tobacco

Balius
horse of: 8 Achilles
gift: 11 immortality

balk 3 bar **4** foil, shun **5** block, check, demur, evade, shirk, spike, stall **6** baffle, defeat, derail, eschew, hinder, impede, recoil, refuse, resist, stymie, thwart **7** inhibit, prevent **8** draw back, hang back, hesitate, obstruct **9** forestall, frustrate **10** shrink from

Balkan 16 Forested mountain
agriculture: 5 grain **6** cotton, grapes, olives **7** tobacco
ancient people: 4 Slav **5** Greek, Roman **8** Illyrian, Thracian
language: 9 Slovenian **10** Macedonian **14** Serbo-Croatian
mountain: 6 Balkan, Massif **7** Rhodope **10** Carpathian **11** Dinaric Alps **13** Transylvanian
religion: 5 Islam **8** Orthodox **13** Roman Catholic
river: 6 Danube, Morava, Vardar
sea boundary: 5 Black **6** Aegean, Ionian **8** Adriatic **13** Mediterranean
state: 6 Greece, Turkey **7** Albania, Romania **8** Bulgaria **10** Yugoslavia

balky 6 mulish, ornery, unruly **7** restive, wayward, willful **8** contrary, perverse, stubborn **9** fractious, obstinate,

pigheaded **10** rebellious, refractory **11** disobedient, intractable **12** recalcitrant, unmanageable

ball 3 hop, orb **4** prom, shot **5** dance, globe **6** pellet, soiree, sphere **7** bullets, globule **8** spheroid **9** cotillion, promenade **11** projectiles

Ball, Lucille
husband: 9 Desi Arnaz
children: 4 Desi **5** Lucie
born: 11 Jamestown NY
roles: 9 Here's Lucy, I Love Lucy **11** The Lucy Show

Balla, Giacomo
born: 5 Italy, Turin
artwork: 8 The Sewer **11** The Mad Woman **18** Speeding Automobile **20** Rhythm of the Violinist **22** Dynamism of a Dog on a Leash **26** The Street Light Study of Light **29** Mercury Passing in Front of the Sun **40** Swifts Paths of Movement and Dynamic Sequences

ballad 3 lay **4** song **5** carol, ditty **6** chanty **8** folk song **12** rhyming story **13** narrative poem **14** narrative verse

Ballad of Reading Gaol, The
author: 10 Oscar Wilde

Ballads and Poems
author: 19 Stephen Vincent Benet

ballast 6 weight **7** balance, control **9** equipoise **10** ballasting, dead weight, makeweight, stabilizer **12** counterpoise **13** counterweight **14** counterbalance **19** stabilizing material

Ballesteros, Severiano
nickname: 4 Seve
sport: 4 golf
nationality: 7 Spanish

ballet 4 Agon **5** Manon, Rodeo **6** Apollo, Parade **7** Giselle, Orpheus **8** Coppelia, Episodes, Ivesiana, Les Noces, Serenade, Swan Lake, The Doves **9** Anastasia, Fancy Free, Interplay, Petrushka, The Jewels **10** La Sylphide, Petrouchka **11** Billy the Kid, Lilac Garden, Soccer Dance, Symphony in C, The Firebird **12** Pillar of Fire, Sailor's Dance, Spring Waters, The Partisans **13** The Nutcracker **14** Romeo and Juliet **15** Concerto Barocco, Fall River Legend, The Rite of Spring **16** Allegro Brillante, La Fille Mal Gardee, Specter of the Rose **17** The Sleeping Beauty **18** Raymonda Variations **19** The Afternoon of a Faun, The Four Temperaments **24** Stravinsky Violin Concerto
ballet company: 5 Kirov, Royal **7** Bolshoi, Joffrey **9** Mariinsky, Maryinsky **11** New York City **13** Ballets Russes **20** Dance Theater of Harlem **21** American Ballet Theater **22** National Ballet of Canada
choreographer: 9 Hanya Holm, Lev Ivanov **10** John Weaver **11** Jules Perrot **12** Agnes de Mille, Igor Moi-

seyev, Marius Petipa, Michel Fokine **13** Jean Dauberval, Jerome Robbins, Leonid Massine **15** Arthur Saint-Leon **16** George Balanchine, Kenneth Mac-Millan **18** August Bournonville, Bronislava Nijinska, Jean Georges Noverre, Sir Frederick Ashton
chorus: 8 ensemble **13** corps de ballet
dancer: 9 Karen Kain **10** Anton Dolin, Marie Lieta, Serge Lifar **11** Allegra Kent, Anna Pavlova, Anthony Blum, Lucile Grahn, Lynn Seymour, Nadia Nerina **12** Fanny Cerrito, Marie Camargo, Peter Martins **13** Alicia Markova, Andre Eglevsky, Anthony Dowell, Carlotta Grisi, Frank Augustyn, Galina Ulanova, Margot Fonteyn, Marie Taglioni, Melissa Hayden, Patricia Neary, Rudolf Nureyev **14** Arthur Mitchell, Cynthia Gregory, Edward Villella, Gelsey Kirkland, Leonide Massine, Maria Tallchief, Suzanne Farrell, Vaslav Nijinsky **15** Jacques D'Amboise, Martine Van Hamel, Maya Plisetskaya, Natalia Makarova, Patricia McBride, Tamara Karsavina **16** Antoinette Sibley, Olga Spessivtseva **17** Alexandra Danilova, Marina Kondratieva **18** Mikhail Baryshnikov
fast movement: 7 allegro
first ballet: 22 Ballet Comique de la Reine
impresario: 12 Marie Rambert **15** Ninette de Valois, Sergei Diaghilev
kick: 9 battement
modern dancer/choreographer: 8 Ted Shawn **9** Eliot Feld **10** Mary Wigman, Paul Draper, Twyla Tharp **11** Anna Sokolow, Antony Tudor, Eric Hawkins, Ruth St Denis **12** Martha Graham **13** Alwin Nikolais, Doris Humphrey, Isadora Duncan **14** Charles Weidman **15** Merce Cunningham
position/step: 4 jete, plie, tour **5** saute **6** releve **7** en avant, fouette, on point, pas seul, turnout **8** batterie, cabriole, en dedans, en dehors, glissade **9** arabesque, developpe, en arriere, entrechat, pas de chat, pas-de-deux, pirouette **10** demi-pointe, port de bras, tour en l'air **11** rond de jambe, terre-a-terre **12** pas de bourree, saut de basque **17** changement de pieds
principal female dancer: 6 etoile **9** ballerina **14** prima ballerina
principal male dancer: 12 danseur noble
skirt: 4 tutu
slow movement: 6 adagio
term: 4 coda **5** barre **6** ballon **14** divertissement

Ball of Fat
author: 15 Guy de Maupassant

balloon 4 grow **5** belly, bloat **6** billow, blow up, dilate, expand **7** distend, enlarge, fill out, inflate, puff out **8** increase, swell out

ballot 4 poll, vote **5** slate **6** ticket, voting **7** polling **13** round of voting **16** list of candidates

ballyhoo 4 hype, puff, push, tout **6** herald, hoopla **7** buildup, promote, puffery, trumpet **8** proclaim **9** advertise, promotion, publicity, publicize **10** hullabaloo, propaganda **11** advertising **15** public relations

balm 5 cream, salve **6** balsam, lotion, solace **7** anodyne, comfort, unguent **8** curative, narcotic, ointment, sedative **9** comforter, emollient **10** palliative **11** restorative **12** tranquilizer

balmy 3 odd **4** calm, fair, mild, soft, warm **5** bland, kooky, weird **6** easing, gentle **7** calming, clement, summery **8** aromatic, fragrant, perfumed, pleasant, redolent, soothing **9** agreeable, ambrosial, eccentric, temperate **10** refreshing, salubrious

Balnibari
    fictional land in: 16 Gulliver's
        Travels
    author: 5 Swift

baloney 3 rot **4** bull, bunk **5** hokum, hooey, stuff **6** bunkum, hot air, humbug **7** hogwash, sausage, spinach **8** claptrap, nonsense, tommyrot **9** poppycock **10** applesauce **11** foolishness

Baloo
    character in: 14 The Jungle Books
    author: 7 Kipling

balsam 3 fir **4** balm **5** cream, salve **7** unguent **8** ointment **9** Impatiens
    varieties: 2 He **3** Fir, She **4** Rose, Wild **6** Garden **8** Zanzibar

Balsam, Martin
    born: 9 New York NY
    roles: 6 Psycho **7** Catch-22 **15** A
        Thousand Clowns, On the Waterfront

Baltic
    language family: 12 Indo-European
    group: 11 Balto-Slavic
    subgroup: 7 Latvian **10** Lithuanian
    canal: 4 Kiel
    port: 4 Kiel, Riga **6** Danzig, Gdansk **7**
        Tallinn

Baltimore
    baseball team: 7 Orioles
    football team: 5 Stars **6** Ravens

Baltimore, David
    field: 12 microbiology
    studied: 11 animal cells **13** viral genetics
    awarded: 10 Nobel Prize

Balto-Slavic
    language family: 12 Indo-European
    branch: 6 Baltic, Slavic

baluster 4 post, rail **6** column, pillar **7** support, upright **8** pilaster

balustrade 7 railing **8** baluster, banister, handrail

Balzac, Honore de

author of: 7 Gobseck **10** La Vendetta **11** Cousin(e) Bette **12** Father Goriot, Le Cousin Pons, Le Pere Goriot **13** Lost Illusions **14** Eugenie Grandet, The Human Comedy **15** The Wild Ass's Skin **16** La Comedie Humaine **23** The Physiology of Marriage

Bamako
    capital of: 4 Mali

Bambi
    author: 11 Felix Salten
    character: 3 Ena **6** Faline, Flower **7** Thumper
    film made by: 6 Disney
    directed by: 9 David Hand

bamboo 4 Sasa **7** Bambusa **9** Shibataea **10** Pseudosasa **11** Arundinaria **13** Phyllostachys **14** Chimonobambusa **15** Semiarundinaria
    varieties: 4 Moso **5** Arrow, Black, Dwarf, Giant, Hardy, Hedge, Henon, Meyer, Pygmy, Simon, Stake **6** Buddha, Common, Forage, Oldham, Sacred, Sickle, Square, Tonkin **7** Allgold, Beechey, Mexican **8** Calcutta, Feathery, Heavenly, Narihira **9** Canebrake, Castillon **10** Red-berried, Square-stem **11** Punting-pole **12** Alphonse Karr, Yellow-groove **13** Dwarf fern-leaf, Fern-leaf hedge, Oriental hedge **14** Chinese-goddess **16** Dwarf white-stripe **17** Silver-stripe hedge **18** Stripe-stem fern-leaf

bamboozle 3 con, gyp **4** coax, dupe, fool, gull, hoax, lure, rook, take **5** cheat, coz-en, trick **6** delude **7** beguile, deceive, defraud, mislead, swindle **8** hoodwink **9** victimize

ban 3 bar **5** debar, taboo **6** banish, enjoin, forbid **7** barring, embargo, exclude **8** disallow, prohibit, stoppage, suppress **9** exclusion, interdict, proscribe, restraint **10** banishment, censorship **11** forbiddance, prohibition, restriction **12** interdiction, proscription

banal 4 dull **5** corny, stale, stock, tired, trite, vapid **6** jejune **7** humdrum, insipid, prosaic **8** bromidic, everyday, ordinary, shopworn **9** hackneyed **10** pedestrian, threadbare, unexciting, unoriginal **11** commonplace, stereotyped **12** cliche-ridden, conventional **13** platitudinous, unimaginative, uninteresting

banality 6 cliche **7** bromide **9** platitude, staleness, triteness **10** insipidity

banana 4 Musa
    varieties: 3 Fe'i **4** Fehi, Koae **5** Dwarf **6** Edible **7** Chinese **9** Flowering **10** Abyssinian, Ladyfinger **12** Canary Island, Chinese dwarf
    similar to: 8 plantain

Bananas
    director: 10 Woody Allen
    cast: 10 Woody Allen **12** Howard Cosell, Louise Lasser **15** Carlos Montalban

Bancroft, Anne
    real name: 23 Anna Maria Louise Italiano
    husband: 9 Mel Brooks
    born: 7 Bronx NY
    roles: 11 Mrs Robinson, The Graduate **15** The Pumpkin Eater, The Turning Point, Two for the Seesaw **16** The Miracle Worker (Oscar)

band 3 set **4** belt, body, club, crew, gang, hoop, join, pack, ring, sash **5** bunch, crowd, group, junta, party, strap, strip, swath, thong, troop, unite **6** caucus, circle, clique, collar, fillet, gather, girdle, league, ribbon, streak, stripe, throng **7** bandeau, binding, circlet, company, society **8** assembly, cincture, ensemble **9** multitude, orchestra, surcingle **10** fellowship, sisterhood **11** association, brotherhood, confederacy, consolidate **13** confederation

bandage 4 bind **5** dress **7** binding, plaster **8** compress, dressing

bandanna, bandana 5 scarf **8** kerchief **10** silk square **11** neckerchief **12** handkerchief

Bandar Seri Begawan
    capital of: 6 Brunei

bandeau 3 bra **4** band **6** fillet **7** binding, circlet **9** brassiere

bandit 4 thug **5** crook, thief **6** badman, outlaw, robber **7** brigand, burglar, footpad, ladrone **8** blackleg **9** desperado, road agent **10** highwayman

bandleader 6 master **7** maestro **8** director **9** conductor
    famous: 11 Glenn Miller, Tommy Dorsey **12** Lawrence Welk

Band of Merry Men
    followers of: 9 Robin Hood

band together 5 unify, unite **6** league **7** combine **10** join forces **11** consolidate

bandy 4 swap **5** trade **6** barter **7** shuffle **8** exchange **9** toss about **11** interchange **16** toss back and forth

bandying 4 swap **5** trade **8** exchange **9** tit for tat **10** quid pro quo **11** give and take

bane 3 woe **4** ruin **5** curse, toxin, venom **6** blight, burden, canker, plague, poison **7** scourge, torment, tragedy **8** calamity, disaster, downfall, nuisance **9** destroyer, detriment, ruination **10** affliction **13** pain in the neck **14** thorn in the side **16** fly in the ointment

baneful 4 evil **6** deadly, malign, woeful **7** harmful, noxious **8** venomous **9** injurious, malignant, poisonous **10** malevolent **11** destructive

bang 3 box, hit, pop, rap, tap **4** beat, blow, boom, clap, cuff, kick, lick, slam, slap, sock **5** burst, clout, crash, knock, smack, thump, whack **6** buffet, charge, report, thrill, thwack, wallop **7** delight **8** good time, headlong, pleasure, suddenly **9** enjoyment, explosion **10** crashingly, excitement

Bangkok
  also: 9 Krung Thep
  capital of: 8 Thailand
  landmark: 5 Wat Po **11** Grand Palace **16** Wat Emerald Buddha
  means: 12 City of Angels
  nickname: 15 Venice of the East
  port: 8 Klongtoi
  river: 10 Chao Phraya

Bangladesh
  other name: 10 East Bengal **12** East Pakistan
  capital/largest city: 5 Dacca
  others: 6 Khulna, Sylhet **7** Comilla, Jessore, Rangpur, Saidpur **8** Jamalpur, Rajshahi **9** Madaripur **10** Chittagong **11** Narayanganj **12** Brahmanbaria
  monetary unit: 4 taka **5** paisa
  island: 10 Sundarbans
  mountain: 15 Chittagong Hills
  highest point: 10 Keokradong
  river: 5 Padna **6** Ganges, Meghna **10** Burhi Ganga, Karnaphuli **11** Brahmaputra
  physical feature:
    bay: 6 Bengal
  people: 7 Bengali
    guerrillas: 11 muktibahini
    leader: 6 Ershad **11** Ziaur Rahman **19** Sheikh Mujibur Rahman
  language: 6 Bihari **7** Bengali, English
  religion: 5 Hindu, Islam
  feature:
    clothing: 4 sari **5** lungi

bangle 3 fob **5** chain, charm **6** armlet, bauble, gewgaw, tinsel **7** bibelot, fribble, trinket **8** bracelet, gimcrack, ornament, wristlet **10** knickknack **11** junk jewelry **14** costume jewelry

Bangui
  capital of: 22 Central African Republic

banish 3 ban, bar **4** drop, oust **5** eject, erase, evict, exile, expel **6** deport, dispel, outlaw, reject, remove **7** cast out, discard, dismiss, exclude, put away, shut out, turn out **8** cast away, dislodge, drive out, get rid of, send away, shake off **9** discharge, eliminate, eradicate, extradite **13** excommunicate **14** send to Coventry

banished person 5 exile **6** emigre, pariah **7** outcast **8** deportee, expellee **10** expatriate **14** deported person **15** displaced person

banishment 3 ban **5** exile **6** ouster **7** removal **8** eviction **9** dismissal, exclusion, expulsion **11** deportation **12** expatriation **14** transportation **15** excommunication

Banjo Eyes
  nickname of: 11 Eddie Cantor

Banjul, Bathurst
  capital of: 6 Gambia

bank 3 bar, row, tip **4** dike, dune, edge, file, flat, fund, heap, hill, keep, line, mass, pile, rank, reef, rise, save, side, tier, tilt **5** amass, array, brink, chain, knoll, mound, ridge, shelf, shoal, shore, slant, slope, stack, store, train **6** barrow, line up, margin, pile up, series, strand, string, supply **7** deposit, parapet, reserve, savings, shallow, terrace **8** keyboard, sandbank **9** exchequer, reservoir, stockpile **10** depository, embankment, repository, storehouse, succession **12** accumulation, trust company **14** savings and loan

Bank Dick, The
  director: 10 Eddie Cline
  cast: 8 W C Fields **9** Una Merkel **15** Cora Witherspoon

banknote 4 bill **9** greenback **11** certificate, legal tender **12** currency note, treasury note **17** silver certificate

bank of pity
  French: 11 mont-de-piete
  literal name for: 10 pawnbroker

bankrupt 5 broke **6** busted, failed, ruined **8** depleted, indigent, in the red, wiped out **9** destitute, exhausted, insolvent, penniless **12** impoverished, without funds

Bankruptcy, A
  author: 20 Bjornstjerne Bjornson

Banks, Ernie
  nickname: 5 Mr Cub
  sport: 8 baseball
  noted for: 7 hitting
  team: 11 Chicago Cubs

banner 4 flag **6** burgee, colors, ensign, record **7** leading, notable, pendant, pennant, winning **8** standard, streamer **9** red-letter **10** profitable **11** outstanding **14** most successful

Bannock
  language family: 10 Shoshonean
  location: 5 Idaho

banquet 4 dine **5** feast, revel **6** dinner, repast **9** symposium

Banquo
  character in: 7 Macbeth
  author: 11 Shakespeare

bantam 3 hen, wee **4** cock, fowl, tiny **5** dwarf, pygmy, runt, small, teeny, weeny **6** little, midget, minute, petite **7** chicken, dwarfed, rooster, stunted **9** miniature **10** diminutive, pocket-size, teeny-weeny **11** Lilliputian, pocket-sized

banter 3 kid, rib **4** dish, josh, mock, ride, twit **5** chaff, jolly, taunt, tease **6** joking, needle **7** jesting, joshing, kid-

ding, rag- ging, ribbing, teasing, waggery **8** badinage, chaffing, raillery, repartee, word play

Banting, Frederick Grant
  field: 8 medicine
  nationality: 8 Canadian
  extracted: 7 insulin
  awarded: 10 Nobel Prize

Bantu
  means: 9 the people
  dwelling: 6 Africa
  tribe: 5 Xosas, Zulus **6** Swazis **7** Basutos, Kalanga

baptism 9 beginning, immersion, sacrament **10** initiation, sprinkling **11** christening **12** introduction, purification **13** rite of passage **16** spiritual rebirth

baptize 3 dub **4** name **8** christen

bar 3 ban, pub, rib, rod **4** band, bank, beam, belt, bolt, cake, curb, flat, line, lock, oust, pale, pole, rail, reef, snag, spar, spit, stay, stop **5** block, catch, check, court, debar, eject, evict, exile, expel, forum, ingot, jimmy, lever, limit, shelf, shoal, slice, sprit, stake, stick, strip, taboo **6** banish, enjoin, fasten, forbid, impede, lounge, paling, ribbon, saloon, secure, streak, stripe, stroke, tavern **7** barrier, block up, canteen, cast out, close up, crowbar, exclude, grating, lock out, measure, prevent, sandbar, shallow, shut out, taproom **8** alehouse, crossbar, disallow, judgment, obstacle, obstruct, preclude, prohibit, restrain, restrict, tribunal **9** barricade, blackball, blacklist, hindrance, long table, lunchroom, restraint, speakeasy **10** constraint, crosspiece, impediment, injunction, limitation **11** obstruction, public house, restriction **14** cocktail lounge, serving counter, stumbling block **15** legal profession

Bara, Theda
  real name: 16 Theodosia Goodman
  nickname: 7 The Vamp
  born: 12 Cincinnati OH
  roles: 6 Carmen, Salome **7** Camille **8** The Vixen **9** Cleopatra **13** A Fool There Was, Madame Du Barry

Barabbas 6 robber **8** murderer

Barak
  father: 7 Abinoam
  summoned by: 7 Deborah
  defeated: 6 Sisera

barb 3 cut, dig, nib **4** cusp, jibe, snag, spur, tine **5** point, prong, spike **6** insult **7** affront, barbule, bristle, prickle, putdown, sarcasm, spicule **9** complaint, criticism **11** badmouthing

Barbados
  capital/largest city: 10 Bridgetown
  others: 7 Oistins **8** Boscabel, Crab Hill, Hastings, Holetown, Portland, Worthing **9** Bathsheba **10** Martin's Bay **11** Belleplaine **12** Speightstown

school: 10 Codrington
head of state: 14 British monarch **15** governor general
mountain: 6 Chalky
highest point: 7 Hillaby
river: 12 Constitution
sea: 8 Atlantic **9** Caribbean
physical feature:
bay: 4 Foul, Long **8** Carlisle
beach: 5 Crane
gully: 12 Welchman Hall
hill: 10 Cherry Tree
point: 5 North, South **6** Ragged **8** Harrison, Kitridge
people: 5 Bajan **9** Barbadian
leader: 5 Adams
language: 7 English
religion: 8 Anglican
place:
airport: 7 Seawell
castle: 8 Sam Lords
church: 7 St Johns
feature:
sea crab: 7 shagger
barbarian 4 boor, hood, lout, punk **5** alien, bully, crude, rowdy, tough, yahoo **6** savage, vandal **7** boorish, hoodlum, lowbrow, peasant, ruffian, uncouth **8** hooligan **9** ignoramus, outlander, roughneck, vulgarian **10** delinquent, illiterate, philistine, provincial, troglodyte, uncultured **11** knownothing **12** uncultivated **15** unsophisticated **16** anti-intellectual
barbaric 4 rude, wild **5** crude **6** coarse, savage, vulgar **7** boorish, uncouth, untamed **9** barbarian, barbarous **10** unpolished **11** ill-mannered, uncivilized
barbarism 7 cruelty **8** savagery **9** brutality **10** inhumanity **11** viciousness
barbarity 7 cruelty **9** brutality **10** savageness **12** ruthlessness
barbarous 4 mean **5** crass, crude, cruel, harsh, rough **6** brutal, coarse, vulgar **7** inhuman, vicious **8** barbaric, impolite **10** outrageous
barber 3 cut **4** trim **5** dress, shave, style **6** Figaro **7** arrange, stylist, tonsure **10** haircutter **11** hairdresser
Barber, Samuel
born: 13 West Chester PA
composer of: 7 Vanessa **10** Dover Beach **16** Adagio for Strings **17** Capricorn Concerto **19** Anthony and Cleopatra, The School for Scandal
Barber of Seville, The
author: 12 Beaumarchais
opera by: 7 Rossini
character: 6 Bazile, Figaro, Rosine, Rosina **8** Almaviva, Bartholo **9** Dr Bartolo **13** Count Almaviva
barbette 5 mound **7** bastion, rampart **8** platform **9** earthwork **10** breastwork
barbiturate 8 euphoria, hypnotic, sedative **10** depressive **13** anesthesiatic **14** barbituric acid

kind: 7 seconal **10** thiopental **11** amobarbital **12** secobarbital **13** phenobarbital
barbule 4 barb **11** feather part
Barchester Towers
author: 15 Anthony Trollope
sequel to: 9 The Warden
character: 7 Mr Slope, Mrs Bold **8** Mr Arabin **9** Dr Proudie, Mr Harding **10** Mrs Proudie **11** Mr Quiverful **13** Canon Stanhope **17** Archdeacon Grantly **18** Signora Vesey-Neroni
bard 4 poet **6** rhymer, writer **8** epic poet, minstrel, poetizer **9** poetaster, rhymester, troubador, versifier **10** poet- singer **13** narrative poet
Bardell, Mrs
character in: 14 Pickwick Papers
author: 7 Dickens
Bardot, Brigitte
husband: 10 Roger Vadim
born: 5 Paris **6** France
roles: 18 And God Created Woman
bare 4 bald, mere, nude, open, show, thin, void, worn **5** basic, blank, empty, naked, offer, plain, scant, stark, strip **6** denude, divest, expose, meager, peeled, reveal, simple, unclad, unmask, unveil, vacant **7** austere, exposed, hapless, uncover, undrape, undress, unrobed **8** disrobed, in the raw, marginal, stripped **9** endurable, essential, unadorned, unclothed, uncolored, uncovered, undressed, unsheathe **10** elementary, just enough, threadbare **11** fundamental, supportable, undecorated, undisguised, unvarnished **12** unelaborated, unornamented **13** unembellished **15** straightforward
barefaced 4 bald, bold, flip **5** brash, fresh, sassy **6** brazen, cheeky, snotty **7** forward **8** flippant, impudent, insolent, palpable **9** shameless, unabashed **11** transparent
barefoot 6 unshod **8** shoeless **9** discalced **10** unsandaled **11** discalceate
Barefoot Boy
author: 21 John Greenleaf Whittier
Barefoot in the Park
director: 8 Gene Saks
based on play by: 9 Neil Simon
cast: 9 Jane Fonda **12** Charles Boyer **13** Robert Redford
barely 4 just **6** almost, hardly **7** faintly, scantly **8** meagerly, only just, scarcely, slightly **9** almost not, just about, sparingly **10** no more than **20** by the skin of one's teeth
bareness 6 nudity **9** bleakness, emptiness, nakedness **10** barrenness
Baresark
origin: 12 Scandinavian
form: 7 warrior
trait: 7 courage
Baretta
character: 7 Rooster **11** Billy Truman,

(Det) Tony Baretta, (Lt) Hal Brubaker
cast: 8 Tom Ewell **11** Robert Blake **12** Edward Grover **15** Michael D Roberts
Tony's pet: 8 cockatoo
named: 4 Fred
barfly 3 sot **4** lush, soak **5** drunk, rummy, souse, toper **7** tippler **8** drunkard **9** alcoholic **11** dipsomaniac
bargain 4 deal, pact **5** steal **6** accord, barter, dicker, haggle, higgle, pledge, treaty **7** compact, entente, good buy, promise **8** contract, covenant, good deal **9** agreement, negotiate **10** settlement **11** arrangement, transaction **13** understanding
French: 9 bon marche
bargain for 6 expect **7** foresee **8** envision, reckon on **11** contemplate
barge 4 bust, scow, ship **6** launch, vessel **7** freight, intrude
barium
chemical symbol: 2 Ba
bark 3 bay, cry, rub, yap, yip **4** flay, hide, howl, hull, husk, peel, rind, roar, skin, woof, yell, yelp **5** crust, scale, shout, strip **6** abrade, arf-arf, bellow, bow-wow, casing, cry out, holler, scrape **7** howling **8** covering, periderm **9** sheathing
Barker, Lex
real name: 25 Alexander Crichlow Barker Jr
wife: 10 Arlene Dahl, Lana Turner
born: 5 Rye NY
roles: 6 Tarzan **11** La Dolce Vita
Barkis
character in: 16 David Copperfield
author: 7 Dickens
Barkley, Catherine
character in: 15 A Farewell to Arms
author: 9 Hemingway
Barlach, Ernst
born: 5 Wedel **7** Germany **8** Holstein
artwork: 9 Expellees **10** Seated Girl, Singing Man **11** Man in a Stock **13** Mater Dolorosa **14** Crippled Beggar, The Hovering One **16** Man Drawing a Sword **25** The Community of the Holy Ones
barn 4 mews **6** corral, stable
Barnabas
companion: 4 Paul
Barnaby Jones
character: 7 J R (Jedediah Romano) Jones **8** Lt Biddle **10** Betty Jones
cast: 9 Mark Shera **10** Buddy Ebsen, John Carter **13** Lee Meriwether
Barnaby Rudge
author: 14 Charles Dickens
character: 8 Mrs Rudge **9** Miss Miggs **10** John Willet **11** Dolly Varden **12** Emma Haredale **13** Edward Chester, Gabriel Varden **14** Reuben Haredale, Simon Tappertit, Sir John Chester **16** Dennis the Hangman, Geoffrey

Haredale
subject: 11 Gordon riots
Barnard, Christiaan
field: 7 surgery **8** medicine
nationality: 12 South African
performed first: 15 heart transplant
Barnard, Edward Emerson
field: 9 astronomy
named for him: 12 red dwarf star
Barnes, Jake
character in: 15 The Sun Also Rises
author: 9 Hemingway
Barney Google
creator: 11 Billy DeBeck
character: 11 Snuffy Smith
baby: 5 Bunky
horse: 9 Spark Plug
Barney Miller
character: 8 (Det) Phil Fish **9** (Det)
Ron Harris **10** (Det Wojo) Wojo-
howicz, (Det) Nick Yamana, (Officer)
Carl Levitt **14** Inspector Luger, (Det)
Arthur Dietrich
cast: 7 Jack Soo **8** Ron Carey, Ron
Glass **9** Abe Vigoda, Hal Linden **11**
Maxwell Gail **12** James Gregory **15**
Steve Landesberg
Barnstock *see* **9** Branstock
Baroja y Nessi, Pio
author of: 15 Caesar or Nothing **23**
The Struggle for Existence **26** Mem-
orias de un Hombre de Accion
barometer
invented by: 10 Torricelli
baroque 6 florid, ornate **10** flamboyant
11 extravagant
Barrack-Room Ballads
author: 14 Rudyard Kipling
barracks 3 BOQ **4** base, camp **7** lodging **8** garrison
barrage 5 blast, burst, salvo, spray **6**
ack-ack, deluge, shower, stream, vol-
ley **7** battery, torrent **8** shelling **9** cannonade, fusillade **10** outpouring **11**
bombardment
barrel 3 keg, tub, tun, vat **4** butt, cask,
drum, tube **8** hogshead
abbreviation: 3 bar, bbl
barren 3 dry **4** arid, dull **5** stale, waste
6 farrow, futile **7** austere, prosaic,
sterile, useless **8** depleted, desolate,
infecund **9** fruitless, infertile **10** lackluster, unfruitful **11** ineffectual, uninspiring, unrewarding **12** unproductive
13 uninformative, uninstructive, uninteresting
barrenness 8 bareness **9** bleakness,
emptiness **10** desolation
barren wilderness 6 desert **9** wasteland
barricade 5 block, fence **7** barrier, bulwark, rampart **8** blockade, obstacle,
obstruct **10** impediment **11** obstruction
Barrie, Sir James M
author of: 7 The Will **8** Mary Rose,

Peter Pan **10** Dear Brutus **13** Quality
Street **15** Margaret Ogilvie, The Wedding Guest **17** Alice Sit-By-the-Fire,
The Little Minister **18** A Kiss for Cinderella, The Twelve- Pound Look **19**
What Every Woman Knows **20** Shall
We Join the Ladies?, The Admirable
Crichton
character: 8 Peter Pan **10** Tinkerbell
11 Captain Hook
Darling children: 4 John **5** Wendy
7 Michael
nurse/Newfoundland dog: 4 Nana
setting: 14 Never-Never Land
barrier 3 bar **4** moat, wall **5** ditch,
fence, hedge **6** hurdle, trench **7** rampart **8** blockade, handicap, obstacle **9**
barricade, hindrance **10** difficulty, impediment, limitation **11** obstruction,
restriction **13** fortification **14** stumbling block
Barrier, The
author: 8 Rex Beach
barring 3 but **4** save **6** except, saving
7 besides **9** excepting, excluding,
other than **11** exclusive of
barrister 6 lawyer **7** counsel **8** advocate, attorney **9** counselor **10** mouthpiece **13** attorney-at-law
barroom 3 bar, pub, **6** bistro, lounge,
saloon, tavern **7** taproom
barrow 4 heap, pile **5** mound **7** tumu-
lus **8** handcart, pushcart **11** wheelbarrow
Barrow, Joe Louis
real name of: 8 Joe Louis
Barry, Gene
real name: 11 Eugene Klass
born: 9 New York NY
roles: 9 Burke's Law **11** Thunder
Road **12** Bat Masterson **16** The
Name of the Game **17** The War of
the Worlds
Barry, John
served in: 16 Revolutionary War
commander of ship: 7 Raleigh **8** Alliance **9** Effingham, Lexington
ship captured: 6 Edward
Barry, Redmond
character in: 11 Barry Lyndon
author: 9 Thackeray
Barry, Sir Charles
architect of: 8 Cliveden **14** City Art
Gallery (Manchester) **18** Houses of
Parliament (London)
Barry Lyndon
author: 25 William Makepeace
Thackeray
character: 12 Redmond Barry **14** Lord
Bullingdon **17** Lady Honoria Lyndon
(Countess of Lyndon) **19** Chevalier
de Balibari
director: 14 Stanley Kubrick
cast: 9 Ryan O'Neal **11** Hardy Kruger
12 Patrick Magee **14** Marisa Berenson
Barrymore, Ethel

real name: 14 Ethel Mae Blythe
brother: 4 John **6** Lionel
born: 14 Philadelphia PA
roles: 11 A Doll's House **14** The Corn
Is Green **16** Portrait of Jennie **19**
Trelawney of the Wells **21** None But
the Lonely Heart, Rasputin and the
Empress
Barrymore, John
real name: 10 John Blythe
brother: 6 Lionel
sister: 5 Ethel
son: 17 John Drew Barrymore
daughter: 14 Diana Barrymore
granddaughter: 4 Drew
nickname: 12 Great Profile
born: 14 Philadelphia PA
roles: 6 Hamlet **7** Don Juan **8** Moby
Dick, Svengali **9** Richard IV **10**
Grand Hotel **11** Beau Brummel **13**
Dinner at Eight **17** Dr Jekyll and Mr
Hyde **21** Rasputin and the Empress
Barrymore, Lionel
real name: 12 Lionel Blythe
brother: 4 John
sister: 5 Ethel
born: 14 Philadelphia PA
roles: 7 The Jest **9** A Free Soul (Oscar), (friend of) Dr Kildare **11** Dr Gillespie **13** Peter Ibbitson, The Copperhead **21** Rasputin and the Empress
Barsabbas *see* **6** Joseph
Barstad, John
character in: 16 A Tale of Two Cities
author: 7 Dickens
Bart, Lily
character in: 15 The House of Mirth
author: 7 Wharton
barter 4 swap **5** trade **8** exchange **11**
interchange
Bartered Bride, The
opera by: 7 Smetana
character: 5 Jenik, Kecal, Micha,
Vasek **7** Marenka
Barth, John
author of: 7 Chimera **12** Giles Goat-
Boy **15** The End of the Road **16** The
Floating Opera, The Sot-Weed Factor
17 Lost in the Funhouse
Barthelme, Donald
author of: 7 Sadness **8** City Life **9**
Great Days, Snow White **12** Sixty
Stories **13** The Dead Father **15** Guilty
Pleasures **18** Come Back Dr Caligari
33 Unspeakable Practices Unnatural
Acts
Bartholdi, Frederic-Auguste
born: 6 Alsace, Colmar
artwork: 13 Lion of Belfort **26** Liberty
Enlightening the World (Statue of
Liberty)
Bartholo, Dr
character in: 18 The Barber of Seville
19 The Marriage of Figaro
author: 12 Beaumarchais
Bartholomew 7 apostle
also called: 9 Nathanael

Bartholomew Fair
author: 9 Ben Jonson

Bartok, Bela
born: 7 Hungary 15 Nagyszentmiklos
composer of: 9 Wrestling 11 Mikrokosmos 12 Divertimento 14 Cantata Profana 15 The Wooden Prince 20 Duke Bluebeard's Castle 21 The Miraculous Mandarin

Bartolommeo, Fra
born: 5 Italy 8 Florence
real name: 31 Bartolommeo di Pagolo del Fattorino
artwork: 5 Jonah 6 Isaiah 13 Salvator Mundi 15 The Last Judgment 17 Vision of St Bernard 24 Madonna della Misericordia 30 The Mystic Marriage of St Catherine

Barton, Benjamin Smith
field: 6 botany
noted for first American: 14 botany textbook

Bartram, John
field: 6 botany
noted for first American: 12 hybrid plants

Baruch
father: 5 Judah 6 Neriah
friend and scribe of: 8 Jeremiah

Baruch, Bernard
9 statesman, financier

basal 3 key 4 easy 5 basic, vital 6 simple 7 initial, minimal, primary 8 cardinal 9 beginning, essential, intrinsic, necessary 10 elementary, lower-level, simplified 11 fundamental, rudimentary 12 prerequisite 13 indispensable

bas bleu 12 bluestocking

base 3 bad, bed, key, low 4 camp, core, foul, mean, post, root, vile 5 basis, dirty, gross, heart, petty, place, stand 6 abject, billet, bottom, craven, ground, impure, locate, scurvy, sinful, sneaky, sordid, source, vulgar, wicked 7 alloyed, corrupt, debased, essence, found on, ignoble, immoral, install, model on, scrubby, situate, station, support 8 backbone, cowardly, degraded, depraved, garrison, infamous, inferior, pedestal, rudiment, shameful, spurious, unworthy 9 dastardly, dissolute, establish, faithless, insidious, nefarious, principle 10 degenerate, derive from, despicable, detestable, evil-minded, foundation, groundwork, iniquitous, villainous 11 adulterated, disgraceful, ignominious, poor quality, scoundrelly 12 black-hearted, contemptible, dishonorable, disreputable, installation, substructure, underpinning, unprincipled 13 discreditable, reprehensible

baseball
term: 3 bag, ERA, fan, RBI, run 4 balk, base, bunt, bush 5 choke, curve, error, fungo, liner, pop-up, slide 6 assist, bat-ter, cellar, double, dugout, duster, inning, on deck, relief (pitcher), rookie, single, slider, triple, umpire, windup 7 blooper, bullpen, catcher, cleanup, fly ball, home run, infield, pickoff, pitcher, rhubarb, rundown, shutout, slugger 8 bean ball, changeup, grounder, keystone, no hitter, outfield, pitchout, southpaw, spitball 9 bleachers, brushback, grand slam, hot corner, infielder, line drive, sacrifice, shortstop 10 bush league, gopher ball, infield fly, outfielder, passed ball 11 bases loaded, knuckleball, pinch hitter, triple crown, World Series 12 Texas leaguer 16 designated hitter, earned run average

Hall of Fame:
1936: 4 Cobb (Ty), Ruth (Babe) 6 Wagner (Honus) 7 Johnson (Walter) 9 Mathewson (Christy)
1937: 4 Mack (Connie) 5 Young (Cy) 6 Lajoie (Nap), McGraw (John), Wright (George) 7 Johnson (Ban), Speaker (Tris) 8 Bulkeley (Morgan)
1938: 8 Chadwick (Henry) 9 Alexander (Grover) 10 Cartwright (Alexander)
1939: 5 Anson (Cap), Ewing (Buck) 6 Gehrig (Lou), Keeler (Willie), Sisler (George) 7 Collins (Eddie) 8 Comiskey (Charlie), Cummings (Candy), Spalding (Albert) 9 Radbourne (Old Hoss)
1942: 7 Hornsby (Rogers)
1944: 7 Kenesaw (M. Landis)
1945: 5 Duffy (Hugh), Kelly (King) 6 Clarke (Fred) 7 Collins (Jimmy), O'Rourke (Jim) 8 Jennings (Hughey), Robinson (Wilbert) 9 Bresnahan (Roger), Brouthers (Dan), Delahanty (Ed)
1946: 5 Evers (Johnny), Plank (Eddie), Walsh (Ed) 6 Chance (Frank), Tinker (Joe) 7 Burkett (Jesse), Chesbro (Jack), Waddell (Rube) 8 Griffith (Clark), McCarthy (Tommy) 9 McGinnity (Joe)
1947: 5 Grove (Lefty) 6 Frisch (Frankie) 7 Hubbell (Carl) 8 Cochrane (Mickey)
1948: 7 Pennock (Herb), Traynor (Pie)
1949: 5 Brown (Mordecai) 7 Nichols (Kid) 9 Gehringer (Charlie)
1951: 3 Ott (Mel) 4 Foxx (Jimmie)
1952: 5 Waner (Paul) 8 Heilmann (Harry)
1953: 4 Dean (Dizzy), Klem (Bill) 6 Barrow (Ed), Bender (Chief), Wright (Harry) 7 Simmons (Al), Wallace (Bobby) 8 Connolly (Tom)
1954: 5 Terry (Bill) 6 Dickey (Bill)
1955: 5 Baker (Frank), Lyons (Ted), Vance (Dazzy) 6 Schalk (Ray) 8 DiMaggio (Joe), Hartnett (Gabby) 10 Maranville (Rabbit)
1956: 6 Cronin (Joe) 9 Greenberg (Hank)
1957: 8 Crawford (Sam), McCarthy (Joe)
1959: 5 Wheat (Zach)
1961: 5 Carey (Max) 8 Hamilton (Billy)
1962: 5 Roush (Edd) 6 Feller (Bob) 8 Robinson (Jackie) 9 McKechnie (Bill)
1963: 4 Rice (Sam), Eppa (Rixey) 5 Flick (Elmer) 8 Clarkson (John)
1964: 4 Ward (Monte) 5 Faber (Red), Keefe (Tim) 6 Grimes (Burleigh), Manush (Heinie) 7 Appling (Luke), Huggins (Miller)
1965: 6 Galvin (Pud)
1966: 7 Stengel (Casey) 8 Williams (Ted)
1967: 5 Waner (Lloyd) 6 Rickey (Branch) 7 Ruffing (Red)
1968: 6 Cuyler (Kiki), Goslin (Goose) 7 Medwick (Joe)
1969: 4 Hoyt (Waite) 6 Musial (Stan) 9 Coveleski (Stan) 10 Campanella (Roy)
1970: 5 Combs (Earle), Frick (Ford) 6 Haines (Jesse) 8 Boudreau (Lou)
1971: 5 Paige (Satchel), Hafey (Chick), Weiss (George) 6 Hooper (Harry), Kelley (Joe) 7 Beckley (Jake) 8 Bancroft (Dave), Marquard (Rube)
1972: 4 Wynn (Early) 5 Berra (Yogi), Gomez (Lefty) 6 Gibson (Josh), Koufax (Sandy), Youngs (Ross) 7 Leonard (Buck) 8 Harridge (Will)
1973: 5 Evans (Billy), Irvin (Monte), Kelly (George), Spahn (Warren), Welch (Mickey) 8 Clemente (Roberto)
1974: 4 Bell (Cool Papa), Ford (Whitey) 6 Conlan (Jocko), Mantle (Mickey) 8 Thompson (Sam) 9 Bottomley (Jim)
1975 5 Kiner (Ralph) 6 Harris (Bucky), Herman (Billy) 7 Averill (Earl), Johnson (Judy)
1976: 5 Lemon (Bob) 6 Connor (Roger) 7 Hubbard (Cal), Roberts (Robin) 9 Lindstrom (Fred) 10 Charleston (Oscar)
1977: 5 Banks (Ernie), Lloyd (Pop), Lopez (Al), Rusie (Amos) 6 Dihigo (Martin), Sewell (Joe)
1978: 4 Joss (Addie) 7 Mathews (Eddie) 8 MacPhail (Larry)
1979: 4 Mays (Willie) 5 Giles (Warren) 6 Wilson (Hack)
1980: 5 Klein (Chuck) 6 Kaline (Al), Snider (Duke), Yawkey (Tom)
1981: 4 Mize (Johnny) 6 Foster (Rube), Gibson (Bob)

1982: 5 Aaron (Hank) **7** Jackson (Travis) **8** Chandler (Happy), Robinson (Frank)
1983: 4 Kell (George) **6** Alston (Walter) **8** Marichal (Juan), Robinson (Brooks)
1984: 5 Reese (Pee Wee) **7** Ferrell (Rick) **8** Aparicio (Luis), Drysdale (Don) **9** Killebrew (Harmon)
1985: 5 Brock (Lou) **7** Vaughan (Arky), Wilhelm (Hoyt) **9** Slaughter (Enos)
1986: 5 Doerr (Bobby) **7** McCovey (Willie) **8** Lombardi (Ernie)
1987: 6 Hunter (Jim "Catfish") **8** Williams (Billy) **9** Dandridge (Ray)
1988: 8 Stargell (Willie)
1989: 5 Bench (Johnny) **7** Barlick (Al) **11** Yastrzemski (Carl) **12** Schoendienst (Red)
1990: 6 Morgan (Joe), Palmer (Jim)
1991: 5 Carew (Rod), Perry (Gaylord), Veeck (Bill) **7** Jenkins (Ferguson), Lazzeri (Tony)
1992: 6 Seaver (Tom) **7** Fingers (Rollie), McGowan (Bill) **9** Newhouser (Hal)
1993: 7 Jackson (Reggie)
1994: 7 Carlton (Steve), Rizzuto (Phil "Scooter") **8** Durocher (Leo)
other player/coach: 7 Jim Rice **8** Pete Rose, Vida Blue **9** Alvin Dark, Bowie Kuhn, Gil Hodges, Hank Bauer, Luis Tiant, Nellie Fox, Nolan Ryan, Ralph Houk, Ron Guidry, Ted Turner, Tommy John **10** Boog Powell, Earl Weaver, Maury Wills, Roger Maris, Sparky Lyle **11** Billy Martin, Dave Kingman, Frank Thomas, George Brett, Mark Fidrych, Mike Schmidt, Rich Gossage **12** Graig Nettles, Dave Winfield, Dennis McLain, Dick Williams, Elston Howard, Ken Griffey Jr, Tommy Lasorda **13** Rocky Colavito, Thurman Munson, Walter O'Malley **14** Keith Hernandez, Peter Ueberroth, Sparky Anderson **15** Rickey Henderson **16** Darryl Strawberry **18** Fernando Valenzuela, George Steinbrenner

baseball leagues
National: 11 Chicago Cubs, New York Mets **13** Atlanta Braves, Houston Astros, Montreal Expos **14** Cincinnati Reds, Florida Marlins, San Diego Padres **15** Colorado Rockies **16** Milwaukee Brewers, St Louis Cardinals **17** Los Angeles Dodgers, Pittsburgh Pirates **18** San Francisco Giants **19** Arizona Diamondbacks **20** Philadelphia Phillies
American: 9 Oakland A's **12** Boston Red Sox, Texas Rangers **13** Anaheim Angels, Detroit Tigers **14** Minnesota Twins, New York Yankees **15** Chicago White Sox, Seattle Mariners,

Toronto Blue Jays **16** Baltimore Orioles, Cleveland Indians, Kansas City Royals, Oakland Athletics **17** Tampa Bay Devil Rays

baseball team
Anaheim: 6 Angels
stadium: 11 Edison Field **7** Anaheim
Atlanta: 6 Braves
stadium: 11 Turner Field
Arizona 12 Diamondbacks
stadium: 15 Bank One Ballpark
Baltimore: 7 Orioles
stadium: 11 Camden Yards
Boston: 6 Red Sox
stadium: 10 Fenway Park
Chicago: 4 Cubs
stadium: 12 Wrigley Field
Chicago: 8 White Sox
stadium: 12 Comiskey Park
Cleveland: 7 Indians
stadium: 11 Jacobs Field
Cincinnati: 4 Reds
stadium: 10 Riverfront **12** Cinergy Field
Colorado: 7 Rockies
stadium: 8 Mile High **10** Coors Field
Detroit: 6 Tigers
stadium: 6 Tiger
Florida: 7 Marlins
stadium: 9 Joe Robbie, Pro Player
Houston: 6 Astros
stadium: 9 Astrodome
Kansas City: 6 Royals
stadium: 8 Kauffman
Los Angeles: 7 Dodgers
stadium: 6 Dodger **18** Los Angeles Coliseum
Milwaukee: 7 Brewers
stadium: 6 County
Minnesota: 5 Twins
stadium: 12 Metropolitan **24** Hubert H Humphrey Metrodome
Montreal: 5 Expos
stadium: 7 Olympic
New York: 4 Mets
stadium: 4 Shea
New York: 7 Yankees
stadium: 6 Yankee
Oakland: 2 A's
stadium: 7 Oakland **8** Coliseum
Philadelphia: 8 Phillies
stadium: 8 Veterans
Pittsburgh: 7 Pirates
stadium: 11 Three Rivers
St Louis: 9 Cardinals
stadium: 13 Busch Memorial
San Diego: 6 Padres
stadium: 8 Qualcomm **10** Jack Murphy
San Francisco: 6 Giants
stadium: 7 3Com Park **15** Candlestick Park
Seattle: 8 Mariners
stadium: 8 Kingdome
Tampa bay: 9 Devil Rays
stadium: 14 Tropicana Field

Texas: 7 Rangers
stadium: 11 The Ballpark
Toronto: 8 Blue Jays
stadium: 7 Sky Dome

baseless 7 unsound **9** unfactual, unfounded **10** groundless, ungrounded **11** unjustified, unsupported **12** without basis **13** unjustifiable **14** uncorroborated **15** unsubstantiated

basement 5 below **6** bottom, cellar **15** underground room

baseness 7 lowness **8** meanness, vileness **9** depravity **11** ignobleness **14** iniquitousness **16** contemptibleness

base of operations
Greek: 6 pou sto

bash 4 blow **5** blast, clout, crack, knock, party, whack **7** clopper **8** winging **9** bacchanal

Bashemath *see* **4** Adah

bashful 3 shy **5** timid **6** demure, modest **8** blushing, reserved, reticent, retiring, sheepish, skittish, timorous **9** diffident, shrinking, uncertain **10** shamefaced **11** constrained, unconfident

bashfulness 7 shyness **10** diffidence **12** sheepishness **14** self-effacement **15** unassertiveness

basic 3 key **4** base, core **5** prime, vital **7** bedrock, primary **8** rudiment **9** essential, intrinsic **10** elementary, foundation **11** fundamental, rudimentary **12** foundational, prerequisite, underpinning

basically
French: 6 au fond

basic ideas 6 basics **7** essence, factors, origins **8** elements, features **9** rudiments **10** principles **11** foundations

basic need 9 essential, necessity, requisite, vital part **10** key element, sine qua non

basic part 4 unit **7** element **9** component **10** ingredient **11** constituent **13** building block

basic quality 6 nature **7** essence **9** principle, substance **12** quintessence

basics 4 ABCs **8** elements **9** rudiments **10** principles **11** nitty-gritty **12** fundamentals

basil
also called: 6 tulasi
botanical name: 6 Ocimum **8** O minimum **10** O basilicum
means: 5 royal **6** kingly, lizard (basilisk)
nickname: 14 kiss-me-Nicholas
origin: 5 India
sacred to: 6 Vishnu **7** Krishna, Lakshmi
symbol of: 4 hate, love
use: 5 pasta, pesto, sauce **10** vegetables

basilica 6 church 10 house of God 14 house of worship

Basilisk
form: 6 dragon

basin 3 pan, tub, vat 4 bowl, dale, dell, font, glen, sink 5 gulch, gully, stoup 6 crater, hollow, lavabo, ravine, tureen, valley 7 dishpan, washtub 8 lavatory, sinkhole, washbowl 9 porringer, washbasin, washstand 10 depression, finger bowl

basis, bases 4 base, root 6 ground 7 bedrock 9 essential, principle 10 foundation, touchstone 11 cornerstone, fundamental 12 underpinning 13 starting point

bask 5 revel, savor 6 relish, wallow 7 delight 8 sunbathe 9 luxuriate 11 warm oneself 12 soak up warmth, toast oneself

basket 5 cesta, crate 6 barrel, hamper 7 carrier, pannier 8 bassinet, canister

basketball
term: 3 key 4 dunk, hoop, pick, post, trap, zone 5 court, guard, lay-up, pivot, point, press, steal 6 assist, basket, center 7 dribble, forward, palming, rebound, referee 8 charging, hook shot, jump shot, sixth man, turnover 9 backboard, backcourt, fast break, field goal, free throw, give-and-go, traveling 11 goal tending, pick-and-roll 12 three-pointer

Hall of Fame:
1959: 5 Allen (Phog; Forrest Clare), Hyatt (Charles), Mikan (George), Olsen (Harold), Stagg (Amos Alonzo), Tower (Oswald) 6 Gulick (Luther), Hickox (Edward), Morgan (Ralph) 7 Carlson (Henry), Kennedy (Matthew) 8 Luisetti (Hank), Meanwell (Walter E), Naismith (James), Schommer (John) 15 Original Celtics
1960: 5 Blood (Ernest) 6 Hanson (Victor), Keaney (Frank), Murphy (Charles), Porter (Henry), Wooden (John) 7 Hepbron (George), Lambert (Ward) 8 Macauley (Ed) 9 McCracken (Branch)
1961: 4 Hoyt (George) 5 Sachs (Leonard), Tobey (David), Walsh (David) 6 Keogan (George), O'Brien (John), Roosma (John) 7 Kurland (Bob), Phillip (Andy), Quigley (Ernest), Trester (Arthur), Wachter (Edward) 8 Borgmann (Bernhard) 9 Steinmetz (Christian) 10 DeBernardi (Forrest), Schabinger (Arthur) 14 Buffalo Germans
1962: 4 Page (Harlan) 6 Sedran (Barney), St John (Lynn) 8 Thompson (John) 9 McCracken (Jack) 10 Morgenweck (Frank)
1963: 4 Reid (William) 7 Gruenig (Robert) 11 New York Rens
1964: 4 Bunn (John) 5 Irish (Ned),

Jones (R William) 6 Foster (Harold), Holman (Nat) 7 Russell (John) 8 Loeffler (Kenneth)
1965: 5 Brown (Walter) 6 Hinkle (Paul), Hobson (Howard), Mokray (William)
1966: 4 Dean (Everett) 8 Lapchick (Joe)
1967: 3 Bee (Clair) 4 Cann (Howard), Gill (Amory) 6 Julian (Alvin)
1968: 3 Iba (Hank; Henry P) 4 Rupp (Adolph F) 6 Taylor (Charles H) 7 Denhart (Henry G) 8 Auerbach (Red; Arnold J)
1969: 6 Davies (Bob) 9 Carnevale (Bernard L)
1970: 5 Cousy (Bob) 6 Pettit (Bob) 10 Saperstein (Abe)
1971: 5 Wells (W R Clifford) 6 Diddle (Edgar A) 7 Douglas (Robert L) 8 Endacott (Paul), Friedman (Max), Gottlieb (Edward)
1972: 5 Drake (Bruce) 6 Ripley (Elmer H), Wooden (John) 7 Beckman (John), Lonborg (Arthur C), Schayes (Dolph)
1973: 6 Fisher (Harry A) 7 Schmidt (Ernest) 8 Podoloff (Maurice)
1974: 6 Liston (Emil) 7 Brennan (Joseph), Russell (Bill) 9 Vandivier (Robert)
1975 4 Gola (Tom) 6 Krause (Edward W) 7 Litwack (Harry), Sharman (Bill)
1976: 4 Gale (Lauren) 6 Baylor (Elgin), Cooper (Charles T) 7 Johnson (Wiliam C), McGuire (Frank)
1977: 5 Fulks (Joe), Hagan (Cliff) 6 Arizin (Paul) 7 Pollard (Jim) 8 Nucatola (John P)
1978: 5 Barry (Sam; Justin M), Meyer (Raymond J) 6 Hickey (Edgar S), Newell (Peter F) 7 Enright (James E) 8 McLendon (John B) 11 Chamberlain (Wilt)
1979: 4 West (Jerry) 5 Lucas (Jerry) 7 Shelton (Everett), Shirley (J Dallas) 8 Harrison (Lester) 9 Robertson (Oscar)
1980: 4 Hepp (Ferenc) 6 Barlow (Thomas B) 7 Kennedy (J Walter) 9 McCutchan (Arad A)
1981: 4 Case (Everett N), Duer (Alva O), Reed (Willis) 5 Greer (Hal) 6 Gaines (Clarence E), Martin (Slater), Ramsey (Frank)
1982: 5 Leith (Lloyd R), Smith (Dean E), Wilke (Louis G) 6 Twyman (Jack) 7 Bradley (Bill) 11 DeBusschere (Dave)
1983: 5 Fagan (Clifford B), Jones (Sam) 6 Steitz (Edward S) 7 Gardner (Jack) 8 Havlicek (John)
1984: 4 Wade (L Margaret) 5 Cervi (Al) 6 Abbott (Senda Berenson), Teague (Bertha F) 8 Anderson (W Harold), Harshman (Marv K), Thurmond (Nate)

1985--1986: 5 Watts (Stanley H) 6 Taylor (Fred R) 7 Holzman (Red), Mihalik (Red) 8 Heinsohn (Tom) 10 Cunningham (Billy)
1986--1987: 5 Barry (Rick) 6 Wanzer (Bobby) 7 Frazier (Walt) 8 Houbregs (Robert J), Maravich (Pete)
1987--1988: 6 Miller (Ralph H), Unseld (Wes) 9 McDermott (Robert), Lovelette (Clyde)
1988--1989: 5 Gates (William "Pop"), Jones (K C) 7 Wilkens (Lenny)
1989--1990 4 Bing (Dave) 5 Hayes (Elvin) 6 Monroe (Earl) 8 Johnston (Neil)
1990--1991: 6 Cowens (Dave), Knight (Bobby), O'Brien (Lawrence F) 8 Fleisher (Lawrence), Gallatin (Harry) 9 Archibald (Nate), Stankovic (Borislav)
1991--1992: 5 Belov (Sergei), White (Nera) 6 Lanier (Bob), Ramsay (Jack) 7 Hawkins (Connie), McGuire (Al) 8 Woolpert (Phillip) 10 Carnesecca (Louie) 13 Harris-Stewart (Lusia)
1992--1993: 5 Issel (Dan) 6 Erving (Julius), Meyers (Ann), Murphy (Calvin), Walton (Bill) 7 Bellamy (Walter), McGuire (Dick) 9 Semjonova (Uljana)
1994: 4 Crum (Denny), Daly (Charles J) 6 Rubini (Cesare) 9 Jeannette (Buddy) 11 Blazejowski (Carol)

other player/coach: 8 Pat Riley 9 Bob McAdoo, Larry Bird 10 Danny Ainge, Kobe Bryant 11 Alex English, Bernard King, Bill Lambeer, Dick Barnett, James Worthy, Kevin McHale, Lew Alcindor, Moses Malone 12 Clyde Drexler, George Gervin, Isaiah Thomas, Larry Johnson, Patrick Ewing, Robert Parish 13 David Robinson, Earvin (Magic) Johnson, Michael Jordan, Scottie Pippen, Terry Cummings 14 Charles Barkley, Hakeem Olajuwon, Shaquille O'Neal 17 Kareem Abdul-Jabbar

basketball team
league: 3 NBA 29 National Basketball Association
Atlanta: 5 Hawks
Boston: 7 Celtics
Charlotte: 7 Hornets
Chicago: 5 Bulls
Cleveland: 9 Cavaliers
Dallas: 9 Mavericks
Denver: 7 Nuggets
Detroit: 7 Pistons
Golden State: 8 Warriors
Houston: 7 Rockets
Indiana: 6 Pacers
Los Angeles: 6 Lakers 8 Clippers
Miami: 4 Heat

Milwaukee: **5** Bucks
Minnesota: **12** Timberwolves
New Jersey: **4** Nets
New York: **14** Knickerbockers
Orlando: **5** Magic
Philadelphia: **5** 76ers **13** Seventy-Sixers
Phoenix: **4** Suns
Portland: **12** Trail Blazers
Sacramento: **5** Kings
San Antonio: **5** Spurs
Seattle: **11** SuperSonics
Toronto: **7** Raptors
Utah: **4** Jazz
Vancouver: **9** Grizzlies
Washington: **7** Wizards
WNBA
Charlotte: **5** Sting
Cleveland: **7** Rockers
Detroit: **5** Shock
Houston: **6** Comets
Los Angeles: **6** Sparks
New York: **7** Liberty
Phoenix: **7** Mercury
Sacramento: **8** Monarchs
Utah: **6** Starzz
Washington: **7** Mystics

Basque
language spoken in: **5** Italy, Spain **6** France

bas-relief
Italian: **12** basso-rilievo

bass **3** low **4** alto **5** basso **7** harmony **8** baritone, bass clef

bass
types: **3** sea **4** rock **5** black **6** calico **7** striped, sunfish **10** largemouth, smallmouth
characteristic: **10** forked-tail **12** spiny-finned

Bassanio
character in: **19** The Merchant of Venice
author: **11** Shakespeare

basso-rilievo **9** bas-relief

Bast, Jacky and Leonard
characters in: **10** Howards End
author: **9** E M Forster

bastard **6** impure **8** inferior, spurious **9** imperfect, irregular, love child **12** natural child **17** illegitimate child

bastardize **6** debase, weaken **7** degrade **9** downgrade

baste **3** sew **4** drip **5** roast **6** cudgel, flavor, stitch, thrash **7** moisten **15** temporary stitch

bastinado **4** beat, blow, cane, drub **5** whale **7** beating **8** drubbing

bastion **4** fort **5** tower **6** pillar **7** bulwark, citadel, rampart **8** barbette, fortress **10** breastwork, stronghold

bat **3** hit, rod **4** cane, clip, club, cuff, mace, slug, sock **5** baton, billy, knock, smack, staff, stick, whack **6** buffet, cudgel, mallet, strike, thwack, wallop **7** clobber **8** bludgeon **9** blackjack, truncheon **10** shillelagh

batch **3** lot **5** bunch, crowd, group, stock **6** amount, number **8** quantity **9** aggregate **10** collection

Bates, Alan
born: **7** England **9** Allestree **10** Derbyshire
roles: **6** Hamlet **8** The Fixer **10** Duet for One, Georgy Girl **12** King of Hearts **13** A Kind of Loving, The Collection, Zorba the Greek **16** An Unmarried Woman **18** An Englishman Abroad, A Prayer for the Dying **22** Far From the Madding Crowd

Bates, Kathy
born: **7** Memphis
roles: **6** Misery **7** Titanic **10** Diabolique, Used People **12** The Late Shift, Men Don't Leave **18** Fried Green Tomatoes

Bates, Miss
character in: **4** Emma
author: **6** Austen

Bateson, William
field: **7** biology
nationality: **7** British
founded: **8** genetics

bath **3** dip, tub **4** wash **5** sauna **6** douche, shower **7** washing **8** ablution, lavement **9** cleansing, immersion, steam bath **10** irrigation
type: **3** hip, mud **4** sitz **5** steam **6** shower, sponge **7** Turkish bath

bathe **3** dip, tub, wet **4** lave, soak, wash **5** douse **6** douche, shower, sponge **7** cleanse **8** irrigate

bathing **3** dip, tub **6** laving, plunge **7** washing **8** swimming **9** ablutions, immersion

bathos **4** corn, mush **5** slush **8** schmaltz **9** mushiness, soppiness **10** maudlinism, slushiness **11** false pathos, mawkishness **14** sentimentalism, sentimentality

bathroom **2** W C **3** can, loo **4** head, john **5** biffy **6** toilet **7** commode, latrine **8** facility, lavatory, men's room, restroom, washroom **10** ladies' room, powder room **11** water closet **14** little boys' room **15** little girls' room

Bathsheba
also: **8** Bathshua
father: **5** Eliam
husband: **5** David, Uriah
son: **7** Solomon
grandfather: **10** Ahithophel

Batman
character: **6** Alfred **7** Egghead, King Tut **8** Catwoman, The Joker **10** Bruce Wayne (Batman), Chief O'Hara, The Penguin, The Riddler **11** Dick Grayson (Robin) **13** Barbara Gordon (Batgirl) **17** Aunt Harriet Cooper **24** Police Commissioner Gordon
cast: **8** Adam West, Burt Ward **9** John Astin **10** Alan Napier, Eartha Kitt, Madge Blake **11** Cesar Romero, Julie Newmar, Victor Buono, Yvonne Craig **12** Frank Gorshin, Neil Hamilton, Stafford Repp, Vincent Price **13** Lee Meriwether **15** Burgess Meredith
city: **10** Gotham City
nickname: **9** Boy Wonder **10** Dynamic Duo **13** Caped Crusader
gimmick: **6** Batlab **8** Batphone **9** Batmobile, Batsignal

Bat Masterson
cast: **9** Gene Barry

baton **3** bat, rod **4** club, mace, wand **5** billy, crook, staff, stick **6** cudgel, fasces **7** crosier, scepter, war club **8** bludgeon, caduceus **9** billy club, truncheon **10** nightstick, shillelagh

batter **4** beat, lash, maul **5** break, crush, pound, smash, smite **6** beat up, buffet, mangle, pummel **7** clobber, shatter

battercake **6** waffle **7** biscuit, pancake

battered **4** shot **6** beat-up, ruined, shabby **8** decrepit **11** dilapidated **12** disreputable

battery **3** set **4** army, band, pack, team **5** block, cadre, force, group, suite, troop **6** caning, cannon, convoy, legion, lineup, outfit, series **7** beating, brigade, company, hitting, hurting, maiming, phalanx, section **8** armament, cannonry, clubbing, division, drubbing, flogging, ordnance, squadron, whipping, wounding **9** cudgeling, spearhead, strapping, thrashing

battle **3** war **4** bout, duel, feud, fray, meet **5** argue, brawl, clash, fight, siege **6** action, affray, combat, debate, engage, tussle **7** contend, contest, crusade, dispute, quarrel, warfare **8** campaign, conflict, skirmish, struggle **9** agitation, encounter, firefight **10** engagement **11** altercation, controversy **13** confrontation

Battle, final
place: **10** Armageddon

battle cry **6** war cry **8** Geronimo, war whoop **9** Rebel yell

Battle Cry
author: **8** Leon Uris

battlefield **5** arena, lists **8** the front, war arena **9** front line **10** battle line, no man's land **11** battlefront **12** battleground

battleground **5** arena, lists **11** battlefield, battlefront

Battle of the Books
author: **13** Jonathan Swift

battle-ready **5** armed **7** arrayed **8** prepared **9** fortified

battleship **4** Iowa **5** Maine **6** Oregon **7** carrier, warship **8** Missouri **9** Ironsides, New Jersey, Wisconsin **10** bluish-gray **11** Dreadnought **12** Constitution
first: **7** Gloire
largest: **6** Yamato
German: **8** Graf Spee

Battus
ruler of: **5** Libya
form: **7** peasant
witness to: **11** cattle theft
thief: **6** Hermes
turned to: **5** stone
cured of: **16** speech impediment

batty 4 nuts **5** crazy, loony, queer, wacko, wacky **6** cuckoo, crazed **7** bat-like, cracked

bauble 3 toy **4** bead **6** geegaw, trifle **7** trinket **8** gimcrack, ornament

Baucis
form: **7** peasant
home: **7** Phrygia
husband: **8** Philemon
offered hospitality to: **4** Zeus **6** Hermes

Baudelaire, Charles
author of: **13** Flowers of Evil **14** Les Fleurs du Mal

Baugh, Sammy
nickname: **13** Slinging Sammy
sport: **8** football
position: **11** quarterback
team: **18** Washington Redskins

Baum, Lyman Frank
author of: **13** The (Wonderful) Wizard of Oz **18** Father Goose His Book, Mother Goose in Prose

Baum, Vicki
author of: **8** Shanghai **10** Grand Hotel, Grand Opera **12** Men Never Know **13** A Tale from Bali, And Life Goes On

Baumer, Paul
character in: **25** All Quiet on the Western Front
author: **8** Remarque

Baumgarner, James
real name of: **11** James Garner

bawdy 4 blue, lewd, sexy **5** dirty, gross, lusty **6** coarse, earthy, ribald, risque, sexual, vulgar **7** raunchy **8** immodest, improper, indecent, off-color **10** indecorous, indelicate, licentious, suggestive

bawdy house 7 brothel **8** bordello, cathouse **10** fancy house, whorehouse **13** sporting house **14** house of ill fame **16** house of ill repute **19** house of prostitution

bawl 3 cry **4** call, howl, roar, wail, weep, yell, yowl **5** shout **6** bellow, clamor, cry out, squall **7** blubber, call out

bawling out 6 rebuke **7** censure, chiding, reproof **8** reproach, scolding **9** reprimand **10** chewing out, upbraiding **11** castigation, reprobation **12** dressing-down, remonstrance **13** tongue-lashing

bawl out 5 scold **6** berate, rail at, rebuke, yell at **7** censure, chew out, reprove, upbraid **8** admonish, reproach **9** castigate, dress down, reprimand **10**

take to task, tongue-lash **14** read the riot act

Bax, Arnold Edward Trevor
born: **6** London **7** England
composer of: **8** Tintagel **13** November Woods **14** Mater Ora Filium **15** The Garden of Fand **27** Overture to a Picaresque Comedy

Baxter, Anne
grandfather: **16** Frank Lloyd Wright
born: **14** Michigan City IN
roles: **8** Applause **11** All About Eve **13** The Razor's Edge

Baxter, Jody
character in: **11** The Yearling
author: **8** Rawlings

Baxter, William Sylvanus
character in: **9** Seventeen
author: **10** Tarkington

bay 3 cry, yap **4** bank, bark, cove, gulf, howl, nook, road, yelp **5** basin, bayou, bight, fiord, firth, inlet, niche, sound **6** alcove, bellow, clamor, lagoon, recess, strait **7** barking, estuary, howling, narrows, yapping, yelling, yelping **9** bellowing **11** compartment **13** natural harbor

bay (at bay) 7 trapped **8** cornered

bay leaf
botanical name: **12** Pimenta acris
expression: **16** to win one's laurels
from tree: **9** bay laurel
  transformation of: **6** Daphne
  tree sacred to: **6** Apollo
  laurel berries called: **10** bacca lauri
  source of: **13** baccalaureate
gives gift of: **8** prophecy
helps girls win back: **12** errant lovers
origin: **5** Italy
protects against: **5** death **6** poison **7** sorcery **11** evil spirits
symbol of: **7** victory (laurel wreath)
use: **4** fish, fowl, meat, soup, stew

bayou 4 slew **5** creek, inlet, marsh, river, swamp **6** outlet, slough, stream **9** backwater **13** stagnant marsh

Bayou State
nickname of: **9** Louisiana **11** Mississippi

Bay Psalm Book
author: **9** John Eliot

Bay State
nickname of: **13** Massachusetts

bazaar 4 fair, mart **6** market **8** carnival, exchange **11** charity fair, charity sale, marketplace

Bazile
character in: **18** The Barber of Seville
author: **12** Beaumarchais

Bazzard, Deputy
character in: **22** The Mystery of Edwin Drood
author: **7** Dickens

BC see **12** before Christ

B C

creator: **10** Johnny Hart
character: **3** Tor **4** Grog **5** Peter **8** anteater **10** Clumsy Carp **11** the Fat Broad
poet: **5** Wiley
era: **11** Neanderthal, prehistoric

BCE 15 before Common Era

be 4 last, live, stay **5** exist, occur **6** befall, endure, happen, remain **7** persist, subsist **8** continue **9** be present, take place **10** come to pass

be absent 4 miss **12** fail to attend

beach 5 coast, shore **6** strand **8** littoral, seashore **10** water's edge

Beach, Rex
author of: **6** The Net **7** Oh Shoot **8** Pardners **9** Going Some **10** Jungle Gold, The Barrier **11** Don Careless, The Spoilers **12** Son of the Gods **13** The Goose Woman, The Ne'er-do-well **15** The Auction Block **17** Alaskan Adventures

beached 7 aground **8** grounded, stranded **11** shipwrecked **12** washed ashore

beacon 4 beam **5** light **6** pharos, signal **7** seamark **8** bale-fire, landmark **9** watch fire **10** lighthouse, watchtower **11** lighted buoy

bead 3 dot **4** blob, drop, pill **5** speck **6** bubble, pellet **7** droplet, globule **8** particle, spherule

be adequate 2 do **6** answer **8** be enough **10** pass muster **12** be sufficient, do well enough **14** be satisfactory

be afraid of 4 fear **5** dread **7** cower at **8** cringe at **10** shrink from

beak 3 neb, tip **4** bill, nose, pike, prow **5** lorum, snout, spout **7** process, rostrum, snozzle **8** hooknose **9** headmaster, proboscis **10** magistrate

beaker 3 cup **5** glass **6** vessel **9** container

beam 3 ray **4** emit, glow, prop, spar, stud **5** brace, glare, gleam, glint, joist, shine, width **6** girder, rafter, streak, stream, timber **7** breadth, expanse, glimmer, glitter, radiate, trestle **8** transmit **9** broadcast, radiation

bean 9 Phaseolus
varieties: **3** goa, pea, soy, wax, yam **4** fava, jack, lima, moth, mung, rice, seim, snap, soja, soya, tick, wild **5** azuki, black, broad, civet, coral, field, green, horse, lubia, pinto, salad, screw, sewee, sieva, snail, sword, tonka **6** butter, castor, common, French, Indian, kaffir, kidney, lablab, locust, manila, mescal, nicker, potato, romano, runner, sacred, string, tepary, velvet, winged, wonder **7** cluster, English, sarawak, Windsor **8** Bovanist, Bush lima, Carolina, Cherokee, European, Egyptian, hyacinth, yard-long **9** algarroba, asparagus, bonavista, dwarf lima, Java

glory **10** dwarf sieva, giant stock, Hottentot's **12** Italian queen, scarlet flame **13** African locust, Florida velvet, Scarlet runner **14** Dutch case-knife **16** white Dutch runner
bean curd: 4 tofu
be a party to 3 aid **4** abet **7** support **9** connive in **11** cooperate in **13** be accessory to, participate in
be apparent 6 appear **7** be clear, be plain **8** be patent **9** be evident, be obvious **10** be manifest
bear 4 bend, drop, give, haul, have, lead, push, show, take, tend, tote, turn, wear **5** abide, admit, allow, apply, brace, brave, bring, brook, carry, curve, drive, force, hatch, press, refer, spawn, stand, whelp, yield **6** affect, aim for, convey, convoy, create, endure, escort, go with, harbor, invite, permit, relate, render, suffer, take on, uphold **7** bolster, cherish, concern, conduct, contain, deliver, develop, deviate, display, diverge, exhibit, pertain, possess, produce, stomach, support, sustain, undergo, warrant **8** bear down, engender, generate, maintain, manifest, shoulder, submit to, tolerate, transfer, underpin **9** accompany, appertain, encourage, germinate, hold close, propagate, put up with, reproduce, touch upon, transport **10** bring forth, keep in mind **11** give birth to, hold up under
bear
  combining form: 4 arct, ursi **5** arcto
  constellation: 4 ursa **9** ursa major, ursa minor
  family: 7 Ursidae
  group of: 6 sleuth
  kind: 3 sun **5** black, brown, koala, malay, panda, polar, sloth **6** kodiak, wombat **7** grizzly **9** roachback, silvertip **10** spectacled, thalarctos
  male: 4 boar
  mythological: 8 Callisto
  order: 9 carnivora
  young: 3 cub
  famous: 6 Smokey
beard 4 dare, defy, face, trap **5** brave **6** corner **7** stubble **8** bristles, confront, whiskers **10** bring to bay **16** five- o'clock shadow
bearded 5 bushy, hairy **6** shaggy **7** bristly, hirsute **8** unshaven **9** whiskered **11** bewhiskered
bear down 4 push **5** press **13** apply pressure
bear down upon 6 assail, attack, come at **7** assault **11** descend upon
Beardsley, Aubrey Vincent
  born: 7 England **8** Brighton
  artwork: 6 Salome **10** Lysistrata **12** Morte d'Arthur
Beard's Roman Women
  author: 14 Anthony Burgess
bearer 5 Atlas **6** holder, porter **7** car-

rier **8** conveyer, producer **9** messenger **13** beast of burden **16** one holding a check
  Spanish: 8 escudero, portador
bear fruit 4 bear **6** mature **7** develop, prosper **8** fructify
bearing 3 air **4** mien, port **5** sense **6** import, manner **7** concern, meaning **8** attitude, behavior, breeding, carriage, demeanor, presence, relation **9** producing, reference, relevance **10** conception, connection, deportment, importance, pertinence **11** application, association, comportment, germination, giving birth, procreation, propagation, reproducing **12** relationship, reproduction, significance **13** applicability
bearing no name 7 unnamed **8** unsigned **9** anonymous
bearings 3 way **6** course **8** position **9** direction **11** orientation **16** sense of direction
bearish 5 cross, gruff, surly, testy **6** crusty, sullen **7** brusque, crabbed, grouchy **8** churlish **9** crotchety, irascible **10** ill-humored, out of sorts **11** ill-tempered, pessimistic **12** cantankerous
bear off 5 seize, steal **6** abduct, convey, kidnap
bear out 5 prove **6** verify **7** confirm **11** corroborate **12** substantiate
Bear State
  nickname of: 8 Arkansas
bear up under 4 bear, take **5** abide, brave, brook, stand **6** endure, suffer **7** stomach, undergo, weather **9** go through, withstand
bear witness 4 back **6** attest **7** confirm, testify **11** corroborate, demonstrate **12** give evidence, substantiate
beast 3 cad, cur, pig, rat **4** ogre **5** brute, swine **6** animal, mammal, savage **8** creature **9** barbarian, quadruped
beastly 3 bad **4** vile **5** awful, cruel, gross, lousy, nasty **6** brutal, coarse, savage **7** bestial, brutish, inhuman, swinish **8** degraded, dreadful, terrible **9** barbarous, loathsome, monstrous **10** abominable, deplorable, disgusting, unpleasant **12** contemptible, disagreeable
beat 3 bat, hit, mix, rap, tap, way **4** area, bang, best, blow, cane, club, drub, flap, flog, flop, lick, maul, path, rout, slap, time, whip, zone **5** clout, count, crush, flail, knock, meter, outdo, pound, pulse, punch, quake, quell, realm, repel, route, shake, smack, smite, strap, throb, whack **6** accent, batter, course, defeat, domain, hammer, master, pummel, quiver, rhythm, rounds, stress, strike, stroke, subdue, switch, thrash, thwack, twitch, wallop **7** cadence, circuit, clobber, conquer, destroy, eclipse,

flutter, pulsate, put down, repulse, scourge, shellac, surpass, trounce, vibrate, win over **8** overcome, vanquish **9** excel over, fluctuate, go pit-a-pat, overpower, palpitate, pulsation, territory **10** win out over **11** predominate, prevail over, triumph over **14** stir vigorously
beat a retreat 6 beat it **7** back off **8** turn tail, withdraw **10** high tail it
beat around the bush 5 dodge, evade, hedge, stall **10** equivocate, mince words
beatific 4 rapt **6** divine, serene **7** angelic, exalted, saintly, sublime **8** blissful, ecstatic, glorious, heavenly **9** rapturous **10** enraptured **14** transcendental
beat it 2 go **3** out **4** away, scat, shoo **5** be off, leave, scram **6** begone, cut out, depart, get out, go away **7** get lost, vamoose **10** hit the road, make tracks
beatitude 5 bliss **7** ecstasy, rapture **8** euphoria, felicity **10** exaltation **11** blessedness, exaltedness, saintliness **13** transcendence **15** transfiguration
Beatles 10 John Lennon, Ringo Starr **13** Paul McCartney **14** George Harrison
  Songs: 6 Taxman **7** Hey Jude, Get Back **10** Nowhere Man, Drive My Car, Revolution **12** Come Together, Dear Prudence, Eleanor Rigby, Rocky Raccoon **13** Twist and Shout **14** A Hard Day's Night, Eight Days A Week **23** Strawberry Fields Forever **24** Lucy in the Sky with Diamonds
  albums: 4 Help **7** Hey Jude, Let It Be **8** Revolver **9** Abbey Road **10** Rubber Soul, White Album **14** A Hard Day's Night, Meet the Beatles **15** Yellow Submarine **17** Yesterday...and Today **18** Magical Mystery Tour **30** Sgt. Pepper's Lonely Hearts Club Band
be at loggerheads 5 clash **7** quarrel **8** disagree
be at odds 6 differ **7** dispute, diverge **8** conflict, disagree
beat rhythmically 3 rap, tap **4** drum **6** tattoo **7** pulsate
Beatrice
  character in: 12 Divine Comedy
  author: 5 Dante
Beatrice
  character in: 19 Much Ado About Nothing
  author: 11 Shakespeare
Beatrice et Benedict
  opera by: 7 Berlioz
Beat the Clock
  host: 10 Bud Collyer
Beattie, Ann
  author of: 11 Distortions **14** Falling in Place **15** The Burning House **19** Secrets and Surprises **20** Chilly Scenes of Winter

Beatty, Ned
born: 10 Louisville
roles: 3 Spy 4 Rudy 9 The Affair 10 The Big Easy, Black Water, Hear My Song 11 Deliverance 14 Prelude to a Kiss

Beatty, Warren
real name: 11 Warren Beaty
sister: 15 Shirley MacLaine
born: 10 Richmond VA
wife: 13 Annette Bening
roles: 4 Reds 5 Bugsy 6 Ishtar 8 Bulworth 9 Dick Tracy 10 Love Affair 11 All Fall Down 13 Heaven Can Wait 14 Bonnie and Clyde 18 Splendor in the Grass 24 The Roman Spring of Mrs Stone
director of: 4 Reds (Oscar) 8 Bulworth

beat up 3 mug 4 lick, maul, whip 6 batter, pummel 7 assault, clobber

beat-up 4 shot 6 shabby 7 worn-out 8 battered 10 broken-down 11 dilapidated

Beaty, Shirley MacLean
real name of: 15 Shirley MacLaine

Beaty, Warren
real name of: 12 Warren Beatty

beau, beaux 3 fop, guy, nob 4 buck, dude, love, stud, toff 5 blade, dandy, flame, lover, Romeo, spark, swain, swell, wooer 6 adorer, escort, fellow, fiance, garcon, squire, steady, suitor 7 admirer, beloved, courter, coxcomb, cupidon, Don Juan, gallant, playboy 8 cavalier, courtier, gay blade, Lothario, paramour, popinjay, true love, young man 9 betrothed, boyfriend, courtesan, gentleman, inamorato, ladies' man 10 sweetheart, young blood 15 gentleman caller, gentleman friend
nickname of: 14 George Brummell

Beauchamp's Career
author: 14 George Meredith

Beau Geste
author: 6 P C Wren 15 Christopher Wren
director: 14 William Wellman
cast: 10 Gary Cooper, Ray Milland 12 Brian Donlevy, Susan Hayward 13 Robert Preston
silent version starred: 12 Ronald Colman
setting: 19 French Foreign Legion

Beaumarchais, Pierre Augustin Caron de
author of: 18 The Barber of Seville 19 The Marriage of Figaro

beau monde 5 elite 6 gentry 7 society 10 upper class, upper crust 11 aristocracy, high society 15 beautiful people

Beaumont, Ned
character in: 11 The Glass Key
author: 7 Hammett

Beauregard, P G T (Pierre Gustave Toutant)
served in: 8 Civil War
side: 11 Confederate
rank: 7 general
ordered firing on: 8 Ft Sumter
battle: 7 Bull Run

beaut 4 lulu, oner 5 daisy, dandy 6 beauty 7 stunner 8 knockout 10 good-looker

beautification 9 adornment 10 decoration 13 embellishment, ornamentation

beautiful 4 fair, fine 5 bonny, great 6 comely, lovely, pretty, seemly, superb, worthy 7 radiant 8 alluring, gorgeous, handsome, pleasing, splendid, very good 9 admirable, beauteous, enjoyable, estimable, excellent, exquisite, first-rate, ravishing, wonderful 10 attractive, stupendous 11 captivating, commendable, fine-looking, good-looking, resplendent 15 pulchritudinous

beautify 4 do up 5 adorn, grace 7 dress up, enhance, gussy up, improve 8 ornament 9 embellish, glamorize

beauty 4 boon, doll 5 asset, beaut, belle, grace, Venus 6 eyeful, looker 7 benefit, feature, goddess, stunner 8 knockout, radiance, splendor 9 advantage, good looks, good thing 10 attraction, excellence, good-looker, loveliness 11 pulchritude 12 handsomeness, magnificence, resplendence 14 attractiveness
goddess of: 6 Graces 7 Gratiae 9 Aphrodite, Charities
god of: 5 Baldr 6 Apollo, Balder, Baldur 7 Angus Og, Phoebus, Pythias 9 Musagetes

Beauvoir, Simone de
author of: 12 The Mandarins, The Second Sex 14 A Very Easy Death, All Said and Done, The Coming of Age, The Prime of Life 17 Ethics of Ambiguity 22 The Force of Circumstance 25 Memoirs of a Dutiful Daughter 34 Brigitte Bardot and the Lolita Syndrome

beaver
young: 3 kit

Beaver State
nickname of: 6 Oregon

be blessed with 3 own 4 have 5 enjoy 7 possess 16 have the benefit of

because 2 so 3 for 4 that, then, thus 5 cause, hence, since 6 whence 7 whereas 8 inasmuch 9 therefore 10 seeing that 11 considering

Bechuanaland
now called: 8 Botswana

Bechuanland see 8 Botswana

beck 3 bid 4 call 7 bidding, summons 9 summoning

Becket
author: 11 Jean Anouilh 18 Alfred Lord Tennyson
director: 14 Peter Glenville
cast: 11 John Gielgud, Peter O'Toole

(King Henry II) 13 Richard Burton (Becket)

Beckett, Samuel
author of: 4 Not I, Play, Watt 6 Embers, Molloy 7 Endgame 8 That Time 9 Footfalls, Happy Days 10 Malone Dies 11 All that Fall, The Lost Ones 13 The Unnameable 15 Waiting for Godot 16 Mercier and Camier 20 Murphy Krapp's Last Tape 25 Stories and Texts for Nothing

Beckmann, Max
born: 7 Germany, Leipzig
artwork: 6 Kasbek 7 Perseus 8 Acrobats, The Night 9 The Actors 11 View of Genoa 12 Charnel House, The Argonauts, The Departure 13 Blindman's Buff, Family Picture 14 Double Portrait 17 David and Bathsheba 18 Odysseus and Calypso 19 Sinking of the Titanic 20 Destruction of Messina 22 The Descent from the Cross

beckon 4 call, coax, draw, lure, pull 6 allure, entice, invite, motion, signal, summon, wave at, wave on 7 attract, gesture 11 gesticulate 14 crook a finger at

be clear 6 appear 7 be plain 8 be patent 9 be evident, be obvious 10 be apparent, be manifest

becloud 3 fog 4 blur, hide, veil 5 befog, cloud 6 muddle, screen, shroud 7 confuse, cover up, eclipse, obscure 8 confound, make hazy, overcast 9 obfuscate 10 camouflage, overshadow 14 make indistinct

become 3 get 4 grow, suit, turn 6 go with 7 enhance, flatter, get to be 8 come to be 9 agree with, begin to be 10 complement 11 be reduced to, turn out to be

become apparent 4 dawn, loom 5 arise 6 appear, crop up, emerge, turn up 7 develop, surface

become bigger 4 grow 5 swell 6 expand 7 develop, enlarge, inflate 8 increase

become irrational 5 break, crack 7 crack up 9 break down, fall apart, go berserk 10 go to pieces 11 lose control 12 lose one's mind

become one 3 wed 4 fuse 5 blend, marry, merge, unite 7 combine 8 coalesce 10 amalgamate 11 consolidate

become seasoned to 5 adapt, inure 6 adjust 8 accustom 9 acclimate, get used to, habituate 15 learn to live with

become smaller 6 lessen, shrink 7 decline, dwindle, shrivel 8 decrease, diminish

become visible 4 loom, show 6 appear, crop up, emerge, show up, turn up 7 surface 11 come to light 12 come into view

becoming 3 apt, fit **4** meet **6** pretty, proper, seemly, worthy **7** fitting **8** suitable **9** befitting, congenial, congruous, enhancing, in keeping **10** attractive, compatible, consistent, flattering, harmonious **11** appropriate, good-looking

Becquerel, Antoine Henri
   field: 7 physics
   nationality: 6 French
   discovered: 13 radioactivity
   awarded: 10 Nobel Prize

bed 3 cot, hay **4** band, bank, base, belt, bunk, crib, lode, plot, sack, seam, zone **5** berth, floor, layer, patch **6** bottom, cradle, pallet **7** deposit, stratum **8** bedstead **10** foundation

bedazzle 4 daze **6** dazzle **7** astound, confuse, enchant, fluster, nonplus, stagger, stupefy **8** befuddle, bewilder, confound, dumfound **9** captivate, overpower, overwhelm **10** disconcert **11** flabbergast **19** sweep one off one's feet

bed chamber 7 bedroom, boudoir

bed down 5 sleep **7** lie down, sack out **8** doss down **10** hit the hay, settle down **11** accommodate, hit the sack

bedeck 4 deck, trim **5** adorn, array **7** garnish **8** decorate, ornament **9** embellish

be deficient in 4 fail, lack, want **7** be scant **9** be short of **10** have too few

be deprived of 4 lack, lose, want

be deserving of 4 earn, rate **5** merit **7** deserve **10** be worthy of **12** be entitled to

bedevil 3 dog **5** annoy, hound, worry **6** badger, harass, pester, plague **9** beleaguer

be devoted to 4 love **5** adore **6** dote on **7** cherish **8** be fond of

bedim 4 blur **6** darken **7** obscure

Bedivere
   character in: 16 Arthurian romance

bedizen 5 adorn, array **6** bedeck, rig out **7** bejewel, costume

bedlam 5 chaos **6** tumult, uproar **7** turmoil **8** madhouse **11** pandemonium

bed of justice
   French: 12 lit de justice

Bedouin, Beduin
   also: 4 Absi, Arab **5** nomad **7** bedawee
   Arabic: 6 badawi
      means: 13 desert dweller
   found in: 5 Egypt, Syria **6** Arabia **11** North Africa
   religion: 5 Islam

bedraggled 4 limp **5** dirty, dowdy, messy, seedy, soggy, tacky, tatty **6** blowsy, frowsy, frumpy, matted, ragtag, sloppy, soiled, untidy **7** unkempt **8** frumpish, sluttish, tattered **10** disarrayed, disordered, disheveled, slatternly, threadbare **11** disarranged **13** draggletailed **14** down-at-the-heels, out-at-the-elbows

bedridden 7 invalid **8** disabled, immobile **13** incapacitated

bedroom 7 boudoir, chamber **10** bedchamber

bedspread 5 quilt **8** bedcover, coverlet **9** comforter

bedstead 3 bed **8** bed frame **10** four poster

bee
   caste: 5 drone, queen **6** worker
   classification: 6 social **8** solitary
   communication: 13 dance language
   family: 6 Apidae **7** Apoidea **8** Bombidae **10** Andrenidae, Halictidae **11** Meliponidae, Xylocopidae **12** Megachilidae
   group of: 5 grist, swarm
   order: 11 Hymenoptera
   scent: 10 pheromones
   variety: 5 mason, miner **6** alkali, cuckoo **8** burrower, honeybee **9** bumblebee, carpenter, plasterer **10** leaf-cutter **11** yellow-faced

beech 5 Fagus
   varieties: 4 Blue **5** Water **6** Copper, Purple **7** Cut-leaf, Weeping **8** American, European, Fern-leaf, Japanese

Beedle, William Franklin, Jr,
   real name of: 13 William Holden

beef 4 heft, kick, meat **5** brawn, gripe, steer **6** cattle, grouch, grouse **7** grumble **8** complain **9** bellyache, complaint, criticize, find fault

Beef State
   nickname of: 8 Nebraska

beefy 5 bulky, burly, hefty **6** brawny, robust **8** thickset **9** strapping

beehive 4 hive **6** apiary **9** busy place **10** powerhouse

Beehive State
   nickname of: 4 Utah

Beekeeping
   god of: 9 Aristaeus

Beelzebub
   character in: 12 Paradise Lost
   author: 6 Milton

be enough 2 do **6** answer **7** suffice

be entitled to 4 rate **5** merit **7** deserve **10** be worthy of **13** be deserving of

beer 3 ale, keg, mum **4** bier, bock, brew, dark, faro, flip, gail, grog, gyle, hops, kvas, malt, mild, quas, scud, suds **5** chang, chica, draft, grout, kvass, lager, light, quass, scuds, stout, weiss **6** bitter, chicha, double, gatter, porter, spruce, stingo, swanky, swipes, wallop, zythum **7** bottled, cerveza, pangasi, pharaoh, Pilsner, tankard, taplash, tapwort **8** bock beer, cervisia, near beer, pilsener **9** microbrew **10** malt liquor
   add to beer: 7 krausen
   bad/inferior beer: 4 tack **5** belch **6** swanky **7** taplash
   brand: 3 Bud **5** Beck's, Coors, Pabst, Piels **6** Corona, Miller, Molson, Stroh's **7** Schlitz **8** Bud Light, Michelob **9** Budweiser, Lowenbrau **10** Miller Lite, Molson Gold **11** Samuel Adams **13** Guinness Stout **14** Pete's Wicked Ale **15** Pabst Blue Ribbon
   cask: 4 butt
   cup: 3 mug **4** toby **5** glass, stein **6** flagon, seidel **7** tankard **8** schooner **9** blackjack
   hot beer and gin: 4 purl
   ingredient: 4 hops, malt **5** yeast **6** barley
   maker: 6 brewer **8** brewster, maltster
   mythological inventor: 9 Gambrinus
   quantity of: 3 keg **4** case **7** six-pack
   small beer: 4 tiff **5** grout
   sour beer: 4 kuas, kvas **5** quash, quass **8** beeregar
   thin beer: 6 pritch, swipes
   Tibetan beer: 5 chang
   warm beer and oatmeal: 6 storry
   with whiskey: 11 Boilermaker

beer-bust 4 toot **5** binge, drunk, spree **6** bender **8** carousal **9** bacchanal

Beery, Noah
   brother: 7 Wallace
   son: 6 Noah Jr
   born: 12 Kansas City MO
   roles: 7 Lord Jim, The Dove **9** Beau Geste **10** The Sea Wolf **14** The Mark of Zorro

Beery, Wallace
   brother: 4 Noah
   nephew: 6 Noah Jr
   wife: 13 Gloria Swanson
   born: 12 Kansas City MO
   roles: 8 The Champ (Oscar) **9** The Bowery, Viva Villa **10** Grand Hotel **11** The Big House **13** Dinner at Eight **14** Treasure Island **15** The Mighty Barnum **16** A Message to Garcia

beet 12 Beta vulgaris
   varieties: 3 Red, Sea **4** Leaf, Wild **5** Sugar **6** Garden, Yellow **7** Spinach
   base of: 6 borsch **7** borscht

Beethoven, Ludwig van
   born: 4 Bonn **7** Germany
   composer of: 5 Laube (sonata) **6** Egmont, Eroica (symphony no 3), Spring (sonata) **7** Fidelio, Leonore **8** Coriolan, Dramatic (sonata), Kreutzer (sonata), Pastoral (symphony no 6), The Storm **9** Moonlight (sonata), Pastorale (sonata), Waldstein (sonata) **10** Bagatellen, Great Fugue (no 133), Pathetique (sonata), Spirit Trio **11** Grosse Fugue (no 133), Harp Quartet (no 74), Namensfeier **12** Appassionata (sonata), Archduke Trio, Konig Stephan **13** Hammerklavier (sonata), Missa Solemnis **15** Emperor Concerto (No 5) **16** Christus am Olberg, The Mount of Olives, The Ruins of Athens **17** Die Ruinen von Athen, Die Weihe des Hauses **18** An

die ferne Geliebte, Rage over a Lost Penny **20** Rasoumoffsky Quartets (no 59) **24** The Creatures of Prometheus **25** Die Geschopfe des Prometheus

beetle
variety: **3** bog, may, sap **4** bark, bean, flea, leaf, mold, moss, pill, rove, sand, stag **5** cedar, click, flour, grain, marsh, penny, tiger, water **6** beaver, diving, flower, fungus, ground, hister, lizard, scarab, spider, weevil **7** bessbug, blister, burying, carrion, firefly, goldbug, goliath, lady- bug, soldier **8** elephant, glow-worm, hercules, Japanese, ladybird, tortoise **9** ant loving, bombadier, burrowing, checkered, fruitworm, goldsmith, grassroot, scavenger, tumblebug, whirligig **10** deathwatch, false clown, longhorned, mammal nest, shiptimber **11** reticulated, trout stream **12** antlike stone, lightning bug **13** feather winged, horseshoe crab

Beetle Bailey
creator/artist: **9** Dik Browne **10** Mort Walker **12** Bob Gustafson
character: **5** Cosmo, Plato **6** Killer, Lt Flap, Lt Fuzz **10** Miss Buxley **12** Gen Halftrack **17** Sgt Orville Snorkel
chef: **6** Cookie
place: **10** Camp Swampy

be evident 6 appear **7** be clear, be plain **8** be patent **9** be obvious **10** be apparent, be manifest

befall 5 ensue, occur **6** betide, chance, follow, happen **10** come to pass **11** materialize

befitting 3 apt, fit **5** right **6** decent, proper, seemly **8** becoming, relevant, suitable **11** appropriate

be fond of 6 dote on **11** be devoted to **12** be in love with

before 3 ere, yet **5** afore, ahead, prior **6** rather, sooner **7** already, earlier, vis-a-vis **8** erewhile, until now **9** in advance, in front of, in sight of **10** face-to-face, previously

before Christ
abbreviation: **2** BC
alternative: **3** BCE **15** before Common Era
Latin: **2** AC **12** ante Christum

beforehand 6 in time, sooner **7** earlier **9** in advance **11** ahead of time

before now 6 in time, sooner **7** earlier **9** in advance

before the fact 6 in time **9** in advance **10** beforehand **11** ahead of time

before the public
Latin: **11** coram populo

befoul 4 soil **5** dirty, smear, stain, sully, taint **6** defile, poison **7** blacken, corrupt, pollute, tarnish **8** besmirch **9** desecrate **11** contaminate

befriend 4 help **6** assist, defend, suc-

cor, uphold **7** comfort, embrace, help out, protect, stand by, stick by, support, sustain, welcome **8** side with **9** give aid to, look after **10** minister to **11** consort with **13** associate with **14** fraternize with, sympathize with **17** take under one's wing

be friends 7 consort **9** associate, pal around **10** fraternize

befringe 3 hem **4** bind, edge, trim **6** border **7** festoon **8** decorate

befuddle 4 daze **5** addle, mix up **6** baffle, muddle, puzzle, rattle **7** confuse, fluster, perplex, stupefy **8** bewilder, confound, unsettle **9** disorient, inebriate, make drunk, make tipsy **10** intoxicate, make groggy **11** disorganize

beg 3 bum, sue **4** pray, shun **5** avert, avoid, cadge, dodge, evade, mooch, parry, plead, shirk **6** escape, eschew, hustle, sponge **7** beseech, entreat, fend off, implore, solicit **8** appeal to, petition, sidestep **9** importune, panhandle **10** supplicate

beg, bey 4 lord **6** prince **8** governor

beget 3 get **4** sire **5** breed, cause, spawn **6** effect, father, lead to **7** produce **8** engender, generate, occasion, result in **9** call forth, procreate, propagate **10** bring about, give rise to

begetter 4 sire **6** father **7** creator **9** generator **10** progenitor

beggar 3 bum, guy **4** chap **5** devil, tramp **6** baffle, fellow **7** almsman, moocher, sponger, surpass **8** beyond **9** challenge, mendicant **10** panhandler

Beggar 7 Lazarus

Beggar's Opera, The
author: **7** John Gay
form: **11** ballad opera
character: **6** Lockit **10** Lucy Lockit **12** Polly Peachum **15** Captain Macheath

begin 5 arise, found, start **6** be born, crop up, emerge, launch, set out **8** break out, commence, embark on, initiate **9** establish, institute, introduce, originate, undertake **10** burst forth, inaugurate **11** set in motion **16** take the first step

beginner 4 babe, tyro **6** author, father, novice, rookie **7** creator, founder, learner, starter, student **8** freshman, neophyte **9** fledgling, greenhorn, initiator, organizer **10** apprentice, originator, prime mover, tenderfoot **11** inaugurator **14** babe in the woods

beginning 3 new **4** germ, seed **5** birth, onset, start **6** embryo, novice, origin, outset, source, spring **7** kickoff, student, untried **8** neophyte, zero hour **9** embryonic, inception, incipient, launching **10** foundation, wellspring **11** preliminary, springboard **12** commencement, fountainhead, inauguration, introduction **13** inexperi-

enced, starting point
Latin: **12** terminus a quo

Beginning of Wisdom, The
author: **19** Stephen Vincent Benet

Beginnings
god of: **5** Janus

begone 3 out **4** away, scat, shoo **5** be off, leave, scram **6** beat it, depart, get out, go away **7** get lost, vamoose

begonia
varieties: **3** Rex, Wax **4** Fern, King, Star, Wild **5** Hardy, Trout **6** Bamboo, Kidney, Shrimp, Winter, Zigzag **7** Bedding, Dewdrop, Elm-leaf, Eyelash, Fuchsia, Leopard, Lily-pad, Swedish **8** Climbing, Fern-leaf, Fireking, Lorraine, Palm-leaf, Pond-lily, Star-leaf, Trailing **9** Alder- leaf, Angel-wing, Beefsteak, Calla-lily, Christmas, Crazy-leaf, Grape-leaf, Grapevine, Hollyhock, Holly- leaf, Honeybear, Iron-cross, Maple-leaf, Miniature, Pennywort, Trout-leaf, Whirlpool **10** Bronze-leaf, Castorbean, Finger-leaf, Guinea-wing, Seersucker, Strawberry **11** Fairy-carpet, Lettuce-leaf, Painted-leaf **12** Blooming-fool, Elephant's Ear, Metallic-leaf **13** Peanut-brittle **14** Hybrid tuberous, Nasturtium-leaf, Youth-and-oldage **15** Winter-flowering **16** Manda's woolly-bear, Philodendron-leaf **17** Miniature pond-lily **18** Trailing watermelon

beg pardon 6 excuse **9** apologize **13** express regret, say one is sorry

be grateful 9 be obliged **10** appreciate, be beholden, be thankful **11** be obligated

begrime 4 soil **5** dirty, muddy, smear, stain, sully **6** smudge, soot up **7** besmear, tarnish

begrimed 5 dirty, grimy, muddy **6** filthy, grubby, soiled **7** unclean **8** unwashed **9** tarnished

begrudge 4 envy **5** covet **6** grudge, resent **11** be jealous of, hold against

beguile 4 dupe, hoax, lull, lure **5** amuse, charm, cheat, cheer, trick **6** delude, divert, occupy, please **7** bewitch, deceive, enchant, ensnare **8** distract, hoodwink **9** bamboozle, captivate, entertain **10** lead astray

beguiling 7 winning, winsome **8** charming, magnetic **9** appealing, disarming **10** bewitching, entrancing **11** captivating **12** ingratiating, irresistible

behalf 3 aid, for **4** part, side **5** favor **7** benefit, by proxy, defense, in aid of, support **8** interest

Behan, Brendan
author of: **10** Borstal Boy, The Hostage **12** The Scarperer **14** The Quare Fellow **25** Confessions of an Irish Rebel

be handed down 4 pass **7** descend **11** be inherited

behave 3 act 13 acquit oneself, deport oneself 14 comport oneself, conduct oneself, control oneself

behavior 4 acts 5 deeds 6 action, habits, manner 7 actions, bearing, conduct, control 8 activity, attitude, demeanor, practice, reaction, response 9 operation 10 deportment 11 comportment, functioning, performance, self-control

behead 9 decollate 10 decapitate, guillotine 15 bring to the block

behest 4 fiat 5 edict, order, say-so 6 charge, decree, ruling 7 bidding, command, dictate, mandate 9 direction, ultimatum 10 injunction 11 instruction

behind 4 rump, seat, slow 5 abaft, after, fanny 8 backward, buttocks, in back of 9 fundament, in arrears 11 to the rear of 12 hindquarters

behind closed doors 7 sub rosa 8 in secret, secretly 9 in private, privately

behindhand 4 late, slow 5 tardy 7 belated 8 backward 10 unpunctual

behind the times 5 passe 7 archaic 9 out-of-date 10 antiquated 12 old-fashioned

behind time 4 late, slow 5 tardy 7 belated, delayed 12 after the fact

behold 3 see 4 heed, look, mark, note, scan, view 5 watch 6 attend, gaze at, look at, notice, regard, survey 7 discern, examine, inspect, observe, stare at, witness 8 look upon 10 scrutinize 11 contemplate 12 pay attention

beholden 5 bound 6 liable 7 obliged 8 indebted 9 obligated 10 answerable, in one's debt 11 accountable, responsible 15 under obligation

behold the man
Latin: 8 ecce homo
said by: 13 Pontius Pilate
spoken of: 6 Christ

behoove 4 suit 5 be apt, befit 6 become, be wise 7 benefit 8 be proper 9 be fitting 11 be advisable, be necessary 13 be appropriate 14 be advantageous

Behring, Emil Adolph von
field: 12 bacteriology
nationality: 6 German
developed: 19 diphtheria antitoxin
awarded: 10 Nobel Prize

beige 3 tan 4 ecru, fawn 6 greige 8 brownish

be ill 3 ail 6 be sick 8 be unwell 12 be indisposed 13 be in ill health

be in a class with 5 equal, match 6 be up to 7 compare 8 approach 10 be as good as 11 compete with 12 be comparable, be on a par with 13 hold a candle to 14 bear comparison

being 4 core, life, soul 5 human 6 living, mortal, nature, person, psyche, spirit 7 essence, persona, reality 8 creature, existing 9 actuality, existence 10 individual, occurrence 11 subsistence

be inherited 4 pass 7 descend 12 be handed down

be in short supply 4 lack, want 8 be scanty, be scarce 9 fall short

be intemperate 7 carouse, debauch 9 dissipate 10 overindulge

be in tune 4 jibe 5 agree, match, tally 6 accord, square 7 conform 9 harmonize

Beirut, Beyrouth
capital of: 7 Lebanon
Phoenician name: 7 Berytus
sea: 13 Mediterranean
settled by: 11 Phoenicians
square: 15 Place des Martyrs

be jealous of 4 envy 6 resent 8 begrudge

Bekesy, Georg von
field: 7 physics
researched: 3 ear 7 cochlea, hearing
awarded: 10 Nobel Prize

Bel 3 god 5 deity

belabor 6 rehash, repeat 7 dwell on 9 reiterate 11 pound away at 12 hammer away at, recapitulate 14 beat a dead horse, go on and on about

Bel-Ami
author: 15 Guy de Maupassant

Belarus
other name: 10 Belorussia 11 Byelorussia, White Russia
capital/largest city: 5 Minsk
head of state: 9 president
government: 8 republic
monetary unit: 5 ruble
river: 5 Dvina 7 Dnieper
physical feature: 13 Pripet Marshes
people: 12 Byelorussian

Belasco, David
author of: 7 DuBarry 15 Madame Butterfly 21 The Return of Peter Grimm 22 The Girl of the Golden West

belated 4 late, slow 5 tardy 6 behind 7 delayed, overdue, past due 8 deferred 10 behindhand, behind time, unpunctual 12 after the fact

belch 4 burp, emit, gush, spew, vent 5 eject, eruct, erupt, expel, issue, spout, spurt, vomit 7 cough up, issuing 8 disgorge, ejection, emission, eruption 9 discharge, roar forth, send forth 10 eructation

Belch, Sir Toby
character in: 12 Twelfth Night
author: 11 Shakespeare

beleaguer 3 vex 5 annoy 6 assail, badger, bother, harass, hector, pester, plague 7 besiege, bombard 8 blockade, surround

bel-esprit 3 wit 12 intellectual

belfry 4 dome 5 spire 7 steeple 9 bell tower, campanile

Belgian Congo see 5 Congo

Belgium
other name: 13 Gallia Belgica 15 Cockpit of Europe 16 Koninkrijk Belgie 17 Royaume de Belgique
capital/largest city: 8 Brussels 9 Bruxelles
others: 2 As 3 Aat, Ans, Ath, Hal, Huy, Mol, Spa 4 Aath, Amay, Asse, Boom, Bree, Doel, Gaud, Geel, Genk, Gent, Hoei, Lier, Looz, Mons, Vise, Waha, Zele 5 Aalst, Alost, Arlon, Ciney, Ecklo, Essen, Eupen, Evere, Genck, Ghent, Heist, Ieper, Jette, Jumet, Liege, Namur, Ronse, Tielt, Uccle, Vorst, Wezet, Ynoir, Ypres 6 Aarlen, Anvers, Bergen, Bilzen, Bruges, Deurne, Izegem, Leuven, Lierre, Merxem, Opwijk, Ostend 7 Antwerp, Ardooie, Berchem, Brabant, Hainaut, Herstal, Hoboken, Ixelles, Leliven, Limburg, Louvain, Malmedy, Mechlin, Roulers, Seraing, Tournai 8 Bastogne, Courtrai, Doorwick, Flanders, Kortrijk, Mouscron, Turnhout, Verviers, Waterloo 9 Antwerpen, Charleroi 10 Anderlecht, Borgerhout, Luxembourg, Quatrebras, Schaerbeek
school: 7 Louvain
division: 5 Liege, Namur 7 Antwerp, Brabant, Hainaut, Limburg 8 Flanders, Wallonia
head of state: 4 king
measure: 3 vat 4 aune, pied 5 carat 6 perche 8 boisseau
monetary unit: 5 belga, franc 7 brabant, centime, crocard
weight: 4 last 5 carat, livre 6 charge 7 chariot 8 esterlin
mountain: 8 Ardennes
highest point: 16 Signal de Botrange
river: 3 Lys 4 Dyle, Leie, Maas, Mark, Yser 5 Boucq, Demer, Lesse, Meuse, Nethe, Rupel, Senne 6 Dender, Escaut, Manjel, Ourthe, Sambre, Semois, Vesdre, Warche 7 Ambleve, Schelde, Scheldt
sea: 5 North
physical feature:
canal: 4 Yser 5 Union 6 Albert 7 Campine
cave: 7 Furfooz 8 Grenelle
forest: 8 Ardennes
plateau: 8 Hohevenn
people: 4 Remi 6 Nervii 7 Belgian, Fleming, Flemish 8 Walloons 9 Bellovaci
artist: 5 Ensor 6 Rubens 7 Delvaux, Van Dyke, Van Eyck 8 Brueghal, Magritte
author: 6 Coster 7 Simenon 9 Verhaeren 10 Conscience, Ghelderode 11 Maeterlinck
composer: 6 Franck
king: 6 Albert 7 Leopold 8 Baudouin
leader: 5 Spaak 9 Tindemans
language: 5 Dutch 6 French, German

7 Flemish
religion: 13 Roman Catholic
place:
    battleground: 5 Bulge **8** Waterloo
    breadhouse: 9 Broodhuis
    castle: 5 Steen
    cathedral: 5 Ghent **13** Saint Rombauts
    city hall: 12 Hotel de Ville
    home for elderly women: 9 Beguinage
    museum: 9 Beaux Arts
    palace: 10 Gruuthuuse
features:
    horse: 9 Brabancon
    lace: 5 fichu **6** Bruges **7** Malines, Mechlin **8** Brussels
    lawn bowling: 6 boules
    linen: 7 brabant
    musical instrument: 8 carillon
    religious procession: 9 Holy Blood
    tapestry: 9 oudenarde
food:
    cheese: 9 Limburger
    gingerbread: 12 pain d'espices
    raisin bread: 8 cramique
    soup: 9 Waterzooi

Belgrade, Beograd
capital of: 10 Yugoslavia
landmark:
    fortress: 10 Kalemegdan
    parliament house: 9 Skupstina
name means: 11 white forest
river: 4 Sava **6** Danube
Roman fort: 10 Singidinum
Serbian: 7 Beograd

Belial
character in: 12 Paradise Lost
author: 6 Milton

belie 4 defy, deny, mask **5** cloak **6** betray, negate, refute **7** conceal, falsify, gainsay **8** disguise, disprove **9** repudiate **10** camouflage, contradict, controvert, invalidate **12** misrepresent

belief 4 view **5** faith, guess, trust **6** theory **7** feeling, opinion **8** judgment, reliance **9** assurance, certitude, deduction, inference **10** assumption, conclusion, confidence, conviction, firm notion, hypothesis, impression, persuasion **11** expectation, presumption, supposition

beliefs 5 canon, creed, dogma, faith, tenet **6** ethics, gospel, morals **8** doctrine, morality **9** principle, teachings **10** conviction, persuasion

believable 8 credible, knowable, possible **9** plausible, thinkable **10** acceptable, convincing, imaginable, supposable **11** conceivable, perceivable

believe 4 hold **5** guess, infer, judge, think, trust **6** assume, credit, deduce, rely on **7** count on, fall for, imagine, presume, suppose, surmise, suspect, swallow, swear by **8** be sure of, consider, depend on, maintain, theorize **9**

speculate **10** conjecture, presuppose, put faith in **11** hypothesize

believe in 5 trust **6** accept, esteem **7** approve, go in for, respect **11** have faith in **16** have confidence in

Believe It or Not
author: 13 Robert L Ripley

believer 7 admirer **8** advocate, disciple, partisan **9** supporter **16** faithful adherent

be like 5 equal, match **8** approach, resemble

Bel-Imperia
character in: 17 The Spanish Tragedy
author: 3 Kyd

Belinda
character in: 16 The Rape of the Lock
author: 4 Pope

belittle 5 knock, scorn **6** deride, malign **7** disdain, put down, run down, sneer at **8** minimize, mitigate, play down, pooh-pooh **9** deprecate, disparage, underrate **10** depreciate, undervalue **11** make light of **13** underestimate **16** cast aspersions on

belittling 5 snide **10** derogatory **11** deprecating, disparaging, unfavorable **12** depreciating **15** uncomplimentary

Belize
other name: 15 British Honduras
capital: 8 Belmopan
largest city/former capital: 10 Belize City
head of state: 13 prime minister **14** British monarch **15** governor-general
monetary unit: 6 dollar
island: 8 Turneffe
mountain range: 4 Maya
highest point: 12 Victoria Peak
river: 3 New **4** Moho **6** Belize, Monkey
sea: 9 Caribbean
physical feature:
    gulf: 8 Honduras
    peninsula: 7 Yucatan
    swamp: 8 mangrove
people: 5 Mayan **6** Indian, Syrian **7** African, Chinese **15** Spanish-American
language: 7 English, Spanish

bell 4 gong, peal **5** chime **6** tocsin **7** ringing **8** carillon **16** tintinnabulation

Bell, Alexander Graham
born: 8 Scotland
inventor of: 9 telephone **14** record cylinder
saying: 24 Mr Watson come here I want you

Bellamann, Henry
author of: 8 King's Row

Bellamy, Edward
author of: 8 Equality **15** Looking Backward

Bellamy, Ralph
born: 9 Chicago IL
roles: 11 Ellery Queen, Mike Barnett **13** The Awful Truth **14** Detective

Story **15** Man Against Crime, State of the Union **19** Sunrise at Campobello

Bellarius
character in: 9 Cymbeline
author: 11 Shakespeare

Bellaston, Lady
character in: 8 Tom Jones
author: 8 Fielding

bell buoy 5 float **6** signal **13** channel marker

belle 4 star **5** queen **6** beauty **7** charmer **12** heart-stopper

Belle Dame Sans Merci, La
author: 9 John Keats

Bellefleur
author: 15 Joyce Carol Oates

Belle Helene, La
also: 14 Beautiful Helen
operetta by: 9 Offenbach

Bellerophon
form: 4 hero
brother: 8 Deliades
son: 11 Hippolochus
home: 7 Corinth
rode: 7 Pegasus
killed: 7 Chimera

Bell for Adano, A
author: 10 John Hersey
director: 9 Henry King
cast: 10 John Hodiak **11** Gene Tierney **13** William Bendix

bellicose see **11** belligerent

belligerence, belligerency 9 animosity, hostility, pugnacity **10** aggression, antagonism **11** bellicosity **12** warmongering **13** combativeness **14** aggressiveness, unfriendliness

belligerent 7 fighter, hostile, martial, warlike, warring **8** attacker, inimical **9** adversary, aggressor, bellicose, combatant, combative, irascible, irritable, truculent **10** aggressive, antagonist, pugnacious, unfriendly **11** bad-tempered, contentious, quarrelsome **12** antagonistic, cantankerous

belligerent state 3 foe **5** enemy **9** aggressor **13** hostile nation

Bellini, Gentile
born: 5 Italy **6** Venice
father: 6 Jacopo
brother: 8 Giovanni
artwork: 24 The Miracle of the True Cross **26** A Procession in St Mark's Square, The Miracle at Ponte di Lorenzo **27** St Mark Preaching in Alexandria **38** A Procession of Relics in the Piazza San Marco

Bellini, Giovanni (Giambellino)
born: 5 Italy **6** Venice
father: 6 Jacopo
brother: 7 Gentile
artwork: 8 St Jerome **16** Venus with a Mirror **18** St Francis in Ecstasy, The Madonna and Child **19** Allegory of Purgatory, The Agony in the Garden, The Barberini Madonna

Bellini, Jacopo
born: **5** Italy **6** Venice
son: **7** Gentile **8** Giovanni
artwork: **11** Crucifixion **16** Christ on
the Cross **35** The Madonna and
Child with Lionello d'Este

Bellini, Vincenzo
born: **5** Italy **7** Catania
composer of: **5** Norma, Zaira **8** Il
Pirata **9** I Puritani **11** La Straniera **12**
La Sonnambula **15** Bianca e Fer-
nando

Bell Jar, The
author: **11** Sylvia Plath

bellow 4 bawl, roar, yell **5** shout,
whoop **6** holler, scream, shriek

Bellow, Saul
author of: **6** Herzog **13** Dean's December, Humboldt's Gift, Mosby's
Memoirs **15** The Last Analysis **16** Mr
Sammler's Planet **18** To Jerusalem
and Back **25** The Adventures of Au-
gie March

Bellows, George Wesley
born: **10** Columbus OH
artwork: **8** Lady Jean **11** Billy Sunday, Edith Cavell, Floating Ice, Up
the Hudson **12** Forty-Two Kids **13**
Men of the Docks **14** Rain on the
River, Stag at Sharkey's **16** The Cliff
Dwellers **18** Emma and her Children
21 Both Members of This Club

Bells Are Ringing
music: **5** Styne
lyric: **5** Green **6** Comden
director: **16** Vincente Minnelli
cast: **9** Fred Clark **10** Dean Martin **12**
Judy Holliday
song: **10** Just in Time **13** The Party's
Over

Bells in Winter
author: **13** Czeslaw Milosz

Bells of St Mary's, The
director: **10** Leo McCarey
cast: **10** Bing Crosby (Father
O'Malley) **12** Henry Travers **13** Ingrid Bergman
sequel to: **10** Going My Way
song: **20** Aren't You Glad You're You

bell tower 5 spire **6** belfry **7** steeple **9**
campanile

Belluschi, Pietro
architect of: **21** Bank of America
Building (San Francisco) **22** Juilliard
School of Music (NYC) **31** Pan
American World Airways Building
(NYC, with Gropius)

bellwether 4 lead **5** doyen, guide, pilot **6** leader **8** director, shepherd **9**
conductor, guidepost, precursor **10**
forerunner, pacesetter **14** standard-
bearer

belly 3 abs, gut, yen **4** guts **5** taste,
tummy **6** bowels, depths, desire, hunger, liking, paunch, vitals **7** abdomen,
insides, midriff, stomach **8** appetite,
interior, recesses **11** breadbasket

bellyache 4 beef, kick **5** gripe **6**
grouch, grouse, squawk **7** grumble **8**
complain **9** tummy ache **11** stomach
ache **12** upset stomach

belong 6 go with **7** concern **8** attach
to, be held by, be part of **9** be owned
by, pertain to **10** be allied to **11** be a
member of **12** be included in **15** be
connected with, be the property of

belongings 4 gear, junk **5** goods, stuff
6 things **7** effects **8** movables **11**
possessions **13** accoutrements, paraphernalia **16** personal property

Beloved
author: **12** Toni Morrison

beloved 4 beau, dear, love, wife **5**
loved, lover **6** adored, fiance, spouse,
steady **7** admired, darling, dearest, fiancee, husband, revered **8** endeared,
esteemed, loved one, precious **9** betrothed, boyfriend, cherished, respected, treasured **10** girlfriend,
sweetheart

below 4 less **5** lower, under **6** in hell
7 beneath, on earth, short of **8** inferior, unworthy **9** at a low ebb, down-
wards **10** downstairs, downstream,
second-rate, underneath **11** at a discount, at the foot of, indifferent, subordinate, underground

below par 3 bad **4** poor **8** inferior **9**
imperfect **10** second-rate **12** below average, not up to snuff

below standard 3 bad **4** poor **5** lousy
6 faulty, shoddy **8** below par, inferior,
slipshod, terrible **9** imperfect **10** second-rate **12** not up to snuff

belt 4 area, band, land, sash, zone **5**
cinch, layer, strip **6** circle, girdle, region, stripe **7** country **8** district, encircle **9** waistband **10** cummerbund

Belushi, James
born: **7** Chicago
roles: **8** Curly Sue **9** Mr. Destiny **13**
Working Stiffs **14** About Last Night
15 Jumpin' Jack Flash **19** Little Shop
of Horrors

Belushi, John
born: **9** Chicago IL
roles: **9** Neighbors **11** Animal House
16 The Blues Brothers **17** Saturday
Night Live

be manifest 6 appear **7** be clear, be
plain **8** be patent **9** be evident, be obvious **10** be apparent

bemoan 3 rue **5** mourn **6** bewail, lament, regret **7** cry over **8** weep over
9 whine over **10** grieve over

bemused 5 dazed, fuzzy **7** muddled,
stunned **8** confused **9** engrossed, stupefied **10** bewildered, dull-witted,
thoughtful **11** preoccupied **12** absent-
minded

be nauseated by 4 hate **5** abhor **6**
detest, loathe **7** despise **8** execrate **9**
abominate **11** can't stomach **13** be

disgusted by, find repulsive, find revolting, find sickening

Benbow, Horace
character in: **9** Sanctuary
author: **8** Faulkner

Ben Casey
character: **12** Dr David Zorba, Dr Ted
Hoffman **13** Nick Kanavaras **14** Dr
Maggie Graham
cast: **8** Sam Jaffe **10** Nick Dennis **12**
Harry Landers, Vince Edwards **14**
Bettye Ackerman

bench 3 pew **4** banc, seat **5** board,
court, stool, table **6** settee **7** counter,
take out, trestle **8** sideline, tribunal **9**
judiciary, workbench, worktable **10**
second team **11** judge's chair, substitutes **12** second string

Benchley, Peter
author of: **4** Jaws **7** The Deep

Benchley, Robert
author of: **14** From Bed to Worse **21**
Benchley Beside Himself, My Ten
Years in a Quandary

benchmark 4 norm **5** gauge, guide,
model **7** example, measure **8** exemplar, paradigm, standard **9** criterion,
principle, prototype, reference, yardstick **10** touchstone

bend 3 arc, bow **4** flex, hook, lean,
loop, mold, sway, turn, warp, wind **5**
crook, curve, defer, force, shape,
stoop, twist, yield **6** accede, attend,
buckle, coerce, compel, crouch, give
in, relent, submit **7** bow down, contort, control, succumb **9** genuflect, influence, surrender **10** buckle down,
capitulate **11** make crooked

Bend in the River, The
author: **9** V S Naipaul

Bendix, William
born: **9** New York NY
roles: **8** Hostages, Lifeboat **11** The
Hairy Ape **13** A Bell for Adano **14**
The Life of Riley **16** Guadalcanal Diary, The Babe Ruth Story

bend to one's own will 4 tame **5**
break, train **6** master, subdue **8** overcome **10** discipline **12** show who's
boss **18** have under one's thumb

beneath 5 below, lower, under **9** covered by **10** inferior to, underneath,
unworthy of **11** subordinate, underground **16** below one's dignity

Benedick
character in: **19** Much Ado About
Nothing
author: **11** Shakespeare

Benedict 5 groom **8** newlywed

benedictine
type: **6** brandy, cognac **7** liqueur
flavor: **4** herb
with brandy: **5** B and B
with bourbon: **9** Twin Hills **13**
Brighton Punch
with whiskey: **10** Frisco Sour

benediction 6 prayer **7** benison **8** blessing **10** invocation **12** consecration **13** closing prayer

benefaction 4 alms, gift **5** grant **7** charity **8** bestowal, donation, offering **9** endowment **10** almsgiving **12** contribution, dispensation, philanthropy

benefactor 5 angel, donor **6** backer, friend, helper, patron **7** sponsor **8** upholder **9** supporter **11** contributor **14** fairy godmother

beneficent 6 benign, kindly **7** liberal **8** generous, salutary **10** beneficial, benevolent, charitable **11** magnanimous **13** philanthropic

beneficial 6 useful **7** good for, healing, helpful **8** valuable **9** favorable, healthful **10** productive, profitable, propitious **12** advantageous, contributive

beneficiary 4 heir **7** grantee, heiress, legatee **8** receiver **9** inheritor, recipient

benefit 3 aid, use **4** gain, good, help **5** asset, avail, serve, value, worth **6** assist, behalf, better, profit **7** advance, be aided, service **8** be helped, be served, blessing, interest **9** advantage, do good for **10** be useful to, betterment, profit from **13** charity affair **18** charity performance

Benet, Stephen Vincent
  author of: 7 America **8** Tiger Joy **11** Western Star **14** John Brown's Body, Thirteen O'Clock, Young Adventure **16** Five Men and Pompey **19** Tales Before Midnight, The Headless Horseman **20** The Beginning of Wisdom **24** The Devil and Daniel Webster

benevolence 7 charity **8** good will, kindness **9** benignity **10** compassion, generosity, kindliness, liberality **13** bountifulness **14** charitableness **15** humanitarianism, kindheartedness

benevolent 3 kin **6** benign, humane, tender **7** liberal **8** generous **9** benignant, bounteous, bountiful, unselfish **10** bighearted, charitable **11** considerate, kindhearted, warmhearted **12** humanitarian **13** compassionate, philanthropic

Bengali
  language family: 12 Indo-European
  branch: 11 Indo-Iranian
  group: 5 Indic
  spoken in: 5 (northern) India

Ben-Hur
  author: 10 Lew Wallace
  character: 4 Iras, Isas **5** Jesus **6** Esther **7** Messala **9** Balthasar, Simonides **11** Judah Ben-Hur
  director: 12 William Wyler
  cast: 11 Jack Hawkins, Stephen Boyd **12** Hugh Griffith **14** Charlton Heston (Judah Ben-Hur)
  setting: 9 Palestine

Oscar for: 5 actor (Heston) **7** picture **8** director **14** cinematography **15** supporting actor (Griffith)

benighted 4 dumb **5** crude, unhip **8** backward, ignorant, untaught **9** primitive, untutored **10** illiterate, uncultured, uneducated, uninformed, unlettered, unschooled **11** empty-headed, know-nothing, uncivilized **12** uncultivated **13** unenlightened

benign 4 good, kind, mild, nice, soft **5** balmy, lucky **6** genial, gentle, humane, kindly, tender **7** affable **8** gracious, harmless, pleasant, salutary **9** favorable, healthful, innocuous, temperate **10** auspicious, benevolent, propitious **11** encouraging, kindhearted, soft-hearted **13** tender-hearted

benignant 4 kind **6** benign, humane, kindly, tender **9** forgiving **10** benevolent **11** kindhearted **13** compassionate, tenderhearted

benignity 8 good will, kindness **10** compassion, kindliness **11** benevolence **15** kindheartedness

Benin
  other name: 17 Republic of Dahomey
  capital: 9 Porto-Novo
  largest city: 7 Cotonou
  others: 4 Pobe **5** Kandi, Kerou, Ketou, Porga **6** Abomey, Ouidah **7** Parakou, Savalou **8** Aplahoue
  government: 30 Military Council of the Revolution
  monetary unit: 5 franc **7** centime
  lake: 5 Aheme **6** Nokoue
  mountain: 7 Atakora
  river: 4 Mono **5** Niger, Oueme **6** Couffo
  sea: 8 Atlantic
  physical feature:
    gulf: 6 Guinea
    plains: 6 Borgou
  people: 3 Fon, Pla **4** Adja, Aizo, Mina, Peul **5** Pedah, Peuhl, Somba **6** Bariba, Fulani, Yoruba **8** Pilapila **9** Dahomeyan
  language: 3 Fon **5** Dendi **6** Bariba, French, Fulani, Yoruba
  religion: 5 Islam **6** tribal **7** animism **13** Roman Catholic
  food:
    tapioca: 4 gari

Benito Cereno
  author: 14 Herman Melville

Benjamin
  father: 5 Jacob
  mother: 6 Rachel
  also known as: 6 Benoni
  brother: 3 Dan, Gad **4** Levi **5** Asher, Judah **6** Joseph, Reuben, Simeon **7** Zebulun **8** Issachar, Naphtali
  sister: 5 Dinah
  descendant of: 11 Benjaminite

Bennet family
  characters in: 17 Pride and Prejudice
  members: 4 Jane, Mary **5** Kitty, Lydia

9 Elizabeth
  author: 6 Austen

Bennett, Arnold
  author of: 8 Accident **10** Clayhanger, Lord Raingo, Milestones, These Twain **11** Buried Alive **13** Hilda Lessways, Riceyman Steps **15** The Old Wives' Tale **18** Anna of the Five Towns

Benny, Jack
  real name: 16 Benjamin Kubelsky
  born: 10 Waukegan IL
  roles: 12 Charley's Aunt **13** Jack Benny Show, To Be or Not To Be **16** Artists and Models

Benoni *see* **8** Benjamin

Benson
  character: 5 Kraus **12** (Lt Gov) Benson DuBois **13** (Gov) Eugene Gatling
  cast: 10 James Noble **11** Inga Swenson **15** Robert Guillaume

bent 4 bias, gift, mind **5** bowed, flair, knack **6** angled, arched, curved, genius, liking, talent **7** ability, aptness, crooked, faculty, hunched, leaning, stooped, twisted **8** aptitude, capacity, facility, fondness, penchant, tendency **9** contorted, endowment **10** attraction, partiality, proclivity, propensity **11** disposition, inclination **12** predilection **14** predisposition

bent into folds 6 fluted, ridged **7** creased, grooved, pleated **8** crinkled, furrowed, puckered, wrinkled **10** corrugated

Benton, Robert
  director of: 14 Kramer vs Kramer (Oscar) **16** Places in the Heart

Benton, Thomas Hart
  born: 8 Neosho MO
  artwork: 7 Bubbles **8** Boomtown **9** Homestead **12** American Life **13** Arts of the West, Cotton Pickers **14** Threshing Wheat **19** Louisiana Rice Fields, The Lord Is My Shepherd

Benue-Congo
  language family: 16 Niger-Kordofanian
  group: 10 Niger-Congo
  includes: 3 Tiv **4** Zulu **5** Bantu, Jukun **6** Chwana, Nyanja **7** Kikongo, Luganda, Swahili

benumb 4 daze, dull **5** blunt **6** deaden **7** stupefy **15** make insensitive

Benvolio
  character in: 14 Romeo and Juliet
  author: 11 Shakespeare

Benz, Karl
  nationality: 6 German
  inventor of: 22 electric ignition engine **26** differential gear automobile
  built first practical: 10 automobile

be obvious 6 appear **7** be clear, be plain **8** be patent **9** be evident **10** be apparent, be manifest

be off 2 go **5** leave, scram **6** beat it, begone, cut out, depart, go away, set out **8** set forth, withdraw **10** make tracks

be of one mind 5 agree **6** accord, concur **10** think alike **11** see eye to eye

be of use 3 aid **4** help **5** serve **6** assist **7** benefit

be on a par with 5 equal **6** be up to **7** compare **10** be as good as **12** be comparable **14** be in a class with

be on the sick list 3 ail **5** be ill **6** be sick **8** be unwell **12** be indisposed **13** be in ill health **17** be under the weather

Beor
son: **4** Bela **6** Balaam

Beothuk (Red Indians)
location: **6** Canada **12** Newfoundland
intermixed with: **7** Naskapi

Beowulf
author: **7** unknown
character: **4** Finn **5** Breca, Hnaef, Oslaf, Scyld **6** Wiglaf **7** Guthlaf, Hengest, Higelac, Hrethel, Unferth **8** Aeschere, Heardred, Hondscio, Hrothgar **9** Hildeburh
great hall: **6** Heorot
monster: **7** Grendel **14** Grendel's mother
tribe: **5** Danes, Geats **8** Frisians
Beowulf tears from Grendel: **3** arm

be part of 4 form **6** make up **8** belong to **9** appertain, pertain to **10** constitute

be patent 6 appear **7** be clear, be plain **9** be evident, be obvious **10** be apparent, be manifest

be pertinent to 4 bear **5** apply, refer **6** affect, relate **7** concern, pertain **9** appertain, touch upon

be plain 6 appear **7** be clear **8** be patent **9** be evident, be obvious **10** be apparent, be manifest

be pleased with 4 like **5** favor **7** approve

bequeath 4 will **5** endow, leave **6** impart **7** consign **8** hand down

bequest 6 legacy **8** bestowal **9** endowment **10** settlement **11** inheritance

berate 5 scold **6** rail at, rebuke **7** bawl out, chew out, reprove, upbraid **8** reproach **9** castigate, criticize, reprimand **10** take to task, tongue-lash

Berber
language family: **11** Afro-asiatic **13** Hamito-Semitic
spoken in: **6** Sahara **11** North Africa

bereave 3 rob **5** strip **6** divest **7** deprive **10** dispossess

Berenice's Hair
constellation of: **13** Coma Berenices

be resigned to 6 accept **8** tolerate

Beret
character in: **16** Giants of the Earth
author: **7** Rolvaag

be revolted by 4 hate **5** abhor **6** de-

test, loathe **7** despise **8** execrate **9** abominate **10** recoil from, shrink from **11** can't stomach **13** find repulsive

berg 4 floe **7** glacier, iceberg, icefloe
South African: **8** mountain
French: **4** neve **5** serac

Berg, Alban
born: **6** Vienna **7** Austria
composer of: **4** Lulu **7** Wozzeck

Bergen, Candace
father: **11** Edgar Bergen
born: **14** Beverly Hills CA
roles: **8** The Group **11** Murphy Brown **15** Carnal Knowledge
husband: **10** Louis Malle

Berger, Thomas
author of: **7** The Feud **9** Neighbors **10** Vital Parts **11** Killing Time **12** Little Big Man, Sneaky People **15** Regiment of Women

Bergman, Ingmar
director of: **14** The Seventh Seal **16** Cries and Whispers, Wild Strawberries **17** Fanny and Alexander **19** Scenes from a Marriage **20** Smiles of a Summer Night

Bergman, Ingrid
born: **6** Sweden **9** Stockholm
children: **12** Pia Lindstrom **18** Isabella Rossellini
roles: **8** Gaslight (Oscar) **9** Anastasia (Oscar), Golda Meir, Joan of Arc, Notorious **10** Casablanca, Intermezzo, Spellbound **17** A Woman Called Golda, The Bells of St Mary's **19** For Whom the Bell Tolls **24** Murder on the Orient Express **25** The Inn of the Sixth Happiness

Berith, Berit, Bris, Brith, Brit 8 covenant **12** circumcision

Berle, Milton
real name: **15** Milton Berlinger
nickname: **11** Uncle Miltie **12** Mr Television
born: **9** New York NY
roles: **17** The Texaco Star Hour **18** Who's Minding the Mint **23** Always Leave Them Laughing

Berlin (East, West)
landmark: **14** Humboldt Castle **15** Gruenwald Castle **16** Berlin Opera House, Markisches Museum **21** Scharlottenburg Castle **29** Kaiser-Wilhelm-Gedachtniskirche
river: **5** Spree
square: **14** Alexander-Platz

Berlin, Elaine
real name of: **9** Elaine May

Berlinger, Milton
real name of: **11** Milton Berle

Berlioz, (Louis) Hector
born: **6** France **13** La Cote St Andre
composer of: **6** Rob Roy, Te Deum **7** Requiem, **8** Herminie, King Lear, Waverley **9** Cleopatra, Nuits d'Ete **10** Le Corsaire, Les Troyens, The Trojans **11** Sardanapale **13** Harold in It-

aly **14** Les Francs Juges, Romeo and Juliet **16** Benvenuto Cellini, Damnation of Faust, Le Carnaval Romain, L'Enfance du Christ **18** Beatrice et Benedict **20** Symphonie Fantastique **28** Symphonie Funebre et Triomphale

Bermuda
other name: **13** Somers Islands
capital/largest city: **8** Hamilton
others: **8** St George
head of state: **14** British monarch **15** governor general
island: **4** Boaz **5** Coney **7** Bermuda, Ireland, Watford **8** Somerset, St Davids **9** St Georges
highest point: **8** Town Hill
sea: **8** Atlantic
physical feature:
harbor: **6** Castle
hill: **5** Gibbs
people:
discoverer: **14** Juan de Bermudez
language: **7** English
religion: **8** Anglican **10** Protestant **15** Church of England
feature:
dancers: **6** Gombey

Bermuda Triangle
bounded by: **7** Bermuda, Florida **9** Melbourne **10** Puerto Rico
site of: **24** mysterious disappearances
of: **5** ships **9** airplanes

Bern, Berne
capital of: **11** Switzerland
landmark: **10** Clock Tower **12** Nydegg Church
river: **3** Aar **4** Aare

Bernard, Henriette-Rosine
real name of: **14** Sarah Bernhardt

Bernhardt, Sarah
real name: **22** Henriette-Rosine Bernard
nickname: **11** Divine Sarah
born: **5** Paris **6** France
roles: **6** Phedre **7** Hernani, Ruy Blas **8** King Lear **14** Queen Elizabeth **17** La Dame aux Camelias

Bernini, Gianlorenzo (Giovanni Lorenzo)
born: **5** Italy **6** Naples
father: **6** Pietro
artwork: **7** Montoya **8** Louis XIV, Vigevano **9** Bellarmine, St Longinus **13** Cathedra Petri, Francis I d'Este, The Assumption **15** Apollo and Daphne **18** Costanza Buonarelli **19** The Rape of Proserpina **21** Saints Andrew and Thomas, The Ecstasy of St Theresa **24** Blessed Lodovica Albertoni **25** Aeneas Anchises and Ascanius
architect of: **12** Santa Bibiana **16** Piazza of St Peter's (Rome) **19** Palazzo Montecitorio **21** Sant' Andrea al Quirinale **22** Palazzo Chigi-Odescalchi **23** Fountain of the Four

Rivers **24** Santa Maria dell' Assunzione

Bernoulli, Daniel
 field: **11** mathematics
 nationality: **5** Swiss
 theory of: **5** gases **6** fluids **18** Bernoulli's Equation

Bernstein, Carl
 author of: **12** The Final Days (with Bob Woodward) **19** All the President's Men (with Bob Woodward)
 newspaper reporter for: **14** Washington Post
 ex: **10** Nora Ephron

Bernstein, Leonard
 born: **10** Lawrence MA
 composer of: **4** Mass **7** Candide, Kaddish **8** Jeremiah **9** Facsimile, Fancy Free, On the Town **13** West Side Story, Wonderful Town **15** The Age of Anxiety, Trouble in Tahiti **16** Chichester Psalms

Beroe
 father: **6** Adonis
 mother: **9** Aphrodite
 nurse of: **6** Semele

Berowne
 character in: **16** Love's Labour's Lost
 author: **11** Shakespeare

Berra, Yogi (Lawrence Peter Berra)
 sport: **8** baseball
 position: **5** coach **7** catcher
 team: **14** New York Yankees

berry 3 egg **4** seed **5** fruit, grain, grape **6** dollar, kernel, tomato, banana **7** currant **8** allspice, bayberry, mulberry **9** blueberry, cranberry, raspberry **10** blackberry, gooseberry, peppercorn, strawberry **11** boysenberry, huckleberry, pomegranate **12** checkerberry
 poisonous: **9** baneberry

Berryman, John
 author of: **8** Recovery **9** Delusions **11** Love and Fame **12** 77 Dream Songs **13** The Dream Songs **16** Berryman's Sonnets **19** The Freedom of the Poet **21** His Toy His Dream His Rest **26** Homage to Mistress Bradstreet

berserk 4 amok, wild **5** crazy **6** insane **7** frantic, violent **8** demented, deranged, frenzied, maniacal, wild-eyed **9** desperate **10** distracted, distraught **12** out of control

Berserker
 origin: **6** Nordic
 form: **7** warrior

berth 3 bed, job **4** bunk, dock, pier, post, quay, slip, spot **5** haven, niche, place, wharf **6** billet, employ, office **8** position **9** anchorage, situation **11** appointment **12** resting place **13** sleeping place

Berthollet, Claude Louis
 field: **9** chemistry
 nationality: **6** French
 researched: **7** ammonia **8** chlorine

Bertram
 character in: **20** All's Well That Ends Well
 author: **11** Shakespeare

Bertram family
 characters in: **13** Mansfield Park
 members: **3** Tom **5** Julia, Maria **6** Edmund **9** Sir Thomas
 author: **6** Austen

beryl
 color: **5** green **6** yellow

Berzelius, Jons Jakob
 field: **9** chemistry
 nationality: **7** Swedish
 developed: **15** chemical symbols
 discovered: **6** cerium **7** silicon, thorium **8** selenium, titanium **9** zirconium
 founded: **15** modern chemistry

be satisfactory 2 do **6** answer **7** suffice **8** be enough **10** be adequate, pass muster **12** be sufficient, do well enough

be scant 4 lack, want **8** be skimpy **9** fall short **14** be insufficient **15** be in short supply

beseech 3 beg **4** pray **6** adjure **7** entreat, implore **9** plead with **10** supplicate

beset 3 dog, set **4** bead, deck, stud **5** annoy, array, hem in, hound, worry **6** assail, badger, harass, pester, plague **7** bedevil, besiege, set upon **8** surround **9** beleaguer, embellish

be sick 3 ail **5** be ill **8** be unwell **12** be indisposed **13** be in ill health

beside 2 by **4** near **5** saved **6** except, nearby, unless **7** abreast, barring, without **8** let alone **9** adjoining, alongside, aside from, other than **10** on a par with, side by side **12** compared with, in addition to

beside oneself 4 wild **6** elated, joyful, joyous, raging **7** berserk, exalted, frantic, furious, ranting **8** agitated, blissful, distrait, ecstatic, frenetic, frenzied **9** delirious, in a frenzy, overjoyed, rapturous **10** distracted, distraught, distressed, enraptured **11** carried away, overwrought, transported **13** out of one's wits

besides 3 but **4** also, save **6** as well, except, saving **7** barring **8** moreover **9** excepting, excluding, other than **11** exclusive of, furthermore

besiege 3 dog **5** annoy, beset, hound **6** assail, badger, harass, pester, plague **7** assault, bedevil **9** beleaguer **10** lay siege to

besmear 4 soil **5** dirty, muddy, smear, stain, sully **6** mess up, slop up, smudge **7** begrime, tarnish **8** besmirch

besmeared 5 dirty, grimy, messy **6** grubby, smudgy **7** muddied, sullied **8** begrimed **10** besmirched

besmirch 4 soil **5** smear, stain, sully,

taint **6** defame, defile **7** blacken, corrupt, debauch, degrade, slander, tarnish **8** discolor, disgrace, dishonor **9** discredit

besotted 5 drunk **6** sodden, soused, wasted, zapped, zonked **7** smashed **9** plastered **10** inebriated, infatuated **11** intoxicated **17** under the influence **20** three sheets to the wind

bespangle 3 dot **4** gild, star, stud **5** adorn, jewel **6** bedeck **7** dress up, festoon, garnish **8** decorate, ornament **9** embellish **10** illuminate

bespatter 4 blot, soil, spot **5** decry, dirty, libel, smear, stain, sully, taint **6** debase, defame, defile, smudge, splash **7** condemn, slander, smotter, tarnish **8** denounce, reproach **9** deprecate, fling dirt **10** calumniate, disapprove

Bessemer, Sir Henry
 nationality: **7** English
 inventor of manufacturing process for: **5** steel

best 3 top **4** most, pick **5** cream, elite **6** choice, finest, nicest, utmost **7** hardest, largest **8** foremost, greatest, superior, topnotch **9** greetings, loveliest, most fully, most of all, unequaled, unrivaled **10** unexcelled **11** compliments, unsurpassed **13** most competent, most desirable, most excellent **14** highest quality, kindest regards

Best, Charles Herbert
 field: **10** physiology
 nationality: **8** Canadian
 discovered: **7** insulin

best group 3 top **5** cream, elite **6** choice **9** chosen few **10** select body **14** cream of the crop, creme de la creme

bestial 5 cruel **6** brutal, savage **7** beastly **8** barbaric, depraved, inhumane, ruthless **9** barbarous, merciless

bestir 4 goad, spur, stir, urge **5** rouse, speed **6** arouse, excite, hasten **7** quicken **8** activate **9** get moving

bestir oneself 5 rouse **8** be active **9** make haste **10** get up early, lose no time **11** keep moving **15** make short work of **19** seize the opportunity

bestow 3 use **4** give, mete **5** apply, award, grant, lay on, spend **6** accord, confer, devote, donate, employ, expend, impart, occupy, render **7** consign, consume, deal out, deliver, hand out, present, utilize **8** dispense, give away **9** apportion **10** settle upon, turn over to

bestowal 4 alms, gift **5** bonus, favor, grant **6** reward **7** charity, present, tribute **8** donation, gratuity, offering **9** endowment **10** conferment, recompense **11** benefaction **12** contribution, dispensation

best society
French: **10** grand monde

Best Years of Our Lives, The
director: **12** William Wyler
based on story by: **15** MacKinlay Kantor
script: **14** Robert Sherwood
cast: **8** Myrna Loy **11** Dana Andrews **12** Teresa Wright, Virginia Mayo **13** Frederic March, Harold Russell **15** Hoagy Carmichael
Oscar for: **5** actor (March) **7** picture **8** director

be sufficient 6 answer **7** suffice **8** be enough **10** be adequate, pass muster **12** do well enough **14** be satisfactory

bet 4 ante, risk **5** stake, wager **6** chance, gamble, hazard, plunge **7** venture **8** make a bet **9** speculate **11** speculation

bete noir 5 bogey **6** plague **7** bugaboo, bugbear **8** anathema, bogeyman **9** annoyance **10** black beast

be thankful 8 thank God **10** appreciate **11** thank heaven **19** thank one's lucky stars

Bethe, Hans Albrecht
field: **7** physics
developed: **8** atom bomb
awarded: **10** Nobel Prize

be the same 5 agree, equal, match **6** equate **7** balance **11** be identical

betide 4 fall **5** occur **6** befall, chance, happen **10** come to pass

betimes 5 early **10** in good time

betoken 4 show **5** augur **6** attest, denote **7** portend, presage, signify **8** foretell

betray 4 dupe, fink, jilt, show, tell **5** rat on, trick **6** expose, reveal, squeal, tell on, unmask **7** abandon, deceive, divulge, lay bare, let down, let slip, sell out, two-time, uncover, violate **8** blurt out, disclose, give away **9** play Judas **10** be disloyal **11** double-cross **12** be unfaithful **13** inform against, play false with **14** break faith with

betrayal 7 perfidy, telling, treason **8** bad faith, sedition, trickery **9** chicanery, deception, duplicity, falseness, treachery, two-timing, violation **10** disclosure, disloyalty, divulgence, revelation **11** double-cross **13** breach of faith, double-dealing **14** unfaithfulness

betrayal of trust 7 falsity, perfidy **8** apostasy, cheating **9** falseness, recreancy **10** disloyalty, infidelity **11** inconstancy **13** deceitfulness, double-dealing, faithlessness **14** unfaithfulness

Betrayer 13 Judas Iscariot

betroth 6 commit, engage, pledge **7** espouse, promise **8** affiance, contract

betrothal 5 troth **8** espousal **10** affiancing, betrothing, engagement

betrothed 6 fiance **7** engaged, fiancee **8** promised **9** affianced

Bettelheim, Bruno
author of: **15** Love Is Not Enough **16** The Informed Heart **20** The Uses of Enchantment

better 3 top **4** more **5** finer, outdo, raise **6** bigger, enrich, exceed, fitter, larger, longer, refine, uplift **7** advance, elevate, enhance, farther, forward, further, greater, improve, mending, promote, surpass, upgrade **8** heighten, improved, increase, outstrip, stronger, superior **9** cultivate, healthier, improving **10** preferable, recovering, strengthen **11** more healthy, progressing

bettering 9 elevation **10** betterment **11** advancement, improvement

betterment 4 good **6** reform **7** benefit **8** revision **9** advantage, amendment, promotion **10** correction, enrichment **11** advancement, improvement **12** amelioration, regeneration **13** rectification **14** reconstruction

better than average 2 A-1 **3** A-OK **4** aces, a-one, fine, good, tops **5** great, prime, super **6** choice, grade-A, superb **7** capital, special **8** peerless, sterling, superior, terrific, top-notch **9** excellent, first-rate, marvelous, matchless, wonderful **10** first-class, inimitable, preeminent, remarkable, tremendous **11** exceptional, outstanding, superlative **12** incomparable **13** extraordinary

between 4 amid **5** among, entre **6** amidst, atwixt, shared **7** betwixt, joining **9** in the midst **10** connecting

between ourselves
French: **9** entre nous
Latin: **8** inter nos

Between the Battles
author: **20** Bjornstjerne Bjornson

between themselves
Latin: **7** inter se

between us 9 entre nous, privately **14** confidentially **15** between you and me **16** between me and thee, between ourselves

betwixt and between 4 so-so **7** average **8** confused **9** in between, undecided **14** halfway between **21** neither one nor the other

Beulah, Land of
place in: **16** Pilgrim's Progress
author: **6** Bunyan

be unlike 4 vary **6** differ **7** deviate, diverge **8** conflict, disagree **12** be at variance, be discordant, be dissimilar

be unwell 3 ail **5** be ill **6** be sick **12** be indisposed **13** be in ill health

be unwilling to pursue
Latin: **13** nolle prosequi

bevel 4 blow, cant, ream, tool **5** angle, bezel, miter, mitre, slant, slope, snape, splay **6** aslant **7** incline, oblique **8** slanting

beverage 3 ade, ale, cup, nog, pop, tea **4** beer, brew, cafe, dram, grog, milk, soda, soup, wine **5** broth, caffe, cider, cocoa, draft, drink, juice, julep, lager, latte, leban, punch, toddy, water **6** bishop, coffee, cordial, eggnog, liquid, liquor, potion **7** limeade, seltzer, spirits, wassail **8** aperitif, cocktail, espresso, expresso, highball, lemonade, libation, potation **9** champagne, chocolate, orangeade **10** cappuccino

Beverley, Constance de
character in: **7** Marmion
author: **5** Scott

Beverly Hillbillies, The
character: **11** Jed Clampett **12** Jane Hathaway, Jethro Bodine **14** Granny Clampett, Milton Drysdale **16** Ellie May Clampett
cast: **9** Irene Ryan, Max Baer Jr, Nancy Kulp **10** Buddy Ebsen **12** Donna Douglas **13** Raymond Bailey

Beverly Hills Cop
director: **11** Martin Brest
cast: **11** Eddie Murphy **13** Judge Reinhold, Lisa Eilbacher

bevy 4 band, body, herd, host, pack **5** brood, covey, crowd, drove, flock, group, horde, party, shoal, swarm **6** clutch, flight, gaggle, school, throng **7** company, coterie **9** gathering, multitude **10** assemblage, collection

bewail 3 rue **5** mourn **6** bemoan, lament, regret **7** cry over, deplore **8** moan over, weep over **10** grieve over

beware 4 mind **6** be wary **7** look out **8** take care, take heed **9** be careful **11** take warning, watch out for **12** be on the alert, guard against **15** take precautions

beware of the dog
Latin: **9** cave canem

bewhiskered 5 bushy, hairy **6** shaggy **7** bearded, bristly, hirsute **8** unshaven **11** mustachioed

bewilder 5 addle, mix up **6** baffle, bemuse, muddle, puzzle **7** confuse, fluster, mystify, nonplus, perplex, stupefy **8** befuddle **10** disconcert

bewildered 7 at a loss, up a tree **8** all at sea, confused **9** perplexed **10** confounded, nonplussed **12** disconcerted

bewilderment 9 confusion **10** perplexity, puzzlement **11** frustration **13** mystification

bewitch 4 jinx **5** charm, spook **6** turn on **7** bedevil, beguile, delight, enchant **8** entrance **9** captivate, enrapture, fascinate **12** cast a spell on **14** put under a spell

bewitched 7 charmed, seduced **8** beguiled **9** bedeviled, enchanted, entranced **10** captivated, enraptured, fascinated, spellbound **11** under a spell

Bewitched
  character: **6** Endora, Serena **7** Maurice **9** Aunt Clara, Esmerelda, Larry Tate **11** Uncle Arthur **12** Abner Kravitz **13** Gladys Kravitz **14** Darrin Stephens **15** Tabitha Stephens **16** Samantha Stephens
  cast: **8** Dick York **9** Paul Lynde **10** David White **11** Dick Sargent, Marion Lorne, Sandra Gould **12** George Tobias, Maurice Evans **13** Alice Ghostley **14** Agnes Moorehead **19** Elizabeth Montgomery

bewitching **8** alluring, charming, enticing, fetching, tempting **9** appealing, beguiling, disarming, seductive **10** enchanting, entrancing **11** captivating, fascinating **12** irresistible

be worthy of **4** earn, rate **5** merit **7** deserve

bey, beg **4** lord **6** prince **8** governor

beyond **2** by **4** over, past **5** above, later, ultra **6** abroad, except, yonder **7** beneath, besides, farther, further, outside, passing **8** superior **9** exceeding, hereafter **10** out of range, out of reach **11** at a distance, in addition to

Beyond Desire
  author: **15** Maxwell Anderson

beyond hope **8** hopeless **9** desperate **10** despairing

Beyond Human Power
  author: **20** Bjornstjerne Bjornson

beyond one's means **10** immoderate **11** extravagant **15** too high on the hog

beyond question **4** sure **6** surely **7** certain, decided, settled **9** certainly, decidedly **10** absolutely, positively **12** without doubt

Bharat (Varsha) *see* **5** India

Bhot *see* **5** Tibet

Bhutan
  other name: **7** Druk-Yul **15** Kingdom of Bhutan, Land of the Dragon
  capital/largest city: **6** Thimbu **7** Thimphu
  others: **4** Paro **12** Phuntsholing **14** Wangdu Phedrang
  government:
    assembly: **7** Tsongdu
  head of state/ government:
    hereditary king: **10** dragon king, druk gyalpo
  other leader:
    spiritual leader: **10** dharma raja
    temporal ruler: **7** deb raja
  monetary unit: **5** paisa, rupee **8** chetrums, ngultrum
  mountain: **5** Black **9** Himalayas **10** Chomo Lhari
  highest point: **10** Kula Kangri
  river: **4** Kuru, Paro **5** Machu, Manas, Pachu, Torsa **6** Amochu, Raidak, Tongsa **7** Sankosh, Thinchu
  physical feature:
    plain: **5** Duars

people: **5** Monpa **6** Bhutia **7** Tibetan **8** Assamese, Nepalese
  dragon people: **7** Drukpas
language: **5** Hindi, Lhoke **7** Tibetan **8** Dzongkha, Nepalese
religion: **15** Tibetan Buddhism
place:
  fortress (dzong): **4** Paro **6** Bya Kar, Tongsa **8** Tashi Cho
feature:
  pony: **6** Tangun

Bianca
  character in: **10** Kiss Me Kate **19** The Taming of the Shrew
  author: **11** Shakespeare

Bianchi, Mose
  born: **5** Italy, Milan
  artwork: **11** Snow in Milan **21** Return from the Festival

bias **4** bent, sway **5** angle, slant **7** bigotry, feeling, leaning **8** tendency **9** fixed idea, prejudice, proneness **10** narrow view, partiality, predispose, proclivity, propensity, unfairness **11** inclination, intolerance **12** diagonal line, one-sidedness, predilection **13** preconception **16** narrow-mindedness, preconceived idea

biased **6** unfair, unjust **7** bigoted, slanted **8** inclined **9** arbitrary **10** intolerant, prejudiced **11** close-minded, opinionated **12** narrow-minded

bibelot **5** curio **7** trinket **8** ornament **9** objet d'art

bible **5** guide **6** manual **8** handbook **9** authority, guidebook **13** reference book

Bible **6** Gospel **7** the Book **8** good book, Holy Writ **10** Scriptures **11** bibliotheca, the Good Book **13** holy scripture **14** Holy Scriptures, sacred writings

Bible, books of
  Old Testament: **3** Job **4** Amos, Ezra, Joel, Osee, Ruth **5** Hosea, Jonah, Jonas, Josue, Kings, Micah, Nahum, Tobit **6** Abdias, Aggeus, Baruch, Daniel, Es- dras, Esther, Exodus, Haggai, Isaiah, Isaias, Joshua, Judges, Judith, Psalms, Samuel, Sirach, Tobias, Wisdom **7** Ezekiel, Genesis, Habacuc, Malachi, Micheas, Numbers, Obadiah **8** Ezechiel, Habakkuk, Jeremiah, Jeremias, Nehemiah, Proverbs **9** Leviticus, Maccabees, Machabees, Malachias, Sophonias, Zacharias, Zechariah, Zephaniah **10** Chronicles **11** Deuteronomy, Song of Songs **12** Ecclesiastes, Lamentations **13** Paralipomenon, Song of Solomon **14** Ecclesiasticus **19** Canticle of Canticles
  New Testament: **4** Acts, John, Jude, Luke, Mark **5** James, Peter **6** Romans **7** Hebrews, Matthew, Timothy **9** Ephesians, Galatians **10** Colossians, Revelation **11** Corinthians,

Philippians **13** Thessalonians, Titus Philemon
  first five books called: **3** Law **5** Torah **10** Pentateuch
  first seven books called: **10** Heptateuch

Bible scholar **7** biblist **9** biblicist

Bible version **5** Douay **6** The Way **7** Vulgate **8** Peshitta **9** Gutenberg, Jerusalem, King James **10** Authorized, New English **11** New American, Rheims-Douay **14** The Living Bible **15** American revised, revised standard

Biblical animal **7** unicorn

Biblical gemstone **6** ligure **7** sardius **8** sardonyx

Biblical instrument **7** sackbut

Biblical length
  reed: **9** six cubits

Biblical measure **3** cab, cor **4** epah, omet, reed, seah **5** cubit, epheh, homer **6** shekel **9** half homer

Biblical personage **9** patriarch

Biblical plant **6** hyssop **12** Rose of Sharon

Biblical precept
  Hebrew: **7** mitsvah, mitzvah

Biblical tree **5** algum, almug **6** storax **7** juniper **8** sycamire **10** gopherwood **11** shittim wood **12** opobalsammum **13** red sandalwood

Biblical weed **4** tare **6** darnel

Biblical weight **6** talent

Biblicist **12** Bible scholar

Bibliotheca **5** Bible **14** sacred writings

Biblist **12** Bible scholar

Bickel, Ernest Frederick McIntyre
  real name of: **13** Frederic March

bicker **4** spar, spat **5** argue, fight **6** haggle **7** dispute, quarrel, wrangle **8** disagree, squabble

bickering **4** spat **5** fight **7** arguing, dispute, quarrel **8** argument, fighting **9** wrangling **10** quarreling, squabbling **12** disagreement

Bickford, Charles
  born: **11** Cambridge MA
  roles: **12** Anna Christie **13** Johnny Belinda **16** Song of Bernadette **18** The Farmer's Daughter

bicycle **4** bike, ride **5** cycle, moped **10** two-wheeler
  invented by: **7** Starley

Bicycle Thief, The
  director: **14** Vittorio De Sica
  cast: **14** Lianella Carell **18** Lamberto Maggiorani

bid **3** ask, say, try **4** call, tell, wish **5** greet, offer, order **6** beckon, charge, demand, direct, effort, enjoin, insist, invite, ordain, summon, tender **7** attempt, command, proffer, propose, request, require **8** call upon, endeavor, instruct, offering, proposal **10** invitation

bidding 4 beck, call **5** offer, order **6** behest, charge, demand, offers **7** command, dictate, mandate, request, summons **8** offering, proposal **9** direction, summoning, tendering **10** injunction, invitation, proffering **11** instruction

bide 4 stay, wait **5** abide, dwell, stand, tarry **6** endure, linger, remain, suffer **8** tolerate **9** put up with

Bierce, Ambrose
author of: **15** Can Such Things Be? **16** In the Midst of Life **19** The Devil's Dictionary

Bierstadt, Albert
born: **7** Germany **8** Solingen
artwork: **11** Laramie Park **13** Mount Corcoran **17** The Rocky Mountains **20** Discovery of the Hudson, Storm on the Matterhorn **21** Sunrise Yosemite Valley **22** Settlement of California **31** Thunderstorm in the Rocky Mountains

bifocal lenses
invented by: **8** Franklin

Bifrost
origin: **12** Scandinavian
form: **6** bridge
bridge of: **4** gods
made of: **7** rainbow
from: **6** Asgard
to: **5** earth

bifurcate 4 fork **5** split **6** branch, divide **7** diverge **8** separate

big 3 top **4** head, high, huge, just, kind, main, vast **5** adult, ample, bulky, chief, great, grown, heavy, husky, large, major, noble, prime, vital **6** heroic, humane, mature **7** eminent, grown-up, haughty, hulking, immense, leading, liberal, mammoth, massive, notable, pompous, sizable, weighty **8** abundant, arrogant, boastful, bragging, colossal, enormous, generous, gigantic, gracious, princely **9** conceited, grandiose, honorable, important, momentous, prominent, strapping **10** benevolent, chivalrous, high-minded, monumental, prodigious **11** magnanimous, pretentious, significant, substantial **12** considerable **13** consequential

Big Apple
nickname of: **11** New York City

Big Bend State
nickname of: **9** Tennessee

Big Chill, The
director: **14** Lawrence Kasdan
cast: **8** Meg Tilly **10** Glenn Close, Kevin Kline **11** Tom Berenger, William Hurt **12** Jeff Goldblum

Big Daddy
character in: **16** Cat on a Hot Tin Roof
author: **8** Williams
played by: **8** Burl Ives

Big E
nickname of: **10** Elvin Hayes

Bigfoot 4 Yeti **9** Sasquatch **17** Abominable Snowman

big guns 4 VIPs **5** brass **6** cannon **7** bigwigs, top dogs **8** big shots, ordnance **9** artillery **14** heavy artillery, high mucky-mucks **15** important people

bighearted 6 lavish **7** liberal **8** generous, handsome, princely, prodigal **9** bounteous, bountiful, unselfish **10** beneficent, benevolent, charitable, free-handed, open- handed, unstinting **11** magnanimous, open-hearted **12** humanitarian

bight 3 bay **4** bend, cave, road

Biglow Papers
author: **18** James Russell Lowell

Big Money, The
author: **13** John Dos Passos

bigness 4 bulk **8** enormity, hugeness **9** amplitude, great size, greatness, largeness, magnitude **11** massiveness

Big O, The
nickname of: **14** Oscar Robertson

bigoted 6 biased **10** intolerant, prejudiced **12** closed- minded, narrow-minded

bigotry 4 bias **6** racism **9** prejudice **10** unfairness **11** intolerance **14** discrimination **16** closed-mindedness, narrow-mindedness

Big Parade, The
director: **9** King Vidor
cast: **11** John Gilbert, Renee Adoree **14** Hobart Bosworth

big shot 3 VIP **4** name **5** mogul, nabob, wheel **6** big gun, bigwig, fat cat, tycoon **7** big deal, magnate, notable **8** somebody **9** big cheese, dignitary, personage **13** high-muck-a-muck, wheeler-dealer

Big Six
nickname of: **16** Christy Mathewson

Big Sky, The
author: **11** A B Guthrie Jr

Big Sky State
nickname of: **7** Montana

Big Sleep, The
author: **15** Raymond Chandler
hero: **13** Philip Marlowe
director: **11** Howard Hawks
cast: **12** Elisha Cook Jr, Lauren Bacall **13** Dorothy Malone, Martha Vickers **14** Humphrey Bogart (Philip Marlowe)
setting: **10** Los Angeles

Big Train
nickname of: **13** Walter Johnson

Big Valley, The
character: **11** Nick Barkley **12** Audra Barkley, Heath Barkley **13** Jarrod Barkley **15** Victoria Barkley
cast: **9** Lee Majors **10** Linda Evans, Peter Breck **11** Richard Long **15** Barbara Stanwyck

bigwig 3 VIP **7** big shot, notable **9** dignitary, personage

bikini 8 two-piece **11** bathing suit
top: **3** bra
bottom **5** thong
topless: **8** monokini
type: **6** string

Bikini 5 atoll **9** Namu islet **10** West Pacific **15** Marshall Islands

bile 4 gall, rage **5** anger, venom, wrath **6** choler, spleen

bilge 3 rot **4** bosh, bull, bunk, tosh **5** hooey, tripe **6** drivel, humbug, jabber, piffle **7** baloney, hogwash, rubbish, twaddle **8** malarkey, nonsense **9** gibberish **10** balderdash **11** foolishness, jabberwocky **13** horsefeathers **16** stuff and nonsense

bilious 4 sick **5** angry, cross, huffy, nasty, testy **6** crabby, cranky, grumpy, queasy, sickly, touchy **7** grouchy, peevish **8** bile- like, greenish, nauseous, petulant, snappish **9** irritable, sickening **10** ill-humored, out of sorts **11** ill-tempered **12** cantankerous **13** short-tempered **15** green at the gills

bilk 3 gyp **4** dupe, gull, rook, take **5** cheat, cozen, trick **6** fleece, rip off **7** deceive, defraud, swindle **8** hoodwink **9** bamboozle, victimize

bill 3 act, fee, law **4** card, chit, list **5** tally **6** agenda, charge, decree, docket, poster, roster, ticket **7** account, catalog, charges, invoice, leaflet, measure, placard, program, statute **8** banknote, brochure, bulletin, calendar, circular, handbill, proposal, register, schedule **9** greenback, inventory, ordinance, reckoning, statement **10** regulation **12** treasury note **13** advertisement **17** silver certificate

billet 3 job **4** base, bunk, camp, digs, note, post **5** berth, house, lodge, place, put up **6** letter, office **7** bed down, lodging, quarter, shelter **8** domicile, dwelling, lodgment, position, quarters **9** residence, situation **11** accommodate, appointment **13** accommodation

billfold see **6** wallet

billiards
player: **11** Willie Hoppe **13** Minnesota Fats, Willie Mosconi

Bill of Divorcement, A
director: **11** George Cukor
cast: **11** Billie Burke **13** John Barrymore **16** Katharine Hepburn

billow 4 roll, wave **5** belly, cloud, crest, surge, swell **6** puff up **7** balloon, breaker

Billy Budd
author: **14** Herman Melville
character: **8** Claggart **11** Captain Vere
opera by: **7** Britten

billyclub 3 bat **5** billy, stick **8** bludgeon **9** truncheon

bin 3 box **4** cart, crib, silo **5** crate, frame, hatch **6** barrel, basket, bunker, hamper, holder, trough, vessel **9** container, inclosure **10** receptacle

binate 4 dual **6** double **7** coupled, two fold **14** growing in pairs

bind 3 rim, tie **4** edge, gird, glue, join, lash, rope, trim, wrap **5** affix, chafe, cover, cramp, force, frame, hitch, paste, stick, strap, tie up, truss **6** attach, border, coerce, compel, encase, fasten, fringe, oblige, secure, swathe **7** bandage, confine, require **8** encumber, obligate **9** prescribe **11** necessitate

binder 4 glue, roux **5** paste **6** cement **8** notebook **9** assurance, guarantee **11** down payment **12** earnest money **17** looseleaf notebook

binding 4 band, face, tape **5** valid **6** edging, ribbon **7** styptic **8** fastener, ligative **9** stringent **10** compulsory, obligatory, peremptory **12** constricting

binge 3 jag **4** bust, orgy, tear, toot **5** blast, drunk, fling, revel, spree **6** bender **7** carouse **8** beer-bust, carousal **11** bacchanalia **12** drunken spree

Bingham, George Caleb
  born: 15 Augusta County VA
  artwork: 13 Stump Speaking **17** The Trapper's Return **18** Verdict of the People **19** The Jolly Flatboatman **20** Raftsmen Playing Cards **31** Fur Traders Descending the Missouri

Bingley, Mr
  character in: 17 Pride and Prejudice
  author: 6 Austen

biochemist 17 biological chemist
  American: 4 Cori **5** Bloch, Moore, Ochoa **7** Axelrod, Lipmann **8** Kornberg
  English: 5 Krebs **6** Porter, Sanger **8** Mitchell
  French: 5 Monod **7** Duclaux
  German: 5 Lynen

biogenesis
  discoverer: 12 Louis Pasteur

biography 3 bio **4** life, vita **6** memoir **7** account, history **9** life story

biologist
  American: 6 Carson, Yerkes **7** Burbank **8** Delbruck
  British: 6 Darwin, Huxley **7** Bateson, Medawar
  French: 5 Jacob, Monod **7** Lamarck
  German: 7 Schwann
  Swiss: 6 Haller

biology
  branch: 6 botany **7** zoology
  classification: 15 Carolus Linnaeus

birch 6 Betula
  varieties: 3 Low, Red **4** Fire, Gray **5** Black, Canoe, Dwarf, Paper, River, Swamp, Sweet, Water, White **6** Cherry, Yellow **7** Monarch **8** Mahogany, Old-field **10** West Indian **13** European white, Japanese white, Young's weeping **14** Japanese cherry

Birches
  author: 11 Robert Frost

bird
  anatomy: 3 bec, neb, nib **4** beak, bill, cere, crop, lora, lore, mala, nape, rump, tail, tuft, wing **5** alula, crest, crown, flank, larum, lorum, pilea, rosta **6** breast, gullet, pecten, pileum, pinion, syrinx, tarsus **7** ambiens, crissum, gizzard, rostrum **8** gigerium, pectines, scapular **9** auchenium, gastraeum **10** cordylanus
  aquatic/water: 3 auk, cob, ern, mew **4** cobb, coot, duck, erne, gony, gull, ibis, loon, rail, shag, skua, sora, swan, teal, tern **5** booby, cahow, crane, diver, goose, grebe, heron, murre, ousel, rotch, snipe, solan, stilt, stork **6** avocet, curlew, cygnet, dipper, fulmar, gannet, godwit, hagdon, jabiru, jacana, osprey, petrel, plover, puffin, rotche, scoter, wigeon **7** anhinga, bidcock, bittern, bustard, dovekey, dovekie, finfoot, mallard, moorhen, pelican, penguin, seriema, skimmer, widgeon **8** alcatras, baldpate, dabchick, flamingo, murrelet, umbrette **9** albatross, baptornis, cormorant, gallinule, guillemot, kittiwake, phalarope, snakebird, spoonbill **10** gaviformes, kingfisher, shearwater, sheathbill, yellowlegs **13** whooping crane
  bird cage/home: 4 cote, mews, nest **5** roost **6** aviary, volary, volery **7** rookery
  bird of freedom: 9 bald eagle
  bird of ill-omen: 5 raven
  bird of Jove: 5 eagle
  bird of June: 7 peacock
  bird of Minerva: 3 owl
  bird of peace: 4 dove
  bird of prey: 3 owl **4** gled, hawk, kite **5** buteo, eagle, glead, glede, harpy, saker **6** condor, elanet, elenet, falcon, musket, osprey, raptor **7** buzzard, goshawk, harrier, kestrel, stooper, vulture **8** caracara **9** accipiter, gyrfalcon, peregrine **11** accipitrine, lammergeier
  bird of wonder/rebirth: 7 phoenix
  carrion-eater: 4 aura **5** urubu **6** condor **7** buzzard, vulture
  class: 4 Aves
  combining form: 3 avi **4** orni **5** ornis **6** ornith **7** ornitho **8** ornithes
  crow family: 3 daw, jay, kae **4** crow, rook **5** crake, raven **6** chough, corbie, magpie **7** corvine, jackdaw
  duck family: 4 clee, coot, lory, smew, teal, wood **5** eider, goose **6** scoter **7** gadwall, mallard, Muscovy, pintail, pochard **8** baldpate, redshank, shoveler **9** merganser **10** bufflehead, canvasback
  extinct: 3 auk, jib, moa **4** dodo, jibi, mamo **5** didus **8** Diatryma **9** aepyornis, apatornis, gastornis, hespornis, solitaire **11** archaeornis
  flightless: 3 emu, ihi, moa **4** dodo, gorb, kagu, kiwi, rhea, weka **5** nandu **6** callow, kakapo, moorup, ratite, takahe **7** apteryx, horling, ostrich, peacock, penguin, roatelo **8** notornis **9** cassowary
  game: 4 duck, guan, rail, sora, teal **5** brant, goose, quail, snipe **6** chukar, colima, grouse, pigeon, plover, turkey **7** bustard, chicken, flapper, gadwall, mallard, pintail, prairie, widgeon **8** baldpate, bobwhite, moorfowl, pheasant, shoveler, tragopan, wildfowl, woodcock **9** merganser, partridge, ptarmigan **10** canvasback
  group of birds: 3 nye **4** bank, bevy, cast, nide, sord **5** aerie, brood, covey, drove, flock, plump **6** covert, flight, gaggle, litter, spring
  largest: 7 ostrich **11** lammergeier
  legendary: 3 roc **6** simurg **7** phoenix, simurgh **9** feng- huang, feng-hwang
  loss of feathers: 7 molting
  smallest: 11 hummingbird
  nocturnal: 3 owl **5** cahow, owlet, potoo **7** bullbat, dorhawk **8** guacharo, nightjar **9** nighthawk, thickknee **10** goatsucker **11** nightingale
  pet: 4 myna **5** mynah **6** canary, parrot, pigeon **8** cockatoo, lovebird, parakeet
  plumage: 8 ptilosis
  poultry: 3 hen **4** duck **5** goose **6** pigeon, turkey **7** chicken, rooster **8** pheasant **14** Cornish game hen
  talking: 4 myna **5** mynah **6** parrot
  wingless: 4 kiwi, weka **7** apteryx
  young: 4 eyas, gull **5** chick, piper, poult, squab **6** gorlin, pullus **7** flapper, nestler **8** birdikin, nestling **9** fledgling
  of Africa: 4 coly, fink, taha, tock **5** crane, paauw **6** barbet, bulbul, cuckoo, jabiru, quelea, whidah **7** courser, finfoot, marabou, ostrich, touraco **8** hornbill, oxpecker, parakeet, umbrette **9** beefeater, broadbill, francolin, napecrest, trochilus **10** hammerhead, weaverbird
  of Antarctic/Arctic: 3 auk **4** gull, knot, skua, xema **5** brant, murre, rotch **6** dunlin, falcon, fulmar, jaeger, rotche **7** dovekey, dovekie, penguin **8** grayling **9** guillemot, gyrfalcon, ptarmigan **10** sheathbill
  of Asia: 4 kora, myna, ruff, smew **5** mynah, pewit, pitta **6** bulbul, chukar, drongo, dunlin, hoopoe, linnet **7** boobook, courser, hill tit, lapwing, peacock, sirgang **8** accentor, dotterel, hornbill, leaf bird, parakeet, tragopan, wheatear **9** brambling, francolin, muted swan
  of Australia: 3 emu **4** kahu, kiwi, koel, koil, lory **5** arara, galah, lowan,

pitta **6** drongo, leipoa **7** boobook, bustard, figbird, grinder, waybung **8** bellbird, bushlark, cockatoo, gang-gang, lorikeet, lyrebird, megapode, manucode, morepork, parakeet, platypus **9** bowerbird, cassowary, coachwhip, cockatiel, frogmouth, pardalote, thornbird **10** kookaburra
of Central America: 4 guan, ibis **5** booby, macaw **6** barbet, jabiru, quezal, toucan **7** bittern, cotinga, jacamar, quetzal, tinamou **8** curassow, puffbird, troupial
of Cuba: 6 trogon **8** tocororo **14** bee hummingbird
of England: 4 kite, rook **9** cormorant **11** carrion crow
of Europe: 3 dar, mag, mew, nun **4** clee, gled, mall, merl, pope, rook, ruff, shag, smew, wren **5** amsel, crake, egret, finch, glede, merle, ousel, ouzel, pewit, pipit, stilt, stork, swift, tarin, terek, whaup **6** cuckoo, dunlin, godwit, grouse, hoopoe, linnet, martin, merlin, missel, redleg, roller, siskin, thrush **7** bittern, bustard, jackdaw, kestrel, lapwing, martlet, ortolan, redwing, ruddock, skylark, sparrow, starnel, wagtail, wryneck **8** bee eater, blackcap, brantail, daychick, dotterel, garganey, nightjar, nuthatch, peesweep, redstart, reedling, starling, throstle, wheatear, whimbrel, whinchat, whinshat, woodcock **9** brambling, chaffinch, crossbill, field fare, gallinule, sheldrake, stonechat **10** chiffchaff, goatsucker, kingfisher, lammergeir, turtledove **11** lammergeier, nightingale, wallcreeper **12** capercaillie
of Hawaii: 2 io **3** ava, ioa, iwa, poe **4** nene, iiwi, koae, mamo, moho, omao **6** parson **7** frigate
of India: 4 baya, kala, koel, koil **5** sarus, shama **6** argala, bulbul, homrai, luggar **7** peacock **8** adjutant, amadavat, pheasant, tragopan **11** red hornbill
of Jamaica: 7 vervain
of Java: 7 sparrow **8** rice bird **9** fruit dove
of Madagascar: 6 drongo **7** anhinga, kirombo, roatelo
of Mexico: 6 jacana
of New Guinea: 9 cassowary **14** bird of paradise
of New Zealand: 3 ihi, kea, moa, poe, tui **4** huia, kaka, kaki, kiwi, koko, kuku, ruru, titi, weka **6** kakapo **7** apteryx **8** morepork, notornis
of North America: 3 ani, auk, tit **4** coot, crow, dove, ibis, lark, loon, pape, rook, sora, stib, swan, tern, wamp, wren **5** booby, brant, colin, crane, egret, finch, grebe, junco, murre, quail, robin, snipe, swift, veery, vireo **6** chebec, cuckoo, cur-

lew, darter, dunlin, fulmar, grouse, hagdon, magpie, martin, oriole, phoebe, plover, shrike, thrush, towhee, turkey, verdin, willet **7** anhinga, bittern, blue jay, catbird, flicker, goshawk, grackle, lapwing, pelican, sparrow, swallow, tanager, warbler **8** bluebird, bobolink, bobwhite, cardinal, grosbeak, killdeer, nuthatch, poorwill, starling, thrasher, titmouse, wheatear **9** blackbird, chickadee, crossbill, goldfinch, gyrfalcon, nighthawk, partridge, sandpiper, snakebird **10** bufflehead, kingfisher, meadowlark, woodpecker **11** hummingbird, mockingbird **12** whippoorwill
of South America: 3 ara, hia **4** anna, guan, jacu, loro, mitu, rhea, soco, toco, yeni **5** egret, macaw, potoo, sylph **6** barbet, chatja, chunga, cracid, jabiru, motmot, sappho, toucan **7** cariama, cotinga, hoatzin, jacamar, limpkin, manakin, seriema, tinamou, warrior **8** boatbill, caracara, curassow, guacharo, hoactzin, screamer, tapacolo, tapaculo, terutero, troupial **9** campanero, trumpeter **11** scarlet ibis
of West India: 3 ani **4** tody
Bird, Larry
sport: 10 basketball
position: 5 coach **7** forward
team: 13 Boston Celtics
from: 7 Indiana
Birdman of Alcatraz
director: 17 John Frankenheimer
cast: 10 Karl Malden **12** Edmond O'Brien, Neville Brand, Thelma Ritter **13** Burt Lancaster (Robert Stroud)
Bird of Paradise
constellation of: 4 Apus
Birds, The
author: 12 Aristophanes
character: 4 Iris **5** Meton **8** Basileia, Cinesias **9** Euelpides **10** King Tereus, Prometheus **12** Peithetairos
Birds, The
director: 15 Alfred Hitchcock
based on story by: 15 Daphne du Maurier
cast: 9 Rod Taylor **11** Tippi Hedren **12** Jessica Tandy **16** Suzanne Pleshette
setting: 10 California
Birds Fall Down, The
author: 15 Dame Rebecca West
Birkin, Rupert
character in: 11 Women in Love
author: 8 Lawrence
Birmingham
football team: 9 Stallions
Birmingham, Stephen
author of: 8 Our Crowd **11** The Grandees **14** The Right People **15** Life at the Dakota

Birnbaum, Nathan
real name of: 11 George Burns
birth 5 blood, start, stock **6** family, origin, source, strain **7** bearing, descent, genesis, lineage **8** ancestry, breeding, delivery **9** beginning, being born, emergence, genealogy, inception, parentage **10** background, beginnings, childbirth, derivation, extraction **11** confinement, parturition **12** commencement
Birth of a Nation, The
director: 10 D W Griffith
cast: 8 Mae Marsh **11** Lillian Gish **14** Henry B Walthall
Birth of Tragedy, The
author: 18 Friedrich Nietzsche
birthstones
January: 6 garnet
February: 8 amethyst
March: 6 jasper **10** aquamarine, bloodstone
April: 7 diamond **8** sapphire
May: 5 agate **7** emerald
June: 5 pearl **7** emerald **9** moonstone **11** alexandrite
July: 4 onyx, ruby **8** star ruby
August: 7 peridot **8** sardonyx **9** carnelian
September: 8 sapphire **10** chrysolite **12** star sapphire
October: 4 opal **5** beryl **10** aquamarine, tourmaline
November: 5 topaz
December: 4 ruby **6** zircon **9** turquoise
biscuit 3 bun **4** cake, roll **5** cooky, scone, wafer **6** bisque, cookie, muffin, parking, simnel **7** cracker, dogbone **8** hardtack, zwieback **9** pale-brown **10** crisp bread, quick bread **15** unglazed pottery
bisect 5 cross, split **8** cut in two **9** cut in half, intersect
bishop 4 abba, pope **5** punch **6** cleric, despot, priest **7** pontiff, prelate, primate **8** overseer **9** clergyman, patriarch **10** chesspiece, high priest
of Rome: 4 pope
Greek: 9 episkopos
means: 8 overseer
district: 7 diocese
headdress: 5 miter, mitre
Bismarck, Otto von
nickname: 14 Iron Chancellor
unified: 7 Germany
chancellor/minister for: 15 Emperor William I
policy: 12 "iron and blood"
bison 4 urus **6** wild ox, wisent **7** aurochs, buffalo
native to: 6 Europe **12** North America
Bissau
capital of: 12 Guinea-Bissau
Bisset, Jacqueline
real name: 22 Jacqueline Fraser Bis-

set

born: 7 England 9 Weybridge
roles: 5 Class 7 Airport, The Deep 11 Day for Night 12 Anna Karenina 16 The Mephisto Waltz 24 Murder on the Orient Express

bistro 3 bar 4 cafe 6 tavern 7 cabaret 9 nightclub 10 supper club
French: 9 estaminet

bit 3 dab 4 chip, drop, iota, mite, snip, whit 5 crumb, grain, pinch, scrap, shred, speck, spell, trace 6 dollop, moment, morsel, paring, trifle 7 droplet, granule, shaving, smidgen 8 fragment, particle 9 short time 10 short while, small piece, smithereen, sprinkling
type: 5 auger, drill 6 gimlet, wimble 7 bradawl 11 brace and bit

bitch 3 nag 5 botch, brood, cheat, fault, shrew, spoil, witch, whine 6 kvetch, virago 7 blunder, bungle, grouse 8 complain, harridan 9 complaint, female dog, termagant

bitchy 4 mean 5 catty, cruel, nasty 6 wicked 7 hateful, vicious 8 spiteful 9 heartless, malicious 10 backbiting, malevolent, vindictive

bite 3 bit, dab, dig, nip 4 gnaw, grip, snip 5 champ, crumb, gnash, prick, scrap, shred, smart, speck, sting, taste 6 morsel, nibble, pierce 7 eat into 8 mouthful, stinging, take hold 10 small piece, tooth wound 12 small portion

biting 5 harsh, sharp 6 bitter 7 caustic, cutting, mordant, nipping 8 piercing, scathing, smarting, stinging 9 sarcastic, trenchant, withering 12 sharp-tongued

bit player 5 extra 6 walk on 14 minor character

bitte 6 please 12 you're welcome 14 I beg your pardon

bitter 4 acid, mean, sour, tart 5 acrid, angry, cruel, harsh, sharp 6 biting, morose, severe, sullen 7 acerbic, caustic, crabbed, painful 8 grievous, piercing, scornful, smarting, spiteful, stinging, wretched 9 rancorous, resentful 10 astringent 11 distressing

bitterness 5 anger, scorn, spite 6 animus, rancor, spleen 7 ill will 8 acerbity, acrimony, sourness 9 animosity, harshness, hostility, malignity, sharpness 10 antagonism, malignancy 11 astringency 12 hard feelings, spitefulness 14 unpleasantness

bitters
type: 6 spirit
flavor: 6 orange 7 gentian
brand: 9 Angostura, Peychaud's

bivalve 4 clam 5 pinna 6 cockle, mussel, mollusk, scallop 8 mollusca 9 pelecypod 13 lamellibranch

bivouac 4 camp 5 tents 10 campground, encampment

bizarre 3 odd 5 kinky, kooky, queer, weird 7 strange, unusual 8 freakish 9 fantastic, grotesque 10 outlandish

Bizet, Georges
real name: 26 Alexandre Cesar Leopold Bizet
born: 5 Paris 6 France
composer of: 4 Roma (suite) 6 Carmen, Patrie 8 Djamileh 11 Don Procopio, L'Arlesienne 12 Jeux d'enfants, Pearl Fishers 14 Children's Games 15 Ivan the Terrible 16 Le Docteur Miracle 18 The Fair Maid of Perth

Bjornson, Bjornstjerne
author of: 4 Arne 7 The King 8 Magnhild 9 A Happy Boy, In God's Way, Lame Hulda, The Editor 10 King Sverre 11 A Bankruptcy, The Bankrupt 12 Sigurd Slembe 14 Arnljot Gelline, Beyond Our Power 15 The Fisher Maiden, The Newly Married 16 Beyond Human Might, Sigurd the Bastard 17 Between the Battles 20 Mary Stuart in Scotland 24 Paul Lange and Tora Parsberg 27 Flags Are Flying in Town and Port

blab 3 rat 6 babble, tattle 7 blabber, prattle 9 tell tales 13 spill the beans 20 let the cat out of the bag

blabber 3 gab, gas, yak 4 blab, bull 5 prate 6 babble, drivel, gabble, gibber, gossip, jabber 7 blather, chatter, palaver, prattle, twaddle 8 blah-blah, chitchat, idle talk 9 jabbering 10 mumbo-jumbo 12 gobbledegook 14 chitter-chatter

blabbermouth 6 gabber, gossip, prater 7 blabber 8 bigmouth, busybody, gossiper, informer, jabberer, liverlip, prattler, quidnunc 9 chatterer 10 chatterbox, talebearer, tattletale 11 rumormonger 12 gossipmonger 13 scandalmonger

black, Black 3 bad, dim, jet 4 dark, evil, grim, inky 5 angry, ebony, murky, Negro, raven, sable 6 dismal, gloomy, som- ber, sullen, wicked 7 colored, furious, hostile, stygian, sunless, swarthy 8 moonless 9 coal-black, lightless, nefarious, unlighted 10 calamitous 11 dark-skinned, threatening 12 Afro-American 13 unilluminated

Black Arrow, The
author: 20 Robert Louis Stevenson

blackball 3 ban, bar, cut 4 snub 5 debar 6 banish, outlaw, reject 7 boycott, exclude, keep out, shut out 8 pass over, turndown 9 blacklist, ostracize, proscribe 11 vote against 12 cold-shoulder 14 send to Coventry

black beast
French: 9 bete noire

blackberry 5 Rubus
variety: 4 Sand 5 Swamp 7 Cut-leaf, Pacific, Running, Sow-teat 9 Evergreen 13 Parsley-leaved 18 Evergreen thornless

Blackberry Winter
author: 12 Margaret Mead

blackbird 3 ani 4 crow, rook 5 raven, slave 6 thrush 7 cowbird, grackle, redwing 8 song bird 9 slave ship 11 slave trader 17 kidnapped islander, plantation laborer
kind: 9 red-winged 12 yellow-headed
family: 8 Turdidae 9 Icteridae

Blackboard Jungle, The
director: 13 Richard Brooks
based on novel by: 10 Evan Hunter
cast: 9 Glenn Ford, Vic Morrow 11 Anne Francis 12 Louis Calhern, Paul Mazursky, Richard Kiley 13 Sidney Poitier 14 Warner Anderson

Black Boy
author: 13 Richard Wright

blacken 5 libel, smear, stain, sully 6 befoul, darken, defame, defile, revile, vilify 7 slander, tarnish 8 besmirch, disgrace, dishonor 9 denigrate, discredit 10 stigmatize

Blackfoot, Blackfeet
language family: 9 Algonkian 10 Algonquian
tribe: 6 Bloods, Kainah, Piegan, Pikuni 7 Siksika
location: 6 Canada 7 Alberta, Montana 12 Saskatchewan

blackguard 3 cad, rat, SOB 5 knave, louse, rogue, scamp 6 rascal 7 bastard, villain 9 miscreant, scoundrel

blackhearted 4 base, vile 6 sinful, wicked 7 ignoble 10 despicable, evil-minded, villainous 11 scoundrelly 12 unprincipled 13 reprehensible

blackjack
also known as: 9 twenty-one
French: 9 vingt-et-un
play against: 6 dealer
additional card: 3 hit

Black Lamb and Grey Falcon
author: 15 Dame Rebecca West

Black Land, The see 5 Egypt

blackleg 7 cheater 8 swindler 9 trickster

blacklist 3 ban, bar 4 shun 5 debar 6 reject 7 exclude, lock out, shut out 8 preclude 9 blackball, ostracize

blacklisting 7 boycott 8 spurning 9 exclusion, ostracism, rejection 12 blackballing

black magic 7 sorcery 10 witchcraft

blackmail 5 force 6 coerce, extort, payoff 7 squeeze, tribute 8 threaten 9 extortion, hush money, shakedown

black mark 4 blot 5 stain 6 bruise 7 blemish, demerit 9 contusion

Blackmore, Richard Doddridge
author of: 10 Lorna Doone 11 Springhaven 13 The Maid of Sker

black mountain see 10 Montenegro

Black Narcissus
author: 11 Rumer Godden
director: 13 Michael Powell 17

Emeric Pressburger
cast: 4 Sabu **11** David Farrar, Deborah Kerr, Jean Simmons
setting: 9 Himalayas

blackness 4 dark **5** gloom, shade **7** dimness **8** darkness

Blackpool, Stephen
character in: 9 Hard Times
author: 7 Dickens

Black Prince, The
author: 11 Iris Murdoch

Blackstone, Sir William
author of: 12 Commentaries (on the Laws of England)

Black Uhlan
nickname of: 12 Max Schmeling

Blackwater State
nickname of: 8 Nebraska

Blackwell, Elizabeth
first American: 11 woman doctor

bladder 3 bag, sac **4** cyst **5** pouch **7** blister, pustule, saccule, utricle **10** receptacle

blade 4 epee, leaf **5** frond, knife, razor, saber, sword **6** cutter, needle, switch **7** scalpel **10** sled runner **11** cutting edge, skate runner

blah 4 bosh, dull, flat, guff, so-so **5** bland, ho-hum, hooey, vapid **6** boring, bunkum, dreary, hot air, humbug **7** blather, eyewash, humdrum, nothing, tedious, twaddle **8** claptrap, lifeless, listless, nonsense **9** gibberish **10** balderdash, monotonous, pedestrian **11** uninspiring **13** characterless, unimaginative, uninteresting, unstimulating

Blaik, Earl H
sport: 8 football
position: 5 coach
team: 4 Army **9** Dartmouth
military rank: 7 colonel

Blair, Eric Arthur
real name of: 12 George Orwell

Blake, Robert
real name: 28 Michael James Vijencio Gubitosi
born: 8 Nutley NJ
roles: 7 Baretta, Our Gang **8** Red Ryder **11** In Cold Blood **12** Little Beaver **23** Tell Them Willie Boy Is Here **24** The Treasure of Sierra Madre

Blake, William
born: 6 London **7** England
author of: 6 Milton, Tiriel **9** Jerusalem **13** The Book of Thel **14** Prophetic Books **15** The Book of Urigen **16** Songs of Innocence **17** Songs of Experience **21** Little Lamb Who Made Thee **23** Marriage of Heaven and Hell, Tiger Tiger Burning Bright
artwork: 6 Milton **9** Book of Job, Jerusalem **11** The Four Zoas **12** Book of Urizen, Divine Comedy **16** Songs of Innocence **17** Songs of Experience **23** Marriage of Heaven and Hell

blamable 10 censurable, deplorable, punishable, reprovable **11** blameworthy **12** reproachable **13** reprehensible

Blamauer, Karoline
real name of: 10 Lotte Lenya

blame 4 onus **5** fault, guilt **6** accuse, burden, charge, rebuke **7** censure, condemn, reproof, reprove **8** reproach **9** castigate, criticism, criticize, liability **10** accusa- tion, disapprove **11** castigation, culpability **12** condemnation, denunciation, remonstrance **13** find fault with, recrimination **14** accountability, responsibility **15** hold responsible

blameless 5 clear **8** innocent, spotless **9** guiltless, not guilty, unspotted, unstained, unsullied, untainted **10** inculpable, not at fault, unblamable **11** unblemished, uncorrupted **13** unimpeachable **14** irreproachable, not responsible

blameless in life
Latin: 12 integer vitae

blame on 7 trace to **8** charge to **9** set down to **11** attribute to **14** lay at the door of

blameworthy 8 blamable **10** censurable, deplorable, punishable, reprovable **12** reproachable **13** reprehensible

blanch 4 fade **6** bleach, whiten **7** lighten **8** turn pale

blanched 3 wan **4** pale **5** ashen, faded **6** chalky, pallid **8** bleached **9** bloodless

bland 4 blah, calm, dull, even, flat, mild **5** balmy, quiet, vapid **6** benign, smooth **7** calming, humdrum, nothing, prosaic, tedious **8** moderate, peaceful, soothing, tiresome, tranquil **9** peaceable, temperate, unruffled **10** monotonous, unexciting, untroubled **11** uninspiring **13** nonirritating, uninteresting, unstimulating

blandish 4 coax, lure, urge **5** charm, tempt **6** cajole, entice, prompt **7** blarney, flatter, wheedle **8** inveigle, persuade

blandishment, blandishments 7 blarney, coaxing **8** cajolery, flattery **9** sweet talk, wheedling **12** ingratiation, inveiglement

Blandois, Monsieur
character in: 12 Little Dorrit
author: 7 Dickens

blank 3 gap **4** dull, idle, void **5** clean, clear, empty, inane, plain, space **6** futile, hollow, unused, vacant, vacuum, wasted **7** useless, vacancy, vacuous **8** unmarked **9** emptiness, fruitless, valueless, worthless **10** empty space, hollowness, profitless **11** meaningless, thoughtless, unrewarding **12** inexpressive **14** expressionless

blanket 4 coat, film **5** cloak, cover, quilt, throw **6** afghan, carpet, mantle,

veneer **7** coating, overlay **8** covering, coverlet **9** comforter

blare 4 honk, peal, roar **5** blast **6** bellow, scream **7** resound, trumpet

blarney 4 fibs, line **5** pitch, spiel **6** hot air **7** coaxing, fawning, snow job, stories **8** cajolery, flattery **9** hyperbole, wheedling **10** inveigling, overpraise, sweet words **12** exaggeration, honeyed words **13** blandishments, overstatement

blase 4 full **5** bored, jaded **6** gorged **7** glutted **9** apathetic, satisfied, saturated, surfeited, unexcited, unmovable **10** insouciant, nonchalant, spiritless, world-weary **11** indifferent, unconcerned **12** uninterested **14** unenthusiastic

Blasko, Bela
real name of: 10 Bela Lugosi

blaspheme 5 curse, swear **6** revile **7** profane **10** take in vain

blasphemous 7 godless, impious, profane, ungodly **10** irreverent **11** irreligious **12** sacrilegious

blasphemy 7 cursing, impiety **8** swearing **9** profanity, sacrilege **11** impiousness, irreverence, profanation

blast 4 bomb, boom, bore, gale, gust, honk, peal, roar, rush, toot **5** blare, bleat, burst, level, shell, surge **6** bellow, blow up, report, scream, shriek **7** explode, resound, torpedo **8** dynamite, eruption **9** discharge, explosion, loud noise **10** detonation **11** sound loudly

blasting material 3 TNT **8** dynamite **9** explosive

blatant 4 loud **5** cheap, clear, crass, crude, gross, harsh, noisy, overt **6** brazen, coarse, tawdry, vulgar **7** blaring, glar- ing, obvious, uncouth **8** flagrant, piercing, unsubtle **9** clamorous, deafening, obtrusive, offensive, prominent, tasteless, ungenteel, unrefined **10** indelicate, unpolished **11** conspicuous, ill-mannered, undignified **12** earsplitting, unmistakable

blather 4 stir **7** chatter, prattle **8** nonsense **9** commotion

Blatty, William P
author of: 11 The Exorcist

Blaue Reiter 10 Blue Riders
group of: 13 German artists

blaze 3 ray **4** beam, burn, fire, glow, rush **5** blast, burst, flame, flare, flash, glare, gleam, shine **6** flames **7** glisten, glitter, shimmer, torrent **8** eruption, outbreak, outburst, radiance **9** explosion **10** brightness, brilliance, effulgence **12** resplendence **13** conflagration

blazer 4 coat **6** jacket **12** sports jacket

blazing 3 hot **5** fiery, afire **6** firing, on fire **7** burning, flaming, flaring, glaring, glowing, intense, shining **8** bursting, bleaming, shooting, shouting **9** brilliant

Blazing Saddles
   director: 9 Mel Brooks
   cast: 9 Mel Brooks **10** Alex Karras, Dom DeLuise, Gene Wilder **11** Slim Pickens **12** Harvey Korman, Madeline Kahn **13** Cleavon Little, John Hillerman **15** David Huddleston

blazon 5 blare, boast **7** trumpet **8** proclaim **10** coat of arms, make public **16** armorial bearings

blazonry 4 arms **5** crest **6** blazon **8** insignia **10** coat of arms **14** heraldic emblem **16** heraldic bearings

bleach 4 fade **6** blanch, whiten **7** lighten, wash out **8** make pale

bleak 3 icy, raw **4** bare, cold, grim **5** chill **6** barren, biting, bitter, dismal, dreary, frosty, gloomy, somber, wintry **7** nipping **8** desolate, piercing **9** cheerless, windswept **10** depressing, forbidding **11** distressing, unpromising **13** weather-beaten

Bleak House
   author: 14 Charles Dickens
   character: 2 Jo (the crossing sweeper) **4** Nemo **5** Guppy, Krook **6** Bucket, Guster **7** Snagsby **8** Ada Clare, Chadband **9** Miss Flite **10** Mrs Jellyby, Turveydrop **11** Dr Woodcourt, Lady Dedlock, Tulkinghorn **12** John Jarndyce **13** Captain Rawdon **14** Harold Skimpole **15** Esther Summerson, Richard Carstone **19** Sir Leicester Dedlock
   satire of: 3 law **6** courts **8** chancery
   case: 19 Jarndyce and Jarndyce

bleakness 8 bareness, grimness **10** barrenness, desolation, dreariness, gloominess **13** cheerlessness

bleat 3 baa, cry, maa **5** whine **7** whimper

bleb 6 bubble **7** blister

bleed 3 run, tap **4** leak, soak **5** drain, valve **6** fleece, suffer **7** diffuse, extract, **8** let blood **9** draw blood, sacrifice **10** hemorrhage, overcharge **12** phlebotomize

Blefuscu
   fictional land in: 16 Gulliver's Travels
   author: 5 Swift

blemish 3 mar, zit **4** blot, blur, flaw, mark, spot **5** spoil, stain, sully, taint **6** blotch, defect, smirch, smudge **7** tarnish **9** disfigure **12** imperfection **13** disfigurement

blend 3 mix **4** fuse **5** merge, unite **6** fusion, go well, merger, mingle **7** amalgam, combine, mixture **8** coalesce, compound, mergence, mingling **9** harmonize **10** amalgamate, complement, concoction **11** combination, incorporate, intermingle

bless 4 give **5** endow, favor, grace, guard, honor **6** anoint, bestow, hal-

low, oblige, ordain **7** baptize, benefit, protect, support **8** dedicate, sanctify **9** watch over **10** consecrate

blessed 4 holy **5** happy, lucky **6** adored, graced, joyful, joyous, sacred **7** endowed, favored, revered **8** blissful, hallowed **9** fortunate, venerated, wonderful **10** felicitous, sanctified **11** consecrated

Blessed Damozel, The
   author: 20 Dante Gabriel Rossetti

blessedness 5 bliss **8** felicity **9** beatitude **11** saintliness

blessing 4 boon, gain, gift, good **5** favor, grace, leave **6** bounty, profit, regard **7** backing, benefit, consent, support **8** approval, sanction **9** advantage, hallowing **10** dedication, good wishes, invocation, permission **11** benediction, concurrence, good fortune **12** consecration, thanksgiving **14** sanctification

blessings 4 joys **5** gifts **6** favors **7** success **8** benefits, delights **10** advantages **11** good fortune

Blifil, Master
   character in: 8 Tom Jones
   author: 8 Fielding

Bligh, Captain William
   character in: 17 Mutiny on the Bounty
   authors: 4 Hall **8** Nordhoff

blight 3 pox, rot **4** harm, kill, ruin, rust **5** blast, crush, curse, decay, smash, spoil, wreck **6** cancer, canker, dry rot, fungus, injure, mildew, plague, thwart, wither **7** cripple, destroy, scourge, shrivel **8** demolish **9** frustrate **10** affliction, corruption, pestilence **12** plant disease **13** contamination

Blimber, Dr
   character in: 12 Dombey and Son
   author: 7 Dickens

blind 4 dull, ruse **5** cover, dodge, front, shade **6** hidden, insane, obtuse, screen **7** obscure, pretext, unaware **8** disguise, heedless, ignorant, mindless, unseeing **9** concealed, deception, senseless, sightless, sun shield, unfeeling, unknowing, unmindful, unnoticed **10** camouflage, insouciant, irrational, masquerade, neglectful, subterfuge, unthinking **11** inattentive, incognizant, indifferent, insensitive, smoke screen, unconcerned, unconscious, unobservant, unobserving **12** imperceptive, uncontrolled, undiscerning, uninterested, unnoticeable, unperceptive, unreasonable **13** unenlightened **14** uncontrollable **15** uncomprehending

blind alley 7 closure, dead-end, impasse **8** blockade, cul-de-sac, dead lock, no escape **9** hindrance, stone wall **10** impassable, standstill **11** obstruction

blinder 4 hood **5** blind, shade **6** screen **7** blinker **9** blindfold

blindfold 6 darken **7** bandage, blinder, obscure **8** covering heedless, reckless **11** strike blind

blind seer 8 Tiresias

blink 4 wink **5** flash, shine, waver **6** fal- ter, flinch, squint **7** flicker, glimmer, shimmer, sparkle, twinkle **9** nictitate, vacillate

blinker(s) 3 eye **6** peeper **7** blinder, flasher, goggles **8** black eye **13** warning signal

blintz, blintze 4 blin **5** crepe **6** blints **7** pancake

blip 3 dot, tap **4** spot **5** bleep, image **6** censor **7** replace

bliss 3 joy **4** glee **6** heaven, luxury **7** delight, ecstasy, rapture **8** gladness, paradise **9** cloud nine, happiness **10** exaltation, jubilation **12** exhilaration

blissful 5 happy **6** divine, joyful, joyous **7** blessed, sublime **8** beatific, ecstatic, glorious, heavenly **9** rapturous

blithe 3 gay **4** airy, glad **5** bold, happy, jolly, merry, sunny **6** casual, cheery, jaunty, jovial, joyous, lively **7** gleeful, radiant **8** carefree, careless, cheerful, debonair, exaltant, heedless, mirthful, uncaring **9** ebullient, sprightly, unfeeling, unmindful **10** blithesome, frolicking **11** indifferent, insensitive, thoughtless, unconcerned, unconscious **12** light-hearted **13** inconsiderate

Blithedale Romance, The
   author: 18 Nathaniel Hawthorne

blithesome 3 gay **5** light, merry, sunny **6** breezy, jaunty, lively **7** buoyant **8** animated, carefree, cheerful **11** free and easy

Blixen-Finecke, Karen
   real name of: 11 Isak Dinesen

blizzard 4 blow, gale **5** blast **6** flurry, squall **7** tempest **8** snowfall **9** snowstorm **11** winter storm

Blizzard State
   nickname of: 11 South Dakota

bloat 5 swell **6** blow up, dilate, expand, puff up **7** balloon, distend, enlarge, inflate

blob 3 dab **4** daub, drop, glob, mass **7** globule, splotch

bloc 4 body, ring, wing **5** cabal, group, union **6** clique **7** combine, faction **8** alliance **9** coalition **11** combination

Bloch, Ernest
   born: 6 Geneva **11** Switzerland
   composer of: 7 Macbeth, Solomon **8** Baal Shem, Schelomo **13** Sacred Service **14** Avodath Hakdesh, Israel Symphony **16** American Symphony **19** Concerto Symphonique **20** Voice in the Wilderness

block 3 bar, jam **4** cube, form, halt, mold **5** brick, check, choke, shape **6**

hinder, impede, re-form, square, stop up, thwart **7** barrier, prevent, reshape **8** blockade, blockage, obstacle, obstruct **9** hindrance **10** impediment **11** obstruction **12** interference

blockade 3 bar, dam **4** dike **5** block, check, levee **6** hurdle **7** barrier, parapet, rampart **8** blockage, obstacle, obstruct, stockade, stoppage **9** barricade, hindrance, roadblock **10** checkpoint, earthworks, impediment **11** obstruction, restriction **13** fortification

blockage 3 jam **8** obstacle **9** hindrance **10** impediment **11** obstruction

blockhead 3 ass, oaf **4** clod, dolt, dope, fool, yutz **5** booby, dummy, dunce, idiot, klutz, moron, ninny **6** dum-dum, nitwit **7** fathead, half-wit, jackass **8** bonehead, dumb-dumb, dummkopf, imbecile, lunkhead, mushhead, numskull **9** harebrain, lamebrain, simpleton **10** chowerhead, dunderhead, nincompoop, noodlehead **12** featherbrain

block out 3 hew **5** carve **6** chisel, devise, map out, sculpt, sketch **7** outline **8** indicate **9** formulate

block up 3 bar **4** clog **6** stop up **7** brick up **9** barricade

blond, blonde 4 fair, gold, pale **5** light **6** flaxen, golden, yellow **8** light tan **9** yellowish **10** fair-haired **11** fair-skinned **12** light-colored

Blonde Bombshell
nickname of: 10 Jean Harlow

Blondell, Joan
husband: 8 Mike Todd **10** Dick Powell
born: 9 New York NY
roles: 8 The Champ **11** Blonde Crazy, Gold Diggers, The Blue Veil **14** Blondie Johnson, The Public Enemy **20** A Tree Grows in Brooklyn

Blondie
creator: 9 Chic Young
character:
husband: 15 Dagwood Bumstead
children: 6 Cookie **9** Alexander **12** Baby Dumpling
boss: 6 Julius **9** Mr Dithers
boss's wife: 4 Cora
neighbor: 11 Herb Woodley **14** Tootsie Woodley
dog: 5 Daisy

blood 4 gore **5** birth, stock **6** family, source, spirit, temper **7** descent, lineage, passion **8** ancestry, heritage, vitality **9** lifeblood **10** extraction, family line, vital fluid, vital force **11** temperament **13** consanguinity **14** vital principle

Blood, field of 8 Aceldama

bloodless 4 pale **5** ashen **6** anemic, pallid **7** insipid **8** blanched, lifeless, peaceful **9** colorless, deathlike, washed out

bloodline 6 family **8** ancestry, pedigree **9** genealogy **10** family tree

Bloodline
author: 13 Sidney Sheldon

bloodshed 4 gore **6** murder, pogrom **7** carnage, killing, slaying **8** butchery, massacre **9** blood bath, blood feud, slaughter **10** mass murder **12** bloodletting, manslaughter **15** spilling of blood

Bloodsmoor Romance, A
author: 15 Joyce Carol Oates

bloodstone
month: 5 March

Blood, Sweat and Tears
author: 17 Winston S Churchill

blood system
part: 5 blood, liver **6** spleen **9** lymph node **10** bone marrow

bloodthirsty 5 cruel **6** bloody, brutal, fierce, savage **7** bestial, demonic, inhuman, vicious **8** barbaric, demoniac, fiendish, pitiless, ruthless **9** atrocious, barbarous, cutthroat, heartless, homicidal, merciless, murdering, murderous **10** demoniacal, sanguinary **11** sanguineous

blood vessel 4 vein **5** aorta **6** artery **7** carotid **9** capillary
prefix: 5 angio

Blood Wedding
author: 19 Federico Garcia Lorca

bloody 3 red **4** gory, rude, vevy **5** cruel, lurid **6** cursed, damned **7** crimson, scarlet **8** bleeding **9** merciless, murderous **10** sanguinary

Bloody Shame *see* **10** Virgin Mary (drink)

bloom 3 bud **4** glow, grow, zest **5** flare, flush, prime, shine, vigor **6** beauty, flow- er, heyday, luster, sprout, thrive **7** blossom, burgeon, develop, prosper, succeed **8** fare well, flourish, fructify, radiance, rosiness, strength **9** bear fruit, flowerage, flowering, germinate **10** blossoming **11** florescence, flourishing

Bloom, Claire
real name: 11 Claire Blume
husband: 10 Rod Steiger
born: 6 London **7** England
roles: 6 Charly **9** Limelight **10** Richard III **15** Look Back in Anger **26** The Spy Who Came in from the Cold

Bloom, Leopold and Molly
characters in: 7 Ulysses
author: 5 Joyce

bloomers 8 knickers, trousers **9** plus fours, underwear **10** underpants **15** knickerbockers

blooming 3 fit **4** pert, rosy **5** utter **6** abloom, robust, strong **7** healthy **8** vigorous **9** healthful **10** blossoming **11** flourishing **12** efflorescent, fit as a fiddle **15** picture of health

blooper 4 goof, slip **5** boner, botch, er-

ror, fluff, gaffe, lapse **6** bobble, booboo, slip-up **7** blunder, mistake, screwup

blossom 4 grow **5** bloom **6** flower, thrive **7** burgeon, develop **8** flourish, progress

Blossomed miraculously 9 Aaron's rod

blossoming 5 bloom **8** blooming, thriving **9** flowering **10** burgeoning, developing **11** florescence, flourishing

blot 3 dry **4** flaw, mark, spot **5** smear, stain, taint **6** absorb, blotch, remove, smirch, smudge, soak up, stigma, take up **7** bad mark, blemish, splotch **8** besmirch **13** discoloration

blotch 4 blot, mark, spot **7** splotch

Blot on the 'Scutcheon, The
author: 14 Robert Browning

blot out 5 erase **6** remove, rub out **7** abolish, eclipse, expunge **9** eliminate, eradicate **10** obliterate

blotting out 7 eclipse, erasing **9** expunging, wiping out **11** eradicating, eradication **12** annihilation, obliterating, obliteration **13** overshadowing

blouse 4 coat **5** drape, tunic, shirt, smock **6** camise, billow **7** blouson **8** casaquin

blow 3 box, hit, jab, pop **4** bang, bash, belt, cuff, gale, gust, honk, jolt, play, puff, sock, toot, wind **5** blast, burst, clout, crack, knock, punch, shock, smack, sound, storm, thump, upset, whack **6** exhale, rebuff, squall, wallop **7** breathe, explode, tempest, tragedy, whistle **8** calamity, disaster, expel air, reversal **9** detriment, windstorm **10** affliction, misfortune **11** catastrophe **14** disappointment

blow from the hand
French: 10 coup de main

blowhard 6 gascon **7** boaster, bragger, egotist **8** braggart **9** big talker **11** braggadocio

blow of mercy
French: 11 coup de grace

blow out 5 burst **7** rupture **10** extinguish

blowsy, blowzy 5 messy **6** frowzy, mussed, sloppy, untidy **7** unkempt **10** disarrayed, disheveled, disordered, disorderly, in disorder **11** disarranged

blow up 5 bloat, burst **6** billow, dilate, expand **7** balloon, distend, enlarge, explode, inflate, puff out **8** dynamite, swell out **12** lose one's cool **14** lose one's temper

Blowup
director: 21 Michelangelo Antonioni
cast: 8 Verushka **10** Sarah Miles **13** David Hemmings **15** Vanessa Redgrave

blowy 5 gusty, windy **6** breezy **7** squally **8** blustery

blubber 3 cry, fat, sob 4 bawl, flab, wail, weep 6 boohoo

Blubber
    author: 9 Judy Blume

bludgeon 3 bat, hit 4 club 5 billy, clout, stick 6 cudgel 7 clobber 9 billy-club, truncheon

blue 3 low, sad 4 aqua, down, navy 5 azure 6 bluish, cobalt, gloomy, indigo, morose 7 doleful 8 cerulean, dejected, downcast, sapphire 9 depressed, turquoise 10 aquamarine, despondent, melancholy 11 downhearted, lapis lazuli, ultra-marine 12 disconsolate 14 down in the dumps, down in the mouth

Blue Angel, The
    director: 17 Josef von Sternberg
    based on novel by: 12 Heinrich Mann
    cast: 10 Kurt Gerron 12 Emil Jannings 15 Marlene Dietrich (Lola-Lola)
    song: 18 Falling in Love Again

Bluebeard
    characteristic: 9 many wives

bluebell 9 Mertensia 18 Mertensia Virginica 21 Campanula rotundifolia
    variety: 7 English, Spanish 8 Virginia 10 Australian, California 11 Clanwilliam

blueberry 9 Vaccinium
    variety: 3 Low 4 Male 5 Swamp 7 Lowbush, Sourtop, Western 8 Creeping, Elliott's, Highbush, Low sweet 9 Late sweet, Rabbit-eye 10 Velvet-leaf 13 Black highbush

blueblood 4 peer 5 noble 8 nobleman 9 patrician, socialite 10 aristocrat, noblewoman 14 peer of the realm

blue-blooded 5 noble, regal, royal 6 titled 7 courtly 8 highbred, wellborn 9 patrician 10 upper-class 12 aristocratic, of royal blood

blue bloods 5 elite, toffs 8 nobility 9 haut monde 10 patricians 11 aristocracy, high society 14 creme de la creme

bluegrass 3 Poa
    varieties: 3 Big 4 Wood 5 Rough, Texas 6 Annual, Canada 7 Bulbous, English 8 Kentucky, Sandberg 10 Rough-stalk

Bluegrass State
    nickname of: 8 Kentucky

Blue Hen State
    nickname of: 8 Delaware

Blue Knight, The
    author: 14 Joseph Wambaugh

Blue Law State
    nickname of: 11 Connecticut

blue-pencil 3 cut 4 edit, trim 6 censor, cut out, delete, digest, reduce 7 abridge, shorten 8 boil down, condense, pare down 9 expurgate 10 abbreviate

blueprint 4 plan 5 chart 6 design, scheme 7 diagram 9 schematic

Blue Riders
    German: 11 Blaue Reiter
    group of: 7 artists

blues 5 dumps 8 doldrums 10 depression, low spirits, melancholy 11 despondency

bluestocking
    French: 7 bas bleu

bluff 3 lie 4 bank, bold, crag, curt, dupe, fake, fool, hoax, liar, open, peak, sham 5 blunt, boast, cliff, faker, frank, fraud, ridge, rough 6 abrupt, candid, crusty, delude, direct, humbug 7 bluffer, boaster, brusque, deceive, fake out, mislead, pretend 8 bragging, headland, headlong, palisade, pretense 9 bamboozle, deception, idle boast, outspoken, precipice, pretender 10 escarpment, forthright, promontory, subterfuge 11 braggadocio, counterfeit, plainspoken 13 unceremonious, straightforward

bluffer 5 bluff, faker, fraud, phony 6 humbug 9 pretender

bluish 7 off-blue 12 somewhat blue

Blume, Claire
    real name of: 11 Claire Bloom

Blume, Judy
    author of: 5 Wifey 6 Deenie 7 Blubber, Forever 19 Then Again Maybe I Won't 22 It's Not the End of the World 26 Tales of a Fourth Grade Nothing 27 Are You There God? It's Me Margaret

Blumenbach, Johann Friedrich
    field: 7 anatomy 10 physiology
    nationality: 6 German
    father of: 20 physical anthropology

blunder 4 goof, slip 5 boner, error, gaffe 6 booboo, bumble, bungle, slip up 7 faux pas, mistake, stagger, stumble 8 flounder 9 gaucherie 11 impropriety, make a booboo 12 indiscretion

blunt 4 curt, dull, numb, open 5 frank, rough, thick 6 abrupt, benumb, candid, deaden, dulled, soften, weaken 7 brusque, lighten, stupefy 8 edgeless, explicit, mitigate, moderate, tactless 9 outspoken, unpointed 10 to the point 11 insensitive, unsharpened 15 straightforward

bluntness 6 candor 10 directness 14 forthrightness 15 plainspokenness

blur 3 dim, fog, run 4 blot, haze, veil 5 bedim, befog, cloud, smear 6 blotch, darken, smudge, spread 7 becloud, obscure, splotch 9 confusion, obscurity

blurb 2 ad 4 rave, spot 5 brief 10 commercial 13 advertisement

blurred 3 dim 5 vague 6 blurry 7 smeared 10 ill-defined, indefinite, indistinct

blurt out 4 blab, sing 7 confess, divulge, let slip 8 give away 9 come clean

blush 5 color, flush 6 redden 7 grow red, turn red 8 rosy tint 9 reddening

blushing 3 coy, red 4 rosy 5 fresh, timid 6 demure, modest 7 colored, bashful, flushed, glowing 8 blooming, sheepish 9 rosaceous 10 embarrassed 11 flourishing

bluster 4 brag, crow, rant 5 bluff, boast, bully, gloat, noise, storm 7 bombast, bravado, crowing, protest, ranting, swagger 8 boasting, gloating, threaten 9 noisy talk 10 swaggering 14 boisterousness

blustery 5 blowy, gusty, windy 6 breezy 7 squally

Blythe, Ethel Mae
    real name of: 14 Ethel Barrymore

Blythe, John
    real name of: 13 John Barrymore

Blythe, Lionel
    real name of: 15 Lionel Barrymore

Boadicea
    Latin name: 8 Boudicca
    queen of: 5 Iceni
    husband: 10 Prasutagus
    ruled: 7 Norfolk (England)
    fought: 6 Romans
    died: 7 suicide

Boanerges
    means: 13 sons of thunder
    name given to: 4 John 5 James

boar
    group of: 7 sounder

board 3 bed 4 deal, feed, food, slat 5 enter, get on, house, lodge, meals, panel, plank, put up 6 batten, billet, embark, go onto 7 council, quarter 8 tribunal 9 clapboard, directors 10 daily meals

board game 4 Clue, Life, ludo 5 chess 7 Othello 8 checkers, cribbage, dominoes, draughts, fanorona, Monopoly, Scrabble 9 Alquerque 10 backgammon 14 Trivial Pursuit 15 Chinese checkers
    Egyptian: 5 Senat
    Korean: 5 Nyout, Pa-tok
    Indian: 7 pachisi 8 parchesi, shatranj 9 ashtapada 10 shaturanga
    Japanese: 2 Go 3 I-go 5 Sho-gi
    Chinese: 6 Ma-jong, wei-ch'i 7 Mahjong, Ma-jongg 8 Mah-jongg
    Swedish: 6 tablut

boast 4 brag, crow, have 5 vaunt 6 flaunt 7 contain, exhibit, possess, show off, talk big 15 blow one's own horn

boaster 6 gascon 7 bragger, egotist 8 blowhard, braggart 9 big talker 11 braggadocio

boastful 5 cocky 7 crowing, pompous, swollen 8 bragging, cocksure, inflated, puffed up, vaunting 9 conceited 11 braggadocio, exaggerated, pretentious **12** vainglorious

boastfulness 7 conceit, egotism **8** bragging **9** cockiness, immodesty, pomposity, vainglory **10** self-praise **11** braggadocio **12** cocksureness

boastful soldier
Latin: **14** miles gloriosus

boat 4 ship **5** craft **6** vessel

Boaz
father: **5** Salma **6** Salmon
wife: **4** Ruth
son: **4** Obed
kinsman of: **5** Naomi **9** Elimelech

bob 3 cut, hop, nod **4** clip, crop, dock, duck, leap, trim **5** dance, shear **6** bounce **7** shorten

Bobadill
character in: **19** Every Man in His Humour
author: **6** Jonson

bobbin 3 pin **4** coil, cord, reel **5** quill, spool **6** piping **7** ratchet, spindle, torchon **8** cylinder

bobcat 3 cat **4** lynx **7** wildcat

Bob Cummings Show, The
later name: **11** Love That Bob
character: **10** Bob Collins **14** Chuck MacDonald **15** Charmaine (Shultzy) Shultz **17** Margaret MacDonald
cast: **9** Ann B Davis **11** Bob Cummings **13** Dwayne Hickman **14** Rosemary DeCamp

Bob Newhart Show, The
character: **12** Elliot Carlin, Emily Hartley, Howard Borden **13** Jerry Robinson, Robert (Bob) Hartley **20** Carol Kester Bondurant
cast: **9** Bill Daily, Jack Riley **11** Peter Bonerz **13** Marcia Wallace **16** Suzanne Pleshette

Boccaccio, Giovanni
author of: **10** Filostrato, Filocopo **11** Life of Dante **12** The Decameron

Boccherini, Luigi
born: **5** Italy, Lucca
composer of: **8** La Divina **9** The Aviary **10** Clementina **11** L'Uccelliera

Boccioni, Umberto
born: **5** Italy **12** Reggio Emilia **16** Reggio di Calabria
artwork: **10** Elasticity **12** The City Rises **15** Charge of Lancers **18** Dynamism of a Cyclist, The Forces of a Street **21** Fusion of Head and Window **30** Unique Forms of Continuity in Space

Bock, Hier
field: **6** botany
nationality: **6** German
founded: **12** modern botany
classified: **6** plants
author of: **15** Neu Kreutterbuch

Bocklin, Arnold
born: **5** Basel **7** Germany

artwork: **13** Pan in the Reeds **16** The Isle of the Dead

Bod see **5** Tibet

bode 4 omen **5** augur **6** herald **7** betoken, ominate, point to, portend, predict, presage, signify **8** forecast, foretell, precurse **9** foreshadow, prefigure

bodega 9 warehouse **12** grocery store

bodice 3 top **5** stays, waist **6** bolero, corset, girdle **7** corsage **8** camisole, corselet **9** stomacher **10** underwaist

bodily 8 corporal, physical

Bodily Harm
author: **14** Margaret Atwood

bodkin 3 awl **4** pick, tool **5** auger, borer, drill, point, probe **6** dagger, lancet, needle, reamer **7** hair pin, piercer **8** puncheon, stiletto

body 3 mob **4** bloc, bulk, form, mass **5** being, build, force, frame, group, shape, stiff, thing, torso, trunk **6** corpse, corpus, figure, league, person, throng **7** cadaver, carcass, combine, council, faction, remains, society **8** assembly, cohesion, congress, deceased, main part, majority, physique, quantity **9** coalition, multitude, stiffness, thickness **10** federation **11** brotherhood, consistency **13** confederation

Body and Soul
director: **12** Robert Rossen
cast: **10** Anne Revere **11** Hazel Brooks, Lilli Palmer **12** John Garfield **13** William Conrad

bodybuilder 12 Charles Atlas **20** Arnold Schwarzenegger

Boeotus
father: **8** Poseidon
mother: **4** Arne

Boer, Boor 6 farmer **9** Afrikaner
language: **9** Afrikaans
ancestry: **5** Dutch
inhabitants of: **9** Transvaal **11** South Africa **15** Orange Free State

Boffin
character in: **15** Our Mutual Friend
author: **7** Dickens

bog 3 fen **4** mire, sink **5** marsh, swamp **6** morass **7** be stuck **8** quagmire, wetlands **9** marshland, swampland

Bogaerde, Derek Van den
real name of: **11** Dirk Bogarde

Bogarde, Dirk
real name: **19** Derek Van den Bogaerde
born: **6** London **7** England **9** Hampstead
roles: **6** Victim **7** Darling **10** The Servant **13** Death in Venice **14** Song Without End, The Night Porter **16** A Tale of Two Cities

Bogart, Humphrey
nickname: **5** Bogie
wife: **12** Lauren Bacall
born: **9** New York NY

roles: **8** Key Largo **10** Casablanca, High Sierra **11** The Big Sleep **14** The Caine Mutiny **15** The African Queen (Oscar) **16** The Maltese Falcon, To Have and Have Not **18** The Petrified Forest **27** The Treasure of the Sierra Madre

Bogdanovich, Peter
director of: **4** Mask **7** Targets, The Trip **9** Paper Moon, Saint Jack **10** Texasville **14** They all Laughed, Picture Windows **18** The Last Picture Show
roles: **7** Targets, The Trip **9** Saint Jack

bogey
term in: **4** golf
song: **18** Colonel Bogey's March

boggle 3 shy **4** balk, muff **5** botch, demure, hover, waver **6** bungle, shrink, wobble **7** blunder, stumble **8** flounder, frighten, hesitate, hold back **9** overwhelm **11** make a mess of

boggy 3 wet **4** soft **5** foggy, mossy, soggy **6** marshy, spongy, swampy **7** squashy

Bogie
nickname of: **14** Humphrey Bogart

Bogota
capital of: **8** Colombia

bogus 4 fake, sham **5** dummy, false, phony **6** ersatz, forged, pseudo **7** feigned, pretend **8** spurious **9** imitation, simulated, synthetic **10** artificial, fraudulent **11** counterfeit, make-believe

Boheme, La
also: **12** Bohemian Life
opera by: **7** Puccini
character: **4** Mimi **7** Colline, Musetta, Rodolfo **8** Marcello **9** Schaunard

bohemian, Bohemian 6 hippie **7** beatnik **10** unorthodox **13** nonconformist **14** unconventional

Bohr, Niels
field: **7** physics
nationality: **6** Danish
developed: **8** atom bomb **13** quantum theory, uranium theory

Boiardo, Matteo Maria
author of: **17** Orlando Innamorato

boil 4 brew, burn, foam, fume, rage, rant, rave, sore, stew, toss **5** chafe, churn, froth, quiver, seethe, simmer, sizzle, well up **7** abscess, bristle, parboil, pustule, smolder **8** furuncle **9** carbuncle, fulminate

boil down 3 cut **6** reduce **7** abridge, cut down, shorten **8** condense, contract **10** abbreviate

boiler 6 copper, geyser, heater, kettle **7** alembic, caldron, furnace

Boilermaker, the
nickname of: **20** James Jackson Jeffries

boisterous 4 loud, wild **5** noisy, rowdy **6** unruly **9** clamorous, out-of-hand **10** disorderly, uproarious **12** obstreperous, uncontrolled, unrestrained

boite, boite de nuit 7 cabaret **9** nightclub

Bojer, Johan
  author of: 12 Folk by the Sea, The Emigrants **14** The Great Hunger, The Power of a Lie **16** Last of the Vikings

bold 3 hot **4** loud, rude **5** brash, brave, fiery, fresh, saucy, vivid **6** brazen, cheeky, daring, flashy, heroic **7** defiant, forward, valiant **8** colorful, creative, fearless, impudent, insolent, intrepid, spirited, stalwart, striking, unafraid, valorous **9** audacious, daredevil, dauntless **10** courageous **11** eye-catching, imaginative, impertinent, indomitable, lionhearted, unshrinking **12** stouthearted **13** adventuresome

boldfaced 5 brash, saucy **6** brassy, brazen **7** forward **8** immodest, impudent, insolent **9** audacious, barefaced, shameless, unabashed

boldness 4 grit **5** nerve, pluck, spunk **6** daring, mettle **7** bravery, courage **8** audacity **9** brashness, hardihood **10** brazenness **11** audaciousness, determination, self- assurance **14** courageousness **15** adventurousness

Bolger, Ray
  born: 12 Dorchester MA
  roles: 9 Scarecrow **10** On Your Toes **13** The Wizard of Oz, Where's Charley

Bolivia
  named for: 12 Simon Bolivar
  capital:
    administrative: 5 La Paz
    legal: 5 Sucre
  largest city: 5 La Paz
  others: 3 Ivo **4** Icla, Itau, Mojo, Saya, Yaco, Yato, Yura **5** Cliza, Llica, Oruro, Quime, Uyuni, Zongo **6** Guaqui, Potosi, Tiraja, Tupiza **8** Pulacayo **9** Santa Cruz **10** Chuquisaca, Cochabamba **11** Vallegrande, Villa Montes
  school: 6 Xavier **8** St Andrew **12** San Francisco
  division: 6 Valles **7** Oriente, Valleys **8** Montanas **9** Altiplano
  measure: 5 league **7** celemin
  monetary unit: 7 centavo **13** peso boliviano
  weight: 5 libra, marco
  lake: 5 Poopo **7** Allagas, Coipasa, Rogagua **8** Titicaca **10** Desaguader
  mountain: 4 Jara **5** Andes, Cusco, Cuzco **6** Pupuya, Sajama, Sorata, Sunsas **7** Illampu **8** Illimani, Mururata, Sansimon, Santiago, Zapaleri **12** Eastern Range, Western Range **18** Cordillera Oriental **20** Cordillera Occidental

highest point: 8 Ancohuma
river: 4 Beni, Yata **5** Abuna, Lauca, Orton **6** Blanco, Ichilo, Itenez, Madidi, Mamore, Mizque, Yacuma **7** Guapore, Machupo **8** Inambari, Itonamas **9** Pilcomayo, Rio Grande, San Miguel **11** Desaguadero, Madre de Dios
physical features:
  lowlands: 6 Llanos
  plateau: 9 Altiplano
  swamp: 6 Izozog
  valley: 5 Yunga
  volcano: 7 Ollague
people: 6 Aymara **7** mestizo, Quechua
  author: 7 Mendoza **8** Arguedas **11** Costa du Rels
  leader: 5 Busch, Sucre **6** Candia, Ortuno, Zamora **7** Bolivar **9** Melgarejo, Paz Zamora, Santa Cruz **10** Barrientos, Estenssoro
language: 6 Aymara **7** Quechua, Spanish
religion: 13 Roman Catholic
place:
  church: 9 St Francis, St Michael **10** San Lorenzo
  monument: 11 La Coronilla
  ruins: 10 Tiahuanaco
  tower: 6 Chulpa
feature:
  animal: 5 llama **6** alpaca, vicuna
  bar/club: 7 boliche
  boat: 5 balsa
  dance/song: 5 cueca **7** huainos, pasillo **8** morenada **9** taquirari **10** palla-palla **11** cacharpayas, wakatokonis
  devil dance: 8 Diablado
  guitar: 8 charango
  skirt: 7 pollera
  wind instrument: 4 kena, sicu **5** erque, quena, tarka **6** pututu **9** pinquillo
  food:
    chicken dish: 14 picante de pollo
    corn: 4 mote
    corn drink: 3 api **14** chicha taratena
    dish: 11 plato paceno **14** sajta de gallina
    dried meat: 7 charque
    pancakes: 7 bunulos
    potato: 5 chuno

Bolkonsky, Andrei
  character in: 11 War and Peace
  author: 7 Tolstoy

Boll, Heinrich
  author of: 8 The Clown **12** The Safety Net **18** Absent Without Leave **21** Group Portrait With Lady **27** The Lost Honor of Katharina Blum **28** Missing Persons and Other Essays

bolster 3 aid **4** help **5** add to, brace **6** assist, cradle, hold up, pillow, prop up, uphold **7** cushion, shore up, sup-

port, sustain **8** buttress, maintain, shoulder **9** reinforce **10** strengthen

bolster one's spirits 5 cheer **7** cheer up, comfort, hearten **8** inspirit **9** buoy one up, encourage

bolt 3 bar, fly, peg, pin, rod, run **4** dart, dash, flee, gulp, jump, leap, lock, roll, rush, tear, wolf **5** bound, brand, catch, dowel, flash, hurry, latch, rivet, scoot, shaft, speed **6** fasten, gobble, hasten, hurtle, length, secure, spring, sprint, stroke **8** fastener **12** swallow whole

bolt down 4 wolf **5** scarf **6** devour, gobble **8** gulp down

bomb 3 dud, egg **4** bust, fail, flop, mine **5** lemon **6** fiasco, fizzle, turkey **7** bombard, grenade, failure, washout

bombard 5 beset, hound, shell, worry **6** assail, attack, batter, harass, pepper, pester, strafe **7** assault, barrage, besiege **8** fire upon **9** cannonade

bombardment 5 blitz, siege **7** air raid, assault, barrage, bombing **10** blitzkrieg

bombast 3 pad **4** puff, rant **6** cotton **7** bluster, fustian, palaver **8** boasting, flummery, rhapsody, tall talk, verbiage **9** bavardage **10** balderdash **12** braggadocio, exaggeration **13** magniloquence, overstatement **14** grandiloquence **17** sesquipedalianism

bombastic 5 tumid, windy, wordy **6** padded, turgid **7** pompous, verbose **8** inflated **12** magniloquent **13** grandiloquent

Bombay
  area: 7 Trombay **8** Salsette **12** Bombay Island
  called: 14 Gateway to India
  creek: 7 Bassein
  landmark: 9 High Court **13** Taj Mahal Hotel **14** Gateway of India **16** Victoria Terminus **17** Rajabai Clock Tower
  rock formation: 10 Deccan Trap
  sea: 7 Arabian

Bona Dea
  also: 5 Fauna
  origin: 5 Roman
  goddess of: 8 chastity **9** fertility
  worshipped by: 5 women
  father: 6 Faunus
  brother: 6 Faunus
  husband: 6 Faunus

bona fide 4 real, true **5** legal **6** actual, honest, lawful **7** genuine, sincere **9** authentic, honorable **10** legitimate **11** in good faith

bon ami 5 lover **8** cleanser. **10** good friend

bonanza 8 gold mine, windfall

Bonanza
  character: 3 Ben **4** Adam, Hoss **5** Candy **7** Hop Sing **9** Little Joe
  family: 10 Cartwright
  cast: 10 Dan Blocker **11** David Ca-

nary, Lorne Greene **13** Michael Landon, Victor Sen Yung **14** Pernell Roberts

ranch: 9 Ponderosa

Bonanza State
nickname of: 7 Montana

bon appetit 14 hearty appetite

Bonario
character in: 7 Volpone
author: 6 Jonson

bonbon 5 candy, sweet **7** fondant **9** sweetmeat **10** confection, sugar candy **13** confectionery **14** chocolate cream

bond, bonds 3 tie **4** cord, knot, link, rope **5** irons, scrip, union **6** chains, pledge **7** compact, fetters, promise **8** affinity, bindings, manacles, security, shackles **9** agreement, guarantee, handcuffs **10** allegiance, attachment, connection, fastenings, obligation **11** certificate, stipulation

Bond, James
actor: 10 Roger Moore **11** Sean Connery **12** Peter Sellers **13** George Lazenby, Pierce Brosnan, Timothy Dalton
appears in: 4 Dr No **9** Golden Eye, Moonraker, Octopussy **10** Goldfinger **11** Thunderball **12** A View To A Kill **13** Licence to Kill, Live and Let Die **15** For Your Eyes Only **16** The Spy Who Loved Me, You Only Live Twice **17** Tomorrow Never Dies **18** Diamonds Are Forever, From Russia with Love, Never Say Never Again, The Living Daylights **22** The Man with the Golden Gun **26** On Her Majesty's Secret Service
author: 10 Ian Fleming
drink: 12 vodka martini **16** shaken not stirred
employer: 3 MI-6 **20** British Secret Service
foe: 7 Blofeld, SPECTRE
office staff: 1 M, Q **14** Miss Moneypenny
university: 6 Oxford
wife: 5 Tracy

bondage 4 yoke **6** chains **7** fetters, serfdom, slavery **8** shackles **9** captivity, servitude, vassalage **11** enslavement

bone
comprise: 8 skeleton
contain: 6 marrow **9** cartilage **11** blood vessel
fitted together by: 5 joint
held by: 8 ligament
pulled by: 6 muscle
specific: 3 rib **4** ulna **5** femur, skull, tibia **6** carpal, fibula, pelvis, radius, sacrum, tarsal **7** humerus, patella, scapula, sternum **8** clavicle, vertebra **9** vertebrae

bone chilling 3 icy **4** cold **5** harsh, sharp **6** arctic, biting, bitter, frigid **7**

cutting, glacial **8** piercing, stinging **11** penetrating **15** teeth-chattering

bonehead 3 ass **4** clod, dolt, fool **5** booby, dunce, idiot, moron, ninny **6** dimwit, nitwit **7** fathead, half-wit **8** dumb- dumb, imbecile, lunkhead **9** blockhead, lamebrain, numbskull **10** dunderhead, nincompoop **11** chowderhead

boner 4 goof, slip **5** error **6** boo-boo, slip-up **7** blooper, blunder, mistake

boneyard 4 dump **7** ossuary **8** Boot Hill, cemetery, junkyard **9** graveyard **10** churchyard **12** burial ground **13** burying ground

Bonheur, Rosa
real name: 19 Marie Rosalie Bonheur
born: 6 France **8** Bordeaux
artwork: 12 The Horse Fair **23** Ploughing in the Nivernais

bonjour 5 hello **7** good day

Bonjour Tristesse
author: 14 Francoise Sagan

bon marche 7 bargain

bon mot 4 quip **7** epigram **9** witticism

Bonn
former capital of: 11 West Germany
landmark: 10 Bundeshaus **11** Munsterkerk
museum: 18 Ludwig van Beethoven
river: 5 Rhine
Roman fort: 15 Castra Bonnensia

Bonnard, Pierre
born: 6 France **16** Fontenay-aux-Roses
artwork: 8 Intimist, Luncheon **9** The Review **13** Nude in the Bath, The Open Window, Women with a Dog **14** After the Shower, Farm at Le Cannet **16** The Breakfast Room **17** The Terrasse Family **22** Figure Before a Fireplace

bonne amie 5 lover **6** friend **10** good friend

bonne nuit 9 good night

bonnet 3 cap, hat **4** cowl, hood, sail **5** cover, toque **7** chapeau, commode **8** headgear **9** headdress

Bonnie and Clyde
director: 10 Arthur Penn
cast: 11 Faye Dunaway (Bonnie Parker), Gene Hackman **12** Warren Beatty (Clyde Barrow) **15** Michael J Pollard

bonny 4 fair **6** comely, lovely, pretty, seemly **7** winning, winsome **8** engaging, fetching, handsome, pleasing **9** beautiful, exquisite, ravishing **10** attractive

bon soir 9 good night **11** good evening

bonus 4 gift **5** prize **6** bounty, reward **7** benefit, premium **8** dividend, gratuity **10** honorarium

Bonus Eventus
also: 7 Eventus
origin: 5 Roman

god of: 4 luck **10** prosperity **11** agriculture

bon vivant 7 epicure, gourmet **8** gourmand, sybarite **10** gastronome

bony 4 lean **5** gaunt, lanky, spare **6** skinny **7** angular, scrawny **11** full of bones **12** skin-and-bones

boo 3 pan **4** hiss **5** taunt **6** deride, heckle, revile **7** catcall **8** ridicule **9** criticize, shout down **11** give the bird **16** give the raspberry

boo-boo 4 goof, slip **5** boner, error **6** slip-up **7** blunder, mistake

boobtube 2 TV **3** box **5** telly **8** idiot box **13** television set

booby 4 bird, dope, fool **5** dummy, dunce, idiot, moron, ninny **6** dimwit, gannet, nitwit **7** fathead, halfwit **8** bonehead, dumb-dumb, imbecile, lunkhead, numskull **9** blockhead, lamebrain, simpleton **10** nincompoop **11** chowderhead

Booby, Lady
character in: 13 Joseph Andrews
author: 8 Fielding

boodle 4 loot, swag **5** booty, bribe, crowd, graft, group **7** plunder **10** collection **11** stolen goods

Boog
nickname of: 10 John Powell

boohoo 3 cry, sob **4** bawl, weep **7** blubber **9** shed tears

book 4 bill, file, list, note, opus, post, tome **5** album, enter, index, slate **6** accuse, charge, engage, enroll, indict, insert, line up, record, tablet, volume **7** catalog, procure, program, put down, reserve **8** mark down, notebook, register, schedule, treatise **9** bound work, write down **10** arrange for **11** publication, written work **16** make reservations

bookish 7 erudite, learned, stilted **8** academic, educated, informed, literary, pedantic, studious, well-read **9** scholarly **11** pedagogical, impractical **12** intellectual

bookkeeper 5 clerk **7** auditor **10** accountant **11** comptroller

booklet 5 folio **7** leaflet, program **8** brochure, circular, pamphlet

Book of Common Prayer
author: 10 Joan Didion

Book of Lights, The
author: 10 Chaim Potok

Book of Manuel
author: 13 Julio Cortazar

Book of Odes
author: 9 Confucius

Book of psalms 12 psalter

Book of Sand, The
author: 15 Jorge Luis Borges

Book of the Duchess, The
author: 15 Geoffrey Chaucer

boom 3 bar **4** bang, beam, gain, grow,

push, roar, spar **5** blast, boost, shaft, spurt **6** growth, rumble, thrive, thrust, upturn **7** advance, develop, prosper, thunder, upsurge **8** flourish, increase **9** expansion, good times

Boom Boom
nickname of: **15** Bernie Geoffrion

boomerang 5 kalie, kiley, kylie, wango **6** atlatl, recoil **7** rebound, womerah, woomera **8** backfire, ricochet, trombush **9** bound back, solitaire **10** projectile

Boomer State
nickname of: **8** Oklahoma

boon 3 fun, gay **4** gift **5** favor, jolly, merry **6** kindly **7** benefit, bequest **8** blessing, donation, offering, pleasant **9** advantage, congenial, convivial, endowment **11** full of cheer, goodnatured

boon companion 3 pal **4** chum **5** buddy, crony **6** friend **7** comrade **8** confrere, intimate **9** confidant **10** bosom buddy

boondocks 4 bush, veld **6** Podunk, sticks **7** boonies, country, outback **8** frontier **9** backwater, backwoods, provinces **10** hinterland **11** backcountry, countryside **12** squaresville **13** nowheresville **14** wide open spaces

Boone, Richard
born: **12** Los Angeles CA
roles: **5** Medic **6** Hombre **7** Paladin **8** The Alamo **11** The Shootist **12** Ten Wanted Men, The Desert Fox **17** Have Gun Will Travel

boonies 6 sticks **7** country **9** backwoods, boondocks, provinces **10** hinterland **11** countryside

boor 3 oaf **4** hick, lout, rube **5** brute, churl, yokel **6** rustic **7** bumpkin, hayseed, peasant **9** vulgarian **10** clodhopper, philistine **11** guttersnipe

boorish 4 rude **5** crude **6** coarse, gauche, oafish, rustic, vulgar **7** loutish, uncouth **9** unrefined **10** unpolished **11** peasantlike

boorishness 8 rudeness **9** surliness, vulgarity **10** bad manners, coarseness, incivility, oafishness **12** churlishness, impoliteness

boost 4 hike, laud, lift, plug, push, rise **5** add to, extol, heave, hoist, pitch, raise, shove, steal, swipe **6** expand, foster, free ad, growth, pickup, praise, upturn, urge on **7** acclaim, advance, develop, elevate, enlarge, forward, further, improve, nurture, promote, root for, support, sustain, upsurge, upswing **8** addition, applause, good word, increase, propound, shoplift **9** expansion, incre- ment, promotion **10** compliment, give a leg up, stick up for **11** development, enlargement, improvement, speak well of

boot
French: **9** chaussure

booth 3 pen **4** coop, nook, tent **5** hutch, stall, stand, table **7** counter **9** cubbyhole, enclosure **11** compartment

Booth, Shirley
real name: **15** Thelma Booth Ford
born: **9** New York NY
roles: **5** Hazel **13** The Matchmaker **19** Come Back Little Sheba (Oscar)

bootleg 5 hooch **7** illegal, illicit **8** unlawful **9** moonshine **12** football play

bootless 6 futile **7** useless **11** ineffective, ineffectual **12** unproductive, unprofitable

bootlick 4 fawn **5** toady **6** cringe, grovel **7** flatter, truckle

bootmaker 7 cobbler **9** shoemaker

booty 4 gain, loot **5** prize **6** boodle, spoils **7** pillage, plunder, takings **8** pickings, winnings

booze 4 bout, soak **5** drink, hooch, spree **6** guzzle, liquor, tipple **7** alcohol, spirits, swizzle **8** cocktail **10** intoxicant **14** drink like a fish
type: **3** gin, rum, rye **4** beer, wine **5** vodka **6** scotch **7** bourbon, whiskey

boozer 3 sot **4** lush **5** drunk, souse, toper **7** tippler **8** drunkard **9** alcoholic, inebriate **11** hard drinker

bordello, bordel 4 stew **5** house **6** bagnio **7** brothel **8** cathouse **10** bawdy house, fancy house, whorehouse **13** sporting house **14** house of ill fame **16** house of ill repute **19** house of prostitution

border 3 hem, rim **4** abut, bind, brim, curb, edge, join, line, pale, trim **5** brink, flank, frame, limit, skirt, touch, verge **6** adjoin, fringe, margin **8** befringe, be next to, boundary, frontier, outskirt **9** extremity, perimeter, periphery **13** circumference

borderline 4 open **5** vague **7** halfway, inexact, obscure, unclear **8** marginal **9** ambiguous, equivocal, uncertain, undecided, unsettled **10** ambivalent, indefinite **11** indefinable, problematic **13** indeterminate

bore 4 drag, drip, sink, tire **5** drill, drive, weary **6** burrow, pierce, tunnel **7** caliber, exhaust, fatigue, wear out **8** gouge out **9** hollow out **10** wet blanket **14** inside diameter

Boreal
pertaining to: **6** Boreas

Boreas
origin: **5** Greek
personifies: **9** north wind
father: **8** Astraeus
mother: **3** Eos
twin sons: **5** Zetes **6** Calais
daughter: **6** Chione **9** Cleopatra

bored 5 jaded **7** wearied **12** discontented, uninterested

boredom 5 ennui **6** tedium **8** doldrums, dullness, monotony **9** weariness **11** tediousness

Borges, Jorge Luis
author of: **8** The Aleph **10** Labyrinths **11** Dreamtigers **13** The Book of Sand **18** A Personal Anthology, In Praise of Darkness **19** Doctor Brodie's Report, Fervor of Buenos Aires **25** A Universal History of Infamy
nationality: **9** Argentina

Borghild
origin: **12** Scandinavian
mentioned in: **8** Volsunga
husband: **7** Sigmund

Borgia, Alfonso de 16 Pope Callistus III

Borgia, Rodrigo de 15 Pope Alexander VI

Borglum, (John) Gutzon
born: **10** Bear Lake ID
artwork: **7** Lincoln **18** Mt Rushmore Memorial, The Mares of Diomedes

Borgnine, Ernest
real name: **18** Ermes Effron Borgnine
wife: **11** Ethel Merman
born: **8** Hamden CT
roles: **5** Marty (Oscar) **8** Barabbas **11** McHale's Navy **12** The Wild Bunch **13** The Dirty Dozen **17** Bad Day at Black Rock **18** From Here to Eternity **20** The Poseidon Adventure

boring 4 dull, flat **5** stale **6** tiring **7** humdrum, insipid, tedious **8** tiresome **9** wearisome **10** monotonous, unexciting **11** repetitious **13** uninteresting

boring tool 3 bit **5** auger, drill **11** brace and bit

Borinquen see **10** Puerto Rico

Boriquen, Borinquen
language family: **8** Arawakan
location: **10** Puerto Rico
related to: **5** Taino

Boris Godunov
author: **16** Alexander Pushkin
opera by: **10** Mussorgsky **12** Shostakovich **14** Rimsky- Korsakov
role: **4** czar, tsar
character: **6** Dmitri, Feodor, Maryna **7** Gregory, Grigory **8** Basmanov, Otrepyev

born 6 innate **7** natural **9** delivered, intuitive **12** brought forth

Born, Max
field: **7** physics
nationality: **7** British
worked on: **13** quantum theory
awarded: **10** Nobel Prize

borne 6 afloat, braved **7** carried, endured **9** put up with, tolerated **11** gone through, went through **12** given birth to

Borneo
other name: **10** Kalimantan
largest city: **12** Bandjermasin
others: **5** Kumai **6** Sambas, Sampit **7** Malinau, Pagatan, Sanggau, Sintang, Tarakan **8** Ketapang **9** Pontianak **10** Balikpapan
division of island:

independent: 6 Brunei
Malaysian state: 5 Sabah **7** Sarawak
part of Indonesia: 10 Kalimantan
measure: 7 gantang
weight: 4 para **6** chapah
mountain: 4 Iran, Raja **5** Saran **6** Kapuas, Muller, Nijaan, Tebang **8** Kinibalu, Schwaner
highest point: 8 Kinabalu
river: 4 Arut, Iwan **5** Bahau, Berau, Kajan, Padas, Pawan **6** Barito, Kapuas, Rajang, Sebuku **7** Kahajan, Mahakam, Mendawi **8** Pembuang
sea: 4 Java, Sulu **7** Celebes **10** South China
physical feature:
  bay: 5 Adang, Kumai **6** Sampit
  cape: 3 Aru **4** Datu **5** Lojar **6** Puting, Sambar **7** Selatan
  port: 4 Miri **5** Balik, Papan **6** Brunei **9** Pontianak **12** Bandjermasin
  strait: 8 Macassar
people: 4 Iban **5** Bukat, Dajak, Dayak, Dusan, Malay, Punan **6** Illano **7** Bakatan, Chinese, Illanum
language: 5 Malay **6** tribal **7** Chinese, English
religion: 5 Islam **7** animism **12** Christianity
feature:
  tree: 5 kapor, kapur **7** billian

Born Yesterday
director: 11 George Cukor
cast: 12 Judy Holliday **13** William Holden **17** Broderick Crawford
Oscar for: 7 actress (Holliday)

Borodin, Alexander
born: 6 Russia **12** St Petersburg
member of: 7 The Five
composer of: 8 Bogatyri **10** Prince Igor **25** In the Steppes of Central Asia

boron
chemical symbol: 1 B
compound: 5 borax

borough 4 burg, town **5** borgo, shire **6** county, parish **7** village **8** district, precinct, province, township **12** municipality
of New York City: 5 Kings, Bronx **6** Queens **8** Brooklyn, Richmond **9** Manhattan **12** Staten Island

Borromini, Francesco
architect of: 10 San Carlino **17** Palazzo Falconieri **20** Sant' Ivo della Sapienza **23** Oratory of San Filippo Neri **24** Collegio di Propaganda Fide **26** San Carlo alle Quattro Fontane (Rome)

borrow 3 get, use **4** copy, take **5** filch, steal, usurp **6** obtain, pilfer, pirate **7** acquire **10** commandeer, plagiarize, take on loan **11** appropriate

Borrow, George Henry
author of: 8 Lavengro **9** Romany Rye, Wild Wales **10** The Zincali **15** The Bible in Spain

Bors, Sir
character in: 16 Arthurian romance

Bosch, Hieronymus
real name: 13 Jerome van Aken **14** Jerome van Aeken **17** Jeroen Anthoiszoon
artwork: 7 Hay-Wain **11** Ship of Fools **14** The Crucifixion **19** Adoration of the Kings **21** The Crowning with Thorns **26** The Garden of Earthly Delights

bosh 3 rot **4** bunk **6** bunkum, drivel **7** twaddle **8** claptrap, nonsense, tommyrot **10** balderdash, tomfoolery **11** foolishness **16** stuff and nonsense

bosky 5 bushy, drunk, shaded, tipsy, treed **6** wooded

Bosnia-Herzegovina
capital/largest city: 8 Sarajevo
others: 4 Neum **5** Tuzla **6** Citluk, Kupres, Lenica, Mostar **8** Prijedor **9** Banja Luka, Bijeljina **10** Srebrenica **12** Bosanski Brod, Siroki Brijeg
head of state: 9 president
monetary unit: 5 dinar
mountain: 11 Dinaric Alps
river: 3 Una **4** Sava **5** Bosna, Drina, Vrbas **7** Neretva
sea: 8 Adriatic
people: 4 Serb **5** Croat **6** Muslim **8** Yugoslav
language: 13 Serbo Croatian
religion: 11 Sunni Muslim **15** Serbian Orthodox

bosom 4 bust, core, dear, soul **5** chest, close, heart, midst **6** breast, center, spirit **7** beloved, nucleus **8** intimate **9** cherished **11** inner circle

bosom buddy 4 chum **5** crony **6** cohort **7** best pal, comrade **8** alter ego, intimate, sidekick **9** companion, confidant **10** best friend

bosomy 5 busty, buxom **6** zaftig **11** full-figured **13** large- breasted

boss 4 head, push **5** chief, order **6** leader, master **7** command, foreman, kingpin, manager **8** employer **9** big cheese, executive **10** supervisor **13** administrator **14** superintendent

bossy 3 cow **9** imperious **10** commanding, tyrannical **11** dictatorial, domineering

Boston
airport: 5 Logan
area: 7 Back Bay **10** Bunker Hill, Fenway Park **11** Faneuil Hall **14** Kennedy Library, Old North Church
baseball team: 6 Red Sox
basketball team: 7 Celtics
dish: 10 baked beans
hockey team: 6 Bruins
landmark: 10 Beacon Hill
leader: 7 Brahmin
nickname: 8 Bean town
river: 7 Charles

Bostonians, The
author: 10 Henry James

Boston Strong Boy
nickname of: 13 John L Sullivan

Boswell, James
author of: 22 The Life of Samuel Johnson

botanist
American: 6 Barton, Carver, Torrey **7** Bartram
Austrian: 6 Mendel
Dutch: 7 DeVries
German: 4 Bock, Cohn
Scottish: 5 Brown
Swedish: 8 Linnaeus
Swiss: 6 Bauhin

botch 3 err, mar **4** blow, fail, flop, flub, goof, hash, mess, muff, ruin **5** spoil **6** bungle, foul up, fumble **7** blunder, butcher, failure, louse up **8** butchery **9** mismanage **11** make a mess of

bother 3 ado, irk, nag, tax, try, vex **4** care, drag, fret, fuss, load, onus, stir **5** annoy, harry, trial, upset, worry **6** dismay, flurry, harass, pester, racket, rumpus, strain, stress, tumult **7** attempt, disturb, problem, trouble **8** disquiet, distress, hardship, headache, irritate, nuisance, vexation **9** aggravate, commotion, hindrance **10** affliction, difficulty, impediment, irritation **11** aggravation, disturbance, encumbrance **12** make an effort **13** inconvenience, pain in the neck **14** responsibility

bothersome 6 taxing, vexing **8** annoying **9** worrisome **10** disturbing **11** aggravating, disquieting, distressing, troublesome **12** inconvenient

Botswana
other name: 12 Bechuanaland
capital/largest city: 8 Gaborone **9** Gaberones
others: 5 Kanye, Orapa, Tsane **6** Serowe **7** Lobatse, Lobotsi, Mochudi, Palapye, Thamaga **10** Molepolole **11** Francistown, Selebi-Pikwe
monetary unit: 4 pula, rand
lake: 3 Dow, Xau **5** Ngami
highest point: 11 Tsodilo Hill
river: 4 Nata, Okwa **5** Chobe, Nosob **6** Cuando, Molopo, Shashi **7** Cubango, Limpopo **8** Botletle, Okovango **9** Okovanggo
physical feature:
  desert: 8 Kalahari
  salt pans: 10 Makarikari
  swamp: 8 Okavango
people: 5 Bantu **6** Tswana **7** Bakatla, Bakwena, Bushman **8** Bamalete, Baralong, Batawana, Batlokwa, Botswana **10** Bamangwato **11** Bangwaketse
language: 5 Bantu, Click **6** Tswana **7** English, Khoisan **8** Setswana

religion: 7 animism **10** Protestant **12** Christianity

Botticelli, Sandro
real name: 30 Alessandro di Mariano dei Filepepi
born: 5 Italy **8** Florence
artwork: 12 Birth of Venus **14** Mystic Nativity **16** Calumny of Apelles **18** Adoration of the Magi **22** Pallas Subduing a Centaur **25** The Madonna of the Magnificat

bottle 3 jar **4** vial **5** flask, phial **6** carafe, flagon, vessel **7** canteen

bottleneck 3 bar, jam **4** clog, stop **5** block **6** detour **7** barrier, embolus **8** blockage, embolism, gridlock, obstacle, stoppage, thrombus **10** congestion, impediment, infarction **11** costiveness, obstruction

bottom 3 can **4** base, core, foot, gist, root, rump, seat, sole **5** basis, belly, cause, fanny, heart, lower **6** center, deeper, depths, ground, lowest, origin, source, spring **7** deepest, essence **8** backside, buttocks, pedestal, riverbed **9** beginning, fundament, principle, rudiments, substance, underpart, underside **10** foundation, mainspring, wellspring **12** quintessence

Bottom
character in: 21 A Midsummer Night's Dream
author: 11 Shakespeare
turned into: 3 ass

bottomless 4 deep **7** abysmal **8** profound **11** measureless **12** immeasurable, unfathomable

Boucher, Francois
born: 5 Paris **6** France
artwork: 9 The Rising **13** Madame Boucher, Reclining Girl **16** Evening Landscape, Rinaldo and Armida, The Toilet of Venus **17** Chinese Tapestries, The Triumph of Venus **18** The Setting of the Sun

boudoir 7 bedroom **10** bedchamber **12** dressing room

bough 4 limb **6** branch

bougie 3 dip, wax **5** light, taper **6** candle, cierge, tallow

boulder, bowlder 3 nob **4** crag, knob, rock **5** block, stone **6** gibber **7** dornick **8** megalith

boulevard 6 avenue **7** parkway **9** concourse

bouleversement 7 turmoil **9** confusion, upsetting **11** overturning

bounce 3 bob, hop, pep **4** bump, life **5** bound, thump, verve, vigor **6** energy, jounce, recoil, spirit **7** rebound **8** dynamism, ricochet, vitality, vivacity **9** animation **10** liveliness

bouncing 3 big **4** full **5** jolly, large, lusty, plump **6** chubby, lively, robust, strong **7** healthy **8** animated, vigorous **12** in good health

bound 3 bob, orb, rim **4** area, edge, jump, leap, line, mark, pale, romp, sure, tied **5** dance, fated, hedge, limit, orbit, range, realm, vault **6** border, bounce, define, domain, doomed, forced, fringe, gambol, liable, prance, region, spring, tied up **7** certain, compass, confine, covered, encased, enclosed, flounce, going to, in bonds, limited, obliged, rebound, secured, trussed, wrapped **8** beholden, boundary, confined, destined, district, encircle, fastened, province, required, resolute, resolved, surround, tethered **9** bailiwick, committed, demarcate, extremity, periphery, territory **10** determined, restrained **11** demarcation **12** circumscribe

boundary 3 rim **4** edge, line, pale **6** border, margin **7** barrier **8** frontier, landmark **9** extremity, periphery **11** demarcation **12** dividing line

boundary line 4 edge **5** bound **6** border **8** sideline

bounder 3 cad, rat **4** heel **5** knave, louse, rogue **6** rascal, rotter **7** caitiff, dastard, villain **9** scoundrel **10** blackguard

Bounderby, Mr
character in: 9 Hard Times
author: 7 Dickens

boundless 4 vast **7** endless, immense **8** infinite, unending **9** limitless, perpetual, unbounded, unlimited **10** without end **11** everlasting, measureless **12** immeasurable, incalculable, unrestricted **13** inexhaustible

bounteous, bountiful 4 free, full, rich **5** ample, large **6** lavish **7** copious, liberal, profuse, teeming **8** abundant, generous, prolific **9** abounding, plenteous, plentiful, unsparing **10** beneficent, benevolent, charitable, munificent, unstinting **11** magnanimous, overflowing

Bountiful, Lady
character in: 17 The Beaux Stratagem
author: 8 Farquhar

bountifulness 10 liberality, generosity **11** benevolence, magnanimity, munificence **14** charitableness **15** humanitarianism

bounty 3 aid **4** gift, help **5** bonus, favor, grant **6** giving, reward **7** charity, present, tribute **8** bestowal, donation, gratuity **9** endowment **10** almsgiving, assistance, generosity, liberality, recompense **11** benefaction, benevolence, munificence **12** contribution, philanthropy **14** charitableness, openhandedness

bouquet 4 odor **5** aroma, scent, spray **7** essence, garland, nosegay, perfume **9** fragrance **11** boutonniere

bouquet garni
ingredient: 5 basil, thyme **6** celery,

savory **7** bay leaf, chervil, parsley **8** rosemary, tarragon

bourbon
variety of: 7 whiskey
origin: 7 America
ingredient: 4 corn
type: 7 blended **8** straight
drink: 9 Mint Julep **10** Boston Sour **11** John Collins **12** Old Fashioned
with Benedictine: 9 Twin Hills
with brandy and Benedictine: 13 Brighton Punch
with Cointreau: 10 Temptation
with rum: 14 Artillery Punch
with sloe gin: 9 Black Hawk
with Southern Comfort: 14 Blended Comfort
with triple sec: 10 Chapel Hill
with vermouth: 9 Allegheny

bourgeois 6 square **7** Babbitt, burgher **8** commoner, ordinary **11** middle-class **12** conventional **13** unimaginative

Bourgeois Gentleman, The
author: 7 Moliere
character: 6 Lucile, Nicole **7** Cleonte, Dorante **8** Coviille, Dorimene **14** Madame Jourdain **16** Monsieur Jourdain

Bourget, Charles Joseph Paul
author of: 11 The Disciple **12** A Cruel Enigma **14** The Night Cometh

Bourgh, Lady Catherine de
character in: 17 Pride and Prejudice
author: 6 Austen

Bourjaily, Vance
author of: 11 The Violated **14** The End of My Life **18** Brill Among the Ruins **22** Now Playing at Canterbury

Bourne Identity, The
author: 12 Robert Ludlum

bout 4 fray, term, tilt, turn **5** brush, clash, cycle, fight, match, set-to, siege, spell, spree **6** affair, battle, course, period, series **7** contest, go-round, scuffle, session, tourney **8** conflict, interval, skirmish, struggle **9** encounter **10** contention, engagement **11** boxing match, embroilment

boutonniere 4 posy **7** nosegay **16** buttonhole flower

bow 3 arc **4** bend, knot, prow, stem **5** agree, curve, defer, front, stoop, yield **6** archer, comply, curtsy, give in, kowtow, relent, salaam, submit, weapon **7** concede, succumb, crescent **9** acquiesce, genuflect, surrender **10** capitulate, forward end **12** genuflection, knuckle under

Bow, Clara
nickname: 6 It Girl
born: 10 Brooklyn NY
roles: 2 It **7** Mantrap **12** The Wild Party

bowdlerize 6 censor **9** expurgate **10** blue-pencil

bow down 5 yield **6** give in, submit **9**

surrender **10** capitulate **12** knuckle under

bowed 4 bent **6** arched, curved, nodded **7** hunched, stooped

bowels 3 gut, pit **4** core, guts, womb **5** abyss, belly, bosom, heart, midst **6** depths, hollow, vitals **7** innards, insides, stomach, viscera **8** entrails, interior, recesses **10** intestines **11** vital organs **13** innermost part

Bowen, Elizabeth
author of: **8** Eva Trout, The Hotel **10** To the North **11** Bowen's Court, Little Girls, The Cat Jumps **12** A World of Love **15** The Heat of the Day, The House in Paris **18** The Death of the Heart

Bowen's Court
author: **14** Elizabeth Bowen

bower 4 jack, joker, nook **5** arbor **6** alcove, anchor, pandal **7** bedroom, chamber, cottage, enclose, retreat, sanctum, shelter **8** dwelling, snuggery

Bowie, David
real name: **16** David Robert Jones
born: **6** London **7** England
roles: **9** Cat People, Labyrinth, The Hunger **20** The Man Who Fell to Earth **24** Merry Christmas Mr Lawrence
wife: **4** Iman
Personae: **11** Aladdin Sane **13** Ziggy Stardust

Bowie Land, Bowie State
nickname of: **8** Arkansas

bowl 4 boat **5** arena, basin **6** cavity, hollow, tureen, valley, vessel **7** dishful, helping, portion, stadium **8** coliseum, deep dish **9** container, porringer **10** depression, receptacle **12** amphitheater

bowler 11 Earl Anthony

bowling
variation: **7** tenpins **8** duckpins, fivepins **10** candlepins
term: **4** miss **5** frame, spare, split **6** strike **10** gutterball
perfect score: **12** three hundred

bow-shape 3 arc **4** arch, bend **5** curve **9** curvature

bow to 5 yield **6** give in, give up, submit **9** acquiesce

box 3 bat, hit, rap **4** belt, cuff, slap, spar **5** booth, caddy, chest, crate, fight, punch, stall, whack **6** buffet, carton, coffer, strike, thwack **8** thumping **9** container **10** receptacle **11** compartment **13** exchange blows

boxer 7 Max Baer **8** Joe Louis **9** Mike Tyson **10** Barney Ross, Gene Tunney, Joe Frazier, Joe Walcott, Leon Spinks **11** Archie Moore, Jack Dempsey, Jack Johnson, Jake LaMotta, Larry Holmes, Muhammad Ali, Sonny Liston **12** Benny Leonard, James Corbett, John Sullivan, Johnny Dundee, Max Schmeling, Mickey Walker, Primo Carnera,

Roberto Duran, Thomas Hearns **13** Carmen Basilio, Ezzard Charles, George Foreman, Hector Camacho, James Jeffries, Rocky Graziano, Rocky Marciano **14** Bob Fitzsimmons, Floyd Patterson, Henry Armstrong **15** Maxie Rosenbloom, Sugar Ray Leonard **16** Evander Holyfield, Sugar Ray Robinson

boy 3 lad **5** youth **8** man child **9** male child, stripling, youngster
French: **6** garcon

Boy
character in: **6** Tarzan
author: **9** Burroughs

boycott 5 spurn **6** reject **7** exclude **8** spurning **9** blackball, blacklist, exclusion, ostracism, ostracize, rejection **12** blackballing, blacklisting

Boyd, James
author of: **5** Drums **8** Long Hunt **9** Roll River **10** Marching On

Boyd, William
born: **13** Hendrysburg OH
roles: **15** Hopalong Cassidy

Boyer, Charles
born: **5** Figeac, France
roles: **7** Algiers **8** Conquest, Gaslight **10** Back Street **11** Lost Horizon **16** The Garden of Allah **19** All This and Heaven Too

boyfriend 3 man **4** beau, date **5** flame, lover, swain, wooer **6** escort, fellow, old man, squire, steady, suitor **7** admirer, beloved, Don Juan **8** cavalier, Lothario, paramour, truelove, young man **9** companion, inamorato **10** sweetheart **15** gentleman caller

boyish 5 boyey, fresh **6** callow, tender **7** boylike, puerile **8** childish, immature, innocent, juvenile, youthful **9** childlike **10** sophomoric

Boylan, Blazes
character in: **7** Ulysses
author: **5** Joyce

Boyle, Robert
field: **9** chemistry
nationality: **7** British
father of: **9** chemistry
advocated: **20** experimental approach
established: **9** Boyle's Law

boylike 5 fresh, young **6** boyish, callow **7** puerile **8** childish, immature, innocent, juvenile, youthful **9** childlike

Boys Town
director: **12** Norman Taurog
cast: **9** Henry Hull **12** Mickey Rooney, Spencer Tracy (Father Flanagan)
Oscar for: **5** actor (Tracy)
sequel: **13** Men of Boys Town
near: **5** Omaha

Boy Wonder
nickname of: **5** Robin **6** Mel Ott

brace 3 duo **4** pair, prop, stay **5** shore, strut, truss **6** bracer, couple, hold up, prop up, steady **7** bolster, bracket,

fortify, prepare, shore up, support, sustain, twosome **8** buttress **9** reinforce, stanchion **10** strengthen **13** reinforcement

bracelet 6 armlet, bangle

bracer 10 stiff drink, stimulator, wristguard **11** invigorator **12** strengthener, strong drink

Brachiosaurus
type: **8** dinosaur, sauropod
location: **10** East Africa **12** United States
period: **8** Jurassic

bracing 8 arousing, reviving **10** energizing, fortifying, refreshing **11** restorative, stimulating **12** exhilarating, invigorating **13** strengthening

Brack, Judge
character in: **11** Hedda Gabler
author: **5** Ibsen

bracken 4 fern **5** brake, brush, ferns **10** underbrush **11** undergrowth

bracket 4 prop, rank, stay **5** brace, class, group, range, shore, strut, truss **6** prop up, status **7** shore up, support **8** category, classify, division, grouping **9** designate, stanchion **10** categorize **11** designation **14** classification

brackish 4 salt **5** briny, salty **6** saline

Bracknell, Lady Augusta
character in: **27** The Importance of Being Earnest
author: **5** Wilde

bract 4 leaf

Bradbury, Ray
author of: **13** Dandelion Wine, Fahrenheit 451 **17** The Illustrated Man **20** The Martian Chronicles **27** Something Wicked This Way Comes

Bradford, Barbara Taylor
author of: **17** A Woman of Substance

Bradford, Richard
author of: **15** Red Sky at Morning

Bradley, Bill (William Warren)
nickname: **10** Dollar Bill
sport: **10** basketball
team: **13** New York Knicks
elected: **7** Senator
from: **9** New Jersey

Bradstreet, Anne
author of: **35** The Tenth Muse Lately Sprung Up in America

Brady Bunch, The
character: **3** Jan **4** Greg **5** Alice, Bobby, Cindy, Peter **6** Marcia **9** Mike Brady **10** Carol Brady
cast: **8** Eve Plumb **9** Ann B Davis **10** Robert Reed, Susan Olsen **13** Barry Williams **14** Mike Lookinland **16** Maureen McCormick **17** Christopher Knight, Florence Henderson

brag 4 crow **5** boast, vaunt **7** big talk, crowing, talk big **8** boasting, bragging **10** exaggerate, self-praise **12** boastfulness, exaggeration **15** blow one's own horn **19** pat oneself on the back

Brage *see* 5 Bragi

Bragg, William Henry and William Lawrence
field: 7 physics
nationality: 7 British
determined: 16 crystal structure
    by: 15 X-ray diffraction
established: 9 Bragg's Law
awarded: 10 Nobel Prize

braggadocio 5 pride 6 egoism, vanity 7 bluster, conceit, swagger 9 cockiness, vainglory 10 pretension 14 self-importance

braggart 7 boaster, bragger 8 blowhard 9 big talker

Bragi
also: 5 Brage
origin: 6 Nordic
god of: 5 music 6 poetry
father: 4 Odin 5 Othin
wife: 4 Idun 5 Iduna, Ithun 6 Ithunn
mother: 3 Fri 5 Frigg, Frija 6 Frigga

Brahe, Tycho
field: 9 astronomy
nationality: 6 Danish
built: 11 observatory

Brahman
country: 5 India
religion: 8 Hinduism
system: 5 caste
rank: 7 highest
function: 6 leader, priest 7 teacher

Brahms, Johannes
born: 7 Germany, Hamburg
composer of: 7 Rinaldo 10 Rain Sonata 11 Triumphlied, Volkslieder 12 Thuner-Sonate 13 German Requiem, Song of Destiny, Song of Triumph 14 Schicksalslied, Song of the Fates, Tragic Overture 15 Gesang der Parzen, Hungarian Dances 19 Liebeslieder Waltzes, Meistersinger Sonata 24 Academic Festival Overture 31 Variations on the St Anthony Chorale

braid 4 knit, lace 5 plait, ravel, twine, twist, weave 7 entwine, wreathe 9 interlace 10 intertwine

brain
part: 7 medulla 8 cerebrum 9 pituitary 10 cerebellum

brainchild 8 creation 9 invention 12 original work 15 imaginative work

braininess 6 genius 9 smartness 10 brightness, brilliance, cleverness 12 intelligence

brainless 4 dumb 6 stupid 7 asinine, foolish, idiotic, moronic, witless 8 mindless 9 imbecilic 10 half-witted 11 lamebrained 12 feeble-minded, simple-minded

brain power 4 mind 9 intellect 12 intelligence 14 mental capacity

Brainworm
character in: 19 Every Man in His Humour
author: 6 Jonson

brainy 5 smart 6 bright, clever 9 brilliant 11 intelligent

brainy group 5 mensa

brake 4 curb, drag, halt, rein, slow, stay, stop 5 check 6 arrest 7 control 9 restraint 10 constraint 11 reduce speed

Bramante, Donato
architect of: 9 Tempietto 14 Belvedere Court (the Vatican), Palazzo Caprini 19 Santa Maria della Pace 21 Santa Maria della Grazie

bramble 4 bush, vine 5 rough, shrub 7 thicket 8 prickers 13 raspberry bush 14 blackberry bush

Bramble, Matthew
character in: 14 Humphry Clinker
author: 8 Smollett

Bran
origin: 5 Welsh
giant king of: 7 Britain
habitat: 3 sea
saint in: 12 Christianity
brother: 9 Evnissyen 10 Manawyddan
sister: 7 Branwen
head buried in: 6 London

branch 3 arm, leg 4 fork, limb, part, wing 5 bough, prong, spray 6 agency, bureau, divide, feeder, member, office, ramify 7 channel, chapter, diverge, radiate, section, segment 8 division, offshoot, separate, shoot off 9 bifurcate, component, extension, tributary 10 department 11 subdivision 12 ramification

branched 6 forked, parted 7 divided 8 extended 9 spread out

Brancusi, Constantin
born: 7 Romania 13 Pestisani Gorj
artwork: 4 Fish 7 Chimera, The Kiss, The Seal 9 Sorceress 10 Adam and Eve, Prometheus 11 Bird in Space, Prodigal Son 12 Flying Turtle, Sleeping Muse 13 Endless Column 20 Sculpture for the Blind

brand 4 blot, kind, make, mark, sear, sign, slur, sort, spot, type 5 class, grade, label, smear, stain, stamp, taint 6 burn in, emblem, smirch, stigma 7 blemish, quality, variety 8 besmirch, disgrace 9 discredit, trademark 10 imputation, stigmatize 11 manufacture

brandish 4 wave 5 shake, swing, wield 6 flaunt, waggle 7 display, exhibit, show off 8 flourish

brand new 4 mint 5 fresh, young 6 unused

Brando, Marlon
born: 7 Omaha NE
roles: 8 Sayonara 10 The Wild One, Viva Zapata 12 Julius Caesar, The Godfather (Oscar refused) 13 Apocalypse Now 15 On the Waterfront (Oscar) 16 Last Tango in Paris 17 Mutiny on the Bounty 21 A Streetcar Named Desire

brandy 6 cognac, grappa, kahlua, kirsch, metaxa 8 Armagnac, Calvados, Tia Maria 9 applejack, Slivovitz 12 Grand Marnier, Peter Heering 14 forbidden fruit
French: 8 eau de vie

Brangwen, Ursula and Gudrun
characters in: 11 Women in Love
author: 8 Lawrence

Branstock
also: 9 Barnstock
origin: 12 Scandinavian
mentioned in: 8 Volsunga
form: 3 oak 4 tree
location: 7 Volsung
house of: 7 Volsung
Odin (Othin) thrusts: 4 Gram 5 sword

Brant, Captain Adam
character in: 22 Mourning Becomes Electra
author: 6 O'Neill

Branwen
origin: 5 Welsh
brother: 4 Bran
husband: 10 Matholwych
son killed by: 9 Evnissyen

Braque, Georges
born: 6 France 18 Argenteuil sur Seine
artwork: 7 Atelier, Grand Nu (Great Nude), The Echo 8 The Table 13 The Portuguese 14 Man with a Guitar 16 Violin and Palette, Violin and Pitcher 18 Woman with a Mandolin

brash 4 bold, rash, rude 5 fresh, hasty, sassy 6 brazen, cheeky, madcap 7 forward 8 careless, heedless, impudent, reckless 9 foolhardy, impetuous, imprudent, know-it-all 10 incautious 11 impertinent, precipitous, smart-alecky 12 unconsidered 13 overconfident

brashness 4 gall 5 brass, cheek, nerve 8 audacity, boldness, chutzpah, temerity 10 brazenness, effrontery 11 forwardness, presumption

Brasilia
capital of: 6 Brazil

brass 4 gall, sand, VIPs 5 cheek, nerve 8 audacity, boldness, chutzpah, officers, temerity 9 impudence 10 brazenness, effrontery 11 forwardness, presumption

Brass, Sampson
character in: 19 The Old Curiosity Shop
author: 7 Dickens

brass instrument 4 tuba 5 bugle 6 cornet 7 trumpet 8 trombone 9 euphonium 10 French horn, sousaphone
ancient: 3 lur 7 Alphorn, buisine, serpent 10 ophicleide

brass tacks 4 crux, meat 7 details 9 realities, substance 10 essentials 11 nitty-gritty 15 sum and substance

brassy 4 bold, loud 5 brash, cheap, cocky, sassy, saucy, showy 6 brazen

7 blaring, forward **8** arrogant, impudent, insolent, overbold **9** barefaced, outspoken, shameless, unabashed **10** unblushing **11** impertinent

brat 3 imp **4** chit **5** whelp **6** hoyden, rascal **9** rude child **10** holy terror **12** spoiled child

Brauhaus 6 tavern **7** brewery

Brautigan, Richard
  author of: 15 Sombrero Fallout **18** The Hawkline Monster **21** Trout Fishing in America **38** The Pill Versus the Springhill Mine Disaster

bravado 7 big talk, blowing, bluster, bombast, bravura, crowing, puffery, swagger **8** boasting, bragging **9** cockiness **10** swaggering **11** braggadocio **12** boastfulness **13** show of courage

brave 4 bear, dare, defy, face, game, take **5** abide, brook, gutsy, stand **6** breast, endure, gritty, heroic, plucky, spunky, suffer **7** doughty, stomach, sustain, undergo, valiant, weather **8** confront, fearless, intrepid, stalwart, tolerate, unafraid, valorous **9** challenge, dauntless, outbrazen, put up with, stand up to, undaunted, withstand **10** courageous **11** lionhearted, unflinching, unshrinking **12** stouthearted

brave deed 4 feat, gest **5** geste **7** exploit **9** heroic act **11** achievement

Brave New World
  author: 12 Aldous Huxley
  character: 4 John **11** Bernard Marx **12** Lenina Crowne, Mustapha Mond

bravery 4 grit **5** pluck, spunk, valor **6** daring, mettle, spirit **7** courage, heroism **8** audacity, boldness **11** intrepidity **12** fearlessness **13** dauntlessness

Bravo, The
  author: 19 James Fenimore Cooper

brawl 3 row **4** fray, tiff **5** broil, clash, fight, melee, scrap, set-to **6** battle, fracas, ruckus, rumpus, uproar **7** dispute, quar- rel, scuffle, wrangle **8** squabble **11** imbroglio **11** altercation, embroilment

brawn 5 might, power **7** muscles, stamina **8** strength **9** beefiness, huskiness **10** robustness, ruggedness, sturdiness **19** muscular development

brawny 5 burly, husky **6** mighty, robust, rugged, strong, sturdy **8** muscular, powerful **9** strapping

Bray, Madeline
  character in: 16 Nicholas Nickleby
  author: 7 Dickens

brazen 4 bold, open **5** brash, saucy **6** brassy, cheeky **7** forward **8** arrogant, immodest, impudent, insolent **9** audacious, barefaced, boldfaced, shameless, unabashed

brazenness 4 gall **5** brass, cheek, nerve **8** audacity, boldness, chutzpah

9 impudence **10** effrontery, fowardness **11** presumption

Brazil
  capital: 8 Brasilia
  former capital: 12 Rio de Janeiro
  largest city: 8 Sao Paulo
  others: 5 Bahia, Belem **6** Recife, Sabara, Santos **7** Vitoria **8** Salvador **9** Ouro Preto, Paranagua **10** Diamantina **11** Porto Alegre **13** Belo Horizonte, Cruzeiro do Sul
  school:
    junior high: 7 ginasio
    senior high: 7 colegio
  measure: 2 pe **4** moio, sack, vara **5** braca, legoa, milha, tonel **6** canada, cuarto, quarto, tarefa **7** garrafa **8** alqueire
  monetary unit: 3 joe **4** reis **5** dobra **7** centara, halfjoe, milreis **8** cruzeiro
  weight: 3 bag **4** onca **5** libra **6** arroba, oitava **7** quilate, quintal **8** tonelada
  island: 6 Maraca, Marajo **7** Bananal, Cardoso, Caviana, Mexiana **8** Comprida
  lake: 4 Aima, Feia **5** Mirim **13** Logo dos Platos
  mountain: 3 Mar **5** Geral, Organ, Piaui **6** Acarai, Gurupi, Parima, Urucum **7** Amambai, Carajas, Gradaus, Oragaos, Roraima **8** Bandeira, Itatiaja, Roncador, Tombador **9** Pacaraima, Sugar Loaf **10** Tumuc-Humac
  highest point: 7 Neblina
  river: 3 Apa, Ica **4** Doce, Geio, Ivai, Jari, Para, Paru, Sono, Tefe **5** Abuna, Anaua, Apore, Capim, Claro, Corua, Icana, Iriri, Itapi, Jurua, Jutai, Manso, Negro, Pardo, Piaui, Preto, Tiete, Turvo, Urubu, Verde, Xingu **6** Ajuana, Amazon, Arinos, Balsas, Branco, Canuma, Contas, Cuiaba, Demini, Grajau, Grande, Gurupi, Ibicui, Iguacu, Japura, Javari, Mearim, Mortes, Mucuri, Parana, Purpus, Ronuro, Sangue, Tacutu, Tibagi, Uatuma, Uaupes **7** Corumba, Iguassu, Madeira, Madiera, Orinoco, Paraiba, Sucuriu, Tapajos, Taquari, Teodoro, Uruguai, Uruguay, Velhass **8** Araguaia, Padauiri, Paracatu, Paraguay, Parnaiba, Solimoes, Tarauaca **9** Tocantins **12** Sao Francisco
  sea: 8 Atlantic
  physical feature:
    bay: 9 All Saints
    cape: 4 Frio **6** Blanco, Buzios, Gurupy, Orange **7** Saotome **8** Saoroque
    dam: 6 Furnas **7** Peixoto
    estuary: 4 Para
    rain forest: 5 selva
    waterfall: 6 Guaira, Iguacu **7** Iguassu **11** Paulo Afonso
  people: 2 Ge **4** Anta **5** Acroa, Arara, Araua, Bravo, Carib, Guana, Negro **6**

Arawak, Caraja **7** Carayan, Javahai, Tariana **8** Botocudo, Chambioa **9** Caucasian, mamelucos, mulattoes **10** Portuguese **11** Tupi-Guarani
  architect: 8 Niemeyer
  artist: 6 Segall **9** Portinari **10** Cavalcenti
  author: 5 Amado, Bilac, Ramos **6** Freyre
  composer: 10 Villalobos
  discoverer: 6 Cabral
  leader: 6 Aranha, Branco, Collor, Franco, Geisel, Medici, Vargas **7** Goulart
  sculptor: 11 Aleijadinho
  language: 10 Portuguese
  religion: 10 Protestant **13** Roman Catholic
  place:
    beach: 7 Ipanema **9** Boa Viagem **10** Copacabana
  feature:
    bird: 4 mitu **5** mitua
    dance: 5 frevo, samba **6** maxixe **9** bossa nova
    fish: 7 piranha
    gourd: 4 cuia
    plantation: 7 fazenda
    slums: 7 favelas
    tree: 5 icica **6** ucuuba **7** arariba
  food:
    dish: 6 vatapa **8** feijoada
    dried salted beef: 7 charque
    drink: 4 acai **9** cafezinho
    tea: 4 mate
    turtle soup: 16 cas quinho de mucua

Brazil
  director: 12 Terry Gilliam
  cast: 8 Ida Lowry **9** Kim Greist **12** Robert De Niro **13** Jonathan Pryce

Brazilian Bombshell
  nickname of: 13 Carmen Miranda

Brazzaville
  capital of: 5 Congo

breach 3 gap **4** gash, hole, rent, rift, slit **5** break, chink, cleft, crack, split **7** crevice, failure, fissure, neglect, opening, rupture **8** defiance, trespass **9** disregard, violation **10** infraction **11** dereliction **12** disobedience, infringement **13** noncompliance, nonobservance, transgression

breach of faith 7 perfidy **8** bad faith, betrayal **9** falseness, treachery, two-timing **10** disloyalty **11** double-cross **13** double-dealing

breach of order 4 riot **6** fracas, mutiny, ruckus, uproar **7** turmoil **8** uprising **9** commotion, rebellion **10** dissension **11** disturbance, pandemonium **18** disturbance of peace

breach of trust 7 falsity, perfidy **9** falseness, treachery **10** disloyalty, infidelity **13** deceitfulness, double-dealing

bread 3 rye **4** food, pita **5** bucks, dough, money, wheat, white **6** staple

9 sourdough **10** livelihood, sustenance **11** staff of life **12** pumpernickel

bread and butter 3 job **6** career, living **7** calling **8** business, vocation **9** life's work **10** livelihood **14** means of support

Bread and Wine
   author: **13** Ignazio Silone

breadbasket 3 gut **5** belly, tummy **6** paunch **7** abdomen, labonza, midriff, Midwest, stomach **11** solar plexus

breadth 4 area, size, span **5** range, reach, scope, width **6** extent, spread **7** compass, expanse, measure, stretch **8** latitude, wideness **9** broadness **10** dimensions **13** extensiveness

break 3 cap, end, fly, gap, off, run, top **4** beat, bust, chip, dash, defy, flee, gash, halt, hole, rend, rent, rest, rift, rive, ruin, snap, stop, tame, tear, tell **5** burst, cease, cleft, crack, crush, erupt, excel, lapse, occur, outdo, pause, sever, shirk, smash, split, train **6** appear, better, breach, chance, cleave, detach, divide, escape, exceed, happen, hiatus, ignore, inform, lessen, master, powder, recess, reveal, soften, subdue, sunder, weaken **7** control, cushion, destroy, disobey, divulge, eclipse, fissure, fortune, give out, lighten, neglect, opening, pull off, respite, run away, rupture, shatter, surpass, suspend, tear off, violate, wipe out **8** announce, bankrupt, burst out, cracking, demolish, diminish, disclose, disjoint, division, fracture, fragment, go beyond, interval, outstrip, overcome, proclaim, renege on, separate, shut down, slip away, splinter **9** dismember, disregard, granulate, interlude, interrupt, make a dash, pulverize, splitting, transcend **10** discipline, disconnect, fall back on, fly the coop, fracturing, impoverish, infringe on, make public, overshadow, separation, shattering, take flight, wrench away **11** discontinue, get away from, opportunity, pay no heed to **12** be derelict in, disintegrate, intermission, interruption, make a getaway, stroke of luck **13** strap for funds **14** bend to one's will, take the force of **15** take to one's heels

breakable 5 frail, shaky **6** flimsy **7** brittle, crumbly, fragile **8** delicate

break apart 7 crumble, shatter **8** collapse **9** fall apart **12** disintegrate, fall to pieces

breakdown 6 mishap **7** crackup, decline, failure **8** analysis, collapse, disorder, division **12** detailed list **13** deterioration **14** categorization

break down 6 divide **7** dissect **8** collapse, separate **9** decompose **11** deteriorate

breaker 4 cask, wave **6** comber **7** crusher **8** boat cask **9** destroyer

break faith with 6 betray **7** do wrong **9** play false **11** double-cross **12** be unfaithful **13** be treacherous **16** sell down the river

Breakfast at Tiffany's
   author: **12** Truman Capote
   director: **12** Blake Edwards
   cast: **10** Buddy Ebsen **12** Mickey Rooney, Patricia Neal **13** Audrey Hepburn (Holly Golightly), George Peppard
   score: **12** Henry Mancini
   song: **9** Moon River

Breakfast Club, The
   director: **10** John Hughes
   cast: **10** Ally Sheedy, Judd Nelson **13** Emilio Estevez, Molly Ringwald **18** Anthony Michael Hall

Breakfast of Champions
   author: **12** Kurt Vonnegut

break free 4 bolt, flee, skip **6** escape **7** get away, make off, run away **9** cut and run **10** fly the coop **12** make a getaway

breakfront 5 hutch **7** cabinet **8** bookcase, cupboard **12** china cabinet

break in 5 train **7** intrude **8** accustom, initiate **9** acclimate, interrupt **10** burglarize **12** indoctrinate

break-in 5 theft **7** robbery **8** burglary, stealing **12** burglarizing **13** housebreaking **19** breaking and entering

Breaking Away
   director: **10** Peter Yates
   screenplay: **11** Steve Tesich
   cast: **10** Paul Dooley **11** Daniel Stern, Dennis Quaid **13** Barbara Barrie **16** Jackie Earle Haley **17** Dennis Christopher
   setting: **7** Indiana **11** Bloomington

break loose 4 bolt, flee, skip **6** escape **7** get away, make off **9** cut and run **10** fly the coop **12** make a getaway

breakneck 4 rash **5** risky **8** reckless, very fast **9** dangerous, daredevil **12** death-defying

break of day 4 dawn **5** sunup **7** dawning, sunrise **8** daybreak **11** crack of dawn

break off 3 end **4** halt **5** cease **6** recess **7** adjourn, snap off, suspend **8** conclude, shut down **11** discontinue

breakout 6 escape, flight **7** getaway **10** decampment

break out 4 bolt, skip **5** begin, erupt **6** escape **7** bust out, get away **10** burst forth, fly the coop **12** make a getaway

Break the Bank
   host: **9** Bert Parks **10** Bud Collyer

break the habit 4 kick, quit, stop **6** eschew, give up **8** renounce, withdraw **14** quit cold turkey

breakthrough 7 advance **11** advancement, improvement, penetration, step forward

breakup 5 split **7** crackup **9** dispersal,

splitting **10** separation **14** disintegration

break with 5 leave **8** be untrue, part from **10** be disloyal **11** divorce from **12** fall away from, separate from

breast 4 bust, core **5** bosom, chest, heart **10** very marrow
   Italian: **5** petto

breastwork 7 bastion, rampart **8** barbette **9** earthwork **13** fortification

breath 4 wind **6** spirit **9** animation, breathing, lifeblood, life force **10** exhalation, inhalation, vital spark **11** divine spark, respiration, vital spirit **12** vitalization

breathe 4 gasp, huff, pant, puff **5** utter **6** impart, murmur **7** respire, whisper **9** draw in air **10** draw breath **15** inhale and exhale

breathe in 6 inhale **7** inspire, respire

breathe out 4 huff, pant, puff **6** exhale, expire **7** respire

breathing 4 live **5** alive **6** living **7** animate **11** respiratory **13** drawing breath

Breathless
   director: **14** Jean-Luc Goddard
   written by: **16** Francois Truffaut
   cast: **10** Jean Seberg **16** Jean-Paul Belmondo
   setting: **5** Paris

breathtaking 7 amazing, awesome **8** exciting **9** startling **10** surprising **11** astonishing

Brecht, Bertolt
   author of: **13** Mother Courage **15** Drums in the Night **18** The Threepenny Opera **21** St Joan of the Stockyards **23** The Caucasian Chalk Circle **27** The Resistable Rise of Arturo Ui **29** The Private Life of the Master Race

Breck, Alan
   character in: **9** Kidnapped
   author: **9** Stevenson

breech 4 rump, seat **6** behind **8** buttocks, haunches, hind part **9** fundament, posterior **12** hindquarters

breeches 5 pants **8** trousers

breed 4 bear, grow, kind, race, sire, sort, type **5** beget, cause, order, raise, spawn, stock **6** family, father, foster, lead to, mother, strain **7** develop, nurture, pro- duce, promote, species, variety **8** generate, multiply, occasion **9** cultivate, give forth, procreate, propagate, reproduce **10** bring forth, give rise to **11** proliferate **16** produce offspring

breeding 4 line **5** grace **6** mating, polish **7** bearing, descent, growing, lineage, manners, raising, rearing **8** ancestry, courtesy, hatching, heredity, pedigree, spawn- ing, training **9** begetting, bloodline, genealogy, gentility, parentage, producing **10** background, extraction, family tree, generation, politeness, production, refinement, upbringing **11** cultivation, germination, multiplying, procreation, propagation **12** reproduction

breeze 4 flit, pass, sail, snap, waft **5** coast, float, glide, sweep **6** zephyr **9** light gust, light wind **10** gentle wind, puff of wind

breezy 3 gay **4** airy, pert, spry **5** blowy, brisk, fresh, gusty, light, merry, pep- py, sunny, windy **6** bouncy, casual, frisky, jaunty, lively **7** buoyant, squally **8** animated, blustery, carefree, cheerful, debonair, spirited **9** energetic, resilient, sprightly, vivacious, windswept **10** blithesome **11** free and easy

Brennan, Walter
   born: 12 Swampscott MA
   roles: 8 Kentucky **12** Come and Get It, The Westerner **13** The Real McCoys **16** To Have and Have Not

Brent, George
   real name: 18 George Brendan Nolan
   wife: 11 Ann Sheridan **14** Ruth Chatterton
   born: 7 Ireland **14** Shannonsbridge
   roles: 7 Jezebel **11** Dark Victory, The Great Lie **17** Forty- Second Street

Bres
   origin: 5 Irish
   king of: 7 Ireland

Breton, Andre
   author of: 5 Nadja **21** Manifesto of Surrealism

Breuer, Marcel
   architect of: 17 IBM Research Center (La Gaude France) **18** UNESCO headquarters (Paris) **25** St John's Abbey and University (Collegeville MN) **26** Whitney Museum of American Art (NYC)
   designed: 5 chair

brevity 9 briefness, pithiness, quickness, shortness, terseness **10** transience **11** conciseness **12** ephemerality, impermanence, succinctness

brew 3 ale **4** beer, boil, cook, form, make, plan, plot, soak, suds **5** begin, drink, hatch, ripen, start, steep, stout **6** cook up, devise, foment, gather, porter, scheme, seethe **7** arrange, brewski, concoct, ferment, mixture, prepare, produce, think up **8** beverage, contrive, initiate **9** formulate, germinate, originate **10** concoction, malt liquor

brewery
   German: 8 Brauhaus

Brian de Bois, Sir
   character in: 7 Ivanhoe
   author: 5 Scott

bribe 3 sop **5** graft **6** buy off, grease, pay off, payola, suborn **9** hush money **10** inducement **11** illegal gift **15**

grease the hand of, grease the palm of
   French: 7 douceur

bric-a-brac 7 baubles, gewgaws **8** bibelots, trinkets **9** gimcracks, kickshaws, ornaments **11** knickknacks

Brick
   character in: 16 Cat on a Hot Tin Roof
   author: 8 Williams

Bricks
   god of: 5 Kulla

bridal 7 nuptial, wedding **8** marriage **11** matrimonial

Bridehead, Sue
   character in: 14 Jude the Obscure
   author: 5 Hardy

Bride of Lammermoor, The
   author: 14 Sir Walter Scott
   character: 10 Lady Ashton, Lucy Ashton, Ravenswood **14** Laird of Bucklaw **16** Sir William Ashton

Brideshead Revisited
   author: 11 Evelyn Waugh
   character: 5 Celia, Julia **8** Cordelia **9** Sebastian **10** Brideshead (Bridey), Rex Mottram **12** Boy Mulcaster, Charles Ryder **13** Lady Marchmain, Lord Marchmain **14** Anthony Blanche

bridge 3 tie **4** band, bind, bond, link, span **5** cross, unify, union **6** go over **7** catwalk, connect, liaison, viaduct **8** alliance, overpass, traverse **9** cross over **10** connection, passageway **11** association, reach across **12** extend across

bridge
   derived from: 5 whist
   type: 7 auction **8** contract
   partnership: 9 East/West **11** North/South
   cards/hand: 8 thirteen
   no cards of a suit: 4 void
   one card of a suit: 9 singleton
   two cards of a suit: 9 doubleton
   rule book by: 5 Goren
   position: 4 east
   action: 3 bid **4** pass
   term: 4 slam **5** trump **6** double, renege, tenace

Bridge of San Luis Rey, The
   author: 14 Thornton Wilder
   character: 5 Clara, Jaime **6** Manuel, Pepita **7** Esteban, Viceroy **9** Uncle Pio **11** La Perichole **14** Brother Juniper **20** Marquesa de Montemayor

Bridge on the River Kwai, The
   director: 9 David Lean
   based on story by: 12 Pierre Boulle
   cast: 11 Jack Hawkins **12** Alec Guinness **13** William Holden **14** Sessue Hayakawa
   Oscar for: 5 actor (Guinness) **7** picture

Bridges, Beau
   real name: 21 Lloyd Vernet Bridges III

father: 5 Lloyd
brother: 4 Jeff
born: 12 Los Angeles CA
roles: 5 Space **8** Norma Rae **11** Signs of Life, The Landlord, The Wild Pair **17** The Fifth Musketeer **20** The Fabulous Baker Boys **25** The Other Side of the Mountain

Bridges, Jeff
   father: 5 Lloyd
   brother: 4 Beau
   born: 12 Los Angeles CA
   roles: 4 Tron **7** Starman **8** King Kong **10** Jagged Edge **12** The Vanishing **13** Kiss Me Goodbye, The Fisher King **14** Against All Odds **18** The Last Picture Show **20** The Fabulous Baker Boys

Bridges, Lloyd
   sons: 4 Beau, Jeff
   born: 12 San Leandro CA
   roles: 7 Sea Hunt **8** Airplane, High Noon

Bridges at Toko-ri, The
   author: 13 James Michener

Bridget
   character in: 19 Every Man in His Humour
   author: 6 Jonson

Bridge Too Far, A
   author: 13 Cornelius Ryan

Bridgetown
   capital of: 8 Barbados

bridle 3 gag **4** curb, rule **5** check **6** arrest, direct, draw up, flinch, hinder, manage, master, muzzle, rear up, recoil **7** con- trol, harness, inhibit, repress **8** draw back, restrain, restrict, suppress **9** constrain, restraint **11** bit and brace, head harness

brief 4 case **5** hasty, pithy, quick, short, swift, terse **6** advise, inform, precis, resume **7** capsule, compact, concise, defense, limited, prepare, summary **8** abridged, abstract, argument, fill in on, fleeting, instruct, succinct **9** condensed, curtailed, momentary, shortened, temporary, thumbnail, transient **10** abridgment, compressed, contention, describe to, short-lived, summarized, transitory **11** abbreviated **12** legal summary

brief account 6 precis, sketch **7** outline, summary **8** anecdote

brier, briar 4 Rosa **5** Rubus, thorn **6** Smilax **7** bramble
   varieties: 3 Cat, Dog, Hag, Saw **4** Bull **5** Green, Horse, Sweet **7** Jackson **8** Austrian **9** Sensitive **14** Austrian copper

brigade 4 crew, team, unit **5** corps, force, group, squad **6** legion, outfit **7** company **9** regiments, squadrons **10** army groups, battalions, contingent, detachment

Brigadoon
   director: 16 Vincente Minnelli

based on Broadway hit by: 14 Lerner and Loewe
cast: 9 Gene Kelly **10** Van Johnson **11** Cyd Charisse
setting: 8 Scotland

brigand 5 thief **6** bandit, gunman, looter, outlaw, pirate, robber, vandal **7** corsair, hoodlum, ruffian, rustler, spoiler **8** marauder, pilferer, pillager **9** buccaneer, cutthroat, desperado, despoiler, plunderer, privateer **10** highwayman

bright 3 gay **4** glad, good, keen, rosy, sage, warm, wise **5** acute, alert, aware, grand, great, happy, jolly, merry, quick, sharp, smart, sunny, vivid **6** astute, blithe, brainy, clever, gifted, joyful, joyous, lively, shrewd **7** beaming, blazing, capable, glowing, healthy, hopeful, intense, lambent, radiant, shining **8** cheerful, dazzling, exciting, gleaming, luminous, lustrous, profound, splendid, talented **9** brilliant, competent, effulgent, excellent, favorable, ingenious, inventive, masterful, promising, sagacious, sparkling, wide-awake **10** auspicious, discerning, glittering, optimistic, perceptive, proficient, propitious, prosperous, remarkable, shimmering, successful **11** clearheaded, illuminated, illustrious, intelligent, light-filled, magnificent, outstanding, quick- witted, resourceful, resplendent **12** exhilarating

brighten 4 lift **5** boost, cheer, light **6** buoy up, lift up, perk up **7** animate, enliven, gladden, lighten **9** make happy, stimulate **10** illuminate

bright-eyed 5 alert, awake **9** wideawake **12** on the qui vive

Bright Flows the River
   author: 14 Taylor Caldwell

brightness 4 glow **5** glare, gleam, shine **6** dazzle, luster **7** glitter, sparkle **8** radiance **9** lightness **10** brilliance, luminosity **12** intelligence

bright spot 3 joy **6** solace **7** comfort **8** pleasure **13** consolation

Brigit
   origin: 5 Welsh
   goddess of: 4 fire **6** wisdom **9** fertility, household **11** agriculture

Brigitte Bardot & the Lolita Syndrome
   author: 16 Simone de Beauvoir

Brill Among the Ruins
   author: 14 Vance Bourjaily

brilliance, brilliancy 4 gift, glow **5** blaze, eclat, gleam, sheen, shine **6** acuity, dazzle, genius, luster, talent, wisdom **7** glitter, shimmer, sparkle **8** grandeur, keenness, radiance, sagacity, splendor **9** alertness, awareness, greatness, ingenuity, intensity, quickness, sharpness, smartness, vividness **10** braininess, brightness, capability, cleverness, competence, effulgence,

excellence, luminosity, perception, profundity, shrewdness **11** discernment, distinction, proficiency **12** intelligence, magnificence, resplendence **13** inventiveness, masterfulness **15** clearheadedness, illustriousness, resourcefulness

brilliant see **6** bright

brim 3 fill, lip, rim **5** brink, flood, ledge, verge **6** border, fill up, margin, well up **8** overflow

brimless hat 3 cap **5** beret **6** beanie **11** stocking cap, tam o'shanter

brimming 4 full **7** flooded, teeming **8** overfull, swarming **11** overflowing

Brimo
   origin: 5 Greek
   form: 7 goddess
   corresponds to: 6 Hecate **7** Demeter **10** Persephone

brine 6 the sea **8** sea water **9** salt water **12** salt solution **14** saline solution **16** pickling solution

bring 4 bear, make, take, tote **5** begin, carry, cause, fetch, force, start **6** compel, convey, create, effect, induce **7** deliver, produce, sell for, usher in **8** convince, engender, generate, initiate, persuade, result in **9** accompany, institute, originate, transport **10** bring about

bring about 2 do **4** form, open **5** begin, cause, found, set up, start **6** attain, create, effect, lead to **7** achieve, execute, produce **8** carry out, generate, initiate, organize **9** establish, institute, succeed at **10** accomplish, effectuate, inaugurate **11** bring to pass, precipitate **18** bring into existence

bring back 6 return **7** restore **8** recreate **9** surrender **10** return with

bring down a peg 5 abase **6** humble **7** mortify **9** humiliate **13** cut down to size

bring down to earth 10 disenchant **11** disenthrall, disillusion, open the eyes **13** break the spell **14** burst the bubble **20** shatter one's illusions

bring forth 4 bear **5** breed, elicit, evoke, hatch, spawn, whelp **7** deliver, produce **9** reproduce **10** make appear **11** give birth to

bring home to 7 blame on, clarify **11** attribute to **15** place emphasis on

bringing together 7 joining, wedding **8** amassing **9** combining, gathering, including **10** assembling, collecting **12** accumulating **13** incorporating

Bringing Up Baby
   director: 11 Howard Hawks
   cast: 9 Cary Grant **14** Charlie Ruggles **16** Katharine Hepburn
   "Baby": 7 leopard

Bringing Up Father
   creator: 13 George McManus
   character: 5 Jiggs **6** Maggie

daughter: 5 Rosie
   brother-in-law: 5 Bimmy
place: 11 Dinty Moore's
favorite dish: 20 corned beef and cabbage

bring into being 4 bear, form, make **5** erect, hatch, spawn, whelp **6** create, design, devise, invent, render **7** concoct, deliver, develop, fashion, produce **8** contrive, generate **9** construct, fabricate, formulate, originate **10** bring forth **11** give birth to

bring into existence 4 form **5** begin, set up, start **6** create **8** organize **9** establish, institute **10** bring about, inaugurate

bring into line 5 adapt **6** adjust **7** conform, shape up **9** harmonize, reconcile **10** discipline **11** accommodate **13** whip into shape

bring into question 11 cast doubt on **18** throw suspicion upon

bring into relief 6 accent, stress **7** dwell on, feature, point up **9** emphasize, press home, underline **10** accentuate, underscore

bring low 5 abase, shame **6** humble **8** cast down **9** denigrate, humiliate

bring off 4 gain **6** attain, effect, secure **7** achieve **10** accomplish

bring to an end 5 cease **6** finish **8** break off, conclude **9** call a halt, terminate **11** discontinue

bring to a standstill 3 end **4** halt, stay, stop **5** block, check **6** arrest **12** bring to a halt

bring to bay 4 trap, tree **6** corner **8** confront, hunt down

bring to bear 5 apply **6** employ **7** utilize **9** implement

bring together 5 amass **6** gather, muster **7** collect, marshal, round up **8** assemble **10** accumulate

bring to light 6 expose, reveal, unveil **7** clarify, divulge, explain, uncover **8** disclose **9** explicate, make known, make plain **10** illuminate, make public

bring to one's senses 3 jar **5** alarm, alert, shock **9** make aware

bring to pass 5 cause **6** create, effect **8** carry out **10** bring about, effectuate

bring to terms 6 settle **7** mediate **9** arbitrate, reconcile

bring to view 5 dig up **6** reveal **7** exhibit, uncover, unearth **8** disclose, retrieve **10** come up with

bring word 4 tell **6** advise, convey, inform, notify, relate, reveal **7** divulge, publish **8** announce, disclose, proclaim **9** apprise of, broadcast, make known, publicize **11** communicate

brink 3 rim **4** bank, brim, edge **5** point, shore, skirt, verge **6** border, margin **9** threshold

briny 4 salt 5 salty 6 saline

brio, con
music: 9 with vigor 10 with spirit

Briseis
origin: 5 Greek
mentioned in: 5 Iliad
father: 18 Briseus of Lyrnessus
husband: 5 Mynes
captured by: 8 Achilles
caused: 7 quarrel
between: 8 Achilles 9 Agamemnon

Briseus
origin: 5 Greek
mentioned in: 5 Iliad
daughter: 7 Briseis
death by: 7 suicide

Brisingamen 8 necklace
origin: 12 Scandinavian
trait: 5 magic
owned by: 5 Freia, Freya

brisk 4 busy, spry 5 alert, fresh, peppy, quick, swift 6 active, breezy, lively, snappy 7 bracing, chipper, dynamic, rousing 8 animated, bustling, spirited, stirring, vigorous 9 energetic, sprightly, vivacious, vivifying 10 refreshing 11 stimulating 12 exhilarating, invigorating

briskness 3 pep 5 vigor 6 energy 8 alac- rity, spryness 9 quickness, swiftness 13 sprightliness

bristle 4 hair, seta 5 quill 7 stiffen, whisker

bristles 5 barbs, setae 6 quills 7 stubble 8 prickles, whiskers

bristletail
variety: 7 jumping 8 firebrat 9 primitive 10 nicoletiid, silverfish

bristly 5 rough 6 barbed, coarse 7 prickly, stubbly 8 unshaven 9 whiskered 11 bewhiskered

Britannia *see* 7 England

British 6 Breton, Briton 7 English 8 Brittany

British Columbia
bordered by: 5 Idaho, Yukon 6 Alaska, Montana 10 Washington 12 Pacific Ocean, United States 20 Northwest Territories
country: 6 Canada
Indian: 5 Haida 6 Nootka, Salish 8 Kwakiutl 9 Tsimshian 10 Bella Coola
island: 9 Vancouver 14 Queen Charlotte
mountain: 5 Coast, Rocky 7 Cascade 8 Columbia 11 Cordilleran 14 Cassiar Omineca
nickname: 2 BC
park: 7 Glacier
rank in size: 5 sixth
river: 6 Fraser
section: 8 province

British Guiana *see* 6 Guyana

British Honduras *see* 6 Belize

British Mythology
god of rebirth/afterlife: 4 Gwyn

chief of gods: 5 Woden
island of paradise: 6 Avalon

Britomart
character in: 15 The Faerie Queene
author: 7 Spenser

Britomartis
origin: 6 Cretan
goddess of: 7 hunters, sailors 9 fishermen
father: 4 Zeus
mother: 5 Carme
corresponds to: 7 Artemis 8 Dictynna

Briton 4 Celt 6 Celtic 7 British

Brittany
coast: 5 Armor
country: 6 France
inhabitant: 5 Celts 6 French, Romans
interior: 6 Argoat
land form: 9 peninsula
language: 6 Breton
other name: 5 Breiz 6 Breton 8 Bretagne

Britten, (Edward) Benjamin
born: 7 England 9 Lowestoft
composer of: 8 Gloriana 9 Billy Budd 10 Paul Bunyan, War Requiem 11 Curlew River, Peter Grimes, Winter Words 12 Owen Wingrave, The Poet's Echo 13 Albert Herring, Death in Venice 14 The Prodigal Son, Turn of the Screw 15 Phantasy Quartet 17 A Ceremony of Carols, A Charm of Lullabies, Sinfonia da Requiem, The Rape of Lucretia 18 Holderlin Fragments 20 Cantata Misericordium 21 A Midsummer Night's Dream, Sonnets of Michelangelo 22 The Burning Fiery Furnace

brittle 7 crumbly, fragile, friable 9 breakable, frangible

broach 4 pose 6 launch, open up, submit 7 advance, bring up, mention, propose, suggest, touch on 9 institute, introduce

broad 4 full, open, wide 5 ample, clear, large, plain, rangy, roomy, thick 7 general, immense, obvious, sizable 8 extended, spacious, sweeping 9 capacious, expansive, extensive, inclusive, outspread, universal, unlimited 10 undetailed 11 far-reaching, nonspecific, wide-ranging 12 all-embracing, encyclopedic 13 comprehensive

broadcast 4 beam, show, talk 5 cable, radio, relay 7 program, send out 8 televise, transmit 9 statement 10 distribute 11 disseminate, put on the air 12 announcement

broaden 5 boost, raise, swell, widen 6 dilate, expand, extend 7 advance, amplify, augment, build up, develop, distend, enlarge, improve, stretch 8 increase 9 intensify, reinforce, spread out 10 strengthen, supplement

broadened 7 dilated, swelled, swollen,

widened 8 enlarged, expanded, extended 9 distended, spread out

broad-minded 7 liberal 8 amenable, catholic, flexible, tolerant, unbiased 9 receptive, unbigoted, undogmatic 11 magnanimous 12 unprejudiced, unprovincial

Broadway Joe
nickname of: 9 Joe Namath

Brobdingnag
fictional land in: 16 Gulliver's Travels
author: 5 Swift

Brobdingnagian 4 huge 5 giant 7 immense, mammoth 8 colossal, enormous, gigantic 10 gargantuan, tremendous 11 elephantine

broccoli 9 vegetable 12 Brassica rapa 16 Brassica oleracea (Botyris Group) 17 Brassica septiceps
variety: 6 Turnip 7 Italian 9 Asparagus, Sprouting

brochure 5 flier 6 folder 7 booklet, leaflet 8 circular, handbill, pamphlet 9 throwaway

Brockton Blockbuster
nickname of: 13 Rocky Marciano

Broglie, Louis Victor de
field: 7 physics
nationality: 6 French
developed: 13 wave mechanics
awarded: 10 Nobel Prize

broil 3 fry 4 bake, burn, cook, sear 5 parch, roast, toast 6 scorch 7 blister

broiler 3 hot, pan 4 rack 5 grill 6 cooker 8 scorcher 12 young chicken

broke 8 bankrupt, strapped, wiped out 9 insolvent, penniless 10 down and out 12 impoverished, on one's uppers, without funds 16 strapped for funds

broken 4 torn 5 rough, split, tamed 6 ruined, uneven 7 crushed, damaged 8 bankrupt, in pieces, ruptured 9 fractured, separated, shattered 10 incomplete 11 fragmentary, interrupted

Broken Commandment, The
author: 14 Toson Shimazaki

broken-down 6 beat-up, ruined 7 rickety, worn-out 8 battered, decrepit 10 ramshackle 11 dilapidated 12 deteriorated

broken-hearted 3 sad 6 gloomy, woeful 7 crushed, doleful, forlorn, unhappy 8 dejected, desolate, downcast, mournful, wretched 9 depressed, long-faced, miserable, sorrowful, woebegone 10 despairing, despondent, melancholy 11 heartbroken 12 disconsolate, inconsolable

Brom Bones
also: 12 Brom Van Brunt
character in: 23 The Legend of Sleepy Hollow
author: 6 Irving

Bromfield, Louis

author of: 11 Early Autumn, Malabar Farm **12** The Rains Came **13** Mrs Parkington, Night in Bombay **14** Wild Is the River **15** The Green Bay Tree **31** The Strange Case of Miss Annie Spragg

bromide 6 cliche **8** banality **9** platitude **10** stereotype **11** trite phrase **19** hackneyed expression

bromidic 4 dull **5** banal, corny, stale, tired, trite, vapid **6** jejune **7** humdrum, insipid **8** ordinary **9** hackneyed **10** pedestrian, unexciting, unoriginal **13** platitudinous, unimaginative

bromine
    chemical symbol: 2 Br

Bromius
    epithet of: 8 Dionysus
    means: 7 thunder

Bronson, Charles
    real name: 16 Charles Buchinsky
    wife: 11 Jill Ireland
    born: 11 Ehrenfeld PA
    roles: 9 Death Wish **13** The Dirty Dozen **14** The Great Escape **16** Battle of the Bulge, The Valachi Papers **19** The Magnificent Seven

Bronte, Anne
    author of: 9 Agnes Grey **23** The Tenant of Wildfell Hall
    pseudonym: 9 Acton Bell

Bronte, Charlotte
    author of: 7 Shirley **8** Jane Eyre, Villette **12** The Professor
    pseudonym: 10 Currer Bell

Bronte, Emily
    author of: 16 Wuthering Heights
    pseudonym: 9 Ellis Bell

Brontes
    member of: 8 Cyclopes

brontophobia
    fear of: 7 thunder

Brontosaurus
    also: 11 Apatosaurus
    type: 8 dinosaur, sauropod
    period: 8 Jurassic

Bronx Bull
    nickname of: 11 Jake La Motta

bronze 3 tan **5** metal **8** brownish, chestnut **10** reddish- tan **12** reddish-brown **13** copper-colored

brooch 3 pin **5** clasp

brood 4 chew, fret, mope, mull, sulk **5** cover, dwell, hatch, spawn, worry, young **6** chicks, family, litter **7** agonize, sit upon **8** children, incubate **9** offspring **10** hatchlings

brook 3 run **4** bear, rill, take **5** abide, allow, creek, stand **6** accept, endure, stream, suffer **7** rivulet, stomach **8** tolerate **9** put up with, streamlet

Brooks, Gwendolyn
    author of: 4 Riot **10** Annie Allen **14** Family Pictures

Brooks, James L

director of: 13 Broadcast News **17** Terms of Endearment (Oscar)

Brooks, Mel
    real name: 14 Melvin Kaminsky
    wife: 12 Anne Bancroft
    born: 10 Brooklyn NY
    director of/roles: 10 Life Stinks, Spaceballs **11** High Anxiety, Silent Movie **12** The Producers **14** Blazing Saddles **17** Young Frankenstein **20** The History of the World

Brooks, Richard
    director of: 10 Fever Pitch **11** Elmer Gantry, In Cold Blood **16** Cat on a Hot Tin Roof, Sweet Bird of Youth **19** Looking for Mr. Goodbar, The Blackboard Jungle **20** The Brothers Karamazov, The Last Time I Saw Paris

broom 4 bush **5** besom, brush, whisk **7** sweeper

broth 5 stock **8** bouillon, consomme **9** clear soup

brothel 4 stew **5** house **6** bagnio, bordel **8** bordello, cathouse **10** bawdy house, fancy house, whorehouse **11** maison close **13** maison de passe, sporting house **14** house of ill fame **16** house of ill repute **19** house of prostitution

brother 3 pal **4** chum, monk, peer **5** buddy, friar **6** cleric **7** comrade, kinsman, part- ner, sibling **8** confrere, landsman, monastic, relative, relation **9** associate, colleague, companion, fellowman **10** countryman **11** male sibling **12** fellow member **13** fellow citizen
    French: 5 frere

brotherhood 4 club **5** amity, lodge **10** fellowship, fraternity, friendship **11** association

Brother Juniper
    character in: 21 The Bridge of San Luis Rey
    author: 6 Wilder

Brothers Karamazov, The
    author: 10 Dostoevsky **17** Fyodor Dostoyevsky
    character: 4 Ivan **6** Dmitri **7** Alyosha (Alexey), Zossima **8** Katerina **9** Grushenka **10** Smerdyakov **15** Fyodor Karamazov

brougham 3 car **8** carriage **10** automobile

brought 6 caused **7** carried, fetched, sold for **8** conveyed **9** conducted, convinced, persuaded

brow 3 rim **4** brim, edge, side **5** brink, verge **6** border, margin **8** boundary, forehead **9** periphery

browbeat 3 cow **5** abash, bully, cower **6** badger, harass, hector **7** henpeck **8** bulldoze, domineer, frighten, threaten **9** terrorize, tyrannize **10** intimidate

browbeater 5 bully **6** despot **7** co-

ercer **9** oppressor, tormenter, tormentor **11** intimidator, petty tyrant

browbeating 8 bullying **11** threatening, tyrannizing **12** intimidation

brown 3 bay, dun, fry, tan **4** buff, cook, drab, fawn, puce, roan, rust **5** beige, camel, cocoa, hazel, khaki, saute, taw- ny, toast, umber **6** auburn, bronze, brunet, coffee, copper, ginger, russet, sorrel, walnut **8** brunette, chestnut, cinnamon, mahogany **9** chocolate, olive drab **10** terra- cotta **11** dirt-colored, sand-colored **12** liver-colored

Brown, Angeline
    real name of: 14 Angie Dickinson

Brown, Berenice Sadie
    character in: 19 A Member of the Wedding
    author: 9 McCullers

Brown, Charles Brockden
    author of: 6 Ormond **7** Wieland **11** Edgar Huntly **12** Arthur Mervyn

Brown, Claude
    author of: 16 The Children of Ham **25** Manchild in the Promised Land

Brown, Dee
    author of: 15 Creek Mary's Blood **24** Bury My Heart at Wounded Knee

Brown, Helen Gurley
    author of: 19 Sex and the Single Girl
    editor of: 12 Cosmopolitan

Brown, Helen Hayes
    real name of: 10 Helen Hayes

Brown, Jim (Jimmy)
    sport: 8 football
    position: 8 fullback
    team: 15 Cleveland Browns
    actor in: 10 Dirty Dozen

Brown, Robert
    field: 6 botany
    nationality: 8 Scottish
    established: 16 Brownian movement

Brown Bomber
    nickname of: 8 Joe Louis

Browne, Dik
    creator/artist of: 9 Hi and Lois **12** Beetle Bailey **16** Hagar the Horrible

Browne, Sir Thomas
    author of: 9 Urn Burial **12** Hydriotaphia **13** Religio Medici **16** The Garden of Cyrus

brownie 3 elf **4** cake, puck **5** fairy, pixie **6** sprite **9** girl scout **10** leprechaun

Browning, Elizabeth Barrett
    author of: 11 Aurora Leigh **14** How Do I Love Thee **16** Casa Guidi Windows **24** Sonnets from the Portuguese

Browning, Robert
    author of: 8 Sordello **10** Paracelsus **11** Pippa Passes **13** Fra Lippo Lippi, My Last Duchess **14** Andrea del Sarto **17** The Ring and the Book **20** The Pied Piper of Hamlin **29** Solilo-

quy of the Spanish Cloister **30** Childe Roland to the Dark Tower Came

brownish 3 tan **5** taupe **6** bronze **8** chestnut **13** copper- colored

Brownlow, Mr
character in: **11** Oliver Twist
author: **7** Dickens

Brownmiller, Susan
author of: **14** Against Our Will

Brown's Descent
author: **11** Robert Frost

browse 3 eat **4** feed, scan, skim, surf **5** graze **6** nibble, peruse, survey **7** dip into, pasture **8** look over **9** check over **11** look through **13** glance through

Bruckner, Anton
born: **7** Austria **9** Ansfelden
composer of: **6** Te Deum **7** Psalm CL **11** Grosse Messe **16** Romantic Symphony **26** Intermezzo for String Quartet

Brueghel, Pieter (the Elder)
born: **5** Breda **8** Flanders
nickname: **14** Peasant Bruegel
sons: **3** Jan **6** Pieter
artwork: **9** Blue Cloak, The Months **10** Dulle Griet (Mad Meg) **12** Fall of Icarus, Peasant Dance, Tower of Babel **14** Children's Games, The Misanthrope **15** Return of the Herd **16** Hunters in the Snow **17** The Triumph of Death **19** Peasant Wedding Dance **21** Peasant Wedding Banquet, The Magpie on the Gallows **22** Massacre of the Innocents **23** The Blind Leading the Blind, The Fall of the Rebel Angels

Brueghel, Jan
born: **8** Brussels, Flanders
nickname: **6** Velvet
father: **13** Pieter Bruegel
artwork: **12** Four Elements **13** Village Street **15** The Garden of Eden (with Rubens) **17** The Battle of Arbela

Brueghel, Pieter (the Younger)
born: **8** Brussels, Flanders
nickname: **12** Hell Brueghel **19** The Infernal Brueghel
father: **13** Pieter Bruegel (the Elder)
artwork: **11** Village Fair **14** The Crucifixion **16** The Burning of Troy

Brugh, Spangler Arlington
real name of: **12** Robert Taylor

bruise 3 mar **4** hurt, mark **5** abuse, wound **6** damage, injure, injury, offend **7** blacken, blemish **8** discolor **9** black mark, contusion **13** discoloration

bruit 3 din **5** noise, rumor **6** clamor, hubbub, racket, report, uproar **7** clangor **10** clattering, noise about **11** voice abroad

Brunei
capital/largest city: **17** Bandar Seri Begawan
others: **4** Labi **5** Badas, Danau, Muara, Seria **6** Bangar, Tutong **7** Kampong **10** Kuala Abang, Kuala Balai **11** Kuala Belait
head of state/government: **6** sultan
island: **6** Borneo **8** Sipitang
mountain: **6** Teraja **9** Ulu Tutong
highest point: **10** Pagon Priok
river: **6** Belait, Brunei, Tutong **9** Temburong
sea: **10** South China
physical feature:
   bay: **6** Brunei
people: **4** Iban **5** Dayak, Malay **7** Chinese, Kadazan
language: **4** Iban **5** Malay **7** Chinese, English
religion: **5** Islam **6** Taoism **7** animism **8** Buddhism **12** Christianity
feature: **3** oil

Brunelleschi, Filippo
architect of: **10** San Lorenzo **11** Pazzi Chapel (Santa Croce), Pitti Palace **12** Santo Spirito **14** Badia Fiesolana **15** Duomo of Florence **16** Palazzo Quaratesi **21** Santa Maria degli Angeli **22** Ospedale degli Innocenti **23** Dome of Florence Cathedral

brunet, brunette 4 dark **5** black **9** brown-eyed, dark brown **10** dark-haired **11** brown-haired, dark-skinned **12** olive-skinned **16** dark-complexioned

Brunhild
origin: **8** Germanic
Scandinavian: **8** Brynhild
character in: **14** Nibelungenlied
queen of: **8** Isenland
husband: **7** Gunther
won by: **9** Siegfried

brunt 4 force **6** impact, stress, thrust **8** violence **9** full force, main shock

brush 4 bush, dust, fern, wash **5** clean, copse, flick, graze, groom, paint, run-in, scrub, sedge, set-to, shine, sweep, touch, whisk **6** battle, bushes, caress, duster, forest, fracas, polish, shrubs, stroke **7** bracken, cleanse, dusting, grazing, meeting, scuffle, thicket, varnish **8** skirmish, woodland **9** encounter, shrubbery, woodlands **10** engagement, underbrush, whisk-broom **11** bush country, undergrowth **12** bristled tool **13** confrontation
type: **4** hair, nail, shoe, wash **5** paint, scrub, tooth **7** clothes

brush aside 6 slight **7** neglect **8** pass over **9** disregard

brush-off 3 cut **4** snub **5** brush **6** rebuff, slight **7** put-down, squelch **9** disregard, rejection **11** repudiation **12** cold shoulder

brusque 4 curt, rude, tart **5** bluff, blunt, gruff, harsh, rough, short **6** abrupt, crusty **7** bearish **8** impolite, ungentle **10** ungracious **12** discourteous **13** unceremonious

Brussels
canal: **9** Charleroi **10** Willebroek
capital of: **7** Belgium
cathedral: **26** Saint Michel and Sainte Gudule
early name: **10** Bruoc-sella
   means: **16** marshy settlement
Flemish: **7** Brussel
French: **9** Bruxelles
headquarters of: **3** EEC **4** NATO **12** Common Market **25** European Economic Community
landmark: **11** Royal Palace **15** Palace of Justice **17** Palace of the Nation
province: **7** Brabant
river: **5** Senne, Zenne
square: **11** Grande Place

brutal 5 crude, cruel, harsh **6** bloody, coarse, fierce, savage **7** brutish, hellish, inhuman, vicious **8** barbaric, pitiless, ruthless **9** atrocious, barbarous, heartless, merciless, unfeeling **10** demoniacal **11** hardhearted, remorseless **12** bloodthirsty

brutality 7 cruelty **8** ferocity, savagery **9** barbarity, harshness **10** inhumanity, savageness **11** brutishness, viciousness **12** ruthlessness

brute 5 beast, demon, devil, fiend, swine **6** animal, savage **7** monster **9** barbarian **10** wild animal **11** cruel person **12** dumb creature

brutish 5 cruel, feral **6** bloody, brutal, fierce, savage **7** inhuman **8** barbaric **9** barbarous, ferocious, unfeeling **11** remorseless

brutishness 8 ferocity, savagery **9** barbarity, brutality **10** bestiality, coarseness, inhumanity, savageness **11** viciousness **15** remorselessness

Brutus
also: **12** Marcus Brutus
character in: **12** Julius Caesar
author: **11** Shakespeare

Bruxelles see **8** Brussels

Bryan, C D B
author of: **12** Friendly Fire **24** Ugly Scenes Beautiful Women

Bryant, Bear (Paul)
sport: **8** football
position: **5** coach
team: **7** Alabama **11** Crimson Tide

Brynhild
origin: **12** Scandinavian
Germanic: **8** Brunhild
husband: **6** Gunnar
won by: **6** Sigurd
position: **8** Valkyrie

Brynhildr Sigrdrifa see **9** Sigrdrifa

Brynner, Yul
real name: **10** Taidje Khan
born: **14** Sakhalin Island
roles: **9** Anastasia, West World **11** The King and I (Oscar) **18** The Ten Commandments **19** The Magnificent Seven **20** The Brothers Karamazov **23** Invitation to a Gunfighter

Brythonic
language family: **12** Indo-European

group: 5 Welsh **6** Breton **7** Cornish, Pictish

Bschliessmayer, Oskar Josef
  real name of: 11 Oskar Werner

Bubba Smith
  nickname of: 17 Charles Aaron Smith

bubble, bubbles 4 bleb, boil, fizz, foam **5** froth **6** burble, fizzle, gurgle, seethe **7** air ball, blister, droplet, globule, sparkle **9** percolate **10** effervesce **13** effervescence

bubbliness 9 fizziness, foaminess **10** ebullience, enthusiasm, frothiness, liveliness **11** high spirits **13** effervescence

bubbling 5 fizzy, foamy **6** frothy **7** fizzing, foaming **9** sparkling **12** effervescent

bubbly 5 fizzy, foamy **6** frothy, lively **7** fizzing, foaming **9** champagne, sparkling **12** effervescent, high-spirited

buccaneer 6 pirate **7** corsair **9** privateer **10** freebooter

Buchan, John (Baron Tweedsmuir)
  author of: 10 John Macnab **11** Greenmantle, Pilgrim's Way **17** John Burnet of Barns **18** The Thirty-Nine Steps

Buchanan, Daisy
  character in: 14 The Great Gatsby
  author: 10 Fitzgerald

Buchanan, Edgar
  born: 13 Humansville MO
  roles: 5 Shane, Texas **7** Arizona **8** Cimarron **9** McLintock **13** Penny Serenade **17** Petticoat Junction **18** Ride the High Country

Buchanan, James
  nickname: 7 Old Buck
  presidential rank: 9 fifteenth
  party: 8 Democrat
  state represented: 2 PA
  defeated: 7 (John Charles) Fremont **8** (Millard) Fillmore
  vice president: 12 (John Cabell) Breckinridge
  cabinet:
    state: 4 (Lewis) Cass **5** (Jeremiah Sullivan) Black
    treasury: 3 (John Adams) Dix **4** (Howell) Cobb **6** (Philip Francis) Thomas
    war: 4 (Joseph) Holt **5** (John Buchanan) Floyd
    attorney general: 5 (Jeremiah Sullivan) Black **7** (Edwin McMasters) Stanton
    navy: 6 (Isaac) Toucey
    postmaster general: 4 (Horatio) King, (Joseph) Holt **5** (Aaron Venable) Brown
    interior: 8 (Jacob) Thompson
  born: 11 Cove Gap PA (near Mercersburg)
  died/buried: 11 Lancaster PA
  education:
    Academy: 8 Old Stone

College: 9 Dickinson
  studied: 3 law
  religion: 12 Presbyterian
  political career: 13 state assembly **24** US House of Representatives
    secretary of: 5 State
    minister: 6 Russia **12** Great Britain
  civilian career: 6 lawyer
  notable events of lifetime/term: 5 Panic (of 1857) **11** English Bill, Pony Express
    raid by: 9 John Brown
    raid on: 12 Harper's Ferry
    Supreme Court case: 9 Dred Scott
  father: 5 James
  mother: 9 Elizabeth (Speer)
  siblings: 4 Jane, John, Mary **5** Maria, Sarah **7** Harriet **9** Elizabeth **11** Edward Young **12** William Speer **16** George Washington
  wife: 4 none
  children: 4 none

Bucharest
  capital of: 7 Romania, Rumania
  founder: 5 Bucur
  landmark: 8 Scinteia **13** Village Museum
  river: 9 Dimbovita
  Rumanian: 9 Bucuresti

Buchinsky, Charles
  real name of: 14 Charles Bronson

buck 3 man **4** beau, deer, dude, kick, male **5** dandy **6** dollar, oppose **7** coxcomb **8** cavalier, gay blade **9** go against **10** young blood

Buck
  character in: 16 The Call of the Wild
  author: 6 London

Buck, Pearl S
  author of: 8 The Exile **9** Other Gods **10** Dragon Seed **12** The Good Earth **13** A House Divided

bucket 3 can, hod, tub **4** cask, pail **5** scoop **6** vessel **7** pailful, pitcher, scuttle **9** container **10** receptacle

Buckeye State
  nickname of: 4 Ohio

buckle 3 sag **4** bend, clip, curl, hasp, hook, warp **5** bulge, catch, clasp **6** cave in, couple, fasten, secure **7** contort, crinkle, crumple, distort, wrinkle **8** belly out, collapse, fastener

buckle down 6 attend **12** apply oneself

Buckley, William F Jr
  author of: 11 Who's on First? **15** God and Man at Yale, God Save the Queen
  editor of: 14 National Review
  wife: 3 Pat
  son: 11 Christopher

Buck Rogers
  creator: 14 Richard Calkins
  character: 5 Alura, Buddy, Dercu, Kayla, Wilma **6** Ardala **10** Killer Kane

bucolic 4 idyl, poem **5** idyll, rural **6**

poetic, rustic **7** eclogue, idyllic, peasant **8** pastoral, shepherd

bud 4 open **5** shoot **6** flower, sprout **7** blossom, burgeon, develop

Bud, Rosa
  character in: 22 The Mystery of Edwin Drood
  author: 7 Dickens

Budapest
  area: 4 Buda, Pest **5** Obuda
  capital of: 7 Hungary
  cathedral: 13 Saint Matthias
  hill: 10 Castle Hill
  island: 6 Csepel
  river: 6 Danube
  Roman town: 8 Aquincum

Buddenbrooks
  author: 10 Thomas Mann

Buddha
  also called: 5 Butsu
  born: 11 Kapilavastu
  father: 11 Suddhodhana
  founded: 8 Buddhism
  means: 15 enlightened one
  message: 6 dharma
  name for: 17 Siddhartha Gautama
  son: 6 Rahula
  tree: 2 bo **5** bodhi
  wife: 9 Yasodhara

Buddhism
  action: 5 karma
  branch: 3 Zen **8** Mahayana **9** Theravada **12** Great Vehicle **14** way of the elders
  doctrine: 6 duhkha **7** nirvana **9** suffering **13** eightfold path **15** four noble truths **17** pratityasamutpada
  founded by: 6 Buddha **17** Siddhartha Gautama
  monk: 7 bhikshu
  nun: 9 bhikshuni
  rebirth: 7 samsara
  religious community: 6 sangha

buddy 3 pal **4** chum, mate **5** amigo, crony **6** cohort, fellow, friend **7** brother, comrade, partner **8** confrere, intimate, playmate, sidekick **9** associate, colleague, companion, confidant **10** playfellow **11** confederate

buddy-buddy 5 close, palsy **6** chummy **8** friendly, intimate **10** palsy-walsy

budge 4 move, push, roll, stir, sway **5** shift, slide **6** change **8** convince, dislodge, persuade **9** dislocate, influence

budget 4 cost, plan **5** funds, means **6** moneys, ration **7** arrange **8** allocate, schedule **9** allotment, allowance, apportion, resources **10** allocation, portion out **12** spending plan **13** financial plan

budgetary 6 fiscal **8** economic, monetary **9** financial, pecuniary

buenas noches 9 good night

bueno 4 good

Buenos Aires
  capital of: 9 Argentina

landmark: 11 Teatro Colon 16 Saavedra Monument, San Martin Theater 17 Wildestein Gallery, Witcomb Art Gallery 18 Church of El Salvador 27 Christopher Columbus Monument
park: 7 Palermo
people: 8 portenos
  means: 15 people of the port
river: 12 Rio de la Plata

buff 3 bug, fan, nut, rub, tan 4 swab 5 freak, hound, maven, mavin, sandy, straw, tawny 6 addict, dauber, polish, smooth, the raw 7 admirer, burnish, devotee, leather 8 bare skin, follower, polisher 9 nakedness, yellowish 10 aficionado, enthusiast 11 buffalo hide, connoisseur 14 yellowish-brown

buffalo 5 bison 6 puzzle 7 mystify 10 intimidate
kind: 7 African 10 Asian water
African: 14 syncerus caffer
Asian water: 14 bubalus bubalis

Buffalo
football team: 5 Bills
hockey team: 6 Sabres

buffer 6 bumper, fender, shield 7 cushion 9 protector

buffet 3 box, hit, jab, rap 4 bang, beat, bump, cuff, meal, push, slap 5 baste, knock, pound, shove, thump 6 pum- mel, strike, supper, thrash, thwack, wallop 7 cabinet, counter 8 credenza 9 cafeteria, sideboard 11 smorgasbord

Buffone, Carlo
character in: 22 Every Man out of His Humour
author: 6 Jonson

buffoon 3 wag 4 fool, zany 5 clown, comic, joker, mimic, Punch 6 jester, madcap 7 Pierrot 8 comedian, funnyman 9 harlequin, pantaloon, prankster, trickster 10 Scaramouch, silly-billy 11 merry-andrew, punchinello, Scaramouche

buffoonery 6 antics, comedy 7 foolery, inanity 8 zaniness 9 asininity, horseplay, silliness, slapstick 10 tomfoolery 11 foolishness, loutishness 12 clownishness, monkeyshines, prankishness 14 clowning around, playing the fool

bug 3 nag 4 flaw, germ 5 annoy, fault, virus 6 badger, bother, defect, insect, pester 7 wiretap 8 drawback, listen in, weakness 9 eavesdrop, Hemiptera 11 Heteroptera
variety: 3 bat, bed, red 4 gnat, lace, leaf, seed, toad 5 negro, plant, shore, stilt, stink, water 6 ambush, damsel, fungus, pirate, ripple 7 boatman, stainer 8 assassin, burrower, creeping 9 royal palm 10 leaf footed 11 ashgray leaf, backswimmer, broadheaded, jumping tree, velvet water 12 velvety shore, water strider, water treader 13 jumping

ground, water measurer, water scorpion 14 scentless plant 17 terrestrial turtle

bugaboo 4 ogre 5 scare 6 fright 7 anxiety

bugbear 4 ogre 5 bogey 6 goblin 7 bugaboo 8 bogeyman 9 bete noire

buggy 4 cart 5 wagon 7 vehicle 8 carriage 10 conveyance

bugle 4 horn 10 instrument

Bugs Bunny
creator: 15 Leon Schlesinger
character: 9 Elmer Fudd
voice of: 8 Mel Blanc
saying: 10 what's up doc

build 4 body, form, make, mold, open 5 begin, brace, erect, forge, found, put up, raise, renew, set up, shape, start, steel 6 create, extend, figure, harden, launch 7 amplify, augment, develop, enhance, enlarge, fashion, greaten, improve, produce 8 embark on, increase, initiate, multiply, physique 9 construct, establish, fabri- cate, institute, intensify, originate, reinforce, structure, undertake 10 inaugurate, strengthen, supplement 11 manufacture, put together 12 construction

building 7 edifice 9 structure 12 construction

building front 6 facade 8 frontage

build up 5 amass 7 develop, promote 8 increase 10 accumulate

Bujold, Genevieve
born: 6 Canada 8 Montreal
roles: 4 Coma 9 Monsignor, Obsession 12 King of Hearts 21 Anne of the Thousand Days

Bujumbura
capital of: 7 Burundi

Bul 17 eighth Hebrew month

bulb 3 bud 4 corm, seed 5 plant, tuber 8 swelling

Bulfinch, Charles
architect of: 7 Capitol (Washington DC) 16 Hartford City Hall (CT) 23 Massachusetts State House (Boston)
style: 7 Federal

Bulgakov, Mikhail
author of: 9 Black Snow 13 The White Guard 14 The Heart of a Dog 19 The Days of the Turbins 21 The Master and Margarita

Bulgaria
capital/largest city: 5 Sofia
others: 3 Lom 4 Rila, Ruse 5 Aytos, Butan, Byclu, Elena, Iskra, Stara, Varna 6 Bleven, Burgas, Devnia, Dulovo, Levsky, Pernik, Pleuna, Pleven, Plevna, Shumen, Shumla, Sliven, Slivno, Widden, Yambol, Zagora 7 Gabrovo, Karlovo, Plovdiv, Sistova, Tirnova 8 Khaskovo, Rustchuk, Svishtov 9 Ruse Vidin, Silistria 11 Kolorovgrad 12 Dimitrovgrad

school: 5 Sofia 7 Plovdiv 13 Veliko Turnovo
measure: 3 oka, oke 5 krine, lekhe, likhe
monetary unit: 3 lev 8 stotinki
weight: 3 oka, oke 5 tovar
mountain: 3 Kom 5 Botev, Pirin, Sapka 6 Balkan, Sredna 7 Vikhren 11 Rila-Rhodope
highest point: 6 Musala 8 Musallah
river: 3 Lom, Vit 4 Arda, Osma 5 Isker, Iskur, Mesta 6 Danube, Marica, Ogosta, Struma, Yantra 7 Maritsa, Stryama, Tundzha
sea: 5 Black
physical feature:
  cape: 5 Emine, Sabla 7 Kuratan
  gulf: 5 Burga
  plateau: 6 Danube
  resort: 9 Pyassatzi 13 Slunchev Bryay
  valley: 7 Maritsa
people: 4 Slav, Turk 5 Gypsy, Pomak, Tatar 6 Bulgar, Slavic 7 Chuvash 9 Cheremiss 10 Macedonian
language: 9 Bulgarian
religion: 5 Islam 24 Bulgarian Eastern Orthodox
place:
  church: 9 St Nedelja
  monastery: 4 Rila 6 Rilski
  monument: 7 Red Army
  mosque: 10 Banya Bashi
  museum: 21 Revolutionary Movement
  square: 5 Lenin
  valley of roses: 8 Kazanluk
feature:
  dance: 4 horo
  holiday: 12 St Georges Day
  newspaper: 17 Rabot Nichesko Delo
food:
  stew: 8 giuvetch

bulge 3 bag, sag 4 bump, lump 5 curve, swell 6 excess 7 distend, project, puff out, sagging 8 protrude, stand out, stick out, swelling, swell out 9 bagginess 10 projection, prominence, protrusion 12 protuberance

bulk 4 body, mass, most, size 6 extent, volume, weight 7 bigness, measure 8 enormity, hugeness, main part, majority, quantity 9 amplitude, greatness, largeness, magnitude, major part, plurality, substance 10 better part, dimensions, lion's share 11 greater part, massiveness, proportions 13 preponderance

bulky 3 big 4 huge 5 large 6 clumsy 7 awkward, hulking, immense, lumpish, massive, sizable, unhandy 8 enormous, ungainly, unwieldy 9 capacious, extensive 10 cumbersome, voluminous 12 unmanageable

bull 2 ox 4 male
male of the: 3 elk 4 seal 5 moose, whale 6 bovine 8 elephant

constellation of: 6 Taurus
Spanish: 4 toro

bulldoze 3 cow **4** bump, fell, push, rage, raze **5** abash, bully, drive, force, level, press, shove **6** coerce, hector, jostle, propel, subdue, thrust **7** buffalo, dragoon, flatten **8** bludgeon, browbeat, domineer, shoulder **9** push about, tyrannize **10** intimidate

Bullen, Frank T
author of: 19 Told in the Dry Watches **22** The Cruise of the Cachalot

bullet 4 ball, lead, shot, slug **7** missile **8** buckshot

bulletin 4 note **6** report **7** account, message, release **8** dispatch **9** statement **10** communique, news report **12** notification **13** communication

Bullet Park
author: 11 John Cheever

bullfighter 6 torero **7** matador, picador **8** Manolete, toreador **9** Escamillo **10** El Cordobes (Manuel Benitez Perez) **15** Miguel Dominguin

Bullion State
nickname of: 8 Missouri

Bullitt
director: 10 Peter Yates
cast: 9 Don Gordon **12** Robert Duvall, Robert Vaughn, Steve McQueen **16** Jacqueline Bisset
setting: 12 San Francisco

bullock 2 ox **4** beef, bull **5** steer

bullocks 4 kine, oxen **5** beefs, bulls **6** beeves, cattle, steers

bull session 3 rap **4** talk **7** gabfest, palaver **8** dialogue **9** discourse **10** discussion **12** conversation **13** confabulation

bull's-eye 5 black **6** center **7** exactly **8** on target **9** dead center, precisely

bully 3 cow **4** good **5** annoy, swell, tough **6** cheers, coerce, despot, harass, hurrah, hurray **7** coercer, right on, ruffian, tread on **8** browbeat, bulldoze, domineer, frighten, ride over, well done **9** oppressor, terrorize, tormentor, tyrannize **10** browbeater, intimidate **11** intimidator

bullying 7 torment **8** coercion **9** despotism **10** harassment, tormenting **11** browbeating, domineering, tyrannizing **12** intimidation

bulrush 5 plant, sedge **7** cattail, papyrus

bulwark 5 guard **7** barrier, parapet, rampart, support, defense **8** mainstay **9** earthwork **10** embankment

Bulwer-Lytton, Edward
author of: 6 Harold, Pelham, Rienzi **9** Richelieu **13** The Coming Race **16** Kenelm Chillingly **18** The Last of the Barons **20** The Last Days of Pompeii

bum 3 beg **4** grub, hobo **5** cadge, idler, mooch, tramp **6** borrow, loafer,

sponge **7** drifter, vagrant **8** derelict, vagabond

bumble 6 bungle **7** blunder, stagger, stumble **8** flounder

Bumble
character in: 11 Oliver Twist
author: 7 Dickens

bumcombe, bunkum 3 rot **4** bosh, bunk **6** drivel **7** twaddle **8** nonsense, tommyrot **10** balderdash **16** stuff-and-nonsense

bump 3 hit, jar, rap **4** bang, blow, butt, hump, jolt, knob, knot, lump, node, poke, slam, slap, sock **5** bulge, clash, crack, crash, gnarl, knock, punch, shake, smack, smash, thump, whack **6** bounce, buf- fet, impact, jostle, jounce, nodule, rattle, strike, wallop **7** collide, run into **8** swelling **9** collision, crash into, smash into **11** excrescence **12** protuberance

bump into 4 meet **7** collide, run into **9** encounter

bumpkin 3 oaf **4** boor, lout **5** churl, yokel **8** ship beam **10** clodhopper

bump off 4 do in, kill, slay **6** murder, rub out **7** execute, gun down **8** dispatch **11** assassinate **12** take for a ride

bumptious 4 bold **5** cocky, pushy **6** brazen **7** forward, haughty **8** arrogant, boastful, cocksure, impudent, insolent **9** bodacious, conceited, obtrusive **10** aggressive, swaggering **11** impertinent, overbearing **12** presumptuous **13** overconfident, self-assertive

bumptiousness 4 gall **5** cheek **8** audacity, boldness **9** impudence **11** forwardness, presumption **12** impertinence **13** obtrusiveness **17** self-assertiveness

bumpy 5 lumpy, rocky, rough **6** uneven **10** undulating

bun 4 coil, knot, roll **8** soft roll **9** sweet roll

Bunaea
epithet of: 4 Hera
refers to: 6 temple

bunch 3 lot, mob **4** band, bevy, gang, heap, herd, host, knot, mass, pack, pile, team **5** array, batch, clump, crowd, flock, group, shock, stack, tribe, troop **6** amount, bundle, gather, huddle, number, string **7** cluster, collect, company **8** assemble, assembly, quantity **9** gathering, multitude **10** assortment, collection, congregate **12** accumulation

bundle 3 lot **4** bale, bind, heap, mass, pack, pile, wrap **5** array, batch, bunch, group, sheaf, stack, truss **6** amount, packet, parcel **7** package **8** quantity **9** multitude **10** assortment, collection **11** tie together **12** accumulation

Bundren family

characters in: 11 As I Lay Dying
member: 4 Anse, Cash, Darl **5** Addie, Jewel **9** Dewey Dell
author: 8 Faulkner

bungalow 5 cabin, house, lodge **7** cottage

bungle 3 mar **4** flub, goof, miff, ruin **5** botch, spoil **6** foul up, mess up, muddle **7** blunder, butcher, do badly, louse up, screw up **8** misjudge **9** mismanage, misreckon **10** miscompute **11** make a mess of, misestimate **12** miscalculate

Bunin, Ivan Alekseyevich
author of: 10 The Village **15** The Elagin Affair **17** The Life of Arseniev **28** The Gentleman from San Francisco

bunk 3 bed, cot, rot **4** bull **5** berth, hokum, hooey, stuff **6** bunkum, hot air, humbug, pallet **7** baloney, blather, bombast, hogwash, inanity, malarky, spinach **8** claptrap, nonsense, tommyrot **9** poppycock **10** applesauce, balderdash **11** foolishness **16** stuff and nonsense

Bunsen, Robert Wilhelm
nationality: 6 German
inventor of: 9 gas burner **10** photo meter **12** Bunsen burner, spectroscope **24** electromechanical battery

Bunshaft, Gordon
architect of: 10 Lever House (NY) **23** Beinecke Rare Book Library (Yale) **33** Hirshhorn Museum and Sculpture Garden (Washington DC) **34** Lyndon Baines Johnson Memorial Library (Austin TX)

Bunyan, John
author of: 10 The Holy War **16** Pilgrim's Progress **25** The Life and Death of Mr Badman **33** Grace Abounding to the Chief of Sinners

buona notte 9 good night

buona sera 11 good evening

buon giorno 7 good day **11** good morning

Buono, Victor
born: 10 San Diego CA
roles: 11 The Stranger **12** Four for Texas **22** Hush Hush Sweet Charlotte **26** Whatever Happened to Baby Jane

buoy 4 bell, lift **5** boost, cheer, float, raise **6** beacon, uplift **7** cheer up, elevate, gladden, lighten **8** brighten **10** keep afloat **14** floating marker

buoyancy, buoyance 4 glee **6** gaiety **7** jollity **8** gladness, vivacity **9** animation, good humor, joviality, lightness, sunniness **10** brightness, cheeriness, enthusiasm, floatiness, joyousness **11** good spirits **12** cheerfulness, exhilaration, floatability **14** weightlessness **16** lightheartedness

buoyant 3 gay **4** glad **5** happy, jolly, light, merry, peppy, sunny **6** afloat, breezy, bright, elated, joyful, joyous, lively **7** hopeful **8** animated, carefree, cheerful, floating, sportive **9** energetic, floatable, sprightly, vivacious **10** blithesome, optimistic, weightless **11** exhilarated, free and easy **12** enthusiastic, lighthearted

buoyed 6 elated **7** exalted, pleased **8** elevated **9** confident, heartened, reassured **10** inspirited

buoy up 4 warm **6** assure, uplift **7** comfort, hearten, inspire **8** inspirit, reassure **9** encourage

Burbank, Luther
field: **7** biology
developed: **13** plant breeding

burble 6 babble, bubble, gurgle, murmur **8** babbling

Burce, Suzanne
real name of: **10** Jane Powell

Burchill, Mr
character in: **19** The Vicar of Wakefield
author: **9** Goldsmith

burden 3 tax, try, vex **4** care, load, onus, pack **5** cargo **6** hamper, hinder, strain, stress, weight **7** afflict, anxiety, freight, oppress, trouble **8** encumber, handicap, hardship, load with, obligate, overload **9** press down, weigh down **10** saddle with **11** encumbrance **14** responsibility

Burden, Jack
character in: **14** All the King's Men
author: **6** Warren

burden of proof
Latin: **12** onus probandi

burdensome 4 hard **5** heavy **6** tiring **7** arduous, onerous **8** wearying **9** Herculean, laborious **10** exhausting

bureau 6 agency, branch, office **7** cabinet, commode, dresser, service, station **8** division **10** chiffonier, department **14** administration, chest of drawers

bureaucrat 8 mandarin, official, politico **9** penpusher **10** politician **11** apparatchik, functionary, rubber stamp **12** civil servant, officeholder **13** public servant

burgee 4 flag **6** banner, colors, ensign **7** pennant

burgeon 3 wax **4** blow, grow, open **5** bloom **6** expand, flower, spread, thrive **7** augment, blossom, develop, enlarge, prosper, shoot up, succeed **8** escalate, flourish, fructify, increase, mushroom, spring up **9** bear fruit **10** effloresce **11** proliferate

Burgess, Anthony
author of: **2** MF **13** Man of Nazareth, Time for a Tiger **14** Enderby Outside, The Wanting Seed **16** A Clockwork Orange, Beard's Roman Women **17** Nothing Like the Sun **20** The End of the World News

burgher 7 citizen **9** bourgeois **11** townsperson

burglar 3 cat **4** yegg **5** thief **6** robber **7** prowler **8** pilferer **9** cracksman, purloiner **12** housebreaker **14** second-story man

burglary 5 theft **6** felony **7** break-in, larceny, robbery **8** filching, stealing **9** pilfering **10** purloining **13** housebreaking **19** breaking and entering

burgundy 3 red **4** wine **5** color **13** reddish-purple

Burgundy
ancient city: **5** Autun
city: **5** Dijon
district: **5** Youne **6** Nievre **7** Cote d' Or **12** Saone-et-Loire
French: **9** Bourgogne
location: **6** France
river: **5** Rhone, Saone
tribe: **9** Burgundii

Buri
origin: **12** Scandinavian
first: **3** god
revealed by: **8** Audhumla **9** Audhumbla

burial 5 rites **7** funeral **9** interment, obsequies **10** entombment, inhumation

burial ground 7 ossuary **8** boneyard, Boot Hill, catacomb, cemetery **9** graveyard **10** churchyard, necropolis **12** potter's field

buried 4 laid, sunk **6** hidden **7** covered, inhumed, immured **9** concealed, deep sixed **10** laid to rest **11** underground

Burke, Francis
character in: **21** The Master of Ballantrae
author: **9** Stevenson

Burkina Faso see **10** Upper Volta

burlap 3 bag **4** hemp, jute **5** cloth **6** fabric **8** material

burlesque 5 farce, spoof **6** comedy, parody, satire **7** mockery, takeoff **8** ridicule, travesty **10** buffoonery, caricature **15** slapstick comedy

burly 3 big **5** beefy, bulky, hefty, large **6** brawny, stocky, strong, sturdy **7** hulking, sizable **8** thickset **9** ponderous, strapping

Burma see **7** Myanmar

burn 3 nip, tan **4** bite, char, fire, glow, hurt, pain, sear, skin **5** be hot, blaze, brown, chafe, flame, flare, flash, parch, prick, scald, singe, smart, smoke, sting **6** abrade, bronze, flames, ignite, kindle, nettle, scorch, scrape, suntan, tingle, wither **7** blister, consume, cremate, flicker, oxidize, prickle, shrivel, smolder, sunburn, swelter **8** abrasion, be ablaze, be on fire, charring, irritate, kindling **9** be flushed, reddening, set fire to, set on fire, use as fuel **10** be feverish,

be in flames, blistering, incandesce, incinerate, irritation, smoldering **12** incineration **13** reduce to ashes

burnable 9 flammable, ignitable **10** combustive **11** combustible, inflammable **13** conflagrative

Burne-Jones, Sir Edward Coley
born: **7** England **10** Birmingham
artwork: **11** Laus Veneris **15** The Golden Stairs **16** The Mirror of Venus **18** The Star of Bethlehem **28** King Cophetua and the Beggar Maid

burner, gas
invented by: **6** Bunsen

Burnett, Carol
born: **12** San Antonio TX
roles: **14** The Four Seasons **19** The Carol Burnett Show

Burnett, Frances H
author of: **20** Little Lord Fauntleroy

Burney, Fanny
author of: **7** Camilla, Diaries, Evelina

Burnham, Daniel Hudson
partner: **16** John Wellborn Root
architect of: **7** Rookery **12** Union Station (Washington DC) **15** Calumet Building **16** Flatiron Building (NYC), Reliance Building **17** Monadnock Building **25** World's Columbian Exposition

burning 3 hot **5** acrid, afire, aglow, eager, fiery, sharp **6** aflame, ardent, biting, fervid, heated, raging, red-hot **7** blazing, boiling, caustic, earnest, fanatic, fervent, flaming, flaring, frantic, glowing, ignited, intense, kindled, painful, pungent, sincere, smoking, zealous **8** flashing, frenzied, piercing, resolute, sizzling, smarting, stinging, tingling **9** corroding, prickling **10** astringent, compelling, flickering, irritating, passionate, smoldering **11** impassioned **12** all-consuming

burnish 3 wax **4** buff **5** rub up, shine **6** polish, smooth

burnished 5 shiny **6** bright, buffed, shined **8** lustrous, polished, smoothed

burnoose 4 cape, robe **5** cloak **6** mantle **7** pelisse

burn out 3 pop **4** blow **7** exhaust **10** exhaustion, extinguish

Burns, George
real name: **14** Nathan Birnbaum
wife: **11** Gracie Allen
born: **9** New York NY
roles: **5** Oh God **12** Going in Style **15** The Sunshine Boys **17** Burns and Allen Show

Burns, Robert
author of: **8** To a Louse, To a Mouse **11** A Red Red Rose, Tam O'Shanter **12** Auld Lang Syne **16** Address to the Deil, Coming Thro the Rye **17** Holy Willie's Prayer **20** Flow Gently Sweet Afton **22** My Heart's in the Highlands **23** The Cotter's Saturday

Night **32** Poems Chiefly in the Scottish Dialect

Burnt Norton
author: **7** T S Eliot

burp 5 belch, eruct **10** eructation

burr 4 buhr, rock **5** notch, stone **9** whetstone **13** pronunciation

Burr
author: **9** Gore Vidal

Burr, Aaron 13 vice president
event: **4** duel
victim: **17** Alexander Hamilton

Burr, Raymond
born: **6** Canada **14** New Westminster **15** British Columbia
roles: **8** Ironside **10** Perry Mason, Rear Window

burro 3 ass **4** mule **6** donkey, onager **7** jackass

Burroughs, Edgar Rice
author of: **15** Tarzan of the Apes

Burroughs, William S
author of: **5** Junky, Queer **6** Junkie **13** The Naked Lunch
member of: **14** Beat Generation

Burroughs, William Seward
nationality: **8** American
inventor of: **13** adding machine
grandson: **17** William S Burroughs (author)

burrow 3 den, dig **4** cave, hole, lair **6** covert, dugout, furrow, tunnel **8** excavate, scoop out **9** hollow out

Burrows, Abe
author of: **41** How to Succeed in Business without Really Trying

bursa 3 bag, sac **5** pouch, purse **6** cavity

bursar 6 purser **7** cashier **9** paymaster, treasurer **10** cashkeeper

burst 3 fly, pop, run **4** bang, bust, rend, rush **5** barge, blast, break, crack, erupt, split, spout **6** blow up, detach, divide, sunder **7** disjoin, explode, rupture, shatter, torrent **8** breaking, break out, cracking, crashing, detonate, eruption, fly apart, fracture, fragment, outbreak, separate, splinter **9** break open, discharge, explosion, gush forth, pull apart, splitting, tear apart **10** detonation, disconnect, outpouring, shattering **11** spring forth **12** disintegrate

burst forth 5 arise, begin, erupt, start **6** arrive, emerge **8** break out, commence

Burstyn, Ellen
real name: **14** Edna Rae Gillooly
born: **9** Detroit MI
roles: **11** The Exorcist **16** Same Time Next Year **18** The Last Picture Show **26** Alice Doesn't Live Here Anymore (Oscar)

Burton, Richard
real name: **22** Richard Walter Jenkins Jr

wife: **15** Elizabeth Taylor
born: **5** Wales **11** Pontrhydfen Wales
roles: **6** Becket, Hamlet **7** Camelot, The Robe **9** Cleopatra **14** My Cousin Rachel **19** The Night of the Iguana, The Taming of the Shrew **21** Anne of the Thousand Days **25** Who's Afraid of Virginia Woolf **26** The Spy Who Came in from the Cold

Burton, Robert
author of: **22** The Anatomy of Melancholy

Burundi
capital/largest city: **9** Bujumbura
others: **5** Ngozi **6** Bururi, Gitega, Kitega, Rutana, Ruyigi **7** Kibumbu, Muyinga
monetary unit: **5** franc **7** centime
lake: **7** Rugwero **8** Tshohoha **10** Tanganyika
mountain: **9** Nyamisana
highest point: **8** Nyarwana
river: **6** Akanya, Ruvuvu, Ruzizi **8** Rukagera **10** Malagarasi
people: **3** Twa **4** Hutu **5** Bantu, Batwa, Pygmy, Tutsi **6** Bahutu, Watusi **7** Barundi
language: **6** French **7** Kirundi, Swahili
religion: **5** Islam **7** animism **10** Protestant **13** Roman Catholic
feature:
    king: **4** mwam
food:
    coffee: **7** Arabica

Burushaski
language spoken in: **7** Kashmir

bury 4 hide **5** cache, cover, inter **6** encase, engulf, entomb, inhume **7** conceal, cover up, enclose, immerse, secrete **8** submerge, submerse **13** lay in the grave **17** consign to the grave

Bury My Heart at Wounded Knee
author: **8** Dee Brown

bush 4 veld **5** brush, hedge, plant, shrub, woods **6** forest, jungle **7** barrens **9** shrubbery, woodlands

Bush, George Herbert Walker
presidential rank: **10** forty-first
party: **10** Republican
state represented: **2** TX **5** Texas
defeated: **7** (Michael) Dukakis
defeated by: **7** (Bill) Clinton
vice president: **6** (James Danforth) Quayle
born: **8** Milton MA
education: **4** Yale **7** Andover
religion: **12** Episcopalian
vacation spot: **5** Maine **13** Kennebunkport
political career: **13** vice president **14** representative **21** Ways and Means Committee
    ambassador to: **2** UN **13** United Nations
    chairman of: **27** Republican National Committee

head of: **3** CIA
liaison with: **5** China
civilian career: **3** oil **14** Zapata Offshore
military career: **5** pilot **6** US Navy
vice president under: **12** Ronald Reagan
notable events of lifetime/term: **7** Gulf War **14** Persian Gulf War **20** Operation Desert Storm
    Supreme Court appointments: **11** David Souter **14** Clarence Thomas
    invasion of: **6** Panama
father: **15** Prescott Sheldon
mother: **13** Dorothy Walker
wife: **13** Barbara Pierce
children: **4** John, Neil **5** Robin (died 1953) **6** George, Marvin **7** Dorothy

bush country 5 scrub, wilds **7** outback **9** wilderness

bushed 4 beat **5** all in, spent, tired, weary **6** done it, pooped **7** drained, wearied, worn out **8** dog tired, fatigued, tired out **9** dead tired, exhausted, played out

bushel
abbreviation: **2** bu **4** bush

bushes 5 brush **6** shrubs **9** brushwood, shrubbery **10** underbrush **11** undergrowth

bushy 5 hairy **6** fluffy, shaggy **7** hirsute **9** overgrown

business 3 job **4** case, duty, firm, line, shop, task, work **5** chore, field, place, point, store, topic, trade **6** affair, career, living, matter, office, racket **7** affairs, calling, company, concern, dealing, factory, mission, problem, pursuit, subject, venture **8** activity, commerce, function, industry, position, province, question, specialty **9** procedure, situation, specialty **10** assignment, bargaining, employment, enterprise, livelihood, occupation, profession, walk of life **11** corporation, negotiation, partnership, transaction, undertaking **13** establishment, manufacturing, merchandising **14** bread and butter, responsibility

businesslike 7 careful, correct, orderly, regular, serious **8** diligent, sedulous, thorough **9** assiduous, efficient, organized, practical **10** methodical, systematic **11** industrious, painstaking **12** professional

Busiris
king of: **5** Egypt
father: **8** Poseidon
mother: **10** Lysianassa

Busoni, Ferruccio
born: **5** Italy **6** Empoli
composer of: **8** Turandot **10** Arlecchino **11** Doctor Faust, Doktor Faust **12** Die Brautwahl **14** Comedy Overture **25** Fantasia Contrappuntistica

bus station 5 depot **8** terminal, terminus

Bus Stop
    director: **11** Joshua Logan
    cast: **9** Don Murray **10** Betty Field **13** Eileen Heckart, Marilyn Monroe **14** Arthur O'Connell

bust 3 nab **4** head, raid **5** bosom, chest, seize **6** arrest, breast, collar **7** capture **9** apprehend, sculpture **12** take prisoner **15** take into custody

Buster Brown
    creator: **10** RF Outcault
    bulldog: **4** Tige
    trademark: **9** sailor hat **10** wide collar

bustle 3 ado, fly **4** dash, flit, fuss, rush, stir, tear, to-do **5** hurry **6** bestir, flurry, hustle, pother, scurry, tumult **7** be quick, fluster, flutter, press on, scamper, scuttle **8** activity, be active, scramble **9** agitation, commotion, make haste **10** excitement, hurly-burly

busy 4 full **6** active, employ, engage, intent, occupy, on duty, work at **7** engaged, labor at, slaving, toiling, working **8** absorbed, bustling, employed, laboring, occupied **9** engrossed, in harness, strenuous **10** hard at work **11** industrious **12** be absorbed in, keep occupied **13** be engrossed in

busybody 3 pry **5** snoop **6** gossip **7** blabber, meddler, Paul Pry **8** telltale **10** chatterbox, newsmonger, talebearer, tattletale **12** blabbermouth **13** scandalmonger

busy place 4 hive **6** warren **7** anthill, beehive

but 3 yet **4** save, than that **5** if not, still **6** except, saving, unless **7** however, outside, that not **9** excepting, other than, otherwise **10** except that **14** on the other hand

Butch Cassidy and the Sundance Kid
    director: **13** George Roy Hill
    cast: **10** Paul Newman (Butch) **13** Katharine Ross (Etta Place), Robert Redford (The Kid)
    score: **13** Burt Bacharach
    Oscar for: **5** score
    song: **27** Raindrops Keep Fallin' on My Head

butcher 4 goof, kill, muff, ruin, slay **5** botch, purge, spoil **6** boggle, bungle, fumble, hack up, hit man, killer, mess up, murder **7** louse up, screw up **8** assassin, decimate, homicide, massacre, murderer **9** liquidate, manhandle, mishandle, slaughter **10** annihilate, hatchet man, liquidator **11** assassinate, exterminate, make a mess of, slaughterer **12** exterminator, massmurderer **15** homicidal maniac

butchery 4 flop, mess **5** botch **8** massacre **9** slaughter

Butes
    father: **6** Boreas **7** Pandion

    mother: **8** Zeuxippe
    brother: **8** Lycurgus **10** Erechtheus
    sister: **6** Procne **9** Philomela
    son: **4** Eryx
    priest of: **6** Athena **8** Poseidon
    member of: **9** Argonauts
    stricken with: **8** insanity
    enticed by: **6** Sirens
    leaped into: **3** sea
    rescued by: **9** Aphrodite

Butkus, Dick (Richard Marvin)
    sport: **8** football
    position: **10** linebacker
    team: **12** Chicago Bears

Butler, Rhett
    character in: **15** Gone With the Wind
    author: **8** Mitchell

Butler, Samuel
    author of: **7** Erewhon **8** Hudibras **16** The Way of All Flesh **20** The Elephant in the Moon

butt 3 end, hit, jab, ram, rap **4** buck, bump, bunt, dupe, goat, mark, push, slap, stub **5** knock, shank, shove, smack, stump, thump **6** bottom, buffet, jostle, object, strike, target, thrust, thwack, victim **8** blunt end **13** laughingstock

buttercup 10 Ranunculus
    variety: **4** Tall **5** Early **6** Common **7** Bermuda, Bulbous, Persian **8** Colombia, Creeping **11** Yellow water

butterfingered 5 inept **6** clumsy **7** awkward **8** bungling **9** maladroit **10** ungraceful

butterfly
    pupa: **9** chrysalis **10** chrysalids **11** chrysalides
    variety: **4** blue **5** giant, nymph, satyr, snout, tiger, zebra **6** alpine, apollo, arctic, kalima **7** alfalfa, budwing, dogface, monarch, peacock, viceroy **9** Baltimore, bathwhite, brimstone, christmas, metalmark, orange tip, wood nymph **10** Parnassian **11** painted lady, spring azure **12** blue mountain, cabbage white, clouded white, silver stripe, white admiral **13** chalkhill blue, mourning cloak, pearl crescent **14** American copper, gulf fritillary, tailed birdwing **15** longtail skipper, regal fritillary **16** black swallowtail, black veined white, camberwell beauty, green veined white, Leonardus skipper, red-spotted purple **18** orchard swallowtail **19** European swallowtail **20** spicebush swallowtail, variegated fritillary **21** great purple hairstreak, questionmark anglewing, white admiral wood nymph

butter up 4 coax **6** cajole **7** flatter, wheedle **8** soft-soap

buttocks 4 buns, butt, rear, rump, seat **5** fanny, nates **6** behind, bottom **7** keister, rear end **8** backside, derriere, haunches **9** fundament, posterior **12** hindquarters

buttonhole 4 halt, slit, stop **6** accost, waylay **7** solicit **8** approach, confront

button one's lip 7 keep mum **10** keep silent **16** keep one's trap shut **18** keep one's lips sealed

Buttons, Red
    real name: **11** Aaron Chwatt
    born: **9** New York NY
    roles: **8** Sayonara **13** The Longest Day **20** The Poseidon Adventure **23** They Shoot Horses Don't They

buttress 4 arch, prop, stay **5** boost, brace, shore, steel **6** prop up **7** bolster, shore up, support **8** abutment, shoulder **9** reinforce, stanchion **10** strengthen

buxom 5 plump **6** bosomy, chesty, robust, zaftig **9** strapping **10** voluptuous **13** large-breasted, well-developed

buy 3 get **4** deal, gain **5** bribe **6** buy off, obtain, pay for, suborn **7** acquire, bargain, corrupt, procure **8** invest in, purchase **9** influence

buy and sell 4 deal **5** trade **6** market

buy off 5 bribe **6** pay off **13** grease the palm

Buzi
    son: **7** Ezekiel

Buz Sawyer
    creator: **8** Roy Crane
    sidekick: **7** Sweeney

Buzuhov, Pierre
    character in: **11** War and Peace
    author: **7** Tolstoy

buzz 3 hum **4** whir **5** drone **6** murmur **7** whisper

by 4 near, over, past **5** along **6** beside, beyond, during, toward **7** through **9** alongside **10** concerning, on or before **11** according to, no later than

by air
    French: **8** par avion

Byam, Roger
    character in: **17** Mutiny on the Bounty
    authors: **4** Hall **8** Nordhoff

Byblis
    father: **7** Miletus
    mother: **6** Cyanea
    twin brother: **6** Caunus
    loved: **6** Caunus
    changed into: **8** fountain

by few words
    Latin: **12** paucis verbis

bygone 4 past **5** olden **6** former, gone by, of yore **7** ancient, earlier **8** departed, obsolete, previous **10** antiquated

by horse
    French: **7** a cheval

Byington, Spring
    born: **17** Colorado Springs CO
    roles: **7** Jezebel **11** Little Women **13** December Bride, Heaven Can Wait **17** Mutiny on the Bounty **20** The Devil and Miss Jones, You Can't

Take It with You **26** The Charge of the Light Brigade

by itself 4 solo **5** alone, aloof, apart **8** isolated **13** unaccompanied

Byng, Admiral
character in: 7 Candide
author: 8 Voltaire

by oneself 4 solo **5** alone, aloof **8** isolated **10** solitarily **13** unaccompanied
Latin: 4 sola **5** solus

by operation of law
Latin: 8 ipso jure

bypass 4 go by **5** avert, avoid, dodge **8** go around **10** circumvent **12** detour around

bypath 3 way **4** lane **5** alley, byway, track, trail **6** bypass **7** footway, pathway, towpath, walkway **8** back road, dirt road, footpath, shortcut, side road **10** beaten path, bridle path, garden path

by-product 8 offshoot **9** aftermath **16** incidental result

by right
Latin: 6 de jure

Byron, Lord (George Gordon)
author of: 7 Don Juan, Manfred **10** The Corsair **19** The Vision of Judgment **20** The Prisoner of Chillon **23** Childe Harold's Pilgrimage

byrrh
type: 8 aperitif
origin: 6 France
flavor: 6 orange **7** quinine

bystander 6 viewer **7** watcher, witness **8** attender, beholder, looker-on, observer, onlooker, passerby **9** spectator

by the book 9 by the rule **13** authoritarian **16** according to Hoyle

by the fact itself
Latin: 9 ipso facto

by the grace of God
Latin: 9 Dei gratia

by the law itself
Latin: 8 ipso jure

by the month
Latin: 9 per mensem

by the rule 9 by the book **11** as specified **13** authoritarian

by the skin of one's teeth 6 barely, hardly **8** only just, scarcely **11** by an eyelash

by the very nature of the deed
Latin: 9 ipso facto

by the way
French: 9 en passant

by virtue and arms
Latin: 13 virtute et armis
motto of: 11 Mississippi

byway 4 lane **5** alley **6** detour, street **8** shunpike

by what right?
Latin: 7 quo jure

byword 3 law, saw **4** rule **5** adage, axiom, maxim, motto, truth **6** dictum, saying, slogan **7** precept, proverb **8** aphorism, apothegm **9** catchword, pet phrase, principle, watchword **10** shibboleth

Byzantine 6 complex **8** scheming **9** expedient, intricate **13** Machiavellian

Byzas
founder of: 9 Byzantium
father: 8 Poseidon

Caan, James
born: **9** New York NY
roles: **6** Misery **9** Dick Tracy, Funny Lady **10** Brian's Song, For the Boys, Rollerball **11** Bulletproof, The Gamblers **12** Brian Piccolo, The Godfather **13** Sonny Corleone **17** Cinderella Liberty

cab 4 hack, taxi **7** taxi cab

Cab 15 Biblical measure

cabal 4 band, plan, plot, ring **5** junta **6** design, league, scheme **7** faction **8** intrigue **10** connivance, conspiracy **11** combination, machination

cabalistic 6 arcane, mystic, occult, secret **7** cryptic, obscure, strange **8** abstruse, esoteric, mystical **10** mysterious, unknowable **11** inscrutable **12** impenetrable, supernatural, unfathomable **16** incomprehensible

cabaret 4 cafe, club **6** bistro **9** nightclub **10** supper club
French: **5** boite **11** boite de nuit

Cabaret
director: **8** Bob Fosse
based on stories by: **20** Christopher Isherwood
cast: **8** Joel Grey **11** Fritz Wepper, Helmut Griem, Michael York **12** Liza Minnelli (Sally Bowles) **14** Marisa Berenson
Oscar for: **7** actress (Minnelli) **8** director **15** supporting actor (Grey)
song: **12** The Money Song

cabbage 16 Brassica oleracea (Capitata Group)
varieties: **3** Cow **4** Deer, Head, Wild **5** John's, Savoy, Skunk **6** Celery **7** Chinese **9** Flowering, Tronchuda **10** Portuguese **11** Yellow skunk **12** Western skunk

Cabecar
language family: **10** Talamancan
location: **9** Costa Rica **12** Sixaola River **14** Central America, Talamanca Plain
intermixed with: **6** Bribri

Cabell, James Branch
author of: **6** Jurgen **12** The High Place **14** Figures of Earth **17** The Cream of the Jest

cabin 3 hut **4** room **5** hutch, lodge, shack **6** shanty **7** cottage **8** bungalow, log cabin, quarters **9** stateroom **11** compartment

cabinet 3 box **4** case, file **5** chest **6** bureau **7** council **8** advisors, cupboard, ministry **10** breakfront, counselors, receptacle **11** china closet **13** advisory board **14** chest of drawers

cable 4 cord, line, rope, wire **5** chain, wires **6** hawser **7** mooring **8** wire line, wire rope **12** electric wire **16** overseas telegram

Cable, George W
author of: **8** Dr Sevier **13** Old Creole Days **15** The Grandissimes

cablegram 4 wire **5** cable **7** message **8** wireless **16** overseas telegram

Cabot, Ephraim
character in: **18** Desire Under the Elms
author: **6** O'Neill

Caca
origin: **5** Roman
goddess of: **6** hearth
corresponds to: **5** Vesta

Cacambo
character in: **7** Candide
author: **8** Voltaire

cache 4 heap **5** hoard, stock, store **8** hideaway **9** stockpile **11** hiding place, secret place

cachet 4 mark, seal **5** stamp, wafer **6** design, slogan **7** capsule

cackle 7 chatter **10** harsh laugh **11** shrill laugh
sound made by: **3** hen **4** chicken

cacophonous 5 harsh **6** off-key **7** grating, jarring, raucous **8** off-pitch, screechy, strident **9** dissonant, out of tune, unmusical **10** discordant **11** unmelodious **12** inharmonious, nonmelodious **13** disharmonious

cacophony 3 din **5** noise **7** discord **9** harshness **10** disharmony, dissonance

cactus
varieties: **3** Cob, Sun **4** Ball, Cane, Chin, Claw, Club, Comb, Crab, Hook, Lace, Leaf, Moon, Rose, Star, Toad, Vine, Yoke **5** Agave, Apple, Brain, Chain, Coral, Crown, Devil, False, Giant, Leafy, Melon, Paper, Plain, Prism, Snake, Spice, Torch **6** Barrel, Button, Cholla, Dagger, Dollar, Easter, Hatpin, Hot-dog, Myrtle, Nipple, Old-man, Orchid, Peanut, Pencil, Ribbon, Spider **7** Cushion, Eve's pin, Feather, Hatchet, Hat-rack, Jumping, Old-lady, Popcorn, Rainbow, Rattail, Redbird, Serpent, Thimble, Whisker **8** Cinnamon, Dumpling, Fishbone, Fishhook, Flapjack, Gold lace, Golf-ball, Hedgehog, Old-woman, Polka-dot, Pond-lily, Snowball, Snowdrop, Starfish, Tortoise, Turk's-cap **9** Bird's nest, Chain-link, Christmas, Cow-tongue, Electrode, Fire-crown, Hairbrush, Lamb's-tail, Mistletoe, New old-man, Organ-pipe, Porcupine, Red orchid, Sea-urchin, Spineless, Teddy-bear, Toothpick, Totem-pole, Turk's-head, White chin **10** Bluebarrel, Candelabra, Cottonpole, Easter-lily, Golden ball, Golden-star, Living-rock, Powder-puff, Silver ball, Strawberry, Unguentine, White torch, Wickerware **11** Frilled lace, Grizzlybear, Joseph's coat, Large barrel, Scarlet ball, Woolly torch **12** Dancing-bones, Golden barrel, Mulecrippler, Scarlet crown, Thanksgiving **13** Colombian ball, Creeping-devil, Dutchman's pipe, Peruvian apple, Peruvian torch, Silver cluster **15** Golden bird's nest **16** Mexican dwarf tree **17** Burbank's spineless **18** Fishhook pincushion

Cacus
form: **5** giant
father: **6** Vulcan
eats: **3** men
killed by: **8** Hercules

cad 3 cur, rat **4** heel, lout **5** churl, knave, louse, rogue **6** rascal, rotter **7** bounder, caitiff, dastard, villain **9** scoundrel

cadaver 4 body **5** stiff **6** corpse **7** remains **8** dead body, deceased

cadaverous 4 pale **5** ashen, gaunt **6** chalky, pallid **7** deathly, ghastly **8** blanched **9** bloodless, deathlike **10** corpselike

caddisfly
variety: **5** micro **8** northern **9** fingernet, primitive, snailcase **10** longhorned, trumpetnet, tubemaking **11** netspinning

Caddoan
tribe: **6** Pawnee **14** Chahiksichhiks

caddy 3 box, can, tin **5** chest **6** coffer

cadence 4 beat, lilt **5** meter, pulse, swing, tempo, throb **6** accent, rhythm **7** measure

Caderousse
character in: **21** The Count of Monte

Cristo
author: 5 Dumas (pere)
cadet 5 plebe **7** recruit, student **11** youngest son **14** military student
cadge 3 beg, bum **5** mooch **6** hustle, peddle, sponge **7** solicit, scrounge **9** panhandle
cadmium
   chemical symbol: 2 Cd
Cadmus
   form: 6 prince
   realm: 9 Phoenicia
   father: 6 Agenor
   mother: 10 Telephassa
   brother: 5 Cilix **7** Phoenix
   sister: 6 Europa
   wife: 8 Harmonia
   son: 8 Illyrius **9** Polydorus
   daughter: 3 Ino **5** Agave **6** Semele **7** Autonoe
   introduced to the Greeks: 7 writing
   founded: 6 Thebes
   planted: 12 dragons teeth
Caduceus
   staff of: 7 Mercury
Caeneus
   also: 6 Caenis
   member of: 9 Argonauts
   gift: 15 invulnerability
   former identity: 6 Caenis
Caenis
   also: 7 Caeneus
   father: 6 Elatus
   violated by: 8 Poseidon
   changed into: 3 man
   subsequent identity: 7 Caeneus
caesar, Caesar 5 ruler **6** despot, kaiser, tyrant **7** emperor **8** autocrat, dictator
Caesar, Julius
   adopted son: 8 Octavian **14** Caesar Augustus
   author of: 13 On the Civil War **14** On the Gallic War
   battle: 4 Zela **5** Munda **7** Durazzo, Thapsus **8** Mytilene **9** Pharsalus **11** Dyrrhachium
   conquered: 4 Gaul
   crossed: 7 Rubicon (river)
   defeated: 6 Pompey
   lover: 9 Cleopatra
   member of: 16 First Triumvirate
   murdered by: 5 Casca **6** Brutus **7** Cassius
   murdered on: 11 Ides of March
   other triumvirs: 6 Pompey **7** Crassus
   saying: 9 Et tu Brute? (Even you Brutus?) **12** Veni vidi vici (I came I saw I conquered)
   wife: 7 Pompeia **8** Cornelia **9** Calpurnia
Caesar, Sid
   partner: 11 Imogene Coca
   born: 9 Yonkers NY
   roles: 15 Your Show of Shows
Caesar and Cleopatra
   author: 17 George Bernard Shaw

Caesar or Nothing
   author: 9 Pio Baroja
caesura 5 break, pause **6** hiatus **12** interruption
cafe 3 bar, inn **5** diner **6** bistro, eatery, nitery, tavern **7** automat, beanery, cabaret **9** cafeteria, chophouse, hash house, lunchroom, nightclub **10** restaurant, supper club **11** bar and grill, coffeehouse, discotheque **12** luncheonette
   French: 9 estaminet
cafe au lait 10 light brown **14** coffee with milk
cafe noir 11 black coffee
cage 3 pen **4** coop **5** pen in **6** coop up, encage, lock up, shut in **7** confine, impound **8** imprison, restrain, restrict **9** enclosure
cagey 3 sly **4** foxy, keen, wary, wily **5** alert, chary, leery, sharp **6** artful, crafty, shifty, shrewd **7** careful, cunning, heedful, prudent **8** cautious, discreet, watchful
Cagliari
   capital of: 8 Sardinia
Cagney, James
   nickname: 5 Jimmy
   born: 9 New York NY
   roles: 7 Ragtime **14** The Public Enemy **17** Yankee Doodle Dandy (Oscar) **19** Man of a Thousand Faces
Cagney and Lacey
   cast: 8 Tyne Daly **11** Sharon Gless
Cain
   father: 4 Adam
   mother: 3 Eve
   brother: 4 Abel, Seth
   home: 4 Eden
   son: 5 Enoch
   killed: 4 Abel
   traveled to: 3 Nod
Caine, Michael
   real name: 24 Maurice Joseph Micklewhite
   born: 6 London **7** England
   roles: 4 Zulu **5** Alfie **6** Sleuth **9** Deathtrap **13** Educating Rita, Jekyll and Hyde **14** The Ipcress File **17** A Shock to the System **19** Hannah and Her Sisters **20** The Man who would be King **21** Dirty Rotten Scoundrels
Caine Mutiny, The
   author: 10 Herman Wouk
   director: 13 Edward Dmytryk
   cast: 7 May Wynn **9** Lee Marvin **10** E G Marshall, Jose Ferrer, Van Johnson **13** Fred MacMurray, Robert Francis **14** Humphrey Bogart (Captain Queeg)
Caingua *see* **7** Guarani
Cairo
   Arab camp: 8 al-Fustat
   Arabic: 9 al-Qahirah
   capital of: 5 Egypt
   island: 5 Rodah **7** Zamalik
   landmark:

   mosque: 7 al-Azhar **11** Muhammed Ali
   statue: 8 Ramses II
   museum: 8 Egyptian
   river: 4 Nile
   Roman fortress: 7 Babylon
   rulers: 5 Turks **7** British, Saladin **8** Fatimids **9** Mamelukes **11** Ismail Pasha, Muhammed Ali **12** Ottoman Turks
   university: 7 Al-Azhar **8** Ain Shams, American
Cairo, Joel
   character in: 16 The Maltese Falcon
   author: 7 Hammett
   played by: 10 Peter Lorre
caitiff 3 cad, cur, rat **4** heel **5** churl, knave, louse, rogue **6** rascal, rotter **7** bounder, dastard, villain **9** scoundrel **10** blackguard
cajole 4 coax **7** beguile, deceive, flatter, wheedle **8** blandish, inveigle, persuade
cajolery 7 blarney, coaxing, fawning **8** flattery, promises, soft soap **9** adulation, sweet talk, wheedling **10** enticement, inveigling, persuasion **11** beguilement **12** blandishment
cake 3 bar, bun, dry **4** lump, mass **5** block, crust, tort **6** cookie, eclair, gateau, harden, pastry, **7** congeal, cupcake, thicken **8** compress, solidify **9** coagulate, sweet roll **11** consolidate
Cakes and Ale
   author: 16 W Somerset Maugham
cakewalk 5 cinch, dance **9** promenade **12** dance contest
calaboose 3 pen **4** jail, stir **6** prison **7** slammer **8** hoosegow
Calah
   founder: 6 Nimrod
Calais
   origin: 5 Greek
   member of: 9 Argonauts
   father: 6 Boreas
   mother: 8 Orithyia
   twin brother: 5 Zetes
calamitous 5 fatal **6** tragic, woeful **7** adverse, baleful, harmful, ruinous, unlucky **8** dreadful **9** blighting **10** disastrous, pernicious **11** cataclysmic, deleterious, destructive, detrimental, distressful, unfortunate **12** catastrophic
calamity 3 ill, woe **4** blow, ruin **5** trial **6** misery, mishap **7** bad luck, failure, ill wind, reverse, scourge, tragedy, trouble, undoing **8** disaster, distress, downfall, hardship **9** adversity, cataclysm, mischance **10** affliction, ill fortune, misfortune **11** catastrophe, tribulation **13** sea of troubles **15** stroke of ill luck
calando
   music: 22 getting weaker and slower
calcium
   chemical symbol: 2 Ca

calculate 4 mean, plan 5 add up, aim at, count, judge, sum up 6 design, devise, figure, intend, reckon 7 compute, measure, predict, project, surmise, work out 8 estimate 9 ascertain, determine 10 conjecture

calculated 7 planned 10 deliberate, purposeful, thought out 11 intentional, prearranged 12 premeditated

calculating 3 sly 4 foxy, wily 6 artful, crafty, shrewd, tricky 7 cunning, devious 8 plotting, scheming 9 designing 10 contriving, intriguing 12 manipulative 13 Machiavellian

calculating machine
invented by: 7 Babbage

calculation 6 answer, result 8 figuring, judgment 9 reckoning 10 estimation 11 computation

calculator 6 abacus 7 counter, thinker 8 computer, reckoner

Calcutta
captured by: 5 Clive
founded by: 23 British East India Company
landmark: 10 Jain Temple 12 Howrah Bridge, Indian Museum 16 Botanical Gardens, Victoria Memorial 17 Zoological Gardens 18 Dakshineswar Temple
opposite city: 6 Howrah
river: 7 Hooghly
state: 10 West Bengal

Calder, Alexander
born: 14 Philadelphia PA
sculptures also called: 7 mobiles 8 stabiles
artwork: 3 Man 5 Whale 6 Spiral 10 Teodelapio 12 Ticket Window 13 La Grande Voile 14 The Brass Family 23 Lobster Traps and Fish Tail

Calderon de la Barca, Pedro
author of: 12 Life Is a Dream

caldron, cauldron 3 pot 6 boiler, kettle

Caldwell, Erskine
author of: 10 Georgia Boy 11 Tobacco Road 14 God's Little Acre

Caldwell, Taylor
author of: 12 Answer as a Man 13 A Pillar of Iron 14 Great Lion of God 17 Testimony of Two Men, The Devil's Advocate 19 Bright Flows the River 20 Glory and the Lightning 22 The Captains and the Kings 24 Dear and Glorious Physician

Caleb Williams
author: 13 William Godwin

Caledonia see 8 Scotland

calendar 4 list 5 chart, diary, table 6 agenda, docket 7 day book, program 8 register, schedule

calf 4 veal 5 dogie 6 weaner 7 leg part
young of: 3 cow 4 bull, seal 5 whale 8 elephant

Calgary
hockey team: 6 Flames

Calhern, Louis
real name: 13 Carl Henry Vogt
born: 10 Brooklyn NY
roles: 8 King Lear 12 Julius Caesar 15 Annie Get Your Gun 16 The Asphalt Jungle 20 The Magnificent Yankee

Calhoun, Rory
real name: 20 Francis Timothy Durgin
born: 12 Los Angeles CA
roles: 8 The Texan 21 Treasure of Pancho Villa 22 How to Marry a Millionaire, Requiem for a Heavyweight

Caliban
character in: 10 The Tempest
author: 11 Shakespeare

caliber 4 bore, rank 5 gifts, merit, place, power, scope, skill, worth 6 repute, talent 7 ability, quality, stature 8 capacity, diameter, eminence, position, prestige 10 capability, competence, estimation, excellence, importance, prominence, reputation 11 achievement, distinction

California
abbreviation: 2 CA 3 Cal 5 Calif
nickname: 6 Golden 8 Eldorado 12 Promised Land
capital: 10 Sacramento
largest city: 10 Los Angeles
others: 4 Lodi 5 Azusa, Chico, Chino, Indio 6 Blythe, Carmel, Covina, Eureka, Fresno, Lompoc, Merced, Oxnard, Pomona, Sonoma, Tulare 7 Alameda, Anaheim, Burbank, Gardena, Needles, Oakland, Salinas, Vallejo, Visalia 8 Altadena, Berkeley, Palo Alto, Pasadena, Redlands, San Diego, Stockton 9 Cucamonga, Long Beach 11 Palm Springs, Santa Monica 12 Beverly Hills, San Francisco, Santa Barbara
college: 3 USC 4 UCLA 5 Mills 6 Pitzer, Pomona 7 Caltech, Chapman, Scripps 8 Stanford, Whittier 10 Occidental, Pepperdine
explorer: 6 Cortez
feature:
  amusement park: 10 Disneyland 15 Knotts Berry Farm
  area: 9 Hollywood 15 Fishermans Wharf
  dam: 6 Hoover, Shasta 7 Boulder
  island prison: 8 Alcatraz
  mill: 7 Sutters
  national park: 7 Redwood, Sequoia 8 Yosemite 11 Kings Canyon 14 Channel Islands, Lassen Volcanic
  parade: 4 Rose
  prison: 6 Folsom 10 San Quentin
tribe: 4 Hupa, Pomo, Yana, Yuki 5 Karok, Maidu, Miwok, Wappo, Wiyot, Yurok 6 Patwin, Shasta, Tolowa, Yokuts 7 Chumash, Luiseno, Salinan, Serrano 8 Diegueno

people: 6 Sutter 10 Earl Warren 11 Robert Frost 13 George S Patton, John Steinbeck 14 William Saroyan
island: 4 Goat, Mare 7 Anacapo, Channel 8 Alcatraz, Catalina, Coronado 9 Farallone
lake: 4 Mono, Soda 5 Clear, Eagle, Owens, Tahoe 6 Salton, Tulare 7 Almanor 8 Elsinore 9 Berryessa
land rank: 5 third
mountain: 4 Muir 5 Coast 6 Lassen, Shasta, Wilson 7 Cascade, Klamath, Palomar, Whitney 10 Peninsular, Transverse 12 Sierra Nevada
  highest point: 7 Whitney
physical feature:
  bay: 8 Monterey, San Diego 12 San Francisco
  cape: 9 Mendocino
  desert: 6 Mohave, Mojave 8 Colorado
  fault: 10 San Andreas
  glacier: 8 Palisade
  sea: 6 Cortez 7 Pacific
  tree: 7 redwood
  valley: 5 Death
  volcano: 6 Lassen
  wind: 7 Collada 8 Santa Ana
president: 13 Richard M Nixon, Ronald W Reagan
river: 3 Eel, Mad, Pit 4 Kern 5 Kings, Owens, Putah, Smith, Stony 6 Little, Merced, Salmon 7 Feather, Klamath, Rubicon, Russian, Salinas, Trinity, Truckee 10 Sacramento, San Jacinto, San Joaquin, Stanislaus
state admission: 11 thirty-first
state bird: 21 California Valley quail
state fish: 21 California golden trout
state flower: 11 golden poppy
state motto: 6 Eureka (I have found it)
state song: 18 I Love You California
state symbol: 11 grizzly bear
state tree: 17 California redwood
baseball team: 6 Angels, Giants, Padres 7 Dodgers 9 Athletics
basketball team: 6 Lakers 8 Clippers 19 Golden State Warriors
football team: 7 Raiders 8 Chargers 11 Forty-Niners

Calinieff, Martin
real name of: 13 Michael Callan

Calinky State
nickname of: 13 South Carolina

calisay
type: 7 liqueur
origin: 5 Spain 9 Catalonia
flavor: 5 herbs 7 quinine

Calkins, Richard
creator/artist of: 10 Buck Rogers

call 3 ask, bid, cry, dub, tag 4 bawl, buzz, hail, name, need, plea, ring, roar, stop, term, yell 5 cause, claim, label, order, phone, rally, right, shout, style, title, visit 6 appeal, ask for, bellow, charge, clamor, cry out, decree, demand, direct, drop in, excuse, gather, halloo, holler, invite, invoke, know as, muster, notice, outcry, pray to, reason, scream, stop by, summon **7** collect, command, contact, convene, convoke, declare, entitle, entreat, grounds, refer to, request, require, specify, stop off, summons, warrant **8** announce, appeal to, assemble, christen, entreaty, identify, instruct, look in on, occasion, petition, proclaim **9** crying out, designate, direction, pay a visit, telephone **10** describe as, invitation, supplicate **11** declaration, instruction **12** announcement, call together, characterize, proclamation, supplication **13** justification

Callan, Michael
  real name: 15 Martin Calinieff
  born: 14 Philadelphia PA
  roles: 9 Cat Ballou **10** The Interns **18** Gidget Goes Hawaiian, The Flying Fontaines **23** The Magnificent Seven Ride

call for 4 need **6** demand, pick up **7** request, require

call forth 4 spur **5** evoke, raise **6** arouse, awaken, excite, incite, invoke, kindle, stir up **7** command, conjure, provoke **8** summon up **9** make aware, stimulate **10** make appear

calling 3 job **4** line, work **5** craft, field, forte, trade **6** career, crying, living, metier, outcry **7** hailing, mission, passion, yelling **8** activity, business, devotion, function, province, shouting, vocation **9** bellowing, crying out, first love, hallooing, life's work, screaming, specialty **10** assignment, attachment, dedication, employment, enthusiasm, livelihood, occupation, profession, walk of life **14** bread and butter, means of support, specialization

calling off 6 ending **7** halting **8** giving up **11** termination **12** backing out of, cancellation

calling oneself thus
  French: 9 soi-disant

Calliope
  member of: 5 Muses
  presided over: 10 epic poetry
  father: 4 Zeus
  mother: 9 Mnemosyne
  son: 7 Orpheus

Callisto
  form: 5 nymph
  attended: 7 Artemis
  loved: 4 Zeus
  changed into: 4 bear
  killed by: 7 Artemis

call off 3 end **4** halt **5** abort **6** cancel, give up **8** postpone **9** back out of, terminate **10** summon away **12** dispense with

Call of the Wild, The
  author: 10 Jack London
  dog: 4 Buck
  master: 12 John Thornton

callous 4 cold, hard **5** cruel, horny, tough **6** inured **8** hardened, uncaring **9** apathetic, heartless, unfeeling **11** hard-hearted, indifferent, insensitive **12** thick-skinned, unresponsive **13** dispassionate, unsympathetic **14** pachydermatous

call out 3 cry **4** bawl, hail, yell **5** shout **6** bellow, cry out, holler, summon **9** challenge

callow 3 raw **5** crude, green, naive **7** artless, awkward, puerile, shallow, untried **8** childish, ignorant, immature, juvenile **9** infantile **10** sophomoric, uninformed, unschooled, unseasoned **11** uninitiated **13** inexperienced **15** unsophisticated

call to 4 hail **5** greet **6** accost, salute **7** address, shout at

call to account 5 chide, scold **6** accuse, charge, rebuke **7** arraign, bawl out, censure, chasten, reprove, upbraid **8** admonish, denounce, reproach **9** criticize, dress down, reprimand **10** take to task **11** remonstrate

call to arms 6 war cry **9** battle cry **11** rallying cry

call to order 4 open **6** muster **7** convene, convoke

call upon 3 ask, bid **4** urge **5** visit **6** charge, enjoin, exhort, invite, invoke **7** beseech, entreat, request, require **8** appeal to, petition, summon up **9** encourage **11** acknowledge

callused 4 hard **5** horny, tough **8** hardened **12** thick- skinned **14** pachydermatous

calm 4 cool, ease, mild **5** allay, balmy, bland, quell, quiet, still **6** becalm, gentle, lessen, pacify, placid, reduce, repose, sedate, serene, smooth, soothe, subdue **7** assuage, collect, compose, cool off, halcyon, mollify, pacific, placate, relaxed, relieve **8** composed, coolness, diminish, mitigate, moderate, peaceful, serenity, tranquil, unshaken **9** alleviate, collected, composure, impassive, placidity, quietness, stillness, unexcited, unruffled **10** cool-headed, motionless, simmer down, smoothness, unagitated, untroubled **11** impassivity, passionless, restfulness, self-control, tranquility, tranquilize, undisturbed, unflappable, unperturbed **12** peacefulness, tranquillity, windlessness **13** imperturbable, self-possessed, stormlessness **14** self- possession **16** imperturbability

calmness 5 poise **6** aplomb **8** coolness, serenity **9** composure, placidity, sangfroid, stillness **10** equanimity, steadiness **11** self-control, tranquility **12** peacefulness, tranquillity **14** presence of mind, self-possession **16** imperturbability

Calpurnia

character in: 12 Julius Caesar
  author: 11 Shakespeare

calumnious 8 libelous **9** maligning, vilifying **10** defamatory, derogatory, slanderous **11** disparaging

calumny 4 barb, slur **5** libel, smear **6** malice **7** slander **8** innuendo **9** aspersion **10** backbiting, defamation, derogation, revilement **11** denigration, deprecation, insinuation **12** backstabbing, calumniation, depreciation, vilification **13** animadversion, disparagement, malicious lies

calvados
  type: 6 brandy
  origin: 6 France **8** Normandy
  flavor: 5 apple
  aged in: 3 oak

Calvary 8 Golgotha
  means: 10 skull place

Calydonian boar
  sent by: 5 Diana
  killed by: 8 Meleager

Calydonian hunt
  pursuit of: 4 boar

Calypso
  form: 5 nymph
  home: 6 Ogygia
  father: 10 Titan Atlas
  detained: 8 Odysseus
    for: 10 seven years

calyx 4 husk **5** sepal

cam 3 cog **4** disk **8** cylinder **10** projection
  located on: 5 shaft, wheel
  motion: 7 rocking **8** circular **12** back and forth

camaraderie 7 jollity **8** bonhomie, good will **10** affability, clubbiness, fellowship, friendship **11** brotherhood, comradeship, sociability **12** congeniality, conviviality, friendliness **13** companionship, esprit de corps **14** good-fellowship

Camarasaurus
  type: 8 dinosaur, sauropod
  location: 12 United States
  period: 8 Jurassic

Cambodia
  other name: 7 Camboja **8** Cambodge **9** Kampuchea
  capital/largest city: 8 Pnom-Penh
  others: 3 Som **4** Ream **5** Takeo **6** Kampot, Kratie, Pursat **7** Kohnieh, Kompong, Kracheh, Rovieng, Samrong **8** Siem Reap, Sisophon **10** Battambang, Stung Treng **11** Kompong Cham **12** Krungkoh Kong **13** Sihanoukville
  head of state: 4 King
  monetary unit: 3 sen **4** quan, riel **6** puttan **7** piaster
  weight: 4 mace, tael
  island: 4 Kong, Rong
  lake: 8 Tonle Sap
  mountain: 3 Pan **7** Dangrek, Dong Rek **8** Cardamom, Elephant

highest point: 10 Phnom Aoral, Phnom Aural
river: 3 San, Sen **5** Sreng **6** Bassac, Chinit, Mekong, Porong, Pursat, Srepok **7** Kamlong, Sekhong **8** Tonle Sap
physical feature:
　bay: 10 Kompongsom
　cape: 5 Samit
　gulf: 4 Siam **8** Thailand
people: 4 Cham, Thai **5** Khmer **7** Chinese **10** Vietnamese
　leader: 6 Pol Pot **8** Sihanouk
language: 5 Khmer **6** French **9** Cambodian **10** Vietnamese
religion: 7 animism **8** Buddhism **12** Christianity
places:
　ruins/temple: 6 Angkor **9** Angkor Wat
feature:
　Communist group: 10 Khmer Rouge
Cambria *see* **5** Wales
cambric 5 cloth, linen **6** cotton, fabric **8** material
camel
　called: 13 beast of burden **15** ship of the desert
　chews: 3 cud
　group: 4 herd
　habitat: 4 Asia **6** Africa, desert
　kind: 7 Arabian **8** Bactrian **9** dromedary
　number of humps: 3 one, two
　species: 6 mammal
　type of: 8 ruminant
　young: 4 calf
camellia
　varieties: 5 Silky **6** Common **8** Mountain, Sasanqua
Camenae
　means: 11 foretellers
　form: 6 nymphs **7** deities
　gift: 8 prophecy
　names: 6 Egeria **8** Carmenta **9** Antevorta, Postvorta
　habitat: 8 fountain
　correspond to: 5 Muses
camera 3 APS, SLR **4** 35mm, view **6** manuel **7** plastic **8** panorama, Polaroid, twin lens **9** automatic **11** large format, range finder **12** medium format **13** point-and-shoot
　brand: 4 Fuji **5** Canon, Kodak, Leica, Nikon, Ricoh **6** Konica, Pentax, Rollei **7** Bronica, Minolta, Olympus **8** Polaroid **10** Hasselblad
　invented by:
　　Kodak: 6 Walker **7** Eastman
　　Polaroid: 4 Land
　　photography: 6 Niepce, Talbot **8** Daguerre
　　film, celluloid: 6 Edison **11** Reichenbach
　　film, transparent: 7 Eastman, Goodwin
　　color photo: 4 Ives

Cameroon
　capital: 7 Yaounde
　largest city: 6 Douala
　others: 3 Wum **4** Bali, Buea, Edea, Tiko **5** Kumba, Lomie, Mamfe **6** Garona, Maroua **7** Batouri, Dschang, Ebolowa, Foumban **8** Victoria **10** N'Gaoundere, N'Kongsamba
　monetary unit: 5 franc **7** centime
　island: 5 Nanny **8** Fernando
　lake: 4 Chad
　mountain: 5 Mbabo **7** Bambuto, Kapsiki, Mandara **8** Batandji **9** Atlantika
　highest point: 8 Cameroon
　river: 3 Dja, Lom **4** Faro, Mbam, Vina **5** Benue, Campo, Cross, Kadei, Mbere, Nyong, N'Goko, Sanga, Shari **6** Djerem, Ivindo, Logone, Sanaga
　sea: 8 Atlantic
　physical feature:
　　cape: 10 Debundscha
　　gulf: 6 Guinea
　　plateau: 7 Adamawa **8** Mambilla
　people: 3 Abo, Edo, Ibo **4** Beti, Bulu, Ekoi, Ijaw, Sara **5** Bantu, Bassa, Kirdi, Pygmy, Tikar **6** Bamoun, Donala, Ewondo, Fulani, Ibibio **7** Bakweri **8** Bamileke
　　Fulani chief: 7 Lamidos
　language: 4 Bulu **5** Bantu, Bassa, Hausa **6** Douala, Ewondo, French, Fulani **7** English **8** Bamileke, Fulfulde
　religion: 5 Islam **7** animism **12** Christianity
　places:
　　home of prime minister: 7 Schloss
Camille
　also: 17 La Dame aux camelias
　author: 14 Alexander Dumas (fils)
　character: 6 Nanine **11** Armand Duval **17** Marguerite Gautier (Camille)
　director: 11 George Cukor
　cast: 10 Greta Garbo (Camille) **12** Henry Daniell, Robert Taylor (Armand) **14** Elizabeth Allan, Laura Hope Crews **15** Lionel Barrymore
Camillo
　character in: 14 The Winter's Tale
　author: 11 Shakespeare
Camirus
　origin: 5 Greek
　grandfather: 6 Helios, Helius
camisole 3 top **4** slip **6** jacket **10** underwaist
camouflage 4 hide, mask, veil **5** blind, cloak, cover, front **6** screen, shroud **7** conceal, cover up **8** disguise **10** masquerade, subterfuge **11** concealment
camouflaged 6 hidden, masked **7** cloaked **8** shrouded **9** concealed, disguised
camp 4 tent **5** tents **7** bivouac, lodging, rough it **8** army base, barracks, quarters **10** pitch a tent
campaign 3 run **4** push **5** drive,

stump **6** action, effort **7** crusade **8** endeavor, movement **9** offensive, operation **11** electioneer, whistle-stop **12** battle series, beat the drums, solicit votes
campanile 6 belfry **9** bell tower
campari
　type: 7 bitters **8** aperitif
　origin: 5 Italy
campground 7 bivouac **8** tent city **16** temporary shelter
Campin, Robert
　born: 8 Flanders
　also known as/identified with: 14 Master of Merode **16** Master of Flemalle
　artwork: 10 St Veronica, The Trinity **13** The Entombment **16** Merode Altarpiece (Merode Triptych) **17** The Virgin and Child **18** The Thief on the Cross
Camptosaurus
　type: 8 dinosaur **10** ornithopod
　location: 12 North America
　period: 8 Jurassic
　characteristic: 10 duck-billed
Camus, Albert
　author of: 4 L'ete **6** Summer **7** The Fall **8** Caligula, The Rebel **9** The Plague **11** A Happy Death, The Stranger **12** Cross Purpose **17** The Myth of Sisyphus
can 3 tin **4** buns, fire, rump, seat **5** fanny, put up **6** bottom **8** backside, buttocks, preserve **9** container, fundament, give the ax
Canaan
　father: 3 Ham
　brother: 4 Cush
　grandfather: 4 Noah
　known as: 12 promised land
　see also **6** Israel
Canada
　capital: 6 Ottawa
　largest city: 8 Montreal
　others: 4 Hull **5** Banff, Laval **6** Dawson, Guelph, London, Oshawa, Quebec, Regina, Sarnia, Val d'or **7** Calgary, Halifax, Moncton, Nanaimo, Sudbury, Toronto, Welland, Windsor **8** Edmonton, Hamilton, Kingston, Moose Jaw, Victoria, Winnipeg **9** Saskatoon, Vancouver **10** Port Arthur, Sherbrooke **11** Fredericton **12** Niagara Falls, Peterborough, Prince Albert, Prince George **13** Charlottetown **21** St Catherines Stratford
　school: 3 UBC **5** Laval **6** McGill, Queens **7** Toronto **8** McMaster, Montreal **9** Concordia, Dalhousie **11** Simon Fraser
　division: 5 Yukon **6** Quebec **7** Alberta, Ontario **8** Manitoba **10** Nova Scotia **12** Newfoundland, New Brunswick, Saskatchewan **15** British Columbia **18** Prince Edward Island **20** Northwest Territories

New division: 7 Nunavut
head of state: 14 British monarch **15** governor general
measure: 3 ton **5** minot, perch, point **6** arpent **7** chainon
island: 4 Read **5** Banks, Bylot, Coats, Devon, Grand, Manan, Parry, Sable **6** Baffin, Breton, Mansel, Middle **7** Belcher **8** Bathurst, Magdalen, Victoria **9** Anticosti, Ellesmere, Vancouver **10** Campobello, Manitoulin **11** Southampton **14** Queen Charlotte
lake: 4 Cree, Erie, Gras, Seul **5** Garry, Huron, Rainy **6** Louise, St John **7** Abitibi, Dubawnt, Nipigon, Ontario, Testlin **8** Kootenay, Manitoba, Okanagan, Reindeer, Superior, Winnipeg **9** Athabaska, Great Bear, Nipissing **10** Great Slave, Mistassini **12** Winnipegosis
mountain: 5 Coast, Royal **6** Robson, Skeena **7** Cariboo, Cascade, Purcell, Rockies, Selkirk, St Elias **8** Columbia, Hazelton, Monashee **9** Mackenzie, Notre Dame, Tremblant **10** Laurentian, Richardson, Shickshock **14** Jacques Cartier
highest point: 5 Logan
river: 3 Hay, Red **4** Peel **5** Liard, Peace, Slave, Yukon **6** Albany, Fraser, Nelson, Nicola, Ottawa, Skeena, St John, Thames, Thelon **7** St Marys **8** Columbia, Gatineau, Kootenay, Petawawa, Saguenay **9** Athabasca, Athapaska, Churchill, Mackenzie, Richelieu **10** Coppermine, St Lawrence **11** Assiniboine, **12** Saskatchewan
sea: 6 Arctic **7** Pacific **8** Atlantic, Labrador
physical features:
　bay: 5 Basin, Fundy, Hecla, James, Minas **6** Baffin, Griper, Hudson, Ungava **8** Georgian
　canal: 3 Soo **7** Welland **10** Wellington
　cape: 5 Canso
　falls: 7 Niagara **9** Horseshoe
　gulf: 10 St Lawrence
　pass: 8 Chilkoot
　peninsula: 5 Gaspe **7** Boothia **8** Labrador, Melville
　plain: 11 Barren lands
　port: 6 Quebec **7** St Johns **8** Hamilton, Victoria **9** Churchill
　strait: 5 Cabot, Davis, Dease **6** Hecate, Hudson **7** Georgia **9** Belle Isle **10** Juan de Fuca
people: 5 Inuit **6** Canuck, Eskimo, French **7** English
　explorer: 5 Cabot **6** Fraser, Joliet **7** Cartier, LaSalle, Selkirk **8** Thompson **9** Champlain, MacKenzie, Marquette
　leader: 4 King, Riel **5** Clark **6** Borden **7** Laurier, Trudeau **8** Campbell, Chretien, Mulroney **9** Macdonald, St Laurent **11** Diefenbaker

language: 6 Eskimo, French **7** English
religion: 8 Anglican **13** Roman Catholic **20** United Church of Canada
places:
　battlefield: 15 Plains of Abraham
　national park: 4 Yoho **5** Banff **6** Jasper **7** Glacier **8** Kootenay **9** Elk Island **10** La Mauricie, Revelstoke **11** Wood Buffalo **12** Prince Albert **13** Waterton Lakes
　resort: 5 Banff **10** Lake Louise
feature:
　airport: 6 Gander
　emblem: 9 maple leaf
　fish: 5 charr, trout
　flower: 10 Juneflower
　police: 8 Mounties **12** Royal Mounted
food:
　soup: 7 rubaboo
canaille 6 proles, rabble **8** riffraff **9** commoners, hoi polloi **11** proletariat **13** great unwashed
canal 4 duct, Erie, Kiel, Suez, tube **5** Grand **6** Panama **7** channel, conduit, passage **8** aqueduct
Canaletto
　real name: 20 Giovanni Antonio Canal
　born: 5 Italy **6** Venice
　artwork: 18 The Stonemason's Yard
canard 4 hoax **5** rumor **7** slander **9** falsehood **12** exaggeration
Canary Islands
　other name: 14 Fortunate Isles **15** Isles of the Blest
　named for: 3 dog **5** canis **6** canine
　capital: 9 Las Palmas **19** Santa Cruz de Tenerife
　largest city: 9 Las Palmas
　others: 4 Icod **6** Laguna **7** Orotava **8** Arrecife, Valverde **12** San Sebastian
　government: 16 overseas province
　of: 5 Spain
　measure: 8 fanegada
　monetary unit: 6 peseta
　island: 4 Roca **5** Clara, Ferro, Lobos, Rocca **6** Gomera, Hierro **7** Inferno, La Palma **8** Graciosa, Tenerife **9** Lanzarote **10** Lanzarotte **11** Gran Canaria **13** Fuerteventura
　mountain: 6 La Cruz **8** El Cumbre, Tenerife
　highest point: 5 Teide, Teyde
　sea: 8 Atlantic
　people: 7 Spanish
　language: 7 Spanish
　religion: 13 Roman Catholic
canasta
　number of players: 4 four
　cards/hand: 6 eleven
　meld: 12 three of a kind
　wild card: 5 deuce, joker
Canberra
　capital of: 9 Australia
　territory: 13 New South Wales **26**

Australian Capital Territory
　lake: 13 Burley Griffin
cancel 4 undo, void **5** abort, annul, erase, quash, scrub **6** delete, offset, recall, recant, repeal, revoke **7** abolish, call off, nullify, rescind, retract, vitiate **8** abrogate, call back, set aside **9** repudiate **10** balance out, bluepencil, do away with, invalidate, neutralize **11** countermand **12** dispense with **13** compensate for **14** counterbalance **18** declare null and void
cancellation 6 repeal **9** abolition **10** abrogation, effacement, rescinding, revocation **11** abolishment, eradication, repudiation, termination
cancer 3 rot **4** crab **6** plague **7** sarcoma, scourge **8** neoplasm, sickness **9** carcinoma **10** malignancy **14** malignant tumor **15** malignant growth
Cancer
　symbol: 4 crab
　planet: 4 Moon
　rules: 4 home **6** family
　born: 4 July, June
Cancer Ward, The
　author: 21 Aleksandr Solzhenitsyn
candelabrum 7 menorah **8** dikerion **9** girandole, trikerion **11** candlestick **12** candleholder
Candia see **5** Crete
candid 4 fair, free, just, open **5** blunt, frank, plain **6** direct, honest **7** genuine, natural, relaxed, sincere, unposed **8** informal, outright, truthful **9** downright, impromptu, outspoken **10** forthright **11** plain spoken, spontaneous, unvarnished **14** extemporaneous **15** straightforward
Candida
　author: 17 George Bernard Shaw
candidate 7 hopeful, nominee **8** aspirant, eligible **9** applicant, contender, job seeker **10** competitor, contestant **11** possibility **15** office seeker
Candid Camera
　host: 9 Allen Funt
　co-host: 11 Bess Myerson **12** Durward Kirby **13** Arthur Godfrey
　tag: 5 smile
Candide
　author: 8 Voltaire
　character: 6 Martin **7** Cacambo **8** Pangloss **9** Cunegonde **11** Admiral Byng **17** Thunder-ten-Tronckh
candidness 6 candor **7** honesty, openess **9** frankness, sincerity **10** directness **12** truthfulness **13** guilelessness
candle 3 dip, wax **5** light, taper **6** bougie, cierge, tallow **9** rush light
candleholder, candlestick 6 sconce **7** menorah **8** dikerion **9** girandole, trikerion **10** chandelier **11** candelabrum
candor 7 honesty **8** fairness, justness, openness **9** bluntness, frankness, sin-

cerity **10** directness **11** artlessness **12** impartiality, truthfulness **14** forthrightness **15** plainspokenness **19** straightforwardness

candy 3 bar **4** kiss **5** cream, fudge, jelly, sweet, taffy **6** bonbon, comfit, dainty, nougat, sweets, toffee **7** brittle, caramel, fondant, gumdrop, praline **8** lollipop **9** chocolate, jellybean, sweetmeat **10** confection **12** all-day sucker **13** confectionery, peanut brittle

cane 3 hit, rap, rod, tan **4** beat, drub, flog, lash, whip **5** baste, flail, smite, staff, stick, whack **6** strike, switch, thrash, wallop **7** trounce **12** walking stick

cane 11 Arundinaria
varieties: 4 Dumb, Wild **5** Arrow, Sugar **6** Rattan, Switch, Tobago, Tonkin **7** Tsingli **8** Southern **11** Spotted dumb **12** Chinese sweet **14** Yellow-leaf dumb

Canea
capital of: 5 Crete

Canetti, Elias
author of: 8 Auto da Fe **12** Tower of Babel **14** Crowds and Power **15** The Torch in My Ear **16** Kafka's Other Trial, The Tongue Set Free

Caniff, Milton
creator/artist of: 10 Dickie Dare **11** Steve Canyon **14** The Gay Thirties **18** Terry and the Pirates

canine 3 cur, dog, fox, pup **4** mutt, wolf **5** hound, hyena, puppy, tooth **6** coyote, cuspid, jackal **7** mongrel **8** eyetooth

canker 4 sore **5** ulcer **6** blight, cancer, lesion **9** mouth sore **12** inflammation

Cannibal Galaxy, The
author: 12 Cynthia Ozick

cannon 3 bit, gun **4** bone **5** carom **6** mortar **7** battery **8** field gun, howitzer, ordnance **9** artillery **10** field piece, mounted gun, pickpocket

Cannon
character: 11 Frank Cannon
cast: 13 William Conrad

Cannon, Dyan
real name: 19 Samille Diane Friesen
husband: 9 Cary Grant
born: 8 Tacoma WA
roles: 6 Shamus **9** Deathtrap **10** Ally McBeal **13** Heaven Can Wait **15** Such Good Friends **19** Bob & Carol & Ted & Alice **23** Revenge of the Pink Panther

cannonade 5 burst, salvo **6** volley **7** barrage, battery **8** shelling **9** fusillade **11** bombardment

canny 4 foxy, wary, wily, wise **5** cagey, sharp **6** artful, astute, clever, crafty, shrewd, subtle **7** careful, cunning, knowing **8** skillful **9** judicious, sagacious **10** convincing **11** circumspect, intelligent **13** perspicacious

Cano, Alonso
born: 5 Spain **7** Granada
artwork: 16 Granada Cathedral (facade) **18** Madonna of the Rosary **20** Immaculate Conception **23** The Seven Joys of the Virgin

canoe 4 boat **5** bungo, kayak **6** dugout **7** pirogue

canoeing
athlete: 11 Marcia Smoke

canon 3 law **4** code, rule **5** dogma, edict, model, order **6** decree **7** pattern, precept, statute **8** doctrine, standard **9** bench mark, criterion, ordinance, principle, yardstick **10** regulation, touchstone

canonical 6 proper **8** accepted, approved, official orthodox **9** authentic, customary **10** authorized, legitimate, recognized, sanctioned **12** conventional **13** authoritative

Canonization, The
author: 9 John Donne

canopy 4 hood **5** cover **6** awning, tester **8** covering

Canova, Antonio
born: 5 Italy **8** Possagno
artwork: 7 Perseus **12** Venus Victrix (Pauline Bonaparte Borghese) **14** Cupid and Psyche **16** Letizia Bonaparte **17** Daedalus and Icarus

Cansino, Margarita Carmen
real name of: 12 Rita Hayworth

cant 4 sham, talk **5** argot, lingo, slang **6** humbug, jargon **8** parlance, pretense **9** hypocrisy **10** lip service, vernacular **11** insincerity **15** pretentiousness **17** sanctimoniousness

cantabile
music: 7 flowing, singing **8** songlike

cantaloupe 5 fruit, melon **9** muskmelon

cantankerous 4 mean **5** cross, huffy, short, sulky, surly, testy **6** crabby, cranky, crusty, grumpy, morose, ornery, sullen, touchy **7** bearish, crabbed, fretful, grouchy, peevish, waspish **8** choleric, churlish, contrary, snappish **9** irascible, irritable, splenetic **10** ill-humored, ill-natured **11** contentious, ill-tempered, quarrelsome **12** disagreeable **13** argumentative

cantatrice 6 singer **9** chanteuse **10** songstress **18** professional singer

canteen 2 PX **4** club **5** flask **6** bottle **10** commissary **11** pocket flask **12** post exchange

canter 4 gait, lope, pace, trot **6** gallop, singer, whiner

Canterbury Tales, The
author: 15 Geoffrey Chaucer
starting point: 9 Southwark, Tabard Inn
goal:
tomb of: 6 Becket
character/tale: 3 Nun **4** Cook, Dyer,

Monk **5** Canon, Friar, Reeve, Webbe **6** Knight, Miller, Parson, Squire, Yeoman **7** Shipman, Tapicer **8** Franklin, Manciple, Merchant, Pardoner, Prioress, Summoner **9** Carpenter, Ploughman **10** Wife of Bath **11** Haberdasher **13** Clerk of Oxford, Sergeant of Law **14** Doctor of Physic

Cantor, Eddie
real name: 21 B Edward Israel Iskowitz
nickname: 9 Banjo Eyes
wife: 9 Ida Tobias
born: 9 New York NY
roles: 7 Whoopee **8** Kid Boots **9** Banjo Eyes

cantor of a synagogue
Hebrew: 5 hazan **6** chazan

Cantos
author: 9 Ezra Pound

can't stand 4 hate **5** abhor **6** detest, eschew, loathe **7** despise **8** execrate **9** abominate, can't abide **11** can't stomach **14** hate the sight of

canvas 4 duck **7** painting **8** painting **9** sailcloth, tarpaulin, tent cloth

canvass 4 poll, scan, sift **5** study, tally **6** survey **7** analyze, discuss, morose, explore, inquiry, inquire, inspect, solicit **8** analysis, campaign, scrutiny **10** evaluation, scrutinize **11** enumeration, exploration, inquire into, investigate, take stock of **13** give thought to, investigation

canyon 3 col, cut, gap **4** draw, pass, wadi, wash **5** break, chasm, cleft, crack, gorge, gulch, gully, notch **6** arroyo, coulee, defile, divide, ravine, valley **7** fissure, opening **8** corridor, crevasse, water gap

cap 3 fez, lid, tam, top **4** acme, seal **5** beret, cover, limit, outdo **6** better, exceed, top off **7** surpass **8** headgear, out-strip **9** headdress **10** visored hat

capability 3 art **4** gift **5** flair, knack, power, skill **6** talent **7** ability, faculty, know-how **8** capacity, efficacy, facility **9** potential **10** attainment, competence, competency **11** proficiency **12** potentiality **13** qualification

capable 3 apt **4** able, deft **5** adept **6** adroit, artful, clever, expert, gifted **7** skilled **8** masterly, skillful **9** competent, effective, ingenious **10** proficient **11** efficacious, intelligent **12** accomplished

capable of assuming legal responsibility
Latin: 8 sui juris

Capable of Honor
author: 10 Allan Drury

capable of managing one's own affairs
Latin: 8 sui juris

capacious 3 big **4** huge, vast, wide **5** ample, broad, large, roomy **7** mammoth, massive **8** gigantic, spacious **9**

expansive, extensive **10** commodious, expandable, tremendous, voluminous **13** amplitudinous

capaciousness 9 amplitude, roominess **12** spaciousness **14** commodiousness

capacitate 5 allow **6** enable, permit **7** empower, qualify **8** make able

capacity 4 mind, role, room, size **5** gifts, limit, might, power, range, scope, space **6** extent, talent, volume **7** ability, faculty **8** aptitude, facility, function, judgment, position, sagacity, strength **9** amplitude, endowment, intellect, potential **10** brain power, capability **11** discernment **12** intelligence, perspicacity **15** maximum contents

caparison 5 adorn, equip **6** bedeck **9** equipment, trappings

cape 4 spit **5** cloak, manta, point, shawl **6** mantle, poncho, serape, tabard, tongue **7** pelisse **8** headland **9** peninsula **10** promontory

Capek, Karel
  author of: 3 R U R **8** Hordubal, Krakatit **9** The Mother **13** Power and Glory **18** The War with the Newts

caper 3 hop **4** jape, jump, lark, leap, romp, skip **5** antic, bound, fling, frisk, prank, spree, stunt, trick **6** bounce, cavort, frolic, gambol, prance **7** caprice **8** escapade **9** adventure, high jinks **10** carrying on **11** shenanigans **14** monkey business

capital 4 cash, fine **5** great, money, super **6** center, riches, superb, wealth **7** supreme **9** excellent, financing, firstrate, majuscule, matchless, principal, resources **10** cash on hand, first-class **11** large letter, wherewithal **12** headquarters **13** working assets **14** available means **15** investment funds, upper-case letter

capital city (of countries)
  of Afghanistan: 5 Kabul
  of Albania: 6 Tirana, Tirane
  of Algeria: 7 Algiers
  of Andorra: 14 Andorra-la-Vella
  of Angola: 6 Luanda
  of Antigua and Barbuda: 7 St John's
  of Argentina: 11 Buenos Aires
  of Armenia: 6 Erivan **7** Yerevan
  of Australia: 8 Canberra
  of Austria: 6 Vienna
  of Azerbaijan: 4 Baku
  of the Bahamas: 6 Nassau
  of Bahrain: 6 Manama
  of Bangladesh: 5 Dacca
  of Barbados: 10 Bridgetown
  of Belarus: 5 Minsk
  of Belgium: 8 Brussels **9** Bruxelles
  of Belize: 8 Belmopan
  of Benin: 9 Porto-Novo
  of Bermuda: 8 Hamilton
  of Bhutan: 6 Thimbu **7** Thimphu
  of Bolivia: 5 La Paz, Sucre
  of Bosnia-Herzegovina: 8 Sarajevo

of Botswana: 8 Gaborone **9** Gaberones
of Brazil: 8 Brasilia
of Brunei: 17 Bandar Seri Begawan
of Bulgaria: 5 Sofia
of Burkina Faso: 11 Ouagadougou
of Burundi: 9 Bujumbura
of Cambodia: 8 Pnom-Penh
of Cameroon: 7 Yaounde
of Canada: 6 Ottawa
of the Canary Islands: 9 Las Palmas **19** Santa Cruz de Tenerife
of Cape Verde: 5 Praia
of the Central African Republic: 6 Bangui
of Chad: 8 Fort-Lamy, N'Djamena
of Chile: 8 Santiago
of China: 6 Peking
of Colombia: 6 Bogota
of Comoros: 6 Moroni
of the Congo: 11 Brazzaville
of Costa Rica: 7 San Jose
of Crete: 5 Canea **8** Iraklion
of Croatia: 6 Zagreb
of Cuba: 6 Havana **8** La Habana
of Cyprus: 7 Nicosia
of Czechoslovakia/ Czech Republic: 6 Prague
of Denmark: 10 Copenhagen
of Djibouti: 8 Djibouti
of the Dominican Republic: 12 Santo Domingo **14** Ciudad Trujillo
of Ecuador: 5 Quito
of Egypt: 5 Cairo
of El Salvador: 11 San Salvador
of England: 6 London
of Equatorial Guinea: 6 Malabo
of Eritrea: 6 Asmara
of Estonia: 7 Tallinn
of Ethiopia: 10 Addis Ababa
of Fiji: 4 Suva
of Finland: 8 Helsinki **11** Helsingfors
of France: 5 Paris
of the Gabon Republic: 10 Libreville
of The Gambia: 6 Banjul **8** Bathurst
of Georgia: 7 Tbilisi
of Germany (East): 10 East Berlin
of Germany (West): 4 Bonn
of Germany (reunited): 5 Berlin
of Ghana: 5 Accra, Akkra
of Greece: 6 Athens
of Greenland: 3 Nuk **8** Godthaab, The Point
of Grenada: 9 St Georges
of Guatemala: 13 Guatemala City
of Guinea: 7 Conakry
of Guinea-Bissau: 6 Bissau
of Guyana: 10 Georgetown
of Haiti: 12 Port-au-Prince
of Honduras: 11 Tegucigalpa
of Hong Kong: 8 Victoria
of Hungary: 8 Budapest
of Iceland: 9 Reykjavik
of India: 8 New Delhi
of Indonesia: 7 Jakarta **8** Djakarta
of Iran: 6 Tehran **7** Teheran
of Iraq: 7 Baghdad
of Ireland: 6 Dublin

of Israel: 9 Jerusalem
of Italy: 4 Roma, Rome
of the Ivory Coast: 7 Abidjan
of Jamaica: 8 Kingston
of Japan: 3 Edo **5** Tokyo
of Java: 7 Jakarta **8** Djakarta
of Jordan: 5 Amman
of Kazakhstan: 7 Alma-Ata
of Kenya: 7 Nairobi
of Kiribati: 6 Tarawa
of Korea (North): 9 Pyongyang
of Korea (South): 5 Seoul
of Kuwait: 10 Kuwait City
of Kyrgyzstan: 7 Bishkek (Frunze)
of Laos: 9 Viengchan, Vientiane
of Latvia: 4 Riga
of Lebanon: 6 Beirut **8** Beyrouth
of Lesotho: 6 Maseru
of Liberia: 8 Monrovia
of Libya: 7 Tripoli
of Liechtenstein: 5 Vaduz
of Lithuania: 5 Vilna **6** Kausas **7** Vilnius
of Luxembourg: 10 Luxembourg
of Macedonia: 6 Skopje
of Madagascar: 10 Tananarive **12** Antananarivo
of Malawi: 8 Lilongwe
of Malaysia: 11 Kuala Lumpur
of Maldives: 4 Male
of Mali: 6 Bamako
of Malta: 8 Valletta
of Mauritania: 10 Nouakchott
of Mauritius: 9 Port Louis
of Mexico: 10 Mexico City
of Moldova: 16 Chisinau, Kishinev
of Monaco: 11 Monaco-Ville
of Mongolia: 9 Ulan Bator
of Montenegro: 7 Cetinje **8** Titograd **9** Podgorica
of Morocco: 5 Rabat **6** Rabbat
of Mozambique: 6 Maputo **15** Lourenco Marques
of Myanmar: 6 Yangon **7** Rangoon
of Namibia: 8 Windhoek
of Nauru: 13 Yaren District
of Nepal: 8 Katmandu **9** Kathmandu
of Netherlands: 8 The Hague **9** Amsterdam
of New Guinea: 11 Port Moresby
of New Zealand: 10 Wellington
of Nicaragua: 7 Managua
of Niger: 6 Niamey
of Nigeria: 5 Abuja, Lagos
of Northern Ireland: 7 Belfast
of Norway: 4 Oslo **11** Christiania
of Oman: 6 Masqat, Muscat
of Pakistan: 9 Islamabad
of Panama: 10 Panama City
of Paraguay: 8 Asuncion
of Peru: 4 Lima
of the Philippines: 6 Manila
of Poland: 6 Warsaw
of Portugal: 6 Lisbon
of Puerto Rico: 7 San Juan
of Qatar: 4 Doha **7** al-Dawha
of Romania: 9 Bucharest
of Russia: 6 Moscow

of Rwanda: 6 Kigali
of Samoa (American): 8 Pago Pago
of Samoa (Western): 4 Apia
of San Marino: 9 San Marino
of Sao Tome and Principe: 7 Sao Tome
of Sardinia: 8 Cagliari
of Saudi Arabia: 6 Riyadh
of Scotland: 9 Edinburgh
of Senegal: 5 Dakar
of Seychelles: 8 Victoria
of Sicily: 7 Palermo
of Sierra Leone: 8 Freetown
of Sikkim: 7 Gangtok
of Singapore: 9 Singapore
of Slovakia: 10 Bratislava
of Slovenia: 9 Ljubljana
of the Solomon Islands: 7 Honiara
of Somalia: 9 Mogadishu **10** Mogadiscio
of South Africa: 8 Cape Town, Pretoria **12** Bloemfontein
of Spain: 6 Madrid
of Sri Lanka: 7 Colombo
of the Sudan: 8 Khartoum
of Suriname: 10 Paramaribo
of Swaziland: 7 Mbabane
of Sweden: 9 Stockholm
of Switzerland: 4 Bern
of Syria: 8 Damascus
of Taiwan: 6 Taipei
of Tajikistan: 8 Dushanbe
of Tanzania: 11 Dar es Salaam
of Thailand: 6 Bankok **7** Bangkok **8** Thonburi **9** Ayutthaya
of Tibet: 5 Lassa, Lhasa
of Togo: 4 Lome
of Tongo: 9 Nukualofa
of Trinidad and Tobago: 11 Port of Spain
of Tunisia: 5 Tunis
of Turkey: 6 Ankara
of Turkmenistan: 9 Ashkhabad
of Tuvalu: 8 Funafuti
of Uganda: 7 Kampala
of Ukraine: 4 Kiev
of United Arab Emirates: 8 Abu Dhabi
of United States: 12 Washington DC
of Uruguay: 10 Montevideo
of Uzbekistan: 8 Tashkent
of Vanuatu: 4 Vila
of Venezuela: 7 Caracas
of Vietnam: 5 Hanoi **6** Saigon
of Wales: 7 Cardiff
of Western Sahara: 6 Al Aiun **7** El Aaiun
of Western Samoa: 4 Apia
of Yemen: 4 Sana, Aden **5** Sanaa
of Yugoslavia: 7 Beograd **8** Belgrade
of Zaire: 8 Kinshasa
of Zambia: 6 Lusaka
of Zimbabwe: 6 Harare **9** Salisbury
capital city (of states) *see state capitals*
capitalism 14 free enterprise
capitalist 5 mogul **6** tycoon **8** investor

9 financier, plutocrat **14** businessperson
capitalize 4 back, fund **5** stake **7** exploit, finance, support, trade on, utilize **8** bankroll, cash in on, profit by **9** subsidize **11** foot the bill **13** make the most of **17** turn an honest penny **23** strike while the iron is hot **24** make hay while the sun shines
capitalize on 7 exploit, utilize **8** profit by **13** turn to account **14** use to advantage
capitol 10 statehouse **11** legislature **15** government house
capitulate 5 yield **6** accede, give in, give up, relent, submit **7** succumb **8** cry quits **9** acquiesce, surrender **11** come to terms, sue for peace **15** lay down one's arms **17** acknowledge defeat, hoist the white flag
capitulation 8 giving in, giving up, quitting, yielding **9** surrender **10** submission

Capote, Truman
  author of: 11 In Cold Blood **12** A Tree of Night **19** Breakfast at Tiffany's **21** other voices other rooms
  character: 14 Holly Golightly
Capp, Al
  real name: 18 Alfred George Caplin
  creator/artist of: 13 Li'l Abner Yokum
Cappotas
  epithet of: 4 Zeus
  means: 8 reliever
Capra, Frank
  director of: 11 Lady for a Day, Lost Horizon **15** State of the Union **17** Arsenic and Old Lace, It's a Wonderful Life, Mr Deeds Goes to Town (Oscar) **18** It Happened One Night (Oscar) **20** You Can't Take It with You (Oscar) **23** Mr Smith Goes to Washington
caprice 3 fad **4** lark, whim **5** antic, caper, craze, fancy, fling, prank, quirk, spree, stunt **6** notion, oddity, vagary **7** impulse **8** crotchet, escapade **10** erraticism **11** peculiarity **12** eccentricity, idiosyncrasy
capricious 6 fickle, fitful, quirky, uneven **7** erratic, faddish, flighty **8** fanciful, skittish, unstable, unsteady, variable, wavering **9** eccentric, impulsive, mercurial, uncertain, undecided **10** changeable, indecisive, irresolute **11** vacillating **12** inconsistent **13** irresponsible **15** shilly-shallying
capriciousness 7 caprice **10** fickleness **11** instability **12** irresolution **13** impulsiveness, inconsistency **15** shilly-shallying

Capricorn
  symbol: 4 goat
  planet: 6 Saturn
  rules: 6 career
  born: 7 January **8** December

capsicum peppers
  origin: 15 tropical America
  color: 3 red **5** green, white **6** violet, yellow
  variety: 5 ancho, chile **7** cayenne, paprika, serrano **8** chipotle, habanero, jalapeno **9** red pepper **11** chili pepper, chili powder, curry powder, sweet pepper
  flavor: 3 hot
  use: 5 chili, curry, pizza **8** barbecue **9** paprikash
capsize 5 upset **6** invert **7** tip over **8** flip over, keel over, overturn, turn over **10** turn turtle
capsule 4 case, pill **6** ampule **7** cockpit **8** covering **9** spore case **12** condensation
captain 4 boss, head **5** chief, pilot **6** leader, master, old man **7** headman, skipper **9** chieftain, commander **10** commandant **12** chief officer **16** company commander **17** commanding officer
  famous: 4 Ahab, Andy, Hook, Kirk, Nemo
Captain Blood
  director: 13 Michael Curtiz
  cast: 10 Errol Flynn **12** Lionel Atwill **13** Basil Rathbone **17** Olivia de Havilland
Captain Carpenter
  author: 15 John Crowe Ransom
Captain Craig
  author: 22 Edwin Arlington Robinson
Captain Hook
  character in: 8 Peter Pan
  author: 6 Barrie
  henchman: Smee
Captain Horatio Hornblower
  author: 10 C S Forester
Captains Courageous
  author: 14 Rudyard Kipling
  director: 13 Victor Fleming
  cast: 12 Mickey Rooney, Spencer Tracy **13** John Carradine, Melvyn Douglas **16** Lionel Barrymore **18** Freddie Bartholomew
  Oscar for: 5 actor (Tracy)
Captain's Daughter, The
  author: 16 Alexander Pushkin
Captain Video and His Video Rangers
  character: 7 Dr Pauli **9** The Ranger **12** Captain Video
  cast: 7 Al Hodge **10** Hal Conklin **11** Don Hastings **13** Richard Coogan
  slogan: 29 Guardian of the Safety of the World
  villain: 4 Atar **7** Nargola **8** Dahoumie, Kul of Eos **9** Dr Clysmok **12** Heng Foo Seeng **14** Mook the Moon Man
  gimmick: 5 Tobor **9** Discatron **11** Atomic Rifle **16** Barrier of Silence, Radio Scillograph **17** Cosmic Ray Vibrator **18** Opticon Scillometer **19** Cloak of Invisibility, Trisonic Com-

pensator

spaceship: 6 Galaxy

caption 5 title 6 legend 7 heading, subhead 8 headline, subtitle 11 explanation

captious 4 mean 5 picky, testy 6 ornery 7 carping, cutting, peevish 8 caviling, contrary, niggling, perverse, petulant, picayune, snappish 9 fractious, querulous 10 belittling, censorious, nitpicking 11 deprecating 12 cantankerous, faultfinding 13 hypercritical

captivate 4 lure 5 charm 6 dazzle, enamor, seduce 7 attract, bewitch, delight, enchant, win over 8 enthrall 9 carry away, enrapture, fascinate, hypnotize, infatuate, mesmerize, transport 13 turn the head of 14 take the fancy of

captivated 7 charmed, pleased 9 delighted, enchanted 10 enraptured, enthralled, spellbound

captivating 7 winning, winsome 8 adorable, charming, dazzling, engaging, fetching, magnetic 9 appealing, beguiling, disarming 10 attractive, bewitching, delightful, enchanting, entrancing 11 enthralling, fascinating, mesmerizing 12 ingratiating, irresistible

captive 3 POW 5 caged 6 penned 7 hostage 8 confined, enslaved, interned, locked up, prisoner 9 oppressed 10 imprisoned, subjugated 12 incarcerated

captivity 7 bondage, holding, slavery 9 servitude 10 detainment 12 imprisonment

capture 3 bag, nab 4 bust, grab, snag, take, trap 5 catch, grasp, pinch, seize, snare 6 arrest, collar, taking 7 bagging, ensnare, procure, seizure, snaring 8 catching, trapping 9 apprehend, collaring, ensnaring, lay hold of 12 apprehension, laying hold of, take prisoner 14 taking prisoner 15 take into custody

Capulet family

characters in: 14 Romeo and Juliet

author: 11 Shakespeare

Capys

father: 9 Assaracus

son: 7 Laocoon 8 Anchises

grandson: 6 Aeneas

founded: 5 Capua

warned against: 11 Trojan horse

car 4 auto, heap 5 buggy, coach, diner, motor 6 boxcar, hot rod, jalopy, wheels 7 flivver, machine, sleeper, vehicle 8 carriage 9 tin lizzie 10 automobile 12 motor vehicle

kind: 4 coal 5 cable, horse, motor 6 cattle, dining, parlor, street 7 baggage, freight, Pullman, railway 8 sleeping

carabiniere 9 policeman

Caracas

birthplace of: 12 Simon Bolivar

capital of: 9 Venezuela

founder: 13 Diego de Losada

museum: 7 Bolivar 8 Criolan 11 Colonial Art, Raul Santana

river: 6 Guaire

carafe 5 flask 6 bottle, vessel 9 container

carapace 4 case 5 shell 6 lorica, shield 7 carapax 8 calipash, covering 11 turtle shell

Caravaggio, Michelangelo Merisi da

born: 5 Italy 10 Caravaggio

artwork: 12 Young Bacchus 14 Burial of St Lucy 16 Raising of Lazarus 17 The Supper at Emmaus 18 Calling of St Matthew, The Life of St Matthew 20 St Matthew and the Angel 21 The Conversion of St Paul 23 The Crucifixion of St Peter 30 The Beheading of St John the Baptist

caravan 4 band, file, line 5 queue, train, troop 6 coffle, column, convoy, parade, string 7 company, cortege, retinue, trailer 9 cavalcade, chain gang, entourage, motorcade 10 procession, wagon train

caravansary 3 inn 5 hotel 8 hostelry

caraway

botanical name: 10 Carum carvi

origin: 6 Europe 9 Asia Minor 14 the Netherlands

liqueur: 6 Kummel

candy-covered caraway seeds: 6 comfit 12 whisky-killer

use: 4 pork, soup, stew 8 rye bread

carbohydrate

consists of: 5 water 6 carbon, oxygen 8 hydrogen 13 carbon dioxide

kinds: 5 sugar 6 simple, starch, xylose 7 complex, glucose, lactose, maltose, sucrose 8 dextrose, fructose 9 cellulose

carbon 4 coal, coke, copy 8 charcoal 9 lampblack

chemical symbol: 1 C

carbon copy 5 clone 7 replica 9 duplicate, facsimile 12 reproduction

carbonize 4 burn, char, sear 5 singe 6 scorch 10 incinerate

carbuncle 4 boil, sore 11 excrescence 12 inflammation

carcass 4 body, bouk, husk, wall 5 shell, stiff, trunk 6 corpse 7 cadaver, carrion, remains 8 dead body, fireball, skeleton 9 framework

carcinoma 5 tumor 6 cancer 8 neoplasm 10 malignancy 15 malignant growth

card 4 bill 6 ticket 7 program 8 postcard

kind: 7 calling, get-well, playing 8 birthday, business, greeting 9 Christmas, Valentine

cardamon

botanical name: 19 Elettaria cardamomum

origin: 4 Asia 5 India 13 southeast Asia

related to: 6 ginger

color: 5 black

use: 5 curry 7 dessert 12 Danish pastry

Cardew, Cecily

character in: 27 The Importance of Being Earnest

author: 5 Wilde

card game 3 loo, war 4 brag, faro, fish, skat, vint 5 ombre, poker, rummy, whist 6 boston, bridge, casino, chemmy, ecarte, euchre, go fish, hearts, memory, piquet, pocher 7 bezique, canasta, cooncan, Old Maid, plafond, primero 8 baccarat, conquian, cribbage, gin rummy, napoleon, patience, pinochle, slapjack 9 blackjack, pelmanism, solitaire, spoil five, twenty-one, vingt-et-un 11 chemin de fer, crazy eights 13 concentration 14 contract bridge 16 beggar-my-neighbor, trente et quarante

card names: 3 ace 4 fool, jack, king, trey 5 deuce, joker, queen

combination of cards: 4 meld

one hand or round: 5 trick

rulebook by: 5 Hoyle

suits: 4 club 5 heart, spade 7 diamond

French: 5 coeur, pique 6 trefle 7 carreau

German: 4 grun, herz, piks 5 karos, treff 6 eichel 7 schelle

Italian: 5 coppa, cuori, fiori, spada 6 denaro, picchi, quadri 7 bastone

Spanish: 3 oro 4 copa 5 basto 6 espada

Cardiff

capital of: 5 Wales

Cardiff Giant 4 hoax 5 relic

cardigan 5 corgi 6 jacket, wampus 7 sweater 10 Welsh corgi

cardinal 3 key, top 4 head, main 5 basic, chief, first, prime, vital 6 cherry, claret, red hat 7 carmine, central, deep-red, highest, leading, primary, scarlet 8 blood-red, dominant, foremost, greatest 9 essential, intrinsic, necessary, paramount, principal, uppermost 10 elementary, preeminent, underlying 11 fundamental, outstanding, predominant, wine-colored 13 indispensable, most important

number suffix: 3 eth

care 3 TLC 4 heed, load, mind, want, wish 5 grief, pains, worry 6 bother, charge, desire, effort, misery, regard, sorrow, strain, stress 7 anguish, anxiety, caution, concern, control, custody, keeping, sadness, thought, trouble 8 distress, give a rap, hardship, nuisance, pressure, vexation 9 annoyance, attention, be worried, diligence, exactness, give a hoot, heartache, vigilance **10** affliction, management, precaution, protection, solicitude **11** application, be concerned, bother about, carefulness, supervision, tribulation, unhappiness **12** ministration, trouble about, watchfulness **13** attentiveness, consideration **14** be interested in, circumspection, discrimination, fastidiousness, meticulousness, responsibility, scrupulousness **17** conscientiousness

Careas 6 eunuch

careen 3 tip, yaw **4** lean, list, sway, tilt, veer **5** heave, slant, slope **7** capsize **8** lean over, overturn

career 3 job **4** line, work **7** calling, pursuit **8** activity, business, lifework, vocation **10** employment, livelihood, occupation, profession, walk of life

care for 4 like, mind, tend **5** fancy **7** oversee **8** attend to, wait upon **9** look after, watch over **10** minister to, provide for

carefree 3 gay **4** glad **5** happy, jolly, sunny **6** breezy, elated, jaunty, joyous **7** buoyant, gleeful, radiant, relaxed, smiling **8** careless, cheerful, jubilant, laughing **9** easygoing **10** full of life, optimistic, untroubled **11** free-and-easy **12** happy-go-lucky, light-hearted, without worry **13** in high spirits **23** without a worry in the world
French: 9 sans souci

careful 4 fine, nice, wary **5** alert, chary, exact, fussy **7** correct, guarded, heedful, mindful, on guard, precise, prudent, tactful **8** accurate, cautious, diligent, discreet, vigilant, watchful **9** attentive, concerned, judicious, observant, regardful **10** fastidious, meticulous, particular, scrupulous, solicitous, thoughtful **11** circumspect, painstaking, punctilious **13** conscientious

carefulness 7 caution **10** steadiness **12** deliberation **14** circumspection

careless 3 lax **4** rash **5** messy, slack **6** casual, sloppy, untidy **7** inexact, offhand **8** heedless, mindless, slapdash, slipshod, slovenly **9** forgetful, imprecise, incorrect, negligent, unmindful **10** disorderly, inaccurate, neglectful, nonchalant, unthinking, untroubled **11** indifferent, thoughtless, unconcerned **12** absent-minded, devilmay-care **13** inconsiderate, lackadaisical

carelessness 6 laxity **7** neglect **9** messiness, slackness **10** inaccuracy, negligence, sloppiness, untidiness **11** imprecision, inexactness **12** heedlessness, indiscretion, slovenliness **13** unmindfulness **14** disorderliness **15** thoughtlessness **16** absentmindedness, irresponsibility

Care of Time, The
author: 10 Eric Ambler

caress 3 hug, pat, pet **5** clasp, touch **6** cuddle, fondle, stroke **7** embrace, petting, toy with **8** fondling, stroking **11** gentle touch

caretaker 6 keeper, porter, warden **7** curator, janitor, steward **8** overseer, watchman **9** concierge, custodian **10** gatekeeper **14** superintendent

careworn 7 haggard, worried **8** fatigued, troubled **11** pessimistic

cargo 4 load **5** goods **6** burden, lading **7** freight **8** shipment **11** consignment, merchandise

Carib
language family: 7 Cariban
location: 7 Guianas **9** Caribbean, Venezuela **12** South America
alleged custom: 11 cannibalism

Cariban
tribe: 5 Carib **6** Acawai, Akawai

Caribbean 3 sea
channel: 7 Yucatan
city: 6 Havana **7** San Juan **8** Santiago **10** Guantanamo **12** Port au Prince **13** Santo Domingo **15** Charlotte Amalie
Indian: 5 Carib **6** Arawak
island: 4 Cuba **5** Aruba, Haiti, Nevis **6** Cayman, Nassau, Tobago, Virgin **7** Antigua, Bahamas, Barbuda, Curacao, Grenada, Jamaica, Leeward **8** Anguilla, Dominica, Trinidad, Windward **9** Saint John **10** Guadeloupe, Hispaniola, Martinique, Montserrat, Puerto Rico, Saint Kitts, Saint Lucia **11** Saint Thomas **12** Saint Vincent **14** Lesser Antilles **15** Greater Antilles **19** Dominican Republic, Netherlands Antilles
language: 6 gullah **10** papiamento
product: 3 rum **5** fruit, spice, sugar **6** coffee

caricature 4 mock **6** parody, satire **7** lampoon, mockery, takeoff **8** satirize, travesty **9** absurdity, burlesque **10** distortion **12** exaggeration

Carker
character in: 12 Dombey and Son
author: 7 Dickens

Carlisle, Kitty
real name: 13 Katherine Conn
husband: 8 Moss Hart
born: 12 New Orleans LA
roles: 13 She Loves Me Not **14** To Tell the Truth **16** A Night at the Opera **19** Murder at the Vanities

Carlton, Steve (Steven Norman)
nickname: 5 Lefty
sport: 8 baseball
position: 7 pitcher
team: 20 Philadelphia Phillies

Carlyle, Thomas
author of: 8 Cromwell **14** Sartor Resartus **17** Frederick the Great **19** The

French Revolution **20** Heroes and Hero-Worship

Carmen
author: 14 Prosper Merimee
opera by: 5 Bizet
setting: 7 Seville
character: 7 Don Jose **9** Escamillo, Frasquita
song: 8 Habanera

Carmen Jones
director: 13 Otto Preminger
based on opera by: 5 Bizet (Carmen)
adaptation by: 18 Oscar Hammerstein II
cast: 11 Pearl Bailey **14** Harry Belafonte **16** Dorothy Dandridge

carmine 3 red **6** cherry **7** crimson, deep red, scarlet **8** blood red **9** bright red

carnage 8 butchery, massacre **9** blood bath, slaughter

carnal 4 lewd **6** erotic, impure, sexual, sinful, wanton **7** fleshly, immoral, lustful, sensual **8** prurient, sensuous, unchaste, venereal **9** lecherous, salacious **10** lascivious, libidinous, voluptuous

Carnegie, Dale
author of: 33 How To Win Friends and Influence People

carnelian
species: 6 quartz

Carnera, Primo
nickname: 13 the Ambling Alp
sport: 6 boxing
class: 11 heavyweight

Carney, Art
real name: 26 Arthur William Matthew Carney
partner: 13 Jackie Gleason
born: 13 Mount Vernon NY
roles: 8 Ed Norton **13** Harry and Tonto (Oscar) **15** The Honeymooners

carnival 4 fair, fete, gala **6** circus **7** holiday, jubilee **8** festival, jamboree, sideshow **9** Mardi Gras **11** celebration

carnivore 3 cat, dog, fox **4** bear, lion, lynx, mink, puma, wolf **5** civet, dingo, fossa, hyena, otter, panda, skunk, tayra, tiger **6** badger, bobcat, coyote, ferret, grison, hyaena, jackal, jaguar, marten, olingo, weasel **7** polecat, raccoon, suricat **8** aardwolf, kinkajou, mongoose **9** meat eater, wolverine **10** cacomistle, coatimundi, flesh eater

carnivorous 9 predatory **10** meateating, predaceous **11** flesh-eating

carol 4 hymn, noel, sing **5** paean **6** warble **8** canticle **9** song of joy **12** song of praise

Caroline Islands
district: 3 Yap **4** Truk **5** Palau **6** Ponape
inhabitant: 10 Polynesian **11** Micronesian
island: 3 Yap **6** Ponape, Ulithi **8**

Nukuroro **10** Babelthuap **14** Kapina-marangi
language: 7 English **10** Polynesian **11** Micronesian
ocean: 7 Pacific

carom 6 bounce, strike **7** collide, rebound, **8** billiard, ricochet **9** bounce off

Caron, Leslie
born: 6 France **19** Boulogne-Billancourt
roles: 4 Gaby, Gigi, Lili **5** Fanny **11** Father Goose **13** Daddy Longlegs **14** The L-Shaped Room **17** An American in Paris

Carothers, Wallace Hume
field: 9 chemistry
discovered: 5 nylon

carousal 4 orgy **5** binge, drunk, spree **7** debauch **9** bacchanal **10** debauchery, saturnalia

carouse 5 drink, party, quaff, revel **6** guzzle, imbibe, tipple **7** roister, wassail **8** live it up **9** make merry **10** go on a binge **11** make whoopee

Carousel (film)
director: 9 Henry King
based on: 6 Liliom
  adaptation by: 21 Rodgers and Hammerstein
cast: 12 Gordon MacRae (Billy Bigelow), Shirley Jones **15** Cameron Mitchell
song: 9 Soliloquy **11** If I Loved You **19** You'll Never Walk Alone

carp 3 nag **5** cavil, chide, decry, knock **6** deride, impugn, jibe at, pick on **7** censure, condemn **8** belittle, complain, reproach **9** criticize, deprecate, disparage, fault-find, find fault **10** disapprove

Carpaccio, Vittore
born: 5 Italy **6** Venice
artwork: 13 Two Courtesans **18** The Dream of St Ursula **19** The Legend of St Ursula **21** St Augustine in his Study **24** St George Killing the Dragon **28** St Augustine's Vision of St Jerome **29** The Arrival of St Ursula at Cologne

carpal
bone of: 5 wrist

carpe diem 11 seize the day **15** enjoy the present

carpenter 6 fitter, joiner **7** builder **8** repairer **10** woodworker **12** cabinetmaker
ant: 10 camponotus
bee: 8 xylocopa
bird: 10 woodpecker
fish: 10 hammerhead
moth: 10 prinoxysus

Carpenter, Harlean
real name: 10 Jean Harlow

carper 6 critic **7** caviler **9** nit-picker **11** fault-finder

carpet 3 mat, rug **4** shag **5** cover,

layer, sheet **7** blanket, matting **8** covering

Carpetbaggers, The
author: 13 Harold Robbins

Carr, Emily
born: 6 Canada **8** Victoria **15** British Columbia
artwork: 3 Sky **8** Big Raven **14** Blunden Harbour, Kispiax Village **15** Woods and Blue Sky **17** Forest Landscape II **36** Cape Mudge An Indian Family with Totem Pole

Carra, Carlo
born: 5 Italy **9** Quargneto
artwork: 13 Lot's Daughters **16** Metaphysical Muse **20** Patriotic Celebration **29** The Funeral of the Anarchist Galli

Carradine, David
father: 4 John
half-brothers: 5 Keith **6** Robert
born: 11 Hollywood CA
roles: 6 Kung Fu **13** Bound for Glory **14** The Serpent's Egg

Carradine, John
real name: 21 Richmond Reed Carradine
son: 5 David, Keith **6** Robert
born: 18 Greenwich Village NY
roles: 9 Cleopatra, Kidnapped **10** Stagecoach **12** Count Dracula **15** The Invisible Man **18** Captains Courageous, The Three Musketeers

Carradine, Keith
father: 4 John
brother: 6 Robert
half-brother: 5 David
born: 10 San Mateo CA
roles: 9 Nashville **10** Pretty Baby

Carraway, Nick
character in: 14 The Great Gatsby
author: 10 Fitzgerald

Carrere, John Merven
partner: 14 Thomas Hastings
architect of: 19 House Office Building (Washington DC) **20** New York Public Library, Senate Office Building (Washington DC) **21** Henry Clay Frick mansion (now Frick Collection NYC)
style: 18 French neo-classical, Spanish Renaissance

carriage 3 air, rig **4** mien **5** buggy, coach, poise, wagon **6** aspect, manner **7** bearing, posture, vehicle **8** attitude, behavior, demeanor, presence **10** appearance, conveyance, deportment **11** comportment

Carrie
author: 11 Stephen King

carried away 7 excited, frantic, seduced **8** ecstatic, frenzied, overcome **9** delirious **10** fascinated, infatuated **11** transported

carrier 3 bus, car **4** rack, wave **5** agent, barge, plane, coach, drain, ferry, train, truck, wagon **6** bearer,

boxcar, pigeon, porter **7** airline, channel, mailman, postman, trucker, vehicle **8** airplane, aircraft, carriage, catalyst, railroad **9** messenger **11** transmitter, wheelbarrow

carrion 5 bones, offal, waste **6** corpse, refuse **7** cadaver, carcass, garbage, remains, wastage **8** crowbait, dead body, leavings

Carroll, Leo G
born: 6 Weedon **7** England
roles: 6 Topper **7** Rebecca **9** Suspicion **10** Spellbound **11** Cosmo Topper **15** A Christmas Carol, The Man from UNCLE, The Paradine Case **16** Father of the Bride, North by Northwest

Carroll, Lewis
real name: 22 Charles Lutwidge Dodgson
author of: 11 Jabberwocky **20** The Hunting of the Shark **22** Through the Looking Glass **28** Alice's Adventures in Wonderland

carrousel 4 ride, tray **8** conveyor **9** quadrille, whirligig **10** tournament **12** merry-go-round

carry 3 lug, run **4** bear, cart, haul, lift, move, prop, ship, take, tote **5** brace, bring, fetch, offer, print, shift, stock **6** convey, hold up, supply, uphold **7** conduct, deliver, display, publish, release, support, sustain **8** displace, maintain, shoulder, transfer, transmit **9** broadcast, transport **10** keep on hand **11** communicate, disseminate

carry away 4 lure **6** abduct, kidnap, seduce **7** attract **9** captivate, fascinate, infatuate, transport

carry off 5 seize, steal **6** abduct, kidnap **7** bear off **9** succeed at **11** get away with

carry out 2 do **6** effect, wind up **7** achieve, execute, fulfill, perform, realize **8** complete, conclude, dispatch **9** discharge, dispose of, succeed at **10** accomplish, bring about **11** bring to pass

carry through 6 effect, finish **7** achieve, develop, execute, fulfill, perform, realize **8** complete, conclude **9** discharge **10** accomplish, consummate, effectuate, perpetuate **13** put into effect

Carson, Rachel Louise
field: 7 biology
studied: 9 pollution
author of: 12 Silent Spring **14** The Sea Around Us **15** The Edge of the Sea

Carstone, Richard
character in: 10 Bleak House
author: 7 Dickens

cart 3 gig, lug **4** bear, dray, haul, move, take, tote, trap **5** bring, carry, fetch, truck, wagon **6** barrow, convey **7** schlepp, trundle, tumbrel **8** curricle, transfer, transmit **9** transport **10** handbarrow, transplant, two-wheeler **11** wheelbarrow

kind: 2 go **3** dog, tip **4** dump, hand, push

carte blanche 7 license **9** a free hand, free reign **10** blank check **12** open sanction **13** full authority **18** unconditional power

cartel 4 OPEC, pool **5** chain, trust **7** combine **8** monopoly **9** syndicate **10** consortium, federation **11** corporation

Carter, Charles
  real name of: 14 Charlton Heston

Carter, James Earl, Jr
  nickname: 3 Hot **5** Jimmy **7** Hotshot
  presidential rank: 11 thirty-ninth
  party: 10 Democratic
  state represented: 2 GA **7** Georgia
  defeated: 4 (Gerald R) Ford **8** (Eugene) McCarthy
  vice president: 7 (Walter Frederick "Fritz") Mondale
  cabinet:
    state: 5 (Cyrus R) Vance **6** (Edmund S) Muskie
    treasury: 6 (G William) Miller **10** (W Michael) Blumenthal
    defense: 5 (Harold) Brown
    attorney general: 4 (Griffin B) Bell **9** (Benjamin R) Civiletti
    interior: 6 (Cecil D) Andrus
    agriculture: 8 (Robert S) Bergland
    commerce: 5 (Juanita Morris) Kreps **9** (Philip M) Klutznick
    labor: 8 (F Ray) Marshall
    HEW: 6 (Patricia Roberts) Harris **8** (Joseph A) Califano (Jr)
    HUD: 6 (Patricia Roberts) Harris **8** (Moon) Landrieu
    transportation: 5 (Brockman) Adams **11** (Neil E) Goldschmidt
    education: 10 (Shirley) Hufstedler
  born: 2 GA **6** Plains
  education: 14 US Naval Academy **26** Georgia Southwestern College **28** Georgia Institute of Technology
  religion: 15 Southern Baptist
  interests: 5 track **6** tennis **7** fishing, hunting **8** football, softball **10** basketball **12** cross country **13** square dancing **17** collecting bottles
    music: 8 folk rock **9** classical
  author: 11 Living Faith **12** Keeping Faith **13** Why Not the Best? **16** Everything to Gain **17** The Blood of Abraham
  political career: 12 state senator
    governor of: 7 Georgia
  civilian career: 12 peanut farmer
  military service: 6 US Navy
  notable events of lifetime/term: 6 SALT II **9** Love Canal, recession **18** Habitat for Humanity
    deaths at: 9 Jonestown
    eruption of: 13 Mount St Helens
    first baby from: 8 test tube
    hostages taken in: 4 Iran

    nuclear accident: 15 Three Mile Island
    pipeline: 5 Alcan
    scandal/investigation: 6 Abscam **9** Bert Lance, Koreagate **11** Billy Carter
    Supreme Court case: 5 Bakke
    treaty: 11 Panama Canal **16** Camp David Accords
  father: 11 James Earl Sr
  mother: 7 Lillian (Gordy)
    nickname: 11 Miss Lillian
  siblings: 6 Gloria **17** William "Billy" Alton **19** Ruth Carter Stapleton
  wife: 8 Rosalynn (Smith)
  children: 7 Amy Lynn **11** John William (Jack) **12** James Earl III (Chip) **13** Donnel Jeffrey (Jeff)
  first lady: 36 Presidential Commission on Mental Health
    author: 19 First Lady from Plains

Carthage see **7** Tunisia

carton 3 box **4** case **5** crate **9** container **11** packing case **12** cardboard box, packing crate **18** cardboard container

Carton, Sydney
  character in: 16 A Tale of Two Cities
  author: 7 Dickens

cartoon 5 comic **6** design, satire, sketch **7** drawing, funnies, picture **8** animated **10** caricature, comic strip

cartoonist 6 artist, drawer **7** gagster **12** caricaturist
  famous: 6 Al Capp, C C Beck, Ted Key **7** Bob Kane, Stan Lee **8** Herblock (Herbert L. Block), Jim Davis, Roy Crane **9** Bud Fisher, Chic Young, Dik Browne, Frank King, Hal Foster, Ham Fisher, Walt Kelly **10** Bob Montana, Gary Larson, Harold Gray, Jimmy Hatlo, Johnny Hart, Joe Shuster, Mort Walker, Paul Conrad, Thomas Nast, Walt Disney **11** Alex Raymond, Bill Mauldin, Dale Messick, David Levine, Ding Darling, Elzie C. Segar, Hank Ketcham, Max Beerbohm, Rollin Kirby **12** Al Hirschfeld, Brad Anderson, Chester Gould, Garry Trudeau, James Thurber, Jeff MacNelly, Jules Feiffer, Milton Caniff, Rube Goldberg, Rudolph Dirks, Virgil Partch **13** Bill Watterson, Charles Addams, Charles Schulz, George McManus, Honore Daumier, Joseph Keppler, Saul Steinberg **14** Homer Davenport, William Hogarth **15** Ernie Bushmiller, Patrick Oliphant, Richard Outcault **16** Benjamin Franklin, George Cruikshank

cartridge 3 dud **4** case, tape **5** blank, shell **6** holder **7** capsule, package **8** cassette, cylinder **9** container

Cartwright, Edmund
  nationality: 7 English
  inventor of: 9 power loom **18** wool-combing machine

carve 3 hew, saw **4** etch, form, hack, mold, rend, turn, work **5** allot, cleve, cut up, model, shape, slash, slice, split **6** chisel, divide, incise, sculpt **7** engrave, fashion, pattern, quarter **8** block out, dissever **9** apportion, sculpture

Carver, George Washington
  field: 9 chemistry
  worked in: 11 agriculture
  studied: 6 peanut **7** soybean **11** sweet potato

carving 5 cameo **8** intaglio, triptych **9** sculpture

caryatid 6 column
  shape of: 12 female figure

Casablanca
  director: 13 Michael Curtiz
  cast: 10 Peter Lorre **11** Claude Rains (Louis), Conrad Veidt, Paul Henreid (Victor Laslo) **12** Dooley Wilson (Sam), **13** Ingrid Bergman (Ilsa Lund) **14** Humphrey Bogart (Rick) **17** Sydney Greenstreet
  Oscar for: 7 picture
  song: 12 As Time Goes By

Casanova 3 cad, rip **4** beau, lech, roue, wolf **5** lover, Romeo, swain, wooer **6** chaser, lecher, suitor **7** admirer, bounder, Don Juan, gallant, rounder **8** cavalier, Lothario, lover boy, paramour **9** ladies' man, libertine, womanizer **10** lady-killer, profligate **11** philanderer

Casby
  character in: 12 Little Dorrit
  author: 7 Dickens

cascade 4 fall, gush, pour, rush **5** chute, falls, surge **6** plunge, rapids, tumble **7** Niagara **8** cataract **9** waterfall

Cascade Range
  location: 9 northwest
  highest peak: 9 Mt. Rainier

case 3 bin, box **4** plea, suit, tray **5** cause, chest, cover, crate, event **6** action, affair, appeal, carton, debate, injury, jacket, matter, sheath, victim **7** cabinet, concern, disease, dispute, episode, example, hearing, housing, inquiry, invalid, lawsuit, overlay, patient, wrapper **8** argument, business, covering, envelope, incident, instance, sufferer **9** condition, container, happening, incidence, sheathing, situation **10** litigation, occurrence, proceeding, protection, receptacle, sick person **11** controversy **12** circumstance, illustration

case in point 7 example **8** instance **12** illustration

Case of Sergeant Grischa, The
  author: 11 Arnold Zweig

Casey
  nickname of: 20 Charles Dillon Stengel

team: 7 Yankees
role: 7 manager

Casey at the Bat
author: 6 Thayer
town: 8 Mudville

Casey Jones 8 engineer, folksong, railroad

cash 5 bills, bread, coins, dough, money **6** change, redeem **8** currency, exchange **9** bank notes **10** paper money **11** legal tender **13** turn into money **14** coin of the realm

cashier 6 banker, bursar, purser, teller **9** treasurer **10** bank teller

cash register
invented by: 4 till **5** Ritty
sign: 6 no sale

casing 4 skin **5** frame **9** sheathing

Casino Royale
author: 10 Ian Fleming

cask 3 keg, tub, tun, vat **4** butt, pipe **6** barrel **8** hogshead

casket 4 case, pall **5** chest **6** coffer, coffin **8** jewel box **11** sarcophagus

Cask of Amontillado, The
author: 13 Edgar Allan Poe
character: 9 Fortunato, Montresor

Cassandra 7 seeress
also: 9 Alexandra
father: 5 Priam
mother: 6 Hecuba
brother: 5 Paris
concubine of: 9 Agamemnon
son: 6 Pelops **9** Teledamus
cursed by: 6 Apollo
violated by: 4 Ajax
killed by: 12 Clytemnestra

Cassatt, Mary
born: 15 Allegheny City PA
artwork: 6 La Loge **7** The Bath **11** The Cup of Tea **12** After the Bath, Woman Bathing **14** Gathering Fruit **15** Reading Le Figaro **20** Girl Arranging Her Hair, Woman and Child Drawing

Cassavetes, John
wife: 12 Gena Rowlands
born: 9 New York NY
roles/films: 8 Husbands **10** The Tempest **13** Rosemary's Baby, The Dirty Dozen **23** A Woman Under the Influence

casserole 4 dish, food, mold **6** tureen, vessel **8** saucepan

Cassio
character in: 7 Othello
author: 11 Shakespeare

Cassiopeia 13 constellation
husband: 7 Cepheus
daughter: 9 Andromeda
offended: 7 Nereids

Cassius
also: 12 Caius Cassius
character in: 12 Julius Caesar
author: 11 Shakespeare

Cass Timberlane
author: 13 Sinclair Lewis
character: 11 Bradd Criley **24** Jinny Marshland Timberlane

cast 3 set, sow **4** fire, form, hurl, look, mien, mint, mold, pick, shed, toss **5** fling, heave, model, pitch, shape, shoot, sling, stamp, throw **6** actors, assign, casing, choose, direct, launch, let fly, propel, sculpt, spread, troupe **7** appoint, company, deposit, diffuse, pattern, players, project, scatter **8** catapult, disperse **9** broadcast, circulate, discharge, launching, semblance **10** appearance, distribute, impression, performers, propulsion **11** disseminate, give parts to **16** dramatis personae

Castalia
origin: 5 Greek
sacred: 6 spring
location: 14 Mount Parnassus
sacred to: 5 Muses **6** Apollo
source of: 11 inspiration

cast aside 4 junk, shed **6** desert, reject **7** abandon, discard, forsake, neglect **8** get rid of, renounce, throw out **9** repudiate, throw away **11** discontinue

cast a spell on 4 hex **4** jinx **5** charm **7** bewitch, conjure, enchant **8** entrance **11** work magic on

cast aspersions on 5 knock, scorn **6** deride, malign **7** disdain, put down, run down, sneer at **8** belittle, poohpooh **9** criticize, disparage **13** find fault with

castaway 3 bum **4** hobo, waif **5** exile, leper, nomad, rover, stray **6** outlaw, pariah **7** Ishmael, outcast, vagrant **8** deportee, derelict, renegade, unperson, vagabond, wanderer **9** foundling, nonperson **10** expatriate **11** beachcomber, offscouring, untouchable **12** down-and-outer **15** knight-of-the-road

cast away 4 junk **6** launch, propel, reject **7** abandon, discard, toss out **8** get rid of, pitch out, throw out **9** throw away

cast down 5 abase, droop, lower **6** abased, deject, droopy, humble, sadden **7** depress, humbled, lowered **8** bring low, dejected, disgrace, saddened **9** depressed, disgraced, humiliate **10** brought low, dishearten, humiliated **11** crestfallen **12** disheartened

caste 4 rank **6** status **7** lineage, station **8** position **9** condition
Hindu: 5 sudra, varna **6** vaisya **7** brahman **9** kshatriya

castigate 5 chide, scold **6** berate, punish, rebuke **7** bawl out, censure, chasten, chew out, correct, reprove, upbraid **8** admonish, chastise, penalize, reproach **9** criticize, dress down, reprimand **10** discipline, take to task **15** call on the carpet **16** haul over the coals

castigation 9 reprimand **10** chastening, correction, discipline, penalizing, punishment **12** chastisement

Castiglione, Baldassare
author of: 20 The Book of the Courtier

castle 4 hall, keep, rook **5** manor, tower, villa **6** palace **7** chateau, citadel, mansion **8** fortress **10** stronghold

Castle, Vernon[1]
wife: 5 Irene **15** ballroom dancers
invented: 10 Castle Walk

Castle, The[2]
author: 10 Franz Kafka
character: 1 K

Castle of Otranto, The
author: 13 Horace Walpole
character: 6 Conrad **7** Alfonso, Manfred, Matilda **8** Isabella, Theodore **12** Father Jerome

Castle Rackrent
author: 14 Maria Edgeworth

cast off 4 shed **6** reject **7** discard, set sail, toss out **8** throw off, throw out **9** repudiate, throw away **11** weigh anchor

Castor and Pollux
also: 6 Gemini **8** Dioscuri **10** Polydeuces, Tyndaridae
form: 8 twin sons
mother: 4 Leda
father: 4 Zeus
sister: 5 Helen **12** Clytemnestra
members of: 9 Argonauts
protectors of: 6 seamen

cast out 4 oust **5** eject, evict, exile, expel **6** banish, reject **7** discard, dismiss, turn out **8** drive out, send away, throw out

cast up 4 spew **5** eject, expel, vomit **6** spew up **7** cough up, throw up **8** disgorge

casual 4 cool, so-so **5** blase, vague **6** chance, random, sporty **7** offhand, passing, relaxed **8** informal **9** easygoing, haphazard, non-dressy, unplanned **10** accidental, fortuitous, incidental, nonchalant, unarranged, undesigned, undirected, unexpected, unforeseen **11** half-hearted, indifferent, unlooked for **13** lackadaisical, serendipitous, unintentional **14** indiscriminate, unpremeditated

Casuals of the Sea
author: 12 William McFee

casualty 4 loss **6** injury, victim **7** injured **8** fatality

casuistry 5 guile **6** deceit **7** fallacy, sophism **8** subtlety **9** Jesuitism, quibbling, sophistry **10** nitpicking **12** equivocation, pettifoggery, speciousness **13** deceptiveness, hair-splitting **14** sophistication

casus belli 10 cause of war

Casy, Jim

character in: 16 The Grapes of Wrath
author: 9 Steinbeck

cat 3 pet **4** puss, whip **5** kitty, pussy, tabby **6** feline, kitten, mouser, tomcat
anatomy: 3 paw **4** loin, nape, rump, tail **5** break, flank, shank **6** feeler **7** dewclaw, leather, whisker **8** vibrissa **10** metatarsus
breed/kind: 3 tom **4** coon, Eyra, lion, lynx, Manx, puma **5** alley, civet, hyena, kitty, Korat, tabby, tiger **6** Angola, angora, bobcat, cougar, jaguar, ocelot, serval **7** Burmese, caracal, cheetah, leopard, linsang, Maltese, panther, Persian, polecat, Siamese, Turkish, wildcat **8** Balinese, Cheshire, Egyptian, ringtail **9** Himalayan, shorthair **10** Abyssinian, chinchilla **11** Russian blue **13** tortoise-shell
combining form: 5 aelur, ailur, felin **6** aeluro, ailuro, felino
Egyptian goddess of: 4 Bast
extinct: 10 saber-tooth
family: 7 Felidae
famous: 6 Morris **8** Cheshire, Garfield, Kilkenny **9** Mehitabel **10** Heathcliff
fastest: 7 cheetah
fear of: 12 aelurophobia, ailurophobia
female: 5 queen **7** lioness, tigress **8** wheencat **9** grimalkin
genus: 5 Felis
grinning: 8 Cheshire
group: 7 clowder, clutter
group of kittens: 6 kendle, kindle
lover: 11 aelurophile, ailurophile
male: 3 gib, tom **6** tomcat
ring-tailed: 6 serval **10** cacomistle
tailless: 4 Manx
young: 6 kitten

cataclysm 4 blow **7** debacle **8** calamity, disaster, upheaval **11** catastrophe, devastation

cataclysmic 4 dire **6** tragic **7** ruinous **10** calamitous, disastrous **12** catastrophic, earth-shaking

catacomb 4 tomb **7** ossuary **8** cemetery **10** passageway **12** burial ground

catafalque 3 box **4** pall **6** casket, coffin

catalog, catalogue 4 file, list, post, roll **5** index **6** record, roster **7** listing **8** classify, register, syllabus, tabulate **9** directory, enumerate, inventory, mail order

Catamitus *see* **8** Ganymede

Cat and Mouse
author: 11 Gunter Grass

catapult 4 cast, hurl, toss **5** fling, heave, pitch, shoot, sling, throw **6** hurtle, onager, propel **9** slingshot **13** hurling engine

cataract 5 falls, flood **6** deluge, rapids **7** cascade, torrent **8** downpour **9** lens cover, waterfall **10** inundation

catastrophe 4 blow **5** havoc **6** mis-

hap, ravage **7** debacle, scourge, tragedy **8** calamity, disaster **9** cataclysm **10** affliction, misfortune **11** devastation

catastrophic 6 tragic **7** ruinous **10** calamitous, disastrous **11** cataclysmic

catcall 3 boo **4** gibe, hiss, hoot, jeer, razz **7** whistle **8** heckling **9** raspberry **10** Bronx cheer

catch 3 bag, bat, get, hit, nab **4** bait, bang, belt, bump, bust, dupe, feel, find, fool, grab, hasp, haul, hoax, hook, lock, lure, make, snag, snap, spot, take, trap **5** booty, break, charm, clasp, crack, get to, grasp, hitch, latch, prize, reach, seize, sense, smack, smite, snare, trick, whack, yield **6** allure, arrest, betray, buffet, collar, corner, corral, dazzle, deceit, delude, descry, detect, expose, fasten, fathom, kicker, snatch, strike, take in, turn on, unmask **7** attract, bewitch, capture, closure, deceive, delight, discern, enchant, ensnare, find out, gimmick, mislead, rasping, seizure **8** catching, come upon, contract, coupling, discover, drawback, enthrall, hoodwink, overtake, perceive, pickings, surprise **9** apprehend, bamboozle, captivate, carry away, enrapture, fastening, intercept, lay hold of, play false, recognize, transport **10** comprehend, understand **11** take captive **12** break out with, come down with, disadvantage, seize and hold, take off guard **14** stumbling block **15** take into custody **18** become infected with

catch-as-catch-can 7 cursory **9** haphazard, hit-or-miss, unplanned **10** disorderly, incomplete **11** superficial, unorganized **12** disorganized, unsystematic

Catcher in the Rye, The
author: 10 J D Salinger
character: 15 Holden Caulfield Phoebe Caulfield

catching 10 contagious, infectious **12** communicable **13** transmittable

catch on to 3 get **5** grasp, savvy **6** absorb, digest, fathom, pick up **10** assimilate, comprehend, get the idea, understand

catch sight of 3 see **4** espy **6** behold, descry, detect, notice **7** discern, make out, observe, pick out **8** perceive

Catch-22
author: 12 Joseph Heller
character: 9 Yossarian
means: 7 paradox

catchword 5 motto **6** byword, cliche, slogan, war cry **8** password **9** battle cry, guide word, pet phrase, watchword **10** shibboleth

categorical 4 flat, sure **7** certain, express **8** absolute, definite, emphatic, explicit **10** pronounced, unreserved

11 unequivocal, unqualified **12** unmistakable **13** unconditional

categorically 10 absolutely, definitely, positively **12** conclusively

categorization 5 order **11** arrangement **14** classification

category 5 class, group **8** division, grouping **14** classification

cater 5 humor **6** pamper, pander, please **7** gratify, indulge, satisfy

caterpillar 4 moth, worm **5** larva **7** cutworm, tractor, webworm **8** hangworm, silkworm, wortworm **9** butterfly, woolybear **10** astragalus

caterwaul 3 cry **4** bawl, howl, wail, yelp **5** whine **6** clamor, scream, shriek, squawk, squeal **7** screech **10** rend the air

catfish 4 barb **5** banjo **6** dorado, madtom, mudcat, sucker **7** ariidae, bluecat **8** bagridae, bullhead, claridae, electric, flathead **9** siluridae **10** channel cat, cuttlefish, mochocidae, plotosidae, spotted cat **11** ictaluridae, pimelodidae, schilbeidae **12** aspredinidae, ostariophysi **14** malapteruridae **16** trichomycteridae

Catfish
nickname of: 9 Jim Hunter

Catfish Row
setting of: 12 Porgy and Bess

catharsis 7 purging, release, venting **9** cleansing **12** purification

Catharsius
epithet of: 4 Zeus
means: 8 purifier

cathartic 5 purge **6** physic **8** aperient, evacuant, laxative **9** castor oil, purgative, purifying

cathedral 3 see **6** church, temple **7** lateran **8** basilica, official **9** authority **10** pontifical
Italian: 5 duomo

Cather, Willa
author of: 9 A Lost Lady, My Antonia, One of Ours, O Pioneers! **13** My Mortal Enemy **16** Shadows on the Rock, The Song of the Lark **18** The Professor's House **23** Sapphira and the Slave Girl **26** Death Comes for the Archbishop

cathode ray tube
abbreviation: 3 CRT
invented by: 7 Crookes

catholic, Catholic 5 broad **7** liberal **9** universal, worldwide **12** all-embracing, all-inclusive **13** comprehensive

cathouse 4 stew **5** house **6** bagnio, bordel **7** brothel **8** bordello **10** bawdy house, fancy house, whorehouse **13** sporting house **14** house of ill fame **16** house of ill repute **19** house of prostitution

Cat Jumps, The
author: 14 Elizabeth Bowen

catlike 5 catty, lithe **7** sinuous **8** stealthy **14** light on the feet

Catlin, George
   born: 13 Wilkes-Barre PA
   artwork: 16 Gallery of Indians

catnap 3 nap **4** doze **6** siesta, snooze **10** forty winks, light sleep

Cato 5 Roman
   Elder: 6 Censor
   younger (grandson): 5 Stoic

Cato
   author: 13 Joseph Addison

Cat on a Hot Tin Roof
   author: 17 Tennessee Williams
   director: 13 Richard Brooks
   cast: 8 Burl Ives (Big Daddy) **10** Jack Carson, Paul Newman (Brick) **14** Judith Anderson **15** Elizabeth Taylor (Maggie)

cats-eye
   species: 11 chrysoberyl
   source: 8 Sri Lanka

cat's paw 4 dupe, pawn, tool **5** patsy **7** fall guy

cattle 4 cows, kine, oxen **5** beefs, bulls, stock **6** beeves, calves, dogies, steers **8** bullocks, milk cows **9** livestock
   family: 7 Bovidae
   group of: 5 drove
   kind: 2 ox **3** yak **4** Zebu **5** Angus **6** Ankole, Jersey **7** Brahman **8** Ayrshire, Guernsey, Hereford, Highland, Holstein **9** Charolais **12** water buffalo **13** Texas Longhorn **16** English Shorthorn, Holstein-Friesian
   young: 4 calf **6** heifer **8** yearling

Catton, Bruce
   author of: 22 A Stillness at Appomattox

catty 4 mean **7** catlike **8** spiteful **9** malicious, malignant **10** malevolent

catwalk 6 bridge **7** walkway **10** passageway

Caucasian
   language branch: 5 Ubykh **9** Daghestan **10** Circassian **11** Khartvelian

Caucon
   brought mysteries to: 8 Messenia

caucus 6 parley, powwow **7** council, meeting, session **8** assembly, conclave **10** conference

caudal 4 back, tail **7** tail-end

cauldron *see* **7** caldron

Caulfield, Holden
   character in: 18 The Catcher in the Rye
   author: 8 Salinger

Caulfield, Joan
   real name: 21 Beatrice Joan Caulfield
   born: 8 Orange NJ
   roles: 8 Dear Ruth **17** My Favorite Husband

causation 4 root **5** cause **6** author, origin, reason, source **7** creator, genesis **8** etiology, inventor, stimulus **9** gener-

ator, invention **10** antecedent, conception, mainspring, originator **11** determinant, inspiration, origination

cause 4 goal, make, root, side **5** ideal, impel, tenet **6** belief, create, effect, incite, lead to, motive, object, origin, reason, source, spring, stir up **7** genesis, grounds, incline, inspire, produce, provoke, purpose **8** etiology, generate, motivate, occasion, stimulus **9** incentive, principle, stimulate **10** aspiration, bring about, conviction, foundation, give rise to, inducement, initiation, mainspring, motivation, persuasion, prime mover **11** bring to pass, inspiration, instigation, precipitate, provocation

cause of war
   Latin: 10 casus belli

cause to appear 6 expose, reveal **7** uncover **8** disclose **12** bring to light **13** bring into view

caustic 3 lye **4** tart **5** acrid, harsh, sharp **6** biting, bitter **7** burning, cutting, erosive, gnawing **8** scathing, stinging **9** corroding, corrosive, sarcastic **10** astringent **11** acrimonious

caution 4 care, heed, warn **5** alarm, alert **6** advise, caveat, exhort, notify, regard, tip-off **7** concern, thought, warning **8** admonish, forewarn, prudence, wariness **9** alertness, restraint, vigilance **10** admonition, discretion, precaution **11** carefulness, forewarning, guardedness, heedfulness, mindfulness **12** deliberation, watchfulness **14** circumspection, put on one's guard

cautionary 7 warning **8** advisory **10** admonitory **11** admonishing

cautious 4 wary **5** alert, cagey **7** careful, guarded, prudent **8** discreet, vigilant, watchful **9** attentive, judicious **11** circumspect

cavalcade 5 troop **6** column, parade **7** caravan, retinue **10** procession

Cavalcade
   director: 10 Frank Lloyd
   based on play by: 10 Noel Coward
   cast: 10 Clive Brook **11** Ursula Jeans **12** Diana Wynyard **13** Herbert Mundin **15** Margaret Lindsay
   Oscar for: 7 picture

cavalier 3 fop **4** beau **5** blade, cocky, dandy, swell **6** hussar, lancer **7** cursory, dragoon, gallant, haughty, offhand, playboy **8** arrogant, courtier, gay blade, horseman, uncaring **9** easygoing **10** cavalryman, disdainful, nonchalant **11** indifferent, thoughtless

cavalry 7 hussars, lancers **8** dragoons **10** mounted men **11** horse troops **13** horse soldiers, mounted troops

cavalryman 6 hussar, lancer **7** dragoon **8** cavalier, horseman **12** horse soldier, horse trooper **14** mounted soldier

cave 3 den **4** lair, sink **6** burrow, cav-

ern, cavity, dugout, grotto, hollow
   growth: 10 stalactite, stalagmite
   explorer: 9 spelunker

caveat 5 alarm, alert, aviso **6** tip-off **7** caution, red flag, warning **8** high sign, red light **10** admonition, danger sign, yellow jack **11** forewarning **12** admonishment, flea in the ear **13** word to the wise **20** handwriting on the wall

caveat emptor 17 let the buyer beware

cave canem 14 beware of the dog

cave in 6 buckle, fall in, give up, submit **7** crumple, give way, implode **8** collapse **10** capitulate **12** fall to pieces

Cavendish, Henry
   field: 7 physics **9** chemistry
   nationality: 7 British
   discovered: 8 hydrogen
   determined composition of: 3 air **5** water **10** nitric acid
   method: 19 Cavendish experiment

cavernous 4 huge, vast **5** roomy **6** gaping **7** chasmal, immense, yawning **8** cavelike, enormous, spacious **10** tremendous

cavil 6 deride **7** nitpick, quibble **8** belittle, complain **9** criticize, deprecate, discredit, disparage, faultfind, find fault **12** pick to pieces

cavity 3 dip, pit **4** bore, dent, hole, sink **5** basin, niche **6** burrow, crater, hollow, pocket, tunnel **7** opening, orifice, vacuity **8** aperture **9** concavity **10** depression, excavation

cavort 4 play, romp **5** bound, caper, frisk **6** frolic, gambol, prance

Cawdor
   author: 15 Robinson Jeffers

Caxtons, The
   author: 12 Bulwer Lytton

Cayuga
   language family: 9 Iroquoian
   location: 4 Ohio **6** Canada **7** New York **8** Oklahoma **9** Wisconsin
   branch of: 10 Six Nations **19** Iroquois Confederacy, League of the Iroquois

CE 9 Common Era

cease 3 end **4** halt, pass, quit, stop **5** abate, pause **6** desist, finish **7** adjourn, die away, forbear, suspend **8** break off, conclude, leave off **9** terminate **11** abstain from, discontinue, refrain from **12** bring to an end

cease-fire 5 truce **9** armistice

ceaseless 7 endless, eternal **8** constant, enduring, unending **9** continual, incessant, permanent, perpetual, unceasing **10** continuous, protracted **11** everlasting, never-ending, unremitting **12** interminable **13** uninterrupted

cease to be 3 die, end **6** die out, expire, vanish **9** disappear, evaporate **13** become extinct

Cecilia (Memoirs of an Heiress)
  author: **11** Fanny Burney

Cecrops
  also: **8** Cecropia
  form: **3** man **6** dragon
  founder of: **6** Attica
  king of: **6** Attica
  father: **14** King Erechtheus
  brother: **6** Metion, Orneus
  wife: **8** Aglaurus
  son: **11** Erysichthon
  daughter: **5** Herse **8** Aglaurus **9** Pandrasos
  renamed Attica: **8** Cecropia

cedar 6 Cedrus
  varieties: **3** red **4** pink, salt **5** Atlas, giant, white **6** Alaska, Cyprus, ground, Mlanje **7** Bermuda, incense, Russian, Spanish **8** Barbados, cigarbox, creeping, Japanese, stinking **10** Ozark white, Port Orford, swamp white, western red, West Indian, Willowmore **11** Clanwilliam, Colorado red, southern red **13** Atlantic white, southern white **14** Chilean incense, Formosa incense **17** California incense

cede 4 give **5** grant, leave, yield **6** tender **7** abandon, deliver, release **8** hand over, transfer **9** deliver up, surrender **10** relinquish

cedez
  music: **8** slow down

Cedric the Saxon
  character in: **7** Ivanhoe
  author: **5** Scott

ceiling 3 top **4** roof **5** cover, limit **6** canopy, cupola, lining **7** maximum **8** altitude **10** upperlimit

Celebes
  also: **8** Sulawesi
  bordered by: **6** Borneo **8** Moluccas **10** Celebes Sea, Kalimantan **12** Flores Strait **14** Makassar Strait
  city: **4** Poso **6** Manado **7** Kendari, Madjene **8** Bonthain, Donggala, Makassar **9** Gorontalo
  location: **9** Indonesia
  people: **4** Bugi, Laki, Mori, Muna, Napu, Palu, Peso, Seko, Wana **5** Besoa, Buton, Toala **6** Bungku, Butung, Parigi, Sadang, Sangir, Toland **7** Banggai, Bolaang, Kabaena, Loinang, Toradja **8** Balantak, Buginese, Mongondu, Rongkong, Sanghike **9** Gorontalo **11** Makassarese
  province: **13** North Sulawesi, South Sulawesi **15** Central Sulawesi **17** Southeast Sulawesi

Celebes ox 4 anoa

celebrate 4 laud **5** bless, cheer, exalt, extol, honor **6** hallow, praise, revere **7** acclaim, applaud, commend, glorify, observe **8** proclaim, sanctify, venerate **9** broadcast, ritualize, solemnize **10** consecrate **11** commemorate **13** ceremonialize

celebrated 5 famed, feted, noted **6** famous, prized **7** eminent, honored, notable, revered **8** lionized, renowned **9** acclaimed, important, prominent, respected, treasured, venerable, well-known **11** illustrious, outstanding **13** distinguished

Celebrated Jumping Frog of Calaveras County, The
  author: **9** Mark Twain

celebration 4 fete, gala **5** feast, party **6** ritual **7** jubilee, revelry **8** carnival, ceremony, festival **9** festivity, hallowing **10** ceremonial, observance **13** commemoration, solemnization **14** sanctification **15** memorialization

celebrity 3 VIP **4** fame, name, note, star **5** glory, wheel **6** bigwig, renown **7** big shot, notable, stardom **8** eminence, luminary **9** dignitary, notoriety, personage **10** notability, popularity, prominence **11** distinction, personality **12** famous person, person of note

celerity 5 haste, hurry, speed **6** hustle **8** alacrity, dispatch, fast clip, fastness, legerity, rapidity **9** briskness, quickness, swiftness **10** expedition, snappiness, speediness **12** precipitance **14** lightning speed **15** expeditiousness

celery seed
  also called: **8** smallage
  origin: **13** Mediterranean
  use: **4** soup **5** salad, sauce **6** pickle **10** vegetables

celestial 3 sky **5** solar **6** astral, divine **7** angelic, elysian, stellar, sublime **8** beatific, blissful, empyrean, ethereal, hallowed, heavenly, seraphic **9** planetary, unearthly **12** astronomical, otherworldly, paradisiacal

celestial being 3 god **5** angel, deity **7** goddess **8** divinity **11** divine being

Celestial City
  place in: **16** Pilgrim's Progress
  author: **6** Bunyan

Celia (Aliena)
  character in: **11** As You Like It
  author: **11** Shakespeare

celibacy 6 purity **8** chastity **9** virginity **10** abstinence, continence **12** bachelorhood, spinsterhood

celibate 4 pure **5** unwed **6** chaste, single **8** bachelor, spinster, virginal **9** abstinent, continent, unmarried

Celine, Louis-Ferdinand
  author of: **12** Guignol's Band **25** Death on the Installment Plan, Journey to the End of the Night

cell
  part: **7** nucleus **8** membrane **9** cytoplasm
  made of: **3** fat **4** salt **5** water **7** protein **9** compounds **12** carbohydrate
  theory of: **7** (Rudolf) Virchow, (Theodor) Schwann

cellar 3 den **4** cave **6** dugout **8** base-

ment **10** downstairs **14** wine collection

Cellini, Benvenuto
  born: **5** Italy **8** Florence
  artwork: **7** Cosimo I, Perseus **13** Bindo Altoviti **18** The Crucified Christ **20** Nymph of Fontainebleau
  autobiography: **22** Life of Benvenuto Cellini

Celsius
  abbreviation of: **1** C

Celt 4 Gaul, Kelt, Manx, Pict, Scot **5** Irish, Welsh **6** Breton, Briton, chisel **8** Scottish **10** Highlander

Celtic 4 Erse
  language group: **6** Gaelic **9** Brythonic
  family: **12** Indo-European
  language of: **5** Gauls

cement 3 fix, set **4** bind, fuse, glue, join, seal, weld **5** paste, stick, unite **6** mortar, secure **8** concrete

cemetery 7 ossuary **8** boneyard, Boot Hill, catacomb **9** graveyard **10** churchyard, necropolis **12** burial ground, memorial park, potter's field **13** burying ground

Cenci, The
  author: **18** Percy Bysshe Shelley

cenobite 4 monk **7** ascetic **8** celibate **9** religious

censor 4 blip, edit **5** amend, bleep, judge, purge **6** critic, delete, excise **7** amender, Bowdler, clean up **8** black out, examiner, reviewer, suppress **9** expurgate, inspector **10** blue-pencil, bowdlerize, expurgator, suppressor **11** bowdlerizer, faultfinder, scrutinizer **12** investigator **17** custodian of morals **25** guardian of the public morals

censorious 5 picky **7** abusive, carping **8** critical **10** defamatory **12** faultfinding

censurable 8 blamable **10** deplorable, punishable, reprovable **11** blameworthy **12** reproachable **13** reprehensible

censure 3 pan, rap **5** chide, scold **6** berate, rebuke **7** bawl out, chew out, chiding, condemn, reproof, reprove, upbraid **8** admonish, denounce, reproach, scolding **9** castigate, complaint, criticism, criticize, reprehend, reprimand **10** admonition, bawling-out, chewing-out, disapprove, upbraiding **11** castigation, disapproval, reprobation **12** condemnation, dressing-down, remonstrance **13** tonguelashing **14** disapprobation **16** rap on the knuckles, take over the coals
  god of: **5** Momos, Momus

census 3 tax **4** data, list, poll **5** count **6** amount, number **11** enumeration **12** registration

Centaur
  form: **3** man **5** horse **7** monster **16** half-man half-horse
  constellation of: **9** Centaurus

famous: 6 Chiron
represents: 11 Sagittarius
Centennial
  author: 13 James Michener
Centennial State
  nickname of: 8 Colorado
center, centre 3 fix, hub, mid **4** axis, core, crux **5** focus, heart, pivot, point **6** direct, gather, middle **7** address, essence, nucleus **8** converge, interior **9** middle **10** focal point **11** concentrate
centered 4 even, true **5** right **7** focused **8** straight **10** pinpointed **12** concentrated
centigrade 5 scale **6** degree **7** celcius **11** thermometer
centigram
  abbreviation of: 2 cg
centiliter
  abbreviation of: 2 cl
centimeter
  abbreviation of: 2 cm
centipede 4 boat **5** shrub **6** earwig, insect **8** chilopod, multiped **9** arthropod **13** muehlenbeckia
central 3 key **4** core, main **5** basic, chief, focal, inner, major, prime **6** inmost, middle **7** leading, midmost, pivotal, primary **8** dominant, foremost, interior **9** essential, paramount, principal **10** middlemost **11** fundamental, predominant **13** most important
Central African Republic
  other name: 11 Ubangi-Chari **20** Central African Empire
  capital/largest city: 6 Bangui
  others: 3 Obo **4** Bria, Ippy **5** Birao, Bouar, Kembe, Ndele, Ngoto, Paoua, Rafai, Zemio **6** Baboua, Bakala, Bozoum, Mbaiki **7** Bambari, Grimari, Zemongo **9** Bangassou, Berberati, Bossangoa, Fort-Sibut
  monetary unit: 5 franc **7** centime
  lake: 4 Chad
  mountain: 5 Karre, Tinga **6** Mongos **9** Dar Challa
  highest point: 11 Kayagangiri
  river: 4 Bomu, Nana **5** Chari, Kotto, Mbari, Mpoko, Ouaka **6** Chinko, Lobaye, Mbomou, Ubangi **11** Upper Sangha
  people: 4 Baya, Sara **5** Banda, Bwaka, Sango **6** Azande, Yakoma **7** Banziri, Mandjia, Nzakara
  language: 5 Sango, Zande **6** French
  religion: 5 Islam **7** animism **12** Christianity **13** Roman Catholic
  place:
    plaza: 13 Edouard Renard
  food:
    tapioca: 6 manioc **7** cassava
Central America
  land form: 7 isthmus
  countries: 6 Belize, Panama **8** Honduras **9** Costa Rica, Guatemala, Nicaragua **10** El Salvador
  bordered by: 6 Mexico, **8** Colombia

12 Caribbean Sea, North America, Pacific Ocean, South America
  capital city: 7 Managua, San Jose **8** Belmopan **10** Panama City **11** San Salvador, Tegucigalpa **13** Guatemala City
  river: 3 New **4** Axul, Coco, Sico, Tuma, Ulua, Wawa **5** Aguan, Chepo, Hondo, Lempa, Wauks **6** Chixoy, Grande, Pasion, Patuca, Sulaco, Waspuk **7** Motagua, Paulaya, San Juan, Sarstun, Segovia **8** Kukalaya **9** Choluteca, Escondido **10** Chucunague **11** Prinzapolca
  lake: 5 Gatun, Guija, Yojoa **7** Atitlan, Managua **9** Nicaragua, Peten Itza
  mountain: 4 Maya, Pija **5** Colon, Huapi, Minas, Pando **6** Dipilto, Gongora, San Blas **8** Brewster, Dar	iense, Isabelia, San Pablo, Santa Ana **9** Esperanza **14** Chirripo Grande
  people: 3 Mam **5** Zambo **6** Indian, Ladino, Quiche **7** mestizo **8** Miskitas **10** Black Carib, Cakchiquel
  animal: 5 tapir **6** agouti **7** opossum, peccary **8** anteater, kinkajou, marmoset **9** armadillo, porcupine, tree sloth **12** howler monkey, spider monkey **14** capuchin monkey
Central Amerind
  language branch: 9 Oto-Mangue **10** Uto-Aztecan **11** Kiowa-Tanoan
central city 8 core city, downtown **9** inner city, urban area **10** metropolis **16** business district, metropolitan area
central idea 3 nut **4** core, crux, gist, meat **5** heart, theme **6** kernel **7** essence **9** main point
centralization 5 focus **11** convergence **13** concentration, consolidation
centralize 5 focus, unify **6** center, gather **7** collect, compact **8** center on, coalesce, converge, pinpoint **9** integrate **10** congregate **11** concentrate, consolidate
central part 4 core, crux, gist, pith **5** heart **6** center, kernel **7** nucleus
century
  abbreviation of: 4 cent
  French: 6 siecle
cephalopod 5 squid **7** mollusk, octopus **8** nautilus **10** cuttlefish
ceramic ware 5 china, glass **7** pottery **8** crockery **9** chinaware, glassware, porcelain, stoneware **10** enamelware **11** earthenware
ceratopsid
  type of: 8 dinosaur
  member: 10 Torosaurus **11** Monoclonius, Triceratops **13** Protoceratops, Styracosaurus **14** Psittacosaurus
Ceratosaurus
  type: 8 dinosaur
  period: 8 Jurassic
Cerberus
  form: 3 dog

  father: 6 Typhon
  mother: 7 Echidna
  sibling: 5 Hydra **7** Orthrus **8** Chimaera **10** Nemean lion **12** Theban Sphinx
  number of heads: 5 three
  guarded: 10 Underworld
Cercopes
  race of: 6 Gnomes
cereal 4 bran, corn, oats, rice, seed **5** grain, grass, gruel, plant, wheat **6** barley, pablum **7** oatmeal, pabulum **8** porridge
cerebellum
  part of: 5 brain
  controls: 7 balance **8** movement
cerebrum
  part of: 5 brain
  controls: 6 seeing **7** hearing, tasting **8** deciding, feelings, learning, smelling, thinking, touching **9** awareness **11** remembering
ceremonial 4 rite **6** formal, ritual **7** liturgy, service **8** ceremony **9** formality, sacrament **10** liturgical, observance **11** celebration, ritualistic
ceremonialize 7 observe **9** celebrate, ritualize **11** commemorate
ceremonious 5 exact, fussy, rigid, stiff **6** formal, proper, solemn **7** careful, correct, pompous, precise **8** starched **9** dignified **10** methodical, meticulous **11** punctilious
ceremony 4 rite **6** custom, nicety, ritual **7** amenity, decorum, pageant, service **8** function, protocol **9** etiquette, formality, propriety **10** observance, politeness **11** celebration, formalities **13** commemoration
Cerenkov, Pavel Alekseevich
  field: 7 physics
  nationality: 7 Russian
  discovered: 12 cause of light **14** Cerenkov effect
Ceres
  origin: 5 Roman
  goddess of: 11 agriculture
  corresponds to: 7 Demeter
certain 4 sure **5** valid **6** secure **7** assured, express, settled, special **8** absolute, cocksure, definite, positive, reliable, specific **9** confident, convinced, satisfied **10** conclusive, individual, inevitable, particular, undeniable, undisputed, undoubtful, undoubting, unshakable **11** indubitable, inescapable, irrefutable, unalterable, unequivocal, unqualified **12** indisputable, unchangeable, unmistakable, wellgrounded **13** bound to happen, incontestable **14** unquestionable **16** incontrovertible
certainly 5 truly **6** indeed, surely **7** for sure **8** of course **9** decidedly **10** absolutely, definitely, positively **11** indubitably, undoubtedly **13** unequivocally,

without a doubt **14** unquestionably **21** beyond a shadow of a doubt

Certain Smile, A
  author: 14 Francoise Sagan

certainty 4 fact **5** faith, trust **6** belief, surety **7** reality, sure bet **8** sureness **9** actuality, assurance, certitude, sure thing **10** confidence, conviction **11** presumption **12** positiveness **13** inevitability **14** conclusiveness, inescapability **17** authoritativeness

certificate 4 deed **6** permit **7** diploma, license, voucher **8** document, warranty **9** affidavit **10** credential **11** testimonial **13** authorization **14** authentication

certification 7 voucher **8** approval **10** validation **11** endorsement **12** confirmation, ratification, verification **13** authorization, corroboration **14** authentication, substantiation

certify 4 aver **5** swear, vouch **6** assure, attest, ratify, second, verify **7** confirm, declare, endorse, support, warrant, witness **8** notarize, sanction, validate **9** authorize, guarantee, testify to **10** underwrite **11** corroborate **12** authenticate, give one's word, substantiate

certitude 5 faith, trust **6** belief, surety **8** reliance, sureness **9** assurance, certainty **10** confidence **12** positiveness **14** conclusiveness

cerulean 4 blue **5** azure **6** cobalt **7** sky blue **9** clear blue

Cervantes Saavedra, Miguel de
  author of: 20 Don Quixote de la Mancha

Cesar Birotteau
  author: 14 Honore de Balzac

cessation 3 end **4** halt, stay, stop **5** pause **6** ending, recess **7** ceasing, halting, respite **8** quitting, stopping, surcease **9** desisting **10** concluding, leaving off, suspension **11** adjournment, breaking off, termination **12** interruption **13** coming to a halt, discontinuing **14** discontinuance

c'est la vie 9 that's life **10** such is life

Cestus
  girdle of: 5 Venus

cetacean 4 apod, orca **5** whale **6** beluga, mammal **7** cetacea, dolphin, dowfish, grampus, narwhal **8** porpoise, sturgeon **9** blue whale **11** baleen whale, killer whale

Cetinje
  capital of: 10 Montenegro

Ceylon *see* **8** Sri Lanka

Cezanne, Paul
  born: 6 France **13** Aix-en-Provence
  artwork: 7 Bathers **11** Card Players **13** The Black Clock, The Railway Out **14** Uncle Dominique **15** La Maison du Pendu **16** The Suicide's House **17** Grandes Baigneuses **19**

Woman with a Coffee Pot **36** Mont-Sainte-Victoire with Large Pine Trees

Chabrier, (Alexis) Emmanuel
  born: 6 Ambert, France
  composer of: 6 Espana **7** L'Etoile **10** Gwendoline **13** Marche Joyeuse **14** Le Roi Malgre Lui **18** King Despite Himself **19** Une Education Manquee

Chad
  other name: 5 Tchad
  capital/largest city: 8 Fort-Lamy, N'Djamena
  others: 3 Ati, Bol, Lai, Mao **4** Fada, Faya, Sarh **5** Mongo **6** Abeche, Bongor **7** Largeau, Moundou **8** Moussoro
  monetary unit: 5 franc **7** centime
  lake: 4 Chad
  mountain: 7 Tibesti, Touside
  highest point: 9 Emi Koussi
  river: 5 Chari **6** Logone **8** Bahraouk
  physical feature:
    plateau: 6 Ennedi
  people: 4 Arab, Daza, Maba, Sara, Teda, Tubu **5** Barma, Hakka, Kreda, Massa **6** Fulani, Kotoko, Toubou, Wadaii **7** Kamadja, Kanembu, Moundan
  language: 4 Sara **5** Turku **6** Arabic, French
  religion: 5 Islam **7** animism **12** Christianity

Chadband
  character in: 10 Bleak House
  author: 7 Dickens

Chadic
  language family: 11 Afroasiatic **13** Hamito-Semitic
  includes: 5 Hausa
  spoken in: 6 Africa **8** Lake Chad

Chadwick, James
  field: 7 physics
  nationality: 7 British
  discovered: 7 neutron
  awarded: 10 Nobel Prize

chafe 3 rub **4** boil, burn, foam, fume, rage, rasp **6** abrade, rankle, scrape, seethe **7** scratch **9** be annoyed **11** be irritated

chaff 3 bug, kid, rag, rib **4** josh, junk, pods, razz, ride, slag, twit **5** dross, hulls, husks, jolly, trash, waste **6** banter, debris, litter, refuse, rubble, shells, shoddy, shucks **7** kidding, ragging, remnant, residue, ribbing, rubbish, waggery **8** badinage, chaffing, leavings, raillery, ridicule **9** sweepings **9** give and take

chaffing 6 banter **7** jesting, joshing, kidding, ragging, ribbing, waggery **8** badinage, raillery

chafing 5 harsh **6** fuming **7** rasping, rubbing **8** abrading, abrasive **10** irritating

Chagall, Marc
  born: 6 Liosno, Liozno, Russia
  artwork: 8 Birthday, Cockcrow **9** The Circus, The Red Sun **10** The Juggler

11 Over Vitebsk **12** The Violinist **14** Double Portrait, I and the Village **16** The Jewish Wedding **17** Lovers with Rooster **20** Paris Through My Window

chagrin 5 shame **6** dismay **8** distress **11** humiliation **13** embarrassment, mortification

chagrined 7 abashed, ashamed **9** mortified **10** humiliated **11** embarrassed

Chahiksichhiks *see* **6** Pawnee

chain 3 fob **5** cable, links **7** shackle **8** necklace **10** metal links **11** linked cable
  abbreviation: 2 ch

Chain, Ernst Boris
  field: 12 biochemistry
  nationality: 7 British
  discovered: 10 penicillin
  worked with: 6 Florey **7** Fleming
  awarded: 10 Nobel Prize

Chained Lady
  constellation of: 9 Andromeda

chains 3 tie **4** bind, lash, moor **5** bonds, irons, tie up, train **6** fasten, fetter, secure, series, string, tether **7** bondage, fetters, manacle, serfdom, shackle, slavery **8** leg irons, manacles, sequence, shackles **9** handcuffs, servitude, thralldom **10** put in irons, succession **11** enslavement, subjugation

chair 4 seat **5** bench, couch, sedan stool **6** chaise, lounge, rocker, settee, throne **7** conduct, ottoman **11** preside over **16** presiding officer

chairman 4 head **5** chair, emcee **6** leader **7** manager, preside, speaker **8** director **9** chairlady, executive, moderator **10** chairwoman, supervisor **11** chairperson, toastmaster **13** administrator **16** presiding officer **18** master of ceremonies

Chair of Forgetfulness
  form: 4 seat
  made of: 5 stone
  location: 10 Underworld

chaise 3 gig **4** shay **5** chair **6** daybed, longue, lounge **7** calesin **8** carriage, duchesse

chalcedony 3 gem **4** onyx, opal, sard **5** agate, prase **6** jasper, plasma, quartz, silica **7** catseye, mineral, opaline, sardius **8** hematite, sardonyx **9** carnelian **10** bloodstone, heliotrope **11** chrysoprase **12** semiprecious **14** silicon dioxide

Chaldean 4 seer **5** magic **6** Syriac **7** Aramaic, semitic **8** magician **9** astrology, enchanter, Nabonidus **10** astrologer, Babylonian, soothsayer **12** Nabopolassar **14** Nebuchadnezzar

chalice 3 cup **5** grail **6** goblet, vessel

chalk 4 draw **6** crayon, pastel, sketch **9** limestone

chalk up 4 earn **5** score **6** attain, charge, credit **7** achieve, ascribe

chalky 3 wan **4** pale **5** ashen, white **6** pallid **7** powdery **8** blanched **9** bloodless

challenge 3 bid, tax, try **4** dare, defy, gage, test **5** doubt, trial **6** demand, impute, summon **7** defiant, dispute, summons **8** question **15** take exception to **20** fling down the gauntlet

chamber 4 diet, hall, room **5** board, court, house, salon **6** office, parlor **7** bedroom, boudoir, council **8** assembly, congress **9** apartment

Chamberlain, Owen
    field: 7 physics
    developed: 8 atom bomb
    awarded: 10 Nobel Prize

Chamberlain, Richard
    real name: 24 George Richard Chamberlain
    born: 12 Los Angeles CA
    roles: 6 Shogun **9** Dr Kildare **10** Wallenberg **13** The Thorn Birds **17** The Bourne Identity **21** The Count of Monte Cristo

Chamberlain, Wilt (Wilton Norman)
    nickname: 6 Dipper **12** Wilt the Stilt
    sport: 10 basketball
    position: 5 coach **6** center
    team: 16 Los Angeles Lakers **17** Philadelphia 76ers **20** Philadelphia Warriors, San Francisco Warriors **21** San Diego Conquistadors

chambermaid
    French: 14 femme de chambre

chambord
    type: 7 liqueur
    origin: 6 France
    flavor: 14 black raspberry

chameleon 4 newt **6** lizard **8** renegade, turncoat **10** fickleness **14** changeableness

champ 4 bite, chew, gnaw **5** chomp, crush, grind, munch **6** crunch **8** champion

champagne 4 fizz **6** bubbly
    type: 4 wine
    drink: 7 the Pope
    with white wine: 8 Cold Duck
    with orange juice: 6 Mimosa
    measure: 6 magnum **8** jeroboam, rehoboam **9** balthazar **10** methuselah, salmanazar **14** Nebuchadnezzar

Champaigne, Philippe de
    born: 7 Belgium **8** Brussels
    artwork: 6 Ex Voto **17** Cardinal Richelieu **26** The Adoration of the Shepherds

champion 3 aid **4** abet, back **6** backer, defend, master, uphold, victor, winner **7** espouse, paladin, paragon, promote, support **8** advocate, defender, fight for, laureate, promoter, speak for, upholder **9** battle for, conqueror, protector, supporter **10** stand up for, vanquisher **11** protagonist, title holder

Champion
    constellation of: 7 Perseus

championship 3 cup **5** crown, title **7** backing, defense, support, winning **8** advocacy, espousal

Chan, Charlie
    creator: 15 Earl Derr Biggers
    actors: 7 E. L. Parks **10** George Kuwa **11** Warner Oland, Sidney Toler **13** Roland Winters, Kamiyama Sojin
    films: 7 The Trap **8** Jade Mask **11** Dead Men Tell **13** Shanghai Cobra, The Chinese Cat, The Black Camel **16** House Without a Key **17** Castle in the Desert, Behind that Curtain

chance 3 try **4** fall, fate, luck, risk **5** lucky, occur **6** befall, danger, gamble, happen, hazard, random **7** attempt, destiny, fortune, turn out, venture **8** accident, jeopardy, occasion **9** come about, fortunate, unplanned **10** accidental, fortuitous, likelihood, likeliness, providence, undesigned, unexpected, unforeseen **11** opportunity, possibility, probability, speculation, unlooked for **12** happenstance **13** unintentional **14** unpremeditated

chance upon 4 find, meet **7** learn of, run into **8** come upon, discover **9** encounter, light upon **10** happen upon **11** stumble upon

chancy 4 iffy **5** dicey, risky **6** touchy, tricky **7** dubious, erratic, unsound **8** doubtful **9** hazardous, uncertain, whimsical **10** capricious, precarious **11** speculative, venturesome **13** problematical, unpredictable

chandelier 11 hanging lamp **12** candleholder **15** lighting fixture

Chandler, Jeff
    real name: 10 Ira Grossel
    born: 10 Brooklyn NY
    roles: 7 Cochise **11** Broken Arrow **17** Merrill's Marauders

Chandler, Raymond
    author of: 11 The Big Sleep **14** The Long Goodbye **16** Farewell My Lovely
    born: 7 England
    character: 13 Philip Marlowe
    screenplay: 13 The Blue Dahlia **15** Double Indemnity **17** Strangers on a Train

Chaney, Lon
    real name: 12 Alonso Chaney
    son: 9 Creighton (Lon Chaney Jr)
    nickname: 19 Man of a Thousand Faces
    born: 17 Colorado Springs CO
    roles: 14 The Unholy Three **18** Tell It to the Marines **20** Hunchback of Notre Dame, The Phantom of the Opera

Chaney, Lon Jr
    real name: 9 Creighton
    father: 3 Lon
    born: 14 Oklahoma City OK

    roles: 6 Lennie **8** The Mummy **10** The Wolf Man **12** Of Mice and Men, Son of Dracula **20** Frankenstein's Monster

change 4 swap, turn, vary **5** alter, coins, shift, trade **6** modify, mutate, recast, reform, silver, switch **7** convert, novelty, remodel, replace, restyle, shuffle, variety, veering **8** pin money, swapping, transfer **9** deviation, diversion, exception, restyling, transform, transmute, turn about, variation **10** alteration, conversion, difference, remodeling, reorganize, revolution, small coins, substitute **11** fluctuation, pocket money, reformation **12** metamorphose, modification, substitution, transmogrify **13** make different, metamorphosis, revolutionize, transmutation, transposition **14** reorganization, transformation **15** transfiguration

changeable 6 fickle, fitful **7** erratic, flighty, mutable, varying **8** unstable, unsteady, variable, volatile **9** deviating, irregular, mercurial, uncertain **10** capricious, inconstant, modifiable, reversible **11** alternating, convertible, fluctuating, vacillating **13** transformable

change in plan
    French: 8 demarche

changeless 4 fast **5** fixed **6** stable **7** abiding, certain, durable, eternal, lasting **8** constant, enduring **9** immutable, steadfast, unvarying **10** unshakable **11** everlasting, unalterable **12** indissoluble

changelessness 9 certainty, constancy, stability **10** durability, permanence **12** immutability **13** steadfastness

change of heart 10 conversion **16** change of attitude

changeover 10 conversion

channel 3 cut **4** gash, lead, send **5** guide, route, steer **6** convey, course, direct, furrow, groove, gutter, strait, trough **7** narrows, passage **11** watercourse **21** avenue of communication

Channing, Carol
    born: 9 Seattle WA
    roles: 10 Hello Dolly **22** Gentlemen Prefer Blondes, Thoroughly Modern Millie

chanson 4 song

Chanson de Roland
    also: 12 Song of Roland
    author: 7 unknown
    character: 4 Aude **6** Turpin **7** Ganelon, Marsile, Olivier **11** Charlemagne, Twelve Peers
    foe: 8 Saracens
    knight: 7 paladin

chant 2 om **3** ode **4** hymn, lied, sing, song **5** carol, croon, dirge, elegy, psalm, theme, trill, troll **6** chorus, intone, melody, monody, strain **7** chanson, chorale, descant **8** canticle, doxology, threnody, vocalize **9** homophony, monophony, offertory, plainsong **11** Gloria Patri **14** Gregorian chant

chanteuse 6 singer (female)

Chants de Maldoror, Les
 author: 18 Comte de Lautreamont

chaos 4 mess **5** furor **6** bedlam, jumble, muddle, tumult, uproar **7** turmoil **8** disarray, disorder, upheaval **9** agitation, commotion, confusion **10** turbulence **11** pandemonium **12** discomposure **14** disarrangement **15** disorganization

Chaos
 origin: 5 Greek
 personifies: 9 confusion

chaotic 7 jumbled, mixed-up, muddled, tangled **8** confused **9** confusing, illogical, turbulent **10** disjointed, incoherent, in disarray **11** unorganized **12** disorganized **13** disharmonious

chap 3 boy, dry, guy, jaw, lad, man, rap **4** chop, gent **5** bloke, buyer, crack, knock, split **6** fellow, redden, split, stroke **7** fissure, roughen **8** customer **9** purchaser

chapbook 7 garland **8** treasury **9** anthology **10** collection **11** florilegium

chapeau 3 hat

chapel 6 church, shrine **7** oratory **9** sanctuary **10** house of God, tabernacle **14** place of worship

chaperon, chaperone 5 guard, watch **6** duenna, escort **7** oversee **8** guardian, shepherd **9** accompany, attendant, custodian, protector, safeguard **11** keep an eye on

chaperoned 7 oversaw **8** attended, escorted **10** supervised **11** accompanied

chapfallen 6 droopy **8** cast down, dejected **9** depressed

chaplain 4 abbe **5** padre, rabbi, vicar **6** cleric, curate, father, parson, pastor, priest, rector **7** Holy Joe **8** minister, preacher, reverend, sky pilot **9** churchman, clergyman **12** ecclesiastic

chaplet 4 band **6** fillet, wreath **7** circlet, coronet

Chaplin, Charlie
 real name: 24 Sir Charles Spencer Chaplin
 nickname: 14 the Little Tramp
 wife: 10 Oona O'Neill **15** Paulette Goddard
 daughter: 9 Geraldine
 born: 6 London **7** England
 director of/roles: 6 The Kid **8** The Tramp **9** Limelight **10** City Lights **11** Modern Times, The Gold Rush **15** Monsieur Verdoux **16** The Great Dictator

Chaplin, Geraldine
 father: 14 Charlie Chaplin

 mother: 17 Oona O'Neill Chaplin
 born: 13 Santa Monica CA
 roles: 12 The Hawaiians **13** Doctor Zhivago

chapter 3 era **4** body, part, span, unit **5** group, phase **6** branch, clause, period **7** episode, portion, section **8** division **9** affiliate **11** subdivision

Chapters of Erie
 author: 10 Henry Adams

char 4 burn, sear **5** singe **6** scorch **9** carbonize **10** incinerate

character 4 part, role, self **5** being, honor **6** makeup, nature, person, traits, weirdo **7** honesty, oddball, persona **8** goodness, morality, original, specimen **9** eccentric, integrity, odd person, qualities, rectitude **10** attributes, individual, one-of-a-kind **11** personality, uprightness **13** individuality, moral strength **15** distinctiveness **16** dramatis personae

characteristic 4 mark **5** trait **6** aspect **7** earmark, feature, quality, typical **8** property, symbolic **9** attribute, mannerism, specialty, trademark **10** emblematic, indicative **11** distinctive, peculiarity **14** distinguishing, representative

characterization 8 portrait **9** depiction, picturing, portrayal **11** delineation, description **12** representing **14** representation

characterize 4 mark **5** class **6** define, depict, typify **7** earmark, portray **8** classify, describe, indicate **9** designate, represent **11** distinguish

characterless 4 weak **5** vague **6** anemic **11** nondescript **13** indeterminate **14** expressionless

Characters of Shakespeare's Plays, The
 author: 14 William Hazlitt

Charcot, Jean Martin
 nationality: 6 French
 father of: 9 neurology

Chardin, Jean Baptiste Simeon
 born: 5 Paris **6** France
 artwork: 7 The Kiss **8** The Grace **14** Young Governess **16** The Copper Cistern **17** Attributes of Music **19** Attributes of the Arts **28** Rayfish Cat and Kitchen Utensils

charge 3 ask, bid, fee **4** care, cost, duty, fill, heap, lade, levy, load, pack, pile, rate, rush, toll **5** beset, blame, debit, exact, onset, order, price, stack, storm, stuff **6** accuse, advice, amount, assail, assess, assign, attack, come at, demand, direct, enjoin, impute, indict, sortie, summon **7** ascribe, assault, bidding, command, control, custody, dictate, expense, keeping, payment, require **8** call upon, instruct, storming **9** attribute, complaint, direction, enjoining, onslaught **10** accusation, allegation, assessment, indictment, in-

junction, management, protection **11** arraignment, incriminate, instruction, safekeeping, supervision **12** delay payment, guardianship, jurisdiction **14** administration, lay the blame for, request payment **15** superintendence **16** put on one's account

chargeable 6 liable **10** answerable **11** responsible

charged 5 taxed, tense **6** blamed, filled, levied, loaded, priced **7** accused, ordered, uptight **8** assessed, attacked, exhorted, mandated, prepared **9** commanded, entrusted **10** accusation, allegation, indictment

Charge of the Light Brigade, The
 author: 18 Alfred Lord Tennyson
 director: 13 Michael Curtiz
 cast: 10 David Niven, Errol Flynn, Nigel Bruce **11** Donald Crisp **13** Patric Knowles **15** Henry Stephenson **17** Olivia de Havilland
 setting: 6 Russia

charger 5 horse, mount, steed **6** vessel **7** accuser, platter **8** warhorse

charge with 5 trust **6** assign, commit **7** consign, entrust **8** delegate, hand over, turn over **9** authorize

chariot 3 car **5** buggy **7** phaeton, vehicle **8** carriage

Charioteer
 constellation of: 6 Auriga

Chariots of Fire
 director: 10 Hugh Hudson
 cast: 7 Ian Holm **8** Ben Cross (Harold Abrahams) **11** John Gielgud, Nigel Havers **12** Ian Charleson (Eric Liddell)
 Oscar for: 5 score (Vangelis) **6** script **7** picture

charisma 5 charm **6** allure, appeal **7** glamour **8** presence, witchery **9** magnetism, sex appeal **10** bewitchery **11** enchantment, fascination **14** attractiveness

charitable 4 kind **6** giving, kindly **7** lenient, liberal **8** generous, gracious, tolerant **9** bounteous, bountiful, forgiving, indulgent **10** almsgiving, benevolent, munificent, open-handed **11** considerate, kindhearted, magnanimous, sympathetic, warmhearted **12** eleemosynary, sympathizing **13** philanthropic, understanding

charitableness 10 liberality **11** benevolence, generousity **12** philanthropy **13** bountifulness **14** openhandedness **15** humanitarianism

Charites *see* **6** Graces

charity 3 aid **4** alms, fund, gift, help, love **6** bounty, giving **7** handout **8** altruism, donating, good will, goodness, humanity, kindness, offering, sympathy **9** benignity, donations, endowment, tolerance **10** alms-giving, assistance, compassion, generosity **11** benefaction, benevolence, fundraising, munificence **12** graciousness, philanthropy **13** contributions, financial help, love of mankind **14** openhandedness

charlatan 4 fake **5** cheat, fraud, quack **7** cozener **8** deceiver, imposter, impostor, swindler **9** trickster **10** mountebank **16** confidence artist

Charles, Nick and Nora
  characters in: 10 The Thin Man
  author: 7 Hammett
  pet dog 4 Asta

Charles O'Malley
  author: 12 Charles Lever

Charleston 5 dance **13** ballroom dance
  capital of: 9 W Virginia

Charlie's Angels
  character: 10 Jill Monroe, John Bosley, Kris Munroe **12** Kelly Garrett **13** Sabrina Duncan **15** Charlie Townsend
  cast: 10 Cheryl Ladd, David Doyle **11** Jaclyn Smith, Kate Jackson **18** Farah Fawcett-Majors
  voice of Charlie: 12 John Forsythe

Charlotte's Web
  author: 7 E B White
  Charlotte: 6 spider
  saved: 6 Wilbur (piglet)

Charly
  director: 11 Ralph Nelson
  based on story by: 11 Daniel Keyes (Flowers for Algernon)
  cast: 10 Leon Janney, Lilia Skala **11** Claire Bloom **13** Dick van Patten **14** Cliff Robertson
  Oscar for: 5 actor (Robertson)

charm 4 draw, grip, lure, take **5** magic, spell **6** allure, amulet, bauble, cajole, engage, please, seduce, turn on **7** attract, beguile, bewitch, conjure, delight, enchant, gratify, sorcery, trinket, win over **8** charisma, enthrall, entrance, ornament, talisman **9** captivate, enrapture, fascinate, magnetism **10** allurement, attraction, cast a spell, lucky piece **11** conjuration, enchantment, fascination, incantation, work magic on

charmer 4 vamp **5** belle, siren **9** enchanter, temptress **11** enchantress, femme fatale, spellbinder

charming 6 lovely **7** likable, winning, winsome **8** alluring, engaging, enticing, fetching, graceful, magnetic, pleasing **9** agreeable **10** attractive, bewitching, delightful, enchanting, entrancing **11** captivating, charismatic, enthralling, fascinating **12** irresistible

charmless 4 dull **5** blunt **6** dreary **9** repulsive, unlikable, unlovable **10** unpleasant **12** disagreeable, unattractive

Charon
  father: 6 Erebus
  mother: 3 Nyx
  occupation: 8 ferryman
  river: 4 Styx

Charops
  epithet of: 8 Hercules
  means: 14 with bright eyes

Charpentier, Gustave
  born: 6 Dieuze, France
  composer of: 6 Julien, Louise **18** Impressions of Italy

chart 3 map, pie **4** plan, plot **5** draft, graph, table **6** design, draw up, lay out, map out, scheme, sketch **7** diagram, outline **8** tabulate **9** blueprint, delineate **10** tabulation

charter 3 let **4** deed, hire, rent **5** grant, lease **6** employ, engage, permit **7** compact, license **8** contract, covenant, sanction **9** agreement, authority, authorize, franchise **10** commission, concession

Charterhouse of Parma, The
  author: 23 Marie Henri Beyle Stendhal
  character: 8 Marietta **10** Count Mosca **11** Clelia Conti **14** Gina Pietranera **16** Fabrizio del Dongo

chartreuse
  type: 7 liqueur
  origin: 6 France **15** Carthusian monks
  flavor: 4 herb
  color: 5 green **6** yellow
  with apricot brandy: 13 Golden Slipper
  with gin: 5 Bijou **9** Green Lady

chary 3 shy **4** wary **5** alert, cagey, leery **7** careful, guarded, heedful, prudent, sparing **8** cautious, hesitant, vigilant, watchful **10** economical, suspicious **11** circumspect, distrustful

Charybdis
  form: 7 monster
  father: 8 Poseidon
  mother: 4 Gaea
  identified with: 9 whirlpool

chase 3 dog **4** hunt, oust, rout, shoo, tail **5** drive, evict, hound, quest, stalk, track, trail **6** dispel, follow, pursue, shadow **7** cast out, go after, hunting, pursuit, repulse, scatter **8** pursuing, run after, send away, stalking, tracking **9** drive away, following **11** put to flight, send packing

Chase, Chevy
  real name: 19 Cornelius Crane Chase
  born: 9 New York NY
  roles: 4 Hero **6** Fletch **8** Foul Play, Vacation **10** Caddyshack **11** Spies Like Us, Three Amigos **17** Saturday Night Live

chasm 3 gap, pit **4** gulf, hold, rift **5** abyss, break, cleft, crack, gorge, gulch, split **6** breach, cavity, crater, divide, ravine **7** fissure **8** crevasse

chasseur 6 hunter

chaste 4 pure **5** clean **6** decent, modest, severe, strict **7** austere, classic, precise, sinless **8** virginal, virtuous **9** continent, righteous, unadorned, unsullied, untainted, wholesome **10** im-

maculate, restrained **11** clean-living, uncorrupted **12** unornamented **13** unembellished

chasten 5 chide, scold **6** berate, punish, rebuke **7** censure, reprove, upbraid **8** admonish, chastise, reproach **9** reprimand **10** discipline, take to task

chastened 7 humbled **8** contrite, penitent **9** repentant **10** remorseful **18** conscience-stricken

chastise 4 beat, flog, whip **5** chide, roast, scold, spank, strap **6** berate, punish, rebuke, thrash **7** censure, chasten, correct, reprove, scourge, upbraid **8** admonish, call down, penalize, reproach **9** castigate, criticize, reprimand **10** discipline, take to task, tongue-lash **15** call on the carpet **16** fulminate against, haul over the coals

chastisement 10 correction, discipline, punishment **11** castigation **12** reprimanding

chastity 6 purity **8** celibacy **9** innocence, virginity **10** abstinence, continence, singleness **12** bachelorhood, spinsterhood **14** abstemiousness
  goddess of: 5 Diana, Fauna **7** Artemis, Bona Dea

chasuble 6 casual **7** garment **8** vestment

Chasuble, Reverend Canon
  character in: 27 The Importance of Being Earnest
  author: 5 Wilde

chat 3 gab, rap **4** talk **5** prate **7** chatter, palaver, prattle **8** chitchat, converse **10** chew the fat, chew the rag, rap session **11** talk session **12** conversation **13** confabulation **16** heart-to-heart talk

chateau 4 wine **6** castle, estate **7** mansion **8** chatelet **12** country house

Chateaubriand, Francois Rene
  author of: 4 Rene **5** Atala **10** Los Natchez, The Martyrs **19** Memoires d'Outre-tombe **24** Memoirs from Beyond the Tomb

Chateau d'If
  prison in: 21 The Count of Monte Cristo
  author: 5 Dumas (pere)

Chateaupers, Phoebus de
  character in: 23 The Hunchback of Notre Dame
  author: 4 Hugo

chattel 4 gear **6** things **7** effects **8** movables **9** trappings **10** belongings **13** accoutrements, paraphernalia **15** personal effects **19** personal possessions

chatter 3 gas **4** blab, talk **5** clank, click, prate **6** babble, gabble, gibber, gossip, jabber, patter **7** blabber, blather, clatter, palaver, prattle, talking, twaddle **8** blabbing, chitchat, idle talk, talk idly **11** confabulate **14** chitterchatter

chatterbox 6 gabber, gasbag, gossip, talker **7** babbler, tattler, windbag **8** jabberer, prattler, tell tale **9** chatterer **10** talebearer, tattle tale **12** blabbermouth, blatherskite, hot-air artist **13** chatterbasket

chatty 5 gabby, gassy, gushy, talky, windy **7** gossipy, gushing, prating, verbose, voluble **8** babbling, chatting, effusive **9** garrulous, jabbering, talkative **10** blabbering, long-winded, loquacious **11** loose-lipped **12** loose-tongued **13** tongue-wagging

Chaucer, Geoffrey
  author of: 18 The Canterbury Tales, Troilus and Criseyde **19** The Book of the Duchess **20** The Legend of Good Women, The Parlement of Fowles

Chauchoin, Claudette Lily
  real name of: 16 Claudette Colbert

chauffeur 6 driver

chaussure 4 boot, shoe **8** footwear

chauvinism 8 jingoism **10** flag-waving, militarism, patriotism **11** nationalism **15** ethnocentricity, superpatriotism

cheap 4 base, easy, mean, poor **5** close, gaudy, petty, tacky, tight **6** common, flashy, meager, paltry, shabby, shoddy, sordid, stingy, tawdry, trashy, two-bit, vulgar **7** ignoble, immoral, miserly **8** costless, gimcrack, indecent, inferior, wretched **9** inelegant, low-priced, penurious, worthless **10** despicable, economical, effortless, in bad taste, reasonable, second-rate **11** inexpensive, tightfisted **12** contemptible

Cheaper by the Dozen
  author: 14 Frank B Gilbreth (with Ernestine Gilbreth Carey)

cheat 3 con, gyp **4** bilk, dupe, fake, foil, fool, gull, hoax, rook, take **5** cozen, crook, fraud, quack, shark, trick **6** baffle, betray, defeat, delude, dodger, escape, fleece, humbug, outwit, thwart **7** deceive, defraud, mislead, swindle **8** chiseler, deceiver, hoodwink, imposter, impostor, swindler **9** bamboozle, charlatan, con artist, frustrate, trickster, victimize **10** circumvent, mountebank **11** shortchange **13** break the rules, double-crosser

check 3 bar, end, fit, gag, tab **4** curb, halt, hold, jibe, mesh, rein, slow, stay, stop, test **5** agree, block, brake, chime, choke, limit, probe, stall, study, tally **6** arrest, bridle, impede, look at, muzzle, peruse, rein in, retard, review, search, survey, thwart **7** barrier, conform, control, examine, explore, harness, inhibit, inspect, perusal, prevent, smother **8** hold back, look into, look over, obstacle, obstruct, restrain, scrutiny, stoppage,

suppress **9** cessation, constrain, frustrate, harmonize, hindrance, restraint **10** circumvent, constraint, correspond, impediment, inspection, limitation, prevention, repression, scrutinize **11** examination, exploration, investigate, obstruction, prohibition, restriction, take stock of **13** investigation **18** bring to a standstill

checkered 4 pied **6** fitful, motley, seesaw, uneven, varied **7** checked, dappled, mottled, piebald **9** irregular, up-and-down **10** inconstant, variegated **11** fluctuating, vacillating **12** particolored

checkmate 4 rout, stop **6** corner, defeat, outwit, stymie, thwart **8** chess win, deadlock **9** frustrate, overthrow **11** countermove

cheder, heder 12 Jewish school

cheek 4 jowl **5** brass, nerve **8** audacity, boldness, temerity **9** arrogance, brashness, impudence, insolence **10** brazenness, effrontery **11** forwardness **12** impertinence

cheep 4 peep **5** chirp, tweet **7** chirrup, chitter, twitter

cheer 3 cry, fun, joy, ole, rah **4** glee, hail, hope, root, warm, yell **5** bravo, shout **6** assure, buoy up, gaiety, hooray, hurrah, huzzah, shriek, uplift **7** acclaim, animate, comfort, delight, enliven, fortify, gladden, hearten, inspire, revelry **8** brighten, buoyance, buoyancy, gladness, optimism, pleasure, reassure, vivacity **9** animation, assurance, encourage, festivity, geniality, joviality, merriment, rejoicing **10** joyfulness, jubilation, liveliness **11** acclamation, high spirits, hopefulness, merrymaking, reassurance **13** encouragement

cheerful 3 gay **4** airy, glad **5** happy, jolly, merry, sunny **6** blithe, breezy, bright, cheery, elated, jaunty, jovial, joyful, joyous, lively **7** buoyant, gleeful **8** gladsome, pleasant **9** agreeable, sparkling, sprightly **10** optimistic **11** in high humor **12** high-spirited, lighthearted

cheerfulness 5 gaity **7** jollity **8** buoyancy, optimism **9** joviality, merriment **10** brightness, cheeriness **11** high spirits **16** lightheartedness

cheerless 3 sad **4** dull, glum, gray, grim **5** bleak **6** dismal, dreary, gloomy, morose, rueful, solemn, somber, sullen, woeful **7** austere, doleful, forlorn, joyless, sunless, unhappy **8** dejected, desolate, dolorous, downcast, funereal, mournful **9** miserable, saturnine, woebegone **10** depressing, despondent, dispirited, lugubrious, melancholy, spiritless, uninviting **11** comfortless, downhearted **12** disconsolate, heavy-hearted

Cheers

location: 3 bar **6** Boston
character: 4 Norm **5** Cliff, Coach, Woody **5** Lilith **7** Rebecca **9** Sam Malone **13** Carla Tortelli, Diane Chambers
cast: 9 Ted Danson **11** George Wendt, Rhea Perlman, Shelley Long **12** Kirstie Alley **13** Kelsey Grammer **14** Woody Harrelson **16** John Ratzenberger

cheer up 5 elate, pep up **6** buoy up **7** comfort, enliven, hearten **8** brighten, inspirit **9** bolster up, encourage **18** bolster one's spirits

cheery 3 gay **5** happy, jolly, merry, sunny **6** bright, joyful **9** sprightly **12** lighthearted

Cheeryble Brothers
  nephew: 5 Frank
  characters in: 16 Nicholas Nickleby
  author: 7 Dickens

cheese
  French: 7 fromage
  kind: 4 bleu, blue, brie, edam, feta, jack **5** brick, colby, cream, gouda, Swiss **6** romano, samsoe **7** cheddar, cottage, fontina, gjetost, gruyere, limburg, munster, ricotta, sapsago, stilton **8** American, bel paese, cheshire, emmental, muenster, parmesan, port wine, raclette **9** camembert, jarlsberg, limburger, port salut, provolone, roquefort **10** caerphilly, Danish blue, Gloucester, gorgonzola, mozzarella, neufchatel **11** emmenthaler, liederkranz, petit suisse, port du salut, wensleydale **12** monterey jack

Cheever, John
  author of: 8 Falconer **10** Bullet Park **16** The Enormous Radio, The World of Apples **17** The Wapshot Scandal **19** The Wapshot Chronicle **20** The Way Some People Live **22** Oh What a Paradise It Seems

Chekhov, Anton
  author of: 6 Ivanov **10** The Sea Gull, Uncle Vanya **15** The Three Sisters **16** The Cherry Orchard

chemical compound 4 acid, base, enol **5** amide, amine, ester, imide **6** isomar, ketone **8** aldehyde

chemical symbols
  actinium: 2 Ac
  aluminum: 2 Al
  antimony: 2 Sb
  argon: 2 Ar
  arsenic: 2 As
  barium: 2 Ba
  boron: 1 B
  bromine: 2 Br
  cadmium: 2 Cd
  calcium: 2 Ca
  carbon: 1 C
  chlorine: 2 Cl
  chromium: 2 Cr
  cobalt: 2 Co
  columbium: 2 Cb

copper: 2 Cu
fluorine: 1 F
gold: 2 Au
hafnium: 2 Hf
helium: 2 He
hydrogen: 1 H
iodine: 1 I
iron: 2 Fe
krypton: 2 Kr
lead: 2 Pb
lithium: 2 Li
magnesium: 2 Mg
manganese: 2 Mn
mercury: 2 Hg
molybdenum: 2 Mo
neon: 2 Ne
nickel: 2 Ni
nitrogen: 1 N
oxygen: 1 O
phosphorus: 1 P
platinum: 2 Pt
plutonium: 2 Pu
potassium: 1 K
radium: 2 Ra
radon: 2 Rn
rhodium: 2 Rh
rubidium: 2 Rb
silicon: 2 Si
silver: 2 Ag
sodium: 2 Na
sulfur: 1 S
thorium: 2 Th
tin: 2 Sn
titanium: 2 Ti
tungsten: 1 W
uranium: 1 U
xenon: 2 Xe
zinc: 2 Zn
zirconium: 2 Zr
chemise 4 slip **5** dress, shift, shirt, smock **6** blouse **7** garment **8** camisole, lingerie, unbelted **12** undergarment
chemist
  American: 4 Urey **5** Tatum **6** Carver **7** Axelrod, Lipmann, Pauling **8** Kornberg, Langmuir, McMillan **9** Carothers **10** Baekleland
  British: 4 Davy **5** Boyle, Chain, Soddy **6** Dalton, Ramsay **7** Faraday **8** Smithson **9** Cavendish, Priestley, Wollaston
  Dutch: 4 Hoff
  French: 5 Curie, Le Bel **6** Cuvier, Dulong **7** Pasteur **9** Gay-Lussac, Lavoisier **10** Berthollet **11** Joliot-Curie
  German: 4 Hahn **5** Krebs **6** Baeyer, Wohler **7** Glauber, Ostwald
  Italian: 8 Avogadro
  Russian: 9 Mendeleev **10** Mendeleyev
  Scottish: 5 Dewar
  Swedish: 7 Scheele **9** Arrhenius, Berzelius
  Swiss: 6 Muller
Chemosh 10 Moabite god
Chennault, Claire L
  served in: 4 WWII **15** Sino-Japanese War

  commander of: 12 Flying Tigers
  general in: 12 Army Air Force
  air advisor to: 13 Chiang Kai-shek
cherchez la femme 15 look for the woman
cheri, cherie 4 dear **10** sweetheart
cherish 4 love **5** honor, nurse, prize, value **6** dote on, esteem, revere, succor **7** care for, idolize, nourish, nurture, shelter, sustain **8** hold dear, treasure, venerate **10** appreciate, take care of
cherished 4 dear **5** loved **7** beloved, darling, dearest **8** favorite, held dear, precious **9** treasured
Cherokee
  language family: 9 Iroquoian
  location: 7 Alabama, Georgia **8** Oklahoma, Virginia **9** Tennessee **13** North Carolina, South Carolina
  associated with: 12 Trail of Tears
  scholar: 7 Sequoya
cherry
  varieties: 3 pie, pin, rum **4** bing, bird, duke, fire, sand, sour, wild **5** black, brush, choke, dwarf, Higan, Naden, sweet **6** bitter, Brazil, ground, Indian, Madden, Oregon, Taiwan, winter **7** bastard, Cayenne, Morello, Nanking, Potomac, prairie, rosebud, sargent, Spanish, St Lucie, wild red, Windsor, Yoshino **8** Barbados, Catalina, oriental, perfumed, Suriname **9** christmas, cornelian, evergreen, Jerusalem, wild black **10** west indian **11** downy ground, Hansen's bush, holly-leaved, western sand **12** clammy ground, European bird, Japanese bush, purple ground **13** European dwarf **14** European ground, false Jerusalem, purple-leaf sand **15** Australian brush **17** Japanese cornelian, Japanese flowering, north Japanese hill
  drink: 6 kirsch
cherry brandy 6 kirsch **12** Peter Heering
Cherry Orchard, The
  author: 12 Anton Chekhov
  character: 4 Anya, Gaev **5** Fiers, Varya, Yasha **7** Pischin **8** Dunyasha, Lopakhin, Trofimov **9** Charlotta **16** Madame Ranevskaya
cherub 4 amor **5** angel, child, cupid, youth **6** moppet **8** amoretto, cherubim **13** heavenly being
cherubic 7 angelic **8** innocent **9** spiritual
Cherubin
  character in: 19 The Marriage of Figaro
  author: 12 Beaumarchais
chervil
  botanical name: 20 Anthriscus cerefolium
  origin: 6 Europe, Russia

  use: 4 soup **5** salad **11** fines herbes, potato salad
Chesapeake
  author: 13 James Michener
Cheshire Cat
  character in: 28 Alice's Adventures in Wonderland
  author: 7 Carroll
chess
  also called: 9 Royal Game
  chess champion: 3 Tal **4** Euwe, Fine **6** Karpov, Lasker, Morphy **7** Fischer, Kashdan, Smyslov, Spassky **8** Alekhine, Kasparov, Philador, Steinitz **9** Anderssen, Botvinnik, Petrosian, Reshevsky **10** Capablanca
  French: 6 echecs
  German: 11 schachspiel
  horizontal rows: 4 rank
  international chess federation: 4 FIDE
  patron goddess/muse: 6 Caissa
  piece: 4 king, pawn, rook **5** queen **6** bishop, castle, knight **8** chessman, material
  Russian: 8 shakhmat
  Spanish: 7 Ajedrez
  term: 3 pin **4** fork, hole **5** check, tempo **6** center **7** isolani, outpost **8** castling, majority, open file, queening, zugzwang **9** checkmate, en passant, promotion **10** fianchetto **11** zwischenzug
  tied game: 4 draw **9** stalemate
  vertical rows: 4 file
chest
  Italian: 5 petto
Chester, Edward
  character in: 12 Barnaby Rudge
  author: 7 Dickens
chesterfield 4 coat, sofa **5** couch **8** overcoat **9** davenport
Chesterton, G K (Gilbert Keith)
  author of: 20 The Man Who Was Thursday **24** The Napoleon of Notting Hill **25** The Innocence of Father Brown
chestnut 8 Castanea
  varieties: 4 Cape, Wild **5** Horse, Water **6** Guiana, Marron **7** Chinese, Spanish **8** American, Eurasian, European, Japanese, Red horse **10** Dwarf horse, Moreton Bay **11** Common horse **12** Chinese water **13** European horse, Japanese horse **15** California horse
chestnut-colored 6 auburn, russet, sienna **8** cinnamon, nut-brown **11** golden-brown, rust-colored **12** reddish-brown
chest of drawers 5 chest **6** bureau, lowboy **7** cabinet, commode, dresser, highboy, tallboy **10** chiffonier
cheval 5 horse
chevalier 4 lord **5** cadet, noble **6** knight **7** gallant **8** cavalier
Chevalier, Maurice

born: 5 Paris 6 France
roles: 4 Gigi 5 Fanny 6 Can-Can 13 The Love Parade, The Merry Widow 18 Love in the Afternoon

chew 4 gnaw 5 champ, crush, grind, munch 6 crunch, nibble 8 ruminate 9 masticate

Chew
character in: 21 The Master of Ballantrae
author: 9 Stevenson

chewing-out 6 rebuke 7 censure, chiding, reproof 8 reproach, scolding 9 reprimand 10 bawling-out, upbraiding 11 castigation, reprobation 12 dressing-down, remonstrance 13 tongue-lashing

chew noisily 4 gnaw 5 chomp, gnash, grind, munch 6 crunch

chew out 5 scold 6 berate, rail at, rebuke 7 bawl out, reprove, upbraid 8 reproach 9 castigate, reprimand 10 take to task, tongue-lash 14 read the riot act

chew the fat 3 gab, gas, jaw, rap, yak 4 blab, chat, chin, talk 5 prate 6 gossip, patter 7 blather, chatter, palaver, prattle, twaddle 8 chitchat, converse, talk idly 10 chew the rag 11 confabulate 14 chitterchatter

chew the rag 4 talk

Cheyenne
language family: 9 Algonkian 10 Algonquian
location: 6 Platte 7 Montana, Wyoming 8 Oklahoma, Red River 9 Minnesota 11 South Dakota
allied with: 7 Arapaho

Cheyenne
character: 6 Smitty 13 Cheyenne Bodie
cast: 7 L Q Jones 11 Clint Walker

chez 4 with 11 at the home of

Chiang Kai-shek
leader of: 5 China 6 Taiwan
ally: 9 Sun Yat-sen
party: 10 Kuomintang 11 Nationalist
defeated by: 10 Communists
wife: 12 Soong Mei-ling

Chibcha (Muisca)
location: 6 Bogota, Panama 8 Colombia 12 South America
associated with: 8 El Dorado

Chibchan
language family: 13 Macro-Chibchan
group: 4 Cuna, Paya, Rama 5 Lenca, Xinca 7 Chibcha

chic 4 tony 5 natty, ritzy, smart, swank 6 classy, modish, snazzy, swanky 7 elegant, stylish, voguish 11 fashionable

Chicago
author: 12 Carl Sandburg

Chicago
airport: 5 O'Hare 6 Midway
baseball team: 4 Cubs 8 White Sox

basketball team: 5 Bulls
downtown area: 4 Loop
football team: 5 Bears
fort: 8 Dearborn
hockey team: 10 Black Hawks
lake: 4 Wolf 7 Calumet 8 Michigan
landmark: 10 Meigs Field, Sears Tower 12 Board of Trade, Comiskey Park, Humboldt Park, Soldier Field, Wrigley Field 13 Shedd Aquarium 15 Lincoln Monument, Merchandise Mart, Newberry Library, Wrigley Building 16 Adler Planetarium 17 Holy Name Cathedral, John Hancock Center 18 Mercantile Exchange, Prudential Building 20 Midwest Stock Exchange 21 Art Institute of Chicago 23 Museum of Contemporary Art 26 Museum of Science and Industry 27 Field Museum of Natural History
mayor: 5 Byrne, Daley 10 Washington
nickname: 9 Windy City
river: 7 Chicago 10 Des Plaines
street: 11 Wacker Drive 13 Chicago Skyway 14 Lake Shore Drive
university: 6 DePaul, Loyola 9 Roosevelt 12 Northwestern 19 University of Chicago 29 Illinois Institute of Technology

chicanery 4 ruse, wile 5 craft, fraud, guile 6 deceit, duping 7 cunning, gulling, knavery, roguery 8 artifice, cozenage, trickery, villainy 9 deception, duplicity, rascality, sophistry 10 craftiness, hocus-pocus, humbuggery, subterfuge 11 hoodwinking 12 pettifoggery 13 double-dealing

chichi 4 arty 5 fussy, showy 6 flashy, frilly, garish, prissy, vulgar 7 finical, pompous, splashy 8 affected, gimcrack, overnice, precious, sissyish 9 arty-tarty, grandiose, nasty-nice 10 flamboyant 11 overrefined, pretentious 12 artsy-craftsy, ostentatious

chick
group of: 5 brood 6 clutch

Chickasaw
language family: 10 Muskhogean
location: 8 Oklahoma 9 Tennessee 11 Mississippi
related to: 7 Choctaw
member of: 19 Five Civilized Tribes

chicken, chickenhearted 3 hen 4 cock, fowl 5 layer, timid 6 afraid, coward, craven, pullet, scared, yellow 7 caitiff, dastard, fearful, gutless, rooster 8 cowardly, poltroon, timorous 9 flinching, fraidy-cat, shrinking 11 lily-livered, yellow-belly 12 fainthearted 13 pusillanimous, yellow-bellied 22 showing the white feather

chickenheartedness 8 timidity 9 cowardice 10 yellowness 11 fearfulness, poltroonery 12 timorousness 13 pusillanimity 16 faintheartedness

chide 5 scold 6 berate, rebuke 7 cen-

sure, chasten, reprove, upbraid 8 admonish, denounce, reproach 9 criticize, find fault, reprimand 10 take to task

chief 3 key 4 boss, head, lord, main 5 first, major, prime, ruler 6 leader, master, ruling 7 captain, highest, leading, monarch, primary, supreme 8 cardinal, chairman, crowning, director, dominant, foremost, greatest, overlord, overseer 9 chieftain, commander, governing, number-one, paramount, potentate, principal, sovereign, uppermost 10 prevailing, ringleader, supervisor 11 outstanding, predominant 12 preponderant 13 administrator

chief good
Latin: 11 summum bonum

chiefly 5 first 6 mainly, mostly 8 above all 9 expressly, in the main, most of all, primarily 10 especially 11 principally 12 particularly 13 predominantly

chieftan 4 boss, head 6 leader 7 captain, head man

chiffonier 6 bureau 7 dresser 8 cupboard 14 chest of drawers

chignon 3 bun 4 knot, roll 6 hairdo 9 hairpiece, hairstyle

child 3 boy, kid, lad, son, tad, tot 4 baby, girl, lass, tyke 5 youth 6 infant, moppet, rug rat 7 toddler 8 daughter, juvenile 9 little one, offspring, youngster

childbearing 5 birth 11 parturition

childbirth 8 delivery 11 confinement, parturition
French: 12 accouchement
goddess of: 4 Upis 5 Parca 6 Lucina, Matuta 7 Artemis 8 Ilithyia 10 Eileithyia

Childe Harold's Pilgrimage
author: 21 George Gordon Lord Byron

Childe Roland to the Dark Tower Came
author: 14 Robert Browning

childhood 5 youth 7 boyhood 8 girlhood 10 school days 11 adolescence, nursery days

childish 5 naive, silly 6 callow, simple 7 asinine, babyish, foolish, puerile 8 immature, juvenile 9 infantile 10 adolescent

childlike 8 childish, immature, innocent 9 ingenuous

child prodigy 7 quiz kid, whiz kid
German: 10 Wunderkind

children 4 boys, kids, sons, tads, tots 5 girls, issue, young 6 babies, result, youth 7 infants, product, progeny 9 daughters, juveniles 11 descendants

Children of God
author: 12 Vardis Fisher

Children of Paradise

director: 11 Marcel Carne
cast: 7 Arletty **11** Albert Remay **14** Pierre Brasseur **17** Jean-Louis Barrault

Child's Garden of Verses, A
author: 20 Robert Louis Stevenson

Chile
other name: 6 Tchile
name means: 21 deepest part of the Earth
capital/largest city: 8 Santiago
others: 4 Boco, Cuya, Lebu, Lota, Ocoa, Tome **5** Angol, Arica, Cobya, Talca **6** Arauco, Calama, Curico, Gatico, Osorno, Ovalle, Serena, Temuco, Vicuna, Yumbel, Yungay **7** Caldera, Chillan, Copiapo, Iquique, Valdiva **8** Coquimbo, Rancagua, Santiago, Vallenar **9** Cauquenes **10** Concepcion, Coquembana, Valparaiso, Vina del Mar **11** Antofagasta, Puerto Montt, Punta Arenas, San Bernardo
measure: 4 vara **5** legua, linea **6** cuadra, fanega
monetary unit: 4 peso **5** libra **6** condor, escudo
weight: 5 grano, libra **7** quintal
island: 3 Luz **4** Prat **5** Byron, Guafo, Hoste, Mocha, Nueva, Nunez, Vidal **6** Chiloe, Chonos, Dawson, Easter, Lennox, Piazzi, Picton, Quilan, Riesco, Stosch, Talcan **7** Angamos, Campana, Hanover, Hermite, Pajaros, Refugio, Tranqui **8** Chauques, Clarence, Huamblin, Nalcayec, Navarino, Traiguen **13** Juan Fernandez **14** Tierra del Fuego
lake: 5 Ranco **6** Yelcho **7** Puyehue, Rupanco **8** Cochrane **10** General Paz, Llanquihue **11** Buenos Aires
mountain: 4 Maca, Toro **5** Chato, Maipo, Maipu, Paine, Potro, Pular, Torre, Yogan **6** Apiwan, Burney, Conico, Jervis, Poquis, Rincon **7** Chaltel, Copiapo, Fitzroy, Palpana, Velluda **8** Cochrane, Tronador, Yanteles **9** Tupungato
highest point: 13 Ojos del Salado
river: 3 Loa **4** Laja, Yali **5** Alhue, Azapa, Bravo, Bueno, Elqui, Lauca, Lluta, Maipo, Maule, Puelo, Rahue, Rapel, Stata, Vitor **6** Biobio, Camina, Choapa, Choros, Cisnes, Colina, Huasco, Limari, Morado, Palena, Poscua, Tolten **7** Copiapo **8** Valdivia
sea: 7 Pacific
physical features:
   bay: 4 Cook, Eyre, Nena, Tarn **5** Lomas, Otway, Sarco **6** Darwin, Inutil, Moreno, Stokes, Tongoy **7** Dyneley, Inglesa, Skyring **8** Desolate
   cape: 4 Dyer, Horn **6** Choros, Falsos, Hornos, Quilan, Tablas **7** Deseado **10** Tres Montes
   channel: 5 Ancho, Cheap **6** Beagle **8** Cockburn, Moraleda
   desert: 7 Atacama

gulf: 5 Ancud, Guafo, Penas **6** Arauco
isthmus: 5 Ofqui
peninsula: 5 Hardy, Lacuy **6** Taitao, Tumbes
point: 4 Toro **5** Gallo, Liles, Lobos, Loros, Morro, Talca, Tetas, Vieja **6** Cachos, Galera, Molles **7** Angamos, Lavapie
strait: 6 Nelson **8** Magellan
volcano: 5 Lanin, Maipo **6** Antuco, Llaima, Oyahue, Tacora **7** Peteroa, Socomap
people: 3 Ona **4** Auca, Inca, Onan **6** Arauca, Chango, Yahgan **7** Mapuche, mestizo, Moluche, Pampean, Patagon, Puegian, Ranquel **8** Alikuluf, Picunche, Tsonecan
   author: 5 Bello **6** Donoso, Neruda **7** Mistral
   conqueror: 7 Valdiva
   explorer: 8 Magellan
   leader: 7 Allende **8** O'Higgins, Pinochet **9** San Martin **10** Alessandri
language: 7 Spanish
religion: 13 Roman Catholic
places:
   copper mine: 12 Chuquicamata
   resort: 8 Portillo **10** Vina del Mar
possession: 12 Easter Island **20** Juan Fernandez Islands
feature:
   cowboy: 5 huaso
   dance: 5 cueca **6** pequen **9** resbalosa
   shrub: 5 litre
   slum: 9 callempas
   tree: 5 rauli
   wind instrument: 4 sicu
food:
   drink: 5 pisco **6** chicha
   hot red pepper: 3 aji
   meat pie: 8 empanada
   soup: 7 cazuela **8** caldillo

chile peppers see **15** capsicum peppers

chill, chilly 3 icy, nip, raw **4** bite, cold, cool, keen **5** aloof, brisk, crisp, fever, harsh, nippy, sharp, stiff, stony **6** arctic, biting, bitter, frigid, frosty, frozen, wintry **7** callous, coolish, cutting, glacial, hostile, iciness, rawness, shivery **8** coolness, uncaring **9** crispness, frigidity, sharpness, unfeeling **10** forbidding, frostiness, unfriendly **11** indifferent, passionless, penetrating **12** unresponsive

chilled 4 cold, iced **6** cooled, frozen **7** frosted **8** hardened **10** dispirited **11** discouraged **12** refrigerated

chilling 3 icy, raw **5** nippy, on ice **6** frigid **7** bracing, cooling **10** unfriendly

Chillingworth, Roger
character in: 16 The Scarlet Letter
author: 9 Hawthorne

chime 4 gong, peal, ring, toll **5** knell, sound **6** jingle, tinkle **7** pealing, ringing **8** carillon, ding-dong, tinkling, tollings **10** set of bells **14** tintinnabulate **16** tintinnabulation

Chimene
character in: 6 The Cid
author: 9 Corneille

chimera 5 dream, fancy **6** bubble, mirage **7** fantasy, monster, phantom **8** daydream, delusion, idle whim, illusion **9** pipe dream **10** self-deceit, she-monster **12** will-o'- the-wisp **13** castle in Spain, fool's paradise, hallucination, self-deception **14** castle in the air **24** figment of one's imagination

Chimera
form: 7 monster
father: 6 Typhon
mother: 7 Echidna
breathes: 4 fire

Chimera
author: 9 John Barth

chimerical 6 absurd, unreal **7** utopian **8** delusive, ethereal, fabulous, fanciful, illusory, mythical quixotic **9** fantastic, imaginary, visionary **10** impossible, phantasmal, **11** nonexistent

chimney 4 flue, tube, vent **5** cleft, gully, spout, stack **6** funnel, hearth **7** opening **9** stovepipe **10** smokestack

chimpanzee 3 ape **6** animal, baboon, monkey

chin 3 gab, jaw, rap **4** chat, talk **7** chatter, palaver **8** chitchat, converse **10** chew the fat, chew the rag **11** confabulate

china 6 dishes, plates **7** pottery **8** crockery **9** chinaware, porcelain, stoneware, tableware **11** ceramicware, earthenware **14** cups and saucers

China
other name: 3 PRC **13** Middle Kingdom **14** Flowery Kingdom **22** People's Republic of China
capital: 6 Peking **7** Beijing
largest city: 8 Shanghai
others: 3 Bai, Noh **4** Ahpa, Amoy, Fuyu, Guma, Hami, Huma, Ipin, Kian, Kisi, Lini, Loho, Luta, Moho, Moyu, Niya, Noho, Omin, Rima, Saka, Sian, Taku, Tali, Tayu, Wuhu, Yaan **5** Chiai, Fusin, Kirin, Koklu, Linyu, Macao, Penki, Shasi, Soche, Taian, Talai, Tihwa, Tuyun, Wuhan, Wusih, Yenan, Yenki, Yulin, Yumen **6** Anshan, Antung, Canton, Dairen, Fuchau, Fuchow, Fushun, Hankow, Harbin, Ilhasa, Kalgan, Loyang, Lushun, Mukden, Nanhai, Ningpo, Singan, Sining, Taipei, Tsinan, Yangku, Yunnan **7** Fuskhih, Hanyang, Kunming, Lanchow, Lioyang, Mengtze, Nanking, Nanning, Paoshan, Peiping, Soochow, Taiyuan, Tatshan, Urumchi, Urumsti, Waichow, Wuchang, Yenping **8** Chinchow, Fengkiek, Fengtien, Hangchow, Kingchow, Nanchang,

Shanghai, Shenyang, Siangtan, Tientsin, Tungchow, Wanchuan, Wanhsien **9** Chungking, Kiangling, Tsingyuan **10** Chiangling, Port Arthur

school: 5 Futan **6** Peking **7** Nanking **8** Hangchow **9** Sun Yat-sen **16** Cheng-tu Technical

division:

province: 5 Honan, Hunan, Hupei, Kansu **6** Anhwei, Fukien, Shansi, Shensi, Yunnan **7** Kiangsi, Kiangsu **8** Chekiang, Kweichow, Shantung, Szechwan, Tientsin, Tsinghai **9** Kwangtung, Manchuria

measure: 3 cho, fan, fen, pau, tou, tun, yan, yin **4** chek, chih, fang, kish, papa, quei, shih, teke, tsan, tsun **5** catty, chang, ching, sheng, shing **6** chupak, gungli, kungho, kungmu, tching **7** kungfen, kungyin **8** kungchih, kungshih, **9** kungching

monetary unit: 4 cash, cent, fyng, mace, tael, tiao, yuan **5** sycee **12** jen nin piao pu

weight: 3 fan, fen, hao, kin, ssu, tan, yin **4** chee, chin, dong, shih, tael, tsin **5** catty, chien, picul, tchin, tsien **6** kungli **7** haikwan, kungfen, kungssu, kungtun **8** kungchin **9** candareen **10** kupingtael

island: 4 Amoy **5** Macao, Matsu, Namki, Taipa **6** Chusan, Hainan, Pratas, Quemoy, Taiwan, Tinian, Yuhwan **7** Coloane, Formosa, Hungtow, Tungsha **8** Ching Hai, Chouchan, Kulangsu

lake: 3 Tai **4** Chao, Na-mu **5** Kaoyu, Oling, Telli **6** Bamtso, Bornor, Ebinor, Erhhai, Khanka, Lopnor, Namtso, Poyang **7** Chaling, Hungtse, Karanor, Kokonor **8** Hulunnor, Montcalm, Taroktso, Tellinor, Tienchih, Tsinghai, Tungting

sea: 6 Yellow **9** East China **10** South China

physical features:

bay: 7 Laichow **8** Hangchow

cape: 7 Olwanpi

channel: 5 Bashi

desert: 4 Gobi **5** Ordos, Shamo **7** Alashan **10** Takla Makan

dry lake: 6 Lopnor

gulf: 5 Pohai **6** Chihli, Tonkin **7** Pechili **8** Liaotung

peninsula: 6 Leichu **7** Luichow **8** Liaotung

plateau: 5 Loess **7** Tibetan

port: 4 Amoy, Wuhu **5** Aigun, Shasi **6** Antung, Canton, Chefoo, Dairen, Ichang, Ningpo, Pakhoi, Swatow, Wuchow **7** Foochow, Hunchun, Luichow, Nanking, Samshui, Santuao, Soochow, Wenchow, Yinkkow, Yungkia **8** Changsha, Hangchow, Kiukiang, Kongmoon, Shanghai, Tengyueh, Tientsin, Tsingtao, Wanhsien **9** Kwangchow, Weihaiwei **10** Tsing-

kiang

strait: 6 Hainan, Taiwan **7** Formosa

people: 3 Han, Yis **4** Huis, Lolo, Miao, Pu-is **5** Hakka, Hoklo, Seres, Sinic **6** Cataia, Chuang, Johnny, Korean, Manchu, Mongol, Serian, Uighun **7** Sinaean, Tibetan

leader: 9 Sun Yat-sen, Zhou Enlai **10** Kublai Khan, Mao Tse-tung **11** Genghis Khan **12** Deng Xiaoping **13** Chiang Kai-shek

philosopher: 6 Lao-tzu **9** Confucius

language: 7 Chinese **8** Mandarin, Shanghai **9** Cantonese

religion: 5 Islam **6** Taoism **8** Buddhism **12** Christianity, Confucianism

place:

palace: 6 Summer **8** Imperial **13** Forbidden City

ruins: 9 Ming Tombs

square: 9 Tiananmen

wonder: 9 Great Wall

feature:

boat: 4 junk

conspirators: 10 Gang of Four

dynasty: 3 Han, Sui **4** Chou, Ch'in, Ming, Sung, T'ang **5** Ch'ing, Shang **6** Manchu

military academy: 7 whompoa

watercolor: 8 shan shiu

China Syndrome, The

director: 12 James Bridges

cast: 9 Jane Fonda **10** Jack Lemmon, Scott Brady **14** Michael Douglas

setting: 17 nuclear power plant

Chinatown

director: 13 Roman Polanski

cast: 10 John Huston **11** Faye Dunaway **13** Jack Nicholson

Oscar for: 10 screenplay

chinaware 6 dishes, plates **7** pottery **8** crockery **9** porcelain, stoneware, tableware **11** ceramicware, earthenware **14** cups and saucers

chine 5 spine **6** dorsum **8** backbone

Chinese book of divination 6 I Ching

Chingachgook

character in: 13 The Pathfinder **20** The Last of the Mohicans

author: 6 Cooper

chink 3 cut, gap **4** gash, hole, rent, rift, ring, slit **5** break, clank, cleft, clink, crack, fault, split **6** breach, jangle, jingle, rattle, tinkle **7** crevice, fissure, opening **8** aperture

Chinook (Flathead)

language family: 9 Chinookan

location: 7 Pacific **10** Washington

ritual: 15 head deformation

Chinookan

tribe: 7 Chinook **8** Flathead

chintzy 5 cheap, close, dowdy, tacky, tatty, tight **6** frowzy, frumpy, shabby, sleazy, stingy **7** miserly **8** grudging, schlocky, stinting **9** niggardly, penuri-

ous **11** closefisted **12** parsimonious **13** penny-pinching

chip 3 bit, cut, hew **4** chop, gash, hack, nick **5** chunk, crumb, flake, scrap, shred, slice, split, wafer **6** chisel, morsel, paring, sliver **7** cutting, shaving, whittle **8** fragment, splinter

chipmunk 4 Chip, Dale **6** chippy, gopher, rodent **8** chipmuck, squirrel **14** ground squirrel **16** chipping squirrel

chipper 3 gay **4** pert, spry **5** alive, brisk, peppy **6** frisky, jaunty, lively **8** animated, carefree, cheerful, spirited **9** easygoing, energetic, sprightly, vivacious **12** high- spirited, light-hearted

Chippewa (Ojibwa, Ojibway)

language family: 9 Algonkian **10** Algonquian

tribe: 4 Cree **6** Ottawa **8** Chippewa **10** Missisauga

location: 6 Canada **9** Lake Huron **11** North Dakota **12** Lake Superior, Niagara Falls

leader: 7 Pontiac

CHiPS

character: 8 (Officer) Jon Baker **10** (Sgt) Joe Getraer **16** (Officer) Frank (Ponch) Poncherello

cast: 10 Robert Pine **11** Erik Estrada, Larry Wilcox

Chirico, Giorgio de

born: 5 Volos **6** Greece

artwork: 15 Enigma of the Hour **19** Enigma of an Afternoon **21** Enigma of an Autumn Night **22** Nostalgia of the Infinite **32** The Melancholy and Mystery of a Street

Chiron

also: 7 Cheiron

form: 7 centaur

father: 6 Cronos, Cronus, Kronos

mother: 7 Philyra

wife: 8 Chariclo

daughter: 6 Endeis

grandson: 6 Peleus

occupation: 7 teacher

chirp 4 peep, sing **5** cheep, chirr, tweet **7** chirrup, chitter, peeping, twitter **8** cheeping

chirrup 4 peep **5** cheep, chirp, tweet **7** chitter, twitter

chisel 3 cut, gyp **4** gull, hoax, rook, tool **5** blade, cheat, slice **6** incise

type: 4 cape, cold, wood **7** v-shaped

Chisel

constellation of: 6 Caelum

chiseler 4 fake **5** cheat, fraud, quack **7** cheater **8** swindler

Chislev 16 ninth Hebrew month

chit 3 IOU, tab **4** note **5** check **7** voucher

chitchat 3 gab **4** chat **5** prate **6** drivel, gossip **7** chatter, palaver, prattle **8** converse **9** small talk **10** chew the fat, chew the rag **11** confabulate **13** confabulation

Chitimacha
language family: 6 Tunica
location: 9 Louisiana
noted for: 8 basketry

chitter 4 peep 5 cheep, chirp, tweet 7 chatter, chirrup, twitter

chitter-chatter 3 gab 4 blab 6 babble, drivel, gabble, jabber 7 blabber, prattle, twaddle 8 chitchat 9 jabbering 16 idle conversation

chivalrous 6 polite 7 courtly, gallant 8 mannerly

chivalry 8 courtesy 9 gallantry 10 knighthood, politeness 11 courtliness

Chivery, Young John
character in: 12 Little Dorrit
author: 7 Dickens

chivy 3 nag 4 hunt, race 5 annoy, chase, chevy, hound, trail, worry 6 badger, bother, harass, pursue 7 scamper, torment

Chlidanope
form: 5 Naiad

Chloe
epithet of: 7 Demeter
means: 5 green

chloride 7 muriate 8 chemical, compound

chlorine
chemical symbol: 2 Cl

chocolate 5 brown, candy, cacao, cocoa, drink 6 bon bon 10 confection

Choctaw
language family: 10 Muskhogean
location: 7 Alabama 11 Mississippi
related to: 9 Chickasaw

Choephoroe
author: 9 Aeschylus
character: 6 Furies 7 Electra, Orestes, Pylades 9 Aegisthus 12 Clytemnestra

choice 3 say 4 A-one, best, fine, pick, vote 5 array, elite, prime, prize, stock, store, voice 6 better, opting, option, select, supply, tip-top 7 display, special, variety 8 choosing, deciding, decision, superior 9 excellent, exclusive, first-rate, preferred, selection, top drawer 10 assemblage, assortment, collection, consummate, discretion, first-class, preferable, preference, well-chosen 11 alternative, appointment, exceptional, superlative 13 determination, extraordinary

choice food 5 treat 8 delicacy

choicest part
French: 14 creme de la creme

choir 4 band 5 quire 6 angels, chorus 7 chorale, singers 10 choristers

Choirboys, The
author: 14 Joseph Wambaugh

choke 3 dam, gag 4 clog, plug 5 block, check, dam up, stuff 6 arrest, bridle, hamper, hinder, impede, plug up, retard, stifle, stop up 7 congest, garrote, inhibit, repress, smother 8 blockade, hold back, obstruct, restrain, strangle, suppress, throttle 9 constrain, constrict, suffocate 10 asphyxiate

choler 3 ire 4 fury, rage 5 anger, wrath 6 spleen, temper

choleric 3 mad 5 angry, irate, testy, vexed 6 cranky, grumpy, shirty, touchy 7 enraged, furious, grouchy, peevish, waspish 8 snappish, wrathful 9 dyspeptic, indignant, irritable, irascible, splenetic 10 infuriated, short-fused 11 contentious, hot-tempered, ill-tempered, thin-skinned 12 cantankerous, sour-tempered 13 quick-tempered, short-tempered

choose 3 opt 4 like, pick, take, wish 5 adopt, elect 6 decide, desire, intend, opt for, prefer, see fit, select 7 call out, embrace, espouse, extract, fix upon, pick out, resolve 8 decide on, settle on 9 determine, single out 10 be inclined 13 commit oneself 14 make up one's mind

choosy 5 fussy, picky 7 finicky 9 selective 10 fastidious, particular 14 discriminating

chop 3 cut, hew, hit, lop 4 blow, chip, crop, cube, dice, fell, gash, hack 5 cut up, mince, slash, slice, split, swipe, whack 6 cleave, cutlet, stroke, sunder 8 fragment, rib slice 9 cotelette, pulverize

Chopin, Frederic Francois
born: 6 Poland 12 Zelazowawola
companion: 10 George Sand
composer of: 5 Etude 7 Ballade 8 Berceuse, Cat Valse, Dog Valse, Fantasie 9 Ecossaise 10 Barcarolle 11 Minute Valse 15 Andante Spianato, Heroic Polonaise (No 6), Raindrop Prelude, Winter Wind Etude 16 Shepherd Boy Etude 17 Impromptu Fantasie, Rondo a la Krakowiak 18 Revolutionary Etude 20 Butterfly's Wings Etude

choral ode
Greek: 7 parodos 8 stasimon

chord 4 cord, line, note, tone 5 music, triad 6 accord, string, tendon 7 cadence, emotion, feeling, harmony 9 harmonize

chore 3 job 4 duty, task, work 5 stint 6 burden, errand, strain 8 farm task, small job 10 assignment 13 household task 14 responsibility

choreography 5 dance 12 stage dancing 16 dance composition

chorister 6 singer 7 changer 8 choirboy

chortle 5 laugh 7 chuckle

chorus 5 choir, unity 6 accord, unison 7 concert, concord, refrain 8 glee club, one voice, response 9 antiphony, consensus, unanimity 11 concordance 12 singing group

chosen 5 elite 6 picked, sorted 7 elected 8 selected 9 picked out

Chosen, The
author: 10 Chaim Potok

Chosen see 5 Korea

Chouans, The
author: 14 Honore de Balzac

chough
group of: 10 chattering

Chowbok
character in: 7 Erewhon
author: 6 Butler

Christ, the see 5 Jesus

christen 3 dip, dub 4 name 6 launch 7 baptize, immerse 8 dedicate, sprinkle 9 designate

Christian
character in: 16 Pilgrim's Progress
author: 6 Bunyan

Christian, Fletcher
character in: 17 Mutiny on the Bounty
authors: 4 Hall 8 Nordhoff

Christian, Linda
real name: 16 Blanca Rosa Welter
husband: 11 Tyrone Power 12 Edmund Purdom
born: 6 Mexico 7 Tampico
roles: 6 Athena 15 Slaves of Babylon 18 Green Dolphin Street

Christiania
capital of: 6 Norway
now called: 4 Oslo

Christie, (Dame) Agatha
author: 7 Curtain 12 The Mousetrap 14 Death on the Nile 15 The Mirror Crack'd 16 Ten Little Indians 19 Murder at the Vicarage 20 And Then There Were None 22 What Mrs McGillicuddy Saw! 23 The Murder of Roger Ackroyd 24 Murder on the Orient Express, Witness for the Prosecution 27 The Mysterious Affair at Styles
character: 6 Mr. Pine 10 Jane Marple 13 Hercule Poirot

Christie, Julie
born: 5 Assam, India 6 Chukua
roles: 7 Darling (Oscar), Shampoo 9 Billy Liar 11 Heat and Dust 13 Doctor Zhivago, Fahrenheit 451, Heaven Can Wait 18 McCabe and Mrs Miller 22 Far From the Madding Crowd

Christine
author: 11 Stephen King

Christmas
also: 4 Noel, Yule 8 Yuletide
feature/symbol: 4 bell, star, tree 5 angel, gifts, holly 6 candle, carols, creche, manger, sleigh, wreath 7 Yule log 8 presents 9 evergreen, mistletoe, snowflake, stockings 10 Santa Claus

Christmas, Joe
character in: 13 Light in August
author: 8 Faulkner

Christmas Carol, A
author: 14 Charles Dickens

character: **7** Tiny Tim **8** Fezziwig **11** Bob Cratchit **12** Marley's Ghost **15** Ebenezer Scrooge

ghosts of: **13** Christmas Past **15** Christmas Future **16** Christmas Present

director: **17** Brian Desmond Hurst

cast: **10** Jack Warner **11** Alastair Sim (Ebenezer Scrooge), Mervyn Johns **14** Michael Hordern **16** Kathleen Harrison

Christopher Robin
character in: **13** Winnie-the-Pooh
author: **5** Milne

chromium
chemical symbol: **2** Cr

chronic 7 abiding, lasting **8** constant, enduring, habitual, periodic **9** confirmed, continual, ingrained, perennial, recurrent, recurring **10** continuous, deep-rooted, deep-seated, inveterate, persistent, persisting **12** intermittent, longstanding

chronicle 3 log **4** epic, list, note, post, saga **5** diary, enter, story **6** annals, docket, record, relate, report **7** account, history, journal, narrate, recount, set down **8** archives **9** narrative **10** chronology

Chronicles of England, Scotland, and Ireland
author: **16** Raphael Holinshed

chronological 5 dated **6** serial **7** ordered, sequent **10** sequential, succeeding, successive **11** consecutive, progressive, time-ordered **12** chronometric, chronoscopic **13** chronographic

chronology 6 annals, record **7** history **9** chronicle **13** order of events

chronometer 5 clock **8** horologe **9** timepiece

chrysanthemum
varieties: **3** Max **4** Corn **5** Daisy, Tansy **6** Nippon **7** Garland **8** Florist's, Tricolor **10** Portuguese

chrysoberyl
variety: **7** cat's-eye **11** alexandrite

chrysolite 4 iron, lava **5** beryl, green, stone **7** yellow **7** mineral, olivine, peridot **8** silicate **9** magnesium **10** aquamarine

chrysoprase
species: **6** quartz
color: **5** green

Chrysothemis
father: **9** Agamemnon
mother: **12** Clytemnestra
brother: **7** Orestes
sister: **7** Electra **9** Iphigenia
daughter: **5** Rhoeo

Chthonian
form: **5** deity **6** spirit
habitat: **10** underworld

Chthonius
member of: **6** Sparti

epithet of: **4** Zeus
means: **15** of the underworld

Chuang-tzu, Chwang-tse
author: **9** Chuang-tzu

chubby 3 fat **5** buxom, plump, podgy, pudgy, stout, tubby **6** chunky, flabby, fleshy, portly, rotund, stocky, zaftig **7** paunchy **8** heavyset, roly-poly, thickset **9** corpulent **10** overweight **15** pleasingly plump

chuck 3 pat, pet, tap **4** cast, toss **5** fling, heave, pitch, sling, throw **6** tickle

chuckle 5 cluck, laugh **6** clumsy **7** cackle, chortle, snicker

chum 3 pal **4** bait **5** buddy, crony **6** cohort, friend **7** comrade **8** intimate, playmate, sidekick **9** companion, confidant **10** bosom buddy, playfellow **11** close friend

chummy 5 close, palsy **7** devoted **8** familiar, friendly, intimate **9** congenial **10** buddy-buddy, palsy-walsy **12** affectionate

chump 4 dolt, dupe, fool, goof, goon, head **5** champ, munch **6** sucker **9** blockhead

chunk 3 gob, wad **4** clod, hunk, lump, mass **5** batch, block, piece **6** nugget, square

chunky 5 beefy, dumpy, lumpy, pudgy, squat, stout, thick **6** chubby, portly, stocky, stodgy, stubby **7** squabby **8** heavyset, thickset **11** thick-bodied

church 4 cult, sect **5** faith **6** belief, chapel, mosque, temple **7** service **8** basilica, religion **9** cathedral, devotions, synagogue **10** house of God, Lord's house, persuasion, tabernacle **11** affiliation **12** denomination **13** divine worship **14** house of worship

Church, Frederick Edwin
born: **10** Hartford CT
artwork: **14** Andes of Ecuador, Falls of Niagara (Niagara Falls) **18** The Heart of the Andes **19** Morning in the Tropics

Churchill, Frank
character in: **4** Emma
author: **6** Austen

Churchill, Sarah
father: **19** Sir Winston Churchill
born: **6** London **7** England
roles: **12** Royal Wedding

Churchill, Winston Spencer
born: **7** England **14** Blenheim Palace
father: **8** Randolph
mother: **12** Jennie Jerome
wife: **16** Clementine Hosier
daughter: **5** Sarah
school: **6** Harrow **9** Sandhurst
captured by: **5** Boers
position: **13** prime minister
author of: **11** Marlborough, My Early Life **14** The World Crisis **17** The Second World War **35** A History of the

English-Speaking Peoples
won: **10** Nobel Prize

churchly 8 clerical, pastoral, priestly **9** parochial **11** ministerial **14** ecclesiastical

churchman 5 vicar **6** bishop, cleric, curate, deacon, parson, pastor, priest, rector **7** prelate **8** chaplain, minister, preacher **9** clergyman **12** ecclesiastic

church official 5 elder **6** beadle, deacon **9** presbyter

churchyard 8 cemetery **9** graveyard **12** burial ground **13** burying ground

churl 3 cad, oaf **4** boor, lout **7** bounder

churlish 4 rude, sour, tart **5** crude, surly, testy **6** crusty, sullen **7** bearish, bilious, boorish, brusque, crabbed, grouchy, ill-bred, uncivil, uncouth, waspish **8** arrogant, captious, choleric, impolite, impudent, insolent, petulant **9** dastardly, insulting, irascible, irritable, obnoxious, rancorous, splenetic **10** unmannerly **11** ill-mannered, ill-tempered, quarrelsome **12** contemptible, discourteous

churn 4 beat, foam, rage, roil, roll, toss, whip **5** heave, shake, swirl, whisk **6** stir up **7** agitate, disturb, pulsate, shake up, vibrate **8** convulse **9** palpitate

chute 5 rapid, slide, slope **7** incline, passage **9** parachute

chutzpa, chutzpah 4 gall **5** brass, cheek, nerve **8** audacity, boldness, temerity **9** brashness, impudence **10** brazenness, effrontery **11** forwardness, presumption

Chwatt, Aaron
real name of: **10** Red Buttons

ciao 2 hi **5** hello **6** so long **7** goodbye **11** see you later

Cicero, Marcus Tullius
lived in: **11** ancient Rome
noted as: **6** author, lawyer, orator **9** statesman **11** philosopher **12** letter writer
position: **6** aedile, consul **7** praetor
author of: **9** De finibus, De oratore **10** De amicitia, De officiis **11** De republica, De senectute, In Catilinam **14** De natura deorum, Pro lege Manilia **23** Tusculanae Disputationes

cicerone 5 guide, pilot **8** conductor **9** explainer

cicisbeo 5 lover

Cid, The
also: **11** Poema del Cid
author: **7** unknown **15** Pierre Corneille
character: **7** Chimene **8** Rodrigue
Cid also called: **14** el Cid Campeador **18** Rodrigo Diaz de Bivar
horse: **7** Babieca

ci-devant 6 former **7** retired **10** heretofore

cierge 3 dip, wax **5** light, taper **6** bougie, candle, tallow

cigar 4 toby **5** claro **6** corona, havana, maduro, stogie **7** cheroot **8** panatela, panetela, perfecto **9** cigarillo, panatella
ingredient: 11 tobacco leaf
part: 6 binder, filler **7** wrapper
made in: 4 Cuba **6** Havana
kept in: 7 humidor

cigarette, cigaret 3 cig, fag **4** biri, rett **5** smoke **6** gasper, grette, reefer **10** coffin nail
ingredient: 3 tar **7** menthol, tobacco **8** nicotine

Cimabue
real name: 11 Cenni di Pepi
born: 5 Italy **8** Florence
artwork attributed: 18 The S Trinita Madonna **29** Madonna Enthroned with St Francis **45** Madonna and Child Enthroned with Angels and Prophets

Cimarron
author: 10 Edna Ferber
director: 13 Wesley Ruggles
cast: 10 Irene Dunne, Richard Dix **13** Estelle Taylor
Oscar for: 7 picture **10** screenplay

Cimarron Strip
character: 8 (US Marshal) Jim Crown **9** Mac Gregor **12** Francis Wilde **17** Dulcey Coopersmith
cast: 10 Randy Boone **12** Jill Townsend, Percy Herbert **13** Stuart Whitman

Cimino, Michael
director of: 11 Heaven's Gate **13** The Deer Hunter (Oscar)

Cimmerian
mentioned by: 5 Homer
form: 10 Westerners
live in: 8 darkness

cinch 4 band, snap **5** girth **6** clinch, ensure, girdle, shoo-in **8** lead-pipe **9** pull tight, sure thing **11** piece of cake

Cincinnati
baseball team: 4 Reds
football team: 7 Bengals

cincture 4 band, belt, cord, sash **6** girdle

cinder 3 ash **4** slag **5** ashes, dross, ember **6** embers, scoria **8** clinkers, iron slag **10** burned coal, burned wood

Cinderella
author: 7 unknown
source: 8 Perrault
character: 14 Fairy Godmother, Handsome Prince **15** Ugly Stepsisters **16** Wicked Stepmother
coach: 7 pumpkin
horses: 9 white mice
footman: 4 frog
loses: 12 glass slipper

cinema 5 films **6** flicks, movies **7** theater **14** motion pictures, moving pictures

cinnamon 5 spice
botanical name: 20 Cinnamomum zeylanicum
variety: 6 cassia, Ceylon **10** zeylanicum
color: 4 buff **5** tawny **6** auburn **8** nut-brown **11** golden- brown, yellow-brown **12** reddish-brown **13** chestnut- brown **14** yellowish-brown
origin: 5 China **7** Vietnam **9** Indonesia **10** East Indies

Cinyras
king of: 6 Cyprus
son: 5 Melus
daughter: 6 Myrrha
introduced worship of: 9 Aphrodite
crime: 6 incest
death by: 7 suicide

cipher 3 nil, zip **4** code, zero **5** aught **6** naught, nobody **7** anagram, nothing, nullity **8** acrostic, goose egg **9** nonentity, obscurity **10** cryptogram **11** cryptograph

Circe
form: 11 enchantress
father: 6 Helios
mother: 5 Perse
brother: 6 Aeetes
son: 6 Agrius **7** Latinus **9** Telegonus
home: 5 Aeaea
turned men into: 4 pigs **5** swine

circle 3 orb, set **4** belt, curl, gird, girt, halo, hoop, knot, loop, reel, ring, turn **5** arena, bound, cabal, crowd, curve, cycle, field, girth, group, hem in, orbit, pivot, range, reach, realm, round, sweep, swing **6** border, bounds, clique, cordon, corona, course, domain, girdle, region, sphere **7** circlet, circuit, company, compass, coterie, enclose, envelop, hedge in, revolve, ringlet, society, theater **8** dominion, encircle, province, sequence, surround **9** bailiwick, encompass, territory, wind about **10** move around, revolution, ring around **11** curve around, progression **12** circumrotate, circumscribe **13** revolve around **14** circumnavigate

Circle 6 gilgal

circlet 4 band, halo, ring **5** tiara **6** diadem, fillet, wreath **7** chaplet, coronet, ringlet

circuit 3 lap, run **4** area, beat, edge, tour, trek, walk **5** jaunt, limit, round, route **6** border, bounds, course, margin, sphere **7** compass, confine, journey **8** circling, frontier, orbiting, pivoting **9** excursion, extremity, perimeter, revolving, territory **10** revolution **13** circumference **14** distance around

circuitous 7 devious, turning, winding **8** circular, indirect, rambling, tortuous, twisting **10** meandering, roundabout, serpentine **12** labyrinthine **14** circumlocutory

circular 4 bill **5** flier, round **6** curved,

notice, rotary **7** coiling, curling, leaflet, rocking, rolling, rounded, turning, winding **8** bulletin, gyrating, handbill, pivoting, spinning, twirling **9** revolving, spiraling, swiveling, throwaway **10** circuitous, ring-shaped **12** announcement **13** advertisement

circulate 4 flow **5** issue, strew **6** circle, course, spread, travel **7** give out, go forth, journey, publish, radiate, scatter **8** announce, disperse, go around, put about **9** broadcast, get abroad, make known, move about, publicize **10** distribute, make public, move around, pass around, put forward **11** disseminate, pass through, visit around **13** make the rounds

circulation 4 flow **6** motion **7** flowing **8** circling, rotation **9** diffusion, radiation **10** dispersion **11** propagation **12** distribution, promulgation, transmission **13** dissemination

circulatory system
part: 4 vein **5** heart **6** artery **9** capillary **15** lymphatic vessel
carries: 6 plasma **9** platelets **13** red blood cells **15** white blood cells

circumcision
Hebrew: 4 Bris, Brit **5** Berit, Brith **6** Berith
performed by: 5 Mohel

circumference 3 rim **4** edge **5** girth **6** border, bounds, fringe, girdle, limits, margin **7** circuit, compass, outline **8** boundary **9** extremity, perimeter, periphery **14** distance around

circumlocution 8 rambling, verbiage **9** garrulity, verbosity, wordiness **10** digression, meandering **14** discursiveness, long-windedness, roundaboutness

circumlocutory 5 wordy **7** diffuse, verbose **8** rambling **9** wandering **10** digressive, discursive, maundering, roundabout

circumnavigate 5 skirt **6** bypass, circle **8** encircle, go around **10** circumvent

circumnavigation 8 circling, skirting **9** bypassing **11** going around **12** encirclement **13** circumvention

circumscribe 3 fix **4** curb **5** check, hem in, limit **6** bridle, circle, corset, define, impede **7** confine, enclose, outline **8** encircle, restrain, restrict, surround **9** constrain, delineate, encompass, proscribe

circumscribed 6 narrow **7** limited **10** restricted

circumscription 5 limit **7** outline **9** hemming in, restraint **10** constraint **11** confinement **12** encirclement **14** restrictedness

circumspect 4 sage, wary **5** alert **7** careful, guarded, prudent **8** cautious, discreet, vigilant, watchful **9** judicious, sagacious, wide-awake **10** deliberate, discerning, particular, thoughtful **13** contemplative, perspicacious **14** discriminating

circumspection 4 care, heed **7** caution **8** prudence **10** discretion, precaution, steadiness **11** carefulness, heedfulness, mindfulness **12** deliberation

circumstance 4 fact, item **5** event, point, thing **6** detail, factor, matter, ritual **7** element **8** ceremony, incident, splendor **9** condition, formality, happening, pageantry **10** brilliance, occurrence, particular, phenomenon **11** vicissitude **12** happenstance, magnificence, resplendence **14** state of affairs

circumstances 5 state **9** situation **11** environment **16** living conditions

circumstantial 4 full **6** minute **7** deduced, hearsay, implied, precise **8** accurate, complete, detailed, explicit, inferred, presumed, thorough **9** secondary **10** blow-by- blow, evidential, exhaustive, extraneous, incidental, particular, unabridged **11** conjectural, inferential, provisional **12** nonessential

circumvent 4 miss, shun **5** avoid, dodge, elude, evade, skirt **6** bypass, circle, escape, outwit, thwart **8** go around **9** frustrate **12** keep away from **14** circumnavigate

circumvention 7 dodging, ducking, eluding, evasion **9** avoidance, bypassing **11** frustration **12** sidestepping

circus 4 ring **5** arena **6** big top, circle, uproar **8** carnival, coliseum **9** spectacle **10** exhibition, hippodrome **11** ampitheater **12** intersection
　act: 5 clown, flyer **7** acrobat, juggler, trapeze **8** side show **9** lion tamer, menagerie **10** equestrian **13** flying trapeze
　famous: 6 Astley **12** Cirque d'Hiver **15** Barnum and Bailey **16** Ringling Brothers

Cist
　form: 9 sacred box
　used for: 8 utensils

cistern 3 box, tub, vat **4** tank, well **6** cavity, vessel **8** aqueduct **9** reservoir

citadel 4 fort **7** bastion, rampart **8** fortress **10** stronghold **13** fortification

citation 4 cite **5** award, honor, kudos, medal, quote **7** example, excerpt, extract, passage **8** instance **9** quotation **12** commendation, illustration **14** official praise

cite 4 name, note **5** honor, quote **6** praise **7** advance, commend, mention, present, refer to, specify **8** allude to, document, indicate **9** enumerate, exemplify **12** bring forward **13** give as example

Cithaeronian *see* **4** Zeus

citified 5 urban **6** urbane **12** cosmopolitan **13** sophisticated

citizen 6 native **7** denizen, subject **8** national, resident **10** inhabitant
　French: 7 citoyen

Citizen Kane
　director: 11 Orson Welles
　script: 11 Orson Welles **17** Herman J Mankiewicz
　cast: 11 Orson Welles **12** Joseph Cotten **13** Everett Sloane **14** Agnes Moorehead
　score: 15 Bernard Herrmann
　sled: 7 Rosebud

citizenry 4 folk **6** people, public **7** society **8** populace **9** community **10** population

citoyen 7 citizen

citrine
　species: 6 quartz
　color: 6 yellow

citron 3 rue **4** lime, rind **5** lemon **6** cedrat, orange, yellow **8** Rutaceae **9** tangerine **10** watermelon **12** citrus medica
　Jewish: 6 ethrog

city 4 burg, town **7** big town **8** denizens, township **9** residents **10** metropolis **11** inhabitants, megalopolis, townspeople **12** municipality **16** incorporated town, metropolitan area

city hall
　French: 12 hotel de ville

City Life
　author: 15 Donald Barthelme

City Lights
　director: 14 Charles Chaplin
　cast: 8 Hank Mann **10** Harry Myers **14** Charlie Chaplin **16** Virginia Cherrill

City of God, The (De Civitate Dei)
　author: 11 St Augustine

City of the Lion *see* **9** Singapore

city slicker 4 dude **8** urbanite **11** cosmopolite **12** sophisticate

City Without Walls and Other Poems
　author: 7 W H Auden

Ciudad Trujillo
　capital of: 17 Dominican Republic

Civ 17 second Hebrew month

civic 5 local **6** public **8** citizen's, communal **9** community

civil 3 lay **4** city **5** civic, state **6** genial, polite, public **7** affable, amiable, citizen, cordial, secular **8** citizen's, communal, decorous, gracious, mannerly, obliging **9** civilized, community, courteous, municipal **10** individual, neighborly, respectful **11** gentlemanly, nonmilitary **12** conciliatory, well-mannered

Civil Disobedience
　author: 17 Henry David Thoreau

civilian 9 lay person **14** private citizen **17** nonmilitary person **18** nonuniformed person

civility 4 tact **7** manners, respect **8**

courtesy **10** affability, amiability, cordiality, good temper, politeness **11** good manners **12** graciousness, pleasantness **13** agreeableness, courteousness **14** respectfulness

civilization 7 culture, society **10** refinement **11** cultivation, worldliness **13** enlightenment **14** sophistication

civilize 5 edify, teach, train **6** inform, polish, refine **7** culture, develop, educate, elevate **8** humanize, instruct **9** cultivate, enlighten **11** acculturate **12** sophisticate

civil law
　Latin: 9 jus civile

Civil War
　admirals: 6 DuPont, Semmes
　battles: 6 Shiloh **7** Bull Run **8** Antietam **9** Nashville, Vicksburg **10** Cold Harbor, Gettysburg **11** Chattanooga, Chickamauga **14** Fredericksburg
　coin: 10 copperhead
　Confederate commanders: 3 Lee **4** Hill, Hood **5** Bragg, Early, Ewell, Mosby, Smith **6** Stuart, Toombs **7** Buckner, Hampton, Jackson **10** Beauregard **12** Breckinridge
　Union commanders: 5 Banks, Buell, Grant, Logan **6** Butler, Custer, Hooker, Porter **7** Sherman, Hancock

clad 6 garbed **7** arrayed, attired, clothed, dressed **9** outfitted

Claggart
　character in: 9 Billy Budd
　author: 8 Melville

claim 3 ask **4** avow, call, plea, take **5** exact, right, title **6** access, affirm, allege, assert, avowal, charge, demand, pick up **7** call for, collect, command, declare, profess, request **8** exaction, insist on, maintain, proclaim **9** assertion, ownership, seek as due, statement **10** allegation, lay claim to, pretension, profession **11** affirmation, declaration, postulation, requirement **12** proclamation, protestation

claimant 6 suitor **9** applicant, pretender **10** petitioner

clairvoyant 7 psychic **8** divining, oracular **9** prescient, prophetic **10** telepathic **11** foreknowing, telekinetic **12** extrasensory, precognitive, psychometric **13** psychokinetic, second-sighted

clam 4 vise **5** clamp, clasp **6** dollar, marine **7** bivalve, mollusk
　kind: 5 pismo, razor **6** butter, quahog **7** geoduck, steamer **10** little neck **11** cherrystone
　part: 4 foot, palp **5** gills, shell, valve **6** mantle, siphon **7** sinuses **8** ligament
　habitat: 3 mud **4** sand
　relative: 6 mussel, oyster

clamber up 5 climb, mount, scale **10** scramble up, struggle up

clamminess 4 damp **7** wetness **8**

dampness, dankness **10** stickiness, sweatiness

clammy 3 wet **4** damp **5** pasty, slimy **6** sticky, sweaty **10** perspiring **11** cold and damp

clamor 3 cry, din **4** call, howl, yell **5** blast, chaos, noise, shout, storm **6** bedlam, bellow, cry out, hubbub, jangle, outcry, racket, rumpus, tumult, uproar **7** bluster, call out, clangor, thunder **8** brouhaha, shouting **9** commotion, hue and cry **10** hullabaloo, vociferate, wild chorus

clamorous 4 loud **5** noisy **10** boisterous, uproarious

clamp 4 clip, grip, vise **5** brace, clasp **6** clench, clinch, fasten, secure **7** bracket **8** fastener

clan 4 gang, knot, line, ring **5** breed, cabal, crowd, group, guild, house, party, stock **6** circle, league, strain **7** company, dynasty, lineage, society **8** alliance, pedigree **10** fraternity **11** affiliation, association, brotherhood, family group, lineal group **12** tribal family

clandestine 6 covert, hidden, masked, secret, veiled **7** cloaked, furtive, private **8** secluded, sneaking, stealthy **9** concealed, secretive, underhand **10** undercover, unrevealed **11** underground, underhanded, undisclosed **12** confidential **13** surreptitious

clang 3 din **4** bong, gong, peal, toll **5** chime, clank, clash, knell **6** jangle **7** clangor, resound, ringing, tolling **8** clashing **10** resounding, ring loudly

clangor 3 din **5** noise **6** clamor, hubbub, jangle, racket, uproar

clank 5 chink, clang, clash, clink **6** jangle, rattle **7** clangor, clatter **8** clashing

clannish 4 cold **5** aloof **6** narrow **7** distant, insular **8** cliquish, snobbish **9** exclusive, parochial, sectarian **10** provincial, restricted, unfriendly **11** unreceptive

Clan of the Cave Bear, The
   author: 9 Jean M Auel

clap 3 bat, hit, rap, tap **4** bang, bump, cast, cuff, dash, hurl, peal, push, roar, rush, slam, slap, swat, toss **5** burst, clack, crack, drive, fling, force, pitch, shove, smack, smite, thump, whack **6** buffet, plunge, propel, strike, thrust, thwack, wallop **7** applaud, clatter **9** explosion **11** set suddenly

claptrap 3 rot **4** bosh, bull, bunk, sham, **5** bilge, hokum, hooey, stuff, trash, tripe **6** bunkum, drivel, hot air, humbug, tinsel **7** baloney, blarney, fustian, hogwash, spinach, twaddle **8** buncombe, nonsense, quackery, tommyrot **9** gaudiness, poppycock, staginess **10** applesauce, flapdoodle, tawdriness, tomfoolery **11** foolishness **15** pretentiousness **16** stuff and nonsense

claque 10 sycophants **15** cheering section

Clare, Ada
   character in: 10 Bleak House
   author: 7 Dickens

claret 3 red **5** blood **7** carmine, deep red, red wine **8** blood-red, Bordeaux, cardinal **11** purplish red, wine-colored

clarification 10 commentary **11** elucidation, explanation, explication **14** further comment
   French: 15 eclaircissement

clarify 5 clear, purge, solve **6** purify, refine **7** clear up, explain, lay open, resolve **9** elucidate, explicate, make clear, make plain **10** illuminate **11** disentangle, shed light on **12** bring to light **18** make understandable

clarinet 4 wind **8** woodwind **11** transposing **13** locorice stick
   mouthpiece: 4 reed
   ancestor: 9 chalumeau
   musician: 12 Benny Goodman

clarion 5 acute, clear, sharp **6** shrill **7** blaring, ringing **8** distinct, piercing, resonant, sonorous, stirring **10** commanding, compelling, imperative **11** high-pitched

Clarissa Harlowe
   author: 16 Samuel Richardson
   character: 8 Miss Howe **11** John Belford **14** Robert Lovelace **20** Colonel William Morden

clarity 6 purity **8** lucidity, radiance **9** clearness, exactness, plainness, precision **10** brightness, brilliance, directness, effulgence, glassiness, luminosity, simplicity **12** explicitness, translucence, transparency **15** intelligibility **17** comprehensibility

Clark, Mark W
   served in: 3 WWI **4** WWII **9** Korean War
   rank: 22 allied commander in Italy **24** commander of forces in Korea **30** chief of staff of army ground forces **42** commander of Allied occupation forces in Austria
   president of: 7 Citadel

Clark, Walter Van Tilburg
   author of: 16 The Ox-Bow Incident

Clarke, Arthur C
   author of: 10 (2010) Odyssey Two **13** (2001) A Space Odyssey, Childhood's End **18** Rendezvous with Rama

clash 4 bang, boil, feud, fray, tiff **5** argue, clang, clank, crash, fight, set-to **6** battle, combat, fracas, jangle, rattle, tussle **7** clangor, clatter, contend, contest, discord, dispute, grapple, jarring, quarrel, wrangle **8** conflict, crashing, friction, skirmish, squabble, struggle **9** altercate, encounter, lock horns **10** antagonism, difference, disharmony, dissidence, opposition **11** cross

swords **12** disagreement **13** exchange blows

clash of arms 5 fight **6** battle, combat **8** conflict, skirmish, struggle **9** encounter **10** engagement

clash with 9 fight with **12** do battle with **14** contend against **15** cross swords with

clasp 3 hug **4** bolt, clip, grip, hasp, hold, hook, link, lock, snap **5** catch, clamp, grasp, latch, press **6** buckle, clinch, clutch, couple, fasten, secure **7** coupler, embrace, grapple, squeeze **8** fastener **9** fastening

clasp in the arms 3 hug **4** hold **6** enfold **7** embrace

class 3 set **4** form, kind, rank, rate, size, sort, type **5** brand, breed, caste, genre, genus, grade, group, index, label, order, state **6** circle, clique, codify, course, lesson, number, sphere, status **7** arrange, catalog, section, session, species, station, variety **8** category, classify, division, pedigree, position **9** condition, designate **10** categorize, pigeonhole, social rank **11** set of pupils **13** social stratum **14** classification **15** departmentalize, graduating group

classic, classical 4 epic **5** model **6** heroic **7** ageless, paragon **8** absolute, accepted, enduring, masterly **9** archetype, excellent, exemplary, first-rate, prototype **10** archetypal, consummate, definitive, first-class, Greco-Roman, prototypal **11** masterpiece, outstanding, traditional **12** ancient Greek, ancient Roman, standard work **13** authoritative, distinguished **14** distinguishing **17** first-class example

classification 4 kind, rank, sort, type **5** class, genus, group, order **6** family, series **7** section, species **8** category, classing, division, grouping, labeling, ordering, taxonomy **9** arranging, gradation **10** assortment, organizing **11** arrangement, designation, disposition **12** categorizing, codification, organization **14** categorization **15** systematization

classified 5 secret **6** sorted **7** classed **8** assorted **10** restricted **11** categorized **12** confidential

classify 3 tag **4** list, rank, rate, size, sort, type **5** brand, class, grade, group, index, label, order, range **6** assort, codify, number, ticket **7** arrange, catalog **8** organize **9** segregate **10** categorize, pigeonhole **11** distinguish

classy 4 chic, posh, tony **5** nifty, nobby, ritzy, smart, swank, swell **6** dressy, modish, spiffy, swanky **7** elegant, genteel, opulent, refined, stylish **8** cultured, polished, tasteful **9** highclass **10** ultrasmart **11** fashionable, in good taste **12** aristocratic, wellmannered

clatter 4 bang 5 clack, clang, clank, clash, clink, clump, crash 6 clamor, jangle, racket, rattle 7 chatter 8 crashing, rattling

clattering 3 din 6 clamor, hubbub, racket, uproar 7 clangor

Claude
real name: 12 Claude Gellee
also called: 14 Claude Lorraine
born: 6 France 9 Champagne
artwork: 7 The Mill 16 Hagar and the Angel 18 Ascanius and the Stag, The Enchanted Castle 27 The Rest on the Flight into Egypt 31 The Embarkation of the Queen of Sheba

Claudel, Paul
author of: 6 L'Otage 10 The Hostage 13 Partage de Midi 15 The Satin Slipper 20 Tidings Brought to Mary

Claudia Quinta
freed: 12 grounded ship
feat proved: 8 chastity

Claudio
character in: 17 Measure for Measure 19 Much Ado About Nothing
author: 11 Shakespeare

Claudius
character in: 6 Hamlet
author: 11 Shakespeare

Claudius the God
author: 12 Robert Graves
sequel to: 9 I Claudius

clause 4 term 7 article, proviso 8 covenant 9 condition, provision 11 proposition, stipulation 13 specification 14 simple sentence

claustrophobia
fear of: 12 closed spaces 14 confined spaces

Clavell, James
author of: 6 Shogun, Tai-Pan 7 King Rat 9 Whirlwind 10 Noble House

clavicle
bone of: 10 collarbone

claw 3 paw 4 foot, grip, maul, tear 5 seize, slash, talon 6 clutch, pincer, scrape 7 scratch 8 lacerate 10 animal nail

Clay, Cassius
former name of: 11 Muhammad Ali

Clayburgh, Jill
born: 9 New York NY
roles: 9 Semi-Tough 12 Starting Over 16 An Unmarried Woman, North Dallas Forty 21 I'm Dancing as Fast as I Can

Clayhanger Trilogy, The
author: 13 Arnold Bennett

clean 3 mop 4 dust, fine, neat, pure, tidy, trim, wash 5 bathe, clear, fresh, moral, order, scour, scrub, sweep 6 bathed, chaste, decent, neaten, tidy up, vacuum, washed 7 cleaned, cleanse, healthy, launder, orderly, perfect, scoured, shampoo, upright 8 cleansed, decorous, flawless, innocent,

sanitary, scrubbed, spotless, unsoiled, virtuous, well-made 9 exemplary, faultless, honorable, laundered, stainless, undefiled, unspotted, unstained, unsullied, untainted, wholesome 10 immaculate, uninfected, unpolluted 11 unblemished 13 unadulterated 14 uncontaminated

cleaner, cleanser 4 soap 5 borax 6 washer 7 ammonia, janitor 8 purifier, scrubber 9 detergent 14 scouring powder

cleaning 7 bathing, washing 8 scouring 9 cleansing, going-over, scrubbing, tidying up 10 laundering

cleanse 3 rid 4 free, wash 5 bathe, clean, clear, erase, flush, scour, scrub 7 absolve, deliver, expunge, launder, release, shampoo 8 sweep out, unburden 9 expurgate

clean-shaven 6 smooth 9 unbearded 11 unwhiskered 12 smooth-shaven

cleansing 7 bathing, healing, purging, washing 8 flushing, scouring 9 expunging, purifying, scrubbing 10 absolution

cleanup 4 gain 6 profit 8 windfall
baseball: 12 fourth batter

clear 3 rid 4 fair, free, keen, make, open 5 alert, clean, empty, gauzy, lucid, plain, sharp, sunny 6 acquit, bright, patent, remove, serene, unstop, wholly 7 absolve, audible, audibly, certain, clearly, evident, express, fly over, glowing, halcyon, hop over, lighten, obvious, plainly, radiant, unblock 8 apparent, brighten, clear-cut, dazzling, definite, distinct, entirely, explicit, gleaming, leap over, luminous, manifest, pass over, pellucid, positive, skip over, unhidden 9 all the way, bound over, brilliant, cloudless, exculpate, exonerate, sparkling, unblocked, unclouded, unimpeded, unmuddled, vindicate, wide-awake 10 articulate, become fair, completely, diaphanous, discerning, distinctly, glistening, pronounced, unconfused, undeniable, unobscured 11 crystalline, inescapable, self-evident, translucent, transparent, unambiguous, unconcealed, undisguised, unequivocal, unqualified 12 articulately, intelligible, recognizable, unencumbered, unmistakable, unobstructed 14 comprehensible 15 distinguishable, straightforward

clearance 4 room, sale 6 margin, permit 7 removal 8 clearing 10 offsetting 11 elimination 13 authorization, certification

clear as day 5 plain 7 obvious 8 apparent, clear-cut, manifest 11 self-evident

clear-cut 4 open 5 exact, lucid, plain 6 patent 7 evident, express, obvious, precise 8 definite, detailed, distinct,

explicit, manifest 10 clear as day, unconfused, undeniable 11 appreciable, conspicuous, self-evident, substantial, unambiguous, undisguised, unequivocal, well-defined 12 crystal-clear, unmistakable 14 comprehensible, understandable 15 straightforward

clearheaded 5 acute, alert, awake, aware, sharp 6 astute 8 rational, sensible 9 on the ball, practical, realistic, wide-awake 10 discerning, insightful, on one's toes, on the stick, perceptive 13 perspicacious

clearheadedness 7 insight 8 sagacity 9 alertness, sharpness 10 perception 11 discernment 12 perspicacity

clearing 5 glade

clearly 6 surely 7 plainly 8 markedly, palpably, patently 9 assuredly, certainly, decidedly, evidently, obviously 10 distinctly, manifestly, noticeably, observably, undeniably 11 beyond doubt, indubitably, perceptibly, undoubtedly 12 recognizably, unmistakably 13 unequivocally 14 beyond question, unquestionably

clearly expressed 8 coherent 10 articulate 11 unambiguous 12 intelligible

clearness 7 clarity 10 brightness, brilliance 12 explicitness 15 unmistakability

clear-sighted 4 sage, wise 5 acute, sharp 6 astute, shrewd 8 piercing 9 judicious, sagacious, sensitive 10 discerning, perceptive 11 intelligent, keen-sighted, penetrating 12 sharp-sighted 13 perspicacious

clear up 6 settle 7 clarify, unsnarl 8 untangle 11 disentangle 12 uncomplicate 13 straighten out

Cleary, Beverly
author of: 6 Ramona 7 Fifteen 12 Henry Huggins 13 Jean and Johnny 15 Beezus and Ramona 16 Sister of the Bride

cleat 5 block, chock, spike, wedge 6 batten 7 bollard

cleavage 3 gap 4 rent, rift, slit 5 cleft, crack, notch, split 6 furrow, trench, trough 7 crevice, fissure, opening 8 crevasse

cleave 3 cut, hew 4 chop, fuse, hack, hold, open, part, plow, rend, rive, slit, tear 5 cling, crack, halve, sever, slash, slice, split, stick, unite 6 adhere, be true, bisect, cut off, detach, divide, furrow, sunder, uphold 7 abide by, chop off, disjoin, lay open, stand by 8 be joined, break off, hold fast, separate 9 disengage, dismember

cleaver 3 axe 4 tool 5 knife ridge

cleft 3 gap 4 rent, rift, slit 5 break, crack, notch, split 6 breach, cloven, cranny, divide, forked, furrow, trench, trough 7 crevice, divided, fissure, notched, opening, slotted 8 aperture, bisected, branched, cleavage, crevasse, division **10** separation **11** indentation

clemency 5 mercy **7** charity **8** humanity, kindness, leniency, mildness, softness, sympathy **9** tolerance **10** compassion, indulgence, moderation, temperance **11** benevolence, forbearance, magnanimity **12** mercifulness, pleasantness **13** forgivingness

clement 4 kind, mild, warm **5** balmy **6** benign, gentle, humane **7** lenient **8** merciful, tolerant **9** not severe, not strict **10** benevolent **13** compassionate

clench 3 set **4** grip **5** clasp, tense **6** clinch, clutch **7** stiffen, tighten **8** fasten on, hold fast **11** grasp firmly, strain tight **12** close tightly

Clennam, Arthur
    character in: 12 Little Dorrit
    author: 7 Dickens

Cleopatra
    queen of: 5 Egypt
    father: 7 Ptolemy
    brother/husband: 7 Ptolemy
    lover: 10 Mark Antony **12** Julius Caesar
    son: 9 Caesarion **15** Alexander Helios **19** Ptolemy Philadelphos
    daughter: 15 Cleopatra Selene
    death by: 3 asp **7** suicide

Cleopatra
    director:
        1934 version: 13 Cecil B DeMille
        1963 version: 17 Joseph L Mankiewicz
    cast:
        1934 version: 13 Henry Wilcoxon, Warren William **16** Claudette Colbert
        1963 version: 11 Rex Harrison **13** Richard Burton, Roddy McDowall **15** Elizabeth Taylor

clergy 6 rabbis **7** clerics, pastors, priests **8** ministry, prelates, the cloth **9** churchmen, clergymen, clericals, ministers, pastorate, preachers, rabbinate, the church, the pulpit **10** priesthood **14** the first estate

clergyman 5 padre, rabbi **6** cleric, father, parson, pastor, priest **7** prelate **8** chaplain, minister, preacher, reverend, sky pilot **9** churchman **13** man of the cloth

cleric 6 parson, pastor **8** chaplain, preacher **9** churchman, clergyman **13** man of the cloth

clerical 6 cleric, filing, office, typing **7** clerkly **8** churchly, of clerks, pastoral, priestly **10** accounting, rabbinical **11** bookkeeping, ministerial **13** record-keeping **14** ecclesiastical

clerical worker 5 clerk **6** typist **9** file clerk **10** bookkeeper, keypuncher **12** office worker **13** data processor

clerk 6 typist **8** salesman **9** file clerk **10** bookkeeper, salesclerk, sales-

woman **11** salesperson **12** office worker

Cleta
    member of: 6 Graces
    worshipped at: 6 Sparta

Cleveland
    baseball team: 7 Indians
    basketball team: 7 Rockers **9** Cavaliers
    football team: 6 Browns

Cleveland, Grover
    name at birth: 22 Stephen Grover Cleveland
    nickname: 5 Grove
    presidential rank: 12 twenty-fourth, twenty-second
    party: 8 Democrat
    state represented: 2 NY
    defeated: 4 (Simon) Wing **6** (Benjamin Franklin) Butler, (James Baird) Weaver, (James Gillespie) Blaine, (John Pierce) St John **7** (John) Bidwell **8** (Belva Ann Bennett) Lockwood, (Benjamin) Harrison
    vice president: 9 (Adlai Ewing) Stevenson, (Thomas Andrews) Hendricks
    cabinet:
        state: 5 (Richard) Olney **6** (Thomas Francis) Bayard **7** (Walter Quinton) Gresham
        treasury: 7 (Daniel) Manning **8** (John Griffin) Carlisle **9** (Charles Stebbins) Fairchild
        war: 6 (David Scott) Lamont **8** (William Crowninshield) Endicott
        attorney general: 5 (Richard) Olney **6** (Judson) Harmon **7** (Augustus Hill) Garland
        interior: 5 (Hoke) Smith, (Lucius Quintus Cincinnatus) Lamar, (William Freeman) Vilas **7** (David Rowland) Francis
    born: 2 NJ **8** Caldwell
    died/buried: 2 NJ **9** Princeton
    education:
        high school: 16 Liberal Institute
    religion: 12 Presbyterian
    interests: 7 fishing **8** shooting **13** gun collecting
    political career:
        mayor of: 7 Buffalo
        governor of: 7 New York
    civilian career: 6 lawyer
    notable events of lifetime/term: 5 Panic (of 1893) **10** gold crisis (of 1895)
        Act: 6 Tariff **14** Dawes Severalty **18** Interstate Commerce
        strike: 7 Pullman
    father: 13 Richard Falley
    mother: 4 Anne (Neal)
    siblings: 7 Ann Neal **9** Mary Allen **11** Susan Sophia, William Neal **12** Richard Cecil **13** Rose Elizabeth **14** Lewis Frederick **20** Margaret Louise Falley
    wife: 7 Frances (Folsom)

children: 4 Ruth **6** Esther, Marion **13** Francis Grover, Richard Folsom

clever 4 able, cute, deft, keen **5** acute, quick, sharp, smart, witty **6** adroit, artful, astute, bright, crafty, expert, shrewd **8** creative, humorous, original **9** ingenious, inventive **11** imaginative, intelligent, quick-witted, resourceful

cleverly 6 deftly **7** sharply, smartly, wittily **8** adroitly, artfully, craftily, expertly **10** creatively, humorously **11** ingeniously, inventively **13** imaginatively, intelligently

cleverness 3 wit **6** acumen **8** ableness, deftness, keenness **9** expertise, ingenuity, quickness, sharpness, smartness **10** adroitness, artfulness, astuteness, brightness, craftiness **12** intelligence, skillfulness **13** inventiveness **15** imaginativeness, quick-wittedness

clew see **4** clue

Clew
    thread in: 9 Labyrinth
    showed way to: 7 Theseus
    given by: 7 Ariadne

cliche 3 saw **6** old saw **7** bromide **8** banality, old story **9** platitude **10** stereotype **11** trite phrase

cliche-ridden 5 corny, stale, tired, trite, vapid **6** jejune **8** bromidic **9** hackneyed **10** unoriginal **13** platitudinous, unimaginative

click 3 tap **4** clap, snap **5** clack, clink, crack **6** rattle **7** crackle

client 5 buyer **6** patron **7** advisee, shopper **8** customer **9** purchaser **17** person represented

cliff 3 tor **4** crag **5** bluff, ledge **8** palisade **9** precipice **10** promontory

Cliff Dwellers see **6** Pueblo

Clift, Montgomery
    real name: 21 Edward Montgomery Clift
    nickname: 5 Monty
    born: 7 Omaha NE
    roles: 9 The Search **10** The Heiress, The Misfits **14** A Place in the Sun **18** From Here to Eternity, Suddenly Last Summer

climactic 7 crucial **8** critical, dramatic **11** sensational, suspenseful

climate 3 air **4** mood, tone **5** pulse **6** spirit, temper **7** quality, weather **8** ambience, attitude **9** character, condition **10** atmosphere **11** disposition, frame of mind, weather zone **12** usual weather **13** weather region **14** general feeling, weather pattern

climax 4 acme, apex, peak **5** crown **6** crisis, height, summit **8** best part, pinnacle **9** high point **10** denouement **11** culmination **12** highest point, turning point **13** critical point, crowning point, decisive point, supreme moment **18** moment of revelation

climb 4 go up, rise **5** mount, scale **6**

ascend, ascent, come up **8** climbing **9** clamber up **10** scramble up

climb down 6 go down **7** descend **8** back down, come down

clinch 3 cap, fix, win **4** bind, bolt, grip, nail **5** cinch, clamp, clasp, close, crown, grasp, screw **6** assure, clutch, couple, decide, fasten, obtain, secure, settle, verify, wind up **7** confirm, grapple **8** complete, conclude, make fast, make sure **9** culminate, establish, finish off **10** grab hold of, hold firmly **12** seize and hold **13** ensure victory

cling 3 hug **4** fuse, grip, hold **5** clasp, grasp, stick **6** adhere, be true, cleave, clutch **7** stand by **8** hang on to, hold fast, hold on to, maintain **9** stay close **10** be constant, be faithful, grab hold of

clinging 6 sticky **7** holding **8** adherent, adhering, adhesive, clasping, cleaving, grasping, gripping, sticking **9** hanging on, holding on **11** holding fast **12** grabbing hold

clinic 9 infirmary **10** polyclinic **13** medical center **15** outpatients' ward

clink 4 ting **5** clack, clank, click **6** jangle, jingle, rattle, tinkle **11** ring sharply

clinkers 4 duds, slag **5** dross, flops **6** cinder, scoria **8** failures

Clinton, William Jefferson
  original last name: 6 Blythe
  nickname: 4 Bill
  presidential rank: 11 forty-second
  party: 10 Democratic
  state represented: 2 AR **8** Arkansas
  defeated: 4 (George) Bush, (Bob) Dole
  vice president: 4 (Albert) Gore
  cabinet:
    state: 11 (Warren) Christopher
    treasury: 7 (Lloyd) Bentsen
    attorney general: 4 (Janet) Reno
    interior: 7 (Bruce) Babbitt
    labor: 5 (Robert) Reich
    HUD: 8 (Henry) Cisneros
  born: 2 AR **4** Hope
  education: 6 Oxford **7** Yale Law **10** Georgetown
  honor: 13 Rhodes Scholar
  political career:
    governor of: 7 Arkansas
    attorney general of: 7 Arkansas
  notable events of lifetime/term: 4 Waco **5** NAFTA **10** Whitewater **13** Anticrime Bill, Rhodes Scholar **15** Branch Davidians **17** Health Security Act
    Supreme Court appointments: 13 Stephen Breyer **17** Ruth Bader Ginsburg
  father: 13 William Blythe
  mother: 12 Virginia Cassidy Blythe
  stepfather: 12 Roger Clinton
  sibling: 12 Roger Clinton

  wife: 13 Hillary Rodham
  children: 7 Chelsea

Clio
  muse of: 7 history

clip 3 bob, cut, fix **4** crop, grip, hook, snip, trim **5** clamp, clasp, shear **6** attach, buckle, clinch, couple, cut off, cut out, fasten, paring, secure, staple **7** cutting, shorten **8** clipping, cropping, cut short, fastener, shearing, snipping

clipper 4 boat, ship **6** cutter, shears **8** aircraft, airplane, sailboat, scissors **9** racehorse

clipping 7 cutting, pruning, snippet **8** trimming

clique 3 set **4** clan, gang **5** crowd, group **6** circle **7** coterie, faction

cliquish 4 cold **5** aloof **7** distant **8** clannish, snobbish **9** exclusive **10** unfriendly **11** unreceptive

cloak 4 cape, hide, mask, robe, veil, wrap **5** cover, tunic **6** mantle, screen, shield, shroud **7** conceal, curtain, pelisse, secrete **8** burnoose, disguise **10** camouflage **11** concealment

cloaked 7 covered, muffled, wrapped **9** disguised

cloaking 7 masking, veiling **8** covering **9** obscuring **10** disguising

cloakroom 8 anteroom, coatroom

clobber 3 hit **4** beat, belt, drub, lick, maul, rout, slug, sock, trim, whip **5** clout, pound, punch, smash, smear, whack **6** batter, beat up, strike, subdue, thrash, wallop **7** conquer, shellac, trounce **8** beat up on, lambaste

clock 5 watch **8** horologe **9** timepiece **11** chronometer

Clockwork Orange, A
  author: 14 Anthony Burgess
  director: 14 Stanley Kubrick
  cast: 12 Patrick Magee **13** Adrienne Corri **15** Malcolm McDowell
  protagonist: 4 Alex

clod 3 oaf, wad **4** boor, dolt, dope, glob, hunk, lout, lump, rube **5** chunk, clown, clump, dummy, dunce, moron, yokel **7** bumpkin, fathead **8** imbecile, numskull **9** blockhead, ignoramus, simpleton

clodhopper 3 oaf **4** boot, clod, hick, lout, rube, slob **5** booby, clown, yokel **6** galoot, lubber, lummox, rustic **7** bumpkin, hayseed, peasant, plowboy, redneck **8** clodpole, lunkhead **9** heavy shoe, hillbilly **10** provincial

clog 4 stop **5** block, check, choke, close, dam up **6** stop up **7** barrier, congest **8** blockage, obstacle, obstruct, stoppage **9** restraint **10** impediment **11** obstruction

clogged 6 choked, halted, jammed **7** clotted, impeded **8** choked up, filled up, hampered, hindered, restrained **10** encumbered, obstructed, overloaded

cloister 4 stoa, walk **5** abbey, aisle **6** arcade, closet, coop up, friary, hole up, immure, shut up, wall up **7** conceal, confine, convent, embower, gallery, nunnery, passage, portico, seclude, walkway **8** shut away **9** colonnade, courtyard, monastery, promenade, sequester **10** ambulatory, passageway

cloistered 5 alone, aloof, apart **6** hidden **7** immured, recluse **8** closeted, confined, detached, isolated, secluded, secreted, separate, solitary **9** concealed, insulated, sheltered, withdrawn **11** dissociated, sequestered

clone 4 copy **5** robot **6** double **7** android, replica **9** automaton, duplicate, replicate **10** carbon copy **12** doppelganger **13** identical copy

close 3 end, hot, pen **4** akin, clog, fast, fill, firm, fuse, halt, join, keen, link, near, neat, nigh, plug, shut, stop, trim, warm **5** alert, block, cease, dense, fixed, humid, muggy, pen in, sharp, short, solid, stuff, tight, unite **6** allied, at hand, clog up, coop up, couple, ending, fill in, fill up, finale, finish, hard by, intent, jammed, loving, narrow, nearby, next to, plug up, recess, secure, shut in, shut up, smooth, stingy, stop up, stuffy, windup **7** adjourn, careful, close up, closing, compact, confine, connect, cramped, crowded, devoted, dismiss, enclose, intense, miserly, pinched, seal off, shut off, similar, stuffed, suspend, teeming **8** attached, blockade, break off, conclude, confined, familiar, friendly, grudging, imminent, intimate, leave off, obstruct, populous, shut down, squeezed, stagnant, stifling, stinting, swarming, thorough, vigilant, watchful **9** attentive, congested, impending, niggardly, penurious, scrimping, terminate **10** almost like, completion, compressed, conclusion, nearly even, nip-and-tuck, resembling, restricted, sweltering, ungenerous **11** almost alike, approaching, approximate, close-fisted, discontinue, forthcoming, impermeable, in proximity, inseparable, nearly equal, neighboring, suffocating, termination, tight-fisted, well-matched **12** bring to an end, impenetrable, parsimonious, unventilated **13** bring together, near to the skin, penny-pinching, uncomfortable **14** thick as thieves

closed 6 secret **7** private **9** exclusive

closed-minded 5 rigid **7** adamant, uptight **8** obdurate, stubborn **9** hidebound, obstinate, pig-headed, unbending **10** inflexible, unyielding **12** intransigent **14** uncompromising

Close Encounters of the Third Kind
  director: 15 Steven Spielberg

cast: 8 Teri Garr **13** Melinda Dillon **15** Richard Dreyfuss **16** Francois Truffaut
score: 12 John Williams

closefisted 4 mean **5** cheap, close, mingy, tight **6** stingy **7** miserly **8** grudging **9** niggardly, penurious **10** economical, ungenerous **11** closehanded, tightfisted **12** parsimonious **13** penny-pinching

close-fitting 4 snug **5** tight **9** skintight **11** constricted, form-fitting **12** constricting, tight-fitting **15** like a second skin

close friend 3 pal **4** chum, mate **5** buddy, crony **6** cohort **7** best pal **8** alter ego, intimate **9** companion, confidant **10** bosom buddy **17** intimate confidant

close loudly 4 bang, clap, slam

closely 6 keenly **7** alertly, sharply **8** intently **9** carefully, heedfully, intensely **10** diligently, vigilantly, vigorously, watchfully **11** attentively

close-mouthed 3 shy **4** cool **5** terse **7** bashful, distant **8** reserved, reticent, retiring, taciturn **9** diffident, secretive, withdrawn **11** tight-lipped **15** uncommunicative

closeness 8 meanness, nearness **10** stinginess **11** familiarity, miserliness **15** tightfistedness

close of day 3 eve **4** dusk, even **6** sunset **7** evening, sundown **8** eventide, gloaming, twilight **9** nightfall

closet 2 WC **4** eury, safe **5** ambry, cuddy **6** covert, hidden, locker pantry, secret, toilet **7** armoire, cabinet, private **8** coatroom, cupboard, imprison, secluded **9** cloakroom, storeroom, visionary **11** speculative, theoretical, unpractical, water closet

close tightly 3 set **4** seal, slam **5** latch **6** clench, secure **13** press together

close to 4 near **6** almost, around **9** just about **12** on the point of **13** approximately

closure 3 lid, tap **4** bung, cork, plug, stop **5** cover **6** ending, faucet, finish, spigot **7** barring, bolting, closing, cloture, locking, sealing, stopper **8** securing, shutting, stoppage **9** cessation **10** conclusion, stoppering **11** termination **14** discontinuance **15** discontinuation

clot 3 gob **4** lump, mass **7** congeal, thicken **8** embolism, solidify, thrombus **9** coagulate, occlusion **11** coagulation

Cloten
character in: 9 Cymbeline
author: 11 Shakespeare

cloth 5 goods **6** fabric **7** textile **8** dry goods, material **9** yard goods **10** piece goods

clothe 3 don **4** case, coat, deck, garb, robe, veil, wrap **5** array, cloak, cloud, cover, drape, dress **6** attire, bedeck, encase, enwrap, outfit, rig out, screen, shroud **7** bedizen, costume, deck out, envelop, sheathe, swaddle **8** accouter

clothed 4 clad **5** robed **6** draped **7** cloaked, couched, covered, dressed, mantled, wearing **8** equipped, provided **9** expressed, furnished

clothes 4 duds, garb, rags, togs, wear **5** dress **6** attire, finery **7** apparel, costume, raiment, regalia **8** clothing, ensemble, garments, wardrobe **11** habiliments

clotheshorse 3 fop **4** dude **5** dandy, model **12** Beau Brummell, fashion plate, man of fashion, sharp dresser **14** woman of fashion

clothing *see* **7** clothes

Clotho
member of: 5 Fates
spinner of: 12 thread of life

cloud 3 dim, mar **4** blur, hide, veil **5** blind, cloak, cover, muddy, shade, sully, upset **6** darken, impair, muddle, screen, shadow, shroud **7** conceal, confuse, curtain, distort, disturb, eclipse, obscure, tarnish **8** overcast **9** discredit, make vague **10** overshadow **11** cast doubt on **14** call to question **19** place under suspicion

cloudburst 6 deluge **8** downpour, rainfall **9** rainstorm

clouded 3 dim **5** dusky, murky **7** blurred, obscure, sullied, tainted, unclear **8** confused, darkened, obscured **10** ill-defined, indistinct

cloudless 4 fair **5** clear, sunny **6** bright **7** halcyon **8** sunshiny **9** unclouded **10** unobscured

Clouds
goddess of: 3 Fri **5** Frigg, Frija **6** Frigga

Clouds, The (Nephelai)
author: 12 Aristophanes
character: 8 Just Plea, Socrates **10** Unjust Plea **11** Strepsiades **12** Pheidippides

cloudy 4 dark, gray, hazy **5** murky, vague **6** dreary, gloomy, leaden, veiled **7** clouded, obscure, sunless, unclear **8** confused, nebulous, overcast **9** confusing, undefined **10** indefinite, mysterious **11** overclouded

Clouet, Jean
born: 8 Flanders
artwork attributed: 13 Guillaume Bude **16** Madame de Canaples, Man with Gold Coins **17** The Count of Brissac, The Dauphin Francis **22** Man with a Book by Petrarch

clout 3 box, hit, jab **4** bash, belt, blow, pull, sock **5** crack, knock, punch, smack, thump, whack **6** wallop **9** influence **10** importance

clove
botanical name: 16 Eugenia aromatica **18** Syzygium aromaticum
origin: 5 Pemba **7** Far East **8** Moluccas, Zanzibar **9** Mauritius **10** Madagascar
use: 3 ham **8** pickling, pomander **16** yellow vegetables

cloven 5 cleft, split **7** divided, notched, slotted **8** bisected

clover 9 Trifolium
varieties: 3 bur, elk, hop, low, pin, red **4** bush, holy, Kura, musk, owl's, tick **5** Alyce, Hubam, lucky, sweet, water, white **6** Alsike, cow hop, indoor, Korean, Ladino, yellow **7** Bukhara, crimson, Italian, mammoth, Mexican, Persian, prairie **8** four-leaf, Japanese, large hop, reversed, small hop, stinking **9** Hungarian **10** strawberry, toothed bur, white Dutch, white sweet **11** yellow sweet **12** silky prairie, subterranean, white prairie **13** European water **16** strawberry-headed

clown 3 wag, wit **4** card, fool, jest, joke, mime, zany **5** comic, cut up, joker **6** jester, madcap **7** buffoon **8** comedian, humorist **9** harlequin, kid around **10** comedienne, fool around **11** funny person, merry-andrew

Clown, The
author: 12 Heinrich Boll

clownishness 6 antics **10** buffoonery, tomfoolery **12** monkeyshines **14** playing the fool

Clowns of God, The
author: 11 Morris L West

cloy 3 gag **4** bore, glut, pall, sate, tire **5** choke, weary **6** benumb, overdo **7** exhaust, satiate, surfeit **8** nauseate, saturate

cloying 5 sweet **6** sugary **9** excessive, satiating **10** saccharine

club 3 bat, hit **4** bash, beat, flog, slug **5** billy, flail, group, guild, lay on, lodge, stick, union **6** batter, buffet, cudgel, league, pommel, pummel, strike **7** society **8** alliance, bludgeon, sorority **9** billyclub, clubhouse, truncheon **10** fraternity, shillelagh, sisterhood **11** affiliation, association, brotherhood, country club

clubhouse 4 club, hall **5** lodge **11** locker rooms **12** meeting house

clue 3 cue, key **4** clew, hint, mark, sign **5** guide, scent, trace **7** glimmer, inkling, pointer **8** evidence **9** indicator, inference **10** indication, intimation, suggestion **11** insinuation

clump 4 bulb, bump, knob, knot, lump, mass, plod, thud **5** batch, bunch, clomp, clunk, copse, group, grove, plunk, shock, stamp, stomp, thump, tramp **6** lumber **7** cluster, thicket **9** aggregate **10** assemblage, collection

clumsiness 9 gawkiness **10** ineptitude **11** awkwardness **12** carelessness, un-

gainliness 13 gracelessness, maladroit-ness

clumsy 5 bulky, crude, gawky, inept, rough **6** klutzy **7** awkward, unhandy **8** bungling, careless, ungainly, unwieldy **9** graceless, makeshift, maladroit, unskilled **10** blundering, cumbersome, ungraceful **11** heavy-handed **12** ill-contrived, unmanageable **14** butterfingered **21** like a bull in a china shop

cluster 4 band, bevy, heap, herd, knot, mass, pack, pile **5** amass, batch, block, bunch, clump, crowd, flock, group, sheaf, shock, swarm **6** gather, muster, throng **7** collect, company **8** assemble, converge **9** aggregate **10** accumulate, assemblage, collection, congregate **12** accumulation, congregation **13** agglomeration **14** conglomeration

cluster around 6 gather **7** collect **10** congregate **12** herd together **13** flock together

clutch 3 hug **4** grip, hold **5** clasp, grasp **6** clench **7** cling to, embrace, squeeze **8** hang on to

clutter 4 fill, heap, mess, pile **5** chaos, strew **6** jumble, litter, tangle **7** scatter **8** disarray, disorder **9** confusion **10** hodgepodge

cluttered 5 messy **7** chaotic, crowded, jumbled, muddled **8** confused, littered **9** scattered **10** disordered, disorderly

Clytemnestra
father: 9 Tyndareus
mother: 4 Leda
brother: 6 Castor, Pollux
sister: 5 Helen **8** Timandra
cousin: 8 Perilaus
husband: 9 Agamemnon
son: 7 Orestes
daughter: 7 Electra, Erigone **9** Iphigenia **12** Chrysothemis
lover: 9 Aegisthus
killed: 9 Agamemnon
killed by: 7 Orestes

coach 3 bus **5** drill, guide, sedan, stage, teach, train, tutor **6** advise, direct, mentor **7** omnibus, trainer **8** carriage, instruct **9** limousine, preceptor **10** automobile, four-in-hand, motor coach, stagecoach **11** four-wheeler, second class **12** economy class **14** private teacher **16** athletic director

coachman 3 fly **4** jehu, whip **5** pilot **6** driver **10** charioteer

Coactrice 14 poisonous snake

coagulate 3 gel, set **4** clot, jell **6** curdle, harden **7** congeal, jellify, thicken **8** solidify

coagulation 3 gob **4** clot, mass **8** clotting, curdling, thrombus **10** thickening

coal 4 ash, bass, char, coke, coom, culm, dust, fuel, slag, smut, swad **5** ember **6** cannel, cinder **7** lignite, clinker **8** charcoal **10** fossil fuel **11** charred wood

box: 3 hod **7** scuttle
made from: 6 carbon
type: 4 hard, soft **7** lignite **10** anthracite, bituminous
mining method: 4 deep **8** opencast **10** strip auger **11** underground
mine: 5 drift, shaft, slope, strip
size: 3 egg, nut, pea **5** stove

coal-black 3 jet **4** dark, inky **5** black, ebony, raven, sable **9** pitch-dark

coalesce 3 mix **4** ally, form, fuse, join, meld **5** blend, merge, unify, unite **6** cohere **7** combine **9** become one, integrate **10** amalgamate, join forces **11** agglutinate, consolidate **12** band together, come together **14** form an alliance

coalition 5 union **6** fusion, league **7** society **8** alliance **9** syndicate **10** federation **11** affiliation, association, combination, confederacy, partnership **12** amalgamation **13** agglomeration, consolidation **14** conglomeration

Coal Miner's Daughter
director: 12 Michael Apted
cast: 9 Levon Helm **11** Sissy Spacek (Loretta Lynn) (Oscar) **13** Tommy Lee Jones **14** Beverly D'Angelo
Oscar for: 7 actress (Spacek)
screenplay: 10 Tom Rickman

Coaluitecan
tribe: 6 Payaya

coarse 4 lewd, rude, vile **5** crass, crude, dirty, gross, harsh, rough **6** common, nubbly, odious, ribald, shaggy, sordid, vulgar **7** boorish, bristly, brutish, ill-bred, loutish, obscene, prickly, uncouth **8** impolite, improper, indecent, scratchy **9** bristling, inelegant, offensive, repulsive, revolting, sandpaper, unrefined **10** disgusting, indecorous, indelicate, lascivious, licentious, scurrilous, unladylike, unpolished **11** foul-mouthed, ill-mannered **12** lacking taste **13** rough-textured, ungentlemanly

coarse-grained 5 crude, harsh, nubby, rough **6** coarse, grainy, shaggy **7** bristly **8** scratchy **9** unrefined **13** rough-textured

coarseness 9 crudeness, grossness, roughness, vulgarity **10** indelicacy, inelegance **11** boorishness **16** lack of refinement

coast 4 skim, slip, waft **5** drift, float, glide, shore, slide, sweep **6** strand **7** seaside **8** glissade, littoral, seaboard, seacoast, seashore **9** shoreline

coaster 3 mat **4** ship, sled, tray **5** wagon **6** cradle, glider, slider **8** toboggan **9** tray stand **13** decanter stand, roller coaster

coat 3 fur **4** hair, hide, pelt, wrap **5** cover, glaze, layer, paint, smear **6** blazer, enamel, encase, jacket, spread **7** coating, encrust, envelop, lacquer, overlay, plaster, slicker, topcoat **8**

covering, laminate, mackinaw, overcoat, raincoat **9** whitewash **10** mackintosh, sports coat

coating 4 coat, film, skin **5** layer, sheet **6** veneer **7** overlay **8** covering, envelope

coat of arms 4 arms **5** crest **6** creast **8** insignia **9** blaconwry **10** escutcheon **14** heraldic emblem **16** armorial bearings

coat of mail 4 mail **5** armor **9** chain mail **11** suit of armor

Coat of Varnish, A
author: 6 C P Snow

coax 6 cajole **7** wheedle **8** butter up, inveigle, soft-soap, talk into **9** sweet-talk

cobalt 4 blue **5** azure **7** element, sky blue **10** bright blue **12** greenish blue
chemical symbol: 2 Co

Cobb, Lee J
born: 9 New York NY
roles: 10 Willy Loman **12** The Virginian **14** Twelve Angry Men **15** On the Waterfront **16** Death of a Salesman

Cobb, Ty (Tyrus Raymond)
nickname: 12 Georgia Peach
sport: 8 baseball
position: 8 outfield
team: 13 Detroit Tigers

cobbler 3 pie **9** bootmaker, shoemaker **12** shoe repairer **16** deepdish fruit pie

cobra
also: 3 asp **5** mamba **11** hooded snake
native to: 4 Asia **6** Africa
kind: 4 king **6** hooded, Indian **8** Egyptian
enemy: 8 mongoose

Coburn, Charles
born: 10 Savannah GA
roles: 9 Boss Tweed **17** The More the Merrier

Coburn, James
born: 8 Laurel NE
roles: 10 Hudson Hawk **11** In Like Flint, Our Man Flint **14** The Great Escape, The Muppet Movie **17** The Nutty Professor **19** The Magnificent Seven

Coca, Imogene
partner: 9 Sid Caesar
born: 14 Philadelphia PA
roles: 15 Your Show of Shows

cock 3 tip **4** knob **5** raise, valve **6** faucet, handle, perk up **7** rooster, stand up **8** cockerel, male bird, set erect **9** bristle up **11** chanticleer **13** turn to one side **16** raise the hammer of **17** draw back the hammer

cockade 4 knot **5** badge **6** ribbon **7** rosette **8** ornament **10** party badge

Cockade State
nickname of: 8 Maryland

cock-and-bull story 3 fib, lie **4** myth, yarn **5** fable **7** fiction, untruth, whop-

per 9 fairy tale, falsehood, fish story, invention, tall story 11 fabrication 13 prevarication

Cockcroft, John Douglas
field: 7 physics
nationality: 7 British
developed: 24 Cockcroft-Walton generator
worked with: 6 Walton
awarded: 10 Nobel Prize

cockeyed 3 mad 4 awry, wild 5 askew, crazy, goofy, inane, nutty, weird 6 absurd, aslant, insane, tilted 7 crooked, foolish, twisted 8 lopsided, sideways 9 irregular, off-center, senseless 10 cockamamie, out of whack, ridiculous, unbalanced 11 nonsensical 12 asymmetrical, preposterous

Cockpit of Europe *see* 7 Belgium

cockscomb 4 comb 5 crest 7 celosia, coxcomb 8 amaranth, caruncle

cocksure 4 pert, smug, vain 5 brash, cocky, pushy 6 cheeky, snooty 8 arrogant, positive 9 assertive, audacious, bumptious, conceited 10 aggressive, swaggering 11 overbearing, self-assured, swell-headed 13 overconfident, self-confident

cocktail 5 drink, fruit, horse 6 shrimp 10 docked tail, semi-formal
type: 4 grog 6 brandy, gibson, gimlet, mai tai, rob roy, zombie 7 Bellini, gin fizz, martini, negroni, sidecar, stinger 8 daiquiri, highball, hot toddy, pink lady 9 cuba libre, hurricane, gin rickey, manhattan, margarita, mint julep, rusty nail 10 bloody mary, tom collins 11 boilermaker, gin and tonic, grasshopper, screwdriver, sloe gin fizz 12 black russian, cosmopolitan, old-fashioned, tom and jerry, whiskey sour 13 planter's punch 15 brandy alexander
mixer: 4 soda 5 tonic, water 7 bitters, seltzer 9 ginger ale
garnish: 4 lime 5 lemon, olive, orange, twist 16 maraschino cherry
stirrer: 7 muddler

cocktail lounge 3 bar 6 saloon, tavern 7 gin mill, taproom

cocky 5 brash, saucy 6 jaunty 8 arrogant, cocksure, impudent 9 conceited, egotistic 10 swaggering

Coco, James
born: 9 New York NY
roles: 11 Sancho Panza 13 Man of La Mancha 21 Last of the Red Hot Lovers

cocoa 5 brown, cacao 9 chocolate 12 hot chocolate

cocoon
covering for: 5 larva
stage: 5 pupal
made of: 4 silk

Cocteau, Jean
author of: 7 Orpheus 8 Antigone 12 Blood of a Poet 18 The Infernal Machine 19 Les Enfants Terribles, Les Parents Terribles 20 The Beauty and the Beast

Cocytus
river in: 5 Hades

coddle 3 pat, pet 4 baby 5 humor, spoil 6 caress, cuddle, dote on, fondle, pamper 7 indulge 11 mollycoddle

code 4 laws 5 rules 6 cipher 7 statute 8 precepts 9 ordinance, standards 10 cryptogram, guidelines, principles 11 cryptograph, proprieties, regulations 13 secret writing 14 secret language

codger 5 crank, miser 6 geezer, oddity, old man 9 eccentric, odd person

codicil 5 rider 8 addendum, addition, appendix 9 extension, subscript 10 postscript, supplement 11 added clause

codify 4 rank, rate 5 grade, group, index, order 7 arrange, catalog 8 classify, organize, tabulate 9 methodize 10 categorize, coordinate, regularize 11 systematize

coelenterate 5 coral, hydra, polyp 6 Medusa 7 acaleph, radiate 8 acalephe 9 jellyfish 10 sea anemone
habitat: 5 ocean 9 salt water

Coelophysis
type: 8 dinosaur, therapod
location: 7 Arizona
period: 8 Triassic

coequal 5 equal 10 coordinate 16 equally important

coequality 6 parity 8 equality, evenness, sameness 10 uniformity 11 equivalency 14 correspondence

coerce 3 cow 4 make 5 bully, drive, force 6 compel, oblige 7 dragoon 8 browbeat, bulldoze, pressure, threaten 9 constrain, strong-arm 10 intimidate

coercer 5 bully 9 oppressor, tormenter, tormentor 10 browbeater 11 intimidator, petty tyrant

coercion 5 force 6 duress 7 threats 8 bullying, pressure 10 compulsion, constraint 11 browbeating 12 intimidation

coercive 8 enforced, forcible 10 compulsory, obligatory 11 threatening

coexist with 12 go hand in hand, go side by side, live together 13 go hand in glove

coffee 6 Coffea 13 Coffea arabica
varieties: 4 Java, Kona, Wild 5 Irish, Mocha 6 Almond, Common 7 Arabian, Arabica, Robusta, Vanilla 8 Liberian, Liberica, Zanzibar 9 Colombian 11 French Roast, Wild robusta 13 Decaffeinated 20 Jamaican Blue Mountain
beverage: 5 decaf, latte 6 kahlua 8 espresso 10 cafe au lait, cappuccino
small cup: 9 demitasse

coffee (black)
French: 8 cafe noir 10 cafe nature

coffee brandy 6 Kahlua 8 Tia Maria
coffee with milk 5 latte
French: 10 cafe au lait

coffer 3 box 4 case 5 chest 9 strong-box 10 depository, repository 13 treasure chest

coffers 5 safes 6 vaults 8 treasury 9 cash boxes 11 money supply

coffin 3 box 4 pall 6 casket 10 catafalque 11 sarcophagus

cog 3 cam, lie 4 gear 5 cheat, cozen, tenon, tooth, wedge, wheel 8 small boat 10 projection

cogent 5 sound, valid 6 potent 7 weighty 8 forceful, powerful 9 effective, trenchant 10 compelling, convincing, persuasive, undeniable 11 meritorious, well-founded 12 well-grounded 16 incontrovertible

cogitate 5 study, think, weigh 6 ponder 7 reflect 8 meditate, mull over, ruminate 9 think over 10 deliberate, think about 11 contemplate, reflect upon 18 consider thoroughly

cogito ergo sum 18 I think therefore I am
said by: 9 Descartes

cognac
type: 6 brandy 7 liqueur
origin: 6 France
brand: 7 Bisquit, Martell 8 Hennessy 10 Remy Martin 11 Courvoisier
label: 2 VO (very old), VS (very special), XO (extra old) 3 XXO (extra extra old) 4 VSOP (very superior old pale) 8 Napoleon (5 year premium)
drink: 9 Andalusia
with Cointreau: 10 Rolls Royce
with Triple Sec: 7 Chicago 10 Rolls Royce
with vodka: 7 Cossack

cognate 4 akin, like 5 alike, close 7 kindred, related, similar 8 familial, parallel, relative 9 affiliate 10 derivative 11 consanguine

cognition 7 knowing 9 awareness, knowledge 11 familiarity 13 comprehension, understanding

cognizance 4 heed, note 5 grasp 6 notice, regard 8 scrutiny 9 attention, awareness, cognition, knowledge 10 perception 11 familiarity, observation, recognition, sensibility 12 apprehension 13 comprehension, consciousness, understanding

cognizant 5 aware 6 posted 7 knowing, mindful 8 familiar, informed, versed in 9 conscious 10 acquainted, conversant, instructed 11 enlightened 13 knowledgeable, understanding

cognomen 4 name 6 handle 7 epithet, moniker, surname 11 appellation, designation

cognoscenti 6 judges 7 experts 8 insiders 11 authorities 12 connoisseurs 14 those in the know

cohere 3 fit, set **4** bind, fuse, glue, hold, jibe, join **5** agree, cling, match, stick, tally, unite **6** cement, concur, square **7** combine, conform, congeal **8** coalesce, coincide, dovetail, solidify **9** coagulate, harmonize **10** correspond **11** consolidate, synchronize **12** hold together **13** stick together

coherence 5 logic, unity **7** clarity, concord, harmony **8** cohesion **9** congruity **10** accordance, conformity, consonance **11** consistency, rationality **12** organization

coherent 5 clear, lucid **7** logical, orderly **8** cohesive, rational **9** congruous, connected, in keeping, organized **10** articulate, consistent, harmonious, meaningful, systematic **11** in agreement **12** intelligible **13** corresponding **14** comprehensible, understandable

cohesion 4 bond **5** union, unity **7** bonding **8** adhesion **10** attraction, solidarity

cohesive 3 set **5** solid **6** sticky **7** viscous **8** cemented, coherent, cohering, sticking **9** connected **11** indivisible, inseparable **12** consolidated **13** agglutinative

Cohn, Ferdinand Julius
  field: 6 botany
  nationality: 6 German
  founded: 12 bacteriology

Cohn, Robert
  character in: 15 The Sun Also Rises
  author: 9 Hemingway

cohort 3 pal **4** chum **5** buddy, crony **6** fellow, friend **7** comrade **8** follower, myrmidon **9** associate, companion **10** accomplice

coif 3 cap **4** hood, veil **6** beggin, burlet, hairdo **8** biggonet, coiffure, skull cap **9** head-dress

coiffed 6 capped, styled **7** dressed **8** arranged

coiffeur 7 stylist **11** hairdresser **15** male hairdresser

coiffure 2 DA, GI **3** bob, bun **4** Afro, coif, perm, shag, trim, updo, wave **6** hairdo **7** beehive, blowcut, comb-out, flattop, haircut, pageboy, upsweep **8** cold wave, cornrows, ducktail **9** hairstyle, permanent, pompadour

coil 4 curl, loop, ring, roll, wind **5** braid, twine, twist **6** circle, spiral, writhe **7** entwine **8** encircle

coin 4 mint **5** hatch, money, piece **6** change, create, devise, invent, make up, silver, strike **7** concoct, dream up, think up **8** conceive **9** fabricate, originate

coin/currency
  of Afghanistan: 3 pul **5** abaze, riyal, rupee **6** abbasi, amania **7** afghani
  of Albania: 3 lek **5** franc **6** qintar **7** quintar
  of Algeria: 5 dinar **7** centime
  of Andorra: 5 franc **6** peseta

of Angola: 6 escudo, kwanza, macuta, macute **7** angolar, centavo
of Argentina: 4 peso **7** centavo **9** argentino
of Armenia: 5 ruble
of Australia: 4 dump, tray, zack **5** pound **6** dollar **8** shilling
of Austria: 4 lira **5** crown, ducat, krone **6** florin, gulden, heller, zehner **8** albertin, groschen, kreutzer **9** schilling
of Azerbaijan: 5 manat
of Bahrain: 5 dinar
of Bangladesh: 4 taka **5** paisa
of Belarus: 5 ruble
of Belgium: 5 belga, franc **7** brabant, centime, crocard
of Benin: 5 franc **7** centime
of Bhutan: 5 paisa, rupee **7** chetrum **8** ngultrum
of Bolivia: 4 peso **7** centavo **9** boliviano
of Bosnia-Herzegovina: 5 dinar
of Botswana: 4 pula, rand
of Brazil: 3 joe **4** reis **5** dobra **7** centara, halfjoe, milreis **8** cruzeiro
of Bulgaria: 3 lev **8** stotinki
of Burkina Faso: 5 franc **7** centime
of Burundi: 5 franc **7** centime
of Cambodia: 3 sen **4** quan, riel **6** puttan **7** piaster
of Cameroon: 5 franc **7** centime
of Canada: 6 loonie, toonie
of Canary Islands: 6 peseta
of Cape Verde: 6 escudo **7** centavo
of Central African Republic: 5 franc **7** centime
of Chad: 5 franc **7** centime
of Chile: 4 peso **5** libra **6** condor, escudo
of China: 4 cash, cent, fyng, mace, tael, tiao, yuan **5** sycee **12** jen nin piao pu
of Colombia: 4 peso, real **6** condor, peseta **7** centavo
of Comoros: 5 franc **7** centime
of Congo: 5 franc **7** centime
of Costa Rica: 5 colon **6** colone **7** centimo
of Crete: 7 drachma
of Croatia: 5 dinar
of Cuba: 4 peso **7** centavo **8** cuarenta
of Cyprus 4 para **5** pound
of Czechoslovakia/ Czech Republic: 5 crown, ducat **6** heller, koruna
of Denmark: 3 one, ora, ore **4** fyrk **5** krone **6** frederik, skilling **9** rigsdaler
of Djibouti: 5 franc **7** centime
of Dominican Republic: 3 oro **4** peso **6** franco
of Ecuador: 5 sucre **7** centavo
of Egypt: 4 fils, kees, para **5** asper, dinar, fodda, gersh, girsh, medin, pound, riyal **6** ahmadi, dirham, foddah, guinea, junayh, maidin, medine, medino **7** piaster, piastre, tallard **8** bedidlik, millieme
of El Salvador: 4 peso **5** colon **7** centavo

of England: 3 ora **4** rial **5** achey, crown, groat, noble, pence, penny, pound **6** bawbee, florin, guinea **7** angelet, hapenny **8** farthing, shilling, sixpence, tuppence, tuppenny **13** pound sterling
of Equatorial Guinea: 6 ekuele, peseta **7** centimo
of Estonia: 3 lat **4** sent **5** kroon **7** estmark
of Ethiopia: 4 besa, birr, harf **5** amole, girsh **6** dollar, kharaf, levant, pataca, talari **7** ashrafi, menelik, plaster, tallero **12** maria theresa
of European Community: 3 ecu
of Fiji: 6 dollar
of Finland: 4 mark **5** penni **6** markka **7** markkaa
of France: 5 franc **7** centime **8** napoleon
of Gabon Republic: 5 franc **7** centime
of the Gambia: 5 pound **6** butbut, dalasi
of Georgia: 5 ruble
of Germany: 4 mark **7** Ostmark, pfennig **12** Deutsche mark
of Ghana: 4 cedi, cidi **5** ackey
of Greece: 5 lepta **7** drachma
of Greenland: 3 ore **5** krone
of Guatemala: 4 peso **7** centavo, quetzal
of Guinea: 4 iliy, syli **5** franc **6** cauris
of Guinea-Bissau: 4 peso **6** escudo **7** centavo
of Haiti: 6 gourde **7** centime
of Honduras: 4 peso **7** centavo, lempira
of Hungary: 4 gara **5** balas, krone, pengo **6** filler, forint, gulden, korona, ongara, ungara
of Iceland: 5 aurar, eyrir, krona **6** kronur
of India: 3 lac, pie **4** anna, fels, lakh, pice, tara **5** abidi, crore, paisa, rupee
of Indonesia: 3 sen **6** rupiah
of Iran: 3 pul **4** asar, gran, lari, rial **5** bisti, daric, dinar, larin, shahi, toman **6** stater **7** ashrafi, kasbeke, pahlavi
of Iraq: 4 fils **5** dinar
of Ireland: 3 rap **4** real **5** pence, pound **6** turney **8** shilling
of Israel: 3 mil **5** agora, agura, pound, pruta **6** agorot, shekel
of Italy: 4 lira, lire, tara **5** grano, paoli, paolo, scudo, soldo **6** danaro, denaro, ducato, sequin **7** testone **8** zecchino **9** centesini
of Ivory Coast: 5 franc **7** centime
of Jamaica: 7 quattie
of Japan: 2 bu **3** mon, rin, rio, sen, shu, yen **4** cash, mibu, oban **5** koban, obang, tempo **6** cobang, ichebu, ichibu, itzebu, kogang **7** itzeboo, itziboo
of Jordan: 4 fils **5** dinar
of Kazakhstan: 5 ruble

of Kenya: 4 cent **5** pound **8** shilling
of Kiribati: 4 cent **6** dollar
of Korea: 3 woh, won **4** chun, hwan, kwan
of Kuwait: 4 fils **5** dinar
of Kyrgyzstan: 3 som
of Laos: 2 at **3** att, kip
of Latvia: 3 lat **4** latu **6** rublis, santim **7** kapeika, santima
of Lebanon: 5 livre, pound **7** piastre
of Lesotho: 4 cent, rand **6** maloti
of Liberia: 4 cent **6** dollar
of Libya: 5 dinar
of Liechtenstein: 5 franc **6** rappen **7** franken
of Lithuania: 3 lit **5** litas, marka **6** centas, fennig **7** ostmark, skatiku **8** auksinas, skatikas
of Luxembourg: 5 franc **7** centime
of Macao: 3 avo **6** pataca, pataco
of Macedonia: 5 denar
of Madagascar: 5 franc **7** centime
of Malawi: 6 kwacha **7** tambala
of Malaysia: 3 sen, tra **4** taro, trah **7** ringgit, tampang
of Maldives: 5 laree, rupee **7** rufiyaa
of Mali: 5 franc **7** centime
of Malta: 4 cent **5** grain, grano, pound
of Mauritania: 5 khoum **7** ouguiya
of Mauritius: 4 cent **5** rupee
of Mexico: 4 onza, peso **5** adobe, claco, tlaco **6** azteca, cuarto, dinero **7** centavo, piaster
of Moldova: 5 ruble
of Monaco: 5 franc **7** centime
of Mongolia: 5 mongo, mungo **6** tugrik **7** tughrik
of Montenegro: 4 para **6** florin **7** perpera
of Morocco: 4 flue, okia, rial **5** floos, franc, okieh, ounce **6** dirham, miskal **8** mouzouna
of Mozambique: 6 escudo **7** centavo, metical
of Myanmar: 3 pya **4** kyat
of Namibia: 4 cent, rand
of Nauru: 4 cent **6** dollar
of Nepal: 4 anna, pice **5** mohar, rupee
of the Netherlands: 4 doit, oord, raps **5** crown, daler, rider, ryder **6** florin, gulden, stiver, suskin **7** daalder, ducaton, escalan, escalin, guilder, stooter, stuiver **8** albertin, ducatoon **9** dubbeltje **12** rijksdaalder **13** albertustaler
of New Guinea: 4 kina, toea
of New Zealand: 4 cent **6** dollar
of Nicaragua: 4 peso **7** centavo, cordoba
of Niger: 5 franc **7** centime
of Nigeria: 4 kobo **5** naira
of Norway: 3 ore **5** krone **6** kroner
of Oman: 3 gaj, gaz **4** rial **5** baiza, ghazi **7** mahmudi
of Pakistan: 4 anna, pice **5** paisa, rupee

of Panama: 4 cent **6** balboa **9** centesimo
of Paraguay: 4 peso **7** centimo, guarani
of Peru: 3 sol **5** libra **6** dinero, reseta **7** centavo
of the Philippines: 4 peso **6** conant, peseta **7** centavo
of Poland: 4 abia **5** dalar, ducat, grosz, marka, zloty **6** fening, groszy, gulden, halerz, korona **8** groschen
of Portugal: 3 avo, joe **4** peca, real **5** conto, crown, dobra, indio, justo, rupia **6** escudo, macuta, octave, pataca, testad, tostao, vintem **7** angalar, centavo, crusado, miereis, moidore, testone **8** equipaga, johannes
of Qatar: 5 riyal **6** dirham
of Rumania: 3 ban, lei, leu, lev, ley **4** bani **5** uncia **6** triens
of Russia: 5 altin, bisti, copec, genga, grosh, kopek, ruble, shaur **6** abassi, copeck, grivna, kopeck, piatak, rouble **7** poltina, valiuta **8** auksinas, deneshka, imperial, polushka **9** poltinnik **10** altininink, chervonets
of Rwanda: 5 franc **7** centime
of San Marino: 4 lira, lire **9** centesimi
of Samoa: 4 tala
of Sao Tome and Principe: 5 dobra **6** escudo **7** centavo
of Sardinia: 7 carline
of Saudi Arabia: 5 girsh, gursh, pound, riyal
of Scotland: 3 ecu **4** demy, doit, lion, mark, rial, ryal **5** bodle, broad, groat, plack, rider, turne **6** bawbee, folles **7** unicorn **8** atchison, hardhead **9** halfpenny **11** bonnetpiece
of Senegal: 5 franc **7** centime
of Sicily: 5 litra, oncia, uncia **6** carlin **7** carline, oncetta
of Sierra Leone: 4 cent **5** leone
of Singapore: 4 cent **6** dollar
of Slovakia: 6 koruna
of Slovenia: 5 tolar
of Solomon Islands: 4 cent **6** dollar
of Somalia: 4 besa **6** somalo **8** shilling **9** centesimi
of South Africa: 4 cent, pond, rand **5** pound **6** florin **7** daalder **9** krugerand
of Spain: 3 cob **4** duro, peso, real **5** dobla **6** cuarto, dinero, doblon, escudo, peseta **7** alfonso, centimo, pistole, realdor **8** doubloon
of Sri Lanka: 4 cent **5** rupee
of Sudan: 5 pound **7** piastre
of Suriname: 4 cent **7** guilder
of Swaziland: 4 rand **9** lilangeni
of Sweden: 3 ore **5** krona, krone **7** carolin **8** skilling **9** rigsdaler
of Switzerland: 5 franc, rappe **6** hallar, rappen **7** angster, centime, duplone **8** baetzner, blaffert
of Syria: 4 lira **5** pound **6** talent **7** piaster

of Taiwan: 4 yuan **6** dollar
of Tajikistan: 5 ruble
of Tanzania: 4 cent **8** shilling
of Thailand: 2 at **3** att **4** baht **5** cutty, fuang, tical **6** pynung, salung, satang **11** bullet money
of Tibet: 5 tanga
of Togo: 5 franc **7** centime
of Tonga: 6 paanga, seniti
of Trinidad and Tobago: 4 cent **6** dollar
of Tunisia: 5 dinar **6** dollar **7** millime
of Turkey: 4 lira, para **5** akcha, asper, attun, kurus, pound, rebia **6** akcheh, sequin, zequin **7** aetilik, beshlik, pataque, piaster **8** medjidie, zecchino
of Turkmenistan: 5 ruble
of Tuvalu: 4 cent **6** dollar
of Uganda: 4 cent **8** shilling
of Ukraine: 6 grivna **10** karbovanet
of United Arab Emirates: 3 fil **6** dirham
of Uruguay: 4 peso **9** centesimo, centisimo
of Uzbekistan: 5 ruble
of Vanuatu: 5 franc **6** dollar
of Venezuela: 4 peso, real **5** medio **6** fuerte **7** bolivar, centimo **8** morocota **10** venezolano
of Vietnam: 2 xu **4** dong **7** piaster
of Western Samoa: 4 sene, tala
of Yemen: 4 fils, rial **5** dinar, riyal
of Yugoslavia: 4 para **5** dinar
of Zaire: 5 zaire **6** makuta
of Zambia: 5 ngwee **6** kwacha
of Zimbabwe: 4 cent **6** dollar
coincide 3 fit **4** jibe, meet **5** agree, cross, match, tally **6** accord, concur, square **7** conform **8** converge, dovetail **9** harmonize **10** correspond **11** synchronize **12** be concurrent, come together **19** occur simultaneously
coincidence 4 fate, luck **6** chance **8** accident **11** concurrence, synchronism **12** happenstance **22** simultaneous occurrence
coincident 10 coexistent, concurrent **12** contemporary, simultaneous **15** contemporaneous
coincidental 6 chance **9** unplanned **10** accidental, contiguous, synchronal **11** concomitant, synchronous **12** happenstance, simultaneous
cointreau
   type: 7 liqueur
   variety: 7 curacao **9** triple sec
   origin: 6 France
   flavor: 6 orange
   drink: 8 Applecar
   with bourbon: 10 Temptation
   with brandy: 7 Sidecar
   with cognac: 11 Rolls Royce
   with gin: 7 Florida **9** White Lady **13** Sweet Patootie **14** Flying Dutchman
   with rum: 8 Acapulco **10** Casa Blanca **11** Beachcomber **12** Blue Hawaiian
   with rye: 10 Temptation

with tequila: 9 Margarita
with whiskey: 16 Canadian Cocktail

Colavito, Rocky (Rocco Domenico)
sport: 8 baseball
team: 16 Cleveland Indians

Colbert, Claudette
real name: 22 Claudette Lily Chauchoin
born: 5 Paris **6** France
roles: 8 Tovarich **9** Cleopatra **14** Palm Beach Story **18** It Happened One Night (Oscar)

cold 3 icy, old **4** cool, dead, flat, hard **5** aloof, brisk, chill, crisp, cruel, faded, faint, gelid, harsh, nippy, polar, sharp, stale, stiff, stony **6** arctic, biting, bitter, chilly, cooled, frigid, frosty, frozen, inured, numbed, remote, severe, snappy, steely, wintry **7** callous, chilled, cutting, distant, frosted, glacial, haughty, nipping, passive, unmoved **8** chilling, coolness, detached, freezing, hardened, piercing, reserved, reticent, stinging, uncaring, unheated, unloving, unwarmed **9** apathetic, heartless, impassive, insensate, unfeeling, unstirred **10** disdainful, forbidding, impervious, insensible, phlegmatic, unfriendly **11** frozen stiff, indifferent, passionless, penetrating, unconcerned, unconscious, unemotional, unexcitable **12** antipathetic, bone-chilling, inaccessible, supercilious, uninterested, unresponsive **13** uninteresting, unsympathetic **14** marrow-chilling, unapproachable **15** teeth-chattering, uncommunicative, undemonstrative **16** chilled to the bone, unimpressionable **18** chilled to the marrow

cold-blooded 4 evil, hard **5** cruel, harsh, stiff, stony **6** brutal, flinty, formal, frigid, inured, savage, steely **7** callous, demonic, inhuman, passive, satanic, unmoved **8** detached, fiendish, hardened, inhumane, pitiless, reserved, ruthless, uncaring **9** barbarous, heartless, impassive, merciless, unfeeling, unpitying, unstirred **10** deliberate, diabolical, disdainful, impervious, implacable, unfriendly, unmerciful, villainous **11** calculating, hard-hearted, indifferent, insensitive, passionless, unconcerned, unemotional, unexcitable **12** bloodthirsty, contemptuous, uninterested, unresponsive **13** disinterested, unimpassioned, unimpressible, unsympathetic **16** unimpressionable

cold-hearted 5 cruel **9** heartless, unfeeling **11** hard-hearted **13** unsympathetic

coldness 5 chill **7** iciness **9** aloofness **10** chilliness, frostiness **12** indifference **13** unfeelingness **14** unfriendliness **15** hardheartedness

Cole, Janet
real name of: 9 Kim Hunter

Cole, Thomas
born: 7 England **13** Bolton-le-Moors
artwork: 8 The Ox-Bow **15** The Voyage of Life **17** The Course of Empire

coleoptera
class: 8 hexopoda
phylum: 10 arthropoda
group: 6 beetle, weevil

Coleridge, Samuel Taylor
author of: 9 Kubla Khan **10** Christabel **14** Dejection An Ode, Lyrical Ballads (with Wordsworth) **19** Biographia Literaria **26** The Rime of the Ancient Mariner

Colette (Sidonie)
author of: 4 Gigi, Sido **5** Cheri **8** Claudine **11** La Vagabonde **14** The Evening Star

coliseum 4 bowl **5** arena **6** circus **7** stadium, theater **9** Colosseum **10** hippodrome **12** amphitheater **14** exhibition hall

collaborate 4 join **5** unite **6** assist, team up **7** collude **9** cooperate **10** join forces **12** work together **14** work side by side

collaborationist 6 puppet **7** traitor **8** quisling

collaborator 4 ally **6** puppet **7** traitor **8** co-worker, quisling, teammate **9** associate, colleague, co-partner **11** confederate

collapse 4 coma, fail, fall, flop, fold **5** faint, swoon **6** attack, buckle, cave-in, fizzle **7** break up, crack-up, crumple, failure, give way, seizure **8** be in vain, buckling, downfall, flounder, keel over, take sick **9** become ill, break down **10** be stricken, break apart, run aground **11** fall through **12** disintegrate, falling apart, fall helpless, fall to pieces **13** come to nothing, sudden illness **14** disintegration **17** become unconscious

collapsed 4 limp **7** caved in, compact **8** deflated, fallen in, folded up **13** disintegrated

Collapse of the Third Republic, The
author: 14 William L Shirer

collapsible 7 folding **8** foldable **10** deflatable

collar 3 nab **4** eton, grab **5** catch, fichu, pinch, seize **6** arrest, bertha **7** capture **9** apprehend, neckpiece **12** take prisoner **15** take into custody

collate 5 order **6** bestow, verify **7** compare **8** assemble, organize **9** integrate **11** put together

collateral 4 bond **5** extra **6** pledge, surety **7** warrant **8** parallel, security, warranty **9** accessory, ancillary, auxiliary, guarantee, insurance, secondary **10** additional, incidental, supporting,

supportive **11** endorsement, subordinate **12** contributory **13** supplementary

collation 3 tea **4** meal **5** lunch **6** brunch, repast, sermon **7** address, reading **8** hotchpot, luncheon, treatise **10** comparison **11** description

colleague 4 mate **6** fellow **7** partner **8** confrere, co-worker, teammate **9** associate, co-partner **11** confederate **12** collaborator, fellow worker

collect 3 get **4** calm, meet **5** amass, raise, rally **6** gather, heap up, muster, obtain, pick up, pile up, summon **7** call for, compile, compose, control, convene, marshal, prepare, receive, solicit **8** assemble, gather up, scrape up **9** aggregate, get hold of **10** accumulate, congregate **11** concentrate, get together

collectanea 8 analects, treasury **9** anthology, gleanings **10** collection, miscellany, selections **11** miscellanea

collected 4 calm, cool **5** quiet **6** placid, poised, serene, steady **8** composed, peaceful, tranquil **9** confident, unruffled **10** cool-headed, restrained **11** level-headed, self-assured, undisturbed, unemotional, unflappable, unperturbed **12** even-tempered **13** self-possessed **14** self-controlled

collection 3 mob **4** bevy, body, gift, heap, mass, pack, pile **5** array, bunch, clump, crowd, drove, flock, group, hoard, store, swarm **6** corpus, jumble, muster, throng **7** cluster, clutter, variety **8** amassing, assembly, oblation, treasury **9** anthology, gathering, offertory, receiving **10** assemblage, assortment, hodgepodge, miscellany, soliciting **11** aggregation, compilation **12** accumulating, accumulation

Collection of Ten Thousand Leaves (Manyoshu)
author: 7 unknown

collective 5 joint **6** common, mutual, united **7** unified **8** combined, gathered **9** aggregate, composite **10** cumulative, integrated **11** accumulated, cooperative

collector 6 grouper **7** dustman **8** antiquer, compiler, composer, gatherer, zamindar **9** assembler **10** garbageman **11** anthologist

Collector, The
author: 10 John Fowles

college 7 academy **8** seminary **9** institute **10** university **11** institution

college-preparatory 4 prep **8** academic **11** liberal-arts **12** nontechnical **13** nonvocational

collegiate 8 academic **10** scholastic, university **11** educational

collide 3 hit **4** meet **5** clash, crash, smash **7** crack up, diverge, run into **8** bump into, conflict, disagree **9** knock into **10** meet head on **11** beat against **13** hurtle against, strike against

Collier, Lucille Ann
real name of: **9** Ann Miller

Collins, Mary Catherine
real name of: **7** Bo Derek

Collins, Mr
character in: **17** Pride and Prejudice
author: **6** Austen

Collins, Wilkie
author of: **6** No Name **12** The Moonstone **15** The Woman in White

collision 4 bump **5** clash, crash, fight, smash **6** battle, combat, impact **7** smash-up **8** accident, conflict, skirmish, struggle **9** encounter **10** engagement **11** clash of arms

colloquial 5 homey, plain **6** casual, chatty, common, folksy **8** everyday, familiar, homespun, informal, ordinary, workaday **9** idiomatic **10** vernacular **14** conversational **15** unsophisticated

colloquy 4 chat, talk **6** caucus, parley **7** council, palaver, seminar **8** commerce, congress, converse, dialogue **9** communion, discourse **10** conference, discussion, rap session **11** interchange, intercourse **12** conversation **13** confabulation

collude 4 plot **7** connive **8** conspire, intrigue **9** cooperate **11** collaborate

collusion 5 fraud **7** treason **8** intrigue **10** complicity, connivance, conspiracy **13** collaboration **15** secret agreement **17** guilty association

Colman, Ronald
born: **7** England **8** Richmond
roles: **9** Beau Geste **10** Arrowsmith **11** A Double Life (Oscar), Lost Horizon **16** A Tale of Two Cities

cologne 5 scent **7** essence, perfume **9** fragrance **11** toilet water

Colomba
author: **14** Prosper Merimee

Colombia
other name: **6** Darien **10** New Granada
capital/largest city: **6** Bogota
others: **3** Ten **4** Amza, Buga, Cali, Mitu, Muzo, Paez, Sipi, Tado, Tolu, Yari **5** Bello, Chinu, Guapi, Neiva, Pasto, Tulua, Tunja **6** Cucuta, Ibaque, Lorica, Quibdo, Sangil, Tumaco **7** Cartago, Ipiates, Leticia, Palmira, Pereira, Popayan **8** Girardot, Maganque, Medellin, Monteria **9** Cartagena, Manizales **10** Santa Marta **11** Bucaramanga **12** Barranquilla, Buenaventura
school: **5** Andes, Valle **20** Instituto Caro y Cuervo **21** Industrial de Santander
measure: **4** vara **7** azumbre, celemin
monetary unit: **4** peso, real **6** condor, peseta **7** centavo
weight: **3** bag **4** saco **5** libra **7** quin-

tal
island: **4** Baru **5** Naipo **6** Fuerte **7** Gorgona, Malpelo **8** Cusachon **9** San Andres **11** Providencia
lake: **4** Tota
mountain: **5** Abibe, Andes, Baudo, Chita, Cocuy, Huila, Pasto **6** Ayapel, Perija, Purace, Tolima, Tunahi **7** Chamusa, del Ruiz **8** Oriengal **10** Santa Marta **17** Central Cordillera, Eastern Cordillera, Western Cordillera
highest point: **14** Cristobal Colon
river: **3** Uva **4** Bita, Meta, Muco, Sinu, Tomo, Yari **5** Cauca, Cesar, Isana, Mesai, Nechi, Pauto, Sucio **6** Amazon, Arauca, Ariari, Atrato, Atroto, Caguan, Pattia, Yapura **7** Apapois, Caqueta, Guainia, Inirida, Truando, Vichada **8** Casanare, Guaviara, Putumayo **9** Magdalena
sea: **7** Pacific **9** Caribbean
physical feature:
cape: **4** Vela **5** Aguja, Marzo, Punta **7** Augusta **8** Gallinas
falls: **10** Tequendama
gulf: **5** Uraba **6** Cupica, Darien, Tibuga **8** Tortugas
inlet: **6** Tumaco
plains: **6** Ilanos
point: **6** Cruces, Lacruz, Solano **8** Caribana, Gallinas
people: **4** Boro, Cuna, Duit, Hoka, Macu, Muso, Muzo, Paez, Tama, Tapa **5** Carib, Catio, Choco, Cofan, Cogui, Cubeo, Guane, Haida, Mocoa, Paeze, Pijao, Seona, Yagua **6** Arawak, Betoya, Calima, Colima, Ingano, Mirana, Saliva, Tahami, Ticunu, Tucano, Tunebo, Witoto, Yahuna **7** Achagua, Andaqui, Chibcha, Chimila, Churoya, Guahibo, Guajiro, Panches, Puinave, Puitoto, Quechua, Shuswap, Tairona, Telembi **8** Coconuco, Guarauno, mestizos, Motilone, Puinavis, Quimbaya, Sinsigas **9** Cocanucos, Coconucan, mulattoes, Panaquita **10** Bellacoola
leader: **7** Bolivar
language: **7** Spanish
religion: **13** Roman Catholic
place:
museum: **4** Gold **8** Colonial
palace: **11** Inquisition
feature:
dance: **7** bambuco **8** merengue
game: **4** tejo
guitar: **5** tiple
poncho: **5** ruana
shoes: **10** alpargatas
shoulder bag: **7** carriel
tree: **8** arboloco
woven hat: **5** jipas

Colombo
capital of: **8** Sri Lanka

colon 4 coin **6** farmer, vitals **7** pioneer, planter, settler, viscera **9** hemistich,

intestine **15** plantation owner, punctuation mark

colonize 5 found, plant **6** gather, settle **7** migrate **8** establish **10** infiltrate

colonnade 3 row **4** stoa **5** porch **6** arcade, piazza **7** portico, terrace **8** cloister **9** peristyle

colony 3 set **4** band, body **5** flock, group, swarm **7** mandate **8** dominion, province **9** community, territory **10** dependency, possession, settlement **12** protectorate **14** satellite state

colophon 6 design, device, emblem **7** insigne **8** insignia **11** inscription

color 3 dye, hue **4** bias, burn, cast, glow, mood, tint, tone, warp, wash **5** bloom, blush, chalk, drift, flame, flush, force, paint, sense, shade, slant, stain, taint, tinge, twist **6** affect, aspect, crayon, effect, import, intent, redden, spirit, stress **7** distort, feeling, meaning, pervert, pigment, redness, skin hue **8** dyestuff, rosiness **9** go crimson, influence, intention, prejudice **10** intimation **11** connotation, implication, insinuation **12** become florid, pigmentation, significance **17** natural complexion

Colorado
abbreviation: **2** CO **4** Colo
nickname: **10** Centennial
capital/largest city: **6** Denver
others: **4** Vail **5** Aspen, Delta, Lamar, Ouray **6** Arvada, Aurora, Denver, Golden, Pueblo, Salida **7** Alamosa, Boulder, Durango, Greeley, Manassa, Manitou **8** Gunnison, Loveland, Trinidad **9** Purgatory, Silverton, Telluride **11** Central City **12** Cripple Creek **13** Grand Junction **15** Colorado Springs
baseball team: **7** Rockies
college: **5** Regis **6** Denver **7** Boulder **17** US Air Force Academy
feature: **11** Four Corners **15** Garden of the Gods **17** Continental Divide
national monument: **8** Dinosaur **14** Great Sand Dunes
national park: **5** Estes **9** Mesa Verde **13** Rocky Mountain
tribe: **3** Ute **7** Arapaho **8** Cheyenne
people: **11** Jack Dempsey **12** Ralph Edwards **14** Scott Carpenter **18** Douglas Fairbanks Sr
lake: **6** Frozen
land rank: **6** eighth
mountains: **5** Longs, Rocky **7** San Juan **9** Pikes Peak **14** Sangre de Cristo
highest point: **6** Elbert
physical feature:
canyon: **5** Black
gorge: **5** Royal
plains: **5** Great
wind: **7** Chinook
river: **4** Gila **5** Yampa **6** Platte **7** Dolores **8** Apishapa, Arikaree, Arkansas, Gunnison **9** Rio Grande **10** Purgatoire

state admission: 12 thirty-eighth
state bird: 11 lark bunting
state flower: 22 Rocky Mountain columbine
state motto: 24 Nothing Without Providence
state song: 22 Where the Columbines Grow
state tree: 18 Colorado blue spruce

colored 4 dyed, hued **5** dusky **6** biased, shaded, tinged, tinted **7** blushed, excused, flushed, glossed, labeled, painted, stained **8** affected, labelled, reddened **9** chromatic, distorted, pigmented **10** influenced, prejudiced **12** complexioned **13** characterized **14** misrepresented

colorful 3 gay **4** loud **5** showy, vivid **6** bright, florid, unique **7** dynamic, graphic, unusual, vibrant, zestful **8** animated, forceful, spirited, vigorous **9** brilliant, full-toned, vivacious **10** compelling, variegated **11** distinctive, interesting, many-colored, picturesque **12** multicolored, particolored

coloring 3 dye **4** tint **5** color, shade, stain **10** coloration, complexion

colorless 3 wan **4** ashy, drab, dull, flat, pale **5** ashen, dingy, faded, pasty, vapid, white **6** anemic, boring, dreary, grayed, pallid, sallow, sickly, undyed **7** ghastly, ghostly, insipid, natural, neutral, prosaic **8** blanched, bleached, lifeless, ordinary, whitened **9** bloodless, washed out **10** cadaverous, lackluster, monotonous, spiritless, unanimated, unexciting, uninspired **11** commonplace **13** uninteresting

Color Purple, The
author: 11 Alice Walker
director: 15 Steven Spielberg
cast: 11 Danny Glover **12** Adolph Caesar, Oprah Winfrey **13** Margaret Avery **14** Whoopi Goldberg

colors 4 flag, jack **6** banner, ensign, pennon **7** pennant **8** standard

colossal 4 huge, vast **5** giant, grand, great **6** mighty **7** extreme, immense, mammoth, massive, titanic **8** enormous, gigantic, imposing **9** exceeding, excessive **10** incredible, inordinate, monumental, prodigious, tremendous **11** extravagant, spectacular **12** awe-inspiring, overwhelming

Colossus of Rhodes
statue of: 6 Apollo

colt 4 foal **5** horse **6** novice **8** equuleus, yearling **9** fledgling, youngster
constellation of: 8 Equuleus

columbium
chemical symbol: 2 Cb

Columbo
character: 9 Lt Columbo
cast: 9 Peter Falk

column 3 row **4** file, line, post **5** pylon, queue, shaft, train **6** parade, pillar, string **7** caravan, phalanx, sup-

port, upright **8** pilaster **9** cavalcade, formation **10** procession **11** vertical row **12** vertical list

columnist 6 writer **7** analyst
famous: 7 Heloise **8** Dear Abby, Herb Caen **9** HL Mencken, Jack Smith **10** Ann Landers **11** Miss Manners **15** Abigail van Buren

coma 6 stupor, torpor **8** collapse **15** unconsciousness

Comanche
language family: 10 Shoshonean
location: 5 Texas **6** Kansas, Mexico **8** Oklahoma
noted as: 8 horsemen

comatose 3 lax **4** dull, idle, lazy **5** inert **6** leaden, torpid **7** drugged, languid, passive **8** inactive, indolent, lifeless, listless, slothful, sluggish **9** apathetic, catatonic, lethargic, stuporous **10** cataleptic, insensible, narcotized, phlegmatic, spiritless **11** indifferent, unconcerned, unconscious **12** unresponsive

comb 4 card, tuft **5** curry, dress, groom, plume, scour, style **6** search **7** arrange, explore, panache, ransack, topknot **8** head tuft, hunt over, untangle **9** cast about, cockscomb, currycomb **11** look through **14** rummage through

combat 5 clash, fight **6** action, attack, battle, oppose, resist **7** contest, go to war, wage war **8** conflict, fighting, skirmish, struggle **9** encounter **10** contention, engagement, war against **11** come to blows, grapple with, make warfare, work against **12** do battle with, march against **13** confrontation **14** military action

Combat
character: 4 Caje (Caddy Cadron) **5** Kirby **8** (Pvt) Braddock **9** Doc Walton, (Lt) Gil Hanley **12** (Sgt) Chip Saunders
cast: 9 Jack Hogan, Rick Jason, Vic Morrow **12** Shecky Greene, Steven Rogers **15** Pierre Jalbert

combatant 7 fighter, soldier, warrior **9** man-at-arms **10** serviceman **11** fighting man

combating 8 battling, clashing, fighting, opposing **9** waging war **10** contention, contesting, opposition, struggling **11** doing battle **13** grappling with **17** coming to blows with

combative 6 bantam **8** militant **9** agonistic, bellicose **10** aggressive, pugnacious **11** belligerent, contentious **12** antagonistic

combativeness 9 hostility, pugnacity **10** antagonism **12** belligerence **14** aggressiveness **15** contentiousness

combination 3 mix **5** alloy, blend, union **6** fusion, league, medley, merger, mixing **7** amalgam, joining, mixture, pooling, variety **8** alliance, blending,

compound **9** coalition, composite, synthesis **10** assortment, coalescing, federation **11** association, composition, confederacy **12** amalgamation **13** confederation

combine 3 mix **4** fuse, join, pool **5** blend, merge, unify, unite **6** couple, league, mingle **8** compound **9** commingle **10** amalgamate, synthesize **11** consolidate, incorporate

combo 4 band **5** group **11** aggregation, combination

comb out 4 curl **5** dress **7** arrange, unsnarl **8** untangle

combustible 8 burnable **9** flammable, ignitable **10** combustive, incendiary **11** inflammable **13** conflagrative

combustion 6 firing **7** burning, flaming **8** ignition, kindling **12** incineration **13** conflagration

combustive 8 burnable **9** flammable, ignitable **11** combustible, inflammable **13** conflagrative

come 2 be, go **3** bud **4** fall, loom, rise **5** arise, issue, occur, range, reach **6** appear, arrive, be made, drop in, emerge, extend, follow, happen, impend, show up, spread, spring, turn up **7** advance, descend, emanate, stretch **8** approach, draw near, go toward, grow to be **9** be a native, germinate, take place **10** be imminent, move toward **11** be a resident, be in the wind, materialize, originate in, spring forth

come about 5 occur **6** chance, happen **7** turn out **10** come to pass

come afterward 5 ensue **6** derive, follow, result **7** succeed

come apart 6 detach **7** disjoin, unstick **8** separate

come back 5 rally **6** answer, retort, return **7** rebound **8** recovery

Come Back Little Sheba
director: 10 Daniel Mann
based on play by: 11 William Inge
cast: 10 Terry Moore **12** Shirley Booth **13** Burt Lancaster
Oscar for: 7 actress (Booth)

come clean 4 sing **5** own up **7** confess **14** unbosom oneself **18** make a clean breast of

come close to 7 verge on **8** approach, border on **11** approximate, nearly equal

comedian 3 wag **4** fool, zany **5** clown, comic, cutup, joker **6** jester, madcap **7** buffoon **8** humorist, jokester **9** prankster **10** comedienne, comic actor **14** practical joker

comedown 4 drop **8** lowering **10** anticlimax

come down 4 dive, drop, fall, sink **6** plunge, tumble **7** descend, plummet **8** decrease

come down a peg 5 deign, stoop **6**

unbend **7** descend **10** condescend **12** lower oneself **13** humble oneself

comedy 3 fun, wit **5** farce, humor **6** banter, joking, pranks, satire **7** foolery, jesting **8** drollery, raillery, travesty **9** burlesque, cutting up, horseplay, silliness **10** buffoonery, pleasantry, tomfoolery **13** fooling around

Comedy of Errors, The
author: **18** William Shakespeare
character: **6** Aegeon, Dromio **7** Adriana, Aemilia, Luciana, Solinus **10** Antipholus

come face to face with 4 meet **8** confront **9** encounter

come first 7 precede, predate **8** antecede, antedate, go before **10** anticipate

come into being 4 dawn, show **5** arise, begin, occur, set in, start **6** appear, be born, crop up, emerge, sprout **8** commence, spring up **9** germinate, originate **11** come to light

come into port 4 dock **5** berth

come into view 4 show **6** appear, come up, emerge, show up **7** surface **11** come to light **13** become visible

come loose 5 let go **6** detach, loosen **7** slip off **8** break off, separate, unfasten **9** break away **10** come undone, come untied, disconnect **11** come unglued, come unstuck

comely 4 fair, nice **5** bonny **6** pretty, proper, seemly, simple **7** correct, fitting, natural, sightly, winning, winsome **8** becoming, blooming, charming, decorous, engaging, fetching, pleasant, pleasing, suitable, tasteful **9** agreeable, appealing, wholesome **10** attractive, unaffected **11** well-favored

come near 4 loom, near **6** appear **8** approach **9** draw close **10** move toward

come-on 4 bait, hook, lure, trap **5** decoy, snare **6** magnet **9** seduction **10** allurement, attraction, bewitchery, enticement, inducement, seducement, temptation **12** inveiglement

comestibles 5 foods **7** edibles **8** victuals **10** foodstuffs, provisions

come to a decision 6 decide, settle **7** resolve **8** conclude **9** determine

come to an understanding 5 agree **6** settle **11** come to terms **12** agree to marry **16** reach an agreement

come to a standstill 4 halt, quit, stop **5** abate, cease **7** die away **8** quit cold

come to blows 5 fight **7** contest **8** do battle **9** square off **12** start to fight

come together 4 meet **5** flock, group, rally **6** gather **7** collect, convene **8** assemble **10** congregate **11** get together

come to light 4 dawn **5** arise **6** appear, crop up, emerge, evolve, show

up, turn up, unfold **7** develop, surface, turn out

come to nothing 4 fail, flop, fold **6** fizzle **8** be in vain, collapse **9** break down **11** fall through **12** come to naught **17** fail to materialize

come to pass 5 ensue, occur **6** arrive, befall, follow, happen **9** take place

come to terms 5 agree, yield **6** give up, settle **7** succumb **8** contract, cry quits **9** make a deal, negotiate, surrender **10** capitulate, compromise **11** come to grips, meet halfway, sue for peace **13** resign oneself **14** strike a bargain **15** lay down one's arms **16** reach an agreement **17** acknowledge defeat, hoist the white flag **18** split the difference

come unglued 6 detach, loosen **8** separate **9** fall apart **11** come unstuck

come unstuck 4 lift **6** detach, loosen **8** break off, unfasten **9** break away, come apart, come loose, fall apart **11** come unglued

come up 4 rise **5** arise **7** quicken, sharpen **8** heighten, increase **9** intensify **10** accelerate, strengthen **12** be referred to

come upon 4 find, meet **7** learn of, run into **8** discover **9** encounter

comfit 5 candy, sweet **9** sweetmeat **10** confection, sugar candy **13** confectionery

comfort 4 calm, ease, help **5** cheer, peace, quiet **6** luxury, relief, solace, soothe, succor, warmth **7** cheer up, compose, console, hearten **8** coziness, opulence, pleasure, reassure, serenity, snugness **9** bolster up, comforter, composure, encourage, well-being **10** cheering up, relaxation **11** consolation, contentment, reassurance **12** satisfaction **13** encouragement, gratification **14** quiet one's fears **16** source of serenity **17** lighten one's burden **18** bolster one's spirits

Comfort, Alex
author of: **11** The Joy of Sex **12** More Joy of Sex

comfortable 4 cozy, easy **6** at ease, at home, serene **7** relaxed **8** adequate, pleasant, suitable **9** agreeable, congenial, contented **10** giving ease, gratifying, untroubled **11** pleasurable, undisturbed **12** satisfactory **16** free from distress

comforter 4 balm, puff **5** quilt, scarf **6** afghan, solace **7** anodyne, blanket, comfort, soother **8** coverlet **10** palliative

comic, comical 4 rich **5** droll, funny, merry, silly, witty **6** absurd, jocose, jovial **7** amusing, jocular, risible **8** farcical, humorous, mirthful **9** facetious, laughable, ludicrous, whimsical **10** ridiculous **11** nonsensical **12** nimblewitted

coming 4 next **6** advent, future, in view, to come **7** arrival, nearing **8** approach, arriving, imminent, on the way **9** advancing, emergence, imminence, impending, in the wind, proximity **10** appearance, occurrence, subsequent **11** approaching, forthcoming, prospective **12** on the horizon **13** materializing

Coming Home
director: **8** Hal Ashby
cast: **9** Bruce Dern, Jane Fonda, Jon Voight **15** Robert Carradine
Oscar for: **5** actor (Voight) **7** actress (Fonda) **10** screenplay

Coming into the Country
author: **10** John McPhee

Coming of Age, The
author: **16** Simone de Beauvoir

Coming of Age in Samoa
author: **12** Margaret Mead

Coming Race, The
author: **18** Edward Bulwer-Lytton

command 3 bid, get **4** boss, call, draw, fiat, grip, head, hold, lead, rule **5** edict, evoke, grasp, guide, order, power **6** adjure, behest, charge, compel, decree, demand, direct, elicit, enjoin, govern, incite, induce, kindle, manage, ordain, prompt, summon **7** call for, conduct, control, deserve, extract, inspire, mastery, provoke, receive, require, summons **8** call upon, instruct, motivate **9** authority, call forth, direction, directive, governing, knowledge, ordinance, supervise, ultimatum **10** administer, be master of, domination, injunction, leadership, management **11** familiarity, instruction, superintend, supervision **12** have charge of **13** comprehension, understanding **14** administration **17** have authority over

commandant 7 captain **9** commander **12** chief officer

commandeer 4 take **5** seize, usurp **8** shanghai **11** appropriate, expropriate

commander 4 boss, head **5** chief, ruler **6** leader **7** manager **8** director **9** conductor

commanding 4 head **5** chief, grand, lofty **6** ruling, senior, strong **7** dynamic, leading, ranking, stately **8** forceful, gripping, imposing, powerful, striking, towering **9** arresting, directing, governing, important, prominent **10** compelling, dominating, impressive **11** controlling, significant **13** authoritative, distinguished, overshadowing

commandment
Hebrew: **7** mitsvah, mitzvah

comme il faut 6 proper **7** fitting **12** as it should be

commemorate 4 hail, mark **5** extol, honor **6** hallow, revere, salute **7** acclaim, glorify, observe **8** venerate **9** celebrate, solemnize **11** acknowledge, memorialize, pay homage to **12** pay tribute to

commence 5 begin, start **8** get going, initiate **10** get started, inaugurate, originated

commencement 4 dawn **5** birth, onset, start **6** outset **7** genesis, morning **9** beginning, first step, inception **10** graduation, initiation **11** origination **12** inauguration **13** graduation day **20** graduation ceremonies

commend 2 OK **4** back, give, laud **5** extol **6** commit, confer, convey, praise **7** acclaim, approve, consign, endorse, entrust, stand by, support **8** delegate, give over, hand over, pass over, relegate, transfer **13** speak highly of

commendable 6 worthy **7** notable **8** laudable **9** admirable, deserving, estimable, exemplary, honorable **10** creditable **11** meritorious **12** praiseworthy

commendation 5 honor **6** praise **7** support **8** approval **10** acceptance **11** acclamation, approbation

commendatory 8 admiring, praising **9** laudatory, praiseful **10** plauditory **13** complimentary **14** congratulatory

commensurate, commensurable 4 even, meet **5** equal **6** square **7** fitting **8** balanced, in accord, parallel, relative, suitable **10** comparable, compatible, consistent, equivalent **11** appropriate, in agreement **13** corresponding, proportionate **14** on a proper scale

comment 4 note, word **6** remark **7** clarify, discuss, explain, expound **8** expand on **9** assertion, criticism, elucidate, shed light, statement, talk about, touch upon, utterance **10** annotation, expression, reflection **11** elucidation, explanation, explication, observation **13** clarification **15** exemplification

commentary 6 review **8** critique, scholium, treatise **9** criticism **10** exposition **11** explanation, explication **12** dissertation **14** interpretation **16** explanatory essay

commentator 6 critic, writer **7** speaker **8** panelist, reporter, reviewer **9** columnist, explainer **10** newscaster **11** interpreter, news analyst

comment upon 7 clarify, clear up, explain **8** spell out **9** delineate, elucidate, explicate, interpret, make plain **10** illuminate, illustrate **14** throw light upon

commerce 5 trade **6** barter **7** trading, traffic **8** business, exchange, industry **12** mercantilism **16** buying and selling **god of: 6** Hermes **7** Mercury

commercial 2 ad **5** sales, trade **8** business **10** mercantile, sales pitch **12** profit-making **13** advertisement **16** buying-and-selling

commingle 3 mix **4** fuse **5** blend,

merge, unify **7** combine **10** amalgamate

commiserate 7 feel for **8** show pity **10** grieve with, lament with **13** express sorrow **14** sympathize with **15** share one's sorrow **17** have compassion for

commiseration 4 pity **8** sympathy **10** compassion, tenderness **13** fellow feeling

commission 3 act, bid, cut, fee **4** duty, hire, name, rank, role, task **5** board, doing, order, piece, power, proxy, trust **6** agency, assign, charge, direct, employ, engage, office **7** appoint, certify, charter, conduct, council, empower, license, mandate, mission, portion, rake-off, stipend, warrant **8** capacity, contract, delegate, dividend, document, exercise, function, position **9** acting out, allotment, allowance, authority, authorize, committal, committee **10** assignment, commitment, committing, delegation, deputation, entrusting, percentage, performing **11** appointment, carrying out, certificate, performance, transacting **12** officer's rank, perpetration **13** authorization, written orders **14** give the go-ahead **15** representatives **16** piece of the action **17** appointment papers, grant officer's rank

commissioner 5 envoy, trier **7** officer, pristaw **8** delegate, official **9** authority, commissar

commissioning 10 assignment, delegation **11** appointment, designation, entrustment **13** authorization

commit 2 do **3** act, put **4** bind, pull **5** enact, place **6** assign, decide, effect, engage, intern, pursue **7** confine, consign, deliver, deposit, entrust, execute, perform, pull off, resolve **8** carry out, give over, obligate, practice, transact, transfer **9** determine **10** make liable, perpetrate **13** participate in **16** institutionalize

commitment 3 vow **4** bond, word **5** stand **6** pledge **7** promise **8** decision, delivery, transfer, warranty **9** assurance, detention, guarantee, liability, restraint **10** assignment, giving over, internment, obligation, resolution **11** confinement, consignment, dispatching **12** imprisonment **13** determination, incarceration **14** responsibility **18** institutionalizing

commit oneself 3 act **7** resolve **8** dedicate, obligate **9** determine

committed 6 active, liable **8** confined, detained, interned **9** concerned, delivered, entrusted, obligated **10** interested, responsive **11** responsible **17** institutionalized

committee 4 body, jury **5** bench, board, group, junta, table **6** bureau, soviet **7** cabinet, council **9** gathering,

syndicate **10** assemblage **12** organization

commode 6 bureau, toilet **7** cabinet, dresser **9** washstand **14** chest of drawers

commodious 5 ample, large, roomy **8** spacious **9** capacious, uncramped **11** unconfining

commodity 4 ware **5** asset, goods, stock **6** staple **7** chattel, holding, product **8** property **9** advantage, belonging **10** possession **11** convenience, merchandise **14** article of trade **17** article of commerce

common 3 bad, low **4** base, lewd, mean, rude, vile **5** brash, cheap, crass, crude, gross, joint, lowly, minor, plain, stock **6** brazen, brutal, coarse, lesser, normal, old-hat, public, ribald, shared, simple, smutty, tawdry, vulgar **7** average, boorish, callous, general, ignoble, ill-bred, loutish, low-bred, obscene, obscure, popular, prosaic, regular, routine, settled, uncouth, unknown, worn-out **8** communal, everyday, familiar, frequent, homespun, impolite, informal, mediocre, middling, nameless, ordinary, plebeian, shameful, standard, workaday, worn thin **9** bourgeois, customary, deficient, household, low-minded, motheaten, obnoxious, offensive, pervasive, shameless, tasteless, unexalted, universal, unnoticed, unrefined, well-known **10** collective, colloquial, despicable, dime-a-dozen, inglorious, threadbare, unblushing, uncultured, unpolished, widespread **11** disgraceful, established, ill-mannered, insensitive, middle-class, oft-repeated, subordinate, traditional, unimportant, widely known, without rank **12** contemptible, conventional, disagreeable **13** garden-variety, insignificant **15** undistinguished

commoners 5 plebs **6** masses **8** plebians

common law
Latin: **13** lex non scripta

commonly 5 often **6** widely **7** as a rule, usually **8** normally, of course **9** generally, in general, most often, popularly, regularly, routinely **10** by and large, familiarly, frequently, habitually, informally, ordinarily, repeatedly **11** customarily **13** traditionally **14** by force of habit, conventionally, for the most part **15** in most instances **17** generally speaking

common people 5 demos, plebs **6** masses **8** populace **9** hoi polloi, plebeians **11** bourgeoisie

commonplace 3 old **4** dull **5** adage, banal, stale, trite, usual **6** cliche, old-hat, truism **7** bromide, general, humdrum, regular, routine, worn-out **8** banality, everyday, familiar, ordinary, standard, worn thin **9** customary, hackneyed, moth-eaten, platitude **10** pedestrian, threadbare, un original, widespread **11** oft-repeated, stereotyped, traditional **12** received idea, run-of-the-mill **13** unimaginative, uninteresting

commonplace book 9 anthology, gleanings, scrapbook

Common Sense
  author: **11** Thomas Paine

common-sense 5 sound **8** everyday, sensible **9** mother wit, practical, pragmatic, realistic **10** no-nonsense **11** down-to-earth, levelheaded, serviceable, utilitarian **12** matter-of-fact

commonwealth 5 state **6** nation **8** republic
  Latin: **10** res publica

commotion 3 ado **4** fuss, stir, to-do **5** furor **6** bustle, racket, ruckus, tumult, uproar **7** clatter, turmoil **9** agitation **10** excitement, hullabaloo **11** disturbance **12** perturbation

communal 5 joint **6** common, mutual, public, shared **9** community **10** collective

commune 3 gab, rap, yak **4** chat, chin, farm, talk, town **5** visit **6** babble, confer, gossip, parley, powwow **7** chatter, palaver, prattle **8** converse, schmooze **9** discourse **10** chew the fat, chew the rag **11** communicate, confabulate **14** shoot the breeze

communicable 8 catching **10** contagious, infectious **12** transferable **13** transmissible, transmittable

communicate 3 say **4** give, show, talk, tell **5** state, write **6** advise, convey, impart, notify, pass on, relate, reveal **7** declare, divulge, exhibit, mention, publish, signify **8** announce, converse, disclose, inform of, proclaim, transmit **9** apprise of, bring word, broadcast, make known, publicize **10** correspond

communication 4 news, note, wire **5** cable **6** letter, missal, report **7** liaison, message, missive, notices, rapport, writing **8** bulletin, dispatch, document, speaking, telegram **9** broadcast, cablegram, directive, statement **10** communique **11** declaration, information **12** conversation, intelligence, proclamation, radio message **13** telephone call **14** correspondence

communicative 4 open **5** frank **6** candid, chatty **7** voluble **8** friendly, outgoing, sociable **9** revealing, talkative **10** expressive, forthright, freespoken, loquacious, revelatory, unreserved **11** informative

communion, Communion 6 accord **7** concord, harmony, rapport, sharing **8** affinity, sympathy **9** agreement **12** the Eucharist **13** communication, contemplation

communique 4 note, wire **5** aviso, cable, flash **6** report, letter, notice **7** epistle, message, missive, release, telegram **8** bulletin, dispatch **9** directive, statement **10** memorandum **12** announcement, intelligence, notification **13** communication

Communist 3 red **6** soviet **7** comrade, marxist **8** Leninist **9** bolshevik, socialist **10** bolshevist **12** totalitarian

Communist Manifesto
  author: **8** Karl Marx **15** Friedrich Engels

community 4 area, folk, town **5** arena, field, group, range, realm, scope **6** locale, people, public, sphere, suburb **7** quarter, society **8** affinity, district, environs, likeness, populace, province, sameness, vicinity **9** agreement, citizenry **10** population, similarity **11** environment, social group **12** commonwealth, neighborhood, surroundings

commute 4 ride, trip **5** alter **6** adjust, change, redeem, soften, switch, travel **7** convert, journey, replace, reverse **8** diminish, exchange, mitigate **9** alleviate, supersede, transform, transmute, transpose **10** substitute **11** transfigure **12** metamorphose, transmogrify

comodo
  music: **9** leisurely

Comoros
  other name: **26** lost pearls of the Indian Ocean
  capital/largest city: **6** Moroni
  others: **6** Bambao **7** Fomboni **8** Dzaoudzi **9** Mutsamudu **11** Mitsamiouli
  monetary unit: **5** franc **7** centime
  island: **6** Moheli **7** Anjouan, Mayotte **12** Grande Comoro
  highest point: **7** Kartala **8** Karthala
  sea: **6** Indian
  physical feature:
    channel: **10** Mozambique
  people: **4** Arab **5** Bantu, Malay **7** African **8** Malagasy
  language: **6** Arabic, French **7** Swahili **8** Malagasy
  religion: **5** Islam **13** Roman Catholic

compact 4 bond, cram, deal, pack, pact, snug, tidy **5** close, dense, press, small, stuff **6** little, treaty **7** bargain, crammed, pressed, squeeze, stuffed **8** alliance, compress, contract, covenant **9** agreement, clustered, concordat **10** compressed **11** arrangement, pack closely **12** concentrated **13** tightly packed, understanding

compactness 7 density **8** snugness **9** smallness **10** littleness **11** compression **13** concentration

companion 3 pal **4** chum, mate **5** buddy, crony **6** escort, friend, helper **7** comrade **9** assistant, associate, attendant

companionable 6 social **7** amiable, cordial **8** friendly, sociable **9** agreeable, congenial, convivial

companionate 4 warm **6** genial **7** cordial **8** amicable, friendly, platonic, suitable **9** accordant, agreeable, consonant, easygoing, nonsexual, spiritual, unfleshly **10** compatible, concordant, harmonious **11** nonphysical, passionless, warm-hearted **12** affectionate **13** companionable

companionship 4 pals **5** chums **7** buddies, company, friends **8** comrades **10** associates, companions, fellowship, friendship **11** camaraderie, comradeship, familiarity, sociability **17** close acquaintance, friendly relations

company 3 mob **4** band, firm, gang **5** bunch, group, guest, party **6** guests, outfit, people, throng **7** callers, concern, friends, society, visitor **8** assembly, comrades, presence, visitors **9** gathering, multitude, syndicate **10** assemblage, companions, fellowship, friendship **11** camaraderie, comradeship, corporation, sociability **12** conglomerate, congregation **13** companionship, establishment **15** business concern

comparable 4 like, up to **5** close, equal **6** akin to **7** similar **8** as good as, parallel **9** a match for, analogous **10** equivalent, on a par with, tantamount **11** approaching, approximate **12** commensurate, in a class with **13** commensurable

comparative 4 near **8** relative **11** approximate

compare 5 equal, liken, match **6** be up to, equate, relate **7** vie with **8** approach, contrast **9** correlate **11** compete with **12** be on a par with **13** hold a candle to **14** be in a class with **20** draw a parallel between

compare notes 6 confer **7** consult **8** talk over **13** exchange views

comparison 7 analogy, kinship **8** contrast, equality, likeness, parallel, relation **10** connection, similarity **11** correlation, resemblance **13** comparability

compartment 3 box, pew **4** brig, cell, crib, hold, hole, nook, room **5** berth, booth, cabin, crypt, niche, stall, vault **6** alcove, bunker, closet **7** chamber, cubicle, section **8** anteroom, roomette **9** cubbyhole **10** pigeonhole **11** antechamber

compass 5 bound, range, reach, scope, sweep **6** domain, extent **8** boundary, province **13** circumference

Compass, Mariner's Compass
  constellation of: **5** Pyxis

Compasses, Pair
  constellation of: **8** Circinus

compassion 4 pity **5** heart **7** empathy, feeling **8** humanity, sympathy **10** ten-

derness **13** commiseration, fellow feeling **17** tender-heartedness
Latin: **12** misericordia

compassionate 4 kind **6** humane **7** pitying **8** merciful **10** benevolent, charitable **11** kindhearted, sympathetic **13** tender-hearted

compatibility 6 accord **7** concord, harmony, rapport **8** affinity **9** agreement, unanimity **12** congeniality **14** like- mindedness

compatible 3 apt, fit **6** seemly **7** fitting **8** in accord, suitable **9** congenial, in keeping **10** like-minded **11** appropriate

compel 4 make **5** drive, force **6** oblige **7** require **11** necessitate

compelled 4 must **5** bound, urged **6** driven, forced **7** coerced, obliged, pressed **8** commanded, dragooned, enforced, impelled, obsessed, pressured, required **11** constrained, overpowered

compelling 7 driving, dynamic **8** forceful **10** commanding **12** overwhelming

compel obedience to 5 force **6** coerce **7** enforce **8** carry out, insist on **10** administer

compendium 4 list **5** brief **6** apercu, digest, precis, survey **7** abstract, capsule, catalog, epitome, summary **8** syllabus, synopsis **9** catalogue **11** abridgement, compilation **12** condensation

compensate 3 pay **5** cover, repay **6** make up, offset, redeem, square **7** balance, pay back, redress **9** indemnify, reimburse **10** make amends, recompense, remunerate **14** counterbalance **15** make restitution

compensation 3 fee, pay **4** gain **5** wages **6** income, profit, return, reward, salary **7** payment, redress **8** benefits, earnings, gratuity **9** indemnity, repayment **10** recompense, settlement **11** restitution **12** remuneration, satisfaction **13** consideration, reimbursement

compete 3 vie **5** fight **6** battle, combat, oppose **7** contend, contest **8** be rivals **9** lock horns, match wits

competence 5 skill **7** ability, know-how, mastery **8** ableness **9** expertise **10** capability, competency, expertness **11** proficiency

competent 3 fit **6** expert, versed **7** skilled, trained **8** skillful **9** efficient, practiced, qualified **10** dependable, proficient **11** experienced, responsible, trustworthy

competition 4 game **5** event, match, rival **7** contest, rivalry, tourney **8** conflict, opponent, struggle **9** contender **10** contention, opposition, tournament

competitive 8 fighting, opposing,

striving **9** combative **10** aggressive, contending

competitor 5 rival **7** fighter **8** opponent **9** adversary, contender **10** contestant, opposition

compilation 4 body **5** group **9** collating, garnering, gathering, mustering **10** assemblage, assembling, assortment, collecting, collection, compendium, marshaling **11** aggregating, aggregation, marshalling **12** accumulating, accumulation

compile 5 amass **6** garner, gather, heap up, muster **7** collate, collect, marshal **8** assemble **10** accumulate

complacent 4 smug **6** at ease **7** content **9** contented **10** self-secure, unbothered, untroubled **13** self-satisfied

complain 3 nag **4** beef, carp, kick, moan, pick **5** cavil, gripe, whine **6** grouch, grouse, squawk **7** grumble **9** bellyache, criticize, find fault **15** state a grievance

complaint 4 beef, kick **5** gripe **6** malady, squawk, tirade **7** ailment, illness, protest **8** debility, disorder, sickness **9** criticism, grievance, infirmity, objection **10** impairment **12** faultfinding **15** dissatisfaction

complaisance 7 pliancy **8** docility **10** affability, amiability, compliance **12** acquiescence

complaisant 4 warm **7** affable, amiable, cordial **8** friendly, gracious, obliging, pleasant, pleasing **9** agreeable, compliant, congenial, easygoing **10** solicitous **11** good-humored, good-natured

Compleat Angler, The
author: **11** Izaak Walton

complement 3 cap **5** crown, match, total, whole **7** balance, perfect **8** ensemble, entirety, parallel, round out **9** aggregate, companion **10** completion, consummate, full amount, full number, supplement **11** counterpart, rounding-out **12** consummation **14** required number

complementary 7 matched **8** integral, opposite **9** companion **10** additional, compatible, completing **11** correlative **12** interrelated, supplemental **13** correspondent, corresponding

complete 3 cap, end **4** full **5** crown, total, utter, whole **6** entire, finish, intact, settle, wrap up **7** achieve, execute, fulfill, perfect, perform, plenary, settled **8** absolute, achieved, carry out, conclude, executed, round out, thorough, unbroken **9** discharge, make whole, performed, polish off, terminate, undivided **10** accomplish, carried out, complement, conclusive, consummate, unabridged **11** consummated **12** accomplished

completed 4 done **5** ended, whole **6** closed, entire, filled **7** matured,

through **8** achieved, finished, realized **9** concluded, executed, fulfilled, perfected **10** terminated, wrapped up **11** consummated **12** accomplished

completeness 8 fullness, richness **9** wholeness **10** perfection **12** thoroughness

completion 3 end **5** close **6** ending, finish, windup **7** closing **9** finishing **10** concluding, conclusion, expiration **11** fulfillment, terminating, termination **12** consummation

complex 4 maze **5** mixed **6** knotty, system **7** network, tangled **8** compound, involved, manifold, multiple, puzzling **9** aggregate, composite, difficult, enigmatic, fixed idea, intricate, obsession **10** perplexing, variegated **11** bewildering, complicated **12** conglomerate, labyrinthian, labyrinthine, multifarious **13** preoccupation

complexion 3 hue **4** look, tone **5** color, guise, image, slant **6** aspect **7** outlook **8** coloring **9** character **10** appearance, coloration, impression **11** countenance, skin texture **12** pigmentation, skin coloring

complexity 6 puzzle **9** intricacy, obscurity **10** bafflement, involution, perplexity **11** crabbedness, elaboration, involvement **12** complication, entanglement **15** inextricability **17** unintelligibility **19** incomprehensibility

compliance 6 assent **7** pliancy **8** docility, giving in, meekness, yielding **9** deference, obedience, passivity **10** conforming, conformity, submission **12** acquiescence, complaisance **13** nonresistance

compliant 8 flexible, yielding **9** agreeable **10** submissive

complicate 4 knot **5** ravel, snarl **6** muddle, tangle **7** confuse, involve **8** confound, entangle **11** make complex **13** make difficult, make intricate

complicated 7 complex **8** involved **9** elaborate, intricate

complication 4 snag **5** hitch **7** dilemma, problem **8** drawback, handicap, obstacle, quandary **9** hindrance **10** difficulty, impediment, perplexity **11** aggravation, obstruction, predicament **12** disadvantage **14** stumbling block

complicity 8 abetment, intrigue, plotting, schemery, scheming **9** collusion, finagling **10** connivance, conspiracy **11** confederacy, contrivance, implication, involvement **12** entanglement

compliment 5 honor, kudos **6** homage, praise **7** tribute **8** flattery **9** adulation, laudation **11** acclamation **12** commendation **14** congratulation

complimentary 4 free **6** gratis **8** admiring, praising **9** adulatory, extolling, laudatory, panegyric, praiseful **10** flattering, gratuitous, plauditory **12** appreciative, commendatory **13** without charge **14** congratulatory

compliments 4 best, laud **5** exalt, extol, toast **6** homage, praise, salute **7** applaud, commend, regards **8** respects **9** greetings **10** best wishes, good wishes **11** salutations **13** felicitations **15** congratulations

comply 3 bow **4** bend, meet, mind, obey **5** defer, yield **6** accede, adhere, follow, give in, submit **7** abide by, conform, consent, fulfill, observe, satisfy **9** acquiesce, surrender

component 4 item, part **5** piece **6** detail, member, module **7** element, modular, segment **8** material **9** composing, elemental, essential, intrinsic **10** elementary, ingredient, particular **11** constituent, fundamental **13** component part

component part 4 item, part **5** piece **6** detail, member **7** element **10** ingredient, particular **11** constituent, fundamental

comport 3 act **4** bear **5** carry **6** acquit, behave, deport **7** conduct

comportment 7 bearing, conduct **8** attitude, behavior, carriage, demeanor, presence **9** acquittal **10** appearance, deportment

comport oneself 3 act **6** behave **13** acquit oneself **14** conduct oneself

compose 4 calm, form, lull, make **5** frame, quell, quiet, relax, shape, write **6** create, devise, make up, pacify, settle, soothe **7** collect, fashion, placate **8** be part of, belong to, comprise, conceive, modulate **9** formulate **10** constitute

composed 4 calm, cool **5** quiet **6** at ease, placid, poised, sedate, serene, steady **8** peaceful, tranquil **9** collected, quiescent, unexcited, unruffled **10** controlled, cool- headed, restrained, unagitated, untroubled **11** level- headed, undisturbed, unemotional, unflappable, unperturbed **12** even-tempered **13** dispassionate, imperturbable **15** undemonstrative

composer 4 bard, poet **6** author, writer **7** creator **8** musician, producer **10** compositor, typesetter

composite 6 mosaic **7** blended **8** combined, compound **10** compounded

composition 4 form, opus, work **5** essay, etude, piece **6** design, layout, make-up, making **7** forming, framing, product, shaping **8** creating, creation, devising, exercise **9** framework, structure **10** concoction, fashioning, organizing, production **11** arrangement, combination, compilation, formulation, preparation **12** constitution, organization **13** configuration

compos mentis 4 sane **13** mentally sound

composure 4 calm, cool, ease **5** poise

6 aplomb **7** control, dignity **8** calmness, coolness, patience, serenity **9** sang-froid **10** equanimity **11** self-control **13** self-assurance, self-restraint **14** cool-headedness, self-possession, unexcitability, unflappability **15** level-headedness **16** even-temperedness, imperturbability

compound 3 mix **4** fuse, make **5** add to, alloy, blend, boost, mixed, union, unite **6** devise, fusion, mingle **7** amalgam, amplify, augment, blended, combine, complex, concoct, enlarge, magnify, mixture, prepare **8** combined, heighten, increase **9** composite, fabricate, formulate, reinforce **10** synthesize **11** combination, complicated, composition, incorporate, put together **12** conglomerate **14** conglomeration

comprehend 3 dig, get **5** catch, grasp, savvy **6** absorb, digest, fathom **7** make out **8** conceive, perceive **9** penetrate **10** appreciate, assimilate, understand

comprehensible 5 clear, plain **7** evident **8** apparent **11** unambiguous **12** intelligible

comprehension 5 grasp **7** insight **9** awareness **10** conception, perception **11** realization **12** acquaintance, appreciation, apprehension **13** consciousness, understanding

comprehensive 4 full **5** broad **7** copious, general, overall **8** complete, sweeping, thorough **9** expansive, extensive, universal **10** exhaustive, widespread **11** compendious **12** all-embracing, all-inclusive

compress 4 cram, pack **5** press **6** reduce, shrink **7** abridge, bandage, compact, curtail, plaster, shorten, squeeze **8** condense, dressing **10** abbreviate

compressed 5 dense **6** jammed, packed **7** crowded **8** squashed, squeezed **9** compacted **12** concentrated

compressed form 6 digest **7** summary **8** cake form, synopsis **10** shortening **11** abridgement, contraction, curtailment **12** abbreviation, condensation

compression 9 narrowing, squeezing, stricture, tightness **10** compaction, constraint **12** constriction

compressor 4 pump **7** presser, reducer **8** squeezer **9** compactor, condenser

comprise 4 form **6** make up **7** compose, contain, include **8** be made of **9** consist of **10** constitute **12** be composed of

compromise 4 risk **5** agree, truce **6** settle **7** balance, compact, imperil **8** endanger, undercut **9** agreement, discredit, embarrass, implicate, make a deal, prejudice **10** adjustment, jeopardize, settlement **11** arrangement,

come to terms, happy medium, make suspect, meet halfway **12** conciliation **13** accommodation, rapprochement **14** make vulnerable, strike a bargain **16** mutual concession **18** split the difference **21** come to an understanding **German: 9** Ausgleich

compromising 7 risking **8** settling **9** adjusting **10** bargaining **11** give and take, making a deal **12** embarrassing, jeopardizing **13** accommodating, coming to terms **14** meeting halfway

Compsognathus
type: 8 dinosaur, theropod
characteristic: 8 smallest
location: 6 Europe **7** Bavaria
period: 8 Jurassic

Compson, Quentin
character in: 14 Absalom Absalom **18** The Sound and the Fury
author: 8 Faulkner

Compson family
characters in: 18 The Sound and the Fury
member: 5 Benjy, Caddy, Jason **7** Candace, Quentin **8** Benjamin
author: 8 Faulkner

compte rendu 6 record, report, review **7** account **15** account rendered

comptroller 7 auditor **9** treasurer **10** accountant, bookkeeper, controller

compulsion 5 force **6** demand, duress, urging **8** coercion, pressure **9** necessity **10** obligation **11** domineering, requirement

compulsive 6 driven, hooked **7** driving, fanatic **8** addicted, habitual **9** compelled, obsessive **10** compelling **14** unable to resist, uncontrollable

compulsory 7 binding **8** coercive, demanded, enforced, forcible, required **9** mandatory, requisite **10** compulsive, imperative, obligatory **11** unavoidable **12** prescriptive

compunction 5 demur, qualm, shame **6** regret, unease **7** anxiety, concern, remorse, scruple **9** misgiving **10** contrition **16** pang of conscience

computation 5 tally, total **8** figuring **9** numbering, reckoning **10** numeration **11** calculation, enumeration

compute 3 add **5** add up, sum up, tally, total **6** figure, reckon **7** count up, work out **9** ascertain, calculate, figure out

computer 5 adder **9** processor **10** calculator
language: 3 Ada, APL **4** Java, LISP, HTML, LOGO **5** ALGOL, BASIC, COBOL **6** Pascal **7** FORTRAN
term: 2 PC **3** bit, bug, CAD, CAM, CPU, DOS, FAQ, RAM, ROM web, www **4** boot, byte, chip, file, hack, icon, spam, Unix **5** CD-Rom, crash, debug, drive, input, modem, mouse, pixel, queue, virus **6** analog, backup, cursor, glitch, hacker, laptop, mem-

ory, online, output, readme, window **7** digital, network, offline, program **8** database, hardware, lightpen, printout, software, terminal **9** hypertext interface, mainframe **10** binary code, floppy disk **11** application, interactive, spreadsheet **12** minicomputer, World Wide Web **13** microcomputer, word processor **14** microprocessor *see also: desktop publishing*

comrade 3 pal **4** ally, chum **5** buddy, crony **6** friend **7** partner **8** confrere, co-worker, helpmate, intimate **9** associate, colleague, companion, confidant **10** bosom buddy **11** confederate **12** collaborator **13** boon companion
Russian: 8 tovarich

comradeship 8 alliance **10** fellowship, friendship **11** association, camaraderie **13** companionship

comte 5 count

Comte Ory, Le
also: **8** Count Ory
opera by: **7** Rossini
character: **13** Countess Adele

Comus
author: **10** John Milton
subtitle: **7** A Masque

Comus
origin: **5** Roman
god of: **7** revelry **8** drinking

con 3 gyp **4** anti, bilk, coax, fool, gull, hoax, lure, rook **5** cheat, cozen, felon, trick **6** delude **7** against, beguile, convict, defraud, mislead, swindle **8** hoodwink, jailbird, prisoner, yardbird **9** bamboozle

Conakry
capital of: **6** Guinea

concatenation 4 link **5** union **6** hookup **7** joining, linking, reunion **8** coupling, junction **10** bracketing, confluence, connection **11** conjunction **12** interlinking **15** interconnection **16** interassociation **18** intercommunication

concave 6 hollow, sunken **8** indented **9** depressed **13** curving inward

conceal 4 hide, mask **5** cloak, cover **6** screen, shield **7** cover up, obscure, secrete **8** disguise **10** camouflage, keep secret

concealed 5 blind, doggo **6** covert, hidden, latent, masked, perdue, secret, veiled **7** cloaked, covered, obscure, unknown, wrapped **8** abstruse, shrouded, ulterior **9** disguised, incognito **11** clandestine

concealment 5 cover **6** hiding **7** hideout, masking **8** covering, hideaway **9** screening, secreting, secretion **10** covering up, under cover

concede 3 own **4** cede **5** admit, agree, allow, grant, yield **6** accept, give up, resign, tender **7** abandon, confess, deliver **8** hand over **9** acquiesce, recognize, surrender, vouchsafe **10** relinquish **11** acknowledge, be persuaded

conceit 3 ego **5** pride **6** vanity **7** ego trip, egotism **8** bragging, self-love **9** vainglory **10** self-esteem **12** boastfulness **14** self-importance

conceited 4 smug, vain **7** stuck-up **8** arrogant, boasting, bragging, puffed up **9** bombastic, overproud, strutting **11** egotistical, swellheaded **12** vainglorious **13** self-important

conceivable 8 credible, knowable, possible **9** thinkable **10** believable, imaginable, supposable **11** perceivable

conceive 4 form **5** frame, hatch, start **6** create, ideate, invent **7** concoct, dream up, imagine, produce, think of, think up **8** consider, contrive, envisage, envision, initiate **9** originate **10** comprehend, understand

concentrate 4 mass **5** amass, bunch, focus, hem in **6** center, gather, heap up, reduce **7** close in, cluster, pay heed, thicken **8** assemble, attend to, condense, converge, fasten on **10** accumulate, congregate **11** bring to bear **12** direct toward

concentrated 5 dense **7** crowded, focused, thought **8** centered **10** compressed

concentration 4 mass **5** focus **7** cluster **9** diligence, gathering, reduction **10** absorption, assemblage, collection, intentness, thickening **11** aggregation, boiling down, convergence, deep thought, engrossment **12** accumulation **13** concentrating, consolidation **14** centralization

concept 4 idea, view **5** image **6** belief, notion, theory **7** opinion, surmise, thought **9** postulate **10** conviction, hypothesis, impression **11** supposition

conception 4 idea **5** birth, image, start **6** notion **7** forming, genesis, inkling, picture **8** creating, devising, hatching **9** beginning, formation, imagining, inception, invention, launching **10** conceiving, concocting, initiation, perception **11** envisioning, formulation, originating **12** apprehension **13** fertilization, understanding **16** becoming pregnant

conceptual 8 abstract **9** visionary **11** conjectural, ideological, speculative, theoretical **12** experimental, hypothetical **15** impressionistic

concern 3 job **4** care, duty, firm, heed **5** chore, house, store, touch, worry **6** affair, affect, charge, matter, occupy, regard **7** anxiety, apply to, company, disturb, involve, mission, trouble **8** bear upon, business, distress, interest, relate to **9** attention, pertain to **10** disconcert, enterprise, solicitude **11** appertain to, corporation, disturbance, involvement, undertaking **12** apprehension **13** consideration, establishment **14** thoughtfulness

concerned 5 upset **6** active, caring,

uneasy **7** alarmed, anxious, engaged, fearful, worried **8** involved, troubled **9** attentive, committed, disturbed **10** disquieted, distressed, interested, solicitous **12** apprehensive **13** participating

concerning 2 of, on, re **3** for **4** as to, over, upon **5** about, anent **7** apropos **8** engaging, touching, worrying **9** affecting, involving, mattering, regarding **10** relating to, respecting

concert 5 union, unity **6** accord, settle **7** concord, harmony **8** teamwork **9** agreement, congruity, unanimity **10** accordance, complicity **11** association, cooperation **13** collaboration **14** correspondence **18** musical performance

concerted 5 joint **6** united **7** planned **8** by assent **10** agreed upon **11** cooperative, prearranged **12** premeditated **13** predetermined

concert hall 5 odeum **6** lyceum **7** theater **9** music hall **10** auditorium **12** symphony hall

concession 5 lease **6** assent **8** giving in, yielding **9** admission, franchise, privilege **10** adjustment, compromise, indulgence **12** acquiescence, modification **14** acknowledgment

Conch
form: **7** trumpet
made of: **5** shell
owned by: **7** Tritons

Conchobar
origin: **5** Irish
king of: **6** Ulster
nephew: **10** Cuchulainn

concierge 7 janitor **9** custodian **10** doorkeeper

conciliate 6 pacify **7** appease, placate **9** make peace, reconcile **11** accommodate

conciliation 11 appeasement, peacemaking **12** propitiation **13** accommodation **14** reconciliation

conciliatory 8 friendly **9** appeasing, pacifying, placatory **10** mollifying, reassuring **11** peacemaking, reconciling **13** accommodative

concise 5 brief, pithy, short, terse **7** compact **8** succinct **9** condensed **10** to the point **11** abbreviated

conciseness 7 brevity **9** terseness **11** compactness **12** condensation, succinctness

conclave 6 parley, powwow **7** council, meeting, session **8** assembly **10** conference, convention **11** convocation **13** secret council

conclude 3 end **4** halt, stop **5** close, infer, judge **6** decide, deduce, effect, finish, gather, reason, settle **7** arrange, resolve, surmise **8** break off, carry out, complete **9** determine, terminate **10** accomplish **11** bring to pass, discontinue **12** draw to a close

concluded 5 bound, ended, guess **6** closed, judged **7** decided, deduced, expired, settled, wound up **9** completed **10** culminated, determined, restrained, terminated

conclusion 3 end **5** close **6** finale, finish, result, upshot, windup **7** finding, outcome **8** decision, judgment **9** agreement, deduction, final part, inference, summation **10** completion, denouement, resolution, settlement, working out **11** arrangement, presumption, termination **13** determination

conclusive 5 clear **6** patent **7** certain, obvious **8** absolute, decisive, definite, manifest, palpable **9** clinching **10** compelling, convincing, undeniable **11** categorical, determining, inescapable, irrefutable **12** demonstrable, unanswerable **13** incontestable, unimpeachable **14** unquestionable **16** incontrovertible

concoct 3 mix **4** brew **5** frame, hatch **6** cook up, create, devise, invent, make up **7** think up **8** compound, contrive **9** fabricate, formulate

concoction 4 brew **5** blend **6** jumble, medley **7** mixture **8** compound, creation **9** invention, potpourri **11** contrivance, fabrication **14** conglomeration

concomitant 7 related **9** accessory, attendant, connected, corollary, secondary **10** additional **12** accompanying, contributing, supplemental **13** complementary

concord 5 amity, peace **6** accord **7** harmony **8** goodwill **9** agreement **10** friendship **11** amicability, cooperation **16** cordial relations **19** mutual understanding

concordance 5 index **6** accord **7** concord **9** agreement, consensus, unanimity **17** meeting of the minds

concordant 6 unison **7** calming **8** agreeing, unifying **9** assenting, consonant **10** concurrent, harmonious

concordat 4 pact **8** covenant **9** agreement

Concorde 3 jet, SST **10** supersonic
   airline **9** Air France **14** British
   Airways

Concordia
   origin: **5** Roman
   goddess of: **5** peace **7** harmony

concourse 7 conflux, joining, linkage, meeting **8** junction **9** amassment **10** assembling, concursion, confluence **11** aggregation, association, convergence **12** congregation, focalization **13** concentration **14** conglomeration **15** flowing together **16** flocking together

concrete 4 real **5** solid **6** cement **7** express, factual, precise **8** definite, distinct, explicit, material, specific, tangible **10** particular **11** fused stones, substantial **12** alloyed rocks

concupiscence 4 itch, lust **6** desire **7** craving, lechery, longing, passion **8** appetite, hot pants, lewdness, satyrism **9** horniness, lubricity, prurience, randiness **10** wantonness **11** goatishness, libertinism, lustfulness **12** sexual desire **13** lecherousness **14** lasciviousness, libidinousness

concur 5 agree, match, tally **6** square **7** conform **8** coincide, hold with **9** be uniform **10** be in accord, correspond **11** go along with **12** go hand in hand

concur in 7 approve **9** agree with **11** go along with

concurrence, concurrency 6 accord **7** concord, consent, harmony **8** approval **9** agreement, consensus, unanimity **10** acceptance, conformity **11** affirmation, coexistence, coincidence, conjuncture, cooperation, synchronism **12** acquiescence **13** collaboration, mutual consent **14** correspondence **15** working together **17** meeting of the minds **22** simultaneous occurrence

concurrent 5 at one **6** allied **7** aligned **8** agreeing, matching **9** congenial, congruous, consonant **10** coexisting, coincident, coinciding, compatible, harmonious **11** in agreement, sympathetic, synchronous **12** commensurate, contemporary, in accordance, simultaneous **13** correspondent, of the same mind **15** contemporaneous

concurring 8 agreeing **10** consenting **11** affirmative, in agreement, synchronous **12** coincidental, simultaneous **13** corresponding

concussion 3 jar **4** blow, bump **5** clash, shock **6** buffet, impact **7** shaking **8** pounding **9** agitation, collision **11** brain injury

condemn 4 damn, doom **5** decry **6** rebuke **7** censure **8** denounce, sentence **9** criticize, proscribe, reprehend **10** disapprove

condemnation 6 rebuke **7** censure, reproof **8** judgment, reproach, sentence **9** criticism **10** conviction, punishment **11** disapproval **12** denunciation, reprehension **14** disapprobation **20** pronouncement of guilt

condensation 6 digest **9** reduction **10** abridgment **13** shortened form **16** condensed version

condense 3 cut **4** trim **6** digest, reduce **7** abridge, compact, liquefy, shorten, thicken **8** boil down, compress, contract, pare down **10** abbreviate, bluepencil **11** concentrate, consolidate, precipitate

condensed form 6 digest, precis **7** summary **8** synopsis **10** shortening **11** abridgment, compression, contraction, curtailment **12** abbreviation

condescend 5 deign, stoop **6** submit, unbend **7** descend, disdain **9** patronize **10** look down on, talk down to **12** come down a peg, lower oneself **13** humble oneself

condescending 7 high-hat **8** superior **10** disdainful **11** overbearing, patronizing

condescension 4 airs **7** disdain, hauteur, modesty **8** humility **9** deference, loftiness **10** humbleness **11** haughtiness **12** graciousness **13** selfabasement **14** self-effacement **19** patronizing attitude **20** assumption of equality **21** high-and-mighty attitude

condign 3 due **4** fair, just, meet **5** right **6** earned, proper, worthy **7** fitting, merited **8** deserved, suitable **9** warranted **11** appropriate

condiment 4 herb **5** sauce, spice **8** dressing, flavorer, seasoner **9** seasoning
   kind: **3** bay **4** dill, mace, mint, sage, salt **5** caper, clove, curry, onion, thyme **6** catsup, garlic, ginger, nutmeg, pepper, pickle, relish **7** caraway, chutney, ketchup, mustard, parsley, oregano, paprika, pimento, tabasco, vinegar **8** cardamon, marjoram, turmeric **9** pimpernel **10** bell pepper, mayonnaise

condition 3 fit **4** term **5** adapt, equip, ready, shape, state, train **6** demand, fettle, malady, status, tone up **7** ailment, prepare, problem, proviso **8** accustom, position, standing **9** agreement, complaint, provision, requisite, situation **10** limitation, make used to, put in shape **11** arrangement, contingency, malfunction, reservation, restriction, stipulation **12** prerequisite **13** circumstances, qualification, state of health **14** state of affairs **15** physical fitness

conditional 7 limited **9** dependent, qualified, tentative **10** contingent, restricted **11** provisional, stipulative **16** with reservations

condolence 4 pity **6** solace **7** comfort **8** sympathy **10** compassion **11** consolation **13** commiseration

Condon, Richard
   author of: **11** Winter Kills **18** Death of a Politician **22** The Manchurian Candidate

condonation 11 forgiveness, overlooking **12** disregarding **13** putting up with

condone 6 excuse, forget, ignore, pardon, wink at **7** absolve, forgive, justify, let pass **8** overlook **9** disregard, put up with

conduce 3 aid **4** help, lead, tend **5** bring, favor, guide **6** effect **7** advance, forward, further, promote **10** contribute

conducive 7 helpful **8** salutary **9** favorable, promotive **10** beneficial **11** expeditious **12** contributive, contributory, instrumental **19** calculated to produce **22** helpful in bringing about

conduct 3 act **4** bear, lead, rule, ways **5** carry, chair, deeds, enact, guide, pilot, steer, usher **6** action, attend, behave, convey, convoy, direct, escort, govern, manage, manner **7** carry on, comport, control, execute, marshal, operate, perform **8** behavior, carry out, dispatch, guidance, regulate, transact **9** accompany, direction, discharge, look after, supervise **10** administer, deportment, government, leadership, management **11** comportment, generalship, preside over, superintend, supervision **14** administration

conduct oneself 3 act **6** behave **13** acquit oneself **14** comport oneself

conductor 3 cad **5** guide **6** carman, escort, leader **7** cathode, channel, maestro, manager **8** aqueduct, batonist, cicerone, conveyor, director, operator, stickman, trainman **9** collector, drum major **10** impresario, supervisor **11** choirmaster, transmitter **13** concert master

conduit 4 duct, main, pipe, tube **5** canal, drain, flume, sewer **6** gutter, trough **7** channel, passage **8** aqueduct **11** watercourse

cone 5 bevel, shape, spire **6** bobbin, conoid, funnel **7** pyramid, volcano **8** pyramid
kind: 3 fir **4** pine **5** larch **7** conifer, retinal **8** ice cream

confabulate 4 chat, talk **6** confer, patter **7** chatter, discuss **8** chitchat, converse, talk idly

confabulation 4 chat, talk **8** chitchat **10** conference, discussion **12** conversation

confection 3 jam **5** candy **6** pastry **7** dessert **8** conserve, delicacy **9** preserves, sweetmeat **10** sugar candy

confectionery 5 candy **6** sweets **7** goodies, pasties **10** sugar candy, sweetmeats

confederacy, Confederacy 3 CSA **4** band, bloc **5** guild, union **6** fusion, league **7** combine, society **8** alliance, the South **9** coalition, syndicate **10** federation **11** association **13** confederation **14** Southern states **18** secessionist states **26** Confederate States of America
capital: 8 Richmond
leader: 14 Jefferson Davis
flag: 12 Stars and Bars
See also **8** Civil War

confederate 4 ally **5** merge, unite **6** cohort, helper **7** abettor, comrade, partner **8** coalesce, coworker **9** accessory, affiliate, associate, colleague, companion **10** accomplice, cooperator, join forces **11** consolidate, helping hand **12** band together, collaborator, right hand man **17** fellow conspirator

Confederates
author: 14 Thomas Keneally

confederation 4 band **5** guild, union **6** fusion, league **7** combine, society **8** alliance **9** coalition, syndicate **10** federation **11** association, confederacy

confer 4 give **5** award **6** accord, parley **7** consult, discuss, palaver **8** converse **9** present to **10** bestow upon **12** compare notes, talk together **15** hold a conference **18** deliberate together

conference 4 talk **6** parley **7** council, meeting, seminar **8** conclave **9** symposium **10** convention, discussion **12** consultation, deliberation

conferment 4 gift **5** award **8** bestowal **12** presentation

confess 3 own **4** avow, sing **5** admit, own up **6** expose, reveal **7** declare, divulge, lay bare **8** blurt out, disclose **9** come clean, make known **11** acknowledge **12** bring to light **14** unbosom oneself **18** make a clean breast of

confessed 6 avowed **8** admitted **9** professed **12** self-declared **14** self-proclaimed

confession 6 avowal, shrift **9** admission **10** disclosure, divulgence, revelation **11** declaration **12** confessional **14** acknowledgment

Confessions of an English Opium Eater
author: 15 Thomas DeQuincey

Confessions of Nat Turner, The
author: 13 William Styron

confidant, confidante 5 crony **6** friend **8** intimate **10** bosom buddy **15** trusty companion

confide 6 impart, reveal **7** confess, divulge, lay bare, let in on, let know **8** disclose **9** make known **12** tell secretly **13** tell privately **14** unbosom oneself

confidence 4 grit, guts **5** faith, nerve, pluck, spunk, trust **6** belief, daring, mettle, secret, spirit **7** courage **8** audacity, boldness, credence, intimacy, reliance **9** certainty, certitude **10** conviction **11** intrepidity **12** self-reliance **13** private matter, self-assurance **14** faith in oneself **17** inside information

confidence man 5 cheat **6** con man **8** swindler **9** charlatan, trickster **10** mountebank

confident 4 bold, sure **5** cocky **6** daring, secure **7** assured, certain **8** cocksure, intrepid, positive **9** convinced, dauntless, expectant **10** optimistic **11** self-assured, self-reliant **13** sure of oneself

confidential 5 privy **6** secret **7** private **8** hush-hush **9** top- secret **10** classified **11** undisclosed **12** off-the-record **16** not to be disclosed

confidentially 7 sub rosa **8** in secret, secretly **9** privately **16** between ourselves **17** behind closed doors
French: 9 entre nous

confiding 6 trusty **7** reliant **8** trustful, trusting **9** confident **11** trustworthy

configuration 4 form **6** design, makeup **11** arrangement, composition

confine 3 pen, tie **4** bind, cage, hold, jail, keep **5** limit **6** coop up, govern, keep in, lock up, shut in, shut up **7** fence in, impound **8** imprison, regulate, restrain, restrict **9** sequester **11** incarcerate **13** hold in custody

confined 4 pent **5** close, tight **6** jailed, narrow **7** cramped **8** locked up **10** imprisoned, restricted

confinement 7 custody, lying in **9** cooping up, detention, restraint **10** childbirth, constraint, limitation, shutting in **11** parturition, restriction **12** accouchement, imprisonment **13** incarceration **15** circumscription

confines 4 edge **6** border, bounds, limits **7** margins **8** precinct **10** boundaries **13** circumference

confirm 5 prove **6** accept, clinch, ratify, uphold, verify **7** agree to, approve, bear out, certify, sustain **8** make firm, validate **9** authorize, establish **11** acknowledge, corroborate, make binding, make certain **12** authenticate, substantiate

confirmation 5 proof **6** assent **8** approval, sanction **9** agreement **10** acceptance, validation **11** affirmation, endorsement **12** ratification, verification **13** corroboration **14** authentication, substantiation

confirmed 3 set **5** fixed **7** chronic **8** hardened, verified **9** ingrained, validated **10** deep-rooted, deep-seated, inveterate, proven true **11** established **12** corroborated **13** authenticated, dyed-in-the-wool, substantiated

confiscate 4 take **5** seize **7** impound, possess, preempt **8** take over **9** sequester **10** commandeer **11** appropriate, expropriate

confiscation 7 seizure **10** impounding, preemption **13** appropriation, commandeering, expropriation

conflagration 4 fire **5** blaze **7** bonfire, inferno **8** conflict, fighting, wildfire **9** brush fire, firestorm, holocaust **10** forest fire, raging fire, wall of fire **11** sea of flames **12** sheet of flame

conflagrative 8 burnable **9** flammable, ignitable **10** combustive, incendiary **11** combustible, inflammable

conflict 4 fray **5** clash, fight, melee, set-to **6** action, battle, combat, fracas, oppose, strife, tussle **7** collide, discord, dissent, scuffle, warfare **8** disa-

gree, division, friction, skirmish, struggle, variance **9** encounter, hostility **10** antagonism, be contrary, difference, dissension, engagement **12** disagreement **13** confrontation **14** be inharmonious **15** be contradictory
Spanish: 9 mano a mano

conflicting 7 warring **8** clashing, opposing **10** ambivalent **13** contradictory

confluence 5 union **7** conflux, joining, linkage, meeting **8** junction, juncture **9** concourse, gathering **10** assembling, concursion **11** association, convergence **13** concentration **14** coming together **15** flowing together

conform 3 fit **4** obey **5** adapt **6** adjust, follow **8** adhere to, jibe with, submit to **9** agree with, reconcile, tally with **10** be guided by, comply with, fall in with, square with **11** acquiesce in **12** correspond to

conformable 8 amenable **9** agreeable, malleable **10** submissive **12** in compliance

conformance 7 harmony **9** agreement **10** accordance, compliance, conformity **13** compatibility

conformation 4 form **5** build, shape **6** figure **7** anatomy **9** formation, framework, structure **11** arrangement **13** configuration

conformist 12 well-adjusted **13** unadventurous

conformity 6 accord, assent **7** harmony **8** likeness **9** agreement, obedience **10** compliance, observance, similarity, submission, uniformity **11** resemblance **12** acquiescence **14** correspondence **15** conventionality

confound 5 amaze, mix up **6** baffle, puzzle, rattle **7** astound, confuse, fluster, mystify, nonplus, perplex, startle **8** astonish, bewilder, dumfound, surprise, unsettle **10** disconcert **11** flabbergast **16** strike with wonder, throw off the scent

confounded 8 confused **10** bewildered, nonplussed **11** dumbfounded **12** disconcerted

confraternity 4 body **5** guild, union **7** society **8** sodality **9** confrairy **11** association, brotherhood

confrere 3 pal **4** ally, chum **5** buddy **6** friend **7** brother, comrade, partner **9** associate, colleague

confront 4 dare, defy, face, meet **5** brave **8** cope with, face up to **9** challenge, encounter, withstand

confrontation 5 clash, run-in, set-to **6** battle, combat, debate **7** contest, dispute, face-off **8** conflict, showdown, skirmish **9** encounter **10** engagement, opposition **11** controversy **17** face-to-face meeting
Spanish: 9 mano a mano

Confucius
  author of: 10 Book of Odes **11** The Analects

confuse 5 addle, befog, mix up, stump **6** baffle, muddle, puzzle, rattle **7** fluster, mistake, mystify, nonplus, perplex **8** befuddle, bewilder, confound, unsettle **10** discompose, disconcert **11** make unclear **12** make baffling **14** make perplexing **17** throw into disorder

confused 5 fazed **6** addled **7** abashed, baffled, chaotic, jumbled, mixed-up, muddled, tangled **8** rambling **9** befuddled, illogical, perplexed, unsettled **10** bewildered, disjointed, distracted, incoherent, nonplussed **11** dumbfounded **12** disconcerted, disorganized **13** disharmonious, heterogeneous

confusing 7 addling **8** baffling, blinding, blurring, dizzying, jumbling, mixing up, muddling **9** deranging, mistaking **10** befuddling, disorderly, flustering, mystifying, perplexing, stupefying **11** bewildering, confounding **13** disconcerting, unintelligible

confusion 4 mess, riot **5** chaos, snarl **6** bedlam, hubbub, jumble, muddle, tangle, tumult, uproar **7** clutter, ferment, turmoil **8** disarray, disorder, madhouse, shambles, upheaval **9** abashment, commotion **10** bafflement, hodgepodge, hullabaloo, perplexity, puzzlement, untidiness **11** disturbance, pandemonium **12** bewilderment, discomposure, stupefaction **13** mystification **14** disarrangement, disconcertment **15** disorganization
French: 14 bouleversement

confutation 6 denial **7** counter **8** negation, rebuttal **10** refutation **13** contradiction

confute 4 deny **5** rebut **6** impugn, oppose, refute **7** counter, gainsay **10** contradict, controvert **12** be contrary to

congeal 3 set **4** clot, jell **6** curdle, freeze, harden **7** stiffen, thicken **8** solidify **9** coagulate **10** gelatinize

congenial 4 like **6** genial, social **7** affable, cordial, kindred, related, similar **8** agreeing, amenable, gracious, pleasant, pleasing, sociable **9** agreeable, convivial **10** compatible, consistent, harmonious, well-suited **11** sympathetic **13** companionable, corresponding
French: 9 en rapport
German: 9 gemutlich

congeniality 7 harmony, rapport **8** affinity **11** sociability **12** conviviality, friendliness, pleasantness **13** compatibility **14** like-mindedness

congenital 6 inborn, inbred, innate, native **7** natural **8** inherent **9** ingrained, inherited, intrinsic **10** hereditary

congested 6 filled, gorged, jammed, packed **7** crowded **9** saturated **11** overcrowded

congestion 3 jam, mob **4** mass **5** snarl **6** pile-up **8** crowding **10** bottleneck **11** obstruction **12** overcrowding

conglomerate 4 heap, mass, pile **5** amass, blend, stack **7** mixture **8** assemble **9** aggregate **10** accumulate, assemblage **12** accumulation **16** large corporation

conglomeration 6 jumble, medley **7** mixture **8** mishmash **9** aggregate, potpourri **10** assortment, collection, hodgepodge **11** aggregation, combination **13** agglomeration

Congo
  other name: 10 Moyen Congo **11** Middle Congo
  capital/largest city: 11 Brazzaville
  others: 3 Ewo **4** Boko **5** Epena, Kayes, Kelle, Okoyo, Sembe **6** Dongou, Komono, Makoua, Matadi, M'Binda, M'Vouti, Ouesso, Sibiti, Zanaga **7** Cabinda, Dolisie, Etoumbi, Gamboma, Kinkala, Loubomo, Loudima, Madingo, Mossaka, Souanke **8** Djambala, Impfondo, Kibangou, Madingou, Mindouli **9** Mossendjo **11** Fort- Rousset, Pointe-Noire **17** Mayombe Escarpment
  school: 13 Marien Ngoubai
  monetary unit: 5 franc **7** centime
  lake: 5 Mweru, Tumba **6** Albert, Nyanza, Upemba **7** Leopold **11** Stanley Pool
  highest point: 6 Leketi
  river: 3 Dja **4** Uele **5** Alima, Congo, Kasal, Kwilu, Lulua, Ngoko, Niari, Sanga, Swilu, Wamba, Zahir, Zaire **6** Kwango, Kwenge, Loange, Lobaye, Lomami, Ogooue, Ubangi **7** Aruwima, Kouilou, Lualaba, Luapula, N'Gounie **8** Itimbiri, Likouala, Lubilash
  sea: 8 Atlantic
  physical feature:
    plateau: 6 Bateke
  people: 3 Rua **4** Akka, Susa, Teke, Vili **5** Amadi, Bantu, Figot, Kongo, Mantu, Pygmy, Sanga, Warua, Zambi **6** Ababua, Bafyot, Bateke, Mbochi, Nzambi, Wabuma **7** Bacongo, Bakongo, Bangala, Batetla, Manyema **10** Binga Pygmy
    discoverer: 3 Cam
  language: 4 Susu **5** Bantu, Fiote **6** French, Kituba **7** Bangala, Lingala
  religion: 5 Islam **7** animism **10** Protestant **13** Roman Catholic
  place:
    church: 9 Saint Anne
    stadium: 5 Eboue
  feature:
    tree: 5 limba

congratulate 4 hail **6** salute **10** compliment, felicitate, wish one joy **11** rejoice with **18** give one's best wishes

28 wish many happy returns of the day

congratulations 6 salute **8** mazeltov **9** blessings, greetings **10** best wishes, good wishes **11** well-wishing **13** felicitations **24** many happy returns of the day

congregate 4 mass **5** amass, flock, swarm **6** gather, throng **7** cluster, collect **8** assemble **12** come together **13** crowd together

congregation 5 crowd, flock, group, horde, laity **6** parish, throng **8** assembly, audience, brethren **9** gathering, multitude **12** parishioners **16** church membership **17** religious assembly

congress, Congress 4 diet **6** caucus **7** council **8** assembly **9** delegates, gathering **10** conference, convention, parliament **11** legislature **14** federal council **15** discussion group, legislative body, national council, representatives **17** chamber of deputies

Congreve, William
  author of: **11** Love for Love **15** The Double-Dealer **16** The Mourning Bride, The Way of the World

congruity 7 harmony **9** agreement, coherence **10** consonance **11** consistency **12** congeniality **13** compatibility **14** correspondence **15** appropriateness

congruous 4 meet **6** seemly **7** apropos **8** becoming, relevant, suitable **9** congenial, consonant, in keeping **10** harmonious **11** appropriate, in agreement **13** corresponding

conifer
  means: **11** cone bearing
  order: **11** coniferales
  class: **10** gymnosperm
  kind: **3** fir, yew **4** pine **5** cedar, larch, pinal **6** ginkgo, pinale, spruce, torrey **7** cypress, hemlock, juniper, redwood, sequoia **8** softwood **9** evergreen

Coningsby
  author: **16** Benjamin Disraeli

conjectural 7 reputed **8** abstract, academic, doubtful, putative, supposed, surmised **11** inferential, speculative, theoretical **12** hypothetical **13** suppositional **14** supposititious

conjecture 4 idea, view **5** fancy, guess, infer, judge, think **6** augury, notion, reckon, theory **7** imagine, opinion, presume, suppose, surmise **8** estimate, forecast, judgment, theorize **9** calculate, deduction, guesswork, inference, speculate, suspicion **10** assumption, guestimate, hypothesis, presuppose **11** guesstimate, hypothesize, speculation, supposition **13** shot in the dark

conjoin 4 join, knit, link **5** touch, unite **7** combine, connect, overlap **8** together **9** associate

conjoined 6 joined, linked, united **7**

knitted, meeting **8** combined, touching **9** connected **10** associated **11** overlapping **14** joined together

conjugal 6 wedded **7** marital, married, nuptial, spousal **9** connubial **11** matrimonial

conjugate 4 join, pair, yoke **5** mated, unite, yoked **6** couple, joined, paired, united **7** connect, coupled, related **9** connected **10** paronymous

conjunction 3 and, but **5** union **7** joining, meeting **11** association, coincidence, combination, concurrence

conjuration 5 charm, spell, trick **11** incantation

conjure 5 allay, charm, raise **6** invoke, summon **7** bewitch, command, enchant **8** call away, call upon **9** call forth **10** cast a spell, make appear **13** make disappear **15** practice sorcery

conjurer 6 wizard **8** magician

conk 3 die, hit **4** bean, blow, fail, head **5** decay, faint, sleep, stall **6** fungus, strike **7** bracket **8** knock out **9** break down **10** straighten

Conn, Katherine
  real name of: **13** Kitty Carlisle

connect 3 tie **4** join **5** hinge, merge, unite **6** attach, couple, relate **7** combine, compare **9** associate, correlate **14** fasten together

connected 4 tied **6** joined, merged, united **7** coupled **8** abutting, adjacent, attached, combined, touching **9** bordering, proximate **10** connecting, contiguous, juxtaposed **12** conterminous **16** fastened together

connected group 5 cycle **6** series **8** sequence **11** progression

Connecticut
  abbreviation: **2** CT **4** Conn
  nickname: **6** Nutmeg **7** Blue Law **9** Freestone **12** Constitution **18** Land of Steady Habits
  capital/largest city: **8** Hartford
  others: **4** Avon **6** Bethel, Canaan, Cos Cob, Darien, Hamden, Mystic, Sharon, Storrs **7** Ansonia, Bristol, Danbury, Enfield, Madison, Meriden, Milford, Niantic, Norwalk, Norwich, Shelton, Tolland, Windsor **8** Guilford, New Haven, Simsbury, Stamford, Westport **9** Greenwich, Naugatuck, New London, Stratford, Waterbury **10** Bridgeport, Manchester, New Britain, Torrington **11** Wallingford
  college: **4** Yale **7** Trinity **8** Hartford, St Joseph, Wesleyan **9** Fairfield **10** Bridgeport, Quinnipiac **11** Connecticut, Sacred Heart **12** U S Coast Guard
  feature: **10** Charter Oak
    museum: **8** PT Barnum
    seaport: **6** Mystic
    theater: **27** American Shakespeare Festival

  tribe: **6** Pequot **7** Mohegan, Niantic **10** Quinnipiac
  people: **8** PT Barnum **9** John Brown **10** Nathan Hale **11** Noah Webster **12** Thomas Hooker **19** Harriet Beecher Stowe
  lake: **10** Candlewood
  land rank: **11** forty-eighth
  mountain: **4** Bear **7** Taconic
    hills: **10** Berkshires
    highest point: **8** Frissell
  physical feature: **15** Long Island Sound
  river: **6** Thames **9** Naugatuck **10** Housatonic **11** Connecticut
  state admission: **5** fifth
  state bird: **5** robin
  state flower: **14** mountain laurel
  state motto: **30** He Who Transplanted Still Sustains
  state song: **12** Yankee Doodle
  state tree: **8** white oak

Connecticut Yankee in King Arthur's Court, A
  author: **9** Mark Twain
  character: **5** Sandy **6** Merlin **8** Alisande, Clarence **11** Morgan le Fay **12** Hello-Central **18** Sir Kay the Seneschal

connection 3 kin, tie **4** bond, link **5** nexus **6** family, friend **7** contact, coupler, kinfolk, kinsman, linkage **8** affinity, alliance, coupling, junction, kinsfolk, relation, relative **9** associate, connector, fastening **10** attachment, kith and kin **11** association, correlation **12** acquaintance, relationship **13** flesh and blood, interrelation

Connelly, Marc
  author of: **16** The Green Pastures
    with Frank Elser: **19** The Farmer Takes a Wife
    with George S Kaufman: **5** Dulcy **11** To the Ladies **17** Beggar on Horseback, Merton of the Movies

Connery, Sean
  real name: **13** Thomas Connery
  born: **8** Scotland **9** Edinburgh
  roles: **6** Marnie **7** The Rock **10** Highlander **14** Robin and Marian **15** The Untouchables **16** The Molly Maguires **20** The Great Train Robbery, The Man Who Would Be King **28** Darby O'Gill and the Little People **29** Indiana Jones and the Last Crusade
    James Bond: **4** Dr No **10** Goldfinger **11** Thunderball **16** You Only Live Twice **18** Diamonds Are Forever, From Russia with Love, Never Say Never Again

connivance 4 plot **5** cabal **6** design, scheme **8** intrigue **9** collusion **10** complicity, conspiracy **11** machination

connive 3 aid **4** abet, plan, plot **5** allow **6** wink at **7** collude **8** conspire **10** be a party to **13** be accessory to, lend oneself to **14** shut one's eyes to

17 be in collusion with, cooperate secretly

conniving 4 wily **6** artful, crafty **7** cunning **8** plotting, scheming **9** designing **10** intriguing **11** calculating

connoisseur 5 judge, maven, mavin **6** expert **7** epicure, gourmet **9** authority **11** cognoscente **17** person of good taste

Connolly, Maureen
nickname: **8** Little Mo
sport: **6** tennis

Connor, Dale
creator/artist of: **9** Mary Worth

connotation 5 drift **6** import, spirit **8** coloring **9** evocation, undertone **10** intimation, suggestion **11** implication, insinuation **12** significance

connote 5 imply **6** hint at **7** suggest **8** intimate **9** insinuate **11** bring to mind

connubial 6 wedded **7** marital, married, nuptial **8** conjugal **11** matrimonial

conquer 4 beat, best, drub, lick, rout, rule, trim, whip **5** floor, quell **6** defeat, humble, master, occupy, subdue, thrash **7** possess, win over **8** overcome, surmount, vanquish **9** overpower, rise above, subjugate **11** prevail over, triumph over **14** get the better of

conqueror 6 victor, winner **7** subduer **8** champion **10** subjugator, vanquisher **12** conquistador

conquest 3 fan **4** sway **5** lover **6** adorer, defeat **7** captive, mastery, triumph, victory, winning **8** adherent, follower, whip hand **9** upper hand **10** ascendancy, conquering, domination, overcoming **11** acquisition, subjugation **12** vanquishment **17** captured territory

Conrad, Joseph
real name: **29** Josef Teodor Konrad Korzeniowski
author of: **6** Chance **7** Lord Jim, Typhoon, Victory **8** Nostromo **13** Almayer's Folly **14** The Secret Agent **15** Heart of Darkness **16** Under Western Eyes **21** An Outcast of the Islands **23** The Nigger of the Narcissus

consanguine 4 akin **7** cognate, kindred, related **8** relative

consanguineous 3 kin **4** akin **7** kindred, related **9** connected **21** having a common ancestor

conscience 8 scruples **10** moral sense, principles **15** ethical feelings **20** sense of right and wrong

conscience-stricken 6 guilty **7** ashamed **8** contrite, penitent **9** chastened, regretful, repentant **10** remorseful **13** guilt-stricken

conscientious 5 exact **6** honest **7** careful, dutiful, ethical, upright **10**

fastidious, meticulous, particular, scrupulous **11** painstaking, responsible, trustworthy **12** conscionable **14** high-principled

conscious 5 aware **7** alert to, alive to, awake to, studied **8** noticing, sensible, sentient **9** cognizant, in the know, observing **10** calculated, deliberate, discerning, perceiving **12** apperceptive, premeditated **13** knowledgeable

consciousness 4 mind **6** senses **8** feelings, thoughts **9** awareness **10** cognizance, perception **11** discernment, sensibility

conscript 3 PFC **4** boot, hire, levy **5** draft **6** call up, employ, engage, enlist, enroll, induct, muster, rookie, seaman, select, take on **7** draftee, impress, private, recruit **8** enlistee, inductee, mobilize, register, selectee, shanghai **9** conscribe **11** buck private

consecrate 5 bless **6** hallow **7** glorify **8** sanctify **10** make sacred **11** immortalize **13** declare sacred

consecrated 4 holy **7** blessed **8** hallowed **10** sanctified

consecutive 6 in turn, serial **8** unbroken **10** continuous, sequential, successive **11** progressive **13** uninterrupted **19** following one another

consensus 6 accord **7** concord **9** unanimity **11** concurrence **13** common consent **14** general opinion **15** majority opinion **16** general agreement

consent 5 agree, allow, yield **6** accede, accept, accord, assent, concur, permit, ratify, submit **7** approve, concede, concord, confirm, endorse **8** approval, sanction **9** acquiesce, agreement **10** acceptance, fall in with, permission **11** concurrence, endorsement, willingness **12** acquiescence, confirmation, ratification

Consenting Adults
author: **12** Peter DeVries

consent to 2 OK **4** okay **6** permit **7** approve **8** accede to **10** concur with **11** acquiesce to, go along with **14** give the go-ahead

consequence 3 end **4** note **5** avail, fruit, issue, value, worth **6** import, moment, result, sequel, upshot **7** account, gravity, outcome **9** aftermath, influence, magnitude, outgrowth **10** importance, notability, prominence, usefulness **11** development, distinction, seriousness **12** significance

consequent 7 ensuing **8** eventual **9** following, resulting

consequential 7 crucial, epochal **8** historic **9** important, momentous **10** meaningful **11** significant

consequently 2 so **4** ergo, then **5** and so, hence, later **9** as a result, therefore **11** accordingly **12** subsequently

conservation 4 care **6** upkeep **9** hus-

bandry **10** careful use, protection **11** maintenance, safekeeping **12** preservation

conservative 5 quiet **6** square **7** oldline **8** cautious, moderate, undaring **9** right-wing **10** nonliberal, unchanging **11** reactionary, right-winger, traditional **13** unprogressive **15** middle-of-the-road **16** opponent of change **17** middle-of-the-roader **22** champion of the status quo

conservatoire 11 music school **12** conservatory, music academy

conservatory 7 nursery **8** hothouse **9** arboretum **10** glasshouse, greenhouse **11** music school **12** music academy **13** conservatoire

conserve 4 save **5** guard **7** care for, cut back, husband, use less **8** maintain, not waste, preserve **9** safeguard **12** use sparingly

consider 4 deem, hold, note **5** gauge, honor, judge, opine, study, think, weigh **6** ponder, regard, review **7** believe, examine, pay heed, respect **8** appraise, envision, hold to be, mull over **9** be aware of, reflect on **10** bear in mind, cogitate on, think about **11** contemplate **12** deliberate on **17** make allowances for **18** turn over in one's mind

considerable 4 tidy **5** ample, great, large **6** goodly **7** notable, sizable **8** not small **9** estimable, important **10** impressive, noteworthy, noticeable, of some size, remarkable **11** a good deal of, significant, substantial

considerably 5 amply **7** greatly, largely, notably, sizably **9** estimably **10** abundantly, noticeably, remarkably **13** significantly, substantially

considerate 4 kind **6** kindly **7** mindful **8** obliging **9** attentive, concerned **10** solicitous, thoughtful

consideration 4 heed, tact **5** cause, honor, point, study **6** factor, ground, motive, notice, reason, regard, review **7** concern, respect, thought **8** interest, judgment **9** attention **10** advisement, cogitation, inducement, kindliness, meditation, reflection, solicitude **11** examination **12** deliberation **13** contemplation **14** thoughtfulness **15** considerateness

consider closely 7 pay heed **11** concentrate **12** pay attention **13** put one's mind to **21** give one's full attention

considered 5 mused **6** deemed, heeded, judged, mulled **7** advised, express, honored, noticed, studied, thought, weighed, willful **8** believed, esteemed, looked on, pondered, regarded, supposed **9** reflected, respected, ruminated **10** deliberate, looked upon, thought out **11** deliberated, entertained, intentional **12** contemplated, premeditated, thought about

consign 5 remit 6 assign, commit, convey, remand 7 deliver, entrust 8 delegate, hand over, relegate, transfer 9 commend to 11 deposit with

consignment 8 delivery, shipment, transfer 10 assignment, committing, consigning, delegation, depositing, entrusting, relegation 11 handing over 12 goods for sale, goods shipped 19 goods sent on approval

consist 3 lie 6 reside 7 contain, include 10 be made up of 11 to be found in 13 be comprised of 14 to be composed of

consistency, consistence 4 body 5 unity 6 makeup 7 density, harmony, texture 8 firmness 9 agreement, coherence, congruity, stiffness, structure, thickness, viscosity 10 accordance, conformity, connection, uniformity 11 compactness, composition, persistence 12 construction, faithfulness, steady effort 13 compatibility, steadfastness 14 correspondence 16 uniform standards 19 constant performance, undeviating behavior

consistent 4 meet 6 steady 7 regular, unified 8 agreeing, constant, of a piece, suitable 9 congenial, congruous, consonant 10 compatible, harmonious, persistent, unchanging 11 in agreement, undeviating 13 correspondent 16 conforming to type

consolation 4 help 5 cheer 6 relief, solace, succor 7 comfort, support 8 easement, soothing, sympathy 10 condolence 11 alleviation, assuagement 13 encouragement

Consolation of Philosophy (De Consolatione Philosophiae)
author: 31 Anicius Manlius Severinus Boethius

console 4 calm, ease 5 cheer 6 soothe, succor 7 comfort, support, sustain 10 lament with, sympathize 11 condole with 13 express sorrow 15 commiserate with 18 express sympathy for

consolidate 4 fuse, join 5 merge, unify, unite 6 league 7 combine, fortify 8 coalesce, compress, condense, federate, make firm, make sure, solidify 9 integrate, make solid 10 amalgamate, centralize, strengthen 11 concentrate, incorporate 12 band together 13 bring together

consolidation 5 union 6 fusion, merger 8 alliance 9 coalition 11 unification 12 amalgamation 13 agglomeration 14 conglomeration

consomme 4 soup 5 broth 9 madrilene

consonance 5 amity, unity 6 accord, unison 7 concord, harmony, oneness 9 agreement, coherence, congruity, unanimity 10 accordance, conformity,

congruence, consonancy 11 concordance, consistency, homogeneity 13 compatibility 14 correspondence, likemindedness

consonant 8 in accord 9 agreeable, congruous, in harmony 10 concordant, consistent 11 in agreement

consort 3 mix 4 club, mate, wife 6 mingle, spouse 7 hang out, husband, pair off, partner 8 go around, sidekick 9 accompany, associate, companion, other half, pal around, rub elbows 10 fraternize 11 keep company

conspicuous 5 clear, great, overt, plain 6 famous, patent 7 eminent, evident, glaring, notable, obvious 8 distinct, flagrant, glorious, manifest, renowned, splendid, striking 9 arresting, brilliant, memorable, notorious, prominent, well-known 10 celebrated, easily seen, remarkable 11 illustrious, outstanding, standing out 13 distinguished, easily noticed, highly visible

conspicuousness 9 celebrity, flagrance, notoriety 10 prominence, visibility 11 obviousness 13 noticeability

conspiracy 4 plot 7 treason 8 intrigue, sedition 9 collusion, treachery 10 connivance, secret plan 11 machination 12 criminal plan 14 treasonous plan

conspirator 7 plotter, schemer, traitor 8 conniver 9 intriguer 10 subversive

conspire 5 unite 6 concur, scheme 7 collude, combine, connive 8 intrigue 9 cooperate, machinate 11 plot treason 12 work together

Constable, John
born: 7 England 12 East Bergholt
artwork: 10 The Haywain 12 Cloud Studies 14 Hadleigh Castle 39 Salisbury Cathedral from the Bishop's Grounds

constancy 6 fealty 7 loyalty 8 devotion 9 fixedness, stability 10 allegiance, permanence 12 faithfulness, immutability 13 dependability, invariability, steadfastness 15 trustworthiness 16 unchangeableness

constant 4 even, true 5 fixed, loyal 6 stable, steady, trusty 7 abiding, devoted, endless, eternal, regular, staunch, uniform 8 diligent, enduring, faithful, resolute, stalwart, unbroken, unvaried 9 ceaseless, continual, immutable, incessant, permanent, perpetual, steadfast, sustained, unceasing, unfailing 10 dependable, invariable, persistent, unchanging, unflagging, unswerving, unwavering 11 everlasting, never-ending, trustworthy, unalterable, undeviating, unrelenting 12 interminable, tried-and-true 13 uninterrupted

Constant Nymph, The
director: 14 Edmund Goulding
cast: 11 Alexis Smith 12 Charles

Boyer, Joan Fontaine 14 Brenda Marshall

constellation 4 host 5 group, rally 6 circle, galaxy, nebula, spiral, throng 7 cluster, company, pattern 9 gathering 10 assemblage, collection 12 spiral nebula 13 configuration 14 island universe
name: 3 Ara, Leo 4 Apus, Crux, Grus, Lynx, Lyra, Pavo, Vela 5 Aries, Cetus, Draco, Hydra, Indus, Lepus, Libra, Lupus, Mensa, Musca, Norma, Orion, Pyxis, Virgo 6 Antlia, Aquila, Auriga, Bootes, Caelum, Cancer, Carina, Corvus, Crater, Cygnus, Dorado, Fornax, Gemini, Hydrus, Octans, Pictor, Pisces, Puppis, Scutum, Taurus, Tucana, Volans 7 Cepheus, Columba, Lacerta, Pegasus, Perseus, Phoenix, Sagitta, Serpens, Sextans 8 Aquarius, Circinus, Equuleus, Eridanus, Hercules, Leo Minor, Scorpius, Sculptor 9 Andromeda, Centaurus, Delphinus, Monoceros, Ophiuchus, Reticulum, Ursa Major, Ursa Minor, Vulpecula 10 Canis Major, Canis Minor, Cassiopeia, Chamaeleon, Horologium, Triangulum 11 Capricornus, Sagittarius, Telescopium 12 Microscopium 13 Canes Venatici, Coma Berenices 14 Camelopardalis, Corona Borealis 15 Corona Australis, Piscis Austrinus 18 Triangulum Australe

consternation 5 alarm, panic, shock 6 dismay, fright, horror, terror 11 trepidation 12 apprehension

constituent 4 atom, part 5 piece, voter 6 factor, member 7 elective, element, essence 8 electing, integral, making up 9 component, formative, principal, supporter 10 appointing, ingredient

constitute 4 form, make, name 5 found, set up 6 create, invest, make up 7 appoint, compose, empower, produce 8 compound, delegate 9 authorize, establish, institute 10 commission

constitution 6 figure, health, make-up, mettle 7 charter, stamina, texture 8 physique, strength, vitality 9 basic laws, formation, structure 10 figuration 11 composition 12 construction 13 configuration 16 governing charter 17 physical condition 21 fundamental principles

constitutional 4 turn, walk 5 basic 6 inborn, ramble, stroll, vested 7 natural, organic 8 inherent, internal, physical 9 chartered, intrinsic 10 congenital 11 fundamental

Constitution State
nickname of: 11 Connecticut

constrain 4 curb, urge 5 check, crush, drive, force, quash 6 coerce, compel, oblige, subdue 7 confine, enforce, put down, repress, squelch 8 hold back, pressure, restrain, restrict, suppress **9** fight down, necessity, strong-arm **14** put the screws on

constrained 3 shy **5** timid **6** forced **7** bashful **8** reserved, reticent **9** compelled, diffident **10** restricted **11** embarrassed

constraint 5 force **6** duress **7** reserve **8** coercion, pressure **9** restraint **10** compulsion, diffidence, inhibition, obligation **11** enforcement **13** necessitation

constrict 4 bind **5** choke, cramp, pinch **6** shrink **7** squeeze **8** compress, contract, strangle **11** strangulate

constriction 7 binding, choking **8** cramping, pinching **9** narrowing, shrinking, squeezing, stricture, tightness **10** constraint, strangling **11** compression, contraction

construct 4 form, make **5** build, erect, frame, set up, shape **6** create, design, devise **7** arrange, fashion **8** organize **9** fabricate, formulate

construction 4 form, make **5** build, style **6** format **7** edifice, raising, reading, rearing, version **8** building, creation, erecting **9** rendition, structure **10** fashioning, production **11** composition, elucidation, explanation, explication, fabrication, manufacture **12** conformation, constructing **13** configuration **14** interpretation **15** putting together

constructive 5 handy **6** useful **7** helpful **8** valuable **9** practical **10** beneficial, productive **12** advantageous

construe 4 read, take **7** explain, make out **8** decipher **9** elucidate, figure out, interpret, translate **10** comprehend, understand

Consuelo
author: 10 George Sand

consul 5 envoy **8** emissary, minister **14** foreign officer, representative **15** diplomatic agent

Consul, The
opera by: 7 Menotti
character: 10 Magda Sorel

consult 6 confer, parley, regard **7** refer to **8** consider, talk over **9** inquire of **11** ask advice of, have an eye to **12** compare notes **13** exchange views **15** discuss together, seek counsel from, take into account **16** seek the opinion of **18** deliberate together

consultant 6 expert **7** adviser, advisor, counsel **9** discusser

consultation 7 council, hearing, meeting, palaver **9** interview **10** conference, discussion **12** deliberation

consumable 6 edible **7** eatable **10** comestible

consume 3 eat **4** gulp **5** drain, eat up, spend, use up, waste **6** absorb, devour, expend, guzzle, ravage **7** de-

plete, destroy, drink up, engross, exhaust **8** demolish, lay waste, squander **9** devastate, dissipate, swallow up **10** annihilate

consumed 4 used **5** burnt, drank, drunk, eaten, spent **6** used up, wasted **7** drained, outworn **8** absorbed, burned up, expended, perished **9** destroyed, engrossed, exhausted, swallowed **10** squandered **11** annihilated

consume greedily 5 eat up, snarf **6** devour, inhale **7** stuff in **8** bolt down, gobble up, gulp down, wolf down **12** swallow whole **13** eat ravenously **14** eat voraciously

consumer 4 user **5** buyer, drain **6** client, patron, waster **7** spender **8** customer **9** purchaser **10** dissipater, squanderer

consummate 2 do **5** sheer, total, utter **6** effect, finish **7** achieve, execute, fulfill, perfect, perform, realize, supreme **8** absolute, carry out, complete, finished, thorough **9** faultless **10** accomplish, bring about, undisputed **11** unmitigated **12** accomplished, unquestioned **13** unconditional **17** through-and-through

consummation 3 end **5** close **6** finish **9** execution **10** attainment, completion, conclusion **11** achievement, culmination, fulfillment, realization **14** accomplishment

consumption 2 TB **3** use **7** using up **9** consuming, depletion **10** exhaustion **11** expenditure, utilization **12** exploitation, tuberculosis

Consus
origin: 5 Roman
god of: 11 good counsel, horse racing
protector of: 5 grain
corresponds to: 3 Ops

contact 4 join, meet **5** reach, touch, union **7** connect, meeting **8** abutment, junction, touching **9** adjacency, get hold of **10** connection **11** association **13** communication **14** get in touch with **15** communicate with

contagion 7 disease **8** epidemic, outbreak **9** infection, spreading **13** contamination

contagious 8 catching **9** spreading **10** infectious, spreadable **12** communicable **13** transmittable

contain 4 curb, hold **5** check **6** embody, hold in **7** control, embrace, enclose, include, inhibit, involve, repress **8** hold back, keep back, restrain, suppress **11** accommodate, incorporate **12** keep the lid on **16** keep within bounds

container 3 bag, box, can, jar, vat **4** pail **6** barrel, bottle, bucket, carton, holder, vessel **10** receptacle

containment 7 control **9** restraint, retention

contaminate 4 foul, soil **5** dirty, spoil,

taint **6** befoul, blight, debase, defile, infect, poison **7** corrupt, pollute **8** besmirch **10** adulterate, make impure

contamination 5 filth **7** fouling, soiling **8** dirtying, foulness, impurity, spoiling **9** dirtiness, poisoning, polluting, pollution, putridity **10** defilement **11** uncleanness **12** adulteration

Conte, Richard
real name: 18 Nicholas Peter Conte
born: 12 Jersey City NJ
roles: 8 Barabbas **13** A Bell for Adano **24** The Greatest Story Ever Told

contemplate 4 note, plan, scan **5** weigh **6** expect, gaze at, intend, ponder, regard, survey **7** examine, imagine, inspect, observe, project, stare at, think of **8** aspire to, envision, mull over, ruminate **9** muse about **10** anticipate, cogitate on, have in view, meditate on, think about **11** reflect upon **12** deliberate on **13** consider fully, look at fixedly, look forward to **14** speculate about **15** view attentively

contemplation 5 study **6** gazing, musing, seeing, survey **7** looking, reverie, thought, viewing **8** scanning, thinking **9** pondering **10** cogitation, inspection, meditation, reflection, rumination **11** examination, observation **12** deliberation **13** consideration

contemplative 6 musing **7** pensive **8** studious **9** engrossed **10** cogitative, meditative, reflective, ruminating, thoughtful **11** speculative **13** introspective, lost in thought

contemporaneous 6 coeval **10** coexistent, coincident, concurrent **11** synchronous **12** contemporary, simultaneous

contemporary 3 new **4** late **6** modern, recent, with-it **7** current **8** advanced, brand-new, up-to-date **10** coexistent, coincident, concurrent, newfangled, present-day **11** ultramodern **12** simultaneous **13** of the same time, up-to-the-minute **15** contemporaneous

contempt 4 hate **5** scorn, shame **6** hatred **7** disdain, disgust **8** aversion, derision, disfavor, disgrace, dishonor, distaste, ignominy, loathing, ridicule **9** antipathy, disregard, disrepute, revulsion **10** abhorrence, repugnance **11** detestation, humiliation

contemptible 3 low **4** base, mean, vile **5** cheap **6** abject, paltry, shabby **8** shameful, unworthy, wretched **9** miserable, repugnant, revolting **10** despicable, detestable, disgusting **11** ignominious

contemptuous 6 lordly **7** haughty, pompous **8** arrogant, derisive, insolent, scornful, snobbish **10** disdainful **12** supercilious **13** condescending, disrespectful

contemptuousness 5 scorn 7 disdain 8 contempt, rudeness 9 arrogance, insolence

contend 3 vie, war 4 aver, avow, hold, spar 5 argue, claim, clash, fight 6 allege, assert, battle, combat, debate, insist, jostle, strive, tussle 7 compete, contest, declare, dispute, grapple, quarrel, wrestle 8 be a rival, maintain, propound, skirmish, struggle 10 put forward

content 4 area, core, gist, load, size, text 5 cheer, happy, heart, ideas, peace 6 at ease, at rest, matter, please, serene, thesis, volume 7 appease, comfort, essence, gratify, insides, meaning, pleased, satisfy, suffice, unmoved 8 capacity, make easy, pleasure, serenity, thoughts 9 contented, gratified, happiness, satisfied, set at ease, substance 10 complacent, untroubled 11 comfortable, contentment, peace of mind, unconcerned 12 satisfaction 13 gratification

contented 5 happy 6 at ease, serene 7 at peace, content, pleased 9 gratified, satisfied 11 comfortable

contentedness 4 ease 5 peace 7 comfort, content 8 pleasure, serenity 9 happiness 11 contentment 12 satisfaction 13 gratification

contention 5 clash, fight 6 battle, combat, strife 7 contest, discord, dispute, rivalry 8 argument, conflict, disunity, fighting, friction, skirmish, struggle, variance 9 assertion, encounter, wrangling 10 dissension, quarreling 11 competition, discordance 12 disagreement 13 confrontation

contentious 5 angry, cross 7 bateful, scrappy 8 captious 9 bellicose 11 pugnacious 11 belligerent, competitive, quarrelsome 12 cantankerous, disputatious 13 argumentative, controversial

contentment 4 ease 5 peace 7 comfort, content 8 pleasure, serenity 9 happiness 12 satisfaction 13 contentedness, gratification

conterminous 8 abutting, adjacent, touching 9 bordering 11 right beside 14 contiguous with

contest 3 war 4 bout, game 5 fight, match 6 battle, combat, debate, oppose, vie for 7 dispute, rivalry, tourney 8 conflict, fight for, object to, struggle 9 battle for, challenge, combat for, encounter 10 compete for, contend for, controvert, engagement, tournament 11 competition, struggle for 12 argue against 14 call in question

contestant 5 rival 6 player 7 entrant, fighter 8 competer, prospect 9 combatant, contender 10 challenger, competitor

context 6 milieu 7 climate, meaning,

setting 8 ambience 9 framework, precincts, situation 10 atmosphere, background, conditions, connection 11 environment 12 relationship, surroundings 13 circumstances 16 frame of reference

contiguous 5 close, handy 6 nearby 7 close-by, tangent 8 abutting, adjacent, next-door, touching 9 adjoining, bordering, in contact 10 juxtaposed 11 neighboring 12 conterminous

continence 6 purity 8 chastity, sobriety 10 abstinence, moderation, temperance 11 forbearance 13 self-restraint

continent 4 Asia, pure 6 Africa, chaste, Europe 7 Eurasia 8 celibate, land mass, mainland, virginal 9 abstinent, Australia, temperate 10 abstemious, Antarctica 12 North America, South America

contingency 7 urgency 8 accident 9 emergency, extremity 10 likelihood 11 possibility, predicament 15 unforeseen event

contingent 9 dependent, subject to 11 conditioned 12 controlled by

continual 7 endless, eternal 8 constant, frequent, habitual, unbroken, unending 9 ceaseless, incessant, perennial, perpetual, recurring, unceasing 10 continuous, persistent 11 everlasting, never-ending, oft-repeated, unremitting 12 interminable 13 uninterrupted

continually 3 aye 4 ever 6 always, steady 7 endless, eternal, forever, on and on 8 steadily 9 recurring 10 constantly, frequently, repeatedly

continuance 4 stay, term 6 extent, period 7 lasting 8 duration 9 extension 10 continuing, permanence 11 adjournment, persistence, protraction 12 continuation, perseverance, prolongation

continuation 6 sequel 8 addition, sequence 9 extension 10 continuing, supplement 11 continuance, protraction 12 prolongation

continue 4 go on, last, stay 5 abide 6 drag on, endure, extend, keep on, keep up, remain, resume, stay on 7 carry on, persist, proceed 9 persevere

continued 6 kept on, kept up, lasted, went on 7 endured 8 extended 9 carried on, persisted, proceeded, prolonged 10 persevered, protracted

continuing 6 steady 7 abiding, eternal, ongoing 8 constant, enduring, extended, unbroken, unending 9 ceaseless, incessant, perpetual, prolonged 10 dragged out, persistent, protracted 11 persevering, unremitting 12 interminable 13 uninterrupted

continuity 4 flow 5 chain 9 continuum 10 succession 11 continuance, progression 12 continuation

continuous 6 linked, steady 7 endless, eternal, lasting 8 constant, enduring, unbroken 9 ceaseless, connected, continual, extensive, incessant, perpetual, prolonged, unceasing 10 continuing, persistent, protracted, successive 11 consecutive, everlasting, persevering, progressive, unremitting 12 interminable 13 uninterrupted

continuum 4 flow 5 chain 8 sequence 10 continuity, succession 11 continuance, progression 12 continuation

contort 4 bend, warp 5 twist 6 deform 7 distort 11 be misshapen

contorted 4 bent 7 crooked, twisted 8 deformed 9 distorted

contortion 7 bending 8 twisting 10 distortion 11 crookedness

contour 4 form 5 lines, shape 6 figure 7 outline, profile 10 silhouette 11 physiognomy

contraband 11 bootlegging 13 smuggled goods 14 illegal exports, illegal imports 15 unlicensed goods 17 black-marketeering 18 prohibited articles 19 unlawful trafficking

contract 3 get 4 pact, take 5 agree, incur 6 absorb, assume, narrow, pledge, reduce, shrink, treaty 7 acquire, compact, develop, dwindle, promise, shorten, tighten 8 compress, condense, covenant, engender 9 constrict, enter into, negotiate, undertake 11 arrangement, come to terms 12 draw together, make a bargain 13 become smaller, legal document 15 sign an agreement 16 written agreement

contracted form 6 digest 7 summary 8 synopsis 9 short form 11 abridgement, compression 12 abbreviation, condensation

contraction 8 decrease 9 drawing in, lessening, narrowing, reduction, shrinkage 10 shortening, shriveling, tightening 11 compression 12 abbreviation, condensation, constriction

contradict 4 deny 5 belie, rebut 6 impugn, oppose, refute 7 confute, counter, dispute, gainsay 8 disprove 10 controvert 12 be contrary to, disagree with

contradiction 6 denial 7 counter 8 negation, rebuttal 10 refutation 11 confutation 12 disagreement

contradictory 8 contrary, opposing 10 discrepant, dissenting, refutatory 11 conflicting, disagreeing 12 antithetical, inconsistent 14 countervailing, irreconcilable

contradistinction 8 contrast 10 difference 13 dissimilarity

contraption 6 device, gadget 9 apparatus, invention 11 contrivance

contrariety 9 deviation 10 difference, divergence 13 contradiction

contrary 5 balky 6 ornery 7 adverse,

counter, froward, hostile, opposed, wayward, willful **8** converse, inimical, opposite, stubborn, untoward **9** disparate, obstinate, unfitting **10** at variance, discordant, headstrong, refractory, unsuitable **11** conflicting, disagreeing, intractable, unfavorable **12** antagonistic, antithetical, disagreeable, inauspicious, incompatible, recalcitrant, unpropitious **13** contradictory **15** at cross purposes, unaccommodating

contrast 6 depart, differ **7** deviate, diverge **8** variance **9** disparity **10** comparison, difference, divergence, unlikeness **11** distinction **12** disagree with **13** differentiate, dissimilarity **15** differentiation, set in opposition

contrasting 8 clashing, dividing, opposing **9** comparing, differing **10** discordant, juxtaposed **14** distinguishing **15** differentiating

contravene 4 deny **5** annul, fight, spurn **6** abjure, breach, combat, disown, negate, offend, oppose, reject, resist **7** disobey, exclude, gainsay, infract, nullify, violate **8** abrogate, disclaim, overstep **9** overreach, repudiate **10** act against, contradict, infringe on, transgress **12** encroach upon **15** trespass against

contretemps 4 spat **5** clash, set-to **7** dispute, quarrel **8** argument, squabble **10** difference, falling out **12** disagreement **18** embarrassing mishap

contribute 4 give **5** endow, grant **6** bestow, confer, donate, lead to **7** advance, forward, hand out, present **9** bear a part, influence **11** have a hand in **13** be conducive to **14** help bring about

contribution 4 alms, gift **5** grant **7** charity, subsidy **8** bestowal, donation, offering **9** endowment **11** benefaction **12** dispensation

contributive 8 valuable **9** favorable **10** beneficial

contributory 9 accessory, ancillary, auxiliary **13** supplementary

contrite 6 rueful **7** humbled **8** penitent **9** chastened, regretful, repentant, sorrowful **10** apologetic, remorseful **18** conscience-stricken

contrition 6 regret **7** penance, remorse **9** atonement, penitence **10** repentance **11** compunction **12** self-reproach **18** qualms of conscience

contrivance 4 plan, plot, tool **5** gizmo, trick **6** design, device, doodad, gadget **7** machine, measure **8** artifice, intrigue **9** apparatus, implement, invention, mechanism, stratagem **10** instrument **11** contraption, machination, thingamajig **12** Rube Goldberg

contrive 4 plan, plot **6** create, design, devise, invent, manage, scheme **7**

concoct **8** maneuver **9** improvise **11** devise a plan **17** effect by stratagem

contrived 7 labored, studied **8** mannered **9** unnatural **10** artificial

contriver 7 creator, deviser **8** designer, inventor **9** architect

control 4 curb, rule, sway **5** brake, steer **6** bridle, charge, govern, manage, master, subdue **7** command, contain, mastery, repress **8** dominate, dominion, regulate, restrain, restrict **9** authority, direction, reign over, restraint, supervise **10** domination, management, manipulate, regulation **11** superintend, supervision, suppressant **12** have charge of, jurisdiction

controlled 5 ruled **6** curbed, steady, swayed **7** checked, managed, powered, servile, subdued **8** directed, governed, held back, kept down, reserved, verified **9** commanded, contained, dominated, moderated, regulated, repressed **10** authorized, regimented, restrained, supervised **11** manipulated

controlling 6 ruling **8** dominant **9** governing **10** commanding **11** influencing, predominant **13** predominating

controversial 7 at issue **8** arguable **9** debatable, polemical **10** disputable **12** questionable **13** causing debate **15** widely discussed **16** open to discussion

controversy 6 debate **7** dispute, quarrel, wrangle **8** argument, squabble **10** contention, discussion, dissension **11** altercation **12** disagreement

controvert 4 deny **5** belie, rebut **6** negate, oppose, refute **7** confute, dispute, gainsay, protest **8** confound, disprove, question **9** challenge, disaffirm **10** contradict, contravene, invalidate **12** give the lie to

contumacious 6 unruly **7** froward **8** contrary, factious, insolent, mutinous, perverse **9** fractious, seditious **10** headstrong, rebellious, refractory **11** disobedient, intractable **12** ungovernable, unmanageable **13** disrespectful, insubordinate

contumely 5 abuse, insult, scorn **7** disdain, obloquy **8** contempt, diatribe, reproach, rudeness **9** arrogance, insolence, invective, pomposity **10** opprobrium, scurrility **11** brusqueness, haughtiness **12** billingsgate, vituperation **15** overbearingness

contusion 4 hurt, mark, sore **5** mouse **6** bruise, injury, shiner **7** blemish **8** abrasion, black eye **9** black mark **13** discoloration **16** black-and-blue mark

conundrum 5 poser, rebus **6** enigma, puzzle, riddle **7** arcanum, mystery, paradox, problem, puzzler, stopper, stumper **11** brain-teaser **13** Chinese puzzle

convalesce 4 mend **5** rally **6** revive **7** improve, recover, restore **8** progress **9** get better **10** recuperate

convalescence 7 recruit **8** recovery **11** restoration **12** recuperation **14** return to health

convene 6 gather, muster, summon **7** collect, convoke, round up **8** assemble **12** call together, come together, hold a session **13** bring together

convenience 3 use **4** ease **6** chance **7** benefit, comfort, service, utility **8** facility, pleasure **9** appliance, enjoyment, handiness, work saver **10** usefulness **11** opportunity **12** availability, satisfaction, suitable time **13** accessibility, accommodation

convenient 5 handy **6** at hand, nearby, suited, useful **7** adapted, helpful **8** suitable **9** easy to use **10** beneficial **11** serviceable **12** advantageous **16** easily accessible

convent 7 nunnery **8** cloister **13** society of nuns

convention 4 code **6** caucus, custom **7** meeting, precept **8** assembly, conclave, congress, practice, propriety, protocol, standard **9** formality, gathering **10** conference, social rule **11** convocation

conventional 5 usual **6** common, normal, proper **7** regular, routine **8** accepted, orthodox, standard **9** customary **11** traditional

converge 4 meet **5** focus **8** approach **11** concentrate **12** come together **13** bring together

convergence 6 accord **8** junction **9** congruity **10** confluence **12** meeting place **14** correspondence

conversant 4 up on **5** aware **6** au fait **7** erudite, privy to, skilled, tutored **8** familiar, informed, sensible, sentient **9** au courant, cognizant, practiced **10** acquainted, proficient **12** well-informed **13** knowledgeable

conversation 3 rap **4** chat, talk **7** gabfest, palaver **8** chit-chat, dialogue **9** discourse, tete-a-tete **11** bull session **13** confabulation
Italian: 13 conversazione

Conversation, The
    director: 18 Francis Ford Coppola
    cast: 10 John Cazale **11** Gene Hackman **13** Allen Garfield

conversational 6 casual, chatty **8** everyday, informal **9** idiomatic **10** colloquial, vernacular

conversazione 12 conversation

converse 3 gab, jaw, rap **4** chat, chin, talk **7** palaver, reverse **8** chitchat, contrary, opposite **10** antithesis, chew the fat, chew the rag **11** confabulate **13** speak together **14** shoot the breeze

conversely 12 contrariwise **14** antithetically, on the other hand

conversion 6 change 10 changeover 12 modification 13 change of heart, metamorphosis, transmutation 14 transformation 15 change in beliefs, transfiguration 16 change of religion

convert 4 turn 6 change, modify, novice 8 neophyte 9 proselyte, transform 11 proselytize

convex 7 bulging, rounded 11 protuberant 13 curved outward

convey 4 bear, cede, deed, give, move, tell, will 5 bring, carry, grant, leave 6 impart, relate, reveal 7 conduct, consign, deliver, divulge 8 bequeath, disclose, dispatch, transfer, transmit 9 confide to, make known, transport 11 communicate

conveyance 3 bus, car, rig, van 4 cart 5 buggy, truck, wagon 7 vehicle 8 carriage, carrying, movement, transfer 9 conveying, transport 12 transmission 14 transportation

convict 3 con 4 doom 5 felon 7 condemn 8 jailbird, prisoner, yardbird 10 find guilty 11 prove guilty 13 declare guilty

conviction 4 view, zeal 5 ardor, creed, dogma, faith, fever, tenet 6 belief, fervor 7 opinion 8 doctrine, judgment, position 9 assurance, certainty, certitude, intensity, principle, viewpoint 10 persuasion 11 earnestness 13 steadfastness

convince 4 sway 6 assure 7 satisfy, win over 8 persuade 9 influence 11 bring around, prevail upon

convincing 5 sound, valid 6 cogent, potent 7 evident 8 assuring, forceful, powerful 9 plausible 10 persuading, persuasive, satisfying

convivial 5 merry 6 genial, jovial 7 affable, festive 8 friendly, sociable 9 agreeable, fun-loving 10 gregarious 13 companionable

convocation 6 caucus, muster, roster 7 council, meeting, roundup 8 assembly, conclave, congress 9 gathering 10 conference, convention 11 ingathering

convoke 4 meet, open 6 gather, muster 8 assemble, converse 11 call to order 12 call together

convolute 4 coil, wave, wavy, wind 5 twirl, twist 6 coiled, rolled, spiral, tangle 7 contort, sinuous, twisted 8 involved, spiraled 9 intricate 11 complicated 12 turn and twist

convolution 4 coil, maze 5 twist 7 coiling, winding 8 twisting 9 labyrinth, sinuosity 10 contortion, undulation 11 sinuousness 12 tortuousness

convoy 5 fleet, usher 6 column, escort 7 conduct 9 accompany, formation, safeguard 10 armed guard, protection

convulse 4 rock, stir 5 laugh, shake, spasm, wring 6 excite 7 agitate, disturb, perturb, trouble 8 double up

convulsion 3 fit 5 spasm 6 tumult 7 seizure 8 outburst, paroxysm 9 agitation, commotion 10 contortion 11 disturbance

convulsive 6 fitful 7 hurtful, rending, shaking 8 exciting, stirring 9 agitating, epileptic, spasmodic, troubling 10 disturbing

Conway, Tim
 real name: 18 Thomas Daniel Conway
 born: 12 Willoughby OH
 roles: 11 McHale's Navy 16 Carol Burnett Show 17 The Steve Allen Show

coo 4 bill 6 babble, gurgle, murmur 20 whisper sweet nothings

Coogan, Jackie
 real name: 16 Jack Leslie Coogan
 wife: 11 Betty Grable
 born: 12 Los Angeles CA
 roles: 6 The Kid 9 Tom Sawyer 11 Oliver Twist, Peck's Bad Boy 15 Huckleberry Finn

cook 3 fix 4 chef, fire, heat, make 5 occur 6 cookie, doctor, happen, seethe 7 concoct, falsify, prepare, process 8 work well 9 improvise
 method: 3 fry 4 bake, boil, brew, sear, stew 5 baste, broil, grill, poach, roast, saute, scald, shirr, steam 6 braise, coddle, simmer 7 parboil, stir-fry 8 barbecue, fricassee

Cooke, Alistair
 author of: 14 One Man's America 18 A Generation on Trial 26 Around the World in Fifty Years
 TV host of: 18 Masterpiece Theatre

cooked sufficiently 4 done 5 ready 7 al dente 11 done to a turn

cookie 3 bar, gal, gul 4 cake, cook 5 wafer 6 person 7 biscuit, brownie 10 shortbread
 type: 4 oreo 5 sugar 7 oatmeal 8 macaroon, molasses 9 girl scout, tollhouse 10 gingersnap, lorna doone 12 peanut butter 13 chocolate chip

cooking, fine/gourmet
 French: 12 haute cuisine

cooking term 3 a la, cut, dot, fry 4 bake, beat, boil, chop, coat, cube, dice, dust, flan, fold, lard, roux, sear, snip, stew, toss, whip 5 aspic, au jus, baste, blend, bread, broil, brush, candy, cream, crepe, devil, dough, flake, glace, glaze, grate, grill, knead, plank, puree, roast, saute, scald, score, shirr, steep, stock, swear, torte 6 au lait, blanch, braise, coddle, devein, dredge, fillet, flambe, fondue, render, simmer, skewer, sliver 7 a la mode, compote, crouton, garnish, goulash, liquefy, parboil, precook, preheat, rissole, scallop, stir-fry 8 aperitif, au gratin, barbecue, conserve, consomme, julienne, marinate, pot roast 9 brochette, demitasse,

drippings, forcemeat, fricassee, lyonnaise, macedoine 10 caramelize, cracklings
 boneless strips of meat/ fish: 6 fillet
 clear soup: 8 bouillon, consomme
 cubed toasted bread: 7 crouton
 food cooked and served in foil or paper: 11 en papillote
 fruit preserve with nuts/raisins: 8 conserve
 fruits in syrup: 7 compote
 in the fashion: 7 a la mode
 remove veins: 6 devein
 skewered meat: 5 kebab 9 brochette
 small cup of black coffee: 9 demitasse
 thin strips: 6 sliver 8 julienne
 with cheese: 8 au gratin
 with ice cream: 7 a la mode
 with juice/with its own juices: 5 au jus
 with milk: 6 au lait

cook up 3 mix 4 brew 5 hatch 6 create, devise, invent, make up 7 concoct, think up 8 compound, contrive 9 fabricate, formulate

cool 3 icy 4 calm, cold 5 aloof, chill 6 chilly, frosty, offish, serene 7 distant, not warm 8 composed, lose heat, make cool, reserved 9 collected, impassive, uncordial, unexcited 10 become cool, cool-headed, deliberate, nonchalant, unfriendly, unsociable, untroubled 11 indifferent, standoffish, undisturbed, unemotional, unflappable 12 slightly cold, somewhat cold, unresponsive 13 dispassionate, imperturbable, self-possessed

cooler 3 ade, can, fan, jug 4 coop, icer, jail 5 drink, icier 6 calmer, icebox, lockup, prison 11 refrigerant 12 refrigerator 14 air conditioner

Cool Hand Luke
 director: 15 Stuart Rosenberg
 cast: 8 J D Cannon 10 Jo Van Fleet, Lou Antonio, Paul Newman 12 Anthony Zerbe, Dennis Hopper 13 George Kennedy 14 Strother Martin
 Oscar for: 15 supporting actor (Kennedy)

Coolidge, Calvin
 name at birth: 18 John Calvin Coolidge
 nickname: 9 Silent Cal
 presidential rank: 9 thirtieth
 party: 10 Republican
 state represented: 2 MA
 succeeded: 7 Harding
 defeated: 5 (Frank Thomas) Johns, (Herman P) Faris, (John William) Davis 6 (William Zebulon) Foster 7 (Gilbert O) Nations, (William James) Wallace 10 (Robert Marion) La Follette
 vice president: 4 none (first term) 5 (Charles Gates) Dawes
 cabinet:
  state: 6 (Charles Evans) Hughes 7

(Frank Billings) Kellogg
treasury: 6 (Andrew William) Mellon
war: 5 (Dwight Filley) Davis, (John Wingate) Weeks
attorney general: 5 (Harlan Fiske) Stone **6** (Charles B) Warren **7** (John Garibaldi) Sargent **9** (Harry Micajah) Daugherty
navy: 5 (Edwin) Denby **6** (Curtis Dwight) Wilbur
postmaster general: 3 (Harry Stewart) New
interior: 4 (Hubert) Work, (Roy Owen) West
agriculture: 4 (Howard Mason) Gore **7** (Henry Cantwell) Wallace, (William Marion) Jardine
commerce: 6 (Herbert Clark) Hoover **7** (William Fairfield) Whiting
labor: 5 (James John) Davis
born: 2 VT **13** Plymouth Notch
died: 2 MA **11** Northampton
buried: 2 VT **8** Plymouth
education:
   College: 7 Amherst
   later studied: 3 law
religion: 17 Congregationalist
vacation spot: 10 Black Hills
author: 32 The Autobiography of Calvin Coolidge
political career: 13 vice president
   state senator/lieutenant governor/governor of: 2 Ma **13** Massachusetts
civilian career: 6 lawyer **17** bank vice president **18** newspaper columnist
notable events of lifetime/term: 22 Pennsylvania coal strike
   Act: 8 Volstead **10** Boulder Dam **11** Immigration **17** Japanese Exclusion
   bribery case: 8 Elks Hill
   conference: 11 Geneva Naval
   flight by: 16 Charles Lindbergh
   Lindbergh's plane: 15 Spirit of St Louis
   Pact: 13 Kellogg-Briand
   trial: 6 Scopes **12** Scopes monkey
quote: 35 (After all) the chief business of America is business **43** Spend less than you make and make more than you spend
father: 10 John Calvin
mother: 8 Victoria (Josephine Moor)
   stepmother: 8 Caroline (Brown)
sibling: 13 Abigail Gratia
wife: 5 Grace (Anna Goodhue)
children: 4 John **6** Calvin
coolness 5 chill **7** dislike, reserve **8** distance **9** aloofness, composure, sangfroid **10** chilliness, detachment, frostiness **11** impassivity **12** indifference **13** lack of emotion, lack of feeling **14** unfriendliness **15** emotionlessness, standoffishness **16** imperturbability, unresponsiveness
coop 3 mew, pen, sty **4** auto, cage,

cote **5** cramp, hutch, roost **6** encase, prison **7** confine **8** imprison **9** enclosure **11** cooperation, cooperative

Cooper, Gary
real name: 16 Frank James Cooper
born: 8 Helena MT
roles: 8 High Noon (Oscar) **9** Beau Geste **12** Sergeant York (Oscar), The Virginian **15** A Farewell to Arms **17** Mr Deeds Goes to Town **19** For Whom the Bell Tolls, The Cowboy and the Lady **20** The Pride of the Yankees **22** North West Mounted Police

Cooper, James Fenimore
author of: 6 The Spy **8** The Bravo, The Pilot **9** Wyandotte **10** The Prairie **11** The Pioneers, The Red Rover **13** The Deerslayer, The Pathfinder, The Water-Witch **20** Leatherstocking Tales, The Last of the Mohicans
character: 4 Cora **5** Alice, Magua, Uncas **7** Hawkeye **11** Natty Bumppo **12** Chingachgook

cooperate 4 join **5** unite **7** go along, pitch in, share in **8** take part **9** join hands **10** act jointly, bear part in, join forces **11** collaborate, participate **12** pull together, work together **14** work side by side

cooperation 7 concert, detente **8** teamwork **9** agreement **10** accordance **11** concurrence, cooperating, give and take, joint action **13** collaboration, participation **15** pulling together, working together

coop up 3 pen **4** cage **5** pen in **6** closet, encage, shut in **7** confine, impound **8** restrain, restrict

coordinate 4 mesh **5** equal, match, order **6** relate **7** arrange, coequal **8** organize, parallel **9** correlate, harmonize **11** correlative, systematize **16** equally important

coordination 4 bond **5** skill **6** accord **7** harmony, liaison **10** adaptation, adjustment **12** equalization, organization **15** synchronization

cop 3 bag, nab, rob, win **4** bull, grab, take **5** bobby, catch, filch, pinch, snare, steal, swipe **6** peeler, pilfer, snatch **7** capture **8** flat foot, gendarme, purchase **9** policeman **11** acquisition, policewoman **13** police officer

cope 4 face, spar **6** handle, hurdle, manage, strive, tussle **7** contend, wrestle **8** struggle **11** hold one's own

copious 4 full **5** ample **6** lavish **7** liberal, profuse **8** abundant, generous **9** bountiful, extensive, plenteous, plentiful

copiousness 6 bounty, plenty, wealth **7** surfeit **8** fullness, plethora **9** abundance, ampleness, plenitude, profusion **10** lavishness, oversupply

Copland, Aaron

born: 10 Brooklyn NY
composer of: 5 Rodeo **9** Quiet City **10** Statements **11** Billy the Kid **12** Connotations **13** Dance Symphony, El Salon Mexico, The Tender Land **15** Outdoor Overture **17** Appalachian Spring **18** Music for a Great City, Music for the Theater

Copley, John Singleton
born: 8 Boston MA
artwork: 11 Samuel Adams **19** The Siege of Gibraltar **21** The Boy with the Squirrel **22** Brook Watson and the Shark, The Death of Major Pierson **26** The Death of the Earl of Chatham

copper
chemical symbol: 2 Cu
copper-colored 5 henna **6** auburn, russet **11** golden-brown, rust-colored **12** reddish-brown

coppice 4 bosk, wood **5** bluff, copse, firth, grove **6** forest, growth **7** boscage, thicket

Coppola, Francis Ford
director of: 12 The Godfather (Part I) (Part II, Oscar) **13** Apocalypse Now, The Cotton Club **15** The Conversation

copse 5 brush, clump, grove **6** forest **7** coppice, thicket **8** woodland

copy 3 ape **4** fake, sham, text **5** clone, mimic, story, Xerox **6** follow, mirror, parody, repeat **7** emulate, forgery, imitate, replica **8** likeness **9** duplicate, facsimile, imitation, photostat, reportage, reproduce **10** carbon copy, manuscript **11** counterfeit, make a copy of **12** reproduction **14** representation **15** written material

coquette 4 vamp **5** flirt, tease **12** heart-breaker

coquettish 3 coy **9** kittenish **11** flirtatious

coral 3 red **4** fire, pink, rose **5** horny, polyp, snake **6** orange, sea fan **8** acropora, hydrozoa, staghorn **9** gorgonian **10** sea feather **12** coelenterata

coram populo 8 publicly **15** before the public

corban 8 offering

Corbett, James (John)
nickname: 12 Gentleman Jim
sport: 6 boxing
class: 11 heavyweight

cord 5 braid, twine **8** thin rope **11** heavy string
   abbreviation: 2 cd

Cordelia
character in: 8 King Lear
author: 11 Shakespeare

cordial 4 warm **6** genial, hearty **7** affable, amiable, sincere **8** friendly, gracious **9** heartfelt **11** good-natured **12** affectionate, wholehearted

cordiality 6 warmth **8** goodwill **9** af-

fection, geniality, sincerity **10** affability, amiability, heartiness **11** amicability, earnestness **12** friendliness,
graciousness, pleasantness **13** agreeableness

cordial relations 5 amity **6** accord **7**
concord, harmony **8** goodwill **9** agreement **10** friendship **11** amicability **15**
entente cordiale

cordon 4 cord, ring, rope **6** circle **8** encircle

cordon bleu 4 bird **5** finch **7** waxbill
10 red cheeked **11** estrildidae
school for: 5 chefs **7** cooking
where: 5 Paris **6** France
founded by: 13 Marthe Distell
means: 10 blue ribbon

core 3 nub, nut **4** crux, gist, guts,
meat, pith **5** heart **6** center, kernel **7**
essence, nucleus **9** substance **10** brass
tacks **11** central part, nitty-gritty **13**
essential part, innermost part **15** sum
and substance

Corelli, Arcangelo
born: 5 Imola, Italy
composer of: 7 La Folia (sonata No
12) **14** Concerti Grossi

coriander
botanical name: 17 Coriandrum sativum
origin: 13 Mediterranean
color: 5 brown, white **6** yellow
flavor: 4 sage **5** cumin **7** caraway **9**
lemon peel
candy: 6 comfit

Corinth, Lovis
born: 6 Tapiau **7** Prussia
artwork: 6 Salome **8** Ecce Homo **10**
Apocalypse **29** The Walchensee with
a Yellow Field

Coriolanus
author: 18 William Shakespeare
character: 8 Cominius, Virgilia,
Volumnia **12** Junius Brutus, Titus
Lartius **14** Tullus Aufidius **15**
Menenius Agrippa, Sicinius Velutus
22 Caius Marcius Coriolanus

cork 3 bob, oak **4** bark, bung, plug,
seal, stop **5** check, close, float **7** confine, filling stopper, stopple **8** restrain,
suppress **10** insulation

corker 3 ace **4** lulu, oner, whiz **7** stopper **8** clencher, striking, top notch **9**
excellent, humdinger **10** remarkable
11 astonishing

corkscrew 4 coil, curl **5** twist **6** spiral
7 winding **10** serpentine **12** bottle
opener

Corleone family
characters in: 12 The Godfather
author: 4 Puzo
member: 5 Fredo, Sonny **7** Don Vito,
Freddie, Michael

corn 4 cure **5** grain **6** callus **7** Zea
Mays **8** preserve, schmaltz **9** vegetable
varieties: 3 Pod **4** Crow, Dent, Rice,

Sand **5** Broom, Flint, Kafir, maize,
Sugar, Sweet **6** Indian, Turkey **8**
Egyptian, Squirrel
bread/cake: 4 pone **7** hoecake **8** tortilla **9** hushpuppy **10** johnnycake
beverage: 7 bourbon, whiskey

Corncracker State
nickname of: 8 Kentucky

Corneille, Pierre
author of: 5 Cinna, Le Cid, Medea,
Medee **6** Horace, The Cid **8** Ni-
comede **9** Polyeucte

Cornelius, Peter von (van)
born: 7 Germany **10** Dusseldorf
artwork: 12 Last Judgment **24** The
Wise and Foolish Virgins **30** The
Four Horsemen of the Apocalypse

Cornell, Katherine
nickname: 21 first lady of the theater
born: 6 Berlin **7** Germany
roles: 8 Dear Liar **9** Saint Joan **18**
Antony and Cleopatra **26** The Barretts of Wimpole Street

corner 3 fix, jam, nab **4** bend, grab,
hole, nail, nook, spot, trap **5** angle,
seize **6** collar, pickle, plight, scrape **7**
dead end, dilemma, impasse **10** blind
alley, pigeonhole **11** predicament

cornerstone 4 base **5** basis **9** principle
10 foundation **11** fundamental

cornet 4 cone, horn **7** trumpet **9**
cornopean

Cornhuskers, The
author: 12 Carl Sandburg

Cornhusker State
nickname of: 8 Nebraska

cornice 4 drip **5** ancon, crown **7** molding, valance **8** astragal

Cornwallis, Charles
also: 10 second Earl **13** first Marquess
nationality: 7 British
served in: 5 India **7** Ireland **18** American Revolution
battle: 8 Yorktown **10** Brandywine
captured: 10 Charleston **12** Philadelphia
surrendered at: 8 Yorktown

Cornwell, David
real name of: 11 John Le Carre

corny 5 banal, hokey, inane, stale,
tired, trite, vapid **6** jejune, square **7**
fatuous, insipid **8** bromidic, ordinary,
shopworn **9** hackneyed **10** threadbare,
unoriginal **11** commonplace, stereotyped **12** cliche-ridden, old-fashioned
13 platitudinous, unimaginative **15**
unsophisticated

corona 4 halo, ring **5** cigar **6** circle,
nimbus

coronet 5 tiara **6** diadem **7** chaplet,
circlet **10** small crown

Corot, Jean-Baptiste-Camille
born: 5 Paris **6** France
artwork: 9 Pastorale **11** Ville
d'Avray, Woman in Blue **15** Woman

with a Pearl **16** The Farnese Garden,
Woman in the Studio **21** Memory of
Mortefontaine **23** Souvenir de Morte-
fontaine

corporal 3 NCO **6** bodily **8** physical **9**
corporeal

corporation 7 combine, company **9**
syndicate **11** association **14** conglomeration

corporeal 6 bodily, mortal **7** worldly **8**
material, physical **11** perceptible **12**
nonspiritual

corps 4 band, crew, team **5** force,
party, squad, troop **6** outfit

corpse 4 body **5** stiff **7** cadaver,
remains **8** dead body

corpselike 4 pale **5** ashen **6** pallid **9**
bloodless, deathlike **10** cadaverous

corpulent 3 fat **5** dumpy, hefty, obese,
plump, pudgy, stout **6** chubby,
chunky, fleshy, portly, rotund **7** lumpish, well-fed **8** roly-poly **10** overweight, well-padded

corral 4 herd **5** pen in **6** shut in **7** enclose, fence in, round up

correct 3 fit, fix **4** true **5** alter, amend,
chide, emend, exact, right, scold **6** adjust, berate, change, modify, proper,
punish, rebuke, remedy, repair, revamp, revise, rework, seemly **7** censure, chasten, factual, fitting, improve,
lecture, perfect, precise, rectify, reprove **8** accurate, admonish, becoming, chastise, flawless, regulate, suitable, unerring **9** castigate, dress down,
faultless, make right, reprimand **10**
acceptable, discipline, take to task **11**
appropriate **12** conventional **16** haul
over the coals, read the riot act to

correction 6 change **8** revision **10** adjustment, alteration, discipline, emendation, punishment **11** castigation,
improvement, reformation **12** chastisement, modification **13** rectification

corrective 7 counter **8** remedial **9** improving **10** palliative, rectifying **11** reformatory, restorative, therapeutic **12**
ameliorative, compensatory **13** counteractive **16** counterbalancing

correctness 8 accuracy **9** exactness,
precision, propriety, rightness **10** exactitude, seemliness **11** suitability **12**
becomingness, flawlessness **13** acceptability

Correggio
real name: 14 Antonio Allegri
born: 5 Italy **6** Emilia **9** Correggio
artwork: 5 Danae **12** Jupiter and Io
14 Leda and the Swan **17** The Rape
of Ganymede **21** The Madonna of St
Francis **23** Adoration of the Shepherds **28** Mystic Marriages of St
Catherine

correlate 7 compare, connect **8** parallel **10** correspond

correlation 8 parallel 10 comparison, connection 14 correspondence

correlative 4 akin 7 related 8 agreeing, parallel 9 analogous 10 comparable, connecting, equivalent 13 corresponding

correspond 3 fit 4 jibe, suit 5 agree, match, tally 6 accord, be like, concur, equate, square 7 conform 8 coincide, dovetail, parallel 9 harmonize 11 communicate, drop a line to, keep in touch

correspondence 4 mail 7 analogy, letters 8 epistles, missives, relation 9 bulletins 10 dispatches, similarity 11 association, communiques, resemblance

corresponding 4 akin 5 alike, equal 7 similar 8 agreeing, matching, tallying 9 according 10 equivalent 11 correlative 12 proportional

corridor 3 way 4 hall, road 5 aisle 6 artery 7 hallway, passage 8 approach 10 passageway

Corridors of Power
    author: 6 C P Snow

corroborate 4 back 5 prove 6 affirm, back up, uphold, verify 7 bear out, certify, confirm, endorse, support, sustain 8 validate 9 vindicate 12 authenticate, substantiate

corroborated 4 backed, proved, proven, upheld 7 factual 8 affirmed, backed up, borne out, verified 9 certified, confirmed, supported, sustained, validated 10 vindicated 11 well-founded 12 well-grounded 13 authenticated, substantiated

corroboration 5 proof 7 support 8 evidence 10 validation 11 affirmation, endorsement, vindication 12 confirmation, verification 13 certification, documentation 14 authentication, substantiation

corroborative 7 proving 9 affirming, backing up, upholding, verifying 10 bearing out, concurring, confirming, supporting, validating 11 affirmative 12 confirmative 14 substantiating

corrode 4 rust 7 oxidize 12 disintegrate

corrosive 4 acid 7 burning, caustic, erosive, mordant 8 abrasive 9 corroding 11 destructive

corrugated 6 fluted, ridged 7 creased, grooved, pleated 8 crinkled, furrowed, puckered, wrinkled 10 crenulated

corrupt 3 low 4 base, evil, mean 5 shady 6 debase, poison, seduce, sinful, wicked 7 crooked, debased, debauch, deprave, immoral, pervert, subvert 8 depraved 9 dishonest, unethical 10 fraudulent, iniquitous 11 contaminate 12 dishonorable, unprincipled, unscrupulous

corruption 4 vice 5 fraud, graft 7 bribery 8 iniquity 9 decadence, depravity, looseness, turpitude 10 debauchery, degeneracy, dishonesty, immorality, perversion, sinfulness, wickedness, wrongdoing 11 malfeasance

corsair 6 pirate, sea dog, Viking 7 brigand, sea wolf 8 marauder, picaroon, sea rover 9 buccaneer, plunderer, privateer, sea looter, sea robber 10 Blackbeard, freebooter 11 Captain Kidd 14 Long John Silver

corset 5 laces 6 girdle 8 corselet 17 foundation garment

Corsica 6 island
    located in: 16 Mediterranean Sea
    capital: 7 Ajaccio
    colony of: 4 Rome
    purchased by: 6 France
    birthplace of: 8 Napoleon
    industry: 7 tourism 10 wine making 12 sheep raising, cheese making

Corsican Brothers, The
    author: 14 Alexandre Dumas (pere)

Cortazar, Julio
    author of: 7 Rayuela 9 A Model Kit, Bestiario, Hopscotch 10 The Winners 12 Book of Manuel, End of the Game 15 All Fires the Fire 18 We Love Glenda So Much

cortege 4 line 5 court, staff, suite, train 6 column, escort, parade, string 7 caravan, company, retinue 9 cavalcade, entourage, following, motorcade 10 attendants, procession 17 funeral procession

corundum
    variety: 4 ruby 8 sapphire, star ruby 12 star sapphire

coruscate 4 beam 5 flash, gleam 7 glimmer, glitter, shimmer, sparkle

Corybant
    attendant of: 6 Cybele

Corythosaurus
    type: 8 dinosaur 10 ornithopod
    period: 10 Cretaceous
    characteristic: 10 duck-billed

Cosby, Bill
    born: 14 Philadelphia PA
    roles: 4 I Spy 8 Ghost Dad 12 The Cosby Show 19 Mother Juggs and Speed, Uptown Saturday Night
    nickname: 3 Cos

Cosby Show, The
    character: 4 Rudy, Theo 6 Denise, Sondra 7 Vanessa 13 Clair Huxtable, (Dr) Cliff (Heathcliff) Huxtable
    cast: 9 Bill Cosby, Lisa Bonet 14 Sabrina LeBeauf 15 Tempestt Bledsoe 18 Malcolm Jamal-Warner 19 Keshia Knight Pulliam, Phylicia Ayers-Rashad

Cosi fan tutte
    also: 11 So Do They All 16 Women Are Like That
    opera by: 6 Mozart
    character: 7 Despina 8 Ferrando 9 Dorabella, Guglielmo 10 Don Alfonso, Fiordiligi

cosmetic 5 blush, liner, paint, rouge 6 makeup, powder 7 mascara, surface 8 artifice, eyeliner, lipstick 9 cold cream, eye shadow 10 foundation, nail polish 11 beautifying 13 eyebrow pencil

cosmic 4 vast 7 immense 8 colossal, enormous, infinite 9 grandiose, universal 10 stupendous, widespread 12 interstellar 14 interplanetary 16 extraterrestrial

cosmopolitan 5 suave 6 urbane 7 worldly 8 traveler 11 broad-minded, worldly-wise 12 globetrotter, sophisticate 13 international, sophisticated

cosmos 5 stars 8 universe 9 macrocosm 10 starry host 13 vault of heaven
    book by: 5 Sagan

Cossack 7 czarist, Russian, trooper 8 horseman 10 cavalry man

cosset 3 pet 6 caress, coddle, fondle, pamper

cost 3 fee, run, tab 4 bill, harm, hurt, loss, pain, take, toll 5 fetch, go for, price, value, worth 6 amount, burden, charge, come to, damage, injure, injury, outlay 7 bring in, expense, penalty, sell for, set back 8 amount to, distress 9 face value, sacrifice, suffering, valuation, weigh down 11 expenditure, market price

Costa-Gavras, Constantine
    director of: 7 Missing

Costard
    character in: 16 Love's Labour's Lost
    author: 11 Shakespeare

Costa Rica
    name means: 9 rich coast
    other name: 19 Land of Eternal Spring
    capital/largest city: 7 San Jose
    others: 5 Canas, Limon, Vesta 6 Boruca, Nicoya 7 Cartago, Golfito, Heredia, Liberia, Negrita 8 Alajuela, Colorado, Guapiles 9 Turrialba 10 Puntarenas
    measure: 4 vara 5 cafiz, cahiz 6 fanega, tercia 7 cajuela, cantaro, manzana 10 caballeria
    monetary unit: 5 colon 7 centimo
    weight: 3 bag 4 caja 5 libra
    island: 4 Cano, Coco
    lake: 6 Arenal
    mountain: 4 Poas 5 Barba, Irazu 6 Blanco 7 Central, Gongora 9 Talamanca, Turrialba 10 Guanacaste
    highest point: 14 Chirripo Grande
    river: 4 Poas 5 Irazu 6 Matina 7 San Juan, Sixaola, Tenoria 8 Tarcoles
    sea: 7 Pacific 9 Caribbean
    physical feature:
        bay: 7 Salinas 8 Coronada
        cape: 5 Velas 6 Blanco 8 Matapalo 10 Santa Elena

crater: 4 Poas
gulf: 5 Dulce **6** Nicoya **8** Papagayo
hot springs spa: 12 Agua Caliente
peninsula: 3 Osa **6** Nicoya
point: 5 Judas **6** Blanca, Burica,
Quepos **7** Cahuito, Galonos,
Guionos, Llerena
valley: 8 Tarcoles **10** Reventazon
people: 4 Voto **6** Boruca, Bribri,
Guaymi **7** Guatuso, mestizo, Spanish
explorer: 8 Columbus, Coronado
language: 7 Spanish
religion: 13 Roman Catholic
place:
shrine: 18 Our Lady of the Angels
theater: 14 Teatro Nacional
feature:
barbecue: 5 asado
dance: 6 torito **9** botijuela, zapate-
ado **11** baile suelto **17** punto
guanacasteco
drum: 8 quijonga
gourd: 4 caro
outdoor concerts: 7 retreta
plantation: 5 finca
wind instrument: 8 chirimia
food:
hearts of palm salad: 7 palmito
pudding: 10 tamal asado
Costello, Lou
real name: 21 Louis Francis Cristillo
partner: 9 Bud Abbott
born: 10 Paterson NJ
roles: 11 Who's on First
costly 4 dear **5** steep, stiff **7** harmful **8**
damaging, precious **9** expensive **10**
disastrous, exorbitant, high-priced **11**
deleterious, extravagant **12** catastrophic
Costner, Kevin
born: 2 CA **10** Los Angeles
films: 3 JFK **9** Silverado, Wyatt Earp
10 Bull Durham, The Postman,
Waterworld **12** The Bodyguard **13**
Field of Dreams, A Perfect World **15**
The Untouchables **16** Dances With
Wolves **24** Robin Hood: Prince of
Thieves
costume 4 garb **5** dress **6** attire, livery,
outfit **7** apparel, clothes, raiment, uniform **8** clothing, garments
costuming 8 disguise **10** masquerade
cot 3 bed, hut, pen **4** coop, crib **5**
cover, stall **7** cottage
cotelette 3 cut **4** chop **5** slice **6** cutlet
coterie 3 set **4** band, camp, clan, club,
crew, gang **5** crowd, group **6** circle,
clique **7** faction
cottage 3 cot, hut **5** lodge, shack **6**
chalet **8** bungalow
Cotten, Joseph
born: 12 Petersburg VA
roles: 8 Gaslight **11** Citizen Kane, The
Third Man **12** Duel in the Sun **14**
Shadow of a Doubt **15** Journey into
Fear **16** Portrait of Jennie **23** The
Magnificent Ambersons

cotton 9 Gossypium
varieties: 3 bog **4** tree, wild **6** kidney, levant, upland **8** lavender **9** sea
island **11** Arizona wild
fabric: 4 duck, jean, lawn, pima **5**
baize, chino, denim, drill, khaki,
lisle, pique, scrim, terry, twill **6** burlap, calico, canvas, chintz, dimity,
madras, muslin, nankin, oxford, poplin, sateen **7** batiste, buckram, cambric, flannel, fustian, gingham, holland, jaconet, oilskin, organdy,
percale, ticking **8** chambray, cre-
tonne, sheeting **9** crinoline, sailcloth
10 broadcloth, hopsacking, printcloth, seersucker, terrycloth **11**
cheesecloth, dotted Swiss
Cotton Club, The
director: 18 Francis Ford Coppola
cast: 9 Diane Lane **11** Richard Gere
12 Gregory Hines
cotton gin
invented by: 7 Whitney
Cotton State
nickname of: 7 Alabama
cottonwood 7 Populus **16** Populus
deltoides
varieties: 5 black, Jack's, swamp **7**
Fremont **9** Rio Grande **10** Wislizenus
11 Great Plains
Cotyleus
epithet of: 9 Asclepius
means: 13 of the hip joint
couch 3 put **4** sofa, word **5** divan,
draft, frame, state, utter, voice **6** daybed, draw up, lounge, phrase, settee **7**
express **8** love seat, set forth **9** davenport **12** chesterfield
couch potato
activity: 7 viewing
loves: 10 television
cougar 3 cat **4** lion, puma **7** panther **9**
catamount **12** mountain lion
cough 4 hack **6** tussis **9** pertussis
cough up 3 pay **5** eject, expel **7** deliver **8** disgorge, hand over **9** surrender **11** regurgitate
Coulomb, Charles Augustin de
field: 7 physics
nationality: 6 French
invented: 14 torsion balance
discovered: 16 inverse square law
council 5 board, panel, synod **7** cabinet, chamber **8** assembly, colloquy,
conclave, congress, ministry **9** committee, gathering, sanhedrin **10** conference, convention **11** convocation
12 congregation **15** representatives
counsel 4 urge, warn **6** advice, advise,
charge, lawyer, prompt **7** call for, caution, opinion, suggest **8** admonish, advocate, attorney, guidance, instruct **9**
barrister, counselor, recommend, solicitor **10** advisement, suggestion **12**
consultation **14** recommendation
counsel house
German: 7 Rathaus

Counsellor-at-Law
director: 12 William Wyler
based on play by: 9 Elmer Rice
cast: 11 Bebe Daniels, Doris Kenyon
12 Isabel Jewell **13** John Barrymore,
Melvyn Douglas, Onslow Stevens
counselor, counsellor 5 tutor **6** lawyer, mentor **7** adviser **8** advocate, attorney, minister **9** barrister, solicitor
10 instructor
counselor-at-law 6 lawyer **8** advocate, attorney **9** barrister, solicitor **10**
mouthpiece
count 4 deem, hold, lord, rate, tell
5 add up, judge, noble, tally, total **6**
impute, look on, matter, number,
reckon, regard **7** ascribe, include, tick
off **8** consider, estimate, look upon,
numerate **9** attribute, enumerate,
numbering, reckoning **10** numeration
11 calculation, computation, enumeration
German: 4 Graf
French: 5 comte
Italian: 5 conte
famous: 7 Dracula **8** Almaviva **11**
Monte Cristo
countenance 3 aid, air **4** back, face,
help, look, mien **5** build, favor **6** aspect, permit, traits, uphold, visage **7**
advance, approve, condone, endorse,
forward, further, profile, promote,
support, work for **8** advocacy, advocate, approval, auspices, champion,
contours, features, presence, sanction
9 promotion **10** appearance, assistance, expression, silhouette **11** approbation, physiognomy **12** championship, moral support **13**
encouragement
counter 3 bar, man **4** defy, disk **5**
piece, stand, table **6** buffet, contra,
offset, oppose, resist **7** against, get
even, hit back, opposed, pay back, reverse **8** contrary, fountain, opposite **9**
fight back, retaliate **11** conflicting **13**
contradictory
counteract 4 curb, undo **5** check, fight
6 defeat, hinder, negate, offset, oppose, resist, thwart **7** assuage, nullify,
repress **8** overcome, restrain **9** alleviate, frustrate, overpower **10** annihilate, contravene, neutralize
counteraction 8 negation **10** offsetting, opposition **13** contravention, nullification **14** neutralization
counteractive 7 adverse **8** inimical **10**
corrective **11** unfavorable **12** antagonistic, neutralizing
counteractor 7 negator **9** nullifier, off-
setter **11** neutralizer
counteragent 3 spy **4** mole **8** antidote
9 antitoxin **10** antipoison **11** double
agent
counterbalance 5 amend, check **6**
cancel, offset, redeem, set off **7** correct, rectify **8** atone for, equalize,

make good, outweigh **9** make up for **10** balance out, neutralize, outbalance, recompense **12** compensation

counterfeit 4 copy, fake, sham **5** bogus, fraud, phony **6** ersatz, forged **7** feigned, forgery **8** spurious **9** facsimile, imitation, simulated **10** artificial, fraudulent, substitute **11** make-believe

Counterfeiters, The
author: **9** Andre Gide

countermand 4 void **5** annul, quash **6** cancel, recall, repeal, revoke **7** abolish, nullify, rescind, retract, reverse **8** abrogate, call back, disenact, override, overrule, set aside, withdraw, write off **12** disestablish

counterpart 4 copy, mate, twin **5** equal, match **6** double, fellow **8** parallel **9** duplicate **11** correlative **12** doppelganger **13** correspondent, spitting image

counterpoise 7 balance **9** stability **11** equilibrium

countersign 4 sign **7** certify, confirm, endorse **8** validate **9** authorize **11** corroborate **12** authenticate

countess
French: **8** comtesse
Italian: **8** contessa

countless 6 myriad, untold **7** endless **8** infinite **9** limitless, unlimited **10** numberless, unnumbered **11** innumerable, measureless **12** immeasurable, incalculable **13** multitudinous

Count of Monte Cristo, The
author: **14** Alexandre Dumas (pere)
character: **6** Albert, Haydee, Morrel **7** Fernand (Comte de Morcerf) **8** Danglars, Mercedes **9** Abbe Faria, Valentine, Villefort **10** Caderousse, Maximilian **12** Edmond Dantes
prison: **10** Chateau d'If

count on 6 expect **7** hope for **10** anticipate

countrified 5 rural **6** rustic **9** backwoods **15** unsophisticated

country 4 area, farm, land **5** realm, rural, state **6** nation, people, public, region, rustic, simple, sticks **7** boonies, farming, kingdom, natives, scenery, terrain **8** citizens, district, homeland, populace **9** backwoods, boondocks, community, landscape, territory **10** fatherland, native land, native soil, population, provincial, rural areas **11** farming area, hinterlands, inhabitants, nationality **12** commonwealth **15** unsophisticated

Country Cousin
author: **16** Louis Auchincloss

Country Girl, The
director: **12** George Seaton
based on play by: **13** Clifford Odets
cast: **10** Bing Crosby, Grace Kelly (Oscar) **11** Anthony Ross **13** William Holden
Oscar for: **7** actress (Kelly)

countryman 4 hick, rube **5** yokel **6** farmer, rustic **7** bumpkin, hayseed, peasant **8** landsman **10** clodhopper, compatriot, provincial

Country of the Pointed Firs, The
author: **15** Sarah Orne Jewett

country place 4 farm **5** manor **6** estate

countryside 6 sticks **7** boonies **9** backwater, backwoods, boondocks, rural area **10** hinterland

count up 3 add **5** tally, total **6** reckon **7** compute **9** calculate

count upon 6 expect **7** foresee **10** anticipate

coup 3 act **4** blow, deed, feat **6** stroke **12** master stroke

coup de grace 9 deathblow **11** mercy stroke **12** decisive blow **15** finishing stroke
literally: **11** blow of mercy

coup de main 14 surprise attack **17** sudden development
literally: **15** blow from the hand

coup d'etat 6 mutiny **8** uprising **9** overthrow, rebellion **10** revolution, subversion

coup de theatre 15 theatrical trick

coup d'oeil 11 quick glance
literally: **14** stroke of the eye

Couperin, Francois (Le Grand)
born: **5** Paris **6** France
composer of: **9** La Sultane, Les Fastes (de la grande et ancienne) **13** Concert Royaux **16** Apotheose de Lulli, Pieces de Clavecin **17** Lecons des Tenebres **20** Les Follies Francoises **31** Le Parnasse on l'Apotheose de Corelli

couple 3 duo, tie **4** bind, join, link, pair, yoke **5** hitch **6** fasten **7** connect, doublet, twosome **10** man and wife **11** man and woman **14** husband and wife

coupler 4 link, lock **5** clasp, hitch **6** buckle **8** fastener **9** fastening

Couples
author: **10** John Updike

coupling 5 clasp, hatch **6** hookup, yoking **7** joining, pairing **8** hitching **9** attaching, fastening **10** attachment, connecting, connection

courage 4 grit, guts, sand **5** nerve, pluck, spunk, valor **6** daring, mettle **7** bravery **8** boldness **9** derring-do, fortitude **11** intrepidity **12** fearlessness **13** dauntlessness **16** stout-heartedness

courageous 4 bold **5** brave, manly **6** dogged, heroic **7** dashing, doughty, gallant, valiant **8** fearless, intrepid, resolute, stalwart, unafraid, valorous **9** dauntless **10** chivalrous **11** indomitable **12** bold-spirited **13** stronghearted

Courbet, Jean Desire Gustave
born: **6** France, Ornans

artwork: **16** The Artist's Studio, The Stonebreakers **17** The Burial at Ornans **19** The Peasants of Flagey **25** Self-Portrait with a Black Dog

courier 4 mule **5** envoy **6** herald, legate, runner **7** Gabriel, mailman, Mercury, postman **8** emissary **9** go-between, harbinger, messenger, postrider **11** herald angel, internuncio

course 3 run, way **4** flow, gush, mode, path, pour, race, road **5** march, orbit, round, route, surge, track **6** action, circle, method, policy, stream **7** channel, circuit, classes, conduct, lessons, passage, subject **8** behavior, lectures, sequence **9** direction, procedure, unfolding **10** curriculum, racecourse, trajectory **11** development, progression

court 3 bar, woo **4** hall, quad, seek, suit, yard **5** bench, manor, plaza, staff, train **6** atrium, castle, homage, induce, invite, palace, pursue, wooing **7** address, attract, chateau, cortege, council, flatter, hearing, meeting, provoke, retinue, session **8** advisers, assembly, audience, blandish, fawn upon, pander to, respects, run after **9** entourage, following **10** attendants, quadrangle **13** solicitations

Courtenay, Tom
born: **4** Hull **7** England
roles: **9** Billy Liar **10** The Dresser **36** The Loneliness of the Long Distance Runner

courteous 4 kind, mild **5** civil **6** polite **7** refined, tactful **8** gracious, mannerly, well-bred **10** diplomatic, respectful, soft-spoken **11** considerate, well-behaved **12** well-mannered

courtesy 5 favor **7** manners, regards, respect **8** civility, kindness, respects **9** deference, gallantry, gentility **10** indulgence, politeness, refinement **11** cultivation **12** graciousness **13** consideration

courtier 4 beau **7** gallant **8** cavalier **9** attendant **18** gentleman-in-waiting

Courtier, The
author: **21** Baldassare Castiglione

Court Jester
director: **11** Melvin Frank **12** Norman Panama
cast: **9** Danny Kaye **11** Glynis Johns **13** Basil Rathbone **14** Angela Lansbury

courtly 5 suave **6** polite **7** elegant, gallant, genteel, refined, stately **8** debonair, decorous, highbred, ladylike, mannerly, polished **9** civilized, courteous, dignified **10** chivalrous **11** blueblooded, gentlemanly **12** aristocratic **14** silk-stockinged

courtship 4 suit **6** wooing **14** keeping company

Courtship of Eddie's Father, The
character: **4** Tina **10** Tom Corbett **12** Eddie Corbett, Norman Tinker **13**

Mrs Livingston
cast: 9 Bill Bixby **11** Brandon Cruz, James Komack **12** Miyoshi Umeki **15** Kristina Holland

Courtship of Miles Standish, The
author: 24 Henry Wadsworth Long-fellow
character: 9 John Alden, Priscilla

courtyard 4 area, quad **6** atrium **9** curtilage, enclosure **10** quadrangle

cousin 7 kinsman **8** relation, relative **9** kinswoman

Cousin Bette
author: 14 Honore de Balzac
character: 6 Crevel **7** Adeline **10** Baron Hulot **11** Mme Marneffe **13** Hortense Hulot, Marechal Hulot **14** Lisbeth Fischer **23** Count Wenceslas Steinbock

Cousin Pons
author: 14 Honore de Balzac

Cousy, Bob
nickname: 12 Mr Basketball
sport: 10 basketball
position: 5 guard
team: 13 Boston Celtics

couturier, couturiere 8 designer **9** midinette **10** dressmaker, seamstress

cove 3 bay **5** inlet **6** lagoon **7** estuary

covenant 3 vow **4** bond, oath, pact **6** pledge, treaty **7** bargain, promise **8** contract **9** agreement **15** solemn agreement
Hebrew: 4 Brit **5** Berit, Brith **6** Berith

Covenant, The
author: 13 James Michener

cover 3 cap, lid, top **4** case, hide, hood, mask, veil, wrap **5** cloak, cross, guard, lay on, put on, quilt **6** asylum, clothe, defend, embody, enwrap, jacket, refuge, report, screen, sheath, shield, shroud, take in, tell of **7** binding, blanket, conceal, contain, defense, embrace, envelop, include, involve, obscure, overlay, protect, put over, secrete, sheathe, shelter, wrapper, write up **8** comprise, deal with, describe, disguise, envelope, pass over, traverse **9** chronicle, comforter, eiderdown, encompass, sanctuary **10** camouflage, comprehend, encasement, protection **11** concealment, hiding place

coverage 7 payment **8** analysis **9** indemnity, reporting **10** protection, publishing **11** description **12** broadcasting **13** reimbursement

covered 4 clad **6** hidden **7** aimed at, cloaked, guarded, insured **8** included, overlaid, screened **9** blanketed, concealed, protected, sheltered, traversed **10** overspread

covering 6 casing, sheath **7** wrapper **8** envelope, wrapping **11** descriptive, explanatory **12** introductory

coverlet 5 quilt, throw **6** afghan,

spread **7** blanket **9** bedspread, comforter

Coverly, Sir Roger de
character in: 12 The Spectator
authors: 6 Steele **7** Addison

covert 6 hidden, secret, veiled **7** sub rosa, unknown **9** concealed, disguised **11** clandestine **13** surreptitious

cover up 4 hide, mask, veil **6** hush up **7** conceal **8** disguise, keep back, suppress, withhold **9** gloss over, whitewash

cover-up 4 mask **5** blind **6** screen **8** disguise **9** whitewash **11** concealment

covet 4 want **5** crave, fancy **6** desire **7** long for

covetous 6 greedy **7** craving, envious, jealous, lustful, selfish **8** desirous, grasping, yearning **9** mercenary, rapacious **10** avaricious

covetousness 4 envy **5** greed **7** avarice **8** jealousy, rapacity **10** greediness **12** graspingness **13** mercenariness

covey 4 bevy **5** flock, group **6** family

cow 4 beef **5** abash, Bossy, bully, deter, Elsie, scare **6** bovine, cattle, dismay **7** terrify **8** browbeat, bulldoze, frighten, threaten **9** terrorize **10** discourage, dishearten, intimidate, make cringe
young: 4 calf **6** heifer

coward 3 cad **5** sissy **6** craven **7** caitiff, chicken, dastard, milksop **8** poltroon **11** Milquetoast, mollycoddle, yellow-belly

Coward, Sir Noel
author of: 8 Hay Fever **9** Cavalcade **10** Sigh No More **12** Blithe Spirit, Private Lives **14** In Which We Serve, Nude with Violin **15** Design for Living

cowardliness 8 timidity **10** yellowness **12** irresolution **13** pusillanimity, spinelessness **18** chicken-heartedness

cowardly 5 shaky, timid **6** afraid, craven, yellow **7** anxious, chicken, fearful, gutless, nervous **8** timorous **9** dastardly, tremulous **10** frightened **11** lily-livered **12** apprehensive, faint-hearted, uncourageous **13** pusillanimous, yellow-bellied **14** chicken-hearted

Cowardly Lion
character in: 13 The Wizard of Oz
author: 4 Baum
played by: 8 Bert Lahr

cowboy 6 drover, gaucho **7** vaquero **8** buckaroo **10** roughrider **12** bronco-buster, cattle-herder

cowed 5 fazed **7** abashed, crushed, subdued **8** dismayed **11** intimidated **12** disconcerted **14** under one's thumb

cower 5 crawl, quail, toady **6** cringe, flinch, grovel, recoil, shrink **7** tremble, truckle **8** bootlick, draw back

cowl 4 cope, hood **5** cloak

Cowley, Malcolm
author of: 12 Exile's Return **16** A Second Flowering **27** And I Worked at the Writer's Trade **28** The Dream of the Golden Mountains

coworker 7 partner **8** teammate **9** associate, colleague **10** accomplice **11** confederate **12** collaborator

Cowper, William
author of: 7 The Task **11** The Cast-Away

Cowperwood, Frank
character in: 8 The Titan **12** The Financier
author: 7 Dreiser

coxcomb 3 fop **4** beau **5** dandy **8** popinjay

coy 3 shy **5** timid **6** demure, modest **7** bashful, prudish **8** blushing, sheepish, skittish, timorous **9** diffident, kittenish, shrinking **10** coquettish, overmodest

Coyote State
nickname of: 11 South Dakota

cozen 3 con, gyp **4** bilk, coax, dupe, gull, rook **5** cheat, trick **6** fleece **7** deceive, defraud, swindle, wheedle **9** bamboozle, victimize

cozener 4 fake **5** cheat, fraud, quack **6** con man **8** deceiver, swindler **9** charlatan, trickster **10** mountebank **13** confidence man

coziness 6 warmth **7** comfort **8** intimacy, snugness **11** contentment

cozy 4 easy, snug **5** comfy, homey **7** restful **8** homelike, relaxing **9** gemutlich, simpatico **11** comfortable **16** snug as a bug in a rug
French: 6 intime

Cozzens, James Gould
author of: 12 Guard of Honor **15** By Love Possessed

CPA 7 auditor **10** accountant, book-keeper **25** certified public accountant

crab 4 carp **5** crank, gripe, grump **6** grouch, grouse **8** complain, sourball **9** shellfish **10** crustacean, curmudgeon
constellation of: 6 Cancer

Crabbe, Buster
real name: 20 Clarence Linden Crabbe
nickname: 16 King of the Serials
born: 9 Oakland CA
roles: 6 Tarzan **10** Buck Rogers **11** Flash Gordon **15** King of the Jungle

crabbed 4 mean, sour **6** cranky, morose **7** grouchy, peevish, pinched **8** churlish, spiteful **9** irascible, irritable, rancorous

crabby 5 cross, testy **6** cranky, touchy **7** grouchy, peevish **8** petulant, snappish **9** irritable **10** ill-humored, out of sorts **11** ill-tempered **12** cantankerous

crack 3 gag, jab, pop **4** chip, clap, gash, gibe, jest, joke, quip, rent, rift,

slit, snap **5** break, burst, cleft, split,
taunt **6** cleave, insult, report **7**
crackle, crevice, fissure, give way,
rupture, thunder **8** fracture, splinter **9**
break down, wisecrack, witticism **10**
go to pieces

cracked 3 mad **4** daft, nuts **5** crazy,
nutty **6** crazed, insane **8** demented,
deranged, unhinged **10** unbalanced **12**
mad as a hatter **13** off one's rocker,
out of one's head **14** off one's trolley
15 mad as a March hare

cracker 5 snack, wafer **7** biscuit, redneck **10** party favor **11** backsettler **12**
backwoodsman

crackerjack 2 A-1 **3** ace **4** a-one, fine
5 super **6** superb, tip-top **8** splendid,
terrific **9** excellent, fantastic, first-rate,
wonderful **10** first-class

Cracker State
nickname of: 7 Georgia

crackle 4 snap **5** craze, crink **9** crepi-
tate

crackpot 3 nut, odd **4** fool, kook **5**
balmy, crank, flake, freak, kinky,
kooky, loony, nutty, wacko **6** freaky,
insane, looney, madman, maniac,
weirdo **7** dingbat, foolish, lunatic,
oddball **9** character, eccentric, screwball **11** impractical

cracksman 4 yegg **7** burglar **10** cat
burglar **14** second- story man

crackup 5 crash, smash, split, wreck **6**
mishap, pileup **7** breakup, debacle,
smashup **8** accident, calamity, collapse, disaster **9** breakdown, collision,
splitting **10** exhaustion, shellshock **11**
catastrophe, prostration **14** disintegration

cradle 3 hug **4** crib, font, rock **6** cuddle, enfold, origin, source, spring **7**
nursery, snuggle **8** bassinet, fountain
10 birthplace, wellspring **12** fountainhead

craft 3 art **4** boat, ruse, ship, wile **5**
guile, knack, plane, skill, trade **6** deceit, vessel **7** ability, calling, cunning,
know-how, mastery, perfidy, pursuit **8**
airplane, artifice, business, commerce,
deftness, fineness, industry, intrigue,
trickery, vocation **9** adeptness, chicanery, deception, duplicity, expertise,
technique **10** adroitness, artfulness,
competency, craftiness, employment,
expertness, handicraft, occupation **11**
proficiency

craftiness 4 ruse, wile **5** guile **7** cunning, slyness **8** artifice, foxiness,
scheming, trickery, wiliness **9** chicanery **10** artfulness **11** machination

craftsman 4 hand **5** smith **6** worker,
wright **7** artisan **8** mechanic

crafty 3 sly **4** foxy, wily **5** canny,
sharp **6** artful, astute, shifty, shrewd,
tricky **7** cunning, devious **8** guileful,
plotting, scheming **9** deceitful, deceptive, designing, dishonest, underhand,

unethical **10** intriguing, perfidious,
suspicious **11** calculating

crag 3 tor **4** rock **5** bluff, cliff **9** precipice

craggy 5 rocky, rough, sheer, steep,
stony **6** abrupt, jagged, ragged, rugged, snaggy **7** scraggy **8** bouldery **9**
rockbound **10** rock-ribbed **11** precipitous

Crain, Jeanne
born: 9 Barstow CA
roles: 5 Pinky **6** Margie **9** State Fair
17 Cheaper by the Dozen **19** A Letter to Three Wives

cram 3 jam **4** fill, pack **5** crowd, force,
grind, press, stuff **7** congest, squeeze
8 compress **9** overcrowd, study hard

Cram, Ralph
architect of: 17 US Military Academy
(West Point) **29** Cathedral of Saint
John the Divine (NYC)
style: 13 Gothic Revival

crammed 4 full **6** filled, packed **7**
studied, stuffed **9** jam- packed **11**
overflowing, well-stocked

cramp 4 pang **5** block, check, crick,
limit, spasm **6** hamper, hinder, stitch,
stymie, thwart **7** prevent, seizure **8**
handicap, obstruct, restrain, restrict **9**
frustrate **12** charley horse

cramped 5 close, tight **6** narrow **7**
compact, pinched **8** confined **10** compressed, restrained, restricted

Cranach, Lucas (Lukas) (the Elder)
born: 7 Kronach, Germany
artwork: 6 Luther **10** Adam and Eve
11 Crucifixion **14** Apollo and Diana
15 Rest on the Flight **18** The Judgment of Paris **22** Duke and Duchess
of Saxony

Cranaus
king of: 6 Athens, Attica
wife: 6 Pedias
daughter: 6 Atthis, Cranae
renamed Athens: 6 Attica

cranberry 9 Vaccinium **19** Vaccinium
vitis-idaea **20** Vaccinium macrocarpon
varieties: 3 bog **4** rock, tree **5** large,
small **8** American, European, high-
bush, mountain **10** Australian

crane 4 bird, boom **5** davit, heron **7**
derrick **10** wading bird
group of: 5 sedge, siege
constellation of: 4 Grus

Crane, Bob
born: 11 Waterbury CT
roles: 12 Colonel Hogan, Hogan's Heroes

Crane, Hart
author of: 9 The Bridge **14** White
Buildings

Crane, Ichabod
character in: 23 The Legend of Sleepy
Hollow
author: 6 Irving

Crane, Roy

creator/artist of: 9 Buz Sawyer,
Wash Tubbs **11** Captain Easy

Crane, Stephen
author of: 11 The Open Boat **20** The
Red Badge of Courage **23** Maggie: A
Girl of the Streets **24** The Bride Comes to Yellow Sky

Cranford
author: 10 Mrs Gaskell

cranium 4 head **5** skull **6** noggin **8**
brain box, brainpan **9** brain case

crank 4 turn, whim **5** brace, winch
6 grouch, handle **7** fanatic **8** crotchet
9 eccentric

cranky 5 cross, testy **6** crabby, touchy
7 bearish, grouchy, peevish, waspish
8 captious, petulant **9** crotchety, irascible, splenetic **10** ill-humored, out of
sorts **11** ill-tempered **12** cantankerous

cranny 3 gap **4** nook, slit **5** break,
chink, cleft, crack, notch, split **7** crevice, fissure **8** cleavage

crash 3 din **4** bang, boom, bump, dash,
ruin **5** crack, slump, smash, wreck **6**
hurtle, invade, pileup, plunge, racket,
slip in, topple, tumble **7** bumping,
clangor, clatter, collide, crackup, decline, failure, hitting, intrude, setback,
shatter, smashup, sneak in **8** accident,
smashing, toppling, tumbling **9** collision, recession **10** bankruptcy, depression, shattering

crass 3 crude, cruel, gross **6** coarse,
oafish, vulgar **7** boorish **8** uncaring **9**
inelegant, unfeeling, unrefined **10** unpolished **11** hardhearted, insensitive
13 unsympathetic

crassness 9 crudeness, grossness, vulgarity **10** coarseness, inelegance, oafishness **11** boorishness **13** insensitivity

Cratchit, Bob
character in: 15 A Christmas Carol
author: 7 Dickens
son: 7 Tiny Tim

crate 3 box, car **4** auto, case, pack **5**
plane **6** jalopy, pallet **8** airplane **9**
container

crater 3 pit **4** hole **6** cavity **10** depression

cravat 3 tie **5** ascot, scarf, stock **7**
necktie **11** neckerchief

crave 4 need, want **5** covet **6** desire **7**
hope for, long for, pine for, require,
sigh for, wish for **8** yearn for **9** hunger for, lust after, thirst for **11** hanker
after, have a yen for **13** have a fancy
for

craven 3 low **4** base **5** timid **6** scared,
yellow **7** fearful, lowdown **8** cowardly, timorous **9** dastardly **10** frightened **11** lily-livered **12** mean-spirited
13 pusillanimous **14** chicken-hearted

craving 3 yen **4** need **6** desire, hunger,
thirst **7** longing **9** hankering

Crawford, Broderick

real name: 24 William Broderick Crawford
wife: 11 Jan Sterling
born: 14 Philadelphia PA
roles: 6 The Mob 10 The Interns 12 Of Mice and Men 13 Born Yesterday, Highway Patrol 14 All the King's Men (Oscar)

Crawford, Henry
character in: 13 Mansfield Park
author: 6 Austen

Crawford, Joan
real name: 17 Lucille Fay Le Sueur
husband: 12 Franchot Tone 18 Douglas Fairbanks Jr
daughter: 6 Cheryl 9 Christina
born: 12 San Antonio TX
biography: 13 Mommie Dearest
roles: 8 The Women 10 Grand Hotel 13 Mildred Pierce (Oscar) 26 What Ever Happened to Baby Jane

crawl 4 drag, inch, poke, worm 5 creep, mosey 6 squirm, wiggle, writhe 7 slither, wriggle

Crawley, Rawdon
character in: 10 Vanity Fair
author: 9 Thackeray

crayon 5 chalk, draft 6 pastel, pencil, sketch 7 drawing 8 charcoal

craze 3 fad 4 rage 5 furor, mania 6 dement 7 derange, passion, unhinge 11 infatuation

crazed 3 mad 6 insane 7 cracked, lunatic 8 demented, deranged

crazy 3 mad, odd 4 avid, daft, gaga, keen, nuts, wild 5 nutty, rabid, silly, weird 6 absurd, far-out, insane, stupid, unwise 7 berserk, bizarre, cracked, excited, foolish, frantic, idiotic, strange, touched, unusual, zealous 8 demented, deranged, maniacal, peculiar, uncommon, unhinged 9 fanatical, foolhardy, imprudent, laughable, senseless 10 hysterical, infatuated, outrageous, passionate, ridiculous, unbalanced 11 smitten with 12 enthusiastic, mad as a hatter 13 out of one's head 15 mad as a March hare

creak 4 rasp 5 grate, grind 6 scrape, screak, squeak 7 screech

Creakle
character in: 16 David Copperfield
author: 7 Dickens

cream 3 top 4 beat, best, drub 5 elite 6 choice, flower 7 the pick, trounce 8 greatest, off-white 14 creme de la creme

Cream, Arnold Raymond
real name of: 10 Joe Walcott

cream of the cream
French: 14 creme de la creme

Cream of the Jest, The
author: 17 James Branch Cabell

creamy 5 thick, foamy 6 smooth, yellow 8 emulsive

crease 4 fold 5 crimp, pleat, ridge 6 furrow, pucker, ruffle, rumple 7 crimple, crinkle, wrinkle 9 corrugate 11 corrugation

create 4 form, make, mold 5 cause, erect, found, set up 6 design, devise, invent 7 appoint, concoct, develop, fashion 8 conceive, contrive, organize 9 construct, establish, fabricate, formulate, institute, originate

creation 5 world 6 making, nature 8 building, devising, erection, founding 9 all things, formation, handiwork, invention 10 brainchild, conception, concoction, fashioning, production 11 development, fabrication, institution, origination 12 construction 13 establishment

Creation
author: 9 Gore Vidal

creative 8 fanciful, original 9 ingenious, inventive 11 imaginative, resourceful

creator 5 maker 6 author, father, framer 7 founder 8 begetter, designer, inventor, producer 9 architect, generator, initiator 10 originator

creature 3 man 4 bird, fish 5 beast, human 6 animal, insect, mammal, mortal, person 7 critter, reptile 9 earthling, quadruped 10 individual, vertebrate 12 invertebrate

credence 5 faith, trust 6 belief, credit 8 reliance 9 certainty, certitude 10 confidence 11 reliability 13 believability 14 acceptableness, dependableness 15 trustworthiness

credentials 6 permit 7 diploma, license, voucher 9 reference 11 certificate, testimonial 13 authorization

credenza 5 shelf, table 6 buffet 8 bookcase 9 sideboard

credible 6 likely 7 tenable 8 possible, probable, reliable 9 plausible, thinkable 10 believable, dependable, imaginable, reasonable 11 conceivable, trustworthy

credit 3 buy 4 time 5 glory, honor, trust 6 accept, assign, esteem, rely on 7 acclaim, ascribe, believe, fall for, swallow 9 allowance, attribute, recognize 10 prepayment 11 acknowledge, recognition 12 commendation 14 acknowledgment

creditable 6 worthy 8 laudable 9 admirable, estimable, reputable 11 commendable, meritorious, respectable 12 praiseworthy

credo 4 code, rule 5 maxim, motto, tenet 8 doctrine 10 philosophy

credulous 5 naive 8 gullible, trusting 9 believing 12 overtrustful, unsuspecting, unsuspicious 13 unquestioning 15 unsophisticated

Cree
language family: 9 Algonkian 10 Algonquian

tribe: 10 Plains Cree 13 Woodlands Cree
location: 6 Canada 8 Manitoba
related to: 8 Chippewa

creed 5 dogma 6 belief, canons, gospel 8 doctrine

creek 3 run 4 rill 5 brook 6 branch, spring, stream 7 freshet, rivulet 10 millstream, small river

Creek
language family: 10 Muskhogean
location: 7 Alabama, Florida, Georgia 11 Mississippi
leader: 8 Red Eagle 15 William McIntosh 20 Alexander McGillivray

Creek Mary's Blood
author: 8 Dee Brown

creep 4 inch, worm 5 crawl, sneak, steal 6 dawdle, squirm, writhe 7 slither, wriggle

creeper 3 ivy 4 bird, iron, vine, worm 5 snake 7 climber, crawler, grapnel, trailer

creepy 4 eery 5 eerie, scary 6 crawly, spooky, uneasy 12 apprehensive

cremate 4 burn, char, fire, sear 5 roast 6 ignite, kindle, scorch 8 enkindle 10 incinerate 11 conflagrate 17 consume with flames

creme de banane
type: 7 liqueur
flavor: 6 banana
color: 6 yellow

creme de cacao
type: 6 brandy 7 liqueur
origin: 6 France
flavor: 9 chocolate
color: 5 brown, white
drink: 11 Fifth Avenue
with rum: 6 Panama
with tequila: 8 Toreador
with vodka: 9 Ninotchka 11 Russian Bear 12 Velvet Hammer, White Russian

creme de cassis
type: 7 liqueur
origin: 6 France 8 Burgundy
flavor: 12 black currant
with gin: 8 Parisian

creme de fraise
type: 7 liqueur
flavor: 10 strawberry

creme de framboise
type: 7 liqueur
flavor: 9 raspberry

creme de la creme 3 top 4 best 5 cream, elite 6 choice, flower 8 choicest, very best 12 choicest part 15 cream of the cream

creme de menthe
type: 7 liqueur
flavor: 4 mint
color: 5 green, white
with brandy: 7 Stinger

with cream: 11 Grasshopper
with gin: 6 Caruso, Virgin
creme de noyau
type: 7 liqueur
flavor: 6 almond
creme de violette
type: 7 liqueur
flavor: 7 violets
color: 8 lavender
creme Yvette
type: 7 liqueur
origin: 12 United States
flavor: 7 violets
with gin: 9 Union Jack
Crenna, Richard
born: 12 Los Angeles CA
roles: 9 Death Ship 13 Our Miss Brooks, The Real McCoys
Creole 6 patois 7 criollo, dialect, Haitian 10 West Indian
Creole State
nickname of: 9 Louisiana
Creon
king of: 6 Thebes 7 Corinth
father: 9 Lycaethus, Menoeceus
sister: 7 Jocasta
daughter: 6 Creusa, Glauce
nephew: 7 Oedipus 8 Eteocles 9 Polynices
niece: 6 Ismene 8 Antigone
defeated: 18 Seven against Thebes
crescendo
music: 22 gradually getting louder
abbreviation: 5 cresc
crescent 3 arc, bow 4 arch 5 curve 8 half-moon
crescit eundo 15 it grows as it goes
motto of: 9 New Mexico
Cressida
also: 8 Criseyde 9 Crisseyde
based on characters of: 7 Bryseis 8 Chryseis
setting: 9 Trojan War
loved: 7 Troilus
deserted Troilus for: 8 Diomedes
crest 3 tip, top 4 apex, arms, comb, peak, tuft 5 crown, plume 6 emblem, height, summit 7 topknot 8 pinnacle 10 coat of arms, escutcheon
crestfallen 8 dejected, downcast 9 depressed, woebegone 10 despondent, dispirited 11 discouraged, downhearted, low-spirited 12 disappointed, disheartened
Cretaceous period
dinosaur from: 9 Euhelopus, Iguanodon 10 Allosaurus, Antrodemus 11 Anatosaurus, Ankylsaurus, Deinonychus, Gorgosaurus, Triceratops 12 Lambeosaurus, Ornithomimus 13 Albertosaurus, Corythosaurus, Hypselosaurus, Hypsilophodon, Palaeoscincus, Protoceratops, Struthiomimus, Styracosaurus, Tyrannosaurus 14 Psittacosaurus, Thescelosaurus 15 Parasaurolophus, Procheneosaurus

Cretan bull
also: 15 Marathonian bull
form: 4 bull
son: 8 Minotaur
captured on: 5 Crete
captured by: 8 Hercules
roamed: 8 Marathon
recaptured by: 7 Theseus
Cretan Mythology
goddess of fishermen/hunters/ sailors: 11 Britomartis
corresponds to Greek: 7 Artemis
goddess of the sea: 8 Dictynna
maze: 9 labyrinth
monster: 8 Minotaur
Crete
other name: 5 Kriti 6 Candia
capital/largest city: 5 Canea 8 Iraklion
others: 3 Hag 4 Lato 5 Khora, Sitia, Zakro 6 Anoyia, Candia, Khania, Lisamo, Mallia, Meleme, Retimo 7 Malerni 8 Kastelli, Nikolaos, Sphakion 9 Heraclion, Heraklion, Rethymnon, Tympakion 11 Palaiophora
government: division of: 6 Greece
monetary unit: 7 drachma
mountain: 3 Ida 5 Dikte, Phino 6 Juktas 7 Lasithi, Madaras 8 Leuka Ori, Theodore, Thriphte 9 Psiloriti
highest point: 3 Ida
sea: 5 Crete 6 Aegean 13 Mediterranean
physical feature:
bay: 4 Suda 5 Kanca 6 Kisamo, Mesara
cape: 4 Buza 5 Liano 6 Salome, Sidero, Spatha 7 Stavros 8 Lithinon, Sidheros
gulf: 6 Khania 9 Merabello
people: 7 Candiot, Cretans, Minoans 9 Caphtorim, Sphakiots 11 Philistines
artist: 7 El Greco
author: 11 Kazantzakis
conqueror: 8 Metellus
king: 5 Minos
language: 5 Greek 6 Minoan 7 Linear A, Linear B
religion: 14 Greek Orthodoxy
place:
ruins: 15 Palace at Knossos
Creusa
also: 6 Glauce
father: 5 Creon, Priam 8 Cychreus 10 Erechtheus
mother: 6 Hecuba
husband: 6 Aeneas 7 Telamon
son: 3 Ion 8 Ascanius
bride of: 5 Jason
killed by: 5 magic, Medea
crevasse 3 gap 4 rift 5 abyss, break, chasm, cleft, gorge, gulch, gully, split 6 breach, divide 7 fissure
crevice 4 rent, rift, slit 5 chasm, cleft, crack, split 6 breach 7 fissure 8 crevasse, fracture
crew 3 men, mob 4 band, body, herd,

mass, pack, team 5 corps, force, group, hands, horde, party, squad, troop 6 seamen, throng 7 company, haircut, sailors 8 mariners 9 multitude, seafarers 10 assemblage, complement
crib 3 bed, bin, cot, hut, key 4 pony, trot 5 cheat, shack, stall, steal 6 creche, manger 7 purloin 8 bassinet 10 plagiarize
cribbage
scorer: 3 peg
score kept on: 5 board
points/game: 8 sixty-one
third hand: 4 crib
jack: 7 his nobs
Crich, Gerald
character in: 11 Women in Love
author: 8 Lawrence
Crichton, Michael
author of: 5 Congo 6 Sphere 8 Airframe 9 Rising Sun 10 Disclosure 12 Jurassic Park 14 The Terminal Man 15 Eaters of the Dead 18 The Andromeda Strain 20 The Great Train Robbery
cricket
players/team: 6 eleven
equipment: 3 bat 4 bail, ball 5 stump 6 wicket
position: 5 gully, mid on, slops 6 bowler, long on, mid off 7 batsman, fine leg, long off 8 third man 9 mid wicket, square leg 10 cover point, extra cover, silly mid on 11 silly mid off 12 wicket keeper 13 deep mid wicket 16 backward short leg
lines: 7 creases
period of play: 4 over 7 innings
championship game: 9 test match
England/Australia match: 8 the Ashes
cricket
variety: 4 bush, cave, fair, sand, tree 5 camel, field, house 6 ground 9 Jerusalem, pygmy mole
Cries and Whispers
director: 12 Ingmar Bergman
cast: 10 Liv Ullmann 12 Ingrid Thulin 16 Harriet Andersson
crime 3 sin 4 tort 5 wrong 6 felony 7 misdeed, offense, outrage 8 foul play, iniquity, villainy 10 misconduct, wrongdoing 11 abomination, lawbreaking, malfeasance, misdemeanor 13 transgression
Crime and Punishment
author: 16 Fyodor Dostoevsky
character: 5 Sonya 6 Dounia 7 Porfiry 9 Razumihin 11 Raskolnikov
criminal 4 hood 5 crook, felon, wrong 6 guilty, outlaw 7 crooked, culprit, illegal, illicit, lawless 8 culpable, offender, unlawful, wasteful 9 felonious, senseless, wrongdoer 10 abominable, delinquent, indictable, lawbreaker, malefactor, outrageous,

villainous **11** blameworthy, disgraceful, lawbreaking **12** transgressor

crimp 4 curl, fold, kink, wave **5** clamp, flute, frill, frizz **7** crinkle, frizzle, wrinkle **8** obstacle

crimple 4 curl **6** pucker **7** crinkle, crumple, wrinkle **9** corrugate

crimson 3 red **4** ruby **5** blush, flush **6** redden **7** carmine, scarlet

cringe 4 duck **5** cower, dodge, quail, toady **6** blench, flinch, grovel, recoil, shrink **7** truckle

cringing 6 abject **7** fawning, ignoble, servile, wincing **8** cowering, toadying **9** flinching, groveling, shrinking, sniveling

crinkle 5 crush **6** rumple, rustle **7** crumple, wrinkle

crinkly 4 wavy **5** curly, kinky **6** crimpy, frizzy **7** cockled, crimped, crimply, puckery, ruffled, rumpled, twisted, wrinkly **8** crimpled, frizzled, puckered, wrinkled **9** shriveled

crinoline 4 hoop **5** skirt **9** hoopskirt, petticoat **10** underskirt

cripple 4 gimp, halt, harm, maim, stop **6** damage, impair **7** disable **8** make lame, paralyze **9** hamstring **10** debilitate, inactivate **12** incapacitate

crisis 6 climax **9** emergency

crisp 5 brisk, fresh, nippy, sharp, terse, witty **6** candid, chilly, crispy, lively, snappy **7** bracing, brittle, crunchy, pointed **8** incisive **9** energetic, sparkling, vivacious **10** potato chip, refreshing **12** invigorating

crisscross 4 awry **5** cross **8** confused, traverse

Crisseyde *see* **8** Cressida

Cristillo, Louis Francis
real name of: **11** Lou Costello

criterion 3 law **4** norm, rule **5** gauge, model **7** example, measure **8** standard **9** guidepost, precedent, principle, yardstick **10** touchstone

critic 5 judge, mavin, scold **6** carper, censor, expert, rapper **7** analyst, arbiter, knocker, reviler **8** attacker, reviewer, vilifier, virtuoso **9** authority, backbiter, detractor, evaluator **10** antagonist, criticizer **11** cognoscente, commentator, connoisseur, faultfinder

critical 5 fussy, grave, hairy, picky, risky, vital **6** urgent **7** carping, crucial, finicky, judging, nagging, serious **8** caviling, decisive, perilous, pressing **9** dangerous, harrowing, hazardous, judicious, momentous, sensitive **10** analytical, censorious, derogatory, diagnostic, nitpicking, precarious **11** disparaging **12** disapproving, faultfinding

critical situation 3 jam **4** mess **6** crisis, pickle **7** straits, trouble **8** hot water **9** deep water **10** difficulty **11** predicament

critical stage 5 H-hour **6** climax, crisis **9** emergency

critical success
French: **13** succes d'estime

criticism 4 fire, flak, slam **5** blame, knock **6** review **7** censure, comment **8** analysis, critique, judgment **9** aspersion, stricture **10** commentary, evaluation **12** faultfinding

criticize 4 carp, fuss, pick **5** cavil, nag at **7** censure, nitpick, reprove **8** denounce, reproach **9** disparage

critique 6 review **8** analysis

Crna Gora *see* **10** Montenegro

croak 3 caw, die **4** kill, moan, roup **7** grumble, kick off **8** complain, harsh cry **13** kick the bucket

Croatia
capital/largest city: **5** Zagreb
others: **4** Knin **5** Split, Zadar **6** Osijek, Rijeka (Fiume) **7** Vukovar, Sibenik **8** Karlovac, Varazdin, Vinkovci **9** Dubrovnik **10** Kostajnica
head of state: **9** president
government: **9** democracy
monetary unit: **5** dinar
mountain: **10** Julian Alps **11** Styrian Alps
sea: **8** Adriatic
people: **5** Serbs **6** Croats **7** Muslims **9** Yugoslavs
language: **8** Croatian **10** Serbo Croat
religion: **17** Catholic Christian, Orthodox Christian

Crocetti, Dino Paul
real name of: **10** Dean Martin

crock 3 jar, pot **4** olla **9** container

crockery 5 china **6** dishes, plates **7** pottery **8** clayware **9** chinaware, tableware **11** ceramic ware, earthenware **14** cups and saucers

Crock of Gold
author: **13** James Stephens

crocodile 4 croc **6** cayman, gavial, lizard **7** reptile, asurian

crocus
varieties: **4** fall, wild **5** dutch **6** autumn, scotch **7** Chilean, saffron **8** tropical **9** celandine **12** iris-flowered

Crome Yellow
author: **12** Aldous Huxley

Crommyonian sow
also: **5** Phaea
killed by: **7** Theseus

Cromwell, Oliver
also: **13** Lord Protector
served in: **15** English Civil War
fought against: **8** Charles I **9** Cavaliers
fought for: **10** Parliament, Roundheads
regiment: **9** Ironsides
battle: **6** Naseby, Oxford **7** Preston **11** Marston Moor

crone 3 hag **5** witch **6** beldam **7** beldame, old wife

Cronus
also: **6** Cronos, Kronos
form: **5** Titan
father: **6** Uranus
mother: **4** Gaea
sister: **4** Rhea
wife: **4** Rhea
son: **4** Zeus **5** Hades **8** Poseidon
daughter: **4** Hera **6** Hestia **7** Demeter
corresponds to: **6** Saturn

crony 3 pal **4** ally, chum, mate **5** buddy **6** bunkie, cohort, friend **7** comrade **8** bunkmate, intimate, shipmate, sidekick **9** accessory, associate, companion, old friend **10** accomplice, bosom buddy **11** confederate **12** acquaintance, collaborator **13** coconspirator

Cronyn, Hume
wife: **12** Jessica Tandy
born: **6** London **7** Canada, Ontario
roles: **13** The Fourposter **17** Phantom of the Opera **19** Sunrise at Campobello

crook 3 arc, bow **4** bend, hook, thug, turn **5** angle, cheat, curve, knave, thief, twist **6** bandit, outlaw, robber **7** burglar **8** criminal, swindler **9** curvature, embezzler

crooked 4 awry, bent, wily **5** askew, bowed, shady **6** crafty, curved, hooked, shifty, sneaky, spiral, warped, zigzag **7** corrupt, sinuous, twisted, winding **8** criminal, deformed, tortuous, twisting, unlawful **9** deceitful, deceptive, dishonest, distorted, nefarious, unethical **10** fraudulent, meandering, perfidious, serpentine **11** underhanded **12** dishonorable, unscrupulous

crookedness 10 dishonesty **11** deviousness **13** deceitfulness, double-dealing

Crookes, William
nationality: **7** British
invented: **8** thallium **10** radiometer **11** Crookes tube

croon 3 hum **4** sing **6** murmur, warble

crop 3 bob, cut, lop **4** clip, snip, trim **5** prune, shear, yield **6** growth **7** harvest, reaping **8** cut short, gleaning **9** gathering **10** production

crop-raising 7 farming, tillage **11** agriculture **12** agribusiness, truck farming **15** market gardening

crop up 5 arise, ensue, occur **6** appear **7** develop, surface **11** come to light

croquet
equipment: **4** ball, hoop **6** mallet, wicket
variation: **5** roque
term: **5** rover
site: **4** lawn

Crosby, Bing
real name: **17** Harry Lillis Crosby
partner: **7** Bob Hope **10** Hedy Lamarr **13** Dorothy Lamour

nickname: 8 Der Bingle
wife: 8 Dixie Lee **12** Kathryn Grant
born: 8 Tacoma WA
roles: 10 Going My Way (Oscar), Holiday Inn **11** High Society **14** The Country Girl, White Christmas **17** The Bells of St Mary's **22** Christmas in Connecticut
    Road to: 3 Rio **4** Bali **7** Morocco **8** Hong Kong, Zanzibar **9** Singapore

cross 3 mad, mix, tau **4** crux, ford, meet, rood **5** angry, blend, erase, gruff, surly, testy, trial **6** burden, cancel, cranky, delete, go over, hybrid, ordeal, shirty, touchy **7** amalgam, annoyed, athwart, grouchy, oblique, peevish, trouble, waspish **8** captious, choleric, churlish, contrary, crucifix, distress, intermix, pass over, petulant, snappish, traverse **9** adversity, crotchety, half-breed, hybridize, intersect, irascible, irritable, querulous, splenetic, strike out, suffering **10** affliction, difficulty, ill-humored, interbreed, misfortune, obliterate, out of sorts, transverse **11** combination, ill-tempered, intractable, tribulation **12** cantankerous, disagreeable, intersecting

crossbar 3 bar **4** spar **5** sprit **6** stripe
crossbreed 3 mix **8** intermix **9** hybridize **10** interbreed
cross-fertilize 9 hybridize
crossing 4 pass **7** mixture, passage **8** blocking, opposing, traverse **9** thwarting **10** traversing **11** hybridizing, intersection **13** hybridization
cross over 4 span **5** cross **6** bridge **8** traverse
crosspiece 3 bar **4** spar **5** sprit
cross-pollinate 9 hybridize
crossroad 12 intersection, turning point
cross swords 5 clash, fight **6** battle, combat, tussle **7** contend, contest **8** skirmish
crossways 7 athwart **12** transversely
crosswise 6 across **7** athwart **8** sideways, traverse **10** transverse
crotchet 3 tat **4** bent, whim **5** habit, quirk, trait **6** foible, hang-up, oddity, vagary, whimsy **7** caprice **8** quiddity **9** mannerism **10** erraticism **11** peculiarity **12** eccentricity, idiosyncrasy, irregularity **14** characteristic
crotchety 3 odd **5** fussy **6** cranky **7** erratic, grouchy **8** contrary, peculiar **9** eccentric
crouch 4 bend, duck **5** cower, squat, stoop **6** cringe, recoil, shrink **9** hunch over **10** hunker down **11** scrooch down, scrunch down
crow 3 daw, jay, kae **4** blow, brag, rook **5** boast, crake, exult, gloat, raven, strut, vaunt **6** cackle, chough, corbie, magpie **7** corvine, jackdaw,

rejoice, swagger, triumph, trumpet **8** jubilate **14** cock-a-doodle-doo
group of: 6 murder
Crow
  constellation of: 6 Corvus
Crow
  language family: 6 Siouan
  tribe: 9 River Crow **12** Mountain Crow
  location: 7 Montana, Wyoming
  related to: 7 Hidatsa
crowbar 3 bar, pry **5** jimmy, lever
crowd 3 jam, mob, set **4** cram, gang, herd, host, mass, push **5** crush, flock, group, horde, press, shove, surge, swarm **6** circle, claque, clique, gather, huddle, legion, throng **7** cluster, coterie, elbow in, squeeze **8** assemble **9** gathering, multitude **10** assemblage, congregate **11** concentrate **12** congregation
Crowd, The
  director: 9 King Vidor
  cast: 9 Bert Roach **11** James Murray **15** Eleanor Boardman
crowded 4 full **6** filled, jammed, mobbed, packed **7** crammed, teeming **8** swarming, thronged **9** congested, jampacked **11** overflowing
crowd out 8 displace **9** overwhelm
crown 3 cap, top **4** acme, apex, head, pate, peak **5** crest, tiara **6** climax, diadem, noggin, noodle, summit, top off, wreath, zenith **7** chaplet, circlet, coronet, fulfill, garland, perfect, royalty **8** complete, monarchy, pinnacle, round out **11** sovereignty
Crowne, Lenina
  character in: 13 Brave New World
  author: 6 Huxley
crowning point 3 cap, tip **4** apex, peak **6** summit, vertex, zenith **8** pinnacle
crown of thorns 4 bane **5** cross **6** burden, ordeal **7** torment **8** vexation **10** affliction **11** tribulation
crow over 5 gloat **9** brag about **10** boast about
crucial 5 grave **6** knotty, urgent **7** serious, weighty **8** critical, decisive, pressing **9** essential, important, momentous **11** determining, significant
Crucible, The
  author: 12 Arthur Miller
crude 3 raw **5** crass, gross, rough **6** coarse, vulgar **7** obscene, sketchy, uncouth **9** imperfect, tasteless, unrefined **10** incomplete, unfinished, unpolished, unprepared **11** uncompleted, undeveloped, unprocessed
crudeness 7 rawness **8** bad taste **9** crassness, grossness, obscenity, vulgarity **10** coarseness, indelicacy **13** tastelessness
cruel 6 brutal, savage **7** inhuman, vicious **8** inhumane, pitiless, ruthless,

sadistic **9** heartless, merciless, unfeeling **10** unmerciful **11** cold-blooded, hardhearted, remorseless **15** uncompassionate
cruelty 6 sadism **8** ferocity, savagery **9** barbarity, brutality **10** bestiality, inhumanity **11** viciousness **12** ruthlessness **13** heartlessness
cruet 3 jar, jug **6** bottle **7** urceole **9** dispenser
cruise 4 sail, scud, skim **5** coast, drift, float, glide, sweep **6** stream, voyage **7** seafare **8** navigate
Cruise, Tom
  original name: 21 Thomas Cruise Maypother
  born: 10 Syracuse NY
  wife: 10 Mimi Rogers **12** Nicole Kidman
  films: 4 Taps **6** Top Gun **7** The Firm, Rain Man **8** Cocktail **10** Far and Away **11** Endless Love, A Few Good Men **12** Jerry Maguire, The Outsiders **13** Days of Thunder, Risky Business **15** The Color of Money **16** All the Right Moves **17** Mission Impossible **21** Born on the Fourth of July, Interview with a Vampire
crumb 3 bit, ort **5** grain, scrap, shred, speck **6** morsel, sliver **8** fragment, particle
crumble 5 crush, decay, grate, grind **6** powder **8** fragment, splinter **9** decompose, pulverize **12** disintegrate
crumbly 7 brittle, friable **9** breakable
Crummles, Vincent
  character in: 16 Nicholas Nickleby
  author: 7 Dickens
crummy 5 awful, lousy **6** rotten **8** terrible
crumple 4 fall **5** crush **6** cave in, crease, pucker, rumple **7** crimple, crinkle, wrinkle **8** collapse **9** corrugate
crunch 4 chew, gnaw **5** chomp, gnash, grind, munch **7** squeeze **8** showdown **9** masticate
Cruncher, Jerry
  character in: 16 A Tale of Two Cities
  author: 7 Dickens
crunchy 3 dry **5** crisp **6** crispy **7** crackly
crusade 5 drive, rally **8** campaign, movement
Crusader 6 knight, zealot **7** pilgrim, Templar **8** champion **11** Hospitaller
Crusades
  time: 10 Middle Ages
  cry: 8 deus vult
  foe: 4 turk **7** infidel, Saladin, saracen
  leader: 7 Tancred
  port: 4 Acre
crush 4 mash **5** break, press, quash, quell, smash **6** enfold, quench, squash, subdue **7** crumble, crumple, embrace, put down, shatter, squeeze, squelch **8** compress, overcome, sup-

press **9** granulate, overpower, overwhelm, pulverize **10** extinguish

crushed 3 sad **5** cowed **6** broken, mashed, woeful **7** abashed, doleful, forlorn, pressed, put down, quashed, quelled, smashed, subdued **8** crumbled, crumpled, dejected, desolate, overcame, overcome, quenched, squashed, squeezed, wretched **9** flattened, miserable, squelched, woebegone **10** compressed, despondent, pulverized, suppressed **11** overpowered, overwhelmed **12** disconsolate, extinguished, inconsolable **13** brokenhearted

crushing 7 mashing **8** decisive, quelling, smashing **10** shattering **11** humiliating, putting down, stamping out, suppression **12** obliterating, overwhelming **13** pulverization

crust 4 coat, gall, hull, rind, scab **5** brass, nerve, shell **6** harden **7** coating **8** chutzpah, covering, pie shell **9** impudence **11** pastry shell

crustacean 4 crab, flea **5** louse, prawn **6** isopod, shrimp **7** lobster **8** barnacle, crawfish, crayfish **9** shellfish, water flea

crusty 4 curt **5** blunt, gruff, rough, short, stern, surly, testy **6** abrupt, crabby, cranky, shirty, snippy, sullen **7** brusque, peevish, waspish **8** choleric, snappish, snippety **9** irascible, splenetic **10** ill-natured **11** ill-tempered **13** short-tempered

crux 3 nub **4** core, gist **5** basis, heart **7** essence **9** essential **10** brass tacks **11** nitty-gritty

cry 3 beg, sob, sue **4** bawl, call, hawk, howl, keen, moan, plea, roar, wail, weep, yell, yelp **5** blare, cheer, groan, mourn, plead, shout, utter, whoop **6** appeal, bellow, blazon, boohoo, clamor, hurrah, huzzah, lament, outcry, prayer, scream, shriek, snivel **7** blubber, call out, exclaim, implore, request, screech, trumpet, whimper **8** entreaty, petition, proclaim **9** advertise, importune **10** adjuration, promulgate **11** exclamation **12** solicitation, supplication

Cry, the Beloved Country
  author: 9 Alan Paton
  locale: 11 South Africa

cry out 4 bark, bawl, call, howl, roar, yell **5** shout **6** bellow, clamor, holler **7** exclaim **8** proclaim **9** ejaculate

cry over 5 mourn **6** bemoan, bewail, lament

crypt 4 tomb **5** vault **8** catacomb **9** mausoleum, sepulcher

cryptic 4 dark **5** vague **6** arcane, hidden, occult, secret **7** obscure, strange **8** esoteric, mystical, puzzling **9** ambiguous **10** cabalistic, mysterious, perplexing **11** enigmatical

cryptogram 4 code **6** cipher

cryptograph 4 code **6** cipher, encode

crystal 3 ice **5** clear, flake, glass, lucid **6** quartz **7** diamond **8** stemware **9** glassware, snowflake, watch part **10** rhinestone **11** transparent

crystallize 3 fix, gel **4** firm, jell **5** candy **6** harden **8** solidify **9** granulate

Csonka, Larry (Lawrence Richard)
  nickname: 9 Lawnmower
  sport: 8 football
  position: 8 fullback
  team: 13 Miami Dolphins, New York Giants

cub 3 boy, pup **4** bear, lion **5** scout, whelp **6** novice **8** reporter **9** youngling, youngster **10** apprentice

Cuba
  other name: 18 pearl of the Antilles
  capital/largest city: 6 Havana **8** Le Habana
  others: 5 Bauta, Colon, Duabi, Guane, Manes **6** Baines, Bayamo, Gibara, Guines, Mayari **7** Antilla, Baracoa, Fomento, Holguin, Holquin, Jiguani, Niquero, Palmira, Sanhuis **8** Artemisa, Camaguey, Cardenas, Guaimaro, Guayabal, Marianao, Matanzas, Nuevitas, Varadero, Yaguajay **9** Cabaiguan, Camajuani, Cienfuego **10** Cienfuegos, Guanabacoa, Guantanamo, Manzanillo, Santa Clara **11** Campechuela, Pinar del Rio, Puerto Padre **12** Ciego de Avila **13** Sagua de Tanamo **14** Sancti Spiritus, Santiago de Cuba **17** Aguada de Pasajeros, Consolacion del Sur
  measure: 4 vara **5** bocoy, cocoy, tarea **6** cordel, fanega **10** caballeria
  monetary unit: 4 peso **7** centavo **8** cuarenta
  weight: 5 libra **6** tercio
  island: 5 Pines, Pinos **6** Sabana **8** Camaguey, Juventud **9** Canarreos **17** Jardines de la Reina
    cay: 4 Coco **5** Largo **6** Romano **7** Guajaba, Rosareo, Sabinal **8** Cantiles **9** San Felipe **10** Santa Maria
  mountain: 6 Copper **7** Cristal, Maestra, Organos **8** Camaguey, Trinidad **9** Las Villas **11** Pinar del rio **12** Guaniguanico **14** Sancti-Spiritus
  highest point: 8 Turquino
  river: 4 Zaza **5** Cauto **8** San Pedro
  sea: 8 Atlantic **9** Caribbean
  physical feature:
    bay: 4 Nipe, Pigs **6** Jiguey **8** Cochinos **10** Buena Vista, Guantznamo
    cape: 4 Cruz **5** Maisi **8** Lucrecia **10** Corrientes, San Antonio
    channel: 8 Nicholas **9** Old Bahama
    falls: 3 Toa **7** Agabama, Caburni
    gulf: 6 Mexico **7** Cazones **8** Anamaria, Batabano **12** Guancanayabo
    inlet: 4 Broa **10** Corrientes
    peninsula: 6 Zapata
    point: 7 Guarico
    swamp: 6 Zapata

  people: 5 Carib, Negro, Taino, white **6** Arawak **7** Ciboney, mestizo **8** Ciboneye
    conqueror: 9 Velazquez
    explorer: 8 Columbus
    leader: 6 Castro **7** Batista **10** Che Guevara
  language: 7 Spanish
  religion: 13 Roman Catholic
    cult: 6 Chango, Yemaya
  places:
    castle: 5 Morro
    cathedral: 8 Santiago
  feature:
    dance: 5 conga, rumba **6** danzon, rhumba **8** guaracha, pachanga
    harvest: 5 zafra
    peasant: 7 guajiro
    tree: 5 jique, jiqui
    witch doctor: 7 nanigos
  food:
    dish: 6 paella
    drink: 4 pina

cubbyhole 4 nook **5** niche **6** cranny **10** pigeonhole **11** compartment

cube of deep-fried pork
  American Spanish: 10 cuchifrito

cubic centimeter
  abbreviation: 4 cu cm

cubic dekameter
  abbreviation: 5 cu dkm

cubic foot
  abbreviation: 4 cu ft

cubic inch
  abbreviation: 4 cu in

cubicle 3 bay **4** cell, nook **5** booth, niche **6** alcove, carrel, recess

cubic meter
  abbreviation: 3 cu m

cubic millimeter
  abbreviation: 4 cu mm

cubic yard
  abbreviation: 4 cu yd

cubit 15 Biblical measure

cuchifrito 19 cube of deep-fried pork

Cuchulainn
  origin: 5 Irish
  hero of: 6 Ulster
  uncle: 9 Conchobar
  guarded house of: 10 Smith Culan
  killed by: 6 Lugaid

cuckoo 3 ani **4** bats, bird, fool, gaga, nuts **5** balmy, batty, crazy, daffy, dotty, goofy, loony, nutty, silly, wacky **6** screwy **7** idiotic **9** screwball **12** crackbrained **13** off one's rocker **14** off one's trolley

cucumber 14 Cucumis sativus
  varieties: 3 bur **4** mock, star, wild **6** bitter, pickle **7** prickly, serpent **9** squirting **13** African horned

cuddle 3 hug, pet **5** clasp **6** caress, curl up, fondle, huddle, nestle, nuzzle **7** cling to, embrace, lie snug, snuggle

Cuddly Dudley
  nickname of: 11 Dudley Moore

cudgel 4 club **5** baton, staff, stick **8** bludgeon **9** billy club, blackjack, truncheon **10** shillelagh **12** quarterstaff

cue 3 key, tip **4** clue, hint, sign **6** signal **7** inkling **10** intimation, suggestion **11** insinuation

cuff 3 box, hit, rap **4** blow **5** clout, smack, thump, whack **6** thwack, wallop

cui bono 10 for what use, of what good **15** for whose benefit

cuisine 4 fare, food, menu **5** table **6** viands **7** cookery, cooking, edibles **8** victuals, vittles **11** comestibles

Cukor, George
  director of: 7 Camille **8** Adam's Rib, Gaslight, The Women **10** My Fair Lady (Oscar) **11** A Double Life, A Star Is Born, Little Women **13** Born Yesterday, Dinner at Eight **14** Romeo and Juliet **16** David Copperfield **18** A Bill of Divorcement **20** The Philadelphia Story

cul-de-sac 6 pocket **7** dead-end, impasse **10** blind alley

cull 4 junk, pick, sift, take **5** dross, glean, scrap, trash, waste **6** choose, divide, garner, gather, jetsam, reject, second, select, winnow **7** castoff, collect, discard, excerpt, extract, leaving **8** abstract, scouring, separate **9** segregate

culminate 3 cap, end, top **5** crown, end up **6** climax, finish, result, top off, wind up **8** complete, conclude **9** terminate **10** consummate

culmination 4 acme, apex, peak **6** apogee, climax, height, zenith **7** epitome **8** pinnacle **10** conclusion **11** fulfillment, realization **12** consummation

Culp, Robert
  born: 10 Berkeley CA
  roles: 4 I Spy **20** Greatest American Hero

culpability 4 onus **5** blame, fault, guilt **9** liability **14** accountability, responsibility

culpable 6 guilty, liable **7** at fault, to blame **8** blamable **10** censurable **11** blameworthy

culprit 5 felon **6** sinner **8** criminal, evildoer, offender **9** miscreant, wrongdoer **10** lawbreaker, malefactor **12** transgressor

cult 4 sect **7** faction, zealots **8** admirers, devotees, devotion **9** disciples, followers **10** admiration

cultivable 6 arable **7** fertile, friable **8** farmable, plowable, tillable

cultivate 3 dig, hoe, sow **4** farm, grow, plow, seek, till, weed **5** court, plant, spade **6** enrich, garden **7** acquire, advance, develop, elevate, enhance, improve

cultivated 3 dug **4** fine, grew, hoed **6** farmed, forked, sought, spaded, tilled,

weeded **7** courted, planted **8** advanced, cultured, elevated, enhanced, enriched, finished, improved, polished **9** developed

cultivation 5 grace **6** polish, sowing **7** farming, manners, tilling **8** agronomy, planting **9** elevation, gardening, gentility, good taste, husbandry **10** refinement **11** agriculture

culture 3 art **5** music **7** the arts **8** learning **9** erudition, knowledge **10** enrichment, literature, refinement **12** civilization **13** enlightenment **15** accomplishments

Culture and Anarchy
  author: 13 Matthew Arnold

cultured 7 elegant, erudite, genteel, learned, refined **8** polished, well-bred, well-read **11** enlightened **12** accomplished, well-educated **13** sophisticated

culture medium 4 agar **8** agar-agar

culvert 5 ditch, drain, sewer **6** trench **7** channel, conduit, fox-hole

cumbersome 5 bulky, hefty **6** clumsy **7** awkward **8** cumbrous, ungainly, unwieldy **9** ponderous **12** unmanageable

cum grano salis 15 not too seriously **16** with a grain of salt

cumin
  botanical name: 14 Cuminum cyminum
  other name: 6 comino, jiraka, kummel
  origin: 5 Egypt
  family: 7 parsley
  symbol of: 5 greed
  guards against straying: 7 pigeons **8** chickens, husbands
  use: 4 fish, meat, rice, soup, stew **5** bread, curry **6** cheese **7** pickles, sausage **8** potatoes **11** chili powder

cum laude 10 with praise

Cummings, E. E. (Edward Estlin)
  author of: 12 in just spring **15** The Enormous Room **17** Tulips and Chimneys **18** Chansons Innocentes

Cummings, Robert
  real name: 29 Clarence Robert Orville Cummings
  born: 8 Joplin MO
  roles: 8 King's Row **14** Dial M for Murder **18** The Bob Cummings Show

cumulate 5 amass **6** gather, heap up, pile up **10** accumulate

cumulative 7 amassed, piled up **8** additive, heaped up **9** aggregate **10** collective **12** accumulative, conglomerate

Cunegonde
  character in: 7 Candide
  author: 8 Voltaire

cunning 3 art, sly **4** foxy, wily **5** canny, craft, guile, knack, skill **6** artful, crafty, deceit, genius, shifty, shrewd, talent, tricky **7** ability, devious, finesse, slyness **8** aptitude, arti-

fice, deftness, foxiness, guileful, subtlety, trickery, wiliness **9** chicanery, deceitful, deception, deceptive, dexterity, duplicity, ingenious, underhand **10** adroitness, artfulness, cleverness, craftiness, expertness, shrewdness **11** deviousness **13** Machiavellian
  god of: 6 Hermes

Cunning Little Vixen, The
  opera by: 7 Janacek

cup 3 cup **5** glass, grail, stein **6** beaker, goblet, vessel **7** chalice, tankard **8** half pint, schooner
  abbreviation: 1 c

Cup
  constellation of: 6 Crater

cupbearer of gods 8 Ganymede

cupboard 6 buffet, bureau, closet **7** armoire, cabinet **9** sideboard, storeroom **10** chiffonier **11** china closet **12** clothespress

Cupid 6 cherub
  also: 4 Amor
  origin: 5 Roman
  god of: 4 love
  mother: 5 Venus
  corresponds to: 4 Eros
  features: 3 bow **5** arrow, wings

cupidity 5 greed **7** avarice, avidity **8** rapacity **10** greediness **11** selfishness **12** covetousness, graspingness **13** concupiscence, insatiability, rapaciousness **14** avariciousness **15** acquisitiveness

cupola 4 dome, roof **5** tower, vault **6** belfry, turret **7** ceiling

cur 3 cad **4** mutt **5** rogue **6** rascal, varlet, wretch **7** mongrel, varmint, villain **9** scoundrel **10** blackguard

curacao
  type: 7 liqueur
  origin: 19 Netherlands Antilles
  flavor: 6 orange
  with gin: 8 Blue Moon, Napoleon **9** Blue Devil **14** Flying Dutchman
  with rum: 6 Mai-Tai **8** Blue Lady **12** Blue Hawaiian
  with vodka: 8 Aqueduct

curate 5 vicar **6** cleric, deacon, parson, pastor, priest, rector **8** minister, preacher **9** churchman, clergyman **12** ecclesiastic

curative 4 balm **7** healing **11** restorative

curator 5 doyen **6** keeper **7** steward **8** director, overseer **9** caretaker, custodian

curb 3 rim **4** edge, rein **5** brink, check, ledge, limit **6** border, bridle, halter, retard, slow up **7** control, harness, inhibit, repress, slacken **8** hold back, moderate, restrain, restrict, slow down, suppress **9** curbstone, hindrance, restraint **10** decelerate, limitation **11** restriction, retardation

curdle 3 rot **4** clot, curd, sour, turn **5** decay, go bad, go off, spoil **7** clabber, congeal, ferment, putrefy, thicken **8** putresce, solidify **9** coagulate **11** deteriorate

cure 3 dry **4** heal, salt **5** smoke **6** remedy **8** antidote, make well, preserve **10** corrective

cure-all 4 balm **6** elixir, remedy **7** panacea **10** catholicon

cured 5 dried **6** healed, mended, smoked **8** made well, remedied **9** preserved, recovered

Curie, Marie Sklodowska and Pierre
field: 7 physics **9** chemistry
discovered: 6 radium **8** polonium **13** radioactivity
awarded: 10 Nobel Prize
daughter: 5 Marie (Joliot-Curie, Nobelist)

curio 7 bibelot, trinket **9** bric-a-brac, objet d'art

curiosity 5 freak, sight **6** marvel, oddity, prying, rarity, wonder **7** novelty **8** interest, nosiness **10** phenomenon, rare object **11** questioning **15** inquisitiveness

curious 3 odd **4** nosy, rare **5** funny, novel, queer, weird **6** prying, quaint, unique **7** bizarre, strange, unusual **8** peculiar, singular, snooping, uncommon **9** inquiring, searching **11** inquisitive, questioning

curl 4 coil, lock, wave, wind **5** crimp, frizz, swirl, twirl, twist **6** spiral **7** frizzle, ringlet, scallop **8** curlicue **9** corkscrew

curled 3 set **5** kinky, waved, wound **6** coiled, frizzy, permed, spiral **7** crimped, frizzed, twisted **8** crinkled, scrolled **9** curlicued

curlicue 4 coil **5** twist **6** spiral **8** flourish

curly 4 wavy **5** kinky **6** frizzy **7** rippled **8** crinkled **9** ringleted

curmudgeon 4 crab **5** crank, grump **6** grouch **8** grumbler, sourball

currant 5 Ribes
varieties: 3 red **5** black, fetid, skunk, squaw, stink **6** alpine, cherry, common, garden, Indian, Sierra **7** Buffalo **8** Missouri, mountain, swamp red **9** chaparral, wild black **11** northern red **12** bristly black **13** American black, European black, northern black, white-flowered **15** California black

currency 4 cash, coin **5** bills, money, vogue **6** specie **7** coinage **9** bank notes **10** acceptance, popularity, prevalence **12** predominance, universality

current 3 now **4** flow, flux, mood, tide **5** draft, drift, trend **6** modern, spirit, stream, with-it **7** feeling, in style, in vogue, popular, present **8** existing, tendency, up-to-date **9** prevalent, zeitgeist **10** atmosphere, present-day, pre-

vailing **11** inclination **12** contemporary, undercurrent

current of air 4 wind **5** draft **6** breeze, zephyr

curricle 3 gig **4** cart, trap **6** chaise **8** carriage

curry powder
origin: 5 India
ingredient: 5 cumin **6** cloves **8** capsicum, turmeric **9** coriander, fenugreek, red pepper **13** cayenne pepper
use: 5 kebab, kebob, kofta, malai **6** kormas **7** curries **8** meat loaf, vindaloo, zucchini **11** potato salad

curse 3 vex **4** bane, cuss, damn, oath **5** blast, cross, swear, trial **6** burden, ordeal, plague, whammy **7** afflict, condemn, evil eye, scourge, swear at, torment, trouble **8** anathema, denounce, execrate, swearing, vexation **9** annoyance, blasphemy, damnation, evil spell, expletive, obscenity, profanity **10** affliction, execration, misfortune **11** imprecation, malediction, tribulation **12** anathematize, denunciation

cursory 5 brief, hasty, quick, swift **6** casual, random **7** hurried, offhand, passing **8** careless **9** desultory, haphazard **11** inattentive, perfunctory, superficial

curt 4 rude **5** bluff, blunt, gruff, short, terse **6** abrupt, crusty, snappy **7** brusque, summary **8** petulant **10** peremptory

curtail 3 cut **4** clip, trim **6** reduce **7** abridge, shorten **8** condense, contract, cut short, decrease, diminish, pare down **10** abbreviate

curtailed 3 cut **7** checked, concise, cut back, reduced, slashed **8** abridged, cut short **9** shortened **10** retrenched

curtailment 7 cutback, cutting, halting, pruning **8** clipping, decrease, trimming **9** lessening, reduction, restraint **10** limitation, shortening **11** abridgement, contraction **12** abbreviation, condensation

curtain 3 end **4** mask, veil **5** blind, cover, drape, shade, sheet **6** screen, shroud **7** conceal, drapery, hanging **8** portiere

Curtis, Tony
real name: 15 Bernard Schwartz
wife: 10 Janet Leigh
daughter: 8 Jamie Lee
born: 9 New York NY
roles: 7 Houdini, Trapeze **12** The Great Race **13** Some Like It Hot **14** The Defiant Ones **16** The Great Imposter **18** The Boston Strangler **22** The Sweet Smell of Success

Curtius
also: 6 Marcus
volunteered as: 17 sacrificial victim

Curtiz, Michael
director of: 10 Casablanca (Oscar), The Sea Hawk **12** Captain Blood **13**

Mildred Pierce **14** Life with Father **17** Yankee Doodle Dandy **24** The Adventures of Robin Hood (with William Keighley) **26** The Charge of the Light Brigade **34** The Private Lives of Elizabeth and Essex

curtsy, curtsey 3 bob, bow, dip **5** honor **6** homage **9** obeisance, reverence **11** bend the knee

curvature 3 arc **4** arch, bend **5** crook **6** bowing

curve 3 arc, bow, ess **4** arch, bend, coil, hook, loop, turn, wind **5** crook, twist **6** spiral, swerve

curved 4 bent **5** bowed **6** arched, looped, turned

curved span 3 bow **4** arch, dome **5** vault **6** bridge

Curve of Binding Energy, The
author: 10 John McPhee

curving 4 bent **5** bowed **6** arched **7** bending, looping, turning, winding **8** twisting

curving inward 6 hollow, sunken **7** concave **8** hollowed **9** depressed

curving outward 5 bowed **6** convex **7** bulging, rounded **8** bellying **11** protuberant

Cuscatlan *see* **10** El Salvador

Cush
father: 3 Ham
grandfather: 4 Noah
brother: 6 Canaan
son: 6 Nimrod
Hebrew for: 8 Ethiopia

cushion 3 mat, pad **4** damp **5** quiet **6** dampen, deaden, muffle, pillow, soften, stifle **7** bolster **8** suppress

Cushitic
language family: 11 Afro-Asiatic **13** Hamito-Semitic
branch: 6 Somali **8** Gallinya
spoken in: 7 Somalia **8** Ethiopia, Tanzania

cusp 4 apex, barb, horn, peak **5** angle, point, tooth **6** corner

custard 4 flan, fool **5** creme **6** junket **7** dessert, pudding **8** flummery **10** blanc-mange, zabaglione

Custer, George A
served in: 8 Civil War **10** Indian Wars
side: 5 Union
battle: 13 Little Big Horn
defeated: 11 Black Kettle
defeated by: 10 Crazy Horse

custodian 6 duenna, keeper, warden **7** janitor **8** chaperon, guardian, watchman **9** attendant, caretaker, chaperone, concierge **14** superintendent

custody 4 care **5** watch **6** charge **9** detention **10** possession, protection **11** confinement, safekeeping, trusteeship **12** conservation, guardianship, preservation

custom 4 form, mode **5** habit, usage **7** fashion **10** convention

customarily 7 as a rule, usually **8** commonly, normally **9** generally, regularly **10** frequently, habitually, ordinarily **13** traditionally

customary 5 usual **6** common, normal, wonted **7** general, regular, routine, typical **8** everyday, habitual, ordinary **10** accustomed **11** traditional **12** conventional

customer 5 buyer **6** client, patron **7** habitue, shopper **9** purchaser

customs 4 duty, levy, toll **6** excise, tariff **9** import tax **10** assessment

cut 3 mow, saw **4** chop, clip, crop, cube, dice, fall, gash, hack, move, nick, pare, part, rent, rive, slit, snip, snub, trim **5** carve, cross, lance, mince, piece, prune, sever, share, shave, shear, slash, slice, split, wound **6** bisect, course, delete, divide, furrow, hollow, ignore, incise, pierce, reduce, sunder, trench **7** abridge, channel, curtail, decline, dissect, opening, passage, portion, section, segment **8** condense, contract, decrease, diminish, incision, lacerate **9** abatement, intersect, lessening, reduction, shrinkage **10** abbreviate, diminution, excavation, shortening **11** contraction, curtailment, indentation

cut and run 4 bolt, flee, skip **6** escape **7** abscond, get away, make off, run away **8** slip away **9** break free **10** break loose, fly the coop **12** make a getaway

cut apart 7 dissect **9** anatomize

cutback 8 decrease, trimming **9** reduction **11** abridgement, curtailment

cut back 4 trim **5** prune **6** reduce **7** abridge, curtail **8** decrease

cut costs 4 save **5** skimp, stint **6** scrimp **7** husband **8** conserve, downsize **9** economize **15** tighten one's belt

cut down 4 kill, trim **5** limit **6** lessen, reduce **7** abridge, curtail, destroy, disable, remodel, shorten **8** condense, decrease, diminish, restrict **10** abbreviate

cut-down form 6 digest, precis **7** summary **8** synopsis, trimming **10** shortening **11** abridgement, contraction, curtailment **12** abbreviation, condensation

cut down to size 5 abase **6** humble **7** mortify **8** belittle, bring low, disgrace **9** humiliate **13** bring down a peg

cute 5 sweet **6** dainty, pretty **7** darling, lovable **8** adorable, handsome, precious **9** beautiful **10** attractive

cut expenses 4 save **5** skimp, stint **6** scrimp **8** conserve **9** economize **12** pinch pennies **15** tighten one's belt

cut in half 5 halve **6** bisect

cut in two 5 halve, sever **6** bisect

cutlet 3 cut **4** chop **5** slice **9** cotelette, croquette

cut off 4 dock, trim **5** apart, sever **6** detach, remove **7** chop off, divorce, isolate **8** amputate, divorced, isolated, separate **10** disconnect

cut out 2 go **4** blow, exit **5** be off, erase, leave, scram, split **6** beat it, delete, depart, escape, excise, go away, remove, set out **7** abolish **8** designed, get rid of, set forth **9** eliminate **10** do away with, hit the road, make tracks **11** exterminate, take a powder

cut short 4 clip, crop, dock, trim **7** abridge, shorten **8** truncate **10** abbreviate

cutter 4 boat **5** blade, hewer, knife **6** sledge, sleigh, tailor **11** cutting edge

cutthroat 5 cruel **6** outlaw **7** brigand, hoodlum, ruffian **8** ruthless **9** merciless

cutting 3 raw **4** acid, cold **5** harsh, nasty, sharp **6** biting, bitter **7** acerbic, caustic, nipping, pruning, searing **8** clipping, derisive, piercing, scathing, smarting, snubbing, stinging, trimming **9** reduction, sarcastic, stringent **11** abridgement, acrimonious, compression, contraction, curtailment, disparaging, penetrating **12** abbreviation, condensation

cutting edge 5 blade **8** vanguard **9** forefront

cutting off 8 severing **9** severance **10** detachment, separation **13** disconnection, disengagement

cutting remark 3 dig **4** gibe, jeer **5** taunt

Cuttle
character in: 12 Dombey and Son
author: 7 Dickens

cut up 4 chop, hack, maim, rend **5** caper, carve, halve, mince, slash, slice, split **6** cleave, deface, deform, divide **7** portion, quarter **8** dissever, mutilate **9** apportion, kid around **10** fool around **11** clown around, play the fool

Cuvier, Georges
field: 7 geology, zoology
nationality: 6 French
founded: 12 paleontology **18** comparative anatomy

Cybele
also: 9 Dindymene **10** Berecyntia, Magna Mater **11** Great Mother **12** Mater Turrita **17** Great Idaean Mother
origin: 8 Phrygian **9** Asia Minor
goddess of: 6 nature
priest: 5 Galli **10** Corybantes
corresponds to: 3 Ops **4** Rhea
epithet: 6 Antaea

Cyclades 3 Dos, Zea **4** Keos, Nios, Sira, Syra **5** Delos, Melos, Naxos,

Paros, Siros, Syros, Tenos, Tinos **6** Andros **7** Amorgos, islands, Kythnos **13** Aegean islands

cycle 3 run **6** series **8** sequence **10** succession **11** progression **14** connected group

cyclone 4 gale, gust, wind **5** storm **7** tornado, twister, typhoon **9** whirlwind, windstorm
Australian: 10 willy-nilly

Cyclone (Cy)
nickname of: 15 Denton True Young

Cyclops, Cyclopes
form: 5 giant
number of eyes: 3 one
father: 6 Uranus
mother: 2 Ge
blinded by: 8 Odysseus

Cycnus
father: 4 Ares
killed in: 4 duel
killed by: 8 Hercules
changed into: 4 swan

cylinder 3 can, tin **4** drum, pipe, roll, tube **5** spool **6** barrel, column, pillar, piston, platen, roller **13** piston chamber

cylindrical 5 round **6** tarete **7** tubular **8** columnar

Cymbeline
author: 18 William Shakespeare
character: 6 Cloten, Imogen **7** Iachimo, Pisanio **9** Bellarius **17** Leonatus Posthumus

Cymru see **5** Wales

cynic 7 scoffer, skeptic **9** pessimist **10** misogynist **11** faultfinder, misanthrope

cynical 8 derisive, sardonic, scoffing, scornful, sneering **9** misogynic, sarcastic, skeptical **12** misanthropic

cypress 8 Taxodium **9** Cupressus
varieties: 3 toy **4** bald, berg, pond **5** false, Gowen, Modoc, Piute **6** Bhutan, Hinoki, Lawson, MacNab, Nootka, Sawara, summer, Tecate **7** African, Arizona, Italian, Mexican, Sargent **8** Cuyamaca, golf-ball, Monterey, mourning, Siskiyou, standing **9** Guadalupe, Mendocino, Montezuma, red summer, Santa Cruz **10** Portuguese, tennis-ball **12** Chinese swamp **18** rough-barked Arizona **19** smooth-barked Arizona

Cyprian see **9** Aphrodite

Cyprus
biblical name: 6 Kittim
capital/largest city: 7 Nicosia
city: 6 Paphos **7** Kyrenia, Larnaca **8** Limassol **9** Famagusta
monetary unit: 4 para **5** pound
mountain: 7 Kyrenia, Troodos
highest point: 7 Olympus
river: 6 Pedias
sea: 13 Mediterranean
physical feature:
  bay: 8 Episkopi
  cape: 4 Gata **5** Greco **7** Andreas,

Arnauti **9** Kormakiti
peninsula: 6 Karpas
plain: 8 Mesaoria **9** Messaoria
people: 5 Greek, Turks **9** Cypriotes
ruler: 5 Turks **6** Greeks, Romans **7**
British **9** Egyptians, Lusignans,
Venetians **10** Byzantines **11** Phoenicians
language: 5 Greek **7** Turkish
religion: 5 Islam **6** Muslim **13** Greek
Orthodoxy **16** Eastern Orthodoxy

Cyrano de Bergerac
director: 13 Michael Gordon
author: 13 Edmond Rostand
cast: 10 Jose Ferrer (Cyrano), Mala
Powers **13** William Powers
character: 6 Roxane **22** Christian de
Neuvillette
setting: 5 Paris
Oscar for: 9 best actor (Ferrer)

Cyrano de Bergerac, Savinien
author of: 25 Voyages to the Moon
and the Sun
play based on his life by: 13 Edmond Rostand

cytology
study of: 5 cells

czar, tsar 4 king **5** ruler **6** caesar, despot, tyrant **7** emperor, monarch **8** dictator, overlord **9** potentate, sovereign

czarina 7 empress

czaristic 10 autocratic **11** all-powerful,
dictatorial, monarchical

Czechoslovakia/Czech Republic
see also **8** Slovakia
capital/largest city: 5 Praha **6** Prague
others: 2 As **4** Asch, Brno, Cheb,
Most **5** Brunn, Nitra, Opava, Plzen,
Tabor, **6** Aussig, Bilina, Kladno, Kosice, Pilsen, Presov, Sadowa, Trnava,
Vsetin **7** Budweis, Jihlava, Liberec,
Olomouc, Ostrava, Teplitz **8** Carlsbad, Jachymov, Karlsbad **9** Press-
burg **10** Austerlitz, Bratislava, Konig-
gratz **11** Reichenberg
university: 7 Charles
division: 7 Bohemia, Moravia, Silesia
8 Ruthenia, Slovakia
measure: 3 Lan **4** Mira **5** Korec, Liket, Stopa **6** Merice, Strych
monetary unit: 5 crown, ducat **6**
heller, Koruna
mountain: 3 Erz, Ore **5** Giant, Tatra
6 Sumava **7** Sudeten, Sudetes **8**
Krkonose **10** Carpathian
highest point: 7 Gerlach **11** Gerlachovka
river: 2 Uh, **3** Mze, Vag, Vah **4** Dyje,
Eger, Elbe, Gran, Hron, Ipel, Iser,
Labe, Nisa, Oder, Odra, Ohre, Olse,
Waag **5** Becva, Dunaj, March, Nitra,
Slana, Tisza **6** Danube, Moldau, Morava, Ondava, Sazava, Torysa, Vltava
7 Laborec, Luznice **8** Berounka

physical feature:
plateau: 8 Bohemian **11** Sudeten-
land
people: 4 Slav **5** Czech **6** Slovak **8**
Bohemian, Moravian
author: 5 Capek, Hasek, Havel **7**
Kundera, Seifert
composer: 6 Dvorak **7** Janacek,
Martinu, Smetana
director: 11 Milos Forman
philosopher/reformer: 8 Come-
nius, John Huss
language: 5 Czech **6** German, Magyar, Slovak **7** Russian **9** Hungarian
religion: 6 Uniate **8** Lutheran **9** Orthodoxy **13** Roman Catholic
place:
castle: 8 Hradcany
cathedral: 7 St Vitus **10** St Nicholas
resort/spa: 8 Carlsbad, Piestany **9**
Marienbad **10** Luhacovice **11** Kar-
lovy Vary **14** Marianske Lazne
square: 9 Wenceslas
feature:
dance: 5 polka **6** redowa, talian **7**
furiant
gymnastics festival: 11 spartakiada
song: 7 Ma Vlast
food:
beer: 6 pilsen
sausage: 5 parky **6** vursty

dab 3 bit, pat, tap **6** stroke **7** smidgen, soupcon

dabble 5 slosh **6** fiddle, putter, splash **7** spatter, toy with **8** sprinkle

dabbler 7 amateur, trifler **10** dilettante **12** experimenter **15** nonprofessional

da capo
music: **22** repeat from the beginning
abbreviation: **2** DC

Dacca
capital of: **10** Bangladesh

d'accord 2 OK **6** agreed **7** granted

Dactyls
also: **7** Daktyls
dwellers of: **8** Mount Ida

dad 2 da, pa **3** pop **4** papa, pops, sire **5** daddy, pappy, pater **6** father, parent **11** the old man

Daedalus
occupation: **9** architect
father: **6** Metion
son: **5** Iapyx **6** Icarus
nephew: **5** Talos **6** Perdix
killed: **5** Talos
built: **9** labyrinth
for: **5** Minos
made: **5** wings

Daedalus, Stephen *see* **30** Portrait of the Artist as a Young Man

daffodil 9 Narcissus **24** Narcissus pseudonarcissus
varieties: **3** sea **6** winter **8** Peruvian **9** petticoat **13** hoop-petticoat

daft 3 mad **4** loco **5** balmy, batty, crazy, daffy, dizzy, goofy, loony, nutty, silly, wacky **6** cuckoo, insane, screwy **7** foolish, lunatic, witless

Dagan
origin: **12** Mesopotamian
god of: **5** earth **11** agriculture
corresponds to: **5** Dagon

dagger 4 dirk, snee **5** blade, knife **6** weapon **7** poniard **8** stiletto **11** snickersnee

Dagon
origin: **10** Philistine, Phoenician
god of: **5** earth **11** agriculture
corresponds to: **5** Dagan

Daguerre, Louis J M
nationality: **6** French
inventor of: **11** photography **13** daguerreotype

Dagwood 8 sandwich
see also **7** Blondie

dahlia

varieties: 3 sea **4** tree **6** common, garden **7** bedding **8** bell tree **10** candelabra

Dahomey, Republic of *see* **5** Benin

daily 7 diurnal, per diem **9** circadian, quotidian

Daimler, Gottlieb
nationality: **6** German
inventor of: **10** carburetor, motorcycle **14** gasoline engine **18** gasoline automobile **25** compression ignition engine

daimyo 4 lord **10** feudal lord

dainty 4 fine **5** fussy, tasty **6** choice, choosy, lovely, pretty, savory **7** choosey, elegant, refined **8** delicate, pleasing **9** beautiful, delicious, exquisite **10** attractive, fastidious, particular

Daira
father: **7** Oceanus

dais 5 stage **6** podium **7** rostrum **8** platform

daisy 6 Bellis **23** Chrysanthemum frutescens **25** Chrysanthemum leucanthemum
varieties: **4** blue, cape, high, lazy **5** crown, giant, globe, oxeye, Paris, veldt, white **6** butter, Easter, Nippon, shas- ta, sleepy, Tahoka **7** African, English, painted, seaside, turfing **8** Dahlberg, mountain, panamint **9** Barberton, Englemann, Swan River, Transvaal **10** Kingfisher, Michaelmas, Portuguese **11** Clanwilliam, Livingstone, Namaqualand **12** Boston yellow, double orange **15** blue-eyed African

Daisy Miller
author: **10** Henry James
character: **10** Giovanelli **12** Winterbourne

Dakar
capital of: **7** Senegal

Dakota (Sioux)
language family: **6** Siouan
tribe: **5** Teton **6** Lakota, Nakota, Santee **7** Yankton **8** Sisseton, Wahpeton, Wiciyela **9** Wahpekute, Yanktonai **11** Mdewakanton
location: **7** Montana **9** Minnesota **11** North Dakota, South Dakota
leader: **4** Gall **10** Crazy Horse **11** Sitting Bull **13** Jashunca-Uiteo
noted for: **15** military prowess
deity: **10** Wakan Tanka

dale 4 dell, dene, glen, vale **6** dingle, hollow, valley

D'Alembert
author of: **12** Encyclopedia

Dali, Salvador
born: **5** Spain **7** Figuras
artwork: **10** Last Supper **17** Atomic Leda and Swan **19** Persistence of Memory **22** Accommodations of Desire **24** Christ of St John of the Cross

Dalibor
opera by: **7** Smetana
character: **6** Milada

Dallas
airport: **23** Dallas-Fort Worth Regional
basketball team: **4** Mavs **9** Mavericks
football team: **7** Cowboys
landmark: **15** Turtle Creek Park **16** Museum of Fine Arts **19** Dallas Theater Center **25** Margo Jones Memorial Theater
river: **7** Trinity
stadium: **10** Cotton Bowl
university: **3** SMU **13** Bishop College **17** Southern Methodist

Dallas
character: **7** JR Ewing **9** Jack Ewing, Jenna Wade, Jock Ewing, Miss Ellie, Ray Krebbs **10** Bobby Ewing **11** Christopher, Cliff Barnes, Mandy Winger, Mark Graison **12** Digger Barnes **13** Clayton Farlow, John Ross Ewing, Sue Ellen Ewing **16** Donna Culver Krebs **17** Pamela Barnes Ewing **22** Eleanor Southworth Ewing
cast: **8** John Beck **9** Dack Rambo, Linda Gray **10** Howard Keel **11** Larry Hagman, Steve Kanaly, Susan Howard **12** Ken Kercheval, Patrick Duffy **16** Barbara Bel Geddes, Priscilla Presley **17** Victoria Principal
ranch: **9** Southfork
business: **3** oil **8** Ewing Oil

dalliance 6 affair, toying **7** romance **8** fiddling, trifling **10** flirtation, lovemaking

dally 3 toy **4** play **5** flirt **6** dawdle, loiter, trifle

Dalmatia *see* **10** Yugoslavia

Dalmatian (dog) 5 spots **12** firehouse dog **13** black and white

Dalton, John
field: **7** physics **9** chemistry
nationality: **7** British
formulated: **12** atomic theory

first: 18 atomic weights table
described: 14 color blindness

dam 3 bar, cow **4** clog, mare, plug, stop, wall **5** bitch, block, check **6** bridle, hinder, hold in, impede, plug up, stanch, stop up **7** barrier, block up, confine, congest, inhibit, repress, stopper, stuff up **8** blockade, hold back, obstruct, restrain **9** barricade, hindrance **11** obstruction

damage, damages 3 mar **4** cost, harm, hurt, loss **6** impair, injure, injury, ravage **10** impairment, reparation, settlement **11** destruction **12** compensation, despoliation

damaging 7 harmful, hurtful, ruinous **9** injurious **11** destructive, detrimental

Damascus
 ancient kingdom: 8 Aramaean
 Arabic: 7 Dimashq
 capital of: 5 Syria
 monastery: 22 Suleiman the Magnificent
 mosque: 5 Great **7** Umayyad
 mount: 6 Qasyun
 museum: 8 National **9** Qasr al-Azm
 river: 4 Awaj **6** Barada
 rulers: 5 Arabs, Timur **6** Romans **7** Mongols, Saladin **8** Assyrian **9** Caliphate, Seleucids **12** Ottoman Turks **15** Byzantine Empire **17** Alexander the Great
 tomb: 7 Saladin

Damastes *see* **10** Procrustes

Dame Pliant
 character in: 12 The Alchemist
 author: 6 Jonson

Damia
 spirit of: 9 fertility

damn 4 doom **5** blast **6** rail at **7** censure, condemn **8** denounce **9** criticize, disparage

damned 4 lost **6** cursed, darned, doomed, fallen **7** doggone, dratted, godless **8** accursed, doggoned **9** condemned, execrated, reprobate **12** unregenerate

Damocles
 of: 8 Syracuse
 offended: 9 Dionysius
 seated under: 14 suspended sword

Damon
 friend: 7 Pythias

damp 3 wet **4** curb, dank, dash, dewy, dull, mist **5** check, foggy, humid, misty, moist, muggy, rainy, soggy, spoil **6** clammy, deaden, hamper, hinder, reduce, soaked, sodden **7** depress, drizzly, inhibit, sopping, wettish **8** dankness, diminish, dripping, humidity, moisture, restrain **9** mugginess, restraint **10** clamminess, discourage **14** discouragement

dampen 3 wet **4** mute **7** moisten, wet down

dampen one's spirits 5 daunt, un-

man **6** deject **7** depress **10** discourage, dishearten

damper 4 curb, mute **8** obstacle **9** hindrance, restraint **10** constraint, impediment, wet blanket **14** discouragement

damsel 4 girl, lass **6** maiden **9** young lady

damselfly
 varieties: 8 forktail **10** civilbluet **11** black-winged, broad-winged **12** narrow-winged, spread-winged, violet dancer

dam up 4 clog, plug **5** block, choke **6** plug up, stop up **7** congest **8** obstruct

Dan
 means: 5 judge
 father: 5 Jacob
 mother: 6 Bilhah
 brother: 3 Gad **4** Levi **5** Asher, Judah **6** Joseph, Reuben, Simeon **7** Zebulun **8** Benjamin, Issachar, Naphtali
 sister: 5 Dinah
 descendant of: 6 Danite

Dana *see* **4** Danu

Dana, Richard Henry
 author of: 21 Two Years Before the Mast

Danae
 form: 6 maiden
 father: 8 Acrisius
 mother: 8 Eurydice
 imprisoned by: 8 Acrisius
 lover: 4 Zeus
 son: 7 Perseus

Danai
 members of: 6 Greeks **7** Argives

Danaides
 daughters of: 6 Danaus
 number of daughters: 5 fifty

Dan August
 character: 9 (Sgt) Joe Rivera **14** (Sgt) Charles Wilentz **16** (Chief) George Untermeyer
 cast: 9 Ned Romero **10** Norman Fell **12** Burt Reynolds **15** Richard Anderson

Danaus
 ruler of: 5 Argos
 father: 5 Belus
 twin brother: 8 Aegyptus
 daughters called: 8 Danaides
 number of daughters: 5 fifty

dance 3 hop, jam **4** ball, jump, leap, prom, reel, skip **5** lindy, party, polka, twist **6** bounce, cavort, frolic, gambol, prance, square **7** fox-trot, perform **8** cakewalk **9** jitterbug **10** Charleston **11** Boston waltz **12** choreography, Virginia reel **15** hesitation waltz
 Renaissance/17th century: 3 jig **5** galop, gigue **6** branle, pavane, redowa **7** bourree, gavotte, lancers, lavolta, mazurka **8** canaries, chaconne, courante, galliard, rigadoon, rigaudon, tourdion **9** allemande, passepied, polonaise, sarabande **10** danse basse, danse haute

18th century: 6 minuet **9** cotillion **11** contre danse **12** country dance
19th century: 5 waltz **9** quadrille
early 1900's: 7 foxtrot, one-step, two-step **8** bunny hug **10** turkey trot **11** grizzly bear
1920's: 5 tango **6** shimmy, toddle **10** Charleston **11** black bottom
1930's: 4 shag **5** conga, rumba, samba, Suzy-Q **7** pecking **8** big apple, lindy hop, trucking **9** jitterbug
1940's: 5 mambo **6** cha-cha
1950's and 1960's: 4 frug, go-go **5** twist **6** monkey **9** rock-'n'-roll
1970's: 5 disco
1980's: 7 lambada
1990's: 8 macarena
Argentine: 5 tango
Austrian: 13 schuhplattler
Balinese: 6 legong
Brazilian: 5 samba **6** maxixe **7** lambada
Cuban: 5 conga, rumba **6** cha-cha
Czech: 5 polka
Dominican: 8 marengue, merengue
folk: 6 Morris **7** maypole
French: 6 can-can **8** galliard **9** ecossaise
German: 11 schottische
Indian: 6 kathak **8** manipuri **9** kathakali **13** bharata nat yam
Japanese: 6 bugaku **7** dengaku **8** sarugaku
 dance/theater: 2 no **3** noh **6** kabuki
Mexican: 3 hat
Polish: 7 mazurka **9** krakoviak, polonaise **11** varsovienne
Scottish: 5 sword
Siamese: 10 wayang wong
Spanish: 4 jota **6** bolero **8** flamenco **9** sevillana **10** seguidilla
modern dancer/choreographer: 4 Juba **8** Ted Shawn **9** Eliot Feld, Gene Kelly, Ray Bolger **10** Alvin Ailey, Mary Wigman, Paul Draper, Twyla Tharp **11** Anna Sokolow, Antony Tudor, Eric Hawkins, Fred Astaire, Irene Castle, Ruth St Denis **12** Bill Robinson, Ginger Rogers, Martha Graham, Vernon Castle **13** Alwin Nikolais, Doris Humphrey, Isadora Duncan **14** Charles Weidman **15** Merce Cunningham
see also **6** ballet

dance of death
 French: 12 danse macabre

Dandelion Wine
 author: 11 Ray Bradbury

dander 3 ire **5** anger, Irish **6** temper

Dandie Dinmont terrier 24 soft-coated wheaten terrier, Staffordshire bull terrier, West Highland white terrier

dandy 3 fop **4** beau, dude, fine **5** beaut, great, super, swell **6** beauty, superb **7** coxcomb, peacock **8** terrific **9** excellent **12** clotheshorse

danger 4 risk **5** peril **6** hazard, menace, threat **8** jeopardy **12** endangerment

dangerous 5 hairy, risky **6** chancy, unsafe **8** menacing, perilous **9** hazardous **10** precarious **11** threatening, treacherous

danger signal 5 alarm, alert **7** red flag, warning

dangle 3 sag **4** drag, hang, sway **5** droop, swing, trail **6** depend **7** draggle, hang out, suspend **8** hang down, hang over **9** oscillate

Daniel
   Babylonian name: 12 Belteshazzar
   companion: 7 Meshach **8** Abednego, Shadrach

Daniel Boone
   character: 5 Mingo **6** Yadkin **11** Cincinnatus, Israel Boone, Jemima Boone **12** Rebecca Boone
   cast: 6 Ed Ames **10** Fess Parker **11** Albert Salmi, Dal McKennon, Darby Hinton **13** Patricia Blair **18** Veronica Cartwright

Danielovitch, Issur
   real name of: 11 Kirk Douglas

dank 3 wet **4** cold, damp **5** humid, moist, muggy, soggy **6** chilly, clammy, sodden, sticky

danke 8 thank you

danke schon 16 thank you very much

dankness 4 damp **7** wetness **8** dampness, humidity **9** humidness, moistness, mugginess **10** clamminess

Danner, Blythe
   born: 14 Philadelphia PA
   roles: 8 Betrayal **15** The Great Santini **16** Man Woman and Child
   daughter: 14 Gwyneth Paltrow

Danny Deever
   story in: 18 Barrack-Room Ballads
   author: 14 Rudyard Kipling

Danny Thomas Show, The
   character: 6 Clancy **12** Uncle Tonoose **13** Danny Williams, Linda Williams, Rusty Williams, Terry Williams **16** Mrs Kathy Williams **18** Uncle Charley Halper
   cast: 9 Sid Melton **10** Rusty Hamer **11** Hans Conried **12** Marjorie Lord, Penney Parker **13** Sherry Jackson **16** Angela Cartwright

danse macabre 12 dance of death

Dante (Alighieri)
   author of: 9 Vita Nuova **15** The Divine Comedy
      Divine Comedy Part I: 10 The Inferno
      Divine Comedy Part II: 9 Purgatory **10** Purgatorio
      Divine Comedy Part III: 8 Paradise, Paradiso
   heroine: 8 Beatrice
   guide: 6 Virgil

Dantes, Edmond

character in: 21 The Count of Monte Cristo
   author: 5 Dumas (pere)

Danton, Ray
   born: 9 New York NY
   roles: 14 I'll Cry Tomorrow **18** The George Raft Story **27** The Rise and Fall of Legs Diamond

Danu
   also: 4 Dana
   origin: 5 Irish
   mother of: 14 Tuatha De Danann

Danvers, Mrs
   character in: 7 Rebecca
   author: 9 Du Maurier
   played by: 14 Judith Anderson

Daphnaea
   epithet of: 7 Artemis
   means: 11 of the laurel

Daphne
   form: 5 nymph
   father: 5 Ladon **6** Peneus
   pursued by: 6 Apollo **9** Leucippus
   changed into: 7 bay tree

Daphnis
   occupation: 7 cowherd **8** shepherd
   father: 6 Hermes
   originated: 14 pastoral poetry
   blinded by: 5 Nomia

Daphnis and Chloe
   characters in: 12 Greek romance
   author: 6 Longus

Daphnis et Chloe
   ballet by: 5 Ravel
   choreographer: 12 Michel Fokine

dapper 4 neat, trim **5** natty, smart **6** jaunty, modish, spiffy, sporty, spruce **7** stylish

dapple 3 dab, dot **4** spot **6** mottle

dappled 7 flecked, mottled, spotted **10** variegated

Darcy, Fitzwilliam
   character in: 17 Pride and Prejudice
   author: 6 Austen

Dardanus
   father: 4 Zeus
   mother: 7 Electra
   twin brother: 6 Iasion
   wife: 6 Myrina
   son: 12 Erechthonius
   ancestor of: 7 Trojans

dare 3 bet **4** defy **5** taunt **7** venture **9** challenge **11** provocation

daredevil 4 bold, rash **5** risky **8** heedless, reckless, stuntman **9** audacious, breakneck, risk-taker **11** adventurous, Evel Knievel **12** death-defying, devil-may-care **13** adventuresome

daredevilry 6 daring **8** rashness **9** derring-do **10** imprudence **12** carelessness, heedlessness, recklessness **13** foolhardiness

Dar es Salaam
   former capital of: 8 Tanzania

Darien see **8** Colombia

daring 4 bold, game **5** brave **6** plucky

7 bravery, courage, gallant, valiant **8** audacity, boldness, intrepid **9** audacious, dauntless, undaunted **10** courageous **11** adventurous, venturesome **13** audaciousness **15** adventurousness

daring deed 4 feat **7** exploit **11** achievement

dark 3 dim **4** deep, evil, inky **5** angry, black, bleak, dingy, dusky, murky, night, shady **6** dismal, dreary, gloomy, hidden, opaque, secret, somber, sullen, wicked **7** evening, joyless, obscure, ominous, shadowy, sunless **8** eventide, frowning, hopeless, overcast, sinister, twilight **9** concealed, nightfall, nighttime, sorrowful **10** forbidding **11** threatening **12** discouraging **13** disheartening

darken 3 dim, dye **4** tint **5** cloud, color **6** sadden **7** blacken, obscure **8** dispirit

darkened 3 dim **5** dusky, unlit **6** cloudy, gloomy **7** clouded **9** blackened, tenebrous, unlighted **10** blacked out **13** unilluminated

darkening 7 eclipse, shading **8** clouding, lowering **9** obscuring, shadowing **10** blackening **12** clouding over

Dark Frontier, The
   author: 10 Eric Ambler

dark-hued 5 black, dusky, ebony, raven **6** somber **7** swarthy

Dark Is Light Enough, The
   author: 14 Christopher Fry

Dark Lady, The
   author: 16 Louis Auchincloss

Dark Laughter
   author: 16 Sherwood Anderson

darkness 4 dusk **5** night, shade **7** dimness, evening **8** eventide, twilight **9** blackness, nightfall, nighttime

Darkness at Noon
   author: 14 Arthur Koestler

Darkness Visible
   author: 14 William Golding

Dark Victory
   director: 14 Edmund Goulding
   cast: 10 Bette Davis **11** George Brent **12** Ronald Reagan **14** Humphrey Bogart **19** Geraldine Fitzgerald
   remade as: 11 Stolen Hours

darling 4 cute, dear, love **5** loved, sweet **6** adored, lovely **7** beloved, dearest, lovable **8** adorable, charming, precious **9** cherished **10** attractive, enchanting, sweetheart **11** captivating

Darling
   director: 15 John Schlesinger
   cast: 11 Dirk Bogarde **13** Julie Christie **14** Laurence Harvey
   Oscar for: 6 script **7** actress (Christie)

Darling, Wendy
   character in: 8 Peter Pan
   author: 6 Barrie

darn 4 damn, dang, dash, drat, mend **5** blast, patch, sew up **6** hang it, stitch

7 consarn, doggone, goldang **8** confound **10** confound it

Darnay, Charles
character in: **16** A Tale of Two Cities
author: **7** Dickens

darnel 12 Biblical weed

Darnell, Linda
real name: **20** Monetta Eloyse Darnell
born: **8** Dallas TX
roles: **12** Blood and Sand, Forever Amber **14** The Mark of Zorro **17** Unfaithfully Yours

Darren, James
real name: **13** James Ercolani
born: **14** Philadelphia PA
roles: **6** Gidget **13** The Time Tunnel

dart 3 run **4** bolt, dash, flit, jump, leap, race, rush, tear **5** bound, fling, hurry, spear, spurt **6** hasten, spring, sprint **7** javelin, missile **10** projectile

D'Artagnan
character in: **18** The Three Musketeers
author: **5** Dumas (pere)

Dartle, Rosa
character in: **16** David Copperfield
author: **7** Dickens

Darwin, Charles
author of: **15** The Descent of Man **18** The Origin of Species **20** The Voyage of the Beagle
studied: **16** Galapagos Islands
field: **6** nature **7** biology
nationality: **7** British
theory of: **9** evolution **16** natural selection
ship: **6** Beagle

dash 3 bit, run, zip **4** bolt, dart, drop, elan, foil, hurl, race, ruin, rush, slam, tear, zeal **5** bound, crash, flair, fling, hurry, oomph, pinch, smash, speed, spoil, throw, touch, verve, vigor **6** dampen, energy, hasten, pizazz, spirit, splash, sprint, thrust, thwart **7** a little, panache, shatter, soupcon, spatter **8** splatter, splinter, vivacity **9** animation, frustrate **10** disappoint, discourage

dashing 4 bold **5** brave **6** daring, plucky **7** gallant **8** fearless, spirited, unafraid **9** audacious, impetuous **10** courageous **13** swashbuckling

dash one's hopes 5 daunt, unman **6** deject **7** depress **8** dispirit **10** discourage, dishearten

Dashwood, Elinor and Marianne
characters in: **19** Sense and Sensibility
author: **6** Austen

Da Silva, Howard
real name: **17** Harold Silverblatt
born: **11** Cleveland OH
roles: **8** Oklahoma **12** Sergeant York **14** The Great Gatsby **20** Abe Lincoln in Illinois

Dass, Secundra
character in: **21** The Master of

Ballantrae
author: **9** Stevenson

dastard 3 cad **6** coward, craven **7** bounder, caitiff, chicken **8** poltroon **11** yellow-belly

dastardly 3 low **4** base, mean, vile **6** sneaky **8** cowardly, shameful **9** atrocious **10** despicable

data 4 dope, info **5** facts, input **7** dossier, figures **8** evidence **9** documents **11** information

Datchery, Mr
character in: **22** The Mystery of Edwin Drood
author: **7** Dickens

date 3 age, era **5** court, epoch, stage **6** escort, period **7** partner, take out **9** companion, originate **10** engagement, rendezvous **11** appointment

date 18 Phoenix dactylifera
varieties: **5** cliff **6** Ceylon **7** Chinese **9** Jerusalem **12** Canary Island

dated 5 passe **6** old hat **8** obsolete, outmoded **9** out-of-date **10** antiquated **12** old-fashioned **13** unfashionable

daub 4 blot, coat, soil, spot **5** cover, dirty, paint, smear, stain **6** blotch, smirch, smudge **7** splotch

Daudet, Alphonse
author of: **6** Sappho **15** The Woman of Arles **17** Letters from My Mill **18** Tartarin of Tarascon

Daughter of the Regiment, The
opera by: **9** Donizetti

Daumier, Honore
born: **6** France **10** Marseilles
artwork: **7** Bathers **9** Gargantua **12** Men of Justice **13** Bluestockings **14** The Washerwoman **16** The Good Bourgeois **18** The Legislative Body **19** Professors and Pupils **20** Stories from Antiquity **21** The Third-Class Carriage

daunt 3 cow **4** dash, faze **5** abash, alarm, scare **6** deject, dismay, menace, subdue **7** depress, unnerve **8** affright, browbeat, frighten, threaten **10** discourage, dishearten, intimidate

dauntless 4 bold **5** brave, gutsy **6** daring, heroic **7** gallant, valiant **8** fearless, resolute, unafraid, valorous **10** courageous **12** stouthearted

dauntlessness 4 grit, guts, sand **5** nerve, pluck, spunk, valor **6** daring, mettle **7** bravery, courage, resolve **8** boldness **9** fortitude **10** resolution **12** fearlessness, resoluteness **16** stoutheartedness

Davers, Lady
character in: **6** Pamela
author: **10** Richardson

David 6 statue
by: **12** Michelangelo
site: **8** Florence
size: **6** heroic

David

king of: **6** Israel
father: **5** Jesse
wife: **6** Maacah, Michal **7** Abigail, Ahinoam, Haggith **9** Bathsheba
son: **5** Amnon **7** Absalom, Chileab, Solomon **8** Adonijah
daughter: **5** Tamar
brother: **5** Eliab **7** Shammah **8** Abinadab
sister: **7** Abigail
friend: **5** Abner **8** Jonathan
nephew: **5** Amasa
city of: **9** Bethlehem, Jerusalem
anointed by: **6** Samuel
killed: **7** Goliath
wrote: **6** Psalms
comforter: **7** Abishag
conspirators against: **4** Joab **8** Abiathar, Adonijah
pertaining to: **7** Davidic

David, Jacques-Louis
born: **5** Paris **6** France
artwork: **6** Mme de Verninac **15** The Death of Marat **19** The Oath of the Horatii **23** The Coronation of Napoleon **26** View of the Luxembourg Gardens **31** The Intervention of the Sabine Women

David Copperfield
author: **14** Charles Dickens
character: **3** Ham **6** Barkis, Mr Dick **7** Creakle **8** Traddles **9** Mr Spenlow, Uriah Heep **10** Aunt Betsey, Little Em'ly, Mr Micawber, Rosa Dartle, Steerforth **11** Dora Spenlow, Little Emily, Mr Murdstone, Mr Wickfield, Mrs Gummidge **13** Clara Peggotty **14** Agnes Wickfield, Betsey Trotwood
director: **11** George Cukor
cast: **8** W C Fields **10** Madge Evans **11** Frank Lawton, Roland Young **13** Basil Rathbone, Edna May Oliver **15** Lionel Barrymore **16** Maureen O'Sullivan **18** Freddie Bartholomew

David Harum
author: **19** Edward Noyes Westcott

Davies, Arthur Bowen
born: **7** Utica NY
artwork: **5** Dream **8** Unicorns **9** Crescendo **13** Every Saturday **15** Dancing Children, Sacramental Tree **17** Along the Erie Canal **18** Leda and the Dioscuri

Davies, Marion
real name: **19** Marion Cecilia Douras
lover: **21** William Randolph Hearst
born: **10** Brooklyn NY
roles: **12** Cain and Mable **13** Runaway Romany **15** Tillie the Toiler

Da Vinci, Leonardo
born: **5** Italy, Vinci
artwork: **8** Mona Lisa **10** La Gioconda **13** The Last Supper **15** The Annunciation **19** The Battle of Anghiari **21** The Adoration of the Magi

Davis, Bette

real name: 18 Ruth Elizabeth Davis
husband: 11 Gary Merrill
born: 8 Lowell MA
roles: 7 Jezebel (Oscar) **9** Dangerous (Oscar), The Letter **10** Now Voyager, The Old Maid **11** All About Eve, Dark Victory **14** Of Human Bondage, The Little Foxes **18** The Petrified Forest **22** Hush Hush Sweet Charlotte **26** What Ever Happened to Baby Jane?

Davis, H L
author of: 14 Honey in the Horn

Davis, Ossie
wife: 7 Ruby Dee
born: 9 Cogdell GA
author: 16 Purlie Victorious
roles/films: 7 Jamaica **15** A Raisin in the Sun **18** No Time for Sergeants **19** Cotton Comes to Harlem

Davis, Sammy Jr
wife: 8 May Britt
group: 14 Will Master Trio
born: 9 New York NY
autobiography: 7 Yes I Can
roles: 11 Mr Wonderful **12** Porgy and Bess **20** The Benny Goodman Story

Davis, Stuart
born: 14 Philadelphia PA
artwork: 4 Visa **9** Eggbeater **11** Lucky Strike, Ready to Wear **11** Owh! In Sao Pao **12** The Mellow Pad **14** Colonial Cubism **15** Cigarette Papers

Davy, Humphrey
field: 9 chemistry
nationality: 7 British
isolated: 5 boron **6** barium, sodium **7** calcium **8** chlorine **9** magnesium, potassium, strontium
invented: 8 Davy lamp **10** miner's lamp

dawdle 4 idle, loaf **5** dally, delay **6** loiter **10** dillydally **12** putter around **13** procrastinate

dawdler
French: 7 flaneur

dawdling
French: 8 flanerie

dawn 4 rise **5** begin, birth, occur, start, sunup **6** advent, appear, Aurora, emerge, origin, strike, unfold **7** develop, sunrise **8** commence, daybreak, daylight **9** beginning, emergence, inception, unfolding **12** commencement
god of: 8 Heimdall
goddess of: 3 Eos **6** Aurore, Matuta

dawning 5 sunup **7** morning, sunrise **8** daybreak, daylight

Dawn Patrol, The
director: 14 Edmund Goulding
cast: 10 David Niven, Errol Flynn **11** Donald Crisp **13** Basil Rathbone **14** Melville Cooper **15** Barry Fitzgerald

day 3 age, era **4** date, time **5** epoch **6** period

Day, Clarence (Jr)
author of: 14 God and My Father, Life with Father, Life with Mother

Day, Doris
real name: 18 Doris von Kappelhoff
born: 12 Cincinnati OH
autobiography: 19 Doris Day Her Own Story
roles: 10 Pillow Talk **12** Calamity Jane **13** The Pajama Game **15** Move Over Darling, The Doris Day Show **23** Please Don't Eat the Daisies

daybed 5 couch **6** lounge **12** chaise longue

day book 3 log **5** diary **6** agenda **7** journal **8** calendar, schedule

daybreak 4 dawn, morn **5** sunup **7** sunrise

daydream 4 muse **5** fancy **7** fantasy, imagine, reverie **9** fantasize **10** woolgather **14** castle in the air

Day for Night
director: 16 Francois Truffaut
cast: 15 Jean-Pierre Leaud **16** Francois Truffaut, Jacqueline Bisset, Jean-Pierre Aumont
Oscar for: 11 foreign film

daylight 4 dawn **5** sunup **7** morning, sunrise **8** full view, openness, sunlight, sunshine

Days and Nights
author: 17 Konstantin Simonov

day's end 3 een, eve **4** dusk, even **6** sunset **7** evening, sundown **8** gleaming, twilight **9** nightfall

Days of Heaven
director: 14 Terrence Malick
cast: 9 Linda Manz **10** Sam Shepard **11** Brooke Adams, Richard Gere
Oscar for: 14 cinematography

Days of Wine and Roses
director: 12 Blake Edwards
cast: 9 Lee Remick **10** Jack Lemmon **11** Jack Klugman **15** Charles Bickford
score: 12 Henry Mancini

daze 4 numb, stun **5** amaze, shock **6** benumb, dazzle, excite, muddle, stupor **7** astound, confuse, stagger, startle, stupefy **8** astonish, bewilder, surprise **9** disorient, electrify **11** flabbergast **12** astonishment, bewilderment, blow one's mind **14** discombobulate

dazed 5 woozy **6** groggy **7** confused, dazzled, stunned **9** befuddled, stupefied **10** bewildered, punch-drunk

dazzle 3 awe **4** blur, daze **5** blind **6** excite **7** confuse, overawe **9** electrify, overpower, overwhelm

dazzling 7 radiant **8** blinding **9** sparkling **10** impressive, staggering **11** coruscating **12** breathtaking, electrifying, overwhelming **14** flabbergasting

deacon 6 cleric **9** churchman, clergyman **12** ecclesiastic

deactivate 6 defuse **9** switch off **10** neutralize

Dead, The
author: 10 James Joyce

dead, the dead 4 beat, cold, dull, flat **5** depth, exact, midst, quiet, spent, tired, total, utter, vapid **6** entire, middle, unused **7** defunct, expired, extinct, insipid, precise, useless, utterly, worn-out **8** abruptly, absolute, complete, deceased, entirely, inactive, lifeless, obsolete, perished, stagnant, suddenly, thorough, unerring **9** exhausted, inanimate, inorganic **10** absolutely, completely, lackluster, unemployed, unexciting **11** ineffectual, inoperative **12** unproductive, unprofitable
Latin: 8 ad patres
god of: 6 Osiris **7** Veiovis

dead body 5 stiff **6** corpse **7** cadaver, remains

deaden 4 dope, drug, dull, mute, numb **5** abate, blunt **6** lessen, muffle, soothe, subdue, weaken **7** assuage, smother **8** diminish, mitigate, moderate **9** alleviate **11** anesthetize

deadened 5 muted **6** dulled, numbed **7** muffled, subdued

Dead Father, The
author: 15 Donald Barthelme

Dea Dia
origin: 5 Roman
goddess of: 11 agriculture
corresponds to: 13 Acca Laurentia

deadlock 7 impasse **8** standoff **9** stalemate **10** standstill

deadly 3 wan **4** dull **5** ashen, awful, fatal, fully, undue **6** boring, lethal, mortal, pallid **7** awfully, baneful, destroy, extreme, ghostly, tedious, totally **8** dreadful, entirely, horribly, terrible, terribly, tiresome **9** excessive, malignant, wearisome **10** cadaverous, completely, implacable, inordinate, relentless, thoroughly **11** destructive, unrelenting

deadpan 5 sober **8** detached **9** impassive **10** poker-faced **11** unemotional **13** straight-faced

dead ringer 4 copy, mate, twin **6** double **9** duplicate **11** counterpart **12** doppelganger **13** spitting image

Dead Souls
author: 12 Nikolai Gogol

dead to the world 6 asleep **7** out cold **9** konked out **10** fast asleep, slumbering **11** sound asleep

dead weight 7 ballast **9** inert mass

Dead Zone, The
author: 11 Stephen King

deal 3 act **4** give, hand **5** round, see to, trade, treat **6** behave, handle, market **7** bargain, concern, deliver, dole out, give out, mete out, oversee **8** consider, dispense **9** agreement,

apportion 10 administer, distribute **11** arrangement **12** distribution **13** apportionment

dealer 5 agent **6** monger, trader, vendor **8** merchant **10** trafficker **11** distributor

dealing, dealings 5 trade **7** traffic **8** business, practice **9** relations, treatment **12** transactions

dealing out 8 dividing **9** allotting, bestowing **10** conferring, consigning, dispensing **12** apportioning, distributing

Dea Marica *see* **6** Marica

Dean, Dizzy (Jay Hanna)
  sport: 8 baseball
  position: 7 pitcher
  team: 16 St Louis Cardinals
  part of: 12 Gashouse Gang
  brother: 4 Paul

Dean, James (Jimmy)
  real name: 14 James Byron Dean
  born: 8 Marion IN
  roles: 5 Giant **10** East of Eden **18** Rebel Without a Cause

Deane, Seneca
  character in: 7 Babbitt
  author: 5 Lewis

Dean's December
  author: 10 Saul Bellow

dear 4 love **5** angel, loved **6** costly **7** beloved, darling **8** esteemed, favorite, precious **9** cherished, expensive, respected **10** sweetheart
  French: 5 cheri **6** cherie

Dear Antoine
  author: 11 Jean Anouilh

Dear Brutus
  author: 12 James M Barrie

dearest 7 beloved, darling

dearth 4 lack **7** paucity **8** scarcity, shortage **10** deficiency

death, Death 5 dying **6** demise **7** decease, passing **9** departure **10** expiration, grim reaper
  goddess of: 3 Hel **7** Berchta, Perchta **10** Ereshkigal

Death Be Not Proud
  author: 9 John Donne

death blow
  French: 11 coup de grace

Death Comes for the Archbishop
  author: 11 Willa Cather
  character: 7 Jacinto **9** Kit Carson **16** Bishop Jean Latour **20** Father Joseph Vaillant

death-dealing 5 fatal **6** lethal, mortal **7** killing **11** destructive

death-defying 4 bold, rash **5** risky **6** daring **8** reckless **9** audacious, breakneck, daredevil

Death in the Family, A
  author: 9 James Agee
  filmed as: 13 All the Way Home

Death in Venice
  director: 15 Luchino Visconti

author: 10 Thomas Mann
  cast: 9 Mark Burns **11** Dirk Bogarde **14** Marisa Berenson

deathless 7 eternal **8** immortal **9** perpetual **11** everlasting

deathlike 3 wan **4** pale **5** ashen **6** pallid **7** ghastly **9** bloodless **10** cadaverous, corpselike

deathly 4 very **7** extreme, intense **8** terrible **9** extremely **12** overwhelming **15** resembling death

Death of a Salesman
  director: 12 Laslo Benedek
  author: 12 Arthur Miller
  character: 4 Biff **5** Happy, Linda **7** Bernard, Charley **8** Uncle Ben **10** Willy Loman
  cast: 13 Frederic March, Kevin McCarthy **14** Mildred Dunnock **15** Cameron Mitchell

Death of Ivan Ilyich, The
  author: 10 Leo Tolstoy

Death of the Gods, The
  author: 17 Dmitri Merejkowski

Death of the Heart
  author: 14 Elizabeth Bowen

Death on the Nile
  author: 14 Agatha Christie

Death Takes a Holiday
  director: 14 Mitchell Leisen
  cast: 11 Guy Standing **13** Evelyn Venable, Frederic March (Death)

Death Valley Days
  host: 12 Robert Taylor, Ronald Reagan **13** Dale Robertson **14** Stanley Andrews

debacle 4 rout, ruin **5** havoc, wreck **8** collapse, disaster, downfall **9** breakdown, cataclysm, overthrow, ruination **10** bankruptcy **11** catastrophe, devastation, dissolution **12** vanquishment **14** disintegration

debar 3 ban **6** reject **7** exclude, keep out **8** preclude, prohibit **9** blackball, blacklist

debark 4 land

debarment 7 removal **8** omission **9** exception, exclusion, exemption, rejection **11** elimination, prohibition **12** nonadmission

debase 5 lower **6** befoul, defile **7** corrupt, degrade **8** disgrace, dishonor **9** desecrate **10** adulterate **11** deteriorate **16** impair the worth of **18** reduce the quality of

debased 4 vile **6** impure **7** corrupt, defiled, lowered **8** degraded, depraved **9** debauched, disgraced, dissolute, perverted **10** degenerate, dissipated **11** adulterated

debasement 9 decadence, depravity **10** corruption, debauchery, degeneracy, immorality, perversion **13** dissoluteness

debatable 4 iffy **6** unsure **7** dubious **8** arguable, doubtful **9** uncertain, unde-

cided **10** disputable **12** questionable **13** problematical

debate 5 argue **6** ponder **7** discuss, dispute, reflect **8** argument, cogitate, consider, hash over **10** cogitation, deliberate, discussion, meditation, reflection, think about **12** deliberation, meditate upon **13** consideration

debauch 4 orgy **5** revel, spree **6** debase **7** carouse, corrupt, deprave, revelry, subvert **8** carousal **9** bacchanal **10** lead astray, saturnalia

debauched 4 lewd **6** wanton **7** corrupt, debased, immoral **8** degraded, depraved, perverse, vitiated **9** abandoned, corrupted, dissolute, lecherous, led astray, pervert- ed, reprobate, shameless **10** degenerate, dissipated, lascivious, libidinous, licentious, profligate **12** disreputable

debauchery 6 excess **11** dissipation **12** immoderation, intemperance **14** self-indulgence

DeBeck, Billy
  creator/artist of: 12 Barney Google **20** Parlor Bedroom and Sink

debilitate 6 weaken **7** wear out **8** enervate **10** devitalize, make feeble **17** deprive of strength

debilitated 5 frail **6** feeble, infirm **7** worn out **8** delicate, weakened **9** enervated **11** devitalized

debilitation 8 handicap, weakness **9** infirmity **10** affliction, disability, impairment, inadequacy **11** disablement

debility 7 fatigue, frailty **8** asthenia, handicap, senility, weakness **9** infirmity, lassitude, weakening **10** affliction, enervation, exhaustion, feebleness, impairment, invalidism, sickliness **11** decrepitude, prostration

debit 4 debt **6** red ink **7** account, payable **9** liability **10** balance due, obligation **11** ledger entry, shortcoming

debonair 5 suave **6** dapper, jaunty, urbane **7** buoyant, elegant, genteel, refined **8** carefree, charming, gracious, well-bred **9** sprightly **11** free and easy **12** lighthearted **13** sophisticated

Deborah 11 Hebrew judge
  companion: 7 Rebekah
  summoned: 5 Barak

debouch 5 drain **6** emerge, let out **7** flow out **9** discharge

debris 4 crap, junk **5** dreck, dregs, dross, ruins, scrap, trash, waste **6** litter, rubble, shards **7** clutter, garbage, rubbish **8** detritus, wreckage **9** fragments

debt 4 bill **5** debit **7** arrears **9** liability **10** obligation **15** deferred payment, that which is owed

debunk 4 bare **5** strip **6** expose, send up, show up, unmask **7** deflate, lampoon, take off, uncloak, uncover

8 ridicule, satirize **9** burlesque, demystify, disparage **13** demythologize

Debussy, Claude Achille
  born: 6 France **15** St Germain-en-Laye
  composer of: 5 La Mer **6** Gigues, Iberia, Images **8** Estampes **9** Nocturnes, Printemps **11** Clair de Lune **13** En Blanc et Noir **15** Children's Corner, L'Enfant prodigue **16** La Demoiselle Elue, Suite Bergamasque **17** Rondes de Printemps, The Blessed Damozel **18** Pelleas et Melisande **24** The Girl with the Flaxen Hair **26** Prelude a l'apres-midi d'un faune **28** Prelude to the Afternoon of a Faun

debut 9 coming out **12** presentation

decadence 5 decay **7** decline **10** corruption, debasement, degeneracy, immorality **12** degeneration **13** deterioration

decadent 7 corrupt, debased, immoral **8** decaying, depraved, perverse **9** debauched, dissolute, perverted **10** degenerate
  French: 11 fin de siecle

Decalogue 15 Ten Commandments

Decameron, The
  author: 17 Giovanni Boccaccio

decamp 7 move off, run away, take off **8** march off, sneak off

decampment 6 escape, flight **7** getaway

decant 4 pour **7** draw off, pour out

decanter 6 bottle, carafe, vessel

decathlon winner 11 Bruce Jenner

Decatur, Stephen
  served in: 11 Algerine War, Barbary Wars **13** Tripolitan War **19** War of Eighteen Twelve
  commander of ship: 12 United States
  defeated ship: 10 Macedonian (British)
  saying: 22 "Our country right or wrong"

decay 3 rot **5** spoil **7** corrode, putrefy, rotting **8** spoiling **9** decompose **12** disintegrate, putrefaction **13** decomposition
  goddess of: 4 Hour **5** Horae

decayed 3 bad **6** putrid, rotted, rotten, ruined **7** corrupt, gone bad, spoiled **10** decomposed **12** deteriorated **13** disintegrated

deceased *see* **4** dead

deceit 5 fraud **8** cheating, trickery **9** duplicity **10** dishonesty, trickiness **11** fraudulence **13** double-dealing **15** underhandedness **17** misrepresentation

deceitful 5 false **6** crafty, sneaky, tricky **7** cunning **9** dishonest, insincere **11** duplicitous, treacherous, underhanded **12** hypocritical **13** double-dealing, untrustworthy

deceive 3 con **4** fool **5** cheat, put on, trick **6** delude **7** defraud, mislead, swindle

deceiver 4 fake **5** cheat, fraud, quack **6** con man **7** cozener **8** impostor, swindler **9** charlatan, trickster **10** mountebank **13** confidence man

decelerate 5 brake **8** slow down

deceleration 7 braking, slowing

December
  event: 11 Pearl Harbor (7), Winter solstice (21, 22)
  flower: 5 holly **9** narcissus
  French: 8 Decembre
  gem: 4 ruby **6** zircon **9** turquoise
  German: 8 Dezember
  holiday: 8 Hanukkah **9** Boxing Day (26), Christmas (25) **16** Saint Nicholas Day (6)
  Italian: 8 Dicembre
  number of days: 9 thirty-one
  origin of name: 5 decem (Latin meaning ten)
  place in year:
    Gregorian: 7 twelfth
    Roman: 5 tenth
    Julian: 7 twelfth
  Spanish: 9 Diciembre
  Zodiac sign: 9 Capricorn **11** Sagittarius

decency 7 decorum, modesty **9** propriety **14** respectability **15** appropriateness

decent 4 fair, nice **5** ample **6** proper, seemly **7** correct, fitting **8** adequate, gracious, obliging, passable, suitable **9** courteous **10** acceptable, sufficient **11** appropriate **12** satisfactory **13** accommodating

deception 3 con **4** scam **5** fraud, sting, trick **7** cunning, slyness **8** artifice, illusion, trickery **9** duplicity, falseness, hypocrisy, treachery **10** craftiness, dishonesty, sneakiness, trickiness **11** fraudulence, insincerity **13** deceitfulness, double-dealing **15** underhandedness **17** untrustworthiness

deceptive 5 phony **9** dishonest **10** fraudulent, misleading

decibel
  abbreviation: 2 dB

decide 4 rule **5** elect, judge **6** choose, decree, select, settle **7** resolve **9** determine

decided 4 firm **7** certain **8** clear-cut, definite, emphatic, resolute **9** assertive **10** deliberate, determined, unwavering **12** indisputable, strong-willed, unhesitating, unmistakable **14** unquestionable

decidedly 9 certainly **10** absolutely **11** indubitably, undoubtedly **12** indisputably, unmistakably **13** unequivocally **14** unquestionably

decidedness 7 purpose, resolve **10** resolution **12** resoluteness **13** determination **14** purposefulness

decide on 5 adopt, elect **6** choose, opt for, select, settle **7** appoint, arrange, embrace, espouse, pick out **8** settle on **9** deter- mine, establish, single out

decigram
  abbreviation: 2 dg

deciliter
  abbreviation: 2 dL

decimate 6 reduce **7** destroy **8** massacre **9** slaughter **13** greatly reduce

decimeter
  abbreviation: 2 dm

decipher 4 read **5** solve **6** decode, deduce, render **7** decrypt, dope out, explain, make out, unravel **8** construe, untangle **9** interpret, translate **12** cryptanalyze

decision 6 decree, ruling **7** finding, outcome, purpose, resolve, verdict **8** judgment **10** conclusion, resolution **12** resoluteness **13** determination **14** purposefulness

decisive 4 firm **5** final **8** absolute, definite, positive, resolute **10** conclusive, convincing, definitive, determined, undeniable **12** indisputable

decisive blow 9 deathblow **11** coup de grace

decisiveness 7 purpose, resolve **10** resolution **12** resoluteness **14** purposefulness

decisive point 3 nut **4** core, crux, gist **5** basis, heart **6** kernel **7** essence **9** essential

deck 4 garb, trim **5** adorn, array, dress, prank **6** clothe, doll up, enrich, outfit, tog out **7** apparel, bedizen, festoon, furbish, garnish, gussy up **8** accouter, beautify, ornament, spruce up **9** embellish

Decker, Mary
  sport: 7 running
  married name: 6 Slaney

deck out 5 adorn, array, dress **6** attire, clothe, fit out, outfit, rig out **7** costume

declaim 4 rail **5** orate **6** recite **7** inveigh **9** sermonize **11** pontificate

declaration 6 avowal, notice **8** document **9** assertion, statement, testimony **10** deposition **11** affirmation, attestation, publication **12** announcement, notification, proclamation **14** acknowledgment

declare 4 show **6** affirm, reveal **7** express **8** announce, proclaim **9** pronounce

declare null and void 6 cancel, repeal, revoke **7** abolish, rescind, retract **8** abrogate, set aside **9** repudiate **10** invalidate **11** countermand

declare untrue 4 deny **9** repudiate **10** contradict

decline 3 ebb **4** drop, fail, flag, sink, wane **5** decay, slump, spurn **6** balk at, eschew, lessen, refuse, reject, weaken, worsen **7** dwindle **8** decrease, diminish, downfall **9** downgrade, downswing **11** deteriorate **13** deterioration

Decline and Fall
author: **11** Evelyn Waugh

Decline and Fall of the Roman Empire, The
author: **12** Edward Gibbon

declivity 4 drop **5** slant, slope **6** plunge **7** descent

decompose 3 rot **5** decay, spoil **7** putrefy **8** separate **10** go to pieces **12** disintegrate

decomposed 6 putrid, rotted, rotten **7** decayed, spoiled **9** putrefied **13** disintegrated

decontaminate 6 purify **9** disinfect, sterilize

decor 13 ornamentation

decorate 4 trim **5** adorn, array, honor **7** festoon, garnish **8** beautify, ornament **9** embellish

decorated 5 fancy **6** decked, ornate **7** adorned, trimmed **8** bedecked **9** bemedaled, bedizened, garnished **10** ornamented **11** embellished

decoration 4 trim **5** award, badge, medal **6** emblem, ribbon **7** garnish **8** ornament, trimming **9** adornment **13** embellishment, ornamentation **14** beautification

decorous 3 fit **6** decent, polite, proper, seemly **7** correct **8** becoming, mannerly, suitable **9** dignified **10** respectful **11** appropriate

decorum 4 tact **5** taste **7** dignity **8** good form **9** gentility, propriety **10** politeness **14** respectability

decoy 4 bait, lure **5** plant, snare **6** allure, come-on, entice **10** enticement, inducement **11** smoke screen

decrease 4 drop, ease, loss **5** abate, taper **6** lessen, reduce **7** cutback, decline, dwindle, fall-off, slacken, subside **8** diminish **9** abatement, dwindling, lessening, reduction **10** de-escalate, diminution **12** de-escalation

decree 3 law **5** edict, order **6** dictum, ruling **7** command, mandate, statute **8** proclaim **9** authorize **12** proclamation

decrepit 7 rickety **8** battered **10** broken-down **11** dilapidated

decrescendo
music: **22** gradually getting softer
abbreviation: **4** decr

decry 7 censure, condemn **8** denounce **9** criticize, deprecate, disparage

Dedalus, Stephen
character in: **7** Ulysses **30** Portrait of the Artist as a Young Man
author: **5** Joyce

dedicate 6 commit, devote, launch, pledge **7** address, present **8** inscribe

dedication 8 devotion **10** commitment

11 devotedness **16** prefatory address **20** prefatory inscription

Dedlock, Sir Leicester and Lady
characters in: **10** Bleak House
author: **7** Dickens

deduce 5 infer **6** gather, reason **8** conclude **10** comprehend, understand

deduct 4 take **6** remove **8** subtract, take from, withdraw **10** decrease by

deduction 5 guess **6** belief, credit, rebate **7** removal **8** analysis, decrease, discount, judgment, markdown, rollback **9** abatement, allowance, exemption, gathering, inference, lessening, reasoning, reduction **10** assumption, concession, conclusion, diminuition, hypothesis, reflection, taking away, withdrawal **11** calculation, presumption, speculation, subtraction, supposition **13** comprehension, consideration, understanding **14** interpretation

Dee, Ruby
real name: **14** Ruby Ann Wallace
husband: **10** Ossie Davis
born: **11** Cleveland OH
roles: **15** A Raisin in the Sun **16** Purlie Victorious

Dee, Sandra
real name: **13** Alexandra Zuck
husband: **8** Bobby Darin
born: **9** Bayonne NJ
roles: **6** Gidget **12** A Summer Place **15** Tammy Tell Me True

deed 3 act **4** feat **5** title **6** action, effort **11** achievement **14** accomplishment

deeds are manly, words are womanish
Italian: **24** fatti maschii parole femine
motto of: **8** Maryland

deem 4 hold, view **5** judge, think **6** regard **7** believe **8** consider

de-emphasize 8 play down **9** underplay

deep 3 far, sea **4** dark, late, lost, rich, wise **5** far in, midst, ocean, vivid **6** astute, strong **7** extreme, intense, learned **8** absorbed, immersed, involved, profound, resonant, sonorous **9** engrossed, sagacious **10** discerning **11** intelligent **13** philosophical

Deep, The
author: **13** Peter Benchley

deeply 6 richly **7** acutely, gravely, greatly, vividly **8** entirely **9** intensely, seriously **10** completely, profoundly, resonantly, sonorously, thoroughly **12** passionately

deeply felt 6 ardent, fervid **7** earnest, fervent, intense, sincere, zealous **9** heartfelt **10** passionate **11** impassioned **12** wholehearted

deepness 10 profundity

deep-rooted 7 abiding, lasting **8** enduring **9** confirmed, ingrained

deep-seated 7 abiding, lasting **8** enduring **9** confirmed, ingrained

deep thought 10 absorption, brown study, intentness **11** engrossment **13** concentration

deep water 3 jam **4** mess **5** ocean **6** pickle **7** trouble **8** distress **10** difficulty **11** dire straits, predicament **12** over one's head

deer
young: **4** fawn
female: **3** doe
male: stag

Deer Hunter, The
director: **13** Michael Cimino
cast: **10** John Cazale, John Savage **11** Meryl Streep **12** Robert De Niro **17** Christopher Walken
Oscar for: **7** picture **8** director **15** supporting actor (Walken)

Deerslayer, The
author: **19** James Fenimore Cooper
first of: **20** Leatherstocking Tales
character: **4** Hist **5** Hetty **6** Judith **9** Hurry Harry **11** Natty Bumppo (Deerslayer) **12** Chingachgook, Thomas Hutter

de-escalate 5 limit **6** lessen, narrow **8** contract, minimize

deface 3 mar **4** mark, scar **5** spoil **6** bruise, damage, impair, injure **9** disfigure

de facto 4 real **6** actual, really **8** actually

defalcate 8 embezzle **14** misappropriate

defamation 5 libel **7** calumny, slander **12** vilification **13** disparagement

defamatory 8 libelous **9** vilifying **10** calumnious, derogatory, slanderous **11** disparaging

defame 5 libel **6** malign, vilify **7** degrade, slander **8** derogate **9** denigrate, discredit, disparage **10** calumniate

Defarge, Madame
character in: **16** A Tale of Two Cities
author: **7** Dickens

default 10 nonpayment

defeat 4 foil, loss, rout **5** cream, crush, elude, quell **6** baffle, thwart **7** conquer, setback, shellac, trounce **8** confound, overcome, vanquish **9** frustrate, overpower, overthrow, overwhelm, thwarting **11** frustration **14** disappointment

defeated 4 beat **5** upset **6** beaten, bested, licked, routed **7** outdone, whipped, worsted **8** overcame **9** conquered, overthrew, put to rout **10** frustrated, overthrown **11** overpowered, overwhelmed **12** hors de combat

defect 4 flaw, scar, spot **5** break, crack, fault, stain **6** blotch, foible **7** blemish, default, failing, frailty **8** omission, weakness **10** deficiency **11** shortcoming **12** imperfection **14** incompleteness

defective 6 broken, faulty, flawed

7 lacking, wanting **8** abnormal, impaired **9** deficient, imperfect, subnormal **10** inadequate, out of order **11** inoperative **12** insufficient

Defence of Poetry
    author: **18** Percy Bysshe Shelley

defend 5 guard **6** secure, shield, uphold **7** endorse, protect, shelter, stand by, support, sustain **8** advocate, champion, maintain, preserve **9** safeguard

defender 8 advocate, champion, guardian, upholder **9** protector, supporter

Defender of the Faith
    Latin: **13** Fidei Defensor
    title of: **17** English sovereigns

Defenders, The
    character: **10** Joan Miller **14** Helen Donaldson, Kenneth Preston **15** Lawrence Preston
    cast: **10** E G Marshall, Robert Reed **11** Joan Hackett, Polly Rowles

defense 4 care **5** guard **7** custody, support **8** advocacy, security **9** barricade, safeguard, upholding **10** protection, stronghold **11** maintenance, safekeeping **12** preservation **13** fortification, justification

defenseless 7 unarmed **8** helpless **10** on one's back, vulnerable, weaponless **11** unprotected, unresisting

defensible 3 fit **5** valid **6** proper **7** tenable **8** sensible, suitable **9** allowable, excusable **10** admissible, condonable, forgivable, pardonable, vindicable **11** justifiable, permissible, supportable, warrantable

defer 4 obey **5** delay, table, yield **6** accede, give in, put off, shelve, submit **7** respect, suspend **8** postpone **10** capitulate

deference 5 honor **6** esteem, regard **7** respect **9** obedience, reverence **12** capitulation **13** consideration

deferential 5 civil **6** polite **7** dutiful **8** obedient, reverent **9** courteous, regardful **10** respectful, submissive **11** acquiescent, considerate, reverential

deferment 4 stay **5** delay **9** extension **12** postponement

deferral 5 pause **6** hiatus, recess **8** abeyance **10** suspension **12** postponement **14** discontinuance

defiance 9 hostility, obstinacy, rebellion **12** disobedience **14** rebelliousness

defiant 4 bold **9** truculent **10** aggressive, rebellious **11** disobedient, provocative

Defiant Ones, The
    director: **13** Stanley Kramer
    cast: **10** Tony Curtis **11** Lon Chaney Jr **12** Cara Williams **13** Charles McGraw, Sidney Poitier, Theodore Bikel
    Oscar for: **10** screenplay

deficiency 4 flaw **6** defect **7** failing, frailty **8** shortage, weakness **10** inadequacy **11** shortcoming **12** imperfection **13** insufficiency

deficient 4 weak **6** flawed **7** lacking, short on **8** inferior **9** defective **10** inadequate **11** substandard **12** insufficient **14** unsatisfactory

deficit 8 shortage **9** shortfall **10** deficiency

de fide 10 of the faith

defile 4 soil **5** dirty, smear, spoil, stain, taint **6** befoul, debase **7** degrade, profane, tarnish **8** besmirch, disgrace, dishonor **9** desecrate

defiled 5 dirty **6** fouled, impure, soiled **7** debased, dirtied, stained, sullied, tainted, unclean **8** befouled, polluted, ravished, smirched, violated **9** blackened, corrupted, tarnished **10** besmirched **12** contaminated

define 5 state **7** clarify, explain, specify **8** describe, spell out **9** delineate, designate

definite 3 set **4** sure **5** exact, fixed **7** certain, precise **8** clear-cut, positive

definitely 5 truly **6** indeed, surely **7** for sure, no doubt **9** assuredly, certainly, decidedly, doubtless, expressly **10** absolutely, decisively, explicitly, positively, undeniably **11** indubitably, inescapably, unavoidably, undoubtedly **12** unmistakably **13** categorically, unequivocally **14** unquestionably **16** incontrovertibly

definiteness 8 sureness **9** certainty, precision **10** exactitude **11** unambiguity

definition 6 limits **7** clarity, purpose **11** description **15** distinctiveness

definitive 5 exact **7** decided, perfect **8** complete, decisive, reliable **10** conclusive, consummate

deflate 6 reduce **7** flatten **8** contract **9** devaluate

deflect 6 divert, swerve

Defoe, Daniel
    author of: **6** Roxana **11** Colonel Jack **12** Moll Flanders **14** Robinson Crusoe **23** A Journal of the Plague Year

DeForest, Lee
    invented/worked on: **10** audion tube, television **13** sound pictures

deform 3 mar **4** maim **5** twist **6** mangle **7** blemish, contort, distort **9** disfigure

deformation 9 deformity **10** distortion **12** malformation **13** disfigurement

deformed 6 marred, warped **7** defaced, mangled, spoiled, twisted **8** crippled **9** misshapen, monstrous **10** disfigured

defraud 3 con **4** bilk, rook **5** cheat **6** fleece, rip off **7** swindle

defray 3 pay **5** cover **11** foot the bill

deft 3 apt **4** able, sure **5** quick **6** adroit, expert **8** skillful **9** dexterous

deftness 5 knack, skill **7** ability **8** facility **9** adeptness, dexterity, handiness **10** adroitness, competency **11** proficiency **12** skillfulness

defunct 4 dead **7** extinct

defy 5 spurn **6** oppose, resist **7** disdain **8** confront **9** challenge, disregard, withstand

degage 4 easy **8** detached **10** disengaged **13** unconstrained

Degas, (Hilaire Germain) Edgar
    born: **5** Paris **6** France
    artwork: **14** The Ballet Class, The Morning Bath **15** Ballet Rehearsal **16** The Millinery Shop **17** The Glass of Absinth **23** Woman with Chrysanthemums **30** The Little Fourteen-Year-Old Dancer

degeneracy 9 decadence, depravity **10** debasement, debauchery, immorality, perversion **11** dissolution

degenerate 3 rot **4** base, sink, vile **5** decay **6** revert, wanton, wicked, worsen **7** corrupt, debased, decline, go to pot, immoral, pervert, vicious **8** decadent, degraded, depraved **9** abandoned, backslide, debauched, dissolute, perverted **10** dissipated, go downhill, profligate, retrograde, retrogress **11** deteriorate, hit the skids **12** disintegrate

degeneration 7 decline **9** depravity **10** corruption, debasement, immorality, perversion **11** degradation, dissolution, viciousness **13** deterioration

degradation 8 disgrace **11** humiliation

Degradation of the Democratic Dogma, The
    author: **10** Henry Adams

degrade 5 lower, shame **6** debase, demote **7** corrupt **8** disgrace, dishonor

degraded 4 vile **6** wicked **7** corrupt, debased, lowered **8** depraved, shameful, unworthy **9** debauched, perverted, reprobate **10** degenerate **11** undignified **12** unregenerate

degrading 3 low **6** menial **8** shameful **11** humiliating

degree 4 mark, step, unit **5** grade, level, order, phase, point, stage **8** division, interval
    abbreviation: **3** deg

De Guiche, Lillian
    real name of: **11** Lillian Gish

de gustibus non est disputandum 29 there is no disputing about tastes

De Havilland, Joan de Beauvoir
    real name of: **12** Joan Fontaine

De Havilland, Olivia
    sister: **12** Joan Fontaine
    born: **5** Japan, Tokyo
    roles: **7** Melanie **10** The Heiress (Oscar) **11** The Snake Pit **12** Captain Blood, To Each His Own (Oscar) **14** Anthony Adverse, My Cousin Rachel **15** Gone With the Wind, Hold Back

the Dawn **16** Light in the Piazza **22** Hush Hush Sweet Charlotte **24** The Adventures of Robin Hood

dehydrate 3 dry **5** parch **6** dry out

dehydrated 3 dry **7** parched, thirsty **8** dried-out **9** shriveled **10** desiccated

deification 7 worship **8** idolatry **10** exaltation **13** glorification

deify 5 exalt **7** glorify, idolize, worship

Deighton, Len
   author of: **4** SS-GB **14** The Ipcress File **15** Funeral in Berlin **16** Catch a Falling Spy

deign 4 deem **5** stoop **6** see fit **7** consent **8** think fit **10** condescend

Dei gratia 15 by the grace of God

Deiphobus
   father: **5** Priam
   mother: **6** Hecuba
   brother: **6** Hector
   wife: **5** Helen
   killed by: **8** Menelaus

Deirdre
   origin: **5** Irish
   husband: **6** Naoise
   father-in-law: **6** Usnach
   uncle: **9** Conchobar

Deirdre of the Sorrows
   author: **19** John Millington Synge

deity, the Deity 3 god **4** idol **7** goddess, godhead, Jehovah **8** Almighty, divinity, immortal, Olympian

deja vu 11 already seen

dejected 3 low, sad **4** blue, down **7** doleful, unhappy **8** desolate **9** depressed, sorrowful **10** despondent, dispirited, spiritless **11** discouraged, downhearted, low-spirited **12** disconsolate, disheartened

dejection 5 gloom **7** sadness **10** depression, low spirits, melancholy **11** despondency **15** dispiritedness, downheartedness

dejeuner 5 lunch

de jure 7 by right **14** according to law

dekagram
   abbreviation: **3** dkg

dekaliter
   abbreviation: **3** dkL

dekameter, decameter
   abbreviation: **3** dkm

Dekker, Thomas
   author of: **11** Westward Ho! (with John Webster) **20** The Shoemaker's Holiday

de Kooning, Willem
   born: **9** Rotterdam **14** The Netherlands
   artwork: **5** Woman **8** Painting **15** Woman and Bicycle

Delacroix, Eugene
   born: **6** France **18** Charenton-St Maurice
   artwork: **8** Paganini **14** Women of Algiers **15** Massacre at Chios **16** The

Barque of Dante **19** Chopin and George Sand **20** Dante and Virgil in Hell **22** Liberty at the Barricades, The Death of Sardanapalus

Delaroche, Paul
   born: **5** Paris **6** France
   artwork: **24** The Death of Queen Elizabeth, The Death of the Duke of Guise **26** The Execution of Lady Jane Grey **36** Children of Edward Imprisoned in the Tower

Delaunay, Robert
   born: **5** Paris **6** France
   artwork: **5** Disks **6** Cities, Rhythm **7** Runners, Windows **10** Cathedrals **11** City of Paris, Eiffel Tower **14** The Cardiff Team **19** Cosmic Circular Forms **28** Simultaneous Prismatic Windows

Delaware
   abbreviation: **2** DE **3** Del
   nickname: **5** First **7** Blue Hen, Diamond
   capital: **5** Dover
   largest city: **10** Wilmington
   others: **5** Acoma, Lewes **6** Easton, Newark, Smyrna **7** Briston, Elsmere, Milford **8** Claymont **9** New Castle **10** Georgetown
   college: **6** Wesley **10** Brandywine, Wilmington **12** Goldey Beacom
   feature: **10** Winterthur **15** Old Swedes Church **17** E I du Pont de Nemours
   tribe: **4** Leni **5** Lenni **6** Lenape, Munsee
   people: **10** Howard Pyle
   island: **7** Fenwick
   land rank: **10** forty-ninth
   physical feature:
      bay: **8** Delaware, Rehoboth
      sea: **8** Atlantic
   river: **8** Delaware **9** Christina, Nanticoke **10** Brandywine
   state admission: **5** first
   state bird: **14** blue hen chicken
   state flower: **12** peach blossom
   state motto: **22** Liberty and Independence
   state song: **11** Our Delaware
   state tree: **13** American holly

Delaware (Lenni-Lenape)
   language family: **9** Algonkian **10** Algonquian
   tribe: **5** Munsi, Unami **6** Munsee **11** Unalachtigo
   location: **7** New York **8** Delaware **9** Manhattan, New Jersey **10** Long Island **12** Pennsylvania, Staten Island
   leader: **7** Tamanen, Tammany
   deity: **11** Kitanitowet

delay 4 slow, stay **5** check, table, tarry **6** dawdle, detain, hamper, hinder, hold up, impede, linger, put off, retard, shelve **7** inhibit, slowing, suspend **8** dawdling, obstruct, postpone, reprieve, stoppage, tarrying **9** deferment, lingering, loitering **10** suspen-

sion **12** postponement, prolongation **13** procrastinate

delayed 4 late **6** put off, slowed **7** held up, stalled, tarried **8** arrested, deferred, detained, retarded **9** postponed, slackened **12** dillydallied **14** procrastinated **15** dragged one's feet

Delbruck, Max
   field: **7** biology **17** molecular genetics
   researched: **20** genetic recombination
   awarded: **10** Nobel Prize

delectable 5 tasty, yummy **8** pleasant **9** agreeable, delicious, enjoyable **10** delightful, gratifying **11** pleasurable

delegate 3 rep **4** give, name **5** agent, envoy, proxy **6** assign, charge, deputy **7** entrust **8** give over, transfer **9** authorize, designate **10** commission **14** representative

delegation 11 designation, entrustment **13** authorization, commissioning

delete 3 cut **4** omit **5** erase **6** cancel, remove

deleterious 7 harmful, hurtful, ruinous **9** dangerous, injurious **11** destructive, detrimental

Delia
   festival of: **6** Apollo

deliberate 4 easy, slow, wary **5** weigh **6** confer, debate **7** careful, discuss, examine, express, planned, prudent, willful **8** cautious, cogitate, consider, measured, meditate, mull over **9** leisurely, unhurried **10** calculated, considered, purposeful, thoughtful **11** circumspect, contemplate, intentional, prearranged **12** premeditated

deliberate together 6 confer **7** consult, discuss

deliberation 4 care **6** debate **10** conference, discussion, steadiness **11** calculation, carefulness, forethought **13** premeditation **14** circumspection

Delibes, C P (Clement Philibert) Leo
   born: **6** France **14** St Germain-du-Val
   composer of: **5** Lakme **6** Sylvia **8** Coppelia **10** Le Roi l'a dit

delicacy 4 tact **5** taste **7** frailty **8** accuracy, elegance, fineness, softness, weakness **9** fragility, frailness, lightness, precision **10** perfection, smoothness **11** savoir-faire, sensibility, sensitivity, unsoundness **13** consideration, exquisiteness, sensitiveness **14** discrimination

delicate 4 fine, soft **5** frail, muted **6** ailing, dainty, feeble, flimsy, infirm, minute, savory, sickly, touchy, unwell **7** careful, elegant, fragile, refined, subdued, tactful **8** detailed, luscious, tasteful, ticklish, weakened **9** breakable, delicious, difficult, exquisite, palatable, sensitive, toothsome **10** appetizing, diplomatic, fastidious, perishable, precarious, scrupulous **11** debilitated

Delicate Balance, A
author: **11** Edward Albee

delicious 5 tasty, yummy **6** joyful, savory **8** charming, luscious, pleasant **9** palatable **10** appetizing, delectable, delightful **11** pleasurable **13** mouthwatering

delight 3 joy **5** amuse, charm, cheer, revel **6** please **7** enchant, gratify, rapture **8** pleasure **9** enjoyment, fascinate, happiness **13** gratification

delighted 6 elated **7** pleased, psyched **8** ecstatic **9** enchanted **10** captivated, enraptured, enthralled **11** on cloud nine

delightful 6 peachy **7** amiable, amusing **8** charming, engaging, pleasing **9** agreeable, congenial, enjoyable **10** enchanting **11** pleasurable **12** entertaining

delight in 4 love **5** adore, eat up, enjoy, fancy, savor **6** dote on, relish **7** cherish **8** treasure **10** appreciate

Delilah
lover: **6** Samson
betrayed: **6** Samson

delineate 4 draw **5** draft **6** define, depict, design, lay out, sketch **7** outline, portray **8** describe **9** represent **12** characterize

delineation 9 depiction, portrayal **11** description **12** illustration **14** representation **16** characterization

delineavit 6 he drew (this) **7** she drew (this)

delinquency 7 misdeed **10** misconduct, negligence **11** dereliction, misbehavior **19** neglect of obligation

delinquent 3 due **4** late **6** remiss **7** hoodlum, misdoer, overdue **8** derelict **9** in arrears, miscreant, negligent, wrongdoer **10** neglectful

delirious 6 raving **7** excited, frantic **8** ecstatic, frenzied **10** incoherent **11** carried away **13** hallucinating

delirium 5 fever **6** frenzy, raving **7** madness, ranting **8** insanity **10** brain fever

Deliro
character in: **22** Every Man Out of His Humour
author: **6** Jonson

Delisle, Guillaume
field: **9** geography
nationality: **6** French
founder of: **15** modern geography

Delius, Frederick
born: **7** England **8** Bradford
composer of: **5** Paris **6** Koanga **7** Eventyr, Irmelin **8** Sea-Drift **9** Brigg Fair **10** Appalachia **11** A Mass of Life, Sur les Cimes **17** Fennimore and Gerda **20** North Country Sketches **22** A Village Romeo and Juliet, Over the Hills and Far Away

deliver 3 aim, say **4** bear, deal, free,

give, save **5** bring, carry, throw, utter **6** convey, direct, launch, rescue, strike **7** release, set free **8** give over, hand over, liberate, proclaim, turn over **9** surrender **10** emancipate

deliverance 6 rescue **7** release **9** salvation **10** liberation **12** emancipation

Deliverance
director: **11** John Boorman
author: **11** James Dickey
cast: **8** Ronny Cox **9** Jon Voight, Ned Beatty **12** Burt Reynolds
song: **13** Dueling Banjos

deliver up 4 cede, give **5** grant, yield **8** fork over, hand over, transfer **9** surrender **10** relinquish

delivery 8 transfer **11** transferral, transmittal **12** transmission

delivery service 3 DHL, UPS **4** USPS **5** FedEx **8** Airborne **11** Express mail

dell 4 dale, dene, glen, vale **5** glade **6** dingle, hollow, valley

Della Robbia, Luca
born: **5** Italy **8** Florence
artwork: **8** Cantoria (Singing Gallery) **12** The Ascension **13** Altman Madonna **15** Madonna and Child, The Resurrection

Dello Joio, Norman
born: **9** New York NY
composer of: **7** The Ruby **12** Psalm of David **15** New York Profiles, The Trial at Rouen, Triumph of St Joan **20** Proud Music of the Storm, The Lamentation of Saul

Delon, Alain
born: **6** France, Sceaux
roles: **10** Purple Noon, The Leopard **13** The Black Tulip **14** Is Paris Burning? **19** Rocco and His Brothers

Delphic
pertains to: **6** Apollo, Delphi

Delphic oracle
oracle of: **6** Apollo
located at: **6** Delphi
priestess: **6** Pythia

Delphinia
festival of: **6** Apollo

Del Rio, Dolores
real name: **21** Lolita Dolores Negrette
born: **6** Mexico **7** Durango
roles: **11** The Fugitive **13** Madame duBarry **15** Flying Down to Rio, Journey into Fear, Maria Candelaria

Delta Wedding
author: **11** Eudora Welty

delude 3 con **4** dupe, fool **5** put on, trick **7** deceive, mislead

deluge 4 bury, glut **5** drown, flood, spate, swamp **6** engulf **7** barrage, torrent **8** inundate, overflow, submerge **10** inundation

DeLuise, Dom
born: **10** Brooklyn NY
roles: **5** Fatso **6** The End **11** Silent Movie **14** Blazing Saddles

delusion 8 illusion **9** misbelief **10** aberration **11** derangement **13** hallucination, irrationality, misconception, self-deception

Delusions, Etc. of John Berryman
author: **12** John Berryman

deluxe 4 fine, posh **5** grand **6** choice, classy **7** elegant **8** splendid **9** luxurious

delve 5 probe **6** search **7** examine, explore **8** look into

demagogue 6 ranter **7** hothead, spouter **8** agitator, fomenter, inflamer **9** firebrand, haranguer **10** incendiary, malcontent, tub-thumper **12** rabble-rouser, troublemaker

demand 4 call, need, want **5** exact, order **7** command, require **11** requirement

demanding 4 hard **5** harsh, rigid **6** strict **8** exacting **9** difficult

demantoid
species: **6** garnet

demarche 4 gait, plan

demean 5 lower, shame **6** debase, humble **7** degrade **8** disgrace **9** humiliate

demeanor 4 mien **6** manner **7** bearing, conduct **8** behavior, presence **10** appearance, deportment **11** comportment

demented 3 mad **4** nuts **5** crazy **6** crazed, cuckoo, insane **7** lunatic **8** deranged

dementia praecox 13 schizophrenia

dementophobia
fear of: **8** insanity

demesne 4 land **5** realm **6** domain, estate **8** property

Demeter
origin: **5** Greek
goddess of: **5** earth **9** fertility
protectress of: **8** marriage **11** social order
father: **6** Cronus
mother: **4** Rhea
daughter: **10** Persephone
corresponds to: **5** Brimo, Ceres **8** Despoena
epithet: **5** Chloe, Lusia, Mysia **6** Antaea, Erinys, Stiria **7** Chamyne, Thesmia **8** Stiritis **9** Anesidora, Thermasia **11** Carpophorus **13** Thesimophorus

Demetrius
character in: **21** A Midsummer Night's Dream
author: **11** Shakespeare

De Mille, Agnes
choreographer of: **5** Rodeo **15** Fall River Legend

DeMille, Cecil B
director of: **9** Cleopatra **18** The Ten Commandments **22** The Greatest Show on Earth
niece: **5** Agnes (choreographer)

Demiphon
form: 4 king
sacrificed: 7 maidens
to prevent: 6 plague
demise 3 end 4 fall, ruin 5 death 7 decease, passing 8 collapse 10 expiration
demobilization 7 release 9 discharge 10 disbanding
demobilize 7 disband, release 9 discharge
Democoon
father: 5 Priam
birth: 12 illegitimate
killed by: 8 Odysseus
democracy 8 equality, fairness
Democracy
author: 10 Henry Adams
Democracy in America
author: 19 Alexis de Tocqueville
Democratic Party
symbol: 6 donkey
president belonging to: 4 Polk 6 Carter, Pierce, Truman, Wilson 7 Clinton, (Lyndon Baines) Johnson, Jackson, Kennedy 8 Buchanan, Van Buren 9 Cleveland, (Franklin D) Roosevelt
Democratic Republican Party
president belonging to: 5 (John Quincy) Adams 6 Monroe 7 Madison 9 Jefferson
demode 8 outmoded 13 unfashionable
demoiselle 4 girl
demolish 4 raze, ruin 5 level, total, wreck 7 destroy 9 devastate
demolition 6 razing 8 leveling, wrecking 11 destruction
demon 3 imp 4 jinn, ogre 5 afrit, devil, fiend, genie, harpy, jinni, lamia, satan, troll 6 afreet, dybbuk, goblin 7 incubus, monster, vampire, warlock 8 go-getter, succubus
demonic, demoniacal 6 hectic 7 frantic, hellish 8 devilish, fiendish, frenzied
demonstrable 7 evident 8 apparent, manifest, palpable 11 supportable
demonstrate 4 show 5 march, prove, teach 6 parade, picket, reveal 7 display, exhibit, explain 8 describe, manifest 9 establish 10 illustrate
demonstration 5 march, rally 6 parade 7 display 9 picketing 10 exhibition, exposition, expression 12 illustration, presentation 13 manifestation
demonstrative 7 gushing 8 effusive 12 affectionate
demonstrativeness 9 gushiness 12 effusiveness, emotionalism
demoralize 8 dispirit 9 undermine 10 disconcert, discourage, dishearten 11 disorganize
de mortuis nil nisi bonum 26 of the dead say nothing but good

demos 5 plebs 6 masses, people 7 commons 8 populace 9 commoners
demote 4 bust 5 abase 7 degrade
Dempsey, Jack (William Harrison)
nickname: 13 Manassa Mauler
sport: 6 boxing
class: 11 heavyweight
demur 5 qualm 6 object 7 protest, scruple 8 disagree 9 misgiving, objection 10 hesitation 11 compunction
demure 3 shy 4 prim 6 modest 7 bashful 8 reserved
demurrer 5 doubt, qualm 7 dissent, protest, scruple 8 objector, question, rebuttal 9 challenge, exception, misgiving, objection, protester, protestor, stricture 11 compunction 12 remonstrance
den 4 lair 5 haunt, study 6 hotbed 7 hangout, library, retreat, shelter 9 sanctuary
denial 7 refusal 9 disavowal, disowning, rejection 10 disclaimer
denigrate 4 soil 5 abuse, smear, sully 6 defame, dump on, malign, revile, vilify 7 asperse, blacken, degrade, run down, slander, traduce 8 backbite, badmouth, belittle, besmirch, tear down 9 call names, discredit, disparage, downgrade 10 calumniate, stigmatize
De Niro, Robert
born: 9 New York NY
roles: 4 Heat 6 Brazil 8 Cape Fear, Sleepers 10 A Bronx Tale, Angel Heart, Awakenings, Goodfellas, Raging Bull (Oscar), Taxi Driver 11 Mean Streets 13 The Deer Hunter 14 New York New York, The Godfather II 15 The King of Comedy, The Untouchables, True Confessions 17 Bang the Drum Slowly
denizen 7 dweller 8 resident 10 inhabitant
Denmark
other name: 17 Kongeriget Danmark
capital/largest city: 9 Kobenhavn 10 Copenhagen
others: 3 Hov 4 Hals, Koge, Nibe, Ribe, Soro 5 Arhus, Kosor, Vejle 6 Aarhus, Abenra, Alborg, Dorsor, Dragor, Nyberg, Odense, Skagen, Struer, Viborg 7 Aalborg, Esbjerg, Horsens, Kolding, Morsens, Randers 8 Ballerup, Elsinore, Gentofte, Glostrup, Hillerod, Naestred, Roskilde, Slagelse 9 Haderslev, Helsingor, Svendborg 10 Fredericia 13 Frederikshavn
school:
university institute of: 18 Theoretical Physics
folk high school: 14 folkehojskoler
continuation school: 11 efterskoler
division: 3 Fyn 7 Jutland, Lolland 9 Schleswig, Sjaelland
measure: 3 ell, fod, mil, pot 4 alen, favn, last, rode 5 album, anker,

kande, linje, paegl, tomme 6 achtel, paegel, skeppe 7 landmil, oltonde, ortonde, skieppe, viertel 8 fjerding 9 ottingkar 10 korntonmde
monetary unit: 3 one, ora, ore 4 fyrk 5 krone 8 frederik, skilling 9 rigsdaler
weight: 2 es 3 lod, ort, vog 4 last, mark, pund, unze 5 carat, kvint, pound, quint, tonde 6 toende 7 centner, lispund, quintin 8 lispound, skippund 9 skibslast, skippound 10 bismerpund
island: 2 Oe 3 Als, Fyn, Mon, Rum, Thy 4 Aaro, Aero, Fano, Fohr, Moen, Mors, Romo 5 Baago, Faero, Faroe, Funen, Laeso, Samso, Sando 6 Amager, Sandoy, Sejero, Sudero 7 Faeroes, Falster, Hesselo, Laaland, Lolland, Seeland, Zealand 8 Bornholm, Eysturoy, Sudhuroy 9 Greenland, Langeland, Sjaelland 10 Vendsyssel
lake: 6 Arreso
hill: 12 Ejer Bavnehoj 14 Himmelbjaerget
highest point: 12 Yding Skovhoj
river: 3 Asa 4 Holm, Omme, Stor 5 Skive, Susaa, Varde 6 Gelsaa, Gudena, Vorgod 7 Gudenaa, Lilleaa, Lonborg
sea: 5 North 6 Baltic 7 Oresund 8 Atlantic, Kattegat 9 Skagerrak
physical feature:
fjord: 3 Ise 4 Isse 5 Lamme
inlet: 3 Ise 5 Fjord, Vejle 6 Nissum, Odense 7 Horsens, Logstor 8 Limfjord, Mariager
peninsula: 7 Jutland
strait: 7 Otesund 8 Kattegat 9 Skagerrak
people: 4 Dane, Jute 5 Angle 6 Cimbri, Eskimo, German, Ostmen, Teuton, Viking 12 Scandinavian
astronomer: 10 Tycho Brahe
author: 11 Isak Dinesen 21 Hans Christian Andersen
founder: 4 Axel 7 Absalon
king: 4 Hans, Knud 6 Canute 8 Frederik 9 Christian 10 Gorm the Old 15 Harold Bluetooth
philosopher: 11 Kierkegaard
physicist: 9 Niels Bohr
queen: 9 Margrethe 12 Thyra Danebod
sculptor: 11 Thorvaldsen
teacher: 4 Kold
language: 4 Odan 6 Danish, German 8 Faeroese 11 Greenlander
religion: 19 Evangelical Lutheran
place:
airport: 7 Kastrup
castle: 7 Egeskov 8 Kronborg 13 Frederiksborg
museum: 6 Rebild 9 Glyptotek 11 Thorvaldsen 15 Rosenborg Castle
park: 10 Langelinie 13 Tivoli Gardens

royal palace: 11 Amalienborg
statue: 13 Little Mermaid
stock exchange: 5 Borse 6 Borsen
feature:
 dance: 6 sextur
 drink: 5 glogg 7 aquavit
 beer: 6 Tuborg 9 Carlsberg
food:
 cheese: 3 Ost 4 Blue, Tybo 5 Es-
 rom, Samso 6 Samsoe 7 Havarti,
 Mycella
 meat patty: 11 frikadeller
 pudding: 15 rodgrod med flode

Dennis, Patrick
 author of: 10 Auntie Mame

Dennis, Sandy
 real name: 16 Sandra Dale Dennis
 born: 10 Hastings NE
 roles: 12 Any Wednesday 15 A Thousand Clowns 18 Up the Down Staircase 25 Who's Afraid of Virginia
 Woolf?

Dennis the Hangman
 character in: 12 Barnaby Rudge
 author: 7 Dickens

Dennis the Menace
 creator: 11 Hank Ketcham
 character: 9 Mrs Elkins 10 John Wilson 12 Eloise Wilson, George Wilson, Joey McDonald, Martha Wilson
 13 Alice Mitchell, Henry Mitchell,
 Tommy Anderson 14 Dennis Mitchell
 dog: 4 Ruff
 cast: 8 Gil Smith, Jay North 10 Billy
 Booth, Gale Gordon, Sara Seeger 11
 Gloria Henry, Irene Tedrow, Sylvia
 Field 12 Joseph Kearns 15 Herbert
 Anderson

denomination 4 name, sect, size 5
class, value 8 category, grouping 10
persuasion 11 designation

denotation 4 mark, name, sign 6
symbol 7 meaning 10 indication

denote 4 mark, mean, name 6 signal 7
signify 8 indicate

denouement 3 end 6 finale, upshot 7
outcome 8 solution 10 conclusion 11
termination

denounce 6 accuse, vilify 7 censure,
condemn 9 criticize

denouncement 7 censure 12 condemnation, denunciation

de novo 4 anew 5 again 6 afresh 16
from the beginning

dense 4 dull, dumb, slow 5 close,
heavy, thick 6 stupid 7 compact,
crowded, intense 8 ignorant 9 dimwitted 10 compressed 11 thickheaded 12
concentrated, impenetrable

Densher, Merton
 character in: 17 The Wings of the
 Dove
 author: 5 James

density 4 mass 6 weight 7 opacity 8
dullness, solidity 9 stupidity, thickness 10 obtuseness, opaqueness 11
compactness

dent 3 pit 4 nick 6 hollow 10 depression 11 indentation

denude 4 bare 5 strip 6 divest 7 lay
bare 8 unclothe

denuded 4 bare 5 naked 6 barren 8
stripped 9 unclothed, uncovered

denunciation 7 censure 12 condemnation, denouncement 13 attack
against

Denver
 basketball team: 7 Nuggets
 football team: 4 Gold 7 Broncos

deny 6 refuse, refute 7 disavow 8 disallow, disclaim 9 disaffirm 10 contradict

deny oneself 5 avoid, forgo 6 eschew, give up, refuse 7 abstain, forbear 8 renounce 9 sacrifice

deny responsibility 7 disavow

Deo gratias 13 thanks be to God

Deo volente 10 God willing

DePalma, Brian
 director of: 6 Carrie 8 Scarface 11
 Carlito's Way, Raising Cain 13
 Dressed to Kill 15 The Untouchables
 17 Mission Impossible 20 Bonfire of
 the Vanities

depart 2 go 4 exit 5 leave 6 embark 7
deviate, digress, entrain

departed 4 dead, gone, late, left, past,
went 6 at rest, bygone 7 gone off 8
gone away 10 passed away 11 gone
to glory 12 late-lamented 20 gone the
way of all flesh

depart for 8 leave for 9 adjourn to,
set off for, set out for 10 head toward, move toward

depart hastily 3 fly 4 flee 5 elope 6
decamp, escape 7 abscond 9 skedaddle

department 4 unit 6 branch, bureau,
sector 7 section 8 district, division,
province

departure 4 exit 5 going 6 exodus 7
leaving 9 deviation 10 digression, divergence

depend 4 rely, rest 5 count, hinge 6
hang on

dependable 4 sure, true 5 loyal 6
steady, trusty 7 trusted 8 faithful, reliable 9 steadfast, unfailing 11 trustworthy

dependence 5 trust 8 reliance 10 confidence, dependency

dependency 10 dependence

dependent 7 reliant

depict 4 draw, limn 5 carve, chart,
draft, paint 6 define, detail, map out,
recite, record, relate, sculpt, sketch 7
diagram, narrate, picture, portray, recount 8 describe 9 chronicle, delineate, dramatize, represent, verbalize 10
illustrate 12 characterize

depiction 6 sketch 7 drawing, picture
8 portrait 9 picturing, portrayal 11 delineation 12 illustration 14 representation 16 characterization

deplete 5 drain, use up 6 lessen, reduce 7 consume, exhaust 8 decrease
10 impoverish

depleted 5 empty, spent, waste 6 barren, used up 7 drained, emptied, reduced, worn out 8 bankrupt, consumed, expended, lessened 9
exhausted, infertile 10 unfruitful

deplorable 5 awful 8 wretched 9 miserable 11 blameworthy 13 reprehensible 17 deserving reproach

deplore 5 mourn 6 bemoan, bewail,
lament 7 censure, condemn 9 grieve
for 12 disapprove of

deport 3 act 4 oust 5 carry, exile, expel 6 banish, behave 7 cast out 10
expatriate 14 conduct oneself

deported person 2 DP 5 exile 8 deportee 10 expatriate 14 banished person

deportment 7 conduct 8 behavior, demeanor 11 comportment

depose 4 oust 6 unseat 8 dethrone 16
remove from office

deposit 3 put 4 pile 5 place 7 put
down, set down 8 sediment 10 accumulate 11 down payment, give in
trust, installment 12 accumulation 14
partial payment

deposition 7 deposit 9 statement, testimony 11 declaration 12 accumulation

depository 4 bank, safe 5 vault 6 museum 7 library 8 archives 10 storehouse

depot 4 dump 7 station 8 terminal,
terminus 10 bus station 15 railroad
station 20 military storage place

depraved 4 vile 6 wicked 7 corrupt,
debased 8 degraded 9 debauched,
perverted 10 degenerate

depravity 8 vileness 9 decadence 10
corruption, debasement, debauchery,
degeneracy, immorality, perversion,
wickedness 11 degradation, dissolution

deprecate 6 insult 7 condemn, protest
8 belittle, object to, play down 10 depreciate 15 take exception to

deprecated 7 defamed, put down 8
despised 9 belittled, derogated, disdained

deprecation 4 slur 5 abuse 7 protest,
put-down 9 aspersion 10 aspersions,
belittling, defamation, derogation 11
disapproval 12 condemnation 13 disparagement

deprecatory 8 critical 9 insulting, maligning, vilifying 10 belittling, defamatory, derogatory, slanderous 11 disparaging 12 disapproving

depreciate 5 scorn 7 run down 8 belittle, diminish 9 denigrate, disparage,

downgrade, lose value **13** reduce in value, lower the value

depreciation 5 scorn **7** disdain **8** contempt **9** criticism, deflation **10** belittling, disrespect **11** devaluation **13** disparagement

depredation 4 sack **6** rapine, ravage **7** looting, pillage, plunder, robbery, sacking **8** spoiling **9** marauding **10** brigandage, ravishment, spoliation **11** desecration, devastation, freebooting, laying waste

depress 5 lower **6** deject, lessen, reduce, sadden, weaken **7** cut back **8** diminish, dispirit **9** press down **10** dishearten **14** lower in spirits

depressed 3 sad **4** blue **7** unhappy **8** dejected, downcast **10** despondent, dispirited, melancholy **11** low-spirited **12** disconsolate, inconsolable

depressing 3 sad **6** gloomy **8** lowering **9** dejecting, saddening **10** oppressing **11** casting down, dispiriting, melancholic, pushing down **12** discouraging, pressing down, weighing down **14** causing sadness

depression 5 gloom **6** dimple, hollow **7** sadness **9** dejection, recession **10** desolation, melancholy **11** despondency, indentation, melancholia **14** discouragement **15** downheartedness, economic decline

deprive 5 strip **6** divest **8** take from **10** confiscate, dispossess

deprived 8 divested, stripped **11** handicapped **12** dispossessed, impoverished **13** disadvantaged **15** underprivileged

deprive of honor 5 abase, shame, sully **6** defame **7** blacken, tarnish **8** disgrace, dishonor **9** discredit **10** stigmatize

deprive of strength 6 hinder, weaken **7** disable, wear out **8** enervate, enfeeble, handicap **10** debilitate, devitalize

de profundis 13 from the depths

depth 6 timbre **8** deepness **10** profundity **19** downward measurement **24** perpendicular measurement

depths 4 deep **6** bowels **8** interior, recesses

deputation 9 committee **10** commission, delegation **15** representatives

deputize 6 assign **7** appoint **8** delegate **10** commission

deputy 4 aide **5** agent, envoy, proxy **6** second **8** delegate, emissary, minister **9** alternate, assistant, go-between, messenger, middleman, surrogate **10** ambassador, substitute **11** pinch hitter **12** spokesperson **14** representative **15** second-in-command

DeQuincey, Thomas
  author of: 19 The English Mail-Coach **31** On the Knocking at the Gate in Macbeth **32** Confessions of an English Opium-Eater

derail 3 bar **4** balk, foil **5** block, check, spike **6** hinder, impede, thwart **7** inhibit, prevent **8** obstruct **14** throw off course

deranged 3 mad **5** crazy **6** insane **8** demented **10** irrational, unbalanced

derangement 6 lunacy **7** madness **8** insanity **9** craziness **11** peculiarity **13** irrationality, mental illness **14** mental disorder

Der Bingle
  nickname of: 10 Bing Crosby

Derby 4 race
  site: 5 Epsom **8** Kentucky **14** Churchill Downs

Derek, Bo
  husband: 4 John
  roles: 3 Ten (10) **6** Bolero, Tarzan

derelict 3 bum **4** hobo **5** tramp **6** remiss **7** outcast, vagrant **8** careless, deserted **9** abandoned, negligent **10** delinquent, neglectful

dereliction 7 failure, neglect **9** disregard **10** negligence **11** delinquency **13** noncompliance, nonobservance

De rerum natura
  author: 9 Lucretius

deride 4 mock **5** scoff, scorn **7** sneer at **8** ridicule

de rigueur 11 fashionable **16** strictly required

derision 5 scorn **7** disdain, mockery **8** ridicule, sneering

derivation 5 stock **6** origin, source **7** descent, getting, lineage **8** ancestry, deriving, heritage **9** acquiring, etymology, parentage **10** background, beginnings, extraction **21** historical development

derive 4 gain **5** arise, enjoy, glean **6** obtain **7** descend **8** stem from **9** originate

dermaptera
  class: 8 hexapoda
  phylum: 10 arthropoda
  group: 6 earwig

dermatitis 4 rash **6** eczema **9** psoriasis **12** inflammation

Dern, Bruce
  born: 9 Chicago IL
  roles: 6 Marnie, Tattoo **10** Coming Home, Family Plot **11** Black Sunday **13** The Wild Angels **14** The Great Gatsby **22** The King of Marvin Gardens

dernier 4 last **5** final **8** ultimate

dernier cri 9 latest cry **10** latest word **13** latest fashion

derogate 4 blot **5** taint **6** smirch **8** disgrace **9** disparage

derogation 4 blot **5** odium, stain **7** blemish **8** contempt, disfavor, disgrace, ignominy **9** disesteem, disrepute **10** disrespect **11** humiliation **13** disparagement

derogatory 9 injurious **10** belittling **11** disparaging, unfavorable **12** unflattering **15** uncomplimentary

derrick 3 rig **5** crane, hoist, tower **9** framework
  kind: 3 oil **6** sheers **7** gin-pole
  part: 3 gin, leg **4** boom, mast **6** pulley **7** guy line

derring-do 6 daring **8** audacity, boldness **11** daredevilry **12** daredeviltry, recklessness **15** venturesomeness

dervish 5 fakir **6** Muslim **7** ascetic

De Sapientia Veterum
  author: 12 Francis Bacon

Descartes, Rene
  author of: 17 Discourse on Method
  field: 11 mathemathics
  nationality: 6 French
  developed: 18 analytical geometry
  quote: 13 Cogito ergo sum **18** I think therefore I am
  pertaining to: 9 Cartesian

descend 3 dip **4** drop, pass **5** slant, slope, swoop **6** go down, invade **7** incline **8** come down, inherited **11** come in force **12** be handed down, move downward

descendant 5 issue, scion **7** progeny **9** offspring

descend upon 6 assail, attack, charge **7** assault, set upon **12** bear down upon

descent 4 drop, fall, raid **5** slant, slope **6** origin **7** assault, decline, lineage **8** ancestry **9** declivity, incursion **10** coming down **11** sneak attack, sudden visit

describe 4 draw **5** trace **6** depict, detail, recite, relate **7** explain, mark out, narrate, outline, portray, recount, speak of **9** delineate **10** illustrate **12** characterize

description 3 ilk **4** kind, sort, type **5** brand, class, genus **6** manner, nature **7** account, species, variety **9** depiction, narration, portrayal **12** illustration **16** characterization

descry 3 see **4** spot **6** behold, notice **7** discern, observe, pick out **8** discover **12** catch sight of

Desdemona
  character in: 7 Othello
  author: 11 Shakespeare

desecrate 6 defile **7** profane, violate **8** dishonor

desecration 8 dishonor **9** violation **10** defilement **11** profanation

desert 3 dry **4** arid, wild **5** leave, waste **6** barren **7** abandon, forsake **8** desolate, untilled **9** infertile, wasteland **10** arid region **11** run away from, uninhabited **12** uncultivated **16** barren wilderness
  world: 4 Gobi, Thar **6** Gibson, Lib-

yan, Mohave, Nubian, Sahara, Syrian **7** Arabian, Atacama, Kara Kum, Painted, Sonoran **8** Kalahari **9** Patagonia **10** Great Sandy **11** Death Valley

watering spot: 5 Oasis

deserted 4 AWOL, left **5** empty **6** lonely, vacant **7** cast off, forlorn, reneged **8** defected, desolate, forsaken, marooned **9** abandoned, absconded **12** quit one's post **14** left in the lurch

desertedness 9 emptiness **10** desolation **13** uncrowdedness

Deserted Village, The
author: 15 Oliver Goldsmith

desertion 8 quitting **9** forsaking **11** abandonment **14** relinquishment

desertlike 3 dry **4** arid, sere **5** sandy **6** barren **7** dried up, parched **9** waterless

deserts 3 due **5** worth **6** reward **7** payment

deserve 4 rate **5** merit **7** warrant **9** earn as due **10** be worthy of, qualify for **12** be entitled to **13** be deserving of

deserving 6 worthy **9** qualified

deserving reproach 8 blamable **10** deplorable, punishable, reprovable **11** blameworthy **12** reproachable **13** reprehensible

De Sica, Vittorio
director of: 15 The Bicycle Thief **27** The Garden of the Finzi-Continis

desiccate 5 dry up, parch **6** wither **7** shrivel **9** dehydrate

design 3 aim, end **4** draw, form, goal, plan, plot **5** draft, motif, set up **6** devise, intend, scheme, sketch, target **7** destine, diagram, drawing, fashion, outline, pattern, project, purpose **8** conceive, intrigue **9** blueprint, intention, objective **11** arrangement **14** draw up plans for

designate 4 call, name, term **5** elect, label **6** assign, choose, select **7** appoint, signify, specify **8** identify, indicate, nominate, pinpoint

designation 5 label **6** naming **10** delegation **11** appointment **13** specification **14** identification

designer 7 creator, deviser, planner **9** contriver **10** originator

designing 4 wily **6** artful, crafty **7** cunning **8** plotting, scheming **9** conniving

desirable 4 fine **8** in demand, pleasing **9** advisable **10** beneficial **11** worth having **12** advantageous

desire 3 yen **4** need, urge, want, wish **5** crave **6** ask for, hunger, thirst **7** craving, longing, long for, request **8** yearning, yearn for **9** hunger for, thirst for

Desire Under the Elms
author: 12 Eugene O'Neill

character: 4 Eben **5** Peter **6** Simeon **11** Abbie Putnam **12** Ephraim Cabot

desirous 4 avid, keen **5** eager **7** hopeful, longing, wishful **8** yearning

desist 4 stop **5** cease **6** lay off **7** suspend **8** leave off **11** discontinue, refrain from

Desk Set
director: 10 Walter Lang
cast: 8 Gig Young **11** Dina Merrill **12** Joan Blondell, Spencer Tracy **16** Katharine Hepburn

desolate 3 sad **4** bare, ruin **5** bleak, empty **6** barren, grieve, ravage, sadden **7** depress, destroy, forlorn **8** dejected, demolish, deserted, distress, downcast, forsaken, lay waste, wretched **9** abandoned, depressed, devastate, miserable, sorrowful **10** despondent, discourage, dishearten, melancholy **11** downhearted, uninhabited

desolating 6 tragic **7** ruinous **8** dreadful, grievous, terrible **10** calamitous, horrendous **11** devastating **12** catastrophic

desolation 4 ruin **6** misery, sorrow **7** sadness **8** bareness, distress, solitude **9** bleakness, dejection, emptiness, seclusion **10** barrenness, depression, dreariness, loneliness, melancholy, wilderness **11** destruction, devastation, unhappiness **12** solitariness

despair 5 gloom, trial **6** burden, ordeal **9** lose heart **10** depression, have no hope **11** despondency, lose faith in **12** hopelessness **14** discouragement

despair of 5 doubt **8** give up on **10** have no hope

desperado 4 thug **5** rowdy **6** bandit, gunman, outlaw **7** brigand, convict, hoodlum, ruffian **8** criminal, fugitive, hooligan **9** terrorist **10** lawbreaker

desperate 4 dire, rash, wild **5** grave, great **6** daring, urgent **7** extreme, frantic, serious **8** critical, hopeless, reckless, wretched **9** dangerous, incurable **10** beyond hope, despairing, despondent

Desperate Hours, The
director: 12 William Wyler
cast: 8 Gig Young **11** Dewey Martin, Martha Scott **13** Arthur Kennedy, Frederic March **14** Humphrey Bogart

Desperately Seeking Susan
director: 14 Susan Seidelman
cast: 7 Madonna **15** Rosanna Arquette

desperation 7 despair **12** hopelessness, recklessness

despicable 4 base, mean, vile **10** detestable, outrageous **11** disgraceful **12** contemptible **13** reprehensible

despise 5 abhor, scorn **6** detest, loathe **7** contemn, disdain, dislike **10** look down on

despoil 3 rob **4** loot **6** ravage **7** pillage, plunder

despoiler 6 looter, robber, vandal **7** brigand **8** pillager **9** plunderer

despondency 5 gloom **6** dismay **7** despair, sadness **9** dejection, pessimism **10** depression, desolation, low spirits, melancholy **11** melancholia **12** hopelessness **14** discouragement **15** downheartedness

despondent 3 low **4** blue, down **8** dejected, downcast, hopeless **9** depressed **11** discouraged, downhearted **12** disconsolate, disheartened

despot 4 czar, tsar **6** tyrant **8** autocrat, dictator **9** oppressor

despotic 9 imperious **10** autocratic, tyrannical **11** dictatorial **13** authoritarian

despotism 7 tyranny **9** autocracy **10** absolutism

dessert 3 pie **4** cake, nuts, tart **5** fruit, sweet, treat **6** pastry **7** cobbler **8** ice cream **11** final course

destination 3 aim, end **4** goal, plan **6** object, target **7** purpose **8** ambition **9** objective **11** journey's end

destiny 3 lot **4** fate **5** karma, moira **6** future, kismet **7** fortune **9** necessity
goddess of: 5 Fates, Morae, Parca **6** Moerae, Moirai, Parcae

destitute 4 poor **5** broke, needy **6** busted **8** indigent **9** penniless **15** poverty-stricken

destitution 4 lack, want **6** penury **7** beggary, poverty **9** indigence, privation **11** extreme want **13** pennilessness **14** impoverishment

destroy 4 ruin **5** waste, wreck **6** ravage **8** demolish **9** devastate

destroy completely 3 end **4** rase, raze **5** total **7** abolish, wipe out **8** lay waste **9** eradicate, extirpate, liquidate **10** annihilate, obliterate **11** exterminate

destroyer 4 bane **6** blight, killer **7** gunboat, warship **10** affliction **11** annihilator

destruct 3 gut **4** raze, ruin **5** wreck **7** despoil, destroy, wipe out **8** decimate, demolish, desolate, pull down, tear down **9** devastate **10** lay in ruins

destruction 4 ruin **5** havoc **8** wreckage, wrecking **10** demolition **11** devastation

destructive 7 harmful, hurtful, ruinous **8** damaging **9** injurious **11** detrimental, devastating **15** not constructive

Destry Rides Again
director: 14 George Marshall
based on a story by: 8 Max Brand
cast: 12 Brian Donlevy, James Stewart **15** Marlene Dietrich **16** Charles Winninger

song: 35 See What the Boys in the Back Room Will Have

desultory 4 idle **6** casual, chance, fitful, random **7** aimless, cursory **9** haphazard **10** without aim **11** unconnected

detach 5 sever **6** loosen **7** unhitch **8** separate, unfasten **9** disengage **10** disconnect **11** disentangle

detached 4 fair **5** aloof **7** distant, neutral, severed **8** reserved, unbiased **9** impartial, objective, separated, uncoupled, unhitched **10** disengaged, fairminded, unfastened **11** indifferent, unconnected **12** disconnected, unprejudiced **13** disinterested, dispassionate **French: 6** degage

detachment 4 unit **5** force **8** coolness, fairness, severing **9** aloofness, isolation, severance **10** cutting off, neutrality, separation **11** objectivity **12** impartiality, indifference **13** disconnection, disengagement, preoccupation **16** special task force

detail 4 fact, iota, item **6** aspect, relate **7** appoint, feature, itemize, recount, respect, specify **9** component, delineate, designate, enumerate **10** detachment, particular **11** special duty **13** assign to a task, particularize **14** special service **20** particular assignment

detailed 6 minute **8** itemized, thorough **10** item by item **12** point by point

detailed list 9 breakdown **11** itemization **14** categorization

detain 4 hold, slow, stop **5** delay **6** arrest, hinder, retard, slow up **7** confine **8** slow down **13** keep in custody

detainment 7 custody, holding **9** detention **11** confinement **12** imprisonment **13** incarceration

detect 3 see **4** espy, note, spot **5** catch **6** notice **7** observe, uncover **8** discover, perceive

detectable 10 noticeable **11** appreciable, discernible, perceivable, perceptible **13** ascertainable

detective 2 PI **3** tec **6** shamus, sleuth **7** gumshoe **10** private eye **12** investigator **19** special investigator

detectives 5 Kojak **7** Columbo, Matlock **8** Sam Spade, Magnum P.I. **9** James Bond, Nancy Drew, Hardy Boys **10** Bertha Cool, Goldfinger, Mike Hammer, Miss Marple, Perry Mason **11** Charlie Chan, Ellery Queen **13** Hercule Poirot, Father Dowling, Philip Marlowe **14** Sherlock Holmes **15** Jessica Fletcher

detention 7 custody, holding **9** keeping in **10** detainment **11** confinement, holding back **12** imprisonment **13** incarceration

deter 4 stop **5** daunt **6** divert, hinder,

impede **7** prevent **8** dissuade **10** discourage

deteriorate 3 ebb **4** fade, wane **5** decay, lapse **6** worsen **7** crumble, decline, fall off **10** degenerate **12** disintegrate

deteriorated 6 shabby **7** rickety **8** decaying, worsened **9** crumbling **10** broken-down, tumble-down **11** dilapidated, in disrepair **13** disintegrated

deterioration 5 decay, lapse **6** fading, waning **7** decline **9** crumbling, decadence, worsening **12** degeneration, dilapidation **14** disintegration

determination 4 grit **5** pluck, power, spunk **6** fixing **7** finding, resolve, verdict **8** boldness, decision, judgment, settling, solution, tenacity **9** reasoning, resolving **10** conclusion, resolution **11** determining, persistence **12** perseverance, resoluteness **13** act of deciding, steadfastness **16** stick-to-itiveness

determine 5 learn **6** affect, decide, detect, settle **7** control, find out, resolve **8** conclude, discover, regulate **9** ascertain, establish, figure out, influence **15** come to a decision, give direction to

determined 7 dead set, decided, settled **8** found out, obdurate, resolute, stubborn **9** obstinate, tenacious **10** figured out **11** ascertained, established **15** come to a decision

deterrent 4 curb **5** check **9** hindrance, restraint **14** discouragement

detest 4 hate **5** abhor **6** loathe **7** despise **10** recoil from **16** dislike intensely

detestable 4 vile **6** odious **7** hateful **9** abhorrent, loathsome, obnoxious, offensive, repulsive, revolting **10** disgusting, unpleasant **12** disagreeable

detestation 4 hate **6** hatred **7** disgust, dislike **8** aversion, distaste, loathing **9** antipathy, repulsion, revulsion **10** abhorrence, repugnance

dethrone 4 oust **6** depose, unseat

detonate 4 fire **5** blast, burst, erupt, go off, shoot **6** blow up, ignite, report, set off **7** explode **8** touch off **9** discharge, fulminate

detonation 5 blast, burst **6** report **9** discharge, explosion

detour 5 skirt **6** bypass, byroad, divert **7** digress **9** deviation, diversion **10** digression

detract 5 lower **6** lessen, reduce **8** diminish **12** subtract from, take away from

detraction 4 flaw **11** shortcoming **12** disadvantage

detractor 5 enemy **6** critic **8** opponent **9** adversary, belittler, slanderer **10** antagonist, bad mouther, disparager

detriment 4 harm, loss **6** damage, injury **10** impairment **12** disadvantage

detrimental 7 adverse, harmful **8** damaging **9** injurious **10** pernicious **11** deleterious, destructive, unfavorable **15** disadvantageous

Detroit
baseball team: 6 Tigers
basketball team: 5 Shock **7** Pistons
football team: 5 Lions
hockey team: 8 Redwings

de trop 7 too many, too much **8** in the way **9** not wanted

Deucalion
father: 10 Prometheus
mother: 7 Pronoia
wife: 6 Pyrrha
son: 6 Hellen
founded: 9 human race
after: 6 deluge

deus ex machina 15 god from a machine **18** improbable solution

Deus vobiscum 12 God be with you

Deus vult 8 God wills (it)
cry of: 9 Crusaders

devaluate 6 lessen, reduce **7** deflate, degrade **10** depreciate

devaluation 4 drop **7** decline **12** depreciation

devalue 5 lower, taint **6** debase, defile, infect **7** cheapen, corrupt, degrade, pervert, pollute, revalue **8** mark down **9** devalu- ate, underrate, write down **10** adulterate, degenerate, demonetize, depreciate, remonetize **11** contaminate

devastate 4 ruin **5** level, spoil, waste, wreck **6** ravage **7** despoil, destroy **8** demolish, desolate, lay waste

devastating 7 ruinous **8** damaging **9** injurious **10** calamitous, disastrous **11** cataclysmic, destructive, detrimental **12** catastrophic

devastation 4 ruin **9** ruination **10** demolition **11** destruction

develop 4 grow **5** print, ripen **6** evolve, expand, finish, flower, mature, pick up, unfold **7** acquire, advance, amplify, augment, broaden, build up, convert, enlarge, improve, process, turn out **8** contract, energize **9** cultivate **10** come to have **11** come to light, elaborate on

development 5 event **6** growth, result **7** advance, history **8** progress **9** evolution

deviant 4 warp **5** shift **7** deviate, pervert **8** aberrant, abnormal **9** deflected, divergent

deviate 4 part, vary, veer **5** stray **6** depart, swerve, wander **8** go astray **9** sidetrack, turn aside

deviation 6 change **7** veering **8** rambling, straying **9** wandering **10** aberration, digression, divergence **11** abnormality, fluctuation

device 4 plan, plot, ploy, ruse, wile

5 angle, trick **6** design, gadget, scheme **7** gimmick **8** artifice, strategy **9** apparatus, invention, mechanism, stratagem **11** contraption, contrivance

devil, the Devil 3 guy **5** rogue, Satan, thing **6** Azazel, fellow, wretch **7** hellion, Lucifer, ruffian, serpent, villain **8** creature **9** Archfiend, Beelzebub, scoundrel **11** unfortunate **12** spirit of evil **13** mischief-maker **16** prince of darkness

Devil and Daniel Webster, The
author: **19** Stephen Vincent Benet
director: **15** William Dieterle
character: **5** Devil **7** Webster **9** Mr Scratch
cast: **10** James Craig **11** Anne Shirley **12** Edward Arnold, Walter Huston
score: **15** Bernard Herrmann
Oscar for: **5** score
also titled: **18** All That Money Can Buy

devilish 4 evil **6** wicked **7** demonic, heinous, impious, satanic, vicious **8** demoniac, fiendish **9** nefarious **10** demoniacal, diabolical, villainous

devil-may-care 4 bold, rash, wild **5** risky **6** daring, rakish **8** heedless, reckless **9** audacious, daredevil

devil's advocate
Latin: **16** advocatus diaboli

Devil's Advocate
author: **14** Taylor Caldwell

Devil's Disciple, The
author: **17** George Bernard Shaw

Devine, Andy
real name: **16** Jeremiah Schwartz
born: **11** Flagstaff AZ
roles: **7** Jingles **9** Andy's Gang **14** Wild Bill Hickok

devious 3 sly **4** wily **6** sneaky, tricky **7** crooked **9** deceitful, dishonest **11** treacherous **12** dishonorable **13** double-dealing

devise 4 plot **5** forge, frame **6** design, invent, map out **7** concoct, prepare, think up **8** block out, conceive, contrive **9** construct, formulate

deviser 6 author, framer **7** creator, planner **8** inventor **9** architect, contriver **10** originator

devitalize 4 kill **6** deaden, weaken **8** enervate **10** debilitate

DeVito, Danny
born: **9** Neptune, NJ
wife: **11** Rhea Perlman
roles: **4** Taxi **5** Twins, Hoffa **6** Tin Men **7** Matilda **9** Get Shorty **11** Mars Attacks **13** Batman Returns, War of the Roses **14** Ruthless People **22** Throw Mamma From the Train

devoid 5 empty **6** barren **7** lacking, wanting, without **8** bereft of **9** destitute **11** unblest with

devote 5 apply **6** direct **7** address, utilize **8** dedicate **10** consecrate, give

over to **11** concentrate **15** give oneself up to **22** center one's attentions on

devoted 4 fond, true **5** loyal **6** ardent, loving **7** earnest, staunch, zealous **8** adhering, faithful **9** dedicated, steadfast **10** passionate, unwavering **17** strongly committed

devotedness 8 devotion **10** commitment, dedication **13** attentiveness **17** earnest attachment

devoted to luxury 9 epicurean, sybaritic **10** hedonistic, voluptuous

devotee 3 fan **6** rooter **7** booster, groupie **8** adherent, advocate, champion, disciple, follower **10** aficionado, enthusiast

devotion, devotions 4 love, zeal **5** ardor, piety **6** fealty, regard **7** loyalty **8** fondness, holiness **9** adherence, godliness, reverence **10** allegiance, commitment, concern for, dedication, devoutness, meditation **11** religiosity **12** faithfulness, spirituality **13** attentiveness, prayer service **15** religious fervor **17** earnest attachment **19** religious observance

De Voto, Bernard A
author of: **21** Across the Wide Missouri

devour 7 stuff in **8** bolt down, gobble up, gulp down, knock off, wolf down **9** go through **10** read widely **14** eat voraciously **15** absorb oneself in, consume greedily **16** read compulsively, take in ravenously **17** become engrossed in

devout 5 pious **6** ardent **7** earnest, fervent, intense, serious, zealous **8** orthodox, reverent **9** religious **10** passionate, worshipful

devoutness 5 piety **8** devotion, holiness **9** godliness, reverence **12** spirituality **15** religious fervor

DeVries, Hugo
field: **6** botany
nationality: **5** Dutch
researched: **8** heredity, mutation

DeVries, Peter
author of: **16** Consenting Adults **24** Slouching Toward Kalamazoo

dew 8 moisture **12** condensation **18** droplets of moisture

Dewar, James
field: **7** physics **9** chemistry
nationality: **8** Scottish
liquified: **8** hydrogen
solidified: **8** hydrogen
developed: **7** cordite **10** Dewar flask **12** liquid oxygen

Dewey, George
served in: **18** Spanish-American War
battle: **9** Manila Bay
destroyed: **12** Spanish fleet

Dewhurst, Colleen
husband: **12** George C Scott
born: **6** Canada **8** Montreal

roles: **12** The Nun's Story **18** Desire Under the Elms **22** A Moon for the Misbegotten

De Wilde, Brandon
born: **10** Brooklyn NY
roles: **3** Hud **5** Shane **11** All Fall Down

dewy 4 damp **5** moist **7** bedewed

dexterity 8 deftness, facility **9** handiness **10** adroitness, nimbleness **11** manual skill, proficiency

dexterous 4 able, deft **5** agile, quick **6** active, adroit, gifted, nimble **8** skillful **9** efficient, ingenious **11** resourceful

diabolic, diabolical 4 evil, foul **6** wicked **7** baleful, demonic, heinous, impious, satanic, vicious **8** devilish, fiendish **9** monstrous, nefarious **10** malevolent, villainous

diadem 4 halo **5** crown, tiara **7** circlet, coronet **8** headband

diagnosis 5 study **8** analysis, scrutiny **11** examination **13** investigation, medical report **16** scientific report **22** conclusion from symptoms, specification of illness

diagonal line 4 bias **5** angle, slant

diagram 3 map **4** plan **5** chart **6** sketch **7** drawing, outline **9** breakdown **11** line drawing **12** illustration **14** representation **15** rough projection

dialect 5 argot, idiom, lingo **6** accent, jargon, patois **8** localism **10** vernacular **11** regionalism **13** colloquialism, provincialism **15** language variety

Dial M for Murder
director: **15** Alfred Hitchcock
based on play by: **14** Frederick Knott
cast: **10** Grace Kelly, Ray Milland **14** Robert Cummings

dialogue, dialog 4 talk **5** lines **6** parley, speech **8** conclave **10** conference **12** conversation **14** verbal exchange **15** personal meeting **16** formal discussion

diamond
characteristic: **7** hardest
color: **4** blue, pink **9** blue-white **12** canary yellow
element: **6** carbon
famous: **4** Hope **6** Jonker **8** Cullinan, Idol's Eye, Koh-i-Noor **9** Excelsior **12** Star of Africa **15** Star of the East **17** Star of Sierra Leone
quality: **3** cut **4** fire **5** color **7** clarity **10** brilliance
source: **5** Congo, India **6** Africa, Borneo, Brazil, Guyana **8** Tanzania **9** Australia, Venezuela **11** South Africa, Soviet Union **12** South America **15** South West Africa
weight: **5** carat, point

Diamond State
nickname of: **8** Delaware

Diana
origin: **5** Roman

goddess of: 4 moon **6** slaves **7** hunting

protectress of: 5 women

corresponds to: 6 Phoebe **7** Artemis

epithet: 10 Nemorensis

means: 10 of the grove

Diana of the Crossways
author: 14 George Meredith
character: 9 Mr Warwick **11** Diana Merion, Percy Dacier **12** Lady Dunstane **14** Thomas Redworth **15** Lord Dannisburgh

diaphanous 5 filmy, gauzy, lucid, sheer **6** flimsy, limpid **8** gossamer, pellucid **11** translucent, transparent

diary 3 log **7** daybook, journal **9** chronicle **12** daily journal **14** day-to-day record

Diary of Anne Frank, The
author: 9 Anne Frank
director: 13 George Stevens
cast: 6 Ed Wynn **9** Lou Jacobi **10** Diane Baker **13** Millie Perkins, Richard Beymer **14** Shelley Winters (Mrs Van Daan) **17** Joseph Schildkraut (Father Frank)
Oscar for: 17 supporting actress (Winters)

Diasia
festival of: 4 Zeus

diatribe 6 tirade **9** contumely, invective **11** castigation **12** vituperation **13** stream of abuse **14** bitter harangue **18** accusatory language **19** violent denunciation

dice 4 chop, cube **5** bones, cubes, cut up, mince
singular: 3 die

Dick, Mr
character in: 16 David Copperfield
author: 7 Dickens

Dickens, Charles
author of: 9 Hard Times **10** Bleak House **11** Oliver Twist **12** Barnaby Rudge, Dombey and Son, Little Dorrit **14** Pickwick Papers **15** A Christmas Carol, Our Mutual Friend **16** A Tale of Two Cities, David Copperfield, Martin Chuzzlewit, Nicholas Nickleby **17** Great Expectations **19** The Old Curiosity Shop **22** The Mystery of Edwin Drood

dicker 4 deal **6** haggle, higgle, outbid **7** bargain, chaffer, quibble, wrangle **8** beat down, talk down, underbid **9** negotiate **17** drive a hard bargain

Dickey, James
author of: 9 The Zodiac **11** Deliverance **16** Strength of Fields **17** Buckdancer's Choice

Dickinson, Angie
real name: 13 Angeline Brown
husband: 13 Burt Bacharach
born: 6 Kulm ND
roles: 8 Rio Bravo **11** Police Woman **13** Dressed to Kill **19** The Sins of Rachel Cade

Dick Tracy
creator: 12 Chester Gould
character: 8 BO Plenty, Moonmaid **12** Gravel Gertie **13** Sparkle Plenty **16** Jeremiah Truehart
wife: 12 Tess Truehart
daughter: 11 Bonny Braids
assistant: 9 Pat Patton
protege: 6 Junior
villain: 5 Itchy **6** B-B Eyes **7** Flattop, Flyface, Measles, Mumbles, The Brow, The Mole **8** The Blank **9** Pruneface, The Midget, The Rodent
equipment: 16 two-way wrist radio

Dick Van Dyke Show, The
character: 9 Alan Brady, Rob Petrie **11** Jerry Helper, Laura Petrie, Sally Rogers **12** Buddy Sorrell, Melvin Cooley, Millie Helper **13** Ritchie Petrie
cast: 9 Rose Marie **10** Carl Reiner, Jerry Paris **13** Larry Matthews, Richard Deacon **14** Mary Tyler Moore, Morey Amsterdam **17** Ann Morgan Guilbert

dictate 4 rule **5** edict, order **6** decree, dictum, direct, enjoin, impose, ordain, ruling, urging **7** bidding, counsel, lay down, mandate **8** set forth **9** determine, ordinance, prescribe, prompting, pronounce, stricture **11** exhortation, inclination, requirement

dictator 4 czar, duce, tsar **6** caesar, despot, fuhrer, kaiser, tyrant **7** emperor **8** autocrat **13** absolute ruler
Argentinian: 5 Peron
German: 6 Hitler
Italian: 9 Mussolini
Russian: 5 Lenin **6** Stalin
Spanish: 6 Franco
Ugandan: 7 Idi Amin

dictatorial 6 lordly **7** haughty, willful **8** absolute, arrogant, despotic **9** arbitrary, imperious, unlimited **10** autocratic, peremptory, tyrannical **11** categorical, domineering, magisterial, overbearing **12** supercilious, unrestricted **13** authoritative **17** inclined to command

diction 7 wording **8** delivery, rhetoric, verbiage **9** elocution **10** intonation, use of idiom, vocabulary **11** enunciation, phraseology, verbal style **12** articulation **13** choice of words, pronunciation **16** turn of expression **17** command of language **18** manner of expression

dictum 3 saw **4** fiat **5** adage, axiom, edict, maxim, order **6** decree, saying, truism **7** dictate, precept, proverb **11** commandment **13** pronouncement **15** dogmatic bidding **22** authoritative statement

Dictys
occupation: 9 fisherman

found: 5 chest
containing: 5 Danae **7** Perseus

didactic 7 donnish, preachy **8** academic, edifying, pedantic, tutorial **9** doctrinal, homiletic, pedagogic **10** expository, moralizing **11** educational, instructive, lecturelike, overbearing **12** prescriptive **17** inclined to lecture

didactics 8 teaching **9** education, teachings **10** pedagogics **11** instruction

Diderot, Denis
author of: 12 Encyclopedia **13** Rameau's Nephew

Didion, Joan
author of: 8 Salvador **10** White Album **14** Play It as It Lays **19** A Book of Common Prayer **24** Slouching Toward Bethlehem

Dido
queen of: 8 Carthage
father: 5 Mutto
brother: 9 Pygmalion
sister: 4 Anna
husband: 8 Sychaeus
lover: 6 Aeneas
corresponds to: 6 Elissa

Dido and Aeneas
opera by: 7 Purcell
character: 4 Dido (Queen of Carthage) **6** Aeneas

die 3 ebb, rot **4** ache, fade, fail, long, pass, stop, wane **5** croak, yearn **6** depart, expire, go flat, pass on, perish, recede, run out, wither **7** be eager, decline, die away, go stale, run down, subside **8** fade away, melt away, pass away, pass over, wear away **9** be anxious, break down, lose force, lose power, meet death **10** degenerate, want keenly **11** come to an end, suffer death **12** wish ardently **13** come to one's end, desire greatly, go to one's glory, kick the bucket **14** leave this world, pine with desire, become inactive **15** slowly disappear **17** become inoperative
plural: 4 dice

die away 4 fade **5** abate, cease **8** diminish

die down 5 abate **7** subside **8** diminish, slack off

die out 6 vanish **9** cease to be, disappear **13** become extinct

Diesel, Rudolf
field: 11 engineering
invented: 12 Diesel engine

diet 5 board, synod **7** edibles, nurture **8** congress, victuals **9** nutriment, nutrition **10** assemblage, convention, parliament, provisions, sustenance **11** comestibles, convocation, legislature, nourishment, subsistence **12** eating habits, eat sparingly **13** eating regimen, lawmaking body **14** eat judiciously **15** eat abstemiously, eat restrictedly, general assembly

16 limitation of fare, regulate one's food **17** bicameral assembly **18** nutritional regimen, representative body, restrict one's intake

Dietrich, Marlene
 real name: **22** Maria Magdalene Dietrich
 born: **7** Germany
 roles: **8** Lola Lola **11** Blonde Venus **12** The Blue Angel **15** Rancho Notorious **16** Destry Rides Again, The Garden of Allah **17** The Scarlet Empress **24** Witness for the Prosecution

Dietrich von Bern
 origin: **8** Germanic
 king of: **10** Ostrogoths
 Latin name: **9** Theodoric

Diety 3 Bel, God **4** Baal **6** Marduk, Molech, Moloch, Yahweh **7** Chemosh, Jehovah **10** Anammelech **11** Adrammelech

Dieu et mon droit 13 God and my right
 motto of: **18** royal arms of England

differ 5 demur **7** dispute, dissent **8** be unlike, contrast, disagree **9** take issue **10** be distinct, depart from, stand apart **11** be disparate, deviate from, diverge from **12** be at variance, be dissimilar, stand opposed

difference 4 spat **5** clash, set-to **7** dispute, quarrel **8** argument, contrast, squabble **9** deviation, disparity, variation **10** divergence, falling out, unlikeness **11** contrariety, contretemps, discrepancy, distinction **12** disagreement **13** contradiction, dissimilarity, dissimilitude **17** contradistinction, lack of resemblance

different 4 rare **6** divers, sundry, unique, unlike **7** bizarre, diverse, foreign, several, strange, unusual, various **8** aberrant, atypical, distinct, manifold, not alike, peculiar, separate, singular, uncommon **9** anomalous, disparate, divergent, other than, unrelated **10** dissimilar, individual, variegated **11** contrasting, distinctive, diversified, not ordinary **12** not identical **13** miscellaneous **14** unconventional

differential 8 contrast **11** distinction

differentiate 6 set off **8** contrast, separate, set apart **11** distinguish, draw the line **12** discriminate **13** make different

differentiation 8 contrast **10** comparison, separation **11** discernment, distinction

differing 6 unlike **7** variant **8** distinct, opposing **9** deviating, disparate, dissident, divergent **10** dissenting, dissimilar **11** contrasting, disagreeing

difficult 4 grim, hard **5** hairy, rough, tough **6** knotty, thorny, trying, unruly, uphill **7** arduous, complex, forward, not easy, onerous, tedious, willful **8** critical, exacting, perverse, stubborn,

ticklish, toilsome **9** demanding, enigmatic, fractious, Herculean, intricate, laborious, obstinate, Sisyphean, strenuous, wearisome **10** burdensome, exhausting, fastidious, formidable, inflexible, perplexing, unyielding **11** bewildering, complicated, hard to solve, intractable, troublesome **12** hard to manage, hard to please, obstreperous, rambunctious, recalcitrant, unmanageable **13** hard to satisfy, problematical, unpredictable **14** hard to deal with **15** unaccommodating

difficulty 3 jam, rub **4** mess, snag **5** trial **6** crisis, muddle, pickle, puzzle **7** barrier, dilemma, problem, straits, trouble **8** hot water, obstacle, quandary, tough job **9** deep water, hindrance, intricacy **10** impediment, perplexity, rough going, uphill work **11** arduousness, obstruction, predicament **12** hard sledding **13** laboriousness **14** stumbling block **15** troublesomeness **17** critical situation

diffidence 7 reserve, shyness **8** meekness, timidity **9** hesitancy, timidness **10** constraint, humbleness, insecurity, reluctance **11** bashfulness **12** introversion, sheepishness, timorousness **14** extreme modesty **15** unassertiveness **19** lack of self-assurance, retiring disposition

diffident 3 shy **6** modest **7** anxious, bashful **8** doubtful, hesitant, reserved, reticent, retiring **11** distrustful, unassertive **12** apprehensive

diffuse 5 wordy **7** verbose **8** rambling **9** desultory, dispersed, scattered, spread out, wandering **10** digressive, discursive, disjointed, long-winded, maundering, meandering, roundabout **14** circumlocutory, extended widely, unconcentrated, vaguely defined **15** not concentrated **18** lacking conciseness

diffuseness 8 rambling **9** prolixity, verbosity, wandering, wordiness **10** dispersion **11** indirection **14** circumlocution, long-windedness

diffusion 6 spread **8** rambling, verbiage **9** dispersal, prolixity, verbosity, wordiness **10** maundering, scattering **11** indirection, profuseness **14** circumlocution, discursiveness, disjointedness, roundaboutness

dig 3 jab **4** gibe, jeer, like, poke, prod, slur **5** aside, drive, gouge, punch, taunt **6** exhume, thrust **7** put-down, salvage, unearth **8** disinter, excavate, pinpoint, retrieve, scoop out **9** extricate, find among, hollow out **10** come up with, excavation, wry comment **11** bring to view **12** verbal thrust **13** cutting remark, search and find

digest 3 dig **5** grasp **6** absorb, fathom, precis, resume **7** realize, summary **8** abstract, dissolve, synopsis **10** abridg-

ment, appreciate, assimilate, comprehend, understand **12** condensation, take in wholly **14** take in mentally

digestive system
 component: **5** liver, mouth, teeth **6** tongue **7** stomach **8** appendix, pancreas **9** esophagus, intestine **11** gall bladder **13** salivary gland

dig in 3 eat **4** root **5** begin, embed, imbed, plant **6** anchor **7** pitch in **8** entrench, go to work **10** begin to eat **12** apply oneself

digit 3 one, six, two, toe **4** five, four, nine, unit, zero **5** light, seven, three **6** cipher, figure, finger, number **7** integer, numeral

dignified 5 proud **6** august, proper **7** upright **8** decorous, reserved **9** honorable **10** upstanding **11** circumspect **13** distinguished **14** self-respecting

dignify 5 raise **6** uplift **7** elevate, inflate, promote

dignitary 3 VIP **7** notable **8** luminary **9** personage **12** person of note

dignity 5 honor **7** decorum, majesty, station **9** loftiness, solemnity **10** augustness, importance **11** comportment, stateliness **12** high position, lofty bearing **13** proud demeanor **14** self-possession

digress 5 stray **6** back up, wander **7** deviate **8** divagate **9** turn aside **15** go off on a tangent **17** depart from subject

digression 6 detour **8** straying **9** departure, deviation, diversion, wandering **10** divagation, divergence, side remark **12** obiter dictum

digressive 7 diffuse **9** wandering **10** disjointed, maundering, roundabout **11** off the point **14** circumlocutory

dig up 6 locate **7** find out, root out, uncover, unearth **8** discover **9** ferret out **12** bring to light

dike 4 bank **5** levee, ridge **10** embankment

Dike *see* **4** Dice

dikerion 11 candelabrum, candlestick **12** candleholder

dilapidated 4 shot **6** beat-up, ruined, shabby **7** rickety, run-down, worn-out **8** battered, decaying, decrepit **10** broken-down, ramshackle, tumble-down **11** in disrepair **12** deteriorated, falling apart **15** falling to pieces

dilate 4 swell, widen **6** expand, extend **7** broaden, distend, enlarge, inflate, puff out **9** make wider

dilation 8 swelling, widening **9** expansion **10** broadening, distension, distention

dilatory 4 lazy, slow **5** tardy **6** remiss **8** dawdling, indolent, slothful, sluggish **9** negligent, reluctant **10** phlegmatic **13** lackadaisical **15** inclined to delay, procrastinating

dilemma 4 bind **6** crunch, plight **7** impasse, problem **8** deadlock, quandary **9** stalemate **11** predicament **13** Hobson's choice **15** difficult choice

dilettante 7 amateur, dabbler, trifler **12** experimenter **16** cultured hobbyist

diligence 4 zeal **8** industry **10** commitment, dedication **11** persistence **12** perseverance

diligent 6 active **7** careful, earnest, patient, zealous **8** plodding, sedulous, studious, thorough, untiring **9** assiduous, concerted **10** persistent **11** hardworking, industrious, painstaking, persevering **12** pertinacious **15** well-intentioned

dill 4 anet
botanical name: 17 Anethum graveolens
origin: 9 Asia Minor **13** Mediterranean
family: 7 parsley
guards against: 7 Evil Eye **10** witchcraft
use: 6 sauces **7** pickles **10** vegetables

Dillon, Matt
roles: 3 Tex **10** Rumblefish **12** The Outsiders

dillydally 3 lag **4** idle, loaf **5** dally, delay **6** dawdle, loiter **8** kill time **9** waste time **10** fool around **13** procrastinate

Dilsey
character in: 18 The Sound and the Fury
author: 8 Faulkner

dilute 4 thin, weak **6** reduce, temper, watery, weaken **7** diffuse, diluted, thin out **8** decrease, diminish, make weak, mitigate, weakened **9** attenuate, liquidify, water down **10** add water to, adulterate, thinned out **11** adulterated, make thinner, watered down

diluted 4 weak **6** dilute, watery **8** weakened **10** thinned out **11** adulterated, watered down

dilution 8 thinning **9** weakening **12** watering down

dim 3 low **4** hazy, soft, weak **5** dusky, faint, foggy, murky, muted, vague **6** blurry, feeble, gloomy, remote **7** blurred, clouded, muffled, shadowy **8** darkened, nebulous, obscured **9** not bright, tenebrous **10** adumbrated, ill-defined, indefinite, indistinct, intangible **13** unilluminated

DiMaggio, Joe
nickname: 9 Joltin Joe
sport: 8 baseball
position: 8 outfield
team: 14 New York Yankees
wife: 13 Marilyn Monroe

dime-a-dozen 6 common **7** humdrum **8** ordinary, workaday **9** plentiful **10** ubiquitous **11** commonplace **12** easy to come by **13** garden-variety **15** undistinguished

dimension, dimensions 4 bulk, mass, size **5** range, scope, width **6** extent, height, length, volume, weight **7** measure **9** amplitude, greatness, magnitude, thickness **10** importance, proportion **11** massiveness **12** measurements **14** physical extent

diminish 3 ebb **4** wane **5** abate, lower **6** lessen, narrow, reduce, shrink **7** decline, dwindle, fall off, shorten, shrivel, subside **8** decrease, peter out **9** be reduced **11** make smaller **13** become smaller

diminuendo
music: 22 gradually getting softer
abbreviation: 3 dim

diminution 6 ebbing, waning **7** decline **8** decrease, lowering **9** dwindling, lessening, reduction, shrinkage **10** falling off, shortening, shriveling, subsidence **11** petering out, slacking off

diminutive 3 wee **4** tiny **5** elfin, short, small, teeny **6** little, minute, petite, slight **7** pet name, stunted **8** dwarfish, half-pint, nickname **9** miniature, short form **10** pocket-size, undersized, vest-pocket **11** lilliputian, small-scale, unimportant **13** insignificant **14** inconsiderable

Dimmesdale, Arthur
character in: 16 The Scarlet Letter
author: 9 Hawthorne

dimness 4 dusk **5** gloom, shade **8** darkness **14** indistinctness

dimwit 4 fool **5** dummy, dunce, idiot, moron **6** cretin, nitwit **7** dingbat, dullard, dumbell, pinhead **8** dumbbell, dummkopf, imbecile, meathead, numskull **9** birdbrain, blockhead, ding-a-ling, lamebrain, numbskull, simpleton **11** chowderhead, knucklehead

dim-witted 4 dull, dumb **5** dense **6** stupid **7** foolish, idiotic, moronic, witless **8** retarded **9** cretinous, imbecilic

din 4 stir, to-do **5** bruit **6** babble, clamor, hubbub, racket, ruckus, tumult, uproar **7** clangor **9** commotion **10** clattering, hullabaloo

Dinah
father: 5 Jacob
mother: 4 Leah
brother: 3 Dan, Gad **4** Levi **5** Asher, Judah **6** Joseph, Reuben, Simeon **7** Zebulun **8** Benjamin, Issachar, Naphtali
violated by: 7 Shechem

dine 3 eat, sup **4** feed **5** feast, lunch **6** fall to, supper **7** banquet, partake **9** breakfast, eat dinner **10** break bread, gluttonize, have dinner **11** gourmandize **14** take sustenance

Dine see **6** Navajo

Dinesen, Isak
real name: 18 Karen Blixen-Finecke
author of: 9 Last Tales **11** Out of Af-

rica **12** Winter's Tales **16** Seven Gothic Tales

dinghy 5 skiff **7** rowboat **8** sailboat **9** small boat

dingy 4 dull **5** dusty, grimy, murky, tacky **6** dismal, dreary, gloomy, shabby **12** dirty and drab

dining room
French: 12 salle a manger

dinner 4 food, meal **5** feast **6** repast, supper **7** banquet
French: 8 dejeuner **10** table d'hote

Dinner at Eight
director: 11 George Cukor
author: 10 Edna Ferber **14** George S Kaufman
cast: 8 Lee Tracy **10** Jean Harlow **11** Billie Burke **12** Wallace Beery **13** John Barrymore, Marie Dressler **15** Lionel Barrymore

dinosaur
means: 14 fearfully great, terrible lizard
subclass: 11 Archosauria
characteristic: 7 diapsid **14** teeth in sockets, two-arched skull **18** three-element pelvis
group: 11 Saurischian **13** Ornithischian
  flesh-eating biped: 8 therapod
  plant-eating quadruped: 8 sauropod
  plant-eating biped: 10 ornithopod
  armored: 10 ceratopsid
of Africa: 9 Iguanodon **13** Brachiosaurus **17** Heterodontosaurus
of Asia: 13 Hypselosaurus, Protoceratops
of Europe: 9 Iguanodon **12** Plateosaurus **13** Compsognathus, Hypselosaurus, Hypsilophodon
of North America: 10 Diplodocus, Edmontonia, Nodosaurus **11** Anatosaurus, Anchisaurus, Gorgosaurus, Monoclonius, Saurolophus, Scolosaurus, Stegosaurus, Triceratops **12** Ankylosaurus, Camarasaurus, Camptosaurus, Coelophysics, Lambeosaurus, Paleoscincus **13** Brachiosaurus, Styracosaurus, Tyrannosaurus **14** Thescelosaurus **15** Parasaurolophus, Procheneosaurus
of South America: 12 Pisanosaurus
fictional: 4 Puff **6** Barney **12** Jurassic Park

dint 4 push, will **5** drive, force, labor, might, power **6** charge, effort, energy, strain, stress **8** endeavor, exertion, strength, struggle **10** insistence **12** forcefulness **13** determination **14** relentlessness

diocese 3 see **7** eparchy **9** bishopric **14** church district
jurisdiction of: 6 bishop

Diomedes
king of: 6 Thrace
father: 4 Ares **6** Tydeus

mother: 6 Cyrene **7** Deipyle
member of: 7 Epigoni
kept: 9 wild mares
fed mares on: 10 human flesh
death planned by: 8 Hercules

Dione
consort of: 4 Zeus

Dionysia
festival of: 8 Dionysus

Dionysus *see* **7** Bacchus

Dioscuri *see* **15** Castor and Pollux

dip 4 bail, dish, dunk, sink, skim, soak
5 droop, ladle, scoop, slope, spoon **6**
dabble, dish up, peruse, shovel **7** decline, descend, dish out, run over **8**
drop down, glance at, submerge, turn
down **13** study slightly **14** immerse
briefly, lift by scooping, try tentatively
15 incline downward

dip into 4 scan, skim **5** ladle **6**
browse, peruse **7** deplete **8** look over
13 glance through, make inroads in

Diplodocus
type: 8 dinosaur, sauropod
period: 8 Jurassic
location: 12 North America

diplomacy 4 tact **5** craft, skill **7** finesse **8** delicacy, prudence, subtlety
10 artfulness, discretion **11** maneuvering, savoir-faire **13** statesmanship **14**
foreign affairs **16** artful management
18 foreign negotiation **21** international
politics

diplomat 5 envoy **6** consul **7** attache
8 emissary, minister **9** statesman **10**
ambassador, negotiator **12** interlocutor
13 tactful person
acceptable: 12 persona grata
unacceptable: 15 persona non grata

diplomatic 5 adept, suave **6** artful, urbane **7** attuned, politic, prudent, tactful **8** discreet **9** sensitive, strategic **13**
ambassadorial **14** foreign-service **15**
state-department

Dipper
nickname of: 15 Wilt Chamberlain

Dipsas
form: 7 serpent

dipsomaniac 3 sot **4** lush, soak, wino
5 drunk, rummy, souse, toper **6** barfly, boozer **7** tippler **8** drunkard **9** alcoholic, inebriate

diptera
class: 8 hexapoda
phylum: 10 arthropoda
group: 7 true fly

Dirae *see* **6** Furies

dire 4 grim **5** awful, grave **6** dismal,
urgent, woeful **7** crucial, extreme,
fearful, ominous, ruinous **8** critical,
dreadful, horrible, terrible **9** appalling,
desperate, harrowing, ill-boding, ill-
omened **10** calamitous, disastrous,
portentous **11** apocalyptic, cataclysmic
12 catastrophic, inauspicious

direct 3 aim **4** head, lead, urge **5**
blunt, clear, focus, frank, guide, order,
pilot, usher **6** advise, candid, charge,
enjoin, handle, head-on, honest, manage **7** address, command, conduct,
control, earmark, forward, level at,
oversee, pointed, sincere, train at **8**
explicit, indicate, instruct, navigate,
personal **9** conduct to, designate, firsthand, intend for, supervise **10** administer, face-to-face, forthright, point-
blank, show the way, unmediated **11**
plain-spoken, point the way, point toward, preside over, superintend **15**
straightforward

direction 3 aim, ENE, ESE, NNE,
NNW, SSE, SSW, way, WNW, WSW
4 bent, care, east, path, west **5** drift,
north, order, route, south, track, trend
6 charge, course, recipe **7** bearing,
command, control, current **8** guidance, headship, tendency **9** alignment
10 guidelines, leadership, management, regulation **11** inclination, instruction, line of march, supervision
12 line of action, prescription, surveillance **13** line of thought **14** administration, point of compass **15** superintendence

directive 5 ukase **8** bulletin **9** statement **10** communique **11** declaration
12 instructions, proclamation **13** communication

directly 4 soon **6** at once, openly **7** exactly, frankly **8** candidly, honestly, in
person, promptly, straight **9** forthwith,
precisely, presently, right away **10**
face-to-face, in a beeline, personally
11 immediately, momentarily **12** in
plain terms, not obliquely, unswerv-
ingly **13** unambiguously, unequivocally **14** as the crow flies **15** in a
straight line **16** as soon as possible **17**
on a straight course, straightforwardly

directness 6 candor **9** bluntness,
frankness **10** candidness **14** forthrightness **19** straightforwardness

direct opposite 7 reverse **8** converse
10 antithesis

director 4 boss, head **5** chief **6** leader,
master **7** curator, foreman, manager **8**
chairman, governor, overseer **9** commander, conductor, organizer **10** controller, supervisor **13** administrator **14**
superintendent

dirge 6 lament **7** requiem **8** threnody **9**
death song **10** burial hymn, death
march **11** funeral song **13** mournful
sound **19** mournful composition

dirigo 7 I direct
motto of: 5 Maine

dirk 3 sny **4** snee, stab **5** knife, skean
6 dagger, skiver **7** poniard
origin: 8 Scotland

Dirks, Rudolph
creator/artist of: 12 Hans and Fritz
17 Captain and the Kids **19** The
Katzenjammer Kids

dirt 3 mud **4** dust, loam, mire, muck,
scum, slop, smut, soil, soot **5** dross,
earth, filth, grime, humus, offal, rumor, slime, trash **6** gossip, ground, refuse, sludge, smudge **7** garbage, rubbish, scandal, slander **8** impurity,
leavings, vileness **9** excrement, indecency, obscenity, profanity, sweepings
10 foul matter, moral filth, scurrility
11 pornography, scuttlebutt, squalidness **12** scabrousness **13** salaciousness **14** defamatory talk **15** filthy substance, unclean language **17**
sensational expose

dirt-cheap 6 a steal **7** bargain **11** inexpensive **14** very reasonable **15** bargain-basement

dirty 4 base, foul, hard, lewd, mean,
soil, spot, vile **5** grimy, messy,
muddy, nasty, smear, stain, sully **6**
coarse, filthy, grubby, mess up, muck
up, risque, rotten, shabby, slop up,
smudge, smudgy, smutty, soiled, sordid, untidy, vulgar **7** begrime, besmear, blacken, corrupt, crooked, devious, illegal, illicit, immoral, low-
down, muddied, obscene, pollute,
squalid, sullied, tarnish, unclean **8** befouled, begrimed, indecent, off-color,
polluted, prurient, scabrous, unwashed **9** besmeared, deceitful, difficult, dishonest, tarnished, unsterile **10**
despicable, fraudulent, licentious, perfidious, unpleasant, villainous **11** distasteful, treacherous **12** contemptible,
disagreeable, dishonorable, pornographic, unscrupulous **14** morally unclean

Dirty Dozen, The
director: 13 Robert Aldrich
cast: 8 Jim Brown **9** Lee Marvin **10**
Robert Ryan, Trini Lopez **11** Clint
Walker **13** George Kennedy **14**
Charles Bronson, Ernest Borgnine,
John Cassavetes, Richard Jaeckel **16**
Donald Sutherland

Dis
also: 8 Dis Pater
means: 5 Hades
god of: 10 underworld
corresponds to: 5 Orcus, Pluto

dis 6 insult **9** disparage

disability 5 minus **6** defect **8** handicap, weakness **9** infirmity, unfitness
10 affliction, impairment, impediment,
inadequacy **11** shortcoming **12** debilitation, disadvantage **16** disqualification

disable 6 damage, hinder, impair,
weaken **7** cripple **8** handicap **12** incapacitate

disabled
French: 12 hors de combat

disabuse 8 set right **9** relieve of **10**
disenchant **11** disillusion, set straight

disaccord 7 discord **10** disharmony **12**
disagreement **15** incompatibility

disacknowledge 4 deny **6** disown **7** disavow **8** disallow, disclaim **9** repudiate

disadvantage 4 flaw **6** burden **7** trouble **8** drawback, handicap, hardship, nuisance, weakness **9** detriment, hindrance, in arrears, weak point **10** impediment **12** weak position **13** inconvenience **16** fly in the ointment

disadvantaged 8 deprived, emergent, emerging, troubled **10** struggling **11** handicapped **12** impoverished **14** underdeveloped **15** underprivileged

disadvantageous 7 harmful **9** injurious **11** detrimental, inadvisable, inexpedient, undesirable, unfavorable, unfortunate

disaffect 4 wean **8** alienate, estrange **10** drive apart

disaffected 5 upset **7** hostile **8** agitated, inimical **9** alienated, disturbed, estranged, withdrawn **10** unfriendly **11** belligerent, discomposed, disgruntled, quarrelsome **12** antipathetic, discontented, dissatisfied **14** irreconcilable

disaffection 7 dislike **8** aversion, distaste **9** antipathy **10** alienation, discontent, disloyalty **12** estrangement

disaffirm 4 deny **5** annul **6** disown **7** decline, disavow **8** abnegate, disclaim, forswear, renounce **9** repudiate **15** wash one's hands of

disaffirmation 6 denial **9** annulment, disavowal **10** abnegation, disclaimer **11** repudiation **12** renunciation **13** contradiction

disagree 4 vary **5** clash, upset **6** depart, differ **7** deviate, diverge, make ill **8** be unlike, conflict, distress **9** discomfit **10** disconcert, stand apart **11** be injurious, fail to agree, not coincide **12** be at variance, be discordant, be dissimilar **13** cause problems **14** be unreconciled **15** be at loggerheads, differ in opinion **16** oppose one another, think differently

disagreeable 5 cross, harsh, nasty, surly, testy **7** grating, grouchy, peevish **8** churlish, petulant **9** difficult, irascible, irritable, obnoxious, offensive, repellent, repugnant, repulsive, unamiable, unwelcome **10** disgusting, ill-natured, uninviting, unpleasant **11** acrimonious, bad-tempered, displeasing, distasteful, ill-tempered, uncongenial, unpalatable **13** uncomfortable

disagreeing 6 at odds **7** deviant, varying **8** clashing **9** deviating, differing, disputing **10** quarreling **11** conflicting **13** at loggerheads

disagreement 5 clash, fight **7** discord, dispute, quarrel **8** argument, squabble, variance **9** deviation, disaccord, disparity, diversity **10** difference, divergence, falling-out, unlikeness **11** discrepancy, incongruity **13** dissimilarity, dissimilitude, lack of harmony **15** incompatibility **16** misunderstanding

disallow 4 deny, veto **6** abjure, forbid, refuse, reject **8** prohibit **9** repudiate

disallowance 4 veto **6** denial **7** refusal **9** rejection **11** prohibition, repudiation

disallowed 6 vetoed **7** abjured, refused **8** rejected **9** forbidden **10** repudiated **12** inadmissible, unacceptable

disappear 2 go **3** end **4** exit, fade, flee **5** leave **6** be gone, depart, die out, retire, vanish **8** be no more, fade away, melt away, withdraw **9** evaporate **12** be lost to view, cease to exist, leave no trace **13** cease to appear, cease to be seen **14** become obscured, cease to be known, pass out of sight **15** vanish from sight

disappearance 9 vanishing **11** evanescence **16** passing from sight

disappoint 4 foil **6** hinder, sadden, thwart **7** chagrin, let down, mislead **9** frustrate **10** dishearten **11** disillusion

disappointing 11 frustrating **12** unfulfilling **13** dissatisfying **14** unsatisfactory

disappointment 3 dud **4** bomb, loss **6** defeat, fiasco, fizzle **7** failure, letdown, setback, washout **8** disaster **9** the knocks **11** frustration **13** unfulfillment, unrealization **15** disillusionment, dissatisfaction

disapprobation 7 censure **8** disfavor **9** criticism, disesteem, objection **11** disapproval, displeasure **12** condemnation **15** dissatisfaction

disapprove 4 veto **5** decry **6** refuse, reject **7** censure, condemn, deplore, dislike **8** denounce, disallow, object to, turn down **9** criticize, deprecate, disparage, frown upon **10** think ill of **13** look askance at, regard as wrong **14** discountenance, refuse assent to **15** take exception to **16** find unacceptable, view with disfavor

disapprove of 7 censure, condemn, deplore **8** object to

disarm 4 move, sway **5** charm **6** entice **7** attract, bewitch, enchant, win over **8** convince, persuade **9** captivate, fascinate, influence, prevail on

disarming 7 melting, winning, winsome **8** charming, magnetic **9** appealing, beguiling, ingenuous, seductive **10** bewitching, entrancing **11** captivating **12** ingratiating, irresistible

disarrange 5 mix up, upset **6** jumble, mess up, muddle, ruffle, rumple **7** confuse, scatter **8** disarray, dishével, disorder, displace, put askew, scramble **11** disorganize **13** put out of order **14** turn topsy-turvy

disarranged 5 messy **6** mussed, sloppy, untidy **7** jumbled, ruffled, rumpled, tousled, unkempt

8 uncombed **9** cluttered **10** disarrayed, disheveled, disordered, disorderly, in disorder **11** in a shambles

disarrangement 4 mess **5** chaos, mix-up, upset **6** jumble, mixing, muddle **7** clutter **8** disarray, disorder, scramble, shambles **9** confusion, messiness, messing up **10** disharmony, disruption, sloppiness, untidiness **12** dishevelment **14** disorderliness **15** disorganization, heaping together

disarray 5 chaos, mix-up, upset **6** jumble **7** clutter **8** disorder, scramble, shambles **9** confusion, messiness **10** disharmony, sloppiness, untidiness **12** dishevelment **14** disarrangement **15** disorganization

disarrayed 5 messy **6** mussed, sloppy, untidy **7** chaotic, jumbled, mixed up **10** disheveled, disordered, disorderly, in disorder **11** disarranged

disarticulate 6 detach **7** unhinge **8** disjoint, disunite, separate **9** disengage, dislocate **10** disconnect **13** put out of joint

disarticulated 5 apart **7** divided **8** unhinged **9** disunited, separated **10** disengaged, disjointed, dislocated, unattached **11** unconnected **12** disconnected **13** helter-skelter

disassemble 7 disband, scatter **8** disperse **9** knock down, take apart

disassociate 7 divorce **8** separate **10** disconnect **12** disaffiliate

disassociation 5 break, split **6** schism **7** divorce **8** division **10** separation

disaster 4 harm **5** wreck **6** blight, fiasco **7** scourge, tragedy, trouble **8** accident, calamity **9** adversity, cataclysm, ruination **10** misfortune **11** catastrophe, great mishap **12** misadventure

disastrous 4 dire **5** fatal **6** tragic **7** adverse, hapless, harmful, ruinous **8** dreadful, grievous, ill-fated, terrible **9** harrowing **10** calamitous, desolating, horrendous, ill-starred **11** destructive, devastating, unfortunate **12** catastrophic, inauspicious

disavow 4 deny **6** abjure, disown, recant, reject **7** gainsay, retract **8** denounce **9** repudiate **10** contradict

disavowal 6 denial **8** demurrer **9** rejection **10** abjuration, disclaimer, refutation **11** repudiation **13** contradiction

disband 7 adjourn, dismiss, scatter **8** disperse, dissolve **11** disassemble

disbelief 5 doubt **7** dubiety **8** distrust, mistrust, unbelief **10** skepticism **11** incredulity **12** doubtfulness **14** lack of credence

disbelieve 5 doubt **6** refuse, reject **7** suspect **8** discount, distrust **9** discredit, unbelieve **10** misbelieve

disbeliever 7 atheist, skeptic 8 apostate

disbursable 7 payable 9 available, spendable 10 expendable

disburse 6 lay out, pay out 7 fork out 8 allocate, shell out 10 distribute

disbursement 6 outlay 7 payment 8 spending 9 paying out 10 dispensing 11 expenditure 12 dispensation, distribution

discard 4 drop, dump, junk, shed 5 scrap 6 remove, shelve 7 abandon, weed out 8 get rid of, jettison, throw out 9 cast aside, dispose of, eliminate, throw away 10 relinquish 11 thrust aside 12 dispense with, have done with 14 throw overboard

discarded 6 dumped, junked 7 cast off, dropped 8 deserted, forsaken, rejected, scrapped 9 abandoned, cast aside, tossed out 10 jettisoned, left behind, thrown away

discern 3 see 4 espy 6 behold, descry, detect, notice 7 make out, observe, pick out 8 perceive 9 ascertain 12 catch sight of

discernible 7 visible 8 apparent 10 detectable, noticeable 11 perceivable, perceptible

discerning 4 sage, wise 5 acute, sharp 6 astute, shrewd 8 piercing 9 judicious, sagacious, sensitive 10 perceptive 11 intelligent, keen-sighted, penetrating 12 clear-sighted, sharp-sighted 13 perspicacious 14 discriminating

discernment 6 acumen, senses 7 insight 8 feelings, sagacity, thoughts 10 cognizance, discretion, perception 11 distinction 13 consciousness, judiciousness 14 discrimination 15 differentiation

discharge 3 axe, can 4 emit, fire, flow, free, gush, ooze, oust, sack, shot 5 blast, burst, eject, expel, exude, issue, let go, shoot 6 bounce, firing, launch, lay off, let fly, propel, report, set off 7 cashier, dismiss, explode, fire off, project, release, seepage, set free, trigger 8 activate, detonate, drainage, emission, get rid of, liberate, throw off, touch off 9 allow to go, exploding, explosion, firing off, fusillade, give forth, pour forth, secretion, send forth, terminate 10 activating, detonating, detonation, triggering 11 send packing, suppuration 13 give the gate to, walking papers 14 demobilization 15 release document 16 remove from office

disciple 3 nut 5 freak, pupil 7 admirer, convert, devotee, pursuer, student 8 adherent, believer, follower, neophyte, partisan 9 proselyte, supporter 10 aficionado 11 afficionado

Disciple, The
  author: 11 Paul Bourget

Disciples see 8 Apostles

disciplinarian 8 martinet 13 authoritarian 16 stickler for rules, strict taskmaster

disciplinary 8 punitive 9 punishing 10 corrective 13 authoritarian

discipline 5 drill, prime, rigor, train 6 method, punish 7 break in, chasten, regimen 8 chastise, drilling, instruct, practice, training 9 schooling 11 preparation 14 indoctrination 15 prescribed habit, teach by exercise 16 course of exercise

disclaim 4 deny 6 disown 7 decline, disavow 8 abnegate, forswear, renounce 9 disaffirm, repudiate

disclaimer 6 denial 8 demurrer 9 disavowal 10 abnegation 11 repudiation 12 renunciation

disclose 4 bare, leak, show, tell 6 expose, impart, reveal, unveil 7 divulge, lay bare, publish, uncover 9 broadcast, make known 10 make public 11 communicate 12 bring to light 13 allow to be seen, bring into view, cause to appear

disco 4 club 5 agogo, dance 7 cabaret 9 dance club, nightclub

discolor 4 spot 5 stain, tinge 6 bleach, streak 7 tarnish

discoloration 4 blot, mark, spot 5 smear, stain 6 blotch, bruise, smudge 7 blemish 9 contusion

discolored 4 doty 5 dingy, dirty, faded, livid 6 soiled, tinged 7 bruised, stained 9 tarnished

discomfit 5 upset 6 thwart 7 chagrin 8 confound, distress 9 embarrass, frustrate 10 disconcert

discomfited 5 upset 6 uneasy 7 ashamed 8 thwarted 9 chagrined, ill at ease 10 distressed 11 embarrassed 12 disconcerted

discomfiture 7 anxiety 9 agitation, confusion 10 uneasiness 11 disquietude, distraction, nervousness 12 discomposure, perturbation 13 embarrassment

discomfort 3 try 4 ache, hurt, pain 5 trial 6 misery 7 malaise, trouble 8 disquiet, distress, hardship, nuisance, soreness, vexation 9 annoyance, discomfit, embarrass 10 affliction, discompose, irritation, make uneasy 11 disquietude

discompose 5 abash, upset 6 rattle 7 agitate, confuse, disturb, fluster, nonplus, perturb, trouble, unnerve 8 disquiet, distract, distress, unsettle 9 discomfit, embarrass 10 disconcert

discomposed 5 upset 6 jolted, rocked, shaken, uneasy 7 anxious, nervous, worried 8 agitated, confused, troubled 9 disturbed, flustered, perturbed 10 disquieted, distracted 11 discomfited, uncollected

discomposure 6 flurry 7 anxiety 8 disquiet 9 agitation, confusion 10 discomfort, uneasiness 11 awkwardness, disquietude, distraction, nervousness 12 discomfiture, perturbation 13 embarrassment 17 self-consciousness

disconcert 5 abash, annoy, upset 6 raffle, ruffle 7 agitate, confuse, disturb, nonplus, perturb, trouble 8 unsettle 10 discompose

disconcerted 5 fazed, upset 7 annoyed, rattled, ruffled 8 agitated, confused, troubled 9 disturbed, perturbed, thrown off, unsettled 10 distracted, nonplussed

disconcertment 8 rattling 9 abashment, agitation, confusion 11 disturbance 12 discomposure

disconnect 6 detach 8 separate, uncouple 9 disengage

disconnected 5 split 6 cut off 7 jumbled, mixed-up, severed 8 confused, detached, rambling 9 illogical, separated, uncoupled 10 disengaged, disjointed, incoherent, irrational, unattached, unfastened 12 disorganized

disconnection 8 severing 9 severance 10 cutting off, detachment, separation 13 disengagement

disconsolate 3 sad 4 blue, down 6 woeful 7 crushed, doleful, forlorn, unhappy 8 dejected, desolate, downcast, wretched 9 depressed, miserable, sorrowful, woebegone 10 despondent, dispirited, melancholy 11 discouraged, low-spirited, pessimistic 12 heavyhearted, inconsolable 13 brokenhearted 14 down in the dumps, down in the mouth

discontent 9 displease 10 discomfort, disgruntle 11 displeasure, unhappiness 15 dissatisfaction

discontented 5 bored 7 fretful, unhappy 9 miserable, regretful 10 displeased, malcontent 11 disgruntled 12 dissatisfied

discontinuance 3 end 4 halt, stop 6 ending, recess 7 ceasing, halting 8 abeyance, giving up, quitting, stoppage, stopping, surcease 9 cessation, desisting 10 concluding, leaving off, suspension 11 abandonment, breaking off, termination

discontinue 3 end 4 drop, quit, stop 5 cease 6 desist, give up 7 abandon, abstain, suspend 8 break off, leave off 9 interrupt, terminate 10 put an end to

discontinuous 8 discrete, episodic, sporadic 9 segmented, spasmodic 10 occasional 11 interrupted 12 disconnected, intermittent

discord 6 strife 7 dispute 8 clashing, conflict, disunity, division, friction 9 cacophony, harshness, wrangling 10 contention, disharmony, dissension, dissonance, quarreling 11 being at odds, differences, discordance 12 disagreement, grating noise 13 lack of concord **15** incompatibility **16** unpleasant sounds

goddess of: 4 Eris **9** Discordia

discordance 6 strife **7** discord, dispute **8** clashing, conflict, disunity, division, friction **9** wrangling **10** contention, disharmony, dissension, quarreling **12** disagreement **15** incompatibility

discordant 6 at odds **9** disparate, dissonant **10** at variance, discrepant **11** conflicting, disagreeing **12** unharmonious

Discordia

origin: 5 Roman

goddess of: 7 discord

corresponds to: 4 Eris

discount 3 cut **5** break **6** rebate **7** cut rate **9** abatement, allowance, deduction, exemption, reduction **10** concession **11** subtraction

discountenance 7 condemn, despise, disdain, dislike **8** object to **9** frown upon **10** disapprove, think ill of **12** look down upon **13** look askance at, regard as wrong **14** hold in contempt **15** take exception to

discourage 4 do in **5** daunt, deter, unman **6** deject, dismay **7** depress, unnerve **8** decimate, dispirit, dissuade, keep back, restrain **9** disparage, prostrate **10** dishearten, disincline, divert from **13** advise against, dash one's hopes **17** dampen one's spirits

discouraged 4 low **7** daunted **8** dejected, downcast, hopeless **9** depressed **10** despondent, dispirited **11** downhearted, pessimistic **12** disconsolate, disheartened

discouragement 4 curb **5** gloom, worry **6** damper, dismay **7** despair **8** obstacle **9** dejection, hindrance, pessimism, restraint **10** constraint, depression, impediment, low spirits, melancholy, moroseness **11** despondency **12** hopelessness, lack of spirit **13** consternation **15** downheartedness

discourse 3 gab **4** chat, talk **5** essay **6** confer, sermon, speech **7** address, discuss, lecture, oration **8** colloquy, converse, dialogue, diatribe, harangue, treatise **10** discussion **11** intercourse **12** conversation, dissertation, talk together **16** formal discussion

Discourse on Method

author: 13 Rene Descartes

discourteous 4 rude **5** fresh, surly **6** cheeky **7** boorish, ill-bred, uncivil, uncouth **8** impolite, impudent, insolent **9** uncourtly, ungallant **10** ill-behaved, ungracious, unladylike, unmannerly **11** ill-mannered, impertinent **13** disrespectful, ungentlemanly

discourtesy 8 rudeness **9** impudence, insolence **10** incivility **11** boorishness **12** impoliteness

discover 3 see **4** find, spot **5** dig up **6** detect, locate, notice **7** discern, find

out, learn of, realize, root out, uncover, unearth **8** come upon, perceive **9** ascertain, determine, ferret out, light upon, recognize **10** chance upon **11** gain sight of, stumble upon **12** bring to light

discredit 4 deny, slur **5** abuse, smear, sully, taint **6** debase, defame, demean, reject, smirch, vilify **7** degrade, dispute, tarnish, vitiate **8** disallow, disgrace, dishonor, disprove, question **9** challenge, disparage, undermine **10** prove false, stigmatize **16** shake one's faith in **17** drag through the mud

discreditable 8 shameful, shocking **9** appalling **10** outrageous, scandalous **11** disgraceful, ignominious **12** dishonorable, disreputable

discreet 6 polite **7** careful, politic, prudent, tactful **8** cautious **9** judicious, sensitive **10** diplomatic, thoughtful **11** circumspect

Discreet Charm of the Bourgeoisie, The

director: 10 Luis Bunuel

cast: 11 Fernando Rey **14** Delphine Seyrig, Stephane Audran

Oscar for: 11 foreign film

discrepancy 3 gap **8** variance **9** disparity **10** difference, divergence **11** discordance, incongruity **12** disagreement **13** dissimilarity, inconsistency

discrepant 6 at odds **8** contrary, opposing **9** disparate **10** at variance, discordant, dissimilar, refutatory **11** conflicting, contrasting, disagreeing **12** antithetical, inconsistent **13** contradictory **14** countervailing, irreconcilable

discrete 7 several, various **8** detached, distinct, separate **9** different **10** unattached **11** disjunctive, independent **12** disconnected, unassociated **13** discontinuous

discretion 4 tact **6** acumen, option **8** judgment, prudence, sagacity, volition **9** good sense **10** preference **11** discernment, inclination **12** good judgment, predilection **13** judiciousness, sound judgment **14** discrimination **15** power of choosing **16** individual choice

discretionary 8 optional **9** voluntary **10** nonbinding **11** nonrequired, unnecessary **12** nonrequisite, unimperative **13** nonobligatory

discriminate 7 disdain **8** separate **11** distinguish **12** disfranchise **13** differentiate

discriminating 5 acute **6** astute, biased, shrewd **7** bigoted, refined **9** judicious, sensitive **10** cultivated, discerning, fastidious **11** intelligent, prejudicial **13** perspicacious **15** differentiating

discrimination 4 bias **5** taste **6** acumen **7** bigotry **8** inequity, judgment, keenness, sagacity **9** prejudice **10** as-

tuteness, discretion, favoritism, refinement, shrewdness **11** discernment, distinction **12** perspicacity **21** differential treatment

discursive 7 diffuse **8** rambling **9** wandering **10** circuitous, digressive, longwinded, meandering, roundabout

discursiveness 8 rambling **10** digression, meandering **14** circumlocution

discuss 6 debate, parley, review **7** dissect, examine, speak of **8** consider, talk over **9** talk about **13** converse about, exchange views **14** discourse about

discussion 3 rap **4** talk **6** debate, parley, powwow, review **7** inquiry **8** analysis, argument, colloquy, dialogue, scrutiny **9** discourse **10** hashing-out **11** disputation **12** deliberation **13** consideration, investigation

disdain 4 snub **5** abhor, scorn, spurn **6** deride, detest, loathe **7** despise, dislike **8** contempt, distaste **9** frown upon **10** abhorrence, brush aside, disrespect **11** intolerance **12** icy aloofness, look down upon **14** deem unbecoming, discountenance

disdained 7 derided, scorned, spurned **8** abhorred, despised **10** deprecated, disparaged **14** held in contempt

disdainful 4 cold **5** aloof **7** haughty, high-hat **8** derisive, scornful, superior **11** overbearing, patronizing **12** contemptuous, supercilious **13** condescending

disease 6 malady **7** ailment, illness **8** sickness **9** ill health, infirmity **10** affliction **15** morbid condition **16** physical disorder

disembark 4 land **7** deplane, detrain, pile out **10** leave a ship **11** get off a ship

disenchant 6 put off **7** turn off **8** alienate, disabuse, turn away **9** undeceive **11** disenthrall, disillusion **12** open one's eyes **13** break the spell **15** burst one's bubble **16** bring down to earth

disencumber 3 rid **8** unburden **9** disburden, extricate **11** disentangle

disengage 5 sever **6** detach **7** disjoin **8** separate **9** extricate **10** disconnect

disengaged 7 unmoved **8** detached **9** apathetic, disjoined, separated **11** indifferent, uncommitted, unconcerned **12** disconnected, unresponsive

French: 6 degage

disengagement 6 apathy **8** severing **9** severance, unconcern **10** detachment, separation **12** indifference **13** disconnection **16** unresponsiveness

disentangle 4 free **6** detach, loosen, remove **7** unravel **9** extricate

disenthrall 9 undeceive **10** disenchant **11** disillusion **12** open one's eyes

13 break the spell **15** burst one's bubble **16** bring down to earth

disesteem 7 dislike **8** disfavor **9** disrepute **11** disapproval, displeasure **14** disapprobation

disfavor 5 odium **7** dislike, ill turn **8** disgrace, ignominy **9** disesteem, disregard **10** disrespect, disservice, harmful act **11** disapproval, discourtesy, displeasure **14** disapprobation **15** dissatisfaction **16** unacceptableness

disfigure 3 mar **4** maim, scar **5** cut up **6** damage, deface, deform, impair **7** blemish, scarify **8** make ugly, mutilate

disfigurement 4 blot, flaw, mark, scar, spot **6** blotch, defect **7** blemish **12** imperfection

disfranchise, disenfranchise 15 deprive of a right **19** discriminate against

disgorge 4 spew **5** eject, expel, spout, vomit **6** cast up, spew up **7** cough up, throw up **8** dislodge **9** discharge **10** vomit forth **11** regurgitate

disgrace 4 blot **5** abase, shame, stain, taint **6** debase, smirch **7** blemish, degrade, eyesore, scandal, tarnish **8** contempt, derogate, disfavor, dishonor, ill favor, reproach **9** discredit, disparage, disrepute, embarrass, humiliate **13** embarrassment, in the doghouse **14** bring shame upon

disgraceful 3 low **4** base, mean, vile **6** odious **8** infamous, shameful, shocking, unseemly, unworthy **9** appalling, degrading, obnoxious **10** despicable, detestable, inglorious, outrageous, scandalous, unbecoming **11** ignominious, opprobrious **12** dishonorable, disreputable **13** discreditable, reprehensible

disgruntled 5 sulky, testy, vexed **6** grumpy, shirty, sullen **7** grouchy, peevish **8** petulant **9** irritated **10** displeased, malcontent **12** discontented, dissatisfied

disguise 4 garb, hide, mask, pose, sham, veil **5** blind, cloak, cover, feign, getup, guise **6** facade, muffle, screen, shroud, veneer **7** conceal, cover-up, dress up, falsify **8** pretense, simulate **9** costuming, dissemble, gloss over **10** camouflage, false front, masquerade **11** concealment, counterfeit **12** misrepresent **13** false identity **15** false appearance

disguised 6 masked, veiled **7** cloaked **9** dressed up, incognito **10** undercover **11** camouflaged **14** unrecognizable

disgust 5 repel **6** appall, hatred, offend, put off, revolt, sicken **7** dislike **8** aversion, contempt, distaste, loathing, nauseate **9** antipathy, disrelish, repulsion, revulsion **10** abhorrence, repugnance **11** detestation, displeasure **12** disaffection **13** be repulsive to, cause aversion **15** turn one's stomach

disgusting 4 vile **5** hasty **6** horrid, odious **7** hateful **9** abhorrent, appalling, loathsome, offensive, repellent, repugnant, repulsive, revolting, sickening **10** abominable, despicable, nauseating **12** reprehensible

dish 4 dole, fare, food **5** ladle, place, plate, scoop, serve, spoon **6** recipe, saucer, vessel **7** bowlful, dishful, edibles, helping, platter, portion, serving **8** dispense, plateful, transfer, victuals **10** comestible **11** shallow bowl

dishabille 7 undress **8** bathrobe, disarray, disorder, informal, negligee **9** housecoat

disharmonious 7 chaotic **8** clashing, confused **9** dissonant, illogical **10** discordant, incoherent **11** conflicting, contentious **12** incompatible **13** heterogeneous

disharmony 5 chaos **6** strife **7** discord **8** clashing, conflict, disarray, disunity, division, friction **9** cacophony, confusion, disaccord, harshness **10** contention, dissension, dissonance **11** discordance **12** disagreement, grating noise **15** disorganization, incompatibility

dishearten 4 dash, faze **5** abash, crush, daunt **6** deject, dismay, sadden **7** depress **8** dispirit **10** discourage

disheartened 3 low **6** dismal **8** dejected, desolate, downcast **9** depressed **10** despondent, dispirited **11** discouraged **12** disconsolate

disheartening 4 dark **7** adverse **8** hopeless **11** dispiriting **12** discouraging, inauspicious

disheveled 5 messy **6** blowsy, frowzy, mussed, sloppy, untidy **7** ruffled, rumpled, tousled, unkempt **8** uncombed **10** bedraggled, disarrayed, disorderly, in disorder **11** disarranged

dishevelment 5 chaos, mix-up, upset **6** jumble **7** clutter **8** disarray, disorder, scramble, shambles **9** messiness **10** sloppiness, untidiness **14** disarrangement **15** disorganization

dishonest 5 false **7** corrupt, crooked **8** cheating, specious, spurious, two-faced **9** deceitful, deceptive, faithless, insincere, not honest **10** fraudulent, mendacious, misleading, perfidious, untruthful **11** underhanded **12** disingenuous, false-hearted, unprincipled, unscrupulous **13** untrustworthy

dishonesty 8 cheating **9** duplicity, falseness, mendacity **10** corruption **11** crookedness **12** speciousness **14** untruthfulness

dishonor 4 blot **5** abase, odium, shame, stain, sully **6** debase, defame, infamy, insult, slight, stigma **7** affront, blacken, blemish, degrade, offense, scandal, tarnish **8** disfavor, disgrace, ignominy **9** discredit, disparage, disre-

pute, humiliate, ill repute **10** derogation, stigmatize **11** discourtesy, humiliation **12** bring shame on **14** public disgrace

dishonorable 4 base **7** debased, ignoble **8** shameful **10** despicable **12** contemptible, disreputable **13** reprehensible

dishonorableness 4 blot **5** odium, shame, stain **6** stigma **7** blemish **8** disfavor, disgrace, ignominy **9** discredit, disrepute, ill repute **10** derogation **11** humiliation

dishonoring 8 disgrace **10** debasement **11** degradation, humiliation

dish up 3 dip **5** ladle, serve, spoon **7** dish out, serve up

disillusion 6 clue in **8** disabuse **9** undeceive **10** disenchant **11** disenthrall **13** break the spell, open the eyes of **14** burst the bubble **16** bring down to earth

disinclination 8 aversion **9** hesitancy **10** reluctance **13** indisposition, unwillingness

disincline 5 deter **8** dissuade, keep back, restrain **10** discourage, divert from **13** advise against **16** attempt to prevent

disinclined 5 loath **6** averse **8** hesitant **9** reluctant, unwilling **10** indisposed

disinfect 6 purify **7** cleanse **8** sanitize **9** kill germs, sterilize **13** decontaminate **15** destroy bacteria

disinfectant 9 germicide **10** antiseptic, germ killer **11** bactericide

disinherit 6 cut off, disown **15** deprive of rights

disintegrate 7 break up, crumble, shatter **8** splinter **9** fall apart **10** break apart, go to pieces

disintegration 4 ruin **5** decay **7** breakup, erosion **8** biolysis **9** crumbling **10** dispersion, dissolving, separation **11** decomposing **12** falling apart **13** decomposition, deterioration, pulverization

disinter 5 dig up **6** exhume **7** unearth

disinterest 6 apathy **9** disregard, unconcern **12** indifference

disinterested 7 neutral, outside **8** unbiased **9** impartial **10** impersonal, uninvolved **12** free from bias, unprejudiced **13** dispassionate

disinterment 9 digging up **10** exhumation, unearthing

disjecta membra 15 disjointed parts **16** scattered members

disjoin 4 part, undo **5** break, sever **6** detach, divide **8** disunite, separate **9** disengage

disjoint 6 detach **7** unhinge **8** disunite, separate **9** dislocate **10** disconnect **13** disarticulate

disjointed 5 apart, split **7** chaotic, divided, jumbled, mixed-up, tangled

8 confused, detached, rambling **9** illogical, spasmodic **10** incoherent, irrational, unattached **11** unconnected **12** disconnected, disorganized **13** discontinuous, disharmonious, helter-skelter, heterogeneous **14** disarticulated

disjointedness 8 rambling **11** indirection **14** discursiveness **16** disconnectedness

disjointed parts
Latin: **14** disjecta membra

disk, disc 3 cam **4** aten, coin, dial, face, plow, puck **5** plate, wafer, wheel **6** harrow, record, sequin **7** discuss **8** diskette **9** cultivate, videodisc **11** discotheque
type: **4** hard **5** fixed **6** floppy **8** magnetic **10** Winchester

dislike 4 hate **5** abhor, scorn **6** animus, detest, enmity, hatred, loathe, malice, rancor **7** despise, disdain, disgust, not like **8** aversion, distaste, loathing, object to **9** abominate, animosity, antipathy, hostility, repulsion, revulsion **10** abhorrence, antagonism, repugnance **11** abomination, detestation **12** disaffection

disliked 5 hated **7** loathed, unloved **8** abhorred, despised, detested **10** abominated

dislike intensely 4 hate **5** abhor **6** detest, loathe **7** despise **9** abominate **10** recoil from

dislocate 6 uproot **7** unhinge **8** disjoint, disunite, separate **9** disengage **10** disconnect **13** disarticulate, put out of joint

dislodge 4 oust **5** eject, expel **6** dig out, dispel, remove, uproot **7** disturb **8** displace, force out **9** extricate **11** disentangle

disloyal 6 untrue **8** recreant **9** faithless, seditious, undutiful **10** inconstant, perfidious, subversive, traitorous, unfaithful **11** treacherous, treasonable **12** dishonorable

disloyalty 7 falsity, perfidy, treason **8** apostasy, betrayal, sedition **9** falseness, rebellion, recreancy, treachery **10** infidelity, subversion **11** inconstancy **12** insurrection **13** breach of trust, deceitfulness, double-dealing, faithlessness **14** lack of fidelity, perfidiousness, unfaithfulness **15** betrayal of trust, breaking of faith **18** subversive activity

dismal 3 sad **4** drab, grim, poor **5** awful, bleak **6** dreary, gloomy, morbid, rueful, somber, woeful **7** abysmal, doleful, forlorn, joyless, unhappy, very bad, visaged **8** dejected, desolate, dolorous, downcast, dreadful, hopeless, horrible, mournful, terrible **9** cheerless, depressed, long-faced, sorrowful, woebegone **10** abominable, despondent, in the dumps, lugubrious, melancholy **11** pessimistic **12** discon-

solate, disheartened, heavy-hearted **13** unmentionable **14** down-in-the-mouth

dismantle 5 strip **6** denude, divest **9** take apart

dismay 3 cow **5** abash, alarm, daunt, dread, panic, scare **6** appall, fright, horror, put off, terror **7** anxiety, concern, horrify, unnerve **8** affright, distress, frighten **10** disappoint, discourage, dishearten, intimidate **11** disillusion, trepidation **12** apprehension, exasperation, intimidation, perturbation **13** consternation **14** disappointment, discouragement **15** disillusionment

dismayed 7 abashed, daunted **8** appalled **10** confounded, nonplussed **12** disconcerted

dismember 4 limb **6** hack up **8** disjoint **16** tear limb from limb

dismiss 3 can **4** fire, free, oust, sack **5** let go **6** bounce, excuse, reject **7** adjourn, cashier, disband, discard, release **8** disclaim, disperse, dissolve, lay aside, liberate, pink-slip, set aside **9** disregard, eliminate, repudiate, send forth, terminate **10** permit to go **11** send packing **12** allow to leave, put out of a job, put out of mind **14** give the heave-ho **17** remove from service, give walking papers **19** discharge from office

dismissal 6 firing **7** release **9** discharge, dispersal, disregard **10** disclaimer **11** adjournment, repudiation

Disney
theme parks **10** Disneyland, EuroDisney **15** Disneyland Paris, Tokyo Disneyland, Walt Disney World

Disney, Walt
creator/artist of: **5** Goofy, Pluto **10** Donald Duck **11** Mickey Mouse, Minnie Mouse

disobedience 8 defiance **9** rebellion **10** resistance **13** noncompliance, nonconformity **14** rebelliousness

disobedient 6 unruly **7** defiant, forward, haughty, wayward **8** contrary, mutinous, perverse, stubborn **9** fractious, insurgent, obstinate, seditious, undutiful **10** disorderly, rebellious, refractory, unyielding **11** intractable **12** noncompliant, recalcitrant, ungovernable, unmanageable, unsubmissive **13** insubordinate

disobey 4 defy **5** break **6** ignore, resist **7** violate **8** overstep **9** disregard **10** infringe on, transgress **11** go counter to **12** rebel against

disoblige 5 annoy **6** bother **7** trouble **13** inconvenience

disobliging 4 rude **8** churlish **9** unhelpful **13** inconsiderate

disorder 4 mess, riot **5** chaos **6** fracas, jumble, malady, muddle, ruckus, uproar **7** ailment, clutter, disease, illness, turmoil **8** disarray, sickness **9**

commotion, complaint, confusion **10** affliction, disruption, dissension **11** disturbance **13** indisposition, minor uprising **14** disarrangement **15** disorganization

disordered 7 jumbled **8** confused, messed up **9** haphazard **11** disarranged **12** disorganized

disorderliness 4 mess **5** chaos **6** muddle **8** disarray **9** confusion **10** disruption **14** disarrangement **15** disorganization

disorderly 3 bad **4** awry, wild **5** amiss, messy, noisy, rowdy **6** sloppy, unruly, untidy **7** chaotic, jumbled, lawless, riotous, unkempt, wayward **8** careless, confused, improper, pell-mell, rowdyish, slipshod, slovenly, unlawful, unsorted **10** boisterous, disheveled, disordered, disruptive, rebellious, straggling, topsy-turvy **11** disarranged **12** disorganized, disreputable, obstreperous, unrestrained, unsystematic **13** helter-skelter, undisciplined **14** rough-and-tumble, unsystematized

disorganization 4 mess **5** chaos, upset **6** jumble, muddle **7** clutter **8** disarray, disorder, shambles **9** confusion, messiness **10** disharmony, disruption, sloppiness, untidiness **12** dishevelment **14** disarrangement, disorderliness

disorganize 5 mix up, upset **6** jumble, mess up, muddle **7** confuse, scatter **8** disarray, disorder, put askew, scramble **10** disarrange **13** put out of order **14** turn topsy-turvy

disorganized 5 messy, upset **7** chaotic, jumbled, mixed-up, muddled **8** confused, rambling **9** haphazard, illogical **10** disordered, disorderly, incoherent, in disarray, irrational **12** unsystematic **16** at sixes and sevens

disoriented 7 mixed-up **8** confused, unstable **10** distracted, out of joint, out of touch **11** not adjusted

disown 4 deny **6** reject **7** cast off, disavow, forsake **8** denounce, disclaim, renounce **9** repudiate **10** disinherit **17** refuse to recognize **19** refuse to acknowledge

disparage 4 mock **6** demean, slight **7** put down, run down **8** belittle, derogate, ridicule **9** denigrate, discredit, underrate **10** depreciate, undervalue **11** detract from

disparagement 5 abuse, libel **7** slander **8** ridicule **9** criticism **10** belittling, defamation, derogation, detraction **11** denigration, putting down **12** vilification **17** defamatory remarks

disparaging 5 snide **10** belittling, derogatory **11** unfavorable **15** uncomplimentary

disparate 6 at odds, unlike **9** different **10** at variance, discordant, discrepant, dissimilar **11** contrasting

disparity 3 gap **8** contrast, imparity, variance **10** difference, divergence, inequality, unlikeness **11** discrepancy, incongruity **12** disagreement, dissemblance **13** contradiction, disproportion, dissimilarity, dissimilitude, inconsistency

dispassion 6 apathy **8** coolness **10** detachment **12** indifference

dispassionate 4 calm, cool, fair **6** serene **7** neutral, unmoved **8** composed, detached, unbiased **9** collected, impartial, unexcited, unruffled **10** impersonal, uninvolved **11** levelheaded, undisturbed, unemotional **12** unprejudiced **13** disinterested, imperturbable

dispatch 4 item, kill, post, slay **5** flash, haste, piece, speed, story **6** finish, letter, murder, report, settle, wind up **7** bump off, execute, forward, message, missive, send off **8** alacrity, bulletin, carry out, celerity, complete, conclude, expedite, massacre, rapidity **9** finish off, quickness, slaughter, swiftness **10** communique, expedition, promptness, put an end to, put to death **11** assassinate, news account **12** send on the way **14** execute quickly, summarily shoot, swift execution **15** make short work of, transmit rapidly **16** carry out speedily, dispose of rapidly **18** telegraphic message **21** official communication

Dis Pater *see* **3** Dis

dispel 4 rout **5** allay, expel, repel **6** banish, remove **7** diffuse, dismiss, resolve, scatter **8** drive off **9** dissipate, drive away, eliminate **10** put an end to **11** disseminate **13** make disappear

dispensable 8 nonvital **9** accessory, extrinsic, secondary **10** disposable, expendable, extraneous **11** superfluous, unessential, unimportant, unnecessary **12** nonessential

dispensation 6 decree **8** approval, bestowal, division **9** allotment, diffusion, exemption, meting out **10** allocation, conferment, credential, dealing out, dispensing, permission, reparation **11** consignment, designation **12** apportioning, distribution, remuneration **13** authorization, dissemination

dispense 6 confer **7** dole out, mete out **8** allocate **9** apportion **10** administer, distribute

dispense with 4 drop, dump, junk, shed **5** scrap **6** shelve **7** abandon, discard **9** dispose of

dispensing 9 bestowing, doling out, meting out **10** allocating, conferring **12** distributing

dispersal 7 breakup, parting **9** dismissal **10** breaking up, scattering **12** distributing, distribution

disperse 4 rout **6** dispel **7** diffuse, disband, scatter, send off **8** drive off **9**

dissipate **10** distribute **11** disseminate **13** send scurrying **16** spread throughout

dispersed 7 diffuse **9** scattered, spread out **10** dissipated **11** distributed **14** extended widely, unconcentrated

dispersion 9 dispersal **10** disbanding, scattering **11** dissipation **12** distribution

dispirit 5 cloud **6** darken, deject, sadden **7** depress **10** demoralize, dishearten

dispirited 3 sad **4** blue, down, glum **5** moody **6** morose **7** forlorn, unhappy **8** dejected, downcast, listless **9** cheerless, depressed **10** melancholy **11** crestfallen, demoralized, discouraged, downhearted, pessimistic **12** disconsolate, disheartened **14** down in the dumps, down in the mouth, unenthusiastic

dispiriting 4 cold, dark **6** chilly, dismal, gloomy **9** dampening **10** depressing **12** discouraging **13** disheartening

displace 4 bump, move, oust **5** shift **6** unseat **7** replace **8** crowd out, dislodge, force out, supplant **9** dislocate, supersede

displaced person 2 DP **5** exile **6** emigre **7** refugee **8** expellee **10** expatriate

display 4 show **6** reveal **7** exhibit **8** manifest **10** exhibition **11** demonstrate, make visible **12** presentation **13** bring into view, demonstration, manifestation **15** put in plain sight

display case 7 cabinet, vitrine **8** showcase

displease 3 irk **5** annoy, pique **6** offend **7** disturb, incense, provoke **8** irritate

displeasing 8 annoying **9** loathsome, offensive, repellent, repugnant **10** irritating **11** distasteful, distressing **12** disagreeable

displeasure 5 wrath **7** dislike **8** vexation **9** annoyance **10** irritation **11** disapproval, indignation **15** dissatisfaction

disport 3 act **4** play, romp **5** amuse, caper, sport **6** divert, frolic, gambol **7** display, pastime **9** amusement, entertain **10** recreation **13** entertainment

disposal 5 array, order, power **7** command, control, dumping, junking, pattern, ridding **8** grouping, riddance **9** authority, clearance, direction, placement **10** discarding, government, management, regulation, settlement **11** arrangement, destruction, disposition, supervision **12** distribution, organization, throwing away **13** authorization, configuration, juxtaposition **14** administration

dispose 4 rank **5** array, order, place **7** arrange, deal out, incline **8** classify,

get rid of, motivate, organize **9** be willing **10** distribute

dispose of 4 dump **5** scrap **6** unload **7** discard **8** get rid of, throw out **9** cast aside, throw away

disposition 6 nature, spirit **7** control **8** bestowal, grouping, tendency **9** placement **11** arrangement, inclination, temperament **12** distribution, organization **14** predisposition **15** final settlement

dispossess 4 oust **5** evict, expel **8** take away, take back **9** deprive of

disproportionate 7 unequal **9** disparate **10** dissimilar, unbalanced

disprove 6 refute **9** discredit **10** controvert

disputable 7 dubious **8** doubtful **9** debatable, uncertain **12** questionable **14** controvertible

disputant 5 rival **7** opposer **8** opponent **9** adversary **10** antagonist, competitor, contestant

disputation 6 debate, review **8** argument, dialogue **10** discussion

dispute 4 feud **5** argue, clash, doubt **6** debate, impugn **7** quarrel, wrangle **8** argument, question, squabble **9** bickering, challenge **10** contradict **11** altercation, controversy **12** disagreement

disputed 6 argued **8** wrangled **9** debatable, in dispute, quarreled **10** in question, unverified **12** questionable **13** controversial **15** unsubstantiated

disqualification 5 minus **8** handicap **10** disability **11** shortcoming **13** ineligibility

disqualify 7 disable **9** make unfit **17** declare ineligible, deny participation

disquiet, disquietude 3 awe **6** unease **7** anxiety **8** distress **9** agitation **10** uneasiness **11** fretfulness, trepidation **12** apprehension, discomposure, perturbation **13** consternation

disquieted 6 uneasy **7** anxious, worried **9** concerned **10** distressed **12** apprehensive

disquieting 6 vexing **8** annoying **9** troubling, upsetting **10** bothersome, disturbing, irritating, perturbing, unsettling **11** distressing **13** disconcerting

disquisition 8 tractate, treatise **9** discourse, monograph **12** dissertation

disregard 6 ignore **8** overlook **11** pay no heed to **13** lack of respect **14** take no notice of **15** lack of attention **16** willful oversight

disregardful 8 careless, heedless **9** unmindful **11** insensitive, thoughtless **13** inconsiderate

disreputable 5 shady **8** infamous, shameful, shocking **9** notorious **10** scandalous **11** disgraceful **12** dishonorable, unprincipled **14** not respectable, of bad character

disrespect 6 insult **8** contempt, dishonor, rudeness **9** disregard **11** discourtesy, irreverence **12** impoliteness

disrespectful 4 rude **8** impolite **11** impertinent **12** contemptuous, discourteous

disrobe 5 strip **7** undress **16** divest of clothing

disrupt 5 upset **9** interrupt **13** interfere with **17** throw into disorder

disruption 5 upset **8** disorder **9** confusion **11** disturbance **12** interference, interruption **14** disarrangement **15** disorganization

dissatisfaction 4 veto **7** protest **9** rejection **10** discontent **11** disapproval, displeasure, unhappiness

dissatisfied 7 unhappy **10** displeased **12** discontented

dissect 5 study **7** analyze, lay open **8** cut apart, separate **9** anatomize, break down

dissemble 4 hide, mask **5** feign **7** conceal **8** disguise **10** camouflage **11** dissimulate

disseminate 6 spread **7** diffuse, scatter **8** disperse **9** broadcast, circulate

dissemination 9 diffusion, dispersal, spreading **10** scattering **12** broadcasting, distribution

dissension 7 discord, dispute **8** conflict, disunity, division **9** rebellion **10** contention, disharmony, quarreling **11** discordance **12** disagreement **14** rebelliousness

dissent 6 object, oppose **7** discord, protest **8** disagree **10** difference, dissension, opposition **12** disagreement **14** withhold assent **16** withhold approval

dissenter 5 rebel **9** dissident, protester **13** nonconformist

dissenting 9 differing, dissident **11** disagreeing

dissertation 6 memoir, thesis **8** tractate, treatise **9** discourse, monograph **12** disquisition

disservice 4 harm, hurt **5** wrong **6** injury **7** bad turn **9** injustice

dissever 3 saw **4** hack, rend **5** carve, sever, slash, slice, split **6** cleave, divide **8** disunite, separate

dissident 5 rebel **8** agitator, opposing **9** differing, dissenter **10** dissenting **11** disagreeing

dissimilar 6 unlike **8** distinct **9** different, disparate

dissimilarity 8 contrast, variance **9** disparity **10** difference, dissonance, divergence, inequality, unlikeness **11** discrepancy **12** disagreement **13** inconsistency **17** lack of resemblance

dissimilitude 8 variance **9** disparity

10 difference, unlikeness **11** incongruity **12** disagreement **17** lack of resemblance

dissimulate 4 hide, mask **7** conceal **8** disguise **9** dissemble **10** camouflage

dissipate 5 waste **6** dispel **7** carouse, deplete, scatter **8** disperse, misspend, squander **11** fritter away, overindulge **13** be intemperate **14** spend foolishly

dissipated 6 wasted **8** misspent **9** abandoned, debauched, dispelled, dispersed, dissolute, scattered **10** squandered **11** intemperate **12** disreputable **13** frittered away

dissipater 5 waste **7** wastrel **8** prodigal **10** profligate, squanderer **11** spendthrift

dissipation 6 excess **7** wasting **9** dispersal **10** debauchery, dispelling, scattering **11** dissolution, loose living **12** immoderation, intemperance **14** disintegration, frittering away, self-indulgence

dissociate 8 separate **10** disconnect **12** break off with

dissociation 7 breakup **10** separation

dissolute 5 loose **7** corrupt, immoral **9** abandoned, debauched **10** dissipated **12** unrestrained

dissolution 9 annulment **10** separation **11** termination **14** disintegration

dissolve 3 end, run **4** fade, melt, thaw, void **5** annul, sever **6** finish, render, soften, vanish **7** break up, disband, liquefy, thaw out **8** abrogate, conclude, evanesce **9** disappear, dissipate, terminate **10** deliquesce **12** disintegrate **13** dematerialize

dissonance 5 clash **7** discord **9** cacophony, harshness **10** difference, disharmony **11** discordance **12** disagreement **13** dissimilarity

dissonant 5 harsh **7** grating, hostile, jarring, raucous, warring **8** clashing, jangling **10** discordant, discrepant **11** cacophonous, disagreeing, incongruent, incongruous, unmelodious **12** incompatible, inconsistent, inharmonious **13** contradictory **14** irreconcilable

dissuade 9 urge not to **10** discourage **13** advise against, persuade not to

distance 3 gap **4** span **7** reserve, stretch **8** coldness, coolness, interval **9** aloofness, formality, restraint, stiffness **11** reservation **16** intervening space

distant 3 far **4** cold, cool **5** aloof **6** far-off, remote **7** faraway **8** detached, reserved **10** far-removed, restrained, unfriendly **11** standoffish **17** not closely related

Distant Mirror, A
author: **15** Barbara W Tuchman

distaste 7 disgust, dislike **8** aversion **9** antipathy **10** repugnance **11** displeasure

distasteful 9 loathsome, repugnant **10** disgusting, unpleasant **11** displeasing **12** disagreeable

distastefulness 13 offensiveness **14** unpleasantness **16** disagreeableness

distasteful work 8 drudgery **11** menial labor

distend 5 bloat, bulge, swell **6** billow, expand **7** inflate, puff out **8** swell out

distended 4 full, taut **5** puffy, tumid **7** blown up, bloated, dilated, swelled, swollen **8** enlarged, expanded, extended, inflated, patulant **9** edematous, stretched

distill 7 draw out, extract **8** condense, vaporize **9** draw forth, evaporate

distillate 7 essence, extract **11** concentrate **13** concentration

distilled 9 condensed, extracted, vaporized **10** evaporated

distinct 5 clear, lucid, plain **7** diverse, supreme **8** clear-cut, definite, explicit, separate **9** different **10** dissimilar, individual **11** unmitigated, well-defined **12** not identical, unmistakable **13** extraordinary **14** unquestionable

distinction 6 renown **8** contrast, eminence **9** greatness **10** difference, excellence, importance, notability, prominence, separation **11** discernment, preeminence, superiority **12** differential **14** discrimination **15** differentiation

distinctive 6 unique **7** special **8** atypical, original, singular, uncommon **9** different **10** individual **13** extraordinary **14** characteristic

distinctiveness 7 clarity **9** character **10** definition, uniqueness **11** personality **13** individuality

distingue 13 distinguished

distinguish 6 decide, define **7** discern **8** set apart **9** single out **10** make famous **12** characterize, discriminate **13** differentiate, make prominent, make well known **14** make celebrated **15** make distinctive, note differences

distinguished 5 grand, great **6** famous, superb **7** elegant, eminent, notable, refined **8** renowned, splendid **9** acclaimed, dignified, distingue, prominent **10** celebrated **11** illustrious, magnificent
French: 9 distingue

distort 6 deform **7** contort **8** misshape **9** disfigure **11** misconstrue **12** misrepresent **15** twist out of shape, twist the meaning

distorted 4 awry **5** askew **6** belied, loaded, warped **7** altered, colored, crooked, twisted **8** cockeyed, deformed, wrenched **9** contorted, falsified, grotesque, irregular, misshapen, misstated, perverted **13** unsymmetrical **14** misrepresented **15** misproportioned

distortion 7 skewing 8 twisting 10 aberration, caricature 11 crookedness, deformation 12 malformation 17 misrepresentation

distract 5 amuse, craze, worry 6 divert, madden 7 agitate, confuse, disturb, perplex, torment, trouble 8 bewilder, disorder 9 entertain

distracted 3 mad 4 wild 6 amused, crazed, insane, raving 7 frantic, pleased, puzzled 8 agitated, confused, deranged, diverted, frenzied, harassed, heedless, occupied 9 disturbed, stirred up 10 bewildered, distraught, irrational 11 entertained, turned aside

distraction 5 fazed, upset 6 frenzy 7 frantic, madness, pastime, rattled, ruffled 8 agitated, confused 9 amusement, diversion, unsettled 10 distraught, distressed, nonplussed, recreation 11 desperation 12 disconcerted 13 entertainment 14 mental distress

distractive 9 confusing 10 disturbing, unsettling 11 distressing, troublesome

distraught 3 mad 7 anxious, frantic 8 agitated, frenzied, seething 10 distracted, distressed 13 beside oneself

distress 4 need, pain, want 5 agony, upset 6 danger, grieve 7 anguish, disturb, torment, torture, trouble 14 acute suffering

distressed 5 upset 7 anxious, fearful, frantic, grieved, unhappy, worried 8 agitated, troubled 9 anguished, concerned, disturbed, tormented 10 distracted, distraught

distressing 5 acute 7 nagging, painful 8 grievous 9 agonizing, upsetting 10 disturbing, tormenting, unpleasant 11 displeasing, troublesome, unfortunate 13 uncomfortable

distribute 5 allot, class 6 divide, parcel 7 arrange, catalog, deliver, dole out, give out, scatter 8 classify, dispense, disperse, separate, tabulate 9 apportion, circulate, methodize, spread out 11 disseminate, systematize

distribution 7 sorting 8 division, grouping 9 allotment, spreading 10 allocation, dispersion, scattering 11 arrangement, circulation, disposition 12 organization 13 apportionment, dissemination

distribution center
French: 8 entrepot

district 4 area, ward 6 parish, region 8 precinct 12 neighborhood

distrust 5 doubt 7 suspect 8 question 9 misgiving, suspicion 11 lack of faith

distrustful 3 shy 4 wary 5 leery 7 dubious, jealous 8 cautious, doubtful, doubting 9 diffident 10 suspicious, untrusting 11 incredulous, mistrustful 12 disbelieving

disturb 5 annoy, upset, worry 6 bother 7 disrupt, perturb, trouble 8 distress, unsettle 9 dislocate, interrupt, intrude on 10 disarrange 11 disorganize

disturbance 5 upset, worry 6 bother, hubbub, ruckus, tumult, uproar 7 rioting, turmoil 8 disorder, distress, outbreak 9 annoyance 11 distraction 12 interruption, perturbation

disturbance of peace 4 riot 6 fracas, ruckus, uproar 7 turmoil 8 disorder 9 commotion 13 breach of order

disturbed 5 upset 6 uneasy 7 annoyed, anxious, nervous, rattled 8 agitated, confused, troubled 9 perturbed 10 disquieted 11 discomfited 12 disconcerted

disunion 7 divorce 8 division 9 secession 10 separation 14 disintegration

disunite 4 part 6 divide 7 divorce 8 separate 9 disengage 10 disconnect 12 disintegrate 13 disarticulate

disunited 6 parted 8 diverged, divorced, unallied 9 came apart, dispersed, separated 10 uncombined 13 disassociated

disunity 6 strife 7 discord 8 clashing, conflict, division, friction 9 wrangling 10 contention, dissension, separation 11 being at odds, discordance 12 disagreement 15 incompatibility

ditat Deus 11 God enriches
motto of: 7 Arizona

ditch 3 pit 4 junk 5 scrap 6 hollow, trench 7 abandon, discard 8 get rid of 10 excavation

dither 4 flap, fuss 5 tizzy, waver, whirl 6 bother, flurry, lather, quiver, shiver, thrill 7 fluster, tremble, twitter 8 hesitate 9 agitation, commotion, confusion, vacillate, vibration 10 excitement

Dithyrambus
epithet of: 8 Dionysus
means: 20 child of the double door

ditty 3 lay 4 song, tune 6 ballad 7 refrain

Dius Fidius
origin: 5 Roman
god of: 5 oaths 11 hospitality 20 international affairs
corresponds to: 6 Sancus 10 Semo Sancus

divagation 8 straying 9 wandering 10 digression, divergence

divan 4 book, hall, poem, room, salon, seat, sofa 5 couch, court 6 canape, daybed, leewan, lounge, settee 7 chamber, council, ottoman, davenport

dive 4 dash, fall, jump, leap 5 lunge 6 plunge 7 gin mill 9 honky-tonk, shabby bar 15 sleazy nightclub

Diver, Dick and Nicole
characters in: 16 Tender Is the Night
author: 10 Fitzgerald

diverge 6 differ, swerve 7 deflect,

deviate 8 be at odds, conflict, disagree, separate, split off

divergence 7 parting 8 conflict, rambling, straying, variance 9 deviation, disparity, wandering 10 difference, separation 11 discrepancy, incongruity 13 dissimilarity, inconsistency

divergent 8 separate 9 different 11 conflicting, disagreeing 12 drawing apart, splitting off

diverse 6 sundry, varied 8 eclectic, far-flung, opposite 9 different, differing, disparate 10 dissimilar 11 conflicting, of many kinds 13 contradictory

diversified 6 divers 7 various 8 manifold 9 different, unrelated 13 miscellaneous

diversify 4 vary 7 diffuse 8 divide up 9 spread out, variegate

diversion 5 hobby 7 pastime 9 amusement, avocation 10 deflection 11 distraction, drawing away 12 turning aside
French: 14 divertissement

diversity 7 variety 8 variance 10 assortment, difference 13 heterogeneity

divert 5 amuse 7 deflect 8 distract 9 entertain, sidetrack, turn aside

diverting 7 amusing 10 deflecting 11 distracting 12 entertaining, sidetracking

divertissement 9 diversion 13 entertainment

divest 3 rid 4 free 5 strip 7 deprive, disrobe, peel off, take off 8 get out of 10 dispossess 14 remove clothing

divest oneself of 6 give up 7 take off 8 get rid of, give over, hand over, put aside, strip off 9 surrender 10 relinquish

divide 4 part, sort 5 share, split 7 arrange, deal out, divvy up 8 allocate, classify, disunite, separate 9 apportion, partition 10 distribute, put in order

divide and rule
Latin: 14 divide et impera
maxim of: 11 Machiavelli

divided 5 apart, split 6 parted 8 meted out 9 disunited, separated 10 unattached 11 apportioned 12 disconnected, portioned out

divide et impera 13 divide and rule
maxim of: 11 Machiavelli

divide in two 5 halve, split 6 bisect 8 cut in two, separate 9 cut in half 10 break in two 11 split in half 18 split down the middle

dividing line 4 edge 5 brink, verge 6 border, margin 8 boundary 9 threshold

divination 5 guess 6 augury 8 prophecy 10 conjecture, foreboding, prediction, prescience 11 premonition, soothsaying 15 prognostication

divine 4 holy 5 guess 6 fathom, sacred

7 predict, surmise, suspect **8** forecast, foretell, heavenly, prophesy **9** admirable, celestial, excellent, marvelous, wonderful

divine being 3 god **5** deity **7** goddess **8** divinity **14** celestial being

Divine Comedy
    author: 14 Dante Alighieri
    part: 7 Inferno **8** Paradiso **10** Purgatorio
    guide: 6 Virgil **8** Beatrice

diviner 4 seer **5** augur **10** soothsayer **14** prognosticator

Divine retribution
    goddess of: 7 Nemesis **8** Adrastea

Divine Sarah
    nickname of: 14 Sarah Bernhardt

divining rod 4 twig, wand **5** dowse **9** doodlebug

divinity 3 god **5** deity **7** goddess **8** holiness, religion, theology **9** theosophy **12** science of God **14** celestial being

division 4 part, unit, wing **5** split **6** branch **7** discord, divider, section **8** disunion, variance **9** partition **10** department, difference, divergence, separation **11** splitting up **12** disagreement

divorce 4 rift **5** split **6** breach, divide **7** rupture **8** disunite, separate **9** segregate **10** dissociate, separation

divulge 4 tell **6** impart, relate, reveal **8** disclose **9** make known **11** communicate

divulgence 7 telling **8** exposure **9** imparting **10** disclosure, giving away, laying open, revelation **13** communication **15** bringing to light **17** bring out in the open

divulge to 4 tell **6** advise, inform, notify, reveal **7** apprise **8** acquaint, disclose **9** enlighten, make aware **11** familiarize **13** spill the beans **20** let the cat out of the bag

Dix, Otto
    born: 7 Germany **11** Unterhausen
    artwork: 6 The War **7** The City **12** The Procuress **15** Sylvia von Harden **18** Parents of the Artist **39** Prague Street Dedicated to My Contemporaries

Dixie Dugan
    creator: 8 J P McEvoy **13** John H Striebel

dizzy 5 fleet, giddy, quick, rapid, shaky, swift **6** whirly **7** confuse, reeling **8** bewilder, unsteady **9** make giddy **11** lightheaded, vertiginous **12** make unsteady

Djawa *see* **4** Java
Djebel al-Tarik *see* **9** Gibraltar
Djibouti
    other name: 16 French Somaliland **39** The French Territory of the Afars and the Issas
    capital/largest city: 8 Djibouti
    others: 5 Obock **6** Dikhil **8** Tadjoura

    9 Ali-Sabieh
monetary unit: 5 franc **7** centime
lake: 4 Abbe **5** Assal
mountain: 5 Gouda
    highest point: 9 Moussa Ali
sea: 3 Red
physical feature:
    gulf: 4 Aden **8** Tadjoura
    strait: 11 Bab el-Mandeb
people: 4 Afar, Arab **5** Issas **6** French **8** European
language: 4 Afar **6** Arabic, French, Somali
religion: 5 Islam

do 3 act **4** fare **5** clean, cover, get on, serve, visit **6** behave, finish, look at, stop in **7** achieve, arrange, carry on, conduct, execute, fulfill, make out, perform, prepare, proceed, suffice **8** be enough, carry out, complete, conclude, organize **10** accomplish, administer, bring about, put in order **13** travel through **14** be satisfactory, comport oneself, conduct oneself

do a favor 4 help **6** assist, oblige **7** help out **11** accommodate, do a kindness

do away with 3 end **4** junk, kill, void **5** erase, quash **6** banish, cancel, cut out, give up, remove, repeal, revoke, rub out **7** abolish, blot out, nullify, rescind, weed out, wipe out **8** abrogate, stamp out, throw out **9** eliminate, eradicate, terminate **10** annihilate, put an end to **11** exterminate

Dobbin, Captain William
    character in: 10 Vanity Fair
    author: 9 Thackeray

Dobie Gillis, The Many Loves of
    character: 11 Zelda Gilroy **13** Maynard G Krebs **14** Herbert T Gillis, Milton Armitage, Winifred (Winnie) Gillis **15** Thalia Menninger **19** Chatsworth Osborne Jr
    cast: 9 Bob Denver **11** Frank Faylen, Sheila James, Tuesday Weld **12** Warren Beatty **13** Dwayne Hickman **14** Florida Friebus, Stephen Franken
    Dobie imitated pose of: 7 Thinker

do business 4 deal **5** trade **10** buy and sell

docile 4 tame **7** willing **8** obedient, obliging **9** agreeable, compliant, tractable **10** manageable **11** complaisant

docility 7 pliancy **8** meekness **9** passivity **10** placidness **12** acquiescence, complaisance **13** nonresistance

dock 4 crop, join, pier, quay **5** berth, wharf **6** couple, cut off, deduct, hook up, link up **7** landing **8** cut short **10** waterfront **12** come into port **13** subject to loss **14** fasten together

dock 5 Rumux
    varieties: 3 Bur **4** Sour **5** Green **6** Golden **7** Prairie, Spinach, Tanner's, Western **8** Patience **9** Purple-wen **10** Giant water

docket 4 bill, card, list **5** slate **6** agenda, lineup, roster **7** program **8** calendar, schedule **9** timetable **14** things to be done **15** order of business

doctor 2 GP, MD **3** PhD **5** alter, treat **6** change **7** dentist, falsify, surgeon **9** internist, osteopath, physician **10** podiatrist, tamper with **11** pathologist **12** gynecologist, obstetrician, pediatrician, psychiatrist, veterinarian **15** ophthalmologist **17** apply medication to **19** general practitioner, medical practitioner

Doctor Brodie's Report
    author: 15 Jorge Luis Borges

Doctor Faustus
    author: 10 Thomas Mann **18** Christopher Marlowe

Doctor Grimshaw's Secret
    author: 18 Nathaniel Hawthorne

Doctor J
    nickname of: 12 Julius Erving

Doctorow, E L
    author of: 7 Ragtime **15** The Book of Daniel

Doctor's Dilemma, The
    author: 17 George Bernard Shaw

Doctor Zhivago
    director: 9 David Lean
    author: 14 Boris Pasternak
    cast: 10 Omar Sharif (Zhivago), Rod Steiger **12** Alec Guinness, Tom Courtenay **13** Julie Christie (Lara) **14** Rita Tushingham **15** Ralph Richardson **16** Geraldine Chaplin

doctrinaire 5 rigid **6** mulish **8** absolute, dogmatic, stubborn **9** arbitrary, imperious, pigheaded **10** bullheaded, inflexible, pontifical **11** dictatorial, opinionated, overbearing, stiff-necked **12** narrow-minded **13** authoritarian **14** disciplinarian

doctrinal 8 didactic, dogmatic, edifying, tutorial **11** educational, instructive **12** prescriptive

doctrine 5 dogma, tenet **6** belief, gospel **7** precept **8** teaching **9** principle **10** conviction, philosophy

document 6 back up, record, verify **7** certify, support **9** legal form **10** instrument **12** give weight to, substantiate **13** official paper

documentation 5 proof **7** support **8** evidence **12** verification **13** corroboration **14** substantiation

doddering 4 weak **6** feeble, senile **7** shaking **8** decrepit **9** tottering, trembling

dodge 4 duck, wile **5** avoid, elude, evade, hedge, trick **6** device, swerve **7** fend off **8** sidestep **9** jump aside, stratagem, turn aside **10** equivocate **11** machination

dodging 7 ducking, eluding, evading

8 shunning **12** sidestepping **13** circumventing

Dodgson, Charles Lutwidge
 real name of: 12 Lewis Carroll

Dodoma
 capital of: 8 Tanzania

Dodsworth
 director: 12 William Wyler
 author: 13 Sinclair Lewis
 character: 4 Fran **12** Arnold Israel **14** Edith Cortright, Renee de Penable **15** Samuel Dodsworth **16** Kurt von Obersdorf **17** Major Clyde Lockert
 cast: 9 Mary Astor, Paul Lukas **10** David Niven **12** Walter Huston **14** Ruth Chatterton

doer 6 dynamo **7** hustler **8** activist, go-getter **12** active person

doff 4 bare, drop, junk, shed **5** scrap, strip **6** put off, remove **7** abandon, cast off, discard, disrobe, take off, toss off, undress **8** throw off, throw out **9** eliminate, step out of **10** do away with

dog 3 cur, pup **4** heel, mutt **5** beast, puppy **6** canine **7** mongrel, villain **9** scoundrel **10** blackguard
 Alaskan: 5 husky **8** malamute, malemute
 anatomy: 3 hip, lip, pad, paw, toe **4** arch, back, hock, loin, rump, stop **5** cheek, crest, croup, flews, skull **6** carpus, dewlap, muzzle, stifle, tarsus **7** brisket, cushion, knuckle, occiput, pastern, withers **8** heelknob, shoulder **10** metacarpus, metatarsus
 Australian: 5 dingo **8** warragal
 barkless: 7 basenji
 breed:
  herding group: 5 pulik **6** briard, collie **12** border collie **13** bearded collie **14** German Shepherd **15** Belgian malinois, Belgian sheepdog, Belgian tervuren **16** Shetland sheepdog **18** Cardigan Welsh corgi, Old English sheepdog, Pembroke Welsh corgi **19** Australian cattle dog, Bouviers des Flandres
  hound group: 6 beagle, borzoi, saluki **7** basenji, harrier, whippet **9** dachshund, greyhound **10** bloodhound, otter hound **11** Afghan hound, basset hound, Ibizan hound **12** pharaoh hound **14** Irish wolfhound **15** English foxhound **16** American foxhound **17** Norwegian elkhound, Scottish deerhound **18** Rhodesian ridgeback **20** black and tan coonhound
  nonsporting group: 6 poodle **7** bulldog **8** chow chow, keeshond **9** dalmatian, lhasa apso **10** keeshonden, schipperke **11** Bichon frise **13** Boston terrier, French bulldog **14** Tibetan spaniel, Tibetan terrier
  sporting group: 6 vizsla **7** pointer **8** Brittany **10** weimaraner **11** Irish setter **12** field spaniel, Gordon set-

ter **13** cocker spaniel, English setter, Sussex spaniel **14** Clumber spaniel **15** golden retriever **17** Irish water spaniel, Labrador retriever **19** flat-coated retriever **20** American water spaniel, curly-coated retriever, English cocker spaniel, Welsh springer spaniel **22** Chesapeake Bay retriever, English springer spaniel **23** German wire-haired pointer **24** German short-haired pointer **25** wirehaired pointing griffon
  terrier group: 10 fox terrier **11** bull terrier, Skye terrier **12** Cairn terrier, Irish terrier, Welsh terrier **13** border terrier **14** Norfolk terrier, Norwich terrier, wire fox terrier **15** Airedale terrier, Lakeland terrier, Scottish terrier, Sealyham terrier **16** Kerry blue terrier, smooth fox terrier **17** Australian terrier, Bedlington terrier, Manchester terrier **18** Jack Russell Terrier, miniature schnauzer **20** Dandie Dinmont terrier **24** soft-coated wheaten terrier, Staffordshire bull terrier, West Highland white terrier **28** American Staffordshire terrier
  toy group: 3 pug **7** Maltese, shih tzu **8** papillon **9** chihuahua, pekingese, toy poodle **11** pomeranian **12** Japanese chin, silky terrier **13** affenpinscher **15** Brussels griffon **16** Italian greyhound, Yorkshire terrier **17** English toy spaniel, Manchester terrier, miniature pinscher **26** Cavalier King Charlea Spaniel
  working group: 5 akita, boxer **7** mastiff, samoyed **8** kuvaszok **9** great Dane, St Bernard **10** komondorok, rottweiler **11** bullmastiff **12** Newfoundland **13** great Pyrenees, Siberian husky **14** giant schnauzer **15** Alaskan malamute **16** doberman pinscher **17** standard schnauzer **18** Bernese mountain dog, Portuguese water dog

Buster Brown's: 4 Tige
Charles, Nick and Nora's: 4 Asta
Chinese: 7 shih tzu
coach: 9 dalmatian
combining form: 3 cyn **4** cani, cyno
constellation: 12 Canis Majoris
Dorothy's: 4 Toto
family: 7 Canidae
FDR's: 4 Fala **5** Falla
female: 3 dam, gip, gyp **4** slut **5** bitch, brach **7** brachet
genus: 5 Canis
group: 4 pack **5** leash **6** kennel
"His Master's Voice": 6 Nipper
Hungarian: 4 puli **6** kuvasz, vizsla
Indian: 5 dhole
Japanese: 5 akita
Little Orphan Annie's: 5 Sandy
male: 3 dog

movie/TV: 4 Asta, Lady **5** Benji, Tramp **6** Lassie **9** Old Yeller, Rin Tin Tin
mythical: 8 Cerberus
Nixon's: 8 Checkers
Punch and Judy's: 4 Toby
Russian: 6 borzoi **7** samoyed
star: 6 Sirius **8** Canicula
Thin Man movies, in: 4 Asta
Welsh: 5 corgi
wild: 5 adjag, dhole, dingo, guara, rabid **6** jackal **7** agouara **8** cimarron
young: 3 pup **5** puppy, whelp

Dogberry
 character in: 19 Much Ado About Nothing
 author: 11 Shakespeare

Dog Day Afternoon
 director: 11 Sidney Lumet
 cast: 8 Al Pacino **10** John Cazale **14** Charles Durning

dogged 8 stubborn **9** tenacious **10** determined, persistent **11** unremitting

dogie 4 calf **14** motherless calf

dogies 6 calves, cattle **16** motherless calves

dogma 5 credo, tenet **7** beliefs **8** doctrine **9** teachings **10** philosophy, principles **11** convictions

dogmatic 6 biased **8** stubborn **9** arbitrary, doctrinal, imperious, obstinate **10** prejudiced **11** dictatorial, domineering, opinionated

Dog Star
 constellation of:
  Hunting Dogs: 13 Canes Venatici
  Larger Dog: 10 Canis Major
  Smaller Dog: 10 Canis Minor

dogwood 6 Cornus
 varieties: 5 Brown, Creek, False, Giant, Silky, Stiff **6** Pagoda, Poison **7** Chinese **8** American, Jamaican, Mountain, Panicled, Redosier, Siberian, Tatarian **9** Blood-twig, Flowering, Tartarian **10** Golden-twig, West Indian **11** Round-leaved **13** White Mountain

Doha, al-Dawha
 capital of: 5 Qatar

do in 4 kill **6** murder **7** destroy, exhaust, tire out

Doktor Faust
 opera by: 6 Busoni
 character: 5 Faust **14** Duchess of Parma **14** Mephistopheles

dolce
 music: 7 sweetly

dolce far niente 18 pleasing inactivity **20** it is sweet to do nothing

dolce vita 9 sweet life

Dol Common
 character in: 12 The Alchemist
 author: 6 Jonson

doldrums 5 blues, dumps, gloom **10** depression, melancholy

dole 4 deal, give **5** share **6** parcel

7 charity, handout, welfare **9** allotment **10** allocation **13** apportionment

doleful 3 sad **6** dismal, dreary, gloomy, woeful **7** joyless, unhappy **9** sorrowful

dolente
music: **9** sorrowful

dole out 4 give, mete **5** allot **6** parcel **7** portion **8** allocate, dispense **9** apportion **10** distribute

doling out 7 dealing **9** allotment, parceling **10** allocation, assignment **12** distribution **13** apportionment

doll 5 dolly, dummy, honey **6** beauty, puppet **7** darling, rag doll **8** baby doll, figurine, golliwog **9** teddy bear **10** marionette, sweetheart **11** pretty child

dollar 3 one **4** bean, bill, buck, coin, note, skin, yuan **5** money, tater, token **6** single **7** ironman, smacker **8** cartwheel, simolean

Dollar A Second
host: **9** Jan Murray

Dollar Bill
nickname of: **11** Bill Bradley

dollop 3 dab **4** blob, dash, lump **11** small amount

Doll's House, A
author: **11** Henrik Ibsen
character: **8** Krogstad **10** Nora Helmer **11** Torvald Helmer

dolly 3 toy **4** cart, doll **9** plaything **15** wheeled platform

dolor 5 grief **6** sorrow **7** anguish, sadness

dolorous 3 sad **6** rueful, woeful **7** doleful, tearful, unhappy **8** dejected, downcast, grievous, mournful, pathetic, pitiable, wretched **9** anguished, cheerless, harrowing, miserable, sorrowful, woebegone **10** calamitous, despondent, lamentable, melancholy **11** distressing **12** disconsolate, heavyhearted **13** grief-stricken

Dolphin
constellation of: **9** Delphinus

Dolphin, The
author: **12** Robert Lowell

dolt 4 clod, fool, jerk **5** idiot, moron **6** nitwit **7** half-wit, jackass **8** bonehead, imbecile, numskull **9** blockhead

doltish 4 dumb, slow **5** thick **6** simple, stupid **7** asinine, foolish, idiotic, moronic, witless **8** ignorant, retarded **9** brainless, imbecilic **10** half-witted, slow-witted **12** dunderheaded, muddleheaded, simple-minded **13** rattlebrained **14** featherbrained

domain 4 area, fief, land **5** field **6** empire, estate, region, sphere **7** kingdom **8** dominion, property, province **9** bailiwick, territory

Dombey and Son
author: **14** Charles Dickens
character: **4** Paul **5** Toots **6** Carker, Cuttle **8** Florence, Mr Dombey **9** Dr

Blimber, Walter Gay **11** Joe Bagstock, Susan Nipper **12** Cousin Feenix, Edith Granger, Solomon Gills

dome
Italian: **5** duomo

Domenichino
real name: **16** Domenico Zampieri
born: **5** Italy **7** Bologna
artwork: **11** Hunt of Diana **16** Monsignor Agucchi **18** The Four Evangelists, The Life of St Cecilia **23** Last Communion of St Jerome **30** Landscape with Tobias and the Angel

domestic 4 cook, maid, tame **6** au pair, butler, native **7** endemic, servant **8** homemade, houseboy **9** attendant, home-grown **10** indigenous, not foreign **11** housebroken, native-grown, not imported **12** domesticated, hearthloving **13** household help

domesticated 4 tame **11** housebroken

domicile 4 home **6** house **8** dwelling **9** residence **14** legal residence

dominance 4 edge **8** hegemony **9** advantage, authority, upper hand **10** precedence **11** preeminence, superiority

dominant 5 chief, major **6** ruling **8** superior **9** principal **10** commanding **11** controlling, outstanding **13** authoritative, most important, most prominent

dominate 4 rule **5** dwarf **6** direct, govern **7** command, control **8** domineer **9** tower over **11** preside over

dominating 6 lordly, ruling **7** topmost **8** dominant **9** directing, governing, principal, prominent **10** commanding **11** controlling, domineering, outstanding **12** advantageous **13** authoritative, most important **15** most outstanding

domination 4 rule **5** power **7** command, control, mastery **9** authority **11** superiority

domineer 7 control **8** dominate, lord over **9** dictate to, tyrannize

domineering 8 arrogant, despotic, dogmatic **9** imperious **10** commanding, oppressive, tyrannical **11** dictatorial, overbearing **13** authoritative

Dominican Republic
capital/largest city: **12** Santo Domingo **14** Ciudad Trujillo
others: **4** Azua, Bani, Moca, Pena, Polo **5** Bonao, Cotui, Nagua, Neiba, Nizao, Sosua **6** Higuey, La Vega, Oviedo **7** Sanchez **8** Barahona, Santiago **11** Puerto Plata **17** San Pedro de Macoris **21** San Francisco de Macoris
measure: **3** ona **5** tarea **6** fanega
monetary unit: **3** oro **4** peso **6** franco
island: **5** Beata, Saona **8** Altovelo, Catalina **10** Hispaniola
lake: **10** Enriquillo
mountain: **4** Tina **5** Gallo, Neiba **7** Baoruco, Central **8** Bahoruco, Oriental **13** Sententrional

highest point: **6** Duarte
river: **4** Yuna **5** Ozama **11** Yaque del Sur **13** Yaque del Norte
sea: **8** Atlantic **9** Caribbean
physical feature:
bay: **4** Ocoa, Yuma **5** Neiba **6** Rincon, Samana **7** Isabela **8** Calderas, Escocesa
cape: **5** Beata, Falso **6** Cabron, Engano **7** Caucedo, Isabela, Macoris
valley: **4** Real **5** Neyba
people: **5** Negro, Taino **6** Indian **7** mulatto, Spanish **9** Caucasian
discoverer: **8** Columbus
language: **6** French **7** English, Spanish
religion: **13** Roman Catholic
feature:
dance: **8** merengue
religious pilgrimage: **8** romerias
food:
dessert: **8** pinonate
fish/meat pastry: **10** pastelitos
stew: **8** sancocho

dominion 4 land, rule **5** realm **6** domain, empire, region **7** command, mastery **9** authority, supremacy, territory **11** sovereignty **12** jurisdiction
Hindu: **3** raj

Dominus 3 God **4** Lord

Dominus vobiscum 16 the Lord be with you

don 4 wear **5** put on **6** pull on **7** dress in, get into

Don
origin: **5** Welsh
form: **7** goddess
son: **7** Gwydion
daughter: **8** Arianrod

dona 4 lady **5** madam

Dona Flor and Her Two Husbands
author: **10** Jorge Amado

Donalbain
father: **6** Duncan
brother: **7** Malcom

Donald Duck
creator: **10** Walt Disney
character:
girlfriend: **5** Daisy
nephew: **4** Huey **5** Dewey, Louie
uncle: **7** Scrooge

Donar
origin: **8** Germanic
god of: **7** thunder

donate 4 give **6** bestow **7** present **8** bequeath **10** contribute **11** make a gift of

Donatello
real name: **15** Donato di Niccolo
born: **5** Italy **9** Florence
artwork: **5** David **6** St Mark **7** Zuccone **8** Jeremiah, St George **11** Gattamelata **12** Mary Magdalen **19** Judith and Holofernes, St John the Evangelist **22** Cavalcanti Annunciation

donation 4 gift 7 present 12 contribution

Don Careless
author: 8 Rex Beach

Don Carlos
author: 14 Johann Schiller
opera by: 5 Verdi
character: 7 Rodrigo 8 Philip II 9 Don Carlos 13 Princess Eboli 15 Grand Inquisitor 17 Elizabeth de Valois

Dondi
creator: 8 Gus Edson 10 Irwin Hasen
dog: 7 Queenie

done 5 ready 8 finished, prepared 9 completed 12 cooked enough 18 cooked sufficiently

done for 4 dead, gone, over, sunk 5 all up, ended, kaput, spent 6 beaten, doomed, ruined 7 all over, damaged, through 8 finished 9 exhausted

done in 4 beat 5 all in, slain, spent, tired, weary 6 bushed, killed, pooped 7 drained, wearied, worn out 8 dog tired, fatigued, murdered, tired out 9 bone weary, dead tired, played out 10 knocked off

Don Giovanni
also: 7 Don Juan 15 The Rake Punished
opera by: 6 Mozart
setting: 7 Seville
character: 7 Masetto, Zerlina 9 Donna Anna, Leporello 10 Don Ottavio 11 Donna Elvira 15 The Commendatore

Donizetti, Gaetano
born: 5 Italy 7 Bergamo
composer of: 10 Anna Bolena, La Favorita 11 Don Pasquale 12 Elixir of Love, Maria Stuarda 13 L'elisir d'amore, Marino Faliero, Torquato Tasso 14 Lucrezia Borgia 15 Roberto Devereux 16 Linda di Chamounix 17 Lucia di Lammermoor 21 Daughter of the Regiment

Don Juan 3 man 4 beau, wolf 5 Romeo, swain, wooer 6 fellow, squire, steady, suitor 7 admirer, courter, gallant, pursuer 8 Casanova, lothario, lover boy, paramour, young man 9 boyfriend, Lochinvar 10 lady-killer 15 gentleman caller

Don Juan
author: 21 George Gordon Lord Byron
character: 6 Haidee 9 Donna Inez 10 Donna Julia

donkey 3 ass 4 fool, mule 5 burro, idiot 7 jackass

Donlevy, Brian
wife: 12 Marjorie Lane
born: 7 Ireland 11 Portadown
roles: 9 Beau Geste 15 The Great McGinty 21 Two Years Before the Mast

Donn, Arabella

character in: 14 Jude the Obscure
author: 5 Hardy

donna 4 lady 5 madam

Donna Reed Show, The
character: 9 Jeff Stone, Mary Stone 10 Donna Stone 11 Dr Alex Stone, Midge Kelsey, Trisha Stone 12 Dr Dave Kelsey
cast: 8 Bob Crane, Carl Betz 9 Ann McCrea, Donna Reed 12 Paul Peterson 13 Patty Peterson 14 Shelley Fabares

Donne, John
author of: 7 Sermons 10 The Ecstasy, The Extasie 11 Holy Sonnets 15 Death Be Not Proud, Songs and Sonnets, The Canonization 20 Paradoxes and Problems 30 A Valediction Forbidding Mourning

donnish 7 preachy 8 academic, didactic, pedantic 9 pedagogic

Donnithorne, Arthur
character in: 8 Adam Bede
author: 5 Eliot

donnybrook 3 row 4 fray 5 brawl, fight, melee, set-to 6 affray, dustup, fracas, ruckus, rumpus 7 ruction, scuffle 8 skirmish 10 free-for-all 19 knock-down-and-drag-out

donor 5 giver 10 benefactor 11 contributor 12 humanitarian 14 philanthropist

do-nothing 5 idler 6 loafer 14 good-for-nothing

do not prosecute
Latin: 13 nolle prosequi

do not repeat
Latin: 12 non repetatur

Don Pasquale
opera by: 9 Donizetti
character: 6 Norina 7 Ernesto 11 Dr Malatesta

Don Quixote de la Mancha
also: 38 El ingenioso hidalgo Don Quijote de la Mancha
author: 17 Miguel de Cervantes (Saavedra)
character: 10 Pedro Perez 11 Sancho Panza 17 Dulcinea del Toboso
horse: 9 Rosinante
musical: 13 Man of La Mancha

doodad 5 gizmo 6 device, gadget 8 ornament 9 doohickey 10 decoration 11 contraption, contrivance, thingamabob, thingamajig 15 whatchamacallit

doohickey 5 gizmo, thing 6 device, dingus, gadget, object, widget 7 dojiggy, whatsis 8 dojigger 9 thingummy 11 thingamabob, thingamajig 14 thingamadoodle 15 whatchamacallit

Dooley, Thomas Anthony
founded: 6 MEDICO 31 Medical International Corporation
worked in: 13 Southeast Asia

doolie 4 USAF 8 freshman

Doolittle, Eliza

character in: 9 Pygmalion 10 My Fair Lady
author: 4 Shaw

doom 3 end, lot 4 fate, ruin 5 death, judge 7 condemn, convict, destiny, portion, verdict 8 judgment 10 Armageddon 11 destruction, Judgment Day 13 consign to ruin, end of the world, pronouncement 15 resurrection day, the Last Judgment 17 mark for demolition

doomed 5 fated 6 damned, ruined 8 ill-fated 9 condemned

doomsday 11 Judgment Day 13 Day of Judgment, end of the world 15 the Last Judgment

do one's best 3 try 6 strive 7 attempt 8 endeavor, go all out 9 take pains 12 make an effort 13 give all one has 15 knock oneself out

Doonesbury
creator: 12 Garry Trudeau
character: 2 B D 5 Honey, Rufus 6 Calvin, Zonker 7 Boopsie 9 Uncle Duke 12 Joanie Caucus 14 Mark Slackmeyer 18 Michael J Doonesbury

door 4 exit 5 entry 6 egress, portal 7 hallway, ingress 8 entrance 11 entranceway

doorway 5 entry 7 ingress, opening 8 entrance

Doorways
god of: 5 Janus

dope 3 pot, tip 4 drip, drug, fool, jerk, junk, nerd, news 5 creep, drugs, dummy, klutz, scoop 6 heroin, sedate, uppers 7 downers, opiates 8 additive 9 narcotics, narcotize, substance 10 antiseptic, astringent, medication 11 anesthetize, preparation 12 disinfectant 17 inside information

dope fiend 4 head, user 5 doper, freak 6 addict, junkie 7 hophead 8 cokehead 10 dope addict, drug abuser, drug addict

do penance 5 atone 7 expiate 10 make amends

dopey 4 dumb 6 leaden, stupid, torpid 7 asinine, idiotic, witless 8 comatose, mindless, sluggish 9 brainless, lethargic 10 dull-witted, slow-witted, slumberous 11 block-headed, thickheaded 12 simple-minded

Doppelganger 6 double 13 ghostly double
literally: 12 double-walker

Doppler, Christian Johann
field: 7 physics
nationality: 8 Austrian
discovered: 13 Doppler Effect

Dorcas
also called: 7 Tabitha
revived by: 5 Peter
hometown: 5 Joppa

Doris
father: 7 Oceanus

mother: 6 Tethys
husband: 6 Nereus
mother of: 7 Nereids

dormancy 7 latency **8** inaction **10** inactivity, quiescence, somnolence **11** hibernation

dormant 4 idle **8** inactive, sleeping **9** quiescent, somnolent **11** hibernating

Dorothy
character in: 13 The Wizard of Oz
author: 4 Baum
dog: 4 Toto

Dorset, Bertha and George
characters in: 15 The House of Mirth
author: 7 Wharton

dorsum 5 chine, spine **8** backbone

dose 2 OD **3** cut, nip **4** dram, pill, shot, slug **5** quota, share, slice **6** amount, needle, ration, tablet **7** capsule, measure, portion, section, segment **8** division, overdose, quantity **9** allotment, allowance, daily dose, injection **10** percentage

Dos Passos, John
author of: 3 U S A **11** The Big Money **13** Three Soldiers **16** Nineteen Nineteen **17** Manhattan Transfer **22** The Forty-Second Parallel

dossier 4 file **5** brief **6** record **9** portfolio **14** detailed report

Dostoevsky, Fyodor Mikhailovich
author of: 8 The Idiot **9** The Double **10** The Gambler **12** The Possessed **18** Crime and Punishment **20** The Brothers Karamazov **23** Notes from the Underground

dot 3 dab **4** mark, spot **5** fleck, point, speck **6** dapple, period **7** stipple **9** small spot

dotage 8 senility **15** second childhood **16** feeblemindedness

dote 8 be senile, fuss over

dote on 5 adore, prize, spoil, value **6** pamper **7** cherish, indulge **8** fuss over, treasure **15** lavish affection

doting 4 fond **6** loving **9** indulgent, pampering **12** affectionate

double 4 dual, twin **5** clone **6** paired **7** replica, two-part **8** two-sided **9** ambiguous, duplicate **10** dead ringer **11** again as much, counterpart, meant for two, twice as much **12** twice as great **13** multiply by two, spitting image **15** increase twofold
German: 12 Doppelganger

Double, The
author: 16 Fyodor Dostoevsky

double-cross 5 rat on **6** betray, do dirt, tell on, turn in **7** abandon, deceive, let down, sell out, two-time **8** denounce, inform on, run out on, snitch on **9** play Judas **10** be disloyal **13** be treacherous, inform against, play false with **14** break faith with **16** blow the whistle on, sell down the river

double-crosser 5 cheat **7** traitor **8** betrayer, deceiver, informer

Double-Dealer, The
author: 15 William Congreve

double-dealing 5 false **6** deceit, sneaky, tricky **7** crooked, devious, perfidy **8** bad faith, betrayal, disloyal **9** deceitful, duplicity, falseness, treachery, two-timing **10** disloyalty, perfidious, sneakiness **11** crookedness, double-cross, duplicitous, treacherous **12** dishonorable **13** breach of faith, faithlessness

double entendre 12 off-color joke, risque remark **18** ambiguous statement

double entente 9 ambiguity

Double Indemnity
director: 11 Billy Wilder
cast: 13 Fred MacMurray **15** Barbara Stanwyck, Edward G Robinson
script: 9 James Cain **15** Raymond Chandler

Double Life, A
director: 11 George Cukor
cast: 10 Signe Hasso **12** Edmond O'Brien, Ronald Colman **14** Shelley Winters
Oscar for: 5 actor (Colman)
script: 10 Ruth Gordon **11** Garson Kanin

double meaning 9 ambiguity
French: 13 double entente **14** double entendre

doublet 4 pair **5** tunic **6** couple, jacket **10** two of a kind

double-talk 4 bunk, jazz **5** hokum **6** bunkum, drivel, gabble, jabber **7** baloney, blather, palaver, prattle, twaddle **8** flimflam, flummery, nonsense **9** gibberish **10** balderdash, hocus-pocus, mumbo jumbo **11** obfuscation **12** gobbledygook

double-walker
German: 12 Doppelganger

Double X
nickname of: 9 Jimmy Foxx

doubt 5 qualm **6** wonder **7** suspect **8** distrust, mistrust, question **9** misgiving, skeptical, suspicion **10** be doubtful, indecision **11** uncertainty **12** apprehension **13** feel uncertain **14** waver in opinion **15** have doubts about **16** lack confidence in, lack of conviction

Doubter *see* **6** Thomas

doubtful 5 vague **7** dubious, obscure, suspect, unclear **9** tentative, uncertain, undecided, unsettled **10** hesitating, irresolute, suspicious **11** unconvinced **12** inconclusive, questionable

doubtfulness 5 doubt **7** dubiety **8** distrust, mistrust, unbelief **9** disbelief, suspicion **10** skepticism **11** incredulity **14** lack of credence

Doubting *see* **6** Thomas

doucement
music: 6 gently

douceur 3 tip **5** bribe **8** gratuity **9** sweetness

dough 4 cash, duff, spud **5** bread, crust, money, paster **6** batter, change, leaven, noodle **8** doughboy **11** infantryman

doughnut 4 cake, tire **5** bagel, torus **6** cymbal, dunker, sinker **7** beignet, cruller, twister

doughty 4 bold **5** brave **6** strong **8** fearless, intrepid, unafraid **9** confident, dauntless **10** courageous, determined **12** stout-hearted

Douglas, Archibald
character in: 7 Marmion
author: 5 Scott

Douglas, Kirk
real name: 17 Issur Danielovitch
son: 7 Michael
born: 11 Amsterdam NY
roles: 8 Champion **9** Spartacus **10** The Vikings **11** Lust for Life **14** Detective Story, Seven Days in May **17** The Glass Menagerie, Young Man with a Horn **18** Letter to Three Wives **22** Mourning Becomes Electra

Douglas, Lloyd C
author of: 7 The Robe **23** The Magnificent Obsession

Douglas, Melvyn
real name: 23 Melvyn Edouard Hesselberg
wife: 12 Helen Gahagan
born: 7 Macon GA
roles: 3 Hud **9** Ninotchka **10** Being There

Douglas, Michael
father: 4 Kirk
roles: 4 Coma **7** The Game **10** Disclosure, Wall Street (Oscar) **11** Star Chamber **13** Basic Instinct **14** Jewel of the Nile **15** Fatal Attraction **16** The China Syndrome, The Perfect Murder **17** Romancing the Stone

dour 4 sour **6** gloomy, morose, solemn, sullen **9** cheerless **10** forbidding, unfriendly

Douras, Marion Cecilia
real name of: 12 Marion Davies

douse 4 soak **5** souse **6** drench **7** immerse **8** saturate, submerge **15** plunge into water

Dove, Noah's
constellation of: 7 Columba

Dover Beach
author: 13 Matthew Arnold

dovetail 4 jibe, join **5** match, tally, unite **8** coincide **9** harmonize **11** fit together **12** interlocking

dowager 5 widow **6** relict **7** elderly

dowdy 4 drab **5** tacky **6** frumpy, shabby, sloppy **8** slovenly **12** unattractive

dowel 3 peg, pin, rod **4** pole **5** stick **7** spindle

down 3 ill **4** blue, deck, drop, fell, gulp, sick **5** drink, floor **6** ailing **7** put away, swallow **8** dejected, downcast, feathers **9** depressed **10** dispirited **12** disheartened

down-and-out 4 sick **5** broke **9** penniless **12** impoverished, on one's uppers **13** incapacitated **15** under the weather

downcast 3 low, sad **4** blue **7** unhappy **8** dejected **9** cheerless, depressed **11** discouraged **12** disconsolate, disheartened

downfall 4 fall, ruin **6** shower **8** collapse, downpour **9** rainstorm, ruination **10** rain shower **11** destruction

downgrade 4 drop **5** lower **6** debase **7** decline, descent, way down **8** belittle, minimize **9** declivity, denigrate, devaluate **10** depreciate

downhearted 3 sad **7** unhappy **8** dejected, downcast **9** depressed, sorrowful **10** dispirited **11** discouraged **12** disheartened

downheartedness 5 gloom **6** dismay **7** despair, sadness **9** dejection, pessimism **10** depression, low spirits, melancholy **11** despondency **12** hopelessness **14** discouragement

down in the dumps 4 blue, glum **6** gloomy **7** in a funk **9** depressed **10** despondent **13** in the doldrums

down in the mouth 3 sad **6** dismal, woeful **7** joyless, unhappy **8** dejected, downcast **9** depressed, sorrowful, woebegone **10** lugubrious **12** disconsolate

downpayment 6 binder **7** advance, deposit **9** money down

downpour 6 shower **9** rainstorm **10** cloudburst, rain shower

downright 4 open **5** blunt, frank, total, utter **6** candid, direct, honest, really **7** in truth, plainly, sincere, utterly **8** absolute, actually, complete **9** out-and-out **10** aboveboard, completely, thoroughly **12** unmistakably **13** thoroughgoing, unequivocally **15** straightforward

Downright
   character in: 19 Every Man in His Humour
   author: 6 Jonson

downstairs 5 below **6** cellar **8** basement **10** first floor **11** ground floor

down the drain 4 gone, lost **9** up in smoke **12** out the window

down-to-earth 5 crass, plain, sober, solid **6** casual, coarse, earthy, simple **7** relaxed **8** informal, sensible **9** practical, pragmatic, realistic **10** hardheaded, hard-boiled, no-nonsense **11** plain-spoken, substantial **12** matter-of-fact, unidealistic **13** unsentimental

downtown 9 inner city, urban area **10** center city, metropolis **16** business district, metropolitan area

downtrodden 9 exploited, oppressed **10** tyrannized **11** subservient **12** harshly ruled

downturn 3 dip, sag **4** drop, fall, skid, slip **5** slide, slump **6** plunge, waning **7** decline, reverse, setback **8** decrease **9** downslide, downswing, downtrend, dwindling, recession **10** depression, diminution **12** degeneration **13** deterioration

Down Under *see* **9** Australia

down with
   French: 4 a bas

downy 4 soft **5** fuzzy, nappy, plumy, quiet **6** fleecy, fluffy **7** cunning, knowing **8** feathery **9** featherbed

do wrong 3 err, sin **8** go astray **9** misbehave **10** transgress

Doyle, Sir Arthur Conan
   see also **14** Holmes, Sherlock
   author of: 13 The Sign of Four **15** A Study in Scarlet, The White Company **25** The Hound of the Baskervilles **26** Adventures of Sherlock Holmes
   character: 10 Irene Adler **12** Dr John Watson **13** Mycroft Holmes **14** Sherlock Holmes **17** Inspector Lestrade, Professor Moriarty

doze 3 nap **6** catnap, siesta, snooze **10** forty winks, light sleep **12** sleep lightly

dozy 4 lazy **6** drowsy, sleepy **7** languid **9** lethargic, somnolent

D P 5 exile **6** emigre **7** outcast, refugee **8** deportee **10** expatriate **14** banished person, deported person **15** displaced person **16** political refugee

drab 4 dull, gray **5** dingy **6** dismal, dreary, gloomy, somber **9** cheerless, dull brown **10** lackluster

drabness 8 dullness **9** dinginess **10** dreariness, gloominess **13** colorlessness

Dracula
   author: 10 Bram Stoker
   character: 8 Dr Seward **10** Mina Murray **12** Count Dracula, Dr Van Hesling, Lucy Westenra **14** Arthur Holmwood, Jonathan Harker

draft 4 drag, gulp, haul, pull, wind **5** drink **6** breeze, induct, sketch **7** diagram, outline, swallow **9** conscript, induction **10** money order **11** postal order, rough sketch **12** conscription, current of air **15** military service **16** drawing from a cask **18** preliminary version **22** call for military service

drafty 6 breezy, chilly

drag 3 lug **4** bore, haul, pull **5** bring, crawl, trail **6** dredge **7** be drawn **9** inch along **10** creep along, move

slowly, spoilsport, wet blanket **11** party-pooper

Dragnet
   character: 8 (Sgt) Ed Jacobs **9** (Sgt) Ben Romero, (Sgt) Joe Friday **10** (Officer) Bill Gannon, (Officer) Frank Smith
   cast: 8 Jack Webb **9** Herb Ellis **11** Harry Morgan **12** Ben Alexander **14** Barney Phillips **16** Barton Yarborough
   setting: 10 Los Angeles

Dragon 14 Leviathan
   constellation of: 5 Draco

drag on 4 last **6** endure, keep on, keep up **7** persist **8** continue **9** persevere

drag one's feet 5 crawl, creep **6** dawdle **9** waste time **10** move slowly **13** procrastinate

dragonfly
   varieties: 5 biddy **6** darner **7** skimmer **8** clubtail, grayback **9** amberwing **12** elisa skimmer

Dragon Seed
   author: 10 Pearl S Buck

Dragon's teeth
   sown by: 6 Cadmus
   location: 6 Thebes
   grew into: 8 warriors

dragoon 5 bully, force **6** coerce, compel **7** trooper **8** browbeat, bulldoze, cavalier, horseman, pressure **9** strongarm **10** cavalryman **12** horse soldier, horse trooper **14** mounted soldier

drag through the mud 5 smear, sully, taint **6** debase, defame, smirch, vilify **7** degrade, tarnish, vitiate **8** disgrace, dishonor **9** discredit, disparage **10** stigmatize

drain 3 sap **4** drag, pipe, tube **5** empty, sewer, use up **6** outlet, strain **7** channel, conduit, debouch, deplete, flow out, pump off **8** empty out **9** depletion, discharge, dissipate **10** impoverish

drainage 4 flow **9** discharge

drained 4 beat **5** all in, empty, spent, tired, weary **6** bushed, done in, pooped, used up **7** emptied, wearied, worn out **8** con- sumed, depleted, dog tired, expended, fatigued, finished, tired out **9** dead tired, enervated, exhausted, played out

Drake, Stan
   creator/artist of: 21 The Heart of Juliet Jones

Drake, Temple
   character in: 9 Sanctuary
   author: 8 Faulkner

dram
   abbreviation: 2 dr

drama 4 play **6** acting **8** the stage **9** direction, vividness **10** excitement, the theater **11** mise-en-scene **15** dramatic quality, intense interest, theatrical

piece
god of: 7 Bacchus
dramatic 8 striking **9** climactic, emotional **10** theatrical **11** sensational, suspenseful **12** melodramatic **13** for the theater
dramatics 6 acting **7** emoting **9** theatrics **10** dramaturgy, stagecraft **11** hamming it up, histrionics, thespianism
dramatis personae 4 cast **6** actors **7** players **10** performers **16** cast of characters, list of performers
dramaturgy 5 drama **7** theater **10** stagecraft **11** dramatic art
Drambuie
type: 7 liqueur
origin: 8 Scotland
flavor: 5 herbs, honey
with scotch: 9 Rusty Nail
drape 4 deck, garb, veil, wrap **5** adorn, array, cloak, cover, dress **6** attire, bedeck, enrobe, enwrap, shroud, swathe, wrap up **7** apparel, bedight, envelop, festoon, sheathe, swaddle **8** enshroud, enswathe
drastic 4 dire, rash **7** bizarre, extreme, radical **8** dreadful **9** dangerous **10** outlandish **11** deleterious
Dravidian
language group: 3 Kui **5** Ghond, Tamil **6** Teluga **8** Kanarese **9** Malayalam
spoken in: 5 India **6** Ceylon **8** Sri Lanka
draw 3 get, tie, tow **4** drag, etch, haul, limn, lure, pick, pull, take **5** charm, draft, drain, evoke, infer, write **6** allure, come-on, deduce, elicit, entice, extend, make up, siphon, sketch **7** attract, distort, draw out, extract, make out, pick out, pull out, pump out, stretch, suck dry, take out, wrinkle **8** contract, deadlock, elongate, protract **9** attenuate, pull along, stalemate **10** attraction, bring forth, enticement, inducement, make appear **14** make a picture of
draw away 2 go **5** leave **6** go back, shrink **7** retreat **8** withdraw
drawback 8 handicap, obstacle **9** detriment, hindrance **10** impediment **12** disadvantage **14** stumbling block
draw back 6 flinch, recoil **7** back off, retreat **8** move away, withdraw
draw close 3 hug **4** come, near **6** arrive, enfold **7** embrace **8** approach, come nigh, gain upon **10** move toward
drawers 5 pants **6** shorts **7** panties **8** bloomers, calzoons, trousers **9** pantalets, underwear **10** underpants
draw forth 5 evoke **6** elicit **7** distill, extract
drawing 5 study **6** sketch **7** lottery,

picture **9** depiction, selection **11** delineation **12** illustration
drawing apart 8 dividing **9** diverging **10** separating **12** splitting off
drawing out 9 expansion, extension **10** elongation, stretching **11** attenuation, lengthening, protraction **12** prolongation
drawing power 4 pull **6** allure, appeal **9** magnetism **10** attraction, enticement **11** fascination
drawing room 5 salon **6** parlor **10** living room **11** sitting room **13** reception room
drawn out 4 long **7** lengthy **8** extended **9** elongated, prolonged **10** lengthened, protracted
draw out 5 educe, evoke **6** elicit, expand, extend, extort **7** distill, enlarge, extract, prolong, spin out, stretch **8** elongate, lengthen, protract **9** attenuate, call forth **10** stretch out
draw the line 5 limit **8** contrast, separate **12** fix a boundary **13** differentiate
draw to a close 3 end **6** finish **8** conclude **11** come to an end
draw together 4 herd, mass, pack **5** bunch, crowd, flock, group **6** gather, huddle **7** cluster, collect, tighten **8** assemble, compress, contract **9** constrict **10** congregate
draw up 3 map **5** draft **6** make up, map out **7** charter, diagram, outline **9** blueprint
draw up plans 5 draft **6** design, sketch **7** outline
dray 4 cart **5** wagon **7** tipcart, tumbrel **8** dumpcart
dread 4 fear **5** awful **6** fright, terror **7** anguish, anxiety, cower at, fearful **8** alarming, cringe at **10** be afraid of, horrifying, shrink from, terrifying **11** fearfulness, frightening, trepidation **12** apprehension **20** anticipate with horror
dreaded object
French: 9 bete noire
dreadful 5 awful **6** tragic **7** fearful **8** alarming, horrible, shocking, terrible **9** frightful **11** distressing
dream 3 joy **4** goal, hope, muse, wish **5** think **6** desire, vision **7** delight, fantasy, hope for, incubus, reverie, think up **8** consider, pleasure, prospect **9** nightmare **11** expectation, have as a goal **13** look forward to, lost in thought
Dream Merchants, The
author: 13 Harold Robbins
Dream of the Golden Mountains, The
author: 13 Malcolm Cowley
Dreams
god of: 6 Icelus, Oniros **7** Oneiros **8** Morpheus **9** Phantasus

Dream Songs, The
author: 12 John Berryman
dream up 5 frame, hatch **6** create, invent **7** concoct **8** conceive, contrive
dreamy 4 airy **5** blank, empty, vague **6** absent, musing, unreal **8** ethereal, fanciful, illusory, soothing **9** fantastic, wonderful **10** delightful **11** preoccupied, unrealistic **13** unsubstantial **14** out of this world
dreariness 9 bleakness **10** desolation, dismalness, gloominess, melancholy **13** cheerlessness
dreary 3 sad **4** drab **5** bleak **6** dismal, gloomy **7** forlorn **8** mournful **9** cheerless **10** depressing, melancholy
dregs 6 rabble **7** deposit, grounds, residue **8** canaille, riffraff, sediment **9** settlings, worst part **11** lower depths
Dreiser, Theodore
author of: 8 The Titan **12** Sister Carrie, The Financier **17** An American Tragedy
drench 3 wet **4** soak **5** douse **8** saturate
dress 4 curl, deck, do up, garb, gown, robe, trim **5** adorn, frock, groom, treat **6** attire **7** apparel, arrange, bandage, cleanse, clothes, comb out, costume, garnish **8** clothing, decorate, ornament **9** disinfect, embellish **12** put on clothes **13** clothe oneself
Dressed to Kill
director: 12 Brian De Palma
cast: 10 Nancy Allen **11** Keith Gordon **12** Michael Caine **14** Angie Dickinson
dressed up 7 adorned, duded up **8** costumed, dolled up, tarted up **9** decorated, disguised, in costume **10** ornamented **11** embellished
dresser 6 bureau **7** cabinet, commode **8** cupboard **10** chiffonier **14** chest of drawers
dressing-down 6 rebuke **7** censure, chiding, reproof **8** reproach, scolding **9** reprimand **10** bawling-out, chewing-out, upbraiding **11** castigation, reprobation **12** remonstrance **13** tongue-lashing
dressing-gown
French: 13 robe-de-chambre
dressmaker 9 couturier, midinette **10** couturiere, seamstress
dress up 5 adorn **6** doll up **7** enhance, improve **8** beautify, ornament, spruce up **9** embellish, embroider, smarten up **10** exaggerate
Dreyfuss, Richard
born: 10 Brooklyn NY
roles: 4 Jaws **6** Tin Men **8** Stakeout **9** The Big Fix, Stand by Me **14** Mr. Holland's Opus, The Goodbye Girl (Oscar) **15** Moon Over Parador **16** American Graffiti **20** Postcards from the Edge **24** Down and Out in Bev-

erly Hills **29** Close Encounters of the Third Kind **31** The Apprenticeship of Duddy Kravitz

dribble 4 drip, kick **6** bounce **7** drizzle, trickle **11** fall in drops, run bit by bit

driblet 4 drip, drop, tear **7** droplet, globule

dried up 4 arid **7** drained, parched **9** prunelike, shriveled **10** dehydrated, desiccated

drift 3 aim **4** flow, gist, heap, mass, pile **5** amass, amble, sense **6** course, gather, object, pile up, ramble, stream, wander **7** current, meander, meaning, purpose, scatter **8** movement **9** direction, intention, objective **10** accumulate **11** implication, peregrinate **12** accumulation, be borne along

drifter 3 bum **4** hobo **5** idler, tramp **6** loafer **8** derelict, vagabond **16** ne'er-do-well

drill 4 bore **5** punch, train **6** pierce **8** exercise, practice, puncture, training, work with **10** boring tool, repetition **11** instruction **17** repeated exercises
type: 4 hand **5** twist **8** electric

drilling 4 rote **6** boring **8** practice, training **9** schooling **10** discipline **11** preparation

drink 3 sip **4** gulp, swig **5** booze, taste, toast **6** absorb, imbibe, ingest, salute, take in **7** alcohol, swallow **8** beverage, libation **9** partake of, the bottle **10** alcoholism **11** drunkenness **15** alcoholic liquor **17** liquid refreshment
type of: 3 cup, fix **4** fizz, flip, mull, puff, sour **5** daisy, julep, punch, shrub, sling, smash **6** cooler, frappe, rickey **7** cob- bler, stinger **8** highball

drinker 3 sot **4** lush, wino **5** dipso, drunk, rummy, souse **6** bibber, boozer, sponge **7** guzzler, imbiber, tippler, waterer **8** drunkard **9** alcoholic, inebriate

drink in 6 absorb, digest, soak up, take in **10** assimilate **14** immerse oneself

Drinking
god of: 5 Comus

drinking spree 4 orgy, toot **5** binge, drunk **6** bender **8** beer-bust, carousal **9** bacchanal

drink up 4 gulp **5** quaff **6** absorb, guzzle, soak up **7** consume, swallow

drip 3 ass **4** bore, jerk, nerd **5** creep, dummy, klutz **6** splash **7** dribble, driz- zle, trickle **8** sprinkle

dripping 3 wet **4** damp **5** soggy, soaked, sodden **10** soaking wet

drive 4 goad, lead, mean, move, prod, push, ride, rush, spur, urge **5** force, guide, impel, motor, press, steer, surge **6** co- erce, compel, incite, intend, outing **7** advance, conduct, go by car, impulse, operate, suggest **9** ambition, campaign, motivate **9** ex- cursion, insinuate, trip by car, urge along **10** motivation

drive apart 8 alienate, estrange **9** disaffect

drive away 4 rout, shoo **5** chase, deter, repel **6** rebuff **7** repulse **8** alienate **11** put to flight, send packing

drive home 7 impress **8** hammer at

drivel 5 drool **6** babble, ramble, slaver **7** dribble, slobber **8** babbling, nonsense, rambling **9** gibberish **12** talk nonsense **13** senseless talk, talk foolishly

drive out 4 fire **5** chase, depel, eject, evict, exile, expel, force, roust **6** compel, remove **7** dismiss, repulse **8** discharge, exorcise

driver 6 cowboy, drover **8** herdsman **9** chauffeur

drizzle 3 fog **4** mist, rain **7** dribble **8** sprinkle

drizzly 3 wet **4** damp **5** foggy, misty, rainy

Dr Jekyll and Mr Hyde
author: 20 Robert Louis Stevenson
character: 5 Poole **10** Mr Utterson **13** Dr Henry Jekyll **14** Dr Hastie Lanyon

Dr Kildare
character: 14 Dr James Kildare **18** Dr Leonard Gillespie
cast: 13 Raymond Massey **18** Richard Chamberlain
hospital: 12 Blair General

Dr No
author: 10 Ian Fleming

droll 5 funny **7** offbeat, strange **8** humorous **9** eccentric, laughable, whimsical **12** oddly amusing

drollery 3 wit **5** humor **6** banter, comedy, whimsy **7** jesting

Dromio
character in: 17 The Comedy of Errors
author: 11 Shakespeare

drone 3 hum **4** buzz, whir **5** idler **6** loafer **7** vibrate **8** parasite **9** murmuring, vibration **10** lazy person

drool 6 drivel, slaver **7** dribble, slobber **8** salivate **15** water at the mouth

droop 3 dim, sag **4** flag, sink **5** lower **6** weaken, wither **8** diminish, hang down **9** lose vigor **14** hang listlessly **15** incline downward

droopy 4 bent, blue, down, limp **5** baggy, bowed, slack **6** dashed, pining **7** doleful, sagging, subdued **8** cast down, dangling, dejected, downcast **9** depressed, dispirited, spiritless, world-weary **11** downhearted, hanging down, languishing **14** down in the mouth

drop 3 can, dab **4** bead, dash, deck, dive, drip, fall, fell, fire, omit, sack, sink, tear **5** abyss, floor, leave, lower, pinch, slide, slope, smack, trace **6** give up, lessen, plunge **7** abandon, decline, descend, descent, dismiss, dribble, driblet, dwindle, forsake, globule, plummet, slacken, smidgen, soupcon, trickle **8** decrease, diminish, leave out, lowering **9** declivity, discharge, knock down, precipice, terminate **10** sprinkling **12** bring to an end **13** fail to include **15** cease to consider, fail to pronounce

drop anchor 4 dock, moor **5** tie up

drop in 4 call, come **5** visit **6** appear, come by, look in, show up, stop by, turn up **7** stop off **9** pay a visit

droplet 4 bead, drip, tear **7** driblet, globule **8** spherule

droplets of moisture 3 dew, fog **4** mist **5** sweat **12** condensation

drop out 4 quit **5** leave **6** resign, retire

dross 4 scum, slag **5** waste **6** cinder, scoria **8** clinkers, impurity

drought, drouth 4 lack, need, want **6** dearth **7** aridity, paucity **8** scarcity, shortage **10** deficiency, dry weather, lack of rain **13** insufficiency

drover 6 cowboy, driver **7** cowpoke **8** herdsman, shepherd **10** cowpuncher

drown 4 soak **5** flood **6** deluge, drench, engulf **7** immerse **8** inundate, overcome, submerge **9** overpower, overwhelm, suffocate, swallow up **10** asphyxiate

drowse 3 nap, nod **4** doze, laze **5** dover, drone, sleep **6** snooze **7** slumber **8** languish **10** sleepiness

drowsy 4 dozy, lazy, slow **5** tired **6** sleepy **7** languid **8** hypnotic, listless, sluggish, soothing **9** lethargic, somnolent, soporific

Dr Strangelove or How I Learned to Stop Worrying and Love the Bomb
director: 14 Stanley Kubrick
cast: 9 Peter Bull **10** Keenan Wynn **11** Slim Pickens **12** George C Scott, Peter Sellers **14** James Earl Jones, Sterling Hayden

drub 3 hit **4** beat, cane, flog, whip **5** whale **6** thrash **9** bastinado

drubbing 6 caning **7** beating, licking, tanning **9** trouncing **11** shellacking

drudge 4 grub, hack, plod, toil **5** labor, slave **6** lackey, menial, toiler **7** grubber **8** inferior, struggle **9** underling **11** subordinate

drudgery 4 toil **5** grind **7** travail **8** hack work **11** menial labor **15** distasteful work

Druk-Yul see **6** Bhutan

drum 3 din, keg, rap, tap, tub **4** beat, cask, roar, roll **5** expel, force **6** barrel, harp on, rumble, tattoo **7** dismiss, pulsate **8** drive out, hammer at **9** discharge, drive home, reiterate **11** beat a tattoo, din in the ear, reverberate

Drums
author: 9 James Boyd

Drums Along the Mohawk
author: 14 Walter D Edmonds
character: 4 Lana **9** Blue Black, John Wolff **11** Joseph Brant, Mark Demooth **12** Mrs McKlennan **13** Gilbert Martin **20** Magdelena Borst Martin

drunk 3 sot **4** bust, lush, soak **5** binge, rummy, souse, tipsy, toper **6** barfly, bender, looped, sodden, soused, stewed, zapped, zonked **7** smashed **8** beer-bust, besotted, carousal **9** alcoholic, plastered **10** inebriated **11** dipsomaniac, intoxicated **13** drinking spree, under the influence

drunkard 3 sot **4** lush, soak, wino **5** rummy, souse, toper **6** barfly **9** alcoholic **11** dipsomaniac

drunkenness 10 alcoholism **11** inebriation **12** intoxication

Drury, Allen
author of: 14 Capable of Honor, Return to Thebes **15** The Promise of Joy **16** Advise and Consent **19** Come Nineveh Come Tyre

Druse 5 Syria **6** Muslim **7** Lebanon

dry 4 arid, blot, dull, wipe **5** droll **6** boring, low-key **7** deadpan, parched, tedious, thirsty **8** rainless **9** dehydrate, desiccate, shrivel up, wearisome **10** dehydrated, monotonous **13** uninteresting

Dryad
form: 5 deity, nymph
location: 5 woods

dry as dust 4 arid, dull, sere **7** parched **8** pedantic, withered **9** shriveled **13** unimaginative

Dryden, John
author of: 10 All for Love **11** Mac Flecknoe **14** Annus Mirabilis **15** Alexander's Feast, Marriage-a-la-Mode **20** Absalom and Achitophel, Essay on Dramatic Poesy, The Hind and the Panther **22** Fables Ancient and Modern

dry goods 5 cloth, goods **6** fabric **8** material **9** yard goods **10** piece goods

dryness 7 aridity, drought **8** aridness **11** dehydration

Dry Salvages
author: 7 T S Eliot

dry up 6 wither **7** shrivel **9** dehydrate, desiccate, evaporate

Dr Zhivago
author: 14 Boris Pasternak
character: 4 Lara
setting: 17 Russian Revolution

dual 6 double **7** twofold, two-part

dub 4 call, name **5** label **6** knight **7** baptize **8** christen, nickname **9** designate

Dubai
part of: 3 UAE

dubiety 5 doubt **8** unbelief **9** disbelief **10** skepticism **11** incredulity **12** doubtfulness **14** lack of credence

Dubin's Lives
author: 14 Bernard Malamud

dubious 5 shady **6** unsure **7** suspect **8** doubtful **9** skeptical, uncertain **10** suspicious, unreliable **11** unconvinced **12** questionable, undependable **13** untrustworthy

Dublin
brewery: 8 Guinness
capital of: 7 Ireland
Irish: 8 Dubh Linn (black pool) **15** Baile Atha Cliath (town of the Hurdle Ford)
landmark: 10 Four Courts **11** Custom House **12** Abbey Theater, Christ Church, Dublin Castle **13** Leinster House **18** Kilmainham **19** St Patrick's Cathedral
mountain: 7 Wicklow
museum: 8 National **10** James Joyce
park: 7 Phoenix
river: 6 Liffey
rulers: 7 English, Vikings
scene of: 12 Easter Rising (1916)
university: 14 Trinity College

Dubliners
author: 10 James Joyce

DuBois, Blanche
character in: 21 A Streetcar Named Desire
author: 8 Williams

Du Bois, W E B
founded: 5 NAACP
author of: 19 The Souls of Black Folk

Dubonnet
type: 8 aperitif
origin: 6 France
ingredient: 7 quinine, red wine
with gin: 3 BVD **8** Napoleon
with rum: 10 Bushranger

duc 4 duke

Duccio di Buoninsegna
born: 5 Italy **6** Sienna
artwork: 6 Maesta **18** The Rucellai Madonna (attributed)

duce, il duce 6 despot, leader, tyrant **8** dictator **9** Mussolini

Duchamp, Marcel
born: 6 France **8** Normandy **10** Blainville
artwork: 5 LHOOQ **9** Given That **11** Etant Donnes **12** Bicycle Wheel **13** The Large Glass (The Bride Stripped Bare by Her Bachelors Even) **24** Nude Descending a Staircase **37** The King and Queen Surrounded by Swift Nudes

Duchess of Malfi, The
author: 11 John Webster
character: 6 Bosola **7** Antonio **8** Giovanna **9** Ferdinand **11** The Cardinal

duck 4 clee, coot, lory, smew, teal, veer **5** avoid, dodge, drake, eider, elude, evade, goose, ruddy, shirk, stoop **6** canard, canvas, crouch, gannet, Peking, scoter, swerve **7** gadwall,

mallard, Muscovy, pintail, pochard **8** baldpate, freckled, redshank, shelduck, shoveler, sidestep, submerge **9** merganser, whistling **10** bufflehead, canvasback **11** wood steamer **13** give the slip to
male: 5 drake
group of: 5 brace

Duck Soup
director: 10 Leo McCarey
cast: 5 Chico, Harpo, Zeppo **7** Groucho (Rufus T Firefly) **12** Louis Calhern, Raquel Torres **14** Margaret Dumont
setting: 9 Freedonia

duct 4 pipe, tube **6** vessel **7** channel, conduit

ductile 6 docile, pliant, supple **7** elastic, plastic, pliable, tensile **8** amenable, bendable, flexible, formable, moldable, shapable, swayable **9** adaptable, compliant, malleable, tractable **10** extensible, manageable, submissive **11** complaisant, manipulable, stretchable, susceptible

dud 3 dog **4** bomb, bust, flop, hash **5** botch, lemon, loser **6** bummer, fiasco, fizzle **7** clinker, debacle, failure, washout **11** lead balloon, miscarriage **14** disappointment

dude 3 fop **4** beau **5** dandy **7** peacock **11** city dweller, city slicker **12** Beau Brummell

Dudevant, Aurore
real name of: 10 George Sand

duds 4 togs **5** flops **6** attire **7** apparel, clothes, fizzles, threads **8** clothing, failures, garments

due 4 owed **5** ample, owing **6** enough, proper, unpaid **7** fitting, merited **8** adequate, becoming, deserved, expected, plenty of, rightful, suitable **9** in arrears, scheduled **10** sufficient **11** appropriate, outstanding

duel
French: 15 affaire d'honneur

Duel, The
author: 15 Alexander Kuprin

duenna 8 guardian **9** attendant, chaperone, custodian, protector

dues 4 fees **7** charges **10** assessment

Duessa
character in: 15 The Faerie Queene
author: 7 Spenser

duet 3 duo, two **4** pair **6** couple **7** twosome

Dufy, Raoul
born: 6 France **7** Le Havre
artwork: 7 The Palm **15** Riders in the Wood **16** Chateau and Horses **18** Deauville Racetrack, Posters at Trouville

dugout 3 den **4** cave **5** canoe **6** cavity, hollow **7** shelter

Duino Elegies
author: 16 Rainer Maria Rilke

Dukas, Paul
born: **5** Paris **6** France
composer of: **6** La Peri **18** Ariane et
Barbe-Bleue **19** Ariadne and Bluebeard **22** The Sorcerer's Apprentice

duke
French: **3** duc

Duke
nickname of: **9** John Wayne

Duke, Patty (Patty Duke Astin)
real name: **13** Anna Marie Duke
husband: **9** John Astin
born: **10** Elmhurst NY
roles: **11** Helen Keller **16** The Miracle
Worker, The Patty Duke Show, Val-
ley of the Dolls

Dukenfield, William Claude
real name of: **8** W C Fields

Duke Snider
nickname of: **11** Edwin Snider

dulcet 7 lyrical, musical, tuneful **8**
pleasing, sonorous **9** melodious **11**
mellifluous

Dulcinea del Toboso
character in: **10** Don Quixote
author: **9** Cervantes

dull 4 slow **5** blunt, dense, muted,
quiet, thick, trite, vapid **6** boring, obtuse, stupid **7** muffled, not keen, prosaic, subdued, vacuous **8** deadened,
inactive, not brisk, not sharp **9** dim-
witted **10** indistinct, lackluster, uneventful **13** unimaginative, uninteresting

Dull
character in: **16** Love's Labour's Lost
author: **11** Shakespeare

dullard 4 dolt **5** dummy, dunce **6** nitwit **7** halfwit **8** dumbbell, imbecile

Dullea, Keir
born: **11** Cleveland OH
roles: **12** David and Lisa **18** Butterflies Are Free **27** Two Thousand
One: A Space Odyssey

dullness 6 idiocy, tedium **8** dumbness,
lethargy, monotony, slowness **9** bluntness, ignorance, stupidity, vapidness
10 boringness, imbecility, obtuseness
11 tediousness **13** dim-wittedness **15**
thick-headedness

dull-witted 5 dazed, fuzzy **7** bemused, muddled, stunned **8** confused
9 stupefied

Dulong, Pierre-Louis
field: **7** physics **9** chemistry
nationality: **6** French
discovered: **19** nitrogen trichloride
studied: **4** heat **13** atomic weights

duly 6 on time **8** properly, suitably **9**
correctly **10** deservedly, punctually,
rightfully **13** appropriately **15** at the
proper time

Dumaine
character in: **16** Love's Labour's Lost
author: **11** Shakespeare

Dumas, Alexandre (fils)

author of: **7** Camille **11** Le Demi-
Monde **17** La Dame aux Camelias **21**
The Lady of the Camellias
Camille inspired: **10** La Traviata
opera by: **5** Verdi

Dumas, Alexandre (pere)
author of: **17** The Queen's Necklace
18 The Three Musketeers **19** The
Man in the Iron Mask **21** The Count
of Monte Cristo **22** The Vicomte de
Bragelonne

Du Maurier, Daphne
author of: **7** Rebecca **10** Jamaica Inn
11 Don't Look Now **14** My Cousin
Rachel **15** Frenchman's Creek **19**
The House on the Strand

Du Maurier, George
author of: **6** Trilby **10** The Martian
13 Peter Ibbetson

dumb 3 mum **4** dull, mute **5** dense,
dopey **6** silent, stupid **7** foolish, aphasic **8** aphasiac **9** dim-witted **13** unintelligent **17** incapable of speech

dumbbell 3 ass, oaf **4** clod, dolt, dope,
fool **5** booby, clown, dummy, dunce,
idiot, moron, ninny **6** dimwit, nitwit **7**
dullard, halfwit **8** dumb-dumb,
dummkopf, imbecile, lunkhead, meathead, numskull **9** birdbrain, blockhead, ignoramus, lamebrain, numbskull, simpleton **10** noodlehead

dumbfound, dumfound 4 stun **5**
amaze **7** startle **8** astonish **11** flabbergast

dumbfounded 5 agape **6** amazed **7**
stunned **9** astounded, stupefied **10** astonished, speechless **11** openmouthed **13** flabbergasted

dumbness 6 idiocy **8** dullness **9** asininity, stupidity, thickness **10** imbecility **11** witlessness **12** wordlessness **14**
speechlessness **15** thickheadedness

dumbstruck 5 agape **6** amazed, gaping **7** riveted **9** awestruck, stupefied
10 speechless **11** electrified, openmouthed **13** flabbergasted

dump 3 hut **4** hole, toss **5** empty,
hovel, shack **6** shanty, unload **8** get
rid of, junkyard **9** dispose of **10** refuse pile **11** rubbish heap

dumpy 5 squat **7** lumpish **13** short
and stout

Dunaway, Faye
real name: **18** Dorothy Faye
Dunaway
born: **8** Bascom FL
roles: **6** Barfly, Milady **7** Network
(Oscar) **8** The Champ **9** Chinatown
13 Mommie Dearest **14** Bonnie and
Clyde **15** Towering Inferno **17** The
Four Musketeers **18** The Three Musketeers

Duncan
character in: **7** Macbeth
author: **11** Shakespeare

Duncan, Sandy
born: **11** Henderson TX

roles: **8** Peter Pan **9** Funny Face **12**
The Boyfriend

dunce 4 fool **5** dummy, idiot, moron **6**
dimwit, nitwit **8** imbecile, numskull **9**
blockhead, numbskull, simpleton

Dunciad, The
author: **13** Alexander Pope

dune 4 bank **5** mound **8** sandbank,
sandpile

dunk 3 dip, sop **4** duck, soak **5** bathe,
douse, drown, slosh, souse, steep **6**
deluge, drench, engulf, plunge **7** baptize, immerse **8** inundate, saturate,
submerge

Dunne, John Gregory
author of: **11** Dutch Shea Jr **18** Quintana and Friends

Dunnock, Mildred
born: **11** Baltimore MD
roles: **8** Baby Doll **12** The Nun's
Story **14** The Corn Is Green **16** Butterfield Eight, Cat on a Hot Tin Roof,
Death of a Salesman

duo 4 pair **5** combo **6** couple **7** twosome **11** combination

duomo 4 dome **9** cathedral

dupe 4 fool, pawn **5** patsy, trick **6**
humbug, sucker **7** cat's paw, deceive,
fall guy, mislead **8** hoodwink **9** bamboozle

duplicate 4 copy **5** clone, match **6** repeat **7** replica **8** parallel **9** facsimile,
imitation, make again, photocopy,
photostat **10** carbon copy **12** reproduction

duplicity 5 fraud, guile **6** deceit **7** cunning **9** deception, falseness **10** dishonesty **13** deceitfulness

Du Pont Labs
founder: **17** E I du Pont de Nemours
inventor of: **5** nylon **6** Teflon **7** Gore-
Tex

Duquesnoy, Francois
born: **8** Brussels, Flanders
nickname: **11** Il Fiammingo
artwork: **8** St Andrew **9** St Susanna

dur
musical term: **5** major **8** major key

durability 7 stamina **8** strength **9** endurance, toughness **10** sturdiness

durable 5 sound, tough **6** strong,
sturdy **7** lasting **8** enduring **11** long-
wearing, substantial

Durand, Asher Brown
born: **18** Jefferson Village NJ
artwork: **14** Kindred Spirits

Durant, Will and Ariel
authors of: **20** The Story of Philosophy **21** Rousseau and Revolution **22**
The Story of Civilization

Durante, Jimmy
real name: **19** James Francis Durante
nickname: **10** Schnozzola **15** Inka
Dinka Doo Man
born: **9** New York NY

roles: 5 Jumbo **21** It's a Mad Mad Mad Mad World

duration 4 term **6** extent, period **11** continuance **12** continuation

Durdles
character in: **22** The Mystery of Edwin Drood
author: **7** Dickens

Durer, Albrecht
born: **7** Germany **9** Nuremberg
artwork: **10** Adam and Eve, Apocalypse, The Triumph **11** Wehlsch Pirg **12** Four Apostles, Large Passion, Melancholia I **13** Castle of Trent **15** Life of the Virgin **18** St Jerome in his Study **19** Virgin with the Siskin **21** Christ Among the Doctors **22** Knight Death and the Devil **24** Crowned Death on a Thin Horse **25** The Feast of the Rose Garlands **28** The Festival of the Rose Garlands

duress 5 force **6** threat **8** coercion, pressure **10** compulsion, constraint

Durgin, Francis Timothy
real name of: **11** Rory Calhoun

during litigation
Latin: **12** pendente lite

Durocher, Leo
nickname: **9** Leo the Lip
sport: **8** baseball
position: **7** manager
team: **11** Chicago Cubs **13** New York Giants **15** Brooklyn Dodgers
saying: **18** Nice guys finish last

Durrenmatt, Friedrich
author of: **5** Traps **8** The Visit **9** The Pledge, The Quarry **13** The Physicists **21** The Judge and His Hangman **27** The Marriage of the Mississippi

Durrie, James and Henry
character in: **21** The Master of Ballantrae
author: **9** Stevenson

dusk 6 sunset **7** sundown **8** twilight **9** nightfall

dusky 3 dim **4** dark **5** murky **6** cloudy, gloomy, veiled **7** swarthy **8** dark-hued

dust 4 dirt, lint **5** brush, motes **8** sprinkle

duster 3 rag **4** coat, robe **5** brush, cloth, whisk **9** housecoat **10** whisk broom

Dutch Guiana see **8** Suriname

Dutch Shea, Jr
author: **16** John Gregory Dunne

dutiful 5 loyal **8** diligent, faithful, obedient **9** compliant **13** conscientious

duty 3 tax **4** levy, onus, task **6** charge, excise, tariff **7** customs **8** business, function, province **10** assignment, obligation **14** responsibility

Duval, Armand
character in: **7** Camille
author: **5** Dumas (fils)

Duvall, Robert
born: **10** San Diego CA
roles: **4** MASH **10** The Apostle **11** Falling Down, Godfather II **12** Lonesome Dove, The Godfather **13** Apocalypse Now, Days of Thunder, Tender Mercies (Oscar) **15** The Great Santini, True Confessions **16** The Handmaid's Tale, The Scarlet Letter **18** To Kill a Mockingbird

Duvall, Shelley
born: **9** Houston TX
roles: **6** Popeye **9** Nashville **10** The Shining, Three Women **15** Brewster McCloud

Dvorak, Antonin
born: **11** Nelahozeves **14** Czechoslovakia
composer of: **5** Dumky **6** Hymnus, Te Deum **8** Carnival (overture) **10** St Ludmilla **11** Stabat Mater **15** American Quartet, From the New World (Symphony in E Minor) **16** The Specter's Bride **17** The Bells of Zlonice

dwarf 3 dim, elf, imp **4** baby, tiny **5** fairy, gnome, pixie, pygmy, small, troll **6** bantam, goblin, petite, sprite **8** diminish **9** miniature **10** diminutive, leprechaun, overshadow

dwarfish 4 wee **4** tiny **5** pygmy, short, small **6** bantam, little, midget **7** compact, squatty **10** diminutive, undersized **13** foreshortened

dweeb 4 fool, geek, nerd, wonk **5** grind

dwell 4 live **5** abide **6** harp on, reside **7** inhabit **10** linger over

dwelling 4 home **5** abode, house **8** domicile **9** residence **10** habitation

dwelling place 4 home **5** abode, house **7** habitat, lodging **8** domicile **9** residence **10** habitation **14** living quarters

dwell on 6 accent, stress **7** feature, iterate **9** emphasize, press home

dwindle 4 fade, wane **6** lessen, shrink **7** decline **8** decrease, diminish **13** become smaller

dye 4 tint **5** color, shade, stain **8** coloring **10** coloration

dyed-in-the-wool 9 confirmed, ingrained **10** deep-rooted, inveterate **11** established

dyestuff 14 coloring matter

dynamic 5 vital **6** active **7** driving **8** forceful, powerful, vigorous **9** energetic

dynamism 3 pep **4** life **5** verve, vigor **6** energy, spirit **8** vitality, vivacity **9** animation **10** liveliness

dynamite 4 raze, ruin **5** blast, trash, wreck **6** blow up, charge **7** destroy, shatter, wipe out **8** decimate, demolish **9** devastate, dismantle, eradicate, explosive **10** annihilate, extinguish, obliterate **11** exterminate

dynamo 4 doer **7** hustler **8** activist, go-getter **9** generator **12** active person **14** bundle of energy, mover and shaker

Dynasts, The
author: **11** Thomas Hardy
subject: **17** Napoleon Bonaparte

dynasty 4 line **5** crown, reign **6** regime **7** lineage, regency **8** dominion, hegemony, kingship, monarchy, regnancy **9** authority **10** government, suzerainty **11** ruling house **12** jurisdiction **14** administration

Dynasty
character: **9** Dex Dexter, Jeff Colby **12** Alexis (Morel Carrington Colby) Dexter **14** Adam Carrington **15** Blake Carrington **16** Amanda Carrington, Steven Carrington **17** Krystle Carrington **18** Dominique Devereaux, Krystina Carrington **21** Fallon Carrington Colby
cast: **9** John James **10** Linda Evans **11** Joan Collins **12** John Forsythe
setting: **6** Denver **8** Colorado
hotel: **8** La Mirage

dyspeptic 4 mean **6** crabby, grumpy, ornery, shirty, touchy **7** grouchy, waspish **8** choleric **9** crotchety, fractious, irascible, irritable **10** ill-humored, ill-natured **11** bad-tempered, contentious, hot-tempered **12** cantankerous, sour-tempered **13** short-tempered

each 3 per **4** a pop **5** every **6** apiece **7** that one, this one **8** everyone, separate **12** respectively

Eagels, Jeanne
born: 12 Kansas City MO
roles: 4 Rain **8** Jealousy **9** The Letter **13** Sadie Thompson **14** Man Woman and Sin

eager 3 hot **4** agog, avid, keen **6** ardent, fervid, intent, raring **7** athirst, earnest, excited, fervent, intense, longing, zealous **8** desirous, diligent, resolute, spirited, yearning **9** ambitious, hungering, impatient, thirsting **10** aggressive, passionate **11** hardworking, impassioned, industrious, persevering **12** enterprising, enthusiastic

eagerly 6 avidly, keenly **8** ardently, desiring, fervidly, intently **9** anxiously, earnestly, fervently, zealously **16** enthusiastically

eagerness 4 zeal, zest **5** ardor **6** fervor **7** avidity **9** readiness **10** enthusiasm **11** willingness

eagle
young: 6 eaglet

Eagle
constellation of: 6 Aquila

Eakins, Thomas
born: 14 Philadelphia PA
artwork: 11 Agnew Clinic **13** Mrs Edith Mahon **14** The Gross Clinic **24** Max Schmitt in a Single Scull

ear
section: 5 inner, outer **6** middle
part: 4 drum **5** anvil, canal **6** hammer **7** cochlea, stirrup **8** hair cell **14** eustachian tube

earl 4 lord, peer **5** noble **8** nobleman
wife: 8 countess

earlier 6 before, in time, sooner **9** before now, in advance **10** beforehand **11** ahead of time **13** before the fact

earliest 5 first **6** oldest, primal **7** ancient, initial, primary, soonest **8** original, primeval **9** beginning, primitive **10** aboriginal, indigenous **11** fundamental

Earl of Baltimore
nickname of: 10 Earl Weaver

Earl the Pearl
nickname of: 10 Earl Monroe

early 5 first **6** primal **7** ancient, archaic, betimes, initial, too soon, very old **8** primeval **9** in advance, prema-

ture, primitive **10** beforehand, in good time, primordial **11** ahead of time, prehistoric, prematurely

Early Autumn
author: 14 Louis Bromfield

early man 6 Peking **9** Cro-Magnon, Steinheim **11** Neanderthal **18** Trobriand Islanders **24** Australopithecus robustus **25** Australopithecus africanus

earmark 3 tag **4** band, hold, sign **5** allot, label, stamp, token, trait **6** aspect, assign, dogear **7** feature, put away, quality, reserve **8** allocate, property, set aside **9** attribute, designate **11** peculiarity, singularity **14** characteristic

earn 3 get, net **4** draw, gain, make, rate, reap **5** clear, merit **6** attain, pick up, secure **7** achieve, collect, deserve, realize, receive, warrant **9** bring home **12** be entitled to

earn as due 4 rate **5** merit **7** deserve **10** be worthy of **12** be entitled to **13** be deserving of

earnest 4 firm **5** eager, fixed, grave, sober, staid **6** ardent, fervid, honest, intent, sedate, solemn, stable, steady, urgent **7** devoted, fervent, intense, serious, sincere, zealous **8** constant, diligent, resolute, spirited, vehement **9** ambitious, assiduous, heartfelt, insistent **10** deeply felt, determined, passionate, purposeful, thoughtful **11** hard-working, impassioned, industrious, persevering **12** enthusiastic, wholehearted

earnest request 4 plea **6** appeal **8** entreaty, petition **11** importunity **12** supplication

earnings 3 pay **5** wages **6** income, salary **7** payment, profits **8** proceeds, receipts, takehome **12** compensation

Earnshaw, Catherine
character in: 16 Wuthering Heights
author: 6 Bronte

ear-splitting 7 blaring **8** piercing **9** clamorous, deafening **10** thunderous

earth 3 sod **4** clay, dirt, dust, land, loam, soil, turf **5** terra **6** ground **7** topsoil
god of: 3 Geb, Keb **5** Dagan, Dagon **10** Trophonius
goddess of: 2 Ge **4** Gaea, Gaia **6** Hecate, Hekate, Tellus

earthen pot
Spanish: 4 olla

earthenware 5 china **7** pottery **8** clayware, crockery **11** ceramic ware

earthly 6 bodily **7** mundane, secular, ungodly, worldly **8** feasible, material, physical, possible, temporal **9** corporeal, practical **10** imaginable **11** conceivable, terrestrial **12** nonspiritual **13** materialistic

earthquake 5 quake, seism, shock **6** tremor **8** temblor, upheaval **11** earth tremor

earth tremor 5 quake, seism, shock **6** tremor **8** temblor, upheaval **10** earthquake

earthy 5 bawdy, crude, dirty, funky, gross, lusty, rough **6** coarse, filthy, ribald, robust, smutty, vulgar **7** obscene, peasant, raunchy **8** indecent **9** primitive, unrefined **10** unblushing, uncultured **12** uncultivated

Earwicker family
characters in: 13 Finnegans Wake
author: 5 Joyce

earwig
variety: 5 black **6** little **10** long horned

ease 4 calm, rest, slip **5** abate, allay, poise, quiet, slide, still **6** aplomb, lessen, luxury, pacify, plenty, relief, repose, solace, soothe **7** assuage, comfort, console, leisure, lighten, mollify, relieve **8** diminish, easement, easiness, facility, maneuver, mitigate, palliate, security, serenity **9** abundance, affluence, alleviate, composure, disburden, readiness **10** confidence, prosperity, relaxation **11** assuagement, naturalness, peace of mind, restfulness **12** tranquillity, unconstraint **13** luxuriousness, move carefully, relaxed manner **14** effortlessness, handle with care, unaffectedness

easel 5 frame, stand **6** tripod

easement 4 ease **6** relief, solace, succor **7** comfort **8** soothing **10** right of way **11** assuagement

easily 5 by far **6** freely, surely **7** clearly, handily, lightly, plainly, readily **8** facilely, smoothly, with ease **9** certainly **10** far and away, undeniably **11** beyond doubt, undoubtedly **12** effortlessly, with facility **13** without a hitch **14** beyond question, without trouble **17** without difficulty **23** beyond the shadow of a doubt

easily embarrassed 3 shy 5 timid 7 bashful 8 blushing, skittish, timorous 9 diffident, shrinking 11 constrained, unconfident

easily noticed 5 clear, plain 6 patent 7 evident, glaring, obvious, visible 8 flagrant, striking 9 arresting, prominent 10 noticeable 11 conspicuous, outstanding

easily ruffled 9 emotional, excitable 11 hot-tempered 13 quick-tempered

easiness 4 ease 10 equanimity, simplicity 11 naturalness 12 indifference 13 impassiveness

East, the 4 Asia 9 the Orient 10 the Far East 11 the Near East 17 Eastern Hemisphere

East Bengal *see* 10 Bangladesh

East Berlin
former capital of: 11 East Germany

East Coker
author: 7 T S Eliot

Eastern Slavic
language family: 12 Indo-European
group: 11 Balto-Slavic
branch: 6 Slavic
language: 7 Russian 9 Ukrainian 12 White Russian

Easter Parade
director: 14 Charles Walters
based on musical by: 12 Irving Berlin
cast: 9 Ann Miller 11 Fred Astaire, Judy Garland 12 Peter Lawford

East Germany *see* 11 Germany, East

East Indies *see* 8 Malaysia 9 Indonesia

Eastman, George
nationality: 8 American
founder of: 14 Eastman Kodak Co
inventor of: 9 Kodak film 11 Kodak camera 20 transparent photo film

East of Eden
author: 13 John Steinbeck
director: 9 Elia Kazan
cast: 8 Burl Ives 9 James Dean 10 Jo Van Fleet 11 Julie Harris 13 Raymond Massey
Oscar for: 17 supporting actress (Van Fleet)
characters: 4 Abra, Adam, Aron 5 Caleb, Trask

East wind
associated with: 5 Eurus 9 Volturnus

Eastwood, Clint
born: 14 San Francisco CA
roles: 7 Firefox, Rawhide 10 Dirty Harry, Hang Em High, Unforgiven 11 Magnum Force, The Dead Pool 12 Coogan's Bluff, Kelly's Heroes, Sudden Impact 13 A Perfect World 14 Play Misty for Me 15 In The Line of Fire, Where Eagles Dare 17 A Fistful of Dollars, Any Which Way You Can, High Plains Drifter 18 Escape from Alcatraz, For a Few Dollars More 21 Two Mules for Sister Sara

23 The Good the Bad and the Ugly 25 The Bridges of Madison County
director of: 10 Unforgiven (Oscar) 12 Sudden Impact 13 Absolute Power, A Perfect World 14 Play Misty For Me 25 The Bridges of Madison County 32 Midnight in the Garden of Good and Evil
mayor of: 6 Carmel

easy 4 calm, mild, open, soft 5 cushy, frank, light, naive 6 benign, calmly, candid, docile, easily, gentle, secure, serene, simple 7 lenient, natural, not hard, relaxed, restful, wealthy 8 affluent, carefree, composed, friendly, gracious, gullible, informal, outgoing, painless, peaceful, pleasant, scarcely, serenely, tranquil, unforced, well-to-do, yielding 9 compliant, indulgent, leisurely, luxurious, tractable, unworried 10 effortless, peacefully, permissive, unaffected, untroubled 11 comfortable, comfortably 12 not difficult, unsuspicious 13 accommodating, unconstrained

easygoing 4 calm 6 casual 7 offhand, patient, relaxed 8 carefree, laidback 9 unruffled, unworried 10 insouciant, nonchalant 11 unconcerned, unexcitable 12 even-tempered, happy-go-lucky, mild-tempered

Easy Rider
director: 12 Dennis Hopper
cast: 10 Karen Black, Peter Fonda 11 Luana Anders 12 Dennis Hopper, Robert Walker 13 Jack Nicholson

easy to use 7 adapted, helpful 9 adaptable 10 convenient 11 serviceable 12 advantageous, user friendly

eat 3 sup 4 bolt, dine, feed, gulp, rust, take 5 feast, lunch 6 devour, gobble, ingest, nibble 7 consume, corrode 8 dispatch, dissolve, wear away, wolf down 9 breakfast, take a meal, waste away 10 break bread, gormandize 14 take sustenance 15 take nourishment

eatable 4 food 6 edible 8 fit to eat 10 comestible, consumable

eat away 4 rust 5 erode 7 corrode, oxidize

eating habits 4 diet 7 regimen

eat into 4 bite 5 erode 6 nibble 7 consume, corrode 8 wear away 9 swallow up

eat one's fill 5 feast, gorge 6 pig out 7 banquet 10 stuff oneself

eat rapidly 4 bolt, gulp, wolf 5 scarf 6 gobble 12 swallow whole

eat up 5 enjoy, savor 6 devour, relish 7 consume, swallow 9 delight in, rejoice in 13 be pleased with, get a kick out of 14 take pleasure in

eat voraciously 6 cram in, devour, gobble 7 stuff in 8 bolt down, gulp down, wolf down 10 gormandize 12 swallow whole

eau, eaux 5 water

eau de vie 6 brandy 11 water of life

eaves 8 overhang

eavesdrop 3 bug, pry, spy, tap 5 snoop 6 attend, harken 7 monitor, wiretap 8 listen in, overhear 9 bend an ear 11 cock one's ear 14 strain one's ears 15 prick up one's ears

ebb 5 abate, go out 6 go down, lessen, recede, shrink, weaken 7 decline, dwindle, retreat, slacken, subside 8 decrease, diminish, fade away, fall away, flow away, flow back, move back, withdraw 9 waste away 10 degenerate 11 deteriorate

ebony 3 jet 4 dark, inky 5 black, raven, sable 8 hardwood 9 coal-black 15 Diospyros Ebenum
varieties: 5 Green, Texas 8 Macassar, Mountain 10 East Indian, Queensland

Ebsen, Buddy
real name: 23 Christian Rudolph Ebsen Jr
born: 12 Belleville IL
roles: 12 Barnaby Jones, Davy Crockett 21 The Beverly Hillbillies

ebullience 3 zip 7 elation 8 buoyancy 9 animation 10 enthusiasm, exuberance, joyousness, liveliness 11 high spirits 12 exhilaration 13 effervescence

ebullient 6 elated, joyful, joyous 9 exuberant 10 exhilarated 12 effervescent, enthusiastic, high-spirited

ecce homo 12 behold the man
said by: 13 Pontius Pilate
spoken of: 6 Christ

eccentric 3 nut, odd 4 kook, rash, sick 5 curio, flake, funny, kooky, nutty, queer, weird 6 freaky, insane, quaint, unique, weirdo 7 bizarre, curious, erratic, oddball, offbeat, strange, unusual, weirdie 8 aberrant, abnormal, crackpot, freakish, peculiar, quixotic, singular, uncommon 9 character, irregular, odd person, off center, parabolic, psychotic, screwball, unnatural, whimsical 10 capricious, elliptical, outlandish, unorthodox 13 extraordinary 14 unconventional

eccentricity 6 oddity, whimsy 7 caprice 9 deviation, queerness 10 aberration 11 abnormality, peculiarity, strangeness 12 idiosyncrasy, irregularity

ecclesiastic, ecclesiastical 5 rabbi, vicar 6 cleric, curate, deacon, parson, pas- tor, priest, rector 7 prelate 8 chaplain, churchly, clerical, minister, pastoral, preacher 9 churchman, clergyman, episcopal, parochial, religious

echelon 4 file, line, rank, rung, tier 5 grade, level 6 office 8 position 9 authority, hierarchy

Echidna 8 anteater
feature: 5 snout

echinoderm 9 sea animal

characteristic: 10 spiny shell

form: 6 radial

kind: 6 cystid **7** crinoid **8** starfish **9** sea urchin **10** basket star **11** sea cucumber

echo 3 ape **4** copy, ring **5** match **6** follow, mirror, parrot, repeat **7** imitate, reflect, resound **8** parallel, simulate **9** duplicate, reproduce, take after **11** reverberate **13** reverberation

Echo

form: 5 nymph

location: 8 mountain

loved: 9 Narcissus

loved by: 3 Pan

changed into: 4 echo

eclair 6 pastry **7** dessert **9** creampuff

eclaircissement 11 explanation **13** clarification, (the) Enlightenment

eclat 4 fame, pomp **5** glory, honor **6** praise, renown, repute **7** acclaim, display, success

eclipse 3 dim **4** hide, loss, mask **5** cloak, cover, excel, outdo **6** darken, exceed **7** blot out, conceal, erasing, masking, obscure, surpass, veiling, wipe out **8** cloaking, clouding, covering, outrival, outshine **9** darkening, shadowing, transcend **10** obliterate, overshadow, tower above **11** blotting out, diminishing, eradicating, obscuration **12** annihilation, obliteration **13** overshadowing

eclogue 4 idyl, poem **5** idyll **7** bucolic **8** dialogue, pastoral

Eclogues

author: 6 Vergil, Virgil

ecole 6 school

economic 6 fiscal **8** material, monetary **9** budgetary, financial, pecuniary **10** productive **12** distributive

economical 5 chary, cheap **6** frugal, modest, saving **7** careful, prudent, sparing, spartan, thrifty **8** economic **9** low-priced, niggardly, penurious, scrimping **10** reasonable **11** closefisted, tightfisted **12** parsimonious

economic decline 8 downturn **9** recession **10** depression

economics

term: 3 GNP **5** labor **7** capital, Marxism, surplus **8** property **9** commodity, Communism, inflation, Keynesian, recession **10** capitalism, monetarist, supply-side **11** bourgeoisie, central bank, competition, consumption, marketplace, proletariat, stagflation **12** distribution, econometrics, fiscal policy, interest rate, laissez-faire, mercantilism **14** federal deficit, macroeconomics, microeconomics, monetary policy **17** trickledown theory **20** gross national product

economist

American: 6 George, Hansen, Sumner, Veblen **7** Commons **8** Friedman,
Laughlin **9** Greenspan **10** Schumpeter

British: 4 Mill **5** Smith **6** Keynes **7** Malthus, Ricardo **8** Marshall

French: 3 Say **7** Quesnay

German: 4 Marx **7** Schacht

Italian: 6 Pareto

Scottish: 5 Smith

economize 4 save **5** pinch, skimp, stint **6** scrimp **7** husband **8** be frugal, conserve, cut costs **9** be prudent **10** avoid waste **11** cut expenses **12** be economical, use sparingly **14** be parsimonious **15** practice economy, tighten one's belt

economizing 10 conserving **11** cutting down **13** penny-pinching **14** belt-tightening **15** pinching pennies **18** tightening one's belt

economy 6 thrift **8** prudence **9** frugality **10** providence **11** thriftiness **15** financial status, productive power

ecstasy 3 joy **5** bliss **6** frenzy, thrill, trance **7** delight, emotion, madness, rapture **8** delirium, gladness, pleasure **9** cloud nine, happiness, transport **10** enthusiasm, exultation

ecstatic 4 glad, rapt **5** happy **6** elated, joyful, joyous **7** exalted, excited **8** blissful **9** delighted, delirious, ebullient, entranced, overjoyed, rapturous **10** enraptured **11** transported **12** enthusiastic **13** beside oneself

Ecuador

name means: 7 equator

other name: 5 Quito

capital: 5 Quito

largest city: 9 Guayaquil

others: 4 Jama, Loja, Napo, Puyo, Tena **5** Guano, Manta, Pajan, Pinas, Piura, Pojan, Yaupi **6** Ambato, Cuenca, Ibarra, Tulcan, Zaruma **7** Azogues, Cayambe, Guamote, Guapulo, Machala, Pelileo, Pillaro, Salinas **8** Riobamba **10** Esmeraldas, Portoviejo

division: 5 Costa **6** Sierra **7** Oriente

measure: 5 libra **6** cuadra, fanega

monetary unit: 5 sucre **7** centavo

weight: 5 libra

island: 4 Puna, Wolf **5** Colon, Mocha, Pinta **6** Baltra, Chaves, Darwin, Pinzon, Rabida, Wenman **7** Isabela, La Plata, Sante Fe, Tortuga **8** Espanola, Floreana, Genovesa, Marchena, Santiago **9** Culpepper, Galapagos, Santa Cruz **10** Fernandina, Santa Maria **11** San Salvador **12** San Cristobal

mountain: 5 Andes **6** Condor, Sangay **7** Cayambe **8** Antisana, Cotopaxi **9** Cotacachi, Pichincha

highest point: 10 Chimborazo

river: 4 Coca, Mira, Napo **5** Cocoa, Daule, Paute, Pindo, Tigre **6** Blanco, Guayas, Tumbes, Zamora **7** Conambo, Curaray, Jubones, Pastaza, Puyango **8** Aguarico, Bobonaza, Cononaco, Naranjal, Putumayo **9** San
Miguel **10** Esmeraldas, Nangaritza **12** Guaillabamba

sea: 7 Pacific

physical feature:

bay: 5 Manta **7** Isabela **9** Elizabeth **11** Santa Elenas **15** Ancon de Sardinas

cape: 4 Rosa **6** Pasado **8** Marshall, Puntilla **10** San Lorenzo

channel: 7 Jambeli

gulf: 9 Guayaquil, Pichincha

peninsula: 10 Santa Elena

point: 4 Jama **5** Essex **6** Galera **9** Albemarle **10** Christobal

people: 4 Cara, Cixo, Inca **5** Ardan, Aucas, Macoa, Maina, Palta, Quitu, Yumbo **6** Canelo, Jibaro, Jivaro, Puruha **7** Cayapas, Jivaros, mestizo, mulatto **8** Barbacoa, Colorado, Montuvio, Serranos **9** Montubios

artist: 4 Egas **8** Santiago **9** Caspicara **10** Guayasamin

author: 6 Espejo **14** Carrera Andrade

conqueror: 7 Pizarro **10** Benalcazar **11** Huayna-Capac

god: 5 umina

leader: 6 Alfaro, Flores **10** Plaza Lasso, Rocafuerte **12** Garcia Moreno **13** Velasco Ibarra

language: 6 Jibaro **7** Quechua, Spanish

religion: 13 Roman Catholic

feature:

animal: 6 vicuna

dictator: 8 caudillo

estate: 8 hacienda

festival: 5 Yamor

hat: 6 Panama **8** jipijapa, toquilla

tree: 5 balsa

food:

baked guinea pig: 3 cuy

corn tamale: 6 humita

drink: 6 chicha

marinated raw shrimp/fish: 7 ceviche, seviche

potato/cheese patty: 11 llapingacho

potato soup: 5 locro

ecumenical 6 global **7** general **8** catholic **9** communist, planetary, universal, worldwide **10** heavenwide **11** communalist **12** all-embracing, all-including, all-inclusive, all-pervading, collectivist, cosmopolitan **13** communitarian, comprehensive, international

eczema 4 rash **8** eruption **10** dermatitis **12** inflammation

eddy 6 vortex **9** maelstrom, whirlpool **14** countercurrent

Eddy, Nelson

partner: 17 Jeanette MacDonald

born: 12 Providence RI

roles: 9 Rose Marie **15** Naughty Marietta **16** Northwest Outpost

Eden 8 Paradise

see also **4** Adam

Eden, Anthony 10 Earl of Avon 13 prime minister

Eden, Barbara
role: 7 Jeannie
TV: 15 I Dream of Jeannie
costar: 11 Larry Hagman

edentate 5 manis, sloth 7 antbear 8 aardvark, anteater 9 armadillo, toothless

Edgar Huntly
author: 20 Charles Brockden Brown

edge 3 hem, rim 4 bind, inch, line, side, trim 5 bound, brink, creep, limit, sidle, slink, sneak, steal, verge 6 border, fringe, margin 7 contour, outline 9 extremity, periphery, threshold 12 boundary line, dividing line, move sideways

Edgeworth, Maria
author of: 7 Belinda 11 The Absentee 14 Castle Rackrent

edging 3 hem 4 trim 5 limit 6 border, fringe, margin, ruffle 7 binding, curbing, salvage 8 boundary, fringing, trimming

edgy 5 sharp, testy 7 anxious, nervous 8 snappish 9 excitable, impatient, irascible, irritable 10 highstrung

edible 7 eatable 10 comestible, consumable, digestible 12 fit to be eaten, nonpoisonous 13 safe for eating

edict 3 law 4 bull, fiat 5 order, ukase 6 decree, dictum, ruling 7 command, dictate, mandate, statute 8 enactment, manifesto, ordinance, prescript 10 injunction, regulation 12 proclamation, public notice 13 pronouncement 14 pronunciamento

edification 8 guidance, teaching 9 direction, education, elevation, uplifting 11 advancement, information, instruction 13 enlightenment 14 indoctrination

edifice 8 building 9 structure 12 construction

edify 5 teach 6 inform 7 educate, improve 8 instruct 9 enlighten

edifying 8 didactic, tutorial 11 educational, instructive 12 enlightening

Edinburgh
bay: 12 Firth of Forth
capital of: 8 Scotland
Celtic: 11 Dune-eideann (Eidin's Fort)
church: 7 St Giles
landmark: 14 Holyrood Palace 15 Edinburgh Castle
port: 5 Leith
rocks: 10 Castle Rock 11 Arthur's Seat

Edison, Thomas Alva
nickname: 17 Wizard of Menlo Park
home: 11 Menlo Park, NJ
inventor of: 6 (wax cylinder) record 9 light bulb, (quadruplex) telegraph 10 phonograph 11 kinetoscope, stock ticker 14 movie projector 16 incandescent lamp 18 automatic telegraph (transmitter and receiver) 21 flexible celluloid film 22 alkaline storage battery

edit 5 adapt, emend 6 censor, polish, redact, revise 7 abridge, clean up, correct, expunge, rewrite, touch up 8 annotate, condense, copy-edit, rephrase 9 expurgate 10 blue-pencil, bowdlerize

edition 4 book, copy, kind 5 issue 6 number 7 imprint, version 8 printing 9 redaction

editor 2 ed 6 writer 7 newsman, reviser 8 compiler, redactor 10 journalist

Edmonds, Walter D
author of: 8 Rome Haul 19 Drums Along the Mohawk

Edmonton
hockey team: 6 Oilers

Edmontonia
type: 8 dinosaur 10 ornithopod
location: 12 North America

Edmund Campion
author: 11 Evelyn Waugh

Edom
name given: 4 Esau
descendants: 8 Edomites

Edson, Gus
creator/artist of: 5 Dondi 8 The Gumps

Ed Sullivan Show, The
regular cast: 17 June Taylor Dancers 23 Ray Bloch and His Orchestra
noted appearances: 7 Beatles, Bob Hope 9 Topo Gigio (mouse) 10 Walt Disney 11 Senor Wences 12 Elvis Presley 14 Martin and Lewis

educate 5 coach, edify, teach, train, tutor 6 inform, school 7 develop 8 civilize, instruct 9 enlighten

education 5 study 7 culture 8 learning, pedagogy, teaching, training, tutelage 9 didactics, erudition, knowledge, schooling 10 pedagogics 11 cultivation, edification, information, instruction, scholarship 13 enlightenment

Education of Henry Adams, The
author: 10 Henry Adams

educe 5 evoke 6 elicit, extort 7 draw out, extract 8 bring out 9 draw forth 12 bring to light

Edward II
author: 18 Christopher Marlowe

Edwards, Blake
director of: 3 SOB, Ten 14 The Pink Panther, Victor Victoria 18 Days of Wine and Roses 19 Breakfast at Tiffany's
wife: 12 Julie Andrews

Edwards, Vince
real name: 18 Vincent Edward Zoimo
roles: 8 Ben Casey 13 Devil's Brigade 14 The Desperadoes 15 Three Faces of Eve

Edwin Drood, The Mystery of
author: 14 Charles Dickens
character: 7 Durdles, Mr Tatar, Rosa Bud 8 Mr Sapsea 10 John Jasper, Mr Datchery 11 Mr Grewgious 12 Mr Crisparkle 13 Deputy Bazzard 14 Helena Landless, Miss Twinkleton, Mr Honeythunder 15 Neville Landless

eel 6 conger
young: 5 elver

eerie 3 odd 5 queer, weird 6 creepy, spooky, uneasy 7 bizarre, fearful, ghostly, ominous, strange, uncanny 10 mysterious, portentous 11 frightening 12 apprehensive

Eeyore 6 donkey
character in: 13 Winnie-the-Pooh
author: 5 Milne

efface 4 raze 5 erase 6 cancel, delete, excise, rub out 7 blot out, destroy, expunge, wipe out 9 eradicate, extirpate 10 annihilate, obliterate

effect, effects 4 fact, gist, make 5 cause, drift, force, goods, power, tenor, truth 6 action, assets, attain, create, impact, import, intent, result, sequel, things, upshot, weight 7 achieve, essence, execute, meaning, outcome, perform, produce, purport, reality, realize 8 carry out, chattels, efficacy, function, holdings, movables, validity 9 actuality, aftermath, execution, furniture, influence, intention, operation, outgrowth, trappings 10 accomplish, bring about, impression 11 commodities, consequence, development, enforcement, general idea, implication, possessions 12 significance 14 accomplishment

effective 4 real 6 active, actual, cogent, moving, potent, strong, useful 7 capable, current, dynamic, telling 8 a reality, eloquent, forceful, forcible, incisive, powerful, striking 9 activated, competent, effectual, efficient, operative 10 compelling, convincing, impressive, persuasive, productive, successful 11 efficacious, influential, in operation, serviceable

effectiveness 5 power 6 effect, impact 7 potency 8 efficacy, strength 9 influence 10 efficiency, usefulness 14 serviceability

effectual 6 acting, active, useful 7 working 8 adequate 9 effective, efficient, operative 11 efficacious, functioning

effectuate 6 effect 7 achieve, execute, realize 8 carry out, complete 9 discharge 10 accomplish, consummate, perpetrate 12 carry through 13 put into effect

effeminate 7 unmanly 8 sissyish, womanish 9 sissified

effervesce 4 fizz, foam 5 froth 6 bubble, fizzle 7 sparkle

effervescence 3 zip **4** dash, fizz, life **5** froth, vigor **6** fizzle, gaiety, spirit **7** foaming **8** bubbling, buoyancy, vitality, vivacity **9** animation, fizziness **10** bubbliness, bubbling up, ebullience, enthusiasm, liveliness

effervescent 3 gay **5** fizzy, merry **6** bubbly, lively **7** fizzing, foaming **8** animated, bubbling **9** ebullient, exuberant, sparkling, vivacious **13** irrepressible

effete 5 spent **6** barren, wasted **7** sterile, worn-out **8** decadent, depraved **9** enervated, exhausted **10** degenerate, unprolific **12** unproductive

efficacious 9 effective, effectual, efficient

efficacy 6 impact **10** efficiency **13** effectiveness

efficiency 5 skill **6** energy **8** efficacy, facility **9** apartment **10** competence **11** proficiency **13** effectiveness

efficient 3 apt **7** capable **8** skillful **9** competent, effective, effectual **10** productive, proficient, timesaving, unwasteful, work-saving **11** crackerjack, efficacious, workmanlike **12** businesslike

effigy 4 doll **5** dummy, image **6** puppet, statue **8** likeness, straw man **9** mannequin, scarecrow **10** marionette **14** representation

effluence 6 efflux **7** outflow, outpour **8** effluent **9** discharge

effluent 5 waste **6** efflux, sewage **7** outflow **9** effluence

effluvium 4 aura, odor, ooze, reek **5** vapor **6** efflux, flatus **8** outgoing

efflux 7 outflow **8** effluent, emission **9** discharge, effluence

effort 3 try **4** toil, work **5** force, labor, pains, power **6** energy, strain, stress **7** attempt, travail, trouble **8** endeavor, exertion, industry, struggle **11** elbow grease

effortless 4 easy **6** facile, simple, smooth **8** graceful, painless **12** not difficult **13** uncomplicated

effortlessness 4 ease **8** easiness, facility **9** readiness **12** painlessness

effrontery 4 gall **5** brass, cheek, nerve **8** audacity, temerity **9** arrogance, brashness, impudence, insolence **10** brazenness **11** presumption **12** impertinence **13** shamelessness
Yiddish: 7 chutzpa **8** chutzpah

effulgence 6 dazzle **8** radiance, splendor **10** brilliance **12** resplendence

effulgent 6 bright **7** radiant **8** dazzling, splendid **9** brilliant **11** resplendent

effusive 5 gushy **6** lavish **7** copious, gushing, profuse **8** ebullient, expansive, exuberant **10** unreserved **11** extravagant, free-flowing, overflowing **12** unrestrained

eft 4 newt **5** again **6** lizard **9** afterward

egalitarian 10 democratic **11** equal-rights **14** constitutional

egalite 8 equality

Egeria
  instructed: 4 Numa **5** nymph **7** advisor

egg 3 ova, roe **4** bomb, goad, mine, oval, ovum, seed, spur **6** embryo, fellow, incite, person **7** albumen **9** instigate, stimulate

Eggar, Samantha
  born: 6 London **7** England
  roles: 12 The Collector, Walking Stick **15** Doctor Doolittle, The Lady in the Car **16** The Molly Maguires

egghead 8 highbrow **13** intellectual

Eggleston, Edward
  author of: 15 The Circuit Rider **19** The Hoosier Schoolboy **22** The Hoosier Schoolmaster

egg on 4 abet, back, goad, spur **6** exhort, incite **8** talk into **9** encourage

egg-shaped 4 oval **5** ovoid **7** oviform **10** elliptical

Egmont
  author: 12 Johann Goethe

egocentric 8 egoistic **11** egomaniacal, egotistical, on an ego trip, self-seeking, self-serving **12** narcissistic, self-absorbed, self-centered, self-involved, self-obsessed **13** self-concerned **14** megalomaniacal, stuck on oneself **18** wrapped up in oneself

egoism 6 vanity **8** self-love **10** narcissism **14** self-absorption, self-importance **16** overweening pride, self-centeredness

egoist 10 narcissist, selfish one **13** selfish person **18** self-centered person

Egoist, The
  author: 14 George Meredith

egoistic 7 selfish **12** narcissistic, self-centered

egotism 6 vanity **7** conceit **8** bragging, smugness **9** arrogance, immodesty, vainglory **10** self-praise **11** braggadocio **12** boastfulness

egotist 6 gascon **7** boaster, peacock **8** blowhard, braggart **9** swaggerer **11** braggadocio

egotistic 4 vain **10** egocentric **12** self-centered **13** self-important

egregious 5 gross **7** extreme, glaring, heinous **8** flagrant, grievous, shocking **9** monstrous, notorious **10** outrageous **11** intolerable **12** insufferable

egress 4 exit, vent **5** issue **6** escape, outlet, way out **7** leakage, outflow, seepage **8** aperture **9** departure, discharge **10** passage out, withdrawal

Egypt
  other name: 3 UAR **5** Kemet **6** Tomeri **11** The Two Lands **12** The Black Land
  capital/largest city: 5 Cairo

  others: 3 Tor **4** Edfu, Gaza, Giza, Idfu, Said, Suez **5** Altur, Aswan, Tanta **6** Boolak, Dumyat, Faiyum, Quseir, Safaga, Sallum **7** Alemein, Memphis, Raschid, Rosetta, Zagazig **8** Damietta, Hurghada, Ismailia, Mansurah **10** Alexandria
  school: 5 Cairo **7** Al-Azhar **8** American
  division: 5 Lower, Nubia, Upper
  measure: 3 apt, dra, hen, rob **4** arab, dira, draa, khet, nief, ocha, roub, theb, wudu **5** abdat, ardab, cubit, farde, fedan, keleh, kerat, kilah, sahme **6** artaba, aurure, baladi, kantar, keddah, robhah, schene **7** choryos, daribah, malouah, roubouh, toumnah **8** kassabah, kharouba **10** diramimari, diribaladi
  monetary unit: 4 fils, kees, para **5** asper, dinar, fodda, gersh, girsh, medin, pound, riyal **6** ahmadi, dirham, foddah, guinea, junayh, maidin, medine, medino **7** piaster, piastre, tallard **8** bedidlik, millieme
  weight: 3 kat, ket, oka, oke **4** dera, heml, khar, okia, rotl **5** artal, artel, deben, kerat, minae, minas, okieh, pound, ratel, uckia **6** hamlah, kantar **7** drachma, quintal
  island: 4 Roda **6** Philae **7** Shadwan **11** Elephantine
  lake: 4 Edku, Idku **5** Qarun **6** Maryut, Moeris, Nasser **7** Manzala **8** Burullus, Mareotis
  mountain: 5 Sinai, Uekia **6** Gharib **13** Shayib al-Banat
  highest point: 8 Katerina **9** Katherina
  river: 4 Bahr, Nile
  Nile branch: 7 Rosetta **8** Damietta
  sea: 3 Red **13** Mediterranean
  physical feature:
    cape: 4 Sudr **5** Banas **8** Rasbanas
    desert: 3 Tih **5** Dakla, Scete, Sinai, Skete **6** Libyan, Nubian, Sahara **7** Arabian
    gulf: 4 Suez **5** Aqaba
    isthmus: 4 Suez
    oasis: 4 Siwa **6** Dakhel, Dakhla, Kharga **7** Farafra, Khargeh **8** Bahariya **9** Bahariyeh **12** Wahel-Khargeh
    peninsula: 5 Sinai **6** Pharos
    plain: 7 Asaseff
    plateau: 3 Tih
  people: 3 Kem **4** Arab, Copt, Misr, Wafd **5** Gippy, Gyppy, Gypsy, Nilot **6** Ababda, Berber, Hyksos, Nubian, Tasian **7** Mizraim, Pharian **8** Badarian, Bisharin, Memphian
    leader: 5 Jawar, Sadat **6** Nasser **7** Mubarak, Saladin **10** King Farouk **11** Ismail Pasha, Mohammed Ali, Tawfiq Pasha
    pharaoh: 5 Khufu, Menes, Zoser **6** Khafre, Ptulol, Ramses **8** Horemheb, Menkaure **9** Akhenaten, Amenemhet, Amenhotep **10** Men-

tuhotep **11** Tutankhamen
queen: 9 Cleopatra, Nefertari, Nefertiti **10** Hatshepsut, Hetepheres
language: 6 Arabic, French **7** English
for liturgy: 6 Coptic
religion: 5 Islam **18** Coptic Christianity
ancient god: 2 Ra **3** Geb, Nut, Shu **4** Aton, Atum, Isis, Ptah, Seth **5** Horus, Thoth **6** Anubis, Hathor, Osiris, Tefnut **8** Nephthys
place:
dam: 4 Sadd, Sudd **5** Aswan **6** Assuan
mosque: 5 Rifai **9** Alabaster **11** Sultan Hasan
palace: 6 Kubbeh
pyramids: 4 Giza **5** Khufu **6** Cheops **7** Saqqara
ruins: 5 Miroe **6** Abydos, Sphinx, Thebes **7** Memphis **8** Berenice **9** Abu Simbel **13** Valley of Kings, Valley of Tombs
temple: 4 Idfu **5** Edoon, Luxor, Thoth **6** Abydos, Karnak, Osiris **7** Dendera
feature:
dynasty: 5 Saite **7** Ayyubid, Fatimid **8** Mameluke **9** Ptolemaic
long robe: 10 gallabiyea
peasant: 6 fellah **8** fellahin **9** fellaheen
sacred bird: 4 benu, ibis **5** bennu
sailboat: 7 felucca
statue: 6 Sphinx **15** Colossi of Memnon
food:
bean: 5 lotus
beer: 6 zythum
bread: 6 herisa
dish: 3 ful
drink: 4 bosa, boza **5** bozah
Egyptian
language family: 11 Afro-Asiatic **13** Hamito-Semitic
later form: 6 Coptic
Egyptian cross 4 ankh
Egyptian Mythology
deities: 6 Ennead
eight gods: 3 Heh **6** Ogdoad
goddess of evil: 7 Sekhmet
goddess of fertility: 2 Io **4** Isis
goddess of law/righteousness: 4 Maat
goddess of love/joy/music/dance: 6 Hathor
goddess of sky: 3 Nut
goddess personifying sky: 6 Hathor
god of bricks: 5 Kulla
god of creation: 4 Ptah
god of dead/Nile: 6 Osiris
god of earth: 3 Geb, Keb
god of ocean: 3 Nun **4** Nunu
god of sun: 2 Ra, Re **5** Horus
corresponds to Greek: 10 Harcorates
god of tombs/embalming: 6 Anubis
god of wisdom/magic/learning:

5 Thoth
corresponds to Greek: 6 Hermes
immortal spirit: 2 Ka
judge of dead: 6 Osiris
king of dead: 6 Osiris
king of gods: 4 Amen, Amon **5** Ammon **6** Amen Ra, Amon Ra
corresponds to Greek: 4 Zeus
corresponds to Roman: 4 Jove **7** Jupiter
personification of femininity: 5 Neith
corresponds to Greek: 6 Athena
ram god: 5 Khnum
vulture: 7 Nekhbet
Ehrlich, Paul
field: 12 bacteriology
nationality: 6 German
studied: 6 toxins **8** immunity **10** antitoxins
discovered: 9 salvarsan
coined term: 12 chemotherapy
awarded: 10 Nobel Prize
Eichmann in Jerusalem
author: 12 Hannah Arendt
eiderdown 4 puff **5** cover, quilt **8** coverlet **9** comforter **10** featherbed
Eight and a Half, 8 1/2
director: 15 Federico Fellini
cast: 10 Anouk Aimee **16** Claudia Cardinale **19** Marcello Mastroianni
Eighteen Seventy-Six, 1876
author: 9 Gore Vidal
Eijkman, Christiaan
nationality: 5 Dutch
discovered: 19 antineuritic vitamin
researched: 8 beriberi
awarded: 10 Nobel Prize
Einstein, Albert
birthplace: 3 Ulm
field: 7 physics
theory of: 10 relativity **14** uranium fission
awarded: 10 Nobel Prize
Eire see **7** Ireland
Eisenhower, Dwight David
nickname: 3 Ike
changed name from: 21 David Dwight Eisenhower
presidential rank: 12 thirty-fourth
party: 10 Republican
state represented: 2 NY
defeated: 4 (Eric) Hass, (Harry Flood) Byrd **5** (Farrell) Dobbs **6** (Darlington) Hoopes, (William Ezra) Jenner **7** (Stuart) Hamblen, (Thomas Coleman) Andrews **8** (Enoch Arden) Holtwick, (Vincent William) Hallinan **9** (Adlai Ewing) Stevenson
vice president: 5 (Richard Milhous) Nixon
cabinet:
state: 6 (Christian Archibald) Herter, (John Foster) Dulles
treasury: 8 (George Magoffin) Humphrey, (Robert Bernard) Anderson

defense: 5 (Thomas Sovereign) Gates (Jr) **6** (Charles Erwin) Wilson **7** (Neil Hesler) McElroy
attorney general: 6 (William Pierce) Rogers **8** (Herbert) Brownell (Jr)
postmaster general: 11 (Arthur Ellsworth) Summerfield
interior: 5 (Douglas) McKay **6** (Frederick Andrew) Seaton
agriculture: 6 (Ezra Taft) Benson
commerce: 5 (Sinclair) Weeks **7** (Frederick Henry) Mueller, (Lewis Lichtenstein) Strauss
labor: 6 (Martin Patrick) Durkin **8** (James Paul) Mitchell
HEW: 5 (Oveta Culp) Hobby **6** (Marion Bayard) Folsom **8** (Arthur Sherwood) Flemming
born: 9 Denison TX
died: 12 Washington DC
buried: 9 Abilene KS
education: 9 West Point **17** US Military Academy
religion: 12 Presbyterian
interest: 4 golf **6** flying **7** fishing, hunting **8** football, painting
vacation spot: 2 CA **11** Palm Springs
author: 11 Waging Peace **15** Crusade in Europe **16** Mandate for Change **27** At Ease: Stories I Tell to Friends
political career: 4 none (prior to presidency)
civilian career:
president of: 18 Columbia University
military service: 7 general **9** World War I **10** World War II **16** Army Chief of Staff
supreme commander of: 6 Allies **15** European Defense (NATO) **18** US occupation forces (Europe)
head of: 18 Joint Chiefs of Staff
notable events of lifetime/term: 4 D-Day, NATO
Acts: 11 Civil Rights
battle of the: 5 Bulge
conference: 7 Big Four **10** NATO Summit **11** Paris Summit
Cuba taken over by: 11 Fidel Castro
invasion: 8 Normandy
trial/execution of: 14 Ethel Rosenberg **15** Julius Rosenberg
USSR shot down: 9 U-Two plane
father: 10 David Jacob
mother: 3 Ida (Elizabeth Stover)
siblings: 3 Roy **4** Earl, Paul **5** Edgar **6** Arthur, Milton
wife: 5 Marie (Geneva Doud)
nickname: 5 Mamie
children: 10 Doud Dwight **15** John Sheldon Doud
ejaculate 4 howl, yell, yelp **5** shout **6** bellow, cry out **7** exclaim **10** vociferate
ejaculation 3 cry **4** howl, yell, yelp **5** shout **6** bellow, outcry, shriek, squeal

7 screech **11** exclamation **12** vociferation

eject 4 emit, oust, spew **5** evict, exile, expel, exude, spout **6** banish, bounce, deport, remove **7** cast out, kick out, spit out, turn out **8** disgorge, drive out, force out, throw out **9** discharge **10** dispossess

ejection 4 gush **5** spurt **6** ouster **7** issuing, removal **8** emission, eruption, eviction **9** dismissal, expelling, expulsion **10** banishment **11** throwing out

Ekdal, Hjalmar
   character in: 11 The Wild Duck
   author: 5 Ibsen

eke 3 add **4** also **7** augment, enlarge, stretch **8** increase, lengthen, likewise, moreover **10** in addition, supplement

elaborate 5 fancy, gaudy, showy **6** expand, flashy, garish, ornate **7** clarify, complex, elegant, labored, specify **8** involved, overdone **9** embellish, intricate **10** add details **11** complicated, painstaking **12** ostentatious **13** particularize

elaborate on 6 expand **7** amplify, develop **9** embellish **10** supplement **11** expatiate on

elaboration 11 added detail, rounding out **12** augmentation **13** amplification, embellishment

Elaine
   character in: 16 Arthurian romance
   called: 8 lily maid
   home: 7 Astolat
   lover: 8 Lancelot
   son: 7 Galahad
   father: 6 Pelles

Elais
   father: 5 Anius
   mother: 7 Dorippe
   changed things into: 3 oil

elan 4 dash, zeal **5** flair, verve, vigor **6** energy, spirit **8** vivacity **9** animation **10** enthusiasm

eland 3 elk **8** antelope **11** taurotragus

elapse 4 go by, pass **5** lapse **6** pass by, roll by, slip by **7** glide by, slide by **8** slip away **9** intervene

elastic 6 pliant, supple **7** pliable, rubbery, springy **8** flexible, tolerant, yielding **9** adaptable, recoiling, resilient **10** rebounding, responsive **11** complaisant, stretchable **12** recuperative **13** accommodating

elate 5 cheer, exalt **6** excite, lift up, please **7** animate, delight, elevate, enliven, gladden, gratify, inspire **10** exhilarate

elated 4 glad **5** happy, proud **6** joyful, joyous **7** exalted, excited, gleeful, pleased **8** animated, blissful, ecstatic, jubilant **9** overjoyed, rejoicing **10** delightful **11** exhilarated **13** in high spirits **18** flushed with success

elation 3 joy **4** glee **5** pride **7** triumph

8 gladness **9** happiness **10** excitement, exultation, jubilation **12** cheerfulness

elbow grease 4 work **5** force, labor **6** effort, energy, muscle **8** exertion, hard work **11** application

elbow in 4 push **5** force, press, shove **6** horn in **7** crowd in

El Cordobes (Manuel Benitez Perez)
   sport: 12 bullfighting

elder 4 head **5** older **6** senior **8** old-timer **9** firstborn, patriarch, presbyter **14** church official **15** church dignitary
   French: 4 aine

elder, elderberry 8 Sambucus
   varieties: 3 Box **4** Blue **5** Dwarf, Sweet **6** Ground, Poison, Yellow **8** American, European, Stinking **10** Red-berried **11** American red, European red **15** Pacific Coast red

elderly 3 old **4** aged **9** venerable **11** over the hill **13** past one's prime

Eldorado
   nickname of: 10 California

Eleanor and Franklin
   author: 11 Joseph P Lash

Eleazar
   father: 4 Dodo **5** Aaron, Elind, Mahli **6** Parosh **7** Phineas **8** Abinadab
   mother: 8 Elisheba
   brother: 5 Abihu, Nadab **7** Ithamar
   succeeded: 5 Aaron

elect 4 pick **5** adopt **6** choose, opt for, select, take up **7** embrace, espouse, fix upon, pick out **8** decide on, settle on **9** single out

election 4 poll, vote **6** choice, option, voting **7** resolve **8** decision **9** balloting, selection **10** resolution **11** alternative **13** determination

electioneer 3 run **5** stump **8** campaign **11** whistle-stop **12** beat the drums, solicit votes

elective 8 optional **9** selective, voluntary **11** not required **12** open to choice, passed by vote **13** discretionary, not obligatory

Electra
   author: 9 Euripides, Sophocles
   character: 7 Orestes, Pylades **8** Dioscuri **9** Aegisthus **12** Clytemnestra
   father: 9 Agamemnon
   mother: 12 Clytemnestra
   brother: 7 Orestes
   sister: 9 Iphigenia **12** Chrysothemis
   husband: 7 Pylades
   son: 5 Medon **9** Strophius

electric 7 dynamic, rousing **8** exalting, exciting, spirited, stirring **9** inspiring, thrilling **10** full of fire **11** galvanizing, power-driven, stimulating **12** electrifying, soul-stirring

electric battery
   invented by: 5 Volta

electricity measure 3 ohm **4** volt, watt **5** joule **6** ampere **10** horsepower

Electric Kool-Aid Acid Test, The
   author: 8 Tom Wolfe

electrify 4 daze, stir, stun **5** amaze, rouse **6** dazzle, excite, fire up, thrill **7** animate, astound, quicken, startle **8** astonish, surprise **9** fascinate, galvanize, stimulate **18** take one's breath away

electrifying 8 dazzling, shocking, stunning **10** astounding, stupefying **11** astonishing

electromagnet
   invented by: 8 Sturgeon

Electryon
   king of: 7 Mycenae
   father: 7 Perseus
   mother: 9 Andromeda
   brother: 6 Mestor **9** Sthenelus
   wife: 5 Anaxo
   son: 9 Licymnius
   daughter: 7 Alcmene
   grandson: 8 Hercules

eleemosynary 10 altruistic, beneficent, benevolent, charitable **13** philanthropic **15** non-profitmaking

elegance 5 class, grace, taste **6** purity **7** balance **8** delicacy, grandeur, richness, symmetry **10** refinement **12** gracefulness **13** exquisiteness, luxuriousness, sumptuousness

elegant 4 fine, rich **5** grand **6** classy, dapper, lovely, ornate, polite, urbane **7** classic, courtly, genteel, refined, stylish **8** artistic, charming, debonair, delicate, graceful, gracious, handsome, polished, tasteful, well-bred **9** beautiful, dignified, exquisite, luxurious, sumptuous **10** attractive, cultivated **11** fashionable, symmetrical **16** wellproportioned

elegiac 3 sad **8** funereal, mournful **10** melancholy

elegy 7 requiem, sad poem **11** funeral song **14** melancholy poem **16** lament for the dead **17** poem of lamentation, song of lamentation **22** melancholy piece of music

Elegy Written in a Country Churchyard
   author: 10 Thomas Gray

Elektra *see* **7** Electra

element, elements 3 air **4** fire **5** earth, water **6** basics, member, milieu **7** essence, factors, origins **8** original **9** basic part, basic unit, component, rudiments **10** basic ideas, ingredient, principles, simple body **11** constituent, environment, foundations, native state, subdivision **13** building block, component part, natural medium **14** natural habitat

elemental 5 basal, basic **10** elementary **11** fundamental, rudimentary

elementary 4 easy **5** basal, basic,

crude, first, plain **6** simple **7** primary **8** original **9** elemental, primitive **11** fundamental, rudimentary, undeveloped **13** uncomplicated

elephant
group of: **4** herd
types: **5** Asian **7** African
features: **5** trunk, tusks
famous: **5** Babar, Dumbo
elephant boy: **4** Sabu **6** mahout
extinct: **7** mammoth **8** mastodon
produce: **5** ivory

elephantine 4 huge **7** immense, mammoth, titanic **8** colossal, enormous, gigantic **9** ponderous **10** gargantuan, tremendous **14** Brobdingnagian

Elephant Man, The
director: **10** David Lynch
cast: **8** John Hurt **11** John Gielgud, Wendy Hiller **12** Anne Bancroft **14** Anthony Hopkins

Eleusinian mysteries
in memory of: **10** Persephone
in honor of: **7** Bacchus, Demeter
celebrated at: **6** Athens **7** Eleusis
founded by: **8** Eumolpus
god of: **7** Bacchus

elevate 4 lift **5** boost, cheer, elate, heave, hoist, raise **6** better, excite, lift up, move up, perk up, refine, uplift **7** advance, animate, dignify, enhance, ennoble, improve, inspire, promote, upraise **8** heighten **9** place high **10** exhilarate, raise aloft

elevated 4 high **5** lofty **6** raised **7** exalted **8** improved, uplifted **9** prominent **10** heightened

elevation 4 hill, lift, rise **5** boost **6** ascent, height **8** altitude, mountain **9** acclivity, bettering, high place, promotion **10** prominence, refinement **11** advancement, cultivation, improvement

elevator 4 cage, lift, silo, wing **5** hoist **7** granary **10** dumbwaiter
inventor: **4** Otis

elevator brake
invented by: **4** Otis

elf 4 puck **5** fairy, gnome, pixie, troll **6** goblin, sprite **7** brownie, gremlin **9** hobgoblin **10** leprechaun

elfin 3 fey, wee **4** tiny **7** pixyish **9** fairylike **10** diminutive

Elgar, Sir Edward William
born: **7** England **10** Broadheath
composer of: **8** Falstaff **9** Cockaigne, Froissart **11** Caractacus, The Kingdom **11** The Apostles **14** The Black Knight, The Light of Life **16** Enigma Variations **19** Pomp and Circumstance, The Banner of St George, The Dream of Gerontius **30** Scenes from the Bavarian Highlands

Eli
son: **6** Hophni **7** Phineas
home: **6** Shiloh **10** high priest
teacher of: **6** Samuel

Eli, Eli, Lama sabachthani
means: **31** My God My God why hast thou forsaken me?

Elia *see* **11** Lamb, Charles

elicit 5 cause, educe, evoke, exact, fetch, wrest **6** derive, extort **7** draw out, extract **9** call forth, draw forth **10** bring forth **12** bring to light

elide 4 omit, slur **5** annul **6** delete **7** neglect **8** slur over, suppress **9** eliminate, strikeout **10** abbreviate

Eliezar
father: **5** Moses
mother: **8** Zipporah
brother: **7** Gershom

eligible 6 proper **7** fitting **8** suitable **9** desirable, qualified **10** acceptable, applicable, authorized, worthwhile **11** appropriate

Elihu
brother: **5** David
friend: **3** Job **6** Bildad, Zophar **7** Eliphaz

Elijah 7 prophet
opposed: **4** Ahab, Baal **7** Jezebel
successor: **6** Elisha

Elimelech
wife: **5** Naomi

eliminate 4 drop, omit, oust **5** eject, erase, exile, expel **6** banish, cut out, delete, except, reject, remove, rub out **7** abolish, cast out, dismiss, exclude, weed out **8** get rid of, leave out, stamp out, throw out **9** eradicate **10** annihilate, do away with **11** exterminate

Eliot, George
real name: **13** Mary Anne Evans
author of: **6** Romola **8** Adam Bede **11** Middlemarch, Silas Marner **17** The Mill on the Floss

Eliot, John
author of: **12** Bay Psalm Book

Eliot, T S
author of: **9** East Coker, Gerontion, Hollow Men **11** Burnt Norton, Dry Salvages **12** Ash Wednesday, Four Quartets, The Waste Land **13** Little Gidding, The Sacred Wood **16** The Family Reunion **20** Murder in the Cathedral **27** Sweeney Among the Nightingales **28** The Love Song of J Alfred Prufrock
inspiration for: **4** Cats

Eliphaz
father: **4** Adah, Esau
friend: **3** Job **5** Elihu **6** Bildad, Zophar

Elisabeth *see* **9** Elizabeth

Elisha 7 prophet
home: **11** Abelmeholah
succeeded: **6** Elijah

elite 3 top **4** best **5** cream **6** choice, flower **7** bigwigs, society, the pick, wealthy **8** big shots, notables **9** haut monde **10** blue bloods, personages,

select body, upper class **11** aristocracy, celebrities, high society **14** creme-de-la-creme

elixir 6 potion, remedy **7** essence, extract, panacea, spirits **8** tincture **11** concentrate **17** alcoholic solution

Eliza
character in: **14** Uncle Tom's Cabin
author: **5** Stowe

Elizabeth
husband: **9** Zacharias, Zechariah
son: **14** John the Baptist

Elizabeth I
queen of: **7** England
father: **10** Henry Tudor **14** Henry the Eighth
mother: **10** Anne Boleyn
sister: **4** Mary **10** Bloody Mary
brother: **14** Edward the Sixth
advisor: **5** Cecil **8** Burghley **10** Walsingham
suitor: **5** Essex **6** Dudley **9** Leicester
victory over: **13** Spanish Armada

Elizabeth II
father: **14** George the Sixth
mother: **9** Elizabeth
husband: **17** Philip Mountbatten
son: **6** Andrew, Edward **7** Charles
daughter: **4** Anne
daughter-in-law: **5** Diana, Sarah (Fergie)

Elizabeth the Queen
author: **15** Maxwell Anderson

elk
group of: **4** gang

Ellas *see* **6** Greece

Ellerbee, Linda 6 writer **10** newscaster
book: **11** And So It Goes

Ellice Islands *see* **6** Tuvalu

Ellington, Duke
real name: **22** Edward Kennedy Ellington
born: **12** Washington DC
composer of: **10** Mood Indigo **14** Creole Love Call, Creole Rhapsody, Hot and Bothered **17** Concerto for Cootie **18** Black and Tan Fantasy

Elliot family
characters in: **10** Persuasion
member: **4** Anne **7** William **9** Elizabeth, Sir Walter
author: **6** Austen

Ellison, Harlan
author of: **7** Paingod **10** Spider Kiss **13** A Boy and His Dog **16** Deathbird Stories **19** Approaching Oblivion **20** Alone Against Tomorrow

Ellison, Ralph
author of: **12** Invisible Man

elm 5 Ulmus
varieties: **3** red **4** bush, cork, rock, vase, wych **5** cedar, Dutch, dwarf, globe, wahoo, water, white **6** Exeter, horned, Jersey, moline, Scotch, willow, winged **7** Belgian, Chinese, Cor-

nish, English, Holland **8** American, fern-leaf, Guernsey, Japanese, Siberian, slippery, tabletop, wheatley **9** September **10** camperdown, Chichester, Huntingdon, smooth-leaf **11** small-leaved **13** European white

Elmer Gantry
   author: 13 Sinclair Lewis
   director: 13 Richard Brooks
   cast: 10 Dean Jagger **11** Jean Simmons **12** Shirley Jones **13** Arthur Kennedy, Burt Lancaster
   Oscar for: 5 actor (Lancaster) **17** supporting actress (Jones)

elocution 6 speech **7** diction, oratory **10** intonation **11** enunciation **12** articulation **13** pronunciation **14** public speaking

Elohim 3 God

Eloisa to Abelard
   author: 13 Alexander Pope

Elon 11 Hebrew judge

elongate 6 extend **7** draw out, prolong **8** lengthen, protract **10** stretch out

elongated 4 long **8** drawn out, extended **9** prolonged **10** attenuated, lengthened, protracted **12** stretched out

eloquence 5 force, grace **7** fluency, oratory **8** rhetoric **9** elocution, speakwell, vividness **10** expression **12** silver tongue
   god of: 4 Ogma **6** Ogmios **7** Mercury

eloquent 5 vivid **6** moving, poetic **8** emphatic, forceful, spirited, stirring, striking **10** articulate, passionate, persuasive **11** impassioned

El Salvador
   other name: 9 Cuscatlan
   capital/largest city: 11 San Salvador
   others: 6 Cutuco, Izalco **7** Corinto, Metapan **8** Acajutla, Libertad, Santa Ana, Usulutan **9** San Miguel, Sonsonate **10** San Vicente, Santa Tecla **11** Union-Cutuco **12** Chalatenango
   school: 15 Jose Simeon Canas **16** Alberto Masferrer
   measure: 4 vara **5** cafiz, cahiz **6** fanega **7** batella, botella, cantara, manzana
   monetary unit: 4 peso **5** colon **7** centavo
   weight: 3 bag **4** caja **5** libra
   lake: 5 Guiha, Guija **8** Ilopango **10** Coatepeque
   mountain: 6 Izalco
   highest point: 8 Santa Ana
   river: 5 Jiboa, Lempa, Lopaz **6** Torola **7** de la Paz **9** Goasoaran **17** Grande de San Miguel
   sea: 7 Pacific
   physical feature:
     bay: 10 Jiquilisco
     coast: 6 Balsam
     gulf: 7 Fonseca
     point: 7 Amapala **8** Remedios
     valley: 7 Hamacas

   people: 5 Lenca, Pipil **6** Indian, Mangue **7** mestizo, Spanish **9** Matagalpa
     artist: 8 Salarrue **10** Mejia Vides
     author: 8 Salarrue **14** Antonio Gavidia
     conqueror: 8 Alvarado
     leader: 6 Osorio **8** Jose Arce **13** Matias Delgado **15** Manuel Rodriguez **17** Hernandez Martinez
     philosopher/journalist: 9 Masferrer
   language: 7 Spanish
   religion: 13 Roman Catholic
   place:
     ruins: 7 Tazumal
   feature:
     blouse: 9 volcanena
     dance: 7 pasillo **15** los historiantes
     drum: 8 huehuetl
     estate: 5 finca
     musical instrument: 7 caramba
   food:
     bread: 10 quesadilla
     cheese pancake: 6 pupusa

Elscheimer, Adam
   born: 7 Germany **15** Frankfurt am Main
   artwork: 17 Tobias and the Angel **21** The Stoning of St Stephen **24** Rest on the Flight into Egypt

else 3 and, too **4** also, more **5** if not, other **7** besides, instead **9** different, otherwise **10** additional, contrarily, in addition

elsewhere 4 away **6** except **7** absence, not here

Elsinore
   castle in: 6 Hamlet **7** Denmark
   author: 11 Shakespeare

Elton, Mr
   character in: 4 Emma
   author: 6 Austen

elucidate 6 detail **7** clarify, clear up, explain, expound **8** describe, spell out **9** delineate, explicate, interpret, make plain **10** illuminate, illustrate **11** comment upon **14** throw light upon

elucidation 7 account **10** commentary **11** description, explanation, explication **13** clarification **14** interpretation **15** exemplification

elude 4 shun **5** avoid, dodge, evade **6** escape, slip by **10** circumvent, fight shy of **11** get away from, keep clear of

eluding 7 dodging, ducking, evading, evasion **8** avoiding **9** avoidance **12** escaping from, sidestepping **13** circumventing **15** getting away from

Elul 16 sixth Hebrew month

elusive 4 foxy, wily **6** crafty, shifty, tricky **7** evasive **8** baffling, puzzling, slippery **11** hard to catch, hard to grasp

elusory 4 wily **6** shifty **7** devious, dodging, elusive, evasive, hedging **8** slippery **9** ambiguous, deceitful,

deceptive, equivocal **10** misleading **12** equivocating

Elvsted, Thea
   character in: 11 Hedda Gabler
   author: 5 Ibsen

elysian 7 sublime **8** blissful, empyreal, empyrean, ethereal, heavenly **9** celestial, unearthly **12** otherworldly, paradisiacal

Elysium
   also: 17 islands of the blest
   afterworld of the: 7 blessed

Elytis, Odysseus
   real name: 19 Odysseus Alepoudelis
   author of: 10 Seemly It Is **20** Heroic and Elegiac Song

emaciated 4 lank, lean, thin **5** gaunt **6** sickly, skinny, wasted **7** haggard, scrawny, wizened **8** skeletal, starving, underfed **10** cadaverous **14** undernourished

emanate 4 flow, rise, stem, well **5** exude, issue **6** spring **7** give off, proceed **8** come from **9** come forth, originate, send forth

emanation 6 coming **7** arising, flowing, issuing **8** effusion **9** effluence, radiation, springing **10** exhalation **11** coming forth

emancipate 4 free **7** manumit, release, set free, unchain **8** liberate, unfetter **9** unshackle **12** set at liberty

emancipation 7 freedom, liberty **10** liberation **11** manumission **12** independence

emasculate 4 geld **5** alter **6** soften, weaken **8** castrate **9** undermine **10** devitalize

Emaux et Camees
   author: 16 Theophile Gautier

Embalming
   god of: 6 Anubis

embankment 4 bank, dike, wall **5** levee

embargo 3 ban **8** shutdown, stoppage **10** impediment, inhibition, injunction, quarantine, standstill **11** prohibition, restriction **12** interdiction, proscription **16** restraint of trade

embark 5 begin, board, start **6** launch, set out **7** enplane, entrain **8** commence, go aboard **9** board ship, enter upon

embark on 5 begin, start **8** approach, commence, initiate, set about **9** enter upon, undertake

embarras de richesses 13 overabundance **21** embarrassment of riches

embarrass 4 faze **5** abash, shame, upset **6** rattle **7** agitate, chagrin, confuse, fluster, mortify, nonplus **8** distress **9** discomfit **10** discompose **13** make ill at ease **14** discountenance **17** make self-conscious

embarrassed 7 abashed **8** red-faced

9 chagrined, mortified **10** nonplussed **11** discomfited **13** self-conscious

embarrassing 7 awkward **8** confused, crushing **9** bothering **10** disturbing, mortifying, unpleasant **12** demoralizing, discomfiting **13** discomforting, disconcerting, uncomfortable

embarrassment 4 blot **5** stain **6** smirch **7** blemish, scandal, tarnish **8** disgrace **9** discredit **19** financial difficulty

embattled 8 fighting **9** embroiled, fortified **11** battle-ready, hard-pressed

embed 3 fix, set **4** bond **5** plant **6** fasten **8** ensconce **9** establish

embedded 3 set **5** fixed **6** bonded **7** engaged, planted **8** immersed, inserted **9** ensconced **11** established

embellish 4 gild **5** adorn, color **6** set off **7** dress up, enhance, fancy up, garnish, gussy up **8** beautify, decorate, ornament **9** elaborate, embroider **10** exaggerate

embellished 6 ornate **7** adorned, flowery **8** brocaded **9** decorated **10** beautified, elaborated, ornamented, rhetorical **11** embroidered

embellishment 5 frill **6** accent **7** garnish **8** furbelow, ornament, trimming **9** adornment **10** decoration, embroidery **11** elaboration **14** beautification **15** fuss and feathers

ember 3 ash **4** slag **6** cinder **7** clinker **8** live coal

embezzle 4 bilk, rook **5** cheat, filch **6** fleece **7** defraud, swindle **9** defalcate **14** misappropriate

embezzler 5 cheat, crook, thief **8** swindler

Embezzler, The
    author: **16** Louis Auchincloss

embitter 4 sour **6** rankle **7** envenom **10** make bitter **11** make cynical **13** make rancorous, make resentful **15** make pessimistic

Embla
    origin: **12** Scandinavian
    first: **5** woman
    made by: **4** gods
    made from: **4** tree

emblem 4 sign **5** badge **6** design, device, symbol **8** colophon, hallmark, insignia

emblematic 7 typical **8** symbolic **10** indicative **11** distinctive **14** characteristic, representative

embodiment 6 avatar **7** epitome, essence **14** representation **15** exemplification, personification

embody 4 fuse **5** blend, merge **6** typify **7** collect, contain, embrace, express, include, realize **8** manifest, organize **9** exemplify, personify, represent, symbolize **10** assimilate **11** consolidate, incorporate **12** substantiate

embolden 7 fortify, hearten, inspire **8** inspirit **9** encourage

emboldened 6 poised **7** assured, unfazed **9** confident, heartened, unabashed **10** courageous, encouraged, inspirited

embonpoint 9 plumpness, stoutness **15** in good condition

emboss 4 knob, knot, stud **5** adorn, chase **6** indent **7** engrave, exhaust **8** decorate

embossed 4 bold **6** raised **7** adorned, antique, knotted **8** engraved, indented **9** decorated, exhausted

embrace 3 hug **5** adopt, clasp, cover, grasp **6** accept, embody **7** contain, espouse, include, involve **8** comprise **9** encompass **10** comprehend **11** consolidate, incorporate

embroider 5 color **7** dress up **9** elaborate, embellish, fabricate **10** exaggerate **11** romanticize

embroidery 8 tapestry **9** adornment, gros point **10** crewelwork, decoration, needlework, petit point **11** imagination **12** exaggeration **13** ornamentation

embroil 4 trap **6** enmesh **7** ensnare, involve **8** entangle **10** complicate

embroiled 8 enmeshed **9** embattled, entangled **11** hard-pressed

embroilment 3 row **4** fray, tilt **5** brawl, brush, clash, melee **6** fracas, ruckus, rumpus, uproar **7** scuffle **8** conflict, disorder, struggle **9** confusion, imbroglio **10** contention **11** altercation **12** entanglement

embryo 3 bud, egg **4** germ **5** fetus, larva, ovule **6** budding, source **8** immature, rudiment **9** beginning **11** rudimentary, undeveloped

embryonic 5 rough **6** unborn **7** nascent **8** immature, inchoate **9** beginning, imperfect, incipient **10** incomplete, unfinished **11** rudimentary, undeveloped

emend 4 edit **6** change, revise **7** correct, improve, rectify

emendation 8 revision **10** alteration, correction **11** improvement

emerald
    species: **5** beryl
    source: **4** Muzo **5** Egypt, India **6** Chivor **8** Colombia, Rhodesia, Zimbabwe **11** South Africa, Soviet Union **13** Ural Mountains
    color: **5** green

Emerald City
    setting in: **13** The Wizard of Oz
    author: **4** Baum

Emerald Isle *see* **7** Ireland

emerge 3 run **4** dawn, emit, flow, gush, loom, pour, rise **5** arise, issue **6** appear, come up, crop up, escape, stream, turn up **7** develop, surface **9** come forth, discharge **11** come to

light **12** come into view **13** become visible **14** become apparent, become manifest

emergence 4 dawn **7** dawning **10** appearance **11** development **13** coming to light, manifestation **15** materialization

emergency 5 pinch **6** crisis **7** urgency **8** exigency **11** contingency, predicament **16** unforeseen danger

Emergency
    character: **8** (Dr) Joe Early, (Paramedic) John Gage **9** (Paramedic) Roy DeSoto **11** (Nurse) Dixie McCall **13** (Dr) Kelly Brackett
    cast: **10** Bobby Troup, Kevin Tighe **11** Julie London **12** Robert Fuller **16** Randolph Mantooth

Emerson, Ralph Waldo
    nickname: **13** Sage of Concord
    author of: **4** Fate **6** Brahma, Nature **10** Friendship, The Rhodora **12** Compensation, Self-Reliance **14** The Concord Hymn **18** The American Scholar
    philosophy: **17** Transcendentalism

emeute 4 riot

emigrant 6 wanderer, wayfarer **10** expatriate

Emigrants, The
    author: **10** Johan Bojer

emigrate 4 move, quit **5** leave **6** depart, remove **7** migrate

emigration 5 exile **6** exodus **12** expatriation

emigre 2 DP **5** alien, exile **7** evacuee, refugee **8** defector, emigrant, expellee, fugitive **9** immigrant **10** expatriate **15** displaced person **16** political refugee

Emile
    author: **19** Jean Jacques Rousseau
    treatise on: **9** education

Emilia
    character in: **7** Othello
    husband: **4** Iago
    author: **11** Shakespeare

eminence 4 fame, hill, note, peak, rise **5** bluff, cliff, glory, knoll, ridge **6** height, repute, summit, upland **7** hillock, hummock **8** mountain, standing **9** celebrity, elevation, greatness, high place, high point **10** excellence, importance, notability, prominence, promontory, reputation **11** distinction, preeminence **12** elevated rank, high position, public esteem **15** conspicuousness

eminence grise 15 unofficial power
    literally: **12** gray eminence

eminent 3 top **5** grand, great, noted **6** famous, signal, utmost **7** exalted, notable, unusual **8** elevated, esteemed, glorious, imposing, laureate, renowned **9** important, memorable, paramount, prominent, well-known **10** celebrated, noteworthy, preeminent, remarkable **11** high-ranking, illustrious, outstanding **13** distinguished, extraordinary

emir 4 amir, Arab, Turk **5** chief, emeer, ruler **6** leader, prince **9** chieftain, commander, dignitary

emissary 5 agent, envoy **6** deputy, herald, legate **7** courier **8** delegate **9** go-between, messenger **10** ambassador **14** representative

emission 5 fumes, smoke, waste **8** ejection, emitting, impurity, issuance, voidance **9** discharge, emanation, excretion, expulsion, extrusion, pollutant **10** sending out **11** throwing out **12** transmission

emit 4 beam, give, shed, vent **5** expel, issue **7** cast out, excrete, secrete, send out **8** dispatch, throw out, transmit **9** discharge, give forth, pour forth

Emma
   author: **10** Jane Austen
   character: **7** Mr Elton **9** Miss Bates, Mrs Weston **11** Jane Fairfax **12** Harriet Smith, Robert Martin **13** Emma Woodhouse **14** Frank Churchill **15** George Knightley

Emmanuel 7 Messiah **11** Jesus Christ
   means: **9** God with us

emollient 3 oil **4** balm **5** balmy, cream, salve **6** lotion **7** calming, easeful, healing, unguent **8** allaying, lenitive, ointment, relaxing, soothing **9** assuasive, lubricant, relieving **10** palliative **11** alleviative, restorative

emolument 3 fee, pay **4** gain, wage **6** income, profit, salary **7** benefit, stipend **9** advantage **10** honorarium **12** compensation, remuneration

emotion 4 fear, hate, heat, love, zeal **5** anger, ardor, pride **6** fervor, sorrow, warmth **7** concern, despair, passion, sadness **8** jealousy **9** agitation, happiness, sentiment, vehemence **10** excitement **12** satisfaction

emotional 4 warm **5** fiery **6** ardent, moving **7** fervent, zealous **8** stirring, touching **9** excitable, impetuous, thrilling, wrought-up **10** high-strung, hysterical, passionate, responsive, vulnerable **11** impassioned, sentimental, tear-jerking **12** enthusiastic, heartwarming, heart-rending, soul-stirring **13** demonstrative, temperamental **14** hypersensitive

emotionalism 8 hysteria **9** gushiness, hysterics, melodrama, theatrics **11** mawkishness **13** melodramatics, show of emotion **14** sentimentality **17** demonstrativeness

emotionless 6 stolid **7** unmoved **9** apathetic, impassive, unfeeling **11** passionless, unemotional

emperor, empress 4 czar, king, shah **5** queen, ruler **6** caesar, kaiser, mikado, sultan **7** czarina, monarch, sultana **9** sovereign **14** dowager empress

Emperor Jones, The
   author: **12** Eugene O'Neill
   character: **4** Jeff **8** Smithers **11** Brutus Jones

Emperor's New Clothes, The
   author: **21** Hans Christian Andersen

emphasis 6 accent, stress, weight **7** feature **10** focal point **12** accentuation, underscoring

emphasize 6 accent, stress **7** dwell on, feature, iterate, point up **9** press home, punctuate, underline **10** accentuate, underscore

emphatic 4 flat **6** marked, strong **7** certain, decided, express, telling **8** absolute, decisive, definite, distinct, forceful, striking, vigorous **9** assertive, insistent, momentous **10** pronounced, undeniable, unwavering, unyielding **11** categorical, conspicuous, significant, unequivocal, unqualified **12** unmistakable

empire 4 rule **5** realm **6** domain **8** dominion, imperium **11** sovereignty **12** commonwealth

Empire State
   nickname of: **7** New York

Empire State of the South
   nickname of: **7** Georgia

Empire Strikes Back, The
   director: **13** Irvin Kershner
   cast: **10** Kenny Baker, Mark Hamill (Luke Skywalker) **11** David Prowse, Peter Mayhew **12** Alec Guinness, Carrie Fisher (Princess Leia), Harrison Ford (Han Solo) **14** Anthony Daniels (C3P0) **16** Billy Dee Williams (Lando Calrissian)
   sequel to: **8** Star Wars
   sequel: **15** Return of the Jedi

empirical 9 firsthand, practical, pragmatic **12** experiential, experimental

employ 3 use **4** hire **5** apply **6** devote, engage, occupy, retain, take on **7** service, utilize **8** exercise, keep busy, put to use **9** make use of **10** commission, employment **12** retainership

employee 6 member, worker **8** hireling **9** job holder, underling **10** wage earner

employer 4 boss, firm **6** outfit **7** company **8** business **10** proprietor **12** organization **13** establishment

employment 3 job, use **4** line, task, work **5** chore, field, trade, using **6** employ **7** calling, pursuit, service **8** business, exercise, exertion, vocation **9** employing **10** engagement, occupation, profession **11** application, utilization **13** preoccupation

emporium 5 store **6** bazaar, market **9** warehouse **10** large store **12** general store **15** department store

empower 4 vest **5** allow, endow **6** enable, invest, permit **7** license **8** delegate, sanction **9** authorize **10** commission

empress 5 queen, ruler **7** czarina, monarch, sultana, tsarina **9** sovereign

emprise 7 venture **9** adventure **10** enterprise **11** undertaking

emptied 6 used up **7** drained, vacated **8** consumed, depleted, finished **9** evacuated, exhausted

emptiness 4 void **6** vacuum **7** vacancy **8** bareness **10** barrenness, desolation, hollowness

empty 4 bare, dump, flow, idle, void **5** banal, drain, inane **6** futile, hollow, vacant **7** aimless, debouch, insipid, pour out, shallow, trivial, vacuous **8** evacuate **9** discharge, frivolous, worthless **10** unoccupied **11** meaningless, purposeless, unfulfilled, uninhabited **13** insignificant

empty space 3 gap **4** void **5** blank **6** cavity, lacuna, vacuum **7** vacancy

empyrean 7 elysian, sublime **8** blissful, heavenly **9** celestial **12** paradisiacal

emu
   also: **4** emeu
   form: **4** bird
   habitat: **9** Australia
   characteristic: **9** nonflying, three toed

emulate 3 ape **4** copy **5** mimic, rival **6** follow **7** imitate

emulative 5 model **9** exemplary

enable 3 aid **5** allow **6** assist, permit **7** benefit, empower, qualify, support **8** make able **10** capacitate, facilitate **15** make possible for

enact 4 pass **6** decree, ratify **7** approve **8** proclaim, sanction **9** authorize, institute, legislate **11** pass into law **12** vote to accept

enactment 3 law **4** bill **5** canon, edict, ukase **6** decree **7** statute **9** ordinance, prescript **11** legislation **12** proclamation, ratification

enamel 4 coat **5** paint **7** coating **10** nail polish **12** glossy finish, tooth coating

enamor 5 charm **6** allure, attach, draw to, excite **7** bewitch, enchant **8** enthrall, entrance **9** captivate, enrapture, fascinate, infatuate **12** take a fancy to

enamored 6 in love **7** amorous **8** lovesick **10** infatuated

en arriere 8 backward

en avant 6 onward **7** forward

en bloc 8 as a whole

encage 3 pen **4** cage **5** pen in **6** coop up, lock up, shut in **7** confine **8** restrain **11** incarcerate

encamp 4 camp **7** bivouac **9** set up camp **10** pitch a tent

encampment 4 camp **5** tents **7** bivouac **8** tent city

encase 4 wrap **5** cover **6** enfold, enwrap **7** enclose, envelop, sheathe

enceinte 8 pregnant

Enceladus
form: **5** giant
hit by: **5** stone
stone flung by: **6** Athena
location: **6** Sicily
buried under: **9** Mount Etna

enchain 7 enslave, shackle **8** enthrall **11** put in chains **13** hold in bondage

enchant 3 hex **5** charm **7** bewitch, delight **8** enthrall, entrance **9** captivate, enrapture, fascinate, hypnotize, mesmerize, transport **14** cast a spell over **16** place under a spell

enchanted 7 charmed, pleased **9** bewitched, delighted, entranced **10** captivated, enraptured, enthralled, spellbound **11** under a spell

enchanting 8 charming, pleasant **9** agreeable, wonderful **10** bewitching, delightful, entrancing **11** captivating, enthralling, fascinating, hypnotizing **12** spellbinding **15** casting a spell on **17** casting a spell over

enchantment 5 spell **6** allure, appeal **9** magnetism **10** attraction **11** captivation, fascination

enchantress 4 vamp **5** siren, witch **7** charmer, vampire **9** sorceress, temptress **10** seductress **11** femme fatale

Enchiridion
author: **11** St Augustine

encircle 4 gird, ring, wall **5** fence, hem in **6** circle, girdle **7** enclose, wreathe **8** surround **9** encompass **12** circumscribe

enclose, inclose 4 ring **6** circle, girdle, insert, wall in **7** close in, fence in, include **8** encircle, surround **9** encompass, send along **12** circumscribe

enclosed area 4 quad **5** court, patio **6** atrium **9** courtyard **10** quadrangle

enclosure 3 sty **4** cage, coop, jail, wall **5** fence, hedge, stall **6** corral, kennel, pigsty **7** paddock, wrapper **8** envelope, stockade **9** cartridge, inclosure **10** receptacle

encomium 5 kudos, paean **6** eulogy **7** plaudit, tribute **8** citation **9** laudation, panegyric **11** acclamation

encompass 4 hold, ring **5** cover, hem in **6** circle, embody, girdle, take in, wall in **7** contain, embrace, enclose, fence in, include, involve, touch on **8** comprise, encircle, surround **11** incorporate **12** circumscribe

encounter 4 bout, face, meet **5** brush, clash, fight **6** affray, battle, combat, endure, fracas, suffer **7** run into, sustain, undergo **8** come upon, confront, meet with, skirmish **9** clash with **10** chance upon, engagement, experience **11** grapple with **12** do battle with, meet and fight, skirmish with **13** confrontation **14** contend against, engage in combat, hostile meeting **18** come face to face with

Encounters with the Archdruid
author: **10** John McPhee

encourage 3 aid **4** help, spur, sway **5** boost, cheer, egg on, favor, impel, rally **6** assist, exhort, foster, induce, prompt **7** advance, forward, further, hearten, inspire, promote **8** embolden, inspirit, reassure **10** give hope to

encouragement 4 lift **5** boost **6** praise **7** backing, support **11** approbation, encouraging, reassurance **12** shot in the arm **13** reinforcement

encroach 6 invade **7** impinge, intrude, overrun, violate **8** infringe, overstep, trespass **9** break into, interfere **10** transgress **11** make inroads

encumber 3 tax **4** lade, load **6** burden, hinder, impede, saddle **8** handicap, load down, obstruct, slow down **9** weigh down **13** inconvenience

encumbrance 4 load, onus **6** burden **9** hindrance **10** impediment **11** obstruction **13** inconvenience

Encyclopedia
author: **9** D'Alembert **12** Denis Diderot

encyclopedic 5 broad **7** erudite **9** scholarly, universal **10** exhaustive **11** wide-ranging **13** comprehensive **15** all-encompassing

end 3 aim **4** edge, goal, halt, kill, ruin, stop **5** cease, close, death, issue, limit, scrap **6** border, demise, design, effect, ending, finale, finish, object, result, run out, upshot, windup **7** destroy, outcome, purpose, remnant **8** boundary, conclude, fragment, leave off, leftover, terminus **9** cessation, eradicate, extremity, finish off, intention, objective, terminate **10** annihilate, completion, conclusion, denouement, expiration, extinction, extinguish, put an end to, settlement **11** consequence, culmination, destruction, exterminate, fulfillment, termination **12** annihilation, consummation, draw to a close **13** extermination **19** bring down the curtain

endanger 4 risk **6** expose, hazard **7** imperil **8** threaten **10** compromise, jeopardize **11** put in danger

endear 8 make dear **10** ingratiate **11** make beloved

endearment 7 pet name **9** sweet talk **10** loving word **12** sweet nothing **13** fond utterance

endeavor 3 aim, job, try **4** seek, work **5** essay, labor **6** aspire, career, effort, strive, work at **7** attempt **8** exertion, interest, striving, struggle, vocation **9** take pains, undertake **10** do one's best, enterprise, occupation **11** undertaking **12** make an effort **13** preoccupation

ended 4 done, over **6** ceased, closed, halted, runout **7** expired, stopped, wound up **8** finished, over with,

resulted **9** completed, concluded, destroyed **10** terminated **11** annihilated **12** discontinued, exterminated

Enderby
author: **14** Anthony Burgess

end from which
Latin: **12** terminus a quo

ending 3 end **5** close **6** finale, finish, windup **9** cessation **10** completion, conclusion, expiration **11** culmination, termination **12** consummation

ending point
Latin: **14** terminus ad quem

Ending Up
author: **12** Kingsley Amis

endless 7 eternal **8** constant, infinite, unbroken, unending **9** boundless, continual, perpetual, unlimited **10** continuous, persistent, without end **11** everlasting, measureless, never-ending **12** interminable **13** uninterrupted

endlessly 7 forever **10** constantly **11** ceaselessly, continually, perpetually **12** continuously
Latin: **11** ad infinitum

endocrine system
component: **5** ovary **6** testes, thymus **7** adrenal, thyroid **9** pituitary **11** parathyroid

endocuticle
consists of: **6** chitin

end of the century
French: **11** fin de siecle

End of the Road, The
author: **9** John Barth

end of the world 8 doomsday **10** Armageddon **11** Judgment Day **13** Day of Judgment **15** the Last Judgment

End of the World News, The
author: **14** Anthony Burgess

endorse, indorse 2 OK **4** back, sign **6** affirm, ratify, second **7** approve, certify, support **8** advocate, champion, sanction, validate, vouch for **9** authorize, recommend **11** countersign, stand behind, subscribe to **14** lend one's name to

endorsement 2 OK **7** support **8** approval **9** signature **10** acceptance **12** commendation, ratification **14** seal of approval **16** official sanction

endow 4 will **5** award, bless, equip, favor, grace, grant, leave **6** accord, bestow, confer, invest, supply **7** furnish, provide **8** bequeath, settle on

endowed 6 graced **7** blessed, favored **8** bestowed, enriched, provided **10** bequeathed

endowment 4 gift **5** award, flair, grant **6** legacy, talent **7** ability, bequest, faculty **8** aptitude, donation **9** attribute **10** capability **11** benefaction, natural gift

end to which
Latin: **14** terminus ad quem

endue 5 dress, endow, equip, indue,

put on **6** bestow, clothe, outfit, supply **7** furnish

endurable 8 bearable **9** tolerable **11** sustainable

endurance 7 stamina **8** strength, tenacity **9** fortitude, hardihood, stability **10** durability, permanence, resolution **11** durableness, persistence **12** immutability, perseverance, staying power **13** tenaciousness **14** changelessness **16** stick-to-itiveness

endure 4 bear, last, live **5** brave, brook, stand **6** live on, remain, suffer **7** persist, prevail, sustain, undergo, weather **8** continue, cope with, tolerate **9** go through, withstand **10** experience **11** bear up under, countenance

enduring 7 abiding, durable, eternal, lasting **8** constant, unending **9** immutable, permanent, steadfast **10** changeless, continuing, unchanging **11** everlasting, long-lasting **12** indissoluble

Endymion
    author: 9 John Keats
    form: 5 youth
    father: 8 Aethlios
    mother: 6 Calyce
    loved by: 4 Moon **6** Selene
    son: 5 Epeus, Paeon **7** Aetolus
    number of daughters: 5 fifty
    granddaughter: 7 Hyrmina

enemy 3 foe **5** rival **7** nemesis **8** armed foe, attacker, opponent **9** adversary, assailant, detractor **10** antagonist, competitor

Enemy of the People, An
    author: 11 Henrik Ibsen

energetic 5 alert, brisk, peppy, zippy **6** active, lively, robust **7** dynamic **8** animated, forceful, restless, spirited, vigorous **9** go-getting **11** hardworking, high-powered, industrious, quick-witted **12** enthusiastic

energize 7 animate, enliven, quicken **8** vitalize **9** galvanize, stimulate **10** invigorate, strengthen

energy 2 go **3** pep, vim, zip **4** elan, zeal, zest **5** drive, force, power, verve, vigor **6** hustle **8** dynamism, vitality, vivacity **9** animation **10** enterprise, liveliness

enervate 3 fag **4** bush, tire **5** weary **6** tucker, weaken **7** deplete, disable, exhaust, fatigue, wash out **8** enfeeble **9** prostrate **10** debilitate, devitalize **13** sap one's energy

enervated 5 spent **6** effete, wasted **7** languid, worn-out **8** fatigued, listless, sluggish, unmanned, unnerved, weakened **9** enfeebled, exhausted, lethargic, washed out **11** debilitated, devitalized, emasculated

enervation 7 fatigue **9** tiredness, weariness **10** exhaustion

en famille 11 in the family

Enfants Terribles, Les
    author: 11 Jean Cocteau

enfant terrible 16 indiscreet person **17** incorrigible child **19** irresponsible person

enfeeble 3 sap **6** impair, weaken **8** enervate **10** debilitate

enfin 7 finally **8** in the end **12** in conclusion

enfold 4 veil, wrap **5** cloak, cover **6** encase, enwrap, shroud **7** blanket, contain, embrace, enclose, envelop, sheathe **8** surround

enforce 5 apply, exact **6** defend, impose **7** execute, support **8** carry out, insist on **9** implement **10** administer

enforcement 5 force **6** duress **7** defense, support **8** coercion, pressure **9** execution **10** compulsion, constraint, imposition, obligation **11** carrying out **13** necessitation, strengthening **14** implementation

engage 4 hire **6** absorb, combat, employ, occupy, pledge, retain, secure, take on **7** betroth, engross, involve, partake, promise, war with **8** affiance, embark on, set about, takepart **9** enter into, fight with, undertake **10** commission **11** busy oneself, participate **12** give battle to **15** take into service

engaged 5 hired, in use **6** active, took on **7** partook, pledged, secured **8** absorbed, employed, involved, occupied, promised, retained, took part **9** affianced, betrothed, engrossed, undertook **10** embarked on **11** entered into, particpated **15** took into service

engagement 3 gig, job **4** bout, date, duty, fray, post **5** banns, berth, brush, fight, troth **6** action, battle, billet, combat **7** contest, meeting, scuffle **8** conflict, position, skirmish **9** betrothal, encounter, situation **10** affiancing, commitment, employment, obligation **11** appointment, arrangement

engage pleasantly 5 amuse, charm **6** divert, please **7** beguile, delight **8** enthrall, interest **9** entertain

engaging 7 likable, lovable, winning, winsome **8** charming, fetching, pleasing **9** agreeable, appealing, disarming **10** attractive, enchanting **11** captivating **12** ingratiating

engender 5 beget, breed, cause **7** produce **8** generate, occasion **10** bring about, give rise to **11** precipitate

engine
    inventor:
        of compression ignition: 7 Daimler
        of electric ignition: 4 Benz
        of gas (compound): 10 Eickemeyer
        of gasoline: 7 Brayton, Daimler
        of piston steam: 4 Watt **8** Newcomen

engineer 5 pilot **6** driver, hogger **7** builder, hoghead, planner **8** maneu-

ver, motorman, operator **10** accomplish

England
    other name: 6 Albion **7** Britain **9** Britannia
    capital/largest city: 6 London
    others: 3 Ely **4** Bath, Deal, Hull, Ryde, Ware, York **5** Blyth, Brent, Derby, Dover, Erith, Flint, Leeds, Ripon, Truro, Wigan **6** Barnet, Bolton, Bootle, Camden, Durham, Ealing, Exeter, Henley, Jarrow, Leyton, Oldham, Oxford, Yeovil **7** Bristol, Bromley, Burnley, Chelsea, Croydon, Enfield, Grimsby, Halifax, Hornsey, Ipswich, Lambeth, Newport, Norwich, Preston, Salford, **8** Bradford, Brighton, Cornwall, Coventry, Dewsbury, Hastings, Plymouth **9** Cambridge, Greenwich, Liverpool, Newcastle, Sheffield **10** Birmingham, Manchester **15** Stratford-on-Avon
    school: 4 Eton **5** Leeds, Rugby **6** Harrow, London, Oxford **9** Cambridge, Sandhurst **23** London School of Economics
    division: 4 Avon, Kent **5** Devon, Essex, **6** Dorset, Durham, Surrey, Sussex **7** Norfolk, Suffolk **8** Cheshire, Cornwall, Somerset **9** Hampshire, Wiltshire, Yorkshire **10** Derbyshire, East Sussex, Humberside, Lancashire, Merseyside, Shropshire, West Sussex **11** Oxfordshire, Tyne and Wear **12** Bedfordshire, Lincolnshire, Warwickshire, West Midlands **13** Hertfordshire, Staffordshire, West Yorkshire **14** Cambridgeshire, Leicestershire, Northumberland, North Yorkshire, South Yorkshire **15** Buckinghamshire, Gloucestershire, Nottinghamshire **16** Northamptonshire **20** Hereford and Worcester
    head of state: 4 king **5** queen **7** monarch
    measure: 3 cut, lea, pin, rod, ton, tun, vat **4** acre, bind, butt, comb, coom, foot, gill, goad, hand, hank, heer, hide, inch, last, line, mile, nail, pace, palm, peck, pint, pipe, pole, pool, rood, rope, sack, seam, span, trug, typp, wist, yard, yoke **5** bodge, chain, coomb, cubit, digit, float, floor, fluid, hutch, jugum, minim, ounce, perch, point, prime, quart, skein, stack, truss **6** barrel, bovate, bushel, cranne, fathom, firkin, gallon, hobbet, hobbit, league, manent, oxgang, pottle, runlet, square, strike, sulung, thread, tierce **7** auchlet, furlong, kenning, quarter, rundlet, seamile, spindle, tertian, virgate **8** carucate, chaldron, hogshead, landyard, puncheon, quadrant, standard
    monetary unit: 3 ora **4** rial **5** ackey, crown, groat, noble, pence, penny, pound, sprat, unite **6** bawbee, florin, guinea, seskin **7** angelet, hapenny **8**

farthing, shilling, sixpence, tuppence

weight: 3 bag, kip, tod, ton **4** keel, last, mast, maun **5** barge, fagot, grain, pound, score, stone, truss **6** bushel, cental, fangot, fother, fotmal, pocket **7** quarter, sarpler

island: 3 Man **4** Holy **5** Farne, Lundy, Wight **6** Coquet, Mersea, Scilly, Thanet, Tresco, Walney **7** Bardsey, Channel, Hayling, Ireland, Sheppey **8** Anglesea, Anglesey, Foulness, Holyhead

lake: 8 Grasmere **9** Ennerdale, Ullswater, Wastwater **10** Buttermere, Windermere **12** Derwentwater **13** Coniston Water

mountain: 5 Black **7** Pennine, Snowdon **8** Cambrian, Cumbrian

   hill: 6 Formby, Lizard, Mendip **7** Brendon, Cemmaes, Trevose

highest point: 11 Scafell Pike

river: 3 Cam, Dee, Don, Esk, Exe, Lea, Nen, Ure, Wye **4** Aire, Avon, Eden, Lune, Nene, Nidd, Ouse, Penk, Tame, Tees, Till, Tyne, Wear, Yare **5** Anker, Colne, Deben, Stour, Swale, Tamar, Tawar, Trent, Tweed **6** Humber, Kennet, Mersey, Rother, Severn, Thames, Wharfe, Witham **7** Derwent, Parrett, Waveney, Welland **8** Torridge **9** Yorkshire **12** Wensum Ribble

sea: 5 Irish, North **6** Celtic **8** Atlantic

physical feature:

   bay: 3 Tor **4** Lyme, Wash **5** Start **6** Mounts **7** Bigbury **8** Bideford, Cardigan, Falmouth, Tremadoc, Weymouth

   chalk cliffs: 5 Dover

   channel: 6 Solent **7** Bristol, English **8** Spithead

   firth: 6 Solway

   forest: 5 Arden **6** Exmoor **8** Dartmoor, Sherwood

   point: 4 Naze **5** Lynas, Morte, Sales **6** Dodman, Lizard, Prawle **8** Hartland, Landsend

   region: 5 Weald **8** Midlands **10** West Riding **11** North Riding **12** Lake District

   valley: 4 Coom, Eden, Tees, Tyne **5** Combe, Coomb **6** Coquet

people: 4 Celt, Pict **5** Jutes, Norse, Saxon **6** Angles, Briton, Norman, Viking

   artist: 6 Romney, Turner **7** Hogarth **8** Reynolds, Rossetti **9** Constable **12** Gainsborough

   author: 3 Kyd **4** Bede, Hume, Pope, Shaw **5** Auden, Bacon, Blake, Burke, Byron, Defoe, Donne, Eliot, Hardy, Joyce, Keats, Scott, Swift, Waugh, Wilde, Woolf **6** Austen, Bronte, Bunyan, Conrad, Dryden, Gibbon, Jonson, Milton, Newton, Ruskin, Sterne, Thomas **7** Boswell, Chaucer, Dickens, Kipling, Marlowe, Shelley, Spenser,

Walpole **8** Browning, Fielding, Lawrence, Sheridan, Smollett, Tennyson, Trollope **9** Churchill, Coleridge, Stevenson, Thackeray **10** Galsworthy, Richardson, Thomas More, Wordsworth **11** Shakespeare

   king: 3 Hal **4** Cnut, John, Lear **5** Henry, James **6** Alfred, Arthur, Canute, Edmund, Edward, Egbert, George, Harold **7** Charles, Richard, Stephen, William **9** Cymbeline **18** Richard Coeur de Lion **19** Richard the Lionheart

   leader: 4 Eden, Grey, Lamb, Peel, Pitt **5** Heath, Major **6** Attlee, Wilson **7** Baldwin, Balfour, Canning, Fitzroy, Spencer, Stanley, Walpole **8** Disraeli, Stanhope, Thatcher **9** Cavendish, Churchill, Gladstone, Grenville, MacDonald, Macmillan **10** Palmerston, Wellington **11** Chamberlain, Douglas-Home, Lloyd George

   queen: 3 Mab **4** Anne, Bess, Jane, Mary **7** Eleanor **8** Boadicea, Victoria **9** Catherine, Charlotte, Elizabeth, Guinivere **10** Bloody Mary **11** Jane Seymour

language: 7 English

religion: 6 Jewish **8** Anglican **9** Methodist, Unitarian **13** Roman Catholic **15** Church of England

place:

   bridge: 5 Tower **6** London **11** Westminster

   cathedral: 4 York **6** Exeter **7** St Pauls **8** St Albans **9** Salisbury **10** Canterbury, Winchester **16** Westminster Abbey

   clock: 6 Big Ben

   fortification: 12 Hadrian's Wall

   museum: 4 Tate **7** British **9** Ashmolean **17** Madame Tussauds Wax

   palace: 7 St James, Windsor **10** Buckingham **12** Hampton Court

   racetrack: 5 Ascot

   ruins: 10 Stonehenge

   street: 4 Grub **5** Fleet **12** Threadneedle **16** Piccadilly Circus

   tower: 6 London

feature:

   dance: 6 morris

food:

   bacon: 6 gammon, rasher **7** streaky

   beer: 5 grout, stout

   cookie: 7 biscuit

   dessert: 6 trifle **11** plum pudding

   dish: 12 fish and chips **14** Cornish pasties **15** bubble and squeak **16** Yorkshire pudding

   drink: 3 ale, tea **6** squash

English, Julian

   character in: 20 Appointment in Samarra

   author: 5 O'Hara

English Mail-Coach, The

   author: 15 Thomas DeQuincey

engrave 3 cut **4** etch **5** carve, stamp **6** chisel **7** decorate, stipple

engraving 3 cut, die **5** print, stamp **7** etching, gravure **9** woodblock **11** copperplate, lithography **12** photogravure

engross 4 hold **6** absorb, arrest, engage, occupy, take up **7** immerse, involve **9** preoccupy

engrossed 4 busy, deep **6** intent **7** engaged **8** absorbed, immersed, involved, occupied **11** preoccupied

engrossing 8 engaging, exciting **9** absorbing, arresting, thrilling **10** intriguing **11** captivating, fascinating, interesting

engrossment 9 immersion **10** absorption, intentness **11** involvement **13** concentration, preoccupation

engulf 4 bury **5** swamp **6** deluge **7** envelop, immerse, overrun **8** inundate, submerge **9** swallow up

enhance 4 lift **5** add to, boost, raise **7** augment, elevate, magnify **8** heighten, redouble **9** embellish, intensify **10** complement

enhancement 11 heightening, improvement **15** intensification

Enid

   character in: 12 The Mabinogion **15** Idylls of the King **16** Arthurian romance

   husband: 7 Geraint

   known for: 9 constancy

   author: 8 Tennyson

enigma 6 puzzle, riddle, secret **7** mystery **8** question **9** conundrum **10** perplexity

enigmatic, enigmatical 7 cryptic, elusive **8** baffling, puzzling **9** ambiguous, equivocal, secretive **10** mysterious, perplexing **11** inscrutable, paradoxical **12** unfathomable **14** indecipherable

Eniwetok 5 atoll

   location: 15 Marshall Islands

   known for: 5 A bomb, H bomb (tests)

enjoin 3 ask, ban, bar, beg, bid **4** urge, warn **6** advise, charge, direct, forbid **7** command, counsel, entreat **8** admonish, call upon, instruct, prohibit, restrain, restrict **9** interdict, proscribe

enjoy 3 own **4** have, like **5** eat up, fancy, savor **6** admire, relish **7** possess **9** delight in, rejoice in **10** appreciate **11** think well of **13** be blessed with, be pleased with, get a kick out of **14** take pleasure in **16** have the benefit of

enjoyable 8 pleasant, pleasing **9** agreeable, fun-filled, rewarding **10** delightful, gratifying, satisfying **11** pleasurable

enjoyment 3 fun, joy **4** zest **5** gusto, right **6** relish **7** benefit, delight **8** blessing, exercise, good time, pleasure

9 advantage, amusement, diversion, happiness, privilege **10** possession, recreation **11** prerogative **12** satisfaction **13** entertainment, gratification

enlarge 4 grow **5** add to, swell, widen **6** expand, extend **7** amplify, augment, broaden, develop, expound, inflate, magnify **8** elongate, increase, lengthen, multiply **9** discourse, elaborate, expatiate

enlarged 7 swollen, widened **8** expanded, extended, inflated **9** amplified, broadened, distended, elongated, magnified

enlargement 6 growth **8** addition, increase, swelling, widening **9** expansion, extension, inflation **10** broadening, elongation **11** development, elaboration, expatiation, lengthening **12** augmentation **13** amplification, magnification **14** multiplication

enlighten 5 edify **6** advise, inform, wise up **7** apprise, clarify, educate **8** civilize, instruct **9** make aware **10** illuminate **12** sophisticate

enlightenment 8 learning **9** erudition, knowledge **11** edification, instruction
French: 15 Eclaircissement
German: 10 Aufklarung

enlist 4 join **6** engage, enroll, join up, obtain, secure, sign up **7** procure, recruit **8** register **9** volunteer **19** gain the assistance of

enlistment 9 signing up **10** admittance, enrollment, recruiting

enliven 4 fire **5** pep up, renew **6** excite, vivify, wake up **7** animate, cheer up, quicken **8** brighten, vitalize **10** make lively, rejuvenate

enlivened 7 revived **8** animated, vivified **9** refreshed **11** invigorated

en masse 7 in a body **8** as a group, as a whole, in a group, together **11** all together

enmesh 4 trap **5** catch, snare, snarl **6** tangle **7** embroil, ensnare, entwine, involve **8** entangle

enmity 6 animus, hatred, malice, rancor, strife **7** ill will **8** acrimony, bad blood **9** animosity, antipathy, hostility **10** bitterness

Ennead 7 dieties
origin: 8 Egyptian
number: 4 nine

ennoble 5 raise **6** refine **7** dignify, elevate

ennui 6 apathy, tedium **7** boredom, languor **9** lassitude, weariness **12** indifference, listlessness
Latin: 12 taedium vitae

Enoch
father: 4 Cain **5** Jared
son: 10 Methuselah
grandfather: 4 Adam

Enoch Arden
author: 18 Alfred Lord Tennyson

character: 8 Annie Lee **9** Philip Ray **10** Miriam Lane

enology *see* **8** oenology

enormity 8 baseness, evilness, hugeness, vastness, vileness, villainy **9** depravity, immensity, largeness, malignity **10** wickedness **11** heinousness, viciousness **12** enormousness **13** atrociousness, monstrousness, offensiveness **14** outrageousness

enormous 4 huge, vast **7** immense, mammoth, massive, titanic **8** colossal, gigantic **10** gargantuan, prodigious, tremendous **11** elephantine **14** Brobdingnagian

enormousness 8 enormity, hugeness, vastness **9** amplitude, immensity, largeness **11** massiveness

Enormous Room, The
author: 10 e e cummings

Enos
father: 4 Seth
grandfather: 4 Adam

enough 5 ample, amply **6** plenty **7** copious **8** abundant, adequate, passably **9** tolerably **10** abundantly, adequately, competence, plentitude, reasonably, sufficient **11** ample supply, full measure, sufficiency **12** sufficiently **14** satisfactorily

enounce 8 set forth **9** enunciate **10** articulate

en passant 8 by the way **9** chess term, in passing

enrage 5 anger **6** madden **7** incense, inflame **9** aggravate, infuriate **11** make furious **13** make one see red **14** throw into a rage **17** make one's blood boil

enraged 3 mad **5** angry, irate **7** angered, furious, violent **8** incensed, inflamed, maddened, provoked **9** irritated **10** aggravated, infuriated **11** exasperated

en rapport 8 in accord **9** congenial **10** in sympathy **11** in agreement

enrapture 5 charm **6** thrill **7** beguile, bewitch, delight, enchant **8** enthrall, entrance, hold rapt **9** captivate, transport

enraptured 4 rapt **8** beatific, blissful, ecstatic **9** delighted, enchanted **10** enthralled **11** transported

enravel 5 snare, snarl, twist **6** enmesh, tangle **7** ensnare, ensnarl, entwine **8** entangle **10** intertwine

enrich 5 adorn, endow **6** refine **7** elevate, enhance, fortify, improve, upgrade **8** make rich **9** embellish **10** ameliorate **11** make wealthy **15** feather one's nest

enroll 4 join **5** admit, enter **6** accept, engage, enlist, join up, sign up, take on **7** recruit **8** register

enrollment 6 roster **9** enrolling, signing up **10** admittance, enlistment, recruiting **12** registration **13** matriculation

en route 8 on the way **9** in transit, on the road

ensconce 4 bury, hide, seat **5** lodge **6** settle **7** conceal, secrete, shelter **9** establish

ensemble 5 getup **6** attire, outfit, troupe **7** company, costume **8** assembly, entirety, grouping, totality **9** aggregate

ensign 4 flag, jack, mark, sign **5** badge **6** banner, colors, emblem, pennon, symbol **7** pennant **8** insignia, standard

enslave 6 addict, subdue **7** capture, control, enchain, shackle **8** dominate, enthrall **9** indenture, subjugate **13** hold in bondage, put in shackles

enslavement 4 yoke **6** chains, thrall **7** bondage, serfdom, slavery **9** captivity, servitude, thralldom, vassalage **11** subjugation

ensnare 4 trap **5** catch **6** enmesh, entrap, tangle **7** enravel **8** entangle

Ensor, James
born: 6 Ostend **7** Belgium
artwork: 8 Intrigue **19** Bourgeois Living Room **25** Entry of Christ into Brussels **26** The Tribulations of St Anthony **29** Self-Portrait Surrounded by Masks

enstatite
source: 5 Burma, Mogok

ensue 6 derive, follow, result **7** succeed **10** come to pass **13** come afterward

ensuing 8 eventual **9** following, resulting **10** consequent, succeeding

en suite 6 in a set **9** in a series **12** in succession

ensure, insure 5 guard **6** assure, clinch, secure **7** protect, warrant **8** be sure of, make safe, make sure **9** guarantee, safeguard **13** make certain of

entail 6 demand **7** call for, include, involve, require **8** occasion **11** incorporate, necessitate

entangle 4 trap **5** catch, mix up, snare, snarl **6** enmesh, foul up, muddle, tangle **7** confuse, embroil, enravel, ensnare, involve **8** encumber **9** embarrass, implicate **10** complicate, compromise, intertwine

entanglement 5 mixup, snarl **6** foul-up, muddle **7** problem **9** confusion, imbroglio **10** difficulty, entrapment **11** embroilment **12** complication

entente 4 pact **6** accord, treaty **7** compact **8** alliance, covenant **9** agreement, consensus, unanimity **10** consortium **12** conciliation **13** rapprochement, understanding **14** likemindedness

entente cordiale 21 friendly understanding

enter 4 go in, join, list, post **6** arrive,

come in, record **8** enlist in, enroll in, inscribe, pass into, set out on, trespass **9** penetrate, sign up for **10** embark upon, take part in

enterprise 4 push, task, zeal **5** drive, vigor **6** daring, effort, energy, spirit **7** attempt, program, project, venture **8** ambition, boldness, campaign, endeavor, industry **9** alertness, eagerness, ingenuity, operation **10** enthusiasm, initiative **11** undertaking, willingness **14** aggressiveness **15** adventurousness

enterprising 4 bold, keen **5** alert, eager **6** active **7** earnest, zealous **8** intrepid **9** ambitious, energetic, inventive, wide-awake **10** aggressive **11** hardworking, industrious, self-reliant, up-and-coming, venturesome **12** enthusiastic

entertain 4 heed **5** admit, amuse, charm **6** absorb, divert, foster, harbor, please, ponder, regale **7** beguile, delight, dwell on, engross, imagine, nurture, support **8** consider, enthrall, interest, muse over, play host **10** cogitate on, give a party, have guests, keep in mind, think about **11** contemplate **13** keep open house

entertainer 4 host **5** actor **6** amuser, artist, dancer, singer **7** hostess **8** magician, musician **9** performer

entertaining 3 fun **7** amusing, hosting **8** charming, pleasing **9** beguiling, diverting, enjoyable **10** delightful, hostessing **11** playing host **12** having guests **14** having people in

entertainment 3 fun **4** play **7** novelty, pastime **8** good time, pleasure **9** amusement, diversion, enjoyment **10** recreation **11** distraction **12** satisfaction
French: 14 divertissement

enter upon 5 begin **6** assume **9** undertake

enthrall, enthral 5 charm, rivet **6** seduce, thrill **7** beguile, bewitch, enchant, enslave **8** entrance, intrigue, transfix **9** captivate, enrapture, fascinate, hypnotize, overpower, spellbind, subjugate, transport **13** keep in bondage **14** put into slavery

enthralled 4 rapt **8** beguiled, enslaved **9** bewitched, enchanted, entranced, in bondage, intrigued **10** captivated, enraptured, fascinated, hypnotized, spellbound, subjugated

enthusiasm 4 love, rage, zeal, zest **5** ardor, craze, hobby, mania **6** fervor, relish **7** elation, passion **8** devotion, interest, keenness **9** diversion, eagerness **10** excitement, exuberance, hobbyhorse **11** distraction, pet activity **12** anticipation

enthusiast 3 bug, fan, nut **4** buff **5** freak **6** addict **7** devotee, fanatic **10** aficionado

enthusiastic 5 eager **6** ardent, fervid **7** fervent, zealous **8** spirited **9** exuberant **10** passionate, unstinting **11** unqualified **12** wholehearted

entice 4 coax, lure **5** tempt **6** allure, incite, induce, seduce **7** attract, beguile, wheedle **8** inveigle, persuade

enticement 4 bait, draw, lure **6** allure **9** seduction, siren song **10** attraction, temptation

entire 4 full **5** gross, total, whole **6** in toto, intact **8** absolute, complete, thorough, unbroken **9** undamaged **10** unimpaired **12** all-inclusive

entirely 5 fully **6** wholly **7** totally, utterly **10** absolutely, altogether, completely, thoroughly **12** unreservedly **13** unqualifiedly
French: 9 tout a fait

entitle 3 dub, tag **4** call, name **5** allow, label, style, title **6** enable, permit **7** qualify **9** authorize, designate **12** make eligible

entity 4 body **5** being, thing **6** matter, object **7** article **8** creature, presence, quantity **9** real thing, structure, substance **10** individual

entomb 4 bury **5** inter **7** confine

entombment 6 burial **9** interment **10** inhumation

Entommeures, Frere Jean des
  character in: 22 Gargantua and Pantagruel
  author: 8 Rabelais

entourage 5 court, staff, suite, train **6** convoy, escort **7** cortege, retinue **9** followers, following **10** associates, attendants, companions

entrails 4 guts **5** offal **6** bowels **7** innards, insides, viscera **10** intestines

entrance 4 door, gate **5** charm, entry, way in **6** access, entree, portal **7** beguile, bewitch, delight, doorway, gateway, gladden, ingress, opening **8** approach, coming in, enthrall **9** captivate, enrapture, fascinate, hypnotize, mesmerize, spellbind, transport **10** admittance, appearance, passageway **12** introduction

entranced 4 rapt **7** charmed **8** beguiled **9** entralled, rapturous **10** enraptured, fascinated, spellbound **11** carried away, transported

entranceway 5 entry, foyer, way in **7** doorway, ingress **8** entryway **9** front hall, vestibule

entrancing 6 lovely **8** adorable, charming **9** appealing, beautiful, beguiling, disarming **10** bewitching, delightful **11** captivating, fascinating **12** irresistible

entrap 3 bag, nab **4** hook, land, nail **5** catch, snare, tempt **6** allure, collar, drag in, draw in, entice, rope in, seduce, suck in **7** beguile, capture, ensnare **8** inveigle

entreat 3 beg **6** adjure, enjoin, exhort **7** beseech, implore, request **8** appeal to, petition **9** importune, plead with **10** supplicate

entreaty 4 plea **6** appeal, prayer **8** petition **11** importunity **12** supplication

entree 4 pull **5** entry **6** access **7** ingress **8** entrance, main dish **9** admission **10** acceptance, admittance, main course

entremets 8 side dish

entrench, intrench 3 fix, set **4** root **5** dig in, embed, plant **6** anchor **7** implant, ingrain, install, solidly **8** ensconce **12** establish

entrenched leaders 11 ruling class **12** powers that be **13** Establishment **14** power structure

entre nous 9 between us, privately **14** confidentially **15** between you and me **16** between me and thee, between ourselves **18** in strict confidence

entrepot 5 depot **9** warehouse **18** distribution center

entrepreneur 7 manager **8** director **9** organizer **10** impresario **11** coordinator

entrust, intrust 5 trust **6** assign, commit **7** consign **8** delegate, hand over, turn over **9** authorize **10** charge with

entrustment 10 delegation **13** authorization, commissioning

entry 3 way **4** door, gate, item, memo, note **5** foyer, way in **6** access, entree, minute, portal, record **7** account, doorway, gateway, ingress, jotting **8** approach, entrance **9** admission, vestibule **10** admittance, appearance, competitor, contestant, memorandum, passageway **11** entranceway **12** entrance hall, introduction, registration

entwine, intwine 4 fold, lace, wind **5** braid, plait, twine, twist, weave **9** interlace **10** interweave

enumerable 6 finite **7** limited **11** denumerable

enumerate 3 add **4** cite, list **5** add up, count, sum up, tally, total **6** detail, number, relate **7** count up, recount, specify, tick off **8** numerate, spell out, tabulate

enumeration 4 list **5** tally **7** account, listing **8** adding up, addition, citation, tallying, totaling **9** checklist, detailing, numbering, reckoning, summing up **10** counting up, recounting, tabulation, ticking off **11** spelling out

enunciate 5 sound, speak, voice **8** vocalize **10** articulate **15** utter distinctly **16** pronounce clearly

enunciation 6 accent, speech **7** diction **9** utterance **12** articulation **13** pronunciation

envelop 4 hide, veil, wrap **5** cloak, cover **6** encase, enfold, engulf, enwrap, shroud, swathe **7** blanket, conceal, contain, enclose, obscure, sheathe, swaddle **8** encircle, surround **9** encompass

envelope 5 cover **6** jacket **8** covering, wrapping

envenom 4 sour **6** rankle **8** embitter **13** make poisonous

enviable 5 lucky **8** salutary **9** agreeable, covetable, desirable, excellent, fortunate **10** beneficial **12** advantageous

envious 5 green **7** jealous **8** covetous, grudging, spiteful **9** jaundiced, resentful

enviousness 4 envy **8** jealousy **10** resentment **12** covetousness **13** resentfulness **19** the green-eyed monster

environment 5 locale, medium, milieu **7** climate, element, habitat, setting **8** ambience **9** situation **10** atmosphere, background **12** surroundings **13** circumstances
French: 11 mise en scene

environs 6 exurbs **7** suburbs **8** vicinity **9** outskirts, precincts **11** outer limits **12** outlying area **15** surrounding area

envisage 5 fancy **7** dream of, dream up, imagine, picture **8** conceive, envision **9** conjure up, visualize **11** contemplate **13** conceptualize **14** have a picture of **16** picture to oneself

envoy 5 agent **6** deputy, legate **7** attache, courier **8** delegate, emissary, minister **9** messenger, middleman **10** ambassador **12** intermediary **14** representative

envy 5 greed, spite **6** resent **8** begrudge, grudging, jealousy **10** resentment **11** be jealous of, enviousness, malevolence **12** covetousness **13** resentfulness **16** be spiteful toward **19** the green-eyed monster

enwrap 6 absorb, engage, enrobe **7** engross, envelop **9** preoccupy

Enyo
  origin: 5 Greek
  goddess of: 3 war
  companion of: 4 Ares
  member of: 6 Graeae, Graiae
  corresponds to: 7 Bellona

enzyme 7 protein **8** molecule **13** macromolecule
  function: 8 catalyst
  acts on: 9 substrate
  kind: 5 amino, malic **6** lactic, lipase, pepsin, rennin, urease **7** amylase, glucose, trypsin **8** aldehyde, glutamic, glycolic, lipozyme, thrombin, xanthine **9** cellulase **12** ribonuclease

eon 3 age, era **8** eternity, long time **9** many years **15** one billion years

Eos
  origin: 5 Greek
  goddess of: 4 dawn
  father: 8 Hyperion

  mother: 5 Theia
  brother: 6 Helios
  sister: 6 Selene
  husband: 8 Astraeus, Tithonus **10** Eosophorus
  son: 6 Memnon **8** Phaethon, Zephyrus **10** Eosophorus
  horse: 6 Lampos **8** Phaethon
  mother of: 5 stars, winds
  corresponds to: 6 Aurore **7** Hermera

Epha, Ephah, Epheh 15 Biblical measure

ephemeral 5 brief **7** passing **8** fleeting, flitting, fugitive, temporal **9** fugacious, momentary, temporary, transient **10** evanescent, fly-by-night, inconstant, nondurable, short-lived, transitory, unenduring **11** impermanent **21** here today gone tomorrow

ephemeroptera
  class: 8 hexapoda
  phylum: 10 arthropoda
  group: 6 mayfly

Ephraim
  father: 6 Joseph
  mother: 7 Asenath
  brother: 8 Manasseh
  blessed by: 5 Jacob
  descendant of: 10 Ephraimite

Ephraimi 16 Greek unical codex

epic 4 saga **5** drama, great, noble **6** fabled, heroic **7** exalted, storied **8** fabulous, imposing, majestic **9** legendary **10** heroic poem, superhuman **14** larger than life

Epicaste *see* **7** Jocasta

epicure 7 glutton, gourmet **8** gourmand, hedonist, sybarite **9** bon vivant **10** gastronome

epicurean 4 rich **6** lavish **7** gourmet, sensual **8** hedonist, Lucullan, sybarite **9** libertine, luxurious, sybaritic **10** hedonistic, sensualist, voluptuary, voluptuous **11** intemperate **13** self-indulgent

epidemic 4 rife **6** plague **7** rampant, scourge **8** catching, outbreak, pandemic **9** contagion, infection, pervasive, prevalent **10** infectious, pestilence, prevailing **11** far-reaching

Epigoni
  sons of: 18 Seven against Thebes

epigram 4 quip **5** adage, maxim **6** bon mot **8** aphorism, apothegm **9** witticism

epilogue 4 coda **5** rider **7** codicil **8** addendum **9** afterword **10** supplement **12** final section

Epione
  husband: 9 Asclepius

episcopal 8 churchly, diocesan, pastoral **12** ecclesiastic(al)

episode 4 part **5** event, scene **6** affair, period **7** chapter, passage, section **8** incident **9** adventure, happening,

milestone **10** experience, occurrence **11** installment

Episode of Sparrows, An
  author: 11 Rumer Godden

episodic 7 halting **8** rambling **9** segmented, wandering **10** digressive, discursive, meandering **13** discontinuous

epistle 6 letter **7** message, missive **10** encyclical

Epistle to a Godson and Other Poems
  author: 7 W H Auden

Epistle to Dr Arbuthnot
  author: 13 Alexander Pope

Epithalamion
  author: 13 Edmund Spenser

epithet 5 curse **6** insult **8** nickname **9** blasphemy, expletive, obscenity, sobriquet **10** ascription **11** appellation, designation

Epithet
  of Aphrodite: 6 Acraea, Scotia **7** Doritis, Erycina, Limenia **8** Melaenis, Nymphaea, Pandemos **9** Migonitis **11** Aphrogeneia, Apostrophia
  of Apollo: 6 Loxias **7** Acesius, Agraeus, Agyieus, Carneus, Phyteus, Spodius **8** Grynaeus **9** Parnopius, Smintheus **10** Alexicacus, Archegetes, Boedromius, Delphinius **11** Argyrotoxus, Epibaterius **12** Platanistius
  of Ares: 8 Enyalius **14** Gynaecothoenas
  of Argus: 8 Panoptes
  of Artemis: 6 Orthia **7** Eurippa, Laphria, Limnaea, Pyronia **8** Aeginaea, Agrotera, Calliste, Caryatis, Daphnaea **9** Hemerasia, Lygodesma **10** Polymastus **11** Leucophryne
  of Asclepius: 8 Cotyleus
  of Athena: 4 Alea **5** Meter, Xenia **6** Ergane, Itonia, Polias **7** Agoraea, Cissaea, Paeonia, Pronaus, Pronoea **8** Anemotis, Poliates, Zosteria **9** Oxyderces, Parthenia, Poliuchus, Promachus **10** Axiopoenus, Chalinitis, Cyparissia **11** Promachorma
  of Cybele: 6 Antaea
  of Demeter: 5 Chloe, Lusia, Mysia **6** Antaea, Erinys, Stiria **7** Chamyne, Thesmia **8** Stiritis **9** Anesidora, Thermasia **11** Carpophorus **12** Thesmophorus
  of Dionysus: 6 Lyaeus **7** Bromius, Cresius **8** Thyoneus, Triambus **9** Pyrigenes **11** Dithyrambus, Mitrephorus
  of Hera: 6 Anthea, Bunaea **8** Henioche **9** Prodromia
  of Hercules: 7 Charops **8** Buphagus **9** Ipoctonus
  of Hermes: 6 Dolius **8** Agoraeus **9** Spelaites **10** Criophorus **11** Argiphontes **12** Argeiphontes, Psychopompus
  of Icelus: 8 Phobetor

of Juno: 6 Moneta **7** Curitis, Pronuba, Sospita

of Jupiter: 5 Ultor **7** Elicius, Pluvius

of Mopsus: 9 Ampycides

of Nestor: 7 Nelides

of Odin: 7 Alfader, Alfadir

of Odysseus: 10 Laertiades

of Persephone: 11 Carpophorus

of Pheriphetes: 9 Corynetes

of Poseidon: 11 Ennosigaeus, Hippocurius **12** Prosclystius

of Rhea: 6 Antaea

of Sinis: 12 Pityocamptes

of Vulcan: 8 Mulciber

of Zeus: 5 Areus, Soter **6** Aqueus, Areius, Nemean, Philus **7** Alastor, Apemius, Ctesius, Lycaeus, Polieus, Stenius **8** Agoraeus, Aphesius, Apomyius, Cappotas, Cosmetas, Dodonian, Herceius, Leucaeus, Tropaean **9** Aegiochus, Chthonius, Coccygius, Hecaleius, Lecheates, Mechaneus **10** Cataebates, Catharsius, Coryphaeus, Homagyrius, Laphystius, Meilichius **11** Eleutherius **12** Panhellenius

epitome 4 peak **5** ideal, model **6** height **7** essence, summary **9** summation **10** embodiment **12** typification **14** representation **15** exemplification, sum and substance

e pluribus unum 12 out of many one
motto of: 12 United States

epoch 3 age, era **4** time **6** period **8** interval

epochal 7 weighty **8** historic **9** important, momentous **11** significant **13** consequential

Eppie
character in: 11 Silas Marner
author: 5 Eliot

Eppie
nickname of: 10 Ann Landers

Epstein, Sir Jacob
born: 9 New York NY
artwork: 4 Adam **7** Genesis **8** Ecce Homo, Einstein **9** Rock Drill **10** Visitation **11** Night and Day, Paul Robeson **12** Behold the Man, Joseph Conrad **13** Haile Selassie **14** Consummatum Est **19** Social Consciousness **20** Monument to Oscar Wilde, St Michael and his (the) Devil

equable 4 calm, even **5** sunny **6** placid, serene, stable, steady **7** regular, uniform **8** constant, pleasant, tranquil, unvaried **9** agreeable, easygoing, unruffled **10** consistent, dependable, unchanging **11** goodnatured, predictable, unexcitable, unflappable **12** even-tempered **13** imperturbable

equably
Latin: 9 pari passu

equal 4 even, like, peer **5** match **7** matched, the same, uniform **8** balanced, be even to, equalize, jibe with, of a piece, parallel **9** agree with, identical, tally with **10** accord with, comparable, equate with, equivalent, square with, tantamount **11** balance with, be the same as, correlative, counterpart, symmetrical **12** commensurate, correspond to, proportional **13** be identical to, corresponding, evenly matched, one and the same

equality 6 parity **7** balance, justice **8** evenness, fair play, fairness, sameness **10** similarity, uniformity **11** equivalency **12** impartiality **13** fair treatment **14** correspondence
French: 7 egalite

Equality
author: 13 Edward Bellamy

Equality State
nickname of: 7 Wyoming

equalization 7 balance **9** stability **11** equilibrium **14** counterbalance
German: 9 Ausgleich

equalize 7 balance **9** make equal **11** make uniform **13** compensate for

equal to 3 fit **4** able, up to **5** adept **7** capable **8** adequate, master of **9** competent, qualified

equanimity 4 cool **5** poise **6** aplomb **8** calmness, coolness **9** composure, sangfroid **10** steadiness **11** self-control, tranquility **12** tranquillity **14** presence of mind, self-possession **16** imperturbability

equate 5 liken, match **7** average, balance, compare, even out **8** equalize, equal out **9** think of as **10** consider as **14** be commensurate, be equivalent to **17** be proportionate to

Equatorial
language family: 16 Andean-Equatorial
group: 8 Arawakan **11** Tupi-Guarani

Equatorial Guinea
other name: 13 Spanish Guinea
capital/largest city: 6 Malabo
others: 4 Bata **9** Rio Benito
division: 5 Bioko **7** Rio Muni
monetary unit: 6 ekuele, peseta **7** centimo
island: 5 Bioko **6** Pagalu **7** Corisco **11** Chico Elobey **12** Grande Elobey
mountain: 5 Mitra
highest point: 11 Santa Isabel
river: 5 Mbini
physical feature:
  gulf: 6 Guinea
people: 4 Bubi, Fang **5** Benge, Combe **6** Bujeba **10** Fernandino
  explorer: 2 Po
  leader: 12 Nguema Biyogo
language: 4 Bubi, Fang **7** Spanish **13** pidgin English
religion: 7 animism **10** Protestant **13** Roman Catholic

equilibrium 7 balance **8** symmetry **9** equipoise, stability **14** sense of balance

equip 3 rig **5** stock **6** fit out, outfit, supply **7** appoint, furnish, prepare, provide **8** accoutre **9** caparison, provision

equipage 4 gear **6** outfit **8** carriage **9** equipment **13** accoutrements

equipment 4 gear **5** stuff **6** tackle **8** equipage, material, materiel, supplies **9** apparatus **11** furnishings, outfittings **13** accoutrements, paraphernalia

equipoise 7 balance **9** stability **11** equilibrium

equitable 3 due **4** fair, just **6** proper **8** unbiased **9** impartial **10** evenhanded, reasonable **12** unprejudiced

equity 4 cash **5** value **6** assets, profit **7** justice **8** fairness, justness **9** cash value **10** investment **12** fair dealings, impartiality **14** evenhandedness, fairmindedness, reasonableness

equivalency 6 parity **7** balance **8** equality **10** coequality, uniformity **14** correspondence

equivalent 4 even, peer **5** equal, match **8** of a piece, parallel **9** the same as **10** comparable, tantamount **11** correlative, counterpart, equal amount

equivocal 4 hazy **5** vague **7** dubious **8** doubtful **9** ambiguous, enigmatic, imprecise, qualified, uncertain, undecided **10** ambivalent, indefinite, suspicious **11** nonspecific **12** undetermined **13** indeterminate

equivocate 5 dodge, evade, fudge, hedge, stall **9** pussyfoot **10** mince words **11** be ambiguous, prevaricate **13** avoid the issue **16** straddle the fence **17** beat around the bush

equivocating 6 shifty **7** devious, dodging, elusive, elusory, evasive, hedging **8** stalling **9** ambiguous, deceptive, equivocal **10** misleading **11** dissembling

ERA
abbr. for: 16 earned run average (baseball) **20** equal rights amendment (failed)

era 3 age **4** time **5** epoch **6** period **8** interval

eradicate 5 erase **6** remove **7** abolish, blot out, destroy, expunge, wipe out **8** get rid of **9** eliminate, extirpate, liquidate **10** annihilate, do away with, extinguish, obliterate **11** exterminate

eradication 7 erasure, removal **9** abolition **11** blotting out, destruction, elimination **12** obliteration

erase 6 delete, remove, rub out **7** expunge, scratch **8** wipe away **9** eliminate, eradicate, strike out

Erasistratus
field: 10 physiology
nationality: 5 Greek
described: 5 brain, heart

Erasmus, Desiderius

author of: 14 Encomium Moriae **16** The Praise of Folly

Erato
muse of: **10** love poetry

Ercolani, James
real name of: **11** James Darren

erect 5 build, put up, raise, rigid, stiff **6** unbent **7** stand up, upright **8** straight, vertical **9** construct, unstooped **12** place upright

erection 7 raising **8** building **9** putting up **11** fabrication **12** construction

eremite 4 monk **6** essene, hermit **7** ascetic, recluse **9** anchorite, religious

Erewhon
author: **12** Samuel Butler
title spelled backwards, modified: **7** nowhere
character: **5** Higgs **6** Strong **7** Chowbok **8** Arowhena

erg
metric unit of: **4** work **6** energy

ergo 4 work **6** hence **7** because **9** therefore **11** accordingly

Eriboea
husband: **6** Aloeus

Ericson 4 Leif
son of: **10** Eric the Red
discovered: **7** Vinland
home: **6** Norway

Erie 4 lake, port **5** canal **9** Iroquoian

Erigone
father: **7** Icarius **9** Aegisthus
mother: **12** Clytemnestra
brother: **6** Aletes
death by: **7** suicide

Erin *see* **7** Ireland

Erin go bragh 14 Ireland forever

Erinys
also: **6** Furies
epithet of: **7** Demeter
means: **4** fury

Eris
origin: **5** Greek
goddess of: **7** discord
brother: **4** Ares
threw: **14** apple of discord
corresponds to: **9** Discordia

Eritrea
capital/largest city: **6** Asmara
others: **5** Assab, Keren **6** Ghinda **7** Massawa
formerly division of: **8** Ethiopia
river: **5** Mareb
highest point: **5** Soira
strait: **11** Bab el Mandeb
sea: **3** Red
language: **7** Amharic
religion: **5** Islam **6** Coptic, Muslim

Erlking
origin: **8** Germanic **12** Scandinavian
form: **6** spirit
personifies: **6** nature
works: **8** mischief
poem by: **6** Goethe
song by: **8** Schubert

ermine 3 fur **4** duty, rank **6** weasel **7** ermalin **8** position

Ernani
opera by: **5** Verdi
setting: **6** Aragon
character: **6** Ernani **11** Donna Elvira

Ernst, Max
born: **5** Bruhl **7** Germany
co-founder of: **7** Dadaism **10** Surrealism
artwork: **7** Moon Man **8** Lady Bird **11** A Little Calm, Femme Oiseau **12** The Whole City **13** The Table Is Set, Totem and Taboo **14** Lunar Asparagus

erode 3 eat **5** spoil, waste **6** ravage **7** corrode, despoil, eat away **8** wear away **12** disintegrate

Eros
origin: **5** Greek
god of: **4** love
mother: **9** Aphrodite
corresponds to: **4** Amor **5** Cupid

erosion 8 abrasion, ravaging **9** corrosion **10** eating away **11** wearing away, wearing down

erosive 7 burning, caustic **9** corrosive

erotic 3 hot **4** lewd, sexy **5** bawdy, lusty **6** ardent, carnal, impure, ribald, risque, sexual, wanton **7** amatory, amorous, obscene, raunchy **8** immodest, indecent, unchaste **9** salacious **10** lascivious, passionate, suggestive

err 3 sin **6** mess up, slip up **7** blunder, do wrong **8** go astray **9** be in error, misbehave **10** transgress **12** make a mistake, miscalculate **13** slip from grace

errand 4 duty, task **6** office **7** mission **10** assignment

errant 5 wrong **6** arrant, astray, erring, roving **7** erratic, wayward **8** mistaken, straying **9** incorrect, wandering, wayfaring **11** adventurous

errare humanum est 12 to err is human

erratic 3 odd **5** queer **6** fitful **7** strange, unusual, wayward **8** aberrant, abnormal, peculiar, shifting, unstable, variable **9** eccentric, unnatural **10** capricious, changeable **11** vacillating **12** inconsistent **13** unpredictable

erroneous 5 false, wrong **6** all wet, faulty, untrue **7** off base, unsound **8** mistaken, spurious **9** incorrect, unfounded **10** fallacious, inaccurate **12** full of hot air **13** unsupportable

error 4 flaw **5** boner, botch, fault **6** boo-boo, bungle, howler **7** blooper, fallacy, mistake **9** oversight **10** inaccuracy **13** misconception **14** miscalculation **15** misapprehension **16** misunderstanding **17** misinterpretation

ersatz 4 fake, sham **5** bogus, phony **9** imitation, pretended, synthetic **10** artificial, not genuine **11** counterfeit

Erse 4 Celt, Gael, Scot **5** Irish **6** Celtic, Gaelic **7** Ireland **8** Scottish **10** Highlander

erstwhile 2 ex **4** past **6** bygone, former **7** onetime **8** previous

eruct 4 burp **5** belch

eructation 4 burp **5** belch

erudite 4 wise **7** learned, sapient **8** cultured, literate, well-read **9** scholarly **10** cultivated, thoughtful, well-versed **11** intelligent **12** well-educated, well-informed, well-reasoned

erudition 5 skill **7** culture **8** learning, literacy **9** education, expertise, knowledge, schooling **10** refinement **11** cultivation, learnedness, scholarship **12** book learning **13** enlightenment

Erulus
king of: **5** Italy
mother: **7** Feronia
gift: **10** three lives

erupt 4 emit, gush, vent **5** eruct **6** blow up **7** explode **8** break out, throw off **9** be ejected, discharge, flow forth, pour forth **10** belch forth, burst forth

eruption 4 rash **6** eczema **7** flare-up, gushing, venting **8** ejection, emission, outbreak, outburst **9** blowing up, discharge, explosion **10** dermatitis, outpouring **11** breaking out **12** flowing forth, inflammation, pouring forth **13** belching forth, bursting forth

Erving, Julius
nickname: **7** Doctor J
sport: **10** basketball
position: **7** forward
team: **11** New York Nets **15** Virginia Squires **25** Philadelphia Seventy-Sixers

Erymanthian boar
form: **4** boar
plagued: **7** Arcadia
captured by: **8** Hercules

erythrophobia
fear of: **8** blushing

Esau
also called: **4** Edom
father: **5** Isaac
mother: **7** Rebekah
twin brother: **5** Jacob
wife: **6** Judith **8** Makalath
son: **7** Eliphaz
birthright sold to: **5** Jacob

escadrille 6 armada **8** flotilla, squadron

escalate 4 rise **5** boost, mount, swell **6** ascend, expand, extend, step up **7** advance, amplify, broaden, elevate, enlarge, magnify **8** increase **9** intensify **10** accelerate, aggrandize

Escalus
character in: **17** Measure for Measure
author: **11** Shakespeare

escapade 4 lark **5** antic, caper, fling, prank, revel, spree, trick **7** caprice **8** mischief **9** adventure **11** high old time

escape 3 lam **4** bolt, exit, flee, flow, gush, leak, seep, shun, skip **5** avert, avoid, dodge, elude, issue, skirt **6** efflux, egress, emerge, eschew, exodus, flight, stream **7** abscond, emanate, getaway, leakage, make off, outflow, outpour, run away, seepage **8** breakout, emission, outburst, slip away, steal off **9** be emitted, break free, cut and run, discharge, diversion, effluence, pour forth **10** break loose, decampment, fly the coop **11** avoid danger, deliverance, distraction, extrication, safe getaway **12** make a getaway

escargot 5 snail

escarpment 4 bank, crag **5** bluff, cliff, ridge, slope **8** headland, palisade **9** precipice **10** promontory

eschew 4 shun **5** avoid, forgo **6** give up **7** forbear **9** keep shy of **11** abstain from **12** steer clear of

eschewal 7 refusal **8** forgoing, shunning **9** avoidance **10** abnegation, abstention, self-denial **11** forbearance **13** nonindulgence **16** nonparticipation

Escoffier, Auguste
nationality: **6** French
profession: **4** chef
worked in: **4** Ritz **6** London

escort 4 date, take **5** guard, guide, train, usher **6** squire **7** company, conduct, cortege, retinue **8** chaperon **9** companion, conductor, entourage **10** attendants, lead the way

escritoire 4 desk **5** table **9** secretary **10** secretaire **11** writing desk

escutcheon 4 arms **5** crest **6** shield **10** coat of arms **16** armorial bearings *see also* **8** Heraldry

Eskimo (Eskimantsic, Askkimey, Inuit, Yuit)
tribe: **5** Aleut
location: **6** Alaska, Arctic, Canada **9** Greenland
noted for: **7** fishing **9** mechanics

Eskimo-Aleut
language branch: **5** Aleut, Yupik
spoken in: **6** Alaska **7** Siberia **15** Aleutian Islands

Esmeralda
character in: **23** The Hunchback of Notre Dame
author: **4** Hugo

esoteric 6 arcane, covert, hidden, occult, secret, veiled **7** cloaked, cryptic, obscure, private **8** abstruse, mystical **9** concealed, enigmatic, recondite **10** inviolable, mysterious **11** inscrutable, undisclosed **12** confidential **16** incomprehensible

ESP 7 insight **9** foresight, intuition **10** sixth sense **11** premonition, second sight **12** clairvoyance **22** extrasensory perception

espanol 7 Spanish **13** Spanish person **15** Spanish language

especial *see* **7** special

especially 6 really **7** notably **9** expressly, intensely, primarily, unusually **10** singularly, uncommonly **11** exclusively, principally **12** particularly, specifically **13** exceptionally, outstandingly **15** extraordinarily

espiegle 7 playful, roguish

espieglerie 12 playful trick

esplanade 4 mall, path, walk **5** drive **9** boardwalk **10** quadrangle

espousal 7 backing, support, wedding **8** adoption, advocacy, marriage, taking up **9** betrothal, promotion **10** supporting **12** championship

espouse 3 wed **4** back, tout **5** adopt, boost, marry **6** take up **7** embrace, further, promote, support **8** advocate, champion, side with **10** stand up for

espressivo
music: **12** expressively
abbreviation: **4** espr

esprit de corps 10 fellowship, group pride, group unity, high morale, solidarity, team spirit **11** camaraderie

espy 3 see, spy **4** spot, view **6** behold, descry, detect, locate, notice **7** discern

essay 3 try **5** paper, theme, tract **6** effort, take on **7** article, attempt, venture **8** critique, endeavor, treatise **9** editorial, undertake **10** commentary, experiment **11** make a stab at, undertaking **12** dissertation, take a crack at, take a fling at **14** make an effort at **16** short composition

Essay on Criticism, An
author: **13** Alexander Pope

Essay on Man, An
author: **13** Alexander Pope

Essays
author: **12** Francis Bacon

Essays in Criticism
author: **13** Matthew Arnold

esse 5 being **9** existence

essence 4 core, germ, gist, pith, soul **5** heart, point, scent **6** elixir, nature, spirit **7** cologne, extract, meaning, perfume, spirits **8** tincture **9** fragrance, lifeblood, principle, substance **11** concentrate, toilet water **12** basic quality, quintessence, significance **15** sum and substance

essential, essentials 3 key **4** main **5** basic, vital **6** basics, needed **7** crucial, leading **8** cardinal, inherent **9** basic need, important, ingrained, intrinsic, necessary, necessity, principal, requisite, rudiments, vital part **10** key element, principles **11** fundamental, nitty-gritty **12** fundamentals **13** indispensable

essential ingredient 9 necessity **10** sine qua non **22** indispensable component

establish 3 fix **4** form, open, show **5** begin, found, prove, set up, start **6**

create, settle, uphold, verify **7** confirm, implant, install, justify, situate, sustain, warrant **8** initiate, organize, validate **9** institute **10** bring about, inaugurate, make secure **11** corroborate, demonstrate **12** authenticate **16** win acceptance for **18** bring into existence

established 6 common **7** regular **8** accepted, familiar **9** customary **10** recognized

establishment, Establishment 4 firm **5** plant **6** office, outfit, system **7** company, concern, factory **8** building, business, creation, founding **9** formation, setting up **10** foundation **11** corporation, development, instituting, institution, ruling class **12** organization, powers that be **13** bringing about

estaminet 4 cafe **6** bistro

estate 4 rank, will **5** class, grade, manor, money, order, state **6** assets, legacy, status, wealth **7** bequest, fortune, station **8** compound, holdings, property **9** condition, situation **10** belongings, plantation **11** inheritance **12** country place

esteem 4 deem, hold **5** honor, judge, prize, think, value **6** admire, reckon, regard, revere **7** believe, cherish, respect **8** approval, consider, estimate, look up to, treasure, venerate **9** calculate, reverence **10** admiration, set store by, veneration **12** appreciation **13** think highly of **16** favorable opinion, hold in high regard **18** attach importance to

esteemed 5 great, noted **6** prized, valued, worthy **7** admired, eminent, honored, notable, revered **9** admirable, important, respected **10** looked up to, preeminent **11** illustrious **13** distinguished, well thought of **14** highly regarded

Estella
character in: **17** Great Expectations
author: **7** Dickens

Estevez, Ramon
real name of: **11** Martin Sheen

Esther
author: **10** Henry Adams

Esther
Persian name of: **8** Hadassah
father: **7** Abihail
grandfather: **6** Shimei
cousin: **8** Mordecai
husband: **9** Ahasuerus
displaced: **6** Vashti
enemy: **5** Haman
holiday: **5** Purim

Esther Waters
author: **11** George Moore

esthetic 7 refined **8** artistic **9** sensitive **10** cultivated, fastidious **12** aesthetic **14** discriminating

estimable 4 good **6** prized **7** admired, revered **8** laudable **9** admirable, honorable, important, reputable, respected, treasured **10** worthwhile **11** commendable **12** praiseworthy **14** highly regarded

estimate 4 view **5** assay, guess, judge, opine, think, value **6** assess, belief, fig- ure, reckon **7** believe, opinion, surmise **8** appraise, conclude, consider, evaluate, judgment, thinking **9** appraisal, calculate, reckoning **10** assessment, conjecture, evaluation **11** calculation

estimation 4 view **6** belief, esteem, regard **7** opinion, respect **8** approval, judgment **9** appraisal, reckoning **10** admiration, evaluation **13** consideration

estimator 7 analyst **8** assessor **9** appraiser, evaluator **10** calculator

Estonia
  capital/largest city: 7 Tallinn
  others: 5 Narva, Paide, Parnu, Tartu, Valga **6** Dorpat **7** Petseri **8** Paldiski **11** Kohtla-Jarve
  government: 8 republic
  measure: 3 tun **4** elle, liin, sund, toll, toop **5** verst **6** sagene, versta **7** kulimet **8** tonnland
  monetary unit: 3 lat **4** sent **5** kroon **7** estmark
  weight: 4 lood, nael, puud
  island: 4 Dago, Muhu **5** Kihnu, Oesel, Saare **6** Sarema, Vormsi **7** Hiiumaa **8** Saaremaa
  lake: 5 Pskov **6** Peipus **9** Vortsjarv
  highest point: 8 Munamagi
  river: 3 Ema **5** Narva, Parnu
  sea: 6 Baltic
  physical feature:
    gulf: 4 Riga **5** Parnu **7** Finland
    strait: 4 Irbe
  people: 4 Esth, Finn **5** Aesti **6** Jewish **8** Estonian **9** Ukrainian **11** Belorussian
  language: 5 Tartu **10** Finno-Ugric
  religion: 8 Lutheran

estop 3 bar **4** fill, plug, stop **7** prevent **8** obstruct

esto perpetua 17 may she live forever
  motto of: 5 Idaho

Estragon
  character in: 15 Waiting for Godot
  author: 7 Beckett
  French for: 8 tarragon

estrange 4 part **8** alienate **9** disaffect **10** antagonize, dissociate, drive apart

estranged 5 aloof **6** cut off **7** distant **8** detached, divorced **9** alienated, separated **10** unfriendly

estrangement 8 coolness **10** alienation **12** disaffection

estuary 5 firth, inlet **10** river mouth, tidal basin

eta 10 Greek vowel **22** estimated time of arrival

etagere 7 whatnot **11** open shelves

etc (&c) 4 et al **7** and so on, whatnot

8 et cetera, whatever **9** and others **10** and so forth, and the rest

etch 3 cut, fix **5** carve, stamp **7** corrode, engrave, impress, scratch

Eteocles
  father: 7 Oedipus
  mother: 7 Jocasta **10** Euryganeia
  uncle: 5 Creon
  brother: 9 Polynices
  sister: 6 Ismene **8** Antigone
  son: 8 Laodamas
  slain by: 9 Polynices

eternal 7 abiding, endless **8** constant, immortal, infinite, timeless, unending **9** ceaseless, continual, perpetual **10** persistent, relentless, without end **11** everlasting, never-ending **12** interminable **13** uninterrupted

eternity 4 Zion **6** Heaven **7** forever, nirvana **8** infinity, paradise **11** ages and ages, endlessness, eons and eons, immortality **12** New Jerusalem, the hereafter, the next world **13** the afterworld **14** the world to come, time without end **15** everlasting life

Ethan Frome
  author: 12 Edith Wharton
  character: 5 Zeena **7** Zenobia **12** Mattie Silver

Ethanim 18 seventh Hebrew month

ether 5 ester, ethyl, ozone, vapor **7** diethyl, solvent **10** anesthetic **11** refrigerant

ethereal 4 airy, rare **6** aerial **7** elusive, refined, sublime **8** delicate, rarefied **9** celestial, exquisite, unearthly, unworldly

ethical 4 fair, just **5** moral, right **6** decent, kosher, proper **7** correct, fitting, upright **8** virtuous **9** honorable **10** aboveboard, scrupulous **15** straightforward **17** open and aboveboard

ethical feelings 9 integrity **10** conscience, moral sense **16** incorruptibility

ethics, ethic 8 morality **9** integrity, moral code **10** conscience, principles **11** moral values, sense of duty **14** moral standards, rules of conduct

Ethics of Ambiguity
  author: 16 Simone de Beauvoir

Ethiopia
  Biblical name: 4 Cush
  other name: 9 Abyssinia
  capital/largest city: 10 Addis Ababa
  others: 3 Edd **4** Axum, Bako, Dori, Goba, Gore, Thio **5** Adola, Adowa, Aduwa, Aksum, Assab, Awash, Dimtu, Elfud, Harar, Jidda, Jimma, Kecha, Meroe, Mojjo **6** Antalo, Asmara, Dessye, Dunkur, Gondar, Harrar, Makale, Napata **7** Ankober, Gambela, Gardula, Magdala, Massawa, Nakamti **8** Dire Dawa, Lalibala, Mustahil
  school: 13 Haile Selassie
  division: 5 Tigre **6** Amhara, Ogaden

  former division: 7 Eritrea
  measure: 3 tat **4** cubi, kuba **5** derah, messe **6** cabaho, sinjer, sinzer, tanica **7** entelam, farsakh, farsang, ghebeta
  monetary unit: 4 besa, birr, harf **5** amole, girsh **6** dollar, kharaf, levant, pataca, talari **7** ashrafi, menelik, plaster, tallero **12** maria theresa
  weight: 3 pek **4** kasm, natr, oket, rotl **5** alada, artal, mocha, neter, ratel, wakea **6** wogiet **8** farasula **9** mutagalla
  island: 6 Dahlak
  lake: 3 Abe **4** Tana **5** Abaya, Shola, Tanna, Tsana, Tzana, Zeway **6** Dambea, Dembea **7** Rudolph **8** Stefanie **11** The Blue Nile
  mountain: 4 Amba, Batu, Guge, Guna, Talo **5** Ahmar, Choke **9** Rasdashan
  highest point: 9 Ras Deshen
  river: 3 Omo **4** Baro, Dawa, Gibe, Gila, Juba **5** Abbai, Akoho, Albai, Awash, Fafan, Mareb, Mofer, Rahad, Webbe **6** Tekeze **7** Tacazze, Takkaze **8** Gashgash, Shebante **11** The Blue Nile
  sea: 3 Red
  physical feature:
    desert: 17 Danakil Depression
    falls: 7 Tisisat **8** Blue Nile
    valley: 4 Rift
  people: 4 Afar, Agau, Beja, Doko, Kafa, Kala, Saho, Shoa **5** Afara, Agows, Galas, Galla, Negro, Tigre **6** Abigar, Amhara, Annuak, Gondar, Hamite, Harari, Sidama, Sidamo, Somali, Tigrai, Wolamo **7** Cushite, Danakil, Donakus, Falasha, Somalis **8** Assamite, Blemmyes **10** Abyssinian, Troglodyte
  leader: 7 Menelik **8** Mengistu **13** Haile Selassie
  language: 3 Giz **4** Afar, Agow, Geez, Saho **5** Geeze, Ghese, Smali, Tigre **6** Arabic, Harari **7** Amharic, English, Italian, Russian **8** Gallinya, Irob-Saho, Tigrinya
  religion: 5 Islam **7** Falasha, Judaism **18** Ethiopian Orthodoxy
  place:
    cathedral: 8 St George
    hall: 6 Africa
    palace: 7 Jubilee **9** Menelik II
    park: 4 Lion
  feature:
    flower: 7 brayera
    game: 5 dulla **8** shum-shir
    garment: 4 toga **5** kamis **6** barnos, chamma, netela, shamma
    tree: 4 koho, koso **5** cusso
  food:
    banana: 4 musa **6** ensete
    beer: 5 talla
    bread dish: 6 injera
    cereal: 4 teff

honey liquor: 3 tej
spicy sauce: 3 wat
ethnic 6 native, racial, unique **8** cultural, national, original **10** indigenous

ethnic group
of Afghanistan: 5 Aimak, Aymak, Kafir, Nuris **6** Baloch, Baluch, Chahar, Durani, Hasara, Hazara, Kaffir, Kirgiz, Pathan, Tajiks, Uzbeks **7** Beluchi, Belucki, Ghilzai, Pakhton, Pakhtun, Pashtun, Pukhtun, Pushtun, Sistani, Taimani, Taimuri, Taliban **8** Jamshidi, Siah Push **9** Firuzkuhi, Safed Push, Safid Push
of Albania: 3 Geg **4** Cham, Gheg, Gueg, Tost **6** Arnaut, Arnout **8** Illyrian, Skipetar
of Algeria: 4 Arab **6** Berber, Kabyle, Shawai, Tuareg **7** Haratin
of Andorra: 7 Catalan
of Angola: 5 Bantu, Kongo, Lundu **6** Chokwe, Herero, Mbundi, Ovambo **7** Bakongo, Kangela, Kikongo **8** Kimbundu, Kwangare **9** Ovinbundu **12** Nyaneka-Humbi
of Antigua and Barbuda: 7 African, British **8** Lebanese **10** Portuguese
of Argentina: 3 Api **4** Lule **5** Vejoz **6** Abipon, Vilela **7** Guarani, Puelche, Ranquel, Taluhet **8** Querandi, Querendy
of Armenia: 5 Armen, Ermyn, Gomer, Hadji
of Australia: 3 Abo **4** Koko, Mara, Wong **5** Anzac, Bieri, Binge, Maori, Myall **6** Aranda, Arunta, Aussie, Binghi, Digger, Kipper, Papuan **7** Arawong, Billjim, Ilpirra **8** Antipode, Barkinji, Euahlayi, Warragal, Warrigal **9** Aborigine **10** Austroloid, Melanesian, Sandgroper **12** Jindyworobak
of Austria: 4 Pole **5** Croat, Czech, Gypsy **6** German **7** Slovene **9** Hungarian
of Azerbaijan: 5 Azeri **11** Azerbaijani
of the Bahamas: 5 black **7** Haitian
of Bahrain: 4 Arab **6** Indian **7** Persian **8** European **9** Pakistani
of Bangladesh: 7 Bengali
of Barbados: 5 Bajan **9** Barbadian
of Belarus: 12 Byelorussian
of Belgium: 4 Remi **6** Nervii **7** Belgian, Fleming, Flemish, Walloon **9** Bellovaci
of Benin: 3 Fon, Pla **4** Adja, Aizo, Mina, Peul **5** Pedah, Peuhl, Somba **6** Bariba, Fulani, Yoruba **8** Pilapila **9** Dahomeyan
of Bhutan: 5 Monpa **6** Bhutia **7** Tibetan **8** Assamese, Nepalese
of Bolivia: 6 Aymara **7** mestizo, Quechua
of Borneo: 4 Iban **5** Bukat, Dajak, Dayak, Dusan, Malay, Punan **6** Ilano **7** Bakatan, Chinese, Illanum
of Bosnia-Herzegovina: 4 Serb **5** Croat **8** Yugoslav
of Botswana: 5 Bantu **6** Tswana

7 Bakatla, Bakwena, Bushman **8** Bamalete, Baralong, Batawana, Batlokwa, Botswana **10** Bamangwato **11** Bangwaketse
of Brazil: 2 Ge **4** Anta **5** Acroa, Arara, Araua, Bravo, Carib, Guana, Negro **6** Arawak, Caraja **7** Carayan, Javahai, mulatto, Tariana **8** Botocudo, Chambioa, mameluco **9** Caucasian **10** Portuguese **11** Tupi-Guarani
of Bruneii: 4 Iban **5** Dayak, Malay **7** Chinese, Kadazan
of Bulgaria: 4 Slav, Turk **5** Gypsy, Pomak, Tatar **6** Bulgar, Slavic **7** Chuvash **9** Cheremiss **10** Macedonian
of Burkina Faso: 4 Bobo, Lobi, Samo **5** Bella, Bissa, Dyula, Fulbe, Hausa, Mande, Marka, Mossi, Puchl **6** Fulani, Senufo, Tuareg **7** Grunshi, Voltaic, Yatenga **8** Mandingo **9** Gourounsi **15** Bunsansi Gambaga
of Burundi: 3 Twa **4** Hutu **5** Bantu, Batwa, Pygmy, Tutsi **6** Bahutu, Watusi **7** Barundi
of Cambodia: 4 Cham, Thai **5** Khmer **7** Chinese **10** Vietnamese
of Cameroon: 3 Abo, Edo, Ibo **4** Beti, Bulu, Ekoi, Ijaw, Sara **5** Bantu, Bassa, Kirdi, Pygmy, Tikar **6** Bamoun, Donala, Ewondo, Fulani, Ibibio **7** Bakweri **8** Bamileke
of Canada: 6 Canuck, Eskimo, French, Innuit **7** English
of the Canary Islands: 7 Spanish
of Cape Verde: 6 Creole **7** African, mulatto **8** European **10** Portuguese
of Central African Republic: 4 Baya, Sara **5** Banda, Bwaki, Sango **6** Azande, Yakoma **7** Banziri, Mandjia, Nzakara
of Chad: 4 Arab, Daza, Maba, Sara, Teda, Tubu **5** Barma, Hakka, Kroda, Massa **6** Fulani, Kotoko, Toubou, Wadaii **7** Kamadja, Kanembu **8** Moundang
of Chile: 3 Ona **4** Auca, Inca, Onan **6** Arauca, Chango, Yahgan **7** Mapuche, mestizo, Moluche, Pampean, Patagon, Puegian, Ranquel **8** Alikuluf, Picunche, Tsonecan
of China: 3 Han, Yis **4** Huis, Lolo, Miao, Pu-is **5** Hakka, Hoklo, Seres, Sinic **6** Cataia, Chuang, Johnny, Korean, Manchu, Mongol, Serian, Uighun **7** Sinaean, Tibetan
of Colombia: 4 Boro, Cuna, Duit, Hoka, Macu, Muso, Muzo, Paez, Tama, Tapa **5** Carib, Catio, Choco, Cofan, Cogui, Cubeo, Guane, Haida, Mocoa, Paeze, Pijao, Seona, Yagua **6** Arawak, Betoya, Calima, Colima, Ingano, Mirana, Saliva, Tahami, Ticunu, Tucano, Tunebo, Witoto, Yahuna **7** Achagua, Andaqui, Chibcha, Chimila, Churoya, Guahibo, Guajiro, mestizo, mulatto, Panches,

Puinave, Puitoto, Quechua, Shuswap, Tairona, Telembi **8** Coconuco, Guarauno, Motilone, Puinavis, Quimbaya, Sinsigas **9** Cocanucos, Coconucan, Panaquita **10** Bellacoola
of Comoros: 4 Arab **5** Bantu, Malay **7** African **8** Malagasy
of the Congo: 3 Rua **4** Akka, Susa, Teke, Vili **5** Amadi, Bantu, Figot, Kongo, Mantu, Pygmy, Sanga, Warua, Zambi **6** Ababua, Bafyot, Bateke, Mbochi, Nzambi, Wabuma **7** Bacongo, Bakongo, Bangala, Batetla, Manyema **10** Binga Pygmy
of Costa Rica: 4 Voto **6** Boruca, Bribri, Guaymi **7** Guatuso, mestizo, Spanish
of Crete: 6 Cretan, Minoan **7** Candiot **8** Sphakiot **9** Caphtorim **10** Philistine
of Croatia: 4 Serb **5** Croat **8** Yugoslav
of Cuba: 5 Carib, Negro, Taino **6** Arawak **7** Ciboney, mestizo **8** Ciboneye **9** Caucasian
of Czechoslovakia/Czech Republic: 4 Slav **5** Czech **6** Slovak **8** Bohemian, Moravian
of Denmark: 4 Dane, Jute **5** Angle **6** Cimbri, Eskimo, German, Ostmen, Teuton, Viking **12** Scandinavian
of Djibouti: 4 Afar, Arab **5** Issas **6** French **8** European
of Dominican Republic: 5 Negro, Taino **6** Indian **7** mulatto, Spanish **9** Caucasian
of Ecuador: 4 Cara, Cixo, Inca **5** Ardan, Aucas, Macoa, Maina, Palta, Quitu, Yumbo **6** Canelo, Jibaro, Jivaro, Puruha **7** Cayapas, Jivaros, mestizo, mulatto **8** Barbacoa, Colorado, Montuvio, Serranos **10** Montubious
of Egypt: 3 Kem **4** Arab, Copt, Misr, Wafd **5** Gippy, Gyppy, Gypsy, Nilot **6** Ababda, Berber, Hyksos, Nubian, Tasian **7** Mizraim, Pharian **8** Badarian, Bisharin, Memphian
of El Salvador: 5 Lenca, Pipil **6** Indian, Mangue **7** mestizo, Spanish **9** Matagalpa
of England: 4 Celt, Jute, Pict **5** Norse, Saxon **6** Angles, Briton, Norman, Viking
of Equatorial Guinea: 4 Bubi, Fang **5** Benge, Combe **6** Bujeba **10** Fernandino
of Estonia: 4 Esth, Finn **5** Aesti **6** Jewish **8** Estonian **9** Ukrainian **11** Belorussian
of Ethiopia: 4 Afar, Agau, Beja, Doko, Kafa, Kala, Saho, Shoa **5** Afara, Agows, Galas, Galla, Negro, Tigre **6** Abigar, Amhara, Annuak, Gondar, Hamite, Harari, Sidama, Sidamo, Somali, Tigrai, Wolamo **7** Cushite, Danakil, Donakus, Falasha **8** Assamite, Blemmyes **10** Abyssinian, Troglodyte
of Fiji: 6 Fijian, Indian **7** Chinese

10 Melanesian, Polynesian **11** Micronesian

of Finland: 3 Jew, Vod, Vot, Yak **4** Avar, Finn, Hame, Lapp, Turk, Veps **5** Fioun, Gypsy, Ijore, Inger, Suomi, Vepse, Zyrin **6** Magyar, Ostiak, Ostyak, Tarast, Tavast, Ugrian **7** Lappish, Mordvin, Permiak, Samoyed, Uralian **8** Cheremis, Estonian, Karelian, Livonian, Swekoman **9** Tavastian **11** Karjalaiset, Suomalaiset

of France: 5 Frank

of the Gabon Republic: 4 Fang **6** Adouma, Bakota, Bateke, Echira, Okande, Omyene **7** Eshiras **8** Bandjabi, Bapounou

of The Gambia: 4 Fula, Jola **5** Foula, Wolof **6** Fulani **8** Mandingo, Serahuli **9** Seranuleh

of Georgia: 5 Azeri **7** Russian **8** Armenian, Georgian, Ossetian

of Germany: 3 Hun **4** Slav, Sorb, Wend **5** Saxon

of Ghana: 2 Ga **3** Ewe **4** Akan, Akim, Akra, Aksa **5** Ahafo, Brong, Inkra **7** Akwapim, Ashanti, Dagomba, Maprusi **11** Mole-Dagbani

of Gibraltar: 6 Jewish **7** British, Italian, Maltese, Spanish **10** Portuguese

of Greece: 5 Greek **6** Achean, Dorian, Ionian **7** Aeolian, Hellene

of Greenland: 3 Ita **6** Eskimo **8** European

of Grenada: 5 Negro **6** Indian

of Guatemala: 3 Mam **4** Chol, Itza, Ixil, Maya **5** Xinca **6** Caribe, Quiche **7** ladinos, mestizo, Pocomam **13** Guatemaltecos

of Guinea: 4 Koma, Loma, Nalu, Susu, Toma **5** Kissi, Manon **6** Fulani, Guerzi **7** Landoma, Malinke **8** Kouranke, Landuman **11** Kissi-Sherbo **12** Guerze- Kpelle

of Guinea-Bissau: 6 Fulani **7** Balanta, Balante, mulatto **8** Mandingo, Mandyako

of Guyana: 6 Akawai, Arawak, Creole, Taruma **7** African, Chinese, mulatto **10** Portuguese

of Haiti: 5 Taino **7** African, mulatto

of Honduras: 4 Maya, Paya, Sumo, Ulva **5** Carib, Lenoa, Pipil **6** Tauira **7** Jicaque, mestizo, Miskito **8** Mosquito

of Hong Kong: 5 Hakka, Haklo, Punti, Tanka **7** British, Chinese **8** American, Japanese **9** Cantonese **10** Portuguese

of Hungary: 3 Hun **4** Serb **5** Croat, Gypsy **6** Cigany, Magyar, Slovak, Ugrian

of Iceland: 6 Celtic, Viking **8** Norseman **9** Norwegian

of India: 2 Ao **3** Gor **4** Bhil **5** Aryan **6** Badaga, Pathan **7** Sherani **9** Dravidian **10** Andamanese

of Indonesia: 4 Dyak **5** Batak, Dayak, Malay **6** Battak, Papuan, Toraja **7** Chinese, Igorots **8** Acehnese, Achi-

nese, Balinese, Javanese, Madurese, Sudanese **11** Minang Kabau

of Iran: 3 Lur, Tat **4** Arab, Kurd, Turk **5** Medes **6** Galcha, Gilani, Jewish, Shugni **7** Baluchi, Persian **8** Armenian, Bactrian, Bartangi, Parthian, Scythian **9** Bakhtiari **11** Azerbaijani, Mazandarani

of Iraq: 4 Arab, Kurd **7** Bedouin

of Ireland: 4 Celt, Erse, Gael **5** Irish **6** Celtic **9** Hibernian

of Israel: 3 Jew **4** Arab **5** Druze **10** Circassian

of Italy: 5 Latin **6** Sabine **7** Italian, Lombard **8** Etruscan

of Ivory Coast: 3 Abe, Dan, Kru, Kwa **4** Akan, Bete, Dida, Guro, Koua, Lobi, Wobe **5** Abron, Abure, Attie, Baule, Guere, Mande, Mossi **6** Baoule, Lagoon, Senufo, Senufu **7** Kroumen, Malinke, Voltaic **8** Dan-Gouro **10** Anyi-Baoule **11** Lobi-Kulango **12** Agnis-Ashanti

of Jamaica: 7 African, Chinese **10** East Indian

of Japan: 3 Eta **6** Korean **8** Japanese, Okinawan **10** Buramkumin

of Java: 5 Krama, Kromo **6** Kalang **8** Javanese, Madurese, Sudanese

of Jordan: 4 Arab, Kurd **7** Bedouin, Checher **8** Armenian, Assyrian **10** Circassian **11** Palestinian

of Kazakhstan: 6 Kazakh

of Kenya: 3 Luo **4** Arab, Meru **5** Bantu, Elgey, Galla, Kamba, Kisii, Luhya, Masai, Nandi, Tugen **6** Kikuyu, Ogaden, Somali **7** Baluyha, Hamitic, Hilotic, Kipsigi, Swahili, Turkana **8** Kalenjin, Marakwet

of Kiribati: 8 Banabans **10** Polynesian **11** Micronesian

of Korea: 6 Korean

of Kuwait: 4 Arab **5** Iraqi, Saudi **6** Indian **7** Bedouin **8** Egyptian **9** Pakistani **11** Palestinian

of Kyrgyzstan: 5 Uzbek **6** Kyrgyz **7** Kirghiz

of Laos: 2 Lu **3** Kha, Lao, Man, Meo, Tai, Yao, Yun **4** Miao, Thai **5** Hmong **8** Lao Teung **10** Phoutheung

of Latvia: 3 Kur, Liv **4** Balt, Cour, Lett **7** Latgale, Latvian, Russian, Zemgale

of Lebanon: 4 Arab **9** Canaanite **10** Phoenician **11** Palestinian

of Lesotho: 4 Zulu **5** Bantu, Tembu **6** Basuto **7** Basotho

of Liberia: 2 Gi **3** Gio, Kra, Kru, Kwa, Vai, Vei **4** Gola, Kroo, Krou, Loma, Mano, Toma **5** Bassa, Gibbi, Gissi, Grebo **6** Gbande, Kpelle, Kpuesi, Krooby, Kruman **7** Krooboy, Krooman **8** Mandingo **15** Americo-Liberian

of Libya: 4 Arab, Tebu **6** Berber, Tuareg **7** Gaetuli **8** Getulans, Harratin

of Liechtenstein: 8 Alamanni, Ale-

manni

of Lithuania: 4 Balt, Lett, Pole **5** Zhmud **6** Jewish, Litvak **7** Aistian, Russian, Yatvyag **10** Lithuanian, Samogitian **11** Belorussian

of Luxembourg: 6 French, German **12** Luxembourger

of Macao: 6 Macaon **7** Chinese **10** Portuguese

of Macedonia: 4 Turk **8** Albanian **10** Macedonian

of Madagascar: 4 Arab, Bara, Hova **5** Malay **6** Merina, Tanala **7** African **8** Betsileo, Mahafaly, Malagasy, Sakalava **9** Antaimoro, Antaisaka, Antandroy, Tsimihety **10** Indonesian, Polynesian **13** Betsimisaraka

of Malawi: 3 Yao **4** Sena **5** Bantu, Lomwe, Ngoni **6** Cheiva, Maravi, Ngonde, Nyanja **7** Tumbuka

of Malaysia: 4 Iban **5** Dayak, Malay **6** Indian **7** Chinese, Kadazan **9** Pakistani, Sri Lankan **10** Bangladesh, Indonesian

of Maldives: 4 Arab **6** Indian **9** Sinhalese **10** Singhalese

of Mali: 3 Bwa **4** Fula, Kyan, Moor, Peul **5** Dogon, Dyula, Fulbe, Marka **6** Berber, Dognon, Fulani, Senufo, Tuareg **7** Bembara, Fellata, Malinke, Miniaka, Songhai, Soninke **8** Khasonke, Mandingo, Senoulfo

of Malta: 7 Maltese

of Mauritania: 4 Arab, Fula, Moor **5** Black, Fulbe, Wolof **6** Bafour, Berber, Fulani **7** African, Soninke, Tukulor **8** Sarakole **9** Sarakolle **10** Toucouleur **12** Halphoolaren

of Mauritius: 6 Creole, French, Indian **7** African, Chinese **8** European **13** Indo-Mauritian

of Mexico: 3 Ixe, Mam, Mie, Ser **4** Chol, Cora, Jova, Meco, Mixe, Pame, Pima, Roto, Seri, Teca, Teco, Texo, Xova **5** Aztec, Chizo, Chora, Mayan, Nahua, Opata, Otomi, Zoque **6** Eudeve, Indian, Mixtec, Pueblo, Toltec, Zotzil **7** Chincha, mestizo, Nahuatl, Nayarit, Spanish, Tehueco, Tepanec, Totonac, Zacatec, Zapotec **8** Lagunero, Mazateca, Tezcucan, Totonaco, Tzapotec, Yucateco, Zacateco, Zapoteca **9** Tlascalan **10** Coahuiltec, Cuitlateco, Tarahumara

of Moldova: 7 Gagauzi **8** Moldovan **9** Moldovian

of Monaco: 6 French **7** Italian **10** Monegasque

of Mongolia: 5 Oirat, Tungu **6** Buryat, Darbet, Khoton, Mongol **7** Kazakhs, Khalkha **8** Tuvinian **9** Dariganga

of Montenegro: 4 Serb, Slav **11** Montenegrin

of Morocco: 4 Arab, Moor **6** Berber, French **7** Spanish

of Mozambique: 3 Yao **5** Bantu, Chopi, Lomue, Lomwe, Macua,

Makua, Ngoni, Nguni, Shona **6** Maravi, Thouga **7** Maconde, Makonde **10** Portuguese

of Myanmar: 4 Shan **7** Burmese, Siamese

of Namibia: 4 Nama **5** Bantu **6** Damara, Herero, Ovambo, Tswara **7** Bushman, Colored **8** Okavango **9** Hottentot

of Nauru: 7 Chinese **10** Melanesian, Polynesian **11** Micronesian

of Nepal: 3 Rai **4** Aoul **5** Limbu, Magar, Murmi, Newar, Tharu **6** Gurkha, Gurung, Nepali, Sherpa, Tamang **7** Bhutias, Kiranti **8** Gorkhali, Nepalese

of the Netherlands: 5 Dutch **7** Frisian **9** Hollander **10** Surinamese **12** Netherlander **13** South Moluccan

of New Guinea: 5 Pygmy **6** Papuan **7** Negrito **10** Melanesian

of New Zealand: 3 Ati **5** Arawa, Dutch, Maori **7** British, Ringatu **10** Polynesian

of Nicaragua: 4 Mico, Mixe, Rama, Smoo, Ulva **5** Cukra, Diria, Lenca, Sambo, Toaca **6** Mangue **7** mestizo, Miskito **8** Mosquito **9** Matagalpa

of Niger: 4 Daza, Idjo, Idyo, Idzo, Peul, Teda **5** Hausa, Warri **6** Djerma, Fulani, Kanuri, Songha, Toubou, Tuareg **13** Djerma-Songhai

of Nigeria: 3 Abo, Aro, Djo, Ebo, Edo, Ibo, Ijo, Tiv, Vai **4** Beni, Bini, Eboe, Efik, Egba, Ejam, Ekoi, Idyo, Igbo, Ijaw, Nupe **5** Angas, Benin, Gwari, Hausa **6** Chamba, Fulani, Ibibio, Kanuri, Yoruba **11** Hausa-Fulani

of Norway: 4 Lapp **5** Samme **6** Nordic, Viking

of Oman: 4 Arab

of Pakistan: 5 Sindi, Wazir **6** Afridi, Bengal, Mahsud, Pathan, Puktun, Sindhi **7** Baluchi, Brahuis, Punjabi, Pushtun, Sherani **8** Khattack, Shinwari, Yusefazi **11** Mohammedzai

of Panama: 4 Cuna **5** Choco **6** Guaymi **7** mestizo

of Qatar: 4 Arab **6** Pushtu, Yemeni **7** Baluchi, Iranian **9** Pakistani

of Romania: 6 Dacian **8** Romanian, Rumanian

of Russia: 4 Slav **5** Kulak **6** Jewish, Soviet, Velika **7** Chukchi, Latvian, Russian, Turkmen **8** Armenian, Estonian, Georgian, Siberian, Ukrainian **10** Lithuanian **11** Belorussian

of Rwanda: 3 Twa **4** Hutu **5** Batwa, Pygmy, Tutsi **6** Bahutu, Watusi **7** Batutsi

of Samoa: 6 Samoan **10** Polynesian

of San Marino: 7 Italian **11** San Marinese

of Sao Tome and Principe: 7 African **10** Portuguese **11** Cape Verdean

of Saudi Arabia: 4 Arab **7** Bedouin

of Scotland: 4 Gael, Pict, Scot **5** Norse

of Senegal: 4 Lebu, Peul, Soce **5** Diola, Dyola, Foula, Laobe, Peulh, Serer, Wolof **6** Fulani, Serere **7** Bambara, Malinke, Tukuler, Tukulor **8** Mandingo

of Seychelles: 5 Asian **6** Creole, French, Indian **7** African, Chinese

of Sicily: 5 Elymi, Sican, Sicel **6** Sicani, Siculi

of Sierra Leone: 3 Vai **4** Kono, Loko, Susu **5** Bulom, Kissi, Limba, Mande, Mendi, Temne **6** Creole, Fulani, Syrian **7** Gallina, Koranko, Kuranko, Sherbro, Yalunka **8** Lebanese, Mandingo

of Sikkim: 4 Rong **5** Bhote **6** Bhotia, Bhutia, Indian, Lepcha **7** Tibetan **8** Nepalese **9** Mongoloid

of Singapore: 5 Malay **6** Indian **7** Chinese **9** Malaysian, Pakistani, Sri Lankan

of Slovakia: 5 Czech **6** Slavic, Slovak **9** Hungarian

of Slovenia: 7 Slovene

of the Solomon Islands: 7 Chinese **8** European **10** Melanesian, Polynesian

of Somalia: 3 Sab **4** Asha **5** Galla **6** Hawiya, Isbaak, Somali **7** Danakil, Hamitic, Marehan, Samaale, Shuhali **8** Rahanwin

of South Africa: 4 Boer, Yosa, Zulu **5** Asian, Bantu, Namas, Nguni, Pondo, Sotho, Swazi, Tembu, Venda **6** Damara, Kaffir **7** African, British, Bushmen, English, Swahili **8** Bechuana, Coloured, Khoikhoi, San Xhosa **9** Afrikaner, Hottentot

of Spain: 4 Pict **5** Diego, Gente, Latin **6** Basque, Espana **7** Catalan, Espanol, Iberian **8** Galician, Gallegos, Maragato

of Sri Lanka: 5 Malay, Tamil, Vedda **6** Veddah, Weddah **7** Burgher, Mahinda, Malabar **8** Eurasian **9** Cingalese, Dravidian, Sinhalese **10** Ginghalese **12** Bandaranaike

of the Sudan: 3 Bor, Dor, Fur **4** Arab, Bari, Beri, Bobo, Daza, Egba, Fula, Golo, Nuba, Nuer, Poul, Sere **5** Anuak, Bongo, Dinka, Fulah, Hausa, Joluo, Junje, Mosgu, Mossi, Negro, Tibbu, Volta **6** Acholi, Azande, Gurusi, Hamite, Lotuho, Makari, Nilote, Nubian, Senufo, Surhai, Taureg **7** Balante, Baqqara, Gubayna, Jaaliin, Nilotes, Shilluk, Songhai, Songhay, Songhoi, Sourhai **8** Kababish, Mandingo, Menkiera **9** Sarakille **10** Gurmantshi, Shaiquiyya

of Suriname: 4 Boni, Bush, Trio **5** Djuka, Dutch **6** Creole, Wayana **7** African, Chinese **10** Amerindian, Boschneger, West Indian **11** Asian Indian

of Swaziland: 5 Asian, Bantu, Swazi **10** Eurafrican

of Sweden: 4 Lapp **5** Norse, Swede **6** Viking

of Switzerland: 5 Swiss, **6** Franks **8** Alamanni, Alemanni, Italians **12** Rhaeto-Romans

of Syria: 4 Arab, Kurd, Turk **5** Alawi, Aptal, Druse, Druze **6** Afshar, Aissor, Aushar, Avshar, Awshar **7** Amorite, Ansarie, Bedouin, Nosaris, Saracen, Shemite **8** Ansarieh, Armenian **9** Ansariyah **10** Circassian **12** Khachaturian

of Taiwan: 4 Yami **5** Hakka, Hoklo **7** Chinese, Malayan **9** Fukienese, Taiwanese **10** Indonesian, Polynesian **12** Kwangtungese

of Tajikistan: 5 Tajik, Uzbek **7** Tadzhik

of Tanzania: 2 Ha **4** Arab, Gogo, Goma, Haya, Hehe **5** Asian, Bantu, Masai **6** Arusha, Chagga, Sukuma, Wagogo, Wagoma **7** African, Makonde, Sambara, Sandawe, Shirazi, Swahili, Wabunga, Zongora **8** Nyakyusa, Nyamwezi

of Thailand: 3 Lao, Mon **4** Lawa, Shan, Thai **5** Malay **6** Indian, Khymer **7** Chinese, Siamese **9** Cambodian **10** Vietnamese

of Tibet: 5 Asian, Balti, Bodpa, Drupa **6** Bhotia, Champa, Drokpa, Khamba, Khambu, Mongol, Panaka, Sherpa, Tangut **7** Bhotiya, Bhutani, Gyarung, Taghlik, Tibetan

of Togo: 3 Ana, Ewe, Twi **4** Mina **5** Hausa **6** Akposa, Kabrai **7** Bassari, Cabrais, Kabrais, Ouatchi **8** Konkomba, Kotokoli, Lotokoli

of Tongo: 10 Polynesian

of Trinidad and Tobago: 5 Irish **6** French, Indian, Syrian **7** African, Chinese, English, Spanish **8** European, Lebanese **10** East Indian, Portuguese, Venezuelan **11** Asian Indian **13** Latin American

of Tunisia: 4 Arab **6** Berber, Jewish

of Turkey: 4 Arab, Kurd, Turk **6** Seljuk

of Turkmenistan: 7 Turkmen **10** Turkmenian

of Tuvalu: 6 Samoan **10** Polynesian

of Uganda: 4 Alur, Gisu, Soga, Teso **5** Ateso, Bantu, Chiga, Ganda, Langi, Lango, Nkole, Pygmy **6** Acholi, Ankole, Bagisu, Bakiga, Basoga, Batoro **7** Baganda, Banyoro, Bunyoro, Hamitic, Lugbara, Nilotic, Sudanic **9** Nyoro-Toro **10** Banyankole, Karamojong

of Ukraine: 7 Russian **9** Ukrainian

of United Arab Emirates: 4 Arab **6** Indian **7** African, Iranian **9** Pakistani **10** South Asian

of Uruguay: 4 Yaro **5** Swiss **6** Indian **7** Italian, mestizo, Russian, Spanish **8** Charruas

of Uzbekistan: 5 Uzbek

of Vanuatu: 8 European **10** Melanesian, Polynesian **11** Micronesian

of Venezuela: 4 Bare, Pume **5** Bello, Carib, pardo, zambo **6** Arawak,

Creole, Timote **7** Charoya, Guahibo, Kaliana, mestizo, mulatto, Otomaca, Timotex **8** Caquetio, Guarauno, Matilone **11** Maquiritare

of Vietnam: 3 Hoa, Man, Meo, Tai, Tay **4** Cham, Kinh, Nung, Thai **5** Khmer, Malay, Muong **7** Chinese **8** Annamese, Annamite **9** Cambodian **10** montagnard, Vietnamese

of Wales: 4 Celt, Kelt **5** Cymry, Kymry, Welsh **7** Brython, Silures, Taffies **8** Awabokal, Cambrian **9** Siluridan

of Western Sahara: 4 Arab **6** Berber

of Western Samoa: 6 Samoan **10** Melanesian, Polynesian

of Yemen: 4 Arab **5** Zaidi **6** Shafai, Yemeni **8** Yemenite

of Yugoslavia: 4 Serb, Slav **5** Croat **7** Bosnian, Slovene **8** Albanian, Croatian **9** Hungarian **10** Macedonian **11** Montenegrin **13** Herzegovinian

of Zaire: 4 Kuba, Luba, Yaka **5** Bantu, Bashi, Bemba, Kongo, Lulue, Lunda, Mongo, Pygmy **6** Azande, Baluba, Watusi **7** Bakongo, Nilotes, Tshokwe **8** European, Mangbetu, Sudanese

of Zambia: 4 Lozi **5** Bantu, Bemba, Ngoni, Tonga

of Zimbabwe: 3 Ila **4** Sena **5** Asian, Bantu, Bemba, Sotho, Tongo, white **6** Indian **7** Barotse, Chinese, English, Mashoma, Mashona, Ndebele **8** Coloured, Japanese, Matabele **9** Afrikaner **10** Balakwakwa

etiquette 5 usage **7** decorum, manners **8** behavior, courtesy, good form, protocol **9** amenities, gentility, good taste **10** civilities, politeness **11** conventions, proprieties **15** rules of behavior

etoile 4 star **9** ballerina

Etruscan
native of: (ancient) **7** Etruria
location: 7 Tuscany
king: 7 Tarquin **11** Lars Porsena

Ettarre
character in: 16 Arthurian romance

ET The Extra-Terrestrial
director: 15 Steven Spielberg
cast: 10 Dee Wallace **11** Henry Thomas, Peter Coyote **13** Drew Barrymore **17** Robert MacNaughton

et tu, Brute 13 and thou Brutus
spoken by: 12 Julius Caesar

etymology 7 history **10** derivation

Etzel
origin: 8 Germanic
mentioned in: 14 Nibelungenlied
represents: 6 Attila
wife: 9 Kriemhild

Eucharist 8 viaticum **9** Communion, sacrament **13** Holy Communion

euchre
number of players: 3 two **4** four **5** three
derived from: 8 triomphe

five tricks won: 5 march
jack of trump: 10 right bower
second highest trump: 9 left bower

Euclid
field: 11 mathematics
nationality: 5 Greek
founder of: 8 geometry
author of: 8 Elements

Eugene Onegin
author: 16 Alexander Pushkin
opera by: 11 Tchaikovsky
character: 4 Olga **6** Lensky, Onegin **7** Tatyana **12** Prince Gremin, Tatyana Larin **14** Vladimir Lensky

Eugenie Grandet
author: 14 Honore de Balzac
character: 5 Nanon **7** Charles, Eugenie **11** Mme d'Aubrion

Euhelopus
type: 8 dinosaur, sauropod
period: 10 Cretaceous

Euler, Leonhard
field: 7 physics **11** mathematics
nationality: 5 Swiss
first: 12 calculus book

eulogize 4 hail, laud, tout **5** boost, exalt, extol **7** acclaim, commend, glorify, magnify **9** celebrate **10** compliment, panegyrize **12** pay tribute to, praise highly

eulogy 5 paean **6** homage **7** hosanna, plaudit, tribute **8** citation, encomium **9** laudation, panegyric **10** high praise **11** acclamation

Eumenides
author: 9 Aeschylus
character: 6 Apollo, Athene, Furies **7** Orestes
see **6** Furies

Eunice
son: 7 Timothy

Eunomia
member of: 5 Horae
personifies: 5 order

Eunuch 6 Biztha, Careas, Zethar **7** Abagtha, Harbona, Mehuman **8** castrato

Eunuch, The
author: 7 Terence

euphemism 11 prudishness, refined term **12** delicate term, overdelicacy **13** prudish phrase **14** mild expression, overrefinement

euphoria 7 ecstasy, elation, rapture **9** well-being

Euphrosyne
member of: 6 Graces

Euphues
character in: 20 Euphues and His England **22** Euphues The Anatomy of Wit
author: 4 Lyly

Euripides
author of: 3 Ion **5** Medea **6** Hecuba **7** Electra, Orestes **8** Alcestis, Heracles **10** Andromache, Heraclidae,

Hippolytus, Phoenissae, The Bacchae **13** The Suppliants **14** The Trojan Women **16** Iphigenia in Aulis **17** Iphigenia in Tauris **21** The Children of Heracles

Europa
also: 6 Europe
father: 6 Agenor
mother: 10 Telephassa
brother: 5 Cilix **6** Cadmus **7** Phoenix
son: 5 Minos **8** Sarpedon **12** Rhadamanthus
daughter: 5 Crete
abducted by: 4 Zeus

Europe *see* **6** Europa

Europe
country: 5 Italy, Malta, Spain, Wales **6** France, Greece, Latvia, Monaco, Norway, Poland, Russia, Sweden **7** Albania, Andorra, Armenia, Austria, Belarus, Belgium, Croatia, Denmark, England, Estonia, Georgia, Germany, Hungary, Iceland, Ireland, Romania, Ukraine **8** Bulgaria, Portugal, Scotland, Slovakia, Slovenia **9** Lithuania, Macedonia, San Marino **10** Azerbaijan, Luxembourg, Yugoslavia **11** Byelorussia, Netherlands, Switzerland, Vatican City **13** Czech Republic, Liechtenstein **14** Czechoslovakia **17** Bosnia Herzegovina
city: 4 Bern, Bonn, Oslo, Rome **5** Paris, Sofia, Vaduz **6** Athens, Dublin, Lisbon, London, Madrid, Monaco, Moscow, Prague, Tirana, Vienna, Warsaw **7** Cardiff **8** Belgrade, Brussels, Budapest, Helsinki, Valletta **9** Amsterdam, Bucharest, Edinburgh, Reykjavik, San Marino, Stockholm **10** Bratislava, Copenhagen, Luxembourg **14** Andorra la Vella
river: 3 Don **4** Ebro, Elbe, Oder **5** Loire, Neman, Rhine, Rhone, Seine, Tagus, Volga **6** Danube, Thames **7** Dnieper, Pechora, Vistula **8** Dniester
island: 3 Man **4** Skye **5** Crete, Malta **6** Faeroe, Sicily **7** Corsica, Iceland, Ireland **8** Balearic, Sardinia **12** British Isles
mountain/mountain range: 4 Alps **7** Balkans **8** Caucasus, Pyrenees **9** Apennines **11** Carpathians **12** Sierra Nevada
highest point: 11 Mount Elbrus
lowest point: 10 Caspian Sea
sea: 4 Aral, Azov, Kara **5** Black, North, White **6** Aegean, Baltic **7** Caspian, Marmara **8** Adriatic **13** Mediterranean
people: 3 Hun **4** Gael, Pict, Serb **5** Celts, Croat, Danes, Dutch, Jutes, Kymry, Marur, Poles, Scots, Slavs, Tatar, Welsh **6** Czechs, Franks **7** Basques, Britons, Gypsies, Iberian, Magyars, Slovaks, Slovene **8** Alamanni, Cossacks, Tyrolean, Walloons
language: 5 Czech, Irish **6** Basque, Danish, French, Gaelic, German, Pol-

ish, Slovak **7** English, Italian, Romance, Russian, Spanish, Swedish **8** Germanic **9** Bulgarian, Portugese **11** Balto-slavic

religion: **5** Islam **6** Jewish, Muslim **8** Anglican, Lutheran **9** Methodist **10** Protestant **12** Presbyterian **13** Dutch Reformed, Greek Orthodox, Roman Catholic **15** Church of England, Eastern Orthodox

holiday: **11** Bastille Day, National Day **12** Guy Fawkes Day **13** Liberation Day, St Patricks Day **14** Queens Birthday **15** Independence Day **19** Heroes of the Republic

Eurus
origin: **5** Greek
personifies: **8** east wind **13** southeast wind

Euryale
member of: **7** Gorgons

Euryanthe
opera by: **5** Weber
character: **6** Adolar **7** Lysiart **9** Eglantine

Euryclea
nurse of: **10** Telemachus

Eurydamas
member of: **9** Argonauts

Eurydice
also: **7** Agriope
form: **5** dryad
husband: **7** Orpheus
daughter: **8** Themiste
pursued by: **9** Aristaeus

Eurynome
father: **7** Oceanus
mother: **6** Tethys
sister: **6** Thetis
daughters: **6** Graces

Eurysthenes
origin: **7** Spartan
father: **11** Aristodemus
twin brother: **7** Procles
shared: **6** throne
shared throne with: **7** Procles

Eurystheus
king of: **6** Tiryns **7** Mycenae
father: **9** Sthenelus
mother: **7** Nicippe
cousin: **8** Hercules
son: **9** Perimedes
imposed: **6** labors
  number of labors: **6** twelve
  imposed on: **8** Hercules

Euterpe
member of: **5** Muses
muse of: **5** music **11** lyric poetry

evacuate 4 quit **5** leave **6** desert, remove, vacate **7** abandon, forsake, move out, take out **8** order out **12** withdraw from

evade 4 duck, shun **5** avoid, dodge, elude, hedge, parry **6** escape, eschew **7** fend off **8** sidestep **10** circumvent, equivocate **12** steer clear of

evaluate 4 rate **5** assay, gauge, judge,

value, weigh **6** assess, size up **8** appraise, estimate

evaluation 4 test **8** analysis, judgment **9** appraisal **10** assessment, estimation

evaluator 5 judge **6** critic, tester **7** analyst, arbiter **8** assessor, reviewer **9** appraiser, estimator

evanesce 6 vanish **8** fade away, pass away **9** disappear, dissipate, evaporate

evanescence 9 vanishing **10** fading away **12** ephemerality **13** disappearance **14** transitoriness

evanescent 8 fleeting **9** ephemeral, transient **10** short- lived, transitory

evangel 6 gospel

Evangeline
author: **24** Henry Wadsworth Longfellow
character: **17** Gabriel Lajeunesse **23** Evangeline Bellefontaine

evangelist 4 John, Luke, Mark **7** apostle, Matthew **8** disciple, minister, preacher, reformer **9** apostolic, missioner, soul-saver **10** missionary, revivalist **12** Bible Thumper, propagandist, proselytizer **17** religious crusader

Evan Harrington
author: **14** George Meredith
character: **6** Louisa **10** Jack Raikes **11** Rose Jocelyn **12** Tom Cogglesby **13** Count de Saldar, Juliana Bonner **14** Caroline Strike **15** Andrew Cogglesby, Ferdinand Laxley, Melville Jocelyn **16** Countess de Saldar, Harriet Cogglesby **21** Melchisedek Harrington

Evans, Dame Edith
born: **6** London **7** England
roles: **8** Tom Jones **11** A Doll's House **13** The Whisperers **14** The Chalk Garden **27** The Importance of Being Earnest

Evans, Mary Anne
real name of: **11** George Eliot

Evans, Maurice
born: **6** Dorset **7** England **10** Dorchester
roles: **9** Saint Joan **13** Rosemary's Baby **14** Man and Superman, Romeo and Juliet **15** Heartbreak House, Planet of the Apes **17** The Devil's Disciple **18** Gilbert and Sullivan **19** Androcles and the Lion

evaporate 5 dry up **6** dispel, vanish **7** scatter **8** dissolve, evanesce, fade away, melt away, vaporize **9** dehydrate, desiccate, disappear, dissipate

evasion 7 dodging, ducking, eluding **8** shunning **9** avoidance **12** sidestepping **13** circumventing, shrinking from **15** attempt to escape

evasive 6 shifty **7** devious, dodging, elusive, elusory, hedging **9** ambiguous, deceitful, deceptive, equivocal **10** misleading **11** dissembling **12** equivocating

Eva Trout
author: **14** Elizabeth Bowen

eve 4 dusk **6** female, sunset **7** evening, sunset **8** eventide **9** day before

Eve
husband: **4** Adam
son: **4** Abel, Cain, Seth
home: **4** Eden

Evelina
author: **11** Fanny Burney

even 4 calm, fair, flat, just, true **5** equal, flush, level, plane, plumb **6** placid, smooth, square, steady **7** balance, equable, flatten, regular, the same, uniform **8** balanced, constant, equalize, matching, parallel, straight, unbiased **9** equitable, identical, impartial, make flush, unruffled, unvarying **10** straighten, unwavering **11** make uniform, unexcitable **12** eventempered, make parallel **13** dispassionate

evening 3 e'en, eve **4** dusk, even **6** sunset **7** day's end, sundown **8** eventide, gloaming, twilight **9** nightfall **10** close of day

evenly matched 5 equal **8** of a piece **9** identical **10** well suited **13** one and the same

evenness 7 balance **8** calmness, equality, fairness, flatness, sameness **9** placidity **10** regularity, smoothness, steadiness, uniformity **11** equivalency

event 4 bout, game **7** contest, episode **8** incident, occasion **9** happening, milestone **10** experience, occurrence, tournament **11** competition

even-tempered 4 calm **6** serene **7** equable, patient **11** good-natured, unflappable **12** mild-tempered, well-adjusted

eventful 7 crucial, epochal, fateful, notable, weighty **8** critical, exciting, historic **9** important, memorable, momentous, thrilling **10** noteworthy **11** significant **13** consequential, unforgettable

eventide 4 dusk **6** sunset **7** evening, sundown **8** gloaming, twilight **9** nightfall

eventual 5 final, later **6** coming, future **7** ensuing **8** imminent, ultimate, upcoming **9** following, impending, resulting **10** consequent, subsequent **11** prospective

eventually 6 one day **7** finally **8** in the end, sometime **10** ultimately **12** in the long run **13** sooner or later **17** in the course of time **20** when all is said and done

even up 3 tie **5** align **8** make even **10** straighten

Eve of St Agnes, The
author: **9** John Keats

ever 5 at all **6** always **7** forever **9** at any time, eternally, in any case **10** at all times, constantly **11** incessantly, perpetually **12** continuously

Everdene, Bathsheba
character in: **22** Far From the Madding Crowd
author: **5** Hardy

Everglade State
nickname of: **7** Florida

evergreen 3 fir, yew **4** pine **5** heath, holly **6** jujube, laurel, myrtle, needle, privet **7** arbutus, casiope, conifer, jasmine, juniper **8** camellia, hawthorn, oleander, rosemary **9** mistletoe, sugarbush **11** conebearing **12** rhododendrum

Evergreen State
nickname of: **10** Washington

everlasting 7 durable, endless, eternal, lasting, tedious, undying **8** constant, immortal, infinite, timeless, tiresome **9** ceaseless, continual, incessant, perpetual, unceasing, wearisome **10** continuous, ever-living **11** long-lasting, never-ending **12** imperishable, interminable **14** indestructible

evermore 6 always **7** forever **9** eternally **10** for all time **13** everlastingly

ever upward
Latin: **9** excelsior
motto of: **7** New York (state)

everybody
French: **11** tout le monde

everyday 4 dull **5** daily, stock, trite, usual **6** common, square **7** mundane, regular, routine **8** familiar, ordinary, workaday **9** customary, hackneyed, quotidian **11** commonplace, day after day, established, stereotyped **12** conventional, run-of-the-mill **13** unimaginative

Everyman
author: **7** unknown
character: **3** God **5** Death, Goods **6** Beauty **7** Kindred **8** Strength **9** Good Deeds, Knowledge, Messenger **10** Fellowship

every man for himself
French: **12** sauve qui peut

Every Man in His Humour
author: **9** Ben Jonson
character: **6** Kitely **7** Bridget **8** Bobadill, Wellbred **9** Brainworm, Downright **13** Edward Knowell **14** Justice Clement

Every Man out of His Humour
author: **9** Ben Jonson
character: **6** Deliro **7** Fungoso, Sordido **9** Macilente, Sogliardo **10** Puntarvolo **12** Carlo Buffone **15** Fastidious Brisk

everyone
French: **11** tout le monde

everywhere 7 all over **10** every place, far and near, far and wide, throughout **11** extensively, in all places, uni-

versally **12** the world over, ubiquitously **14** to the four winds

evict 4 oust **5** eject, expel **6** remove **7** kick out, turn out **8** dislodge, get rid of, throw out **10** dispossess

evidence 4 fact, sign **5** proof, token **7** exhibit, grounds **9** testimony **10** indication **11** affirmation **12** confirmation, illustration **13** corroboration, documentation, material proof **14** authentication, substantiation **15** exemplification

evident 5 clear, plain **6** patent **7** certain, obvious, visible **8** apparent, manifest, tangible **10** noticeable, undeniable **11** conspicuous, perceptible **12** demonstrable, unmistakable **14** unquestionable **24** plain as the nose on your face

evidently 7 clearly, plainly **9** assumedly, certainly, doubtless, obviously **10** apparently, undeniably **11** doubtlessly **12** unmistakably **14** unquestionably **16** to all appearances

evil 3 bad, sin **4** base, vice, vile **5** venal **6** sinful, wicked **7** heinous, immoral, vicious **8** baseness, iniquity, sinister **9** depravity, malicious, malignant, nefarious, turpitude **10** corruption, immorality, iniquitous, malevolent, pernicious, villainous, wickedness, wrongdoing **12** blackhearted, unprincipled, unscrupulous
goddess of: **7** Sekhmet

evildoer 6 sinner **7** culprit, villain **9** miscreant, wrongdoer **10** malefactor **12** transgressor

evil-minded 4 base **5** nasty **6** wicked **7** ignoble, immoral **8** depraved **10** despicable, iniquitous, villainous **12** dishonorable, unprincipled

evilness 6 malice **7** cruelty **8** villainy **9** barbarity, malignity **10** sinfulness, wickedness

evince 4 show **6** convey, reveal **7** display, exhibit, express **11** communicate, demonstrate **12** give evidence

Evius see **7** Bacchus

Evnissyen
origin: **5** Welsh
brother: **4** Bran **10** Manawyddan
sister: **7** Branwen
caused: **3** war
    between: **5** Irish **7** British
killed: **6** nephew

evoke 4 stir **5** rouse, waken **6** arouse, awaken, call up, elicit, excite, induce, invite, invoke, summon **7** produce, provoke, suggest **9** call forth, conjure up, stimulate **10** bring forth

evolution 4 rise **6** change, growth **8** fruition, increase **9** expansion, unfolding **10** maturation **11** development, enlargement, progression **13** metamorphosis
founder of theory: **13** Charles Darwin

forerunner of theory: 12 Charles Lyell **18** Chevalier de Lamarck

evolve 4 grow **5** ripen **6** expand, mature, unfold, unroll **7** develop, enlarge **8** increase

Ewell, Tom
real name: **14** Yewell Tompkins
born: **11** Owensboro KY
roles: **8** Adam's Rib **9** State Fair **14** The Great Gatsby **16** Tender Is the Night, The Seven Year Itch

ewer 3 jug, urn **5** basin **6** vessel **7** pitcher

Ewing, Patrick
sport: **10** basketball
team: **13** New York Knicks **15** Georgetown Hoyas

exacerbate 3 irk **5** anger **6** deepen, worsen **7** inflame, magnify, provoke, sharpen **8** heighten, increase, irritate **9** aggravate, intensify **10** exaggerate **12** fan the flames **16** pour oil on the fire **17** add insult to injury **18** add fuel to the flames **19** rub salt into the wound

exact 4 take, true **5** claim, force, mulct, right, wrest **6** compel, demand, extort, strict **7** careful, correct, extract, literal, precise, require, squeeze **8** accurate, clear-cut, exacting, explicit, specific **9** on the head, on the nose **10** methodical, meticulous, scrupulous, systematic **11** painstaking, punctilious, to the letter, unequivocal

exacting 4 hard **5** harsh, rigid, stern, tough **6** severe, strict, trying **7** arduous **8** critical **9** demanding, difficult, hard-nosed, strenuous, unbending, unsparing **10** hard-headed, meticulous, no-nonsense

exactly 4 just **5** fully, quite, truly **6** indeed, just so, wholly **7** quite so **8** entirely, of course, strictly **9** assuredly, certainly, correctly, literally, precisely **10** absolutely, accurately, definitely, explicitly, that's right **12** specifically

exactness 8 accuracy **9** precision **10** exactitude **12** accurateness

exact satisfaction 6 avenge, punish **7** get back, get even, revenge **9** retaliate **14** get one's own back

exaggerate 5 boast **6** overdo **7** amplify, lay it on, magnify, stretch **9** embellish, embroider, enlarge on, overstate **11** hyperbolize

exaggerated 7 extreme, intense **10** inordinate, overstated **14** overemphasized

exalt 4 laud **5** cheer, elate, extol, honor **6** praise, uplift **7** acclaim, applaud, commend, elevate, ennoble, glorify, inspire, magnify, worship **8** venerate **9** celebrate, stimulate **10** exhilarate, make much of **12** pay tribute to

exaltation 4 high **5** bliss, glory, honor **6** praise **7** dignity, ecstasy, elation, rapture, tribute, worship **8** grandeur, nobility, praising **9** happiness, panegyric, transport **10** eulogizing, exultation, veneration **11** celebration, deification **12** exhilaration

exalted 2 up **5** grand, happy, lofty, noble **6** august, elated, lordly **7** excited, notable **8** blissful, ecstatic, elevated, glorious, inspired, uplifted **9** dignified, honorable, rapturous, venerable **10** heightened **11** high-ranking, illustrious, magnificent

exaltedness 5 bliss **6** height **7** ecstasy, elation, heights, rapture **8** highness, nobility **9** elevation, loftiness, transport

examination 4 exam, quiz, test **5** assay, audit, final, orals, probe, study **6** review, survey **7** midterm, perusal **8** analysis, scrutiny **10** inspection **11** looking over **13** investigation **15** physical checkup

examine 4 pump, quiz, scan, test, view **5** audit, grill, probe, query, study **6** peruse, ponder, review, survey **7** explore, inspect, observe **8** consider, look into, look over, question **10** scrutinize **11** inquire into, interrogate, investigate, take stock of

examiner 6 tester **8** inquirer, reviewer, surveyor **12** interrogator, investigator

example 5 ideal, model **6** sample **7** paragon, pattern **8** exemplar, specimen, standard **9** archetype, prototype **11** case in point **12** illustration **14** representation **15** exemplification

exasperate 3 bug, irk, vex **4** rile **5** anger, annoy, chafe, pique **6** bother, enrage, harass, madden, offend, rankle, ruffle **7** incense, provoke, turn off **8** irritate **9** aggravate, infuriate **15** try one's patience

exasperating 7 irksome **8** annoying **9** vexatious **10** irritating **11** infuriating

Excalibur 5 sword
  drawn from: 5 stone
    by: 6 Arthur
  given by: 5 Nimue **7** Viviane **13** Lady of the Lake

ex cathedra 12 from the chair **13** with authority **22** from the seat of authority

excavate 3 dig **4** mine **5** dig up, gouge **6** burrow, cut out, dig out, furrow, groove, quarry, tunnel **7** uncover, unearth **8** scoop out **9** hollow out **11** make a hole in

excavation 3 dig, pit **4** hole, mine, sump **5** ditch, grave, shaft, space **6** cavity, dugout, trench, trough **7** digging, opening

exceed 4 pass **5** excel **6** go over, outrun, overdo **7** outpace, outrank, surpass **8** go beyond, outreach, outrival, outstrip, surmount **9** come first, overshoot, transcend **10** be superior **11** predominate

exceedingly 4 very **6** vastly **7** greatly, notably **9** amazingly, eminently, extremely, supremely, unusually **10** enormously, especially, unwontedly, very highly **11** excessively **12** immeasurably, impressively, inordinately, preeminently, surpassingly **13** astonishingly, outstandingly, superlatively **15** extraordinarily

excel 5 outdo **6** exceed **7** prevail, surpass **8** outrival, outstrip **9** rank first **10** tower above **11** predominate, take the cake **20** walk off with the honors

excellence 5 merit **7** quality **8** eminence **9** greatness **10** perfection **11** distinction, high quality, preeminence, superiority **13** transcendence

excellent 4 aces, A-one, fine, tops **5** great, nifty, prime, super, swell **6** bang-up, choice, grade A, superb **7** capital, classic, notable **8** peerless, sterling, superior, terrific, top-notch **9** admirable, exemplary, first-rate, matchless, superfine, wonderful **10** first-class, preeminent, tremendous **11** exceptional, outstanding, superlative

excelsior 10 ever upward
  motto of: 7 New York (state)

Excelsior State
  nickname of: 7 New York

except 3 ban, bar, but **4** omit, save **6** enjoin, excuse, exempt, reject, remove, saving **7** barring, besides, exclude, shut out **8** count out, disallow, pass over **9** eliminate, excepting, excluding, other than **11** exclusive of

excepted 6 exempt **7** excused **8** excluded **11** not included

exception 6 oddity, rarity **7** anomaly, removal **8** omission **9** debarment, deviation, exclusion, exemption, isolation, rejection, seclusion **10** difference, leaving out, separation **11** elimination, peculiarity, repudiation, segregation, shutting out, special case **12** disallowment, irregularity, renunciation **13** inconsistency

exceptional 3 odd **4** rare **5** great, queer **6** unique **7** special, strange, unusual **8** aberrant, abnormal, atypical, freakish, peculiar, singular, superior, terrific, uncommon, unwonted **9** anomalous, excellent, irregular, marvelous, unheard of, unnatural, wonderful **10** first-class, inimitable, noteworthy, out-of-sight, phenomenal, remarkable **11** outstanding **12** incomparable **13** extraordinary, unprecedented **17** better than average

exception to the rule 7 anomaly **11** abnormality **12** irregularity

excerpt 4 part **5** piece **7** extract, portion, section **8** abstract, fragment **9** quotation, selection **13** quoted passage

excess 4 glut **5** extra, flood, spare **7** residue, surfeit, surplus, too much

8 fullness, overflow, plethora **9** avalanche, excessive, profusion, remainder, repletion **10** inundation, lavishness, oversupply **11** undue amount **13** overabundance **14** superabundance

excessive 5 undue **6** excess **7** extreme, profuse, too much **8** needless **9** senseless **10** immoderate, inordinate **11** exaggerated, extravagant, superfluous, unnecessary **12** overabundant, unreasonable **16** disproportionate

excessively 5 enorm **7** greatly **9** extremely, intensely **11** exceedingly, fanatically **12** boisterously, exorbitantly, inordinately **14** overabundantly

exchange 4 swap **5** trade **6** barter, switch **8** bandying, trade off **9** tit for tat **10** quid pro quo **11** convert into, give-and-take, interchange, reciprocate, reciprocity

exchange blows 3 box **5** clash, fight **6** battle, combat, tussle **7** contend, contest, grapple **8** skirmish **11** cross swords

exchange of viewpoints 6 debate, parley **8** dialogue **10** conference, discussion

exchange premium 4 agio

exchange views 6 confer, debate **7** consult, discuss **8** consider, talk over **12** compare notes

excise 3 tax **4** duty **6** cut off, cut out, impost, remove **7** extract **8** pluck out **9** eradicate, surcharge

excitable 4 edgy **5** jumpy **7** jittery, nervous **8** feverish, frenzied, skittish **9** flappable, hotheaded **10** highstrung, passionate **11** combustible, inflammable

excite 4 fire, move, whet **5** evoke, pique, rouse, waken **6** arouse, awaken, elicit, foment, incite, kindle, spur on, stir up, thrill **7** agitate, animate, inflame, provoke **8** energize **9** electrify, galvanize, instigate, stimulate, titillate **13** get a kick out of

excited 4 daft **5** afire, astir **6** ablaze **7** aroused **8** agitated, ecstatic, frenzied, inflamed, turned on **9** disturbed, stirred up **10** magnetized **11** electrified

excitement 3 ado **4** flap, stir, to-do **5** furor, kicks **6** action, flurry, frenzy, hoopla, thrill, tumult **7** elation, ferment, flutter, turmoil **8** activity, brouhaha, interest **9** adventure, agitation, animation, commotion, fireworks **10** enthusiasm **11** stimulation

exciting 5 spicy **6** moving, risque **7** rousing, zestful **8** dazzling, stirring **9** affecting, impelling, inspiring, thrilling **11** hair-raising, provocative, sensational, stimulating, titillating **12** breathtaking, electrifying **13** spine-tingling

exclaim 4 howl, yell **5** shout **6** bellow,

cry out **7** call out **8** proclaim **9** ejaculate **10** vociferate

exclamation 3 cry **4** howl, yell, yelp **5** shout **6** bellow, outcry, shriek, squeal **7** screech **9** expletive **11** ejaculation **12** interjection, vociferation

exclamation of:
   approval: 3 ole, rah **5** bravo
   despair: 4 alas **5** alack **7** woe is me
   dicovery: 3 aha, oho
   disdain: 3 duh, hah, tsk **4** bosh, bunk, pooh
   disgust: 3 bah, ugh **4** damn, darn, drat, pfui, rats **5** shoot **6** humbug, phooey
   joy: 3 yay **4** whee, yeah **6** hooray, hurrah, hurray **7** whoopie
   pain: 4 ouch **5** yipes
   relief: 4 phew, whew
   other: 3 fie, hah, hey, tut, wow **4** oops, scat, shoo, ta-da **5** voila **6** hoopla
   bacchanalian cry: 4 evoe

exclude 3 ban, bar **4** omit, oust **5** eject, evict, expel **6** banish, except, forbid, refuse, reject, remove **7** boycott, keep out, rule out, shut out **8** disallow, leave out, prohibit, set aside, throw out **9** blackball, repudiate **13** shut the door on

excluding 3 but **4** save **6** except, saving **7** banning, barring, besides **9** excepting, other than **10** keeping out

exclusion 6 ouster **7** barring, refusal, removal **8** ejection, eviction **9** debarment, dismissal, expelling, expulsion, rejection, restraint **10** banishment, keeping out, preclusion, prevention **11** prohibition, throwing out **12** nonadmission

exclusive 4 full, posh, sole **5** aloof, total **6** closed, entire, single **7** private **8** absolute, clannish, cliquish, complete, snobbish, unshared **9** undivided, selective **10** restricted **11** restrictive

exclusive of 3 but **4** save **6** except, saving **7** barring, besides **9** excepting, excluding, other than

excommunicate 3 ban **4** oust **5** eject, expel **6** banish, remove **8** unchurch **12** anathematize

excommunication 3 ban **6** ouster **8** anathema **10** banishment **12** proscription

excoriate 4 flay **5** curse **6** berate, revile **7** censure **8** denounce, execrate **9** skin alive

excrescence 4 bump, hump, knob, knot, lump **5** bulge, gnarl **6** nodule **8** swelling **10** protrusion **12** protuberance

excrete 4 void **5** expel **8** evacuate **9** discharge, eliminate

excruciating 5 acute **6** fierce, severe **7** cutting, extreme, intense, racking, violent **9** agonizing, exquisite, torturous

10 lacerating, tormenting, unbearable **11** unendurable **12** insufferable

exculpate 5 clear **6** acquit, excuse, pardon **7** absolve **9** exonerate, let one off, vindicate

excursion 4 hike, ride, tour, trek, trip, walk **5** drive, jaunt, sally, tramp **6** cruise, flight, junket, outing, ramble, sortie, stroll, voyage **10** expedition **12** pleasure trip

excusatory 9 defensive **10** apologetic **11** extenuatory, vindicatory **13** justificatory

excuse 4 free **5** alibi, clear, spare **6** acquit, defend, exempt, let off, pardon, reason **7** absolve, condone, defense, explain, forgive, indulge, justify, release **8** argument, bear with, mitigate, overlook, palliate, pass over **9** disregard, exculpate, exemption, exonerate, extenuate, gloss over, let one off, relieve of, vindicate, whitewash **10** absolution **11** exoneration, vindication **12** apologize for **13** justification **16** make allowance for **17** accept one's apology

execrable 4 vile **5** awful **8** dreadful, terrible **9** atrocious, revolting **10** abominable

execrate 4 hate **5** abhor **6** detest, loathe **7** despise **9** abominate, can't stand, excoriate **10** shrink from **11** can't stomach **12** be revolted by **13** be nauseated by, find repulsive **15** be disgusted with **20** regard with repugnance

execration 4 hate **6** hating **7** disgust **8** loathing **9** despising, repulsion, revulsion **10** repugnance **11** abomination, detestation

execute 2 do **3** act **4** kill, play, slay **5** enact **6** effect, murder, render **7** achieve, enforce, fulfill, perform, realize, sustain **8** carry out, complete, massacre **9** discharge **10** accomplish, administer, consummate, effectuate, perpetrate, put to death **11** assassinate **12** carry through **13** put into effect

execution 5 doing **7** killing, slaying **9** discharge, effecting, rendition **10** completion **11** achievement, carrying out, fulfillment, performance, realization, transaction **14** accomplishment, administration, implementation, interpretation, putting to death

executioner 6 hit man, killer, slayer **7** butcher, hangman **8** assassin, murderer

Executioner's Song, The
   author: 12 Norman Mailer
   subject: 11 Gary Gilmore

executive 3 CEO, CFO **4** suit **7** manager **8** chairman, director, overseer **9** president **10** leadership, managerial, supervisor **11** directorial, supervisory **13** administrator **14** administrative, superintendent

executives 5 suits **7** leaders **8** managers, officers **9** directors **13** governing body **14** administration

executor 4 doer **5** agent **9** performer **13** administrator

exegesis 10 exposition **11** explanation **14** interpretation **18** explication de texte

exemplar 5 ideal, model **7** example, pattern **8** original, specimen, standard **9** archetype, prototype

exemplary 5 ideal, model **6** sample **7** typical **8** laudable, sterling **9** admirable, emulative, estimable, nonpareil **10** noteworthy **11** commendable, meritorious **12** illustrative, praiseworthy **14** characteristic, representative

exemplification 7 epitome, essence, example **8** citation, evidence **10** embodiment **11** case in point **12** illustration **13** documentation **14** representation **15** personification

exemplify 6 depict, embody, typify **8** instance **9** epitomize, personify, represent **10** illustrate **11** demonstrate **12** characterize

exempli gratia 6 such as **10** for example **19** for the sake of example
   abbreviation: 2 eg

exempt 4 free **5** clear, freed, spare **6** except, excuse, immune, pardon, spared **7** absolve, cleared, excused, release, relieve **8** absolved, excepted, relieved **9** not liable, privilege **10** privileged

exemption 6 excuse **7** expense, freedom, release **8** immunity **9** allowance, deduction, exception **10** absolution **12** dispensation

exercise 3 use **4** show **5** apply, drill, exert, teach, train, tutor, wield **6** employ, school, warm-up **7** break in, develop, display, execute, exhibit, perform, prepare, program, utilize, workout **8** accustom, aerobics, carry out, ceremony, movement, practice, training **9** discharge, inculcate, schooling **10** daily dozen, discipline, employment, gymnastics, isometrics **11** application, demonstrate, give lessons, performance, utilization **12** calisthenics **14** do calisthenics

exert 3 use **5** apply, wield **6** employ, expend **7** utilize **8** exercise, put forth, resort to **9** discharge, make use of **11** put in action, set in motion

exertion 4 toil, work **5** labor, pains **6** effort, energy **7** travail, trouble **8** activity, endeavor, industry, strength, struggle **11** application, elbow grease

ex facie 9 on the face **10** apparently **11** from the face

ex facto 8 actually **15** according to fact

exhalation 4 puff **6** breath, wheeze,

whoosh **10** expiration **12** breathing out

exhale 4 huff, pant, puff **6** expire **7** breathe, respire **10** breathe out

exhaust 3 fag, tax **4** bush, poop, tire **5** drain, empty, spend, use up **6** expend, finish, strain, weaken **7** consume, deplete, disable, draw off, draw out, fatigue, wear out **8** enervate, overtire **9** dissipate **10** debilitate, devitalize, run through **13** sap one's energy

exhausted 4 beat, gone **5** all in, spent **6** bushed, done in, pooped, used up **7** drained, emptied, wearied, worn out **8** bankrupt, consumed, depleted, expended, fatigued, finished, tired out **9** dead tired, enervated, played out **11** devitalized **12** impoverished

exhausting 5 tough **6** tiring, uphill **7** arduous **8** toilsome **9** difficult, fatiguing, Herculean, laborious, Sisyphean, wearisome **10** burdensome

exhaustion 7 fatigue, using up **8** draining, spending **9** depletion, tiredness, weariness **10** enervation **11** consumption

exhaustive 6 all-out **7** in-depth **8** complete, profound, sweeping, thorough **9** intensive **12** all-embracing, all-inclusive **13** comprehensive

exhibit 3 air **4** show **6** flaunt, parade, reveal, unveil **7** display **8** brandish **9** put on view **10** exhibition, exposition, make public **11** demonstrate **12** bring to light **13** public showing

exhibition 4 show **5** array **7** display, exhibit, showing **9** unveiling **10** exposition **13** demonstration, public showing

exhibitionist 7 flasher, show-off **15** attention-seeker

exhilarate 4 lift **5** cheer, elate **6** excite, perk up **7** animate, delight, enliven, gladden, hearten, quicken **9** stimulate **10** invigorate

exhilaration 6 gaiety **7** delight, elation **8** gladness, vivacity **9** animation **10** exaltation, excitement, joyousness, liveliness **11** high spirits **16** lightheartedness

exhort 3 bid **4** goad, prod, spur, urge **5** egg on, press **6** advise, enjoin **7** beseech, implore **8** admonish, advocate, appeal to, persuade **9** encourage, plead with, recommend **14** give a pep talk to

exhortation 6 sermon, urging **7** bidding, lecture, pep talk **8** dictates, harangue, prodding **9** prompting

exhumation 9 digging up **12** disinterment **13** disentombment

exhume 5 dig up **8** disinter

exigency 3 fix, jam **5** needs, pinch **6** crisis, pickle, plight, scrape, strait **7** demands **8** hardship, quandary

9 emergency, extremity, urgencies **10** difficulty **11** constraints, contingency, necessities, predicament **12** circumstance, requirements

exigent 5 vital **6** urgent **8** critical, exacting, pressing **9** demanding, difficult, necessary

exile 2 DP **4** oust **5** eject, expel **6** banish, deport, emigre, pariah **7** outcast, refugee **8** drive out, expellee **9** expulsion **10** banishment, expatriate

Exile, The
author: **9** Pearl Buck

exiled person 5 exile **6** emigre **7** outcast **8** expellee **10** expatriate

Exile's Return
author: **13** Malcolm Cowley

exist 4 last, live, stay **5** abide, ensue, occur **6** endure, happen, obtain, remain **7** breathe, prevail, survive

existence 4 life **5** being **7** reality **8** presence, survival **9** actuality, animation, endurance **11** continuance, materiality, subsistence, tangibility

existent 4 real **5** alive **6** actual, extant, living **7** present **8** existing, tangible **9** surviving, to be found **11** in existence

existing 4 real **5** being **6** actual, extant, living **7** ongoing, present **9** existence, surviving, to be found **10** continuing, prevailing **11** established, in existence **12** accomplished

exit 4 blow **5** go out, leave, split **6** cut out, depart, egress, escape, exodus, way out **7** retreat **8** withdraw **9** departure **10** withdrawal **11** take a powder

ex libris 15 out of the books of **16** from the library of

ex nihilo nihil fit 25 out of nothing nothing is made **27** nothing is created from nothing

exocuticle
consists of: **9** sclerotin

exodus 4 exit **5** exile **6** flight, hegira **9** departure, migration **10** emigration, going forth

Exodus
author: **8** Leon Uris
story of founding of: **6** Israel

exonerate 4 free **5** clear **6** acquit **7** absolve, forgive **9** exculpate, vindicate **12** find innocent

exoneration 8 clearing **10** absolution **11** exculpation, vindication

exorbitant 4 dear **5** undue **6** costly **7** extreme **8** enormous **9** egregious, excessive, expensive, out-of-line **10** high-priced, inordinate, oppressive, outrageous, overpriced **11** extravagant **12** extortionate, preposterous, unreasonable

exorcise 5 expel **7** cast out **8** get rid of

Exorcist, The
author: **18** William Peter Blatty
director: **15** William Friedkin

cast: **8** Lee J Cobb **10** Linda Blair **11** Jason Miller, Max von Sydow **12** Ellen Burstyn
Oscar for: **10** screenplay

exoskeleton
of insect: **5** shell **8** body wall
part: **10** epicuticle, exocuticle **11** endocuticle

exoteric 4 open **6** public, simple **7** popular **8** exterior, external, outsider

exotic 5 alien **6** quaint, unique **7** foreign, strange, unusual **8** colorful, peculiar, striking **9** different, not native **10** from abroad, intriguing, outlandish, unfamiliar **11** exceptional **13** not indigenous

expand 4 grow, open **5** swell, widen **6** dilate, evolve, extend, fatten, spread, unfold, unfurl, unroll **7** amplify, augment, develop, distend, enlarge, inflate, magnify, stretch, unravel **8** heighten, increase, multiply **9** outspread, spread out **10** aggrandize

expanded 4 grew **5** grown **7** dilated, swelled, swollen, widened **8** enlarged, extended, unfolded, unfurled, unrolled **9** augmented, broadened, increased, outspread, spread out, stretched **10** heightened **11** aggrandized

expanse 4 area **5** field, range, reach, space, sweep **6** extent **7** breadth, compass, stretch **9** magnitude

expansion 6 growth **8** dilation, increase, swelling, widening **9** enlarging, extension, spreading **10** amplifying, distention, magnifying, stretching **11** development, enlargement, lengthening, multiplying **12** augmentation **13** amplification

expansive 4 free, open, vast, wide **5** broad **6** genial **7** affable, amiable, general, liberal **8** effusive, generous, outgoing **9** bounteous, bountiful, capacious, extensive, exuberant **10** voluminous **11** extroverted, far-reaching, uninhibited, unrepressed, wide-ranging **12** unrestrained **13** comprehensive

expatiate 6 expand **7** amplify, enlarge, expound **9** discourse, elaborate

expatriate 2 DP **5** exile **6** emigre, pariah **7** outcast, refugee **15** displaced person

expatriation 5 exile **9** expulsion **10** banishment

expect 5 guess, trust **6** assume, demand, plan on, reckon **7** believe, count on, foresee, hope for, imagine, look for, presume, require, suppose, surmise **8** envision, reckon on, rely upon **9** calculate **10** anticipate, bargain for, conjecture, reckon upon **11** contemplate **13** look forward to

expectancy 11 expectation **12** anticipation

expectant 4 agog **5** eager, ready **7** anxious, hopeful, waiting **9** expecting

10 looking for, optimistic **12** anticipating, apprehensive

expectation 4 hope **5** trust **6** belief, chance **8** prospect, reliance **9** assurance **10** confidence, expectancy, likelihood **11** presumption **12** anticipation **13** contemplation

expedient 4 help, wise **5** means **6** resort, tactic, useful **7** benefit, helpful, measure, politic, selfish, stopgap **9** advantage, advisable, conniving, desirable, effective, judicious, makeshift, opportune, practical, strategem **10** beneficial, instrument, profitable, worthwhile **11** calculating, self-seeking, self-serving **12** advantageous **14** self-interested

expedite 4 rush **5** hurry **6** hasten **7** advance, forward, further, promote, quicken, speed up **8** dispatch **10** accelerate, facilitate **11** precipitate, push through

expedition 4 trek **6** voyage **7** journey, mission **8** campaign, voyagers **9** explorers, travelers, wayfarers **10** enterprise **11** adventurers, exploration

expeditious 4 fast **5** alert, awake, hasty, quick, rapid, ready, swift **6** prompt, snappy, speedy **7** instant **8** punctual **9** effective, immediate **10** bright-eyed **11** efficacious

expel 4 fire, oust, sack, spew, void **5** eject, evict, exile **6** banish, bounce, remove **7** cashier, cast out, dismiss, drum out, excrete **8** dislodge, drive out, evacuate, force out, throw out **9** discharge, eliminate

expellee 2 DP **5** exile **14** banished person **15** displaced person

expend 3 pay **4** give **5** drain, empty, spend, use up **6** donate, lay out, pay out **7** consume, exhaust, fork out, wear out **8** disburse, dispense, shell out, squander **9** dissipate, go through **10** contribute

expendable 7 payable **9** available, forgoable, spendable **10** consumable, extraneous **11** disbursable, dispensable, replaceable, superfluous **12** nonessential **14** relinquishable

expended 5 spent **6** used up **7** drained, emptied, paid out **8** consumed **9** disbursed, exhausted **10** dissipated

expenditure 3 use **4** cost **5** price **6** charge, outlay, output **7** payment **8** exertion, expenses, spending **9** expending, paying out **10** employment, money spent **11** application, consumption **12** disbursement

expense 4 cost, rate **5** drain, price **6** amount, charge, figure, outlay **9** depletion, quotation

expensive 4 dear **6** costly **9** excessive **10** exorbitant, high-priced, immoderate, overpriced **11** extravagant **12** un-economical, unreasonable **15** beyond one's means

experience 3 see **4** bear, feel, know, meet, view **5** doing, event, sense **6** affair, behold, endure, suffer **7** episode, observe, sustain, undergo **8** exposure, incident, perceive, practice, training **9** adventure, encounter, go through, happening, seasoning, withstand **10** occurrence **11** familiarity, live through, observation **17** personal knowledge **18** firsthand knowledge

experienced 4 able, wise **6** expert, master **7** capable, knowing, skilled, trained, veteran **8** seasoned **9** competent, efficient, practical, qualified **10** well-versed **11** worldly-wise **12** accomplished **13** sophisticated

experiential 9 empirical, firsthand, practical

experiment 4 test **5** assay, flier, trial **6** feeler, try out **7** analyze, examine, explore, venture **8** analysis, research **11** examination, investigate **12** seek proof for, verification **13** investigation **14** mess around with

experimental 3 new **4** test **5** fresh, rough, trial **7** radical **9** tentative **10** conceptual, first-draft **11** conjectural, speculative **13** developmental, trial-and-error

experimentation 7 testing **8** analysis, research **10** experiment **11** examination, exploration **13** investigation, trial and error

experimenter 6 tester **10** researcher **15** experimentalist

expert 3 ace, apt, pro, wiz **4** able, deft, whiz **5** adept, crack, doyen, maven, mavin, shark **6** adroit, artist, facile, master, wizard **7** artiste, capable, perfect, skilled, trained, veteran **8** masterly, skillful, virtuoso **9** authority, competent, masterful, practiced, qualified **10** first-class, past-master, proficient, specialist **11** connoisseur, crackerjack, experienced **12** accomplished, professional **13** knowledgeable **French: 6** au fait

expertise 5 savvy, skill **7** know-how **10** expertness **12** special skill **14** specialization **15** professionalism

expertness 5 savvy, skill **7** ability, know how **8** training **9** expertise **10** capability, competence, experience **11** proficiency **12** special skill **13** qualification **14** accomplishment, specialization **15** professionalism

expiate 7 appease **8** atone for **13** make amends for **16** pay the penalty for

expiation 6 amends, shrift **7** penance **9** atonement **11** appeasement **16** paying the penalty

expiration 3 end **5** death, dying **6** demise, ending, finish **7** passing, closing **8** decrease, exhaling **10** conclusion **11** termination **12** breathing out

expire 3 die, end **5** cease, lapse **6** finish, perish, run out **7** decease, kick off, succumb **8** conclude, pass away **9** terminate **11** come to an end, discontinue **13** kick the bucket **14** give up the ghost

expired 4 dead, died **6** lapsed, ran out, run out **7** defunct, laspsed **8** deceased, lifeless, perished **10** passed away **11** came to an end, come to an end **14** gave up the ghost

explain 6 fathom **7** clarify, clear up, justify, resolve **8** describe, spell out **9** elucidate, explicate, interpret, make clear, make plain **10** account for, illuminate, illustrate **11** demonstrate, rationalize **14** give a reason for **20** give an explanation for

explainer 6 critic **7** analyst **8** reviewer **10** translator **11** commentator, interpreter

explanation
French: 15 eclaircissement

explicate 7 analyze, clarify, develop, explain **8** annotate **9** elucidate, interpret **10** elucidated, illuminate, illustrate

explication 8 analysis **10** commentary **11** elucidation, explanation **12** illumination **13** clarification **14** interpretation

explication de texte 8 exegesis **11** explanation **14** interpretation **17** literary criticism

explicit 5 blunt, clear, exact, frank, plain **6** candid, direct **7** certain, express, pointed, precise **8** absolute, definite, distinct, specific **9** outspoken **10** unreserved **11** categorical, unequivocal, unqualified **15** straightforward **16** clearly expressed

explicitness 7 clarity **9** clearness, precision **11** unambiguity

explode 5 belie, blast, burst, erupt, go off **6** blow up, expose, refute, set off **7** destroy **8** detonate, disprove **9** discredit, repudiate **10** invalidate, prove false, prove wrong **11** burst loudly **12** utter noisily **14** burst violently, express noisily **18** discharge violently **19** burst out emotionally

exploit 4 feat **5** abuse **6** misuse **7** utilize **8** profit by, put to use **9** adventure, brave deed, heroic act, make use of **10** daring deed **11** achievement **12** capitalize on **14** accomplishment, use to advantage **15** take advantage of **16** make selfish use of **21** take unfair advantage of **22** turn to practical account

exploited 6 abused **7** ill used, misused **11** downtrodden **15** took advantage of **16** taken advantage of

exploration 5 probe **7** inquiry **8** scrutiny **9** discovery **10** expedition, experiment **11** examination **12** scouting trip **13** investigation

explore 3 try **5** plumb, probe, scout **6** survey, try out **7** analyze, examine, feel out, pry into **8** look into, research, traverse **9** delve into, penetrate, range over **10** scrutinize, search into, travel over **11** inquire into, investigate, reconnoiter **14** experiment with

explorer
American: 4 Byrd, Pike **5** Boone, Clark, Lewis, Peary, Perry
Australian: 4 Hume **5** Sturt **6** Stuart **8** Mitchell
British: 4 Bell, Cook, Park **5** Baker, Bligh, Bruce, Cabot, Davis, Drake, Grant, Puget, Scott, Smith, Speke **6** Baffin, Burton, Hudson, Lander **7** Raleigh, Stanley **8** Franklin **9** Frobisher, MacKenzie, Vancouver **11** Livingstone
Danish: 6 Bering **7** Niebuhr
Dutch: 6 Tasman **7** Barents, Le Maire **8** Schouten **10** Linschoten
French: 6 Joliet **7** Cartier, Jolliet, La Salle **9** Champlain, Marquette **12** Bougainville
Italian: 8 Columbus **9** Marco Polo, Verrazano **15** Amerigo Vespucci
Moslem: 10 Ibn Battuta
Norwegian: 8 Amundsen
Portuguese: 3 Cam, Cao **4** Dias, Diaz **6** Cabral, Da Gama **7** Almeida **8** Covilhao, Magellan **11** Albuquerque **23** Prince Henry the Navigator
Russian: 10 Middendorf **11** Przhevalsky
Spanish: 6 Balboa, Cortes, De Soto **7** Pizarro **8** Coronado, Orellana, Valdivia **11** Ponce de Leon
Swedish: 12 Nordenskjold
Viking: 10 Eric the Red **11** Leif Ericson

explosion 3 fit **4** clap **5** blast, burst, crack **6** report **7** tantrum **8** eruption, outbreak, outburst, paroxysm **9** blowing up, discharge **10** detonation **11** fulmination

explosive 3 TNT **5** shaky, tense **6** touchy **7** cordite, keyed up **8** critical, dynamite, perilous, strained, ticklish, unstable, volatile **9** dangerous, emotional, gelignite **10** ammunition, precarious **12** pyrotechnics **13** nitroglycerin

exponent 6 backer **8** advocate, champion, defender, promoter **9** expounder, proponent, spokesman, supporter **12** propagandist

export 7 send out **8** dispatch **10** sell abroad **11** foreign sale **12** ship overseas

expose 4 bare, risk, show **5** brand, offer, strip **6** betray, denude, divest, hazard, let out, reveal, submit **7** display, divulge, exhibit, imperil, let slip,

subject, uncover, unearth **8** denounce, disclose, endanger **10** jeopardize, reveal to be **12** acquaint with, bring to light **16** leave unprotected

expose 6 baring **8** exposure **10** divulgence, revelation

exposed 4 open **5** bared **8** divulged, laid open, revealed, unmasked **9** denounced, disclosed, displayed, uncovered, unearthed **11** unprotected, unsheltered

exposition 4 expo, fair, mart, show **6** bazaar, market **7** account, display, exhibit, picture **8** exegesis **9** trade fair, trade show **10** commentary, exhibition, world's fair **11** description, elucidation, explanation, explication **12** illustration, presentation **13** clarification, demonstration **14** interpretation

expostulate 5 argue **6** enjoin, exhort, object, reason **7** caution, counsel, protest **8** forewarn **9** plead with **11** remonstrate **13** cry out against, reason against **14** inveigh against

exposure 4 view **5** vista **6** expose **7** outlook, frontage, prospect **9** divulging, unmasking **10** disclosure, divulgence, laying bare, laying open, revelation, subjection, submission, uncovering **11** perspective **12** public notice **15** bringing to light

expound 6 defend, uphold **7** explain **8** describe **9** elucidate, explicate, hold forth, make clear

express 3 say **4** fast, show, word **5** clear, couch, exact, lucid, plain, quick, rapid, speak, state, swift, utter, vivid, voice **6** convey, direct, evince, phrase, relate, reveal **7** certain, declare, divulge, exhibit, nonstop, precise **8** definite, describe, disclose, evidence, explicit, forceful, specific, vocalize **9** high-speed, make known, verbalize **10** articulate, particular **11** categorical, communicate, unequivocal **12** put into words

expression 4 look, mien, term, tone, word **5** idiom, style **6** airing, aspect, phrase, saying **7** emotion, meaning, stating, venting, voicing, wording **8** language, locution, phrasing, relating, speaking, uttering **9** assertion, eloquence **10** appearance, modulation **11** countenance, declaration, enunciation, phraseology **12** articulation, setting forth, turn of phrase **13** communication

expressionless 5 blank, empty **6** vacant **7** deadpan **12** inexpressive

expressive 5 vivid **6** moving **7** telling **8** eloquent, forceful, poignant, powerful, striking **9** effective **10** compelling, indicative, meaningful, thoughtful **11** significant **14** characteristic

expressly 7 clearly, plainly **9** decidedly, pointedly, precisely, specially

10 definitely, distinctly, explicitly **12** particularly, specifically **13** categorically, unequivocally **18** in no uncertain terms

express sorrow 3 cry **4** weep **6** grieve, lament **7** condole, console **10** sympathize **11** commiserate

expropriate 4 take **5** seize **8** take over **10** commandeer, confiscate **11** appropriate

expropriation 7 seizure **10** arrogation, taking over **12** confiscation **13** commandeering

expulsion 5 exile **6** ouster **7** ousting, removal **8** ejection, eviction **9** debarment, discharge, dismissal, exclusion, expelling **10** banishment **11** elimination, prohibition, throwing out **12** proscription

expunge 5 erase **6** delete, efface, rub out **7** blot out, destroy, wipe out **9** eradicate, strike out **10** obliterate

expurgate 3 cut **4** blip, edit **5** bleep, purge **6** censor, cut out, delete, excise, remove **8** bleep out **10** bluepencil, bowdlerize

exquisite 4 fine **5** dainty **6** choice, lovely, superb **7** elegant, perfect **8** delicate, flawless, peerless, precious, splendid **9** admirable, excellent, faultless, matchless **10** consummate, fastidious, impeccable, meticulous **11** superlative **12** incomparable **14** discriminating

exquisiteness 6 beauty **8** delicacy, elegance, fineness **10** loveliness, perfection **12** flawlessness

extant 6 living **7** present **8** existent, existing **9** surviving, to be found **11** in existence

Extasie, The
author: 9 John Donne

extemporaneous 5 ad-lib **7** offhand **9** extempore, impromptu **10** improvised, off the cuff, unprepared **11** extemporary, spontaneous, unrehearsed **12** without notes **13** without notice **14** unpremeditated **15** spur-of-the-moment **19** off the top of one's head

extemporary 5 ad-lib **9** extempore, impromptu **10** improvised, off the cuff, unprepared **14** extemporaneous **19** off the top of one's head

extempore 5 ad-lib **7** offhand **9** impromptu **10** improvised, off the cuff, unprepared **11** extemporary, unrehearsed **12** without notes **14** extemporaneous, unpremeditated **15** spur-of-the-moment **19** off the top of one's head

extemporize 5 ad-lib **6** make up **9** improvise **14** speak impromptu **15** speak off the cuff

extend 4 give **5** grant, offer, widen **6** bestow, expand, impart, put out, spread, submit **7** advance, amplify, augment, broaden, draw out, enlarge, hold out, proffer, prolong, stretch **8** continue, elongate, increase, lengthen, protract, reach out **10** make longer, stretch out **12** stretch forth

extended 4 long **7** widened **8** drawn out, enlarged, expanded, thorough, unfolded, unfurled **9** broadened, continued, extensive, prolonged, spread out **10** lengthened, protracted, widespread **12** stretched out **13** comprehensive

extending 8 full form **9** expansion **10** drawing out, elongation, proffering, stretching **11** enlargement, lengthening **12** putting forth

extension 3 arm, ell **4** wing **5** annex, delay **6** branch, length, outlay **7** adjunct **8** addition, appendix, increase **9** appendage, expansion, outgrowth **10** drawing out, proffering **11** enlargement, lengthening **12** continuation, postponement, prolongation

extensive 4 huge, long, vast, wide **5** broad, great, large **7** lengthy **8** enormous, extended, far-flung, thorough **9** capacious, universal **10** protracted, voluminous **12** all-inclusive, considerable **13** comprehensive

extensiveness 4 span **5** range, reach, scope **6** extent, spread **7** breadth, compass, expanse, stretch

extent 4 area, size, time **5** range, reach, scope, sweep **6** amount, degree, length **7** breadth, compass, expanse, stretch **8** duration **9** amplitude, magnitude **10** dimensions

extenuate 6 excuse, temper **7** explain, justify, qualify **8** mitigate, moderate

extenuating 9 lessening, tempering **10** mitigating, moderating, qualifying **11** attenuating, diminishing, explanatory, justifiable

exterior 4 face, skin **5** alien, outer, shell **6** exotic, facade, finish, manner **7** bearing, coating, foreign, outside, outward, surface **8** covering, demeanor, external **9** extrinsic, outer side, outermost **10** extraneous **11** superficial

exterminate 3 zap **4** kill **5** erase, waste **7** abolish, destroy, expunge, root out, wipe out **8** demolish, massacre **9** eliminate, eradicate, slaughter **10** annihilate, extinguish

external 5 alien, outer **7** foreign, outside, outward, surface **8** exterior **9** extrinsic, outermost **10** extraneous **11** superficial

extinct 4 dead, gone, lost **6** put out **7** defunct, died out, gone out **8** quenched, vanished **12** extinguished

extinction 5 death **7** eclipse **9** wiping out **11** destruction, eradication **13** disappearance

extinguish 3 end, zap **4** dash, do in, kill **5** crush, douse, quash **6** cancel,

dispel, put out, quench, stifle **7** abolish, blow out, destroy, smother, wipe out **8** demolish, snuff out **9** eliminate, eradicate, suffocate

extinguished 6 put out **7** gone out **8** quenched **15** no longer burning

extirpate 5 erase **7** abolish, destroy, extract, pull out, root out, wipe out **8** demolish **9** eradicate **10** annihilate, extinguish, obliterate **11** exterminate

extol 4 laud **6** praise **7** acclaim, applaud, commend, glorify **8** eulogize **9** celebrate **10** compliment **16** sing the praises of

extort 5 educe, exact **6** coerce, elicit **7** extract **9** shake down

extortion 5 force, graft **6** payola, ransom **7** threats, tribute **8** coercion **9** blackmail, hush money, shakedown **14** forced payments

extortionate 5 undue **7** extreme **9** excessive, out-of-line **10** exorbitant, inordinate **12** unreasonable

extra 4 more **5** spare **7** adjunct, further, surplus **9** accessory, auxiliary, redundant, unusually **10** additional, attachment, complement, especially, remarkably, uncommonly **11** superfluous, unnecessary **12** additionally, appurtenance, particularly, supplemental **13** exceptionally **15** extraordinarily

extract 3 get **4** cite, cull **5** educe, evoke, exact, glean, juice, quote, wrest **6** choose, deduce, derive, elicit, obtain, pry out, remove, select **7** copy out, distill, draw out, essence, excerpt, passage, pull out, root out, take out **8** abstract, bring out, citation, pluck out, press out, separate **9** extirpate, extricate, quotation, selection **10** distillate, squeeze out **11** concentrate

extraction 5 stock **7** descent, removal **8** ancestry **10** derivation, drawing out, pulling out

extraneous 5 alien **6** exotic **7** foreign, strange **9** extrinsic, unrelated **10** immaterial, incidental, irrelevant, not germane **11** superfluous **12** adventitious, inadmissible, nonessential, not pertinent **13** inappropriate

extraordinary 3 odd **4** rare **5** queer **6** unique **7** amazing, notable, strange, unusual **8** uncommon **9** fantastic, monstrous, unheard of **10** incredible, phenomenal, remarkable **11** exceptional **12** unbelievable **13** inconceivable

extraterrestrial 2 ET **3** Alf **6** cosmic **10** outer-space **12** interstellar, otherworldly **14** interplanetary

extravagance 5 folly, waste **6** excess **7** caprice **9** absurdity **10** profligacy **11** prodigality, squandering, unrestraint **12** immoderation, improvidence, overspending, recklessness, wastefulness **13** excessiveness **14** capriciousness **16** inordinate outlay, unreasonableness

extravagant 4 wild **6** absurd, costly, unreal **7** foolish **8** fabulous, lavishly, prodigal, spending, wasteful **9** excessive, expensive, fantastic, high-flown, imprudent **10** exorbitant, high-priced, immoderate, inordinate, openhanded, outlandish, outrageous, overpriced, profligate **11** improvident, spendthrift, squandering **12** overspending, preposterous, unreasonable, unrestrained

extravaganza 4 fair **5** opera **6** ballet **7** pageant **8** carnival, operetta **9** spectacle, stage show **10** exposition, vaudeville **11** opera bouffe, spectacular **12** Broadway show, opera comique, son et lumiere, wild west show **14** phantasmagoria **17** sound and light show

extreme 3 end **5** depth **6** excess, height, severe **7** intense, radical, unusual **8** advanced, boundary, farthest, uncommon **9** excessive, extremity, nth degree, outermost, very great **10** avant-garde, immoderate, inordinate, outrageous **11** exaggerated, extravagant, most distant **13** extraordinary

extremely 4 very **5** quite **7** awfully **8** terribly **9** curiously, intensely, unusually **10** abnormally, especially, freakishly, peculiarly, remarkably, singularly, uncommonly **11** exceedingly, excessively, unnaturally **12** immoderately, surprisingly **13** exceptionally **15** extraordinarily

extremely painful 7 racking **9** agonizing, torturous **10** tormenting, unbearable **11** intolerable, unendurable **12** excruciating, insufferable

extremity 3 arm, end, leg, tip, toe **4** edge, foot, hand, limb **5** bound, brink, limit, reach **6** border, finger, margin **7** confine, extreme **8** boundary, terminus **9** outer edge, periphery

extricate 4 free **5** loose **6** get out, rescue **7** deliver, release **8** liberate, untangle **9** disengage **11** disencumber, disentangle **12** wriggle out of

extrication 6 escape **7** loosing, release **10** liberation **11** deliverance **13** disengagement **15** disentanglement

extrinsic 5 alien **7** foreign **9** accessory **10** accidental, extraneous, incidental **11** dispensable **12** nonessential

extrovert 7 show-off **13** exhibitionist **14** life of the party **17** hail-fellow-well-met

extroverted 8 outgoing, sociable **9** expansive **10** gregarious **12** unrestrained

extrude 4 spew **5** eject, expel **7** project, push out **8** force out, protrude, stickout **9** thrust out

exuberance 3 zip **4** elan, life, zeal **5** vigor **6** energy, spirit **8** buoyancy, vitality, vivacity **9** animation, eagerness **10** enthusiasm, excitement, liveliness **13** effervescence, sprightliness

exuberant 4 lush, rich **5** eager

6 lavish, lively **7** copious, excited, profuse, zealous **8** abundant, animated, spirited, vigorous **9** bounteous, energetic, luxuriant, plenteous, plentiful, sprightly **12** enthusiastic **13** superabundant

exudation 3 sap, tar **4** ooze **5** pitch, sweat **7** leakage, seepage **8** bleeding, drainage **9** discharge, excretion

exude 4 drip, emit, ooze **5** sweat **7** secrete **9** discharge

exult 4 crow **5** gloat, glory **7** rejoice **8** be elated **10** be jubilant, jump for joy **11** be delighted **13** be exhilarated **15** be in high spirits

exultant 5 happy **6** elated, joyful **7** crowing **8** boasting, ecstatic, euphoric, gloating, jubilant **9** rapturous, rejoicing **10** triumphant

exultation 3 joy **7** elation, ovation, rapture, triumph **9** rejoicing **10** jubilation

Eyck, Jan van
  born: 8 Flanders, Maaseyck **10** Maastricht
  artwork: 9 Timotheos **15** Ghent Altarpiece **18** Adoration of the Lamb, The Man in a Red Turban, The Virgin in a Church **20** The Arnolfini Marriage **24** Arnolfini Wedding Portrait **29** The Madonna with Chancellor Rolin **30** The Madonna with Canon van der Paele

eye 3 orb **4** scan, view **5** sight, study, taste, watch **6** behold, gaze at, look at, peeper, regard, survey, take in, vision **7** inspect, observe, stare at **8** eyesight, glance at **10** perception, scrutinize **14** discrimination
  part: 4 iris, lens, rods **5** cones, nerve, pupil **6** cornea, muscle, retina **11** blood vessel

eyeful 4 doll **5** beaut, peach, Venus **6** beauty **7** stunner **8** knockout **10** good-looker **13** beautiful girl **14** beautiful woman

eyeglass, eyeglasses 4 lens **5** specs **6** eyecup, lenses **7** goggles, monocle **8** bifocals, cheaters, contacts, pincenez **9** lorgnette **10** spectacles

Eye of the Needle
  author: 10 Ken Follett

eyesight 4 eyes **5** sight **6** vision

eyewitness 5 gaper, gazer **6** gawker, viewer **7** witness **8** attester, attestor, beholder, informer, looker-on, observer, onlooker, passerby **9** bystander, spectator, testifier **10** rubberneck

eyre 4 lake, tour **7** circuit

Ezekiel
  father: 4 Buzi

Ezra
  father: 7 Seraiah

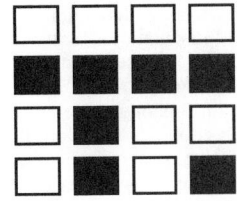

Fabares, Ruby Bernadette Nanette
  real name of: **13** Nanette Fabray
  aunt of: **14** Shelley Fabares
fable 3 fib, lie **4** hoax, myth, tale, yarn
  6 legend **7** fiction, leg-pull, parable,
  romance, untruth, whopper **8** allegory
  9 fairy tale, falsehood, invention, tall
  story **11** fabrication
fabled 6 unreal **7** storied **8** fabulous,
  fanciful, mythical **9** imaginary, legendary **10** fictitious **12** mythological
Fables
  author: **5** Aesop **16** Jean de La Fontaine
  ends with: **5** moral
  feature: **4** hare **8** tortoise **10** sour
  grapes
Fabray, Nanette
  real name: **28** Ruby Bernadette
  Nanette Fabares
  partner: **9** Sid Caesar
  born: **10** San Diego CA
  roles: **7** Baby Nan **12** The Band
  Wagon **13** Sid Caesar Hour **15** High
  Button Shoes, Our Gang comedies
fabric 5 cloth, frame, stuff **6** makeup **7**
  textile, texture **8** dry goods, material **9**
  framework, structure, substance, yard
  goods **10** foundation **12** organization,
  substructure **14** infrastructure, super-
  structure
  cotton: **4** duck **5** denim, drill, scrim,
  terry **6** burlap, calico, canvas, chintz,
  dimity, madras, muslin, oxford, poplin **7** batiste, buckram, flannel, gingham, organdy, percale, ticking **8**
  chambray **9** crinoline, sailcloth **10**
  broadcloth, printcloth, seersucker **11**
  cheesecloth, dotted Swiss
  linen: **6** canvas, damask **7** butcher,
  cambric **8** birds-eye **9** huckaback
  natural: **4** jute, silk, wool **5** linen **6**
  cotton **8** asbestos
  silk: **3** raw **4** tram **7** organza **8** organzie **9** organzine
  synthetic: **5** nylon, orlon, rayon **6**
  olefin **7** acetate, acrylic **9** polyester
  type: **4** felt, lace, lame **5** crepe,
  gauze, moire, serge, voile **6** damask,
  faille, jersey, melton, velour, velvet **7**
  brocade, chiffon, flannel, foulard,
  gingham, taffeta **8** chenille, cordu-
  roy, tapestry **9** gabardine, velveteen
  wool: **4** felt **5** crepe, serge, tweed,
  twill **6** boucle, covert, faille, melton,
  woolen **7** challis, doeskin, Donegal,
  worsted **8** homespun, Shetland **9** Astrakhan, gabardine, sharkskin **10**
  hopsacking **11** Harris tweed, herringbone
    from goats: **8** cashmere
    sheep: **5** Iraqi **6** Hirrik, merino,
    Romney, Somali **7** Lincoln **8** Cots-
    wold, Tatarian **9** Hampshire,
    Southdown **10** Corriedale, Dorset
    Down, Dorset Horn, Shropshire,
    Sikkim Bera **13** Hampshire Down
    other wool-bearing animals:
      5 camel, llama **6** alpaca, vicuna
fabricate 4 fake, form, make **5** build,
  erect, feign, forge, frame, hatch, shape
  6 design, devise, invent, make up **7**
  compose, concoct, falsify, fashion,
  produce, trump up **8** assemble, contrive, simulate **9** construct, embroider,
  formulate **11** counterfeit, manufacture
fabrication 3 fib, lie **4** myth, yarn **5**
  fable **6** makeup **7** fiction, forgery, untruth **8** building, creation, erection **9**
  fairy tale, falsehood, invention **10** assemblage, concoction, fashioning, production **11** composition, manufacture
  12 constructing, construction **13** prevarication **16** cock-and-bull story
Fabritius, Carel
  real name: **13** Carel Pietersz
  born: **14** Midden-Beemster, The Netherlands
  artwork: **11** View of Delft **12** The
  Goldfinch **19** The Raising of Lazarus
fabulous 5 great **6** fabled, superb **7**
  amazing, storied **8** fanciful, invented,
  mythical, smashing **9** fantastic, imaginary, legendary, marvelous, wonderful
  10 apocryphal, astounding, fictitious,
  incredible, stupendous **11** astonishing,
  spectacular **12** mythological, unbelievable **13** extraordinary
facade 4 face, mask **6** veneer **8** frontage, pretense **9** front view **10** false
  front **13** building front
face 3 air, mug, pan **4** coat, gall, grit,
  look, pout, puss, sand **5** brass, cheek,
  cover, front, image, nerve, pluck,
  spunk **6** aspect, daring, facade, kisser,
  mettle, repute, visage **7** bravado, dignity, front on, grimace, obverse, overlay, surface **8** boldness, confront,
  features, forepart, frontage, good
  name, overlook, prestige **9** encounter,
  hardihood, impudence, semblance **10**
  appearance, confidence, effrontery, expression, give toward, look toward,
  reputation, turn toward **11** countenance, physiognomy, self-respect
Face
  character in: **12** The Alchemist
  author: **6** Jonson
facet 3 cut **4** part, side **5** angle, phase,
  plane **6** aspect **7** surface
facetious 5 comic, droll, funny, witty
  6 clever, jocose, joking, jovial **7**
  amusing, comical, jesting, jocular,
  playful **8** humorous **12** wisecracking
face-to-face 6 direct **8** one-on-one,
  personal **9** firsthand
facile 3 apt **4** glib **5** adept, handy,
  quick, slick **6** adroit, artful, casual,
  clever, fluent, smooth **7** cursory, shallow **8** careless, skillful **10** effortless,
  proficient **11** superficial
facilitate 3 aid **4** ease **6** foster, help
  in, smooth **7** advance, forward, further, lighten, promote, speed up **8** expedite, simplify **10** accelerate, make
  easier
facility 3 aid **4** bent, ease **5** knack,
  means, skill **7** aptness, fluency **8** deftness, easiness, resource **9** advantage,
  appliance, dexterity, readiness **10**
  adroitness, capability, competence, efficiency, expertness, smoothness **11**
  convenience, proficiency **14** effortlessness, practicability
facsimile 3 fax **4** copy **5** clone, xerox
  7 replica, reprint **8** likeness **9** duplicate, imitation, photostat **10** transcript
  12 reproduction
fact 3 act **4** deed **5** event, truth **6** verity **7** reality **8** incident, specific **9** actuality, certainty, happening, thing
  done **10** occurrence, particular **12** circumstance
faction 3 set **4** bloc, gang, ring, sect,
  side, unit **5** cabal, clash, group, split
  6 breach, circle, clique, schism, strife
  7 combine, coterie, discord, rupture,
  section **8** conflict, division, minority,
  sedition **9** rebellion **10** contention,
  disruption, dissension, dissidence, insurgency, quarreling **11** subdivision
  12 disagreement **13** splinter group **15**
  incompatibility
factious 7 warring **8** divisive, fighting,
  mutinous **9** alienated, bickering, combative, estranged **10** contending, rebellious **11** belligerent, contentious,

disaffected, disagreeing, dissentious, quarrelsome **12** disputatious **13** at loggerheads, insubordinate **15** insurrectionary **16** at sixes and sevens

factitious 4 sham **5** phony **9** pretended, synthetic, unnatural **10** artificial **12** manufactured

factor 4 part **5** agent, cause **6** reason **7** element **9** component, influence **11** constituent **12** circumstance **13** consideration

factory 4 mill, shop **5** plant, works **8** workshop **11** manufactory

factotum 4 aide **6** Figaro **8** handyman **9** gal Friday, guy Friday, man Friday **10** girl Friday **12** right-hand man **15** jack-of-all-trades

factual 4 real, true **5** exact, plain **6** actual **7** certain, correct, genuine, literal **8** accurate, concrete, definite, faithful **9** authentic, unadorned **10** scrupulous, verifiable

faculty, faculties 4 bent, gift, wits **5** flair, knack, power, skill **6** genius, reason, talent **7** quality **8** aptitude, capacity, function, penchant, teachers **9** adeptness, endowment **10** capability, professors **12** mental powers, skillfulness **13** teaching staff

fad 4 mode, rage, whim **5** craze, fancy, mania, vogue **6** whimsy **7** fashion **10** dernier cri, latest word **11** latest thing

faddish 2 in **6** trendy **10** innovative **11** fashionable

fade 3 die, dim, ebb **4** blur, dull, fail, flag, pale, wane **5** droop, taper **6** bleach, lessen, recede, whiten, wither **7** crumble, decline, dwindle, fall off, grow dim, shrivel **8** diminish, dissolve, evanesce, languish, make pale, melt away, pass away **9** disappear, dissipate, evaporate, lose color

fade away 3 die, ebb **6** recede **7** subside **8** diminish

faded 4 drab, dull, pale **5** dingy **6** grayed **7** died out **8** bleached, dwindled, whitened, withered **9** colorless, shriveled, washed out

Faerie Queene, The
  author: 13 Edmund Spenser
  character: 3 Una **5** Guyon **6** Duessa **8** Artegall, Gloriana (the Faerie Queen) **9** Archimago, Britomart **12** Prince Arthur **14** Red Cross Knight

Fafnir
  origin: 12 Scandinavian
  form: 6 dragon
  father: 8 Hreidmar
  brother: 5 Otter, Regin
  killed: 8 Hreidmar
  killed by: 6 Sigurd

fag 4 bush, butt, poop, tire, weed **5** weary **6** tucker **7** exhaust **9** cigarette

Fagin
  character in: 11 Oliver Twist
  author: 7 Dickens

Fahrenheit
  abbreviation: 1 F
Fahrenheit 451
  author: 11 Ray Bradbury
Fahrenheit, Gabriel Daniel
  field: 7 physics
  nationality: 6 German
  invented: 16 thermometer scale **18** alcohol thermometer, mercury thermometer

fail 3 die, ebb **4** bomb, flag, flop, fold, wane **5** abort, crash, droop, flunk **6** desert, slip up **7** decline, dwindle, forsake, founder, give out, go under, let down, misfire **8** be in vain, collapse, fade away, languish, lay an egg, miscarry **9** disappear, fall short, fizzle out **10** end in smoke, go bankrupt, not succeed, run aground **11** be stillborn, come to grief, deteriorate, fall through, go up in smoke, miss the mark **12** come to naught, turn out badly **13** come to nothing **15** go out of business **16** meet one's Waterloo, meet with disaster

fail at 11 fall short of **12** be defeated in, not succeed at **16** be unsuccessful at

failed
  French: 6 manque
failing 4 weak **5** fault, shaky **6** defect, ebbing, foible, waning **7** folding, frailty **8** drooping, flagging, giving up, slipping, weakness **9** deficient, dwindling, giving out, weakening, weak point **10** deficiency, going under **11** shortcoming **12** unsuccessful **13** insufficiency

fail to include 4 drop, omit **5** elide **8** leave out, pass over

failure 3 dud **4** bomb, flop, mess, ruin **5** botch, crash, loser **6** fizzle, mishap, muddle, turkey **7** decline, default, failing, folding, misfire, washout **8** collapse, downfall **9** breakdown, ruination **10** bankruptcy, ne'er-do-well

Fainall, Mrs
  character in: 16 The Way of the World
  author: 8 Congreve

faint 3 dim, low **4** pale, soft, thin, weak **5** dizzy, faded, frail, giddy, muted, small, swoon, timid **6** dulcet, feeble, little, meager, remote, slight, subtle, torpid **7** fearful, fragile, languid, muffled, obscure, pass out, worn out **8** black out, collapse, cowardly, delicate, drooping, fatigued, timorous **9** exhausted, inaudible, lethargic, whispered **10** indistinct **11** lightheaded, lily-livered, vertiginous **13** inconspicuous **17** lose consciousness

fainthearted 4 weak **5** timid **6** feeble **8** cowardly **10** irresolute **11** halfhearted, indifferent, lily-livered

faintheartedness 9 cowardice **12**

cowardliness, yellow streak **13** pusillanimity, yellow feather **17** pusillanimousness **18** chickenheartedness

fair 4 fine, just, pale, so-so **5** blond, bonny, sunny **6** blonde, bright, comely, creamy, decent, honest, justly, kosher, lovely, medium, pretty, proper, square **7** average, cricket, legally, not dark, upright **8** adequate, candidly, carnival, honestly, mediocre, middling, moderate, ordinary, passable, pleasant, rainless, squarely, sunshiny, unbiased **9** beautiful, cloudless, equitable, ethically, honorable, honorably, impartial, justified, objective, tolerable, unclouded **10** aboveboard, attractive, evenhanded, exhibition, legitimate, pretty good, reasonable, truthfully **11** indifferent, respectable **12** forthrightly, light-colored, lightskinned, on the up-and-up, run-of-the-mill, satisfactory, unprejudiced **13** disinterested, dispassionate **19** according to the rules

Fair, A A
  pseudonym of: 18 Erle Stanley Gardner

Fairbanks, Douglas
  real name: 17 Douglas Elton Ulman
  wife: 12 Mary Pickford
  son: 18 Douglas Fairbanks Jr
  born: 8 Denver CO
  roles: 9 Robin Hood **11** The Iron Mask **14** The Black Pirate, The Mark of Zorro **16** The Thief of Bagdad **18** The Three Musketeers **23** The Private Life of Don Juan

Fairbanks, Douglas Jr
  father: 16 Douglas Fairbanks
  wife: 12 Joan Crawford
  born: 9 New York NY
  roles: 8 Gunga Din **12** Little Caesar **15** Sinbad the Sailor **16** That Lady in Ermine **17** Catherine the Great **18** The Prisoner of Zenda **19** The Corsican Brothers

fair dealing 7 honesty **8** fairness **15** trustworthiness

Fairfax, Gwendolen
  character in: 27 The Importance of Being Earnest
  author: 5 Wilde

Fairfax, Jane
  character in: 4 Emma
  author: 6 Austen

Fairfax, Mrs
  character in: 8 Jane Eyre
  author: 15 Charlotte Bronte

Fair Land, Fair Land
  author: 11 A B Guthrie Jr

fairly 5 fully **6** justly, rather, really **7** rightly **8** actually, honestly, passably, properly, somewhat, squarely **9** equitably, honorably, so to speak, tolerably **10** absolutely, completely, moderately, positively, reasonably **11** impartially, objectively **12** evenhand-

edly, legitimately **15** dispassionately **19** in a manner of speaking
Latin: 9 pari passu

fairness 7 balance, honesty, justice **8** equality, fair play **11** objectivity **12** impartiality **14** even-handedness **16** equal opportunity

fair play 7 cricket, justice **8** equality, fairness **12** impartiality **16** equal opportunity

fair-skinned 4 pale **5** blond, light **6** blonde **17** light-complexioned

fairy 3 elf **5** pixie **6** sprite **10** leprechaun

fairy tale 3 fib **4** myth **5** fable **6** legend **7** fantasy, fiction **8** tall tale **9** invention **16** fabrication **16** cock-and-bull story, Mother Goose story
German: 7 Marchen

fait accompli 16 accomplished fact, thing already done

faith 4 sect **5** creed, trust **6** belief, church, fealty **7** loyalty, promise **8** credence, fidelity, reliance, religion, security **9** assurance, certainty, certitude, constancy **10** confidence, conviction, obligation, persuasion

faithful 4 true **5** close, exact, loyal, tried **6** honest, strict, trusty **7** devoted, factual, precise, similar, staunch, upright **8** accurate, constant, lifelike, reliable, resolute, truthful **9** steadfast **10** dependable, scrupulous, true-to-life, unswerving, unwavering, verifiable **11** trustworthy **13** conscientious, incorruptible

faithfulness 6 fealty **7** loyalty **8** devotion, fidelity **9** constancy **10** allegiance **11** reliability **13** steadfastness

faithless 5 false **6** fickle **8** disloyal **10** inconstant, perfidious, unreliable **11** treacherous **13** untrustworthy

faithlessness 5 doubt **7** perfidy **9** disbelief, falseness, treachery **10** disloyalty, fickleness, infidelity, skepticism **11** inconstancy **13** unreliability **14** perfidiousness, unfaithfulness

fake 4 hoax, ruse, sham **5** bogus, dodge, dummy, faker, false, feign, forge, fraud, phony, put-on, quack, trick **6** deceit, forged, humbug, poseur, pseudo **7** falsify, forgery, not real, pretend, trump up **8** artifice, contrive, deceiver, delusion, imposter, invented, simulate, specious, spurious **9** charlatan, concocted, contrived, deception, dissemble, fabricate, imitation, imposture, pretender, simulated **10** artificial, fabricated, fictitious **11** contrivance, counterfeit, dissimulate, fabrication, make-believe

faker 5 fraud, phony **6** humbug **8** imposter **9** charlatan, pretender

fakir 5 Hindu **6** Muslim **7** ascetic, dervish

falcon 4 eyas **5** hobby, saker **6** desert, lanner, merlin **7** goshawk, kestrel, prairie, shaheen, tiercel **8** caracara, falconet **9** gyrfalcon, peregrine
cover eyes: 4 seel

Falcon and the Snowman, The
author: 13 Robert Lindsey
director: 15 John Schlesinger
cast: 8 Sean Penn (Andrew Daulton Lee, the Snowman) **13** Timothy Hutton (Christopher John Boyce, the Falcon)

Falconer
author: 11 John Cheever

Falconet, Etienne-Maurice
born: 5 Paris **6** France
artwork: 9 The Bather **12** Bathing Nymph **13** Milo of Crotona, Peter the Great **19** Pygmalion and Galatea

falconry 7 hawking
equipment: 4 lure **5** cadge **6** jesses **7** creance

Falk, Lee
creator/artist of: 10 The Phantom **19** Mandrake the Magician

Falk, Peter
born: 9 New York NY
roles: 7 Columbo **9** Murder Inc **12** The Great Race **13** Murder by Death, Wings of Desire **17** The Cheap Detective **19** Pocketful of Miracles **21** It's a Mad Mad Mad Mad World, Robin and the Seven Hoods

fall, falls 3 die, ebb, err, sin **4** drop, plop, ruin, slip, wane **5** droop, lapse, occur, slope, slump, spill **6** autumn, crop up, defeat, happen, perish, plunge, topple, tumble **7** be slain, be taken, capture, cascade, cheapen, come off, crumple, decline, descend, descent, falling, plummet, sinking, succumb **8** cataract, collapse, come down, decrease, diminish, disgrace, downfall, drop down, dropping, go astray, hang down, lowering **9** crash down, overthrow, reduction, surrender, take place, waterfall **10** capitulate, come to pass, corruption, debasement, depreciate, diminution, subsidence, subversion, transgress **11** be destroyed, harvest time **12** capitulation, depreciation, Indian summer **15** loss of innocence

Fall, The
author: 11 Albert Camus

Falla, Manuel de
born: 5 Cadiz, Spain
composer of: 11 El Amor Brujo, La Atlantida, La Vida Breve, Life Is Short **14** Fantasia Betica **15** Love the Magician **19** The Three-Cornered Hat **21** El sombrero de tres picos **25** Nights in the Gardens of Spain

fallacious 5 false, wrong **6** faulty, flawed, untrue **8** delusive, mistaken **9** deceptive, erroneous, illogical, incorrect **10** inaccurate, misleading, untruthful

fallacy 4 flaw **5** catch, error, fault **7** mistake, pitfall **8** delusion, illusion **9** misbelief **10** faultiness **11** false belief, false notion **13** inconsistency, misconception **15** misapprehension

fall apart 5 decay **7** break up, crumble, shatter **8** fragment, splinter **10** go to pieces **11** fragmentize **12** disintegrate

fall away 4 fade, wane **5** abate **7** drop off, slacken, subside **8** mitigate, taper off

fall back 6 recede **7** back off, retreat

fallen 4 dead **5** loose, slain **6** ousted, ruined, sinful **7** debased, deposed, dropped, immoral, spilled, toppled, tumbled **8** sprawled **9** butchered, disgraced, massacred, turned out **10** discharged, overthrown **11** slaughtered

fallen short
French: 6 manque

fall for 7 believe, swallow

fall guy 4 dupe, pawn, tool **5** patsy **7** cat's-paw

fallible 5 frail, human **6** faulty, mortal, unsure **9** imperfect **10** unreliable

fall in drops 4 drip, rain **7** dribble, drizzle **8** sprinkle

falling apart 6 ruined, shabby **7** rickety, run-down **8** decaying, decrepit **9** crumbling **10** broken-down, collapsing, ramshackle, tumbledown **11** dilapidated **13** deteriorating

Falling in Place
author: 10 Ann Beattie

falling into decay 6 ruined, shabby **7** rotting, run-down **8** decrepit **9** crumbling, moldering **10** broken-down, tumbledown **11** dilapidated, in disrepair **13** deteriorating

falling off 3 ebb **4** fall, wane **7** decline **8** decrease **9** dwindling, lessening, reduction **10** diminution **13** deterioration

falling out 4 spat **7** dispute, quarrel **8** argument, squabble **10** difference **12** disagreement

fall in with 6 concur **7** conform **8** accede to **9** acquiesce **11** go along with

fall off 4 drop, wane **6** lessen, plunge, reduce, topple **7** decline, drop off, plummet, slacken, subside **8** decrease, diminish, moderate, peter out

Fall of the House of Usher, The
author: 13 Edgar Allan Poe
character: 8 Narrator **13** Madeline Usher, Roderick Usher

fallow 4 arid, idle **5** inert **6** barren, unused **7** dormant, unsowed, worn out **8** depleted, inactive, untilled **9** exhausted, unplanted **10** unfruitful **12** uncultivated, unproductive

fall short 6 be less, fail at, give up **9** be lacking, lag behind **10** have too few **11** fail to reach, miss the mark **12** be inadequate **14** be insufficient

fall to one's lot 4 fall 5 occur 6 befall, chance, happen 7 turn out 9 come about 10 come to pass

fall upon 5 fly at 6 assail, attack, dive at 7 embrace, lunge at, set upon 8 thrust at, tuck into

false 4 fake, sham 5 bogus, phony, wrong 6 ersatz, faulty, forged, pseudo, tricky, unreal, untrue 7 devious, feigned, inexact, invalid, unsound 8 delusive, disloyal, mistaken, spurious, two-faced 9 deceitful, deceiving, deceptive, dishonest, erroneous, faithless, imitation, incorrect, unfounded 10 apocryphal, artificial, factitious, fallacious, inaccurate, inconstant, misleading, not correct, perfidious, traitorous, unfaithful, untruthful 11 counterfeit, make-believe, treacherous 12 hypocritical 13 double-dealing

false front 4 mask, sham, show 6 facade, screen, veneer 8 pretense

false-hearted 8 two-faced 9 deceitful, deceiving, faithless 10 perfidious 13 double-dealing, untrustworthy

falsehood 3 fib, lie 5 lying, story 6 canard, deceit 7 fiction, figment, perfidy, perjury, untruth, whopper 8 bad faith, white lie 9 deception, duplicity, hypocrisy, invention, mendacity 10 dishonesty, distortion, inaccuracy 11 dissembling, fabrication, insincerity 12 misstatement, two-facedness 13 deceptiveness, dissimulation, double-dealing, falsification 17 misrepresentation

falseness 5 fraud 6 deceit 7 perfidy 9 duplicity, treachery 10 dishonesty 12 spuriousness 13 deceitfulness, double-dealing, faithlessness 14 untruthfulness

falsified 5 false, phony 6 forged, made-up 7 assumed 10 fictitious

falsify 4 fake 5 belie, rebut 6 doctor, misuse, refute 7 confute, distort, pervert 8 disprove 10 tamper with 12 misrepresent

Falstaff
opera by: 5 Verdi
character: 4 Anne 6 Fenton, Pistol 7 Dr Caius 8 Bardolph 11 Dame Quickly 12 Mistress Ford, Mistress Page 15 Mistress Quickly, Sir John Falstaff

Falstaff, Sir John
character in: 12 Henry IV Part I 13 Henry IV Part II 22 The Merry Wives of Windsor
author: 11 Shakespeare

falter 3 lag 4 halt, reel 5 demur, waver 6 dodder, mumble, shrink, teeter, totter 7 shamble, shuffle, stagger, stammer, stumble, stutter 8 hesitate 9 fluctuate, vacillate 10 dillydally 11 be undecided 12 be irresolute, show weakness 14 blow hot and cold

fame 4 note 5 eclat, glory 6 renown, repute 7 laurels 8 eminence, prestige 9 celebrity, notoriety 10 notability, popularity, prominence, reputation 11 distinction, preeminence 15 illustriousness

famed 5 noted 6 famous 7 notable 8 renowned 9 prominent, well-known 10 celebrated

familiar 3 pal 4 bold, chum, cozy, free, snug 5 buddy, close, crony, known, stock, usual 6 chummy, common, friend 7 forward, general 8 accepted, amicable, at home in, everyday, frequent, friendly, habitual, informal, intimate, ordinary, seasoned, versed in 9 abreast of, brotherly, confidant, customary, fraternal, gemutlich, intrusive, simpatico, skilled in, well-known 10 accessible, accustomed, acquainted, apprised of, conversant, proverbial, unreserved 11 cognizant of, commonplace, impertinent, traditional 12 confidential, conventional, hand and glove, no stranger to, proficient at 13 boon companion, companionable, disrespectful 15 taking liberties

familiarity 4 ease 5 amity, skill 7 know-how, mastery 8 coziness, intimacy 9 closeness, impudence, indecorum, knowledge, unreserve 10 casualness, chumminess, cognizance, disrespect, experience, fellowship, fraternity, friendship 11 association, brotherhood, conversance, forwardness, impropriety, informality, naturalness, presumption, proficiency 12 acquaintance, impertinence, unconstraint, undue liberty, unseemliness 13 brotherliness, comprehension, intrusiveness, understanding, undue intimacy 16 acquaintanceship

familiarize 4 edify, teach, tutor 6 inform, orient (oneself), school, season 7 educate 8 accustom, acquaint, instruct 9 enlighten, habituate, inculcate 11 acclimatize

family 3 kin, set 4 clan, kind, line, race, sept 5 blood, breed, brood, class, group, house, issue, order, stock, tribe 7 dynasty, kinfolk, kinsmen, lineage, progeny 8 ancestry, category, division, kinsfolk 9 forebears, genealogy, offspring, parentage, relations, relatives 10 extraction, kith and kin 11 forefathers 14 classification
goddess of: 6 Cardea

Family Affair
character: 4 Jody 5 Buffy, Cissy 8 Mr (Giles) French 9 Bill Davis
cast: 10 Brian Keith 11 Anissa Jones, Kathy Garver 14 Sebastian Cabot 15 Johnnie Whitaker

family line 4 tree 7 lineage 8 ancestry 9 blood line, genealogy, parentage

Family Moskat, The
author: 19 Isaac Bashevis Singer
Family Reunion, The
author: 7 T S Eliot
Family Ties
character: 4 Nick 5 Ellen 6 Skippy 10 Alex Keaton 11 Elyse Keaton 12 Andrew Keaton, Steven Keaton 13 Mallory Keaton 14 Jennifer Keaton
cast: 9 Marc Price 11 Michael J Fox, Tina Yothers 12 Michael Gross 14 Justine Bateman 20 Meredith Baxter-Birney

family tree 7 lineage 8 ancestry, pedigree 9 blood line, genealogy

famine 4 lack, want 6 dearth, hunger 7 paucity, poverty 8 scarcity 9 depletion 10 deficiency, exhaustion, famishment, meagerness, scantiness, starvation 11 destitution, half rations, short supply 13 acute shortage, extreme hunger, insufficiency

famished 6 hungry 7 starved

famous 5 noted 7 eminent, notable 8 far-famed, renowned, well-known 9 notorious, prominent 10 celebrated 11 conspicuous, illustrious 13 distinguished

famous person 4 name, star 7 notable 8 luminary, somebody 9 celebrity, personage, superstar 11 personality

fan 3 bug, nut 4 buff 5 fiend, freak 6 addict, rooter, zealot 7 booster, fanatic 8 follower, partisan

fanatic 5 crazy 6 maniac, zealot 7 hothead, radical 8 activist, militant 9 extremist 10 enthusiast 24 member of the lunatic fringe

fanaticism 6 fervor 8 activism, zealotry 9 dogmatism, extremism, monomania, obsession 10 enthusiasm, radicalism 11 extreme zeal, militantism 12 intemperance 13 ruling passion 15 opinionatedness

fancied 5 liked 6 dreamt, took to, unreal 7 assumed, desired, dreamed, thought 8 imagined, supposed 9 conceived, imaginary, preferred

fanciful 3 odd 6 unreal 7 bizarre, curious, flighty, unusual 8 fabulous, humorous, illusory, mythical, quixotic, romantic 9 eccentric, fantastic, imaginary, invective, legendary, visionary, whimsical 10 apocryphal, capricious, chimerical, fictitious 11 imaginative

fanciful talk 7 blarney 9 hyperbole, tall tales 11 fish stories 12 exaggeration

fancy 3 yen 4 fine, idea, like, want 5 crave, dream, enjoy, favor, opine, showy, taste, think 6 assume, custom, deluxe, de-sire, florid, liking, notion, ornate, relish, rococo, take it, take to, vagary, vision, whimsy 7 baroque, caprice, conceit, dream of, elegant, fantasy, figment, gourmet, imagine, leaning, longing, long for, picture, presume, reverie, special, suppose, surmise, suspect, unusual **8** be fond of, crotchet, daydream, fondness, illusion, not plain, penchant, superior, weakness, yearn for **9** elaborate, epicurean, expensive, hankering, superfine **10** be bent upon, conceive of, conjecture, decorative, high-priced, ornamental, partiality **11** distinctive, exceptional, extravagant, gingerbread, hanker after, have a mind to, imagination, inclination **12** have an eye for, predilection **13** be pleased with, take a liking to

fancy house 4 stew **5** house **6** bagnio **7** brothel **8** bordello, cathouse **10** bawdy house, whorehouse **13** sporting house **14** house of ill fame **16** house of ill repute **19** house of prostitution

fang 4 claw, nail, root, take, tang, tusk **5** prong, seize, tooth **6** obtain **7** capture, procure **8** eyetooth **9** chelicera

fanny 3 bum **4** buns, rump, seat, tush **6** behind, bottom **8** backside, buttocks, derriere **9** fundament

Fanny
    author: 9 Erica Jong

Fanny
    character in: 13 Joseph Andrews
    author: 8 Fielding

fan out 7 scatter **8** disperse **9** spread out

fantasize 5 dream, fancy **7** imagine **8** daydream

fantastic 3 mad, odd **4** huge, wild **5** antic, crazy, great, queer, weird **6** absurd, superb **7** amazing, bizarre, extreme, strange **8** enormous, fabulous, fanciful, freakish, illusory, quixotic, romantic, terrific **9** grotesque, imaginary, marvelous, visionary, wonderful **10** chimerical, far-fetched, incredible, irrational, outlandish, ridiculous, tremendous **11** extravagant, implausible, sensational **12** preposterous, unbelievable

fantasy 4 mind **5** dream, fancy **6** mirage, notion, vision, whimsy **7** caprice, chimera, fiction, figment, phantom, reverie **8** daydream, illusion, phantasm **9** imagining, invention, nightmare, unreality **10** apparition **11** fabrication, imagination, make-believe, supposition **13** hallucination, realm of dreams, visionary idea

Fantasy Island
    character: 6 Tattoo **8** Mr Roarke
    cast: 16 Herve Villechaize, Ricardo Montalban

far 4 afar, much **6** deeply, remote, way-off, yonder **7** distant, greatly **11** beyond range, out-of-the-way **12** considerably, immeasurably, incomparably

Faraday, Michael
    field: 7 physics **9** chemistry

worked in: 11 electricity
    developed: 9 generator **12** electrolysis
    liquified: 8 chlorine
    discovered: 6 carbon **7** benzene **24** electromagnetic induction
    named for him: 5 farad

far and near 10 every place, everywhere, far and wide **11** in all places

far and wide 10 every place, everywhere, far and near **11** in all places

Far Away and Long Ago
    author: 8 W H Hudson

farce 4 sham **6** parody **7** mockery **8** drollery, nonsense, pretense, travesty **9** absurdity, burlesque, horseplay, low comedy **10** buffoonery, tomfoolery **11** broad comedy, make-believe **12** harlequinade **14** ridiculousness

farceur 3 wag **5** joker

farcical 5 droll, funny, silly **6** absurd, stupid **7** asinine, comical, foolish **8** humorous **9** laughable, ludicrous, senseless **10** irrational, ridiculous

fare 2 do **3** fee **4** diet, food, menu **5** board, get on, rider, table **6** charge, client, manage **7** make out, perform, regimen, turn out **8** customer, get along, victuals **10** provisions **11** comestibles, ticket price **12** food and drink, passage money **15** paying passenger **20** cost of transportation

farewell 6 so long **7** good-bye, parting **8** Godspeed **9** departing, departure **11** leave-taking, parting wish, valediction **17** parting compliment
    French: 5 adieu **8** au revoir
    German: 14 auf Wiedersehen
    Hawaiian: 5 aloha
    Italian: 4 ciao **5** addio **11** arrivederci
    Japanese: 8 sayonara
    Latin: 4 vale
    Spanish: 5 adios

Farewell to Arms, A
    author: 15 Ernest Hemingway
    character: 13 Frederic Henry **16** Catherine Barkley

far-fetched 7 dubious **8** doubtful, strained, unlikely **10** cockamamie, improbable **11** implausible **12** preposterous, unconvincing

Far From the Madding Crowd
    author: 11 Thomas Hardy
    character: 10 Fanny Robin, Gabriel Oak **12** Sergeant Troy **14** Farmer Boldwood **17** Bathsheba Everdene
    setting: 6 Wessex

farina 4 meal, mush **5** flour **6** cereal, pollen, starch **8** semolina

farm 3 sow **4** plow, reap **5** plant, ranch, tract **6** grange, spread **7** harvest **9** cultivate **10** plantation **11** till the soil **12** country place

farmable 6 arable **7** friable **8** plowable, tillable **10** cultivable

farm animal 2 ox **3** cow, ewe, hen,

hog, pig, ram, sow **4** bull, goat **5** beast, brute, horse, sheep **7** chicken, rooster

farm boundaries
    god of: 8 Silvanus, Sylvanus

farmer 6 grower, raiser, reaper **7** granger, planter, rancher **8** agrarian **9** harvester **10** agronomist, husbandman **12** sharecropper **13** agriculturist, truck gardener **15** tiller of the soil

farming
    god of: 4 Thor

far-off 6 remote **7** distant, far-away **11** unreachable **12** inaccessible **13** unforeseeable

farouche 3 shy **6** fierce, sullen **10** unsociable

far-out 3 mad **4** wild **5** crazy, weird **7** bizarre, strange **10** outlandish **14** fantastic

Far Pavilions, The
    author: 6 M M Kaye

Farragut, David
    served in: 8 Civil War **10** Mexican War **19** War of Eighteen Twelve
    captured: 9 Mobile Bay **10** New Orleans
    saying: 30 Damn the torpedoes full speed ahead

far-reaching 4 wide **5** broad **8** sweeping **9** expansive, extensive, universal, unlimited **11** wide-ranging

Farrell, James T
    author of: 11 Judgment Day **12** Studs Lonigan, Young Lonigan **29** The Young Manhood of Studs Lonigan

far-removed 6 far-off, remote **7** distant, faraway

farrow 6 barren **7** piglets, sterile **9** infertile **10** unpregnant

Farrow, Mia
    real name: 27 Maria de Lourdes Villier Farrow
    father: 10 John Farrow
    mother: 16 Maureen O'Sullivan
    husband: 11 Andre Previn **12** Frank Sinatra
    companion: 10 Woody Allen
    born: 12 Los Angeles CA
    roles: 5 Zelig **11** John and Mary, Peyton Place **12** The Hurricane **13** Rosemary's Baby **14** The Great Gatsby **16** Allison MacKenzie **19** Hannah and Her Sisters **20** The Purple Rose of Cairo

far side 4 back **7** reverse **8** back side

Far Side, The
    creator/artist: 10 Gary Larson

farsighted 4 wise **5** acute **6** shrewd **7** prudent **9** farseeing, hyperopic, judicious, prescient, provident **10** forehanded, foreseeing **11** clairvoyant, levelheaded

farther 6 beyond, deeper, longer **7** further, remoter **9** lengthier **10** more remote **11** more distant, more removed

farthermost 7 extreme 8 farthest, furthest 11 furthermost, most distant

farthest 3 end 4 most 7 extreme, longest 8 furthest, remotest, ultimate 9 uttermost 11 farthermost, furthermost

fascia 4 band, sash 5 board, strip 6 fillet, girdle, ribbon, tissue 7 bandage 8 membrane 9 dashboard

fascinate 5 charm, rivet 6 absorb, allure 7 beguile, bewitch, delight, enchant, engross 8 enravish, enthrall, entrance, transfix 9 captivate, enrapture, overpower, spellbind 14 hold spellbound

fascinating 8 alluring, charming, gripping, riveting 9 absorbing, beguiling 10 bewitching, delightful, enchanting, engrossing, entrancing 11 captivating, enthralling, interesting 12 overpowering, spellbinding

fascination 4 draw, lure 5 charm 6 allure 9 magnetism 10 attraction 11 captivation

fascism 6 Nazism 9 autocracy, oligarchy 10 plutocracy 11 corporatism, police state 13 corporativism 14 corporate state 15 totalitarianism 17 national socialism 21 right-wing dictatorship

fascist 8 dictator 9 Mussolini, rightwing 10 black shirt, brown shirt, repressive, tyrannical 11 dictatorial, doctrinaire 12 storm trooper

fashion 3 air, fad, hew, way 4 form, make, mode, mold, rage 5 carve, craze, forge, frame, habit, shape, style, tenor, trend, usage, vogue 6 create, custom, design, devise, manner 7 compose, pattern, produce 8 attitude, behavior, contrive, demeanor 9 construct, fabricate 10 convention 11 manufacture

fashionable 2 in 3 hip 4 chic 5 smart 6 modish, with-it 7 current, in style, in vogue, popular, stylish, voguish 9 in fashion 10 all the rage, prevailing
French: 9 de rigueur

fashionable world
French: 10 grand monde

fashion designer 4 (Christian) Dior 5 Kenzo, (Jean) Patou, Prada 6 Adolfo, (Georgio) Armani, Lanvin, Poiret, (Coco) Chanel 7 Galanos, (Gianni) Versace, Halston, Missoni, (Pierre) Balmain 8 Givenchy 9 Courreges, Mary Quant, Valentino 10 Balenciaga, Donna Karan, Mainbocher, Perry Ellis 11 Calvin Klein, Emilio Pucci, Ralph Lauren 12 Liz Claiborne, Lucien Lelong, Norman Norell, Pierre Cardin, Schiaparelli 13 Karl Lagerfeld, Rudi Gernreich 14 Pauline Trigere 15 Claire McCardell 16 Gloria Vanderbilt, Yves Saint-Laurent
Empress Eugenie's: 5 (Charles Frederick) Worth
Marie Antoinette's: 10 Rose Bertin
Empress Josephine's: 19 Louis Hippolyte Leroy

fashioned 4 made 5 built 6 formed, framed, molded, shaped, styled 7 adapted, crafted, created, devised, managed, modeled 9 contrived, patterned 11 constructed 12 accommodated

fashion plate 4 dude 5 dandy 12 Beau Brummell, clotheshorse, man of fashion, sharp dresser 14 woman of fashion

fast 4 firm, taut, true, wild 5 ahead, brisk, fleet, fully, hasty, loose, loyal, quick, rapid, rigid, swift, tight 6 famish, firmly, fly- ing, rakish, secure, speedy, stable, starve, steady, wanton, winged 7 abiding, devoted, durable, fasting, fast day, fixedly, hastily, hurried, immoral, lasting, lustful, quickly, rapidly, solidly, soundly, staunch, swiftly, tightly 8 constant, enduring, faithful, fastened, go hungry, immodest, reckless, resolute, securely, speedily, unfading 9 debauched, dissolute, hurriedly, immovable, immovably, in advance, permanent, resistant, steadfast 10 completely, dissipated, firmly tied, lascivious, licentious, profligate, starvation, stationary, unswerving, unwavering 11 accelerated, expeditious, extravagant, intemperate, pleasuremad, tenaciously 12 hunger strike, ineradicable, lickety-split

Fast, Howard
author of: 9 Spartacus 11 Freedom Road 13 The Immigrants 15 Citizen Tom Paine

fasten 3 bar, fix, pin, tie, wed 4 bind, bolt, clip, fuse, hold, hook, join, lash, link, lock, moor, snap, weld, yoke 5 affix, clamp, clasp, dowel, focus, hitch, close, latch, rivet, screw, stick, truss, unite 6 adhere, anchor, attach, button, cement, couple, direct, pinion, secure, solder, tether 7 connect 8 dovetail 11 put together

fastener 3 peg, pin, tie 4 clip, glue, grip, hook, line, nail, snap, tack 5 catch, clamp, clasp, cleat, latch, screw, strap, truss 6 buckle, button, cement, staple, thread, zipper 7 bracket 8 barrette 9 fastening, safety pin, thumbtack 10 clothespin, connection, hook and eye

fastening 4 snap 5 clasp 8 coupling 9 attaching 10 attachment, connection

fasten together 3 tie 4 dock, join 6 couple, hook up, link up

fastidious 5 fussy, picky 6 choosy, dainty, proper, queasy 7 finicky 8 exacting, precious 9 difficult, squeamish 10 meticulous, particular 11 overprecise, overrefined, persnickety 12 hard to please, overdelicate 13 hypercritical

Fastidious Brisk
character in: 22 Every Man out of His Humour
author: 6 Jonson

fastidiousness 4 care 12 exactingness 14 discrimination 15 persnicketiness

fat 4 full, oily 5 beefy, fatty, flush, heavy, obese, palmy, plump, pudgy, stout, suety 6 chubby, fleshy, grease, greasy, portly, rotund 7 copious, fertile, lumpish, paunchy, replete, stuffed 8 abundant, blubbery, chockful, fruitful, thickset, unctuous 9 animal fat, corpulent, fortunate, lucrative, plenteous, plentiful, rewarding 10 overweight, potbellied, productive 11 wellstocked 12 remunerative

fatal 6 deadly, lethal, mortal 7 ruinous 8 terminal, virulent 10 calamitous, disastrous 11 destructive 12 catastrophic, causing death

fatalism 8 stoicism 11 resignation 12 acquiescence, helplessness 13 powerlessness 14 predestination

fatality 5 death 8 casualty 9 lethality, mortality 10 deadliness, malignancy 11 banefulness

fatal woman see 11 femme fatale

fate 3 lot 4 doom 5 karma, moira 6 effect, future, kismet, upshot 7 chances, destiny, fortune, outcome, portion 8 prospect 10 providence 11 consequence 12 will of heaven 14 predestination

fated 4 sure 5 bound, meant 6 doomed 7 certain 8 destined

fateful 5 fatal 7 crucial, ominous 8 critical, decisive 9 momentous 10 disastrous, portentous 11 significant

Fates
also: 5 Morae 6 Moerae, Moirai, Parcae
named: 6 Clotho 7 Atropos 8 Lachesis
goddesses of: 7 destiny
number of goddesses: 5 three
called: 12 weird sisters
parents: 4 Zeus 5 Night 6 Themis

father 3 dad, pop 4 abbe, cure, papa, sire 5 beget, begin, daddy, found, hatch, maker, padre, pater 6 author, create, design, old man, parson, pastor, priest 7 creator, founder 8 ancestor, begetter, designer, engender, forebear, inventor, preacher 9 architect, confessor, originate, procreate 10 forefather, male parent, originator, progenitor
French: 4 pere

Father 4 Abba

Father, The
author: 16 August Strindberg

Father Knows Best
character: 11 Jim Anderson 13 Betty Anderson (Princess), Kathy Anderson (Kitten) 15 James Anderson Jr (Bud) 16 Margaret Anderson
cast: 9 Billy Gray, Jane Wyatt 11 Ro-

bert Young **12** Lauren Chapin **13** Elinor Donahue

atherland 6 Heimat, patria, patrie **8** homeland **10** birthplace, motherland, native land, native soil **13** mother country, native country

atherly 6 benign, kindly, tender **8** parental, paternal **9** indulgent **10** beneficent, benevolent

ather of his country
Latin: **12** Pater Patriae

ather of stars/wind 8 Astraeus

ather of the Bride
director: **16** Vincente Minnelli
cast: **11** Billie Burke, Joan Bennett, Leo G Carroll **12** Spencer Tracy **15** Elizabeth Taylor
sequel: **21** Father's Little Dividend

ather of the family
Latin: **13** paterfamilias

ather of the Rivers see **4** Nile

athers and Sons
author: **12** Ivan Turgenev
character: **5** Katya, Pavel **6** Arkady, Vasily **8** Bazaroff, Fenichka **9** Kirsanoff **15** Madame Odintzoff

fathom 5 probe **6** divine, follow **7** hunt out, root out, uncover, unravel **8** discover **9** ferret out, figure out, penetrate **10** comprehend, understand **16** get to the bottom of

fathom
abbreviation: **4** fath

fatigue 3 fag **4** bush, tire **5** drain, weary **6** tedium, tucker, weaken **7** exhaust, languor, wear out **8** enervate, overtire **9** heaviness, lassitude, tiredness, weariness **10** debilitate, drowsiness, enervation, exhaustion **12** debilitation, listlessness **13** overtiredness

fatigued 4 beat **5** all in, jaded, spent, tired, weary **6** bushed, done in, fagged, pooped **7** worn out **8** dog-tired, weakened **9** dead tired, enervated, exhausted, overtaxed **10** overworked **11** debilitated, tuckered out

fatiguing 6 tiring **7** arduous, tedious **8** tiresome **9** wearisome **10** exhausting

Fatima
character in: **9** Bluebeard

fatti maschii, parole femine 29 deeds are manly words are womanish
motto of: **8** Maryland

fatty 4 oily **5** lardy, suety **6** greasy **7** buttery **8** blubbery **9** shortened

fatuous 5 inane, silly, vapid **6** obtuse, simple, stupid **7** asinine, foolish, idiotic, moronic, puerile, vacuous, witless **8** besotted, imbecile **9** brainless, senseless **10** ridiculous

faucet 3 tap **4** cock **5** spout, valve **6** nozzle, outlet, spigot **7** bibcock

Faulkland
character in: **9** The Rivals
author: **8** Sheridan

Faulkner, William

author of: **7** The Bear **8** Sartoris **9** Sanctuary, The Hamlet **10** The Reivers **11** As I Lay Dying **13** Light in August **15** Absalom Absalom! **17** Intruder in the Dust **18** The Sound and the Fury

fictional county: **13** Yoknapatawpha

fault 3 bug, sin **4** flaw, slip, snag **5** blame, crime, error, guilt, stain, taint, wrong **6** defect, foible, glitch, impugn **7** blemish, blunder, censure, failing, frailty, misdeed, mistake, offense, reprove **8** drawback, weakness **9** criticize, infirmity, oversight, weak point **10** deficiency, impediment, negligence, peccadillo, wrongdoing **11** culpability, dereliction, misdemeanor, shortcoming **12** imperfection, indiscretion **13** answerability, transgression **14** accountability, responsibility

faultfind 3 nag **4** beef, carp, kick **5** cavil, gripe, knock **6** deride, squawk **7** nitpick **8** complain **9** criticize

faultfinder 3 nag **4** bear, crab **5** crank **6** carper, censor, critic, grouch **7** caviler, grouser **8** quibbler, sorehead **9** derogator, detractor, Mrs Grundy, nitpicker **10** bellyacher, complainer, curmudgeon, fuddy-duddy, fussbudget

faultfinding 4 beef, kick **5** gripe **6** squawk **7** beefing, carping, griping, kicking, nagging **9** complaint, criticism, squawking **10** nitpicking **11** complaining, criticizing

faultless 5 ideal **7** correct, perfect **8** accurate, flawless **9** exemplary **10** immaculate, impeccable **11** unblemished **13** unimpeachable **14** irreproachable, without blemish

faulty 3 bad **4** awry **5** amiss, false, wrong **7** injured, unsound **8** impaired, inferior, mistaken **9** defective, deficient, erroneous, imperfect, incorrect **10** inadequate, out of order, unreliable **14** unsatisfactory

faun
form: **5** deity, satyr **7** goat-man
location: **5** rural

Fauna see **7** Bona Dea

Faunus
origin: **5** Roman
form: **5** deity
location: **5** woods
also called: **5** Inuus **6** Fatuus
king of: **6** Latium
father: **5** Picus
son: **7** Latinus
corresponds to: **3** Pan

Faure, Gabriel Urbain
born: **6** France **7** Pamiers
composer of: **5** Dolly **6** Pavane **7** Ballade, Mirages, Requiem, Shylock **8** Penelope **9** Fantaisie, Promethee **12** Le Jardin Clos **13** La Chanson d'Eve **14** La Bonne Chanson **18** L'Horizon Chimerique, Pelleas et

Melisande **21** Masques et Bergamasques

Faust
author: **12** Johann Goethe
character: **6** Wagner **8** Gretchen **10** Homunculus **11** Helen of Troy **14** Mephistopheles

Faust
opera by: **6** Gounod
character: **6** Siebel **8** Valentin **10** Marguerite **14** Mephistopheles

Faustulus
vocation: **8** herdsman, shepherd
raised: **5** Remus **7** Romulus

faute de mieux 24 for lack of something better

faux pas 4 goof **5** boner, error, gaffe, lapse **6** boo-boo, howler, slip-up **7** blooper, blunder, mistake **9** false step **11** impropriety **12** indiscretion

favela 4 slum **10** shanty town

Favell, Jack
character in: **7** Rebecca
author: **9** Du Maurier

Favonius
origin: **5** Roman
personifies: **8** west wind

favor 3 aid **4** abet, back, gift, help, like **5** be for, fancy, humor **6** assist, esteem, foster, oblige, pamper, prefer, succor, uphold **7** approve, commend, endorse, go in for, indulge, kind act, memento, present, service, support **8** advocacy, approval, courtesy, espousal, good deed, good turn, goodwill, largesse, look like, resemble, sanction, side with, souvenir **9** encourage, patronage, patronize, smile upon, take after, use gently **10** act of grace, use lightly **11** accommodate, approbation, be partial to, benefaction, countenance, good opinion **12** be the image of, championship, commendation, dispensation, kindly regard **13** accommodation, goodwill token

favorable 4 fair, good, kind **6** benign, timely **7** helpful, hopeful **8** amicable, friendly, salutary **9** approving, conducive, opportune, promising **10** auspicious, beneficial, convenient, propitious **11** predisposed, serviceable, sympathetic **12** advantageous, commendatory, well-disposed

favorable opinion 6 esteem, regard **7** respect **8** approval **10** admiration **12** appreciation

favorably disposed 7 willing **8** amenable, inclined, obliging **9** agreeable **11** sympathetic

favorite 3 pet **5** fancy, jewel **6** choice **7** darling, special **9** best-liked, preferred **11** front-runner, most popular **13** fair-haired one **14** apple of one's eye

favoritism 4 bias **10** partiality **12** one-sidedness, partisanship

Fawley, Jude and Drusilla
characters in: **14** Jude the Obscure
author: **5** Hardy

fawn 5 toady **6** pander **7** flatter, truckle **8** pay court **9** be servile, seek favor **12** be obsequious, bow and scrape

fawning 7 servile **8** flattery, toadying **9** adulating, adulation, truckling **10** flattering, obsequious **11** sycophantic **12** ingratiating **14** obsequiousness

fax 4 send **8** transmit **9** facsimile

faze 4 fret **5** abash, daunt, upset, worry **6** bother, flurry, rattle **7** disturb, fluster, perturb **8** confound **9** discomfit, embarrass **10** discompose, disconcert

fazed 5 upset **7** abashed, ruffled **8** agitated, bothered, confused **9** chagrined, unsettled **10** confounded, distracted, nonplussed **11** embarrassed **12** disconcerted

FBI, The
character: **10** Arthur Ward **21** Inspector Lewis Erskine
cast: **12** Philip Abbott **16** Efrem Zimbalist Jr

fealty 7 loyalty **8** devotion, fidelity **9** adherence, constancy **10** allegiance, attachment **12** faithfulness

fear 3 awe **4** care **5** alarm, bogey, dread, panic, qualm, worry **6** dismay, esteem, fright, horror, phobia, revere, terror, threat, wonder **7** anxiety, bugaboo, bugbear, concern, quaking, specter **8** affright, venerate **9** cowardice, nightmare, reverence, shudder at, tremble at **10** be afraid of, be scared of, feel awe for, foreboding, take fright, veneration **11** trepidation **12** apprehension, perturbation **13** consternation **14** be frightened of

fearful 4 dire **5** awful, dread, eerie, lurid, timid **6** afraid, aghast, horrid, scared, uneasy **7** alarmed, anxious, ghastly, macabre, nervous, ominous, panicky, worried **8** alarming, dreadful, horrible, shocking, sinister, skittish, terrible, timorous **9** appalling, concerned, diffident, frightful, tremulous **10** formidable, frightened, portentous, terrifying **11** distressing, frightening, intimidated **12** apprehensive, fainthearted **13** panic-stricken **14** chicken-hearted

fearfulness fear **5** alarm, dread, panic **6** fright, terror **7** anguish, anxiety **8** timidity **11** trepidation **12** apprehension

fearless 4 bold **5** brave **6** daring, gritty, heroic, plucky **7** doughty, gallant, valiant **8** intrepid, unafraid, valorous **9** audacious, confident, dauntless, unabashed, undaunted **10** courageous, undismayed **11** adventurous, indomitable, lionhearted, unflinching, unshrinking, venturesome, without fear **12** stout-hearted

fearlessness 4 grit **5** pluck, valor **7** bravery, courage **8** boldness **10** confidence **13** dauntlessness

Fear of Flying
author: **9** Erica Jong

feasible 6 doable, viable **7** fitting, politic **8** possible, suitable, workable **9** advisable, desirable **10** achievable, attainable, reasonable **11** appropriate, conceivable, practicable

feast 4 dine, fete **5** festa, gorge **6** bounty **7** banquet, holiday, jubilee, surplus **8** feast day, festival **9** bacchanal, saint's day **10** gluttonize, gormandize, have a feast, rich supply **11** celebration, eat one's fill, elegant meal, wine and dine

feat 3 act **4** deed, task **6** action, stroke **7** exploit, triumph **8** maneuver **9** adventure **10** attainment, enterprise **11** achievement, performance, tour de force **14** accomplishment

feather 4 down, kind, sort **5** adorn, eider, pinna, plume, quill **7** bristle, plumage, variety **9** character, turn an oar

featherbrained 4 dumb **5** silly **6** simple, stupid **7** foolish, witless **9** brainless **12** muddleheaded, simple-minded **13** rattle-brained **14** scatterbrained

feather in one's cap 5 honor **6** credit **11** distinction

feather one's nest 6 enrich **15** fill one's pockets

feature, features 3 see **4** mark, star **5** fancy, trait **6** aspect, play up, visage **7** display, earmark, imagine, picture, present, quality **8** envision, hallmark, headline, main item, property **9** attribute, character, highlight, specialty, spotlight **10** conceive of, lineaments **14** characteristic

February
event: **4** Lent **5** Purim **8** Leap year **9** Mardi Gras **12** Ash Wednesday, Groundhog Day (2)
flower: **6** violet **8** primrose
French: **7** Fevrier
gem: **8** amethyst
German: **7** Februar
holiday: **9** Candlemas (2) **13** President's Day Valentine's Day (14) **14** Chinese New Year **16** Lincoln's Birthday (12) **19** Washington's Birthday (22)
Italian: **8** Febbraio
Latin: **6** Februa
number of days: **10** twenty-nine (every 4 years) **11** twenty-eight
origin of name: **7** Februus
  Roman god of: **12** purification
place in year:
  Gregorian: **6** second
  Roman: **7** twelfth
Spanish: **7** Febrero
Zodiac signs: **6** Pisces **8** Aquarius

Fechner, Gustav Theodore

nationality: **6** German
founder of: **22** experimental psychology

fecit 6 he made (it) **7** she made (it)

feckless 3 lax **5** slack **6** remiss **8** careless, heedless **9** negligent, worthless **10** neglectful **11** thoughtless **13** irresponsible

Fecundity
goddess of: **5** Freia, Freya

Fed
Federal Reserve System: **6** the Fed
FBI agent: **4** G-man **6** feebie, fibbie
Treasury agent: **4** T-man
head: **14** Alan Greenspan

Federalist Party
president belonging to: **5** Adams **10** Washington

federate 5 unite **7** combine **12** join together

federation 5 union **6** league **7** combine **8** alliance **9** coalition, syndicate **10** sisterhood **11** association, brotherhood, confederacy **12** amalgamation **13** confederation

fee 4 fare, hire, toll, wage **5** price **6** charge, salary, tariff **7** payment, stipend **9** emolument **10** commission, honorarium **12** compensation, remuneration **13** consideration

feeble 4 flat, lame, poor, puny, tame, thin, weak **5** faint, frail, vapid **6** ailing, flabby, flimsy, infirm, meager, paltry, senile, sick- ly, slight **7** fragile, insipid **8** decrepit, delicate, disabled, impotent, weakened **9** colorless, declining, doddering, enervated, enfeebled, forceless, not strong, powerless **10** inadequate, spiritless, wishy-washy **11** debilitated, ineffective, ineffectual

feeble-minded 4 dull, dumb **6** senile, stupid **7** moronic **8** backward, childish, retarded **9** imbecilic, senseless, subnormal **10** half-witted, weak-minded **12** mentally slow

feeble-mindedness 6 dotage, idiocy **8** dullness, senility, slowness **9** denseness, stupidity **11** retardation

feed 3 eat **4** fare, fuel, mash **5** cater, feast, graze **6** devour, fodder, forage, foster, viands **7** augment, bolster, consume, gratify, nourish, nurture, pasture, satisfy, support, sustain **8** maintain, take food, victuals **9** encourage, foodstuff, provender **10** minister to, provisions, strengthen **11** comestibles, nourishment, wine and dine

feeder 6 branch **7** channel **9** tributary

feel 3 paw, see **4** know **5** grope, press, probe, reach, sense, think, touch **6** fin- ger, fumble, handle, makeup, notice **7** believe, discern, feeling, observe, palpate, texture **8** perceive **9** be aware of, be moved by, character, sensation **10** comprehend, experience, manipulate, suffer from, understand

11 be convinced, be stirred by, be touched by, composition

feel aversion toward 4 hate **5** abhor **6** detest **7** despise **9** abominate, can't abide, can't stand **11** can't stomach **12** be revolted by **13** find repugnant, find repulsive **14** view with horror

feeler 7 antenna **8** proposal, tentacle **10** experiment **12** trial balloon

feel indebted 10 appreciate, be beholden, be grateful **13** feel obligated

feeling 4 aura, pity, view, zeal **5** ardor, gusto, sense, verve **6** fervor, spirit, thrill, warmth **7** concern, emotion, opinion, passion **8** attitude, instinct, reaction, response, sympathy **9** affection, awareness, intuition, sensation, sentiment, vehemence **10** atmosphere, compassion, enthusiasm, impression **11** earnestness, inclination, point of view, sensibility, sensitivity

feeling life is wearisome
Latin: **12** taedium vitae

feelings 3 ego **5** pride **8** emotions, passions **10** self- esteem **13** sensibilities, sensitivities **16** susceptibilities

feel pain 4 ache, hurt **5** smart **6** suffer **7** agonize **9** be in agony **11** be tormented **12** be in distress

Feenix, Cousin
character in: **12** Dombey and Son
author: **7** Dickens

feet 4 dogs, pads, paws **5** hoofs **6** hooves **8** gunboats, tootsies

feign 4 fake, sham **5** forge, put on **6** affect, assume, cook up, invent, make up **7** concoct, pretend **8** simulate **9** fabricate **11** counterfeit, make a show of, make believe

feigned 4 fake, sham **5** bogus, phony **6** ersatz **8** spurious **9** imitation, insincere, pretended, simulated **10** artificial **11** counterfeit, make-believe

feint 4 hoax, mask, move, pass, ploy, ruse, wile **5** blind, bluff, dodge, trick **6** gambit **7** pretext **8** artifice, maneuver, pretense **9** stratagem **10** subterfuge **13** feigned attack

Feldman, Marty
born: **6** London **7** England
roles: **11** Silent Movie **17** Young Frankenstein **24** The Last Remake of Beau Geste

feldspar
varieties: **8** sunstone **9** amazonite, moonstone

felicitate 4 hail **6** salute **10** wish one joy **11** rejoice with **12** congratulate **18** give one's best wishes **28** wish many happy returns of the day

felicitations 3 joy **6** cheers **9** blessings, greetings **10** best wishes, good wishes **11** compliments, salutations **12** pat on the back **15** congratulations **24** many happy returns of the day

felicitous 3 apt **5** happy **6** joyful, joy-

ous **7** fitting, germane, well-put **8** inspired, pleasing, relevant, suitable, well-said **9** effective, fortunate, pertinent **10** propitious, well-chosen **11** appropriate

felicity 5 bliss, charm, grace, knack, skill **6** heaven, nicety **7** aptness, delight, ecstasy, fitness **8** paradise **9** beatitude, happiness **12** blissfulness **13** effectiveness **15** appropriateness

Felix the Cat
creator: **11** Pat Sullivan

fell 4 raze **5** level **7** cut down, destroy, hew down **8** demolish **9** knock down, prostrate

Feller, Bob (Robert)
nickname: **11** Rapid Robert
sport: **8** baseball
position: **7** pitcher
team: **16** Cleveland Indians

Fellini, Federico
director of: **8** Amarcord, Casanova, La Strada **11** La Dolce Vita **15** Nights of Cabiria **18** Juliet of the Spirits

fellow 3 boy, guy, mac, man, pal **4** chap, chum, dude, gent, mate, peer **5** equal **6** friend **7** comrade, consort **8** coworker **9** associate, colleague, companion **10** compatriot

fellow conspirator 4 ally **6** cohort **7** abettor **8** henchman **9** accessory **11** confederate **12** collaborator

fellow creature 5 human **6** mortal, person **10** individual

fellow feeling 6 regard **7** empathy, kinship **8** affinity, fondness **10** attraction, partiality

fellowship 5 amity **7** society **8** intimacy **10** affability, cordiality, fraternity, friendship **11** amicability, association, brotherhood, comradeship, familiarity, sociability **12** friendliness **13** companionship

felon 5 crook, cruel, thief **6** fierce, outlaw, wicked **7** convict, illegal, villain, whitlow **8** criminal, gangster, jailbird, murderer **10** law-breaker, malefactor **11** public enemy **12** inflammation

felony 5 arson, crime **6** murder **7** assault, misdeed, offense, robbery **8** burglary **9** blackmail **10** kidnapping, wrongdoing **12** capital offense

female 3 cow, dam, hen, sow **4** girl, mare **5** bitch, tabby, woman **6** heifer **7** distaff, womanly **8** feminine, ladylike **9** womanlike

feminine 4 soft **5** woman **6** dainty, female, gentle **7** distaff, girlish, womanly **8** delicate, ladylike **10** femalelike, like a woman **14** of the female sex

femininity 8 softness **10** femaleness, gentleness **11** girlishness, womanliness **12** feminineness **13** female quality

femme 4 wife **5** woman

femme de chambre 9 lady's maid **11** chambermaid

femme fatale 4 vamp **5** siren **7** charmer **10** fatal woman, seductress **11** enchantress

femur
bone of: **5** thigh **8** upper leg

fen 3 bog **4** moor, sump **5** marsh, swale, swamp **6** bottom, morass, slough **7** lowland, wetland **8** quagmire

fence 3 pen **4** coop, duel, gird, rail **5** hedge, hem in **6** corral, secure, wall in **7** barrier, confine, palings **8** encircle, palisade, stockade, surround **9** barricade, encompass **11** cross swords

fencing
equipment: **4** epee, foil, mask **5** saber, sword **8** plastron
part of weapon: **5** blade, forte, guard **6** foible, handle, medium, pommel
term: **3** hit **5** prime, sixte, touch **6** octave, quarte, quinte, tierce **7** en garde, on guard, seconde, septime
deceptive move: **5** feint
movement: **4** beat **5** lunge, parry **6** double, fleche, thrust **7** advance, cutover, recover, retreat, riposte **9** disengage **11** froissement

fend 2 do **5** avert, avoid, parry, repel, shift **6** manage **7** keep off, make out, provide, repulse, support, survive, ward off **8** push away

fender 3 pad **4** curb **5** guard **6** buffer, bumper, shield, sluice **7** cushion, railing **9** fireguard, protector **10** cowcatcher, fire screen, protection, wheel guard

fend off 5 avert, dodge, evade, parry, repel **6** escape **7** ward off **8** sidestep, stave off

fennel
botanical name: **17** Foeniculum vulgare
family: **7** parsley
varieties: **3** dog **4** wild **5** giant **8** Florence **9** common dog **11** common giant
mythical aid to: **9** fortifier **11** aphrodisiac, slenderizer **12** rejuvenation, stops hiccups **16** restores eyesight
use: **4** duck, fish **5** bread, rolls **7** chicken **8** apple pie **16** seafood casserole

Fenrir
also: **6** Fenris
origin: **12** Scandinavian
form: **4** wolf **7** monster
father: **4** Loki
mother: **9** Angerboda, Angrbodha, Angurboda
sister: **3** Hel
brother: **11** Iormungandr, Jormungandr **14** Midgard Serpent
ate: **4** Odin **5** Othin
killed by: **5** Vidar

Fenris *see* 6 Fenrir

Fenton
 character in: 22 The Merry Wives of Windsor
 author: 11 Shakespeare

feral 4 wild 6 brutal, deadly, ferine, fierce, savage 7 bestial, untamed, vicious 9 ferocious 12 uncultivated 14 undomesticated

Ferber, Edna
 author of: 5 Giant, So Big 8 Cimarron, Show Boat 9 Ice Palace, Stage Door (with George S Kaufman) 13 Dinner at Eight (with George S Kaufman), Saratoga Trunk 14 The Royal Family (with George S Kaufman)

Ferdinand
 king of: 5 Spain
 wife: 8 Isabella
 patron of: 8 Columbus

Ferdinand
 character in: 10 The Tempest
 author: 11 Shakespeare

Ferdinand
 character in: 16 Love's Labour's Lost
 author: 11 Shakespeare

Ferdinand the Bull
 author: 9 Munro Leaf
 disliked: 12 bullfighting

Ferd'nand
 creator: 3 Mik 13 Dahl Mikkelsen

Feria
 origin: 5 Roman
 form: 7 holiday

Fermat, Pierre de
 field: 11 mathematics
 nationality: 6 French
 discovered: 16 analytic geometry

ferment 4 foam, mold, sour, turn 5 froth, yeast 6 enzyme, fester, leaven, seethe, tumult, unrest, uproar 7 agitate, inflame, smolder, turmoil 8 bubble up, disquiet 9 agitation, commotion, leavening 10 disruption, effervesce, turbulence 11 be turbulent, fomentation

fermented 6 soured, worked 7 seethed 8 agitated

Fermi, Enrico
 field: 7 physics
 nationality: 7 Italian
 developed: 10 atomic bomb 20 uranium fission theory
 awarded: 10 Nobel Prize

fern
 varieties: 3 air, cup, lip, man, oak, saw 4 ball, blue, claw, deer, dish, felt, fire, gold, hand, iron, king, lace, lady, male, moss, nest, pine, sago, tara, tree, wall, wart, wood 5 beard, beech, chain, cloak, fancy, glade, glory, grape, grass, hedge, holly, marsh, plume, royal, strap, swamp, sweet, sword, table, water, whisk 6 adder's, bamboo, basket, Boston, button, carrot, coffee, cotton, cuplet, dagger, ladder, meadow, mother, rib-

bon, shield, silver, tongue, turnip, winter 7 bladder, boulder, brittle, bulblet, crested, emerald, feather, Fee's lip, fragile, Goldie's, hacksaw, Halberd, hammock, leather, New York, ostrich, parsley, peacock, rainbow, walking 8 bear-foot, bear's-paw, cinnamon, climbing, elk's-horn, fishtail, floating, florist's, fragrant, hairy lip, Hartford, licorice, mosquito, Nebraska, Savannah, snuffbox, soft tree, staghorn 9 asparagus, bird's-nest, black tree, blond tree, Christmas, common cup, deer's-foot, downy wood, flowering, glossy cup, hare's foot, long beech, sensitive, vegetable, Venus hair, viscid lip, wavy cloak, woolly lip 10 Alabama lip, Boott's wood, broad beech, deer-tongue, Duff's sword, erect sword, five-finger, hay-scented, lady ground, maidenhair, scented oak, shoestring, silver tree, silver-back, silver-lace, silver-leaf, slender lip, strawberry, upside-down, woolly tree 11 Braun's holly, coastal wood, Coville's lip, crested felt, crested wood, dwarf Boston, elephant-ear, Fendler's lip, hart's-tongue, interrupted, Jamaica gold, leatherleaf, leatherwood, narrow beech, netted chain, Northern oak, Parry's cloak, Pursh's holly, rabbit's-foot, rattlesnake, Sierra water, walking leaf 12 Adder's-tongue, American wall, berry bladder, Clinton's wood, Dudley's holly, Eaton's shield, English hedge, Hawaiian tree, Java staghorn, limestone oak, mountain wood, Northern lady, resurrection, Southern lady, squirrel-foot, toothed sword, Western holly, Western sword 13 California lip, Cleveland's lip, Dudley's shield, European chain, fan maidenhair, Fendler's cloak, Florida ribbon, leathery grape, Malay climbing, mountain holly, Northern holly, prickly shield, Prince-of-Wales, spinulose wood, Tasmanian tree, triangle water, Virginia chain, wild bird's nest 14 Anderson's holly, Australian tree, bulblet bladder, California gold, common staghorn, dissected grape, dwarf asparagus, hen-and-chickens, imbricate sword, silver-king tree, West Indian tree 15 American parsley, California cloak, California holly, Delta maidenhair, East Indian holly, European parsley, mountain bladder, mountain parsley 16 black-stemmed tree, daisy-leaved grape, Farley maidenhair, Tassel maidenhair, Tracy's maidenhair 17 Bermuda maidenhair, brittle maidenhair, climbing bird's nest, walking maidenhair 18 Aleutian maidenhair, American maidenhair, Barbados maidenhair, Northern maidenhair, Trailing maidenhair, Tri-

angular staghorn 20 Australian maidenhair, California maidenhair

fernet-branca
 type: 8 aperitif
 origin: 5 Italy
 flavor: 4 herb

Fern Hill
 author: 11 Dylan Thomas

ferocious 6 brutal, deadly, fierce, savage 7 bestial, brutish, enraged, violent 8 fiendish, maddened, ravening, ruthless 9 atrocious, barbarous, merciless, murderous, predatory, rapacious 10 relentless 11 cold-blooded 12 bloodthirsty

ferocity 7 cruelty 8 savagery 9 barbarity, brutality, harshness 10 fierceness, inhumanity, savageness 11 brutishness, viciousness 12 ruthlessness

Ferrer, Jose
 real name: 33 Jose Vincente Ferrer de Otero y Cintron
 wife: 8 Uta Hagen 15 Rosemary Clooney
 son: 6 Miguel
 born: 8 Santurce 10 Puerto Rico
 roles: 7 I Accuse 9 Joan of Arc 11 Moulin Rouge, Ship of Fools 14 The Caine Mutiny 16 Cyrano de Bergerac (Oscar), Lawrence of Arabia 24 The Greatest Story Ever Told

ferret out 5 dig up 6 detect 7 find out, root out, uncover, unearth 8 discover 9 ascertain

fertile 4 rich 5 loamy 6 fecund 8 creative, fruitful, original, prolific 9 fructuous, ingenious, inventive, luxuriant, plenteous 10 fecundated, fertilized, fructified, generative, productive, vegetative 11 imaginative, resourceful 12 reproductive

Fertility
 god of: 7 Bacchus, Mutinus 8 Lupercus, Picumnus
 goddess of: 4 Isis 5 Fauna 6 Athena, Athene, Brigit, Libera, Pallas, Saitis, Tellus 7 Astarte, Berchta, Bona Dea, Demeter, Perchta 11 Tritogeneia 12 Pallas Athena 16 Alalcomean Athena

fertilize 6 enrich, manure 8 fructify 9 fecundate, pollinate 10 impregnate, inseminate

fertilizer 4 dung, muck 5 guano, niter 6 manure, potash 7 compost 8 bonemeal, dressing 10 enrichener 14 superphosphate

fervent 4 keen 5 eager, fiery 6 ardent, devout, fervid, fierce, hearty, heated 7 burning, earnest, intense, zealous 8 spirited, vehement 9 heartfelt 10 passionate 11 impassioned, warmhearted 12 enthusiastic, wholehearted

fervid 5 eager 6 ardent, raging 7 burning, earnest, fanatic, fervent, intense, zealous 8 spirited 10 passionate 11 impassioned 12 all-consuming

fervor 4 fire, zeal, zest 5 ardor, gusto,

piety, verve **6** warmth **7** passion **9** animation, eagerness, intensity, vehemence **10** devoutness, enthusiasm, heartiness **11** earnestness, seriousness **14** purposefulness

Feste
clown in: **12** Twelfth Night
author: **11** Shakespeare

Fester see **12** Addams Family

fester 3 rot, vex **4** fret, gall, grow, rile **5** chafe, pique **6** nettle, plague, rankle **7** blister, form pus, inflame, putrefy, smolder, torment **8** irritate, ulcerate **9** intensify, suppurate

festering 6 putrid **7** rotting **8** infected, inflamed, rankling **10** putrefying **11** suppurating

festina lente 15 make haste slowly

festival 4 fete, gala **5** feast **6** fiesta **7** gala day, holiday, jubilee **8** carnival, jamboree **11** celebration, festivities

Festival of
Adonis: **6** Adonia
Apollo: **5** Delia **8** Didymaea **9** Delphinia **12** Daphnephoria
Athena: **6** Lenaea **8** Diipolia **9** Pyanepsia **11** Oschophoria
Attica: **13** Rural Dionysia **14** Lesser Dionysia
Bacchus: **11** Bacchanalia
Boeotians: **7** Daedala **13** Little Doedala
Demeter: **5** Haloa
Dionysus: **5** Haloa **8** Dionysia
flowers: **11** Anthesteria
Greeks: **6** Heraea **9** Pyanepsia **11** Scirophoria, Skirophoria **13** Thesmorphoria
Persephone: **5** Haloa
Roman: **8** Floralia, Matralia **9** Lemuralia, Liberalia **10** Larentalia, Lupercalia, Matronalia, Parentalia, Saturnalia
spring: **11** Anthesteria
wine: **11** Anthesteria
Zeus: **6** Diasia **8** Didymaea

festive 3 gay **4** gala **5** jolly, merry **6** festal, joyous **7** larkish, playful **8** sportive **9** convivial **10** frolicsome **11** celebratory **12** lighthearted

festivity 3 joy **4** fete, gala **5** feast, mirth **6** fiesta, gaiety, levity **7** fanfare, jollity, jubilee, revelry **8** festival, jamboree **9** merriment, rejoicing **11** celebration, merrymaking

festoon 3 lei **4** swag **5** chain, curve **6** wreath **7** garland, hanging **8** decorate

fetch 3 get **4** cost **5** bring, go for, yield **6** afford, obtain **7** procure, realize, sell for **8** amount to, retrieve

fetching 6 divine, lovely **8** adorable, becoming, charming, engaging, pleasing **9** appealing **10** attractive, delightful **11** captivating

fete 4 gala **5** feast, party, treat **6** regale **7** banquet, holiday **8** carnival, festival **9** bal masque **11** celebration, garden party, wine and dine **13** fete champetre

fete champetre 11 garden party **15** outdoor festival

fetid 4 foul, gamy, rank **5** fusty, moldy, musty, nasty **6** putrid, rancid, rotten **7** noisome, stenchy, tainted **8** mephitic, stifling, stinking **9** stenchful **10** malodorous **11** ill-smelling, suffocating

fetish 4 idol, joss **5** charm, craze, image, mania, totem **6** amulet, scarab **7** passion **8** idee fixe, talisman **9** obsession **10** golden calf, phylactery **11** magic object **12** superstition **13** preoccupation

fetter 4 bind, bond, cage, curb, yoke **5** chain, tie up **6** duress, hamper, hinder, hobble, impede, shut in, tether **7** confine, durance, manacle, pin down, shackle, tie down, trammel, truss up **8** bracelet, encumber, handcuff, hold back, restrain **9** hindrance, restraint **13** put into bilbos **15** bind hand and foot

feud 3 row **4** fuss, spat, tiff **5** argue, brawl, clash, set-to **6** affray, bicker, breach, enmity, fracas, schism, strife **7** discord, dispute, faction, ill will, quarrel, rupture, wrangle **8** argument, bad blood, be at odds, clashing, conflict, disagree, squabble, vendetta **9** animosity, bickering, hostility **10** falling out **11** altercation, controversy **12** disagreement, hard feelings
famous: **6** McCoys **9** Hatfields

Feud, The
author: **12** Thomas Berger

feudal lord
Japanese: **6** daimyo

Feuerbach, Anselm
born: **6** Speyer **7** Germany
artwork: **9** Iphigenia **15** Judgment of Paris, Plato's Symposium **18** The Fall of the Titans

fever 4 fire, heat **5** ardor, craze, flush, furor **6** desire, frenzy, warmth **7** ferment, illness, pyrexia **8** delirium, sickness **9** agitation **10** enthusiasm, excitement **11** temperature **12** restlessness

feverish 3 hot **5** fiery **6** ardent, red-hot **7** burning, excited, fanatic, febrile, fervent, fevered, flushed, parched, pyretic, zealous **8** frenzied, inflamed, restless **9** impatient, overeager, wrought-up **10** high-strung, passionate **11** impassioned

few 4 rare, some, thin **5** scant **6** meager, paltry, scanty, scarce, skimpy, sparse, unique **7** handful, limited, not many, several, unusual **8** exiguous, piddling, sporadic, uncommon **9** hardly any **10** infrequent, occasional **11** scarcely any, small number **13** infinitesimal, insignificant **14** inconsiderable

Fezziwig
character in: **15** A Christmas Carol
author: **7** Dickens

fiance, fiancee 6 future **7** engaged, pledge **8** intended, promised **9** affianced, betrothed, bride-to-be, groom-to-be **10** bride-elect, groom-elect

fiasco 4 bomb, flop **5** botch **6** fizzle **7** debacle, washout **8** disaster **10** nonsuccess

fiat 3 act, law **4** rule **5** edict, order, ukase **6** decree, dictum, ruling **7** command, mandate **11** commandment

fiat lux 15 let there be light

fib 3 lie **5** hedge **7** fiction, untruth **8** white lie **9** half-truth, invention **10** equivocate **11** fabrication, harmless lie, prevaricate **13** falsification, prevarication, tell a white lie **15** stretch the truth **17** misrepresentation

fiber 4 hemp, jute, silk **5** fibre, linen, nylon, rayon, shred, sinew, sisal **6** cotton, dacron, manila, nature, strand, thread **7** quality, texture **8** filament **9** character, polyester, structure

fibrolite
source: **5** Burma, Mogok

fibula
bone of: **8** lower leg

fickle 5 giddy **6** fitful **7** erratic, flighty **8** shifting, unstable, unsteady, variable, volatile, wavering **9** frivolous, mercurial, spasmodic, whimsical **10** capricious, changeable, inconstant, irresolute, unreliable **11** fluctuating, light-headed, vacillating **12** inconsistent **13** feather-headed, unpredictable, untrustworthy **14** feather-brained

fiction 3 fib, lie **4** play, tale, yarn **5** fable, novel **7** fantasy, forgery, novella, romance, whopper **8** tall tale **9** falsehood, invention, narrative **10** concoction, short novel, short story **11** fabrication, imagination, made-up story **12** storytelling **13** prevarication **16** cock-and-bull story

fictional 6 made-up **8** invented, literary **9** mythical **9** storybook **10** fictitious **11** theoretical **12** hypothetical

fictitious 4 fake, sham **5** bogus, false, phony **6** forged, made-up, unreal, untrue **7** assumed, feigned **8** fanciful, invented, mythical, spurious **9** imaginary, legendary, simulated, trumped-up, unfounded **10** apocryphal, artificial, fabricated, fraudulent, not genuine **11** counterfeit **14** supposititious

fiddle 3 bow, saw, toy **4** fool **5** cheat, dally, fraud **6** dawdle, monkey, potter, putter, tamper, trifle, violin **7** falsify, finagle, fritter, swindle **9** deception **10** fool around, mess around **12** monkey around

Fidei Defensor 18 Defender of the Faith
title of: **17** English sovereigns

Fidelio
  opera by: **9** Beethoven
  character: **5** Rocco **7** Leonora (Fidelio), Pizarro **8** Fernando **9** Florestan

fidelity 5 honor **6** fealty **7** honesty, loyalty, probity **8** accuracy, devotion **9** adherence, closeness, constancy, exactness, good faith, integrity, precision, sincerity **10** allegiance, exactitude **11** earnestness, reliability, staunchness **12** faithfulness, truthfulness **14** correspondence **15** trueheartedness, trustworthiness

Fides
  origin: **5** Roman
  personifies: **9** good faith

fidget 4 fret, fuss, jerk, stew, toss **5** chafe, worry **6** jiggle, squirm, twitch, wiggle, writhe **7** twiddle, wriggle

fidgety 5 antsy, fussy, jerky, jumpy **6** uneasy **7** jittery, nervous, restive, squirmy, twitchy, unquiet **8** restless **9** impatient, irritable, tremulous **12** apprehensive

fief 4 land **6** domain, estate **9** territory

field 3 lea **4** area, grab, lawn, line, mead, turf, yard **5** arena, catch, court, front, glove, green, heath, lists, orbit, range, reach, realm, scope, sward, sweep **6** circle, common, course, domain, extent, meadow, pick up, region, sphere **7** acreage, calling, diamond, expanse, pasture, run down, stretch **8** clearing, province, retrieve, spectrum **9** bailiwick, grassland, territory **10** department, occupation, profession **12** battleground

Field, Sally
  born: **10** Pasadena CA
  roles: **5** Sybil **6** Gidget **8** Norma Rae (Oscar) **9** Punchline, Surrender **12** The Flying Nun **14** Murphy's Romance **15** Absence of Malice **16** Places in the Heart (Oscar) **18** Smokey and the Bandit

Fielding, Cecil
  character in: **15** A Passage to India
  author: **7** Forster

Fielding, Henry
  author of: **6** Amelia **7** Shamela **8** Tom Jones, Tom Thumb **12** Jonathan Wild **13** Joseph Andrews

Field of Blood 8 Aceldama

Fields, W C
  real name: **23** William Claude Dukenfield
  born: **14** Philadelphia PA
  roles: **5** Poppy **8** Micawber **11** The Bank Dick **16** David Copperfield **17** My Little Chickadee **27** Never Give a Sucker an Even Break

Fields of Mourning
  location: **10** underworld
  inhabited by: **14** shades of lovers
    lovers who died by: **7** suicide

Fields of Visions, The
  author: **12** Wright Morris

fiend 5 beast, brute, demon, devil, Satan **6** dybbuk **7** incubus, monster, villain **8** succubus **9** barbarian, hellhound, scoundrel **10** evil spirit **12** wicked person **14** devil incarnate **16** prince of darkness

fiendish 4 evil, foul **5** cruel **6** wicked **7** demonic, heinous, impious, satanic, vicious **8** barbaric, demoniac, devilish **9** monstrous, nefarious **10** demoniacal, diabolical, villainous

fierce 4 fell, wild **5** cruel, feral, fiery **6** bru-tal, fervid, raging, savage, strong **7** enraged, extreme, fearful, fervent, furious, intense, leonine, untamed, violent **8** horrible, menacing, powerful, ravening, ravenous, terrible, tigerish, uncurbed, vehement **9** barbarous, bellicose, ferocious, impetuous, merciless, truculent, unbridled, voracious **10** immoderate, inordinate, passionate **11** threatening **12** bloodthirsty, overpowering, overwhelming, unrestrained
French: 8 farouche

fierceness 4 zeal **7** passion **8** ferocity, wildness **9** pugnacity, vehemence **10** savageness

fiery 5 afire, angry, irate **6** ablaze, alight, ardent, fervid, fierce, red-hot, torrid **7** blazing, burning, febrile, fervent, fevered, flaming, glaring, glowing, peppery, pyretic, violent, zealous **8** choleric, feverish, flashing, headlong, inflamed, spirited, vehement, wrathful **9** excitable, hotheaded, impetuous, impulsive, irascible, irritable **10** full of fire, high-strung, mettlesome, passionate, sweltering **11** hottempered, impassioned, precipitate **12** enthusiastic

fiesta 4 fete, gala **5** feast, party **6** picnic **7** funfair **8** carnival, feast day, festival, jamboree **9** saint's day **10** block party, observance, street fair **11** celebration **13** com-memoration **15** festive occasion

fig 5 Ficus
  varieties: **3** keg, sea **4** bush, cape, Java, Zulu **5** cedar, clown, Congo, rusty **6** common, Devil's, exotic, golden, Indian, Kaffir, Mysore, sacred **7** Barbary, cluster, oak-leaf, spotted, weeping **8** climbing, creeping, Dracaena, mulberry, sycamore **9** Hottentot, mistletoe, strangler **10** East Indian, fiddle-leaf, glossy-leaf, little-leaf, Moreton Bay, Philippine **11** Port Jackson **16** West Indian laurel

Figaro
  character in: **18** The Barber of Seville **19** The Marriage of Figaro
  author: **12** Beaumarchais

fight 3 box, row, war **4** bout, duel, feud, fray, grit, spar, spat, tiff, tilt, wage **5** ar-gue, brawl, brush, clash, event, joust, match, melee, pluck, round, scrap, set-to **6** battle, bicker, combat, engage, fracas, mettle, oppose, resist, spirit, strife, tussle **7** carry on, conduct, contend, contest, discord, dispute, go to war, quarrel, repulse, scuffle, tourney, wage war, wrangle **8** confront, dogfight, gameness, skirmish, squabble, struggle **9** bickering, encounter, pugnacity, scrimmage, toughness, wrangling **10** contention, difference, dissension, prizefight, strive with, tournament **11** altercation, armed action, battle royal, bellicosity, clash of arms, controversy **12** belligerency, do battle with, rise up in arms, struggle with **13** armed conflict, combativeness, confrontation, exchange blows, pitched battle

fight back 7 counter, get even, hit back, pay back **9** retaliate **10** strike back **13** counterattack

fighter 5 boxer **7** soldier, sparrer, warrior **8** pugilist, scrapper **9** combatant **10** militarist **11** belligerent

fighting 3 war **4** fray **5** brawl, melee **6** action, battle, bicker, combat, rumpus, tumult, tussle **7** contest, dispute, quarrel, warfare **8** battling, brawling, conflict, skirmish, squabble **9** bickering, disputing **10** engagement, quarreling, squabbling **11** clash of arms, controversy, hostilities

Fighting Marine
  nickname of: **10** Gene Tunney

fighting men 4 army **6** legion, troops **7** legions, militia **8** military, soldiers, soldiery **13** military force **15** military machine

fighting spirit 9 animosity, hostility, pugnacity **10** antagonism **11** bellicosity **12** belligerence **14** aggressiveness

fight shy of 5 avoid, dodge, elude, evade, skirt **6** escape **8** sidestep

figment 5 fable, fancy, story **6** canard **7** fantasy, fiction, product **8** creation **9** falsehood, invention **10** concoction **11** fabrication

figuration 4 form **7** outline **9** formation, structure **12** constitution

figurative 6 florid, ironic, ornate **7** flowery **8** humorous, symbolic **9** satirical **10** not literal **11** allegorical **12** hyperbolical, metaphorical

figure, figures 3 cut, man, sum **4** body, cast, cost, foot, form, mark, plan, rate, sign, sums **5** add up, adorn, build, count, digit, force, frame, guess, judge, mo-tif, price, shape, think, total, tot up, value, woman **6** amount, appear, assess, cipher, design, device, emblem, factor, leader, number, person, reckon, schema, symbol **7** anatomy, believe, compute, contour, count up, diagram, drawing, imagine, notable, numeral, outline, pattern, presume, suppose **8** appraise, be placed, eminence, estimate, ornament, physique, presence **9** calculate, character, diversify, embellish, have a part, personage, play a part, quotation, variegate **10** arithmetic, conjecture, shine forth, silhouette **11** be mentioned, be prominent **12** calculations, computations, illustration

figurehead 4 tool **5** dummy, front, token **6** cipher, puppet **8** ornament **9** nonentity

figure out 6 reckon **7** compute, find out, work out **8** discover **9** ascertain, calculate, determine

figure roughly 5 guess **6** reckon **8** estimate **11** approximate, make a stab at

figure up 3 add **5** add up, total, tot up **6** reckon **7** compute, count up **9** calculate

figurine 7 bibelot **8** ornament **9** statuette

Fiji
capital/largest city: 4 Suva
others: 3 Mba **4** Mbua **5** Navua **6** Labasa **7** Lautoka, Nausori, Vaileka, Vunisea **8** Korolevu, Savusavu **9** Singatoka
school: 12 South Pacific
head of state: 14 British monarch **15** governor general
monetary unit: 6 dollar
island: 4 Ngau **6** Ovalau, Rotuma, Yasawa **7** Kandavu, Taveuni **8** Viti Levu **9** Vanua Levu
highest point: 8 Victoria **9** Tomaniivi
river: 4 Rewa **8** Ndreketi
sea: 4 Koro **7** Pacific
people: 6 Fijian, Indian **7** Chinese **10** Melanesian, Polynesian **11** Micronesian
language: 5 Hindi **6** Fijian **7** English
religion: 5 Hindu, Islam **9** Methodist **13** Roman Catholic
feature:
cluster houses: 5 mbure

filament 4 hair, line, wire **5** fiber, fibre **6** cilium, ribbon, strand, string, thread

filbert 7 Corylus
varieties: 3 red **4** cork, Momi, plum **5** azure, China, giant, Greek, joint, Nikko, noble, white **6** alpine, balsam, Fraser, Korean, needle, Scotch, silver, summer **7** cascade, Douglas, lowland, Spanish **8** Algerian, Japanese, Sakhalin, Southern **9** Himalayan, Shasta Red **10** dwarf Nikko, Santa Lucia **11** bristle-cone **13** Pacific silver **14** Southern balsam

filch 3 cop, rob **4** copy, crib, hook, lift **5** boost, heist, steal, swipe **6** pilfer, pirate **7** purloin **8** arrogate **10** plagiarize **11** appropriate, expropriate

file 3 row **4** data, line, list, rank, tier **5** ap-ply, chain, index, put in, queue,

store **6** drawer, folder, record, stacks, string **7** catalog, dossier, put away, records, request **8** archives, classify, petition **9** catalogue, chronicle
type: 4 mill, nail, rasp, wood **5** round **9** half-round **13** three-cornered

filial 7 dutiful, sonlike **10** daughterly, respectful

fill 3 act **4** cram, glut, lade, load, meet, pack, puff, sate **5** crowd, gorge, lay by, lay in, serve, stock, store **6** answer, as-sign, blow up, charge, dilate, do duty, expand, infuse, make up, occupy, outfit, supply, take up **7** distend, execute, furnish, inflate, pervade, preside, provide, satiate, satisfy, suffuse, surfeit **8** carry out, function, permeate, saturate **9** discharge, provision, replenish **10** full amount, impregnate, overspread

filled in 7 stood in **9** completed, **11** substituted

filled out 6 marked **7** matured **9** completed

fillet 4 band **5** slice, strip **6** ribbon **7** bandeau, circlet

fillip 3 tap **4** flip, snap, toss **5** flick, tonic **6** buffet **8** stimulus

Fillmore, Millard
presidential rank: 10 thirteenth
party: 4 Whig
state represented: 2 NY
defeated: 5 no one
succeeded upon death of: 6 Taylor
vice president: 4 none
cabinet:
State: 7 (Daniel) Webster, (Edward) Everett
Treasury: 6 (Thomas) Corwin
War: 6 (Charles Magill) Conrad
Attorney General: 10 (John Jordan) Crittenden
Navy: 6 (William Alexander) Graham **7** (John Pendleton) Kennedy
Postmaster General: 4 (Nathan Kelsey) Hall **7** (Samuel Dickinson) Hubbard
Interior: 6 (Alexander Hugh Holmes) Stuart
born: 7 Locke NY
died/buried: 9 Buffalo NY
education:
college: 4 none
studied: 3 law
religion: 9 Unitarian
interests: 5 civic
first chancellor of University of: 7 Buffalo
founder: 22 Buffalo General Hospital **24** Buffalo Historical Society
author: 21 Millard Fillmore Papers
political career: 13 state assembly, Vice President **24** US House of Representatives
civilian career: 6 lawyer (New York Supreme Court) **7** teacher **10** wool

carder **12** cloth dresser
notable events of lifetime/term: 25 Compromise of Eighteen-Fifty
act: 13 Fugitive Slave
father: 9 Nathaniel
mother: 6 Phoebe (Millard)
siblings: 5 Cyrus, Julia **11** Phoebe Maria **12** Almon Hopkins, Calvin Turner **13** Charles DeWitt **14** Darius Ingraham, Olive Armstrong
wife: 7 Abigail (Powers) **8** Caroline (Carmichael McIntosh)
children: 11 Mary Abigail **13** Millard Powers

fill with air 5 bloat **6** billow, blow up, expand **7** balloon, distend, inflate, puff out **8** swell out

fill with dread 5 alarm, panic **6** dismay **7** perturb, terrify, unnerve **8** disquiet, frighten

fill with gloom 6 darken, sadden **8** dispirit

fill with wonder 3 awe **5** amaze **7** astound **8** astonish **9** fascinate

film, films 4 cine, coat, haze, mist, skin, veil **5** cloud, flick, movie, sheet, shoot **6** cinema, flicks, movies, screen **7** coating **8** membrane

filmy 3 dim **4** fine, hazy, thin **5** gauzy, misty, sheer, wispy **8** cobwebby, finespun, gossamer **10** diaphanous, see-through

fils 3 son

filter 4 leak, ooze, seep **5** drain, exude, sieve **6** effuse, purify, refine, screen, strain **7** clarify, cleanse, dribble, trickle, well out **8** filtrate, strainer

filth 3 mud **4** dirt, dung, mire, muck, porn, slop, smut **5** offal, slime, slush, trash **6** manure, ordure, refuse, sewage, sludge **7** carrion, excreta, garbage, squalor **8** impurity, lewdness, ribaldry, vileness **9** excrement, grossness, indecency, nastiness, obscenity, pollution **10** corruption, defilement, immorality, indelicacy, putridness **11** pornography, squalidness **13** contamination **14** suggestiveness

filthy 4 foul, vile **5** black, dirty, grimy, gross, messy, nasty **6** grubby, impure, odious, soiled **7** defiled, dirtied, obscene, smirchy, squalid, unclean **8** befouled, slovenly, unwashed **9** repulsive **10** besmirched, disgusting **12** contaminated

finagle 3 con, gyp **4** plot, rook **5** cheat, mulct, trick **6** chisel, fleece, scheme, wangle **7** defraud, swindle **8** engineer, intrigue, maneuver

final 4 last, rear **6** ending, latest **7** closing, extreme **8** complete, decisive, finished, hindmost, rearmost, terminal, thorough, ultimate **10** concluding, conclusive, definitive, exhaustive, hindmost **11** irrevocable, terminating **12** unappealable, unchangeable

13 determinative
French: **7** dernier

finale 3 end **5** close, finis **6** finish, windup **7** curtain **8** epilogue, last part, swan song **10** conclusion **11** culmination, termination

final limit
Latin: **14** terminus ad quem

finally 6 lastly **10** eventually, inexorably, ultimately **11** inescapably **12** conclusively, definitively, in conclusion **16** incontrovertibly
French: **5** enfin
Latin: **10** ad extremum

final section 4 coda **5** rider **6** ending **7** last act **8** addendum, epilogue **9** afterword **10** conclusion

final settlement 8 solution **11** disposition

finance 6 pay for **7** banking **8** accounts **9** economics **10** underwrite

financial backer 5 angel **6** patron **7** sponsor **9** supporter **10** benefactor

financial support 7 backing, subsidy **10** assistance **12** contribution

financier 5 angel **6** backer, banker, broker **7** rich man **10** capitalist **11** millionaire, underwriter

Financier, The
author: **15** Theodore Dreiser
character: **12** Aileen Butler, Edward Butler **15** Henry Cowperwood **16** Frank A Cowperwood **23** Lillian Semple Cowperwood

Finch, Peter
real name: **15** Peter Ingle-Finch
born: **6** London **7** England
roles: **7** Network (Oscar) **11** Lost Horizon **12** The Nun's Story **15** The Pumpkin Eater **18** Sunday Bloody Sunday

Finchley, Sondra
character in: **17** An American Tragedy
author: **7** Dreiser

find 3 get, see, win **4** earn, espy, gain, meet, rule, spot **5** award, catch, dig up, judge, learn **6** attain, come by, decide, decree, detect, expose, locate, regain **7** achieve, acquire, adjudge, bargain, bonanza, discern, get back, godsend, good buy, hit upon, procure, recover, uncover, unearth **8** bump into, come upon, discover, disinter, lucky hit, meet with, retrieve, windfall **9** ascertain, determine, discov-ery, encounter, pronounce, repossess **10** adjudicate **11** acquisition

fin de siecle 8 decadent **15** end of the century

find fault 3 nag **4** beef, carp **5** blame, cavil, gribe **6** grouse, squawk **7** nitpick **8** complain **9** bellyache, criticize, disparage **10** disapprove

find guilty 5 blame **6** indict **7** condemn, convict **8** sentence **9** implicate

finding 6 decree, ruling **7** verdict **8** decision

find innocent 5 clear **6** acquit **9** exonerate

find out 5 learn **6** detect, locate **7** uncover, unearth **8** discover **9** ascertain, determine, establish

find repulsive 4 hate **5** abhor **6** detest, loathe **7** despise **8** execrate, recoil at **9** abominate

fine 4 airy, chic, fair, keen, neat, nice, rare, thin **5** bonny, clear, dandy, gauzy, mulct, nifty, sharp, sheer, silky, small, smart, sunny, swell **6** assess, bonnie, bright, charge, choice, comely, dainty, flimsy, ground, lovely, minute, modish, pretty, silken, slight, spiffy, subtle, superb **7** damages, elegant, forfeit, fragile, penalty, perfect, powdery, precise, refined, slender, stylish, tenuous **8** cobwebby, delicate, ethereal, flawless, gossamer, handsome, penalize, pleasant, polished, powdered, rainless, skillful, splendid, superior, tasteful **9** admirable, beautiful, brilliant, cloudless, excellent, exquisite **10** assessment, attractive, consummate, diaphanous, fastidious, pulverized, swimmingly **11** excellently, exceptional, lightweight, magnificent, transparent, well-favored **12** accomplished **13** hairsplitting, unsubstantial
music: **3** end

fine clothes 8 glad rags **10** Sunday best **16** best bib and tucker

fine-looking 4 fair **5** bonny **6** bonnie, comely, lovely, pretty, seemly **8** gorgeous, handsome **9** beauteous, beautiful, exquisite, ravishing **10** attractive **11** resplendent **15** pulchritudinous

fineness 6 beauty **8** delicacy, elegance, thinness **10** perfection, smoothness **12** flawlessness **13** exquisiteness

fine points 3 art **7** finesse, nuances **8** niceties **10** subtleties **11** refinements **12** distinctions

finer 6 better **8** superior

finery 6 frills, tinsel **7** baubles, gaudery, gewgaws **8** frippery, spangles, trinkets **9** trappings, trimmings **13** paraphernalia

finesse 4 ruse, tact, wile **5** craft, dodge, guile, savvy **7** cunning **8** artifice, delicacy, intrigue, trickery **9** deception, stratagem **10** artfulness, discretion, subterfuge
French: **11** savoir-faire

fine workmanship 8 delicacy **9** precision **13** craftsmanship

finger 3 paw **4** feel, poke, ring **5** digit, index, punch, thumb, touch **6** caress, feeler, handle, middle, pinkie, pollex **7** pointer, squeeze, toy with, twiddle **8** identify, play with **10** manipulate

finicky 5 fussy, picky **6** choosy **8** niggling **10** fastidious, meticulous, nit-

picking, overprecise, particular, pernickety **11** persnickety **14** discriminating, overparticular

finish 3 end **4** coat, face, gild, goal, kill, last, seal, stop **5** cease, close, glaze, use up **6** clinch, defeat, devour, ending, finale, settle, veneer, wind up **7** achieve, coating, consume, curtain, destroy, fulfill, get done, lacquer, realize, surface, varnish **8** carry out, complete, conclude, dispatch, epilogue, exterior, get rid of, knock off, make good **9** discharge, eradicate, objective, polishing, terminate **10** accomplish, completion, conclusion, consummate, denouement **11** discontinue, exterminate, termination

finished 4 full **5** ended, final, ideal, whole **6** entire, urbane **7** classic, elegant, perfect, refined, shapely, skilled, trained, well-set **8** complete, flawless, polished, well-bred **9** beautiful, completed, concluded, exquisite, faultless **10** consummate, cultivated, impeccable **11** consummated **12** accomplished

finishing stroke 9 death blow
French: **11** coup de grace

finish off 4 kill, slay **7** destroy, execute, wipe out **8** complete, dispatch **9** eradicate, polish off **10** annihilate **11** exterminate

finite 7 bounded, limited **8** confined, temporal **9** countable **10** measurable, restricted, short-lived, terminable **13** circumscribed

Finland
other name: **5** Suomi **15** Suomen Tasavalta
capital/largest city: **8** Helsinki **11** Helsingfors
others: **3** Aba, Abo, Kem **4** Kemi, Ouli, Oulu, Ouou, Pori, Vasa **5** Enare, Espoo, Kotka, Lahti, Rauma, Turku, Vaasa **6** Imatra, Kuopio **7** Joensuu, Kajaani, Kokkola, Mikkeli, Tampere, Tapiola **9** Jyvaskyla, Mariehamn, Rovaniemi **12** Lappeenranta
measure: **5** kannu, verst **6** fathom, kannor **8** otlinger, skalpund, tunnland
monetary unit: **4** mark **5** penni **6** markka
island: **5** Aland, Karlo **6** Aaland **7** Hailuto **9** Vallgrund **10** Ahvenanmaa
lake: **3** Juo, Muo **4** Kemi, Kiui, Nasi, Oulu, Puru, Pyha, Simo **5** Enara, Enare, Hauki, Inari, Kalla, Lappa, Lesti, Puula, Saima **6** Ladoya, Lentua, Saimaa, Sounne, Syvari **7** Koitere, Nilakka, Pielien **9** Kallavesi, Pielavesi
mountain: **7** Laltiva **10** Saari Selka
highest point: **6** Haltia **11** Haldetsokka
river: **4** Kala, Kemi, Kymi, Oulu, Pats, Simo, Teno **5** Ivalo, Lotta, Ounas, Siika, Torne **6** Iijoki, Lapuan, Muonio, Pasvik, Tornoi, Vuoski **7** Kitinen **8** Kokemaki

sea: 6 Baltic **8** Atlantic
physical feature:
  gulf: 7 Bothnia, Finland
  isthmus: 7 Karelia
  peninsula: 13 Fennoscandian
people: 3 Jew, Vod, Vot, Yak **4** Avar,
  Finn, Hame, Lapp, Turk, Veps **5**
  Fioun, Gypsy, Ijore, Inger, Suomi,
  Vepse **6** Magyar, Ostiak, Ostyak,
  Tarast, Tavast, Ugrian, Zyrian **7** Lappish, Mordvin, Permiak, Samoyed,
  Uralian **8** Cheremis, Estonian, Karelian, Livonian, Swekoman **9** Tavastian **11** Karjalaiset, Suomalaiset
  athlete: 10 Paavo Nurmi
  composer: 8 Sibelius
  designer: 9 Marimekko
language: 4 Avar, Lapp **5** Karel,
  Ugric, Vogul **6** Magyar, Ostyak,
  Tarast **7** Finnish, Olonets, Samoyed,
  Swedish **8** Estonian **10** Olonetsian
religion: 19 Evangelical Lutheran
place:
  canal: 6 Saimaa
  castle: 10 Saint Olaf's **11** Olavin-
    linna
  fortress: 8 Sveaborg **11** Suomen-
    linna
  memorial: 8 Sibelius
  pine ridge: 10 Punkaharju
feature:
  game: 9 pesapallo
food:
  dish: 11 Karelian pie
  fruit: 16 yellow cloudberry
  liqueur: 9 Mesimarja
Finn
  also: 5 Fionn **13** Fionn MacCumal
  origin: 5 Irish
  king of: 4 gods **14** Tuatha De Da-
    nann
  son: 6 Ossian
  father: 5 Cumal **6** Comhal
Finnegans Wake
  author: 10 James Joyce
  family: 9 Earwicker
Finney, Albert
  wife: 10 Anouk Aimee
  born: 7 England, Salford
  roles: 5 Annie **7** Scrooge **8** Tom
    Jones **10** The Dresser **12** Shoot the
    Moon **13** Two for the Road **17** Un-
    der the Volcano **29** Saturday Night
    and Sunday Morning
Finnish Mythology *see* **21** Scandinavian Mythology
Finno-Ugric
  language family: 6 Uralic
  Finnic group: 4 Lapp **6** Votyak, Zyr-
    yan **7** Finnish, Mordvin, Permian **8**
    Estonian **9** Cheremiss
  Ugric group: 5 Vogul **6** Ostyak **7** Ob-
    Ugric **9** Hungarian
Fionn, Fionn MacCumal *see* **4** Finn
fiord, fjord 5 firth, inlet **7** estuary
  location: 6 Norway
fir 4 pine **5** cedar, larch **6** alpine, bal-

sam, linden, spruce **7** conifer, cypress,
douglas **9** evergreen
Firbolg
  origin: 5 Greek, Irish
  defeated by: 9 Fomorians
  ousted by: 4 gods **14** Tuatha De Da-
    nann
fire 3 can, vim **4** bake, boot, burn,
  cook, dash, dump, elan, hurl, oust,
  sack, stir **5** ardor, blaze, eject, flame,
  flare, flash, force, gusto, let go, light,
  power, punch, rouse, salvo, shell,
  shoot, spark, verve, vigor **6** arouse,
  bounce, depose, excite, fervor, foment, genius, ignite, incite, kindle,
  luster, spirit, stir up, vivify, volley **7**
  animate, bombard, bonfire, cashier,
  dismiss, inferno, inflame, inspire,
  project, quicken, sniping, trigger **8** enfilade, fervency, inspirit, radiance,
  splendor, vivacity **9** broadside, cannonade, discharge, eagerness, fusillade, galvanize, holocaust, instigate,
  intensity, stimulate, vehemence **10**
  brilliance, effulgence, enthusiasm **11**
  bombardment, earnestness, inspiration
  13 conflagration, sharpshooting **15**
  imaginativeness
  god of: 4 Loki **5** Ishum **6** Vulcan **10**
    Hephaestus, Hephaistos
  goddess of: 6 Brigit
Fire and Ice
  author: 11 Robert Frost
firearm 3 gun, rod **5** piece, rifle **6** pistol **7** shotgun **8** revolver **10** machine
  gun **12** shooting iron **13** submachine
  gun **20** Saturday-night special
firefight 5 clash **6** battle, combat **8**
  skirmish
firefly 8 glowworm, lampyrid **9** candle-
  fly **12** lightning bug
Fire Next Time, The
  author: 12 James Baldwin
fire off 5 eject, shoot **6** launch **8** detonate **9** discharge
Fireside Theatre
  host: 9 Jane Wyman **11** Frank Wis-
    bar, Gene Raymond
Firestarter
  author: 11 Stephen King
fire up 4 fuel, rile **5** anger, light, rouse
  6 arouse, excite, ignite, incite, kindle
  7 animate, enthuse, inspire **8** activate,
  energize, irritate, vitalize **9** galvanize,
  stimulate
firm 4 bent, fast, grim, hard, taut **5**
  close, dense, fixed, house, rigid,
  rocky, solid, stiff, stony, tight, tough **6**
  dogged, flinty, intent, moored, rooted,
  secure, stable, steady, steely **7** compact, company, dead set, decided, earnest, serious, settled, staunch **8** anchored, business, constant, definite,
  fearless, obdurate, resolute, resolved,
  unshaken **9** confirmed, hard-nosed,
  immovable, obstinate, steadfast, tenacious, unbending **10** adamantine,

compressed, determined, inexorable,
inflexible, invincible, persistent, unwavering, unyielding **11** corporation,
established, partnership, unalterable,
unfaltering, unflinching **12** conglomerate, indissoluble, organization **13** establishment
firmament 3 air, sky **5** ether, space,
  vault **6** canopy, welkin **7** heavens, the
  blue, the void **10** outer space
firmness 8 tenacity **9** obstinacy **10** resolution **11** persistence, staunchness
  12 resoluteness **13** determination, inflexibility, steadfastness
first 4 head, main **5** basic, prime, start,
  vital **6** before,eldest, maiden, outset,
  primal, rather, sooner **7** highest, leading, premier, primary, ranking, supreme **8** earliest, foremost, original,
  primeval, superior **9** beginning, essential, inception, initially, paramount,
  primitive, principal **10** aboriginal, elementary, preeminent, preferably, primordial **11** fundamental, rudimentary
  12 commencement, introduction, introductory
first among equals
  Latin: 16 primus inter pares
first appearance 4 dawn **5** debut **9**
  beginning **12** introduction
firstborn 5 elder, older **6** eldest, oldest
Firstborn, The
  author: 14 Christopher Fry
First Circle
  author: 23 Aleksandr Solzhenitsyn Jr
first god *see* **8** god, first
firsthand 6 direct **8** personal **9** empirical **10** unmediated **12** experimental
First Lady of the Theater
  nickname of: 10 Helen Hayes **16**
    Katherine Cornell
first-line 4 main **5** chief **7** primary **8**
  foremost
first moving thing
  Latin: 12 primum mobile
first-rate 3 ace **4** A-one, best, fine,
  tops **5** crack, elite, great, prime **6**
  choice, finest, select **7** top-hole **8**
  splendid, superior, top-notch, very
  good **9** admirable, estimable, excellent, exclusive, nonpareil, top drawer,
  topflight, wonderful **10** noteworthy,
  stupendous **11** commendable, outstanding **12** above-average, incomparable **13** distinguished
First State
  nickname of: 8 Delaware
first step 5 start **9** beginning **12** commencement
firth 5 fjord, inlet **7** estuary
fiscal 8 economic, monetary **9** budgetary, financial, pecuniary
fish 3 net **4** cast, hook, hunt **5** angle,
  grope, seine, trawl, troll **6** ferret,
  search **7** rummage
fish

class: 7 Agnatha 12 Osteichthyes 14 Chondrichthyes

fin: 4 anal, tail 6 caudal, dorsal, median, paired, pelvic 7 adipose, ventral 8 pectoral

kind: 3 cod, eel, gar, ray 4 bass, carp, hake, opah, pike, tuna 5 brill, perch, shark, skate, sword, trout 6 bichir, blenny, marlin, minnow, mullet, salmon, tarpon 7 anchovy, catfish, dogfish, dolphin, hagfish, herring, lamprey, piranha, sunfish 8 bluefish, cavefish, crayfish, flounder, goldfish, lungfish, mackerel, menhaden, moray eel, pilchard, sea horse, squirrel, sturgeon 9 killifish, pygmy goby, swordfish 10 coelacanth, flying fish, paddlefish, rabbit fish, rocksucker, whale shark 11 anemonefish, electric eel, electric ray, lanternfish, longnose gar 13 butterflyfish 14 largemouth bass

part: 3 fin 4 gill 5 scale 6 cirrhi 10 gas bladder 11 swim bladder 12 rete mirabile

shellfish:
> **crustacean:** 4 crab 6 shrimp 7 lobster 8 blue crab, king crab, snow crab 9 langouste 11 langoustine 13 Dungeness crab, horseshoe crab
>
> **mollusk:** 4 clam 6 mussel, oyster, quahog 8 surf clam 9 horse clam, razor clam 11 geoduck clam

young: 3 fry 10 fingerling

Fisher, Bud
creator/artist of: 11 Mutt and Jeff

Fisher, Carrie
father: 11 Eddie Fisher
mother: 13 Debbie Reynolds
role: 12 Princess Leia
films: 7 Shampoo 8 Star Wars 12 This Is My Life 16 The Blues Brothers 17 When Harry Met Sally 18 The Return of the Jedi 19 The Empire Strikes Back, Hannah and Her Sisters
author: 20 Postcards from the Edge

Fisher, Ham
creator/artist of: 10 Joe Palooka

Fisher, Vardis
author of: 10 The Mothers 13 Children of God 17 The Testament of Man

fisherman 5 eeler 6 angler, caster, jacker, netter, seiner 7 trawler, troller 8 piscator 9 flycaster, Waltonian 17 the compleat angler

Fishermen
goddess of: 11 Britomartis

Fishes
constellation of: 6 Pisces

fish story 3 fib, lie 7 fiction, whopper 9 falsehood, tall story 16 cock-and-bull story

fishy 3 odd 4 dull 5 blank, queer, shady, weird 6 vacant 7 dubious, strange, suspect 8 doubtful, peculiar, slippery 9 dishonest 10 farfetched, glassy-eyed, improbable, suspicious, unreliable 11 exaggerated, extravagant 12 questionable, unscrupulous 14 expressionless

fission 7 atomize 8 breaking, cleavage, scission 9 severance, splitting 10 breaking up, sunderance 12 disseverance, reproduction

fissure 3 gap 4 rift, slit 5 chink, cleft, crack, gully, split 6 breach, cranny, groove, hiatus 8 aperture, cleavage

fit 4 able, good, hale, meet, ripe, suit, well, whim 5 adapt, agree, alter, burst, equal, equip, hardy, match, ready, right, shape, sound, spasm, spell, train 6 access, accord, adjust, become, concur, enable, in trim, mature, primed, proper, robust, seemly, strong, timely, worthy 7 adapted, apropos, capable, caprice, conform, correct, empower, fashion, healthy, prepare, qualify, rectify, seizure, toned up, trained 8 apposite, becoming, coincide, crotchet, decorous, eligible, graduate, grand mal, outbreak, outburst, paroxysm, petit mal, prepared, relevant, suitable 9 calibrate, competent, consonant, deserving, efficient, explosion, harmonize, initiated, opportune, pertinent, qualified 10 acceptable, applicable, capacitate, convenient, convulsion, correspond, seasonable 11 appropriate, capacitated

fitful 4 weak 6 broken, random, uneven 7 erratic 8 listless, off-and-on, periodic, sporadic, unsteady, variable 9 irregular, spasmodic 10 capricious, changeable, convulsive 11 fluctuating 12 disconnected, intermittent

fitness
Hebrew: 7 kashrut 8 kashruth

fit out 4 robe 5 array, dress, equip 6 attire, clothe, supply 7 appoint, deck out, prepare

fitting 3 apt 4 meet 6 proper, seemly 8 decorous, suitable 9 congruous 11 appropriate
French: 11 comme il faut

fit to be eaten 6 edible 9 palatable 10 comestible, consumable, digestible

fit together 4 join 5 hinge, unite 6 hook up 7 connect 8 dovetail 9 interlock 10 articulate

Fitzgerald, Barry
real name: 20 William Joseph Shields
born: 6 Dublin 7 Ireland
roles: 10 Going My Way 11 The Quiet Man 19 How Green Was My Valley

FitzGerald, Edward
author of: 24 The Rubaiyat of Omar Khayyam (translation)

Fitzgerald, F Scott
wife: 10 Zelda Sayre
author of: 10 The Crack-Up 13 The Last Tycoon 14 The Great Gatsby 16 Tender Is the Night 18 This Side of Paradise 24 The Beautiful and the Damned
coined term: 7 Jazz Age

Fitzgerald, George Francis
field: 7 physics
nationality: 5 Irish
theory of: 24 electromagnetic radiation

Fitzgerald, Geraldine
born: 6 Dublin 7 Ireland
roles: 11 Dark Victory 12 Ah Wilderness, Rachel Rachel 15 Watch on the Rhine 16 Wuthering Heights 24 Long Day's Journey into Night

Fitzsimmons, Bob (Robert Prometheus)
sport: 6 boxing

Fitzsimmons, Maureen
real name of: 12 Maureen O'Hara

Five, The
group of: 16 Russian composers
member: 3 Cui 7 Borodin 9 Balakirev 10 Mussorgsky 14 Rimsky-Korsakov

Five Easy Pieces
director: 11 Bob Rafelson
cast: 10 Karen Black 11 Fannie Flagg 12 Susan Anspach 13 Jack Nicholson 14 Billy Breen Bush, Sally Struthers

Five Men and Pompey
author: 19 Stephen Vincent Benet

five-o'clock shadow 5 beard 7 stubble 8 bristles, whiskers

fix 3 jam, put, set 4 bind, make, mend, mess, moor, spot 5 place, rivet 6 adjust, anchor, attach, decide, fasten, harden, impose, muddle, pickle, plight, repair, scrape, secure, settle 7 congeal, connect, correct, dilemma, impasse, implant, patch up, prepare, rebuild 8 assemble, hot water, make fast, make firm, quandary, regulate, renovate, set right, solidify 9 establish, prescribe, retaliate, stabilize 10 difficulty 11 consolidate, involvement, predicament 12 entanglement

fixation 5 quirk 6 fetish 7 complex 8 crotchet, delusion 9 monomania, obsession 13 preoccupation

fixed 3 set 4 fast, firm 5 rigid, still 6 intent, rooted, stable, steady 8 constant, fastened, resolute, unpliant 9 immovable, unbending 10 determined, inflexible, motionless, persistent, stationary, unwavering

fixed idea 4 bias 5 slant 9 obsession 13 preconception
French: 8 idee fixe

fixedness 8 firmness 9 constancy, stability 10 immobility 12 immutability 16 unchangeableness

fixed regard 7 staring 9 diligence 10 absorption, intentness 11 engrossment 13 concentration

Fixer, The
   author: 14 Bernard Malamud
fixing 6 repair 7 mending, mooring, placing, putting, setting 8 deciding, imposing, righting, riveting, settling, trimming 9 adjusting, anchoring, attaching, fastening, hardening, preparing, repairing 10 adjustment, assembling, congealing, connecting, correcting, implanting, rectifying, regulating, regulation 11 determining, prescribing, solidifying, stabilizing 12 establishing 13 consolidating
fixture 6 addict 7 devotee, habitue, regular 8 equipage 9 apparatus, appendage, appliance, equipment 10 attachment 11 appointment 12 appurtenance 13 paraphernalia
fix up 4 plan 6 design, devise 7 arrange, prepare 8 renovate, schedule
fix upon 4 pick 6 choose, opt for, select 7 call out, extract, pick out
fizz 4 foam 5 froth 7 bubbles 11 carbonation 13 effervescence
fizziness 9 foaminess 10 bubbliness, frothiness 13 effervescence
fizzing 6 bubbly 7 foaming 8 bubbling 9 sparkling 12 effervescent, effervescing
fizzle 3 dog, dud 4 bomb, fail, flop, hiss, mess 5 abort, botch 6 bubble, fiasco, gurgle, muddle, turkey 7 failure, founder, misfire, sputter, washout 8 collapse, disaster, miscarry
fizzy 6 bubbly 8 bubbling 9 sparkling 12 effervescent
flabbergast 4 stun 5 amaze, shock 6 puzzle 7 astound, stagger, stupefy 8 astonish, bewilder, bowl over, confound, overcome 9 dumbfound
flabbergasted 5 agape 6 amazed, gaping 9 awestruck, stupefied 10 astonished, dumbstruck, spellbound 11 dumbfounded 12 hornswoggled 13 thunderstruck
flabby 4 lame, limp, soft, weak 5 baggy, slack 6 doughy, effete, feeble, flimsy, floppy, spongy 7 flaccid 8 impotent, listless, yielding 9 enervated, inelastic 10 out of shape, spiritless 11 adulterated, emasculated
flag 3 ebb, sag 4 fade, fail, pall, sink, tire, wane, warn, wave, wilt 5 abate, faint, slump 6 banner, colors, dodder, emblem, ensign, signal, totter 7 decline, give way, pennant, subside, succumb 8 grow weak, languish, Old Glory, standard, streamer 9 grow weary, Union Jack 12 Stars and Bars 15 Stars and Stripes
flagellant 7 ascetic 8 penitent 13 self-mortifier
flagon 3 gun, jug, mug 4 ewer 5 flask, stein 6 bottle, carafe, vessel 7 canteen 8 schooner
flagrant 5 gross, sheer 6 arrant, bra-

zen, crying 7 blatant, glaring, heinous, obvious 8 immodest 9 audacious, barefaced, flaunting, monstrous, notorious, shameless 10 outrageous, scandalous 11 conspicuous
Flaherty, Margaret (Pegeen)
   character in: 24 Playboy of the Western World
   author: 5 Synge
flail 4 beat, lash, whip 5 swing 6 thresh 7 scourge
flair 4 bent, dash, feel, gift 5 knack, style, taste, touch, verve 6 genius, talent 7 faculty, feeling, panache 8 aptitude, capacity 9 ingenuity 11 discernment
flake 3 bit 4 chip, peel 5 fleck, layer, patch, scale, sheet, strip 7 chip off, crumble, peel off, shaving 8 scale off
flaky 4 bats, gaga, nuts 5 balmy, batty, crisp, daffy, dotty, goofy, loony, nutty, scaly, short, wacky 6 scabby, screwy, scurfy 8 scabious, squamous 9 eccentric 10 flocculent
flamboyant 4 wild 5 gaudy, jazzy, showy 6 flashy, florid, garish, ornate, rococo 7 baroque, dashing 8 colorful, exciting 10 theatrical 11 sensational 12 ostentatious
flame 4 beau, fire, glow 5 ardor, blaze, blush, flare, flash, flush, glare, gleam, light, lover, spark, swain 6 fervor, ignite, kin-dle, redden, warmth 7 passion 8 fervency 9 affection, boyfriend, intensity 10 enthusiasm, excitement, girlfriend, sweetheart 13 conflagration
flaming 5 afire, fiery 6 ablaze, alight, ardent, bright, fervid, stormy 7 blazing, burning, fervent, glaring, glowing, igneous, intense, shining, violent 8 flagrant, vehement 9 brilliant, egregious 10 passionate, smoldering 11 conspicuous, inflammable
flammable 7 igneous 10 combustive, incendiary 11 combustible, inflammable
flan 3 pie 4 gust, puff, tart 6 expand, pastry 7 custard, dessert 12 creme caramel
flanerie 8 dawdling, idleness
flaneur 5 idler 6 loafer 7 dawdler
flank 3 hip 4 edge, line, loin, side, wing 5 cover, skirt 6 border, fringe, haunch, screen, shield
Flannagan, John Bernard
   born: 7 Fargo ND
   artwork: 6 New One, Not Yet 9 Beginning 11 Dragon Motif 15 Triumph of the Egg 16 Jonah and the Whale
flap 3 bat, fly, tab 4 bang, beat, flop 5 apron, shake, skirt 6 lappet 7 agitate, banging, flutter, vibrate 9 oscillate
flare 4 burn, glow 5 blaze, erupt, flame, flash, glare, gleam, taper, torch, widen 6 blow up, dilate, expand, ignite, signal, spread 7 bell out,

broaden, distend, explode, stretch 8 boil over, break out 9 coruscate 10 incandesce
flash 4 glow, wink 5 blaze, blink, burst, flame, flare, glare, gleam, jiffy, shake, shine, spark, touch, trice 6 minute, moment, second, streak 7 flicker, glimmer, glisten, glitter, instant, sparkle 8 instance, outburst, radiance 9 coruscate 10 occurrence 11 coruscation, fulmination, scintillate 13 incandescence
Flash Gordon
   creator: 8 Dan Berry 11 Alex Raymond 12 Austin Briggs
   character: 11 Emperor Ming 12 Princess Aura
   companion: 4 Dale
   portrayed by: 12 Buster Crabbe
flashy 4 loud 5 gaudy, jazzy, showy, smart 6 garish, sporty, tawdry, tinsel, vulgar 7 raffish 8 dazzling 9 bedizened 10 flamboyant, tricked out 11 pretentious 12 ostentatious
flask 6 bottle 7 canteen 9 container
flat, flats 3 low 4 dead, dull 5 clear, equal, flush, level, marsh, plain, plane, prone, shoal, shoes, stale, total, vapid 6 direct, planar, smooth, supine 7 blowout, exact-ly, insipid, laid low, leveled, levelly, loafers, prairie, regular, shallow 8 absolute, complete, definite, lowlands, positive, puncture, thorough, unbroken 9 apartment, downright, precisely, prostrate, reclining, recumbent, tasteless 10 flavorless, horizontal, peremptory 11 unequivocal, unpalatable, unqualified 12 deflated tire, horizontally, unmistakable
flatfish 3 ray 4 sole 5 brill, fluke 6 turbot 7 halibut, sand dab, sunfish, teleost 8 flounder
Flathead see 5 Salis 7 Chinook
flatness 8 dullness 9 levelness, staleness 10 insipidity 13 tastelessness 14 flavorlessness
flatten 4 deck, even, fell 5 crush, floor, level, plane 6 defeat, ground, smooth 7 deflate 8 compress, overcome 9 overwhelm, prostrate
flatter 4 fool, laud 5 court, extol, honor, toady 6 become, cajole, delude 7 adulate, beguile, deceive, mislead, wheedle 8 blandish, bootlick, butter up, eulogize, soft-soap 9 brown-nose, sweet-talk, truckle to 10 compliment,overpraise, panegyrize
flatterer 5 toady 6 fawner, yes man 8 eulogist, truckler, wheedler 9 sycophant 10 bootlicker 11 lickspittle 13 apple-polisher
flattering 7 lauding 8 praising 9 extolling, favorable, laudatory 10 gratifying 13 complimentary
flattering attention 5 court 7 fawning

flattery 6 eulogy **7** blarney, fawning, snow job **8** cajolery, encomium, jollying, soft soap, toadying, toadyism **9** adulation, panegyric, servility, truckling, wheedling **10** sycophancy **12** blandishment **14** obsequiousness

Flaubert, Gustave
author of: 8 Salammbo **12** Madame Bovary **21** A Sentimental Education **24** The Temptation of St Anthony

flaunt 3 air **4** brag, wave **5** boast, sport, strut, vaunt **6** blazon, dangle, parade **7** exhibit, show off **8** brandish, flourish **9** advertise, broadcast

flavor 4 aura, lace, soul, tang, tone **5** gusto, imbue, savor, spice, style, tenor **6** aspect, infuse, lacing, relish, season, spirit **7** essence, instill **8** ambience, piquancy **9** attribute, seasoning

flavorful 4 rich **5** nutty, sapid, spicy, tangy, tasty, zesty **6** savory **7** peppery, piquant **8** aromatic **9** palatable, toothsome **10** appetizing

flavoring 4 herb, salt **5** spice **6** pepper **7** essence, extract, vanilla **8** additive, seasoner **9** chocolate, condiment, seasoning

flavorless 4 dull, flat, thin, weak **5** bland, stale, vapid **6** watery **7** insipid **9** tasteless

flaw 3 mar **4** blot, harm, spot, vice **5** error, fault, speck, stain **6** blotch, deface, defect, foible, impair, injure, injury, smudge, weaken **7** blemish, failing, fallacy, frailty, mistake **8** weak spot, weakness **9** deformity, disfigure **10** compromise, defacement **11** shortcoming **12** imperfection **13** disfigurement

flawed 6 faulty **8** impaired **9** defective, imperfect

flawless 5 sound **7** perfect **9** errorless, faultless **10** immaculate, impeccable

flawlessness 8 accuracy **10** perfection **11** correctness **14** immaculateness

flay 4 bark, pare, peel, skin **5** scalp, scold, strip **6** assail, fleece, punish, rebuke **7** plunder, upbraid **9** castigate, excoriate **11** decorticate

flea
varieties: 3 bat, dog, rat **5** mouse **6** rodent **9** carnivore **10** sticktight

fleck 3 dot, jot **4** drop, mark, mole, spot **5** flake, speck **6** bespot, dapple, mottle, streak, tittle **7** blemish, freckle, spatter, speckle, stipple **8** particle, small bit **9** bespeckle **10** besprinkle

Fledermaus, Die
also: 6 The Bat
operetta by: 7 (Johann) Strauss
character: 5 Adele, Falke, Frank **6** Alfred **9** Rosalinda **14** Prince Orlofsky **18** Baron von Eisenstein

fledgling 4 tyro **6** novice **8** beginner,

freshman 9 greenhorn **10** apprentice, tenderfoot

flee 4 shun, skip **5** avoid, dodge, elude, evade, split **6** decamp, desert, vanish **7** abscond, fly away, make off **8** speed off **9** cut and run, disappear **10** fly the coop

fleece 3 gyp **4** bilk, dupe, gull, rook, wool **5** cheat, cozen, trick **7** deceive, defraud, swindle **9** bamboozle, victimize

fleet 3 run **4** band, fade, fast, flow, navy, skim, spry, swim, unit **5** agile, array, brief, creek, drift, float, hasty, inlet, light, quick, rapid, shift, ships, short, swift **6** abound, active, armada, nimble, number, speedy, sudden, vanish **7** caravan, cursory, hurried **8** flotilla, squadron **9** disappear, momentary, transient **10** evanescent, transitory **11** expeditious **13** instantaneous

fleeting 5 brief, quick **7** passing **8** flitting, fugitive, temporal **9** ephemeral, fugacious, momentary, temporary, transient **10** evanescent, perishable, transitory **11** impermanent, precarious, unenduring

Fleming, Alexander
field: 12 bacteriology
nationality: 7 British
discovered: 10 penicillin
awarded: 10 Nobel Prize

Fleming, Henry
character in: 20 The Red Badge of Courage
author: 5 Crane

Fleming, Ian
author of: 4 Dr No **9** Moonraker **10** Goldfinger **11** Thunderball **12** Casino Royale **13** Live and Let Die **15** For Your Eyes Only **16** The Spy Who Loved Me, You Only Live Twice **18** From Russia with Love **20** Chitty Chitty Bang Bang
character: 1 M, Q **6** Oddjob **7** Blofeld, SPECTRE (organization) **9** James Bond **14** Miss Moneypenny **15** Auric Goldfinger

Fleming, Victor
director of: 13 The Wizard of Oz **14** Treasure Island **15** Gone With the Wind (Oscar) **18** Captains Courageous

flesh 3 fat, man **4** body, meat, pulp **5** brawn, power, vigor **6** embody, fatten, people **7** fatness, fill out, mankind, realize **8** humanity, physique, strength **9** carnality, substance **10** sensuality **11** materiality **13** individualize, particularize

flesh and blood 3 kin **4** real **5** a body, child **6** family **7** kindred **8** children **9** corporeal, offspring, relations, relatives **10** kith and kin **11** substantial

flesh-eating 9 predatory **10** predaceous **11** carnivorous

fleshy 3 fat **5** beefy, obese, plump, stout, tubby **6** chubby, portly, rotund, stocky **7** paunchy **8** roly-poly, thickset **9** corpulent, succulent **10** overweight, potbellied

Fletcher, Louise
born: 12 Birmingham AL
roles: 17 The Cheap Detective **25** One Flew Over the Cuckoo's Nest (Oscar)

Fletcher, Susannah Yolande
real name of: 12 Susannah York

flex 4 bend **5** curve

flexible 4 mild, soft **5** lithe **6** docile, genial, gentle, limber, pliant, supple **7** amiable, ductile, elastic, plastic, pliable, springy **8** bendable, yielding **9** adaptable, compliant, malleable, resilient, tractable **10** changeable, extensible, manageable, responsive, submissive **11** complaisant

Flibbertigibbet
character in: 10 Kenilworth
author: 5 Scott

flick 4 film **5** brush, graze, movie, sweep, whisk

Flicka
nickname of: 17 Frederica Von Stade

Flicka 5 horse
in: 14 My Friend Flicka

flicker 4 flit, glow, sway **5** blaze, flame, flare, flash, gleam, glint, shake, spark, throb, trace, waver **6** quaver, quiver, waggle **7** flutter, glimmer, glisten, glitter, modicum, pulsate, shimmer, sparkle, tremble, vestige, vibrate, wriggle **8** undulate **9** coruscate, fluctuate, oscillate, scintilla, vacillate

Flickertail State
nickname of: 11 North Dakota

flicks 5 films **6** cinema, grazes, movies, sweeps, whisks **7** brushes

flier 4 bill **5** pilot **6** notice **7** aviator, leaflet, venture **8** brochure, bulletin, circular, handbill **10** experiment **12** announcement **13** advertisement

flight 4 rout, rush, wing **5** flock **6** escape, exodus, flying, hegira **7** fleeing, retreat, soaring, winging **8** squadron **10** withdrawal **11** aeronautics

flighty 5 dizzy, giddy **6** fickle **8** quixotic, reckless, unstable, volatile **9** frivolous, mercurial, whimsical **10** capricious, changeable, inconstant, indecisive, irresolute **11** harebrained, impractical, light-headed, thoughtless **13** irresponsible **14** scatterbrained

flimsy 4 poor, thin, weak **5** cheap, filmy, frail, gauzy, petty, sheer **6** feeble, shab-by, shoddy, sleazy, slight, trashy **7** foolish, fragile, ill-made, shallow, trivial **8** cobwebby, delicate, gossamer, trifling **9** frivolous, worthless **10** diaphanous, inadequate, jerry-built, ramshackle **11** dilapidated, superficial **13** unsubstantial

flinch 3 fly, shy **4** jerk **5** cower, quail, quake, start, wince **6** blench, cringe, falter, quaver, quiver, recoil, shiver, shrink **7** contort, grimace, retreat, shudder

fling 2 go **3** try **4** ball, bash, cast, dash, emit, hurl, lark, toss **5** eject, expel, heave, pitch, sling, spree, trial **6** let fly, propel **7** attempt **8** bit of fun **11** precipitate

Flintstones, The
   character: 7 Pebbles **8** Bamm Bamm **11** Betty Rubble **12** Barney Rubble **14** Fred Flintstone **15** Dino the Dinosaur, Wilma Flintstone
   voice: 8 Alan Reed, Mel Blanc **10** Don Messick **12** Bea Benaderet, Gerry Johnson **13** Jean Vander Pyl
   city: 7 Bedrock
   creator: 12 Hanna-Barbera

Flintwinch
   character in: 12 Little Dorrit
   author: 7 Dickens

flinty 4 cold, hard **5** cruel, harsh, stern, stony **6** inured, steely **7** callous **8** hardened **10** unyielding **11** hardhearted, insensitive

flip 3 tap **4** bold, pert, spin, toss, turn **5** brash, flick, fresh, throw, thumb **6** cheeky, fillip **8** impudent, insolent, turn over **9** unabashed

flippant 4 glib, pert, rude **5** brash, lippy, saucy **6** cheeky, nimble **7** voluble **8** impudent, insolent, trifling **9** bumptious, frivolous, talkative **11** impertinent **12** presumptuous **13** disrespectful

Flipper
   character: 8 Bud Ricks **10** Sandy Ricks **11** Porter Ricks
   cast: 10 Brian Kelly, Luke Halpin **11** Tommy Norden
   Flipper played by: 4 Suzy

flirt 3 toy **4** play, vamp **5** dally, tease **6** trifle **8** coquette **12** heartbreaker

flit 4 dart, scud, skim, wing **5** speed **6** hasten, scurry **7** flicker, flutter

Flitch of Bacon, The
   author: 16 William Ainsworth

Flite, Miss
   character in: 10 Bleak House
   author: 7 Dickens

flivver 3 car **4** auto, heap **5** motor **6** jalopy, wheels **7** machine, vehicle **8** motorcar **9** tin lizzie **10** automobile

float 3 bob **4** waft **5** drift, hover, slide **6** bear up, buoy up, hold up, launch **8** levitate

floating 4 free **5** awash, loose **6** adrift, afloat, errant **7** buoyant, wafting **8** drifting **9** fluctuant, wandering **10** unattached

flock 2 go **3** mob, run **4** band, bevy, gang, herd, mass, pack, rush **5** bunch,

crowd, crush, drove, group, surge, troop **6** clique, gather, huddle, muster, stream, throng **7** cluster, company, coterie **8** converge **9** gathering, multitude **10** assemblage, collection, congregate **11** aggregation **12** congregation
   of fish: 6 school
   of game birds: 5 covey
   of geese: 6 gaggle
   of insects: 5 swarm
   of lions: 5 pride
   of seals or whales: 3 pod
   of young birds: 5 brood

flocks
   god of: 3 Pan

flock together 6 gather, mingle **7** convene **8** assemble **9** associate **10** congregate

flog 4 beat, cane, club, cuff, drub, hide, lash, maul, whip **5** birch, flail, smite, strap **6** cudgel, paddle, strike, switch, thrash **7** scourge **8** lambaste **9** horsewhip **10** flagellate

flood 4 flow, glut, gush, tide **6** deluge, drench, shower, stream **7** cascade, current, torrent **8** downpour, flow over, inundate, overflow, saturate, submerge, wash over **9** overwhelm **10** cloudburst, inundation, outpouring, oversupply
   period before: 12 antediluvian

Flood
   author: 16 Robert Penn Warren

flooded 6 flowed, surged **7** deluged, glutted, overran, swamped **8** drenched, engulfed **9** inundated, outpoured, washed out **10** downpoured, overflowed

floor 2 KO **4** base, deck, fell, kayo, tier **5** level, stage, story **6** bottom, ground **7** minimum, parquet **8** base rate, flooring, pavement **9** prostrate

flop 4 bomb, bust, drop, fail, fold, plop **5** close **6** fiasco, fizzle, topple, tumble, turkey **7** failure, go under, shutter, washout **8** disaster, lay an egg **14** disappointment

Flora
   origin: 5 Roman
   goddess of: 7 flowers

floral 6 bloomy **7** verdant **8** blossomy **9** botanical **10** herbaceous

Floralia
   origin: 5 Roman
   form: 8 festival

Florence
   artist: 6 Giotto **7** Cimabue **8** Ghiberti **9** Donatello **10** Michelozzi **11** della Robbia **12** Brunelleschi, Michelangelo
   capital of: 7 Tuscany **15** Firenze province
   cathedral/church: 10 San Lorenzo, San Miniato, Santa Croce **18** Santa Maria del Fiore
   Italian: 7 Firenze

landmark: 5 David, Pieta **6** Uffizi **8** Bargello **11** Pitti Palace **12** Ponte Vecchio **13** Boboli Gardens **14** Loggia dei Lanzi, Palazzo Vecchio **19** Piazza della Signoria **22** Baptistry of San Giovanni, Ospedale degli Innocenti
mountain: 9 Apennines
religious reformer: 10 Savonarola
river: 4 Arno
ruler: 5 Goths **6** Medici, Romans **8** Lombards **9** Etruscans **15** Byzantine Empire
tomb of: 7 Galileo, Rossini **11** Machiavelli **12** Michelangelo **15** Lorenzo de Medici

florescence 5 bloom **9** flowerage **10** blossoming

florid 4 rosy **5** gaudy, ruddy, showy **6** blowsy, hectic, ornate, rococo **7** baroque, flowery, flushed, reddish **8** inflamed, red-faced, rubicund, sanguine **9** elaborate **10** flamboyant, ornamented **12** ostentatious **13** grandiloquent

Florida
   abbreviation: 2 FL **3** Fla
   nickname: 6 Flower **8** Sunshine **10** Peninsular
   capital: 11 Tallahassee
   largest city: 12 Jacksonville
   others: 4 Tice **5** Cocoa, Miami, Ocala, Tampa **7** Hialeah, Orlando, Palatka, Sebring **8** Sarasota **9** Bradenton, Palm Beach, Pensacola **10** Clearwater **11** Brooksville, Coral Gables, Gainesville, St Augustine **12** Daytona Beach, Ft Lauderdale, St Petersburg
   baseball team: 7 Marlins
   college: 4 Nova **5** Barry, Miami, Tampa **6** Eckerd **7** Rollins, Stetson
   explorer: 11 Ponce de Leon
   feature:
      amusement park: 5 Epcot **10** Marineland **11** Disney World
      canal: 5 Miami **7** Tamiami
      museum: 8 Ringling
      national park: 10 Everglades
   tribe: 3 Ais **5** Ocale, Utina **6** Calusa, Chatot, Potano **7** Timucua **8** Seminole
   people: 5 conch **7** cracker, Osceola
   island: 7 Bahamas, Sanibel **8** Biscayne
      key: 4 Long, Vaca, West **5** Largo **7** Big Pine **8** Biscayne **9** Sugarloaf
   lake: 4 Dora **6** Apopka, Harney, Jessup, Newnan **7** Ledwith **8** Arbuckle **9** Kissimmee **10** Okeechobee
   land rank: 12 twenty-second
   physical feature:
      bay: 8 Biscayne **9** Apalachee **10** Waccasassa
      cape: 5 Sable **7** Kennedy **9** Canaveral
      gulf: 6 Mexico
      sea: 8 Atlantic
      springs: 6 Silver **7** Rainbow

swamp: 10 Everglades, Okefenokee
river: 6 Banana, Indian **7** Aucilla, Manatee, Scambia, St Johns, Suwanee **9** Ochlawaha **12** Apalachicola
state admission: 13 twenty-seventh
state bird: 11 mockingbird
state fish: 16 Atlantic sailfish
state mammal: 7 dolphin
state flower: 13 orange blossom
state motto: 12 In God We Trust
state song: 11 Swanee River **14** Old Folks at Home
state tree: 13 sabal palmetto **15** cabbage palmetto

florilegium 7 garland **8** chapbook, treasury **9** anthology

Florizel
character in: 14 The Winter's Tale
author: 11 Shakespeare

floruit 12 he flourished **13** she flourished

flotilla 5 fleet **6** armada

Flotow, Friedrich von
born: 7 Germany **11** Mecklenburg
composer of: 6 Martha **11** Die Matrosen **19** Alessandro Stradella

flotsam 4 junk **6** debris, refuse **7** garbage **8** castoffs

flounce 3 hem **4** edge, leap, skip, trim, trip **5** bound, caper, frill, stamp, stomp, storm, strut **6** bounce, edging, fringe, gambol, prance, ruffle, sashay, spring **7** valance **8** furbelow, ornament, skirting, trimming

flounder 4 fish, flop, halt, limp **5** lurch, waver **6** falter, hobble, muddle, totter, tumble, wallow, welter **7** blunder, shamble, stagger, stumble **8** flatfish, hesitate, struggle

Flounder, The
author: 11 Gunter Grass

flourish 4 curl, dash, grow, pomp, rant, show, turn **5** bloom, bluff, get on, shake, strut, sweep, swing, swish, twirl, twist, wield **6** flaunt, flower, hot air, parade, splash, thrive, waving **7** blossom, bravado, burgeon, cadenza, fanfare, fustian, glitter, prosper, shaking, succeed, swagger **8** boasting, brandish, curlicue, fare well, get ahead, swinging, vaunting, wielding **9** agitation, grace note, thrashing **10** decoration **11** braggadocio, brandishing, fanfaronade, ostentation **12** appoggiatura **13** embellishment, magniloquence, swashbuckling **14** grandiloquence

flourishing 8 swinging, swishing, thriving, wielding **9** flaunting **10** prospering, successful **11** brandishing

flout 3 rag **4** defy, mock, twit **5** chaff, scorn, spurn, taunt **6** gibe at, insult

flow 3 jet, run **4** flux, gush, pass, pour, rush, seep, tide **5** drain, drift, float, flood, glide, issue, spout, spurt, surge, sweep, swirl, train **6** abound, course, deluge, efflux, effuse, filter, plenty,
rapids, stream **7** cascade, current, debouch, torrent, well out **8** effusion, millrace, plethora, sequence **9** abundance, discharge, effluence, emanation **10** outpouring, succession **11** debouchment, progression

flower 3 bud **4** best, blow, open, pick, posy **5** bloom, cream, elite, ripen **6** mature **7** blossom, bouquet, burgeon, develop, nosegay, prosper **8** flourish **11** aristocracy

flower arranging, art of
Japanese: 7 ikebana

Flower Fables
author: 15 Louisa May Alcott

flowering 4 peak **5** bloom **6** height, heyday **8** blooming, maturing **10** blossoming, developing, prospering **11** flourishing

Flowering Judas
author: 19 Katherine Anne Porter

flowers
goddess of: 5 Flora

Flowers of Evil
author: 17 Charles Baudelaire
French title: 14 Les Fleurs du Mal

Flower State
nickname of: 7 Florida

flowery 5 fancy **6** floral, florid, ornate **8** blooming **10** blossoming, burgeoning, euphuistic, figurative, florescent, ornamental, rhetorical **11** embellished **12** efflorescent, magniloquent **13** grandiloquent

Flowery Kingdom *see* **5** China

flowing 4 flux **5** fluid **6** ebbing, fluent, smooth **7** current, copious, gliding, running **8** abundant **9** liquefied, plentiful **10** continuity, pouring out, proceeding

fluctuate 4 sway, vary, veer **5** shift, swing, waver **6** dawdle, falter, wobble **8** hesitate, undulate **9** alternate, oscillate, vacillate **10** dillydally

fluctuation 5 shift **6** change **7** veering **8** shifting, swinging **9** deviation, variation **11** alternation, oscillation, vacillation

flue 3 net **4** barb, down, pipe, tube, vent **5** fluff, fluke, shaft **6** funnel **7** channel, chimney, passage **9** smokejack

fluent 4 glib **5** vocal **6** facile **7** voluble **8** effusive, eloquent **9** garrulous, talkative **10** articulate, effortless

fluff 3 err, nap **4** down, flub, fuzz, lint, miss, puff, slip, soft **5** botch, floss, froth, primp **6** forget **7** blunder **8** feathers

fluffy 5 downy, fuzzy, nappy, wooly **6** fleecy, woolly **8** feathery

fluid 6 liquid, watery **7** unfixed **8** flexible, floating, shifting, solution, unstable **9** adaptable, liquefied, unsettled **10** adjustable, changeable, indefinite

fluid ounce
abbreviation: 4 fl oz

fluke 3 hap **5** freak **6** chance **7** miracle **8** accident, windfall **9** mischance **11** vicissitude **12** stroke of luck

flummery 7 dessert, pudding **9** gibberish **10** doubletalk, mumbo jumbo **11** obfuscation

flunky 6 lackey, menial, minion **7** servant **9** attendant, underling

fluorine
chemical symbol: 1 F

flurry 3 ado **4** fuss, gust, heat, puff, stir **5** alarm, fever, flush, haste, panic **6** breeze, bustle, pother, rattle, shower, squall, tumult **7** agitate, confuse, disturb, fidgets, fluster, flutter, perturb **8** confound, disquiet **9** agitation, commotion, confusion **10** discompose, disconcert, turbulence **11** disturbance, hurry-scurry, trepidation **12** discomposure, perturbation, restlessness

flush 4 even, glow, swab, tint, wash **5** bloom, blush, color, elate, flood, level, rinse, scour, scrub, shock, spray **6** access, dampen, deluge, douche, drench, excite, puff up, tremor **7** animate, flutter, glowing, impulse, moisten, redness, wash out **8** rosiness, rosy glow, squarely, strength **9** freshness, make proud, ruddiness **10** exultation, jubilation

flushed 3 hot, red **4** rosy, ruby **5** aglow, **6** florid, torrid **7** crimson, excited, scarlet **8** blushing, feverish **10** prosperous

flushed with success 5 proud **6** elated

fluster 4 daze **5** shake, upset **6** dither, flurry, hubbub, muddle, ruffle **7** agitate, confuse, disturb, flutter, perplex, per-turb, startle, turmoil **8** befuddle, bewilder **9** agitation, commotion, confusion, discomfit **10** discompose, disconcert **12** bewilderment, discomfiture, discomposure **14** discombobulate

flute 4 fife, fold, pipe, roll, tube, wind **5** crimp **6** furrow, groove **7** piccolo, whistle **8** recorder **9** wine glass **14** champagne glass

flutter 3 bob **4** flap, flit, soar, stir, wave, wing **5** hurry, shake, throb **6** flurry, quiver, ripple, thrill, tremor, wobble **7** beating, flitter, fluster, pulsate, tremble, twitter **8** flapping, tingling **9** agitation, commotion, confusion, palpitate, sensation, vibration **12** perturbation

fluvial 7 aquatic

fluviatile 7 aquatic

flux 4 flow, tide **5** flood **6** course, motion, stream, unrest **7** current **8** mutation, shifting **10** alteration, transition **11** fluctuation **12** modification **14** transformation

fly 4 flap, flee, sail, skip, soar, wave, wing **5** coast, float, glide, hover, hurry, split, swoop **6** hasten, hustle **7** flutter, run away, take off, vibrate **8** take wing, undulate

fly
varieties: 3 bat, bot **4** blow, deer, dung, gnat, horn, moth, rust, sand **5** beach, black, crane, dance, drone, flesh, fruit, horse, house, march, marsh, midge, mydas, punky **6** bee fly, cactus, maggot, pomace, robber, stable, tsetse, warble, window **7** chalcid, seaweed, skipper, soldier, tachima **8** lousefly, mosquito, stiletto **9** leaf miner **10** flat-footed, fungus gnat, humpbacked **11** thickheaded **14** black scavenger

fly apart 5 burst **6** blow up **7** explode, shatter **8** detonate, fragment

fly at 6 assail, attack

fly-by-night 5 shady **6** shifty **7** crooked **8** unstable, untrusty **9** dishonest **10** unreliable **12** disreputable, undependable **13** irresponsible, untrustworthy

Flying Dutchman, The
opera by: 6 Wagner
character: 4 Erik **5** Senta **6** Daland **11** The Dutchman

Flying Fish
constellation of: 6 Volans

Flying Nun, The
character: 9 Sister Ana **11** Sister Sixto **13** Carlos Ramirez **14** Mother Superior **15** Sister Bertrille **16** Sister Jacqueline
cast: 10 Sally Field **12** Alejandro Rey, Linda Dangcil, Marge Redmond **14** Shelly Morrison **17** Madeleine Sherwood

fly in the ointment 5 hitch **7** problem, trouble **8** drawback, nuisance **9** hindrance **10** impediment **12** disadvantage

Flynn, Errol
real name: 17 Leslie Thomas Flynn
born: 6 Hobart **8** Tasmania **9** Australia
roles: 10 The Sea Hawk **12** Captain Blood **14** Too Much Too Soon **15** The Sun Also Rises **24** The Adventures of Robin Hood **26** The Charge of the Light Brigade

fly off the handle 6 see red

fly the coop 4 bolt, flee **6** escape, run off **7** abscond, get away, make off, run away, skip out, take off

foal 4 cade, colt **5** filly, young **9** fledgling

foam 4 fizz, head, scum, suds **5** froth, spume **6** lather **7** sparkle **8** bubbling **13** effervescence

foaming 5 sudsy **6** bubbly, frothy **7** lathery **8** bubbling, frothing

foamy 5 fizzy **6** frothy **7** lathery **8** bubbling **9** sparkling **12** effervescent

fob 5 chain, medal, strap **6** ribbon **8** ornament **9** medallion

focal 3 key **4** main **5** chief **7** central, pivotal **8** foremost **9** principal

Foch, Ferdinand
served in: 3 WWI
nationality: 6 French
rank: 7 marshal **16** commander-in-chief
battle: 5 Marne, Somme

Foch, Nina
real name: 20 Nina Consuelo Maud Fock
born: 6 Leyden **11** Netherlands
roles: 9 Spartacus **14** Executive Suite, Song to Remember **17** An American in Paris, My Name Is Julia Ross **18** The Ten Commandments

Fock, Nina Consuelo Maud
real name of: 8 Nina Foch

focus 3 aim, fix, hub **4** core **5** haunt, heart **6** adjust, center, direct, middle, resort **7** nucleus, retreat **8** converge **9** limelight, spotlight **10** rendezvous **11** concentrate **12** headquarters

focusing 6 aiming **9** adjusting, centering, directing **10** adjustment, converging **11** pinpointing **13** concentrating

fodder 4 feed, food **6** forage, silage **7** rations **9** provender

foe 5 enemy, rival **8** attacker, opponent **9** adversary, assailant, combatant, contender, disputant **10** antagonist, competitor

fog 3 dim **4** daze, haze, smog, soup **5** brume, cloud **6** darken, muddle, stupor, trance **7** confuse, obscure, pea soup, perplex **8** bewilder **9** murkiness **10** cloudiness **12** bewilderment

Fogg, Phileas
character in: 26 Around the World in Eighty Days
author: 10 Jules Verne
valet: 12 Passepartout

foggy 3 dim **4** dark, hazy **5** dusky, filmy, fuzzy, misty, murky, musty, soupy, vague **6** cloudy, smoggy, spacey **7** brumous, clouded, obscure, shadowy, unclear **8** confused, nebulous, overcast, vaporous **9** beclouded **10** indistinct

foible 4 kink **5** quirk **6** defect, whimsy **7** failing, frailty **8** crotchet, weak side, weakness **9** infirmity **10** deficiency **11** shortcoming **12** imperfection

Foible
character in: 16 The Way of the World
author: 8 Congreve

foil 3 nip **4** balk, film, leaf **5** check, flake, match, sheet, wafer **6** hinder, lamina, set off, thwart **7** enhance, prevent **8** backdrop, contrast **9** frustrate

10 antithesis, complement, supplement **11** correlative, counterpart

foist 6 impose, unload **7** palm off, pass off

fold 3 hug, lap, pen, sty **4** bend, curl, sect, tuck, wrap, yard **5** clasp, close, crimp, flock, group, layer, pleat **6** corral, crease, dog-ear, double, encase, enfold, fur-row, gather, parish, pucker, ruffle, rumple, wrap up **7** crinkle, crumple, embosom, embrace, entwine, envelop, flounce, overlap, wrinkle **8** barnyard, compound, doubling, stockade **9** community, corrugate, enclosure **12** congregation

folder 7 booklet, leaflet **8** brochure, circular, pamphlet **9** portfolio

foliage 6 leaves **7** leafage, verdure

folklore 5 myths **6** fables **7** legends **10** traditions

folks 3 kin **6** family, people **7** kinsmen, parents **8** everyone **9** relatives **10** kith and kin

folksy 6 casual, chatty **8** familiar, friendly, homespun, informal, sociable **10** neighborly **14** conversational **15** unsophisticated

folk tale
German: 7 Marchen

Follett, Ken
author of: 14 Eye of the Needle **15** On Wings of Eagles, The Key to Rebecca **22** The Man from St Petersburg

follow 3 dog **4** copy, heed, hunt, mind, note, obey, tail **5** aim at, chase, grasp, hound, stalk, trace, track, trail, watch **6** attend, notice, pursue, regard, shadow, take up **7** cherish, emulate, imitate, observe, replace, succeed **8** practice, supplant **9** accompany, cultivate, prosecute **10** comprehend, understand

follower 3 fan **4** tail **5** pupil, toady **6** chaser, hunter, shadow, stooge **7** admirer, apostle, convert, devotee, protege, pursuer, servant, stalker **8** adherent, advocate, disciple, hanger-on, henchman, parasite, partisan, retainer, servitor **9** accessory, attendant, dependent, proselyte, satellite, supporter, sycophant

following 4 next **5** below, suite, train **6** public **7** ensuing, retinue **8** audience **9** adherents, clientele, entourage, partisans, patronage **10** attendance, consequent, sequential, subsequent, succeeding, successive **11** consecutive

Follow the Fleet
director: 12 Mark Sandrich
cast: 11 Fred Astaire **12** Ginger Rogers **13** Randolph Scott **21** Harriet Hilliard Nelson
song: 11 We Saw the Sea **13** Let Yourself Go **24** Let's Face the Music and Dance

follow-up 7 ensuing 8 sequence 9 aftermath 10 subsequent

folly 6 idiocy, levity 7 inanity, mistake 8 nonsense, trifling 9 absurdity, asininity, frivolity, giddiness, silliness 10 imbecility, imprudence, tomfoolery 11 doltishness, fatuousness, foolishness 12 indiscretion 13 brainlessness, irrationality, senselessness

foment 4 goad, spur, urge 5 rouse 6 arouse, excite, foster, incite, kindle, stir up 7 agitate, inflame, promote, provoke, quicken 8 irritate 9 aggravate, galvanize, instigate, stimulate 10 exacerbate

fond 5 naive 6 ardent, doting, loving, tender 7 amorous, devoted 8 desirous, enamored, harbored, held dear 9 cherished, indulgent, preserved, sustained 10 infatuated, passionate 11 impassioned, sentimental 12 affectionate 16 overaffectionate

Fonda, Henry
wife: **16** Margaret Sullavan
son: **5** Peter
daughter: **4** Jane
born: **13** Grand Island NE
roles: **7** Jezebel, Warlock **8** Fail Safe **10** Fort Apache, In Harm's Way, The Best Man, The Lady Eve **12** On Golden Pond (Oscar) **13** Mister Roberts, Ox-Bow Incident, The Longest Day **14** Twelve Angry Men, Young Mr Lincoln **16** Advise and Consent, Battle of the Bulge, How the West Was Won, The Grapes of Wrath **18** The Boston Strangler **19** My Darling Clementine, The Immortal Sergeant **21** Sometimes a Great Notion

Fonda, Jane
father: **5** Henry
brother: **5** Peter
husband: **9** Ted Turner, Tom Hayden **10** Roger Vadim
born: **9** New York NY
roles: **5** Julia, Klute (Oscar) **10** Barbarella, Coming Home (Oscar) **11** A Doll's House **12** Any Wednesday, On Golden Pond **13** China Syndrome **17** Barefoot in the Park **23** They Shoot Horses Don't They?

Fonda, Peter
father: **5** Henry
sister: **4** Jane
born: **9** New York NY
roles: **7** The Trip **9** Easy Rider **13** The Wild Angels

fondle 3 hug, neck, pet 4 neck. 5 spoon 6 caress, cuddle, nestle, nuzzle, smooch, stroke 7 embrace, make out 8 canoodle 10 bill and coo

fondness 4 bent, care, love 5 ardor, fancy 6 desire, liking 7 passion 8 devotion, penchant, weakness 9 affection 10 attachment, partiality, preference, propensity, tenderness 11

amorousness, inclination 12 predilection 14 susceptibility

fond utterance 9 sweet talk 10 endearment 12 sweet nothing

Fons
origin: **5** Roman
god of: **7** springs

fons et origo 15 source and origin

Fontaine, Joan
real name: **25** Joan de Beauvoir de Havilland
sister: **17** Olivia de Havilland
husband: **11** Brian Aherne
born: **5** Japan, Tokyo
roles: **3** Ivy **7** Ivanhoe, Rebecca **8** Casanova, Gunga Din, Jane Eyre, The Women **9** Suspicion (Oscar) **12** The Devil's Own **15** Frenchman's Creek, September Affair **16** Tender Is the Night, The Constant Nymph

Fontanne, Lynn
husband: **10** Alfred Lunt
born: **6** London **7** England
roles: **8** The Visit **9** Quadrille, The Pirate **10** The Sea Gull **13** O Mistress Mine **15** Design for Living **18** The Great Sebastians **19** The Taming of the Shrew

food 4 chow, feed, grub 5 board 6 fodder, forage, silage, viands 7 edibles, nurture, pasture, rations 8 eatables, victuals 9 nutrition, pasturage, provender 10 provisions, sustenance 11 comestibles, nourishment, subsistence

food, miraculous 5 manna

fool 3 ass, con, oaf 4 bilk, clod, dolt, dupe, gull, hoax, jest, joke 5 cheat, chump, clown, cozen, cut up, dummy, dunce, feign, goose, idiot, klutz, moron, nin-ny, tease, trick 6 diddle, fleece, frolic, hum-bug, jester, nitwit, rip off, stooge 7 beguile, buffoon, deceive, defraud, half-wit, Pierrot, pretend 8 bonehead, dummkopf, flimflam, hoodwink, imbecile, lunkhead, meathead, numskull 9 bamboozle, blockhead, harlequin, ignoramus, numbskull, simpleton 10 dunderhead, nincompoop, scaramouch 11 Punchinello

fool around 3 toy 4 idle 5 clown, dally 6 dawdle, loiter, trifle

foolhardy 4 rash 5 brash, hasty 6 madcap 8 careless, heedless, reckless 9 daredevil, hotheaded, impetuous, imprudent, impulsive 10 headstrong, incautious 11 harebrained, thoughtless

foolish 5 inane, silly 6 absurd, stupid, unwise 7 asinine, fatuous, idiotic, moronic, witless 9 brainless, imbecilic, imprudent, ludicrous, senseless 10 boneheaded, incautious, indiscreet, ridiculous 12 preposterous 13 irresponsible, unintelligent

foolishness 5 folly 6 idiocy, lunacy 8 unwisdom 9 absurdity, asininity, pu-

erility, silliness, stupidity 10 imbecility, imprudence 11 fatuousness, witlessness 12 childishness, extravagance, indiscretion 13 brainlessness, senselessness 14 ridiculousness 15 injudiciousness 16 irresponsibility, preposterousness

Fool of Quality, The
author: **11** Henry Brooke

foot 3 dog, pad, paw 4 base, hoof 6 bottom, tootsy 7 trotter 8 infantry 10 foundation
abbreviation: **2** ft

football
term: **3** end 4 bomb, down, draw, flat, punt, sack 5 blitz, guard, zebra 6 center, fumble, option, pocket, safety, tackle 7 audible, bootleg, flanker, holding, kickoff, lateral, offside, platoon, reverse, rollout, shotgun 8 clipping, gridiron, halfback, turnover 9 crackback, field goal, nose guard, scrimmage, touchback 10 conversion, cornerback, linebacker, nose tackle 11 quarterback 12 encroachment

Hall of Fame:
1963: 4 Bell (Bert), Carr (Joe), Hein (Mel), Mara (Tim) **5** Baugh (Sammy), Clark (Dutch), Halas (George), Henry (Pete) **6** Hutson (Don), Nevers (Ernie), Thorpe (Jim) **7** Hubbard (Cal), Lambeau (Curly), McNally (John Blood) **8** Nagurski (Bronko), Marshall (George P)
1964: 5 Lyman (Link) **6** Healey (Ed), Hinkle (Clarke), Rooney (Art) **7** Trafton (George) **9** Conzelman (Jimmy), Michalske (Mike)
1965: 6 Graham (Otto), Grange (Red) **7** Luckman (Sid) **8** Driscoll (Paddy), Fortmann (Daniel J), Van Buren (Steve) **10** Chamberlin (Guy), Waterfield (Bob)
1966: 3 Ray (Hugh "Shorty") **5** Guyon (Joe), Owens (Steve) **6** Dudley (Bill), Herber (Arnie), McAfee (George), Turner (Clyde "Bulldog") **8** Kiesling (Walt)
1967: 5 Brown (Paul E), Layne (Bobby) **6** Reeves (Dan), Strong (Ken) **7** Bidwill (Charles W), Tunnell (Emlen) **8** Bednarik (Chuck), Stydahar (Joe)
1968: 6 Hirsch (Elroy), Motley (Marion), Trippi (Charley) **7** Battles (Cliff), Donovan (Art), Millner (Wayne) **13** Wojciechowicz (Alex)
1969: 5 Neale (Earle "Greasy"), Perry (Joe) **7** Edwards (Albert Glen "Turk") **8** Stautner (Ernie) **9** Nomellini (Leo)
1970: 5 Fears (Tom), Pihos (Pete) **9** McElhenny (Hugh) **12** Christiansen (Jack)
1971: 5 Brown (Jim) **6** Hewitt (Bill), Kinard (Frank "Bruiser"), Tittle (Y A) **8** Lombardi (Vince) **10** Robustelli

(Andy) **11** Van Brocklin (Norm)
1972: 4 Hunt (Lamar) **6** Matson (Ollie), Parker (Ace) **9** Marchetti (Gino)
1973: 5 Berry (Raymond) **6** Parker (Jim) **7** Schmidt (Joe)
1974: 4 Lane (Dick "Night Train") **5** Groza (Lou "The Toe") **6** George (Bill) **7** Canadeo (Tony)
1975: 5 Brown (Roosevelt), Moore (Lenny) **6** Connor (George) **7** Lavelli (Dante)
1976: 4 Ford (Len) **6** Taylor (Jim) **8** Flaherty (Ray)
1977: 5 Gregg (Forrest), Starr (Bart) **6** Sayers (Gale), Willis (Bill) **7** Gifford (Frank)
1978: 6 Ewbank (Weeb), Wilson (Larry) **7** Alworth (Lance), Leemans (Tuffy) **8** Nitschke (Ray)
1979: 3 Mix (Ron) **4** Lary (Yale) **6** Butkus (Dick), Unitas (Johnny)
1980: 4 Otto (Jim) **5** Jones (David "Deacon"), Lilly (Bob) **8** Adderley (Herb)
1981: 5 Davis (Willie), Ringo (Jim) **6** Badgro (Morris "Red"), Blanda (George)
1982: 4 Huff (Sam) **5** Musso (George), Olsen (Merlin) **6** Atkins (Doug)
1983: 4 Bell (Bobby) **6** Gilman (Sid) **8** Mitchell (Bobby), Warfield (Paul) **9** Jurgensen (Sonny)
1984: 5 Brown (Willie) **6** Taylor (Charley) **9** McCormack (Mike) **11** Weinmeister (Arnie)
1985: 6 Gatski (Frank), Namath (Joe) **7** Rozelle (Pete), Simpson (OJ) **8** Staubach (Roger)
1986: 6 Lanier (Willie), Walker (Doak) **7** Hornung (Paul), Houston (Ken) **9** Tarkenton (Fran)
1987: 6 Csonka (Larry), Dawson (Len), Greene (Joe), Langer (Jim), Upshaw (Gene) **7** Johnson (John Henry), Maynard (Don)
1988: 3 Ham (Jack) **4** Page (Alan) **5** Ditka (Mike) **11** Biletnikoff (Fred)
1989: 4 Wood (Willie) **5** Shell (Art) **6** Blount (Mel) **8** Bradshaw (Terry)
1990: 6 Griese (Bob), Harris (Franco), Landry (Tom) **7** Lambert (Jack), St Clair (Bob) **8** Buchanan (Buck) **9** Hendricks (Ted)
1991: 5 Jones (Stan) **6** Hannah (John) **7** Schramm (Tex) **8** Campbell (Earl), Stenerud (Jan)
1992: 5 Davis (Al) **6** Barney (Lem), Mackey (John) **7** Riggins (John)
1993: 4 Noll (Chuck) **5** Fouts (Dan), Walsh (Bill) **6** Little (Larry), Payton (Walter)
1994: 5 Grant (Bud), Kelly (Leroy), Smith (Jackie), White (Randy) **7** Dorsett (Tony), Johnson (Jimmy)
other player/coach: 8 Don Shula, Kyle Rote **9** Amos Stagg, Dan Marino, Earl Blaik, Jerry Rice, Lou Lit-

tle, **10** Bear Bryant, Bruce Smith, Bubba Smith, Joe Montana, Joe Paterno, Ken Stabler, Larry Brown, Troy Aikman, Walter Camp, Warren Moon **11** Ahmad Rashad, Craig Morton, Deion Sanders, Earl Morrall, Floyd Little, Jim Plunkett, Knute Rockne, Reggie White **12** Bud Wilkinson, Joe Thiesmann, Ozzie Newsome, Roman Gabriel, William Perry **13** Ara Parseghian, Eric Dickerson, **14** Lawrence Taylor, Lydell Mitchell

football bowl games 3 Sun **4** Rose **5** Aloha, Gator, Peach, Sugar, Super **6** Citrus, Copper, Cotton, Fiesta, Orange **7** Holiday, Liberty **10** Bluebonnet, California **12** Independence

football leagues
National Football League (NFL): 11 New York Jets **12** Buffalo Bills, Chicago Bears, Detroit Lions **13** Dallas Cowboys, Denver Broncos, Miami Dolphins, New York Giants **14** Atlanta Falcons, Los Angeles Rams **15** Baltimore Ravens, Cleveland Browns, Green Bay Packers, Seattle Seahawks, Tennessee Oilers (formerly Houston) **16** Kansas City Chiefs, Minnesota Vikings, New Orleans Saints, Phoenix Cardinals (formerly St Louis), San Diego Chargers **17** Cincinnati Bengals, Indianapolis Colts (formerly Baltimore), Los Angeles Raiders (formerly Oakland) **18** New England Patriots, Philadelphia Eagles, Pittsburgh Steelers, Tampa Bay Buccaneers, Washington Redskins **23** San Francisco Forty-Niners

United States Football League (USFL): 10 Denver Gold **12** Chicago Blitz **14** Baltimore Stars, Boston Breakers **15** Houston Gamblers, Oakland Invaders, Oklahoma Outlaws, Tampa Bay Bandits **16** Arizona Wranglers, Memphis Showboats, Michigan Panthers, Orlando Renegades, Portland Breakers **17** Jacksonville Bulls, Los Angeles Express, New Jersey Generals, Philadelphia Stars **18** Washington Federals **19** Birmingham Stallions **21** San Antonio Gunslingers

football team (NFC)
Atlanta: 7 Falcons
  stadium: 11 Georgia Dome
Chicago: 5 Bears
  stadium: 12 Soldier Field
Dallas: 7 Cowboys
  stadium: 6 Texas
Detroit: 5 Lions
  stadium: 17 Pontiac Silverdome
Green Bay: 7 Packers
  stadium: 9 Milwaukee **12** Lambeau Field
Los Angeles: 4 Rams
  stadium: 7 Anaheim
Minnesota: 7 Vikings
  stadium: 9 Metrodome

New Orleans: 6 Saints
  stadium: 18 Louisiana Superdome
New York: 6 Giants
  stadium: 6 Giants
Philadelphia: 6 Eagles
  stadium: 8 Veterans
Phoenix: 9 Cardinals
  stadium: 8 Sun Devil
  formerly in: 7 St Louis
San Francisco: 11 Forty-Niners
  stadium: 15 Candlestick Park
Tampa Bay: 10 Buccaneers
  stadium: 5 Tampa
Washington: 8 Redskins
  stadium: 14 Robert F Kennedy
football team (AFC)
Buffalo: 5 Bills
  stadium: 4 Rich
Cincinnati: 7 Bengals
  stadium: 10 Riverfront
Cleveland: 6 Browns
  stadium: 9 Cleveland
Denver: 7 Broncos
  stadium: 8 Mile High
Houston: 6 Oilers
  stadium: 9 Astrodome
Indianapolis: 5 Colts
  stadium: 11 Hoosier Dome
  formerly in: 9 Baltimore
Kansas City: 6 Chiefs
  stadium: 9 Arrowhead
Los Angeles: 7 Raiders
  stadium: 16 Memorial Coliseum
  formerly in: 7 Oakland
Miami: 8 Dolphins
  stadium: 9 Joe Robbie
New England: 8 Patriots
  stadium: 7 Foxboro
New York: 4 Jets
  stadium: 6 Giants
Pittsburgh: 8 Steelers
  stadium: 11 Three Rivers
San Diego: 8 Chargers
  stadium: 8 San Diego
Seattle: 8 Seahawks
  stadium: 8 Kingdome

footfall 3 pad **4** pace, step **5** tread **8** footstep
foothold 4 grip, hold **7** support **8** purchase
footloose 4 free **8** carefree **9** fancyfree **10** unattached **11** uncommitted **12** unencumbered
footnote 5 gloss **9** reference **10** annotation **11** explanation **12** afterthought
footnote abbreviations 2 ca, ms, nd, qv **3** mss **4** et al, ibid **5** et seq, infra, op cit, pseud, supra **6** loc cit
footpad 5 thief **6** bandit, mugger, outlaw, robber **10** highwayman
footpath 4 lane, ramp **5** jetty, trail **8** sidewalk
foot soldiers 8 infantry **10** fusilliers, musketeers
footstool 6 buffet **7** hassock, ottoman **8** footrest

footwear
  French: **9** chaussure

fop 4 beau, dude **5** dandy, swell **7** coxcomb **8** popinjay **9** prettyboy **11** Beau Brummel

foppish 4 vain **5** gaudy, showy **6** ornate **7** finical **8** affected, dandyish **9** dandified **12** ostentatious **13** overelaborate

forage 4 feed, food, hunt, raid, seek **6** fodder, ravage, search, silage **7** despoil, explore, pasture, plunder, rummage **8** scavenge, scrounge **9** pasturage, provender **10** provisions

foray 4 raid **5** sally **6** attack, inroad, invade, ravage, thrust **7** pillage, plunder, venture **8** invasion **9** incursion **10** expedition **11** depredation

forbear 4 quit, stop **5** cease, forgo **6** desist, endure, eschew, forego, give up, suffer **7** abstain, refrain **8** abnegate, renounce, tolerate

forbearance 4 pity **5** mercy **6** pardon **8** clemency, eschewal, leniency, meekness, mildness, patience **9** endurance, tolerance **10** abstention, abstinence, continence, indulgence, moderation, submission, temperance **11** longanimity, resignation **12** mercifulness

forbearing 6 denial **7** lenient, refusal **8** eschewal, tolerant **9** indulgent **10** abnegation, abstention, abstinence, permissive, refraining **13** nonindulgence **16** nonparticipation

forbid 3 ban, bar **4** veto **5** taboo **6** enjoin, hinder, impede, oppose, refuse, reject **7** exclude, gainsay, inhibit, obviate, prevent **8** disallow, obstruct, preclude, prohibit, restrain **9** interdict, proscribe

forbiddance 3 ban **4** no-no **5** taboo **7** barring, embargo **9** exclusion, interdict **11** prohibition **12** interdiction, proscription

forbidden 4 no-no, tabu **5** taboo **6** banned **8** debarred **10** prohibited, proscribed
  German: **8** verboten

forbidden fruit
  type: **6** brandy **7** liqueur
  origin: **7** America
  flavor: **5** honey **6** orange **10** grapefruit

forbidding 4 dour, grim, ugly **6** odious **7** hideous, ominous **8** horrible, sinister **9** abhorrent, offensive, repellent, repulsive **10** unfriendly, unpleasant **11** prohibitive, prohibitory, threatening **12** disagree-able, inhospitable **14** unapproachable

force 3 pry, vim **4** army, body, coax, crew, drag, gang, make, pull, push, team, unit, urge **5** break, clout, corps, drive, group, impel, might, power, press, squad, value, vigor, wrest **6** coerce, compel, duress, effect, elicit, energy, enjoin, extort, impact, import, impose, induce, oblige, propel, stress, thrust, weight, wrench **7** cogency, intrude, meaning, obtrude, potency, require, squeeze, stamina **8** charisma, coercion, division, efficacy, emphasis, momentum, persuade, pressure, squadron, strength, validity, violence, vitality **9** animation, battalion, constrain, magnetism, overpower, puissance **10** attraction, compulsion, constraint, detachment **11** necessitate, weightiness **12** significance **13** effectiveness
  Latin: **3** vis

forced 5 slave **7** binding, coerced, labored, obliged **8** affected, enslaved, grudging, mannered, required, strained **9** compelled, impressed, insincere, mandatory, unwilling **10** artificial, compulsory, obligatory **11** constrained, involuntary

forceful 5 pithy, valid, vivid **6** cogent, potent, robust, strong, virile **7** dynamic, intense **8** emphatic, powerful, puissant, vigorous **9** effective, energetic **10** impressive

forceless 4 weak **8** impotent

force measurement 4 dyne **6** newton **7** poundal

Force of Circumstance
  author: **16** Simone de Beauvoir

Force of Destiny, The
  also: **17** La Forza del Destino
  opera by: **5** Verdi
  character: **7** Leonora **8** Don Carlo **9** Don Alvaro

forcible 8 coercive **10** compulsory

ford 3 car **4** span, wade **5** cross, shoal **6** bridge, stream **7** passage **8** crossing, tin lizzy

Ford, Gerald Rudolph
  born: **17** Leslie Lynch King Jr
  adopted by/named after: **10** step father
  nickname: **5** Jerry **7** Mr Clean
  presidential rank: **12** thirty-eighth
  party: **10** Republican
  state represented: **2** MI
  defeated: **5** no one
  elected to neither: **10** presidency **14** vice presidency
  vice president: **11** (Nelson A) Rockefeller
  cabinet:
    state: **9** (Henry A) Kissinger
    treasury: **5** (William E) Simon
    defense: **8** (Donald H) Rumsfeld **11** (James) Schlesinger
    attorney general: **4** (Edward H) Levi **5** (William B) Saxbe
    interior: **6** (Rogers Clark Ballard) Morton, (Thomas S) Kleppe **8** (Stanley K) Hathaway
    agriculture: **4** (Earl Lauer) Butz **6** (John A) Knebel
    commerce: **4** (Frederick B) Dent **6** (Rogers Clark Ballard) Morton **10** (Elliot L) Richardson
    labor: **5** (W J) Usery (Jr) **6** (John T) Dunlop **7** (Peter J) Brennan
    HEW: **7** (F David) Mathews **10** (Caspar W) Weinberger
    HUD: **4** (James T) Lynn **5** (Carla Anderson) Hills
    transportation: **7** (William T) Coleman (Jr) **8** (Claude S) Brinegar
  born: **7** Omaha NE
  education:
    University: **8** Michigan
    Law School: **4** Yale
  religion: **12** Episcopalian
  interests: **4** golf **6** boxing, skiing **8** football, swimming
  vacation spot: **2** CO **4** Vail
  author: **21** Portrait of the Assassin (with John R Stiles) **27** A Time To Heal: An Autobiography
  political career: **13** vice president **19** House minority leader **24** US House of Representatives
  civilian career: **6** lawyer
    assistant football coach at: **4** Yale
  military service: **6** US Navy **10** lieutenant, World War II
  notable events of lifetime/term: **9** recession **12** Bicentennial
    assassination attempts on: **4** Ford
    clemency for: **12** draft dodgers, draft evaders
    kidnapping/trial/conviction of: **11** Patty Hearst
    scandal: **8** Lockheed **10** Hays Affair
    talks: **4** SALT
  quotes: **19** I am a Ford not a Lincoln **41** Indebted to no man{hp}---{hp}the president of all the people **50** Our long national nightmare is over Our constitution works
  father:
    natural: **15** Leslie Lynch King
    adoptive: **17** Gerald Rudolph Ford
  mother: **7** Dorothy (Gardner King Ford)
  siblings:
    half-brothers: **12** James Francis **13** Thomas Gardner **14** Richard Addison
  wife: **9** Elizabeth (Bloomer Warren)
    nickname: **5** Betty
  children: **4** John **5** Susan **6** Steven **7** Michael

Ford, Glenn
  real name: **11** Gwyllyn Ford
  wife: **13** Eleanor Powell
  born: **6** Canada, Quebec
  roles: **4** Rage **5** Gilda, Jubal **6** Santee **8** Cimarron **11** The Rounders **14** Is Paris Burning? **17** Interrupted Melody **18** Don't Go Near the Water **19** The Blackboard Jungle **23** Teahouse of the August Moon

Ford, Harrison
  born: **9** Chicago IL
  roles: **7** Frantic, Witness **8** Star Wars

11 Blade Runner 15 Return of the Jedi 16 American Graffiti 19 Raiders of the Lost Ark 20 The Empire Strikes Back 30 Indiana Jones and the Temple of Doom

Ford, John
author of: 13 Perkin Warbeck 17 'Tis Pity She's a Whore 19 The Lover's Melancholy

Ford, John
director of: 10 Stagecoach 11 The Informer (Oscar), The Quiet Man (Oscar) 12 The Hurricane, The Searchers 13 Grapes of Wrath (Oscar), Mister Roberts (with Mervyn LeRoy), The Lost Patrol 17 The Long Voyage Home 19 How Green Was My Valley (Oscar), My Darling Clementine 27 The Man Who Shot Liberty Valence

Ford, Thelma Booth
real name of: 12 Shirley Booth

Ford and Mistress Ford
characters in: 22 The Merry Wives of Windsor
author: 11 Shakespeare

Ford automobiles 3 LTD 5 Edsel, Pinto, T-Bird 6 Model T, Taurus 7 Mustang 11 Thunderbird

fore 5 front 7 frontal 8 anterior, headmost

forearm 4 ulna 5 prime, ready 7 prepare

forebear 8 ancestor, begetter 10 antecedent, procreator, progenitor

foreboding 4 omen 5 dread 6 augury, boding 7 portent 9 intuition, misgiving 10 prescience, prognostic 11 premonition 12 apprehension, presentiment

forecast 5 augur 6 augury, divine, expect 7 outlook, portend, predict, presage, project 8 envisage, envision, prophesy 9 calculate, prevision, prognosis 10 anticipate, conjecture, prediction, prescience, projection 11 extrapolate 12 anticipation, precognition, presentiment 13 prognosticate 15 prognostication

forefather 6 author 8 ancestor, begetter 9 patriarch, precursor 10 antecedent, originator, procreator, progenitor 12 primogenitor

forefront 4 fame, head, lead 8 vanguard 9 celebrity

foreign 5 alien 6 exotic, remote 7 distant, strange, unknown, unusual 8 imported 9 barbarous, extrinsic, irregular, unrelated 10 extraneous, heathenish, introduced, irrelevant, outlandish, unfamiliar 11 incongruous, inconsonant, unconnected 12 antipathetic, inadmissible, inapplicable, incompatible, inconsistent 13 inappropriate 16 uncharacteristic

Foreign Correspondent
director: 15 Alfred Hitchcock
cast: 10 Joel McCrea, Laraine Day 13

George Sanders 14 Robert Benchley 15 Albert Basserman, Herbert Marshall

foreigner 5 alien, pagan 6 emigre 8 newcomer, outsider, stranger 9 barbarian, immigrant, nonnative, outlander
German: 9 Auslander

foreign officer 6 consul 8 diplomat, minister 10 ambassador 14 representative 15 charge d'affaires

foreknowledge 9 intuition, prevision 10 prescience 11 premonition 12 anticipation, apprehension, clairvoyance, precogni-tion, presentiment

foreman 4 boss 7 manager 8 chairman, overseer 9 president, spokesman 10 supervisor 11 coordinator 14 superintendent

foremost 4 head, main 5 chief, vital 7 capital, leading, supreme 8 cardinal 9 essential, paramount, principal 10 preeminent

forerunner 4 omen, sign 5 token 6 augury, herald 7 portent, presage 8 ancestor 9 harbinger, precursor, prototype 10 progenitor, prognostic 11 predecessor, premonition

foresee 5 augur 6 divine, expect 7 predict, presage 8 envision, prophesy 10 anticipate 13 prognosticate

foreshadow 5 augur 7 presage, promise 9 prefigure

foresight 6 wisdom 8 planning, prudence, sagacity 9 prevision 10 discretion, precaution, prescience, providence, shrewdness 12 anticipation, clairvoyance, perspicacity, precognition, preparedness 13 premeditation 14 farsightedness

forest 4 bush, wood 5 copse, grove, stand, woods 6 jungle 7 thicket 8 wildwood, woodland 10 timberland, wilderness

forestall 5 avert, avoid, block, deter 6 thwart 7 head off, obviate, prevent, ward off 8 preclude 10 anticipate, circumvent, counteract

Forester, C S (Cecil Scott)
author of: 6 The Gun 14 A Ship of the Line 15 Payment Deferred, The African Queen 24 Captain Horatio Hornblower

forests
god of: 3 Pan 7 Silenus, Virbius
pertaining to: 6 silvan, sylvan
nymph: 5 dryad

foretell 5 augur 6 divine 7 portend, predict, presage 8 prophesy, soothsay 9 apprehend 13 prognosticate

forethought 4 heed 7 caution 8 prudence, sagacity, wariness 10 discretion, precaution, providence, shrewdness 11 carefulness 12 anticipation, deliberation 13 consideration, premed-

itation 14 circumspection, farsightedness

forever 6 always 9 eternally, undyingly 10 constantly 11 ceaselessly, continually, incessantly, perpetually, unceasingly 12 interminably 13 everlastingly, unremittingly
Latin: 11 in perpetuum

forewarn 4 bode 5 alert 6 advise, notify, signal, tip off 7 caution, portend, presage, prewarn 8 cry havoc

foreword 7 preface, prelude 8 preamble, prologue 12 introduction

Forewords and Afterwords
author: 7 W H Auden

for example
Latin: 2 eg 13 exempli gratia

forfeit 4 fine, miss 5 waive, waste, yield 6 waiver 7 damages, default, let slip, penalty 8 squander 9 surrender 10 assessment

Forfeit
author: 11 Dick Francis

forge 4 copy, form, make 5 clone, shape 6 devise, hearth, smithy 7 falsify, fashion, furnace, imitate, produce, turn out 8 contrive, simulate 9 fabricate, ironworks 11 counterfeit, manufacture

forgery 4 copy, fake, hoax, sham 5 clone, fraud 7 cloning 9 deception, imitation 11 counterfeit, fraudulence 13 falsification 14 counterfeiting 17 misrepresentation

forget 6 slight 7 neglect 8 overlook, pass over 9 disregard

forgetful 6 remiss 7 out of it 8 amnesiac, careless, heedless, mindless 9 negligent, oblivious, unmindful 10 neglectful 11 inattentive

forget-me-not 8 Myosotis
varieties: 5 white 6 alpine, garden 7 Chinese 8 creeping

forgive 5 clear 6 acquit, excuse, pardon 7 absolve, condone, release, set free 8 overlook, reprieve 9 discharge, exculpate, exonerate

forgiveness 6 pardon 7 amnesty 9 remission 10 absolution

forgiving 6 benign, kindly 8 excusing 9 benignant, pardoning 11 kindhearted

forgo 4 skip 5 waive, yield 6 eschew, give up 8 abnegate, renounce 9 sacrifice, surrender 10 relinquish

fork 4 bend, stab 5 angle, elbow, split 6 branch, crotch, divide, impale, pierce, ramify, skewer 7 diverge, trident 8 division 9 bifurcate, pitchfork 10 divergence, separation 11 bifurcation 12 intersection

forked 5 cleft, tined 6 horned, zigzag 7 angular, divided, pronged 8 branched 9 ambiguous, deceitful, equivocal 10 bifurcated

For Kicks
author: **11** Dick Francis
fork out 5 spend **6** expend **8** disburse, dispense
for lack of something better
French: **12** faute de mieux
forlorn 4 lone **6** abject, bereft, dismal, dreary, lonely **7** unhappy **8** bereaved, dejected, deserted, desolate, forsaken, helpless, hopeless, lonesome, pathetic, pitiable, solitary, wretched **9** abandoned, depressed, desperate, destitute, forgotten, miserable, woebegone **10** despairing, despondent, dispirited, friendless **11** comfortless **12** disconsolate, inconsolable **13** brokenhearted
form 3 cut, hew, way **4** body, cast, kind, make, mode, mold, plan, rite, rule, sort, trim, type **5** being, brand, build, carve, class, forge, found, frame, genre, genus, guise, habit, image, model, order, phase, set up, shape, stamp, style, usage **6** aspect, chisel, create, custom, design, devise, fettle, figure, manner, matrix, person, ritual, sculpt, system **7** acquire, anatomy, compose, conduct, contour, decorum, develop, fashion, fitness, harmony, liturgy, manners, outline, pattern, produce, species, variety **8** ceremony, comprise, contract, likeness, physique, practice, presence, rough-hew, symmetry **9** character, construct, establish, etiquette, fabricate, framework, propriety, sculpture, semblance, structure **10** appearance, constitute, deportment, figuration, proceeding, proportion, regularity **11** arrangement, description, incarnation, manufacture, orderliness, shapeliness **12** denomination **13** configuration, manifestation **15** conventionality
formal 4 cool, prim **5** aloof, fancy, fixed, grand, legal, rigid, smart, stiff **6** dressy, lawful, proper, solemn, strict **7** distant, outward, pompous, prudish, regular, settled, stilted, stylish **8** decorous, definite, expli-cit, external, official, positive, reserved, starched **9** customary **10** ceremonial, inflexible, prescribed **11** ceremonious, highfalutin, perfunctory, punctilious, ritualistic, standoffish, straitlaced **12** conventional **13** authoritative **14** uncompromising
formal discussion 6 debate, parley **8** dialogue **10** conference
formality 4 rite **6** custom, motion, ritual **7** decorum, reserve **8** ceremony, coolness **9** etiquette, propriety, punctilio **10** ceremonial, convention **15** conventionality
Forman, Milos
director of: **7** Amadeus (Oscar), Ragtime **25** One Flew Over the Cuckoo's Nest (Oscar)
formation 3 set **6** makeup **7** genesis **8**

building, creation **9** structure **10** generation, production **11** arrangement, composition, development, fabrication, manufacture **12** organization **13** configuration, constellation, establishment
formative 7 plastic, shaping **9** sensitive **10** accessible **11** susceptible **13** determinative **14** impressionable
former 2 ex **4** gone, past **5** olden, prior **6** bygone, gone by, lapsed, of yore, whilom **7** ancient, earlier, elapsed, old-time, quondam **8** anterior, previous **9** aforesaid, erstwhile, preceding **10** antecedent, first-named **14** aforementioned
French: **8** ci-devant
formerly 4 once **5** of old **6** ere now, lately, of yore, whilom **7** long ago **8** hitherto **9** anciently **10** originally, previously
former student 6 alumna **7** alumnus, dropout **8** graduate
formidable 6 taxing **7** awesome, fearful, mammoth, onerous **8** alarming, dread-ful, imposing, menacing, terrific **9** dangerous, demanding, difficult **10** forbidding, impressive, portentous, terrifying **11** threatening **12** overpowering, overwhelming
formless 5 vague **9** amorphous, shapeless
Formosa see **6** Taiwan
formula 4 cant, plan, rule **5** chant **6** cliche, recipe, saying, slogan **7** precept **9** blueprint, guideline, platitude, principle, rigmarole **10** pleasantry **11** incantation **12** prescription
formulate 5 draft, frame, state **6** define, devise, invent **7** compose, itemize, specify **11** systematize **13** particularize
Fornax
origin: **5** Roman
goddess of: **6** baking
fornication 8 adultery
for one's country
Latin: **9** pro patria
Forrest, Nathan Bedford
served in: **8** Civil War
side: **11** Confederate
known for: **12** cavalry raids
forsake 4 deny, drop, flee, quit **5** leave, spurn, waive, yield **6** abjure, depart, desert, give up, reject, resign, vacate **7** abandon, cast off, disavow, discard, lay down **8** abdicate, disclaim, go back on, jettison, part with, renounce **9** repudiate, surrender **10** relinquish
forsaken 4 bare **5** empty **8** deserted, desolate, rejected **9** abandoned, discarded, neglected **11** uninhabited
Forsete see **7** Forseti
Forseti
also: **7** Forsete

origin: **12** Scandinavian
god of: **7** justice
father: **5** Baldr **6** Balder, Baldur
mother: **5** Nanna
dwelling place: **7** Glitnir
Forster, E M (Edward Morgan)
author of: **7** Maurice **10** Howards End **14** A Room with a View **15** A Passage to India **17** The Longest Journey **22** Where Angels Fear to Tread
member of: **15** Bloomsbury Group
forswear 4 deny **5** spurn **6** abjure, disown, eschew, give up, recant, reject, revoke **7** disavow, gainsay, retract **8** abdicate, disclaim, renounce, take back **9** disaffirm, repudiate **10** contravene
Forsyte Saga, The
author: **14** John Galsworthy
trilogy including: **5** To Let **10** In Chancery **16** The Man of Property
character: **3** Jon **4** June **5** Fleur **6** Dartie **7** Annette **8** Winifred **9** Old Jolyon **11** Young Jolyon **12** Irene Forsyte **13** Soames Forsyte **14** Philip Bosinney
Forsythe, John
real name: **17** John Lincoln Freund
born: **12** Penn's Grove NJ
roles: **5** Topaz **7** Dynasty, Madame X **11** In Cold Blood **14** Bachelor Father, Charlie's Angels **15** Blake Carrington **16** And Justice for All **19** The Trouble with Harry **23** Teahouse of the August Moon
fort 4 base, camp **6** castle **7** bastion, bulwark, citadel, station **8** fastness, garrison **10** stronghold
forte 4 bent **5** knack, skill **6** talent **8** strength **9** specialty **11** proficiency
music: **4** loud
abbreviation: **1** f
forth 5 ahead **6** onward **7** outward
forthcoming 5 handy, on tap **6** at hand **7** helpful **8** imminent **9** available, impending **10** accessible, obtainable, openhanded **11** approaching, cooperative, prospective
for the greater glory of God
Latin: **19** ad majorem Dei gloriam
for the public good
Latin: **14** pro bono publico
for the time being
Latin: **10** pro tempore
For the Time Being
author: **7** W H Auden
for this purpose only
Latin: **5** ad hoc
forthright 4 open **5** blunt, frank **6** candid, direct, openly **7** bluntly, frankly, up-front **8** candidly, directly, straight **9** outspoken **10** truthfully **11** outspokenly, plain-spoken **15** straightforward **17** straightforwardly
forthrightness 6 candor **7** honesty **8**

openness **9** frankness, sincerity **19** straightforwardness

forthwith 4 ASAP, stat **6** at once, pronto **7** quickly **8** directly, in a jiffy, promptly, right off **9** instantly **11** immediately **12** straightaway

fortification 5 tower **7** bastion, bulwark, citadel, rampart **8** fortress, garrison **9** earthwork **10** breastwork, stronghold

fortify 4 lace **5** boost, brace, cheer **6** buoy up, enrich, harden, secure, shield, urge on **7** build up, bulwark, hearten, protect, shore up, stiffen, support, sustain **8** buttress, embolden, garrison, reassure **9** encourage, reinforce, stimulate **10** invigorate, strengthen

fortissimo
music: **8** very loud
abbreviation: **2** ff

fortitude 4 dash, grit, guts, sand **5** nerve, pluck, spunk, valor **6** daring, mettle, spirit **7** bravery, courage, heroism, prowess **8** backbone, boldness, firmness, tenacity **9** endurance, hardihood **10** resolution **11** intrepidity **12** fearlessness, resoluteness **13** dauntlessness, determination

Fortitude
author: **11** Hugh Walpole

Fort-Lamy
former name of: **8** N'Djamena
capital of: **4** Chad

fortress 7 bastion, bulwark, citadel, rampart **8** buttress **9** acropolis **10** stronghold

Fortress, The
author: **11** Hugh Walpole

fortuitous 5 happy, lucky, stray **6** casual, chance, random **9** haphazard, hit-or-miss **10** accidental, incidental, undesigned, unexpected, unintended, unpurposed **11** inadvertent **12** adventitious **13** serendipitous, unintentional **14** unpremeditated

fortuity 6 chance **8** accident **12** happenstance

Fortuna
origin: **5** Roman
goddess of: **7** fortune
corresponds to: **5** Tyche

fortunate 4 fair, rich, rosy **5** happy, lucky, palmy **6** benign, bright, timely **7** blessed, booming, favored, halcyon, well-off **8** well-to-do **9** favorable, opportune, promising **10** auspicious, convenient, felicitous, profitable, propitious, prosperous, successful **11** encouraging, flourishing **12** advantageous, providential

Fortunate Isles *see* **13** Canary Islands

Fortunato
character in: **20** The Cask of Amontillado
author: **3** Poe

fortune, fortunes 3 lot **4** doom, fate, luck, mint, pile, star **5** karma, means **6** chance, es-tate, income, kismet, riches, wealth **7** bonanza, capital, destiny, godsend, portion, revenue **8** accident, fatality, gold mine, good luck, lady luck, opulence, property, treasure, windfall **9** affluence, haphazard, substance **10** prosperity, providence **11** dame fortune **12** circumstance **13** circumstances
goddess of: **5** Tyche **7** Fortuna

Fortunes of Nigel, The
author: **14** Sir Walter Scott

fortuneteller 4 seer **5** augur, Gypsy, sibyl **6** medium, oracle **7** palmist, prophet **8** magician **10** soothsayer **11** chiromancer, clairvoyant **12** crystal gazer

for two
French: **5** a deux

Forty Days of Musa Dagh, The
author: **11** Franz Werfel

42nd Parallel, The
author: **13** John Dos Passos

Forty-Second Street
director: **10** Lloyd Bacon
cast: **9** Guy Kibbee, Una Merkel **10** Dick Powell, Ruby Keeler **11** Bebe Daniels, George Brent **12** Ginger Rogers, Warner Baxter
choreographer: **13** Busby Berkeley
song: **15** Young and Healthy **17** Forty-second Street **19** Shuffle Off to Buffalo **28** You're Getting to Be a Habit with Me

Forty Thieves, The
story in: **13** Arabian Nights
character: **7** Ali Baba
code word: **10** Open Sesame

forty winks 3 nap **4** doze **6** catnap, snooze

forum 6 medium, outlet **7** rostrum, seminar **8** platform **9** symposium **10** colloquium

forward, forwards 3 out **4** back, bold **5** ahead, brash, fresh, relay, sassy **6** assist, brazen, cheeky, hasten, onward, pass on, send on, spread **7** advance, frontal, further, go-ahead, promote, quicken, re-route **8** anterior, champion, immodest, impudent, insolent, up-to-date **9** advancing, barefaced, intrusive, offensive, presuming, readdress, shameless **10** accelerate, unmannerly **11** impertinent, progressive **12** enterprising, presumptuous **13** overconfident
French: **7** en avant

forwardness 4 gall **5** brass, cheek **8** audacity, boldness **10** brazenness, effrontery **11** presumption **13** bumptiousness, obtrusiveness

for what use
Latin: **7** cui bono

For Whom the Bell Tolls
author: **15** Ernest Hemingway

director: **7** Sam Wood
character: **5** Maria, Pablo, Pilar **6** Andres, Rafael **7** Anselmo, El Sordo **8** Augustin, Fernando **12** Robert Jordan
cast: **10** Gary Cooper **12** Akim Tamiroff **13** Ingrid Bergman, Joseph Calleia, Katina Paxinou **15** Arturo de Cordova
score: **11** Victor Young
Oscar for: **17** supporting actress (Paxinou)

for whose benefit
Latin: **7** cui bono

For Your Eyes Only
author: **10** Ian Fleming

Forza del Destino, La *see* **17** Force of Destiny, The

Fosse, Bob
director of: **5** Lenny **7** Cabaret (Oscar) **11** All That Jazz

fossil 4 fogy, rock **5** fogey, oldie, relic, stone **7** imprint, antique **9** remainder **13** petrification

foster 3 aid **4** back, feed, rear, tend **5** favor, nurse, raise **6** foment, harbor, mother, rear up, take in **7** advance, bring up, care for, cherish, forward, further, nourish, nurture, promote, protect, support, sustain **8** advocate, befriend, hold dear, sanction, side with, treasure **9** encourage, patronize, stimulate **11** accommodate, countenance

Foster, Alicia Christian
real name of: **11** Jodie Foster

Foster, Harold
creator/artist of: **6** Tarzan **13** Prince Valiant

Foster, Jodie
real name: **21** Alicia Christian Foster
born: **7** Bronx NY
roles: **7** Contact **8** Maverick **9** Tom Sawyer **10** Taxi Driver, The Accused (Oscar) **11** Bugsy Malone **13** Little Man Tate **20** The Silence of the Lambs (Oscar)

Foster, Stephen Collins
born: **15** Lawrenceville PA
composer of: **11** Swanee River **13** Camptown Races **16** Beautiful Dreamer **17** My Old Kentucky Home, The Old Folks at Home **27** Jeanie with the Light Brown Hair

Foucault, Jean Bernard Leon
field: **7** physics
nationality: **6** French
proved: **19** Earth spins on its axis
measured: **15** velocity of light
named for him: **8** pendulum **16** Foucault currents

Foucault's Pendulum
author: **10** Umberto Eco

foul 3 wet **4** base, clog, evil, lewd, soil, vile **5** dirty, foggy, grimy, gross, gusty, misty, muddy, murky, nasty, rainy, sully, taint **6** choked, cloudy, coarse, defile, filthy, grubby, odious, putrid, risque, scurvy, smelly, smutty, soiled, sordid, stormy, tangle, turbid, vulgar, wicked **7** abusive, begrime, drizzly, ensnare, hateful, heinous, impeded, obscene, pollute, profane, smeared, squalid, squally, stained, sullied, tangled, unclean **8** begrimed, besmirch, blustery, ensnared, entangle, immodest, indecent, infamous, stinking, unseemly **9** atrocious, besmeared, entangled, insulting, loathsome, monstrous, nefarious, notorious, obnoxious, repulsive, revolting **10** abominable, bedraggled, detestable, disgusting, encumbered, flagitious, indelicate, malodorous, putrescent, scurrilous, villainous **11** blasphemous, disgraceful **12** contemptible

foul-mouthed 4 lewd, rude, vile **5** dirty, gross **6** coarse, filthy, vulgar **7** abusive, obscene, profane **9** offensive **10** indelicate

foul play 5 crime **6** murder **8** violence **9** treachery

foul-smelling 4 rank **5** acrid, fetid, musty **6** putrid, smelly **7** noisome, reeking **8** stinking **10** malodorous

foul up 3 mar **4** goof, muff, ruin **5** botch, mix up, spoil **6** bungle, mess up, muddle **7** blunder, butcher, confuse, louse up, screw up **9** mismanage

found 4 base, rear, rest **5** build, erect, raise, set up, start **6** create, ground, locate, settle **7** develop, sustain **8** colonize, organize **9** construct, establish, institute, originate

foundation 3 bed **4** base, foot, fund, rock, root **5** basis, cause **6** bottom, cellar, ground, motive, origin, reason, source **7** charity, premise, purpose, support **8** basement, creation, pedestal **9** endowment, rationale **10** assumption, groundwork, settlement **11** benefaction, institution **12** commencement, installation, philanthropy, substructure, underpinning **13** establishment, justification **14** infrastructure, understructure

foundational 3 key **4** base, core **5** basic, prime **7** primary **9** essential **10** elementary

foundation garment 6 corset, girdle **8** corselet

founder 4 fall, limp, reel, sink, trip **5** abort, drown, lurch, swamp **6** author, father, go down, go lame, hobble, perish, plunge, sprawl, topple, tumble **7** break up, builder, capsize, creator, go under, planner, stagger, stumble, succumb **8** collapse, miscarry **9** architect, organizer, shipwreck **10** originator, strategist **12** disintegrate

foundered 4 sank **6** failed **7** beached, swamped **8** capsized, went down **9** collapsed

founding 5 birth **8** creation, settling **9** beginning **11** institution, origination **12** introduction, organization **13** establishment

found on 6 base on **7** model on **8** stem from **10** derive from **11** establish on

fountain 3 jet **4** flow, gush, well **5** birth, cause, spout **6** cradle, feeder, origin, reason, source, spring **7** genesis **8** purveyor, supplier **9** beginning, reservoir, upswelling **10** derivation, wellspring

fountainhead 4 font **6** origin, source, spring **9** beginning **10** wellspring

Fountainhead, The
   author: 7 Ayn Rand
   character: 11 Howard Roark
   profession: 9 architect

fourgon 3 van **7** tumbril

Four Horsemen of the Apocalypse, The
   author: 19 Vicente Blasco Ibanez
   based on: 10 Revelation

400 Blows, The
   director: 16 Francois Truffaut
   cast: 10 Albert Remy **13** Claire Maurier **14** Patrick Auffray **15** Jean-Pierre Leaud

Four Quartets
   author: 7 T S Eliot

Four-Season Recreation State
   nickname of: 7 Vermont

fourth class mail 10 parcel post

fourth dimension 4 time

fourth estate 5 press **10** journalism

fowl 3 hen **4** cock, duck, game **5** banty, capon, chick, goose, quail **6** bantam, grouse, pigeon, turkey **7** chicken, cornish, leghorn, poultry **8** duckling

Fowles, John
   author of: 8 Mantissa, The Magus **10** The Aristos **12** Daniel Martin, The Collector **13** The Ebony Tower **25** The French Lieutenant's Woman

fox 9 scavenger
   young: 3 kit, pup
   group of: 5 leash, skulk

Fox (Mesquakie, Red Earth People)
   language family: 9 Algonkian **10** Algonquian
   location: 4 Iowa **9** Wisconsin
   allied with: 4 Sauk **8** Kickapoo

Fox, Fontaine
   creator/artist of: 16 Toonerville Folks **18** Toonerville Trolley

foxglove 9 digitalis
   varieties: 5 false, rusty **6** common, yellow **7** Grecian, Mexican **10** downy false **12** willow-leaved

foxiness 5 guile **7** cunning, slyness **8** artifice, trickery, wiliness **10** craftiness, shrewdness

fox-trot 5 dance **13** ballroom dance

Foxx, Jimmy (James Emory)
   nickname: 7 Double X
   sport: 8 baseball
   team: 12 Boston Red Sox **21** Philadelphia Athletics

Foxx, Redd
   real name: 16 John Elroy Sanford
   born: 9 St Louis MO
   roles: 13 Sanford and Son **19** Cotton Comes to Harlem

foxy 3 sly **4** wily **5** canny, sharp, slick **6** artful, astute, clever, crafty, shifty, shrewd, sneaky, tricky **7** cunning, devious, oblique **8** guileful, scheming, stealthy **9** conniving, deceitful, deceptive, designing, insidious, underhand **10** intriguing

foyer 4 hall **5** lobby **6** loggia **8** anteroom **9** vestibule **11** antechamber

fracas 3 row **4** fray, to-do **5** brawl, broil, clash, fight, melee, scrap **6** battle, ruckus, rumpus, strife, uproar **7** scuffle **9** imbroglio **10** donnybrook, free-for-all **11** altercation, embroilment

fraction 3 bit, few **4** chip **5** crumb, piece, ratio, scrap **6** morsel, trifle **7** cutting, portion, section, segment, shaving **8** fragment, particle, quotient **10** proportion **11** subdivision

fractious 5 cross, huffy **6** shirty, touchy, unruly **7** fretful, grouchy, peevish, pettish, waspish, wayward, willful **8** contrary, perverse, petulant, shrewish, snappish **9** irascible, irritable, querulous **10** rebellious, refractory **11** quarrelsome **12** disputatious, recalcitrant, unmanageable

fracture 4 rend, rift **5** break, crack, fault, sever, split **6** breach, cleave **7** disrupt, rupture, shatter **8** cleavage, division **9** severance **10** separation

Fra Diavolo, ou L'Hotellerie de Terracine
   also: 31 Brother Devil or The Inn at Terracina
   comic opera by: 5 Auber
   character: 7 Lorenzo, Zerlina **11** Lady Allcash, Lord Allcash **17** Marquis di San Marco

fragile 4 soft, weak **5** crisp, frail **6** dainty, feeble, flimsy, infirm, sleazy, slight, tender **7** brittle, crumbly, friable, rickety, shivery **8** decrepit, delicate **9** breakable, ephemeral, frangible, splintery **10** evanescent, tumbledown **11** dilapidated **13** unsubstantial

fragility 7 frailty **8** delicacy, weakness **9** frailness **10** feebleness **11** brittleness **12** frangibility

fragment 3 bit **4** chip, snip **5** crumb, cut up, piece, scrap, shard, shred, trace **6** chop up, divide, morsel **7** break up, crumble, portion, remnant, section, segment, shatter, vestige **8** disunite, fraction, separate, splinter, survival **12** disintegrate

fragmentary 6 broken, choppy **7** scrappy **8** detached **9** piecemeal, scattered, segmented **10** disjointed, fractional, incomplete, unfinished **12** disconnected

Fragonard, Jean-Honore
  born: 6 France, Grasse
  artwork: 8 The Swing **10** Stolen Kiss, The Bathers, The Warrior **12** Le Billet Doux **14** Progress of Love **16** La Chemise Enlevee **18** Storming the Citadel **40** Coresus Sacrificing Himself to Save Callirhoe

fragrance 4 aura, balm **5** aroma, scent **7** bouquet, incense, perfume **9** redolence, sweetness

fragrant 5 balmy, spicy **7** odorous **8** aromatic, perfumed, redolent **11** odoriferous

Fragrant Harbor *see* **8** Hong Kong

frail 4 puny, weak **6** feeble, flimsy, infirm, sleazy, slight, weakly **7** brittle, crumbly, fragile, rickety, shivery **8** decrepit, delicate, fallible **9** breakable, frangible, splintery **10** perishable, vulnerable **11** dilapidated **13** unsubstantial

frailness 8 delicacy, weakness **9** fragility **11** unsoundness

frailty 3 sin **4** flaw, vice **5** fault **6** defect, foible **7** blemish, failing **11** fallibility **12** imperfection **14** susceptibility

Fra Lippo Lippi
  author: 14 Robert Browning

frame 3 rim, set **4** body, case, cast, form, make, mold, mood, plan **5** build, draft, hatch, humor, set up, shape, state **6** border, casing, design, devise, edging, figure, indite, invent, map out, nature, scheme, sketch, system, temper **7** anatomy, backing, chassis, concoct, contour, housing, outline, setting **8** attitude, conceive, contrive, mounting, organize, physique, skeleton **9** formulate, structure **11** disposition, scaffolding, systematize, temperament **12** constitution, construction

frame of mind 4 mood **7** climate **8** attitude **10** atmosphere **11** disposition

framer 6 author, shaper **7** creator, planner **10** formulator

framework 5 shell, truss **7** carcass **8** skeleton, template **9** structure **10** foundation **11** scaffolding **14** infrastructure

Framley Parsonage
  author: 15 Anthony Trollope

France
  other name: 4 Gaul
  anthem: 14 La Marseillaise
  capital/largest city: 5 Paris
  others: 4 Nice, St.-Lo **5** Brest, Lille, Lyons, Rouen, Vichy **6** Amiens, Calais, Cannes, Carnac, Cognac, Dieppe, Grasse, Nantes, Prades, Rheims **7** Antibes, Avignon, Bayonne, Dunkirk,

Le Havre, Les Baux **8** Bordeaux, Boulogne, Chartres, Grenoble, Poitiers, Toulouse **9** Cherbourg, Roquefort **10** La Rochelle, Marseilles, Saint-Denis, Strasbourg **12** Saint-Nazaire **13** Aix-en- Provence, Fontainebleau
  school: 8 Grenoble, Saint Cyr, Sorbonne **10** Montpelier
  division: 5 Anjou, Bearn, Berry, Maine, Savoy **6** Alsace, Artois, Marche, Poitou **7** Gascony, Guienne, Picardy **8** Auvergne, Bordeaux, Brittany, Burgundy, Dauphine, Flanders, Lorraine, Lyonnais, Normandy, Provence, Touraine **9** Aquitaine, Champagne, Languedoc **11** Ile de France **12** Bourbonnaise, Franche-Comte
  measure: 3 pot, sac **4** aune, mine, muid, pied, velt **5** arpen, carat, ligne, minot, pinte, point, pouce, velte **6** arpent, hemine, league, quarte, setier
  monetary unit: 5 franc **7** centime
  weight: 3 sol **4** gros, kilo, once **5** carat, livre, pound, tonne **6** gramme **7** tonneau **8** esterlin **9** esterling
  island: 2 Re **3** Yeu **4** Cite **5** Groix, Hyere **6** Comoro, Oleron, Tahiti, Ushant **7** Corsica, Leeward, Reunion **8** Windward **10** Guadeloupe, Martinique **12** New Caledonia
  lake: 6 Annecy, Cazaux, Geneva
  mountain: 4 Jura **5** Pelat **6** Vosges **8** Ardennes, Pyrenees **10** French Alps **11** Pic Montcalm
  highest point: 5 Blanc **9** Mont Blanc
  river: 3 Lys **4** Oise, Yser **5** Aisne, Eiser, Isere, Loire, Meuse, Rhine, Rhone, Saone, Seine **7** Garonne, Gironde
  sea: 5 North **8** Atlantic **13** Mediterranean
  physical feature:
    bay: 6 Biscay **7** Arachon
    beach: 4 Utah **5** Omaha
    cape: 5 Hague, Talma
    channel: 7 English **8** La Manche
    gulf: 4 Lion
  people: 6 Franks
    artist: 5 Corot, David, Degas, Manet, Monet **6** Braque, Ingres, Millet, Renoir, Seurat **7** Cezanne, Daumier, Gauguin, Matisse, Utrillo **8** Pissarro **9** Delacroix, Fragonard, Gericault
    author: 4 Gide, Hugo, Zola **5** Camus, Dumas **6** France, Proust, Racine, Sartre, Villon **7** Moliere **8** Rabelais, Rousseau, Voltaire **9** Corneille, Descartes, Giraudoux, Montaigne **10** Baudelaire
    composer: 5 Bizet, Ravel, Satie **6** Franck, Gounod **7** Berlioz, Debussy, Poulenc
    king: 5 Henri, Louis **6** Clovis, Philip **7** Charles **9** Hugh Capet **11** Charlemagne **13** Louis Philippe **14** Henry of Navarre

    leader: 6 Danton, Petain **7** Colbert, Mazarin **8** de Gaulle, D'Estaing, Pompidou **9** Joan of Arc, Richelieu **10** Mitterrand **11** Robespierre **17** Napoleon Bonaparte
    queen: 7 Eugenie **9** Josephine **13** Marie de Medici **15** Marie Antoinette
  language: 6 French
  expressions: 6 deja vu **7** apropos, detente, en masse, faux pas, vis-a-vis **8** de riguer **9** bete noire, c'est la vie, coup d'etat **10** bon appetit **11** coup de grace, joie de vivre, raison d'etre, savoir faire, tour de force **12** carte blanche, cause celebre, je ne sais quoi, nouveau riche, fait accompli **14** creme de la creme, noblesse oblige
  religion: 5 Islam **7** Judaism **8** Huguenot **10** Protestant **13** Roman Catholic
  place:
    cathedral: 6 Rheims **8** Chartres **9** Madeleine, Notre Dame **10** Sacre-Coeur **14** Sainte-Chapelle **15** Mont-Saint-Michel
    chapel: 8 Ronchamp
    gardens: 9 Tuileries
    hall of mirrors: 16 Galerie des Glaces
    museum: 6 Louvre
    palace: 6 Elysee **10** Luxembourg, Versailles **12** Grand Trianon, Petit Trianon, **13** Fontainebleau
    prison: 8 Bastille
    racetrack: 6 Le Mans **7** Auteuil **10** Longchamps
    resort: 3 Pau **5** Vichy **6** Cannes, Menton **7** Antibes, Mentone, Riviera **8** Biarritz, Chamonix, Grenoble **9** Cote d'Azur **11** Aix-les-Bains
    section of Paris: 8 Left Bank **9** Right Bank **10** Montmartre, Rive Droite, Rive Gauche **12** Latin Quarter
    street: 13 Champs-Elysees **17** Place de la Concorde
    woods: 14 Bois de Boulogne **15** Bois de Vincennes
  possession: 12 French Guiana
    island: 6 Futuna, Hoorne, Wallis **7** Reunion **8** Miquelon **10** Guadeloupe, Martinique **11** Saint Pierre **12** New Caledonia **15** French Polynesia
  feature:
    airport: 4 Orly **9** Le Bourget **15** Charles de Gaulle
    bicycle race: 12 Tour de France
    dance: 5 gavot **6** branle, canary, cancan **7** boutade, gavotte
    fortification: 11 Maginot Line
    holiday: 11 Bastille Day
    monument: 13 Arc de Triomphe **14** Tomb of Napoleon
    national theater: 16 Comedie Francaise
    sightseeing boat: 12 bateau mou-

che
tower: 6 Eiffel
food:
cheese: 4 bleu, Brie **6** bonbel **7** boursin **8** Muenster **9** camembert, marcillat, port-salut, Roquefort **11** coulommiers
dessert: 6 mousse
dish: 4 pate **5** crepe **6** canape, quiche **7** souffle **8** escargot, piperade, pot au feu **9** cassoulet, tournedos **14** pate de foie gras
drink: 6 cognac **8** bordeaux, burgundy **9** champagne
french fries: 12 pommes frites
pastry: 7 brioche **8** napoleon **9** croissant
soup: 8 a l'oignon **13** bouillabaisse
steak: 7 bifteck
France, Anatole
real name: 30 Jacques Anatole Francois Thibault
author of: 5 Thais **12** Golden Verses **13** My Friend's Book, Penguin Island **17** The Gods Are Athirst **20** The Revolt of the Angels **25** Le Crime de Sylvestre Bonnard **27** At the Sign of the Reine Pedauque
franchise 5 grant, right **6** ballot **7** charter, freedom, license **8** immunity, suffrage **9** privilege **10** permission **11** prerogative **13** authorization
Franciosa, Anthony
real name: 14 Anthony Papales
born: 9 New York NY
wife: 14 Shelley Winters
roles: 12 The Naked Maja **13** A Hatful of Rain, Long Hot Summer, Name of the Game, Wild Is the Wind **15** Assault on a Queen
Francis, Dick
author of: 4 Bolt, Risk **5** Nerve, Proof **6** Banker, Reflex **7** Break In, Enquiry, Forfeit, Rat Race **8** Dead Cert, For Kicks, Slayride, Trial Run, Twice Shy, Whip Hand **9** Bonecrack, The Danger, Knockdown **10** Blood Sport, High Stakes, In the Frame **11** Smokescreen **12** Flying Finish
Franck, Cesar
born: 5 Liege **7** Belgium
composer of: 4 Ruth **5** Hulda **6** Psyche **7** Rebecca **8** Ghiselle **9** Les Djinns **10** Les Eolides, Redemption **13** La Tour de Babel, Les Beatitudes, The Beatitudes **16** Le Chasseur Maudit **17** The Accursed Hunter
Franco, Francisco
dictator of: 5 Spain
title: 10 el caudillo
party: 7 falange, fascist
followers: 11 fifth column
frank 4 bold, free, open **5** clear, plain, round **6** candid, direct, honest, patent **7** artless, evident, genuine, natural, sincere, up-front **8** apparent, distinct, explicit, manifest **9** downright, ingen-

uous, outspoken **10** aboveboard, forthright, unreserved **11** plainspoken, transparent, unambiguous, undisguised, unequivocal **12** unmistakable **15** straightforward
Frank, Anne
author of: 19 The Diary of Anne Frank
Frankenstein
author: 17 Mary Godwin Shelley
character: 7 Clerval, Justine, William **9** Elizabeth **10** The Monster **12** Robert Walton **18** Victor Frankenstein
Franklin, Benjamin
author of: 20 Poor Richard's Almanack
inventor of: 12 lightning rod **13** bifocal lenses, Franklin stove
frankness 6 candor **7** honesty **8** openness **9** bluntness, sincerity **10** directness **11** artlessness **13** guilelessness **14** forthrightness **19** straightforwardness
frantic 3 mad **4** wild **5** crazy, rabid **6** hectic, insane, raging, raving **7** berserk, excited, furious, nervous, violent **8** agitated, deranged, frenetic, frenzied **9** delirious **10** distracted, distraught, infuriated **11** impassioned, overwrought **12** ungovernable
Frasier
network: 3 NBC
cast: 5 Eddie (dog) **10** Peri Gilpin (Roz), Jane Leeves (Daphne) **11** John Mahoney (Martin) **13** Kelsey Grammer (Frasier) **15** David Hyde Pierce (Niles)
characters: 5 Eddie **8** Roz Doyle **10** Niles Crane, Daphne Moon **11** Martin Crane **12** Frasier Crane
spinoff of: 6 Cheers
fraternal 6 hearty, loving, social **7** devoted, kindred, related **8** amicable, friendly **9** brotherly **11** warmhearted **12** affectionate **14** consanguineous
fraternity 4 clan, club **5** Greek, union **6** circle, clique, league **7** company, coterie, kinship, society **8** alliance **9** coalition **10** federation **11** association, brotherhood, confederacy, propinquity **13** brotherliness, consanguinity, interrelation
Fraternity
author: 14 John Galsworthy
fraternize 3 mix **5** unite **6** concur, hobnob, mingle **7** combine, consort **8** coalesce **9** associate, cooperate, harmonize, pal around, socialize **10** sympathize **11** confederate
Fratres Arvales see **5** Arval
frau 4 lady, wife **12** married woman
fraud 4 fake, hoax, hype, ruse, sham **5** cheat, craft, guile, knave, quack, rogue, trick **6** deceit, humbug, rascal **7** swindle **8** artifice, cheating, cozenage, impostor, swindler, trickery **9** charlatan, chicanery, con artist, decep-

tion, duplicity, impos-ture, pretender, stratagem, swindling, treachery **10** dishonesty, mountebank, subterfuge **11** counterfeit, four-flusher, machination **13** dissimulation
fraudulence 6 deceit **8** trickery **9** deception **13** deceitfulness, deceptiveness **17** misrepresentation
fraudulent 4 sham, wily **5** bogus, false **6** crafty, tricky **7** crooked, cunning, knavish **8** cheating, guileful, spurious **9** deceitful, deceptive, dishonest **11** counterfeit, treacherous, underhanded **12** dishonorable, unprincipled
fraught 4 full **5** heavy, laden **6** filled, loaded **7** charged, replete, teeming **8** attended, pregnant **9** abounding
fraulein 4 miss **9** young lady **14** unmarried woman
fray 3 rub **4** fret, fuss, riot, spat, tiff **5** brawl, chafe, fight, melee, ravel, set-to **6** bat-tle, combat, fracas, rumble, rumpus, strain, tatter, tumult, tussle **7** contest, dispute, frazzle, quarrel, scuffle, warfare, wear out, wrangle **8** conflict, skirmish, squabble **9** bickering, commotion **10** contention, dissension, engagement **11** altercation, controversy **12** disagreement
Frazer, Sir James G
author of: 14 The Golden Bough
freak 3 fad, odd **4** kink, turn, whim **5** craze, fancy, humor, queer, quirk, sport, twist **6** marvel, oddity, vagary, whimsy, wonder **7** anomaly, bizarre, caprice, erratic, monster, strange, unusual **8** crotchet, mutation, peculiar **9** curiosity, deviation **10** aberration **11** abnormality, monstrosity **12** irregularity
freakish 3 odd **5** queer, weird **7** bizarre, strange, unusual **8** peculiar, singular, uncommon **9** eccentric, fantastic **10** outlandish **13** extraordinary
Frederick
character in: 11 As You Like It
author: 11 Shakespeare
Frederick I
nickname: 10 Barbarossa
position: 16 Holy Roman Emperor
dynasty: 12 Hohenstaufen
wife: 7 Beatrix
battle: 7 Legnano
Frederick the Great
nickname: 8 Old Fritz
position: 13 King of Prussia
invaded: 7 Silesia
war: 13 Seven Years' War **18** Austrian Succession
free 3 big, lax **4** able, bold, easy, idle, idly, open, save **5** clear, extra, let go, loose, rid of, spare **6** daring, devoid, exempt, giving, gratis, lavish, parole, ransom, redeem, unbond, uncage, wanton **7** allowed, assured, forward, liberal, loosely, manumit, release, un-

chain, unleash **8** at no cost, careless, costless, devoid of, familiar, fearless, generous, handsome, immune to, informal, let loose, liberate, prodigal, released, unfasten **9** abandoned, audacious, available, boundless, bounteous, bountiful, confident, delivered, discharge, disengage, dissolute, expansive, extricate, footloose, lacking in, leisurely, liberated, permitted, unblocked, unbridled, unchained, unclogged, unimpeded, unmuzzled, unshackle **10** autonomous, bighearted, carelessly, chargeless, emancipate, gratuitous, licentious, manumitted, munificent, openhanded, unattached, unconfined, unfettered, unhampered, unoccupied, unreserved, unshackled **11** emancipated, enfranchise, independent, uncluttered, uncommitted, uninhibited, unrepressed **12** enfranchised, overfamiliar, uncontrolled, unencumbered, unobstructed, unrestrained **13** complimentary, unceremonious, unconstrained

free-and-easy 6 breezy, casual, jaunty **7** buoyant, relaxed **8** debonair, informal **12** lighthearted, presumptuous, unrestrained **13** unconstrained

freed 6 exempt, loosed, spared **7** cleared, excused **8** absolved, let loose, released, relieved **11** emancipated

freedom 4 play **5** range, scope, sweep, swing **6** candor, margin **7** abandon, license, release **8** autonomy, boldness, latitude, openness, rudeness **9** bluntness, frankness, impudence, indecorum **10** directness, disrespect, liberation **11** abandonment, forwardness, impropriety, inormality, manumission, naturalness, sovereignty, unrestraint **12** emancipation, impertinence, unconstraint **13** downrightness **14** unreservedness **15** enfranchisement

Freedom of the Poet, The
   author: **12** John Berryman

free-flowing 7 copious, gushing, profuse **8** effusive

free-for-all 3 row **4** fray **5** brawl, fight, melee, scrap **6** affray, fracas, ruckus, tussle **7** rhubarb, ruction, wrangle **9** brannigan **10** donnybrook

free from bias 7 neutral **9** impartial, unbigoted **12** unprejudiced **13** disinterested

free from moisture 3 dry **4** arid, sere **5** parch **6** dry out **7** parched **8** dried out, rainless **9** dehydrate **10** dehydrated, desertlike, desiccated

free hand 12 carte blanche, open sanc-tion **13** full authority

free rein 12 carte blanche, open sanction **13** full authority

free-spoken 6 chatty **7** voluble **9** talkative **10** loquacious, unreserved **13** communicative

Free State
   nickname of: **8** Maryland

Freestone State
   nickname of: **11** Connecticut

Free to Choose
   author: **14** Milton Friedman (with Rose Friedman)

Freetown
   capital of: **11** Sierra Leone

freeze 3 nip **4** bite, cool, halt, stop **5** chill, frost, sting **6** arrest, benumb, harden, pierce **7** ceiling, congeal, terrify **8** glaci-ate, solidify **11** anesthetize, refrigerate, restriction

freezing 3 icy **6** arctic, frigid **7** glacial

Frege, Gottlieb
   field: **11** mathematics
   nationality: **6** German
   founded: **13** symbolic logic

Freia see **5** Freya

freight 4 haul, lade, load, ship **5** cargo, carry, goods **6** burden, charge, convey, lading **7** baggage, cartage, luggage, portage **8** transmit, truckage **9** transport **10** conveyance **13** transshipment

Freischutz, Der
   also: **11** The Marksman
   opera by: **5** Weber
   character: **3** Max **6** Agathe, Caspar, Samiel

Freki
   origin: **12** Scandinavian
   form: **4** wolf
   owner: **4** Odin **5** Othin
   received: **4** food
   exception: **4** meat
   fellow wolf: **4** Geri

French, Daniel Chester
   born: **8** Exeter NH
   artwork: **7** (seated) Lincoln (at Lincoln Memorial) **21** The Minute Man of Concord

French-American
   French: **9** Franglais

French civil code 12 Code Napoleon

French Connection, The
   director: **15** William Friedkin
   cast: **11** Fernando Rey, Gene Hackman (Popeye Doyle), Roy Scheider
   Oscar for: **5** actor (Hackman) **7** editing, picture **8** director **10** screenplay
   sequel: **21** The French Connection II

French-English
   French: **9** Franglais

French Guinea see **6** Guinea

French Indonesia see **7** Vietnam

French is spoken here
   French: **18** ici on parle francais

French Lieutenant's Woman, The
   director: **10** Karel Reisz
   author: **10** John Fowles
   cast: **9** Leo McKern **11** Hilton McRae, Jeremy Irons, Meryl Streep
   script: **12** Harold Pinter

French national anthem 12 Marseillaise

French national theater 16 Comedie Francaise

French parliament
   formal sessions: **12** lit de justice

French Somaliland see **8** Djibouti

French Sudan, Soudan see **4** Mali

French Togoland see **4** Togo

frenzied 3 mad **4** wild **7** excited, frantic, furious **8** agitated, ecstatic **9** delirious

frenzy 3 fit **4** fury **5** craze, furor, mania, state **6** access **7** mad rush, madness, seizure, turmoil **8** delirium, hysteria, outburst **9** obsession, transport **11** distraction

Frenzy
   director: **15** Alfred Hitchcock
   cast: **8** Jon Finch **10** Anna Massey **11** Barry Foster **16** Barbara Leigh-Hunt

frequency 9 iteration **10** recurrence, regularity, repetition **11** persistence, reiteration

frequent 5 daily, haunt, usual **6** common, wonted **7** regular **8** constant, everyday, familiar, habitual, numerous, ordinary, resort to **9** continual, customary, incessant, perpetual, recurrent **10** accustomed **11** reiterative

frequently 5 often **7** usually **8** ofttimes **9** generally **10** constantly, habitually, ordinarily, repeatedly **11** continually, customarily, incessantly, perpetually, recurrently

frere 4 monk **5** friar **7** brother

Frescobaldi, Girolamo
   born: **5** Italy **7** Ferrara
   composer of: **13** Fiori Musicali **14** Musical Flowers

fresh 3 fit, hot, new **4** bold, cool, fair, keen, late, pert, pure, rare, rosy, rude **5** alert, brisk, chill, clear, green, nervy, novel, ready, ruddy, sassy, saucy, stiff, sweet **6** active, biting, brassy, brazen, bright, cheeky, lively, modern, recent, rested, snotty, unique, unused, unworn **7** bracing, cutting, forward, glowing, just out, nipping, strange, uncured, undried, unfaded, untried, unusual **8** assuming, blooming, brand-new, creative, flippant, gleaming, impudent, insolent, original, stinging, unabated, undimmed, unsalted, unsmoked, unwilted, up-to-date **9** energetic, inventive, obtrusive, refreshed, sparkling, undecayed, unpickled, unspoiled, unwearied, wholesome **10** meddlesome, new-fangled, refreshing, unfamiliar, unimpaired, unwithered **11** flourishing, invigorated, modernistic, smartalecky, untarnished **12** presumptuous, unaccustomed

freshen 4 wash **5** brace, calve, clean, groom, renew **6** air out, breeze, desalt, revive **7** cool off, sweeten **8** renovate, spruce up **9** deodorize

freshet 5 crest, flood **11** overflowing

Freshman, The
  director: **9** Sam Taylor **12** Fred Newmeyer
  cast: **11** Harold Lloyd **13** Jobyna Ralston **14** Brooks Benedict

Fresnel, Augustin Jean
  field: **7** physics
  nationality: **6** French
  worked in: **6** optics

fret 3 eat, rub, vex **4** fray, fume, gall, gnaw, mope, pine, pout, stew, sulk **5** brood, chafe, erode, sulks, worry **6** abrade, lament, ruffle, tatter **7** agonize, corrode, fidgets **8** disquiet, distress, irritate, vexation, wear away **9** annoyance, excoriate **10** irritation **11** displeasure, peevishness **12** discomposure

fretful 5 cross, huffy, sulky, tense **6** cranky, shirty, touchy **7** grouchy, nervous, peevish, pettish, waspish **8** contrary, petulant, snappish **9** crotchety, irritable, querulous **11** complaining **12** cantankerous

fretfulness 5 worry **6** unease **7** anxiety **10** crankiness **11** peevishness **12** irritability

Freud, Sigmund
  lived in: **6** Vienna
  collaborator: **6** Breuer
  disciple: **4** Jung **5** Adler
  daughter: **4** Anna
  method: **15** free association **19** dream interpretation
  coined: **2** id **8** superego **14** psychoanalysis
  author of: **13** Totem and Taboo **22** Interpretation of Dreams **37** Group Psychology and the Analysis of the Ego, Jokes and Their Relation to the Unconscious

Freund, John Lincoln
  real name of: **12** John Forsythe

Frey
  also: **5** Freyr
  origin: **12** Scandinavian
  god of: **5** peace **8** marriage **10** prosperity
  race: **5** Vanir
  father: **5** Niord, Njord
  home: **7** Alfheim

Freya
  also: **5** Freia
  origin: **8** Teutonic
  goddess of: **4** love **6** beauty **9** fecundity
  race: **5** Vanir
  leader of: **9** Valkyries
  father: **5** Niord, Njord

Fri *see* **5** Frigg

friable 7 crumbly **9** breakable, frangible

friar
  French: **5** frere

Friar Lawrence
  character in: **14** Romeo and Juliet
  author: **11** Shakespeare

Friar Tuck
  character in: **9** Robin Hood

friary 5 abbey **6** priory **8** cloister **9** hermitage, monastery

friction 6 strife **7** chafing, discord, grating, quarrel, rubbing **8** abrasion, bad blood, conflict, fretting **9** animosity, attrition, hostility **10** antagonism, contention, dissension, dissidence, opposition, resentment, resistance **12** disagreement **13** counteraction

Friday
  character in: **14** Robinson Crusoe
  author: **5** Defoe

Friday
  from: **5** Freya, Frigg
  heavenly body: **5** Venus
  French: **8** vendredi
  Italian: **7** venerdi
  Spanish: **7** viernes
  German: **7** freitag

Friedan, Betty
  author of: **19** The Feminine Mystique
  co-founder of: **3** NOW **28** National Organization for Women

Friedkin, William
  director of: **11** The Exorcist **19** The French Connection (Oscar)

Friedman, Milton
  author of: **12** Free to Choose (with Rose Friedman) **20** Capitalism and Freedom

Friedrich, Caspar David
  born: **7** Germany **10** Greifswald
  artwork: **22** The Cross on the Mountains **26** Man and Woman Gazing at the Moon, The Ruined Monastery of Eldena, Two Men Contemplating the Moon

friend 3 pal **4** ally, beau, chum, date, mate **5** amigo, buddy, crony, lover **6** backer, cohort, escort, fellow, intime, minion, patron **7** brother, comrade, consort, partner **8** adherent, advocate, confrere, co-worker, defender, favorite, follower, henchman, intimate, mistress, myrmidon, paramour, partisan, playmate, retainer, sidekick, soul mate **9** associate, bedfellow, colleague, companion, confidant, copartner, supporter **10** benefactor, encourager, playfellow, well-wisher **12** acquaintance
  French: **3** ami **4** amie **9** bonne amie
  Spanish: **5** amiga, amigo

friendliness 5 amity **8** bonhomie, good will **9** geniality **10** affability, amiability, cordiality, fraternity **11** amicability, camaraderie, sociability **14** neighborliness **16** companionability

friendly 4 kind **6** allied, ardent, benign, chummy, clubby, genial, kindly, loving, social **7** affable, amiable, cordial, devoted, helpful **8** amicable, fa-

miliar, generous, gracious, intimate, salutary **9** brotherly, convivial, favorable, fortunate, fraternal, opportune **10** accessible, auspicious, beneficial, hospitable, neighborly, not hostile, propitious **11** kindhearted, sympathetic, warmhearted **12** advantageous, affectionate **13** companionable

Friendly, Fred W
  president of: **7** CBS News
  collaborator: **13** Edward R. Murrow
  show: **8** See It Now

Friendly Fire
  author: **8** C D B Bryan

Friendly Islands *see* **5** Tongo

friendly understanding
  French: **15** entente cordiale

friend of the court
  Latin: **12** amicus curiae

Friends
  network: **3** NBC
  cast: **10** Lisa Kudrow **11** Matt LeBlanc **12** Courteney Cox, Matthew Perry **14** David Schwimmer **15** Jennifer Aniston
  characters: **10** Ross Geller **11** Rachel Green **12** Chandler Bing, Phoebe Buffay, Monica Geller **13** Joey Tribbiani

friendship 5 amity **6** accord, comity **7** concord, harmony **8** close tie, goodwill, intimacy, sympathy **10** consonance, cordiality, fellowship, fraternity **11** brotherhood, comradeship, familiarity **12** amicableness **13** companionship, understanding **14** neighborliness **16** acquaintanceship

Frigg
  also: **3** Fri **5** Frija **6** Frigga
  origin: **8** Teutonic
  goddess of: **3** sky **6** clouds **8** marriage
  husband: **4** Odin **5** Othin
  race: **4** Asar **5** Aesir

Frigga *see* **5** Frigg

fright 4 fear, funk **5** alarm, dread, panic, scare **6** dismay, horror, terror, tremor **7** anxiety, concern, flutter, quaking **8** cold feet **9** misgiving, quivering, the creeps **10** the jitters, the willies **11** disquietude, palpitation, trepidation **12** apprehension, intimidation, perturbation **13** consternation

frighten 5 alarm, daunt, scare, shock **6** affray, excite **7** agitate, horrify, petrify, startle, terrify **8** disquiet **9** terrorize **10** intimidate

frightened 6 afraid, scared **7** alarmed, panicky **9** horrified, petrified, terrified **10** terrorized

frightening 5 awful, dread **7** fearful **8** alarming, dreadful **10** horrifying, terrifying **11** hair-raising

frightful 5 awful, lurid, nasty **6** grisly, horrid **7** baleful, extreme, fearful, ghastly, hideous, macabre, ogreish **8** alarming, dreadful, fearsome, freakish, gruesome, horrible, horrific, shocking, sinister, terrible, terrific **9** appalling, loathsome, monstrous, offensive, repellent, repulsive, revolting **10** abominable, detestable, disgusting, horrendous **12** insufferable

frigid 3 icy, raw **4** cold, cool, prim **5** aloof, bleak, gelid, stiff **6** biting, bitter, chilly, formal, frosty **7** austere, cutting, distant, glacial, nipping **8** freezing, piercing **10** forbidding **11** straitlaced **12** unresponsive

frigidity 7 iciness **8** coldness **9** aloofness **10** frostiness **16** unresponsiveness

Frija *see* **5** Frigg

frill 3 air **5** extra **6** edging, fringe, ruffle **7** flounce **8** falderal, frippery, furbelow, ornament **9** gathering, mannerism **10** decoration **11** affectation, superfluity **13** embellishment

fringe 3 hem, rim **4** edge, mane **5** limit, skirt **6** border, edging, margin, tassel **7** enclose, outline, selvage **8** decorate, frontier, skirting, surround, trimming **9** embellish, periphery

frisk 3 hop **4** jump, lark, leap, romp, skip, trip **5** bound, caper, cut up, dance, sport **6** bounce, cavort, frolic, gambol, prance, search, spring **7** disport, examine, inspect, ransack **8** look over

frisky 4 spry **5** agile, peppy **6** active, lively, nimble **7** jocular, playful, waggish **8** animated, mirthful, prankish, spirited, sportive **9** vivacious **10** frolicsome, rollicking

fritter 4 blow **5** use up, waste **7** deplete, pancake **8** fool away, idle away, squander **9** dissipate

fritter away 4 blow **5** waste **6** misuse **8** misspend, squander **9** dissipate

fritter away time 4 idle **6** dawdle **10** dillydally

Fritzi Ritz
  aunt to: 5 Nancy
  creator: 15 Ernie Bushmiller **16** Larry Whittington
  character: 4 Phil **5** Nancy, Rollo **6** Sluggo

frivolity 3 fun **4** jest, play **5** folly, sport **6** levity, whimsy **7** abandon **8** airiness, dallying, frippery **9** emptiness, flippancy, giddiness, lightness **10** fickleness, triviality, wantonness **11** flightiness **15** thoughtlessness

frivolous 4 airy, vain **5** barmy, dizzy, emp- ty, inane, light, minor, petty, silly **6** flimsy, frothy, paltry, slight, stupid **7** fatuous, flighty, foolish, trivial, witless **8** careless, flippant, heedless, niggling, piddling, trifling **9** brainless, imprudent, pointless, senseless, unserious, worthless **10** insouciant **11** extravagant, harebrained, impractical, improvident, nonsensical,

superficial, unimportant **13** insignificant, rattlebrained **14** shallowbrained

frizzle 4 curl **5** crimp

frock 4 coat, gown, robe, suit **5** cloak, dress, smock **6** blouse **7** cassock, soutane **8** chasuble, surplice, vestment **9** clericals **10** canonicals

frog 3 pad, pod **4** knot, wood **5** frosh, hitch, track **6** holder, peeper, toggle **7** crawler, croaker, cushion, leopard, tadpole **8** bullfrog, fastener, pickerel, pollywog **9** amphibian, plow frame **12** flower holder

Frogs, The
  author: 12 Aristophanes
  character: 5 Pluto **6** Charon **7** Bacchus **8** Dionysus, Hercules, Xanthias **9** Aeschylus, Euripides

Froissart, Jean
  author of: 8 Meliador **10** Chronicles

frolic 3 fun **4** lark, play, romp, skip **5** act up, antic, caper, frisk, mirth, prank, sport, spree **6** cavort, gaiety, gambol **7** disport, jollity, make hay **8** escapade **9** amusement, festivity, joviality, merriment **10** buffoonery, pleasantry, recreation, skylarking, tomfoolery **11** merrymaking **13** entertainment

frolicsome 5 antic, jolly, merry **6** cheery, jaunty, lively **7** playful **8** cheerful, mirthful, prankish **9** sprightly **12** lighthearted

Frollo, Claude
  character in: 23 The Hunchback of Notre Dame
  author: 4 Hugo

from 2 de, ex, of **3** for, fro **5** off of, out of **7** against **8** starting **9** beginning

from abroad 5 alien **6** exotic **7** foreign **8** imported

fromage 6 cheese

from behind
  Latin: 6 a tergo

From Here to Eternity
  director: 13 Fred Zinnemann
  author: 10 James Jones
  cast: 9 Donna Reed **11** Deborah Kerr **12** Frank Sinatra, George Reeves **13** Burt Lancaster **14** Ernest Borgnine **15** Montgomery Clift
  setting: 11 Pearl Harbor
  Oscar for: 7 picture **8** director **12** screenwriter **15** supporting actor (Sinatra) **17** supporting actress (Reed)

from inside
  Latin: 7 ab intra

from outside
  Latin: 7 ab extra

From Russia With Love
  author: 10 Ian Fleming

from scratch 4 anew **14** from ground zero **16** from the beginning **20** from fresh ingredients

from side to side 4 over, sway **5**

cross **7** athwart, swaying, zigzag **12** back and forth

from the beginning
  Latin: 5 ab ovo **6** de novo **8** ab initio

from the chair
  Latin: 10 ex cathedra

from the depths
  Latin: 11 de profundis

from the face
  Latin: 7 ex facie

from the fact
  Latin: 7 de facto

from the founding of the city
  Latin: 13 ab urbe condita

from the library of
  Latin: 8 ex libris

from the seat of authority
  Latin: 10 ex cathedra

front 3 air, top **4** face, fore, head, lead, mask, mien **5** first **6** facade, give on, regard **7** bearing, initial, look out **8** anterior, carriage, demeanor, presence, pretense, trenches, vanguard **9** beginning, semblance

Front, The
  director: 10 Martin Ritt
  cast: 10 Lloyd Gough, Woody Allen, Zero Mostel **13** Joshua Shelley, Michael Murphy **16** Herschel Bernardi

frontage 7 outlook **8** exposure, prospect

frontier 4 edge **5** march, verge **6** border, limits **7** extreme, marches **8** boundary, confines, outposts **9** backlands, backwoods, outskirts, perimeter **10** hinterland **11** territories

front matter 8 foreword **9** title page **12** introduction **15** table of contents **20** introductory material

Front Page, The
  author: 8 Ben Hecht **16** Charles MacArthur
  director: 11 Billy Wilder **14** Lewis Milestone
  actor: 9 Mae Clarke, Mary Brian, Pat O'Brien **10** Jack Lemmon, David Wayne **12** George E Stone, Carol Burnett **13** Adolphe Menjou, Allen Garfield, Susan Sarandon, Walter Catlett, Walter Matthau **14** Charles Durning **15** Andrew Pendleton, Vincent Gardenia **19** Edward Everett Horton
  character: 4 Earl **5** Burns, Grant, Hildy, Peggy **6** Walter **7** Hartman, Johnson **8** Williams

frost 4 rime **5** chill **7** iciness **8** coolness, distance **9** aloofness, cold spell, frigidity **10** chilliness, glaciality **13** inhospitality **14** unfriendliness

Frost, Robert
  author of: 7 Birches **10** Fire and Ice, Home Burial **11** Mending Wall **13** Brown's Descent **15** The Road Not Taken **17** After Apple-Picking **21** The

Death of the Hired Man **30** Stopping by Woods on a Snowy Evening

frostiness 3 nip **4** bite **5** chill **7** iciness **8** coldness, coolness **9** crispness, frigidity, hoariness, sharpness **10** chilliness, wintriness

frosting 3 mat **4** trim **5** glass, icing **7** cooling, topping **8** chilling, divinity, freezing, trimming **13** embellishment, ornamentation

frosty 3 icy **4** cold, cool **5** bleak, chill, hoary **6** frigid, wintry **8** freezing

froth 4 bosh, fizz, foam, fume, head, scum, suds, surf **5** spume, trash, yeast **6** lather, trivia **7** bubbles, rubbish **8** flummery, frippery, nonsense, trumpery, whitecap **9** frivolity **10** balderdash, triviality **12** fiddle-faddle

frothy 5 fizzy, foamy, light **6** bubbly **7** trivial **9** frivolous **15** inconsequential

froward 5 balky **6** unruly **7** wayward, willful **8** contrary, perverse, stubborn **9** difficult, fractious, obstinate **10** headstrong, refractory **11** disagreeing, intractable **12** recalcitrant **13** contradictory **15** unaccommodating

frown 4 fret, mope, muse, pout, sulk **5** glare, scowl **6** glower, ponder **14** discountenance

frowning 4 dark **5** angry **6** gloomy, somber, sullen **8** scowling **9** glowering

frown upon 7 condemn, dislike **8** object to **14** discountenance

frowsy, frowzy 5 fusty, musty, stale **6** sloppy, untidy **7** tousled, unkempt **8** slovenly

frozen 3 icy **4** cold, iced, numb **5** chill, gelid, polar **6** arctic, chilly, cooled, wintry **7** chilled, clogged, glacial, stymied **8** benumbed, hibernal, icebound **10** obstructed, stalemated **11** frostbitten, immobilized **12** refrigerated

fructify 5 bloom **6** sprout, thrive **7** blossom, prosper, succeed **8** flourish

frugal 4 slim **5** scant, tight **6** skimpy, stingy **7** ascetic, sparing, thrifty **9** niggardly, penny-wise **10** abstemious, economical, unwasteful **12** parsimonious

frugality 6 thrift **7** economy **8** prudence, stinting **9** parsimony **10** scantiness, stinginess **11** thriftiness **12** cheeseparing **13** niggardliness, pennypinching **16** parsimoniousness

fruit 4 crop **5** award, issue, yield, young **6** effect, profit, result, return, reward, upshot **7** benefit, harvest, outcome, produce, product, progeny, revenue **8** earnings **9** advantage, emolument, offspring, outgrowth **10** production **11** consequence **12** remuneration

fruitful 6 fecund **7** fertile **8** blooming, prolific, yielding **9** effective **10** pro-

ductive, profitable, successful **11** efficacious **12** advantageous, fructiferous

fruition 8 maturity, ripeness **10** attainment **11** achievement, fulfillment, realization **12** consummation, satisfaction **13** actualization, gratification **15** materialization

fruitless 4 arid, vain **5** empty, inept **6** barren, futile, hollow **7** sterile, useless **8** abortive, bootless, nugatory **9** infertile, pointless, worthless **10** profitless, unavailing, unprolific **11** incompetent, ineffective, ineffectual, inoperative, purposeless, unrewarding **12** unproductive, unprofitable, unsuccessful **13** inefficacious

fruit trees
  goddess of: 6 Pomona

frumpy 4 drab **5** dowdy **8** slovenly **10** slatternly **12** unattractive

frustrate 3 bar **4** balk, foil **5** block, check, upset **6** baffle, cancel, defeat, hinder, impede, thwart **7** counter, cripple, fluster, inhibit, nullify, prevent **8** dispirit, obstruct, prohibit, suppress **9** forestall, hamstring, undermine **10** circumvent, disappoint, disconcert, discourage, dishearten

frustration 6 defeat **7** balking, chagrin, failure, foiling, letdown **8** futility **9** hindrance, thwarting **10** bafflement, inhibition, nonsuccess **11** obstruction **12** discomfiture, interference **13** contravention, counteraction **14** disappointment, nonfulfillment **15** dissatisfaction

fry 4 cook **5** brown, grill, saute **7** frizzle **9** fricassee

fry 4 fish **5** child, young **8** children, small fry

Fry, Christopher
  author of: 9 Yard of Sun **12** The Firstborn **13** Venus Observed **20** The Dark Is Light Enough **21** The Lady's Not for Burning

frying pan 3 wok **6** frypan **7** browner, griddle, skillet

fuchsia
  varieties: 4 cape, tree **5** hardy **10** California **11** honeysuckle

fuddled 5 bosky, dopey, drunk, tipsy **6** boozed, groggy **7** maudlin, muddled, sozzled, tippled **8** confused **9** stupefied **10** inebriated **11** intoxicated

fudge 3 lie **4** bosh, fake **5** candy, cheat, evade, hedge, hunch, patch, welch **7** falsify, penuche **8** divinity

fuel 3 fan, gas, oil **4** coal, feed, fire, wood **5** light, means, stoke **6** charge, fill up, fodder, ignite, incite, kindle **7** impetus, inflame, sustain **8** activate, energize, gasoline, material, recharge, stimulus **9** petroleum, stimulate **10** ammunition, motivation, sustenance **11** inspiration, wherewithal

fugitive 4 hobo **5** brief, exile, hasty,

nomad, rover, short, tramp **6** errant, fading, flying, loafer, outlaw **7** cursory, elusive, erratic, escaped, escapee, fleeing, hurried, passing, refugee, runaway, summary, vagrant **8** apostate, deserter, escaping, fleeting, flitting, renegade, shifting, unstable, vagabond, volatile, wanderer **9** ephemeral, fugacious, itinerant, momentary, straggler, temporary, transient, uncertain **10** evanescent, expatriate, short-lived, transitory **11** impermanent

Fugitive, The
  character: 9 Donna Taft **11** Fred Johnson (one-armed man) **12** (Lt) Philip Gerard **13** (Dr) Richard Kimble
  cast: 10 Barry Morse, Bill Raisch **12** David Janssen **15** Jacqueline Scott

fuhrer, Fuhrer, der fuhrer 4 Nazi **6** Hitler, leader, tyrant **8** dictator **11** Adolf Hitler

fulfill 2 do **4** heed, keep, meet, obey, suit **6** answer, effect, follow, redeem **7** achieve, execute, observe, perfect, perform, realize, satisfy **9** discharge, establish, implement **10** accomplish, consummate, effectuate

fulfillment, fulfilment 7 delight **8** crowning, pinnacle, pleasure **9** execution, happiness **10** attainment, completion **11** achievement, contentment, culmination, realization **12** effectuation, satisfaction **13** contentedness, establishment, gratification **14** accomplishment, implementation

Fulks, Sarah Jane
  real name of: 9 Jane Wyman

full 3 big **4** rich, very, wide **5** ample, broad, flush, laden, large, plump, quite, round, sated, total, whole **6** entire, gorged, in- tact, loaded, mature, packed, rotund **7** brimful, crammed, exactly, fraught, glutted, heaping, maximum, perfect, plenary, replete, shapely, stuffed, teeming **8** brimming, bursting, complete, resonant, swarming, thorough **9** abounding, capacious, perfectly, precisely, saturated, surfeited **10** unabridged, voluminous

full amount 3 all, sum **5** total, whole **8** entirety, totality **9** aggregate **10** complement

full-bodied 3 fat **4** rich **5** ample, lofty **6** hearty, mature, robust **9** flavorful **10** meaningful

Fuller, R Buckminster
  architect of: 10 US Pavilion (Expo '67 Montreal) **13** Dymaxion House
  form: 12 geodesic dome

full-fledged 5 adept **6** expert, mature **7** skilled, trained **8** complete, masterly, schooled **9** qualified, topflight **10** proficient **11** experienced **13** authoritative

full form 9 extension **10** elongation **11**

enlargement **12** augmentation **13** amplification

full-grown 4 ripe **5** adult, manly, of age, matured, womanly **9** developed

full measure 6 enough, plenty **9** abundance, plenitude **10** competence **11** sufficiency

Full Moon
author: 11 P G Wodehouse

fullness 7 satiety **8** richness **9** amplitude, roundness, satiation **12** completeness **14** voluminousness

full of fire 7 rousing **8** electric, exciting, spirited **9** thrilling **11** galvanizing, stimulating **12** electrifying, soul-stirring

full of life 5 vital **8** animated, spirited, vigorous **9** ebullient, energetic, exuberant, vivacious

full of pep 5 vital **6** lively **8** animated

full of vim and vigor 5 peppy **6** lively **11** invigorated

full view 7 the open **8** daylight, openness

fully 5 amply, quite **6** richly, wholly **7** totally, utterly **8** entirely **9** copiously, perfectly **10** abundantly, altogether, completely, positively, throughout **11** plentifully **12** sufficiently **13** substantially

fully realized 7 perfect **8** achieved, complete, executed, finished **9** completed, perfected, performed **11** consummated **12** accomplished

fulminate 4 boil, rage, rant **7** explode **8** denounce

fulminate against 5 roast **6** berate **7** scourge **8** call down, chastise **9** castigate

fulmination 7 violent **8** bursting, eruption **9** discharge, explosion

fulsome 3 fat **4** foul **5** suave **6** lavish, odious **7** cloying, lustful, noisome, obscene **8** overdone, unctuous **9** excessive, obnoxious, offensive, repulsive, tasteless **10** disgusting, obsequious

Fulton, Robert
nationality: 8 American
inventor of: 9 steamboat (Clermont), submarine **12** Fulton's folly **13** marine torpedo

fumble 3 err, mar **4** blow, muff **5** grope, spoil **6** bobble, boggle, bollix, bungle, goof up, mess up, muddle **7** butcher, louse up, screw up **9** mishandle

fume 3 gas **4** boil, burn, emit, foam, haze, puff, rage, rant, rave, reek, waft **5** exude, scent, smell, smoke, stink, vapor **6** bil-low, exhale, miasma, seethe, stench **7** carry on, explode, flame up, flare up, smolder **10** exhalation

fun 3 gas **4** ball, game, jest, lark, play, romp, trip **5** antic, blast, cheer, mirth, prank, sport, spree **6** frolic, gaiety,

joking **7** jollity, revelry, whoopee **8** escapade, good time, pleasure **9** amusement, diversion, enjoyment, horseplay, joviality, merriment **10** buffoonery, recreation, relaxation, skylarking, tomfoolery **11** distraction, playfulness, waggishness **13** entertainment

Funafuti
capital of: 6 Tuvalu

function 3 act, job **4** duty, fete, gala, help, role, task, work **5** feast, field, niche, party, place, power, range, scope, serve **6** affair, behave, do duty, office, soiree, sphere **7** banquet, benefit, concern, faculty, operate, perform, purpose **8** activity, business, capacity, ceremony, occasion, province **9** festivity, objective, operation, reception **13** entertainment

functional 6 useful **7** working **8** operable **9** operative, practical **11** serviceable, utilitarian

functionary 8 employee, official **10** bureaucrat **13** administrator

functioning 5 in use **6** active, at work, usable **7** working **9** effectual, operating, operative

fund 3 pot **4** bank, foot, lode, mine, pool, vein, well **5** endow, float, fount, hoard, kitty, stock, store **6** pay for, spring, supply **7** finance, nest egg, reserve, savings, support **8** treasure **9** endowment, patronize, reservoir **10** foundation, investment, repository, storehouse, underwrite **12** accumulation

fundament 3 can **4** buns, rump, seat **5** fanny **6** behind, bottom **8** backside, buttocks, haunches **9** posterior **12** hindquarters

fundamental 3 key **4** ABC's, base, main **5** axiom, basic, basis, chief, first, major, vital **7** central, crucial, element, primary **8** cardinal, integral **9** component, essential, necessary, principal, principle, requisite **10** elementary, foundation, groundwork, underlying **11** cornerstone **13** indispensable

funds 4 cash, jack, pelf **5** bread, dough, lucre, means, money, moola **6** assets, income, wampum, wealth **7** capital, scratch **8** finances, property **9** resources **11** wherewithal

funeral 4 wake **5** rites **6** burial **7** requiem **9** cremation, interment, obsequies **10** entombment, inhumation

funeral song 5 dirge, elegy **6** lament **7** requiem **8** threnody **11** lamentation

funereal 3 sad **4** grim **5** weepy **6** dismal, dreary, gloomy, solemn, somber, woeful **7** doleful **8** desolate, dirgeful, grieving, mournful **9** cheerless, woebegone **10** depressing, lachrymose, lugubrious **13** brokenhearted

fun-filled 5 happy **6** joyful, joyous **8**

pleasant, pleasing **9** enjoyable **10** delightful **11** pleasurable

Fungoso
character in: 22 Every Man Out of His Humour
author: 6 Jonson

fungus, fungi 4 mold, myco, rust, smut **5** ergot, yeast **6** mildew **7** truffle **8** mushroom **9** toadstool **11** thallophyte

fun-loving 5 jolly, merry **6** genial, jovial **7** affable **8** sociable **9** convivial **10** gregarious

funnel 4 cone, duct, flue, pipe, pour **5** focus, shaft **6** direct, filter, siphon **7** channel, chimney, conduit **9** stovepipe **10** smokestack, ventilator **11** concentrate

funny 3 odd **5** antic, comic, droll, merry, queer, weird, witty **6** absurd, jocose **7** amusing, bizarre, comical, curious, jesting, jocular, offbeat, strange, unusual, waggish **8** farcical, humorous, mirthful, peculiar, sporting, uncommon **9** diverting, facetious, hilarious, laughable, ludicrous **10** outlandish, ridiculous

Funny Girl
director: 12 William Wyler
cast: 8 Lee Allen **10** Kay Medford, Omar Sharif **11** Anne Francis **13** Walter Pidgeon **15** Barbra Streisand (Fanny Brice)
score: 9 Jule Styne **10** Bob Merrill
sequel: 9 Funny Lady
song: 6 People **18** Don't Rain on My Parade

funnyman 3 wag, wit **4** card, fool, mime, zany **5** clown, comic, joker **6** jester, madcap **7** buffoon **8** comedian, humorist, jokester **9** harlequin

fuoco, con
music: 8 with fire

fur 3 fox **4** down, hair, lamb, mink, pelt, seal **5** coney, lapin, otter, sable **6** beaver, fleece, jaguar, kit fox, nutria, rabbit, red fox **7** blue fox, cheetah, leopard, muskrat, opossum, raccoon **8** black fox, cross fox, squirrel, white fox **9** silver fox **10** animal skin, chinchilla **11** karakul lamb, Persian lamb **13** broadtail lamb **14** mouton-dyed lamb

furbelow 5 frill **6** fringe **7** falbala, flounce **8** trimming

furbish 4 buff **5** renew, shine **6** polish **7** burnish **8** renovate

Furiae *see* **6** Furies

Furies
5 Dirae **6** Erinys, Furiae, Semnai **7** Alecto, Erinyes, Megaera **9** Eumenides, Tisiphone
form: 7 spirits
sex: 6 female
mother: 4 Gaea
father: 6 Uranus
born of the blood of: 6 Uranus

Greek name: 6 Erinys **7** Erinyes **9** Eumenides

Roman name: 5 Dirae **6** Furiae

furious 3 mad **4** wild **5** angry, fiery, irate, rabid **6** enrage, fierce, fuming, raging, savage, stormy **7** intense, rampant, violent **8** frenetic, frenzied, heedless, maddened, provoked, reckless, up in arms, vehement, wrathful **9** fanatical, irascible, turbulent **10** infuriated, passionate, tumultuous, unbalanced **11** tempestuous **12** ungovernable, unrestrained

furl 4 coil, curl, fold, roll, wrap **5** truss **6** curl up, fold up, furdle, roll up, spiral

furlong
   abbreviation: 3 fur

furnace 4 kiln, oven **5** forge, stove **6** boiler, heater **11** incinerator

Furnace
   constellation of: 6 Fornax

furnish 3 arm, rig **4** gird, give, vest **5** array, dress, endow, equip, favor, fit up, grant, stock **6** fit out, outfit, purvey, render, supply **7** appoint, indulge, prepare, provide **8** accoutre, bestow on, decorate **9** provision **11** accommodate

furnishings 5 decor **9** equipment **11** accessories **12** haberdashery

furnish room for 5 lodge, put up **6** billet **7** shelter **11** accommodate

furniture 7 effects **8** chattels, movables, property **11** possessions **12** appointments

furor 3 fad **4** flap, rage, to-do, word **5** craze, mania, noise, thing, vogue **6** fervor, frenzy, hoopla, lunacy, raving, uproar **7** fashion, madness, passion **8** brouhaha, insanity, reaction **9** agitation, commotion, obsession, transport **10** dernier cri, enthusiasm, excitement, fanaticism

furrow 3 cut, dig, rut **4** knit, line, plow, rift, seam **5** cleft, crack, ditch, ridge, track **6** crease, groove, pucker, trench, trough **7** channel, crevice, fissure, wrinkle **10** depression **11** corrugation

furry 4 soft **5** downy, hairy, scary **6** cuddly, fleecy, pelted, shaggy **8** fearsome, horrible **11** hair-raising

further 3 aid, new, too, yet **4** also, back, help, more **5** again, extra, favor, fresh, other, spare, speed **6** abroad, assist, back up, beyond, foster, hasten, oblige, to boot, yonder **7** advance, afar off, besides, farther, for-

ward, promote, quicken, stand by, work for **8** champion, expedite, likewise, moreover **9** accessory, ancillary, auxiliary, encourage, propagate **10** accelerate, additional, strengthen **11** accommodate **12** additionally, contributory, supplemental **13** supplementary

furtherance 3 aid **4** help, lift **5** favor **6** succor **7** advance, defense, support **8** advocacy, interest **9** patronage, promotion **10** assistance **11** advancement, cooperation, countenance **12** championship

furthering 3 aid **6** aiding, growth **8** abetting, advocacy, espousal **9** assisting, fostering, promoting, promotion **10** assistance, supporting **11** advancement, encouraging, propagating, propagation **12** accelerating, acceleration, encouragement **13** strengthening

furthermore 3 too **4** also **6** as well, to boot **7** besides **8** likewise, moreover **10** in addition **12** additionally

furthermost 7 extreme **8** farthest **11** farthermost

furtive 3 sly **4** wily **5** shady **6** covert, crafty, hidden, masked, secret, shifty, sneaky, unseen, veiled **7** cloaked, elusive, evasive, private **8** secluded, shrouded, skulking, sneaking, stealthy **9** collusive, secre-tive, underhand **10** mysterious, undercover, unrevealed **11** clandestine **12** confidential **13** surreptitious **14** conspiratorial

fury 3 fit, hag, ire, pet **4** gall, huff, rage, snit **5** force, might, shrew, vixen, wrath **6** attack, choler, frenzy, spleen, virago **7** assault, bluster, dudgeon, hellcat, tantrum **8** acerbity, acrimony, ferocity, outburst, severity, she-devil, spitfire, violence **9** intensity, termagant, vehemence, virulence **10** excitement, fierceness, turbulence **11** impetuosity

fuse 4 join, link, meld, melt, weld, wick **5** blend, merge, smelt, torch **6** league, mingle, solder **7** combine **8** coalesce, federate, ignition, solidify **9** associate, detonator **10** amalgamate, assimilate **11** confederate, consolidate, incorporate, intermingler

fusillade 4 hail, rain **5** salvo, spray **6** volley **7** barrage, battery **8** drumfire, enfilade **9** broadside, cannonade **11** bombardment

fusion 5 blend, union **6** league **7** combine, melding, melting, merging **8** alliance, blending, compound, smelting **9** coalition, synthesis **10** commixture,

dissolving, federation **11** association, coalescence, combination, commingling, confederacy, unification **12** amalgamation, intermix-ture, liquefaction **13** agglomeration, confederation

fuss 3 ado, nag **4** carp, fool, fret, fume, pomp, spat, stew, stir, tiff, to-do **5** annoy, cavil, labor, set-to, worry **6** bother, bustle, excite, fidget, flurry, hubbub, hustle, niggle, pester, pother, potter, putter, rattle, scurry, tinker **7** agitate, confuse, dispute, fluster, flutter, nitpick, quarrel, quibble, perturb, trouble, turmoil **8** ceremony **9** agitation, commotion, confusion **10** disconcert, hurly-burly, turbulence **11** disturbance, superfluity **12** perturbation **15** ceremoniousness

   Yiddish: 7 tzimmes

fuss over 6 dote on

fussy 4 busy **6** ornate **7** finical, finicky, nervous **8** bustling, critical, exacting **9** assiduous, cluttered, crotchety, demanding, squeamish **10** compulsive, fastidious, meticulous, nitpicking, oldmaidish, particular, scrupulous **11** painstaking, persnickety

fusty 5 moldy, musty, stale **6** foisty, rancid, stuffy **8** obsolete **9** out of date **10** malodorous **12** old fashioned

Futabatei, Shimei
   author of: 16 The Drifting (Floating) Cloud

futile 4 idle, vain **5** empty, petty **7** trivial, useless **8** abortive, bootless, nugatory, trifling **9** frivolous, fruitless, valueless, worthless **10** profitless, unavailing **11** ineffective, ineffectual, unimportant **12** unprofitable, unsuccessful **13** insignificant

future 4 hope **5** after, later **6** coming, lat-ter, morrow, offing, to come **7** by-and-by, ensuing, outlook **8** eventual, prospect, tomorrow, ultimate **9** following, hereafter, impending, projected **10** in prospect, subsequent, succeeding **11** anticipated, expectation, opportunity, prospective **12** anticipation

   Spanish: 6 manana

Future Shock
   author: 12 Alvin Toffler

fuzz 4 down, lint **5** fluff **6** police

fuzzy 3 dim **4** hazy **5** downy, foggy, linty, misty, murky, vague, wooly **6** fluffy, frizzy, woolly **7** blurred, obscure, shadowy, unclear **8** confused **9** pubescent **10** indefinite, indistinct

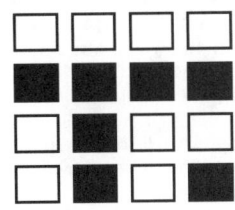

gab 3 jaw, rap, yak **4** blab, chat **5** prate **6** babble, gibber, gossip, jabber, patter **7** baloney, blarney, blather, chatter, prattle **8** chitchat, idle talk, talk idly **10** balderdash **12** conversation

gabble 3 rap **4** blab **5** prate **6** babble, drivel, gossip, jabber **7** blather, chatter, prattle, twaddle **8** babbling, chitchat, idle talk **9** gibbering, jabbering **10** blathering, chattering **14** chitter-chatter

gabfest 3 rap **4** chat, talk **7** palaver **8** chitchat **10** discussion **12** conversation **13** confabulation

gable 4 edge, peak, roof, wall **6** detail, dormer, pinion **7** aileron **8** pediment, triangle

Gable, Clark
real name: 17 William Clark Gable
wife: 13 Carole Lombard
nickname: 7 The King
born: 7 Cadiz OH
roles: 7 Red Dust **8** Saratoga **10** The Misfits **11** Rhett Butler **15** Gone With the Wind **18** It Happened One Night (Oscar)

Gabo, Naum
real name: 17 Naum Neemia Pevsner
born: 6 Russia **7** Brainsk
founder: 14 Constructivism
artwork: 6 Column **11** Spiral Theme **16** Sculptural Models **19** Kinetic Construction **24** Variations of Spheric Theme

Gabon Republic
capital/largest city: 10 Libreville
others: 4 Oyem **5** Bongo, Kango **6** Mitzic, Moanda, Mouila, Omvane **7** Makokou, Mounana **9** Lambarene **10** Port-Gentil **11** Franceville
monetary unit: 5 franc **7** centime
lake: 7 Anengue, Azinguo
mountain: 5 Mpele **7** Chaillu, Cristal, Mikongo **8** Balaquri, Birougou
highest point: 8 Iboundji
river: 4 Como **6** Abanga, Ivindo, Ogooue **7** Ngounie
sea: 8 Atlantic
physical feature:
    cape: 5 Lopez
people: 4 Fang **6** Adouma, Bakota, Bateke, Echira, Okande, Omyene **7** Eshiras **8** Bandjabi, Bapounou
    leader: 3 Mba **5** Bongo
philanthropist: 16 Albert

Schweitzer
language: 6 French
religion: 5 Islam **7** animism **10** Protestant **13** Roman Catholic
feature:
    tree: 6 okoume
food: 6 manioc **9** Dika bread

Gabor, Eva
mother: 5 Jolie
sister: 5 Magda **6** Zsa Zsa
born: 7 Hungary **8** Budapest
roles: 4 Gigi **10** Green Acres **12** My Man Godfrey **13** A Royal Scandal, Forced Landing **15** Youngblood Hawke **18** The Truth About Women **20** The Last Time I Saw Paris

Gabor, Zsa Zsa
real name: 9 Sari Gabor
mother: 5 Jolie
sister: 3 Eva **5** Magda
husband: 10 Nick Hilton **13** George Sanders
born: 7 Hungary **8** Budapest
roles: 4 Lili **11** Moulin Rouge **14** Lovely To Look At **20** The Story of Three Loves

Gaborone, Gaberones
capital of: 8 Botswana

Gabriel 9 archangel
means: 8 man of God **11** God is strong
spoke to: 4 Mary **9** Zacharias, Zechariah

Gad
father: 5 Jacob
mother: 6 Zilpah
brother: 3 Dan **4** Levi **5** Asher, Judah **6** Joseph, Reuben, Simeon **7** Zebulun **8** Benjamin, Issachar, Naphtali
sister: 5 Dinah
descendant of: 6 Gadite

gadget 4 tool **6** device, doodad, jigger **7** gimmick, novelty **9** accessory, doohickey **10** attachment **11** contraption, contrivance, thingamabob, thingamajig

Gaea
also: 2 Ge **4** Gaia
origin: 5 Greek
goddess of: 5 earth
husband: 6 Uranus
children: 6 Pontus, Titans, Uranus **7** Cyclops, Erinyes **9** mountains **13** Hecatonchires
son: 6 Nereus **7** Iapetus, Oceanus
daughter: 4 Rhea **5** Theia **6** Phoebe,

Tethys, Themis **9** Mnemosyne
corresponds to: 6 Tellus

Gaelic
language family: 12 Indo-European
branch: 4 Erse **6** Celtic
subgroup: 4 Manx **5** Irish **8** Scottish

gaffe 4 goof **5** boner **6** boo-boo **7** blunder **11** impropriety **12** indiscretion
French: 7 faux pas **9** gaucherie

gag 4 hoax, hush, jest, joke, stop **5** block, choke, heave, retch **6** muffle, muzzle, stifle **7** cloture, foolery, silence, smother **8** stoppage, suppress **9** horseplay, restraint **13** facetiousness

Gaia see **4** Gaea

gaiety, gayety 3 fun **4** show **5** mirth **6** frolic, tinsel **7** elation, glitter, jollity, spirits **8** airiness, frippery, trumpery, vivacity **9** amusement, animation, brummagem, gaudiness, merriment, showiness **10** brightness, brilliance, garishness, jauntiness, joyousness, liveliness **11** celebration, merrymaking **12** cheerfulness, colorfulness, exhilaration, sportiveness **13** effervescence, sprightliness

gain, gains 3 add, bag, get, hit, net, win **4** jump, leap, plus, reap **5** bloom, bonus, fetch, glean, put on, reach, wages, yield **6** attain, come to, gather, income, obtain, pick up, profit, return, salary, secure, thrive **7** achieve, acquire, blossom, capture, collect, improve, procure, produce, prosper, recover, revenue **8** addition, arrive at, black ink, dividend, earnings, flourish, increase, overtake, proceeds, winnings **9** accretion, advantage, increment **10** attainment **11** improvement **12** accumulation, compensation, remuneration

Gaines, Ernest J
author of: 33 The Autobiography of Miss Jane Pittman

gainful 4 rich **6** paying **9** lucrative **10** productive, profitable **12** remunerative

gainfully 8 usefully **10** profitably **11** lucratively **12** productively **14** remuneratively

gain recognition 9 establish

gainsay 4 deny **6** abjure, oppose, refute **7** disavow, dispute **9** repudiate **10** contradict, controvert

Gainsborough, Thomas
born: 7 England, Sudbury

artwork: 10 The Blue Boy **14** The Morning Walk **15** Mr and Mrs Andrews, The Hon Mrs Graham **16** Viscount Ligonier **26** Peasant Girl Gathering Sticks

gait 4 pace, step, walk **5** tread **6** stride **7** bearing **8** carriage **10** deportment
French: 8 demarche

gaiter 4 boot, shoe, spat, vamp **5** chaps, strad **6** gaskin, hugger, puttee **7** legging **8** cuttikin, overshoe

gala 3 gay **5** grand, party **7** benefit, festive, opulent **8** festival, majestic, splendid **9** festivity, glamorous, sumptuous **10** ceremonial, fancy-dress, glittering **11** celebration, celebratory, magnificent, spectacular, star-studded
French: 4 fete

Galahad
character in: 16 Arthurian romance
father: 8 Lancelot
mother: 6 Elaine
quest: 9 Holy Grail
symbol of: 6 purity **8** nobility

Galatea
form: 6 maiden, statue **8** sea nymph
father: 6 Nereus
mother: 5 Doris
courted by: 10 Polyphemus
lover: 4 Acis
killed: 4 Acis
statue carved by: 9 Pygmalion
brought to life by: 9 Aphrodite
son: 6 Paphos

gale 3 fit **4** blow, gust, stir **6** flurry, squall, tumult, uproar **7** cyclone, tempest **8** eruption, outbreak, outburst **9** agitation, commotion, windstorm

Galileo Galilei
nationality: 7 Italian
birthplace: 4 Pisa
inventor of: 6 sector **11** thermometer
studied: 6 motion **8** pendulum
discovered: 18 Jupiter's satellites
constructed: 9 telescope
formulated: 18 law of falling bodies
author of: 8 Dialogue **10** Discourses **18** The Starry Messenger
condemned for: 6 heresy

gall 3 bug, irk, vex **4** bile, flay, fret, miff, rile **5** anger, annoy, brass, chafe, cheek, gripe, nerve, score, sting, venom **6** abrade, bruise, enrage, harass, injure, nettle, offend, rancor, ruffle, spleen **7** affront, incense, provoke, rub sore **8** acrimony, audacity, boldness, irritate, rudeness, temerity **9** animosity, assurance, displease, excoriate, impudence, insolence, malignity, sauciness, virulence **10** bitterness, brazenness, effrontery, exacerbate, exasperate **11** presumption

gallant 3 fop **4** bold, dude, game, stud **5** blood, brave, dandy, gutsy, noble, suave, swell **6** daring, heroic, kindly, plucky, polite, urbane **7** courtly, dashing, valiant **8** cavalier, fearless, gay

blade, intrepid, mannerly, obliging, resolute, stalwart, valorous, well-bred **9** attentive, courteous, dauntless **10** chivalrous, courageous, thoughtful **11** considerate, gentlemanly, lionhearted **12** stouthearted

gallantries 10 attentions **11** compliments **12** pleasantries

gallantry 4 grit, sand **5** nerve, pluck, valor **6** daring, mettle, spirit **7** bravery, courage, dashing, heroism, prowess, suavity **8** chivalry, courtesy, urbanity **9** derring-do, fortitude, gentility **10** politeness **11** courtliness, intrepidity **12** fearlessness, resoluteness **13** attentiveness, dauntlessness, determination **14** courageousness

gallery 4 stoa **5** salon **6** arcade, loggia, piazza **7** balcony, passage, portico **8** cloister, corridor **9** bleachers, colonnade, mezzanine, triforium **10** ambulatory, grandstand, passageway

Gallia Belgica see **7** Belgium

galliano
type: 7 liqueur
origin: 5 Italy
flavor: 5 herbs, spice
color: 6 yellow
with creme de cacao: 14 Golden Cadillac
with rum: 9 Bossa Nova
with vodka: 16 Harvey Wallbanger

gallinule 3 hen **4** coot, fowl, rail, sora **7** moorhen **8** dabchick, hyacinth, rallidae, ricebird, swamphen

Gallipoli
director: 9 Peter Weir
cast: 7 Mark Lee **8** Bill Kerr **9** Mel Gibson **11** Robert Grubb

gallivant, galavant 3 gad **4** kite, roam, rove **5** jaunt, range, stray **6** ramble, travel, wander **7** gallant, meander, traipse, **8** gad about **9** philander

gallon
abbreviation: 3 gal

gallop 3 fly, hie, jog, run **4** bolt, dart, dash, flit, race, rush, scud, skim, trot, whiz **5** bound, hurry, scoot, shoot, speed, whisk **6** hasten, scurry, spring, sprint **7** mad dash, scamper, scuttle, tear off **8** fast clip, fast gait **9** skedaddle

Galloping Ghost
nickname of: 9 Red Grange

gallows 4 rope **5** noose **6** gibbet, halter **8** scaffold

galore 7 aplenty, to spare

galosh, galoche 4 boot, clog, shoe **6** arctic, patten, rubber **8** overshoe

Galsworthy, John
author of: 5 To Let **6** Strife **7** Justice **9** Loyalties **10** In Chancery **11** The Skin Game **13** A Modern Comedy **14** The Forsyte Saga **15** End of the

Chapter **16** The Man of Property **22** Indian Summer of a Forsyte

Galt, John
character in: 13 Atlas Shrugged
author: 7 Ayn Rand

galvanize 4 fire, move, stir, wake **5** rally, rouse, treat **6** arouse, awaken, charge, excite, foment, spur on, thrill **7** inspire, provoke, quicken **8** activate, energize, vitalize **9** electrify, stimulate

galvanizing 7 rousing **8** electric, exciting, spirited **9** inspiring, thrilling **11** stimulating **12** electrifying, soul-stirring

Galveston Giant
nickname of: 11 Jack Johnson

Gamaliel
father: 6 Simeon **8** Pedahzur
grandfather: 6 Hillel
taught: 4 Paul

Gambia
capital/largest city: 6 Banjul **8** Bathurst
others: 5 Bakau, Basse, Mansa **7** Bintang, Brikama, Kuntaur **10** Georgetown
monetary unit: 5 butut, pound **6** dalasi
island: 7 Ft James, St Mary's **8** Elephant
river: 3 Bao **6** Gambia **7** Bintang, Nianija **9** Sandougou
sea: 8 Atlantic
people: 4 Fula, Jola **5** Foula, Wolof **6** Fulani **8** Mandingo, Serahuli **9** Seranuleh
language: 4 Fula **5** Wolof **6** Fulani **7** English, Malinke **8** Mandingo
religion: 5 Islam **10** Protestant **13** Roman Catholic

gambit 4 ploy, ruse **5** feint, trick **6** scheme **8** artifice, maneuver **9** stratagem

gamble 3 bet **4** back, risk **5** flyer, wager **6** chance, hazard, toss-up **7** trust in, venture **9** speculate **11** speculation, uncertainty

gambler 5 dicer, shark, sharp, sport **6** banker, bettor, bookie, dealer, player **7** hustler **8** gamester, hazarder **10** speculator

Gambler, The
author: 16 Fyodor Dostoevsky
character: 6 Astley, Polina **10** The General **11** Mlle Blanche **15** Marquis de Grieux **16** Alexey Ivanovitch **22** Antonida Tarasyevitchev

gambol 3 hop **4** leap **5** bound, caper, frisk, sport, vault **6** bounce, cavort, frolic, prance, spring **7** disport, rollick

game 3 bad, fun **4** golf, halt, lame, lark, play, polo, pool, prey, romp **5** antic, brave, cocky, darts, gimpy, jacks, match, rugby, sport, spree **6** boccie, boxing, daring, frolic, gaiety, gambol, heroic, plucky, quarry, soccer, spunky, squash, tennis **7** archery,

bowling, contest, crooked, croquet, curling, fencing, frisbee, gallant, hawking, hunting, hurling, jai alai, limping, pastime, tourney, valiant, willing **8** baseball, crippled, deformed, disabled, fearless, football, handball, hobbling, intrepid, lacrosse, ping pong, resolute, skittles, spirited, valorous, wild fowl **9** amusement, badminton, billiards, dauntless, diversion, festivity, merriment, wrestling **10** basketball, courageous, determined, horseshoes, ice-skating, lawn tennis, recreation, tournament, volleyball **11** competition, distraction, merrymaking, racquetball, table tennis, unflinching **12** shuffleboard **13** entertainment, incapacitated, roller-skating
>   **board game: 4** Clue, Life, ludo **5** chess **7** Othello **8** checkers, cribbage, dominoes, draughts, fanorona, Monopoly, Scrabble **10** backgammon **14** Trivial Pursuit
>>   **Chinese: 6** Ma-jong, wei-ch'i **7** mahjong **8** Mah-jongg
>>   **Egyptian: 5** Senat
>>   **Indian: 7** pachisi **8** parchesi, shatranj **9** ashtapada, parcheesi **10** shaturanga
>>   **Japanese: 2** Go **3** I-go **5** Sho-gi
>>   **Korean: 5** Nyout, Pa-tok
>>   **Swedish: 6** tablut
>   **card game: 3** loo, war **4** brag, fish, skat, vint **5** ombre, poker, rummy, tarot, whist **6** boston, bridge, casino, chemmy, ecarte, euchre, go fish, hearts, memory, piquet, pocher **7** bezique, canasta, cooncan, old maid, plafond, primero **8** baccarat, conquian, cribbage, gin rummy, napoleon, patience, pinochle, slapjack **9** blackjack, pelmanism, solitaire, spoil five, twenty-one **11** chemin de fer, crazy eights **13** concentration **14** contract bridge **16** beggar-my-neighbor, trente et quarante

gamete 3 egg **4** ovum **5** sperm **6** oocyte, zygote **8** germ cell, oosphere **12** spermatozoan, spermatozoon

Gamow, George
>   **field: 7** physics **9** cosmology
>   **proponent of: 13** big bang theory
>   **deciphered: 11** genetic code
>   **proposed: 13** quantum theory
>   **established: 17** Gamow-Teller theory

Gamp, Sarah
>   **character in: 16** Martin Chuzzlewit
>   **author: 7** Dickens

gamut 3 ken **5** reach, scope, sweep **6** extent **7** compass, purview

Gandhi
>   **director: 19** Richard Attenborough
>   **cast: 11** Ben Kingsley **13** Candice Bergen
>   **Oscar for: 5** actor (Kingsley) **7** picture

gang 3 mob **4** band, body, crew, pack, pals, ring, team **5** chums, crowd, flock, group, party, relay, shift, squad, troop **6** clique, outfit **7** buddies, company, coterie, cronies, friends, phalanx **8** comrades **9** coworkers, neighbors **10** associates, classmates, companions, contingent, detachment **11** schoolmates

gangster 4 goon, hood, thug **5** crook, felon, tough **6** bandit, gunman **7** hoodlum, mafioso, mobster, ruffian **8** criminal, hooligan **9** racketeer

Gant, Eugene
>   **character in: 17** Look Homeward Angel, Of Time and the River
>   **author: 5** Wolfe

Ganymede
>   **also: 9** Catamitus
>   **cupbearer of: 4** gods

gap 3 cut **4** gash, hole, rent, rift, slit, slot, void **5** abyss, break, chasm, chink, cleft, crack, gulch, gully, notch, pause **6** breach, canyon, cavity, divide, hiatus, lacuna, ravine, recess, vacuum, valley **7** crevice, fissure, interim, opening **8** aperture, crevasse, fracture, interval, puncture **9** disparity, interlude **10** difference, divergence **12** intermission, interruption

gape 4 gasp, gawk, gaze, ogle, part, peer, yawn **5** split, stare **6** cleave, expand **7** fly open **8** wide open, separate **10** rubberneck

gaping 6 astare **7** gawking, staring, yawning **13** rubbernecking

garb 3 rig **4** gear, gown, robe, suit, togs **5** dress, getup, habit **6** attire, finery, livery, outfit **7** apparel, clothes, costume, raiment, uniform, vesture **8** clothing, garments, vestment, wardrobe **9** trappings **11** habiliments

garbage 4 dirt, junk **5** offal, swill, trash, waste **6** debris, litter, refuse **7** carrion, rubbish **9** sweepings

garbage in, garbage out 4 GIGO
>   **term in: 9** computers

garble 5 mix up **6** jumble **7** confuse, distort **8** fragment

Garbo, Greta
>   **real name: 21** Greta Louisa Gustaffson
>   **born: 6** Sweden **9** Stockholm
>   **roles: 4** Love **7** Camille **8** Conquest, Mata Hari **9** Ninotchka **10** Grand Hotel **12** Anna Christie, Anna Karenina **13** Queen Cristina, Two-Faced Woman **14** The Painted Veil **16** Flesh and the Devil

Garcia Lorca, Federico
>   **author of: 5** Yerma **12** Blood Wedding, Gypsy Ballads **19** House of Bernarda Alba

Garcia Marquez, Gabriel
>   **author of: 9** Leaf Storm **23** The Autumn of the Patriarch **25** One Hundred Years of Solitude

garcon 3 boy **6** waiter **7** servant

garden 4 Eden, lawn, plot, yard **7** Arcadia **8** paradise **10** Gethsemane
>   **type: 4** herb, rock, rose **5** truck **6** flower, formal **7** kitchen **9** botanical, vegetable

gardenia
>   **varieties: 5** crape **9** butterfly

Garden of the Finzi Continis, The
>   **director: 14** Vittorio De Sica
>   **author: 14** Giorgio Bassani
>   **cast: 10** Fabio Testi **11** Romolo Valli **12** Helmut Berger **14** Dominique Sanda **15** Lino Capolicchio
>   **Oscar: 11** foreign film

Garden of the West
>   **nickname of: 6** Kansas

garden party
>   **French: 13** fete champetre

gardens
>   **god of: 9** Vertumnus
>   **goddess of: 5** Venus

Garden State
>   **nickname of: 9** New Jersey

garden variety 5 plain **6** common, simple **7** regular **8** everyday, familiar, ordinary **11** commonplace

Gardner, Ava
>   **husband: 9** Artie Shaw **12** Frank Sinatra, Mickey Rooney
>   **born: 12** Smithfield NC
>   **roles: 7** Mogambo **8** Show Boat **9** Mayerling, Naked Maja **10** On the Beach **15** The Sun Also Rises **18** Snows of Kilimanjaro **19** The Barefoot Contessa, The Night of the Iguana

Gardner, Erle Stanley
>   **character: 9** Paul Drake **10** Perry Mason **11** Della Street **14** Hamilton Burger
>   **also wrote as: 6** A A Fair

Gardner, John
>   **author of: 7** Grendel **12** October Light **14** Nickel Mountain, The Art of Living, The King's Indian **17** Michelsson's Ghosts **20** The Sunlight Dialogues, The Wreckage of Agathon

Gareth
>   **character in: 16** Arthurian romance

Garfield, James Abram
>   **presidential rank: 9** twentieth
>   **party: 10** Republican
>   **state represented: 2** OH
>   **defeated: 3** (Neal) Dow **6** (James Baird) Weaver, (John Wolcott) Phelps **7** (Winfield Scott) Hancock
>   **vice president: 6** (Chester Alan) Arthur
>   **cabinet:**
>>   **state: 6** (James Gillespie) Blaine
>>   **treasury: 6** (William) Windom
>>   **war: 7** (Robert Todd) Lincoln
>>   **attorney general: 8** (Isaac Wayne) MacVeagh
>>   **navy: 4** (William Henry) Hunt
>>   **postmaster general: 5** (Thomas Lemuel) James

interior: 8 (Samuel Jordan) Kirkwood
born: 2 OH **6** Orange **8** log cabin
died: 9 Elberon NJ
died by: 13 assassination
buried: 11 Cleveland OH
education:
  seminary: 6 Geauga
  college: 5 Hiram (Eclectic Institute)
  8 Williams
  studied: 3 law
religion: 17 Disciples of Christ
political career: 8 US Senate (declined seat) **11** state Senate **24** US House of Representatives
civilian career: 6 lawyer **7** teacher **11** lay preacher
military service: 6 US Army **8** Civil War **12** major general
notable events of lifetime/term:
  exposure of: 15 Star Route frauds
father: 7 Abraham
mother: 5 Eliza (Ballou)
siblings: 4 Mary **5** James **6** Thomas **9** Mehitabel
wife: 8 Lucretia (Rudolph)
  nickname: 5 Crete
children: 4 Mary **5** Abram, Eliza **6** Edward **12** James Rudolph **13** Harry Augustus, Irvin McDowell

Garfield, John
real name: 15 Julius Garfinkle
born: 9 New York NY
roles: 6 Juarez **10** Humoresque **11** Body and Soul **26** The Postman Always Rings Twice

Gargamelle
character in: 22 Gargantua and Pantagruel
author: 8 Rabelais

Gargantua and Pantagruel
author: 16 Francois Rabelais
character: 7 Panurge **10** Gargamelle, Grangosier, Picrochole **23** Frere Jean des Entommeures

gargantuan 4 huge, vast **5** great **7** hulking, immense, mammoth, massive, titanic **8** colossal, enormous, gigantic, lubberly, towering **9** herculean, monstrous, overgrown **10** prodigious, stupendous, tremendous **11** elephantine **13** amplitudinous

Gargery, Joe
character in: 17 Great Expectations
author: 7 Dickens

garish 4 loud **5** cheap, gaudy, showy **6** brassy, bright, flashy, tawdry, tinsel, vulgar **7** blatant, glaring **9** flaunting, obtrusive **11** pretentious **12** ostentatious **13** overelaborate

garland 3 bay, lei **4** halo **5** crown **6** corona, diadem, fillet, laurel, wreath **7** chaplet, circlet, coronet, festoon **8** chapbook, headband, treasury **9** anthology **10** collection **11** florilegium

Garland, Hamlin

author of: 18 Main-Travelled Roads **20** Rose of Dutcher's Coolly

Garland, Judy
real name: 11 Frances Gumm
husband: 7 Sid Luft **16** Vincente Minnelli
daughter: 9 Lorna Luft **12** Liza Minnelli
costar: 12 Mickey Rooney
born: 13 Grand Rapids MN
roles: 7 Dorothy **11** A Star Is Born, Babes in Arms **12** Easter Parade **13** The Wizard of Oz **14** The Harvey Girls **15** A Child Is Waiting, Meet Me in St Louis

garlic
botanical name: 13 Allium sativum
origin: 4 Asia **13** Mediterranean
charm against: 7 poverty, witches **13** whooping cough
use: 4 fish, fowl, meat **5** salad **10** vegetables **13** Italian dishes, salad dressing
varieties: 4 crow, hog's, wild **5** bear's, false, field, giant, grace, mouse, stag's, sweet **6** levant **7** serpent, society, Spanish, striped **8** daffodil, oriental **11** great-headed, round-headed **16** fragrant-flowered

Garm
origin: 12 Scandinavian
form: 8 watchdog
watches over: 3 Hel
location: 8 Niflheim

garment, garments 4 garb, gear, togs **5** dress, habit **6** attire, outfit **7** apparel, clothes, costume, raiment **8** clothing, vestment **10** habiliment

garner 4 reap **5** amass, hoard **6** gather, heap up **7** acquire, collect **8** assemble **10** accumulate

Garner, James
real name: 15 James Baumgarner
born: 8 Norman OK
roles: 8 Maverick, Sayonara **11** Jim Rockford **12** Bret Maverick, Hour of the Gun **13** Darby's Rangers, Rockford Files **14** Murphy's Romance, Victor Victoria **23** Support Your Local Sheriff **25** The Americanization of Emily

garnet
varieties: 6 syrope **9** almandite, demantoid, hessonite, rhodolite **12** grossularite
month: 7 January

garnish 4 deck, gild, trim **5** adorn, array **6** bedeck, doll up, set off **7** festoon, furbish, smarten **8** beautify, decorate, emblazon, ornament, spruce up, trimming **9** adornment, embellish, embroider **10** decoration **13** embellishment

garret 4 loft **5** attic

garrison 4 fort **5** guard **6** patrol, secure **7** battery, bivouac, brigade, platoon, station **8** division, regiment,

squadron **10** detachment, escadrille **13** fortification

garrulity 8 verbiage **9** loquacity, prosiness, verbosity, wordiness **13** talkativeness

garrulous 5 gabby, windy, wordy **6** chatty **7** gossipy, prating, verbose, voluble **8** babbling, chattery, effusive **9** prattling, talkative **10** loquacious

Garry Moore Show, The
cast: 9 Allen Funt, Denise Lor, John Byner, Ken Carson **11** Chuck McCann, Marion Lorne **12** Carol Burnett, Durward Kirby, Jackie Vernon, Pete Barbutti **13** Dorothy Loudon

Garson, Greer
born: 7 Ireland **10** County Down
roles: 10 Mrs Miniver (Oscar) **11** Madame Curie **12** Her Twelve Men **13** Mrs Parkington, Random Harvest **14** Goodbye Mr Chips **16** That Forsyte Woman **17** Pride and Prejudice **19** Sunrise at Campobello

gas 4 fuel, fume **5** vapor **6** petrol **7** essence

gascon 7 boaster, bragger, egotist **8** blowhard, braggart **9** swaggerer **11** braggadocio

gasconade 4 brag, crow **5** boast **7** bravado **8** boasting **11** braggadocio

gash 4 hack, rend, rent, slit, tear **5** carve, cleft, crack, lance, slash, slice, split, wound **6** cleave, incise, pierce **7** dissect, fissure, quarter **8** incision, lacerate

Gaskell, Elizabeth
author of: 4 Ruth **8** Cranford **10** Mary Barton **13** North and South **24** The Life of Charlotte Bronte

Gaslight
director: 11 George Cukor
cast: 10 Terry Moore **12** Charles Boyer **13** Dame May Whitty, Ingrid Bergman **14** Angela Lansbury **15** Halliwell Hobbes

Gasoline Alley
creator: 9 Bill Perry, Frank King **10** Dick Moores
character: 3 Eve **4** Adam, Hope **6** Clovia, Gideon, Nubbin **7** Chipper, Gabriel **10** Walt Wallet
wife: 14 Phyllis Blossom
children: 4 Judy **5** Corky **7** Skeezix
daughter-in-law: 9 Nina Clock
dog: 5 Punky

gasp 4 gulp, pant, puff **5** blurt **6** suck in, wheeze **10** vociferate

gastronome 7 epicure, gourmet **9** bon vivant

gastronomy 9 epicurism

gastropod, gasteropod 4 slug **5** cowry, snail, whelk **6** cowrie, limpet, nerite **7** abalone, mollusk **8** univalve

gate 3 tap **5** crowd, house, valve **6** portal, sluice, spigot **7** doorway

8 audience, hatchway **9** turnstile **10** attendance

gateau 4 cake **7** dessert

gatekeeper 5 guard **6** porter **7** St. Peter **8** watchman

Gates, Horatio
  served in: 16 Revolutionary War **18** French and Indian War
  battle: 6 Camden **8** Saratoga
  defeated: 8 Burgoyne
  defeated by: 10 Cornwallis

gateway 4 adit **5** entry **6** access, portal **7** doorway, opening **8** entrance, entryway **10** passageway

Gath 14 Philistine city

gather 4 fold, mass **5** amass, group, infer, learn, pleat, shirr, stack **6** assume, deduce, heap up, muster, pile up, pucker, ruffle **7** cluster, collect, convene, marshal, observe **8** assemble, conclude **9** stockpile **10** accumulate, congregate, understand **11** concentrate

gathering 3 mob **4** gang, pack **5** bunch, crowd, crush, drove, flock, horde, party, press **6** throng **7** company, meeting, roundup, turnout **8** assembly, conclave **9** concourse, multitude **10** assemblage, collection, conference, convention **11** aggregation, convergence, convocation **12** accumulation, congregation **13** concentration

gather together 4 herd **5** amass, hoard, rally **6** muster **7** collate, collect, compile, marshal, round up, sweep up **8** assemble, shepherd **9** aggregate, stockpile **10** accumulate, congregate

Gatling, Richard Jordan
  nationality: 8 American
  inventor of: 10 machine gun **16** steam-powered plow

gatophobia
  fear of: 4 cats

gauche 5 inept **6** clumsy, oafish **7** awkward, boorish, ill-bred, uncouth **8** bungling, plebeian, tactless **9** inelegant, maladroit, tasteless, unrefined **10** blundering, uncultured, ungraceful, unmannerly, unpolished **11** proletarian **13** ungentlemanly

gaucherie 5 gaffe **7** blunder, faux pas **11** impropriety **12** indiscretion

Gaudeamus igitur 22 Let us therefore be joyful

gaudy 4 loud, sham **5** cheap, showy, vivid **6** flashy, flimsy, garish, tawdry, tinsel, vulgar **7** glaring, intense **8** colorful, dazzling, lustrous, striking **9** brilliant, sparkling, tasteless, worthless **10** bespangled, glittering **11** pretentious **12** ostentatious

gauge, gage 4 rate, size **5** guess, judge, meter **6** assess **7** adjudge, measure **8** appraise, estimate, evalu-

ate, standard **9** ascertain, calculate, criterion, yardstick **11** measurement
  type: 4 ring **5** bevel

Gauguin, Paul Eugene Henri
  born: 5 Paris **6** France
  artwork: 9 Nevermore **12** The Tahitians **13** The White Horse **15** The Yellow Christ **18** Horsemen on the Beach **23** The Vision after the Sermon (Jacob Wrestling with the Angel) **25** Be in Love and You Will Be Happy **26** The Spirit of the Dead Watching **36** Where Do We Come From? Who Are We? Where Do We Go?
  book: 6 Noa Noa

Gaul *see* **6** France

gaunt 4 bony, grim, lank, lean, slim, thin **5** bleak, lanky, spare **6** barren, meager, skinny, wasted **7** haggard, pinched, scraggy, scrawny, slender, spindly, starved **8** deserted, desolate, forsaken, raw-boned, skeletal, withered **9** emaciated, shriveled **10** cadaverous, forbidding **14** spindle-shanked

Gauss, Carl Friedrich
  field: 7 physics **9** astronomy **11** mathematics
  nationality: 6 German
  worked in: 9 magnetism **11** electricity **12** number theory
  named for him: 9 Gauss's Law

Gautier, Marguerite
  character in: 7 Camille
  author: 5 Dumas (fils)

Gautier, Theophile
  author of: 6 La Peri **7** Giselle **8** Albertus **11** Young France **13** Emaux et Camees **16** Enamels and Cameos **20** Mademoiselle de Maupin, The Romance of the Mummy
  doctrine: 14 Art for art's sake

gauzy 5 filmy, sheer **6** flimsy, sleazy **10** diaphanous **11** translucent, transparent

gave up 4 quit **5** ceded **7** dropped, forsook, yielded **8** forswore, resigned **9** abandoned, abdicated, forfeited, renounced **11** surrendered **12** discontinued, relinquished

Gawain
  character in: 16 Arthurian romance
  opponent: 11 Green Knight

gawk 4 gape, gaze, peer **10** rubberneck

gawky 6 clumsy, klutzy **7** awkward, lumpish **8** bungling, fumbling, lubberly, ungainly, unwieldy **9** all thumbs, graceless, ham-fisted, ham-handed, maladroit **10** blundering, ungraceful

gay 3 fun **4** airy, glad **5** happy, jolly, merry, showy, sunny, vivid **6** blithe, bright, cheery, elated, frisky, genial, jaunty, jocose, jovial, joyful, joyous, lively, social **7** buoyant, chipper, coltish, dashing, festive, gleeful, glowing, intense, jocular, playful, smiling, wag-

gish **8** animated, cheerful, colorful, exultant, gladsome, humorous, jubilant, lustrous, skittish, spirited, splendid, sportive, volatile **9** brilliant, convivial, frivolous, hilarious, rejoicing, sparkling, sprightly, sumptuous, vivacious **10** flamboyant, frolicsome, glittering, homosexual, insouciant, theatrical, variegated **12** effervescent, lighthearted, multicolored

Gay, John
  author of dialogue/lyrics for: 15 The Beggar's Opera

Gay, Walter
  character in: 12 Dombey and Son
  author: 7 Dickens

gay blade 3 fop **4** beau **5** blade, dandy **7** playboy **8** cavalier **9** ladies' man **12** boulevardier, man-about-town

Gay Divorcee, The
  director: 12 Mark Sandrich
  cast: 10 Alice Brady, Erik Rhodes **11** Betty Grable, Fred Astaire **12** Ginger Rogers **19** Edward Everett Horton
  song: 11 Continental, Night and Day

Gay-Lussac, Joseph
  field: 7 physics **9** chemistry
  nationality: 6 French
  discovered: 24 law of combining gas volumes
  invented: 10 hydrometer

Gaynor, Mitzi
  real name: 20 Franceska Mitzi Gerber
  husband: 8 Jack Bean
  born: 9 Chicago IL
  roles: 8 Les Girls **10** Golden Girl **12** Anything Goes, South Pacific **14** The Joker Is Wild **32** There's No Business Like Show Business

gaze 3 eye **4** gape, ogle, peek, peer, scan **5** glare, lower, stare, study, watch **6** behold, glance, glower, peruse, regard, survey **7** examine, inspect, observe, witness **8** look long, pore over, scrutiny **10** rubberneck, scrutinize **11** contemplate

gaze at 4 view **5** watch **6** behold, look at **7** stare at **8** look upon **11** contemplate

gazpacho 4 soup
  ingredients: 6 onions **7** peppers **8** tomatoes **9** cucumbers

Gazza Ladra, La
  also: 17 The Thieving Magpie
  opera by: 7 Rossini

Ge *see* **4** Gaea

gear 3 cam, rig **4** duds, garb, togs **5** dress, tools **6** attire, outfit, tackle, things **7** apparel, clothes, rigging **8** clothing, cogwheel, flywheel, garments, material, property **9** apparatus, equipment, trappings **10** belongings, implements **11** accessories, instruments **12** contrivances **13** accoutrements, paraphernalia

Geb
  also: 3 Keb

origin: 8 Egyptian
god of: 5 earth
daughter: 4 Isis
son: 6 Osiris
sister: 3 Nut

Geer, Will
born: 11 Frankfort IN
roles: 7 Grandpa **10** The Waltons **11** In Cold Blood

Gehenna 4 hell

Gehrig, Lou (Henry Louis)
nickname: 9 Iron Horse
sport: 8 baseball
position: 9 first base
team: 14 New York Yankees

Geist 4 mind **6** spirit

gelatin 4 agar, glue **5** aspic, gelee, jelly **6** glutin, pectin **7** protein, sericin

gelatinize 3 set **4** jell **7** congeal, stiffen, thicken **9** coagulate

gelatinous 7 colloid, viscous **8** muculent **9** jelly-like

geld 5 alter **8** castrate **10** emasculate

gelid 3 icy **6** frigid, frozen **8** freezing

gem 4 dear, doll, rock **5** beaut, bijou, jewel, peach, prize **6** marvel, wonder **8** treasure
type: 4 jade, opal, ruby, sard **5** agate, amber, beryl, coral, pearl, topaz **6** garnet, pyrope, quartz, spinel, zircon **7** apatite, cat's-eye, citrine, diamond, emerald, jadeite, kunzite, olivine, peridot **8** amethyst, corundum, feldspar, hematite, lazurite, nephrite, sapphire, steatite, sunstone **9** almandite, amazonite, carnelian, demantoid, enstatite, fibrolite, malachite, moonstone, morganite, rhodolite, scapolite, spodumene, tiger's-eye, turquoise **10** aquamarine, bloodstone, chalcedony, hessionite, rose quartz, tourmaline **11** alexandrite, chrysoberyl, chrysocolla, chrysoprase, lapis lazuli, rock crystal, topaz quartz **12** grossularite

Gemini
symbol: 5 twins
planet: 7 Mercury
rules: 14 communications
born: 3 May **4** June
twins: 6 Castor, Pollux

Gemini Contenders, The
author: 12 Robert Ludlum

Gem State
nickname of: 5 Idaho

gemutlich 4 easy **9** agreeable, congenial, simpatico **11** comfortable

gendarme 9 policeman

gender 3 sex **4** kind, male, sort, type **5** class **6** female, neuter **8** feminine **9** masculine

genealogy 4 line **5** birth, house, stock **7** lineage **8** ancestry, pedigree **9** parentage **10** derivation, extraction

Gene Autry Show, The
cast: 10 Pat Buttram

horse: 8 Champion
theme song: 20 Back in the Saddle Again

general 5 basic, broad, usual, vague **6** common, normal, public, wonted **7** blanket, current, generic, inexact, natural, overall, popular, regular, typical **8** everyday, frequent, habitual, ordinary, pandemic, sweeping **9** customary, extensive, imprecise, panoramic, prevalent, universal, worldwide **10** accustomed, collective, ecumenical, prevailing, widespread **11** unspecified **12** conventional, nonexclusive, nontechnical **13** comprehensive, miscellaneous

General Electric Theater
host: 12 Ronald Reagan

general idea 4 gist **5** drift, tenor **6** effect, import **7** purport **10** impression **11** implication

generality 6 cliche, truism **9** platitude **12** universality **14** collectiveness **17** miscellaneousness **18** indiscriminateness

generalization 3 law **5** axion **7** bromide **9** inference, statement

generalize 5 infer, judge **8** conclude

generally 5 often **6** always, mainly, mostly **7** as a rule, chiefly, largely, usually **9** currently, typically **10** frequently, habitually, ordinarily, repeatedly **11** extensively, principally, universally

general/military leader
American:
Revolutionary War: 3 (Light Horse Harry) Lee **5** Allen, Barry, Gates, Jones, Wayne **6** Arnold, Greene, Marion, Morgan **10** Washington
War of 1812: 4 Hull **5** Perry, Scott **7** Decatur
Mexican War: 5 Scott **6** Kearny
Civil War: 3 Lee **5** Early, Grant, Meade **6** Thomas, (JEB) Stuart **7** Forrest, Pickett, Sherman, (Stonewall) Jackson **8** Farragut, Sheridan **9** McClellan **10** Beauregard, Longstreet
Indian Wars: 6 Custer **7** Houston **10** Crazy Horse
WWI: 4 Sims **8** Mitchell, Pershing
WWII: 4 King **5** Clark **6** Arnold, Halsey, Nimitz, Patton **7** Bradley, Merrill **8** Marshall, Stilwell **9** Chennault, Doolittle, MacArthur **10** Eisenhower, Wainwright
Korean War: 5 Clark **9** MacArthur
Vietnam War: 6 Abrams **12** Westmoreland
Gulf War: 6 Powell **11** Schwarzkopf
British: 4 Byng, Haig, Howe, Slim **5** Wolfe **6** French, Gordon, Harris, Nelson, Wavell **7** Allenby, Clinton, Dowding, Wingate **8** Braddock, Burgoyne, Cromwell, Jellicoe, Lawrence

9 Alexander, Kitchener **10** Cornwallis, Montgomery, Wellington **11** Marlborough, Mountbatten
Carthagenian: 8 Hannibal **13** Hamilcar Barca
French: 3 Ney **4** Foch **5** Murat **6** Giraud, Joffre, Petain, Roland **7** Nivelle **8** De Gaulle, Montcalm, Napoleon **9** Lafayette **10** Bernadotte
German: 5 Kluck **6** Moltke, Paulus, Rommel, Scheer **7** Blucher, Goering, Tirpitz **8** Bismarck, Goebbels, Guderian **9** Rundstedt **10** Falkenhayn, Hindenburg, Kesselring, Ludendorff, Schlieffen **17** Frederick the Great
Israeli: 5 Dayan
Japanese: 10 Tojo Hideki **15** Yamamoto Isoroku
Macedonian: 7 Ptolemy **8** Philip II **9** Alexander (the Great)
Norman: 7 William (the Conqueror)
Roman: 5 Sulla **6** Brutus, Pompey, Seneca, Trajan **7** Crassus, Hadrian, Lepidus **8** Gracchus, Octavian (Caesar Augustus), Tiberius **9** Vespasian **10** Flamininus, Mark Antony **11** Gaius Marius **12** Julius Caesar **15** Cassius Longinus, Scipio Africanus **18** Tarquinius Superbus
Russian: 6 Zhukov **7** Kutuzov, Voronov **8** Brusilov, Kerensky, Kornilov, Samsonov **9** Bagration **10** Timoshenko, Vasilevsky

generate 4 bear, coin, form, make, sire **5** beget, breed, cause, frame, spawn, yield **6** create, evolve, father, induce, invent **7** develop, fashion, produce **8** contrive, engender, fructify, occasion **9** construct, fabricate, fecundate, fertilize, institute, originate, procreate, propagate, reproduce **10** effectuate, impregnate **11** proliferate

generation 3 kin **4** clan, line, race **5** breed, house, issue, stock, tribe **6** family, growth, strain **7** genesis, lineage, progeny **8** breeding, creation **9** begetting, causation, evolution, formation, offspring **10** production **11** development, engendering, origination, procreation, propagation **12** impregnation, reproduction **13** fertilization, proliferation

generic 6 common **7** general **8** sweeping **9** universal **10** collective **11** generalized, unspecified **12** nonexclusive **13** comprehensive **14** nonrestrictive

generosity 6 bounty **7** charity **8** altruism, courtesy, kindness, largesse **9** abundance, nobleness **10** liberality **11** benevolence, hospitality, magnanimity

generous 5 ample, large, lofty, noble **6** humane, lavish **7** copious, liberal **8** abundant, effusive, obliging, princely, prodigal **9** bounteous, bountiful, honorable, plenteous, plentiful, plethoric, unselfish, unstinted **10** altruistic, beneficent, benevolent, bighearted, charitable, freehanded, free-giving, high-minded, hospitable, munificent, open-handed, ungrudging, unstinting **11** considerate, extravagant, magnanimous, overflowing **12** humanitarian, largehearted, unrestricted **13** accommodating, philanthropic

genesis 4 rise, root **5** birth **6** origin **8** creation **9** begetting, beginning, inception **10** generation **11** engendering **12** commencement

geneticist
American: 5 Temin **6** Morgan, Muller

genetics
science of: 8 heredity
researcher: 6 Mendel

Genghis Khan
also: 11 Jenghiz Khan
name means: 14 universal ruler
position: 13 Mongol emperor
defeated: 6 Russia **10** Chin empire
occupied: 6 Peking

genial 3 gay **4** glad, kind, warm **5** civil, happy, jolly, merry, sunny **6** bright, cheery, hearty, jaunty, jocund, jovial, joyful, joyous, kindly, lively, social **7** affable, amiable, chipper, cordial, festive **8** cheerful, friendly, gracious, mirthful, pleasant, sociable **9** agreeable, congenial, convivial, courteous, expansive, sparkling, vivacious **10** neighborly **12** lighthearted **13** companionable

geniality 10 affability, cordiality **11** sociability **12** conviviality, friendliness **13** expansiveness

genius 3 ace, wit **4** bent, gift, mind, whiz **5** brain, flair, knack **6** expert, master, wisdom **7** faculty, insight, prodigy **8** aptitude, judgment, penchant, sagacity, wizardry **9** ingenuity, intuition, invention **10** mastermind, perception, proclivity, propensity **11** imagination, percipience **12** intelligence, predilection **13** understanding

Genius, The
author: 15 Theodore Dreiser

genius loci 16 guardian of a place

genre 4 kind, sort, type **5** breed, class, genus, group, order, style **6** school **7** fashion, species, variety **8** category, division **11** description **14** classification

genteel 4 tony **5** civil, elite, ritzy, swank, swell **6** modish, poised, polite, urbane **7** courtly, elegant, high-hat, refined, stylish **8** cultured, decorous, ladylike, mannerly, polished, wellbred **9** courteous, high-class, hightoned, patrician **10** cultivated, wellspoken **11** fashionable, gentlemanly, highfalutin, over-refined, pretentious **12** aristocratic, silk-stocking, thoroughbred

gentian 8 Gentiana
varieties: 5 blind, green, horse **6** alpine, bottle, closed, Sierra, yellow

7 crested, fringed, prairie, spurred **8** Catesby's, soapwort, stemless **9** Mendocino **10** pine barren

gentil 4 kind **5** noble **6** gentle

gentile
Yiddish: 3 goy
man: 7 shegetz
woman: 6 shiksa

gentility 6 polish **7** decorum, suavity **8** breeding, chivalry, civility, courtesy, urbanity **9** gallantry, propriety, punctilio **10** refinement **11** cultivation, savoir-faire **12** mannerliness

gentle 3 low **4** calm, easy, kind, meek, mild, soft, tame **5** balmy, bland, light, quiet **6** benign, broken, docile, kindly, placid, serene, slight, smooth, tender **7** lenient, pacific, subdued **8** harmless, merciful, moderate, peaceful, tolerant, tranquil **9** indulgent, temperate, tractable **10** manageable, thoughtful, untroubled **11** considerate, sympathetic **12** domesticated **13** compassionate, tenderhearted
French: 6 gentil

gentleman 3 don, guy, man, one **4** chap, gent **5** swell **6** fellow, person, squire **7** esquire, hidalgo **8** cavalier **9** caballero, chevalier, patrician **10** aristocrat, individual

Gentleman Jim
nickname of: 12 James Corbett

gentlemanly 6 polite **7** courtly, gallant, refined **8** cultured, decorous, mannerly, polished, well-bred **9** courteous, dignified **10** cultivated

Gentleman's Agreement
director: 9 Elia Kazan
based on novel by: 12 Laura Z Hobson
cast: 10 Anne Revere **11** Celeste Holm, Gregory Peck **12** John Garfield **14** Dorothy McGuire
Oscar for: 7 picture **17** supporting actress (Holm)

Gentlemen Prefer Blondes
author: 9 Anita Loos

gentleness 8 calmness, docility, mildness, serenity, tameness **10** compassion, tenderness **12** mercifulness, peacefulness, tractability

gentle wind 4 waft **6** breath, breeze, zephyr

gently 6 easily, kindly, meekly, mildly, softly, tamely **7** amiably, lightly **8** benignly, placidly, smoothly, tenderly **9** gradually **10** delicately, moderately, pleasantly, soothingly **15** compassionately, sympathetically

gentry 5 elite **7** society **8** nobility **10** blue bloods, gentlefolk **11** aristocracy, aristocrats

genuflect 4 bend **6** kowtow

genuine 4 open, pure, real, true **5** frank, naive, plain, solid **6** actual, candid, hon- est, proven, simple **7** art-

less, earnest, natural, sincere **8** bona fide, sterling, true-blue **9** authentic, guileless, heartfelt, ingenuous, simon-pure, unalloyed, veritable **10** legitimate, unaffected **13** unadulterated **15** straightforward, unsophisticated

genuineness 7 honesty **9** frankness, sincerity **10** candidness, simplicity **11** artlessness **13** guilelessness **14** unaffectedness **19** straightforwardness

genus 4 kind, sort, type **5** class, group **7** variety **8** category, division **14** classification

geologist
British: 4 Hall
German: 6 Werner
Scottish: 6 Hutton

geoponics 7 tillage **8** agronomy **9** husbandry **10** agronomics **11** agriculture, cultivation

George Burns and Gracie Allen Show, The
character: 9 Mr Beasley (Mailman) **11** Harry Morton **13** Blanche Morton
theme song: 8 Love Nest

Georgetown
capital of: 6 Guyana

Georgia (former Soviet Union)
capital/largest city: 7 Tbilisi
others: 6 Batumi **7** Kutaisi, Rustavi, Sukhumi
division: 7 Ossetia **8** Abkhazia, Adzharia
head of state: 9 president
government: 8 republic
monetary unit: 5 ruble
mountain: 8 Caucasus
river: 4 Kura **5** Rioni
sea: 5 Black
people: 5 Azeri **7** Russian **8** Armenian, Georgian, Ossetian **9** Abkhazian
language: 8 Georgian
religion 14 Georgian Church **15** Russian Orthodox

Georgia (US)
abbreviation: 2 GA
nickname: 5 Peach **7** Cracker **21** Empire State of the South
capital/largest city: 7 Atlanta
others: 4 Rome **5** Jesup, Macon **6** Albany, Athens, Dalton, Plains, Sparta **7** Augusta, Conyers, Conde, Decatur, Griffen, Vidalia **8** Columbus, La-Grange, Marietta, Moultrie, Savannah, Valdosta, Waycross **9** Brunswick **11** College Park, Gainesville, Thomasville **13** Andersonville
college: 4 Tift **5** Clark, Emory, Paine **6** Mercer **7** Atlanta, Spelman **8** Wesleyan **9** Morehouse **10** Agnes Scott **11** Georgia Tech
explorer: 15 James Oglethorpe
feature: 16 Little White House
amusement park: 19 Six Flags Over Georgia
national cemetery: 13 Anderson-

ville
national monument: 8 Ocmulgee
11 Fort Pulaski 13 Fort Frederica
tribe: 5 Creek, Guale, Yuchi 6 Chiaha,
Oconee, Uchean 7 Yamasee 8
Hitchiti
people: 6 Ty Cobb 7 cracker 10
Bobby Jones 11 Juliette Low 15 Erskine Caldwell 16 Margaret Mitchell
18 Joel Chandler Harris
island: 3 Sea 6 Jekyll, Sapelo 7 Ossa-
baw 10 Cumberland
lake: 6 Lanier, Martin 7 Harding, Not-
tely 8 Bankhead, Hartwell, Sinclair
land rank: 11 twenty-first
mountain: 5 Stone 7 Lookout 8 Ken-
nesaw 9 Blue Ridge 11 Alleghenies
13 High Point Peak
   highest point: 17 Brasstown Bald
   Peak
physical feature:
   sea: 8 Atlantic
   springs: 4 Warm
   swamp: 10 Okefenokee
president: 11 Jimmy Carter
river: 3 Pea 5 Flint 6 Etowah, Oconee,
Pigeon 7 Conecuh, Satilla, St Mary's,
Tugaloo 8 Altamaha, Ocmulgee,
Ogeechee, Savannah, Suwannee 9
Chattooga 13 Chattahoochie
state admission: 6 fourth
state bird: 13 brown thrasher
state fish: 14 largemouth bass
state flower: 12 Cherokee rose
state motto: 6 Wisdom 20 Justice
and Moderation
state song: 7 Georgia
state tree: 7 live oak

Georgia Peach
nickname of: 6 Ty Cobb

Georgics, The
author: 6 Vergil, Virgil

Geraint
character in: 16 Arthurian romance
wife: 4 Enid

geranium 11 Pelargonium
varieties: 3 ivy 4 fish, lime, mint,
pine, rock, rose, show, wild 5 apple,
fancy, house, lemon, regal, zonal 6
almond, alpine, cactus, jungle, nutmeg, orange 7 apricot, bedding, coconut, feather, hanging, knotted,
polecat 8 crowfoot, fern-leaf, horse-
hoe 9 beefsteak, oak-leaved 10 California, gooseberry, peppermint,
strawberry, sweetheart, village-oak
11 grape-leaved, herb-scented, ma-
ple-leaved, rose-scented 12 silver-
leaved, southernwood, sweet-scented
13 black-flowered, pansy-flowered,
pheasant's-foot 14 Lady Washington,
little-leaf rose 15 mint-scented rose
16 Martha Washington 17 English
finger-bowl

Gerber, Franceska Mitzi
real name of: 11 Mitzi Gaynor

Gerd, Gerda

origin: 12 Scandinavian
husband: 4 Frey 5 Freyr

Gere, Richard
roles: 5 Yanks 10 Breathless, Cotton
Club 11 Pretty Woman 12 Days of
Heaven 14 American Gigolo 19
Looking for Mr Goodbar 22 An Officer and a Gentleman
former wife: 13 Cindy Crawford
cause 5 Tibet

germ 3 bud, bug, egg 4 ovum, root,
seed 5 ovule, spark, spore, virus 6
embryo, origin, source, sprout 7 microbe, nucleus, seed bud 8 bacillus,
offshoot, rudiment 9 bacterium, beginning 12 fountainhead 13 microorganism

German 3 Hun 4 balt, Goth 5 boche,
heine, jerry, kraut, Saxon 6 Teuton 7
tedesco 8 Prussian, Teutonic 9 deut-
scher
article: 3 das, dem, den, der, des, die,
ein 4 eine, eins
empire: 5 reich
pronoun: 3 ich, mir, sie, uns
man: 4 herr
storm and stress: 13 sturm und
drang
thank you: 5 danke 10 danke schon
toast: 6 prosit 10 gesundheit
woman: 4 frau 8 fraulein

German-Dutch
language family: 12 Indo-European
branch: 8 Germanic
group: 15 Western Germanic
language: 9 Low German 10 High
German

germane 3 apt, fit 6 native, proper 7
apropos, fitting, related 8 material,
relative, relevant, suitable 9 connected, intrinsic, pertinent 10 applicable 11 appropriate 12 appertaining

germaneness 9 relevance 10 pertinence 13 applicability 15 appropriateness

Germanic
language family: 12 Indo-European
group: 6 Gothic 15 Western Germanic

Germanic Mythology
chief of gods: 5 Wotan
   corresponds to Scandinavian: 4
   Odin
dwarf: 15 Rumpelstiltskin
dwarves: 8 Niblungs 9 Nibelungs
emperor: 15 Dietrich von Bern
epic: 14 Nibelungenlied
goddess of clouds/sky/marriage: 3
Fri 5 Frigg, Frija 6 Frigga
goddess of death/fertility: 7
Berchta, Perchta
goddess of love/ beauty/fecundity:
5 Freya
goddess of moon/ witch: 5 Holle
god of thunder: 5 Donar
god of winter sports: 4 Ullr 5 Uller
hero: 6 Sigurd 9 Siegfried

heroine: 6 Gudrun, Kudrun 7
Guthrun 8 Brunhild 9 Kriemhild
king: 7 Siggeir
king of dwarves: 8 Alberich
knight of the holy grail: 9 Lohengrin
magic cloak: 9 Tarnkappe
maidens: 9 Valkyries
nature spirit: 7 Eriking
nymph: 7 Lorelei, Lurelei
water spirit: 3 Nix

German is spoken here
German: 25 hier wird Deutsch gesprochen

German literary movement (18th
cent) 13 sturm und drang

Germany (see also *Germany, East* and
Germany, West)
capital: 6 Berlin
government leader: 10 chancellor,
Helmut Kohl
monetary unit: 12 Deutsche mark
people: 3 Hun 4 Slav, Sorb, Wend 5
Saxon
   artist: 4 Marc 5 Durer 7 Barlach,
   Cranach, Gropius, Holbein 9 Grunewald 14 Mies van der Rohe
   author: 4 Mann, Marx 5 Grass 6
   Brecht, Elsner, Goethe 7 Johnson,
   Lessing 8 Hochhuth
   composer: 4 Bach 5 Weill 6
   Brahms, Handel, Wagner 7 Strauss
   8 Schumann 9 Beethoven, Hindemith 11 Mendelssohn
   conductor: 5 Henze 6 Walter 9
   Klemperer 11 Furtwangler, Stockhausen
   historical leader: 6 Hitler, Kaiser 8
   Bismarck 10 Barbarossa
   Prussian noble: 6 Junker
   religious leader: 6 Luther
language: 6 German 10 High German
11 Hochdeutsch
religion: 8 Lutheran 10 Protestant 13
Roman Catholic 17 Evangelical
Church
food:
   bread: 12 pumpernickel
   dish: 9 lebkuchen
   dumpling: 6 knodel
   frankfurter: 15 wiener wurstchen
   fruit bread: 7 stollen
   ham: 11 Westphalian
   potato salad: 14 kartoffelsalat
   pot roast: 11 sauerbraten
   sausage: 5 wurst 9 blutwurst, bratwurst 10 brockwurst, knackwurst,
   leberwurst
   sole: 8 seezunge

Germany, East (former) (see also
Germany)
capital/largest city: 10 East Berlin
others: 4 Jena 5 Halle, Waren 6 Er-
furt, Weimar 7 Cottbus, Dresden,
Leipzig, Meissen, Potsdam, Rostock,
Schwedt, Wannsee, Zwickau 9
Frankfurt, Magdeburg 10 Anger-
munde, Warnemunde, Wittenberg
11 Neustrelitz 13 Karl-Marx-Stadt

(Chemnitz)
school: 8 Humboldt
division: 6 Saxony **9** Thuringia **11** Brandenburg, Mecklenburg **12** Saxony-Anhalt
government: 11 Volkskammer (Peoples' Chamber)
monetary unit: 4 mark **7** Ostmark, pfennig
lake: 6 Muritz
mountain: 3 Ore **4** Harz **10** Erzgebirge
highest point: 11 Fichtelberg
river: 4 Elbe, Oder **5** Havel, Saale, Spree **6** Neisse, Warnow
sea: 6 Baltic
physical feature:
　forest: 10 Thuringian
　place: 10 Berlin Wall **17** Checkpoint Charlie
　castle: 9 Sans Souci
　church: 8 St Thomas **12** Thomaskirche
　city center: 13 Karl Marx Platz **14** Alexanderplatz, Neubrandenberg
　comic opera: 12 Komische Oper
　gate: 11 Brandenburg
　museum: 7 Zwinger **8** Pergamon **10** Goethe Haus
　opera house: 18 Deutsche Staatsoper
　feature:
　　china: 7 Dresden
　　fair: 7 Leipzig
　　theater company: 16 Berliner Ensemble

Germany, West (former) (see also *Germany*)
capital: 4 Bonn
largest city: 10 West Berlin
others: 4 Kiel **5** Essen, Mainz, Trier **6** Aachen, Bochum, Bremen, Kassel, Lubeck, Minden, Munden, Munich **7** Cologne, Hamburg, Hanover, Krefeld, Munster **8** Augsburg, Biberach, Dortmund, Duisberg, Duisburg, Freiburg, Mannheim, Solingen **9** Darmstadt, Karlsruhe, Nuremberg, Oldenburg, Stuttgart, Wiesbaden, Wuppertal **10** Dusseldorf, Heidelberg, Steingaden **11** Saarbrucken **12** Oberammergau **13** Gelsenkirchen **15** Frankfurt am Main **16** Mulheim an der Ruhr
school: 4 Bonn **7** Hamburg **10** Heidelberg **16** Ludwig- Maximilian
division: 4 Saar **5** Baden, Hesse **6** Bremen **7** Bavaria **9** Rhineland **10** Palatinate, Westphalia **11** Lower Saxony, Wurttemberg **17** Schleswig-Holstein
head of government: 10 chancellor
monetary unit: 4 mark **7** pfennig **12** Deutsche mark
island: 11 East Frisian **12** North Frisian
lake: 9 Constance **11** Inner Alster, Outer Alster
mountain: 4 Harz **8** Feldberg

11 Black Forest **12** Bavarian Alps
highest point: 9 Zugspitze
river: 3 Ems **4** Elbe, Main, Nahe, Ruhr, Saar, Wese **5** Donau, Rhine, Weser **6** Danube, Neckar **7** Moselle, Pegnitz
sea: 5 North **6** Baltic
physical feature:
　canal: 4 Kiel **10** Mittelland
　forest: 5 Black **7** Bohemia **9** Teu Toburg
　place: 17 Checkpoint Charlie
　botanical garden: 18 Pflantzen und Blumen
　boulevard: 14 Kurfurstendamm
　church: 12 Frauenkirche (Cathedral of Our Lady) **13** Kaiser Wilhelm **16** Gadachtniskirche
　city center: 11 Marienplatz
　fortress: 9 Marksburg
　fountain: 14 Schoner Brunnen
　garden: 10 Englischer
　hall: 9 Beethoven
　museum: 8 Residenz **9** Durer Haus **12** Schatzkammer **14** Alte Pinakothek
　opera house: 18 Deutsches Opern Haus
　park/zoo: 18 Hagenbecks Tierpark
　residential district: 11 Hansa Vierte **12** Hanse Viertel
　resort (on Baltic): 10 Travemunde
　theater: 9 Cuvillies
feature:
　beer cellar: 11 bierkellern
　beer garden: 10 biergarten
　beer hall: 10 bierhallen
　beer room: 10 bierstuben
　cars: 3 BMW **4** Opel **7** Porsche **10** Volkswagen **12** Mercedes-Benz
　children: 6 kinder
　city hall: 5 Romer **7** Rathaus
　festival: 11 Oktoberfest
　folk songs: 11 volkslieder
　kitchen: 5 kuche
　old city: 8 Altstadt
　pre-Lent carnival: 8 Fasching
　secondary school: 9 gymnasium
　states: 6 lander
　wine street: 11 Weinstrasse
germicide 11 bactericide **12** disinfectant

Germinal
author: 9 Emile Zola
germinate 3 bud **4** blow, open **5** bloom, shoot **6** flower, push up, sprout **7** blos- som, burgeon, develop **8** generate, spring up, vegetate
germination 9 sprouting **11** propagation

Gershom
father: 5 Moses
mother: 8 Zipporah
brother: 12 Eliezer
Gershwin, George
born: 10 Brooklyn NY
partner/lyricist: 11 Ira Gershwin
composer of: 9 Funny Face **11** Of

Thee I Sing **12** Porgy and Bess **13** Cuban Overture **14** Rhapsody in Blue **15** Strike Up the Band **17** An American in Paris

Gertrude
character in: 6 Hamlet
author: 11 Shakespeare
husband: 8 Claudius
widow of: 6 Hamlet
Gervin, George
nickname: 6 Iceman
sport: 10 basketball
team: 15 San Antonio Spurs
Gesta Romanorum
author: 7 unknown
gestation 9 evolution, pregnancy **10** epigenesis, generation, incubation, maturation **11** development, propagation
gesticulate 3 nod **4** wink **5** nudge, shrug **6** beckon, motion, signal **8** indicate **9** pantomime
gesture 3 nod **4** sign, wave, wink **5** nudge, shrug, touch **6** beckon, motion, signal **8** courtesy, dumb show, flourish, high sign **9** formality, pantomime **13** demonstration
get 3 bag, fix, net, wax, win **4** beat, coax, earn, gain, grab, grip, grow, have, hear, move, reap, sway, take, turn **5** annoy, catch, fetch, glean, grasp, learn, reach, seize, sense, upset **6** arrive, attain, baffle, become, collar, come by, come to, enlist, entrap, fathom, follow, induce, obtain, pick up, pocket, prompt, puzzle, secure, snatch, suborn, take in, turn to **7** achieve, acquire, capture, confuse, contact, dispose, ensnare, go after, incline, inherit, mystify, perplex, prepare, procure, realize, receive, wheedle, win over **8** bewilder, confound, contract, irritate, perceive, persuade **9** influence, transport **10** comprehend, disconcert, predispose, understand
get a kick out of 4 like **5** eat up, enjoy, fancy, savor **6** relish **10** appreciate
getaway 6 escape, exodus, flight **10** decampment
get done 2 do **6** finish **8** complete **10** accomplish
get even 6 avenge **7** counter, hit back, pay back, revenge **9** retaliate
Gethsemane 6 garden
get into 3 don **5** enter, put on
get in touch with 5 reach **7** contact
get lost 4 scat, shoo **5** be off, leave, scram **6** beat it, begone, depart, go away **7** vamoose
get one's dander up 4 gall, rile **5** anger **6** enrage, madden, nettle, ruffle **7** incense, inflame, outrage **9** infuriate
get out of bed 4 rise **5** arise **12** rise and shine
get rid of 4 drop, dump, junk, shed **5**

get rid of 4 drop, dump, junk, shed **5** ditch, scrap **6** banish, cut out, delete, remove, unload **7** abolish, discard, weed out **8** jettison, stamp out, throw out **9** eliminate, eradicate **10** annihilate **11** exterminate

Get Smart
character: 5 Hymie (CONTROL robot) **7** Agent 99, Carlson, Starker **8** Larrabee, The Chief (Thaddeus) **12** Maxwell Smart (Agent 86) **15** Conrad Siegfried
cast: 8 Don Adams **9** King Moody **10** Stacy Keach **11** Dave Ketchum, Dick Gautier, Edward Platt **12** Bernie Kopell **13** Barbara Feldon **14** Robert Karvelas
Max worked for: 7 CONTROL
foe: 4 KAOS

get the better of 4 foil, rout **5** crush, quell **6** baffle, defeat, thwart **7** conquer **8** confound, overcome **9** frustrate, overthrow

get the upper hand of 5 quell **6** master **7** conquer **8** dominate, overcome, surmount

get the worst of 4 fail, fall, lose

Getting Even
author: 10 Woody Allen

get to 5 reach **8** approach

get-together 2 do **3** bee **4** meet **5** agree, party, visit **6** affair, gather, hobnob **7** meeting **8** assemble, assembly **9** gathering

getup 3 rig **6** attire, outfit **7** costume **8** disguise, ensemble

get up 4 find, rise **5** arise, rouse, stand **8** assemble

get used to 5 adapt, inure **6** adjust **8** accustom **9** acclimate, habituate

gewgaws 7 baubles, doodads, trifles **8** trinkets **9** bric-a-brac, gimcracks, kickshaws, ornaments **11** knickknacks

Ghana
other name: 9 Gold Coast
capital/largest city: 5 Accra, Akkra
others: 3 Oda **4** Axim, Fian, Keta, Tala, Tema **5** Bawku, Enchi, Lawra, Legon, Sampa, Yapei **6** Dunkwa, Karaga, Kpandu, Kumasi, Nsawam, Obuasi, Swedru, Tamale, Tarkwa, Wasipe **7** Antubia, Damongo, Mampong, Prestea, Sekondi, Sunyani, Winneba **8** Akosombo, Kintampo, Takoradi **9** Cape Coast **15** Sekondi-Takoradi
school: 6 Kumasi **9** Cape Coast
monetary unit: 4 cedi **5** ackey
lake: 5 Volta **8** Bosumtwi
mountain: 12 Akwapim Hills
highest point: 8 Afadjato
river: 3 Oti, Pra **4** Daka, Tano **5** Afram, Volta **7** Ankobra, Kulpawn **10** Black Volta, White Volta
sea: 8 Atlantic
physical feature:
gulf: 6 Guinea

people: 2 Ga **3** Ewe **4** Akan, Akim, Akra, Aksa **5** Ahafo, Brong, Inkra **7** Akwapim, Ashanti, Dagomba **8** Mamprusi **11** Mole-Dagbani
language: 2 Ga **3** Ewe, Gur, Kwa, Twi **5** Fanti, Hausa **7** Dagomba, English
religion: 5 Islam **7** animism **13** Roman Catholic
feature:
castle: 14 Christiansborg
dam: 8 Akosombo
national dress: 5 kente

ghastly 3 wan **4** grim, ugly **5** ashen, pasty, weird **6** dismal, glassy, grisly, horrid, odious, pallid **7** fearful, ghostly, haggard, hideous, uncanny **8** blanched, dreadful, gruesome, horrible, shocking, spectral, terrible **9** appalling, colorless, deathlike, frightful, ghostlike, loathsome, repellent, repulsive, revolting **10** cadaverous, corpselike, forbidding, horrendous, lackluster, terrifying

Ghiberti, Lorenzo
born: 5 Italy **8** Florence
artwork: 9 St Matthew, St Stephen **15** Gates of Paradise (baptistry doors) **16** St John the Baptist **19** The Sacrifice of Isaac

ghost 4 hint **5** demon, shade, spook, trace **6** goblin, shadow, sprite, wraith **7** banshee, chimera, phantom, specter **8** phantasm **9** hobgoblin, phantasma, semblance **10** apparition, suggestion **12** Doppelganger **13** manifestation **15** materialization

Ghost and Mrs Muir, The
character: 11 Candice Muir, Martha Grant **12** Jonathan Muir **13** Claymore Gregg **14** Mrs Carolyn Muir **18** Captain Daniel Gregg
TV cast: 8 Reta Shaw **9** Hope Lange **13** Edward Mulhare **14** Harlen Carraher, Kellie Flanagan **19** Charles Nelson Reilly
setting: 11 Gull Cottage
director: 17 Joseph L Mankiewicz
movie cast: 8 Edna Best **11** Gene Tierney, Rex Harrison **13** George Sanders

Ghostbusters
director: 11 Ivan Reitman
screenplay: 10 Dan Aykroyd **11** Harold Ramis
cast: 10 Bill Murray, Dan Aykroyd **11** Harold Ramis **15** Sigourney Weaver

ghostly 4 pale **5** eerie, weird **6** spooky, unreal **7** ghastly, phantom, shadowy, uncanny **8** illusive, spectral **9** unearthly **10** phantasmal, wraithlike **11** phantomlike **12** supernatural

ghostly double
German: 12 Doppelganger

Ghosts
author: 11 Henrik Ibsen
character: 7 Manders **12** Oswald

Alving **14** Jacob Engstrand, Mrs Helen Alving **15** Regina Engstrand

ghoulish 5 eerie, scary, weird **7** demonic, hellish, macabre, ogreish, satanic **8** diabolic, fiendish, gruesome, infernal, sinister **9** monstrous **10** horrifying, zombielike **11** hair-raising, necrophilic

Giacometti, Alberto
born: 11 Switzerland **12** Stampa-Tessin
artwork: 3 Dog **7** The Cage **8** Caroline **10** City Square **11** Head of Diego, Man Pointing **14** Reclining Woman **17** The Palace at Four Am **19** Hands Holding the Void

Gianni Schicchi
opera by: 7 Puccini
character: 11 Buoso Donati

giant 3 big **4** huge **5** titan **7** Goliath, spanker, thumper, whopper **8** behemoth, colossus, strapper **9** Gargantua **14** Brobdingnagian

Giant
director: 13 George Stevens
author: 10 Edna Ferber
cast: 9 James Dean **10** Chill Wills, Rock Hudson **11** Jane Withers **12** Carroll Baker **15** Elizabeth Taylor
setting: 5 Texas
Oscar for: 8 director

Giant see **8** Gigantes

giant people 6 Anakim

Giants in the Earth
author: 9 O E Rolvaag
character: 3 Ole **5** Beret **8** Per Hansa **9** Anna Marie **12** Hans Kristian **15** Peder Victorious

gibber 3 gab **4** blab **5** prate **6** babble, gabble, jabber **7** blabber, blather, chatter, prattle **8** chitchat

gibberish 4 blab, bosh **6** babble, drivel, gabble **7** blather, twaddle **8** nonsense **10** balderdash, double-talk, flapdoodle, hocus-pocus, mumbo-jumbo **12** gobbledegook

Gibbon, Edward
author of: 33 The (History of the) Decline and Fall of the Roman Empire

gibbous 6 convex, curved, humped **7** bulging, rounded, swollen **8** swelling **10** humpbacked, protuberant

Gibbs family
characters in: 7 Our Town
member: 6 George **7** Rebecca
author: 6 Wilder

gibe, jibe 3 rag **4** jeer, mock, quip, razz, twit **5** chaff, flout, knock, toast, scoff, sneer, taunt **6** deride, needle, rail at **7** mockery, poke fun, sarcasm **8** brickbat, derision, ridicule, taunting **9** criticism, wisecrack

Gibraltar
other name: 11 rock of Tarik **13** Djebel al-Tarik **15** rock of Gibraltar

largest city: 9 Gibraltar
government: 18 British crown colony
head of government: 15 governor general
mountain: 6 Misery
sea: 13 Mediterranean
physical feature:
  bay: 5 Ceuta, Rosia, Sandy **6** Catlan **9** Algeciras
  cliffs: 17 Pillars of Hercules
  people: 6 Jewish **7** British, Maltese, Spanish **8** Italians **10** Portuguese
  language: 7 English, Spanish
  feature: 12 King's Bastion
  gardens: 7 Alameda **11** Barbary apes

Gibson, Mel
  roles: 6 Mad Max **9** Gallipoli, The Bounty **10** Braveheart **12** Lethal Weapon **14** The Road Warrior **26** The Year of Living Dangerously

Giddens, Regina
  character in: 14 The Little Foxes
  author: 7 Hellman

giddy 5 dizzy, faint, silly **6** fickle, fitful **7** awesome, erratic, flighty, muddled, reeling **8** careless, dizzying, fainting, fanciful, reckless, swimming, unsteady, volatile, whirling **9** befuddled, frivolous, impulsive, mercurial, whimsical **10** capricious, changeable, inconstant **11** hare-brained, harum-scarum, lightheaded, thoughtless, vacillating, vertiginous **12** inconsistent, overpowering **13** irresponsible, rattlebrained

Gide, Andre
  author of: 13 The Immoralist **15** Strait Is the Gate **17** The Counterfeiters **18** Lafcadio's Adventure (The Vatican Swindle) **19** The Pastoral Symphony

Gideon 11 Hebrew judge
  father: 5 Joash, Ophra
  son: 9 Abimelech
  also called: 9 Jerubbaal

Gidget
  character: 5 Larue **10** Anne Cooper, John Cooper **16** Francine (Gidget) Lawrence **21** Professor Russ Lawrence
  cast: 9 Don Porter **10** Peter Deuel, Sally Field **11** Betty Conner **13** Lynette Winter
  film role: 9 Sandra Dee

Gielgud, Sir John
  born: 6 London **7** England
  roles: 6 Arthur, Becket, Hamlet **7** Macbeth **9** Saint Joan **26** The Barretts of Wimpole Street **27** The Importance of Being Earnest

gift 3 aid, dot, fee, sop, tip **4** alms, bent, boon, dole, help, turn **5** award, bonus, bribe, craft, dower, dowry, favor, flair, forte, graft, grant, knack, power, prize, skill **6** genius, legacy, talent, virtue **7** aptness, bequest, faculty, handout, largess, premium,
present, quality, tribute **8** aptitude, capacity, donation, facility, gratuity, offering, property **9** attribute, endowment, expertise, ingenuity **10** adroitness, capability, competency **11** benefaction, proficiency **12** contribution **13** consideration, qualification

gifted 4 able, deft **5** adept, crack, handy, quick, slick **6** adroit, bright, clever, expert, facile, master, wizard **7** capable, skilled **8** finished, masterly, polished, superior, talented **9** brilliant, ingenious, inventive, practiced, qualified **10** proficient **11** crackerjack, experienced, resourceful **12** accomplished

Gift From the Sea, The
  author: 19 Anne Morrow Lindbergh

gig 3 job **4** trap **5** stint **6** chaise **7** dogcart **8** carriage, curricle **10** engagement

Gigantes
  single member: 5 giant
  father: 6 Uranus
  mother: 4 Gaea
  heads of: 3 men
  bodies of: 8 serpents
  attacked: 4 gods

gigantic 4 huge, vast **5** bulky, jumbo **6** mighty **7** hulking, immense, lumpish, mammoth, massive, titanic **8** colossal, enormous, lubberly, towering, unwieldy **9** herculean, monstrous, ponderous, strapping **10** gargantuan, prodigious, stupendous, tremendous, voluminous **11** elephantine

giggle 6 cackle, hee-hee, simper, tee-hee, titter **7** chuckle, snicker, snigger, twitter

Gigi
  director: 16 Vincente Minnelli
  based on story by: 7 Colette
  cast: 8 Eva Gabor **11** Leslie Caron **12** Louis Jourdan **15** Hermione Gingold, Jacques Bergerac **16** Maurice Chevalier
  score: 14 Lerner and Loewe
  Oscar for: 7 picture **8** director
  song: 4 Gigi **15** I Remember It Well **25** Thank Heaven for Little Girls **29** The Night They Invented Champagne

Gilbert, Cass
  architect of: 14 US Customs House (NYC) **17** Woolworth Building (NYC) **20** Supreme Court Building (Washington DC) **21** Minnesota State Capitol (St Paul) **22** George Washington Bridge

Gilbert, John
  real name: 11 John Pringle
  wife: 9 Ina Claire **11** Leatrice Joy **13** Virginia Bruce
  born: 7 Logan UT
  roles: 4 Love **12** The Big Parade **13** The Merry Widow **15** A Woman of Affairs **16** Flesh and the Devil

Gilbert, William
field: 7 physics
nationality: 7 British
father of: 11 electricity
named for him: 27 CGS unit of magnetomotive force

Gilbert, W S, and Sullivan, Arthur Seymour
  composers of: 7 Ivanhoe **8** Iolanthe, Patience **9** Ruddigore, The Mikado **11** H M S Pinafore, Princess Ida, The Sorcerer, Trial by Jury **12** The Grand Duke **13** The Gondoliers, Utopia Limited **19** The Yeoman of the Guard **20** The Pirates of Penzance **24** Thespis or The Gods Grown Old
  produced by: 10 D'Oyly Carte
  devotees: 9 Savoyards

Gilbert Islands *see* **8** Kiribati

Gil Blas (of Santillane)
  author: 11 Alain LeSage
  character: 6 Scipio **11** Don Alphonso

Gilbreth, Frank B, Jr
  author of: 17 Cheaper by the Dozen (with Ernestine Gilbreth Carey)

gild 4 bend **5** slant, twist **7** cover up, stretch, touch up **10** exaggerate

Gilded Age, The
  authors: 9 Mark Twain **19** Charles Dudley Warner

gilded youth
  French: 13 jeunesse doree

Gileadite password 10 Shibboleth

Giles Goat-Boy
  author: 9 John Barth

Gilgal 5 wheel **6** circle

Gilgamesh
  origin: 8 Sumerian
  king of: 4 Uruk **5** Erech
  servant: 6 Enkidu
  event: 5 flood

gill
  abbreviation: 2 gi

Gilligan's Island
  character: 7 Skipper (Jonas Grumby) **8** Gilligan **9** Mrs Howell (Lovey), Professor (Roy Hinkley) **11** Ginger Grant **14** Mary Ann Summers **17** Thurston Howell III
  cast: 9 Bob Denver, Dawn Wells, Jim Backus **10** Alan Hale Jr, Tina Louise **14** Natalie Schafer, Russell Johnson
  ship: 6 Minnow

Gills, Solomon
  character in: 12 Dombey and Son
  author: 7 Dickens

gimcrack 5 bijou, curio **6** bauble, gewgaw, trifle **7** trinket, whatnot **8** kickshaw, ornament **9** bagatelle, plaything **10** knickknack **11** contrivance, thingamabob, thingamajig

gimmick 4 plan, ploy, ruse, wile **5** angle, dodge, stunt **6** design, device, gadget, scheme **7** wrinkle **9** stratagem **10** subterfuge **11** contrivance

gin
  origin: 11 Netherlands

ingredient: 4 sloe **6** grains **12** juniper berry

type: 6 Geneva **8** Plymouth **9** London dry

drink: 5 Allen **6** Gibson, gimlet **7** Belmont, Bennett, gin Fizz, swizzle **8** Pink Lady **9** Gin Rickey **10** Tom Collins **11** Alabama Fizz, gin and tonic **12** Grand Passion **14** Casino Cocktail

with anisette: 8 Snowball **11** Bachio Punch

with apricot brandy: 14 Boston Cocktail

with brandy: 15 Bermuda Highball

with Chartreuse: 5 Bijou **9** Green Lady

with cherry brandy: 14 Singapore Sling

with Cointreau: 7 Florida **9** White Lady **13** Sweet Patootie **14** Flying Dutchman

with creme de cacao: 9 Alexander

with creme de cassis: 8 Parisian

with creme de menthe: 6 Caruso, Virgin

with creme Yvette: 9 Union Jack

with Curacao: 8 Blue Moon, Napoleon **9** Blue Devil **14** Flying Dutchman

with Dubonnet: 3 BVD **8** Napoleon

with Grand Marnier: 7 Red Lion

with grapefruit juice: 8 Salty Dog

with kirsch, kirschwasser: 7 Florida **10** Lady Finger

with onions: 6 Gibson

with orange juice: 5 Abbey **13** Orange Blossom

with Pernod: 7 Dubarry

with rum: 3 BVD

with scotch: 12 Barbary Coast

with sherry: 11 Renaissance

with strawberries: 10 Bloodhound

with Swedish Punch: 5 Biffy

with vermouth: 5 Bijou, Bronx, Tango **6** Caruso **7** Bermuda, Cabaret, Martini **10** Bloodhound

with vodka: 15 Russian Cocktail

ginger 3 pep, tan **5** brown, spice **6** energy

varieties: 3 red **4** wild **5** crape, crepe, shell, torch, white **6** canton, common, Kahili, orchid, spiral, yellow **9** butterfly **10** small shell, variegated

botanical name: 8 Zingiber **12** Z officinales

Sanskrit: 9 singabera

origin: 4 Asia **5** China, India **7** Jamaica

use: 6 tongue **7** vinegar **9** beef stock **11** baked dishes, gingerbread **12** chicken stock

gingerly 6 warily **7** charily, timidly **8** daintily **9** carefully, finically, guardedly, heedfully, mincingly, prudently **10** cautiously, delicately, discreetly, hesitantly, vigilantly, watchfully **11** squeamishly **12** fastidiously, suspiciously **13** circumspectly

gingham 5 cloth **6** cotton, fabric, striped **8** chambray **9** checkered

gin mill 3 bar **4** dive **6** saloon, tavern **9** honky-tonk, roadhouse

Ginnungagap
origin: 12 Scandinavian
void filled with: 4 mist
between: 9 Nifelheim **10** Muspelheim

Ginsberg, Allen
author of: 4 Howl **7** Kaddish **10** Planet News **11** Mind Breaths **16** The Fall of America **20** Reality and Sandwiches

Giordano, Umberto
born: 5 Italy **6** Foggia
composer of: 6 Fedora **8** Mala Vita **13** Andrea Chenier **14** Madame Sans-Gene

Giorgione da Castelfranco
born: 5 Italy **12** Castelfranco
artwork: 10 The Tempest **13** Ordeal of Moses, Sleeping Venus **17** Judgment of Solomon **19** The Concert Champetre (disputed) **20** The Three Philosophers **23** Adoration of the Shepherds

Giotto di Bondone
born: 5 Italy **8** (near) Florence
artwork attributed: 17 Ognissanti Madonna **31** Presentation of Christ in the Temple **32** St Francis Surrounded by his Brothers

Giovanelli
character in: 11 Daisy Miller
author: 5 James

Giovanni's Room
author: 12 James Baldwin

giraffe
constellation of: 14 Camelopardalis
kin: 5 okapi
other name: 10 camelopard

girandole 11 candelabrum, candlestick **12** candleholder

Girardon, Francois
born: 6 France, Troyes
artwork: 13 Bathing Nymphs **14** Galley of Apollo, Virgin of Troyes **16** Rape of Persephone **17** (tomb for) Cardinal Richelieu **23** Apollo Tended by the Nymphs

Giraudoux, Jean
author of: 5 Bella **6** Judith, Ondine, Racine **7** Electra **12** Amphitryon 38 **15** Tiger at the Gates **18** Madwoman of Chaillot **20** My Friend from Limousin

gird 3 pen, tie **4** belt, girt, loop, ring **5** brace, hem in, hitch, steel, strap, truss **6** circle, fasten, girdle, harden, secure, wall in **7** besiege, confine, enclose, fortify, hedge in, prepare, stiffen, sustain, tighten **8** blockade, buttress, encircle, lay siege, surround **9** encompass **10** strengthen **12** circumscribe

girder 4 beam **5** brace, truss **6** binder, rafter **7** support, tie-beam

girdle 3 hem **4** band, belt, ring, sash **5** girth, hedge, stays **6** bodice, circle, corset **7** baldric, circlet, contour **8** boundary, cincture, corselet **9** surcingle, waistband **10** cummerbund **12** waist cincher **17** foundation garment

girl 4 bird, cook, help, lass, maid, minx, miss **5** angel, chick, nymph, wench **6** damsel, kitten, lassie, maiden, pigeon, virgin **7** baggage, colleen, darling, fiancee, ingenue, nymphet **8** daughter, domestic, handmaid, lady love, mistress, scullion **9** affianced, betrothed, inamorata, lady's maid, soubrette **10** sweetheart **11** maidservant
French: 10 demoiselle, jeune fille

girl Friday 4 aide **6** helper **9** assistant, secretary **10** amanuensis **12** office worker **23** administrative assistant

girlfriend 6 steady **7** beloved, sweetie **8** best girl **10** one and only, sweetheart

Girl in a Swing
author: 12 Richard Adams

girlish 8 girl-like, maidenly, youthful **10** maidenlike

Girl of the Golden West, The
opera by: 7 Puccini
setting: 8 Gold Rush **10** California
character: 6 Minnie **7** Johnson, Sheriff

Girl Scouts
founded by: 11 Juliette Low
abbr: 5 GSUSA
rank: 7 brownie **10** tenderfoot

girt 4 belt, bind, gird, ring **5** bound, girth **6** belted, circle, girdle, ringed **7** circled, girdled **9** encircled

girth 5 cinch **9** perimeter **10** saddle band **13** circumference

Giselle
ballet by: 4 (Adolphe Charles) Adam

Gish, Lillian
real name: 12 Lillian Gishi **15** Lillian de Guiche
born: 13 Springfield OH
roles: 8 La Boheme **10** Enoch Arden **11** Annie Laurie, Intolerance, Way Down East **12** Duel in the Sun **13** Scarlet Letter **14** Broken Blossoms **16** Portrait of Jennie **17** Orphans of the Storm, The Birth of a Nation

Gissing, George
author of: 5 Demos **13** New Grub Street **14** The Nether World

gist 3 nut **4** core, crux, meat, pith **5** drift, force, heart, sense, tenor, theme **6** burden, center, effect, import, kernel, marrow, spirit **7** essence, purport **8** main idea **9** main point, substance **11** implication **12** significance

give 3 buy, pay, tip **4** bend, ease, emit, hire, lend, show, sink **5** admit, allot, allow, apply, award, bribe, deign, endow, grant, issue, leave, offer, relax, utter, voice, yield **6** accord, addict, afford, assign, attach, bestow, bounce, commit, confer, convey, devote, donate, enable, enrich, hand to, impart, loosen, notify, open on, permit, recede, relent, render, shrink, supply, tender, unbend, vest in **7** concede, consign, deliver, entrust, fork out, furnish, hand out, let know, present, proffer, provide, requite, retreat, slacken **8** announce, bequeath, collapse, dispense, exchange, fork over, hand over, lead on to, make over, move back, put forth, shell out **9** apportion, break down, dispose of, equip with, favor with, look out on, present to, pronounce, subscribe, surrender, vouchsafe **10** articulate, become soft, compensate, contribute, deliquesce, distribute, recompense, remunerate, resilience, supply with **11** communicate, flexibility, provide with, springiness

give aid to 4 help **6** assist, succor **7** help out **8** befriend **9** look after **10** minister to

give a leg up 3 aid **4** help, lift **5** boost, hoist, raise **6** assist **7** elevate

give and take 8 exchange **10** compromise **11** interchange, reciprocity

give a pep talk to 4 goad, prod, spur **5** press **6** exhort **9** encourage

give a reason for 7 clarify, clear up, explain, justify **9** elucidate **10** account for

give as security 4 pawn **6** pledge **7** deposit, pay down, put down

give away 6 bestow, betray, donate, reveal **7** hand out

give birth 4 bear **5** hatch **6** create, invent **7** deliver, develop **9** originate **10** bring forth

give confidence to 7 inspire **8** embolden, inspirit **9** encourage

give courage 5 brace **6** buck up **7** hearten **8** inspirit, motivate

give energy to 7 animate, enliven **8** activate, energize, vitalize **9** stimulate **10** invigorate

give enjoyment 5 amuse, charm **6** divert, please **7** beguile, delight **8** enthrall **9** entertain

give forth 4 emit, gush **5** exude, issue **7** send out **8** throw off, transmit **9** discharge

give full attention 7 pay heed **8** fasten on **11** concentrate

give in 5 defer, yield **6** accede, cave in, submit **7** succumb **9** surrender **10** capitulate **12** knuckle under

give in to 7 yield to **9** indulge in, partake of **16** abandon oneself to

give leave 3 let **5** allow **6** permit **8** sanction **9** authorize **14** give permission

give moral support to 3 aid **4** abet,

back, help **6** assist, uphold **7** support, sustain **8** sanction **9** encourage

given 3 apt **4** wont **5** prone **6** likely, wonted **7** awarded, donated, granted, offered **8** accorded, bestowed **9** committed, conferred, entrusted, presented **10** accustomed, handed over, in the habit **11** contributed **13** furnished with, made a donation, presented with **17** made a contribution

give new life to 3 fan **4** fire **6** awaken, revive **8** revivify **10** rejuvenate **11** reincarnate

give oneself to 8 dedicate **10** buckle down, consecrate

give one's word 3 vow **5** swear **6** assure, pledge **7** certify, promise, warrant **9** guarantee

give one walking papers 3 axe, can **4** fire, oust, sack **5** let go **6** bounce, lay off **7** cashier, dismiss, release **8** get rid of **9** discharge, terminate **11** give the gate, send packing

give out 4 quit, tell, tire **6** assign, inform, reveal, run out **7** divulge, dole out, mete out **8** allocate, announce, disclose, dispense, proclaim **9** apportion, broadcast, parcel out **10** distribute, make public, portion out **11** disseminate

give over 4 cede **5** yield **9** surrender **10** relinquish

give permission 3 let **5** allow **6** accede, permit **7** approve **8** sanction **9** acquiesce, authorize, give leave

give rise to 4 sire **5** breed, cause **6** lead to **7** produce **8** engender, generate, occasion **9** call forth **10** bring about

give support to 3 aid **4** abet **5** serve **6** defend, prop up, second **7** bolster, comfort, sustain **8** buttress, champion **10** contribute, minister to, provide for, stick up for

give the go-ahead 4 okay **5** order **6** direct **7** appoint, charter, empower **8** contract **9** authorize **10** commission

give the lie to 5 belie **8** disprove **9** repudiate **10** contradict, controvert

give the raspberry 3 boo, pan **4** razz **6** deride, hoot at **8** ridicule **11** give the bird **17** give the Bronx cheer

give the right to 5 allow **6** permit **7** entitle, qualify **9** authorize

give the slip 4 duck **5** avoid, dodge, elude, evade

give up 4 cede, drop, lose, quit, skip **5** forgo, let go, waive, yield **6** eschew, resign **7** abandon, forfeit, forsake **8** abdicate, forswear, renounce **9** sacrifice, surrender **10** relinquish **11** discontinue

give up the ghost 3 die **6** expire, pass on, perish **7** decease **8** pass away **15** breathe one's last

give vent 4 free **5** let go **7** release **8** let loose, liberate **12** give free rein

give way 4 fall **6** buckle, cave in **7** crumple **8** collapse **10** break apart

giving birth 7 bearing **8** creating, creation, delivery, hatching **9** inventing, invention **10** childbirth, delivering **11** originating, origination, parturition

giving up 7 refusal **8** dropping, quitting, yielding **9** resigning **10** abandoning, abdicating, abdication, abstinence, continence, forbearing, forfeiting, forfeiture, self-denial **11** abandonment, forswearing, resignation **12** renunciation, surrendering **14** relinquishment

gizmo 4 tool **6** device, doodad, gadget **7** whatsis **9** apparatus, implement, invention, mechanism **10** instrument **11** contraption, contrivance, thingamabob, thingamajig

glacial 3 icy, raw **4** cold **5** chill, gelid, polar **6** arctic, biting, bitter, frigid, frosty, frozen, wintry **7** hostile **8** freezing, inimical, piercing **9** congealed **10** disdainful, unfriendly **12** antagonistic, bone-chilling, contemptuous

Glackens, William James
born: 14 Philadelphia PA
artwork: 9 Promenade **11** Chez Mouquin **15** Nude with an Apple **16** Washington Square (A Holiday in the Park) **17** Luxembourg Gardens

glad 5 happy **6** elated, joyful, joyous **7** elating, gleeful, pleased, tickled **8** blissful, cheerful, cheering, pleasing, rejoiced **9** contented, delighted, joygiving **10** delightful, entrancing, gratifying **11** exhilarated, tickled pink **12** exhilarating

gladden 5 cheer, elate **6** please **7** animate, cheer up, delight, enliven, gratify, hearten, rejoice **8** inspirit, pleasure **9** make happy **10** exhilarate

gladdened 5 happy **6** joyful, joyous **8** cheerful

glade 4 dell, glen, lawn, vale, wood **5** grove, marsh, vista **6** canada, hollow, valley **7** opening **8** clearing

gladness 3 joy **4** glee **5** bliss, cheer, mirth **7** delight, gaiety, jollity **8** pleasure **9** happiness **10** joyfulness **11** contentment **12** cheerfulness

glad rags 5 array **6** attire, finery **10** Sunday best

Gladsheim
origin: 12 Scandinavian
palace of: 4 Odin **5** Othin
location: 8 Valhalla

gladsome 3 gay **5** happy, merry **6** cheery, joyful, joyous **8** cheerful **12** lighthearted

glamor, glamour 5 charm, magic **6** allure **7** glitter, romance **8** illusion **9** adventure, challenge, magnetism **10**

excitement **11** enchantment, fascination **14** attractiveness

glamorous, glamourous 8 alluring, charming, dazzling, exciting, magnetic **10** attractive, bewitching, enchanting **11** captivating, charismatic, fascinating

glance 4 kiss, peek, peep, scan, skim, slip **5** brush, graze, shave, touch **6** bounce, careen, squint **7** glimpse, rebound **8** ricochet **9** brief look, quick look, quick view
French: **6** apercu

glance through 4 scan, skim **6** browse, peruse **7** dip into **8** look over **9** check over

gland
part of: **15** endocrine system
type: **4** duct **8** ductless
kind: **3** oil **5** sweat **7** adrenal, thyroid **8** pancreas **9** pituitary **11** parathyroid
ductless gland secretes: **8** hormones

glare 4 glow **5** blaze, flame, flare, flash, gleam, glint, gloss, lower, scowl, sheen **6** dazzle, glower **7** flicker, glimmer, glisten, glitter, radiate, shimmer, sparkle, twinkle **8** radiance **9** angry look, black look, dirty look **10** brightness, harsh light, luminosity **12** resplendence

glaring 4 rank **5** gross, harsh, vivid **6** arrant, bright, strong **7** blatant, flaring, intense, obvious **8** blinding, dazzling, flagrant, piercing **9** audacious, brilliant, egregious **10** glittering, outrageous, shimmering **11** conspicuous, penetrating, resplendent, unconcealed, undisguised **12** unmistakable

Glasgow, Ellen
author of: **10** Vein of Iron **12** Barren Ground **13** In this Our Life, Sheltered Life **18** They Stooped to Folly **20** The Romantic Comedians

glass 6 beaker, goblet **7** chalice, tumbler **10** tumblerful
type of: **4** fizz, sour **5** flute, tulip **6** jigger, sherry **7** balloon, collins, cordial, red wine, snifter **8** cocktail, highball **9** champagne, white wine **10** hollow-stem, pousse cafe **12** old-fashioned

glasshouse 7 nursery **8** hothouse **10** greenhouse **12** conservatory

glassiness 7 clarity **8** dullness, flatness **9** shininess **10** brilliance, luminosity **12** lifelessness, transparency

Glass Key, The
author: **15** Dashiell Hammett
character: **9** Shad O'Rory **10** Janet Henry, Opal Madvig, Paul Madvig **11** Ned Beaumont **12** Senator Henry **13** Bernie Despain

Glass Menagerie, The
director: **12** Irving Rapper
author: **17** Tennessee Williams
character: **5** Laura **6** Amanda **12** Tom

Wingfield
cast: **9** Jane Wyman **11** Kirk Douglas **13** Arthur Kennedy **16** Gertrude Lawrence

glassware 5 agata **6** aurene **7** crystal, favrile, steuben, vitrics **8** amerina, stemware
worker: **7** glazier

glassy 4 dull **5** clear, shiny **6** glazed, smooth **8** lifeless **10** glittering **11** transparent

Glauber, Johann Rudolf
field: **9** chemistry
nationality: **6** German
prepared: **12** tartar emetic **13** sodium sulfate (Glauber's salt) **16** hydrochloric acid

Glaucus
god of: **3** sea
father: **5** Minos
ally of: **7** Trojans
loved by: **5** Circe **6** Scylla **10** Amphitrite

glaze 4 blur **5** gloss **6** enamel, finish **7** grow dim, varnish **8** film over **9** glass over

glazed 4 iced **5** filmy **6** coated, glassy, shined, smooth **7** glossed, sugared **8** enameled, lustrous, polished **9** burnished, varnished

Glazunoff, Alex K (Glazunov, Alexander Konstantinovich)
born: **6** Russia **12** St Petersburg
composer of: **10** Chopiniana, The Seasons **11** Stenka Razin **13** Hymn to Pushkin **15** Memorial Cantata

gleam 3 bit, jot, ray **4** beam, drop, glow, hint, iota **5** blink, flare, flash, glare, glint, gloss, grain, sheen, shine, spark, speck, trace **6** luster, streak **7** flicker, glimmer, glimpse, glisten, glitter, inkling, shimmer, sparkle, tiny bit, twinkle **8** least bit, radiance **9** coruscate **10** brightness, brilliance, effulgence **11** coruscation, scintillate

gleaming 5 clear, shiny **6** bright, flashy, glossy **7** shining, radiant **8** dazzling, glinting, luminous, lustrous, polished, splendid **9** brilliant, burnished, sparkling **10** glistening

glean 4 cull **5** amass **6** gather, pick up **7** harvest **10** accumulate **13** piece together **14** scrape together

gleanings 8 analects, extracts **10** miscellany, selections **11** collectanea, miscellanea **15** commonplace book

Gleason, Jackie
real name: **18** Herbert John Gleason
nickname: **15** Mr Saturday Night
born: **10** Brooklyn NY
roles: **5** Gigot **6** The Toy **10** The Hustler **11** Life of Riley, The Poor Soul **12** Ralph Kramden **15** Joe the Bartender, The Honeymooners **17** Don't Drink the Water, Jackie Gleason Show, The Time of Your Life **22**

Requiem for a Heavyweight **24** Reggie Van Gleason the Third

glebe 3 sod **4** clod, land, plot, soil **5** earth, field **6** termon **8** kirktown **10** church land

glee 3 joy **5** mirth, verve **6** gaiety **7** delight, ecstasy, jollity, rapture **8** gladness, hilarity, laughter **9** joviality, merriment **10** exultation, jocularity, joyfulness, joyousness, liveliness **11** playfulness **12** cheerfulness, exhilaration, sportiveness **13** jollification, sprightliness

glee club 6 chorus **12** singing group **13** choral society

gleeful 3 gay **4** glad **5** happy, jolly, merry **6** elated, jocund, jovial, joyful, joyous, lively **7** festive **8** blissful, cheerful, exultant, mirthful **9** delighted **11** exhilarated **12** lighthearted

Gleipnir
origin: **12** Scandinavian
chain that bound: **6** Fenrir, Fenris

glen 4 dale, dell, vale **6** bottom, hollow

Glencaire Cycle
author: **12** Eugene O'Neill

glib 4 oily **5** gabby, quick, ready, suave **6** facile, fluent, smooth **7** devious, voluble **8** flippant, slippery, unctuous **9** insincere, talkative

glide 3 run **4** flow, roll, sail, skim, slip, soar **5** coast, drift, float, issue, skate, slide, steal **6** elapse, stream **7** proceed **8** glissade

glider 5 swing **7** aviator **9** sailplane **10** hydroplane

glimmer 3 bit, ray **4** beam, drop, glow, hint **5** blink, flare, flash, glare, gleam, grain, shine, speck, trace **7** flicker, glimpse, glisten, glitter, shimmer, sparkle, twinkle **9** coruscate, scintilla **10** flickering, intimation **11** scintillate

glimpse 3 see, spy **4** espy, peek, peep, spot **6** glance, peek at, peep at, squint **9** brief look, quick look, quick view **12** catch sight of, fleeting look
French: **6** apercu

Glinka, Mikhail Ivanovich
born: **6** Russia **8** Smolensk
composer of: **12** Ivan Sussanin, Karaminskaya **13** Jota Aragonesa **18** Russlan and Ludmilla

glint 4 gaze, look, peep **5** flash, gleam, sheen, shine, stare **6** glance **7** appear, glimmer, glimpse, glisten, glitter, shim- mer, sparkle, twinkle **9** coruscate **11** scintillate

glissade 5 coast, glide, slide

glissando
music: **7** sliding

glisten 4 glow **5** flash, gleam, glint, shine **7** flicker, glimmer, glister, glitter, radiate, shimmer, sparkle, twinkle **9** coruscate **11** scintillate

glitter 4 fire, glow, pomp, show **5**

flare, flash, gleam, glint, sheen, shine **6** luster, thrill, tinsel **7** beaming, display, glamour, glimmer, glisten, radiate, sparkle, twinkle **8** grandeur, radiance, splendor **9** pageantry, showiness **10** brilliance, excitement, refulgence **11** electricity

glittering 6 bright **7** radiant, shining **8** luminous, lustrous **9** brilliant, sparkling **11** coruscating

gloaming 4 dusk **7** evening **8** twilight

gloat 4 bask, brag **5** exult, strut, vaunt **7** revel in, swagger, triumph **8** crow over **9** glory over

global 5 world **6** all-out **7** general **9** planetary, unbounded, universal, unlimited, worldwide **10** widespread **13** comprehensive, international **16** intercontinental

globe 3 orb **4** ball **5** Earth, world **6** planet, sphere **7** globule **8** spheroid, spherule **9** biosphere

globule 4 ball, bead, bleb, blob, drop **5** globe **6** bubble, pellet, sphere **7** blister, droplet **8** particle, spheroid

glogg
    type: 5 punch
    origin: 6 Sweden

gloom 3 woe **4** dark, dusk, murk **5** blues, dolor, grief, shade **6** misery, sorrow **7** despair, dimness, sadness, shadows **8** darkness, distress, doldrums **9** blackness, dejection, dinginess, duskiness, murkiness, obscurity **10** cloudiness, depression, gloominess, low spirits, melancholy, mopishness, moroseness, oppression **11** despondency, forlornness, unhappiness **12** hopelessness **13** cheerlessness **16** disconsolateness, heavy-heartedness

gloomy 3 dim, sad **4** dark, dour, down, dull, glum, grim, mopy, sour **5** dusky, moody, mopey, murky, shady **6** cloudy, dismal, dreary, morbid, morose, shaded, somber **7** doleful, forlorn, shadowy, sunless, unhappy **8** dejected, desolate, downcast, frowning, funereal, overcast **9** cheerless, depressed, heartsick, miserable, sorrowful, woebegone **10** chapfallen, despondent, dispirited, ill-humored, melancholy **11** comfortless, crestfallen, discouraged, downhearted, low-spirited, pessimistic **12** disconsolate, disheartened, heavy-hearted **13** in the doldrums **14** down in the dumps, down in the mouth

Gloria in Excelsis Deo 22 Glory in the highest to God

Gloriana
    character in: 15 The Faerie Queene
    author: 7 Spenser

Gloriana
    opera by: 7 Britten
    character: 10 Elizabeth I **11** Earl of Essex

glorification 7 worship **8** devotion **9**

adoration, adulation **10** exaltation, veneration **13** magnification

glorify 4 laud **5** adore, deify, exalt, extol, honor **6** praise, revere **7** beatify, dignify, elevate, ennoble, idolize, worship **8** canonize, enshrine, sanctify, venerate **9** celebrate, glamorize **10** consecrate **11** apotheosize, immortalize, romanticize

glorious 4 fine **5** grand, great, noble, noted **6** august, divine, famous, superb **7** eminent, glowing, honored, notable, radiant, shining, stately, sublime, supreme **8** dazzling, gorgeous, imposing, lustrous, majestic, renowned, splendid **9** beautiful, brilliant, dignified, excellent, marvelous, sparkling, wonderful **10** celebrated, delightful, impressive, preeminent **11** illustrious, magnificent, resplendent **12** praiseworthy **13** distinguished

glory 4 fame, mark, name **5** boast, honor, revel, vaunt **6** esteem, homage, praise, renown, repute **7** dignity, majesty, worship **8** blessing, eminence, grandeur, nobility, prestige, splendor **9** adoration, celebrity, gratitude, solemnity, sublimity **10** admiration, excellence, notability, veneration **11** benediction, distinction, preeminence, stateliness **12** magnificence, resplendence, thanksgiving **14** impressiveness **15** illustriousness

Glory in the highest to God
    Latin: 19 Gloria in Excelsis Deo

gloss 4 glow, mask, veil **5** cloak, color, glaze, gleam, japan, sheen, shine **6** enamel, excuse, luster, polish, veneer **7** cover up, lacquer, shimmer, varnish **8** annotate, disguise, mitigate, radiance **9** whitewash **10** annotation, brightness, brilliance, commentary, smooth over **11** explain away, explanation, rationalize **12** luminousness, treat lightly **14** interpretation

gloss over 4 hide, mask, veil **7** conceal, cover up **9** dissemble, whitewash **12** misrepresent

glossy 5 photo, shiny, showy, silky, sleek, slick **6** bright, satiny, smooth **7** picture, shining **8** gleaming, lustrous, magazine, polished **9** burnished

glove 3 kid **4** cuff, mitt **5** catch, thumb **6** gusset, mitten, muffle **7** chevron **8** gauntlet

glow 4 fill, heat **5** ardor, bloom, blush, color, flush, gleam, gusto, shine **6** fervor, thrill, tingle, warmth **7** flicker, glimmer, glisten, glitter, radiate, shimmer, smolder, twinkle **8** radiance **9** eagerness, intensity, radiation, reddening, vividness **10** brightness, enthusiasm **11** earnestness

glower 4 pout, sulk **5** frown, glare, lower, scowl, stare

glowing 3 hot, red **4** rave **5** ruddy, vivid **6** ardent, bright, florid, raving **7**

fervent, flaming, flushed **8** ecstatic, exciting **9** rhapsodic, thrilling **10** passionate **11** luminescent, sensational, stimulating **12** enthusiastic

Glubbdubdrib
    fictional land in: 16 Gulliver's Travels
    author: 5 Swift

Gluck, Christoph Willibald (von)
    born: 7 Bavaria **8** Neumarkt
    composer of: 5 Orfeo **6** Armide **7** Alceste **13** Paride ed Elena **14** Echo et Narcisse **17** Iphigenie en Aulide **18** Iphigenie en Tauride

glue 3 fix, gum **5** affix, epoxy, paste, putty, stick **6** adhere, cement, fasten, mortar **7** plaster, stickum **8** adherent, adhesive, concrete, fixative, mucilage **11** agglutinate

gluey 5 gooey, gummy, mucid, ropey, slimy, tacky, thick, **6** sticky, viscid **7** stringy, viscous **8** adhesive **12** mucilaginous

glum 6 gloomy, morose **8** dejected **9** cheerless **10** melancholy **14** down in the mouth

glut 4 bolt, clog, cram, drug, fill, gulp, jade, load, sate **5** choke, flood, gorge, stuff **6** burden, deluge, devour, excess, gobble **7** congest, overeat, satiate, surfeit, surplus **8** gobble up, obstruct, overdose, overfeed, overload, plethora, saturate **10** gormandize, oversupply, saturation **11** obstruction, superfluity **13** overabundance, supersaturate **14** superabundance **15** supersaturation

glutinous 5 gluey, bummy, mucid, ropey, slimy, tacky, thick **6** sticky, viscid **7** viscous **8** adhesive **10** gelatinous **12** musilaginous

glutton 3 hog, pig **6** gorger **7** stuffer **8** gourmand **9** chowhound, overeater **10** belly-slave **11** gormandizer, trencherman

gluttonous 6 greedy **7** hoggish, piggish, swinish **8** edacious, grasping, ravening, ravenous **9** excessive, voracious **10** insatiable, omnivorous **11** intemperate

gluttony 8 rapacity, voracity **10** overeating **11** gourmandism, hoggishness, piggishness **12** gormandizing, intemperance, ravenousness **13** voraciousness

gnarled 6 knotty, rugged, snaggy **7** crooked, knotted, nodular, twisted **8** leathery, wrinkled **9** contorted, distorted **11** full of knots **13** weatherbeaten

gnash 4 gnaw **5** chomp

gnat 7 no-see-um
    group of: 5 cloud, horde

gnaw 4 bite, chew, fret, gall **5** chafe, chomp, eat at, grate, graze, munch, worry **6** browse, crunch, harrow, nibble, rankle **7** torment, trouble **8**

distress, nibble at, ruminate **9** eat away at, masticate

gnome 3 elf **4** pixy **5** dwarf, troll **6** goblin, sprite **10** leprechaun

gnostic 4 sage, wise **6** clever, shrewd **7** knowing **8** mandaean, simonian **10** insightful

gnothi seauton 11 know thyself

gnu 7 brindle **8** antelope **10** wildebeest
type: 5 C gnou **9** C taurinus **12** Connochaetes

go 3 act, end, fit, fly, pep, run, try, vim **4** blow, dash, elan, fare, flee, flow, jibe, lead, life, pass, quit, stir, turn, wend, work **5** agree, begin, be off, blend, drive, force, get on, lapse, leave, reach, scram, slide, split, steam, tally, trial, verve, vigor, whirl **6** accord, beat it, be used, belong, chance, decamp, depart, effort, elapse, energy, expire, extend, mettle, pass by, repair, result, retire, spirit **7** advance, attempt, be given, be known, comport, fall out, glide by, move out, operate, perform, proceed, slip off, take off, turn out, vamoose, work out **8** ambition, endeavor, function, move away, progress, slip away, sneak off, spread to, start for, steal off, vitality, vivacity, withdraw **9** animation, harmonize, terminate, transpire **10** enterprise, experiment, initiative

goad 4 move, prod, push, spur, urge, whet **5** drive, egg on, impel, press, prick, set on **6** arouse, exhort, fillip, incite, motive, propel, stir up **8** pressure, stimulus **9** constrain, incentive, stimulant, stimulate **10** cattle prod, inducement, motivation **11** instigation

goal 3 aim, end **4** home, mark, wire **5** point, score, tally **6** design, intent, object, target **7** end line, purpose **8** ambition, goal line, terminus **9** intention, objective **10** finish line

go along with 5 usher **6** assent, convoy, escort **8** accede to, shepherd **9** accompany, agree with, chaperone, consent to **10** comply with

go ashore 4 land **6** debark **9** disembark

go astray 3 err, sin **6** wander **7** deviate, do wrong **9** misbehave **10** transgress **13** fall from grace

goat 3 kid **4** buck, butt **5** billy, nanny **6** victim **7** fall guy **9** scapegoat **11** whipping boy **13** laughingstock
breed: 6 Angora, Chamal, Nubian, Saanen **7** Granada **8** La Mancha **10** Toggenburg **11** Anglo-Nubian **12** French Alpine **13** British Alpine
combining form: 4 aego **5** capri
family: 7 Bovidae
female: 3 doe **5** capra, nanny **7** doeling
genus: 5 Capra
goat-boy: 5 Giles
goat-milk cheese: 7 chevret

goat-man: 5 satyr
god: 3 Pan **5** satyr **7** Aegipan
group of: 4 herd **5** tribe
hair: 5 kasha, tibet
hair of Angora goat: 6 mohair
male: 4 buck **5** billy
meat: 7 cabrito
star: 7 capella
young: 3 kid

Goat, Horned Goat
constellation of: 11 Capricornus

goat god 3 Pan **5** satyr

go away 3 ebb **4** fade, scat, wane **5** abate, leave, scram **6** depart, lessen, retire **8** withdraw **9** disappear

gob 3 dab, tar **4** clot, glob, lump, mass **6** sailor **7** Jack Tar

go back 7 return **7** retreat

gobble 3 caw **4** bolt, gulp, wolf **5** raven, stuff **6** cackle, devour, gabble, gaggle **8** bolt down, cram down, gulp down

gobbledygook 4 bosh, bunk, cant, tosh **6** jargon **7** rubbish, twaddle **8** buncombe, nonsense, tommyrot **9** gibberish, moonshine **10** balderdash, double-talk, hocus-pocus, mumbo jumbo **11** foolishness **12** fiddle-faddle

gobble up 6 devour **8** bolt down, gulp down, wolf down

go before 7 precede, predate **8** antecede, antedate **9** come first, go ahead of **10** anticipate

go-between 5 agent, envoy, fixer, proxy **6** deputy, second **7** arbiter **8** delegate, emissary, mediator **9** messenger, middleman, moderator **10** arbitrator, interceder, negotiator **12** intermediary **13** intermediator **14** representative

goblet 3 cup **5** glass **6** vessel **7** chalice

goblin 4 ogre **5** bogey, demon, troll **7** gremlin **8** bogeyman

Gobseck
author: 14 Honore de Balzac

go by 4 pass **6** elapse, pass by, roll by, rush by, slip by **7** glide by, slide by **8** slip away

go by car 4 ride **5** drive, motor

go-cart 4 cart **5** buggy **6** barrow **8** carriage, handcart, pushcart, stroller **11** wheelbarrow

go crimson 4 burn, glow **5** blush, color, flame, flush **6** redden

God, god 4 Lord **5** Allah, deity **6** Elohim, Jahveh, Yahweh **7** Holy One, Jehovah, Skaddai **8** divinity, the Deity **9** Our Father **10** the Creator, the Godhead **11** divine being, God Almighty, the Almighty **13** the Omnipotent, the Omniscient **14** the All-Merciful, the Man Upstairs **15** the Supreme Being
Hebrew: 6 Adonai
Latin: 7 Dominus

god, first

origin: 12 Scandinavian
known as: 7 Forsete, Forseti

God and Man at Yale
author: 17 William F Buckley Jr

God and my right
French: 14 Dieu et mon droit
motto of: 18 royal arms of England

God be with us
German: 10 Gott mit uns

God be with you
Latin: 12 Deus vobiscum

Godbole, Professor
character in: 15 A Passage to India
author: 7 Forster

Goddard, Jean-Luc
director of: 10 Breathless

Goddard, Paulette
real name: 10 Marion Levy
husband: 14 Charlie Chaplin **15** Burgess Meredith **18** Erich Maria Remarque
born: 11 Great Neck NY
roles: 11 Modern Times, Unconquered **15** So Proudly We Hail **16** Standing Room Only, The Great Dictator **19** Diary of a Chambermaid

Goddard, Robert Hutchings
nationality: 8 American
inventor of: 12 rocket engine **22** liquid propellant rocket

Godden, Rumer
author of: 8 The River **14** Black Narcissus, Kitchen Madonna **16** The Peacock Spring **18** In This House of Brede, The Greengage Summer **19** An Episode of Sparrows **23** The Battle of Villa Fiorita

God enriches
Latin: 9 ditat Deus
motto of: 7 Arizona

Godfather, The
author: 9 Mario Puzo
family: 8 Corleone
director: 18 Francis Ford Coppola
cast: 8 Al Pacino (Michael) **9** James Caan (Sonny) **10** John Cazale (Fredo), John Marley, Talia Shire **11** Diane Keaton **12** Marlon Brando (Don Vito Corleone), Richard Conte, Robert Duvall **14** Sterling Hayden **17** Richard Castellano
Oscar for: 5 actor (Brando) **7** picture **10** screenplay
sequel: 18 The Godfather Part II

Godfather, The, Part II
director: 18 Francis Ford Coppola
cast: 8 Al Pacino **10** John Cazale, Talia Shire **11** Diane Keaton **12** Lee Strasberg, Robert DeNiro, Robert Duvall
Oscar for: 7 picture **10** screenplay **15** supporting actor (DeNiro)
sequel to: 12 The Godfather

godforsaken 5 bleak **6** lonely, remote **8** deserted, desolate, wretched **9** abandoned, neglected

god from a machine
Latin: **13** deux ex machina

God is with us
German: **10** Gott mit uns

godless 4 evil **6** wicked **7** heathen, impious, profane, ungodly **8** agnostic, depraved **9** atheistic **10** unhallowed **11** blasphemous, irreligious, unrepentant, unrighteous **12** sacrilegious, unsanctified

godlessness 7 atheism **8** apostasy, unbelief **9** disbelief **10** irreligion

godlike 4 holy **5** godly, pious **6** deific, divine, sacred **8** immortal, olympian

godliness 5 piety **8** devotion, holiness **9** reverence **10** devoutness **12** spirituality

godly 4 good, holy **5** moral, pious **6** devout, divine, sacred **7** devoted, saintly **8** faithful, hallowed, reverent **9** believing, God-loving, pietistic, religious, righteous, spiritual **10** God-fearing, sanctified **11** consecrated, pure in heart, reverential

go down 3 ebb **4** drop, fade, wane **5** abate, lower, slide **6** lessen, plunge, reduce, weaken **7** descend, plummet, slacken, subside **8** decrease, diminish, moderate

God Save the Queen
author: **17** William F Buckley Jr

God's Grace
author: **14** Bernard Malamud

God's Little Acre
author: **15** Erskine Caldwell

Godthaab
capital of: **9** Greenland

God willing
Latin: **10** Deo volente

God wills it
Latin: **8** Deus vult
cry of: **9** Crusaders

Goes, Hugo van der
born: **5** Ghent **8** Flanders
artwork: **7** The Fall **14** The Lamentation **19** The Death of the Virgin **21** The Adoration of the Magi **22** The Adoration of the Child **26** The Adoration of the Shepherds

Goethe, Johann
author of: **5** Faust **6** Egmont **24** The Sorrows of Young Werther **29** Wilhelm Meister's Apprenticeship

go-getter 4 doer **7** hustler **8** achiever, live wire

go-getting 7 driving, dynamic **8** forceful, hustling **9** ambitious, assertive, energetic **10** aggressive **11** hard-driving, hard-working, industrious

Gogol, Nikolai
author of: **7** The Nose **9** Dead Souls **10** Taras Bulba **11** The Overcoat **19** The Inspector-General

go hand in hand 5 match, tally **6** concur, square **7** coexist **9** accompany

go hungry 4 fast **6** famish, starve **7** abstain

Going My Way
director: **10** Leo McCarey
cast: **10** Bing Crosby (Father O'Malley) **12** Gene Lockhart **15** Barry Fitzgerald
Oscar for: **4** song **5** actor (Crosby) **7** picture **8** director **15** supporting actor (Fitzgerald)
song: **15** Swinging on a Star

gold 3 bar **4** gilt **5** aurum, ingot **6** beauty, nugget, purity, yellow **7** bullion **8** goodness, goodwill, humanity, kindness **11** beneficence
chemical symbol: **2** Au

gold and silver
Spanish: **9** oro y plata
motto of: **7** Montana

Gold Bug, The
author: **13** Edgar Allan Poe

Gold Coast see **5** Ghana **11** Sierra Leone

golden 4 best, gilt, rosy **5** blest, blond, great, happy, palmy **6** bright, gilded, joyous, timely **7** aureate, halcyon, richest, shining **8** beatific, glorious, happiest, splendid **9** favorable, opportune, priceless, promising **10** auspicious, delightful, propitious, seasonable **11** exceptional, flourishing, resplendent **12** advantageous, bright-yellow **13** extraordinary

Golden Age
first age of: **3** man
world ruled by: **6** Cronus, Saturn

Golden Ass, The
author: **14** Lucius Apuleius
character: **4** Milo **5** Fotis **6** Lucius **8** Charites, Pamphile **9** Lepolemus **10** Thrasillus

Goldenberg, Emmanuel
real name of: **15** Edward G Robinson

Golden Bough, The
branch of: **9** mistletoe
sacred to: **10** Proserpina
used by: **6** Aeneas
at shrine of: **5** Diana **7** Virbius
author: **15** Sir James G Frazer

Golden Bowl, The
author: **10** Henry James
character: **8** Mr Verver **12** Maggie Verver, Mrs Assingham **13** Prince Amerigo **14** Charlotte Stant

Golden Boy
nickname of: **11** Paul Hornung

golden brown 3 tan **5** tawny, toast **6** sienna **7** tobacco **8** chestnut

Golden Cockerel, The
also: **8** Le Coq d'Or **15** Zolotoy Petushok
opera by: **14** Rimsky-Korsakov
character: **9** King Dodon **14** Queen of Shemaka

golden egg-layer

form: 5 goose
made of: **4** gold

Golden Fleece
made of: **4** gold
kept at: **7** Colchis
kept by: **10** King Aeetes
stolen by: **5** Jason **9** Argonauts
accomplice: **5** Medea

Golden Legend
author: **13** William Caxton

goldenrod 8 Solidago
varieties: **5** sweet, white **6** Wreath **7** seaside **8** blue- stem, European **10** California

Golden State
nickname of: **10** California

golden youth
French: **13** jeunesse doree

goldfinch
group of: **5** charm

Goldfinger
director: **11** Guy Hamilton
author: **10** Ian Fleming
cast: **9** Gert Frobe (Auric Goldfinger) **10** Bernard Lee (M) **11** Lois Maxwell (Miss Moneypenny) **12** Harold Sakata (Oddjob), Shirley Eaton **13** Honor Blackman (Pussy Galore), Sean Connery (James Bond, 007)

Golding, William
author of: **8** Free Fall **13** A Moving Target **14** Lord of the Flies, Rites of Passage **15** Darkness Visible

gold mine 7 bonanza **10** mother lode

Gold Rush, The
director: **14** Charlie Chaplin
cast: **9** Mack Swain, Tom Murray **11** Georgia Hale **14** Charlie Chaplin (Little Tramp)
setting: **5** Yukon

Goldsmith, Oliver
author of: **18** She Stoops to Conquer, The Deserted Village **19** The Vicar of Wakefield

goldwasser
form: **7** liquor
origin: **6** France **7** Germany
flavor: **4** herb **5** spice **7** caraway
flecked with: **8** gold leaf

golf
average number strokes to reach a hole: **3** par
ball in another's path: **6** stymie
championship: **6** US Open **9** Grand Slam **11** British Open **17** Masters' Tournament
club: **4** iron, wood **6** driver, putter **7** brassie **8** long iron **9** sand wedge, short iron **10** middle iron **13** pitching wedge
club carrier: **6** caddie
course also called: **5** links
golf ball formerly called: **6** guttie **8** feathery
hole scored in one stroke: **3** ace **9** hole-in-one
one stroke less than par: **6** birdie

one stroke more than par: 5 bogey
part of the course: 3 cup, tee **4** hole
5 apron, green, rough **6** bunker, hazard **7** fairway **8** sand trap
position: 3 lie
stance: 4 open **6** closed, square **7** address
two strokes less than par: 5 eagle
type of competition: 5 match, skins
6 stroke
uprooted turf: 5 divot
warning cry: 4 fore

golfer 8 Ben Hogan, Ernie Els, Lee Elder, Sam Snead **9** Carol Mann, Hale Irwin, Patty Berg, Tom Watson **10** Betsy Rawls, Bobby Jones, Deane Beman, Gary Player, Hubie Green, Jim Demaret, Judy Rankin, Lee Trevino, Nancy Lopez, Tiger Woods **11** Ben Crenshaw, Billy Casper, Byron Nelson, Calvin Peete, Donna Caponi, Gene Sarazen, Julius Boros, Tom Weiskopf, Walter Hagen **12** Arnold Palmer, Jack Nicklaus, Joanne Carner, Johnny Miller, Mickey Wright, Sandra Haynie **14** Cary Middlecoff, Kathy Whitworth **16** Roberto DeVicenzo **19** Susie Maxwell Berning **20** Severiano Ballesteros **21** Babe Didrikson Zaharias

Golgotha 7 Calvary
means: 10 skull place

Goliath 5 giant
home: 4 Gath **9** Philistia
slain by: 5 David
weapon: 9 slingshot

golliwogg 3 toy **4** doll **9** plaything

Gomer Pyle USMC
character: 5 Bunny **7** Frankie **9** Corp Boyle **11** Duke Slayter, (Sgt) Vince Carter
cast: 9 Jim Nabors, Roy Stuart **10** Ted Bessell **11** Frank Sutton **12** Ronnie Schell **13** Barbara Stuart

Gomorrah
destroyed with: 5 Sodom **6** Zeboim **10** Admah

Gondoliers, The
operetta by: 18 Gilbert and Sullivan
character: 4 Luiz **5** Tessa **7** Casilda **8** Gianetta **13** Marco Palmieri **15** Duke of Plaza-Toro **16** Giuseppe Palmieri

gone 3 ago, out **4** away, dead, left, lost, past **6** absent, ruined, used up **7** defunct, died out, extinct, missing **8** departed, finished, hopeless, vanished **11** disappeared

Goneril
character in: 8 King Lear
author: 11 Shakespeare

Gone With the Wind
author: 16 Margaret Mitchell
character: 5 Mammy **6** Big Sam, Prissy **7** Dr Meade **10** Ellen (Robillard) O'Hara **11** Gerald O'Hara, Honey Wilkes, India Wilkes **12** Ashley Wilkes, Aunt Pittypat, Belle Watling **13** Scarlett O'Hara, Tarleton

twins 15 Mrs Merriweather **21** Melanie Hamilton Wilkes
Scarlett's husband: 11 Rhett Butler **12** Frank Kennedy **15** Charles Hamilton
Scarlett's children: 4 Emma, Wade **6** Bonnie
Scarlett's sister: 7 Carreen, Suellen
director: 13 Victor Fleming
cast: 9 Ona Munson **10** Clark Gable (Rhett Butler) **11** Evelyn Keyes, Vivien Leigh (Scarlett O'Hara) **12** Leslie Howard (Ashley Wilkes) **13** Ann Rutherford **14** Hattie McDaniel (Mammy), Thomas Mitchell (Gerald O'Hara) **16** Butterfly McQueen (Prissy) **17** Olivia de Havilland (Melanie Hamilton Wilkes)
score: 10 Max Steiner
Oscar for: 7 actress (Leigh), picture **8** director **12** screenwriter **17** supporting actress (McDaniel)
producer: 14 David O Selznick

good 3 ace, fit, new **4** best, boon, fine, full, gain, kind, pure, real **5** ample, crack, favor, great, large, merit, moral, pious, prize, right, solid, sound, sunny, valid, value, worth **6** adroit, choice, devout, entire, genial, honest, humane, kindly, lively, newest, profit, proper, seemly, select, tiptop, useful, virtue, wealth, worthy **7** adapted, benefit, capable, capital, dutiful, fitting, genuine, godsend, healthy, orderly, service, sizable, skilled, success, upright, welfare **8** adequate, becoming, blessing, bonafide, cheerful, complete, decorous, gracious, innocent, interest, kindness, obedient, obliging, pleasant, precious, reliable, salutary, skillful, smartest, sociable, splendid, suitable, thorough, topnotch, valuable, virtuous, windfall **9** admirable, advantage, agreeable, authentic, convivial, deserving, efficient, enjoyable, enjoyment, excellent, exemplary, expensive, favorable, first-rate, happiness, healthful, honorable, priceless, qualified, religious, righteous, unsullied, untainted, wholesome, wonderful **10** altruistic, beneficent, beneficial, benevolent, excellence, first-class, legitimate, proficient, prosperity, sufficient, worthwhile **11** appropriate, commendable, considerate, improvement, kindhearted, substantial, sympathetic, well-behaved **12** advantageous, considerable, praiseworthy, satisfactory **13** companionable, conscientious, righteousness
French: 3 bon **4** bien
Spanish: 5 bueno
German: 3 gut

Good as Gold
author: 12 Joseph Heller

Good Book 5 Bible

good breeding 5 grace **6** polish

7 manners **9** gentility **10** refinement **11** cultivation

good buy 4 deal **5** steal **7** bargain

goodby, goodbye 3 bye **6** bye-bye, bye now, so long **7** parting, send-off **8** farewell, Godspeed **9** departure **10** separation **11** be seeing you, leavetaking, see you later **12** God be with you **15** till we meet again
French: 5 adieu **8** au revoir
German: 14 auf Wiedersehen
Hawaiian: 5 aloha
Italian: 4 ciao **5** addio **11** arrivederci
Japanese: 8 sayonara
Latin: 4 vale
Spanish: 5 adios **12** hasta la vista

Goodbye, Mr Chips
director: 7 Sam Wood
author: 11 James Hilton
cast: 11 Greer Garson, Paul Henreid (von Henreid), Robert Donat
Oscar for: 5 actor (Donat)
character: 7 Mr Chips **10** Mrs Wickett **12** Kathy Bridges
school: 10 Brookfield

Goodbye Girl, The
director: 11 Herbert Ross
based on play by: 9 Neil Simon
cast: 11 Marsha Mason **13** Quinn Cummings **15** Richard Dreyfuss
Oscar for: 5 actor (Dreyfuss)

Good Companions, The
author: 11 J B Priestley

good counsel
god of: 6 Consus

good day
French: 7 bonjour
German: 8 guten tag
Spanish: 10 buenos dias
Italian: 10 buon giorno

good deal 3 buy **5** steal **7** bargain

good deed 8 kindness **11** benefaction **12** philanthropy
Hebrew: 7 mitsvah, mitzvah

Good Earth, The
author: 10 Pearl S Buck
character: 4 O-Lan **6** Nung En **7** Nung Wen, The Fool **8** Wang Lung **11** Pear Blossom **12** Lotus Blossom
director: 14 Sidney Franklin
cast: 8 Keye Luke, Paul Muni **10** Tilly Losch **11** Jessie Ralph, Luise Rainer **14** Walter Connolly **15** Charley Grapewin
Oscar for: 7 actress (Rainer)

good feelings 3 era **8** good will **11** benevolence **12** friendliness

good form 9 etiquette, good taste **10** politeness **11** good manners

good-for-nothing 5 idler **6** loafer **7** useless **9** no-account, shiftless, worthless

good fortune 4 luck **7** bonanza **8** fortuity, lady luck, windfall **9** blessings **10** lucky break

good friend
French: **6** bon ami **9** bonne amie

good health 5 vigor **7** fitness **8** vitality **10** robustness

Goodhue, Bertram Grosvenor
architect of: **13** St Bartholomew (NYC) **14** St Thomas Church (NYC) **25** Chapel at US Military Academy (West Point), National Academy of Sciences (Washington DC) **28** Nebraska State Capitol Building (Lincoln)
style: **13** Gothic Revival **15** Spanish Colonial

good humor 10 affability, amiability, cheeriness, kindliness, mellowness **12** cheerfulness, complaisance, pleasantness **15** kindheartedness

good-humored 4 mild, warm **6** cheery, genial, gentle, kindly, mellow **7** affable, amiable **8** cheerful, pleasant **9** congenial, easygoing **11** complaisant

good-looker 3 fox **4** doll, hunk **5** beaut, Venus **6** Adonis, beauty, eyeful **7** stunner **8** knockout **11** handsome Dan

good-looking 4 fair, foxy, sexy **5** bonny **6** comely, lovely, pretty **8** alluring, clean-cut, gorgeous, handsome, stunning **9** beauteous, beautiful, exquisite, ravishing **10** attractive, bewitching, enchanting **11** captivating, eye-catching, well-favored **15** pulchritudinous

good looks 6 beauty **10** comeliness, loveliness **11** pulchritude **12** handsomeness **14** attractiveness

good luck
Yiddish: **8** mazel tov

goodly 4 tidy **5** ample, large **7** sizable **11** substantial **12** considerable

good manners 8 courtesy **9** amenities, etiquette, gentility **10** politeness, refinement

good name 4 face **5** image **10** reputation **11** self-respect

good nature 6 warmth **9** geniality, good humor **10** affability, amiability, cordiality, likability **12** complaisance, pleasantness **13** agreeableness

good-natured 4 warm **5** sunny **6** genial, kindly **7** affable, amiable **8** cheerful, friendly, obliging, pleasant **9** agreeable, congenial, easygoing **11** complaisant, good-humored, warmhearted **13** accommodating

goodness 3 boy, gee, hey, say, wow **5** favor, honor, mercy, merit, piety, value, worth, wowee **6** profit, purity, virtue **7** benefit, decorum, gee whiz, heavens, honesty, probity, service **8** boy-oh-boy, devotion, gracious, kindness, morality **9** advantage, innocence, integrity, land alive, landsakes, nutrition, propriety, rectitude **10** generosity, kindliness, sakes alive, usefulness **11** benevolence, nourishment

12 virtuousness **13** righteousness, wholesomeness **14** heavens to Betsy

good night
French: **7** bon soir **9** bonne nuit
German: **9** gute nacht
Spanish: **12** buenas noches
Italian: **10** buona notte

good opinion 6 esteem, regard **7** respect **8** approval **10** admiration

good person 4 dear, love **5** angel **7** darling **10** sweetheart

goods 4 gear **5** cloth, stock, wares **6** fabric, things **7** effects, fabrics **8** chattels, material, movables, property, textiles **9** inventory, trappings **11** commodities, furnishings, merchandise, possessions **13** appurtenances, paraphernalia

good sense 6 brains, wisdom **8** judgment **12** intelligence

good taste 10 refinement **11** cultivation, discernment **14** discrimination

good-tempered 5 sunny **7** amiable, smiling **8** cheerful **12** sweet-natured

good time 3 fun **9** amusement, diversion, enjoyment **13** entertainment

good times 4 boom **8** fat years

good turn 5 favor **7** service **8** good deed

goodwill 5 amity **8** kindness **9** benignity **10** cordiality, kindliness **11** amicability, benevolence **12** friendliness **15** kindheartedness

good wishes 4 best **5** favor **6** regard **7** consent, regards **8** approval, blessing, respects, sanction **11** compliments

Goodwood, Caspar
character in: **18** The Portrait of a Lady
author: **5** James

good word 6 praise **10** compliment **11** approbation **12** commendation **14** congratulation

Goodyear, Charles
nationality: **8** American
developed: **16** vulcanized rubber

goof 3 err **4** boob, flub, fool, mess **5** botch, error, gum up **6** bollix, booboo, bungle, fumble, slip up **7** blunder, mistake **9** oversight

Goolagong Cawley, Evonne
sport: **6** tennis
heritage: **19** Australian Aborigine

go on all fours 5 crawl, creep

goose
young: **7** gosling
group of: **5** flock, skein **6** gaggle

goose egg 3 nil, zip **4** zero **5** aught **6** cipher, naught **7** nothing **11** horse collar

go over 5 audit, check **6** review **7** examine, inspect **10** scrutinize **11** investigate

Gopher State
nickname of: **9** Minnesota

Gorbachev, Mikhail Sergeyevich
party: **9** Communist
country: **4** USSR **6** Russia **31** Union of Soviet Socialist Republics
born: **9** Stavropol **10** Privolnoye **16** Krasnogvardeisky
education: **21** Moscow State University
political career: **9** Politburo **16** General Secretary **20** Agriculture Secretary **23** Stavropol Communist Party **35** Deputy Supreme Soviet Central Committee
policy: **8** glasnost **11** perestroika
distinguishing characteristic: **19** strawberry birthmark (head)
wife: **15** Raisa Maksimovna
occupation: **7** teacher
daughter: **5** Irisa
occupation: **6** doctor **9** physician
grandchild: **6** Oksana

Gorcey, Leo
born: **9** New York NY
roles: **4** Spit **10** Bowery Boys **11** Dead End Kids

Gordimer, Nadine
author of: **11** July's People **12** The Lying Days **13** A Guest of Honor **15** Burger's Daughter **16** A Soldier's Embrace **21** The Late Bourgeois World
award: **10** Nobel Prize

Gordon, Ruth
real name: **15** Ruth Gordon Jones
husband: **11** Garson Kanin
born: **11** Wollaston MA
roles: **11** Where's Poppa? **13** Rosemary's Baby **14** Harold and Maude **17** Inside Daisy Clover **20** Abe Lincoln in Illinois

gore 5 blood **7** carnage **8** butchery **9** bloodshed, slaughter

Gore, Albert
born: **10** Washington (DC)
wife: **6** Tipper **13** Mary Elizabeth
children: **5** Sarah **6** Albert **7** Karenna, Kristin
education: **7** Harvard **10** Vanderbilt
profession: **10** journalist
author of: **17** Earth in the Balance
political career: **6** Senate **13** vice president **22** House of Representatives

Gorgas, William Crawford
field: **8** medicine
position: **18** army surgeon general
conquered: **7** malaria **11** yellow fever
location: **11** Panama Canal

gorge 3 gap, ire **4** bolt, cram, craw, dale, dell, fill, glen, glut, gulp, pass, sate, vale **5** abyss, anger, blood, chasm, cleft, gulch, gully, mouth, stuff, wrath **6** canyon, defile, devour, gobble, gullet, hatred, hollow, muzzle, nausea, ravine, throat **7** disgust, indulge, overeat, satiate **8** crevasse **9** animosity, esophagus, repulsion, revulsion **10** gluttonize, gormandize, repugnance **11** overindulge

gorgeous 4 fine, rich **5** grand **6** bright, costly, lovely **7** elegant, opulent, shining **8** dazzling, glorious, imposing, splendid, stunning **9** beautiful, brilliant, exquisite, luxurious, ravishing, sumptuous **10** attractive, glittering, impressive **11** good-looking, magnificent, resplendent, splendorous **13** splendiferous

Gorgons
form: **7** maidens **8** monsters
names: **6** Medusa, Stheno **7** Euryale, Sthenno
father: **7** Phorcys
mother: **4** Ceto
protectress: **6** Graeae, Graiae
hair of: **6** snakes
hands of: **5** brass
turned viewers to: **5** stone

Gorgosaurus
type: **8** dinosaur, theropod
location: **7** Alberta **12** North America
period: **10** Cretaceous

gorilla
group of: **4** band
studied by: **10** Dian Fossey

Gorky, Arshile
real name: **21** Vosdanig Manoog Adokian
born: **7** Armenia **11** Khorkomvari
artwork: **5** Agony **15** Diary of a Seducer **17** Making the Calendar **21** The Artist and his Mother, Water of the Flowery Hill **22** The Liver is the Cock's Comb

Gorky, Maxim (Maksim)
real name: **25** Alekseimaksimovich Peshkov
author of: **7** V I Lenin **11** My Childhood **14** The Lower Depths **18** The Small Town Okurov **20** City of the Yellow Devil, Twenty-six Men and a Girl **27** The Life of Matthew Kozhemyakin

gormandize 5 feast, raven **6** devour

gory 5 scary **6** bloody, creepy **9** murderous **10** horrifying, sanguinary, terrifying **11** bloodsoaked, ensanguined, frightening **12** bloodstained, bloodthirsty **13** bloodcurdling

gospel, Gospel 5 credo, creed **8** doctrine **11** the good news, the last word **12** the final word **13** the whole truth, ultimate truth
the first four books of the New Testament: **4** Luke, John, Mark **7** Matthew

Gospel writers 4 John, Luke, Mark **7** Matthew **9** synoptist

gospodin (Russian) 2 Mr **6** Mister

gossamer 5 filmy, gauzy, sheer **8** cobwebby **10** diaphanous **13** insubstantial

gossip 4 news **6** babble, report, tattle **7** comment, hearsay, prattle, scandal, twaddle **8** idle talk **10** backbiting **12** tittle-tattle **13** newsmongering

gossiper 3 pry **4** blab **5** prate, snoop, yenta **6** gabble, magpie, meddle, tattle **7** babbler, meddler, prattle, snooper, tattler **8** busybody **9** chatterer **10** chatterbox, newsmonger, talebearer, tattletale **11** rumormonger **12** blabbermouth, gossipmonger **13** scandalmonger

Go Tell It on the Mountain
author: **12** James Baldwin

Gothic
language family: **12** Indo-European

go through 4 bear **6** endure, suffer **7** sustain, undergo **9** encounter, withstand **10** experience

go to 3 see **5** visit **6** attend **8** appear at, frequent

go to bed 6 retire, turn in **7** lie down, sack out **8** flake out **9** hit the hay **10** call it a day, hit the sack **11** catch some z's

go to pieces 5 break, crack **7** break up, crack up, crumble, give way, shatter **8** splinter **9** break down, fall apart **11** lose control **12** disintegrate

go to work on 6 attack, tackle **8** set about **9** undertake

go to wrack and ruin 5 decay **7** crumble **9** fall apart **12** disintegrate

Gotterdammerung 17 Twilight of the Gods
see: **8** Ragnarok

Gott mit uns 11 God be with us, God is with us

gouge 5 carve, drill, scoop **6** chisel, extort **10** overcharge

gouge out 5 drill **6** hollow **8** carve out, scoop out **9** chisel out, hollow out **10** whittle out

Gould, Chester
creator/artist of: **9** Dick Tracy

Gould, Elliott
real name: **16** Elliott Goldstein
wife: **15** Barbra Streisand
born: **10** Brooklyn NY
roles: **4** MASH **11** Little Murders **14** The Long Goodbye **15** California Split, Getting Straight **19** Bob & Carol & Ted & Alice

Goulding, Edmund
director of: **10** Grand Hotel **11** Dark Victory **17** The Dawn Patrol

go under 4 fail, fall, sink **9** go belly up **10** go bankrupt

Gounod, Charles Francois
born: **5** Paris **6** France
composer of: **5** Faust **6** Gallia, Sappho, Te Deum **8** Cinq-Mars, Mireille **9** La Colombe, Polyeucte **10** Mors et Vita **11** Marie Stuart, Stabat Mater **13** La Reine de Saba **14** Romeo and Juliet **16** La Nonne Sanglante, Phile-

mon et Baucis **17** La Tribute de Zamora **18** Le Medecin Malgre Lui

gourd 4 pepo **9** Cucurbita
varieties: **3** ash, ivy, rag, wax **4** club **5** snake, white **6** bitter, bottle, dipper, sponge, teasel, viper's **7** fig-leaf, Malabar, serpent, trumpet **8** calabash, hedgehog, Missouri **9** dishcloth **10** goareberry, gooseberry, knobkerrie, silver-seed **11** sugar- trough **12** Hercules'-club **14** scarlet-fruited

gourmand 7 glutton **8** big eater **9** bon vivant, chowhound **11** gormandizer, trencherman

gourmet 7 epicure **9** bon vivant **10** gastronome **11** connoisseur, gastronomer **12** gastronomist

gourmet cooking
French: **12** haute cuisine

gout 5 style, taste **10** preference

govern 3 run **4** boss, curb, form, head, lead, rule, sway, tame **5** check, guide, pilot, steer **6** bridle, direct, manage **7** command, control, incline, inhibit, oversee **8** dominate, restrain **9** influence, supervise **10** administer, discipline, hold in hand **11** hold in check, superintend **13** be at the helm of **14** pull the strings **16** keep under control **17** exercise authority **18** be in the driver's seat

governed 3 led **5** ruled **6** guided **7** steered, subject **8** directed **9** dependent **10** controlled, supervised **12** administered **13** superintended

governing 6 ruling **7** curbing, guiding, heading, leading, swaying **8** bridling, checking, managing, piloting, reigning, steering **9** directing, inclining **10** inhibiting, management, overseeing **11** controlling, influencing, restraining, supervision **13** administering **14** administrating, administration, superintending

governing body 10 government, management, parliament **12** powers that be **14** administration **16** board of directors, board of governors **18** executive committee

government 3 law **4** rule **5** state **6** regime **7** command, control **8** dominion, guidance **9** authority, direction **10** domination, management, regulation **11** supervision **13** governing body, statesmanship **14** administration
absence of: **7** anarchy
absolute: **7** czarism, tsarism, tyranny **9** autocracy, despotism
by the best: **11** aristocracy
by church: **9** theocracy
by elders: **12** gerontocracy
by technologists: **11** technocracy
by few: **9** oligarchy
by mob: **10** ochlocracy
by people: **9** democracy
by rich: **10** plutocracy
by three: **8** triarchy **11** triumvirate

by two: 7 biarchy 10 duumvirate
by women: 8 gynarchy 10 matriarchy

governor
Turkish: 3 bey
Barbary States: 3 dey

Gowan
character in: 12 Little Dorrit
author: 7 Dickens

go with 6 convey, convoy, escort 7 conduct 9 accompany

gown 4 robe 5 dress, frock 10 nightdress

goy 6 non-Jew 7 Gentile

Goya (y Lucientes, Francisco Jose de)
born: 5 Spain 13 Fuente de todos
artwork: 8 Proverbs 10 Disparates 11 Tauromaquia 12 Los Caprichos, The Naked Maja 15 Majas on a Balcony 17 The Disasters of War 21 Charles IV and his Family

grab 3 bag, nab 4 grip, hold, pass 5 catch, clasp, grasp, lunge, pluck, seize 6 clutch, collar, snatch 7 capture

grace 4 deck, love, tact, trim 5 adorn, charm, endow, exalt, favor, honor, mercy, merit, piety, skill, taste 6 beauty, bedeck, enrich, pardon, polish, set off, virtue 7 charity, culture, decorum, dignify, dress up, elevate, enhance, garnish, glorify, manners, smarten, suavity 8 beautify, clemency, decorate, elegance, felicity, fluidity, God's love, holiness, lenience, ornament, reprieve, sanctity, spruce up, urbanity 9 embellish, endowment, etiquette, exemption, extra time, God's favor, good looks, propriety 10 aggrandize, comeliness, devoutness, excellence, indulgence, refinement 11 cultivation, forgiveness, lissomeness, pulchritude, saintliness, willowiness 12 dispensation, gracefulness, mannerliness, mercifulness 14 accomplishment, divine goodness
French: 11 savoir faire

graceful 5 lithe 6 comely, limber, lovely 7 elegant, lissome, shapely, sinuous, willowy 8 delicate 9 beautiful, lithesome, sylphlike 10 attractive 11 light-footed

gracefulness 8 delicacy, fluidity 10 suppleness 11 lissomeness

graceless 5 gawky, inept 6 clumsy 7 awkward 10 ungraceful 11 heavyhanded

Graces
also: 7 Gratiae 9 Charities
goddesses of: 6 beauty
father: 4 Zeus
mother: 6 Eurynome
names: 4 Auxo 5 Cleta 6 Aglaia, Thalia 7 Phaenna 8 Hegemone 10 Euphrosyne

gracious 2 my 3 boy, gee, wow 4 kind 5 civil, mercy, oh boy 6 benign, hu-

mane, kindly, polite, tender, ye gods 7 affable, amiable, clement, cordial, courtly, gee whiz, lenient, my stars 8 friendly, goodness, merciful, obliging, pleasant 9 benignant, courteous, landsakes 10 benevolent, charitable, chivalrous, hospitable 11 good heavens, good natured, kindhearted 13 compassionate 14 heavens to Betsy

gradation 4 step 5 stage 6 degree 7 shading 8 grouping, ordering 9 arranging 11 arrangement 12 organization 14 classification

grade 4 bank, even, hill, mark, ramp, rank, rate, sort, step 5 brand, caste, class, level, order, pitch, place, slope, stage, value 6 degree, estate, rating, smooth, sphere, status 7 flatten, incline, quality, station 8 classify, gradient, position, standing 9 acclivity, condition, declivity, intensity

grade-A 2 A-1 4 aces, a-one, fine, tops 5 grade, great, prime, super 6 choice, superb, tip-top 7 capital 8 peerless, sterling, superior, top-notch 9 excellent, first-rate, matchless, superfine 10 first-class, preeminent, tremendous 11 outstanding, superlative

Gradgrind, Thomas and Louisa
characters in: 9 Hard Times
author: 7 Dickens

gradient 4 ramp, tilt 5 pitch, slant, slope 6 ascent 7 incline, leaning 9 steepness 11 inclination

gradual 4 slow 6 gentle, steady 7 regular 8 measured 9 graduated, piecemeal 10 continuous, deliberate, drop-by-drop, inch-by-inch, step-by-step, successive 11 incremental, progressive 13 imperceptible, slow-but-steady 14 little-by-little

graduate 5 grade 6 alumna 7 alumnus, mark off 9 calibrate 10 measure out 14 grant a degree to, receive a degree

Graduate, The
director: 11 Mike Nichols
cast: 12 Anne Bancroft (Mrs Robinson) 13 Dustin Hoffman, Katharine Ross 14 Murray Hamilton, William Daniels
score: 17 Simon and Garfunkel
Oscar for: 8 director

Graeae
also: 6 Graiae
goddesses of: 3 sea
number: 5 three
names: 4 Enyo 5 Deino 9 Pemphredo
father: 7 Phorcys
mother: 4 Ceto
sisters: 7 Gorgons
protectresses of: 7 Gorgons
personified: 6 old age
three shared: 6 one eye 8 one tooth
eye stolen by: 7 Perseus
corresponds to: 4 Enyo

Graeme, Alison

character in: 21 The Master of Ballantrae
author: 9 Stevenson

Graf 5 count

graffito, graffiti 4 name 6 slogan 7 drawing, scratch 8 scribble 10 defacement

graft 3 bud 4 join, last, slip, swag 5 booty, infix, inset, plant, scion 6 bribes, payola, splice, spoils, sprout 7 bribery, implant, ingraft, payoffs, plunder, rake-off 8 kickback 9 hush money 10 corruption, transplant 12 implantation 13 inserted shoot

Graham, Bruce
architect of: 17 John Hancock Center (Chicago)

Grahame, Kenneth
author of: 19 The Wind in the Willows

Graiae *see* 6 Graeae

grain 3 bit, dot, jot, rye 4 atom, corn, dash, iota, mite, oats, seed, whit 5 crumb, grist, maize, ovule, pinch, spark, speck, touch, trace, wheat 6 barley, cereal, kernel, millet, morsel, pellet, tittle, trifle 7 granule, modicum 8 fragment, molecule, particle 9 scintilla
abbreviation: 2 gr
god of: 7 Robigus
goddess of: 6 Ribigo

Grain Coast *see* 11 Sierra Leone

Grainger, Percy Aldridge
born: 9 Australia, Melbourne
composer of: 14 Country Gardens 17 Handel in the Strand 19 Rosenkavalier Ramble

gram
abbreviation of: 1 g

Gram
origin: 12 Scandinavian
mentioned in: 8 Volsunga
form: 5 sword
owned by: 7 Sigmund
used by: 6 Sigurd
killed by: 6 Fafnir

grand 2 A-1 3 big 4 fine, full, good, head, huge, keen, main 5 chief, fancy, great, large, lofty, noble, regal, royal, showy, super, swell 6 august, choice, groovy, kingly, lordly, superb 7 dashing, elegant, exalted, haughty, mammoth, opulent, pompous, queenly, stately, sublime, supreme 8 arrogant, complete, elevated, fabulous, glorious, imperial, imposing, majestic, palatial, princely, real cool, real gone, smashing, splendid, striking, terrific 9 admirable, dignified, excellent, first-rate, grandiose, luxurious, marvelous, principal, sumptuous, wonderful 10 impressive, monumental, out-of-sight 11 highfalutin, magnificent, pretentious, sensational 12 ostentatious 13 comprehensive, distinguished

Grand Canyon State
   nickname of: **7** Arizona

grande dame 9 great lady

grandee 5 noble **8** nobleman **9** blue
   blood **10** aristocrat

Grandees
   author: **17** Stephen Birmingham

grandeur 4 fame, pomp **5** glory, state
   6 luster **7** dignity, majesty **8** eminence, nobility, splendor **9** celebrity,
   loftiness, solemnity, sublimity **10** augustness, excellence, importance **11**
   distinction, stateliness **12** magnificence, resplendence **14** impressiveness

Grand Hotel
   author: **9** Vicki Baum
   character: **9** Miss Flamm **12** Baron
      Gaigern **14** Dr Otternschlag, Otto
      Kringelein **27** Herr Generaldirektor
      Preysing **32** Elisaveta Alexandrovna
      Grusinskaya
   director: **14** Edmund Goulding
   cast: **10** Greta Garbo **12** Joan Craw-
      ford, Wallace Beery **13** John Barry-
      more **15** Lionel Barrymore
   setting: **6** Berlin

Grand Illusion
   director: **10** Jean Renoir
   cast: **5** Dalio **7** Carette **9** Dita Parlo,
      Jean Gabin **13** Pierre Fresnay **16** Er-
      ich von Stroheim

grandiloquent 5 lofty **6** florid, turgid
   7 flowery, pompous, stilted, swollen **8**
   inflated **9** bombastic, grandiose, high-
   flown **10** rhetorical **11** highfalutin,
   pretentious **12** high-sounding, magniloquent

grandiose 5 grand **7** pompous,
   splashy **8** affected **9** high-flown **10**
   flamboyant, theatrical **11** extravagant,
   highfalutin, pretentious

Grand Marnier
   type: **6** brandy, cognac **7** liqueur
   origin: **6** France
   flavor: **6** orange
   with gin: **7** Red Lion

grand monde 10 great world **11** best
   society **16** fashionable world

grand prix 10 grand prize

grand prize
   French: **9** grand prix

Grange, Red (Harold)
   nickname: **14** Galloping Ghost
   sport: **8** football
   team: **11** U of Illinois **12** Chicago
      Bears

Granger, Edith
   character in: **12** Dombey and Son
   author: **7** Dickens

Grangosier
   character in: **22** Gargantua and
      Pantagruel
   author: **8** Rabelais

Granite State
   nickname of: **12** New Hampshire

grant 4 boon, cede, gift, give **5** admit,
   allot, allow, award, endow, favor,
   yield **6** accord, assign, bestow, confer,
   donate, permit **7** agree to, bequest,
   concede, consent, deal out, largess,
   present, subsidy, tribute **8** accede to,
   allocate, bestowal, dispense, donation,
   gratuity, offering **9** allotment, allowance, apportion, consent to, endowment, vouchsafe **10** assignment, concession, indulgence **11** benefaction **12**
   contribution, presentation **13** appropriation

Grant, Cary
   real name: **23** Archibald Alexander
      Leach
   wife: **10** Dyan Cannon **13** Barbara
      Hutton
   born: **7** England **8** Bristol
   roles: **6** Topper **9** Dream Wife,
      Houseboat **10** Indiscreet **11** Blonde
      Venus, Father Goose **13** To Catch a
      Thief **14** Bringing Up Baby, Monkey
      Business, The Bishop's Wife **15** She
      Done Him Wrong **16** North by
      Northwest **17** Arsenic and Old Lace,
      I Was a Male War Bride **18** Opera-
      tion Petticoat **20** The Philadelphia
      Story **21** None But the Lonely Heart

Grant, Lee
   real name: **21** Lyova Haskell Rosen-
      thal
   born: **9** New York NY
   roles: **7** Shampoo **10** Plaza Suite **11**
      Peyton Place, The Landlord **14** De-
      tective Story **19** In the Heat of the
      Night **20** Divorce American Style

Grant, Ulysses Simpson
   real name: **17** Hiram Ulysses Grant
   nickname: **3** Sam **4** Lyss **27** Uncondi-
      tional Surrender Grant
   presidential rank: **10** eighteenth
   party: **10** Republican
   state represented: **2** IL
   defeated: **5** (David) Davis, (James)
      Black **6** (Charles) O'Conor **7** (Hor-
      ace) Greeley, (Horatio) Seymour **9**
      (William Slocomb) Groesbeck
   vice president: **5** (Thomas W) Ferry
      (acting) **6** (Henry) Wilson (died in
      office 1875), (Schuyler) Colfax
   cabinet:
      state: **4** (Hamilton) Fish **9** (Elihu
         Benjamin) Washburne
      treasury: **7** (Alexander Turney)
         Stewart, (Benjamin Helm) Bristow,
         (Lot Myrick) Morrill **8** (George
         Sewall) Boutwell **10** (William
         Adams) Richardson
      war: **4** (Alphonso) Taft **7** (James
         Donald) Cameron, (John Aaron)
         Rawlins, (William Worth) Belknap
      attorney general: **4** (Alphonso)
         Taft, (Ebenezer Rockwood) Hoar
         7 (Amos Tappan) Akerman **8**
         (George Henry) Williams **10** (Ed-
         wards) Pierrepont
      navy: **5** (Adolph Edward) Borie **7**

(George Maxwell) Robeson
      postmaster general: **5** (James No-
         ble) Tyner **6** (Marshall) Jewell **8**
         (James William) Marshall, (John
         Angel James) Creswell
      interior: **3** (Jacob Dolson) Cox **6**
         (Columbus) Delano **8** (Zachariah)
         Chandler
   born: **15** Point Pleasant OH
   died: **15** Mount McGregor NY
   buried: **9** New York NY
   education: **9** West Point **17** US Mili-
      tary Academy
   religion: **9** Methodist
   author: **24** Personal Memoirs of US
      Grant **30** Around the World with
      General Grant
   political career:
      secretary of: **3** War (interim ap-
         pointment)
   civilian career: **6** farmer
   military service: **6** US Army **8** Civil
      War **10** Mexican War **18** Illinois Vol-
      unteers **20** Commander of Union
      Army
   notable events of lifetime/career: **5**
      Panic (of 1873) **11** Black Friday
      (gold panic) **16** Custer's Last Stand
      Act: **10** Salary Grab
      conspiracy: **11** Whiskey Ring
      scandal: **14** Credit Mobilier
   quote: **60** "No terms except uncondi-
      tional and immediate surrender can
      be accepted"
   father: **9** Jesse Root
   mother: **6** Hannah (Simpson)
   siblings: **5** Clare **10** Orvil Lynch **11**
      Mary Frances **13** Samuel Simpson,
      Virginia Paine
   wife: **5** Julia (Boggs Dent)
   children: **5** Ellen **9** Jesse Root **13**
      Frederick Dent **14** Ulysses Simpson

granted
   French: **7** d'accord

grantee 8 receiver **9** recipient **11** beneficiary

grant immunity to 4 free **5** clear,
   spare **6** except, excuse, exempt **7** absolve, release, relieve **9** privilege

grantor 5 giver **8** bestower **10** benefactor

granulate 5 crush **6** powder **9** pulverize **11** crystallize

granulated 6 ground **7** crushed **8**
   powdered **10** pulverized **12** crystal-
   lized

granule 5 grain **7** crystal **8** particle

grape 5 Vitis **13** Vitis vinifera
   varieties: **3** cat, red, sea **4** amur,
      blue, bush, cape, rock, sand, tail **5**
      bear's, bunch, frost, Javan, sugar,
      veldt **6** canyon, Damson, Miller, Ore-
      gon, pigeon, possum, summer, win-
      ter **7** African, Bullace, catbird,
      chicken, Concord, Spanish **8** Euro-
      pean, mountain **9** evergreen, pan-
      handle, river-bank **10** silver-leaf **11**

southern fox **13** sweet mountain

wine: 5 Gamay **6** Cayuga, Duriff, Merlot, Muscat, Shiraz **7** Barbera, Catawba **8** Baco Noir, Dolcetto, Labrusca, Nebbiolo, Verduzzo **9** Aglianico, Fume Blanc, Huxelrebe, Pinot Noir, Primitivo, Trebbiano, Zinfandel **10** Chardonnay, Sangiovese **11** Chenin Blanc, Petite Sirah, Pinot Bianco, Seyval Blanc **13** Cabernet Franc, Montepulciano **14** Sauvignon Blanc **15** Gewurztraminer **17** Cabernet Sauvignon **20** Johannisberg Riesling

Grapes of Wrath, The
author: 13 John Steinbeck
character: 4 Noah **6** Connie, Ma Joad, Pa Joad **7** Jim Casy, Tom Joad **12** Rose of Sharon
director: 8 John Ford
cast: 10 Henry Fonda **11** Jane Darwell **12** Dorris Bowden **13** John Carradine **15** Charley Grapewin
Oscar for: 17 supporting actress (Darwell)

graphic 4 seen **5** clear, drawn, lucid, vivid **6** visual **7** painted, printed, visible, written **8** distinct, explicit, forcible, lifelike, pictured, striking **9** pictorial, realistic, trenchant **10** expressive **11** descriptive, picturesque **12** illustrative

grappa
type: 6 brandy **7** liqueur
origin: 5 Italy
made from: 9 grape pulp

grapple 4 face, grip, hold, meet **5** catch, clasp, fight, grasp, seize **6** breast, clutch, combat, engage, fasten, tackle, take on **7** contend, grapnel, wrestle **8** confront, deal with, do battle, make fast, struggle **9** encounter, large hook, lay hold of **11** hold tightly

grasp 3 get, ken **4** grab, grip, hold, sway, take **5** catch, clasp, infer, power, range, reach, savvy, scope, seize, sense, skill, sweep **6** clinch, clutch, deduce, fathom, follow, master, snatch, take in, talent **7** catch at, compass, control, embrace, grapple, mastery, seizing, seizure **8** clutches, gripping, perceive **9** handclasp, knowledge, seize upon **10** comprehend, perception, understand **13** comprehension, understanding

grasping 5 venal **6** greedy **7** hoggish, miserly, selfish, wolfish **8** covetous **9** mercenary, predatory, rapacious **10** avaricious **11** acquisitive

graspingness 5 greed **7** avarice **8** rapacity, venality **10** greediness **12** covetousness

grass
varieties: 3 cup, cut, dog, eel, elk, mat, nut, oat, oil, pin, rib, rye, Uva **4** barn, bear, bent, blue, chee, cord, crab, deer, fish, hair, lace, love, Lyme, moor, Nard, palm, Para, rice, rush, silk, star, tape, worm, yard **5** arrow, Bahia, beach, beard, Brome, Carib, China, cloud, curly, Ditch, fever, goose, lemon, Means, Melic, Mondo, natal, quack, sedge, shave, shore, Smilo, spike, squaw, Sudan, sword, Vasey, wheat, white, witch, zebra **6** Aleppo, alkali, basket, Bengal, Buffel, Canary, carpet, Dallis, Dudder, finger, gallow, Guinea, Indian, Korean, Manila, Napier, orange, orchid, Pampas, Rescue, Rhodes, ribbon, ripple, scurvy, signal, starry, switch, Tobosa, velvet, vernal, viper's, Zoysia **7** Bermuda, Brahman, Bristle, Buffalo, Esparto, Harding, Johnson, Kleberg, Pangola, poverty, pudding, quaking, Ravenna, sea lyme, serpent, tall oat, Wallaby, Widgeon **8** Angleton, blue-eyed, blue love, Boer love, elephant, fountain, hairy cup, lazy- man's, molasses, Ree wheat, sand love, scorpion, tuber oat **9** blue conch, centipede, common rye, hairy crab, hare's-tail, Hungarian, Malojilla, Mascarene, Oregon rye, rancheria, tall wheat, water star, yellow nut **10** Amur silver, beavertail, big quaking, blue finger, citronella, English rye, false wheat, golden-eyed, Indian rice, Italian rye, Korean lawn, Kuma bamboo, purple-eyed, rabbit-foot, rabbit-tail, reed canary, tufted hair, Washington, western rye, yellow-eyed **11** annual beard, branched cup, desert wheat, domestic rye, dwarf meadow, feather love, giant finger, green needle, Lehmann love, Nepal silver, Pentz finger, prairie cord, ringed beard, St Augustine, sweet vernal, Texas needle, Texas winter, weeping love **12** Common carpet, crested wheat, crinkled hair, European dune, Indian basket, Japanese lawn, Japanese love, Korean velvet, perennial rye, slender wheat, squirreltail, western wheat **13** American beach, Australian rye, billion-dollar, European beach, Himalaya fairy, Japanese sedge, little quaking, Paraguay Bahia, plains bristle, Siberian wheat **14** African Bermuda, bluebunch wheat, Japanese carpet, Pensacola Bahia, perennial veldt, pubescent wheat, Saint Augustine, stiff-hair wheat **15** European feather, Wilmington Bahia **16** creeping windmill, Pacey's English rye **17** Australian feather, intermediate wheat, Mediterranean salt, Transvaal dog-tooth **18** Australian windmill, California blue-eyed, Mexican everlasting **19** Fairway crested wheat **20** standard crested wheat

Grass, Gunter
author of: 6 Floods **8** Dog Years **10** The Tin Drum **11** Cat and Mouse, The Flounder **16** Local Anaesthetic **18** The Meeting at Telgte **20** From the Diary of a Snail **33** Headbirths or The Germans Are Dying Out

grasshopper
variety: 5 pygmy **6** meadow, monkey **7** katydid **10** band winged, cone headed, long-horned, slant-faced **11** bush katydid, leaf-rolling, short-horned **12** shield-backed, spur-throated

grassland 3 lea **4** farm, vale, veld **5** field, pampa, plain, range, veldt **6** meadow **7** pasture, prairie, savanna **8** farmland, flatland, savannah **10** plantation

grate 3 irk, jar, rub, vex **4** bars, burr, buzz, gall, rasp **5** annoy, chafe, clack, grill, grind, mince, shred **6** abrade, gnaw at, hearth, rankle, scrape, scream, screen **7** firebed, firebox, grating, lattice, scratch, screech **8** irritate **9** fireplace, pulverize **10** exasperate, firebasket **11** latticework

grateful 7 obliged **8** beholden, indebted, thankful **9** gratified, obligated **12** appreciative

gratefulness 6 thanks **9** gratitude **12** appreciation, thankfulness

Gratiae *see* **6** Graces

Gratiano
character in: 19 The Merchant of Venice
author: 11 Shakespeare

gratification 3 joy **4** glee, kick **5** bliss **6** relish, solace, thrill **7** comfort, delight, ecstasy, elation, rapture **8** gladness, humoring, pleasing, pleasure, soothing **9** enjoyment, happiness, transport **10** indulgence, jubilation, satisfying **11** contentment, enchantment **12** exhilaration, satisfaction

gratified 5 happy **7** content, pleased **9** satisfied **11** comfortable

gratify 4 suit **5** amuse, favor, humor **6** coddle, divert, pamper, please, regale, soothe, thrill, tickle **7** appease, delight, enchant, flatter, gladden, indulge, refresh, satisfy **8** enthrall, entrance, interest, recreate **9** enrapture, entertain, transport **10** compliment, exhilarate

gratifying 8 humoring, pleasant, pleasing, soothing **9** agreeable, enjoyable, indulging, pampering, rewarding **10** delightful, satisfying **11** pleasurable

grating 4 bars, fret, grid **5** grate, harsh, raspy **6** creaky, grille, shrill **7** jarring, lattice, rasping, raucous, squeaky, tracery, trellis **8** abrasive, annoying, filigree, fretwork, gridiron, jangling, piercing, scraping, strident **9** offensive, vexatious **10** discordant, gate of bard, irritating, unpleasant **11** cacophonous, displeasing, high-pitched **12** disagreeable, exacerbating, exasperating

grating noise 7 discord, rasping 8 grinding 9 cacophony, harshness 10 disharmony, dissonance

gratis 4 free 10 gratuitous, on the house 13 complimentary, without charge

gratitude 6 thanks 10 obligation 11 recognition 12 appreciation, beholdenness, gratefulness, thankfulness, thanksgiving 14 acknowledgment

gratuitous 4 free 6 gratis, wanton 7 donated, willing 8 baseless, unproven 9 unfounded, voluntary 10 free of cost, groundless, irrelevant, unasked for, unprovoked 11 conjectural, impertinent, presumptive, spontaneous, uncalled for, unjustified, unwarranted 13 complimentary, unrecompensed

gratuity 3 tip 4 gift 8 donation
French: 7 douceur 9 pourboire

Graustark
author: 20 George Barr McCutcheon

grave 4 dour, sage, tomb 5 acute, crypt, mound, quiet, sober, staid, vault, vital 6 gloomy, sedate, solemn, somber, urgent 7 crucial, earnest, ossuary, serious, subdued, weighty 8 catacomb, cenotaph, critical, frowning, pressing 9 dignified, important, long-faced, mausoleum, momentous, sepulcher 10 thoughtful 11 burial ground, grim visaged, significant 13 consequential, philosophical 16 last resting place, place of interment
music: 6 solemn 7 serious

Graves, Robert
author of: 9 I Claudius, King Jesus 14 Claudius the God 15 The White Goddess 16 Goodbye to All That

graveyard 7 charnel, ossuary 8 boneyard, boot hill, cemetery 10 churchyard, necropolis 12 memorial park, potter's field 13 burying ground

gravitate 4 fall, head, move, sink, tend 6 settle 7 be drawn, descend, incline 8 converge, zero in on 9 be prone to 10 lean toward

gravity 4 pull 6 danger, import, moment 7 concern, dignity, urgency 8 calmness, enormity, grimness, serenity, sobriety 9 emergency, magnitude, solemnity, staidness 10 attraction, gloominess, importance, sedateness, solemnness, somberness 11 consequence, earnestness, gravitation, seriousness 12 significance, tranquillity 13 consideration, crucial nature 14 critical nature, pull of the earth, thoughtfulness 16 mutual attraction

gray, grey 3 dun 4 ashy, dark, drab, pale 5 ashen, foggy, hoary, misty, murky, slate 6 cloudy, dismal, gloomy, silver, somber 7 clouded, grayish, grizzly, neutral, silvery, sunless 8 overcast 9 cheerless, pearl-gray 10 depressing, gray-haired, gray-headed 11 dove-colored, hoary-headed 12 mouse-colored, silver-haired 13 salt and pepper

Gray, Harold
creator/artist of: 17 Little Orphan Annie

Gray, Thomas
author of: 32 Elegy Written in a Country Churchyard

grayness 4 murk 6 pallor 8 drabness 9 bleakness 10 somberness

Grayson, Kathryn
real name: 19 Zelma Kathryn Hedrick
born: 14 Winston-Salem NC
roles: 8 Show Boat 10 Kiss Me Kate 13 Anchors Aweigh, The Desert Song 15 The Vagabond King

graze 3 rub 4 crop, rasp, skim, skin 5 brush, grind, swipe 6 abrade, browse, bruise, glance, scrape 7 pasture, scratch 8 abrasion, eat grass 16 turn out to pasture

grease 4 fat, oil 4 balm, lard 5 salve 6 anoint, tallow 7 unguent 8 ointment 9 drippings, lubricant, lubricate

grease the palm 3 tip 5 bribe 6 buy off, pay off

greasy 3 fat 4 oily, waxy 5 fatty, lardy, slick 7 buttery 8 slippery, slithery 10 lardaceous, oleaginous

great 3 apt, big 4 able, a-one, cool, fine, good, high, huge, kind, many, phat, vast, well 5 chief, crack, grand, grave, gross, heavy, large, noble, noted, super, swell 6 adroit, choice, expert, famous, groovy, humane, loving, strong, superb 7 awesome, crucial, decided, eminent, extreme, grandly, immense, leading, mammoth, notable, serious, titanic, weighty 8 abundant, colossal, critical, enormous, esteemed, fabulous, generous, gigantic, glorious, gracious, manifold, renowned, skillful, smashing, splendid, superbly, superior, terrific, very well 9 boundless, countless, cyclopean, excellent, fantastic, first-rate, important, marvelous, momentous, monstrous, prominent, unlimited, wonderful 10 altruistic, celebrated, gargantuan, high-minded, inordinate, out-of-sight, prodigious, proficient, pronounced, remarkable, splendidly, stupendous, tremendous, voluminous 11 crackerjack, excellently, extravagant, illustrious, magnanimous, magnificent, outstanding, sensational, significant, superlative, wonderfully 12 considerable 13 consequential, distinguished, inexhaustible, magnificently, multitudinous 14 out of this world

Great Ajax
origin: 5 Greek
hero of: 9 Trojan War

greater 4 more 5 finer 6 better, bigger, larger 8 superior

Great Escape, The
director: 11 John Sturges

cast: 11 James Coburn, James Garner 12 Steve McQueen 13 David McCallum 14 Charles Bronson 15 Donald Pleasance 19 Richard Attenborough
setting: 7 Germany, POW camp

greatest 4 best, most 5 ultra 6 picked, select, utmost 7 extreme, highest, maximal, maximum, noblest, supreme 8 champion 9 first-rate 11 superlative, unsurpassed

Greatest Show on Earth, The
director: 13 Cecil B DeMille
cast: 11 Betty Hutton, Cornel Wilde 12 James Stewart 13 Dorothy Lamour, Gloria Grahame 14 Charlton Heston
Oscar for: 7 picture

Great Expectations
author: 14 Charles Dickens
character: 3 Pip 7 Estella 9 Compeyson, Mr Jaggers 10 Joe Gargery 12 Abel Magwitch, Miss Havisham 13 Herbert Pocket
director: 9 David Lean
cast: 9 John Mills 11 Martita Hunt 12 Alec Guinness, Bernard Mills 13 Valerie Hobson 16 Francis L Sullivan

Great Gatsby, The
author: 16 F Scott Fitzgerald
character: 9 Jay Gatsby 11 Tom Buchanan 12 Myrtle Wilson, Nick Carraway 13 Daisy Buchanan

Great God Brown, The
author: 12 Eugene O'Neill

great lady
French: 10 grande dame

Great Lake 4 Erie 5 Huron 7 Ontario 8 Michigan, Superior

Great Land
nickname of: 6 Alaska

greatly 6 vastly 7 largely, notably 8 markedly, mightily, very much 9 immensely 10 abundantly, enormously, infinitely, powerfully, remarkably 12 considerably, immeasurably, tremendously

great mishap 5 wreck 6 blight, fiasco 7 tragedy 8 calamity, disaster 9 cataclysm, ruination 11 catastrophe

greatness 8 eminence, nobility 9 loftiness 10 excellence, importance, notability, prominence 11 preeminence, superiority 12 magnificence 15 illustriousness

Great Profile
nickname of: 13 John Barrymore

Great Railway Bazaar, The
author: 11 Paul Theroux

great world
French: 10 grand monde

Great Ziegfeld, The
director: 14 Robert Z Leonard
cast: 8 Myrna Loy 10 Fanny Brice 11 Frank Morgan, Luise Rainer (Anna Held) 13 Virginia Bruce, William

Powell

Oscar for: 7 actress (Rainer), picture

grebe 4 bird, fowl, loon **5** diver **6** dipper **7** henbill **8** dabchick **9** hell-diver **10** water witch

Grecco, Al

    character in: 20 Appointment in Samarra

    author: 5 O'Hara

Greco, El Greco

    real name: 23 Domenikos Theotokopoulos

    born: 5 Crete **6** Candia

    artwork: 7 Espolio (Disrobing of Christ), Laocoon **12** View of Toledo **19** Cleaning of the Temple **20** Healing of the Blind Man **21** Burial of the Count Orgaz **27** Christ Stripped of his Garments **28** San Ildefonso at his Writing Desk **29** Cardinal Fernando Nino de Guevara **42** Christ Driving the Money-Changers from the Temple

Greece

    other name: 5 Ellas **16** Hellenic Republic

    capital/largest city: 6 Athens

    others: 4 Enor **5** Canea, Corfu, Pylos, Volos **6** Delphi, Patras, Sparta **7** Chalcis, Corinth, Olympia, Piraeus **8** Salonika, Thessaly **9** Epidaurus, Gallipoli **10** Herakleion **11** Hermoupolis

    school: 5 Crete **6** Athens, Patras, Thrace **8** Ioannina, Salonika

    division: 6 Attica, Epirus, Thrace **7** Boeotia **8** Thessaly **9** Macedonia

    measure: 3 pik **4** bema, piki, pous **5** baril, chous, cubit, diote, doron, maris, pekhe, podos, pygon, xylon **6** acaena, bacile, barile, cotula, dichas, gramme, hemina, koilon, lichas, milion, orgyia, palame, pechys, schene, xestes **7** amphora, bacvhel, chenica, choenix, cyathos, diaulos, metreta, stadium, stremma **8** condylos, daktylos, dekapode, dolichos, medimnos, medimnus, metretes, palaiste, plethron, plethrum, stathmos **9** hemiekton, oxybaphon

    monetary unit: 5 lepta **7** drachma

    weight: 3 mna, oke **4** mina, obol **5** livre, pound **6** diobol, kantar, obolos, obolus, talent **7** chalcon, drachma **8** diobolon

    island: 3 Ios **5** Chios, Corfu, Crete, Delos, Melos, Naxos, Paros, Samos, Syros, Tenos, Thera, Zante **6** Andros, Euboea, Ionian, Ithaca, Lemnos, Lesbos, Patmos, Rhodes, Skyros, Thasos **7** Mykonos **8** Cyclades, Mytilene, Skiathos, Skopelos **9** Alonnisos **10** Cephalonia, Dodecanese, Samothrace **16** Northern Sporades

    lake: 5 Karla, Volve **6** Copais, Kopais, Prespa, Voweis **8** Ioannina, Koroneia, Vistonis **9** Trichonis, Vegoritis

    mountain: 3 Ida **4** Idhi, Oeta, Oite,

Ossa **5** Athos **6** Ithome, Peleon, Pelion, Pindus **7** Grammos, Helicon, Rhodope **8** Hymettos, Smolikas, Taygetos, Taygetus **9** Parnassus **10** Hagion Oros, Lycabettus, Pentelicus

    highest point: 7 Olympus

    river: 4 Arta **6** Peneus, Struma, Vardar **7** Hellada, Maritsa **8** Achelous, Aliakmon

    sea: 5 Crete **6** Aegean, Ionian **7** Mirtoon **13** Mediterranean

    physical feature:

        gulf: 7 Corinth, Saronic

        peninsula: 6 Balkan **10** Chalcidice **12** Peloponnesus

        plain: 7 Boeotia **8** Thessaly

        plateau: 7 Arcadia

        valley: 5 Nemea

    people: 5 Greek **6** Achean, Dorian, Ionian **7** Aeolian, Hellene

        artist: 7 El Greco

        author: 5 Homer **6** Hesiod, Pindar **8** Menander **9** Aeschylus, Euripides, Sophocles **11** Kazantzakis **12** Aristophanes

        god: 4 Ares, Hera, Leto, Zeus **5** Cupid **6** Apollo, Cronus, Hermes, Hestia **7** Artemis, Demeter **8** Dionysus, Poseidon **9** Aphrodite **10** Hephaestus, Persephone **12** Pallas Athena **13** Phoebus Apollo

        historian: 9 Herodotus **10** Thucydides

        king: 11 Constantine

        lawmaker: 5 Draco, Solon **8** Lycurgus, Pericles

        leader: 10 Papandreou

        mathematician: 6 Euclid **10** Archimedes, Pythagoras

        mythological: 5 Atlas, Helen, Jason, Medea, Medusa **7** Ariadne, Chimera, Pandora, Pegasus, Perseus, Theseus **8** Achilles, Heracles, Minotaur, Odysseus **9** Agamemnon, Andromeda, Iphigenia, King Minos **10** Prometheus **11** Bellerophon

        orator: 11 Demosthenes

        philosopher: 5 Plato **8** Socrates **9** Aristotle

        physician: 11 Hippocrates

        sculptor: 5 Myron **7** Phidias **10** Praxiteles

        tycoon: 7 Onassis

    language: 5 Greek

    religion: 14 Greek Orthodoxy

    place:

        ruins: 5 Delos, Pella, Pylos, Samos **6** Delphi, Sparta, Thebes, Tiryns **7** Corinth, Eleusis, Elevsis, Knossos, Mycenae, Olympia **9** Acropolis, Epidaurus, Parthenon **13** Palace of Minos

    feature:

        coffeeshop: 7 kaphene

        marketplace: 5 agora

        port 7 Piraeus

        presidential guard: 7 Evzones

        village square: 7 plateia

    food:

        dish: 4 gyro **7** baklava, mousaka **8** moussaka, souvlaki, dolmades **10** shish kabob

        liquor: 4 ouzo

        wine: 7 retsina

greed 7 avarice, avidity, craving **8** cupidity, rapacity **11** itching palm, money-hunger, piggishness, selfishness **12** covetousness **13** rapaciousness **14** avariciousness

greediness 7 avarice **8** gluttony, rapacity, voracity **12** covetousness, graspingness **15** acquisitiveness

greedy 4 avid **5** eager **6** ardent, hungry **7** anxious, burning, craving, fervent, hoggish, piggish, selfish, swinish, wolfish **8** covetous, famished, grasping, ravenous **9** devouring, impatient, mercenary, predatory, rapacious, thirsting, voracious **10** avaricious, gluttonous, insatiable **11** acquisitive, money-hungry **12** gormandizing

Greek

    language family: 12 Indo-European

    ancient branch: 5 Attic, Doric, Ionic **6** Aeolic

Greek alphabet 5 alpha **4** beta **5** gamma **5** delta **7** epsilon **4** zeta **3** eta **5** theta **4** iota **5** kappa **6** lambda **2** mu **2** nu **2** xi **7** omicron **2** pi **3** rho **5** sigma **3** tau **7** upsilon **3** phi **3** chi **3** psi **5** omega

Greek Anthology, The

    author: 8 Cephalas, Meleager

Greek measure 4 mina **5** cubit **6** obolos, talent **7** drachma, stadion

Greek Mythology

    afterworld of the blessed: 7 Elysium

    amber islands: 10 Electrides

    architect of labyrinth: 8 Daedalus

    blood-sucking monster: 5 Lamia

    cupbearer to the gods: 8 Ganymede **9** Catamitus

    dragon: 8 basilisk

    drink of the gods: 6 nectar

    eagle/lion monster: 7 griffin, griffon, gryphon

    enchantress: 5 Circe

    female warrior: 6 Amazon

    fire-breathing monster: 7 Chimera

    first man: 12 Alalcomeneus

    food/drink/perfume of the gods: 8 ambrosia

    the Furies: 5 Dirae **6** Erinys, Furiae, Semnai **7** Erinyes **9** Eumenides

        names: 7 Allecto, Megaera **9** Tisiphone

    goat god: 7 Aegipan

    goddess of beauty: 6 Graces **7** Gratiae **9** Charities

        names: 4 Auxo **5** Cleta **6** Aglaia, Thalia **7** Phaenna **8** Hegemone **10** Euphrosyne

    goddess of childbirth: 8 Ilithyia **10** Eileithyia

corresponds to Roman: **6** Lucina
goddess of the dawn: 3 Eos
   corresponds to Roman: **6** Aurora
goddesses of destiny: 5 Fates, Morae **6** Moerae, Moirai
   names: **5** Moira **6** Clotho **8** Lachesis
   corresponds to Roman: **6** Parcae
goddess of discord: 4 Eris
   corresponds to Roman: **9** Discordia
goddess of divine punishment/ recklessness: 3 Ate
goddess of divine retribution: 8 Adrastea
goddess of the earth: 2 Ge **4** Gaea, Gaia
   corresponds to Roman: **6** Tellus
goddess of earth/fertility: 7 Demeter
   corresponds to Roman: **5** Ceres
goddess of earth/Hades: 5 Brimo **6** Hecate, Hekate
goddess of fortune: 5 Tyche
   corresponds to Roman: **7** Fortuna
goddess of healing: 4 Iaso
goddess of health: 6 Hygeia
   corresponds to Roman: **5** Salus
goddess of the hearth: 6 Hestia
   corresponds to Roman: **5** Vesta
goddess of justice: 4 Dice, Dike **6** Astrea **7** Astraea
goddesses of literature/the arts: 5 Muses **7** the Nine **8** Pierides **10** Castalides
   names: **4** Clio **5** Aoede, Erato, Mneme **6** Melete, Thalia, Urania **7** Euterpe **8** Calliope **9** Melpomene **10** Polyhymnia **11** Terpsichore
   corresponds to Roman: **7** Camenae
muse of astronomy: 6 Urania
muse of dancing/choral song: 11 Terpsichore
muse of history: 4 Clio
muse of idyllic poetry/comedy: 6 Thalia
muse of love poetry: 5 Erato
muse of meditation: 6 Melete
muse of memory: 5 Mneme
muse of music/lyric poetry: 7 Euterpe
muse of poetry/epic: 8 Calliope
muse of sacred music/dance: 10 Polyhymnia
muse of song: 5 Aoede
muse of tragedy: 9 Melpomene
goddess of love/beauty: 6 Urania **7** Cyprian, Paphian **8** Cytherea **9** Aphrodite **10** Anadyomene
   corresponds to Roman: **5** Venus
goddess of memory: 9 Mnemosyne
goddess of the night: 3 Nyx
goddess of peace: 5 Irene
   corresponds to Roman: **3** Pax
goddess of the rainbow: 4 Iris
goddess of sailors: 5 Brizo
goddess of the sea: 10 Amphitrite
goddesses of the sea: 6 Graeae,

Graiae
   names: **4** Enyo **5** Deino **9** Pemphredo
goddesses of seasons/growth/ decay/social order: 4 Hour **5** Horae
   names: **4** Dice, Dike **5** Carpo, Irene **6** Thallo **7** Eunomia
goddess of spring flowers: 6 Thallo
goddess of summer fruit: 5 Carpo
goddess of victory: 4 Nike
   corresponds to Roman: **6** Athena **8** Victoria
goddess of war: 4 Enyo
   corresponds to Roman: **7** Bellona
goddess of wisdom/fertility/arts/ warfare: 6 Athena, Athene, Pallas, Saitis **11** Tritogeneia **12** Pallas Athena **18** Alalcomenean Athena
   corresponds to Roman: **7** Minerva
goddess of youth/spring: 4 Hebe
god of beekeeping/winemaking/ husbandry: 9 Aristaeus
god of censure/ridicule: 5 Momos, Momus
god of dreams: 6 Icelus, Oniros **7** Oneiros **8** Morpheus
god of earth: 10 Trophonius
god of Eleusinian mysteries: 7 Bacchus
god of erotic desire: 7 Himeros
god of fire/metalworking/ handicrafts: 10 Hephaestus, Hephaistos
   corresponds to Roman: **6** Vulcan
god of the heavens: 4 Zeus
   corresponds to Roman: **4** Jove **7** Jupiter
   corresponds to Egyptian: **4** Amen, Amon **5** Ammon **6** Amen Ra, Amon Ra
god of light/healing/music/poetry/ prophecy/beauty: 6 Apollo
god of love: 4 Eros
   corresponds to Roman: **4** Amor **5** Cupid
god of male power/procreation: 7 Priapus
   corresponds to Roman: **7** Mutinus
god of marriage: 5 Hymen **9** Hymenaeus
   corresponds to Roman: **8** Talassio
god of medicine/healing: 9 Asclepius
   corresponds to Roman: **11** Aesculapius
god of oaths: 6 Horcus
god of recovery from illness: 11 Telesphorus
god of sea/caused earthquakes: 8 Poseidon
   corresponds to Roman: **7** Neptune
god of shepherds/flocks/pastures/ forests: 3 Pan **7** Sinoeis
god of sleep: 6 Hypnos, Hypnus
   corresponds to Roman: **6** Somnus
god of the sun: 6 Helios **8** Hyperion
   corresponds to Roman: **3** Sol
god of the underworld: 6 Infiri

god of war: 4 Ares **8** Theritas
   corresponds to Roman: **4** Mars
god of wine/fertility/drama: 5 Evius **7** Bacchus **8** Dionysus
Gorgon monster: 6 Medusa
hundred-headed monster: 5 Ladon **8** Typhoeus
islands of the blessed: 10 Hesperides
man/horse monster: 7 centaur
messenger of gods/god of roads/ commerce/invention/cunning/ thieves: 6 Hermes
   corresponds to Roman: **7** Mercury
monster that asked riddles: 6 Sphinx
monsters that turn people to stone: 7 Gorgons
moon goddess/huntress/virgin: 6 Phoebe, Selene **7** Artemis
   corresponds to Roman: **5** Diana
   corresponds to Cretan: **11** Britomartis
nine-headed water serpent: 5 Hydra
nymph: 7 Calypso
one-eyed giant: 7 Cyclops
oracle of Apollo: 13 Delphic oracle
personification of death: 4 Mors **8** Thanatos
personification of punishment/ revenge: 5 Poena, Poine
personification of soul: 6 Psyche
physician to gods of Olympia: 5 Paeon
prophetess: 9 Alexandra, Cassandra
queen of heaven: 4 Hera, Here
   corresponds to Roman: **4** Juno
race of gods: 6 Titans
   names: **4** Rhea, Thia **5** Coeus, Crius **6** Cronus, Phoebe, Tethys, Themis **7** Iapetus, Oceanus **8** Hyperion **9** Mnemosyne
river god: 6 Asopus, Peneus, Simois **7** Inachus, Pelegon **8** Achelous
river in Hades: 4 Styx **5** Lethe **7** Acheron, Cocytus
   ferryman: **6** Charon
river of forgetfulness: 5 Lethe
ruler of the winds: 6 Aeolus
satyr/god of the forest: 7 Silenus
sea god: 6 Nereus, Triton **7** Glaucus, Phorcys, Proteus
sea monster: 6 Scylla
seer: 6 Mopsus **8** Tiresias
serpent: 6 dipsas
serpent of darkness: 5 Apepi **7** Apophis
seven against Thebes: 6 Tydeus **8** Adrastus, Capaneus **9** Polynices **10** Amphiaraus, Hippomedon **13** Parthenopaeus
seven sisters: 8 Pleiades
   names: **4** Maia **6** Merope **7** Alcyone, Celaeno, Electra, Sterope, Taygete
sorceress: 5 Medea
spirits of disease/evil/old age/death: 5 Keres
**three-headed dog that guards un-

derworld: **8** Cerberus
twins: **8** Dioscuri **15** Castor and Pollux
two-headed serpent: **11** Amphisbaena
underworld: **5** Hades,
  corresponds to Roman: **3** Dis **5**
  Orcus, Pluto **8** Dis Pater
underworld darkness: **6** Erebus
underworld spirit: **9** Chthonian
virgin huntress: **8** Atalanta, Atalante
whirlpool: **9** Charybdis
winged horse: **5** Arion **7** Pegasus
woman/beast monster: **6** Python **8**
  Delphyne
woman/bird monster: **5** Harpy
woman/serpent monster: **7** Echidna
wood nymph: **5** dryad
Greek uncial codex **4** Syri **6** Regius **8**
Ephraemi **9** Laudianus, Vaticanus **10**
Sinaiticus **11** Basiliensis **12** Alexandri-
nus, Sangallensis **13** Koridethianus
green **3** raw **4** jade, lawn, lime, turf **5**
crude, heath, olive, rough, sward,
young **6** callow, campus, common,
tender, unripe **7** awkward, emerald,
verdant, verdure **8** greenish, gullible,
ignorant, immature, inexpert, not
cured, not dried, pea-green, sea-green,
unsmoked, untanned, unversed **9**
blue-green, credulous, grassplot, lime-
green, unfledged, unskilled, untrained
10 aquamarine, chartreuse, golf
course, grass-green, greensward, kelly-
green, olive green, uninformed, unmellowed, unpolished, unseasoned **11**
cobalt green, forest green,
undeveloped, yellow-green **12** easily
fooled, green-colored, not fully aged,
putting green, village green **13** inexperienced, undisciplined **14** underdeveloped **15** unsophisticated
Green Acres
  character: **7** Mr Haney **8** Eb Dawson
  10 Fred Ziffel, Sam Drucker **11** Doris
  Ziffel, Hank Kimball, Lisa Douglas
  20 Oliver Wendell Douglas
  cast: **8** Eva Gabor, Fran Ryan **9** Alvy
  Moore, Frank Cady, Tom Lester **10**
  Pat Buttram **11** Eddie Albert **13** Barbara Pepper, Hank Patterson
  pig: **6** Arnold
  town: **11** Hooterville
green at the gills **6** queasy, sickly **7**
bilious **8** nauseous **9** nauseated, sickening
greenback **4** bill **8** banknote **12** treasury note **15** legal-tender note **17** silver
certificate
Green Bay
  football team: **7** Packers
Green Bay Tree, The
  author: **14** Louis Bromfield
Greene, Graham
  author of: **11** The Third Man **12**
  Brighton Rock, Ways of Escape **14**
  The Human Factor **16** Monsignor

Quixote **17** The End of the Affair,
The Ministry of Fear, Travels with
My Aunt **19** The Heart of the Matter,
The Power and the Glory
Greene, Joe
  nickname: **7** Mean Joe
  sport: **8** football
  position: **7** lineman
  team: **18** Pittsburgh Steelers
Greene, Lorne
  born: **6** Canada, Ottawa **7** Ontario
  roles: **5** Adama **7** Bonanza **11** Peyton
  Place **12** Autumn Leaves, The Buccaneer **13** Ben Cartwright **16** The Silver Chalice **19** Battlestar Galactica
Greene, Nathanael
  served in: **16** Revolutionary War
  rank: **16** brigadier general **20** quartermaster general
  battle: **7** Cowpens, Trenton **12** Eutaw
  Springs, Hobkirk's Hill **18** Guilford
  Court House
green-eyed monster **4** envy **8** jealousy **12** covetousness
Green for Danger
  director: **13** Sidney Gilliat
  cast: **7** Leo Genn **9** Sally Gray **11** Alastair Sim **12** Rosamund John,
  Trevor Howard
greenhorn **4** rube, tyro **6** novice,
rookie **7** learner **8** beginner, neophyte,
newcomer **9** fledgling **10** apprentice,
tenderfoot **14** babe in the woods
Green Hornet, The
  character: **4** Kato **9** Britt Reid (The
  Green Hornet)
  cast: **8** Bruce Lee **11** Van Williams
  car: **11** Black Beauty
  creator: **11** Bert Whitman
  sidekick: **4** Kato
Green House, The
  author: **16** Mario Vargas Llosa
Greening of America, The
  author: **12** Charles Reich
greenish **6** sickly **7** bilious
Greenland
  alternate name: **14** Kalaalit Nunaat
  capital/largest city: **3** Nuk **8** Godthaab, The Point
  others: **4** Etah, Nord **5** Thule **6**
  Ivigut, Umanak **7** Godhavn, Ivigtut
  10 Nanortalik **11** Julianehaab **12** An-
  gmagssalik, Sukkertoppen **14** Chris-
  tianshaab
  government: **20** home rule under
  Denmark
  monetary unit: **3** ore **5** krone
  island: **5** Disko
  mountain: **5** Forel, Payer **7** Khardyu
  8 Peterman **15** Petermannsbjerg
  highest point: **9** Gunnbjorn
  16 Gunnbjornsfjaeld
  sea: **6** Arctic **9** Greenland
  physical feature: **9** Inland Ice
    bay: **5** Disko **6** Baffin **8** Melville
    cape: **4** Jaal **6** Grivel, Walker **8** Bis-
    marck, Brewster, Farewell, Lowen-

orn **11** Morris Jesup
  glacier: **10** Jacobshavn
  strait: **5** Davis **7** Denmark
  people: **3** Ita **6** Eskimo **8** European
  explorer: **10** Eric the Red
  language: **6** Danish, Eskimo **11**
  Greenlandic
  religion: **19** Evangelical Lutheran
  feature:
    airbase: **4** Etah **5** Thule
    animal: **7** caribou
Green Mansions
  author: **8** W H Hudson
  character: **4** Rima **5** Nuflo **6** Mr Abel
Greenmantle
  author: **10** John Buchan
Green Mountain State
  nickname of: **7** Vermont
Greenough, Horatio
  born: **8** Boston MA
  artwork: **20** George Washington **18**
  The Chanting Cherubs
Green Pastures, The
  author: **12** Marc Connelly
Greenstreet, Sydney
  born: **7** England **8** Sandwich
  roles: **9** The Fat Man **10** Casablanca
  16 The Maltese Falcon **19** Passage to
  Marseilles
green with envy **7** envious, jealous **8**
covetous
greet **4** hail, meet **5** admit **6** accept,
accost, salute **7** receive, speak to, welcome **9** smile upon, recognize **10** bid
welcome
greeting **6** salute **7** welcome **8** salut-
ing **9** reception, welcoming **10** salutation **12** introduction, presentation
greetings **4** best **5** hello **7** regards **8**
respects **10** best wishes, good wishes,
salutation **11** compliments, remembrance, well-wishing **13** felicitations
  Latin: **5** salve
gregarious **6** genial, lively, social **7** affable **8** friendly, outgoing, sociable **9**
convivial, talkative, vivacious **11** extroverted **13** companionable
gremlin **3** imp **5** demon, gnome **6** goblin
Grenada
  other name: **11** Isle of Spice
  capital/largest city: **9** St Georges
  others: **8** Sauteurs
  head of state: **14** British monarch
  15 governor general
  island: **8** Windward **9** Carriacou **10**
  Grenadines
  lake: **10** Grand Etang
  highest point: **11** St Catherine
  sea: **9** Caribbean
  physical feature:
    bay: **9** St Georges'
  people: **5** Black, Negro **6** Indian
    discoverer: **8** Columbus
  language: **7** English
  religion: **8** Anglican **10** Protestant **13**
  Roman Catholic

food:
spice: 4 mace **6** nutmeg
grenade 7 missile **9** pineapple
Grendel
character in: 7 Beowulf
author: 11 John Gardner
Grewgious, Mr
character in: 22 The Mystery of Edwin Drood
author: 7 Dickens
Grey, Joel
real name: 8 Joel Katz
born: 13 Cleveland Ohio
roles: 7 Cabaret, George M **13** Come September **23** The Seven Percent Solution
Grey, Zane
author of: 18 Valley of Wild Horses **20** The Spirit of the Border **21** Riders of the Purple Sage, The Last of the Plainsmen
greyhound
group of: 5 leash
Greystoke, Lord
real identity of: 6 Tarzan
griddle cake 6 blintz, waffle **7** crumpet, hot cake, pancake **8** corncake, flapcake, flapjack **10** battercake **11** flannel cake **13** buckwheat cake
French: 5 crepe **12** crepe suzette
German: 11 pfannkuchen
Hungarian: 10 palacsinta
Indian: 8 chapatty
Gride, Arthur
character in: 16 Nicholas Nickleby
author: 7 Dickens
grief 3 woe **4** care **5** agony, worry **6** burden, misery, ordeal, sorrow **7** anguish, anxiety, concern, despair, remorse, sadness, trouble **8** distress, grieving, hardship, nuisance, vexation **9** grievance, heartache, suffering **10** affliction, desolation, discomfort, heartbreak **11** despondency, tribulation **12** wretchedness **13** inconvenience
griefstricken 7 joyless, unhappy **8** saddened, wretched **9** sorrowful **13** brokenhearted
Grieg, Edvard Hagerup
born: 6 Bergen, Norway
composer of: 5 I Host **8** Bergljot, In Autumn, Peer Gynt **11** Lyric Pieces **12** Landjaenning **14** Fra Holbergs Tid, Lyriske Stykker **15** Sigurd Jorsalfar **16** From Holberg's Time **17** Recognition of Land **18** Foran Sydens Kloster **22** At a Southern Convent Gate
grievance 4 beef, hurt **5** wrong **6** injury **7** outrage **8** hardship, iniquity **9** complaint, injustice **10** affliction, bone to pick, disservice
grieve 3 cry, rue, sob **4** moan, pain, wail, weep **5** be sad, mourn **6** bemoan, deject, harass, lament, sadden, sorrow **7** afflict, agonize, depress, op-

press, torture **8** disquiet, distress **10** discomfort **11** be anguished
grieve over 5 mourn **6** bemoan, bewail, lament **7** cry over **8** moan over, weep over
grievous 3 sad **5** acute, grave, harsh, heavy **6** severe, tragic, woeful **7** crucial, glaring, harmful, heinous, painful, serious, very bad **8** critical, shameful, shocking **9** agonizing, appalling, atrocious, monstrous, nefarious, sorrowful **10** burdensome, calamitous, deplorable, iniquitous, lamentable, outrageous, unbearable **11** destructive, distressing, intolerable, significant **12** insufferable **13** heartbreaking
griffin
also: 7 griffon, gryphon
form: 7 monster
head of: 5 eagle
wings of: 5 eagle
body of: 4 lion
guards of: 4 gold
location: 7 Scythia
Griffith, Andy
real name: 20 Andrew Samuel Griffith
born: 8 Mt Airy NC
roles: 7 Matlock **13** Will Stockdale **15** A Face in the Crowd, Angel in My Pocket **18** No Time for Sergeants **19** The Andy Griffith Show
Griffith, D W
director of: 11 Intolerance **14** Broken Blossoms **17** Orphans of the Storm, The Birth of a Nation
Griffith, Hugh
born: 5 Wales **8** Anglesey **10** Marian Glas
roles: 6 Ben-Hur **8** Lucky Jim, Tom Jones
griffon see **7** griffin
grill 3 fry **4** cook, grid, pump, quiz, sear **5** broil, query **7** broiler, grating, griddle **8** gridiron, question **9** crossbars **11** interrogate **12** cross-examine
grim 4 foul, hard, ugly **5** cruel, harsh, lurid, stern, sulky **6** brutal, fierce, gloomy, grisly, grumpy, horrid, morose, odious, severe, somber, sullen **7** austere, ghastly, hideous, inhuman, macabre, squalid, vicious **8** dreadful, fiendish, gruesome, horrible, resolute, scowling, shocking, sinister **9** appalling, ferocious, frightful, heartless, loathsome, merciless, obstinate, repellent, repugnant, repulsive, revolting **10** determined, forbidding, implacable, inexorable, relentless, unyielding
grimace 4 face **5** scowl, smirk, sneer **6** glower **7** wry face
French: 4 moue
grime 4 dirt, dust, smut, soil, soot **5** filth **6** smudge
Grimhild
origin: 12 Scandinavian

mentioned in: 8 Volsunga
form: 9 sorceress
husband: 5 Giuki, Gjuki
daughter: 6 Gudrun, Kudrun **7** Guthrun
son: 6 Gunnar
tricked Sigurd to marry: 6 Gudrun, Kudrun **7** Guthrun
Grimm Brothers (Jakob and Wilhelm)
editors of: 15 Hansel and Gretel **16** Grimm's Fairy Tales
grim reaper 5 death **12** angel of death
grim-visaged 8 frowning, scowling **9** long-faced **10** stern-faced
grin 4 beam **5** smile, smirk **6** rictus, simper **11** crack a smile
grind 4 file, grit, mill, rasp, whet **5** chore, crush, gnash, grate **6** abrade, drudge, polish, powder, scrape **7** crammer, hard job, plodder, sharpen, slavery **8** bookworm, drudgery **9** granulate, pulverize, triturate
Gringoire
character in: 23 The Hunchback of Notre Dame
author: 4 Hugo
grip 3 bag **4** grab, hilt, hold **5** clasp, grasp, rivet, seize **6** clench, clutch, handle, retain, snatch, valise **7** attract, control, impress, mastery, satchel **8** clutches, hold fast, suitcase **9** gladstone, handclasp, handshake, retention, spellbind **10** domination, perception
gripe, gripes 4 beef, carp, fret, kick, pain, pang, rail **5** cavil, colic, spasm, whine **6** cramps, grouch, grouse, kvetch, mutter, squawk, twinge, twitch **7** grumble, protest, whining **8** complain, distress, grousing, bellyache, complaint, find fault, grievance, grumbling **10** affliction
Grisham, John
author of: 7 The Firm **9** The Client **10** The Chamber, The Partner **11** A Time to Kill **12** The Rainmaker **14** The Runaway Jury **15** The Pelican Brief, The Street Lawyer
movie: 7 The Firm
actors: 9 Tom Cruise **11** Gene Hackman
movie: 9 The Client
actors: 13 Tommy Lee Jones, Susan Sarandon **17** Jeanne Tripplehorn
movie: 15 The Pelican Brief
actors: 12 Julia Roberts **16** Denzel Washington
grisly 4 foul, gory, grim **5** lurid **6** horrid, odious **7** ghastly, hideous, macabre **8** dreadful, gruesome, horrible, shocking, sinister **9** abhorrent, appalling, frightful, loathsome, repellent, repugnant, repulsive, revolting **10** abominable, forbidding, horrendous
grit 3 rub **4** dirt, dust, guts, muck,

rasp, sand, soot **5** filth, gnash, grate, nerve, pluck, spunk **6** crunch, mettle, scrape **7** courage, stamina **8** backbone, tenacity **9** fortitude **10** doggedness, resolution **12** perseverance **13** determination, grind together

Grizzly Bear State 10 California

groan 4 howl, moan, roar, wail **5** bleat, crack, creak, whine **6** bellow, bemoan, lament, murmur, squeak **7** grumble, screech, whimper **8** complain

grocery store
Spanish: **6** bodega

groggy 5 dazed, dizzy, dopey, shaky, woozy **6** addled, punchy **7** muddled, reeling, stunned **8** confused, sluggish, unsteady **9** befuddled, lethargic, perplexed, stupefied **10** bewildered, punch-drunk, staggering

groom 4 comb, wash **5** boots, brush, curry, dress, drill, preen, prime, primp, train, valet **6** flunky, lackey, spouse **7** clean up, consort, develop, educate, footman, freshen, hostler, husband, prepare, refresh, rub down, servant **8** exercise, initiate, make neat, make tidy, practice, spruce up **9** currycomb, make ready, stableboy **10** bridegroom, manservant **12** indoctrinate **13** livery servant

groove 3 cut, rut, use **4** rule **5** flute, habit, score, usage **6** custom, furrow, gutter, hollow, trench **7** channel, cutting, scoring **8** practice **9** procedure **10** beaten path, convention **11** corrugation **12** fixed routine, second nature

grope 3 paw **5** probe **6** finger, fumble **7** fish for, venture **9** feel about **11** feel one's way, move blindly, try one's luck **13** search blindly

Gropius, Walter
architect of: **5** Fagus (factory) **7** Bauhaus (Dessau) **13** Pan Am Building (NYC) **31** Harvard University Graduate Center

gross 3 bag, big, fat **4** bulk, earn, huge, lewd, mass, rank, reap, vast **5** bulky, crude, great, heavy, large, obese, plain, sheer, total, utter, whole **6** carnal, coarse, earthy, entire, pick up, ribald, smutty, sordid, take in, vulgar **7** glaring, heinous, immense, lump sum, massive, obscene, obvious, titanic, uncouth **8** colossal, complete, enormous, flagrant, gigantic, improper, indecent, manifest, unseemly, unwieldy **9** aggregate, downright, egregious, lecherous, monstrous, offensive, unrefined **10** gargantuan, indelicate, lascivious, licentious, outrageous, overweight, prodigious, stupendous **11** unequivocal, unmitigated, unqualified

grossness 7 obesity **8** hugeness, lewdness, ribaldry **9** crudeness, heaviness, indecency, obscenity, roughness, vul-

garity **10** coarseness, indelicacy, inelegance **14** lasciviousness

grossularite
species: **6** garnet

grotesque 3 odd **4** wild **5** antic, weird **6** absurd, exotic, far-out, rococo, way-out **7** baroque, bizarre, strange **8** deformed, fanciful, peculiar **9** contorted, distorted, eccentric, fantastic, misshapen, odd-shaped, unnatural **10** outlandish **11** extravagant, incongruous **12** preposterous

grotto 4 cave **6** burrow, cavern, hollow, recess, tunnel **8** catacomb

grouch 3 cry **4** beef, carp, crab, fret, kick, mope, pout, rail, sulk **5** cavil, crank, gripe, growl, moper, whine **6** grouse, mutter, pouter **7** grumble, killjoy, protest **8** complain, grumbler **9** bellyache, find fault **10** complainer, curmudgeon, spoilsport, wet blanket

grouchy 5 cross, testy **6** crabby, cranky, grumpy, touchy **8** snappish **10** ill-humored, out of sorts **11** ill-tempered **12** cantankerous **13** short-tempered

ground, grounds 3 set, sod **4** area, base, call, dirt, farm, land, loam, soil, turf, yard **5** acres, basis, beach, cause, dregs, drill, earth, field, found, lawns, realm, teach, train **6** campus, domain, estate, excuse, inform, motive, object, reason, region, secure, settle, sphere, strand **7** account, confirm, deposit, dry land, educate, founder, gardens, habitat, prepare, purpose, support, terrain **8** district, exercise, firm land, initiate, instruct, occasion, organize, practice, premises, property, province, sediment, the earth **9** arguments, bailiwick, establish, fix firmly, institute, principle, rationale, settlings, territory **10** discipline, inducement, real estate, terra firma **11** pros and cons **12** indoctrinate **14** considerations

grounded 5 based **6** kept in, taught **7** aground, beached, bounded, drilled, founded, secured, trained **8** informed, prepared, stranded **9** foundered, initiated **10** kept at home, instructed, restricted **11** disciplined, established **12** washed ashore **13** indoctrinated

grounding 8 training **9** education **10** background, experience **11** preparation **14** indoctrination **15** familiarization

groundless 4 idle **5** empty, false **6** faulty, flimsy, unreal, untrue **8** baseless, needless, unproved **9** erroneous, illogical, imaginary, unfounded **10** chimerical, fallacious, gratuitous **11** uncalled for, unjustified, unsupported, unwarranted **13** unjustifiable, without reason

groundwork 4 base, root **5** basis **6** cradle, ground, origin, source, spring **7** bedrock, footing, grounds, taproot **8**

keystone, learning, planning, practice, training **9** spadework **10** foundation **11** cornerstone, fundamental, preparation **12** fundamentals, underpinning **14** apprenticeship, indoctrination

group 3 set **4** band, clan, file, gang, herd, pack, sift, size, sort **5** align, bunch, class, crowd, flock, grade, hoard, index, party, place, range, swarm, tribe, troop **6** as- sign, branch, circle, clique, family, hobnob, league, line up, mingle, throng **7** arrange, catalog, cluster, combine, company, consort, coterie, faction, marshal, section, species, variety **8** classify, division, graduate, organize, register **9** associate, gathering **10** assemblage, collection, coordinate, detachment, fraternity, fraternize **11** aggregation, alphabetize, association, brotherhood, subdivision **12** congregation **14** classification, representation

Group, The
author: **12** Mary McCarthy

grouping 7 sorting **8** arraying, ordering **10** assemblage, assortment **11** arrangement, disposition **12** distribution, organization

group of performers 6 troupe **7** company **8** ensemble

Group Portrait of a Lady
author: **12** Heinrich Boll

grouse 4 beef, crab, fret, fume, fuss, kick **5** gripe **6** grouch, mutter, squawk, take on **7** carry on, grumble **8** complain, gamebird **9** bellyache

grove 4 bosk **5** brake, copse **6** forest, pinery, timber **7** coppice, orchard, thicket, wood lot **8** wildwood, woodland **9** shrubbery **10** plantation

grovel 4 fawn **5** cower, crawl, stoop, toady **6** cringe, kowtow, snivel **7** flatter, truckle **8** bow and scrape **13** demean oneself, humble oneself **14** lick the boots of

groveling 6 abject **7** fawning, servile **8** cowering, crawling, cringing, toadying **9** kowtowing, truckling **11** bootlicking **17** bowing and scraping

grow 4 bud, sow, wax **5** boom, farm, rise, till **5** bloom, breed, plant, raise, ripen, surge, swell, widen **6** become, expand, extend, flower, garden, mature, spread, sprout, thrive **7** advance, amplify, blossom, develop, enlarge, fill out, get to be, improve, magnify, produce, prosper, shoot up, stretch, succeed **8** come to be, flourish, fructify, increase, mushroom, progress, spring up, vegetate **9** cultivate, germinate, propagate, skyrocket **10** aggrandize

Growing Up in New Guinea
author: **12** Margaret Mead

growl 4 fret, snap **5** croak, grind, gripe, groan, grunt, snarl, whine **6**

grouse, murmur, mutter, rumble **7** grumble **8** complain, talk back

grown-up 3 big, man **4** lady, ripe **5** adult, of age, woman **6** mature, senior **7** worldly **9** full-blown, full-grown, gentleman **11** full-fledged **13** sophisticated

growth 4 crop, hump, lump, rise **5** gnarl, prime, surge, swell, tumor **6** sowing, spread **7** advance, harvest, produce, success **8** increase, maturity, planting, progress **9** expansion, extension, flowering, increment **10** burgeoning, matureness, production, prospering **11** advancement, cultivation, development, enlargement, excrescence, flourishing, improvement, propagation **12** augmentation, mass of tissue **13** amplification
goddess of: 4 Hour **5** Horae

Groza, Lou
nickname: 6 The Toe
sport: 8 football
team: 15 Cleveland Browns

grub 3 bum, dig **4** food, toil, worm **5** cadge, dig up, larva, mooch, slave **6** drudge, sponge **7** rummage

grubber 5 slave **6** drudge, toiler **7** laborer

grubby 4 foul **5** dirty, grimy, messy, muddy, nasty, seedy, tacky **6** beat-up, filthy, frowzy, frumpy, shabby, shoddy, sloppy, smudgy, soiled, sordid **7** squalid, unclean, unkempt **8** begrimed, slovenly, unwashed **9** besmeared **10** bedraggled

grudge 4 envy **5** pique, spite **6** animus, hatred, malice, rancor, resent **7** dislike, ill will **8** aversion, begrudge **9** animosity **10** resentment **11** malevolence **12** hard feelings

grudging 7 envious **8** hesitant, spiteful **9** reluctant, resentful, unwilling **10** ungenerous **13** penny-pinching

grueling 4 hard **6** brutal, tiring **7** racking **9** fatiguing, punishing, torturous **10** exhausting

gruesome 4 gory, grim **5** awful **6** grisly, horrid **7** fearful, ghastly, hideous, macabre **8** horrible, shocking, terrible **9** frightful, loathsome, repellent, repulsive, revolting **10** forbidding, horrendous, horrifying **13** blood-curdling, spine-chilling

gruff 4 curt, rude, sour, tart **5** bluff, blunt, harsh, husky, raspy, rough, sharp, short, stern, sulky, surly **6** abrupt, croaky, crusty, grumpy, hoarse, ragged, sullen **7** bearish, brusque, caustic, crabbed, cracked, grouchy, peevish, throaty, uncivil, waspish **8** churlish, guttural, impolite, snarling, strident **9** bristling, insulting **10** ill-humored, ill-natured, ungracious **11** ill-tempered **12** discourteous

grumble 4 fret **5** chafe, gripe, growl **6**

grouch, grouse, mutter **8** complain **9** find-fault

grump 4 crab **5** crank **6** grouch **8** grumbler, sourball **10** curmudgeon

grumpy 4 sour **5** moody, sulky, surly, testy **6** crabby, cranky, crusty, sullen **7** grouchy, peevish, pettish **8** churlish **9** irritable, splenetic **10** ill-humored, out of humor, out of sorts **11** disgruntled, ill-disposed, ill-tempered **12** cantankerous

grunt 3 cry **4** bark, call, gasp, howl **5** burro, croak, groan, snort, utter **6** bellow, grouch, mumble, murmur, mutter, shriek **7** howling, whisper **8** complain **9** ululation **11** foot soldier, infantryman

Grunwald, Matthais (Grunewald, Mathis)
real name: 23 Mathis Gothardt Neithardt
born: 7 Germany **8** Wurzburg
artwork: 14 The Crucifixion **15** The Resurrection **20** Altarpiece at Isenheim

Grushenka
character in: 20 The Brothers Karamazov
author: 11 Dostoyevsky

Gryce, Percy
character in: 15 The House of Mirth
author: 7 Wharton

gryphon *see* **7** griffin

Guam
capital: 5 Agana
largest city: 8 Tamuning
others: 4 Agat, Apra, Toto, Yigo **5** Magua **6** Dededo, Merizo **8** Inarajan, Mangilao, Mongmong, Sinajana, Talofofo, Tamuning **9** Barrigada, Finegayan, Santa Rita
member of: 7 Mariana (islands)
mountain: 5 Tenjo
highest point: 6 Lamlam
sea: 7 Pacific **10** Philippine
people: 7 Spanish **8** American, Chamorro, Filipino **11** Micronesian
  explorer: 8 Magellan
  ruler: 5 Japan, Spain **12** United States
language: 7 English **8** Chamorro
religion: 16 Roman Catholicism
feature: 7 typhoon **9** coral reef
Air Force base: 8 Andersen
product: 5 copra **6** banana, papaya

guarantee, guaranty 4 avow, bail, bond, pawn, word **5** swear **6** affirm, allege, assure, attest, avowal, insure, pledge, surety **7** deposit, endorse, promise, sponsor, testify, voucher, warrant **8** contract, covenant, security, vouch for, warranty **9** agreement, answer for, assurance, insurance, testimony **10** collateral, underwrite **11** affirmation, endorsement, word of honor **12** give one's word

guard 4 mind, save, tend **5** watch **6** at-

tend, convoy, defend, escort, patrol, picket, screen, secure, sentry, shield, warder **7** conduct, defense, protect, shelter **8** defender, garrison, guardian, keep safe, preserve, security, sentinel, watchdog, watchman **9** bodyguard, concierge, custodian, guardsman, protector, safeguard, watch over **10** doorkeeper, gatekeeper, protection **12** preservation **13** keep watch over

guard against 6 beware **10** look out for **11** take warning, watch out for

guarded 4 wary **5** cagey, chary, leery **7** careful, heedful, mindful, prudent **8** cautious, discreet, hesitant **9** in custody, protected, tentative **10** restrained, suspicious, under guard **11** circumspect, on one's guard

guardian 5 guard **6** convoy, escort, keeper, patrol, patron, picket, sentry, warden, warder **7** curator, trustee **8** advocate, champion, defender, sentinel, shepherd, wardsman, watchdog **9** attendant, bodyguard, caretaker, conductor, custodian, preserver, protector, safeguard, vigilante **10** benefactor **11** conservator **13** friend at court, guardian angel **14** legal custodian

guardian of a place
Latin: 10 genius loci

guardianship 4 care **6** charge **7** custody, keeping **10** protection **11** safekeeping, supervision, trusteeship

Guatemala
capital/largest city: 13 Guatemala City
others: 4 Ocos **5** Coban, Vieja **6** Chahal, Chisec, Cuilco, Flores, Iztapa, Jalapa, Salama, Solola, Tacana, Tecpan, Yaloch, Zacapa **7** Antigua, Cuilapa, Jutiapa, San Jose **8** Progreso **9** Escuintla, Tiquisate **10** Livingston **11** Totonicapan **13** Puerto Barrios, Quezaltenango **14** San Pedro Carcha **16** Chichicastenango
school: 9 San Carlos
measure: 4 vara **6** cuarta, tercia **7** cajuela, manzana **10** caballeria
monetary unit: 4 peso **7** centavo, quetzal
weight: 4 caja **5** libra
lake: 5 Dulce, Guija, Peten **6** Izabal **7** Atitlan **9** Amatitlan, Peten Itza
mountain: 4 Agua, Mico **5** Fuego, Madre **6** Pacaya, Tacana **7** Atitlan, Toliman **8** La Candon, Las Minas **10** Acatenango, Santa Maria **12** Cuchumatanes
highest point: 8 Tajumuko **9** Tajamulco
river: 4 Azul **5** Bravo, Dulce, Lapaz **6** Belize, Chixoy, Negino, Pasion, Samala **7** Chiapas, Motagua, Sarstun, Sastoon **8** Polochic, Rio Dulce, Sarstoon **10** Usumacinta
sea: 7 Pacific **8** Atlantic **9** Caribbean
physical feature:
  bay: 8 Amatique

gulf: 8 Honduras
people: 3 Mam **4** Chol, Itza, Ixil, Maya **5** Xinca **6** Caribe, Quiche **7** ladinos, mestizo, Pocomam **13** Guatemaltecos
language: 6 Quiche **7** Spanish
religion: 13 Roman Catholic
place:
  church: 10 Santo Tomas
  ruins: 5 Mayan, Tikal **8** Uaxactun
feature:
  bird: 7 quetzal
  clarinet: 8 chirimta
  dance: 5 elson **8** guarimba
  flute: 3 xul
  military dictator: 8 Caudillo
food:
  dish: 6 pepian **10** enchiladas **13** gallo en chicha
  fruit: 4 anay
guava 7 Psidium **16** Psidium guineense
  varieties: 5 apple **6** common, purple, yellow **7** Cattley, Chilean **9** pineapple **10** Costa Rican, strawberry **13** yellow cattley **16** purple strawberry, yellow strawberry

Gudrun
  also: 6 Kudrun **7** Guthrun
  origin: 12 Scandinavian
  mentioned in: 8 Volsunga
  father: 5 Giuki, Gjuki **6** Hertel
  mother: 8 Grimhild
  brother: 6 Gunnar
  husband: 4 Atli **6** Herwig, Sigurd
  killed: 4 Atli
  corresponds to: 9 Kriemhild

guess 4 deem, view **5** fancy, judge, opine, think **6** assume, belief, deduce, divine, gather, reckon, regard, theory **7** believe, daresay, feeling, imagine, opinion, predict, suppose, surmise, suspect, venture **8** conclude, estimate, theorize **9** postulate, speculate, suspicion **10** assumption, conjecture, divination, hypothesis, prediction **11** hypothesize, make a stab at, postulation, presumption, speculation, supposition
guesswork 7 surmise **10** conjecture, hypothesis **11** supposition **13** shot in the dark
guest 5 diner **6** caller, client, friend, inmate, lodger, patron, roomer **7** boarder, company, habitue, invitee, patient, visitor **8** customer **9** sojourner **10** frequenter **14** paying customer

Guest, Edgar A
  author of: 12 A Heap of Livin'
Guest, Judith
  author of: 14 Ordinary People
Guevara 3 Che **7** Ernesto
  born: 9 Argentina
  active in: 15 Cuban Revolution
  friend: 6 Castro
  role in: 5 Evita
  killed in: 7 Bolivia
guffaw 4 howl **6** scream **10** belly laugh, horse laugh

guidance 3 tip **4** clue, help, hint, lead **6** advice, escort **7** conduct, counsel, pointer **8** auspices **9** direction **10** leadership, management, protection, suggestion **11** information, instruction, supervision **12** intelligence **13** enlightenment
guide 4 lead, rule **5** model, pilot, steer, usher **6** beacon, convoy, direct, escort, govern, handle, leader, manage, marker, master, mentor **7** adviser, command, conduct, control, example, marshal, monitor, oversee, pattern, steerer, teacher **8** chaperon, cicerone, director, engineer, helmsman, landmark, lodestar, maneuver, polestar, regulate, shepherd, signpost **9** accompany, attendant, conductor, counselor **10** manipulate
guidebook 5 bible **6** manual **8** Baedeker, handbook **13** reference book
Guidry, Ron (Ronald Ames)
  nickname: 18 Louisiana Lightning
  sport: 8 baseball
  position: 7 pitcher
  team: 14 New York Yankees
guild 5 hansa, hanse, order, union **6** league **7** company, society **8** alliance **9** coalition **10** craft union, federation, fraternity, labor union, sisterhood, trade union **11** association, brotherhood, confederacy, corporation
Guildenstern
  character in: 6 Hamlet
  author: 11 Shakespeare
guile 5 craft, fraud **6** deceit, tricks **7** cunning, slyness **8** artifice, strategy, trickery, wiliness **9** chicanery, deception, duplicity, treachery **10** artfulness, craftiness, dishonesty, hankypanky, stratagems, trickiness **11** fraudulence **13** sharp practice
guileless 4 open **5** frank, naive **6** candid, honest, simple **7** artless, natural, sincere **8** harmless, innocent, truthful **9** ingenuous, innocuous **10** aboveboard, unaffected **11** undesigning, unoffending **15** straightforward, unselfconscious, unsophisticated
guilelessness 6 candor **9** innocence, sincerity **10** candidness, directness **11** artlessness **13** ingenuousness
guilt 3 sin **4** blot, vice **5** shame, wrong **6** infamy, stigma **7** misdeed **8** disgrace, dishonor, misdoing, trespass **9** black mark, turpitude **10** guiltiness, misconduct, sinfulness, wrongdoing **11** criminality, culpability, degradation, delinquency, dereliction, humiliation, misbehavior, self-disgust **13** transgression
guiltless 4 good, pure **5** clean **6** chaste **7** angelic, sinless **8** innocent, unfallen, virtuous **9** blameless, childlike, faultless **10** immaculate, inculpable, unblamable **11** uncorrupted
  French: 12 sans reproche

guilt-stricken 7 ashamed **18** conscience-stricken
guilty 5 sorry, wrong **6** erring, sinful **7** ashamed, corrupt, hangdog, immoral **8** blamable, contrite, criminal, culpable, penitent, sheepish **9** offensive, regretful, repentant **11** blameworthy **18** conscience-stricken
Guinea
  other name: 12 French Guinea **13** Rivieres du Sud
  capital/largest city: 7 Conakry
  others: 4 Boke, Fria, Labe **5** Beyla **6** Dabola, Kankan, Kindia **7** Dubreka, Siguiri **8** Kerouane **9** Kouroussa, Nzerekore
  measure: 7 jacktan
  monetary unit: 4 iliy, syli **5** franc **6** cauris
  weight: 4 akey, piso, uzan **5** benda, seron **6** quinto **8** aguirage
  island: 3 Los **5** Tombo **7** Tristao
  mountain: 4 Loma **6** Tamgue **11** Fouta Djalon
  highest point: 5 Nimba
  river: 4 Milo **5** Kogon, Niger **6** Bafing, Faleme, Gambia **7** Kolente, Senegal **8** Konkoure, Tinkisso **13** Great Scarcies
  sea: 8 Atlantic
  physical feature:
    cape: 5 Verga
  people: 4 Koma, Loma, Nalu, Susu, Toma **5** Kissi, Manon **6** Fulani, Guerzi **7** Landoma, Malinke **8** Kouranke, Landuman **11** Kissi-Sherbo **12** Guerze-Kpelle
  language: 5 Fulbe, Mande **6** Arabic, French, Fulani **7** English
  religion: 5 Islam **7** animism
  feature:
    plant: 11 globeflower
    tree: 4 akee **5** dalli
Guinea-Bissau
  other name: 16 Portuguese Guinea
  capital/largest city: 6 Bissau
  others: 4 Buba **5** Catio, Farim **6** Bafata, Bolama, Cacheu, Cacine, Dandum, Mansoa **7** Bissora, Bubaque, San Joav **9** Fulacunda **10** Nova Lamego **11** Madina do Boe, Madine do Boe, Sao Domingos
  monetary unit: 4 peso **6** escudo **8** centavos
  island: 4 Roxa **6** Orango **7** Bijagos, Formosa
  river: 4 Geba **6** Cacheu, Mansoa **7** Corubal
  sea: 8 Atlantic
  people: 6 Fulani **7** Balanta, Balante, mulatto **8** Mandingo, Mandyako
  language: 5 Fulah **7** Balante, Crioulo **8** Mandingo **10** Portuguese **21** Cape Verde-Guinea Creole
  religion: 5 Islam **7** animism **12** Christianity
Guinevere
  character in: 16 Arthurian romance

husband: 6 Arthur
lover: 8 Lancelot

Guinness, Sir Alec
born: 6 London **7** England
roles: 8 Star Wars **11** Oliver Twist **13** Doctor Zhivago **14** Our Man in Havana, The Ladykillers **15** A Passage to India, Ben Obi Wan Kenobi, Lavender Hill Mob **16** Lawrence of Arabia **17** Great Expectations **21** Kind Hearts and Coronets **22** Tinker Tailor Soldier Spy **23** The Bridge on the River Kwai (Oscar)

guise 4 garb, mode **5** dress, habit **6** attire **7** apparel, clothes, costume, fashion **8** clothing, disguise, pretense **10** masquerade

Gulag Archipelago, The
author: 23 Aleksandr Solzhenitsyn Jr

gulch 3 gap **4** rift **5** abyss, chasm, cleft, crack, gorge, gully, split **6** arroyo, breach, divide, ravine **8** crevasse

gulf 4 cove, rent, rift **5** abyss, chasm, cleft, firth, fjord, gully, inlet, split **6** canyon, lagoon **7** estuary, opening **8** crevasse **10** separation

gull 3 gyp **4** dupe, rook **5** cozen, trick **7** deceive, defraud, sea gull, sea bird, swindle **9** bamboozle, victimize

gullet 3 maw **4** craw, crop **5** belly, gorge, tummy **6** dewlap, throat **7** abdomen, channel, stomach, weasand **9** beer belly, esophagus

gullible 5 green, naive **6** simple **8** innocent, trustful, trusting **9** credulous **11** easily duped **12** easily fooled, overtrusting, unsuspicious **13** easily cheated, inexperienced **14** easily deceived **15** unsophisticated

Gulliver's Travels
author: 13 Jonathan Swift
character: 14 Lemuel Gulliver
visited: 6 Laputa, Yahoos **8** Blefuscu, Lilliput, Luggnagg **9** Balnibari **10** Houyhnhnms **11** Brobdingnag **12** Glubbdubdrib

gully 3 gap **5** ditch, gorge, gulch **6** defile, furrow, gutter, ravine, trench **7** channel **11** small canyon, small valley, watercourse **13** drainage ditch

gulp 4 bolt, swig, wolf **5** quaff, swill **6** devour, guzzle **7** swallow, toss off **8** mouthful

gulp down 4 bolt **6** devour, gobble **7** swallow **8** gobble up, wolf down

gum 5 wax **5** latex, resin **6** chicle **8** mucilage **10** Eucalyptus
varieties: 3 cup, red **4** blue, cape, gray, rose, snow, sour **5** apple, black, cider, coral, giant, gully, Karri, Manna, sug- ar, swamp, sweet **6** cotton, Deane's, desert, gimlet, salmon, snappy, Tupelo **7** Barbary, cabbage, Fuchsia, maiden's, Morocco, scarlet, spotted **8** Formosan, Lehmann's, mountain, scribbly, spinning **9** forest red, Murray red, steedman's **10** Australian, candle-bark, red-spotted, Sydney blue, Timor white, tumble-down, urn-fruited **11** Blakely's red, blue weeping, salmon white, small-leaved, strickland's **12** lemon-scented, red-flowering, silver-dollar **13** American sweet, Oriental sweet, Tasmanian blue, Tasmanian snow **14** yellow-flowered **15** Omeo round-leaved, round-leaved snow **16** rough-barked manna, scarlet-flowering **17** heart-leaved silver **20** silver-leaved mountain

gummed 5 glued, gummy, stuck **6** sticky **8** adhering, adhesive

Gummidge, Mrs
character in: 16 David Copperfield
author: 7 Dickens

gummy 5 gluey, gooey, gunky **6** gloppy, sticky, viscid **7** rubbery, viscous **8** adhesive **10** gelatinous **12** mucilaginous

gumption 3 zip **4** dash, push **5** drive, spunk, verve **6** energy, hustle, pizazz, spirit **7** courage **10** enterprise, get-up-and-go, initiative **12** forcefulness **14** aggressiveness **15** resourcefulness

gumshoe 3 tec **4** dick **6** shamus **9** detective **10** private eye **12** investigator

gun 3 aim, gat, rod, try **4** Colt, hunt, iron **5** piece, rifle, shoot **6** cannon, Magnum, mortar, musket, pistol **7** attempt, carbine, firearm, Gatling, go after, Long Tom, shotgun **8** howitzer, ordnance, revolver **9** automatic, Big Bertha, derringer, equalizer, flintlock, forty-five, twenty-two, Remington **10** fieldpiece, machine gun, six-shooter, three-fifty, Walther PPK, Winchester **11** blunderbuss, thirty-eight, trusty-rusty **12** fowling piece, muzzle loader, shooting iron **13** Kentucky rifle **14** artillery piece, Smith and Wesson
invented by:
  breechloader: 8 Thornton
  magazine: 9 Hotchkiss
  silencer: 5 Maxim

Gunga Din
story in: 18 Barrack-Room Ballads
author: 14 Rudyard Kipling
director: 13 George Stevens
cast: 8 Sam Jaffe **9** Cary Grant **12** Joan Fontaine **14** Victor McLaglen **18** Douglas Fairbanks Jr
setting: 5 India
remade as: 13 Soldiers Three **14** Sergeants Three

gunman 6 bandit, outlaw, robber, sniper **7** hoodlum **9** assailant, desperado, holdup man

Gunn, Ben
character in: 14 Treasure Island
author: 9 Stevenson

Gunnar
origin: 12 Scandinavian
father: 5 Giuki, Gjuki

mother: 8 Grimhild
sister: 6 Gudrun, Kudrun **7** Guthrun
wife: 8 Brynhild
Brynhild won by: 6 Sigurd

Gunsmoke
character: 3 Sam (the bartender) **8** Doc (Dr Galen) Adams **10** Quint Asper **11** Newly O'Brien **12** Chester Goode, Festus Haggen, Kitty Russell (Miss Kitty) **18** Marshall Matt Dillon **24** Clayton Thaddeus (Thad) Greenwood
cast: 9 Ken Curtis **10** Buck Taylor, Roger Ewing **11** Amanda Blake, James Arness **12** Burt Reynolds, Dennis Weaver, Glenn Strange, Milburn Stone
setting: 9 Dodge City
saloon: 10 Longbranch

Guns of August, The
author: 15 Barbara W Tuchman

Guns of Navarone, The
director: 12 J Lee Thompson
based on novel by: 15 Alistair MacLean
cast: 10 David Niven **11** Gregory Peck, James Darren **12** Anthony Quinn, Stanley Baker **13** Anthony Quayle

Gunther
origin: 8 Germanic
mentioned in: 14 Nibelungenlied
king of: 8 Burgundy
wife: 8 Brunhild
sister: 9 Kriemhild
killed by: 9 Kriemhild

Guppy
character in: 10 Bleak House
author: 7 Dickens

gurgle 5 plash **6** babble, bubble, burble, murmur, ripple **7** sputter **8** bubbling, gurgling

guru 5 guide **6** leader, master **7** teacher **9** preceptor **11** instructor

gush 3 gab, gas, jet, run **4** blab, bull, rush, well **5** issue, prate, spout, spurt **6** bab- ble, burble, drivel, hot air, splash, squirt, stream **7** baloney, blabber, blather, chatter, pour out, prattle, rubbish, torrent, twaddle **8** nonsense, outburst, rattle on **10** outpouring **11** mawkishness **12** emotionalism **14** sentimentalism, talk effusively **16** run off at the mouth

gushiness 12 effusiveness, emotionalism **17** demonstrativeness

gushing 6 lavish **7** pouring, profuse **8** effusive, spurting **10** flattering **11** free-flowing **12** demonstative, unrestrained **16** overenthusiastic

gushy 8 effusive **12** unrestrained **13** demonstrative **16** overenthusiastic

gussy up 5 adorn **7** dress up, enhance **8** beautify, decorate, ornament **9** embellish

gust 3 fit **4** blow, puff, wind **5** blast, burst, draft **6** breeze, flurry, squall,

zephyr **8** outbreak, outburst, paroxysm **9** explosion

Guster
character in: **10** Bleak House
author: **7** Dickens

gusto 3 joy **4** zeal, zest **5** savor **6** fervor, relish **7** delight **8** appetite, pleasure **10** enthusiasm **12** appreciation,
exhilaration, satisfaction

gusto, con
music: **9** with style, with taste

gusty 5 blowy, windy **6** breezy **7**
squally **8** blustery

gut 4 raze **5** belly, clean, level, tummy
6 bowels, paunch, ravage **7** abdomen,
consume, midriff, stomach, viscera **8**
entrails, lay waste **9** bay window,
beer belly, spare tire **10** disembowel,
eviscerate, intestines, midsection **11**
breadbasket

guten abend 11 good evening

Gutenberg
nationality: **6** German
inventor of: **11** movable type
printer of: **14** Gutenberg Bible

guten morgen 11 good morning

guten tag 7 good day

Guthrie, A B Jr
author of: **6** Arfive **9** The Big Sky **10**
The Way West **13** The Last Valley
16 Fair Land Fair Land, The Blue
Hen's Chick, The Thousand Hills

Guthrun see **6** Gudrun

Gutman, Casper
character in: **16** The Maltese Falcon
author: **7** Hammett

guts 4 dash, grit **5** nerve, pluck, spunk
6 bowels, daring, mettle, spirit, vitals
7 bravado, bravery, courage, gizzard,
innards, insides, viscera **8** audacity,
backbone, boldness **9** fortitude **10**
intestines **11** intrepidity

gutsy 4 game **5** brave **6** heroic, plucky
7 doughty, valiant **8** fearless, intrepid,
stalwart, unafraid, valorous **9** dauntless, undaunted **10** courageous
11 lionhearted, unflinching **12** stouthearted

guttural 3 low **4** deep **5** gruff, harsh,
husky, raspy, thick **6** hoarse **7** throaty
8 croaking **12** inarticulate

guy 3 boy, joe, kid, man **4** body, chap,
dude, gent, rope **5** bloke, human,
joker **6** fellow, hombre, person **8**
blighter, up-holder **9** supporter **10** individual

Guyana
name means: **12** land of waters
other name: **13** British Guiana
capital/largest city: **10** Georgetown
others: **7** Charity **8** Hyde Park, Ro-
signol **9** Jonestown, Mackenzie
island: **6** Leguan **8** Wakenaam
mountain: **5** Amuku, Ariwa, Kamoa
6 Akarai, Kanuku **7** Caburai **9** Pacaraima
highest point: **7** Roraima
river: **5** Waini **6** Barama **7** Amakura,
Baruima, Berbice **8** Demerara, Ma-
zaruni, Rupununi **9** Essequibo **10**
Burro-Burro
ocean: **8** Atlantic
physical feature:
falls: **5** Great, Tiger **7** Kamaria **8**
Kaieteur **9** Serikoeng **10** Surwak-
wima **15** Fredrik Willem IV
people: **6** Akawai, Arawak, Creole,
Taruma **7** African, Chinese, mulatto
10 Portuguese
language: **5** Hindi **7** English
religion: **5** Hindu, Islam **8** Anglican
13 Roman Catholic

Guy Fawkes
author: **16** William Ainsworth

Guy Mannering
author: **14** Sir Walter Scott

Guyon
character in: **15** The Faerie Queene
author: **7** Spenser

Guys and Dolls
director: **17** Joseph L Mankiewicz
based on story by: **11** Damon Runyon
cast: **10** Stubby Kaye **11** Jean Simmons **12** Frank Sinatra, Marlon
Brando, Vivian Blaine
setting: **11** New York City
score: **12** Frank Loesser
song: **11** Luck Be a Lady **12** Guys
and Dolls **26** Sit Down You're Rocking the Boat

guzzle 4 bolt, swig **5** quaff, swill **6** de-

vour, imbibe, tipple **7** toss off **8** gulp
down

guzzler 5 drunk **6** boozer **7** imbiber,
tippler **8** devourer, drunkard **9** alcoholic

Gwawl
origin: **5** Welsh
mentioned in: **10** Mabinogion
rival of: **5** Pwyll
sought hand of: **8** Rhiannon

Gwydion
origin: **5** Welsh
son: **14** Llew Llaw Gyffes
sister: **9** Arianhrod
lover: **9** Arianhrod

Gwyn
origin: **7** British
god of: **7** rebirth **9** afterlife

Gyas
companion of: **6** Aeneas

Gyes see **5** Gyges

Gygaea, Gyge
form: **5** nymph
location: **4** lake

Gyges
also: **4** Gyes
member of: **13** Hecatonchires

gymnasium 5 arena **6** circus **7** stadium **10** hippodrome

gymnast 10 Olga Korbut **13** Mary Lou
Retton, Nadia Comaneci

gymnastics 9 exercises **10** acrobatics
11 contortions **16** physical training

Gynaecothoenas
epithet of: **4** Ares
means: **17** feasted by the women

gynophobia
fear of: **5** women

gyp 3 con **4** bilk, burn, fake, hoax,
rook, scam, soak **5** cheat, cozen,
fraud, phony, trick **6** diddle, fleece,
humbug, ripoff **7** con game, defraud,
swindle **8** flimflam, hoodwink **9** bamboozle, deception

gypsy
Italian: **7** zingara, zingaro

gyrate 5 swirl, twirl, wheel, whirl **6**
circle, rotate, spiral **7** revolve **9** pirouette **10** spin around

habeas corpus 11 have the body **23** produce the person in court
legal writ guards against: 19 illegal imprisonment

habiliments 4 garb, wear **5** dress **6** attire, outfit **7** clothes, costume, raiment, regalia **8** clothing, wardrobe **9** vestments

habit 3 rut, way **4** garb, gear, robe, rule, wont **5** dress, trait, usage **6** attire, custom, groove, livery, manner, outfit **7** apparel, clothes, costume, garment, leaning, raiment, routine, uniform, vesture **8** clothing, fondness, habitude, nun's wear, practice **9** mannerism, trappings **10** beaten path, convention, observance, partiality, proclivity, propensity **11** habiliments, inclination, peculiarity **12** predilection, second nature **13** accoutrements, fixed practice **14** matter of course, predisposition **15** behavior pattern

habitat 3 pad **4** digs, home, spot, zone **5** abode, haunt, place, range, realm, roost **6** domain, locale, milieu, region **7** housing, lodging, setting, terrain **8** domicile, dwelling, home base, lodgment, precinct, quarters **9** territory **10** habitation **11** environment, natural home **12** place of abode **13** dwelling place **14** stamping ground **15** natural locality **17** native environment

habitation 3 pad **4** digs, home **5** abode, haunt, house, roost **6** colony **7** habitat, housing, lodging, shelter, tenancy **8** domicile, dwelling, lodgment, quarters **9** community, occupancy, residence **10** occupation, settlement **12** place of abode **13** dwelling place, temporary stay **16** place of residence

Habit of Being, The
author: 15 Flannery O'Connor

habitual 5 fixed, usual **6** common, normal, wonted **7** chronic, natural, regular, routine, typical **8** addicted, constant, expected, familiar, frequent, periodic, repeated **9** confirmed, continual, customary, incessant, ingrained, perpetual, recurrent **10** accustomed, deep-rooted, deep-seated, inveterate, methodical, systematic **11** established, traditional **12** conventional, second nature **14** by force of habit

habitual practice 4 wont **5** habit **6** custom

habituate 5 adapt, drill, imbue, inure, train **6** harden, school, season **7** break in, instill **8** accustom, initiate **9** inculcate **10** discipline, make used to **12** indoctrinate

habitue 7 regular **10** frequenter **13** regular patron **15** frequent visitor **16** constant customer

hacek 13 inverted caret **15** diacritical mark

hack 3 cab, cut, hew, nag **4** bark, chip, chop, gash, plug, rasp, slit, taxi **5** coach, cut up, notch, slash, slice, whack **6** cleave, mangle **7** hackney, taxicab **8** lacerate, mutilate **9** cart horse, dray horse, scribbler, workhorse **10** cough drily, cut roughly, draft horse, hired horse, shaft horse **11** common horse, penny-a-liner **12** hackney coach, worn-out horse **13** carriage horse **16** grubstreet writer **18** horse-drawn carriage

hackle 3 peg **4** card, comb, hack, hook, ruff **5** curry, plume, quill **6** heckle, mangle **7** bristle, feather, plumage

Hackman, Gene
born: 15 San Bernardino CA
roles: 8 Superman **11** Popeye Doyle **14** Bonnie and Clyde **15** The Conversation **19** The French Connection (Oscar) **20** The Poseidon Adventure

hackneyed 4 dull, worn **5** banal, inane, stale, stock, trite, vapid **6** common, jejune **7** cliched, humdrum, insipid, routine, worn-out **8** bromidic, ordinary, shopworn, well-worn **9** moth-eaten **10** pedestrian, threadbare, uninspired **11** commonplace, stereotyped **12** conventional **13** platitudinous, unimaginative

Hadassah 6 Esther

Hades 4 hell
also: 3 Dis **5** Pluto **10** lower world, Underworld
corresponds to: 5 Orcus
god of: 5 Orcus, Pluto
goddess of: 6 Hecate, Hekate

Haenigsen, Harry
creator/artist of: 5 Penny **7** Our Bill

hafnium
chemical symbol: 2 Hf

hag 3 bat, nag **4** drab, fury **5** biddy, crone, frump, harpy, shrew, vixen, witch **6** beldam, gorgon, ogress, vi-

rago **7** hellcat **8** battle-ax, harridan **9** termagant

Hagar
servant of: 5 Sarah
husband: 7 Abraham
son: 7 Ishmael

Hagar the Horrible
creator: 9 Dik Browne

Hagen
origin: 8 Germanic
mentioned in: 14 Nibelungenlied
killed by: 9 Kriemhild
killed: 9 Siegfried

Haggadah 7 parable **8** anecdote
source: 6 Talmud
read at: 5 seder **8** Passover

haggard 4 beat, wild, worn **5** gaunt, spent, tired, upset, weary **6** bushed, fagged, pooped, raging, wasted **7** ranting **8** careworn, drooping, fatigued, flagging, frenzied, harassed, harrowed, overcome, toilworn, wild-eyed **9** exhausted, woebegone **10** hollow-eyed **11** debilitated, overwearied, overwrought, tuckered out, wild-looking **12** tired-looking

Haggard, H Rider
author of: 3 She **17** King Solomon's Mines
noted phrase: 18 She who must be obeyed

haggle 6 barter, bicker, dicker, higgle **7** bargain, dispute, quarrel, quibble, wrangle **8** beat down, squabble

Hagiographa
Hebrew: 7 Ketubim

hagiographer 19 writer of saints' lives

Hagman, Larry
mother: 10 Mary Martin
born: 13 Weatherford TX
roles: 6 Dallas **7** J R Ewing **15** I Dream of Jeannie

Hahn, Otto
field: 9 chemistry
nationality: 6 German
discovered: 13 protoactinium **14** nuclear isomers
awarded: 10 Nobel Prize

Haida
language family: 6 Masset, Na-Dene **10** Skidegatta
tribe: 7 Kaigani
location: 6 Alaska **15** British Columbia **21** Queen Charlotte Islands

related to: 7 Tlingit **9** Tsimshian
associated with: 9 totem pole **13** wood sculpture

hail 3 ave **4** call **5** cheer, exalt, extol, greet, hello, honor, shout **6** accost, call to, esteem, salute **7** acclaim, address, applaud, commend, glorify, receive, shout at, usher in, welcome **8** cry out to, eulogize, greeting **9** accosting **10** calling out, compliment, panegyrize, salutation **11** make welcome
German: 4 heil
Latin: 3 ave **5** salve

Hailey, Arthur
author of: 5 Hotel **6** Wheels **7** Airport **12** In High Places **14** Final Diagnosis **16** The Moneychangers

hail-fellow-well-met 8 familiar, friendly, intimate, outgoing, sociable **9** extrovert **10** gregarious

Hail Mary
Latin: 8 Ave Maria **12** rosary prayer

Hail the Conquering Hero
director: 14 Preston Sturges
cast: 10 Ella Raines **12** Eddie Bracken **14** Raymond Walburn **15** William Demarest **16** Franklin Pangborn

hail to victory
German: 8 sieg heil

Hair
writers: 9 James Rado **11** Gerome Ragni
composer: 13 Galt MacDermot
character: 3 Hud **4** Woof **6** Berger, Claude, Crissy, Dionne, Jeanie, Sheila
songs: 4 3500 **8** Aquarius **9** Ain't Got No **12** Colored Spade **17** Manchester England

hair 3 fur, mop **4** coat, down, iota, mane, pelt, wool **5** bangs, curls, locks **6** fleece **7** tresses **8** ringlets **12** narrow margin
loss: 8 alopecia, baldness

haircut, hairdo 3 bob, bun, cut **4** Afro, clip, crop, fade, perm, shag, trim, updo **5** bangs, braid, butch, swirl **6** boogie, mohawk **7** beehive, buzzcut, chignon, cornrow, crewcut, flattop, fuzz cut, natural, pachuco, page boy, pigtail, shingle, tonsure, upsweep **8** bouffant, brushcut, coiffure, ducktail, ponytail, razorcut **9** barbering, hairstyle, permanent, pompadour **10** feathercut, french knot

haircutter 6 barber **11** hairdresser, hair stylist

hairdresser 8 coiffeur **9** coiffeuse **10** beautician, haircutter **11** beauty salon **12** beauty parlor
French: 8 coiffeur

hair-raising 5 eerie **7** bristle **8** exciting **9** thrilling **10** terrifying **11** astonishing **12** breathtaking, electrifying **13** horripilation, spine-tingling

hairsplitting 4 fine **6** minute, subtle **7** carping **8** caviling, delicate, hairline,

niggling **9** minuscule, quibbling **10** nitpicking, unapparent **12** faultfinding, overcritical **13** imperceptible, inappreciable, infinitesimal **15** inconsequential

hairy 5 bushy, furry, wooly **6** fleecy, pilose, shaggy, woolly **7** hirsute

Hairy Ape, The
author: 12 Eugene O'Neill

Haiti
name means: 15 mountainous land
other name: 12 Santo Domingo
capital/largest city: 12 Port-au-Prince
others: 5 Aquin, Furcy, Limbe **6** Hinche, Jacmel, St Marc **7** Jeremie, Leogane, Saltrou **8** Gonaives, Kenscoff, Les Cayes **10** Cap-Haitien
monetary unit: 6 gourde **8** centimes
island: 5 Vache **6** Gonave, Tortue **7** Navassa, Tortuga **8** Caymites **10** Hispaniola **14** Grande Cayemite **15** Greater Antilles
lake: 8 Saumatre
mountain: 4 Nord **5** Cahos **6** Macaya, Noires **7** Lahotte **8** Troudeau
highest point: 7 La Selle, Laselle
river: 9 Guayamoul **10** Artibonite
sea: 8 Atlantic **9** Caribbean
physical feature:
  gulf: 6 Gonave
  passage: 8 Windward
people: 5 Taino **7** African, mulatto
  discoverer: 8 Columbus
  liberator: 19 Toussaint Louverture
  ruler: 7 Papa Doc **8** Duvalier
language: 6 Creole, French, patois
religion: 6 voodoo **13** Roman Catholic
feature:
  dance: 5 mambo
  festival: 9 Mardi Gras
  fortress: 10 La Ferriere **24** Citadelle du Roi Christophe
  security force: 8 bogeymen **15** Tontons Macoutes
food:
  sweet potato: 6 batata

Hakenkreuz 11 hooked cross **12** Nazi swastika

HAL
character in: 14 Two Thousand One (2001)
author: 6 Clarke

Halas, George
nickname: 8 Papa Bear
sport: 8 football
position: 5 coach
team: 12 Chicago Bears

halcyon 4 calm, fair **5** happy, quiet, sunny **6** blithe, golden, hushed, joyous, placid, serene **7** pacific **8** carefree, cheerful, peaceful, tranquil **9** cloudless, contented, reposeful, unclouded, unruffled **10** unagitated, untroubled

hale 3 fit **4** well **5** hardy, sound **6** hearty, robust, rugged, sturdy **7**

healthy, in shape **8** vigorous **9** energetic, in the pink, strapping **10** able-bodied, robustious **12** in fine fettle

Hale, Edward Everett
author of: 21 The Man Without a Country
hero: 11 Phillip Nolan

Hale, George Ellery
field: 9 astronomy
initiated: 20 Mt Palomar Observatory
invented: 17 spectroheliograph

Hale, Nathan, 7 patriot
hanged as a: 3 spy

Hale-Bopp 5 comet

Haley, Alex
author of: 5 Roots **26** The Autobiography of Malcolm X

Haley, Jack
born: 8 Boston MA
roles: 6 Tin Man **13** The Wizard of Oz

half 4 part, some **6** all but, barely, fairly, feebly, halved, in part, meager, partly, rather, scanty, skimpy, slight, weakly **7** divided, faintly, limited, partial, portion, section **8** fraction, middling, moderate, passable, passably, slightly **9** deficient, imperfect, partially, tolerable, tolerably **10** fractional, inadequate, incomplete, moderately, relatively **12** fifty percent, inadequately, insufficient, pretty nearly **13** after a fashion, comparatively **14** insufficiently

half-asleep 6 drowsy, groggy, unwary **7** out-of-it, unaware **8** sluggish **9** not-with-it, oblivious

half-hearted 4 cold, cool, tame **5** blase, faint **7** languid, passive **8** listless, lukewarm **9** apathetic, lethargic **10** ambivalent, irresolute, lackluster, phlegmatic, spiritless, unaspiring **11** indifferent, perfunctory **13** lackadaisical **14** unenthusiastic

half homer 15 Biblical measure

half-moon 3 arc, bow **4** arch **5** curve **8** crescent

Half Moon 4 ship
of: 11 Henry Hudson

halfway 6 almost, in part, medial, medium, middle, midway, nearly, partly, rather **7** midmost **8** somewhat **9** partially, to a degree **10** middlemost, moderately **11** equidistant, in the middle **12** intermediate, pretty nearly, to some extent **13** in some measure **18** between two extremes

half-wit 4 dolt, dope, fool **5** dummy, dunce, idiot, moron, ninny **6** dimwit, nitwit **7** dullard **8** dumb-dumb, imbecile, numskull **9** blockhead, numbskull, simpleton **10** nincompoop **15** mental defective, mental deficient

half-witted 4 dumb **5** silly **6** stupid **7** asinine, foolish, idiotic, moronic **9** dimwitted, imbecilic, senseless

11 lamebrained 12 feeble-minded, simple-minded

hall 5 entry, foyer, lobby 6 arcade 7 chamber, gallery, hallway, passage 8 anteroom, club room, corridor, entrance 9 vestibule 10 auditorium, dining hall, passageway 11 antechamber, banquet hall, concert hall, waiting room 12 amphitheater, assembly room, meeting place 13 reception room

Hall, Diane
real name of: 11 Diane Keaton

Hall, James
field: 7 geology 9 chemistry
nationality: 7 British
founded: 12 geochemistry 19 experimental geology

Hall, James Norman
author of: 17 Mutiny on the Bounty
co-author: 15 Charles Nordhoff

Hallel 6 praise 16 liturgical prayer

Haller, Albrecht von
field: 7 biology
nationality: 5 Swiss
founded: 15 modern neurology

Haller, Harry
character in: 11 Steppenwolf
author: 5 Hesse

Halley, Edmund
field: 9 astronomy
nationality: 7 British
discovered: 12 Halley's Comet

hallmark 4 sign 5 badge, stamp 6 device, emblem, symbol 14 characteristic

halloo 3 cry 4 call, hail, yell 5 shout 6 cry out, holler

hallow 5 bless 7 respect 8 dedicate, sanctify, venerate 10 consecrate

hallowed 4 holy 6 sacred 7 blessed, honored 9 beatified, dedicated 10 sacrosanct, sanctified 11 consecrated

Halloween
date: 7 October (31)
also called: 13 All Hallows Eve
symbol: 7 pumpkin 12 jack-o-lantern
saying: 12 trick or treat

hallucination 5 dream 6 mirage, vision 7 chimera, fantasy, figment 8 delusion, illusion 9 nightmare 10 aberration, apparition 14 phantasmagoria

hallway 4 hall 5 entry, foyer 7 passage 8 corridor, entryway 10 passageway

halo 6 aurora, corona, luster, nimbus 7 aureole, dignity, majesty 8 grandeur, holiness, radiance, sanctity, splendor 9 solemnity, sublimity 11 ring of light 12 chromosphere, luminousness, magnificence, resplendence 13 spiritual aura 15 illustriousness

Hals, Franz
born: 7 Antwerp, Holland
artwork: 9 Gypsy Girl 10 Hille Bobbe (The Witch of Haarlem) 13 The Jolly Toper 14 Jacobus Zaffius 15 The Merry Company 19 The Laughing Cavalier 22 Portrait of a Standing Man 24 The Regents of the Almshouse 26 Yonker Ramp and his Sweetheart 28 The Regentesses of the Almshouse 33 The Banquet of the St George Civic Guard

Halsey, William F
served in: 3 WWI 4 WWII
rank: 12 fleet admiral
battle: 9 Leyte Gulf 11 Philippines 14 Solomon Islands

halt 3 end 4 balk, curb, foil, quit, rest, rout, stay, stem, stop, wait, whoa 5 abate, block, brake, break, cease, check, close, crush, delay, pause, quash, quell, stall, tarry 6 bridle, cut off, defeat, draw up, hamper, hinder, impede, linger, pull up, recess, rein in, scotch, subdue, thwart, wind up 7 heave to, inhibit, prevent, put down, repress, respite, squelch, suspend, time out 8 break off, breather, choke off, don't move, hang fire, interval, knock off, leave off, overturn, prohibit, restrain, restrict, shut down, suppress, vanquish 9 cessation, frustrate, interlude, interrupt, overthrow, terminate 10 call it a day, extinguish, shut up shop, standstill, suspension 11 come to a halt, come to a stop, discontinue, hold in check, termination 12 intermission, interruption, throttle down 13 spike one's guns 14 breathing spell, discontinuance

halting 6 ending 7 curbing 8 episodic, hesitant, stopping 9 faltering, stumbling 10 calling off, discursive, suspending 11 restraining, terminating 13 discontinuous 14 calling a halt to, putting a stop to

halting place
Spanish: 6 posada

halutz 7 pioneer 26 person who emigrates to Israel

halve 6 bisect 9 cut in half 10 split in two 13 divide equally

ham 6 emoter 9 overactor 20 amateur radio operator

Ham
character in: 16 David Copperfield
author: 7 Dickens

Ham
father: 4 Noah
brother: 5 Shem 7 Japheth
son: 3 Put 4 Cush 6 Canaan 7 Misraim
descendant of: 6 Hamite

Hamadryad
form: 5 dryad
spirit of: 4 tree

Haman
served: 9 Ahasuerus also see 6 Esther

Hamill, Mark
born: 9 Oakland CA
roles: 8 Star Wars 13 Luke Skywalker 15 Return of the Jedi 20 The Empire Strikes Back

Hamilton
capital of: 7 Bermuda

Hamilton, Alexander
1st Secretary:, 8 Treasury
slain by: 9 Aaron Burr
in: 4 duel

Hamilton, Charles
character in: 15 Gone With the Wind
author: 8 Mitchell

Hamilton, Iain
composer of: 6 Aurora 7 Alastor 8 Sinfonia 9 Pharsalia 11 The Bermudas 18 Threnos In Time of War 20 The Royal Hunt of the Sun 21 The Catiline Conspiracy

Hamilton, Margaret
real name: 23 Margaret Hamilton Meserve
born: 11 Cleveland OH
roles: 4 Cora 13 The Wizard of Oz 23 The Wicked Witch of the West

Hamito-Semitic
language also known as: 11 Afro-Asiatic
branch: 6 Berber, Chadic 7 Semitic 8 Cushitic, Egyptian

hamlet 4 burg 7 village 8 hick town, tank town 10 crossroads 11 whistle stop 12 one-horse town, small village 13 jerkwater town

Hamlet
author: 18 William Shakespeare
character: 7 Horatio, Laertes, Ophelia 8 Claudius, Gertrude, Polonius, The Ghost 11 Rosencrantz 12 Guildenstern
soliloquy: 13 To be or not to be
skull: 6 Yorick
castle: 8 Elsinore
setting: 7 Denmark
director: 15 Laurence Olivier
cast: 11 Basil Sydney, Felix Aylmer, Jean Simmons 12 Eileen Herlie 15 Laurence Olivier
Oscar for: 5 actor (Olivier) 7 picture

Hamlet, The
author: 15 William Faulkner
character: 4 Eula, Jody 6 Labove 8 Ab Snopes 9 V K Ratliff 10 Flem Snopes, Mink Snopes, Will Varner 11 Isaac Snopes 12 Henry Armstid

Hamlin, Vincent T
creator/artist of: 8 Alley Oop

Hammarskjold, Dag 7 Swedish 13 United Nations 16 secretary-general

hammer 3 hit, tap 4 bang, form, make, nail 5 drive, forge, knock, pound, punch, shape, whack 6 pummel, rammer, strike 7 beat out, fashion
type: 4 claw, jack, tack 5 gavel, steam 6 mallet, sledge 8 ballpeen 10 pile driver 12 upholsterers

Hammer, Mike

detective created by: 14 Mickey Spillane

hammered 5 drunk **6** banged, beaten, shaped **7** knocked, pounded, whipped, wrought **8** battered, repeated **10** terrorized

Hammett, Dashiell
  author of: 10 Red Harvest, The Thin Man **11** The Glass Key **12** The Dain Curse **16** The Maltese Falcon
  character: 4 Asta (dog) **8** Sam Spade **11** Miles Archer, Nick Charles, Nora Charles **13** Continental Op

hamper 3 gag **4** balk, curb, stem **5** block, check, stall **6** fetter, hinder, hog-tie, hold up, impede, muzzle, retard, thwart **7** inhibit, prevent, shackle **8** encumber, handicap, obstruct, restrain, restrict **9** frustrate **13** interfere with

Hampton, Hope
  nickname: 22 The Duchess of Park Avenue
  born: 14 Philadelphia PA
  roles: 8 Star Dust **13** Lawful Larceny, The Road to Reno **16** The Price of a Party

hamstring 6 impair, muscle, tendon **7** cripple, disable **8** handicap **10** debilitate

Hamsun, Knut
  author of: 3 Pan **6** August, Hunger **8** Victoria **9** Mysteries, Vagabonds **16** Children of the Age **18** The Growth of the Soil

Hananiah *see* **8** Shadrach

hand, hands 3 aid, man, paw **4** care, fist, give, help, hold, lift, mitt, palm, pass **5** guide, power, reach **6** assist, charge, convey, helper, menial, script, worker **7** command, control, custody, deliver, keeping, laborer, ovation, present, support, workman **8** auspices, dominion, employee, guidance, handyman, hired man, longhand, meat-hook **9** assistant, associate, authority, hired hand **10** assistance, domination, management, minister to, penmanship, possession, turn over to, workingman **11** calligraphy, furnish with, handwriting, supervision **12** jurisdiction **13** member of a crew **15** burst of applause, manual extremity, round of applause

handbag 3 bag **4** grip **5** purse **6** clutch, valise **7** satchel **8** moneybag, reticule **10** pocketbook, portmanteau

handbill 5 flier, tract **6** notice **7** leaflet **8** bulletin, circular **12** announcement **13** advertisement

handbook 5 bible **6** manual **8** baedeker **9** guidebook, vade mecum **13** reference book

handcart 4 cart **6** barrow **8** pushcart **10** handbarrow **11** wheelbarrow

handcuffs 5 cuffs, irons **6** chains **7**

fetters **8** manacles, shackles **9** bracelets

hand down 4 will **5** leave **6** hand on, pass on **8** bequeath

Handel, George Frederick (Georg Friedrich)
  born: 5 Halle **7** Germany
  lived in: 7 England
  composer of: 4 Nero, Saul **5** Serse, Silla, Siroe, Teseo **6** Admeto, Alcina, Almira, Esther, Flavio, Jeptha, Joseph, Ottone, Samson, Semele, Xerxes **7** Amadigi, Athalia, Deborah, Lotario, Messiah, Rinaldo, Rodrigo, Solomon, Tolomeo **8** Atalanta, Berenice, Hercules, Scipione, Theodora **9** Agrippina, Radamisto, Rodelinda, Tamerlano **10** Alessandro, Belshazzar, Floridante, Water Music **12** Giulio Cesare, Il Pastor Fido, Muzio Scevola **13** Israel in Egypt, Riccardo Primo **14** Acis and Galatea, Fireworks Music **15** Alexander's Feast, Judas Maccabaeus **16** Hornpipe Concerto **19** Julius Caesar in Egypt, Ode for St Cecilia's Day **22** The Royal Fireworks Music **23** Hallelujah Organ Concerto, The Harmonious Blacksmith **24** The Triumph of Time and Truth

handful 7 minimum, modicum **10** scattering, smattering, sprinkling, thimbleful, tiny amount **11** scant amount, small number **13** small quantity

handgun 3 rod **5** piece, rifle **6** pistol, weapon **7** firearm, shotgun **8** revolver **9** automatic, twenty-two **12** shooting iron **20** Saturday night special

handicap 4 curb **5** limit **6** burden, defect, hamper, hinder, impede, retard, thwart **7** barrier, inhibit, repress, shackle **8** deafness, drawback, encumber, hold back, lameness, obstacle, restrain, restrict, suppress **9** blindness, detriment **10** difficulty, impediment, inhibition, limitation **11** encumbrance, restriction, shortcoming **12** disadvantage **13** inconvenience **14** stumbling block

handicapped 7 limited **8** burdened, disabled, held back, hindered, impaired, retarded **10** encumbered, restrained, restricted **13** disadvantaged

handicrafts
  god of: 10 Hephaestus, Hephaistos

handicraftsman 7 artisan **10** handworker **12** handicrafter

handiness 7 utility **8** deftness **9** dexterity **10** adroitness, usefulness **11** convenience **12** availability **13** accessibility

hand in glove 5 as one **10** side by side **13** close together

handle 3 paw, ply, run, tag, use **4** feel, grip, hilt, hold, knob, name, poke, pull, sell, work **5** carry, grasp, guide,

knead, pilot, pinch, shaft, shank, steer, swing, touch, treat **6** caress, CB name, deal in, employ, finger, fondle, manage, market, pick up, stroke **7** care for, command, conduct, control, massage, moniker, operate, paw over, trade in, utilize **8** cognomen, deal with, maneuver **9** traffic in **10** manipulate, take care of **11** appellation, merchandise **12** offer for sale **13** bring into play

handout 4 alms, dole **7** freebie **19** something for nothing

hand out 4 deal, give **5** grant **6** bestow, confer, donate **7** dole out, mete out, present **8** dispense **9** apportion **10** contribute, distribute

hand over 4 cede **5** grant, yield **6** give up, tender **7** abandon, release **8** transfer **9** deliver up, surrender **10** relinquish

handsome 4 fair **5** ample, bonny, noble **6** benign, comely, lovely, pretty **7** elegant, liberal, sightly, sizable, stately **8** abundant, generous, gracious, imposing, merciful, princely, splendid, stunning, tasteful **9** beauteous, beautiful, bountiful, exquisite, unselfish **10** attractive, benevolent, big-hearted, impressive, sufficient, well- formed **11** fine-looking, good-looking, magnanimous **12** considerable, easy to look at, humanitarian **13** compassionate, easy on the eyes **16** well-proportioned

hand to hand
  Spanish: 9 mano a mano

handy 4 deft, near, nigh **5** adept, on tap **6** adroit, at hand, clever, expert, on call, on hand, useful, wieldy **7** capable, helpful, skilled **8** skillful **9** available, competent, dexterous, easy to use, efficient, practical **10** accessible, convenient, manageable, obtainable, proficient **11** at one's elbow, close at hand, in readiness, ready to hand, serviceable **12** accomplished **14** nimble-fingered **15** within easy reach **16** easily accessible **17** at one's beck and call

hang 3 bow, sag **4** drop, gist, rest **5** affix, hinge, knack, lie in, lower, lynch, point, trail **6** append, attach, dangle, depend **7** incline, meaning, suspend, thought **8** lean over, let droop, repose in, string up, turn upon **9** be pendant, be pendent **11** be dependent, be subject to, bend forward, swing freely **12** be contingent, bend downward **13** revolve around **15** die on the gallows, fasten from above **16** execute by hanging, send to the gallows

hangdog 6 abject **7** ashamed **8** defeated, degraded, hopeless, resigned, wretched **9** miserable **10** browbeaten, chapfallen, humiliated, shamefaced **11** crestfallen, embarrassed, intimidated **13** guilty-looking

hang down 3 sag **5** droop
hanger-on 7 admirer, groupie **8** follower **9** sycophant
hanging object
Japanese: **8** kakemono
hang loosely 3 bag, sag **5** droop
hangout 3 den **5** haunt
hang out 3 mix **4** live **5** dwell **6** hobnob, loiter, mingle, reside **7** consort **9** associate, be friends, pal around, run around **10** fraternize, hang around **11** keep company
hanker after 4 want **5** covet, crave, fancy **6** desire **7** long for, pine for **8** aspire to, yearn for **9** lust after **11** have a yen for, have an eye on, hunger after, thirst after
hankering 3 yen **4** itch, urge **6** aching, desire, hunger, pining, thirst **7** craving, longing **8** yearning
Hanna-Barbera
creators of: **6** Top Cat **7** Jetsons **8** Yogi Bear **11** Tom and Jerry **15** Quickdraw McGraw **16** Huckleberry Hound **14** The Flintstones
Hannah
husband: **7** Elkanah
son: **6** Samuel
Hanoi
capital of: **7** Vietnam **12** North Vietnam
river: **3** Red **4** Yuan **7** Song Koi
delta: **6** Tonkin
airport: **6** Gia Lam
Hans Brinker
author: **5** (Mary Elizabeth Mapes) Dodge
character: **4** Raff **5** Gleck, Hilda **6** Gretel **7** Boekman, Mevrouw
feature: **12** silver skates
Hansel and Gretel
author: **13** Grimm Brothers (Jakob and Wilhelm)
opera by: **11** Humperdinck
character: **5** Witch
feature **4** oven **16** gingerbread house
Hans Kristian
character in: **16** Giants of the Earth
author: **7** Rolvaag
Hanson, Howard
born: **7** Wahoo NE
composer of: **5** Sacra (symphony No 5) **6** Nordic (symphony No 1) **7** Requiem (symphony No 4) **8** Romantic (symphony No 2) **10** Merry-Mount
haphazard 6 casual, chance, fitful, random **7** aimless, chaotic **8** careless, on-and-off, slapdash, sporadic **9** arbitrary, hit-or-miss **10** accidental, disordered, disorderly, fortuitous, undesigned, undirected, unthinking **11** purposeless, unorganized **12** disorganized, unmethodical, unsystematic **14** indiscriminate, unpremeditated **15** catch-as-catch-can
hapless 6 cursed, jinxed, no-good, rot-

ten, woeful **7** forlorn, unhappy, unlucky **8** accursed, hopeless, ill- fated, luckless, wretched **9** miserable **10** ill-starred **11** star-crossed, unfortunate
happen 5 arise, ensue, occur **6** appear, befall, betide, crop up, result **7** turn out **8** become of, spring up **9** be borne by, be the case, come about, eventuate, take place, transpire **10** be one's fate, come to pass **11** be endured by **12** be suffered by **13** be one's fortune, fall to one's lot, present itself
happening 4 case **5** event **6** advent, affair, matter **7** episode **8** accident, incident, occasion **9** adventure, incidence **10** experience, occurrence, proceeding **11** vicissitude **12** circumstance, happenstance **20** just one of those things
happenstance 4 luck **6** chance **8** accident, fortuity
happiness 3 joy **4** glee **5** bliss, cheer, mirth **6** gaiety **7** comfort, content, delight, ecstasy, elation, jollity, rapture **8** blessing, felicity, gladness, pleasure **9** beatitude, enjoyment, merriment, rejoicing, transport **10** cheeriness, exuberance, exultation, jubilation **11** blessedness, contentment, high spirits **12** cheerfulness, satisfaction **13** gratification **16** lightheartedness, sense of well-being
happy 3 fit, gay **4** glad, meet **5** lucky **6** elated, joyful, joyous, timely **7** content, fitting, gleeful, pleased, tickled **8** blissful, cheerful, cheering, ecstatic, exultant, jubilant, pleasant, pleasing **9** agreeable, contented, delighted, exuberant, favorable, fortunate, gratified, opportune, overjoyed, rapturous, rhapsodic **10** auspicious, convenient, delightful, felicitous, gratifying, propitious, seasonable **11** exhilarated, tickled pink, transported **12** advantageous **13** in high spirits **15** in seventh heaven
Happy Days
character: **6** Arnold, Fonzie **10** Ralph Malph **11** Potsie Weber **12** Chachi Arcola **14** Pinky Tuscadero **15** Chuck Cunningham **16** Alfred Delvecchio, Arthur Fonzarelli, Howard Cunningham, Joanie Cunningham, Leather Tuscadero, Marion Cunningham, Richie Cunningham
cast: **8** Roz Kelly **9** Donny Most, Erin Moran, Pat Morita, Ron Howard, Scott Baio, Tom Bosley **10** Al Molinaro, Marion Ross, Suzi Quatro **12** Henry Winkler **13** Anson Williams, Gavan O'Herlihy **15** Randolph Roberts
happy-go-lucky 6 blithe **7** buoyant, flighty, relaxed **8** carefree, careless, feckless, heedless, skittish **9** easygoing, unworried **10** insouciant, noncha-

lant, optimistic, untroubled **11** free-and-easy, unconcerned **12** devil- may-care, light-hearted **13** irresponsible **14** scatterbrained **23** without a worry in the world
harangue 6 speech, tirade **7** lecture, oration **8** diatribe, scolding **9** contumely, sermonize **12** denunciation, vituperation
Harare
capital of: **8** Zimbabwe
harass 3 cow, irk, vex **4** bait, ride **5** annoy, beset, bully, harry, hound, tease, worry **6** attack, badger, bother, heckle, hector, pester, plague **7** assault, bedevil, besiege, disturb, torment **8** browbeat, distress, irritate **9** persecute **10** discommode, exasperate, intimidate **14** raid frequently
harbinger 4 clue, omen **5** token **6** herald, symbol **7** portent **8** signaler **9** announcer, first sign, precursor **10** forerunner, indication, proclaimer
Harbonna 6 eunuch
harbor 3 bay **4** cove, dock, feel, goal, hide, hold, keep, pier, port, quay **5** basin, haven, house, inlet, lodge, wharf **6** asylum, billet, foster, lagoon, refuge, retain, shield, take in **7** care for, cling to, conceal, nurture, protect, quarter, retreat, shelter **8** hideaway, keep safe, maintain, muse over, terminus **9** brood over, sanctuary **11** concealment, destination, hiding place **12** give refuge to **13** bear in the mind, terminal point **18** protected anchorage
Harcorates *see S* Horus
hard 3 sad **4** cold, firm, mean, ugly **5** cruel, eager, harsh, heavy, rigid, rough, solid, stern, stiff, stony, tight, tough **6** bitter, brutal, fierce, firmly, keenly, knotty, severe, steely, strict, strong, sullen, thorny, unkind **7** angrily, arduous, callous, closely, complex, cryptic, eagerly, earnest, harmful, heavily, hostile, hurtful, inhuman, intense, onerous, sharply, solidly, tightly, to heart, vicious, violent, willing, zealous **8** animated, baffling, critical, diligent, exacting, fiercely, forceful, forcibly, hardened, intently, involved, pitiless, powerful, puzzling, rocklike, ruthless, severely, spirited, spiteful, steadily, strongly, stubborn, untiring, venomous, vigorous **9** arduously, assiduous, bellicose, confusing, difficult, earnestly, energetic, furiously, Herculean, insulting, intensely, intricate, laborious, malicious, merciless, painfully, rancorous, seriously, strenuous, stringent, unbending, unpliable, unsparing, violently, wearisome **10** burdensome, diligently, forcefully, formidable, impervious, implacable, inexorable, inflexible, lamentable, melancholy, oppressive, perplexing, persistent, powerfully,

relentless, resolutely, rigorously, tormenting, unbearable, unflagging, unfriendly, unpleasant, untiringly, unyielding, vigorously, vindictive **11** acrimonious, agonizingly, assiduously, belligerent, bewildering, complicated, distressing, emotionally, hardhearted, industrious, insensitive, intolerable, laboriously, persevering, troublesome, unceasingly, unmalleable, unrelenting, unremitting, unsparingly **12** antagonistic, cantankerous, determinedly, disagreeable, enterprising, impenetrable, persistently, relentlessly, thick-skinned, unfathomable, unflaggingly **13** conscientious, disheartening, distressfully, energetically, indefatigable, industriously, with much anger **14** uncompromising, with much sorrow **15** conscientiously **16** with all one's might **18** with strong feelings

hard-and-fast 3 set **6** strict **7** binding **8** exacting, rigorous **9** mandatory, unbending **10** compelling, compulsory, inflexible, obligatory, undeniable, unyielding **11** irrevocable, unalterable, unremitting **12** indisputable **13** incontestable **14** uncompromising

Hardcastle family
  characters in: 18 She Stoops to Conquer
  author: 9 Goldsmith

hard drinker 3 sot **4** lush, soak, wino **5** drunk, rummy, souse, toper **6** barfly, boozer **7** guzzler, imbiber, tippler **8** drunkard **9** alcoholic **11** dipsomaniac **14** problem drinker **16** two-fisted drinker

harden 3 dry, gel, set **4** cake, fire, firm **5** adapt, adjust, blunt, enure, inure, steel **6** anneal, freeze, season, temper **7** calcify, callous, congeal, fortify, petrify, stiffen, thicken, toughen **8** accustom, solidify **9** fossilize, make tough, reinforce **10** discipline, invigorate, strengthen **11** crystallize, turn to stone **12** restrengthen **13** make unfeeling

hard feelings 5 anger **6** grudge, hatred, rancor **7** ill will **8** acrimony **9** animosity, hostility **10** antagonism, bitterness **12** spitefulness

hardheaded 4 cool **5** balky **6** astute, mulish, poised, shrewd **7** willful **8** contrary, sensible, stubborn **9** immovable, objective, obstinate, pigheaded, practical, pragmatic, realistic, unbending, unfeeling **10** coolheaded, impersonal, inflexible, refractory, selfwilled, unyielding **11** down-to-earth, intractable, tough-minded, unemotional, unflappable **14** self-controlled

hardhearted 4 cold, hard, mean **5** cruel, stony **6** brutal, Hannah **7** callous, inhuman **8** pitiless, ruthless, uncaring **9** heartless, merciless, unfeeling, unpitying, unsparing **11**

coldblooded, indifferent, insensitive, remorseless, unforgiving **12** cruelhearted, thick-skinned **13** unsympathetic

hardihood 4 grit **5** pluck, spunk **6** mettle **7** courage **8** strength **9** endurance, fortitude **10** resolution **12** resoluteness

Harding, Warren Gamaliel
  presidential rank: 11 twenty-ninth
  party: 10 Republican
  state represented: 2 OH
  defeated: 3 (James Middleton) Cox, (William Wesley) Cox **4** (Eugene Victor) Debs **7** (Aaron Sherman) Watkins **8** (Robert Charles) Macauley **11** (Parley Parker) Christensen
  vice president: 8 (Calvin) Coolidge
  cabinet:
    state: 6 (Charles Evans) Hughes
    treasury: 6 (Andrew William) Mellon
    war: 5 (John Wingate) Weeks
    attorney general: 9 (Harry Micajah) Daugherty
    navy: 5 (Edwin) Denby
    postmaster general: 3 (Harry Stewart) New **4** (Hubert) Work, (William Harrison) Hays
    interior: 4 (Albert Bacon) Fall, (Hubert) Work
    agriculture: 7 (Henry Cantwell) Wallace
    commerce: 6 (Herbert Clark) Hoover
    labor: 5 (James John) Davis
  born: 9 Corsica OH (now Blooming Grove)
  died: 2 CA (while in office) **12** San Francisco
  buried: 8 Marion OH
  education:
    College: 11 Ohio Central
  religion: 7 Baptist
  interests: 5 poker
    played musical instrument: 6 cornet **7** helicon
  political career: 8 US Senate **15** Ohio State Senate
  lieutenant governor of: 4 Ohio
  civilian career: 9 publisher **13** schoolteacher **15** newspaper editor **17** insurance salesman
  notable events of lifetime/term:
    Act: 21 Fordney-McCumber Tariff
    peace treaty with: 7 Austria, Germany, Hungary
    scandal: 10 Teapot Dome (oil)
    Treaty: 9 Five-Power, Nine-Power **16** Four-Power Pacific
  father: 11 George Tryon
  mother: 6 Phoebe (Elizabeth Dickerson)
    stepmother: 4 Mary (Alice Severns) **6** Eudora (Kelley Luvisi)
  siblings: 11 George Tryon **12** Mary Clarissa **14** Charity Malvina, Phoebe Caroline **15** Abigail Victoria **16**

Charles Alexander, Eleanor Priscilla
  wife: 8 Florence (Kling DeWolfe)
  children:
    illegitimate daughter: 21 Elizabeth Ann Christian (by mistress Nan Britton)

hardly 4 just, only **6** barely, rarely **7** faintly, in no way **8** not often, not quite, scarcely **9** almost not, by no means **10** in no manner, uncommonly **12** certainly not, infrequently **13** not by any means **15** not by a great deal

hardnosed 4 hard **5** harsh, rigid, stern, tough **6** severe, shrewd, strict **8** critical, hard-line, exacting, stubborn **9** demanding, unbending, unsparing **10** hardheaded, inflexible, nononsense, unyielding **11** calculating, intractable **12** unsentimental **14** uncompromising

Hardouin-Mansart, Jules
  architect of: 8 Orangery (Versailles) **12** Chateau du Val (St Germain-en-Laye), Grand Trianon (Versailles), Place Vendome (Paris) **15** Chateau de Clagny (Versailles) **16** Galerie des Glaces (Hall of Mirrors at Versailles), Les Invalides (Church of the Dome, Paris)

hard-pressed 7 harried, put-upon **9** embattled **10** overworked

hardship 3 woe **4** load **5** agony, grief **6** burden, misery, ordeal, sorrow **7** problem, travail, trouble **8** handicap **9** adversity, privation, suffering **10** affliction, difficulty, misfortune **11** cross to bear, encumbrance, tribulation, unhappiness **12** wretchedness

hard sledding 8 tough job **10** difficulty, tough going, uphill work **11** arduousness **13** laboriousness

hard times 4 bust **5** slump **8** bad times **9** recession **10** depression

Hard Times
  author: 11 Studs Terkel

Hard Times
  author: 14 Charles Dickens
  character: 9 Sissy Jupe **10** Mrs Sparsit **11** Mr Bounderby **12** Tom Gradgrind **14** James Harthouse **15** Louisa Gradgrind, Thomas Gradgrind **16** Stephen Blackpool

hard to catch 3 sly **4** foxy, wily **6** crafty, shifty, tricky **7** elusive, evasive **8** slippery

hard to grasp 6 arcane **7** complex, elusive **8** abstruse, baffling, puzzling, slippery **9** difficult, enigmatic **10** perplexing **16** incomprehensible

hard to manage 6 unruly **7** froward, willful **8** perverse, stubborn **9** difficult, fractious, obstinate **10** inflexible, refractory, unyielding **11** intractable **12** obstreperous, unmanageable

hard to please 5 fussy, picky **7** exigent, finicky **8** critical **10** fastidious, meticulous, particular

Hardwick, Elizabeth
author of: **11** Simple Truth **12** A View of My Own **15** Sleepless Nights **20** Seduction and Betrayal

Hardwicke, Sir Cedric
born: **3** Lye **7** England
roles: **14** On Borrowed Time **21** Livingstone and Stanley **36** A Connecticut Yankee in King Arthur's Court

hardwood 4 wood **8** leadwood
kind: **3** ash, elm, oak **4** teak **5** beech, birch, maple **6** cherry, linden, walnut **7** hickory **8** mahogany, rosewood, sycamore

hardworking 8 diligent, sedulous **9** assiduous **11** industrious, persevering **12** enterprising **13** conscientious

hardy 3 fit **4** hale **5** tough **6** hearty, mighty, robust, rugged, strong, sturdy **7** healthy **8** stalwart, vigorous **9** strapping **10** able-bodied **12** in fine fettle **13** physically fit **15** in good condition

Hardy, Oliver
partner: **10** Stan Laurel
born: **8** Harlem GA
roles: **8** Pardon Us **9** Saps at Sea **10** Way Out West

Hardy, Thomas
author of: **10** The Dynasts **14** Jude the Obscure **20** The Return of the Native **21** Tess of the D'Urbervilles **22** Far from the Madding Crowd, The Mayor of Casterbridge
mythical county: **6** Wessex
represents: **11** Dorsetshire

hare
constellation of: **5** Lepus
group of: **4** down, husk

harebrained 5 silly, wacko, wacky **7** asinine, flighty, foolish **8** skittish **9** dimwitted, senseless **10** half-witted **11** empty-headed **12** simple-minded **13** rattlebrained **14** featherbrained, scatterbrained

Haredale, Reuben
character in: **12** Barnaby Rudge
author: **7** Dickens

harem 5 serai, wives **6** purdah, serail, senana, zenana **8** love nest, seraglio **10** concubines
room: **3** oda
guard: **6** eunuch

Hargreaves, James
nationality: **7** English
inventor of: **13** spinning jenny

Harker, Jonathan
character in: **7** Dracula
author: **6** Stoker

harlot 3 pro **4** bawd, doxy, jade, pros, slut, tart **5** whore **6** chippy, wanton **7** jezebel, trollop **8** call girl, mistress, strumpet **9** courtesan, kept woman **10** prostitute **11** fallen woman **12** painted woman, scarlet woman, streetwalker

Harlow, Jean
real name: **16** Harlean Carpenter
nickname: **15** Blonde Bombshell

born: **12** Kansas City MO
roles: **7** Red Dust **8** Riffraff, Saratoga **9** Bombshell, China Seas **11** Hell's Angels, Libeled Lady **13** Dinner at Eight

harm 3 ill, mar, sin **4** evil, hurt, maim, pain, ruin, vice **5** abuse, agony, havoc, spoil, wound, wrong **6** damage, debase, deface, ill-use, impair, injure, injury, malice, misuse, trauma **7** blemish, cripple, degrade, scourge **8** aggrieve, calamity, hardship, iniquity, maltreat, mischief, villainy **9** adversity, detriment, disfigure, suffering, undermine **10** defacement, immorality, impairment, misfortune, sinfulness, wickedness **11** destruction, devastation, malevolence **12** do violence to **13** deterioration, maliciousness

harmful 3 bad **7** adverse, baneful, hurtful, ruinous **8** damaging **9** dangerous, injurious, unhealthy **10** pernicious **11** deleterious, destructive, detrimental, unhealthful, unwholesome **17** counterproductive

harmless 4 mild, safe **6** benign, gentle **7** sinless **8** innocent, nontoxic **9** blameless, guiltless, incorrupt, innocuous, peaceable **10** not hurtful **11** inoffensive **12** not dangerous **15** unobjectionable

harmlessness 6 safety **9** innocence **10** gentleness **11** nontoxicity **12** nonvirulence **13** innocuousness **15** inoffensiveness

Harmon, Young John
character in: **15** Our Mutual Friend
author: **7** Dickens

Harmonia
father: **4** Ares
mother: **9** Aphrodite
husband: **6** Cadmus
daughter: **3** Ino

harmonious 5 sweet **6** dulcet **7** amiable, cordial, unified **8** amicable, friendly, in accord, matching **9** agreeable, congenial, in harmony, melodious **10** compatible, consistent, euphonious, likeminded **11** coordinated, harmonizing, in agreement, mellifluous, sympathetic **12** synchronized **13** sweet-sounding **17** agreeably combined

harmonium 9 reed organ

harmonize 3 fit **4** jibe, mesh **5** agree, blend, chime, tally **6** accord, adjust, attune **7** conform **8** be in tune **9** reconcile **10** complement, correspond, go together **13** sing in harmony

harmony 5 amity, order, peace, unity **6** accord **7** balance, concord **8** matching, symmetry, sympathy **9** agreement, unanimity **10** conformity, fellowship, friendship, proportion **11** amicability, cooperation, correlation, parallelism **12** congeniality, coordination, mutual regard **13** compatibility,

mutual fitness **14** like-mindedness **15** organic totality **17** good understanding **19** harmonious relations, pleasing consistency **21** concurrence in opinions

Harmony
goddess of: **9** Concordia

harness 4 curb, rein, tugs, yoke **5** lines, reins, rig up **6** bridle, collar, employ, halter, muzzle, straps, tackle, traces **7** exploit, hitch up, utilize **8** restrain **9** caparison, trappings **12** put in harness, render useful **13** control and use, turn to account **14** make productive **22** direct to a useful purpose

Harper, Joe
character in: **9** Tom Sawyer
author: **5** Twain

harp on 7 dwell on **9** reiterate **18** repeat persistently

Harpy
form: **7** monster
head of: **5** woman
body of: **4** bird
father: **7** Thaumas
mother: **7** Electra
names: **5** Aello **7** Celaeno, Ocypete, Podarge

harridan 3 hag **5** crone, shrew, witch **6** virago **8** battle-ax, old crone **12** mean old woman

harried 5 upset **7** worried **8** harassed, troubled **10** distraught

Harris, Joel Chandler
author of: **10** Uncle Remus (His Songs and Sayings)
character: **7** Brer Fox, tar baby **8** Brer Bear **10** Brer Rabbit

Harris, Julie
real name: **14** Julia Ann Harris
born: **18** Grosse Pointe Park MI
roles: **6** Harper **10** East of Eden, I Am a Camera **11** The Haunting **14** A Shot in the Dark, The Hiding Place **19** The Last of Mrs Lincoln **21** The Member of the Wedding **22** Requiem for a Heavyweight **27** And Miss Reardon Drinks a Little

Harris, Richard
born: **7** Ireland **8** Limerick
roles: **7** Camelot **8** Cromwell **15** A Man Called Horse **16** The Molly Maguires, This Sporting Life **17** Mutiny on the Bounty, The Guns of Navarone **20** The Cassandra Crossing **26** The Return of a Man Called Horse

Harris, Roy
composer of: **16** Folksong Symphony **17** American Portraits **27** When Johnny Comes Marching Home (overture)

Harrison, Benjamin
nickname: **3** Ben **9** Little Ben
presidential rank: **11** twenty-third
party: **10** Republican
state represented: **2** IN

defeated: 4 (Clinton Bowen) Fisk **6** (James Langdon) Curtis **7** (Robert Hall) Cowdrey **8** (Albert) Redstone, (Alson Jenness) Streeter, (Belva Ann Bennett) Lockwood **9** (Grover) Cleveland
vice president: 6 (Levi Parsons) Morton
cabinet:
  state: 6 (James Gillespie) Blaine, (John Watson) Foster
  treasury: 6 (Charles) Foster, (William) Windom
  war: 6 (Stephen Benton) Elkins **7** (Redfield) Proctor
  attorney general: 6 (William Henry Harrison) Miller
  navy: 5 (Benjamin Franklin) Tracy
  postmaster general: 9 (John) Wanamaker
  interior: 5 (John Willock) Noble
  agriculture: 4 (Jeremiah McLain) Rusk
born: 11 North Bend OH
died/buried: 14 Indianapolis IN
education:
  prep school: 14 Farmer's College
  University: 21 Miami University of Ohio
  later studied: 3 law
religion: 12 Presbyterian
interests: 7 fishing, hunting **8** swimming
author: 17 This Country of Ours **20** Views of An Ex- President
political career: 8 US Senate
  city attorney: 12 Indianapolis
  reporter of: 19 Indiana supreme court
  secretary of: 31 Republican state central committee
civilian career: 6 lawyer **12** law professor
military service: 8 Civil War **16** brigadier general
notable events of lifetime/term:
  Act: 16 Dependent Pension, Sherman Anti-Trust **21** Sherman Silver Purchase
  Tariff: 8 McKinley
father: 9 John Scott
mother: 9 Elizabeth (Ramsey Irwin)
siblings: 8 Mary Jane **9** John Irwin, John Scott **10** Anna Symmes, James Irwin **12** James Findlay **13** Carter Bassett **14** Archibald Irwin
  half sisters: 9 Elizabeth **13** Sarah Lucretia
wife: 4 Mary (Scott Lord Dimmick) **8** Caroline (Lavinia Scott)
children: 9 Elizabeth, Mary Scott **15** Russell Benjamin

Harrison, Lou
born: 10 Portland OR
composer of: 8 Rapunzel, Solstice **13** Changing World **15** Four Strict Songs, Johnny Appleseed **17** The Perilous Chapel **19** Almanac of the Seasons **22** At the Tomb of Charles Ives

Harrison, Peter
architect of: 11 Brick Market (Newport RI), King's Chapel (Boston) **14** Redwood Library (Newport RI), Touro Synagogue (Newport RI)

Harrison, Rex
real name: 21 Reginald Carey Harrison
nickname: 8 Sexy Rexy
wife: 10 Kay Kendall **11** Lilli Palmer **13** Rachel Roberts
born: 6 Huyton **7** England
roles: 9 Cleopatra **10** My Fair Lady (Oscar) **12** Blithe Spirit, Henry Higgins **14** Doctor Dolittle **16** The Foxes of Harrow **17** Unfaithfully Yours **18** The Ghost and Mrs Muir **20** Anna and the King of Siam

Harrison, Wallace K
architect of: 13 Lincoln Center (NYC) **14** Socony Building (NYC) **17** Rockefeller Center (NYC) **22** Metropolitan Opera House (NYC) **25** United Nations Headquarters (NYC) **34** Nelson A Rockefeller Empire State Plaza (Albany NY), ALCOA Building (Pittsburgh, with Max Abramovitz)

Harrison, William Henry
nickname: 6 Old Tip **22** The Washington of the West
presidential rank: 5 ninth
party: 4 Whig
state represented: 2 OH
defeated: 6 (James G) Birney **8** (Martin) Van Buren
vice president: 5 (John) Tyler
cabinet:
  state: 7 (Daniel) Webster
  treasury: 5 (Thomas) Ewing
  war: 4 (John) Bell
  attorney general: 10 (John Jordan) Crittenden
  navy: 6 (George Edmund) Badger
  postmaster general: 7 (Francis) Granger
born: 2 VA **17** Charles City County **18** Berkeley plantation
died: 12 Washington DC
buried: 11 North Bend OH
education: 16 privately tutored (at home)
  College: 13 Hampden-Sydney (did not graduate)
  later studied: 8 medicine
religion: 12 Episcopalian
political career: 8 US Senate **11** state Senate **24** US House of Representatives
  governor of: 16 Indiana Territory
  minister: 8 Columbia
civilian career: 6 farmer **7** soldier
military service: 6 US Army **12** major general **19** War of Eighteen Twelve
  battle: 6 (the) Thames **8** Lake Erie **10** Tippecanoe
notable events of lifetime/term: 24 Land Act of Eighteen Hundred
  campaign slogan: 21 Tippecanoe and Tyler too
  treaty of: 10 Greenville
father: 8 Benjamin
mother: 9 Elizabeth (Bassett)
siblings: 3 Ann **4** Lucy **5** Sarah **8** Benjamin **9** Elizabeth **13** Carter Bassett
wife: 4 Anna (Tuthill Symmes)
children: 8 Benjamin **9** John Scott **10** Mary Symmes **11** Anna Tuthill **12** James Findlay, William Henry **13** Carter Bassett, Lucy Singleton **16** Elizabeth Bassett, John Cleves Symmes

Harrow 10 prep school
rival: 4 Eton

harrowing 7 fearful, painful **8** alarming, chilling **9** traumatic, upsetting **10** disturbing, terrifying, tormenting **11** distressing, frightening **13** bloodcurdling

harry 3 irk, vex **4** bait, gall, raid, ride, sack **5** annoy, beset, bully, haunt, hound, tease, worry **6** badger, bother, harass, heckle, hector, pester, plague **7** disturb, pillage, plunder, torment, trouble **8** distract, distress, irritate **9** terrorize **10** exasperate, intimidate **16** attack repeatedly

harsh 4 hard, mean **5** cruel, raspy, rough, sharp, stern **6** bitter, brutal, hoarse, severe, shrill, unkind **7** abusive, caustic, glaring, grating, jarring, rasping, raucous, squawky **8** piercing, pitiless, ruthless, scratchy, strident, ungentle **9** Draconian, heartless, merciless, too bright, unmusical, unsparing **10** discordant, overbright, unpleasant, vindictive **11** cacophonous, hardhearted **12** uncharitable, unharmonious

harshness 5 rigor **7** cruelty, discord **9** brutality, cacophony, raspiness, roughness, sternness, stridency **10** dissonance, shrillness, unkindness **12** ungentleness **13** heartlessness **14** unpleasantness **15** hardheartedness

Hart, Johnny
creator/artist of: 2 B C **13** The Wizard of Id

Hart, Moss
author of: 15 Once in a Lifetime **20** You Can't Take It with You (with George S Kaufman) **21** The Man Who Came to Dinner (with George S Kaufman)

Harte, Bret
author of: 20 The Luck of Roaring Camp **22** The Outcasts of Poker Flat

Hartford
hockey team: 7 Whalers

Harthouse, James
character in: 9 Hard Times
author: 7 Dickens

Hartley, Vivian Mary
real name of: **11** Vivien Leigh

harum-scarum 5 giddy **6** wildly **7** erratic, flighty, foolish **8** careless, confused **9** aimlessly, haphazard, impetuous, impulsive, unplanned, unsettled **10** bewildered, recklessly, unreliable **11** haphazardly, harebrained, impulsively **12** absent-minded, capriciously, disorganized, inconsistent, undependable **13** rattlebrained **14** featherbrained, scatterbrained

Harun ar-Rashid 6 caliph **7** Baghdad **13** Arabian Nights

harvest 3 cut, mow **4** crop, gain, pick, reap **5** amass, fruit, pluck, yield **6** gather, haying, mowing, output, result, return, reward **7** benefit, collect, cutting, picking, produce, product, reaping **8** fruition, gleaning, proceeds **9** aftermath, amassment, gathering, outgrowth **10** accumulate, collection, harvesting **12** accumulation **13** season's growth

harvest time 4 fall **6** autumn **8** maturity **12** Indian summer

Harvey
director: **11** Henry Koster
based on play by: **9** Mary Chase
cast: **6** rabbit **8** Peggy Dow **12** James Stewart (Elwood P Dowd) **13** Cecil Kellaway, Josephine Hull
Oscar for: **17** supporting actress (Hull)

Harvey, Laurence
real name: **19** Larushka Misch Skikne
wife: **16** Margaret Leighton
born: **9** Lithuania, Yomishkis
roles: **7** Darling **12** Life at the Top, Room at the Top **14** Of Human Bondage, Summer and Smoke **16** Butterfield Eight **17** Walk on the Wild Side

Harvey, William
field: **7** anatomy
nationality: **7** British
discovered: **18** circulation of blood

Hasen, Irwin
creator/artist of: **5** Dondi **9** Goldbergs **11** Wonder Woman **12** Green Lantern

hash out 6 review **7** discuss **8** consider, talk over

hasp 4 lock **5** catch, clasp, latch **7** closure **8** fastener

Hassam, (Frederick) Childe
born: **12** Dorchester MA
artwork: **13** Southwest Wind **14** Summer Sunlight, Washington Arch **15** Against the Light **23** Boston Commons at Twilight

hassle 3 bug, row, vex **5** annoy, fight, harry, hound, scrap, set-to **6** badger, battle, bother, harass, tussle **7** contest, dispute, quarrel **8** argument, conflict, squabble, struggle **9** persecute

hassock 4 boss, pess, seat, tuft, weed **5** bunch, chair, group, trush **6** buffet, plants, tuffet **7** ottoman, tussock **9** footstool, vegetable

hasta la vista 6 good-by, so long **7** goodbye **12** until I see you **16** until we meet again

hasta manana 13 until tomorrow **14** see you tomorrow

haste 4 rush **5** hurry, speed **8** celerity, dispatch, rapidity, rashness **9** fleetness, quickness, swiftness **10** expedition, speediness, undue speed **11** hurriedness **12** recklessness **13** careless hurry, impetuousness, impulsiveness, precipitation

hasten 3 fly, run **4** bolt, dart, dash, flit, jump, race, rush **5** egg on, hurry, impel, speed, whisk **6** hustle, incite, scurry, sprint, urge on **7** advance, drive on, hurry on, hurry up, promote, quicken, scamper, scuttle, speed up **8** expedite, make time **10** accelerate, lose no time **11** go full blast, precipitate, push forward **12** step on the gas **13** go on the double **14** step right along **15** go like lightning, make short work of, work against time **20** go hell-bent for leather

hastily 4 fast **5** apace **6** pronto, rashly **7** quickly **8** promptly, speedily **9** hurriedly, like a shot, posthaste, summarily **10** carelessly, heedlessly, recklessly, too quickly **11** impetuously, impulsively, on the double **12** lickety-split, straightaway **13** precipitately, thoughtlessly **18** hell-bent for leather **20** like greased lightning, on the spur of the moment

Hastings, Thomas see **17** Carrere, John Merven

hasty 4 fast, rash **5** brief, fleet, quick, rapid, swift **6** abrupt, prompt, rushed, speedy **7** cursory, hurried, passing **8** fleeting, headlong, heedless, reckless **9** impetuous, impulsive, momentary **10** breathless **11** precipitate, superficial, unduly quick **12** quick as a wink **19** without deliberation

hat
French: **7** chapeau

hatch 4 plan, plot **5** frame **6** cook up, create, design, devise, evolve, invent, make up **7** concoct, dream up, fashion, produce, think up **8** conceive, contrive **9** construct, fabricate, formulate, improvise, originate **10** bring forth **11** give birth to, manufacture

hatchlings 5 brood, young **6** chicks **9** offspring

hate 5 abhor, dread, venom **6** animus, detest, enmity, hatred, loathe, malice, rancor **7** be sorry, despise, dislike, wince at **8** acrimony, aversion, be sick of, distaste, execrate, loathing **9** abominate, animosity, antipathy, be tired of, disliking, hostility, not care to **10** abhorrence, be averse to, feel sick at, recoil from, repugnance, resentment, shrink from **11** abomination, be hostile to, be reluctant, be unwilling, detestation, malevolence, wish to avoid **12** be repelled by **14** have no taste for, hold in contempt, revengefulness, vindictiveness **16** bear malice toward, have no stomach for **17** feel disinclined to, not have the heart to **19** regard as distasteful

hateful 4 evil, foul, mean, ugly, vile **5** nasty **6** odious, sinful, wicked **7** heinous **8** infamous, scornful **9** abhorrent, atrocious, loathsome, monstrous, obnoxious, offensive, repellent, repugnant, revolting, sickening **10** abominable, deplorable, despicable, detestable, disdainful, disgusting, forbidding, full of hate, irritating, unbearable, unpleasant, villainous **11** distasteful, intolerable, unendurable **12** contemptible, contemptuous, insufferable **13** objectionable

Hathaway, Anne
husband: **11** Shakespeare

Hathor
origin: **8** Egyptian
goddess of: **3** joy **4** love
symbol: **4** ears, head **5** horns
patron of: **5** dance, music
personifies: **3** sky

Hat on the Bed, The
author: **9** John O'Hara

hatred 4 hate **5** venom **6** animus, enmity, malice, rancor **7** disgust, dislike, ill will **8** acrimony, aversion, bad blood, distaste, loathing **9** animosity, antipathy, hostility, revulsion **10** abhorrence, antagonism, bitterness, repugnance, resentment **11** abomination, detestation, malevolence **14** revengefulness, vindictiveness

haughtiness 4 airs **5** pride **7** conceit, hauteur **8** snobbery **9** arrogance **10** snootiness **13** condescension **14** disdainfulness, high-handedness **16** superciliousness

haughty 5 aloof **6** lordly, snooty, uppish, uppity **7** high- hat, stuck-up **8** arrogant, scornful, snobbish **9** conceited, officious **10** disdainful, high-handed, hoity-toity **11** highfalutin, overbearing, overly proud, patronizing, swell-headed **12** contemptuous **13** condescending, high and mighty

haul 3 bag, lug, tow, tug **4** cart, drag, draw, gain, jerk, move, pull, swag, take, tote, yank **5** booty, bring, carry, catch, fetch, heave, truck, yield **6** convey, profit, remove, reward, spoils, wrench **7** capture, takings **9** transport

haunches 4 buns, rear, rump, seat **5** nates **7** rear end **8** buttocks **9** fundament, posterior **12** hindquarters

haunt 3 vex **5** beset, worry **6** live in, obsess, plague, prey on **7** disturb, terrify, torment, trouble, weigh on **8** distress, frequent, frighten **9** hang out at, preoccupy, terrorize **10** hang around, hover about, loiter near, visit often **11** beat a path to **12** linger around

haunts 3 den **4** cave, hole, lair, nest **6** burrow **7** hangout **8** hideaway **9** waterhole **10** rendezvous **12** meeting place **14** gathering place **15** stamping grounds

Hauptmann, Gerhart
   author of: 10 Before Dawn, The Weavers

haute couture 11 high fashion

haute cuisine 11 fine cooking **14** gourmet cooking

hauteur 5 swank **7** conceit, disdain **8** snobbery **9** arrogance, loftiness **10** snootiness **11** haughtiness **12** affectedness, snobbishness **13** condescension **14** disdainfulness, high-handedness **16** superciliousness **19** patronizing attitude

haut monde 5 elite **10** blue bloods, upper class, upper crust **11** aristocracy, high society **14** creme de la creme

Havana
   capital of: 4 Cuba
   gulf: 6 Mexico
   landmark: 15 Cabaret Parisien **16** Castillo del Morro **17** Castillode la Punta, Jose Marti Monument **18** Castillo de los Atares, Castillo de la Fuerza, Garcia Lorca Theater **19** Maximo Gomez Monument **21** Latinamericano Stadium **22** Academy of Science of Cuba
   river: 10 (Rio) Almendares
   Spanish: 8 La Habana

Havasupai, Supai
   location: 7 Arizona **11** Grand Canyon
   related to: 7 Yavapai **8** Hualapai

have 3 buy, eat, get, own, use **4** bear, fool, gain, gull, hold, host, keep, make, must **5** beget, carry, cheat, drink, enjoy, force, grasp, ought, smoke, trick **6** accept, affirm, compel, harbor, obtain, outwit, permit, retain, suffer **7** achieve, acquire, defraud, exhibit, possess, realize, receive, swindle **8** comprise, maintain, manifest, outsmart, perceive, tolerate **9** encompass, encounter, partake of, recognize, victimize **10** comprehend, experience, understand

have a go at 3 try **6** hazard, tackle **7** attempt **8** give a try **9** undertake **10** give a whirl **12** take a crack at, take a whack at

have a good opinion of 5 favor **6** admire, revere **7** approve, respect **9** believe in **10** appreciate

have a hand in 7 advance, forward **9** influence **10** take part in **12** contribute to **13** be conducive to, participate in **14** help bring about

have an eye on 4 want **5** covet,

crave, fancy **6** desire **7** long for, pine for **8** aspire to, yearn for **9** lust after **11** have a yen for

have a yen for 4 want **5** covet, crave **6** desire **7** long for, wish for **8** yearn for **9** lust after **11** hanker after **13** have a fancy for

have bearing on 5 apply, refer **6** relate **7** concern, pertain **9** appertain, touch upon **13** be pertinent to, have respect to

have done with 4 drop, junk, shed **7** abandon, discard **9** dispose of **10** relinquish **12** dispense with

have faith in 5 trust **6** rely on **9** believe in **16** have confidence in

have guests 8 play host **9** entertain **10** give a party **13** keep open house **16** offer hospitality

Have Gun Will Travel
   character: 6 Hey Boy **7** Hey Girl, Paladin
   cast: 6 Lisa Lu **7** Kam Tong **12** Richard Boone
   setting: 12 San Francisco **13** Hotel Carleton

have in mind 4 mean, want, wish **6** desire, intend **10** think about

haven 4 port **5** cover **6** asylum, harbor, refuge **7** hideout, retreat, shelter **8** hideaway **9** sanctuary

have no hope 6 give up **7** despair **11** be desperate

have plenty 6 abound, be rich **8** flourish, overflow **10** be numerous, have enough **11** be plentiful **14** be well supplied **18** have more than enough

have the body
   Latin: 12 habeas corpus
   legal writ guards against: 19 illegal imprisonment

have too few 4 lack, want **7** be scant **9** fall short **13** be deficient in, have a dearth of **14** have a paucity of **15** be in short supply, have a scarcity of, not have enough of

having life 5 alive, vital **6** living, viable **7** animate

having the means 3 fit **4** able **6** fitted **7** capable, equal to **8** adequate **9** qualified **12** being solvent **20** having the wherewithal

Havisham, Miss
   character in: 17 Great Expectations
   author: 7 Dickens

havoc 4 ruin **5** chaos **8** calamity, disaster, disorder, upheaval **9** cataclysm, ruination **11** catastrophe, destruction, devastation **12** wrack and ruin **16** widespread damage

Havoc, June, 7 actress
   sister: 12 Gypsy Rose Lee
   dramatized as: 5 Gypsy
   billed as: 8 Baby June

Hawaii

abbreviation: 2 HI
nickname: 5 Aloha **15** Sandwich Islands **20** Paradise of the Pacific
capital/largest city: 8 Honolulu
others: 3 Ewa **4** Aiea, Hana, Hilo, Laie, Paia **5** Kapaa, Kapaa, Lihue, Maili **6** Kailua, Kekaha **7** Kahului, Kaneohe, Lanikae, Wahiawa, Waianae, Wailuku
college: 9 Chaminade, Hawaii Loa **12** Brigham Young **13** Hawaii Pacific
dance: 4 hula
explorer: 4 Cook **7** Gaetano
feature:
   district: 7 Lahaina
   national park: 9 Haleakala **15** Hawaii Volcanoes
festivity: 4 luau
food: 3 poi **4** taro
foreigner: 5 haole
gift: 3 lei
greeting: 5 aloha
goddess: 4 Pele
king: 10 Kamehameha
medicine man: 6 Kahuna
musical instrument: 3 uke **7** ukulele, ukelele
native woman: 6 wahine
people: 5 Don Ho **9** Hiram Fong **10** Polynesian **11** Sanford Dole, Bette Midler **12** Daniel Inouye, Father Damien
porch: 5 lanai
queen 12 Liliuokalani
island name: 4 Kure **9** Kahoolawe
   big isle: 6 Hawaii
   friendly isle: 7 Molokai
   garden isle: 5 Kauai
   gathering place: 4 Oahu
   house of the sun: 9 Haleakala
   mystery isle: 6 Niihau
   pineapple isle: 5 Lanai
   valley isle: 4 Maui
lake: 5 Waiau
land rank: 12 forty-seventh
mountain: 3 Kea, Loa **5** Kaala **6** Kohala, Kohala, Koolau **7** Kamakou, Waianae **8** Maunaloa **9** Lanaihale
   highest point: 8 Maunakea
physical feature:
   bay: 5 Pohue **6** Halawa, Kiholo, Mamala **7** Kamohio, Kaneohe, Waiagua **8** Kawaihae, Maunalua
   beach: 7 Waikiki
   canyon: 6 Waimea
   channel: 3 Aua **5** Kaiwi **6** Kalohi **7** Pailolo
   crater: 7 Kilauea **9** Punchbowl
   desert: 3 Kau
   harbor: 5 Pearl
   promontory: 11 Diamond Head
   valley: 3 Iao **5** Manoa
   volcano: 7 Kilauea **8** Maunakea, Maunaloa **9** Haleakala
state admission: 8 Fiftieth
state bird: 4 nene **13** Hawaiian goose
state flower: 5 lehua **11** red hibiscus **15** scarlet hibiscus

state motto: 44 The Life of the Land is Perpetuated in Righteousness
state song: 11 Hawaii Ponoi **12** Our Own Hawaii
state tree: 5 kukui **9** candlenut

Hawaii
author: 13 James Michener

Hawaiian swimmer 14 Duke Kahanamoku

Hawaii Five-O
character: 4 Kono **5** Wo Fat **8** Ben Kokua **11** Chin Ho Kelly **13** Danny Williams **14** Steve McGarrett
cast: 4 Zulu **7** Kam Fong **8** Jack Lord **11** Khigh Dhiegh **12** Al Harrington **14** James MacArthur

hawk 4 bird, sell, vend **6** falcon, peddle **8** militant **9** accipiter, warmonger
young: 4 eyas
group of: 4 cast

Hawk, Sir Mulberry
character in: 16 Nicholas Nickleby
author: 7 Dickens

Hawkes, John
author of: 10 Second Skin **11** The Cannibal, The Lime Twig **12** The Beetle Leg **15** The Blood Oranges

Hawkeye 11 Natty Bumppo
author: 6 Cooper

Hawkeye Pierce 4 Mash **8** Alan Alda

Hawkeye State
nickname of: 4 Iowa

Hawkins, Jim
character in: 14 Treasure Island
author: 9 Stevenson

Hawkline Monster, The
author: 16 Richard Brautigan

Hawks, Howard
director of: 8 Red River, Rio Bravo, Scarface **11** The Big Sleep **12** Sergeant York **13** His Girl Friday **14** Bringing Up Baby **16** To Have and Have Not, Twentieth Century

Hawn, Goldie
husband: 12 Gus Trinkonis
born: 12 Washington DC
roles: 7 Laugh-In, Shampoo **8** Foul Play **12** Cactus Flower **13** Private Benjamin **18** Butterflies Are Free

hawser 4 line, rope **5** cable **7** mooring

hawthorn 9 Crataegus
varieties: 5 water, yeddo **6** Indian **7** English

Hawthorne, Nathaniel
author of: 13 The Marble Faun **14** Twice-told Tales **16** The Scarlet Letter **20** Mosses from an Old Manse **24** The House of the Seven Gables

Haydee
character in: 21 The Count of Monte Cristo
author: 5 Dumas (pere)

Haydn, Franz Joseph
born: 6 Rohrau **7** Austria
called: 9 Papa Haydn
composer of: 7 The Bird, The Joke

10 Gypsy Rondo, The Seasons **11** The Creation **12** Emperor's Hymn, Wild Band Mass **13** The Apothecary **14** Lord Nelson Mass, Theresienmesse **15** Mass in Time of War **16** Il Mondo della Luna, Mariazellermesse **17** The World of the Moon **38** The Seven Last Words of Our Savior on the Cross
quartet: 3 Sun **4** Bird, Frog, Lark, Tost **5** Dream, Razor, Witch **6** Fifths, Maiden **7** Emperor, Erdoedy, Russian, Sunrise, The Bell, The Hunt **8** Farmyard, Horseman, The Jokes **9** The Donkey **14** The House on Fire, The Row in Vienna
symphony: 4 Fire **5** Paris **6** Le Midi, Le Soir, Loudon, Merkur, Oxford, The Hen **7** Evening, Le Matin, Mercury, Morning, Salomon, The Bear, The Hunt **8** Abschied, Alleluia, Drum Roll, Farewell, Military, Mourning, Surprise, The Clock, The Queen, The Storm **9** Children's, Christmas **10** La Passione, La Tempesta, The Miracle, The Passion **11** The Imperial **12** Der Philosoph, Maria Theresa, The Afternoon **13** Auf dem Anstand **14** The Philosopher **15** The Schoolmaster, Trauersymphonie, With the Horn Call **17** At the Hunting Place **18** Mit dem Hornersignal

Hayes, Elvin
nickname: 4 Big E
sport: 10 basketball
team: 8 San Diego **14** Houston Rockets

Hayes, Helen
real name: 15 Helen Hayes Brown
nickname: 29 First Lady of the American Theater
son: 14 James MacArthur
roles: 7 Airport **9** Anastasia **22** The Sin of Madelon Claudet (Oscar)

Hayes, Rutherford B (Birchard)
nickname: 8 Rud Hayes
presidential rank: 10 nineteenth
party: 10 Republican
state represented: 2 OH
defeated: 5 (Green Clay) Smith **6** (James B) Walker, (Peter) Cooper, (Samuel Jones) Tilden
vice president: 7 (William Almon) Wheeler
cabinet:
state: 6 (William Maxwell) Evarts
treasury: 7 (John) Sherman
war: 6 (Alexander) Ramsey **7** (George Washington) McCrary
attorney general: 6 (Charles) Devens
navy: 4 (Nathan) Goff (Jr) **8** (Richard Wigginton) Thompson
postmaster general: 3 (David McKendree) Key **7** (Horace) Maynard
interior: 6 (Carl) Schurz

born: 10 Delaware OH
died/buried: 9 Fremont OH
education:
preparatory school: 4 Webb
College: 6 Kenyon
Law School: 7 Harvard
religion: 9 Methodist
political career: 24 US House of Representatives
city solicitor of: 10 Cincinnati
governor of: 4 Ohio
civilian career: 6 farmer, lawyer
military service: 6 US Army **8** Civil War **12** Ohio infantry **18** brevet major general
notable events of lifetime/term: 10 Depression (of 1873) **15** railroad strikes (of 1877) **18** civil service reform **24** specie payments resumption **Act: 26** Bland-Allison Silver Purchase
father: 10 Rutherford
mother: 6 Sophia (Birchard)
siblings: 7 Lorenzo **11** Sarah Sophia **13** Fanny Arabella
wife: 4 Lucy (Ware Webb)
children: 5 Fanny **9** James Webb (renamed Webb Cook) **11** George Crook **12** Manning Force, Scott Russell **14** Joseph Thompson, Sardis Birchard (renamed Birchard Austin) **15** Rutherford Platt

hayseed 4 hick, rube **5** yokel **6** rustic **7** bumpkin, peasant **10** clodhopper

Hayward, Susan
real name: 14 Edythe Marrener
husband: 10 Jess Barker
born: 10 Brooklyn NY
roles: 11 I Want to Live (Oscar) **14** I'll Cry Tomorrow, My Foolish Heart **18** With a Song in My Heart **23** Smash Up The Story of a Woman

Hayworth, Rita
real name: 22 Margarita Carmen Cansino
husband: 7 Aly Khan **10** Dick Haymes **11** Orson Welles
born: 10 Brooklyn NY
roles: 5 Gilda **9** Cover Girl **14** Separate Tables **17** Miss Sadie Thompson, You'll Never Get Rich

hazan 18 cantor of a synagogue

hazard 3 bet **4** dare, luck, risk **5** fluke, guess, offer, peril, stake, wager **6** chance, danger, expose, gamble, menace, mishap, submit, threat **7** advance, daresay, imperil, pitfall, presume, proffer, suppose, venture **8** accident, chance it, endanger, jeopardy, theorize, threaten, throw out **9** mischance, speculate, tempt fate, volunteer **10** conjecture, jeopardize, misfortune **11** coincidence, hypothesize, imperilment, take a chance, trust to luck **12** endangerment, happenstance, stroke of luck

Hazard of New Fortunes, A
author: 18 William Dean Howells

hazardous 4 iffy **5** risky, shaky **6** chancy, unsafe, unsure **7** dubious, unsound **8** doubtful, insecure, perilous, unstable **9** dangerous, uncertain **10** precarious, unreliable **11** speculative, threatening **13** untrustworthy

haze 3 fog **4** daze, film, mist, pall, veil **5** cloak, cloud, smoke, vapor **6** mantle, muddle, screen **9** fogginess **12** befuddlement, bewilderment **16** state of confusion

hazel 3 nut **4** tree **5** brown, shrub, tawny **8** brownish **14** yellowish-brown
   varieties: 4 tree **5** Chile, witch **6** winter **7** Chinese, Turkish **8** American, European, Japanese **11** spike winter **12** Chinese witch **13** Japanese witch **15** buttercup winter

Hazel
   character: 12 George Baxter, Harold Baxter **13** Dorothy Baxter
   cast: 9 Don DeFore **12** Shirley Booth, Whitney Blake **13** Bobby Buntrock
   creator: 6 Ted Key

hazelnut 7 Corylus
   varieties: 6 beaked **7** Chinese, Turkish **8** American, European, Japanese

Hazlitt, William
   author of: 6 essays **17** The Spirit of the Age **32** The Characters of Shakespeare's Plays

hazy 3 dim **5** dusky, faint, filmy, foggy, misty, murky, smoky, vague **6** bleary, blurry, cloudy, smoggy, veiled **7** bleared, general, muddled, obscure, unclear **8** confused, nebulous, overcast **9** ambiguous, uncertain **10** ill-defined, indefinite

head 2 go, IQ **3** aim, CEO, end, hie, tip, top **4** acme, apex, bent, boss, czar, duce, font, fore, gift, jefe, king, lead, main, mind, peak, rise, rule, tsar, turn, well **5** begin, brain, chief, crest, crown, drive, first, front, guide, pilot, prime, queen, ruler, start, steer **6** climax, crisis, direct, genius, govern, honcho, launch, leader, manage, origin, ruling, source, spring, summit, talent, vertex, zenith **7** ability, admiral, captain, command, conduct, control, foreman, general, go first, highest, leading, make for, manager, marshal, monarch, precede, premier, primary, proceed, ranking, supreme, topmost **8** aptitude, be head of, big wheel, capacity, chairman, dictator, director, dominant, foremost, fountain, fruition, headmost, initiate, judgment, managing, pinnacle, start off, superior, suzerain, upper end **9** acuteness, beginning, commander, commodore, extremity, forefront, front rank, governing, intellect, introduce, mentality, paramount, potentate, president, principal, sovereign, supervise, uppermost **10** administer, be master of,

birthplace, cleverness, commandant, commanding, conclusion, first place, gray matter, inaugurate, lead the way, move toward, perception, preeminent, supervisor, wellspring **11** be at the helm, controlling, culmination, discernment, forward part, highest rank, officiate at, preside over, superintend, take the lead, termination **12** apprehension, field marshal, fountainhead, guiding light, place of honor, take charge of, take the reins, turning point, utmost extent **13** administrator, go at the head of, most prominent, prime minister, understanding **14** chief executive, highest ranking, superintendent **15** be in the vanguard, make a beeline for, quickness of mind **16** commander-in-chief, direct one's course, inevitable result **17** commanding general, have authority over **18** be in the driver's seat, chairman of the board, go in the direction of **21** chief executive officer

head
   contains: 4 eyes **5** brain, mouth, skull **9** braincase **10** optic nerve **12** ocular muscle **13** cranial cavity, lacrimal organ, orbital cavity **14** buccaval cavity

headache 5 trial **6** strain, stress **7** problem, trouble **8** migraine, nuisance **10** affliction, difficulty **13** inconvenience, pain in the neck

headdress 3 cap, hat **6** bonnet **7** chapeau **12** headcovering

headgear 3 cap, fez, hat, tam **4** cowl, hood, kepi, topi, veil **5** beret, busby, crown, derby, miter, mitre, opera, shako, shawl, snood, straw, terai, tiari, topee, toque **6** beanie, boater, bonnet, bowler, cloche, fedora, helmet, mobcap, panama, sailor, trilby, turban **7** bicorne, biretta, chapeau, hardhat, homberg, pillbox, porkpie, stetson, **8** babushka, kerchief, mantilla, nightcap, skullcap, snap-brim, sombrero, tarboosh, tricorne, yarmulke **9** stovepipe, sunbonnet, ten-gallon **10** pith helmet **11** deerstalker, dolly varden

headland 4 bank, crag **5** bluff, cliff **8** palisade **9** precipice **10** promontory

headlong 6 abrupt **8** abruptly, heedless, pell-mell, reckless **9** headfirst, impetuous **10** heedlessly, recklessly **11** impetuously, precipitate, precipitous **13** head over heels, precipitously

headman 5 chief **6** leader **7** foreman **8** alderman, princeps **9** commander **10** councilman, supervisor **14** public official

head-on 6 direct **7** frontal **10** face-to-face

headshrinker 6 shrink **7** analyst **12** psychiatrist **13** psychoanalyst

headstrong 4 rash **6** dogged, mulish,

unruly **7** defiant, froward, willful **8** contrary, obdurate, reckless, stubborn **9** hotheaded, imprudent, impulsive, obstinate, pigheaded **10** bullheaded, incautious, refractory **11** intractable **12** incorrigible, recalcitrant, ungovernable, unmanageable **14** uncontrollable **22** bent on having one's own way

heady 4 hard **6** potent, strong **8** alluring, exciting, inviting, stirring, tempting **9** seductive, thrilling **10** high-octane **11** high-voltage, tantalizing **12** exhilarating, intoxicating

heal 4 cure, knit, mend **5** right, salve, treat **6** heal up, remedy, settle, soothe **7** compose, get well, improve, recover, rectify, relieve **8** heal over, make well **9** alleviate, make whole, reconcile **10** conciliate, convalesce, recuperate **11** set to rights **14** make harmonious, return to health **20** restore good relations

healed 4 knit **5** cured **6** mended **7** got well **8** relieved

healing 6 curing **7** mending **8** knitting, soothing **9** emollient, improving, restoring **10** making well **11** restorative **13** strengthening
   god of: 6 Apollo **7** Phoebus, Pythius **9** Asclepius, Musagetes **11** Aesculapius
   goddess of: 4 Iaso

health 5 vigor **7** fitness, stamina **8** strength, vitality **9** hardihood, hardiness, well-being **10** robustness **16** general condition **17** physical condition
   goddess of: 6 Hygeia

healthful 7 healthy **8** hygienic, salutary **9** wholesome **10** beneficial, nourishing, nutritious, salubrious **12** healthgiving, invigorating

healthiness 6 health **9** good shape, soundness **10** good health, robustness **12** salutariness **13** good condition, healthfulness, wholesomeness **14** salubriousness

healthy 3 fit **4** hale **5** hardy, sound **6** hearty, robust, strong, sturdy **8** vigorous **9** in the pink **10** able-bodied **12** in fine fettle **18** sound of mind and limb

heap 3 gob, lot **4** fill, gobs, hunk, load, lots, lump, mass, mess, pack, pile, slew **5** amass, award, batch, bunch, flood, group, mound, ocean, slews, stack, store, world **6** accord, assign, bundle, deluge, engulf, gather, jumble, load up, oceans, oodles, pile up, plenty, worlds **7** barrels, cluster, collect, mete out, present **8** good deal, inundate, pour upon **9** abundance, gathering, great deal, multitude, profusion **10** assemblage, collection, shower upon **11** aggregation, concentrate **12** accumulation **13** agglomeration

heap up 5 amass 6 pile up 7 stack up 10 accumulate

hear 4 heed 5 admit, favor, grant, judge, learn 6 attend, be told, gather, look on 7 approve, concede, examine, find out, receive, witness 8 accede to, appear at, discover, hear tell, hold with, listen to 9 acquiesce, ascertain, hearken to 10 understand 11 acknowledge

hear!
French: 4 oyez
cry used by: 10 court crier
precedes: 5 trial 12 proclamation

hearing 5 probe, sound 6 review 7 council, earshot, inquiry 8 audience 9 interview 10 conference 11 examination, questioning 12 consultation 13 interrogation, investigation

hearken to 4 heed, mark, mind 6 attend 8 listen to 11 take to heart 14 pay attention to

Hearns, Thomas
nickname: 6 Hitman
sport: 6 boxing
class: 12 middleweight, welterweight

hearsay 4 talk 5 rumor 6 gossip, report 8 idle talk 9 grapevine 11 scuttlebutt

heart 3 hub, nub 4 base, core, crux, guts, love, meat, mood, pith, root, soul 5 humor, pluck, spunk, valor 6 center, daring, desire, kernel, middle, nature, source, spirit 7 bravery, charity, courage, emotion, essence, nucleus, stomach 8 audacity, backbone, boldness, clemency, feelings, firmness, fondness, gameness, interior, main part, sympathy 9 affection, fortitude, gallantry, inner part, rudiments, sentiment, tolerance 10 brass tacks, compassion, enthusiasm, essentials, foundation, gentleness, indulgence, manfulness, principles, resolution, tenderness, true nature 11 busiest part, central part, disposition, forgiveness, nitty-gritty, temperament 12 fearlessness, fundamentals, quintessence, resoluteness 13 audaciousness
part: 5 aorta, valve 6 atrium 7 chamber 9 ventricle
pumps: 5 blood

heartache 3 woe 4 pain 5 grief 6 misery, sorrow 7 anguish, sadness, torment, trouble 8 distress 9 suffering 11 tribulation, unhappiness

heartbreaker 4 vamp 5 flirt, tease 8 coquette

Heartbreak House
author: 17 George Bernard Shaw

hearten 4 abet 5 cheer 6 assure, solace 7 animate, cheer up, comfort, console, enliven, gladden 8 brighten, embolden, energize, inspirit, reassure 9 encourage 10 invigorate

heartening 7 hopeful 9 favorable 10 auspicious, reassuring 11 encouraging

heartfelt 4 deep, full 5 total 6 ardent, devout, entire, honest 7 earnest, fervent, genuine, intense, sincere 8 complete, profound, thorough 10 keenly felt 12 all-inclusive, wholehearted

hearth 4 home 5 abode, house 8 fireside 9 fireplace, household 10 family life 12 family circle 13 chimney corner
goddess of: 4 Caca 5 Salus, Vesta 6 Hestia

Heart Is a Lonely Hunter, The
author: 15 Carson McCullers
character: 8 Mr Singer 9 Mick Kelly 10 Dr Copeland, Jake Blount 11 Biff Brannon

heartless 4 cold, mean 5 cruel 6 brutal, savage, unkind 7 callous, inhuman, unmoved 8 pitiless, ruthless, uncaring 9 unfeeling, unpitying, unstirred 10 unmerciful 11 coldhearted, cold-blooded, hardhearted, insensitive 12 cruelhearted, unresponsive 13 unsympathetic

Heart of Darkness
author: 12 Joseph Conrad
character: 5 Kurtz 7 Marlowe

Heart of Dixie
nickname of: 7 Alabama

Heart of Juliet Jones, The
creator: 9 Stan Drake
character: 3 Eve

Heart of Midlothian, The
author: 14 Sir Walter Scott

Heart of the Matter, The
author: 12 Graham Greene
character: 5 Yusef 6 Wilson 7 Mrs Rolt 9 Mrs Scobie 11 Major Scobie

heart-stopper 5 belle 6 beauty 7 charmer, stunner 8 knockout 10 good-looker 13 beautiful girl 14 beautiful woman

hearty 4 hale, warm, well 5 ample, hardy, sound 6 lively, robust, strong 7 cordial, genuine, healthy, profuse, sincere, zestful 8 complete, effusive, generous, thorough, vigorous 9 heartfelt, unbounded 10 unreserved 12 enthusiastic, unrestrained, wholehearted 13 physically fit

hearty appetite
French: 10 bon appetit

Heaslop, Ronald
character in: 15 A Passage to India
author: 7 Forster

heat 3 fry 4 bake, boil, cook, sear, stew, warm, zeal 5 ardor, broil, roast, steam 6 braise, climax, fervor, height, simmer, stress, thrill, warmth, warm up 7 hotness, make hot, passion, rapture, swelter 8 fervency, hot spell, warmness 9 eagerness, intensity, transport 10 enthusiasm, excitement 12 bring to a boil

heated 3 hot 5 angry, fiery, irate 6 bitter, fierce, raging, stormy 7 excited, fervent, furious, intense, violent 8 frenzied, inflamed, vehement 9 emotional 10 infuriated, passionate 11 impassioned, tempestuous

heated discussion 7 dispute 8 argument 10 war of words 11 controversy 12 disagreement

heath 5 Erica
varieties: 4 Tree 5 Berry, Besom, Irish, Otago, Spike 6 Dorset, Scotch, Spring 7 Cornish, Fringed, Spanish, Twisted 9 Cranberry 11 Cross-leaved

Heathcliff
character in: 16 Wuthering Heights
loved: Cathy
author: 6 Bronte

heathen 3 goy 4 boor 5 pagan 6 savage 7 atheist, gentile, infidel 8 agnostic, idolator 9 barbarian, ignoramus 10 polytheist, troglodyte, unbeliever 11 non-believer 17 uncivilized native

heather 7 Calluna
varieties: 3 Bog, Red 4 Bell, Snow 5 Beach, False, White 6 French, Golden, Scotch 8 Corsican, Mountain 9 Christmas 11 White winter 13 Mediterranean 18 Everblooming French

heat up 3 fan, zap 4 goad, nuke, warm, whet 6 arouse 7 enhance, sharpen 8 increase 9 aggravate, intensify 10 strengthen

heave 3 peg, pry, sob 4 arch, blow, cast, emit, fire, hurl, lift, moan, pant, puff, puke, toss 5 boost, bulge, chuck, eject, fling, groan, hoist, lever, pitch, raise, retch, sling, surge, swell, throw, vomit 6 dilate, drag up, draw up, exhale, expand, haul up, launch, let fly, propel, pull up, tilt up, yank up 7 elevate 8 thrust up 9 discharge, palpitate 11 regurgitate

heaven, Heaven, the Heavens 3 wow 4 Zion 5 bliss, glory, mercy, space 6 my oh my, utopia 7 delight, ecstasy, Elysium, my stars, nirvana, Olympus, rapture 8 boy oh boy, goodness, land sake, paradise, Valhalla 9 afterlife, dreamland, next world, Shangri-la 10 afterworld, Beulah Land, life beyond, outer space, perfection, sheer bliss 11 enchantment, the Holy City, world beyond, world to come 12 eternal bliss, good gracious, New Jerusalem, the City of God, the firmament 13 Abraham's bosom, Elysian fields, seventh heaven 14 heavens to Betsy, our eternal home 15 life everlasting, our Father's house, the heavenly city 16 goodness gracious, Isle of the Blessed, supreme happiness, the abode of saints, the Celestial City, the vault of heaven 17 complete happiness, the wild blue yonder 18 Island of the Blessed, the celestial sphere, the heavenly kingdom, the kingdom of Heaven 19 the celestial expanse 21 the happy hunting ground

god of: 2 An **3** Anu **4** Jove, Zeus **7** Jupiter

Heaven Can Wait (1943)
director: 13 Ernst Lubitsch
cast: 9 Don Ameche **11** Gene Tierney **12** Marjorie Main **13** Charles Coburn

Heaven Can Wait (1978)
director: 9 Buck Henry **12** Warren Beatty
cast: 10 Dyan Cannon, Jack Warden **12** Warren Beatty **13** Julie Christie
remake of: 17 Here Comes Mr Jordan

heavenly 6 divine **7** angelic, blessed, saintly, sublime **8** beatific, blissful

Heavens and Earth
author: 19 Stephen Vincent Benet

Heaven's My Destination
author: 14 Thornton Wilder

heavy 3 big, fat, sad **4** deep, dull, full, hard, lazy, slow **5** broad, bulky, dense, grave, gross, harsh, hefty, large, obese, plump, rough, stout, thick **6** clumsy, coarse, deadly, dreary, fierce, gloomy, leaden, pained, portly, raging, rugged, savage, solemn, strong, sturdy, torpid, woeful **7** awesome, complex, copious, doleful, forlorn, furious, intense, joyless, languid, lumpish, massive, notable, onerous, profuse, roaring, ruinous, serious, tearful, tedious, violent, weighty **8** abundant, agonized, burdened, crushing, cumbrous, damaging, dejected, desolate, downcast, forceful, grieving, grievous, imposing, lifeless, listless, mournful, pedantic, profound, seething, sluggish, stricken, tiresome, unwieldy **9** apathetic, cheerless, corpulent, depressed, difficult, excessive, extensive, harrowing, important, injurious, laborious, lethargic, lumbering, miserable, momentous, ponderous, rampaging, sorrow- ful, turbulent, wearisome **10** burden- some, calamitous, cumbersome, dis- tressed, full of care, immoderate, impressive, inordinate, melancholy, monotonous, noteworthy, oppressive, overweight, pernicious, phlegmatic, unbearable, unstinting **11** crestfallen, deleterious, destructive, detrimental, distressing, extravagant, intemperate, intolerable, unrelenting, unremitting **12** considerable, disconsolate, hard to endure, overwhelming, unrestrained **13** consequential, grief- stricken, of great import **16** laden with sorrows **18** of great consequence

heavy-handed 5 harsh **6** clumsy **7** awkward **8** bungling **9** graceless, maladroit **10** blundering, oppressive, ungraceful

heavyhearted 3 sad **4** glum **6** dismal, gloomy, morose **7** doleful, forlorn, joyless, unhappy **8** dejected, downcast **9** cheerless, depressed, sorrowful **10**

despondent, melancholy **11** downhearted **14** down in the dumps, down in the mouth

Hebe
goddess of: 5 youth **6** spring
father: 4 Zeus
mother: 4 Hera
brother: 4 Ares
husband: 8 Hercules
handmaiden to: 4 gods
corresponds to: 8 Juventas

Hebrew alphabet
or: 5 aleph
b/v: 4 beth
g: 5 gimel
d: 6 daleth
h: 2 he **5** cheth
v/w: 3 vav
z: 5 zayin
y/j/i: 3 yod
k/kh: 4 kaph
l: 5 lamed
m: 3 men
n: 3 nun
`: 4 ayin
p/f: 2 pe
k: 4 koph
r: 4 resh
sh/s: 4 shin
s: 3 sin **4** sadi **6** samekh
t: 3 tav **4** teth

Hebrew Judge 4 Ehud, Elon, Jair, Tola **5** Abdon, Ibzan **6** Gideon, Samson, Samuel **7** Deborah, Othniel, Shamgar **8** Jephthah

Hebrew months
first: 4 Ahib, Nisn **6** Ehanim, Tishri
second: 3 Bul, Civ **4** Iyar **7** Heshvan
third: 5 Sivan **6** Kislev
fourth: 5 Tebet **6** Tammuz, Tebeth
fifth: 2 Ab **7** Shelbat
sixth: 4 Adar, Elul **6** Veadar
seventh: 4 Abib **5** Nisan **6** Tishri **7** Ethanim
eighth: 3 Zif **4** Iyer **11** Marcheshvan
ninth: 5 Sivan **7** Chislev
tenth: 6 Tabeth, Tammuz
eleventh: 2 Ab **6** Shebat
twelfth: 4 Adar, Elul

he carved it
Latin: 8 sculpsit

Hecate
also: 6 Hekate
goddess of: 5 earth, Hades
associated with: 6 hounds **7** sorcery **10** crossroads
corresponds to: 5 Brimo

heckle 3 boo **4** bait, hiss, hoot, mock, razz, ride, twit **5** annoy, bully, chivy, harry, hound, taunt **6** badger, harass, harrow, hector, jeer at, molest, needle **7** provoke **9** shout down

Heckle and Jeckle 7 magpies **8** cartoons

hectare
abbreviation of: 2 ha

hectic 3 mad **4** wild **6** stormy **7** cha-

otic, frantic, furious **8** feverish, frenetic, frenzied, headlong **9** breakneck, turbulent **10** tumultuous

hectoliter
abbreviation of: 2 hl

hectometer
abbreviation of: 2 hm

hector 4 bait, ride **5** bully, harry, hound, tease, worry **6** badger, harass, needle, plague **7** torment, swagger **8** browbeat

Hector
father: 5 Priam
mother: 6 Hecuba
brother: 5 Paris
sister: 9 Cassandra
wife: 10 Andromache
son: 8 Astyanax
hero of: 9 Trojan War
killed by: 8 Achilles

Hecuba
also: 5 Maera **6** Hecabe
father: 5 Atlas
husband: 5 Priam **8** Tegeates
son: 5 Paris **6** Hector **7** Helenus, Polites, Troilus **9** Deiphobus, Polydorus
daughter: 6 Creusa **7** Laodice **8** Polyxena **9** Cassandra
changed into: 3 dog **5** bitch
hound of: 7 Icarius

Hecuba
author: 9 Euripides
character: 8 Odysseus, Polyxena **9** Agamemnon, Polydorus **10** Polymestor

Hedda Gabler
author: 11 Henrik Ibsen
character: 10 Judge Brack **11** Hedda Tesman, Thea Elvsted **12** George Tesman **13** Eilert Lovberg **17** Miss Juliana Tesman

heder 12 Jewish school

hedge 3 hem **4** duck, edge, ring, wall **5** bound, dodge, evade, fence, guard, hem in, limit **6** border, margin, shut in, waffle **7** barrier, enclose, mark off, outline **8** encircle, hedgerow, surround **9** be evasive, delineate, demarcate, insurance, pussyfoot, temporize **10** equivocate, protection **11** delineation, row of bushes **12** compensation **13** circumference, fence of shrubs **14** beg the question, counterbalance **17** beat around the bush

he died
Latin: 5 obiit

he does not pursue
Latin: 14 non prosequitur

hedonist 8 Sybarite **9** debauchee, libertine **10** dissipater, profligate, sensualist, voluptuary **14** pleasure seeker

hedonistic 7 sensual **9** epicurean, libertine, sybaritic **10** voluptuous **11** intemperate **13** self-indulgent **15** pleasure-seeking

he drew this
Latin: 10 delineavit

heed 4 care, mind, obey 5 bow to, pains, study 6 concur, follow, hold to, notice, regard 7 defer to, observe, perusal, respect, yield to 8 accede to, consider, listen to, prudence, scrutiny, submit to 9 attention, be ruled by, give ear to 10 bear in mind comply with, precaution, take note of 11 carefulness, examination, heedfulness, mindfulness, observation, take to heart 12 take notice of 13 attentiveness 14 fastidiousness, meticulousness, pay attention to, scrupulousness 17 conscientiousness

heedful 4 wary 5 alert, aware, cagey, chary 7 alive to, careful, mindful, prudent 8 cautious, discreet, vigilant, watchful 9 attentive, concerned, conscious

heedless 3 lax 4 rash 5 slack 6 remiss, unwary 7 foolish, unaware, witless 8 careless, mindless, reckless, uncaring 9 foolhardy, frivolous, impetuous, imprudent, negligent, oblivious, unheeding, unmindful 10 incautious, neglectful, unthinking, unwatchful 11 harebrained, improvident, inattentive, thoughtless, unconcerned, unobservant, unobserving 12 happy-go-lucky 14 scatterbrained

heedlessly 5 blind 6 rashly 8 headlong 9 foolishly, witlessly 10 carelessly, mindlessly, recklessly 11 frivolously, impetuously, impulsively, negligently, unmindfully 12 neglectfully, unthinkingly 13 inattentively, thoughtlessly, unconcernedly 15 inconsiderately, uncooperatively

heedlessness 8 rashness 9 unconcern 10 negligence 11 inattention, unawareness 12 carelessness, indiscretion, mindlessness, recklessness 13 unmindfulness 15 thoughtlessness 16 irresponsibility

heel 3 cad, cur, end, rat 4 list, rind, tilt 5 churl, crust, louse 6 rotter 7 bounder, caitiff, dastard

he engraved it
    Latin: 8 sculpsit

Heep, Uriah
    character in: 16 David Copperfield
    author: 7 Dickens

he flourished
    Latin: 7 floruit

hefty 3 big 5 beefy, bulky, burly, heavy, husky, large, stout 6 brawny, hearty, mighty, robust, rugged, strong, sturdy 7 hulking, massive, sizable, weighty, well-fed 8 muscular, powerful, stalwart, thickset 9 corpulent, strapping 11 substantial

hegemony 7 control 9 authority, dominance, influence, supremacy

Heggen, Thomas
    author of: 9 Mr Roberts

hegira 6 exodus, flight 7 journey

he himself said it
    Latin: 9 ipse dixit

Heidi 4 girl
    location: 9 Swiss Alps
    author 12 Johanna Spyri
    friend: 5 Peter

Heifetz, Jascha
    born: 6 Russia
    instrument: 6 violin

height 4 acme, apex, hill, peak, rise 5 bluff, cliff, crest, knoll, limit, mound, tower 6 apogee, heyday, summit, zenith 7 hilltop, maximum, plateau 8 altitude, eminence, highland, highness, mountain, palisade, pinnacle, tallness, ultimate 9 elevation, extremity, flowering, high point, loftiness, supremacy 10 perfection, promontory 11 culmination 12 consummation, upward extent, utmost degree, vantage point

heighten 5 raise 7 elevate 8 increase 9 aggravate, intensify

heil 4 hail

Heimberger, Eddie Albert
    real name of: 11 Eddie Albert

Heine, Heinrich
    author of: 9 Atta Troll 11 Book of Songs 19 Germany A Winter's Tale

Heinlein, Robert
    author of: 10 Double Star 16 Starship Troopers 20 The Green Hills of Earth 22 Stranger in a Strange Land 23 The Moon Is a Harsh Mistress

heinous 4 evil, foul, vile 5 gross, nasty 6 grisly, horrid, odious, sinful, wicked 7 beastly, ghastly, hideous, inhuman, vicious 8 infamous, shocking, terrible 9 abhorrent, atrocious, loathsome, monstrous, nefarious, offensive, repugnant, repulsive, revolting, sickening 10 abominable, deplorable, despicable, detestable, disgusting, iniquitous, outrageous, scandalous, villainous 11 disgraceful, distasteful 12 contemptible 13 objectionable, reprehensible

heinousness 4 evil 7 outrage 8 atrocity, baseness, enormity, foulness, savagery, vileness, villainy 9 barbarity, depravity, malignity 10 inhumanity 13 loathsomeness, monstrousness 14 outrageousness

heir, heiress 7 legatee 9 inheritor 10 inheritrix 11 beneficiary, inheritress 12 heir apparent 15 heir presumptive

Heiress, The
    director: 12 William Wyler
    based on novel by: 10 Henry James
        film title: 16 Washington Square
    cast: 13 Miriam Hopkins 15 Montgomery Clift, Ralph Richardson 17 Olivia de Havilland
    score: 12 Aaron Copland
    Oscar for: 7 actress (de Havilland)

Hekate see 6 Hecate

Hel
    origin: 12 Scandinavian

    goddess of: 5 death
    rules: 8 Niflheim 10 underworld
    father: 4 Loki
    mother: 9 Angerboda, Angrbodha, Angurboda
    brother: 6 Fenrir, Fenris 11 Iormungandr, Jormungandr 14 Midgard Serpent
    color of body: 4 blue 5 flesh
    home of: 4 dead

Helen
    father: 4 Zeus
    mother: 4 Leda
    brother: 6 Castor, Pollux
    sister: 8 Timandra 12 Clytemnestra
    husband: 8 Menelaus
    abducted by: 5 Paris
    carried off to: 4 Troy
    abduction caused: 9 Trojan War
    quote: 33 the face that launched a thousand ships

Helena
    character in: 20 All's Well That Ends Well 21 A Midsummer Night's Dream
    author: 11 Shakespeare

helicopter
    invented by: 8 Sikorsky
    also: 8 autogyro 9 eggbeater

Helios
    origin: 5 Greek
    god of: 3 sun
    father: 8 Hyperion
    mother: 4 Thia
    children: 5 Circe 6 Aeetes 8 Phaethon
    corresponds to: 3 Sol

heliotrope 12 Heliotropium
    varieties: 6 garden, winter, yellow 7 seaside

helium
    chemical symbol: 2 He

hell, Hell 5 agony, grief, Hades 6 misery, the pit 7 Abaddon, anguish, despair, Gehenna, inferno, remorse, torment 8 Appolyons, hell fire, the abyss 9 martyrdom, perdition, suffering 10 lake of fire 12 hopelessness, wretchedness 13 bottomless pit, Satan's kingdom, the lower world, the underworld 14 place of the lost, the Devil's house, the nether world, the shades below 15 everlasting fire, home of lost souls, infernal regions 16 abode of the damned

Hellen
    king of: 8 Thessaly
    father: 9 Deucalion
    mother: 6 Pyrrha
    wife: 6 Orseis
    son: 5 Dorus 6 Aeolus, Xuthus
    ancestor of: 8 Hellenes

Hellenic Republic see 6 Greece

Heller, Joseph
    author of: 7 Catch-22 10 Good as Gold 17 Something Happened

hellion 5 devil, rogue, scamp 9 scoundrel 13 mischief-maker

hellish 4 foul, vile **5** awful **6** brutal **7** hateful **8** accursed, damnable, dreadful, horrible, infernal **9** atrocious, revolting **10** abominable, disgusting

Hellman, Lillian
   author of: 5 Maybe **10** Pentimento **13** Scoundrel Time **14** The Little Foxes, Toys in the Attic **15** Watch on the Rhine **16** The Children's Hour **17** An Unfinished Woman **22** Another Part of the Forest

hello
   French: 7 bonjour
   German: 8 guten tag
   Spanish: 10 buenos dias
   Hebrew 6 shalom
   Italian: 4 ciao **10** buon giorno
   Latin: 3 ave

Hello-Central
   character in: 36 A Connecticut Yankee in King Arthur's Court
   author: 5 Twain

help 3 aid **4** back, balm, calm, care, crew, cure, ease, gift, lift, save **5** allay, emend, force, guide, hands, salve, serve, staff **6** advice, advise, assist, give to, menial, relief, remedy, rescue, soothe, succor, uphold **7** advance, backing, console, correct, endorse, further, helpers, improve, nurture, promote, rectify, relieve, servant, service, stand by, support, welfare, workers, workmen **8** advocate, befriend, champion, domestic, factotum, farmhand, guidance, laborers, maintain, mitigate, retainer, retrieve, side with **9** alleviate, chip in for, employees, encourage, extricate, lend a hand, make whole, promotion, put at ease, underling, workhands, work force **10** ameliorate, apprentice, assistance, assistants, bring round, corrective, friendship, go to bat for, hired hands, kind regard, minister to, preventive, protection, stick up for **11** advancement, benevolence, cooperation, endorsement, furtherance, good offices, helping hand, make healthy, restorative **12** bring through, contribute to, contribution, hired helpers, intercede for **13** collaboration, cooperate with, encouragement, take the part of

helper 3 aid **4** aide **5** angel **6** backer, deputy, patron, second **7** adjunct, partner, servant **8** adjutant, advocate, champion, confrere, co-worker, employee, retainer **9** assistant, associate, auxiliary, colleague, man Friday, right hand, supporter **10** accomplice, aide-de-camp, apprentice, benefactor, girl Friday **11** confederate, helping hand, subordinate **12** collaborator, right-hand man **13** good samaritan **14** fairy godmother

helpful 4 fine, good, kind, nice **6** usable, useful **8** obliging, splendid, valuable **9** excellent, favorable, practical **10** beneficial, profitable, supportive

11 considerate, cooperative, serviceable **12** advantageous, constructive **13** accommodating

helping hand 3 aid **4** aide, hand **5** boost **6** assist, hand up, helper, succor **7** abettor, support **9** assistant **10** assistance

helplessness 8 weakness **9** impotence, inability, infirmity **10** dependence, feebleness, ineptitude **12** incapability, incompetence, inefficiency **13** powerlessness, vulnerability

Helsinki
   capital of: 7 Finland

hem 3 box, rim **4** bind, brim, edge, welt **5** bound, brink, skirt, verge **6** border, edging, fringe, impede, margin, turn up **7** confine, enclose, stammer, stutter, turning **8** compress, encircle, restrain, surround

he made it
   Latin: 5 fecit

hem in 4 best **5** fence **7** besiege, confine, enclose **8** encircle, surround

Hemingway, Ernest
   author of: 9 In Our Time **14** A Moveable Feast **15** A Farewell to Arms, The Sun Also Rises **16** To Have and Have Not **18** Islands in the Stream, The Old Man and the Sea **19** For Whom the Bell Tolls **21** The Snows of Kilimanjaro **34** The Short Happy Life of Francis Macomber

hemlock 5 Tsuga **15** Conium maculatum
   varieties: 5 Dwarf, Water **6** Canada, Ground, Poison **7** Siebold, Spotted, Western **8** Carolina, Japanese, Mountain

hemp 14 Cannabis sativa
   varieties: 3 Bog **5** Cuban, Sisal **6** Deccan, Indian, Manila **7** African **8** Deckaner **9** Bowstring, Mauritius **10** New Zealand **13** Colorado River **15** Ceylon bowstring, Indian bowstring **16** African bowstring

hen
   young: 6 pullet **7** lobster

Henchard, Michael
   character in: 22 The Mayor of Casterbridge
   author: 5 Hardy

henchman 4 goon, thug **6** flunky, lackey, minion, stooge, yes-man **7** gorilla **8** hanger-on, hireling, retainer **9** attendant, bodyguard **10** hatchet man, lieutenant **12** right- hand man, strong-arm man

Henderson, Marge
   creator/artist of: 10 Little Lulu

henna 3 dye **5** rinse **6** auburn, russet **8** cinnamon **11** rust-colored **12** reddish-brown **13** copper-colored

henpecked 4 meek **5** timid **6** docile **8** obedient **10** browbeaten, submissive, wife-ridden **11** unassertive

Henry, Frederic
   character in: 15 A Farewell to Arms
   author: 9 Hemingway

Henry Esmond
   author: 16 William Thackeray
   character: 5 Frank **7** Beatrix **9** Lord Mohun **10** Father Holt **11** James Stuart **12** Rachel Esmond **13** Francis Esmond

Henry IV
   author: 18 William Shakespeare
   character: 7 Hotspur **11** Prince Henry, Thomas Percy **14** Edmund Mortimer, Sir Walter Blunt **15** John of Lancaster, Mistress Quickly, Sir John Falstaff **18** Earl of Westmoreland, King Henry the Fourth

Henry V
   author: 18 William Shakespeare
   character: 7 Dauphin, Montjoy **15** Charles the Sixth (King of France) **17** Princess Katharine
   director: 15 Laurence Olivier
   cast: 11 Leslie Banks **12** Robert Newton **13** Renee Asherson **15** Laurence Olivier

Henry VI
   author: 18 William Shakespeare
   character: 6 Edward (Prince of Wales) **7** Charles (Dauphin of France), Eleanor, Louis XI (King of France) **8** Lady Bona, Lady Grey **9** Joan of Arc **10** Lord Talbot **11** Bolingbroke **12** John Beaufort, Lord Clifford, Lord Hastings **13** Henry Beaufort, Joan La Pucelle **15** Margaret of Anjou, Margery Jourdain **16** Bastard of Orleans, Cardinal Beaufort
      duke: 4 York (Richard Plantagenet) **7** Bedford, Suffolk **8** Somerset **10** Gloucester
      earl: 7 Suffolk, Warwick **9** Salisbury
      Richard Plantagenet's son: 6 Edmund, Edward, George **7** Richard

Henry VIII
   author: 18 William Shakespeare
   character: 7 Cranmer **8** Gardiner **10** Anne Boleyn **12** Thomas Wolsey **14** Queen Katharine, Thomas Cromwell **16** Cardinal Campeius
      duke: 7 Norfolk, Suffolk **10** Buckingham

Henze, Hans Werner
   born: 7 Germany **10** Westphalia
   composer of: 6 Ariosi, Ondine **8** King Stag **10** El Cimarron **11** Konig Hirsch **12** The Bassarids, The Young Lord **14** Being Beauteous **15** The Runaway Slave **17** Boulevard Solitude **18** Der Prinz von Homburg, The Raft of the Medusa **19** Elegy for Young Lovers **48** The Long and Weary Journey to the Flat of Natasha Ungeheur

Heorot
   great hall in: 7 Beowulf

he painted it
Latin: **6** pinxit

Hepburn, Audrey
real name: **19** Audrey Hepburn-Ruston
husband: **9** Mel Ferrer
born: **7** Belgium **8** Brussels
roles: **6** Ondine **7** Charade, Sabrina **9** Bloodline, Funny Face **10** My Fair Lady **11** War and Peace **12** Roman Holiday (Oscar), The Nun's Story **13** Green Mansions, Wait Until Dark **18** Love in the Afternoon **19** Breakfast at Tiffany's

Hepburn, Katharine
co-star: **12** Spencer Tracy
born: **10** Hartford CT
roles: **7** Desk Set, Holiday **8** Adam's Rib **10** Alice Adams, Pat and Mike, Summertime **12** Morning Glory (Oscar), On Golden Pond (Oscar), The Rainmaker **14** Woman of the Year **15** The African Queen, The Lion in Winter (Oscar) **18** Suddenly Last Summer **20** The Philadelphia Story **23** Guess Who's Coming to Dinner (Oscar) **24** Long Day's Journey into Night

Hephaestus
also: **10** Hephaistos
father: **4** Zeus
mother: **4** Hera
god of: **4** fire **11** handicrafts **12** metalworking
vocation: **5** smith
wife: **9** Aphrodite
corresponds to: **6** Vulcan

Hephzibah
husband: **8** Hezekiah
son: **8** Manasseh

Hepzibah see **9** Hephzibah

Hera
also: **4** Here
origin: **5** Greek
queen of: **6** Heaven
father: **6** Cronos, Cronus, Kronos
mother: **4** Rhea
brother: **4** Zeus
husband: **4** Zeus
son: **4** Ares
daughter: **9** Eilithyia **10** Hephaestus
birthplace: **5** Samos
festival: **7** Daedala
counterfeit: **7** Nephele
corresponds to: **4** Juno
epithet: **6** Anthea, Bunaea **8** Henioche **9** Prodromia

Heracles see **8** Hercules

Heracles, Children of
author: **9** Euripides
character: **6** Hyllus, Iolaus **7** Alcmene, Macaria **8** Demophon **10** Eurystheus

Heracles, Madness of
author: **9** Euripides
character: **4** Hera **5** Lycus **6** Megara **7** Theseus **8** Heracles **10** Amphitryon

Herakles see **8** Hercules

herald 4 clue, omen, sign **5** crier, envoy, token, usher **6** augury, inform, report, reveal, symbol **7** courier, divulge, portent, presage, publish, usher in, warning **8** announce, forecast, foregoer, foretell, proclaim **9** advertise, harbinger, indicator, make known, messenger, precursor, prefigure, publicize **10** forerunner, indication, proclaimer **11** bruit abroad, communicate, give voice to, predecessor **13** give tidings of

heraldic emblem 4 arms **5** crest **8** blazonry, insignia **10** coat of arms

heraldry
also called: **4** arms **10** coat of arms
band: **3** bar **4** bend, fess, orle
black: **5** sable
blue: **5** azure
border: **4** orle
bottom: **4** base
center: **5** fesse
coat of arms of cities/countries/colleges: **14** impersonal arms
coat of arms on shield/crest/helmet/motto: **19** armorial achievement
colors: **8** tincture
concerns family's: **8** heritage **9** genealogy
described as: **9** blazoning
divided diagonally: **7** per bend
divided vertically and horizontally: **9** quartered
expert: **8** armorist
for holding shield: **10** supporters
fur: **4** vair **6** ermine
gold/yellow: **2** or
green: **4** vert
helmet top: **5** crest
horizontal band: **4** fess
illegitimacy mark: **5** baton **6** baston **11** bar sinister **12** bend sinister
intrafamily distinctions: **12** differencing
daughter: **7** lozenge
eldest son: **5** label
younger son: **7** cadency
left part: **8** sinister
main figure: **6** charge **8** ordinary **14** heraldic device
metal: **2** or **6** argent
motto in: **6** scroll
orange: **5** tenne
placed on lord's: **6** banner, shield **8** garments **14** horse trappings
portrayed as: **6** emblem, symbol
position: **7** courant, dormant, passant, rampant, salient **8** couchant, trippant
purple: **7** purpure
red: **5** gules
red-purple: **8** sanguine
right part: **6** dexter
shield: **10** escutcheon
sunshade: **8** mantling
held by: **6** wreath
made of: **4** silk
surface/background: **5** field
top: **5** chief
two or more colors: **16** lines of partition
vertical band: **4** pale
wavy: **4** ente, onde, unde
when worn by followers: **5** badge **6** livery
white/silver: **6** argent

herb 4 drug **5** plant, spice **6** annual, physic **7** herbage, perfume **8** aromatic, biennial, medicine **9** flavoring, perennial, seasoning, succulent
kind: **3** bay, rue **4** corn, dill, hemp, mint, rose, sage **5** anise, basil, curry, chili, grass, onion, peony, thyme, wheat **6** catnip, celery, chives, clover, fennel, garlic, pepper, sesame **7** boneset, caraway, ginseng, lavender, mustard, oregano, parsley **8** camomile, licorice, rosemary, tarragon **9** buttercup, marijuana, spearmint **10** peppermint **11** wintergreen

Herbert, George
author of: **9** The Temple

Herbert, Victor
born: **6** Dublin **7** Ireland
composer of: **14** Babes in Toyland, Hero and Leander **15** Naughty Marietta

herbivorous 10 vegetarian **11** planteating **14** noncarnivorous

Herceius
epithet of: **4** Zeus
means: **14** of the courtyard

herculean, Herculean 4 hard **5** burly, hefty, tough **6** brawny, mighty, robust, rugged, strong, sturdy **7** arduous, onerous **8** muscular, powerful, toilsome, wearying **9** difficult, fatiguing, laborious, strapping, strenuous **10** burdensome, exhausting, formidable, prodigious **12** backbreaking

Hercules
also: **7** Alcides **8** Heracles, Herakles **9** Carnopian
father: **4** Zeus
mother: **7** Alcmene
cousin: **10** Eurystheus
wife: **4** Hebe **6** Megara **8** Deianira
son: **5** Lamus **6** Hyllus **8** Telephus **11** Therimachus
daughter: **7** Macaria
teacher: **6** Chiron
gift: **8** strength
performed: **6** labors
number of labors: **6** twelve
epithet: **7** Charops **8** Buphagus **9** Ipoctonus
corresponds to: **6** Sancus **10** Semo Sancus

Hercyna
form: **5** nymph
location: **8** fountain
playmate: **10** Persephone

herd 3 lot, mob **4** army, band, body, gang, goad, host, lead, mass, pack,

spur 5 array, bunch, crowd, drive, drove, flock, force, group, guide, horde, party, press, rally, swarm, tribe, troop **6** gather, huddle, legion, muster, number, throng **7** cluster, collect, company, convene, round up **8** assemble, assembly, conclave **9** gathering, multitude **10** assemblage, collection **11** convocation **12** congregation

Herds
god of: 8 Silvanus, Sylvanus
herdsman 6 cowboy, driver, drover **7** cowpoke **8** shepherd

Herdsman
constellation of: 6 Bootes

herd together 5 flock, group **6** gather **7** cluster, collect **10** congregate **12** band together

hereafter 5 limbo **6** heaven **8** paradise **9** afterlife, from now on, next world, Purgatory **10** afterworld, future life, henceforth, life beyond, ultimately **11** in the future, world to come **12** at a later date, at a later time, henceforward, subsequently **14** life after death **15** heavenly kingdom

here and there 6 around **11** at intervals **18** in this place and that
Latin: 6 passim

Here Comes Mr Jordan
director: 13 Alexander Hall
cast: 11 Claude Rains, Evelyn Keyes, Rita Johnson **16** Robert Montgomery
remade as: 13 Heaven Can Wait

hereditary 6 inborn, inbred **7** genetic **9** ancestral, heritable, inherited **10** congenital, handed-down **11** established, inheritable, traditional

here lies
Latin: 8 hic jacet

heresy 7 dissent, fallacy **8** apostasy **10** dissension, heterodoxy, iconoclasm, irreligion **11** unorthodoxy **13** nonconformity **15** unsound doctrine

heretic 7 skeptic **8** apostate, recreant, recusant, renegade **9** dissenter **10** backslider **11** freethinker, misbeliever **12** deviationist **13** nonconformist

heretical 7 radical **9** dissident **10** unorthodox **12** iconoclastic **13** nonconforming, nonconformist **14** unconventional

heretofore
French: 8 ci-devant

Hereward the Wake
author: 15 Charles Kingsley

Hergesheimer, Joseph
author of: 8 Java Head **19** The Three Black Pennys

heritage 6 estate, legacy **7** portion **9** patrimony, tradition **10** birthright **11** inheritance **16** family possession

Hermaphroditus
father: 6 Hermes
mother: 9 Aphrodite

loved by: 8 Salmacis
joined with: 8 Salmacis
became: 8 bisexual

Hermes
origin: 5 Greek
occupation: 6 herald
messenger of: 4 gods
father: 4 Zeus
mother: 4 Maia
son: 3 Pan **6** Prylis **7** Abderus, Daphnis **14** Hermaphroditus
birthplace: 7 Arcadia
god of: 4 luck **5** roads, sleep **6** dreams, wealth **7** cunning, thieves **8** commerce **9** fertility, invention, merchants
invented: 4 lyre
sandals had: 5 wings
epithet: 6 Dolius **8** Agoraeus **9** Spelaites **10** Criophorus **11** Argiphontes **12** Argeiphontes, Psychopompus
corresponds to: 5 Thoth **7** Mercury

hermetic 6 mystic, occult **7** obscure **8** abstruse, airtight, esoteric, mystical **9** recondite

Hermia
character in: 21 A Midsummer Night's Dream
author: 11 Shakespeare

hermine, L'
author: 11 Jean Anouilh

Hermione
character in: 14 The Winter's Tale
author: 11 Shakespeare

Hermione
father: 8 Menelaus
mother: 5 Helen
husband: 7 Orestes
son: 9 Tisamenus

hermit 7 eremite, recluse **8** cenobite, monastic, solitary **9** anchorite **11** desert saint **14** solitudinarian **16** religious recluse

hermitage 5 abbey **6** friary, priory **7** convent, retreat **8** cloister **9** monastery

hero, heroine 4 idol, star **7** gallant **8** brave man, champion, great man, male lead, male star, noble man **9** daredevil, daring man, main actor **10** adventurer, leading man **11** protagonist, valorous man **12** man of courage, man of the hour **13** chivalrous man, popular figure **15** fearless fighter, idealized person, intrepid warrior, legendary person

Hero
character in: 19 Much Ado About Nothing
author: 11 Shakespeare

Hero
vocation: 9 priestess
priestess of: 9 Aphrodite
lover: 7 Leander
death by: 7 suicide **8** drowning

Herod Antipas
father: 13 Herod the great

mother: 8 Malthace
grandfather: 9 Antipater
wife: 8 Herodias
half brother: 6 Philip
beheaded: 14 John the Baptist

Herodias
husband: 6 Philip **12** Herod Antipas
daughter: 6 Salome

Herodotus
called: 15 Father of History
wrote history of: 11 Persian Wars

Herod Philip
daughter: 6 Salome

heroic 4 bold, epic **5** brave, grand, noble **6** daring **7** classic, exalted, gallant, Homeric, valiant **8** elevated, fearless, highbrow, inflated, intrepid, mythical, resolute, valorous **9** bombastic, dauntless, dignified, grandiose, high-flown, legendary, undaunted **10** chivalrous, courageous **11** exaggerated, extravagant, lionhearted, pretentious, unflinching **12** mythological, ostentatious, stouthearted

heroic act 4 feat **7** exploit **9** brave deed

heroism 5 valor **6** daring **7** bravery, courage, prowess **8** boldness, chivalry, nobility **9** fortitude, gallantry **11** intrepidity **12** fearlessness **13** dauntlessness **14** courageousness **15** lionheartedness

Herophilus
field: 7 anatomy
nationality: 5 Greek
experimented with: 15 post-mortem exams

Heros
author: 8 Menander

herpetophobia
fear of: 8 reptiles

Herrenvolk 10 master race

Herrick, Robert
author of: 10 Hesperides **20** Corinna's Going A Maying **26** Gather ye rosebuds while ye may

Herriman, George
creator/artist of: 8 Krazy Kat

Herschel, William
field: 9 astronomy
nationality: 7 British
discovered: 6 Uranus

Hersey, John
author of: 7 The Wall **9** Hiroshima **13** A Bell for Adano, The Conspiracy **22** My Petition for More Space

Hertz, Heinrich
field: 7 physics
nationality: 6 German
discovered: 13 electric waves **18** wireless telegraphy
named for him: 13 hertzian waves
unit of: 9 frequency

Herzog
author: 10 Saul Bellow

he sculptured it
Latin: **8** sculpsit

Hesiod
author of: **8** Theogony **12** Works and Days

hesitancy 10 indecision, reluctance, unsureness **11** uncertainty, vacillation **12** irresolution

hesitant 5 loath **6** unsure **7** halting **8** doubtful, wavering **9** diffident, faltering, reluctant, tentative, uncertain, undecided **10** hesitating, indecisive, irresolute **11** half- hearted, hanging back, vacillating **15** shilly-shallying **17** lacking confidence, sitting on the fence

hesitate 4 balk, halt **5** delay, pause, shy at, waver **6** falter **7** scruple, stick at **8** be unsure, hang back **9** stickle at, vacillate **10** dillydally, shrink from, think twice **11** be reluctant, be uncertain, be undecided, be unwilling, stop briefly **12** be irresolute, shilly-shally **16** straddle the fence

hesitating 8 doubtful, hesitant **10** indecisive, irresolute, on the fence

he speaks
Latin: **8** loquitur

Hesperia
also: **5** Italy **16** Iberian Peninsula

Hesperides
author: **13** Robert Herrick

Hesperides
form: **6** nymphs
guarded: **12** golden apples
guarded with: **5** Ladon **6** dragon
names: **5** Aegle **6** Hestia **7** Erythea, Hespera **8** Arethusa **9** Hespereia, Hesperusa
islands of the: **7** blessed
form of: **6** heaven

Hess, Victor Francis
field: **7** physics
discovered: **10** cosmic rays
awarded: **10** Nobel Prize

Hesse, Hermann
author of: **6** Demian **9** Rosshalde **10** Siddhartha **11** Steppenwolf **12** Magister Ludi **14** Peter Camenzind **15** Beneath the Wheel **16** Death and the Lover, Journey to the East, The Glass Bead Game

Hesselberg, Melvyn Edouard
real name of: **13** Melvyn Douglas

Hessian
native of: **5** Hesse **7** Germany
soldier: **9** mercenary
aided: **7** British
in: **16** Revolutionary War

Hestia
origin: **5** Greek
goddess of the: **6** hearth
father: **6** Cronos, Cronus, Kronos
mother: **4** Rhea
corresponds to: **5** Vesta

Heston, Charlton
real name: **13** Charles Carter
born: **10** Evanston IL
roles: **5** El Cid, Moses **6** Ben-Hur (Oscar) **15** Planet of the Apes **18** The Ten Commandments **21** The Agony and the Ecstasy **22** The Greatest Show on Earth

heterogeneous 5 mixed **6** motley, unlike, varied **7** diverse, jumbled **8** assorted **9** composite, disparate, divergent, unrelated **10** dissimilar, variegated **11** diversified **13** miscellaneous

hew 2 ax **3** cut, lop **4** chop, form, hack, mold **5** carve, model, prune, sever, shape **6** chisel, cut out, devise **7** cut down, fashion, whittle **8** chop down **9** sculpture

He Who Gets Slapped
author: **14** Leonid Andreyev

he wrote it
Latin: **8** scripsit

hex 4 harm, jinx, sign **5** curse, spell, witch **6** hoodoo, voodoo, whammy **7** bewitch, enchant, evil eye, ill wind, possess **8** sorcerer **9** sorceress **11** malediction

Hexateuch 27 first six books of Old Testament
see also **7** Books of **12** Old Testament

heyday 4 acme **5** bloom, crest, flush, prime, vigor **6** zenith **9** flowering, salad days

Heyerdahl, Thor
author of: **7** Kon-Tiki **16** The Ra Expeditions

Hi and Lois
creator: **9** Dik Browne **10** Mort Walker
character:
  brother: **12** Beetle Bailey
  children: **3** Dot **4** Chip **5** Ditto **6** Trixie
  dog: **4** Dawg
  friend: **7** Thirsty

hiatus 3 gap **4** void **5** blank, break, lapse, space **6** lacuna, vacuum **7** interim **8** interval **10** disruption **12** interruption

Hiawatha, The Song of
author: **24** Henry Wadsworth Longfellow
character: **5** Nahma **7** Kwasind, Nokomis, Wenonah **8** Mondamin **9** Chibiabos, Minnehaha **11** Mudjekeewis **12** Pau-Puk-Keewis, Pearl-Feather

hibernate 5 sleep **6** retire **8** withdraw **13** become dormant

hibernating 6 asleep **7** dormant **8** inactive, sleeping **9** quiescent

Hibernia *see* **7** Ireland

hibiscus
varieties: **7** Chinese **8** Hawaiian, Japanese

hic jacet 8 here lies

hick 4 boor, rube **5** yokel **6** rustic **7** hayseed

Hickock, James B 5 scout **7** marshal
called: **8** Wild Bill

hickory 5 Carya
varieties: **4** Pale, Sand **5** Broom, Swamp, Water **6** Pignut **7** Chinese **8** Mountain, Shagbark **9** Mockernut, Shellbark **10** White-heart **12** Small-fruited

Hicks, Edward
born: **11** Attleboro PA
artwork: **19** The Peaceable Kingdom

hidden away 6 buried, cached **7** stashed **8** closeted, pocketed, secluded, secreted **9** concealed **10** out of sight **11** stashed away **12** inaccessible, undiscovered

hidden meaning 6 enigma, puzzle, riddle, secret **7** mystery

hidden motive
French: **13** arriere pensee

hide 4 mask, pelt, skin, veil **5** cache, cloak, cloud, cover **6** lie low, screen, shroud **7** conceal, curtain, leather, obscure, repress, seclude, secrete **8** disguise, suppress

hideaway 7 hideout, retreat **11** hiding place, secret place

hideous 4 grim, ugly, vile **5** awful **6** horrid, odious **7** ghastly, macabre **8** dreadful, gruesome, horrible, shocking **9** abhorrent, appalling, frightful, grotesque, loathsome, monstrous, repellent, repugnant, repulsive, revolting, sickening **10** abominable, detestable, disgusting, horrendous

hiding place 5 cache **8** hideaway **9** hidey hole **10** repository **11** secret place

Hieronimo
character in: **17** The Spanish Tragedy
author: **3** Kyd

hier wird Deutsch gesprochen 18 German is spoken here

Higgins, Henry
character in: **9** Pygmalion **10** My Fair Lady
author: **4** Shaw

Higgs
character in: **7** Erewhon
author: **6** Butler

high 3 gay, top **4** main, tall **5** aloft, chief, far up, grand, great, jolly, lofty, merry, noble, prime, sharp, undue, way up **6** alpine, august, elated, jovial, joyful, joyous, shrill **7** capital, eminent, exalted, excited, extreme, gleeful, leading, notable, playful, primary, serious, soaring, soprano **8** cheerful, elevated, exultant, foremost, imposing, jubilant, mirthful, peerless, piercing, strident, superior, towering, uncurbed **9** ascendant, excellent, excessive, exuberant, important, overjoyed, principal, prominent, unbridled, uppermost **10** exorbitant, immoderate, inordinate, preeminent **11** cloud-capped, exaggerated, exhilarated, extravagant, high-pitched, illustrious, intemperate, predominant, significant, sky- scraping **12** earsplitting, high-reaching, lighthearted, unreasonable, unrestrained **13** consequential, distinguished

high-and-mighty 5 lofty **6** lordly **7** haughty **8** arrogant **9** imperious **11** overbearing

highborn 5 noble **8** highbred, well-born **9** patrician **10** of high rank, upper-class **12** aristocratic, of high degree, silk-stocking **13** of gentle blood

highbred 5 noble, regal **6** lordly **7** refined **8** highborn, wellborn **9** patrician **11** aristocracy, blue-blooded

highbrow 4 snob **5** brain **7** bookish, Brahmin, egghead, elitist, erudite, scholar, thinker **8** cultured, mandarin, snobbish **9** scholarly **10** cultivated, double-dome, mastermind **12** intellectual **13** knowledgeable

highest good
Latin: **11** summum bonum

highest point
Latin: **11** ne plus ultra

high fashion
French: **12** haute couture

high-flown 4 wild **5** lofty, proud **6** absurd, florid, lordly, turgid, unreal **7** flowery, orotund, pompous **8** elevated, fabulous, inflated **9** bombastic, excessive, fantastic, grandiose **10** flamboyant, immoderate, inordinate, outrageous **11** exaggerated, extravagant, highfalutin, pretentious, sententious **12** magniloquent, preposterous, presumptuous, unreasonable, unrestrained **13** grandiloquent, self-important

High German
language family: **12** Indo-European
branch: **8** Germanic
group: **15** Western Germanic
subgroup: **11** German-Dutch
division: **6** German **7** Yiddish

high-hat 5 aloof **6** formal, la-di-da, snooty **7** haughty **8** snobbish **12** supercilious

highjinks, hijinks 6 antics, capers, pranks, stunts **11** shenanigans **12** monkeyshines

highland, Highlands 4 rise **7** heights, plateau, uplands **8** headland **9** tableland **10** promontory **11** hill country **17** mountainous region
refers especially to: **8** Scotland
dance: **5** fling

highlight 4 peak **6** accent, climax, stress **7** feature, point up **9** emphasize, high point, underline **10** accentuate, focal point, make bright

highly qualified 3 fit **4** able **7** trained **8** eligible, prepared, skillful **9** practiced **10** proficient **11** experienced **12** accomplished

highly regarded 6 prized **7** admired, revered **8** esteemed **9** respected, treasured **13** well thought of

highly valued 4 dear **5** loved **6** adored **7** beloved, revered **8** esteemed, precious **9** cherished, treasured

highly visible 7 glaring, obvious **8** distinct **9** prominent **11** conspicuous, outstanding

high-minded 4 fair, just **5** lofty, moral, noble **6** honest, worthy **7** ethical, sincere, upright **8** truthful, virtuous **9** exemplary, honorable, reputable, righteous, uncorrupt **10** chivalrous, idealistic, principled, scrupulous **13** conscientious, square-dealing

High Noon
director: **13** Fred Zinnemann
cast: **10** Gary Cooper (Will Kane), Grace Kelly **12** Lloyd Bridges **14** Thomas Mitchell
score: **14** Dimitri Tiomkin
Oscar for: **5** actor (Cooper)

high old time 4 ball, lark **5** fling, revel, spree **8** escapade

high-pitched 5 acute, sharp **6** shrill **7** clarion, squeaky **8** piercing

high place 3 tor **4** hill, peak, rise **5** aerie, bluff, cliff, knoll, ridge **6** height, summit, upland **7** hillock, hummock, plateau **8** eminence, mountain **9** elevation **10** prominence, promontory

high point, highest point 3 cap, top **4** acme, apex, peak **5** crest, crown **6** apogee, climax, height, heyday, summit, tiptop, vertex, zenith **8** eminence, pinnacle **9** flowering **10** prominence **11** culmination

high position 4 note **8** eminence, high rank, standing **9** supremacy **10** ascendancy, importance, notability, prominence **11** distinction, preeminence

high-powered 7 driving, dynamic **8** forceful **9** ambitious, assertive, energetic, go-getting **10** aggressive **11** hard- driving

high praise 5 kudos, paean **6** eulogy **7** hosanna, plaudit **8** encomium **9** laudation, panegyric **11** acclamation

high-priced 4 dear, high **6** costly, pricey **9** expensive **10** exorbitant, overpriced **11** extravagant

high-principled 5 moral, noble **6** chaste, honest, worthy **7** ethical, upright **9** honorable, reputable **10** idealistic **11** responsible, trustworthy **13** conscientious

high quality 5 merit **7** quality **9** greatness **10** excellence, perfection **11** distinction, superiority

high-ranking 3 top **5** grand, great, lofty, regal, royal **6** august **7** eminent, exalted, supreme **8** elevated, es-

teemed, imposing **9** important, paramount, venerable **10** preeminent **11** illustrious **13** distinguished

High Sierra
director: **10** Raoul Walsh
cast: **9** Ida Lupino **10** Alan Curtis, Joan Leslie **13** Arthur Kennedy **14** Humphrey Bogart (Mad Dog Earle)
remade as: **17** Colorado Territory **19** I Died a Thousand Times

high society 5 elite **6** jet set **9** haut monde, top drawer **11** aristocracy **14** creme de la creme
French: **9** haut monde

High Society
director: **14** Charles Walters
cast: **10** Bing Crosby, Grace Kelly **11** Celeste Holm **12** Frank Sinatra, Louis Calhern **14** Louis Armstrong
score: **10** Cole Porter
remake of: **20** The Philadelphia Story
song: **8** True Love **10** Did You Evah? **16** You're Sensational

high-speed 4 fast **5** quick, rapid, swift **6** speedy **7** express

high-spirited 5 vital **6** lively **8** animated **9** exuberant, vivacious **12** effervescent, enthusiastic

high spirits 5 vigor **6** gaiety **7** delight, elation **8** gladness, vitality, vivacity **9** animation **10** enthusiasm, exaltation, excitement, joyousness, liveliness **12** exhilaration **16** lightheartedness

high-strung 4 edgy **5** jumpy, moody, tense **6** uneasy **7** jittery, nervous, uptight **8** neurotic, restless, skittish **9** emotional, excitable, impatient, wrought-up **10** hysterical **13** oversensitive, temperamental **14** easily agitated, hypersensitive

High Tor
author: **15** Maxwell Anderson

highway 7 freeway, parkway, thruway **8** hard road, highroad, main road, speedway, turnpike **9** paved road **10** expressway, interstate, main artery **12** four-lane road, thoroughfare
British: **9** coach road, royal road **12** King's highway **13** Queen's highway

highwayman 5 crook, thief **6** bandit, outlaw, robber **7** brigand, footpad

hike 4 rise, roam, rove, trek, walk **5** leg it, march, raise, tramp **6** draw up, hoof it, jerk up, pull up, ramble, trudge, wander **7** hitch up, raise up **8** addition, increase **9** expansion **10** escalation **12** augmentation **13** journey on foot **14** go by shank's mare

hilarious 3 gay **5** jolly, merry, noisy **6** jocund, jovial, joyful, joyous, lively **7** comical, gleeful, riotous **8** jubilant, mirthful **9** exuberant, laughable, very funny **10** boisterous, hysterical, rollicking, uproarious, vociferous **11** exhilarated **12** high-spirited **13** highly amusing **14** laugh- provoking

hilarity 3 fun, gig, joy **4** glee, riot **5**

laugh, mirth, noisy **6** comedy, gaiety, giggle, levity **7** chortle, chuckle, jollity **8** hysteria, laughter **9** amusement, funniness, joviality, jubilance, merriment **10** exuberance **12** exhilaration, humorousness **14** uproariousness

Hilbert, David
field: **8** geometry **11** mathematics
nationality: **6** German
formulated: **12** modern axioms

Hilda Lessways
author: **13** Arnold Bennett

hill 4 bank, dune, heap, pile, ramp, rise **5** bluff, butte, cliff, climb, grade, knoll, mound, mount, slope **6** height **7** hillock, hilltop, hummock, incline, upgrade **8** eminence, foothill, highland, hillside **9** acclivity, declivity, downgrade, elevation **10** prominence, promontory

Hill, Arthur
born: **6** Canada **7** Melfort **12** Saskatchewan
roles: **13** All the Way Home **15** The Ugly American **17** Look Homeward Angel **25** Who's Afraid of Virginia Woolf?

Hill, George Roy
director of: **8** The Sting (Oscar) **23** The World According to Garp **29** Butch Cassidy and the Sundance Kid

Hillary, Edmund
born: **10** New Zealand
climbed: **9** Mt. Everest
explored: **9** South Pole

Hiller, Arthur
director of: **25** The Americanization of Emily

hillock 4 hill, rise **5** knoll, mound **7** hummock **8** eminence

Hill Street Blues
character: **5** LaRue, Renko **9** Bobby Hill, Jablonski, Joe Coffey, Lucy Bates **10** Fay Furillo, Mick Belker, Washington **11** (Lt) Norman Buntz **12** Howard Hunter, (Captain) Frank Furillo **13** Henry Goldblum **14** Joyce Davenport
cast: **8** Joe Spano **10** Bruce Weitz, Ed Marinaro, Kiel Martin **11** Betty Thomas, Charles Haid, Dennis Franz **12** Robert Prosky **13** James B Sikking, Michael Warren, Veronica Hamel **14** Taurean Blacque **15** Daniel J Travanti

Hilton, James
author of: **11** Lost Horizon **14** Good-Bye Mr Chips

Himalayas 9 mountains
countries **5** India, Nepal, Tibet, **6** Bhutan **8** Pakistan
peak: **7** Everest **9** Annapurna
native: **6** sherpa
Climber: **7** Hillary **13** Tenzing Norkay
legendary creature: **4** yeti **17** Abominable Snowman

Hind see **5** India

Hind and the Panther, The
author: **10** John Dryden

Hindemith, Paul
born: **5** Hanau **7** Germany
composer of: **8** The Demon **9** Cardillac **10** Heriodiade **12** Ludus Tonalis, Neues vom Tage, News of the Day **13** Sancta Susanna **14** Cupid and Psyche, Mathis Der Maler **15** In Praise of Music **17** Murder Hope of Women **18** Die Harmonie der Welt, Nobilissima Visione **19** The Four Temperaments **23** Morder Hoffnung der Frauen

hinder 3 bar **4** curb, foil, stay, stop **5** block, check, delay, deter, spike, stall **6** arrest, detain, fetter, hamper, hobble, hog-tie, hold up, impede, retard, stifle, stymie, thwart **7** inhibit **8** encumber, handicap, hold back, obstruct, restrain, slow down **9** frustrate, hamstring **13** interfere with

Hindi
language family: **12** Indo-European
branch: **11** Indo-Iranian
group: **5** Indic
official language of: **5** India

hindmost 4 last, rear **7** tail end **12** farthest back

hindpart 4 tail **6** far end **7** rear end **8** backside, buttocks, haunches **9** afterpart, posterior

hindquarters 4 rear, rump **7** rear end, tail end **8** back legs, backside, buttocks, haunches **9** posterior

hindrance 3 bar **4** clog, curb, snag **5** catch **6** fetter **7** barrier, shackle **8** blockade, blockage, handicap, obstacle **9** barricade, restraint, retardant **10** constraint, difficulty, impediment, limitation **11** encumbrance, obstruction, restriction **12** interference **14** stumbling block

hinge 4 hang, rest, turn **5** pivot, swing **6** depend **7** be due to **9** arise from **10** result from **11** be subject to, emanate from **13** revolve around

hint 3 bit, jot, tip **4** clue, idea, iota **5** grain, imply, pinch, tinge, touch, trace, whiff **6** little, notion, tip off **7** inkling, pointer, signify, soupcon, suggest, whisper **8** allusion, indicate, innuendo, intimate, insinuate, suspicion **10** impression, indication, intimation, smattering, suggestion **11** implication, indirection, insinuation **12** flea in the ear, slight amount **13** word to the wise

hinted 7 implied, oblique **8** implicit, indirect **9** suggested

hinterland 6 sticks **7** boonies, country **8** interior, midlands **9** backwater, backwoods, boondocks, rural area **11** countryside

Hippalectryon
form: **7** monster

head and forelegs of: **5** horse
legs, tail and body of: **4** cock

Hippocampus
form: **7** monster
body of: **5** horse
tail of: **4** fish

Hippocrene
form: **6** spring
location: **12** Mount Helicon

hippodrome 5 arena **6** circus **7** stadium **8** coliseum

Hippogriff
form: **7** monster
combined: **5** horse **7** griffin

Hippolyte
also: **7** Antiope **9** Hippolyta
queen of: **7** Amazons
husband: **7** Theseus
son: **10** Hippolytus
Hercules stole her: **6** girdle

Hippolytus
author: **9** Euripides
character: **7** Artemis, Phaedra, Theseus **9** Aphrodite

Hippolytus
father: **7** Theseus
mother: **9** Hippolyta
stepmother: **7** Phaedra
loved by: **7** Phaedra
killed by: **8** Poseidon

hire 3 fee, get, let, pay **4** cost, gain, rent **5** lease, wages **6** charge, employ, engage, income, obtain, profit, retain, reward, salary, secure, take on **7** appoint, charter, payment, procure, stipend **8** earnings, receipts **9** emolument **10** recompense **12** compensation, remuneration

hireling 4 goon, thug **6** flunky, lackey, menial, minion, stooge **7** gorilla **8** henchman, retainer **9** strong-arm **10** hatchet man

Hiroshima
author: **10** John Hersey

hirsute 5 bushy, downy, hairy, nappy, wooly **6** shaggy, woolly **7** bearded, bristly, prickly, unshorn **8** bristled, unshaven **9** whiskered **11** bewhiskered

His Girl Friday
director: **11** Howard Hawks
cast: **9** Cary Grant **12** Gene Lockhart, Ralph Bellamy **15** Rosalind Russell
remake of: **12** The Front Page

Hispania see **5** Spain

hiss 3 boo **4** mock, razz **6** deride, heckle, hoot at, jeer at, revile **7** catcall, scoff at, sneer at **9** shout down **10** Bronx cheer **16** give the raspberry

histology
study of: **6** tissue

historian
American: **4** Webb **5** Adams **6** Brooks, De Voto, Durant, Fisher, Miller, Nevins, Sparks, Turner **7** Morison, Parkman, Taussig, Tuch-

man **8** Bancroft, Channing, Prescott, Robinson **10** Hofstadter
British: 4 Bede (the Venerable) **6** Gibbon, Turner **7** Toynbee **8** Macaulay **9** Trevelyan
Chinese: 10 Ssu-ma Ch'ien, Ssu-Ma Kuang
French: 5 Bayle, Blanc, Bloch, Taine **7** Braudel **8** Mabillon, Michelet, Voltaire **11** Tocqueville
German: 5 Ranke **7** Mommsen **8** Spengler **10** Burckhardt, Treitschke
Greek: 8 Polybius **9** Herodotus **10** Thucydides
Islamic: 8 al Tabari **10** Ibn Khaldun
Italian: 4 Polo, Vico **5** Croce **11** Machiavelli **12** Guicciardini
Latin: 4 Livy **7** Sallust, Tacitus
Scottish: 7 Carlyle

historic 5 famed **7** notable **8** renowned **9** memorable, well-known **10** celebrated **11** outstanding

historical 4 past, real, true **6** actual, bygone, former **7** ancient, factual **8** attested, recorded **9** authentic **10** chronicled, documented

historical period 3 age, era **4** date, time **5** epoch, stage

history 4 epic, saga, tale **5** story **6** annals, change, growth, record, resume, review **7** account, the past **8** old times **9** chronicle, days of old, narration, narrative, portrayal, tradition, yesterday **10** bygone days, days of yore, olden times, the old days, yesteryear **11** bygone times, development, former times, local events, major events, world events **12** actual events **13** an unusual past, human progress **14** military action, national events, recapitulation **15** political change

History of Colonel Jacque, The
  author: 11 Daniel Defoe
History of Henry VII
  author: 12 Francis Bacon
History of Mr Polly, The
  author: 7 H G Wells
  character: 6 Miriam **8** Uncle Jim **13** The Plump Woman
History of the English-Speaking Peoples, A
  author: 17 Winston S Churchill
His Toy, His Dream, His Rest
  author: 12 John Berryman

histrionics 4 fuss **6** acting, tirade **7** bluster, bombast **8** outburst **9** dramatics, hamminess, staginess, theatrics **10** dramaturgy, playacting **11** performance, rodomontade **13** melodramatics, temper tantrum, theatricality **16** ranting and raving

hit 3 bat, jab, lob, rap, tap **4** bang, bash, beat, belt, blow, boon, bump, butt, clip, club, coup, cuff, damn, drub, find, flog, hurt, move, pelt, poke, slam, slap, slug, sock, stir, swat **5** abash, baste, clout, crack, crush, flail, knock, paste, pound, punch, reach, rouse, smack, smash, smite, thump, touch, upset, whack **6** affect, arouse, assail, attack, attain, batter, cudgel, effect, impact, incite, pommel, revile, strike, thrash, thwack, wallop, winner **7** achieve, assault, censure, clobber, condemn, execute, godsend, impress, inflame, provoke, quicken, realize, shatter, success, triumph, trounce, victory **8** arrive at, bang into, blessing, bring off, denounce, lambaste, overcome, reproach **9** criticize, deal a blow, devastate, lash out at, overwhelm, sensation, smash into **11** collide with, connect with, deal a stroke, strike out at **12** go straight to **13** make a bull's-eye, send to the mark **14** popular success, strike together **16** mount an offensive

hit back 7 counter, get even, pay back **9** fight back, retaliate **10** strike back

hitch 3 tie, tug **4** curb, draw, halt, haul, hike, jerk, knot, loop, pull, snag, stop, yank, yoke **5** catch, check, clamp, delay, raise, tying **6** attach, couple, fasten, mishap, secure, tether **7** bracket, connect, harness, joining, mistake, problem, trouble **8** coupling, handicap, make fast, obstacle **9** attaching, fastening, hindrance, mischance, restraint **10** connection, difficulty, impediment, limitation **11** restriction **12** complication, interruption, loop together, put in harness **14** stumbling block

Hitchcock, Alfred
  director of: 6 Frenzy, Marnie, Psycho **7** Rebecca, Vertigo **8** Lifeboat, The Birds **9** Notorious, Suspicion **10** Family Plot, Rear Window, Spellbound **13** To Catch a Thief **14** Dial M for Murder, Shadow of a Doubt **15** The Lady Vanishes **16** North by Northwest **17** Strangers on a Train **18** The Thirty-Nine Steps **19** The Trouble with Harry **20** Foreign Correspondent

hither 2 on **4** here, near **5** close **6** closer, nearby, nearer, onward **7** close by, forward **8** over here **11** to this place **12** to the speaker

hitherto 6 ere now, hereto **7** thus far, till now, up to now **8** until now **10** before this, heretofore

Hitler, Adolf
  author of: 9 Mein Kampf

hit man 6 killer, slayer **8** assassin, hired gun, murderer **11** executioner **12** exterminator

Hitman
  nickname of: 12 Thomas Hearns
hit-or-miss 3 lax **6** casual, fitful **7** aimless, cursory **8** slapdash **9** haphazard **10** incomplete **11** purposeless, superficial, unorganized **12** unsystematic **15** catch-as-catch-can

hive 3 hub **5** heart **6** center, colony **7** cluster **9** busy place **11** swarm of bees

H M S Pinafore
  subtitle: 23 The Lass That Loved a Sailor
  operetta by: 18 Gilbert and Sullivan
  character: 11 Dick Deadeye **14** Ralph Rackstraw **15** Captain Corcoran, Little Buttercup, Sir Joseph Porter **17** Josephine Corcoran

Hoagland, Edward
  author of: 15 African Calliope **17** The Tugman's Passage

hoar 3 old **4** aged, rime **5** frost, moldy, mushy, passe, stale, white **6** old hat **7** ancient, antique, elderly, grayish **8** grizzled **9** out of date

hoard 4 fund, heap, mass, pile **5** amass, buy up, cache, lay up, store **6** save up, supply **7** acquire, collect, lay away, reserve **8** quantity **9** amassment, gathering, stockpile, store away **10** accumulate, collection **12** accumulation

hoarse 5 gruff, harsh, husky, raspy, rough **6** croaky **7** cracked, rasping, raucous, throaty **8** gravelly, guttural, scratchy

hoary 3 old **4** aged, gray, hoar **5** dated, passe, white **6** grayed, old hat **7** ancient, antique, grizzly **8** grizzled, whitened **9** out-of-date **11** gray with age **12** white with age

hoax 3 gyp **4** bilk, dupe, fake, fool, gull, yarn **5** bluff, cheat, cozen, fraud, prank, spoof, trick **6** canard, delude, humbug, take in **7** deceive, defraud, fiction, mislead, swindle **8** hoodwink **9** bamboozle, chicanery, deception, fish story, victimize **10** hocus-pocus

Hoban, James
  architect of: 13 The White House, Great Hotel (Washington, DC)

Hobbes, Thomas
  author of: 9 Leviathan

Hobbit, The
  prelude to: 14 Lord of the Rings
  author: 10 J R R Tolkien
  character: 5 Bilbo **7** Baggins
  wizard:: 7 Gandalf

hobble 4 bind, gimp, halt, limp **5** block, check, cramp **6** fetter, hamper, hinder, hog-tie, impede, lumber, stymie, thwart, toddle **7** inhibit, manacle, shackle, shamble, shuffle, stagger, stumble **8** encumber, handicap, hold back, lame gait, obstruct, restrain, restrict **9** constrain, frustrate, hamstring **10** uneven gait, walk lamely **13** interfere with

hobby 7 pastime, pursuit **8** sideline **9** amusement, avocation, diversion **10** relaxation **13** entertainment **14** divertissement

hobbyhorse 5 hobby 7 pastime 8 interest, toy horse 9 diversion 10 enthusiasm 11 distraction 12 rocking horse

hobgoblin 3 imp 4 ogre 5 bogey 6 goblin 7 bugaboo, bugbear 9 betenoire

hobnob 3 mix 4 club 6 mingle 7 consort, hang out 9 associate, rub elbows 10 fraternize

hobo 3 beg, bum 5 stiff, tramp 6 beggar, cadger, loafer 7 drifter, migrant, moocher, vagrant 8 derelict, vagabond, wanderer 9 scrounger 11 beachcomber

hoc est 6 this is

Ho Chi Minh City
　formerly: 6 Saigon
　river: 6 Saigon
　delta: 6 Mekong
　former capital of: 9 Indochina 11 Cochin China 12 South Vietnam

hockey
　athlete: 8 Bobby Orr, Brad Park 9 Bobby Hull, Ken Dryden, Mike Bossy 10 Doug Harvey, Eddie Shore, Ed Giacomin, Gordie Howe, Guy Lafleur, Ray Bourque, Rod Gilbert, Stan Mikita 11 Bobby Clarke, Brian Leetch, Denis Potvin, Eric Lindros, Jean Ratelle, Mark Messier 12 Emile Francis, Jean Beliveau, Marcel Dionne, Mario Lemieux, Phil Esposito, Wayne Gretzky 13 Bernard Parent, Jacques Plante, Larry Robinson, Pat La Fontaine 14 Alex Delvecchio, Maurice Richard 15 Bernie Geoffrion 18 Yvan Serge Courneyer

hockey team
　Anaheim: 11 Mighty Ducks
　Atlanta: 9 Thrashers
　Boston: 6 Bruins
　Buffalo: 6 Sabres
　Calgary: 6 Flames
　Carolina: 10 Hurricanes
　Chicago: 10 Black Hawks
　Columbus: 11 Blue Jackets
　Dallas: 5 Stars
　Detroit: 8 Red Wings
　Edmonton: 6 Oilers
　Florida: 8 Panthers
　Hartford: 7 Whalers
　Los Angeles: 5 Kings
　Montreal: 9 Canadiens
　New Jersey: 6 Devils
　New York: 7 Rangers 9 Islanders
　Ottawa: 8 Senators
　Philadelphia: 6 Flyers
　Phoenix: 7 Coyotes
　Pittsburgh: 8 Penguins
　Quebec: 9 Nordiques
　St Louis: 5 Blues
　San Jose: 6 Sharks
　Tampa Bay: 9 Lightning
　Toronto: 10 Maple Leafs
　Vancouver: 7 Canucks
　Washington: 8 Capitals
　Winnipeg: 4 Jets

hocus-pocus 4 bosh, bull, hoax, sham 5 chant, charm, cheat, magic, spell 6 bunkum, deceit, fakery, humbug 7 con game, hogwash, rubbish, swindle 8 delusion, flimflam, tommyrot, trickery 9 deception, moonshine, poppycock 10 dishonesty, flapdoodle, hanky-panky, magic spell, magic words, mumbo jumbo, subterfuge 11 bewitchment, incantation, legerdemain, magic tricks 12 fiddle-faddle, magic formula 13 sleight of hand

Hoder
　also: 5 Hodur
　origin: 12 Scandinavian
　brother: 5 Baldr 6 Balder, Baldur
　father: 4 Odin 5 Othin
　killed: 5 Baldr 6 Balder, Baldur

hodgepodge, hotchpotch 3 mix 4 hash, mess, olio 6 jumble, medley, muddle 7 melange, mixture 8 mishmash 9 composite, confusion, patchwork, potpourri 10 miscellany

Hoff, Jacobus Hendricus van't
　field: 9 chemistry
　nationality: 5 Dutch
　researched: 7 gas laws 10 carbon atom 14 thermodynamics
　awarded: 10 Nobel Prize

Hoffman, Dustin
　born: 12 Los Angeles CA
　roles: 5 Lenny 6 Ishtar 7 Tootsie 8 Papillon 10 Ratso Rizzo 11 The Graduate 12 Little Big Man 14 Kramer vs Kramer (Oscar), Midnight Cowboy 19 All the President's Men

Hofmann, Hans
　born: 7 Germany 11 Weissenberg
　artwork: 6 Spring 7 The Gate 13 Effervescence 14 Fantasia in Blue, Magenta and Blue 16 Sanctum Sanctorum

Hofstadter, Richard
　author of: 14 The Age of Reform

hog 3 pig, sow 4 arch, boar, trim 5 broom, sheep, swine 6 gorger, porker 7 baconer, glutton, take all 9 razorback 10 locomotive

Hogan, Paul
　country: 9 Australia
　roles: 10 Mick Dundee 15 Crocodile Dundee

Hogan's Heroes
　character: 7 (Peter) Newkirk 8 Lt Carter 10 Sgt (Hans) Schultz 11 Louis LeBeau 14 Col Robert Hogan 15 Col Wilhelm Klink
　cast: 8 Bob Crane 10 John Banner, Larry Hovis 11 Robert Clary 13 Richard Dawson 15 Werner Klemperer

Hogarth, William
　born: 6 London 7 England
　artwork: 12 Captain Coram 14 A Rake's Progress 15 Marriage a la Mode, The Beggar's Opera 16 A Harlot's Progress 19 Garrick as Richard III

hogshead 3 keg, tun, vat 4 butt, cask, drum 6 barrel

hogwash 3 rot 4 bull, bunk 5 hokum, hooey, stuff 6 bunkum, drivel, hot air, humbug 7 baloney, blather, spinach, twaddle 8 claptrap, nonsense, tommyrot 9 poppycock 10 applesauce 11 foolishness 13 horsefeathers 16 stuff and nonsense

hoi polloi 6 rabble, the mob 7 the herd 8 canaille, populace, riffraff, the crowd, the plebs 9 the masses, the proles, the vulgar 10 commonalty 12 the multitude 14 the lower orders, the proletariat, the rank and file 15 the common people, the lower classes, the working class

hoist 4 lift 5 heave, raise, run up 6 bear up, pull up, take up, uplift 7 elevate, raise up, upraise 9 bear aloft

Hokusai, Katsushika
　born: 3 Edo 5 Japan, Tokyo
　artwork: 5 Crabs, Manga 10 Waterfalls 11 Chushingura 25 Thirty-six Views of Mount Fuji

Holabird, William
　partner: 11 Martin Roche
　architect of: 12 Gage Building 13 Cable Building, Crerar Library (City Hall, Chicago) 14 Tacoma Building 15 McClurg Building 17 Marquette Building

Holbein, Hans (the Elder)
　born: 7 Germany 8 Augsburg
　son: 11 Hans Holbein (the Younger)
　artwork: 11 St Sebastian 14 Fountain of Life 18 Kaisheim Altarpiece 31 Presentation of Christ in the Temple

Holbein, Hans (the Younger)
　born: 7 Germany 8 Augsburg
　father: 11 Hans Holbein (the Elder)
　artwork: 7 Erasmus 9 Henry VIII 11 Jane Seymour 12 Dance of Death 13 The Dead Christ

hold 4 bear, bind, bond, curb, deem, grip, halt, have, hilt, keep, knob, lock, prop, rule, stay, sway, take, urge 5 block, brace, carry, check, clasp, cling, count, defer, grasp, guard, limit, offer, power, shaft, shore, stall, stand, stick, strap, think, unite, watch 6 adhere, affirm, assert, assume, cleave, clinch, clutch, deduct, detain, direct, enfold, handle, hinder, hold up, join in, manage, occupy, reckon, regard, retain, submit, take in, tender, thwart, uphold 7 advance, believe, carry on, command, conduct, confine, contain, control, declare, embrace, enclose, enforce, execute, hold off, include, inhibit, mastery, possess, present, presume, prevent, profess, propose, protect, repress, reserve, support, suppose, surmise, suspend, toehold, venture 8 advocate, conceive, conclude, consider, engage in, foothold, handhold, hold back, hold down, leverage, maintain, obligate, postpone, purchase, put forth, restrain, restrict, set aside, suppress, withhold **9** advantage, anchorage, authority, be in force, dominance, forestall, frustrate, influence, keep valid, ownership, stay fixed, stick fast **10** ascendancy, attachment, desist from, domination, possession, put forward, understand **11** accommodate, preside over

hold a candle to 5 equal, match **6** be up to **7** compare **8** approach **10** be as good as **11** come close to, compete with **12** be comparable **14** bear comparison

hold against 6 resent **8** begrudge

hold back 3 lag **4** curb, deny, keep, slow **5** check, dally, limit, stall **6** arrest, bridle, falter, refuse **7** contain, inhibit, keep out, reserve, retrain **8** hesitate, keep back, maintain, restrain, withhold **9** constrain

hold close 3 hug **5** clasp **6** cuddle, harbor **7** cherish, embrace, snuggle

Holden, William
   real name: 23 William Franklin Beedle Jr
   nickname: 4 Bill
   born: 9 O'Fallon IL
   roles: 6 Picnic **7** Network, Sabrina **9** Golden Boy **13** Born Yesterday **14** The Country Girl **15** Stalag Seventeen (Oscar), Sunset Boulevard **23** The Bridge on the River Kwai

hold fast 4 fuse, hold **5** cling, stick **6** adhere

hold firmly 4 grip **5** clasp, grasp **6** clench, clinch, clutch **10** grab hold of

hold forth 5 orate **7** expound **9** discourse, expatiate, speechify

hold in abeyance 5 table **6** recess, shelve **7** suspend **8** lay aside, postpone

hold in bondage 7 control, enchain, enslave, entrall **8** dominate **9** subjugate **12** make a slave of

holdings 6 assets **8** property **10** securities **11** commodities

hold in high regard 5 honor, prize, value **6** admire, esteem, revere **7** cherish, respect **8** look up to, treasure, venerate **10** rate highly, set store by **13** think highly of **18** attach importance to

hold one's own 4 cope **6** manage **7** contend **11** be a match for **20** maintain one's position **22** keep one's head above water

hold rapt 5 charm **7** beguile, bewitch, enchant **8** enthrall, entrance **9** captivate, enrapture, fascinate, spellbind, transport

hold to 4 bind **8** obligate

hold together 4 bind, fuse, glue, hold, join **5** cling, stick, unite **6** ce-

ment, cohere **7** combine **11** consolidate

holdup 3 rob **4** bear, halt, stay, stop **5** delay, heist, steal, theft **6** hijack, retain, uphold **7** robbery, stickup, support, sustain **8** stoppage **9** hindrance **12** interruption

hold up 4 prop, slow **5** block, brace, check, delay **6** bear up, detain, endure, hinder, impede, manage **7** bolster, present, stand up, support, sustain **8** keep back, obstruct **13** rob at gunpoint

hold up under 4 bear **6** endure, manage **8** tolerate

hold warmly 3 hug **5** clasp **6** cuddle **7** embrace, snuggle

hole 3 den, gap, pit **4** brig, cage, cave, flaw, keep, lair, rent, slit, slot **5** break, crack, fault, shaft **6** breach, burrow, cavern, cavity, crater, defect, dugout, lockup, pocket, prison, tunnel **7** dungeon, fallacy, opening, orifice, slammer **8** aperture, dark cell, puncture **9** concavity, open space **10** depression, excavation **11** discrepancy, hollow place, indentation, perforation **13** inconsistency

Holgrave, Mr
   character in: 24 The House of the Seven Gables
   author: 9 Hawthorne

holiday 3 gay **4** fete, gala **5** feria **6** cheery, fiesta, joyful, joyous, junket, outing **7** festive, holy day, jubilee **8** cheerful, feast day, festival, vacation **11** celebrating, celebration, merrymaking
   American: 6 Easter **8** Arbor Day, Labor Day **9** Christmas (Dec 25), Halloween (Oct 31) **10** Father's Day, Good Friday, Mother's Day **11** Columbus Day, Election Day, Memorial Day, New Year's Day (Jan 1), Veterans' Day (Nov 11) **12** Children's Day, Thanksgiving **15** Independence Day (July 4), St Valentine's Day (Feb 14) **23** National Grandparents' Day
   birthday: 8 Lincoln's **11** Robert E Lee's (Jan 19), Washington's **17** Martin Luther King's (Jan 15)
   Hawaiian: 13 Kamehameha Day (June 11)
   British: 8 Hogmanay (Dec 31) **9** Boxing Day (Dec 26) **11** Harvest Home **12** Guy Fawkes Day (Nov 5), Twelfth Night (Jan 5) **14** Queen's Birthday (June) **15** Commonwealth Day (May 24), Mothering Sunday **19** Feast of Saint Swithin (July 15)
   Canadian: 11 Victoria Day **14** Queen's Birthday, Remembrance Day
   Chinese: 7 New Year **15** Lantern Festival **17** Confucius' Birthday (Sept 28) **18** Dragon Boat Festival
   French: 11 Bastille Day (May 14)
   German: 11 Oktoberfest

   Greek: 7 Genesia **11** Feast of Pots
   Indian: 4 Holi **6** Basant, Diwali (New Year) **17** Hindu fire festival **22** Mahatma Gandhi's Birthday (Oct 2)
   Irish: 16 Saint Patrick's Day (March 17)
   Italian: 13 Liberation Day (April 25)
   Japanese: 11 Hina-Matsuri **12** Children's Day (May 5), Feast of Dolls (March 3) **15** Constitution Day (May 3) **17** Girls' Doll Festival
   Jewish: 5 Purim **6** Sukkot **7** Shavuot, Sukkoth **8** Hanukkah, Passover **9** Yom Kippur **12** Rosh Hashanah **20** Hamishah Assar B'Shevat, The New Year of the Trees **21** Feast of the Tabernacles
   Korean: 6 Ch'usok
   Latin American: 12 Day of the Race
   Moslem: 7 Mouloud **8** Id-al-Adha, Id-al-Fitr **12** Maulid-an-Nabi **14** month of Ramadan
   religious: 6 Advent **7** Lady Day (Mar 25) **8** Epiphany, Shabuoth **9** Candlemas, Mardi Gras, Martinmas (Nov 11), Pentecost **10** Whitsunday **11** All Souls' Day (Nov 2) **12** Ascension Day, Ash Wednesday, Feast of Weeks **13** Shrove Tuesday, Trinity Sunday **15** Annunciation Day (Mar 25) **16** Feast of All Saints **20** Feast of Corpus Christi **23** Day of Our Lady of Guadalupe (Dec 12) **27** Purification of the Virgin Mary **30** Feast of the Immaculate Conception (Dec 8)
   Roman: 7 Feralia **10** Saturnalia
   Scottish: 8 Hogmanay **12** Candlemas Day **19** Festival of the Virgin
   South American: 21 Simon Bolivar's Birthday (July 24)
   Sri Lankan: 5 Wesak
   Soviet Union: 6 May Day (May 1) **14** Lenin's Birthday (April 22) **39** Day of the Great October Socialist Revolution (Nov 7)
   Swedish: 13 Santa Lucia Day (Dec 13)
   Thai: 11 Visakha Puja
   Vietnamese: 3 Tet

holiness 8 sanctity **9** godliness **10** sacredness **11** blessedness, saintliness

Holland see **11** Netherlands

holler 4 bark, roar, yell **5** gripe, shout **6** bellow, cry out, grouse **8** complain **9** hue and cry

Holliday, Judy
   real name: 11 Judith Tuvim
   born: 9 New York NY
   roles: 8 Adam's Rib **13** Born Yesterday (Oscar) **15** Bells Are Ringing

Hollinshed, Raphael
   author of: 37 Chronicles of England Scotland and Ireland

hollow 3 dip, low, rut **4** cave, dale, deep, dell, dent, dull, glen, hole, sink, vain, vale, void **5** ditch, empty, false, muted **6** cavern, cavity, crater, dig out, dimple, furrow, futile, groove, pocket, sunken, vacant, vacuum, valley **7** channel, concave, useless **8** crevasse, empty out, excavate, gouge out, indented, not solid, nugatory, rumbling, scoop out, specious, unfilled **9** cavernous, concavity, deceptive, depressed, fruitless, pointless, valueless, worthless **10** depression, profitless, sepulchral, unavailing, unresonant **11** indentation, meaningless, nonresonant **12** unprofitable **13** curving inward, disappointing, reverberating **14** expressionless, unsatisfactory **15** inconsequential

Holloway, Stanley
born: **6** London **7** England
roles: **10** My Fair Lady **15** Alfred Doolittle **18** The Lavender Hill Mob

Hollow Men
author: **7** T S Eliot

hollowness 4 void **6** vacuum **7** vacancy **9** emptiness

hollow out 4 bore **5** drill **6** dig out **8** carve out, gouge out, scoop out **9** chisel out **13** tunnel through

holly 4 Ilex
varieties: **3** box, sea **4** dune **5** Cuban, Dutch, dwarf, false, Furin, Kashi, swamp, Tsuru **6** desert, horned, Oregon, Sarvis, Soyogo, summer **7** African, Chinese, English, Georgia, Madeira **8** American, European, hedgehog, Japanese, Kurogane, mountain **9** box- leaved, Highclere, miniature, moonlight, porcupine, Singapore **10** Costa Rican, luster-leaf, West Indian **11** large-leaved, Puerto Rican, screw-leaved **12** Canary Island, gold hedgehog, myrtle-leaved, smooth-leaved **14** silver hedgehog

hollyhock 6 mallow **7** Antwerp, figleaf **8** biennial **9** ficifolia, Malvaceae **10** alcea rosea

Hollywood's Mermaid
nickname of: **14** Esther Williams

Hollywood Squares
host: **9** Jon Bauman **12** John Davidson **13** Peter Marshall
regular: **8** Wally Cox **10** Joan Rivers **13** Cliff Arquette (Charley Weaver), Shadoe Stevens

Holmes, Oliver Wendell
author of: **12** Old Ironsides **30** The Autocrat of the Breakfast Table

Holmes, Sherlock
address: **11** (221B) Baker Street
appears in: **13** The Sign of Four **14** The Naval Treaty **15** A Study in Scarlet, The Speckled Band **16** Scandal in Bohemia, The Blue Carbuncle, The Copper Beeches **18** The Red-Headed League, The Solitary Cyclist **22** Hound of the Baskervilles
assistants: **21** Baker Street Irregulars
author: **16** (Sir) Arthur Conan Doyle
brother: **7** Mycroft
femme fatale **10** Irene Adler

foe: **17** Professor Moriarty
hat: **11** deerstalker
hobby: **6** violin
housekeeper/landlady: **9** Mrs Hudson
keeps tobacco in: **7** slipper **14** Turkish slipper
police: **17** Inspector Lestrade
sidekick: **12** Dr John Watson

Holmwood, Arthur
character in: **7** Dracula
author: **6** Stoker

holocaust 4 ruin **5** havoc **6** ravage **7** bonfire, carnage, inferno, killing **8** butchery, genocide, massacre **10** deadly fire, mass murder **11** devastation **12** annihilation **13** conflagration

Holofernes
character in: **16** Love's Labour's Lost
author: **11** Shakespeare

Holofernes
general of: **14** Nebuchadnezzar
killed by: **6** Judith

Holst, Gustav Theodore
born: **7** England **10** Cheltenham
composer of: **7** Savitri **10** Egdon Heath, Ode to Death, The Planets **11** Hammersmith **12** St Paul's Suite **13** Fugal Concerto **14** The Hymn of Jesus, The Perfect Fool **16** Somerset Rhapsody **17** The Cloud Messenger **19** Hymns from the Rig-Veda

holy 4 pure **5** godly, moral, pious **6** adored, devout, divine, sacred, solemn **7** angelic, blessed, from God, revered, saintly, sinless **8** faithful, hallowed, heavenly, reverent, virtuous **9** from above, guileless, religious, righteous, spiritual, undefiled, unspotted, unstained, unworldly, venerated, worshiped **10** heaven-sent, immaculate, inviolable, sacrosanct, sanctified, worshipped **11** consecrated, pure in heart, uncorrupted
Latin: **7** sanctus

Holy Ark
Hebrew: **10** Aron Kodesh

holy of holies
Latin: **16** sanctum sanctorum

Holy one *see* **5** Jesus

Holy Spirit, Holy Ghost 9 Paraclete **13** presence of God **23** third person of the Trinity
Latin: **15** Spiritus Sanctus
Greek: **12** Hagion Pneuma

holy war
Arabic: **5** jehad, jihad

Holy Willie's Prayer
author: **11** Robert Burns

Homadus
form: **7** centaur
killed by: **8** Hercules

homage 5 honor **6** esteem, praise, regard **7** respect, tribute, worship **8** devotion **9** adoration, adulation, deference, obeisance, reverence **10** exaltation, veneration **13** glorification

Homagyrius
epithet of: **4** Zeus
means: **9** assembler

hombre 3 man

home 5 abode, haunt, haven, house **6** asylum, cradle, refuge **7** habitat, hangout **8** domicile, dwelling, hospital **9** orphanage, poorhouse, residence **10** habitation, native land, sanatorium **11** institution **12** fountainhead **13** dwelling place, home sweet home **14** stamping ground **16** place of residence **18** natural environment **25** place where one hangs one's hat

Home Burial
author: **11** Robert Frost

homegrown 5 local **6** native **8** domestic **10** indigenous

Home Is the Sailor
author: **10** Jorge Amado

homelike 4 cozy **5** comfy, homey **6** simple **8** cheerful, domestic, familiar, informal, inviting **11** comfortable

homely 4 cozy, drab, snug **5** comfy, homey, plain **6** modest, rustic, simple **7** artless, natural **8** everyday, familiar, homelike, homespun, ordinary, uncomely **9** graceless **10** ill-favored, provincial, unaffected, unassuming, ungraceful, unhandsome **11** comfortable **12** plain-looking, unattractive **13** unpretentious

Homer
author of: **5** Iliad **7** Odyssey

Homer, Winslow
born: **8** Boston MA
painter of: **9** seascapes
artwork: **9** High Cliff **10** Breezing Up, Eight Bells **11** Marine Coast, Northeaster, The Life Line **13** The Fog Warning, The Gulf Stream **21** Inside the Bar Tynemouth, Prisoners from the Front

home rule 8 autonomy **11** sovereignty **12** independence **14** self-government

homespun 5 plain **6** folksy, homely, modest, native, simple **7** artless, natural **8** down-home, homemade **9** handwoven **10** hand-loomed, unaffected **11** hand-crafted, hand-wrought **13** unpretentious

homey 4 cozy **6** casual, folksy **8** down-home, homelike, homespun, informal **15** unsophisticated

homicide 6 killer, murder, slayer **7** slaying **8** foul play, murderer, regicide, vaticide **9** bloodshed, man killer, manslayer, matricide, parricide, patricide, uxoricide **10** fratricide **11** infanticide **12** manslaughter

homiletic 7 preachy **8** didactic **10** moralizing

homily 6 sermon **7** lecture **10** preachment **11** exhortation

homogeneous 4 akin, pure **7** kindred, similar, uniform, unmixed **8** all alike, constant, of a piece **9** identical, unvarying **10** consistent **13** of the same kind, unadulterated

homology 7 analogy **8** likeness, relation **10** similarity **12** relationship **14** correspondence

Honduras
name means: 6 depths
capital/largest city: 11 Tegucigalpa
others: 4 Tela, Yoro **5** Copan, Danli, Lapaz **6** Roatan **7** Gracias, La Ceiba **8** Trujillo, Yuscaran **9** Choluteca, Juticalpa **10** El Progreso **11** Comayaguela **12** Puerto Cortes, San Pedro Sula
measure: 4 vara **5** milla **6** mecate **7** cajuela
monetary unit: 4 peso **7** centavo, lempira
island: 3 Bay **5** Bahia, Utila **6** Roatan **7** Bonacca, Guanaja
lake: 5 Criba, Yojoa **6** Brewer
mountain: 4 Pija **6** Agalta **7** Celaque **9** Esperanza
highest point: 8 Las Minas
river: 4 Coco, Sico, Ulua **5** Aguan, Lempa, Negro, Tinto, Wanks **6** Patuca, Sulaco **7** Olancho, Paulaya, Segovia **8** Guiavope, Santiago **9** Choluteca **10** Chamelecon
sea: 7 Pacific **8** Atlantic **9** Caribbean
physical feature:
  coast: 5 North **8** Mosquito **10** Costa Norte
  gulf: 7 Fonseca **8** Honduras
  port: 7 Laceiba **8** Trujillo
people: 4 Maya, Paya, Sumo, Ulva **5** Carib, Lenca, Pipil **6** Tauira **7** Jicaque, mestizo, Miskito **8** Mosquito
  discoverer: 8 Columbus
  farmer: 9 campesino
language: 7 English, Spanish
religion: 13 Roman Catholic
place:
  ruins: 5 Copan **8** Tenampua
  feature:
    bird: 9 zenzontle
    dance: 5 sique **7** mascaro
    estate: 10 latifundia
    farm: 6 milpas **10** minifundia
    musical instrument: 7 caramba, marimba
    tree: 8 cockspur
  food:
    beans: 8 frijoles
    beef dish: 6 tapado
    corn: 5 maize
    stuffed corn cake: 10 naca tamale
    tripe stew: 8 mondongo
hone 4 long, moan, pine, tool, whet **5** stroke, strope, whine, yearn **6** hanker, grumble, mutter, sharpen **9** whetstone

Honegger, Arthur
born: 5 Havre **6** France
nationality: 5 Swiss
member of: 6 Les Six, The Six
composer of: 5 Rugby **6** Judith **7** L'Aiglon **8** Antigone **9** The Eaglet

10 Le Roi David **13** Pastorale d'ete **18** Jeanne d'Arc au Bucher, Liturgical Symphony **19** Pacific Two-Thirty-One

honest 4 fair, just, open, real, true **5** blunt, frank, legal, plain, solid, valid **6** candid, decent, lawful, proper, square **7** artless, ethical, genuine, sincere, upright **8** bona fide, clear-cut, faithful, innocent, reliable, straight, true-blue, truthful, virtuous **9** authentic, blameless, guileless, honorable, ingenuous, reputable, righteous **10** aboveboard, dependable, forthright, law-abiding, legitimate, on the level, principled, reasonable, scrupulous, unaffected, unreserved **11** plainspoken, trustworthy, undisguised **12** on the up-and-up, tried and true **13** conscientious, fair and square **15** straightforward, unsophisticated **16** as good as one's word, straight-shooting **17** open and aboveboard
  honest man: 10 Abe Lincoln
  Searcher: 8 Diogenes

honesty 4 word **5** honor **7** probity **8** fairness, good name, morality, scruples, veracity **9** innocence, integrity, rectitude, sincerity **10** principles **11** just dealing, uprightness **12** faithfulness, reputability, truthfulness **13** guiltlessness, square dealing **15** trustworthiness **16** incorruptibility, straight shooting

honeybee
classification: 6 social
live in: 4 hive **6** colony
headed by: 5 queen
male: 5 drone
laborer: 6 worker
food-gatherer: 7 forager
gather: 6 nectar, pollen
produce: 5 honey
queen's food: 10 royal jelly
pertaining to: 5 apian
keeper: 8 apiarist

honeyed 4 kind **5** sweet **6** sugary **7** cloying, fawning **10** flattering, saccharine **12** ingratiating **13** complimentary

honeyed words 4 line **7** blarney **8** cajolery, flattery, soft soap **9** sweet talk

Honey in the Horn
author: 7 H L Davis

Honeymooners, The
character: 8 Ed Norton **12** Alice Kramden, Ralph Kramden, Trixie Norton
cast: 8 Jane Kean **9** Art Carney **12** Sheila MacRae **13** Audrey Meadows, Jackie Gleason, Joyce Randolph
Ralph's job: 9 bus driver
Ed's job: 5 sewer
lodge: 8 Raccoons
Saying: 16 You're the greatest **38** One of these days Alice, pow, right in the kisser

honeysuckle 8 Lonicera **19** Aquilegia canadensis, Justicia californica **24** Rhododendron prinophyllum
varieties: 3 fly **4** bush, cape **5** coral, giant, grape, hairy, swamp **6** desert, French, purple, yellow **7** Arizona, Jamaica, trumpet **8** Himalaya, Japanese, swamp fly, Tatarian **9** chaparral, Tartarian **10** yellow cape **11** European fly **12** giant Burmese, long-flowered, South African **13** Hall's Japanese

Honeythunder, Mr
character in: 22 The Mystery of Edwin Drood
author: 7 Dickens

Hong Kong
name means: 13 incense harbor **14** fragrant harbor
capital: 8 Victoria
largest city:
  section: 7 Kowloon **8** Hong Kong, Victoria
others: 4 Tai O **5** Tai Po **8** Aberdeen, Pingshan, Yuenlong **9** Shataukok **10** Sheungshui
division: 7 Kowloon **8** Hong Kong **14** New Territories
government: 18 British crown colony
head of state: 14 British monarch **15** governor general
island: 5 Lamma **6** Lan Tao, Lantau, Middle, Poi Toi **8** Hong Kong **9** Ap Lei Chau **11** Stonecutter
mountain: 6 Castle **8** Victoria
highest point: 9 Tai Mo Shan
river: 5 Pearl **6** Canton **8** Sham Chun
sea: 10 South China
physical feature:
  bay: 4 Mirs **6** Quarry **7** Kowloon, Repulse **9** Deep Water
  harbor: 4 Tolo **8** Aberdeen, Hong Kong, Victoria
  peak: 8 Victoria
  peninsula: 7 Kowloon
people: 5 Hakka, Haklo, Punti, Tanka **7** British, Chinese **8** American, Japanese **9** Cantonese **10** Portuguese
language: 7 Chinese, English **9** Cantonese
religion: 5 Hindu, Islam **6** Taoism **8** Buddhism **12** Christianity
feature:
  airport: 6 Kai Tak
  clothing: 6 samfoo **9** cheongsam
  houseboat: 6 sampan
  rock: 5 Amahs **6** Sha Tin
  temple: 18 Ten Thousand Buddhas

Honiara
capital of: 14 Solomon Islands

honi soit qui mal y pense 31 shamed be the one who thinks evil of it
  motto of: 16 Order of the Garter

honk 4 toot **5** blare, blast **7** trumpet

honky-tonk 4 dive **7** gin mill **9** roadhouse, nightclub

honor 3 pay **4** cash, fame, laud, note, take **5** adore, exalt, extol, favor, glory, grant, leave, power, right, truth, value **6** accept, admire, credit, esteem, homage, praise, redeem, regard, renown, repute, revere, virtue **7** acclaim, commend, decency, dignify, glorify, honesty, liberty, probity, respect, tribute, worship **8** eminence, fairness, good name, goodness, justness, look up to, make good, pleasure, prestige, sanction, venerate, veracity **9** adoration, celebrity, constancy, deference, greatness, integrity, principle, privilege, rectitude, reverence, sincerity **10** admiration, compliment, exaltation, good report, importance, notability, permission, prominence, veneration **11** acknowledge, approbation, distinction, pay homage to, recognition, think much of, uprightness **12** commendation, faithfulness, high standing, pay tribute to, truthfulness **13** authorization, bow down before, glorification, have regard for, honorableness, make payment on **14** high-mindedness, scrupulousness **15** illustriousness, trustworthiness **17** a feather in one's cap, conscientiousness

honorable 4 good **5** noble, title **6** decent, honest, lordly, square **7** upright **9** elevated, reputable, respected **10** creditable **11** distinctive, illustrious, respectable, trustworthy **12** considerable **13** distinguished

hood 4 cowl, lout, punk **5** bully, rowdy, scarf, tough **6** vandal **7** hoodlum, ruffian **8** hooligan **9** barbarian, roughneck **10** delinquent **12** headcovering, neighborhood

Hood, Raymond
  architect of: 11 RCA Building (Rockefeller Center) **17** Daily News Building (NYC) **18** McGraw-Hill Building (NYC) **22** Chicago Tribune Building **24** American Radiator Building
  style: 13 International

hoodlum 4 hood, punk, thug **5** crook, rowdy, tough **6** gunman **7** bruiser, gorilla, mobster, ruffian **8** criminal, gangster, hooligan, plug-ugly **9** desperado, strong arm **10** delinquent

hoodwink 3 gyp **4** dupe, fool, gull, hoax, rook **5** cheat, cozen, trick **7** deceive, defraud, mislead, swindle **8** inveigle **9** bamboozle, victimize

hook 3 arc, bag, bow, nab, net **4** arch, bend, bill, curl, gaff, grab, loop, take, trap, wind **5** angle, catch, crook, curve, elbow, fluke, hitch, latch, seize, snare **6** buckle, collar, fasten, peavey, secure **7** capture, crampon, ensnare, grapnel, grapple, pothook **8** crescent, make fast **9** horseshoe

Hooke, Robert
  field: 7 physics **9** astronomy
  nationality: 7 British

discovered: 9 Orion star **15** Jupiter rotation **20** moon's center of gravity **21** earth's center of gravity
  invented: 10 microscope
  named for him: 15 law of elasticity

hooked 8 addicted **9** compelled, obsessive **10** compulsive, habituated **14** uncontrollable

hooked cross
  German: 10 Hakenkreuz

hook up 4 ally, dock, join **5** hinge **6** couple, link up **7** connect **8** assemble **10** articulate **11** fit together **14** fasten together

hooligan 4 hood, lout, punk **5** bully, rowdy, tough **6** vandal **7** hoodlum, ruffian **9** barbarian, roughneck **10** delinquent

hoopla 4 hype **8** ballyhoo **9** promotion, publicity **10** hullabaloo, propaganda **11** advertising **15** public relations

Hoosier Schoolmaster, The
  author: 15 Edward Eggleston

Hoosier State
  nickname of: 7 Indiana

hoot 3 boo, din **4** bawl, blow, hiss, honk, howl, jeer, moan, mock, razz, roar, wail, yelp, yowl **5** shout, sneer, taunt, whoop **6** bellow, chorus, cry out, deride, outcry, racket, scream, shriek, shrill, tumult, uproar **7** catcall, cry down, scoff at, screech, sing out, sneer at, snicker, ululate, wailing, whistle **8** proclaim, shouting **9** caterwaul, commotion, raspberry, screaming, snicker at **10** Bronx cheer, screeching

Hoover, Herbert Clark
  nickname: 13 Great Engineer **14** Great Secretary **17** Great Humanitarian **18** Great Public Servant
  presidential rank: 11 thirty-first
  party: 10 Republican
  state represented: 2 CA
  defeated: 5 (Alfred Emanuel) Smith **6** (George William) Norris, (Norman) Thomas, (William Frederick) Varney, (William Zebulon) Foster **8** (Verne L) Reynolds
  vice president: 6 (Charles) Curtis
  cabinet:
    state: 7 (Henry Lewis) Stimson
    treasury: 5 (Ogden Livingston) Mills **6** (Andrew William) Mellon
    war: 4 (James William) Good **6** (Patrick Jay) Hurley
    attorney general: 8 (William DeWitt) Mitchell
    navy: 5 (Charles Francis) Adams
    postmaster general: 5 (Walter Folger) Brown
    interior: 6 (Ray Lyman) Wilbur
    agriculture: 4 (Arthur Mastick) Hyde
    commerce: 6 (Robert Patterson) Lamont, (Roy Dikeman) Chapin

labor: 4 (William Nuckles) Doak **5** (James John) Davis
  born: 12 West Branch IA
  died: 13 New York City NY
  buried: 12 West Branch IA
  education:
    University: 8 Stanford
  religion: 5 Quaker **16** Society of Friends
  interests: 7 fishing
  vacation spot: 10 Camp Hoover **11** Rapidan Camp **22** Shenandoah National Park
  author: 7 Memoirs **11** On Growing Up **14** An American Epic **16** Years of Adventure **18** Principles of Mining, The Great Depression **20** America's First Crusade **21** American Individualism, The Challenge to Liberty **24** The Ordeal of Woodrow Wilson **25** The Problems of Lasting Peace **26** The Cabinet and the Presidency **28** Addresses Upon the American Road **51** The State Papers and Other Public Writings of Herbert Hoover
  political career: 19 US Food Administrator
    head of: 23 American Relief Committee **28** Commission for Relief in Belgium
    director: 38 General Relief and Reconstruction of Europe
    member/chairman: 22 Supreme Economic Council
    secretary of: 8 Commerce
    chairman of: 17 Hoover Commissions
  civilian career: 6 author **14** mining engineer **18** consulting engineer
  notable events of lifetime/term: 15 Great Depression
    conference: 11 London Naval
    crash of: 11 stock market
    independence for: 11 Philippines
    Tariff: 11 Hawley-Smoot
  named for him: 11 Hoover apron, Hoover plate (clean plate), Hooverville (shantytown)
  father: 10 Jesse Clark
  mother: 6 Huldah (Randall Minthorn)
  siblings: 3 May **13** Theodore Jesse
  wife: 3 Lou (Henry)
  children: 10 Allan Henry **12** Herbert Clark
  first lady:
    vice president of: 10 Girl Scouts

hop 3 bob **4** ball, jump, leap, prom, romp, skip, step, trip **5** bound, caper, dance, frisk, mixer, vault **6** bounce, gambol, prance, soiree, spring **7** Humulus
  varieties: 4 Wild **5** False **6** Common **8** European, Japanese

hope 3 yen **4** help, wish **5** crave, dream, faith, fancy, trust **6** aspire, belief, chance, desire, expect, hunger, rescue, yen for **7** believe, count on, craving, dream of, longing, long for **8**

ambition, daydream, feel sure, optimism, prospect, reckon on, reliance, yearn for, yearning **9** assurance, hankering, have faith, hunger for, salvation, take heart **10** anticipate, aspiration, assumption, be bent upon, confidence, conviction, expectancy **11** be confident, contemplate, expectation, have an eye to, possibility, presumption, reassurance, saving grace **12** anticipation, be optimistic, heart's desire **13** encouragement, have a fancy for, look forward to **14** have a hankering **17** great expectations **18** have one's heart set on **19** look on the bright side

Hope, Anthony
  real name: 21 Sir Anthony Hope Hawkins
  author of: 15 Rupert of Hentzau **18** The Prisoner of Zenda

Hope, Bob
  real name: 16 Leslie Townes Hope
  co-star: 10 Bing Crosby **13** Dorothy Lamour
  born: 6 Eltham **7** England
  roles:
    Road to: 3 Rio **4** Bali **6** Utopia **7** Morocco **8** Hong Kong, Zanzibar **9** Singapore
  performed for: 3 USO

hopeful 7 assured, in hopes **8** cheering, sanguine, trusting **9** confident, expectant, favorable, fortunate, promising **10** auspicious, heartening, of good omen, optimistic, propitious, reassuring **11** encouraging **12** anticipative

hopeless 3 sad **4** lost, vain **6** abject, futile **7** forlorn, useless **8** dejected, downcast **9** depressed, incurable, pointless **10** beyond help, despairing, despondent, impossible, melancholy, past remedy **11** downhearted, heartbroken, irreparable, irrevocable, pessimistic, sick at heart **12** beyond recall, disconsolate, heavyhearted, irredeemable, irreversible **13** grief-stricken, irretrievable **14** down in the mouth, sorrow-stricken

hopelessness 7 despair **8** futility **9** pessimism **11** uselessness

Hopi (Hopitu, Moki)
  language family: 10 Shoshonean
  location: 7 Arizona
  adapted culture of: 6 Pueblo
  ceremony: 10 snake dance

Hopkins, Anthony
  born: 5 Wales **10** Port Talbot
  roles: 10 Audrey Rose **11** A Doll's House **12** Young Winston **14** The Elephant Man **15** The Lion in Winter

Hopper, Edward
  born: 7 Nyack NY
  artwork: 10 Nighthawks **18** Early Sunday Morning, House by the Railroad **19** Second Story Sunlight **20**

Sunlight in a Cafeteria **21** Lighthouse at Two Lights

Horae
  also: 5 Hours
  goddesses of: 5 decay **6** growth **7** seasons **11** social order
  names: 4 Dice, Dike **5** Irene **7** Eunomia

Horatio
  character in: 6 Hamlet
  author: 11 Shakespeare

Horatio
  character in: 17 The Spanish Tragedy
  author: 3 Kyd

Horatius
  origin: 5 Roman
  defended: 6 bridge
    over: 5 Tiber
    against: 9 Etruscans

horde 3 mob **4** band, gang, host, pack **5** bunch, crowd, crush, drove, party, swarm, tribe, troop **6** legion, throng **7** company **8** assembly **9** gathering, multitude **10** assemblage **12** congregation

Horgan, Paul
  author of: 10 Whitewater **13** Lamy of Santa Fe **18** The Thin Mountain Air

horizon 4 area **5** field, range, realm, scope, vista, world **6** bounds, domain, sphere **7** compass, expanse, outlook, purview, stretch **8** frontier, prospect **11** perspective

horizontal 4 even, flat **5** flush, level, plane, plumb, prone **6** supine **8** parallel (to something) **9** lying down, prostrate, reclining, recumbent **14** flat on one's back

horizontal support 3 tie **4** beam **5** brace, joist **6** girder, header, lintel **8** crossbar

hormone 4 ACTH **5** auxin **6** cortin **7** estrone, insulin, steroid **8** endocrin, estrogen, galactin, lactogen, secretin **9** adrenalin, cortisone **12** progesterone, testosterone

horn 4 tusk **5** cornu, point, spike **6** antler **11** excrescence
  brass instrument: 4 oboe, tuba **5** bugle **6** cornet **7** bassoon, trumpet **8** alto horn, baritone, clarinet, trombone **9** euphonium, saxophone **10** French horn, mellophone, sousaphone **11** English horn

Horn of Africa see **7** Somalia

Hornung, Paul
  nickname: 9 Golden Boy
  sport: 8 football
  position: 6 runner **11** placekicker
  team: 15 Green Bay Packers

horny 4 hard **5** tough **7** callous, lustful **8** callused, hardened **12** thick-skinned **14** pachydermatous

horologe 5 clock **9** timepiece **11** chronometer

horoscope see **9** astrology

horrendous 4 gory **5** awful **6** horrid **7** ghastly, hideous **8** dreadful, horrible, shocking, terrible **9** appalling, frightful, repellent, repulsive, revolting **10** horrifying

horrible 3 bad **4** foul, rank, vile **5** awful, nasty **6** grisly, horrid, odious **7** ghastly, hideous **8** dreadful, gruesome, shocking, terrible, unsavory **9** abhorrent, appalling, atrocious, frightful, harrowing, loathsome, monstrous, obnoxious, repellent, repulsive, revolting, sickening **10** abominable, despicable, detestable, disgusting, forbidding, nauseating, unbearable, unpleasant **11** disquieting, distasteful, unspeakable **12** disagreeable, insufferable

horrid 3 bad **4** foul, grim, ugly **5** awful, nasty, rough **6** bratty, horror, shaggy, wicked **7** fearful, hideous **8** dreadful, gruesome, horrible, shocking, terrible **9** bristling, frightful, offensive, revolting, vexatious **10** abominable, detestable, unpleasant **11** troublesome **12** disagreeable

horrific 4 dire **5** awful **7** fearful, ghastly **8** dreadful, horrible, shocking, terrible **9** appalling

horrified 6 aghast **8** appalled **9** petrified, terrified **10** frightened **13** thunderstruck **14** terror-stricken

horrify 5 daunt, repel, shock **6** appall, dismay, revolt, sicken **7** disgust, petrify, terrify **8** affright, disquiet, frighten, nauseate **10** disconcert, dishearten **11** make one sick **15** make one turn pale **18** make one's flesh creep **22** make one's hair stand on end

horrifying 5 awful, dread **8** alarming, dreadful **10** terrifying **11** frightening, hair-raising

horror 3 woe **4** fear **5** alarm, crime, dread, panic **6** dismay, hatred, misery, terror **7** anguish, cruelty, disgust, dislike, outrage, torment **8** atrocity, aversion, distaste, distress, hardship, loathing **9** antipathy, awfulness, privation, repulsion, revulsion, suffering **10** abhorrence, affliction, discomfort, inhumanity, repugnance **11** abomination, detestation, hideousness, trepidation **12** apprehension, terribleness, wretchedness

horror-struck 6 aghast **7** fearful **8** appalled **9** horrified, terrified **10** frightened **13** scared to death

hors de combat 8 disabled **13** out of the fight

hors d'oeuvre 3 dip **6** canape, relish, tidbit **9** antipasto, appetizer **10** finger food

horse 4 colt, foal, hack, jade, mare, plug, pony, sire, stud **5** bronc, filly, mount, pacer, pinto, steed **6** bronco, dobbin, equine, nellie **7** cavalry, charger, cow pony, gelding, hackney, hussars, lancers, mustang, palfrey, trotter **8** cossacks, dragoons, galloper, stallion, troopers, yearling **9** broodmare, racehorse **10** cavalrymen, draft horse **12** horse cavalry, horse marines, quarter horse, thoroughbred **13** horse soldiers, mounted troops **15** mounted troopers, mounted warriors

Achilles': 7 Xanthus

Alexander the Great's: 10 Bucephalus

anatomy: 4 hock, hoof, loin, mane, tail **5** croup, flank, shank **6** cannon, gaskin, haunch, stifle **7** coronet, crupper, fetlock, gambrel, nostril, pastern, withers **11** throatlatch

Australian: 5 myall **8** warragal, warrigal, yarraman

breed: 6 Morgan, Nubian, Tarpan **7** Arabian, Belgian, mustang **8** Galloway, Shetland **9** Appaloosa, Percheron Clydesdale, Lippizaner **12** Narragansett, Standardbred, Thoroughbred **15** Tennessee-Walker

Bellerophon's: 7 Pegasus

Caligula's: 9 Incitatus (made a senator)

castrated: 7 gelding

color: 3 bay, dun **4** gray, pied, roan, zain **5** morel, pinto **6** calico, dapple, sorrel **7** piebald **8** chestnut, palomino, schimmel (gray)

combining form: 4 eque, equi **5** hippo

Dick Turpin's: 9 Black Bess

Don Quixote's: 9 Rosinante

family: 7 Equidae **9** Miohippus, Orohippus

female: 3 dam **4** mare **5** filly

French: 6 cheval

gear: 3 bit **4** rein, tack **6** saddle **7** blinder, harness, snaffle **9** surcingle **11** saddlecloth

Gen Custer's: 8 Comanche

Gen Grant's: 10 Cincinnati

Gen Robert E Lee's: 9 Traveller

Gen Sherman's: 6 Rienzi

genus: 5 equus

Gulliver's Travels: 9 Houyhnhnm

kind: 3 cob **4** race **6** bronco, hunter, jumper **7** charger, mustang, palfrey, quarter, trotter **8** destrier

legendary: 6 Trojan

Lone Ranger's: 6 Silver

male: 4 colt **8** stallion

measure: 4 hand

Mohammed's: 7 Alborak

movie/story: 6 Flicka **8** Champion **11** Black Beauty **14** National Velvet **16** The Black Stallion

Napoleon's: 7 Marengo

Odin's: 8 Sleipnir

Orlando's: 11 Vegliantino

pace: 4 lope, trot **5** amble **6** canter, gallop

pair of: 4 span, team **6** tandem

race: 5 derby, plate **6** exacta **7** pick

six **8** claiming, handicap **9** allowance **11** daily double, sweepstakes **12** steeplechase, weight-for-age

> **Triple Crown: 7** Belmont **9** Preakness **13** Kentucky Derby

riding show: 8 gymkhana

riding sport: 4 polo

Rinaldo's: 6 Bayard

Roy Rogers': 7 Trigger

Siegfried's: 5 Grani

small: 4 pony

Stonewall Jackson's: 12 Little Sorrel

Tom Mix's: 4 Tony

Tonto's: 5 Scout

television: 4 Mr. Ed

three: 6 random, troika **7** unicorn

Wellington's (at Waterloo): 10 Copenhagen

wild: 5 fuzzy **6** bramby, kumrah, outlaw, tarpan **7** jughead **8** bangtail, fuzztail, warragal, warrigal

Will Rogers': 8 Soapsuds **10** Bootlegger

winged: 7 Pegasus

young: 4 colt, foal **5** filly **8** yearling

horseback riding

> **athlete: 11** Frank Chapot **17** William Steinkraus

horse collar 3 zip **4** zero **5** aught, zilch **6** cipher, naught **8** goose egg

Horse Knows the Way, The

> **author: 9** John O'Hara

horseman 5 groom, rider **6** hussar, jockey, lancer, ostler **7** cossack, dragoon, hostler, trainer, trooper **9** postilion, stableboy, stableman **10** cavalryman, equestrian, roughrider **11** horse marine, stable owner **12** equestrienne, horse breeder, horse soldier, stable keeper **14** cavalry soldier, horseback rider, mounted trooper

horseplay 6 pranks **7** foolery **9** cutting up **10** buffoonery, tomfoolery **13** fooling around, horsing around

horse racing

> **jockey: 8** Del Insko **11** Bill Hartack, Eddie Arcaro **12** Angel Cordero, Bill Haughton, Laffit Pincay, Steve Cauthen **13** Johnny Longden, Stanley Dancer **15** Willie Shoemaker
>
> **god of: 6** Consus

Horseshoe Robinson

> **author: 12** John P Kennedy

horse soldier 6 hussar, lancer **7** dragoon, trooper **8** cavalier, horseman **10** cavalryman

horse trooper 6 hussar, lancer **7** dragoon, Mountie **8** cavalier, horseman **10** cavalryman **12** horse soldier **14** mounted soldier **16** mounted policeman

Horton, Edward Everett

> **sidekick of: 11** Fred Astaire
>
> **born: 10** Brooklyn NY
>
> **roles: 15** Cinderella Jones, Her Primitive Man **18** Springtime for Henry

Horus

origin: 8 Egyptian

god of: 3 sun

Greek name: 10 Harcorates

symbol: 6 falcon

mother: 4 Isis

father: 6 Osiris

enemy: 3 Set **4** Seth

hosannas 4 yeas **5** kudos **6** bravos, cheers, paeans **7** acclaim, hurrahs, huzzahs, yippees **8** applause **10** hallelujas **11** halleluiahs

hose, hosiery 5 socks **6** nylons, tights **7** anklets, argyles, hosiery **9** knee-highs, pantyhose, stockings **10** bobbysocks

Hosea

> **father: 5** Beeri

hospitable 4 open, warm **6** genial **7** cordial **8** amenable, amicable, friendly, gracious, sociable, tolerant **9** agreeable, convivial, receptive, welcoming **10** accessible, gregarious, openhanded, openminded, responsive **12** approachable

hospital 4 home **6** asylum, clinic **7** sick bay **8** pavilion, rest home **9** infirmary **10** polyclinic, sanatorium **11** nursing home **13** medical center

> **French: 9** hotel Dieu

hospital, private

> **French: 13** maison de sante

hospitality 5 cheer **6** warmth **7** welcome **8** openness **9** geniality **10** cordiality, heartiness, kindliness **11** amicability, sociability **12** congeniality, conviviality, friendliness **13** Gemutlichkeit **14** hospitableness, neighborliness **15** warmheartedness

> **god of: 6** Sancus **10** Dius Fidius, Semo Sancus

host, hostess 3 lot, mob **4** army, band, body, crew, gang, mess **5** array, crowd, drove, emcee, group, horde, party, swarm, troop **6** legion, throng **7** company, maitre d', meeting **8** conclave, congress, hosteler, hotelier, landlord, welcomer **9** gathering, innkeeper, multitude **10** confluence, convention, headwaiter, party giver, proprietor **11** convocation, hotel keeper **12** congregation, head waitress, hotel manager, proprietress, receptionist **17** restaurant manager **18** master of ceremonies **20** mistress of ceremonies

hostage 6 pledge **7** captive **8** prisoner

Hostage, The

> **author: 12** Brendan Behan

hostel 3 inn **4** hall **5** hotel, lodge **7** hospice, lodging, shelter **8** hospital, hostelry

hostile 3 icy **4** cold, mean, ugly **5** angry, at war, enemy, testy **6** at odds, at outs, bitter, chilly, cranky, malign, touchy, unkind **7** opposed, vicious, warring **8** battling, clashing, contrary, fighting, opposing, snappish, spiteful, venomous **9** bellicose, bristling, dissident, malicious, malignant, truculent **10** contending, ill-natured, malevolent, on bad terms, unfriendly **11** belligerent, contentious, disagreeing, ill-disposed, quarrelsome **12** antagonistic, cantankerous, disagreeable, disputatious, incompatible **13** argumentative, at loggerheads, unsympathetic

hostile act 4 raid **6** strike, threat **7** assault, offense **8** act of war, invasion **9** hostility, incursion **10** aggression

hostile nation 3 foe **5** enemy **7** invader

hostility 3 war **4** duel, feud, fray, hate **5** anger, clash, fight, venom **6** battle, combat, enmity, fracas, hatred, malice, rancor, spleen **7** contest, dispute, ill will, scuffle, warfare, warring **8** act of war, argument, battling, conflict, fighting **9** animosity, antipathy, bickering **10** antagonism, bitterness, contention, dissidence, opposition, state of war **11** altercation, malevolence, viciousness **12** belligerence, contrariness, disagreement **14** unfriendliness, vindictiveness

hot 3 new, top **4** good, late, live, near, warm **5** fiery, fresh, nippy, sharp **6** ardent, baking, biting, fervid, fierce, heated, hectic, latest, molten, raging, recent, red-hot, stormy, sultry, torrid **7** boiling, burning, earnest, excited, furious, intense, melting, peppery, piquant, popular, pungent, searing, violent **8** agitated, animated, broiling, feverish, frenzied, roasting, scalding, sizzling, steaming, vehement, very warm **9** emotional, excellent, scorching, simmering, very close, wrought-up **10** attractive, blistering, passionate, smoldering, successful, sweltering **11** electrified, fast-selling, most popular, radioactive, sought after, tempestuous **12** incandescent **14** fast and furious, highly seasoned, in close pursuit

hot air 7 bombast **8** rhetoric **9** hyperbole **12** exaggeration **13** overstatement

hotel de ville 9 a city hall
  literally: 16 mansion of the city

hotel Dieu 9 a hospital **12** mansion of God

Hotel New Hampshire, The
  author: 10 John Irving

hothouse 6 tender **7** fragile, nursery **8** delicate **10** glasshouse, greenhouse **12** conservatory **13** over-protected

hot temper 4 fire **5** anger **6** pepper **8** acrimony **9** short fuse

hot-tempered 7 peppery **9** emotional, excitable **13** easily ruffled, quick-tempered

hot water 3 jam **4** mess **6** pickle **7** trouble **10** difficulty **11** predicament

Houghston, Walter
  real name of: 12 Walter Huston

hound 3 dog, fan, nag, nut, pup **4** bait, buff, hunt, mutt, tail **5** annoy, chase, doggy, freak, harry, lover, pooch, puppy, stalk, track, trail, whelp, worry **6** addict, badger, canine, follow, harass, hector, keep at, needle, pester, pursue **7** bedevil, poochie **9** keep after **10** aficionado, hunting dog **11** afficionado
  dog breed: 6 beagle, borzoi, saluki **7** basenji, harrier, whippet **9** dachshund, greyhound **10** bloodhound, otter hound **11** Afghan hound, basset hound, Ibizan hound **12** pharaoh hound **14** Irish wolfhound **15** English foxhound **16** American foxhound **17** Norwegian elkhound, Scottish deerhound **18** Rhodesian ridgeback **20** black and tan coonhound
  group of: 3 cry **4** mute, pack

Hound of the Baskervilles, The
  author: 19 Sir Arthur Conan Doyle
  character: 8 Dr Watson **14** Sherlock Holmes **19** Sir Henry Baskerville

hour 3 day **4** span, time **5** space **6** period **8** interval
  abbreviation: 2 hr

Hour *see* **5** Horae

house, House 4 clan, firm, hall, home, keep, line, shop **5** abode, board, lodge, put up, store **6** billet, church, family, garage, harbor, strain, temple **7** Commons, company, concern, contain, council, descent, dynasty, lineage, quarter, shelter, theater **8** ancestry, assembly, audience, building, business, congress, domicile, dwelling **9** ancestors, household, residence **10** auditorium, family tree, habitation, hippodrome, opera house, spectators **11** accommodate, concert hall, corporation, legislature, noble family, partnership, royal family **12** business firm, lower chamber, meeting place, organization **13** dwelling place, establishment
  god of: 8 Silvanus, Sylvanus

housebreaker 5 thief **6** robber **7** burglar **8** pilferer **9** purloiner **10** cat burglar **14** second-story man

housebreaking 5 theft **7** break-in, robbery **8** burglary, stealing **12** burglarizing **19** breaking and entering

House Divided, A
  author: 9 Pearl Buck

House for Mr Biswas, A
  author: 9 V S Naipaul

household 4 home **5** house **6** family, hearth, menage **8** of a house **9** for a house **10** for a family, for home use **12** family circle
  goddess of: 6 Brigit

household gods 5 lares, Roman **7** penates

household help 4 cook, maid **7** foot-

man, steward **8** domestic, gardener, handyman, houseboy **9** charwoman, chauffeur, domestics, majordomo, nursemaid **11** housekeeper

household of three
  French: 12 menage a trois

House of Atreus, The
  author: 9 Aeschylus
  character: 7 Electra, Orestes **9** Aegisthus, Agamemnon, Cassandra **12** Clytemnestra

house of health
  French: 13 maison de sante

House of Mirth, The
  author: 12 Edith Wharton
  character: 8 Lily Bart, Mr Selden **9** Gus Trenor **10** Judy Trenor, Mr Rosedale, Percy Gryce **12** Bertha Dorset, George Dorset

House of the Seven Gables, The
  author: 18 Nathaniel Hawthorne
  character: 10 Mr Holgrave **14** Phoebe Pyncheon **16** Clifford Pyncheon **20** Judge Jaffrey Pyncheon, Miss Hepzibah Pyncheon

house of worship 6 chapel, church, mosque, temple **8** basilica **9** cathedral, synagogue **10** house of God, Lord's house, tabernacle

housewife 4 wife **8** hausfrau **9** homemaker **11** housekeeper

housing 4 case, home **5** abode, house **6** casing, jacket, sheath, shield **7** lodging, shelter **8** covering, domicile, dwelling, envelope, lodgment, quarters **9** enclosure, residence **10** habitation **14** accommodations

Housman, A E
  author of: 14 A Shropshire Lad

Houston
  baseball team: 6 Astros
  basketball team: 6 Comets **7** Rockets
  canal: 11 Houston Ship
  channel: 12 Buffalo Bayou
  football team: 6 Oilers **8** Gamblers
  landmark: 4 NASA **12** Alley Theater **14** Jesse Jones Hall **22** Manned Spacecraft Center **29** San Jacinto Battlefield Monument
  battleship: 5 Texas
  named after: 10 Sam Houston
  planned by: 7 A C Allen, J K Allen
  stadium: 9 Astrodome
  street: 15 Old Spanish Trail
  university: 4 Rice **12** Texas Medical **13** Texas Southern

Houston, Sam
  position: 9 US Senator
  governor of: 5 Texas **9** Tennessee
  president of: 15 Republic of Texas
  served in: 9 Creek Wars **15** Texas Revolution
  battle: 10 San Jacinto
  defeated: 9 Santa Anna

Houyhnhnms
  race of horses in: 16 Gulliver's

Travels
author: 5 Swift
hovel 3 hut **4** dump, hole **5** cabin, shack **6** shanty
hover 4 flit, hang **5** float, haunt, pause, poise, waver **6** attend, falter, seesaw **7** flitter, flutter **9** fluctuate, hang about, vacillate
Hovhaness, Alan
born: 12 Somerville MA
composer of: 10 Magnificat
how
Latin: 7 quo modo
Howard, Catherine
husband: 9 Henry VIII
number: 5 fifth
fate: 8 beheaded
Howard, Ron
born: 2 OK **6** Duncan
roles: 4 Opie **9** Happy Days **16** American Graffiti, Richie Cunningham **19** The Andy Griffith Show
director of: 6 Cocoon, Gung Ho, Splash, Willow
Howard, Sidney
author of: 13 The Silver Cord **22** They Knew What They Wanted
Howard, Trevor
born: 7 England **12** Cliftonville
roles: 6 The Key **13** Ryan's Daughter, Sons and Lovers **14** Brief Encounter **23** The Invincible Mr Disraeli
Howards End
author: 9 E M Forster
character: 9 Jacky Bast **10** Paul Wilcox, Ruth Wilcox **11** Henry Wilcox, Leonard Bast **13** Charles Wilcox, Helen Schlegel **16** Margaret Schlegel, Theobald Schlegel
how are you
German: 8 wie geht's **9** wie geht es
Howe, Elias
nationality: 8 American
invented: 13 sewing machine
Howells, William Dean
author of: 12 Indian Summer **15** A Modern Instance **20** A Hazard of New Fortunes, The Rise of Silas Lapham
How Green Was My Valley
author: 16 Richard Llewellyn
director: 8 John Ford
character: 6 Marged **7** Bronwen **10** Beth Morgan **11** Iestyn Evans **12** Gwilym Morgan
  Morgan children: 4 Davy, Huur, Ivor, Owen **5** Ianto **6** Gwilym **8** Angharad
cast: 7 Anna Lee **9** John Loder **11** Donald Crisp **12** Maureen O'Hara **13** Roddy McDowall, Walter Pidgeon
Oscar for: 7 picture **8** director **15** supporting actor (Crisp)
howl 3 bay, cry **4** bark, hoot, roar, wail, yell, yelp, yowl **5** groan, shout, whine **6** bellow, clamor, cry out, outcry, scream, shriek, uproar **7** ululate

howler 4 goof **5** error **6** boo-boo **7** blooper, blunder, mistake
How To Win Friends and Influence People
author: 12 Dale Carnegie
hoyden 3 imp **4** brat, chit **6** tomboy
Hoyle, Edmund 9 authority, (card games)
Hoyle, Fred
field: 9 astronomy
nationality: 7 British
developed: 17 steady-state theory
Hoyt, Rosemary
character in: 16 Tender Is the Night
author: 10 Fitzgerald
Hsitsang see **5** Tibet
Hualapai
language family: 5 Yuman
location: 7 Arizona
related to: 7 Yavapai **9** Havasupai
hub 3 nub **4** axis, core **5** focus, heart, pivot **6** center, middle **10** focal point
Hubble, Edwin Powell
field: 9 astronomy
studied: 15 galactic nebulae
named for him: 14 Hubble constant, space telescope
hubbub 3 din **4** fuss, stir, to-do **5** noise **6** babble, bedlam, bustle, clamor, pother, racket, ruckus, tumult, uproar **7** ferment, turmoil **8** disorder **9** agitation, commotion, confusion, hue and cry **10** hullabaloo, hurly-burly **11** disturbance, pandemonium **12** perturbation
Hubert
creator: 11 Dick Wingert
huckleberry 9 Vaccinium **11** Gaylussacia
varieties: 2 He **3** Box, Red **4** Blue, Shot **5** Black, Dwarf, Hairy, Squaw, Sugar **6** Garden **8** Thin-leaf **9** Evergreen **10** California, Little-leaf
Huckleberry Finn (The Adventures of)
author: 9 Mark Twain
character: 3 Jim **9** Tom Sawyer **12** Widow Douglas **13** Judge Thatcher
huckster 5 adman **6** badger, hawker, kidder, seller, vendor **7** haggler, peddler
Hud
director: 10 Martin Ritt
cast: 10 John Ashley, Paul Newman **12** Patricia Neal **13** Melvyn Douglas **14** Brandon de Wilde
Oscar for: 7 actress (Neal) **15** supporting actor (Douglas)
huddle 4 heap, herd, mass, mess **5** bunch, crowd, group **6** cuddle, curl up, jumble, medley, muddle, nestle, throng **7** cluster, collect, meeting, snuggle **8** converge, disarray, disorder **9** confusion, gathering **10** conference, discussion, hodge-podge **12** think session

Hudibras
author: 12 Samuel Butler
character: 6 Ralpho **8** Crowders **9** Sidrophel
Hudson, Rock
real name: 12 Roy Scherer Jr
co-star: 8 Doris Day
born: 10 Winnetka IL
roles: 5 Giant **10** Pillow Talk **15** A Farewell to Arms, McMillan and Wife **20** Magnificent Obsession
Hudson, W H
author of: 13 Green Mansions, The Purple Land **17** Far Away and Long Ago
bird-girl: 4 Rima
hue 4 cast, tint, tone **5** color, shade, tinge **8** tincture **10** coloration
hue and cry 4 call, howl, roar, yell, yowl **5** alarm, alert, shout, storm **6** bellow, clamor, hubbub, outcry, shriek, uproar **7** thunder **10** cry of alarm, hullabaloo
huff 3 pet **4** fury, rage, snit **7** bad mood, dudgeon, outrage **8** ill humor, vexation **9** annoyance, petulance **10** fit of anger, fit of pique, resentment
huffy 4 curt, hurt **5** angry, cross, irate, moody, sulky, surly, testy **6** cranky, grumpy, moping, morose, shirty, sullen, touchy **7** in a snit, peevish, waspish, wounded **8** churlish, offended, petulant, snappish **9** glowering, in a lather, in a pucker, irritable, querulous, rancorous, resentful, sensitive **10** ill-humored, out of sorts **11** disgruntled, quarrelsome, thin-skinned **12** discontented **14** easily offended, hard to live with, hypersensitive
hug 4 hold **5** clasp **6** clutch, cuddle, nestle **7** cling to, embrace, snuggle, squeeze **9** hold close, hover near **11** keep close to **13** cling together, follow closely **15** parallel closely, press to the bosom
huge 4 vast **5** giant, great, jumbo **6** mighty **7** immense, mammoth, massive, titanic **8** colossal, enormous, gigantic, imposing **9** cyclopean, extensive, herculean, leviathan, monstrous **10** gargantuan, monumental, prodigious, staggering, stupendous **11** elephantine, extravagant, spectacular **12** overwhelming **14** Brobdingnagian
hugeness 4 bulk **8** enormity, vastness **9** great size, immensity, largeness, magnitude **11** massiveness
Huggins, Charles Brenton
field: 10 physiology
researched: 6 cancer **12** chemotherapy
awarded: 10 Nobel Prize
Hughes, Langston
author of: 9 The Big Sea **12** One-Way Ticket **13** The Weary Blues **19** Shakespeare in Harlem **20** The Panther and the Lash

Hughes, Richard
author of: 18 A High Wind in Jamaica

Hughes, Thomas
author of: 19 Tom Brown's Schooldays

Hugh the Drover
opera by: 15 Vaughan Williams
character: 4 Mary 12 The Constable 14 John the Butcher

Hugin
origin: 12 Scandinavian
form: 5 raven
owned by: 4 Odin 5 Othin
personifies: 7 thought
duty: 10 newsbearer
other raven: 5 Munin

Hugo, Victor
author of: 7 Ruy Blas 13 Les Miserables 16 Notre Dame de Paris 23 The Hunchback of Notre Dame
character: 6 Javert 9 Esmeralda, Quasimodo 15 Jean Valjean

hulk 4 ship 5 giant, wreck 8 behemoth

hulking 3 big 5 bulky, heavy, husky 7 massive 8 powerful, unwieldy 9 oversized, ponderous 10 cumbersome

hull 3 pod 4 case, husk, peel, rind, skin 5 shell, shuck 7 coating 8 carapace 9 epidermis, tegmentum 10 integument

Hull, Isaac
served in: 19 War of Eighteen-Twelve
sunk ship: 9 Guerriere (British)
commander of ship: 12 Constitution

hullabaloo 3 din 4 stir 5 babel 6 bedlam, clamor, hubbub, ruckus, tumult, uproar 9 confusion 11 pandemonium
Yiddish: 7 tzimmes

hum 4 buzz, purr, whir 5 croon, drone, thrum 6 be busy, bustle, intone, murmur, thrive 7 buzzing, droning, purring, vibrate 8 be active, whirring 9 vibration 10 faint sound 13 be in full swing

human 3 man 5 of man, of men 6 gentle, humane, kindly, mortal, person 7 hominid, like man, manlike 8 merciful, personal 10 anthropoid, individual 11 Homo sapiens, sympathetic

Human Comedy, The
author: 14 Honore de Balzac, William Saroyan

Human Condition, The
author: 12 Hannah Arendt

humane 4 kind 5 human 6 kindly, tender 7 pitying 8 merciful 9 unselfish 10 benevolent, bighearted, charitable, goodwilled 11 magnanimous, sympathetic, warmhearted 12 humanitarian 13 compassionate, philanthropic

Human Factor, The
author: 12 Graham Greene

humanitarian 4 kind 6 humane 8 generous 10 altruistic, benevolent, charitable 11 kind-hearted 12 large-hearted 13 compassionate, philanthropic 14 philanthropist

humanity 3 man 4 love 5 mercy 6 people 7 charity, mankind, mortals 8 goodwill, kindness, sympathy 9 humankind, humanness, mortality 10 compassion, gentleness, humaneness, kindliness, tenderness 11 benevolence, Homo sapiens, human beings, human nature, magnanimity 12 the human race 13 brotherly love, fellow feeling 15 warmheartedness 16 fraternal feeling

humanum est errare 12 to err is human

Humbert Humbert
character in: 6 Lolita
author: 7 Nabokov

humble 3 low 4 meek, poor 5 abase, abash, crush, lower, lowly, plain, shame 6 common, debase, demean, demure, gentle, modest, shabby, simple, subdue 7 chasten, conquer, degrade, mortify, obscure, put down 8 bring low, derogate, disgrace, dishonor, inferior, ordinary, plebeian, pull down, wretched 9 bring down, embarrass, humiliate, make lowly, miserable 10 inglorious, low-ranking, make humble, obsequious, put to shame, respectful, unassuming 11 deferential, subservient, unimportant, unpresuming 12 self-effacing, take down a peg 13 insignificant, unpretentious 14 unostentatious 15 inconsequential, undistinguished

humbled 5 cowed 7 abashed, debased, subdued 9 conquered, disgraced 10 brought low, humiliated

Humboldt, Alexander von
nationality: 6 German
originator of: 7 ecology 10 geophysics

Humboldt's Gift
author: 10 Saul Bellow

humbug 3 fib, gyp, lie 4 bull, bunk, dupe, fake, fool, gull, hoax, liar, lies, sham 5 cheat, cozen, dodge, faker, fraud, hokum, lying, quack, spoof, trick 6 bunkum, con man, deceit, fibber, phooey, take in 7 beguile, blather, cheater, deceive, falsify, fiction, forgery, mislead, rubbish, sharper, swindle 8 artifice, claptrap, flimflam, flummery, hoodwink, impostor, nonsense, perjurer, pretense, swindler, trickery 9 bamboozle, charlatan, deception, fabricate, falsehood, hypocrisy, hypocrite, imposture, mendacity, poppycock, trickster 10 balderdash, hocus-pocus, mountebank, pretension 11 counterfeit, make-believe 12 equivocation, misrepresent 13 confidence man, double-dealing, falsification 15 pretentiousness

humdinger 4 lulu, oner 5 dandy, doozy 6 beauty, hummer, marvel 8 Jim dandy, superior 10 ripsnorter 12 lollapalooza 13 extraordinary

humdrum 4 blah, dull, dumb, flat 5 banal, trite 6 boring, common, dreary 7 insipid, mundane, routine, tedious, trivial 8 everyday, lifeless, mediocre, ordinary, tiresome, wearying 9 hackneyed, unvarying, wearisome 10 monotonous, pedestrian, uneventful, unexciting, uninspired 11 commonplace, indifferent, uninspiring 12 conventional, run-of-the-mill 13 unexceptional, uninteresting

humerus
bone of: 8 upper arm

humid 4 damp, dank 5 moist, muggy, soppy 6 clammy, steamy, sticky, sultry

humidity 4 smog 8 dampness, moisture 9 mugginess 10 stickiness

humiliate 5 abash, crush, shame 6 debase, humble, subdue 7 chagrin, chasten, degrade, mortify, put down 8 belittle, bring low, disgrace, dishonor 9 discomfit, embarrass 11 make ashamed 13 bring down a peg

humiliated 7 abashed, crushed, debased, humbled 8 degraded 9 chagrined, disgraced, mortified

humiliation 5 shame 7 chagrin 8 disgrace, dishonor 9 abasement 10 debasement 11 degradation 12 discomfiture 13 embarrassment, mortification

humility 7 modesty, shyness 8 meekness, timidity 9 lowliness 10 demureness, diffidence, humbleness 11 bashfulness 13 self-abasement 17 unpretentiousness

hummock 4 hill, rise 5 knoll, mound 7 hillock, tussock

Humologumena 17 New Testament books

humor 3 wit 4 baby, gags, mood, puns 5 farce, jests, jokes, spoil 6 cajole, comedy, joking, pamper, parody, satire, soothe, suffer, temper, whimsy 7 appease, flatter, foolery, fooling, indulge, jesting, mollify, placate, spirits, waggery 8 drollery, give in to, jocosity, low humor, nonsense, raillery, ridicule, tolerate, travesty, wordplay 9 burlesque, funniness, low comedy, put up with, slapstick, wittiness 10 buffoonery, caricature, comicality, comply with, high comedy, jocoseness, jocularity, tomfoolery, wisecracks, witticisms 11 broad comedy, disposition, foolishness, frame of mind, go along with 12 monkeyshines 13 ludicrousness 14 ridiculousness

humorist 3 wag, wit 4 card 5 comic 8 comedian

humorous 5 comic, droll, funny, witty 6 jocose 7 amusing, comical, jocular, waggish 8 farcical, mirthful, sportive

9 facetious, laughable, ludicrous, satirical, whimsical **10** ridiculous **11** nonsensical, rib-tickling **13** sidesplitting

hump 4 arch, bend, bump, knob, lift, lump, rise **5** bulge, hunch, knurl, mound, put up, tense **8** swelling **9** convexity **10** projection, prominence **11** excrescence

Humperdinck, Engelbert
born: **4** Bonn **7** Germany
composer of: **10** The Miracle **15** Hansel and Gretel

Humphry Clinker
author: **19** Tobias George Smollet
character: **10** Mr Dennison **12** Jerry Melford, Lydia Melford **14** George Dennison, Matthew Bramble **15** Winifred Jenkins **18** Miss Tabitha Bramble **26** Lieutenant Obadiah Lismahago

Humpty Dumpty
character in: **12** nursery rhyme **22** Through the Looking Glass
author: **7** Carroll

hunch 4 arch, bend, clue, hump, idea **5** tense **7** feeling, glimmer, inkling **8** good idea **9** intuition, suspicion **10** foreboding **11** premonition **12** presentiment

Hunchback of Notre Dame, The
author: **10** Victor Hugo
character: **9** Esmeralda, Gringoire, Quasimodo **12** Claude Frollo **20** Phoebus de Chateaupers

hunched 4 bent **7** crooked, slumped, stooped **9** contorted

hundredweight
abbreviation: **3** cwt

Hungary
capital/largest city: **8** Budapest
others: **4** Gyor, Pecs **5** Harta **6** Mohacs, Sopron, Szeged **7** Komarom, Miskolc, Szentes **8** Dubrecen, Kaposuar, Szegedin **9** Kecskemet **10** Albertirsa **11** Nagykanizsa, Szombathely
measure: **3** ako **4** yoke **5** itcze, marok, metze **7** huvelyk
monetary unit: **4** gara **5** balas, krone, pengo **6** filler, forint, gulden, korona, ongara, ungara
weight: **7** vamfont **8** vammazsa
island: **8** Margaret
lake: **5** Ferto **7** Balaton, Velence **9** Blatensee **10** Neusiedler, Plattensee
mountain: **4** Alps, Bukk **5** Matra, Tatra **6** Bakony, Mecsek, Vertes **7** Cserhat, Gerecse **8** Borzsony, Zempleni **9** Korishegy **10** Carpathian
highest point: **5** Kekes
river: **3** Mur, Sio **4** Duna, Raab, Raba, Sajo, Zala **5** Bodva, Drava, Drave, Ipoly, Kapos, Koros, Maros, Tarna, Tisza **6** Danube, Henrad, Poprad, Szamos, Theiss, Zagyva **7** Vistula **8** Berretyo
physical feature:
    canal: **3** Sio **6** Sarviz

forest: **6** Bakony
plain: **6** Puszta
port: **5** Fiume
people: **3** Hun **4** Serb **5** Croat, Gypsy **6** Cigany, Magyar, Slovak, Ugrian
    composer: **5** Lehar, Liszt **6** Bartok, Kodaly
    national hero: **5** Arpad
    playwright: **6** Molnar
language: **6** German, Magyar, Slovak **8** Croatian **9** Hungarian **10** Finno-Ugric
religion: **8** Lutheran **9** Calvinism **13** Roman Catholic **16** Eastern Orthodoxy
place:
    church: **32** Gothic Coronation Church of Matthias
    ruins: **8** Aquincum
    square: **6** Heroes
    tomb: **14** Turbe of Gul Baba **16** Father of the Roses
feature:
    dance: **3** kos **7** czardas **10** varsoviana
    dog: **4** puli
    musical instrument: **8** taragata **9** czimbalom
food:
    dish: **6** gulyas **7** goulash **15** chicken paprikas
    pastry: **4** rete **5** torte
    wine: **5** Tokay **10** Bulls Blood
hunger 3 yen **4** itch, love, lust, want, wish **5** crave, greed **6** desire, famine, hanker, liking, relish, thirst **7** burn for, craving, itch for, long for, pant for **8** appetite, fondness, voracity, yearn for, yearning **9** hankering, lust after **10** greediness, starvation **11** have a yen for, thirst after **12** malnutrition, ravenousness
hungry 5 eager **6** greedy **7** starved **8** ravenous, starving **9** voracious
hunk 3 gob, wad **4** clod, glob, lump, mass **5** block, chunk, piece **6** gobbet **7** portion **8** quantity
hunt 4 seek **5** chase, probe, shoot, stalk, trace, track, trail **6** course, follow, pursue **7** explore, go after, look for **8** ferret out, drive out **9** ferret out, search for, try to find **11** go in quest of, inquire into **14** riding to hounds **20** leave no stone unturned
Hunt, Richard Morris
architect of: **8** Biltmore (Asheville NC) **11** Marble House (Newport RI), The Breakers (Newport RI) **12** Lenox Library (NYC) **14** Studio Building (NYC) **19** National Observatory (Washington DC) **22** William Vanderbilt House (NYC) **23** Metropolitan Museum of Art (NYC)
hunter
constellation of: **5** Orion
French: **8** chasseur
Hunter, Jim

nickname: **7** Catfish
sport: **8** baseball
position: **7** pitcher
team: **14** New York Yankees **16** Oakland Athletics
Hunter, Kim
real name: **8** Jane Cole
born: **9** Detroit MI
roles: **16** Stairway to Heaven, The Seventh Victim **21** A Streetcar Named Desire
Hunting
god of: **7** Verbius
goddess of: **5** Diana **7** Artemis
Hunting Dogs
constellation of: **13** Canes Venatici
hurdle 4 jump, leap, snag, wall **5** bound, clear, fence, hedge, vault **6** hazard **7** barrier **8** obstacle, surmount **9** hindrance, roadblock **10** difficulty, impediment, spring over **11** obstruction **12** interference **14** stumbling block
hurl 4 cast, toss **5** chuck, fling, heave, pitch, sling, throw **6** launch, let fly, propel **7** fire off, project **9** discharge
hurly-burly 4 stir **5** furor **6** action, bustle, hubbub, hustle, uproar **8** activity **9** commotion **10** hullabaloo
hurrah, hurray 4 fine, good **5** bravo, cheer, great, huzza **6** huzzah, salute **7** acclaim, hosanna **9** excellent, halleluia, wonderful **10** exaltation, hallelujah
hurricane 7 cyclone, monsoon, tempest, typhoon **9** windstorm
Hurricane, The
director: **8** John Ford
cast: **7** Jon Hall **9** Mary Astor **12** C Aubrey Smith **13** Dorothy Lamour, Raymond Massey
setting: **9** Manikoora
hurried 4 fast **5** hasty **6** hectic, rushed, speedy **7** cursory, frantic **8** careless, feverish, frenetic, headlong, slapdash, slipshod **9** breakneck, haphazard, impulsive **11** precipitate, superficial
hurry 3 ado, zip **4** bolt, dart, dash, fuss, goad, prod, rush, stew, whiz **5** egg on, haste, speed **6** flurry, hasten, hustle, push on, scurry, tumult, urge on **7** drive on, flutter, press on, scuttle, speed up, turmoil **8** make time, move fast, pressure, scramble, step on it **9** commotion, go quickly, make haste, step along **10** accelerate, get a move on, get hopping, lose no time, make tracks **11** come quickly, get cracking, go like a shot, go like sixty **12** step on the gas **13** go like the wind **14** cover the ground **15** hustle and bustle
hurt 3 cut, mar **4** ache, balk, burn, foil, harm, lame, maim, mark, maul, pain, pang, scar **5** agony, block, check, grief, limit, lower, pique, smart, spike, sting, stung **6** aching, bruise, damage,

deface, dismay, grieve, hamper, hinder, impair, impede, injure, lessen, mangle, marked, miffed, misery, morose, narrow, offend, oppose, pained, piqued, reduce, retard, thwart, weaken **7** agonize, bruised, chagrin, cripple, crushed, damaged, disable, exclude, inhibit, injured, mangled, painful, scarred, scratch, torment, torture, trouble, wounded **8** aggrieve, crippled, decrease, dejected, diminish, disabled, dismayed, distress, encumber, hold back, minimize, mutilate, obstruct, offended, preclude, restrain, smarting, soreness, wretched **9** aggrieved, annoyance, chagrined, dejection, disfigure, forestall, frustrate, heartsick, indignant, miserable, mortified, mutilated, resentful, scratched, suffering **10** discomfort, distressed, heartbreak, melancholy, resentment **11** aggravation, crestfallen, heartbroken **12** disheartened, wretchedness **13** embarrassment, mortification

Hurt, John
    born: 7 England **22** Chesterfield Derbyshire
    roles: 5 Alien **8** Partners **9** I Claudius (TV; Caligula) **14** The Elephant Man **15** Midnight Express

Hurt, William
    roles: 8 Body Heat **9** Gorky Park **10** Eyewitness **11** The Big Chill **13** Broadcast News **20** Kiss of the Spider Woman, Children of a Lesser God

hurtful 5 cruel **6** deadly **7** abusive, baleful, harmful **8** crushing, improper, stinging, wounding **9** injurious

hurtle 3 fly, hie, run, zip **4** bolt, dart, dash, race, rush, tear, whiz **5** bound, lunge, scoot, shoot, speed, spurt, whisk **6** charge, gallop, plunge, scurry **7** scamper, scuttle **11** go like a shot **13** go like the wind **14** go lickety-split

husband 3 man **4** keep, mate, save **5** amass, groom, hoard, hubby, store **6** old man, retain, save up, spouse **7** consort **8** conserve, maintain, preserve, set aside **10** accumulate, bridegroom, married man

husbandry 7 farming **9** geoponics **11** agriculture, crop- raising **12** conservation
    god of: 9 Aristaeus

hush 4 calm **5** quell, quiet, shush, still **6** shut up, soothe **7** be quiet, be still, keep mum, mollify, silence **8** be silent, pipe down, quietude **9** quiet down, quietness, stillness **10** knock it off **11** tranquility **12** peacefulness, tranquillity

hushed 4 calm **5** quiet, still **6** calmed, gentle, lulled, silent **7** allayed, quieted, soothed, stifled **8** pacified, silenced, tranquil **12** tranquilized **13** tranquillized

hush money 5 bribe **6** payoff, payola **7** tribute **9** blackmail, extortion

huskiness 5 brawn **9** beefiness **10** hoarseness, robustness, ruggedness, sturdiness **11** muscularity

husky 3 big **5** beefy, burly, gruff, harsh, hefty, plump, rough, solid, stout, thick **6** brawny, coarse, hoarse, robust, stocky, strong, sturdy **7** cracked, grating, rasping, raucous, throaty **8** athletic, croaking, guttural, muscular, powerful, thickset **9** strapping **10** overweight **12** strong as an ox **15** broad-shouldered

husky, **8** Siberian
    work: 7 sled dog

hussar 8 cavalier, horseman **10** cavalryman **12** horse soldier, horse trooper **14** mounted soldier

hussy 4 bawd, jade, minx, slut, tart **5** wench, whore **6** harlot, wanton **7** baggage, trollop **8** strumpet **9** brash girl, lewd woman, saucy miss **10** adulteress, loose woman, prostitute **11** brazen woman, fallen woman **12** scarlet woman **17** woman of easy virtue

hustle 3 ado, fly **4** bolt, dart, dash, fuss, prod, push, rush, stir, toss **5** elbow, hurry, nudge, scoot, shove, throw **6** bounce, bustle, flurry, hasten, hubbub, jostle, scurry, tumult **7** flutter, scuttle, speed up, turmoil **8** make time, scramble, shoulder, step on it **9** commotion, make haste, step along **10** lose no time **11** hurry-scurry, move quickly **12** be aggressive

hustler 4 doer **6** con man, dynamo, hooker **8** go-getter, live-wire, swindler **10** prostitute **12** streetwalker

Hustler, The
    director: 12 Robert Rossen
    cast: 10 Paul Newman **11** Piper Laurie **12** George C Scott **13** Jackie Gleason (Minnesota Fats)

Huston, John
    director of: 8 Key Largo **10** The Misfits **11** Moulin Rouge **12** Prizzi's Honor **13** Asphalt Jungle **15** The African Queen **16** The Maltese Falcon **19** The Night of the Iguana **27** The Treasure of the Sierra Madre (Oscar)
    father: 12 Walter Huston
    wife: 11 Evelyn Keyes
    born: 8 Nevada MO
    daughter: 8 Anjelica
    roles: 9 Chinatown **11** Winter Kills

Huston, Walter
    real name: 15 Walter Houghston
    son: 10 John Huston
    born: 6 Canada **7** Toronto
    roles: 9 Dodsworth **18** All That Money Can Buy **27** The Treasure of the Sierra Madre

hut 4 shed **5** cabin, hutch, shack **6** lean-to, shanty **7** cottage, shelter

hutch 3 pen, sty **4** cage, coop, cote, crib, shed **5** stall **9** enclosure

Hutchinson, A S M
    author of: 13 If Winter Comes

Hutton, Betty
    real name: 18 Betty June Thornburg
    born: 13 Battle Creek MI
    roles: 15 Annie Get Your Gun **19** Greatest Show on Earth

Hutton, James
    field: 7 geology
    nationality: 8 Scottish
    founder of: 7 geology

Hutton, Timothy
    father: 9 Jim Hutton
    roles: 4 Taps **6** Daniel **14** Ordinary People **22** The Falcon and the Snowman

Huxley, Aldous
    author of: 11 Crome Yellow **13** Brave New World **17** Point Counter Point
    brother: 6 Julian

Huxley, Julian
    field: 7 biology
    nationality: 7 British
    promoted theory of: 9 evolution

Huygens, Christiaan
    nationality: 5 Dutch
    invented: 13 pendulum clock
    discovered: 12 Saturn's rings
    formulated: 17 wave theory of light

hyacinth 10 Hyacinthus **20** Hyacinthus orientalis
    varieties: 4 musk, pine, star, wild, wood **5** Dutch, grape, Roman, water **6** common, garden, meadow, nutmeg, starry, summer, Tassel **7** feather, peacock **11** common grape

Hyacinthus
    father: 7 Amyclas
    daughter: 7 Orthaea
    loved by: 6 Apollo **8** Zephyrus
    killed by: 5 quoit **6** discus
    from his blood sprang: 6 flower
        petals marked: 4 AI-AI
        means: 4 alas

Hyades
    also: 5 Hyads **10** Palilicium
    form: 6 nymphs
    father: 5 Atlas **7** Oceanus
    mother: 6 Tethys **7** Pleione
    sisters: 8 Pleiades
    nurtured: 8 Dionysus
    placed among: 5 stars

hybrid 5 cross **7** amalgam, mixture **9** composite, half- breed **10** crossbreed

hybridize 5 cross **14** cross-fertilize, cross-pollinate

Hydra
    form: 12 water serpent
    number of heads: 4 nine
    killed by: 8 Hercules

hydrangea
    varieties: 4 Wild **6** French, Peegee **8** Climbing

hydrogen
chemical symbol: **1** H
hydrophobia 6 rabies
fear of: **5** water
Hygeia
father: **9** Asclepius
goddess of: **6** health
corresponds to: **5** Salus
hygienic 4 pure **5** clean **7** aseptic,
healthy, sterile **8** germ- free, harmless,
salutary, sanitary **9** healthful, wholesome **10** salubrious, unpolluted **11**
disease-free, disinfected, uninjurious
12 prophylactic **14** uncontaminated
Hylaeus
form: **7** centaur
born on: **5** cloud
Hymen
also: **9** Hymenaeus
god of: **8** marriage
holds: **5** torch
corresponds to: **8** Talassio
hymenoptera
class: **8** hexapoda
phylum: **10** arthropoda
group: **3** ant, bee **4** wasp **6** chacid,
sawfly **12** ichneumon fly
hymn 5 paean, psalm **6** anthem **12**
song of praise **14** devotional song **17**
song in praise of God
Hymn to Proserpine
author: **24** Algernon Charles Swinburne
Hypatia
author: **15** Charles Kingsley
hyper 7 keyed-up **10** high-strung, over-
active
hyperbole 8 metaphor **11** enlargement
12 exaggeration **13** magnification,
overstatement **14** figure of speech
hyperbolize 6 overdo **7** amplify, magnify, stretch **9** embroider, overstate **10**
exaggerate
hyperborean 6 arctic **8** freezing,
northern **13** septentrional

Hyperborean
inhabitant of: **8** Paradise
Hyperion
also: **6** Helios
form: **5** Titan
father: **6** Uranus
mother: **4** Gaea
sister: **5** Theia
son: **6** Helios
daughter: **3** Eos **6** Selene
corresponds to: **6** Apollo
Hyperion
author: **9** John Keats **24** Henry Wadsworth Longfellow
hypersensitive 6 touchy **9** emotional
13 temperamental
Hypnos
also: **6** Hypnus
god of: **5** sleep
father: **6** Erebus
mother: **3** Nyx
brother: **8** Thanatos
corresponds to: **6** Somnus
hypnotic 9 soporific **11** mesmerizing
12 spellbinding
hypnotize 7 control **9** mesmerize,
spellbind
hypocrisy 6 deceit, fakery **7** falsity **9**
duplicity, mendacity, phoniness **10**
dishonesty **11** dissembling, insincerity
12 two-facedness
hypocrite 5 phony **8** deceiver **9** pretender **10** dissembler
Hypocrite 15 whited sepulcher
hypocritical 5 false, phony **7** feigned
8 feigning, two- faced **9** deceitful, deceptive, dishonest, insincere, truthless
11 counterfeit
hyporchema
form: **9** choral ode
origin: **5** Greek
honored: **6** Apollo **8** Dionysus
hypothalamus
regulates: **15** body temperature
located in: **5** brain

hypothesis 6 theory, thesis **7** premise,
theorem **8** proposal **9** assertion, postulate **10** assumption, conclusion,
conjecture **11** explanation, guesstimate, presumption, proposition, speculation, supposition
hypothesize 5 infer **6** assume **7** imagine, presume, suppose **8** theorize **9**
postulate, speculate **10** conjecture
hypothetical 7 assumed, dubious **8**
possible, supposed **9** imaginary, uncertain **10** contingent, postulated **11**
conditional, conjectural, presumptive,
speculative, theoretical **12** questionable **13** suppositional
Hypselosaurus
type: **8** dinosaur, sauropod
location: **6** France **8** Mongolia
period: **10** Cretaceous
Hypsilophodon
type: **8** dinosaur **10** ornithopod
location: **7** England
period: **10** Cretaceous
Hyrie
transformed into: **4** swan
hyssop 8 Hyssopus **18** Hyssopus offi-
cialis
varieties: **5** anise, giant, water **9** blue
giant **10** nettle-leaf **11** fennel giant,
purple giant, yellow giant **12** Mexican giant **13** fragrant giant, wrinkled
giant
Hyssop 13 Biblical plant
hysteria 3 fit **5** panic **6** frenzy **8** delirium
hysterical 5 crazy, droll **6** absurd,
crazed, raving **7** amusing, comical **8**
farcical, frenzied, worked-up **9** laughable, ludicrous, wrought-up **10** distracted, distraught, ridiculous, uproarious **11** carried away, overwrought,
wildly funny **13** beside oneself, out of
one's wits **14** uncontrollable
hysterics 3 fit **12** emotionalism

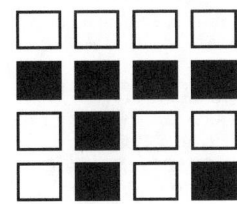

I, Claudius
author: **12** Robert Graves
story of: **36** Tiberius Claudius Drusus Nero Germanicus (Emperor of Rome) (on Masterpiece Theater) actors: **8** John Hurt **11** Derek Jacobi, Sheila White **12** Brian Blessed, Sian Phillips **14** Patrick Stewart, Margaret Tyzack

I, the Jury
author: **14** Mickey Spillane
hero: **10** Mike Hammer

I Am a Fugitive from a Chain Gang
director: **11** Mervyn LeRoy
cast: **8** Paul Muni **11** Helen Vinson **13** Glenda Farrell, Preston Foster

I am unwilling to contend
Latin: **14** nolo contendere

Ibanez, Vicente Blasco
author of: **30** The Four Horsemen of the Apocalypse

Iberian Peninsula
also: **8** Hesperia
comprising: **5** Spain **8** Portugal

Ibsen, Henrik
author of: **6** Ghosts **8** Peer Gynt **11** A Doll's House, Hedda Gabler, Rosmersholm, The Wild Duck **16** The Master Builder **18** An Enemy of the People, John Gabriel Borkman

I came, I saw, I conquered
Latin: **12** veni vidi vici
author: **12** Julius Caesar

Icarus
father: **8** Daedalus
built: **5** wings
flew too near: **3** sun
death by: **8** drowning

ICC 28 Interstate Commerce Commission

ice 3 gem **4** berg, floe, gems, rime **5** chill, frost, glace **6** freeze, icicle, jewels **7** crystal, dessert, glacier, jewelry, sherbet **8** diamonds **11** refrigerant, refrigerate

ice-cold 3 icy **4** cold **5** gelid, polar **6** arctic, bitter, frigid, frosty, wintry **7** chilled, frosted, glacial, subzero **8** chilling, freezing, Siberian, unheated, unwarmed **9** stone-cold, supercold **11** hyperborean, supercooled **12** bone-chilling

ice cream 7 dessert, sherbet **4** soda **5** glace **6** frappe, sundae **7** dessert, parfait, sherbet, spumoni, tortoni

Iceland
other name: **15** Lydveldid Island
capital/largest city: **9** Reykjavik
others: **3** Hof **6** Geysir **7** Akranes, Husavik **8** Akureyri, Keflavik, Kopasker **9** Kopavogur **10** Hveragerdi, Isafjordur **12** Siglufjordur **13** Hafnarfjordur, Neskaupstadur, Seydisfjordur
government:
general assembly: **7** Althing
measure: **3** set **4** alin **5** almud **6** almenn, ferfet, pattur **7** fathmur, fermila, oltunna
weight: **4** pund **5** pound, tunna **6** smjors
island: **7** Heimaey, Surtsey, Westman
lake: **6** Myvatn **10** Thorisvatn **14** Thingvallavatn
mountain: **5** Jokul **10** Orafajokul
volcano: **4** Laki **5** Askja, Hekla, Katla **7** Surtsey
highest point: **17** Hvannadalshnjukur
river: **5** Hvita **7** Fnjoska, Thjorsa **15** Jokulsa a Fjollum
sea: **9** Greenland **13** North Atlantic
physical feature:
fjord: **4** Eyja
geyser: **5** gryla **6** geysir **11** Great Gusher
glacier: **6** Jokull **11** Orafajokull, Vatnajokull
plain: **15** Skeidharasandur
waterfall: **8** Godafoss, Gullfoss **9** Dettifoss
people: **6** Celtic, Viking **8** Norseman **9** Norwegian
first settler: **8** Arnarson
hero: **4** Bele, Eric, Leif **10** Sigurdsson
language: **5** Norse **9** Icelandic
religion: **19** Evangelical Lutheran
place:
national shrine: **11** Thingvellir
feature:
airport: **9** Kopavogur
bird: **4** gull **6** falcon **9** gyrfalcon
literary genre: **4** saga
wrestling: **5** glima
food:
dish: **4** skyr, svio **7** bloomor **8** harofisk

Iceman
nickname of: **12** George Gervin

Iceman Cometh, The
author: **12** Eugene O'Neill
role: **6** Hickey

Ice Palace
author: **10** Edna Ferber

ice skating
athlete: **9** Janet Lynn, John Curry **10** Carol Heiss, Dick Button, Eric Heiden, Sonja Henie **11** Sheila Young **12** Peggy Fleming, Tara Lipinski **13** Dorothy Hamill, Scott Hamilton **14** Linda Fratianne

ich dien 6 I serve
motto of: **13** Prince of Wales

I Ching 30 ancient Chinese book of divination

ichor
form: **5** fluid
in veins of: **4** gods

Ichthyocentaur
form: **8** creature
location: **3** sea
head/torso: **5** human
legs: **5** horse
tail: **4** fish

iciness 4 cold **5** chill **9** frigidity **10** chilliness, frostiness, wintriness **12** slipperiness

ici on parle francais 18 French is spoken here **19** here one speaks French

icky 5 gluey, gooey, gross, gucky, gummy, mushy, nasty, tacky, weepy **6** sticky, syrupy, viscid **7** maudlin, viscous **8** bathetic **9** glutinous, offensive, repulsive, revolting **10** disgusting **12** mucilaginous

icon, ikon 4 idol **5** image **6** effigy, figure, statue **7** picture **8** likeness **11** sacred image

iconoclast 5 rebel **7** radical, upstart **9** dissenter **13** nonconformist, revolutionary

icy 3 raw **4** cold, cool **5** aloof, gelid **6** arctic, chilly, frigid, frosty, frozen, glazed, sleety, wintry **7** distant, glacial, haughty, hostile **8** chilling, freezing, slippery **9** impassive **10** forbidding, unfriendly **11** coldhearted, unemotional

Ida
form: **5** nymph
watched over: **4** Zeus
mount: **5** Crete **7** Phrygia

Idaea
form: **5** nymph
domain: **8** Mount Ida

husband: 7 Phineus **9** Scamander
son: 6 Teucer

Idaho
abbreviation: 2 ID **3** Ida
nickname: 3 Gem
capital/largest city: 5 Boise
others: 4 Buhl **5** Malad, Nampa **6**
Moscow **7** Orofino, Rexburg **8** Caldwell, Lewiston **9** Pocatello, Twin
Falls **10** Idaho Falls **11** Coeur
d'Alene
college: 17 Northwest Nazarene
explorer: 13 Lewis and Clark
feature: 9 Sun Valley **17** Continental
Divide
  dam: 5 Oxbow **8** Brownlee
  national monument: 16 Craters of
  the Moon
tribe: 5 Banak, Shake **6** Cayuse, Paiute, Spokan **7** Bannock, Kutenai,
Spokane **8** Kalispel, Nez Perce, Sahaptin, Shoshone, Shoshoni **9** Shos-
honee **11** Coeur d'Alene
people: 9 Ezra Pound, Sacagawea **11**
Chief Joseph **17** William Edgar Borah
lake: 4 Bear **5** Grey's **6** Priest **11**
Coeur d'Alene, Pend Oreille **22**
American Falls Reservoir
land rank: 10 thirteenth
mountain: 4 Ryan **5** Rocky **6** Rhodes,
Taylor, Tetons **7** Cabinet **8** Ban-
nocks, Big Baldy, Bluenose, Saw-
tooth **9** Wasatches **10** Clearwater **11**
Beaverheads, Bitterroots **13** Selkirk
Ranges
  highest point: 5 Borah
physical feature:
  falls: 5 Moyie **8** Shoshone **9** Upper
  Mesa
  springs: 4 Soda **6** Hooper **7** Lava-
  hot
river: 4 Bear **5** Boise, Snake, St Joe **6**
Locksa, Salmon **7** Payette, Spokane
8 Kootenai **11** Coeur d'Alene, Pend
Oreille
state admission: 10 forty-third
state bird: 16 mountain bluebird
state flower: 7 syringa
state motto: 13 It Is Perpetual **16** Let
It Be Perpetual
state song: 15 Here We Have Idaho
state tree: 16 western white pine

Idas
father: 8 Aphareus
mother: 5 Arene
brother: 7 Lynceus
wife: 8 Marpessa
daughter: 9 Cleopatra

idea 4 clue, hint, view **6** belief, notion
7 concept, feeling, inkling, insight,
opinion, outlook, thought **8** approach,
proposal, solution **9** sentiment **10**
conception, conclusion, conviction,
impression, indication, intimation,
suggestion **12** apperception, appreciation **13** approximation, mental pic-

ture, understanding **14** interpretation,
recommendation

ideal 3 aim **4** hero, idol **5** dream,
model **7** epitome, optimal, pattern,
perfect **8** exemplar, last word, paradigm, standard, ultimate **9** archetype,
criterion, excellent, exemplary, faultless, matchless, objective **10** impeccable **11** inspiration

idealism 8 optimism **9** meliorism **10**
utopianism **11** romanticism

idealist 7 dreamer, utopian **8** romantic
9 Pollyanna, stargazer, visionary **11**
romanticist **13** perfectionist

idealized 6 dreamy **7** utopian, wishful
8 fanciful, illusory, romantic **10** optimistic **11** pie-in-the-sky, unrealistic **13**
insubstantial

idea man 7 advisor **8** inventor **9** innovator **10** consultant **12** entrepreneur

idee fixe 9 fixed idea
music: 14 recurring motif

idem 24 the same as previously given
28 the same as previously mentioned

identical 4 twin **7** uniform **8** selfsame, very same **9** duplicate **15** interchangeable **17** indistinguishable

identification 2 ID **5** badge, label **6**
dogtag **7** license **8** passport **9** detection **10** connection, revelation **11** affiliation, association, credentials, pinpointing, recognition **12** confirmation,
verification **13** ascertainment

identify 4 know **5** place **6** finger, verify **7** combine, pick out, specify **9** associate, designate, determine, recognize, single out **11** distinguish

identifying device 4 logo, mark, sign
5 badge **6** emblem, ensign, symbol **8**
insignia, logotype

identity 4 name, self **6** accord **7** harmony, oneness, rapport **9** unanimity
11 delineation, duplication, personality **13** individuality **15** differentiation,
distinctiveness

ideology 5 dogma, ethos **6** ideals, theory **7** program **8** doctrine **9** rationale
10 principles

Ides of March, The
author: 14 Thornton Wilder

id est 6 that is
abbreviation: 2 ie

idiocy 5 folly **6** lunacy **7** fatuity, inanity, madness, suicide **8** insanity **9** absurdity, asininity, cretinism, mongol-
ism, stupidity **11** foolishness **13**
foolhardiness, senselessness

idiom 5 argot, lingo, slang **6** brogue,
jargon, patois, phrase, speech **7** dialect **8** language, localism, parlance **10**
vernacular **13** colloquialism

idiomatic 6 common **8** informal, ordinary **10** vernacular **14** conversational

idiosyncrasy 3 tic **5** quirk **6** oddity **7**
anomaly **9** mannerism **11** distinction,
peculiarity **12** eccentricity

idiot 3 ass **4** boob, dolt, dope, fool,
jerk **5** cluck, dummy, dunce, moron,
ninny **6** cretin, dimwit, nitwit **7** half-
wit **8** dumbbell, numskull **9** blockhead, numbskull, simpleton **10** nincompoop

Idiot, The
author: 16 Fyodor Dostoevsky
character: 7 Myshkin **11** Mme
Epanchin **14** Aglaya Epanchin, Par-
fen Rogozhin **16** Natasya Filipovna
19 Ganya Ardalionovitch **22** Prince
Lef Nicolaievitch

idiotic 5 crazy, dopey, nutty **6** absurd,
addled, stupid **7** asinine, doltish, foolish, moronic **9** foolhardy, imbecilic,
senseless **10** half-witted, irrational, ridiculous **12** feebleminded **13** rattlebrained

I direct
Latin: 6 dirigo
motto of: 5 Maine

idle 4 laze, lazy, loaf, vain **5** empty, inert, petty, vapid, waste, while **6**
drowsy, fallow, futile, otiose, putter,
torpid, unused **7** aimless, fritter, jobless, languid, trivial, useless, wait out
8 baseless, bootless, fool away, inactive, indolent, listless, slothful, sluggish, trifling **9** at leisure, enervated,
fruitless, lethargic, out of work, pointless, somnolent, valueless, worthless
10 not working, unemployed, unoccupied **11** unimportant **12** unproductive
15 unsubstantiated

idleness 5 sloth **7** inertia **8** laziness,
lethargy **9** indolence **10** inactivity **11**
joblessness, languidness **12** sluggishness, unemployment
French: 8 flanerie

idler 3 bum **6** loafer **7** drifter, vagrant
10 ne'er-do-well
French: 7 flaneur

idol 4 hero, icon **5** relic **6** effigy, statue
7 darling **8** artifact **9** superstar **10**
simulacrum, golden calf **11** graven
image, inspiration

idolatry 5 mania **7** madness, passion,
worship **8** devotion **9** adoration, obsession **10** veneration **11** idolization,
infatuation **12** image worship **13** preoccupation

idolization 7 worship **9** adulation, reverence **10** exaltation, veneration

idolize 5 adore, deify, honor, prize **6**
admire, revere **7** worship **8** treasure,
venerate **9** reverence **11** apotheosize

Idomeneo, re di Creta
also: 20 Idomeneus King of Crete
opera by: 6 Mozart
character: 4 Ilia **7** Electra **8** Ida-
mante, Poseidon

Idomeneus
king of: 5 Crete
father: 9 Deucalion

I don't know what
French: 12 je ne sais quoi

I Dream of Jeannie
  character: 7 Jeannie **9** Dr Bellows **10** (Captain) Tony Nelson **11** Gen Peterson, (Captain) Roger Healey **13** Amanda Bellows
  cast: 9 Bill Daily **11** Barbara Eden, Hayden Rorke, Larry Hagman **13** Barton MacLane, Emmaline Henry
  Tony's job: 9 astronaut

idyllic 6 rustic, sylvan **7** bucolic **8** arcadian, pastoral, peaceful, romantic **9** unspoiled

Idylls of the King, The
  author: 18 Alfred Lord Tennyson
  based on story of: 10 King Arthur

if 2 an **6** though **7** whether **8** although, provided **9** condition, supposing **10** even though **11** stipulation, supposition

iffy 4 moot **5** risky **6** chancy, unsure **7** dubious, erratic **8** arguable, doubtful **9** debatable, uncertain, undecided, unsettled, whimsical **10** capricious, disputable, unresolved **11** conjectural, speculative **12** questionable **13** problematical, unpredictable

If Winter Comes
  author: 13 A S M Hutchinson

if you please
  French: 12 s'il vous plait

ignitable 8 burnable **9** flammable **10** combustive, incendiary **11** combustible, inflammable **13** conflagrative

ignite 4 burn, fire **5** blaze, flame, light **6** blow up, kindle **7** explode, inflame **8** take fire, touch off **9** catch fire, set fire to, set on fire **11** catch on fire

ignoble 3 low **4** base, foul, mean, vile **6** craven **7** debased, heinous **8** cowardly, degraded, depraved, indecent, infamous, inferior, shameful, unworthy **9** dastardly, nefarious **10** degenerate, despicable **11** disgraceful **12** contemptible, dishonorable **13** discreditable, pusillanimous **14** unconscionable

ignominious 3 low **5** sorry **6** abject **8** grievous, shameful, wretched **9** degrading **10** despicable, inglorious, unbearable **11** disgraceful, humiliating **12** dishonorable, disreputable **13** discreditable

ignominy 5 shame **6** infamy **8** contempt, disgrace, dishonor **11** degradation, humiliation

ignoramus 4 fool **5** dunce **6** nitwit **7** low-brow **8** numskull **9** numbskull, simpleton **10** illiterate **11** know-nothing

ignorance 9 confusion **10** illiteracy **11** unawareness **12** backwardness **13** obliviousness, unfamiliarity **15** unenlightenment

ignorant 4 dumb **5** naive **6** stupid **7** asinine, blind to, fatuous, shallow, unaware **8** innocent, untaught **9** in the dark, unknowing, unlearned, un-

trained, untutored, unworldly **10** illiterate, uneducated, uninformed, unlettered, unschooled **11** insensitive, uncognizant **12** unperceptive **13** irresponsible, unenlightened, unintelligent **15** unknowledgeable

ignore 4 omit, skip, snub **5** scorn **6** eschew, slight **7** neglect **8** overlook, pass over **9** disregard

Igraine
  character in: 16 Arthurian romance
  son: 6 Arthur
  by: 14 Uther Pendragon

Iguanodon
  type: 8 dinosaur **10** ornithopod
  means: 11 iguana tooth
  found by: 13 Gideon Mantell
  location: 6 Africa, Europe, Sussex **7** Belgium, England
  period: 10 Cretaceous
  characteristic: 10 duck-billed

ikebana
  Japanese: 21 art of arranging flowers

Ile de France see **9** Mauritius

Ilha Formosa see **6** Taiwan

Iliad, The
  author: 5 Homer
  character: 5 Paris, Priam **6** Hector **8** Achilles, Menelaus **9** Agamemnon, Patroclus **11** Helen of Troy
  subject: 9 Trojan War

Iliniwek see **8** Illinois

Ilion
  Greek name for: 11 ancient Troy

Ilium
  Latin name for: 11 ancient Troy

ill, ills 3 woe **4** evil, foul, harm, sick, vile **5** abuse, cross, no way, surly, trial **6** ailing, damage, hardly, injury, laid up, malady, malice, nowise, plague, poorly, sickly, sorrow, unkind, unwell, wicked **7** ailment, cruelty, disease, failing, harmful, invalid, not well, ominous, outrage, peevish, trouble, unlucky, unsound **8** diseased, mischief, scarcely, sinister, vengeful **9** afflicted, complaint, infirmity, malicious, unhealthy **10** affliction, disturbing, foreboding, indisposed, misfortune, wickedness **11** abomination, acrimonious, malefaction, threatening, unfavorable **12** inauspicious, unpropitious **15** under the weather

ill-advised 4 dumb, rash **5** hasty, silly **6** myopic, stupid, unwise **7** foolish **9** foolhardy, ill-judged, impolitic, imprudent, misguided, senseless **10** indiscreet, unthinking **11** injudicious **12** shortsighted **13** ill-considered, irresponsible

ill-at-ease 3 shy **4** edgy **6** on edge, uneasy **7** abashed, fidgety, nervous **8** bothered, troubled **9** disturbed, nonplused, perturbed **10** disquieted, nonplussed **11** discomfited, discomposed, embarrassed **12** disconcerted **13** self-

conscious, uncomfortable **15** discountenanced

ill-boding 4 dire **7** ominous **9** ill-omened **11** apocalyptic **12** inauspicious

ill-bred 4 rude **5** crude **7** boorish, uncivil, uncouth **8** churlish, impolite **10** unmannerly **11** ill-mannered **12** discourteous

ill-defined 3 dim **4** hazy **5** faint, murky **6** blurry **7** blurred, clouded, shadowy **8** nebulous, obscured **10** indistinct

illegal 5 wrong **6** banned **7** illicit **8** criminal, not legal, outlawed, unlawful **9** felonious, forbidden **10** actionable, prohibited, proscribed **12** illegitimate, unauthorized, unsanctioned **13** against the law

illegible 7 unclear **8** obscured **9** scribbled **10** unreadable **14** indecipherable, undecipherable, unintelligible

illegitimate 7 bastard, illegal, illicit, lawless, natural **8** baseborn, improper, unlawful **10** prohibited **11** misbegotten, unwarranted **12** unauthorized, unsanctioned

ill-fated 6 doomed, jinxed **7** hapless, unlucky **8** blighted, luckless **9** ill-omened **10** ill-starred

ill-favored 4 ugly **5** plain **6** homely **8** unlovely **9** repulsive, unsightly **12** disagreeable, unattractive

ill-fortune 6 mishap **7** bad luck **8** calamity, disaster, hardship **9** adversity **10** misfortune **11** catastrophe

ill health 6 malady **7** ailment, disease, illness **8** sickness **9** infirmity

ill-humored 5 sulky, testy **6** crabby, grumpy, sullen **7** grouchy **10** in a bad mood, unfriendly, unsociable

illiberal 5 petty, small **6** biased, narrow **7** bigoted **9** hidebound **10** brassbound, intolerant, prejudiced, ungenerous **11** opinionated, small-minded **12** narrow-minded, short-sighted

illicit 7 illegal, lawless **8** criminal, improper, not legal, unlawful **9** felonious **10** prohibited **11** black-market, clandestine **12** illegitimate, not permitted, unauthorized **13** against the law, impermissible **15** under-the-counter

Illinois
  abbreviation: 2 IL **3** Ill
  nickname: 4 Tall **6** Sucker **7** Prairie **13** Land of Lincoln
  capital: 11 Springfield
  largest city: 7 Chicago
  others: 4 Pana **5** Alton, Cairo, Elgin, Flora, Olney, Pekin **6** Albion, Berwyn, Canton, Herrin, Joliet, Peoria, Skokie **7** Batavia, Decatur, Genesco, Mendota, Nokomis **8** Evanston, Rockford, Waukegan **9** Centralia **10** Barrington **11** Bloomington
  college: 4 Knox **5** Barat **6** Aurora, DePaul, Eureka, Loyola, Olivet,

Quincy, Shimer **7** Bradley, Chicago, Wheaton **8** Millikin **9** Augustana **12** Northwestern **16** Illinois Wesleyan **23** Illinois Institute of Tech
explorer: 6 Joliet **7** Jolliet **9** Marquette
feature: 10 stockyards
  airport: 5 O'Hare
  museum: 18 Science and Industry
  seaway: 10 St Lawrence
  trail: 7 Lincoln
tribe: 3 Fox **4** Sauk **9** Kaskaskia
people: 9 Black Hawk, Jack Benny **10** Jane Addams, Walt Disney **12** Carl Sandburg **15** Ernest Hemingway **18** Engineer Casey Jones **20** William Jennings Bryan
lake: 3 Fox **5** Grass **7** Calumet **8** Michigan, Pistakee
land rank: 12 twenty-fourth
mountain: 6 Ozarks
  highest point: 12 Charles Mound
physical feature:
  hills: 7 Shawnee
president: 14 Abraham Lincoln
river: 4 Ohio, Rock **5** Spoon **6** Wabash **7** Chicago, Elkhorn **8** Big Muddy, Illinois, Mackinaw, Sangamon **9** Kaskaskia **10** Des Plaines **11** Mississippi
state admission: 11 twenty-first
state bird: 8 cardinal
state flower: 6 violet
state motto: 29 State Sovereignty, National Union
state song: 8 Illinois
state tree: 7 burl oak **8** white oak

Illinois (Iliniwek)
language family: 9 Algonkian **10** Algonquian
tribe: 6 Peoria **7** Cahokia, Tamaroa **9** Kaskaskia, Moingwena **10** Michigamea
location: 4 Iowa, Ohio **7** Indiana **8** Illinois, Michigan, Missouri **9** Wisconsin
built: 12 Cahokia Mound
murdered: 7 Pontiac
related to: 5 Miami **6** Ojibwa **7** Ojibway

illiterate 7 witless **8** childish, ignorant, unversed **9** unlearned, untutored **10** amateurish, incoherent, uneducated, uninformed, unlettered, unreliable, unschooled **11** not educated, uninitiated, unscholarly **12** uninstructed **13** unenlightened, ungrammatical **15** unknowledgeable

ill-made 6 shoddy **7** awkward **8** deformed, inferior **9** makeshift, malformed **10** jerry-built, jury-rigged **15** misproportioned

ill-mannered 4 rude **5** crude **6** coarse **7** boorish, ill-bred, loutish, uncivil **8** impolite **9** offensive, ungallant **10** ill-behaved, ungracious **12** discourteous **13** disrespectful

ill-natured 4 sour **5** cross, nasty, surly **6** bitter, cranky, malign **7** caustic, grouchy, peevish **8** captious, churlish, spiteful, venomous **9** crotchety, irascible, irritable, malignant, rancorous, splenetic **10** ill-humored, unfriendly **11** acrimonious, contentious, quarrelsome **12** antagonistic, cantankerous

illness 6 malady **7** ailment, disease **8** disorder, sickness **9** complaint, ill health, infirmity **10** affliction, disability, poor health **11** malfunction **13** indisposition

illogical 4 wild **5** crazy, dopey, nutty, silly, wacky **6** absurd, far-out, screwy **7** asinine, offbeat, unsound **9** erroneous, senseless **10** fallacious, irrational, off-the-wall, ridiculous **11** incongruent, incongruous, nonsensical, unreasoning **12** inconsistent, preposterous, unreasonable **13** contradictory

ill-omened 4 dire **7** adverse, ominous **9** ill-boding **11** apocalyptic, unfavorable **12** inauspicious, unpropitious

ill-smelling 4 foul, high, olid, rank **5** fetid, fusty **6** putrid, rancid, smelly, stinky, strong **7** reeking **8** stinking **10** malodorous

ill-starred 4 dire **5** fatal **6** tragic **7** adverse **8** ill-fated **10** calamitous, disastrous **11** unfortunate **12** catastrophic, inauspicious

ill-suited 5 inapt **8** mismated, unsuited **9** misjoined, unfitting **10** ill-adapted, ill-matched, malapropos, mismatched, unbecoming, unsuitable **11** incongruous, unbefitting, uncongenial **12** incompatible, inconsistent **13** inappropriate

ill-tempered 4 mean, rude, sour **5** angry, cross, harsh, nasty, testy **6** bitter, cranky, shirty **7** acerbic, furious, grouchy, peevish, waspish **8** choleric, churlish, petulant **9** crotchety, irascible, irritable **10** bad-natured, ill-humored, ill-natured, in a bad mood, unpleasant **11** acrimonious **12** cantankerous

ill-treatment 4 harm **5** abuse **6** ill-use, injury, misuse **7** cruelty **13** mortification

illuminate 5 edify, light **7** clarify, enhance, explain, light up **8** brighten, illumine, instruct, spell out **9** elucidate, enlighten, exemplify, irradiate, make clear **12** throw light on **13** cast light upon

illuminated 3 lit **5** lit up **6** bright **7** lighted **9** clarified, decorated, illumined **10** brightened, elucidated, irradiated

illumination 6 lights, wisdom **7** insight **8** lighting **9** education, knowledge **10** illumining, lighting up, perception, revelation **11** edification, information, instruction, irradiation **13** comprehension, enlightenment

Illuminations, Les
  author: 13 Arthur Rimbaud
illumined 3 lit **7** lighted **8** luminous **11** illuminated
ill-use 4 harm, hurt **5** abuse **6** injure, misuse **7** assault, cruelty, harming **8** maltreat, mistreat **10** bodily harm **12** maltreatment, mistreatment
illusion 5 error, fancy **6** mirage, vagary, vision **7** caprice, chimera, fallacy **8** delusion, phantasm **9** deception, false idea, misbelief, semblance, unreality **10** apparition, false image, hocus-pocus, humbuggery, impression **11** false belief, fata morgana **13** hallucination, misconception, misimpression **15** misapprehension
illusive 5 false **6** unreal **7** phantom, seeming **8** apparent, chimeric, fanciful, fantastic, illusory **9** deceptive **10** ostensible **11** illusionary
illusory 4 sham **5** false **6** unreal **7** seeming **8** apparent, delusive, fanciful, illusive, spurious **9** deceptive, erroneous, imaginary **10** fallacious, misleading, ostensible **11** counterfeit, unrealistic **13** hallucinatory
illustrate 4 show **6** define **7** clarify, explain, picture, point up, portray **8** decorate, ornament **9** bring home, delineate, elucidate, emphasize, make clear, represent **10** illuminate **11** demonstrate **12** pictorialize, throw light on **16** make intelligible
illustration 5 image, plate **6** figure **7** drawing, example, picture **8** instance, specimen **9** portrayal **10** photograph **14** representation **15** exemplification
illustrious 5 famed, great, noted **6** famous **7** eminent, honored, notable **8** glorious, lustrous, peerless, renowned, splendid **9** acclaimed, brilliant, exemplary, matchless, prominent **10** celebrated **11** magnificent **13** distinguished
illustriousness 8 grandeur **9** greatness **11** distinction **12** magnificence
ill will 4 gall **5** anger, spite **6** animus, enmity, hatred, malice, rancor, spleen **7** dislike **8** acrimony, aversion, bad blood, loathing **9** animosity, antipathy, hostility **10** abhorrence, antagonism, bitterness, contention **11** malevolence **12** hard feelings, spitefulness
ill wind 7 bad luck **8** bad break, hard luck **9** adversity, mischance **10** misfortune
Illyrius
  father: 6 Cadmus
Ilmarinen
  origin: 7 Finnish
  form: 10 blacksmith
  hero in: 8 Kalevala
  forged: 5 Sampo
  Sampo's owner: 5 Louhi
I Love Lucy
  character: 9 Fred Mertz **10** Ethel

Mertz **11** Little Ricky, Lucy Ricardo **12** Ricky Ricardo

cast: 9 Desi Arnaz **11** Lucille Ball, Vivian Vance **14** William Frawley

Ricky's club: 7 Babaloo **9** Tropicana

Il Penseroso
author: 10 John Milton
companion piece: 8 L'Allegro

image 4 copy, icon, idea, idol **6** double, effigy, fetish, figure, memory, simile, statue, symbol, visage **7** concept, picture, replica **8** likeness, metaphor, portrait **9** depiction, duplicate, facsimile, mirroring, semblance **10** photograph, reflection, simulacrum **11** countenance, delineation, incarnation **12** recollection, reproduction **13** mental picture **14** figure of speech, representation

imaginable 8 feasible **9** thinkable **11** conceivable

imaginary 4 sham **5** fancy, phony **6** made-up, unreal **7** fancied, fiction, figment **8** delusion, fabulous, fanciful, illusion, illusory, invented, mythical, romantic **9** fantastic, figmental, legendary **10** factitious, fictitious **11** counterfeit, make-believe

imagination 5 fancy **7** cunning, thought **9** ingenuity, invention **10** astuteness, creativity, enterprise **12** creativeness **13** inventiveness **14** thoughtfulness **15** creative thought, resourcefulness

imaginative 6 clever **7** unusual **8** creative, inspired, original **9** ingenious, inventive **10** innovative **11** resourceful **12** enterprising **16** off the beaten path, out of the ordinary

imagine 5 fancy, guess, infer, judge **6** assume, gather **7** believe, dream up, picture, presume, pretend, project, suppose, surmise, suspect **8** conceive, envisage, envision **9** fantasize, visualize **10** conjecture

imbecile 3 ass **4** dolt, dope, fool, jerk **5** dummy, dunce, idiot, moron, ninny **6** nitwit **7** dingbat **8** dumbbell **9** blockhead, simpleton **10** nincompoop

imbecilic 4 dumb **5** inane, silly **6** absurd, stupid **7** asinine, foolish **8** careless, mindless **11** thoughtless

imbecility 6 idiocy **8** dullness, dumbness **9** asininity, stupidity, thickness **16** simplemindedness

imbibe 4 swig, tope **5** drink, quaff **6** guzzle, ingest, tipple **7** consume, partake, swallow **8** chugalug, toss down, wash down

imbiber 3 sot **4** wino **5** drunk, toper **7** drinker, tippler **8** consumer, drunkard, ingester

imbroglio 3 row **4** fray **5** brawl, broil, clash, fight, melee, scrap **6** fracas, ruckus, rumpus, uproar **7** scuffle **8** argument **9** confusion **11** altercation,

embroilment **12** entanglement **13** embarrassment

imbue 4 fill, fire, tint **5** bathe, color, endow, steep, tinge **6** arouse, infuse **7** animate, impress, ingrain, inspire, instill, pervade, suffuse **8** permeate, tincture **9** inculcate

Imhotep
father: 4 Ptah
mother: 7 Sekhmet
position: 6 scribe, vizier, writer **9** architect, physician
architect of pyramid: 8 Sakkarah

imitate 3 ape **4** copy, mime **5** mimic **6** mirror, parody, parrot **7** emulate, pass for **8** look like, simulate **9** duplicate, represent **10** caricature **11** counterfeit, impersonate

imitation 4 fake, mock, sham **5** aping, phony **6** ersatz, parody **7** man-made, mimicry, takeoff **8** travesty **9** burlesque, facsimile, semblance, simulated, synthetic **10** adaptation, artificial, caricature, impression, similarity, simulation **11** counterfeit, duplication, make-believe **12** reproduction **13** impersonation **14** representation

Imitation of Christ, The
author: 13 Thomas a Kempis

immaculate 4 pure **5** clean, ideal **6** chaste, intact, virgin **7** perfect, saintly, sinless **8** flawless, innocent, spotless, unsoiled, virginal, virtuous **9** faultless, guiltless, shipshape, stainless, unstained, unsullied **11** spic and span, untarnished **13** above reproach, unimpeachable **14** irreproachable **15** unexceptionable

immanent 6 inborn, inbred, innate **7** natural **8** inherent **9** ingrained, intrinsic **10** congenital, deep-rooted, deep-seated, indigenous, indwelling **11** instinctive, instinctual

Immanuel 7 Messiah **11** Jesus Christ
means: 9 God with us

immaterial 7 ghostly, shadowy, trivial **8** bodiless, ethereal, mystical, noumenal, spectral, trifling, unbodied **9** spiritual, unearthly **10** evanescent, extraneous, impalpable, intangible, irrelevant, of no moment **11** disembodied, incorporeal, not relevant, unimportant **12** extramundane, extrasensory **13** insignificant, insubstantial, unsubstantial **14** of no importance **15** inconsequential, of little account

immature 5 green, young **6** callow, unripe **7** babyish, kiddish, puerile **8** childish, juvenile, unformed, youthful **9** embryonic, half-grown, infantile, not mature, pubescent **10** unfinished, unmellowed **11** out of season, rudimentary, undeveloped **16** wet behind the ears

immeasurable 7 endless, immense **8** infinite **9** boundless, limitless, unbounded, unlimited **10** fathomless **11**

illimitable, inestimable, measureless, never-ending **12** incalculable, interminable, unfathomable **13** inexhaustible

immediate 4 near, next, nigh **5** close, hasty, local, swift **6** abrupt, nearby, prompt, recent, speedy, sudden **7** express, instant, nearest **8** adjacent, punctual **9** proximate, undelayed **10** contiguous **13** instantaneous

immediately 3 now **4** ASAP, stat **9** instantly, right away **10** this minute **12** without delay
French: 11 tout de suite

immemorial 5 olden **7** ageless, ancient **8** dateless, hallowed, timeless **9** ancestral, legendary, venerable **11** time-honored **12** long-standing, mythological **15** long-established

immense 4 huge, vast **5** great **7** mammoth, massive **8** colossal, enormous, gigantic **9** extensive, monstrous **10** prodigious, stupendous, tremendous **11** measureless **14** Brobdingnagian

immensity 8 enormity, hugeness, vastness **9** largeness **12** enormousness

immerse 3 dip **4** duck, dunk, sink, soak **5** bathe, douse, lower, steep **6** absorb, drench, engage, occupy, plunge **7** engross **8** submerge

immerse briefly 3 dip **4** dunk

immersion 7 bathing, dunking **8** drowning **10** absorption, submersion **11** engrossment, involvement, submergence **13** concentration, preoccupation

immigrant 5 alien **7** migrant, settler **8** colonist, newcomer **9** foreigner, nonnative

immigrate 6 move to, settle **7** migrate **8** colonize

imminent 4 near **7** looming **8** menacing, perilous **9** immediate, impending **10** near at hand **11** approaching, close at hand, threatening

immobile 4 fast **5** fixed, quiet, rigid, stiff, still **6** at rest, laid up, rooted, secure, stable, static **7** riveted **9** immovable, not moving, quiescent, steadfast **10** motionless, stationary, stock-still **11** unbudgeable **13** incapacitated

immobilize 3 fix, set **4** stud **6** disarm, freeze, splint **7** disable **8** paralyze, transfix **12** incapacitate

immoderate 5 undue **7** extreme **8** whopping **9** excessive, unbridled **10** exorbitant, gargantuan, inordinate, prodigious **11** extravagant, intemperate, uncalled-for **12** unreasonable, unrestrained **14** unconscionable

immoderation 6 excess **10** debauchery **11** dissipation, prodigality, unrestraint **12** extravagance, intemperance, recklessness **13** excessiveness **14** prodigiousness

immodest 4 lewd, vain **5** gross, loose **6** brazen, coarse, risque, wanton **7**

pompous 8 boastful, braggart, indecent, inflated, unchaste **9** bombastic, conceited, shameless **10** indecorous, indelicate, peacockish, suggestive **11** exaggerated, pretentious **12** self-centered

immoral 4 evil, lewd **5** dirty, wrong **6** sinful, wicked **7** corrupt, heinous, obscene, raunchy, vicious **8** depraved, indecent, infamous, prurient **9** debauched, dissolute, nefarious, salacious, unethical **10** dissipated, iniquitous, licentious, profligate **12** pornographic, unprincipled

Immoralist, The
author: **9** Andre Gide

immorality 3 sin **4** evil **9** decadence, depravity, indecency, obscenity, prurience **10** corruption, debasement, degeneracy, sinfulness **13** salaciousness

immortal 3 god **6** divine **7** abiding, eternal, undying **8** enduring **9** deathless **11** everlasting **12** imperishable

Immortals 6 giants, greats, titans **7** the gods **8** demigods **13** all-time greats
Greek/Roman: 8 pantheon

immovable 3 icy, set **4** cold, fast **5** fixed **6** dogged, secure, steely, stolid **7** adamant, settled **8** detached, fastened, immobile, obdurate, resolute, stubborn **9** heartless, impassive, unfeeling **10** inexorable, inflexible, stationary, unbendable **11** coldhearted, unbudgeable **12** unchangeable **13** unimpressible, unsympathetic **16** unimpressionable

immune 4 free, safe **5** clear **6** exempt **9** protected, resistant **12** invulnerable **13** unsusceptible

immunity 7 freedom **9** exemption **10** resistance **16** unsusceptibility

immure 3 hem, pen **4** cage, coop, jail, wall **6** entomb, intern, wall in, wall up **7** confine, enclose, seclude **8** cloister, imprison **11** incarcerate

immutability 9 endurance, stability **14** changelessness

immutable 4 firm **5** fixed, solid **6** stable **7** lasting **8** constant, enduring **9** permanent, unaltered, unvarying **10** changeless, inflexible, unchanging **11** unalterable **12** unchangeable, unmodifiable **14** intransmutable **16** incontrovertible

Imogen
character in: **9** Cymbeline
author: **11** Shakespeare

imp 3 elf **4** brat **5** demon, devil, gnome, pixie, scamp **6** goblin, hoyden, rascal, sprite, urchin **7** upstart **9** hobgoblin **10** evil spirit, leprechaun

impact 4 jolt **5** brunt, crash, force, shock, smash **6** burden, effect, thrust **7** contact **9** collision, influence **10** concussion **11** implication **12** repercussion

impair 3 mar **4** harm, hurt **6** damage, hinder, injure, lessen, reduce, weaken, worsen **7** cripple, subvert, vitiate **8** decrease, enervate, enfeeble, undercut **10** debilitate **11** detract from

impaired 6 broken, faulty, flawed **7** damaged **9** defective, deficient, imperfect

impairment 4 flaw, harm **5** fault **6** damage, defect, injury, malady **7** ailment, illness **8** debility, disorder, handicap, sickness, weakness **9** detriment, hindrance, infirmity **10** disability, impediment, inadequacy **12** debilitation

impale 3 fix, pin **4** gore, stab, tack **5** affix, stick **8** transfix **10** run through

impart 4 give, lend, tell **5** grant, offer, share **6** accord, afford, pass on, relate, render, report, reveal **7** confide, consign, deliver, divulge, mention **8** bestow on, confer on, disclose, dispense **9** make known **10** contribute **11** communicate

impartial 4 fair, just **7** neutral **8** detached, unbiased **9** equitable, objective **10** evenhanded, fair-minded, open-minded **11** nonpartisan **12** unprejudiced **13** disinterested, dispassionate

impartiality 7 justice **8** equality, fair play, fairness **10** detachment, neutrality **11** objectivity

impasse 4 snag **7** dead end, dilemma **8** cul-de-sac, deadlock, quandary, standoff **9** stalemate **10** blind alley, bottleneck, standstill **11** predicament

impassioned 5 eager, fiery **6** ardent, heated **7** earnest, excited, fervent, intense, rousing, zealous **8** animated, forceful, inspired, stirring

impassive 4 calm, cool **5** aloof, stony **6** sedate, stolid **7** stoical, unmoved **8** reserved **9** apathetic, untouched **10** impervious, insensible, phlegmatic **11** emotionless, indifferent, inscrutable, unemotional, unperturbed **13** dispassionate, imperturbable, unimpressible **16** unimpressionable

impassiveness 8 coldness **9** aloofness, stolidity **12** indifference **15** emotionlessness

impassivity 6 apathy **8** coolness, stoicism **9** aloofness, stolidity **10** dispassion **15** emotionlessness **16** imperturbability

impatient 4 edgy **5** fussy, hasty, itchy, rabid, tense, testy **6** ardent, touchy **7** annoyed, anxious, brusque, hurried, nervous, peevish, restive **8** agitated, feverish, restless **9** excitable, irascible, irritable, irritated **10** high-strung, intolerant, passionate **12** enthusiastic

impeach 4 slur **6** accuse, assail, attack, charge, impugn, indict **7** arraign, slander **8** badmouth, belittle, question **9** challenge, discredit, disparage, incul-

pate **11** incriminate **16** call into question

impeccable 7 perfect **8** flawless **9** blameless, excellent, faultless **10** immaculate **11** unblemished **12** irreprovable, unassailable **13** unimpeachable **14** irreproachable **15** unexceptionable

impecunious 4 poor **5** broke, needy **6** hard-up **7** pinched **8** bankrupt, indigent **9** destitute, insolvent, penniless **10** down-and-out, straitened **12** impoverished **15** poverty-stricken

impede 5 block, check, delay, deter, stall **6** arrest, halter, hamper, hinder, retard, stymie, thwart **7** disrupt, inhibit **8** hold back, obstruct, slow down **9** frustrate, interrupt, sidetrack **13** interfere with

impediment 4 flaw **5** block, delay **6** defect **7** barrier **8** blockage, drawback, handicap, obstacle **9** deformity, hindrance **10** detraction **11** obstruction **12** interference **14** stumbling block

impedimenta 4 gear **7** baggage **9** equipment **13** accoutrements, paraphernalia

impel 4 goad, prod, push, spur, urge **5** drive, force **6** compel, incite, induce, prompt **7** require **8** motivate **9** constrain, stimulate **11** necessitate

impend 4 brew, hang, loom **5** hover, lower **6** menace **8** approach, draw near, overhang, threaten

impending 4 near **6** coming **7** brewing, looming **8** imminent, menacing, oncoming **9** immediate **11** approaching, forthcoming, threatening

impenetrable 5 dense, solid, thick **6** sealed **7** elusive, obscure **8** puzzling **9** insoluble **10** impassable, impervious, insensible, intangible, inviolable, mysterious, unpalpable **11** inscrutable, unenterable **12** inaccessible, inexplicable, invulnerable, unfathomable **16** incomprehensible

impenitent 4 lost **6** inured **7** callous, defiant **8** hardened, obdurate **9** unashamed **10** uncontrite **11** remorseless, unrepentant, unrepenting **12** incorrigible, unapologetic **13** irreclaimable

imperative 6 urgent **7** crucial, needful **8** critical, pressing **9** essential, mandatory, necessary, requisite **10** compulsory, obligatory **12** unavoidable

imperceptible 5 minor, scant, small **6** hidden, minute, slight, subtle **7** minimal **8** academic **10** indistinct **12** undetectable, unnoticeable **13** infinitesimal, insignificant, unappreciable, unperceivable **14** inconsiderable

imperceptive 5 blind **9** unfeeling **11** insensitive, unobservant **12** inpercipient, unperceptive **13** unsympathetic

imperfect 6 faulty, flawed **8** deformed, fallible, impaired **9** blemished, defective

imperfection 4 flaw **5** fault **6** defect **7** blemish **8** weakness **9** deformity **10** faultiness, impairment, inadequacy **11** fallibility, shortcoming **13** insufficiency **14** incompleteness

imperial 5 bossy **6** feudal, lordly **8** despotic **9** arbitrary, imperious **10** autocratic, high-handed, peremptory, repressive, tyrannical **11** dictatorial, domineering, magisterial, overbearing **13** authoritarian

Imperial Presidency, The
   author: **20** Arthur M Schlesinger Jr

imperil 4 risk **6** chance, expose, gamble, hazard **8** endanger **10** compromise, jeopardize **13** put in jeopardy

imperious 5 bossy, lofty **6** lordly **7** haughty **8** arrogant, despotic, imperial **10** autocratic, commanding, peremptory, tyrannical **11** dictatorial, domineering, overbearing **13** high-and-mighty

imperiousness 9 arrogance, loftiness **11** haughtiness

imperishable 6 stable **7** durable, lasting **14** indestructible

imperium 4 rule **5** realm **6** domain, empire **8** dominion **11** sovereignty

impermanent 7 passing **8** fleeting, fugitive, not fixed, unstable **9** ephemeral, temporary, transient **10** evanescent, transitory, unenduring

impermeable 5 dense, solid, tight **6** opaque **9** nonporous **10** impervious, waterproof

impersonal 4 dead **6** remote **7** general, inhuman, neutral **8** detached, lifeless, soulless **9** impartial, impassive, inanimate, inorganic, objective **10** spiritless **11** perfunctory **13** disinterested, dispassionate

impersonate 3 ape **4** copy, mime **5** mimic **6** pose as **7** imitate, portray **9** personify, represent **11** pretend to be **12** masquerade as

impertinence 4 sass **5** cheek, sauce **7** affront **8** audacity, boldness, rudeness **9** freshness, impudence, insolence, sauciness **10** cheekiness, disrespect, effrontery, incivility **11** irrelevance **17** disrespectfulness, inappropriateness

impertinent 4 rude **5** fresh, surly **6** brassy, brazen, smarty **7** uncivil **8** arrogant, impudent, insolent **9** extrinsic, insulting, unrelated **10** extraneous, immaterial, irrelevant, not germane, peremptory, unmannerly **11** unimportant **12** discourteous, presumptuous **13** disrespectful, inappropriate **14** beside the point

imperturbability 5 poise **6** aplomb **8** calmness, coolness **9** composure, sangfroid **10** equanimity, steadiness **11** self-control, tranquility **12** tranquillity **14** presence of mind, self-possession

imperturbable 4 calm, cool **6** sedate, serene **8** composed **9** collected, impassive, unanxious, unfazable, unruffled **10** impervious **11** levelheaded, undisturbed, unexcitable, unflappable, unflustered **13** dispassionate, unsusceptible

impervious 6 closed **8** immune to **11** impermeable **12** impenetrable, inaccessible, invulnerable **14** unapproachable

impetuosity 8 rashness **11** spontaneity, unrestraint **12** recklessness **13** impulsiveness **14** capriciousness

impetuous 4 rash **5** hasty **6** abrupt, stormy **7** rampant, violent **8** forcible, headlong, vehement **9** impulsive **10** capricious, inexorable, relentless, unexpected **11** precipitate **14** unpremeditated

impetus 4 prod, push, spur **5** boost, drive, force, start **6** motive **7** impulse **8** momentum, stimulus **9** impulsion, incentive **10** motivation, propulsion **11** moving force, stimulation

impiety 9 blasphemy, sacrilege **10** disrespect, irreligion **11** irreverence, ungodliness

impinge 7 intrude, obtrude, violate **8** encroach, infringe, trespass **10** transgress

impious 7 godless, immoral, profane, ungodly **8** apostate, renegade **9** perverted **10** iniquitous, irreverent **11** blasphemous, irreligious **12** iconoclastic, sacrilegious **13** disrespectful

impiousness 7 impiety **9** blasphemy, sacrilege **10** disrespect **11** irreverence, ungodliness

impish 5 elfin **7** implike, puckish, roguish **8** prankish, rascally, sportive **11** mischievous

implacable 10 inexorable, inflexible, relentless, unamenable **11** intractable, unrelenting **12** unappeasable, unpacifiable **14** irreconcilable, uncompromising

implant 3 fix, set, sow **4** root **5** embed, graft, imbed, inlay, teach **6** infuse, insert **7** impress, instill **8** entrench **9** establish, inculcate **10** impregnate

implausible 8 doubtful, unlikely **9** illogical, senseless **10** far-fetched, improbable, incredible, outrageous, ridiculous **12** preposterous, unbelievable, unreasonable **13** inconceivable

implement 4 tool **5** begin, enact, piece, start **6** device **7** achieve, article, fulfill, realize, utensil **8** activate, carry out **9** apparatus, appliance, equipment, materials **10** accomplish, bring about, instrument **11** set in motion **13** put into effect

implicate 7 connect, embroil, ensnare, involve **8** entangle **9** associate, inculpate **11** incriminate

implication 6 effect **7** outcome **8** innuendo, overtone **9** inference **10** connection, intimation, suggestion **11** association, connotation, consequence, insinuation, involvement **12** entanglement, ramification, significance

implicit 5 total **6** hinted, innate **7** certain, implied, staunch **8** absolute, complete, inferred, inherent, profound, resolute **9** deducible, steadfast, suggested **10** understood, unreserved, unshakable **13** unquestioning

implied 5 tacit **7** oblique **8** indirect **9** implicity, indicated

implode 11 burst inward **17** compress violently

implore 3 beg **4** urge **6** obtest **7** beseech, entreat **9** importune, plead with **10** supplicate

imply 4 hint, mean **6** denote **7** bespeak, betoken, connote, presume, signify, suggest **8** evidence, indicate, intimate **9** insinuate **10** presuppose

impolite 4 rude **7** ill-bred, uncivil **9** impolitic, unfitting, ungenteel, unrefined **10** undecorous, unmannerly **12** discourteous **13** disrespectful, inconsiderate

impoliteness 8 rudeness **10** bad manners, incivility **11** boorishness, discourtesy

import 6 burden, moment, thrust **7** meaning **9** overtones **10** importance **11** connotation, implication **12** ramification, significance

importance 4 rank **5** value, worth **6** esteem, import, moment, repute, weight **7** stature **8** eminence, position **9** influence, relevance **11** consequence, seriousness, weightiness **12** significance **13** essentialness, momentousness

Importance of Being Earnest, The
   author: **10** Oscar Wilde
   character: **12** Cecily Cardew, Jack Worthing, Letitia Prism **16** Gwendolen Fairfax **17** Algernon Moncrieff (Algy) **20** Lady Augusta Bracknell **21** Reverend Canon Chasuble

important 5 great, major **7** leading, notable, seminal, serious, weighty **8** creative, esteemed, foremost, original **9** momentous, prominent **10** imperative, meaningful, preeminent, remarkable **11** distinctive, influential, significant **13** consequential

imported 5 alien **6** exotic **7** foreign **9** not native

importunate 7 begging **8** pleading **9** imploring **10** entreating, persistent **11** troublesome **12** supplicating

importune 3 beg, sue **4** pray **5** plead **6** adjure, exhort **7** beseech, entreat, implore **8** appeal to, petition **10** supplicate

importunity 4 plea 6 appeal 7 request 8 entreaty, petition 12 supplication

impose 3 set 4 levy 5 apply, enact, foist, force, lay on 6 peddle, slap on 7 command, dictate, inflict, palm off, place on 9 establish, institute, introduce, prescribe 10 thrust upon

impose upon 5 annoy 6 bother, illuse 8 ill-treat, maltreat, mistreat 15 take advantage of

imposing 5 grand, lofty 7 massive, stately 8 majestic, striking, towering 10 commanding, impressive, monumental 11 outstanding 12 awe-inspiring

imposition 5 abuse 6 burden, ill use 8 foisting 10 obligation 15 taking advantage

impossible 8 stubborn 9 insoluble 10 unbearable, unsolvable, unyielding 11 intolerable, intractable, not possible 12 insufferable, intransigent, unachievable, unanswerable, unattainable, unimaginable, unmanageable 13 inconceivable 16 out of the question

impost 3 fee, tax 4 duty, fine, toll 6 charge, excise, tariff 10 assessment

impostor 4 sham 5 cheat, duper, fraud, phony, quack 6 con man 7 bluffer, shammer 8 deceiver 9 charlatan, defrauder, pretender, trickster 10 dissembler, mountebank 11 counterfeit, flimflam man, masquerader, pettifogger 12 impersonator

imposture 4 fake, hoax, play, ruse, sham 5 cheat, fraud, trick 6 deceit, humbug 7 forgery, swindle 8 artifice, delusion, pretense, quackery 9 deception, falsehood, imitation 10 pretension 11 charlatanry, counterfeit, fraudulence 12 charlatanism 13 impersonation, mountebankery

impotence 8 weakness 9 paralysis 10 disability, incapacity, inefficacy 12 helplessness 13 powerlessness 14 ineffectuality 15 ineffectiveness

impotent 4 weak 5 frail 6 feeble 7 hapless 8 disabled, feckless, helpless 9 paralyzed, powerless 11 ineffective

impound 3 pen 4 cage 5 pen in, seize 6 coop up, encage, lock up, shut in 7 confine 13 hold in custody

impoverish 4 bust, ruin 5 break, drain 6 beggar, pauper, reduce 7 deplete, exhaust 8 bankrupt, make poor 9 pauperize 18 send to the poorhouse

impoverished 4 poor 6 abject, barren, bereft, effete, used up 7 drained, sterile, wanting, worn out 8 depleted, indigent, wiped out 9 destitute, exhausted 10 down-and-out, pauperized 11 impecunious 12 unproductive, without means

impractical 6 sloppy, unwise 8 careless, quixotic, romantic 10 loose-ended, starry-eyed 11 unrealistic 12

disorganized 13 helter-skelter, unintelligent

imprecation 5 curse 8 anathema 11 malediction

impregnable 6 mighty, potent, strong, sturdy 8 powerful 10 invincible 12 invulnerable, unassailable, unattackable 13 unconquerable

impregnate 3 wet 4 soak 5 steep 6 dampen, drench, imbrue, infuse 7 moisten, suffuse 8 fructify, inundate, permeate, saturate 9 fecundate, fertilize 10 inseminate

impresario 7 manager, sponsor 8 director 9 conductor, organizer 12 entrepreneur

impress 4 grab, move, stir, sway 5 reach, touch 6 affect, excite, sink in, strike 8 bedazzle 9 electrify, influence, overpower, overwhelm

impression 4 idea, mark, mold, view 5 hunch, stamp, trace, track 6 belief, effect, impact, notion 7 contour, feeling, impress, imprint, opinion, outline, surmise 9 influence, reception, sensation 10 conviction 11 indentation 13 understanding

impressionable 8 gullible, passible, sentient 9 affective, receptive 10 vulnerable 11 suggestible

impressive 5 grand 6 august, moving 8 exciting, imposing, majestic, striking 9 memorable, thrilling 11 magnificent, outstanding 12 awe-inspiring, overpowering, soul-stirring 13 unforgettable

imprimis 15 in the first place

imprint 3 fix 4 etch, mark, sign 5 infix, press, stamp, title 6 indent 7 engrave, impress 8 inscribe 9 engraving 10 depression, impression 11 indentation

imprison 3 pen 4 jail 6 coop up, engage, entomb, immure, lock up 7 confine, fence in, impound, shackle 8 restrain 9 constrain 11 hold captive, incarcerate

improbable 8 doubtful, unlikely 9 illogical 11 implausible 12 unreasonable 13 unforeseeable

improbable solution in a play's plot
Latin: 13 deus ex machina

impromptu 6 sudden 7 offhand 9 impulsive, makeshift, on the spot 10 improvised, off the cuff, unexpected, unprepared 11 spontaneous, unrehearsed 14 extemporaneous, unpremeditated, without warning 15 spur-of-the-moment 16 extemporaneously, on a moment's notice 19 off the top of one's head

improper 4 lewd 5 inapt, unfit 8 indecent, off-color, unseemly 9 ill-suited, irregular 10 indecorous, malapropos, out of place, suggestive, unbecoming,

unsuitable 12 inharmonious 13 inappropriate, unconformable
French: 5 outre

impropriety 5 gaffe 7 blunder, faux pas 9 gaucherie, indecorum, vulgarity 10 bad manners 11 boorishness 12 impoliteness, indiscretion

improve 4 help 5 rally 6 better, enrich, repair 7 correct, develop, enhance 9 cultivate 10 ameliorate, recuperate

improvement 4 gain 6 reform, repair 7 advance, upswing 8 additive, progress 9 amendment 10 betterment, emendation, refinement 11 advancement, enhancement, reclamation 12 amelioration 14 reconstruction

improvidence 10 imprudence 11 prodigality 12 extravagance, wastefulness 13 shiftlessness 16 shortsightedness

improvident 6 lavish 8 prodigal, reckless, wasteful 9 imprudent, negligent, unthrifty 10 thriftless 11 extravagant, spendthrift 12 shortsighted 14 unparsimonious

improvise 5 ad-lib 6 make up, wing it 11 extemporize

improvised 5 ad-lib 7 devised, offhand 8 invented 9 concocted, contrived, dreamed-up, extempore, hatched-up, impromptu, makeshift 10 off-the-cuff, originated, unprepared 11 extemporary, spontaneous, unrehearsed 12 extemporized 14 extemporaneous, unpremeditated 15 improvisational, spur-of-the- moment

imprudent 4 rash 5 crazy, dopey 6 unwise 7 foolish 8 heedless, mindless, untoward 9 foolhardy 10 ill-advised, incautious, indiscreet, unthinking 11 inadvisable, injudicious, thoughtless 13 ill-considered

impudence
Yiddish: 7 chutzpa 8 chutzpah

impudent 4 bold, rude 5 brash, fresh, nervy, saucy 6 brazen, cheeky 7 forward, upstart 8 impolite, insolent 9 bumptious, shameless 11 impertinent, smart-alecky, wiseacreish 12 discourteous 13 disrespectful

impugn 4 deny 5 knock, libel 6 assail, attack, berate, negate, oppose 7 asperse, slander 8 denounce, question 9 challenge, criticize 10 contradict 14 call in question, cast aspersions 16 call into question

impugnment 7 slander 10 aspersions

impulse 4 bent, goad, push, spur, urge, whim 5 drive, fancy, force 6 desire, motive, notion, thrust, whimsy 7 caprice, impetus, whimsey 8 instinct, momentum, movement, stimulus, stirring 9 incentive 10 incitement, motivation 11 inclination, inspiration, instigation

impulsive 4 rash 7 driving, offhand 8

forceful, forcible, notional **9** impelling, impetuous, impromptu, unplanned, whimsical **10** capricious, incautious, propellant, propelling **11** involuntary, spontaneous **12** devil-may-care **13** unpredictable **14** extemporaneous, unpremeditated **15** spur-of-themoment

impulsiveness 8 rashness **11** impetuosity, spontaneity, unrestraint **12** recklessness, whimsicality **14** capriciousness

impunity 8 immunity **9** clearance, exemption, privilege **10** absolution **11** prerogative **12** dispensation

impure 4 foul, lewd **5** dirty **6** coarse, filthy, smutty **7** debased, defiled, immoral, lustful, noisome, noxious, obscene, sullied, tainted, unclean **8** degraded, devalued, immodest, improper, indecent, polluted, prurient, unchaste, vitiated **9** lecherous, salacious, unrefined **10** indecorous, indelicate, libidinous, licentious **11** adulterated, depreciated, unwholesome **12** contaminated

impurity 5 alloy, dross, filth, taint **8** foulness **9** dirtiness, pollutant, pollution **10** adulterant, corruption, defilement **11** contaminant, taintedness, uncleanness **12** adulteration **13** contamination, foreign matter **15** unwholesomeness

imputation 6 charge **10** accusation, allegation, ascription **11** attribution

impute 5 refer **6** assign, charge, credit, relate **7** ascribe **9** attribute

inability 10 inaptitude, incapacity, ineptitude **12** helplessness, incapability, incompetence **13** maladroitness, powerlessness

in absence
Latin: **10** in absentia

in absentia 9 in absence

inaccessible 9 not at hand **11** unreachable **12** unattainable, unobtainable **14** unapproachable

in accord 9 agreeable, approving, in harmony, of one mind **10** concurring, consenting **11** in agreement
French: **9** en rapport

inaccuracy 4 goof, slip **5** error, fault, wrong **6** boo-boo **7** blunder, erratum, fallacy, mistake **9** unclarity **10** faultiness **11** imprecision, inexactness **13** incorrectness, unreliability **14** fallaciousness

inaccurate 3 off **5** false, wrong **6** faulty **7** inexact **8** mistaken **9** erroneous, imprecise, incorrect, off target **10** fallacious, unreliable **11** not on target, off the track **13** wide of the mark

inaction 8 abeyance, deferral, dormancy, dullness, idleness **9** cessation, indolence **10** inactivity, quiescence, somnolence, suspension **11** complacency

inactive 4 dull, idle, lazy **5** inert, quiet, still **6** low-key, otiose, static, torpid, unused **7** dormant, languid **8** indolent, slothful, sluggish **9** do-nothing, easygoing, leisurely, sedentary, somnolent **10** on the shelf **11** inoperative **12** out of service

inactivity 4 rest **5** quiet **6** disuse **7** inertia **8** dormancy, idleness, inaction **9** stillness **10** quiescence

in actuality
Latin: **6** in esse

in addition 3 and, too **4** also, more, plus, then **5** above, added, again, extra **6** as well, beyond **7** besides, further **8** moreover **10** additional **12** additionally, supplemental

inadequacy 4 lack **7** failing **10** deficiency, impairment **11** shortcoming **13** insufficiency

inadequate 5 inept, short, unfit **6** meager, scanty, too raw **7** lacking, not up to, wanting **8** below par, unfitted **9** deficient, imperfect, incapable **11** incompetent, unqualified **12** insufficient

inadmissible 10 disallowed, extraneous **11** intolerable **12** not permitted, unacceptable **14** nonpermissible

in advance 6 before, in time, sooner **7** earlier **9** before now **10** beforehand **11** ahead of time **13** before the fact

inadvertent 7 unmeant **10** accidental, fortuitous, unintended, unthinking **11** involuntary **13** unintentional **14** unpremeditated

inadvisable 5 risky **6** chancy, unwise **9** impolitic, imprudent **10** ill-advised **11** inexpedient, injudicious, inopportune

in aeternum 7 forever

in agreement
French: **9** en rapport

inalienable 6 sacred **8** absolute, defended, inherent **9** protected **10** inviolable, sacrosanct **12** unassailable **13** unforfeitable, unimpeachable

in all
Latin: **6** in toto

in all places 10 every place, everywhere, far and near, far and wide

in a low voice
Latin: **9** sotto voce

inamorata 4 lady, love **5** lover **7** beloved, darling **8** ladylove, mistress, paramour, truelove **10** sweetheart

inane 4 dumb **5** dopey, empty, silly, vapid **6** absurd, jejune, stupid **7** asinine, fatuous, foolish, idiotic, insipid, shallow, vacuous **9** pointless, senseless **10** ridiculous, unthinking **11** meaningless, nonsensical **13** unintelligent

inanimate 4 cold, dead, dull **5** inert **6** asleep, stolid **8** lifeless, soulless **9** inorganic, insensate, nonliving, senseless, unfeeling **10** insensible, insentient **11** unconscious

inanity 6 drivel **7** hogwash, vacuity **8** nonsense, vapidity **9** absurdity, asininity, silliness **11** foolishness **13** pointlessness, senselessness **14** ridiculousness

Inanna
origin: **8** Sumerian
goddess of: **3** war **4** love
sister: **10** Ereshkigal
realm: **6** heaven
corresponds to: **6** Ishtar **7** Astarte, Mylitta **9** Ashtoreth

in any case 6 anyhow, anyway **9** at any rate **10** in any event

inapplicable 5 unfit **6** not apt **8** unsuited **10** inapposite, irrelevant, not germane, unsuitable **12** incompatible, not pertinent **13** inappropriate

inappropriate 5 inapt **8** ill-timed, improper, unsuited **9** unfitting **10** indecorous, in bad taste, out of place, unbecoming, unsuitable **11** incongruous **12** incompatible, infelicitous
French: **10** mal a propos

inapt 8 improper, unseemly, unsuited **9** ill-suited, incorrect, unfitting **11** incongruous **13** inappropriate

inaptness 9 inability, ineptness **10** clumsiness, inaptitude, ineptitude **12** incompetence **13** maladroitness **14** unskillfulness

in arrears 4 late **7** overdue **10** delinquent

inarticulate 4 dumb, mute **7** babbled, blurred, garbled, mumbled **8** confused, wordless **9** paralyzed **10** incoherent, indistinct, speechless, tongue-tied **12** inexpressive **14** unintelligible **15** uncommunicative

inartistic 9 graceless, inelegant, tasteless **10** ungraceful **11** unaesthetic **12** unattractive

in a series
French: **7** en suite

in a set
French: **7** en suite

in attendance 4 here **7** present, serving **9** appearing, caring for, on the spot, waiting on **12** accompanying, looking after, taking care of

inattention 6 apathy **10** negligence **12** carelessness **14** lack of interest **16** absentmindedness, unresponsiveness

inattentive 7 unaware **8** careless, heedless **9** forgetful, negligent, unmindful **10** distracted **11** daydreaming, thoughtless, unobservant **12** absentminded

inaugurate 5 set up, start **6** induct, launch **7** instate, kick off, usher in **8** initiate **9** institute, undertake **10** embark upon **11** set in action

inauguration 5 start **9** beginning, induction **10** dedication **11** origination **12** commencement

inaugurator 6 author, father **7** creator, founder, starter **9** initiator, organizer **10** originator, prime mover

inauspicious 7 unlucky **9** ill-chosen, ill-omened **10** badly timed, disastrous **11** unfavorable, unfortunate, unpromising **12** infelicitous, unpropitious

in a vacuum
Latin: **7** in vacuo

in bad faith
Latin: **8** mala fide

in being
Latin: **6** in esse

inborn 5 basic **6** inbred, innate, native **7** natural **8** inherent **9** inherited, intrinsic, intuitive **10** congenital **11** fundamental, instinctive **14** constitutional

inbred 6 inborn, innate, primal **7** natural **8** inherent **9** ingrained, inherited, intrinsic, intuitive **10** congenital, deep-rooted, deep-seated, hereditary, indwelling **11** instinctive, instinctual **12** deeply rooted **14** constitutional

Inca
language family: **7** Quechua
location: **4** Peru **5** Chili **7** Bolivia, Ecuador **9** Argentina **12** South America
leader: **7** Huascar **8** Topa Inca **9** Atahualpa, Pachacuti **10** Manco Capac **11** Huayna Capac
conquered by: **7** Pizarro
ruins: **11** Machu Picchu, Sacsahuaman, Tambo Machay

incalculable 7 dubious **8** infinite **9** countless, uncertain **11** inestimable, innumerable, measureless, uncountable **12** immeasurable, incomputable **13** unforeseeable, unpredictable

incandesce 4 burn, glow **5** flare, flash

incandescent 7 dynamic, glowing, radiant **8** electric, galvanic, magnetic, white-hot **9** brilliant **11** high-powered **12** electrifying **13** scintillating

incantation 3 hex **4** jinx **5** chant, charm, magic, spell **6** voodoo **7** sorcery **8** wizardry **10** black magic, hocus-pocus, invocation, mumbo-jumbo, necromancy, witchcraft **11** abracadabra, conjuration

incapable 5 inept, unfit **6** unable **8** helpless, impotent, inferior **9** powerless, unskilled, untrained **10** inadequate **11** incompetent, ineffective, inefficient, unqualified

incapacitate 4 maim, undo **5** lay up **7** cripple, disable **8** enfeeble, handicap, paralyze, sideline **9** make unfit **10** disqualify **13** make powerless **14** put out of action **15** render incapable

incapacitated 6 laid up **8** crippled, disabled, disarmed, helpless, stricken **9** hamstrung, paralyzed, sidelined **10** on the shelf, prostrated **11** immobi-

lized, out of action **12** hors de combat **14** flat on one's back

incapacity 7 illness **8** sickness **9** crippling **10** deficiency, disability **12** incapability

incarcerate 3 pen **4** jail **6** commit, coop up, immure, intern, lock up **7** confine, impound **8** imprison, restrain

incarceration 9 detention **10** commitment, internment **11** confinement, durance vile **12** imprisonment **18** institutionalizing

incarnate 8 embodied, manifest **9** personify **10** actualized, in the flesh **11** objectified, personified

Incarnations
author: **16** Robert Penn Warren

incautious 4 rash **5** brash **6** unwary **8** careless, heedless, reckless **9** hotheaded, impetuous, imprudent, impulsive, overhasty **10** headstrong, indiscreet, unthinking **11** injudicious, thoughtless

incendiary 8 agitator, arsonist **12** inflammatory

incense 3 ire **5** anger **6** burn up, enrage, madden **7** inflame, provoke **9** infuriate, make angry **13** make indignant
spice: **6** stacte

incensed 3 mad **5** angry, irate **6** fuming, raging **7** enraged, furious **8** burned up, inflamed, outraged, provoked **9** affronted, indignant **10** infuriated

incentive 4 lure, spur **6** come-on, motive **8** stimulus **10** enticement, inducement, motivation **11** inspiration **13** encouragement

inception 5 birth, debut, onset, start **6** origin, outset **7** arrival **9** beginning **12** commencement, inauguration

incessant 8 constant, unbroken, unending **9** ceaseless, continual, perpetual, unceasing **10** continuous, persistent **11** everlasting, unrelenting, unremitting **12** interminable **13** uninterrupted

inch
abbreviation: **2** in

In Chancery
author: **14** John Galsworthy
part of trilogy: **11** Forsyte Saga

inchoate 7 budding, nascent **8** formless, unformed, unshaped **9** amorphous, beginning, embryonic, incipient, shapeless **10** commencing, disjointed, uncohesive **11** unorganized **12** disconnected

incidence 4 rate **5** range, scope **6** extent **8** occasion **9** frequency, happening **10** commonness, occurrence, phenomenon **11** routineness

incident 5 clash, event, scene **6** affair **7** episode, related **8** occasion **9** hap-

pening **10** incidental, occurrence **11** contretemps, disturbance

incidental 5 minor **9** accessory, secondary **10** extraneous, unexpected **11** subordinate, unlooked-for

incidentally 7 apropos, by the by **8** by the way **9** in passing **14** speaking of that **15** parenthetically **21** while we're on the subject

incidentals 6 extras **8** minutiae **10** minor items **11** accessories, odds and ends **13** appurtenances

incinerate 4 burn **7** consume, cremate **9** carbonize **13** reduce to ashes

incineration 6 firing **7** burning, flaming **8** ignition, kindling **9** cremation **10** combustion **13** carbonization

incinerator 4 oven **6** burner **7** furnace

incipient 7 budding, nascent **8** inchoate **9** beginning, embryonic, fledgling, promising **10** developing, half-formed **11** rudimentary

in circulation 4 rife **6** abroad, around **7** at large **9** all around **11** going around **12** spread around **14** around and about **15** making the rounds

incise 4 etch **5** carve **7** cut into, engrave

incision 3 cut **4** scar, gash, nick, slit **5** cleft, notch, score, slash, slice, wound **6** furrow

incisive 4 curt, keen **5** acute, brisk, crisp, sharp **6** biting, shrewd **7** cutting, express, mordant, precise, probing, summary **8** analytic, piercing **9** trenchant, well-aimed **10** perceptive **11** intelligent, penetrating

incite 4 goad, prod, stir **5** drive, egg on, impel, rouse **6** arouse, excite, fire up, foment, induce, prompt, stir up, urge on **7** actuate, agitate, inflame, provoke **8** activate **9** instigate, stimulate

incitement 6 urging **7** arousal, driving, goading **8** egging on, exciting, firing up, stirring **9** agitating, fomenting, inflaming, prompting, provoking **10** activation, stirring up **11** provocation, stimulation

incivility 8 rudeness **9** barbarism, impudence, indecorum, surliness, vulgarity **10** bad manners, coarseness, disrespect **11** boorishness, discourtesy, misbehavior, uncouthness **12** impoliteness, tactlessness **14** unpleasantness

inclement 3 raw **4** foul **5** harsh, nasty, rough **6** bitter, severe, stormy **7** violent **11** tempestuous

inclination 3 bow, dip, nod **4** bend, bent, hill, rake, rise **5** grade, pitch, slant, slope **6** liking **7** bending, leaning, sloping **8** fondness, lowering, penchant, tendency **9** acclivity, inclining, proneness **10** preference, proclivity, propensity **11** disposition **12** predilection **14** predisposition

incline 3 bow **4** bend, cant, hill, lean, like, rake, seem, tend, tilt, wont **5** be apt, enjoy, pitch, slant, slope **6** prefer **7** decline **8** be likely, gradient **9** acclivity **10** lean toward **11** bend forward, have a mind to

inclined 3 apt **5** prove **6** liable, likely **7** given to **10** disposed to **11** predisposed

incline downward 3 dip, sag **4** sink **5** droop, slant, slope

inclined to delay 4 slow **5** tardy **6** remiss **8** dawdling, dilatory, sluggish **9** reluctant **12** foot-dragging **13** dilly-dallying **15** procrastinating

include 5 cover **6** enfold, entail, take in **7** contain, embrace, involve, subsume **8** comprise **9** encompass **10** comprehend **11** incorporate

inclusive 7 general, overall **8** sweeping, taking in **9** embracing, including **10** comprising, encircling **11** surrounding **12** encyclopedic **13** comprehending, comprehensive, incorporating **15** all-encompassing

incognito 7 unknown, unnamed **8** nameless **9** concealed, disguised, protected **10** in disguise, uncredited, undercover, unrevealed **11** undisclosed **12** unidentified **14** unacknowledged, unrecognizable

incognizant 6 obtuse **7** unaware **8** ignorant, unseeing **9** unknowing **13** unconscious of **15** uncomprehending

incoherent 7 muddled, unclear **8** confused, rambling **9** illogical **10** disjointed, irrational **11** bewildering, nonsensical **12** inconsistent **14** unintelligible

In Cold Blood
    author: 12 Truman Capote
    director: 13 Richard Brooks
    cast: 11 Paul Stewart, Robert Blake, Scott Wilson **12** John Forsythe

income 5 means, wages **6** salary **7** revenue **8** earnings **9** emolument **10** livelihood

income, annual
    French: 5 rente

incomparable 8 peerless **9** matchless, unequaled, unrivaled **10** inimitable **11** ne plus ultra, superlative **12** transcendent **13** beyond compare **14** unapproachable

incompatibility 6 strife **7** discord **8** friction, variance **9** disaccord, wrangling **10** antagonism **11** being at odds, discordance **13** lack of harmony

incompatible 6 at odds **7** jarring **8** clashing, contrary, unsuited **10** at variance, discordant, mismatched **11** disagreeing, incongruous, uncongenial **12** antagonistic, inconsistent, inharmonious **13** contradictory, inappropriate

incompetency 9 inability, unfitness **10** ineptitude **11** lack of skill **12** inefficiency **15** ineffectiveness

incompetent 5 inept, unfit **8** inexpert **9** incapable, unskilled, untrained **11** ineffective, ineffectual, inefficient, unqualified **14** lacking ability

incomplete 6 broken **7** partial, wanting **9** defective, deficient **10** unfinished **11** fragmentary

incompleteness 8 omission **10** deficiency **11** shortcoming **15** unfinished state

incomprehensible 7 obscure **8** abstruse, baffling **9** confusing **10** befuddling **11** bewildering, inscrutable, ungraspable **12** impenetrable, unfathomable **14** unintelligible **19** beyond comprehension, beyond understanding

incomprehension 10 bafflement, puzzlement **12** bewilderment **19** failure to understand

inconceivable 7 strange **8** unlikely **10** improbable, incredible **11** unthinkable **12** beyond belief, unbelievable, unimaginable **14** highly unlikely

in conclusion
    French: 5 enfin

inconclusive 4 open **9** unsettled **10** indecisive, indefinite, unresolved, up in the air **11** not definite **12** unconvincing, undetermined **13** indeterminate

incongruity 8 variance **9** disparity **10** aberration, disharmony, divergence **11** abnormality, discrepancy **13** dissimilarity, inconsistency, unsuitability **17** inappropriateness

incongruous 3 odd **6** far-out **8** contrary **10** at variance, discrepant, out of place, outlandish, unsuitable **11** conflicting, disagreeing **12** incompatible, inconsistent, out of keeping **13** contradictory, inappropriate **14** irreconcilable

inconsequential 5 petty **6** slight **7** trivial **8** nugatory, picayune, piddling, trifling **9** valueless **10** negligible, of no moment **11** meaningless, unimportant **13** insignificant **15** of no consequence

inconsiderable 5 light, minor, petty, small **6** little, modest, paltry, slight **7** minimal, trivial **8** picayune, trifling **9** no big deal **10** negligible **11** unimportant **13** insignificant, no great shakes **15** inconsequential

inconsiderate 4 rash, rude **6** remiss, unkind **7** uncivil **8** careless, impolite, tactless, uncaring **9** negligent **10** ungracious, unthinking **11** insensitive, thoughtless **12** disregardful, uncharitable

inconsistency 8 variance **9** disparity **10** difference, divergence **11** discrep-

ancy, incongruity **12** disagreement **13** dissimilarity

inconsistent 6 fickle **7** erratic, wayward **8** contrary, notional, unstable, variable **9** changeful, dissonant **10** changeable, discrepant, inconstant, irresolute **11** inaccordant, incongruous, inconsonant, vacillating **12** incompatible, inharmonious **13** contradictory, unpredictable **14** irreconcilable

inconsolable 7 crushed **8** dejected, desolate, wretched **9** miserable **10** despondent **12** disconsolate **13** brokenhearted

inconsonant 10 discordant **12** out of keeping, unharmonious

inconspicuous 3 dim **5** faint, muted **6** modest **9** unnoticed **10** unapparent, unassuming **11** unobtrusive **12** not egregious, unnoticeable **14** unostentatious

inconstancy 10 fickleness, infidelity **11** instability **14** capriciousness, changeableness, unfaithfulness

inconstant 6 fickle, untrue **7** erratic **8** cavalier, disloyal, unstable **9** mercurial **10** capricious, changeable, unfaithful **11** interrupted, uncommitted, undedicated, unsteadfast

incontinence 8 rashness **12** recklessness **13** lack of control **16** irresponsibility

incontinent 8 unchaste **12** unrestrained

incontrovertibility 8 sureness **9** certainty **12** absoluteness, definiteness **13** undeniability **14** irrefutability, conclusiveness **15** indisputability **16** incontestability **17** unquestionability

incontrovertible 9 apodictic **10** unarguable, undeniable **11** established, irrefutable **12** indisputable **14** beyond question, unquestionable

inconvenience 6 bother, put out **7** trouble **8** hardship, headache, nuisance **9** annoyance, disoblige, put one out **10** discomfort **13** be a nuisance to, pain in the neck

inconvenient 7 awkward, unhandy **8** annoying, tiresome, untimely **10** bothersome, burdensome **11** distressing, inopportune, troublesome

Incoronazione di Poppea, L'
    also: 22 The Coronation of Poppaea
    opera by: 10 Monteverdi
    character: 4 Nero **6** Ottone **7** Ottavia

incorporate 4 fuse **6** embody, work in **7** include **10** amalgamate, assimilate **11** consolidate

incorporated 6 united **8** embodied, included **11** amalgamated, assimilated **12** consolidated

incorporeal 6 occult, unreal **7** ghostly, phantom **8** bodiless **9** spiritual, unearthly, unfleshly, unworldly **10** immaterial, intangible **11** disembodied **12** supernatural **13** insubstantial

incorrect 5 false, wrong **6** untrue **7** inexact **8** mistaken **9** erroneous **10** fallacious, inaccurate

incorrectness 5 error **9** wrongness **10** inaccuracy **12** carelessness, slovenliness

incorrigible 6 unruly **8** hardened, hard-core, hopeless **10** beyond help, delinquent **11** intractable **12** beyond saving, past changing, unmanageable **14** uncontrollable

incorrigible child
French: **14** enfant terrible

incorruptible 4 pure **6** honest **7** upright **8** reliable **9** faultless, righteous **10** unbribable **11** trustworthy **14** irreproachable

increase 3 wax **4** grow **5** add to, swell **6** enrich, expand **7** advance, augment, burgeon, enhance, enlarge **8** multiply **12** become larger

increasing 7 growing **9** enlarging, expansion, extending, extension **10** drawing out **11** enlargement **12** augmentation

incredible 6 absurd **7** amazing, awesome **10** astounding, farfetched, remarkable **11** astonishing **12** preposterous, unbelievable, unimaginable **13** extraordinary, inconceivable

Incredible Hulk, The
character: **9** Jack McGee **11** David Banner
cast: **9** Bill Bixby **10** Jack Colvin **11** Lou Ferrigno

incredulous 7 dubious **8** doubtful **9** skeptical **10** suspicious **11** distrustful **12** disbelieving

increment 4 gain, rise **5** raise **6** growth, profit **7** benefit **8** addition, increase **9** accretion **10** supplement **11** enlargement **12** accumulation, appreciation, augmentation **13** proliferation

incriminate 5 blame **6** accuse, charge, indict

incrimination 5 blame **7** charges **10** accusation, indictment

incubate 3 set, sit **4** plot **5** breed, brood, clock, cover, hatch **6** scheme **7** develop, gestate, sit upon **8** generate

incubus 5 demon **8** bad dream **9** nightmare

inculcate 5 drill, imbue, infix, teach, train **6** impart, infuse **7** implant, impress, instill **8** instruct **9** brainwash, condition, enlighten **10** indoctrinate

inculpable 5 clear **8** innocent **9** blameless, guiltless, not guilty **10** not at fault, unblamable **14** not responsible

incur 6 arouse, assume, incite, stir up **7** acquire, bring on, involve, provoke **8** bring out, contract, fall into

incurable 8 cureless, hopeless **9** cease-less **10** beyond cure, inveterate, relentless, unflagging **12** incorrigible, irremediable **13** dyed-in-the-wool, uncorrectable

incursion 4 push, raid **5** foray **6** attack, inroad, sortie **7** assault **8** invasion **11** advance into, impingement **12** encroachment, infiltration

indebted 5 bound **7** bounden **8** beholden, grateful, thankful **9** obligated **10** chargeable **11** accountable **15** under obligation

indebtedness 4 debt **5** debit **7** arrears **9** liability **10** balance due, obligation **11** liabilities

indecency 10 immorality **12** unseemliness **13** offensiveness, salaciousness **14** indecorousness

indecent 4 blue, lewd, rude **5** bawdy, dirty **6** filthy, smutty, vulgar **7** ignoble, ill-bred, immoral, obscene, uncivil **8** immodest, improper, prurient, unseemly **9** offensive, salacious **10** in bad taste, indecorous, indiscreet, licentious, unbecoming **11** unwholesome **12** pornographic

Indecent Obsession, An
author: **17** Colleen McCullough

indecipherable 7 cryptic **9** enigmatic, illegible **10** unreadable **11** inscrutable

indecision 5 doubt **6** acrisy **7** dilemma, swither **8** wavering **10** hesitation **11** fluctuation, vacillating, vacillation, uncertainty **12** irresolution

indecisive 4 weak **7** dubious, unclear **8** doubtful, hesitant, wavering **9** confusing, debatable, mercurial, uncertain, unsettled **10** disputable, hesitating, irresolute, wishy-washy **11** halfhearted, vacillating **12** inconclusive **13** indeterminate **17** blowing hot and cold

indecorous 5 gross **6** sinful, wicked **7** ill-bred **8** immodest, improper, low-class, unseemly **9** unfitting **10** unbecoming, unsuitable **11** blameworthy **13** inappropriate, reprehensible

indecorum 8 bad taste **9** immodesty, indecency, vulgarity **11** impropriety **12** impoliteness, unseemliness

indeed 5 truly **6** in fact, really **7** for sure, in truth **8** actually, to be sure **9** certainly, in reality, veritably **10** positively, to be honest, undeniably **11** joking apart **13** in point of fact, with certainty **14** to tell the truth **15** as a matter of fact, without question **16** strictly speaking

indefatigable 6 dogged **7** staunch **8** diligent, sedulous, tireless, untiring **9** energetic **10** persistent, unflagging, unwearying **11** persevering, unfaltering **13** inexhaustible

indefensible 8 improper, vincible **9** pregnable, untenable **10** vulnerable **11** defenseless, inexcusable, unpro-tected, unspeakable **12** open to attack, unpardonable **13** unjustifiable

indefinite 3 dim **5** vague **6** unsure **7** inexact, obscure, unknown **8** doubtful **9** ambiguous, amorphous, limitless, tentative, uncertain, unsettled **10** ill-defined, indecisive, indistinct, inexplicit **11** illimitable, measureless, unspecified **12** undetermined **13** indeterminate

indefiniteness 6 vagary **9** ambiguity, vagueness **10** indecision **11** uncertainty **12** equivocation

indelible 4 fast **5** fixed, vivid **7** lasting **8** deep-dyed **9** ingrained, memorable, permanent **10** unerasable **11** unremovable **12** ineradicable **13** unforgettable

indelicate 4 lewd, rude **5** broad, crude, gross **6** clumsy, coarse, risque, vulgar **7** awkward, obscene **8** immodest, improper, indecent, off-color, unseemly **9** offensive, unrefined **10** indecorous, indiscreet, suggestive, unbecoming

in demand 7 popular **9** desirable **11** sought after

indemnification 7 payment **10** recompense, reparation **12** compensation

indemnify 3 pay **5** atone, cover, repay **6** insure, secure **7** pay back, protect, rectify, requite, satisfy **8** make good **9** make right, make up for, reimburse **10** compensate, make amends, recompense, remunerate **15** make restitution

indemnity 7 redress **8** coverage, security **9** insurance, repayment **10** protection **11** restitution **12** compensation **15** indemnification

indent 5 notch, set in **6** recess **7** set back

indentation 3 bay, cut, pit **4** dent, nick **5** gouge, inset, niche, notch, score **6** cavity, furrow, pocket, recess **8** incision **9** concavity **10** depression

indented 6 hollow, sunken, zigzag **7** concave, notched **9** depressed

indenture 4 bind **8** contract **10** apprentice

indentured 5 bound **10** contracted **11** apprenticed

independence 7 freedom, liberty **8** autonomy **10** liberation **11** sovereignty **12** emancipation, self-reliance **14** self-government **17** self-determination

independent 4 free **7** solvent, well-off **8** affluent, separate, unallied, well-to-do **9** apart from, exclusive, on one's own, sovereign, uncoerced, well-fixed **10** autonomous, well-heeled **11** self-reliant, unconnected **12** unassociated, uncontrolled **13** self-directing, self-governing, unconstrained **15** individualistic, self-determining

indescribable 9 ineffable 11 beyond words, indefinable, unutterable 12 overwhelming 13 inexpressible 17 beyond description 20 beggaring description

indestructible 8 enduring 9 permanent 11 everlasting, infrangible, unbreakable 12 imperishable

indeterminate 5 vague 7 obscure, unclear 8 not clear 9 ambiguous, uncertain, undefined 10 indefinite, perplexing, unresolved 11 problematic, unspecified 12 undetermined, unstipulated

index 4 clue, mark, sign 5 proof, token 7 catalog, symptom 8 evidence, glossary, register 9 catalogue, indicator 10 indication 13 manifestation 16 alphabetical list

Index Librorum Prohibitorum 22 index of prohibited books

index of prohibited books
  Latin: 25 Index Librorum Prohibitorum

India
  other name: 4 Hind 6 Bharat 12 Bharat Varsha
  capital: 8 New Delhi
  largest city: 8 Calcutta
  others: 4 Agra, Gaya, Pune 5 Dacca, Poona, Surat 6 Bombay, Jaipur, Kanpur, Lahore, Madras, Madura, Mysore, Nagpur 7 Banaras 8 Kolhapur, Mandalay, Mirzapur, Shahpura, Srinagar 9 Ahmedabad, Bangalore, Hyderabad 10 Darjeeling
  division: 3 Goa 5 Assam, Bihar, Jammu 6 Kerala, Orissa, Punjab, Sikkim 7 Gujarat, Haryana, Kashmir, Manipur, Tripura 8 Nagaland 9 Karnataka, Meghalaya, Rajasthan, Tamil Nadu 10 West Bengal 11 Daman and Diu, Maharashtra, Pondicherry 12 Uttar Pradesh 13 Andhra Pradesh, Madhya Pradesh 15 Himachal Pradesh
  measure: 3 ady, gaz, gez, jow, lan 4 byee, coss, depa, doph, hath, koss, kunk, raik, rati, seit, taun, tola 5 bigha, covid, crosa, denda, depoh, drona, erosa, garce, hasta, krosa, parah, ratti, salay, yojan 6 adhaka, amunam, covido, cudava, dumbha, geerah, moolum, mushti, ouroub, palgat, parran, prasha, ropani, tipree, unglee, yojana 7 dhanush, gavyuti, khahoon, niranga, prastha 8 okthabah
  monetary unit: 3 lac, pie 4 lakh, pice 5 abidi, rupee
  weight: 3 mod, pai, vis 4 drum, hoen, kona, pala, pank, pice, ruay, tael, tali, tola, wang, yava 5 adpad, candy, hubba, maund, tical 6 karsha 8 mangelin
  island: 6 Agatti, Chilka 7 Andaman, Minicoy, Nicobar 8 Amindivi 9 Laccadive 11 Lakshadweep

lake: 5 Jheel, Lonar, Wular 6 Chilka, Colair, Dhebar, Kolair 7 Kolleru, Pulicat, Pushkar, Sambahr
mountain: 8 Aravalli 9 Broad Peak, Distaghil, Himalayas, Karakoram, Nanda Devi, Rakaposhi 10 Gasherbrum, Masherbrum 11 Nanga Parbat 12 Eastern Ghats, Kanchenjunga, Western Ghats
  hills: 4 Chin, Naga 5 Khasi 6 Lushai 7 Nilgiri
highest point: 12 Godwin Austen
river: 3 Son 4 Beas, Kosi, Tapi 5 Gogra, Indus, Jumna, Tapti 6 Gandak, Ganges, Jhelum, Kaveri, Kistna, Sutlej, Yamuna 7 Cauveri, Cauvery, Chambal, Damodar, Hooghly, Krishna, Narbada, Narmada 8 Godavari, Mahanadi 10 Bhagirathi 11 Brahmaputra
sea: 6 Indian 7 Arabian
physical feature:
  bay: 6 Bengal
  cape: 7 Comorin
  desert: 4 Thar 9 Rajasthan
  forest: 3 Gir
  gulf: 5 Kutch 6 Cambay, Mannar
  pass: 9 Karakoram
  plain: 12 Indo-Gangetic
  plateau: 6 Deccan 7 Shillon 11 Chota Nagpur
  rains: 7 monsoon
  strait: 4 Palk
  swamp: 9 Sundarban 11 Rann of Kutch
  valley: 13 Vale of Kashmir
people: 2 Ao 3 Gor 4 Bhil 5 Aryan 6 Badaga, Pathan 7 Sherani 9 Dravidian 10 Andamanese
  caste: 3 Jat 5 Sudra 6 Rajput, Shudra 7 Brahman, Brahmin, Harijan, Maratha, Vaishya 9 Kshatriya 11 Untouchable
  dynasty: 5 Gupta, Mogul 6 Maurya, Rajput 8 Marathas 14 Delhi Sultanate
  god: 4 Kali, Rama, Siva 5 Durga, Laxmi, Shiva 6 Brahma, Kumara, Vishnu 7 Ganesha, Hanuman, Krishna, Lakshmi 9 Kartikeya 10 Subramanya
  ruler: 5 Akbar, Asoka, Babur, Timur 7 Humayun 8 Hyder Ali, Jahangir 9 Aurangzeb, Shah Jahan 11 Rajiv Gandhi, Tippu Sultan 12 Indira Gandhi 13 Queen Victoria 15 Jawaharlal Nehru, Mohandas K (Mahatma) Gandhi 18 Chandragupta Maurya
language: 4 Urdu 5 Hindi, Oriya, Tamil 6 Sindhi, Telugu 7 Bengali, English, Kannada, Malayam, Marathi, Punjabi 8 Assamese, Gujarati, Kashmiri, Sanskrit 9 Malayalam
religion: 4 Sikh 5 Hindu, Islam, Parsi 7 Jainist, Judaism 8 Buddhism 11 Zoroastrian 12 Christianity
place:

  cathedral: 10 Saint Thome
  fortress: 3 Red 11 Saint George
  mausoleum: 8 Taj Mahal
  minaret: 9 Qutb Minar
  mosque: 10 Jama Masjid
  park: 6 Maidan
  president's residence: 17 Rashtrapati Bhavan
  railway station: 8 Victoria
  shrine: 7 Raj Ghat
  street: 7 Raj Path 11 Chowringhee, Marine Drive 12 Chandni Chauk 14 Connaught Place
  temple: 5 Birla 6 Ellora, Golden 7 Kailasa 10 Ajanta Cave
feature:
  dance: 6 nautch 7 cantico
  religious text: 7 Rig Veda
  shrine: 5 stupa
food:
  beer: 5 apong
  bread: 7 chapati
  liquor: 4 soma, sura 5 shrab
  tea: 5 assam

Indian
  constellation: 5 Indus

Indiana
  abbreviation: 2 IN 3 Ind
  nickname: 7 Hoosier
  capital/largest city: 12 Indianapolis
  others: 4 Gary, Peru 6 Brazil, Goshen, Hobart, Jasper, Kokomo, Marion, Muncie, Wabash 7 Elkhart, Ft Wayne, Hammond, LaPorte, Whiting 8 Columbus, Richmond 9 Lafayette, Mishawaka, South Bend, Vincennes 10 Evansville, Huntington, Logansport, Terre Haute 11 Bloomington, East Chicago 12 Connorsville, Michigan City
  college: 4 Ball 6 Bethel, Butler, DePauw, Goshen, Marion, Purdue, Wabash 9 Notre Dame 10 Evansville, Valparaiso
  explorer: 7 La Salle
  feature: 10 New Harmony 12 Indian mounds
    national memorial: 14 Lincoln boyhood
  tribe: 3 Wea 5 Miami 7 Shawnee
  people: 7 Hoosier 10 Cole Porter, Eugene Debs, Gus Grissom, Red Skelton 12 Wilbur Wright 15 Booth Tarkington, Theodore Dreiser 18 James Whitcomb Riley
  lake: 5 Clear, James 6 Monroe 7 Manitou, Wawasee 8 Michigan 9 Mansfield 11 Maxinkuckee
  land rank: 12 thirty-eighth
  mountain: 13 Greensfort Top
  physical feature:
    cave: 9 Wyandotte
  river: 4 Ohio 5 White 6 Maumee, Wabash 8 Kankakee 10 Tippecanoe, Whitewater
  state admission: 10 nineteenth
  state bird: 8 cardinal
  state flower: 5 peony 6 zinnia

state motto: 19 Crossroads of America

state song: 28 On the Banks of the Wabash Far Away

state tree: 5 tulip **11** tulip poplar

Indiana

basketball team: 6 Pacers

Indiana

author: 10 George Sand

character: 4 Noun **7** Delmare **13** Rodolphe Brown **15** Raymon de Ramiere

Indianapolis

football team: 5 Colts

Indic

language family: 12 Indo-European

branch: 11 Indo-Iranian

subgroup: 5 Hindi, Oriya **6** Nepali, Sindhi **7** Bengali, Marathi, Pakrits, Panjabi **8** Assamese, Gujarati, Kashmiri **9** Sinhalese

indicate 4 mean, show, tell **5** imply **6** denote, evince, record, reveal **7** bespeak, point to, signify, specify, suggest **8** point out, register, stand for **9** be a sign of, designate, establish, make known, represent, symbolize

indication 4 clue, hint, mark, omen, sign **5** token **6** augury, boding, signal **7** gesture, mention, portent, presage, showing, symptom, telling, warning **8** evidence, pointing **9** foretoken **10** foreboding, indicating, intimation, signifying, suggestion **11** designation, premonition **13** demonstration, manifestation

indicative 8 symbolic **10** denotative, emblematic, evidential, expressive, indicatory, suggestive **11** connotative, designative, significant, symptomatic **13** symptomatical **14** characteristic, representative

indicator 4 clue **5** guide **7** pointer **10** indication

indict 4 cite **6** accuse, charge, have up, impute, pull up **7** arraign, bring up, impeach **9** criminate, inculpate, prosecute **11** incriminate **13** prefer charges

indifference 6 apathy **7** disdain, neglect **8** coldness, no import **9** aloofness, unconcern **10** negligence, paltriness, triviality **11** disinterest, impassivity, inattention, insouciance, nonchalance **12** carelessness, unimportance **13** impassiveness, insensibility, insensitivity **14** insignificance, lack of interest

indifferent 4 cool, fair, rote, so-so **5** aloof **6** medium, modest **7** average, unmoved **8** detached, mediocre, middling, moderate, ordinary, passable **9** apathetic, impassive, not caring, unmindful **10** impervious, insensible, insouciant, nonchalant, second-rate, uninspired **11** commonplace, perfunctory, unconcerned **12** uninterested **13** insusceptible **15** undistin-

guished **17** betwixt and between, neither good nor bad

indigence 4 need, want **6** penury **7** beggary, poverty **9** pauperism, privation **11** destitution, dire straits **13** pennilessness

indigenous 6 native **7** endemic **8** domestic, homebred **9** home-grown **10** aboriginal **13** autochthonous, originating in

indigent 4 poor **5** needy **6** hard-up, in need, in want **7** pinched **8** badly off **9** destitute, moneyless, penniless **12** impoverished **15** poverty-stricken

indiges

title in: 4 Rome

suggests: 11 deification

for service to: 7 country

indigestible 4 rich **13** unassimilable

indignant 3 mad **4** sore **5** angry, huffy, irate, riled **6** fuming, miffed, peeved, piqued, put off, put out **8** incensed, offended, provoked, steaming, worked up, wrathful **9** resentful, wrought up **10** displeased, infuriated **15** on one's high horse

indignation 3 ire **4** fury, huff, rage **5** pique, wrath **6** animus, choler, dismay, uproar **7** umbrage **8** vexation **9** annoyance **10** irritation, resentment **11** displeasure

indignity 4 slur **5** abuse **6** insult, slight **7** affront, offense, outrage **8** dishonor, rudeness **9** injustice **11** discourtesy, humiliation **12** mistreatment **13** slap in the face

indigo 3 dye **4** blue **8** dark blue, deep blue, navy blue **10** Indigofera

varieties: 4 wild **5** false **7** bastard **8** wild blue **9** blue false **10** plains wild, white false **12** prairie false **13** fragrant false

indirect 5 vague **6** remote, zigzag **7** crooked, devious, distant, evasive, hedging, oblique, winding **8** rambling, tortuous **9** ancillary, secondary **10** circuitous, derivative, digressive, discursive, incidental, meandering, roundabout, unintended **13** unintentional

indirection 8 rambling **10** digression, meandering, zigzagging **14** circuitousness, circumlocution, roundaboutness

indiscernible 6 hidden **9** invisible **10** indistinct **12** undetectable, unnoticeable **13** imperceptible

indiscreet 6 unwise **7** foolish **8** careless, tactless, unseemly **9** foolhardy, ill-judged, impolitic, imprudent, tasteless, untactful **10** incautious **11** improvident, injudicious, thoughtless, unbefitting, uncalled-for **12** undiplomatic **13** inconsiderate, uncircumspect

indiscretion 8 rashness **10** imprudence **12** carelessness, heedlessness, recklessness, tactlessness **13** foolhardiness, insensitivity **15** thoughtlessness **16** irresponsibility

indiscriminate 6 motley, random **7** aimless, chaotic, jumbled, mongrel **8** confused, slapdash, unchoosy **9** haphazard, hit-or-miss **10** hodgepodge **11** promiscuous, unselective **12** disorganized, unsystematic **16** higgledy-piggledy, undistinguishing

in disorder 5 messy **6** blowsy, frowsy, mussed, sloppy, untidy **7** ruffled, rumpled, tousled, unkempt **8** uncombed **10** disarrayed, disheveled, disordered, disorderly **11** disarranged

indispensable 5 basic, vital **6** needed **7** crucial, needful **8** required **9** essential, mandatory, necessary, requisite **10** compulsory, imperative, obligatory **11** fundamental

indispensable condition

Latin: 10 sine qua non

indispensable element 9 basic need, essential, necessity, requisite **10** sine qua non **11** requirement

indisposed 3 ill **5** loath **6** ailing, averse, laid up, sickly, unwell **7** opposed **8** hesitant, taken ill **9** bedridden, reluctant, unwilling **10** not oneself **11** disinclined **15** under the weather

indisposition 5 upset **6** malady **7** ailment, illness **8** sickness **9** complaint, ill health

indisputable 4 sure **7** assured, certain, decided, evident, obvious **8** absolute, apparent, clear-cut, definite, positive **10** conclusive, unarguable, undeniable **11** indubitable, irrefutable **12** unassailable, unmistakable **13** incontestable **14** unquestionable **16** incontrovertible **20** beyond a shadow of doubt

indissoluble 5 fixed **7** abiding, lasting **8** constant, enduring **9** immutable, indelible, permanent, perpetual **11** everlasting **12** imperishable, ineradicable

indistinct 3 dim **4** weak **5** faint, muddy, murky, vague **6** cloudy, hidden **7** blurred, clouded, muffled, obscure, shadowy, unclear **8** confused, nebulous, puzzling **9** ambiguous, enigmatic, illegible, inaudible, uncertain **10** ill-defined, incoherent, indefinite, mysterious, out of focus **11** not distinct **13** indeterminate **14** indecipherable, unintelligible **16** incomprehensible

indistinguishable 7 obscure, unclear **9** invisible **10** indistinct, unapparent **12** unnoticeable, unobservable **13** a carbon copy of, identical with, imperceptible, inconspicuous, indiscernible

individual 6 person, unique **7** one's own, private, special, unusual **8** distinct, especial, original, personal, separate, singular, somebody, specific, uncommon **9** different, exclusive **10** particular **11** distinctive, independent

12 personalized **14** characteristic, unconventional

individuality 6 cachet **10** uniqueness **11** distinction, singularity, specialness **13** particularity **15** distinctiveness

individually 4 each **5** apart **6** apiece, singly **8** a la carte, uniquely **10** one at a time, peculiarly, personally, separately **12** respectively **13** distinctively **18** characteristically

Indochina 9 peninsula
   includes: 4 Laos **6** Malaya **7** Myanmar, Vietnam **8** Cambodia, Thailand

indoctrinate 5 brief, drill, teach, train, tutor **6** infuse, school **7** educate, implant, instill **8** initiate **9** brainwash, inculcate **12** propagandize

indoctrination 5 drill **8** drilling, teaching, training **9** education, schooling **10** initiation, instilling **11** inculcation, instruction

Indo-European
   language branch: 5 Greek **6** Celtic, Italic **7** Romance **8** Albanian, Armenian, Germanic **9** Anatolian, Tocharian **11** Balto-Slavic, Indo-Iranian

Indo-Iranian
   language family: 12 Indo-European
   ancient: 7 Avestan **8** Sanskrit **10** Old Persian
   modern Iranian: 5 Indic, Tajik **6** Pashto **7** Baluchi, Kurdish, Persian
   modern Indic: 4 Pali **5** Hindi, Oriya **6** Nepali, Sindhi **7** Bengali, Marathi, Panjabi **8** Assamese, Gujarati, Kashmiri **9** Sinhalese

indolence 5 sloth **7** inertia, languor, laxness **8** idleness, laziness **10** inactivity

indolent 4 lazy **5** inert, slack **7** lumpish **8** dawdling, dilatory, inactive, listless, slothful, sluggish **9** do-nothing, easygoing, lethargic, shiftless **13** lackadaisical

indomitable 6 dogged **7** doughty, staunch, valiant **8** cast-iron, fearless, intrepid, resolute, stalwart, stubborn **9** dauntless, steadfast, undaunted **10** courageous, formidable, invincible, unwavering, unyielding **11** insuperable, persevering, unflinching, unshrinking **12** invulnerable, unassailable **13** indefatigable, irrepressible, unconquerable

Indonesia
   other name: 9 Nusantara **12** Tanah Airkita **21** Netherlands East Indies
   capital/largest city: 7 Jakarta **8** Djakarta
   others: 5 Bogor, Medan **6** Malang, Manado **7** Bandung **8** Macassar, Semarang, Surabaya **9** Hollandia, Palembang, Surakarta **10** Jogjakarta, Yogyakarta **11** Banjarmasin
   measure: 5 depah, depoh
   monetary unit: 3 sen **6** rupiah
   weight: 5 catty, ounce, thail **6** soekoe

island: 3 Aru **4** Bali, Buru, Java **5** Ambon, Ceram, Seram, Spice, Sumba, Timor **6** Bangka, Borneo, Flores, Lombok, Madura, Tidore **7** Belawan, Celebes, Morotai, Sumatra, Sumbawa, Ternate **8** Belitung, Moluccas, Sulawesi **9** Halmahera, New Guinea **10** Kalimantan **11** Lesser Sunda **12** Greater Sunda
lake: 4 Toba **5** Ranau **6** Towuti
river: 4 Hari, Musi, Solo **5** Rokan **6** Asahan, Barito, Kampar **7** Brantas, Kaptuas **9** Indrogiri, Mamberamo, Martapura
sea: 4 Java, Savu **5** Banda, Ceram, Timor **6** Flores, Indian **7** Arafura, Celebes, Molucca, Pacific **10** Philippine, South China
physical feature:
   strait: 5 Sunda **7** Makasar, Malacca **8** Makassar
   volcano: 6 Slamet **8** Krakatoa
people: 5 Batak, Dayak, Dyaks, Malay **6** Papuan, Toraja **7** Battaks, Chinese, Igorots **8** Acehnese, Achinese, Balinese, Javanese, Madurese, Sudanese **11** Minang Kabau
   leader: 7 Suharto, Sukarno
language: 5 Tetum **6** Bahasa, Igorot **7** English, Gyarung, Malayan **8** Balinese, Chamorro, Javanese, Madurese, Sudanese **10** Indonesian, Polynesian
religion: 5 Hindu, Islam **7** animism **8** Buddhism **12** Christianity, Confucianism
place:
   palace: 6 Kraton
   pyramid: 5 Stupa **9** Borobudur
   shrine: 6 Dagoba, Kraton
   feature:
      cap: 5 pitji
      cloth: 5 batik
      jacket: 6 kebaja
      lizard: 12 Komodo dragon
      scarf: 9 selendang
      shadow play: 6 wajang, wayang
      skirt: 4 kain **6** sarong
      tree: 4 supa
   food:
      ceremonial dinner: 9 selamatan

indoors 6 at home, inside, shut in, shut up, within **10** in the house **11** sequestered

Indo-Pacific
   language subgroup: 4 Kate **5** Kiwai **7** Andaman, Merauke **8** Highland, Tasmania **9** Ekari-Moni, Hollandia, Timor-Alor **10** New Britain **12** Astrolabe Bay, Bougainville **14** Vogelkop-Kamoro **16** Eastern New Guinea, Northern Salomons **17** Northern Halmahera

indorse *see* **7** endorse

In Dubious Battle
   author: 13 John Steinbeck

indubitable 4 sure **7** certain **9** undoubted **10** conclusive **11** irrefutable,

unequivocal **12** indisputable, unmistakable **14** unquestionable **16** incontrovertible

indubitably 6 surely **7** for sure **8** of course **9** certainly, doubtless **10** for certain **11** undoubtedly **12** without doubt **14** unquestionably, with no question

induce 3 get **4** coax, spur, sway **5** cause, impel **6** arouse, effect, incite, lead to, prompt **7** actuate, bring on, dispose, incline, inspire, produce, provoke, win over **8** activate, motivate, occasion, persuade **9** encourage, influence, instigate, prevail on **10** bring about, bring round, give rise to **11** prevail upon, set in motion

inducement 4 bait, goad, spur **5** cause **6** ground, motive, reason **8** stimulus **9** incentive **10** allurement, attraction, enticement, incitement, persuasion, temptation **11** inspiration, instigation, provocation

induct 5 crown, draft, frock **6** enlist, invest, lead in, ordain, sign up **7** bring in, install, instate, usher in **8** enthrone, initiate, register **9** conscript, establish, introduce **10** consecrate, inaugurate

in due course 4 then **6** thence **10** eventually **11** accordingly **15** at the proper time **19** in the fullness of time

indulge 4 baby **5** favor, humor, serve, spoil, treat **6** coddle, cosset, oblige **7** appease, cater to, gratify, yield to **8** pander to **9** give way to **11** accommodate, go along with, mollycoddle

indulgence 6 excess, luxury **8** kindness, lenience, patience **9** allowance, benignity, tolerance **10** compassion, debauchery, profligacy, sufferance **11** dissipation, forbearance, forgiveness **12** extravagance, graciousness, immoderation, intemperance **13** understanding **14** permissiveness

indulgent 4 kind **6** benign, tender **7** clement, lenient, patient, sparing **8** humoring, obliging, tolerant, yielding **9** easygoing, forgiving, pampering **10** forbearing, permissive **11** complaisant, forebearing **12** conciliatory **13** understanding

Indus
   constellation near: 4 Grus, Pavo
   river in: 4 Asia **5** India, Tibet **8** Pakistan
   into: 10 Arabian Sea

industrious 4 busy **6** active **7** zealous **8** diligent, occupied, sedulous, tireless **9** assiduous, energetic **10** productive, purposeful, unflagging **11** hardworking, painstaking, persevering, unremitting **12** businesslike, enterprising **13** indefatigable

industry 2 go **4** toil, zeal **5** field, labor, trade **6** bustle, energy, hustle **8** activity, business, commerce, hard work **9** assiduity, diligence **10** enterprise **11** application, manufacture **12** perseverance, sedulousness **13** assiduousness **15** industriousness **16** indefatigability

inebriate 3 sot **4** lush, soak, wino **5** drunk, rummy, souse, toper **6** barfly, boozer **7** tippler **8** drunkard **9** alcoholic **11** dipsomaniac

inebriated 4 high **5** drunk, oiled, tight, tipsy **6** bombed, loaded, potted, stoned, tanked, zonked **7** drunken, smashed, sozzled, wrecked **8** besotted **9** befuddled, plastered **10** in one's cups **11** intoxicated **12** drunk as a lord **17** under the influence **20** three sheets to the wind

ineffable 5 ideal **6** divine, sacred **9** spiritual **10** indefinite, untellable **11** indefinable, unspeakable, unutterable **12** transcendent **13** indescribable, inexpressible **14** incommunicable, transcendental

in effect 6 active **8** a reality **9** activated, effective, operative **11** in operation

ineffective 4 vain, weak **6** futile **7** useless **8** impotent **9** fruitless, incapable, powerless, worthless **10** inadequate **11** inefficient, inoperative, not much good, of little use **12** unproductive

ineffectual 4 lame, vain, weak **5** inept **6** feeble, futile **7** hapless, useless **8** impotent **10** inadequate, not up to par, profitless, unavailing **11** incompetent, ineffective, inefficient **12** unproductive, unprofitable, unsuccessful **13** inefficacious **14** unsatisfactory

inefficient 5 inept, slack **6** futile **8** slipshod **9** pointless, unskilled **10** inadequate **11** incompetent, indifferent, ineffective, ineffectual **12** not efficient, unproductive **13** inefficacious **14** good-for-nothing

inelegance 9 crudeness, grossness, roughness, vulgarity **10** coarseness **13** tastelessness

inelegant 4 ugly **6** coarse, common **8** inferior **9** tasteless, unrefined **10** ungraceful

ineligible 5 unfit **10** unentitled, unsuitable **11** not eligible, unqualified **12** disqualified, unacceptable

ineluctable 4 sure **5** fated **7** certain **10** ineludible, inevasible, inevitable, inexorable, sure as fate, unevadable **11** inescapable, irrevocable, unavoidable, unstoppable **13** unpreventable

inept 5 empty, inane, silly, unapt **6** clumsy **7** asinine, awkward, fatuous, foolish **8** bungling **9** maladroit, pointless, senseless, unfitting, unskilled, untrained **10** out of place, unsuitable **11** incompetent, ineffective, ineffectual, inefficient, nonsensical, unqualified **13** inappropriate, inefficacious

ineptitude 9 inability **10** clumsiness, inadequacy **11** awkwardness **12** incompetence **14** ineffectuality **15** ineffectiveness

inequality 8 imparity, inequity **9** disparity, diversity, prejudice **10** difference, divergence, favoritism, unfairness, unlikeness **11** inconstancy, unequalness **12** irregularity, variableness **13** disproportion, dissimilarity, dissimilitude

inequity 4 bias **9** injustice, prejudice **10** favoritism, inequality, unfairness **14** discrimination

ineradicable 7 lasting **9** indelible, permanent **10** inerasable **12** ineffaceable **14** indestructible

inert 4 dull, numb **5** slack, still **6** leaden, static, supine, torpid **7** languid, passive **8** immobile, inactive, listless, sluggish **9** impassive, inanimate, quiescent **10** motionless, phlegmatic, stationary

inertia 6 apathy, stupor, torpor **7** languor **8** dullness, inaction, laziness, lethargy **9** indolence, inertness, lassitude, passivity, torpidity, weariness **10** inactivity, supineness **11** passiveness **12** listlessness, sluggishness

inertness 6 apathy **8** lethargy **9** passivity **10** quiescence **12** sluggishness **14** motionlessness

inescapable 4 sure **7** certain, evident **8** manifest, positive **10** inevitable **11** ineluctable, predestined, unavoidable

in esse 7 in being **11** in actuality **16** actually existing

inestimable 7 sumless **8** precious **9** priceless **10** invaluable **11** beyond price, measureless **12** immeasurable, incalculable, unmeasurable

inevitable 4 sure **5** fated **7** certain **8** destined **10** ineludible **11** ineluctable, inescapable, predestined, unavoidable **13** predetermined, unpreventable

inexact 3 off **6** faulty, sloppy **8** careless, slovenly **9** defective, imperfect, imprecise **10** inaccurate, unspecific **11** approximate

in exactly the same words
Latin: **19** verbatim et literatim

inexcusable 10 unbearable **11** intolerable, unallowable **12** indefensible, unforgivable, unpardonable **13** unjustifiable

inexhaustible 7 endless **8** infinite, tireless, unending **9** boundless **13** indefatigable **15** measurelessness

in existence 5 alive **6** extant, living **8** existent, existing **9** surviving, to be found

inexorable 4 firm **5** cruel, stiff **6** dogged **7** adamant **8** obdurate, pitiless, ruthless **9** immovable, merciless, unbending **10** adamantive, determined, inflexible, relentless, unyield-

ing **11** inescapable, intractable **12** irresistible **14** uncompromising

inexpedient 6 futile, unwise **7** useless **11** detrimental, impractical, inadvisable, injudicious, undesirable **13** not worthwhile **15** disadvantageous

inexpensive 5 cheap **8** moderate **9** low-priced **10** economical, reasonable **13** nominal-priced, popular-priced

inexpensive table wine
French: **12** vin ordinaire

inexperienced 5 fresh, green, naive **6** callow **7** untried **8** inexpert, unversed **9** unfledged, unskilled, untrained, untutored **10** unfamiliar, unschooled, unseasoned **11** uninitiated, unpracticed **12** unaccustomed, unacquainted, unconversant **15** unsophisticated

inexpert 5 inept **6** clumsy, gauche **7** awkward **8** bungling **9** incapable, maladroit **10** amateurish, unpolished, unskillful **11** incompetent, ineffective, inefficient, unqualified **14** unaccomplished

inexplicable 8 abstruse, baffling, puzzling **9** insoluble **10** insolvable, mysterious, mystifying, perplexing **11** enigmatical, inscrutable **12** unfathomable, unaccountable, unexplainable **14** undecipherable **16** incomprehensible

inexpressive 5 blank, empty **6** vacant **14** expressionless

in extenso 12 at full length

in extremis 9 near death **11** in extremity **15** on the outer edges **19** at the uttermost limit

in extremity
Latin: **10** in extremis

in fact
Latin: **7** de facto

infallible 4 sure **7** assured, certain, perfect **8** flawless, inerrant, positive, reliable, surefire, unerring **9** apodictic, faultless, foolproof, unfailing **10** dependable, impeccable **11** irrefutable **13** unimpeachable **16** incontrovertible

infamous 3 low **4** base, evil, foul, vile **6** odious, sinful, sordid, wicked **7** corrupt, heinous, ignoble, immoral, knavish **8** damnable, recreant, shameful **9** abhorrent, monstrous, nefarious, notorious **10** abominable, detestable, iniquitous, of evil fame, outrageous, perfidious, profligate, scandalous, scurrilous, villainous **11** disgraceful, of ill repute, opprobrious, treacherous **12** dishonorable, disreputable

infamy 4 evil **5** odium, shame **7** scandal **8** contempt, disgrace, dishonor, ignominy, villainy **9** discredit, disesteem, disrepute, notoriety **10** corruption, opprobrium, wickedness **11** abomination **13** despicability, notoriousness

infancy 6 cradle, nonage **8** babyhood,

inflict

minority **9** beginning, childhood, inception **10** immaturity

infant 3 kid **4** babe, baby **5** child **7** neonate, newborn, preemie, toddler **8** nursling, suckling

infantile 7 babyish **8** childish, juvenile **9** childlike, infantine **10** infantlike, sophomoric

infantryman 6 Zouave **7** dogface, dragoon **8** chasseur, doughboy, sorefoot **11** foot soldier

infatuated 7 charmed, smitten **8** beguiled, enamored, inflamed, obsessed **9** bewitched, enchanted, entranced **10** captivated, enraptured, enthralled, spellbound **11** carried away, intoxicated **12** having a crush

infatuation 4 rave **5** craze, crush, folly, mania **6** desire **7** passion **9** obsession, puppy love **10** enthusiasm **11** fascination, foolishness **12** passing fancy

infect 4 ruin **5** spoil, taint, touch **6** blight, damage, poison **7** afflict, corrupt **9** indispose, influence **11** contaminate

infected 6 impure, morbid, septic **7** corrupt, tainted **8** cankered, diseased, poisoned **12** contaminated

infection 6 blight **7** disease **9** contagion, virulence **11** suppuration

infectious 8 catching, epidemic, virulent **9** catchable, infective, spreading **10** compelling, contagious, inoculable **11** captivating **12** communicable, irresistible

infecund 6 barren, farrow **7** sterile **9** infertile **12** unproductive

infer 4 deem **5** glean, guess, judge, opine **6** deduce, gather, reason, reckon **7** presume, suppose, surmise **8** conclude **9** speculate **10** conjecture

inference 4 clue **10** intimation, suggestion **11** insinuation

inferior 4 poor **6** junior **8** low-grade, mediocre **9** secondary **10** low-quality, second-rate, subsidiary **11** indifferent, subordinate, subservient, substandard **12** not up to snuff

infernal 4 vile **5** awful, black, lower **6** cursed, Hadean, nether **7** heinous, hellish, Stygian, vicious **8** accursed, damnable, devilish, fiendish, horrible, terrible **9** atrocious, execrable, malicious, monstrous, nefarious, Plutonian **10** abominable, demoniacal, diabolical, flagitious, horrendous, iniquitous
also: 9 Tartarean
refers to: 10 underworld

inferno 4 hell, oven **5** abyss, Hades **6** hotbox, the pit, Tophet **7** furnace, roaster, sizzler **8** hellfire, hellhole, scorcher **9** perdition **10** lower world, underworld **11** netherworld **12** fiery furnace **13** nether regions **15** infernal regions **16** fire and brimstone, the bottomless pit

Inferno
part I of: 12 Divine Comedy
author: 14 Dante Alighieri

infertile 4 arid, bare **6** barren, effete, fallow **7** drained, sterile **8** depleted, desolate, impotent, infecund **9** exhausted, fruitless **10** unfruitful, unprolific **12** unproductive **13** nonproductive

infest 4 team **5** beset, crawl, creep, swarm **6** abound, infect, plague, ravage **7** overrun, torment **9** crawl with, swarm with

infestation 6 plague, ravage **9** lousiness, pervasion **11** overrunning **12** overswarming

in few words
Latin: 12 paucis verbis

infidel 5 pagan **6** savage **7** atheist, heathen, heretic, skeptic **8** agnostic, apostate, idolater **9** barbarian **10** unbeliever **11** nonbeliever

infidelity 6 breach **7** falsity, perfidy **8** adultery, betrayal **9** disregard, violation **10** disloyalty, infraction **12** nonadherence **13** nonobservance, transgression **14** unfaithfulness

infiltrate 4 leak, seep **5** imbue, steep **6** absorb, seep in **7** pervade **8** colonize, permeate **9** insinuate, penetrate

infinite 4 vast **5** great **7** endless, immense **8** enormous **9** boundless, limitless, unbounded, unlimited **10** tremendous, without end **11** illimitable, measureless **12** immeasurable, incalculable, interminable **13** inexhaustible **15** uncircumscribed

infinitesimal 3 wee **4** puny, tiny **6** minute **10** diminutive, negligible **11** microscopic **13** imperceptible, inappreciable, insignificant, undiscernible **14** extremely small, inconsiderable

infinity 7 forever **8** eternity **10** infinitude, perpetuity **11** endlessness, eternal time **12** sempiternity **13** boundlessness, limitlessness **14** illimitability **15** everlastingness, immeasurability, incalculability, measurelessness **16** inexhaustibility **19** incomprehensibility

Infiri
gods of: 10 underworld

infirm 3 ill **4** weak, worn **5** anile, frail, shaky **6** ailing, feeble, poorly, sickly **7** failing, fragile, unsound **8** decrepit, disabled, helpless, unstable, weakened **9** doddering, emaciated, enervated, enfeebled, powerless **11** debilitated **12** strengthless

infirmary 6 clinic **7** sick bay **8** hospital

infirmity 4 flaw **5** fault **6** defect, malady **7** ailment, failing, frailty, illness **8** debility, disorder, handicap, sickness **9** fragility, frailness **10** deficiency, disability, infirmness **11** instability **12** debilitation, imperfection, unstableness **13** indisposition, vulnerability

in flagrante delicto 8 in the act **9** red-handed

inflame 4 fire, rile **5** craze, rouse **6** arouse, enrage, excite, heat up, ignite, incite, kindle, madden, stir up, work up **7** agitate, incense, provoke **8** enkindle **9** electrify, stimulate **10** intoxicate

inflamed 3 mad **5** angry, irate, riled **6** crazed, fuming, roused **7** aroused, enraged, excited, fired up, furious, incited **8** agitated, incensed, provoked, reddened **9** steamed up, stirred up **10** infuriated **11** intensified

inflame with love 6 enamor **9** enrapture, impassion, infatuate

inflammable 5 fiery **8** choleric, volatile **9** excitable, flammable, ignitable, impetuous, overhasty, sensitive **10** high-strung, incendiary **11** combustible, precipitate **12** inflammatory

inflammation 4 acne, fire, gout, sore **6** canker, firing **7** arousal, chafing **8** bursitis, ignition, kindling, soreness, sore spot, swelling **9** agitation **10** incitement, irritation **13** conflagration, rabblerousing
suffix: 4 itis

inflammatory 5 fiery, rabid **8** arousing, enraging, inciting, mutinous, volcanic **9** demagogic, explosive, insurgent **10** incendiary, rebellious **11** combustible, fulminating, inflammable, intemperate, provocative **13** rabble-rousing, revolutionary

inflate 5 bloat, swell **6** blow up, dilate, expand, fill up, pump up **7** distend, improve, puff out **10** appreciate **11** rise in value

inflated 5 blown, gassy, tumid, wordy **6** blew up, turgid **7** bloated, blown up, dilated, flowery, pompous, swollen, verbose **8** boastful, enlarged, expanded **9** bombastic, distended, overblown, swelled up **10** rhetorical, swelled out **11** exaggerated, pretentious

inflection 4 tone **5** tenor **6** accent **10** modulation **11** enunciation, tone of voice **12** articulation **13** pronunciation

inflexible 4 firm, hard, taut **5** fixed, rigid, solid, stiff **6** dogged, mulish **7** adamant **8** obdurate, resolute, stubborn **9** hidebound, immovable, immutable, ironbound, obstinate, pigheaded, stringent, tenacious, unbending, unplastic **10** adamantine, determined, headstrong, impervious, implacable, inexorable, unwavering, unyielding **11** hard and fast, intractable, not flexible, unmalleable **12** unchangeable **14** uncompromising

inflict 4 dump **5** lay on, wreak **6** impose, unload **7** put upon **9** visit upon

10 administer, perpetrate **11** bring to bear

inflorescence 5 bloom **6** flower **7** blossom, cluster **8** blooming **9** flowering **10** blossoming
type: 4 cyme **5** spike, umbel **6** corymb, raceme, spadix **7** panicle **9** capitulum **14** verticillaster

influence 4 hold, move, pull, stir, sway **5** clout, guide, impel, power **6** arouse, effect, incite, induce, prompt, weight **7** act upon, actuate, control, dispose, incline, inspire, mastery, potency, provoke **8** dominion, leverage, persuade, pressure, prestige **9** advantage, authority **10** ascendancy, domination, predispose

influential 6 moving, potent, strong **7** leading, weighty **8** forceful, powerful, puissant **9** effective, effectual, important, inspiring, momentous **10** activating **11** efficacious, significant **12** instrumental **13** consequential

influx 5 entry **6** inflow **7** arrival, indraft, ingress **9** flowing in, incursion, inpouring **10** converging, inundation **12** infiltration

in force 6 extant **7** en masse **8** in

inform 3 rat **4** fink, tell **5** edify **6** advise, clue in, notify, snitch, squeal, tattle, tell on, tip off **7** apprise, let know **8** acquaint, denounce, forewarn, report to **9** declare to, enlighten **11** communicate, familiarize, serve notice **14** blow the whistle

inform against 5 rat on **6** betray, fink on, tell on **7** sell out **8** denounce, squeal on **11** double-cross **16** blow the whistle on

informal 4 easy **6** casual, simple **7** natural, offhand **8** familiar **9** easygoing, not formal **10** unofficial **11** spontaneous **12** come-as-you-are **13** unceremonious, unconstrained **14** unconventional

informal preliminary conference
French: **10** pourparler

informant 6 source **7** adviser, tipster **8** appriser, informer, notifier, reporter **9** announcer, spokesman **10** respondent **11** enlightener, horse's mouth, spokeswoman

information 4 data, news **5** facts, notes **6** notice, papers, report **7** account, tidings **8** briefing, bulletin, evidence, material **9** documents, knowledge, materials **10** communique **11** fact-finding **12** announcement, intelligence, notification **13** enlightenment

informed 4 told, up on, wise **5** aware, posted, talked, taught, warned **7** abreast, advised, knowing, learned, tattled **8** apprised, betrayed, educated, notified, reported, snitched, up to date **9** au courant, permeated **10** acquainted, instructed **11** enlightened, intelligent **13** knowledgeable

informer 3 rat **4** fink **5** Judas **6** canary **7** blabber, stoolie, tattler, traitor **8** betrayer, mouchard, snitcher, squealer **11** stool pigeon

Informer, The
author: **13** Liam O'Flaherty
director: **8** John Ford
cast: **10** Una O'Connor **11** Wallace Ford **12** Heather Angel **13** Margot Grahame, Preston Foster **14** Victor McLaglen
score: **10** Max Steiner
remade as: **7** Up Tight

infraction 6 breach **8** trespass **9** violation **10** peccadillo **11** lawbreaking **12** disobedience, encroachment, infringement, unobservance **13** nonobservance, transgression

infrastructure 4 base, root **5** basis **6** bottom, fabric, ground **7** bedrock, footing, support **9** framework, substrate **10** foundation, groundwork, substratum **12** substructure, underpinning **14** understructure

infrequent 3 few **4** rare **6** fitful, seldom, unique **7** unusual **8** sporadic, uncommon **9** spasmodic **10** occasional **16** few and far between

infringe 5 break **6** butt in, invade **7** disobey, impinge, infract, intrude, violate **8** encroach, overstep, trespass **10** contravene, transgress

in front 5 ahead, first **6** before **7** forward

in full possession of one's faculties
Latin: **12** compos mentis

infuriate 3 vex **4** gall, rile **5** anger, chafe **6** enrage, madden, offend **7** incense, inflame, outrage, provoke **8** irritate **9** aggravate, burn one up, make angry **10** exasperate **15** raise one's dander

infuriating 7 irksome **8** annoying, enraging **9** maddening, provoking **10** irritating **11** aggravating **12** exasperating, inflammatory

infuse 5 imbue **7** fortify, implant, inspire, instill **8** impart to, pour into **9** inculcate, insinuate, introject

in futuro 11 in the future

Inge, William
author of: **6** Picnic **7** Bus Stop **19** Come Back Little Sheba **26** The Dark at the Top of the Stairs

in general 7 as a rule, usually **10** by and large, on the whole

ingenious 4 deft **6** adroit, clever, crafty, expert, shrewd **7** cunning **8** masterly, original, skillful, stunning **9** brilliant, dexterous, inventive, masterful **11** resourceful

ingenuity 5 flair, skill **7** cunning, know-how, mastery **8** aptitude, deftness, facility **9** adeptness, dexterity, expertise, sharpness **10** adroitness, as-

tuteness, brilliance, cleverness, shrewdness **11** imagination **12** good thinking, skillfulness **13** ingeniousness, inventiveness **15** imaginativeness, quick-wittedness, resourcefulness

ingenuous 4 open **5** frank, naive **6** direct, honest **7** artless, genuine, natural, up front **8** trusting **9** guileless **10** unaffected **11** openhearted **13** simplehearted **15** straightforward, unsophisticated **16** straight-shooting

ingenuousness 7 naivete **8** openness **9** frankness **11** artlessness

ingest 3 eat **4** gulp, take **5** drink **6** absorb, devour, imbibe, take in **7** consume, swallow **8** gulp down

inglorious 3 low **4** base, evil, mean, vile **6** odious **7** corrupt, heinous, ignoble **8** depraved, flagrant, infamous, shameful, shocking **9** atrocious, degrading, nefarious **10** despicable, detestable, outrageous, scandalous **11** disgraceful, ignominious, opprobrious **12** contemptible, dishonorable

in good condition
French: **10** embonpoint

in good health 2 OK **4** fine, hale, well **6** hearty, robust, tiptop **7** healthy **8** all right, blooming, vigorous **9** full of pep, in the pink **17** full of vim and vigor

in good time 5 early **7** betimes **11** ahead of time

ingot 3 bar **5** block

ingrained 4 deep, firm **5** fixed **6** inborn, inbred, innate, rooted **8** inherent, thorough **9** confirmed, implanted, indelible, intrinsic **10** deep-rooted, deep-seated, inveterate **14** constitutional

Ingram, Blanche
character in: **8** Jane Eyre
author: **6** Bronte

ingratiating 4 oily **5** sweet **6** genial, smarmy **7** affable, amiable, cordial, fulsome, gushing, likable, lovable, winning, winsome **8** charming, engaging, friendly, gracious, magnetic, pleasing, unctuous **9** appealing, congenial **10** attractive, enchanting, obsequious, oleaginous, personable, persuasive **11** captivating, good-humored, self-serving **12** presumptuous

ingratiation 7 blarney **8** flattery **9** sweet talk **12** inveiglement **13** blandishments

ingratitude 14 ungratefulness **18** lack of appreciation

ingredient 4 part **6** aspect, factor **7** element, feature **9** component, essential, principle **11** constituent, contributor **12** integral part

Ingres, Jean-Auguste-Dominique
born: **6** France **9** Montauban
artwork: **9** Odalisque, The Source **13**

Mme Moitessier **14** The Turkish Bath **15** Valpincon Bather **16** Roger and Angelica **17** The Vow of Louis XIII **21** Comtesse d'Haussonville **25** The Ambassadors of Agamemnon **26** The Vow of Louis the Thirteenth

ingress 5 entry, way in **6** access **8** entrance

inhabit 5 lodge **6** live in, occupy, people, settle, tenant **7** dwell in **8** populate, reside in

inhabitant 6 inmate, lessee, lodger, native, renter, tenant **7** boarder, citizen, denizen, dweller, settler **8** occupant, occupier, resident, villager **9** inhabiter

inhalation 4 gasp **5** sniff **6** breath **11** breathing in

inhale 5 sniff, snuff **6** suck in **7** inspire, respire **9** breathe in, inbreathe

inherent 6 inborn, inbred, innate, native **7** natural **9** essential, ingrained, intrinsic **10** deep-rooted, hereditary, inveterate **11** inalienable, inseparable **14** constitutional

inherit 3 get **6** be left, come by **7** acquire **8** come into **9** come in for **10** fall heir to

inheritance 6 devise, estate, legacy **7** bequest **8** bestowal, heritage **9** endowment, patrimony **10** bequeathal, birthright

inherited 8 came into, heirloom, unearned **10** handed down

inheritor 4 heir **7** legatee **11** beneficiary

Inherit the Wind
   director: 13 Stanley Kramer
   based on play by: 10 Robert E Lee **14** Jerome Lawrence
   cast: 8 Dick York **9** Gene Kelly **10** Elliot Reid **11** Harry Morgan **12** Spencer Tracy (Clarence Darrow) **13** Frederic March (William Jennings Bryan) **16** Florence Eldridge

inhibit 3 bar, gag **4** curb, stop **5** block, check **6** arrest, enjoin, forbid, hinder, impede, muzzle **7** control, harness, prevent, repress, smother **8** hold back, obstruct, prohibit, restrain, restrict, suppress **9** constrain **11** hold in leash

inhibited 4 cold **6** barred, curbed, frigid **7** bridled, checked, guarded **8** hindered, reserved **9** repressed **10** controlled, obstructed, restrained **11** constrained, discouraged, held in check **12** unresponsive **14** under restraint

inhibition, inhibitions 5 check **7** reserve **8** blockage **9** misgiving, restraint, stricture **10** constraint, impediment **11** guardedness, mental block, obstruction, restriction **12** constriction **17** self-consciousness

in high spirits 2 up **3** gay **5** happy,

merry **6** elated, jaunty, joyful, joyous **7** buoyant **8** carefree, ecstatic, exultant, jubilant **9** overjoyed **11** exhilarated, on cloud nine **13** up in the clouds **15** on top of the world

in hoc signo vinces 26 in this sign shalt thou conquer
   motto of: 19 Constantine the Great **from vision of: 5** cross

inhospitable 4 cold, cool, rude **5** aloof **6** unkind **7** distant, hostile **8** impolite **10** unfriendly, ungracious, unobliging, unsociable **11** standoffish, uncongenial, unreceptive, unwelcoming **12** discourteous, unneighborly **13** inconsiderate **14** unapproachable **15** unaccommodating

inhuman 5 cruel **6** brutal, savage **7** brutish, satanic, vicious **8** barbaric, demoniac, fiendish, pitiless, ruthless, venomous **9** barbarous, heartless, malignant, merciless, monstrous, unfeeling **10** diabolical, malevolent **11** coldhearted, cold-blooded, hardhearted

inhumane 6 brutal, savage **7** inhuman **8** fiendish, pitiless, ruthless **9** barbarous, heartless, merciless, unfeeling, unpitying **10** unmerciful **11** coldblooded, hardhearted **12** bloodthirsty **13** unsympathetic

inhumanity 6 sadism **7** cruelty **8** atrocity, savagery **9** barbarism, barbarity, brutality **11** brutishness, heinousness, malevolence, viciousness **12** fiendishness, ruthlessness **13** heartlessness, mercilessness **15** coldbloodedness **16** bloodthirstiness

inhumation 6 burial **9** interment **10** entombment

inimical 5 toxic **6** at odds **7** harmful, hateful, hostile, hurtful, ruinous **8** venomous, virulent **9** dangerous, illwilled, injurious, on the outs, poisonous, rancorous **10** unfriendly **11** acrimonious, deleterious, destructive, detrimental, ill-disposed **12** antagonistic, antipathetic, disputatious **13** at loggerheads, at sword's point

inimitable 4 rare **6** unique **7** supreme **8** peerless **9** matchless, nonpareil, unequaled, unmatched, unrivaled **10** consummate, preeminent, unexcelled **11** superlative, unsurpassed **12** incomparable, unparalleled **13** beyond compare

iniquitous 4 base, evil, vile **6** sinful, wicked **7** corrupt, debased, immoral, vicious **8** depraved, infamous **9** nefarious **10** evil-minded **12** blackhearted **13** reprehensible

iniquity 3 sin **4** evil, vice **5** wrong **6** infamy **7** knavery, outrage, roguery **8** inequity, villainy **9** depravity, evildoing, flagrancy, turpitude **10** corruption, dishonesty, immorality, miscreancy, profligacy, sinfulness, unfairness, unjustness, wickedness,

wrongdoing **11** abomination **13** transgression **14** gross injustice **15** unrighteousness

in isolation
   Latin: 7 in vacuo

initial 5 first **6** maiden, primal **7** opening, primary **8** germinal, original, starting **9** beginning, inaugural, incipient **10** commencing, initiatory **12** introductory

initiate 4 haze, open **5** begin, found, set up, start **6** induct, invest, launch, take in **7** bring in, install, kick off, receive, usher in **8** be opened, commence, get going, set afoot, set going **9** enter upon, establish, institute, introduce, originate **10** inaugurate, lead the way **11** break ground, get under way, take the lead **12** acquaint with **13** blaze the trail **15** familiarize with **16** lay the first stone, lay the foundation **19** start the ball rolling

initiation 5 onset, start **6** outset **7** genesis, opening **8** entrance, guidance, outbreak, starting **9** beginning, inception, induction **10** admittance, initiating, ushering in **11** inculcation **12** commencement, inauguration, introduction **14** indoctrination **15** formal admission

initiative 4 lead **8** dynamism **9** first move, first step **10** creativity, enterprise, get-up-and-go, leadership **11** originality **12** forcefulness **14** aggressiveness

in its original place
   Latin: 6 in situ

inject 3 put **4** pump **5** force, imbue, infix **6** infuse, insert **7** instill, throw in **8** intromit **9** interject, introduce **11** interpolate

injection 4 hypo, shot **7** booster, vaccine **9** antitoxin, insertion **10** hypodermic **11** inoculation, vaccination **12** shot in the arm

injudicious 4 dumb, wild **5** crazy **6** stupid, unwise **7** foolish, unsound **8** heedless, reckless **9** audacious, foolhardy, hotheaded, imprudent, senseless **10** self-willed, unsuitable **11** inadvisable

injunction 4 writ **5** edict, order **7** command **10** admonition, court order

Injun Joe
   character in: 9 Tom Sawyer
   author: 9 Mark Twain

injure 3 mar **4** harm, hurt, lame, maim **5** abuse, spoil, stain, sting, sully, wound, wrong **6** bruise, damage, debase, deface, deform, impair, malign, mangle, misuse, offend, scathe **7** afflict, affront, blemish, violate, vitiate **8** do harm to, ill-treat, lacerate, maltreat, mutilate **9** disfigure

injured 4 hurt, lame **6** abused, harmed, maimed, marred, piqued **7** bruised, damaged, defaced, grieved, scathed, wounded, wronged **8** crippled, deformed, impaired, insulted, offended **9** afflicted, affronted, aggrieved **10** disfigured

injurious 7 abusive, adverse, harmful, hurtful, noxious, ruinous **8** damaging, inimical **9** corrosive **10** calamitous, disastrous, pernicious **11** deleterious, destructive, detrimental

injury 3 cut **4** blow, gash, harm, hurt, stab **5** abuse, wound **6** bruise, damage, lesion **7** affront, outrage, scratch **9** aspersion, contusion, indignity, injustice **10** affliction, defamation, detraction, disservice, impairment, laceration, mutilation **12** vilification

injustice 3 sin **4** bias, evil **5** wrong **6** injury **7** bigotry, offense, tyranny **8** foul play, inequity, iniquity **9** prejudice, unjust act **10** disservice, favoritism, inequality, infraction, partiality, unfairness, unjustness, wrongdoing **11** malpractice, persecution **12** encroachment, infringement, partisanship **13** transgression

in keeping 6 normal **7** natural **8** becoming **9** congruous, consonant **10** consistent **11** appropriate, in agreement **12** in compliance, in conformity

inkling 3 cue, tip **4** clue, hint, idea **6** notion **7** glimmer, whisper **8** innuendo **9** suspicion, vague idea **10** conception, glimmering, indication, intimation, suggestion **11** insinuation, supposition

inky 3 jet **4** dark **5** black, raven, sable **7** stygian **9** coal-black

inlet 3 bay **4** cove, gulf **5** bight, fiord, firth, fjord **6** harbor, strait **7** estuary, narrows **9** waterway

in line 4 even **6** in a row **7** aligned, in order **8** queued up, straight **12** under control

in loco 7 in place **16** in the proper place

in loco parentis 16 replacing a parent **19** in the place of a parent

inmate 3 con **5** felon **6** lodger, tenant **7** convict, denizen **8** prisoner, resident **10** inhabitant

in medias res 19 in the middle of things **21** in the middle of the story

in memoriam 10 in memory of **13** as a memorial to, to the memory of

In Memoriam A H H
author: 18 Alfred Lord Tennyson

in memory of
Latin: 10 in memoriam

In Memory of W B Yeats
author: 7 W H Auden

inmost 5 inner **6** inside **7** central **8** interior **9** innermost

in motion 5 afoot, astir **6** active, moving **7** on the go, working **8** under way **9** on the move, operating, operative **10** responsive

In My Father's Court
author: 19 Isaac Bashevis Singer

inn 5 hotel, lodge, motel, serai **6** hostel, imaret, tavern **7** hospice, pension **8** hostelry **9** roadhouse **11** caravansary, public house
French: 7 auberge
Spanish: 6 posada

innards 4 guts **6** bowels, vitals **7** gizzard, insides, viscera **10** intestines **14** liver and lights

innate 6 inborn, inbred, native **7** natural **8** inherent **9** essential, ingrained, inherited, intrinsic, intuitive **10** congenital, hereditary, indigenous **11** instinctive **14** constitutional

inner 6 hidden, inside, inward, mental, middle **7** central, private, psychic **8** esoteric, interior, internal, personal **9** concealed, emotional, spiritual, unobvious **10** more secret **12** more intimate **13** psychological

inner circle 4 core **5** bosom, cadre, heart **6** center **7** nucleus

inner city 8 core city, downtown **9** urban area **10** city limits, metropolis **11** central city **16** metropolitan area

Inner Mongolia
other name: 9 Neimenggu, Neimengku
capital: 6 Hohhot **7** Huhehot
desert: 4 Gobi
tent: 4 yurt

innermost 6 inmost, secret **7** deepest **10** deep-rooted, deep-seated **11** most private **12** most intimate, most personal

innermost part 4 core, crux, pith, soul **6** center, kernel **7** essence, nucleus

Inness, George
born: 10 Newburgh NY
artwork: 7 The Monk **14** Home of the Heron, Peace and Plenty **16** Delaware Water Gap **17** The Delaware Valley **19** The Lackawanna Valley

Innisfail see **7** Ireland

innkeeper 4 host, oste **6** tapper, venter **7** padrone **8** boniface, hosteler, hotelier, landlord, publican **10** proprietor **12** maitre d'hotel, restaurateur

innocence 6 purity **7** naivete **8** chastity **9** freshness **10** clean hands, simplicity **11** artlessness, sinlessness **12** incorruption, spotlessness **13** blamelessness, guilelessness, guiltlessness, impeccability, inculpability, ingenuousness, stainlessness **14** immaculateness

innocent 3 tot **4** baby, naif, open, pure, tyro **5** clean, naive **6** chaste, honest, novice, simple **7** artless, ingenue, sinless, upright **8** harmless, pristine, spotless, virginal, virtuous **9** blameless, childlike, faultless, greenhorn, guileless, guiltless, ingenuous, innocuous, little one, stainless, uncor-

rupt, undefiled, unstained, unsullied, unworldly, well-meant **10** artless one, immaculate, impeccable, inculpable, tenderfoot, young child **11** inoffensive, unblemished, uncorrupted, unmalicious, unoffending **12** unsuspicious **13** meaning no harm, unimpeachable **14** above suspicion, irreproachable **15** unsophisticated
Latin: 12 integer vitae

Innocents, The
director: 11 Jack Clayton
based on story by: 10 Henry James (The Turn of the Screw)
cast: 11 Deborah Kerr, Megs Jenkins **13** Peter Wyngarde **15** Michael Redgrave
script: 12 Truman Capote **16** William Archibald

Innocents Abroad, The
author: 9 Mark Twain (Samuel Clemens)

innocuous 4 dull, mild **5** banal, empty, trite, vapid **6** barren **7** insipid **8** harmless, innocent, painless **9** pointless **11** commonplace, inoffensive, meaningless

innocuousness 6 safety **9** blandness, innocence **12** harmlessness **15** inoffensiveness

in no uncertain terms 7 clearly, plainly **9** expressly **10** definitely, distinctly **13** categorically, unequivocally

innovation 5 shift **7** novelty **8** updating **10** alteration, dernier cri, new measure, remodeling, renovation **11** institution, latest thing **12** commencement, inauguration, introduction, streamlining **13** modernization

innovator 7 deviser, planner **9** contriver **10** instigator, originator **11** inaugurator

Inns of Court 8 Gray's Inn **11** Inner Temple, Lincoln's Inn **12** Middle Temple **14** legal societies
in: 6 London
member: 9 barrister

innuendo 4 hint **7** whisper **8** overtone **9** inference **10** imputation, intimation **11** implication, insinuation

innumerable 6 myriad **8** numerous **9** countless **10** numberless, unnumbered **12** incalculable **13** multitudinous

Ino
also: 9 Leucothea
goddess of: 3 sea
father: 6 Cadmus
mother: 8 Harmonia
sister: 5 Hgave **6** Semele **7** Autonoe
husband: 7 Athamas
son: 8 Learchus **10** Melicertes
stepson: 7 Phrixus
stepdaughter: 5 Helle
saved: 8 Odysseus
cared for infant: 8 Dionysus
changed into: 10 sea goddess

inoculate 5 imbue, shoot **6** infuse, inject, insert **7** implant, instill **8** immunize **9** inculcate, vaccinate

inoculation 4 shot **6** needle **7** booster **9** injection **10** hypodermic **11** vaccination **12** immunization

inoffensive 4 mild, safe **5** bland **7** neutral **8** harmless, innocent **9** endurable, innocuous, tolerable **10** sufferable **11** unoffending **15** unobjectionable

inoffensiveness 6 safety **9** innocence **10** neutrality **12** harmlessness **13** innocuousness

in one's debt 7 obliged **8** beholden, indebted **9** obligated **15** under obligation

in one's own person
　　Latin: **16** in propria persona
in one's own place
　　Latin: **7** suo loco
in one's own right
　　Latin: **7** suo jure
in one's rightful place
　　Latin: **7** suo loco

inoperable 6 broken **10** broken down, unworkable **11** ineffective

in operation 5 in use **7** in force, working **8** in effect **9** operating, operative

inoperative 4 dead, down **8** inactive **10** not working, out of order

inopportune 7 awkward **8** ill-timed, untimely **10** badly timed, ill-advised, unsuitable **11** troublesome, undesirable, unfavorable, unfortunate **12** inauspicious, incommodious, inconvenient, unpropitious, unseasonable **13** inappropriate **15** disadvantageous

in order 2 OK **4** neat, tidy **6** proper **7** correct, perfect **8** all right

inordinate 5 undue **6** lavish, wanton **7** extreme, profuse, surplus **8** needless, overmuch, shocking **9** excessive **10** deplorable, exorbitant, immoderate, irrational, outrageous, scandalous **11** disgraceful, extravagant, intemperate, overflowing, superfluous, uncalled-for, unnecessary **12** unreasonable, unrestrained **13** superabundant **14** super-saturated, unconscionable **16** disproportionate

inordinately 6 overly, unduly **9** extremely **11** excessively **12** immoderately, outrageously, prodigiously **13** extravagantly, intemperately, superfluously, unnecessarily

inorganic 4 dead **7** mineral **8** lifeless **9** inanimate, nonliving **10** artificial

in passing
　　French: **9** en passant
in perpetuum 7 forever
in petto 11 in the breast **12** not disclosed

in pieces 6 broken **7** asunder, smashed **8** in shreds, sundered **9** torn apart **13** in smithereens

in place
　　Latin: **6** in loco, in situ
in plain sight 7 exposed, obvious **10** in full view, noticeable **12** out in the open **17** in front of one's nose
in posse 11 potentially **13** in possibility
in possibility
　　Latin: **7** in posse
In Praise of Darkness
　　author: **15** Jorge Luis Borges
in propria persona 15 in one's own person

inquest 5 probe **7** autopsy, delving, hearing, inquiry, probing **8** necropsy **10** postmortem **11** inquisition **13** investigation

inquire 3 ask **5** probe, query, study **6** search **7** examine, explore, inspect **8** check out, look into, look over, question **9** track down **10** look deeper, scrutinize **11** investigate

inquirer 5 asker, snoop **6** seeker **7** auditor, querier, quizzer, student **8** pollster, searcher **9** catechist **10** inquisitor, questioner **12** interlocutor, interrogator, investigator

inquiry, enquiry 4 hunt, quiz **5** probe, query, quest, study **6** search, survey **7** inquest **8** analysis, question, research, scrutiny **9** interview **10** inspection **11** examination, exploration, inquisition, questioning **13** interrogation, investigation

inquisitive 4 nosy **6** prying, snoopy **8** meddling, snooping **9** inquiring, intrusive, searching **10** meddlesome, too curious **11** interfering, overcurious, questioning

in re 13 in the matter of
in reality
　　Latin: **7** de facto
in rem 15 against the thing
　　of a legal proceeding: 18 against the property
in rerum natura 19 in the nature of things
in retreat 10 backing off, retreating **11** withdrawing, backing away
in reverse 8 backward **9** backing up **22** in the opposite direction

insalubrious 7 harmful, noisome, noxious **8** inimical, virulent **9** injurious, unhealthy **10** pernicious **11** deleterious, detrimental, unhealthful, unwholesome

insane 3 mad **4** bats, daft, dumb, loco, nuts, wild, zany **5** balmy, batty, crazy, loony, manic, nutty, potty **6** absurd, crazed, raving **7** berserk, bizarre, bonkers, cracked, foolish, idiotic, lunatic, tetched, touched, unsound **8** demented, frenzied, maniacal, unhinged **9** eccentric, imbecilic, imprudent, insensate, paranoiac, psychotic, senseless **10** ridiculous, un-

balanced **11** injudicious **12** mad as a hatter, off one's chump, round the bend, unreasonable **13** off one's rocker, out of one's head, out of one's mind, out of one's wits, schizophrenic **15** bats in the belfry, mad as a March hare, stark staring mad **17** nutty as a fruitcake

insanity 5 folly, mania **6** idiocy, lunacy, raving **7** madness **8** dementia, paranoia **9** aberrance, absurdity, craziness, monomania, psychosis, stupidity **10** aberration **11** derangement, foolishness, unsoundness **12** loss of reason **13** hallucination, mental illness, schizophrenia, senselessness

insatiable 8 ravenous **9** insatiate, limitless, voracious **10** bottomless, gluttonous, implacable, omnivorous **12** unappeasable, unquenchable

inscribe 3 pen **4** etch, mark, seal, sign **5** blaze, brand, carve, write **6** chisel, incise, letter, scrawl **7** engrave, impress, imprint **8** scribble **9** autograph

inscription 5 motto, title **6** legend, rubric **7** address, caption, epigram, epitaph, heading, titulus, writing **8** colophon, epigraph, graffiti **9** engraving, lettering **10** dedication

inscrutable 6 arcane, hidden, masked, veiled **7** deadpan, elusive **8** baffling, puzzling **9** concealed, enigmatic **10** mysterious, mystifying, perplexing, poker-faced, unknowable, unreadable, unrevealed **12** inexplicable, unfathomable, unsearchable **14** indecipherable, unintelligible **16** incomprehensible

In Search of Identity
　　author: **12** Anwar el-Sadat

insect 3 ant, bee, bug, fly **4** flea, gnat, moth, pest, wasp **5** aphid, imago **6** bedbug, beetle, cicada, earwig, hornet, mantis, mayfly, vermin **7** chigger, cricket, firefly, katydid, ladybug, termite **8** horsefly, housefly, lacewing, mosquito **9** arthropod, butterfly, cockroach, dragonfly **10** silverfish **11** grasshopper
　　study of: 10 entomology
　　young: 4 grub, pupa **5** larva, nymph **6** larvae, maggot **9** chrysalis **11** caterpillar
　　anatomy: 4 palp **5** cerci, notum **6** cercus, feeler, labium, labrum, ocelli, thorax **7** antenna, maxilla, ocellus **8** antennae, mandible, maxillae **9** proboscis, spiracles **10** ovipositor **11** exoskeleton

insectivore 4 mole **5** shrew **6** desman, tenrec **7** moon rat **8** alamiqui, anteater, hedgehog **9** solenodon

insecure 4 weak **5** frail, risky, shaky **6** infirm, unsafe, unsure, wobbly **7** dubious, exposed, not firm, not sure, rickety, unsound **8** critical, doubtful, in danger, perilous, unstable, unsteady **9** dangerous, diffident, hazardous, in a bad way, tottering, unassured, uncertain, under fire **10** endangered, precarious, ramshackle, unreliable, unshielded, vulnerable **11** defenseless, dilapidated, unprotected, unsheltered

insecurities 4 risk **5** peril **6** danger, hazard **7** pitfall **8** jeopardy **11** contingency

insecurity 5 doubt **9** self-doubt, shakiness **10** diffidence, unsafeness **11** dubiousness, incertitude, instability, uncertainty **12** doubtfulness, endangerment, insecureness, unsteadiness **13** vulnerability **14** precariousness **15** defenselessness, lack of assurance **16** apprehensiveness

insensate 4 cold **5** cruel **6** brutal **8** inhumane **9** heartless, unfeeling **11** unconscious

insensibility 4 coma **5** swoon **6** apathy, torpor, trance **8** blackout, dullness, lethargy, numbness, obduracy, oblivion, stoicism **9** analgesia, catalepsy **10** anesthesia, obtuseness **12** incognizance, indifference, mindlessness **13** insensitivity, unfeelingness **15** unconsciousness

insensible 4 cold **9** insensate, senseless **11** unconscious

insensitive 4 cold, dead, numb **5** blase **7** callous **8** hardened **9** apathetic, impassive, insensate, unaware of, unfeeling **10** impervious, insensible **11** indifferent, unconcerned **12** thick-skinned **15** uncompassionate

insensitiveness 8 rudeness **10** coarseness, indelicacy **12** tactlessness **13** insensibility, insensitivity **17** inconsiderateness

inseparable 8 attached **11** indivisible, unseverable **12** indissoluble

insert 3 add **5** embed, enter, imbed, infix, inlay, inset, pop in, put in, set in **6** infuse, inject, push in, tuck in **7** drive in, implant, intrude, place in, press in, slide in, stick in, stuff in, wedge in **8** thrust in **9** interject, interlard, interpose, introduce **10** put between **11** interpolate, intersperse

insertion 2 ad **5** entry, graft, inlay, inset **7** implant **11** insinuation, parenthesis **12** interjection **13** advertisement

inset 4 gore **5** embed, godet, imbed, inlay, panel **6** insert **9** insertion

in seventh heaven 6 elated, joyful, joyous **8** ecstatic, euphoric **9** exuberant, rapturous **11** on cloud nine **13** up in the clouds

inside 2 in **5** inner **6** inmost, inward, secret **7** private **8** cliquish, esoteric, interior, internal, intimate **9** inner part, inner side, innermost **12** confidential

inside information 3 tip **10** inside dope

inside out 9 backwards **10** in disorder, topsy turvy **11** wrong side to

insides 4 guts **6** bowels, vitals **7** gizzard, innards, viscera **10** intestines

insidious 3 sly **4** foxy, wily **5** shady **6** artful, covert, crafty, sneaky, subtle, tricky **7** crooked, cunning, devious, furtive **8** guileful, slippery, sneaking, stealthy **9** concealed, deceitful, designing, disguised, secretive, underhand **10** contriving, perfidious, pernicious, undercover, undetected **11** clandestine, deleterious, treacherous, underhanded **12** disingenuous, falsehearted **13** Machiavellian, surreptitious

insight 6 acumen **9** intuition **10** perception **11** discernment, penetration **12** apprehension, perceptivity, perspicacity **13** comprehension, intuitiveness **14** perceptiveness
French: **6** apercu

insignia 3 bar **4** mark, sign, star **5** badge, medal, patch **6** emblem, stripe, symbol **7** chevron, epaulet, oak leaf **10** decoration **13** badge of office

insignificance 8 puniness **9** pettiness, smallness **10** meagerness, triviality **11** irrelevance **12** unimportance

insignificant 4 puny **5** petty, small **6** flimsy, meager, minute, paltry **7** trivial **8** niggling, not vital, nugatory, picayune, piddling, trifling **9** minuscule, worthless **10** immaterial, irrelevant, negligible, of no moment, second-rate **11** indifferent, meaningless, unimportant **12** nonessential **13** small potatoes **14** inconsiderable **15** inconsequential, of little account, of no consequence **18** not worth mentioning

insincere 5 false, lying **6** untrue **7** devious, evasive **8** guileful, two-faced, uncandid **9** deceitful, dishonest, equivocal **10** fraudulent, perfidious, untruthful **11** dissembling **12** disingenuous, hypocritical, mealymouthed **13** dissimulating, double-dealing

insincerity 4 sham **6** deceit **8** pretense, uncandor **9** deception, falseness, hypocrisy, mendacity **11** affectation, shallowness, unfrankness **12** uncandidness **13** artificiality **16** disingenuousness

insinuate 5 imply **6** inject, insert **7** asperse, let fall, suggest, wheedle, whisper **8** intimate **10** ingratiate **11** worm one's way

insinuation 4 hint **8** allusion, infusion, innuendo **9** aspersion, insertion, intrusion **10** allegation, imputation, intimation, suggestion **11** implication, penetration **12** ingratiation, interjection

insipid 4 arid, blah, drab, dull, flat, lean **5** banal, bland, empty, inane, stale, trite, vapid **6** barren, boring, jejune, stupid **7** prosaic **8** lifeless, zestless **9** pointless, savorless, tasteless,

wearisome **10** monotonous, namby-pamby, wishy-washy **11** commonplace **12** unappetizing **13** characterless, uninteresting

insist 4 aver, hold, urge, warn **5** claim, vouch **6** assert, demand, exhort, repeat, stress **7** caution, command, contend, persist, protest, require **8** admonish, maintain **9** reiterate **10** asseverate **13** lay down the law **14** take a firm stand **15** stand one's ground

insistence 6 demand, urging **7** urgency **8** exigency, pressure **9** clamoring **11** persistence **12** perseverance **14** imperativeness

insistent 4 firm **7** adamant **8** emphatic, repeated, stubborn **9** assertive, demanding **10** determined, unyielding **11** unrelenting

in situ 7 in place **18** in its original place

insolence 4 gall **7** disdain, hauteur **8** audacity **9** arrogance, impudence **10** brazenness, disrespect, effrontery, incivility, lordliness **11** haughtiness, presumption **12** disobedience, impertinence, impoliteness **13** bumptiousness, imperiousness **14** unmannerliness **16** superciliousness

insolent 4 rude **5** fresh, nervy **6** brazen, cheeky **7** defiant, galling, haughty **8** arrogant, impolite, impudent **9** audacious, bumptious, insulting **10** disdainful, outrageous, unmannerly **11** impertinent, overbearing **12** contemptuous, discourteous, presumptuous, supercilious **13** disrespectful

insoluble 12 inexplicable, unanswerable **13** undissolvable, unexplainable **14** undecipherable **16** incomprehensible

insolvent 5 broke **6** ruined **8** bankrupt, wiped out **9** destitute, moneyless, penniless **10** down-and-out, out of money **11** impecunious **12** impoverished, overextended

insomnia 11 nuit blanche, pervigilium, wakefulness **12** insomnolence **13** sleeplessness

insouciant 4 airy **5** perky **6** breezy, casual, jaunty **7** buoyant, offhand **8** carefree, debonair, flippant **9** easygoing, mercurial, unruffled, sans souci, whimsical **10** capricious, nonchalant, untroubled **11** free and easy, indifferent, unconcerned **12** devil-may-care, happy-go-lucky, lighthearted

inspect 3 eye **4** scan **5** probe, study **6** peer at, peruse, review, survey **7** examine, explore, observe **8** pore over **10** scrutinize **11** contemplate, investigate, reconnoiter

inspection 4 scan **5** audit, check, probe, study **6** review, survey **7** perusal **8** checking, scrutiny **9** appraisal, oversight **11** examination

inspector 7 analyst, auditor 8 analyzer, examiner, overseer, reviewer 9 appraiser, detective 11 scrutinizer 12 investigator
   famous: 3 Fix, Fox 4 Japp 5 Queen 6 Alleyn, Bucket, Gerard, Gideon, Javert 7 Maigret 8 Clouseau, Lestrade 9 Dalgliesh

Inspector-General, The
   author: 12 Nikolai Gogol
   character: 4 Anna, Osip 5 Maria 26 Ivan Alexandrovich Hlestakov 35 Anton Antonovich Skvoznik-Dmukhanovsky

inspiration 4 idea, spur 5 fancy, flash 6 motive 7 impulse 8 afflatus, stimulus 9 incentive, influence, prompting 10 compulsion, incitement, motivation, revelation 13 encouragement

inspire 4 fire, stir 5 cause, exalt, impel, rouse 6 arouse, excite, induce, prompt, vivify 7 animate, enliven, hearten, produce, promote, provoke, quicken 8 embolden, engender, enkindle, illumine, inspirit, motivate, occasion 9 encourage, galvanize, influence, stimulate 10 give rise to, illuminate

inspired 3 apt 5 fired, moved 6 elated 7 elegant, exalted, excited, incited, touched, well-put 8 creative, original, prompted 9 impressed, ingenious, inventive, motivated 10 encouraged, felicitous, influenced, stimulated, well-chosen 11 exhilarated, imaginative 13 well-expressed

inspiring 5 grand 6 moving 7 awesome 8 eloquent, stirring 9 affecting, brilliant 10 impressive 11 encouraging, magnificent, stimulating

inspirit 5 boost, cheer, rouse 6 buoy up, uplift 7 animate, comfort, enliven, hearten, inspire 9 encourage, give a lift

in spite of himself
   French: 9 malgre lui

instability 8 wavering, weakness 9 hesitancy 10 fitfulness, hesitation, indecision, insecurity 11 flightiness, fluctuation, inconstancy, vacillation 12 irresolution, unstableness, unsteadiness 13 changeability, inconsistency, mercurialness, vulnerability 14 capriciousness, changeableness

install, instal 3 lay 4 seat 5 crown, embed, imbed, lodge, plant 6 induct, invest, locate, move in, ordain 7 arrange, emplace, instate, receive, situate, station, usher in 8 coronate, initiate, position 9 establish 10 inaugurate, set in place

   installation 5 plant 6 agency 8 facility 9 formation, induction 10 foundation, initiation, ordination 11 appointment, institution, investiture 12 inauguration, military base, organization 13 establishment

installment 4 part, unit 5 issue 6 laying 7 chapter, payment, section, segment 8 division, fragment, locating

instance 4 case, time 6 sample 7 example 8 occasion, specimen 9 precedent, prototype 10 antecedent 11 case in point 12 circumstance, illustration

instant 5 flash, jiffy, quick, trice 6 abrupt, minute, moment, prompt, second, sudden 8 premixed 9 immediate, on the spot, precooked, twinkling 10 ready-to-use 11 split second 12 unhesitating

instantaneous 5 rapid, swift 6 abrupt, direct, prompt, speedy, sudden 9 immediate 13 quick as a flash

instantaneously 6 at once 7 quickly, rapidly 8 in a flash, in no time, instanter, right now 9 on the spot, right away 11 immediately 21 in the twinkling of an eye

instantly 6 at once 7 quickly 8 directly, in a flash, promptly, right now 9 instanter, on the spot 10 here and now 11 immediately 12 quick as a wink, without delay 15 instantaneously 17 without hesitation

instar
   insect period between: 5 molts 7 molting

in statu quo 17 in the state in which (something is or was)

Instauratio Magna
   author: 12 Francis Bacon

instead 6 in lieu, rather 10 in its place

instigate 4 goad, spur, urge 5 begin, rouse, start 6 foment, incite, kindle, prompt, stir up 7 provoke 8 initiate 9 stimulate 10 bring about 11 set in motion

instigator 6 shaper 7 inciter 9 architect, innovator 10 prime mover, ringleader

instill, instil 4 pour 5 mix in, teach 6 impart, induce 7 implant, inspire 8 engender 9 inculcate

instinct 4 gift 5 knack 6 genius, nature 7 faculty 8 aptitude, capacity, tendency 9 intuition, mother wit 10 proclivity

instinctive 6 inborn, inbred, innate, native 7 natural 8 inherent, inspired 9 automatic, impulsive, intuitive, unlearned 10 deep-seated, unacquired 11 instinctual, involuntary, spontaneous

institute 4 pass 5 begin, enact, found, set up, start 6 ordain, school 7 academy, college, society 8 commence, get going, initiate, organize 9 establish, introduce, originate, prescribe, undertake 10 constitute, foundation, inaugurate 11 association, get under way 13 put into effect 14 bring into being

institution 4 rite 5 habit, usage 6 custom, prison, ritual, school 7 academy,

college, company, fixture 8 bughouse, madhouse, nuthouse, seminary 9 institute 10 convention, crazy house, foundation, university 11 association 12 organization 13 establishment

institutionalize 6 commit, detain 7 confine, put away 8 imprison 11 incarcerate

in strict confidence 7 sub rosa 9 between us, entre nous, privately 14 confidentially 15 between you and me 16 between me and thee, between ourselves

instruct 3 bid 5 brief, coach, drill, guide, order, teach, train, tutor 6 advise, direct, inform, notify, school 7 apprise, command, educate 8 acquaint 9 catechize, enlighten 12 indoctrinate

instruction 8 coaching, guidance, pedagogy, teaching, training, tutelage, tutoring 9 education 11 instructing 14 indoctrination

instructions 4 rule 5 maxim, moral, motto 6 advice, homily, lesson 7 precept 9 direction, guideline 11 explanation, information 12 prescription 13 specification 14 recommendation

instructive 8 didactic, edifying 11 educational 12 enlightening

instructor 3 don 4 guru 5 coach, guide, tutor 6 mentor 7 counsel, maestro, teacher, trainer 8 educator, lecturer 9 governess, pedagogue, preceptor, professor 10 schoolmarm 12 schoolmaster 13 schoolteacher 14 schoolmistress

instrument 4 deed, tool 5 agent, grant, means, paper 6 agency, device, gadget, medium 7 charter, machine, utensil, vehicle 8 contract 9 apparatus, appliance, equipment, expedient, implement, mechanism 11 contrivance

Instrument, The
   author: 9 John O'Hara

instrumental 5 vital 6 active, useful 7 crucial, helpful 8 a means to, decisive, valuable 9 assisting, conducive, effective, effectual, essential 10 functional 12 contributory

instrumentality 5 force, means 6 agency, charge 9 influence, mediation 12 intervention

insubordinate 6 unruly 7 defiant 8 insolent, mutinous 9 fractious 10 disorderly, rebellious, refractory 11 disobedient, intractable, uncompliant 12 recalcitrant, ungovernable, unsubmissive

insubordination 6 mutiny, revolt 7 anarchy 8 sedition 9 rebellion 10 dissention, insurgence, unruliness 12 disobedience, insurrection 13 noncompliance 14 refractoriness

insubstantial 4 airy, weak 5 frail, shaky, small 6 flimsy, modest, paltry, slight, unreal 7 fragile, trivial, unsound **8** baseless, bodiless, delicate, ethereal, gossamer, piddling, trifling, unstable **9** imaginary, visionary **10** groundless, immaterial, impalpable, intangible **12** apparitional **14** inconsiderable

in succession
French: **7** en suite

insufferable 7 hateful **8** dreadful **10** abominable, detestable, disgusting, outrageous, unbearable **11** intolerable, unendurable, unspeakable **13** insupportable

insufficiency 4 lack, need, want **6** dearth **7** drought, paucity **8** scarcity, shortage **10** deficiency, inadequacy, meagerness, scantiness **11** undersupply

insufficient 6 scanty, skimpy, sparse **7** lacking, wanting **8** impotent **9** deficient, not enough **10** inadequate **11** incompetent **14** unsatisfactory

insular 5 petty **6** biased, narrow **7** bigoted, limited **8** isolated **9** illiberal, insulated, parochial **10** intolerant, prejudiced, provincial **12** narrow-minded

insulate 5 cover **6** cut off, detach, enisle, shield **7** cushion, isolate, protect, seclude **8** separate **9** segregate, sequester **10** disconnect

insult 3 cut **4** slap **5** abuse, cheek, scorn **6** deride, offend, slight **7** affront, offense, outrage **8** be rude to, belittle, rudeness **9** disparage, impudence, indignity **11** discourtesy, lese majesty

insulting 4 rude **5** nasty **7** abusive, uncivil, vicious **8** impolite, insolent **9** invidious, offensive **10** defamatory, derogatory **11** disparaging **12** discourteous **13** disrespectful

insuperable 8 crushing **9** defeating **10** impassable, impossible, invincible, unbeatable, unyielding **12** inexpugnable, overpowering, overwhelming **13** overmastering, unconquerable **14** insurmountable

insurance 6 policy **8** coverage, security, warranty **9** assurance, guarantee, indemnity

insure 6 secure **10** underwrite

insurgent 5 rebel **7** lawless **8** mutineer, mutinous, partisan, renegade, resister, revolter **9** breakaway, dissident, guerrilla **10** disorderly, rebellious **11** disobedient **13** insubordinate, revolutionary, revolutionist **15** insurrectionist

insurmountable 8 hopeless, too great **10** unbeatable **11** beyond reach, insuperable **13** unconquerable

insurrection 4 riot **6** mutiny, revolt, rising **8** outbreak, uprising **9** rebellion **10** insurgence, revolution

intact 4 safe **5** sound, whole **6** unhurt **7** perfect **8** complete, integral, unbroken, unharmed **9** undamaged, uninjured, untouched **10** in one piece, unimpaired **11** in good shape **15** without a scratch

intangible 5 vague **7** elusive, shadowy **8** abstract, ethereal, fleeting, fugitive **9** transient **10** accidental, evanescent, immaterial, impalpable **11** abstraction, untouchable **12** imponderable **13** imperceptible, insubstantial

integer 5 digit, whole **6** entity, figure, number **7** numeral **11** whole number

integer vitae 8 innocent **15** blameless in life

integral 4 full **5** basic, total, whole **6** entire, intact **7** perfect, rounded **8** complete, finished, inherent **9** component, essential, fulfilled, necessary, requisite **10** fulfilling **11** constituent, well-rounded **13** indispensable

integrate 3 mix **4** fuse **5** blend, merge, unify, unite **6** mingle **7** combine **8** intermix **10** amalgamate **11** desegregate **13** bring together

integrated 6 entire, joined, linked, united **7** blended, merged, unified, unitary **8** combined **9** composite, undivided **10** harmonized, reconciled **11** coordinated, synthesized **12** desegregated, unsegregated

integration 5 union **6** fusion, mixing **8** blending **9** combining, synthesis **11** combination **12** assimilation **13** desegregation

integrity 5 unity **6** purity, virtue **7** decency, honesty, probity **8** cohesion, morality, strength **9** character, coherence, principle, rectitude, wholeness **11** reliability, self-respect, uprightness **12** completeness

integument 4 coat, hide, husk, rind, skin **5** shell, **7** coating, cuticle, epiderm, exoderm **8** covering, envelope, membrane

integumentary system
component: **4** hair, skin **5** nails

intellect 3 wit **4** mind **5** brain, sense **6** brains, wisdom **7** thinker **9** cognition, mentality **10** perception **11** mental power, rationality **12** intellectual, intelligence **13** consciousness, understanding

intellectual 4 sage **5** brain **6** brainy, mental, pundit, savant **7** bookish, egghead, scholar, thinker **8** abstract, academic, cerebral, highbrow, longhair, mandarin, rational, studious **9** intellect, of the mind, reasoning, scholarly **10** thoughtful **11** intelligent
French: **9** bel-esprit

intelligence 4 dope, news **6** acumen, advice, brains, notice, report, wisdom **7** tidings **8** sagacity **9** intellect, knowledge **10** advisement, shrewdness **11** information **12** notification, perspicacity **13** comprehension, understanding

intelligent 4 keen, sage, wise **5** alert,

canny, quick, sharp, smart **6** astute, brainy, bright, clever, shrewd **7** knowing, prudent **8** informed, sensible, thinking **9** brilliant, sagacious **10** perceptive, thoughtful **11** clearheaded, quick-witted, sharp-witted **12** well-informed **13** perspicacious

intelligentsia 5 mensa **7** academe **8** thinkers **10** ivory tower **13** intellectuals

intelligible 5 clear, lucid **7** evident, obvious **8** apparent, clear-cut, coherent, definite, distinct **11** unambiguous, well-defined **12** unmistakable **14** comprehensible, understandable

intemperance 10 alcoholism, insobriety **11** dissipation, drunkenness, inebriation **12** immoderation, recklessness **13** excessiveness **16** irresponsibility

intemperate 5 harsh **6** brutal, rugged, severe **7** extreme, violent **8** bibulous, uncurbed **9** dissolute, excessive, inclement **10** dissipated, gluttonous, immoderate, inordinate **11** extravagant, inabstinent, incontinent **12** unrestrained **13** overindulgent

intend 3 aim **4** mean, plan, wish **6** aspire, design, expect **7** project, propose, resolve **9** calculate, determine **10** have in mind **11** contemplate

intended 5 meant **6** fiance, future **7** engaged, fiancee, implied, willful **8** proposed, purposed **9** affianced, betrothed, bride-to-be, groom-to-be, voluntary **10** calculated, deliberate **11** intentional

intense 4 deep, keen **5** acute, sharp **6** ardent, potent, strong **7** burning, earnest, extreme, fervent, violent **8** emphatic, forceful, forcible, powerful, vehement **10** passionate **12** concentrated, considerable

intensely 4 very **5** hotly **6** deeply, keenly **7** acutely, eagerly, vividly **8** ardently, heatedly, terribly **9** extremely, fervently, seriously, violently, zealously **10** forcefully, powerfully, profoundly, vehemently, vigorously **11** excessively, exquisitely, strenuously **12** considerably, passionately **13** energetically

intensify 5 boost **6** deepen, worsen **7** magnify, quicken, sharpen **8** escalate, heighten, increase, redouble **9** aggravate, reinforce **10** accelerate, strengthen

intensifying 9 worsening **10** increasing, magnifying, redoubling, sharpening **11** aggravating, heightening, reinforcing **12** exacerbating **13** strengthening

intensity 4 zeal **5** ardor, depth, force, power, vigor **6** energy, fervor **7** emotion, passion, potency **8** severity, strength **9** magnitude, vehemence **11** earnestness **12** forcefulness

intensive 6 all-out 7 growing, radical 8 complete, sweeping, thorough 10 exhaustive, increasing 11 comprehensive 12 concentrated 13 thoroughgoing

intent 3 aim, end, set 4 bent, gist, plan 5 drift, fixed 6 burden, design, import, steady 7 earnest, intense, meaning, purport, purpose 8 absorbed, piercing, resolved 9 engrossed, insistent, intention, steadfast, substance, tenacious, unbending 10 determined, unwavering 11 preoccupied 12 concentrated, significance, undistracted 13 determination, premeditation

intention 3 aim, end 4 goal, plan 6 design, intent, object, target 7 purpose, resolve 9 objective 10 resolution 13 determination

intentional 6 willed 7 planned 8 designed, intended 9 voluntary 10 calculated, deliberate, purposeful 12 contemplated, premeditated 13 done on purpose

intently 6 deeply, raptly 9 fervently, zealously 10 absorbedly 11 attentively 12 passionately 18 without distraction 22 with undivided attention

intentness 10 absorption 11 engrossment 13 concentration

inter 4 bury 5 inurn 6 entomb, inhume 7 inearth, lay away 9 lay to rest 11 ensepulcher

interact 4 join, mesh 5 coact, unite 6 engage 7 combine, conjoin 8 dovetail 9 cooperate, interlace, intermesh, interplay, interwork 10 coordinate, interreact

inter alia 16 among other things

inter alios 17 among other persons

interbreed 3 mix 5 cross 8 intermix 10 crossbreed

intercede 5 plead 6 step in 7 mediate, speak up 9 arbitrate, interpose, intervene, offer help 12 offer support 14 put in a good word 16 lend a helping hand

intercept 3 nab 4 grab, stay, stop, take 5 catch, seize 6 ambush, arrest, cut off, detain 7 deflect, reroute

intercessor 5 agent 6 bishop, broker 8 advocate, mediator 9 go-between, middleman 12 intermediary, spokesperson

interchange 5 shift 6 switch 7 trading 8 exchange, junction, swapping, transfer 9 alternate, crossover 10 substitute 11 give and take, reciprocity

interchangeable 8 parallel, tradable 9 analogous 10 equivalent, switchable, synonymous 12 exchangeable, transposable 13 corresponding

interconnected 8 adjacent 10 contiguous, juxtaposed 12 conterminous, labyrinthine

intercourse 4 talk 5 trade 6 coitus,

parley 7 pairing, traffic 8 colloquy, commerce, congress, coupling, dealings, exchange 9 communion, discourse, relations 10 connection, copulation 12 conversation 14 communications, correspondence

interdict 3 ban, bar 5 taboo 6 enjoin, forbid 7 barring, censure 8 prohibit, restrain, restrict 9 proscribe 11 forbiddance, prohibition 12 proscription

interdiction 3 ban 7 barring 11 forbiddance, prohibition 12 proscription

interest, interests 4 gain, good, part, weal 5 bonus, hobby, share, stake, touch, yield 6 absorb, affect, behalf, divert, engage, notice, profit, regard 7 attract, benefit, concern, holding, involve, pastime, portion, pursuit, service 8 dividend 9 advantage, attention, avocation, curiosity, preoccupy, suspicion 10 absorption, investment 11 engrossment 13 preoccupation

interested 6 active 7 engaged 8 diverted 9 committed, concerned 10 fascinated, responsive

interesting 7 curious 8 engaging, magnetic, pleasing, riveting, striking 9 absorbing, appealing, arresting 10 attractive, suspicious 11 fascinating, stimulating 12 entertaining

interfere 3 jar, mix 6 butt in, horn in, meddle, rush in, step in 7 counter, intrude 8 conflict 9 frustrate, intercede, interpose, intervene 11 get in the way 14 be a hindrance to, be an obstacle to, be inconsistent, stick in one's oar

interference 3 bar 6 static 8 clashing, conflict, friction, invasion, meddling 9 collision, hindrance, intrusion 12 interception, interruption, intervention

interfere with 6 hinder, impede, thwart 7 disrupt 9 interrupt

interim 7 stopgap 8 interval, meantime, temporal 9 interlude, temporary, tentative 10 pro tempore 11 provisional

interior 4 bush 5 inner 6 inmost, inside, inward 8 internal 9 backwoods, heartland, innermost, upcountry 10 hinterland

Interiors
    director: 10 Woody Allen
    cast: 10 E G Marshall 11 Diane Keaton 12 Marybeth Hurt 13 Geraldine Page 15 Kristin Griffith 16 Maureen Stapleton
    screenplay: 10 Woody Allen

interject 5 put in 6 inject, insert, slip in 7 force in, sneak in, throw in 9 interpose, introduce 11 interpolate

interjection 2 ah, er, lo, oh, ow, um 3 aha, cry, fie, hey, huh, ugh, wow 4 ahem, alas, darn, dear, drat, egad, gosh, heck, jeez, oops, ouch, phew, rats 5 aside, golly, zowie 6 eureka, hooray, hurrah, hurray 7 gee-whiz, jeepers 9 insertion 11 ejaculation, ex-

clamation 13 interpolation, interposition

interlace 3 mix 4 knit, link 5 braid, plait, twine, twist, weave 7 wreathe 9 alternate 10 intertwine, interweave 11 intersperse

interlaced 5 woven 6 linked, twined 7 braided, knitted, plaited, twisted 8 entwined, latticed, wreathed 9 interknit 10 interwoven 11 intertwined 12 interspersed

interlocutor 8 minstrel 9 converser, dialogist 12 interrogator 14 man in the middle

interlope 6 invade, meddle 7 intrude, obtrude 8 encroach, infringe, trespass 9 interfere

interloper 7 invader, meddler 8 intruder, outsider 10 interferer, trespasser 11 gatecrasher 15 persona non grata

interlude 5 break, event, letup, pause 6 recess 7 episode, respite 8 incident, interval 12 intermission 14 breathing spell

intermediary 6 midway, umpire 7 referee 8 bridging, mediator 9 go-between, in-between, mediating, middleman 10 arbitrator 11 adjudicator, arbitrating

intermediate 3 mid 4 fair, mean, so-so 6 median, medium, middle, midway 7 average, halfway, mediate, midmost 8 mediocre, middling, moderate 11 intervening

interment 6 burial 7 funeral 10 entombment, inhumation

Intermezzo
    director: 13 Gregory Ratoff
    cast: 8 Edna Best 12 Leslie Howard 13 Cecil Kellaway, Ingrid Bergman

interminable 6 prolix 7 endless 8 infinite, unending 9 boundless, ceaseless, incessant, limitless, perpetual, unlimited 10 continuous, long-winded 11 illimitable 12 long-drawn-out

intermingle 3 mix 4 fuse 5 blend, merge, mix up, unite 6 commix 7 combine 8 emulsify, intermix 9 commingle, interfuse, interlace 10 amalgamate, homogenize, interblend 12 conglomerate

intermission 3 gap 4 halt, rest, stop 5 break, pause 6 hiatus, recess 7 interim 8 interval, stoppage 9 interlude 10 suspension

intermittent 6 fitful 8 on and off, periodic, sporadic 9 irregular, recurrent, spasmodic 10 occasional 13 discontinuous 15 on-again-off-again

intermix 3 mix 5 blend, cross, mix in 6 mingle 10 crossbreed, interbreed 11 intermingle, intersperse

intern 6 commit, detain 7 confine, impound 8 imprison, restrain

internal 5 inner, state 6 inmost 8 domestic, interior **9** executive, political, sovereign **12** governmental **14** administrative

international 9 worldwide **12** cosmopolitan

international affairs
  god of: 6 Sancus **10** Dius Fidius, Semo Sancus

Internet
  terms: 3 AOL, FAQ, FTP, net, URL, web, WWW **4** chat, host, link, post **5** cyber, flame, Lycos, Yahoo, e-mail, TCP/IP **6** dial-up, Gopher, online, server, Usenet, Excite **7** browser, Web site **8** firewall, Username **9** hypertext, newsgroup, webmaster, Alta-Vista **11** interactive **12** search engine, World Wide Web
  based on: 7 ARPAnet

internment 9 detention **10** commitment, impounding **11** confinement **12** imprisonment

inter nos 16 between ourselves

interpolate 3 add **5** put in **6** inject, insert, work in **7** implant, intrude, stick in, throw in, wedge in **8** sandwich **9** insinuate, interject, interlard, interline, intervene, introduce **11** intercalate, intersperse

interpose 6 butt in, impose, inject, insert, meddle, step in **7** intrude, mediate, obtrude **9** arbitrate, insinuate, intercede, interfere, interject, interrupt, intervene, negotiate **11** come between, interpolate

interpret 3 see **4** read, take **6** accept, define, render, reword **7** clarify, explain, make out, restate, unravel **8** construe, decipher **9** elucidate, explicate, figure out, make clear, puzzle out, translate **10** account for, paraphrase, understand

interpretation 7 reading, version **8** analysis **9** rendition **10** commentary **11** explanation **12** construction

interpreter 7 analyst **9** explainer **10** translator **11** commentator

interrelated 9 companion, connected **10** compatible, correlated **13** complementary, correspondent, corresponding

interrelation 10 connection **11** association, correlation **12** relationship

interrogate 3 ask **4** test **5** grill, probe, query **7** examine **8** question **9** catechize **11** investigate **12** cross-examine **18** give the third degree

interrogation 4 quiz **5** probe, query **7** inquiry **8** grilling, querying, question, quizzing **9** catechism, inquiring **11** examination, inquisition, questioning

interrupt 4 stop **5** sever **7** cut in on, disjoin, disturb **8** break off **9** break in on, intersect, punctuate **10** disconnect **11** discontinue **13** interfere with

interrupted 6 broken, cut off, halted

7 checked, stalled, stopped **8** arrested, broke off, deferred **9** broken off, disturbed, suspended **11** broke in upon, intercepted **12** discontinued

interruption 3 gap **4** halt, rift, stop **5** break, pause **6** hiatus, lacuna **9** hindrance, interlude **11** obstruction **12** interference, intermission **13** disconnection, discontinuity

inter se 15 among themselves **17** between themselves

intersect 4 meet **5** cross **6** bisect, divide **7** overlap **8** crosscut, transect, traverse **9** cut across **10** crisscross

intersection 6 corner **8** crossing, junction **10** crossroads **11** interchange

intersperse 3 dot, mix **5** strew **6** mingle, pepper **7** bestrew, scatter, wedge in **8** disperse, intermix, sprinkle **9** broadcast, interfuse, interject, interlard, interpose **11** intercalate, interpolate *(areola)*

interstice 4 slit, slot **5** crack, space **7** opening, orifice **8** aperture, interval

intertwine 4 lace **5** braid, plait, twine, twist, weave **7** entwine **8** entangle **9** interlace

interval 3 gap **4** gulf, rest, rift **5** break, cleft, pause, space, spell **6** breach, hiatus, recess, season **7** interim, opening **9** interlude **10** interspace, separation **12** intermission, interruption

intervene 4 pass **6** befall, butt in, step in **7** break in, intrude, mediate **9** arbitrate, intercede, interfere, interpose, interrupt, take place **10** come to pass **11** come between

intervention 9 butting in, intrusion, mediation **10** breaking in, stepping in **11** arbitration **12** intercession, interference **13** interposition **14** intermediation

interview 4 chat, talk **6** parley **7** meeting **8** audience **10** conference, evaluation, round table **11** questioning **12** consultation, conversation

interweave 3 mix **4** fuse, join, knit, lace, link **5** blend, braid, plait, twine, twist **6** splice **7** wreathe **9** interlace, interknit **10** intertwine **11** intersperse

intestinal 5 inner **7** enteric **8** internal, visceral

intestines 4 guts **6** bowels **7** insides, viscera **8** entrails

in the air 2 up **5** above, aloft **7** skyward **8** all about, in the sky, overhead **10** everywhere **11** in the clouds

in the doghouse 9 in bad odor **10** in disfavor, in disgrace, in ill favor **11** in disrepute

in the end 6 one day **7** finally **8** sometime **10** eventually, ultimately **13** sooner or later **17** in the course of time
  French: 5 enfin

in the family
  French: 9 en famille

in the first place
  Latin: 8 imprimis

in the future
  Latin: 8 in futuro
  Spanish: 6 manana

In the Heat of the Night
  director: 13 Norman Jewison
  cast: 8 Lee Grant **10** Rod Steiger **11** Warren Oates **13** Sidney Poitier (Virgil Tibbs)
  score: 11 Quincy Jones
  Oscar for: 5 actor (Steiger) **7** picture **10** screenplay

in the know 9 cognizant **11** on the inside **13** fully informed, knowledgeable **23** having inside information

in the manner of
  French: 3 a la

in the matter of
  Latin: 4 in re

in the meantime
  Latin: 9 ad interim

in the middle of things
  Latin: 11 in medias res

in the midst of 5 among **7** amongst **12** surrounded by **13** in the middle of

in the nature of things
  Latin: 13 in rerum natura

in the neighborhood of 6 almost, around, nearly **7** close to **9** generally, just about **10** more or less, not far from **13** approximately **15** in the vicinity of

in the place cited
  Latin: 6 loc cit **10** loco citato

in the place of a parent
  Latin: 14 in loco parentis

in the same manner that
  Latin: 7 quo modo

in the same place
  Latin: 4 ibid **6** ibidem

in the state in which
  Latin: 10 in statu quo

in the style of
  French: 7 a la mode

in the very act of committing the crime
  Latin: 18 in flagrante delicto

in the vicinity of 4 near **6** almost, around, nearly **7** close to **9** just about **10** more or less, not far from **13** approximately **19** in the neighborhood of

in the way
  French: 6 de trop

in the whole
  Latin: 6 in toto

in the work cited
  Latin: 5 op cit **11** opere citato

in the year of the reign
  Latin: 9 anno regni

in the year of the world
  Latin: 9 anno mundi

In This House of Brede
author: **11** Rumer Godden

in this sign shalt thou conquer
Latin: **16** in hoc signo vinces
motto of: **19** Constantine the Great
from vision of: **5** cross

intimacy 5 amity **6** caring, warmth **8** dearness, fondness **9** affection, closeness **10** chumminess, endearment, fraternity, lovemaking, tenderness **11** brotherhood, camaraderie, familiarity **12** friendliness

intimate 3 pal **4** chum, dear, deep, hint **5** bosom, buddy, close, crony, imply, rumor **6** allude, direct **7** guarded, private, special, suggest **8** detailed, familiar, indicate, personal, profound, thorough **9** cherished, confidant, first-hand, innermost, insinuate **12** confidential
French: **6** intime

intimately 7 closely **8** secretly, very well **9** privately **10** familiarly, personally **11** essentially **13** intrinsically **14** confidentially

intimation 4 clue, hint, sign **5** rumor **7** inkling, portent **8** allusion, innuendo **10** indication, suggestion **11** insinuation **13** veiled comment

Intimations of Immortality
author: **17** William Wordsworth

intime 4 cozy **8** intimate

in time 6 before, sooner **7** earlier **9** before now, in advance **10** beforehand, eventually **11** ahead of time **13** before the fact, sooner or later

intimidate 3 cow **5** alarm, bully, daunt, scare **6** coerce, menace, subdue **7** buffalo, terrify **8** browbeat, frighten **9** terrorize

intimidated 5 cowed, fazed **6** scared **7** crushed, daunted, subdued **10** browbeaten, frightened, terrorized

intimidation 7 tyranny **8** bullying, coercion **9** despotism **11** browbeating, terrorizing, tyrannizing **12** scare tactics

intimidator 5 bully **6** despot **7** coercer **9** oppressor, tormenter, tormentor **10** browbeater

into 2 in, to **5** among **6** inside, toward, within **7** against

intolerable 7 hateful, racking **9** abhorrent, agonizing, excessive, loathsome, torturous **10** abominable, outrageous, unbearable **11** unendurable **12** excruciating, insufferable, unreasonable **13** insupportable

intolerance 4 bias **6** racism **7** bigotry **8** weak spot **9** no stomach, prejudice **10** chauvinism, xenophobia **12** low tolerance **16** hypersensitivity, narrow-mindedness

Intolerance
director: **10** D W Griffith
cast: **8** Mae Marsh **11** Lillian Gish

12 Robert Harron **17** Constance Talmadge

intolerant 7 bigoted, hostile, jealous **9** fanatical, parochial, resentful, sectarian **10** prejudiced, xenophobic **11** mistrustful **12** chauvinistic, closed-minded, narrow-minded

intonation 4 tone **5** pitch **6** accent **8** chanting **10** modulation, inflection

intone 3 hum, say **4** song **5** chant, croon, drawl, mouth, speak, utter, voice **6** murmur, recite **8** intonate, modulate, singsong, vocalize **9** enunciate, pronounce **10** articulate

in toto 5 in all, uncut **6** entire, wholly **7** totally **8** as a whole, entirely, outright **10** completely, in the whole, unabridged **11** all together, uncondensed

intoxicant 3 gin, rum **4** beer, grog, wine **5** booze, drink **6** liquor, tipple, whisky **7** alcohol, spirits, whiskey **8** cocktail, highball **9** inebriant

intoxicated 4 high, rapt **5** drunk, oiled, tight, tipsy **6** bombed, elated, loaded, stewed, stinko, stoned, zonked **7** drunken, exalted, smashed, wrecked **9** delighted, enchanted, entranced, plastered **10** enthralled, inebriated, infatuated, in one's cups **11** exhilarated, transported

intoxicating 4 hard **5** heady **6** potent **7** elating **9** alcoholic, spiritous **11** inebriating **12** exhilarating

intoxication 3 joy **5** bliss **7** elation, rapture **8** euphoria **9** poisoning, tipsiness **10** excitement, insobriety **11** drunkenness, inebriation **12** befuddlement, stupefaction

intractable 6 mulish, ornery, unruly **7** froward, willful **8** obdurate, perverse, stubborn **9** fractious, obstinate **10** headstrong, inflexible, refractory **11** unmalleable **12** contumacious, incorrigible, ungovernable, unmanageable **14** hard to cope with, uncontrollable

intransigent 7 diehard **8** obdurate, stubborn **9** steadfast, unmovable **10** inflexible, iron-willed, unyielding **11** intractable, unbudgeable **14** uncompromising

intrepid 4 bold **5** brave **6** daring, heroic **7** doughty, valiant **8** fearless, resolute, valorous **9** audacious, dauntless **10** courageous, undismayed **11** adventurous

intrepidity 4 guts **5** spunk, valor **6** mettle **7** bravery, courage **8** backbone **9** fortitude, sangfroid **12** fearlessness **13** dauntlessness

intricacy 10 complexity **11** involvement **12** complication, entanglement **15** complicatedness

intricate 6 knotty, tricky **7** complex, devious, tangled **8** involved **9** entangled **11** complicated

intrigue 3 spy **4** fire, plot **5** amour **6**

absorb, arrest, scheme **7** attract, collude, knavery, romance **8** conspire, enthrall, scheming **9** fascinate, machinate, titillate **10** conspiracy, love affair **11** machination **13** double-dealing **15** interest greatly, tickle one's fancy

intriguer 7 cheater, plotter, schemer **8** conniver, finagler **9** trickster **10** machinator, wirepuller **11** conspirator, Machiavelli, manipulator

intriguing 8 engaging, exciting **9** absorbing, beguiling **11** captivating, enthralling, fascinating, interesting

intrinsic 5 basic, per se **6** inborn, inbred, innate, native **7** natural **8** inherent **9** essential, ingrained **10** indigenous, underlying **11** fundamental

introduce 3 add **4** show, urge **5** begin, offer, put in, start **6** create, expose, import, inform, infuse, insert **7** advance, bring in, kick off, lead off, present, propose, sponsor, throw in **8** acquaint, initiate, lead into **9** establish, institute, interject, interpose, make known, originate, recommend **10** put forward **11** familiarize, interpolate

introduction 6 change **7** novelty, opening, preface, prelude **8** foreword, preamble, prologue **9** insertion, precursor **10** bringing in, conducting, innovation, ushering in **11** instituting, institution

introductory 7 initial **9** beginning, prefatory **10** initiatory, precursory **11** acquainting, preliminary **13** get-acquainted

introspection 8 brooding **10** meditation, reflection, rumination **12** deliberation, self-analysis, self-scrutiny **13** contemplation, soul-searching **15** self-examination, self-observation, self-questioning

introspective 7 pensive **10** reflective **13** contemplative, lost in thought

introversion 7 reserve **8** brooding **10** constraint, diffidence, withdrawal **13** introspection

introvert 5 loner **7** brooder, thinker **13** contemplative, private person

introverted 3 shy **5** stiff **8** reserved **9** inhibited, repressed, withdrawn **10** antisocial, restrained **13** inner-directed, introspective

intrude 4 push **6** butt in, impose, meddle, thrust **7** obtrude **8** encroach, trespass **9** interfere, interlope, interpose, intervene

intruder 10 encroacher, interferer, interloper, intervener, trespasser **11** gate-crasher

Intruder in the Dust
author: **15** William Faulkner

intrusive 4 nosy **5** pushy **6** prying, snoopy **8** in the way, invasive **9** hindering, obtrusive, officious, unwel-

come 10 meddlesome **11** impertinent, interfering, interruptive

intuition 5 flash, hunch **7** insight, surmise **8** instinct **9** guesswork, telepathy **10** sixth sense **11** second sight **12** clairvoyance, precognition

intuitive 6 inborn, inbred, innate, native **7** natural, psychic **10** telepathic **11** clairvoyant, instinctive, intuitional, nonrational **12** extrasensory

Inuit *see* **6** Eskimo

inundate 4 glut **5** drown, flood, swamp **6** deluge, drench, engulf **8** load down, overcome, overflow, saturate, submerge **9** overwhelm **10** overburden, overspread

inundation 4 glut **5** flood **6** deluge **9** avalanche

in unison 5 as one **8** in chorus **9** all at once **11** all together

inure 5 adapt, steel, train **6** adjust, custom, harden, season, temper **7** toughen **8** accustom **9** acclimate, get used to, habituate **10** discipline, naturalize, strengthen **11** acclimatize, desensitize, familiarize **12** become used to **15** learn to live with **16** become hardened to

in use 8 employed **9** operating **11** functioning, operational

in vacuo 9 in a vacuum **11** in isolation

invade 5 flood, limit **6** assail, attack, engulf, infect, infest **7** assault, overrun, violate **8** permeate, restrict, strike at, trespass **9** intrude on, march into, penetrate

invader 6 raider **8** attacker, intruder, marauder **9** aggressor, assailant **10** trespasser

invalid 4 null, sick, void, weak **5** false **6** ailing, infirm, sickly, unwell **7** amputee, cripple, unsound, useless **8** disabled, not valid, nugatory, weakened **9** enfeebled, forceless, illogical, paralytic, powerless, worthless **10** dead letter, fallacious, paraplegic **11** debilitated, ineffective, inoperative, unsupported **12** unconvincing **13** incapacitated, unsupportable **14** good-for-nothing, valetudinarian

invalidate 5 annul **6** cancel, refute, repeal, weaken **7** nullify, vitiate **8** abrogate, make void, undercut **9** discredit, undermine **11** countermand

invalidation 7 voiding **9** annulment **10** abrogation **12** cancellation **13** nullification

invaluable 4 rare **6** choice **9** priceless **11** beyond price, inestimable

invariable 7 uniform **8** constant **9** immutable, unfailing, unvarying **10** changeless, consistent, unchanging, unwavering **11** unalterable, undeviating **12** unchangeable

invariably 4 ever **6** always **7** forever **9** every time, uniformly **10** all the time,

constantly **11** perpetually, universally **15** in every instance **16** without exception

invasion 4 raid **5** foray **6** attack, breach, inroad, sortie **7** assault **8** trespass **9** incursion, intrusion, onslaught **10** aggression, juggernaut, usurpation **11** penetration **12** encroachment, infiltration, infringement, overstepping

Invasion of the Body Snatchers
director:
   1956 version: 9 Don Siegel
   1978 version: 13 Philip Kaufman
cast:
   1956 version: 10 Dana Wynter, Larry Gates **11** King Donovan **13** Kevin McCarthy
   1978 version: 11 Brooke Adams **12** Jeff Goldblum, Leonard Nimoy **16** Donald Sutherland

invective 4 rant **5** venom **6** insult **7** censure, railing, sarcasm **8** diatribe **9** contumely **10** execration, harsh words, revilement **11** verbal abuse **12** billingsgate, denunciation, vilification, vituperation

inveigh 4 rail, slam **5** abuse, knock, scold **6** rebuke, revile **7** censure, put down, run down, upbraid **8** belittle, denounce, harangue, reproach **9** castigate, criticize, dress down **10** vituperate

inveigh against 5 abuse **6** defame, rail at, revile **7** protest **8** denounce **9** castigate

inveigle 4 coax, lure **5** tempt, trick **6** allure, cajole, entice, rope in, seduce, suck in **7** beguile, ensnare, flatter, mislead, wheedle **8** persuade, softsoap **9** bamboozle, sweet-talk

inveiglement 7 coaxing **8** cajolery, flattery **9** wheedling **10** enticement, persuasion **13** blandishments

invent 4 coin **6** cook up, create, devise, make up **7** concoct, develop, fashion, think up, trump up **8** conceive, contrive **9** conjure up, fabricate, formulate, originate **10** come up with **11** put together

invented 6 fabled, made up **8** fabulous, fanciful, mythical **9** fantastic, imaginary, legendary **10** apocryphal, fictitious

Inventing America
author: **10** Garry Wills

invention 3 lie **4** fake, sham **6** design, device, gadget **7** fiction, forgery, machine **8** creation, trumpery **9** apparatus, discovery, fertility, implement, ingenuity, inventing **10** concoction, creativity, production **11** contraption, contrivance, development, fabrication, imagination, originality, origination **13** dissimulation, inventiveness, prevarication **15** resourcefulness

invention
god of: **6** Hermes

inventive 6 bright, clever **9** ingenious **11** resourceful

inventiveness 9 ingenuity **10** cleverness, creativity **11** imagination, originality **15** imaginativeness

inventor 5 maker **6** author **7** creator, deviser **8** engineer, producer, tinkerer **9** architect, generator, innovator **10** discoverer, originator
of air brake: **12** Westinghouse
of automobile: **7** Daimler
of barometer: **10** Torricelli
of camera: **7** Eastman
of cotton gin: **7** Whitney
of cylinder lock: **4** Yale
of dynamite: **5** Nobel
of elevator: **4** Otis
of gyrocompass: **6** Sperry
of helicopter: **8** Sikorsky
of linotype: **12** Mergenthaler
of machine gun: **7** Gatling
of movable type: **9** Gutenberg
of phonograph, incandescent lamp, mimeograph, dictating machine, fluoroscope: **6** Edison
of photography: **6** Niepce, Talbot **8** Daguerre
of Polaroid: **4** Land
of quick-freezing: **8** Birdseye
of reaper: **9** McCormick
of radio: **7** Marconi
of revolver: **4** Colt
of rocket engine: **7** Goddard
of sewing machine: **4** Howe
of sleeping car: **7** Pullman
of steamboat: **6** Fulton
of steam engine: **4** Watt
of steam locomotive: **10** Stephenson
of telegraph: **5** Morse
of telephone: **4** Bell
of wireless telegraph: **7** Marconi
of vulcanized rubber: **8** Goodyear

inventory 4 roll **5** goods, index, stock **6** roster, supply **7** catalog **8** register, schedule **9** stock list **10** accounting **11** merchandise, stock-taking

inverse 8 backward, contrary, converse, indirect, inverted, opposite, reversed **11** back to front, bottom-to-top, right-to-left

inversion 7 turning **8** reversal **9** ectropion, turnabout **10** transposal **12** resupination **13** transposition

inverted 7 inverse **8** bottom up **10** upside-down

invest 4 fill, garb, give **5** adorn, allot, array, color, cover, dress, endow, imbue **6** clothe, devote, enable, enrich, infuse, supply **7** appoint, license **8** set aside **9** apportion

investigate 4 sift **5** probe, query, study **6** survey **7** analyze, dissect, explore, inspect **8** ask about, look into, pore over, question, research **9** anatomize, delve into **10** scrutinize

investigation 5 probe, study **6** review, search, survey **7** anatomy, inquiry **8** analysis, research, scrutiny **10** dissection, inspection **11** fact-finding

investigator 6 shamus **7** analyst, gumshoe **8** examiner, inquirer, observer **9** detective **10** private eye, researcher

investment 4 ante, risk **5** share, stake **7** venture **8** offering

inveterate 6 inured **7** adamant, chronic, diehard **8** constant, habitual, hardened **9** confirmed, incurable, ingrained, recurrent, steadfast **10** continuous, deep-rooted, deep-seated **11** established **12** long-standing, unregenerate **15** unreconstructed

invidious 7 vicious **8** spiteful **9** insulting, malicious, offensive, rancorous, resentful, slighting **10** malevolent

invigorate 4 stir **5** brace, cheer, liven, pep up, renew, rouse, zip up **6** jazz up, vivify **7** animate, enliven, fortify, refresh, restore **8** energize, vitalize **9** stimulate **10** exhilarate, rejuvenate, strengthen

invigorated 6 braced **7** revived **8** animated, restored, vivified **9** energized, full of pep, quickened, refreshed **10** stimulated **11** rejuvenated **12** strengthened **17** full of vim and vigor

invigorating 7 bracing **9** animating, healthful **10** energizing, enlivening, quickening, refreshing, vitalizing **11** restorative, stimulating **12** rejuvenating **13** strengthening

invincible 10 unbeatable **11** impregnable, indomitable, insuperable **12** invulnerable, undefeatable **13** irrepressible, unconquerable **14** insurmountable

in vino veritas 18 in wine there is truth

inviolable 4 holy, pure **6** chaste, divine, sacred, secret **7** blessed **8** hallowed **9** dedicated, inviolate, undefiled **10** sacrosanct **11** consecrated, impregnable, trustworthy **12** impenetrable, invulnerable, unassailable **13** incorruptible

inviolate 4 pure **6** intact, sacred, secret **8** hallowed **9** unaltered, unchanged, undefiled, unstained **10** inviolable, sacrosanct

invisible 6 covert, hidden, unseen, veiled **7** obscure **9** concealed, unseeable **10** unapparent **13** imperceptible, undiscernible

Invisible Man
  author: 12 Ralph Ellison

Invisible Man, The
  author: 7 H G Wells
  character: 4 Hall **6** Dr Kemp, Marvel **7** Griffin **11** Colonel Ayde

invitation 3 bid **4** call, lure **5** offer **7** bidding, summons **8** open door **9** challenge **10** allurement, enticement, inducement, temptation **12** solicitation

invite 3 bid **4** call, lure, urge **5** tempt

6 entice, induce **7** attract, solicit, welcome **9** encourage

inviting 4 warm **8** alluring, charming, engaging, enticing, magnetic, tempting **9** appealing, welcoming **10** attractive, intriguing

invocation 4 plea **6** appeal, orison, prayer **8** petition **9** summoning **12** supplication

in vogue 2 in **6** modish **7** a la mode, current, in style, stylish **9** in fashion **11** fashionable **12** le dernier cri

invoke 3 beg, use **5** apply **6** ask for, employ **7** beseech, conjure, entreat, implore, pray for **8** call upon, petition, resort to **9** appeal for, call forth, implement, importune, introduce **10** supplicate

involuntary 6 forced, reflex **7** coerced **8** unchosen, unwilled **9** automatic, reluctant, unwilling **10** compulsory **11** inadvertent, instinctive, spontaneous, unconscious **13** unintentional **15** against one's will

involve 5 imply, mix up **6** commit, engage, entail, wrap up **7** contain, embroil, include **8** comprise, depend on, entangle **9** implicate, preoccupy

involved 7 complex, engaged, mixed up, wound up **8** absorbed, immersed **9** committed, elaborate, embroiled, engrossed, entangled, intricate, wrapped up **10** implicated **11** complicated, preoccupied

involve deeply 5 mix up **6** absorb, commit, wrap up **7** embroil, engross, immerse **8** entangle **9** implicate, preoccupy

invulnerable 10 formidable, invincible, unbeatable **11** impregnable, indomitable, insuperable **12** imperishable, inexpugnable, unassailable, undefeatable **13** unconquerable, undestroyable

inward, inwards 5 inner **6** mental, toward **7** going in, ingoing, private **8** incoming, interior, inwardly, personal **9** spiritual, the inside **10** interiorly

in what way
  Latin: 7 quo modo

in which case 4 then, when **6** thence **9** whereupon **11** accordingly **12** at which point

In Which We Serve
  director: 9 David Lean **10** Noel Coward
  script: 10 Noel Coward
  cast: 9 John Mills **10** Noel Coward **12** Bernard Miles, Celia Johnson

in wine there is truth
  Latin: 13 in vino veritas

Io
  father: 7 Inachus
  husband: 9 Telegonus
  loved by: 4 Zeus
  son: 7 Epaphus

  changed into: 6 heifer
  color of heifer: 5 white
  guarded by: 5 Argus
  pursecuted by: 6 gadfly
  sent by: 4 Hera
  corresponds to: 4 Isis

iodine
  chemical symbol: 1 I

Iolanthe
  author: 9 W S Gilbert

Iole
  father: 7 Eurytus
  loved by: 8 Heracles
  captive of: 8 Heracles, Hercules

Ion
  author: 9 Euripides
  character: 6 Apollo, Athene, Crensa, Xuthus

ion 15 charged particle
  part of: 8 molecule
  charge: 8 negative, positive
  loses or gains: 8 electron
  called: 5 anion **6** cation **12** dissociation

Ionesco, Eugene
  born: 7 Romania, Slatina
  author of: 9 The Lesson, The Chairs **10** Rhinoceros **14** The Bald Soprano

iota 3 bit, jot **4** atom, spot, whit **5** shred, spark, speck **7** smidgin **8** particle **9** scintilla **11** faint degree, small amount **15** tiniest quantity

IOU 4 chit, debt, note **6** marker **10** obligation **12** promise to pay **14** promissory note

Iowa
  abbreviation: 2 IA
  nickname: 7 Hawkeye
  capital/largest city: 9 Des Moines
  others: 4 Ames **5** Amana, Mason, Perry **6** Algona, Keokuk, Le Mars, Marion, Newton **7** Anamosa, Clinton, Dubuque, Ft Dodge, Ottumwa **8** Waterloo **9** Davenport, Ft Madison, Marquette, Mason City, Sioux City **10** Burlington, Cedar Falls, West Branch **11** Cedar Rapids **12** Marshalltown **13** Council Bluffs
  college: 3 Coe **5** Corot, Drake, Loras **7** Cornell, Parsons **8** Grinnell, Wartburg **12** Iowa Wesleyan
  explorer: 6 Joliet **7** Jolliet **9** Marquette **13** Lewis and Clark
  feature: 13 Amana Colonies **17** first apple orchard
    church: 11 Little Brown
    national historical site: 13 Herbert Hoover
    national monument: 12 Effigy Mounds
    state fair: 4 Iowa
  tribe: 3 Fox **4** Sauc **5** Ioway, Omaha **9** Muscoutin, Winnebago
  people: 7 Hawkeye **9** Grant Wood **10** John L Lewis **11** Billy Sunday **15** Buffalo Bill Cody, Charles Ringling
  lake: 5 Clear, Storm **6** Spirit **7** Rath-

bun **11** East Okoboji, West Okoboji
land rank: 11 twenty-fifth
president: 13 Herbert Hoover
river: 4 Iowa **5** Cedar, Floyd, Skunk **8**
Big Sioux, Missouri **9** Des Moines **11**
Mississippi, Nishnabotna **12** Wap-
sipinicon
state admission: 11 twenty-ninth
state bird: 16 eastern goldfinch
state flower: 8 wild rose
state motto: 45 Our Liberties We
Prize and Our Rights We Will Maintain
state song: 13 The Song of Iowa
state tree: 3 oak

Iowa, Ioway
language family: 6 Siouan
location: 4 Iowa
related to: 3 Oto **8** Missouri

Iphigenia
father: 9 Agamemnon
mother: 12 Clytemnestra
brother: 7 Orestes
sister: 7 Electra **12** Chrysothemis
saved by: 7 Artemis

Iphigenia in Aulis
author: 9 Euripides
character: 8 Achilles, Menelaus **9** Agamemnon **12** Clytemnestra

Iphigenia in Tauris
author: 9 Euripides
character: 5 Thoas **6** Athena **7** Orestes, Pylades

Iphigenie en Aulide
also: 16 Iphigenia in Aulis
opera by: 5 Gluck
character: 7 Artemis, Calchas **8** Achilles **9** Agamemnon **12** Clytemnestra

Iphigenie en Tauride
also: 17 Iphigenia in Tauris
opera by: 5 Gluck
character: 5 Diana, Thoas (King of
Scythia) **7** Orestes, Pylades **9** the Furies

ipse dixit 15 he himself said it **21** assertion without proof
ipsissima verba 8 verbatim **12** the
very words
ipso facto 15 by the fact itself **24** by
the very nature of the deed
ipso jure 14 by the law itself **16** by
operation of law
IRA 19 Irish Republican Army **27** Individual Retirement Account

Iraklion
capital of: 5 Crete

Iran
name means: 15 land of the Aryans
earlier name: 5 Media **6** Persia
capital/largest city: 6 Tehran **7** Teheran
others: 3 Qum **4** Shah **5** Ahwaz, Urmia **6** Abadan, Bandar, Kashan,
Meshed, Shiraz, Tabriz **7** Birjand,
Hamadan, Isfahan, Mashhad, Zahi-
dan **11** Bandar Abbas
supreme head of state: 5 faghi **17**

religious guardian
measure: 3 gaz, zar, zer **4** cane **5**
gareh, kafiz, makuk, qasab **6** charac,
chebel, ghalva **7** capicha, chenica,
farsakh, mansion, mishara **8** parasang, piamaneh, stathmos
monetary unit: 3 pul **4** asar, gran,
rial **5** bisti, daric, dinar, larin, shahi,
toman **6** stater **7** ashrafi, pahlavi
weight: 3 ser **4** dung, rotl, seer **5** abbas, artel, pinar, ratel **6** batman, dirhem, karwar, miscal, nimman **7** abbassi **8** tcheirek
lake: 5 Niris, Tasht, Tuzlu, Urmia **6**
Sahweh, Sistan **7** Maharlu **8** Nemekser, Urumiyeh
mountain: 6 Elburz, Zagros
highest point: 8 Demavend
river: 4 Aras **5** Araks, Atrak, Atrek,
Karun, Safid, Sefid **6** Gargan
sea: 7 Arabian, Caspian
physical feature:
   desert: 9 Dasht-i-Lut **11** Dasht-i-
   Kavir
   gulf: 4 Oman **7** Persian
   strait: 6 Hormuz
people: 3 Lur, Tat **4** Arab, Kurd,
Turk **5** Medes **6** Galcha, Gilani, Jewish, Shugni **7** Baluchi, Persian **8** Armenian, Bactrian, Bartangi, Parthian,
Scythian **9** Bakhtiari **11** Azerbaijani,
Mazandarani
   mister: 4 agha
   dynasty: 5 Qajar **7** Arsacid, Pahlavi, Safavid **8** Parthian, Seleucid
   9 Sassanian **10** Achaemenid
   statesman, mathematician, poet:
   11 Omar Khayyam
   ruler: 5 Abbas, Cyrus **6** Darius,
   Xerxes **10** Rafsanjani **23** Shah Mohammed Reza (Riza) Pahlavi **25**
   Ayatollah Ruhollah Khomeini
language: 4 Luri, Zend **5** Farsi, Turki
6 Arabic **7** Baluchi, Kurdish, Persian
8 Armenian **11** Azerbaijani
religion: 5 Baha'i, Islam **7** Judaism **9**
Shia Islam **11** Zoroastrian **12** Christianity
place:
   dam: 5 Karaj
   mosque: 4 Shad **5** Royal **12** Mas-
   jidi-i-Shah **18** Madreseh Chahar
   Bagh
   ruins: 4 Susa **10** Persepolis
feature: 13 Peacock Throne
   head cloth: 6 chador **7** chawdar
   parliament: 6 majlis
   underground water channel: 5
   qanat
food: 5 kabob
   soured milk: 4 mast
   stuffed vegetables/leaves: 5
   dolma **6** dolmeh

Iraq
capital/largest city: 7 Baghdad
others: 2 Ur **3** Kut **5** Al Faw, Amara,
Ashur, Basra, Erbil, Mosul, Najaf,
Qurna **6** Hillah, Kirkuk, Tikrit **7** Kar-

bala, Mandali, Samarra, Umm Qasr
8 Al Zubair
division:
   ancient: 5 Akkad, Sumer **7** Assyria
   9 Babylonia **11** Mesopotamia
monetary unit: 4 fils **5** dinar
lake: 6 al-Milh **7** Sanniya **8** al-
Hammar
mountain: 6 Qalate, Zagros **7**
Qaarade **9** Kurdistan
highest point: 7 Halgurd
river: 6 Diyala, Hawran, Tigris **8**
Great Zab **9** al-Ubayyid, Euphrates,
Little Zab **13** Shatt-al-Arab
physical feature:
   desert: 6 Syrian **8** al-Hajava
   gulf: 7 Persian
people: 4 Arab, Kurd **7** Bedouin
leader: 6 Faisal, Sargon **7** Abbasid,
Hussein, Ottoman **9** Hammurabi
13 Harun al-Rashid, Saddam Hussein **14** Nebuchadnezzar **16** Abbasid Caliphate
language: 5 Farsi **6** Arabic **7** Kurdish, Persian, Turkish
religion: 5 Islam **12** Christianity
place:
   ancient: 14 Hanging Gardens
   arch: 9 Ctesiphon
   mosque: 5 Great **9** Kadhimain
   ruins: 2 Ur **7** Babylon, Nineveh,
   Samarra
   Sumerian temple tower: 8 Ziggu-
   rat
feature:
   marketplace: 4 souk
   war: 4 Gulf **11** Desert Storm **12**
   Desert Shield

irascibility 8 acerbity **9** bad temper,
crossness, testiness **10** crabbiness,
crankiness **11** peevishness, waspishness **12** irritability **16** cantankerous-
ness
irascible 5 cross, testy **6** cranky,
grumpy, ornery, touchy **7** grouchy,
peevish, waspish **8** choleric **9** irritable, splenetic **10** ill-humored **11** bad-
tempered, hot-tempered, intractable
12 cantankerous
irate 3 mad **5** angry, livid, rabid, riled,
vexed **6** galled **7** angered, annoyed,
enraged, furious **8** burned up **9** indignant, irritated **10** infuriated
ire 4 fury, rage **5** anger, wrath **6** choler
7 outrage, umbrage **8** vexation **10** resentment **11** indignation

Ireland
other name: 4 Eire, Erin **5** Ierne **8**
Hibernia **9** Innisfail **11** Emerald Isle
capital/largest city: 6 Dublin
others: 4 Cobh, Cork, Erne, Suir,
Tara **5** Adare, Ennis, Sligo **6** Bangor,
Galway, Lurgan, Mallow, Tralee, Ulster **7** Athlone, Belfast, Donegal,
Dundalk, Kildare, Wexford **8** Drog-
heda, Kilkenny, Limerick **9** Craiga-
von, Tipperary, Waterford **10**
Queenstown **11** Londonderry

school: 7 Trinity
division: 4 Cork, Down, Mayo **5** Clare, Kerry, Meath **6** Antrim, Armagh, Galway, Tyrone, Ulster **7** Donegal, Kildare, Wexford, Wicklow **8** Kilkenny, Limerick **9** Fermanagh, Killarney, Tipperary, Waterford **11** Londonderry
   ancient: 6 Ulster **7** Munster **8** Connacht, Leinster
head of government: 9 taoiseach (prime minister)
measure: 4 mile **6** bandle **8** crannock
monetary unit: 3 rap **4** real **5** pence, pound **6** turney **8** shilling
island: 3 Man **4** Aran, Bear, Holy, Tory **5** Clare, Clear, Magee **6** Achill, Saltee, Whiddy **7** Blasket, Gorumna, Rathlin **8** Aranmore, Inisheer **9** Inishmore **10** Inishbofin
lake: 3 Doo, Key, Ree, Tay **4** Conn, Derg, Erne, Mask **5** Allen, Barra, Capra, Gowna, Leane, Lough, Neagh **6** Boderg, Cooter, Corrib, Ennell **7** Dromore, Gougane, Oughter, Sheelin **9** Killarney
mountain: 5 Galty **6** Croagh, Mourne **7** Errigal, Muckish, Patrick, Wicklow **8** Comeragh **10** Benna Beola, Twelve Bens, Twelve Pins **13** Knockmealdown **19** Macgillycuddy's Reeks
highest point: 13 Carrantuohill
river: 3 Lee, May **4** Bann, Deel, Erne, Nore, Suir **5** Boyne, Clare, Feale, Flesk, Foyle, Laune **6** Bandon, Barrow, Corrib, Liffey, Slaney **7** Kenmare, Munster, Shannon **10** Blackwater
sea: 5 Irish **8** Atlantic
physical feature:
   bay: 4 Clew **5** Sligo **6** Bantry, Dingle, Galway, Tralee **7** Donegal, Dundalk
   cape: 5 Clear
   channel: 5 North **9** St George's
   cliffs: 5 Moher
   point: 6 Cahore **8** Carnsore
people: 4 Celt, Erse, Gael **6** Celtic **9** Hibernian
   author: 4 Shaw **5** Behan, Burke, Joyce, Swift, Synge, Wilde, Yeats **6** O'Casey, Steele **7** Beckett, O'Connor **8** O'Faolain, Sheridan, Stephens **9** Goldsmith, O'Flaherty **13** St John Gogarty
   leader: 4 Tone **6** Devlin, Valera **7** Grattan, Parnell, Redmond **8** O'Connell **9** Brian Boru **12** Saint Patrick
   legend: 9 Cuchulain **11** Finn MacCool
language: 4 Erse **5** Irish **6** Gaelic **7** English
religion: 8 Anglican **13** Roman Catholic
feature:
   airport: 7 Shannon
   castle: 4 Tara **7** Blarney

crystal: 9 Waterford
dance: 3 jig **4** reel
game: 7 hurling
lottery: 16 Irish Sweepstakes
manuscript: 11 Book of Kells
museum: 10 James Joyce
political movement: 8 Sinn Fein
race: 10 Irish Derby
relic: 13 Ardagh Chalice
revolutionary society: 6 Fenian
stone: 7 Blarney
street: 8 O'Connell
theater: 5 Abbey
food:
   beer: 5 stout
Ireland forever
   Gaelic: 11 Erin go bragh
I Remember Mama
   director: 13 George Stevens
   based on play by: 13 John Van Druten
   cast: 10 Ellen Corby, Irene Dunne, Philip Dorn **12** Oscar Homolka **16** Barbara Bel Geddes
   setting: 12 San Francisco
Irene
   member of: 5 Horae, Hours
   personifies: 5 peace
   corresponds to: 3 Pax
iridescence 7 glitter **11** opalescence, pearliness **12** nacreousness, play of colors
iridescent 5 shiny **7** glowing **8** colorful, nacreous **9** prismatic **10** changeable, opalescent **11** rainbowlike
iris
   varieties: 3 fan, red **4** roof, wall, wild **5** Dutch, dwarf, house **6** copper, German, orchid, Sierra, Spuria, violet, yellow **7** African, bearded, crested, English, Evansia, Lamance, peacock, Persian, Prairie, Spanish, walking **8** Japanese, mourning, Siberian, stinking **9** beachhead, beardless, butterfly, Palestine **10** snake's-head
Iris
   goddess of: 7 rainbow
   messenger of: 4 gods
   father: 7 Thaumas
   mother: 7 Electra
   sisters: 7 Harpies
   husband: 8 Zephyrus
Irish 4 Erse **4** Celtic, dander, Gaelic, temper
   accent: 6 brogue
   death spirit: 7 banshee
   flower: 8 shamrock
   girl: 7 colleen
   king: 9 Brian Boru
   legislature: 4 Dail
   saint: 7 Patrick
   society: 8 Sinn Fein
   theater: 5 Abbey
Irish gods 14 Tuatha De Danann
Irishman 4 Celt, Gael, Kelt, Mick **5**

Paddy **7** Irisher **9** Hibernian, orangeman **10** bogtrotter
Irish Mythology
   cats: 8 Kilkenny
   fairies: 4 Side
   god of love/beauty/youth: 7 Angus Og
   god of poetry/eloquence: 4 Ogma
   god of sea: 8 Manannan
   gods: 14 Tuatha De Danann
   hero: 10 Cuchulainn
   invaders/ancestors: 9 Milesians
   king: 4 Bres **5** Ronan **9** Conchobar **10** Matholwych
   king of gods: 4 Finn **5** Fionn
   pirate/demon: 8 Fomorian
   sea goddess: 3 Ler, Lir
   spirit: 4 Puca **5** Pooka
      corresponds to British: 4 Puck
irk 3 bug, vex **4** gall **5** annoy **6** bother, pester, ruffle **7** provoke **8** irritate
irksome 5 pesky **6** plaguy, vexing **7** plaguey, tedious **8** annoying, tiresome, wearying **9** difficult, provoking, vexatious, wearisome **10** bothersome, irritating, nettlesome **11** troublesome
iron
   chemical symbol: 2 Fe
Iron Age
   period of: 4 time
   followed age of: 6 Bronze
ironclad 5 fixed **6** strict **9** immutable, permanent **10** inexorable, inflexible, rigoristic, unchanging **11** irrevocable, unalterable **12** irreversible, unchangeable, unmodifiable
Iron Horse
   nickname of: 9 Lou Gehrig
ironic, ironical 3 odd **5** funny, weird **6** biting **7** abusive, caustic, curious, cutting, mocking, strange **8** derisive, sardonic, sneering, stinging **9** facetious, insincere, pretended, sarcastic **10** surprising, unexpected **11** implausible, incongruous **12** inconsistent **13** contradictory
irons 5 bonds **6** chains **7** fetters, presses, smooths **8** manacles, shackles **9** golf clubs, handcuffs **10** restraints
Ironside
   character: 7 (Det Sgt) Ed Brown **10** Mark Sanger **11** Fran Belding **12** Eve Whitfield **14** Robert Ironside
   cast: 11 Don Galloway, Don Mitchell, Raymond Burr **13** Elizabeth Baur **15** Barbara Anderson
irony 7 mockery, sarcasm **9** absurdity **11** incongruity, indirection **12** contrariness **13** facetiousness **14** implausibility
Iroquoian
   tribe: 6 Cayuga, Mohawk, Oneida, Seneca **8** Cherokee, Iroquois, Onandaga **9** Tuscarora **12** Kaniengehaga
Iroquois
   language family: 9 Iroquoian
   tribe: 6 Cayuga, Mohawk, Oneida,

Seneca **8** Onondaga **9** Tuscarora
location: **6** Canada **7** New York **11**
Connecticut **13** Massachusetts
leader: **11** Cornplanter, Joseph Brant
formed: **10** Six Nations **19** League of
the Iroquois
supernatural force: **6** Orenda
prophet: **10** Ganiodaiyo

irrational 6 absurd **7** foolish, unsound
8 baseless **9** illogical, unfounded **10**
ill-advised, unthinking **11** nonsensical,
unreasoning **12** unreasonable

irreclaimable 4 lost **6** wicked **7** corrupt, debased **9** abandoned, reprobate
12 disreputable, irredeemable, irreformable **16** beyond redemption

irreconcilable 7 opposed **12** incompatible, inconsistent, intransigent, un-
adjustable, unappeasable, unbridge-
able

irreformable 6 wicked **7** corrupt **9**
abandoned, reprobate, shameless
11 unrepentant **12** disreputable **13** irreclaimable

irrefutable 10 undeniable **12** indisputable, not refutable **13** proof positive
14 unquestionable **16** incontrovertible

irrefutably 6 surely **10** definitely, positively, undeniably **12** conclusively,
indisputably **13** incontestably **14** unquestionably **16** incontrovertibly

irregular 3 odd **5** bumpy, queer, rough
6 broken, uneven **7** crooked, unusual
8 aberrant, abnormal, improper, peculiar, singular **9** anomalous, desultory,
eccentric, haphazard, not smooth, out
of line, unaligned, unfitting **10** indecorous, unexpected, unsuitable **12** asymmetrical, unmethodical, unsystematic
13 inappropriate, nonconforming **14**
unconventional **16** uncharacteristic

irregularity 7 anomaly **9** asymmetry,
deviation **10** aberration, divergence,
unevenness **11** abnormality, peculiarity **12** constipation, eccentricity

irrelevant 5 inapt **7** foreign, off base **9**
unfitting, unrelated **10** extraneous, immaterial, malapropos, not apropos,
not germane **11** impertinent, unconnected **12** nonpertinent **14** beside the
point

irreligion 7 atheism **8** apostasy, unbelief **9** disbelief **11** godlessness

irreligious 6 unholy **7** godless, impious, profane, ungodly **8** agnostic **9**
atheistic **10** irreverent **11** unbelieving
12 not religious, sacrilegious

irremediable 8 hopeless **9** incurable
11 irreparable **12** beyond remedy

irreparable 9 unfixable **10** remediless
12 irremediable, irreversible **13** beyond redress, uncompensable, uncorrectable

irreplaceable 6 unique **9** essential **13**
indispensable

irrepressible 7 vibrant **8** bubbling,

galvanic, undamped **9** ebullient **10**
boisterous, full of life **11** tempestuous
12 unquenchable **13** unsquelchable
14 uncontrollable, unrestrainable

irreproachable 8 flawless **9** blameless, faultless, stainless, unspotted **10**
impeccable, inculpable **11** unblemished **12** above reproof, without fault
13 unimpeachable

irresistible 8 alluring, enticing **9** beck-
oning, seductive **10** enchanting, superhuman **11** tantalizing **12** overpowering, overwhelming

irresolute 4 weak **6** fickle, unsure **8**
doubtful, hesitant, unsteady, wavering
9 faltering, uncertain, undecided, unsettled **10** changeable, hesitating, indecisive, unresolved **11** vacillating

irresolution 5 doubt **9** hesitancy **10**
hesitation, indecision

irresponsibility 8 rashness **10** immaturity, imprudence **11** foolishness
12 carelessness, heedlessness, indifference, indiscretion, recklessness **13** unreliability **15** thoughtlessness, unde-
pendability **17** untrustworthiness

irresponsible 4 rash **7** foolish **8** careless, immature, reckless **9** imprudent,
overhasty **10** capricious, incautious,
unreliable **11** harebrained, indifferent,
injudicious, thoughtless **12** undependable **13** ill-considered, untrustworthy
14 not responsible, scatterbrained

irresponsible person
French: **14** enfant terrible

irreverence 7 impiety **9** blasphemy,
sacrilege **10** irreligion

irreverent 5 saucy **6** brazen **7** impious, profane **8** critical, impudent,
sneering **9** debunking, shameless,
skeptical, slighting **11** blasphemous,
disparaging, irreligious **12** nose-
thumbing **13** disrespectful

irrevocable 5 final **10** conclusive **11**
unalterable **12** irreversible, unchangeable

irritability 6 spleen **8** acerbity, edginess **9** crossness, huffiness, petulance,
testiness **10** crabbiness, crankiness,
impatience **11** fretfulness, peevishness, short temper, waspishness **12**
irascibility

irritable 5 testy **6** grumpy, touchy **7**
fretful, grouchy, peevish, pettish,
waspish **8** snappish **9** impatient, irascible **10** ill-humored **11** easily vexed,
ill-tempered

irritate 3 irk, vex **5** anger, annoy,
chafe, peeve **6** nettle, worsen **7** inflame, provoke **8** make sore **9** aggravate, make angry **10** exasperate

irritated 3 mad, raw **4** sore **5** cross,
irked, irate, testy, vexed **6** chafed,
crabby, galled, miffed, peeved,
piqued, put out **7** annoyed, burning,
nettled, peevish **8** burned up, choleric, incensed, inflamed, provoked **9**

impatient, irascible **10** aggravated **11**
exasperated

irritating 5 acrid, harsh, rough **7** caustic, chafing, galling, irksome, rasping
8 abrasive, annoying **9** provoking,
vexatious **10** bothersome **11** infuriating, troublesome **12** exasperating

irritation 6 bother **7** chafing **8** distress, vexation **9** annoyance **10** discomfort **11** irksomeness

irruption 4 raid **5** break, foray **6** inroad **7** upsurge **8** bursting, invasion
9 incursion, intrusion

Irving, John
author of: **16** A Widow for One Year
18 The Cider-House Rules **19** A
Prayer for Owen Meany **20** The Hotel New Hampshire **23** The World
According to Garp

Irving, Washington
author of: **11** Salmagundi **12** Rip Van
Winkle **13** The Sketch Book **23** The
Legend of Sleepy Hollow

Isaac
father: **7** Abraham
mother: **5** Sarah
brother: **7** Ishmael
wife: **7** Rebekah
son: **4** Esau **5** Jacob
birthplace: **5** Gerar
burial place: **9** Machpelah
blessed: **5** Jacob
sacrificed at: **6** Moriah

Isaac of York
character in: **7** Ivanhoe
author: **5** Scott

Isabella
character in: **17** Measure for Measure
author: **11** Shakespeare

Isaiah
means: **12** Jehovah saves
father: **4** Amoz
son: **11** Shearzashub **18** Maharshalal-
hashbaz

Iscariot see **5** Judas

Isenstein
origin: **12** Scandinavian
home of: **8** Brunhild
location: **8** Isenland

I serve
German: **7** ich dien
motto of: **13** Prince of Wales

Iseult, Isolde, Isolt
character in: **16** Arthurian romance
lover: **7** Tristan **8** Tristram
betrothed to: **8** King Mark

I shall rise again
Latin: **8** resurgam

Isherwood, Christopher
author of: **10** I Am a Camera **13** Berlin Stories **17** Down There on a Visit
character: **11** Sally Bowles

Ishmael
narrator in: **8** Moby Dick
author: **8** Melville

Ishmael

father: 7 Abraham
mother: 5 Hagar
means: 11 God will hear
brother: 5 Isaac
son: 5 Kedar **7** Kedemah
descendant of: 10 Ishmaelite

Ishtar
also: 7 Mylitta
origin: 8 Assyrian **10** Babylonian
goddess of: 3 war **4** love
queen of: 6 heaven
corresponds to: 6 Inanna **7** Astarte
9 Ashtoreth

Isis
origin: 8 Egyptian
goddess of: 9 fertility
hieroglyphic symbol: 6 throne
husband: 6 Osiris
brother: 6 Osiris
son: 5 Horus
father: 3 Geb, Keb
mother: 3 Nut
horns of: 3 cow
headdress: 9 solar disk
corresponds to: 2 Io

Islam
adherent: 4 Sufi **5** Shiah **6** Moslem, Muslim, Shiite, Wahabi **7** Sunnite **8** Islamite **9** Mussulman **10** Mohammedan
crusade: 5 Jahad, Jihad
deity: 5 Allah
flight from Mecca: 6 hegira
founder/prophet: 8 Mohammed, Muhammad
holy city: 5 Mecca **6** Medina
other names: 9 Moslemism **13** Mohammedanism
pilgrimage to Mecca: 4 hadj
priest: 4 imam
scripture: 5 Koran

Islamabad
capital of: 8 Pakistan

Islamic 6 Moslem, Muslim **10** Mohammedan

island 4 isle **5** atoll, haven, islet, oasis **6** refuge **7** enclave, retreat, shelter **9** sanctuary

Islands of the Blessed *see* **10** Hesperides

isle, islet 3 ait, cay, key **4** holm **5** atoll, islet **6** island

Isle of Cloves *see* **8** Tanzania

Isle of Spice *see* **7** Grenada

Isleta (Tuei)
language family: 6 Pueblo, Tanoan
location: 9 New Mexico, Rio Grande

isn't that so?
French: 9 n'est-ce pas?
German: 9 nicht wahr?

isolate 6 banish, detach, enisle **7** seclude **8** insulate, separate, set apart **9** segregate, sequester **10** disconnect, place apart, quarantine

isolated 4 lone, solo **5** alone, apart **6** cut off, lonely, remote, unique **7** insular, removed **8** detached, secluded, set

apart, solitary **9** separated, unrelated **10** segregated **11** out-of-the-way, quarantined, sequestered

isolation 7 privacy **8** solitude **9** aloneness, apartness, hermitism, seclusion **10** desolation, detachment, insularity, insulation, quarantine, separation **11** confinement, segregation **12** separateness

isoptera
class: 8 hexapoda
phylum: 10 arthropoda
group: 7 termite **8** white ant

Ispahan
also: 7 Isfahan **8** Aspadana
location: 4 Iran
capital of: 6 Persia
river: 8 Zayandeh

I Spy
character: 13 Kelly Robinson **14** Alexander Scott
cast: 9 Bill Cosby **10** Robert Culp
Kelly's cover: 9 tennis bum

Israel
former name: 5 Jacob
means: 12 soldier of God
wrestled with: 5 angel

Israel
other name: 4 Zion **6** Canaan, Yishuv **9** Palestine **12** Promised Land
capital: 9 Jerusalem
largest city: 12 Tel Aviv-Jaffa
others: 4 Acre, Elat, Gaza **5** Eilat, Elath, Haifa, Holon, Jaffa, Jenin **6** Ashdod, Bat Yam, Dimona, Hebron, Nablus **7** Netanya, Rehovot, Tel Aviv **8** Nazareth, Ramallah, Ramat Gan **9** Beersheba, Bene Beraq, Bethlehem
school: 6 Hebrew **14** Technion-Israel **26** Weizmann Institute of Science
division: 5 Judea, Negev, Sinai **7** Galilee **8** West Bank **9** Gaza Strip **12** Golan Heights
government:
legislature: 7 Knesset
political parties: 5 Labor, Likud, Mapam
measure: 3 cab, car, hin, kab, kor **4** bath, ezba, omer, reed **5** cubit, donum, dunam, ephah, ganeh, homer, kaneh
monetary unit: 3 mil **5** agora, agura, pound, pruta **6** agorot, shekel
lake: 5 Huleh **7** Dead Sea **8** Kinneret, Tiberias **12** Sea of Galilee
mountain: 4 Nafh, Sagi **5** Harif, Ramon, Tabor **6** Atzmon, Carmel, Hatira
highest point: 5 Meron **6** Meiron
river: 4 Qarn **5** Faria, Malik, Sareq **6** Hadera, Jordan, Kishon, Qishon, Sarida, Yarkon, Yarmuk **7** Lakhish
sea: 3 Red **4** Dead **7** Galilee **13** Mediterranean
airline: 4 El Al
physical feature:
bay: 5 Haifa

desert: 5 Negev, Sinai
gulf: 5 Aqaba
plain: 5 Judea **6** Sharon **7** Zebulun **9** Esdraelon
people: 3 Jew **4** Arab **5** Druze **10** Circassian
ancient: 6 Hebrew
immigrant: 4 olim
Jew born in Israel: 5 sabra
leader: 4 Eban, Meir **5** Begin, Dayan, Herzl, Peres, Rabin **6** Ben-Zvi, Eshkol **7** Sharett **8** Weizmann **9** Ben- Gurion
language: 6 Arabic, French, Hebrew **7** English, Yiddish
religion: 5 Baha'i, Islam **7** Judaism **12** Christianity
place:
church: 13 Holy Sepulcher
gates to Old Jerusalem: 3 New **4** Dung, Zion **5** Jaffa **6** Herod's **8** Damascus **10** St Stephen's
mosque: 13 Dome of the Rock
mount: 4 Zion **6** Olives, Scopus
shrine: 3 Bab **4** Book **11** Wailing Wall, Western Wall **18** Garden of Gethsemane
tomb: 9 Sanhedrin **10** King David's
way of sorrows: 11 Via Dolorosa
feature: 14 Dead Sea Scrolls
collective village: 7 kibbutz **9** kibbutzim
cooperative village: 6 moshav **8** moshavim
dance: 4 hora
movement: 7 Zionism
Palestinian uprising: 8 intifada
peace agreement: 16 Camp David Accords
tree: 5 judas
wave of immigration: 5 aliya **6** aliyot
food:
dish: 4 pita **6** hummus **7** falafel

Israel, tribes of 3 Dan, Gad **4** Levi **5** Asher, Judah **6** Joseph, Reuben, Simeon **7** Zebulun **8** Benjamin, Issachar, Naphtali

Israel-born
Hebrew: 5 sabra

Israelite 3 Jew **6** Hebrew, Jewish, Semite **7** Judaist **8** Hebraist
descended from: 5 Jacob
king: 4 Ahab, Elah, Jehu, Omri, Saul **5** David, Hosea, Nadab, Zimri

Issachar
father: 5 Jacob
mother: 4 Leah
brother: 3 Dan, Gad **4** Levi **5** Asher, Judah **6** Joseph, Reuben, Simeon **7** Zebulun **8** Benjamin, Naphtali
sister: 5 Dinah
descendant: 11 Issacharite

Is Sex Necessary?
author: 7 E B White **12** James Thurber

issuance 8 emission **9** allotment, discharge, emanation **12** dispensation, distribution

issue 4 gush, rise, stem **5** allot, arise, ensue, erupt, go out, heirs, spout, yield **6** emerge, follow, number, result, spring **7** dispute, emanate, flow out, give out, outcome, outflow, pass out, problem, proceed, product, progeny **8** children, dispense, drainage, eruption, granting, heritors, issuance, question **9** circulate, discharge, effluence, grow out of, offspring, posterity, pour forth **10** distribute, outpouring **11** consequence, descendants, publication **12** dispensation, distributing

Istanbul
  area: 7 Beyoglu **8** Stamboul
  capital of: 6 Turkey
  formerly: 9 Byzantium **14** Constantinople
  landmark: 10 Hippodrome **11** Hagia Sophia **12** Galata Bridge **14** Bosporus Bridge **26** Palais de la Culture d'Istanbul
  mosque: 3 New **8** Mihrimah **9** Yeni Camii **11** Suleymaniye
  museum: 13 Topkapi Palace **14** Archaeological **20** Turkish and Islamic Art
  rulers: 4 Rome **6** Athens, Darius, Rhodes, Sparta **8** Persians, Suleiman **9** Macedonia **11** Latin Empire **12** Ottoman Turks **15** Byzantine Empire, Turkish Republic **19** Constantine the Great
  sea: 5 Black **7** Marmara **8** Bosporus **10** Golden Horn

isthmus 4 neck, spit **5** point, strip **6** narrow, strait, tongue **7** narrows
  name: 4 Suez **6** Panama **7** Corinth

I sustain the wings
  Latin: 12 sustineo alas
  motto of: 10 US Air Force

Italic
  language family: 12 Indo-European
  branch: 5 Latin, Oscan **7** Umbrian

italics 11 slanted type

Italy
  also: 8 Hesperia
  capital/largest city: 4 Roma, Rome
  others: 4 Pisa **5** Genoa, Milan, Padua, Turin, Udine **6** Amalfi, Ancona, Assisi, Naples, Rimini, Savona, Venice, Verona **7** Bologna, Bolzano, Brescia, Catania, Messina, Palermo, Ravenna, Taranto, Trieste **8** Florence
  division: 6 Apulia, Latium, Marche, Molise, Umbria, Veneto **7** Abruzzi, Liguria, Tuscany **8** Calabria, Campania, Lombardy, Piedmont **10** Basilicata **12** Valle d'Agosta **13** Emilia-Romagna **17** Trentino-Alto Adige **19** Friuli-Venezia Giulia
    independent enclave: 9 San Marino **11** Vatican City
  measure: 3 pie **4** orna **5** palma, palmo, punto, salma, stero **6** barile,

miglie, moggio, rubbio, tomolo **7** braccio, secchio **8** giornata, quadrato

monetary unit: 4 lira, lire, tara **5** grano, paolo, soldo **6** danàro, denaro, ducato **7** testone **8** zecchino **9** centesini

weight: 5 carat, libra, oncia, pound **6** denaro, libbra

island: 4 Elba **5** Capri, Egadi, Eolie **6** Ischia, Istria, Linosa, Lipari, Sicily, Ustica **7** Aeolian, Trieste, Vulcano **8** Lampione, Sardinia **9** Borromean, Lampedusa, Stromboli **10** Isola Bella **11** Pantelleria

lake: 4 Como, Iseo, Nemi **5** Garda **6** Albano, Lesina, Lugano, Varano **7** Bolsena, Perugia **8** Maggiore **9** Bracciano, Trasimeno

mountain: 4 Alps, Etna, Visa **5** Amaro, Blanc, Corno, Somma **6** Cimone, Ortles **9** Apennines, Dolomites, Maritimes **11** Gennargentu **12** Gran Paradiso **16** Abruzzi Apennines
  Alps: 6 Apuane, Carnic, Julian, Otztal **7** Bernina **8** Ligurian **9** Lepontine
  volcano: 4 Etna **7** Vulcano **8** Vesuvius **9** Stromboli

highest point: 4 Rosa

river: 2 Po **4** Adda, Agri, Arno, Liri, Nera, Reno, Sele, Taro **5** Adige, Crati, Mannu, Oglio, Parma, Piave, Salso, Stura, Tiber, Tirso **6** Aniene, Belice, Isonzo, Mincio, Ofanto, Panaro, Rapido, Sangro, Simeto, Tanaro, Tevere, Ticino **7** Biferno, Bradano, Chienti, Metauro, Montone, Ombrone, Pescara, Rubicon, Secchia, Trebbia **8** Volturno

sea: 6 Ionian **8** Adriatic, Ligurian **10** Tyrrhenian **13** Mediterranean

physical feature:
  bay: 6 Naples
  channel: 5 Malta
  grotto: 4 Blue
  gulf: 5 Gaeta, Genoa **6** Venice **7** Salerno, Taranto **11** Manfredonia
  hills of Rome: 7 Caelian, Viminal **8** Aventine, Palatine, Quirinal **9** Esquiline **10** Capitoline
  lagoon: 6 Venice
  pass: 5 Resia **6** Maloja **7** Bernina, Brenner, Simplon **9** Mont Cenis **13** Saint Gotthard **17** Great Saint Bernard
  resort: 14 Italian Riviera
  strait: 6 Sicily **7** Messina, Otranto **9** Bonifacio

people: 7 Italian
  ancient: 5 Latin, Remus **6** Sabine **7** Lombard, plebian, Romulus **8** Etruscan **9** patrician
  architect: 5 Nervi, Ponti, Salvi **6** Vasari **7** Alberti, Guarini, Juvarra, Vignola **8** Ammanati, Bramante, Palladio **9** Borromini, De Sanctis **12** Brunelleschi, Michelangelo
  artist: 5 Balla, Carra **6** Batoni,

Gaulli, Guardi, Titian **7** Bellini, Chirico, Cimabue, Cortona, Da Vinci, Raphael, Tiepolo, Uccello **8** Carracci, Mantegna, Masaccio, Severini **9** Benvenuti, Canoletto, Giorgione **10** Botticelli, Caravaggio, Modigliani, Tintoretto **11** Buoninsegna, Fra Angelico **12** Michelangelo **13** Giotto Bondone **14** della Francesca

  composer: 5 Verdi **7** Bellini, Cavalli, Corelli, Puccini, Rossini, Vivaldi **8** Mascagni, Piccinni **9** Donizetti, Scarlatti **10** Monteverdi, Palestrina **11** Leoncavallo

  emperor: 4 Nero, Otho **5** Galba, Nerva, Titus **6** Trajan **7** Hadrian **8** Caligula, Claudius, Commodus, Domitian, Octavian, Tiberius **9** Caracalla, Vespasian, Vitellius **10** Diocletian **11** Constantine **13** Antoninus Dius **14** Caesar Augustus, Marcus Aurelius

  film director: 6 de Sica **7** Fellini **8** Visconti **9** Antonioni **10** Bertolucci, Rossellini, Wertmuller, Zeffirelli

  god: 4 Juno, Mars **5** Ceres, Diana, Janus, Lares, Venus **6** Apollo, Vulcan **7** Bacchus, Jupiter, Minerva, Neptune, Penates **8** Quirinus

  Italian author: 3 Eco **4** Levi **5** Bembo, Bruno, Pulci, Tasso **6** Artino, Vasari **7** Ariosto, Bassani, Deledda, Moravia **8** Bandello, Petrarch **9** Boccaccio, D'Annunzio, Sannazaro **10** Cavalcanti, Guinicelli, Metastasio, Pirandello, Straparola **11** Castiglione, Machiavelli **12** Guicciardini, Michelangelo **14** Dante Alighieri

  Latin author: 4 Cato, Livy, Ovid **5** Pliny, Varro **6** Cicero, Gallus, Horace, Seneca, Vergil, Virgil **7** Donatus, Juvenal, Martial, Plautus, Sallust, Tacitus, Terence **8** Boethius, Catullus, Lucilius, St Jerome **9** St Ambrose, Suetonius **11** St Augustine

  ruler: 4 Moro **6** Cavour, Enrico **7** Mazzini **9** Mussolini **10** Berlinguer **14** Victor Emmanuel **15** Alcide de Gasperi

  ruler/military leader: 5 Sulla **6** Brutus, Pompey, Seneca **7** Crassus, Lepidus **8** Gracchus **10** Mark Antony **12** Gaius Marious, Julius Caesar **15** Cassius Longinus, Scipio Africanus **18** Tarquinius Superbus

  old ruling family: 4 Este **6** Borgia, Medici, Sforza **8** Visconti

  sculptor: 6 Canova, Marini, Pisano **7** Bernini, Bologna, Cellini **8** Antelami, Boccioni, Ghiberti **9** Donatello, Sansovino **10** Giacometti, Pollaiuolo, Verrocchio **11** Della Robbia **12** Michelangelo

wife: 7 Poppaea 9 Agrippina, Messalina 13 Livia Drusilla
language: 5 Ladin, Latin 6 French, German 7 Italian, Slovene 8 Friulian 9 Sardinian
expressions: 4 ciao 5 bella 10 primadonna
religion: 13 Roman Catholic
place:
  arch: 11 Constantine
  baths: 9 Caracalla
  bridge: 5 Sighs 12 Ponte Vecchio
  cathedral/church: 5 Siena 7 St Mark's, Vatican 8 San Marco, St Peter's 13 Sistine Chapel
  fountain: 5 Trevi
  museum: 5 Duomo 6 Uffizi 8 Bargello, National 10 Capitoline 11 Pitti Palace, Villa Giulia 16 Gallerio Borghese
  opera house: 7 La Scala
  palace: 5 Doges
  road: 9 Appian Way
  ruins: 5 Forum 7 Capitol, Pompeii 8 Pantheon 9 Catacombs, Colosseum 11 Herculaneum 13 Circus Maximus
  steps: 7 Spanish
  tower: 18 Leaning Tower of Pisa
feature:
  unification movement: 12 Risorgimento
food:
  cheese: 6 romano 7 fontina, ricotta 8 parmesan
  dish: 5 pizza 6 scampi 7 gnocchi, lasagna, lasagne, polenta, ravioli, risotto 9 antipasti, antipasto 17 chicken cacciatora, cacciatore
  ice cream: 6 gelato 7 spumoni
  meat: 6 salami 9 pepperoni 10 mortadella, prosciutto
  soup: 8 caciucco 10 minestrone
  wine: 7 Chianti
itch 3 yen 4 ache, long, pine 5 crave, crawl, creep, yearn 6 desire, hanker, hunger, thirst, tickle 7 craving, prickle 8 appetite, have a yen, pruritis, tingling, yearning 9 hankering
it does not follow
  Latin: 11 non sequitur
item 4 unit 5 entry, piece, point, story, thing 6 detail, matter, notice, report 7 account, article, feature, subject 8 dispatch, notation 9 paragraph 10 particular 11 news article
itemization 4 list 7 listing 11 enumeration
itemize 6 detail 7 specify 8 spell out 9 enumerate
items of business 4 list 6 agenda, docket 7 program 8 schedule
iterate 6 repeat 7 restate 9 reiterate
It Girl
  nickname of: 8 Clara Bow
it grows as it goes

Latin: 12 crescit eundo
  motto of: 9 New Mexico
Ithaca
  ancient home of: 8 Odysseus, Penelope
  modern home of: 7 Cornell (University)
It Happened One Night
  director: 10 Frank Capra
  cast: 8 Alan Hale, Ward Bond 10 Clark Gable 11 Roscoe Karns 14 Walter Connolly 16 Claudette Colbert
  Oscar for: 5 actor (Gable) 7 actress (Colbert), picture 8 director
  remade as: 16 Eve Knew Her Apples 20 You Can't Run Away from It
I think therefore I am
  Latin: 13 cogito ergo sum
  said by: 9 Descartes
itinerant 5 nomad, rover 6 roamer, roving 7 migrant, nomadic, roaming, vagrant 8 vagabond, wanderer, wayfarer 9 footloose, transient, traveling, wandering, wayfaring 11 peripatetic
itinerary 3 log 5 diary, route 6 course 7 account, circuit, day book, journal 8 schedule 9 timetable 10 travel plan
it is not clear; it is not evident
  Latin: 9 non liquet
it is not lawful; it is not permitted
  Latin: 8 non licet
it is sweet to do nothing
  Italian: 14 dolce far niente
It's a Gift
  director: 13 Norman Z McLeod
  cast: 8 W C Fields 9 Baby LeRoy, Tommy Bupp 10 T Roy Barnes 13 Charles Sellon, Morgan Wallace 14 Kathleen Howard
  remake of: 17 It's the Old Army Game
It's a Wonderful Life
  director: 10 Frank Capra
  cast: 9 Donna Reed 11 Beulah Bondi 12 Henry Travers, James Stewart 13 Gloria Grahame 15 Lionel Barrymore
  remade as: 22 It Happened One Christmas
itsy-bitsy 3 wee 4 tiny 5 dwarf, pygmy, small, teeny 6 bantam, little, minute, petite 9 miniature, miniscule 10 diminutive, teeny-weeny 11 microscopic, pocket-sized
It Takes a Thief
  character: 8 Noah Bain 12 Alister Mundy, Wallie Powers 14 Alexander Mundy
  cast: 11 Edward Binns, Fred Astaire 12 Robert Wagner 13 Malachi Throne
Itza
  language family: 6 Toltec
  location: 6 Mexico 7 Chichen, Yucatan 14 Central America
Iulus *see* 8 Ascanius

Ivan 4 czar, tsar 8 the Great 11 the Terrible 18 grand duke of Muscovy
  English equivalent: 4 John
  personifies: 6 Russia
Ivanhoe
  author: 14 Sir Walter Scott
  character: 7 Rebecca 8 Guilbert 9 Robin Hood 10 Lady Rowena 11 Isaac of York 12 King Richard I 14 Cedric the Saxon, Sir Brian de Bois 16 Wilfred of Ivanhoe 19 King Richard the First
Ivanhoe, Burle Icle
  real name of: 8 Burl Ives
I've Got a Secret
  host: 10 Bill Cullen, Garry Moore, Steve Allen
Ives, Burl
  real name: 16 Burle Icle Ivanhoe
  nickname: 17 Wayfaring Stranger
  born: 6 Hunt IL
  roles: 8 Big Daddy 10 East of Eden 13 The Big Country 14 Our Man in Havana 16 Cat on a Hot Tin Roof 18 Desire Under the Elms
Ives, Charles
  born: 9 Danbury CT
  composer of: 11 Putnam's Camp 13 Concord Sonata 19 Washington's Birthday 20 Central Park in the Dark 21 The Unanswered Question 23 Three Places in New England
ivory 4 tusk 6 dentin
  source: 6 walrus 8 elephant
  used for: 4 dice 9 piano keys 13 billiard balls
  color: 5 cream 8 off-white
Ivory Coast
  capital/largest city: 7 Abidjan
    new capital: 12 Yamoussoukro
  others: 3 Man 4 Divo 5 Daloa, Tabou 6 Adzobe, Bonoua, Bouake, Danane, Gagnoa 7 Korhogo, Odienne, Seguela 8 Dimbokro 9 Agboville, Bondoukou, Sassandra 10 Abengourou 11 Grand Bassam 14 Ferkessedougou
  monetary unit: 5 franc 7 centime
  highest point: 5 Nimba
  river: 3 Bia 5 Komoe, Komoe 7 Bandama, Cavally 9 Sassandra
  ocean: 8 Atlantic
  physical feature:
    cape: 6 Palmas
    gulf: 6 Guinea
    lagoon: 3 Aby 5 Ebrie
    wind: 9 harmattan
  people: 3 Abe, Dan, Kru, Kwa 4 Akan, Bete, Dida, Guro, Koua, Lobi, Wobe 5 Abron, Abure, Attie, Baule, Guere, Mande, Mossi 6 Baoule, Lagoon, Senufo, Senufu 7 Dan Guro, Kroumen, Malinke, Voltaic 10 Anyi-Baoule 11 Lobi-Kulango 12 Agnis-Ashanti
  language: 4 Akan 6 Dioula, French
  religion: 5 Islam 7 animism 13 Roman Catholic

place:
    canal: 5 Vridi
    dam: 7 Bandama
    game reserve: 9 Sassandra
    feature: 7 kola nut

Ivory Coast *see* **11** Sierra Leone

ivory-towered 6 remote **8** academic, romantic **11** conjectural, impractical, theoretical, unrealistic **12** hypothetical

ivy 6 Cissus, Hedera **15** Kalmia latifolia
    varieties: 3 fan, red **4** baby, tree **5** grape, Irish, Nepal, water **6** aralia, Baltic, Boston, canary, devil's, German, ground, marine, parlor, poison, spider, switch **7** colchis, English, Italian, Madeira, Mexican, parsley, Persian, Swedish **8** Algerian, American, coliseum, fragrant, Japanese, red-flame **9** bird's-foot, ghost-tree, heart-leaf **10** five-leaved, Kenilworth, variegated **12** Hagenburger's **13** Solomon Island **14** miniature grape **15** Gloire-de-Marengo

Ivy League colleges 4 Yale **5** Brown **7** Cornell, Harvard **8** Columbia **9** Dartmouth, Princeton **12** Pennsylvania (Penn)

I Want to Live!
    director: 10 Robert Wise
    cast: 12 Simon Oakland, Susan Hayward (Barbara Graham) **13** Theodore Bikel **15** Virginia Vincent
    score: 12 Johnny Mandel
    Oscar for: 7 actress (Hayward)

I will defend
    Latin: 6 tuebor

IWW 8 Wobblies **10** labor union **27** Industrial Workers of the World
    leader: 4 Debs **6** DeLeon **7** Haywood

members: 6 miners **9** lumbermen **16** migratory workers

Ixion
    king of: 8 Lapithae
    wife: 3 Dia
    son: 9 Pirithous
    children: 8 centaurs
    loved: 4 Hera
    punished by: 4 Zeus
    bound to: 5 wheel

Iyar 17 second Hebrew month

Iynx
    father: 3 Pan
    mother: 4 Echo

Izmir
    formerly: 6 Smyrna
    location: 6 Turkey **9** Aegean Sea **11** Gulf of Izmir
    settle by: 7 Ionians **8** Aeolians
    ruled by: 13 Ottoman Empire

izzard 3 zed, zee

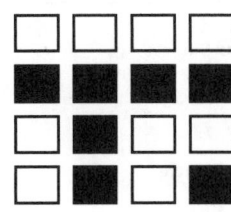

ja 3 yes

jab 3 cut, dig, hit, rap, tap **4** belt, blow, bump, clip, goad, lick, pelt, plug, poke, poke, prod, sock, stab, swat **5** elbow, nudge, paste, swing **6** strike, stroke

jabber 3 gab, gas **4** blab **5** clack, prate **6** babble, cackle, drivel, gibber, gossip, hot air, patter, ramble, rattle, raving **7** blabber, blather, chatter, gushing, maunder, palaver, prating, prattle, ranting, twaddle, twattle **8** chitchat, idle talk, nonsense, talk idly **9** gibberish **10** maundering **14** chitter-chatter

jack 4 flag **5** knave, money **6** ensign, sailor

jackass 3 ass **4** fool, mule **5** burro, dummy, idiot **6** donkey

Jack Benny Show, The
  cast: 8 Mel Blanc **9** Dennis Day, Don Wilson **11** Frank Nelson **13** Artie Auerbach, Eddie (Rochester) Anderson **14** Mary Livingston
  Jack's car: 7 Maxwell
  Jack played: 6 violin

jacket 4 case, coat **5** cover **6** blazer, casing, folder, sheath **7** wrapper **8** envelope, mackinaw, wrapping **9** container, enclosure, short coat, sport coat **10** dinner coat **11** windbreaker

Jackson, Andrew
  nickname: 10 Old Hickory
  presidential rank: 7 seventh
  party: 10 Democratic
  state represented: 2 TN **9** Tennessee
  defeated: 4 (Henry) Clay **5** (John Quincy) Adams
  vice president: 7 (John Caldwell) Calhoun **8** (Martin) Van Buren
  cabinet:
    state: 6 (Louis) McLane **7** (John) Forsyth **8** (Martin) Van Buren **10** (Edward) Livingston
    treasury: 5 (William John) Duane **6** (Louis) McLane, (Samuel Dulucenna) Ingham **8** (Levi) Woodbury
    war: 4 (Lewis) Cass **5** (John Henry) Eaton
    attorney general: 5 (Roger Brooke) Taney **6** (Benjamin Franklin) Butler **7** (John McPherson) Berrien
    navy: 6 (John) Branch **8** (Levi) Woodbury **9** (Mahlon) Dickerson
    postmaster general: 5 (William Taylor) Barry **7** (Amos) Kendall

  born: 8 Waxhaw SC
  died/buried: 11 Nashville TN
  education:
    college: 4 none
    studied: 3 law
    admitted to: 3 bar
  religion: 12 Presbyterian
  political career: 8 US Senate **24** US House of Representatives
    judge: 22 Tennessee Superior Court
  civilian career: 6 lawyer
  military service: 12 major general **16** brigadier general
    defeated: 6 Creeks **9** Cherokees
    captured: 9 Pensacola
    military governor of: 7 Florida
  notable events of lifetime/term:
    battle: 5 Alamo **10** New Orleans
    fought: 5 duels
    scandal/wife suspected of: 6 bigamy
    war: 8 Creek War **13** Revolutionary **16** First Seminole War **19** War of Eighteen Twelve
  father: 6 Andrew
  mother: 9 Elizabeth (Hutchinson)
  siblings: 4 Hugh **6** Robert
  wife: 6 Rachel (Donelson Robards)
  children:
    adopted: 11 wife's nephew **15** Andrew Jackson Jr

Jackson, Anne
  husband: 10 Eli Wallach
  born: 10 Millvale PA
  roles: 3 Luv **10** The Typists

Jackson, Charles
  author of: 14 The Lost Weekend

Jackson 5 4 Tito **6** Jackie, Marlon **7** Michael **8** Jermaine
  songs: 3 ABC **10** I'll Be There **12** I Want You Back **14** The Love You Save

Jackson, Glenda
  born: 7 England **10** Birkenhead
  roles: 10 Elizabeth R **11** Women in Love (Oscar) **13** A Touch of Class (Oscar) **14** The Music Lovers **16** Mary Queen of Scots **18** Sunday Bloody Sunday
  politics: 11 Labour Party **18** Member of Parliament

Jackson, Jesse Louis
  title: 8 Reverend
  party: 10 Democratic
  born: 12 Greenville SC
  education: 20 University of Illinois **26** Chicago Theological Seminary **49** North Carolina Agricultural and Technical State College
  religion: 7 Baptist
  political career: 17 Democratic primary
  civilian career: 4 SCLC **9** PUSH Excel **13** Operation PUSH **20** Operation Breadbasket **24** National Rainbow Coalition **37** Southern Christian Leadership Conference

Jackson, Michael
  born: 2 IN **4** Gary
  father: 6 Joseph
  mother: 9 Katherine
  siblings: 4 Tito **5** Janet, Randy **6** Jackie, La Toya, Marlon **7** Maureen **8** Jermaine
  wife: 16 Lisa Marie Presley
  trademark: 5 glove
  recordings: 3 Bad **7** Triumph, Victory **8** Thriller **9** Dangerous **10** Off the Wall
  film: 6 The Wiz
  group: 8 Jacksons **11** Jackson Five

Jackson, Reggie
  nickname: 13 Mister October
  sport: 8 baseball
  position: 8 outfield
  known for: 7 hitting
  team: 9 Oakland A's **14** New York Yankees **16** California Angels

Jackson, Shirley
  author of: 10 The Lottery **28** We Have Always Lived in the Castle

Jackson, Stonewall (Thomas)
  served in: 8 Civil War **10** Mexican War
  side: 11 Confederate
  battle: 7 Bull Run **8** Antietam, Richmond **9** Seven Days **14** Fredericksburg **16** Chancellorsville, Shenandoah Valley

Jacksonville
  football team: 5 Bulls **7** Jaguars

Jacob
  father: 5 Isaac
  mother: 7 Rebekah
  brother: 4 Esau
  wives: 4 Leah **6** Rachel
  concubines: 5 Bilah **6** Zilpah
  son: 3 Dan, Gad **4** Levi **5** Asher, Judah **6** Joseph, Reuben, Simeon **7** Zebulun **8** Benjamin, Issachar, Naphtali
  daughter: 5 Dinah

dream of: 6 ladder
wrestled with: 5 angel
name changed to: 6 Israel
burial place: 9 Machpelah

Jacob, Francois
field: 7 biology
nationality: 6 French
discovered: 3 RNA
awarded: 10 Nobel Prize

jacuzzi 4 bath **9** whirlpool

jade
species: 7 jadeite **8** nephrite
source: 5 Burma, China **6** Mexico **7** Mogaung **10** New Zealand **12** United States

jaded 5 blase, bored, sated, spent, stale, tired, weary **6** cloyed, dulled, fagged **7** glutted, satiate, spoiled, wearied, worn-out **8** dog-tired, fatigued, overused, satiated, shopworn, tired out **9** exhausted, played out, surfeited **11** overwearied **12** overindulged

jadeite
variety: 4 jade

jagged 5 jaggy, rough, spiny **6** barbed, broken, craggy, nicked, ridged, rugged, snaggy, spiked, thorny, uneven, zigzag **7** angular, bristly, cragged, notched, pointed, spinous, studded **8** indented, serrated **9** irregular, knifelike **10** crenulated, saw-toothed **12** sharp-toothed

Jagger, Mick
born: 12 Dartford, Kent (UK)
musician for: 13 Rolling Stones
songs: 8 Star, Star, Lady Jane **9** Start Me Up **10** Brown Sugar, The Citadel, She's So Cold, Wild Horses **11** Ruby Tuesday **12** Paint It Black **13** Get Off My Cloud **14** Honky Tonk Woman **15** Jumpin' Jack Flash
body feature: 4 lips
wife: 6 Bianca
companion: 9 Jerri Hall

Jaggers, Mr
character in: 17 Great Expectations
author: 7 Dickens

jaguar 3 cat **5** tiger **6** feline **7** panther **8** uturuncu

jail 3 bag, can, jug, nab, pen **4** book, brig, bust, cell, keep, stir **5** clink, pinch, pound, run in, seize **6** arrest, collar, cooler, lockup, prison, take in **7** arraign, bring in, capture, confine, dungeon, slammer **8** bastille, big house, hoosegow, imprison, stockade **9** apprehend, black hole, calaboose, guardroom, workhouse **10** guardhouse **11** incarcerate, reformatory **12** halfway house, penitentiary, reform school, station house **13** hold in custody, police station **14** detention house **16** penal institution **17** house of correction

jailbird 3 con **5** felon, lifer **7** convict **8** prisoner

jailer 5 guard, screw **6** gaoler, keeper, warden **7** turnkey **9** custodian

Jair 11 Hebrew judge

Jakarta, Djakarta
capital of: 9 Indonesia

Jake's Thing
author: 12 Kingsley Amis

jalopy 3 car **4** auto, heap **5** motor **6** wheels **7** flivver, machine, vehicle **8** motorcar **9** tin lizzie **10** automobile

jam 3 fix, mob, ram, sea **4** army, cram, herd, host, mess, pack, push, stop **5** block, cease, crowd, crush, drove, flock, horde, pinch, press, shove, stall, stick, stuff, swarm, tie-up, wedge **6** arrest, edge in, pickle, plight, scrape, strait, throng, thrust, work in, worm in **7** congest, dilemma, foist in, force in, squeeze, suspend, trouble **8** hot water, obstruct, quandary, sandwich **9** interrupt, multitude, overcrowd **11** malfunction, predicament **13** agglomeration

Jamaica
name means: 18 land of wood and water
capital/largest city: 8 Kingston
others: 6 May Pen **8** Ocho Rios **9** Morant Bay, Port Maria, Port Royal **10** Mandeville, Montego Bay **11** Port Antonio, Spanish Town **12** Saint Ann's Bay, Savanna-la-Mar
head of state: 14 British monarch **15** governor general
monetary unit: 7 quattie
island: 4 Navy **15** Greater Antilles
mountain: 8 Sir John's
highest point: 4 Blue
river: 5 Black, Cobre, Great, Minho, White **9** Rio Grande
sea: 8 Atlantic **9** Caribbean
physical feature: 13 Portland Bight
area: 14 Cockpit Country
bay: 4 Buff, Hope, Long **6** Morant **9** Discovery **10** Black River, Bluefield's, Old Harbour
point: 6 Galina **8** Portland **9** North East, North West, South East **11** North Negril, South Negril
people: 7 African, Chinese **10** East Indian
ancient: 6 Arawak **7** Ciboney
discoverer: 8 Columbus
leader: 5 Seaga **6** Garvey, Manley **10** Bustamente
language: 7 Creole **7** English
religion: 7 Baptist **8** Anglican **9** Methodist **11** Church of God, Rastafarian **13** Roman Catholic
place:
beach: 11 Doctor's Cave
botanical garden: 4 Hope
racetrack: 12 Caymanas Park
feature:
evil spirits: 7 duppies
guerrilla fighters: 7 Maroons
tree: 4 poui **5** cedar, ceiba, mahoe, saman **6** cassia, guango **7** logwood **8** mahogany **9** casuarina, poinciana **10** silkcotton **11** lignum vitae
witch doctor: 8 obeah man
food:
coffee: 12 Blue Mountain
drink: 3 rum **4** jake **8** tia maria
fruit: 5 guava, mango **6** pawpaw
spicy soup: 9 pepper pot

jamboree 2 do **4** bash, gala **5** party, revel, spree **6** fiesta, frolic **7** blowout, jubilee, shindig **8** carnival, carousal, festival **9** festivity **11** celebration
French: 4 fete **13** fete champetre

James 7 apostle
also called: 12 James the Less
father: 7 Zebedee **8** Alphaeus
brother: 4 John, Levi **5** Judas
disciple of: 5 Jesus
killed by: 12 Herod Agrippa
with John called: 13 sons of thunder

James, Henry
author of: 11 Daisy Miller, The American **13** The Bostonians, The Golden Bowl **14** Roderick Hudson, The Ambassadors **15** The Aspern Papers **16** Washington Square **17** The Turn of the Screw, The Wings of the Dove **18** The Portrait of a Lady **19** Princess Casamassima

James, P D
author of: 12 Cover Her Face **13** Innocent Blood **15** Unnatural Causes **17** Devices and Desires **21** Shroud for a Nightingale **22** Death of an Expert Witness
character: 13 Adam Dalgliesh

James the Less see **5** James

jammed 4 full **5** stuck **6** filled, loaded, massed, packed, rammed, wedged **7** blocked, crammed, crowded, crushed, pressed, stuffed **8** overfull, squeezed **10** obstructed, sandwiched **11** overcrowded

Janacek, Leos
born: 8 Hukvaldy **14** Czechoslovakia
composer of: 5 Mladi, Youth **6** Jenufa **9** In the Mist **10** Taras Bulba **13** Katya Kabanova **14** Glagolitic Mass **17** On an Overgrown Path **18** The Makropoulos Case **21** From the House of the Dead, The Cunning Little Vixen **24** The Diary of One Who Vanished, The Excursions of Mr Broucek

Jane
character in: 6 Tarzan
author: 9 Burroughs

Jane Eyre
author: 15 Charlotte Bronte
character: 5 Mason **7** Mrs Reed **10** Grace Poole, Mary Rivers, Mrs Fairfax **11** Adele Varens, Bertha Mason, Diana Rivers **12** Bessie Leaven, St John Rivers **13** Blanche Ingram **15** Edward Rochester
school: 6 Lowood
house: 10 Thornfield

director: 15 Robert Stevenson
cast: 11 Orson Welles **12** Joan Fontaine **14** Margaret O'Brien
jangle 3 din, jar **4** ring **5** annoy, chime, clang, clank, clash, crash, upset **6** jingle, racket, rattle **7** clangor, clatter, grate on **8** irritate **9** cacophony **11** reverberate **13** reverberation **14** tintinnabulate
janitor 5 super **6** porter **8** handyman **9** caretaker, custodian, janitress **11** cleaning man **12** cleaning lady **13** cleaning woman **14** maintenance man, superintendent
Janssen, David
　real name: 16 David Harold Meyer
　born: 9 Naponee NE
　roles: 6 Harry O **11** The Fugitive **14** Richard Diamond **15** Dr Richard Kimble
January
　event: 15 Inauguration Day (every 4 years)
　flower: 8 snowdrop **9** carnation
　French: 7 Janvier
　gem: 6 garnet
　German: 6 Januar
　holiday: 8 Epiphany (6) **11** New Year's Day (1) **12** Twelfth Night (5)
　Italian: 7 Gennaio
　number of days: 9 thirty-one
　origin of name: 5 Janus
　　Roman god of: 5 doors **8** doorways **10** beginnings
　place in year:
　　Gregorian: 5 first
　　Julian/Roman: 8 eleventh
　Spanish: 5 Enero
　Zodiac sign: 8 Aquarius **9** Capricorn
Janus
　origin: 5 Roman
　god of: 8 doorways **9** rising sun **10** beginnings, setting sun
Japan
　other name: 5 Nihon **6** Nippon
　name means: 18 Land of the Rising Sun
　capital/largest city: 3 Edo **5** Tokyo
　others: 4 Kobe, Naha **5** Kyoto, Osaka **6** Nagoya, Sendai **7** Fukuoka, Niigata, Sapporo **8** Kanazawa, Kawasaki, Nagasaki, Yokohama **9** Hiroshima, Kagoshima **10** Kitakyushu
　school: 4 Chuo, Keio **5** Hosei, Kyoto, Nihon, Tokyo **6** Sophia, Waseda **7** Fukuoka **8** Doshisha
　head of state: 7 emperor
　measure: 2 go **3** boo, cho, djo, fun, inc, ken, kin, kon, rin, shi, sho, sun, tan **4** hiro, isse, kati, koku, niyo, shoo **5** carat, catty, issho, ittan, momme, picul, shaku **6** kwamme **8** hiyak-kin **9** hiyak-hiro **11** komma-ichida, kujira-shaku
　monetary unit: 2 bu **3** mon, rin, rio, sen, shu, yen **4** cash, mibu, oban **5** koban, obang, tempo **6** cobang, ichebu, ichibu, itzebu, kobang **7** itze-boo, itziboo

weight: 2 mo **3** fun, kon, rin **4** kati, kwan **5** carat, catty, momme **8** hiyakkin
island: 3 Iki, Izu, Oki, Tsu **4** Oita, Sado, Yaku **5** Amami, Awaji, Bonin, Hondo, Kuril, Rebun, Sikok **6** Honshu, Kiushu, Kyushu, Loochu, Marcus, Riukiu, Tanega, Tyukyu **7** Cipango, Hachijo, Iwo Jima, Okinawa, Rishiri, Shikoko, Shikoku, Volcano **8** Hokkaido, Miyajima, Okigunto, Okushiri, Tsushima, Yakujima
lake: 4 Biwa, Suwa, Toya **6** Towada **8** Kutchawa, Shikotsu
mountain: 3 Uso, Zao **5** Asahi, Asama, Hondo, Yesso **6** Asosan, Enasan, Hiuchi, Kiusiu, Yariga **7** Hakusan, Kujusan, Tokachi **8** Fujiyama **9** Japan Alps
highest point: 4 Fuji **7** Fujisan
river: 4 Tone, Yalu **8** Ishikari, Tonegawa **11** Shinano- gawa
sea: 3 Suo **5** Japan **6** Inland **7** Amakusa, Okhotsk, Pacific **8** Tsushima
physical feature:
　bay: 3 Ise **4** Miku, Tosa, Yedo **5** Amori, Mutsu, Osaka, Otaru, Tokyo **6** Ariake, Atsumi, Sendai, Suruga, Toyama, Wakasa **7** Uchiura
　cape: 3 Iro, Oki, Oma, Toi **4** Daio, Esan, Jizo, Mela, Mino, Noma, Nomo, Sada, Sawa, Shio, Soya, Suzu **5** Erimo, Kyoga, Rurui **6** Todoga **7** Shiriya **8** Ashizuri, Shakotan **12** Muroto Nojima
　channel: 3 Kii **5** Bungo
　current: 5 Japan **7** Okhotsk **8** Kuro Shio
　divine wind: 8 kamikaze
　gulf: 6 Sagami
　plain: 4 Nobi **5** Kanto
　strait: 4 Soya **5** Korea, Osumi **6** Nemuro, Tanega, Tokara **7** Tsugaru **8** Tsushima **9** La Perouse
people: 3 Eta **6** Korean **8** Japanese, Okinawan **9** Buramkumin
　ancient: 4 Ainu **5** Jomon, Yayoi
　artist: 4 Okyo **5** Buson, Jocho, Korin, Taiga, Unkei **6** Buncho, Eitoku, Kenzan, Koetsu, Reisai, Sesshu, Sesson, Shubun **7** Baiitsu, Choshun, Foujita, Gyokudo, Hokusai, Josetsu, Sanraku, Sharaku, Sotatsu, Utamaro **8** Harunobu, Kiyonaga, Motonobu **9** Hiroshige, Mitsunobu
　author: 5 Basho **7** Abe Kobo **8** Mori Ogai **11** Ueda Akinari **12** Ihara Saikaku, Mishima Yukio, Sakyo Komatsu **13** Natsume Soseki, Zeami Motokiyo **14** Shimazaki Toson, Tsubouchi Shoyo **15** Motoori Norinaga, Murasaki Shikibu **16** Fujiwara Nokisaki, Kawabata Yasunari **17** Tanizaki Junichiro **19** Chikamatsu Monzaemon

dynasty: 5 Meiji, Taira **6** Yamato **8** Fujiwara, Minamoto
leader: 4 Hojo **5** Kammu, Meiji **6** Go-Toba, Ieyasu **7** Akihito, Go-Daigo **8** Hirohito, Nobunaga, Yoritomo **9** Hideyoshi, Yoshimasa **10** Tojo Hideki, Yoshimitsu **11** Hara Takashi, Ito Hirobumi **12** Tanaka Kakuei **13** Konoe Fumimaro, Shotoku Taishi **14** Yoshida Shigeru **15** Ashikaga Takauji **18** Matsukata Mayayoshi
legendary ruler: 5 Jimmu, Jingo **7** Izanagi
shogunate: 8 Ashikaga, Kamakura, Tokugawa
language: 8 Japanese
　alphabet/characters: 4 kana **5** kanji **8** hiragana, katakana
　dialect: 5 Kanto
religion: 6 Tendai **7** Shingon **8** Buddhism **9** Shintoism **12** Confucianism
place:
　castle: 4 Nijo
　hall: 5 Hoodo **7** Phoenix **12** Golden Buddha
　mausoleum: 4 Ojin **7** Nintoku
　palace: 7 Akasaka, Katsura
　shrine: 5 Heian **11** Itsukushima **16** Grand Shrine of Ise
　temple: 6 Kotoku **7** Byodoin, Horyuji, Ryoanji, Senso-ji, Todaiji **8** Enkakuji, Kenchoji, Kofukuji **9** Kinkakuji **13** Asakusa Kannon
feature:
　abacus: 7 soroban
　bed: 5 futon
　clothing: 6 kimono
　festival: 13 Cherry Blossom
　firm: 4 Sony **5** Honda **6** Mitsui, Nissan, Toyota, Yasuda **7** Iwasaki **8** Sumitomo **10** Mitsubishi
　flower arranging: 7 ikebana
　painting style: 4 kano, tosa **5** nanga, nisee, onnae, rarae, rimpa, shijo **6** chinso, otokoe, sesshu, ukiyoe **7** konpeki, nihonga, yamatoe
　paper folding art: 7 origami
　poem: 4 waka **5** haiku, tanka
　puppet theater: 7 bunraku
　rush floor covering: 6 tatami
　sport: 4 judo **6** karate **13** sumo wrestling
　statue: 8 Daibutsu **11** Great Buddha
　tea ceremony: 7 chanoyu
　theater: 2 no **3** noh **6** kabuki
　the way of the warrior/code of honor: 7 bushido
　tree: 6 bonsai
　wood block print: 6 ukiyoe
food:
　beverage: 4 sake **8** green tea
　dish: 5 sushi **7** sashimi, tempura **8** sukiyaki, teriyaki, yakitori
　noodle: 4 soba
Japanese

independent language of: 5 Japan **13** Ryukyu Islands

jape 4 gibe, joke **5** antic, caper, prank **7** mockery

Japheth
father: 4 Noah
brother: 3 Ham **4** Shem

Jaques
character in: 11 As You Like It
author: 11 Shakespeare

jar 3 din, jug, pot, urn **4** bong, bray, buzz, daze, faze, jolt, rock, stir, stun **5** blare, blast, brawl, clang, clank, crash, crock, flask, floor, quake, shake, shock, throw, upset **6** beaker, bottle, impact, jangle, jiggle, joggle, racket, rattle, vessel **7** agitate, astound, clangor, clatter, confuse, disturb, fluster, perturb, shake up, startle, stupefy, trouble, upheave, vibrate **8** befuddle, bewilder, bleating, canister, clashing, convulse, decanter, demijohn, disquiet, distract, unsettle **9** agitation, cacophony, container **10** concussion, discompose, disconcert, receptacle **11** discordance
Spanish: 4 olla

jargon 4 bosh, bull, bunk, cant **5** argot, fudge, hooey, idiom, lingo, prate, usage **6** babble, brogue, drivel, patois, pidgin, piffle **7** baloney, blabber, blather, dialect, fustian, hogwash, prattle, rubbish, twaddle **8** folderol, malarkey, nonsense, parlance, tommyrot, verbiage **9** gibberish, moonshine, poppycock, rigmarole **10** balderdash, flapdoodle, hocus-pocus, rigamarole, vernacular, vocabulary **11** abracadabra, jabberwocky, phraseology, shibboleths **12** gobbledygook, lingua franca **14** grandiloquence

Jarley, Mrs
character in: 19 The Old Curiosity Shop
author: 7 Dickens

Jarndyce, John
character in: 10 Bleak House
author: 7 Dickens

jarring 4 rude **5** harsh, rough **6** jangly **7** grating, jolting, rasping, shaking **8** clashing, grinding, jangling, rattling, strident **9** dissonant, wrenching **10** discordant **12** nerve- racking **13** nerve-wracking

Jarry, Alfred
author of: 7 King Ubu **11** Ubu in Chains **13** Ubu the Cuckold

jasmine 8 Jasminum
varieties: 4 blue, cape, rock, star **5** crape, night, royal **6** orange, yellow **7** Arabian, Chilean, Italian, Spanish **8** Carolina, cinnamon, Japanese, Paraguay, pinwheel, primrose, windmill **9** angel-wing **10** Catalonian, Madagascar **11** Confederate

Jason
leader of: 9 Argonauts

father: 5 Aeson
mother: 8 Alcimede, Polymede
half-brother: 6 Pelias
son: 5 Thoas **6** Euneus, Pheres **7** Medeius **8** Mermerus, Tisander **9** Alcimenes, Thessalus
daughter: 7 Eriopis
teacher: 6 Chiron **7** centaur, Cheiron
retrieved: 12 Golden Fleece
ship: 4 Argo
loved by: 5 Medea
loved: 6 Glauce

Jasper, John
character in: 22 The Mystery of Edwin Drood
author: 7 Dickens

jaundiced 5 blase, bored **6** bitter **7** cynical, envious, hostile, jealous **8** covetous, doubting, satiated **9** green-eyed, resentful, skeptical **10** embittered, suspicious **11** mistrustful

jaunt 4 spin, tour, trip **6** airing, flight, junket, outing, ramble, stroll **9** adventure, excursion, promenade, short trip **10** expedition

jaunty 4 airy, neat, trim **5** natty, perky **6** blithe, bouncy, breezy, dapper, lively, sporty, spruce **7** buoyant **8** carefree, debonair **9** sprightly, vivacious **12** lighthearted, high-stepping, high-spirited

Java
other name: 5 Djawa
capital/largest city: 7 Jakarta **8** Djakarta
others: 5 Bogor, Dessa **6** Kediri, Malang **7** Bandung, Batavia **8** Semarang, Surabaja, Surabaya **9** Surakarta **11** Djokjakarta **13** Pelabuhanratu
government: 17 island of Indonesia
measure: 3 kan **4** paal, rand **5** palen
weight: 4 amat, pond, tali **5** pound **6** soekel
island: 4 Bali **5** Sunda **6** Lombok, Madura
mountain: 4 Amat, Gede **5** Lawoe, Murjo, Prahu **6** Raoeng, Slamet **8** Soembing
highest point: 6 Semuru **7** Semeroe
river: 4 Solo **7** Brantas
sea: 4 Java **6** Indian **7** Pacific
physical feature:
plateau: 4 Ijen
strait: 5 Sunda
people: 5 Krama, Kromo **6** Kalang **8** Javanese, Madurese **9** Sundanese
dynasty: 7 Mataram **9** Majapahit, Srivijaya
language: 4 Kavi, Kawi **5** Malay **6** Sassak **8** Balinese, Madurese, Sudanese **16** Bahasa Indonesian
religion: 5 Hindu, Islam **7** animism **8** Buddhism
place:
temple: 6 Chandi, Thandi **9** Borobudur, Prambanan
feature:
cloth: 3 kat **5** batik, kapok

dance: 7 seri mpi
dancer: 6 bedoyo
fishing boat: 4 prau
ornamental dagger: 4 kris
puppet play: 6 wajang, wayang
food:
fruit: 6 durian, lomboy, nangca **7** gondang

javelin 4 dart **5** lance, shaft, spear **10** projectile

jaw 3 gab, rap **4** chat, chin, talk **7** jawbone, palaver **8** chitchat, converse, mandible **10** chew the fat, chew the rag **11** confabulate

Jaws
author: 13 Peter Benchley
director: 15 Steven Spielberg
cast: 10 Robert Shaw **11** Roy Scheider **12** Lorraine Gary **15** Richard Dreyfuss
score: 12 John Williams
Oscar for: 5 score

Jayhawker State
nickname of: 6 Kansas

jazz musician 8 Art Tatum **9** Bud Powell **10** Miles Davis **11** Lester Young **12** Benny Goodman, John Coltrane **13** Charles Mingus, Charlie Parker, Duke Ellington, Thelonius Monk **14** Dizzy Gillespie, Louis Armstrong, Ornette Coleman, Wynton Marsalis

jealous 4 wary **7** anxious, envious, mindful **8** covetous, grudging, watchful **9** concerned, green-eyed, regardful, resentful **10** possessive, protective, suspicious **11** mistrustful, mistrusting **12** apprehensive

jealousy 4 envy **8** distrust, jaundice, mistrust **9** suspicion **10** resentment **12** covetousness **14** possessiveness **16** green-eyed monster
color: 5 green

Jebus
city captured by: 5 David
renamed: 9 Jerusalem
inhabitant: 8 Jebusite

jeer 3 boo, bug, dig, rap **4** barb, hiss, hoot, mock, razz, slam, slur **5** abuse, flout, hound, knock, scoff, scorn, sneer, taunt, whoop **6** deride, harass, heckle, hector, insult, revile **7** catcall, laugh at, mockery, obloquy **8** derision, ridicule, scoffing **9** aspersion, contumely, poke fun at, whistle at

Jeffers, Robinson
author of: 5 Medea, Tamar **6** Cawdor **8** Solstice **9** Dear Judas **12** Roan Stallion **14** Thurso's Landing **18** The Women at Point Sur **21** The Tower Beyond Tragedy

Jefferson, Thomas
nickname: 16 Sage of Monticello
presidential rank: 5 third
party: 20 Democratic-Republican
state represented: 2 VA
defeated: 5 (John) Adams **8** (Charles

Cotesworth) Pinckney
vice president: 4 (Aaron) Burr **7** (George) Clinton
cabinet:
  state: 7 (James) Madison
  treasury: 6 (Samuel) Dexter **8** (Albert) Gallatin
  war: 8 (Henry) Dearborn
  attorney general: 6 (Caesar Augustus) Rodney **7** (Levi) Lincoln **12** (John) Breckenridge
  navy: 5 (Robert) Smith
born: 2 VA **14** Shadwell estate **15** Goochland (Albemarle) County
died/buried: 10 Monticello
education: 14 William and Mary
interests: 6 violin **7** writing **11** agriculture **12** architecture
favorite foods: 10 French food **11** French wines
vacation: 12 Poplar Forest
author: 25 Declaration of Independence, Notes on the State of Virginia **39** A Summary View of the Rights of British America
political career: 8 governor **16** House of Burgesses **19** Virginia legislature **25** Declaration of Independence, Second Continental Congress
  secretary of: 5 state
  minister to: 6 France
civilian career: 6 farmer, lawyer
notable events of lifetime/term:
  expedition: 13 Lewis and Clark
  prohibition of: 19 importation of slaves
  purchase: 9 Louisiana
father: 5 Peter
mother: 4 Jane (Randolph)
siblings: 4 Jane, Lucy, Mary **6** Martha **8** Randolph **9** Anna Scott, Elizabeth **10** Peter Field
wife: 6 Martha (Wayles Skelton)
children: 4 Mary **6** Martha
Jeffersons, The
  character: 8 Florence **9** Tom Willis **11** Helen Willis **12** Harry Bentley **15** George Jefferson, Lionel Jefferson, Louise Jefferson, Ralph the Doorman **20** Jenny Willis Jefferson
  cast: 9 Mike Evans **10** Damon Evans, Marla Gibbs, Roxie Roker **11** Ned Wertimer **12** Paul Benedict **13** Franklin Cover, Isabel Sanford **14** Sherman Hemsley **15** Berlinda Tolbert
  George's business: 11 dry cleaning
  spinoff from: 14 All in the Family
Jeffreys, Harold
  field: 7 physics **9** astronomy
  nationality: 7 British
  explained: 7 weather
  studied: 10 Earth's core **11** solar system
Jeffries, James Jackson
  nickname: 14 The Boilermaker
  sport: 6 boxing
  class: 11 heavyweight

jehad, jihad 6 strife **7** holy war **8** struggle
Jehioada
  father: 7 Paseach
  son: 7 Benaiah
  means: 12 Jehovah knows
Jehoshaphat
  father: 3 Asa **6** Ahitub, Nimshi, Parnah
  mother: 8 Jehorani
  means: 13 Jehovah judges
Jehovah 3 god **4** YHWH **5** diety
Jehu
  father: 6 Hanani **11** Jehoshaphat **14** reckless driver
jejune 4 dull **5** banal, inane, stale, trite, vapid **7** humdrum, insipid, puerile **8** ordinary **9** hackneyed **10** pedestrian, unexciting, unoriginal, wishy-washy **11** commonplace **12** conventional **13** uninteresting
jell 3 gel, jam, set **4** clot, firm **5** jelly **7** congeal, thicken **9** coagulate **10** gelatinize
Jellyby, Mrs
  character in: 10 Bleak House
  author: 7 Dickens
jellyfish 5 hydra, polyp, softy **6** coward, medusa, nettle **7** sunfish **8** weakling **10** ctenophore, pantywaist **11** milquetoast, mollycoddle **12** coelenterate, invertebrate, siphonophore **18** Portuguese man-of-war
je ne sais quoi 13 I don't know what **18** indefinable quality
Jenner, Bruce
  sport: 13 track and field
  known for: 9 decathlon
  won: 8 Olympics
Jenner, Edward
  nationality: 7 British
  discovered: 11 vaccination **19** smallpox inoculation
Jenney, William Le Baron
  architect of: 21 Home Insurance Building (Chicago)
jeopardize 4 risk **6** expose, hazard **7** imperil **8** endanger **10** compromise **11** put into danger
jeopardy 4 risk **5** peril **6** danger, hazard **8** exposure, unsafety **9** liability **10** insecurity **11** imperilment **12** endangerment **13** vulnerability **14** precariousness
Jephthah 11 Hebrew judge
  father: 6 Gilead
Jeremiah
  father: 7 Hilkiah **10** Habazaniah
  daughter: 7 Mamutal
  grandson: 7 Jehohaz
  friend, scribe: 6 Baruch
jerk 3 ass, tic, tug **4** dope, dupe, fool, pull, snap, yank **5** dummy, dunce, idiot, klutz, pluck, shake, spasm, start, twist **6** quiver, reflex, thrust, twitch,

wrench **7** tremble **8** convulse **9** trembling
jerky 4 beef, meat **5** jolty, jumpy **6** choppy, elboic, jouncy **7** biltong, charqui, fidgety, twitchy **9** dried beef, spasmodic, twitching
Jeroboam
  father: 5 Joash, Nebat
  successor: 9 Zachariah
Jerry
  (British): 6 German
jerry-built 4 weak **5** frail, run-up, shaky, tacky **6** faulty, flimsy, shoddy, sleazy **7** rickety, unsound **8** gimcrack, slipshod, thrown-up, unstable **9** cheap-jack, defective **10** ramshackle **13** unsubstantial **14** thrown-together
jersey 3 cow **5** maillot, shirt **6** tricot **7** sweater **8** camisole, guernsey, pullover **10** undershirt
Jersey Joe
  nickname of: 10 Joe Walcott
Jerusalem
  author: 12 William Blake
Jerusalem
  former name: 5 Jebus
  pool of: 6 Siloam **8** Bethesda
Jerusalem
  Arabic: 14 Bayt al-Muqaddas
  capital of: 6 Israel
  Hebrew: 12 Yerushalayim
  hills: 7 Judaean
  landmark: 6 al-Aqsa **11** Wailing Wall, Western Wall **12** Israel Museum **13** Dome of the Rock **14** Dead Sea Scrolls **15** Shrine of the Book **17** Rockefeller Museum **24** Church of the Holy Sepulcher
  mount: 6 Olives, Scopus
  river: 6 Kidron
  ruler: 5 Arabs, David, Herod **6** Persia, Romans **7** British, Saladin, Seljuks, Solomon **8** Ayyubids, Fatimids, Ptolemy I **9** Crusaders, Maccabees, Mamelukes **10** Canaanites **12** Antiochus III **13** Pontius Pilate **15** Byzantine Empire **17** Alexander the Great, Antiochus the Third
  street: 11 Via Dolorosa
Jerusalem Delivered
  author: 13 Torquato Tasso
Jervis, Mrs
  character in: 6 Pamela
  author: 10 Richardson
jessamine 8 Jasminum
  varieties: 3 day **5** night, poet's **6** orange, yellow **12** willow-leaved **13** night-blooming **14** Carolina yellow
Jesse
  father: 4 Obed
  grandfather: 4 Boaz
  grandmother: 4 Ruth
  great-grandfather: 5 Rahab
  son: 5 David, Eliab **7** Shammah **8** Abinadab
jest 3 gag, pun **4** fool, game, gibe, jape, joke, josh, quip **5** act up, crack,

laugh, prank, tease, trick **6** banter, bon mot **9** wisecrack, witticism **10** crack jokes, pleasantry **11** horse around

jester 3 wag, wit **4** card, fool, mime, zany **5** clown, comic, joker, mimer, mimic **6** madcap, mummer **7** buffoon **8** comedian, funnyman, humorist, quipster **9** harlequin **10** motley fool **11** merry-andrew, pantomimist, punchinello

jesting 6 joking **7** teasing **8** sportive **9** bantering, unserious **12** wisecracking

Jesus
also called: 7 Holy One, Messiah **8** Nazarene, Son of God **9** the Christ **12** Man of Sorrows **13** Prince of Peace **14** Savior Anointed
mother: 4 Mary
stepfather: 6 Joseph
birthplace: 9 Bethlehem
lived in: 8 Nazareth
death place: 9 Jerusalem
buried by: 17 Joseph of Arimathea
disciples: 4 John, Jude **5** James, Peter, Simon **6** Andrew, Philip, Thomas **7** Matthew **12** James the Less **13** Judas Iscariot **20** Bartholomew Nathanael
secret follower: 9 Nicodemus
famous discourse: 16 Sermon on the Mount

jet 4 gush **5** flush, issue, shoot, spout, spray, spurt, surge, swash **6** effuse, nozzle, rush up, squirt, stream **7** sparger, sprayer, Spritze, syringe **8** atomizer, fountain, shoot out, Spritzer **9** discharge, sprinkler

Jethro
daughter: 8 Zipporah
son-in-law: 5 Moses

Jetsons, The
character: 5 Astro **10** Jane Jetson, Judy Jetson **11** Elroy Jetson **12** George Jetson **13** Cosmo G Spacely
voices: 8 Mel Blanc **10** Daws Butler, Don Messick, Janet Waldo **13** George O'Hanlon **14** Penny Singleton

jettison 4 dump **5** eject, scrap **6** unload **7** cast off, discard **8** throw out **9** discharge, eliminate, pitch over, throw over **13** toss overboard

jetty 4 dike, dock, mole, pier, quay, slip **5** black, ebony, groin, levee, raven, sable, wharf **6** bridge **7** sea wall **8** buttress **10** breakwater

jeu de mots 3 pun **11** play on words

jeu d'esprit 9 witticism **17** witty literary work
literally: 12 play of spirit

jeune fille 4 girl **9** young girl **13** unmarried girl

jeunesse doree 11 gilded youth, golden youth

Jew 6 Essene, Hebrew, Judean, Semite **7** Edomite, Judaist, Moabite **8** Hebraist, Sephardi **9** Israelite

jewel 3 ace, gem, pip **4** bead, dear, find, ring, whiz **5** honey, pearl, prize, stone, tiara **6** bangle, bauble, brooch, locket, winner **7** earring, pendant, trinket **8** bracelet, knockout, necklace, ornament, pure gold, treasure **9** humdinger, lavaliere **10** topnotcher **11** crackerjack, masterpiece

jewelry 4 gems, gold **6** silver **7** bangles, gewgaws, regalia **8** trinkets **10** adornments **14** precious stones

Jewett, Sarah Orne
author of: 26 The Country of the Pointed Firs

Jewish 6 Hebrew, Judaic **7** Hebraic, Semitic
bread: 5 matzo **6** matzoh **7** challah
candelabrum: 7 menorah
ceremonial robe: 5 kitel
color: 5 white
coming of age: 10 bar mitzvah, bat mitzvah
dietary laws: 7 kashrut **8** kashruth
fit to eat: 6 kosher
not fit to eat: 4 tref
group: 8 Hadassah **9** B'nai B'rith
holy day/festival: 5 Purim, seder **6** Sukkot **7** Shavuot **8** Chanukah, Hanukkah, Passover **9** Yom Kippur **12** Rosh Hashanah
law/scripture: 5 Torah **6** Gemara, Talmud, Tanach **7** Mishnah
liturgical prayer: 6 Yigdal **8** Kol Nidre
recited on eve of: 9 Yom Kippur
marriage canopy: 6 chupah
months:
1st: 6 Tishri
2nd: 7 Heshvan
3rd: 6 Kislev
4th: 5 Tevet
5th: 6 Shevat
6th: 4 Adar
7th: 5 Nisan
8th: 4 Iyar
9th: 5 Sivan
10th: 6 Tammuz
11th: 2 Av
12th: 4 Elul
prayerbook: 6 mahzor, siddur **7** machzor
quarter: 6 ghetto, mellah
school: 5 heder **6** cheder
skullcap: 5 kipah **8** yarmulka
service to commemorate the dead: 6 Yizkor
synagogue: 4 shul **5** schul
toast: 8 mazel tov

Jewkes, Mrs
character in: 6 Pamela
author: 10 Richardson

Jew of Malta, The
author: 18 Christopher Marlowe
character: 7 Abigail, Barabas **8** Ithamore **15** Governor of Malta

Jezebel
director: 12 William Wyler
cast: 10 Bette Davis, Fay Bainter,

Henry Fonda **11** Donald Crisp, George Brent **15** Margaret Lindsay
Oscar for: 7 actress (Davis) **17** supporting actress (Bainter)

Jezebel
father: 7 Ethbaal
husband: 8 King Ahab
daughter: 8 Athaliah
opposed: 6 Elijah
killed: 6 Naboth
father-in-law: 4 Omri

jib 3 arm, shy **4** balk, boom, sail, tack **5** demur, gigue, stick **6** recoil **7** scruple

jibe 2 go **3** fit **4** mesh, tack **5** agree, fit in, match, shift, tally **6** accord, concur, square **7** conform **8** coincide, dovetail **9** harmonize **10** correspond, go together **11** fit together

jiffy 3 sec **4** jiff **5** flash, shake, trice **6** minute, moment, second **7** half a mo, instant **9** twinkling **10** nanosecond **11** microsecond, millisecond, split second

jigger 4 dram, shot **5** glass **6** device, doodad, gadget, object **7** bicycle, gimmick, measure **9** doohickey, shot glass **10** boneshaker **11** contraption, thingumabob

jiggle 4 jerk **5** shake **6** bounce, fidget, joggle, jostle, twitch, wiggle **7** agitate, wriggle

jihad *see* **5** jehad

jilt 5 leave **6** betray, desert **7** forsake, let down **12** break off with **17** break an engagement

Jim
character in: 15 (The Adventures of) Huckleberry Finn
author: 5 Twain

jimmy 3 bar, pry **5** force, lever **7** crowbar

jingle 4 ring **5** clang, clank, clink, ditty **6** jangle, tinkle **7** clatter, ringing **8** doggerel, facetiae, limerick **10** catchy poem, catchy song **12** product theme **13** reverberation **14** commercial tune **16** tintinnabulation

Jingle, Alfred
character in: 14 Pickwick Papers
author: 7 Dickens

jingoism 10 chauvinism, flag-waving, patriotics **11** nationalism **14** overpatriotism, spread-eagleism **15** superpatriotism **16** ultranationalism

jinn 3 imp **5** afrit, demon, genie, jinni **6** afreet, spirit **8** jinniyeh

jinx 3 hex **5** curse **6** plague, whammy **7** bugaboo, bugbear, evil eye, ill wind, nemesis **9** evil spell
French: 9 bete noire

jitney 3 bus, cab

jitterbug 5 dance, lindy **8** lindy hop **12** boogie-woogie

jitters 6 shakes **7** anxiety, fidgets, jimjams, shivers, willies **9** jumpiness, quivering, shakiness, tenseness, the creeps, whim-whams **10** uneasiness **11** butterflies, fidgetiness, nervousness **12** skittishness **13** heebie- jeebies **16** screaming-meemies

jittery 5 jumpy **6** uneasy **7** anxious, nervous

Jivaro, Shuara, Jibaro
tribe: 6 Achual, Antipa **8** Aguaruna, Huambiza
location: 4 Peru **7** Ecuador **12** South America
noted for: 7 tsantsa (shrunken heads)

Joab
mother: 7 Zeruiah
brother: 6 Asahel **7** Abishai
commanded: 10 David's army
killed: 5 Abner, Amasa **7** Absalom
killed by: 7 Benaiah
conspired to overthrow: 5 David

Joad family
characters in: 16 The Grapes of Wrath
members: 2 Ma, Pa **3** Tom **4** Noah **6** Connie **12** Rose of Sharon
author: 9 Steinbeck

job 3 lot **4** care, duty, part, role, spot, task, work **5** chore, craft, field, place, quota, share, stint, trade, trust **6** affair, career, charge, errand, living, metier, office, output **7** calling, concern, mission, opening, portion, product, pursuit **8** activity, business, capacity, contract, exercise, function, position, province, vocation **9** allotment, piecework, situation **10** assignment, commission, engagement, enterprise, livelihood, occupation, profession **11** achievement, appointment, performance, undertaking **14** accomplishment, responsibility

Job 8 sufferer
father: 8 Issachar
friend: 5 Elihu **6** Bildad, Zophar **7** Eliphaz

job holder 6 worker **8** employee, hireling

job seeker 7 hopeful **8** aspirant **9** applicant, candidate

Jocasta
also: 8 Epicaste
queen of: 6 Thebes
father: 9 Menoeceus
brother: 5 Creon
husband: 5 Laius **7** Oedipus
son: 7 Oedipus **8** Eteocles **9** Polynices
daughter: 6 Ismene **8** Antigone
death by: 7 hanging, suicide

Jochebed
father: 4 Levi
husband: 5 Amram
nephew: 5 Amram
son: 5 Aaron, Moses

jockey 5 Baeza, Krone **6** Arcaro, Pincay **7** Cauthen, Cordero, Cruguet, Hartack **8** McCarron, McHargue, Turcotte **9** Shoemaker, Velasquez

jocose 3 fun **4** arch **5** comic, droll, funny, jolly, merry, witty **6** joking, jovial **7** amusing, comical, jesting, jocular, playful, roguish, teasing, waggish **8** humorous, mirthful, prankish, sportive **9** facetious

jocular 3 gay **5** droll, funny, jolly, merry, witty **6** jocose, jocund, joking, jovial **7** amusing, jesting, playful, roguish, rompish, waggish **8** humorous, mirthful, prankish, sportive **9** facetious **10** frolicsome **12** entertaining, lighthearted

jocund 5 jolly, merry **6** breezy, cheery, elated, jovial, lively **8** cheerful, debonair, pleasant **9** easygoing **10** untroubled **12** happy-go-lucky, lighthearted

Joel
means: 12 Jehovah is God
father: 4 Nebo **6** Samuel **7** Azariah, Pedaiah, Pethuel
brother: 6 Nathan

Joe Palooka
creator: 9 Ham Fisher **11** Tony DiPreta
character:
children: 3 Joe **5** Buddy **7** Joannie
friend: 9 Little Max **10** Jerry Leemy
manager: 11 Knobby Walsh
valet: 6 Smokey
wife: 8 Anne Howe
profession: 5 boxer

jog 3 bob, jar, tug **4** jerk, pull, rock, stir, trot, yank **5** nudge, shake, twist **6** bounce, jiggle, jostle, jounce, prompt, twitch, wrench **7** actuate, animate **8** activate, energize **9** stimulate

jogger 4 memo **6** layboy, runner **7** trotter **8** reminder **10** memorandum

Johannesburg
airport: 8 Jan Smuts
area: 4 Rand **9** Transvaal
capital of: 11 South Africa
landmark: 13 Carlton Centre **14** Africana Museum **16** Union Observatory **17** Zoological Gardens **20** Melrose Bird Sanctuary
township: 6 Soweto **7** Lenasia **10** Nancefield
university: 13 Rand Afrikaans, Witwatersrand

John
father: 7 Zebedee
brother: 5 James
son: 5 Peter
called, with brother: 9 Boanerges **13** sons of thunder
pertaining to John or his writings: 9 Johannine

John Barleycorn
personification of: 6 liquor **7** whiskey

John Brown's Body
author: 19 Stephen Vincent Benet

John Bull
personification of: 7 England **10** Englishman

John Gabriel Borkman
author: 11 Henrik Ibsen

John Mark *see* **4** Mark

Johnny Belinda
director: 13 Jean Negulesco
cast: 8 Lew Ayres **9** Jane Wyman **15** Charles Bickford
Oscar for: 7 actress (Wyman)

Johnny Cash Show, The
cast: 9 Jim Varney **10** Howard Mann **11** Carl Perkins, Steve Martin **14** June Carter Cash, Tennessee Three **15** Statler Brothers **32** Mother Maybelle and the Carter Family

Johnny-come-lately 8 newcomer **9** latecomer **10** new arrival **11** late arrival

Johnny U
nickname of: 12 Johnny Unitas

Johns, Glynis
born: 8 Pretoria **11** South Africa
roles: 11 Mary Poppins **13** The Sundowners **17** A Little Night Music **26** Around the World in Eighty Days

Johns, Jasper
born: 9 Augusta GA
artwork: 4 Flag **6** Studio, Target **8** Watchman **10** Fool's House **12** Device Circle **13** Painted Bronze (Beer Cans) **14** The Barber's Tree **19** Target with Four Faces **22** Target with Plaster Casts

Johnson, Andrew
presidential rank: 11 seventeenth
party: 8 Democrat
state represented: 2 TN
defeated: 5 no one
succeeded upon death of: 7 Lincoln
vice president: 4 none
cabinet:
state: 6 (William Henry) Seward
treasury: 9 (Hugh) McCulloch
war: 7 (Edwin McMasters) Stanton **9** (John McAllister) Schofield
attorney general: 5 (James) Speed **6** (William Maxwell) Evarts **8** (Henry) Stanbery
navy: 6 (Gideon) Welles
postmaster general: 7 (Alexander Williams) Randall **8** (William) Dennison
interior: 5 (John Palmer) Usher **6** (James) Harlan **8** (Orville Hickman) Browning
born: 9 Raleigh NC
died: 16 Carter's Station TN
buried: 13 Greeneville TN
education: 9 no college **12** self-educated
political career: 8 US Senate **13** vice president **22** House of Representatives
only president to be: 9 impeached (1868)
found: 9 not guilty
mayor of: 11 Greeneville (TN)

governor of: 9 Tennessee
civilian career: 6 tailor
military service: 8 Civil War **12** US Volunteers **16** brigadier general
   military governor of: 9 Tennessee
notable events of lifetime/term: 14 Reconstruction
   Purchase: 6 Alaska
father: 5 Jacob
mother: 4 Mary (McDonough)
   stepfather: 15 Turner Dougherty
sibling: 7 William
wife: 5 Eliza (McCardle)
children: 4 Mary **6** Andrew, Martha, Robert **7** Charles

Johnson, Don
born: 10 Flatt Creek (MO)
roles: 7 Melanie **8** Dead-Bang, Paradise **9** Miami Vice, Cease Fire **11** Guilty as Sin **16** In Pursuit of Honor, The Long Hot Summer
wife: 15 Melanie Griffith

Johnson, Earvin
nickname: 5 Magic
sport: 10 basketball
position: 5 guard
team: 16 Los Angeles Lakers

Johnson, Jack (John Arthur)
nickname: 11 Little Artha **14** Galveston Giant
sport: 6 boxing
class: 11 heavyweight

Johnson, Lyndon Baines
nickname: 3 LBJ **15** Landslide Lyndon
presidential rank: 11 thirty-sixth
party: 10 Democratic
state represented: 2 TX
succeeded upon death of: 7 Kennedy
defeated: 4 (Earle Harold) Munn, (Eric) Hass **6** (John) Kasper **7** (Clifton) DeBerry **9** (Barry Morris) Goldwater
vice president: 4 none (first term) **8** (Hubert Horatio) Humphrey
cabinet:
   state: 4 (David Dean) Rusk
   treasury: 4 (Joseph William) Barr **6** (Clarence Douglas) Dillon, (Henry Hamill) Fowler
   defense: 8 (Clark McAdams) Clifford, (Robert Strange) McNamara
   attorney general: 5 (William Ramsey) Clark **7** (Robert Francis) Kennedy **10** (Nicholas deBelleville) Katzenbach
   postmaster general: 6 (Lawrence Francis) O'Brien, (William Marvin) Watson **9** (John Austin) Gronouski
   interior: 5 (Stewart Lee) Udall
   agriculture: 7 (Orville Lothrop) Freeman
   commerce: 5 (Cyrus Rowlett) Smith **6** (John Thomas) Connor, (Luther Hartwell) Hodges **10** (Alexander Buel) Trowbridge
   labor: 5 (William Willard) Wirtz

   HEW: 5 (Wilbur Joseph) Cohen **7** (John William) Gardner **10** (Anthony Joseph) Celebrezze
   HUD: 4 (Robert Colwell) Wood **6** (Robert Clifton) Weaver
   transportation: 4 (Alan Stevenson) Boyd
born: 11 (near) Stonewall TX
died/buried: 13 (near) Johnson City TX
education:
   teachers' college: 19 Southwest Texas State
   law school: 10 Georgetown
religion: 17 Disciples of Christ
vacation spot: 8 LBJ Ranch
author: 15 The Vantage Point
political career: 8 US Senate **13** vice president **24** US House of Representatives
civilian career: 7 teacher
military service: 6 US Navy **10** World War II **11** World War Two
notable events of lifetime/term: 9 race riots **12** Great Society
   act: 11 Civil Rights **12** Voting Rights **19** Economic Opportunity
   assassination of: 14 Robert F Kennedy **18** Martin Luther King Jr
   capture of: 6 Pueblo
   Pueblo captured by: 10 North Korea
   treaty: 23 Nuclear Non-Proliferation
   war: 7 Vietnam **11** Arab-Israeli
father: 7 Sam Ealy
mother: 7 Rebekah (Baines)
siblings: 10 Sam Houston **12** Lucia Huffman **13** Josefa Hermine, Rebekah Luruth
wife: 7 Claudia (Alta Taylor)
   nickname: 8 Lady Bird
children: 9 Lynda Bird **10** Luci Baines
First Lady:
   responsible for: 24 Highway Beautification Act
   author: 16 A White House Diary

Johnson, Philip Cortelyou
architect of: 10 Glass House (New Canaan CT), Wiley House (New Canaan CT) **12** Hodgson House (New Canaan CT) **13** Pennzoil Place (Houston TX) **14** Bolssonas House (New Canaan CT) **16** Amon Carter Museum (Ft Worth TX) **17** Sheldon Art Gallery (Lincoln NE) **18** A T and T Headquarters (NYC), Kline Science Center (Yale) **19** New York State Theater (Lincoln Center)

Johnson, Samuel
author of: 8 Rasselas, The Idler **18** The Lives of the Poets **22** The Vanity of Human Wishes **30** Dictionary of the English Language

Johnson, Walter
nickname: 8 Big Train
sport: 8 baseball

position: 7 pitcher
team: 18 Washington Senators

John the Baptist
father: 9 Zechariah
mother: 9 Elizabeth
descendant of: 5 Aaron
precurser of: 5 Jesus **10** the Messiah

joie de vivre 11 joy of living **19** delight in being alive

join 3 hug, mix **4** abut, ally, band, bind, fuse, glue, link, meet, pool **5** affix, brush, chain, enter, graze, marry, merge, paste, reach, skirt, stick, touch, unify, unite **6** adjoin, attach, bridge, cement, cohere, couple, fasten, scrape, solder, splice **7** combine, connect, verge on **8** border on, enlist in, enroll in, federate, hold fast **9** associate, cooperate, syndicate **10** amalgamate, fraternize **11** confederate, consolidate **12** conglomerate

joined 3 met, wed **4** tied **5** bound, fused, glued, mated, yoked **6** allied, bonded, linked, merged, paired, seamed, united, welded **7** coupled, married, related, spliced **8** attached, cemented, combined, enlisted, fastened **9** bracketed, connected **10** associated, hand-in- hand, integrated **11** hand-in-glove

join forces 4 ally **5** merge, unite **6** league, team up **7** combine **8** coalesce **9** affiliate, cooperate **11** consolidate **12** band together

joint 4 hock, knee, knot, link **5** elbow, hinge, nexus **6** allied, common, mutual, shared, united **7** knuckle, unified **8** combined, communal, coupling, junction, juncture **9** associate, community, conjoined, corporate, unanimous **10** associated, collective, connection, hand-in- hand, like-minded **11** coalitional, conjunctive, cooperative **12** articulation, consolidated **13** collaborative
kind:
   ball and socket: 3 hip **8** shoulder
   fused: 5 skull **11** base of spine
   hinged: 4 knee **5** elbow
   unfused: 3 hip, jaw **4** knee **5** elbow **8** shoulder

joint action 7 concert **8** teamwork **11** cooperating, cooperation, give-and-take **13** collaboration, participation

joint effort 7 concert **8** teamwork **11** cooperation **13** collaboration

jointly 8 arm in arm, in common, in unison, mutually, together, unitedly **10** conjointly, hand-in-hand, side by side **12** collectively **13** in association, in conjunction

join together 3 wed **4** fuse, weld **5** marry, unify, unite **6** solder **9** integrate **10** amalgamate **11** consolidate, incorporate

join up 6 enlist, enroll, sign up **9** volunteer

joist 4 beam 5 brace 6 timber 7 support

joke 3 gag, pun, wit 4 butt, dupe, fool, gibe, goof, gull, jape, jest, josh, lark, mock, quip 5 antic, caper, cinch, clown, farce, prank, put-on, roast, tease, trick 6 banter, bon mot, deride, frolic, gambol, gibe at, jeer at, parody, satire, take in, target, trifle, whimsy 7 buffoon, bumpkin, chortle, lampoon, laugh at, nothing, scoff at, smile at, snicker 8 anecdote, badinage, pooh-pooh, pushover, repartee, ridicule, town fool, travesty 9 burlesque, diversion, horseplay, simpleton, wisecrack, witticism 10 pleasantry 11 horse around, monkeyshine 13 facetiousness, laughingstock

joker 3 wag, wit 4 snag, trap, zany 5 catch, clown, hitch, mimic, rider, snare, trick 6 jester, madcap 7 codicil, pitfall, punster 8 addendum, comedian, funnyman, humorist 10 subterfuge, supplement 11 wisecracker French: 7 farceur

jokester 3 wag 5 comic, cutup, joker 8 comedian 9 prankster

Joliba *see* 5 Niger

Joliot-Curie, Frederic
  field: 9 chemistry
  nationality: 6 French
  discovered: 23 artificial radioisotopes
  awarded: 10 Nobel Prize
  wife: 16 Irene Joliot-Curie

Joliot-Curie, Irene
  field: 7 physics
  nationality: 6 French
  discovered: 23 artificial radioisotopes
  awarded: 10 Nobel Prize
  husband: 14 Frederic Joliot
  father: 11 Pierre Curie
  mother: 10 Marie Curie

jollity 3 fun 4 glee, play, romp 5 cheer, mirth, revel, sport 6 frolic, gaiety 7 revelry, whoopee 8 hilarity 9 amusement, festivity, jocundity, joviality, merriment, pleasure 10 jocularity 11 merrymaking 12 conviviality

jolly 3 gay 5 droll, funny, happy, merry 6 jocund, jovial 7 gleeful, jocular, playful 8 cheerful, mirthful, sportive 9 fun-loving 10 delightful, rollicking 12 high-spirited

Jolly Roger 11 pirate's flag 18 skull and crossbones

jolt 3 bob, jar, jog 4 bump, jerk, jump, stun 5 lurch, quake, shake, shock, start, throw, upset 6 bobble, bounce, jiggle, joggle, jostle, jounce, quiver, trauma, twitch 7 disturb, perturb, setback, shake up, shaking, startle 8 convulse, reversal 9 agitation, take aback 11 thunderbolt

Joltin' Joe
  nickname of: 11 Joe DiMaggio

Jonah
  father: 7 Amittai

swallowed by: 9 large fish
  preached in: 7 Nineveh
  hometown: 10 Gathhepher

Jonathan
  means: 11 Jehovah gave
  father: 4 Jada, Saul 6 Joiada, Kereah 8 Abiathar
  friend: 5 David
  son: 9 Meribkaal 12 Mephibosheth

Jonathan Livingston Seagull
  author: 11 Richard Bach

Jonathan Wild
  author: 13 Henry Fielding

Jones, Carolyn
  born: 10 Amarillo TX
  roles: 8 Morticia 15 The Addams Family

Jones, Inigo
  architect of: 11 Queen's House (Greenwich) 14 Banqueting Hall (Whitehall Palace, London)
  restoration: 16 St Paul's Cathedral

Jones, James
  author of: 7 Whistle 14 The Thin Red Line 15 Some Came Running 18 From Here to Eternity

Jones, James Earl
  born: 11 Arkabutla MS
  roles: 6 The Man 7 Othello 8 Star Wars 15 The Emperor Jones 17 The Great White Hope
  voice of: 10 Darth Vader

Jones, John Paul
  served in: 11 Russian navy 16 Revolutionary War 21 British merchant marine
  commander of ship: 6 Ranger 10 Providence 15 Bonhomme Richard
  defeated ship: 7 Serapis
  saying: 23 "I have not yet begun to fight"

Jones, Shirley
  husband: 11 Jack Cassidy, Marty Ingels
  born: 10 Smithton PA
  roles: 8 Carousel, Oklahoma 11 Elmer Gantry, The Music Man 18 The Partridge Family

Jones, Tom
  born: 5 Wales 10 Pontypridd
  songs: 7 Delilah 9 She's a Lady 11 Thunderball 13 Love Me Tonight 15 Letter to Lucille 16 What's New Pussycat 21 Green Green Grass of Home

Jong, Erica
  author of: 5 Fanny 12 Fear of Flying 18 At the Edge of the Body 20 How to Save Your Own Life

jonquil 4 bulb, lily 8 daffodil 9 narcissus

Jonson, Ben
  author of: 6 The Fox 7 Sejanus, Volpone 11 A Tale of a Tub 12 The Alchemist 15 Bartholomew Fair 18 Every Man in His Humo(u)r 21

Every Man out of His Humo(u)r 23 Epicene or the Silent Woman

Jordan
  other name: 24 Hashemite Kingdom of Jordan
  capital/largest city: 5 Amman
    ancient name: 12 Philadelphia
  others: 4 Krak, Ma'an, Salt 5 Aqaba, Ariha, Irbid, Jenin, Karak, Kerak, Sarga, Zarga, Zerke 6 Bethel, Hebron, Jarash, Jerash, Madaba, Nablus, Ramtha 7 Al-Aqaba, Bethany, El-Kerak, El Zerga, Jericho, Kirmoab, Nabulus, Samaria 8 Al-Khalil, Ram Allah 9 Bethlehem, Jerusalem
  school: 7 yarmouk
  division: 8 East Bank, West Bank 11 Transjordan
  ancient state: 4 Edom, Moab 5 Ammon, Judah 6 Gilead
  head of state: 11 King Hussein
    wife: 4 Noor (nee Lisa Walaby)
  monetary unit: 4 fils 5 dinar
  mountain: 3 Hor 4 Nebo 5 Bukka, Dabab 6 Ataiba, Gilead, Mubrak
  highest point: 9 Jabal Ramm, Jebel Ramm
  river: 6 Jordan, Yarmuk 11 Nahr-az-Zarga
  sea: 3 Red 4 Dead 7 Galilee 13 Mediterranean
  physical feature:
    desert: 6 Syria
    gulf: 5 Aqaba
    plateau: 11 Transjordan
    valley: 4 Ghor 9 Great Rift
    wind: 7 Khamsin
  people: 4 Arab, Kurd 7 Bedouin, Checher 8 Armenian, Assyrian 10 Circassian 11 Palestinian
    ancient: 8 Armonite 9 Nabataean
    ruler: 5 Talal 6 Faisal, Greeks, Romans 7 Hussein 8 Abdullah, Selucidas 9 Crusaders 10 Ibn Hussein, Nabataeans 12 Ottoman Turks 18 Abdullah Ibn Hussein
    tribe: 5 Qaysi 6 Yamani
  language: 6 Arabic
  religion: 5 Islam 13 Greek Orthodox
  place:
    canal: 8 East Gher
    ruins: 5 Ajlun, Petra 6 Jarash 7 Al Karak
  feature:
    headdress: 8 kaffiyeh
    village headman: 7 mukhtar
    village square: 5 sahah
  food:
    dessert: 7 baklava
    pastry: 7 katayif

Jordan, Robert
  character in: 19 For Whom the Bell Tolls
  author: 9 Hemingway

Jormungandr
  also: 10 Jormungand 11 Iormungandr 14 Midgard Serpent
  origin: 12 Scandinavian

form: 7 serpent
father: 4 Loki
mother: 9 Angerboda, Angrbodha, Angurboda
brother: 6 Fenrir, Fenris
sister: 3 Hel
wrapped around: 5 world
killed by: 4 Thor
death place: 6 Vigrid
killed: 4 Thor

Jo's Boys
author: 15 Louisa May Alcott
sequel to: 11 Little Women

Joseph
father: 4 Bani **5** Aseph, Jacob **10** Mattathias
mother: 6 Rachel
brother: 3 Dan, Gad **4** Levi **5** Asher, Judah **6** Reuben, Simeon **7** Zebulun **8** Benjamin, Issachar, Naphtali
wife: 4 Mary **7** Asenath
stepson: 5 Jesus
also called: 20 Barsabbas of Arimathea **21** Barsabbas of Arimathaea
buried: 5 Jesus
slave of: 8 Potiphar

Joseph Andrews
author: 13 Henry Fielding
character: 5 Fanny **9** Lady Booby **11** Mrs Slipslop, Parson Adams, Peter Pounce **13** Pamela Andrews

josh 3 guy, kid, rag, rib **4** dish, haze, jape, jest, jive, joke, quiz, razz, ride, twit **5** chaff, jolly, put on, roast, tease **6** banter, needle **8** ridicule

Joshua
means: 18 Jehovah is salvation
father: 3 Nun
succeeded: 5 Moses
captured: 7 Jericho, Lachish
hid spies: 5 Rahab

jostle 3 jab **4** bump, butt, poke, prod, push **5** crowd, elbow, shove **7** collide **8** shoulder **10** hit against, run against **12** knock against

jot 3 bit, dot **4** iota, list, mite, note, snip, whit **5** enter, speck, trace **6** record, trifle **7** modicum, one iota, put down, set down, smidgen, snippet **8** flyspeck, particle, register, scribble, take down **9** scintilla

Jo the crossing sweeper
character in: 10 Bleak House
author: 7 Dickens

jotting 4 memo, note **6** doodle **8** scribble **10** memorandum, scribbling

Jotun
origin: 12 Scandinavian
form: 5 giant
conflicts with: 4 gods
enemy: 4 Asar **5** Aesir

Joule, James Prescott
field: 7 physics
nationality: 7 British
established law of: 20 conservation of energy
named for him: 10 unit of work

jounce 3 bob **6** bounce **7** rebound **8** ricochet

Jourdain, Monsieur
character in: 21 The Bourgeois Gentleman **22** Le Bourgeois Gentilhomme
author: 7 Moliere

Jourdan, Louis
real name: 11 Louis Gendre
born: 6 France **9** Marseille
roles: 4 Gigi **6** Can Can **9** Octopussy **15** The Paradine Case **23** Three Coins in the Fountain **24** Letter from an Unknown Woman

journal 3 log **5** album, daily, diary, paper, sheet **6** annual, ledger, memoir, record, weekly **7** almanac, daybook, gazette, history, logbook, monthly, tabloid **8** calendar, magazine, notebook, register, yearbook **9** chronicle, newspaper, quarterly, scrapbook **10** chronology, confession, memorandum, memory book, periodical, record book **11** account book, daily record, publication **13** autobiography

journalism 15 the fourth estate

journalist 6 author, editor, writer **7** byliner, diarist, newsman **8** reporter **9** columnist, newswoman **12** newspaperman **13** correspondent **14** newspaperwoman

Journal of the Plague Year, A
author: 11 Daniel Defoe

journey 3 fly, way **4** roam, rove, sail, tour, trek, trip, wend **5** jaunt, quest, route, tramp **6** course, cruise, flight, junket, outing, ramble, roving, travel, voyage, wander **7** circuit, meander, odyssey, passage, transit **8** divagate, navigate, sightsee, vagabond **9** excursion, itinerary, take a trip, wandering **10** divagation, expedition, pilgrimage **11** peregrinate **13** peregrination

Journey Into Fear
author: 10 Eric Ambler

journey's end 4 goal **9** objective **11** destination

joust 4 tilt **5** combat, jostle **7** contend, contest, tourney **8** run a tilt **10** contention, tournament

Jove see **7** Jupiter

jovial 3 gay **5** jolly, merry, sunny **6** blithe, cheery, hearty, jocose, jocund **7** buoyant, gleeful, jocular, playful, zestful **8** cheerful, humorous, laughing, mirthful, sportive **9** convivial, fun-loving, hilarious **10** delightful, frolicsome, rollicking

joviality 3 fun **4** glee **5** cheer, gaity, mirth **7** delight, jollity, revelry **8** buoyancy **9** jocundity, merriment **10** joyfulness, liveliness **11** high spirits

jowl 3 jaw **5** cheek, chops **6** muzzle **8** mandible

joy 3 gem **4** glee **5** jewel, pride, prize **6** gaiety **7** delight, ecstasy, elation, rapture **8** gladness, pleasure, treasure **9** enjoyment, happiness **10** excitement, exultation, jubilation **11** contentment, delectation **12** cheerfulness, exhilaration, satisfaction
goddess of: 6 Hathor

Joyce, James
author of: 7 Ulysses **9** Dubliners **13** Finnegans Wake **31** A Portrait of the Artist as a Young Man

joyful 4 glad, rosy **5** happy **6** bright, elated **7** blessed, pleased **8** cheerful, ecstatic, exultant, gladsome, jubilant, pleasing **9** delighted, full of joy, overjoyed **10** delightful, enraptured, gratifying, heartening **11** pleasurable, transported **12** heartwarming

joyless 3 sad **4** glum, grim **5** black **6** dismal, gloomy, morbid, woeful **7** doleful, forlorn, unhappy **8** dejected, desolate, dolorous, downcast, mournful **9** cheerless, depressed, sorrowful, woebegone **10** despondent, in the dumps, lugubrious, melancholy **11** downhearted, pessimistic **12** disconsolate, heavyhearted **14** down in the mouth

joy of living
French: 11 joie de vivre

Joy of Sex, The
author: 11 Alex Comfort

joyous 3 gay **4** glad **5** happy, merry **7** festive, gleeful **8** cheerful, gladsome, mirthful **9** rapturous, wonderful **10** delightful, gratifying, heartening **11** pleasurable **12** heartwarming, lighthearted

joyousness 4 glee **8** gladness **9** happiness, merriment **10** blitheness, exuberance **11** high spirits **16** lightheartedness

jubilant 3 gay **4** glad **5** happy, jolly, merry **6** blithe, cheery, elated, enrapt, joyful, joyous **7** buoyant, charmed, gleeful, pleased, radiant, smiling **8** cheerful, ecstatic, exultant, gladsome, laughing, mirthful **9** delighted, delirious, exuberant, gladdened, gratified, overjoyed, rapturous, rejoicing, rhapsodic **10** blithesome, captivated, enraptured **11** exhilarated, intoxicated, tickled pink **12** happy as a lark, lighthearted **13** in high spirits

jubilation 5 bliss **9** rejoicing **11** celebration **12** exhilaration

jubilee 2 do **4** bash, fete, gala **5** blast, party **6** frolic, revels **7** blowout, holiday, revelry, shindig **8** festival, winging **9** festivity **10** jubilation, observance **11** anniversary, celebration, merrymaking **12** conviviality **13** commemoration

Judah
father: 5 Jacob
mother: 4 Leah
brother: 3 Dan, Gad **4** Levi **5** Asher, Judah **6** Joseph, Reuben, Simeon **8**

Benjamin, Issachar, Naphtali
sister: 5 Dinah
wife: 5 Shuah
son: 2 Er **4** Onan **5** Perez, Zerah **6** Baruch, Shelah
daughter-in-law: 5 Tamar
last king of: 8 Zedekiah
descendant of: 8 Judahite

udah, tribes of *see* **14** Israel, tribes of

udas
brother: 5 James
also called: 8 Thaddeus
disciple of: 5 Jesus

udas Iscariot 8 betrayer
disciple of: 5 Jesus
betrayed: 5 Jesus
replaced by: 8 Matthias

ude 7 apostle
brother: 5 James

ude the Obscure
author: 11 Thomas Hardy
character: 10 Jude Fawley **12** Arabella Donn, Sue Bridehead **14** Drusilla Fawley **16** Little Father Time **17** Richard Phillotson

udge 3 try **4** deem, find, hear, rank, rate **5** fancy, gauge, guess, infer, juror, value, weigh **6** assess, assume, censor, critic, decide, deduce, expert, reckon, regard, review, rule on, settle, size up, umpire **7** adjudge, analyze, arbiter, believe, conduct, discern, imagine, justice, referee, resolve, suppose, surmise **8** appraise, assessor, conclude, consider, estimate, official, reviewer **9** appraiser, arbitrate, ascertain, authority, determine, evaluator, moderator **10** adjudicate, arbitrator, conjecture, magistrate **11** adjudicator, connoisseur, distinguish **12** pass sentence

udgment, judgement 4 view **5** sense, taste **6** acumen, belief, decree, ruling **7** finding, opinion, verdict **8** decision, estimate, sentence **9** appraisal, deduction, valuation **10** assessment, conclusion, conviction, discretion, perception, persuasion, shrewdness **11** arbitration, discernment, percipience **14** discrimination, perceptiveness

udgment at Nuremberg
director: 13 Stanley Kramer
cast: 11 Judy Garland **12** Spencer Tracy **13** Burt Lancaster **14** Richard Widmark, William Shatner **15** Marlene Dietrich, Montgomery Clift **16** Maximilian Schell (Oscar)

udgment Day 8 doomsday **13** end of the world **14** day of reckoning **15** the Last Judgment

udgment Day
author: 13 James T Farrell

udgment of Paris *see* **5** Paris

udicial 5 legal **8** imposing, juristic,

majestic, official **9** magistral **11** magisterial **13** distinguished

judiciary 5 bench, court **11** court system

judicious 4 just, sage, wise **5** acute, sober, sound **6** astute, shrewd **7** knowing, politic, prudent, tactful **8** sensible **9** sagacious **10** diplomatic, discerning, percipient, reasonable, reflective, thoughtful **11** levelheaded **13** perspicacious **14** discriminating

judiciousness 4 tact **6** acumen, wisdom **8** prudence, sagacity **9** good sense **10** discretion **11** discernment, percipience **12** perspicacity **14** discrimination

Judique, Mrs Tanis
character in: 7 Babbitt
author: 5 Lewis

Judith
husband: 4 Esau
killed: 10 Holofernes

Judith Paris
author: 11 Hugh Walpole

jug 3 jar, urn **4** ewer **5** crock, stein **6** bottle, carafe, flagon, vessel **7** pitcher, tankard **8** decanter, demijohn **9** container

juggle 4 redo **5** alter **6** modify **7** falsify **8** disguise, fool with **9** keep aloft **10** manipulate, meddle with, reorganize, tamper with, tinker with **12** misrepresent

juggler 5 cheat **6** jester **8** conjuror, deceiver, jongleur, magician, shuffler **15** prestidigitator

Juice
nickname of: 9 O J Simpson

juicy 3 wet **4** lush, racy **5** fluid, lurid, moist, pulpy, runny, sappy, spicy, vivid **6** fluent, liquid, risque, watery **7** flowing, graphic **8** colorful, dripping, exciting, luscious **9** succulent, thrilling **10** intriguing **11** captivating, fascinating, picturesque, provocative, sensational, tantalizing

Jules and Jim
director: 16 Francois Truffaut
cast: 10 Henri Serre **11** Marie Dubois, Oskar Werner **12** Jeanne Moreau

Julia
character in: 20 Two Gentlemen of Verona
author: 11 Shakespeare

Julia
character: 10 Corey Baker, Eddie Edson, Julia Baker **11** Hannah Yarby **14** Earl J Waggedorn, Marie Waggedorn **15** Dr Morton Chegley
cast: 10 Lloyd Nolan, Marc Copage **11** Betty Beaird, Michael Link **12** Eddie Quillan, Lurene Tuttle, Paul Winfield **14** Diahann Carroll

Julia
director: 13 Fred Zinnemann
based on story by: 14 Lillian

Hellman (Pentimento)
cast: 9 Jane Fonda (Lillian Hellman) **11** Hal Holbrook **12** Jason Robards (Dashiell Hammett) **15** Vanessa Redgrave (Julia) **16** Maximilian Schell
Oscar for: 12 screenwriter **15** supporting actor (Robards) **17** supporting actress (Redgrave)

Julius Caesar
author: 18 William Shakespeare
character: 6 Brutus (Marcus Brutus), Portia **7** Cassius (Gaius Cassius) **9** Calpurnia **10** Mark Antony (Marcus Antonius)
director: 17 Joseph L Mankiewicz
cast: 10 James Mason **11** Deborah Kerr, Greer Garson, John Gielgud **12** Edmond O'Brien, Louis Calhern, Marlon Brando

July
flower: 8 larkspur **9** water lily
French: 7 Juillet
holiday: 11 Bastille Day (14), Dominion Day (1) **15** Independence Day (4) **16** Saint Swithin's Day (15)
gem: 4 ruby
German: 4 Juli
Italian: 6 Luglio
number of days: 9 thirty-one
origin of name: 12 Julius Caesar
place in year:
Gregorian: 7 seventh
Roman: 5 fifth
Spanish: 5 Julio
Zodiac sign: 3 Leo **6** Cancer

jumble 3 mix **4** heap, mess, olio, stew **5** bunch, chaos, mix up, pitch, snarl **6** ball up, medley, muddle, pile up, tangle, tumble **7** clutter, farrago, melange, mixture, scatter **8** disarray, mishmash **9** aggregate, confusion, patchwork, potpourri **10** hodgepodge, miscellany, salmagundi **11** gallimaufry **12** accumulation **14** conglomeration

jumbled 5 messy **7** chaotic, mixed up, snarled, tangled **8** confused **9** cluttered, illogical **10** disjointed, incoherent **11** disarranged **12** disconnected, disorganized

jumbo 4 huge, vast **5** giant **6** mighty **7** immense, mammoth, titanic **8** colossal, enormous, gigantic, towering **9** cyclopean, monstrous, oversized **10** monumental, stupendous **11** elephantine, mountainous

jump 3 hop **4** buck, leap, pass, skip **5** boost, bound, pitch, start, surge, vault, wince **6** ambush, attack, blench, bounce, flinch, gambol, go over, hurdle, prance, recoil, spring, switch, upturn, zoom up **7** advance, barrier, digress, maunder, overrun, upsurge **8** fall upon, obstacle **9** barricade, increment, skyrocket **10** impediment **11** obstruction **12** augmentation

jumper 4 frog, sled, toad **5** dress, horse, shirt, smock **6** blouse, hopper, jacket, leaper **7** overall **8** coverall, kangaroo

jump for joy 5 exult **7** rejoice

jumpy 5 nervy, shaky **6** goosey, uneasy **7** alarmed, anxious, fidgety, fretful, jittery, nervous, panicky, twitchy, uptight **8** aflutter, agitated, fluttery, skittish **9** trembling, twitching **10** frightened **12** apprehensive

junction 6 linkup **7** conflux, joining **10** confluence, crossroads **11** concurrence, convergence, interchange **12** intersection

juncture 4 pass, seam **5** joint **6** crisis, linkup, moment **7** closure, joining, meeting **8** interval, occasion **10** confluence, connection **11** convergence, point in time **12** intersection **13** critical point

June
  characteristic: 8 weddings
  event: 12 Midsummer Day (24), Midsummer Eve (23) **14** summer solstice (21)
  flower: 4 rose
  French: 4 Juin
  gem: 5 pearl **9** moonstone **11** alexandrite
  German: 4 Juni
  holiday: 7 Flag Day (14) **10** Father's Day (third Sunday) **13** Kamehameha Day (11) **22** Jefferson Davis' birthday (3)
  Italian: 6 Giugno
  number of days: 6 thirty
  origin of name: 4 Juno (Roman goddess) **6** Junius (Roman clan) **8** juniores (youths)
  place in year:
    Gregorian: 5 sixth
    Roman: 6 fourth
  saying: 24 What is so rare as a day in June
  Spanish: 5 Junio
  Zodiac sign: 6 Cancer, Gemini

jungle 4 bush, wild **5** woods **10** rain forest, wilderness **11** undergrowth **12** swampy forest, virgin forest

Jungle, The
  author: 13 Upton Sinclair
  character: 3 Ona **5** Jonas **6** Marija **8** Elzbieta **12** Jurgis Rudkus **13** Antanas Rudkus
  criticism of: 19 meat-packing industry

Jungle Books, The
  author: 14 Rudyard Kipling
  character: 3 Kaa **5** Akela, Baloo, Hathi **6** Buldeo, Messau, Mowgli **8** Bagheera **9** Shere Khan **11** Gray Brother

Jungle Jim
  creator: 11 Alex Raymond
  character: 4 Joan, Kolu

junior 5 later, lower, minor, newer **6** lesser **7** younger **8** inferior **9** secondary **11** subordinate

juniper 9 Juniperus

varieties: 4 ashe, plum **5** Greek, Irish, shore **6** common, ground, needle, Polish, Sierra, Syrian **7** African, incense, prickly, Sargent **8** creeping, drooping, mountain, red-berry, Waukegan **9** alligator, blue-spire, Himalayan, prostrate **10** California **11** cherrystone **12** Canary Island, sweetfruited **13** Rocky Mountain

junk 4 dump **5** scrap, trash, waste **6** debris, litter, refuse **7** clutter, discard, garbage, rubbish, rummage **8** castoffs, oddments, throw out **9** dispose of, throw away **11** odds and ends

junket 4 tour, trip **7** journey **9** excursion

Juno
  origin: 5 Roman
  queen of: 6 heaven
  father: 6 Saturn
  brother: 7 Jupiter
  husband: 7 Jupiter
  son: 4 Mars
  protectress of: 5 women **8** marriage
  epithet: 6 Lucina, Moneta **7** Curitis, Pronuba, Sospita
  festival: 10 Matronalia
  corresponds to: 4 Hera, Here

Juno and the Paycock
  author: 10 Sean O'Casey

junta 5 cabal **7** council **9** committee **18** military government

Jupe, Sissy
  character in: 9 Hard Times
  author: 7 Dickens

Jupiter
  also: 4 Jove
  god of: 5 light **7** heavens, weather **9** lightning **11** thunderbolt
  epithet: 5 Ultor **7** Elicius, Pluvius
  corresponds to: 4 Zeus

Jupiter
  position: 5 fifth
  satellite: 2 Io **6** Europa **8** Amalthea, Callisto, Ganymede
  characteristic: 7 red spot

Jura 11 Swiss canton **13** mountain range

Jurassic period
  dinosaur from: 10 Diplodocus **11** Apatosaurus, Stegosaurus **12** Brontosaurus, Camarasaurus, Camptosaurus, Ceratosaurus, Megalosaurus **13** Brachiosaurus, Compsognathus, Ornitholestes

Jurgen
  author: 17 James Branch Cabell

Jurgens, Curt
  also: 11 Curd Jurgens
  born: 6 Munich **7** Germany
  roles: 12 The Blue Angel **16** The Spy Who Loved Me

jurisdiction 3 say **4** area, beat, rule, sway, zone **5** field, range, reach, scope **6** bounds, domain, sphere **7** circuit, command, compass, control, quarter **8** district, dominion, hegem-

ony, latitude, precinct, province **9** authority, bailiwick **10** legal right **11** prerogative

jurist 5 judge **6** lawyer **7** counsel, justice **8** advocate, attorney **9** barrister, counselor, solicitor **10** magistrate **12** legal adviser **13** attorney-at-law

jury 5 panel, peers **6** assize, twelve **9** committee, makeshift, veniremen

jury-rigged 9 improvised, makeshift, temporary

jus 3 law **5** right

jus civile 8 civil law

jus gentium 12 law of nations

jus naturale 11 law of nature

jus sanguinis 12 right of blood (law) citizenship of child is same as: **7** parents

jus soli 11 right of land, right of soil (law) citizenship of child based on place of: **5** birth

just 3 but, due **4** fair, firm, good, only, sane **5** fully, moral, quite, solid, sound **6** at most, barely, decent, hardly, honest, lately, merely, proper, simply, strong, worthy **7** condign, ethical, exactly, fitting, logical, merited, only now, upright **8** adequate, balanced, deserved, entirely, narrowly, recently, scarcely, sensible, suitable, unbiased **9** befitting, blameless, equitable, honorable, impartial, justified, objective, perfectly, precisely, reputable, righteous, unbigoted, uncorrupt **10** aboveboard, absolutely, acceptable, completely, evenhanded, fair-minded, high-minded, no more than, nothing but, not long ago, principled, reasonable, scrupulous, upstanding **11** appropriate, justifiable, trustworthy, well-founded **12** conscionable, open to reason, unprejudiced, well-grounded **13** conscientious, disinterested, dispassionate

just about 6 almost, around, barely, nearly **7** close to **10** not far from **12** on the point of **13** approximately

Just Above My Head
  author: 12 James Baldwin

just a moment ago
  French: 11 tout a l'heure

justice 5 honor, right, truth **6** amends, equity, the law, virtue **7** honesty, payment, penalty, probity, redress **8** fair play, fairness, goodness, legality **9** atonement, integrity, rightness **10** correction, lawfulness, legitimacy, reparation **11** just desserts, proper cause, uprightness **12** chastisement, compensation, equitability, remuneration, satisfaction **13** due punishment, equitableness, justification, righteousness **17** constitutionality
  god of: 7 Forsete, Forseti
  goddess of: 4 Dice, Dike **6** Astrea **7** Astraea

Justice
  author: **14** John Galsworthy
Justice Clement
  character in: **19** Every Man in His
    Humour
  author: **6** Jonson
justice to all
  Latin: **15** justitia omnibus
  motto of: **18** District of Columbia
justifiable 9 excusable **10** defensible
  11 explanatory, extenuating, support
  able
justification 5 alibi **6** excuse **7** apology, defense, pretext, support **8** sanction **10** accounting, adjustment, validation **11** explanation, vindication **12**
  confirmation **13** rectification **14** reconciliation

justification for existence
  French: **11** raison d'etre
justify 6 back up, defend, excuse, uphold **7** bear out, confirm, explain,
  support, sustain, warrant **8** sanction,
  validate **9** vindicate **10** account for,
  prove right
justitia omnibus 12 justice to all
  motto of: **18** District of Columbia
just now
  French: **11** tout a l'heure
just the same 6 anyhow, anyway **12**
  nevertheless
just the thing 7 apropos **8** suitable
  11 appropriate **12** exactly right
Justus *see* **5** Titus
jut 5 bulge **6** beetle, extend **7** poke out,
  project **8** overhang, protrude, shoot

out, stand out, stick out **13** thrust
forward
jute 19 Corchorus capsularis
  varieties: **5** Bimli, China, Tossa,
    white **7** bastard **10** Bimlipatum
juvenile 5 child, minor, young, youth
  6 boyish, callow, infant, junior **7** girlish **8** childish, immature, teenager,
  youthful **9** childlike, pubescent, stripling, youngster **10** adolescent, sophomoric **15** unsophisticated
juxtaposed 6 next to **8** adjacent,
  touching **9** proximate **10** contiguous,
  side by side **12** conterminous
juxtaposition 5 touch **7** balance, contact **8** contrast, nearness **9** adjacency,
  proximity **10** apposition, contiguity

K
   character in: 9 The Castle
   author: 5 Kafka
Ka
   origin: 8 Egyptian
   form: 6 spirit
   trait: 11 immortality
kabob 5 cabab, cobob, kabab, kebab, kebob **7** shaslik **8** shashlik **9** shashlick
Kabul
   capital of: 11 Afghanistan
Kafka, Franz
   author of: 7 Amerika **8** The Trial **9** The Castle **16** The Metamorphosis
kahlua
   type: 6 brandy
   origin: 6 Mexico
   flavor: 6 coffee
   with rum: 10 Black Maria
   with tequila: 9 Brave Bull
   with vodka: 12 Black Russian
Kahn, Albert
   architect of: 15 River Rouge Plant **17** Highland Park Plant **20** Athletic Club Building (Detroit) **21** General Motors Building (Detroit)
Kahn, Louis Isadore
   architect of: 16 Kimbell Art Museum (Ft Worth TX) **23** Yale Center for British Art **24** Yale University Art Gallery **28** Phillips Exeter Academy Library (NH) **31** Richards Medical Research Building (U of PA) **33** Salk Institute for Biological Studies (La Jolla CA)
Kahn, Madeline
   born: 8 Boston MA
   roles: 5 Cosby **9** Paper Moon **10** What's Up Doc? **14** Blazing Saddles **17** Young Frankenstein
kaiser 5 ruler **7** emperor, Wilhelm **8** autocrat
kakemono 6 scroll **13** hanging object
kale 16 Brassica oleracea (Acephala Group)
   varieties: 3 sea **4** Ruvo, tall, tree **6** Indian, Scotch **7** cabbage, Chinese, Italian, kitchen **8** Siberian **9** flowering, Tronchuda **10** decorative, ornamental, Portuguese **13** dwarf Siberian **16** ornamental-leaved
kaleidoscopic 6 mobile, motley **7** protean **8** shifting, unstable, variable **9** checkered **10** changeable, variegated

11 fluctuating, many colored, rainbowlike, vacillating **12** ever-changing
Kaleva 8 folk hero
   origin: 7 Finnish **8** Estonian
Kali
   also: 3 Uma **5** Durga **7** Parvati
   husband: 4 Siva **5** Shiva
   festival: 6 dewali
   goddess of: 5 death **7** disease
Kalimantan see **6** Borneo
Kalki
   author: 9 Gore Vidal
Kampala
   capital of: 6 Uganda
Kampuchea see **8** Cambodia
Kandinsky, Wassily (Vasily)
   born: 6 Moscow, Russia
   artwork: 7 Striped **8** Twilight **10** Black Lines **11** Impressions **12** Blue Mountain (no 84), Compositions, Violet Orange **13** Black Relation **14** Improvisations **15** Capricious Forms **17** Bavarian Mountains, The Street in Murnau **23** Painting with White Border
Kanga
   character in: 13 Winnie the Pooh
   author: 5 Milne
   child: 3 Roo
kangaroo
   young: 4 joey
   group of: 3 mob **5** troop
Kaniengehaga see **6** Mohawk
Kansas
   abbreviation: 2 KS **4** Kans
   nickname: 5 Wheat **9** Jayhawker, Sunflower **15** Garden of the West
   capital: 6 Topeka
   largest city: 7 Wichita
   others: 4 Hays, Iola **5** Colby, Dodge **6** Salina **7** Abilene, Chanute, Emporia, Liberal **8** Atchison, Lawrence **9** Great Bend **10** Belleville, Hutchinson, Kansas City **11** Coffeeville, Leavenworth **12** Junction City
   college: 5 Baker, Tabor **7** Bethany **8** Sterling, Washburn
   explorer: 8 Coronado
   feature: 16 Eisenhower Center
     fort: 5 Riley, Scott
     Indian training school: 16 Haskell Institute
     penitentiary: 11 Leavenworth
     reservoir: 11 Tuttle Creek
   tribe: 3 Kaw **4** Pani **5** Kansa, Kiowa,

Osage **6** Pawnee **7** Arapaho, Wichita **8** Cheyenne, Comanche, Kickapoo
   people: 7 Jayhawk **11** Damon Runyon **13** Amelia Earhart, Karl Menninger **14** Walter Chrysler **15** Edgar Lee Masters
   lake: 6 Cheney, Kerwin, Neosho **7** Milford
   land rank: 10 fourteenth
   mountain:
     highest point: 9 Sunflower
   physical feature:
     plains: 5 Great, Osage
   president: 17 Dwight D Eisenhower
   river: 3 Kaw **6** Kansas **8** Arkansas, Cimarron, Missouri **9** Smoky Hill **10** Republican
   state admission: 12 thirty-fourth
   state bird: 17 western meadowlark
   state flower: 9 sunflower
   state motto: 29 To the Stars Through Difficulties
   state song: 14 Home on the Range
   state tree: 10 cottonwood
Kansas City
   baseball team: 6 Royals
   football team: 6 Chiefs
   landmark: 12 Union Station **22** Nelson-Atkins Art Gallery
   river: 6 Kansas **8** Missouri
Kant, Immanuel
   author of: 20 Critique of Pure Reason
Kantor, MacKinlay
   author of: 13 Andersonville
Karloff, Boris
   real name: 17 William Henry Pratt
   born: 7 Dulwich, England
   roles: 12 Frankenstein
karma 3 act **4** aura, deed, duty, fate, rite **5** force, power **6** action, kismet, spirit **7** destiny **9** vibration
Kasdan, Lawrence
   director of: 11 The Big Chill
Kashmiri
   language family: 12 Indo-European
   branch: 11 Indo-Iranian
   group: 5 Indic
   spoken in: 5 (northern) India
kashruth, kashrut 7 fitness **17** Jewish dietary laws
Katharina
   character in: 19 The Taming of the Shrew
   author: 11 Shakespeare
Katmandu, Kathmandu
   capital of: 5 Nepal

Katzenjammer Kids
also: 17 Captain and the Kids
creator: 12 Rudolph Dirks
character: 4 Hans 5 Fritz, Momma 10 der Captain 12 der Inspector

Kaufman, George S
author of:
with Edna Ferber: 9 Stage Door 13 Dinner at Eight 14 The Royal Family
with Moss Hart: 15 Once in a Lifetime 20 You Can't Take It with You 21 The Man Who Came to Dinner

Kay (Sir Kay)
character in: 16 Arthurian romance
foster brother: 6 Arthur

Kaye, Danny
real name: 19 David Daniel Kaminski
born: 10 Brooklyn NY
wife: 10 Sylvia Fine
roles: 14 The Court Jester 19 The Inspector General 21 Hans Christian Andersen 26 The Secret Life of Walter Mitty

Kaye, M M
author of: 9 Trade Wind 12 Death in Kenya 15 Death in Zanzibar, Shadow of the Moon, The Far Pavilions

Kazakhstan
capital/largest city: 7 Alma-Ata
others: 9 Karaganda 13 Petropavlovsk, Semipalatinsk
head of state: 9 president
government: 8 republic
monetary unit: 5 ruble
sea: 4 Aral 7 Caspian
physical feature: 7 steppes 12 Lake Balkhash
people: 6 Kazakh
language: 6 Kazakh

Kazan, Elia
director of: 10 East of Eden, Viva Zapata 15 On the Waterfront (Oscar) 18 Splendor in the Grass 19 Gentleman's Agreement (Oscar) 20 A Tree Grows in Brooklyn 21 A Streetcar Named Desire

Kazantzakis, Nikos
author of: 13 Zorba the Greek 14 Freedom or Death, The Greek Passion 25 The Last Temptation of Christ

kazoo 5 bazoo, zarah 6 hewgag 11 eunuch flute
French: 8 mirliton

Keach, Stacy
real name: 18 Walter Stacy Keach Jr
born: 10 Savannah GA
brother: 5 James
roles: 3 Doc 6 Luther 10 Mike Hammer 24 Twinkle Twinkle Killer Kane

Kearny, Stephen Watts
served in: 10 California, Mexican War
commander of: 13 Army of the West

occupied: 9 New Mexico
battle: 10 San Gabriel, San Pasqual

Keaton, Buster
real name: 19 Joseph Francis Keaton
born: 7 Piqua KS
roles: 6 Go West 7 College 10 The General 12 The Cameraman

Keaton, Diane
real name: 9 Diane Hall
born: 12 Los Angeles CA
roles: 4 Reds 7 Sleeper 8 Baby Boom 9 Annie Hall (Oscar) 12 Shoot the Moon, The Godfather 13 The Good Mother 14 Play It Again Sam 19 Looking for Mr Goodbar 20 The Little Drummer Girl

Keats, John
author of: 5 Lamia 8 Endymion, Hyperion, Isabella 11 Ode to Autumn, Ode to Psyche 14 Ode on Indolence 15 Ode on Melancholy, The Eve of St Agnes 16 Ode on a Grecian Urn 17 Ode to a Nightingale 20 La Belle Dame Sans Merci 31 On First Looking into Chapman's Homer

Kedemah
also called: 5 Kedar
father: 7 Ishmael
mother: 5 Hagar
descendant of: 8 Kedarite

Keel (of Argo)
constellation of: 6 Carina

Keel, Howard
real name: 17 Harry Clifford Leek
costar: 14 Kathryn Grayson
born: 11 Gillespie IL
roles: 6 Dallas, Kismet 8 Show Boat 10 Kiss Me Kate 13 Clayton Farlow 15 Annie Get Your Gun 27 Seven Brides for Seven Brothers

Keeler, Ruby
husband: 8 Al Jolson
costar: 10 Dick Powell
born: 6 Canada 7 Halifax
roles: 15 Footlight Parade 17 Forty-Second Street 32 Gold Diggers of Nineteen Thirty Three

keel over 5 faint, swoon, upset 7 capsize, tip over 8 collapse, fall down, fall flat, flip over, overturn, turn over 10 turn turtle

keen 4 avid, fine 5 acute, alert, eager, sharp 6 ardent, astute, clever, fervid, fierce, shrewd 7 earnest, excited, fervent, intense, zealous 8 incisive 9 impatient, paper thin, razorlike 10 discerning 11 finely honed, impassioned, penetrating, quick-witted 12 enthusiastic 13 perspicacious 14 discriminating

Keene, Carolyn
created: 18 Nancy Drew mysteries
father 17 Edward Stratemeyer

keen-eyed 5 alert 8 vigilant, watchful 9 attentive, eagle- eyed, observant, sharp-eyed, wide-awake

keen-minded 5 acute, sharp, smart 6

astute, clever, shrewd 10 perceptive 11 penetrating

keenness 4 zeal, zest 5 ardor 6 acumen, fervor 7 passion 9 acuteness, eagerness, sharpness 10 astuteness, cleverness, enthusiasm, excitement, shrewdness 11 discernment 12 anticipation, intelligence, perspicacity

keen-sighted 4 sage, wise 5 acute, sharp 6 astute, shrewd 8 piercing 9 eagle-eyed, judicious, sagacious, sharp-eyed 10 discerning 11 intelligent, penetrating 12 clear-sighted, sharp-sighted 13 perspicacious

keep 3 bar 4 clog, fort, have, heap, hold, mind, pile, stay 5 abide, block, carry, cramp, delay, deter, guard, honor, lay in, place, stack, stall, stand, stick, stock, store, tie up, tower 6 arrest, castle, detain, donjon, endure, hamper, hinder, hobble, hold up, impede, living, pay for, remain, retain, retard 7 care for, carry on, citadel, deposit, furnish, inhibit, observe, possess, prevent, shackle, support, sustain 8 conserve, continue, encumber, fortress, hang on to, hold back, maintain, obstruct, preserve, restrain 9 celebrate, constrain, hamstring, persevere, persist in, ritualize, safeguard, solemnize, watch over 10 accumulate, daily bread, livelihood, provide for, stronghold, sustenance 11 commemorate, maintenance, memorialize, subsistence 12 room and board 13 fortification

keep an eye on 5 watch 7 oversee 9 chaperone, look after, watch over

keep apart 7 isolate 8 separate 9 segregate

keep at bay 7 beat off, fend off, ward off 8 stave off

keep back 5 check, delay 6 detain, hold up, retain 8 withhold

keep busy 3 use 6 employ, engage, occupy 7 utilize

keep clear of 4 shun 5 avoid, dodge, elude, evade, skirt 6 escape

keep company 4 date 6 court 7 consort, hang out 8 go around, go steady 9 accompany, associate 10 fraternize, go together

keeper 5 guard, nurse 6 duenna, escort, jailer, sentry, warden 7 curator 8 chaperon, guardian, retainer, sentinel, wet nurse 9 attendant, bodyguard, caretaker, chaperone, custodian, governess, nursemaid, protecter, protector 11 conservator, nurserymaid 13 guardian angel

keep in mind 8 consider, remember 10 think about

keep mum 13 button one's lip

keep off 7 fend off, stay off, ward off 8 stave off

keep one's counsel 12 remain silent **13** button one's lip

keep open 8 hold open **16** leave unscheduled

keep out 6 reject **8** prohibit **9** blackball, blacklist

keep out of sight 4 hide **5** cover **6** lay low, lie low **7** conceal, cover up, secrete **10** camouflage

keep private 4 hide **7** conceal, reserve **8** withhold

keepsake 5 relic, token **6** emblem, memory, symbol **7** memento **8** memorial, reminder, souvenir **11** remembrance **18** token of remembrance

keep secret 4 hide **6** hush up **7** conceal, cover up **8** suppress, withhold

keep silent 10 remain dumb **15** not breathe a word

keep steady 5 poise **7** balance **9** stabilize

keep to 5 cling, stick **6** adhere, be true, cleave, hold to **7** be loyal, stand by **8** maintain

keg 3 tub, tun, vat **4** butt, cask, drum, tank **6** barrel **7** rundlet **8** hogshead, puncheon **9** container, kilderkin

Keller, Helen
born: **4** deaf **5** blind
teacher: **12** Anne Sullivan
play and film: **16** The Miracle Worker
author: **13** William Gibson
actors: **9** Patty Duke **12** Anne Bancroft
both won: **6** Oscars

Kellerman, Sally
born: **11** Long Beach CA
roles: **4** MASH **15** Hot Lips Houlihan

Kelly, Gene
real name: **17** Eugene Curran Kelly
born: **12** Pittsburgh PA
roles: **7** Pal Joey **9** Brigadoon, On the Town **13** Anchors Aweigh **15** Singin' in the Rain **17** An American in Paris **18** The Three Musketeers

Kelly, Grace
husband: **21** Prince Rainier Grimaldi
nickname: **11** Ice Princess
born: **14** Philadelphia PA
princess of: **6** Monaco
roles: **7** Mogambo **8** High Noon **10** Rear Window **11** High Society **13** To Catch a Thief **14** Dial M for Murder, The Country Girl (Oscar)

Kelly, Walt
creator/artist of: **4** Pogo

kelp 3 ash **4** agar, alga, leag **5** varec, varic, wrack **7** seaweed
source of: **4** soda **6** iodine **9** potassium

Kelpie
origin: **8** Scottish
form: **5** horse **6** spirit
habitat: **4** lake **5** river

causes: **8** drowning
warns of: **8** drowning

Kelvin
abbreviation: **1** K

Kelvin, William Thomson
field: **7** physics **11** mathematics
nationality: **7** British
worked on: **4** heat **11** electricity
invented: **12** electrometer, galvanometer **13** tide predictor
named for him: **22** Kelvin temperature scale

Kempis, Thomas a
author of: **20** The Imitation of Christ

Keneally, Thomas
author of: **12** Confederates **14** Schindler's List

Kenilworth
author: **14** Sir Walter Scott
character: **6** Alasco, Dudley (Earl of Leicester) **10** Amy Robsart **12** Wayland Smith **13** Richard Varney **14** Queen Elizabeth **15** Flibbertigibbet **16** Edmund Tressilian

Kennedy, Arthur
real name: **17** John Arthur Kennedy
born: **11** Worcester MA
roles: **6** Becket **9** All My Sons **11** Peyton Place **12** Blind Victory **16** Death of a Salesman

Kennedy, Frank
character in: **15** Gone With the Wind
author: **8** Mitchell

Kennedy, John Fitzgerald
nickname: **3** JFK **4** Jack
presidential rank: **11** thirty-fifth
party: **10** Democratic
state represented: **2** MA
defeated: **5** (Richard Milhous) Nixon
vice president: **7** (Lyndon Baines) Johnson
cabinet:
  state: **4** (David Dean) Rusk
  treasury: **6** (Clarence Douglas) Dillon
  defense: **8** (Robert Strange) McNamara
  attorney general: **7** (Robert Francis) Kennedy
  postmaster general: **3** (James Edward) Day **9** (John Austin) Gronouski
  interior: **5** (Stewart Lee) Udall
  agriculture: **7** (Orville Lothrop) Freeman
  commerce: **6** (Luther Hartwell) Hodges
  labor: **5** (William Willard) Wirtz **8** (Arthur J) Goldberg
  HEW: **8** (Abraham Alexander) Ribicoff **10** (Anthony Joseph) Celebrezze
born: **11** Brookline MA
died: **8** Dallas TX
  died by: **13** assassination
  assassinated by: **6** (Lee Harvey) Oswald

buried: **25** Arlington National Cemetery
education:
  prep school: **6** Choate
  University: **7** Harvard **9** Princeton **23** London School of Economics
religion: **13** Roman Catholic
interests: **7** sailing **8** football **13** touch football
vacation spot: **9** Cape Cod MA **13** Hyannis Port MA
author: **15** Strategy of Peace, Why England Slept **17** Profiles in Courage (Pulitzer Prize)
political career: **9** US Senator **24** US House of Representatives
civilian career: **17** newspaper reporter
military service: **6** US Navy **10** lieutenant **11** World War Two
  commander of: **6** PT boat
notable events of lifetime/term: **9** Bay of Pigs **10** Berlin Wall, Peace Corps **18** Cuban missile crisis
  march: **11** Civil Rights
  treaty: **14** Nuclear Test-Ban
  quote: **17** Ich bin ein Berliner (I am a Berliner) **35** We stand today on the edge of a New Frontier **61** Ask not what your country can do for you ask what you can do for your country
father: **13** Joseph Patrick
mother: **4** Rose (Fitzgerald)
siblings: **4** Jean **6** Eunice, Joseph **8** Kathleen, Patricia, Rosemary **11** Edward Moore **13** Robert Francis
wife: **10** Jacqueline (Lee Bouvier)
  nickname: **6** Jackie
  second marriage to: **7** Onassis
children: **14** John Fitzgerald (John-John, JFK Jr.), Patrick Bouvier (died in infancy) **15** Caroline Bouvier

Kennicott, Dr Will and Carol
characters in: **10** Main Street
author: **5** Lewis

Kentucky
abbreviation: **2** KY
nickname: **9** Bluegrass **11** Corncracker
capital: **9** Frankfort
largest city: **10** Louisville
others: **5** Berea **6** Corbin, Hazard **7** Ashland, Glasgow, Newport, Paducah, Shively **8** Danville **9** Covington, Henderson, Lexington, Owensboro **12** Bowling Green, Hopkinsville, Madisonville
college: **5** Berea **6** Centre **7** Ashbury, Brescia **8** Ursuline **12** Transylvania
explorer: **11** Daniel Boone
feature: **7** Obelisk
  birthplace: **14** Abraham Lincoln
  fort: **4** Knox
  national park: **11** Mammoth Cave
  race: **13** Kentucky Derby
  racetrack: **14** Churchill Downs
  trail: **10** Wilderness
tribe: **7** Shawnee **8** Cherokee,

Iroquois
people: 11 corncracker, John M Harlan **13** Louis Brandeis **16** Frederick M Vinson, Robert Penn Warren
lake: 8 Kentucky **10** Cumberland
land rank: 13 thirty-seventh
mountain: 4 Pine **10** Cumberland
  highest point: 5 Black **8** Big Black
physical feature:
  basin: 9 Bluegrass
  cave: 7 Mammoth
  gap: 10 Cumberland
  plain: 7 Coastal
  plateau: 10 Cumberland
president: 14 Abraham Lincoln
  Confederate president: 14 Jefferson Davis
river: 3 Dix **4** Ohio, Salt **5** Green **6** Barren **7** Licking **8** Big Sandy, Kentucky **9** Tennessee **10** Cumberland **11** Mississippi
state admission: 9 fifteenth
state bird: 8 cardinal
state flower: 9 goldenrod
state motto: 26 United We Stand Divided We Fall
state song: 17 My Old Kentucky Home
state tree: 10 coffee tree **11** tulip poplar **12** yellow poplar

Kenya
capital/largest city: 7 Nairobi
others: 5 Nyeri, Thika, Wajir **6** Kisumu, Kitale, Lodwar, Moyale, Nakuru, Webuye **7** Eldoret, Kericho, Malindi, Mandera, Mombasa, Nanyuki **9** Lokitaung
measure: 4 wari
monetary unit: 4 cent **5** pound **8** shilling
island: 5 Manda, Patta
lake: 6 Magadi, Nakuru, Natron, Rudolf **7** Turkana **8** Naivasha, Victoria
mountain: 5 Elgon, Kulai, Nyira, Nyiru **6** Matian **7** Logonot **8** Aberdare
  highest point: 5 Kenya **6** Kinyaa **9** Kirinyaga
river: 3 Lak **4** Athi, Dawa, Kuja, Tana **5** Nzoia **6** Galana **8** Turkwell
sea: 6 Indian
physical feature:
  bay: 7 Formosa
  desert: 6 Chalbi
  escarpment: 3 Mau
  gulf: 9 Kavirondo
  highlands: 5 Kenya, Kisii, Luyla **7** Kericho
  plain: 4 Kano
  plateau: 5 Nandi, Yatta **6** Elgeyo
  valley: 9 Great Rift
people: 3 Luo **4** Arab, Meru **5** Bantu, Elgey, Galla, Kamba, Kisii, Luhya, Masai, Nandi, Tugen **6** Kikuyu, Ogaden, Somali **7** Baluhya, Hamitic, Hilotic, Kipsigi, Swahili, Turkana **8** Kalenjin, Marakwet
  god: 4 Ngai
  leader: 5 Mboya **12** Jomo Kenyatta

13 Daniel Arap Moi
language: 3 Luo **5** Bantu, Luhya, Masai **6** Kikuyu **7** English, Swahili **8** Guyerati **10** Hindustani
religion: 5 Islam **7** animism **8** Anglican **13** Roman Catholic
place:
  archeological excavation: 11 Gamble's Cave
  mosque: 5 Khoja
  museum: 9 Fort Jesus
  national park/wildlife preserve: 4 Meru **5** Nyeri, Tsavo **6** Arusha **7** Manyara, Nairobi, Samburu **8** Aberdare, Amboseli **10** Lake Nakuru, Mount Kenya, Rift Valley
  ruins: 4 Gedi
feature:
  garment: 5 kanga **7** kitenge
  round house: 6 shamba
  secret organization: 6 Mau Mau
  tree: 6 ayieke, baobab
food:
  fish: 7 tilapia
  wine: 5 tembo

Kepler, Johannes
nationality: 6 German
invented: 14 convex eyepiece **21** astronomical telescope
formulated:
  three laws of planetary motion (Kepler's Laws): 10 law of areas **11** harmonic law **24** elliptical orbit of planets
author of: 14 Astronomia nova, Harmonice mundi **16** Rudolphine Tables **23** Mysterium cosmographicum **30** Epitome astronomiae Copernicanae

kerchief 5 cloth, scarf **7** muffler **8** babushka, bandanna, kaffiyah, neckwear **9** headpiece, neckcloth **11** neckerchief **12** handkerchief

Keres
origin: 5 Greek
spirits of: 4 evil **5** death **6** old age **7** disease

Keres-Siouan
language branch: 5 Keres **7** Caddoan **9** Iroquoian **11** Siouan-Yuchi

kernel 3 nub, nut, pip, pit **4** core, germ, gist, pith, seed **5** grain, stone **6** center, marrow **7** nucleus **12** quintessence

Kerouac, Jack
author of: 6 Big Sur **9** On the Road **13** The Dharma Bums **16** Lonesome Traveler

Kerr, Deborah
real name: 22 Deborah Jane Kerr-Trimmer
born: 8 Scotland **11** Helensburgh
roles: 11 Edward My Son, The King and I **12** The Hucksters **13** The Sundowners **14** Separate Tables, The Chalk Garden **18** From Here to Eternity **19** The Night of the Iguana **20** Heaven Knows Mr Allison

Kesey, Ken
author of: 21 Sometimes a Great Notion **25** One Flew Over the Cuckoo's Nest

Ketcham, Hank
creator/artist of: 15 Dennis the Menace

kettle 3 pan, pot, tub, vat **6** boiler, teapot, tureen **8** cauldron, crucible, saucepan

Ketubim 8 writings **11** Hagiographa

Keturah
husband: 7 Abraham

kewpie 4 doll
originator: 9 Rose O'Neil **13** carnival prize

key 3 cue, fit **4** clue, gear, mode, suit **5** adapt, light, point, scale **6** adjust, answer, direct, opener **7** address, finding, meaning, pointer **8** indicant, solution, tonality **9** indicator **10** exposition, indication, resolution **11** elucidation, explanation, explication, translation **14** interpretation

Key, Ted
creator/artist of: 5 Hazel

keyboard instrument 5 organ, piano **6** spinet **8** psaltery, virginal **9** harmonium **10** clavichord, pianoforte **11** harpsichord

keyed up 5 tense **7** excited, nervous **8** volatile **9** emotional, explosive

key element 9 essential, vital part **18** primary constituent **20** indispensable element

Key Largo
director: 10 John Huston
based on story by: 15 Maxwell Anderson
cast: 12 Claire Trevor, Lauren Bacall **14** Humphrey Bogart **15** Edward G Robinson, Lionel Barrymore
Oscar for: 17 supporting actress (Trevor)

Keynes, John Maynard
author of: 44 The General Theory of Employment Interest and Money

keynote 3 nub **4** core, gist, pith **5** heart, theme **6** marrow **7** essence, nucleus, pattern **8** main idea, quiddity **9** substance **11** nitty-gritty, salient idea **12** central point

keystone 4 base, crux, root **5** basis **8** gravamen, linchpin **9** principle **10** foundation, mainspring

Keystone State
nickname of: 12 Pennsylvania

Key to Rebecca, The
author: 10 Ken Follett

KGB 4 USSR **14** security police **18** intelligence agency

Khachaturian, Aram Ilich
born: 6 Tiflis **7** (Soviet) Georgia
composer of: 6 Gayane **9** Spartacus **12** Song of Stalin

khaki 5 cloth **6** fabric **7** uniform **9** olive-drab **14** yellowish- brown

khan, kahn 3 inn **4** lord **5** chief, ruler **6** prince **7** emperor **9** chieftain, sovereign **11** caravansary
  famous: 3 Aga, Ali **4** Yuan **6** Kublai **7** Genghis **8** Ghenghis

Khartoum
  capital of: 5 Sudan

Khayyam, Omar
  born: 6 Persia
  famous as: 4 poet **9** statesman **13** mathematician
  name means: 9 tentmaker
  author of: 11 The Rubaiyat

Khoisan
  language spoken by: 3 San **7** Bushmen **9** Khoikhoin **10** Hottentots
  includes: 5 Hatsa **7** Sandawe
  distinguishing sound: 5 click

Khomeini, Ruholla
  title: 9 ayatollah
  ruled: 4 Iran

Khruschev, Nikita
  premier of: 4 USSR
  followed: 8 Bulganin
  preceded: 7 Kosygin

Khyber Pass
  between: 8 Pakistan and **11** Afghanistan
  range: 9 Hindu Kush

kibbutz 10 collective **11** Israeli Farm

kibitzer 3 pry **5** prier, snoop **6** butt-in **7** advisor, meddler, snooper, watcher **8** busybody, onlooker **9** buttinsky

kick 3 fun, hit, out, pep, vim **4** beef, boot, dash, fret, fume, fuss, life, punt, snap, tang, zest **5** eject, force, gripe, growl, power, punch, verve, vigor **6** flavor, grouch, grouse, object, recoil, remove, return, strike, stroke, thrill **7** boot out, cast out, grumble, fly back, protest, rebound, sparkle, turn out **8** backlash, complain, jump back, piquancy, pleasure, pungency, reaction, throw out, vitality **9** amusement, animation, complaint, enjoyment, find fault, grievance, intensity, make a fuss, objection **10** excitement, spring back **11** give the gate, remonstrate, send packing, show the door **12** protestation **13** gratification, remonstration

Kickapoo
  language family: 9 Algonkian **10** Algonquian
  location: 5 Texas **6** Kansas, Mexico **9** Chihuahua, Wisconsin
  related to: 3 Fox, Sac **4** Sauk

kickback 3 cut **5** bribe, graft, share **6** boodle, payoff, payola **9** hush money **10** commission, percentage, protection, recompense **12** compensation, remuneration **15** protection money

kick downstairs 4 bust **6** demote **7** degrade

kickoff 5 start **7** opening **9** beginning, inception, launching **12** inauguration

kick out 4 oust **5** eject, evict, expel **8** throw out **9** discharge

kicks 3 fun **7** thrills **8** pleasure **10** excitement **11** stimulation

kick upstairs 5 boost **7** advance, elevate, promote

kid 3 rag, rib, tot **4** baby, fool, gull, jest, joke, josh, mock, ride, tyke **5** bluff, child, cozen, harry, put on, tease, trick, youth **6** delude, infant, moppet, plague, shaver, squirt **7** beguile, deceive, laugh at, mislead **8** goat hide, goatskin, hoodwink, juvenile, ridicule, teenager, yearling **9** bamboozle, billy goat, little one, make fun of, nanny goat, offspring, young goat, youngster **10** adolescent **11** goat leather, young person **12** little shaver

Kid, The
  nickname of: 11 Ted Williams **13** William Bonney (Billy)

kid around 5 clown, cut up **10** fool around, play around **11** clown around

Kidd, William 13 pirate captain
  born: 8 Scotland
  end: 6 hanged

Kidder, Margot
  born: 6 Canada **11** Yellow Knife
  roles: 7 Sisters **8** Lois Lane, Superman **14** Some Kind of Hero **19** The Amityville Horror

Kiddush 6 prayer **8** blessing **14** sanctification

kidnap 5 seize, steal **6** abduct, hijack, snatch **7** bear off, capture, impress, skyjack **8** bear away, carry off, shanghai **10** run off with **11** make off with **13** hold for ransom

Kidnapped
  author: 20 Robert Louis Stevenson
  character: 9 Alan Breck **10** Rankeillor **12** David Balfour **15** Ebenezer Balfour

Kigali
  capital of: 6 Rwanda

Kiley, Richard
  born: 9 Chicago IL
  roles: 7 Redhead **13** Man of La Mancha **16** Advise and Consent

Kilimanjaro, Mount
  in 6 Africa **8** Tanzania
  feature: 15 highest in Africa
  see also **9** Hemingway

Kilkenny Cats
  origin: 5 Irish
  form: 4 cats
  number: 3 two
  left after fight: 5 tails

kill 4 beat, do in, halt, hang, ruin, slay, stay **5** break, check, drown, erase, lynch, quell, shoot, waste **6** behead, defeat, murder, poison, rub out, stifle **7** bump off, butcher, cut down, destroy, execute, garrote, silence,

smother, squelch, wipe out **8** blow away, dispatch, get rid of, knock off, massacre, strangle, string up **9** dismember, finish off, shoot down, slaughter, suffocate **10** asphyxiate, decapitate, disembowel, extinguish, guillotine, put a stop to, put an end to, put to death **11** assassinate, burn to death, electrocute, exterminate **13** mortally wound

killer 6 hit man, slayer **7** butcher **8** assassin, murderer **11** executioner **12** exterminator

Killers, The
  director: 13 Robert Siodmak
  based on story by: 15 Ernest Hemingway
  cast: 10 Ava Gardner **12** Edmond O'Brien **13** Burt Lancaster

killer whale 4 orca **7** grampus **11** Orcinus orca

killing 4 coup **5** fatal **6** big hit, deadly, lethal, mortal, murder **7** bonanza, cleanup, deathly, hanging, slaying, success, suicide **8** butchery, fatality, homicide, lynching, massacre, regicide, shooting, smash hit, stabbing, windfall **9** bloodshed, execution, garroting, martyrdom, matricide, murderous, patricide, poisoning, slaughter, uxoricide **10** cleaning up, decimation, fratricide, immolation, impalement, sororicide, strangling **11** crucifixion, devastating, elimination, infanticide **12** annihilation, death-dealing, decapitation, excruciating, guillotining, manslaughter, master stroke, stroke of luck, violent death **13** electrocution, extermination, strangulation **17** capital punishment

Killing Fields
  director: 11 Roland Joffe
  based on article by: 15 Sydney Schanberg (The Death and Life of Dith Pran)
  cast: 10 Haing S Ngor **12** Sam Waterston
  setting: 8 Cambodia
  Oscar for: 15 supporting actor (Ngor)

Killing Time
  author: 12 Thomas Berger

killjoy 6 grouch **8** grumbler, sourball, sourpuss **9** Cassandra, gloomy Gus, worrywart **10** complainer, malcontent, spoilsport, wet blanket **11** crapehanger, party-pooper

kill time 4 idle **6** dawdle **9** waste time **10** fool around

Kilmer, Joyce
  author of: 5 Trees

kiln 3 ost **4** bake, burn, fire, oast, oven **5** drier, glaze, stove, tiler **7** furnace **8** calciner, limekiln **9** oasthouse

kiloliter
  abbreviation: 2 kL

kilometer
  abbreviation: 2 km

Kim
  author: 14 Rudyard Kipling
  character: 9 Mahbub Ali **11** Tibetan Lama **12** Kimball O'Hara **16** Colonel Creighton **22** Hurree Chunder Mookerjee

kimono 4 gown, robe
  traditional costume of: 5 Japan
  sash: 3 obi
  ornament: 7 netsuke

kin 4 akin, clan, kith, race **5** folks, tribe **6** family, people **7** kinfolk, kinsmen, related **8** clansmen, kinfolks **9** next of kin, relations, relatives, tribesmen **10** kith and kin **11** connections, consanguine, distaff side, spindle side **13** flesh and blood **14** kissing cousins

kind 3 ilk **4** cast, make, mold, sort, type **5** brand, breed, caste, civil, class, genre, genus, style **6** benign, gentle, kidney, kindly, nature, polite, strain, tender **7** amiable, cordial, variety **8** amicable, friendly, generous, gracious, merciful, obliging **9** courteous **10** bighearted, charitable, neighborly, thoughtful **11** considerate, description, designation, good-hearted, good-humored, good-natured, softhearted, sympathetic, warmhearted, well-meaning **12** affectionate, well-disposed **13** accommodating, compassionate, tenderhearted, understanding
  French: 6 gentil

kindhearted 4 good, warm **6** benign, gentle, humane, kindly, loving **7** helpful **8** amicable, generous, gracious, merciful **10** altruistic, charitable, thoughtful **11** considerate, good-hearted, good-natured, softhearted, sympathetic, warmhearted, well-meaning **12** affectionate, humanitarian **13** accommodating, compassionate, philanthropic, tenderhearted, understanding

kindheartedness 5 mercy **8** altruism, goodness, goodwill, humanity, sympathy **10** compassion, humaneness, tenderness **11** benefaction, benevolence, magnanimity **12** graciousness, philanthropy **13** consideration, understanding, unselfishness **14** charitableness **15** humanitarianism

kindle 4 fire, goad, prod, stir, urge, whet **5** awake, light, rouse, waken **6** arouse, excite, foment, ignite, incite, induce, stir up **7** agitate, animate, inflame, inspire, provoke, quicken, sharpen **8** enkindle **9** call forth, intensify, set fire to, set on fire, stimulate **10** invigorate

kindling 4 fuel **5** brush, paper, twigs **6** firing, tinder **7** burning, flaming **8** firewood, igniting, ignition, lighting, shavings **9** brushwood **10** combustion, enkindling

kindly 4 good, warm **6** benign, gentle, gently, humane, tender, warmly **7**

amiable, amiably, civilly, cordial, devoted, patient **8** amicable, amicably, benignly, friendly, generous, gracious, humanely, merciful, tenderly **9** cordially, courteous **10** benevolent, bighearted, charitable, charitably, generously, graciously, mercifully, neighborly **11** considerate, good-humored, good-natured, magnanimous, softhearted, sympathetic, warmhearted, well-meaning **12** affectionate, benevolently, bigheartedly, humanitarian **13** compassionate, considerately, good-humoredly, good-naturedly, magnanimously, philanthropic, softheartedly, tenderhearted, understanding, warmheartedly, well-meaningly **14** affectionately, well-manneredly **15** compassionately, sympathetically, tenderheartedly, understandingly **17** philanthropically

kindness 3 aid **4** gift, help **5** favor, grace, mercy **6** bounty **7** charity **8** good deed, good turn, goodness, goodwill, humanity, patience, sympathy **9** tolerance **10** act of grace, assistance, compassion, generosity, humaneness, kind office, toleration **11** benefaction, beneficence, benevolence, magnanimity **12** act of charity, graciousness, philanthropy **13** consideration, understanding, unselfishness **14** charitableness **15** humanitarianism

Kind of Anger, A
  author: 10 Eric Ambler

kindred 4 akin, like **5** alike **6** allied, united **7** related, similar **8** agreeing, familial, matching **9** accordant, analogous, congenial, simpatico **10** harmonious, resembling **11** consanguine, sympathetic **13** corresponding

kine 4 cows, oxen **6** cattle **9** livestock

kinfolk 3 kin **6** family **7** kinsmen **8** clansmen **9** relations, relatives **10** kith and kin

king 3 HRH **5** liege, ruler **7** monarch **8** suzerain **9** potentate, protector, sovereign **10** His Majesty **11** crowned head, royal person, the anointed **18** defender of the faith
  Latin: 3 rex

king/emperor/dynasty
  of Afghanistan: 5 Barakzai
  of Albania: 3 Zog **9** Ahmet Zogu
  of Algeria: 3 bey, dey **6** disawa **8** Jugurtha **9** bevlerbay, Masinissa
  of Austria: 7 Charles, Francis **9** Ferdinand, Habsburgs **10** Franz Josef
  of Bahrain: 9 al-Khalifa
  of Belgium: 7 Leopold **8** Baudouin
  of China: 3 Han, Sui **4** Chou, Ch'in, Ming, Sung, T'ang **5** Ch'ing, Shang **6** Manchu
  of Crete: 5 Minos
  of Denmark 4 Hans, Knud **6** Canute **8** Frederik **9** Christian **10** Gorm the Old **15** Harold Bluetooth

  of Egypt: 5 Khufu, Menes, Zoser **6** Farouk, Khafre, Ptulol, Ramses **7** Saladin **8** Horemheb, Menkaure **9** Akhenaten, Amenemhet, Amenhotep **10** Mentuhotep **11** Tutankhamen
  of England: 3 Hal **4** Cnut, John, Lear **5** Henry, James **6** Alfred, Arthur, Canute, Edmund, Edward, Egbert, George, Harold **7** Charles, Richard, Stephen, William **9** Cymbeline **18** Richard Coeur de Lion **19** Richard the Lionheart **21** Richard the Lionhearted
  of France: 5 Henri, Louis **6** Clovis, Philip **7** Charles **8** Napoleon **9** Hugh Capet **11** Charlemagne **21** Richard the Lionhearted **13** Louis Philippe **14** Henry of Navarre
  of Germany: 6 Kaiser **7** Wilhelm **9** Frederick **10** Barbarossa
  of Greece: 5 Creon **6** Atreus **7** Theseus **8** Menelaus **10** Agammemnon **11** Constantine
  of India: 5 Akbar, Asoka, Babur, Gupta, Mogul, Timur **6** Maurya, Rajput **7** Humayun **8** Hyder Ali, Jahangir, Marathas **9** Aurangzeb, Shah Jahan **11** Tippu Sultan **14** Delhi Sultanate **18** Chandragupta Maurya
  of Iran: 5 Abbas, Cyrus, Qajar **6** Darius, Xerxes **7** Arsacid, Pahlavi, Safavid **8** Parthian, Seleucid **9** Sassanian **10** Achaemenid **15** Shah Reza Pahlavi
  of Iraq: 6 Faisal, Sargon **7** Hussein **9** Hammurabi **13** Harun al-Rashid **14** Nebuchadnezzar
  of Ireland: 9 Brian Boru
  of Italy/Rome: 4 Nero, Otho **5** Galba, Nerva, Titus **6** Trajan **7** Hadrian **8** Caligula, Claudius, Commodus, Domitian, Octavian, Tiberius **9** Caracalla, Vespasian, Vitellius **10** Diocletian **11** Constantine **13** Antoninus Dius **14** Caesar Augustus, Marcus Aurelius, Victor Emmanuel
  of Japan: 5 Jimmu, Jingo, Meiji, Taira **6** Yamato **7** Akihito, Izanagi **8** Ashikaga, Fujiwara, Hirohito, Kamakura, Minamoto, Tokugawa
  of Java: 7 Mataram **9** Majapahit, Srivijaya
  of Jordan: 5 Talal **6** Faisal **7** Hussein **8** Abdullah, Selucidas **10** Ibn Hussein, Nabataeans
  of Korea: 2 Yi **4** Choe **5** Ki-tse, Koryo **6** Chi-tsi, Chi-tzu, Tangun
  of Kuwait: 5 Ahmad, Sabah, Salem **7** Mubarak **12** Jaber al-Ahmed, Sabah al-Salim **15** Abdullah al-Salim
  of Liechtenstein: 7 Florian **13** Francis Joseph **16** von Liechtenstein
  of Luxembourg: 8 Sigefroi, Wencelas **12** Jean l'Aveugle **21** House of Nassau-Weilburg
  of Madagascar: 6 Merina
  of Malawi: 6 Maravi
  of Maldives: 4 Didi

of Mexico: 10 Maximilian
of Monaco: 5 Louis 6 Albert, Honore 7 Antoine, Charles, Rainier 9 Florestan
of Mongolia: 8 Jahangir, Jehangir 10 Kublai Khan, Tsendenbal 11 Genghis Khan
of Morocco: 7 Alawite, Almohad 9 Almoravid
of Nepal: 8 Mahendra 9 Tribhuwan 10 Birenda Bir 12 Bikram Sha Dev 17 Prithwi Narayan Sha
of the Netherlands: 7 William
of Nigeria: 3 Ife, Nok, Oyo 5 Benin 6 Fulani 10 Kanem- Borno
of Norway: 4 Olaf, Olav 5 Olave, Oscar 6 Haakon, Harold, Magnus, Sverre
of Peru: 7 Huascar 9 Atahualpa 10 Manco Capac
of Poland: 5 Piast 7 Casimir, Jagello 8 Augustus
of Portugal: 6 Manuel, Philip, Sancho 7 Alfonso 9 Ferdinand, Sebastian 23 Prince Henry the Navigator
of Qatar: 18 Ahmad bin Ali al-Thani 22 Khalifa bin Hamad al-Thani
of Rumania: 5 Carol 7 Michael
of Russia: 4 Ivan, Paul 5 Peter 6 Alexis 7 Michael 8 Nicholas 9 Alexander 12 Boris Godunov
of Sardinia: 12 Charles Felix 13 Charles Albert 14 Victor Emmanuel
of Saudi Arabia: 4 Fahd, Saud 6 Faisal, Khalid 7 Ibn Saud 9 Abdul Aziz
of Scotland: 5 David, James 6 Duncan 7 Kenneth, Macbeth, Malcolm, Stuarts, William 9 Alexander 14 Robert the Bruce 19 Bonnie Prince Charlie
of Sicily: 4 Eryx 5 Bomba, Henry, Peter, Roger 7 Charles, Cocalus, Leontes 9 Ferdinand, Frederick
of Spain: 6 Pelayo, Philip, Ramiro, Sancho, Witiza 7 Alfonso, Almohad, Charles, Umayyad 8 al-Mansur, Reccared, Roderick 9 Almoravid, Ferdinand, Leovigild 10 Juan Carlos 11 Abd al-Rahman, Reccosvinth
of Swaziland: 3 Kbe 5 Nyama 6 Mswati, Sozisa 7 Sobhuza
of Sweden: 4 Vosa, Wasa 5 Oscar 6 Gustav 8 Gustavus 10 Carl Gustav 12 Gustav Adolph 13 Charles Gustav 22 Jean Baptiste Bernadotte
of Syria: 5 Rezin 6 Faisal, Hazael 8 Benhadad 9 Antiochus
of Thailand: 4 Rama 7 Chakkri, Mongkut 10 Chao Phraya 12 Prahjadhipok 13 Chulalongkorn 17 Bhumibol Adulyadej
of Tongo: 11 George Tupou 14 Taufaahau Tupou
of Tunisia: 6 Hafsid 7 Fatimid 8 Aghlabid, Almohade 10 Husseinite
of Turkey: 8 Mausolus
of Uganda: 6 Mutesa, Mwanga 8 Kabarega

of Upper Volta: 4 Naba 5 Mogho
of Zimbabwe: 9 Lobengula, Mzilikaze

King, Frank
creator/artist of: 13 Gasoline Alley

King, Martin Luther
born: 7 Atlanta, Georgia
died: 7 Memphis 9 Tennessee
wife: 12 Coretta Scott
career: 8 minister (Southern Baptist), activist
notable moments: 17 "I Have A Dream" speech 26 march from Selma to Montgomery

King, Stephen
author of: 2 It 4 Cujo 6 Carrie, Misery 9 Christine, Salem's Lot, The Stand 10 Night Shift, The Shining 11 Firestarter, Pet Sematary, The Dead Zone 12 Skeleton Crew, The Dark Tower 16 Different Seasons, The Tommyknockers

King and I, The
director: 10 Walter Lang
cast: 10 Rita Moreno, Yul Brynner 11 Deborah Kerr 12 Martin Benson
score: 21 Rodgers and Hammerstein
from the book: 20 Anna and the King of Siam
song: 12 Shall We Dance? 16 Getting to Know You, Hello Young Lovers 18 Something Wonderful

King Arthur
opera by: 7 Purcell
character: 6 Merlin, Osmond, Oswald 8 Emmeline, Philadel 14 Duke of Cornwall

kingdom 4 land 5 duchy, field, realm, state 6 domain, empire, nation, sphere 7 country, dukedom 8 dominion, monarchy 9 territory 12 principality

King John
author: 18 William Shakespeare
character: 6 Elinor 9 Constance 11 Prince Henry 13 Hubert de Burgh 15 Blanch of Castile, Lewis the Dauphin 16 Arthur of Bretagne Cardinal Pandulph, William Longsword, William Mareshall 19 Philip Faulconbridge, Robert Faulconbridge

King Kong
director: 13 Merian C Cooper 17 Ernest B Schoedsack
cast: 7 Fay Wray 10 Bruce Cabot 11 James Flavin 12 Noble Johnson 15 Robert Armstrong
setting (final scene): 19 Empire State Building
score: 10 Max Steiner

King Lear
author: 18 William Shakespeare
character: 5 Edgar, Regan 6 Edmund 7 Goneril 8 Cordelia 10 Earl of Kent 12 Duke of Albany, King of France 14 Duke of Cornwall 16 Earl of Gloucester

kingly 5 grand, noble, regal, royal 6

august, lordly, mighty 7 queenly, stately 8 absolute, despotic, glorious, kinglike, imperial, majestic, princely, splendid 9 imperious, monarchal, patrician, sovereign 10 autocratic, commanding, tyrannical 11 magnificent 12 awe- inspiring

Kingman, Dave
nickname: 4 Kong
sport: 8 baseball
position: 8 outfield 9 first base
team: 11 Chicago Cubs, New York Mets 14 New York Yankees, San Diego Padres 16 California Angels 18 San Francisco Giants

king of gods 4 Amen, Amon, Finn, Zeus 5 Ammon, Enlil, Fionn, Wotan 6 Marduk 7 Jupiter 8 Merodach 12 Baal Merodach 13 Fionn MacCumal

King of Hearts
character in: 28 Alice's Adventures in Wonderland
author: 7 Carroll

King of Righteousness 11 Melchizedek

Kingsley, Ben
roles: 6 Gandhi (Oscar) 8 Betrayal 14 Schindler's List

Kingsley, Charles
author of: 7 Hypatia 10 Alton Locke 11 Westward Ho! 14 The Water Babies 15 Hereward the Wake

King Solomon's Mines
author: 13 H Rider Haggard
character: 5 Twala 6 Gagool, Umbopa 14 Sir Henry Curtis 15 Allan Quatermain, Captain John Good

King's Row
author: 14 Henry Bellamann
director: 7 Sam Wood
cast: 10 Betty Field 11 Ann Sheridan, Claude Rains 12 Ronald Reagan 13 Charles Coburn 14 Judith Anderson, Robert Cummings
score: 21 Erich Wolfgard Korngold
character: 11 Drake McHugh, Elise Sandor 13 Randy Monaghan 14 Cassandra Tower, Parris Mitchell

Kingston
capital of: 7 Jamaica

kink 4 coil, flaw, knot, pang 5 cramp, crick, crimp, frizz, gnarl, hitch, quirk, snarl, spasm, twist 6 defect, foible, glitch, oddity, tangle, twinge, vagary 7 crinkle, frizzle 8 crotchet 9 queerness, stiffness, weirdness 10 difficulty 11 peculiarity, singularity 12 charley horse, complication, eccentricity, freakishness, idiosyncrasy, imperfection

kinky 3 odd 4 sick, wiry 5 kooky, queer 6 frizzy, matted, quirky, twisty 7 bizarre, deviant, frizzly, knotted, strange, tangled, twisted, unusual 8 aberrant, abnormal, crinkled, freakish, frizzled, peculiar, perverse 9 eccentric, unnatural **10** unorthodox **13** idiosyncratic

Kinshasa
  capital of: **5** Zaire

kinsman 3 sib, son **4** aunt, heir **5** child, uncle **6** cousin, father, mother, parent, sister **7** brother **8** daughter, landsman, relation, relative **9** offspring **10** countryman **11** grandfather, grandmother **13** blood relation, blood relative

Kiowa
  language family: **6** Tanoan
  location: **6** Plains **7** Montana **8** Colorado, Oklahoma
  allied with: **7** Arapaho **8** Comanche **11** Kiowa Apache
  deity: **5** Taime

Kiowa Apache
  language family: **12** Shapwailutan
  location: **6** Plains

Kipling, Rudyard
  author of: **3** Kim **8** Gunga Din, Mandalay **11** Danny Deaver **12** The Seven Seas **13** Just So Stories, The Jungle Book **18** Barrack-Room Ballads, Captains Courageous

Kipps
  author: **7** H G Wells

Kirchhoff, Gustav Robert
  field: **7** physics
  nationality: **6** German
  discovered: **6** cesium **8** rubidium
  developed: **12** spectroscope
  named for him: **19** electric circuit laws

Kirchner, Ernst Ludwig
  born: **7** Germany **13** Aschaffenburg
  artwork: **11** Street Scene **12** Street Berlin **13** Moonlit Winter **21** Self-portrait with Model

Kirghiz *see* **10** Kyrgyzstan

Kiribati
  other name: **14** Gilbert Islands
  capital/largest city: **6** Tarawa
  others: **5** Betio **7** Bairiki, Bonriki **9** Bikenibeu
  school: **12** South Pacific
  monetary unit: **4** cent **6** dollar
  island: **5** Flint, Ocean **6** Banaba, Canton, Malden, Tarawa **7** Abemama, Fanning, Gilbert, Marakei, Nonouti, Phoenix, Vostock **8** Caroline, Starbuck **9** Christmas, Enderbury, Tabiteuea **10** Butaritari, Equatorial, Washington **12** Northern Line, Southern Line
  sea: **7** Pacific
  people: **8** Banabans **10** Polynesian **11** Micronesian
  language: **6** Samoan **7** English **10** Gilbertese
  religion: **5** Baha'i **8** Anglican **9** Methodist **11** Church of God **13** Roman Catholic **19** Seventh Day Adventist

kirsch, kirschwasser
  type: **6** brandy **7** liqueur

origin: **6** France **7** Germany **11** Switzerland
  flavor: **6** cherry
  with gin: **7** Florida **10** Lady Finger
  with vodka: **12** Volga Boatman

kismet 3 end, lot **4** doom, fate **5** karma, moira **7** destiny, fortune, portion **8** God's will **10** Providence **11** will of Allah **12** circumstance **13** inevitability **14** predestination

kiss 4 buss, neck **6** smooch, salute **8** osculate

Kiss for Cinderella, A
  author: **12** James M Barrie

Kissinger, Henry
  born: **6** Fuerth **7** Germany
  career: **9** statesman **11** businessman **16** Secretary of State
  won: **10** Nobel Prize

kit 3 rig **4** gear **5** tools **6** outfit, tackle, things **7** devices **8** supplies, utensils **9** equipment, trappings **10** implements, provisions **11** furnishings, impediments, instruments, necessaries **13** accoutrements, paraphernalia

Kitasato, Shibasaburo
  field: **12** bacteriology
  nationality: **8** Japanese
  isolated: **7** anthrax, tetanus **9** dysentery **13** bubonic plague
  developed: **19** diphtheria antitoxin

kitchen 6 bakery, cocina, galley **7** cuisine **8** cookroom, scullery **9** bakehouse, cookhouse

Kitchener, Horatio Herbert
  also: **18** first Earl Kitchener
  nationality: **7** British
  served in: **7** Boer War **15** South African War
  battle: **8** Khartoum, Omdurman
  governor of: **8** the Sudan
  commander in chief of: **5** India **12** Egyptian army
  consul general of: **5** Egypt

kitel 20 Jewish ceremonial robe
  color: **5** white

Kitely
  character in: **19** Every Man in His Humour
  author: **6** Jonson

kittenish 3 coy **7** playful **10** coquettish

Klamath
  language family: **8** Penutian
  location: **6** Oregon **10** California
  related to: **5** Modoc **6** Cayuse, Molala

Klee, Paul
  born: **11** Switzerland **14** Munchenbuchsee
  artwork: **9** Locksmith **11** Ad Parnassum **18** Barbarian Sacrifice, Demon above the Ships **20** The Twittering Machine **22** Revolution of the Viaduct **23** Dance-Play of the Red Skirts **24** Dance Monster to my Soft Song **35** The Vocal Fabric of the Singer Rosa Silber

Kleist, Heinrich von
  author of: **11** Penthesilea **14** The Marquise of O **16** The Broken Pitcher **18** The Prince of Homburg

Kline, Kevin
  roles: **4** Dave **8** In and Out **11** The Big Chill **13** Sophie's Choice **16** A Fish Called Wanda **17** Pirates of Penzance

Klugman, Jack
  born: **14** Philadelphia PA
  roles: **6** Quincy **12** Oscar Madison, The Odd Couple

klutz 5 dummy **9** blockhead **11** satchelfoot **13** fumblefingers

klutzy 4 dumb **6** clumsy, stupid **7** awkward **9** graceless

knack 4 bent, gift, turn **5** flair, forte, skill **6** genius, talent **7** ability, faculty, finesse **8** aptitude, capacity, facility **9** dexterity, expertise, ingenuity, quickness, readiness **10** adroitness, capability, cleverness, competence, efficiency, propensity **11** inclination, proficiency **13** dexterousness

knave 3 cad, cur, dog, rat **4** jack (cards) **5** phony, rogue, scamp **6** con man, rascal, rotter, varlet, wretch **7** bounder, culprit **8** scalawag, swindler **9** charlatan, con artist, reprobate, scoundrel **10** blackguard **11** rapscallion **14** good for nothing

knee breeches 8 breeches, jodhpurs, knickers **9** plus fours **14** knickerbockers

kneel 3 bow **6** curtsy, kowtow, salaam **7** bow down **9** genuflect **13** make obeisance **16** prostrate oneself

knell 4 peal, ring, toll **5** chime, sound **6** stroke **7** pealing, ringing, tolling

Knickerbocker Holiday
  author: **15** Maxwell Anderson

knickknack, nicknack 3 toy **6** bauble, gewgaw, trifle **7** bibelot, trinket **8** frippery, gimcrack **9** bagatelle, bric-a-brac, plaything **11** thingamajig

knife 3 cut **4** dirk, shiv, stab **5** blade, slash, wound **6** cutter, pierce **7** cut down, cutlery **8** cut apart, lacerate, mutilate
  type: **3** pen **4** jack **5** bowie, bread, putty, table **6** dagger, paring, pocket **7** butcher, carving, hunting, machete, palette, pruning, scalpel **8** skinning, stiletto, surgical **11** switchblade

knight 4 hero **7** fighter, gallant, paladin, soldier, Templar, warrior **8** cavalier, champion, defender, guardian, horseman, Lancelot **9** gentleman, man-at-arms, protecter, protector **10** equestrian, vindicator

Knight
  character in: **18** The Canterbury Tales
  author: **7** Chaucer

Knightley, George

character in: **4** Emma
author: **6** Austen
Knights, The
author: **12** Aristophanes
character: **5** Demus **6** Nicias **11** Demosthenes **20** Cleon the Paphlagonian
knit 3 tat **4** ally, bind, draw, join, knot, link **5** braid, plait, twist, unify, unite, weave **6** attach, crease, fasten, furrow, stitch **7** connect, crochet, wrinkle **10** intertwine, interweave **12** draw together
knob 3 nub **4** bulb, bump, grip, hold, hump, knot, knur, lump, node, snag **5** bulge, gnarl, knurl, latch, lever, swell **6** handle, nubbin **8** handhold, swelling, tubercle **9** convexity **10** projection, prominence, protrusion **12** protuberance, protuberancy
knock 3 bat, hit, pat, rap, tap **4** bang, beat, belt, blow, bomb, bump, clip, cuff, dash, kick, lick, push, slam, slap, sock, swat, thud **5** abuse, cavil, clout, crack, crash, decry, pound, punch, smack, smash, smite, thump, whack **6** batter, carp at, defeat, hammer, jostle, murder, peck at, pummel, strike, stroke, thwack, wallop **7** censure, condemn, failure, setback **8** belittle, lambaste **9** criticism, criticize, deprecate, disparage, reprehend **12** condemnation, faultfinding, reprehension
knock down 4 deck, down, drop, fell **5** floor **7** flatten **8** bowl over, discount **9** take apart **11** disassemble
knock off balance 6 rattle **7** shake up **8** unsettle **9** take aback **11** disorganize
knockout 2 KO **4** doll **5** beaut, Venus **6** beauty, eyeful **7** stunner
knock out of shape 4 maul **5** crush **6** batter, beat up, mangle
knoll 4 hill, rise **5** mound
knot 3 bun **4** bump, frog, heap, hump, loop, lump, mass, pack, pile, star, tuft **5** braid, bunch, clump, group, hitch, knurl, plait, twist **6** bundle, circle **7** cat's-paw, chignon, cluster, epaulet, rosette **8** ornament **9** gathering **10** assemblage, collection, intertwist **13** interlacement
type: **3** bow, top **4** flat, slip **5** slide **6** double, single, square **7** running **8** hangman's, overhand, shoulder, surgeon's **9** half-hitch **11** figure-eight, midshipman's
Knots Landing
character: **9** Abby Ewing, Gary Ewing **10** Greg Sumner **11** Valene Ewing **12** Mac Mackenzie **14** Karen Mackenzie, Paige Forrester
cast: **10** Donna Mills, Joan Van Ark **11** Julie Harris, Kevin Dobson, Michelle Lee **13** William Devane **14** Douglas Sheehan, Ted Shackelford **17** Nicolette Sheridan

knotty 4 hard **5** bumpy, rough, tough **6** coarse, flawed, knobby, knurly, rugged, snaggy, thorny, tricky, uneven **7** complex, gnarled, knurled, nodular **8** baffling, involved, puzzling, ticklish, unsmooth **9** blemished, difficult, intricate **10** perplexing **11** complicated, troublesome **12** rough-grained **13** coarse-grained, problematical
know 3 see **6** be sure, be wise, notice **7** be smart, discern, make out, realize **8** identify, perceive **9** apprehend, be assured, be aware of, be certain, be close to, get wise to, recognize **10** be informed, be positive, understand **11** be confident, be sagacious, be thick with, distinguish, feel certain, have down pat, have no doubt **12** discriminate, have down cold, have the ear of **13** be cognizant of, be intelligent, have knowledge, rub elbows with **14** be familiar with
knowable 9 thinkable **11** conceivable, discernible, perceivable **14** understandable
Knowell, Edward
character in: **19** Every Man in His Humour
author: **6** Jonson
know for sure 9 be certain **10** be positive
know-how 3 art **4** bent, gift **5** craft, flair, knack, savvy, skill **6** talent **7** ability, mastery **8** aptitude, capacity, deftness **9** adeptness, expertise, knowledge, technique **10** adroitness, capability, competence, experience, expertness **11** proficiency **12** skillfulness **15** professionalism
French: **11** savoir-faire
knowing 4 deep, wise **5** aware, canny, sharp, smart, sound **6** astute, brainy, bright, clever, shrewd **7** erudite, fraught, learned, sapient **8** academic, educated, eloquent, highbrow, literary, profound, schooled, sensible **9** conscious, judicious, revealing, sagacious **10** discerning, expressive, meaningful, perceptive, percipient, scholastic, widely read **11** enlightened, intelligent, significant **12** intellectual, well-informed **13** comprehending, knowledgeable, perspicacious, philosophical, sophisticated, understanding
knowing how to live
French: **11** savoir-vivre
knowing just what to do
French: **11** savoir-faire
know-it-all 5 brash **13** overconfident
knowledge 3 ken, tip **4** data, hint, lore, news **5** sense **6** memory, notice, report, wisdom **7** inkling, mention, tidings **8** learning **9** awareness, education, erudition, schooling, statement **10** cognizance, intimation, perception **11** cultivation, declaration, familiarity, information, realization, recognition,

revelation, scholarship **12** announcement, book learning, intelligence, notification **13** communication, comprehension, consciousness, enlightenment, pronouncement
god of: **4** Odin **5** Othin
knowledgeable 3 hip **4** up on **8** at home in, versed in **12** familiar with, well-informed **14** acquainted with, conversant with
French: **9** au courant
knowledge of the world
French: **11** savoir-vivre
known 5 noted, plain **6** common, famous, patent **7** evident, obvious, popular **8** apparent, definite, distinct, familiar, manifest, palpable **9** notorious, prominent **10** celebrated, recognized **11** self-evident
know thyself
Greek: **13** gnothi seauton
knuckle under 5 yield **6** give in, submit **7** bow down **9** surrender **10** capitulate
knurled 5 bumpy, lumpy **6** gnarly, knobby, knotty, knurly, nubbly, ridged **7** bulging, gnarled, knotted, nodular
koala
family: **9** marsupial
habitat: **9** Australia
food: **10** eucalyptus
resembles: **9** small bear
kin of: **6** wombat
Koch, Robert
field: **12** bacteriology
nationality: **6** German
isolated: **2** TB **12** tuberculosis
awarded: **10** Nobel Prize
Kodaly, Zoltan
born: **7** Hungary **9** Kecskemet
composer of: **9** Hary Janos **11** Czinka Panna, Missa Brevis, Szekely Fono **14** Budavari Te Deum **15** Dances of Galanta **17** Dances of Marosszek, Peacock Variations, Psalmus Hungaricus **28** The Spinning Room of the Szekelys
Koestler, Arthur
author of: **14** Darkness at Noon **15** The Sleepwalkers
Kohinoor, Koh-i-noor 7 diamond **6** (106) carats
from: **5** India
part of: **18** British Crown Jewels
kohoutek 5 comet
named for: **15** Czech astronomer
Kojak
character: **5** (Det) Rizzo **7** (Det) Stavros **9** (Lt) Theo Kojak **10** (Det) Saperstein **11** Frank McNeil **12** (Lt) Bobby Crocker
cast: **9** Dan Frazer **10** Vince Conti **11** Kevin Dobson, Mark Russell **12** Telly Savalas **13** George Savalas (Demosthenes)

trademark: 8 lollipop
phrase: 14 Who loves ya baby?

Kollwitz, Kathe
  real name: 12 Kathe Schmidt
  born: 10 Konigsberg **11** East Prussia
  artwork: 3 War **5** Death, Pieta **11**
    Proletariat **13** Weavers' Revolt
    (Weaver's Rebellion) **14** Mother and
    Child, The Peasants' War **18** Death
    Seizing a Woman

Kol Nidre 4 vows **8** promises **22** Jewish liturgical prayer
  recited on eve of: 9 Yom Kippur

Kong
  nickname of: 11 Dave Kingman

Kon-Tiki
  author: 13 Thor Heyerdahl
  name of: 4 raft

kook 3 nut **5** crazy, flake, loony,
  wacko **6** cuckoo, weirdo **7** dingbat **8**
  crackpot **9** ding-a-ling, eccentric, fruitcake, harebrain, screwball **10** crackbrain

Koran 5 Islam, Quran **9** Word of God
  10 Sacred book
  revelations to: 8 Mohammed
  division: 4 sura
  dictated by: 7 Gabriel **9** archangel

Korea
  other name: 6 Chosen **17** land of
    morning calm
  capital:
    North Korea: 9 Pyongyang
    South Korea: 5 Seoul
  largest city: 5 Seoul
  others: 5 Masan, Mokpo, Pusan,
    Sinpo, Suwon, Taegu, Wonju **6**
    Chonju, Inchon, Kangso, Kunsan,
    Taejon, Wonsan **7** Hanyang, Hung-
    nam, Kaesong, Kangson, Kwangju **8**
    Chongjin, Chunchon, Kimchaek
  school: 5 Busan **6** Yonsei **7** Hanyang
    8 Kim Chaek, Kyung Hee **9** Kim II
    Sung
  division:
    ancient: 5 Silla **6** Chosen **7** Ko-
      guryo, Paekche
  monetary unit: 3 woh, won **4** chun,
    hwan, kwan
  weight: 3 won
  island: 4 Chin, Koje **5** Cheju, Sinmi **6**
    Anmyon, Huksan, Namhae **7** Tok-
    chok **8** Quelpart **10** Paengnyong
  mountain: 4 Wang **5** Chiri, Halla **6**
    Kwanmo, Sobaek **7** Diamond, Kye-
    bang, Nangnim, Taebaek **8** Chang-
    pai, Hamgyong, Myohyang **9** Paektu-
    san **10** Kumgang-san
  highest point: 6 Paektu **9** Paektu-san
  river: 3 Han, Kin, Kum, Kun, Nam **4**
    Lobk, Yalu **5** Amnok, Imjin, Tumen
    6 Namhan, Pukhan, Somjin, Soyang,
    Yesong **7** Naktong, Taedong **8**
    Changjin, Youngsan **9** Chongchon
  sea: 5 Japan **6** Yellow **9** East China
  physical feature:
    bay: 5 Korea **6** Yongil **7** Kanghwa,

Kyonggi **9** Tongjoson
  cape: 4 Musu
  point: 7 Changgi **8** Changsan
  strait: 5 Korea
  valley: 7 Naktong
  people: 6 Korean
    artist: 8 Chong Son **10** Kimtlong-do
    dynasty: 2 Yi **4** Choe **5** Koryo
    leader: 6 Sejong **8** Yi Sung-gy **9**
      Kim II Sung **11** Chun Doo Hwan,
      Syngman Rhee **12** Park Chung Hee
    legendary leader: 5 Ki-tse **6** Chi-
      tse, Chi-tzu, Tangun
    poet: 10 Hwang Chini
  Unification Church Leader 12 Sun
    Myung Moon
  language: 6 Korean
    alphabet: 6 hangul
  religion: 6 Taoism **7** animism **8** Bud-
    dhism **9** Chondogyo **12** Christianity,
    Confucianism
  place:
    palace: 8 Kyongbok
    temple: 7 Haein-sa **17** Hall of Eter-
      nal Life
    tomb: 14 Dancing Figures
  feature:
    clothing: 5 chima
    game: 3 yut **5** akoan **6** ho-hpai **7**
      kol-ye-si **9** ryong-hpai, sang-ryouk
      10 ke-pouk-hpai, sin-syo-tyen **12**
      tjak-ma- tchi-ki **15** kko-ri-pouk-
      tchi-ki
    martial art: 9 tae-kwon-do
    musical instrument: 6 chaing **7**
      kayagum, komungo
    porcelain: 7 Celadon
    porch: 4 maru
    pottery: 8 pun-chong
  food:
    bean curd: 4 tubu
    hot pickle: 6 kimchi
    meat-filled dumpling: 5 mandu
    noodle: 5 kuksu

Korman, Harvey
  born: 9 Chicago IL
  roles: 11 High Anxiety **13** Danny
    Kaye Show **14** Blazing Saddles **16**
    Carol Burnett Show

Kornberg, Arthur
  field: 12 biochemistry
  sythesized: 3 DNA, RNA **15** ribonu-
    cleic acid **20** deoxyribonucleic acid
  awarded: 10 Nobel Prize

kosher 5 right **6** proper **7** ethical **8** fit
  to eat **10** aboveboard **12** on the up
  and up

Kosinski, Jerzy
  author of: 5 Steps **7** Cockpit **9** Blind
    Date **10** Being There **11** Passion Play
    12 The Devil Tree **14** The Painted
    Bird

Kowalski, Stanley
  character in: 21 A Streetcar Named
    Desire
  wife: 6 Stella
  sister-in-law: 7 Blanche
  author: 8 Williams

kowtow 4 bend, fawn **5** cower, stoop,
  toady **6** bow low, cringe, curtsy,
  grovel, salaam **7** truckle **8** bootlick,
  butter up, softsoap **9** genuflect **11** apple-polish **12** bow and scrape **16**
  prostrate oneself

kowtowing 7 fawning, servile **8** toadying **9** groveling **10** obsequious

Kraken
  origin: 9 Norwegian
  form: 7 monster
  habitat: 3 sea
  caused: 10 whirlpools

Kramer, Stanley
  director of: 10 On the Beach **11** Ship
    of Fools **14** Inherit the Wind, The
    Defiant Ones **19** Judgment at Nurem-
    berg

Kramer vs Kramer
  director: 12 Robert Benton
  based on novel by: 11 Avery Cor-
    man
  cast: 10 Howard Duff **11** Justin
    Henry, Meryl Streep **13** Dustin Hoff-
    man, Jane Alexander
  Oscar for: 5 actor (Hoffman) **7** pic-
    ture **8** director **10** screenplay **17** sup-
    porting actress (Streep)

Krantz, Judith
  author of: 8 Scruples **13** Princess
    Daisy **16** I'll Take Manhattan, Mis-
    tral's Daughter

Krazy Kat
  creator: 14 George Herriman
  character:
    cop: 12 Offissa B Pupp
    mouse: 6 Ignatz
  prop: 5 brick
  place: 4 jail **14** Coconino County **24**
    Kelly's Exclusive Brick Yard

Krebs, Hans Adolf
  field: 9 chemistry
  nationality: 6 German
  discovered: 15 citric acid cycle
  awarded: 10 Nobel Prize

Kreisler, Fritz
  born: 6 Vienna **7** Austria
  composer of: 7 Allegro **10** Pr-
    aeludium **15** Caprice Viennois **16**
    Tambourin Chinois

Kreutzer, Rodolphe
  born: 6 France **10** Versailles
  composer of: 16 Etudes ou Caprices

Kreutzer Sonata, The
  author: 10 Leo Tolstoy
  character: 13 Mme Pozdnishef,
    Trukhashevsky **16** Vasyla Pozdnishef

Krieg 3 war

Kriemhild
  origin: 8 Germanic
  mentioned in: 14 Nibelungenlied
  brother: 7 Gunther
  husband: 9 Siegfried
  slew: 5 Hagan **7** Gunther
  avenged: 6 murder **9** Siegfried
  corresponds to: 6 Gudrun, Kudrun **7**
    Guthrun

Kristin Lavransdatter
author: **12** Sigrid Undset

Kronos *see* **6** Cronus

Krook
character in: **10** Bleak House
author: **7** Dickens

Kropp, Albert
character in: **25** All Quiet on the Western Front
author: **8** Remarque

krypton
chemical symbol: **2** Kr

Kuala Lumpur
capital of: **8** Malaysia

Kubla Khan
author: **15** Samuel Coleridge
city: **6** Xanadu
river: **4** Alph

Kubrick, Stanley
director of: **6** Lolita **9** Spartacus **11** Barry Lyndon **12** Paths of Glory **13** Dr Strangelove (or How I Learned to Stop Worrying and Love the Bomb) **16** A Clockwork Orange **30** Two Thousand and One A Space Odyssey

kudos **4** fame **5** award, glory, honor, prize **6** esteem, praise, renown, repute **7** acclaim, plaudit **8** citation, prestige **9** celebrity, laudation **10** admiration, decoration **12** commendation **14** celebratedness

Kudrun *see* **6** Gudrun

Kukla, Fran & Ollie
hostess: **11** Fran Allison
puppet: **5** Kukla, Ollie (Oliver J Dragon) **8** Mercedes **9** Cecil Bill **10** Col Crackie **11** Beulah Witch **12** Olivia Dragon **13** Delores Dragon **14** Fletcher Rabbit **18** Mme Ophelia Oglepuss

kummel
origin: **7** Germany
flavor: **7** caraway

kumquat **10** Fortunella
varieties: **4** oval **5** round **6** Marumi, Nagami **16** Australian desert

Kung Fu
character: **8** Master Po **9** Master Kan **14** Kwai Chang Caine
cast: **8** Keye Luke **9** Philip Ahn **11** Radames Pera **14** David Carradine
Caine raised in: **13** Shaolin Temple

kunzite
species: **9** spodumene

Kupka, Frank (Frantisek)
born: **6** Opocno **7** Bohemia **14** Czechoslovakia
artwork: **12** Black Accents, The Cathedral **16** Etude pour la Fugue **17** Fugue in Red and Blue **23** Fugue in Two Colors Amorpha **25** Philosophical Architecture

Kuprin, Aleksandr
author of: **7** The Duel **10** Yama the Pit

Kurosawa, Akira
director of: **3** Ran **8** Rashomon **12** Seven Samurai

Kurtz
character in: **15** Heart of Darkness
author: **6** Conrad

Kuwait
name means: **9** small fort
capital/largest city: **10** Kuwait City
others: **6** Ahmadi **7** Hawalli **8** Abdullah, al-Jahrah, Fahaheel, Shuwaykh **9** al-Shuayba **12** Mena al- Ahmadi, Mina Abd Allah, Mina al-Ahmadi
head of state: **4** emir
monetary unit: **4** fils **5** dinar
island: **5** Warba **7** Bubiyan, Failaka
physical feature:
bay: **6** Kuwait **12** Khor Abdullah
duststorm: **4** kaus
gulf: **7** Persian
oasis: **6** Jahrah
people: **4** Arab **5** Iraqi, Saudi **6** Indian **7** Bedouin **8** Egyptian **9** Pakistani **11** Palestinian
ruling family: **5** Sabah
sheikh (Sabah family): **5** Ahmad, Salem **7** Mubarak **12** Jaber al-Ahmed, Sabah al-Salim **15** Abdullah al-Salim
religion: **5** Islam
war: **4** Gulf **11** Desert Storm, Persian Gulf **12** Desert Shield
enemy: **4** Iraq **13** Saddam Hussein

Kwa
language family: **16** Niger-Kordofanian
group: **10** Niger-Congo
includes: **3** Ewe, Ibo, Twi **4** Bini, Nupe, Togo **6** Yoruba **7** Dahomey

Kwakiutl
language family: **8** Wakashan
location: **6** Canada **15** British Columbia, Vancouver Island **20** Queen Charlotte Island
related to: **6** Nootka **10** Bellabella
noted for: **10** totem poles **15** Cannibal Society, wooden sculpture
called: **14** potlatch people

Kwanza, Kwanzaa **15** harvest festival
celebrated by: **16** African-Americans

Kyd, Thomas
author of: **17** The Spanish Tragedy

Kyrgyzstan
formerly: **10** Kirghiz SSR
capital/largest city: **6** Frunze **7** Bishkek
head of state: **9** president
government: **8** republic
monetary unit: **3** som
mountain: **8** Tian Shan
people: **5** Uzbek **6** Kyrgyz **7** Kirghiz, Russian
language: **6** Turkic **7** Kirghiz, Russian
religion: **6** Muslim **10** Sunni Islam

Kyrie eleison **13** Lord have mercy

Laban
  father: 7 Bethuel
  grandfather: 5 Nahor
  daughter: 4 Leah 6 Rachel
  sister: 7 Rebekah
  son-in-law: 5 Jacob

label 3 tag 4 mark, name, note, seal, sign, slip 5 brand, stamp, tally, title 6 define, docket, ticket 7 earmark, mark off, sticker 8 classify, describe 9 designate 10 denominate, put a mark on 11 appellation, designation, inscription 12 characterize 13 specification 14 classification, identification 16 characterization

labor, labour 4 plod, toil, work 5 slave, sweat 6 drudge, effort, suffer 7 agonize, travail, workers, workmen 8 drudgery, exertion, laborers, manpower, plodding, plug away, struggle 9 employees, grind away, work force 10 birth pangs, childbirth, menial work, smart under 11 birth throes, manual labor, parturition 12 accouchement, be affected by, be burdened by, be troubled by 13 be the victim of 14 employ one's time, work like a slave

labored 5 heavy, stiff 6 clumsy, forced, wooden 7 awkward, cramped, halting, studied 8 drawnout, overdone, strained 9 contrived, difficult, laborious, maladroit, ponderous, unnatural 13 self-conscious, unspontaneous

laborer 4 esne, hand, peon, serf 6 coolie, drudge, menial, toiler, worker 7 plodder, workman 8 handyman, hired man, hireling, workhand 9 hired hand 10 roustabout, wage earner, workingman 11 proletarian 12 manual worker 16 blue- collar worker

laborious 4 hard 6 brutal, severe, uphill 7 arduous, irksome, labored, onerous, wearing, rigorous, tiresome, toilsome, wearying 9 demanding, difficult, effortful, fa- tiguing, herculean, strenuous, wearisome 10 burdensome, oppressive, struggling 11 troublesome

laboriously 4 hard 9 arduously 14 with difficulty 15 with great effort

laboriousness 5 trial 8 tough job 10 difficulty, rough going, uphill work 11 arduousness 12 hard sledding 15 troublesomeness

labor omnia vincit 15 work conquers all
  motto of: 8 Oklahoma

Labors of Hercules *see* 8 Hercules

labyrinth 3 web 4 knot, maze 5 snarl 6 jungle, morass, riddle, tangle 7 complex, network 9 intricacy, mare's nest 10 complexity, perplexity, wilderness 11 convolution

Labyrinth
  form: 4 maze
  location: 5 Crete
  built by: 8 Daedalus
  for: 9 King Minos
  challenged by: 7 Theseus
  he was aided by: 7 Ariadne
  with: 6 thread
  housed: 8 Minotaur

Lacaille, Nicholas Louis de
  field: 9 astronomy
  nationality: 6 French
  mapped: 14 constellations

lace 3 tie 4 beat, bind, cane, dope, lash, whip 5 braid, cinch, close, flail, spank, spike, strap, tie up, truss 6 dope up, fasten, flavor, infuse, punish, secure, tether, thrash 7 fortify, spice up, suffuse, tighten 8 chastise, make fast, make taut 10 strengthen 11 add liquor to 12 add spirits to, draw together, give a beating

Lacedaemon
  founder of: 6 Sparta
  father: 4 Zeus
  mother: 8 Taygete
  wife: 6 Sparta
  son: 7 Amyclas
  daughter: 8 Eurydice
  descendants: 5 Helen 6 Castor, Pollux 8 Dioscuri 9 Hippocoon, Tyndarius 12 Clytemnestra

lacerate 3 cut, rip 4 gash, hurt, pain, scar, stab, tear 5 lance, sever, slash, slice, wound 6 deface 7 agonize, scratch, torment, torture 8 distress, give pain, puncture 10 excruciate 11 inflict pain

lacerating 5 acute 6 fierce, severe 7 cutting, extreme, intense, violent 12 excruciating

laceration 3 cut, rip 4 tear 5 wound 10 mutilation

Lachaise, Gaston
  born: 5 Paris 6 France
  artwork: 12 Standing Nude 13 Standing Woman 14 Floating Figure

Lachesis
  form: 4 Fate
  holds: 12 thread of life
  determines: 6 length 7 destiny

lachrymose 3 sad 5 teary, weepy 6 crying 7 maudlin, tearful, weeping 8 mournful 10 melancholy

lack 4 miss, need, want 6 dearth 7 absence 8 omission, scarcity, shortage 9 be missing, be short of, depletion, neediness, privation, scantness 10 deficiency, exhaustion 11 deprivation, fall short of 12 be inadequate 13 be caught short, be deficient in 14 be found wanting, be insufficient

lackadaisical 4 idle 7 languid, loafing 8 lifeless, listless, mindless 9 apathetic, lethargic, unexcited 10 inanimated, phlegmatic, spiritless, unaspiring, uninspired 11 indifferent, languishing, unambitious, unconcerned, unexcitable, unmotivated 12 uninterested 13 dillydallying

lackey 4 page 5 slave, toady, usher, valet 6 butler, flunky, helper, menial, minion, squire, waiter 7 servant, steward 8 employee, follower, hanger-on, hireling, inferior, retainer 9 assistant, attendant, cupbearer, mercenary, underling

lacking 7 needing, wanting 9 deficient 10 inadequate 12 falling short, insufficient
  French: 6 manque

lackluster 4 blah, dead, drab, dull 5 bland, muted 6 boring, dreary, leaden, pallid, somber 7 humdrum, nothing, prosaic, subdued 8 lifeless, mediocre, ordinary 9 colorless 10 lusterless 11 commonplace 12 run-of-the-mill 13 uninteresting

lack of conviction 5 doubt 8 question 9 misgiving 10 hesitation, indecision 11 uncertainty
  trait of: 14 Doubting Thomas

lack of faith 5 doubt 7 atheism 8 distrust, mistrust 9 disbelief, suspicion

lack of feeling 6 apathy 8 coldness, numbness 11 impassivity 15 emotionlessness, hardheartedness, passionlessness

lack of interest 5 ennui 6 apathy 7 boredom 9 unconcern 12 indifference

lack of respect 8 contempt, rudeness

9 disregard **10** disrespect **11** discourtesy, irreverence **12** impoliteness

lack of skill 9 inability **10** clumsiness, ineptitude **11** awkwardness **12** incompetency

Laclos, Pierre Choderlos de
author of: **22** Les Liaisons Dangereuses

Lacombe, Lucien
director: **10** Louis Malle
cast: **12** Pierre Blaise **13** Aurore Clement **16** Holger Lowenadler

laconic 4 curt **5** blunt, brief, pithy, short, terse **7** compact, concise, pointed, spartan, summary **8** succinct **9** condensed **10** to the point **12** concentrated **14** sparing of words

lacquer 4 coat **5** glaze **7** coating, shellac, varnish

lacrimoso
music: **7** tearful

lacrosse
Indian name: **9** bagataway
circle around goal: **6** crease
played with: **6** crosse **14** pouched racquet
players/team: **3** ten
position: **6** goalie **9** attackman **10** defenseman, midfielder
term: **6** riding **8** clearing

lacuna 3 gap, pit **4** gulf, hole, void **5** blank, break, crack, ditch, pause, space **6** breach, cavity, hiatus **7** caesura, fissure, interim, opening, vacancy **8** interval, omission **10** interstice, suspension **12** interruption **13** discontinuity

lacustrine 7 aquatic **8** riparian **11** lake-growing **12** lake-dwelling

lacy 4 fine **5** filmy, gauzy, meshy, netty, sheer, webby **6** barred, frilly, netted, porous, webbed **7** gridded, netlike **8** cobwebby, delicate, filigree, gossamer, lacelike, retiform **9** filigreed **10** diaphanous, reticulate **11** latticelike, transparent

lad 3 boy, kid **5** sprig, youth **6** shaver, sprout **8** juvenile, young man **9** schoolboy, stripling, young chap, youngster **11** young fellow

Ladd, Alan
son: **5** David **6** Alan Jr
co-star: **12** Veronica Lake
born: **12** Hot Springs AR
roles: **5** Shane **13** The Blue Dahlia **14** The Great Gatsby, This Gun for Hire

ladies' man 4 beau, stud **5** spark **6** escort, gigolo **7** playboy **8** cavalier, gay blade

Ladino
also: **7** Judezmo **12** Judeo-Spanish
spoken by: **9** Sephardim
based on: **10** Old Spanish
script: **6** Hebrew **7** mestizo

Ladoga, Lake

largest in: **6** Europe
located in: **6** Russia

La Dolce Vita
director: **15** Federico Fellini
cast: **9** Lex Barker, Nadia Gray **10** Anouk Aimee **11** Anita Ekberg **19** Marcello Mastroianni

ladrone 5 thief **6** bandit, outlaw

lady 4 wife **5** woman **6** female, matron, spouse **7** duchess, peeress **8** baroness, countess **10** aristocrat, noblewoman **11** gentlewoman, marchioness, viscountess, woman of rank **13** well-bred woman
German: **4** frau
Italian: **5** donna
Spanish/Portuguese: **4** dona

Lady Chatterley's Lover
author: **10** D H Lawrence
character: **7** Mellors **19** Constance Chatterley

Lady Eve, The
director: **14** Preston Sturges
cast: **10** Henry Fonda **13** Charles Coburn **14** Eugene Pallette **15** Barbara Stanwyck, William Demarest

Lady for a Day
director: **10** Frank Capra
based on story by: **11** Damon Runyon
cast: **9** Guy Kibbee, May Robson **13** Warren William
remade as: **19** Pocketful of Miracles

Lady from Dubuque, The
author: **11** Edward Albee

Lady from the Sea, The
author: **11** Henrik Ibsen

Lady in Chair
constellation of: **10** Cassiopeia

ladylike 5 civil **6** modest, polite, proper **7** courtly, elegant, genteel, refined **8** cultured, decorous, mannerly, polished, well-bred **9** courteous, dignified **10** cultivated **11** respectable **12** well mannered **13** well brought up

Lady of the Camellias, The see **7** Camille

Lady of the Lake, The
author: **14** Sir Walter Scott
character: **9** Allan Bane **11** Roderick Dhu **12** Ellen Douglas **13** Malcolm Graeme **14** James Fitz-James, James of Douglas

Lady Oracle
author: **14** Margaret Atwood

lady's maid
French: **14** femme de chambre

Lady's Not for Burning, The
author: **14** Christopher Fry

lady's-slipper, lady-slipper
varieties: **4** pink **5** showy **6** orchid **8** mountain, ram's-head **9** two-leaved **10** small white **11** large yellow, small yellow

Lady Vanishes, The
director: **15** Alfred Hitchcock

cast: **9** Paul Lukas **13** Dame May Whitty **15** Michael Redgrave **16** Margaret Lockwood

Lady Windermere's Fan
author: **10** Oscar Wilde
character: **10** Mrs Erlynne **14** Lord Darlington, Lord Windermere **18** Lord Augustus Lorton

Laertes
son: **8** Odysseus

Laertes
character in: **6** Hamlet
sister: **7** Ophelia
father: **8** Polonius
author: **11** Shakespeare

La Farge, John
born: **9** New York NY
artwork: **14** Maua Our Boatman **17** The Muse of Painting **18** Red and White Peonies

La Fayette, Comtesse de
author of: **19** La Princesse de Cleves

Lafayette, Marquis de
also: **38** Marie Joseph Paul Yves Roch Gilbert du Motier
nationality: **6** French
served in: **14** July Revolution **16** French Revolution **18** American Revolution
battle: **8** Yorktown **10** Brandywine

Lafcadio's Adventures (The Vatican Swindle)
author: **9** Andre Gide

La Fontaine, Jean de
author of: **6** Fables

lag 4 drag, halt, inch, limp, snag **5** dally, delay, hitch, tarry, trail **6** be idle, be late, be slow, dawdle, falter, hold up, linger, loiter, trudge **7** be tardy, setback, slacken, stagger **8** be behind, hang back, slowdown **9** be overdue, inch along **10** drag behind, slackening **11** slowing down **12** bide one's time, take one's time **13** falling behind, procrastinate

laggard 4 mope, poke, slow, slug **5** idler, snail, tardy **6** loafer, remiss **7** dallier, dawdler, lounger **8** lingerer, loiterer, potterer, putterer, slowfoot, slowpoke, sluggard, sluggish **9** donothing, straggler **12** dilly-dallier **13** stick-in-the-mud

lagniappe, lagnappe 3 tip **4** gift, perk **5** bonus, favor, prize **7** largess, memento, present **8** gratuity, largesse **9** pourboire

Lagos
former capital of: **7** Nigeria

Lahr, Bert
real name: **14** Irving Lahrheim
born: **9** New York NY
roles: **12** Cowardly Lion **13** The Wizard of Oz

laic 3 lay **5** civil **6** laical **7** amateur, popular, profane, secular, worldly **8** temporal **11** nonclerical, nonpastoral

12 secularistic **13** inexperienced **15** nonprofessional **17** nonecclesiastical

lair 3 den, lie, mew **4** hole, nest **5** cover, haunt **6** burrow, cavern, covert **7** hideout, retreat **8** hideaway **9** sanctuary **12** resting place

laissez-faire, laisser-faire 8 hands off **9** let them be, unconcern **12** indifference **14** let-alone policy, live and let live **15** noninterference, nonintervention

laissez-passer 4 pass **6** permit **11** allow to pass

Laius
king of: **6** Thebes
father: **8** Labdacus
great-grandfather: **6** Cadmus
wife: **7** Jocasta
son: **7** Oedipus
killed by: **7** Oedipus

Lajeunesse, Gabriel
character in: **10** Evangeline
author: **10** Longfellow

lake
of Afghanistan: **7** Helmand **13** Hamud-i-Helmand
of Albania: **4** Ulze **5** Matia, Ohrid **6** Prespa **7** Ochrida, Scutari, Shkoder **8** Ohridsko
of Algeria: **5** Hodna **6** Sabkha **7** Cherqui, Fedjadj, Meirhir **10** Azzel Matti, Meherrhane
of Andorra: **11** Engolasters
of Argentina: **6** Viedma **7** Cardiel, Fagnano, Musters **11** Buenos Aires, Mar Chiquita, Nahuel Huapi
of Armenia: **3** Van **5** Sevan, Urmia **8** Urumiyah
of Australia: **4** Eyre **5** Carey, Cowan, Frome, Moore, Wells **6** Austin, Barlee, Bulloo, Dundas, Harris, Mackay **7** Amadeus, Blanche, Everard, Torrens **8** Carnegie, Gairdner **9** MacDonald **10** Yammayamma **14** Disappointment
of Austria: **6** Almsee **7** Fertoto, Mondsee **8** Bodensee, Traunsee **9** Constance **10** Neusiedler
of Benin: **5** Aheme **6** Nokoue
of Bolivia: **5** Poopo **7** Allagas, Coipasa, Rogagua **8** Titicaca **10** Desaguader
of Botswana: **3** Dow, Xau **5** Ngami
of Brazil: **4** Aima, Feia **5** Mirim **13** Logo dos Platos
of Burundi: **7** Rugwero **8** Tshohoha **10** Tanganyika
of Cambodia/Kampuchea: **8** Tonle Sap
of Cameroon: **4** Chad
of Canada: **4** Cree, Erie, Gras, Seul **5** Garry, Huron, Rainy **6** Louise, St John **7** Abitibi, Dubawnt, Nipigon, Ontario, Testlin **8** Kootenay, Manitoba, Okanagan, Reindeer, Superior, Winnipeg **9** Athabaska, Great Bear, Nipissing **10** Great Slave, Mistassini **12** Winnipegosis

of Central African Republic: **4** Assa
of Chad: **4** Chad
of Chile: **5** Ranco **6** Yelcho **7** Puyehue, Rupanco **8** Cochrane **10** General Paz, Llanquihue **11** Buenos Aires
of China: **3** Tai **4** Chao, Na-mu **5** Kaoyu, Oling, Telli **6** Bamtso, Bornor, Ebinor, Erhhai, Khanka, Lopnor, Namtso, Poyang **7** Chaling, Hungtse, Karanor, Kokonor **8** Hulunnor, Montcalm, Taroktso, Tellinor, Tienchih, Tsinghai, Tungting
of Colombia: **4** Tota
of the Congo: **5** Mweru, Tumba **6** Albert, Nyanza, Upemba **7** Leopold **11** Stanley Pool
of Costa Rica: **6** Arenal
of Denmark **6** Arreso
of Djibouti: **4** Abbe **5** Assal
of Dominican Republic: **10** Enriquillo
of Egypt: **4** Edku, Idku **5** Qarun **6** Maryut, Moeris, Nasser **7** Manzala **8** Burullus, Mareotis
of El Salvador: **5** Guiha, Guija **8** Ilopango **10** Coatepeque
of England: **8** Grasmere **9** Ennerdale, Ullswater, Wastwater **10** Buttermere, Windermere **12** Derwentwater **13** Coniston Water
of Estonia: **5** Pskov **6** Peipus **9** Vortsjarv
of Ethiopia: **3** Abe **4** Tana **5** Abaya, Shola, Tanna, Tsana, Tzana, Zeway **6** Dambea, Dembea, Rudolf **8** Blue Nile, Stefanie
of Finland: **3** Juo, Muo **4** Kemi, Kiui, Nasi, Oulu, Puru, Pyha, Simo **5** Enara, Enare, Hauki, Inari, Kalla, Lappa, Lesti, Puula, Saima **6** Ladoya, Lentua, Saimaa, Sounne, Syvari **7** Koitere, Nilakka **8** Pielinen **9** Kalavesi, Pielavesi
of France: **6** Annecy, Cazaux, Geneva
of Gabon Republic: **7** Anengue, Azinguo
of Germany, East: **6** Muritz
of Germany, West: **9** Constance **11** Inner Alster, Outer Alster
of Ghana: **5** Volta **8** Bosumtwi
of Greece: **5** Karla, Volve **6** Copais, Kopais, Prespa, Voweis **8** Ioannina, Koroneia, Vistonis **9** Trichonis, Vegoritis
of Grenada: **10** Grand Etang
of Guatemala: **5** Dulce, Guija, Peten **6** Izabal **7** Atitlan **9** Amatitlan, Peten Itza
of Haiti: **8** Saumatre
of Honduras: **5** Criba, Yojoa **6** Brewer
of Hungary: **5** Ferto **7** Balaton, Velence **9** Blatensee **10** Neusiedler, Plattensee
of Iceland: **6** Myvatn **10** Thorisvatn **14** Thingvallavatn
of India: **5** Jheel, Lonar, Wular **6** Chilka, Colair, Dhebar, Kolair **7** Kol-

leru, Pulicat, Pushkar, Sambahr
of Indonesia: **4** Toba **5** Ranau **6** Towuti
of Iran: **5** Niris, Tasht, Tuzlu, Urmia **6** Sahweh, Sistan **7** Maharlu **8** Nemekser, Urumiyeh
of Iraq: **6** al-Milh **7** Sanniya **8** al-Hammar
of Ireland: **3** Doo, Key, Ree, Tay **4** Conn, Derg, Erne, Mask **5** Allen, Barra, Carra, Gowna, Leane, Lough, Neagh **6** Boderg, Cooter, Corrib, Ennell **7** Dromore, Gougane, Oughter, Sheelin **9** Killarney
of Israel: **5** Huleh **7** Dead Sea **8** Kinneret, Tiberias **12** Sea of Galilee
of Italy: **4** Como, Iseo, Nemi **5** Garda **6** Albano, Lesina, Lugano, Varano **7** Bolsena, Perugia **8** Maggiore **9** Bracciano, Trasimeno
of Japan: **4** Biwa, Suwa, Toya **6** Towada **8** Kutchawa, Shikotsu
of Kazakhstan: **8** Balkhash
of Kenya: **6** Magadi, Nakuru, Natron, Rudolf **7** Turkana **8** Naivasha, Victoria
of Lebanon: **5** Quran **6** Qirawn
of Lithuania: **5** Dysna
of Luxembourg: **8** Haut Sure
of Macedonia: **5** Ohrid **6** Prespa **7** Ochrida
of Madagascar: **5** Itasy **7** Alaotra, Kinkony
of Malawi: **5** Nyasa **6** Chilwa, Malawi
of Mali: **2** Do **4** Debo **5** Garou **7** Korarou **9** Faguibine
of Mexico: **7** Chapala, Texcoco **9** Patzcuaro
of Mongolia: **3** Uvs **5** Har Us **6** Bor Nor **7** Ghirgis, Ubsa Nor **8** Airik Nor, Durga Nor, Hobsogol, Khara Usu **9** Khubsugul, Khukhu-Nur **10** Khirgis Nor
of Montenegro: **7** Scutari, Shkoder
of Mozambique: **5** Nyasa **6** Chuali, Nyassa **8** Nhavarre
of Myanmar: **4** Inle
of Nauru: **11** Buada Lagoon
of the Netherlands: **7** Haarlem **10** Ijsselmeer **11** Grevelingen, Hazinguliet
of New Zealand: **3** Ada **4** Gunn, Ohau **5** Hawea, Taupo **6** Pukaki, Pupuke, Te Anau, Tekapo, Wanaka **7** Brunner, Diamond, Kanieri, Okareka, Rotorua **8** Okataina, Paradise, Rotoaira, Wakatipi **9** Manapouri
of Nicaragua: **7** Managua **9** Nicaragua
of Niger: **4** Chad
of Nigeria: **4** Chad
of the Nile: **4** Tana **5** Kyoga, Tsana **6** Albert, Edward, Nasser **8** Victoria
of Norway: **4** Alte **5** Ister, Mjosa, Snasa **6** Femund **7** Rostavn, Tunnsjo
of Panama: **5** Gatun
of Paraguay: **4** Vera, Ypoa **8** Ypa-

carai
of Peru: 8 Titicaca
of Poland: 5 Goplo, Mamry **8** Niego-cin, Sniardwy **13** Stettin Lagoon
of Puerto Rico: 5 Loiza **6** Carite **8** Dos Bocas **9** Caonillas, Guatajaca
of Romania: 5 Sinoe **6** Snagov
of Russia: 3 Seg **4** Azov, Kola, Neva **5** Byelo, Chany, Elton, Erara, Ilmen, Lacha, Onega, Vozhe **6** Baikal, La-doga **10** Caspian Sea
of Rwanda: 4 Kivu **5** Ihema **6** Buf-era, Bulera, Mohasi **7** Rugwero, Ruh-nodo **8** Mugesera, Tshohoha
of Sardinia: 6 Omodeo
of Scotland: 3 Awe, Dee, Lin, Tay **4** Earn, Fyne, Gair, Gare, Linn, Ness, Oich, Ryan, Sloy **5** Duich, Leven, Lochy, Lough, Morar, Maree, Nevis **6** Laggan, Linnhe, Lomond **7** Kat-rine, Rannoch, St Marys
of Senegal: 6 Guiers
of Sicily: 7 Pergusa **8** Camarina
of Slovenia: 4 Bled
of Spain: 4 Lago **9** Albrifera
of the Sudan: 2 No **4** Chad, Toad **6** Nasser
of Sweden: 4 Ster **5** Asnen, Malar, Silja, Vaner **6** Vanern, Vatter, Wen-nen **7** Hielmar, Malaren, Vattern **8** Dalalven **9** Hjalmaren
of Switzerland: 3 Uri, Zug **4** Biel, Thon, Thun **5** Ageri, Leman, Morat **6** Bienne, Brienz, Geneva, Lugano, Sarnen, Wallen, Zurich **7** Hallwil, Lucerne, Lungern **8** Maggiore, Vierw-ald **9** Bielersee, Constance, Neucha-tel, Sarnersee, Thunersee
of Syria: 5 Merom **7** Djeboid **8** Tibe-rias
of Tanzania: 5 Eyasi, Nyasa, Rukwa **6** Malawi, Natron, Nyassa **7** Man-yara **8** Victoria **10** Tanganyika
of Thailand: 9 Nong Lahan
of Tibet: 3 Aru, Bam, Bum, Nam **4** Mema, Tosu **5** Jagok, Tabia **6** Dag-tse, Garhur, Kashun, Nam Iso, Sel-ing, Tangra, Yamdok **7** Kyaring, Terinam, Tsaring, Zilling **8** Jiggitai **9** Tengrinor **11** Manasarowar
of Tunisia: 6 Achkel, Djerid **7** Bizerte
of Turkey: 3 Tuz, Van **7** Egridir **8** Beysehir
of Uganda: 5 Kioga, Kyoga **6** Albert, Edward, George **8** Victoria
of the United States: 4 Erie, Mead **5** Huron, Tahoe **6** Cayuga, Finger, George, Itasca, Oneida, Seneca **7** Il-iamma, Ontario **8** Michigan, Superior **9** Champlain, Great Salt, Salton Sea, Teshekpuk, Winnebago **10** Okeecho-bee **11** Yellowstone **13** Pontchar-train, Wallenpaupack, Winnipesau-kee **14** Lake of the Woods
of Uruguay: 5 Merin, Mirim **18** Em-balse del Rio Negro
of Venezuela: 9 Maracaibo, Tacarigua

of Wales: 4 Bala **6** Vyrnwy
of Yugoslavia: 4 Bled **5** Ohrid **6** Prespa **7** Ochrida, Scutari
of Zaire: 4 Kivu **5** Mweru, Tumba **6** Albert, Edward, Upemba **9** Mai-Ndombe **10** Tanganyika
of Zambia: 5 Mweru **6** Kariba **9** Bangweulu **10** Tanganyika
of Zimbabwe: 4 Kyle **6** Kariba

Lake, Veronica
real name: 29 Constance Frances Ma-rie Ockelman
co-star: 8 Alan Ladd
born: 10 Brooklyn NY
roles: 13 The Blue Dahlia **14** I Mar-ried a Witch, This Gun for Hire **16** Sullivan's Travels

Lake Isle of Innisfree, The
author: 7 W B Yeats

L'Allegro
author: 10 John Milton
companion piece: 11 Il Penseroso

Lalo, (Victor Antoine) Edouard
born: 5 Lille **6** France
composer of: 7 Namouna **8** Le Roi d'Ys **11** The King of Ys **15** Spanish Symphony **18** Symphonie Espagnole

lama 4 monk **6** priest
in: 7 Lamaism
high priest: 9 Dalai Lama
locale: 5 Tibet

Lamar, Ruby
character in: 9 Sanctuary
author: 8 Faulkner

Lamarck, Jean B
field: 7 biology
forerunner of theory of: 9 evolution
author of: 21 Philosophie Zoologique

La Mare, Walter de
author of: 16 Memoirs of a Midget

Lamarr, Hedy
real name: 21 Hedwig Eva Maria Kiesler
born: 6 Vienna **7** Austria
roles: 7 Ecstasy **16** Samson and Deli-lah

Lamas, Fernando
wife: 10 Arlene Dahl **14** Esther Wil-liams
son: 7 Lorenzo
born: 9 Argentina **11** Buenos Aires
roles: 13 The Merry Widow **16** Dan-gerous When Wet **23** The Girl Who Had Everything

Lamb, Charles
author of: 12 Essays of Elia **13** Dream Children **20** Tales From Shakespeare **25** A Dissertation upon Roast Pig **31** Specimens of English Dramatic Poets
pseudonym: 4 Elia
sister: 4 Mary

lambaste 4 beat, drub, lick, pelt, whip **5** scold, smear **6** berate, defeat, pum-mel, rebuke, subdue, thrash, wallop **7** bawl out, censure, chew out, clobber, cuss out, shellac, trounce **8** bludgeon,

denounce, vanquish **9** castigate, dress down, light into, overwhelm, repri-mand

lambent 6 bright **7** radiant, shining **8** luminous, lustrous **10** flickering, shimmering

Lambert, Constant
born: 6 London **7** England
composer of: 9 Horoscope, Rio Grande **14** Romeo and Juliet **17** Mu-sic for Orchestra **27** Summer's Last Will and Testament

lame 4 game, halt, weak **5** sorry **6** clumsy, feeble, flimsy, infirm, maimed; uncool **7** failing, halting, hobbled, limping, unsound, wanting **8** crippled, deformed, disabled **9** defi-cient, faltering **10** inadequate **11** inef-fectual **12** insufficient, unconvincing, unpersuasive **14** unsatisfactory

lamebrain 3 ass, sap **4** fool **5** booby, dunce, idiot, moron, ninny **6** dimwit, nitwit **7** fathead, half-wit **8** bonehead, dumb-dumb, imbecile, lunkhead, numskull **9** blockhead, numbskull **10** dunderhead, nincompoop **11** chow-derhead

lamebrained 4 dumb **6** stupid **7** asi-nine, foolish, idiotic, moronic **8** crack-pot **9** dimwitted, imbecilic **10** half-witted **12** feeble-minded, simple-minded

Lamech
father: 9 Methusael **10** Methuselah
wives: 4 Adah **6** Zillah
son: 5 Jabal, Jubal **9** Tubalcain
daughter: 6 Naamah

lament 3 cry, sob **4** moan, wail, weep **5** dirge, mourn **6** bewail, outcry, plaint, regret **7** deplore, keening, req-uiem, whimper **8** mourning **9** death song **11** condole with, lamentation **12** funeral music **13** complain about **14** express pity for, show concern for, sympathize with **15** commiserate with

lamentable 4 dire **6** woeful **7** piteous **8** dreadful, grievous, pathetic, pitiable, shameful, terrible, wretched **9** miser-able **10** deplorable **11** distressing, re-gret- table, unfortunate **13** dishearten-ing, heart- breaking

Lamia
author: 9 John Keats

Lamia
form: 7 monster
characteristic: 12 blood-sucking

La Motta, Jake (Jacob)
nickname: 9 Bronx Bull
sport: 6 boxing
class: 12 middleweight
movie biography: 10 Raging Bull

Lamour, Dorothy
real name: 23 Mary Leta Dorothy Kau- meyer
trademark: 6 sarong
co-star: 7 Bob Hope **10** Bing Crosby
born: 12 New Orleans LA

roles:
Road to: 3 Rio **4** Bali **6** Utopia **7** Morocco **8** Hong Kong, Zanzibar **9** Singapore

L'Amour, Louis
author of: 5 Hondo, Lando **7** Sackett, Shalako **8** Conagher **10** Key-Lock Man, Rivers West **14** The Californios, The Daybreakers **15** Westward the Tide **16** How the West Was Won, Over on the Dry Side **21** The Man from Broken Hills, To the Far Blue Mountains

lamp 4 bulb **5** light, torch **6** beacon **7** blinker, lantern **9** headlight, spotlight **10** chandelier, floodlight, Kleig light, night light **11** searchlight **12** ceiling light, reading light **14** ceiling fixture
invented by:
arc: 6 Staite
incandescent: 6 Edison
incandescent frosted: 6 Pipkin
incandescent gas: 8 Langmuir
Kleig: 7 Kleigel
mercury vapor: 6 Hewitt
miner's safety: 4 Davy
neon: 6 Claude

Lampedusa, Giuseppe di
author of: 10 The Leopard

lampoon 5 farce, put-on, spoof, squib **6** parody, satire, send up **7** mockery, takeoff **8** diatribe, ridicule, satirize, travesty **9** broadside, burlesque **10** caricature, pasquinade **11** make light of

Lamus
father: 8 Hercules
mother: 7 Omphale
attacked: 5 ships

Lamy of Santa Fe
author: 10 Paul Horgan

lanai 4 deck **5** porch **7** terrace, veranda

Lancaster 17 English royal house
faction in: 13 War of the Roses
founder: 11 John of Gaunt
symbol: 7 red rose

Lancaster, Burt
real name: 22 Burton Stephen Lancaster
born: 9 New York NY
roles: 5 Moses **9** All My Sons, Local Hero **11** Elmer Gantry (Oscar) **12** Atlantic City, The Rainmaker **13** The Rose Tattoo **14** Seven Days in May **16** Sorry Wrong Number **17** Birdman of Alcatraz **18** From Here to Eternity **19** Come Back Little Sheba, Sweet Smell of Success

lance 4 gaff, pike **5** shaft, spear **7** assegai, halberd, harpoon, javelin

Lancelot, Launcelot
character in: 16 Arthurian romance
also called: 13 Lancelot du Lac
father: 3 Ban
son: 7 Galahad
lover: 6 Elaine **9** Guinevere
home: 10 Joyous Gard

lancer 8 cavalier, horseman **10** cavalryman **12** horse soldier, horse trooper **14** mounted soldier

Lanchester, Elsa
real name: 17 Elizabeth Sullivan
husband: 15 Charles Laughton
born: 7 England **8** Lewisham
roles: 15 Come to the Stable **22** The Bride of Frankenstein **24** Witness for the Prosecution **25** The Private Life of Henry VIII **31** The Private Life of Henry the Eighth

land 3 get, lea, nab, net **4** area, dirt, dock, gain, grab, lawn, loam, moor, park, soil, take, ward, zone **5** acres, catch, earth, grass, green, humus, light, put in, realm, seize, shire, snare, state, tie up, tract **6** alight, anchor, canton, clinch, colony, county, debark, domain, empire, fields, ground, meadow, nation, parish, realty, region, secure **7** acreage, capture, country, descend, dry land, grounds, kingdom, pasture, section, set down, subsoil, terrain, win over **8** come down, district, dominion, farmland, homeland, location, mainland, make land, make port, precinct, property, province, republic, vicinity **9** cornfield, disembark, grassland, lay anchor, lay hold of, lead one to, reach land, territory **10** bring one to, carry one to, come to land, drop anchor, fatherland, motherland, native land, native soil, real estate, settle down, settlement, terra firma, wheat field **11** countryside, put into port **12** commonwealth, put into shore, real property, village green **13** the old country

Landau, Lev Davidovitch
field: 7 physics
nationality: 7 Russian
discovered: 12 liquid helium **14** ferromagnetism
awarded: 10 Nobel Prize

landed property 5 manor **6** estate **8** compound **12** countryplace

land force 4 army **6** legion, troops **7** legions **8** infantry, soldiers, soldiery **9** artillery

Landless, Neville and Helena
characters in: 22 The Mystery of Edwin Drood
author: 7 Dickens

landlord 5 owner **6** holder, squire **8** landlady **9** landowner, possessor **10** freeholder, landholder, proprietor **13** property owner **14** lord of the manor

landmark 8 keystone, monument, signpost **9** benchmark, guidepost, highlight, high point, milestone, watershed **11** cornerstone **12** turning point **16** historic building

Landmarks
god of: 8 Terminus

Land of Enchantment
nickname of: 9 New Mexico

Land of Lincoln
nickname of: 8 Illinois

Land of Opportunity
nickname of: 8 Arkansas

Land of Sky-blue Waters
nickname of: 9 Minnesota

Land of Steady Habits
nickname of: 11 Connecticut

Land of Ten Thousand Lakes
nickname of: 9 Minnesota

Land of the Dakotas
nickname of: 11 North Dakota

Land of the Midnight Sun
nickname of: 6 Alaska

Landon, Michael
real name: 20 Eugene Maurice Orowitz
born: 13 Forest Hills NY
roles: 7 Bonanza **15** Highway to Heaven **19** Little Joe Cartwright **20** I Was a Teenage Werewolf **23** Little House on the Prairie

landscape 4 view **5** scene, sight, vista **6** aspect **7** scenery **8** panorama, prospect **9** spectacle **10** rural scene, scenic view **14** natural scenery

landscape architect 7 Le Notre, Olmsted

landsman 10 countryman **13** fellow citizen

Landsteiner, Karl
field: 8 medicine **9** pathology
distinguished: 10 blood types
identified: 8 RH factor
awarded: 10 Nobel Prize

lane 3 way **4** pass, path, road **5** alley, byway, drive, route, track, trail **6** access, avenue, bypath, course **7** passage, roadway **8** alleyway, approach, footpath **10** passageway

Lang, Walter
director of: 7 Desk Set **11** The King and I

Lange, Jessica
born: 9 Cloquet MN
roles: 7 Country, Frances, Tootsie **8** Cape Fear, King Kong **11** All That Jazz **16** Crimes of the Heart **26** The Postman Always Rings Twice

Langella, Frank
born: 9 Bayonne NJ
roles: 7 Dracula **23** The Diary of a Mad Housewife

Langland, William
author of: 12 Piers Plowman

Langmuir, Irving
field: 9 chemistry
invented: 15 atomic blowtorch **17** gas-tungsten lights
awarded: 10 Nobel Prize

language 4 cant, jive **5** argot, idiom, lingo, prose, slang, words **6** jargon, patois, speech, tongue **7** cursing, cussing, dialect, diction, wording **8** parlance, rhetoric, swearing, verbiage **9** discourse, elocution, profanity **10** ex-

pression, use of words, vernacular, vocabulary **11** imprecation, phraseology, profane talk **12** mother tongue, native tongue **13** colloquialism **14** public speaking, self-expression **16** manner of speaking, mode of expression **17** oral communication, reading and writing, verbal intercourse
of Afghanistan: 4 Dari **5** Farsi **6** Afghan, Pashto, Pushtu **7** Balochi, Baluchi, Persian
of Albania: 3 Geg **4** Cham, Gheg, Hish, Tosk **5** Greek **8** Albanian
of Algeria: 6 Arabic, Berber, French, Zenata **7** Senhaja
of Andorra: 6 French **7** Catalan, Spanish
of Angola: 5 Bantu **8** Kimbundu, Oumbundu **9** Ovimbundu **10** Portuguese
of Antigua and Barbuda: 7 English
of Argentina: 7 Spanish
of Armenia: 7 Russian **8** Armenian
of Australia: 6 Yabber **7** English **9** aborigine (dialects)
of Austria: 5 Czech **6** German, Magyar **8** Croatian **9** Slovenian
of Azerbaijan: 6 Turkic
of the Bahamas: 6 Creole **7** English
of Bahrain: 4 Urdu **5** Farsi **6** Arabic **7** English, Persian
of Bangladesh: 6 Bihari **7** Bengali, English
of Barbados: 7 English
of Belgium: 5 Dutch **6** French, German **7** Flemish
of Benin: 3 Fon **5** Dendi **6** Bariba, French, Fulani, Yoruba
of Bermuda: 7 English
of Bhutan: 5 Hindi, Lhoke **7** Tibetan **8** Dzongkha, Nepalese
of Bolivia: 6 Aymara **7** Quechua, Spanish
of Borneo: 5 Malay **7** Chinese, English
of Bosnia-Herzegovina: 13 Serbo Croatian
of Botswana: 5 Bantu, Click **6** Tswana **7** English, Khoisan **8** Setswana
of Brazil: 10 Portuguese
of Brunei: 4 Iban **5** Malay **7** Chinese, English
of Bulgaria: 9 Bulgarian
of Burkina Faso: 4 Bobo, Lobi, More, Samo **5** Dyula, Mande, Mossi **6** French
of Burundi: 6 French **7** Kirundi, Swahili
of Cambodia/Kampuchea: 5 Khmer **6** French
of Cameroon: 4 Bulu **5** Bantu, Bassa, Hausa **6** Douala, Ewondo, French, Fulani **7** English **8** Bamileke, Fulfulde
of Canada: 6 Eskimo, French **7** English
of Canary Islands: 7 Spanish

of Cape Verde: 7 Crioulo **10** Portuguese **13** Verdean Creole
of Central African Republic: 5 Sango, Zande **6** French
of Chad: 4 Sara **5** Turku **6** Arabic, French
of Chile: 7 Spanish
of China: 7 Chinese **8** Mandarin, Shanghai **9** Cantonese
of Colombia: 7 Spanish
of Comoros: 6 Arabic, French **7** Swahili **8** Malagasy
of Congo: 4 Susu **5** Bantu, Fiote **6** French, Kituba **7** Bangala, Lingala
of Costa Rica: 7 Spanish
of Crete: 5 Greek **6** Minoan **7** Linear A, Linear B
of Croatia: 8 Croatian **10** Serbo Croat
of Cuba: 7 Spanish
of Cyprus: 5 Greek **7** Turkish **8** Armenian
of Czechoslovakia/Czech Republic: 5 Czech **6** German, Magyar, Slovak **7** Russian **9** Hungarian
of Denmark: 4 Odan **6** Danish **8** Faeroese **11** Greenlander
of Djibouti: 4 Afar **6** Arabic, French, Somali
of Dominican Republic: 6 French **7** English, Spanish
of Ecuador: 6 Jibaro **7** Quechua, Spanish
of Egypt: 6 Arabic, Coptic, French **7** English
of El Salvador: 7 Spanish
of England: 7 English
of Equatorial Guinea: 4 Bubi, Fang **6** pidgin **7** Spanish
of Eritrea: 7 Amharic
of Estonia: 5 Tartu **10** Finno-Ugric
of Ethiopia: 3 Giz **4** Afar, Agow, Geez, Saho **5** Geeze, Ghese, Smali, Tigre **6** Arabic, Harari **7** Amharic, English, Italian, Russian **8** Gallinya, Irob-Saho, Tigrinya
of Fiji: 5 Hindi **6** Fijian **7** English
of Finland: 4 Avar, Lapp **5** Karen, Ugric, Vogul **6** Magyar, Ostyak, Tarast **7** Finnish, Olonets, Samoyed, Swedish **8** Estonian **10** Olenetsian
of France: 6 French
of Gabon Republic: 6 French
of The Gambia: 4 Fula **5** Wolof **6** Fulani **7** English, Malinke **8** Mandingo
of Georgia: 8 Georgian
of Germany: 6 German **10** High German **11** Hochdeutsch
of Ghana: 2 Ga **3** Ewe, Gur, Kwa, Twi **5** Fanti, Hausa **7** Dagomba, English
of Gibraltar: 7 English, Spanish
of Greece: 5 Greek
of Greenland: 6 Danish, Eskimo **11** Greenlandic
of Grenada: 7 English
of Guatemala: 6 Quiche **7** Spanish
of Guinea: 5 Fulbe, Mande **6** Arabic, French, Fulani **7** English

of Guinea-Bissau: 5 Fulah **7** Balante, Crioulo **8** Mandingo **10** Portuguese **21** Cape Verde--Guinea Creole
of Guyana: 5 Hindi **7** English
of Haiti: 6 Creole, French, patois
of Honduras: 7 English, Spanish
of Hong Kong: 7 Chinese, English **9** Cantonese
of Hungary: 6 German, Magyar, Slovak **8** Croatian **9** Hungarian **10** Finno-Ugric
of Iceland: 5 Norse **9** Icelandic
of India: 4 Urdu **5** Hindi, Oriya, Tamil **6** Sindhi, Telugu **7** Bengali, English, Kannada, Malayam, Marathi, Punjabi **8** Assamese, Gujarati, Kashmiri, Sanskrit **9** Malayalam
of Indonesia: 5 Tetum **6** Bahasa, Igorot **7** English, Gyarung, Malayan **8** Balinese, Chamorro, Javanese, Madurese, Sudanese **10** Indonesian, Polynesian
of Iran: 4 Luri, Zend **5** Farsi, Turki **6** Arabic **7** Baluchi, Kurdish, Persian **8** Armenian **11** Azerbaijani
of Iraq: 5 Farsi **6** Arabic **7** Kurdish, Persian, Turkish
of Ireland: 4 Erse **5** Irish **6** Gaelic **7** English
of Israel: 6 Arabic, French, Hebrew **7** English
of Italy: 5 Ladin, Latin **6** French, German **7** Italian, Slovene **8** Friulian **9** Sardinian
of Ivory Coast: 4 Akan **6** Dioula, French
of Jamaica: 6 Creole **7** English
of Japan: 5 Kanto **8** Japanese
of Java: 4 Kavi, Kawi **5** Malay **6** Sassak **8** Balinese, Madurese, Sudanese **16** Bahasa Indonesian
of Jordan: 6 Arabic
of Kazakhstan: 6 Kazakh
of Kenya: 3 Luo **5** Bantu, Luhya, Masai **6** Kikuyu **7** English, Swahili **8** Buyerati **10** Hindustani
of Kiribati: 6 Samoan **7** English **10** Gilbertese
of Korea: 6 Korean
of Kuwait: 6 Arabic
of Kyrgyzstan: 6 Turkic **7** Kirghiz
of Laos: 3 Lao, Man, Meo **6** French **7** English
of Latvia: 7 Lettish
of Lebanon: 6 Arabic, French, Syriac **7** English, Turkish **8** Armenian
of Lesotho: 5 Sotho **7** English, Sesotho
of Liberia: 3 Kru, Kwa **5** Mande **7** English
of Libya: 6 Arabic, Berber **7** English, Italian
of Liechtenstein: 6 German **10** Alemannish
of Lithuania: 5 Zmudz **6** Baltic **10** Lithuanian
of Luxembourg: 6 French, German **7** English **13** Letzeburgesch

of Macao: 7 Chinese, English **9** Cantonese **10** Portuguese
of Macedonia: 10 Macedonian
of Madagascar/Malagasy Republic: 6 French **8** Malagasy, Malgache
of Malawi: 3 Yao **4** Cewa **5** Bantu, Ngoni, Tonga **6** Nyanja **7** English, Tumbuka **8** Chichewa **10** Chitumbuka
of Malaysia: 4 Bugi, Dyak **5** Malay, Tamil **6** Battok, Rejang **7** Chinese, English, Lampong, Niasese **8** Achinese, Javanese, Makassar **14** Bahasa Malaysia
of Maldives: 6 Arabic, Divehi
of Mali: 5 Dogon, Dyula, Feulh, Mande, Marka **6** Berber, French, Fulani **7** Bambara, Malinke, Senoufo, Songhai
of Malta: 7 English, Italian, Maltese
of Mauritania: 4 Fula **5** Wolof **6** Arabic, French **7** Phoolor, Tukulor **8** Fulfulde, Mandingo **9** Sarakolle **10** Hassaniyya
of Mauritius: 4 Urdu **5** Hindi, Tamil **6** Creole, French **7** English
of Mexico: 5 Mayan, Otomi **6** Mixtec **7** Mazahua, Mazatec, Nahuatl, Spanish, Totonac, Zapotec **8** Tarascan
of Moldova: 8 Romanian **9** Moldovian
of Monaco: 6 French **7** English, Italian **10** Monegasque
of Mongolia: 6 Kazakh **16** Khalkha Mongolian
of Montenegro: 13 Serbo-Croatian
of Morocco: 6 Arabic, Berber, French **7** Spanish
of Mozambique: 3 Yao **5** Makua **6** Nyanji, Thonga **7** Swahili **10** Portuguese
of Myanmar: 3 Lai **4** Chin, Kuki, Pegu, Shan **5** Karen **6** Kachin **7** Burmese
of Namibia: 5 Bantu **6** German **7** English, Khoisan **9** Afrikaans
of Nauru: 7 English, Nauruan
of Nepal: 6 Nepali, Newari **7** English
of the Netherlands: 5 Dutch **7** English, Frisian
of New Guinea: 4 Motu **7** English **16** Melanesian Pidgin
of New Zealand: 5 Maori **7** English
of Nicaragua: 7 English, Spanish
of Niger: 5 Hausa, Mande **6** Djerma, French, Fulani, Tuareg **8** Mandingo, Tamashek
of Nigeria: 3 Ibo **4** Efik, Igbo **5** Hausa **6** Yoruba **7** English
of Norway: 4 Lapp **5** Norse **6** Bokmal **7** Nynorsk, Riksmal **8** Landsmal, Samnorsk **9** Landsmaal, Norwegian
of Oman: 4 Urdu **5** Hindi **6** Arabic **7** Baluchi
of Pakistan: 4 Urdu **6** Pushtu, Sindhi **7** Baluchi, Bengali, English, Punjabi
of Panama: 7 English, Spanish
of Paraguay: 6 German **7** Guarani, Spanish

of Peru: 6 Aymara **7** English, Quechua, Spanish
of the Philippines: 4 Moro **5** Bicol, Bikol **6** Ibanag **7** Cebuano, English, Ilocano, Spanish, Tagalog, Visayan **8** Filipino **9** Pampangan, Philipino **10** Samar-Leyte **13** Bamboo-English **14** Panay-Hiligayon
of Poland: 6 Kaszub, Polish **10** Pomeranian
of Polynesia: 4 Niue, Uvea **5** Maori **6** Samoan, Tongan **7** Austral, Tagalog, Tokelau **8** Hawaiian, Tahitian **9** Marquesan, Tuamatuan **10** Mangarevan
of Portugal: 10 Portuguese
of Qatar: 6 Arabic
of Romania: 6 French, Magyar **7** Russian **8** Romanian, Rumanian **9** Hungarian
of Russia: 5 Evenk **6** Buriat, Kalmyk **7** Finnish, Russian **8** Ossetian
of Rwanda: 6 French **7** Swahili **11** Kinyarwanda
of Samoa: 6 Samoan **7** English
of San Marino: 7 Italian
of Sao Tome and Principe: 10 Portuguese
of Sardinia: 7 Italian
of Saudi Arabia: 6 Arabic
of Scotland: 4 Erse **6** Celtic, Gaelic, Keltic, Lallan **7** English, Lalland
of Senegal: 5 Wolof **6** French
of the Seychelles: 6 Creole, French **7** English
of Sierra Leone: 4 Krio **5** Limba, Mende, Mendi, Temne **6** Creole **7** English
of Singapore: 5 Malay, Tamil **7** Chinese, English **8** Mandarin
of Slovakia: 6 Slovik Slovak
of Slovenia: 7 Slovene
of the Solomon Islands: 7 English **13** Pidgin English **16** Melanesian Pidgin
of Somalia: 6 Arabic, Somali **7** English, Italian
of South Africa: 4 Taal, Zulu **5** Bantu, Hindi, Nguni, Sotho, Swazi, Tamil, Venda, Xhosa **6** Telegu, Thonga **7** English, Khoisan, Ndebele, Sesotho **8** Bujarati, Fanakalo **9** Afrikaans **13** Kitchen-Kaffir
of Spain: 6 Basque **7** Catalan, Spanish **8** Balearic, Galician **9** Castilian, Valencian
of Sri Lanka: 4 Pali **5** Tamil **7** English **9** Sinhalese
of Sudan: 2 Ga **3** Efe, Ewe, Ibo, Kru, Vak, Vei **4** Efik, Mole, Tshi **6** Arabic, Nubian, Yoruba **7** English **8** Mandango, Mandingo **9** Ta Bedawie
of Suriname: 5 Carib, Dutch, Hindi **6** Arawak **7** English **8** Javanese, Taki-Taki **10** Hindustani **11** Sranan Tongo **12** Sranang Tongo
of Swaziland: 5 Ngumi **7** English, Siswati **9** Afrikaans **10** Portuguese
of Sweden: 4 Lapp **7** Swedish

of Switzerland: 5 Ladin **6** French, German **7** Italian **8** Romansch **14** Switzerdeutsch
of Syria: 6 Arabic, French, Syriac **7** Aramaic, English, Kurdish, Turkish **8** Armenian
of Taiwan: 4 Amon, Amoy **5** Hakka, Kuo Yu **6** Minnan **9** Taiwanese **15** Mandarin Chinese
of Tajikistan: 5 Tajik **7** Tadzhik
of Tanzania: 5 Bantu **6** Arabic **7** English, Khoisan, Nilotic, Swahili **8** Cushitic, Gujarati
of Thailand: 3 Lao, Tai **4** Ahom, Shan, Thai **5** Kadai **7** Bangkok, English **9** Krung Thep **12** Chinese Malay
of Tibet: 5 Balti **6** Ladkhi **7** Bhutani, Bodskad **8** Sanskrit **9** Bhutanese
of Togo: 3 Ana, Ewe, Twi **4** Mina **5** Hausa **6** French, Kabrai, Kabrie **7** Bassari, Dagomba, Quatchi **8** Kotokoli, Lotocoli
of Tonga: 6 Tongan **7** English
of Trinidad and Tobago: 6 French **7** Chinese, English, Spanish **10** Portuguese **12** French Patois
of Tunisia: 6 Arabic, Berber, French
of Turkey: 6 Arabic **7** Kurdish, Turkish
of Turkmenistan: 6 Turkic **10** West Turkic
of Tuvalu: 6 Samoan **7** English **8** Tuvaluan **10** Polynesian
of Uganda: 5 Ateso, Ganda **7** English, Luganda, Swahili
of Ukraine: 9 Ukrainian
of United Arab Emirates: 5 Farsi **6** Arabic **7** English, Persian
of Uruguay: 7 Italian, Spanish
of Uzbekistan: 5 Uzbek
of Vanuatu: 6 French **7** Bislama, English **16** Melanesian Pidgin
of Venezuela: 4 Pume **7** Spanish
of Vietnam: 3 Yue **4** Cham **5** Khmer, Rhade **6** French **7** Chinese, English **9** Cantonese **10** Vietnamese
of Wales: 5 Welsh **6** Celtic, Cymric, Keltic, Kymric **7** Cymraeg, English
of Western Sahara: 16 Hassaniyya Arabic
of Western Samoa: 6 Samoan **7** English
of Yemen: 6 Arabic
of Yugoslavia: 7 Bosnian, Slovene **8** Albanian, Croatian **9** Hungarian, Slovenian **10** Macedonian **11** Montenegrin **13** Herzegovinian, Serbo-Croatian
of Zaire: 5 Bantu **6** French **7** Chiluba, Kikongo, Lingala, Swahili **8** Sudanese, Tshiluba
of Zambia: 4 Lozi **5** Bemba, Lunda, Tonga **6** Luvale, Nyanja **7** English **9** Afrikaans
of Zimbabwe: 3 Ila **5** Bantu, Shona **7** English, Ndebele

language, artificial
of James Cooke Brown: 6 Loglan

of Hans Freudenthal: 6 Lincos **13** Lingua Cosmica
of Alexander Gode: 11 Interlingua
of C K Ogden: 12 Basic English
of J M Schleyer: 7 Volapuk
of Jean Francois Sudre: 8 Solresol
of L L Zamehof: 9 Esperanto
language, extinct 6 Dacian, Hattic, Lycian, Lydian, Palaic **7** Cornish, Elamite, Hittite, Hurrian **8** Etruscan, Illyrian, Phrygian, Sumerian, Thracian, Urartian **9** Dalmatian **15** Cuneiform Luwian **18** Hieroglyphic Luwian
languid 4 dull, slow, weak **5** faint, heavy, inert, shaky, spent, weary **6** feeble, infirm, leaden, sickly, supine, torpid **7** rickety, unsound, worn-out **8** drooping, fatigued, inactive, lifeless, listless, sluggish, unstable **9** apathetic, declining, doddering, enervated, exhausted, inanimate, lethargic, trembling, unhealthy **10** indisposed, spiritless **11** debilitated **12** on the decline **13** lackadaisical
languidness 6 apathy, torpor **7** inertia **8** lethargy **12** listlessness, sluggishness **13** indisposition
languish 3 ebb **4** fade, fail, flag, wane, wilt **5** covet, droop, faint **6** desire, hunger, sicken, thirst, wither **7** dwindle, long for, pine for, sigh for **8** diminish, give away, take sick, yearn for **9** become ill, break down, hanker for, hunger for, thirst for, waste away **10** go downhill **11** deteriorate, have a yen for, hunger after **12** be desirous of **13** go into decline
Languish, Lydia
character in: 9 The Rivals
author: 8 Sheridan
languor 5 ennui **6** torpor **7** inertia **8** dullness, hebetude, lethargy **9** indolence, lassitude, torpidity, weariness **10** dispassion, dreaminess **11** languidness, leisureness **12** lifelessness, listlessness, sluggishness
lank 4 bony, lean, limp, thin **5** gaunt, spare **6** skinny, slight **7** angular, scrawny **8** straight
lanky 4 bony, lean **5** gaunt, gawky, rangy, spare, weedy **6** skinny **7** angular, scrawny **8** gangling, rawboned **11** tall and thin
La Nouvelle Heloise
author: 10 J J Rousseau
Lansbury, Angela
born: 6 London **7** England
roles: 4 Mame **8** Gaslight **10** JB Fletcher **11** Sweeney Todd **14** Murder She Wrote **15** Jessica Fletcher **22** The Manchurian Candidate
Laocoon
vocation: 6 priest
father: 5 Priam
mother: 6 Hecuba
sons: 3 two (unnamed)
warned: 7 Trojans

warned of: 11 Trojan horse
killed by: 11 sea serpents
Laomedon
king of: 4 Troy
father: 4 Ilus
wife: 6 Strymo
son: 5 Priam **6** Lampus **7** Clytius **8** Hicetaon, Tithonus
daughter: 7 Hesione **8** Themiste
Laos
other name: 7 Lan Xang **23** land of a million elephants
capital/largest city: 9 Viengchan, Vientiane
others: 4 Nape **5** Pakse, Xieng **6** Paklay **7** Thakhek **11** Savannakhet, Xiang Khoang **12** Luang Prabang **14** Louangphrabang
school: 12 Sisavangvong
measure: 3 bak
monetary unit: 2 at **3** att, kip
mountain: 3 Lai, Loi, San **4** Copi, Khat **5** Atwat **6** Khoung, Tiubia **15** Annam Cordillera
highest point: 3 Bia **7** Phou Bia
river: 3 Noi **4** Done **5** Khong **6** Mekong, Sebang
physical feature:
   plain: 4 Jars
   plateau: 8 Bolovens
people: 2 Lu **3** Kha, Lao, Man, Meo, Tai, Yao, Yun **4** Miao, Thai **5** Hmong **8** Lao Teung **10** Phoutheung
   leader: 7 Fa Ngoun **13** Souphanouvong **14** Souligna Vongsa, Souvanna Phouma
language: 3 Lao, Man, Meo **6** French **7** English
religion: 7 animism **8** Buddhism **17** Theravada Buddhism
feature:
   Buddhist priest: 5 bonze
   Communist guerrilla group: 9 Pathet Lao
   musical instrument: 5 khene
   temple: 3 wat
   trail: 9 Ho Chi Minh
Laothoe
concubine of: 5 Priam
son: 6 Lycaon **9** Polydorus
Lao-tzu, Lao-tze, Lao-Tse, Lao-tsze
author of: 10 Tao Te Ching
founder of: 6 Taoism
lap 3 sip **4** lick, wash **5** awash, drink, plash, slosh **6** babble, bubble, gurgle, lick up, murmur, ripple, splash, tongue
La Paz
administrative capital of: 7 Bolivia
Laphria
epithet of: 7 Artemis
Laphystius
epithet of: 4 Zeus
lapidary 11 stonecutter
expert in: 4 gems
lapis lazuli 9 azure-blue **17** semiprecious stone

species: 8 lazurite
source: 10 Badakhshan **11** Afghanistan
Laplace, Pierre S
field: 7 physics **9** astronomy
nationality: 6 French
hypothesis of: 18 nebular solar system
Lapland
region of: 6 Norway, Sweden **7** Finland
peninsula: 4 Kola
native: 4 Lapp
herders of: 8 reindeer
lapse 3 gap, sag **4** drop, fall, flaw, go by, loss, sink, slip, stop, wane **5** boner, break, cease, droop, error, fault, pause, slump **6** breach, elapse, expire, hiatus, laxity, pass by, period, recede, recess, run out, slip by, wither, worsen **7** blunder, decline, descent, failing, failure, faux pas, interim, passage, relapse, respite, subside **8** collapse, downfall, elapsing, interval, omission, slip away **9** backslide, disregard, interlude, oversight, slump down, terminate **10** degenerate, falling off, forfeiture, infraction, negligence, peccadillo, regression **11** backsliding, delinquency, dereliction, deteriorate, shortcoming **12** degeneration, intermission, interruption, lose validity **13** deterioration, process of time, slight mistake **14** become obsolete, fall into disuse
lapsus linguae 16 a slip of the tongue
Laputa 12 Flying Island
inhabitants: 11 visionaries
in: Gulliver's Travels
lar *see* **5** lares
Lara
character in: 9 Dr Zhivago
author: 9 Pasternak
larboard 8 left side
same as: 4 port
larceny 5 fraud, theft **7** bilking, forgery, looting, robbery, sacking **8** burglary, cheating, fleecing, stealing **9** extortion, pilferage, pilfering, swindling **10** absconding, peculation, plagiarism, purloining **11** defalcation, depredation **12** embezzlement, grand larceny, petit larceny, petty larceny, safecracking **13** appropriation, housebreaking **16** misappropriation
larder 5 cuddy **6** pantry, spence **7** buttery **8** food room **9** stillroom, storeroom **10** supply room **11** storage room
Lardner, Ring
author of: 11 The Love Nest, You Know Me Al **12** Treat Em Rough **16** Gullible's Travels
Larentalia
origin: 5 Roman
event: 8 festival
lares

form: 7 spirits
watched over: 5 house **6** hearth **9** community **10** crossroads
single member: 3 lar
companions: 7 penates
correspond to: 8 Dioscuri

large 3 big, fat **4** high, huge, vast, wide **5** ample, broad, grand, great, heavy, hulky, obese, plump, roomy **6** goodly, mighty, portly, rotund **7** copious, immense, liber- al, massive, sizable **8** colossal, enormous, gigantic, imposing, man-sized, outsized, spacious, sweeping, towering **9** boundless, capacious, expansive, extensive, giantlike, kingsized, limitless, monstrous, overgrown, ponderous, strapping, unlimited, unstinted **10** exorbitant, gargantuan, stupendous **11** extravagant, far- reaching, magnificent, substantial **12** considerable **13** comprehensive **14** Brobdingnagian

large-hearted 8 generous **10** altruistic, benevolent, charitable **12** humanitarian **13** philanthropic

largely 6 mainly, mostly, widely **7** chiefly, greatly **9** generally, primarily **10** on the whole **11** extensively, principally **12** considerably **13** predominantly, substantially **14** for the most part, to a great extent

large-scale 3 big **4** epic, huge, vast, wide **5** broad, great **6** all-out, heroic, mighty **8** colossal, far-flung, gigantic **9** extensive, monstrous **10** gargantuan, stupendous, tremendous **11** far-reaching, wide-ranging **15** allencompassing

largess, largesse 3 aid **4** boon, gift, help **5** favor, mercy **6** bounty, reward **7** charity, payment **8** bestowal, donation, gratuity, kindness, offering **9** benignity **10** assistance, generosity **11** benefaction, benevolence **12** philanthropy, remuneration

large store 8 emporium **11** supermarket **15** department store

largo
music: 4 slow **14** dignified tempo

lark 3 gag **4** game, jape, romp, whim **5** antic, caper, fling, prank, spree, trick **6** frolic, gambol **7** caprice **8** escapade **11** high old time **12** sportiveness
group of: 10 exaltation

larkspur 9 Consolida **10** Delphinium
varieties: 4 Tall **5** Dwarf **6** Rocket

La Rochefoucauld, Francois
author of: 6 Maxims **7** Maximes

larva
insect stage after: 3 egg
insect stage before: 4 pupa
legless: 6 maggot

lascivious 4 foul, lewd **5** bawdy, dirty, gross, lurid **6** coarse, filthy, impure, rib- ald, sordid, vulgar, wanton **7** immoral, lustful, obscene, ruttish, squalid **8** depraved, immodest, im-proper, indecent, prurient **9** lecherous, salacious, shameless **10** indelicate, licentious, unblushing **11** dirty-minded, unwholesome

lash 3 fix, hit, tie **4** beat, bind, blow, flog, moor, rope, whip **5** brace, curse, flail, hitch, knock, leash, pound, scold, smack, strap, thong, tie up, truss **6** attach, be- rate, buffet, fasten, hammer, pinion, revile, secure, strike, stroke, tether, thrash, whip up **7** lecture, scourge, upbraid **8** lambaste, make fast **9** castigate, horsewhip **10** take to task, tongue-lash **11** rail against **13** cat-o'- nine-tails

Lash, Joseph P
author of: 18 Eleanor and Franklin

lashed together 4 tied **5** bound **6** tied up **7** secured, trussed **8** fastened

lash out at 5 fly at **6** assail, attack, strike **8** fall upon

Las Palmas
capital of: 13 Canary Islands

lass 4 girl, maid, miss **5** wench **6** damsel, female, lassie, lovely, maiden, pretty, virgin **7** colleen **10** schoolgirl, young woman

Lasser, Louise
father: 8 S J Lasser
husband: 10 Woody Allen
born: 9 New York NY
roles: 22 Mary Hartman Mary Hartman

lassie 4 girl, lass, maid **6** maiden **7** colleen **10** young woman

Lassie
character: 5 Timmy **9** Doc Weaver **10** Jeff Miller, Paul Martin, Ruth Martin **11** Corey Stuart, Ellen Miller **12** Gramps Miller **17** Sylvester (Porky) Brockway
cast: 10 Jan Clayton, Jon Provost, Jon Shepodd, Robert Bray **11** Arthur Space, Tommy Rettig **12** Donald Keeler, June Lockhart **14** Cloris Leachman, George Chandler **15** George Cleveland
type of dog: 6 collie

lassitude 5 ennui **6** apathy, torpor **7** boredom, fatigue, inertia, languor, malaise **8** debility, doldrums, dullness, lethargy, weakness **9** faintness, indolence, tiredness, torpidity, weariness **10** droopiness, drowsiness, enervation, exhaustion, feebleness, supineness **11** languidness, prostration **12** indifference, lack of energy, listlessness, sluggishness

lasso 4 lash, rope **5** catch, noose, reata, riata, thong **6** lariat

last 3 end **4** go on, keep, live, stay, wear **5** abide, after, exist, final, stand **6** behind, ending, endure, extend, finale, finish, hold on, hold up, remain, utmost **7** carry on, closing, extreme, finally, hold out, outlive, outwear, persist, stand up, subsist, survive, tail-ing **8** at the end, continue, doomsday, farthest, final one, furthest, hindmost, hold good, in back of, maintain, rearmost, terminal, terminus, trailing, ultimate **9** in the rear, persevere **10** Armageddon, concluding, conclusion, conclusive, eventually, terminally, ultimately **11** crack of doom, crucial time **12** in conclusion, tagging along **13** Day of Judgment
French: 7 dernier

Last Analysis, The
author: 10 Saul Bellow

Last Days of Pompeii, The
author: 18 Edward Bulwer-Lytton
character: 4 Ione **5** Nydia **7** Arbaces, Glaucus **9** Apaecides

Last Frontier
nickname of: 6 Alaska

lasting 4 firm **5** fixed, solid **7** abiding, chronic, durable, eternal **8** constant, enduring, immortal, lifelong, longterm **9** incessant, lingering, long-lived, permanent, perpetual, steadfast, unceasing **10** continuing, deep-rooted, deep-seated, perdurable, persistent, protracted **11** established, neverending **12** indissoluble **14** indestructible, of long duration **17** firmly established

Last Lion, The
author: 17 William Manchester

lastly 6 at last **7** finally, to sum up **8** after all, in the end **10** on the whole **12** in conclusion **19** all things considered **33** taking everything into consideration

Last of the Barons, The
author: 18 Edward Bulwer-Lytton

Last of the Mohicans, The
author: 19 James Fenimore Cooper
character: 5 Magua, Uncas **9** Cora Munro **10** Alice Munro **11** Natty Bumppo **12** Chingachgook **18** Major Duncan Heyward

last part 3 end **6** ending, finale, finish **8** third act **10** denouement **12** final chapter

Last Picture Show, The
director: 16 Peter Bogdanovich
based on story by: 13 Larry McMurtry
cast: 10 Ben Johnson **11** Jeff Bridges **12** Ellen Burstyn **13** Eileen Brennan **14** Cloris Leachman, Cybill Shepherd, Timothy Bottoms
Oscar for: 15 supporting actor (Johnson) **17** supporting actress (Leachman)

Last Puritan, The
author: 15 George Santayana

La Strada
director: 15 Federico Fellini
cast: 11 Aldo Silvana **12** Anthony Quinn **15** Giulietta Masina, Richard Basehart

score: 8 Nino Rota
Oscar for: 11 foreign film

last resort
French: 8 pis aller

Last Tango in Paris
director: 18 Bernardo Bertolucci
cast: 12 Marlon Brando **14** Maria
Schneider

Last Things
author: 6 C P Snow

Last Valley, The
author: 11 A B Guthrie Jr

Last Waltz, The
director: 14 Martin Scorsese
cast: 7 The Band **8** Bob Dylan **9** Neil
Young **10** The Staples **11** Eric Clap-
ton, Muddy Waters, Neil Diamond,
Van Morrison **12** Joni Mitchell **13**
Emmylou Harris

last word
French: 10 dernier cri

latch 3 bar **4** bolt, clip, hasp, hook,
lock, loop, shut, snap **5** catch, clamp,
close **6** buckle, button, clinch, fasten,
secure **8** make fast **9** fastening

late 3 new **4** dead, gone, slow **5** fresh,
tardy **6** held up, put off, recent **7** delayed, newborn, overdue, tardily **8** departed, detained, dilatory, passed on **9**
after time, postponed **10** behindhand,
behind time, dilatorily, unpunctual **16**
recently deceased

late arrival 7 laggard **8** lateness, newcomer **9** immigrant, latecomer, tardi-
ness **16** Johnny-come-lately

Late George Apley, The
author: 10 J P Marquand

lately 6 of late **7** just now **8** latterly,
recently, right now **9** currently, presently, yesterday **10** not long ago **13** a
short time ago

Late Mattia Pascal, The
author: 15 Luigi Pirandello

latency 8 abeyance, deferral, dormancy, inaction **10** quiescence, suspension

Late Night with David Letterman
feature: 11 Ask Mr Melman **15** Stupid Pet Tricks **18** Brush with Greatness, Stupid People Tricks
bandleader: 10 Paul Shafer
city: 7 New York

latent 6 covert, hidden **7** abeyant, dormant, lurking, passive **8** inactive,
sleeping **9** concealed, potential, quiescent, suspended, unaroused, unexposed **10** in abeyance, intangible, unapparent, unrealized **11** not manifest,
undeveloped, unexpressed **13** inconspicuous

later 4 next **5** since **6** behind, in time,
mature **7** ensuing, tardily **8** in a
while, in sequel **9** afterward, following, presently, thereupon **10** consequent, more re- cent, most recent,
subsequent, succeeding, successive,

thereafter **11** after a while, consecutive **12** subsequently, successively, toward the end

lateral 4 side **5** sided **7** flanked,
oblique, sloping **8** edgeways, edgewise, flank- ing, sidelong, sideward,
sideways, sidewise, skirting, slanting

latest fashion
French: 10 dernier cri

lather 4 foam, head, scum, soap, suds
5 froth, spume, sweat **6** soap up **8**
make foam, soapsuds **9** make froth
11 shaving foam

Latin
language family: 12 Indo-European
branch: 6 Italic
group: 7 Romance
subgroup: 6 French **7** Catalan, Italian, Romansh, Spanish **8** Romanian
9 Provencal **10** Portuguese **13**
Rhaeto- Romanic

Latino, Latina 8 Hispanic **13** Latin
American

Latinus
king of: 6 Latium
father: 6 Faunus
mother: 6 Marica
wife: 5 Amata
daughter: 7 Lavinia

latitude 5 range, scope, sweep **6** leeway, margin **7** license **8** free play **9**
amplitude, elbowroom, full swing **10**
indulgence, liberality **11** opportunity,
unrestraint **12** independence **15** freedom of action, freedom of choice **16**
unrestrictedness

Latona *see* **4** Leto

La Tour, Georges de
born: 3 Vic **6** France **8** Lorraine
artwork: 7 Peasant **10** The New Born
12 Peasant's Wife, The Card Cheat
15 St Peter Penitent **16** The Fortune
Teller **18** The Denial of St Peter **23**
The Education of the Virgin **31** St
Sebastian Tended by the Holy
Women

Latrobe, Benjamin Henry
architect of: 9 US Capitol **15** Sedge-
ley Mansion (PA) **18** Baltimore Cathedral **22** Philadelphia Waterworks
style: 12 Greek Revival, Neoclassical
13 Gothic Revival

latter 3 end **4** last **5** final, later **6** ending, latest, modern **7** ensuing **8** terminal **10** most recent, subsequent, succeeding, successive **13** last-mentioned
15 second-mentioned

lattice 4 fret, grid **5** frame, grate **6**
grille, screen **7** framing, grating, network, trellis, webwork **8** fretwork,
openwork **9** framework, reticulum **11**
trelliswork **12** reticulation

Latvia
former name: 30 Latvian Soviet Socialist Republic
capital/largest city: 4 Riga
others: 5 Cesis, Libau **6** Dvinsk, Li-

bava, Tukums **7** Jelgava, Jurmala,
Liepaja, Rezekne **8** Dunaberg, Duna-
burg, Valmiera **9** Ventspils **10** Daugavpils
government: 8 republic
measure: 3 let **4** stof **5** stoff, verst **6**
arshin, kulmet **7** verchoc, verchok **8**
krouchka, pourvete **9** deciatine, lofstelle, pourvette **10** tonnseteel
monetary unit: 3 lat **4** latu **6** rublis,
santim **7** kapeika, santima
weight: 9 liespfund
lake: 7 Aluksne
river: 4 Ogre **5** Gauja, Venta **6** Salaca
7 Daugava, Lielupe **12** Western
Dvina
sea: 6 Baltic
physical feature:
cape: 8 Domesnes
gulf: 4 Riga
strait: 4 Irbe
people: 3 Kur, Liv **4** Balt, Cour, Lett
7 Latgale, Latvian, Russian, Zemgale
former ruler: 15 Teutonic Knights
language: 7 Lettish
religion: 8 Lutheran **13** Roman Catholic

laud 5 extol, honor **6** praise **7** acclaim,
commend, glorify

laudable 5 model, noble **8** sterling **9**
admirable, estimable, excellent, exemplary **10** creditable **11** commendable,
meritorious **12** praiseworthy **13** unimpeachable **17** deserving of esteem **18**
worthy of admiration

laudation 6 praise **7** acclaim **8** applause, approval **11** approbation **12**
commendation

laudatory 8 admiring, honoring, praising **9** adulatory, approving, extolling,
favorable **10** eulogistic, eulogizing,
flattering, glorifying **11** acclamatory,
approbatory, celebratory, encomiastic,
panegyrical **12** commendatory **13**
complimentary

laugh 4 glee, ha-ha, ho-ho, howl, roar
5 mirth **6** cackle, giggle, guffaw, titter
7 break up, chortle, chuckle, snicker,
snigger **10** bellylaugh, horselaugh **12**
express mirth **14** roll in the aisle, split
one's sides

laughable 5 comic, dopey, droll,
funny, inane, merry, silly, witty **6** absurd, stupid **7** amusing, asinine, comical, foolish, risible **8** farcical, tickling
9 diverting, grotesque, hilarious, ludicrous **10** outlandish, outrageous, ridiculous **11** rib-tickling **12** preposterous
13 sidesplitting

Laugh-In, Rowan & Martin's
regular: 8 Dan Rowan **9** Gary Owens,
Judy Carne, Ruth Buzzi **10** Dick
Martin, Goldie Hawn, Larry Hovis,
Lily Tomlin **11** Arte Johnson, Henry
Gibson **12** Jo Anne Worley **13** Eileen
Brennan
saying: 10 Sock it to me **15** Here

come de judge, You bet your bippy **24** Beautiful downtown Burbank **31** Look that up in your Funk and Wagnalls

laughingstock 3 ass **4** butt, dupe, fool, joke **8** fair game **11** figure of fun

laugh off 6 deride **7** dismiss, put down **8** belittle, ridicule **9** disparage

laughter 3 joy **4** glee **5** mirth **6** gaiety **7** jollity, revelry **8** hilarity **9** joviality, merriment **11** merrymaking **12** conviviality, exhilaration

Laughton, Charles
 wife: 14 Elsa Lanchester
 born: 7 England **11** Scarborough
 roles: 9 Rembrandt **10** Jamaica Inn **13** Les Miserables **15** Ruggles of Red Gap, The Paradine Case **16** Advise and Consent **17** Mutiny on the Bounty **23** Barretts of Wimpole Street, The Hunchback of Notre Dame **24** Witness for the Prosecution **25** The Private Life of Henry VIII (Oscar)

launch 4 fire, hurl **5** begin, eject, float, found, impel, shoot, start, throw **6** let fly, propel, unveil **7** fire off, project, send off **8** catapult, initiate, premiere, put to sea **9** cast forth, discharge, establish, institute, introduce, set afloat **10** embark upon, inaugurate, set forth on **11** set in mo- tion, venture upon **13** thrust forward **15** set into the water

launder 4 soak, wash **5** clean, rinse, scour, scrub **7** cleanse, wash out **11** wash and iron

Launfal
 knight of: 10 round table

Laura
 director: 13 Otto Preminger
 cast: 11 Clifton Webb, Dana Andrews, Gene Tierney **12** Vincent Price **14** Judith Anderson

laurel 6 Kalmia, Laurus **13** Laurus nobilis **14** Ficus benjamina **15** Cordia alliodora
 varieties: 3 bog, pig **4** pale **5** black, dwarf, great, sheep **6** Alpine, cherry, ground, Indian, purple, Sierra, spurge, tropic **7** Chinese, English, red-twig, weeping, western **8** American, drooping, Himalaya, Japanese, mountain, Portugal **9** Tasmanian **10** Australian, California, variegated **11** Alexandrian

Laurel, Stan
 real name: 22 Arthur Stanley Jefferson
 partner: 11 Oliver Hardy
 born: 7 England **9** Ulverston
 roles: 8 Pardon Us **9** Saps at Sea **10** Way Out West

laurels 4 fame **5** award, glory, honor, kudos, prize **6** credit, praise, renown, reward **7** acclaim, tribute **8** accolade, applause, citation **9** celebrity **10** deco-

ration, popularity **11** acclamation, distinction, recognition **12** commendation **15** illustriousness

Laurie
 also: 16 Theodore Laurence
 character in: 11 Little Women
 author: 6 Alcott

laus Deo 11 praise to God **13** praise be to God

lavation 7 bathing, washing **8** ablution, cleaning **9** cleansing

lavender 4 herb, mint **5** aspic, behen, lilac, spick, spike **6** purple **7** inkroot **8** amethyst, stichado **9** lavendula
 represents: 6 purity
 uses: 6 sachet **7** perfume **8** medicine **9** cosmetics

laver 11 footed basin

Laverne and Shirley
 character: 12 Frank De Fazio **13** Carmine Ragusa, Lenny Kolowski, Mrs Edna Babish, Shirley Feeney **14** Laverne De Fazio **15** Andrew (Squiggy) Squiggman
 cast: 10 Eddie Mekka, Phil Foster **12** Betty Garrett, David L Lander **13** Cindy Williams, Michael McKean, Penny Marshall
 girls worked in: 12 Shotz Brewery
 theme song: 23 Making Our Dreams Come True
 spinoff from: 9 Happy Days

Lavinia
 father: 7 Latinus
 mother: 5 Amata
 husband: 6 Aeneas

lavish 4 free, lush, wild **5** plush, waste **6** shower **7** copious, opulent, pour out, profuse **8** abundant, effusive, generous, prodigal, squander **9** bounteous, bountiful, dissipate, excessive, exuberant, impetuous, luxuriant, plenteous, plentiful, sumptuous, unsparing **10** immoderate, munificent, profligate, unstinting **11** extravagant, fritter away, intemperate, overindulge, overliberal, spend freely **12** give overmuch, greathearted, overwhelming, unrestrained, without limit

lavishness 6 bounty **8** lushness, opulence **9** profusion **10** luxuriance **11** munificence, prodigality **12** extravagance, immoderation **13** bountifulness, plenteousness, sumptuousness

Lavoisier, Antoine
 field: 9 chemistry
 nationality: 6 French
 founder: 15 modern chemistry
 named: 6 oxygen **8** hydrogen

law 3 act **4** bill, code, fuzz, rule, writ **5** axiom, bylaw, canon, dogma, edict, model, truth **6** decree, police **7** justice, mandate, precept, statute, theorem **8** absolute, legality, standard **9** criterion, enactment, gendarmes, legal form, ordinance, postulate, principle **10** civil peace, convention, due proc-

ess, invariable, regulation **11** commandment, formulation, fundamental, orderliness, working rule **13** jurisprudence, standing order **14** generalization, rules of conduct **15** legal profession
 Latin: 3 jus
 goddess of: 4 Maat

law-abiding 6 honest **7** upright **9** honorable **10** aboveboard, principled

lawbreaker 3 con **4** hood, thug **5** crook, felon **6** outlaw **7** convict, culprit **8** criminal, jailbird, offender, scofflaw **9** miscreant, wrongdoer **10** delinquent, malefactor, recidivist **11** perpetrator **12** transgressor

lawful 3 due **5** legal, licit **6** proper, titled **7** allowed, granted **8** rightful **9** legalized, statutory, warranted **10** authorized, legitimate, prescribed **11** legitimized, permissible **15** legally entitled **16** legally permitted

lawless 6 unruly, wanton **7** chaotic, defiant, illegal, riotous, wayward **8** anarchic, mutinous, unlawful, wide open **9** insurgent, out of hand, unbridled **10** disorderly, licentious, rebellious, refractory, ungoverned **11** disobedient, lawbreaking, terroristic **12** disorganized, freewheeling, illegitimate, noncompliant, unrestrained **13** insubordinate, transgressive **14** uncontrollable

lawlessness 5 chaos **7** anarchy **8** disorder

lawn 4 park, turf, yard **5** glade, grass, sward **7** grounds, terrace **10** grassy plot, green field, greensward, meadowland **12** grassy ground

law of a place
 Latin: 7 lex loci

Law of Moses 5 Torah **10** Pentateuch **15** Ten Commandments

law of nations
 Latin: 10 jus gentium

law of nature
 Latin: 11 jus naturale

Lawrence, Carol
 real name: 16 Carol Maria Laraia
 husband: 12 Robert Goulet
 born: 13 Melrose Park IL
 roles: 5 Maria **13** West Side Story

Lawrence, D H
 author of: 10 The Rainbow **11** Women in Love **13** Sons and Lovers **20** Lady Chatterley's Lover

Lawrence, Ernest Orlando
 field: 7 physics
 invented: 9 cyclotron
 awarded: 10 Nobel Prize

Lawrence, Gertrude
 real name: 29 Alexandra Dagmar Lawrence Klasen
 born: 6 London **7** England
 roles: 9 Pygmalion **11** The King and I **17** The Glass Menagerie

Lawrence, T E
  also: 16 Lawrence of Arabia
  served in: 3 WWI 10 Arab Revolt
  advisor to: 6 Faisal 12 Husayn Ibn Ali
  fought against: 5 Turks 8 Ottomans
  author of: 20 Seven Pillars of Wisdom

Lawrence of Arabia
  director: 9 David Lean
  cast: 10 Jose Ferrer, Omar Sharif 11 Claude Rains, Jack Hawkins, Peter O'Toole (T E Lawrence) 12 Alec Guin- ness, Anthony Quinn 13 Anthony Quayle
  Oscar for: 7 picture 8 director 14 cinematography

Lawrence Welk Show, The
  champagne lady: 8 Alice Lon 11 Norma Zimmer
  cast: 7 Aladdin 11 Larry Hooper, Myron Floren 12 Bobby Burgess 13 Barbara Boylan, Lennon Sisters
  Welk played: 9 accordion

lawyer 6 jurist, legist 7 counsel, shyster 8 advocate, attorney 9 barrister, counselor, solicitor 10 mouthpiece, prosecutor 11 pettifogger 12 legal advisor 14 special pleader 15 ambulance chaser

lax 4 hazy, limp, weak 5 agape, loose, slack, vague 6 casual, flabby, floppy, remiss 7 cryptic, flaccid, inexact, lenient, not firm, relaxed 8 careless, derelict, droop- ing, heedless, nebulous, slipshod, uncaring, yielding 9 confusing, imprecise, negligent, oblivious, undutiful, unheeding, unmindful 10 ill-defined, incoherent, neglectful, permissive 11 hanging open, indifferent, thoughtless, unconcerned 12 loosemuscled, unstructured 13 irresponsible 15 unconscientious

laxness 7 neglect 9 looseness, slackness 10 negligence 11 imprecision 12 carelessness, indifference

Laxness, Halldor Kiljan
  author of: 12 Iceland's Bell 14 The Atom Station 17 Independent People 25 The Great Weaver from Kashmir
  won: 10 Nobel Prize

lay 3 air, bet, put, set 4 bear, fell, fine, form, give, laic, lend, levy, make, plan, poem, raze, rest, seat, song, tune 5 align, allot, apply, ditty, exact, floor, hatch, level, offer, place, stage, wager 6 assess, assign, ballad, charge, demand, depict, devise, gamble, ground, hazard, impose, impute, laical, layout, locate, melody, repose, strain 7 amateur, arrange, concoct, contour, deposit, dispose, forward, present, produce, profane, proffer, refrain, secular, set down, situate, station 8 allocate, assemble, beat down, give odds, inexpert, organize, oviposit, position 9 attribute, elucidate, enunci-

ate, formulate, knock down, knock over, prostrate, roundelay, situation 10 cause to lie, topography 11 arrangement, disposition, nonclerical, orientation, put together 12 conformation 13 configuration, inexperienced, nonspecialist 14 partly informed, unprofessional 15 nonprofessional 17 nonecclesiastical

lay at the door of 6 assign 7 ascribe 8 charge to 9 attribute

lay bare 4 bare, show 6 expose, reveal, unmask, unveil, unwrap 7 divulge, exhibit, publish, uncover 8 disclose 9 broadcast, make known 10 make public 11 communicate

lay down arms 5 yield 6 give up 7 succumb 8 cry quits 9 surrender 10 capitulate 11 come to terms, sue for peace 13 declare a truce 17 acknowledge defeat

layer 3 bed, lap, ply 4 coat, fold, leaf, seam, slab, tier, zone 5 level, plate, scale, sheet, stage, story 6 lamina 7 stratum 9 thickness

layman 4 laic 6 sister 7 amateur, brother 8 outsider 9 churchman 10 catechumen 11 churchwoman, communicant, parishioner 15 nonprofessional 16 member of the flock

layoff 4 fire 6 firing, idling, ouster, the axe 7 dismiss, release, sacking, the boot, the gate, the sack 8 pink slip, shutdown 9 closedown, discharge, dismissal, hard times, the bounce 10 cashiering, depression, the heave-ho 11 furloughing, termination 12 unemployment 13 disemployment, walking papers 20 discharge temporarily

lay off 7 dismiss, forfeit, release, set free 8 get rid of, liberate 9 discharge, terminate 11 give the gate, send packing

Lay of the Last Minstrel, The
  author: 14 Sir Walter Scott
  character: 8 Margaret, The Dwarf 13 Lady Buccleuch, Lord Cranstoun 17 Master of Buccleuch 19 Ghost of Michael Scott 21 Sir William of Deloraine

lay on 6 bestow, confer, supply 7 present, provide

lay open 4 open 6 expose, open up 7 clarify 9 make plain 18 make understandable

layout 4 form, plan 5 chart, draft, dummy, model, motif, spend 6 design, expend, pay out, sketch, spread 7 diagram, drawing, fork out, outline, pattern 8 disburse, shell out 9 blueprint, delineate, placement, spread out, structure 11 arrangement, composition

lay waste 4 ruin 5 level, wreck 6 ravage 7 despoil, destroy, wipe out 8 demolish, desolate 9 devastate, eradicate 10 annihilate, obliterate

Lazarus 6 beggar
  means: 8 God helps
  sister: 4 Mary 6 Martha
  hometown: 7 Bethany
  resurrected by: 5 Jesus

Lazarus
  author: 14 Leonid Andreyev

Lazarus, Mell
  creator/artist: 5 Momma 9 Miss Peach

lazurite
  variety: 11 lapis lazuli

lazy 3 lax 4 idle, slow 5 inert, slack 6 drowsy, sleepy, torpid 7 laggard, languid 8 inactive, indolent, listless, slothful, sluggish 9 apathetic, easygoing, lethargic, shiftless 10 languorous, slow-moving 13 unindustrious 15 unwilling to work

lazy person 5 drone, idler 6 loafer 14 good-for-nothing

l'chaim, l'chayim 5 toast 6 Hebrew, to life

Leachman, Cloris
  born: 11 Des Moines IA
  roles: 7 Phyllis 11 High Anxiety 12 Kiss Me Deadly 17 Young Frankenstein 18 Mary Tyler Moore Show, The Last Picture Show

lead 2 go 3 aim, top 4 clue, draw, edge, have, head, hero, hint, live, lure, pass 5 charm, excel, guide, model, outdo, pilot, steer, tempt 6 allure, convey, direct, en- tice, extend, induce, manage, margin, pursue, seduce 7 advance, attract, bring on, command, conduct, control, example, go first, incline, issue in, marshal, pioneer, precede, proceed, produce, stretch, surpass, undergo 8 domineer, go before, guidance, moderate, outstrip, persuade, priority, result in, shepherd, star part 9 advantage, come first, direction, go through, headliner, influence, plurality, rank first 10 branch into, experience, first place, indication, precedence, precedency, set the pace, show the way, tend toward 11 antecedence, be in advance, leading role, preside over, protagonist

lead
  chemical symbol: 2 Pb
  mineral: 10 fiedlerite
  ore: 6 galena, pyrite

lead astray 4 dupe, lure 6 delude 7 beguile, deceive, ensnare, mislead 19 lead up the garden path

leaden 4 dark, dull, glum, gray 5 inert, murky 6 dreary, gloomy, numbed, somber, torpid 7 grayish, languid 8 burdened, careworn, darkened, deadened, listless, sluggish, unwieldy 9 depressed, inanimate 10 cumbersome, hard to move

leader 4 boss, guru, head 5 chief, guide, mogul 6 bigwig, honcho, master, mentor, tycoon 7 captain, foreman, kingpin, magnate, manager, pioneer, prophet **8** director, superior **9** chieftain, commander, conductor, godfather, pacemaker, patriarch **10** forerunner, pacesetter, pathfinder, supervisor **11** frontrunner, torchbearer, trailblazer

leadership 4 helm, lead, sway **5** reins, wheel **7** command, primacy **8** charisma, guidance, headship, hegemony **9** captaincy, supremacy **10** domination, mastership **11** managership, preeminence, stewardship **12** directorship, governorship, guardianship, self-reliance **13** ability to lead, self-assurance **14** administration **15** managerial skill, superintendency **17** authoritativeness

leading 3 top **4** head, main **5** basic, chief, first, great, prime **6** ruling **7** advance, guiding, initial, leadoff, notable, primary, ranking, stellar, supreme, topmost **8** advanced, dominant, foremost **9** directing, essential, governing, nonpareil, paramount, principal, prominent, sovereign, unrivaled **10** motivating, preeminent, underlying **11** controlling, outstanding, pacesetting **12** unchallenged, unparalleled **13** most important **14** quintessential **15** most influential, most significant

lead on 4 goad **5** egg on **6** entice **7** mislead, support **9** encourage **19** lead up the garden path

lead the way 4 lead, show, take **5** guide **6** escort **7** conduct

leaf 4 flip, foil, page, skim **5** blade, bract, folio, frond, green, inset, petal, sheet, thumb **6** browse, glance, insert, needle **7** foliole, lamella, leaflet **9** cotyledon, extension, turn green **10** lamination **12** sheet of metal
edge: 5 erose **7** crenate, dentate
angle: 4 axil
aperture: 5 stoma
kind: 5 calyx, petal, sepal **7** corolla

leaflet 2 ad **4** bill **5** flier, flyer, tract **6** folder, notice **7** booklet, handout **8** brochure, bulletin, circular, handbill, pamphlet **9** broadside, throwaway **10** broadsheet **12** announcement **13** advertisement

league 4 ally, band **5** cabal, group, guild, merge, union **6** cartel **7** combine, compact, company, network, society **8** alliance **9** coalition **10** conspiracy, federation, frater- nity, join forces **11** association, confederacy, confederate, consolidate, cooperative, partnership **13** collaboration, confederation, confraternity

Leah
means: 7 wild cow
father: 5 Laban
husband: 5 Jacob
sister: 6 Rachel

slave: 6 Zilpah
son: 4 Levi **5** Judah **6** Reuben, Simeon **7** Zebulun **8** Issachar
daughter: 5 Dinah
burial place: 9 Machpelah

leak 3 ebb, rip **4** blab, gash, hole, ooze, rent, rift, seep, vent **5** break, chink, cleft, crack, drain, exude, fault, spill **6** breach, efflux, escape, filter, let out, reveal, take in **7** confide, crevice, divulge, dribble, fissure, let slip, opening, outflow, rupture, seepage **8** aperture, disclose, draining, give away, puncture **9** discharge, percolate **10** interstice, make public **11** be permeable, perforation **12** admit leakage **16** let enter or escape

leakage 5 issue **7** outflow, seepage **9** discharge

Leakey, Louis S Bazett
field: 12 anthropology
discovered: 8 early man
worked at: 8 Tanzania **12** Olduvai Gorge
wife: 4 Mary
son: 7 Richard

lean 3 aim, bow, tip **4** bend, cant, lank, list, poor, rely, rest, slim, tend, thin, tilt **5** gaunt, lanky, lurch, scant, slant, slope, small, spare, weedy **6** barren, depend, meager, modest, nonfat, prefer, scanty, skinny, sparse, svelte **7** angular, count on, incline, recline, scraggy, scrawny, slender, spindly, trust in, willowy **8** exiguous, rawboned, resort to, skeletal **9** emaciated **10** inadequate, set store by **11** be partial to, have faith in, prop oneself **12** insufficient, seek solace in **14** rest one's weight, support oneself

Lean, David
director of: 10 Summertime **11** Oliver Twist **13** Doctor Zhivago, Ryan's Daughter **15** A Passage to India **16** Lawrence of Arabia (Oscar) **17** Great Expectations **23** The Bridge on the River Kwai (Oscar)

Leander
loved: 4 Hero
swam nightly: 10 Hellespont
death by: 8 drowning

leaning 4 bent, turn **5** slant **7** relying **8** affinity, tendency **9** proneness **10** dependence, partiality, preference, proclivity, propensity **11** inclination **14** predisposition

leap 3 hop **4** jete, jump, romp, rush, skip **5** bound, caper, frisk, vault **6** bounce, cavort, frolic, gambol, hasten, hurtle, prance, spring **7** hop over **8** jump over **9** bound over, saltation **10** hurtle over, jump across, spring over

Lear, Norman
TV producer of: 5 Maude **13** The Jeffersons **14** All in the Family

Learchus
father: 7 Athamas

mother: 3 Ino
killed by: 7 Athamas

learn 3 con **4** hear **6** detect, master, pick up **7** find out, uncover, unearth **8** discover, memorize **9** ascertain, determine, ferret out **10** become able **12** find out about

learned 4 deep, wise **7** erudite **8** cultured, educated, informed, lettered, literate, profound, schooled, well-read **9** scholarly **10** cultivated **12** accomplished, intellectual, well-educated **13** knowledgeable

Learned, Michael
roles: 5 Nurse **10** The Waltons

learner 4 tyro **5** pupil, tutee **6** novice, rookie **7** draftee, recruit, scholar, student, trainee **8** beginner, disciple, enlistee, follower, freshman, neophyte **9** fledgling, greenhorn, novitiate, proselyte, schoolboy **10** apprentice, schoolgirl, tenderfoot **11** schoolchild

learning 4 lore **5** study **6** wisdom **7** culture **8** teaching **9** education, erudition, knowledge, schooling **11** cultivation, edification, information, instruction, scholarship **13** comprehension, enlightenment, understanding

Learning
god of: 5 Thoth

Leary, Timothy
phrase: 19 Tune in, turn on, drop out

leash 4 curb, lead, line, rein, ruin **5** strap, thong **6** bridle, choker, fasten, hold in, stifle, string, tether **7** contain, control, harness **8** restrain, suppress

leatherneck 6 gyrene, marine

Leather-Stocking Tales
author: 19 James Fenimore Cooper
includes: 10 The Prairie **11** The Pioneers **13** The Deerslayer, The Pathfinder **20** The Last of the Mohicans
hero of: 7 Hawkeye **10** Pathfinder, The Trapper **11** Natty Bumppo **13** The Deerslayer **15** Leather-stocking **16** Le Longue Carabine

leave 2 go **3** fly **4** cede, exit, flee, jilt, keep, quit, will **5** allot, be off, cause, endow, forgo, going, split, waive, yield **6** assign, bug out, commit, decamp, depart, desert, eschew, forego, give up, legate, move on, recess, resign, retain, set out **7** abandon, abscond, bequest, consent, consign, deposit, entrust, forsake, holiday, let stay, liberty, parting, produce, push off, release, respite, retreat, sustain, take off, time off **8** approval, bequeath, farewell, furlough, generate, give over, maintain, result in, sanction, shove off, vacation **9** allowance, apportion, departure, hotfoot it, let remain, surrender, tolerance **10** concession, depart from, embark from, go away from, indulgence, permission, relinquish, retire from, sabbatical, sufferance, withdrawal **11** bid farewell, endorsement **13** absent oneself, understanding

leave a ship 4 land **6** debark **8** go ashore **9** disembark **11** abandon ship

leave behind 4 jilt **6** desert, vacate **7** abandon, discard, forsake **8** evacuate **9** cast aside **10** relinquish **11** outdistance

leave cold 4 bore **12** leave unmoved **15** leave unaffected

Leave It To Beaver
character: **11** June Cleaver, Ward Cleaver **12** Eddie Haskell, Wally Cleaver **13** Beaver (Theodore) Cleaver
cast: **7** Tony Dow **9** Ken Osmond **12** Hugh Beaumont, Jerry Mathers **18** Barbara Billingsley

leave off 3 end **4** halt, quit, stop **5** cease **6** desist, finish **7** suspend **8** conclude **11** discontinue, refrain from

leave out 4 drop, omit **6** except, reject **7** exclude

Leaves of Grass
author: **11** Walt Whitman

leave suddenly 3 fly **4** flee **6** cut out, decamp, run off **7** abscond, make off, run away, rush off, take off **11** take a powder **15** be off and running

leave-taking 4 exit **5** adieu **7** goodbye, leaving, parting, send-off **8** au revoir, farewell **9** departure **10** withdrawal

leave undone 4 quit **6** give up **7** abandon, forsake, neglect **8** give up on

Lebanon
ancient name: **9** Phoenicia
capital/largest city: **6** Beirut **8** Beyrouth
others: **3** Sur **4** Arca, Tyre **5** Ehden, Halba, Hamat, Sahle, Saida, Sayda, Sidon, Sofar, Zahla, Zahle **6** Byblos, Ghazir, Juniye, Tibnin **7** Baalbek, Batroun, Bsherri, Rachaya, Tripoli, Zgharta **8** Djezzine, El Hermel, Hasbaiya, Merjuyun **9** Broummana, Marjayoun **10** Beited Dine, Heliopolis
ancient city: **8** Carthage
school: **4** Arab **8** American, Lebanese **11** Saint Joseph
division:
ancient: **4** Tyre **5** Arwad, Sidon **6** Byblos, Jubayl
monetary unit: **5** livre, pound **7** piastre
lake: **5** Quran **6** Qirawn
mountain: **4** Mzar **5** Aruba **6** Hermon **7** Lebanon, Sannine **8** Kadischa, Kenisseh **9** Kennisseh **10** al- Mukammal **11** Anti-Lebanon
highest point: **7** es Sauda **13** Qurnat al-Sawda
river: **3** Dog, Joz **5** Barid, Kebir, Lycos **6** Auwali, Barada, Damour, Litani **7** Hasbani, Leontes, Orontes **8** Kasemieh

sea: **13** Mediterranean
physical feature:
cape: **10** Pigeon Rock **11** Ras esh Shiqa **12** Qadisha Gorge
plain: **4** Bika **5** Bekaa
valley: **5** Beqaa **6** al-Biqa **9** Great Rift
wind: **7** khamsin
people: **4** Arab **11** Palestinian
ancient: **9** Canaanite **10** Phoenician
leader: **6** Bashir, Sarkis **7** Chamoun **8** Franjieh **9** al-Din Maan **11** Amin Gemayel **13** Bashir Gemayel
poet: **11** Kahlil Gibran
rulers: **5** Arabs **6** French, Greeks, Romans **8** Hittites, Ottomans, Persians **9** Assyrians, Crusaders, Egyptians, Mamelukes **11** Babylonians
language: **6** Arabic, French, Syriac **7** English, Turkish **8** Armenian
religion: **5** Druse, Druze, Islam **8** Maronite, Melchite **10** Protestant **11** Monophysite **12** Christianity **13** Greek Catholic **14** Greek Orthodoxy **17** Armenian Orthodoxy
place:
dam: **5** Qarun
ruins: **7** Baalbek **15** Temple of Bacchus, Temple of Jupiter
feature:
Christian group: **10** Phalangist
dance: **6** dabkeh, dabkey
tree: **5** cedar
food:
dish: **6** kibbeh **8** tabouleh
drink: **4** arak **6** arrack

Le Bel, Joseph Achille
field: **9** chemistry
nationality: **6** French
founded: **15** stereochemistry

Le Bourgeois Gentilhomme
author: **7** Moliere
character: **7** Cleonte, Dorante **9** M Jourdain **16** Monsieur Jourdain

Le Carre, John
real name: **13** David Cornwell
author of: **11** A Perfect Spy **13** Smiley's People **18** The Looking Glass War **19** A Small Town in Germany **20** The Little Drummer Girl **21** The Honorable Schoolboy **22** Tinker Tailor Soldier Spy **26** The Spy Who Came in from the Cold

lechayim, lehayim 6 to life

lecherous 4 lewd **5** randy **6** carnal **7** goatish, lustful, ruttish **8** prurient **9** sala- cious, satyrlike **10** lascivious, libidinous, licentious, lubricious

lechery 4 lust **8** lewdness **9** carnality, prurience **10** satyriasis **11** lustfulness, nym- phomania **13** salaciousness **14** lasciv- iousness

Le Cid
author: **9** Corneille
composer: **21** Leconte Dehisle, Charles **13** Jules Massenet

Leconte de Lisle, Charles
author of: **14** Poemes Antiques, Poemes Barbares

Le Corbusier
real name: **23** Charles Edouard Jeanneret
architect of: **10** La Tourette (monastery) **15** Notre Dame du Haut (Ronchamp France) **16** Unite d'Habitation (Marseilles)
planned city of: **10** Chandi garh (capital of the Punjab)
style: **6** Purism **12** New Brutalism

lecture 4 talk **5** chide, scold, speak **6** homily, preach, rail at, rebuke, sermon, speech **7** address, censure, chiding, expound, oration, reading, re proof, reprove, upbraid, warning **8** admonish, call down, harangue, moralize, reproach **9** discourse, hold forth, reprimand, sermonize, talking-to **10** preachment, take to task **12** chastisement, disquisition, remonstrance

lecture hall 9 classroom **10** auditorium **12** amphitheater, assembly hall

lecturelike 7 donnish, preachy **8** academic, didactic, pedantic **9** homiletic **10** moralizing

LED 18 light emitting diode **19** alphanumeric display

Leda
father: **8** Thestius
husband: **9** Tyndareus
lover: **4** swan, Zeus
son: **6** Castor, Pollux **8** Dioscuri **10** Polydeuces
daughter: **5** Helen **6** Phoebe **8** Philonoe, Timandra **12** Clytemnestra

Leda and the Swan
author: **7** W B Yeats

ledge 4 sill, step **5** ridge, shelf **6** mantel, offset **8** foothold, shoulder **10** projection **11** mantelpiece, mantelshelf, outcropping

Lee, Bruce
born: **12** San Francisco
son: **7** Brandon
roles: **7** Marlowe **11** Fists of Fury, Game of Death **14** The Green Hornet, Enter the Dragon **17** Return of the Dragon, Chinese Connection **24** Bruce Lee: Curse of the Dragon

Lee, Christopher
born: **6** London
roles: **5** Jocks **6** Albino, Serial **7** The Girl **8** Caravans **9** Shaka Zulu, The Keeper, The Gorgon **10** Dark Places **11** Eye for an Eye, Horror Hotel, Moulin Rouge, Killer Force **12** Count Dracula, The Wicker Man, The Oblong Box, Scream of Fear **13** The Death Train **14** Treasure Island **15** Journey of Horror **16** Castle of Fu Manchu, The Creeping Flesh, A Tale of Two Cities **17** The Four Musketeers **23** Return from Witch Mountain

25 The Hound of the Baskervilles **30** The Private Life of Sherlock Holmes

Lee, Gypsy Rose
born: 7 Seattle
author of: 5 Gypsy **8** Doll Face **15** Lady of Burlesque
roles: 11 The Stripper, My Lucky Star **13** Screaming Mimi

Lee, Harper
author of: 18 To Kill a Mockingbird

Lee, Johnny
born: 8 Alta Loma (TX)
roles: 11 Urban Cowboy **12** School Spirit

Lee, Henry
nickname: 15 Light Horse Harry
served in: 16 Revolutionary War
member of: 10 US Congress **19** Continental Congress
governor of: 8 Virginia
suppressed: 16 Whiskey Rebellion
son: 7 Robert E

Lee, Peggy
born: 9 Jamestown (ND)
roles: 7 Mr. Music **13** The Jazz Singer **15** Pete Kelly's Blues **18** Ladies Sing the Blues

Lee, Robert E
father: 5 Henry **15** Light Horse Harry
born: 11 Stratford VA **18** Westmoreland County
wife: 21 Mary Ann Randolph Custis
served in: 8 Civil War **10** Mexican War
commander of: 22 Army of Northern Virginia
suppressed raid: 9 John Brown **12** Harper's Ferry
battle: 7 Bull Run **8** Antietam **10** Gettysburg **14** Fredericksburg **16** Chancellorsville, Seven Days' Battles
surrendered at: 20 Appomattox Court House
president of: 17 Washington College

Lee, Spike
original name: 17 Sheldon Jackson Lee
born: 2 GA **7** Atlanta
wife: 17 Tonya Linette Lewis
films: 8 Malcolm X **10** School Daze **11** Jungle Fever **15** Do the Right Thing, She's Gotta Have It
company: 18 Forty Acres and A Mule
ads for: 4 Nike

Lee, Stan 10 cartoonist
of: 9 Spider-Man

leek 18 Allium ampeloprasum
emblem of: 5 Wales
varieties: 4 lily, rose, sand, wild **5** lady's **6** meadow

leer 4 ogle **5** fleer, smirk **6** goggle

leery 4 wary **5** cagey, chary **6** unsure **7** guarded **8** cautious, doubtful, hesitant **9** skeptical, undecided **10** suspicious **11** circumspect, distrustful, mistrustful

Leeuwenhoek, Anton van

field: 10 microscopy
father of: 12 microbiology
discovered: 13 red blood cells

leeway 4 play **5** scope, slack **6** margin **7** cushion, headway, reserve **8** headroom, latitude **9** allowance, clearance, elbow room, extra time, tolerance **11** flexibility **13** room for choice **14** margin for error **15** maneuverability

left behind 7 vacated **8** deserted, forsaken, forsook **9** abandoned, discarded, evacuated **12** relinquished

leftover 6 excess, legacy, unused **7** overage, residue, surplus, uneaten **8** leavings, oddments, residual, survivor **9** carry-over, remainder, remaining

left-wing 7 leftist, liberal, radical **9** socialist **11** progressive

left-winger 7 leftist, liberal, radical **9** socialist **11** progressive

Lefty
nickname of: 5 Gomez **12** Steve Carlton

leg 3 gam, lap, pin **4** limb, part, post, prop **5** brace, femur, shank, stage, stump, tibia **6** column, fibula, member, pillar **7** portion, section, segment, stretch, support, upright

legacy 4 gift **6** devise, estate **7** bequest, vestige **8** heirloom, heritage, leftover, survivor **9** carry-over, throwback, tradition **10** birthright, hand-me-down **11** inheritance

legal 4 fair **5** licit, of law, valid **6** kosher, lawful **7** cricket **8** forensic, judicial, juristic, rightful **9** courtroom, juridical **10** legiti- mate, sanctioned **11** permissible

legal advisor 6 lawyer **7** counsel **8** advocate, attorney **9** barrister, counselor, so licitor **13** attorney-at-law **14** counselor-at-law

legal form 4 writ **8** document **10** instrument

legality 8 validity **9** licitness **10** lawfulness, legitimacy **17** constitutionality

legalization 8 sanction **9** enactment **10** permission, validation **13** authorization **14** legitimization

legalize 5 enact **6** permit **8** sanction, validate **9** authorize **10** legitimize

legal residence 4 home **8** domicile, dwelling

legal tender 4 cash **5** money **8** currency

legate 5 agent, envoy **6** deputy **8** emissary **14** representative

legatee 4 heir **7** heiress **9** inheritor **11** beneficiary

legation 7 embassy, mission **8** ministry **9** consulate **10** delegation **11** chancellery

legend 3 key **4** edda, lore, myth, saga, tale **5** fable, motto, story, title **7** caption, fiction, proverb **8** folklore **11** inscription

legendary 5 famed **6** fabled, famous, mythic **7** storied **8** fabulous, fanciful, mythical **9** imaginary **10** apocryphal, celebrated, fictitious, proverbial

Legend of Good Women, The
author: 15 Geoffrey Chaucer
character: 4 Dido **5** Medea **6** Thisbe **7** Alceste, Ariadne, Lucrece, Phyllis **9** Cleopatra, Hypsipyle, Philomela **12** Hypermnestra

Legend of Sleepy Hollow, The
author: 16 Washington Irving
character: 12 Brom Van Brunt (Brom Bones), Ichabod Crane **16** headless horseman, Katrina Van Tassel

Leger, Fernand
born: 6 France **8** Argentan
artwork: 8 Bargeman **10** Adam and Eve, The Wedding, Three Women **11** The Builders, The Cyclists, The Mechanic, The Stairway **14** The Great Parade **15** Le Grand Dejeuner **16** Contrasting Forms, Nudes in the Forest **21** Butterflies and Flowers

legerdemain 7 cunning **8** deftness, jugglery, juggling, trickery **9** deception **10** adroitness, artfulness **11** maneuvering **13** sleight of hand **16** prestidigitation

legible 4 neat **5** clear, plain **7** visible **8** clear-cut, distinct, readable **12** decipherable **14** comprehensible, understandable

legion 3 mob, sea **4** army, host, mass **5** corps, drove, horde, spate, swarm **6** myriad, throng, troops **7** brigade **8** division **9** multitude

leg irons 5 bonds, irons **6** chains **7** fetters **8** shackles

legislation 3 act **4** bill **6** ruling **7** measure, statute **9** amendment, enactment, law making, ordinance

legislator 7 senator **8** alder man, delegate, lawgiver, lawmaker **10** councilman **11** assemblyman, congressman **13** congresswoman **14** representative **15** parliamentarian

legislature 4 diet **5** house **6** senate **7** chamber, council **8** assembly, congress **10** parliament

legitimacy 8 legality, validity **10** lawfulness **11** correctness, genuineness **12** authenticity, rightfulness **15** appropriateness

legitimate 4 fair, just, true **5** legal, licit, sound, valid **6** lawful, proper **7** correct, genuine, logical, tenable **8** rightful **9** authentic, justified, plausible **10** believable, reasonable **11** appropriate, well-founded

leg-pull 4 hoax **9** deception **13** practical joke

Legree, Simon 13 cruel overseer
character in: 14 Uncle Tom's Cabin
author: 5 Stowe

LeGuin, Ursula K

author of: 13 Lathe of Heaven 14 Rocannon's World 15 The Dispossessed 16 Always Coming Home 21 The Left Hand of Darkness

Lehar, Franz (Ferencz)
  born: 7 Komarno (then Hungary, now Czechoslovakia)
  composer of: 9 Gipsy Love 13 The Merry Widow 20 The Count of Luxembourg

Lehmbruck, Wilhelm
  born: 7 Germany 9 Meiderich
  artwork: 11 Rising Youth 12 Man Flung Down, Praying Woman, Seating Youth 13 Kneeling Woman, Standing Woman, Standing Youth

Leigh, Janet
  husband: 10 Tony Curtis
  daughter: 14 Jamie Lee Curtis
  born: 8 Merced CA
  roles: 6 Psycho, The Fog 10 The Vikings 11 Little Women, Touch of Evil

Leigh, Vivien
  real name: 17 Vivian Mary Hartley
  husband: 15 Laurence Olivier
  born: 5 India 10 Darjeeling
  roles: 11 Ship of Fools 12 Anna Karenina 13 Blanche du Bois, Scarlett O'Hara 14 Waterloo Bridge 15 Gone With the Wind (Oscar) 17 That Hamilton Woman 21 A Streetcar Named Desire (Oscar), Roman Spring of Mrs Stone

Leighton, Margaret
  husband: 12 Max Reinhardt 14 Laurence Harvey, Michael Wilding
  born: 7 England 10 Barnt Green 14 Worcestershire
  roles: 12 The Go-Between 13 The Winslow Boy 14 Separate Tables 19 The Night of the Iguana

leisure 4 ease, rest 6 recess, repose 7 holiday, respite, time off 8 free time, vacation 9 diversion, idle hours, spare time 10 recreation, relaxation

leisurely 4 idle, slow 6 casual, slowly 7 languid, relaxed, restful 9 unhurried 10 slow-moving 11 lingeringly, unhurriedly 12 without haste 13 lackadaisical

Lemmon, Jack
  real name: 18 Jack Uhler Lemmon III
  wife: 11 Felicia Farr
  born: 8 Boston MA
  roles: 7 Missing 10 April Fools 12 Grumpy Old Men, Save the Tiger (Oscar), The Apartment, The Great Race, The Odd Couple 13 China Syndrome, Mister Roberts, Some Like It Hot 18 Days of Wine and Roses, Under the Yum-Yum Tree 19 How to Murder Your Wife

lemon 11 Citrus limon
  varieties: 4 wild 5 dwarf, giant, Meyer, water 6 garden, wonder 9 wild water 12 Chinese dwarf

14 American wonder
  slang for: 3 dud 9 defective

lemures
  form: 6 ghosts
  characteristic: 10 maleficent 11 troublesome

lend 4 give, loan 6 impart, in vest, supply 7 advance, furnish 10 contribute

lend a hand 3 aid 6 assist 7 help out

lend assistance 3 aid 4 abet, help 6 succor 7 relieve 16 give a helping hand

lend one's name to 7 endorse, support 9 recommend

length 3 run 4 span, term, time 5 piece, range, reach 6 extent, period 7 com- pass, measure, portion, section, segment, stretch 8 distance, duration, end to end 9 longitude, magnitude 11 elapsed time, measurement

lengthen 3 pad 5 add to 6 expand, extend, let out, pad out 7 augment, drag out, draw out, fill out, prolong, spin out, stretch 8 elongate, flesh out, increase, protract 9 attenuate, string out

lengthening 8 full form 9 extending, extension 10 elongation, stretching 11 extenuation, protraction 12 prolongation

lengthy 5 windy, wordy 6 padded, prolix 7 endless 8 drawn out, extended, over- long, rambling 9 elongated, extensive, garrulous, long-drawn, prolonged 10 digressive, discursive, long- winded, protracted 12 interminable

leniency 5 mercy 7 charity 8 clemency 9 tolerance 10 compassion 11 forbearance, magnanimity 12 mercifulness 13 forgivingness

lenient 4 kind, mild, soft 6 gentle 7 clement, liberal, patient, sparing 8 merciful, moderate, tolerant 9 easygoing, forgiving, indulgent 10 benevolent, charitable, forbearing, permissive 11 kindhearted, soft-hearted, sympathetic 13 compassionate, tender-hearted

Lenin, Vladimir Illyich
  surname: 7 Ulyanov
  also called: 7 Nikolai
  founder of: 10 Bolshevism
  leader of: 17 Russian Revolution
  premier of: 4 USSR

Lenni-Lenape see 8 Delaware

Lennon, John
  born: 9 Liverpool (UK)
  songs: 5 Woman 6 Mother 9 Stand By Me 10 Jealous Guy
  see also 7 Beatles

Lenny
  director: 8 Bob Fosse
  cast: 8 Jan Miner 11 Stanley Beck 13

Dustin Hoffman (Lenny Bruce) 14 Valerie Perrine (Honey Harlowe)

Leno, Jay
  host of: 14 The Tonight Show
  author of: 9 Headlines (Books I-IV) 17 Leading with My Chin

Le Notre, Andre
  landscape architect of: 6 Clagny 9 Tuileries 10 Ver sailles 12 Saint Germain 13 Fontainebleau 22 Chateau de Vaux-le-Vicomte

lens
  invented by:
    achromatic: 7 Dollond
    bifocal: 8 Franklin
    fused bifocal: 6 Borsch

Lenya, Lotte
  real name: 16 Karoline Blamauer
  husband: 9 Kurt Weill
  born: 7 Austria, Hitzing
  roles: 5 Jenny 18 From Russia with Love, The Seven Deadly Sins, The Three-penny Opera

Leo
  symbol: 4 lion
  planet: 3 Sun
  rules: 7 romance 10 creativity
  born: 4 July 6 August

Leonard, Elmore
  author of: 4 Swag 5 Glitz, Stick 6 Hombre 7 La Brava 9 Cat Chaser, Gold Coast, Gunsights, The Hunted 10 Mr Majestyk 12 The Big Bounce 14 Fifty-Two Pick-Up, Valdez Is Coming 16 Double Dutch Treat, The Bounty Hunters 18 Forty Lashes Less One

Leonato
  character in: 19 Much Ado About Nothing
  author: 11 Shakespeare

Leoncavallo, Ruggiero
  born: 5 Italy 6 Naples
  composer of: 8 Serafita 10 I Pagliacci

Leontes
  character in: 14 The Winter's Tale
  author: 11 Shakespeare

Leonteus
  leader of: 6 Greeks
  leader at: 4 Troy
  suitor of: 5 Helen

leopard 3 cat 7 panther 10 spotted cat
  group of: 4 leap

Leo the Lip
  nickname of: 11 Leo Durocher

lepidoptera
  class: 8 hexapoda
  phylum: 10 arthropoda
  group: 4 moth 9 butterfly

leprechaun 3 elf, imp 5 dwarf, gnome 6 sprite 12 little person

Ler
  also: 3 Lir
  origin: 5 Irish
  personifies: 3 sea

son: 8 Manannan
corresponds to: 4 Llyr

Lerner, Alan J.
born: 7 New York
author of: 4 Gigi **7** Camelot **9** Brigadoon **10** My Fair Lady **17** An American in Paris
composer of: 7 Tribute **15** The Little Prince
producer of: 14 Paint Your Wagon

Lesage, Le Sage, Alain
author of: 7 Gil Blas **8** Turcaret

Lesbos
island in: 6 Aegean
home of: 6 Sappho

Lescaze, William
architect of: 18 Borg-Warner Building (Chicago) **38** Philadelphia Savings Fund Society Building

Lescot, Pierre
architect of: 10 Cour Carree **20** Fontaine des Innocents
rebuilding of: 6 Louvre

lese-majeste, lese majesty 5 crime **7** treason
against: 12 king's dignity

Lesotho
other name: 10 Basutoland
capital/largest city: 6 Maseru
others: 4 Roma **5** Joels **6** Leribe, Morija **7** Quthing, Sekakes **8** Mafeteng, Matsieng **9** Marakabei, Qachas Nek, Semonkong **10** Butha Buthe, Mokhotlong, Thaba Bosiu **11** Mohales Hoek **12** Sehlabathebe, Teyateyaneng
head of state: 4 king
monetary unit: 4 cent, rand
mountain: 6 Maloti, Maluti **7** Central **8** Injasuti, Machache **10** Ben Macdhui **11** Drakensberg, Thaba Putsoa
highest point: 16 Thabana Ntlenyana
river: 5 Senqu **6** Orange, Tugela **7** Caledon **9** Makhaleng
physical feature:
gorge: 5 Oxbow
people: 4 Zulu **5** Bantu, Tembu **6** Basuto **7** Basotho
leader: 7 Moshesh **9** Mosheshwe **10** Moshoeshoe **14** Leabua Jonathan
language: 5 Sotho **7** English, Sesotho
religion: 7 animism **13** Roman Catholic **18** Lesotho Evangelical
feature:
blanket: 4 kobo
house: 8 rondavel
water project: 11 Malibamatso

less 5 fewer **6** barely, little **7** smaller **8** meagerly, slighter **10** not as great **11** more limited

lessen 3 ebb **4** ease, sink, thin, wane **5** abate, lower **6** dilute, reduce, shrink **7** abridge, decline, dwindle, lighten, slacken, subside **8** contract, decrease, diminish, mitigate, wind down **9** alleviate **10** depreciate

lessening 6 waning **8** decrease, dilution **9** abatement, deduction, dwindling, reduction, shrinkage **10** diminution, lightening, mitigation, shortening, slackening **11** abridgement, alleviation, contraction, diminishing, slacking off **12** abbreviation, condensation, depreciation

Lesseps, Ferdinand 8 engineer **9** Suez Canal

lesser 4 less **5** minor **7** humbler, smaller **8** inferior, slighter **9** secondary **11** sec- ondarily

Lessing, Doris
author of: 8 Shikasta **16** The Four-Gated City **17** The Golden Notebook **20** The Sirian Experiments **21** The Children of Violence **37** Marriages Between Zones Three Four and Five **42** The Making of the Representative for Planet Eight

lesson 5 class, drill, guide, model, moral, study **6** caveat, notice, rebuke **7** cau- tion, example, message, reading, segment, warning **8** exemplar, exercise, homework **9** deterrent **10** admonition, advisement, assignment, punishment, recitation, Scriptures **11** instruction **12** remonstrance

Lestrade, Inspector
character in: 14 (The Adventures of) Sherlock Holmes
author: 10 Conan Doyle

let 4 make, rent **5** admit, allow, cause, grant, lease, leave **6** enable, permit, sublet, suffer **7** approve, charter, concede, empower, endorse, hire out, license, warrant **8** sanction, sublease, tolerate **9** authorize

let
term in: 6 tennis
serve touches: 3 net

let down 4 drop **5** lower **6** betray **8** push down **10** disappoint **11** disillusion

letdown 3 rue **4** balk, blow **6** fizzle, regret **7** chagrin, set back **8** comedown **10** anticlimax, bafflement, bitter pill, dashed hope, discontent **11** frustration **12** blighted hope, discomfiture **13** mortification **14** disappointment, disenchantment, disgruntlement **15** disillusionment, dissatisfaction

let fall 4 drop **5** let go **7** release

let fly 4 cast, hurl **5** eject, fling, heave, sling, throw **6** launch, propel

let go 3 axe, can **4** fire, free, lose, oust, sack **6** bounce, give up

lethal 5 fatal, toxic **6** deadly, mortal **7** baneful, killing **8** venomous, virulent **9** dan gerous, malignant, poisonous **11** destructive **13** mortally toxic

lethargic 4 dull, idle, lazy **5** inert **6** drowsy, sleepy, torpid **7** languid, passive **8** comatose, indolent, listless, slothful, sluggish **9** apathetic, enervated, somnolent, soporific **10** dispir-

ited, lackluster, unspirited **11** debilitated, indifferent

lethargy 5 sloth **6** apathy, stupor, torpor **7** inertia, languor **8** dullness, laziness **9** indolence, lassitude, torpidity **10** drowsiness, inactivity **12** indifference, listlessness, slothfulness, sluggishness

Lethe
form: 5 river
location: 5 Hades
caused: 13 forgetfulness

let in 5 admit **7** receive **12** allow to enter

let loose 4 free **5** let go **6** let fly **7** release, set free, unleash **8** give vent, liberate **12** give free rein

Leto
also: 6 Latona
father: 5 Coeus
mother: 6 Phoebe
son: 6 Apollo
consort: 4 Zeus
daughter: 5 Diana **7** Artemis

let off 5 let go **6** acquit, excuse, exempt **7** release, set free **8** liberate **9** discharge

let slip 6 betray, expose, reveal **7** divulge, uncover **8** blurt out, disclose, give away

Let's Make a Deal
host: 9 Monty Hall
announcer: 10 Jay Stewart

letter 4 note **7** epistle, message, missive **8** dispatch, document **9** substance **10** billet-doux

Letter, The
director: 12 William Wyler
based on story by: 15 Somerset Maugham
cast: 10 Bette Davis **14** Frieda Inescort **15** Gale Sondergaard, Herbert Marshall, James Stephenson
setting: 6 Malaya

Letterman, David
Host of: 26 Late Show with David Letterman

letter ordering imprisonment
French: 14 lettre de cachet
carried seal of: 4 king **9** sovereign

letters 8 learning **9** erudition **10** literature **13** belles lettres

Letters from the Underground
author: 16 Fyodor Dostoevsky

Letter to Three Wives, A
director: 17 Joseph L Mankiewicz
cast: 10 Ann Sothern **11** Jeanne Crain, Jeffrey Lynn, Kirk Douglas, Paul Douglas **12** Linda Darnell, Thelma Ritter
Oscar for: 6 script **8** director

let the buyer beware
Latin: 12 caveat emptor

let the people rule
Latin: 13 regnat populus
motto of: 8 Arkansas

let there be light
Latin: **7** fiat lux

lettre de cachet 26 letter ordering imprisonment **28** letter under the sovereign's seal

lettuce 7 Lactuca
varieties: **3** cos **5** chalk, frog's, lamb's, water **6** Boston, garden, miner's **7** iceberg, prickly, romaine **8** escarole **9** asparagus **11** common lamb's

letup 4 lull **5** pause **6** relief **7** respite **8** decrease, interval, slowdown, stopping, surcease, vacation **9** abatement, cessation, interlude, lessening, remission **10** slackening **11** retardation

Let Us Now Praise Famous Men
author: **9** James Agee

Let us therefore be joyful
Latin: **15** Gaudeamus igitur

Le Vau, Louis
architect of: **6** Louvre **10** Versailles **12** Hotel Lambert **22** Chateau de Vaux-le-Vicomte **24** College des Quatres Nations

levee 3 dam **4** bank, dike, pier, quay, wall **5** ditch, jetty, ridge, wharf **6** durbar **9** reception **10** embankment

level 3 aim, bed **4** even, flat, rank, raze, tied, vein, zone **5** align, floor, flush, grade, layer, plane, point, stage, story, wreck **6** direct, height, lay low, reduce, smooth, topple **7** aligned, even out, flatten, landing, on a line, station, stratum, uniform **8** equalize, make even, position, tear down, together **9** devastate, elevation, knock down **10** consistent, horizontal, on a par with, unwrinkled **11** achievement, neck and neck **12** on an even keel

level-headed 4 sage **5** sound **6** poised, stable, steady **7** prudent **8** balanced, cautious, composed, sensible **9** collected, judicious, practical, unruffled **10** cool-headed, dependable, thoughtful **11** circumspect **12** eventempered **13** dispassionate **14** self-controlled

levelheadedness 6 aplomb **9** good sense, soundness, stability **10** equanimity **11** common sense **13** judiciousness

Levene, Sam
real name: **12** Samuel Levine
born: **6** Russia
roles: **12** Guys and Dolls **13** Nathan Detroit **15** The Sunshine Boys

lever 3 bar, pry **5** jimmy, raise **7** crowbar

Lever, Charles
author of: **14** Charles O'Malley

Leverrier, Urbain Jean Joseph
field: **9** astronomy
nationality: **6** French
co-discovered: **7** Neptune
worked with: **14** John Couch Adams

Levi
father: **5** Jacob **6** Melchi, Symeon
mother: **4** Leah
son: **6** Kohath, Merari **7** Gershom
brother: **3** Dan, Gad **5** Asher, Judah **6** Joseph, Reuben, Simeon **7** Zebulun **8** Benjamin, Issachar, Naphtali
sister: **5** Dinah
violated: **5** Dinah
also called: **7** Matthew
descendant of: **6** Levite

Leviathan 6 dragon **10** sea monster
means: **13** spirally bound
represents: **14** terrible powers

Leviathan
author: **12** Thomas Hobbes

Levin, Ira
author of: **6** Sliver **13** Rosemary's Baby **16** The Stepford Wives

Levin, Konstantin
character in: **12** Anna Karenina
author: **7** Tolstoy

Levi-Strauss, Claude
method: **13** structuralism
author of: **13** Mythologiques, The Savage Mind **16** Tristes Tropiques **22** Structural Anthropology **29** Elementary Structures of Kinship

Levitch, Joseph
real name of: **10** Jerry Lewis

levity 3 fun **5** mirth **6** joking, whimsy **8** hilarity, trifling **9** flippancy, frivolity, lightness, silliness **10** jocularity, pleasantry, triviality **11** flightiness, foolishness **16** lightheartedness

levy 3 fee, tax **4** duty, make, toll, wage **5** draft, exact, start **6** assess, call up, charge, demand, enlist, excise, impose, muster, pursue, tariff **7** carry on, collect **9** calling up, conscript, prosecute **10** assess ment, imposition **12** conscription

Levy, Marion
real name of: **15** Paulette Goddard

Lew Archer, Private Detective
author: **13** Ross MacDonald

lewd 5 bawdy **6** ribald, risque, vulgar, wanton **7** goatish, immoral, lustful, obscene **8** indecent, prurient **9** lecherous, libertine, salacious **10** lascivious, libidinous, licentious, lubricious **11** Rabelaisian **12** pornographic

Lewis, C S
author of: **10** Perelandra **13** Prince Caspian, The Last Battle **14** Surprised by Joy, The Silver Chair, Til We Have Faces **17** The Horse and His Boy **18** The Magician's Nephew **19** The Screwtape Letters **20** Out of the Silent Planet **21** The Chronicles of Narnia **25** The Voyage of the Dawn Treader **29** The Lion the Witch and the Wardrobe

Lewis, Jerry
real name: **13** Joseph Levitch
partner: **10** Dean Martin
born: **8** Newark NJ

roles: **8** The Caddy **10** The Bellboy, The Sad Sack **11** Cinderfella **12** The Geisha Boy **16** Artists and Models **17** The Nutty Professor **20** The Disorderly Orderly

Lewis, Sinclair
author of: **7** Babbitt **9** Dodsworth **10** Arrowsmith, Main Street **11** Elmer Gantry **14** Cass Timberlane

lexicon 5 gloss, index **8** code book, glossary, synonymy, wordbook, wordlist **9** thesaurus, wordstock **10** dictionary, vocabulary **11** concordance, onomasticon

lex loci 11 law of a place

lex non scripta 9 common law **12** unwritten law

lex scripta 10 statute law, written law

Leyden, Lucas (Lukas) van
born: **6** Leiden, Leyden **14** The Netherlands
artwork: **12** Last Judgment **14** The Card Players, The Game of Chess **26** Mohammed and the Murdered Monk

Lhasa
capital of: **5** Tibet

liability 4 debt, drag, duty, onus **5** debit, minus **6** arrear, burden **8** drawback, handicap, obstacle **9** hindrance **10** impediment, obligation **11** encumbrance, shortcoming **12** disadvantage, indebtedness **13** inconvenience **14** responsibility, stumbling block

liable 3 apt **4** open **5** prone **6** likely **7** exposed, ripe for, subject **8** disposed, inclined **9** obligated, sensitive **10** answerable, chargeable, vulnerable **11** accountable, responsible, susceptible

liaison 4 bond, link **5** amour, union **7** contact **8** alliance, intrigue, mediator **9** ad- venture, dalliance, go-between **10** connection, flirtation, love affair **11** association, cooperation, interchange **12** coordination, entanglement **13** communication

liar 6 fibber **8** perjurer **9** falsifier **10** fabricator **11** story teller **12** prevaricator

libation 4 wine **5** drink, water **6** liquid **8** ambrosia, beverage, offering, potation **9** sacrifice

libel 4 slur **5** smear **6** defame, malign, revile, vilify **7** asperse, blacken, calumny, obloquy, slander **8** derogate **9** aspersion, discredit, disparage **10** calumniate, defamation **12** vilification

Libeled Lady
director: **10** Jack Conway
cast: **8** Myrna Loy **10** Jean Harlow **12** Spencer Tracy **13** William Powell **14** Walter Connolly
remade as: **9** Easy to Wed

Libera
origin: **7** Italian
goddess of: **4** wine **9** fertility, vineyards

husband: 5 Liber
corresponds to: 10 Persephone
liberal 5 ample, broad **6** casual, lavish
7 leftist, lenient **8** abundant, advanced, flexible, generous, handsome, left-wing, prodigal, reformer, tolerant, unbiased **9** bounteous, bountiful, impartial, not strict, plenteous, reformist, unbigoted, unspar- ing **10** fairminded, forbearing, left-winger, munificent, not literal, openhanded, open-minded, unrigorous, unstinting **11** broad-minded, enlightened, extravagant, libertarian, magnanimous, progressive **12** freethinking, humanitarian, open to reason, unprejudiced **14** latitudinarian

liberal arts
7 trivium: 5 logic **7** grammar **8** rhetoric
10 quadrivium: 5 music **8** geometry **9** astronomy **10** arithmetic
liberality 10 generosity **11** benevolence, munificence **12** philanthropy **13** bountifulness **14** openhandedness
liberate 5 let go **6** let out, redeem, rescue, spring **7** absolve, deliver, manumit, release, set free **8** let loose **9** discharge, disengage, extricate, unshackle **10** emancipate **11** disencumber
liberated 5 freed, let go **7** rescued, set free **8** let loose, released **10** discharged, extricated **11** emancipated
liberation 6 escape, rescue **7** freedom, freeing, release **8** delivery **9** letting go, releasing **11** manumission **12** emancipation

Liberia
capital/largest city: 8 Monrovia
others: 4 Sino **5** Gribo, Rebbo **6** Bopora, Gbanga, Harper, Kakata **7** Bgarnga, Kolahun, Nanakru, Tappita, Vonjama **8** Buchanan, Garraway, Marshall, Nanakaru, Sass Town **9** Grand Cess, River Cess, Roysville **10** Careysburg, Green ville, Sanoquelli **11** Robertsport **12** Sanniquellie
school: 7 Liberia **10** Cuttington **15** Our Lady of Fatima **16** Booker Washington
  religious school/secret society: 4 poro **5** sande
measure: 4 kuba
monetary unit: 4 cent **6** dollar
mountain: 3 Uni **4** Bong, Putu **5** Niete, Nimba **9** Bomi Hills
highest point: 6 Wutivi
river: 4 Cess, Lofa, Mano **5** Duobe, Lotta, Manna, Morro, Sinoe **6** Cestos, Douobe **7** Cavalla, Cavally **8** San Pedro **9** Saint John, Saint Paul, Sehnkwehn
sea: 8 Atlantic
physical feature:
  wind: 9 harmattan
people: 2 Gi **3** Gio, Kra, Kru, Kwa, Vai, Vei **4** Gola, Kroo, Krou, Loma,

Mano, Toma **5** Bassa, Gibbi, Gissi, Grebo **6** Gbande, Kpelle, Kpuesi, Krooby, Kruman **7** Krooboy, Krooman **8** Mandingo **15** Americo-Liberian
  leader: 3 Doe **6** Tubman **7** Roberts, Tolbert
  language: 3 Kru, Kwa **5** Mande **7** English
  religion: 5 Islam **7** animism **10** Protestant **12** Christianity
  feature:
    clothing: 5 lappa
    rubber plantation: 9 Firestone

Libertas
origin: 5 Roman
personifies: 7 liberty
liberte egalite fraternite 25 liberty equality fraternity
motto of: 16 French Revolution
liberties 6 misuse **7** license **9** violation **10** distortion **11** familiarity, impropriety **13** falsification
libertine 4 goat, lewd, rake, roue **5** loose, satyr **6** lecher, wanton **7** immoral, lustful, seducer **8** unchaste **9** debauchee, dissolute, lecherous, reprobate, womanizer **10** immoralist, lascivious, libidinous, licentious, profligate, sensualist, voluptuary
liberty 5 leave, right **7** freedom, license **8** autonomy, delivery, free time, furlough, sanction, vacation **9** privilege **10** liberation, permission, shore leave **11** citizenship, manumission **12** carte blanche, dispensation, emancipation, independence **15** enfranchisement **17** self- determination

liberty equality fraternity
French: 24 liberte egalite fraternite
motto of: 16 French Revolution
Libra
symbol: 6 scales **7** balance
planet: 5 Venus
rules: 8 marriage
born: 7 October **9** September
Libreville
capital of: 13 Gabon Republic
Libya
capital/largest city: 7 Tripoli
  summer capital: 8 Benghazi
others: 4 Homs, Marj, Surt **5** Beida, Darna, Derna, Khums, Kufra, Sebha, Sidri, Zawia **6** Garian, Murzuq, Tobruk **7** Es Sidar, Gharyan, Misrata **8** Ajdabiya, Misurata, Rashanuf **12** Marsa el Brega
school: 7 Alfateh **9** Garyounis
division: 6 Fezzan **9** Cyrenaica **12** Tripolitania
measure: 3 dra, pik, saa **4** kele **5** bozze, donum, jabia, teman, uckia **6** barile, gorraf, misura **7** mattaro, termino **8** kharouba
weight: 4 kele **6** gorraf **8** kharouba
monetary unit: 5 dinar
mountain: 5 Green **13** Jabal al Akh-

dar, Tibesti Massif
highest point: 9 Bette Peak
sea: 13 Mediterranean
physical feature:
  desert: 6 Libyan, Sahara **9** Calanscio
  gulf: 5 Bomba, Sidra, Sirte
  oasis: 4 Ghat **5** Kufra, Sebha **7** Tazerbo **8** Al-Kufrah, Ghudamis
  plain: 6 al Marj, Gefara **7** Jaffara
  plateau: 12 Gebel Nefuisa, Jabal Nafusah
  wind: 6 ghibli
people: 4 Arab, Tebu **6** Berber, Tuareg **7** Gaetuli lans, Harratin
  leader: 6 Battus **7** Jalloud, Qadhafi **8** Aegyptus **9** al- Qaddafi, Karamanli **13** Idris al-Senusi
  religious leader: 8 al-Senusi
  ruler: 4 Rome **5** Italy **6** Greece **9** Phoenicia **12** Ottoman Turks
language: 6 Arabic, Berber **7** English, Italian
  alphabet: 8 tifinagh
religion: 5 Islam
feature: 14 Tropic of Cancer
  clothing: 5 lanaf **9** barracano
  festival: 3 Mez **7** Fantasi
  Islamic law: 6 sharia
  leader: 6 sheikh
  ruins: 11 Leptis Magna
food:
  dish: 5 bazin **8** couscous
  red pepper: 6 filfil
license 3 let **4** pass, visa **5** allow, grant, leave, right **6** enable, laxity, permit **7** anarchy, approve, certify, charter, empower, endorse, freedom, liberty, warrant **8** accredit, audacity, disorder, latitude, passport, sanction, temerity **9** admission, allowance, authorize, franchise, looseness, privilege, slackness **10** brazenness, commission, debauchery, unruliness **11** certificate, free passage, lawlessness, libertinism, presumption, safe- conduct **12** carte blanche, dispensation, recklessness
licentious 4 lewd **5** dirty, loose **6** amoral, sleazy, wanton **7** brutish, goatish, immoral, lawless, lustful, raunchy, ruttish **8** depraved, prodigal **9** abandoned, debauched, dissolute, excessive, lecherous, libertine, salacious **10** dissipated, lascivious, libidinous, lubricious, profligate, ungoverned **11** promiscuous **12** unprincipled, unrestrained, unscrupulous **13** irresponsible, unconstrained
licentiousness 7 abandon **8** lewdness **10** immorality, wantonness
licit 5 legal, legit, valid **6** kosher, lawful **9** allowable, statutory **10** acceptable, admissible, authorized, legitimate, sanctioned **11** permissible **12** authorizable, sanctionable **14** constitutional
lick 3 bit, dab, hit, jot, lap **4** beat, blow, drub, fire, hint, iota, rout, slap, snip, sock, suck, whip **5** crack,

punch, sally, shred, spank, speck, taste, touch, trace **6** defeat, ignite, kindle, master, sample, stroke, subdue, thrash, tongue, wallop **7** clobber, conquer, modicum, smidgen, trounce **8** outmatch, overcome, particle, vanquish **9** overpower, overthrow, scintilla, subjugate **10** smattering **12** denunciation

lid 3 cap, top **4** cork, curb, plug **5** cover, limit **7** ceiling, maximum, stopper, stopple **9** operculum, restraint

lie 3 fib **4** loll, rest, stay **5** abide, exist, range, story **6** belong, deceit, extend, inhere, lounge, obtain, remain, repose, sprawl **7** falsify, fiction, perjury, recline, romance, untruth **8** misstate, tall tale **9** deception, embellish, embroider, fabricate, falsehood, invention **10** equivocate **11** fabrication, prevaricate **12** equivocation **13** falsification, prevarication **17** misrepresentation

Liechtenstein
capital/largest city: 5 Vaduz
others: 4 Haag **6** Balzer, Eschen, Iradug, Schaan **7** Balzers, Bendern, Nendeln, Planken, Triesen **12** Schellenberg
division:
  ancient province: 6 Rhaeti **7** Rhaetia
government:
  legislature: 7 Landtag
monetary unit: 6 rappen **7** franken
mountain: 4 Alps **8** Naafkopf, Rhatikon **12** Three Sisters
highest point: 15 Vorder-Grauspitz
river: 5 Rhine
physical feature:
  valley: 6 Lavena, Samina
people: 8 Alemanni
  leader: 7 Florian **15** Francis Joseph II **16** von Liechtenstein
language: 6 German **10** Alemannish
religion: 13 Roman Catholic
place:
  castle: 9 Gutemburg, Gutenberg
feature:
  legendary dwarf: 10 wildmannli
  wine: 7 Vaduzer

lie down 6 retire **7** go to bed, recline **8** take a nap **11** take a snooze **15** catch forty winks

life 4 path, soul, zest **5** being, human, plant, story, verve, vigor **6** animal, career, course, energy, memoir, person, spirit **8** creature, duration, life span, lifetime, lifework, organism, survival, vitality, vivacity **9** animation, biography, existence, life story, longevity **11** subsistence **13** autobiography
French: 3 vie

Life Before Man
author: 14 Margaret Atwood

Lifeboat
director: 15 Alfred Hitchcock
cast: 10 John Hodiak **12** Mary Ander-

son **13** William Bendix **16** Tallulah Bankhead

life-giving 5 vital **9** vivifying **12** invigorating

life jacket 7 Mae West

lifeless 4 dead, dull, flat, late **5** inert, stiff, vapid **6** boring, hollow, static, torpid, wooden **7** defunct **8** deceased, departed, inactive, lifeless, sluggish **9** colorless, inanimate **10** lackluster, spiritless

lifelessness 5 death **7** inertia **8** dullness, limpness, vapidity **9** blandness **10** flaccidity, inactivity **13** colorlessness

Life Magazine
founder: 9 Henry Luce

Life of Dante
author: 17 Giovanni Boccaccio

Life of Emile Zola
director: 15 William Dieterle
cast: 8 Paul Muni **11** Donald Crisp **12** Gloria Holden **15** Gale Sondergaard **17** Joseph Schildkraut (Dreyfus)
Oscar for: 7 picture

Life of Man, The
author: 14 Leonid Andreyev

Life of Riley, The
character: 4 Babs **6** Dangle, Junior **8** Peg Riley **9** Jim Gillis **10** Cunningham, Digby (Digger) O'Dell **11** Waldo Binney **13** Chester A Riley **14** Honeybee Gillis
cast: 9 John Brown, Lanny Rees, Sid Tomack **10** Tom D'Andrea **12** Emory Parnell, Wesley Morgan **13** Gloria Winters, Jackie Gleason, Lugene Sanders, Robert Sweeney, William Bendix **14** Gloria Blondell, Rosemary DeCamp **16** Douglas Dumbrille, Marjorie Reynolds, Sterling Holloway

Life of Samuel Johnson, The
author: 12 James Boswell

life of the party 7 show-off **9** extrovert **13** exhibitionist **17** hail-fellow-well-met

Life on the Mississippi
author: 9 Mark Twain

life span 4 life **8** lifetime **14** life expectancy

Life Studies
author: 12 Robert Lowell

Life With Father
author: 13 Clarence Day Jr
director: 13 Michael Curtiz
cast: 9 ZaSu Pitts **10** Irene Dunne **11** Edmund Gwenn **13** William Powell **15** Elizabeth Taylor
setting: 11 New York City

lifework 6 career **7** calling **8** vocation **10** livelihood, occupation, profession

lift 4 high, palm, pick, rear, rise, soar, take **5** boost, climb, exalt, filch, heave, hoist, pinch, raise, steal, swipe **6** ascend, ascent, banish, cancel, pilfer, pirate, pock- et, remove, revoke,

snatch, thieve, uplift, vanish **7** elation, elevate, purloin, raise up, raising, rescind, scatter, upraise **8** disperse **9** disappear, dissipate, float away **10** ascendance, move upward, plagiarize, put an end to **11** appropriate, countermand, inspiration, make off with, reassurance **12** give a boost to, shot in the arm **13** encouragement, enheartenment

ligament
holds: 5 bones

Ligeia
author: 13 Edgar Allan Poe
character: 19 Lady Rowena Trevanion

light 3 gay **4** airy, beam, easy, fair, fall, find, fire, glow, lamp, land, pale, puny, side, soft, stop **5** aglow, angle, blaze, blond, faint, flame, funny, glare, guide, happy, jolly, match, model, perch, petty, put on, roost, shine, slant, small, spare, spark, sunny, torch **6** alight, aspect, beacon, blithe, bright, candle, chance, frugal, gentle, get off, ignite, jaunty, kindle, luster, meager, paltry, scanty, settle, simple, slight, turn on **7** amusing, buoyant, chipper, clarify, come off, descend, get down, gleeful, insight, lantern, lighten, lighter, lucifer, not dark, not rich, paragon, radiant, radiate, sparkle, sunbeam, trivial **8** approach, attitude, bleached, blondish, brighten, carefree, cheerful, come upon, discover, dismount, ethereal, exemplar, gossamer, graceful, illumine, jubilant, luminous, meet with, moderate, moonbeam, not heavy, paradigm, radiance, sportive, step down, switch on, trifling, untaxing **9** brilliant, catch fire, direction, encounter, frivolous, irradiate, light-hued, set fire to, sprightly, stumble on, sylphlike, viewpoint **10** abstemious, brightness, brilliance, burdenless, come across, come to rest, effortless, effulgence, floodlight, happen upon, illuminate, light-toned, luminosity, manageable, restricted, set burning, weightless **11** conflagrate, elucidation, illuminated, information, make radiant, superficial, undemanding, underweight **15** inconsequential
god of: 6 Apollo **7** Mithras, Phoebus, Pythius **8** Heimdall **9** Musagetes
Latin: 3 lux
measurement: 7 candela **11** candlepower

light-colored 4 pale **5** beige, blond **6** blonde, flaxen, pastel **7** neutral, whitish **9** yellowish

light-complexioned 4 fair, pale **12** white-skinned

lighten 4 buoy, ease, lift **5** abate, allay, blaze, elate, flare, flash, gleam, shine **6** buoy up, lessen, reduce, revive, temper, unload, uplift **7** assuage, enliven, gladden, inspire, light up, relieve **8** brighten, mitigate, moderate, unburden **9** alleviate, coruscate, disburden, irradiate **10** illuminate, make bright **11** become light, disencumber, make lighter, scintillate

light-filled 5 sunny **6** bright **7** well-lit **11** illuminated

lighthearted 3 gay **4** airy, glad **5** jolly, merry, sunny **6** blithe, cheery, joyful, joyous, lively **7** buoyant, cheered, chipper **8** carefree, cheerful, sanguine **9** sprightly **10** insouciant, untroubled **11** free and easy **12** effervescent

lightheartedness 3 joy **4** glee **5** mirth **8** gladness **9** happiness, merriment **10** blitheness, exuberance, joyfulness, joyous ness **11** high spirits

Light in August
author: **15** William Faulkner
character: **8** Doc Hines, Joe Brown **9** Lena Grove, McEachern **10** Byron Bunch **12** Joanna Burden, Joe Christmas

lightless 4 dark **5** black, murky **7** stygian **9** unlighted **13** unilluminated

lightly 6 airily, easily, gently, nimbly, softly, thinly, weakly **7** blandly, faintly, quickly, readily, swiftly, timidly **8** blithely, fac- ilely, gingerly, meagerly, slightly, sparsely **9** buoyantly, sparingly **10** carelessly, flippantly, hesitantly, moderately **11** frivolously, slightingly **13** indifferently, thoughtlessly, unconcernedly, without effort **14** without concern

lightness 8 airiness, radiance **10** brightness, fluffiness, luminosity **12** illumination, luminousness

lightning rod
invented by: **8** Franklin

light of day 8 daylight, sunlight, sunshine

light sleep 3 nap **4** doze **6** catnap, snooze **10** forty winks

light wind 4 waft **6** breeze, zephyr **10** gentle wind **11** breath of air

Lightwood, Mortimer
character in: **15** Our Mutual Friend
author: **7** Dickens

lignum vitae 10 wood of life
tree species: **8** Guaiacum

likable, likeable 4 nice **6** genial **7** amiable, lovable, winsome **8** charming, engaging, loveable, pleasant, pleasing **9** agreeable, appealing, simpatico **10** attractive **11** complaisant, sympathetic

like 4 akin, care, dote, same, wish **5** enjoy, equal, fancy, favor, savor **6** admire, allied, choose, esteem, relish **7** approve, cognate, endorse, matched, related, similar, support, uniform **8** be fond of, parallel, selfsame, think fit **9** analogous, congru- ent, have a mind, identical **10** comparable, equivalent,

homologous, resembling **11** be partial to, much the same **12** feel in clined, have a crush on, take a shine to **13** cor- responding, find agreeable **14** take plea- sure in

Like a Bulwark
author: **13** Marianne Moore

likelihood 8 prospect **10** good chance **11** possibility, probability **12** potentiality

likely 3 apt, fit **4** able **6** liable, proper **8** credible, destined, inclined, probable, probably, rational, reliable, suitable **9** befitting, plausible, promising, qualified **10** believable, presumably, reasonable **11** appropriate, verisimilar **16** in all probability

like-mindedness 6 accord **7** concord, harmony, rapport **8** affinity **9** agreement **12** congeniality **13** compatibility

likeness 5 image, model, study **6** effigy **7** analogy, picture, replica **8** affinity, portrait **9** agreement, depiction, facsimile, portrayal, rendition, semblance **10** similarity, similitude **11** delineation, resemblance **14** correspondence, representation

likes 9 favorites **10** prejudices **11** preferences **12** inclinations, partialities

likewise 3 and, eke, too **4** also **5** ditto **6** as well **7** be sides, equally, the same **8** moreover **9** similarity **10** in addition

liking 4 bent **5** fancy, taste **7** leaning **8** affinity, appetite, fondness, penchant, soft spot, weakness **9** affection **10** partiality, preference, proclivity, propensity **11** inclination **12** predilection

Li'l Abner
creator: **6** Al Capp
character: **5** Pappy **7** Salomey (pig), Wolf Gal **10** Joe Btfsplk, Mammy Yokum, Marryin' Sam **11** Adam Lazonga, Hairless Joe **12** Lena the Hyena, Tobacco Rhoda **13** Joanie Phoanie **14** Daisy Mae Scragg, Evil-Eye Flee gle, Stupefyin' Jones **15** Fearless Fosdick, Henry Cabbage Cod, Lonesome Polecat, Moonbeam McSwine **16** General Bullmoose, Sir Cecil Cesspool **17** Sen Jack S Phogbound **18** J Roaringham Fatback **21** Appassionata von Climax
brewery: **23** Big Barnsmell's Skonk Works
event: **15** Sadie Hawkins Day
juice: **16** Kickapoo Joy Juice
kingdom: **14** Lower Slobbovia
mountain: **11** Onnecessary
animal: **6** Schmoo
people: **7** kygmies
place: **8** Dogpatch
railroad: **11** West Po'k Chop
ruler: **14** King Nogoodnick

lilac 7 Syringa
varieties: **4** late, vine, wild **6** common, Indian, summer **7** Chinese, cut-

leaf, Persian **9** Himalayan, Hungarian **12** Japanese tree **16** Catalina mountain

Lili
director: **14** Charles Walters
cast: **9** Mel Ferrer **11** Leslie Caron, Zsa Zsa Gabor **16** Jean-Pierre Aumont

Lilies of the Field
director: **11** Ralph Nelson
cast: **8** Lisa Mann **10** Lilia Skala **13** Sidney Poitier
Oscar for: **5** actor (Poitier)

Liliom
author: **12** Ferenc Molnar
source for: **8** Carousel

lillet
type: **8** aperitif
origin: **6** France
flavor: **6** orange
color: **3** red **5** white

Lilliput
fictional land in: **16** Gulliver's Travels
inhabitants: **10** tiny people
author: **5** Swift

lilliputian 3 wee **4** tiny **5** dwarf, short, small, teeny, weeny **6** little, midget, minute, petite **9** miniature **10** diminutive, teeny-weeny **11** pocket-sized

Lilongwe
capital of: **6** Malawi

lily 6 Lilium
varieties: **3** Alp, cow, day, pig **4** Arum, bell, boat, corn, fawn, fire, flax, herb, palm, pine, pond, rain, roan, rock, sand, Sego, star, toad, wood **5** adobe, Aztec, blood, bugle, calla, coast, cobra, crane, Cuban, fairy, globe, glory, Gray's, Ifafa, lemon, magic, natal, queen, regal, royal, showy, snake, spear, swamp, sword, tiger, torch, trout, water, wheel **6** Alpine, Amazon, Canada, Crinum, desert, Easter, eureka, ginger, hidden, Kaffir, Marhan, meadow, one-day, orange, Oregon, shasta, Sierra, spider, sunset, tartar, turban, voodoo, yellow, Zephyr **7** African, Bermuda, chamise, checker, garland, leopard, madonna, Nankeen, panther, redwood, thimble, toad-cup, triplet, trumpet, western **8** Atamasco, Barbados, bluebead, Carolina, climbing, Columbia, flamingo, gloriosa, Guernsey, Humboldt, Jacobean, Japanese, long's red, Mariposa, Martagon, Michigan, mountain, paradise, Peruvian, plan tain, Siberian, Solomon's, St Bruno's, St James's, turk's cap **9** alligator, avalanche, butterfly, caucasian, celestial, chaparral, checkered, Eucharist, Kamchatka, naked-lady, orange-cup, pineapple, pinewoods, pot-of-gold, red ginger, red spider, St Joseph's **10** belladonna, blackberry, blue funnel,

fairy water, giant water, globe spear, gold-banded, Josephine's, orange-bell, pink Easter, pygmy water, royal water, small tiger, St Bernard's, Washington, white water, wild yellow, yellow-bell, yellow pond **11** African corn, Amazon water, blue African, candlestick, dwarf ginger, golden-rayed, milk-and-wine, Palmer spear, Scarborough, southern red, yellow water **12** African blood, Chinese white, golden spider, prickly water, resurrection, speckled wood, white trumpet **13** Bermuda Easter, cape blue water, Chinese sacred, Egyptian water, fragrant water, India red water, lavender globe, magnolia water, minor Turk's-cap, per fumed fairy, pink porcelain, scarlet ginger, showy Japanese, tuberous water, wild orange-red **14** Chinese-lantern, lesser Turk's-cap, little Turk's-cap, Santa Cruz water, yellow Turk's-cap **15** Australian water, backhouse hybrid, golden hurricane, scarlet Turk's-cap **16** American Turk's cap, Bellingham hybrid, Cape Cod pink water, fragrant plantain, Japanese Turk's-cap, western orange-cup **17** midsummer plantain **18** European white water, seer sucker plantain **20** narrow-leaved plantain

lily-livered 6 afraid, craven, scared, yellow **7** chicken, fearful, gutless **8** cowardly **9** dastardly **12** fainthearted **13** pusillanimous, yellow-bellied **14** chicken-hearted, chicken-livered **22** showing the white feather

lily-white 4 good, pure **6** biased, decent, proper, racist **7** bigoted, upright **8** all-white, innocent, virtuous **9** blameless, exclusive, exemplary, faultless, guiltless, honorable, righteous **10** impeccable, inculpable, prejudiced, segregated, upstanding **11** uncorrupted **12** unintegrated **13** unimpeachable **14** discriminatory, irreproachable

Lima
  capital of: 4 Peru
  foothills of: 5 Andes
  founder: 7 Pizarro
  nickname: 11 city of kings
  ocean: 7 Pacific
  port: 6 Callao
  river: 5 Rimac
  square: 12 Plaza de Armas
limb 3 arm, gam, leg, pin **4** part, spur, twig, wing **5** bough, shoot, sprig **6** branch, member **9** appendage, extension, outgrowth **10** projection, prosthesis
limber 5 agile, lithe, relax **6** loosen, pliant, supple **7** bending, elastic, lissome, pliable **8** flexible **9** lithesome, malleable
lime 18 Citrus aurantifolia
  varieties: 3 key **4** wild **7** Mexican,

Persian, Rangpur, Spanish **8** Mandarin **10** West Indian **14** Australian wild **15** Australian round **16** Australian desert, Australian finger

Limenia
  epithet of: 9 Aphrodite
  means: 11 of the harbor
Limerick
  county in: 7 Ireland
  gave name to: 12 nonsense poem
  rhyme scheme: 5 aabba
  popularized by: 10 Edward Lear
limit 3 end **4** curb **8** boundary, end point, restrain, ultimate **13** breaking point
limitation 4 curb **5** quota **8** boundary, decrease **9** lessening, reduction, restraint **10** shortening **11** abridgement, restriction, shortcoming **13** qualification, specification
limited 5 fixed **6** finite, narrow **7** bounded, cramped, defined, minimal, special **8** confined **9** delimited, specified **10** controlled, restrained, restricted **13** circumscribed
limitless 7 endless, eternal, unbound **8** infinite, unending **9** boundless, unlimited **11** measureless **12** immeasurable
limits 3 rim, top **4** curb, edge **5** bound, check, quota **6** border, define, fringe, margin, narrow **7** ceiling, confine, delimit, inhibit, maximum, qualify **8** confines, frontier, restrain, restrict **9** perimeter, periphery, prescribe, restraint **10** boundaries **11** limitations **12** restrictions
limn 4 draw **6** sketch **7** picture **9** delineate
Limnaea
  epithet of: 7 Artemis
  means: 9 of the lake
limp 3 lax **4** gimp, halt, soft, weak **5** crawl, loose, skulk, slack **6** droopy, falter, flabby, floppy, hobble **7** flaccid **8** drooping, lameness, yielding **9** dead tired, enervated, exhausted
limpid 4 pure **5** clear, lucid **8** clear-cut, pellucid, vitreous **11** crystalline, perspicuous, translucent, transparent, unambiguous **15** straightforward

Lincoln, Abraham
  nickname: 9 Honest Abe **20** Illinois Rail Splitter
  presidential rank: 9 sixteenth
  party: 4 Whig **10** Republican
  state represented: 2 IL
  defeated: 4 (John) Bell **7** (John Charles) Fremont, (Stephen Arnold) Douglas **9** (George Brinton) McClellan **12** (John Cabell) Breckinridge
  vice president: 6 (Hannibal) Hamlin **7** (Andrew) Johnson
  cabinet:
    state: 6 (William Henry) Seward
    treasury: 5 (Salmon Portland) Chase **9** (Hugh) McCulloch, (William Pitt) Fessenden

  war: 7 (Edwin McMasters) Stanton, (Simon) Cameron
  attorney general: 5 (Edward) Bates, (James) Speed
  navy: 6 (Gideon) Welles
  postmaster general: 5 (Montgomery) Blair **8** (William) Dennison
  interior: 5 (Caleb Blood) Smith, (John Palmer) Usher
  born: 2 KY **8** log cabin **11** Larue County **17** Sinking Spring farm
  died: 12 Washington DC, Fords Theater
    died by: 13 assassination
    assassinated by: 15 John Wilkes Booth
  buried: 13 Springfield IL
  education:
    educated by: 4 self
    studied: 3 law
  interests: 7 theater
    received patent for: 25 adjustable buoyant chambers (for lifting boats)
  political career: 16 state legislature **24** US House of Representatives
  civilian career: 6 lawyer **8** surveyor **10** postmaster
  military service:
    War: 9 Black Hawk
    US Army: 7 private
    captain of company of: 10 volunteers
  notable events of lifetime/term: 8 Civil War **24** Emanci pation Proclamation
    Act: 9 Homestead, Income Tax, Judiciary **12** Conscription
    debates: 14 Lincoln-Douglas
    speech: 17 Gettysburg Address
  father: 6 Thomas
  mother: 5 Nancy (Hanks)
    stepmother: 5 Sarah (Bush Johnston)
  siblings: 5 Sarah **6** Thomas
    stepbrother: 4 John
    stepsister: 7 Matilda **9** Elizabeth
  wife: 4 Mary (Ann Todd)
  children: 6 Thomas **10** Robert Todd **11** Edward Baker **14** William Wallace

Lind, James
  field: 8 medicine
  nationality: 8 Scottish
  eliminated: 6 scurvy
Lindbergh, Anne Morrow
  author of: 14 Gift from the Sea **15** Bring Me a Unicorn **16** North to the Orient **19** War Within and Without
linden 5 Tilia
  varieties: 6 Indoor **7** Crimean **8** American, Japanese **9** Mongolian **10** Manchurian **11** Large-leaved **13** Pendent silver **19** Small-leaved European
lindy 5 dance **8** lindy hop **9** jitterbug
  nickname for: 16 Charles Lindbergh
line, lines 4 card, cord, dash, draw,

file, idea, mark, note, part, race, rank, rope, rule, tier, word **5** align, array, breed, cable, craft, front, house, model, queue, range, score, slash, stock, trade **6** belief, border, column, crease, family, furrow, letter, method, metier, policy, report, scheme, series, stance, strain, strand, streak, stripe, system, thread **7** calling, circuit, conduit, contour, cordage, example, lineage, marshal, outline, pattern, purpose, pursuit, queue up, routine, towline, wrinkle **8** ancestry, business, dialogue, doctrine, fishline, ideology, inscribe, position, postcard, trenches, vanguard, vocation **9** conductor, crow's foot, direction, frontline, genealogy, intention, principle **10** barricades, convention, firing line, livelihood, long stroke, occupation, procession, profession, underscore **11** demarcation

lineage 4 line **5** blood, stock **7** descent **8** ancestry, heredity, pedigree **9** genealogy, parentage **10** derivation, extraction

linen
  fabric: 6 canvas, damask **7** butcher, cambric **8** birds-eye **9** huckaback
  plant: 4 flax
  finest from: 7 Belgium, Ireland
  processing term: 6 shives, sliver **7** carding, hackled, retting **8** beetling, breaking, rippling, spinning **9** scutching

line of march 4 path **5** route, track **11** parade route

line of reasoning 4 case **7** premise **8** argument **10** hypothesis

line up 4 book **5** align **6** engage, even up **7** arrange, procure, program, queue up **8** schedule **9** form a line, put in a row **10** arrange for

line-up 5 slate **6** roster **8** schedule

linger 3 lag **4** idle, last, stay, wait **5** dally, delay, tarry, trail **6** dawdle, hang on, loiter, remain **7** persist, survive **9** die slowly **10** dillydally, hang around

lingering 4 slow **7** abiding, chronic, delayed, lagging, lasting, staying, waiting **8** dawdling, delaying, dragging, drawn out, dwelling, enduring, hovering, tarrying **9** loitering, remaining **10** protracted, sauntering **15** procrastinating

lingo 4 cant, talk **5** argot, idiom, slang **6** jargon, patois, tongue **7** dialect **8** language, parlance **10** vernacular

linguist 8 polyglot **10** grammarian, translator **11** etymologist, interpreter, philologist, phonetician, phonologist, semanticist **12** morphologist **13** lexicographer

liniment 4 balm **5** salve **7** unguent **8** ointment **9** emollient

link 3 tie **4** bind, bond, fuse, loop, ring

5 group, joint, tie in, unite **6** couple, relate, splice **7** bracket, combine, conjoin, connect, involve, liaison **8** junction, relation **9** associate, implicate **10** connection, connective **11** association **12** interconnect, relationship

linkage 3 tie **4** bond **6** hookup **10** connection **11** affiliation, association, correlation

link up 4 dock, join **6** couple, hook up **7** connect **9** affiliate **14** fasten together

Linnaeus, Carolus
  field: 6 botany
  nationality: 7 Swedish
  developed: 8 taxonomy **18** nomenclature system

linotype
  invented by: 12 Mergenthaler

Linton, Edgar
  character in: 16 Wuthering Heights
  author: 6 Bronte

Linus
  vocation: 4 poet **8** musician
  father: 6 Apollo
  mother: 8 Psamathe
  inventor of: 6 melody, rhythm
  identified with: 5 crops **9** withering **10** harvesting
  student: 8 Hercules
  killed by: 8 Hercules

lion 3 cat **6** cougar **7** wildcat **9** celebrity **12** man of the hour **15** king of the jungle
  group of: 5 pride
  constellation of: 3 Leo

lionhearted 4 bold **5** brave **6** heroic **7** valiant **8** fearless, intrepid, stalwart, unafraid, valorous **9** audacious, dauntless **10** courageous **11** indomitable **12** stouthearted
  see **8** Richard I

Lion in Winter, The
  director: 13 Anthony Harvey
  cast: 10 Jane Merrow **11** Peter O'Toole (Henry II) **13** Timothy Dalton **14** Anthony Hopkins **16** Katharine Hepburn (Eleanor of Aquitaine)
  Oscar for: 7 actress (Hepburn)

lionize 5 exalt **6** admire, praise, revere **7** acclaim, adulate, ennoble, flatter, glorify **8** enshrine, eulogize **9** celebrate, glamorize **10** aggrandize **11** immortalize

lion's share 4 bulk, most **8** majority **9** major part **11** greater part **13** preponderance

lip 3 lap, rim **4** brim, edge, kiss, lick, wash **5** apron, mouth, spout, utter **6** labial, labium, margin **8** backtalk, labellum **9** insincere **10** embouchure, mouthpiece **11** superficial

Lipchitz, Jacques
  real name: 17 Chaim Yakob Lipchiz
  born: 9 Lithuania **11** Druskieniki **12** Druskininkai
  artwork: 4 Head **6** Bather, Figure **7**

Harpist **9** Sacrifice **10** Prometheus **11** Benediction, Joie de Vivre **12** Peace on Earth **14** Man with a Guitar **15** Acrobats on a Ball, Man with Mandolin, Song of the Vowels **17** Notre Dame de Liesse, Sailor with a Guitar **19** Pierrot with Clarinet, Return of the Prodigal **24** Virgin of the Inverted Heart

Lipizzaner 11 stocky horse
  bred in: 7 Austria
  color: 5 white
  used in: 8 dressage **18** jumping exhibitions

Lipmann, Fritz Albert
  field: 12 biochemistry
  discovered: 9 Coenzyme A
  awarded: 10 Nobel Prize

Lippi, Filippino
  born: 5 Italy, Prato
  father: 15 Fra Filippo Lippi
  artwork: 20 The Vision of St Bernard **24** The Life of St Thomas Aquinas **26** The Lives of Sts Philip and John

Lippi, Fra Filippo
  born: 5 Italy **8** Florence
  son: 9 Filippino
  artwork: 15 Madonna and Child, The Feast of Herod **19** The Tarquinia Madonna **21** Coronation of the Virgin **25** The Madonna Adoring Her Child

liqueur 5 booze, drink, hooch **7** alcohol, potable, spirits **8** bever age, potation **9** aqua vitae, drinkable, inebriant, moonshine **10** intoxicant
  almond: 8 amaretto
  anise: 8 absinthe
  apple: 8 calvados
  apricot: 10 abricotine
  caraway: 6 kummel **7** aquavit
  chocolate: 12 creme de cacao
  citrus: 10 goldwasser, liquor d'or
  coffee: 6 Kahlua
  grape: 6 Metaxa
  herb: 6 pernod **7** raspail **10** vielle cure **11** fiori alpini
  honey: 8 Drambuie
  medicinal: 11 Benedictine
  mint: 13 creme de menthe
  orange: 6 strega **7** curacao **9** cointreau **12** Grand Marnier
  raspberry: 9 framboise

liquid 5 drink, fluid **6** melted, molten, thawed **7** potable **8** beverage, solution

liquidate 3 hit, pay **4** kill **5** clear, erase, waste **6** cancel, murder, pay off, rub out, settle, wind up **7** abolish, break up, destroy, wipe out **8** close out, conclude, demolish **9** discharge, dispose of, eradicate, put to rest, terminate **10** account for, do away with **11** assassinate

liquor 3 gin, rum, rye **5** booze, broth, hooch, juice, sauce, vodka **6** brandy, liquid, redeye, rotgut, Scotch **7** bourbon, extract, spirits, whiskey **9** drippings, moonshine **10** inebriants

11 intoxicants
measure: 4 pint, pony, shot **5** fifth, quart **6** jigger, magnum
symbol: 14 John Barleycorn

Lir *see* **3** Ler

Lisbon
capital of: 8 Portugal
landmark:
 castle: 11 Saint George
 monastery: 9 Jeronimos
 square: 10 Black Horse
 tower: 5 Belem
Moorish name: 7 Lixbuna
ocean: 8 Atlantic
Portuguese: 6 Lisboa
river: 5 Tagus
Roman name: 14 Felicitas Julia
rulers: 5 Moors **6** French, Romans **7** British, Germans, Spanish **11** Phoenicians

lissome 5 agile, lithe, quick **6** limber, lively, nimble, pliant, supple **7** slender **8** flexible, graceful **9** lithesome, sprightly **11** light-footed

list 3 tip **4** bend, heel, lean, roll, tilt **5** index, slant, slate, slope, table **6** careen, muster, record, roster **7** catalog, in cline, leaning **8** register, schedule, tabulate **9** catalogue, inventory

listen 4 hark, hear, heed, list **6** attend **7** give ear, hearken **8** give heed, listen in, overhear **9** be all ears, bend an ear, eavesdrop **10** take notice **12** pay attention

listener 3 ear **6** hearer **7** auditor **10** overhearer **12** eavesdropper

Lister, Joseph
field: 7 surgeon **8** medicine
nationality: 7 British
pioneer of: 17 antiseptic surgery

listless 4 down, dull, lazy **6** dreamy, drowsy, leaden, mopish, torpid **7** languid **8** in active, indolent, lifeless, sluggish **9** apathetic, enervated, lethargic, soporific **10** phlegmatic, spiritless **11** indifferent, unconcerned **12** uninterested **13** lackadaisical

Liston, Charles
nickname: 5 Sonny
sport: 6 boxing
class: 11 heavyweight

Liszt, Franz (Ferencz)
born: 7 Hungary, Raiding
teacher: 6 Czerny
daughter: 6 Cosima
son-in-law: 6 Wagner
composer of: 5 Dante (symphony), Faust (symphony) **8** Christus **9** Psalm XIII **10** Nuages gris **13** Psalm Thirteen **17** Years of Pilgrimage **18** Annees de Pelerinage **19** Hungarian Rhapsodies **22** The Legend of St Elizabeth

litany 4 list **7** account, catalog, recital **9** catalogue, narration, rendition **10** recitation, repetition **11** description, enumeration

literacy 7 culture **8** learning **9** erudition **11** edification, eruditeness, learnedness, scholarship **12** intelligence **13** enlightenment

literal 4 real, true **5** exact **6** actual, direct, honest, strict **7** correct, factual, precise, prosaic **8** accurate, faithful, reliable, truthful, verbatim **9** authentic **10** adlitteram, dependable, meticulous, scrupulous, un-disputed **11** trustworthy, undeviating, word-for-word **12** matter-of-fact **13** authoritative, conscientious, unimaginative, unimpeachable

literary 6 poetic **7** bookish, of books **8** artistic, lettered, literate **12** intellectual

literate 7 learned **8** cultured, educated, lettered, literary, schooled, well-read **12** well-informed **13** knowledgeable

literati 9 highbrows **12** connoisseurs **13** intellectuals **14** intelligentsia

literature 4 lore **5** books, works **6** papers, theses **7** letters **8** classics, writings **9** treatises **11** scholarship **12** publications **13** belles lettres, dissertations

lithe 5 agile **6** limber, nimble, pliant, supple **7** lissome, pliable **8** bendable, flexible, graceful

Lithgow, John
roles: 9 Footloose **17** Terms of Endearment **19** Third Rock From the Sun **21** Harry and the Hendersons **23** The World According to Garp **29** The Adventures of Buckaroo Banzai

lithium
chemical symbol: 2 Li

Lithuania
other/former name: 5 Litva **7** Lietuva **33** Lithuanian Soviet Socialist Republic
capital/largest city: 5 Vilna **6** Kaunas **7** Vilnius
others: 4 Balt, Lett **5** Aesti, Kouno, Memel **6** Kovnac **7** Jel gava, Palanga, Telsiai **8** Ignalina, Kapsukas, Klaipeda, Siauliai **9** Panevezys **10** Elektrenai
government: 8 republic
monetary unit: 3 lit **5** marka **6** centas **7** ostmark, skatiku **8** auksinas
lake: 5 Dysna
mountain: 15 Samogitian Hills
highest point: 9 Juozapine
river: 5 Neman, Neris, Rusne **6** Dubysa, Nieman, Viliya **7** Nemunas, Nevezis, Nevezys **8** Pregolya
sea: 6 Baltic
physical feature:
 lagoon: 8 Courland, Kuronian
people: 4 Balt, Lett **5** Zhmud **6** Jewish, Litvak, Polish **7** Aistian, Russian, Yatvyag **10** Lithuanian, Samogitian **11** Belorussian
language: 5 Zmudz **6** Baltic **10** Lithuanian

religion: 8 Lutheran **13** Roman Catholic

litigation 4 suit **7** contest, dispute, lawsuit **10** contention, day in court **11** controversy, disputation, legal action, prosecution

litter 3 bed **4** heap, junk, lair, mess, nest, pile **5** issue, strew, trash, young **6** de- bris, jumble, pallet, refuse **7** bedding, clutter, kittens, progeny, puppies, rubbish, scatter **8** leavings **9** offspring, stretcher

little 3 bit, dot, jot, wee **4** dash, drop, hint, iota, mean, mild, tiny, whit **5** brief, crumb, elfin, faint, fleet, hasty, never, petty, pinch, pygmy, quick, scant, short, small, speck, trace **6** bantam, hardly, meager, minute, narrow, paltry, petite, rarely, seldom, skimpy, slight, trifle **7** minimum, modicum, not much, passing, stunted, trivial **8** dwarfish, fragment, inferior, mediocre, not at all, not often, particle, piddling, pittance, scarcely, slightly, some what, trifling, unworthy **9** by no means, deficient, hardly any, itsy- bitsy, itty-bitty, miniature, momentary, pint-sized, third- rate, worthless **10** diminutive, inflexible, negligible, short-lived, suggestion, undersized **11** commonplace, Lilliputian, microscopic, of no account, opinionated, pocket-sized, scarcely any, small amount, unimportant **12** insufficient, run-of-the-mill, short-sighted **13** infinitesimal, insignificant, next to nothing

Little America
on: 10 Antarctica **12** Ross Ice Shelf
bases established by: 11 Admiral Byrd

Little Annie Rooney
creator: 14 Darrell McClure

Little Artha
nickname of: 11 Jack Johnson

Little Bighorn 5 river **7** Wyoming
battle site of: 5 Sioux **6** Custer, Dakota **8** Cheyenne
called: 16 Custer's last stand
see also **13** Custer, George A.

Little Big Man
author: 12 Thomas Berger
director: 10 Arthur Penn
cast: 11 Faye Dunaway **12** Martin Balsam **13** Dustin Hoffman (Jack Crabb) **14** Chief Dan George **15** Richard Mulligan

little by little
French: 7 peu a peu
Spanish: 9 poco a poco

Little Caesar
director: 11 Mervyn LeRoy
cast: 13 Glenda Farrell **15** Edward G Robinson (Rico) (Caesar Enrico Bandello) **18** Douglas Fairbanks Jr

Little Corporal 8 Napoleon

Little Dipper 11 star cluster
  in: **9** Ursa Minor **10** Little Bear
Little Dorrit
  author: **14** Charles Dickens
  character: **3** Amy (Little Dorrit), Tip
  4 Rugg **5** Casby, Fanny, Flora,
  Gowan **6** Affery, Merdle, Pancks, Rigaud (Blandois) **7** Meagles **8** Mr F's
  Aunt **9** Mrs Merdle **10** Flintwinch **13**
  Arthur Clennam, William Dorrit **16**
  Monsieur Blandois, Young John
  Chivery
Little Drummer Girl, The
  author: **11** John Le Carre
Little Emily, Little Em'ly
  character in: **16** David Copperfield
  author: **7** Dickens
Little Fox
  constellation of: **9** Vulpecula
Little Foxes, The
  author: **14** Lillian Hellman
  character: **13** Regina Giddens
  director: **12** William Wyler
  cast: **10** Bette Davis (Regina) **12** Teresa Wright **14** Richard Carlson **15**
  Herbert Marshall
  prequel: **22** Another Part of the Forest
Little Gidding
  author: **7** T S Eliot
Little House on the Prairie
  author: **18** Laura Ingalls Wilder
  character: **6** Albert **7** Dr Baker **8** Rev
  Alden **9** Mr Edwards **10** Andy Garvey, Lars Hanson, Nels Oleson **11**
  Adam Kendall, Alice Garvey, Mary
  Ingalls **12** Grace Ingalls, Laura In-
  galls, Nellie Oleson, Willie Oleson **13**
  Carrie Ingalls, Harriet Oleson **14**
  Charles Ingalls, Eva Beadle Simms,
  Jonathan Garvey **15** Caroline Ingalls
  cast: **10** Dabbs Greer, Kevin Hagen
  11 Karl Swenson, Merlin Olsen,
  Richard Bull **12** Hersha Parady, Ka-
  ren Grassle, Victor French **13** Alison
  Arngrim, Linwood Boomer, Michael
  Landon **14** Melissa Gilbert **15**
  Jonathon Gilbert, Sidney Greenbush,
  Wendy Turnbeaugh **16** Brenda Turn-
  beaugh, Charlotte Gilbert, Lindsay
  Greenbush **17** Katherine McGregor,
  Matthew Laborteaux, Patrick Laborteaux **18** Melissa Sue Anderson
  setting: **6** Winoka **9** Minnesota, Plum
  Creek **11** Walnut Grove
Little John
  character in: **9** Robin Hood
Little King, The
  creator: **10** Otto Soglow
  technique: **9** pantomine
little-known 6 unsung **7** obscure, unnoted **10** unrenowned
Little Learning, A
  author: **11** Evelyn Waugh
Little Lord Fauntleroy
  author: **15** Frances H Burnett

Little Lulu
  creator: **14** Marge Henderson
Little Match Girl, The
  author: **21** Hans Christian Andersen
Little Men
  author: **15** Louisa May Alcott
Little Mermaid, The
  author: **21** Hans Christian Andersen
Little Minister, The
  author: **12** James M Barrie
Little Mo
  nickname of: **15** Maureen Connolly
Little Nemo in Slumberland
  creator: **11** Winsor McCay
  character: **6** Dr Pill **8** cannibal, princess
    clown: **4** Flip
    dog: **6** Blutch
little one 3 tot **4** babe, baby, tyke **5**
  child **6** infant, wee one **7** toddler
Little Orphan Annie
  creator: **10** Harold Gray
  character:
    foster father: **13** Daddy Warbucks
    dog: **5** Sandy
    saying: **13** Leapin' Lizards
little people 5 elves **6** dwarfs **7** fairies, midgets **11** leprechauns
Little Prince, The
  author: **21** Antoine de Saint-Exupery
Little Rhody
  nickname of: **11** Rhode Island
Little Rock see **8** Arkansas
Little Tramp
  nickname of: **14** Charlie Chaplin
Little Women
  author: **15** Louisa May Alcott
  character: **6** Laurie (Theodore Laurence), Marmee **10** John Brooke **14**
  Professor Bhaer
    March sisters: **2** Jo **3** Amy, Meg **4**
    Beth
  director:
    1933 version: **11** George Cukor
    1949 version: **11** Mervyn LeRoy
  cast (1933): **9** Paul Lukas **10** Frances
  Dee, Jean Parker **11** Joan Bennett **16**
  Katharine Hepburn (Jo)
  cast (1949): **9** Mary Astor **10** Janet
  Leigh **11** June Allyson **12** Peter Lawford **14** Margaret O'Brien **15** Elizabeth Taylor
liturgical 6 ritual **10** ceremonial **11**
  ceremonious, sacramental
liturgy 4 mass, rite **6** ritual **7** service,
  worship **8** ceremony, services **9** communion, sacrament
lituus
  form: **5** staff
  shape: **7** crooked
Lityerses
  father: **9** King Midas
  held: **15** reaping contests
  killed: **6** losers
livable, liveable 4 cozy, snug **5**
  comfy, homey **8** bearable, passable,

pleasant, suitable **9** agreeable, endurable, enjoyable, habitable, tolerable **10**
acceptable, convenient, gratifying, satisfying, worthwhile **11** comfortable
live 2 be **3** hot **4** bunk, feed, stay **5**
abide, afire, aglow, alive, dwell, exist,
fiery, lodge, quick, stand, vital **6**
ablaze, active, aflame, alight, at hand,
billet, bodily, endure, hold on, living,
obtain, occupy, red-hot, remain, reside, settle, thrive **7** animate, at issue,
be alive, blazing, breathe, burning,
current, flaming, fleshly, going on, ignited, persist, prevail, subsist, survive
8 existent, flourish, get ahead, get
along, have life, increase, multiply,
physical, pressing, take root, up- to-
date, white-hot **9** breathing, corporeal
10 draw breath
live and keep well
  Latin: **11** vive valeque
Live and Let Die
  author: **10** Ian Fleming
live dissolutely 7 carouse, debauch **9**
  dissipate **11** overindulge
livelihood 3 job **5** trade **6** career, living, metier **7** calling, support, venture
8 business, position, vocation **9** situation **10** enterprise, line of work, occupation, profession, sustenance **11**
maintenance, subsistence, undertaking
liveliness 3 pep, zip **4** brio, elan **5**
vigor **7** agility **8** alacrity, vitality, vivacity **9** animation, briskness, eagerness **10** ebullience, nimbleness **13**
sprightliness
lively 5 alert, brisk, eager, peppy,
perky, vivid **6** active, ardent, bouncy
7 buoyant, excited, fervent, intense **8**
animated, spirited, vigorous **9** energetic, excitable, sprightly, vivacious
12 enthusiastic
liven 4 buoy **5** cheer, elate, pep up **6**
perk up, vivify **7** animate, delight, enliven, fortify, gladden, hearten, punch
up, quicken **8** brighten, embolden, energize, inspirit **10** exhilarate, invigorate, strengthen
liver
  stores: **8** glycogen
  color: **3** red **5** brown
  produces: **4** bile **10** blood cells
Livermore Larruper
  nickname of: **7** Max Baer
livery 4 garb, suit **5** dress **6** attire **7**
costume, raiment, regalia, uniform **8**
clothing **9** vestments
Lives of a Bengal Lancer
  director: **13** Henry Hathaway
  cast: **10** Gary Cooper **12** Franchot
  Tone **14** Sir Guy Standing **15** Richard Cromwell
Lives of the Poets, The
  author: **13** Samuel Johnson
live through 4 know **7** survive, undergo **9** go through **10** experience

livid 3 mad 4 pale 5 angry, irate, riled, vexed 6 fuming, galled, purple, raging 7 bruised, enraged, furious 8 contused, incensed, inflamed, outraged, provoked, wrathful 9 indignant, steamed up, ticked off 10 discolored, infuriated 11 exasperated 12 black-and-blue

living 3 job 4 life, live, work 5 alive, being, quick, trade 6 active, bodily, career, extant, income 7 animate, calling, fleshly, going on, organic, venture 8 business, embodied, enduring, existent, existing, material, up-to-date, vocation 9 animation, breathing, corporeal, existence, incarnate, life-style, operative, permanent, remaining, surviving, way of life 10 employment, enterprise, having life, in the flesh, line of work, livelihood, occupation, persisting, prevailing, profession, subsisting, sustenance 11 maintenance, subsistence 13 drawing breath

living being 8 creature, organism

living conditions 10 atmosphere 11 environment 13 circumstances

living picture
French: 13 tableau vivant

living quarters 4 home 5 abode, house 6 billet 7 housing, lodging, shelter 8 domicile, dwelling, quarters 9 apartment, residence 10 habitation 13 dwelling place

Livy
also: 11 Titus Livius
author of: 13 Ab urbe condita 26 From the Foundation of the City

lizard 3 dab, eft, uma 4 adda, gila, newt, seps, tegu, uran 5 agama, anole, anoli, gecko, idler, shrink 6 aguana, dragon, iguana, komodo, moloch 7 lounger, monitor, reptile, saurian 8 dinosaur, lacerata, scorpion 9 alligator, blind worm, chameleon, crocodile, galliwasp 10 chuckwalla, glass snake, horned toad, salamander 11 gila monster 12 Komodo dragon
characteristic: 6 scales 7 molting 9 oviparous 11 cold-blooded 12 regeneration
constellation of: 7 Lacerta

llama 6 alpaca, kechua, mammal, vicuna 7 guanaco 8 ungulate 13 Peruvian sheep

llano 11 grassy plain
in: 12 South America

Llewellyn, Richard
author of: 19 How Green Was My Valley

Llew Llaw Gyffes
origin: 5 Welsh
father: 7 Gwydion
mother: 9 Arianrhod
wife: 10 Blodenwedd
curses bestowed by: 9 Arianrhod

Lloyd
origin: 5 Welsh

form: 8 magician
cast spells upon: 7 Pryderi

Lloyd, Harold
born: 10 Burchard NE
roles: 9 Feet First 10 Safety Last 11 The Freshman 13 The Kid Brother

Lloyd Webber, Andrew
born: 6 London
Composer of: 4 Cats 5 Evita 6 Jeeves 12 Song and Dance 13 Aspects of Love 15 Tell Me on a Sunday 16 Starlight Express 20 Jesus Christ Superstar, The Phantom of the Opera 39 Joseph and the Amazing Technicolor Dreamcoat

Llud
also: 4 Ludd, Nudd
origin: 5 Welsh
king of: 7 Britain
rid kingdom of: 6 plague
famous for: 10 generosity

Llyr
origin: 5 Welsh
son: 10 Manawyddan
corresponds to: 3 Ler, Lir

load 3 try, vex 4 care, fill, haul, heap, lade, pack, pile 5 cargo, crush, stack, stuff, worry 6 burden, hamper, hinder, lad- ing, misery, strain, weight 7 afflict, carload, freight, oppress, trouble 8 capacity, contents, encumber, handicap, pressure, shipload, shipment 9 overwhelm, plane load, truckload, wagonload, weigh down 10 affliction, deadweight, depression, misfortune, oppression 11 encumbrance

loads 4 lots, much 5 heaps, piles, scads 6 oodles, plenty 14 more than enough

loaf 4 idle, loll 5 dally 6 be lazy 7 goof off 8 kill time, malinger 9 do nothing, gold brick, laze about, waste time 10 take it easy 12 lounge around

loafer 3 bum 4 shoe 5 idler 6 no-good 7 laggard, shirker, sponger, wastrel 8 deadbeat, loiterer, sluggard 9 goldbrick, lazybones 10 lazy person, malingerer, ne'er-do- well 11 couch potato 12 lounge lizard 15 drugstore cowboy
French: 7 flaneur

loan 4 lend 5 allow 6 credit 7 advance, lending 8 mortgage 9 advancing

loath 4 loth 6 averse 7 against, counter, hostile, opposed 8 inimical 9 reluctant, resisting, unwilling 10 indisposed, set against 11 disinclined

loathe 4 hate 5 abhor, scorn 6 detest, eschew 7 deplore, despise, disdain, dislike 9 abominate 10 blench from, flinch from, recoil from, shrink from 11 keep clear of, shy away from 12 draw back from 14 be unable to bear, find disgusting, view with horror 16 have no stomach for

loathing 4 hate 5 odium 6 hatred 7

disgust, dislike 8 aversion, distaste 9 antipathy, repulsion, revulsion 10 abhorrence, repugnance 11 abomination, detestation

loathsome 4 foul, mean, rank, vile 5 nasty 6 odious 7 hateful 9 abhorrent, invidious, obnoxious, offensive, repugnant, re- pulsive, revolting, sickening 10 abominable, despicable, detestable, disgusting, nauseating, unbearable 11 distasteful

lobby 5 foyer 8 anteroom, politick 9 vestibule 11 antechamber, pull strings, waiting room 12 entrance hall

lobscouse 4 meat 8 hardtack 10 vegetables 11 sailor's stew

local 6 narrow, native, nearby 7 insular, limited 8 citywide, confined, regional 9 adjoining, homegrown, parochial, sectional 10 provincial 11 territorial 12 neighborhood 13 circumscribed

locale 4 area, site, spot, zone 6 region 7 quarter, section, setting 8 locality, location, precinct, province, vicinity 12 neighborhood

locality 4 area, site, spot, zone 5 place 6 locale, region 7 quarter, section 8 district, location, precinct, province, vicinity 9 territory 12 neighborhood

locate 3 fix, put 4 find, live, post, seat, stay 5 dwell, place 6 detect, move to, reside, settle 7 deposit, discern, hit upon, set down, situate, station, uncover, unearth 8 come upon, meet with, pinpoint 9 establish, ferret out, light upon, search out, stumble on, track down 10 settle down 12 put down roots

location 4 site, spot 5 place 6 locale 8 district, position 9 situation 11 whereabouts 12 neighborhood

Lochinvar
character in: 7 Marmion
bride: 5 Ellen
author: 5 Scott

Loch Ness
in: 8 Scotland
home of: 6 Nessie 7 monster

lock 3 bar, dam, pen 4 bang, bolt, cage, coil, curl, grab, grip, hank, hold, hook, jail, join, link, tuft 5 catch, clamp, clasp, grasp, latch, seize, skein, tress, unite 6 clinch, coop up, fasten, lock up, secure, shut in 7 confine, embrace, entwine, grapple, impound, padlock, ringlet 8 dock gate, imprison 9 canal gate, fastening, floodgate, interlink 10 intertwine, sluice gate 11 incarcerate

lock, cylinder
invented by: 4 Yale

Lockhart, Gene
daughter: 12 June Lockhart
granddaughter: 11 Ann Lockhart
born: 6 Canada, London 7 Ontario
roles: 12 Madame Bovary 16 Death

of a Salesman **19** The Inspector General **20** Abe Lincoln in Illinois

lock horns 4 feud, tiff **5** argue, brawl, clash, fight **7** dispute, quarrel, wrangle **8** squabble **9** altercate

Lockit 4 Lucy
  character in: 12 Beggar's Opera
  author: 3 Gay

lockup 3 jug, pen **4** jail, stir **5** clink, pokey **6** cooler, prison **7** slammer **8** big house, hoosegow **11** reformatory **12** penitentiary

lock up 3 pen **4** cage, jail **6** coop up, secure **7** confine, impound **8** imprison, restrain, restrict **11** incarcerate

Lockyer, Joseph Norman
  field: 9 astronomy
  nationality: 7 British
  discovered: 6 helium

loco citato 15 in the place cited
  abbreviation: 6 loc cit

locomotive
  invented by:
    electric: 4 Vail
    experimental: 6 Fenton, Hedley **10** Stephenson, Trevithick
    first US: 6 Cooper
    practical: 10 Stephenson

locust 7 Robinia
  varieties: 4 moss **5** black, honey, mossy, swamp, sweet, water **6** clammy, yellow **7** African, bristly **8** ship-mast **10** West Indian **13** Allegheny moss, South American

locution 4 term **5** idiom, trope, usage **6** phrase, saying **7** wording **8** idiolect, phrasing **9** set phrase, utterance, verbalism **10** expression **11** phraseology, regionalism **12** turn of phrase **14** figure of speech

lode 3 bed **4** seam **7** deposit

lodge 3 bed, hut **4** camp, file, room, stay **5** cabin, catch, hotel, house, motel, put up **6** billet, harbor, resort, submit **7** cottage, quarter, shelter, sojourn **8** register

lodging 4 room **8** quarters **13** accommodation

Loewe, Frederick
  born: 6 Vienna
  Composer of: 4 Gigi **7** Camelot **8** Galateya **9** Brigadoon **10** My Fair Lady **14** Paint Your Wagon **15** The Little Prince

loft 3 lob **5** attic, pop up **6** belfry, garret **7** balcony, gallery, hit high, mansard **8** top floor **9** attic room, throw high **10** clerestory

loftiness 5 pride **9** arrogance **11** haughtiness **13** imperiousness **16** superciliousness

Lofting, Hugh
  author of: 10 Dr Dolittle

lofty 4 cold, high, tall **5** aloof, grand, great, noble, proud **6** lordly, mighty, remote, snooty **7** distant, eminent, ex-

alted, haughty, leading, soaring, stately, stuck-up, sublime **8** arrogant, eleva- ted, glorious, imposing, insolent, majestic, puffed-up, scornful, snobbish, superior, towering **9** conceited, dignified, imperi- ous, important **10** disdainful, hoity-toity, preeminent **11** high ranking, illustrious, patronizing **12** high-reaching **13** condescending, distinguished, high-and-mighty, self-important

lofty bearing 7 dignity, majesty **10** augustness **11** stateliness

log 5 block, diary, stump **6** docket, lumber, record, timber **7** account, daybook, journal, logbook **8** calendar, schedule

Logan, Mount
  in: 5 Yukon **12** St. Elias range
  highest mt. in: 6 Canada

loges 5 boxes **7** balcony **9** mezzanine

loggia 5 lanai, porch **6** arcade, piazza **7** balcony, gallery

logic 5 sense **6** reason **7** cogency **8** analysis, argument **9** coherence, deduction, good sense, induction **10** dialectics

logical 5 clear, sound, valid **6** cogent, likely **7** germane **8** coherent, rational, relevant, sensible **9** deducible, pertinent, plausible **10** analytical, consistent, most likely, reasonable **11** enlightened, intelligent **13** well-organized

logos 4 word **5** ratio **6** saying, speech **7** thought **9** discourse, reckoning **10** proportion

logy 4 dull **5** inert, tired, weary **6** drowsy, groggy, sleepy, torpid **8** comatose, life- less, listless, sluggish **9** enervated, inanimate, lethargic **10** phlegmatic **12** hebetudinous

Lohengrin
  opera by: 6 Wagner
  character: 4 Elsa **6** Ortrud **9** Gottfried (Duke of Brabant) **25** Count Frederick of Telramund

Lohengrin
  origin: 8 Germanic
  knight of: 9 Holy Grail
  father: 8 Parsifal, Parzival

loiter 4 idle, laze, loaf, loll, lurk **5** dally, skulk, slink, tarry **6** dawdle **10** dillydally, hang around **11** hover around **12** shilly-shally

Loki
  origin: 12 Scandinavian
  mentioned in: 9 Lokasenna
  god of: 4 fire
  son: 6 Fenrir, Fenris
  daughter: 3 Hel
  fathered: 10 Jormungand **11** lormungandr, Jormungandr **14** Midgard Serpent
  mother of his children: 9 Angerboda, Angrbodha, Angurboda
  caused death of: 5 Baldr **6** Balder,

Baldur
  form: 5 giant
  extorted treasure from: 7 Andvari
  function: 4 evil **6** strife **7** discord **8** mischief

Lolita
  author: 15 Vladimir Nabokov
  character: 6 Lolita **14** Humbert Humbert
  director: 14 Stanley Kubrick
  based on novel by: 15 Vladimir Nabokov
  cast: 7 Sue Lyon (Lolita) **10** James Mason (Humbert Humbert) **12** Peter Sellers **14** Shelley Winters

loll 3 sag **4** drag, drop, flap, flop, idle, lean, loaf **5** droop, relax, slump **6** dangle, dawdle, lounge, repose, slouch, sprawl **7** goof off, recline **8** flop over, languish

Lollobrigida, Gina
  born: 5 Italy **7** Subiaco
  roles: 7 Trapeze **14** Anne of Brooklyn, The Wayward Wife **15** Solomon and Sheba **20** Buona Sera Mrs Campbell **27** The World's Most Beautiful Woman

Loman, Willy
  character in: 16 Death of a Salesman
  author: 6 Miller
  epitome of: 8 salesman

Lombard, Carole
  real name: 15 Jane Alice Peters
  husband: 10 Clark Gable
  born: 11 Fort Wayne IN
  roles: 12 My Man Godfrey **13** Nothing Sacred, To Be Or Not To Be **16** Twentieth Century

Lome
  capital of: 4 Togo

London
  airport: 7 Gatwick **8** Heathrow, Stansted
  architect: 4 Wren
  area: 4 Soho **6** Camden **7** Brixton, Chelsea, Holborn, Pimlico **8** Vauxhall **9** Bayswater, Belgravia, Islington, Southwark **10** Bloomsbury, Kensington, Paddington, Shoreditch **11** Notting Hill, St John's Wood **13** Knightsbridge
  capital of: 7 England **12** Great Britain **13** United Kingdom
  landmark: 6 Big Ben **8** Hyde Park **9** Whitehall, Wimbledon **11** Regent's Park, Saint James's, Tate Gallery, Tower Bridge **12** Covent Garden, London Bridge **13** British Museum, Tower of London **14** British Library, Speaker's Corner **15** National Gallery, Trafalgar Square **16** Buckingham Palace, Piccadilly Circus, Westminster Abbey **17** Kensington Gardens, Royal Festival Hall, Westminster Palace **18** Houses of Parliament **19** Saint Paul's Cathedral **23** Victoria and Albert Museum

police: 7 bobbies
  established by: 13 Sir Robert Peel
prime minister's residence: 16 Ten
  Downing Street
river: 6 Thames
Roman name: 9 Londinium
subway: 11 Underground

London, Jack
  author of: 9 White Fang **10** The Sea
  Wolf **16** The Call of the Wild

lone 4 only, sole **5** alone **6** single,
  unique **8** isolated, singular, solitary,
  unpaired **9** unabetted **10** individual,
  unattended, unescorted **13** companionless, unaccompanied

loneliness 9 isolation, seclusion **12**
  lonesomeness, solitariness **14** friend-
  lessness

**Loneliness of the Long Distance
Runner, The**
  author: 12 Alan Sillitoe
  director: 14 Tony Richardson
  cast: 11 Avis Bunnage, Peter Madden
  12 Tom Courtenay **15** Michael Redgrave

lonely 6 remote **7** forlorn **8** deserted,
  desolate, forsaken, hermitic, isolated,
  lonesome, secluded, solitary, unsocial
  9 by oneself, reclusive, withdrawn **10**
  friendless, unattended **11** uninhabited,
  unpopulated **12** unfrequented **13**
  companionless, unaccompanied

Lone Ranger, The
  character: 5 Tonto
  cast: 8 John Hart **12** Clayton Moore
  14 Jay Silverheels
  horse: 5 Scout **6** Silver
  saying: 8 kemo sabe
  Lone Ranger used: 13 silver bullets
  theme: 19 William Tell Overture

lonesome 5 alone, aloof **6** lonely **7**
  forlorn, insular **8** desolate, detached,
  forsaken **9** alienated, withdrawn **10**
  friendless, unfriended **13** companionless

Lone Star State
  nickname of: 5 Texas

long 4 hope, lust, pine, sigh, want,
  wish **5** covet, crave, yearn **6** aspire,
  hanker, hunger, thirst **7** lengthy, spun
  out **8** drawn-out, extended, have a
  yen, in length, unending **9** elongated,
  extensive, prolonged **10** be bent on,
  protracted **11** far-reaching, have a desire **12** from end to end, interminable,
  outstretched

Long, Crawford Williamson
  field: 8 medicine
  first used: 5 ether

Longaville
  character in: 16 Love's Labour's Lost
  author: 11 Shakespeare

Long Day's Journey into Night
  author: 12 Eugene O'Neill
  director: 11 Sidney Lumet
  cast: 13 Dean Stockwell **14** Jason Ro-

bards Jr **15** Ralph Richardson **16**
Katharine Hepburn

Longest Day, The
  director: 10 Ken Annakin **12** Andrew
  Marton, Bernard Wicki
  cast: 9 John Wayne, Mel Ferrer **10**
  Henry Fonda, Red Buttons, Robert
  Ryan, Rod Steiger **12** Peter Lawford
  setting: 4 D-Day **8** Normandy (Allied
  invasion)

long-faced 4 glum **6** dismal, gloomy **7**
  doleful, unhappy **8** dejected, mournful
  10 lugubrious **14** down in the mouth

Longfellow, Henry Wadsworth
  author of: 8 Hyperion, (The Song of)
  Hiawatha **10** Evangeline **15** Paul Revere's Ride **18** Tales of a Wayside
  Inn **21** The Wreck of the Hesperus
  27 The Courtship of Miles Standish

longing 3 yen **4** wish **6** ardent, pining,
  thirst **7** craving, wishful **8** desirous,
  yearning **9** hankering, hungering **10**
  aspiration **11** languishing

long-lasting 7 chronic, lengthy, tedious **8** enduring, extended **9** prolonged
  10 continuing, protracted

long live
  French: 4 vive

long past 3 old **5** olden **6** gone by, of
  yore **7** ancient, long ago **8** long gone

long-standing 4 long **5** hardy, hoary
  6 rooted **7** abiding, ancient, chronic,
  durable, lasting **8** enduring, habitual,
  hallowed, unfading **9** confirmed, continual, long-lived, perennial, perpetual, venerable **10** continuous, deep-
  rooted, deep-seated, inveterate, persistent, persisting **11** long-lasting,
  time-honored **15** long-established

Longstreet, James
  served in: 8 Civil War
  side: 11 Confederate
  battle: 7 Bull Run **10** Gettysburg **11**
  Chickamauga **14** Fredericksburg **18**
  Wilderness Campaign
  after war joined: 11 Republicans
  US minister to: 6 Turkey

Long Voyage Home, The
  director: 8 John Ford
  based on play by: 12 Eugene O'Neill
  cast: 9 Ian Hunter, John Wayne **13**
  Wilfrid Lawson **14** Thomas Mitchell
  15 Barry Fitzgerald

long-wearing 5 tough **6** strong,
  sturdy **7** durable, lasting **8** enduring
  11 substantial

long-winded 5 wordy **6** prolix **7**
  lengthy, tedious, verbose **8** rambling
  9 garrulous **10** digressive, discursive

long-windedness 8 rambling **9** garrulity, prolixity, verbosity, wordiness **14**
  discursiveness

look 3 air, see **4** cast, face, gape, gaze,
  mien, ogle, peek, peep, scan, seem,
  show, view **5** front, glare, guise,
  sight, stare, study, watch **6** appear,
  behold, glance, regard, survey **7** bear-

ing, examine, exhibit, glimpse **8** demeanor, manifest, once-over, presence, scrutiny **10** appearance, be
directed, cut a figure, expression,
scrutinize **11** contemplate, counte
nance, observation

look after 4 help **6** assist, defend **7**
  help out, protect **10** minister to **11**
  watch out for **17** take under one's
  wing

look askance at 7 condemn **8** object
  to **9** frown upon **10** disapprove **14**
  discountenance **15** take exception to
  16 find unacceptable, view with disfavor

look at 3 see **4** view **6** behold, notice,
  regard **7** examine, inspect, witness **10**
  scrutinize

Look Back in Anger
  director: 14 Tony Richardson
  based on play by: 11 John Osborne
  cast: 7 Mary Ure **10** Edith Evans **11**
  Claire Bloom **13** Richard Burton **15**
  Donald Pleasance

look down on 7 despise, disdain **9**
  frown upon, patronize **10** condescend
  13 put on airs with **14** hold in contempt

looker-on 6 viewer **7** watcher, witness
  8 beholder, observer, onlooker **9** bystander, spectator

look for 4 seek **5** await **6** expect, pursue **7** hunt for **9** search for **10** anticipate

look for the woman
  French: 15 cherchez la femme

look forward to 5 await **6** expect **7**
  long for, wait for **9** pin hope on **10**
  anticipate **17** count the days until

Look Homeward, Angel
  author: 11 Thomas Wolfe
  character: 7 Ben Gant **9** Eliza Gant
  10 Eugene Gant, Laura James, Oliver
  Gant **15** Margaret Leonard

look in the eye 4 defy, face **5** brave
  8 confront **9** challenge

look into 5 probe **7** examine, explore
  10 scrutinize **11** inquire into, investigate

lookout 4 heed **5** guard, scout, vigil **6**
  patrol, sentry **7** spotter **8** observer,
  sentinel, watchdog, watchman **9** alertness, attention, awareness, readiness,
  vigilance **10** precaution **11** guardedness, mindfulness, watchkeeper **12**
  surveillance, watchfulness

look out 4 mind **6** beware **8** take care,
  watch out **9** be careful, be on guard
  11 take warning **12** be on the alert

look over 4 scan, skim **5** judge **6** assess, peruse, survey **7** dip into **8** appraise, evaluate **13** browse through,
  glance through

look through 4 scan, skim **6** browse,
  peruse **7** dip into **8** look over **9** check
  over **13** glance through

look toward 7 count on **10** anticipate **13** look forward to

look upon 3 see **4** view **6** be hold, gaze at, look at **7** observe, stare at

look upon as 4 deem, hold **5** count, judge, think **6** regard, view as **7** account, believe **8** consider, take to be

look up to 5 honor **6** admire, esteem, revere **7** respect **8** venerate

loom 4 hulk, rise, soar **5** tower **6** appear, ascend, emerge **8** stand out **9** take shape

loom, power
invented by: **10** Cartwright

loop 3 eye **4** bend, coil, curl, furl, ring, roll, turn **5** braid, curve, noose, plait, twirl, twist, whorl **6** circle, eyelet, spiral **7** opening, ringlet **8** aperture, encircle, loophole **10** wind around **11** convolution, curve around

Loos, Anita
author of: **22** Gentlemen Prefer Blondes

loose 4 fast, free, lewd, undo, wild **5** freed, let go, slack, untie, vague **6** freely, loosen, unbind, undone, untied, wanton **7** immoral, inexact, loosely, release, set free, slacken, unbound, uncaged, unchain, unleash, unloose, unyoked **8** careless, heedless, liberate, not tight, rakehell, unbridle, unchaste, unfasten, unjoined, untether **9** abandoned, debauched, dissolute, imprecise, liberated, libertine, unbridled, unchained, unleashed, unmanacle, un shackle **10** dissipated, inaccurate, licentious, not binding, profligate, unattached, unexacting, unfastened, unfettered, unhandcuff, untethered **11** not fastened, unconnected **12** unimprisoned **13** unconstrained

loose-fitting 4 limp **5** baggy, loose, slack **6** draped, droopy **7** sagging **9** overlarge, oversized

loosely connected 5 jerky **6** fitful **8** episodic, rambling **9** spasmodic, wandering **10** digressive, discursive, meandering

loosen 3 lax **4** ease, free, undo **5** break, relax, untie **6** limber, unbend, unbind **7** release, relieve, slacken, unchain, unscrew **8** liberate, unbuckle, unfasten, work free **10** emancipate

looseness 8 fastness, lewdness, wildness **9** slackness, vagueness **10** debauch- ery, immorality, inaccuracy, profligacy, wantonness **11** dissipation, dissolution, imprecision **12** carelessness, heedlessness, inexactitude **14** licentiousness

loot 3 rob **4** haul, raid, sack, swag, take **5** booty, prize, strip **6** boodle, fleece, pilfer, ravage, spoils **7** pillage, plunder, ransack **11** stolen goods

looter 5 thief **6** robber, vandal **7** brigand **8** pillager **9** despoiler, plunderer

lop 3 cut **4** chip, chop, crop, dock, flop, sned, snip, trim **5** droop, prune, sever **6** cut off, deduct, detach, remove, slouch **7** cut back **8** amputate, truncate

Lopez, Nancy
sport: **4** golf
husband: **9** Ray Knight
plays: **8** baseball

lopsided 4 awry **5** askew **6** aslant, tipped, uneven **7** crooked, leaning, listing, slanted, tilting, unequal **8** cockeyed, inclined, slanting **9** irregular **10** asymmetric, off- balance, unbalanced **15** disproportional **16** disproportionate

loquacious 5 gabby, talky, windy, wordy **6** blabby, chatty, prolix **7** prating, verbose, voluble **8** babbling, chattery **9** garrulous, prattling, talkative **10** chattering, long-winded

loquitur 8 he speaks **9** she speaks

lord 4 king **5** chief, crown, ruler **6** leader, master **7** monarch **8** overlord, seign- ior, superior **9** commander, landowner, sovereign **10** landholder, proprietor
Japanese: **6** daimyo
Turkish: **3** beg, bey

Lord
Latin: **7** Dominus

Lord be with you, the
Latin: **15** Dominus vobiscum

Lord have mercy
Greek: **12** Kyrie eleison

Lord Jim
author: **12** Joseph Conrad
character: **5** Stein **6** Marlow **9** Dain Waris **14** Gentleman Brown

lordliness 7 disdain **8** contempt **9** arrogance, insolence, loftiness **11** haughtiness **13** imperiousness **16** superciliousness

lordly 4 cold **5** aloof, bossy, grand, lofty, noble, proud, regal **6** august, remote, snooty **7** distant, elegant, eminent, exalted, haughty, stately, stuck-up **8** arrogant, despotic, imposing, majestic, princely, puffed-up, scornful, snobbish **9** conceited, dignified, imperious, sumptuous **10** disdainful, hoity-toity, tyrannical **11** dictatorial, domineering, magisterial, magnificent, patronizing **13** condescending, high-and-mighty, self- important

Lord of the Flies
author: **14** William Golding

Lord of the Rings, The
author: **10** J R R Tolkien
creatures: **3** elf, ent, orc **5** dwarf **6** hobbit

Lord Weary's Castle
author: **12** Robert Lowell

lore 7 beliefs, legends **10** traditions

Lorelei

also: **7** Lurelei
origin: **8** Germanic
form: **5** nymph
dwelling place: **5** cliff, Rhine
lured: **7** boatmen
caused shipwrecks by: **7** singing

Lorelei Lee
role in: **22** Gentlemen Prefer Blondes
played by: **6** Monroe **8** Channing
song: **27** Diamonds Are a Girl's Best Friend

Loren, Sophia
real name: **14** Sofia Scicolone
husband: **10** Carlo Ponti
born: **4** Rome **5** Italy
roles: **5** El Cid **8** Two Women (Oscar) **9** Arabesque, Houseboat **13** Man of La Mancha **14** The Black Orchid **18** Desire Under the Elms **20** Marriage Italian Style **21** A Countess from Hong Kong, The Pride and the Passion

Lorentz, Hendrik Anton
field: **7** physics
nationality: **5** Dutch
discovered: **17** special relativity
named for him: **21** Lorentz transformation **34** Lorentz- Fitzgerald Length Contraction
awarded: **10** Nobel Prize

Loring, Eugene
choreographer of: **11** Billy the Kid

Lorna Doone
author: **11** R D Blackmore
character: **8** John Ridd **9** Tom Faggus **11** Carver Doone **13** Sir Ensor Doone **14** Jeremy Stickles **15** Reuben Huckaback

Lorre, Peter
real name: **16** Laszlo Lowenstein
born: **7** Hungary **9** Rosenberg
roles: **1** M **6** Mr. Moto **7** Mad Love **9** Joel Cairo **10** Casablanca, The Verdict **12** The Big Circus **14** Three Strangers **16** The Maltese Falcon **18** Crime and Punishment, The Mask of Dimitrios

Lorry, Jarvis
character in: **16** A Tale of Two Cities
author: **7** Dickens

Los Angeles
airport: **3** LAX **7** Burbank **23** Los Angeles International
area: **5** Watts **6** Bel Air, Downey, Venice **7** Anaheim, Compton, Norwalk **8** Mar Vista, Pasadena, Torrance, Westwood **9** Brentwood, Hollywood, Inglewood, Long Beach **10** Culver City **11** Century City, Garden Grove, Palos Verdes, Santa Monica **12** Beverly Hills, Marina del Rey **16** Pacific Palisades
San Fernando Valley: **6** Encino **7** Tarzana, Van Nuys, Ventura **10** Northridge **11** Sherman Oaks
baseball team: **7** Dodgers
basketball team: **6** Lakers, Sparks

8 Clippers
football team: 4 Rams 7 Express, Raiders
hockey team: 5 Kings
landmark: 5 Forum 10 Disneyland 11 Civic Center, Getty Museum, Watts Towers 12 Griffith Park 13 Farmers' Market, Hollywood Bowl, Hollywood Park, La Brea Tar Pits, Magic Mountain 15 Knott's Berry Farm 16 Bonaventure Hotel 17 Norton Simon Museum 22 Grauman's Chinese Theater 23 Griffith Park Observatory
mountains: 10 San Gabriel 11 Santa Monica
nickname: 15 City of the Angels
street: 4 Vine 10 Rodeo Drive 12 Olvera Street 15 Mulholland Drive 16 Van Nuys Boulevard 17 Wilshire Boulevard 18 Hollywood Boulevard 20 Santa Monica Boulevard
university: 3 USC 4 UCLA 7 Caltech 10 Pepperdine 17 Occidental College 31 California Institute of Technology
lose 4 fail, miss 6 forget, ignore, mislay 7 confuse, forfeit 8 misplace 9 fail to win, stray from 10 be the loser, fail to heed 11 be thrown off 12 be defeated in, be deprived of, suffer loss of, take a licking
lose control 5 break, crack 7 crack up 9 fall apart 10 go to pieces 15 go off the deep end
lose faith 6 give up 7 despair 9 lose heart 10 have no hope 18 become disenchanted
lose force 3 die 7 run down 9 lose power
lose heart 6 give up 7 de spair 17 become discouraged
lose one's cool 12 fly into a rage 13 become enraged, throw a tantrum 14 lose one's temper 15 fly off the handle
loser 4 flop 7 failure 8 defeated 9 conquered 10 vanquished
lose track of 4 lose 9 let escape 11 lose sight of
lose vigor 4 flag 5 droop 6 sicken, weaken, wither 7 decline
Losing Battles
author: 11 Eudora Welty
loss 4 ruin 5 wreck 6 defeat, losing 7 licking, removal, undoing 8 overturn, riddance, wrecking 9 abolition, mislaying, privation 10 amount lost, demolition, extinction, forfeiture, misplacing, number lost 11 bereavement, deprivation, destruction, dissolution, eradication, expenditure, extirpation
loss of life 5 death 8 fatality 9 mortality
lost 5 stray 6 absent, astray, killed, ruined, wasted 7 lacking, mislaid, missing, misused, strayed, wrecked 8 absorbed, murdered, perished, vanished, wiped out 9 abolished, destroyed, en-

grossed, misplaced, off- course 10 demolished, eradicated, extirpated, gone astray, misapplied, squandered 11 annihilated, misdirected, obliterated, preoccupied 12 exterminated
Lost Honor of Katharina Blum, The
author: 12 Heinrich Boll
Lost Horizon
author: 11 James Hilton
character: 10 Hugh Conway, Rutherford 12 Henry Barnard, Miss Brinklow 14 Father Perrault 20 Captain Mallison Chang
director: 10 Frank Capra
cast: 5 Margo 8 H B Warner, Sam Jaffe 9 Jane Wyatt 10 John Howard 12 Isa- bel Jewell, Ronald Colman 14 Thomas Mitchell 19 Edward Everett Horton
setting: 5 Tibet
Lost Illusions
author: 11 Honore de Balzac
Lost in America
director: 12 Albert Brooks
cast: 12 Albert Brooks, Julie Hagerty
Lost in Space
character: 5 Robot 7 Don West 12 Judy Robinson, Will Robinson 13 Pen- ny Robinson 14 Dr Zachary Smith 16 Maureen Robinson 16 Prof John Rob- inson
cast: 9 Billy Mumy 11 Guy Williams, Mark Goddard 12 June Lockhart, Marta Kristen 14 Jonathan Harris 16 Angela Cartwright
ship: 9 Jupiter II
Lost in the Funhouse
author: 9 John Barth
Lost in the Stars
author: 15 Maxwell Anderson
lost in thought 7 pensive 8 absorbed 9 engrossed, wrapped up 13 contemplative, in a brown study, introspective
Lost Lady, A
author: 11 Willa Cather
Lost Ones, The
author: 13 Samuel Beckett
Lost Patrol, The
director: 8 John Ford
cast: 8 Alan Hale 11 Wallace Ford 12 Boris Karloff 14 Victor McLaglen
score: 10 Max Steiner
Lost Weekend, The
author: 14 Charles Jackson
director: 11 Billy Wilder
cast: 9 Jane Wyman, Mary Young 10 Frank Falen, Ray Milland 11 Philip Terry 12 Doris Dowling 13 Howard da Silva
Oscar for: 5 actor (Milland) 7 picture 8 director 10 screenplay
lot 4 fate, lots, many, much, plot 5 field, patch, quota, share, straw, tract 6 oceans, oodles, ration 7 counter,

measure 8 beaucoup, property 9 allotment, allowance, great deal
Lot
grandfather: 5 Terah
father: 5 Haran
uncle: 7 Abraham
son: 5 Ammon
hometown: 5 Sodom
rescued by: 6 angels
fled to: 4 Zoar
lothario 3 rip 4 rake, roue, wolf 5 lover, Romeo, sheik 6 lecher 7 Don Juan, seducer, swinger 8 Casanova, lover- boy 9 debauchee, debaucher, libertine, womanizer 10 lady-killer, profligate, sensualist 11 philanderer, skirt-chaser
Lothario
character in: 15 The Fair Penitent
author: 4 Rowe
Loti, Pierre
author of: 18 An Iceland Fisherman
pseudonym of: 5 Viaud
lotion 4 balm, wash 5 salve 6 liquid 7 unction, unguent 8 cosmetic, liniment, ointment, solution 9 demulcent, emollient, freshener, skin cream 10 after-shave, astringent 11 conditioner, embrocation, moisturizer
Lotis
form: 5 nymph
changed into: 4 tree 5 lotus
lotophagi
means: 11 lotus-eaters
lots 4 much 5 heaps, loads, plots, scads 10 quantities
lotus 7 Nelumbo 13 Nymphaea lotus
varieties: 4 blue 5 water, white 6 sacred 8 American, Egyptian 10 East Indian
lotus-eaters 9 lotophagi
appear in: 7 Odyssey
loud 5 gaudy, noisy, showy, vivid 6 bright, flashy, garish 7 blatant, booming, intense, splashy 8 colorful, sonorous 9 clam- orous, deafening 10 resounding, stentorian, thundering, vociferous 11 ear-piercing, loud-mouthed 12 earsplitting, ostentatious
loud sound 4 bang, boom, clap, honk, howl, peal, roar, slam, toot 5 blare, blast, burst, crash 6 bellow, report, scream, shriek 7 clatter, thunder 9 explosion 10 detonation
Lou Grant
character: 6 Animal 8 Joe Rossi 10 Art Donovan 11 Charlie Hume 12 Billie Newman 15 Margaret Pynchon
cast: 10 Jack Bannon, Mason Adams 11 Edward Asner, Linda Kelsey 12 Robert Walden 13 Nancy Marchand 14 Darryl Anderson
paper: 17 Los Angeles Tribune
spinoff of: 18 Mary Tyler Moore Show
Louis, Joe
real name: 14 Joe Louis Barrow

nickname: 11 Brown Bomber
sport: 6 boxing
class: 11 heavyweight
Louis, Morris
  born: 11 Baltimore MD
  artwork: 4 Veil **5** Signa **7** Stripes **8** Unfurled **15** Mountains and Sea
Louise
  opera by: 11 Charpentier
  character: 6 Julian
Louisiana
  abbreviation: 2 LA
  nickname: 5 Bayou, Sugar **6** Creole **7** Pelican
  capital: 10 Baton Rouge
  largest city: 10 New Orleans
  others: 5 Houma **6** Bunkie, Gretna, Kenner, Minden, Monroe, Ruston **7** Bastrop **8** Bogalusa **9** Lafayette, Opelousas **10** Alexandria, Shreveport **11** Lake Charles
  college: 3 LSU **6** Loyola, Tulane **7** Dillard, Newcomb **9** Grambling
  explorer: 7 La Salle **9** Iberville **13** Pierre Lemoyne
  feature:
    area: 5 bayou **13** French Quarter
    festival: 9 Mardi Gras
    music: 4 jazz
    stadium: 9 Sugar Bowl
    street: 7 Bourbon
  tribe: 4 Adai, Ioni, Rees, Waco **5** Caddo, Haini, Washa **6** Eyeish, Pawnee **7** Andarko, Arikara, Atakapa **8** Ovachita **9** Bayogoula, Nachitoch
  people: 5 Cajun **6** Creole **7** Acadian, pelican **8** Huey Long **14** Lillian Hellman, Louis Armstrong
  island: 5 Avery
  lake: 3 Iat **4** Iatt **5** Caddo, Clear, Cross, Larto, White **6** Borgne, Saline **8** Darbonne, Maurepas **9** Bistineau, Calcasieu, Catahoula **10** False River **13** Pontchartrain
  land rank: 11 thirty-first
  mountain:
    highest point: 8 Driskill
  physical feature: 15 Head of the Passes **17** coastal marshlands
    delta: 11 Mississippi
    gulf: 6 Mexico
    salt domes: 11 Five Islands
  river: 3 Red **5** Amite, Bayou, Pearl **6** Tensas **8** Ouachita **11** Mississippi
  state admission: 10 eighteenth
  state bird: 19 eastern brown pelican
  state flower: 8 magnolia
  state motto: 5 Union **7** Justice **10** Confidence
  state song: 15 Give Me Louisiana **16** You Are My Sunshine
  state tree: 11 bald cypress
Louisiana Lightning
  nickname of: 9 Ron Guidry
lounge 4 flop, idle, laze, loaf, loll, rest, sofa **5** couch, dally, divan, lobby, relax, sleep, slump **6** dawdle, daybed, repose, slouch, sprawl **7** recline,

slumber **8** kill time, languish **9** davenport, do nothing, lie around, vestibule **10** dillydally, stretch out, take it easy **12** chaise longue
lourd
  music: 5 heavy
Lourenco Marques
  capital of: 10 Mozambique
louse 3 cad, rat **4** heel **5** churl, knave **6** rascal, rotter, vermin **8** parasite **9** scoundrel
louse up 3 mar **4** goof, muff, ruin **5** botch, spoil **6** bungle, foul up, mess up **7** butcher, do badly, screw up **9** mismanage **11** make a mess of
lousy 3 bad **4** mean **5** awful, nasty **6** crummy, rotten, shabby, unkind **7** hateful, vicious **8** dreadful, inferior, infested, terrible **9** unethical, worthless **10** pediculous, second-rate, unpleasant **12** contemptible
lout 3 ape, oaf **4** boor, clod **5** booby, churl, clown, dummy, dunce, klutz, yokel **6** lummox, rustic **7** bumpkin, dullard
loutish 4 rude **5** crude **6** coarse, gauche, oafish, vulgar **7** boorish, uncouth **9** unrefined **10** unpolished **11** peasantlike
lovable, loveable 4 cute **5** sweet **6** cuddly, lovely, taking **7** darling, winning, winsome **8** adorable, charming, engaging, fetching **9** endearing **10** enchanting **11** captivating
Lovberg, Eilert
  character in: 11 Hedda Gabler
  author: 5 Ibsen
love 3 man **4** beau, bent, dear, girl, mind, turn **5** adore, amity, amour, angel, ardor, enjoy, fancy, flame, honey, lover, savor, taste, woman **6** admire, bask in, choice, esteem, fellow, relish **7** beloved, charity, cherish, concord, darling, dearest, emotion, leaning, passion, rapture, revel in, sweetie **8** affinity, be fond of, devotion, fondness, goodwill, hold dear, loved one, mistress, paramour, penchant, precious, sympathy, treasure, truelove, weakness **9** adoration, affection, boyfriend, delight in, inamorata, rejoice in, sentiment **10** admiration, appreciate, attachment, cordiality, friendship, girlfriend, partiality, proclivity, solicitude, sweetheart, sweetie pie, tenderness **11** amorousness, benevolence, brotherhood, inclination, infatuation **12** be enamored of, congeniality, predilection
  god of: 4 Amor, Eros **5** Cupid **7** Angus Og
  goddess of: 5 Freia, Freya, Venus **6** Hathor, Inanna, Ishtar **7** Astarte, Mylitta **9** Aphrodite
Love, the Magician
  also: 11 El Amor Brujo
  ballet by: 5 Falla

love affair 5 amour **7** liaison, romance **14** affaire de coeur
Love Boat, The
  character: 3 Ace **10** (Cruise Director) Julie McCoy **11** (Dr) Adam Bricker, (Purser Burl) Gopher Smith **14** (Captain) Merrill Stubing **15** (Bartender) Isaac Washington
  cast: 8 Ted Lange **10** Fred Grandy **11** Lauren Tewes **12** Bernie Kopell, Gavin MacLeod
  ship: 15 Pacific Princess
love child 7 bastard **12** natural child **17** illegitimate child
love conquers all
  Latin: 15 omnia vincit amor
loved one 4 love, wife **5** lover **6** fiance, spouse **7** be loved, dearest, fiancee, husband **9** boyfriend **10** girlfriend, sweetheart **12** family member
Love for Three Oranges, The
  opera by: 9 Prokofiev
Love in the Afternoon
  director: 11 Billy Wilder
  cast: 10 Gary Cooper **13** Audrey Hepburn **16** Maurice Chevalier
  setting: 5 Paris
Lovelace, Richard
  author of: 18 To Althea from Prison **23** To Lucasta Going to the Wars
loveliness 6 beauty **9** good looks **11** pulchritude **14** attractiveness
lovely 4 cute, fine, good **5** sweet **6** comely **7** elegant, lovable, winning, winsome **8** adorable, alluring, charming, engaging, fetching, handsome, pleasant, pleasing **9** agreeable, beautiful, endearing, enjoy- able, exquisite **10** attractive, delightful, en- chanting **11** captivating, fascinating **12** irresistible
Love Machine, The
  author: 16 Jacqueline Susann
Love Me Tonight
  director: 15 Rouben Mamoulian
  cast: 8 Myrna Loy **14** Charlie Ruggles **16** Maurice Chevalier **17** Jeanette MacDonald
  score: 14 Rodgers and Hart
  song: 4 Mimi **5** Lover **14** Isn't It Romantic
love of country
  Latin: 11 amor patriae
Love of One's Neighbor
  author: 14 Leonid Andreyev
lover 3 fan, man, nut **4** beau, buff, dear, girl, love **5** flame, freak, honey, Romeo, swain, woman, wooer **6** fellow, suitor **7** admirer, beloved, darling, devotee, Don Juan, fanatic, sweetie **8** Casanova, follower, Lothario, loved one, lover boy, mistress, paramour, truelove **9** boyfriend, inamorata **10** aficionado, enthusiast, girlfriend, sweetheart **11** afficionado
  French: 6 bon ami **9** bonne amie
  Italian: 8 cicisbeo

Lovers and Other Strangers
director: **8** Cy Howard
cast: **8** Gig Young **9** Anne Meara, Bea Arthur **11** Anne Jackson **13** Bonnie Bedelia, Harry Guardino **14** Cloris Leachman, Michael Brandon **17** Richard Castellano

love seat 4 sofa **5** couch **6** settee **13** courting chair

lovesick 7 amorous **8** yearning **10** moonstruck

Love's Labour's Lost
author: **18** William Shakespeare
character: **4** Dull **5** Maria **7** Berowne, Costard, Dumaine **8** Rosaline **9** Ferdinand, Katherine **10** Holofernes, Jaquenetta, Longaville **16** Princess of France **18** Don Adriano de Armado

Love Song of J Alfred Prufrock, The
author: **7** T S Eliot

Love Story
author: **10** Erich Segal

Love-wit
character in: **12** The Alchemist
author: **6** Jonson

loving 4 fond, kind, warm **6** ardent, caring, doting, erotic, tender **7** amatory, amorous, devoted **8** enamored, friendly **10** benevolent, passionate, solicitous **11** sympathetic, warm hearted **12** affectionate

loving word 9 sweet talk **10** endearment **12** sweet nothing

low 4 base, blue, deep, down, evil, glum, mean, soft, vile **5** awful, cruel, dirty, dumpy, faint, gross, lower, lowly, muted, prone, quiet, short, small, squat **6** brutal, coarse, common, cruddy, crummy, fee- ble, gentle, gloomy, humble, hushed, little, paltry, scurvy, softly, sordid, stubby, stumpy, sunken, vulgar, wicked **7** coastal, concave, corrupt, doleful, heinous, muffled, obscene, quietly, snubbed, squalid, subdued, unhappy **8** cowardly, degraded, dejected, depraved, downcast, inferior, low-lying, low-slung, mediocre, murmured, sawed-off, soothing, terrible, trifling, undersea, unworthy **9** dastardly, depressed, lethargic, nefarious, prostrate, repugnant, repulsive, submarine, submerged, truncated, unethical, whispered **10** abominable, despicable, despondent, dispirited, melancholy, outrageous, scandalous **11** ignominious, scoundrelly, underground, unimportant **12** contemptible, disheartened, dishonorable **14** down in the mouth

Low, Juliette
founder of: **10** Girl Scouts

lowbred 4 non-u **6** coarse, common, vulgar **7** lowbrow, peasant **10** lowerclass, uncultured

low-down 4 base, mean **5** dirty **10**

despicable 12 contemptible **13** reprehensible

Lowell, James Russell
author of: **12** The Cathedral **15** The Biglow Papers **16** A Fable for Critics **21** The Vision of Sir Launfal

Lowell, Robert
author of: **8** Day by Day **9** Skunk Hour **10** The Dolphin **11** Life Studies **15** For the Union Dead **16** Lord Weary's Castle

lower 3 cut, dim **4** damp, drop, duck, mute, pare, sink, sulk **5** frown, glare, pared, prune, scowl **6** deduct, glower, lop off, muffle, reduce, soften, subdue **7** curtail, depress, immerse, let down, put down, reduced, repress, shorten **8** decrease, diminish, grow dark, lessened, make less, pare down, pull down, submerge, take down, tone down **9** curtailed, decreased, make lower, pared down **10** abbreviate, diminished

lower-case letter 9 minuscule **11** small letter

lower-class 4 poor **6** common **7** lowbred, lowbrow, peasant **9** unrefined **10** blue-collar **12** working-class

lower classes 6 proles, rabble **8** canaille, riffraff **9** hoi polloi, peasantry **11** proletariat **13** the common herd, working people **16** the great unwashed

lower depths 4 pits, scum **5** dregs **6** rabble **8** canaille, riffraff **14** scum of the earth

Lower Depths, The
also called: **11** At the Bottom **14** A Night's Lodging
author: **10** Maxim Gorky

lower in rank 4 bust **6** demote **7** degrade

lower in spirits 6 deject, sadden **7** depress **8** dispirit **10** dishearten

low-key 4 soft **5** loose, muted **6** gentle, subtle **7** muffled, relaxed, subdued **8** laid-back, softened, soft-sell **9** modulated, toned-down **10** lowpitched, restrained **11** low- pressure, understated, unobtrusive **14** unostentatious

lowliness 8 baseness **9** obscurity **10** humbleness

lowly 3 low **6** humble, modest, simple, softly **7** ignoble, low born, lowbred, obscure **8** baseborn, plebeian **10** unassuming **11** proletarian **13** unpretentious

low-minded 4 lewd, vile **5** crude, gross **6** coarse, smutty, vulgar **7** obscene, uncouth **9** obnoxious, offensive **11** disgraceful **12** contemptible

low point, lowest point 4 base, foot, zero **5** depth, nadir, worst **6** bottom **7** perigee **10** rock bottom

low-priced 5 cheap, token **6** budget,

modest 7 bargain, cut-rate, low-cost, nominal, reduced **8** closeout, moderate **9** dirt-cheap **10** discounted, economical, marked-down, reasonable **11** inexpensive **15** bargain-basement

low-ranking 5 minor, petty **11** subordinate, unimportant

low-spirited 3 low, sad **4** blue, down, glum **6** gloomy, morose, woeful **7** doleful, forlorn, unhappy **8** dejected, desolate, downcast **9** depressed, heartsore, sorrowful, woebegone **10** despondent, dispirited, melancholy **11** crestfallen, discouraged, downhearted **12** disconsolate, disheartened **14** down-in-the-mouth

low spirits 4 funk **5** gloom **6** dismay, sorrow **7** despair **8** dejected **9** pessimism **10** depression, desolation, melancholy, moroseness **11** despondency **12** hopelessness **14** discouragement **15** downheartedness

Loy, Myrna
real name: **13** Myrna Williams
co-star: **13** William Powell
born: **13** Raidersburg MT
roles: **10** The Thin Man **11** Nora Charles **17** Cheaper by the Dozen **22** The Best Years of Our Lives

loyal 4 firm, true **6** trusty **7** devoted, dutiful, staunch **8** constant, faithful, reliable, resolute, true-blue **9** steadfast **10** dependable, scrupulous, unswerving, unwavering **11** trustworthy **12** tried and true

loyalist 4 tory **12** conservative

Loyalties
author: **14** John Galsworthy

loyalty 6 fealty **8** devotion, fidelity, firmness **9** adherence, constancy **10** allegiance **11** reliability, staunchness **12** faithfulness **13** dependability, steadfastness **15** trustworthiness

lozenge 4 drop, pill **6** tablet, troche **8** pastille **9** cough drop

Luanda
capital of: **6** Angola

Lubitsch, Ernst
director of: **9** Ninotchka **13** Heaven Can Wait, To Be or Not To Be

Lucas, Charlotte
character in: **17** Pride and Prejudice
author: **6** Austen

Lucas, George
director of: **8** Star Wars **16** American Graffiti

Lucentio
character in: **19** The Taming of the Shrew
author: **11** Shakespeare

Lucerne
German: **6** Luzern
river: **5** Reuss
landmark: **9** Hofkirche **11** Am Rhyn House **15** Mariahilf Church

Lucia di Lammermoor

opera by: 9 Donizetti
based on novel by: 14 Sir Walter Scott
   called: 20 The Bride of Lammermoor

Luciana
character in: 17 The Comedy of Errors
author: 11 Shakespeare

Luciani, Albino 13 Pope John Paul I **20** Pope John Paul the First

lucid 5 clear **6** bright, direct, normal **7** certain, precise, radiant, shining **8** accurate, apposite, dazzling, luminous, lustrous, pellucid, positive, rational, specific **9** brilliant, sparkling **10** articulate, perceptive, responsive, to the point **11** clearheaded, crystalline, illuminated, resplendent, transparent **12** crystal clear, intelligible **13** clear thinking, scintillating, well-organized **14** comprehensible, understandable **15** straightforward

Lucifer
means: 5 Satan **11** fallen angel, light bearer **13** friction match

Lucina
origin: 5 Roman
goddess of: 10 childbirth
corresponds to: 4 Juno **8** Ilithyia **10** Eileithyia

Lucio
character in: 17 Measure for Measure
author: 11 Shakespeare

luck 3 lot **4** fate **5** karma **6** chance, kismet **7** destiny, fortune, success, triumph, victory **8** accident, fortuity, good luck, Lady Luck **11** good fortune, piece of luck **12** happenstance
god of: 12 Bonus Eventus

lucky 4 good **5** happy **6** in luck, timely **7** blessed, favored **9** favorable, fortunate, opportune, promising **10** auspicious, beneficial, felicitous, of good omen, propitious **12** providential

Lucky Jim
author: 12 Kingsley Amis

lucky piece 4 tiki **5** charm **6** amulet, grigri **8** shamrock, talisman **10** lucky charm **11** rabbit's foot

lucrative 7 gainful **8** fruitful **10** beneficial, high-income, high-paying, profitable **11** moneymaking **12** remunerative

Lucretia
husband: 26 Lucius Tarquinius Collatinus
raped by: 16 Sextus Tarquinius
death by: 7 suicide

Lucretius
author of: 13 De rerum natura **19** On the nature of things

Lucullan 4 rich **6** lavish **7** gourmet **9** epicurean, luxurious

Lucy Show, The
also: 9 Here's Lucy
character: 9 Kim Carter **10** Lucy

Carter **11** Craig Carter **12** Harry Conners, Vivian Bagley **13** Mary Jane Lewis, Sherman Bagley **14** Lucy Carmichael **15** Chris Carmichael, Harrison Cheever, Jerry Carmichael, Theodore J Mooney **18** Harrison Otis Carter
cast: 9 Ralph Hart **10** Candy Moore, Dick Martin, Gale Gordon, Lucie Arnaz, Roy Roberts **11** Desi Arnaz Jr, Lucille Ball, Vivian Vance **12** Jimmy Garrett **13** Mary Jane Croft

ludicrous 4 wild **5** comic, crazy, funny **6** absurd, far-out **7** amusing, comical **8** farcical **9** laughable **10** outlandish, ridiculous **11** nonsensical **12** preposterous

Ludlum, Robert
author of: 15 The Matlock Paper **17** The Bourne Identity, The Parsifal Mosaic, The Road to Gandolfo **18** The Osterman Weekend **19** The Gemini Contenders **20** The Rhinemann Exchange **23** The Chancellor Manuscript, The Scarlatti Inheritance

Luftwaffe 9 air weapon **18** German Nazi air force

lug 3 tow, tug **4** bear, drag, draw, haul, pull, tote **5** carry, heave **9** transport

luggage 4 bags, gear **6** trunks **7** baggage, effects, valises **9** suitcases **13** accouterments

Luggnagg
fictional land in: 16 Gulliver's Travels
author: 5 Swift

Lugnasad
origin: 5 Irish
feast date: 11 August first

Lugosi, Bela
real name: 10 Bela Blasko
born: 5 Lugos **7** Hungary
roles: 7 Dracula **21** Murders in the Rue Morgue

lugubrious 4 dour, glum **6** gloomy, morose, rueful, somber, woeful **7** doleful, elegiac **8** dolorous, downcast, funereal, mournful **9** miserable, sorrowful, woebegone **10** depressing, melancholy

Luke
birthplace: 7 Antioch
companion: 4 Paul
occupation: 9 physician
wrote: 6 Gospel

lukewarm 4 cool, mild, warm **5** aloof, tepid **8** detached, uncaring **9** apathetic, temp- erate **11** halfhearted, indifferent, per- functory, unconcerned **12** uninterested **13** lackadaisical **14** unenthusiastic **15** body-temperature, room- temperature

lull 3 gap **4** calm, ease, halt, hush **5** break, pause, quell, quiet, still **6** hiatus, la- cuna, pacify, recess, soothe, subdue **7** assuage, caesura, compose,

mollify, respite **8** breather, calmness **9** interlude **12** brief silence, interruption

Lully, Jean-Baptiste
born: 5 Italy **8** Florence
composer of: 4 Atys, Isis **6** Persee, Psyche, Roland, Thesee **7** Alceste, Phaeton **10** Le Sicilien, Proserpine **11** Bellerophon **13** Acis et Galatee, Amadis de Gaule, L'Amour medecin **14** Acis and Galatea, Armide et Renaud, Le mariage force **16** Cadmus et Hermione **17** Achille et Polyxene, Cadmus and Hermione **19** Achilles and Polyxene **20** Les Amants magnifiques **22** Le Bourgeois Gentilhomme, Monsieur de Pourceaugnac

lulu 3 pip **4** oner **5** dandy, doozy **8** Jim Dandy **9** allowance, humdinger, wonderful **10** remarkable

lumber 3 log **4** plod, wood **5** barge, clump, stamp **6** boards, planks, trudge, waddle **7** shamble, shuffle **8** flounder **9** fell trees

Lumber State
nickname of: 5 Maine

Lumet, Sidney
director of: 7 Network, Serpico **13** The Pawnbroker **14** Twelve Angry Men **15** Dog Day Afternoon **24** Long Day's Journey Into Night

luminary 3 VIP **5** light, wheel **6** bigwig **7** big shot, notable **8** somebody **9** celebrity, dignitary, personage **10** luminosity **11** illuminator

luminescent 5 aglow **7** glowing **8** gleaming, luminous **9** twinkling **10** flickering, glimmering, glistening, shimmering **11** fluorescent **14** phosphorescent

luminosity 4 glow **5** gleam, sheen, shine **6** luster **8** radiance **10** brightness, brilliance

luminous 6 bright **7** glowing, radiant, shining **8** lustrous **9** brilliant **10** irradiated **11** illuminated, luminescent **15** reflecting light

lump 3 gob, mix **4** bump, cake, clod, fuse, heap, hunk, knob, knot, mass, node, pile, pool **5** amass, batch, blend, bunch, chunk, clump, group, knurl, merge, tumor, unite **6** gather, growth, nodule **7** collect, combine, compile **8** assemble, swelling **9** aggregate **10** protrusion, tumescence **11** excrescence **12** protuberance

lumpish 4 dull, slow **5** bulky, dumpy, heavy, lumpy **6** clumsy **7** awkward **8** clod dish, ungainly, unwieldy **9** corpulent **10** cumbersome, overweight

Lumpkin, Tony
character in: 18 She Stoops to Conquer
author: 9 Goldsmith

lump together 4 fuse, pool **7** combine **10** amalgamate **11** consolidate, incorporate

Luna

personifies: 4 moon
Greek: 6 Selene

lunacy 5 folly, mania **6** idiocy **7** madness **8** dementia, insanity **9** absurdity, asininity, craziness, silliness, stupidity **10** imbecility, imprudence, insaneness **11** foolishness **13** foolhardiness, senselessness

lunatic 3 mad, nut **4** daft, loco **5** batty, crazy, loony, nutty, potty **6** cuckoo, in- sane, madman, maniac, screwy **7** bonkers, cracked, touched **8** crackers, demented, demo niac, deranged, maniacal, unhinged **9** psychotic, senseless **10** irrational, psychopath, reasonless, unbalanced **11** crazy person, mentally ill, not all there **12** crackbrained, insane person, psychopathic, round the bend **13** off one's rocker, of unsound mind, out of one's mind

lunch
French: 8 dejeuner

luncheonette 4 cafe **5** diner **7** beanery **8** snack bar **9** hash house, lunchroom **10** coffee shop **11** eating house **12** lunch counter, sandwich shop

lunchroom 4 cafe **5** diner, grill **8** snack bar **9** cafeteria **12** luncheonette

lunge 3 cut, jab **4** dash, dive, pass, rush, stab **5** hit at, lurch, swing, swipe **6** attack, charge, plunge, pounce, thrust **7** set upon **8** fall upon, strike at **9** make a pass

lunkhead 3 ass **4** dope, fool **5** booby, dunce, idiot, moron, ninny **6** dimwit, nitwit **7** fat head, halfwit **8** bonehead, dumb-dumb, imbecile, numskull **9** blockhead, lamebrain, numbskull **10** dunderhead, nincompoop **11** chowderhead

Lunt, Alfred
wife: 12 Lynn Fontanne
born: 11 Milwaukee WI
roles: 12 The Guardsman **13** The Ragged Edge

Lupercalia
origin: 5 Roman
event: 8 festival
honoring: 6 Faunus **8** Lupercus
to procure: 9 fertility

Lupercus
origin: 5 Roman
god of: 9 fertility
corresponds to: 3 Pan **6** Faunus

Lupino, Ida 7 actress **8** director
husband: 10 Howard Duff **12** Collier Young, Louis Hayward
born: 6 London **7** England
roles: 8 Devotion **10** The Hard Way **12** Junior Bonner, Women's Prison **13** Escape Me Never **15** Strange Intruder **17** On Dangerous Ground **18** The Light That Failed, While the City Sleeps

lurch 4 cant, keel, list, reel, roll, sway, tilt, toss **5** lunge, pitch, slant **6** ca-

reen, plunge, swerve, teeter, totter **7** incline, stagger, stumble

Lurch 6 butler
on: 15 The Addams Family

lure 4 bait, coax, trap **5** bribe, decoy, snare, tempt **6** allure, cajole, come-on, entice, induce, seduce **7** attract, beguile **8** cajolery, persuade **9** fascinate, tantalize **10** allurement, attraction, enticement, inducement, temptation **11** drawing card **12** blandishment

Lurelei see **7** Lorelei

lurid 4 gory, grim **5** eerie, fiery, vivid **6** bloody **7** carmine, flaming, ghastly, glaring, glowing, graphic, scarlet, shining **8** dramatic, rubicund, sanguine, shocking **9** appalling, bright-red **11** sensational **12** melodramatic **13** bloodcurdling

lurk 4 hide **5** prowl, skulk, slink, sneak **9** lie in wait

Lusaka
capital of: 6 Zambia

luscious 5 tasty **6** savory **7** scented **8** aromatic, fragrant, perfumed **9** delicious, flavorful, succulent, toothsome **10** appetizing, delectable **13** mouthwatering

lush 4 posh, rich **5** dense, fancy, grand **6** ornate **7** elegant, profuse **8** abundant, pro lific, splendid **9** elaborate, luxuriant, lux- urious, sumptuous **11** flourishing, magnificent

lust 5 covet, crave **6** be lewd **7** craving, lechery, passion **8** lewdness **9** carnality, hunger for, sexuality **10** satyriasis **14** lasciviousness, libidinousness

lust after 4 want **5** covet, crave **6** desire **11** have a yen for, have an eye on, hunger after, thirst after

luster 4 fame, glow **5** gleam, glory, gloss, honor, merit, sheen, shine **6** dazzle **7** burnish, glimmer, glitter, sparkle **8** prestige, radiance **9** radiation **10** brightness, brilliance, luminosity, notability, refulgence **11** distinction **12** luminousness, resplendence **15** illustriousness

lusterless 3 dim, wan **4** dead, drab, dull, flat **5** faded, matte, muted **7** prosaic **9** colorless, tarnished

Lust for Life
author: 11 Irving Stone
director: 16 Vincente Minnelli
based on story by: 11 Irving Stone
cast: 11 James Donald, Kirk Douglas (Vincent Van Gogh), Pamela Brown **12** Anthony Quinn (Gaugin)
Oscar for: 15 supporting actor (Quinn)

lustful 4 lewd **6** carnal **8** prurient **9** lecherous, salacious **10** lascivious, libidinous

lustrous 6 bright, glossy **7** glowing, radiant, shining **8** dazzling, gleaming,

luminous, polished **9** burnished, effulgent **10** glistening **11** coruscating, illuminated **12** incandescent

lusty 4 hale **5** husky, sound **6** brawny, hearty, robust, rugged, sturdy, virile **7** healthy **8** vigorous **9** exuberant, strapping **10** full of life **11** uninhibited **12** unrestrained, wholehearted **13** irrepressible

Lutetia
Latin: 5 Paris

Luther, Martin
born: 7 Germany **8** Eisleben
author: 16 Ninety-Five Theses **27** On the Freedom of a Christian Man **46** Address to the Christian Nobility of the German Nation **51** A Prelude Concerning the Babylonian Captivity of the Church
excommunicated by: 8 Pope Leo X **15** Pope Leo the Tenth
summoned before: 11 Diet of Worms
founded: 11 Lutheranism, Reformation **13** Protestantism

lux 5 light

Luxembourg
other name: 9 Luxemburg **13** Lucilinburhuc
name means: 10 little fort
capital/largest city: 10 Luxembourg
others: 4 Hamm **5** Roodt, Wiltz **6** Mersch, Remich **7** Kopstal, Lintgen, Petange, Redange, Vianden **8** Capellen, Clervaux, Diekirch, Frisange **9** Dudelange **10** Echternach, Ettel bruck, Hesperange, Larochette **11** Differdange, Wormeldange **12** Grevenmacher, Troisvierges, Wasserbillig **14** Esch-sur-Alzette
division: 6 Esleck **7** Bon Pays, Gutland, Oesling
measure: 5 fuder
monetary unit: 5 franc **7** centime
lake: 8 Haut Sure
mountain: 8 Ardennes
highest point: 8 Huldange **9** Burgplatz **11** Wemperhardt
river: 3 Our **4** Sure, Syre **5** Alert, Clerf, Eisch, Mosel, Sauer, Wiltz **6** Chiers **7** Alzette, Moselle **8** Petrusse **11** Ernz Blanche
physical feature:
  plateau: 4 Bock **8** Ardennes, Lorraine
  valley: 7 Moselle
people: 6 French, German **12** Luxembourger
  ruler: 8 Sigefroi, Wencelas **12** Jean l'Aveugle **21** House of Nassau-Weilburg
  saint: 10 Willibrord
language: 6 French, German **7** English **13** Letzeburgesch
religion: 13 Roman Catholic
food:
  pastry: 20 les pensees brouillees

luxuriant 4 lush, rank **5** dense, fancy, grand **6** florid, ornate **7** elegant, flowery, profuse, teeming **8** abundant, splendid **9** elaborate, exuberant, luxurious, overgrown, sumptuous **10** flamboyant **11** extravagant, flourishing, magnificent

luxuriate 4 bask **6** relish **7** delight **8** wallow in **9** indulge in

luxurious 4 rich **5** grand **6** costly, effete **7** elegant, wealthy **8** decadent, pampered **9** enjoyable, expensive, indulgent, sumptuous **10** gratifying **11** comfortable, pleasurable

luxuriousness 4 ease **6** luxury **7** comfort **8** richness **10** costliness **13** sumptuousness

luxury 5 bliss **6** heaven, riches, wealth **7** delight **8** paradise, pleasure **9** enjoyment **10** high living, indulgence **12** extravagance, nonessential, nonnecessity, satisfaction **13** gratification

LXX *see* **15** Septuagint

Lycaon
 king of: 7 Arcadia
 father: 8 Pelasgus
 son: 8 Maenalus, Tegeates
 tested: 4 Zeus
 turned into: 4 wolf

Lycidas
 author: 10 John Milton
 elegy for: 10 Edward King

Lycus
 king of: 6 Thebes **7** Cilicia

father: 7 Pandion **9** Chthonius
mother: 5 Pylia
brother: 7 Nycteus
wife: 5 Dirce
niece: 7 Antiope
son: 5 Lycus
succeeded: 8 Sarpedon
killed by: 6 Zethus **7** Amphion **12** Antiope's sons

Lydia
 kingdom in: 9 Asia Minor
 king: 7 Croesus
 queen: 7 Omphale
 capital: 6 Sardis
 conquered by: 8 Persians

lying down 5 in bed, prone **6** supine **7** napping, resting **8** snoozing **9** reclining, recumbent **10** taking a nap **13** taking a snooze

Lyle, Albert Walter
 nickname: 6 Sparky
 sport: 8 baseball
 position: 7 pitcher
 team: 12 Boston Red Sox **14** New York Yankees
 author of: 11 The Bronx Zoo

Lyly, John
 author of: 20 Euphues and His England **22** Euphues the Anatomy of Wit

lynch 4 hang **6** gibbet **8** string up

Lynde, Paul

born: 13 Mount Vernon OH
roles: 12 Bye Bye Birdie **16** Hollywood Squares **17** Beach Blanket Bingo **18** Under the Yum-Yum Tree

lynx 3 cat **6** bobcat **7** wildcat

Lyonnesse
 place: 12 near Cornwall **16** Arthurian romance
 birthplace of: 8 Tristram
 fate: 11 sunk into sea

Lyre
 constellation of: 4 Harp, Lyra
 star: 4 Vega

lyric, lyrical 6 poetic **7** lilting, melodic, musical, singing, tuneful **8** songlike **9** melodious **10** euphonious **11** mellifluent, mellifluous **13** sweetsounding

Lyrical Ballads
 author: 17 William Wordsworth **21** Samuel Taylor Coleridge

lyrics 4 poem **5** words

Lysander
 character in: 21 A Midsummer Night's Dream
 author: 11 Shakespeare

Lysistrata
 author: 12 Aristophanes
 character: 7 Lampito **8** Cinesias, Cleonice, Myrrhine **10** Magistrate **14** Old Men of Athens (Chorus)

M
- **director: 9** Fritz Lang
- **cast: 10** Peter Lorre **11** Inge Landgut **12** Ellen Widmann **15** Gustav Grundgens
- **setting: 6** Berlin

Mabinogian
- **origin: 5** Welsh
- **tales of: 7** romance

macabre 4 grim **5** eerie, weird **6** grisly, horrid **7** ghastly, ghostly **8** dreadful, gruesome, horrible, horrific **9** frightful, ghostlike, unearthly **11** frightening

Macao
- **other name: 5** Ao-men, Macau
- **territory of: 8** Portugal
- **monetary unit: 3** avo **6** pataca, pataco
- **island: 5** Taipa **7** Coloane
- **highest point: 5** Hag-Sa
- **river: 5** Pearl **6** Canton
- **sea: 10** South China
- **people: 7** Chinese, Macaoan **10** Portuguese
- **language: 7** Chinese, English **9** Cantonese **10** Portuguese
- **religion: 6** Taoism **8** Buddhism **13** Roman Catholic
- **place:**
  - **street: 11** Praia Grande
- **feature:**
  - **houseboat: 6** sampan

Macareus
- **father: 6** Aeolus
- **mother: 7** Encrete
- **sister: 6** Canace

MacArthur, Douglas
- **served in: 3** WWI **4** WWII **9** Korean War, World War I **10** World War II **11** World War One, World War Two
- **commander of: 15** Rainbow (42nd) Division **19** United Nations forces **24** US Army forces in the Pacific
- **rank: 15** five-star general **16** army chief of staff
- **battle: 5** Luzon, Pusan **6** Inchon **9** New Guinea **11** Leyte Island, Philippines **14** Bismark Islands, Solomon Islands **15** Bataan Peninsula **16** Admiralty Islands, Corregidor Island
- **accepted surrender of: 5** Japan
- **surrender occurred aboard: 8** Missouri
- **chairman of: 13** Remington Rand
- **author of: 13** Reminiscences

- **smoked: 11** corncob pipe
- **saying: 12** "I shall return"

Macbeth
- **author: 18** William Shakespeare
- **character: 6** Banquo, Duncan (King of Scotland) **7** MacDuff, Malcolm **11** Lady Macbeth **12** Three Witches
- **title: 5** thane
- **domain: 6** Glamis
- **director: 13** Roman Polanski
- **cast: 8** Jon Finch **10** Martin Shaw **13** Nicholas Selby **14** Francesca Annis

Maccabees
- **title of: 5** Judas
- **patriarch: 10** Mattathias
- **means: 8** hammerer
- **holiday: 8** Hanukkah

MacDonald, John D
- **author of: 11** Condominium
- **character: 11** Travis McGee

MacDonald, Ross
- **real name: 13** Kenneth Millar
- **author of: 8** The Chill **10** Black Money **13** The Blue Hammer **14** The Goodbye Look
- **character: 9** Lew Archer

MacDowell, Edward Alexander
- **born: 9** New York NY
- **composer of: 9** Sea Pieces **11** To a Wild Rose **13** Fireside Tales **15** Poems after Heine **16** Hamlet and Ophelia, New England Idylls, Woodland Sketches **17** Idylls after Goethe

MacDuff
- **character in: 7** Macbeth
- **author: 11** Shakespeare

mace
- **origin: 9** Indonesia
- **from same tree as: 6** nutmeg
- **tree: 17** Myristica fragrans
- **use: 4** fish **7** seafood **9** cherry pie, pound cake **16** chicken fricassee

Macedonia
- **capital/largest city: 6** Skopje
- **head of state: 9** president
- **government: 8** republic
- **monetary unit: 5** denar
- **river: 6** Struma, Vardar
- **people: 4** Turk **9** Albanian **10** Macedonian
- **language: 10** Macedonian
- **religion: 27** Macedonian Orthodox Christian

macerate 4 fade, mash, pulp, soak **5** souse, steep **6** shrink, soften, squash, wither **7** decline, liquefy, shrivel

8 dissolve, emaciate, fluidize, permeate, saturate **9** liquidize, waste away **10** lose weight

MacGraw, Ali
- **real name: 12** Alice MacGraw
- **husband: 8** Bob Evans **12** Steve McQueen
- **born: 12** Pound Ridge NY
- **roles: 7** Dynasty **9** Love Story **10** The Getaway **13** The Winds of War **15** Goodbye Columbus

Macheath, Captain
- **character in: 12** Beggar's Opera
- **author: 3** Gay
- *see* Threepenny Opera

ma chere 6 my dear

Machiavelli, Niccolo
- **author of: 9** The Prince **11** The Art of War **16** Discourses on Livy
- **home: 8** Florence
- **The "Prince": 12** Cesare Borgia

Machiavellian 6 amoral, crafty **7** cunning, devious **8** scheming **9** deceitful, designing **10** perfidious **11** self-serving, treacherous, underhanded **12** falsehearted, unscrupulous

machination 4 plot, rule, ruse **5** dodge **6** design, device, scheme **8** artifice, intrigue, maneuver **9** stratagem **10** conspiracy **11** contrivance

machine 3 set **4** army, body, camp, club, gang, pool, ring **5** corps, crowd, force, group, setup, trust, union **6** device, system **7** combine, coterie, faction, society **9** apparatus, appliance, machinery, mechanism, structure **11** association **12** organization **13** establishment

machine gun
- **invented by: 7** Gatling
- **improved by: 5** Maxim **9** Hotchkiss

machinery 4 gear **5** setup, tools **6** agency, makeup, system, tackle, wheels **9** apparatus, mechanism, resources, structure **12** contrivances, organization

macho 5 he-man, manly **6** strong, virile

Machpelah
- **location: 6** Hebron
- **burial place of: 4** Leah **5** Isaac, Jacob, Sarah **7** Abraham, Rebekah

Machu Picchu 5 ruins
- **of: 5** Incas
- **in: 4** Peru

Macilente
character in: **22** Every Man out of His
Humour
author: **6** Jonson
MacInnes, Helen
author of: **13** North from Rome **14**
Above Suspicion **16** Decision at Delphi **17** The Venetian Affair **21** The
Salzburg Connection
macintosh, mackintosh 7 slicker **8**
raincoat **10** waterproof
Mack, Connie
real name: **30** Cornelius Alexander
McGillicuddy
sport: **8** baseball
position: **7** manager
team: **21** Philadelphia Athletics
MacKellar
character in: **21** The Master of Ballantrae
author: **9** Stevenson
mackerel
young: **5** spike **6** tinker **7** blinker
mackinaw 4 coat **6** jacket **8** overcoat
Mack the Knife see **15** Three Penny
Opera
MacLaine, Shirley
real name: **19** Shirley MacLean Beaty
brother: **12** Warren Beatty
born: **10** Richmond VA
roles: **6** Can Can **10** Being There **11**
Irma La Douce **12** Sweet Charity,
The Apartment **15** Some Came Running, The Turning Point, Two for the
Seesaw **16** The Children's Hour **17**
Terms of Endearment (Oscar) **19** The
Trouble with Harry **20** The Bliss of
Mrs Blossom
MacMurray, Fred
wife: **9** June Haver
born: **10** Kankakee IL
roles: **11** My Three Sons **12** The
Apartment **14** Above Suspicion, The
Caine Mutiny **15** Double Indemnity
20 The Miracle of the Bells
macrocosm 6 cosmos, nature **7**
heavens **8** creation, universe **9** firmament
mad 4 avid, daft, loco, nuts, wild **5** angry, balmy, crazy, irate, nutty **6** ardent, crazed, cuckoo, fuming, insane,
miffed, screwy, ticked **7** cracked, enraged, excited, fanatic, furious, in a
huff, lunatic, riled up, teed off,
touched **8** crackers, demented, deranged, frenzied, incensed, maniacal,
provoked, unhinged, up in arms,
worked up, wrathful **9** devoted to,
non compos, seeing red, ticked off,
wrought up **10** distracted, distraught,
infatuated, infuriated, in love with, irrational, unbalanced **11** boiling over,
exasperated, impassioned, not all
there **12** enthusiastic, round the bend
13 beside oneself, in high dudgeon,
not quite right, off one's rocker, out
of one's mind

Madagascar
other name: **16** Malagasy Republic
capital/largest city: **10** Tananarive **12**
Antananarivo
others: **6** Tulear **7** Majanga, Nossibe,
Toliary **8** Manakara, Tamatave **9**
Faradofay, Mananjory, Toamasina **10**
Antsirabe **11** Antsiranana, Diego-
Suarez, Fort Dauphin
measure: **7** gantang
monetary unit: **5** franc **7** centime
island: **6** Barren, Radama **7** Nossi-Be
11 Sainte-Marie **12** Chesterfield
lake: **5** Itasy **7** Alaotra, Kinkony
mountain: **4** Boby **9** Ankaratra **12**
High Plateaus, Tsiafajavona **17**
Tsaratanana Massif
highest point: **11** Maromokotro
river: **5** Ikopa, Mania, Sofia **7** Man-
goky, Mangoro, Onilahy **8** Ivoloina,
Manambao, Mananara **9** Betsiboka,
Manambolo **10** Manarandra **11** Tsiri-
bihina
ocean: **6** Indian
physical feature:
bay: **6** Radama **8** Antongil **9** Maha-
jamba **10** Sahamalaza
cape: **5** Amber **10** Saint-Andre **11**
Sainte-Marie **14** Saint-Sebastien
channel: **10** Mozambique
lagoon: **9** pangalane
plateau: **9** Ankaizina
people: **4** Arab, Bara, Hova **5** Malay
6 Merina, Tanala **7** African **8** Betsileo, Mahafaly, Malagasy, Sakalava
9 Antaimoro, Antaisaka, Antandroy,
Tsimi-hety **10** Indonesian, Polynesian
13 Betsimisaraka
dynasty: **6** Merina
leader: **9** Ratsiraka, Tsiranana **11**
Ranamantsoa
language: **6** French **8** Malagasy, Malgache
religion: **5** Islam **7** animism **10** Protestant **13** Roman Catholic
place:
market: **4** Zoma
royal estate: **4** Rova
feature:
animal: **4** zebu **5** lemur **6** foussa
musical instrument: **11** jego
vaotavo
proverb: **8** hainteny
shawl: **5** lamba
food:
vegetable: **7** brettes
madam, madame 3 Mrs **4** dame,
lady **6** matron **7** dowager **8** mistress
German: **4** Frau
Spanish: **6** senora
Italian: **5** donna **7** signora
Spanish/Portuguese: **4** dona
Madame Bovary
author: **15** Gustave Flaubert
character: **10** Emma Bovary, Leon
Dupuis **13** Charles Bovary **17** Rodolphe Boulanger
Madame Butterfly

also: **15** Madama Butterfly
opera by: **7** Puccini
character: **5** Bonze **6** Suzuki **9** Cho-
Cho-San, Cio-Cio-San, Sharpless **14**
Prince Yamadori **19** Lieutenant Pinkerton
aria: **7** Un beldi
mad as a hatter 3 mad **4** daft, nuts **5**
crazy, nutty **6** insane **7** cracked,
touched **8** demented, deranged, unhinged **10** unbalanced **13** off one's
rocker, out of one's head **14** off one's
trolley **15** mad as a March hare **17**
nutty as a fruitcake
mad as a March hare 3 mad **4** daft,
nuts **5** crazy, nutty **6** insane **7**
cracked, touched **8** demented, deranged, unhinged **10** unbalanced **12**
mad as a hatter **13** out of one's head
14 off one's trolley **17** nutty as a
fruitcake
madcap 4 rash, wild, zany **5** brash,
clown, giddy, joker **6** unruly **7** erratic,
flighty, foolish **8** reckless **9** hotheaded, impetuous, impulsive, senseless **10** incautious **11** impractical,
thoughtless **12** unconsidered **13** inconsiderate, undisciplined
madden 3 vex **4** gall **5** anger, craze,
pique, upset **6** enrage, frenzy **7** derange, incense, inflame, outrage, provoke, torment, unhinge **9** aggravate,
infuriate, unbalance **10** exasperate
made 5 built **6** formed **7** created **8**
composed, produced **9** assembled, developed **10** fabricated **11** constructed
12 manufactured
madeira
type: **4** wine **6** brandy **7** liqueur **8**
aperitif
origin: **7** Madeira
Madeira Islands
capital: **7** Funchal
city: **5** Monte
island: **6** Grande **7** Dezerte, Madeira
8 Desertas **9** Selvagens **10** Porto
Santo
ocean: **8** Atlantic
owned by: **8** Portugal
stone aqueduct: **7** levadas
wine: **4** Bual **5** Tinta, Tinto **6** Canary,
Gomera **7** Malmsey, Marsala, Sercial
8 Verdelho
made-up 5 false **7** assumed, created **8**
fanciful, invented **9** fictional, imaginary, pretended, thought-up **10** fictitious **11** make-believe, theoretical **12**
hypothetical
Mad Hatter
character in: **28** Alice's Adventures in
Wonderland
author: **7** Carroll
madhouse 6 asylum, bedlam, uproar
7 turmoil **8** loony bin, nuthouse
Madison, James
nickname: **23** Father of the Constitution

presidential rank: 6 fourth
party: 20 Democratic-Republican
state represented: 2 VA
defeated: 7 (DeWitt) Clinton **8** (Charles Cotesworth) Pinckney
vice president: 5 (Elbridge) Gerry **7** (George) Clinton
cabinet:
   state: 5 (Robert) Smith **6** (James) Monroe
   treasury: 6 (Alexander James) Dallas **8** (Abraham Alfonse Albert) Gallatin, (George Washington) Campbell, (William Harris) Crawford
   war: 6 (James) Monroe, (William) Eustis **8** (William Harris) Crawford **9** (John) Armstrong
   attorney general: 4 (Richard) Rush **6** (Caesar Augustus) Rodney **7** (William) Pinkney
   navy: 5 (William) Jones **8** (Paul) Hamilton **13** (Benjamin Williams) Crowninshield
born: 12 Port Conway VA **16** King George County
died/buried: 2 VA **12** Orange County **16** Montpelier estate
education:
   tutored at home by: 15 Rev Thomas Martin
   school: 15 Donald Robertson
   college of: 9 New Jersey (now Princeton University)
religion: 12 Episcopalian
interests: 3 law **11** agriculture **14** natural history
author: 16 Federalist Papers (with Hamilton and Jay) **24** Memorial and Remonstrances **29** Journal of the Federal Convention
political career: 24 US House of Representatives **25** Second Continental Congress
   secretary of: 5 state
   signed: 12 Constitution
civilian career: 6 farmer **7** planter
military service:
   colonel of: 19 Orange County militia
notable events of lifetime/term: 19 War of Eighteen Twelve
   battle of: 10 New Orleans
   treaty of: 5 Ghent
   Washington DC burned by: 7 British
father: 5 James
mother: 7 Eleanor (Rose Conway)
siblings: 5 Sarah **6** Reuben **7** Ambrose, Catlett, Francis, William **9** Elizabeth **11** Nelly Conway **13** Frances Taylor
wife: 8 Dorothea (Payne Todd)
   nickname: 6 Dolley
first lady:
   saved: 11 state papers **25** George Washington's portrait
madman 3 nut **5** loony **6** maniac

7 lunatic **8** demoniac **9** psychotic **10** psychopath
Mad Max
   director: 12 George Miller
   cast: 9 Mel Gibson
   sequel: 14 The Road Warrior **17** Beyond Thunderdome (with Tina Turner)
madness 6 lunacy, oddity **8** delusion, dementia, illusion, insanity **9** craziness **11** derangement
Madonna
   nickname: 15 The Material Girl
   husband: 8 Sean Penn
   recordings: 7 Madonna **8** True Blue **11** Like A Prayer, Like A Virgin
   films: 9 Dick Tracy **11** Truth or Dare **12** Who's That Girl **14** Body of Evidence **16** Shanghai Surprise **17** A League of Their Own **23** Desperately Seeking Susan
   tour: 6 Girlie **13** Blond Ambition
   books: 3 Sex
Madrid
   area: 9 Salamanca **19** Ciudad Universitaria
   capital of: 5 Spain
   landmark: 14 National Palace **18** Biblioteca Nacional
     bull ring: 22 Plaza de Toros Monumental
     museum: 5 Prado
   mountain: 18 Sierra de Guadaramma
   river: 10 Manzanares
   square: 10 Plaza Mayor **11** Plaza del Sol **13** Plaza de Espana
   street: 13 Paseo del Prado
Madwoman of Chaillot
   author: 13 Jean Giraudoux
maelstrom 4 eddy **5** shoot, swirl **6** bedlam, rapids, tumult, uproar, vortex **7** riptide, torrent **8** disorder, madhouse, undertow, upheaval **9** confusion, whirlpool **10** white water **11** pandemonium
   location: 8 Norway
maenad, menad 5 lenae **7** bacchae, bassara **8** clodones, thyiades **9** bacchante **10** mimallones
   companion of: 7 Bacchus **8** Dionysus
Maeterlinck, Maurice
   author of: 8 The Blind **11** The Blue Bird, The Intruder **19** Pelleas and Melisande
ma foi 6 my word, really **7** my faith
magazine 6 weekly **7** arsenal, journal, monthly **9** quarterly **10** periodical, powder room **13** military depot, munitions room
Magdalene *see* Mary
magenta 6 maroon **7** carmine, crimson, fuchsia **9** vermilion **12** purplish rose **13** reddish purple
Maggie: A Girl of the Streets
   author: 12 Stephen Crane
maggot 4 grub, worm **5** larva **8** mealworm

Magi
   also called: 7 wise men **11** astrologers
   followed: 15 Star of Bethlehem
   visited: 5 Jesus
   gifts: 4 gold **5** myrrh **12** frankincense
   singular: 5 magus
magic 4 lure **5** charm, spell **6** hoodoo, voodoo **7** sorcery **8** charisma, jugglery, witchery, wizardry **9** occultism, voodooism **10** allurement, black magic, demonology, divination, hocus-pocus, witchcraft **11** captivation, conjuration, enchantment, fascination, legerdemain, the black art **12** entrancement **13** sleight of hand **16** prestidigitation
   god of: 5 Thoth
Magic
   nickname of: 13 Earvin Johnson
Magic Flute, The
   also: 14 Die Zauberflote
   opera: 6 Mozart
   character: 6 Pamina, Tamino **8** Papagena, Papageno, Sarastro **10** Monostatos **12** Queen of Night
magician 5 magus **6** shaman, wizard **7** juggler, warlock **8** conjurer, sorcerer **9** alchemist **11** illusionist, medicine man, necromancer, witch doctor **12** escape artist **15** prestidigitator
Magic Mountain, The
   author: 10 Thomas Mann
   character: 6 Naphta **7** Clavdia **11** Hans Castorp, Settembrini **15** Joachim Ziemssen
magisterial 9 imperious **10** autocratic, peremptory **11** dictatorial, domineering, overbearing **13** condescending
Magister Ludi: The Glass Bead Game
   author: 12 Hermann Hesse
magistrate 2 JP **5** judge **7** prefect **17** justice of the peace
Magna Carta 7 charter
   forced by: 6 barons
   upon: 8 King John
   at: 9 Runnymede
   guaranteeing: 14 civil liberties
magna cum laude 15 with great praise
Magna Graecia 27 ancient Greek colonies in Italy
Magna Mater 3 Ops **4** Rhea **6** Cybele
Magnani, Anna
   nickname: 10 Nannerella
   roles: 8 Open City **13** The Rose Tattoo (Oscar) **15** The Fugitive Kind **21** Secret of Santa Vittoria
magnanimous 7 liberal **8** generous, princely **9** forgiving, unselfish **10** altruistic, beneficent, charitable **12** largehearted **13** philanthropic
magnate 3 VIP **5** giant, mogul, nabob **6** big gun, bigwig, leader, tycoon **7** big shot, notable **8** big wheel, great

man **9** celebrity **13** empire builder, industrialist

magnesium
chemical symbol: **2** Mg

magnetic 8 alluring, charming, inviting **9** of a magnet, seductive **10** attractive, enchanting, entrancing, persuasive **11** captivating, charismatic, fascinating **12** irresistible

magnetism 4 lure **5** charm **6** allure **8** charisma **9** mesmerism, seduction **10** allurement, attraction, enticement **11** captivation, enchantment, fascination

magnification 5 honor **7** worship **9** adoration, blowing up, expansion, inflation, reverence **11** acclamation, enlargement, idolization **12** exaggeration **13** amplification, glorification, overstatement

magnificence 4 pomp **5** glory, state **6** luxury **7** glitter, majesty, royalty **8** grandeur, richness, splendor **10** brilliance **13** sumptuousness

magnificent 4 fine **5** grand, noble **6** august, superb **7** elegant, exalted, stately, sublime **8** glorious, imposing, majestic, splendid **9** brilliant, exquisite, wonderful **10** commanding, impressive **11** resplendent **12** transcendent **13** extraordinary

Magnificent Ambersons, The
director: **11** Orson Welles
based on novel by: **15** Booth Tarkington
cast: **7** Tim Holt **10** Anne Baxter **12** Joseph Cotten **14** Agnes Moorehead **15** Dolores Costello

Magnificent Obsession, The
author: **13** Lloyd C Douglas

Magnificent Seven, The
director: **11** John Sturges
cast: **10** Brad Dexter, Eli Wallach, Yul Brynner **11** James Coburn **12** Robert Vaughn, Steve McQueen **13** Horst Buchholz **14** Charles Bronson
setting: **6** Mexico
score: **14** Elmer Bernstein
remake of: **12** Seven Samurai
sequel: **16** Return of the Seven **20** Magnificent Seven Ride

magnify 4 laud **5** adore, boost, exalt, extol **6** blow up, double, expand, praise, puff up, revere **7** acclaim, amplify, enlarge, glorify, greaten, inflate, stretch, worship **8** heighten, maximize, overrate **9** embroider, overstate, reverence **10** exaggerate

magniloquence 7 bombast, fustian **8** euphuism, tumidity **9** pomposity, turgidity **10** orotundity **11** fanfaronade, grandiosity **14** grandiloquence **15** pretentiousness

magniloquent 5 tumid, windy, wordy **6** turgid **7** pompous, verbose **8** inflated **9** bombastic **13** grandiloquent

magnitude 4 bulk, fame, mass, size **6** extent, renown, repute, volume **7** big-

ness, expanse, measure **8** eminence, enormity, hugeness, vastness

magnolia
varieties: **4** ashe, star **6** saucer **7** Chinese **8** southern, umbrella **11** great-leaved

Magnum, P. I.
character: **2** TC **4** Rick **7** Higgins **12** Thomas Magnum
cast: **10** Tom Selleck **12** Roger E Mosley **13** John Hillerman
setting: **6** Hawaii

Magog
father: **7** Japheth

Magritte, Rene Francois Ghislain
born: **7** Belgium **8** Lessines
artwork: **14** La Belle Captive, The False Mirror, The Key of Dreams **15** Memory of a Voyage **18** L'Empire des Lumieres (The Empire of Light), The Menaced Assassin

Magua
character in: **20** The Last of the Mohicans
author: **6** Cooper

Magus see **4** Magi

Magwitch, Abel
character in: **17** Great Expectations
author: **7** Dickens

Magyar 9 Hungarian

Mahican see **7** Mohican

mah-jongg 4 game
origin: **7** Chinese
play piece: **4** tile
suit: **3** bam, dot **5** crack, winds
dragon: **3** red **5** white
term: **4** kong, pung **6** flower

Mahler, Gustav
born: **7** Austria, Bohemia
composer of: **12** Resurrection (symphony No 2) **15** Das Klagendelied **16** Songs of a Wayfarer **17** Das Lied von der Erde, Kindertotenlieder, The Song of the Earth **19** Des Knaben Wunderhorn **28** Lieder eines fahrenden Gesellen

mahogany 4 tree, wood **5** brown **8** hardwood **9** Swietenia **12** reddish-brown
varieties: **3** red **5** swamp, white **7** African, big-leaf, Florida, Senegal, Spanish **8** Honduras, mountain **9** Nyasaland, Venezulan **10** West Indian

Mahon, Christopher
character in: **27** The Playboy of the Western World
author: **5** Synge

mahzor, machzor 16 Jewish prayer book

Maia
member of: **8** Pleiades
place in group: **6** eldest
father: **5** Atlas
mother: **7** Pleione
son: **6** Hermes

maid 6 tweeny **7** servant **8** domestic **9** hired girl, housemaid, lady's maid, nursemaid **10** parlor maid **11** maidservant **12** upstairs maid **13** female servant
French: **6** au pair

maiden, maidenly 4 girl, lass, maid, miss **5** chick, first **6** chaste, damsel, lassie, virgin **7** colleen, girlish, ingenue, initial, untried **8** original, virginal, youthful **9** inaugural, soubrette, unmarried **10** demoiselle, initiatory **12** introductory

Maid Marian
beloved of: **9** Robin Hood

maidservant 4 amah, ayah, char, lass, maid **5** bonne **6** au pair, tweeny **7** abigail **8** charlady, domestic **9** hired girl, lady's maid, tirewoman **10** handmaiden, parlormaid

Maidu
language family: **8** Penutian
location: **10** California
noted for: **8** basketry

mail 4 arms, post **5** armor **6** get out **7** airmail, harness, letters, panoply **8** dispatch, packages **9** postcards **10** send by mail, send by post, suit of mail **11** surface mail **12** mail delivery, put in the mail **13** postal service **14** defensive armor, drop in a mailbox **17** post-office service

Mailer, Norman
author of: **15** An American Dream **16** Armies of the Night **18** The Naked and the Dead **19** The Executioner's Song

Maillol, Aristide
born: **6** France **13** Banyuls-sur-mer
artwork: **5** Night, Torso **7** Le Desir (Desire) **11** Ile de France **12** Young Cyclist **14** Action in Chains, The Three Nymphs **16** The Mediterranean (Seated Woman) **17** Monument to Cezanne, Monument to Debussy **18** Venus with a Necklace

maim 3 cut, rip **4** gash, lame, maul, rend, tear **5** slash, wound **6** deface, hobble, injure, mangle, savage **7** cripple, disable **8** lacerate, mutilate **9** disfigure, dismember, hamstring **12** incapacitate

main 4 head **5** chief, prime, vital **6** urgent **7** capital, central, crucial, leading, primary, special, supreme **8** critical, foremost, pressing **9** essential, important, necessary, paramount, principal, requisite **10** particular, preeminent **11** outstanding, predominant **13** consequential, indispensable

Main, Marjorie
real name: **13** Mary Tomlinson
partner: **12** Wallace Beery **13** Percy Kilbride
born: **7** Acton IN
roles: **7** Dead End **8** Ma Kettle

Maine

abbreviation: 2 ME
nickname: 6 Lumber **8** Pine Tree **10** Wonderland
capital: 7 Augusta
largest city: 8 Portland
others: 4 Bath, Saco **5** Hiram, Orono **6** Auburn, Bangor **7** Kittery **8** Boothbay, Lewiston, Ogunquit **9** Bar Harbor, Biddeford, Brunswick, Skowhegan **10** Waterville **11** Millinocket, Presque Isle
college: 5 Bates, Colby **7** Bowdoin
explorer: 6 Cabots **8** Norsemen
feature: 8 lobsters **19** West Quoddy Headlight
   beach: 10 Old Orchard
   national park: 6 Acadia
   waterway: 18 Allagash Wilderness
tribe: 6 Abnaki **7** Wewenoc
people: 10 downeaster **11** Dorothea Dix **19** Edna St Vincent Millay **24** Henry Wadsworth Longfellow
island: 4 Orrs **8** Mt Desert **10** Campobello
lake: 5 Sebec, Wyman **6** Sebago **8** Rangeley, Schoodic **9** Flagstaff, Moosehead **10** Chesuncook
land rank: 11 thirty-ninth
mountain: 5 Kineo, White **7** Bigelow **8** Cadillac
   highest point: 8 Katahdin
physical feature:
   bay: 5 Casco **9** Penobscot **12** Merrymeeting **13** Passamaquoddy
   sand dunes: 13 Desert of Maine
river: 4 Saco **6** St John **7** St Croix **8** Allagash, Kennebec **9** Aroostook, Kennebago, Penobscot **12** Androscoggin
state admission: 11 twenty-third
state bird: 9 chickadee
state fish: 16 land-locked salmon
state flower: 7 thistle **8** pine cone **22** white pine cone and tassel
state motto: 7 I Direct
state song: 16 State of Maine Song
state tree: 16 eastern white pine

mainly 6 mostly **7** chiefly **8** above all **9** in the main, most of all, primarily **10** on the whole **11** principally **13** predominantly **14** for the most part, in great measure **16** first and foremost
main point 3 nut **4** core, crux, gist, meat **5** basis, heart, theme **6** kernel **7** essence **10** brass tacks **11** nitty-gritty **15** sum and substance
mainspring 5 agent, cause **6** motive **9** incentive **10** motivation
mainstay 4 prop **6** anchor, pillar **7** bulwark **8** backbone, buttress **16** pillar of strength
Main Street
   author: 13 Sinclair Lewis
   character: 14 Carol Kennicott **15** Dr Will Kennicott
maintain 4 aver, avow, hold, keep **5** claim, state, swear **6** affirm, allege, assert, defend, insist, keep up, uphold

7 care for, contend, declare, finance, profess, stand by, support, sustain **8** conserve, continue, preserve **9** keep alive, keep going **10** provide for, take care of
maintenance 4 keep **6** living, repair, upkeep **7** keeping, support **10** livelihood, protection, sustenance **11** safekeeping, subsistence, sustainment **12** conservation, preservation, safeguarding
maison de sante 10 sanitarium **13** house of health
maize 4 corn, milo **5** grain **6** cereal, silage, yellow **7** zea mays **10** Indian corn
majestic, majestical 5 grand, lofty, noble, regal, royal **6** august, famous, superb **7** elegant, eminent, stately, sublime **8** esteemed, glorious, imperial, imposing, princely, renowned, splendid **10** impressive **11** illustrious, magnificent **13** distinguished
majesty 4 pomp **5** glory **6** luster **7** dignity **8** elegance, eminence, grandeur, mobility, splendor **9** elevation, loftiness, solemnity, sublimity **10** augustness **11** distinction, stateliness **12** gloriousness, magnificence **14** impressiveness
major 4 main **5** chief, prime, vital **6** larger, urgent **7** capital, crucial, greater, leading, primary, ranking, serious, supreme **8** critical, foremost, pressing **9** essential, important, necessary, paramount, principal, requisite **10** preeminent **11** outstanding, predominant, significant **13** consequential, indispensable

Major Barbara
   director: 13 Gabriel Pascal
   based on play by: 17 George Bernard Shaw
   cast: 11 Deborah Kerr, Rex Harrison, Wendy Hiller **12** Robert Morley, Robert Newton **14** Sybil Thorndike
majority 4 bulk, mass **8** best part, legal age, maturity **9** adulthood, seniority, womanhood **10** lion's share **13** preponderance
major key (in music)
   German: 3 dur
Major prophets *see* **8** prophets
majuscule 7 capital **11** large letter **13** capital letter **15** upper-case letter
make 3 fix **4** form, kind, mark, meet, pass **5** beget, brand, build, catch, cause, enact, erect, force, frame, impel, press, reach, shape, speak, utter **6** attain, compel, create, devise, draw up, effect, foment, makeup, oblige, render **7** appoint, compose, deliver, dragoon, fashion, produce, require **8** arrive at, assemble, engender **9** cause to be, constrain, construct, establish, fabricate, formation, legislate, pronounce, structure **10** bring about,

fashioning **11** composition, manufacture
make a bet 3 bet **4** risk **5** stake, wager **6** chance, gamble, hazard, plunge **7** venture
make a clean breast of 7 confess, lay bare, own up to **8** blurt out **14** come clean about
make a dash 3 fly, run **4** flee **6** escape **7** get away **8** make a run **10** make a break, take flight **12** make a getaway
make a deal 5 agree **6** settle **10** compromise **11** come to terms, meet halfway **14** strike a bargain
make advances 8 approach, come on to, sound out **11** proposition **13** make overtures, put the moves on
make a fuss over 6 dote on **7** protest **8** crow over
make again 4 copy **6** remake, repeat **9** duplicate **11** reconstruct
make a getaway 4 bolt, flee, skip **6** escape **7** get away, make off, run away **8** make a run, slip away **9** break free, cut and run, make a dash **10** break loose, fly the coop, take flight
make a gift of 4 give **6** donate **7** present **8** bequeath **10** contribute
make allowance for 6 excuse, pardon **7** forgive, indulge **8** bear with, pass over
make amends 5 atone **6** make up, square **7** expiate **9** do penance **10** compensate
make a mess of 3 mar **4** goof, muff, ruin **5** botch, spoil **6** bungle, foul up, mess up **7** butcher, do badly, louse up, screw up **9** mismanage
make a mistake 3 err **4** goof **6** mess up, slip up **12** miscalculate
make an effort 3 try **5** essay **6** strive, work at **7** attempt **8** endeavor
make appear 5 evoke **6** elicit **7** produce **9** conjure up **10** bring forth
make a racket 3 cry **4** howl, yell **5** shout **6** bellow, clamor, holler, scream **7** bluster **8** make a din **10** vociferate **12** raise a rumpus
make a stab at 3 try **5** essay, guess **6** reckon, take on **7** attempt, surmise, venture **8** estimate, give a try **9** undertake **10** conjecture **11** approximate **12** take a crack at, take a fling at
make a stand 9 stand fast **13** refuse to yield **17** fight to the last man
make a statement 6 remark **7** clarify, comment, discuss, explain, expound **9** elucidate, talk about
make aware 4 tell **5** edify **6** advise, inform, notify, reveal **7** apprise **8** acquaint, disclose **9** divulge to, enlighten, introduce **11** familiarize **16** bring to (one's) attention
make away with 3 eat **4** kill, take

5 spend, steal **6** kidnap, murder **7** abolish, consume, destroy **8** carry off, embezzle, get rid of **9** dissipate

make-believe 4 fake, sham **5** false, phony **6** made-up, make-up, unreal **7** assumed, charade, fantasy, feigned, fiction **8** creation, imagined, invented, pretense, spurious **9** fantastic, imaginary, invention, pretended, simulated **10** artificial, fictitious **11** counterfeit, fabrication **13** falsification

make certain of 6 assure, clinch, ensure **8** be sure of **10** make sure of

make damp 5 bedew **6** dampen **7** moisten **8** sprinkle

make dark 3 dim **6** darken **7** blacken, obscure

make different 4 vary **5** alter, amend **6** change, modify, mutate **7** convert, remodel **9** transform, transmute **12** metamorphose

make distinctive 8 set apart **9** single out **11** distinguish **12** characterize **13** differentiate

make easy 4 ease **6** smooth **7** explain, lighten **8** simplify **10** clear a path, facilitate

make eligible 5 allow **6** permit **7** entitle, qualify **9** authorize

make evident 4 show **5** prove **6** reveal **7** exhibit **8** manifest **9** establish, make clear, make plain **11** demonstrate

make fast 3 fix **4** moor **5** affix, tie up **6** attach, fasten, secure **7** connect

make feeble 6 weaken **7** wear out **8** enervate **10** debilitate, devitalize

make furious 5 anger **6** enrage, madden **7** incense, inflame **9** infuriate

make giddy 5 dizzy **12** make unsteady **15** make lightheaded

make good 5 repay **6** arrive, make it **7** fulfill, succeed **11** reach the top **15** make restitution

make happy 5 amuse, cheer, elate **6** please **7** delight, gratify **9** entertain

make haste slowly
Latin: **12** festina lente

make hostile 5 repel **6** offend **7** provoke **8** alienate **10** antagonize

make ill 5 repel **6** infect, revolt, sicken **7** afflict, disgust, repulse **8** disagree, distress, make sick, nauseate **9** discomfit **14** turn the stomach

make ill at ease 5 upset **6** rattle **7** fluster **8** distress **9** discomfit, embarrass **10** disconcert

make impure 4 foul, soil **5** dirty, spoil, taint **6** befoul, blight, defile, infect, poison **7** corrupt, pollute **10** adulterate **11** contaminate

make inroads 6 invade **7** impinge, intrude **8** encroach, infringe, trespass **9** penetrate

make known 4 tell **6** advise, impart,

inform, notify, report, reveal, unveil **7** apprise, divulge, lay bare, publish, uncover **8** disclose **9** broadcast **10** give notice, make public **11** communicate

make less forceful 6 soften, weaken **9** undermine **10** devitalize, emasculate

make light of 8 belittle, minimize, pooh-pooh, sneeze at **9** deprecate, disparage, underrate **10** depreciate, undervalue **13** underestimate

make merry 5 revel **7** carouse, roister **9** celebrate, have a ball **15** paint the town red

make much of·5 honor **6** praise **7** acclaim, applaud, commend, flatter **8** fuss over

make nervous 5 annoy, upset **7** agitate, disturb, perturb, trouble, unnerve **10** disconcert

make off with 4 lift **5** boost, steal, swipe **6** abduct, kidnap, snatch **7** bear off **8** carry off **10** run off with **11** get away with

make one's blood boil 5 anger **6** enrage, madden **7** incense, inflame **9** infuriate

make one's eyes pop 4 stun **5** amaze, shock **6** dazzle **7** stagger, startle **8** astonish **9** electrify **11** flabbergast

make out 3 see **4** espy **6** behold, descry, detect, fill in, notice **7** discern, observe, pick out **8** get along, perceive, write out **12** catch sight of

make plain 7 clarify, clear up, explain, lay open **9** elucidate, explicate, make clear **10** illuminate **11** disentangle, shed light on **12** bring to light

make possible for 5 allow **6** enable, permit **7** empower, qualify **10** capacitate

make public 3 air **4** tell, vent **5** print, utter, voice **6** expose, inform, reveal, spread **7** declare, display, divulge, exhibit, express, give out, publish **8** announce, disclose, proclaim, televise **9** broadcast, circulate, publicize

maker, Maker 3 god **4** poet **5** smith **6** author, forger **7** builder, creator, founder **8** declarer, inventor, producer **9** architect, generator **10** originator **12** manufacturer

make ready 5 prime **7** arrange, forearm, prepare

make reparation for 5 atone, repay **6** pay for **10** compensate, recompense, remunerate

make restitution 5 repay **7** pay back **9** reimburse **10** compensate, recompense

make right 3 fix **5** amend, emend **6** remedy, repair **7** correct, improve, rectify

make self-conscious 5 abash **6** rattle **7** chagrin, fluster **9** discomfit, embarrass **10** disconcert

makeshift 6 make-do **7** standby, stopgap **8** slapdash **9** alternate, expedient, temporary, tentative **10** substitute **11** provisional

make sick 6 revolt **7** disgust **8** nauseate

make smaller 6 lessen, reduce, shrink, take in **8** decrease, diminish

make sure 5 cinch **6** assure, clinch, decide, ensure, secure, settle **9** ascertain **11** double-check

make thinner 4 thin **6** dilute **9** water down **10** adulterate

make tracks 2 go **4** scat, shoo **5** be off, leave, scram **6** beat it, cut out, depart, go away **8** withdraw **10** hit the road

make uncomfortable 3 try **7** agitate, perturb **8** disquiet, distress **9** discomfit, embarrass **10** discompose

make uneasy 6 rattle **7** disturb, perturb, trouble, unnerve **8** disquiet, distress **9** discomfit, embarrass **10** discomfort, discompose, disconcert

make uniform 4 even **5** equal **6** smooth **7** balance **8** equalize **10** straighten

makeup 5 frame **9** character, cosmetics, framework, structure **11** composition, personality **12** constitution, organization

make up 4 form **5** cover **6** invent **7** arrange, concoct **8** assemble **9** improvise, reconcile **10** compensate, constitute **11** put together

make up for 5 atone **7** expiate **8** make good **10** make amends **13** compensate for

make up one's mind 6 decide **7** resolve **9** determine

make use of 3 use **5** apply **6** employ, engage, occupy **7** exploit, utilize **8** keep busy, put to use **13** turn to account

make weary 4 do in, poop, tire **7** exhaust, wear out **9** enervate

makeweight 6 weight **7** ballast

make well 4 cure, heal

make wider 5 widen **6** dilate, expand **7** broaden, stretch **9** spread out

make worse 6 worsen **8** heighten, increase **9** aggravate, intensify **10** exacerbate

making excuses 8 alibiing **9** defending **10** justifying **11** apologizing

Making of the President, The (series)
author: **14** Theodore H White

making the rounds 5 about **6** abroad **11** circulating, going around **13** going the route

Malachi
means: **11** my messenger
identified with: **4** Ezra **8** Mordecai, Nehemiah **10** Zerubbabel

maladroit 5 inept 6 clumsy, gauche 7 awkward, unhandy 8 bumbling, bungling, tactless 9 impolitic, unskilled 10 blundering, left-handed, ungraceful

maladroitness 9 gaucherie, inability 10 clumsiness, ineptitude 11 awkwardness, unhandiness 12 incompetence

malady 7 ailment, disease, illness 8 disorder, sickness 9 affection, complaint, infirmity 10 affliction, disability

mala fide 10 in bad faith, not genuine

malaise 4 pang 5 throb 6 twinge 7 anxiety 8 disquiet 9 lassitude 10 uneasiness, discomfort 11 nervousness

Malamud, Bernard
  author of: 8 The Fixer 9 God's Grace 10 The Natural, The Tenants 11 Dubin's Lives 12 The Assistant

Malaprop, Mrs
  character in: 9 The Rivals
  author: 8 Sheridan

Malawi
  other name: 9 Nyasaland
  capital: 8 Lilongwe
  largest city: 8 Blantyre
  others: 4 Bana 5 Dedza, Limbe, Mzuzu, Zomba 6 Kasese, Mzimba, Salima 7 Chipoka, Chiromo, Deep Bay, Karonga, Katumbi 8 Chikwawa, Chilumbe, Kota Kota, Nkata Bay 9 Monkey Bay 10 Port Herald 12 Fort Johnston, Livingstonia
  monetary unit: 6 kwacha 7 tambala
  lake: 5 Nyasa 6 Chilwa, Malawi
  mountain: 11 Livingstone
  highest point: 6 Mlanje 7 Mulanje
  river: 3 Bua 5 Shire 7 Dwangwa 11 South Rukuru
  physical feature:
    highlands: 5 Shire
    plateau: 5 Nyika
    valley: 5 Shire 9 Great Rift
  people: 3 Yao 4 Sena 5 Bantu, Lomwe, Ngoni 6 Cheiva, Maravi, Ngonde, Nyanja 7 Tumbuka
    dynasty: 6 Maravi
    explorer: 16 David Livingstone
    leader: 5 Banda
  language: 3 Yao 4 Cewa 5 Bantu, Ngoni, Tonga 6 Nyanja 7 English, Tumbuka 8 Chichewa 10 Chitumbuka
  religion: 5 Islam 7 animism 10 Protestant 12 Presbyterian 13 Roman Catholic
  feature:
    village: 5 mudzi

Malaysia
  capital/largest city: 11 Kuala Lumpur
  others: 4 Ipoh, Sibu 5 Anson, Davao, Telok 6 Iloilo, Johore, Kupang, Manado, Penang, Pinang 7 Bintulu, Kuantan, Kuching, Melalap 8 Port Weld, Sandakan 10 Georgetown, Kota Baharu 11 Johor Baharu, Port Dickson 12 Kota Kinabulu 14 Port Swettenham

  division: 5 Sabah 6 Malaya 7 Malacca, Sarawak
  head of state:
    supreme head of state: 18 yang di-pertuan agong
  measure: 3 pau, tun 4 para, pipe, tael, wang 5 parah 6 chupak, parrah 7 gantang
  monetary unit: 3 sen, tra 4 taro, trah 7 ringgit, tampang
  weight: 4 chee, mace, tael, wang 7 tampang
  island: 6 Banggi, Borneo, Labuan, Penang, Pinang, Tioman 7 Pangkor, Sebatik 8 Langkawi 10 Perhentian 11 Balambangan
  mountain: 4 Bulu, Hose, Iban, Iran, Main, Mulu, Niut, Raja 5 Murjo, Niapa, Ophir 6 Blumut, Kapuas, Leuser, Slamet 7 Binaija, Brassey, Crocker 8 Rindjani 11 Gunong Korbu, Gunong Tahan
  highest point: 8 Kinabalu
  river: 5 Klang, Kutai, Perak 6 Barito, Pahang, Rajang, Rejang 7 Sarawak 12 Kinabatangan
  sea: 4 Sulu 7 Celebes 10 South China
  physical feature:
    bay: 5 Labuk
    cape: 5 Sirik
    highlands: 7 Cameron
    passage: 6 Sibutu
    peninsula: 5 Malay
    point: 13 Tanjong Gelang
    strait: 6 Johore 7 Balabac, Malacca
  people: 4 Iban 5 Dayak, Malay 6 Indian 7 Chinese, Kadazan 9 Pakistani, Sri Lankan 10 Bangladesh, Indonesian
  language: 4 Bugi, Dyak 5 Malay, Tamil 6 Battok, Rejang 7 Chinese, English, Lampong, Niasese 8 Achinese, Javanese, Makassar 14 Bahasa Malaysia
    alphabet: 5 tagal
  religion: 5 Hindu, Islam 6 Taoism 7 animism 8 Buddhism 12 Christianity, Confucianism
  place:
    mosque: 8 National
  feature:
    cap: 7 songkok
    cloth: 4 tapa 5 batik
    clothing: 4 baju, malo, sari 5 badju, pareu 6 cabaya, kebaya, sam-foo, sarong 9 cheongsam
    dance: 4 haka, hula 5 joget
    game: 9 sepakraga
    hamlet: 7 kampong
    parish: 5 mukim
    rice paddy: 4 padi
    scarf: 9 selendang
    self-defense: 5 silat
    shadow play: 6 menora
    spirit: 5 hantu
  food:
    drink: 4 kava
    fruit: 6 durian 8 rambutan 10 mangosteen

Malcolm
  character in: 7 Macbeth
  author: 11 Shakespeare

Malcolm X
  original name: 13 Malcolm Little
  born: 7 Omaha NE
  religion: 5 Islam 11 Black Muslim 13 Nation of Islam
  assassinated in: 6 Harlem 11 New York City
  book about: 26 The Autobiography of Malcolm X
    author: 9 Alex Haley
  film about: 8 Malcolm X
    director: 8 Spike Lee

malcontent 4 glum, sour 5 rebel 6 grouch, grumpy, morose, sullen, uneasy 7 grouchy, growler, repiner, restive 8 dejected, downcast, grumbler, restless 9 insurgent, irritable 10 complainer, despondent 11 faultfinder 12 discontented, dissatisfied, faultfinding, hard to please

mal de mer 11 seasickness

Malden, Karl
  real name: 16 Mladen Sekulovich
  born: 6 Gary IL
  roles: 6 Patton 8 Baby Doll 15 On the Waterfront 21 A Streetcar Named Desire 24 The Streets of San Francisco

Maldives
  capital/largest city: 4 Male
  government:
    legislature: 6 Majlis
  monetary unit: 5 laree, rupee
  island: 3 Ari, Gan 4 Addu, Male 5 Rasdu 6 Felidu, Hulele, Mulaku 7 Malcolm, Minicoy, Nilandu 8 Maldives, Suvadiva 9 Fadiffolu, Wilingili 10 Haddummati, Kolumadulu 11 Tiladummati 13 Ihavandiffulu, Miladummadulu 16 North Malosmadulu, South Malosmadulu
  sea: 6 Indian 7 Arabian 9 Laccadive
  physical feature:
    channel: 4 Wadu 7 Kardiva 8 Veimandu 10 Equatorial 11 Eight Degree 17 One and a Half Degree
  people: 4 Arab 6 Indian 9 Sinhalese 10 Singhalese
    ruling family/sultans: 4 Didi
  language: 6 Arabic, Divehi
  religion: 5 Islam
  feature:
    coconut fiber: 4 coir
    dried coconut: 5 copra

male 3 boy, man, ram, tom 4 bull 5 manly, youth 6 tomcat 7 manlike, rooster 8 stallion 9 billy goat, masculine

Male
  capital of: 8 Maldives

male bird 4 cock 5 drake 6 gander 7 rooster

maledict 4 damn 5 curse 8 denounce 9 proscribe 12 anathematize

malediction 5 curse 8 anathema, diatribe 9 damnation, evil spell 10 execration 11 fulmination, imprecation 12 denunciation, proscription

malefactor 5 felon, knave, rogue 6 sinner 7 culprit 8 criminal, evil-doer, offender 9 miscreant, scoundrel, wrongdoer 10 malfeasant

male hairdresser
  French: 8 coiffeur

malentendu 7 mistake 16 misunderstanding

male power
  god of: 7 Priapus

Malevich, Kasimir Severinovich
  born: 4 Kiev 6 Russia
  artwork: 11 Black Square 15 The Knife Grinder 18 Eight Red Rectangles 19 Woman with Water Pails 34 Suprematist Composition White on White

malevolence 4 evil, hate 5 spite 6 enmity, grudge, hatred, malice, rancor, spleen 7 despite, ill will 9 hostility, malignity 10 antagonism, malignance, malignancy 12 spitefulness 13 maliciousness

malevolent 5 surly 6 malign, sullen 7 baleful, vicious 8 sinister, spiteful, venomous 9 invidious, malicious, malignant, rancorous, resentful 10 ill-natured, pernicious, revengeful 11 acrimonious, ill-disposed 14 ill-intentioned

malfeasance 5 crime 8 misdeeds 10 misconduct, wrongdoing

malformation 9 deformity 10 aberration, distortion 11 abnormality, monstrosity, peculiarity 12 grotesquerie, irregularity 13 disfigurement

malformed 7 twisted 8 deformed 9 contorted, distorted, grotesque, irregular, misshapen

malfunction 6 glitch, malady 7 problem 9 complaint

malgre lui 16 in spite of himself

Mali
  other name: 11 French Sudan 12 French Soudan 16 Sudanese Republic
  capital/largest city: 6 Bamako
  others: 3 Gao 5 Kayes, Mopti, Segou 6 Djenne 7 Sikasso 8 Taoudeni, Timbuktu 10 Tombouctou
  division: 5 Sahel 7 Azaouad
  monetary unit: 5 franc 7 centime
  lake: 2 Do 4 Debo 5 Garou 7 Korarou 9 Faguibine
  mountain: 4 Mina 6 Iforas 7 Manding
  highest point: 12 Hombori Tondo
  river: 4 Bani 5 Bagoe, Bakoy, Diaka,

Niger 6 Bafing, Bakoye, Baoule, Faleme 7 Azaouak, Senegal
  physical feature:
    desert: 6 Sahara 8 Chech Erg 10 Sekkane Erg 13 Haricha Hamada
    plateau: 14 Adrar des Iforas
    valley: 5 Niger 7 Tilemsi
  people: 3 Bwa 4 Fula, Kyan, Moor, Peul 5 Dogon, Dyula, Fulbe, Marka 6 Berber, Dognon, Fulani, Senufo, Tuareg 7 Bambara, Fellata, Malinke, Miniaka, Songhai, Soninke 8 Khasonke, Mandingo, Senoulfo
    leader: 4 Umar 5 Keita 6 Traore 9 Mansa Musa
  language: 5 Dogon, Dyula, Feulh, Mande, Marka 6 Berber, French, Fulani 7 Bambara, Malinke, Senoufo, Songhai
  religion: 5 Islam 7 animism
  place:
    ruins: 8 Terhazza
  feature:
    empire: 4 Mali 5 Ghana 7 Bambara, Songhai

malice 4 hate 5 spite, venom 6 enmity, grudge, hatred, rancor 7 ill will 8 acrimony 9 animosity, malignity 10 antagonism, bitterness, evil intent, resentment 11 malevolence 12 spitefulness

malice aforethought
  legal term: 51 planning to commit a crime without just cause or provocation

malicious 7 baleful, harmful, hateful, vicious 8 spiteful 9 invidious, malignant, rancorous, resentful 10 malevolent, revengeful, vindictive 11 acrimonious, ill-disposed

malign 3 bad 4 evil 5 abuse, black 6 defame, revile, vilify 7 baneful, harmful, hateful, noxious, ominous, put down, run down, slander 8 backbite, bad mouth, belittle, derogate, menacing, sinister 9 denigrate, deprecate, disparage, injurious, malicious, malignant 10 malevolent, pernicious, speak ill of 11 deleterious, detrimental, threatening 14 inveigh against

malignancy 5 spite, tumor 6 cancer, malice, rancor 7 ill will, sarcoma 8 acrimony, neoplasm, toxicity 9 carcinoma, hostility, virulence 10 bitterness 11 malevolence, viciousness 12 hard feelings, spitefulness, vengefulness 13 poisonousness

malignant 4 evil 5 fatal, toxic 6 bitter, deadly 7 hateful, hostile, vicious 8 fiendish, spiteful, venomous, virulent 9 invidious, malicious, poisonous, rancorous, resentful 10 diabolical, evil-minded, malevolent, pernicious, revengeful, vindictive 11 acrimonious, ill-disposed

malignant spirit 3 imp 5 demon, devil 7 gremlin

malignity 4 evil 5 spite, venom 6 animus, rancor, spleen 7 ill will 8 acrimony 9 animosity 12 hard feelings, spitefulness, venomousness

malinger 4 loaf 5 dodge, evade, shirk, slack 7 goof off 9 goldbrick

mall 4 yard 5 court, plaza 6 arcade, circus, piazza, square 8 cloister 9 colonnade, esplanade, promenade 10 quadrangle 12 parade ground

Mallarme, Stephane
  author of: 8 Herodias 18 L'Apres Midi d'un faune 19 The Afternoon of a Faun

Malle, Louis
  director of: 10 Pretty Baby 12 Atlantic City 13 Lacombe Lucien 16 Murmur of the Heart
  wife: 13 Candice Bergen

malleable 6 docile, pliant 7 ductile, plastic, pliable 8 flexible, moldable, workable 9 adaptable, compliant, teachable, tractable 10 governable, manageable 12 easily shaped 13 easily wrought 14 impressionable

mallet
  type: 6 rubber, wooden 12 plastic-faced

malnutrition 10 emaciation, starvation 16 undernourishment

malodorous 4 rank 5 acrid, fetid, musty 6 putrid, smelly 7 noisome, reeking 8 stinking 12 foul-smelling

Malone, Dorothy
  real name: 20 Dorothy Eloise Maloney
  husband: 15 Jacques Bergerac
  born: 9 Chicago IL
  roles: 11 Peyton Place 14 Too Much Too Soon 16 Written on the Wind

Malory, Sir Thomas
  author of: 14 Le Morte d'Arthur

Malpighi, Marcello
  field: 10 physiology
  nationality: 7 Italian
  founded: 18 microscopic anatomy

malpractice 10 negligence

Malraux, Andre
  author of: 8 Man's Fate 11 Anti-Memoirs, Days of Wrath, The Royal Way 13 The Conquerors 18 The Voices of Silence

Malta
  capital: 8 Valletta
  largest city: 6 Sliema
  others: 5 Marfa, Mdina, Mgarr, Mosta, Nadut, Paola, Rabat 6 Zejtun 7 Senglea, Zeibrun 8 Cospicua, Floriana, Mellieha, Victoria 10 Birkirkara, Birzebbuga, Vittoriosa
  measure: 4 rotl 5 artal, canna, parto, ratel, salma 6 kantar 7 caffiso
  monetary unit: 4 cent 5 grain, grano, pound
  island: 4 Gozo 5 Malta 6 Comino, Filfla 7 Filfola 9 Cominotto 10 Comminotto

highest point: 12 Dingli Cliffs
sea: 13 Mediterranean
physical feature:
  bay: 7 St Paul's **8** Mellieha **10** Marsaxlokk
  channel: 11 North Comino, South Comino
  harbor: 5 Grand **10** Marsamxett
people: 7 Maltese
  leader: 7 Mintoff **9** Buttigieo **18** Parisot de La Valette
  ruler: 5 Arabs **6** Romans **7** British **8** Napoleon **10** Byzantines **11** Hospitalers, Phoenicians **13** Carthaginians **15** Holy Roman Empire, Knights of St John
language: 7 English, Italian, Maltese
religion: 13 Roman Catholic
feature:
  gondola boat: 7 dghaisa

Maltese Falcon, The
author: 15 Dashiell Hammett
director: 10 John Huston
cast: 9 Mary Astor (Brigid O'Shaughnessy) **10** Peter Lorre (Joel Cairo) **12** Elisha Cook Jr (Wilmer), Gladys George **14** Humphrey Bogart (Sam Spade) **17** Sydney Greenstreet (the Fat Man)
character: 6 Wilmer **8** Sam Spade **9** Joel Cairo **11** Miles Archer **12** Casper Gutman, Floyd Thursby **18** Brigid O'Shaughnessy
remade as: 13 Satan Met a Lady

malt liquor 3 ale **4** beer, bock, brew **5** stout **6** porter

maltreat 4 harm, hurt **5** abuse **6** illuse, injure **8** mistreat

maltreatment 5 abuse **6** ill-use, injury **7** assault, cruelty **10** bodily harm, oppression **11** manhandling, molestation, persecution **12** mistreatment

Malvolio
character in: 12 Twelfth Night
author: 11 Shakespeare

Mama
character: 4 Nels **6** Dagmar, Katrin, TR Ryan **9** Aunt Jenny **10** (Papa) Lars Hansen **11** (Mama) Marta Hansen
cast: 8 Iris Mann **9** Peggy Wood, Ruth Gates **11** Judson Laire, Robin Morgan **12** Rosemary Rice **13** Dick Van Patten, Kevin Coughlin
dog: 6 Willie
based on book: 16 Mama's Bank Account
author: 13 Kathryn Forbes
setting: 12 San Francisco
theme: 12 Holverg Suite **13** The Last Spring

mamma, mama 2 ma **3** mam, mom, mum **4** wife **5** madre, mammy, mater, mommy, mummy, mumsy, woman **6** mother, parent

mammal

bat (chiroptera): 4 tomb **5** fruit, naked, smoky **7** mastiff, vampire **9** fisherman, horseshoe, leaf-nosed, sac-winged, slit-faced, thumbless **10** disk-winged, free-tailed, moustached **11** funnel-eared, hollow-faced, mouse-tailed **12** false vampire, sheath-tailed, sucker-footed, yellow-winged **14** vespertilionid **21** New Zealand short-tailed
carnivore: 3 cat, dog, fox **4** bear, lion, lynx, mink, puma, wolf **5** civet, dingo, fossa, hyena, otter, panda, skunk, tayra, tiger **6** badger, bobcat, coyote, ferret, grison, hyaena, jackal, jaguar, marten, olingo, weasel **7** polecat, raccoon **8** aardwolf, kinkajou, mongoose, suricate **9** wolverine **10** cacomistle, coatimundi
cetacea: 4 gray **5** pilot, right, whale **6** beluga, killer **7** dolphin, rorqual **8** humpback, narwhale, porpoise **10** sperm whale **11** beaked whale **16** bottle-nosed whale
edentata: 5 sloth **8** anteater **9** armadillo, tree sloth
egg-laying: 7 echidna **13** spiny anteater **18** duck-billed platypus
even-toed ungulate: 2 ox **3** elk, hog, pig **4** deer, goat, oxen **5** bison, camel, llama, moose, okapi, sheep **6** alpaca, cattle, duiker, vicuna **7** buffalo, caribou, gazelle, giraffe, guanaco, muntjak, peccary **8** antelope **9** mouse deer **10** chevrotain **12** hippopotamus
hyracoidea: 5 hyrax
insect-eating: 4 mole **5** shrew **6** desman, tenrec **7** gymnure, moon rat **8** hedgehog **9** shrew-mole, solenodon **10** golden mole, otter shrew, water shrew **13** elephant shrew
lagomorpha: 4 hare, pika **6** rabbit
marsupials/pouched: 5 koala **6** cuscus, numbat, possum, wombat **7** opossum, wallaby **8** kangaroo **9** bandicoot, phalanger **14** Tasmanian devil
odd-toed ungulate: 3 ass **5** horse, kiang, tapir, zebra **6** onager, quagga **10** rhinoceros
pinnipedia: 4 seal **6** walrus **7** sea lion
primate: 5 lemur, loris, potto **6** avahis, aye-aye, baboon, galago, gibbon, indris, monkey, people **7** gorilla, tamarin, tarsier **8** marmoset, simpoona **9** orangutan, tree shrew **10** chimpanzee
proboscidea: 8 elephant
rodent: 4 cavy, vole **5** coypu, gundi, hutia, mouse **6** agouti, beaver, coruro, gerbil, gopher, jerboa, nutria **7** blesmol, cane rat, hamster, lemming, mole-rat, rock rat **8** capybara, chipmunk, dormouse, sewellel, spiny rat, squirrel, tucu-tuco, viscacha **9** chozchori, false paca, pacaranas,

porcupine, woodchuck **10** chinchilla, prairie dog, springhare **11** kangaroo rat, pocket mouse, viscacha rat **13** kangaroo mouse **16** Speke's pectinator
sirenia: 6 dugong, sea cow **7** manatee
tubulidentata: 8 aardvark

mammon, Mammon 4 gain, gold **5** money **6** profit, riches, wealth **9** affluence **11** possessions **13** material goods, the god of money

Mammon, Sir Epicure
character in: 12 The Alchemist
author: 6 Jonson

mammoth 4 huge **5** great **6** mighty **7** immense, massive **8** colossal, enormous, gigantic, whopping **9** cyclopean, herculean, monstrous, ponderous, very large **10** gargantuan, monumental, prodigious, stupendous, tremendous **11** elephantine, mountainous

Mammy
character in: 15 Gone With the Wind
author: 8 Mitchell

Mamoulian, Rouben
director of: 13 Love Me Tonight, Silk Stockings **14** Queen Christina, The Mark of Zorro

man 3 boy, guy, one **4** chap, gent, hand, male, soul **5** equip, hubby, human, staff **6** anyone, attend, butler, fellow, fit out, helper, outfit, people, person, spouse, waiter, worker **7** footman, husband, laborer, mankind, someone, subject, workman **8** employee, garrison, handyman, henchman, humanity, liegeman, somebody **9** assistant, gentleman, hired hand, humankind **11** Homo sapiens
Spanish: 6 hombre

Man, first 4 Adam **12** Alalcomeneus
Nordic: 3 Ask

Man, Isle of
capital: 7 Douglas
location: 8 Irish Sea
native: 4 Manx **7** Manxman
Manx cat lacks: 4 tail

Man, Woman and Child
author: 10 Erich Segal

man about town 5 blade **7** playboy **8** cavalier, gay blade **12** boulevardier

manacle, manacles 3 ply, run, use **4** cope, fare, head, rule, work **5** bonds, get on, guide, irons, order, pilot, shift, steer, wield **6** chains, direct, fetter, govern, handle, make go **7** command, conduct, control, operate, oversee, shackle, succeed, survive, work out **8** cope with, deal with, dominate, get along, handcuff, maneuver, shackles **9** bracelets, handcuffs, look after, supervise, watch over **10** accomplish, administer, bring about, manipulate, put in irons, take care of **11** be at the helm, hand-fetters, preside over, put in chains, superintend **12** have charge of, hold the reins

manage 4 care, rule **6** bosses, charge, wheels **7** bigwigs, command, conduct, control, dealing, running, tactics **8** big shots, guidance, handling, ordering, planning, strategy, top brass **9** direction, directors, operation **10** conducting, executives, overseeing, regulation **11** generalship, negotiation, supervision, supervisors, transaction **12** manipulation, organization **14** administration, administrators **15** superintendence

manageable 4 easy **6** docile, pliant, wieldy **8** amenable, flexible **9** compliant, tractable **10** governable, submissive **12** controllable

management 4 boss, head **5** agent, chief **7** foreman, planner **8** overseer **9** budgeteer, majordomo, organizer, tactician **10** impresario, negotiator, supervisor **11** manipulator **13** administrator **14** superintendent

manager 4 boss, head **5** agent, chief **7** foreman, planner **8** overseer **9** budgeteer, majordomo, organizer, tactician **10** impresario, negotiator, supervisor **11** manipulator **13** administrator **14** superintendent

managerial 9 executive **10** management **11** supervisory **14** administrative, organizational

Managua
    capital of: 9 Nicaragua

Manala see **7** Tuonela

Manama
    capital of: 7 Bahrain

manana 6 future **8** tomorrow **11** in the future

Man and Superman
    author: 17 George Bernard Shaw

Manassa Mauler
    nickname of: 11 Jack Dempsey

Manasseh
    father: 6 Joseph
    mother: 7 Asenath
    great uncle: 4 Esau
    grandfather: 5 Jacob
    descendant of: 9 Manassite

man-at-arms 7 fighter, soldier, warrior **9** combatant **10** cavalryman

Manchester, William
    author of: 11 The Last Lion **14** American Caesar **15** Goodbye Darkness

Manchuria
    also: 7 Manchow
    city: 5 Aigun, Hulan, Kirin, Peian, Penki **6** Anshan, Antung, Dairen, Fu-Shun, Hailar, Harbin, Hokang, Mukden, Penchi, Yenchi **7** Hulutao, Ikuliho, Ssuping, Tantung **8** Chinchao, Paicheng, Shenyang **9** Changchun, Chiamussu, Manchouli, Miuchwang **10** Port Arthur **11** Chichihaerh, Mutanchiang
    peninsula: 8 Liaotung
    province: 5 Jehol, Jilin, Kirin **8** Liaoning **12** Heilongjiang, Heilungkiang
    river: 4 Amur, Liao, Yalu **5** Argun, Mutan, Nonni, Tumen **6** Ussuri **7** Sungari
    tribe: 5 Tungu **6** Manchu, Mongol

Mandalay
    found in: 18 Barrack-Room Ballads
    author: 14 Rudyard Kipling

mandamus
    legal term: 48 writ from a superior court commanding that a thing be done
    literally: 9 we command

Mandan
    language family: 6 Siouan
    location: 11 North Dakota
    ceremony: 5 Okipa

Mandarins, The
    author: 16 Simone de Beauvoir

mandate 5 edict, order **6** behest, charge, decree **7** bidding, command, dictate **8** approval, sanction **9** authority, direction, directive **10** commission, dependency **11** instruction, requisition **12** protectorate **13** authorization

mandatory 7 binding, exigent, needful **8** required **9** called for, essential, necessary, requisite **10** compulsory, imperative, obligatory, peremptory

Mandelbaum Gate, The
    author: 11 Muriel Spark

Manderley
    house in: 7 Rebecca
    author: 9 Du Maurier

mandible 3 jaw **4** beak, bill, jowl **7** maxilla **8** lower jaw
    part: 4 mala **5** angle, molar, ramus **6** corpus

Mandrake the Magician
    creator: 7 Lee Falk **9** Phil Davis
    character: 5 Narda **6** Lothar

Manes
    spirits or souls of: 4 dead

Manet, Edouard
    born: 5 Paris **6** France
    artwork: 7 Olympia **8** The Fifer **9** Emile Zola **10** Argenteuil **12** The Guitarist **19** Le Dejeuner sur l'Herbe (Luncheon on the Grass) **25** The Bar at the Folies-Bergeres **31** Execution of the Emperor Maximilian

Manette, Dr and Lucie
    characters in: 16 A Tale of Two Cities
    author: 7 Dickens

maneuver 4 move, plot, ploy **5** dodge, guide, pilot, steer, trick **6** deploy, device, gambit, scheme, tactic **7** finagle **8** arti-fice, contrive, intrigue **9** stratagem **10** manipulate **11** contrivance, machination, pull strings

Man for All Seasons, A
    director: 13 Fred Zinnemann
    based on play by: 10 Robert Bolt
    cast: 9 Leo McKern **10** Robert Shaw **11** Orson Welles, Wendy Hiller **12** Paul Scofield (Sir Thomas More), Susannah York **14** Nigel Davenport **15** Vanessa Redgrave
    Oscar for: 5 actor (Scofield) **7** picture **8** director

man Friday 4 aide **8** adjutant, employee **9** assistant **10** aide de camp **12** right-hand man
    source: 14 Robinson Crusoe

Man from St Petersburg, The
    author: 10 Ken Follett

Man from UNCLE, The
    character: 9 Mr Waverly **12** Napoleon Solo **13** Illya Kuryakin
    cast: 11 Leo G Carroll **12** Robert Vaughn **13** David McCallum
    foe: 6 THRUSH

manful 5 brave **8** resolute **10** courageous

manganese
    chemical symbol: 2 Mn

mangle 3 cut **4** harm, hurt, lame, maim, maul, ruin, tear **5** crush, press, slash **6** damage, impair, injure **7** flatten **8** lacerate, mutilate **9** disfigure

manhandle 4 maul **5** abuse **6** batter **7** rough up **8** maltreat, mistreat **9** pull about, push about **10** knock about, slap around

Manhattan
    director: 10 Woody Allen
    cast: 9 Anne Byrne **10** Woody Allen **11** Diane Keaton, Meryl Streep **13** Michael Murphy **15** Mariel Hemingway

Manhattan Transfer
    author: 13 John Dos Passos

manhood 5 prime **8** legal age, machismo, majority, maleness, maturity, virility **9** adulthood, manliness, mature age **10** manfulness **11** masculinity

mania 4 rage **5** craze **6** frenzy, lunacy, raving **7** craving, madness, passion **8** delirium, delusion, dementia, fixation, hysteria, insanity **9** monomania, obsession **10** aberration, compulsion, enthusiasm, fanaticism **11** fascination, infatuation

maniac 3 ass, nut **4** fool **5** loony **6** cuckoo, madman, nitwit **7** half-wit, lunatic **8** psychotic, screwball, simpleton **10** crackbrain, psychopath

manic 2 up **4** high **7** excited, frantic, hyped up **8** agitated, frenzied, worked up **9** wrought up **10** freaked out, switched on **11** hyperactive

manifest 4 bare, open, show **5** clear, frank, plain **6** candid, evince, expose, patent, reveal, unveil **7** display, divulge, evident, exhibit, express, obvious, uncover, visible **8** apparent, disclose, evidence, indicate, palpable

9 make known **10** noticeable **11** demonstrate, make visible, self-evident, transparent, unconcealed, undisguised

manifestation 4 show **7** display, example, symptom **8** evidence, instance **10** exhibition, expression, indication, revelation **12** illustration, presentation, proclamation, public notice **13** demonstration

manifesto 4 bull **5** edict, ukase **6** notice **9** broadside, statement **10** communique, encyclical **11** declaration **12** announcement, annunciation, notification, proclamation, public notice **13** position paper, pronouncement **14** pronunciamento

manifold 4 many **6** myriad, varied **7** complex, diverse **8** multiple, numerous **9** many-sided, multiform **10** variegated **11** diversified, innumerable **12** multifarious **13** multitudinous

Manila
capital of: **11** Philippines
former name: **8** Maynilad
island: **5** Luzon
landmark: **9** Rizal Park **16** San Agustin Church
river: **5** Pasig
section: **10** Quezon City
university: **10** Santo Tomas

Man in the Gray Flannel Suit, The
author: **11** Sloan Wilson

manipulate 3 pat, ply, use **4** feel, work **5** drive, pinch, wield **6** employ, finger, handle, manage, stroke **7** control, deceive, defraud, massage, operate, squeeze

Manitoba
bay: **6** Hudson
capital: **8** Winnipeg
city: **6** Carman, The Pas **7** Brandon, Caribou, Dauphin, Selkirk **8** Flin Flon, Lynn Lake, Wabowden, Winnipeg **9** Churchill, Killarney, Sherridon, Swan River **10** St Boniface **11** Norway House, York Factory **16** Portage La Prairie
flower: **11** windflower **13** prairie crocus
Indian tribe: **4** Cree **6** Eskimo, Ojibwa **8** Chippewa **10** Assiniboin
lake: **4** God's, Swan **5** Cedar, Moose **6** Island **7** Dauphin, Red Deer **8** Manitoba, Reindeer, St Martin, Waterhen, Winnipeg **9** Granville
mountain: **4** Hart **5** Baldy
name means: **16** lake of the prairies **18** Great Spirit's strait **19** Great Spirit's narrows
nickname: **15** Prairie Province **16** Keystone Province
province of: **6** Canada
river: **3** Red **4** Seal, Swan **5** Hayes **6** Nelson, Roseau, Souris **7** Pembina **8** Winnipeg **9** Churchill **11** Assiniboine **12** Saskatchewan
university: **7** Brandon **10** St Boniface

Mankiewicz, Joseph L
director of: **6** Sleuth **9** Cleopatra **11** All About Eve (Oscar) **12** Guys and Dolls, Julius Caesar **18** The Ghost and Mrs Muir **19** A Letter to Three Wives (Oscar)

mankind 3 man **6** people **7** mortals, persons, society **8** humanity **9** humankind **11** Homo sapiens

manlike 5 macho, manly **6** virile **8** hominoid **9** masculine

manly 4 bold, male **5** brave, hardy, husky, noble **6** brawny, daring, heroic, manful, plucky, robust, strong, sturdy, virile **7** gallant, staunch, valiant **8** athletic, fearless, malelike, muscular, powerful, resolute, stalwart, vigorous **9** masculine, strapping **10** chivalrous, courageous **11** gentlemanly, indomitable, self-reliant **12** stouthearted
Spanish: **5** macho

man-made 4 mock, sham **6** formed **7** crafted, created **8** produced **9** fashioned, ready-made, simulated, synthetic **10** artificial, fabricated, factitious, originated **11** constructed, handcrafted **12** manufactured

Mann, Delbert
director of: **5** Marty (Oscar) **14** Separate Tables

Mann, Thomas
author of: **12** Buddenbrooks **13** Death in Venice, Doctor Faustus **16** The Magic Mountain

manna 4 boon **5** award **6** reward **7** bonanza **16** divine sustenance

mannequin 4 form **5** dummy, model **6** figure

manner 3 air, way **4** form, kind, make, mode, mold, race, rank, sort, type **5** brand, breed, caste, genre, grade, guise, habit, stamp, style **6** aspect, custom, method, strain **7** bearing, conduct, fashion, species, variety **8** behavior, carriage, category, demeanor, practice, presence **9** character **10** appearance, deportment **14** classification

mannered 6 formal **7** stilted, studied **8** affected **9** contrived, unnatural **10** artificial **11** ceremonious

mannerism 4 airs, pose **5** habit **8** pretense **10** pretension **11** affectation, singularity **12** eccentricity, idiosyncrasy

mannerly 5 civil **6** polite **7** courtly, gallant, genteel, refined **8** well-bred **9** courteous **10** chivalrous **11** gentlemanly, well-behaved

manner of living
Latin: **12** modus vivendi

manner of looking at the world
German: **14** Weltanschauung

manner of speaking 7 diction **9** elocution **10** intonation **13** pronunciation

manners 6 polish **7** decorum **8** behavior, breeding, courtesy **9** amenities, deference, etiquette, gallantry, gentility, politesse, propriety **10** deportment, politeness, refinement **11** courtliness

Mannix
character: **9** Joe Mannix, Peggy Fair **10** (Lt) Adam Tobias **13** Lou Wickersham
cast: **10** Gail Fisher, Robert Reed **11** Mike Connors **16** Joseph Campanella

Mannon family
members: **4** Ezra, Orin **7** Lavinia **9** Christine
characters in: **22** Mourning Becomes Electra
author: **6** O'Neill

Manoah
son: **6** Samson

mano a mano 5 alone **8** conflict **13** confrontation, in a small group
literally: **10** hand to hand

Man of a Thousand Faces
nickname of: **9** Lon Chaney

Man of Nazareth
author: **14** Anthony Burgess

Man of Property, The
author: **14** John Galsworthy

Man of Sorrows see **5** Jesus

Manolin
character in: **18** The Old Man and the Sea
author: **9** Hemingway

Manon Lescaut
author: **11** Abbe Prevost

Manor, The
author: **19** Isaac Bashevis Singer

manor house 6 estate, manoir **7** chateau, mansion **11** stately home

manpower 4 help **5** brawn, labor **9** work force, employees

manque 6 failed, missed **7** lacking **11** fallen short, unfulfilled

Mansart, Francois
architect of: **14** Chateau de Berny **18** Hotel de la Vrilliere **33** Church of Sainte Marie de la Visitation
feature: **11** mansard roof

manservant 5 groom, valet **6** butler **7** footman **8** factotum **9** chauffeur

Man's Fate
author: **12** Andre Malraux

Mansfield, Jayne
real name: **14** Vera Jane Palmer
husband: **14** Mickey Hargitay
born: **10** Bryn Mawr PA
roles: **15** Hell on Frisco Bay **26** Will Success Spoil Rock Hunter

Mansfield, Katherine
author of: **5** Bliss **12** The Dove's Nest **14** The Garden Party

Mansfield Park
author: **10** Jane Austen
character: **5** Yates **8** Mrs Grant **9** Mrs Norris, Rushworth **10** Fanny Price

11 Lady Bertram 12 Mary Crawford 13 Henry Crawford 16 Sir Thomas Bertram
> Bertram children: 3 Tom 5 Julia, Maria 6 Edmund

mansion 5 manor, villa 6 castle, estate, palace 7 chateau 10 manor house

manslaughter 6 murder 7 killing 8 homicide

manta 3 ray 4 cape 5 cloak, shawl 9 devilfish

Mantegna, Andrea
> born: 5 Italy 14 Isola di Carturo
> artwork: 9 Parnassus 16 Camera degli Sposi (Bridal Chamber) 18 The Triumph of Caesar, The Triumph of Virtue 20 Madonna della Vittoria

Man That Corrupted Hadleyburg, The
> author: 9 Mark Twain

Mantius
> father: 8 Melampus
> son: 6 Clitus

mantle 4 cape, film, mask, pall, veil 5 cloak, cloud, cover, scarf, tunic 6 canopy, screen, shroud 7 blanket, curtain, wrapper 8 covering, envelope, mantilla

Mantle, Mickey (Charles)
> sport: 8 baseball
> position: 8 outfield
> team: 14 New York Yankees

manual 6 primer 8 handbook, physical, textbook, workbook 9 guidebook 10 done by hand 12 hand-operated, nonautomatic 15 instruction book

manual skill 8 deftness 9 dexterity, handiness 10 adroitness 12 coordination

manufacture 4 form, make, mold 5 build, frame 6 cook up, create, devise, invent, make up 7 concoct, fashion, produce, think up, trump up 8 assemble 9 construct, fabricate 11 mass-produce, put together

manufacturing 8 devising 9 inventing, producing 10 industrial 11 fabricating, nonagrarian

manumission 7 freeing 10 liberation 11 setting free 12 emancipation

manumit 4 free 7 set free 8 liberate 10 emancipate

manure 4 dung 5 feces 6 ordure 7 compost, excreta 8 dressing 10 fertilizer

manuscript 6 script 10 typescript 14 shooting script 15 written document

Manvah
> son: 6 Samson

Man Who Came to Dinner, The
> director: 15 William Keighley
> based on play by: 8 Moss Hart 14 George S Kaufman
> cast: 10 Bette Davis 11 Ann Sheridan, Billie Burke 12 Monty Woolley 13 Richard Travis

Man Who Fell to Earth, The
> director: 12 Nicholas Roeg
> cast: 7 Rip Torn 9 Buck Henry 10 Candy Clark, David Bowie

Man Who Shot Liberty Valence, The
> director: 8 John Ford
> cast: 9 John Wayne, Lee Marvin, Vera Miles 12 Edmund O'Brien, James Stewart

Man Who Was Thursday, The
> author: 12 G K Chesterton

Man Without a Country, The
> author: 17 Edward Everett Hale
> character: 11 Philip Nolan

Manx 3 cat 8 Goidelic
> spoken on: 10 Isle of Man
> manx cat lacks: 4 tail

many 4 a lot, lots 5 a heap, heaps, piles 6 divers, dozens, myriad, scores, sundry 7 numbers, several, various 8 numerous 9 countless 10 a profusion, numberless 11 an abundance, innumerable 13 multitudinous

manzanita 14 Arctostaphylos
> varieties: 4 dune, Ione, Otay 5 hairy, hoary, Morro, Parry, Pecho 6 island, Sonoma, woolly 7 Mexican, Pajarro, pine-mat 8 big-berry, Del Norte, Eastwood, Mariposa, Monterey, shagbark, Stanford 9 Fort Bragg, greenleaf, heart-leaf, little Sur, white-leaf 10 serpentine, silver-leaf 11 brittle-leaf, pink-bracted

Maori
> native of: 10 New Zealand

Mao Tse-Tung
> also: 8 Mao Zedong
> born: 5 China
> leader of: 10 communists
> title: 8 Chairman
> led: 9 Long March
> book: 16 The Little Red Book

map 4 plan, plot 5 chart, graph, ready 6 design, devise, lay out 7 arrange, diagram, prepare, project 8 contrive, organize 9 elevation 10 make a map of, projection 14 representation 18 topographical chart

maple 4 Acer
> varieties: 3 red 4 Amur, hard, rock, soft, vine 5 black, chalk, field, hedge, Nikko, river, sugar, swamp, white 6 Balkan, canyon, Norway, Oregon, parlor, sierra, silver, Triden 7 big-leaf, Florida, Persian, scarlet, striped 8 big-tooth, Drummond, full-moon, Hawthorn, Hornbeam, Japanese, mountain, Shantung, Sycamore, Tatarian 9 ash-leaved, eagle-claw, flowering, paperbark, Schwedler, Tartarian 11 Montpellier 12 Pennsylvania 13 Rocky Mountain, Southern sugar 18 Rocky Mountain sugar

map out 3 map 5 chart, draft 6 devise, lay out 7 diagram, outline 8 block out 9 delineate, formulate

Maputo
> capital of: 10 Mozambique

mar 4 hurt, maim, mark, nick, ruin, scar 5 botch, spoil, stain, taint 6 blight, damage, deface, defile, impair 7 blemish, destroy, scratch 8 diminish, mutilate 9 disfigure

Marabar Caves
> setting in: 15 A Passage to India
> author: 7 Forster

Maranatha
> means: 9 O Lord come

maraschino
> type: 7 liqueur
> origin: 5 Italy
> flavor: 6 cherry
> color: 3 red 5 white

Marathi
> language family: 12 Indo-European
> branch: 11 Indo-Iranian
> group: 5 Indic
> spoken in: 5 (northern) India

Marathonian bull see 10 Cretan bull

marauder 6 looter, pirate, ranger 7 corsair, ravager, spoiler 8 pillager 9 buccaneer, despoiler, guerrilla, plunderer, privateer 10 depradator, freebooter

marble 3 jet 4 vein 5 agate 6 basalt, blotch, mottle, streak 7 calcite 8 dolomite 9 limestone 10 serpentine, travertine 12 anthraconite
> quarry: 7 Carrara

Marble Faun, The
> author: 18 Nathaniel Hawthorne
> character: 5 Hilda 6 Kenyon, Miriam 9 Donatello

marbles
> type: 3 mib, taw 4 aggy, duck, immy, migg 5 agate, monny, scrap 6 commie, glassy, hoodle, marine 7 cat's eye, rainbow, shooter 9 carnelian 16 peppermint stripe
> term: 3 hit 4 shot 6 edgers, ringer 7 bowling, for fair, histing, lagging, lag line, lofting 8 circling, for keeps, hunching 9 pitch line 10 roundsters 11 knuckle down 13 knuckling down

Marc, Franz
> born: 6 Munich 7 Germany
> artwork: 10 Blue Horses 12 Yellow Horses 13 Fighting Forms

Marceline
> character in: 19 The Marriage of Figaro
> author: 12 Beaumarchais

march 2 go 4 hike, rise, step, trek, walk 5 tramp 6 file by, growth, parade 7 advance, proceed 8 progress 9 group walk 10 go directly, procession, walk in step 11 advancement, development, progression 12 martial music

March

event: 9 Mardi Gras 11 Ides of March (15) 12 Ash Wednesday 13 vernal equinox (21)
flower: 7 jonquil 8 daffodil
French: 4 Mars
gem: 10 aquamarine, bloodstone
German: 4 Marz
holiday: 12 St Joseph's Day (19) 13 St Patrick's Day (17)
Italian: 5 Marzo
number of days: 9 thirty-one
origin of name: 4 Mars
  Roman god of: 3 war
place in year:
  Gregorian: 5 third
  Roman: 5 first
saying: 20 Beware the Ides of March 40 March comes in like a lion and goes out like a lamb
Spanish: 6 Marcha
Zodiac sign: 5 Aries 6 Pisces

March, Fredric
real name: 29 Ernest Frederick McIntyre Bickel
born: 8 Racine WI
roles: 11 A Star Is Born 12 Anna Karenina, The Buccaneer 13 Les Miserables 14 Anthony Adverse, Inherit the Wind, Mary of Scotland, Seven Days in May 16 Death of a Salesman 17 Alexander the Great, Dr Jekyll and Mr Hyde (Oscar), The Desperate Hours 18 Death Takes a Holiday 19 The Affairs of Cellini 22 The Best Years of Our Lives (Oscar) 23 Barretts of Wimpole Street

Marchen 8 folk tale 9 fairy tale

March family
members: 2 Jo 3 Amy, Meg 4 Beth 6 Marmee
characters in: 11 Little Women
author: 6 Alcott

March Hare
character in: 28 Alice's Adventures in Wonderland
author: 7 Carroll

Marchmain family
characters in: 19 Brideshead Revisited
author: 5 Waugh

Marciano, Rocky
real name: 23 Rocco Francis Marchegiano
nickname: 19 Brockton Blockbuster
sport: 6 boxing
class: 11 heavyweight

Marconi, Guglielmo
nationality: 7 Italian
nickname: 16 father of wireless
invented/discovered: 5 radio 12 radio signals 16 magnetic detector 30 wireless high frequency telegraph
shared (1919): 20 Nobel Prize for physics

Marcus Welby MD
character: 11 (Dr) Steven Kiley 13 Consuelo Lopez

cast: 11 James Brolin, Robert Young 12 Elena Verdugo

Mardi (and a Voyage Thither)
author: 14 Herman Melville
character: 4 Alma, Jarl, Mohi, Taji 5 Media, Samoa, Yoomy 6 Yillah 7 Annatoo 10 Babbalanja, Braidbeard 11 Queen Hautia

Mardi Gras 7 holiday 8 carnival, festival, jamboree 10 fat Tuesday 13 Shrove Tuesday
king: 3 rex
social club: 5 krewe

Marduk
also: 8 Merodach 12 Baal Merodach
origin: 10 Babylonian
chief of: 4 gods

mare 3 sea 9 brood-mare 11 female horse

mare nostrum 6 our sea
ancient Roman name for: 13 Mediterranean

margin 3 hem, rim 4 edge, side 5 bound, skirt, verge 6 border, fringe, leeway 7 confine 8 boundary 9 allowance, extra room, safeguard

marginal 9 on the edge 11 in the margin 12 barely useful

mariage de convenance 21 marriage of convenience

marigold 7 Tagetes
varieties: 3 big, bur, fig, pot 4 cape, corn, wild 5 Aztec, fetid, field, marsh, water 6 desert, French, signet 7 African 12 sweet-scented

marijuana, marihuana 3 boo, kif, pot, tea 4 hash, hemp, herb, weed 5 bhang, blunt, dagga, ganja, grass, joint 6 buddha, moocah, reefer 7 chronic, hashish 8 cannabis, locoweed, mary jane

Marin, John Cheri (3rd)
born: 12 Rutherford NJ
artwork: 8 Sea Piece 12 Maine Islands 13 Tunk Mountains 16 Beach Flint Island 19 Movement Fifth Avenue 21 Seaside Interpretation 26 Camden Mountain across the Bay

marine 3 sea 5 naval 6 gyrene 7 aquatic, oceanic, of ships, pelagic 8 maritime, nautical, of the sea, seagoing 9 salt-water, seafaring 10 oceangoing 11 leatherneck 13 oceanographic

mariner 3 gob, tar 4 salt 5 pilot 6 sailor, sea dog, seaman 7 boatman 8 deck hand, helmsman, seafarer 9 navigator, yachtsman 10 bluejacket 12 seafaring man 16 able-bodied seaman

Marion, Francis
nickname: 8 Swamp Fox
served in: 16 Revolutionary War
type of warfare: 9 guerrilla
area fought in: 13 South Carolina
battle: 12 Eutaw Springs

marionette 6 puppet 10 fantoccino

famous: 4 Judy 5 Punch 9 Pinocchio
dummy: 13 Mortimer Snerd 15 Charlie McCarthy
maker: 4 Sarg

marital 6 wedded, wifely 7 married, nuptial, spousal 8 conjugal 9 connubial, husbandly 10 of marriage 11 matrimonial

maritime 5 naval 6 marine 7 aquatic, coastal, oceanic, of ships 8 nautical, of the sea, seagoing 9 seafaring

marjoram
botanical name: 8 Majorana, O vulgare, Origanum 16 M hortensis moench
origin: 4 Asia 13 Mediterranean
family: 4 mint
symbol of: 5 honor 9 happiness
charm against: 10 witchcraft
used as: 12 air sweetener
use: 4 eggs, fish, meat 5 salad 8 stuffing 9 vegetable

Marjorie Morningstar
author: 10 Herman Wouk

mark 3 cut, mar, pit 4 dent, goal, harm, heed, line, mind, nick, note, pock, rate, scar, show, sign, spot 5 badge, brand, grade, judge, label, notch, point, proof, score, stain, stamp, token, track 6 attend, bruise, deface, denote, emblem, evince, injure, intent, rating, regard, reveal, streak, symbol, target, typify 7 betoken, blemish, correct, imprint, measure, scratch, signify, suggest, symptom, write in, write on 8 bull's-eye, colophon, disclose, evidence, hallmark, indicate, manifest, point out, standard, stand for 9 be a sign of, criterion, designate, disfigure, objective, symbolize, yardstick 10 impression, indication, touchstone 11 distinguish 12 characterize 13 differentiate

Mark
also: 8 John Mark
mother: 4 Mary
cousin: 8 Barnabas
wrote: 11 Gospel

Mark (King Mark)
character in: 16 Arthurian romance

Mark Antony
also: 14 Marcus Antonius
character in: 12 Julius Caesar
author: 11 Shakespeare

mark down 4 note 5 enter, lower 6 record, reduce 7 put down 9 write down

marked 5 clear, great, noted, plain 6 dotted, scored, severe, showed, spotty, tabbed, tagged, traced 7 branded, labeled, pointed, specked, spotted, stained, tracked 8 destined, speckled, striking, targeted 9 indicated, prominent 10 emphasized, identified, made note of, noticeable, remarkable, singled out 11 conspicuous, distinctive, outstanding **12** considerable **13** distinguished

marker 3 IOU, peg, run, tab **4** chip, flag, sign **5** score **6** etcher, scorer, tablet, ticket **7** counter **8** bookmark, memorial, monument, recorder

market 4 hawk, sell, vend **5** stand **6** bourse, peddle, retail **7** grocery **9** dispose of **10** curb market, meat market **11** butcher shop, grocer's shop, marketplace

marketplace 4 mart **5** agora, arena, plaza **6** bazaar, market, square **8** exchange

Mark of Zorro, The
director: **15** Rouben Mamoulian
cast: **11** Tyrone Power **12** Linda Darnell **13** Basil Rathbone **15** Gale Sondergaard
score: **12** Alfred Newman

mark out 8 describe **9** delineate

marksman 8 dead shot, good shot, sure shot **9** crack shot **12** sharpshooter

marksmanship 3 aim **5** skill **8** accuracy **13** sharpshooting

Marley's Ghost
character in: **15** A Christmas Carol
author: **7** Dickens

Marlow
character in: **7** Lord Jim
author: **6** Conrad

Marlowe
character in: **15** Heart of Darkness
author: **6** Conrad

Marlowe, Christopher
author of: **8** Edward II **13** Doctor Faustus, The Jew of Malta **14** Hero and Leander **15** Edward the Second **19** Tamburlaine the Great

Marmee
character in: **11** Little Women
author: **6** Alcott

Marmion
author: **14** Sir Walter Scott
character: **11** Lord Marmion **13** Ralph de Wilton **14** Clare Fitz-Clare **16** Archibald Douglas **19** Constance de Beverley

Marnie
director: **15** Alfred Hitchcock
cast: **10** Diane Baker **11** Sean Connery, Tippi Hedren

maroon 4 plum, wine **6** desert, strand **7** abandon, forsake, magenta **8** cast away, jettison **9** put ashore **10** cast ashore, terra cotta **11** brownish-red, leave behind **15** leave high and dry

Marple, Miss Jane
detective created by: **14** Agatha Christie

Marquand, J P
author of: **13** Wickford Point **18** The Late George Apley
character: **6** Mr Moto

marquee 4 tent **6** awning, canopy **8** marquise

marred 6 ruined **7** damaged, injured, spoiled **8** impaired **9** blemished, destroyed **10** disfigured

marriage 7 wedding, wedlock **8** nuptials **9** matrimony
god of: **4** Frey **5** Freyr, Hymen **9** Hymenaeus
goddess of: **3** Fri **5** Frigg, Frija **6** Frigga, Tellus

marriage broker
Yiddish: **8** shadchan **9** schatchen

marriage of convenience
French: **19** mariage de convenance

Marriage of Figaro, The
also: **15** Le Nozze di Figaro
opera: **6** Mozart
character: **7** Susanna **8** Countess **9** Cherubino, Dr Bartolo **10** Marcellina **13** Count Almaviva

Marriage of Figaro, The
author: **12** Beaumarchais
character: **6** Figaro **7** Suzanne **8** Cherubin **9** Marceline **10** Dr Bartholo **13** Count Almaviva **16** Countess Almaviva

Marriages Between Zones Three, Four and Five
author: **12** Doris Lessing

married 3 wed **5** mated **6** joined, united, wedded **7** hitched, marital **8** combined, espoused **9** connubial **11** matrimonial, tied the knot

married woman
German: **4** frau

marry 3 wed **7** espouse, make one **10** get spliced, tie the knot **13** join in wedlock **14** join in marriage, lead to the altar, take in marriage

Marryat, Frederick
author of: **11** Peter Simple **16** Mr Midshipman Easy

Mars
also: **6** Mamers, Mavors
origin: **5** Roman
god of: **3** war
mother: **4** Juno
wife: **5** Nerio
epithet: **5** Ultor **8** Gradivus
corresponds to: **4** Ares

Mars
position: **6** fourth
nickname: **9** Red Planet
satellite: **6** Deimos, Phobos

Marseillaise 20 French national anthem

marsh 3 bog, fen **5** swamp **6** morass, slough **7** bottoms, wetland **8** quagmire **9** everglade, marshland, quicksand

Marsh, Dame Ngaio
author of: **9** Dead Water **12** Final Curtain **13** Death at the Bar **14** Enter a Murderer **19** Singing in the Shrouds

character: **10** Troy Alleyn **14** Roderick Alleyn

Marsh, Reginald
born: **5** Paris **6** France
artwork: **9** The Bowery **10** Pip and Flip **14** Why Not Use the El? **16** Tattoo and Haircut **17** Twenty-Cent Haircut

marshal 5 align, array, chief, group, order **6** deploy, draw up, gather, leader, line up, muster **7** arrange, collect, manager, sheriff **8** assemble, director, marechal, mobilize, organize **9** fire chief **10** law officer, supervisor **11** police chief **12** chief officer, field marshal **13** generalissimo

Marshall, George C
served in: **3** WWI **4** WWII **9** Korean War, World War I **10** World War II **11** World War One, World War Two
rank: **12** chief of staff **16** general of the army
author of: **12** Marshall Plan
secretary of: **5** state **7** defense
winner of: **15** Nobel Peace Prize (1953)

Marshall, Penny
husband: **9** Rob Reiner
born: **7** Bronx NY
roles: **5** Myrna **12** The Odd Couple **14** Laverne DeFazio **17** Laverne and Shirley
director: **3** Big

marshy 3 wet **4** miry **5** boggy, fenny, muddy **6** swampy **7** paludal, paludic **11** waterlogged

marsupial 5 koala **6** numbat, possum, wombat **7** cuscuse, opossum, wallaby **8** kangaroo **9** bandicoot, phalanger **14** Tasmanian devil

mart 4 show **6** market **8** exchange **9** trade fair, trade show **10** exposition

Martha
sister: **4** Mary
brother: **7** Lazarus
home: **7** Bethany

martial 7 hostile, Spartan, warlike **8** militant, military **9** bellicose, combative, soldierly **10** pugnacious **11** belligerent, contentious

Martian Chronicles, The
author: **11** Ray Bradbury

Martin, Dean
real name: **16** Dino Paul Crocetti
partner: **10** Jerry Lewis
born: **14** Steubenville OH
roles: **8** Matt Helm, Rio Bravo, The Caddy **9** The Stooge **10** Living It Up **12** Four for Texas, Sailor Beware **14** Toys in the Attic **15** Some Came Running **16** Artists and Models

Martin, Mary
son: **11** Larry Hagman
born: **13** Weatherford TX
roles: **6** I Do I Do **8** Peter Pan **12** Sound of Music, South Pacific

Martin, Steve

born: 6 Waco TX

roles: 7 The Jerk **17** Pennies From Heaven, Saturday Night Live **19** The Man with Two Brains **20** Dead Men Don't Wear Plaid **26** Planes Trains and Automobiles

Martin Chuzzlewit
  author: 14 Charles Dickens
  character: 5 Mercy **7** Charity **8** Tom Pinch **9** Pecksniff, Ruth Pinch, Sarah Gamp **10** Mark Tapley, Mary Graham **15** Jonas Chuzzlewit **17** Anthony Chuzzlewit

martinet 6 despot, tyrant **8** dictator **10** hard master, taskmaster **11** drillmaster, Simon Legree **12** little Caesar **13** authoritarian, drill-sergeant

Marty
  director: 11 Delbert Mann
  cast: 10 Betsy Blair **11** Joe De Santis **14** Ernest Borgnine **15** Esther Minciotti
  Oscar for: 5 actor (Borgnine) **7** picture
  script: 14 Paddy Chayefsky

martyr 5 saint **8** sufferer

martyrdom 5 agony **6** ordeal **7** anguish, torment, torture **9** bitter cup, suffering **10** affliction **11** cup of sorrow **13** crown of thorns

marvel 4 gape **6** be awed, rarity, wonder **7** miracle **8** be amazed **9** spectacle **10** phenomenon

Marvell, Andrew
  author of: 9 The Garden **16** To His Coy Mistress

marvelous, marvellous 4 A-one, fine **5** grand, great, super **6** divine, lovely, superb **7** amazing **8** colossal, fabulous, heavenly, smashing, splendid **9** fantastic, first-rate, wonderful **10** phenomenal, remarkable, stupendous **11** astonishing, magnificent, outstanding, sensational **13** extraordinary

marvelous to relate
  Latin: 13 mirabile dictu

Marwood, Mrs
  character in: 16 The Way of the World
  author: 8 Congreve

Marx, Bernard
  character in: 13 Brave New World
  author: 6 Huxley

Marx, Karl
  author of: 10 Das Kapital **18** Communist Manifesto (with Friedrich Engels)

Marx Brothers 5 Chico (Leonard), Gummo (Milton), Harpo (Adolph, Arthur) Zeppo (Herbert) **7** Groucho (Julius)
  costar: 14 Margaret Dumont
  born: 9 New York NY
  roles: 8 Coconuts, Duck Soup **11** The Big Store **13** Horse Feathers **14** A Day at the Races, Animal Crackers, Monkey Business **16** A Night at the Opera
  Groucho's TV show: 14 You Bet Your Life

Mary 6 Virgin **7** Madonna **8** Holy Mary **9** Magdalene, of Cleopas **10** Virgin Mary **11** Mother of God, Regina Coeli **13** Queen of Heaven **15** Mother of Sorrows **17** Mother of the Church
  mother: 4 Anna, Anne
  husband: 6 Joseph **7** Alpheus, Cleopas
  son: 4 Jude, Mark **5** Jesus, Moses, Simon **12** James the Less
  sister: 6 Martha
  brother: 7 Lazarus **8** Barnabas
  cousin: 9 Elizabeth
  home: 8 Nazareth
  visitor: 7 Gabriel
  flower: 4 lily **8** marigold

Mary
  author: 10 Sholem Asch

Maryland
  abbreviation: 2 MD
  nickname: 4 Free **7** Cockade **12** Old Line State
  capital: 9 Annapolis
  largest city: 9 Baltimore
  others: 5 Essex **6** Easton, Laurel, Towson **8** Aberdeen, Bethesda, Pocomoke **9** Frederick, Ocean City, Rockville **10** Cumberland, Hagerstown, Pikesville **11** Catonsville, College Park
  college: 4 Hood **7** Goucher, St John's **10** Washington **11** Towson State **12** Johns Hopkins **21** Annapolis Naval Academy
  feature:
    fort: 7 McHenry
    national battlesite: 8 Antietam
    presidential retreat: 9 Camp David
    race: 9 Preakness **12** Steeplechase
    racetrack: 5 Bowie **6** Butler, Laurel **7** Pimlico
  tribe: 5 Conoy **9** Nanticoke
  people: 6 Wesort **8** Terrapin **10** Spiro Agnew **11** crawthumper **14** Sargent Shriver **15** Francis Scott Key
    explorer: 7 Calvert
  lake: 8 Patapsco **9** Deep Creek, Loch Raven, Pretty Boy **10** Rocky Gorge **11** Triadelphia
  land rank: 11 forty second
  mountain: 4 Dans **8** Piedmont **9** Blue Ridge **11** Appalachian
    highest point: 8 Backbone
  physical feature:
    bay: 10 Chesapeake
    sea: 8 Atlantic
    swamp: 7 Pocoson
    valley: 5 Great **10** Hagerstown
  river: 3 Elk **7** Chester, Potomac **8** Choptank, Patapsco, Patuxent, Pocomoke **11** Susquehanna
  state admission: 7 seventh
  state bird: 15 Baltimore oriole
  state fish: 11 striped bass
  state flower: 14 black-eyed Susan
  state motto: 22 Manly Deeds Womanly Words **43** Thou Hast Crowned Us With the Shield of Thy Good Will
  state song: 18 Maryland My Maryland
  state tree: 8 white oak

Mary Poppins
  director: 15 Robert Stevenson
  based on story by: 9 P L Travers
  cast: 6 Ed Wynn **11** Dick Van Dyke (Bert), Glynis Johns **12** Julie Andrews **14** David Tomlinson **16** Hermione Baddeley
  score: 13 Robert Sherman **14** Richard Sherman
  Oscar for: 4 song **5** score **7** actress (Andrews) **13** visual effects
  song: 14 Chim-chim-cheree

Mary Queen of Scots
  director: 14 Charles Jarrott
  cast: 12 Trevor Howard **13** Glenda Jackson (Elizabeth I), Timothy Dalton **14** Nigel Davenport **15** Patrick McGoohan, Vanessa Redgrave (Mary of Scotland)

Mary Tyler Moore Show, The
  character: 8 Lou Grant **9** Ted Baxter **12** Gordon (Gordy) Howard, Mary Richards, Sue Ann Nivens **13** Bess Lindstrom **14** Marie Slaughter **15** Murray Slaughter **16** Phyllis Lindstrom, Rhoda Morgenstern **23** Georgette Franklin Baxter
  cast: 8 John Amos **9** Ted Knight **10** Betty White **11** Edward Asner **12** Gavin MacLeod, Georgia Engel **13** Joyce Bulifant, Lisa Gerritsen, Valerie Harper **14** Cloris Leachman
  setting: 11 Minneapolis

Mary Worth
  creator: 8 Carey Orr **9** Dale Allen **10** Dale Connor **13** Allen Saunders
  character: 4 Bill, Slim

Masaccio
  real name: 26 Tommaso di Ser Giovanni di Mone
  born: 5 Italy **27** Castel San Giovanni di Valdarno
  artwork: 14 The Holy Trinity **15** The Tribute Money **24** The Expulsion from Paradise

Mascagni, Pietro
  born: 5 Italy **7** Leghorn
  composer of: 4 Iris **6** Nerone **7** Isabeau **10** Le Maschere **11** L'Amico Fritz **14** Il Piccolo Marat **19** Cavalleria Rusticana

masculine 4 bold, male **5** brave, hardy, husky, macho, manly **6** brawny, daring, manful, plucky, robust, strong, sturdy, virile **7** staunch, valiant **8** athletic, fearless, forceful, intrepid, muscular, powerful, resolute, vigorous **9** strapping **10** courageous **11** indomitable, self-reliant **12** stouthearted

Masefield, John

author of: 7 Cargoes **8** Sea Fever **16** Salt Water Ballads

Maseru
capital of: 7 Lesotho

mash 4 mush **5** crush, paste, puree, smash **6** squash **8** mishmash **9** pulverize

M*A*S*H (TV Series)
character: 10 (Capt) BJ Hunnicut, (Lt Col) Henry Blake, (Maj) Frank Burns **12** (Corp) Radar O'Reilly **13** Father (John) Mulcahy, (Capt Benjamin Franklin) Hawkeye Pierce, (Col) Sherman Potter **14** (Corp) Maxwell Klinger **15** (Maj Margaret) Hot Lips Houlihan **19** (Capt) Trapper John McIntyre **24** (Maj) Charles Emerson Winchester
cast: 8 Alan Alda **9** Jamie Farr **11** Harry Morgan, Loretta Swit, Mike Farrell, Wayne Rogers **12** Gary Burghoff **13** Larry Linville **15** McLean Stevenson **16** David Ogden Stiers **18** William Christopher
war: 6 Korean
MASH stands for: 26 Mobile Army Surgical Hospital
tent: 5 Swamp
theme: 17 Suicide Is Painless

M*A*S*H (Film)
director: 12 Robert Altman
cast: 10 Jo Ann Pflug **11** Elliot Gould (Trapper John McIntyre), Tom Skerritt (B J Hunnicut) **12** Gary Burghoff (Radar O'Reilly), Robert Duvall (Frank Burns) **14** Sally Kellerman (Margaret Hot Lips Houlihan) **16** Donald Sutherland (Hawkeye Pierce)

masjid 6 mosque

mask 4 hide, veil **5** blind, cloak, cover **6** domino, screen, shroud **7** conceal, cover-up, curtain, obscure **8** disguise **9** face guard, false face **10** camouflage, keep secret

Mask
director: 16 Peter Bogdanovich
cast: 4 Cher **10** Eric Stoltz (Rocky Dennis), Sam Elliott

masked 9 concealed, covered up, disguised **10** in disguise, masquerade

Masked Ball, A
also: 17 Un Ballo in Maschera
opera by: 5 Verdi
character:
first version: 9 Count Horn **10** King Gustav **12** Count Ribbing
second version: 3 Sam, Tom **13** Count Riccardo

masking 6 hiding **7** veiling **8** covering **9** eclipsing, obscuring **10** concealing, covering up

Mason, Bertha
character in: 8 Jane Eyre
author: 6 Bronte

Mason, James
wife: 6 Pamela
born: 7 England **12** Huddersfield

roles: 6 Lolita **7** Lord Jim **9** Bloodline **10** Georgy Girl **13** Heaven Can Wait **14** Humbert Humbert, Murder by Decree, The Seventh Veil **15** Prisoner of Zenda **16** North by Northwest **17** The Boys from Brazil

Mason, Marsha
husband: 9 Neil Simon
born: 9 St Louis MO
roles: 10 Chapter Two **11** Blume in Love **14** The Goodbye Girl **15** Max Dugan Returns **17** Cinderella Liberty

Masque of the Red Death, The
author: 13 Edgar Allan Poe

masquerade 4 mask, ruse, veil **5** cloak, cover, guise, trick **6** masque, pose as, screen, shroud **7** cover-up, pretext **8** artifice, pretense **9** bal masque **10** camouflage, masked ball, subterfuge **11** impersonate **12** harlequinade

Masquerade Party
host: 9 Bert Parks **10** Bud Collier **11** Peter Donald **12** Eddie Bracken, Robert Q Lewis **14** Douglas Edwards

mass, Mass 3 jam, lot, mob **4** body, bulk, cake, clot, heap, host, hunk, knot, lump, pack, pile **5** amass, batch, block, bunch, chunk, clump, corps, crowd, crush, group, horde, press, stack, troop **6** bundle, gather, matter, throng, weight **7** collect, pyramid **8** assemble, best part, main body, majority, material **9** aggregate, Eucharist, gathering, plurality **10** accumulate, assemblage, assortment, collection, concretion, congregate, cumulation, lion's share **11** aggregation, consolidate, greater part **12** accumulation, congregation **13** Holy Communion, holy sacrament, preponderance **14** conglomeration

Massachusetts
abbreviation: 2 MA **4** Mass
nickname: 3 Bay **7** Puritan **9** Baked Bean, Old Colony
capital/largest city: 6 Boston
others: 4 Ayer, Lynn, Otis **5** Athol, Barre, Lenox, Salem **6** Agawam, Dedham, Groton, Nahant, Natick, Revere, Saugus, Woburn **7** Belmont, Beverly, Concord, Danvers, Everett, Holyoke, Ipswich, Medford, Peabody, Taunton, Waltham **8** Brockton, Chicopee, Cohasset, Plymouth, Scituate, Yarmouth **9** Arlington, Attleboro, Braintree, Brookline, Cambridge, Lexbridge, Lexington, Worcester **10** Gloucester, New Bedford, Pittsfield **11** Springfield **12** Provincetown, Williamstown
college: 3 MIT **5** Clark, Curry, Smith, Tufts **6** Babson **7** Amherst, Harvard, Simmons, Wheaton **8** Brandeis, Williams **9** Hampshire, Holy Cross, Merrimack, Radcliffe, Wellesley **11** Springfield **12** Mount Holyoke, Northeastern **13** Boston College

feature: 10 Walden Pond **12** Plymouth Rock
national seashore: 7 Cape Cod
village: 13 Old Sturbridge
tribe: 6 Nauset **8** Pocomtuc **10** Wampanoags
people: 8 Pilgrims **9** Amy Lowell, Elias Howe **10** Cyrus Field, Eli Whitney **11** Clara Barton, John Hancock, Samuel Adams, Samuel Morse **12** Henry Thoreau, Robert Lowell, Winslow Homer **13** James Whistler, Joseph Kennedy, Robert Kennedy **14** Emily Dickinson **15** Henry Cabot Lodge **16** Benjamin Franklin, Edward "Ted" Kennedy **17** Ralph Waldo Emerson **18** Bartholomew Gosnold, James Russell Lowell, Nathanial Hawthorne **19** Oliver Wendell Holmes, William Cullen Bryant **21** John Greenleaf Whittier
explorer: 8 Norsemen
island: 5 Duke's **9** Nantucket **13** Chappaquidick **15** Martha's Vineyard
lake: 5 Onota **7** Quabbin, Rohunta, Webster **8** Long Pond **11** Watuppa Pond **16** Assawompsett Pond **17** Chaubunagungamaug
land rank: 10 forty-fifth
mountain: 3 Tom **6** Brodie, Potter **7** Alander, Everett, Taconic **10** Berkshires
highest point: 8 Greylock
physical feature:
bay: 8 Buzzard's
cape: 3 Ann, Cod
sea: 8 Atlantic
president: 9 John Adams **14** Calvin Coolidge **15** John Quincy Adams **21** John Fitzgerald Kennedy
river: 6 Nashua **7** Charles, Concord, Quaboag, Taunton **8** Chicopee **9** Deerfield, Merrimack **10** Blackstone, Housatonic **11** Connecticut
state admission: 5 sixth
state bird: 9 chickadee
state flower: 9 mayflower **15** trailing arbutus
state motto: 37 With the Sword She Seeks Peace Under Liberty **45** By the Sword We Seek Peace But Peace Only Under Liberty
state song: 22 All Hail to Massachusetts
state tree: 11 American elm

massacre 7 butcher, carnage **8** butchery, decimate **9** bloodbath, slaughter **10** mass murder **12** bloodletting

massage 3 rub **4** flex **5** chafe, knead **6** finger, handle, stroke **7** rubbing, rub down, stretch **8** kneading, stroking **10** manipulate **12** manipulation

Massasoit see **10** Wampanoags

Massenet, Jules Emile Frederic
born: 6 France **9** St Etienne
composer of: 5 Le Cid, Manon, Thais **7** Werther **9** Herodiade **11** David Rizzio **12** Don Quichotte **13** Le Roi

de Lahore **21** Le Jongleur de Notre-Dame

masses 6 plebes, proles, rabble, the mob **7** the many **8** the crowd **9** hoi polloi, plebeians **11** the populace, the riffraff **12** the multitude **13** the common herd **14** the proletariat, the rank and file **15** the common people, the lower classes, the working class **16** the great unwashed

massive 4 huge, vast **5** ample, bulky, great, heavy, hefty, massy, solid **7** hulking, immense, mammoth, titanic, weighty **8** colossal, enormous, gigantic, imposing, towering, whopping **9** cyclopean, extensive, monstrous, ponderous **10** gargantuan, impressive, monumental, stupendous **11** elephantine, substantial

massiveness 4 bulk, size **6** volume, weight **7** bigness **8** enormity, hugeness, vastness **9** amplitude, bulkiness, greatness, immensity, largeness, magnitude

mast 4 main, nuts, pole, post, spar **5** spirit, staff, stick, stuff **6** acorns, pillar **9** beechnuts, chestnuts
type: 4 fore, main **6** jigger, mizzen
support: 4 bibb

master 3 ace **4** able, A-one, best, boss, curb, deft, head, lord, main, tame, whiz **5** check, chief, crack, grasp, owner, prime, ruler **6** bridle, choice, expert, genius, gifted, govern, leader, manage, subdue, wizard **7** conquer, control, excel at, head man, manager, primary, skilled, skipper, supreme **8** director, dominate, finished, governor, masterly, overcome, overlord, overseer, regulate, suppress, talented, virtuoso **9** authority, conqueror, craftsman, first-rate, paramount, practiced, principal **10** controller, proficient, supervisor **12** get the hang of, ship's captain

Master Builder, The
author: 11 Henrik Ibsen
character: 5 Hilda **7** Solness

master craftsman 7 artisan **12** masterworker **13** skilled worker

masterful 4 able, deft **5** bossy **6** expert, superb **7** dynamic, skilled **8** finished, forceful, masterly, resolute, skillful, virtuoso **9** excellent **10** commanding **11** domineering, self-reliant **12** accomplished, strong-willed **13** authoritarian, self-confident

masterfulness 6 genius **10** capability, competence, excellence **11** proficiency

Master Melvin
nickname of: 6 Mel Ott

mastermind 4 plan, sage **6** direct, expert, genius, master, pundit, wizard **7** old hand, planner **8** conceive, director, engineer, organize, virtuoso **9** authority, initiator, organizer **10** specialist **11** moving force

Master of Ballantrae, The
author: 20 Robert Louis Stevenson
character: 4 Chew **5** Teach **9** MacKellar **11** Henry Durrie, James Durrie **12** Alison Graeme, Francis Burke, Secundra Dass

master of ceremonies 4 host **5** emcee **11** toastmaster

master of the family
Latin: 13 paterfamilias

masterpiece 5 jewel, prize **7** classic, paragon **8** monument, treasure **9** nonpareil **10** brainchild **11** chef d'oeuvre, ne plus ultra, prizewinner

Masterpiece Theater
host: 13 Alistair Cooke

master race
German: 10 Herrenvolk

Masters, Edgar Lee
author of: 19 Spoon River Anthology

Mastersingers of Nuremberg, The
also: 27 Die Meistersinger von Nurnberg
opera by: 6 Wagner
character: 9 Eva Pogner, Hans Sachs **10** Beckmesser **18** Walther von Stolzing

mastery 4 rule, sway **5** grasp **7** ability, command, control **8** deftness, whip hand **9** dominance, supremacy, upper hand **10** adroitness, attainment, domination, leadership **11** achievement, acquirement, proficiency, superiority **14** accomplishment

masticate 4 chew, gnaw **5** chomp, munch **6** nibble

Mastroianni, Marcello
born: 5 Italy **11** Fontana Liri
roles: 13 Eight and a Half **7** La Notte **11** La Dolce Vita, The Stranger, White Nights **19** Divorce Italian Style

mat 3 dim, pad, rug **4** dead, dull, flat **5** doily, muted **6** carpet, matrix, tangle **7** bedding, bolster, coaster, cushion, support **8** entangle **10** lackluster, lusterless
Japanese: 6 tatami

Mata Hari
real name: 21 Gertrud Margarete Zelle
worked as: 3 spy **6** dancer
worked for: 7 Germans
executed by: 6 French

match 3 fit **4** game, join, mate, meet, pair, peer, suit, twin, yoke **5** adapt, agree, equal, event, unite **6** couple, double, oppose **7** be alike, be equal, combine, connect, contend, contest, vie with **8** parallel **9** companion, duplicate, harmonize **10** correspond, equivalent, tournament **11** competition, counterpart

matched 5 equal **8** of a piece **9** identical **11** coordinated

matching 4 twin **5** equal **6** paired

10 equivalent **11** harmonizing **13** corresponding

matchless 4 rare **7** supreme **8** crowning, foremost, peerless, sterling, superior **9** exemplary, first rate, priceless, paramount, unequaled, unmatched, unrivaled **10** invaluable, preeminent, unbeatable, unexcelled **11** inestimable, superlative, unsurpassed **12** incomparable, unparalleled

matchmaker
Yiddish: 8 shadchan **9** schatchen

mate 3 pal **4** chum, twin, wife **5** buddy, crony, hubby, match **6** couple, friend, spouse **7** cohabit, comrade, consort, husband, pair off, partner **8** copulate, coworker, sidekick **9** associate, colleague, companion, duplicate **10** better half, equivalent **11** confederate, counterpart **12** fellow worker, ship's officer

materfamilias 15 mother of a family

material 5 stuff **6** matter **8** elements **9** substance **12** constituents

materialism 5 greed **12** covetousness **15** acquisitiveness

materialistic 6 greedy **8** covetous, grasping **11** acquisitive, unspiritual

materiality 9 existence **11** tangibility

materialization 5 ghost, shade **6** coming, wraith **7** phantom, specter **9** emergence **10** apparition, appearance **13** manifestation

materialize 4 loom, rise, show **5** bob up, issue, pop up **6** appear, crop up, emerge, turn up **9** come forth **10** burst forth **11** come to light, spring forth **12** come into view

materially 7 vitally **8** palpably, tangibly **9** in the main, seriously **10** monetarily **11** corporeally, essentially, financially, in substance **12** considerably, emphatically **13** significantly, substantially **14** for the most part

material possessions 6 assets, estate, wealth **7** fortune **8** property **10** belongings **12** worldly goods

material proof 8 evidence **13** documentation

materials 4 data **5** cloth, facts, notes, tools **6** stocks, stores, timber **7** fabrics, figures **8** concrete, dry goods, supplies, textiles **9** citations, equipment, machinery, yard goods **10** essentials, piece goods, quotations, references **11** impressions **12** observations **15** bricks and mortar

materiel 4 gear **6** stores **8** supplies **9** equipment, materials **10** provisions **16** military supplies

Mater Matuta see **6** Matuta

maternal 4 fond **6** doting **8** motherly **9** of a mother, shielding **10** motherlike, protective, sheltering

maternity 5 labor **8** delivery

9 pregnancy 10 childbirth, motherhood 11 parturition 12 accouchement, childbearing

mathematical, mathematic 5 exact, rigid **6** strict **7** precise **8** accurate, rigorous, unerring **10** meticulous, scientific, scrupulous **11** punctilious, well-defined **13** computational

mathematician
   American: 5 Aiken **6** Wiener
   British: 6 Newton **7** Babbage
   French: 6 Fermat **9** D'Alembert, Descartes
   German: 5 Frege, Gauss **6** Bessel **7** Hilbert
   Greek: 6 Euclid, Thales **11** Anaximander
   Norwegian: 4 Abel
   Swiss: 5 Euler **9** Bernoulli

Mathewson, Christy
   nickname: 5 Matty **6** Big Six
   sport: 8 baseball
   position: 7 pitcher
   team: 13 New York Giants

Matholwych
   king of: 7 Ireland
   wife: 7 Branwen

matinee 9 early show **16** early performance **20** afternoon performance

Mating Season, The
   author: 11 P G Wodehouse

Matisse, Henri Emile Benoit
   born: 6 France **16** Chateau Cambresis (Le Cateau)
   artwork: 5 Dance, Music **8** The Slave **10** Odalisques **11** Joie de Vivre **12** Harmony in Red, La Serpentine **13** Head with Tiara, The Open Window **15** Bathers by a River, Memory of Oceanie, Woman with the Hat **16** Heads of Jeannette **19** Torso with Arms Raised **20** Goldfish and Sculpture

matriarch 7 dowager **10** female head, grande dame **11** female ruler **12** female leader **13** materfamilias

matriculate 4 join **5** enter **6** enlist, enroll, sign up **7** check in **8** register

matriculation 9 signing up **10** enrollment **12** registration

matrimonial 6 bridal, wedded, wifely **7** marital, married, nuptial, spousal **8** conjugal, hymeneal **9** affianced, connubial, husbandly **11** epithalamic

matrimony 7 wedlock **8** marriage **11** holy wedlock

matrix 3 die **4** cast, form, mold **5** frame, punch, stamp

matron 4 dame **5** madam **7** dowager **8** forelady, mistress, overseer **9** forewoman **10** directress **11** housekeeper **12** married woman **14** superintendent

matter 3 fix **4** gist, snag, text **5** count, drift, event, sense, stuff, theme, thing, topic **6** affair, crisis, import, moment, object, scrape, strait, thesis **7** content,

dilemma, episode, essence, purport, signify, subject, trouble **8** argument, business, elements, exigency, material, obstacle, quandary **9** adventure, emergency, happening, situation, substance **10** difference, difficulty, experience, impediment, importance, occurrence, perplexity, proceeding **11** carry weight, consequence, predicament, transaction **12** circumstance, significance

matter-of-course 5 usual **6** common **7** routine **8** everyday, ordinary, standard **9** customary **11** commonplace, established

matter-of-fact 4 real **5** blunt, frank **6** candid, direct **7** factual, literal, mundane, natural, prosaic **8** ordinary, sensible **9** outspoken, practical, pragmatic, realistic **10** hardheaded, no-nonsense, unaffected, uninspired, unromantic **11** commonplace, common-sense, down-to- earth, straightout **13** unimaginative, unsentimental **15** straightforward

matter-of-factness 10 detachment **11** impassivity **12** practicality **13** impassiveness **17** unimaginativeness

Matter of Time, A
   author: 12 Jessamyn West

Matthau, Walter
   real name: 13 Walter Matthow **23** Walter Matuschanskavasky
   born: 9 New York NY
   roles: 5 Kotch **8** A New Leaf **10** Plaza Suite **11** Pete n Tillie **12** Bad News Bears, Ensign Pulver, Grumpy Old Men,Oscar Madison, The Front Page, The Odd Couple **15** California Suite, The Sunshine Boys **16** The Fortune Cookie **22** A Guide for the Married Man

Matthew 7 apostle
   father: 7 Alpheus
   also called: 4 Levi
   wrote: 6 Gospel

Matthiessen, Peter
   author of: 10 Sand Rivers **14** The Snow Leopard

maturation 6 growth **8** fruition, ripening **9** growing up

mature 4 ripe **5** adult, bloom, grown, manly, of age, ready, ripen **6** flower, grow up, mellow, nubile, virile **7** blossom, develop, grown-up, matured, womanly **8** finished, maturate, seasoned **9** come of age, completed, full-blown, full-grown, perfected, practiced **10** middle- aged **11** become adult, experienced, full-fledged, in one's prime **12** marriageable

Mature, Victor
   born: 12 Louisville KY
   roles: 7 The Robe **11** After the Fox, Kiss of Death **12** Cry of the City, One Million BC **16** Samson and Delilah **19** Androcles and the Lion

matured 3 big **4** aged, ripe **5** adult, grown **6** formed **7** ripened **8** flowered, mellowed, seasoned **9** blossomed, developed, full-blown, full-grown **11** full-fledged

maturity 7 manhood **8** legal age, majority, practice, ripeness **9** adulthood, composure, full bloom, readiness, seasoning, womanhood **10** completion, experience, full growth, maturation, matureness, perfection **11** culmination, fulfillment **12** age of consent

Matuta
   origin: 5 Roman
   goddess of: 3 sea **4** dawn **7** harbors **10** childbirth
   called: 11 Mater Matuta

Maud
   author: 18 Alfred Lord Tennyson

Maude
   character: 5 Carol **7** Phillip **10** Henry Evans **12** Florida Evans, Maude Findlay, Mrs Naugatuck **13** Walter Findlay **14** Dr Arthur Harmon **20** Vivian Cavender Harmon
   cast: 8 Bill Macy, John Amos **10** Conrad Bain **11** Esther Rolle **13** Brian Morrison, Rue McClanahan **14** Beatrice Arthur, Kraig Metzinger **15** Adrienne Barbeau **16** Hermione Baddeley
   spinoff from: 14 All in the Family
   spinoff: 9 Good Times

maudlin 5 gushy, mushy, teary **6** slushy **7** gushing, mawkish, tearful **8** bathetic **9** emotional **10** lachrymose **11** sentimental **13** overemotional

maudlinism 6 bathos **11** mawkishness **14** sentimentalism, sentimentality

Maugham, W Somerset
   author of: 9 The Circle **10** Our Betters **11** Cakes and Ale **12** Miss Thompson **13** The Razor's Edge **14** Of Human Bondage **15** The Constant Wife **18** The Moon and Sixpence **21** Lady Frederick Ashenden

maul 4 beat **5** stomp **6** batter, beat up, bruise, mangle, pummel, thrash **7** rough up **9** manhandle **10** knock about

Mauldin, Bill
   creator/artist of: 7 Up Front **12** Willie and Joe

Mau Mau 13 secret society
   of: 6 Kikuyu
   in: 5 Kenya

maunder 4 loaf **5** drift, run on, stray **6** babble, dawdle, gabble, gibber, ramble, wander **7** blather, meander, prattle, saunter **8** flounder, ramble on, straggle **9** go on and on, hem and haw **10** dillydally

maundering 7 diffuse **8** rambling **9** wandering **10** digressive, disjointed, roundabout **14** drift, run on, stray **6** babble, dawdle, gabble, gibber, ramble, wander **7** blather, meander, prattle, saunter **8** flounder, ramble on, straggle **9** go on and on, hem and haw **10** dillydally

Maupassant, Guy de
  author of: 6 Belami **9** Ball of Fat, Mont-Oriol **11** A Woman's Life, The Necklace **12** Ball of Tallow **16** Mademoiselle Fifi

Mauriac, Francois
  author of: 8 Genitrix **10** The Egoists **12** Viper's Tangle **15** A Kiss to the Leper, The Desert of Love **20** A Woman of the Pharisees

Mauritania
  capital/largest city: 10 Nouakchott
  others: 4 Atar **5** Kaedi, Rosso **6** Fderik **7** Akjoujt **10** Nouadhibou
  division: 5 Sahel **7** Chemama
  monetary unit: 5 khoum **7** ouguiya
  highest point: 11 Kediat Idjil
  river: 7 Senegal
  sea: 8 Atlantic
  physical feature:
    desert: 6 Sahara
    valley: 7 Chemama **12** Senegal River
  people: 4 Arab, Fula, Moor **5** Black, Fulbe, Wolof **6** Bafour, Berber, Fulani **7** African, Soninke, Tukulor **8** Sarakole **9** Sarakolle **10** Toucouleur **12** Halphoolaren
    leader: 4 Luly **5** Salek **6** Daddah **8** Haidalla
    ruler: 6 France **9** Almoravid **14** Kingdom of Ghana
  language: 4 Fula **5** Wolof **6** Arabic, French **7** Phoolor, Tukulor **8** Fulfulde, Mandingo **9** Sarakolle, Hassaniya
  religion: 5 Islam
  place:
    mosque: 5 Grand
  feature:
    beehive hut: 4 ruga
    priest-teacher: 8 marabout
    waterskin: 6 guerba
  food:
    dish: 7 meshuri
    tea: 5 attay

Mauritius
  other name: 11 Ile de France
  capital/largest city: 9 Port Louis
  others: 6 Reduit **8** Curepipe **9** Mahebourg **13** Quartre Bornes **19** Grande Riviere Sud-Est
  head of state: 14 British monarch **15** governor general
  monetary unit: 4 cent **5** rupee
  island: 3 Est **4** Flat **5** Ambre, Cerf's, Morne, Round **7** Agalega, Serpent **9** Mauritius, Rodrigues, Rodriguez, St Brandon **12** Gunner's Quoin **15** Cargados Carajos
  highest point: 27 Piton de la Petite Riviere Noire
  sea: 6 Indian
  people: 6 Creole, French, Indian **7** African, Chinese **8** European

13 Indo-Mauritian
  leader: 8 Jugnauth **9** Ramgoolam
  ruler: 5 Dutch **6** French **7** English
  language: 4 Urdu **5** Hindi, Tamil **6** Creole, French

mausoleum 10 family tomb **11** stately tomb **18** sepulchral monument

mauve 4 plum, puce **5** lilac **6** violet **8** lavender **11** light purple **12** bluish purple

maverick 5 loner **8** yearling **9** dissenter, dissident, eccentric **11** independent **13** individualist, noncomformist

Maverick
  character: 12 Bart Maverick, Bret Maverick **13** Brent Maverick **16** Samantha Crawford **24** Cousin Beauregard Maverick
  cast: 9 Jack Kelly **10** Roger Moore **11** James Garner **13** Diane Brewster, Robert Colbert

maw 4 craw, crop, jaws **5** mouth **6** gullet, muzzle, throat

mawkish 5 gushy, mushy, teary **7** maudlin, tearful **9** emotional, nostalgic, schmaltzy **10** lachrymose **11** sentimental **15** oversentimental

mawkishness 4 mush **5** slush **6** bathos **9** mushiness, soppiness **10** maudlinism, slushiness **14** sentimentalism, sentimentality

maxim 3 saw **4** rule **5** adage, axiom, motto **6** old saw, saying, truism **7** proverb **8** aphorism, apothegm **9** platitude

Maximes
  author: 23 Francois La Rochefoucauld

Maxims of the Law
  author: 12 Francis Bacon

maximum 3 top **4** most **6** utmost **7** highest, largest, maximal, optimum, supreme **8** foremost, greatest **9** paramount **11** unsurpassed

Maxwell, Elsa 6 author **7** hostess **9** socialite **10** party-giver **23** "The hostess with the mostes'"

May
  characteristic: 7 Maypole **13** queen of the May
  flower: 8 hawthorn **15** lily of the valley
  French: 3 Mai
  gem: 7 emerald
  German: 3 Mai
  holiday: 6 May Day (1) **10** Mother's Day (2nd Sunday) **11** Memorial Day (last Monday) **14** Armed Forces Day (3rd Saturday)
  Italian: 6 Maggio
  number of days: 9 thirty-one
  origin of name: 4 Maia
    Roman goddess of: 6 spring
  place in year:
    Gregorian: 5 fifth
    Roman: 5 third
  saying: 27 April showers bring May

flowers
  Spanish: 4 Mayo
  Zodiac sign: 6 Gemini, Taurus

May, Elaine
  real name: 12 Elaine Berlin
  partner: 11 Mike Nichols
  born: 14 Philadelphia PA
  roles: 8 A New Leaf **15** California Suite
  director of: 16 The Heartbreak Kid
  writer/director of: 8 A New Leaf

Maya
  city: 4 Coba **5** Tulum, Uxmal **6** Akumal, Cuello, Izamal **8** Calakmul, Palenque **11** Chichen Itza
  conqueror: 8 Alvarado
  day: 5 uayeb
  language family: 5 Mayan **10** Maya-Quiche
  location: 5 Tikal **6** Belize, Mexico **7** Chiapas, Mayapan, Tabasco, Yucatan **8** Honduras **9** Guatemala **11** Chichen Itza **14** Central America
  month: 5 uinal **6** uninal
  noted for: 9 astronomy **12** architecture **19** hieroglyphic writing
  rain god: 4 Chac **5** Chaac **7** Chac Mol **8** Chac Mool
  ruins: 9 Yaxchilan **20** Temple of Inscriptions
  underworld: 7 Xibalba
  year: 4 haab

maybe 6 mayhap **7** perhaps **8** feasibly, possibly **9** perchance **10** God willing, imaginably **11** conceivably **12** peradventure

Maybe
  author: 14 Lillian Hellman

Mayberry RFD
  character: 5 Alice **7** Aunt Bee **8** Sam Jones **9** Mike Jones **10** Goober Pyle **11** Emmett Clark **13** Howard Sprague, Millie Swanson
  cast: 8 Ken Berry **10** Jack Dodson **11** Buddy Foster, Paul Hartman **13** Alice Ghostley, Arlene Golonka, Frances Bavier, George Lindsey

mayfly
  varieties: 5 small **6** stream **9** burrowing

mayhem 4 maim **6** felony **7** battery, cripple **8** mutilate, violence **9** crippling, dismember **10** mutilation **13** disfigurement

may he rest in peace
  Latin: 16 requiescat in pace

may it do good
  Latin: 6 prosit

Maylie, Mrs and Rose
  characters in: 11 Oliver Twist
  author: 7 Dickens

Mayo, Virginia
  real name: 13 Virginia Jones
  husband: 12 Michael O'Shea
  born: 9 St Louis MO
  roles: 17 The West Point Story

22 The Best Years of Our Lives **26** The Secret Life of Walter Mitty

Mayor of Casterbridge, The
  author: 11 Thomas Hardy
  character: 13 Donald Farfrae, Richard Newson 14 Lucetta Le Sueur 15 Michael Henchard 19 Elizabeth Jane Newson, Susan Henchard-Newson

Mays, Willie
  nickname: 9 Say Hey Kid
  sport: 8 baseball
  position: 11 center field
  team: 11 New York Mets 13 New York Giants 18 San Francisco Giants

may she live forever
  Latin: 12 esto perpetua
  motto of: 5 Idaho

may she rest in peace
  Latin: 16 requiescat in pace

maze 5 snarl 6 jungle, tangle 7 complex, meander, network 9 labyrinth 11 convolution

mazel tov 8 good luck

Mbabane
  capital of: 9 Swaziland

McBeal, Ally *see* 10 Ally McBeal

McCambridge, Mercedes
  real name: 32 Carlotta Mercedes Agnes McCambridge
  born: 8 Joliet IL
  roles: 5 Giant 8 Cimarron 11 Touch of Evil 14 All the King's Men 15 A Farewell to Arms 18 Suddenly Last Summer

McCarey, Leo
  director of: 8 Duck Soup 10 Going My Way (Oscar) 13 The Awful Truth (Oscar) 15 Ruggles of Red Gap 17 The Bells of St Mary's

McCarthy, Mary
  author of: 8 The Group
  sister of: 5 Kevin

McCay, Winsor
  creator/artist of: 23 Little Nemo in Slumberland

McClellan, George B
  nickname: 25 Little Mac the Young Napoleon
  served in: 8 Civil War 10 Mexican War
  side: 5 Union
  commander of: 16 Army of the Potomac
  battle: 8 Antietam 18 Peninsular campaign
  governor of: 9 New Jersey

McCloud
  character: 10 Sam McCloud 13 Chris Coughlin, (Sgt) Joe Broadhurst 14 Peter B Clifford
  cast: 8 JD Cannon 11 Terry Carter 12 Dennis Weaver, Diana Muldaur

McClure, Darrell
  creator/artist of: 17 Little Annie Rooney

McCrea, Joel
  wife: 10 Frances Dee
  born: 12 Los Angeles CA
  roles: 11 Buffalo Bill 14 Palm Beach Story 16 Sullivan's Travels, The Great Man's Lady 17 Reaching for the Sun, The More the Merrier 20 Foreign Correspondent

McCreary, Fainy (Mac)
  character in: 3 USA
  author: 9 Dos Passos

McCullers, Carson
  author of: 17 The Mortgaged Heart 18 Member of the Wedding 21 The Ballad of the Sad Cafe 23 Reflections in a Golden Eye, The Heart Is a Lonely Hunter

McCullough, Colleen
  author of: 13 The Thornbirds 19 An Indecent Obsession

McCutcheon, George Barr
  author of: 9 Graustark

McEvoy, JP
  creator/artist of: 10 Dixie Dugan

McFee, William
  author of: 15 Casuals of the Sea

McGinley, Phyllis
  author of: 12 Three Decades 15 A Pocketful of Wry 24 The Horse Who Lived Upstairs

McHale's Navy
  character: 7 Christy 9 Willy Moss 11 Fuji Kobiaji, Happy Haines 12 Harrison (Tinker) Bell, Lester Gruber 13 Virgil Farrell, (Ensign) Charles Parker, (Lt Cdr) Quinton McHale 14 (Lt) Elroy Carpenter 18 (Capt) Wallace B Binghamton
  cast: 8 Joe Flynn 9 Tim Conway 10 Billy Sands, Gary Vinson, John Wright, Yoshio Yoda 11 Bob Hastings, Edson Stroll 12 Gavin MacLeod 14 Carl Ballantine, Ernest Borgnine

McKenna, Siobhan
  born: 7 Belfast, Ireland
  roles: 11 King of Kings 13 Doctor Zhivago 14 Of Human Bondage 24 Playboy of the Western World

McKim, Charles M
  architect of: 27 Lutheran Church of the Redeemer (Houston)

McKim, Mead, and White
  partners: 13 Stanford White 18 Charles Follen McKim 21 William Rutherford Mead
  architects of: 11 Century Club 14 University Club, Washington Arch 17 Vanderbilt Mansion 18 Columbia University (NYC) 19 Boston Public Library, Pennsylvania Station (NYC), (first) Madison Square Garden (NYC) 21 New York Herald Building, Pierpont Morgan Library (NYC) 31 Madison Square Presbyterian Church
  style: 7 Shingle 18 Italian Renaissance

McKinley, William
  nickname: 13 Major McKinley
  presidential rank: 11 twenty-fifth
  party: 10 Republican
  state represented: 2 OH
  defeated: 4 (Eugene Victor) Debs 5 (Seth Hockett) Ellis, (William Jennings) Bryan 6 (John McCauley) Palmer, (Wharton) Barker 7 (Charles Eugene) Bentley, (John Granville) Woolley, (Jonah Fitz Randolph) Leonard 8 (Charles Horatio) Matchett, (Joseph Francis) Malloney, (Joshua) Levering
  vice president: 6 (Garret Augustus) Hobart 9 (Theodore) Roosevelt
  cabinet:
    state: 3 (John Milton) Hay, (William Rufus) Day 7 (John) Sherman
    treasury: 4 (Lyman Judson) Gage
    war: 4 (Elihu) Root 5 (Russell Alexander) Alger
    attorney general: 4 (Philander Chase) Knox 6 (John William) Griggs 7 (Joseph) McKenna
    navy: 4 (John Davis) Long
    postmaster general: 4 (James Albert) Gary 5 (Charles Emory) Smith
    interior: 5 (Cornelius Newton) Bliss 9 (Ethan Allen) Hitchcock
    agriculture: 6 (James) Wilson
  born: 7 Niles OH
  died: 9 Buffalo NY
    died by: 13 assassination
  buried: 8 Canton OH
  education:
    college: 10 Allegheny
    law school: 6 Albany
  religion: 9 Methodist
  author: 37 The Tariff in the Days of Henry Clay and Since
  political career: 24 US House of Representatives
    governor of: 4 Ohio
  civilian career: 6 lawyer
  military service: 7 captain 8 Civil War 11 brevet major
  notable events of lifetime/term:
    Act: 13 Dingley Tariff
    Peace Conference: 5 Hague
    Treaty of: 5 Paris
    war with: 5 Spain
  father: 7 William
  mother: 5 Nancy (Campbell Allison)
  siblings: 4 Anna, Mary 5 Abner, Helen, James 10 Abbie Celia 12 David Allison 14 Sarah Elizabeth
  wife: 3 Ida (Saxton)
  children: 3 Ida 9 Katherine

McManus, George
  creator/artist of: 12 The Newlyweds 16 Bringing Up Father

McMillan, Edwin Mattison
  field: 7 physics 9 chemistry
  developed: 16 synchrocyclotron
  awarded: 10 Nobel Prize

McMillan and Wife
  character: 7 Mildred 13 Sally McMil-

Ian 14 (Sgt) Charles Enright 15 (Commissioner) Stewart McMillan **cast: 10** John Schuck, Rock Hudson **11** Nancy Walker **15** Susan Saint James

McMurtry, Larry
author of: 10 Texasville **12** Lonesome Dove **14** Horseman Pass By **18** The Last Picture Show

McPhee, John
author of: 16 In Suspect Terrain **20** Coming into the Country **23** The Curve of Binding Energy **26** Encounters with the Archdruid

McQueen, Steve
real name: 21 Terrence Steven McQueen
wife: 10 Ali MacGraw
born: 8 Slater MO **14** Indianapolis IN
roles: 7 Bullitt, The Blob **8** Papillon **14** The Great Escape, The Sand Pebbles **16** The Cincinnati Kid **17** Thomas Crown Affair, Wanted Dead or Alive **19** The Magnificent Seven

McTeague
author: 11 Frank Norris

mea culpa 7 my fault **14** through my fault

Mead, Margaret
author of: 14 My Earlier Years **16** Blackberry Winter **18** Coming of Age in Samoa **20** Growing Up in New Guinea **42** Sex and Temperament in Three Primitive Societies
husband: 14 Gregory Bateson

Meade, Dr and Mrs
characters in: 15 Gone With the Wind
author: 8 Mitchell

Meade, George Gordon
served in: 8 Civil War **10** Mexican War
side: 5 Union
battle: 7 Bull Run **8** Antietam **10** Gettysburg **13** South Mountain **14** Fredericksburg **16** Chancellorsville **18** Peninsular campaign
commander of: 16 Army of the Potomac

meadow 3 lea **4** mead, park **5** field, green **6** forage **7** herbage, pasture, savanna **9** grassland, pasturage

meager 4 bare, lean, slim, thin **5** scant, short, spare, token **6** little, paltry, scanty, scarce, skimpy, slight, sparse **7** scrimpy, slender, stinted, wanting **9** deficient **10** inadequate **12** insufficient **13** insubstantial

meagerness 8 sparsity **9** smallness **10** inadequacy, measliness, scantiness, skimpiness, sparseness **13** insufficiency **14** insignificance

Meagles
character in: 12 Little Dorrit
author: 7 Dickens

meal 4 bran, chow, diet, eats, fare, food, grub, menu **5** feast, flour, grits

6 farina, groats, repast, spread **7** banquet, cooking, cuisine, oatmeal **8** cornmeal, victuals **10** bill of fare **11** nourishment, refreshment

mealymouthed 6 unsure **7** devious **8** hesitant **9** deceptive, insincere

mean 3 low, par, say **4** base, evil, norm, plan, poor, rude, rule, vile, want, wish **5** aim at, cheap, close, cruel, imply, nasty, petty, small, tight, venal **6** denote, flimsy, greedy, hint at, intend, malign, medium, menial, normal, paltry, sleazy, sordid, stingy, tell off, trashy, unfair **7** average, balance, betoken, dream of, drive at, express, hoggish, inhuman, miserly, point to, propose, purpose, regular, resolve, selfish, signify, squalid, suggest, think of, trivial, vicious **8** aspire to, gimcrack, grasping, indicate, inferior, inhumane, intimate, low-grade, picayune, piddling, pitiless, rubbishy, say truly, shameful, standard, stand for, trifling, uncaring, wretched **9** illiberal, low-paying, malicious, mercenary, merciless, miserable, niggardly, penurious, symbolize, unfeeling **10** avaricious, compromise, despicable, have in mind, have in view, jerry-built, low-ranking, malevolent, pinchpenny, second-rate, ungenerous, villainous **11** closefisted, commonplace, disgraceful, happy medium, hardhearted, self-seeking, small-minded, tightfisted, unimportant **12** contemptible, disagreeable, dishonorable **13** insignificant, unsympathetic **15** inconsequential

meander 4 loop, rove, wind **5** snake, stray, twist **6** circle, ramble, spiral, wander, zigzag **8** undulate **9** convolute, corkscrew

meandering 7 devious, sinuous, turning, winding **8** indirect, rambling, tortuous, twisting **9** wandering **10** circuitous, roundabout, serpentine

meaning 3 aim, end **4** gist, goal, hint, meat, pith, plan, view **5** drift, force, point, sense, value, worth **6** burden, design, intent, object, scheme, thrust, upshot **7** content, essence, pointer, purport, purpose **9** intention, substance **10** denotation, indication, intimation, suggestion **11** implication **12** significance **15** sum and substance

meaningful 4 deep **5** meaty, pithy **6** useful **7** pointed, serious **8** eloquent, explicit, pregnant **9** designing, important **10** expressive, gratifying, portentous, purposeful, suggestive, worthwhile **11** significant, substantial **13** consequential

meaningless 5 trite **6** absurd, paltry, stupid **7** aimless, fatuous, foolish, idiotic, shallow, trivial, useless **8** baffling, piddling, puzzling **9** enigmatic, facetious, frivolous, illegible, sense-

less, valueless, worthless **10** incoherent, mystifying, perplexing **11** bewildering, inscrutable, nonsensical, purposeless, unessential, unimportant **12** impenetrable, inexplicable, inexpressive, preposterous **13** insignificant, unsubstantial **14** undecipherable

Mean Joe
nickname of: 9 Joe Greene

means 3 way **4** jack, mode **5** bread, dough, funds, money **6** avenue, course, income, method, resort, riches, wealth **7** capital, dollars, measure, process, revenue **8** property **9** affluence, long green, resources, substance **11** alternative, wherewithal

mean-spirited 3 low **4** base, poor, vile **5** cheap, nasty, petty, small, snide, sorry, tight, venal **6** abject, measly, paltry, scurvy, shabby, sordid, stingy **7** ignoble, miserly, selfish, vicious **8** tightwad, wretched **9** miserable, penurious **10** ungenerous **12** parsimonious

Mean Streets
director: 14 Martin Scorsese
cast: 11 Amy Robinson, David Proval **12** Harvey Keitel, Robert DeNiro

meantime 7 interim **8** interval **9** meanwhile

meanwhile 8 meantime **12** concurrently, in the interim **13** at the same time **14** simultaneously

measurable 10 assessable, computable, mensurable, reckonable **11** appraisable **12** determinable

measure 3 act, law **4** bill, plan, rule, size, step, time **5** bound, clock, gauge, judge, limit, means, plumb, quota, range, scale, scope, share, sound, value **6** amount, assess, course, degree, design, extent, method, resort, scheme, survey **7** portion, project **8** appraise, evaluate, proposal, quantity **9** allotment, allowance, enactment, procedure, restraint, yardstick **10** limitation, moderation, proceeding, temperance

measure, unit of
of Afghanistan: 3 paw, sir **5** jerib, karoh **6** khurds **7** kharwar
of Algeria: 3 pik **5** rebis, tarri **6** termin
of Argentina: 4 sino **5** legua **6** cuadra, lastre **7** manzana
of Australia: 4 arna, naut, saum
of Austria: 4 fass, fuss, joch, mass, muth, yoke **5** halbe, linie, meile, metze, pfiff, punkt **6** achtel, becher, leipoa, seidel **7** klafter, viertel **8** dreiling **12** futtermassel
of Belgium: 3 vat **4** aune, pied **5** carat **6** perche **8** boisseau
of Bolivia: 6 league **7** celemin
of Borneo: 7 gantang
of Brazil: 2 pe **4** moio, sack, vara **5** braca, legoa, milha, tonel **6** canada,

cuarto, quarto, tarefa **7** garrafa **8** alqueire
of Bulgaria: 3 oka, oke **5** krine, lekhe, likhe
of Canada: 3 ton **5** minot, perch, point **6** arpent **7** chainon
of the Canary Islands: 8 fanegada
of Chile: 4 vara **5** legua, linea **6** cuadra **7** fanega
of China: 3 cho, fan, fen, pau, tou, tun, yan, yin **4** chek, chih, fang, kish, papa, quei, shih, teke, tsan, tsun **5** catty, chang, ching, sheng, shing **6** chupak, gungli, kungho, kungmu, tching **7** kungfen, kungyin **8** kungchih, kungshih **9** kungching
of Colombia: 4 vara **7** azumbre, celemin
of Costa Rica: 4 vara **5** cafiz, cahiz **6** fanega, tercia **7** cajuela, cantaro, manzana **10** caballeria
of Cuba: 4 vara **5** bocoy, cocoy, tarea **6** cordel, fanega **10** caballeria
of former Czechoslovakia: 3 lan **4** mira **5** korec, liket, stopa **6** merice, strych
of Denmark: 3 ell, fod, mil, pot **4** alen **5** album, anker, kande, linje, paegl **7** landmil, oltonde, ortonde, skieppe, viertel **8** fjerding **9** ottingkar **10** korntonde
of the Dominican Republic: 3 ona **5** tarea **6** fanega
of Ecuador: 5 libra **6** cuadra, fanega
of Egypt: 3 apt, dra, hen, rob **4** arab, dira, draa, khet, nief, ocha, roub, theb, wudu **5** abdat, ardab, cubit, farde, fedan, keleh, kerat, kilah, sahme **6** artaba, aurure, baladi, kantar, keddah, robhah, schene **7** choryos, daribah, malouah, roubouh, toumnah **8** kassabah, kharouba **10** diramimari, diribaladi
of El Salvador: 4 vara **5** cafiz, cahiz **6** fanega **7** batella, botella, cantara, manzana
of England: 3 cut, ell, lea, pin, rod, ton, tun, vat **4** acre, bind, butt, comb, coom, cran, foot, gill, goad, hand, hank, heer, hide, inch, last, line, mile, nail, pace, palm, peck, pint, pipe, pole, pool, rood, rope, sack, seam, span, trug, typp, wist, yard, yoke **5** bodge, chain, cubit, digit, float, floor, fluid, hutch, jugum, minim, ounce, perch, point, prime, quart, skein, stack, truss **6** barrel, bovate, bushel, cranne, fathom, firkin, gallon, hobbet, hobbit, league, manent, oxgang, pottle, runlet, square, strike, sulung, thread, tierce **7** auchlet, furlong, kenning, quarter, rundlet, seamile, spindle, tertian, virgate **8** carucate, chaldron, hogshead, landyard, puncheon, quadrant, standard
of Estonia: 3 tun **4** elle, liin, sund, toll, toop **5** verst **6** sagene, versta

7 kulimet **8** tonnland
of Ethiopia: 3 tat **4** cubi, kuba **5** derah, messe **6** cabaho, sinjer, sinzer, tanica **7** entelam, farsakh, farsang, ghebeta
of Finland: 5 kannu, verst **6** fathom, kannor **8** ottinger, skalpund, tunnland
of France: 3 pot, sac **4** aune, mine, pied, velt **5** arpen, carat, ligne, minot, pinte, point, pouce, velte **6** arpent, hemine, league, quarte, setier
of Greece: 3 pik **4** bema, piki, pous **5** baril, chous, cubit, diote, doron, maris, pekhe, podos, pygon, xylon **6** acaena, bacile, barile, cotula, dichas, gramme, hemina, koilon, lichas, milion, orgyia, palame, pechys, schene, xestes **7** bacvhel, chenica, choenix, cyathos, diaulos, metreta, stadium, stremma **8** condylos, daktylos, dekapode, dolichos, medimnos, medimnys, metretes, palaiste, plethron, plethrum, stathmos **9** hemiekton, oxybaphon
of Guatemala: 4 vara **6** cuarta, tercia **7** cajuela, manzana **10** caballeria
of Guinea: 7 jacktan
of Honduras: 4 vara **5** milla **6** mecate **7** cajuela
of Hungary: 3 ako **4** hold, yoke **5** itcze, marok, metze **7** huvelyk
of Iceland: 3 set **4** alin **5** almud **6** almenn, ferfet, pottur **7** fathmur, fermila, oltunna
of India: 3 ady, gaz, gez, jow, lan **4** byee, coss, depa, doph, hath, koss, kunk, raik, rati, seit, taun, tola **5** bigha, covid, crosa, danda, depoh, drona, erosa, garce, hasta, krosa, parah, ratti, salay, yojan **6** adhaka, amunam, covido, cudava, cumbha, geerah, moolum, mushti, ouroub, palgat, parran, prasha, ropani, tipree, unglee, yojana **7** dhanush, gavyuti, khahoon, niranga, prastha **8** okthabah
of Indonesia: 5 depah, depoh
of Iran: 3 gaz, zar, zer **4** cane **5** gareh, kafiz, makuk, qasab **6** charac, chebel, ghalva **7** capicha, chenica, farsakh, mansion, mishara **8** parasang, piamaneh, stathmos
of Ireland: 4 mile **6** bandle **8** crannock
of Israel: 3 cab, car, hin, kab, kor **4** bath, ezba, omer, reed **5** cubit, donum, dunam, ephah, ganeh, homer, kaneh
of Italy: 3 pie **4** orna **5** palma, palmo, punto, salma, stero **6** barile, miglie, moggio, rubbio, tomolo **7** braccio, secchio **8** giornata, quadrato
of Japan: 2 go **3** boo, cho, djo, fun, inc, ken, kin, kon, rin, shi, sho, sun, tan **4** hiro, isse, kati, koku, niyo, shoo **5** carat, catty, issho, ittan, momme, picul, shaku **6** kwamme

8 hiyak-kin **9** hiyak-hiro **11** kommaichida, kujira-shaku
of Java: 3 kan **4** paal, rand **5** palen
of Kenya: 4 wari
of Laos: 3 bak
of Latvia: 3 let **4** stof **5** stoff, verst **6** arshin, kulmet **7** verchoc, verchok **8** krouchka, pourvete **9** deciatine, lofstelle, pourvette **10** tonnseteel
of Liberia: 4 kuba
of Libya: 3 dra, pik, saa **4** kele **5** bozze, donum, jabia, teman, uckia **6** barile, gorrah, misura **7** mattaro, termino **8** kharouba
of Luxembourg: 5 fuder
of Madagascar: 7 gantang
of Malaysia: 3 pau, tun **4** para, pipe, tael, wang **5** parah **6** chupak, parrah **7** gantang
of Malta: 4 rotl **5** artal, canna, parto, ratel, salma **6** kantar **7** caffiso
of Mexico: 3 bag, pie **4** alma, onza, vara **5** almud, baril, carga, jarra, labor, legua, libra, linea, marco, sitio **6** adarme, almude, arroba, carega, fanega, ochaua, terceo **7** pulgada, quintal **9** cuarteron, cuartillo **10** caballeria
of Morocco: 4 kala, muhd, rotl, saah, sahh, ueba **5** artal, cadee, gerbe, ratel **6** covado, dirhem, fanega, izenbi, kintar, tangin, tomini **8** quintral
of Myanmar: 2 ly **3** dha, gon, mau, sao, tao, tat **4** byee, phan, seit, taun, that **5** shita, thuoc **6** lamany, palgat **7** chaivai **8** okthabah
of the Netherlands: 2 el **3** aam, ahm, ell, kan, vat **4** duim, mijl, rood, rope **5** anker, roede, wisse **6** bunder, legger, maatje, mutsje, streep **7** schepel **8** mimgelen, steekkan
of Nicaragua: 4 vara **5** cahiz **6** suerte **7** cajuela, manzana **10** cabelleria
of Norway: 3 fot, mal **4** alen **5** kande **6** fathom **7** skieppe **9** korntonde
of Panama: 7 celemin
of Paraguay: 3 pie **4** lino, lira, lire, vara **5** legua **6** cuadra, fanega
of Peru: 4 topo **5** galon **7** celemin **8** fanegada
of the Philippines: 4 loan **5** braza, catty, cavan, chupa, fardo, ganta, picul, punto **6** apatan, balita, lachsa, quinon **7** quilate **8** chinanta
of Poland: 3 cal **4** mila, pret **5** morga, sazen, vloka, wloka **6** cwierc, cwierk, kwarta, lokiec **7** garniec **9** kwarterka
of Portugal: 2 pe **4** bota, moio, vara **5** almud, fanga, geira, linha, milha **6** almude, covado **7** alquier, ferrado, selamin **8** alqueire
of Puerto Rico: 6 cuerda **10** cabelleria
of Rumania: 7 faltche
of Russia: 3 fut, lof **4** duim, fass, loof, pood, quar, stof **5** duime, foute,

korec, korek, ligne, osmin, pajak, st-off, stoof, vedro, verst **6** charka, liniya, osmina, paletz, sagene, stekar, tchast, tsarki, versta, verste **7** archine, arsheen, botchka, chkalik, garnetz, verchoc, verchok **8** boutylka, chetvert, krouchka, kroushka **9** chetverik **10** dessiatine **11** polugarnetz

of Scotland: 3 cop **4** boll, cran, fall, mile, peck, pint, rood, rope, span **5** crane, lippy **6** audlet, davach, firlot, lippie, noggin **7** chalder, choppin **8** mutchkin, stimpart, stimpert **9** particate, shaftment, shathmont

of Sicily: 5 salma **7** caffiso

of Sierra Leone: 4 load **6** kettle

of Somalia: 3 top **4** caba **5** chela, darat, tabla **6** cubito **8** parsalah

of South Africa: 4 vara

of Spain: 3 pie **4** codo, dedo, paso, vara **5** braza, cahiz, carga, legua, medio, palmo, sesma **6** cordel, cuarta, fanega, racion, yugada **7** azumbre, celemin, estadel, pulgada **8** fanegada

of Sri Lanka: 4 para, seer **5** parah **6** amunam, parrah

of Sudan: 2 ud

of Suriname: 7 ketting

of Sweden: 3 aln, fot, ref, tum **4** alar, amar, famn, kapp, last, stop **5** carat, foder, kanna, linje, nymil, spann **6** fathom, jumfru **7** oxhuvud, tunland **8** fjarding, koltunna, tunnland

of Switzerland: 3 imi, pot **4** aune, fuss, muid, pied, zoll **5** lieue, linie, maass, pouce, staab, toise **6** perche, strich **7** klafter, viertel **9** quarteron **10** holzlafter **11** holzklafter

of Syria: 5 makuk **6** garava

of Thailand: 2 wa **3** can, ken, niv, rai, sat, sok, wah **4** cohi, keup, niou, tang **5** kwien, leeng, sesti, vouah **6** kabiet, kanahn **7** chaimeu **8** changawn **9** anukabiet

of Tunisia: 3 saa **4** saah **5** cafiz **6** mettar **8** milerole

of Turkey: 3 dra, oka, pik **4** draa, khat, kile, zira **5** berri, kileh, zirai **6** arshin, chinik, fortin, halebi **7** nocktat

of Uruguay: 4 vara **6** cuadra, suerte

of Venezuela: 5 galon, milla **6** fanega **7** estadel

of Vietnam: 4 gang, phan, thon

of Wales: 5 cover **7** cantred, crannoc, listred

of Yugoslavia: 3 oka, rif **4** akov, ralo **5** donum, khvat, lanaz, plaze, stopa **6** motyka, ralico **9** danoranja

measured 5 equal, exact **6** steady **7** precise, regular, studied, uniform **8** verified **10** calculated, deliberate **11** cold-blooded, intentional, well-planned **12** premeditated **13** predetermined

Measure for Measure

author: 18 William Shakespeare

character: 5 Lucio **6** Angelo, Juliet **7** Claudio, Escalus, Mariana **8** Isabella **9** Vincentio

measureless 7 endless **8** infinite **9** boundless, unlimited **12** immeasurable

measurement 4 area, mass, size **5** depth, width **6** extent, height, length, volume, weight **7** breadth, content, gauging **8** capacity, plumbing, sounding **9** amplitude, appraisal, dimension, magnitude, measuring, reckoning, surveying **10** assessment, estimation, evaluation **11** mensuration

Biblical: 4 omer **5** cubit, ephah **6** shekel

champagne: 6 magnum **8** jeroboam, rehoboam **9** balthazar **10** methuselah, salmanazar **14** Nebuchadnezzar

cloth: 4 bolt

cotton: 4 bale

electricity: 3 ohm **4** volt, watt **5** joule **6** ampere **10** horsepower

energy: 3 BTU **5** joule **7** calorie **11** kilocalorie **18** British thermal unit

firewood: 4 cord

force: 4 dyne **6** newton **7** poundal

gold/jewelry: 5 carat, karat, point

Greek: 4 mina **5** cubit **6** obolos, talent **7** drachma, stadion

gun: 5 gauge **7** caliber

light: 7 candela **11** candlepower

liquor/spirits: 4 pint, pony, shot **5** fifth, quart **6** jigger, magnum

metric system: 5 liter, meter **9** deciliter, decimeter, dekaliter, dekameter, kiloliter, kilometer, nanometer **10** centiliter, centimeter, cubic meter, hectoliter, hectometer, milliliter, millimeter **11** square meter **14** cubic dekameter **15** cubic centimeter, cubic millimeter, square decimeter, square dekameter, square kilometer **16** square centimeter, square hectometer, square millimeter

metric weight: 3 ton **4** gram **5** tonne **7** quintal **8** dekagram, kilogram **9** centigram, hectogram, microgram, milligram

paper: 4 ream **5** quire

pressure: 6 pascal **10** atmosphere

Roman: 2 as **5** cubit, libra **6** pondus **7** stadium

sound: 7 decibel

temperature: 6 degree, Kelvin **7** Celsius **10** Fahrenheit

time: 3 day **4** hour, week, year **5** month, score **6** decade, minute, second **7** century **10** millennium, nanosecond **11** microsecond, millisecond

typography: 2 em, en **4** pica **5** point

unit: 3 cup, rod **4** acre, dram, foot, gill, inch, link, mile, peck, pint, yard **5** chain, minim, ounce, quart **6** barrel, bushel, circle, degree, fathom, gallon **7** furlong, hectare **8** angstrom, hogshead, teaspoon **9** cubic foot, cubic inch, cubic yard, square rod **10** fluid ounce, right angle, square foot, square inch, square mile, square yard, tablespoon **25** international nautical mile

weight: 3 ton **4** dram **5** grain, ounce, pound **7** scruple **8** short ton **9** ounce troy, pound troy **11** pennyweight **13** hundredweight

measure out 6 ration **7** dole out, mete out **9** apportion

meat 3 nut **4** core, fare, food, gist, grub **5** heart, point **6** kernel **7** edibles, essence, nucleus **8** victuals **9** provender, substance **10** provisions, sustenance **11** comestibles, nourishment

mechanic 6 joiner **7** artisan **9** automatic, craftsman, machinist **11** uninspired **12** grease monkey

mechanical 4 cold **7** routine **9** automatic, unfeeling **10** impersonal, self-acting, unthinking **11** instinctive, involuntary, machinelike, perfunctory, unconscious **13** machine-driven

mechanism 4 tool **5** motor, works **7** machine, utensil **9** apparatus, appliance, implement, machinery **10** instrument **11** contrivance

medal 5 award, honor, prize **6** laurel, reward, ribbon, trophy **8** citation **9** medallion **10** decoration

Medawar, Peter Brian
  field: 7 biology
  nationality: 7 British
  discovered: 23 acquired immune tolerance
  awarded: 10 Nobel Prize

meddle 5 mix in **6** butt in, horn in, kibitz **7** intrude, pry into **9** interfere, interlope, intervene **10** tamper with

meddler 3 pry **5** snoop **7** Paul Pry **8** busybody **10** interferer, Nosy Parker

meddlesome 4 nosy **5** pushy **6** prying, snoopy **7** pushing **8** meddling, snooping **9** intrusive, obtrusive, officious **11** impertinent, interfering **12** presumptuous

Medea
  author: 9 Euripides
  character: 5 Creon, Jason **6** Aegeus, Glauce

Medea
  form: 9 sorceress
  father: 6 Aeetes
  mother: 5 Idyia
  aunt: 5 Circe
  brother: 8 Apsyrtus
  sister: 9 Chalciope
  lover: 5 Jason
  son: 6 Medeus, Pheres **8** Mermerus, Tisander **9** Alcimenes, Thessalus
  killed: 7 her sons
  escaped to: 6 Athens

Medeus
  father: 6 Aegeus
  mother: 5 Medea

Media 14 ancient kingdom
  present day: 4 Iran

capital: 8 Ecbatana
King: 6 Darius, Xerxes **9** Ahasueras
inhabitant: 4 Mede **5** Aryan **7** Persian **8** Parthian
media 5 press, radio **9** magazines **10** billboards, journalism, newspapers, television **11** journalists
  singular: 6 medium
medial 4 mean **6** median **7** average
median 3 mid, par **4** mean, norm **5** mesne **6** center, medial, medium, middle **7** average, central, halfway **8** middling, midpoint, moderate **12** intermediate
mediate 6 pacify, step in, umpire **7** referee **8** moderate **9** arbitrate, intercede, interpose, intervene, negotiate, reconcile **10** conciliate, propitiate
mediation 6 parley **10** adjustment, com- promise, discussion **11** arbitration, give- and-take, negotiation, peacemaking **12** conciliation, intercession, intervention, pacification **14** reconciliation
mediator 6 umpire **7** referee **9** go-between, moderator **10** arbitrator, negotiator, peacemaker, reconciler **12** intermediary
medical 7 healing **8** curative, remedial, salutary, sanative **9** medicinal **10** medicative **11** restorative, therapeutic
medical abbreviation
  a c: 11 before meals
  ad lib: 8 as needed **9** as desired
  agit: 5 shake
  aq: 5 water
  b i d: 9 twice a day
  cap: 4 take **7** capsule
  coch: 8 spoonful
  dil: 6 dilute **8** dissolve
  fldxt: 12 fluid extract
  ft: 4 make
  ft mist: 12 make a mixture
  ft pulv: 11 make a powder
  gr: 5 grain
  gt: 4 drop
  gtt: 5 drops
  h s: 9 at bedtime
  in d: 5 daily
  lot: 6 lotion
  mod praesc: 21 in the manner prescribed
  O: 4 pint
  O D: 8 right eye
  O S: 7 left eye
  O U: 9 in each eye
  ol: 3 oil
  p c: 9 after food **10** after meals
  p o: 7 by mouth
  p r n: 25 as circumstances may require
  pil: 3 pill
  pulv: 6 powder
  q i d: 14 four times daily
  rep: 6 repeat
  s o s: 11 if necessary
  ss: 7 one half

  tab: 6 tablet
  t i d: 15 three times daily
  ut dict: 10 as directed
Medical Center
  character: 9 (Dr) Joe Gannon **11** Nurse Wilcox, (Dr) Paul Lochner **13** Nurse Chambers **14** Nurse Courtland, (Dr) Jeanne Bartlett
  cast: 9 James Daly **11** Chad Everett, Chris Hutson **12** Audrey Totter, Jayne Meadows **14** Corinne Camacho
medical practitioner 6 doctor, medico **9** physician
medication 4 balm **5** tonic **6** elixir, remedy **7** nostrum, panacea **8** medicine **10** medicament, palliative **11** restorative
Medici, Giovanni de' 8 Pope Leo X **15** Pope Leo the Tenth
Medici, Giulio 14 Pope Clement VII **21** Pope Clement the Seventh
medicine 4 balm, drug, pill **5** salve, tonic **6** remedy **7** nostrum **10** healing art, medication **11** restorative **12** therapeutics **13** materia medica
  god of: 9 Asclepius **11** Aesculapius
medieval 8 Dark Ages **10** antiquated, Middle Ages **12** old-fashioned **14** pre-Renaissance
mediocre 4 so-so **5** petty **6** common, meager, medium, normal, paltry, slight **7** average **8** inferior, ordinary, passable, trifling **9** tolerable **10** negligible, pedestrian, second-rate **11** commonplace, indifferent, unimportant **12** run-of-the-mill **13** inappreciable, insignificant **14** fair- to-middling, inconsiderable **15** inconsequential, undistinguished
mediocrity 8 poorness **9** pettiness **10** low-quality, meagerness, paltriness, triviality **11** inferiority **12** indifference, ordinariness, unimportance **14** insignificance **15** commonplaceness
meditate 4 muse, plan **5** aim at, study, think **6** devise, ponder **7** concoct, dream of, propose, reflect **8** cogitate, consider, contrive, mull over, ruminate **9** dwell upon **10** deliberate **11** contemplate
meditation 4 yoga **5** study **6** musing, poring **7** mulling, reverie, thought **8** brooding **9** discourse, pondering **10** cogitation, reflection, rumination **12** deliberation **13** consideration, contemplation
Mediterranean
  called by ancient Romans: 11 mare nostrum
  coast: 7 Riviera
  gulf: 5 Lions, Sidra, Tunis **7** Antalya, Catania, Taranto **8** Hammamet **9** Iskenderon
  island: 4 Elba **5** Capri, Corfu, Crete, Ibiza, Malta **6** Cyprus, Euboea, Lesbos, Rhodes, Sicily **7** Corsica, Majorca, Minorca **8** Balearic, Sardinia

  resort: 4 Nice **5** Capri **6** Cannes **7** Riviera **9** Cote d'Azur **10** Costa Brava
  river into: 2 Po **4** Ebro, Nile **5** Rhone
  sea: 5 Black **6** Aegean, Ionian **8** Adriatic, Ligurian **10** Tyrrhenian
  strait: 8 Bosporus **9** Bosphorus, Gibraltar **11** Dardanelles
  wind: 7 mistral, sirocco
medium 3 way **4** form, mean, mode, tool **5** means, organ **6** agency, avenue, common, milieu, normal **7** average, balance, channel, diviner, psychic, setting, vehicle **8** middling, moderate, ordinary **9** go-between, middle way, mid-course **10** atmosphere, compromise, golden mean, instrument, moderation **11** clairvoyant, environment, happy medium **12** crystal-gazer, intermediary, intermediate, middle ground, spiritualist, surroundings **13** fortuneteller **15** instrumentality
The Medium
  composer: 7 Menotti **5** opera
medley 4 hash, mess, olio **6** jumble, mosaic **7** farrago, melange, mixture **8** mishmash, pastiche **9** patchwork, potpourri **10** assortment, hodgepodge, miscellany **11** gallimaufry
Medon
  mentioned in: 5 Iliad **7** Odyssey
  father: 6 Oileus
  mother: 5 Rhene
  position: 6 herald
  friend of: 8 Penelope
  killed by: 6 Aeneas
medulla
  part of: 5 brain
  controls: 6 glands **7** muscles
Medusa
  form: 6 Gorgon
  father: 7 Phorcys
  mother: 4 Ceto
  sisters: 6 Graiae
  loved by: 8 Poseidon
  children: 7 Pegasus **8** Chrysaor
  sight of her caused people to turn to: 5 stone
  killed by: 7 Perseus
meek 4 mild **6** docile, gentle, humble, modest **8** lamblike, retiring, tolerant, yielding **9** compliant, spineless, tractable, weak-kneed **10** spiritless, submissive, unas- suming **11** acquiescent, complaisant, deferential, unassertive, unresisting **13** long-suffering, tenderhearted, unpretentious
meekness 7 pliancy, shyness **8** docility, humility **9** passivity **10** diffidence, humbleness **11** bashfulness **13** nonresistance **14** self-effacement
meet 3 apt, fit **4** abut, face, good, heed, obey **5** cross, equal, greet, match, rally, right **6** adjoin, answer, border, follow, gather, muster, proper, seemly **7** abide by, collect, convene,

execute, fitting, fulfill, observe, perform, respect, run into, satisfy, welcome **8** assemble, becoming, bump into, confront, converge, decorous, opposite, relevant, suitable **9** agreeable, allowable, befitting, congruous, discharge, encounter, intersect, permitted, pertinent **10** admissable, comply with, congregate, felicitous **11** acknowledge, appropriate, permissible **12** come together

meet eye to eye 4 face **8** confront, face up to **11** meet vis- a-vis

meet halfway 6 settle **9** make a deal **10** compromise **11** come to terms **14** strike a bargain **18** split the difference

meet head on 4 face **5** crash **6** oppose **7** collide, crack up **8** confront, face up to **9** challenge, encounter

meeting 4 date **5** group, tryst **6** caucus **7** council **8** assembly, conclave, congress **9** encounter, gathering **10** conference, convention, engagement, rendezvous **11** assignation, convocation, get-together **12** introduction, presentation **13** confrontation

Meeting at Telgte
  author: **11** Gunter Grass

meeting of the minds 7 concert, concord, harmony **9** agreement **11** concordance **13** understanding

meeting place 5 mecca **10** focal point, rendezvous

Meet Me in St Louis
  director: **16** Vincente Minnelli
  cast: **8** Leon Ames, Tom Drake **9** Mary Astor **11** Judy Garland **12** June Lockhart, Marjorie Main **13** Lucille Bremer **14** Margaret O'Brien
  song: **11** Trolley Song **14** The Boy Next Door **33** Have Yourself a Merry Little Christmas

Meet the Press
  moderator: **9** Ned Brooks **10** Bill Monroe **11** Edwin Newman **14** Lawrence Spivak, Martha Rountree

meet with 4 meet **6** endure **7** undergo **8** come upon **9** encounter **10** come across, experience

Mefitis
  also: **8** Mephitis
  prevented: **5** winds
  kind of winds: **7** harmful

Megaera
  member of: **6** Furies

Megamede
  husband: **12** King Thespius
  number of daughters: **5** fifty

Megara
  father: **5** Creon
  husband: **8** Hercules
  son: **11** Therimachus

Mehuman 6 eunuch

Mein Kampf
  author: **11** Adolf Hitler
  means: **7** my fight **8** my battle

Meitner, Lise
  field: **7** physics
  nationality: **8** Austrian
  collaborator: **8** Otto Hahn
  contributed to: **21** atomic bomb development
  discovered: **12** protactinium **16** fission of uranium

Melaenis
  epithet of: **9** Aphrodite
  means: **5** black

melancholia 7 despair **10** depression, desolation, melancholy **11** despondency

melancholy 4 blue, glum **5** blues, dumps, gloom, moody **6** dismal, dreary, gloomy, mopish, morose, somber **7** despair, doleful, forlorn, joyless, unhappy **8** dejected, desolate, doldrums, dolorous, downcast, funereal, mournful **9** cheerless, dejection, depressed, heartsick, moodiness, plaintive **10** calamitous, depressing, depression, despondent, dispirited, gloominess, low spirits **11** despondency, discouraged, downhearted, forlornness, languishing, melancholia, sick at heart, unfortunate **12** disconsolate, heavyhearted **14** down in the dumps, down in the mouth **16** disconsolateness
  French: **6** triste **9** tristesse

melange 3 mix **4** olio **6** jumble, medley **7** mixture **8** compound, mishmash, pastiche **9** pasticcio, patchwork, potpourri **10** assemblage, assortment, hodgepodge, miscellany **11** gallimaufry

Melanippe
  form: **4** foal
  foal born to: **6** Euippe
  transformed into: **4** Arne, girl
  father: **4** Ares
  queen of: **7** Amazons

Melanosaurus
  type: **8** dinosaur
  period: **8** Triassic

Melba, Nellie
  title: **4** dame
  born: **9** Australia
  voice: **7** soprano
  named for her: **10** Melba toast, Peach melba

Melbourne
  bay: **7** Hobson's **11** Port Phillip
  landmark: **20** Flemington Racecourse
  river: **5** Yarra **6** Plenty **9** Mary Creek, Patterson **11** Maribyrnong **12** Diamond Creek **13** Kororoit Creek **14** Dandenong Creek, Gardiner's Creek **16** Moonee Ponds Creek
  state: **8** Victoria
  university: **6** Monash **7** La Trobe

Melchizedek
  means: **19** king of righteousness
  hometown: **5** Salem
  contemporary: **7** Abraham

meld 3 mix **4** fuse, join **5** blend, merge, unite **6** jumble, mingle **7** combine **8** coalesce, intermix, scramble **9** commingle **10** amalgamate, intertwine, interweave **11** consolidate, incorporate, intermingle

Meleager
  father: **4** Ares **6** Oeneus
  mother: **7** Althaea
  uncle: **9** Plexippus
  slew: **14** Calydonian boar
  loved: **8** Atalanta
  killed: **15** mother's brothers
  sisters: **11** Meleagrides

melee 3 row **4** fray, riot **5** brawl, scrap, set-to **6** fracas, rumpus, tussle **7** scuffle **8** disorder, dogfight **9** commotion, fistfight **10** free-for-all **11** altercation, pandemonium

Meliad
  form: **5** nymph
  nymph of: **6** flocks **10** fruit trees

mellifluous 4 soft **5** sweet **6** dulcet, mellow, smooth **7** musical **8** resonant **9** full-toned, melodious **10** euphonious, harmonious, sweet-toned **13** sweet-sounding

Mellors
  character in: **20** Lady Chatterley's Lover
  author: **8** Lawrence

mellow 4 rich, ripe, soft **5** drunk, sweet **6** mature, season, soften **7** matured, relaxed **8** luscious, tolerant **9** delicious **10** full-bodied **11** sympathetic **12** full-flavored **13** compassionate, understanding

mellowness 8 full body, fullness, maturity, richness, ripeness, softness **9** tolerance **10** compassion, smoothness **12** lusciousness, pleasantness

melodic 5 lyric **7** tuneful

melodious 4 rich, soft **5** clear, lyric, sweet **6** dulcet, mellow, smooth **7** melodic, musical, ringing, tuneful **8** resonant **9** full-toned **10** euphonious, sweet-toned **11** mellifluent, mellifluous

melodrama 9 theatrics **12** emotionalism **13** theatricality

melodramatic 5 corny, hammy, hokey, stagy **7** maudlin, mawkish **8** cornball, frenzied **10** flamboyant, histrionic **11** exaggerated, overwrought, sensational, sentimental, spectacular **13** overemotional

melody 3 air **4** aria, song, tune **5** ditty, theme **6** ballad, strain, timbre **7** concord, euphony **10** musicality **11** tunefulness **12** mellifluence **13** melodiousness **14** harmoniousness **15** mellifluousness

melon
  varieties: **4** pear **5** mango, snake, stink **6** casaba, citron, Dudaim, netted, nutmeg, orange, winter **7** Persian, serpent **8** honeydew

10 cantaloupe, preserving, watermelon **11** pomegranate **16** Oriental pickling, Queen Anne's pocket **17** Chinese preserving

Melpomene
member of: **5** Muses
personifies: **7** tragedy

melt 4 fade, fuse, pass, thaw **5** blend, merge, shade, touch **6** affect, disarm, dispel, soften, vanish **7** appease, dwindle, liquefy, mollify, scatter **8** dissolve **9** disappear, dissipate, evaporate, waste away **10** arouse pity, conciliate, propitiate

melt away 5 dry up **8** vaporize **9** evaporate

Melville, Herman
author of: **4** Omoo **5** Mardi, Typee **7** Redburn **8** Moby Dick **9** Billy Budd **12** Benito Cereno **16** The Confidence Man **20** Bartleby the Scrivener

Melville, Julia
character in: **9** The Rivals
author: **8** Sheridan

Melvin and Howard
director: **13** Jonathan Demme
cast: **9** Paul LeMat **12** Jason Robards **15** Mary Steenburgen
Oscar for: **6** script **17** supporting actress (Steenburgen)

member 3 arm, leg, toe **4** foot, hand, limb, part, tail, wing **5** bough, digit, organ, piece, shoot **6** branch, finger, pinion **7** element, portion, section, segment **8** fragment **9** appendage, component, extremity **10** ingredient **11** constituent

member
of the bar: **4** beak **7** counsel **8** advocate, attorney **9** barrister, counselor **10** mouthpiece **12** legal advisor **13** attorney-at-law
of a crew: **4** hand, mate **6** ensign, ganger, gunner, purser, yeoman **7** bowsman, oarsman, steward, swabbie **8** cabin boy, coxswain, deckhand, helmsman **9** first mate, navigator
of faculty: **3** don, PhD **4** prof **5** tutor **6** doctor, master **7** teacher **8** lecturer **9** professor **10** instructor
of family: **3** son **4** aunt **5** niece, uncle **6** cousin, father, mother, nephew, sister **7** brother **8** daughter, grandson **11** grandfather, grandmother **13** granddaughter
of legislature: **4** whip **6** deputy **7** senator, speaker **8** delegate, lawmaker **10** legislator, politician **11** congressman **12** congresswoman **14** representative
of religious order: **3** nun **4** dame, monk **5** Clare, friar, priest **6** father, hermit, Jesuit, sister **7** Alexian, ascetic, brother, Cluniac, Templar **8** Capuchin, cenobite, minister, Trappist **9** Carmelite, Dominican

10 Carthusian, Cistercian, Franciscan **11** Augustinian, Benedictine **14** mother superior

Member of the Wedding, The
author: **15** Carson McCullers
character: **6** Jarvis **11** Janice Evans **13** Frankie Addams, John Henry West **16** Honey Camden Brown **18** Berenice Sadie Brown

membership 4 club **6** league, roster **7** company, society **9** community, personnel **10** connection, fellowship, fraternity **11** affiliation, association, brotherhood

membrane 3 web **4** film, skin **6** lining, sheath **7** coating **8** envelope, pellicle **9** thin sheet **10** integument

memento 5 favor, relic, token **6** record, trophy **8** keepsake, memorial, reminder, souvenir **11** memorabilia, remembrance **12** remembrancer **13** commemoration

memento mori 23 remember that thou must die **31** object serving as a reminder of death

Memnon
origin: **8** Oriental **9** Ethiopian
father: **8** Tithonus
mother: **3** Eos **4** Dawn
brother: **8** Emathion
companions: **10** Memnonides
fought with: **7** Trojans
killed by: **8** Achilles
made immortal by: **4** Zeus
commemorated with: **11** giant statue
at: **6** Thebes

Memnonides see **6** Memnon

memo
French: **11** aide memoire

memoir 4 life **5** diary **7** journal **9** biography, life story **10** adventures **11** confessions, experiences, reflections **13** autobiography, recollections, reminiscences

Memoirs of a Dutiful Daughter
author: **16** Simone de Beauvoir

memorabilia 6 papers **7** records **8** archives **9** documents

memorable 6 famous **7** eminent, notable, salient **8** historic, stirring, striking **9** important, momentous, prominent, red-letter **10** celebrated, impressive, noteworthy, remarkable **11** illustrious, outstanding, significant **13** distinguished, extraordinary, unforgettable

memorandum 4 memo, note **5** brief **6** agenda, minute, record **7** jotting **8** reminder **11** brief report, list of items

memorial 6 homage **7** tribute **8** monument **10** monumental **11** testimonial **13** commemorative

memorialization 11 celebration **13** commemoration

memorialize 4 mark **5** honor

9 celebrate **11** commemorate, pay homage to **12** pay tribute to

memory 4 fame, mark, name, note **5** glory, honor, token **6** esteem, recall, regard, renown, repute **7** memento, respect **8** eminence, keepsake, memorial, prestige, reminder, souvenir **10** estimation, reputa- tion **11** distinction, remembering, remembrance, testimonial **12** recollection, remembrancer, reminiscence **13** commemoration
goddess of: **9** Mnemosyne

Memphis
football team: **9** Showboats

menace 3 cow **4** risk **5** bully, daunt, peril **6** danger, hazard, threat **7** imperil, pitfall, portend, presage, terrify **8** browbeat, endanger, forebode, jeopardy, threaten **9** terrorize **10** intimidate, jeopardize **11** be a hazard to, imperilment **12** endangerment

menacing 7 hostile **9** dangerous **11** belligerent, threatening, treacherous **12** antagonistic

menage a trois 9 threesome **16** household of three

Menander
author of: **5** Heros **13** Perikeiromene **14** The Arbitration, The Misanthrope **16** The Rape of the Lock

Men at Arms
author: **11** Evelyn Waugh

Mencken, H L
author of: **10** Prejudices **19** The American Language
editor of: **10** The Mercury **11** The Smart Set
coined word: **9** booboisie, eclysiast

mend 3 fix **4** cure, darn, heal, knit **5** amend, emend, patch **6** better, reform, remedy, repair, revise **7** correct, improve, rectify, restore, retouch, touch up **8** overhaul, renovate **9** meliorate **10** ameliorate **11** recondition

mendacious 5 false, lying **8** spurious **9** deceptive **10** misleading, untruthful

mendacity 5 fraud, lying **6** deceit **7** falsity, perfidy **9** chicanery, deception, duplicity, falsehood, hypocrisy **10** dishonesty **11** insincerity **13** doubledealing, falsification, prevarication **14** untruthfulness **17** misrepresentation

Mendel, Gregor Johann
field: **6** botany
nationality: **8** Austrian
discovered: **14** laws of heredity
founded: **8** genetics

Mendeleyev (Mendeleev), Dimitri Ivanovich
field: **9** chemistry
nationality: **7** Russian
devised: **11** periodic law **13** periodic table

Mendelssohn, (Jakob Ludwig) Felix
born: **7** Germany, Hamburg
composer of: **6** Elijah, St Paul

7 Athalie, Italian (symphony No 4), Lorelei, Ruy Blas **8** Antigone, Scottish (symphony No 3) **11** Reformation (symphony No 5), The Hebrides **12** Hymn of Praise (symphony No 2) **17** Songs without Words **21** A Midsummer Night's Dream

mendicant 6 beggar **10** alms-seeker, panhandler

Mending Wall
    author: 11 Robert Frost

Menelaus
    king of: 6 Sparta
    father: 6 Atreus
    mother: 6 Aerope
    brother: 9 Agamemnon
    wife: 5 Helen
    son: 11 Megapenthes, Nicostratus
    daughter: 8 Hermione

mene mene tekel upharsin 20 handwriting on the wall **30** numbered numbered weighed divided
    foretells destruction of: 10 Belshazzar
    from Biblical book of: 6 Daniel

menhaden 4 pogy **5** pogie **6** bunker **7** alewife, bugfish, ellfish, fatback, herring, oldwife, sardine **8** bonyfish, hardhead, ladyfish **10** mossbunker

menial 3 low **4** mean **5** drone, lowly, slave, toady **6** abject, drudge, flunky, helper, humble, lackey **7** fawning, ignoble, servant, servile, slavish **8** cringing, employee **9** degrading, groveling, sycophant, truckling, underling **10** apprentice, obsequious **11** bootlicking, subordinate, subservient, sycophantic

menial labor 4 toil **5** grind **8** drudgery

Menjou, Adolphe
    born: 12 Pittsburgh PA
    roles: 9 Golden Boy, Pollyanna **11** A Star Is Born **12** The Front Page **13** A Woman of Paris **15** A Farewell to Arms, State of the Union **16** Little Miss Marker **18** A Bill of Divorcement

Mennonite 4 sect
    oppose: 15 military service
    favor: 10 plain dress
    kin to: 5 Amish

meno
    music: 4 less

Menominee, Menomini, Menomonie
    language family: 9 Algonkian **10** Algonquian
    location: 4 Ohio **7** Indiana **8** Illinois, Michigan **9** Wisconsin

menorah 11 candelabrum, candlestick **12** candleholder
    number of candles: 5 seven

Menotti, Gian-Carlo
    born: 5 Italy **10** Cadigliano
    composer of: 9 The Consul, The Medium **12** The Island God, The Tele-

phone **19** Amelia Goes to the Ball **24** Amahl and the Night Visitors

mens sana in corpore sano 22 a sound mind in a sound body

mental 5 crazy, nutty **6** insane, psycho **7** cracked, lunatic, psychic **8** abstract, cerebral, neurotic, rational **9** disturbed, in the mind, of the mind, psychotic **10** disordered, subjective, unbalanced **11** intelligent, mentally ill **12** intellectual, metaphysical **13** psychological

mental application 9 diligence **10** absorption, intentness **11** deep thought, engrossment, fixed regard **13** concentration **14** close attention

mental disorder 5 quirk **6** lunacy, oddity **7** madness **8** delusion, insanity, neurosis **9** craziness, psychosis **10** aberration **11** abnormality, derangement, mental lapse, peculiarity, strangeness **12** eccentricity, idiosyncrasy **13** schizophrenia **15** manic depression

mental hospital 6 asylum **8** madhouse **11** institution

mental institution 6 asylum **8** madhouse **9** funny farm **12** insane asylum

mentality 4 mind **6** acumen, brains, wisdom **8** judgment, sagacity **9** intellect **10** gray matter, perception **11** discernment **12** intelligence, perspicacity

mental lapse 5 quirk **6** lunacy, oddity **7** madness **8** rambling, straying **9** wandering **10** aberration **11** derangement, peculiarity **12** eccentricity **13** forgetfulness

mentally incapable
    Latin: 15 non compos mentis

mentally sound
    Latin: 12 compos mentis

mention 3 say **4** cite, hint, name, tell **5** imply, state **6** hint at, notice, remark, report, tell of **7** comment, divulge, inkling, narrate, observe, recount, refer to, specify **8** allude to, allusion, disclose, intimate **9** insinuate, make known, reference, statement, touch upon, utterance **10** advisement, indication, suggestion **11** designation, insinuation, observation **12** acquaintance, announcement, notification **13** communication, enlightenment, specification

mentor 4 guru **5** guide, tutor **6** master **7** adviser, monitor, proctor, teacher **9** counselor, preceptor, professor **10** instructor

Mentor
    advisor of: 8 Odysseus
    educated: 10 Telemachus

Mephibosheth
    father: 8 Jonathan
    also called: 9 Meribbaal
    grandfather: 4 Saul
    son: 5 Micha

Mephistopheles
    character in: 5 Faust
    author: 6 Goethe

Mephitis see **7** Mefitis

mer 3 sea

Merab
    father: 4 Saul
    sister: 6 Michal
    brother-in-law: 5 David

mercantile 5 trade **8** business **10** commercial **16** buying-and-selling

mercantilism 5 trade **8** business, commerce, exchange **13** commercialism

Mercedes
    character in: 21 The Count of Monte Cristo
    author: 5 Dumas (pere)

mercenary 5 venal **6** for pay, greedy **7** for gain, selfish **8** covetous, grasping, hireling, monetary **10** avaricious **11** acquisitive, paid soldier **12** hired soldier

merchandise 4 sell **5** goods, stock, trade, wares **6** deal in, market **7** effects, staples **8** huckster **9** advertise, publicize, traffic in **10** belongings, buy and sell, distribute **11** commodities **12** stock in trade

merchant 6 broker, dealer, hawker, jobber, monger, trader, vendor **7** peddler **8** chandler, retailer, salesman **9** purchaser, tradesman **10** saleswoman, shopkeeper, wholesaler **11** storekeeper, tradeswoman

Merchant of Venice, The
    author: 18 William Shakespeare
    character: 6 Portia **7** Antonio, Jessica, Lorenzo, Nerissa, Shylock **8** Bassanio, Gratiano

merci 8 thank you

merci beaucoup 16 thank you very much

merciful 4 kind **6** benign, humane, tender **7** clement, feeling, lenient, pitying, sparing **8** gracious **9** forgiving **10** beneficent **11** kindhearted, softhearted, sympathetic **13** compassionate, understanding

merciless 4 fell **5** cruel, harsh **6** fierce, severe **7** callous, inhuman **8** inhumane, pitiless, ruthless **9** ferocious, heartless, unpitying, unsparing **10** relentless, unmerciful **11** cold-blooded, hardhearted, remorseless, unrelenting

Mercouri, Melina
    husband: 11 Jules Dassin
    born: 6 Athens, Greece
    roles: 7 Topkapi **10** Gaily Gaily **13** Never on Sunday **15** Once Is Not Enough

mercurial 6 fickle, lively, mobile **7** erratic, flighty, kinetic, protean **8** electric, spirited, unstable, variable, volatile **9** impetuous, impulsive **10** capricious, changeable, inconstant

11 fluctuating **13** irrepressible, unpredictable

mercury
chemical symbol: **2** Hg

Mercury
origin: **5** Roman
messenger of: **4** gods
god of: **7** science, thieves **8** commerce **9** eloquence
corresponds to: **6** Hermes, Ogmios

Mercutio
character in: **14** Romeo and Juliet
author: **11** Shakespeare

mercy 4 pity **5** grace **6** lenity **7** charity **8** blessing, clemency, humanity, kindness, lenience, leniency, sympathy **9** good thing, tolerance **10** compassion, humaneness, lucky break **11** benevolence, forbearance, forgiveness, piece of luck **13** commiseration, fellow feeling **15** softheartedness **17** tenderheartedness
Latin: **12** misericordia

Mercy seat *see* **16** Ark of the Covenant

Merdle
character in: **12** Little Dorrit
author: **7** Dickens

mere 4 bald, bare, sole **5** plain, scant, sheer, utter **6** common, paltry **7** mundane **8** nugatory, ordinary, trifling **10** negligible, uneventful **13** commonplace, unmitigated **13** insignificant, unappreciable **14** inconsiderable

mere 6 mother

Meredith, Burgess
wife: **15** Paulette Goddard
born: **11** Cleveland OH
roles: **3** Magic, Rocky **6** Batman (the Penguin) **7** Madame X **8** Foul Play **12** Hurry Sundown, Of Mice and Men **15** Magnificent Doll, Such Good Friends **16** Advise and Consent

Meredith, George
author of: **9** The Egoist **10** Modern Love **14** Evan Harrington **16** Beauchamp's Career **19** Diana of the Crossways **25** The Ordeal of Richard Feverel

merely 3 but **4** just, only **5** quite **6** barely, in part, purely, simply, solely **7** utterly **8** scarcely, wholly **10** absolutely

meretricious 4 mock, sham **5** bogus, false, phony **6** pseudo, shoddy, tawdry **8** delusive, specious, spurious **9** deceptive **10** fraudulent, misleading **11** counterfeit

merge 4 fuse, join, weld **5** blend, unify, unite **6** link up **7** combine **8** coalesce, converge, intermix **9** associate, become one, integrate, interfuse, interlock **10** amalgamate, synthesize **11** confederate, consolidate **12** band together, interconnect

mergence 3 mix **5** blend **7** merging,

mixture **8** mingling **10** concoction **11** combination

Mergenthaler, Ottmar
nationality: **8** American
invented: **8** linotype

merger 5 union **7** wedding **8** marriage **9** coalition **12** amalgamation **13** confederation, consolidation

meridian 3 tip, top **4** acme, apex, brow, peak **5** crest, crown, point, ridge **6** apogee, climax, summit, vertex, zenith **7** heights **8** pinnacle **11** culmination

Merimee, Prosper
author of: **6** Carmen **7** Colomba

merit 4 earn, rate **5** value, worth **6** credit, desert, invite, prompt, talent, virtue **7** ability, benefit, deserve, quality, stature, warrant **8** efficacy **9** advantage **10** be worthy of, excellence, worthiness **11** distinction **12** be entitled to, have a right to **13** justification

merited 3 due **5** rated **6** earned **8** deserved, rightful

meritorious 4 fine **6** worthy **8** laudable **9** admirable, estimable, excellent, exemplary **10** creditable, noteworthy **11** commendable, exceptional **12** praiseworthy

Mermaid Tycoon
nickname of: **14** Esther Williams

Merman, Ethel
real name: **20** Ethel Agnes Zimmermann
husband: **14** Ernest Borgnine
born: **9** Astoria NY
autobiography: **6** Merman
roles: **11** Call Me Madam **12** Anything Goes, Panama Hattie **15** Annie Get Your Gun **16** Stage Door Canteen **21** Alexander's Ragtime Band

Mermerus
father: **5** Jason
mother: **5** Medea

Merope
member of: **8** Pleiades
father: **5** Atlas **8** Oenopion
husband: **7** Polybus **8** Sisyphus **11** Cresphontes, Polyphontes
son: **7** Aepytus
raped by: **5** Orion
raised: **7** Oedipus

merrily 5 gaily **6** gladly **7** briskly, happily, lightly, lustick, quickly **8** blithely, jocundly, jovially, joyfully, joyously **9** festively, gleefully **10** cheerfully, laughingly, mirthfully **11** hilariously, vivaciously **14** lightheartedly

Merrimac *see* **9** Pennacook

merriment 3 fun **4** glee **5** cheer, mirth **6** frolic, gaiety, hoopla, levity **7** good fun, jollity, revelry, whoopee **8** hilarity, laughter **9** amusement, festivity, good humor, jocundity, joviality **10** jocularity, jubilation, liveliness, skylarking **11** celebration, gleefulness,

good spirits, merrymaking **12** conviviality, exhilaration, sportiveness **16** lightheartedness

Merriweather, Mrs
character in: **15** Gone With the Wind
author: **8** Mitchell

merry 3 gay **5** happy, jolly **6** blithe, cheery, jocund, jovial, joyous, lively **7** festive, gleeful, jocular **8** animated, carefree, cheerful, gladsome, laughing, mirthful, partying, reveling, sportive **9** convivial, fun-loving, sprightly, vivacious **10** frolicsome, rollicking, skylarking **12** high-spirited, lighthearted

merrymaking 5 sport **6** frolic, gaiety, hoopla, revels **7** jollity, revelry, whoopee **8** carousal **9** festivity, funmaking, high jinks, merriment, rejoicing, whoop-de-do **10** saturnalia **11** bacchanalia, celebration, festivities **12** conviviality

Merry Wives of Windsor, The
author: **18** William Shakespeare
character: **4** Ford, Page **5** Caius **6** Doctor, Fenton **7** Slender **8** Anne Page **12** Mistress Ford, Mistress Page **15** Mistress Quickly, Sir John Falstaff

mesa 4 hill, peak **5** bench, butte, table **7** plateau, terrace **9** cartouche, tableland

Mescalero
language family: **6** Apache
location: **6** Mexico **9** New Mexico
related to: **5** Lipan **10** Chiricahua

mesh 3 fib, net, web **4** grid, jibe **5** agree, sieve, tally **6** engage, enmesh, grille, plexus, screen **7** connect, engaged, netting, network, webbing, webwork **8** dovetail, interact, lacework, meshwork, openwork **9** grillwork, interlock, inter-mesh **10** coordinate, correspond, interweave, wickerwork **11** fit together, latticework **12** reticulation

Meshach
former name: **7** Mishael
companion: **6** Daniel
friend: **8** Abednego, Shadrach

Mesmer, Franz (Friedrich) Anton
nationality: **6** German
developed: **8** hypnosis

mesmerize 5 charm **7** bewitch **8** enthrall, entrance **9** fascinate, hypnotize, magnetize, spellbind, transport

Mesopotamian mythology
god of agriculture/earth: **5** Dagan
corresponds to Phoenician: **5** Dagon

Mesquakie *see* **3** Fox

mess 3 fix **4** hash, stew **5** mix-up, pinch **6** crisis, jumble, litter, muddle, pickle, plight, scrape, strait **7** clutter, dilemma, trouble **8** disarray, disorder, hot water, mess hall, mishmash, quandary **9** cafeteria, confusion, imbroglio, refectory, situation **10** commissary, difficulty, dining hall, dining room, hodgepodge **11** predicament **14** conglomeration

message 4 news, note, word **5** moral, point, theme **6** letter, notice, report **7** meaning, missive, purport, tidings **8** bulletin, dispatch **9** statement **10** communique, memorandum **12** intelligence **13** communication

mess around with 4 test **6** try out **8** fool with, play with **10** tinker with **14** experiment with

messenger 5 envoy **6** bearer, runner **7** carrier, courier **8** delegate, emissary **9** deliverer, go-between **11** delivery boy, delivery man **12** intermediary

messenger of gods 4 Iris **6** Hermes **7** Mercury

Messiaen, Olivier Eugene Prosper Charles
    born: 6 France **7** Avignon
    composer of: 11 Exotic Birds, Turangalila **13** Chronochromie **20** Le Nativite du Seigneur **22** Quartet for the End of Time **27** Vingt Regards sur l'Enfant Jesus **33** Et expecto resurrectionem mortuorum **41** Transfiguration de Notre Seigneur Jesus Christ

Messiah
    means: 11 anointed one
    see also **10** Jesus

Messick, Dale
    creator/artist of: 19 Brenda Starr Reporter

messiness 5 chaos, mix-up, upset **6** jumble **7** clutter **8** disarray, disorder, scramble, shambles **9** confusion **10** disharmony, sloppiness, untidiness **12** dishevelment **14** disarrangement **15** disorganization

mess up 3 mar **4** goof, muff, ruin **5** botch, spoil **6** bungle, foul up, jumble **7** blunder, butcher, disturb, do badly, louse up, screw up **9** mismanage **10** disarrange **11** disorganize, make a mess of, make an error **12** make a mistake

messy 4 ugly **6** blowsy, frowsy, grubby, sloppy, tricky, untidy **7** awkward, chaotic, jumbled, tangled, unkempt **8** confused, littered **9** cluttered, difficult **10** bedraggled, disheveled, disordered, slatternly, topsy-turvy, unenviable, unpleasant **11** disarranged **12** embarrassing, inextricable **13** uncomfortable

mesto
    music: 8 mournful

metal
    alloy: 5 brass, monel **6** bronze, nickel, niello, pewter, solder
    bar: 3 gad **4** risp **5** ingot
    bolt: 5 rivet
    box: 8 canister
    casting: 3 peg
    classification: 5 light, noble **6** alkali, common **7** coinage **8** platinum, precious **9** rare earth **10** low-melting,

refractory, transition **11** high-melting **14** semiconductors
    clippings: 7 scissel
    coarse: 5 matte
    corrosion: 4 rust
    crude: 3 ore **4** slug
    cymbals: 3 tal
    deposit: 4 lode, vein
    design: 7 chasing
    disk or plate: 4 shim **5** medal, paten **6** platen, sequin
    eyelet: 7 grommet
    filings: 5 lemel
    god of: 6 Vulcan **10** Hephaestus
    heaviest: 6 osmium
    kind: 3 tin **4** gold, iron, lead, zinc **6** barium, cerium, cesium, copper, erbium, nickel, osmium, radium, silver, sodium **7** arsenic, bismuth, calcium, holmium, iridium, lithium, rhodium, silicon, terbium, thulium **8** actinium, aluminum, antimony, europium, lutetium, platinum, rubidium, samarium, selenium, titanium, tungsten **9** beryllium, magnesium, palladium, potassium, ruthenium, strontium **10** molybdenum, phosphorus
    layer: 7 plating
    leaf: 4 foil
    lightest: 7 lithium
    liquid: 7 mercury
    mass: 3 pid **5** ingot **7** bullion
    piece: 4 jack, slug
    refuse: 4 slag **5** dross
    shaper: 5 swage
    suit: 4 mail **5** armor **6** armour
    thread: 4 lame, wire
    trademark: 5 monel
    ware: 4 tole **6** Revere
    worker: 5 smith **6** forger, welder **7** armorer, riveter **8** armourer **9** goldsmith, ironsmith **10** blacksmith **11** coppersmith, silversmith **12** metallurgist

Metalious, Grace
    author of: 11 Peyton Place

metalworking
    god of: 6 Vulcan **10** Hephaestus, Hephaistos

metamorphose 6 change, mutate **7** convert **9** transform **11** transfigure

Metamorphoses
    author: 4 Ovid

metamorphosis 8 mutation **10** alteration, conversion **11** permutation **12** change of form, modification **13** radical change, transmutation **14** transformation **15** series of changes, startling change, transfiguration **18** transmogrification

Metamorphosis, The
    author: 10 Franz Kafka

metaphor 5 image, trope **6** simile **7** analogy **8** metonymy, parallel **11** equivalence **14** figure of speech, representation

metaphysical 5 basic, lofty, vague

6 far-out **7** eternal **8** abstract, abstruse, esoteric, mystical, ultimate **9** essential, high-flown, recondite, universal **10** impalpable, intangible, jesuitical, oversubtle **11** existential, fundamental, ontological, speculative **12** cosmological, intellectual, unanswerable **13** philosophical **15** epistemological

Metaphysics
    author: 9 Aristotle

metaxa
    type: 6 brandy **7** liqueur
    origin: 6 Greece

mete, mete out 5 allot **6** assign, divide **7** deal out, dole out **8** allocate, disburse, dispense **9** apportion, parcel out **10** administer, distribute, measure out

meteoric 4 fast **5** fiery, rapid, swift **6** speedy, sudden **7** blazing, flaming, instant **8** flashing, unabated **10** inexorable **11** ineluctable, unstoppable

meter
    abbreviation: 1 m

method 3 way **4** form, mode, plan, tack **5** means, order, style, usage **6** course, design, manner, scheme, system **7** fashion, formula, process, program, purpose, routine **8** approach, efficacy **9** procedure, technique, viability **13** modus operandi

methodical, methodic 4 neat, tidy **5** exact **7** careful, logical, orderly, precise, regular, uniform **10** analytical, deliberate, meticulous, systematic **12** businesslike **13** well-regulated

methodization 5 order **11** arrangement **12** organization **14** categorization, classification **15** systematization

methodize 5 order **7** arrange **8** classify, organize **11** systematize

Methuselah
    father: 5 Enoch
    son: 6 Lamech
    years lived: 23 nine hundred and sixty-nine
    known as: 9 oldest man

meticulous 4 nice **5** exact, fussy **7** finical, finicky, precise **8** exacting, sedulous **10** fastidious, particular, scrupulous **11** painstaking, punctilious **13** conscientious, perfectionist

meticulousness 4 care **5** pains **12** sedulousness, thoroughness **14** fastidiousness, scrupulousness **17** conscientiousness

metier 3 job **4** area, line, work **5** craft, field, forte, trade **7** calling, pursuit **8** activity, business, lifework, province, vocation **9** specialty **10** employment, livelihood, occupation, profession

meting out 8 alloting **9** bestowing, doling out **10** allocating, conferring, consigning, dealing out, dispensing **11** designating **12** apportioning, distributing, measuring out

Metis
  member of: 6 Titans
  father: 7 Oceanus
  mother: 6 Tethys
  consort of: 4 Zeus
  daughter: 6 Athena
Metropolis
  director: 9 Fritz Lang
  cast: 10 Alfred Abel **12** Brigitte Helm
metropolitan area 4 city **8** core city, downtown, environs **9** inner city, precincts, urban area **10** city limits, metropolis **11** central city **16** business district
mettle 3 vim **4** grit, guts **5** nerve, pluck, spunk, valor, vigor **6** spirit **7** bravery, courage, heroism **8** audacity, backbone, boldness, gameness, temerity **9** derring-do, fortitude, gallantry, manliness **10** enthusiasm, resolution **11** intrepidity **12** fearlessness **13** determination
mettlesome 4 bold, edgy **5** brave, fiery **6** ardent, plucky, spunky **7** gingery, peppery **8** restless, skittish, spirited **9** excitable, impatient **10** courageous, high-strung **12** high-spirited
Mexica *see* **5** Aztec
Mexico
  other name: 8 New Spain
  capital/largest city: 10 Mexico City
  others: 4 Leon **5** La Paz, Taxco **6** Cancun, Celaya, Merida, Oaxaca, Puebla, Toluca **7** Durango, Guaymas, Tampico, Tijuana, Torreon **8** Acapulco, Culiacan, Ensenada, Irapuato, Mazatlan, Mexicali, Saltillo, Veracruz **9** Chihuahua, Matamoras, Monterrey, Queretaro, Salamanca, Zacatecas **10** Hermosillo **11** Guadalajara, Nuevo Laredo **12** Ciudad Juarez, Villahermosa **13** Coatzacoalcos, Piedras Negras, San Luis Potosi **14** Puerto Vallarta **15** Netzahualcoyotl
    ancient city: 4 Tula **7** Texcoco **8** Tlacopan **10** Monte Alban **11** Teotihuacan **12** Tenochtitlan **13** Tula de Allende
  division: 6 Colima, Oaxaca, Puebla, Sonora **7** Chiapas, Durango, Hidalgo, Jalisco, Sinaloa, Tabasco, Yucatan **8** Campeche, Coahuila, Tlaxcala, Veracruz **9** Chihuahua, Michoacan, Nuevo Leon, Zacatecas **13** San Luis Potosi **14** Baja California
  measure: 3 bag, pie **4** alma, onza, vara **5** almud, baril, carga, jarra, labor, legua, libra, linea, marco, sitio **6** adarme, almude, arroba, carega, fanega, ochaua, terceo **7** pulgada, quintal **9** cuarteron, cuartillo **10** caballeria
  monetary unit: 4 onza, peso **5** adobe, claco, tlaco **6** azteca, cuarto, dinero **7** centavo, piaster
  weight: 3 bag **4** onza **5** libra, marco **6** arroba, tercio **7** quintal
  island: 6 Carmen, Cedros **7** San Jose,

Tiburon **8** Cerralvo **10** Tres Marias **13** Espiritu Santo **14** Santa Magdelena, Santa Margarita **15** Angel de la Guarda
  lake: 7 Chapala, Texcoco **9** Patzcuaro
  mountain: 6 Colima, Tacana, Toluca **9** Paricutin **11** Ixtacihuatl, Sierra Madre **12** Popocatepetl **14** Sierra Zacateca **16** Chiapas Highlands **24** Transverse Volcanic Sierra
  highest point: 7 Orizaba **12** Citlaltepetl
  river: 4 Mayo **5** Yaqui **6** Balsas, Fuerte, Grande, Panuco **8** Colorado, Grijalva **10** Papaloapan, Usumacinta **13** Bravo del Norte, Coatzacoalcos, Lerma-Santiago
  sea: 7 Pacific **8** Atlantic **9** Caribbean
  physical feature:
    bay: 8 Campeche **9** Olas Atlas
    cape: 10 Corrientes
    desert: 6 Sonora
    gulf: 6 Mexico **8** Campeche **10** California **11** Tehuantepec
    isthmus: 11 Tehuantepec
    peninsula: 7 Yucatan **14** Baja California
    plain: 7 Tabasco
    plateau: 7 Mexican
    valley: 7 Chiapas
  people: 6 Indian **7** Mestizo, Spanish
    architect: 7 O'Gorman
    artist: 6 Orozco, Rivera, Tamayo **9** Siqueiros
    composer: 6 Chavez
    emperor: 10 Maximilian
    explorer: 6 Cortes, Cortez **7** Cordoba **8** Alvarado, Grijalva
    god: 6 Tlaloc **12** Quetzalcoatl **14** Huitzilopochtl
    leader: 3 Gil **4** Diaz **5** Lopez, Rubio, Villa **6** Calles, Huerta, Juarez, Madero, Valdes, Zapata **7** Obregon **8** Carranza, Iturbide, Portillo, Santa Ana **9** Diaz Ordaz, Montezuma, Rodriguez **13** Madrid Hurtado **16** Salinas de Gortari
    revolutionary/priest: 13 Morelos y Pavon **16** Hidalgo y Costilla
    soldier/explorer: 12 conquistador
    viceroy: 7 Mendoza
    writer: 3 Paz **5** Nervo, Reyes, Yanez **6** Azuela, Guzman, Najera **7** Fuentes
  language: 5 Mayan, Otomi **6** Mixtec **7** Mazahua, Mazatec, Nahuatl, Spanish, Totonac, Zapotec **8** Tarascan
  religion: 13 Roman Catholic
  place:
    cathedral: 10 Assumption
    center of Mexico City: 6 Zocalo **21** Plaza de la Constitucion
    floating gardens: 10 Xochimilco
    museum: 28 Shrine of the Virgin of Guadalupe
    park: 7 Alameda **11** Chapultepec
    ruins: 5 Mitla, Uxmal **8** Palenque **10** Monte Alban **11** Chichen Itza,

Teotihuacan **20** Temple of Quetzalcoatl
    street: 13 Avenida Juarez **16** Paseo de la Reforma
    temple/pyramid: 7 Cholula **8** Castillo
  feature:
    agreement: 5 NAFTA
    Christmas tradition: 6 pinata
    coffee plantation: 5 finca
    empire: 4 Maya **5** Aztec, Olmec **6** Mixtec, Toltec **7** Zapotec
    large estate: 8 hacienda
    musician: 8 mariachi
    small farm/commune: 6 ejidos
    sport: 7 jai alai **12** bullfighting
    tree: 9 sapodilla **11** chicozapote
  food:
    corn cake: 8 tortilla
    dish: 4 mole, taco **5** huevo, pollo **6** tamale **7** burrito, chorizo, taquito, tostada **8** empanada **9** enchilada, guacamole, sopadilla **10** chili verde, quesadilla **11** chimichanga **12** chili relleno
    drink: 6 pulque **7** tequila
Mexico City
  Aztec name: 12 Tenochtitlan
  capital of: 6 Mexico
  landmark: 13 Mercado Merced **15** Chapultepec Park **19** Basilica of Guadalupe
    bull ring: 11 Plaza Mexico
    floating gardens: 10 Xochimilco
    pyramids: 11 Teotihuacan
  square: 6 Zocalo **22** Plaza de las Tres Culturas
  street: 16 Paseo de la Reforma
Meyerbeer, Giacomo
  real name: 17 Jacob Liebmann Beer
  born: 6 Berlin **7** Germany
  composer of: 7 Dinorah **10** Le Prophete, The African, The Prophet **12** Les Huguenots, The Huguenots, The North Star **14** Robert le Diable, Robert the Devil
mezza voce
  music: 9 half voice **10** half volume
mezzo
  music: 4 half
Miami
  bay: 8 Biscayne
  county: 4 Dade
  developer: 7 Flagler
  football team: 8 Dolphins
  museum: 4 Lowe **12** Villa Viscaya
  ocean: 8 Atlantic
  people: 5 Cuban **8** Hispanic
  section: 7 Hialeah **10** Bal Harbour **11** Coral Gables
  stadium: 10 Orange Bowl
  tropical garden: 9 Fairchild
  university: 5 Barry **8** St Thomas
  zoo: 11 Crandon Park
Miami (Twightwee)
  language family: 9 Algonkian **10** Algonquian
  tribe: 3 Wea **5** Miami **10** Piankashaw

location: 4 Ohio **7** Indiana **8** Illinois, Michigan **9** Wisconsin
leader: 12 Little Turtle
allied with: 6 Peoria

Miami Vice
character: 4 Gina **5** Trudy **8** (Capt) Castillo **13** Riccardo Tubbs, Sonny Crockett
cast: 10 Don Johnson **11** Olivia Brown **15** Saundra Santiago **16** Edward James Olmos **20** Phillip Michael Thomas

Micah Clarke
author: 19 Sir Arthur Conan Doyle

Micawber, Mr
character in: 16 David Copperfield
author: 7 Dickens

Michael
author: 17 William Wordsworth

Michael
means: 12 Who is like God
father: 8 Izrahiah **11** Jehoshaphat
son: 4 Omri **8** Zabadiah
also: 9 archangel

Michel
father: 4 Saul
husband: 5 David, Palti
sister: 5 Merab

Michelangelo Buonarotti (Simoni)
architect of: 11 Campidoglio (Capitoline Hill) **12** Medici Chapel (Florence) **13** Farnese Palace **21** Palazzo Medici-Riccardi (Florence) **22** Palazzo dei Conservatori (Capitoline Hill) **24** Convent of San Marco Library
born: 5 Italy **7** Caprese
patron: 12 Pope Julius II **14** Lorenzo d'Medici **19** Pope Julius the Second **21** Lorenzo the Magnificent
artwork: 5 David, Moses, Pieta **6** Brutus, Slaves **7** Bacchus **9** The Victor **10** Holy Family **12** Madonna Pitti **15** The Last Judgment **18** Conversion of St Paul **20** Madonna Seated on a Step, Sistine Chapel Ceiling **21** The Flight of the Lapites, The Martyrdom of St Peter

Michelozzo
architect of: 21 Palazzo Medici-Riccardi (Florence) **24** Convent of San Marco Library

Michelson, Albert A
field: 7 physics
established: 12 speed of light **15** velocity of Earth
awarded: 10 Nobel Prize

Michener, James A
author of: 5 Space **6** Alaska, Hawaii, Iberia, Legacy, Poland **8** Caravans, Sayonara **9** The Source **10** Centennial, Chesapeake **11** The Covenant, The Drifters **16** The Fires of Spring **18** The Bridges at Toko-ri **22** Tales of the South Pacific

Michigan
abbreviation: 2 MI **4** Mich

nickname: 4 Lake **9** Wolverine **10** Automobile **15** Water Wonderland **16** Winter Wonderland
capital: 7 Lansing
largest city: 7 Detroit
others: 4 Caro, Troy **5** Flint, Niles, Wayne **6** Adrien, Alpena, Bad Axe, Monroe, Owosso, Warren, Wassar **7** Bay City, Holland, Jackson, Livonia, Midland, Pontiac, Saginaw, Trenton, Wyoming **8** Ann Arbor, Cadillac, Dearborn, Escanaba, Ironwood, Manistee, Muskegon, Petoskey, Royal Oak **9** Cheboygan, Hillsdale, Kalamazoo, Marquette, Port Huron, Roseville, Wyandotte **10** Birmingham, River Rouge **11** Battle Creek, Grand Rapids **12** Benton Harbor, Traverse City **13** Sault Ste Marie, St Clair Shores
college: 4 Alma, Hope **5** Wayne **6** Adrian, Albion, Calvin, Olivet, Owosso **7** Detroit, Oakland **9** Hillsdale, Kalamazoo, Marygrove
feature:
  bridge: 8 Mackinac
  canal: 3 Soo **12** Sault St Marie
  festival: 12 Holland Tulip
  national park: 10 Isle Royale
  village: 10 Greenfield
tribe: 6 Ojibwa, Ottawa **8** Chippewa **10** Potawatomi
people: 9 Henry Ford, wolverine **11** Bruce Catton, Edgar A Guest, Julie Harris, Ralph Bunche, Ring Lardner **16** Charles Lindburgh
  explorer: 6 Joliet **7** La Salle, Nicolet **9** Marquette **12** Etienne Brule, Sault St Marie
island: 8 Mackinaw
lake: 4 Burt, Erie **5** Clear, Huron, Round, Torch **6** Austin, Devils, Moline **7** Bawbees, St Clair **8** Houghton, Michigan, Superior
land rank: 11 twenty-third
mountain: 6 Copper **7** Gogebic **9** Menominee, Porcupine
  highest point: 12 Mount Curwood
physical feature:
  bay: 7 Saginaw, Thunder **8** Keweenaw, Sturgeon
  straits: 8 Mackinac
president: 10 Gerald Ford
river: 4 Cass **5** Grand, Huron **6** Raisin **7** Detroit, Saginaw, St Clair, St Mary's **8** Escanaba, Muskegon **9** Menominee
state admission: 11 twenty-sixth
state bird: 5 robin
state fish: 5 trout
state flower: 12 apple blossom
state motto: 11 I Will Defend **39** If You Seek a Pleasant Peninsula Look About You
state song: 18 Michigan My Michigan
state tree: 16 eastern white pine

Mickey Mouse
creator: 10 Walt Disney

character: 5 Morty **6** Ferdie **11** Minnie Mouse
cow: 10 Clarabelle

Micklewhite, Maurice Joseph
real name of: 12 Michael Caine

Micmac
language family: 9 Algonkian **10** Algonquian
location: 6 Canada **10** Nova Scotia **12** Newfoundland, New Brunswick **14** Gaspe Peninsula **16** Cape Breton Island **18** Prince Edward Island

microbe 4 germ **5** virus **6** gamete, zygote **8** bacillus, parasite **9** bacterium **10** spirochete **13** microorganism, streptococcus **14** staphylococcus

microbiologist
American: 7 Waksman **9** Baltimore
Dutch: 11 (van) Leeuwenhoek

Micronesia
part of: 7 Oceania
island: 3 Nui **4** Guam, Rota, Truk, Wake **5** Makin, Nauru, Wotho **6** Bikini, Ellice, Majuro, Ponape **7** Gilbert, Mariana **8** Caroline, Kiribati, Marshall

microorganism 3 bug **4** germ **5** virus **7** microbe **8** bacillus, pathogen **9** bacterium

microphobia
fear of: 12 small objects

microscope
invented by:
  compound: 7 Janssen
  electronic: 5 Knoll, Ruska
  field ion: 7 Mueller
single lens model improved by: 11 (van) Leeuwenhoek
  first observed: 8 protozoa **13** red blood cells **19** single-celled animals

microscopic, microscopical 4 tiny **5** teeny **6** atomic, minute **9** invisible **10** diminutive, very little **13** imperceptible, infinitesimal

microscopy
founder: 11 Robert Hooke **13** Jan Swammerdam **16** Marcello Malpighi **19** Anton van Leeuwenhoek

Midas
king of: 7 Phrygia
father: 7 Gordius
gift: 11 golden touch
gift from: 7 Silenus
ears changed to those of: 3 ass
changed by: 6 Apollo

midday 4 noon **7** noonday **8** meridian, noontide, noontime

middle 3 act, gut, hub, mid **4** core, main **5** belly, heart, midst, waist **6** center, course, medial, median, midway, throes **7** central, halfway, midmost, midriff, nucleus, process, stomach **8** midpoint **9** heartland **10** midsection **12** intermediate

Middle Ages
French: 8 moyen age

middle-class 4 mass **8** ordinary **9** bourgeois **10** mainstream, middlebrow

middle Europe
German: 12 Mitteleuropa

middle ground 4 mean **7** balance **8** midpoint **11** equilibrium **12** common ground

Middle Kingdom *see* **5** China

middleman 5 agent **6** broker, dealer, jobber **7** liaison **8** mediator **9** go-between **10** wholesaler **11** distributor, intercessor **12** entrepreneur, intermediary

Middlemarch
author: 11 George Eliot
character: 5 Celia **12** Will Ladislaw **13** Rosamond Viney **14** Dorothea Brooke, Edward Casaubon, Tertius Lydgate **15** Sir James Chettam

middlemost 4 mean **5** inner **6** inmost, median **7** central, midmost **8** interior

middle-of-the-road 8 moderate **10** mainstream

middle-of-the-roader 8 moderate **12** mainstreamer

middle way
Latin: 8 via media

middling 4 fair, so-so **6** medium **7** average, fairish, minimal **8** mediocre, moderate, ordinary, passable **9** tolerable **10** pretty good, second-rate **11** indifferent **12** run-of-the-mill, unremarkable

Midgard
also: 10 Mithgarthr
origin: 12 Scandinavian
means: 10 abode of man
located between: 8 Niflheim **10** Muspelheim
connected to Asgard by: 7 bifrost **13** rainbow bridge
formed from brow of: 4 Ymir

midget 4 doll, runt **5** dwarf, pygmy **6** peewee, puppet, shrimp, squirt **7** manikin **8** half-pint, munchkin, small fry, Tom Thumb **9** pipsqueak **10** fingerling, homunculus **11** hop-o'-my-thumb, lilliputian

Midi 5 skirt **16** the south of France

midlands 8 interior **10** hinterland **13** central region

midmost 5 inner **6** inmost, middle **7** central, pivotal **8** interior **10** middlemost

Midnight Cowboy
director: 15 John Schlesinger
cast: 9 Jon Voight **11** John McGiver, Sylvia Miles **13** Brenda Vaccaro, Dustin Hoffman (Ratso Rizzo)
Oscar for: 7 picture

Midnight Express
director: 10 Alan Parker
cast: 8 John Hurt **9** Bo Hopkins, Brad Davis (Billy Hayes) **10** Randy Quaid **12** Irene Miracle
setting: 13 Turkish prison

score: 14 Giorgio Moroder
Oscar for: 5 score **6** script

midori
type: 7 liqueur
origin: 5 Japan
flavor: 5 melon

midpoint 4 core, mean **5** focus **6** center, middle **15** point of no return

midriff 3 gut **4** guts **5** belly, tummy **6** paunch **7** abdomen, stomach **9** diaphragm **10** midsection **11** breadbasket

midst 3 eye, hub **4** core **5** bosom, heart, thick **6** center, depths, middle **7** nucleus **8** interior

Midsummer Night's Dream, A
author: 18 William Shakespeare
character: 4 Puck (Robin Goodfellow) **6** Bottom, Helena, Hermia, Oberon **7** Theseus, Titania **8** Lysander **9** Demetrius, Hippolyta

midterm 4 exam, test **6** review **11** examination

midwife
French: 11 accoucheuse

mien 3 air **4** look **5** guise, style **6** aspect, manner, visage **7** bearing, feature **8** attitude, behavior, carriage, demeanor, presence **9** semblance **10** appearance, deportment, expression **11** countenance

Mies van der Rohe, Ludwig
architect of: 14 German Pavilion (1929 International Exposition, Barcelona), Lake Shore Drive (apartment towers, Chicago), Tugendhat House (Brno Czechoslovakia) **15** National Gallery (West Berlin), Seagram Building (NYC)
style: 13 International
principle: 10 less is more

miff 3 irk, vex **4** rile **5** anger, annoy, chafe, pique **6** nettle, offend, rankle **7** affront, provoke **8** irritate **9** put one off **10** exasperate **11** make one sore **14** rub the wrong way **15** raise one's dander

Mifune, Toshiro
born: 5 China **8** Tsingtao
roles: 6 Midway, Shogun **8** Rashomon **12** Seven Samurai **13** Throne of Blood

Miggs, Miss
character in: 12 Barnaby Rudge
author: 7 Dickens

might 3 may **5** brawn, clout, force, power, vigor **6** energy, muscle **7** potency, prowess **8** strength **9** influence, lustihood, puissance, toughness **10** capability, competence, durability, robustness, sturdiness **11** capableness **12** forcefulness

mighty 4 able, bold, huge, vast, very **5** brave, hardy, husky, lusty, stout, truly **6** brawny, manful, potent, really, robust, strong, sturdy **7** immense, massive, titanic, valiant **8** colossal, enormous, forceful, gigantic, imposing,

majestic, powerful, puissant, stalwart, towering, valorous, vigorous **9** monstrous, strapping **10** courageous, gargantuan, invincible, monolithic, monumental, prodigious, stupendous **11** elephantine, exceedingly, indomitable, of great size **12** overpowering, particularly **13** exceptionally **14** Brobdingnagian

migrate 4 move, trek **6** travel **7** journey **8** emigrate, relocate, resettle **9** immigrate

migration 4 trek **6** exodus, flight, moving **7** passage **8** diaspora, movement

mikado 5 ruler **7** emperor, monarch **9** sovereign **10** locomotive **15** Japanese emperor

Mikado, The
subtitle: 15 The Town of Titipu
operetta by: 18 Gilbert and Sullivan
character: 4 Ko-Ko **6** Mikado, Peep-Bo, Yum-Yum **7** Katisha, Pooh-Bah **8** Nanki-Poo, Pish-Tush **9** Pitti-Sing

Mikkelsen, Dahl
also: 3 Mik
creator/artist of: 8 Ferd'nand

mikrophobia
fear of: 5 germs

mikvah 16 public ritual bath
used by: 12 Orthodox Jews

mild 4 calm, easy, soft, warm **5** balmy, bland **6** docile, gentle, placid, serene, smooth **7** pacific, summery **8** delicate, moderate, not sharp, pleasant, soothing, tranquil **9** easygoing, emollient, not severe, not strong, temperate **10** forbearing, not extreme, springlike **11** complaisant, uninjurious **12** good-tempered

mildew 4 mold **6** blight, fungus

mildewed 5 fusty, moldy **10** discolored

mildness 8 calmness, delicacy, serenity, softness **9** placidity **10** gentleness, good temper

Mildred Pierce
director: 13 Michael Curtiz
based on novel by: 10 James M Cain
cast: 8 Ann Blyth, Eve Arden **10** Jack Carson **12** Bruce Bennett, Joan Crawford, Zachary Scott
Oscar for: 7 actress (Crawford)

mild-tempered 7 equable, patient **9** easygoing **11** good-natured, unflappable

mile
abbreviation: 2 mi

Miles, Sarah
brother: 11 Christopher
husband: 10 Robert Bolt
born: 7 England **11** Ingatestone
roles: 6 Blow-Up **10** The Servant **11** The Hireling **13** Ryan's Daughter **16** Lady Caroline Lamb

miles gloriosus 15 boastful soldier
Miles Gloriosus
  author: **7** Plautus
Milesian
  origin: **5** Irish
  invaders from: **5** Spain
  invaded: **7** Ireland
  defeated: **14** Tuatha De Danann
  ancestors of: **5** Irish
milestone 7 jubilee **8** milepost, sign-post **10** road marker **11** anniversary **12** red-letter day, turning point
Milestone, Lewis
  director of: **12** Of Mice and Men, The Front Page **13** A Walk in the Sun **17** Mutiny on the Bounty **25** All Quiet on the Western Front (Oscar)
Milestones
  author: **13** Arnold Bennett
milieu 5 scene **7** culture, element, setting **8** ambience, backdrop **10** background **11** environment, mise-en-scene **12** surroundings
militant 7 defiant, extreme, martial, warlike, warring **8** fighting, military **9** assertive, bellicose, combatant, combative **10** aggressive, pugnacious **11** belligerent, contentious **12** disputatious, paramilitary, warmongering **14** uncompromising
military 4 army **5** armed, crisp **6** strict, troops **7** martial, militia, Spartan, warlike **8** generals, soldiers **9** combative, defensive, regulated, soldierly, warmaking **10** regimented **11** armed forces, belligerent, soldierlike
military force 4 army, navy **6** legion, troops **7** legions, militia **8** military, regiment, soldiers, soldiery **9** battalion **11** fighting men **13** fighting force
military machine 4 army **6** legion, troops **11** armed forces **13** fighting force
military rank abbreviation
  admiral: **3** adm
  brigadier general: **2** bg **7** brig gen
  captain: **3** cpt **4** capt
  chief petty officer: **3** CPO
  colonel: **3** col
  commander: **5** comdr
  corporal: **3** cpl
  ensign: **3** ens
  general: **3** gen
  lieutenant: **2** lt **5** lieut
  lieutenant colonel: **3** ltc **5** lt col
  lieutenant general: **5** lt gen **8** lieut gen
  major: **3** maj
  master sergeant: **4** msgt
  non-commissioned officer: **3** nco
  private: **3** pvt
  private first class: **3** pfc
  sergeant: **3** sgt
  sergeant first class: **3** sfc
  sergeant major: **4** smaj **6** sgt maj
  specialist: **4** spec
  staff sergeant: **4** ssgt

military storehouse 6 armory **7** arsenal **8** magazine **9** arms depot **13** ordnance depot **14** ammunition dump
military stores 7 arsenal, weapons **8** ordnance **9** munitions **10** ammunition
military unit 4 army, crew, unit **5** corps, force, squad **6** legion, outfit **7** brigade, company **8** regiment, squadron **9** battalion, task force **10** contingent, detachment
milksop 4 baby, wimp **5** mouse, pansy, sissy, softy **6** coward **7** crybaby, nebbish **8** mama's boy, poltroon, weakling **9** fraidy-cat **10** namby-pamby, pantywaist, scaredy-cat, weak sister **11** milquetoast, mollycoddle
mill 4 roam, teem **5** crush, grind, shape, swarm, works **6** finish, groove **7** factory, meander **8** converge **9** granulate, pulverize
Mill, John Stuart
  author of: **9** On Liberty **14** Utilitarianism **20** The Subjection of Women **28** Principles of Political Economy
Millais, Sir John Everett
  born: **7** England **12** Southampton
  artwork: **7** Bubbles **9** Blind Girl **12** Autumn Leaves, Chill October **13** My First Sermon **18** Lorenzo and Isabella **25** Christ in the Carpenter's Shop **36** Young Men of Benjamin Seizing Their Brides
Millament, Mrs
  character in: **16** The Way of the World
  author: **8** Congreve
Milland, Ray
  real name: **21** Reginald Truscott-Jones
  born: **5** Neath, Wales
  roles: **9** Beau Geste **11** Blonde Crazy **14** Dial M for Murder, The Lost Weekend (Oscar) **22** Bulldog Drummond Escapes
Millay, Edna St Vincent
  author of: **11** Second April **13** The Harp Weaver **19** Make Bright the Arrows **20** A Few Figs from Thistles
millennium 13 thousand years **9** age of gold **21** one-thousandth anniversary
Miller
  character in: **18** The Canterbury Tales
  author: **7** Chaucer
Miller, Ann
  real name: **17** Lucille Ann Collier
  autobiography: **15** Miller's High Life
  born: **9** Chireno TX
  roles: **9** On the Town, Stage Door **10** Hit the Deck, Kiss Me Kate **11** Sugar Babies **16** The Kissing Bandit
Miller, Arthur
  wife: **13** Marilyn Monroe
  author of: **8** The Price **11** The Crucible **12** After the Fall **16** Death of a Salesman **18** A View from the Bridge

Miller, Henry
  author of: **5** Nexus, Sexus **6** Plexus **14** Tropic of Cancer **17** Tropic of Capricorn **18** The Rosy Crucifixion **21** The Colossus of Maroussi
Milles, Carl
  real name: **23** Wilhelm Carl Emil Anderson
  born: **5** Lagga **6** Sweden
  artwork: **5** Diana, Jonah **6** Europa **12** Man and Nature, Playing Bears **13** Peace Monument **15** Orpheus Fountain **18** Meeting of the Waters, Saltsjobaden Church (bronze doors)
millet 16 Panicum miliaceum
  varieties: **3** hog **5** pearl, Sanwa **6** finger, Indian **7** African, foxtail, Italian **8** barnyard, browntop, Japanese **16** Japanese barnyard
Millet, Jean-Francois
  born: **6** France, Gruchy
  artwork: **5** Sower **7** Angelus **11** The Gleaners, The Winnower **14** Potato Planters, The Man with a Hoe **23** Oedipus Taken from the Tree
Millett, Kate
  author of: **6** Flying **14** Sexual Politics
milligram
  abbreviation: **2** mg
milliliter
  abbreviation: **2** mL
millimeter
  abbreviation: **2** mm
Millionaire, The
  character: **14** Michael Anthony
  cast: **12** Marvin Miller
Mill on the Floss, The
  author: **11** George Eliot
  character: **8** Bob Jakin, Mrs Glegg **9** Lucy Deane, Mrs Pullet **11** Philip Wakem, Tom Tulliver **12** Stephen Guest **14** Maggie Tulliver
Mills, Hayley
  real name: **15** Rose Vivian Mills
  father: **4** John
  sister: **6** Juliet
  husband: **11** Ray Boulting
  born: **6** London **7** England
  roles: **8** Tiger Bay **9** Pollyanna **11** Summer Magic **13** The Parent Trap **14** The Chalk Garden **15** The Moon-Spinners **19** In Search of Castaways **20** The Trouble with Angels
Mills, John
  daughter: **6** Hayley, Juliet
  born: **7** England **10** Felixstowe
  roles: **12** Tunes of Glory **13** Ryan's Daughter **14** The Chalk Garden **17** Great Expectations **19** Swiss Family Robinson
Mills, Robert
  architect of: **10** Post Office (Washington DC) **12** Patent Office (Washington DC) **14** Circular Church (Charleston) **15** Unitarian Church (Philadelphia) **16** Treasury Building (Washington DC) **18** Washington

Monument **25** Sansom Street Baptist Church (Philadelphia) **29** Egyptian Revival Monument Church (Richmond VA)
style: 12 Greek Revival
millstream 3 run **4** race **5** brook, canal, creek, river **6** branch
Milne, A A
  author of: 13 Winnie-the-Pooh **20** The House at Pooh Corner
  character: 3 Roo **4** Pooh **5** Kanga **6** Eeyore, Piglet, Tigger **16** Christopher Robin
Milo, Milos
  island of: 6 Greece **8** Cyclades **9** Aegean Sea
  found: 5 Venus **6** statue
  missing: 4 arms
Milosz, Czeslaw
  author of: 11 Native Realm, The Usurpers **13** Bells in Winter **14** Seizure of Power, The Captive Mind
milquetoast 4 wimp **7** milksop, nebbish **11** mollycoddle
Milton
  author: 12 William Blake
Milton, George
  character in: 12 Of Mice and Men
  author: 9 Steinbeck
Milton, John
  author of: 7 Lycidas **8** L'Allegro **11** Il Penseroso **12** Areopagitica, Paradise Lost **15** Samson Agonistes **16** Paradise Regained **29** On the Morning of Christ's Nativity
Milton Berle Show, The
  host: 11 Milton Berle
  regulars: 10 Fatso Marco **11** Arnold Stang, Jack Collins, Milton Frome, Ruth Gilbert **12** Irving Benson **13** Bobby Sherwood
  announcer: 8 Sid Stone **11** Jimmy Nelson **13** Jack Lescoulie
  orchestra: 8 Alan Roth, Billy May **11** Victor Young
  theme: 7 Near You
  Milton Berle's nickname: 12 Mr Television
  sponsor: 5 Buick **6** Texaco
Milwaukee
  baseball team: 7 Brewers
  basketball team: 5 Bucks
  Indian name: 16 Mahn-a-waukee Seepe
  lake: 8 Michigan
  river: 9 Milwaukee, Menomonee, **12** Kinnickinnic
  university: 9 Marquette
mimic 3 ape **4** aper, copy, echo, mime **6** mirror, parrot **7** copycat, copyist, feigner, imitate, take off **8** imitator, simulate **9** reproduce **10** burlesquer **11** counterfeit, impersonate **13** impressionist
Mimir
  origin: 12 Scandinavian
  god of: 3 sea

decapitated by: 5 Vanir
head sent to: 4 Odin **5** Othin
oracle for: 4 Asar **5** Aesir
mimosa 14 Acacia dealbata **18** Albizia Julibrissin
  varieties: 5 Texas **6** golden **7** prairie **8** Egyptian
  cocktail contains: 9 champagne **10** orange juice
mince 4 dice, pose **5** grate, shred **6** refine, soften **7** posture, qualify **8** chop fine, hold back, mitigate, moderate, palliate **9** gloss over, put on airs, whitewash **12** attitudinize **14** affect delicacy, affect primness **15** give oneself airs **16** affect daintiness, soften one's speech **18** cut into small pieces **19** be mealymouthed about **20** cut into tiny particles
mince words 5 dodge, hedge, stall **10** equivocate **11** be ambiguous **13** avoid the issue **17** beat around the bush
mind 4 hate, heed, note, obey, tend, will, wits **5** abhor, bow to, brain, focus, sense, watch **6** brains, choice, detest, eschew, follow, intent, liking, memory, notice, notion, reason, recall, regard, resent, sanity **7** dislike, marbles, observe, opinion, outlook, thought **8** adhere to, attend to, be wary of, judgment, object to, reaction, response, submit to, take care, thinking **9** attention, awareness, be careful, cognition, faculties, intellect, intention, look after, sentiment **10** be cautious, comply with, conception, conclusion, gray matter, impression, perception, propensity, recoil from, reflection, shrink from, take care of **11** acquiesce to, be wary about, inclination, percipience, point of view, rationality, remembrance **12** apprehension, disapprove of, intelligence, recollection, reminiscence, take charge of, take notice of **13** be conscious of, comprehension, concentration, consciousness, consideration, contemplation, look askance at, preoccupation, ratiocination, retrospection, understanding **14** pay attention to
German: 5 Geist
mindful 4 wary **5** aware **7** alert to, alive to, careful, heedful **8** cautious, sensible, watchful **9** cognizant, conscious, observant, regardful **10** absorbed in, open-eyed to, thoughtful **11** attentive to, engrossed in, taken up with **12** occupied with **15** preoccupied with
mindfulness 9 alertness, awareness **10** perception **12** acquaintance **13** attentiveness, consciousness, understanding
mindless 6 insane, obtuse, stupid **7** asinine, doltish, idiotic, unaware, witless **8** careless, heedless **9** apathetic, cretinous, imbecilic, oblivious, unat-

tuned, unheeding **10** neglectful, regardless, sophomoric, unthinking **11** inattentive, indifferent, nonsensical, thoughtless, unobservant, unreasoning **12** disregardful, simple-minded **13** inconsiderate, unintelligent **14** indiscriminate
mine 3 pit **4** fund **5** cache, hoard, shaft, stock, store **6** dig for, quarry, supply, tunnel, wealth **7** extract, reserve **8** dig under, excavate, treasure **9** abundance, booby-trap **10** excavation **12** accumulation
Mineo, Sal
  real name: 14 Salvatore Mineo
  born: 7 Bronx NY
  roles: 5 Giant, Tonka **6** Exodus **18** Rebel Without a Cause, Who Killed Teddy Bear?
mineral 3 jet, ore **4** coal, gold, iron, mica, opal, spar, talc **5** beryl, topaz **6** augite, barite, blende, cerine, copper, galena, garnet, iolite, pinite, rutile, sandix, silver, sphene, spinel, sulfur **7** amesite, apatite, azurite, biotite, bornite, calcite, citrine, coesite, crystal, cuprite, cyanite, element, gahnite, helvite, jadeite, kernite, kunzite, niobite, olivine, prasine, zeolite, zircon **8** asbestos, borocite, chlorite, cinnabar, corundum, dolomite, epsomite, fayalite, feldspar, fluorite, graphite, hematite, lazulite, siderite, sodalite, stibnite, triplite, wellsite **9** aragonite, argentite, carnelian, celestite, cerussite, danburite, fosterite, kaolinite, lawsonite, magnetite, malachite, muscovite, petroleum, phenakite, scapolite, tridymite, turquoise, wulfenite **10** calaverite, chalcedony, orthoclase, pyrrhotite, sphalerite, tourmaline, wolfachite **11** alexandrite, chrysoberyl, melanterite **12** brazilianite, chalcopyrite, fincalconite, fluorapatite **13** rhodochrosite
Minerva
  origin: 5 Roman
  goddess of: 3 war **4** arts **6** wisdom **11** handicrafts
  corresponds to: 6 Athena
mingle 3 mix **4** fuse, join **5** blend, merge, unite **6** hobnob **7** combine, consort **8** coalesce, intermix **9** associate, circulate, commingle, interfuse, interlard, socialize **10** amalgamate, fraternize, intertwine, interweave **11** intermingle, intersperse **12** rub shoulders
miniature 3 wee **4** tiny **5** elfin, pygmy **6** bantam, little, petite **9** minuscule **10** diminutive, pocket-size, small-scale **11** lilliputian, microcosmic, microscopic
minim
  abbreviation: 3 min
minimal 5 token **7** minimum, nominal **13** least possible, unappreciable
minimize 5 dwarf **6** reduce, shrink

8 belittle, mitigate **9** underrate **10** depreciate, undervalue

minimum 4 base **5** basic, least **7** modicum **8** smallest

minister 4 abbe, tend **5** padre, rabbi, serve, vicar **6** answer, cleric, father, oblige, parson, pastor, priest **7** care for, cater to **8** attend to, chaplain, pander to, preacher, reverend **9** clergyman, secretary **10** evangelist, revivalist, take care of **11** accommodate **12** ecclesiastic **13** cabinet member

ministerial 6 cleric **8** churchly, clerical, pastoral, priestly **14** ecclesiastical

ministration 3 aid **4** care **6** charge **7** comfort **9** attention **10** protection **11** supervision

Ministry of Fear, The
  author: 12 Graham Greene

Minnehaha
  character in: 8 Hiawatha
  author: 10 Longfellow

Minnelli, Liza
  father: 8 Vincente
  mother: 11 Judy Garland
  born: 12 Los Angeles CA
  roles: 6 Arthur **7** Cabaret (Oscar) **14** New York New York **16** The Sterile Cuckoo **17** Flora the Red Menace

Minnelli, Vincente
  director of: 4 Gigi (Oscar) **9** Brigadoon **11** Lust for Life **15** Bells Are Ringing, Meet Me in St Louis **16** Father of the Bride **17** An American in Paris

Minnesota
  abbreviation: 2 MN **4** Minn
  nickname: 6 Gopher **9** North Star **19** Land of Sky-blue Waters **22** Land of Ten Thousand Lakes
  capital: 6 St Paul
  largest city: 11 Minneapolis
  others: 3 Ada, Ely **4** Mora **5** Edina **6** Austin, Duluth, Newulm, Winona **7** Babbitt, Bemidji, Fosston, Hibbing, Mankato, Red Wing, St Cloud **8** Brainerd, Moorhead **9** Albertlea, Blue Earth, Richfield, Rochester, Roseville **10** Minnetonka, Robinsdale **11** Bloomington, St Louis Park **14** Brooklyn Center **18** International Falls
  college: 6 Bethel, St Olaf, Winona **7** Bemidji, Hamline **8** Adolphus, Augsburg, Carleton, St Thomas **10** Macalester
  feature:
    monument: 10 Paul Bunyan
    national monument: 9 Pipestone **12** Grand Portage
    national park: 9 Voyageurs'
    Norse artifact: 19 Kensington Rune Stone
  tribe: 5 Sioux **6** Dakota, Ojibwa, Santee **8** Chippewa **9** Menominee
  people: 11 Judy Garland **12** Mayo brothers **13** Harold Stassen, Lauris Norstad, Sinclair Lewis **16** F Scott Fitzgerald
  explorer: 8 Hennepin, Norsemen, Radisson **9** Greysolon **12** Groseilliers **19** Sieur Duluth of du Lhut
  lakes: 3 Red **5** Leech, Rainy **6** Itasca **7** Bemidji **8** Superior **9** Mille Lacs **10** Minnewaska **14** Lake of the Woods, Winnibigoshish
  land rank: 7 twelfth
  mountain: 6 Cuyuna, Mesabi **7** Misquah **9** Vermilion
    highest point: 5 Eagle
  physical feature: 6 Big Bog **14** Northwest Angle
    falls: 9 Minnehaha
  river: 3 Red **5** Rainy **6** Pigeon **7** St Croix, St Louis **9** Des Moines, Minnesota **10** St Lawrence **11** Mississippi
  state admission: 12 thirty-second
  state bird: 10 common loon
  state fish: 7 walleye
  state flower: 14 moccasin flower **24** pink and white lady's slipper
  state motto: 17 The Star of the North
  state song: 13 Hail Minnesota
  state tree: 13 Norway red pine
  baseball team: 5 Twins
  football team: 7 Vikings
  hockey team: 10 North Stars

Minni see **7** Armenia

minor 5 child, light, petty, small, youth **6** infant, lesser, paltry, slight **7** trivial **8** nugatory, picayune, piddling, teenager, trifling **9** secondary, youngster **10** adolescent **11** subordinate, unimportant **13** insignificant **14** inconsiderable **15** inconsequential

minority 4 less **5** youth **6** lesser, nonage **7** boyhood, infancy **8** girlhood **9** childhood, juniority **10** immaturity **11** adolescence

minor-league 4 punk **5** dinky, seedy, tacky **6** cheesy, common, lesser, shabby **8** inferior, small-fry **9** secondary, small-time **10** bush-league, second-rate **13** insignificant

Minos
  king of: 5 Crete
  father: 4 Zeus
  mother: 6 Europa
  brother: 8 Sarpedon **12** Rhadamanthys
  wife: 8 Pasiphae
  daughter: 7 Ariadne, Phaedra
  ordered: 9 Labryinth
  became: 5 judge
    in: 5 Hades

Minotaur
  form: 7 monster
  combined: 3 man **4** bull
  father: 10 Cretan bull
  mother: 8 Pasiphae
  home: 9 Labyrinth
  ate flesh of: 6 humans
  killed by: 7 Theseus

minstrel 4 bard, poet **6** dancer, end

man, lyrist, player, singer **8** comedian, songster **9** blackface, poetaster, serenader, versifier **10** troubadour **11** entertainer **12** interlocutor, vaudevillian **15** song-and-dance man

mint
  varieties: 3 dog, red **4** wood **5** apple, field, lemon, stone, water **6** coyote, dotted, orange, Scotch **7** Meehan's **8** bergamot, Corsican, creeping, Japanese, mountain **9** pineapple
  flavor: 7 menthol **9** spearmint **10** peppermint
  liqueur: 13 creme de menthe
  botanical name: 6 Mentha **8** Labiatae, M spicata **9** M piperita
  origin: 13 Mediterranean
  related herb: 7 oregano **8** marjoram, rosemary
  symbol of: 11 hospitality
  mythical nymph: 6 Mintha
    beloved of: 5 Pluto
    Mintha trod underfoot by: 10 Persephone
  cure for: 7 hiccups
  antidote for: 16 sea serpent stings
  use: 4 lamb **5** salad **6** fruits

Minthe
  form: 5 nymph
  changed into: 9 mint plant
  changed by: 10 Persephone

minuscule 3 wee **4** tiny **5** small **6** minute **10** teeny-weeny **11** small letter **13** infinitesimal **15** lower-case letter

minute 3 wee **4** fine, puny, tiny, wink **5** close, exact, flash, jiffy, petty, scant, shake, teeny, trice **6** breath, little, moment, petite, second, slight, strict **7** careful, instant, minikin, precise **8** detailed, itemized, trifling **9** miniature, twinkling **10** a short time, diminutive, exhaustive, meticulous, negligible, scrupulous **11** lilliputian, microscopic **12** sixty seconds **13** conscientious, imperceptible, inappreciable, infinitesimal, insignificant **14** extremely small, inconsiderable
  abbreviation: 3 min

minute portion 3 bit, sip **4** bite **5** crumb, grain, scrap, shred, speck **6** morsel, sliver **7** swallow **8** fragment, mouthful, particle

minutiae 6 trivia **7** trifles **8** niceties **10** bagatelles, pedantries, subtleties **11** odds and ends, particulars **12** minor details, trivialities **15** particularities

minx 4 jade, slut **5** hussy, huzzy, wench **7** baggage **10** prostitute

Minyades
  daughters of: 6 Minyas

Miolnir
  hammer of: 4 Thor

mir 5 peace, world **21** Russian village commune

mirabile dictu 12 strange to say **17** marvelous to relate

miracle 4 omen, sign **6** marvel, wonder **7** mystery, portent, prodigy **9** divine act, sensation, spectacle **10** phenomenon **11** masterpiece

Miracle of Morgan's Creek, The
director: **14** Preston Sturges
cast: **9** Diana Lynn **11** Betty Hutton **12** Brian Donlevy, Eddie Bracken **15** William Demarest

Miracle on 34th Street
director: **12** George Seaton
based on story by: **15** Valentine Davies
cast: **9** John Payne **11** Edmund Gwenn (Kris Kringle), Natalie Wood **12** Gene Lockhart, Maureen O'Hara, Thelma Ritter
Oscar for: **12** screenwriter **15** supporting actor (Gwenn)

Miracle Worker, The
director: **10** Arthur Penn
cast: **9** Patty Duke (Helen Keller) **10** Victor Jory **11** Inga Swenson **12** Anne Bancroft (Anne Sullivan)
Oscar for: **7** actress (Bancroft) **17** supporting actress (Duke)

miraculous 6 divine **7** amazing, magical **9** marvelous, visionary, wonderful **10** incredible, mysterious, phenomenal, prodigious, remarkable **11** astonishing, astounding, exceptional, spectacular, supernormal **13** extraordinary, preternatural, wonderworking **14** thaumaturgical

miraculous food 5 manna

Miraculous writing
also: **4** mene **5** perez, tekel **8** upharsin
means: **7** divided, weighed **8** numbered
interpreted by: **6** Daniel

mirage 5 fancy **7** fantasy **8** delusion, illusion, phantasm **9** unreality **12** will-o'-the-wisp **13** hallucinations, misconception **14** castle in the air **15** optical illusion

Miranda
character in: **10** The Tempest
author: **11** Shakespeare

Miranda, Carmen
real name: **26** Maria do Carmo Miranda da Cunha
nickname: **18** Brazilian Bombshell
born: **8** Portugal **16** Marco de Canavezes
roles: **10** Copacabana **14** That Night in Rio **15** Weekend in Havana **16** Down Argentine Way **22** Springtime in the Rockies

mire 3 bog, fen, mud **4** cake, muck, ooze, soil **5** marsh, muddy, slime, slush, smear **6** enmesh, sludge **7** begrime, bog down, ensnare, spatter **8** besmirch, entangle, quagmire

Miriam
father: **5** Amram

mother: **8** Jochebed
brother: **5** Aaron, Moses

Miro, Joan
born: **5** Spain **8** Montroig **9** Barcelona
artwork: **9** Help Spain, The Reaper **13** Dutch Interior **14** Constellations **16** Catalan Landscape **19** Dog Barking at the Moon **20** Still Life with Old Shoe **26** Woman and Bird in the Moonlight

mirror 4 copy, show **5** glass, image, model **7** epitome, example, paragon, reflect **8** exemplar, manifest, paradigm, standard **10** reflection **11** cheval glass **12** looking glass

mirth 4 glee **6** gaiety, levity **7** jollity **8** drollery, hilarity, laughter **9** amusement, festivity, happiness, jocundity, joviality, merriment **10** jocularity **11** good spirits, merrymaking, playfulness **12** cheerfulness

mirthful 3 gay **4** glad **5** happy, jolly, merry **6** blithe, jocose, jovial, joyful, joyous **7** gleeful, jocular, risible

mirthless 3 sad **4** dour, glum **6** gloomy, morose **7** joyless, unhappy **8** dejected **9** cheerless, sorrowful **10** in the dumps, melancholy **14** down in the mouth

miry 3 wet **4** oozy **5** boggy, mucky, muddy, slimy, slushy, soggy **6** claggy, swampy **7** sloughy

misadventure 3 ill **4** slip **6** mishap **7** debacle, failure, reverse, setback **8** bad break, calamity, casualty, disaster **9** adversity, mischance **10** infelicity, misfortune **11** catastrophe, contretemps

misanthrope 5 cynic **7** skeptic **9** pessimist **10** misogynist

Misanthrope, Le
author: **7** Moliere
character: **7** Alceste, Arsinoe, Eliante **8** Celimene, Philinte

misanthropic 4 cold **5** surly **6** morose **7** cynical, distant **10** antisocial, unfriendly, unsociable **11** distrustful **12** discourteous, inhospitable, unneighborly, unpersonable, unresponsive **14** unapproachable **15** unaccommodating

misapply 5 abuse **6** misuse **9** misemploy **13** use improperly

misapprehension 5 mixup **7** mistake **11** misjudgment **13** misconception **14** miscalculation **15** false impression, misconstruction **16** misunderstanding **17** misinterpretation

misappropriate 4 bilk **5** abuse, cheat, mulct, steal **6** misuse **7** defraud, purloin, swindle **8** embezzle, misapply, peculate **9** defalcate, misemploy

misappropriation 6 misuse, taking **11** defalcation **12** embezzlement

misbehave 5 act up **7** disobey, do wrong **10** transgress **15** get into mischief

misbehavior 5 lapse **7** misdeed, offense **8** acting up, trespass **9** impudence **10** bad conduct, bad manners, disrespect, misconduct **11** delinquency, dereliction, impropriety, misdemeanor **12** indiscretion **13** transgression **16** obstreperousness, unmanageableness

miscalculate 3 err **8** misjudge **10** guess wrong **11** misestimate

miscalculation 5 error **10** inaccuracy **13** misestimation

miscarriage 4 slip **5** botch **6** fizzle **7** default, failing, failure, misfire, undoing, washout **8** casualty, collapse

miscarry 4 fail **5** abort, botch **6** fizzle, go awry **9** terminate **12** come to naught

miscellanea 8 analects **9** anthology, gleanings, scrapbook **10** collection, miscellany, selections **11** collectanea

miscellaneous 5 mixed **6** divers, motley, sundry, varied **7** diverse, mingled, various **8** assorted, manifold **9** different **11** diversified **13** heterogeneous

miscellaneous collection
Latin/pseudo Latin: **14** omniumgatherum

miscellany 5 blend **6** jumble, medley **7** melange, mixture, variety **8** analects, extracts, mishmash, pastiche **9** anthology, gleanings, potpourri **10** assortment, collection, hodgepodge, salmagundi, selections **11** collectanea, compilation, gallimaufry, miscellanea **14** conglomeration, omnium-gatherum

mischance 6 ill lot, mishap **7** bad luck, ill luck, ill wind **8** accident **9** adversity **10** infelicity, misfortune **12** misadventure

mischief 4 evil **5** wrong **6** injury, malice **7** devilry, knavery, roguery **8** deviltry, foul play, plotting, scheming, villainy **9** depravity, devilment, rascality **10** orneriness, wrongdoing **11** naughtiness, playfulness, roguishness, shenanigans, willfulness **12** prankishness, sportiveness **14** capriciousness

mischief-maker 3 imp **5** demon, devil, scamp **7** gremlin, hellion **9** scoundrel **10** hell-raiser

mischievous 3 sly **5** elfin **6** elfish, impish, malign, vexing, wicked **7** harmful, naughty, noxious, playful, roguish, teasing, vicious, waggish **8** annoying, devilish, prankish, spiteful, sportive **9** injurious, malicious, malignant, uninvited **10** frolicsome, gratuitous, pernicious **11** deleterious, destructive, detrimental, uncalled for **12** exacerbating

misconceive 3 err **4** lose, miss **8** misjudge **12** misinterpret **13** misunderstand

misconception 5 error **8** delusion **11** misjudgment **13** erroneous idea **14** mis- information **15** misapprehension, mis- construction **16** misunderstanding **17** misinterpretation, misrepresentation

misconduct 7 misdeed, misstep **10** mis- prision, peccadillo, wrongdoing **11** delinquency, dereliction, impropriety, malefaction, malfeasance, misbehavior, misdemeanor **13** transgression

misconstrue 7 distort, mistake **8** misjudge **9** misreckon, misrender **12** misapprehend, miscalculate, misinterpret, mistranslate **13** misunderstand

miscreant 3 bum **4** heel **5** knave, scamp **6** bad egg, rascal, sinner, wretch **7** villain **8** evildoer, lost soul, scalawag **9** reprobate, scoundrel **10** blackguard, black sheep, malefactor

misdeed 3 sin **4** slip **5** crime, lapse, wrong **6** felony **7** faux pas, offense, outrage **8** atrocity, trespass **9** violation **10** misconduct, peccadillo **11** malfeasance, misbehavior, misdemeanor **12** indiscretion, infringement **13** transgression

misdemeanor 3 sin **5** crime, fault **7** offense, misdeed **8** disorder **10** peccadillo **11** misbehavior **13** transgression

misdoer 5 crook **8** criminal **9** miscreant, wrongdoer **10** delinquent

mise en scene 6 milieu **7** setting **8** ambience **10** atmosphere, background **11** environment **12** stage setting, surroundings

miser 5 piker **7** hoarder, niggard, Scrooge, skimper **8** tightwad **9** skinflint **10** cheapskate, pinchpenny **12** pennypincher, stingy person

Miser, The
  also: **6** L'Avare
  author: **7** Moliere
  character: **5** Elise **6** Valere **7** Anselme, Cleante, Mariane **8** Harpagon

miserable 3 sad **4** mean **5** inept, needy, sorry **6** abject, scurvy, shabby, sordid, woeful **7** abysmal, crushed, doleful, forlorn, grieved, hapless, unhappy **8** beggarly, degraded, dejected, desolate, dolorous, feckless, inferior, mournful, pathetic, pitiable, rubbishy, very poor, wretched **9** appalling, atrocious, cheerless, depressed, desperate, heartsick, sorrowful, woebegone **10** chapfallen, deplorable, despicable, despondent, heavy- laden, lamentable, second-rate, unbearable **11** crestfallen, heartbroken, unfortunate **12** contemptible, disconsolate, impoverished **13** brokenhearted **14** down in the mouth

Miserables, Les
  author: **10** Victor Hugo
  character: **6** Javert **7** Cosette, Fantine **10** Thenardier **11** Jean Valjean **15** Father Madeleine, Marius Pontmercy **17** Eponine Thenardier

misericordia 5 mercy **10** compassion

miserliness 6 penury **9** frugality, par-

simony **10** stinginess **13** niggardliness, penny-pinching **15** tight-fistedness

miserly 4 mean, near **5** cheap, tight **6** frugal, greedy, meager, stingy **7** selfish **8** grasping, grudging, pinching **9** illiberal, niggardly, penurious, scrimping **10** avaricious, ungenerous **11** closefisted, closehanded, tight-fisted **12** parsimonious **13** penny-pinching

misery 3 woe **4** blow **5** agony, curse, grief, trial **6** ordeal, regret, sorrow **7** anguish, bad deal, bad news, chagrin, despair, sadness, torment, trouble **8** bad scene, calamity, disaster, distress, exaction, hardship **9** dejection, heartache, privation, suffering **10** affliction, bitter pill, depression, desolation, melancholy, misfortune **11** catastrophe, despondency, tribulation **12** wretchedness

Misfits, The
  director: **10** John Huston
  based on story by: **12** Arthur Miller
  cast: **10** Clark Gable, Eli Wallach **12** Thelma Ritter **13** Marilyn Monroe **15** Montgomery Clift

misfortune 4 blow, loss **6** misery, mishap **7** bad luck, reverse, setback, tragedy, trouble **8** calamity, casualty, disaster, downfall, hard luck, hardship **9** adversity, hard times, ruination **10** affliction, ill fortune **11** catastrophe, tribulation **12** misadventure

misgiving, misgivings 4 fear **5** alarm, doubt, dread, qualm, worry **7** anxiety, dubiety **8** disquiet, mistrust **9** suspicion **10** foreboding, skepticism **11** dubiousness, uncertainty **12** apprehension, doubtfulness, presentiment, reservations **14** second thoughts

misguided 5 at sea **6** adrift, faulty, misled, unwise **7** in error **8** mistaken **9** erroneous, imprudent, led astray, off course **10** ill-advised, indiscreet, misadvised **11** injudicious, misdirected, misinformed

mishap 4 slip, snag **5** botch **6** fiasco, slipup **7** reverse, setback **8** casualty, disaster **9** mischance **10** difficulty, misfortune **11** miscarriage **12** misadventure

mishmash 3 mix **4** hash, stew **5** salad **6** jumble, medley, muddle **7** melange **8** mixed bag, pastiche, scramble **9** patchwork **10** assemblage, crazy quilt, hodgepodge, miscellany, salmagundi **14** conglomeration, omnium-gatherum

misinform 7 deceive, mislead **8** misguide **9** misdirect **10** lead astray **12** misrepresent

misinterpret 11 misconstrue **12** misapprehend **13** misunderstand

misinterpretation 13 misconception **16** misunderstanding **17** misrepresentation

misjudge 3 err **7** mistake **10** exaggerate, understate **11** misconceive, mis-

construe **12** misapprehend, miscalculate, misinterpret, overestimate **13** misunderstand, underestimate

mislay 4 lose, miss **8** displace, misplace

mislead 4 dupe, fool, gull **6** betray, delude, entice, seduce, take in **7** beguile, deceive **8** hoodwink, inveigle, misguide **9** bamboozle, misdirect, misinform, play false, victimize **10** lead astray **11** double-cross, string along

misleading 6 luring **8** deluding **9** deceiving **10** misguiding **11** hoodwinking

mismanage 3 mar **4** flub, muff, ruin **5** botch, spoil **6** bollix, bungle, foul up, mess up **7** louse up, screw up **9** mishandle **11** make a hash of, make a mess of

misnomer 8 misusage, solecism **9** barbarism, misnaming **11** malapropism

misogynic 7 cynical **11** woman-hating **12** misanthropic

misogynist 5 cynic **10** woman-hater **11** misanthrope

misplace 4 lose **5** abuse **6** mislay **11** lose track of

misreckon 8 misjudge **10** guess wrong, miscompute **11** misestimate **12** miscalculate

misrepresent 7 falsify, mislead **8** disguise

misrepresentation 7 mockery **8** altering, travesty, twisting **9** burlesque, doctoring **10** caricature, distortion, falsifying **12** adulteration, exaggeration, misstatement **13** falsification

miss 4 blow, girl, lack, lady, lass, lose, loss, maid, muff, skip, slip, want **5** avert, avoid, error, forgo, let go, woman **6** bypass, damsel, escape, forego, lassie, maiden, miscue, pass by **7** blunder, colleen, default, failure, fly wide, let pass, let slip, long for, mistake, neglect, old maid, overrun, pine for **8** leave out, omission, overlook, pass over, senorita, slip up on, spinster, yearn for **9** disregard, fall short, false step, gloss over, go without, overshoot, oversight, surrender, young lady **10** demoiselle, schoolgirl **12** be absent from **13** feel the loss of, mademoiselle

missal 10 prayer book

missed
  French: **6** manque

misshapen 7 twisted **8** deformed **9** contorted, distorted

missile 4 ball, dart **5** arrow, lance, shaft, shell, spear, stone **6** bullet, rocket **7** harpoon, javelin **10** projectile

missing 4 AWOL, gone, lost **6** absent **7** lacking, left out, not here **8** avoiding, skipping **10** longing for, not present **11** overlooking, yearning for **12** disregarding

Missing
director: **22** Constantine Costa-Gavras
cast: **8** John Shea **10** Jack Lemmon
11 Sissy Spacek **13** Melanie Mayron

Missing Persons and Other Essays
author: **12** Heinrich Boll

mission 3 end, job **4** task **5** quest **6**
charge **7** calling, mandate, pursuit **8**
legation, ministry **9** objective **10** assignment, commission, delegation, enterprise **11** raison d'etre, undertaking

Mission
tribe: **7** Chumash, Juaneno, Luiseno
8 Diegueno **9** Costanoan **10** Gabr-
ielino **11** Fernandario
location: **10** California

Mission: Impossible
character: **5** Casey, Paris **10** Rollin
Hand **11** Dana Lambert, James
Phelps **12** Daniel Briggs **13** Barney
Collier **14** Cinnamon Carter, Willie
Armitage
cast: **10** Greg Morris, Peter Lupus,
Steven Hill **11** Barbara Bain, Peter
Graves **12** Leonard Nimoy, Martin
Landau **14** Lynda Day George **15**
Lesley Ann Warren

Mississippi
abbreviation: **2** MS **4** Miss
nickname: **5** Bayou **6** Mudcat **8** Magnolia
capital/largest city: **7** Jackson
others: **6** Biloxi, Helena, Laurel, Tupelo, Winona **7** Belzoni, Corinth,
Grenada, Natchez **8** Bogalusa, Columbus, Gulfport, Meridian **9** Kosciusko, Vicksburg **10** Clarksdale, Pascagoula **11** Hattiesburg **13** Pass
Christian
college: **4** Rust **6** Alcorn **7** Jackson **8**
Belhaven, Millsaps, Tougaloo **11**
Mississippi **12** Blue Mountain, William Carey
feature: **12** Natchez Trace
national military park: **9** Vicksburg
national seashore: **11** Gulf Islands
tribe: **3** Sac **5** Tious **6** Biloxi, Mandan, Tunica **7** Choctaw, Natchez,
Tonikan **8** Chicksaw
people: **11** Eudora Welty **15** William
Faulkner **17** Tennessee Williams
explorer: **6** DeSoto, Joliet **9** Iberville, Marquette
island: **3** Cat **4** Horn, Ship **9** Petit
Bois
lake: **4** Enid **6** Sardis **7** Barnett, Grenada **8** Pickwick **9** Arkabutla, Oka-
tibbee
land rank: **12** thirty-second
highest point: **7** Woodall
physical feature:
delta: **10** Yazoo Basin
hills: **8** Fall Line **9** Tennessee **11**
Loess Bluffs
prairie: **5** Black **7** Jackson
sound: **11** Mississippi
river: **4** Leaf **5** Pearl, Yazoo **8** Big
Black **9** Tombigbee, Yalobusha

10 Homochitto, Pascagoula **11** Mississippi **12** Tallahatchie
state admission: **9** twentieth
state bird: **11** mockingbird
state flower: **8** magnolia
state motto: **14** By Valor and Arms
state song: **13** Go Mississippi
state tree: **8** magnolia

missive 4 note **6** billet, letter **7** epistle,
message **13** communication **14** correspondence

Miss Julie
author: **16** August Strindberg

Miss Lonelyhearts
author: **13** Nathanael West

Missouri
abbreviation: **2** MO
nickname: **5** Ozark **6** Show-Me **7** Bullion **15** Mother of the West
capital: **13** Jefferson City
largest city: **7** St Louis
others: **5** Eldon, Hayti, Lamar, Macon, Rolla **6** Butler, Joplin, Mexico **7**
Bethany, Bolivar, Cameron, Clayton,
Lebanon, Moberly, Sedalia **8** Berkeley, Columbia, Hannibal, Kirkwood,
Sikeston, St Joseph **10** Bonne Terre,
Kansas City **11** Springfield, Warrens-
burg **12** Independence **13** Cape Gi-
rardeau, Webster Groves
college: **5** Avila, Drury **6** Tarkio **7**
Lincoln, St Louis, Webster **8** Stephens **10** Washington **11** Westminster
feature:
dam: **5** Osage
tribe: **3** Fox, Sac **4** Sauk **5** Osage **7**
Shawnee **8** Cherokee, Missouri
people: **7** TS Eliot **9** Mark Twain **10**
Jesse James **11** Omar Bradley **12**
Helen Traubel, Sara Teasdale **13**
John J Pershing, Marianne Moore,
Samuel Clemens **15** Reinhold Niebuhr **22** George Washington Carver
explorer: **6** Joliet **7** La Salle **9** Marquette
lake: **7** Norfolk **9** Tablerock, Taney-
como **10** Bull Shoals **14** Kaysinger
Bluff **15** Lake of the Ozarks
land rank: **10** nineteenth
mountain: **6** Ozarks **10** St Francois
highest point: **8** Taumsauk
physical feature: **8** Bootheel **9** Big
Spring
plains: **4** Till **5** Osage
plateau: **5** Ozark
president: **12** Harry S Truman
river: **4** Salt **5** Grand, Osage, White **6**
Platte **7** Current, Meramec **8** Big
Muddy, Chariton, Missouri **9** Des
Moines, Gasconade, St Francis **11**
Mississippi
state admission: **12** twenty-fourth
state bird: **8** bluebird
state flower: **8** hawthorn
state motto: **41** The Welfare of the
People Shall Be the Supreme Law

state song: **13** Missouri Waltz
state tree: **7** dogwood

Miss Peach
creator: **11** Mell Lazarus
character: **3** Ira **6** Arthur, Lester,
Marcia **8** Francine
place: **9** Kamp Kelly **11** Kelly School

misspend 5 waste **8** squander **9** dissipate, throw away **11** fritter away

misspent 6 wasted **8** depraved **9** debauched, dissolute, idled away **10**
misapplied, profitless, squandered,
thrown away

misstate 5 alter **6** bollix, garble **7** confuse, distort, falsify, pervert **8** mis-
quote **9** misreport **12** misrepresent

misstatement 3 fib, lie **4** tale **5** error
7 falsity, untruth **9** falsehood **13** prevarication **17** misrepresentation

misstep 3 sin **4** goof, slip, vice **5**
boner, error, fault, gaffe, lapse **6** boo-
boo, defect, foul-up **7** blooper, faux
pas, offense, screw-up **11** delinquency, dereliction, shortcoming **12**
indiscretion **13** transgression

miss the mark 4 fail **9** fall short **11**
come up short

miss the point 7 mistake **11** fail to
catch, misconceive **12** misapprehend
13 misunderstand

mist 3 fog **4** haze, murk, smog **5**
steam, vapor **7** drizzle

mistake 4 slip **5** boner, error, gaffe,
mix-up **6** slipup **7** blooper, blunder,
confuse, faux pas, misstep **8** confound, misjudge **9** misreckon, oversight **11** misconstrue, misidentify **12**
misapprehend, miscalculate, misinterpret **13** misunderstand **14** miscalculation
French: **10** malentendu

mistaken 5 at sea, false, wrong **6**
faulty, untrue **7** at fault, in error, unsound **8** deceived **9** erroneous, illogical, incorrect, off course, unfounded
10 fallacious, groundless, inaccurate,
ungrounded **11** unjustified

Mister 3 aga, dom, don, pan, reb, sir **4**
agha, babu, herr **5** sahib, senor **6** senhor, signor **7** mynheer **8** monsieur

Mister Roberts
author: **12** Thomas Heggen
director: **8** John Ford **11** Mervyn Le-
Roy
cast: **8** Ward Bond **10** Henry Fonda,
Jack Lemmon (Ensign Pulver) **11**
Betsy Palmer, James Cagney **13** William Powell
Oscar for: **15** supporting actor (Lemmon)

Mister Saturday Night
nickname of: **13** Jackie Gleason

mistreat 4 harm **5** abuse, bully,
hound, wrong **6** harass, ill-use, injure,
misuse, molest **7** assault, oppress,
outrage, pervert, torment, violate

8 ill-treat, maltreat **9** brutalize, manhandle, mishandle, persecute

mistreatment 5 abuse **6** ill-use, injury **7** assault, cruelty, harming **10** bodily harm, oppression **11** manhandling, molestation, persecution **12** maltreatment

mistress 3 Mrs **4** doxy, lady, Miss **5** lover, Madam **6** matron **8** ladylove, paramour **9** concubine, headwoman, housewife, inamorata, kept woman **10** chatelaine, girlfriend, sweetheart

mistrust 5 doubt, qualm **7** anxiety, dubiety, suspect **8** distrust, question, wariness **9** challenge, chariness, leeriness, misgiving, suspicion **10** disbelieve, skepticism

misty 4 dewy, hazy **5** filmy, foggy, murky **6** cloudy, opaque, steamy **8** nebulous, overcast, vaporous **10** indistinct

misunderstand 7 confuse, misread, mistake **8** misjudge **9** misreckon **11** misconceive, misconstrue **12** misapprehend, miscalculate, misinterpret, miss the point

misunderstanding 4 rift, spat **5** set-to **7** discord, dispute, quarrel, wrangle **8** conflict, squabble **10** difference, dissension, misreading **11** altercation, contretemps, misjudgment **12** disagreement **13** misconception **15** false impression, misapprehension **16** miscomprehension **17** misinterpretation

French: 10 malentendu

misuse 4 harm, hurt **5** abuse, waste, wrong **6** debase, injure **7** corrupt, exploit, outrage, pervert, profane **8** illtreat, maltreat, misapply, mistreat, wrong use **9** misemploy **10** corruption, perversion, prostitute **11** desecration, profanation, squandering **12** ill treatment, maltreatment, mistreatment, prostitution **13** misemployment **14** misapplication **15** take advantage of

Mitchell, Billy (William Lendrum)
    advocate of: 8 air power
    court-martialed for: 15 insubordination
    served in: 3 WWI
    rank: 16 brigadier general
    commander of: 15 US army air forces

Mitchell, Margaret
    author of: 15 Gone With the Wind

Mitchell, Silas Weir
    author of: 9 Hugh Wynne (Free Quaker) **11** Roland Blake

Mitchell, Thomas
    born: 11 Elizabeth NJ
    roles: 7 Our Town **8** Doc Boone **9** The Outlaw **10** Stagecoach **11** Gerald O'Hara, Lost Horizon **15** Gone With the Wind **19** Only Angels Have Wings

Mitchum, Robert

born: 12 Bridgeport CT
    roles: 6 Midway **10** Winds of War **11** Thunder Road **13** Ryan's Daughter, The Longest Day, The Sundowners **15** The Story of G I Joe **16** Farewell My Lovely **20** Heaven Knows Mr Allison

mite 3 bit, jot **4** atom, iota, whit **5** scrap, speck **6** spider **7** smidgen **8** arachnid, particle

Mitford, Jessica
    author of: 21 The American Way of Death **22** Kind and Usual Punishment

Mitford, Nancy
    author of: 14 Noblesse Oblige **16** The Pursuit of Love **18** Love in a Cold Climate
    coined term: 1 U **4** non-U

Mithgarthr see **7** Midgard

Mithras
    origin: 7 Persian
    god of: 5 light, truth
    corresponds to: 3 Sol

mitigate 4 ease **5** allay, blunt **6** lessen, reduce, soften, soothe, temper, weaken **7** assuage, lighten, mollify, placate, relieve **8** diminish, moderate, palliate **9** alleviate, extenuate **10** ameliorate

mitigating 6 easing **8** allaying, blunting, reducing **9** assuaging, lessening, relieving, softening, tempering **10** lightening, moderating, palliating, palliative **11** diminishing, extenuating **12** ameliorating

Mitteleuropa 12 middle Europe

mitzvah, mitsvah 8 good deed **11** commandment

mix 3 add **4** beat, club, fold, fuse, join, stir, whip **5** admix, alloy, blend, merge, put in, unite **6** commix, fusion, hobnob, mingle **7** combine, consort, include, mixture **8** assembly, coalesce, compound, intermix, mingling **9** associate, commingle, interfuse, interlard, introduce, socialize **10** amalgamate, fraternize, intertwine, interweave **11** incorporate, intermingle, intersperse, put together

mixed 4 coed **5** fused **6** hybrid, motley **7** alloyed, blended, inmixed, mingled, mongrel, not pure **8** combined **9** composite, uncertain **10** ambivalent, indecisive, interwoven, variegated **11** adulterated, diversified, half and half, put together **12** conglomerate, inconclusive **13** heterogeneous, male-and-female, miscellaneous

mixed-up 6 addled **7** chaotic, jumbled, muddled, tangled **8** confused, rambling **9** befuddled, illogical, nonplused, perplexed **10** bewildered, disjointed, incoherent, irrational, nonplussed **12** disconnected, disorganized **13** disharmonious, heterogeneous

Mixtec
    tribe: 7 Zapotec

mixture 3 mix **4** hash, stew **5** alloy, blend, union **6** fusion, jumble, medley **7** amalgam, melange **8** compound, mishmash, pastiche **9** admixture, composite, potpourri **10** commixture, hodgepodge, salmagundi **11** association, combination **12** adulteration, amalgamation, intermixture

mixup 4 mess, riot **5** fight, melee, snafu **6** fracas, muddle, tangle **7** mistake **8** disorder **9** confusion, imbroglio **11** misjudgment **14** miscalculation **16** miscomprehension, misunderstanding

mix up 5 addle **6** mess up, muddle **7** confuse, nonplus, perplex **8** befuddle, bewilder **10** disarrange

Mneme
    member of: 5 Muses
    personifies: 6 memory

Mnemosyne
    origin: 5 Greek
    member of: 6 Titans
    goddess of: 6 memory
    father: 6 Uranus
    mother: 4 Gaea
    daughters: 5 Muses

Moab
    son of: 3 Lot
    land near: 7 Dead Sea
    home of: 4 Ruth **5** Naomi

Moabite god 7 Chemosh

moan 3 sob **4** keen, wail **5** groan **6** bemoan, bewail, lament, plaint **7** grumble **11** lamentation

moan over 5 mourn **6** bemoan, bewail, lament **7** cry over **8** weep over **10** grieve over

moat 4 foss **5** ditch, fosse, graff **6** gutter, rundel, trench

mob 4 gang, herd **5** crowd, crush, horde, Mafia, swarm **6** masses, rabble, throng **7** flock to **8** assembly, populace, surround **9** gathering, hoi polloi, multitude, plebeians, syndicate **10** converge on **11** proletariat, rank and file **14** organized crime

mobile 6 active, motile **7** kinetic, movable, nomadic **8** portable, rootless **9** footloose, traveling, wandering **10** ambulatory, locomotive

mobilize 6 call up, muster, summon **7** marshal **8** activate, organize **10** call to arms **11** put in motion

mobster 5 hood **6** hitman **7** hoodlum, Mafioso **8** gangster **10** gang member

Moby Dick
    author: 14 Herman Melville
    character: 4 Ahab **5** Stubb **7** Ishmael **8** Fedallah, Queequeg, Starbuck

mock 3 ape **4** copy **5** belie, mimic, scorn, spurn, taunt **6** deride, insult, jeer at, parody, revile, show up **7** imitate, laugh at, let down, profane, scoff at, sneer at **8** ridicule **9** burlesque, frustrate, make fun of, poke fun at **10** caricature, disappoint, make game of **11** make sport of

mockery 4 joke, sham **5** farce, scorn **7** jeering, mimicry, sarcasm **8** derision, raillery, ridicule, scoffing, travesty **9** burlesque, contumely **10** disrespect, ridiculing **13** laughingstock

Mock Turtle
   character in: 28 Alice's Adventures in Wonderland
   author: 7 Carroll

mode 3 cut, fad, way **4** form, rage, rule **5** craze, means, style, taste, trend, vogue **6** course, custom, manner, method, system **7** fashion, process **8** approach, practice **9** condition, procedure, technique **10** appearance

model 4 cast, copy, form, mold, show, type **5** build, dummy, ideal, shape, sport, style **6** design, mirror, mock-up **7** display, example, fashion, outline, paragon, pattern, perfect, replica, subject, variety, version **8** exemplar, paradigm, peerless, standard **9** archetype, criterion, exemplary, facsimile, mannequin, prototype, simulated **10** simulacrum **14** representation, representative

model on 6 base on **7** found on **10** derive from

mode of operating
   Latin: 2 mo **13** modus operandi

moderate 4 calm, cool, curb, fair, hush, mild, tame **5** abate, chair, sober **6** direct, gentle, lessen, manage, medium, modest, soften, subdue, temper **7** average, careful, conduct, control, oversee **8** diminish, measured, mediocre, middling, ordinary, passable, rational, regulate, restrain, tone down **9** judicious, peaceable, temperate, unruffled **10** not violent, reasonable **11** inexpensive, preside over **12** mainstreamer, medium-priced

moderation 7 abating, economy **8** allaying **9** abatement, frugality, lessening, remission, restraint **10** continence, diminution, mitigation, palliation, relaxation, temperance **11** alleviation, forbearance, self-control **12** moderateness **13** temperateness **14** abstemiousness **19** avoidance of extremes

moderator 8 chairman, mediator **10** chairwoman, negotiator

modern 4 new **6** modish, recent **7** current, in vogue **8** up-to-date **10** present-day **11** fashionable, streamlined **12** contemporary **15** contemporaneous **16** twentieth-century

Modern Comedy, A
   author: 14 John Galsworthy

modernistic 3 neo **6** modern **7** moderne **10** new-fangled **12** contemporary

modernity 5 vogue **7** fashion, new

look, novelty, the rage **8** last word **14** newfangledness **15** contemporaneity **16** new fashionedness

modernize 4 redo **5** renew **6** do over, revamp, update **7** restore **8** redesign, renovate **9** refurbish **10** regenerate, rejuvenate, streamline **11** recondition **13** bring up to date **16** move with the times

modern times 5 today **8** nowadays **10** the present **13** the here and now

Modern Times
   director: 14 Charles Chaplin
   cast: 12 Henry Bergman **14** Charlie Chaplin, Chester Conklin **15** Paulette Goddard **19** Stanley "Tiny" Sandford

modest 3 coy, shy **4** meek, prim **5** plain, quiet, timid **6** demure, humble, proper, simple **7** bashful, limited, nominal, prudish, unshowy **8** blushing, discreet, moderate, reserved, timorous **9** diffident, shrinking **10** unassuming **11** circumspect, constrained, inexpensive, puritanical, straitlaced, unassertive, unobtrusive **12** mediumpriced, not excessive, self-effacing, unpretending **13** unpretentious **14** unostentatious

modesty 7 coyness, prudery, reserve, shyness **8** humility, plainess, timidity **9** propriety, restraint, reticence **10** constraint, demureness, diffidence, humbleness, simplicity **11** bashfulness, naturalness **12** timorousness **14** reasonableness, self-effacement **15** inexpensiveness

modicum 3 bit, dab, jot **4** atom, dash, drop, inch, iota, mite, whit **5** crumb, grain, pinch, scrap, speck, tinge, touch **6** morsel, sliver, snatch, trifle **7** handful, minimum, smidgen **8** fraction, fragment, particle **9** little bit **10** sprinkling **11** small amount **13** small quantity

modification 6 change **8** revision **9** variation **10** adjustment, alteration, conversion, emendation, regulation **14** transformation **15** differentiation

modify 4 redo, vary **5** adapt, alter, limit, lower, remit **6** adjust, change, narrow, reduce, remold, revise, rework, soften, temper **7** control, convert, qualify, remodel, reshape **8** moderate, modulate, restrain, restrict, tone down **9** condition, refashion, transform, transmute **10** reorganize **12** transmogrify

Modigliani, Amedeo
   born: 5 Italy **7** Leghorn, Livorno
   artwork: 10 Seated Nude **13** Reclining Nude, Yellow Sweater **15** Jeanne Hebuterne

modish 2 in **3** now **4** chic **5** natty, nifty, sharp, smart, today **6** dapper, snazzy, spiffy, trendy, with it **7** a la mode, current, faddish, in style, in

vogue, stylish, voguish **9** high-style **11** fashionable **13** up-to-the-minute

Modoc
   language family: 12 Shapwailutan
   division: 10 Lutuamnian
   location: 6 Oregon **10** California
   leader: 14 Chief Kintpuash (Captain Jack)
   related to: 7 Klamath

Modred
   character in: 16 Arthurian romance

Mod Squad, The
   character: 9 Linc Hayes, (Capt) Adam Greer **11** Julie Barnes, Pete Cochran
   cast: 11 Michael Cole, Peggy Lipton, Tige Andrews **19** Clarence Williams III

modulate 4 pass **5** lower **6** accord, attune, change, reduce, soften, temper **8** moderate, progress, regulate, tone down, turn down **9** harmonize

modulation 4 tone **5** pitch **6** accent **9** reduction **10** expression, regulation, transition

modus operandi 15 mode of operating
   abbreviation: 2 mo

modus vivendi 14 manner of living

Mogadishu, Mogadiscio
   capital of: 7 Somalia

mogul 3 VIP **4** czar, lord **5** baron, power, wheel **6** bigwig, tycoon **7** big shot, magnate, notable **8** big wheel **9** personage, potentate

Mohammed
   also: 7 Mahomet, Prophet **8** Muhammad
   born: 5 Mecca
   clan: 6 Hashim
   daughter: 6 Fatima
   deity: 5 Allah
   died: 6 Medina
   father: 8 Abdallah, Abdullah
   father-in-law: 7 Abu Bakr, Abubekr
   flight: 4 hadj **6** hegira, hejira
   follower: 6 Moslem, Muslim, Wahbi **10** Mohammedan
   grandfather: 13 Abd al-Muttalib
   horse: 5 Buraq **7** Alborrak
   mother: 5 Amina
   religion: 5 Islam
   shrine: 5 Kaaba
   son: 7 Ibrahim
      adopted: 3 Ali
   successor: 4 imam **5** calif **6** caliph **7** Abu Bakr
   tribe: 7 Koreish, Quraysh
   uncle: 5 Abbas **8** Abu Talib
   wife: 5 Aisha **6** Ayesha, Safiya **7** Khadija **8** Khadidja, Kadijah

Mohammedan 4 Sufi **6** Moslem, Muslim, Shiite **7** Islamic, Moorish, Sunnite **10** Mahometan, Muhammadan, Muhammedan

Mohave, Mojave
   language family: 5 Yuman
   location: 7 Arizona **10** California

Mohawk (Kaniengehaga)
language family: 9 Iroquoian
location: 6 Canada, Quebec **7** New York **11** Lake Ontario
leader: 8 Hiawatha **11** Joseph Brant
member of: 19 League of the Iroquois

Mohegan, Mohican, Mahican
language family: 9 Algonkian **10** Algonquian
location: 7 New York **9** Wisconsin **11** Connecticut **12** Hudson Valley
leader: 5 Occom, Uncas **12** Chingachgook
allied with: 6 Pequot
with Delaware: 11 Loup Indians, Wolf Indians
subject of novel: 20 The Last of the Mohicans
   author: 19 James Fenimore Cooper

Moira
personifies: 4 fate

moist 3 wet **4** damp, dank, dewy **5** humid, misty, muggy, rainy **6** clammy, drippy, watery **7** aqueous, drizzly, tearful, wettish, wet-eyed **8** dripping, vaporous **10** lachrymose

moisten 3 dew, wet **4** damp, hose, mist, soak **5** spray, water **6** dampen, douche, splash, sponge **8** humidify, irrigate, saturate, vaporize **10** moisturize

moisture 3 dew, wet **4** damp, mist **5** sweat, vapor **7** drizzle, exudate, wetness **8** dampness, dankness, humidity **9** moistness, mugginess **10** wateriness **11** evaporation **12** perspiration

Mojave see **6** Mohave

Moki see **4** Hopi

mold 3 cut, die, ilk **4** cast, form, kind, line, make, rust, sort, turn, type **5** brand, frame, knead, model, shape, stamp, train **6** blight, create, figure, fungus, kidney, lichen, matrix, mildew, render, sculpt, shaper **7** contour, convert, develop, fashion, outline, pattern, quality, remodel **9** character, construct, formation, structure, transform

molding 4 cyma, dado, gula, ogee **5** ovolo

Moldova
other name: 8 Moldavia
capital/largest city: 8 Chisinau, Kishinev
head of state: 9 president
government: 8 republic
monetary unit: 5 ruble
river: 8 Dniester
people: 7 Gagauzi **8** Moldovan **9** Moldavian
language: 8 Romanian **9** Moldavian
religion: 15 Russian Orthodox

moldy 5 fusty, hoary, musty, stale **7** spoiled **8** mildewed

molest 3 irk, vex **4** fret, harm, hurt **5** abuse, annoy, beset, harry, worry **6** attack, bother, harass, hector, injure, pester, plague **7** assault, disturb, torment, trouble **8** maltreat

Moliere (Jean-Baptiste Poquelin)
author of: 6 Scapin **8** Tartuffe, The Miser **10** Amphitryon **13** Le Misanthrope **17** The School for Wives **19** The Imaginary Invalid **20** The School for Husbands **22** Le Bourgeois Gentilhomme

Moll Flanders
author: 11 Daniel Defoe
character: 5 Robin **6** Jemmy E **10** Sea Captain

mollification 8 soothing **9** placation **11** appeasement, assuagement **12** conciliation

mollify 4 calm, curb, dull, ease, lull **5** abate, allay, blunt, check, quell, quiet, still **6** lessen, pacify, reduce, soften, soothe, temper **7** appease, assuage, lighten, placate **8** decrease, mitigate, moderate, palliate, tone down

mollusk 4 clam, slug **5** conch, cowry, murex, snail, squid, whelk **6** chiton, cockle, cowrie, limpet, mussel, oyster, teredo, triton **7** abalone, bivalve, geoduck, octopus, scallop **8** argonaut, nautilus, shipworm **9** shellfish **10** cuttlefish, nudibranch, peri- winkle

mollycoddle 3 pet **4** baby, wimp **5** sissy, spoil **6** cosset, coward, pamper **7** cater to, crybaby, indulge, milksop **8** give in to, mama's boy, weakling **9** cream puff **11** milquetoast, overindulge

Molnar, Ferenc
author of: 6 Liliom **7** The Swan **12** The Guardsman

Moloch 3 god 5 diety
also: 6 Molech
worshiped by: 9 Ammonites

molt 4 cast, shed, slip **6** change, slough **7** castoff, discard, ecdysis **8** exuviate

molten 6 melted, red-hot **7** fusible, igneous, smelted **8** magmatic **9** liquefied

molto
music: 4 very

Moly
form: 4 herb
given to: 8 Odysseus
given by: 6 Hermes
to counteract spells of: 5 Circe

Momaday, N Scott
author of: 18 The House Made of Dawn **21** The Way to Rainy Mountain

moment 5 flash, jiffy, trice, value, worth **6** import, minute, second, weight **7** concern, gravity, instant **8** interest, juncture **9** twinkling **10** importance **11** consequence, weightiness **12** significance

momentary 5 brief, hasty, quick, short **6** sudden **7** instant, passing **8** flashing, fleeting, fugitive, imminent **9** ephemeral, immediate, temporary, transient **10** short-lived, transitory **13** instantaneous

momentous 5 grave **7** crucial, fateful, salient, serious, weighty **8** critical, decisive, eventful **9** essential, important, ponderous **11** far-reaching, influential, significant, substantial **12** earthshaking **13** consequential

momentous occurrence 5 event **8** occasion **9** milestone **12** red-letter day, turning point

momentum 2 go **4** dash, push **5** drive, force, speed, vigor **6** energy, moment, thrust **7** headway, impetus, impulse **8** velocity **10** propulsion

Mommsen, Theodor
author of: 16 The History of Rome

Momus
also: 5 Momos
god of: 7 censure **8** ridicule

Monaco
capital: 11 Monaco-Ville
largest city: 10 Monte Carlo
others: 9 Fontville
division: 9 Fontville **10** Monte Carlo **11** La Condamine, Monaco-Ville
head of government: 15 minister of state
head of state: 6 prince
monetary unit: 5 franc **7** centime
river: 7 Vesubie
sea: 13 Mediterranean
physical feature: 9 Cote d'Azur
people: 6 French **7** Italian **10** Monegasque
   oceanographer: 15 Jacques Cousteau
   prince: 5 Louis **6** Albert, Honore **7** Antoine, Charles, Rainier **9** Florestan
   princess: 10 Grace Kelly
   ruler: 4 Rome **5** Genoa **6** Greece **8** Grimaldi, Saracens **9** Phoenicia
language: 6 French **7** English, Italian **10** Monegasque
religion: 13 Roman Catholic
place:
   beach: 8 Larvotto
   casino: 10 Monte Carlo
   gardens: 6 Exotic
   museum: 12 Oceanography
   park: 18 Princess Antoinette
feature:
   auto race: 15 Monaco Grand Prix

Monaco-Ville
capital of: 6 Monaco

Mona Lisa
also called: 10 La Gioconda
artist: 15 Leonardo da Vinci
noted for: 5 smile
museum: 6 Louvre

monarch 3 HRH **4** czar, doge, emir, khan, king, rani, shah, tsar **5** rajah, ruler, queen **6** caesar, kaiser, prince

7 czarina, emperor, empress, majesty, pharaoh **8** kaiserin, princess **9** chieftain, potentate

monarchical 9 czaristic **10** autocratic **11** dictatorial

monastery 5 abbey **6** friary, priory **7** convent, nunnery, retreat **8** cloister

monastic 7 ascetic, monkish, recluse **8** celibate, hermitic, secluded, solitary **9** cloistral, reclusive, unworldly **10** cloistered, hermitlike **11** sequestered **13** contemplative

mon cher 6 my dear

Moncrieff, Algernon (Algy)
character in: **27** The Importance of Being Earnest
author: **5** Wilde

Mond, Mustapha
character in: **13** Brave New World
author: **6** Huxley

Monday
French: **5** lundi
German: **6** montag
heavenly body: **4** moon
Italian: **6** lunedi
means: **12** day of the moon
Spanish: **5** lunes

Mondrian, Piet
real name: **23** Pieter Cornelis Mondriaan
born: **10** Amersfoort **14** The Netherlands
artwork: **5** Trees **10** The Red Tree **12** Ocean and Pier **17** Evening Landscapes **18** Landscape with a Mill **20** Broadway Boogie-Woogie **29** Composition in Red Yellow and Blue

Monet, Claude Oscar
born: **5** Paris **6** France
artwork: **7** Poplars **9** Haystacks, The Thames **11** Water Lilies **14** Rouen Cathedral **16** Women in the Garden **17** Impression Sunrise **18** Mornings on the Seine **21** The Bridge at Argenteuil

monetary 6 fiscal **9** budgetary, financial, pecuniary, sumptuary

money 4 cash, coin **5** bread, bucks, dough, funds **6** assets, riches, specie, wealth **7** capital, coinage, payment, revenue, scratch **8** currency, hard cash, proceeds **9** affluence, long green **10** collateral, greenbacks **11** wherewithal

money-carrier
French: **12** porte-monnaie

moneyed, monied 4 rich **5** flush, swell **6** flashy, loaded **7** elegant, opulent, solvent, wealthy **8** affluent **10** prosperous

money-grubbing 5 venal **6** greedy **8** covetous, grasping **9** mercenary **10** avaricious

money lender 6 banker, lender, usurer **7** lombard, shylock **9** loanshark **10** pawnbroker

money saved 7 nest egg, savings **10** investment

money spent 6 outlay **7** payment **8** expenses **11** expenditure

Mongolia
other name: **13** Outer Mongolia
capital/largest city: **9** Ulan Bator
others: **5** Kobdo **6** Darhan **10** Choibalsan, Sukhe Bator, Tsetserlik, Uliassutai
ancient capital: **9** Karakoram
government:
legislature: **17** People's Great Hural **18** People's Great Khural
monetary unit: **5** mongo, mungo **6** tugrik **7** tughrik
weight: **3** lan
lake: **3** Uvs **5** Har Us **6** Bor Nor **7** Ghirgis, Ubsa Nor **8** Airik Nor, Durga Nor, Hobsogol, Khara Usu **9** Khubsugul, Khukhu-Nur **10** Khirgis Nor
mountain: **4** Cast, Orog **5** Altai **6** Kentei, Sevrej **7** Ich Ovoo, Khangai, Khentei **8** Tannu-Ola **9** Edrengijn **10** Cagaan Bogd **11** Munky Sardyk **14** Hangayn-Hentiyn, Monch Chajrchan
highest point: **10** Tabun Bogdo
river: **3** Tes **4** Egin, Onon, Tuul, Uldz **5** Kobdo, Tesin **6** Orkhon **7** Kerulen, Selenga, Selenge **8** Dzabkhan, Dzavchan
physical feature:
desert: **4** Gobi **5** Ordos, Shamo
plateau: **8** Mongolia
region: **10** Great Lakes
people: **5** Oirat, Tungu **6** Buryat, Darbet, Khoton, Mongol **7** Kazakhs, Khalkha **8** Tuvinian **9** Dariganga
leader: **8** Jahangir, Jehangir **10** Kublai Khan, Tsendenbal **11** Genghis Khan
ruler: **4** Huns **5** Ching **6** Manchu **7** Kirghiz, Uighurs **8** Hsiung-nu
spiritual/secular ruler: **12** Living Buddha **21** Jebtsun Damba Khutu Khtu
language: **6** Kazakh **16** Khalkha Mongolian
religion: **7** Lamaism **9** Shamanism **15** Tibetan Buddhism
place:
monastery: **6** Gandun
feature:
felt tent: **4** yurt
nomadic herder: **4** arat
food:
fermented mare's milk: **5** airag

Mongolian
language family: **6** Altaic
group: **6** Buryat **7** Khalkha

Mongoose, The
nickname of: **11** Archie Moore

mongrel 3 cur **4** mutt **5** mixed **6** hybrid **7** bastard **8** offshoot **9** anomalous, crossbred **10** crossbreed

moniker 3 tag **4** name **5** label, title **6** eponym, handle **7** epithet, surname **8** cognomen, nickname, taxonomy

9 sobriquet **11** appellation, designation **12** denomination

monitor 2 TV **4** tend **5** guide, teach **6** censor, direct, pickup, police, screen, sensor **7** oversee, proctor, scanner **8** overseer, watchdog **9** supervise **14** disciplinarian

Monkees, The
cast/musician: **9** Davy Jones, Peter Tork **10** David Jones **11** Micky Dolenz, Mike Nesmith

monkey 3 ape, ass, toy **4** butt, dupe, fool, jerk **5** clown, jimmy **6** baboon, fiddle, meddle, simian, tamper, tinker, trifle **7** buffoon, primate **13** laughingstock
group of: **5** troop
god: **7** Hanuman
kind: **3** owl **4** saki, titi **5** aotus, lemur, titis **6** baboon, guenon, howler, langur, rhesus, spider **7** colobus, Goeldi's, guereza, macaque, tamarin, tarsier, uakaris **8** capuchin, mandrill, marmoset, squirrel, talapoin **11** douroucouli

monkey business 6 capers **9** highjinks **11** shenanigans

monkeyshines 6 antics, capers, pranks **7** hijinks **10** buffoonery, tomfoolery **11** foolishness

Monks (Edward Leeford)
character in: **11** Oliver Twist
author: **7** Dickens

monocle 4 quiz **5** glass **7** lorgnon **8** eyeglass

Monoclonius
type: **8** dinosaur **10** ceratopsid
location: **12** North America
characteristic: **6** horned

Monod, Jacques
field: **7** biology
nationality: **6** French
researched: **3** RNA **8** genetics
awarded: **10** Nobel Prize

monograph 8 tractate, treatise **9** discourse **12** disquisition, dissertation

monolith 5 stone **6** column, menhir, pillar, statue **7** obelisk **8** memorial, monument

monologue, monolog 6 screed, sermon, speech **7** address, lecture, oration **9** discourse, soliloquy **11** expatiation **12** disquisition

monopolize 3 own **6** absorb, corner, manage, take up **7** consume, control, preempt **8** arrogate, dominate, regulate, take over **9** cartelize **11** appropriate

monopoly 4 bloc **5** trust **6** cartel, corner **7** combine, control **8** dominion **9** copyright, ownership, syndicate **10** consortium, domination **11** sovereignty **12** jurisdiction **14** proprietorship

Monopoly 9 board game
invented by: **6** Darrow

places: 2 go, RR **4** jail **6** chance **9** Boardwalk, Park Place
piece: 5 hotel, house

monotonous 3 dry **4** dull, flat **5** banal **6** boring, dreary, jejune, stodgy, torpid **7** droning, humdrum, insipid, mundane, prosaic, routine, tedious **8** plodding, singsong, tiresome, toneless, unvaried **9** colorless, soporific, wearisome **10** pedestrian **11** repetitious, somniferous **13** uninteresting

monotony 3 rut **5** ennui **6** tedium **7** boredom, humdrum **8** dullness, flatness, prosaism, sameness **9** iteration **10** dreariness, redundancy, uniformity **11** reiteration, tediousness **13** wearisomeness **14** predictability

Monroe, Earl
nickname: 12 Earl the Pearl
sport: 10 basketball
position: 5 guard
team: 16 Baltimore Bullets **21** New York Knickerbockers

Monroe, James
presidential rank: 5 fifth
party: 20 Democratic-Republican
state represented: 2 VA
defeated: 4 (Rufus) King **5** (John Quincy) Adams
vice president: 8 (Daniel D) Tompkins
cabinet:
  state: 5 (John Quincy) Adams
  treasury: 8 (William Harris) Crawford
  war: 7 (John Caldwell) Calhoun
  attorney general: 4 (Richard) Rush, (William) Wirt
  navy: 8 (Samuel Lewis) Southard, (Smith) Thompson **13** (Benjamin Williams) Crowninshield
born: 2 VA **18** Westmoreland County
died: 13 New York City NY
buried: 10 Richmond VA
education: 14 William and Mary (did not graduate)
religion: 12 Episcopalian
author: 67 A View of the Conduct of the Executive in the Foreign Affairs of the United States
political career: 8 US Senate
  governor of: 8 Virginia
  minister: 5 Spain **6** France **12** Great Britain
  secretary of: 3 war **5** state
civilian career: 6 lawyer
military service: 5 major **7** captain **10** lieutenant **16** Revolutionary War **17** lieutenant colonel
  wounded in Battle of: 7 Trenton
notable events of lifetime/term: 5 Panic (of 1819) **14** Monroe Doctrine
  Agreement: 9 Rush-Bagot
  Compromise: 8 Missouri
  war: 8 Seminole
father: 6 Spence
mother: 9 Elizabeth (Jones)
siblings: 6 Andrew, Spence

9 Elizabeth **11** Joseph Jones
wife: 9 Elizabeth (Kortright)
  nickname: 5 Eliza
children: 11 Maria Hester **14** Eliza Kortright

Monroe, Marilyn
real name: 23 Norma Jean Mortenson Baker
husband: 11 Joe DiMaggio **12** Arthur Miller
born: 12 Los Angeles CA
roles: 7 Bus Stop, Niagara **10** The Misfits **13** Some Like It Hot **16** The Seven-Year Itch **22** Gentlemen Prefer Blondes, How To Marry a Millionaire **23** The Prince and the Showgirl

Monrovia
capital of: 7 Liberia
monseigneur 6 my lord
monsieur 2 Mr **3** sir **6** mister, my lord

Monsieur Beaucaire
author: 15 Booth Tarkington

Monsignor Quixote
author: 12 Graham Greene

monster 4 Fury, gila, ogre, yeti **5** argus, beast, brute, demon, devil, fiend, freak, ghoul, giant, golem, harpy, hydra, lamia, satyr, titan **6** dragon, gorgon, marvel, oddity, savage, threat, wonder, wretch, zombie **7** anomaly, caitiff, centaur, chimera, deviant, grendel, incubus, mammoth, mermaid, vampire, variant, villain **8** bogeyman, colossus, gargoyle, Loch Ness, succubus, werewolf **9** barbarian, curiosity, cutthroat, scoundrel **10** blackguard, phenomenon **11** abnormality, miscreation **12** Frankenstein, lusus naturae

monstrous 4 bald, evil, huge **5** cruel, giant **6** grisly, mighty, odious **7** ghastly, harried, heinous, hideous, hulking, immense, mammoth, obscene, obvious, satanic, titanic, vicious **8** colossal, enormous, fiendish, flagrant, gigantic, gruesome, horrible, outright, shocking **9** atrocious, egregious, nefarious, revolting **10** diabolical, gargantuan, outrageous, prodigious, scandalous, stupendous, tremendous, villainous **14** Brobdingnagian

monstrousness 8 baseness, enormity, evilness, vileness, villainy **9** barbarity, depravity, malignity **10** inhumanity, wickedness **11** heinousness, viciousness **13** atrociousness, offensiveness **14** outrageousness

Montague family
characters in: 14 Romeo and Juliet
author: 11 Shakespeare
member: 5 Romeo

Montaigne, Michel de
author of: 6 Essais, Essays

Montalban, Ricardo
born: 6 Mexico **10** Mexico City
roles: 4 Khan **8** Mr Roarke **9** The

Colbys **13** Fantasy Island **24** Star Trek II The Wrath of Khan

Montalvo, Garcia de
author of: 12 Amadis of Gaul

Montana
abbreviation: 2 MT **4** Mont
nickname: 6 Big Sky **7** Bonanza, Stubtoe **8** Mountain, Treasure
capital: 6 Helena
largest city: 8 Billings
others: 4 Kipp **5** Butte, Havre, Malta **6** Hardin **7** Bozeman, Chinook, Choteau, Forsyth, Glasgow, Roundup **8** Anaconda, Missoula **9** Kalispell **10** Great Falls
college: 7 Carroll **10** Great Falls **13** Rocky Mountain
feature: 17 Continental Divide
  cemetery: 6 Custer
  national park: 7 Glacier **11** Yellowstone
tribe: 4 Cree, Crow, Hohe **5** Sioux **6** Atsima, Atsina, Salish **7** Arapaho, Bannock, Kutenai, Siksika **8** Cheyenne, Chippewa, Flatfoot, Flathead, Shoshone **9** Blackfeet **11** Assiniboine
people: 8 Myrna Loy **9** Will James **10** Gary Cooper **14** Charles Russell **15** Jeannette Rankin
  explorer: 13 Lewis and Clark **16** Pierre Jean de Smet
lake: 5 Tiber **6** Hebgen **8** Flathead, Fort Peck, Medicine **10** Yellowtail **11** Canyon Ferry, Hungry Horse
land rank: 6 fourth
mountain: 4 Ajax **5** Baldy, Cowan, Crazy, Lewis **6** Sphinx, Torrey **7** Bighorn, Big Belt, Hilgard, Purcell, Rockies, Trapper **8** Absaroka, Gallatin, Pentagon, Snowshoe
  highest point: 11 Granite Peak
physical feature: 10 Great Falls
river: 3 Sun **4** Milk **5** Clark, Teton **6** Marias, Powder, Tongue, Willow **7** Madison, Shields **8** Columbia, Kootenai, Missouri **9** Blackfoot **10** Bitterroot **11** Musselshell, Yellowstone
state admission: 10 forty-first
state bird: 17 western meadowlark
state fish: 26 black-spotted cutthroat trout
state flower: 10 bitterroot
state motto: 13 Gold and Silver
state song: 7 Montana
state tree: 13 Ponderosa pine

Montana, Bob
creator/artist of: 6 Archie

Montand, Yves
real name: 7 Ivo Livi
wife: 14 Simone Signoret
born: 5 Italy **14** Monsummano Alto
roles: 1 Z **12** Let's Make Love **14** Is Paris Burning?

montani semper liberi 28 mountaineers are always free men
motto of: 12 West Virginia

Montcalm, Louis Joseph
also: 17 Marquis de Montcalm

nationality: 6 French
served in: 18 French and Indian War
battle: 6 Oswego, Quebec (siege) **8** Carillon **11** Ticonderoga **16** Fort William Henry
killed in battle at: 6 Quebec **15** Plains of Abraham

mont-de-piete 10 pawnbroker
literally: 10 bank of pity

Montenegro
name means: 13 black mountain
other name: 4 Zeta **8** Crna Gora
capital: 7 Cetinje **8** Titograd **9** Podgorica
cities: 3 Bar **5** Kotor, Tivat **6** Niksic, Ulcinj **8** Antivari, Dulcigno, Ivangrad, Pljevlja **10** Hercegnovi **11** Sveti Stefan
division:
    Roman province: 7 Illyria
governed by: 10 Yugoslavia
monetary unit: 4 para **6** florin **7** perpera
lake: 7 Scutari, Shkoder
mountain: 8 Durmitor **11** Dinaric Alps
river: 3 Lim **4** Piva, Tara, Zeta **6** Moraca **7** Ceotina
sea: 8 Adriatic
physical feature:
    gulf: 5 Kotor
people: 4 Serb, Slav **11** Montenegrin
    former ruler (Orthodox bishop): 7 vladike **8** vladika
language: 13 Serbo-Croatian
religion: 16 Serbian Orthodoxy

Monteverdi, Claudio
born: 5 Italy **7** Cremona
composer of: 5 Adone, Orfeo **7** Arianna **14** La Favola d'Orfeo **17** The Fable of Orpheus **21** The Coronation of Poppea **22** L'incoronazione di Poppea **24** Il Ritorno d'Ulisse in patria **34** Il Combattimento di Tancredi e Clorinda

Montevideo
capital of: 7 Uruguay

Montezuma
emperor of: 6 Aztecs
in: 6 Mexico
conquered by: 6 Cortez

Montgomery, Bernard Law
also: 27 (first) Viscount Montgomery of Alamein
author of: 7 Memoirs **17** A History of Warfare
battle: 9 El Alamein
chief: 19 British general staff
commander of: 17 British Eighth Army **32** British occupation forces in Germany
commando raid: 6 Dieppe
deputy supreme commander: 4 NATO
Eighth Army called: 10 Desert Rats
evacuation of: 7 Dunkirk
fought against: 6 Rommel **11** Africa Corps, Afrika Korps

invasion: 6 Sicily **8** Normandy
member: 12 House of Lords
nationality: 7 British
nickname: 5 Monty
served in: 3 WWI **4** WWII

Montgomery, Robert
real name: 17 Henry Montgomery Jr
daughter: 9 Elizabeth
born: 8 Beacon NY
roles: 11 The Big House **13** Night Must Fall **17** Here Comes Mr Jordan

month
1st day: 7 calends
13th or 15th: 4 ides
9th before ides: 5 nones
half: 9 fortnight
next: 7 proximo
preceding: 3 ult(imo)
present: 4 inst(ant)

Month in the Country, A
author: 12 Ivan Turgenev

Mont-Oriol
author: 15 Guy de Maupassant

Montreal
airport: 6 Dorval **8** St Hubert **12** Cartierville
baseball team: 5 Expos
founder: 11 Maisonneuve
hill: 10 Mount Royal
hockey team: 9 Canadiens
island: 5 Jesus **6** Bizard, Perrot **8** Montreal **9** des Soeurs **14** de Boucherville
lake: 7 St Louis
landmark: 12 Place des Arts **13** Molson Stadium **16** Chateau de Ramezay **17** Church of Notre Dame, St Sulpice Seminary **21** Man and His World Exhibit
original name: 10 Ville-Marie
province: 6 Quebec
river: 6 Ottawa **10** St Lawrence **11** des Prairies **14** des Milles Isles
subway: 5 Metro
university: 6 McGill

Montresor
character in: 20 The Cask of Amontillado
author: 3 Poe

Mont Saint Michel and Chartres
author: 10 Henry Adams

Monty
nickname of: 15 Montgomery Clift **17** (General) Bernard Montgomery

monument 4 slab **5** token **6** shrine **7** memento, obelisk, witness **8** cenotaph, memorial, monolith, reminder **9** testament, tombstone **10** gravestone **11** remembrance, testimonial **13** commemoration

monumental 4 huge **5** fatal, heavy **7** awesome, classic, epochal, immense, lasting, massive **8** colossal, decisive, enduring, gigantic, historic, immortal, statuary **9** cyclopean, egregious, memorable **10** horrendous, monolithic,

shattering, stupendous **11** inestimable **12** catastrophic **13** unprecedented

mooch 3 beg, bum **5** cadge **6** hustle, sponge **7** solicit **8** freeload

mood 5 blues, dumps, humor **6** spirit, temper **7** feeling **8** doldrums, vexation **9** condition **10** depression, gloominess, melancholy **11** disposition, melancholia, temperament **14** predisposition **16** hypersensitivity

moody 4 mean **5** sulky, surly, testy **6** crabby, dismal, fickle, gloomy, mopish, morbid, morose, sullen **7** erratic, flighty, peevish, unhappy **8** brooding, dejected, notional, variable, volatile **9** impetuous, impulsive, irascible, irritable, mercurial, saturnine, whimsical **10** capricious, changeable, despondent, inconstant, lugubrious, melancholy **11** pessimistic **12** inconsistent **13** temperamental, unpredictable

Mookerjee, Hurree Chunder
character in: 3 Kim
author: 7 Kipling

moon 4 gape, lamp, luna, roam **5** dream, month, stare **6** dawdle, wander **8** daydream **9** satellite
god of: 3 Sin **5** Nanna **6** Meztli
goddess of: 4 Luna **5** Diana, Holle, Tanit **6** Hecate, Hekate, Phoebe, Selena, Selene, Tanith **7** Artemis, Astarte, Cynthia
full: 9 plenilune
new: 5 prime
waning: 7 waiand

Moon and Sixpence, The
author: 16 W Somerset Maugham

moonless 4 dark **5** black, murky **7** stygian **9** lightless, unlighted **13** unilluminated

Moonlighting
character: 11 Maddie Hayes **12** Agnes Dipesto, David Addison
cast: 11 Bruce Willis **13** Allyce Beasley **14** Cybill Shepherd
detective agency: 8 Blue Moon

Moon Mullins
creator: 12 Frank Willard
character: 4 Kayo **5** Mamie **9** Mushmouth **11** Uncle Willie **15** Lady Plushbottom, Lord Plushbottom **16** Moonshine Mullins

Moon of the Caribbees, The
author: 12 Eugene O'Neill

moonshine 5 hokum **6** bunkum, humbug **7** bootleg **8** clockade, homebrew, malarky, nonsense **10** balderdash, bathtub gin **11** mountain dew

moonstone
species: 8 feldspar
source: 5 Burma, Mogok

Moonstone, The
author: 13 Wilkie Collins
character: 7 Dr Candy **12** Lady Verinder, Sergeant Cuff **13** Franklin Blake **14** John Herncastle, Rachel

Verinder **15** Rosanna Spearman **16** Godfrey Ablewhite

moor 3 fen **4** dock, down, fell, lash, wold **5** affix, berth, chain, heath, marsh, tie up **6** anchor, attach, fasten, secure, steppe, tether, tundra, upland **7** savanna, tie down **8** make fast **9** wasteland

Moore, Archie
nickname: **11** The Mongoose
real name: **18** Archibald Lee Wright
sport: **6** boxing
class: **16** light-heavyweight

Moore, Clement C
author of: **23** A Visit from Saint Nicholas

Moore, Dick
creator/artist of: **13** Gasoline Alley

Moore, Dudley
nickname: **12** Cuddly Dudley
wife: **11** Suzy Kendall, Tuesday Weld
born: **5** Essex **7** England **8** Dagenham
roles: **3** Ten **8** Arthur **8** Lovesick, Six Weeks **9** Bedazzled **13** Micki and Maude **16** Arthur on the Rocks **17** Like Father Like Son
plays: **5** piano

Moore, George
author of: **12** Esther Waters **15** Hail and Farewell

Moore, Henry
born: **7** England **10** Castleford
artwork: **4** Mask **8** Two Forms **9** North Wind **10** Bird Basket **11** Family Group, Head of a Girl **12** Locking Piece **13** Nuclear Energy **15** Reclining Figure **20** Four-Piece Composition

Moore, Marianne
author of: **12** Like a Bulwark, Nevertheless, O To Be a Dragon, Tell Me Tell Me

Moore, Mary Tyler
husband: **11** Grant Tinker
born: **10** Brooklyn NY
roles: **4** Mary **12** Mary Richards **14** Ordinary People **18** The Dick Van Dyke Show **21** The Mary Tyler Moore Show

Moore, Mrs
character in: **15** A Passage to India
author: **7** Forster

Moore, Roger
born: **6** London **7** England
roles: **8** The Saint **12** Simon Templar
as James Bond: **9** Moonraker, Octopussy **13** Live and Let Die **16** The Spy Who Loved Me **22** The Man with the Golden Gun

Moorehead, Agnes
born: **9** Clinton MA
roles: **6** Endora **9** Bewitched **11** Citizen Kane **13** Johnny Belinda **15** Dear Dead Delilah **20** Magnificent Obsession **23** The Magnificent Ambersons

mooring 4 hook, line, rope **5** cable, chain **6** anchor, hawser

moot 4 open **7** eristic **8** arguable, disputed **9** debatable, undecided, unsettled **10** disputable, unresolved **11** conjectural **12** questionable **13** controversial, problematical **14** controvertible

mope 4 fret, pine, pout, sulk **5** brood, worry **6** grieve, grouse, lament, repine **7** grumble **8** languish

Mopsus
occupation: **4** seer
mother: **5** Manto
grandfather: **8** Tiresias
member of: **9** Argonauts
founded: **6** oracle
location: **6** Mallus **7** Cilicia
cofounder: **11** Amphilochus
epithet: **9** Ampycides

moral 3 tag **4** fair, just, pure **5** adage, maxim, motto, noble, right **6** honest, lesson, proper, saying **7** epigram, ethical, message, proverb, saintly **8** aphorism, didactic, personal, virtuous **9** estimable, homiletic, honorable, preaching **10** aboveboard, high-minded, principled **11** meritorious, sermonizing, tendentious **12** conscionable

moral code 5 ethos **6** ethics **9** integrity, standards **10** principles

morale 4 mood **6** spirit, temper **10** confidence, resolution **11** disposition
French: **13** esprit de corps

morality 5 honor **6** ethics, habits, tastes, virtue **7** modesty, probity **8** fairness, goodness **9** integrity, rectitude **10** chasteness **11** uprightness **13** righteousness

moralize 6 preach **7** lecture

moralizing 7 preachy **8** didactic **9** homiletic

morally corrupt 6 effete **8** decadent, depraved **10** degenerate

moral sense 9 integrity **10** conscience

morass 3 bog, fen **4** mire **5** marsh, swamp **6** slough **8** quagmire, wetlands **9** quicksand

morbid 3 sad **4** dour, glum, grim **5** moody **6** gloomy, morose, somber **8** brooding **9** depressed, saturnine **10** despondent, lugubrious **11** melancholic, pessimistic, unwholesome

morbid condition 6 malady **7** ailment, disease, illness **8** sickness **9** infirmity

Morcerf, Comte de (Fernand)
character in: **21** The Count of Monte Cristo
author: **5** Dumas (pere)

mordant 6 biting, bitter **7** acerbic, caustic, cutting, waspish **8** incisive, piercing, scathing, scornful, stinging, venomous, virulent **9** acidulous, mali-

cious, sarcastic, trenchant **11** acrimonious

Mordecai
cousin: **6** Esther
served: **15** Ahasuerus Xerxes
enemy: **5** Haman

more 5 added, extra, other, spare **6** longer **7** further, reserve **10** additional **12** additionally, supplemental **13** supplementary

More, Thomas
author of: **6** Utopia

Moreau, Frederic
character in: **21** A Sentimental Education
author: **8** Flaubert

Moreau, Gustave
born: **5** Paris **6** France
artwork: **7** Orpheus **13** Dance of Salome (Salome Dancing), The Apparition **16** Hesiod and the Muse **18** The Poet and the Siren **19** Oedipus and the Sphinx **27** Diomedes Devoured by His Horses

Morehouse, J Ward
character in: **3** USA
author: **9** Dos Passos

Morel, Paul
character in: **13** Sons and Lovers
author: **8** Lawrence

Moreno, Rita
real name: **20** Rosita Dolores Alverio
born: **7** Humacao **10** Puerto Rico
roles: **13** Pagan Love Song, The Deerslayer, West Side Story **15** Singin' in the Rain

more or less 5 about **6** around **8** somewhat **9** generally, just about **13** approximately

moreover 3 too **4** also **7** besides, further **11** furthermore **12** more than that

mores 4 code **5** ethos, forms, rules **6** usages **7** customs, rituals **9** etiquette, practices, standards **10** traditions **11** conventions, observances, proprieties

more than enough 5 ample **6** excess, plenty **7** copious, profuse **8** plethora **9** abundance, amplitude, bountiful, excessive, profusion **10** oversupply

Morgan, Daniel
served in: **16** Revolutionary War
commander of: **8** riflemen **13** sharpshooters
battle: **7** Cowpens **8** Saratoga **12** Bemis Heights, Freeman's Farm
helped suppress: **16** Whiskey Rebellion

Morgan, Thomas Hunt
founder of: **8** genetics
awarded: **10** Nobel Prize

Morgan family
characters in: **19** How Green Was My Valley
members: **4** Beth, Davy, Huur, Ivor,

Owen **5** Ianto **6** Gwilym **8** Angharad
author: **9** Llewellyn

morganite
color: **4** pink **5** peach

Morgan le Fay
character in: **16** Arthurian romance

Moriarty, Professor
villain in: **14** (The Adventures of) Sherlock Holmes
author: **10** Conan Doyle

moribund 5 dying **6** doomed, waning **10** stagnating

Morier, James
author of: **18** Hajji Baba of Ispahan

morituri te salutamus 28 we who are about to die salute thee
said by: **15** Roman gladiators
said to: **13** Roman emperors

Mork & Mindy
character: **4** Mork **6** Eugene **10** Cora Hudson **13** Mindy McConnel **17** Frederick McConnel
cast: **9** Pam Dawber **11** Conrad Janis **13** Elizabeth Kerr, Robin Williams **14** Jeffrey Jacquet
Mork's planet: **3** Ork
phrase: **8** nanu nanu
spinoff from: **9** Happy Days

Morland, Catherine
character in: **15** Northanger Abbey
author: **6** Austen

Morley, Robert
born: **6** Semley **7** England
roles: **5** Melba **10** Oscar Wilde **11** Beau Brummel, Edward My Son **12** Major Barbara **15** Marie Antoinette, The African Queen **21** The Man Who Came to Dinner

Mormon State
nickname of: **4** Utah

morning 4 dawn **5** early, sunup **7** sunrise **8** daybreak, daylight, forenoon **9** matutinal

morning-glory 7 Ipomoea **10** Calystegia **11** Convolvulus
varieties: **3** red **4** wild **5** beach, dwarf **6** Ceylon, common, silver, woolly, yellow **9** Brazilian **16** Imperial Japanese

Morocco
other name: **7** Barbary **8** Maroquin **9** Al Maghrib **13** Maghrib el Aksa **19** Mauretania Tingitana
capital: **5** Rabat **6** Rabbat
largest city: **10** Casablanca
others: **3** Fes, Fez, Sla **4** Ifni, Safi, Sale, Sali, Taza **5** Ceuta, Oujda, Porte, Saffi **6** Agadir, Meknes, Semara, Tetuan **7** Elarish, Kenitra, Larache, Mazagan, Mililla, Mogador, Tangier, Tetouan **8** Kouribga, Tinerhir **9** Marrakech, Marrakesh **10** Youssoufia **11** Port-Lyautey
division:
disputed territory: **13** Western Sahara
head of state: **4** king

measure: 4 kala, muhd, rotl, saah, sahh, ueba **5** artal, cadee, gerbe, ratel **6** covado, dirhem, fanega, izenbi, kintar, tangin, tomini **8** quintral

monetary unit: 4 flue, okia, rial **5** floos, franc, okieh, ounce **6** dirham, miskal **9** mouzouna

weight: 4 rotl **5** artel, ratel **6** dirhem, kintar **7** quintal

island: 7 Madeira

mountain: 3 Rif **4** Bani **5** Abyla, Atlas, Sarro **8** Tidiguin **9** Anti-Atlas, High Atlas, Jebel-Musa **11** Middle Atlas

highest point: 12 Jebel Toubkal **13** Djebel Toubkal

river: 3 Dra, Ziz **4** Sous **5** Sebou **6** Gheris **7** Tensift **8** Moulouya **9** Oum er Rbia

sea: 8 Atlantic **13** Mediterranean

physical feature:
cape: **3** Nun, Sim **4** Juby, Noun, Rhir **6** Cantin
desert: **6** Sahara
oasis: **8** Tafilelt
plain: **5** Rharb
strait: **9** Gibraltar
valley: **7** Ouergha
wind: **5** leste **9** charqui
people: **4** Arab, Moor **6** Berber, French **7** Spanish
dynasty: **7** Alawite, Almohad **9** Almoravid
leader: **5** Idris **7** Lyautey **8** Hassan II **9** Abd el-Krim
philosopher: **8** Averroes
language: **6** Arabic, Berber, French **7** Spanish
religion: **5** Islam
place:
ruins: **9** Volubilis
feature:
clothing: **4** haik **7** jellaba
hat: **3** fez
Islamic holy war: **5** jehad, jihad
shanty town: **10** bidonville
food:
dish: **8** couscous

moron 3 ass, nut, oaf, sap **4** boob, dolt, dope, fool **5** dummy, dunce, idiot, loony, ninny **6** dimwit, nitwit **7** half-wit, jackass **8** bonehead, dumbbell, dumbhead, imbecile, numskull **9** blockhead, numbskull, simpleton **10** muttonhead, nincompoop

Moroni
capital of: **7** Comoros

Moros
mother: **3** Nyx
personifies: **4** fate

morose 3 low, sad **4** blue, dour, glum, sour **5** cross, moody, sulky, surly, testy **6** cranky, gloomy, grumpy, mopish, solemn, sullen **7** waspish **8** churlish, downcast, mournful **9** depressed, irascible, saturnine **10** despondent, melancholy **11** crestfallen

moroseness 5 gloom **8** glumness

9 pessimism, sulkiness, surliness **10** sullenness

Morpheus
god of: **6** dreams
father: **6** Hypnos

morphology
study of: **9** structure

Morris, Dinah
character in: **8** Adam Bede
author: **5** Eliot

Morris, Willie
author of: **5** Yazoo **10** Good Old Boy **15** North Toward Home

Morris, Wright
author of: **8** Will's Boy **10** Plain's Song **13** Field of Vision, My Uncle Dudley

Morrison, Toni
real name: **19** Chloe Anthony Wofford
author of: **4** Sula, Jazz **7** Beloved, Tar Baby **12** The Bluest Eye **13** Song of Solomon
honor: **10** Nobel Prize **13** Pulitzer Prize

Morrow, Vic
born: **7** Bronx NY
roles: **6** Combat **8** Cimarron **14** God's Little Acre **15** The Twilight Zone **18** Portrait of a Mobster **19** The Blackboard Jungle
daughter: **18** Jennifer Jason Leigh

Morse, Samuel F B
nationality: **8** American
invented: **9** Morse code **17** electric telegraph **24** electromagnetic telegraph

morsel 3 bit, nip, sip **4** bite, drop, iota, whit **5** crumb, grain, piece, scrap, snack, speck, taste, touch, trace **6** dollop, nibble, sliver, tidbit **7** modicum, segment, swallow **8** fraction, fragment, mouthful, particle **9** scintilla

mortal 4 deep, type **5** fatal, grave, human **6** deadly, lethal, living, person, severe **7** earthly, extreme, intense, mundane **8** creature, enormous, fleeting, temporal **9** character, corporeal, ephemeral **10** individual, transitory **12** unimaginable

mortality 7 carnage **8** fatality **9** bloodshed, ephemeral, slaughter **10** transience **11** evanescence **12** impermanence **13** extermination **14** transitoriness

mortar 6 cannon, cement, vessel **7** plaster **8** adhesive

Morte d'Arthur, Le
author: **12** Thomas Malory

Mortgaged Heart, The
author: **15** Carson McCullers

mortification 3 rot **5** decay, shame **7** chagrin, penance **8** ignominy **11** humiliation **12** putrefaction **13** embarrassment

mortified 6 rotted **7** abashed,

ashamed, debased **8** dismayed, festered, tortured **9** chagrined, putrefied **11** discomfited, embarrassed

mortify 3 rot **4** deny, fast **5** abash, decay, shame **6** appall, fester **7** chagrin, horrify, putrefy **9** discomfit, embarrass **10** discipline, disconcert

Mosaic law 10 Pentateuch **15** Ten Commandments

Moscow
  airport: 12 Sheremetyevo
  canal: 11 Moscow-Volga
  capital of: 4 USSR **6** Russia **11** Soviet Union
  hills: 5 Lenin
  landmark: 7 Kremlin **9** Gorky Park, Red Square **12** Lenin Library **13** Izmailovo Park, Sokolniki Park **14** Bolshoi Theater **16** Moscow Art Theater **21** Luzhniki Sports Complex
  museum: 6 Armory **7** Pushkin **10** Historical **16** Tretyakov Gallery **28** Central Museum of the Soviet Army
  river: 5 Setun, Volga, Yauza **6** Moscow
  Russian: 6 Moskva

Moses
  father: 5 Amram
  mother: 8 Jochebed
  sister: 6 Miriam
  brother: 5 Aaron
  wife: 8 Zipporah
  son: 7 Eliezar, Gershom
  father-in-law: 6 Jethro
  received: 15 Ten Commandments
  patriarch of: 10 Israelites
  saw: 11 burning bush
  successor: 6 Joshua
  pertaining to: 6 Mosaic

Moses, Grandma
  real name: 17 Anna Mary Robertson, Mary Anne Robertson
  born: 11 Greenwich NY
  artwork: 23 Out for the Christmas Trees

mosey 4 poke **5** amble **6** stroll **7** saunter, shuffle

Moslem 4 Moor **5** Islam, Sunni **6** Muslim, Shiite **7** Islamic **10** Mohammadan, Muhammadan

mosque 6 temple
  Arabic: 6 masjid, musjid

Mosquito Coast, The
  author: 11 Paul Theroux
  director: 9 Peter Weir
  cast: 11 Helen Mirren **12** Harrison Ford, River Phoenix

Mosquito State
  nickname of: 9 New Jersey

moss
  varieties: 4 ball, club, gold, rose **5** broom, bunch, coral, ditch, fairy, Irish, spike, water **6** Scotch, spring **7** cushion, haircap, peacock, Spanish **8** floating, fountain, Japanese, mat spike **9** dwarf club, flowering **10** little club, pincushion **11** basket spike,

meadow spike, shining club **12** treelet spike **13** Douglas's spike

Mossbauer, Rudolph Ludwig
  field: 7 physics
  nationality: 6 German
  discovered: 15 Mossbauer effect **28** recoil-free gamma ray absorption
  awarded: 10 Nobel Prize

Mosses from an Old Manse
  author: 18 Nathaniel Hawthorne

most 4 best, very **6** degree **7** maximum **9** extremely

most distant point 5 limit, reach **8** boundary **9** extremity **11** ultima Thule

Mostel, Zero
  real name: 16 Samuel Joel Mostel
  born: 10 Brooklyn NY
  roles: 8 The Front **10** Rhinoceros **11** The Enforcer **12** The Producers **15** Du Barry Was a Lady **16** Fiddler on the Roof **17** Panic in the Streets

most important 3 key, top **4** head, main **5** chief **7** central, highest, leading **8** cardinal, dominant, foremost, greatest **9** paramount, principal, uppermost **10** preeminent **11** outstanding, predominant

mostly 6 mainly **7** as a rule, chiefly, greatly, largely **8** above all **9** generally, primarily, specially **10** especially **11** principally **12** particularly **13** predominantly

most prominent 7 leading **8** dominant **10** preeminent **11** outstanding

most successful 6 banner, record **7** winning **10** triumphant **11** outstanding

mote 3 dot **4** iota **5** speck **8** particle **9** scintilla

moth
  varieties: 4 hawk, luna, tent **5** ghost, gypsy, plume, royal, swift, yucca **6** hornet, lappet, miller, urania **7** clothes, emperor, flannel, hook tip, leopard, tussock **8** army worm, forester, imperial, polka dot **9** carpenter, clearwing **10** forest tent **11** pseudosphex **12** African peach **13** American tiger, giant Hercules **14** tropical sphinx **15** Chinese silkworm, glover's silkworm **20** striped morning sphinx

moth-eaten 5 holey **6** old-hat **7** worn-out **8** outmoded **10** antiquated, threadbare **11** dilapidated

mother 3 mom, mum **4** bear, mama, mind, mums, rear, tend **5** beget, breed, mammy, mater, momma, mommy, mummy, nurse, raise **6** origin, source **7** care for, indulge, nurture, old lady, produce, protect **8** conceive, stimulus **10** wellspring **11** inspiration
  French: 4 mere **5** maman
  Spanish: 5 madre
  Italian: 5 mamma
  of wind: 3 Eos

  of stars: 3 Eos
  of gods: 5 Nammu

mother country 8 homeland **10** fatherland, native land, native soil, old country **13** native country

Mother Goose in Prose
  author: 14 Lyman Frank Baum

motherly 4 kind **6** gentle, loving, tender **7** devoted **8** maternal, parental **9** indulgent **10** protective, sheltering

mother of a family
  Latin: 13 materfamilias

Mother of the West
  nickname of: 8 Missouri

mother's helper
  French: 6 au pair

motif 4 form, idea **5** shape, style, theme, topic **6** design, figure, thread **7** pattern, refrain, subject **9** treatment

motion 3 cue, nod **4** flow, flux, move, sign, stir **5** drift **6** action, beckon, signal, stream **7** gesture, kinesis, passage, request **8** mobility, movement, progress **10** indication, suggestion **11** gesticulate, proposition **13** gesticulation **14** recommendation

motionless 4 calm, dead, idle **5** fixed, inert, still **6** at rest, frozen, stable, static **8** immobile, inactive, lifeless, tranquil, unmoving **9** immovable, quiescent **10** stationary, transfixed **11** immobilized **12** unresponsive

motion picture 3 pic **4** cine, film, show **5** flick, movie **6** cinema, talkie **8** flickers **10** photodrama **11** picture show **13** moving picture

motivate 4 goad, move, stir **5** egg on, impel **6** arouse, induce, prompt, stir up, turn on **7** actuate, provoke **8** activate, persuade **9** influence, stimulate

motivation 5 cause **6** reason **7** impetus, impulse **9** causation, impulsion **11** provocation

motive 3 aim, end **4** goal, spur **5** cause **6** design, object, reason **7** grounds, purpose **8** occasion, stimulus, thinking **9** incentive, intention, prompting, rationale **10** enticement, incitement, inducement **11** inspiration, instigation, provocation

motley 4 pied **5** mixed, tabby **6** hybrid, sundry, unlike, varied **7** dappled, piebald, watered **8** assorted, brindled, speckled **9** checkered, composite, different, disparate, divergent, harlequin, patchwork **10** dissimilar, iridescent, polychrome, variegated **11** diversified, incongruous, varicolored **12** multicolored **13** heterogeneous, kaleidoscopic, miscellaneous

motor 3 car **4** auto, ride, tour **5** drive, pilot, wheel **6** engine, turbine **7** machine **8** efferent **10** automobile

motorcar 4 auto, heap **6** jalopy, wheels **7** flivver, machine, vehicle **9** tin lizzie **10** automobile

motor vehicle 3 bus, cab, car, van **4** auto, heap, jeep, limo, taxi **5** motor, sedan, truck, wagon **6** jalopy, jitney, pickup, wheels **7** flivver, hardtop, machine, omnibus, town car, vehicle **9** limousine, tin lizzie **10** automobile **11** convertible

mottled 4 pied **5** tabby **7** blotchy, flecked, piebald, specked **8** brindled, speckled, stippled **10** iridescent, multicolor, variegated **11** varicolored **12** parti-colored **13** kaleidoscopic, polychromatic

motto 3 saw **4** rule **5** adage, axiom, maxim **6** byword, dictum, saying, slogan, truism **7** epigram, precept, proverb **8** aphorism **9** catchword, principle, watchword

moue 4 pout **7** grimace

Moulin Rouge
 director: 10 John Huston
 cast: 10 Jose Ferrer (Toulouse-Lautrec) **11** Suzanne Flon, Zsa Zsa Gabor **12** Eric Pohlmann
 setting: 5 Paris **10** Montmartre

mound 4 bump, dune, heap, hill, pile, rick **5** knoll, mogul, ridge, stack **7** bulwark, hillock, hummock, rampart **9** earthwork **10** embankment **12** entrenchment

Mound Builders
 location: 15 Ohio River Valley **22** Mississippi River Valley
 known for: 13 earthen mounds

mount 3 fit, fix, rig, set, wax **4** go up, grow, pony, rise, soar **5** affix, camel, climb, equip, frame, horse, scale, steed, surge, swell **6** ascend, fit out, outfit, set off **7** augment, charger, climb up, get over, get upon, install, set into **8** elephant, increase, multiply, straddle **9** intensify

mountain 3 alp **4** peak **5** bluff, butte, range, ridge **6** height, massif **7** volcano **8** eminence, highland **9** elevation
 of Afghanistan: 3 Koh **5** Safeo **6** Chagai, Pamirs **7** Nowshak **8** Koh-i-Baba, Safed Koh, Sulaiman **9** Himalayas, Hindu Kush, Istoro Nal **11** Khwaja Amran, Paropamisus
 of Albania: 5 Shala **6** Pindus **8** Koritnjk **10** Mount Korab **12** Albanian Alps
 of Algeria: 5 Aissa, Atlas, Aures, Dahra, Tahat **6** Chelia **7** Ahaggar, Kabylia, Mouydir **8** Djurjura **9** Djurdjura, Tell Atlas **12** Saharan Atlas
 of Andorra: 6 d'Etats **8** l'Estanyo **8** Pyrenees **10** Cataperdis **11** Como Pedrosa
 of Angola: 4 Moco **5** Chela **6** Loviti **16** Humpata Highlands
 of Antigua and Barbuda: 9 Boggy Peak
 of Argentina: 4 Toro **5** Andes, Chato, Laudo, Potro **6** Conico, Pissis, Rin-

con **8** Famatina, Murallon, Olivares, Tronador, Zapaleri **9** Aconcagua, Tupungato **10** Cordillera **13** Ojos del Salado **15** Cerro Mercedario, Sierra de Cordoba
 of Armenia: 6 Ararat, Taurus **8** Karabekh **7** Aladagh **12** Mount Aragats
 of Australia: 3 Ise **4** Blue, Olga, Ossa, Zeil **5** Bruce, Snowy **6** Cradle, Doreen, Garnet, Gawler, Magnet, Morgan **7** Bongong, Gregory **8** Augustus, Brockman, Cuthbert, Herbert, Jusgrave, Mulligan, Surprise **9** Murchison, Kosciusko, Woodroffe **14** Australian Alps **15** New England Range **18** Great Dividing Range
 of Austria: 4 Alps **6** Tirols, Tyrols, Stubai **8** Eisenerz, Rhatikon **9** Dolomites, Kitzbuhel **10** Hohe Tauern **13** Grossglockner **14** Silvretta Group
 of Azerbaijan: 8 Caucasus
 of Bangladesh: 10 Keokradong **15** Chittagong Hills
 of Barbados: 6 Chalky **7** Hillaby
 of Belgium: 8 Ardennes **16** Signal de Botrange
 of Benin: 7 Atakora
 of Bhutan: 5 Black **9** Himalayas **10** Chomo Lhari, Kula Kangri
 of Bolivia: 4 Jara **5** Andes, Cusco, Cuzco **6** Sajama, Sorata, Sunsas **7** Illampu **8** Ancohuma, Illimani, Mururata, Sansimon, Santiago, Zapaleri **12** Eastern Range, Western Range **18** Cordillera Oriental **20** Cordillera Occidental
 of Borneo: 4 Iran, Raja **5** Saran **6** Kapuas, Muller, Nijaan, Tebang **8** Kinabalu, Kinibalu, Schwaner
 of Bosnia-Herzegovina: 11 Dinaric Alps
 of Brazil: 3 Mar **5** Geral, Organ, Piaui **6** Acarai, Gurupi, Parima, Urucum **7** Amambai, Carajas, Gradaus, Neblina, Oragaos, Roraima **8** Bandeira, Itatiaia, Roncador, Tombador **9** Pacaraima, Sugar Loaf **10** Tumuc-Humac
 of Brunei: 6 Teraja **9** Ulu Tutong **10** Pagon Priok
 of Bulgaria: 3 Kom **5** Botev, Pirin, Sapka **6** Balkan, Musala, Sredna **7** Vikhren **8** Musallah **11** Rila-Rhodope
 of Burkina Faso: 4 Tema **8** Nakourou **10** Tenakourou, Tenekourou
 of Burundi: 8 Nyarwana **9** Nyamisana
 of Cambodia: 3 Pan **7** Dangrek, Dong Rek **8** Cardamom, Elephant **10** Phnom Aoral, Phnom Aural
 of Cameroon: 5 Mbabo **7** Bambuto, Kapsiki, Mandara **8** Batandji, Cameroon **9** Atlantika
 of Canada: 5 Coast, Logan, Royal **6** Robson, Skeena **7** Cariboo, Cascade, Purcell, Rockies, Selkirk, Stelias, St Elias **8** Columbia, Hazelton, Monashee **9** Mackenzie, Notre

Dame, Tremblant **10** Laurentian, Richardson, Shickshock **14** Jacques Cartier
 of Canary Islands: 5 Teide, Teyde **6** La Cruz **8** El Cumbre, Tenerife
 of Cape Verde: 4 Cano, Fogo **10** Pico de Cano
 of Central African Republic: 5 Karre, Tinga **6** Mongos **9** Dar Challa **11** Kayagangiri
 of Chad: 7 Tibesti, Touside **9** Emi Koussi
 of Chile: 4 Maca, Toro **5** Chato, Maipo, Maipu, Paine, Potro, Pular, Torre, Yogan **6** Apiwan, Burney, Conico, Jervis, Poquis, Rincon **7** Chaltel, Copiapo, Fitzroy, Palpana, Velluda **8** Cochrane, Tronador, Yanteles **9** Tupungato **13** Ojos del Salado
 of Colombia: 5 Abibe, Andes, Baudo, Chita, Cocuy, Huila, Pasto **6** Ayapel, Perija, Purace, Tolima, Tunahi **7** Chamusa, del Ruiz **8** Oriengal **10** Santa Marta **14** Cristobal Colon **17** Central Cordillera, Eastern Cordillera, Western Cordillera
 of Costa Rica: 4 Poas **5** Barba, Irazu **6** Blanco **7** Central, Gongora **9** Talamanca, Turrialba **10** Guanacaste **14** Chirripo Grande
 of Crete: 3 Ida **5** Dikte, Phino **6** Juktas **7** Lasithi, Madaras **8** Leuka Ori, Theodore, Thriphte **9** Psiloriti
 of Croatia: 10 Julian Alps **11** Styrian Alps
 of Cuba: 6 Copper **7** Cristal, Maestra, Organos **8** Camaguey, Trinidad, Turquino **9** Las Villas **11** Pinar del rio **12** Guaniguanico **14** Sancti-Spiritus
 of Czechoslovakia: 3 Ore **5** Grant, Tatra **5** Sumava **7** Gerlach, Sudeten **8** Krkonose **9** High Tatra **10** Carpathian **11** Gerlachovka
 of Denmark: 12 Ejer Bavnehoj, Yding Skovhoj **14** Himmelbjaerget
 of Djibouti: 5 Gouda **9** Moussa Ali
 of Dominican Republic: 4 Tina **5** Gallo, Neiba **6** Duarte **8** Baoruco, Central **8** Bahoruco, Oriental **13** Septentrional
 of Ecuador: 5 Andes **6** Condor, Sangay **7** Cayambe **8** Antisana, Cotopaxi **9** Cotacachi, Pichincha **10** Chimborazo
 of Egypt: 5 Sinai, Uekia **6** Gharib **8** Katerina **9** Katherina **13** Shayib al-Banat
 of El Salvador: 6 Izalco **8** Santa Ana
 of England: 5 Black **7** Pennine, Snowdon **8** Cambrian, Cumbrian **11** Scafell Pike
 of Equatorial Guinea: 5 Mitra **11** Santa Isabel
 of Ethiopia: 4 Amba, Batu, Guge, Guna, Talo **5** Ahmar, Choke **9** Rasdashan, Ras Deshen
 of Finland: 6 Haltia **7** Laltiva

10 Saari Selka **11** Haldetsokka
of France: 4 Alps, Jura **5** Blanc, Pelat **6** Vosges **8** Ardennes, Pyrenees **9** Mont Blanc **10** French Alps **11** Pic Montcalm
of Gabon Republic: 5 Mpele **7** Chaillu, Cristal, Mikongo **8** Balaquri, Birougou, Iboundji
of Georgia: 8 Caucasus
of Germany: 3 Ore **4** Harz **8** Feldberg **9** Zugspitze **10** Erzgebirge **11** Black Forest, Fichtelberg **12** Bavarian Alps
of Ghana: 8 Afadjato **12** Akwapim Hills
of Gibraltar: 6 Misery
of Greece: 3 Ida **4** Idhi, Oeta, Oite, Ossa **5** Athos **6** Ithome, Peleon, Pelion, Pindus **7** Grammos, Helicon, Olympus, Rhodope **8** Hymettos, Smolikas, Targetos, Taygetus **9** Parnassus **10** Hagion Oros, Lycabettus, Pentelicus
of Greenland: 5 Forel, Payer **7** Khardyu **8** Peterman **9** Gunnbjorn **15** Petermannsbjerg **16** Gunnbjornsfjaeld
of Guatemala: 4 Agua, Mico **5** Fuego, Madre **6** Pacaya, Tacana **7** Atitlan, Toliman **8** La Candon, Las Minas, Tajumuko **9** Tajamulco **10** Acatenango, Santa Maria **12** Cuchumatanes
of Guinea: 4 Loma **5** Nimba **6** Tamgue **11** Fouta Djalon
of Guyana: 5 Amuku, Ariwa, Kamoa **6** Akarai, Kanuku **7** Caburai **9** Pacaraima
of Haiti: 4 Nord **5** Cahos **6** Macaya, Noires **7** Lahotte, Laselle **8** Troudeau
of Honduras: 4 Pija **6** Agalta **7** Celaque **8** Las Minas **9** Esperanza **25** Central American Cordillera
of Hong Kong: 6 Castle **8** Victoria **9** Tai Mo Shan
of Hungary: 4 Alps, Bukk **5** Kekes, Matra, Tatra, Vetes **6** Bakony, Mecsek **7** Cserhat, Gerecse **8** Borzsony, Zempleni **9** Korishegy **10** Carpathian
of Iceland: 4 Laki **5** Askja, Hekla, Jokul, Katla **7** Surtsey **10** Orafajokul **16** Hvannadalshnukur
of India: 8 Aravalli **9** Broad Peak, Distaghil, Himalayas, Karakoram, Nanda Devi, Rakaposhi **10** Gasherbrum, Masherbrum **11** Nanga Parbat **12** Eastern Ghats, Godwin Austen, Kanchenjunga, Western Ghats
of Iran: 6 Elburz, Zagros **8** Demavend
of Iraq: 6 Qalate, Zagros **7** Halgurd, Qaarade **9** Kurdistan
of Ireland: 5 Galty **6** Croagh, Mourne **7** Errigal, Muckish, Patrick, Wicklow **8** Comeragh **10** Benna Beola, Twelve Bens, Twelve Pins **13** Carrantuohill, Knockmealdown **19** Macgillycuddy's Reeks
of Israel: 4 Nafh, Sagi **5** Harif, Meron, Ramon, Tabor **6** Atzmon,

Carmel, Hatira, Meiron
of Italy: 4 Alps, Etna, Rosa, Viso **5** Amaro, Blanc, Corno, Somma **6** Cimone, Ortles **7** Vulcano **8** Vesuvius **9** Apennines, Dolomites, Maritimes, Stromboli **10** Apuane Alps, Carnic Alps, Julian Alps, Otztal Alps **11** Bernina Alps, Gennargentu **12** Gran Paradiso, Ligurian Alps **13** Lepontine Alps **16** Abruzzi Apennines
of Jamaica: 4 Blue **8** Sir Johns
of Japan: 3 Uso, Zao **4** Fuji **5** Asahi, Asama, Hondo, Yesso **6** Asosan, Enasan, Hiuchi, Kiusiu, Yariga **7** Fujisan, Hakusan, Kujusan, Tokachi **8** Fujiyama **9** Japan Alps
of Java: 4 Amat, Gede **5** Lawoe, Murjo, Prahu **6** Raoeng, Semuru, Slamet **7** Semeroe **8** Soembing
of Jordan: 9 Jabal Ramm, Jebel Ramm
of Kenya: 5 Elgon, Kenya, Kulai, Nyira, Nyiru **6** Kinyaa, Matian **7** Logonot **8** Aberdare **9** Kirinyaga
of Korea: 4 Wang **5** Chiri, Halla **6** Kwanmo, Paektu, Sobaek **7** Diamond, Kyebang, Nangnim, Taebaek **8** Chang-pai, Hamgyong, Myohyang **9** Paektu-san **10** Kumgang-san
of Kyrgyzstan: 8 Tian Shan
of Laos: 3 Bia, Lai, Loi, San **4** Copi, Khat **5** Atwat **6** Khoung, Tiubia **7** Phou Bia **15** Annam Cordillera
of Lebanon: 4 Mzar **5** Aruba **6** Hermon **7** es Sauda, Lebanon, Sannine **8** Kadischa, Kenisseh **9** Kennisseh **10** al-Mukammal **11** Anti-Lebanon **13** Qurnat al-Sawda
of Lesotho: 6 Maloti, Maluti **7** Central **8** Injasuti, Machache **10** Ben Macdhui **11** Drakensberg, Thaba Putsoa **16** Thabana Ntlenyana
of Liberia: 4 Bong, Putu **5** Niete, Nimba **6** Wutivi **9** Bomi Hills
of Libya: 5 Green **9** Bette Peak **13** Jabal al Akhdar, Tibesti Massif
of Liechtenstein: 4 Alps **8** Naafkopf, Rhatikon **12** Three Sisters **15** Vorder-Grauspitz
of Lithuania: 9 Juozapine **15** Samogitian Hills
of Luxembourg: 8 Ardennes, Huldange **9** Burgplatz **11** Wemperhardt
of Madagascar: 4 Boby **9** Ankaratra **11** Maromokotro **12** High Plateaus, Tsiafajavona **17** Tsaratanana Massif
of Malawi: 6 Mlanje **7** Mulanje **11** Livingstone
of Malaysia: 4 Bulu, Hose, Iban, Iran, Main, Mulu, Niut, Raja **5** Murjo, Niapa, Ophir **6** Blumut, Kapuas, Leuser, Slamet **7** Binaija, Brassey, Crocker **8** Kinabalu, Rindjani **11** Gunong Korbu, Gunong Tahan
of Mali: 4 Mina **6** Iforas **7** Manding **12** Hombori Tondo
of Mexico: 6 Colima, Tacana, Toluca **7** Orizaba **9** Paricutin **11** Ixtacihuatl,

Sierra Madre **12** Citlaltepetl, Popocatepetl **14** Sierra Zacateca **16** Chiapas Highlands **24** Transverse Volcanic Sierra
of Mongolia: 4 Cast, Orog **5** Altai **6** Kentei, Sevrej **7** Ich Ovoo, Khangai, Khentei **8** Tannu-Ola **9** Edrengijn **10** Cagaan Bogd, Tabun Bogdo **11** Munky Sardyk **14** Hangayn-Hentiyn, Monch Chajrchan
of Montenegro: 8 Durmitor **11** Dinaric Alps
of Morocco: 3 Rif **4** Bani **5** Abyla, Atlas, Sarro **8** Tidiguin **9** Anti-Atlas, High Atlas, Jebel-Musa **11** Middle Atlas **12** Jebel Toubkal **13** Djebel Toubkal
of Mozambique: 5 Binga **7** Lebombo
of Myanmar: 4 Chin, Naga, Pegu, Popa **5** Dawna **6** Arakan, Kachin, Lushai, Patkai **7** Karenni **8** Nattaung, Peguyoma, Saramati, Victoria **10** Tenasserim **11** Hkakabo Razi, Manipur Hill **12** Tanen Taunggi
of Namibia: 9 Brandberg **14** Khomas Highland, Koakoveld Hills
of Nepal: 6 Cho Oyu, Churia, Makalu **7** Everest, Lhotse I, Manaslu, Siwalik **8** Lhotse II **9** Annapurna, Himalayas **10** Dhaulagiri, Gosainthan, Himalchuli **11** Ganesh Himal **12** Kanchenjunga **14** Mahabharat Lekh
of New Guinea: 4 Snow **6** Orange **7** Bismark, Wilhelm **8** Victoria **9** Carstensz **10** Puncak Jaya **11** Owen Stanley **12** Albert Edward
of New Zealand: 4 Cook, Eden, Flat, Owen **5** Allen, Chope, Lyall, Mitre, Ohope, Otari, Young **6** Egmont, Stokes, Tasman **7** Aorangi, Cameron, Coronet, Ernslaw, Huiarau, Pihanga, Ruahine, Ruapehu, Tauhera, Tutamee, Tyndall **8** Aspiring, Richmond, Tauranga **9** Messenger, Murchison, Ngauruhoe, Raukumara, Tongariro **11** Remarkables **12** Southern Alps
of Nicaragua: 4 Leon **5** Negro, Viejo **6** Madera, Telica **7** Managua, Mogoton, Saslaya **9** Momotombo
of Niger: 7 Bagzane, Greboun **9** Air Massif
of Norway: 5 Sogne **6** Kjolen **7** Numedal **8** Blodfjel, Snohetta, Telemark, Ustetind **9** Harteigen, Jotunheim, Langfjell, Ramnanosi **10** Dovrefjell, Galdhoepig, Glitretind, Vibmesnosi **11** Myrdalfjell **12** Galdhopiggen **13** Glittertinden **14** Aardangerjokul, Hallingskarvet, Skagastolstind
of Oman: 4 Qara **5** Green, Hafit, Harim, Nakhl, Tayin **6** al-Sham **8** el-Akhdar **11** Jabal Akhdar **13** Green Mountain
of Pakistan: 3 Pab, Pub **4** Salt **6** Makran **7** Kirthar **8** Himalaya, Safed Koh, Sulaiman **9** Hindu Kush,

Karakoram, Tirich Mir **11** Makran Coast **12** Godwin Austin **13** Central Makran **14** Takht-i-Sulaiman

of Panama: 4 Baru, Maje **5** Chico, Gandi **6** Darien **7** Columan, San Blas, Veragua **8** Chiriqui, Santiago, Tabasara **10** Costa Rican **14** Serrania de Sapo **15** Aspave Highlands **17** Cordillera Central

of Peru: 5 Andes **7** El Misti, Huamina **8** Coropuna **9** Huascaran

of Philippines: 3 Apo, Iba **4** Mayo, Taal **5** Albay, Askja, Hibok, Mayon, Pulog **6** Pagsan **7** Banahao, Canlaon

of Poland: 4 Rysy **5** Tatra **6** Beskid **7** Pieniny, Sudeten **9** Beshchady, High Tatra, Holy Cross **10** Carpathian

of Portugal: 4 Acor, Lapa **5** Gerez, Marao, Mousa **6** Bornes, Peneda **7** Larouco **8** Caramulo **9** Caldeiro, Monchique **11** Pico da Serra **14** Serra da Estrela

of Puerto Rico: 4 Toro **5** Cayey, Punta **6** Yunque **8** Guilarte, Luquilla **10** Torrecilla **17** Cordillera Central

of Romania: 5 Banat, Bihor, Negoi **6** Codrul, Rodnei **7** Apuseni, Balkans, Caliman, Fagaras **8** Pietrosu **9** Moldavian **10** Carpathian, Moldoveanu **17** Transylvanian Alps

of Russia: 5 Altai, Lenin, Sayan, Urals **6** Anadyr, Elbrus, Koryak, Pamirs, Pobedy **7** Belukha, Crimean, Khibiny, Stanovi, Zhiguli **8** Caucasus, Dzhughur, Stanavoi, Tien Shan **9** Kopet Dagh, Narodnaya, Pamir-Alai, Yablonovy **11** Sikhote-Alin, Verkhoyansk

of Rwanda: 7 Mitumba, Virunga **8** Muhavura **9** Karisimbi

of Samoa: 4 Fito, Vaea **5** Alava **6** Savaii **7** Matafao **8** Silisili **9** Rainmaker

of San Marino: 6 Titano **9** Apennines

of Sardinia: 4 Rasu **5** Ferry, Linas **7** Gallura, Limbara **8** Marghine, Serpeddi, Vittoria **11** Gennargentu

of Saudi Arabia: 5 Razih **6** Tuwayq **10** Jebal Sawda

of Scotland: 5 Attow, Ochil **6** Sidlaw **7** Cheviot **8** Ben Nevis, Grampian **9** Ben Lomond, Highlands, Trossachs

of Senegal: 6 Gounou **12** Fouta Djallon

of Sicily: 4 Erei, Etna, Moro, Sori **5** Aetna, Atlas, Erici, Hybla, Iblei, Ibrei **7** Nebrodi, Vulcano **9** Apennines, Le Madonie, Stromboli **10** Peloritani

of Sierra Leone: 4 Loma **9** Bintimani **10** Tingi Hills

of Sikkim: 7 Dongkya, Donkhya **9** Himalayas, Singalili **10** Darjeeling **12** Kanchenjunga

of Singapore: 6 Mandai **7** Panjang **10** Bukit Timah

of Slovakia: 7 Sudetes **8** Low Tatra **9** High Tatra, Slovak Ore **10** Carpathian, Nizke Tatry **11** Visoke Tatry **15** White Carpathian

of the Solomon Islands: 5 Balbi **11** Popomanasiu

of Somalia: 5 Guban **7** Surud Ad **11** Migiurtinia, Ogo Highland

of South Africa: 3 Aux, Kop **5** Table **7** Kathkin **8** Injasuti **9** Stormberg **10** Devil's Peak, Sneeuwberg **11** Drakensberg **12** Giant's Castle **13** Witwatersrand **14** Mont-aux-Sources **15** Great Escarpment

of Spain: 4 Gata **5** Aneto, Rouch, Teide **6** Cuenca, Estats, Europa, Gredos, Magina, Morena, Nethou, Nevada, Teleno, Toledo **7** Alcaraz, Banuelo, Catalan, Cerredo, Demanda, Iberian, La Sagra, Moncayo, Perdido **8** Almanzor, Asturias, Galician, Maladeta, Monegros, Montseny, Mulhacen, Penalara, Pyrenees **10** Albarracin, Cantabrian, Guadarrama, Torrecilla

of Sri Lanka: 5 Pedro **7** Sri Pada **9** Adams Peak **14** Pidurutalagala

of Sudan: 4 Nuba **6** Red Sea **7** Imatong, Kinyeti **9** Dongotona **10** Jabal Marra, Jebel Marra **18** Ethiopian Highlands

of Surinam: 4 Emma **6** Kayser, Oranje **10** Julianatop, Tumuc-Humac, Wilhelmina **13** Eilert's Il Haan, Van Ach Van Wyck **15** Guiana Highlands

of Swaziland: 7 Emlembe **8** Highveld **11** Drakensberg

of Sweden: 4 Sarv **5** Ammar, Kebne **6** Helags, Kjolen, Ovniks, Sarjek **7** Kjollen **10** Kebnekaise

of Switzerland: 3 Dom **4** Alps, Jura, Rigi, Rosa, Todi **5** Adula, Blanc, Cenis, Eiger, Genis, Karpf, Righi **6** Linard, Pizela, Sentis **7** Bernina, Beverin, Grimsel, Pilatus, Rotondo **8** Balmhorn, Jungfrau **9** Weisshorn **10** Diablerets, Matterhorn, St Gotthard, Wetterhorn **11** Burgenstock **12** Dufourspitze **13** Rheinwaldhorn **14** Finsteraarhorn

of Syria: 6 Carmel, Hermon **7** Alawite, Libanus **10** Nusairiyya **11** Anti-Lebanon

of Taiwan: 5 Tatun **6** Tzukao, Yu Shan **7** Taitung **8** Morrison **10** Sinkao Shan **11** Hsin-Kao Shan **15** Chungyang Shanmo

of Tajikistan: 13 Communism Peak

of Tanzania: 4 Kibo, Mero **8** Usambara **11** Kilimanjaro

of Thailand: 5 Dawna, Khieo **6** Phanom **8** Dang Raek, Inthanon, Kao Prawa, Maelamun **9** Khao Luang **11** Bilauktaung, Doi Inthanon

of Tibet: 5 Kamet, Sajum **6** Kailas, Kunlun **7** Bandala, Everest **9** Himalayas, Karakoram

of Togo: 4 Togo **7** Atakora, Baumann, Koronga

of Tunisia: 5 Atlas **6** Chambi, Mrhila **7** Tebessa **8** High Tell, Zaghouan

12 Northern Tell **18** Dorsale Tunnisienne

of Turkey: 2 Ak **3** Ala **4** Alai, Dagh, Kara **5** Hasan, Hinis, Honaz, Murat, Murit **6** Ala Dag, Ararat, Bingol, Bolgar, Pontic, Suphan, Taurus **7** Aladagh, Erciyas **8** Karacali **10** Kackar Dagi

of Uganda: 4 Oboa **5** Elgon **7** Virunga **9** Mufumbiro, Ruwenzori **10** Margherita **18** Mountains of the Moon

of Ukraine: 7 Crimean **10** Carpathian

of United States: 4 Hood **5** Coast, Green, Kenai, Ozark, Rocky, White **6** Alaska, Brooks, DeLong, Elbert, Helena, Mesabi, Pocono, Shasta **7** Cascade, Chugach, Foraker, Harvard, Kilauea, Massive, Olympic, Olympus, Rainier, St Elias, Whitney **8** Catskill, Davidson, Endicott, Katahdin, Mauna Loa, McKinley, Mitchell, Ouachita, St Helens, Wrangell **9** Allegheny, Blue Ridge, Kuskokwim, North Peak, Pike's Peak **10** Black Hills, Blanca Peak, Grand Teton, Washington, Williamson **11** Appalachian, Santa Monica **12** Sierra Nevada **14** Berkshire Hills

of Uruguay: 6 Animas **10** Grand Hills **14** Cuchilla Grande **15** Mirador Nacional

of Vanuatu: 6 Lopevi **11** Tabwemasana

of Venezuela: 3 Pao **4** Pava, Yair **5** Andes, Duida, Icutu **6** Concha, Cuneva, Merida, Parima, Sierra, Yumari **7** Bolivar, Imutaca, Masaiti, Roraima **8** Gurupira **9** Pacaraima **10** Auyan-Tepui **11** Turimiquire **18** Cordillera del Norte

of Vietnam: 6 Badinh, Badink **7** Nindhoa, Ninhhoa **8** Fansipan, Knontran, Ngoklinh, Ngoklink, Tchepone, Tclepore **18** Annamese Cordilera

of Wales: 6 Berwyn **7** Snowdon **8** Cambrian **9** Prescelly **13** Brecon Beacons

of Western Samoa: 4 Fito, Vaea **13** Mauga Silisili

of Yemen: 6 Shuayb, Thamir **7** Djehaff

of Yugoslavia: 5 Karst **6** Balkan **7** Rhodope, Triglav **8** Crna Gora, Durmitor **9** Sar-Pindus **10** Carnic Alps, Julian Alps, Karawanken **11** Dinaric Alps **13** Slovenian Alps **20** Northern Albanian Alps

of Zaire: 7 Crystal, Mitumba, Virunga **9** Ruwenzori **10** Margherita, Nyaragongo **18** Mountains of the Moon

of Zambia: 8 Muchinga **12** Mafinga Hills

of Zimbabwe: 5 Vumba **6** Manica **7** Inyanga **9** Inyangani **11** Chimanimani, Matopo Hills

Mountain
constellation of: **5** Mensa

mountaineers are always free men
Latin: **19** montani semper liberi
motto of: **12** West Virginia

Mountain State
nickname of: **7** Montana **12** West Virginia

Mountbatten, Louis
also: **27** first Earl Mountbatten of Burma
nationality: **7** British
position: **12** first sea lord
supreme allied commander of: **13** Southeast Asia
chief of: **25** British combined operations
viceroy of: **5** India
served in: **3** WWI **4** WWII
directed invasion of: **10** Madagascar
recaptured: **5** Burma

mountebank 5 cheat, fraud, phony, quack **6** con man, humbug **7** hustler, sharper **8** huckster, operator, swindler **9** charlatan, con artist **11** quacksalver

mounted soldier 6 hussar, lancer **7** dragoon **8** cavalier, horseman **10** cavalryman

mourn 3 cry, rue, sob **4** keen, pine, wail, weep **6** bemoan, bewail, grieve, lament, regret, sorrow **7** deplore, despair **8** languish, weep over

mournful 3 sad **5** black, sorry, weepy **6** dismal, rueful, somber, triste, woeful **7** doleful, joyless, unhappy **8** dejected, dirgeful, dolorous, funereal, grevious, saddened **9** depressed, plaintive, sorrowful **10** depressing, dispirited, lamentable, lugubrious, melancholy **11** distressing, melancholic **12** heavy hearted

mourning 3 woe **5** black, crape, dolor, grief, weeds **6** sorrow **7** anguish, despair **8** grieving **9** lamenting, sorrowing **11** bereavement, lamentation

Mourning Becomes Electra
author: **12** Eugene O'Neill
character: **4** Seth **10** Hazel Niles, Peter Niles **16** Captain Adam Brant
Mannon family: **4** Ezra, Orin **7** Lavinia **9** Christine

mourning period
Hebrew: **6** shibah, shivah

mouser 3 cat **4** puss **5** kitty, pussy **6** feline **8** pussycat

Mousetrap, The
author: **14** Agatha Christie

mousseline 6 muslin

mousy 3 shy **4** drab, dull **5** timid, wimpy **7** bashful, fearful **8** timorous **9** colorless, unnoticed, withdrawn **11** unobtrusive **13** inconspicuous

mouth 3 bay, say **4** bell, jaws, lips **5** inlet, speak, voice **6** outlet, portal

7 declare, estuary, opening **8** aperture, propound **9** pronounce

mouthful 3 dab **4** bite **5** taste **6** morsel, nibble

mouthpiece 4 reed **6** lawyer **7** counsel **8** advocate, attorney **9** counselor

mouth-watering 8 inviting, tempting **9** appealing **10** appetizing **11** tantalizing

movable, moveable 4 free **5** loose **6** mobile, motile, moving **8** portable **10** changeable

movables 4 gear **5** goods **7** baggage, effects, luggage **9** equipment **10** belongings **11** impedimenta, possessions **13** accoutrements, paraphernalia

move 2 go **3** act, ask, get **4** bear, deed, fire, lead, pass, ploy, step, stir, sway, turn, urge **5** begin, budge, carry, cause, drive, impel, plead, rouse, shift, touch **6** action, affect, arouse, attack, convey, excite, exhort, incite, induce, motion, prompt, strike, stroke, switch **7** advance, budging, gesture, go ahead, impress, inspire, measure, operate, proceed, propose, provoke, request, suggest **8** function, interest, locomote, maneuver, motivate, persuade, relocate, start off, stirring, transfer, transmit **9** impassion, influence, recommend, stimulate, transport, transpose **10** transplant **11** opportunity

move downward 3 dip **4** dive, drop, fall, sink **6** plunge, tumble **7** decline, descend, plummet **8** decrease

movement 4 part **5** drive, steps, works **6** action, effort, motion **7** crusade, measure, program, section **8** activity, division, gestures, maneuver, progress, stirring **9** agitation, execution, mechanism, operation **10** locomotion **11** undertaking

move out 5 leave **6** depart, vacate **8** evacuate

move quickly 3 fly, run **4** bolt, dash, race, rush, tear **5** hurry **6** hasten, sprint

move sideways 4 edge **5** sidle **8** sidestep

move slyly 4 edge, lurk **5** sidle, skulk, slink, sneak, steal

move up 5 boost, climb, heave, hoist, raise, scale **6** ascend, uplift **7** advance, elevate, promote, upraise

move upward 4 rise, soar **5** climb, mount **6** ascend **7** take off

movie 4 film, show **5** flick **6** cinema **7** feature, picture, showing **9** screening
invented by:
machine: **7** Jenkins
panoramic: **6** Waller
projector: **6** Edison
talking: **14** Warner Brothers

moving 5 motor **6** mobile, motile

8 exciting, poignant, spurring, stirring, touching **9** affecting, inspiring **10** impressive, locomotive, motivating **11** interacting, stimulating

moving about 5 astir **6** active **7** on the go

Moving Target, A
author: **14** William Golding

Mowgli
character in: **14** The Jungle Books
author: **7** Kipling

moxie 4 grit, guts, sand **5** nerve, pluck, spunk **6** mettle, spirit **7** courage, stamina **8** audacity, backbone **9** hardihood, toughness **10** pluckiness **13** dauntlessness

moyen age 10 Middle Ages

Mozambique
capital/largest city: **6** Maputo **15** Lourenco Marques
others: **4** Tete **5** Beira, Pemba, Zumbo **6** Chemba, Nacala, Pafuri, Sofala **7** Nampula **8** Mutarara **9** Inhambane, Quelimane **11** Porto Amelia
school: **15** Eduardo Mondlane
monetary unit: **6** escudo **7** centavo, metical
island: **6** Inhaca **7** Angoche **8** Bazanuto **9** Benguerua
lake: **5** Nyasa **6** Chuali, Nyassa **8** Nhavarre
mountain: **7** Lebombo
highlands: **6** Namuli **9** Gorongosa
highest point: **5** Binga
river: **4** Buzi, Save **5** Lurio, Msalu **6** Rovuma, Ruvuma **7** Ligonha, Limpopo, Lugenda, Messaio, Zambezi **8** Changane
ocean: **6** Indian
physical feature:
cape: **7** Delgado
channel: **10** Mozambique
people: **3** Yao **5** Bantu, Chopi, Lomue, Lomwe, Macua, Makua, Ngoni, Nguni, Shona **6** Maravi, Thouga **7** Maconde, Makonde **10** Portuguese
explorer: **11** Vasco de Gama
leader: **8** Chissano **9** Dos Santos **12** Samora Machel **15** Eduardo Mondlane
language: **3** Yao **5** Makua **6** Nyanji, Thonga **7** Swahili **10** Portuguese
religion: **5** Islam **7** animism **13** Roman Catholic
place:
game reserve: **8** Marromeu **9** Gorongosa, Gorongoza **18** Maputo Elephant Park
reservoir: **11** Cabora Bassa
feature:
bride price: **6** lobolo

Mozart, Wolfgang Amadeus
born: **7** Austria **8** Salzburg
cataloguer: **6** Kochel
composer of: **4** Linz (symphony No 36) **5** Paris (symphony No 31)

6 Prague (symphony No 38) **7** Don Juan, Haffner (symphony No 35), Jupiter (symphony No 41), Requiem, Turkish (concerto) **8** Idomeneo **9** Credo Mass, Mitridate **10** Lucio Silla **11** Don Giovanni, Hunt Quartet, Il Re Pastore, Sparrow Mass **12** A Musical Joke, Cosi Fan Tutte (So Do They All or Women Are Like That), Haydn Quartet, Spatzenmesse **13** The Magic Flute, Trumpet Sonata, Turkish Sonata **14** Coronation Mass, Stadler Quintet, Die Zauberflote **15** Haffner Serenade, La Finta Semplice, Prussian Quartet **16** Dissonant Quartet, La Clemenza di Tito, Posthorn Serenade, Serenata Notturna **17** A Little Night Music **18** Jeunehomme Concerto, La Finta Giardiniera, The Clemency of Titus **19** Bastien und Bastienne, The Marriage of Figaro **20** Eine Kleine Nachtmusik, The Pretender Gardener **21** Der Schauspieldirektor, Ein Musikalischer Spass **22** The Pretending Simpleton **25** Die Entfuhrung aus dem Serail **27** The Abduction from the Seraglio

Mr, Mister
Russian: **8** gospodin
French: **8** monsieur
Yiddish: **3** Reb

Mr B
character in: **6** Pamela
author: **10** Richardson

Mr Basketball
nickname of: **8** Bob Cousy

Mr Britling Sees It Through
author: **7** H G Wells

Mr Cub
nickname of: **10** Ernie Banks

Mr Deeds Goes to Town
director: **10** Frank Capra
cast: **10** Gary Cooper (Longfellow Deeds), Jean Arthur **14** George Bancroft

Mr Ed
character: **9** Carol Post **10** Kay Addison, Wilbur Post **12** Roger Addison **14** Gordon Kirkwood, Winnie Kirkwood
cast: **8** Leon Ames **9** Alan Young **11** Connie Hines, Edna Skinner **12** Larry Keating **18** Florence MacMichael
Mr Ed was: **12** talking horse

Mr Flood's Party
author: **22** Edwin Arlington Robinson

Mr Midnight
nickname of: **10** Steve Allen

Mr Peepers
character: **9** Mrs Gurney **11** Marge Weskit, Mr Remington **12** Harvey Weskit **14** Nancy Remington **15** Robinson Peepers **20** Superintendent Bascom
cast: **8** Wally Cox **9** Gage Clark **11** Ernest Truex, Marion Lorne, Tony Randall **14** Patricia Benoit **16** Georgiann Johnson
Mr Peepers taught: **7** science
school: **13** Jefferson High

Mr Sammler's Planet
author: **10** Saul Bellow

Mrs Dalloway
author: **13** Virginia Woolf
character: **10** Miss Kilman, Peter Walsh, Sally Seton **15** Richard Dalloway **16** Clarissa Dalloway **17** Elizabeth Dalloway

Mrs Miniver
director: **12** William Wyler
cast: **11** Greer Garson **12** Teresa Wright **13** Dame May Whitty, Walter Pidgeon
Oscar for: **7** actress (Garson), picture **8** director **17** supporting actress (Wright)

Mr Smith Goes to Washington
director: **10** Frank Capra
cast: **9** Guy Kibbee **10** Jean Arthur **11** Claude Rains **12** Edward Arnold, James Stewart **14** Thomas Mitchell

Mrs Parkington
author: **14** Louis Bromfield

Mrs Stevens Hears the Mermaids Singing
author: **9** May Sarton

Mrs Warren's Profession
author: **17** George Bernard Shaw

Mr Television
nickname of: **11** Milton Berle

much 3 far **4** a lot, lots **5** about, ample, heaps, loads, often **6** almost, indeed, nearly, overly, rather, scores **7** copious, greatly **8** abundant, good deal, plenty of, quantity, somewhat, striking **9** decidedly, important, plenteous, plentiful, regularly **10** frequently, impressive, noteworthy, oftentimes, satisfying, sufficient, worthwhile **11** appreciable, exceedingly, excessively, sufficiency **12** considerable **13** approximately, consequential

Much Ado About Nothing
author: **18** William Shakespeare
character: **4** Hero **7** Claudio, Don John, Leonato **8** Beatrice, Benedick, Dogberry, Don Pedro

much in little
Latin: **13** multum in parvo

much loved 4 dear **7** beloved, darling, dearest **8** precious **9** cherished, treasured

mucilage 3 gum **4** glue **5** paste **6** cement **8** adhesive

mucilaginous 5 gluey, gummy, gunky **6** gloppy, sticky **8** adhesive

muck 3 mud **4** dirt, dung, gunk, mire, ooze, slop **5** filth, slime **6** sewage, sludge **7** compost, garbage

muck up 4 soil **5** dirty, muddy **7** pollute

mud 4 dirt, muck, soil, wire

Mudcat State
nickname of: **11** Mississippi

muddied 5 dirty, grimy **6** grubby, soiled **7** stained **8** begrimed, confused

muddle 3 fog **4** blow, daze, haze, mess, muff, ruin **5** botch, chaos, mix up, spoil, throw **6** boggle, bungle, fumble, goof up, jumble, mess up, pother, rattle **7** blunder, clutter, confuse, nonplus, stupefy **8** bewilder, confound, disarray, disorder **13** disconcertion **14** disarrangement

muddlebrained 5 inept **7** witless **8** confused **11** lamebrained

muddled 5 fuzzy **7** bemused **8** confused **10** bewildered

muddy 4 dull **5** dirty, grimy, vague **6** filthy, grubby **7** obscure **8** begrimed, confused

muff 5 botch, spoil **6** bungle **10** handwarmer

muffle 3 gag **4** dull, hush, mask, mute, veil, wrap **5** cloak, cover, quell, quiet, still **6** dampen, deaden, shroud, soften, stifle, swathe **7** conceal, enclose, envelop, silence, swaddle

muffled 3 low **4** dull, soft **5** faint, muted **6** dulled, feeble, hushed, veiled **7** cloaked, covered, quelled, quieted, stilled, subdued, swathed, wrapped **8** deadened, shrouded, silenced, softened, swaddled **9** concealed, enveloped, inaudible **10** indistinct, suppressed

mug 3 cup **4** face, puss, toby **5** stein, stoup **6** beaker, flagon, goblet, kisser, visage **7** chalice, tankard, toby jug, tumbler **11** countenance

mugger 8 assailer, attacker **9** assailant, assaulter

mugginess 4 damp **8** dampness, dankness, humidity **9** humidness **10** sultriness **12** oppressiveness

muggy 5 close, humid **6** clammy, steamy, sticky, stuffy, sultry, sweaty **8** steaming, vaporous **10** oppressive, sweltering

mulberry 5 Morus
varieties: **3** red **4** Aino **5** black, paper, white **6** French, Indian **7** Russian **8** American, silkworm

mulct 4 bilk **6** extort **7** defraud, swindle

mule 3 ass **5** burro **6** donkey **7** jackass
group of: **4** span

mulish 5 balky **6** ornery **8** perverse, stubborn **9** fractious, obstinate **10** refractory **11** intractable **12** recalcitrant

mull, mull over 5 study, weigh **6** ponder **8** consider, meditate, pore over, ruminate **10** deliberate

Muller
character in: **25** All Quiet on the Western Front
author: **8** Remarque

Muller, Hermann Joseph

field: 8 genetics
researched: 5 X-rays **8** mutation
awarded: 10 Nobel Prize

Muller, Paul
  field: 9 chemistry
  nationality: 5 Swiss
  established: 16 DDT as insecticide
  awarded: 10 Nobel Prize

Mulligan, Buck
  character in: 7 Ulysses
  author: 5 Joyce

multicolored 10 variegated

multifarious 4 many **5** mixed **6** divers, motley, sundry, varied **7** diverse, protean, several, various **8** manifold, numerous **9** different, multiplex **10** variegated **11** diversified **13** heterogeneous, miscellaneous

multiple 4 many **7** various **8** manifold

multiply 5 add to, beget, breed, raise **6** extend, spread **7** augment, enhance, enlarge, magnify **8** generate, heighten, increase **9** intensify, procreate, propagate, reproduce **11** proliferate

multitude 3 mob **4** army, herd, host, mass, pack, slew **5** array, crowd, crush, drove, flock, flood, horde, troop **6** legion, myriad, scores, throng **7** conflux

multum in parvo 12 much in little **23** a great deal in a small space

mum 4 mute **5** quiet, still, tacit **6** silent **8** taciturn, wordless **9** secretive **12** closemouthed **15** uncommunicative

mumble 5 growl, grunt, mouth **6** murmur, mutter, rumble **7** stammer **9** hem and haw

mumbo jumbo 3 rot **4** blah, bosh, cant, tosh **5** bilge, hokum, hooey, tripe **6** hot air, humbug **7** baloney **8** flummery **9** gibberish, sophistry **10** double talk, hocus pocus **11** doublespeak, jabberwocky, obfuscation **12** fiddle-faddle, gobbledygook, obscurantism

Mummy, The
  director: 10 Karl Freund
  cast: 10 Zita Johann **12** Boris Karloff, David Manners **16** Bramwell Fletcher

munch 4 chew, gnaw **5** champ, chomp, crush, grind **9** masticate

Munch, Edvard
  born: 5 Loten **6** Norway **10** Hedemarken
  artwork: 6 The Cry **7** Puberty, The Kiss **9** The Scream **11** Dance of Life **12** Frieze of Life **21** Death in the Sick Chamber

Munchausen, Baron 4 liar **7** solider **10** adventurer **11** exaggerator

Munchkins
  characters in: 13 The Wizard of Oz
  author: 4 Baum

mundane 5 petty **7** earthly, humdrum, prosaic, routine, worldly **8** day-to-day, everyday, ordinary **9** practical **10** pedestrian **11** commonplace, down-to-earth, terrestrial

Muni, Paul
  real name: 16 Muni Weisenfreund
  born: 7 Austria, Lemberg (now Lvov Ukraine)
  roles: 6 Juarez **8** Scarface **10** The Valiant **12** The Good Earth **14** Clarence Darrow, Inherit the Wind **15** The Last Angry Man **18** The Life of Emile Zola **22** The Story of Louis Pasteur (Oscar) **26** I Am a Fugitive from a Chain Gang

municipal 4 city **5** civic **6** public **9** community **14** administrative

municipality 4 city, town **6** parish **7** village **8** township **9** bailiwick

munificence 6 bounty **7** charity **8** largesse **9** patronage **10** generosity, liberality **11** benefaction, beneficence, benevolence **12** philanthropy **13** bounteousness, bountifulness **14** charitableness **15** humanitarianism

munificent 4 free **6** kindly, lavish **7** liberal, profuse **8** generous, princely **9** bounteous, bountiful **10** altruistic, beneficent, benevolent, charitable, freehanded, open-handed **11** extravagant, magnanimous **12** eleemosynary, humanitarian **13** philanthropic

Munin
  origin: 12 Scandinavian
  form: 5 raven
  owned by: 4 Odin **5** Othin
  personifies: 6 memory
  duty: 10 newsbearer
  other raven: 5 Hugin

Munsters, The
  character: 11 Lily Munster **12** Eddie (Edward Wolfgang) Munster **13** Herman Munster **14** Grandpa Munster, Marilyn Munster
  cast: 7 Al Lewis **9** Pat Priest **10** Fred Gwynne **11** Beverly Owen **12** Butch Patrick **13** Yvonne DeCarlo

Muppet Show, The
  character: 4 Rolf **5** Gonzo **6** Animal, Beaker **7** Scooter **9** Miss Piggy **10** Fozzie Bear **13** Kermit the Frog (Kermie)

Murasaki, Lady
  author of: 14 The Tale of Genji

murder 4 kill, slay **5** abuse, waste **6** mangle, misuse **7** butcher, corrupt, cut down, killing **8** homicide, knock off **9** agonizing, slaughter **10** bastardize, formidable, impossible, oppressive, unbearable **11** assassinate, intolerable **12** manslaughter **13** assassination, very difficult **14** commit homicide, use incorrectly

Murder, She Wrote
  character: 15 Jessica (JB) Fletcher
  cast: 14 Angela Lansbury
  setting: 9 Cabot Cove

murderer 4 Cain **6** killer, slayer **7** butcher **8** assassin, Barabbas, homicide **9** cutthroat

Murder in the Cathedral
  author: 7 T S Eliot

Murder of Roger Ackroyd, The
  author: 14 Agatha Christie

Murder on the Orient Express
  author: 14 Agatha Christie
  detective: 13 Hercule Poirot

murderous 4 gory **5** cruel, rough **6** bloody, brutal, deadly, savage, trying **7** killing **9** dangerous, difficult, ferocious **11** devastating **12** bloodthirsty, disagreeable

Murdoch, Iris
  author of: 7 The Bell **11** Under the Net **12** A Severed Head, The Sea the Sea **14** The Black Prince **15** Nuns and Soldiers **17** The Good Apprentice, The Nice and the Good **20** The Philosopher's Pupil **24** The Book and The Brotherhood **30** The Sacred and Profane Love Machine

Murdstone, Mr
  character in: 16 David Copperfield
  author: 7 Dickens

Murillo, Bartolome (Bartolomeo) Esteban
  born: 5 Spain **7** Seville
  artwork: 13 Angels' Kitchen **14** Death of St Clare **15** The Two Trinities **17** Vision of St Anthony **23** The Immaculate Conception **24** Dream of the Roman Patrician

murk 3 fog **4** haze, mist **5** gloom **6** miasma **7** pea soup **8** darkness

murky 3 dim **4** dark, gray, hazy **5** dusky, foggy, misty **6** cloudy, dismal, dreary, gloomy, somber **7** obscure, sunless **8** lowering, overcast, vaporous **9** cheerless

murmur 3 hum **4** buzz, purl, purr, sigh **5** drone, sough, swish **6** lament, mumble, mutter, rumble, rustle **7** grumble, lapping, whimper, whisper **8** low sound, susurrus **9** complaint, undertone

murophobia
  fear of: 4 mice

Murphy, Eddie
  roles: 3 Raw **13** Trading Places **14** The Golden Child **15** Coming to America, Forty-Eight Hours **16** Beverly Hills Cop **17** Saturday Night Live, The Nutty Professor **19** Beverly Hills Cop Two

Murray, Bill
  roles: 7 Stripes **9** Meatballs **10** Caddyshack **12** Ghostbusters, Groundhog Day **13** The Razor's Edge **17** Saturday Night Live **27** Not Ready for Prime Time Players

Murray, Don
  wife: 9 Hope Lange
  born: 11 Hollywood CA
  roles: 7 Bus Stop **13** A Hatful of Rain

16 The Bachelor Party, The Hoodlum Priest

Murray, Jeanne
  real name of: 13 Jean Stapleton

Murray, Mina
  character in: 7 Dracula
  author: 6 Stoker

Musaeus
  occupation: 4 poet, seer

Musagetes *see* **6** Apollo

Muscat, Masqat
  capital of: 4 Oman

muscle 4 grit, thew **5** bicep, brawn, force, might, power, sinew, vigor **6** energy, flexor, tendon **7** potency, prowess, stamina **8** virility **9** puissance **10** sturdiness **16** muscular strength
  kind: 4 limb **5** axial **6** smooth **7** dynamic, flexors, special, striped **8** postural, striated **9** abductors, extensors, voluntary **11** involuntary
  fuel: 4 food
  action: 4 pull
  specific: 6 rectus **7** deltoid, oblique **8** omohyoid **9** abdominal, abdominis, sartorius **10** pectoralis **11** intercostal, sternohyoid **13** biceps brachii, rectus femoris **14** vastus medialis **15** brachioradialis, vastus lateralis **16** serratus anterior, tensor fascia lata **17** quadriceps femoris **18** transverse thoracic **19** sternocleidomastoid **20** transversus abdominis
  supplementary structure: 6 sheath **10** deep fascia, retinacula **14** synovial bursae, synovial sheath

muscular 3 fit **5** burly, husky, tough **6** brawny, sinewy, strong **8** athletic, powerful **9** strapping

muscular contraction 3 tic **5** cramp, crick, spasm **6** stitch **12** charley horse

musculoskeletal system
  component: 4 bone **6** muscle, tendon **8** ligament

muse 4 mull **6** ponder, review **7** reflect **8** cogitate, consider, meditate, ruminate **9** speculate **10** deliberate **11** contemplate

Musee des Beaux Arts
  author: 7 W H Auden

Muses
  also: 7 the Nine **8** Pierides **10** Castalides
  form: 9 goddesses
  names: 4 Clio (history) **5** Erato (love poetry) **6** Thalia (comedy), Urania (astronomy) **7** Euterpe (music, lyric poetry) **8** Calliope (epic poetry) **9** Melpomene (tragedy) **10** Polyhymnia (sacred poetry) **11** Terpsichore (dance)
  father: 4 Zeus
  mother: 9 Mnemosyne
  corresponds to: 7 Camenae

Musgrave, Thea
  born: 8 Scotland **9** Edinburgh

composer of: 11 The Decision **16** The Five Ages of Man **17** Beauty and the Beast, The Voice of Ariadne

mush 5 slush **6** drivel **8** porridge **14** sentimentalism, sentimentality

mushiness 5 slush **6** bathos **10** sponginess **11** mawkishness **14** sentimentalism, sentimentality

mushroom 4 grow **5** burst, fungi **6** blow up, expand, fungus, spread, sprout **7** burgeon, explode, shoot up **8** flourish, increase, spring up **9** toadstool **11** proliferate
  part: 3 cap **4** veil **5** gills, stalk, tubes, volva **6** button, hyphae, spores **7** annulus, basidia **10** rhizomorph
  non-poisonous: 5 field, honey, morel, table **6** oyster **7** inky cap, parasol **8** puffball, shiitake **9** fairy-ring, morchella, shaggy cap, stinkhorn **10** champignon **11** chanterelle **12** edible bolete, slippery jack **16** old man of the woods
  poisonous: 7 amanita **8** death cap, sickener **9** fly agaric **12** jack-o-lantern **13** devil's boletus **15** destroying angel
  study of: 8 mycology

mushy 4 soft **5** foggy, misty, pappy, pulpy, vague **6** cloudy, quaggy, spongy **7** maudlin, mawkish, squashy, squishy **8** effusive, romantic, squelchy **10** lovey-dovey **11** sentimental, tear-jerking **12** affectionate

Musial, Stan
  nickname: 10 Stan the Man
  sport: 8 baseball
  team: 16 St Louis Cardinals

music 4 song, tune **5** score **6** melody **7** euphony, harmony **8** lyricism **10** minstrelsy **11** tunefulness **13** melodiousness
  god of: 5 Brage, Bragi **6** Apollo **7** Phoebus, Pythius **9** Musagetes

musical 5 lyric, sweet **6** dulcet **7** lilting, lyrical, melodic, tuneful **9** melodious **10** euphonious, harmonious **11** mellifluent

musical instrument 3 lur, sax, saz **4** bass, bell, drum, fife, gong, harp, horn, lute, lyre, oboe, outi, pipe, tuba, viol **5** argul, banjo, bugle, cello, cobza, flute, kazoo, organ, piano, guena, rabob, sansa, shawm, sheng, sitar, viola **6** bagana, chimes, cornet, cymbal, fiddle, guitar, spinet, treble, violin, zither **7** bagpipe, bassoon, cittern, clavier, kithara, marimba, panpipe, pibcorn, piccolo, samisen, strings, tambura, theorbo, timpani, trumpet, ukulele **8** autoharp, bass drum, calliope, clarinet, dulcimer, Jew's harp, mandolin, psaltery, recorder, talharpa, triangle, trombone, virginal **9** accordion, balalaika, castanets, harmonica, harmonium, krummhorn, rommelpot, saxophone, snare

drum, xylophone **10** bongo drums, clavichord, concertina, flugelhorn, French horn, kettledrum, sousaphone, tambourine, vibraphone **11** English horn, harpsichord **12** jouhikantele
  classification: 4 horn, reed, wind **5** brass **6** string **8** keyboard, woodwind **10** electronic, percussion

musical terms
  agitated: 7 agitato
  all players/singers together: 5 tutti
  becoming quicker: 11 accelerando
  continue without a break: 5 segue
  disconnected/each note separate: 8 staccato
  end: 4 fine
  expressively: 10 espressivo
    abbreviation: 4 espr
  fast: 6 veloce **7** allegro
  gentle: 5 soave
  gently: 9 doucement
  getting slower: 10 allargando
  getting weaker and slower: 7 calando
  gradually getting louder: 9 crescendo
    abbreviation: 5 cresc
  gradually getting softer: 10 diminuendo **11** decrescendo
    abbreviation: 3 dim **4** decr
  gradually slowing: 11 rallentando
    abbreviation: 4 rall
  half: 5 mezzo
  half voice/half volume: 9 mezza voce
  heavy: 5 lourd
  in an undertone/in a low voice: 9 sotto voce
  leisurely: 6 comodo
  less: 4 meno
  light: 8 leggiero
  little: 4 poco
  lively: 3 vif
  loud: 5 forte
    abbreviation: 1 f
  moderately slow and even: 7 andante
  more: 3 piu
  mournful: 5 mesto
  not too much: 9 non troppo
  plucked instead of bowed: 9 pizzicato
    abbreviation: 4 pizz
  quick/vivacious: 6 vivace
  repeat from beginning: 6 da capo
    abbreviation: 2 D C
  shaking and quavering/rapid alternation of notes: 5 trill
  silent: 4 tace
  singing/songlike/flowing: 9 cantabile
  sliding: 9 glissando
  slow: 5 lento **6** adagio
  slow dignified tempo: 5 largo
  slow down: 5 cedez
  smooth/connected: 6 legato
  soft: 5 piano
    abbreviation: 1 p
  solemn/serious: 5 grave

sorrowful: 7 dolente
strict time: 10 tempo gusto
sudden accent: 9 sforzando
 abbreviation: 2 sf
sweetly: 5 dolce
tearful: 9 lacrimoso
tenderly: 10 affettuoso
trembling vibrating effect/rapid re-iteration of a single pitch: 7 tremolo
very: 5 molto
very loud: 10 fortissimo
 abbreviation: 2 ff
very soft: 10 pianissimo
 abbreviation: 2 pp
with fire: 8 con fuoco
with spirit/vigor: 7 con brio
with style/taste: 8 con gusto
with the mute: 10 con sordino
musician 4 bard **5** piper **6** artist, player, singer, violer **7** bandman, cellist, drummer, pianist, twanger **8** minstrel, organist, virtuoso **9** performer, trumpeter, violinist **11** saxophonist

Music Man, The
 director: 13 Morton Da Costa
 cast: 12 Buddy Hackett, Shirley Jones (Marian the librarian) **13** Robert Preston (Professor Harold Hill) **15** Hermione Gingold
 setting: 9 River City
 score: 15 Meredith Willson
 song: 15 Till There Was You **19** Seventy-six Trombones

music school 12 conservatory
 French: 13 conservatoire
musing 6 absent, dreamy **7** mulling **8** absorbed **9** pondering **10** meditating, meditative, reflecting, reflective
musjid 6 mosque

Muskogean, Muskhogean
 tribe: 4 Cree **7** Alabama, Alibamu, Choctaw, Natchez **8** Seminole **9** Chickasaw

Muslim *see* **6** Moslem
muslin
 French: 10 mousseline
muss 4 mess **6** foul up, jumble, ruffle, rumple, tangle, tousle **7** crumple, disturb **8** dishevel, disorder **9** bedraggle **10** disarrange
mussed 5 messy **6** frowzy, untidy **7** ruffled, rumpled, tousled, unkempt **8** uncombed **10** disarrayed, disheveled, disordered, disorderly **11** disarranged

Mussorgsky (Moussorgsky), Modest Petrovich
 born: 5 Pskov **6** Russia
 member of: 7 The Five
 composer of: 7 Sunless **10** The Nursery **12** Boris Godunov **13** Khovanshchina **19** Night on Bald Mountain **21** Songs and Dances of Death **22** Pictures at an Exhibition

mustard
 botanical name: 5 B alba **6** B hirta, B nigra **7** B juncea **8** Brassica

also called: 7 sinapis
 origin: 4 Asia **5** China
 use: 6 hotdog, sauces **7** egg roll **9** hamburger **13** salad dressing
muster 4 call **5** amass, raise, rally **6** gather, line up, summon **7** collect, company, convene, convoke, marshal, meeting, round up, turnout **8** assemble, assembly, mobilize **9** convocate, gathering **10** assemblage, confluence, congregate, inspection **11** aggregation **12** accumulation **13** agglomeration
musty 3 old **4** damp, dank, worn **5** banal, dirty, dusty, moldy, stale, tired, trite **6** frousy, frouzy, frowsy, frowzy, old hat, stuffy **7** worn-out **8** familiar, mildewed **9** hackneyed **10** antiquated, threadbare **11** commonplace
mutable 6 fickle **8** flexible, variable **9** adaptable, alterable, mercurial, versatile **10** adjustable, changeable, inconstant, modifiable, permutable **11** convertible, metamorphic **13** transformable
mutate 4 turn **5** alter **6** change **7** convert **9** transform
mutation 6 change **7** anomaly **9** deviation, variation **10** alteration **12** modification **13** metamorphosis **14** transformation **15** transfiguration **18** transmogrification
mutatis mutandis 30 necessary changes having been made
mute 3 mum **4** dumb **5** quiet, tacit **6** silent **8** aphasiac, nonvocal, reserved, reticent **9** unsounded, unuttered, voiceless **10** speechless **12** inarticulate, noncommittal, unpronounced **13** unarticulated **15** uncommunicative
muted 3 dim, low **4** dull, soft, weak **5** quiet **6** dulled, feeble **7** muffled **8** deadened, softened **10** indistinct, lackluster
mutilate 4 lame, maim **6** cut off, deform, excise, mangle **7** butcher, cripple **8** amputate, lacerate, truncate **9** disfigure, dismember
mutineer 5 rebel **9** dissident, insurgent **10** malcontent **15** insurrectionist
mutinous 6 unruly **10** dissenting, rebellious **13** revolutionary

Mutinus
 origin: 5 Roman **7** Italian
 god of: 9 fertility
 fertility in: 8 marriage
 corresponds to: 7 Priapus
mutiny 4 coup **5** rebel **6** revolt, rise up **8** takeover, upheaval, uprising **9** overthrow, rebellion **10** insurgency **12** insurrection

Mutiny on the Bounty
 author: 15 Charles Nordhoff, James Norman Hall
 character: 6 Tehani **9** Roger Byam **12** William Bligh (Captain Bligh) **13** George Stewart **17** Fletcher Christian
 director: 10 Frank Lloyd

 cast: 10 Clark Gable (Fletcher Christian) **12** Eddie Quillan, Franchot Tone **13** Herbert Mundin **15** Charles Laughton (Captain Bligh)
 Oscar for: 7 picture
mutt 3 cur, dog, pup **5** puppy **7** mongrel

Mutt and Jeff
 creator: 7 Al Smith **9** Bud Fisher
 character: 5 A Mutt **6** Cicero **7** Mrs Mutt
mutter 4 carp **5** gripe, growl, grunt **6** grouch, grouse, kvetch, mumble, murmur, rumble **7** grumble, whisper **8** complain
mutual 5 joint **6** common, shared **7** related **8** communal, returned **10** coincident, reciprocal **11** correlative, interactive
mutual understanding 6 accord **9** agreement
muzzle 3 gag **4** bind, curb **5** check, quiet, still **6** bridle, rein in, stifle **7** harness, silence **8** strangle, suppress, throttle

Myanmar
 former name: 5 Burma
 other name: 16 Land of the Pagodas
 capital: 6 Yangon **7** Rangoon
 ancient capital: 3 Ava **4** Pegu **8** Mandalay
 largest city: 7 Rangoon
 others: 2 Ye **3** Ava **4** Pegu **5** Akyab, Bhamo, Katha, Minbu, Namtu, Papun, Prome, Tavoy **6** Hsenwi, Hsipaw, Lashio, Maymyo, Monywa, Shwebo **7** Bassein, Henzada, Pakokku, Toungoo **8** Moulmein, Myingyan
 measure: 2 ly **3** dha, gon, mau, sao, tao, tat **4** byee, phan, seit, taun, that **5** shita, thuoc **6** lamany, palgat **7** chaivai **8** okthabah
 monetary unit: 3 pya **4** kyat
 weight: 2 ta **3** can, pai, vis **4** binh, kyat, ruay, viss **5** behar, candy, ticul **6** abucco **7** peiktha
 lake: 4 Inle
 mountain: 4 Chin, Naga, Pegu, Popa **5** Davna **6** Arakan, Kachin, Lushai, Patkai **7** Karenni **8** Nattaung, Peguyoma, Saramati, Victoria **10** Tenasserim **11** Manipur Hill **12** Tanen Taunggi
 highest point: 11 Hkakabo Razi
 river: 3 Hka **6** Salwin, Sutang **7** Irawadi, Kaladan, Myitnge, Salween, Schweli, Sittang **8** Chindwin, Indawgyi **9** Irrawaddy
 sea: 7 Andaman
 physical feature:
 bay: 4 Siam **6** Bengal, Hunter **7** Heanzay **8** Thailand
 gulf: 8 Martaban
 plateau: 4 Shan
 port: 5 Akyab **7** Bassein, Henzada **8** Moulmein
 people: 2 Ao, Vu, Wa **3** Kaw, Lai,

Lao, Mon, Pyu, Tai, Was **4** Akha, Chin, Juki, Kadu, Laos, Lolo, Miao, Naga, Sema, Shan, Thai, Tsin **5** Karen, Lhota **6** Birman, Burman, Kachin, Peguan, Rengma **7** Akhlame, Burmese, Kakhyen, Palauna, Palaung, Siamese **8** Mon-Khmer **9** Arakanese **12** Tibeto-Berman
language: 3 Lai **4** Chin, Kuki, Pegu, Shan **5** Karen **6** Kachin **7** Burmese, English
religion: 5 Hindu, Islam **8** Buddhism **12** Christianity
place:
  mines: 6 Mawchi **7** Bawdwin
  pagoda: 9 Shwe Dagon
  road: 4 Ledo **5** Burma **9** Stillwell
feature:
  ball game: 7 chin-lon
  festival: 5 Water **6** Lights **10** Thadin-gyut
  silk head band: 10 gaungbaung
  skirt: 6 longyi
  traveling theatrical group: 4 Pwes
My Antonia
  author: 11 Willa Cather
  character: 9 Jim Burden **15** Antonia Shimerda
My Darling Clementine
  director: 8 John Ford
  cast: 7 Tim Holt **8** Ward Bond **10** Henry Fonda (Wyatt Earp) **12** Linda Darnell, Victor Mature (Doc Holliday) **13** Walter Brennan
my dear
  French: 7 ma chere, mon cher
My Fair Lady
  director: 11 George Cukor
  based on play by: 17 George Bernard Shaw (Pygmalion)
  cast: 11 Rex Harrison (Professor Henry Higgins) **13** Audrey Hepburn (Eliza Doolittle) **15** Stanley Holloway **16** Wilfrid Hyde-White
  score: 14 Lerner and Loewe
  Oscar for: 7 picture
  song: 14 The Rain in Spain **24** I Could Have Danced All Night
my faith
  French: 5 ma foi
my fault
  Latin: 8 mea culpa
My Favorite Martian
  character: 8 Tim O'Hara **11** Uncle Martin **15** Mrs Lorelei Brown
  cast: 9 Bill Bixby **10** Ray Walston **13** Pamela Britton
Myles
  king of: 7 Laconia
  invented: 9 grain mill
My Little Margie

character: 7 Charlie **9** Mrs Odetts **11** Mr Honeywell **13** Freddie Wilson **14** Margie Albright, Vernon Albright **15** Roberta Townsend
cast: 9 Don Hayden, Gale Storm **10** Willie Best **12** Clarence Kolb **13** Hillary Brooke **14** Charles Farrell **15** Gertrude Hoffman
my lord
  French: 8 monsieur **11** monseigneur
  Italian: 9 monsignor **10** monsignore
My Man Godfrey
  director: 13 Gregory La Cava
  cast: 10 Alice Brady, Mischa Auer **11** Gail Patrick **13** Carole Lombard, William Powell
myriad 6 untold **7** endless **8** infinite, manifold **9** boundless, countless, limitless, uncounted **11** innumerable, measureless **12** immeasurable, incalculable **13** multitudinous
Myrina
  husband: 8 Dardanus
myrmidon 6 cohort **8** follower, henchman
Myrmidons
  people of: 6 Aegina **8** Thessaly
  created by: 4 Zeus
  created from: 4 ants
  characteristic: 7 warlike
  leader: 6 Peleus **8** Achilles
Myrrha
  also: 6 Smyrna
  father: 11 King Cinyras
  loved: 7 Cinyras
  crime: 6 incest
  son: 6 Adonis
  changed into: 6 myrtle **9** myrrh tree
Myrtilus
  charioteer of: 8 Oenomaus
myrtle 6 Myrtus **10** Vinca minor **14** Myrtus communis **18** Cyrilla racemiflora **23** Umbellularia californica
  varieties: 3 bog, gum, sea, wax **4** cape, Jew's, sand **5** crape, crepe, downy, dwarf, Greek, honey, scent **6** German, Oregon, Polish, willow **7** box sand, classic, running, Swedish **10** Western tea **11** candleberry, Queen's crape, sandverbena **13** Allegheny sand, bracelet honey, California wax **16** Australian willow
Mysia
  epithet of: 7 Demeter
mysophobia
  fear of: 4 dirt
Mysteries of Paris, The
  author: 9 Eugene Sue
Mysteries of Udolpho, The
  author: 15 Mrs Ann Radcliffe

mysterious 4 dark **6** cloudy, covert, hidden, secret **7** cryptic, obscure, strange, unknown **8** baffling, puzzling **9** enigmatic, secretive **10** perplexing, sphinxlike, undercover **11** clandestine, inscrutable **12** impenetrable, inexplicable, supernatural, unfathomable **13** surreptitious **14** undecipherable
Mysterious Stranger, The
  author: 9 Mark Twain
mystery 6 enigma, occult, puzzle, riddle, secret **7** problem, secrecy **9** conundrum, obscurity, symbolism, vagueness **11** ambivalence, elusiveness **12** ineffability, quizzicality **13** ineffableness, mystification
Mystery of Edwin Drood, The see **10** Edwin Drood
mystical, mystic 5 inner **6** hidden, occult **7** cryptic, obscure **8** abstruse, esoteric, ethereal, symbolic **9** enigmatic, secretive **10** cabalistic, symbolical, unknowable **11** inscrutable, nonrational **12** metaphysical, otherworldly **14** transcendental
mystification 9 confusion **10** bafflement, perplexity, puzzlement **12** bewilderment
mystify 4 fool **5** elude **6** baffle, puzzle **7** confuse, deceive, mislead, perplex **8** bewilder, confound **9** bamboozle
myth 3 fib, lie **4** tale, yarn **5** error, fable, story **6** canard, legend **7** fantasy, fiction, hearsay, parable **8** allegory, delusion, illusion, tall tale **9** fairy tale, falsehood **10** shibboleth **13** prevarication
mythical, mythic 6 fabled, unreal **8** illusory **9** imaginary, legendary, pretended **10** conjured-up, fabricated, fantasized, fictitious **13** unsubstantial
mythological, mythologic 6 unreal **8** fabulous, illusory, imagined **9** fantastic, imaginary, legendary, unfactual **10** fictitious
My Three Sons
  character: 11 Chip Douglas, Mike Douglas **12** Steve Douglas **13** Robbie Douglas **18** Katie Miller Douglas, Uncle Charley O'Casey **20** Ernie Thompson Douglas, Michael Francis (Bub) O'Casey
  cast: 8 Don Grady, Tina Cole **12** Tim Considine **13** Fred MacMurray **14** William Frawley **15** Barry Livingston, William Demarest **17** Stanley Livingston
  dog: 5 Tramp
my word
  French: 5 ma foi

nab 4 bust, grab, nail, snag **5** catch, pinch, seize, snare **6** arrest, collar, detain, haul in, pick up, pull in, snatch **7** capture **9** apprehend

nabob 3 VIP **4** lord **5** mogul, nawab **6** deputy, tycoon **7** magnate **8** governor **9** plutocrat **10** capitalist **11** billionaire, millionaire

Nabokov, Vladimir
  author of: **3** Ada **4** Mary, Pnin **6** Lolita **8** Pale Fire

nadir 4 base, zero **5** floor **6** apogee, bottom **7** nothing **8** low point **10** rock bottom **11** lowest point

Nadja
  author: **11** Andre Breton

nag 4 fury, goad, harp **5** annoy, devil, harpy, scold, shrew, vixen **6** badger, bicker, harass, hassle, heckle, hector, nettle, peck at, pester, pick at, pick on, plague, rail at, tartar, virago **7** bedevil, upbraid **8** battle-ax, irritate **9** importune, termagant, Xanthippe

Nahua *see* Aztec

Nahuatl *see* Uto-Aztecan

Naiad
  form: **5** nymph
  location: **5** water

nail 3 fix, pin **4** brad, claw, spad **5** talon **6** fasten, hammer, secure
  part: **3** bed **4** root

Naipaul, V S
  author of: **10** Guerrillas **15** A Bend in the River **17** A House for Mr Biswas **19** The Return of Eva Peron, The Suffrage of Elvira

Nairobi
  capital of: **5** Kenya

naive 4 open **5** green, plain **6** candid, simple, unwary, unwise **7** artless, foolish, natural, unjaded **8** gullible, immature, innocent **9** childlike, credulous, guileless, ingenuous, unspoiled, unworldly **10** unaffected, unassuming **11** susceptible **12** unsuspecting, unsuspicious **15** unsophisticated

naivete, naiveté 6 candor **7** modesty **8** openness **9** credulity, frankness, greenness, innocence, sincerity **10** callowness, simplicity **11** artlessness, foolishness, naturalness **12** childishness, inexperience **13** ingenuousness **14** unaffectedness **16** simplemindedness

naked 4 bald, bare, nude, pure

5 bared, frank, plain, sheer **6** patent, simple, unclad **7** blatant, exposed **8** disrobed, laid bare, manifest, palpable, undraped, wide- open **9** in the buff, unclothed, uncovered, undressed **11** perceptible, unappareled, unqualified, unvarnished **15** in the altogether

Naked and the Dead, The
  author: **12** Norman Mailer

Naked City
  character: **5** Libby **9** (Det) Adam Flint **10** (Det Lt) Dan Muldoon, (Lt) Mike Parker **11** (Det) Jim Halloran, (Sgt) Frank Arcaro **13** Janet Halloran
  cast: **9** Paul Burke **11** Nancy Malone **12** John McIntire **13** Harry Bellaver, Horace McMahon, Suzanne Storrs **15** James Franciscus
  setting: **11** New York City
  theme: **19** Somewhere in the Night

Namath, Joe (Joseph William)
  nickname: **11** Broadway Joe
  sport: **8** football
  position: **11** quarterback
  team: **11** New York Jets

namby-pamby 3 coy **4** dull, prim, weak **5** banal, inane, vapid **6** prissy **7** insipid, mincing, sapless **9** colorless, innocuous, simpering **10** indecisive, wishy-washy **13** characterless

name 3 dub, tag **4** call, term **5** label, title **6** choose, ordain, select **7** appoint, baptize, epithet, specify **8** christen, cognomen, delegate, deputize, nominate, taxonomy **9** authorize, designate, signature, sobriquet **10** commission **11** appellation, designation **12** denomination, nomenclature

nameless 5 minor **7** obscure, unknown, unnamed **9** anonymous, unheard-of, unhonored **12** undesignated

namely
  Latin: **3** viz **9** videlicet

Name of the Game
  character: **8** Andy Hill **9** Joe Sample, Ross Craig **10** Dan Farrell, Jeff Dillon **11** Glenn Howard **12** Peggy Maxwell
  cast: **9** Ben Murphy, Gene Barry **10** Mark Miller **11** Cliff Potter, Robert Stack **13** Tony Franciosa **15** Susan Saint James
  business: **8** magazine **10** publishing

Name of the Rose, The
  author: **10** Umberto Eco

Name That Tune

  host: **9** Red Benson **10** Bill Cullen **12** George de Witt
  orchestra: **11** Harry Salter

Namibia
  other name: **15** South West Africa
  capital/largest city: **8** Windhoek
  others: **6** Tsumeb **8** Luderitz **9** Walvis Bay **10** Oranjemund, Swakopmund **12** Keetmanshoop
  monetary unit: **4** cent, rand
  mountain: **14** Khomas Highland, Koakoveld Hills
  highest point: **9** Brandberg
  river: **4** Fish **6** Cunene, Orange **7** Zambezi **8** Okavango
  sea: **8** Atlantic
  physical feature:
    bay: **6** Walvis
    desert: **5** Namib **8** Kalahari
    region: **12** Caprivi Strip
  people: **4** Nama **5** Bantu **6** Damara, Herero, Ovambo, Tswara **7** Bushman, colored **8** Okavango **9** Hottentot
  language: **5** Bantu **6** German **7** English, Khoisan **9** Afrikaans
  religion: **7** animism **8** Lutheran
  feature:
    homeland: **9** bantustan

Nammu
  origin: **8** Sumerian
  mother of: **4** gods
  personifies: **3** sea

Namtar
  origin: **8** Akkadian, Sumerian
  form: **5** demon
  personifies: **5** death

Nana
  author: **9** Emile Zola

Nana (Nurse) (dog)
  character in: **8** Peter Pan
  author: **6** Barrie

Nancy
  character in: **11** Oliver Twist
  author: **7** Dickens

Nancy
  creator: **15** Ernie Bushmiller
  character: **5** Rollo **6** Sluggo **10** Aunt Fritzi

Nanna
  origin: **12** Scandinavian
  husband: **5** Baldr **6** Balder, Baldur
  habitat: **4** moon

Nannerella
  nickname of: **11** Anna Magnani

nanometer
  abbreviation: **2** nm
Naoise
  origin: **5** Irish
  wife: **7** Deirdre
  uncle: **9** Conchobar
  killed by: **9** Conchobar
  father: **6** Usnach, Usnech
Naomi
  husband: **9** Elimelech
  daughter-in-law: **4** Ruth
  son: **6** Mahlon **7** Chilion
nap 3 nod **4** doze, rest **6** cat nap,
  drowse, siesta, snooze **7** doze off,
  drop off, goof off, shut-eye, slumber **8**
  drift off **10** forty winks
napery 5 doily **6** linens, napkin **10** ta-
  blecloth
Naphtali
  father: **5** Jacob
  mother: **6** Bilkah
  brother: **3** Dan, Gad **4** Levi **5** Asher,
    Judah **6** Joseph, Reuben, Simeon **7**
    Zebulun **8** Benjamin, Issachar
  sister: **5** Dinah
  descendant of: **10** Naphtalite
Napoleon Bonaparte
  also: **9** Napoleon I **18** Emperor of the
    French
  battle: **3** Ulm **5** Eylau **6** Lutzen, Mos-
    cow, Toulon (siege), Wagram **7** Bau-
    tzen, Dresden, Leipzig, Marengo,
    Mondovi **8** Borodino, Waterloo **9**
    Friedland **10** Austerlitz **13** Aspern-
    Essling, Jena-Auerstadt, Peninsular
    War **22** War of the Fifth Coalition
  born: **7** Corsica
  exile to: **4** Elba **11** Saint Helena
  fought against: **7** Kutuzov **10** von
    Blucher, Wellington **14** Barclay de
    Tolly
  French fleet destroyed at: **9** Trafal-
    gar
    destroyed by: **6** Nelson
  laws: **14** Napoleonic Code
  marshal/general under: **3** Ney **5** Mu-
    rat **7** Massena **10** Bernadotte
  position: **7** emperor **11** first consul
    13 consul for life
  tomb: **5** Paris **9** Invalides
  wife: **9** Josephine **20** Marie-Louise of
    Austria
Napoleon of Notting Hill, The
  author: **12** G K Chesterton
narcissism 6 egoism, vanity **7** conceit
  8 self-love **11** egocentrism **16** selfcen-
  teredness
narcissist 6 egoist **7** egotist **11** egocen-
  trist **12** self- absorbed, self-admiring
narcissistic 4 smug, vain **6** vanity **7**
  conceit, selfish **8** egotistic, puffed-up
  9 conceited **10** egocentric, egoistical
  11 egomaniacal, egotistical
narcissus
  varieties: **5** poet's **6** poetaz **7** leedsii,
    trumpet **10** paper-white, polyanthus
    16 primrose peerless

Narcissus
  father: **8** Cephisus
  mother: **8** Leiriope
  loved: **7** himself
  loved by: **4** Echo
  punished by: **9** Aphrodite
  changed into: **6** flower
narcotic 4 drug, morphine **5** opium **6**
  herion, opiate **8** medicine, sedative **9**
  soporific **10** medicament, medication,
  painkiller **12** tranquilizer **14** pharma-
  ceutical
Narragansett
  language family: **9** Algonkian **10** Al-
    gonquian
  location: **11** Connecticut, Rhode Is-
    land
  related to: **7** Niantic
  involved in: **9** Pequot War **14** King
    Philip's War **15** Great Swamp Fight
narrate 6 detail, recite, relate, render,
  repeat, retell **7** portray, recount **8** describe, set forth **9** chronicle **10** tell a
  story **15** give an account of
narration 7 recital, telling **8** relating,
  speaking **9** voice-over **10** recitation,
  recounting **11** chronicling, description
  12 storytelling
narrative 4 tale **5** story **6** report **7** account, recital **8** dialogue, episodic **9**
  anecdotal, chronicle, statement **10** historical **12** storytelling
**Narrative of Arthur Gordon Pym,
The**
  author: **13** Edgar Allan Poe
narrow 3 set **4** fine, slim **5** close,
  scant, small, tight **6** biased, scanty **7**
  bigoted, cramped, pinched, shallow,
  slender, tapered **8** confined, dogmatic,
  isolated, squeezed **9** hidebound, illiberal, parochial **10** attenuated, compressed, intolerant, provincial, restricted **11** constricted, incapacious,
  opinionated, reactionary **12** conservative
narrowing 5 taper **8** tapering **9**
  squeezing **11** compressing **12** constricting
narrow-minded 5 petty **7** bigoted,
  prudish **8** one-sided **9** hidebound, parochial, unworldly **10** provincial **11**
  opinionated, reactionary, straitlaced
  12 conservative **15** unsophisticated
narrow-mindedness 4 bias **7** bigotry
  9 prejudice **10** unfairness **11** intolerance
narrows 4 neck, pass **5** canal **6** ravine,
  strait **7** channel, isthmus, passage
Nasca see **5** Nazca
Nascimento, Edson Arantes do
  real name of: **4** Pele
Nash, Ogden
  author of: **6** Versus **9** Hard Lines **20**
    The Private Dining Room **21** I'm a
    Stranger Here Myself
Nashville

  director: **12** Robert Altman
  cast: **10** Karen Black, Lily Tomlin **11**
    Henry Gibson **12** Ronee Blakley **13**
    Barbara Harris, Michael Murphy **14**
    Keith Carradine **16** Geraldine Chaplin
  Oscar for: **4** song
  song: **6** I'm Easy
Nassau
  capital of: **7** Bahamas
Nasser, Gamal Abdel
  president of: **5** Egypt **18** United Arab
    Republic
nasty 4 foul, mean, vile **5** awful **6** odious **7** beastly, hateful, vicious **8** horrible **9** repellent, revolting **10** abominable, disgusting, nauseating, unpleasant
  11 distasteful **12** disagreeable
Natchez
  language family: **10** Muskhogean
  tribe: **6** Avoyel, Taensa
  location: **11** Mississippi **13** South Car-
    olina
  allied with: **7** Choctaw
  practiced: **14** head flattening
nates 4 buns, rear, rump, seat **7** rear
  end **8** buttocks, haunches **9** fundament, posterior **12** hindquarters
Nathan
  father: **5** Attai
  served: **5** David **7** Solomon
Nathanael, Nathaniel see **5** Jesus **8**
  Apostles **11** Bartholomew
nation 4 host, race **5** realm, state, tribe
  6 empire, people **7** country, kingdom
  8 republic **9** community **11** sovereignty **12** commonwealth
national park
  Alaska: **13** Mount McKinley
  Arizona: **11** Grand Canyon **15** Petri-
    fied Forest
  Arkansas: **10** Hot Springs
  California: **7** Redwood, Sequoia **8** Yo-
    semite **11** Kings Canyon **14** Channel
    Islands, Lassen Volcanic
  Canada: **4** Yoho **5** Banff, Fundy **6**
    Jasper, Kluane **8** Kootenay **9** Auyuit-
    tuq **13** Waterton Lakes
  Colorado: **5** Estes **9** Mesa Verde **13**
    Rocky Mountain
  Florida: **10** Everglades
  Hawaii: **9** Haleakala **15** Hawaii Volca-
    noes
  Kentucky: **11** Mammoth Cave
  Maine: **6** Acadia
  Michigan: **10** Isle Royale
  Minnesota: **9** Voyageurs
  Montana: **7** Glacier **11** Yellowstone
  New Mexico: **15** Carlsbad Caverns
  North Carolina: **19** Great Smoky
    Mountains (with Tennessee)
  North Dakota: **17** Theodore Roose-
    velt
  Oklahoma: **6** Platte
  Oregon: **10** Crater Lake
  South Dakota: **8** Badlands, Wind
    Cave
  Tennessee: **6** Shiloh **13** Cumberland

Gap **19** Great Smoky Mountains (with North Carolina)
Texas: 7 Big Bend **18** Guadalupe Mountains
Utah: 4 Zion **6** Arches **11** Bryce Canyon, Canyonlands, Capital Reef
Virginia: 10 Shenandoah **26** Colonial National Historical
Washington: 7 Olympic **12** Mount Rainier **13** North Cascades
Wyoming: 10 Grand Teton **11** Yellowstone

National Velvet
director: 13 Clarence Brown
cast: 10 Anne Revere **11** Donald Crisp **12** Mickey Rooney **14** Angela Lansbury **15** Elizabeth Taylor
horse: 6 The Pie
Oscar for: 17 supporting actress (Revere)
sequel: 19 International Velvet

native 4 home **5** basic, local, natal **6** inborn, inbred, innate, savage **7** citizen, endemic, natural **8** domestic, inherent, national, paternal **9** aborigine, elemental, homegrown, ingrained, inherited, intrinsic, primitive **10** congenital, countryman, hereditary, indigenous **11** instinctive **12** countrywoman **13** autochthonous

Native Americans
Registered tribes and/or nations, by state:
AL: 11 Poarch Creek
AK: 5 Aleut, Haida **6** Eskimo **7** Tlingit **10** Athabascan, Tsimpshian
AZ: 4 Hopi, Pima **6** Navajo, Apache, Papago **7** Yavapai
CA: 5 Hoopa, Yurok, Karok **6** Paiute **8** Cherokee
CO: 3 Ute
CT: 18 Mashantucket Pequot
FL: 8 Seminole, Cherokee **10** Miccosukee
ID: 7 Bannock **8** Shoshone, Nez Perce
IA: 9 Sac and Fox
KS: 4 Iowa **8** Kickapoo **10** Potawatomi
LA: 9 Coushatta **10** Chitimacha **12** Tunica-Biloxi
ME: 8 Maliseet **9** Penobscot **13** Passamaquoddy
MA: 9 Wampanoag
MI: 6 Ottawa **8** Cherokee, Chippewa **10** Potawatomi
MN: 5 Sioux **8** Chippewa
MS: 7 Choctaw
MO: 4 Crow **5** Sioux **8** Cheyenne **9** Blackfoot **11** Assiniboine
NE: 5 Omaha **9** Winnebago **11** Santee Sioux
NV: 6 Paiute, Washoe **8** Shoshone
NM: 6 Apache, Navajo, Pueblo
NY: 6 Mohawk, Seneca, Oneida **8** Onondaga
NC: 6 Lumbee **8** Cherokee
ND: 5 Sioux **6** Mandan **7** Arikara, Hidatsa **8** Chippewa
OK: 5 Creek, Kiowa, Osage **7** Choctaw **8** Cherokee, Cheyenne, Comanche, Arapaho, Chicasaw
OR: 5 Wasco **6** Siletz, Paiute **11** Warm Springs
RI: 12 Narragansett
SC: 7 Catawba
SD: 5 Sioux
TX: 4 Tiwa **8** Kickapoo **16** Alabama-Coushatta
UT: 3 Ute **6** Navajo **7** Goshute **14** Southern Paiute
WA: 5 Lummi **6** Yakama **8** Quinault
WI 6 Oneida **8** Chippewa **9** Winnebago
WY: 8 Shoshone, Arapahoe
see also Individual Entries

native country 7 country **8** homeland **10** fatherland **13** mother country

native-grown 5 local **8** domestic **9** homegrown **10** indigenous

native land 8 homeland **10** birthplace, fatherland, native soil **13** mother country, native country

native of Israel
Hebrew: 5 sabra

native soil 8 homeland **10** fatherland, native land **13** mother country, native country

Native Son
author: 13 Richard Wright

NATO
members: 5 Italy, Spain **6** Canada, France, Greece, Norway, Turkey **7** Belgium, Denmark, Germany, Iceland **8** Portugal **10** Luxembourg **11** Netherlands **12** United States **13** United Kingdom
proposed: 6 Poland **7** Hungary **13** Czech Republic

natty 4 chic, neat, posh, tidy, trim **5** smart **6** dapper, jaunty, snappy, spruce **7** dashing, modish, stylish **11** fashionable

Natty Bumppo
also: 7 Hawkeye **10** Pathfinder, The Trapper **13** The Deerslayer **15** Leatherstocking **16** Le Longue Carabine
character in: 23 The Leatherstocking Tales
friend: 5 Uncas **12** Chingachgook
author: 6 Cooper

natural 5 plain **6** inborn, native, normal **7** earthly, genuine, regular **8** God-given, inherent **9** essential, intuitive, unstudied **10** unaffected, unmannered **11** instinctive, spontaneous, terrestrial **13** unpretentious **14** characteristic **15** straightforward
in craps: 5 seven **6** eleven

Natural, The
director: 13 Barry Levinson
based on story by: 14 Bernard Malamud
character: 7 Roy Hobbs

cast: 10 Glenn Close **12** Robert Duvall **13** Robert Redford

natural child 7 bastard **9** love child **17** illegitimate child

natural gift 5 flair **6** talent **7** ability, faculty **8** aptitude **9** attribute, endowment

natural habitat 5 range **6** domain, milieu **7** element **9** territory **11** environment

naturalize 5 adapt, adopt **6** adjust **8** accustom **9** acclimate **11** domesticate, familiarize

naturalness 4 ease **9** sincerity **10** simplicity **11** artlessness, genuineness **12** unconstraint **14** unaffectedness

nature 4 bent, kind, mood, sort, type **5** birth, earth, globe, humor, stamp, style, trait **6** cosmos, spirit **7** essence, feature, variety **8** category, creation, instinct, property, universe **9** character **11** disposition, peculiarity **12** constitution **13** particularity **14** characteristic
goddess of: 6 Cybele **9** Dindymene **10** Berecyntia

Nature
author: 17 Ralph Waldo Emerson

naught 3 nil **4** zero **5** nihil, zilch **6** cipher **7** nothing, useless **9** worthless

naughty 3 bad **4** blue **5** bawdy, dirty **6** ribald, risque, vulgar **7** wayward, willful **8** devilish, off-color, perverse **9** fractious, obstinate **11** disobedient, misbehaving, mischievous **12** pornographic, recalcitrant, unmanageable **13** disrespectful

Nauru
other name: 14 Pleasant Island
capital: 13 Yaren District
cities: 3 Boe, Ewa **4** Aiwo, Ijuw **5** Baiti, Buada, Nibok, Uaboe, Yaren **6** Anabar, Anetan, Meneng **7** Anibare **10** Denigomodu
monetary unit: 4 cent **6** dollar
lake: 11 Buada Lagoon
sea: 7 Pacific
physical feature:
 bay: 7 Anibare
 lagoon: 5 Buada
 point: 4 Anna **6** Meneng
people: 7 Chinese **9** Melanesian, Polynesian **11** Micronesian
 explorer: 9 John Fearn
language: 7 English, Nauruan
religion: 10 Protestant **13** Roman Catholic
feature: 9 phosphate

nausea 7 disgust, heaving **8** contempt, loathing, retching, sickness, vomiting **9** repulsion, revulsion **10** queasiness **11** airsickness, biliousness, car sickness, seasickness **12** upset stomach **14** motion sickness, travel sickness

Nausea, Nausee
author: 14 Jean-Paul Sartre

nauseate 5 repel, upset **6** offend,

revolt, sicken **7** disgust, repulse **8** make sick **15** turn one's stomach

nauseated 3 ill **4** sick **5** upset **6** queasy **8** repelled, revolted **9** disgusted

nauseating 9 offensive, repellent, repulsive, revolting, sickening **10** disgusting

nauseous 4 sick **5** upset **6** queasy **9** abhorrent, nauseated, offensive, repellent, repulsive, revolting, sickening, upsetting **10** disgusting, nauseating **12** unappetizing

Nausicaa
father: **8** Alcinous
position: **8** princess
aided: **8** Odysseus

Nausithous
father: **8** Poseidon
mother: **8** Periboea
occupation: **8** helmsman
employer: **7** Theseus
became: **4** king
realm: **8** Phaeacia

nautical 5 naval **6** marine **7** aquatic, boating, oceanic **8** maritime, of the sea, seagoing, yachting

nautical mile
abbreviation: **3** nmi

Nautilus
submarine in: **32** Twenty Thousand Leagues Under the Sea
skipper: **11** Captain Nemo
author: **5** Verne

Navajo, Navaho (Dine)
language family: **10** Athapascan, Athapaskan
location: **4** Utah **7** Arizona **9** New Mexico
noted for: **7** weaving **14** silversmithing
dwelling: **5** hogan

navigate 3 fly **4** ride, sail, ship **5** cross, steer **6** cruise, voyage **8** maneuver, sail over **11** plot a course **12** chart a course

navigation 7 boating, sailing **8** cruising, piloting, voyaging **9** traveling **10** seamanship
god of: **5** Niord, Njord

Navigators Islands *see* **12** Western Samoa

navy 5 fleet **6** armada, convoy **8** flotilla, warships

navy-blue 6 indigo **8** dark blue, deep blue

nay 4 also, deny, vote **5** never **6** denial, refuse **7** against, but also, refusal **8** negative

Nazarene *see* **5** Jesus

Nazarene, The
author: **10** Sholem Asch

Nazca, Nasca
location: **4** Peru **12** South America
noted for: **8** ceramics, textiles **10** Nazca lines (sketches on plain)

Nazi 7 facost
air force: **9** Luftwaffe
swastika: **10** Hakenkreuz
collaborator: **8** quisling
elite guard: **13** schutzstaffel
leader: **4** Hess **6** Hitler **7** Himmler **8** Goebbels
police: **7** gestapo
trials: Nuremberg

N'Djamena
capital of: **4** Chad

Neal, Patricia
husband: **9** Roald Dahl
born: **9** Packard KY
roles: **3** Hud (Oscar) **15** A Face in the Crowd, The Fountainhead **18** The Subject Was Roses

near 4 nigh **5** about, close **6** all but, almost **7** close by, close to, looming **8** approach, come up to, imminent, next door **9** alongside, close with, impending **10** hereabouts **11** approaching, practically, proximately, threatening **13** approximately

nearby 5 close, handy **6** at hand **7** close by **8** next door **9** adjoining **10** accessible, hereabouts

near death
Latin: **10** in extremis

near home 5 close **7** close by **10** hereabouts

nearly 4 nigh **5** about **6** all but, almost **7** close to, roughly **11** practically **13** approximately

nearly equal 5 close **7** similar **10** nip-and-tuck **11** approaching

nearly even 5 close **10** head to head, nip-and-tuck **11** neck and neck

nearness 8 intimacy, vicinity **9** adjacency, closeness, handiness, immediacy, proximity **10** contiguity **11** propinquity **12** availability, neighborhood **13** accessibility, approximation

nearsighted 6 myopic
opposite: **9** hyperopic **10** presbyopic

neat 4 tidy **5** clean, great **6** groovy **7** concise, correct, orderly **8** accurate, exciting, original, straight, striking, succinct **9** competent, dexterous, efficient, ingenious, organized, purposive, shipshape **10** controlled, immaculate, methodical, systematic **11** imaginative, intelligent, uncluttered

neatness 5 order **8** tidiness **11** orderliness **12** organization

Nebraska
abbreviation: **2** NE **4** Nebr
nickname: **4** Beef **8** Antelope **10** Blackwater, Cornhusker **12** Tree-planter's
capital: **7** Lincoln
largest city: **5** Omaha
others: **5** Cozad **6** Gering **7** Kearney **8** Beatrice, Hastings **9** Broken Bow **11** Grand Island, North Platte, Scottsbluff
college: **4** Dana **5** Doane **8** Duchesne, Hastings **9** Creighton **15** Midland Lutheran
feature: **8** Boys' Town
national monument: **11** Scott's Bluff **15** Agate Fossil Beds
tribe: **3** Oto **4** Otoe **5** Kiowa, Omaha, Ponca, Sioux **6** Pawnee
people: **10** Henry Fonda **11** Fred Astaire, Roscoe Pound
lake: **7** Merritt, Sherman, Swanson **10** McConaughy **13** Lewis and Clark
land rank: **9** fifteenth
physical feature: **8** Badlands
hills: **4** Sand **5** Drift, Loess
plains: **5** Great
river: **4** Loup **5** Logan **6** Dismal, Nemaha, Platte **7** Big Blue, Elkhorn **8** Missouri, Niobrara **10** Little Blue, Republican **12** Harlan County
state admission: **13** thirty-seventh
state bird: **17** western meadowlark
state flower: **9** goldenrod
state motto: **20** Equality Before the Law
state song: **17** Beautiful Nebraska
state tree: **3** elm **10** cottonwood

nebris
skin of: **4** fawn

Nebrophonus *see* **5** Thoon

Nebuchadnezzar
father: **12** Nabopolassar
son: **10** Bel shazzar **12** Evilmerodach
same as: **7** Nabucco **14** Nebuchadrezzar
king of: **7** Babylon
conquered: **9** Jerusalem
destroyed: **6** temple
deported: **4** Jews
into: **7** slavery
general: **11** Holophernes

nebula 4 Crab, Ring, Veil **5** Great **6** Lagoon **7** Rosette **9** Horsehead

nebulous 3 dim **4** dark, hazy **5** murky, vague **6** cloudy **7** obscure, unclear **8** confused **9** ambiguous, uncertain **10** impalpable, indefinite, indistinct, intangible **13** indeterminate

necessarily 8 perforce **9** naturally **10** inevitably, inexorably **11** accordingly **12** compulsorily **13** automatically, axiomatically, unqualifiedly **16** incontrovertibly

necessary 6 needed, urgent, wanted **7** crucial, desired, exigent, fitting, needful **8** required **9** called for, essential, requisite **10** compulsory, imperative, obligatory **13** indispensable

necessary changes having been made
Latin: **15** mutatis mutandis

necessitate 5 cause, force, impel **6** compel, demand, oblige **7** call for, enforce, require **9** constrain, prescribe

necessitation 5 cause, force **6** demand, duress **8** coercion, pressure **10** compulsion, constraint, obligation **11** enforcement, requirement

necessity, necessities 4 must, need **6** demand, needed **7** urgency **8** exigency, pressure **9** essential, requisite **10** sine qua non **11** requirement **13** indispensable
Latin: **10** sine qua non

neck 3 pet **4** kiss, nape, pass **6** caress, cervix, cuddle, fondle, smooth, strait **7** channel, isthmus, make out **9** narrowing

neckerchief 5 scarf **8** bandanna, kerchief

necklace 3 tie **5** beads, chain, noose **6** choker, collar, locket, pearls, string **7** jewelry, pendant **8** ornament **9** lavaliere

necktie 3 bow **4** band **5** ascot, black, scarf **6** cravat, string **7** Windsor **10** four in hand **11** half Windsor **12** hangman's rope

necromancer 5 hexer, magus, witch **6** wizard **7** charmer, warlock **8** conjurer, exorcist, magician, sorcerer **9** enchanter, occultist, voodooist **10** soothsayer **13** black magician, thaumaturgist

necromancy 5 magic, spell **7** sorcery **8** black art **10** witchcraft **11** enchantment, foretelling

necrophobia
fear of: **5** death **10** dead bodies

necropolis 8 cemetery **9** graveyard **12** burial ground **13** burying ground

nectar
drink of: **4** gods
gives: **4** life

nee 4 born **11** maiden-named

need 4 lack, want, wish **5** crave, exact **6** demand, penury **7** call for, longing, poverty, require, straits **8** distress, exigency, yearn for **9** essential, extremity, indigence, necessity, requisite **10** bankruptcy, insolvency **11** desideratum, destitution, necessitate, requirement **13** impecuniosity, pennilessness

needed 5 vital **7** crucial **9** essential, necessary, requisite **13** indispensable

needful 7 wishful **8** required **9** essential, necessary, requisite **10** imperative **13** indispensable

needle 3 vex **4** josh, leaf, ride, twit **5** annoy, chaff, harry, taunt, tease **6** badger, harass, hector **7** torment **9** indicator
prefix: **3** acu

needle-shaped 5 sharp **6** peaked, spiked **7** pointed **8** piercing **10** bodkin-like

needless 7 useless **9** excessive, pointless, redundant **10** gratuitous, pleonastic, unavailing **11** dispensable, purposeless, superfluous, uncalled-for, unessential, unnecessary **12** overabundant

needlework 6 sewing **7** basting, brocade, darning, tacking, tatting **8** appli-

que, knitting, quilting **9** stitching **10** embroidery **11** cross stitch, needle point

needy 4 poor **5** broke **6** hard-up, in want **8** indigent, strapped **9** destitute, money less, penniless **10** down-and-out **12** impoverished **15** poverty-stricken

ne'er-do-well 3 bum **5** idler, loser **6** loafer, no-good **7** goof-off, sad sack, wastrel **8** layabout **9** do-nothing, no-account **10** black sheep **14** good-for-nothing

nefarious 3 bad, low **4** base, evil, foul, vile **6** odious, wicked **7** beastly, ghastly, heinous, hellish, ungodly, vicious **8** depraved, devilish, infamous, infernal, shameful **9** atrocious, execrable **10** abominable, despicable, detestable, iniquitous, scandalous, villainous **11** disgraceful, opprobrious, unspeakable **12** dishonorable **13** unmentionable

Nefertem
origin: **8** Egyptian
personifies: **5** lotus
true identity: **4** Ptah

Nefertiti
queen: **5** Egypt
husband: **8** Ikhnaton **9** Amenhotep
nephew: **11** Tutankhamen

negate 4 deny, veto, void **5** quash, quell, rebut **6** defeat, disown, refute, repeal, revoke, squash **7** blot out, destroy, disavow, gainsay, nullify, retract, reverse, squelch, wipe out **8** abrogate, disallow, disclaim, set aside, vanquish **9** overthrow, overwhelm, repudiate **10** contradict, invalidate

negating 7 denying, voiding **8** refuting, revoking **9** reversing **10** cancelling, nullifying **11** disallowing **12** invalidating, setting aside **13** contradicting

negation 6 denial **7** counter **8** reversal **9** rejection **10** abrogation, disclaimer, refutation **11** confutation, repudiation **12** invalidation **13** contradiction, nullification

negative 4 blue, dark **5** bleak **6** at odds, gloomy **7** dubious, opposed **8** contrary, doubtful, downbeat, inimical, opposing, refusing **9** declining, demurring, dissident, jaundiced, objecting, rejecting, reluctant, skeptical, unwilling **10** dissenting, fatalistic **11** disagreeing, pessimistic **12** antagonistic, disapproving **13** uncooperative **14** unenthusiastic

neglect 4 fail, omit **5** let go, shirk **6** forget, ignore, laxity, pass by, pass up, slight **7** abandon, default, laxness, let pass, let ride, let slip **8** be remiss, idleness, let slide, omission, overlook, pass over, shake off **9** disregard, oversight, passivity, slackness **10** inaccuracy, negligence, remissness **11** dere-

liction, inattention, inexactness **12** carelessness, fecklessness, indifference, slovenliness **13** noncompliance, unfulfillment **14** nonpreparation **16** underachievement

neglected 7 dropped, ignored, omitted, shirked, unkempt **8** forsaken, untended **9** abandoned, cast aside, forgotten **10** overlooked, uncared for **11** disregarded

neglectful 4 lazy **5** slack **6** remiss, untrue **8** careless, derelict, heedless **9** forgetful, negligent, oblivious, unheeding, unmindful **10** inconstant, thriftless, unfaithful, unthinking, unwatchful **11** improvident, inattentive, indifferent, respectless, thoughtless, unobservant **12** devil-may-care, disregardant, disregardful, happy-go-lucky **15** procrastinating

negligee, neglige 4 robe **6** kimono **7** wrapper **8** bathrobe, peignoir **9** housecoat **12** dressing gown

negligence 6 laxity **7** neglect **11** disregarded **12** carelessness

negligent 3 lax **5** slack **6** remiss, untidy **8** careless, heedless, slovenly **9** forgetful, unheeding, unmindful **10** neglectful, unthinking, unwatchful **11** inattentive, indifferent, thoughtless, unobservant **13** inconsiderate

negligible 5 minor, petty, small **6** minute, paltry, slight **7** trivial **8** piddling, trifling **11** unimportant **13** insignificant **15** inconsequential

negotiate 4 cash, make, pass **6** barter, cash in, convey, dicker, haggle, handle, manage, redeem, settle **7** arrange, consign, deliver, discuss, get over **8** contract, cope with, deal with, hand over, make over, pass over, sign over, transact, transfer, transmit, turn over **10** bargain for **11** come to terms, meet halfway

negotiation 4 deal **6** treaty **8** argument, haggling **9** dickering **10** bargaining **11** arbitration, arrangement **12** compromising

negotiator 7 arbiter **8** mediator **9** go-between **10** arbitrator **12** intermediary

Nehemiah
father: **5** Azbuk **14** Hachaliah

neigh 5 hinny **6** nicker, whinny

neighbor 4 abut, meet **5** touch **6** adjoin, be near, border, friend **7** conjoin **8** borderer, border on **9** associate **12** acquaintance

neighborhood 4 area, part, side, ward **5** place, range **6** locale, parish, region, sphere **7** quarter, section **8** confines, district, environs, precinct, purlieus, vicinity **9** community

neighboring 4 near, next **5** close **6** at hand, nearby **7** close by **8** abutting, adjacent **9** adjoining, bordering **10** contiguous **11** surrounding **12** circumjacent

neighborly 4 kind **5** civil **6** chummy, kindly, polite **7** affable, amiable, cordial, helpful **8** amicable, friendly, gracious, obliging **9** courteous **10** hospitable **11** considerate, warmhearted **12** well-disposed

Neighbors
  author: **12** Thomas Berger

Neith
  origin: **8** Egyptian
  personifies: **10** femininity
  son: **2** Ra
  corresponds to: **6** Athena

Nekhbet
  origin: **8** Egyptian
  form: **7** vulture
  guardian of: **5** Egypt **10** Upper Egypt

Nelson, Harriet Hilliard
  real name: **14** Peggy Lou Snyder
  husband: **5** Ozzie
  son: **4** Rick **5** David
  born: **11** Des Moines IA
  roles: **30** The Adventures of Ozzie and Harriet

Nelson, Horatio
  also: **14** Viscount Nelson
  nationality: **7** British
  battle: **9** Trafalgar **11** Bay of Abukir **15** Battle of the Nile **16** Cape Saint Vincent **18** Battle of Copenhagen
  defeated: **5** Danes **6** French **7** Spanish
  flagship: **7** Victory
  killed at: **9** Trafalgar
  lover: **16** Emma Lady Hamilton

Nelson, Ozzie
  real name: **18** Oswald George Nelson
  wife: **15** Harriet Hilliard
  son: **4** Rick **5** David
  born: **12** Jersey City NJ
  roles: **30** The Adventures of Ozzie and Harriet

Nemean
  epithet of: **4** Zeus **5** games
  precursor of: **8** Olympics

Nemean lion
  strangled by: **8** Hercules

nemesis 4 ruin **5** match, **6** rival **7** avenger, goddess, justice, revenge, undoing **8** downfall, punisher, Waterloo **9** overthrow, vengeance **10** punishment **11** destruction, retaliation, retribution **16** instrument of fate

nemine contradicente 11 unanimously **18** no one contradicting

nemine dissentiente 11 unanimously **15** no one dissenting

Nemo
  character in: **10** Bleak House
  author: **7** Dickens

Nemo, Captain
  character in: **32** Twenty Thousand Leagues Under the Sea
  author: **5** Verne
  submarine: **8** Nautilus

nene 13 Hawaiian goose

neologism, neology 7 coinage **9** nonce word

neon
  chemical symbol: **2** Ne

neonate 4 baby **6** infant **7** newborn

neophyte 4 tyro **5** pupil **6** novice, rookie **7** amateur, convert, entrant, learner, recruit, student, trainee **8** beginner, disciple, newcomer **9** greenhorn, novitiate, proselyte **10** apprentice, tenderfoot **11** probationer

neoplasm 5 tumor **6** cancer, growth **7** sarcoma **9** carcinoma **10** malignancy **14** carcinosarcoma

Nepal
  other name: **9** Shangri-La
  capital/largest city: **8** Katmandu **9** Kathmandu
  others: **5** Patan, Patna **6** Gurkha **7** Birganj **8** Bhadgaon, Lalitpur **9** Bhaktapur **10** Biratnagar
  university: **9** Tribhuvan
  division: **5** Terai **13** High Himalayas
  monetary unit: **4** anna, pice **5** mohar, paisa, rupee
  mountain: **6** Cho Oyu, Churia, Lhotse, Makalu **7** Manaslu, Siwalik **9** Annapurna, Himalayas **10** Dhaulagiri, Gosainthan, Himalchuli **11** Ganesh Himal **12** Kanchenjunga **14** Mahabharat hekh
  highest point: **9** Mt Everest
  river: **4** Kali, Kosi, Mugu, Seti **5** Babai, Bheri, Rapti, Sarda, Tamur **6** Gandak **7** Karnali **8** Narayani
  physical feature:
    plain: **5** Terai
    valley: **5** Nepal **8** Katmandu
  people: **3** Rai **4** Aoul **5** Bhote, Limbu, Magar, Murmi, Newar, Tharu **6** Bhutia, Gurkha, Gurung, Nepali, Sherpa, Tamang **7** Kiranti, Tibetan **8** Gorkhali, Nepalese
    birthplace of: **6** Buddha **13** Gautama Buddha **17** Siddhartha Gautama
    king: **8** Mahendra **9** Tribhuwan **18** Prithwi Narayan Shah **23** Birenda Bir Bikram Shah Dev
    ruler: **4** Rana **5** Malla **6** Rajput
  language: **6** Nepali, Newari
  religion: **8** Buddhism, Hinduism
  place:
    dam: **6** Gandak
    shrine: **9** Swayambhu **10** Gorakhnath
  feature:
    animal: **3** dzo, yak **7** dzopkyo
    arch: **6** Juddha
    god/goddess: **5** Indra **6** Kumari
    legend: **4** Yeti **17** abominable snowman
    soldiers: **6** Gurkha

Nepali
  language family: **12** Indo-European
  branch: **11** Indo-Iranian
  group: **5** Indic
  spoken in: **5** Nepal

nepenthe 4 drug **5** drink, opium **6** heroin, opiate **7** hashish **8** narcotic

nephrite
  variety: **4** jade

ne plus ultra 4 acme **6** finest **8** ultimate **12** highest point

nepotism 10 favoritism
  patron of: **9** relatives

Neptune
  origin: **5** Roman
  god of: **3** sea
  corresponds to: **8** Poseidon

Neptune
  position: **6** eighth
  satellite: **6** Nereid, Triton
  color: **4** blue
  studied by: **7** Voyager (2)

Nereid
  form: **5** nymph
  location: **3** sea
  father: **6** Nereus

Nereus
  god of: **3** sea
  father: **6** Pontus
  mother: **4** Gaea
  father of: **7** Nereids
  number of Nereids: **5** fifty
  son: **7** Nerites

Nerissa
  character in: **19** The Merchant of Venice
  author: **11** Shakespeare

neritic 7 aquatic, coastal **8** offshore

Nero
  name: **18** Nero Claudius Caesar
  emperor of: **4** Rome
  mother: **9** Agrippina
  father: **19** Domitius Ahenobarbus
  stepfather: **8** Claudius
  tutor: **6** Seneca
  son: **11** Britannicus
  wife: **7** Octavia **13** Poppaea Sabina
  successor: **5** Galba

nerve 4 dash, gall, grit, guts, sass **5** brass, cheek, crust, pluck, spunk, valor **6** mettle, spirit **7** bravery, courage **8** backbone, boldness, coolness, gameness, strength, tenacity **9** arrogance, assurance, derring-do, endurance, flippancy, fortitude, gallantry, hardihood, hardiness, impudence, insolence, sauciness **10** assumption, brazenness, confidence, effrontery, steadiness **11** intrepidity, presumption **12** fearlessness, impertinence, resoluteness **13** determination **16** stoutheartedness

nerveless 4 calm, dead, weak **5** brave, frail, inert **6** feeble, flabby **7** flaccid **8** cowardly **9** powerless **10** courageous **12** fainthearted

nervous 4 wild **5** jumpy, shaky, tense **6** touchy, uneasy **7** alarmed, anxious, excited, fearful, fidgety, jittery, peevish, ruffled **8** feverish, neurotic, skittish, startled, timorous, unstrung **9** delirious, disturbed, excitable, impatient, irritable, sensitive, trembling, tremulous, unsettled **10** high-strung, hysterical **12** apprehensive

nervousness 6 tremor **7** anxiety, flutter, shaking, tension **8** hysteria, timidity **9** agitation, quivering, the creeps, the shakes, trembling, twitching **10** the fidgets, touchiness **11** disturbance, fidgetiness, stage fright **12** apprehension, excitability, irascibility, irritability, perturbation, timorousness **16** hypersensitivity

nervous system
  component: 3 CNS **4** ears, eyes **5** brain, taste, touch **7** ganglia **8** nerve end **10** nerve fiber, spinal cord

nervy 4 bold, firm, rude **5** brash, gutty, gutsy, sassy **6** brassy, brazen, cheeky, gritty, plucky, strong **7** assured, nervous **10** courageous, determined **12** stouthearted

Nesbitt, Cathleen
  born: 7 England **8** Cheshire
  roles: 10 My Fair Lady **18** Upstairs Downstairs **23** Three Coins in the Fountain

Nessus
  form: 7 centaur
  shot by: 8 Hercules
  caused death of: 8 Hercules

n'est-ce pas? 10 isn't that so?

nestle 3 lie, pet **4** live, snug, stay **5** clasp, dwell, lodge **6** bundle, caress, coddle, cosset, cuddle, enfold, fondle, huddle, nuzzle, occupy, remain, settle **7** embrace, inhabit, lie snug, snuggle **8** lie close **10** settle down

Nestor
  origin: 5 Greek
  attributes: 6 oldest, wisest
  father: 6 Neleus
  son: 10 Thasymedes **11** Pisistratus
  epithet: 7 Nelides

net 3 web **4** earn, gain, grab, grid, grip, mesh, snag, take, trap **5** catch, clasp, grate, seize, snare **6** clutch, enmesh, gather, grille, obtain, pick up, screen, snap up, take in **7** acquire, bring in, capture, collect, ensnare, grating, lattice **8** entangle, gather in, gridiron, Internet, meshwork **9** apprehend, grillwork, lay hold of, screening **10** accumulate **11** latticework
constellation of: 9 Reticulum

nether 5 basal, below, lower, under **6** bottom, lowest **8** downward, inferior **9** subjacent **10** bottommost

Netherlands
  other name: 7 Holland **12** Low Countries
  capital/largest city: 9 Amsterdam
  others: 3 Urk **5** Delft, Lisse **6** Almelo, Arnhem, Leiden, Velsen **7** Haarlem, Helmond, Hengelo, Limburg, Tilberg, Tilburg, Utrecht **8** Aalsmeer, Enschede, Ijmuiden, Nijmegen, The Hague **9** Apeldoorn, Dordrecht, Eind-

hoven, Groningen, Rotterdam **12** Scheveningen
  division: 6 Twente **7** Drenthe, Limburg, Utrecht, Zeeland **9** Friesland, Groningen **10** Gelderland, Overijssel **12** North Brabant, North Holland, South Holland **19** Netherlands Antilles
  government:
    legislature: 4 Raad **11** Eerste Kamer, Tweede Kamer
  head of state: 5 queen
  measure: 2 el **3** aam, ahm, ell, kan, vat **4** duim, mijl, rood, rope **5** anker, roede, wisse **6** bunder, legger, maatje, mutsje, streep **7** schepel **8** mimgelen, steekkan
  monetary unit: 4 doit, oord, raps **5** crown, daler, rider, ryder **6** florin, gulden, stiver, suskin **7** daalder, ducaton, escalan, escalin, guilder, stooter, stuiver **8** albertin, ducatoon **9** dubbeltje **12** rijksdaalder **13** albertustaler
  weight: 3 ons **4** last, pond **5** bahar **6** korrel **7** wichtje
  island: 5 Texel **7** Ameland, Frisian **8** Antilles, Vlieland
  lake: 7 Haarlem **10** Ijsselmeer **11** Grevelingen, Havingvliet
  highest point: 11 Vaalserberg
  river: 3 Eem, Lek **4** Leck, Maas, Waal, Ysel **5** Donge, Hunse, Meuse, Rhine, Schie, Yssel **6** Dintel, Dommel, Ijssel, Kromme **7** Scheldt
  sea: 5 North
  physical feature:
    canal: 6 Oranje **7** Juliana, Merwede **8** Drentsch, North Sea **10** Wilhelmina **11** New Waterway
    former bay: 9 Zuider Zee
    port: 9 Europoort
  people: 5 Dutch **7** Frisian **9** Hollander **10** Surinamese **12** Netherlander **13** South Moluccan
    artist: 4 Eyck, Hals **5** Appel, Bosch **7** Van Gogh, Vermeer **8** Mondrian, Ruisdael **9** Rembrandt
    author: 6 Vondel **7** Erasmus, Grotius, Spinoza **8** Vestdijk **9** Anne Frank
    explorer: 6 Tasman
    king: 7 William
    queen: 7 Beatrix, Juliana **10** Wilhelmina
    ruler: 5 Spain **13** House of Orange **15** Holy Roman Empire
    scientist: 7 Huygens **11** Leeuwenhoek
  language: 5 Dutch **7** English, Frisian
  religion: 13 Dutch Reformed, Protestantism **16** Roman Catholicism
  place:
    airport: 8 Schiphol
    bird sanctuary: 9 Waddenzee
    miniature town: 9 Madurodam
    museum: 9 Frans Hals, Stedelijk **11** Mauritshuis, Rijksmuseum

14 Vincent Van Gogh **19** Boymans-van Beuningen
  seat of government: 7 Den Haag **8** The Hague **11** 'sGravenhage
  tower: 14 Schreierstoren
  feature:
    cheese market: 9 kaasmarkt
    earth mounds: 6 terpen
    flower: 5 tulip
    flower parade: 12 Bloemencorso
    pottery: 5 Delft
    reclaimed land: 6 polder
    wooden shoes: 7 klompen
  food:
    cheese: 4 Edam **5** Gouda **6** Leyden **7** cottage
    dish: 10 nasi goreng, rijsttafel
    drink: 3 gin **8** anisette, schnapps
    pea soup: 10 erwtensoep

Netherlands East Indies see **9** Indonesia

netherworld 4 hell **5** Hades **10** underworld **14** infernal region

nettle 3 vex **4** bait, gall, miff, rile **5** annoy, beset, chafe, harry, pique, sting **6** bother, harass, ruffle **7** perturb, prickle, provoke **8** irritate **9** displease **10** exasperate

nettle 6 Urtica
  varieties: 4 dead, dumb, hemp, rock **5** false, flame, hedge, horse, Roman **6** spurge **7** painted **8** stinging **9** white dead **11** spotted dead **12** western horse

network 3 web **4** grid, mesh, trap **5** grate, group, snare **6** grille, scheme, system **7** complex, netting, station

Network
  director: 11 Sidney Lumet
  based on story by: 14 Paddy Chayefsky
  cast: 9 Ned Beatty **10** Peter Finch, Wesley Addy **11** Faye Dunaway **12** Robert Duvall **13** William Holden **16** Beatrice Straight
  Oscar for: 5 actor (Finch) **7** actress (Dunaway) **17** supporting actress (Straight)

networks see **18** Television Networks

neuroptera
  class: 8 hexapoda
  phylum: 10 arthropoda
  group: 7 ant lion, fishfly **8** alderfly, lacewing, snakefly

neurotic 4 sick **7** anxious, intense, nervous **8** abnormal, unstable **9** disturbed, obsessive, unhealthy **10** distraught, immoderate **11** overwrought

neuter 5 fixed **6** barren, fallow, gelded, spayed **7** asexual, sexless, sterile **8** impotent **9** infertile

Neutra, Richard J
  architect of: 15 Mathematics Park (Princeton) **16** Lovell Heath House (Los Angeles CA) **17** von Sternberg House (Northridge CA) **22** Orange County Courthouse (Santa Ana CA)

neutral 4 mean **5** aloof **6** medium, middle, normal, remote **7** average **8** pacifist, peaceful, unbiased **9** impartial, in-between, peaceable, withdrawn **10** achromatic, indefinite, of two minds, unaffected, uninvolved **11** half-and-half, indifferent, nonpartisan, unconcerned **12** fence sitting, intermediate, noncombatant **13** disinterested, dispassionate **14** nonbelligerent, noninterfering **16** nonparticipating **18** noninterventionist

neutralize 4 halt, stop **5** annul, block, check **6** cancel, defeat, impede, negate, offset, stymie **7** balance, disable, nullify, prevent **8** overcome, suppress **9** frustrate, overpower **10** counteract **12** counterpoise, incapacitate **14** counterbalance

neutralizer 7 blocker **9** nullifier **12** counteractor, counteragent **15** counterbalancer

Neuvillette, Christian de
  character in: 16 Cyrano de Bergerac
  author: 7 Rostand

Nevada
  abbreviation: 2 NV **3** Nev
  nickname: 6 Silver **9** Sagebrush
  capital: 10 Carson City
  largest city: 8 Las Vegas
  others: 3 Ely, Nye **4** Elko, Reno **6** Fallon, Nellis, Sparks, Storey, Washoe **7** Boulder, Gerlach **9** Hawthorne, Henderson **11** Weed Heights **12** Virginia City
  explorer: 7 Fremont **13** Jedediah Smith
  feature: 12 Comstock Lode
    dam: 5 Davis **6** Hoover
    hot springs: 4 Tule **9** Punch Bowl, Steam Boat
    national monument: 11 Death Valley
  tribe: 5 Modoc, Washo **6** Digger, Mohave, Paiute **7** Klamath **8** Achomawi, Atsugewi, Shoshone
  lake: 4 Mead, Ruby **5** Tahoe, Weber **6** Mohave, Walker **7** Pyramid **8** Lahontan, Rye Patch **9** Wild Horse
  land rank: 7 seventh
  mountain: 4 East, Pine, Ruby **5** White **7** Rockies, Toiyabe, Wasatch **13** Sierra Nevadas
    highest point: 12 Boundary Peak
  physical feature: 7 geysers **10** hot springs
    basin: 5 Great
    cave: 6 Gypsum
    desert: 7 Sonoran
    plateau: 8 Columbia
  river: 5 Reese **6** Carson, Walker **7** Truckee **8** Colorado, Humboldt
  state admission: 11 thirty-sixth
  state bird: 7 sagehen **16** mountain bluebird
  state flower: 9 sagebrush
  state motto: 16 All for Our Country
  state song: 15 Home Means Nevada

  state tree: 9 pinon pine **15** single-leaf pinon

never 4 ne'er **7** not ever **8** at no time, not at all

never-ending 6 steady **7** abiding, eternal, lasting, nonstop **8** constant, enduring, immortal, infinite, repeated, unbroken **9** ceaseless, continual, incessant, perennial, perpetual, recurring, unceasing **10** continuous, persistent, relentless **11** everlasting, unremitting **12** interminable, undiminished **13** uninterrupted

never-failing 4 firm, sure **6** proven, trusty **7** abiding **8** enduring, reliable **9** steadfast **10** dependable **11** trustworthy, undeviating, unfaltering **12** unhesitating, tried-and-true

nevermore 6 no more **10** never again

Never on Sunday
  director: 11 Jules Dassin
  cast: 11 Jules Dassin, Titos Vandis **14** Georges Foundas, Melina Mercouri
  setting: 6 Greece

nevertheless 3 but, yet **6** anyhow, anyway, even so, though **7** however **8** after all, although **10** contrarily, in any event, regardless **12** contrariwise **15** notwithstanding

Neville, Constance
  character in: 18 She Stoops to Conquer
  author: 9 Goldsmith

new 4 late **5** fixed, fresh, green, novel **6** modern, reborn, recent, remote, unused **7** altered, changed, current, just out, rebuilt, resumed, untried **8** original, reopened, repaired, restored, up-to-date **9** recreated, refreshed, remodeled, renovated, uncharted, unessayed, untouched **10** revivified, unexplored, unfamiliar, ungathered, unseasoned, unventured **11** regenerated, uncollected, unexercised **12** unaccustomed **13** reconstructed, reinvigorated

New Atlantis
  author: 12 Francis Bacon

New Brunswick
  abbreviation: 2 NB
  bay: 5 Fundy, Maces **7** Shepody **9** Chignecto, Miramichi **13** Passamaquoddy
  channel: 5 Minas **10** Grand Manan
  city: 7 Moncton **8** Bathurst **9** Riverview **10** Edmundston, Saint John **11** Fredericton
  island: 4 Deer **6** Miscou **7** Machias **10** Campobello, Grand Manan
  known as: 16 Atlantic province, maritime province
  lake: 5 Grand **8** Oromocto **12** Magagudavic **14** Chiputneticook
  people: 5 Irish **6** French **7** Acadian, English **8** American, Scottish **9** Algonkian **10** Anglo Saxon
  religion: 6 Canaan **7** Baptist **8** Angli-

can **10** Protestant **12** Presbyterian, United Church **13** Roman Catholic
  river: 5 Cains, Green **6** Renous, Salmon **7** Tobique **8** Kedgwick, Nashwak, Oromocto **9** Miramichi, Patapedia, Saint John **10** Nepisiguit, Richibucto, Saint Croix **11** Petitcodiac, Restigouche, Upsalguitch **12** Kennebecasis

New Centurions, The
  author: 14 Joseph Wambaugh

newcomer 4 tyro **5** alien **6** novice **7** entrant **8** intruder, neophyte, outsider, stranger **9** foreigner, immigrant, outlander **10** interloper, trespasser

New Deal Agency 3 AAA, CCC, CWA, FCA, FHA, FSA, NRA, NYA, PWA, REA, SEC, SSB, TVA, WPA **4** FCIC, FDIC, FERA, HOLC, NLRD, USHA

New Delhi
  capital of: 5 India
  designed by: 7 Lutyens
  earlier city: 5 Dilli **8** Dhillika, Din Panah, Kilookai **9** Firozabad **11** Tughlukabad **12** Indraprastha **13** Shah Jahanabad
  invader: 5 Timur **6** Abdali **7** British, Rohilas **8** Marathas **9** Nadir Shah
  landmark: 7 Red Fort **9** India Gate, Qutb Minar **10** Iron Pillar, Jama Masjid **12** Humayun's Tomb **14** Connaught Place **15** Rajghat Memorial **17** Rashtrapati Bhavan (Presidential Palace) **23** Jantar Mantar Observatory **30** Gandhi National Museum and Library
  river: 6 Yamuna
  street: 7 Raj Path (Kingsway)
  university: 15 Jawaharlal Nehru

New England
  capital: 6 Boston **7** Augusta, Concord **8** Hartford **10** Montpelier, Providence
  city: 4 Lynn **5** Barre **6** Bangor, Lowell, Nashua **7** Hyannis, Rutland, Warwick **8** Brockton, Cranston, Lawrence, Lewiston, New Haven, Portland, Stamford **9** Cambridge, Fall River, New London, Pawtucket, Waterbury, Worcester **10** Bridgeport, Burlington, Manchester, Pittsfield, Portsmouth, Woonsocket **11** Brattleboro, Springfield
  football team: 8 Patriots
  Indians: 6 Abnaki, Pequot **7** Mahican, Mohegan, Niantic, Nipmuck, Wangunk **8** Algonkin, Iroquois **9** Algonquin, Pennacook **10** Quinnipiac **12** Narragansett
  lake: 6 Sebago, Tiogue **7** Sunapee **9** Champlain, Moosehead **10** Candlewood **11** Pemaduncook **13** Winnipesaukee
  mountain: 5 Green, White **8** Greylock, Katahdin **9** Berkshire, Mansfield **10** Washington **11** Appalachian
  river: 5 Otter **6** Thames **7** Charles **8** Kennebec, Pawtucket, Winooski

9 Merrimack, Missiquoi, Naugatuck, Pawcatuck, Penobscot, Saint John **10** Housatonic, Providence, Quinnipiac **11** Connecticut **12** Androscoggin
state: 5 Maine **7** Vermont **11** Connecticut, Rhode Island **12** New Hampshire **13** Massachusetts

newfangled 5 novel **6** modern, modish **7** stylish

new-fashioned 6 modern, modish **7** stylish **8** up-to-date

Newfoundland
abbreviation: 4 Nfld
capital: 10 Saint Johns
city: 19 Happy Valley Goose Bay
lake: 7 Jeddore, Melville **8** Meelpaeg **10** Michikamau
mountain: 9 Long Range
river: 5 Eagle **6** Fraser, Gander **8** Exploits, Naskaupi **9** Churchill
section: 8 Labrador

New Granada *see* **8** Colombia

New Guinea
other name: 14 Papua New Guinea
capital/largest city: 11 Port Moresby
others: 3 Lae, Wau **4** Daru **5** Soron, Wewak **6** Aitape, Kikori, Medang, Rabaul **7** Gorolka, Kitbadi
division:
   eastern half of island: 9 Indonesia, Irian Jaya
   western half of island: 14 Papua New Guinea
government: 22 constitutional monarchy
head of state: 14 British monarch **15** governor-general
monetary unit: 4 kina, toea
island: 3 Aru **4** Aroe, Buka **5** Arroe, Ceram, Japen, Jobie, Manus **6** Cretin, Mussau, Ninigo, Waigeu **7** Sainson, Solomon **8** Bismarck, Kiriwina, Schouten, Woodlark **9** Admiralty, Trobriant **10** Louisiande, New Britain, New Ireland **12** Bougainville **14** D'Entrecasteaux
mountain: 4 Snow **6** Orange **8** Bismarck, Victoria **9** Carstensz **11** Owen Stanley **12** Albert Edward
highest point:
   Irian Jaya: 9 Carstensz **10** Puncak Jaya
   Papua New Guinea: 7 Wilhelm
river: 3 Fly **4** Hamu, Hany, Ramu **5** Degul, Sepik **6** Kikori, Purari **7** Amberno, Markham
sea: 5 Ceram, Coral, Sepik **6** Indian **7** Arafura, Pacific, Solomon **8** Bismarck
physical feature:
   bay: 3 Oro **5** Milne **8** Geelvink
   gulf: 4 Huon **5** Papua
   strait: 6 Torres, Vitiaz
people: 5 Pygmy **6** Papuan **7** Negrito **10** Melanesian
   explorer: 15 Jorge de Menesses
   ruler: 7 Germany **9** Australia **12** Great Britain
language: 4 Motu **7** English **16** Mela-

nesian Pidjin
religion: 7 animism **10** Protestant **13** Roman Catholic
feature:
   bird: 7 mudlark **9** cassowary
food:
   dried coconut meat: 5 copra

New Hampshire
abbreviation: 2 NH
nickname: 7 Granite
capital: 7 Concord
largest city: 10 Manchester
others: 5 Dover, Keene **6** Berlin, Durham, Exeter, Nashua **7** Hanover, Laconia **8** Sandwich **9** Claremont, Rochester **10** Portsmouth **12** Bretton Woods
college: 5 Keene **6** Rivier **9** Dartmouth, St Anselms **10** New England
feature: 14 Great Stone Face
   notch: 7 Kinsman, Pinkham **8** Crawford **9** Franconia
tribe: 6 Abnaki **9** Pennacook
people: 11 Robert Frost **12** Daniel French **13** Daniel Webster, Horace Greeley, Mary Baker Eddy
   explorer: 9 Champlain **16** Captain John Smith
island: 4 Star **5** White **6** Shoals **7** Lunging
lake: 5 Squam **7** Ossipee, Sunapee, Umbagog **8** Newfound **10** Winnisquam **13** Winnipesaukee
land rank: 11 forty-fourth
mountain: 5 Flume, White **6** Moriah, Paugus **7** Waumbek **8** Chocorua, Sandwich **9** Franconia, Monadnock **11** Profile Peak **12** Presidential
   highest point: 10 Washington
physical feature:
   bay: 5 Great
president: 14 Franklin Pierce
river: 4 Saco **6** Israel **7** Bellamy **8** Souhegan **9** Merrimack **10** Piscataqua **11** Connecticut, Salmon Falls **12** Androscoggin
state admission: 5 ninth
state bird: 11 purple finch
state flower: 11 purple lilac
state motto: 13 Live Free Or Die
state song: 15 Old New Hampshire **26** New Hampshire My New Hampshire
state tree: 10 paper birch, white birch

Newhart
character: 4 Dick **6** Joanna **7** Michael **9** Stephanie
cast: 9 Mary Frann **10** Bob Newhart, Julia Duffy **12** Peter Scolari

Newhart, Bob
born: 9 Chicago IL
roles: 3 Bob **7** Newhart **10** Cold Turkey **12** George and Leo **17** The Bob Newhart Show
films: 7 catch-22 **8** In and out

New Hebrides *see* **7** Vanuatu

New Jersey

abbreviation: 2 NJ
nickname: 6 Garden **8** Mosquito
capital: 7 Trenton
largest city: 6 Newark
others: 4 Lodi **5** Ewing, Ft Lee **6** Camden, Dumont, Haddon, Kearny, Linden, Nutley, Orange, Rahway, Totowa **7** Bayonne, Cape May, Clifton, Hoboken, Hohokus, Keyport, Madison, Matawan, Netcong, Oradell, Paramus, Passaic, Raritan, Teaneck, Tenafly, Wyckoff **8** Carteret, Cranford, Freehold, Garfield, Hillside, Metuchen, Paterson, Secaucus, Watchung **9** Bridgeton, Elizabeth, Engle wood, Hawthorne, Irvington, Maplewood, Montclair, Ocean City, Princeton **10** Asbury Park, Belleville, Ft Monmouth, Hackensack, Jersey City, Livingston, Long Branch, Morristown, Perth Amboy **11** Bergenfield **12** Atlantic City, Collingswood, New Brunswick
colleges: 4 Drew **6** Upsala **7** Rutgers **8** Caldwell, Monmouth, St Peter's **9** Princeton, Seton Hall **10** Bloomfield **18** Fairleigh-Dickinson
feature: 9 Boardwalk **16** Delaware Water Gap
tribe: 8 Delaware **11** Lenni-Lanape
people: 9 Aaron Burr **11** Joyce Kilmer, Paul Robeson **12** Stephen Crane, Thomas Edison **13** James Lawrence **19** James Fenimore Cooper **21** William Carlos Williams
   explorer: 6 Hudson **9** Verrazano
lake: 6 Mohawk **9** Greenwood, Hopatcong
land rank: 10 forty-sixth
mountain: 8 Piedmont **10** Kittatinny **13** First Watchung **14** Second Watchung
   highest point: 9 High Point
physical feature: 9 Palisades, Sandy Hook
   bay: 8 Delaware
   cape: 3 May
   ocean: 8 Atlantic
president: 15 Grover Cleveland
river: 4 Toms **6** Dennis, Haynes, Hudson, Mantua, Ramapo **7** Mullica, Passaic, Raritan **8** Cohansey, Delaware, Tuckahoe **10** Hackensack
state admission: 5 third
state bird: 16 eastern goldfinch
state flower: 6 violet
state motto: 20 Liberty and Prosperity
state tree: 6 red oak
basketball team: 4 Nets
football team: 8 Generals
hockey team: 6 Devils

Newley, Anthony
wife: 11 Joan Collins
born: 6 London **7** England
roles: 11 Oliver Twist **25** Stop the World I Want to Get Off

41 The Roar of the Greasepaint The Smell of the Crowd

newly 4 anew **6** afresh, lately, of late **7** freshly, just now **8** recently

newly rich person
French: **12** nouveau riche

Newlywed Game, The
host: **10** Bob Eubanks
executive producer: **11** Chuck Barris

Newlyweds, The
creator: **13** George McManus
character: **12** Baby Snookums

Newman, Barnett
born: **9** New York NY
artwork: **7** Abraham, The Wild **8** Onement I **18** Stations of the Cross **19** Vir Heroicus Sublimis

Newman, Christopher
character in: **11** The American
author: **5** James

Newman, John Henry (Cardinal)
author of: **18** Apologia pro Vita Sua

Newman, Paul
wife: **14** Joanne Woodward
born: **11** Cleveland OH
company: **10** Newman's own
roles: **3** Hud **6** Harper, Picnic **8** The Sting, Twilight **10** The Hustler, The Verdict **11** Nobody's Fool **12** Cool Hand Luke **15** Absence of Malice, The Color of Money **16** Cat on a Hot Tin Roof, The Left-Handed Gun, The Long Hot Summer, The Silver Chalice **17** The Hudsucker Proxy **29** Butch Cassidy and the Sundance Kid

New Mexico
abbreviation: **2** NM **4** N Mex
nickname: **8** Sunshine **17** Land of Enchantment
capital: **7** Santa Fe
largest city: **11** Albuquerque
others: **3** Jal **4** Taos **5** Aztec, Belen, Hobbs, Raton **6** Clovis, Deming, Gallup, Grants **7** Artesia, Bananea, Roswell, Socorro, Torreon **8** Carlsbad **9** Las Cruces, Los Alamos **10** Alamogordo **13** Piedras Negras
college: **7** Sante Fe **11** Albuquerque
feature: **11** Four Corners
dam: **5** Butte **8** Elephant
labs: **6** Sandia **17** Los Alamos National
national monument: **10** Aztec Ruins, White Sands **11** Chaco Canyon **17** Gila Cliff Dwelling
national park: **15** Carlsbad Caverns
observatory: **14** Sacramento Peak
tribe: **3** Sia **4** Hano, Piro, Tano, Taos, Tewa, Tiwa, Zuni **5** Acoma, Jemez, Kares, Manso, Pecos, Tiqua, Tonoa **6** Apache, Isleta, Laguna, Navaho, Navajo, Pueblo **7** Anasazi, Picuris **8** Santa Ana **9** Mescalero **12** Santo Domingo
people: **9** Kit Carson, Peter Hurd **11** Bill Mauldin
explorer: **5** Onate **6** de Niza, de

Vaca **8** Coronado
lake: **6** El Vado, Navajo, Sumner **7** Conchas **8** McMillan **10** Alamogordo **13** Elephant Butte
land rank: **5** fifth
mountain: **5** Jemez **6** Sandia **7** Manzano, Mimbres, Rockies, Truchas **8** Mogollon **9** Guadalupe, San Andres **10** Nacimiento, Sacramento **11** Mount Taylor **15** Sangre de Christo
highest point: **11** Wheeler Peak
physical feature:
basin: **8** Tularosa
desert: **15** Jornada de Muerto
plains: **5** Great
river: **3** Ute **4** Gila **5** Pecos **7** San Jose, San Juan **8** Canadian **9** Rio Grande
state admission: **12** forty-seventh
state bird: **10** roadrunner
state fish: **14** cutthroat trout
state flower: **5** yucca
state motto: **15** It Grows as It Goes
state song: **14** O Fair New Mexico **16** Asi es Nuevo Mexico
state tree: **5** pinon **8** tarantah **15** velvet ash pinyon

New Orleans
basketball team: Jazz
event: **9** Mardi Gras, Sugar Bowl **25** International Jazz Festival
football team: **6** Saints
landmark: **7** Cabildo **9** Old Square, Superdome **10** Vieux Carre **12** Pirate's Alley **13** French Quarter
noted for: **4** jazz
people: **5** Cajun **6** Creole **7** Acadian
river: **11** Mississippi
street: **5** Royal **7** Bourbon
university: **6** Loyola, Tulane

news 4 dirt, dope, talk, word **5** flash, libel, piece, rumor, story **6** babble, expose, gossip, report **7** account, article, chatter, hearsay, lowdown, mention, message, release, scandal, slander, tidings **8** bulletin, dispatch, exposure **9** statement **10** communique, disclosure, divulgence, revelation **11** information **12** announcement, intelligence

news account 4 item **5** story **6** report **7** release **8** bulletin, dispatch **10** communique

newsmonger 6 gossip **8** busybody, reporter

News of the Day
also: **12** Neues vom Tage
opera by: **9** Hindemith
character: **5** Laura **7** Eduoard

Newsome, Chadwick
character in: **14** The Ambassadors
author: **5** James

New Spain *see* **6** Mexico

newspaper 3 rag **5** daily, paper, sheet **6** herald, weekly **7** courant, gazette, journal, tabloid, tribune **10** periodical **11** publication

New Testament

books of: **4** Acts, John, Jude, Luke, Mark **5** James, Peter, Titus **6** Romans **7** Hebrews, Matthew, Timothy **8** Philemon **9** Ephesians, Galatians **10** Colossians, Revelation **11** Corinthians, Philippians **13** Thessalonians
books: **12** Humologumena

Newton, Isaac
field: **11** mathematics
nationality: **7** English
discovered laws of: **6** motion **7** gravity **8** calculus
discovered: **13** color spectrum **15** binomial theorem **16** method of fluxions
invented: **21** infinitesimal calculus

New York
abbreviation: **2** NY
nickname: **6** Empire **9** Excelsior
capital: **6** Albany
largest city: **7** New York
others: **3** Rye **4** Rome, Troy **5** Ilion, Islip, Nyack, Olean, Owego, Utica **6** Attica, Auburn, Cohoes, Elmira, Goshen, Ithaca, Oneida, Oswego, Tappan **7** Ardsley, Babylon, Batavia, Buffalo, Congers, Endwell, Geneseo, Hewlett, Mahopac, Merrick, Messena, Mineola, Montauk, Oneonta, Pennyan, Suffern, Syosset, Wantagh, Yaphank, Yonkers **8** Bethpage, Catskill, Endicott, Herkimer, Kingston, Ossining, Pottsdam, Saratoga, Tuckahoe **9** Rochester, Scarsdale **10** Binghamton, Bronxville, Mamaroneck **11** Cooperstown, New Rochelle, Schenectady, White Plains **12** Poughkeepsie
college: **4** Bard, CUNY, Iona, Pace, SUNY **5** Finch, Keuka **6** Hobart, Hunter, Vassar **7** Adelphi, Barnard, Colgate, Cornell, Fordham, St John's **8** Columbia, Skidmore, Syracuse **9** Juilliard, Rochester, West Point **13** Sarah Lawrence **30** Rensselaer Polytechnic Institute
feature:
prison: **6** Attica **8** SingSing
tribe: **4** Erie **6** Cayuga, Mohawk, Oneida, Seneca **7** Mohican, Montauk **8** Iroquois, Onondaga **9** Manhattan,
people: **7** John Jay **8** Walloons **9** Jonas Salk **10** Henry James **11** Rockefeller, Walt Whitman **12** Eugene O'Neill **13** DeWitt Clinton, John Burroughs **14** Herman Melville **15** Peter Stuyvesant **16** Eleanor Roosevelt, Washington Irving **17** Fiorello La Guardia
explorer: **6** Hudson **9** Champlain, Verrazano **16** Dutch West India Co
island: **4** Fire, Long **5** Ellis **6** Staten **7** Bedloe's, Fisher's, Liberty, Shelter, Welfare **8** Thousand **9** Governors, Manhattan
lake: **4** Erie **6** Cayuga, Finger, George, Oneida, Otisco, Otsego, Owasco, Placid, Seneca **7** Conesus, Ontario,

Saranac, Schroon **8** Saratoga **9** Champlain
land rank: 9 thirtieth
mountain: 4 Bear **5** Slide **7** Taconic **9** Catskills **11** Adirondacks
　highest point: 5 Marcy
physical feature:
　bay: 7 Jamaica, Peconic **8** Moriches
　canal: 4 Erie **7** Gowanus
　falls: 7 Niagara
　valley: 6 Mohawk
president: 14 Martin Van Buren **14** Teddy Roosevelt **15** Millard Fillmore **17** Theodore Roosevelt **23** Franklin Delano Roosevelt
river: 4 East **5** Black, Tioga **6** Harlem, Hoosic, Hudson, Mohawk, Oswego **7** Ausable, Genesee, Niagara **10** St Lawrence **11** Susquehanna
state bird: 8 bluebird
state fish: 10 brook trout
state flower: 4 rose
state motto: 9 Excelsior (Ever upward, Still higher)
state tree: 10 sugar maple

New York City
nickname: 6 Gotham **8** Big Apple
airport: 3 JFK **6** Newark **9** La Guardia **12** John F Kennedy
area: 4 Soho **6** Harlem **7** Chelsea, Midtown, Tribeca **8** Broadway **9** Chinatown, Manhattan **10** Stuyvesant **11** Bensonhurst, Brownsville, Little Italy **12** Hell's kitchen **13** Spanish Harlem **16** Greenwich Village **17** Bedford-Stuyvesant
baseball team: 4 Mets **7** Yankees
basketball team: 6 Knicks **7** Liberty **14** Knickerbockers
borough: 5 Bronx **6** Queens **8** Brooklyn, Richmond **9** Manhattan **12** Staten Island
early governor: 10 Stuyvesant
feature:
　building: 11 Empire State
　hall of fame: 8 baseball
　park: 7 Central
　square: 5 Times, Union **6** Herald
　statue: 7 Liberty
　street/avenue: 4 Park, Wall **5** Fifth **7** Madison **8** Broadway
　tomb: 6 Grant's
football team: 4 Jets **6** Giants
former name: 12 New Amsterdam
hockey team: 7 Rangers **9** Islanders
island: 4 City, Long **5** Ellis, Ward's **6** Riker's, Staten **7** Liberty **8** Randall's **9** Governor's, Manhattan, Roosevelt
landmark: 5 Macy's **8** Aqueduct, Bronx Zoo **9** Unisphere **10** Jones Beach **11** Battery Park, Central Park, Coney Island, Penn Station, Shea Stadium, Times Square **12** Carnegie Hall **13** Gracie Mansion, Lincoln Center, Port Authority, Rockaway Beach, Trinity Church, United Nations, Yankee Stadium **14** Waldorf-Astoria **15** NY Public Library, NY

Stock Exchange, Seagram Building, Statue of Liberty **16** Chrysler Building, World Trade Center **17** Arthur Ashe Stadium, Hayden Planetarium, Rockefeller Center, Woolworth Building **18** Astoria Film Studios, Radio City Music Hall **19** Empire State Building, Grand Central Station, Madison Square Garden, St Patrick's Cathedral **22** Metropolitan Opera House **29** Cathedral of Saint John the Divine
mayor: 4 Koch **6** Walker **9** La Guardia
museum: 6 Jewish **7** Whitney **9** Cloisters **10** Guggenheim **12** Cooper-Hewitt, Metropolitan **15** Frick Collection **17** Museum of Modern Art (MoMA) **30** American Museum of Natural History
river: 4 East **6** Harlem, Hudson
street: 6 Bowery **8** Broadway **9** Lexington **10** Park Avenue, Wall Street **11** Central Park, Fifth Avenue, Sutton Place **13** Madison Avenue **17** Forty-Second Street
university: 3 NYU **6** Queens **7** Barnard, Fordham, Yeshiva **8** Brooklyn, Columbia **13** Hunter College **22** Juilliard School of Music **23** City University of New York

New Zealand
native's nickname: 4 Kiwi
other name: 8 Aotearoa **12** Nieuw Zeeland **23** Land of the Long White Cloud
capital: 10 Wellington
largest city: 8 Auckland
others: 5 Leuin, Oreti, Otaki, Taupo **6** Clutha, Foxton, Oamaru, Picton, Timaru **7** Dunedin, Manu Kau, Raetihi, Rotorua **8** Hamilton, Kawakawa, Touranga **9** Lyttelton **10** Queenstown **12** Christchurch, Invercargill, Port Chalmers **13** Port Nicholson **14** Napier-Hastings **15** Palmerston North
school: 5 Otago **6** Massey **7** Waikato **8** Auckland, Victoria **10** Canterbury
division: 11 North Island, South Island
head of state: 14 British monarch **15** governor general
monetary unit: 4 cent **6** dollar
island: 4 Cook, Niue, Otea **5** North, South **6** Bounty, Chatam, Snares **7** Stewart, Tokelau **8** Auckland, Campbell, Kermadec, Puketutu **9** Antipodes **10** Resolution, Three Kings **12** Great Barrier
lake: 3 Ada **4** Gunn, Ohau **5** Hawea, Taupo **6** Pukaki, Pupuke, Te Anau, Tekapo, Wanaka **7** Brunner, Diamond, Kanieri, Okareka, Rotorua **8** Okataina, Paradise, Rotoaira, Wakatipu **9** Manapouri
mountain: 4 Eden, Flat, Owen **5** Allen, Chope, Lyall, Mitre, Ohope, Otari, Young **6** Egmont, Stokes, Tas-

man **7** Cameron, Coronet, Ernslaw, Huiarau, Pihanga, Ruahine, Ruapehu, Tauhera, Tutamoe, Tyndall **8** Aspiring, Richmond, Tauranga **9** Messenger, Murchison, Ngauruhoe, Raukumara, Tongariro **11** Remarkables **12** Southern Alps
highest point: 4 Cook **7** Aorangi
river: 4 Avon **5** Mokau, Waipa **6** Clutha, Rakaia, Tamaki, Waihou, Wairau, Wairoa **7** Waikato, Waitaki **8** Clarence, Manawatu, Wanganui **10** Rangitikei
sea: 6 Tasman **12** South Pacific
physical feature:
　bay: 4 Ohua **5** Evans, Hawke, Lyall **6** Awarua, Cloudy, Golden, Plenty, Tasman **7** Fitzroy, Pegasus, Poverty **8** Halfmoon, Rangaunu
　bight: 7 Karamea **10** Canterbury **13** North Taranaki, South Taranaki
　cape: 4 East, West **5** North **6** Egmont **8** Farewell, Foulwind, Palliser **9** Southwest
　channel: 8 Colville
　falls: 10 Sutherland
　glacier: 3 Fox **6** Tasman **11** Franz Joseph
　gulf: 7 Hauraki
　harbor: 7 Kaipara, Manukau **9** Waitemata
　peninsula: 5 Mahia, Otago
　plains: 10 Canterbury
　sound: 8 Doubtful
　strait: 4 Cook **7** Foveaux
　people: 3 Ati **5** Arawa, Dutch, Maori **7** British, Ringatu **10** Polynesian
　author: 5 Frame **9** Mansfield **10** Ngaio Marsh **12** Ashton-Warner
　explorer: 4 Cook **6** Tasman
　mountain climber: 7 Hillary
language: 5 Maori **7** English
religion: 8 Anglican **9** Methodist **10** Protestant **12** Presbyterian **13** Roman Catholic
place:
　national park: 9 Fiordland, Fjordland, Tongariro
feature:
　animal: 7 tuatara
　bird: 3 kea, tui **4** kiwi, weka **6** takahe **7** apteryx **8** bellbird
　tree: 4 rimu, tawa **5** kauri, matai **6** totara
food:
　fish: 4 mako
　fruit: 4 kiwi **9** tamarillo **17** Chinese gooseberry
next-door 8 adjacent **9** adjoining **10** connecting, contiguous, juxtaposed, side-by-side, **12** conterminous
next to 6 beside **8** abutting, adjacent **9** adjoining, bordering **10** contiguous, juxtaposed **12** conterminous
next world, the 6 Heaven **8** eternity, paradise **12** the hereafter **14** the world to come
Nez Perce (Numipu)

language family: 10 Shahaptian
location: 5 Idaho **6** Oregon **10** Washington
leader: 11 Chief Joseph

Niamey
capital of: 5 Niger

nib 3 end, tip, top **4** apex, peak **5** point **6** height, tiptop, vertex **7** extreme **8** pinnacle **9** extremity

nibble 3 nip **4** bite, chew, gnaw, peck **5** crumb, munch, speck, taste **6** crunch, morsel, peck at, tidbit **8** fragment, particle

Nibelung, ring of
origin: 8 Germanic
mentioned in: 14 Nibelungenlied
stolen by: 8 Alberich

Nibelungenlied
origin: 8 Germanic
form: 4 epic
date written: 17 thirteenth century
related to: 8 Volsunga
author: 7 unknown
character: 5 Etzel (Attila), Hagen **6** Gernot **7** Gunther **8** Brunhild, Dankwart, Giselher **9** Kriemhild, Siegfried
inspired: 6 Wagner

Nibelungs, Niblungs
origin: 8 Germanic, Teutonic
followers of: 9 Siegfried
race: 6 dwarfs
possessed: 8 treasure
captured by: 9 Siegfried
family of: 7 Gunther

Nicaragua
capital/largest city: 7 Managua
others: 4 Leon, Rama **6** Masaya **7** Corinto, Granada **8** Jinotega **9** Matagalpa **10** Bluefields, Chinandega
division: 13 Mosquito Coast
measure: 4 vara **5** cahiz **6** suerte **7** cajuela, manzana **10** cabelleria
monetary unit: 4 peso **7** centavo, cordoba
weight: 3 bag **4** caha, caja **8** tonelada
island: 7 Ometepe
lake: 7 Managua **9** Nicaragua
mountain: 4 Leon **5** Negro, Viejo **6** Madera, Telica **7** Managua, Saslaya **9** Momotombo
highest point: 7 Mogoton
river: 4 Coco, Tuma **5** Wanks **6** Grande, Poteca **7** San Juan **8** Tipitapa **9** Escondido
sea: 7 Pacific **9** Caribbean
physical feature:
  gulf: 7 Fonseca
people: 4 Mico, Mixe, Rama, Smoo, Ulva **5** Cukra, Diria, Lenca, Sambo, Toaca **6** Mangue **7** mestizo, Miskito **8** Mosquito **9** Matagalpa
  author: 5 Dario
  explorer: 6 Davila **7** Cordoba **8** Columbus
  group: 6 Contra **10** Sandinista
  leader: 6 Somoza, Walker, Zelaya

7 Nicardo **8** Chamorro
language: 7 English, Spanish
religion: 13 Roman Catholic
place:
  cathedral: 12 Metropolitan
feature:
  dance: 5 sones **10** zapateados, zarabandas
food:
  beans: 8 frijoles
  dish: 10 naca tamale
  drink: 5 tiste **9** pinolillo
  fruit: 6 zapote

nice 4 deft, fine, good, kind **5** dandy, exact, fussy, great, swell **6** divine, genial, lovely, proper, seemly, strict, subtle **7** amiable, amusing, careful, cordial, correct, finicky, genteel, likable, precise, refined, winning **8** accurate, charming, cheerful, delicate, friendly, gracious, jim-dandy, ladylike, pleasant, pleasing, rigorous, skillful, unerring, virtuous, well-bred **9** agreeable, congenial, excellent, fantastic, marvelous, sensitive, wonderful **10** attractive, delightful, enchanting, entrancing, fastidious, methodical, meticulous, scrupulous **11** interesting, painstaking, pleasurable, punctilious, respectable, sympathetic, warmhearted **13** compassionate, understanding, well brought up **17** overconscientious

Nice and the Good, The
author: 11 Iris Murdoch

nicely 6 neatly **7** exactly, fussily, happily **9** carefully, precisely **10** accurately, critically, pleasantly, unerringly **11** faultlessly, fortunately, opportunely **12** attractively, fastidiously

nicety 4 care, tact **5** flair, grace **6** acumen, polish **7** culture, finesse, insight **8** accuracy, delicacy, elegance, subtlety **9** attention, exactness, precision **10** refinement **11** cultivation, penetration, preciseness, sensitivity **12** per spicacity, subtle detail, tastefulness **13** elaborateness, particularity **14** discrimination, fastidiousness, meticulousness

niche 4 cove, nook, slot **5** berth, trade **6** alcove, cavity, corner, cranny, dugout, hollow, metier, recess **7** calling **8** position, vocation **9** cubby hole **10** depression, pigeon hole **11** proper place **13** hole in the wall

Nicholas Nickleby
author: 14 Charles Dickens
character: 5 Smike **11** Arthur Gride, Newman Noggs **12** Kate Nickleby, Madeline Bray **13** Lord Verisopht, Ralph Nickleby **14** Frank Cheeryble **15** Sir Mulberry Hawk, Vincent Crummles, Wackford Squeers **17** Cheeryble Brothers

Nichols, Mike
Wife: 11 Diane Sawyer

director of: 7 Catch-22 **11** The Birdcage, The Graduate (Oscar) **15** Carnal Knowledge **25** Who's Afraid of Virginia Woolf?

Nicholson, Ben
born: 6 Denham **7** England
artwork: 9 Fireworks **11** White Relief **12** Tuscan Relief **13** Painted Relief **14** At the Chat Botte

Nicholson, Jack
born: 9 Neptune NJ
roles: 4 Wolf **5** Hoffa **6** Batman **8** Ironweed **9** Chinatown, Easy Rider **10** The Shining **11** A Few Good Men, Mars Attacks, The Two Jakes **12** Prizzi's Honor, The Passenger **13** The Last Detail **14** As Good As It Gets (Oscar), Five Easy Pieces **15** Carnal Knowledge **17** Terms of Endearment **20** The Witches of Eastwick **22** The King of Marvin Gardens **25** One Flew Over the Cuckoo's Nest (Oscar) **26** The Postman Always Rings Twice

nicht wahr? 10 isn't that so?

nick 3 cut, jag, mar **4** chip, dent, gash, mark, scar **5** cleft, gouge, notch, score, wound **6** damage, deface, indent, injure, injury **7** marking, scarify, scoring, scratch **8** incision, lacerate **10** depression **11** indentation

nickel
chemical symbol: 2 Ni

Nickel Mountain
author: 11 John Gardner

nickname 6 handle **7** agnomen, epithet, moniker, pet name **8** baby name, cognomen **9** pseudonym, sobriquet **10** diminutive **11** appellation, designation

Nicomachean Ethics
author: 9 Aristotle

Nidhogg
origin: 12 Scandinavian
form: 7 serpent
domain: 8 Niflheim
gnaws on lowest root of: 9 Iggdrasil, Yggdrasil

niello 5 alloy
of: 6 sulfur
with: 4 lead **6** copper, silver
used as: 5 inlay

Nielsen, Carl August
born: 6 Odense **7** Denmark
composer of: 9 Maskarade **12** Saul and David **16** Inextinguishable (symphony No 4)

Nietzsche, Friedrich
author of: 14 The Will to Power **17** Beyond Good and Evil, The Birth of Tragedy **20** Thus Spake Zarathustra

Niflheim
origin: 12 Scandinavian
ruler of: 3 Hel
purpose: 10 punish dead
climate: 3 fog **4** cold **8** darkness

nifty 4 chic, fine, neat, posh **5** natty, smart **6** clever, dapper **7** dashing, stylish **8** splendid **10** attractive **11** fashionable

Niger
other name: **6** Joliba, Kworra, Ramtil
capital/largest city: **6** Niamey
others: **5** Goure **6** Agadex, Agadez, Maradi, Tahoua, Zinder
division:
region: **3** Air **5** Arlit, Sahel
monetary unit: **5** franc **7** centime
lake: **4** Chad
mountain: **7** Bagzane **9** Air Massif
highest point: **7** Greboun
river: **5** Niger **6** Dillia
physical feature:
desert: **6** Sahara
oasis: **6** Kaouar
plateau: **5** Djado **6** Tegama **7** Tchigai **8** Mengueni **11** Adar Doutchi, Djerma Ganda
people: **4** Daza, Idjo, Idyo, Idzo, Peul, Teda **5** Hausa, Warri **6** Djerma, Fulani, Kanuri, Songha, Toubou, Tuareg **13** Djerma-Songhai
conqueror: **13** Usman Dan Fodio
leader: **5** Diori **6** Saibou **7** Ousmane **8** Kountche
language: **5** Hausa, Mande **6** Djerma, French, Fulani, Tuareg **8** Mandingo, Tamashek
religion: **5** Islam **7** animism **12** Christianity
place:
ruins: **6** Agadez
feature:
cavalry: **5** Dosso
empire: **4** Mali **6** Fulani **7** Songhai **10** Kanem-Borno
tree: **6** acacia, baobab

Nigeria
capital: **5** Abuja
largest city: **5** Lagos
new capital: **5** Abuja
others: **3** Aba, Ado, Ede, Isa, Iwo, Jos, Oyo **4** Bida, Bidi, Buea, Kano, Offa, Yola **5** Benin, Bonny, Enugu, Warri, Zaria **6** Burutu, Ibadan, Ilesha, Ilorin, Kachia, Kaduna, Kadune, Kokoto, Mushin, Takoba **7** Calabar, Onitsha, Oshogbo **8** Abeokuta **9** Maiduguri, Ogbomosho **12** Port Harcourt
division: **3** Air, Isa, Oyo **4** Kano, Nupe, Ondo **5** Asben, Benin, Bornu, Ijebu, Ogoja, Warri **6** Biafra, Degema, Owerri, Sokoto **7** Adamawa
monetary unit: **4** kobo **5** naira
lake: **4** Chad
highest point: **7** Dimlang
river: **3** Oli **4** Gana, Yobe **5** Benin, Benue, Cross, Niger **6** Kaduna, Sokoto **7** Calabar, Gongola **8** Komadugu **9** Sambreiro
sea: **8** Atlantic
physical feature:
bight: **5** Benin, Bonny **6** Biafra
delta: **5** Niger
gulf: **6** Guinea
plains: **5** Bornu **9** Hausaland

plateau: **3** Jos, Udi **6** Bauchi
port: **5** Lagos **7** Calabar **8** Harcourt
people: **3** Abo, Aro, Djo, Ebo, Edo, Ibo, Ijo, Tiv, Vai **4** Beni, Bini, Eboe, Efik, Egba, Ejam, Ekoi, Idyo, Igbo, Ijaw, Nupe **5** Angas, Benin, Gwari, Hausa **6** Chamba, Fulani, Ibibio, Kanuri, Yoruba **11** Hausa-Fulani
author: **6** Achebe
British colonial ruler: **6** Goldie, Lugard
kingdom: **3** Ife, Nok, Oyo **5** Benin **6** Fulani **10** Kanem-Borno
leader: **5** Gowon **6** Balewa, Ojukwu, Schick **7** Awolowo, Azikine, Azikiwe, Shagari **8** Obasanjo **9** Babangida **13** Usman dan Fodio
language: **3** Ibo **4** Efik, Igbo **5** Hausa **6** Yoruba **7** English
religion: **5** Islam **7** animism **12** Christianity
place:
dam: **6** Kainji
mosque/walled city: **4** Kano
feature:
dress: **4** riga **7** agbados
tree: **5** abura, afara **6** obeche **10** terminalia
war: **7** Biafran

niggard **4** mean **5** cheap, miser, tight **6** stingy **7** miserly **8** scrimper **9** skinflint **10** ungenerous **12** parsimonious

niggardliness **6** penury **8** meanness **9** closeness, parsimony **10** stinginess **11** miserliness **13** penny-pinching **15** tight-fistedness

niggardly **4** mean, poor **5** cheap, close, sorry, tight **6** flimsy, frugal, meager, measly, paltry, saving, scanty, shabby, stingy, tawdry **7** miserly, scrubby, sparing, thrifty **8** beggarly, grubbing, grudging, stinting, wretched **9** illiberal, mercenary, miserable, penurious **10** hardfisted, second-rate, ungenerous **11** closefisted **12** contemptible, insufficient, parsimonious

niggling **5** fussy, minor, petty, small **7** finicky **8** caviling, nugatory, picayune, piddling, trifling **9** quibbling **10** negligible, nit-picking **12** pettifogging **13** insignificant **15** inconsequential

nigh **4** near **5** close, handy **6** almost, at hand, nearly **7** close by **8** adjacent **9** bordering **11** neighboring, practically

night **4** dark, dusk **7** bedtime, evening, sundown **8** darkness, eventide **9** murkiness, obscurity **13** tenebrousness
goddess of: **3** Nox

nightclub
French: **5** boite **11** boite de nuit

nightfall **4** dark, dusk **6** sunset **7** evening, sundown **8** darkness, eventide, gloaming, moonrise, twilight
French: **10** crepuscule

Night Gallery
host: **10** Rod Serling

Nightingale, Florence
birthplace: **7** England
worked in: **10** Crimean War
founded: **13** modern nursing
nickname: **18** The Lady with the Lamp
first woman to receive: **12** Order of Merit

nightingale
group of: **5** watch

Nightline
host: **9** Ted Koppel

nightly **4** dark **7** evening, obscure **9** nocturnal **11** nocturnally

nightmare **7** incubus **8** bad dream, succubus **13** hallucination

Night of the Iguana, The
director: **10** John Huston
based on play by: **17** Tennessee Williams
cast: **7** Sue Lyon **8** Skip Ward **10** Ava Gardner **11** Deborah Kerr **13** Richard Burton
setting: **6** Mexico

nightshade **16** Solanum dulcamara
varieties: **4** ball **5** black **6** common, deadly, sticky **7** Malabar **8** stinking **9** melon-leaf, poisonous, soda-apple **10** enchanter's

Nights of Cabiria
director: **15** Federico Fellini
cast: **13** Amedeo Nazzari **14** Francois Perier **15** Giulietta Masina
remade as: **12** Sweet Charity

nightstick **3** rod **4** mace, wand **5** baton, staff **6** cudgel **7** scepter **8** bludgeon **9** billy club, truncheon **10** shillelagh

nighttime **4** late **5** night **9** late-night, nighttide, nocturnal

Night to Remember, A
director: **8** Roy Baker
based on story by: **10** Walter Lord
cast: **9** Jill Dixon **11** Kenneth More **13** David McCallum **16** Laurence Naismith
setting: **7** Titanic

nihil **7** nothing

nihilism **5** chaos **6** anomie **7** license **9** amorality, anarchism, emptiness, terrorism **10** alienation, iconoclasm, radicalism, skepticism **11** agnosticism, lawlessness, nothingness **12** nonexistence **16** irresponsibility

nihilist **5** rebel **9** anarchist, terrorist **13** revolutionary

Nihon *see* **5** Japan

Nike
origin: **5** Greek
goddess of: **7** victory
father: **11** Titan Pallas
mother: **4** Styx
brother: **5** Zelos
corresponds to: **6** Athena **8** Victoria

nil 4 none, null, zero **6** cipher, naught **7** nothing, nullity **11** nonexistent

Nile
boat: 5 baris **6** cangia, nuggar, sandal **7** felucca, gaiassa **8** dahabeah
cities: 3 Qus **4** Abri, Argo, Idfu, Isna, Juba, Qina **5** Aswan, Asyut, Cairo, Kokka, Kusti, Luxor, Meroe, Minya, Rejaf, Saite, Tanis, Tanta **6** Atbara, Faiyum **7** Malakel, Mansura, Rosetta **8** Khartoum, Omdurman, Rusayris **9** Was Madani **10** Alexandria
dam: 6 Sannar **9** Aswan High, White Nile
desert bordering: 6 Libyan, Nubian **7** Arabian
falls: 5 Ripon **8** Kabalega **9** Murchison
feature: 6 Sphinx
  pyramid: 4 Giza
  temple: 8 Ramses II **9** Abu Simbel **11** Deir el-Bahri, Medinet Habu
flows into: 13 Mediterranean
flows through: 5 Egypt, Kenya, Sudan, Zaire **6** Rwanda, Uganda **7** Burundi **8** Ethiopia, Tanzania
island: 4 Roda **6** Philae
lake: 4 Tana **5** Kyoga, Tsana **6** Albert, Edward, Nasser **8** Victoria
other name: 4 Hapi **20** The Father of the Rivers
people: 3 Jur, Luo, Lwo, Nuo, Suk **4** Bari, Beja, Golo, Luoh, Madi **5** Nilot **7** Shilluk
plain: 6 Gezira
plant: 4 sudd **5** lotus
starting point: 5 Tsana **8** Victoria
swamp: 4 Sudd
tributary: 4 Arab **5** Rahad, Sobat **6** Atbara, Ghazai, Kagera **7** Rosetta **8** Blue Nile, Damietta **9** Bahr Jebel, White Nile

Niles, Hazel and Peter
characters in: 22 Mourning Becomes Electra
author: 6 O'Neill

nil nisi bonum 21 nothing unless it is good

nil sine numine 27 nothing without the divine will
motto of: 8 Colorado

nimble 4 deft, spry **5** agile, fleet, light, quick, rapid, ready, swift **6** active, expert, lively, prompt, speedy, supple **8** animated, skillful, spirited **9** dexterous, mercurial, sprightly **10** proficient

nimbleness 7 agility **8** alacrity, spryness **9** dexterity, quickness **10** limberness, suppleness

nimble-witted 5 droll, witty **6** clever **11** resourceful

nimbus 4 aura, disk, halo **5** cloud, vapor **7** aureole **8** radiance

Nimitz, Chester
served in: 3 WWI **4** WWII
commander of: 12 Pacific fleet
rank: 12 fleet (five-star) admiral

22 chief of naval operations
battle: 6 Midway **9** Leyte Gulf **13** Philippine Sea

Nimoy, Leonard
born: 8 Boston MA
films: 7 Mr Spock **8** Star Trek **14** Funny About Love **16** Three men and a Baby **17** Mission: Impossible **21** Star Trek: The Voyage Home **22** Star Trek: The Wrath of Khan **24** Star Trek: The Final Frontier **25** Star Trek: The Search for Spock

Nimrod
father: 4 Cush
grandfather: 3 Ham
great grandfather: 4 Noah
founded: 5 Accad, Calah, Resen **7** Nineveh **8** Rehoboth
famed as: 6 hunter

nincompoop 4 boob, dolt, dope, fool, jerk **5** dummy, dunce, idiot, klutz, moron, ninny **6** dimwit, lummox, nitwit **7** half-wit, jackass **8** bonehead, dummkopf, imbecile, lunkhead, numskull **9** blockhead, dumb bunny, harebrain, numbskull, simpleton **10** dunderhead, dunderpate, muddlehead, noodlehead **11** knucklehead, rattlebrain **12** featherbrain, scatterbrain

Nine, the see **5** Muses

Nineteen Eighty-Four
author: 12 George Orwell
character: 4 Syme **5** Julia **6** O'Brien **11** Charrington **12** Winston Smith

1919
author: 13 John Dos Passos

Ninety-Five Theses
author: 12 Martin Luther

Nineveh
founder: 6 Nimrod

Nine worthies
mentioned in: 16 medieval romances
three each of: 4 Jews **6** Pagans **10** Christians
names: 5 David **6** Arthur, Hector, Joshua **11** Charlemagne **12** Julius Caesar **15** Judas Maccabaeus **17** Alexander the Great **18** Godefroy de Bouillon

ninny 3 ass, sap **4** fool, simp **5** booby, dunce, idiot, moron **6** dimwit, nitwit **7** fathead, half-wit **8** bonehead, dumb-dumb, imbecile, lunkhead, numskull **9** blockhead, dumb bunny, lamebrain, numbskull **10** dunderhead, nincompoop **11** chowderhead

Ninotchka
director: 13 Ernst Lubitsch
cast: 9 Ina Claire **10** Bela Lugosi, Greta Garbo **13** Melvyn Douglas
setting: 5 Paris
remade as: 13 Silk Stockings

Ninurta
also: 5 Ninib
origin: 8 Sumerian **10** Babylonian
type of god: 4 hero
personifies: 4 wind **9** south wind

father: 5 Enlil
avenger of: 5 Enlil

Ninus
wife: 9 Semiramis
founder of: 7 Nineveh

Niobe
father: 8 Tantalus
mother: 5 Dione
brother: 6 Pelops
husband: 7 Amphion
children: 9 seven sons **14** seven daughters
children called: 6 Niobid
taunted: 4 Leto
children killed by: 6 Apollo **7** Artemis
changed into: 5 stone
changed by: 4 Zeus

Niord
also: 5 Njord
origin: 12 Scandinavian
god of: 4 wind **10** navigation, prosperity
king of: 5 Vanir
son: 4 Frey **5** Freyr
daughter: 5 Freia, Freya

nip 3 cut, lop **4** bite, clip, crop, dock, grab, grip, ruin, snag, snap, snip **5** blast, check, chill, clamp, clasp, crack, crush, frost, grasp, pinch, quash, seize, sever, shear, snare, tweak **6** benumb, clutch, cut off, freeze, pierce, snatch, sunder, thwart **7** curtail, destroy, shorten, squeeze **8** compress, cut short, demolish **9** frustrate **10** abbreviate

nip-and-tuck 5 close

nip in the bud 7 prevent **8** preclude **9** forestall, frustrate

Nipper, Susan
character in: 12 Dombey and Son
author: 7 Dickens

Nippon see **5** Japan

nippy 3 raw **5** brisk, chill, crisp, sharp **6** biting, chilly **7** cutting

nit-pick 4 carp, pick **5** cavil **9** criticize

nitrate 4 salt **5** ester **6** sodium **9** potassium **10** fertilizer

nitrogen
chemical symbol: 1 N

nitty-gritty 4 core, crux, gist, meat, pith **5** heart **7** essence **9** substance

nitwit 3 ass **4** clod, dolt, fool **5** booby, dummy, dunce, idiot, klutz, moron, ninny **7** fathead, pinhead **8** bonehead, dumb-dumb, imbecile, lunkhead, meathead, numskull **9** birdbrain, blockhead, lamebrain, numbskull **10** dunderhead, nincompoop, noodlehead **11** chowderhead

Niven, David
real name: 21 James David Graham Niven
autobiography: 16 The Moon's a Balloon **21** Bring on the Empty Horses
born: 8 Scotland **10** Kirriemuir

roles: 11 Phileas Fogg **12** Casino Royale, My Man Godfrey **14** The Pink Panther, Separate Tables (Oscar) **16** Stairway to Heaven, Wuthering Heights **18** The Prisoner of Zenda **26** Around the World in Eighty Days

Nix, nixie
origin: 8 Germanic
form: 6 spirit
habitat: 5 water

Nixon, Richard Milhous
presidential rank: 13 thirty-seventh
party: 10 Republican
state represented: 2 CA
defeated: 7 (George Corley) Wallace **8** (Hubert Horatio) Humphrey
vice president: 4 (Gerald Rudolph) Ford **5** (Spiro Theodore) Agnew
cabinet:
  state: 6 (William Pierce) Rogers **9** (Henry A) Kissinger
  treasury: 5 (William E) Simon **6** (George P) Shultz **7** (David Matthew) Kennedy **8** (John Bowden) Connally
  defense: 5 (Melvin Robert) Laird **10** (Elliot L) Richardson **11** (James R) Schlesinger
  attorney general: 5 (William B) Saxbe **8** (John Newton) Mitchell **10** (Elliot L) Richardson **11** (Richard G) Kleindienst
  postmaster general: 6 (Winton Malcolm) Blount
  interior: 6 (Rogers Clark Ballard) Morton, (Walter Joseph) Hinkel
  agriculture: 4 (Earl Lauer) Butz **6** (Clifford Morris) Hardin
  commerce: 4 (Frederick B) Dent **5** (Maurice Hubert) Stans
  labor: 6 (George Pratt) Shultz **7** (James Day) Hodgson, (Peter J) Brennan
  HEW: 5 (Robert Hutchinson) Finch **10** (Caspar W) Weinberger, (Elliot Lee) Richardson
  HUD: 4 (James T) Lynn **6** (George Wilcken) Romney
  transportation: 5 (John Anthony) Volpe **8** (Claude S) Brinegar
born: 2 CA **10** Yorba Linda
died: 7 New York **11** New York City
education:
  college: 8 Whittier
  law school: 14 Duke University
religion: 6 Quaker **16** Society of Friends
interests: 8 football
vacation spot: 11 Key Biscayne (FL), San Clemente (CA)
dog: 8 Checkers **11** King Timahoe
author: 9 Six Crises **10** The Real War **11** Beyond Peace **27** RN: The Memoirs of Richard Nixon
political career: 8 US Senate **13** Vice President **24** US House of Representatives
civilian career: 6 lawyer

military service: 6 US Navy **10** lieutenant, World War II
notable events of lifetime/term:
  Calley court martialed for: 13 Mylai Massacre
  court martial of: 6 Calley
  creation of: 10 Bangladesh
  crisis: 3 oil **6** energy
  embargo on: 3 oil
  first men on: 4 moon
  incident: 11 Wounded Knee
  pardon of Nixon by: 4 Ford
  publication of: 14 Pentagon Papers
  resignation of: 5 Agnew, Nixon
  scandal: 9 Watergate
  student deaths at: 9 Kent State
  treaty: 10 Seabed Arms **32** Nonproliferation of Nuclear Weapons
  trip to: 5 China
  war: 7 Vietnam **10** Middle East **12** East Pakistan
quotes: 31 A respectable Republican cloth coat **35** You won't have Nixon to kick around any more
father: 14 Francis Anthony
mother: 6 Hannah (Milhous)
siblings: 11 Arthur Burdg **12** Harold Samuel **13** Edward Calvert, Francis Donald
wife: 8 (Thelma Catherine) Patricia (Ryan)
  nickname: 3 Pat
children: 5 Julie **8** Patricia
  Julie married: 15 David Eisenhower
  Patricia married: 9 Edward Cox
  Patricia's nickname: 6 Tricia

Njord *see* **5** Niord

no 3 nay, nix, not **4** none, veto
French: 3 non
German: 4 nein
Spanish: 2 no
Italian: 2 no
Russian: 4 nyet

Noah
father: 6 Lamech
grandfather: 10 Methuselah
son: 3 Ham **4** Shem **7** Japheth
grandson: 3 Put **4** Cush **6** Canaan **7** Misraim
great grandson: 6 Nimrod
built: 3 ark
collected: 5 pairs **7** animals
survived: 5 flood
pertaining to: 8 Noachian

Noah's Ark
made of: 10 gopherwood
landfall: 6 Ararat

nob 4 peer, toff **5** swell **9** patrician **10** aristocrat

Nobel, Alfred
nationality: 7 Swedish
invented: 8 dynamite
originated: 10 Nobel Prize

Nobel Prizes
Literature:
  1901: 20 Rene F A

Sully-Prudhomme
1902: 14 Theodor Mommsen
1903: 20 Bjornstjerne Bjornson
1904: 13 Jose Echegaray **15** Frederic Mistral
1905: 17 Henryk Sienkiewicz
1906: 14 Giosue Carducci
1907: 14 Rudyard Kipling
1908: 13 Rudolf C Eucken
1909: 13 Selma Lagerlof
1910: 12 Paul von Heyse
1911: 18 Maurice Maeterlinck
1912: 16 Gerhart Hauptmann
1913: 21 Sir Rabindranath Tagore
1915: 13 Romain Rolland
1916: 19 Verner von Heidenstam
1917: 11 K A Gjellerup **17** Henrik Pontoppidan
1919: 15 Carl F G Spitteler
1920: 10 Knut Hamsun
1921: 13 Anatole France
1922: 25 Jacinto Benavente y Martinez
1923: 18 William Butler Yeats
1924: 17 Wladyslaw S Reymont
1925: 17 George Bernard Shaw
1926: 13 Grazia Deledda
1927: 12 Henri Bergson
1928: 12 Sigrid Undset
1929: 10 Thomas Mann
1930: 13 Sinclair Lewis
1931: 14 Erik A Karlfeldt
1932: 14 John Galsworthy
1933: 10 Ivan A Bunin
1934: 15 Luigi Pirandello
1936: 12 Eugene O'Neill
1937: 17 Roger Martin du Gard
1938: 10 Pearl S Buck
1939: 15 Frans E Sillanpaa
1944: 15 Johannes V Jensen
1945: 15 Gabriela Mistral
1946: 12 Hermann Hesse
1947: 9 Andre Gide
1948: 7 T S Eliot
1949: 15 William Faulkner
1950: 15 Bertrand Russell (Earl Russell)
1951: 14 Par F Lagerkvist
1952: 15 Francois Mauriac
1953: 21 Sir Winston L S Churchill
1954: 15 Ernest Hemingway
1955: 15 Halldor K Laxness
1956: 16 Juan Ramon Jimenez
1957: 11 Albert Camus
1958: 15 Boris L Pasternak
1959: 18 Salvatore Quasimodo
1960: 14 Saint-John Perse
1961: 9 Ivo Andric
1962: 13 John Steinbeck
1963: 13 George Seferis
1964: 14 Jean Paul Sartre
1965: 17 Mikhail A Sholokhov
1966: 10 Nelly Sachs **17** Samuel Joseph (Shmuel Y) Agnon
1967: 19 Miguel Angel Asturias
1968: 16 Yasunari Kawabata
1969: 13 Samuel Beckett
1970: 22 Aleksandr I Solzhenitsyn

1971: **11** Pablo Neruda
1972: **12** Heinrich Boll
1973: **12** Patrick White
1974: **13** Eyvind Johnson **14** Harry Martinson
1975: **14** Eugenio Montale
1976: **10** Saul Bellow
1977: **17** Vicente Aleixandre
1978: **19** Isaac Bashevis Singer
1979: **14** Odysseus Elytis
1980: **13** Czeslaw Milosz
1981: **12** Elias Canetti
1982: **20** Gabriel Garcia Marquez
1983: **14** William Golding
1984: **15** Jaroslav Seifert
1985: **11** Claude Simon
1986: **11** Wole Soyinka
1987: **13** Joseph Brodsky
1988: **13** Naguib Mahfouz
1989: **10** Camilo Cela
1990: **10** Octavio Paz
1991: **14** Nadine Gordimer
1992: **12** Derek Walcott
1993: **12** Toni Morrison
1994: **11** Kenzaburo Oe
1995: **12** Seamus Heaney
1996: **17** Wislawa Szymborska
1997: **7** Dario Fo

Physiology/Medicine:
1901: **15** Emil A von Behring
1902: **13** Sir Ronald Ross
1903: **12** Niels R Finsen
1904: **11** Ivan P Pavlov
1905: **10** Robert Koch
1906: **12** Camillo Golgi **19** Santiago Ramon y Cajal
1907: **16** Charles L A Laveran
1908: **11** Paul Ehrlich **15** Elie Metchnikoff
1909: **11** Emil T Kocher
1910: **14** Albrecht Kossel
1911: **16** Allvar Gullstrand
1912: **12** Alexis Carrel
1913: **14** Charles R Richet
1914: **12** Robert Barany
1919: **11** Jules Bordet
1920: **12** Shack A S Krogh
1922: **12** Otto Meyerhof **14** Archibald V Hill
1923: **13** John J R Macleod **20** Sir Frederick G Banting
1924: **15** Willem Einthoven
1926: **15** Johannes Fibiger
1927: **19** Julius Wagner-Jauregg
1928: **16** Charles J H Nicolle
1929: **17** Christiaan Eijkman **20** Sir Frederick G Hopkins
1930: **15** Karl Landsteiner
1931: **12** Otto H Warburg
1932: **12** Edgar D Adrian **21** Sir Charles Sherrington
1933: **13** Thomas H Morgan
1934: **12** George R Minot **14** George H Whipple, William P Murphy
1935: **11** Hans Spemann
1936: **9** Otto Loewi **13** Sir Henry H Dale

1937: **31** Albert Szent-Gyorgyi von Nagyrapolt
1938: **16** Corneille Heymans
1939: **13** Gerhard Domagk
1943: **9** Henrik Dam **12** Edward A Doisy
1944: **14** Herbert S Gasser, Joseph Erlanger
1945: **11** Ernst B Chain **16** Sir Howard W Florey **19** Sir Alexander Fleming
1946: **14** Hermann J Muller
1947: **9** Carl F Cori **10** Gerty T Cori **16** Bernardo A Houssay
1948: **11** Paul H Muller
1949: **11** Walter R Hess **21** Antonio C de A F Egas Moniz
1950: **12** Philip S Hench **14** Edward C Kendall **16** Tadeus Reichstein
1951: **10** Max Theiler
1952: **14** Selman A Waksman
1953: **13** Fritz A Lipmann, Sir Hans A Krebs
1954: **11** John F Enders **13** Thomas H Weller **17** Frederick C Robbins
1955: **14** Axel H T Theorell
1956: **13** Andre Cournand **15** Werner Forssmann **20** Dickenson W Richards Jr
1957: **11** Daniel Bovet
1958: **12** Edward L Tatum **13** George W Beadle **15** Joshua Lederberg
1959: **11** Severo Ochoa **14** Arthur Kornberg
1960: **13** Peter B Medawar **15** Sir Frank M Burnet
1961: **14** Georg von Bekesy
1962: **12** James D Watson **14** Francis H C Crick **16** Maurice H F Wilkins
1963: **16** Alan Lloyd Hodgkin **18** Sir John Carew Eccles **20** Andrew Fielding Huxley
1964: **11** Feodor Lynen **12** Konrad E Bloch
1965: **10** Andre Lwoff **12** Jacques Monod **13** Francois Jacob
1966: **17** Francis Peyton Rous **21** Charles Brenton Huggins
1967: **10** George Wald **12** Ragnar Granit **20** Haldan Keffer Hartline
1968: **13** Robert W Holley **14** H Gobind Khorana **18** Marshall W Nirenberg
1969: **11** Max Delbruck **14** Alfred D Hershey, Salvador E Luria
1970: **11** Ulf von Euler **13** Julius Axelrod **14** Sir Bernard Katz
1971: **17** Earl W Sutherland Jr
1972: **13** Rodney R Porter **14** Gerald M Edelman
1973: **12** Konrad Lorenz **13** Karl von Frisch **17** Nikolaas Tinbergen
1974: **12** Albert Claude **15** Christian de Duve **16** George Emil-Palade
1975: **12** Howard M Temin **14** Da-

vid Baltimore, Renato Dulbecco
1976: **15** Baruch S Blumberg **22** Daniel Carleton Gajdusek
1977: **13** Andrew Schally, Rosalyn S Yalow **14** Roger Guillemin
1978: **11** Werner Arber **13** Daniel Nathans, Hamilton Smith
1979: **13** Allan M Cormack **17** Godfrey Hounsfield
1980: **11** Jean Dausset **12** George D Snell **15** Baruj Benacerraf
1981: **11** David H Hubel **12** Roger W Sperry **17** Torsten N Wiesel
1982: **9** John R Vane **15** Bengt Samuelsson **17** Sune Karl Bergstrom
1983: **17** Barbara McClintock
1984: **11** Niels K Jerne **13** Cesar Milstein **16** Georges J F Koehler
1985: **13** Michael S Brown **16** Joseph L Goldstein
1986: **12** Stanley Cohen **18** Rita Levi-Montalcini
1987: **14** Susumu Tonegawa
1988: **10** James Black **14** Gertrube B Elion **16** George H Hitchings
1989: **12** Harold Varmas **14** J Michael Bishop
1990: **12** Joseph Murray **14** E Donnall Thomas
1991: **10** Edwin Neher **11** Bert Sakmann
1992: **10** Edwin Krebs **12** Edmond Fisher
1993: **12** Phillip Sharp **14** Richard Roberts
1994: **12** Alfred Gilman **13** Martin Rodbell
1995: **12** Edward B Lewis **14** Eric F Wieschaus
1996: **13** Peter C Doherty **16** Rolf M Ziwkernagel
1997: **16** Stanley B. Prusiner

Chemistry:
1901: **16** Jacobus H van't Hoff
1902: **11** Emil Fischer
1903: **16** Svante A Arrhenius
1904: **16** Sir William Ramsay
1905: **17** J F W Adolf von Baeyer
1906: **12** Henri Moissan
1907: **13** Eduard Buchner
1908: **19** Sir Ernest Rutherford
1909: **14** Wilhelm Ostwald
1910: **11** Otto Wallach
1911: **11** Marie S Curie
1912: **12** Paul Sabatier **14** Victor Grignard
1913: **12** Alfred Werner
1914: **17** Theodore W Richards
1915: **18** Richard Willstatter
1918: **10** Fritz Haber
1920: **13** Walther Nernst
1921: **14** Frederick Soddy
1922: **13** Francis W Aston
1923: **10** Fritz Pregl
1925: **16** Richard Zsigmondy
1926: **15** Theodor Svedberg
1927: **15** Heinrich Wieland

1928: 12 Adolf Windaus
1929: 15 Sir Arthur Harden **19** Hans von Euler-Chelpin
1930: 11 Hans Fischer
1931: 9 Carl Bosch **16** Friedrich Bergius
1932: 14 Irving Langmuir
1934: 11 Harold C Urey
1935: 16 Irene Joliot-Curie **19** Frederic Joliot-Curie
1936: 12 Peter J W Debye
1937: 10 Paul Karrer **17** Sir Walter N Haworth
1938: 11 Richard Kuhn
1939: 14 Adolf Butenandt, Leopold Ruzicka
1943: 14 Georg von Hevesy
1944: 8 Otto Hahn
1945: 16 Artturi I Virtanen
1946: 12 James B Sumner **13** John H Northrop **15** Wendell M Stanley
1947: 17 Sir Robert Robinson
1948: 12 Arne Tiselius
1949: 15 William F Giauque
1950: 9 Kurt Alder, Otto Diels
1951: 13 Glenn T Seaborg **14** Edwin M McMillan
1952: 14 Archer J P Martin, Richard L M Synge
1953: 17 Hermann Staudinger
1954: 13 Linus C Pauling
1955: 17 Vincent du Vigneaud
1956: 15 Nikolai N Semenov **20** Sir Cyril N Hinshelwood
1957: 17 Sir Alexander R Todd (Baron Todd)
1958: 15 Frederick Sanger
1959: 17 Jaroslav Heyrovsky
1960: 13 Willard F Libby
1961: 12 Melvin Calvin
1962: 10 Max F Perutz **12** John C Kendrew
1963: 11 Giulio Natta, Karl Ziegler
1964: 26 Dorothy Mary Crowfoot Hodgkin
1965: 19 Robert Burns Woodward
1966: 15 Robert S Mulliken
1967: 12 Manfred Eigen **15** Sir George Porter **27** Ronald George Wreyford Norrish
1968: 11 Lars Onsager
1969: 9 Odd Hassel **13** Derek H R Barton
1970: 18 Luis Federico Leloir
1971: 15 Gerhard Herzberg
1972: 13 Stanford Moore **18** Christian B Anfinsen, William Howard Stein
1973: 16 Ernst Otto Fischer **17** Geoffrey Wilkinson
1974: 10 Paul J Flory
1975: 14 John W Cornforth, Vladimir Prelog
1976: 16 William N Lipscomb
1977: 13 Ilya Prigogine
1978: 13 Peter Mitchell
1979: 11 Georg Wittig **13** Herbert C Brown

1980: 8 Paul Berg **13** Walter Gilbert **15** Frederick Sanger
1981: 12 Kenichi Fukui **13** Roald Hoffmann
1982: 9 Aaron Klug
1983: 10 Henry Taube
1984: 21 Robert Bruce Merrifield
1985: 11 Jerome Karle **16** Herbert A Hauptman
1986: 8 Yuan T Lee **12** John C Polanyi **16** Dudley Herschbach
1987: 11 Donald J Cram **16** Charles J Pederson
1988: 11 Robert Huber **13** Hartmut Michel **17** Johann Deisenhofer
1989: 10 Thomas Cich **12** Sidney Altman
1990: 10 Elias Corey
1991: 12 Richard Ernst
1992: 13 Rudolph Marcus
1993: 10 Kary Mullis **12** Michael Smith
1994: 10 George Olah
1995: 11 Paul Crutzen, Mario Molina **16** F Sherwood Rowland
1996: 11 Robert F Curl **15** Richard E Smalley, Sir Harold W Kroto
1997: 9 Jens C Skou **10** Paul D Boyer **11** John E Walker

Physics:
1901: 16 Wilhelm K Roentgen
1902: 12 Pieter Zeeman **15** Hendrik A Lorentz
1903: 11 Marie S Curie, Pierre Curie **15** A Henri Becquerel
1904: 11 John W Strutt (Lord Rayleigh)
1905: 13 Philipp Lenard
1906: 16 Sir Joseph Thomson
1907: 16 Albert A Michelson
1908: 15 Gabriel Lippmann
1909: 10 Karl F Braun **16** Guglielmo Marconi
1910: 20 Johannes D van der Waals
1911: 11 Wilhelm Wien
1912: 10 Nils G Dalen
1913: 20 Heike Kamerlingh Onnes
1914: 10 Max von Laue
1915: 16 Sir William H Bragg, Sir William L Bragg
1917: 14 Charles B Barkla
1918: 9 Max Planck
1919: 13 Johannes Stark
1920: 17 Charles E Guillaume
1921: 14 Albert Einstein
1922: 10 Nils H D Bohr
1923: 15 Robert A Millikan
1924: 14 Karl M G Siegbahn
1925: 12 Gustav Hertz, James Franck
1926: 11 Jean B Perrin
1927: 14 Arthur H Compton **15** Charles T R Wilson
1928: 18 Sir Owen W Richardson
1929: 15 Louis V de Broglie
1930: 23 Sir Chandrasekhara V Raman

1932: 16 Werner Heisenberg
1933: 11 Paul A M Dirac **16** Erwin Schrodinger
1935: 16 Sir James Chadwick
1936: 11 Victor F Hess **13** Carl D Anderson
1937: 16 Clinton J Davisson **17** Sir George P Thomson
1938: 11 Enrico Fermi
1939: 15 Ernest O Lawrence
1943: 9 Otto Stern
1944: 11 Isidor I Rabi
1945: 13 Wolfgang Pauli
1946: 12 Percy W Bridgman
1947: 18 Sir Edward V Appleton
1948: 17 Patrick M S Blackett
1949: 12 Hideki Yukawa
1950: 12 Cecil F Powell
1951: 14 Ernest T S Walton **17** Sir John D Cockcroft
1952: 10 Felix Bloch **14** Edward M Purcell
1953: 12 Frits Zernike
1954: 7 Max Born **12** Walther Bothe
1955: 13 Polykarp Kusch, Willis E Lamb Jr
1956: 11 John Bardeen **15** Walter H Brattain **16** William B Shockley
1957: 11 Tsung Dao Lee **12** Chen Ning Yang
1958: 9 Igor Y Tamm **10** Ilya M Frank **15** Pavel A Cherenkov
1959: 11 Emilio Segre **15** Owen Chamberlain
1960: 13 Donald A Glaser
1961: 16 Robert Hofstadter, Rudolf L Mossbauer
1962: 10 Lev D Landau
1963: 11 J Hans Jensen **16** Eugene Paul Wigner **18** Maria Goeppert Mayer
1964: 17 Charles Hard Townes **25** Nikolai Gennadiyevich Basov **30** Aleksandr Mikhailovich Prokhorov
1965: 18 Shinichiro Tomonaga **22** Julian Seymour Schwinger, Richard Phillips Feynman
1966: 13 Alfred Kastler
1967: 17 Hans Albrecht Bethe
1968: 12 Luis W Alvarez
1969: 14 Murray Gell-Mann
1970: 12 Hannes Alfven **15** Louis Eugene Neel
1971: 11 Dennis Gabor
1972: 11 John Bardeen, Leon N Cooper **20** John Robert Schreiffer
1973: 8 Leo Esaki **11** Ivar Giaever **15** Brian D Josephson
1974: 12 Antony Hewish **13** Sir Martin Ryle
1975: 8 Aage Bohr **13** Ben R Mottelson **15** L James Rainwater
1976: 12 Samuel C C Ting **13** Burton Richter
1977: 13 John H Van Vleck, Sir Nevill Mott **15** Philip W Anderson
1978: 12 Arno A Penzias, Peter

Kapitza (Pyotr Kapitsa) **13** Robert W Wilson
1979: 10 Abdus Salam **14** Sheldon Glashow, Steven Weinberg
1980: 9 Val L Fitch **12** James W Cronin
1981: 12 Kai M Siegbahn **14** Arthur Schawlow **19** Nicolaas Bloembergen
1982: 14 Kenneth G Wilson
1983: 14 William A Fowler **25** Subrahmanyan Chandrasekhar
1984: 11 Carlo Rubbia **15** Simon van der Meer
1985: 16 Klaus von Klitzing
1986: 10 Ernst Ruska, Gerd Binner **14** Heinrich Rohrer
1987: 12 K Alex Mueller **13** J Georg Bednorz
1988: 13 Leon M Lederman **14** Melvin Schwartz **15** Jack Steinberger
1989: 11 Hans Dehmelt **12** Norman Ramsey, Wolfgang Paul
1990: 12 Henry Kendall **13** Richard Taylor **14** Jerome Friedman
1991: 12 Pierre Gennes
1992: 13 George Charpak
1993: 12 Joseph Taylor, Russell Hulse
1994: 13 Clifford Shull **17** Bertram Brockhouse
1995: 11 Martin l Perl **15** Frederick Reines
1996: 9 David M Lee **16** Douglas D Osheroff **17** Robert C Richardson
1997: 9 Steven Chu **11** William D Phillips **20** Claude Cohen-Tannoudji

Peace:
1901: 13 Frederic Passy **15** Jean Henri Dunant
1902: 12 Elie Ducommun **18** Charles Albert Gobat
1903: 17 Sir William R Cremer
1904: 27 Institute of International Law
1905: 24 Baroness Bertha von Suttner
1906: 17 Theodore Roosevelt
1907: 12 Louis Renault **14** Ernesto T Moneta
1908: 12 Fredrik Bajer **14** Klas P Arnoldson
1909: 16 Auguste Beernaert **35** Paul H Balluat d'Estournelles de Constant
1910: 24 International Peace Bureau
1911: 12 Alfred H Fried **13** Tobias M C Asser
1912: 9 Elihu Root
1913: 15 Henri La Fontaine
1917: 30 International Red Cross Committee
1919: 13 Woodrow Wilson
1920: 12 Leon Bourgeois
1921: 15 Christian L Lange **19** Karl Hjalmar Branting

1922: 14 Fridtjof Nansen
1925: 13 Charles G Dawes **26** Sir Joseph Austen Chamberlain
1926: 14 Aristide Briand **16** Gustav Stresemann
1927: 12 Ludwig Quidde **17** Ferdinand E Buisson
1929: 12 Frank B Kellogg
1930: 15 (Lars Olof Jonathan) Nathan Soderblom
1931: 10 Jane Addams **20** Nicholas Murray Butler
1933: 15 Sir Norman Angell
1934: 15 Arthur Henderson
1935: 16 Carl von Ossietzky
1936: 19 Carlos Saavedra Lamas
1937: 13 E A Robert Cecil (Viscount Cecil)
1938: 36 Nansen International Office for Refugees
1944: 30 International Red Cross Committee
1945: 11 Cordell Hull
1946: 9 John R Mott **11** Emily G Balch
1947: 21 Friends Service Council **31** American Friends Service Committee
1949: 11 John Boyd Orr (Baron Orr)
1950: 12 Ralph J Bunche
1951: 11 Leon Jouhaux
1952: 16 Albert Schweitzer
1953: 15 George C Marshall
1954: 51 Office of the United Nations High Commissioner for Refugees
1957: 14 Lester B Pearson
1958: 28 Rev Dominique Georges Henri Pire
1959: 16 Philip J Noel-Baker
1960: 14 Albert J Luthuli
1961: 15 Dag Hammarskjold
1962: 13 Linus C Pauling
1963: 25 League of Red Cross Societies **30** International Red Cross Committee
1964: 18 Martin Luther King Jr
1965: 26 United Nations Children's Fund (UNICEF)
1968: 10 Rene Cassin
1969: 30 International Labor Organization (ILO)
1970: 14 Norman E Borlaug
1971: 11 Willy Brandt
1973: 8 Le Duc Tho **15** Henry A Kissinger
1974: 10 Eisaku Sato **12** Sean MacBride
1975: 15 Andrei D Sakharov
1976: 13 Betty Williams **15** Mairead Corrigan
1977: 20 Amnesty International
1978: 10 Anwar Sadat **13** Menachem Begin
1979: 12 Mother Teresa
1980: 19 Adolfo Perez Esquivel
1981: 51 Office of the United Na-

tions High Commissioner for Refugees
1982: 10 Alva Myrdal **19** Alfonso Garcia Robles
1983: 10 Lech Walesa
1984: 17 Bishop Desmond Tutu
1985: 51 International Physicians for the Prevention of Nuclear War
1986: 10 Elie Wiesel
1987: 17 Oscar Arias Sanchez
1988: 31 United Nations peacekeeping troops
1989: 9 Dalai Lama
1990: 16 Mikhail Gorbachev
1991: 13 Aung San Suu Kyi
1992: 15 Rigoberta Menchu
1993: 9 F W de Klerk **13** Nelson Mandela
1994: 11 Yasir Arafat, Shimon Peres **12** Yitzhak Rabin
1995: 13 Joseph Rotblat
1996: 14 Jose Ramos Horta **23** Carlos Filepe, Ximenes Belo
1997: 12 Jody Williams

Economics:
1969: 12 Jan Tinbergen, Ragnar Frisch
1970: 14 Paul A Samuelson
1971: 13 Simon S Kuznets
1972: 13 Kenneth J Arrow, Sir John R Hicks
1973: 15 Wassily Leontief
1974: 12 Gunnar Myrdal **18** Friedrich A von Hayek
1975: 17 Tjalling C Koopmans **18** Leonid V Kantorovich
1976: 14 Milton Friedman
1977: 11 Bertil Ohlin, James E Meade
1978: 13 Herbert A Simon
1979: 14 Sir Arthur Lewis **15** Theodore Schultz
1980: 14 Lawrence R Klein
1981: 10 James Tobin
1982: 14 George J Stigler
1983: 12 Gerard Debreu
1984: 15 Sir Richard Stone
1985: 16 Franco Modigliani
1986: 19 James McGill Buchanan
1987: 12 Robert M Solow
1988: 13 Maurice Allais
1989: 14 Trygve Haavelmo
1990: 12 Merton Miller **13** William Sharpe **14** Harry Markowitz
1991: 11 Ronald Coase
1992: 10 Gary Becker
1993: 11 Robert Fogel **12** Douglas North
1994: 8 John Nash **12** John Harsanyi **14** Reinhard Selten
1995: 14 Robert E Lucas Jr.
1996: 14 James A Mirrlees **15** William S Vickrey
1997: 13 Myron S Scholes, Robert C Merton

nobility 5 elite, lords **7** dignity, majesty, peerage, primacy, royalty **8** breeding, eminence, grandeur, high rank, prestige, splendor **9** gentility, grandness, greatness, loftiness, sublimity, supremacy **10** blue bloods, mightiness, patricians, patriciate, upper crust **11** aristocracy, distinction, exaltedness, preeminence, stateliness, superiority **12** magnificence

nobility obliges
  French: **14** noblesse oblige

noble 3 don **4** high, just, lord, peer **5** famed, grand, great, lofty, moral, regal, royal **6** famous, gentle, honest, knight, lordly, squire, superb, worthy **7** awesome, courtly, eminent, ethical, exalted, grandee, stately, sublime, supreme, upright **8** baronial, cavalier, elevated, glorious, handsome, highborn, imperial, imposing, lordlike, majestic, princely, renowned, selfless, splendid, superior, virtuous **9** chevalier, dignified, estimable, excellent, exemplary, gentleman, honorable, patrician, personage, reputable **10** aristocrat, impressive, preeminent **11** magnanimous, magnificent, meritorious, pureblooded, trustworthy **12** aristocratic, thoroughbred **13** distinguished, incorruptible
  French: **6** gentil

Noble House
  author: **12** James Clavell

nobleman 4 lord, peer **7** grandee **9** patrician **10** aristocrat

noblesse oblige 15 nobility obliges

noblewoman 4 dame, lady, rani **5** begum, queen **6** milady **7** czarina, duchess, empress, peeress, sultana **8** baroness, contessa, countess, maharani, princess **11** marchioness

Nobody Knows My Name
  author: **12** James Baldwin

nock 5 notch
  in: **5** arrow

nocturnal 4 dark **5** night **7** nightly, obscure **8** darkling **9** nighttime

nod 3 bob **4** doze, hail, show, sign **5** agree, greet, lapse, let up **6** assent, beckon, concur, drowse, motion, reveal, salute, signal **7** consent, drop off, fall off, gesture, signify **9** recognize

node 3 bud **4** bump, burl, hump, knob, knot, lump **5** bulge, joint **6** button **8** swelling **10** prominence, tumescence **11** excrescence **12** protuberance

nodule 3 sac, wen **4** bump, cyst, knob, knot, lump, stud **5** bulge **6** growth **8** swelling **9** outgrowth **10** projection, prominence, protrusion, tumescence **11** excrescence **12** protuberance

noel, Noel 4 yule **5** carol **8** yuletide **9** Christmas **13** Christmastide

No Exit
  author: **14** Jean-Paul Sartre

noggin 3 cup, mug **4** bean, head, pate **5** gourd **6** noodle

Noggs, Newman
  character in: **16** Nicholas Nickleby
  author: **7** Dickens

Noguchi, Hideyo
  field: **12** bacteriology
  nationality: **8** Japanese
  isolated: **8** syphilis

noise 3 ado, din **4** bang, blab, boom, echo, pass, roar, stir, wail **5** babel, blare, blast, bruit, rumor, sound, voice **6** bedlam, clamor, hubbub, racket, repeat, report, rumble, tumult, uproar **7** barrage, bluster, clatter, thunder **8** brawling, gabbling, rumbling, shouting **9** cacophony, cannonade, circulate, commotion, discharge **10** dissonance, hullabaloo **11** pandemonium **12** caterwauling, vociferation **13** reverberation

noiseless 5 quiet, still, tacit **6** hushed, silent **9** soundless, voiceless

noisemaker 4 bell, horn **5** siren **6** rattle **7** clacker, clapper, snapper, whistle

noisome 4 foul, rank **5** acrid, fetid, toxic **6** putrid, rotten, smelly **7** baneful, harmful, hurtful, noxious, reeking **8** mephitic, stinking **9** injurious, offensive, poisonous, unhealthy **10** malodorous, nauseating, pernicious **11** deleterious, detrimental **12** evil-smelling

noisy 4 loud **5** alive **6** lively, raging, shrill, stormy **7** blaring, blatant, furious, grating, jarring, rackety **8** animated, piercing, strident **9** clamorous, deafening, dissonant, turbulent **10** boisterous, clangorous, discordant, rampageous, resounding, thundering, thunderous, tumultuous, uproarious **11** cacophonous, tempestuous **12** earsplitting

Nolan, Lloyd
  born: **14** San Francisco CA
  roles: **22** Lieutenant Colonel Queeg **26** The Caine Mutiny Court Martial

Nolde, Emil
  real name: **10** Emil Hansen
  born: **5** Nolde **7** Germany
  artwork: **7** Prophet **10** Papua Youth **11** Tropical Sun **12** The Magicians, The Pentecost **13** The Last Supper, Three Russians **14** Doubting Thomas **20** Life of Maria Aegyptica **22** Christ Among the Children, Christ and the Adulteress

nolens volens 10 willy-nilly **19** whether willing or not

noli me tangere 10 touch me not

nolle prosequi 14 do not prosecute **19** be unwilling to pursue

nolo contendere 21 I am unwilling to contend

no longer able to fight
  French: **12** hors de combat

no longer in existence 4 dead, gone, lost **7** defunct, died out, extinct **8** vanished

Nolte, Nick
  born: **7** Omaha NE
  roles: **5** U-Turn, Weeds **7** The Deep, Cape Fear **10** Cannery Row **11** Lorenzo's Oil, Mother Night **12** I Love Trouble **13** Prince of Tides **14** Rich Man Poor Man **15** Forty-Eight Hours **16** North Dallas Forty

nomad 4 arab, hobo, okie **5** gypsy, mover, rover, stray, tramp **6** roamer **7** migrant, rambler, refugee, runaway, strayer, tuareg, vagrant **8** bohemian, emigrant, migrator, renegade, traveler, vagabond, wanderer **9** immigrant, itinerant, straggler

nomadic 6 roving **7** migrant, roaming, vagrant **8** drifting, vagabond **9** footloose, itinerant, migratory, strolling, traveling, wandering

nom de guerre 5 alias **7** war name **9** pseudonym **11** assumed name

nom de plume 5 alias **7** pen name **9** false name, pseudonym **11** assumed name, writing name

nomenclature 5 lingo, terms **6** jargon, naming **8** glossary, language, taxonomy **10** nomination, vocabulary

nominal 3 low **5** cheap, small **6** puppet **7** minimum, titular, trivial **8** baseless, moderate, official, so-called, trifling **9** pretended, professed, purported, suggested **10** groundless, ostensible, reasonable

nominate 3 tag **4** call, name, pick, term **5** elect, label, style **6** choose, invest, select **7** elevate, install, propose, suggest **9** authorize, recommend

nomination 8 election **9** accession, selection **10** suggestion

nominee 7 hopeful **8** aspirant, eligible **9** applicant, candidate **10** competitor, contestant

nonadjustable 5 fixed, rigid **9** immovable **10** inflexible

nonalcoholic 4 soft **15** nonintoxicating

nonattendance 3 cut **7** absence, truancy **11** absenteeism

nonbeliever 5 cynic, pagan **7** atheist, doubter, heathen, infidel, skeptic **8** agnostic, apostate **10** backslider, empiricist, questioner, unbeliever **11** disbeliever, freethinker **14** doubting Thomas

nonbinding 8 optional **9** voluntary **12** unimperative **13** discretionary

nonce 6 pro tem **7** present **9** time being

nonchalance 9 composure, unconcern **13** offhandedness
  French: **11** insouciance

nonchalant 3 lax **4** cool, idle, lazy **5** blase, slack **6** casual **7** languid, offhand, unmoved **8** careless, heedless, indolent, listless **9** apathetic, collected, easygoing, lethargic, unexcited, unheeding, unmindful, unruffled, unstirred, withdrawn **10** insensible, insouciant, phlegmatic, unaffected

noncombatant 7 neutral **8** civilian

noncommittal 3 mum **4** cool, mute, safe, wary **5** vague **7** careful, evasive, guarded, neutral, politic, prudent **8** cautious, discreet, reserved **9** ambiguous, equivocal, tentative **10** indecisive, indefinite, unspeaking **11** circumspect, temporizing

noncompliance 6 breach **7** failure, neglect **9** disregard **10** resistance **11** dereliction

noncompliant 6 unruly **7** defiant, froward, naughty, wayward **8** contrary, mutinous, perverse, stubborn **9** differing, dissident, fractious, objecting, obstinate, resistant, resistive, undutiful **10** disorderly, dissenting, rebellious, refractory, unorthodox, unyielding

non compos mentis 14 not of sound mind **17** mentally incapable

nonconfirming 7 denying **8** negating, refuting **9** rejecting **10** disavowing **11** disclaiming, repudiating

nonconformist 3 nut **4** beat, card **5** freak, hippy, loner, rebel **6** oddity, weirdo **7** heretic, oddball, radical **8** bohemian, crackpot, deserter, maverick, original, reformer, renegade, vagabond **9** character, dissenter, dissident, eccentric, exception, insurgent, protester, screwball **10** dissenting, iconoclast, rebellious, schismatic **13** individualist, revolutionary

nonconformity 5 quirk **6** oddity **7** anomaly **9** deviation, rebellion **10** aberration, divergence, resistance

noncongenial 6 unlike **8** opposite **9** different, disparate, ill-suited, unrelated **10** dissimilar **11** disagreeing **12** disagreeable, incompatible **13** unsympathetic

nondescript 5 usual, vague **8** ordinary **9** amorphous, colorless **11** stereotyped **12** unimpressive **13** characterless, undistinctive, unexceptional **15** undistinguished

nonentity 4 zero **6** cipher, nobody **7** nothing, no-count, nullity **8** small-fry, unperson **10** mediocrity

nonessential 5 frill **6** luxury, trivia **7** trivial **9** extrinsic, secondary, trimmings **10** accidental, extraneous, incidental, irrelevant, peripheral, subsidiary

nonexclusive 4 open **6** public, shared **7** divided **12** unrestricted

nonexistence 4 lack, void **7** absence **8** oblivion **11** nothingness

nonexistent 4 gone **5** short **6** absent **7** lacking, missing, wanting **11** unavailable **12** insufficient

nonindulgence 7 refusal **8** eschewal, forgoing **9** avoidance, eschewing

10 abstaining, abstention, refraining **11** forbearance **16** nonparticipation

nonirritating 4 calm **5** bland **6** benign **7** calming **8** soothing, tranquil **9** temperate

non licet 13 it is not lawful **16** it is not permitted

non liquet 12 it is not clear **14** it is not evident

nonmaterialistic 9 spiritual **10** idealistic **12** intellectual

nonmember 5 guest **7** outcast, visitor **8** outsider

nonnatural 7 manmade **9** synthetic **10** artificial, fabricated, factitious **12** manufactured

nonobservance 6 breach **7** failure, neglect **9** disregard **11** dereliction **13** noncompliance

non obstante 15 notwithstanding

no-nonsense 4 grim, hard **5** grave, harsh, rigid, sober, stern **6** ardent, intent, severe, solemn, strict **7** earnest, serious **8** critical, diligent, exacting, resolute **9** committed, dedicated, demanding, hardnosed, practical, pragmatic, unbending, unsparing **10** determined, hardheaded, purposeful, sobersided **12** businesslike

nonpareil 5 elite, ideal, model, super **6** symbol, unique **7** epitome, paragon, pattern, supreme **8** exemplar **9** unequaled, unmatched, unrivaled **10** apotheosis **11** exceptional, unsurpassed **13** extraordinary **14** representative

French: **11** ne plus ultra **14** creme de la creme

nonparticipation 7 refusal **8** eschewal, forgoing **9** avoidance, eschewing **10** abstaining, abstention, refraining, sitting out **11** forbearance

nonpartisan 4 fair, just **8** unbiased, unswayed **9** equitable, impartial, objective, unbigoted **10** impersonal, uninvolved **12** freethinking, unaffiliated, unimplicated, uninfluenced, unprejudiced **13** disinterested

nonpermissible 9 forbidden **10** disallowed **11** intolerable **12** inadmissible, unacceptable

nonplus 4 balk, faze, foil, halt, stop **5** abash, stump, upset **6** baffle, bother, dismay, muddle, puzzle, stymie **7** astound, confuse, disturb, mystify, perplex **8** astonish, bewilder, confound, deadlock **9** dumbfound, embarrass **10** disconcert **11** flabbergast **14** discountenance

nonplussed, nonplused 5 at sea, fazed **7** at a loss, baffled, floored, mixed-up, muddled, puzzled, stumped **8** confused **9** befuddled, mystified, unsettled **10** bewildered, confounded **12** disconcerted

nonpoisonous 4 safe **8** nontoxic **11** nonvenomous, nonvirulent

non possumus 8 we cannot

nonpresence 3 cut **7** absence, truancy **11** absenteeism

nonprofessional 3 lay **4** laic **7** dabbler

French: **7** amateur **10** dilettante

non prosequitur 15 he does not pursue

non repetatur 11 do not repeat

nonresident 7 tourist, visitor **9** transient **11** out-of-towner

nonresistance 6 assent **7** pliancy **8** docility, giving in, meekness, yielding **9** deference, obedience, passivity **10** compliance, conforming, conformity, pliability, submission **12** acquiescence, complaisance

nonresistant 4 meek **6** docile, pliant **7** passive, pliable **8** deferent, obedient, yielding **9** compliant **10** conforming, submissive **11** acquiescent, complaisant, deferential

nonscholarly 8 untaught **9** unlearned **10** uneducated, unlettered, unpedantic, unschooled

nonsectarian 10 ecumenical **11** interchurch **16** undenominational **17** nondenominational **19** interdenominational

nonsense 3 rot **4** bosh, bunk **5** folly, trash **6** antics, babble, drivel, joking, piffle **7** baloney, blather, bombast, chatter, fooling, garbage, hogwash, inanity, prattle, rubbish, trifles, twaddle **8** claptrap, flummery **9** absurdity, frivolity, gibberish, high jinks, horseplay, moonshine, silliness, stupidity **10** balderdash, flapdoodle, tomfoolery, triviality **11** foolishness, shenanigans **12** childishness, extravagance **13** facetiousness, ludicrousness, senselessness **14** ridiculousness **15** meaninglessness

nonsensical 4 wild **5** crazy, funny, inane, silly **6** absurd, stupid **7** asinine, comical, foolish **8** farcical **9** facetious, laughable, ludicrous **10** irrational, ridiculous

non sequitur 15 it does not follow

nonspecialized 11 generalized

nonspecific 4 hazy **5** vague **7** general, inexact **9** imprecise, uncertain **10** indefinite, undetailed **11** approximate, generalized

nonspiritual 7 earthly, profane, secular, worldly **8** material, temporal **13** materialistic

nonstop 7 endless, express **8** constant, unbroken **9** incessant **10** continuous, unrelieved **11** unremitting **12** interminable

nonstudious 9 unlearned **10** uneducated, unlettered, unpedantic, unschooled

nontaxable 9 sheltered **10** deductible

nontechnical 6 simple 8 academic 13 uncomplicated

nontypical 7 unusual 8 abnormal, uncommon 9 anomalous, irregular 16 unrepresentative

non-U *see* 12 Mitford, Nancy

nonuniform 5 mixed 6 unlike 7 altered, changed, erratic, unalike 8 changing, variable 9 deviating, different, irregular, multiform 10 dissimilar 11 fluctuating, nonstandard 12 inconsistent

nonvital 9 accessory, extrinsic 10 disposable, expendable, incidental 11 dispensable, superfluous, unessential, unimportant, unnecessary

nonvocational 8 academic

nonvolitional 6 reflex 8 unwilled 9 automatic 11 instinctive, involuntary, spontaneous 12 uncontrolled

noodle 4 bean, head, pate 5 gourd, pasta 6 noggin 8 practice 9 improvise

nook 3 den 4 cove, lair 5 haven, niche 6 alcove, cavity, corner, cranny, dugout, recess, refuge 7 retreat, shelter 8 hideaway 9 cubbyhole 10 depression 11 hiding place

noon 6 midday, zenith 8 high noon, meridian

no one contradicting
  Latin: 19 nemine contradicente

no one dissenting
  Latin: 18 nemine dissentiente

noose 3 tie 4 bond, hang, loop 5 catch, hitch, lasso, snare 6 choker, entrap, halter, lariat, tether

Nootka
  language family: 8 Wakashan
  tribe: 5 Makah 6 Hoiath, Ozette 7 Ahosath, Nitinat 8 Machlath, Otsosath, Tokwaath 9 Ihatisath, Mowachath, Nochalath, Qayokwath, Tsishaath, Yoloilath 10 Hishkwiath, Hochoqtlis, Manohisath, Tlaokwiath 11 Chiqtlisath, Hopachasath, Qiltsamaath
  location: 10 Washington 15 Vancouver Island
  leader: 8 Maquinna 10 Wikaninish
  related to: 5 Makah
  noted for: 7 whaling

Nordhoff, Charles
  author of: 17 Mutiny on the Bounty (with James Norman Hall)

Nordic Mythology *see* 21 Scandinavian Mythology

Norge *see* 6 Norway

noria 10 water wheel

norm 3 par 4 rule, type 5 gauge, model 7 average, measure, pattern 8 standard 9 barometer, criterion, yardstick 12 measuring rod

normal 3 fit, par 4 sane 5 sound, usual 6 steady 7 average, healthy, natural, regular, typical, uniform 8 constant, expected, mediocre, middling, ordinary, rational, reliable, standard 9 incessant, steadfast, unceasing 10 conforming, consistent, continuous, dependable, reasonable, unchanging 11 conformable, rightminded, unremitting 12 conventional 13 uninterrupted 14 representative

Normandy, Normandie
  beach: 4 Gold, Juno, Utah 5 Omaha, Sword
  borders: 7 Picardy 8 Brittany 14 English Channel
  church/shrine: 12 Saint Etienne 15 Mont Saint Michel
  city: 4 Caen, St. Lo 5 Rouen 7 Le Havre 9 Cherbourg
  event: 4 D Day 17 Operation Overlord
  region of: 6 France
  river: 5 Seine

Norma Rae
  director: 10 Martin Ritt
  cast: 9 Pat Hingle 10 Ron Liebman, Sally Field 11 Beau Bridges
  Oscar for: 4 song 7 actress (Field)
  song: 16 It Goes Like It Goes

Norn
  origin: 12 Scandinavian
  form: 6 virgin 7 goddess
  personifies: 4 fate
  original Norn: 5 Urdar
  the three: 4 Urd 5 Skuld 8 Verdandi
  known as: 12 weird sisters

Norris, Frank
  author of: 6 The Pit 8 McTeague 10 The Octopus

Norse Mythology
  abode of man: 7 Midgard 10 Mithgarthr
  afterworld: 6 Manala 7 Tuonela
  began race of giants: 4 Ymir
  blacksmith/hero: 9 Ilmarinen
  boar: 10 Saehrimnir
  bridge of gods: 7 Bifrost
  dragon: 6 Fafnir
  dwarf: 5 Skuld 7 Andvari
  earth is made from: 4 Ymir
  elf: 4 Norn 8 Verdandi
  epic: 8 Kaleva
  final battle: 15 Gotterdammerung 17 Twilight of the Gods
  first god: 4 Buri 7 Forsete, Forseti
  first man: 3 Ask
  first woman: 5 Embla
  folk hero: 8 Kalevala
  giant: 4 Loki 5 Jotun, Thrym 6 Thiazi, Thjazi 7 Skrymir
  giantess: 3 Urd 5 Thokk 9 Angerboda, Angrbodha, Angurboda
  giant's realm: 9 Jotunheim
  goat: 7 Heidrun
  goddesses: 7 Asynjur
  goddess of death: 3 Hel
  goddess of forbidden marriages: 4 Lofn
  goddess of marriage: 4 Frey 5 Freyr
  goddess of peace: 4 Frey 5 Freyr
  goddess of prosperity: 4 Frey
  5 Freyr
  goddess of spring: 4 Idun 5 Iduna, Ithun 6 Ithunn
  goddess of the sea: 3 Ran
  god of beauty/radiance: 5 Baldr 6 Balder, Baldur
  god of dawn: 8 Heimdall
  god of farming: 4 Thor
  god of fire: 4 Loki
  god of knowledge: 4 Odin 5 Othin
    corresponds to Germanic: 5 Wotan
  god of justice: 7 Forseti
  god of light: 8 Heimdall
  god of music: 5 Bragi
  god of navigation: 5 Niord, Njord
  god of poetry: 4 Odin 5 Bragi, Othin
    corresponds to Germanic: 5 Wotan
  god of prosperity: 5 Niord, Njord
  god of rain: 4 Thor
  god of sea: 5 Aegir, Mimir
  god of thunder: 4 Thor
  god of underworld: 8 Niflheim
  god of victory: 3 Tyr
  god of war: 4 Odin 5 Othin
    corresponds to Germanic: 5 Wotan
  god of wind: 5 Niord, Njord
  god of wisdom: 4 Odin 5 Othin
    corresponds to Germanic: 5 Wotan
  hero: 11 Vainamoinen 12 Lemminkainen
  home of dead: 3 Hel
  king: 5 Gjuki
  magician: 11 Joukahainen
  magic necklace: 11 Brisingamen
  misty void: 11 Ginnungagap
  mountain: 11 Hindarfjall
  nature spirit: 7 Eriking
  oak tree: 9 Barnstock, Branstock
  Odin's court/hall: 8 Valhalla
  Odin's father: 3 Bor
  Odin's horse: 8 Sleipnir
  Odin's magic ring: 8 Draupnir
  Odin's palace: 9 Gladsheim
  Odin's raven: 5 Hugin, Munin
  Odin's spear: 6 Gungni
  Odin's throne: 10 Hlidskjalf
  Odin's wolf: 4 Geri 5 Freki
  race of gods: 5 Vanir
  saga: 8 Vulsunga
  sea monster: 6 Kraken
  serpent: 7 Nidhogg 11 Jormungandr
  Sigmund's sword: 4 Gram
  slave: 8 Kullervo
  sorceress: 5 Louhi 8 Grimhild
  Thor's hammer: 7 Miolnir
  Thor's servant: 7 Thialfi
  tree with three roots: 9 Iggdrasil, Yggdrasil
  Valkyrie: 8 Brynhild 9 Brunhilde, Sigrdrifa 11 Brunnehilde
  virgin goddess: 3 Urd 4 Norn 5 Skuld, Urdar 8 Verdandi
  warrior: 8 Baresark 9 Berserker

watchdog: 4 Garm
wolf monster: 6 Fenrir, Fenris
north 5 polar, upper **6** arctic
North America
nation: 4 Cuba **5** Haiti **6** Belize, Canada, Mexico, Panama **7** Bahamas, Jamaica **8** Barbados, Honduras **9** Costa Rica, Guatemala, Nicaragua **10** El Salvador, Puerto Rico, Saint Lucia **12** Saint Vincent, United States **17** Dominican Republic, Trinidad and Tobago **28** Saint Vincent and the Grenadines
desert: 6 Mojave **7** Painted, Sonoran **11** Death Valley
island: 4 Long **6** Baffin, Cayman, Kodiak **7** Antigua, Bermuda, Iceland **8** Aleutian, Catalina, Thousand **9** Antilles, Greenland, Nantucket, Vancouver **10** Cape Breton **12** Newfoundland, Prince Edward **14** Queen Charlotte
ocean/sea/bay: 6 Arctic, Baffin, Bering, Hudson, Mexico **7** Chukchi, Lincoln, Pacific **8** Amundsen, Atlantic, Beaufort, Labrador **9** Caribbean, Greenland **10** California, Chesapeake, St Lawrence
river: 3 Red **4** Ohio **5** Peace, Snake, Yukon **6** Hudson **8** Arkansas, Colorado, Columbia, Missouri **9** Churchill, Mackenzie, Rio Grande **10** St Lawrence **11** Mississippi **12** Saskatchewan
lake: 4 Erie **5** Huron **7** Ontario **8** Michigan, Superior, Winnipeg **9** Great Bear, Nicaragua **10** Great Lakes, Great Slave
mountain range: 5 Ozark, Rocky **6** Alaska **7** Cascade **9** Blue Ridge **10** Laurentian **11** Appalachian, Sierra Madre **12** Sierra Nevada
highest point: 13 Mount McKinley
lowest point: 13 Death Valley
city: 4 Nome **5** Miami **6** Boston, Dallas, Denver, Havana, Ottawa, Quebec **7** Atlanta, Calgary, Chicago, Detroit, Houston, Memphis, New York, Phoenix, Seattle, Toronto **8** Montreal, Portland, San Diego **9** Anchorage, Milwaukee, Reykjavik, Vancouver **10** Kansas City, Los Angeles, Mexico City, New Orleans, Washington **11** Philadelphia, San Antonio, San Francisco
mineral: 3 oil, tin **4** coal, gold, lead, salt, zinc **6** cobalt, copper, nickel, quartz, silver **7** iron ore, mercury, sulphur, uranium **8** aluminum, antimony, asbestos, chromium, platinum, titanium, tungsten **9** magnesium, manganese, petroleum **10** molybdenum, natural gas
Northanger Abbey
author: 10 Jane Austen
character: 8 Mrs Allen **10** John Thorpe **12** James Morland **14** Isabella Thorpe **16** Catherine Morland

Tilney family: 5 Henry **7** Captain, Eleanor, General
North by Northwest
director: 15 Alfred Hitchcock
cast: 9 Cary Grant **10** James Mason **11** Leo G Carroll **12** Martin Landau **13** Eva Marie Saint **17** Jessie Royce Landis
setting (climax): 13 Mount Rushmore
score: 15 Bernard Herrmann
North Carolina
abbreviation: 2 NC **4** N Car
nickname: 7 Tar Heel **8** Old North **10** Turpentine
capital: 7 Raleigh
largest city: 9 Charlotte
others: 4 Bath **6** Durham, Lenoir, Shelby, Wilson **7** Edenton, Hickory, Kinston, New Bern, Roxboro, Tarboro **8** Gastonia **9** Albemarle, Asheville, Goldsboro, Henderson, Kitty Hawk, Lumberton **10** Chapel Hill, Greensboro, Greenville, Kannapolis, Wilmington **11** Statesville, Thomasville, Williamston **12** Fayetteville, Jacksonville, Winston-Salem
college: 4 Duke, Elon **7** Catawba **8** Davidson **10** Wake Forest
feature:
   battle site: 18 Guilford Courthouse
   national park: 19 Great Smoky Mountains (with Tennessee)
   national seashore: 11 Cape Lookout **12** Cape Hatteras
tribe: 3 Eno **5** Coree **6** Cheraw **7** Buffalo, Moratok, Pamlico **8** Chowanoc, Hatteras **9** Tuscarora
people: 6 O Henry (William Sidney Porter) **7** tarheel **11** Billy Graham, Thomas Wolfe **13** Dolley (Dolly) Madison, Edward R Murrow **14** Richard Gatling
   explorer: 6 de Soto **8** de Ayllon **9** Verrazano
island: 7 Roanoke
lake: 6 Norman, Phelps **7** Fontana **8** Waccamaw **12** Mattamuskeet
land rank: 12 twenty-eighth
mountain: 5 Black, Unaka **6** Harris **9** Blue Ridge **10** Great Smoky **13** Clingman's Dome
   highest point: 8 Mitchell
physical feature: 10 Outer Banks **11** French Broad **15** Little Tennessee
   cape: 4 Fear **7** Lookout **8** Hatteras
   plateau: 8 Piedmont
   sea: 8 Atlantic
   sound: 4 Core **5** Bogue **7** Croatan, Pamlico
   swamp: 6 Dismal
president: 9 James Polk **13** Andrew Johnson
river: 3 Haw, Tar **4** Fear **5** Neuse **6** Chowan, Lumber, Peedee, Yadkin **7** Roanoke, Wateree
state admission: 7 twelfth
state bird: 8 cardinal
state fish: 11 channel bass

state flower: 7 dogwood **9** goldenrod
state motto: 20 To Be Rather Than To Seem
state song: 16 The Old North State
state tree: 4 pine
state dance: 4 shag
North Dakota
abbreviation: 2 ND **4** N Dak
nickname: 5 Sioux **11** Flickertail **16** Land of the Dakotas
capital: 8 Bismarck
largest city: 5 Fargo
others: 5 Minot **9** Bottineau, Jamestown, Williston **10** Grand Forks
college: 4 Mary **9** Jamestown
feature:
   dam: 4 Oahe **8** Garrison
   garden: 18 International Peace
   national park: 17 Theodore Roosevelt
tribe: 5 Sioux **6** Mandan **7** Arikara, Hidatsa **8** Chippewa
people: 12 Eric Sevareid
   explorer: 6 Carver **8** Thompson, Varennes **13** Lewis and Clark
lake: 5 Stump **6** Devils **9** Sakakawea
land rank: 11 seventeenth
mountain: 6 Turtle **8** Killdeer **10** Black Butte
   highest point: 10 White Butte
physical feature:
   basin: 9 Williston
   plain: 8 The Slope
   valley: 8 Red River
river: 3 Red **4** Park, Rush **5** Cedar, Goose, Heart, James, Knife, Mouse **6** Souris **7** Deslacs, Pembina **8** Missouri, Cheyenne, Wild Rice **9** Otter Tail **10** Cannonball **11** Yellowstone **12** Boise de Sioux **14** Little Missouri **18** Red River of the North
state admission: 8 fortieth **11** thirtyninth (with South Dakota)
state bird: 17 western meadowlark
state fish: 12 northern pike
state flower: 15 wild prairie rose
state motto: 45 Liberty and Union Now and Forever One and Inseparable
state song: 15 North Dakota Hymn
state tree: 11 American elm
North Dallas Forty
director: 11 Ted Kotcheff
based on story by: 9 Peter Gent
cast: 8 Mac Davis **9** Nick Nolte **11** Dayle Haddon **14** Charles Durning
Northern Crown
constellation of: 14 Corona Borealis
Northern Rhodesia *see* **6** Zambia
North Korea *see* **5** Korea
North Star State
nickname of: 9 Minnesota
North Vietnam *see* **7** Vietnam
Northwest Passage
director: 9 King Vidor
author: 14 Kenneth Roberts
cast: 10 Ruth Hussey **11** Robert

Young **12** Spencer Tracy **13** Walter Brennan

Northwest Territories
  abbreviation: 3 NWT
  borders: 7 Alberta **8** Manitoba **9** Baffin Bay, Hudson Bay **11** Arctic Ocean, Beaufort Sea, Labrador Sea **12** Saskatchewan **15** British Columbia
  city: 6 Inuvik **8** Hay River **9** Fort Smith **11** Yellowknife **12** Frobisher Bay
  country: 6 Canada
  Inuit land: 7 Nunavut
  island: 5 Banks, Devon **6** Baffin **7** Melville **8** Bathurst, Somerset, Victoria **9** Ellesmere **11** King William **13** Prince of Wales, Prince Patrick **14** Queen Elizabeth
  mineral: 3 oil **4** gold, lead, zinc **6** silver **8** tungsten **9** petroleum
  mountain: 21 Mount Sir James MacBrien
  native: 5 Inuit **6** Eskimo
  territory: 8 Franklin, Keewatin **9** Mackenzie

North wind
  associated with: 6 Boreas

Norway
  other name: 5 Norge **20** Land of the Midnight Sun
  capital: 4 Oslo **11** Christiania
  largest city: 4 Oslo
  others: 3 Gol, Nes **4** Bodo, Moss, Odda, Rena, Voss **5** Bjort, Floro, Hamar, Molde, Skien, Skjak, Vadso **6** Bergen, Horton, Larvik, Narvik, Tromso **7** Alesund, Arendal, Drammen, Harstad, Sandnes **8** Aalesund, Kirkenes **9** Stavanger, Trondheim **10** Hammerfest **12** Kristiansand
  division: 3 Amt **4** Oslo **5** Fylke, Troms **6** Bergen, Opland, Tromso **7** Finmark, Hedmark, Ostfold **8** Letemark, Nordland, Rogaland, Vestfold **9** Ostlandet
    former: 11 Kalmar Union
    province called: 6 fylker
  government:
    legislature: 8 Storting
  head of state: 4 king
  measure: 3 fot, mal **4** alen **5** kande **6** fathom **7** skieppe **9** korntonde
  monetary unit: 3 ore **5** krone
  weight: 3 lod **4** mark, pund **10** bismerpund
  island: 4 Vega **5** Bomlo, Donna, Froya, Hitra, Hopen, Senja, Smola, Soroy **6** Alsten, Averoy, Bouvet, Hinnoy, Karmoy, Kvaloy, Solund, Vannoy **7** Gurskoy, Lofoten, Mageroy, Seiland **8** Jan Mayen, Svalbard
  lake: 4 Alte **5** Ister, Mjosa, Snasa **6** Femund **7** Rostavn, Tunnsjo
  mountain: 5 Sogne **6** Kjolen **7** Numedal **8** Blodfjel, Snohetta, Telemark, Ustetind **9** Harteigen, Jotunheim, Langfjell, Ramnanosi **10** Dovrefjell, Galdhoepig, Glitretind, Vibmesnosi **11** Myrdalfjell **14** Aardangerjokul, Hallingskarvet, Skagastolstind
  highest point: 12 Galdhopiggen **13** Glittertinden
  river: 3 Ena **4** Alta, Klar, Otra, Rana, Tana, Teno **5** Bardu, Begna, Glama, Lagen, Orkla, Otter, Rauma, Reisa **6** Glomma, Lougen, Namsen, Pasvik
  sea: 5 North **6** Arctic **7** Barents **8** Atlantic **9** Norwegian, Skagerrak
  physical feature:
    cape: 4 Naze **7** Nordkyn **8** Nordkapp **9** Lindesnes
    fjord: 4 Oslo **5** Sogne
    glacier: 12 Jostedalsbre
    inlet: 2 Is **3** Kob, Ran **4** Alst, Ands, Bokn, Nord, Ofot, Salt, Sunn, Tyri, Vest **5** fiord, fjord, Folda, Lakse, Sogne **6** Bjorna, Hadsel **7** Hortens **9** Trondheim
    plateau: 5 Doure, Dovre, Fjeld **9** Hardanger
  people: 4 Lapp **5** Samme **6** Nordic, Viking
    artist: 5 Munch
    author: 5 Ibsen **6** Hamsun, Undset **7** Holberg **8** Bjornson **9** Wergeland
    composer: 5 Grieg **7** Sinding **8** Svendsen
    explorer: 4 Eric, Leif, Mohn, Sars **6** Nansen **8** Amundsen
    explorer/statesman: 6 Nansen **8** Amundsen **9** Heyerdahl
    king: 4 Olaf, Olav **5** Olave, Oscar **6** Haakon, Harold, Magnus, Sverre
    mathematics: 4 Abel
  Nazi collaborator: 8 Quisling
  Norse god/goddess: 3 Sif, Tyr **4** Frey, Idun, Loki, Odin, Thor **5** Bragi, Freya, Hoder, Woden **6** Balder, Eostre, Frigga, Hermod
    sculptor: 8 Vigeland
  language: 4 Lapp **5** Norse **6** Bokmal **7** Nynorsk, Riksmal **8** Landsmal, Samnorsk **9** Landsmaal, Norwegian
  religion: 19 Evangelical Lutheran **22** National Church of Norway
  place:
    castle: 8 Akershus
    cathedral: 7 Nidaras
    museum: 7 Kon Tiki **10** Viking Ship **15** Polar Expedition
    park: 7 Frogner
  former colony: 7 Vinland
  feature:
    dance: 6 gangar **7** halling **8** springar **9** spingleik
    literature form: 4 edda, saga
  food:
    bread: 8 flat brod
    cheese: 3 Ost **7** gjetost **9** gammelost, Jarlsberg
    drink: 7 aquavit

Norwegian Mythology *see* **21** Scandinavian Mythology

nose
  sense of: 5 smell
  part: 7 nostril **14** olfactory patch

nosegay 4 posy **7** bouquet **10** tussymussy

nosiness 6 prying **9** curiosity **15** inquisitiveness

nostalgia 6 pining, regret **7** longing **11** remembrance **12** homesickness **13** regretfulness

Nostradamus
  name: 7 Michael **17** Michelde Notredame
  occupation: 7 prophet **9** physician **10** astrologer **13** metaphysicist
  wrote: 9 Centuries

Nostromo
  author: 12 Joseph Conrad

nostrum 4 balm, cure, dose, drug **5** draft **6** elixir, physic, potion, remedy **7** cure-all, formula, panacea **8** medicine **9** treatment **10** medicament **12** prescription

nosy, nosey 6 prying, snoopy **7** all ears, curious **8** snooping **9** intrusive **11** inquisitive, overcurious **13** eavesdropping

nota bene 8 note well **10** take notice

notability 4 fame **6** import, moment, renown **8** eminence **9** celebrity **10** importance, prominence **11** consequence, distinction, preeminence **12** significance

notable 3 VIP **4** name **5** famed, wheel **6** biggie, bigwig, famous, marked **7** eminent, salient **8** luminary, renowned, striking **9** celebrity, dignitary, personage, prominent, reputable **10** celebrated, pronounced, remarkable **11** conspicuous, outstanding, personality **13** distinguished

notably 7 visibly **8** markedly **10** distinctly, strikingly **11** prominently **12** unmistakably **13** conspicuously, outstandingly

not alike 8 distinct **9** different, differing, disparate, divergent **10** dissimilar **11** contrasting

notation 5 entry **10** memorandum

not bright 3 dim **4** dark, dull **5** dense, dusky, murky **6** cloudy, stupid **7** clouded **8** obscured **13** unilluminated

notch 3 cut **4** dent, mark, nick, nock **5** grade, level, score **6** degree **7** scoring, scratch **11** indentation

not disclosed
  Italian: 7 in petto

note 4 bill, fame, line, mark **5** bread, draft, enter, green, money, write **6** regard, renown **7** epistle, jot down, lettuce, message, missive, put down, scratch, set down, voucher **8** currency, dispatch, eminence, mark down, perceive **9** bank draft, celebrity, greenback **10** communique, importance, memorandum, prominence, reputation **11** certificate, consequence, distinction

notebook 3 log **5** diary **6** record **7** journal **9** looseleaf
　French: 6 cahier

noted 6 famous **7** eminent **8** renowned **9** prominent, reputable **10** celebrated, remarkable **11** illustrious, outstanding **13** distinguished

Notes from the Underground
　author: 16 Fyodor Dostoevsky

note well
　Latin: 8 nota bene

noteworthy 7 unusual **8** singular **9** important **10** remarkable **11** outstanding, significant, substantial **12** considerable **13** distinguished, exceptionable

not far from 4 near **6** all but, almost, nearly **7** close to **8** not quite **13** approximately

not genuine 4 fake, sham **5** bogus, false, phony **6** ersatz, unreal **7** feigned **8** spurious **9** imitation, insincere, pretended, synthetic **10** artificial, fraudulent **11** counterfeit **12** hypocritical
　Latin: 8 mala fide

not germane 9 extrinsic, unrelated **10** extraneous, immaterial, irrelevant **11** incongruous, inconsonant, unconnected **12** incompatible, nonessential **13** inappropriate

not guilty 5 clear **8** innocent **9** blameless **10** inculpable, unblamable

nothing 3 air, nix, zip **4** none, zero **5** stuff, trash, zilch **6** bauble, bubble, cipher, gewgaw, naught, trifle, trivia **7** duck egg, nullity, rubbish, trinket **8** goose egg **9** bagatelle, obscurity **14** insignificance **16** inconsequentials
　Latin: 5 nihil

nothing is created from nothing
　Latin: 16 ex nihilo nihil fit

nothingness 4 void **5** death **8** oblivion **9** emptiness **10** triviality **12** nonexistence **14** insignificance

Nothing Sacred
　director: 14 William Wellman
　cast: 13 Carole Lombard, Frederic March **14** Walter Connolly
　score: 11 Oscar Levant
　remade as: 10 Living It Up
　script: 8 Ben Hecht

nothing unless it is good
　Latin: 12 nil nisi bonum

nothing without the divine will
　Latin: 13 nil sine numine
　motto of: 8 Colorado

notice 3 eye, see **4** dope, heed, info, mark **5** goods **6** poster, rating, regard, review, take in **7** leaflet, mention, observe, warning **8** brochure, circular, critique, handbill, pamphlet **9** appraisal, attention, knowledge, statement **10** advisement, cognizance, disclosure **11** declaration, information

12 announcement, intelligence **13** advertisement, communication, specification

noticeable 5 clear, plain **7** evident, obvious **8** definite, distinct, manifest, palpable, striking **10** observable **11** appreciable, conspicuous, perceivable, perceptible **12** unmistakable

notification 4 news, word **6** advice, report **7** message, release **8** bulletin, dispatch **9** statement **10** communique **11** information **12** announcement, intelligence **13** communication

notify 4 tell, warn **6** advise, inform **7** apprise, let know **8** acquaint, send word **9** enlighten

not indigenous 5 alien **6** exotic **7** foreign **8** imported **9** nonnative **10** extraneous **11** naturalized

notion 4 idea, view, whim **5** fancy, humor, quirk **6** belief, vagary, whimsy **7** caprice, conceit, concept, opinion **8** crotchet **9** suspicion **10** conception, intimation **12** eccentricity

not native 5 alien **6** exotic **7** foreign **8** imported **10** extraneous **11** naturalized

not of sound mind
　Latin: 15 non compos mentis

not ordinary 4 rare **6** exotic, unique **7** bizarre, foreign, strange, unusual **8** peculiar, singular, uncommon **9** anomalous, different, fantastic **11** distinctive, outstanding **14** unconventional

notoriety 4 blot **5** shame, stain **6** infamy, stigma **7** scandal **8** disgrace, dishonor, ignominy **9** discredit, disrepute **11** degradation

notorious 6 arrant **7** blatant, glaring **8** infamous, renowned **9** egregious **10** celebrated, outrageous **11** outstanding

Notorious
　director: 15 Alfred Hitchcock
　cast: 9 Cary Grant **11** Claude Rains **12** Louis Calhern **13** Ingrid Bergman

not pertinent 9 unrelated **10** extraneous, immaterial, irrelevant **11** incongruous, unconnected **13** inappropriate

not quite 6 all but, almost, nearly

Notre Dame 9 cathedral
　style: 6 Gothic
　location: 5 Paris
　setting for: 20 Hunchback of Notre Dame
　feature: 7 statues **9** gargoyles

not required 8 elective, optional **9** voluntary

not too seriously
　Latin: 13 cum grano salis

Notus
　origin: 5 Greek
　personifies: 9 south wind

not wanted
　French: 6 de trop

notwithstanding
　Latin: 11 non obstante

not working 4 dead **8** inactive **10** unemployed **11** inoperative **12** unresponsive

Nouakchott
　capital of: 10 Mauritania

Noumea
　capital of: 12 New Caledonia

nourish 4 feed **5** nurse **6** suckle **7** nurture, sustain

nourishing 4 rich **6** hearty **7** healthy **9** fostering, nurturing, wholesome **10** nutritious, sustaining **11** maintaining **12** invigorating **13** strengthening

nourishment 4 chow, eats, food, grub, meat **5** bread **6** viands **8** victuals **9** nutriment, nutrition **10** sustenance **11** comestibles

nouveau riche 9 newly rich (person)

Novak, Kim
　real name: 19 Marilyn Pauline Novak
　born: 9 Chicago IL
　roles: 6 Picnic **7** Pal Joey, Vertigo **14** Of Human Bondage **17** Bell Book and Candle **20** The Jeanne Eagels Story **22** The Man with the Golden Arm **31** Amorous Adventures of Moll Flanders

Nova Scotia
　borders: 10 Bay of Fundy **12** New Brunswick **13** Atlantic Ocean **16** Gulf of St Lawrence **20** Northumberland Strait
　city: 5 Truro **6** Sydney **7** Amherst, Halifax **8** Glace Bay, Yarmouth **9** Dartmouth **10** New Glasgow
　country: 6 Canada
　island: 10 Cape Breton
　means: 11 New Scotland
　mineral: 3 oil **4** lead, salt, sand, zinc **6** barite, gravel, gypsum, silver **9** celestite, petroleum **10** natural gas
　mountain: 5 North **8** Cobequid
　part of: 6 Acadia **12** Appalachians **17** Maritime Provinces **18** Atlantic Provinces
　river: 4 Avon **5** Clyde **6** LaHave, Medway, Mersey **7** St Mary's **12** Shubenacadie

novel 3 new **6** unique **7** unusual **8** original, singular, uncommon **9** different **10** innovative, unorthodox **14** unconventional
　French: 5 roman

novelty 5 token **6** bauble, change, gewgaw **7** memento, newness, trinket **8** gimcrack, souvenir, surprise **9** bagatelle, variation **10** innovation, knickknack, uniqueness **11** originality

November
　event: 11 Election Day
　flower: 13 chrysanthemum
　French: 8 Novembre
　gem: 5 topaz
　German: 8 November
　holiday: 11 All Souls' Day (2),

Veterans Day (11) **12** All Saints' Day (1), Guy Fawkes Day (5), Thanksgiving (4th Thursday)
Italian: 8 Novembre
number of days: 6 thirty
origin of name: 5 novem (Latin meaning nine)
place in year:
  Gregorian: 8 eleventh
  Roman: 5 ninth
Spanish: 9 Noviembre
Zodiac sign: 7 Scorpio **11** Sagittarius

novice 4 tyro **5** pupil **7** amateur, learner, student **8** beginner, disciple, newcomer **9** greenhorn **10** apprentice, tenderfoot

Novum Organum
  author: 12 Francis Bacon

novus ordo seclorum 24 a new order of the ages is born
  author: 6 Vergil, Virgil
  work: 8 Eclogues
  motto of: 11 US Great Seal

Now, Voyager
  director: 12 Irving Rapper
  cast: 10 Bette Davis **11** Claude Rains, Janis Wilson, Paul Henreid **12** Gladys Cooper
  score: 10 Max Steiner

now and then 8 on-and-off, periodic, sometime, sporadic **9** irregular, sometimes, temporary **10** infrequent, occasional **11** irregularly **12** infrequently, occasionally, periodically, sporadically

Nox, Nyx
  goddess of: 5 night

noxious 4 foul **6** deadly, lethal, putrid **7** baneful, beastly, harmful, hurtful, noisome **8** damaging, virulent **9** injurious, loathsome, poisonous, revolting **10** abominable, disgusting, pernicious, putrescent **11** deleterious **12** foul-smelling

nth degree 5 limit **6** utmost **7** extreme

nuance 5 shade, touch **6** nicety **7** finesse **8** delicacy, fineness, keenness, subtlety **9** sharpness, variation **10** modulation, refinement **11** discernment

nub 4 core, crux, gist, hump, knob, knot, lump, node **5** bulge, heart **6** kernel **7** essence **8** swelling **10** projection, prominence, tumescence **11** nitty-gritty **12** protuberance

nubbin 3 ear **4** corn, lump, stub **5** bulge, fruit, piece, stump **10** diminutive

Nubbles, Kit
  character in: 19 The Old Curiosity Shop
  author: 7 Dickens

nubbly 5 lumpy, rough **6** coarse, knobby, pebbly

nucleus 3 nub **4** core, pith, seed **5** heart **6** center, kernel

nude 3 raw **4** bare **5** bared, naked **6** unclad **7** exposed **8** in the raw, stripped **9** unadorned, unarrayed, unclothed, uncovered, undressed
French: 9 au naturel

nudge 3 jab, jog, nod **4** bump, jolt, poke, prod, push **5** elbow, press, punch, shove, touch **6** jostle, motion, signal **8** indicate

nugatory 4 idle **5** empty **6** hollow, otiose, paltry **7** trivial, useless **8** piddling, trifling **9** meritless, valueless, worthless **10** profitless **11** ineffectual **12** functionless **15** inconsequential

nugget 4 hunk, lump **5** chunk, piece

nuisance 4 bore, fret, hurt, pain, pest **5** curse, thorn, worry **6** blight, bother, burden, plague **7** scourge, torment, trouble **8** handicap, vexation **9** annoyance, grievance **10** affliction, irritation, misfortune, pestilence **11** aggravation, botheration **13** inconvenience

Nuk
  capital of: 9 Greenland

Nukualofa
  capital of: 5 Tonga

null 2 NG **4** void **6** no good **7** invalid **9** valueless, worthless **10** immaterial **11** inoperative, nonexistent, unimportant **13** insignificant

nullification 6 repeal **7** voiding **8** recision **9** abolition, annulment **10** abrogation, rescinding **11** abolishment **12** cancellation, invalidation

nullify 4 veto, void **5** annul **6** cancel, repeal, revoke **7** abolish, rescind, retract **8** abrogate, make void, override, set aside **10** invalidate

nullity 6 cipher, naught **7** nothing **9** nonentity

numb 4 dead **6** frozen **8** deadened **9** insensate, unfeeling **10** insensible, narcotized **12** anesthetized

number 3 mob, sum, tot **4** army, bevy, book, herd, host, mass, part **5** array, bunch, count, crowd, digit, group, issue, swarm, tally, total **6** amount, cipher, figure, reckon, scores, symbol **7** chapter, company, compute, edition, foliate, integer, numeral, passage, section **8** division, estimate, magazine, numerate, paginate, quantity **9** abundance, aggregate, calculate, character, enumerate, multitude, paragraph, quarterly **10** assemblage, quantities **13** preponderance

numbered numbered weighed divided
  Aramaic: 21 mene mene tekel upharsin
  called: 16 writing on the wall
  foretells destruction of: 10 Belshazzar
  Biblical book of: 6 Daniel

numberless 6 myriad **7** copious, umpteen **8** unending, zillions **9** countless, plenteous, unbounded, uncounted

11 illimitable, uncountable **12** immeasurable **13** multitudinous

numbness 8 deadness **11** insentience

numeral 5 digit **6** cipher, figure, letter, number, symbol **7** integer **9** character

numerate 3 add **5** count, tally, total **6** number, reckon **7** compute, tick off **9** calculate

numerophobia
  fear of: 7 numbers

numerous 4 many **6** myriad **7** copious, profuse **8** abundant **9** plentiful **13** multitudinous

Numidia see **7** Algeria

Numipu see **8** Nez Perce

Numitor
  king of: 9 Alba Longa
  father: 5 Proca
  brother: 7 Amulius
  daughter: 10 Rhea Silvia
  grandson: 5 Remus **7** Romulus

numskull, numbskull 3 sap **4** dolt, dope, fool, jerk **5** dummy, dunce, idiot, klutz, ninny **6** dimwit, nitwit **7** dullard, half-wit **8** bonehead, dummkopf, imbecile, lunkhead, silly ass **9** blockhead, simpleton **10** dunderhead, muttonhead, nincompoop, noodlehead **11** chowderhead, knucklehead **12** scatterbrain

Nun see **4** Nunu

nuncio 5 envoy **6** legate **8** diplomat, minister **9** messenger **10** ambassador **11** papallegate **14** representative

nunnery 5 abbey, order **6** priory **7** cenacle, convent **8** cloister **9** hermitage, monastery **10** sisterhood

Nun's Story, The
  director: 12 Fred Zinneman
  based on story by: 12 Kathryn Hulme
  cast: 10 Dean Jagger, Edith Evans, Peter Finch **13** Audrey Hepburn, Peggy Ashcroft **15** Colleen Dewhurst

Nunu
  also: 3 Nun
  origin: 8 Egyptian
  god of: 5 ocean
  personifies: 5 chaos

nuptial 7 marital **8** conjugal, hymeneal **9** connubial **11** matrimonial

nuptials 7 wedding **8** marriage **9** espousals, hymeneals **12** matrimonials

Nurmi, Paavo
  nickname: 13 The Flying Finn
  sport: 5 track
  won: 8 Olympics

nurse 4 feed **5** nanny, treat **6** attend, doctor, foster, harbor, remedy, sister, succor, suckle **7** care for, nourish, nurture, promote **8** attend to, guardian **9** attendant, cultivate, encourage, governess
Hindi/Indian: 4 ayah
Orient: 4 amah

famous: 11 Edith Cavell, Sister Kenny **19** Florence Nightingale

nursery 6 hotbed **9** incubator, preschool **10** greenhouse, schoolroom **12** conservatory, kindergarten

nursery rhyme character 3 Tom **4** Jack, Jill, Mary **5** Peter, Polly **6** Bo-Peep **8** King Cole **9** Jack Sprat **10** Jack Horner, Miss Muffet **11** Mother Goose **12** Humpty Dumpty **13** Little Boy Blue, Mother Hubbard

nurture 4 feed, mess, rear, tend **5** breed, raise, teach, train, tutor **6** foster, school **7** bring up, develop, educate, nourish, prepare, sustain, victual **8** instruct, maintain **9** cultivate, provision **10** discipline, strengthen

Nusantara *see* **9** Indonesia

nut 3 fan, pit **4** buff, seed **5** freak, idiot, loony, stone **6** madman, maniac, zealot **7** devotee, fanatic, lunatic, oddball **8** crackpot **9** eccentric, screwball **10** aficionado, enthusiast, psychopath **11** afficionado

Nut
  origin: 8 Egyptian
  goddess of: 3 sky

nut-brown 5 tawny **6** auburn, brunet **8** brunette, cinnamon

Nutcracker, The
  also: 13 Shchelkunchik
  ballet by: 11 Tchaikovsky
  based on fairy tale by: 11 ETA

Hoffmann
  contains: 17 Waltz of the Flowers **24** Dance of the Sugarplum Fairy
  characters: 4 mice **5** Clara, Fritz **6** prince **10** nutcracker **11** toy soldiers **12** Drosselmeyer **14** Sugarplum Fairy

nutmeg
  botanical name: 17 Myristica fragrans
  from same plant as: 4 mace
  origin: 9 Indonesia
  use: 5 punch **6** eggnog **8** desserts **10** vegetables **11** baked dishes

Nutmeg State
  nickname of: 11 Connecticut

nutriment 4 chow, eats, fare, feed, food, meat, mess **5** board **6** fodder, forage **7** aliment, edibles **8** eatables, victuals **9** foodstuff, groceries, provender **10** provisions, sustenance **11** nourishment

nutrition 4 chow, feed, food, grub **6** fodder, forage, silage **7** edibles, rations **8** eatables **9** groceries, pasturage, provender **10** foodstuffs, provisions, sustenance **11** nourishment, subsistence

nutritious 9 wholesome **10** nourishing, sustaining

nuts 3 mad **4** bats, daft **5** balmy, crazy, dotty, loony, potty, wacko, wacky **6** insane **7** bananas, bonkers, cracked, touched **8** demented, deranged, unhinged **10** unbalanced

nutty 3 mad **4** daft **5** balmy, crazy, dippy, dotty, goofy, inane, loony, silly, wacko, wacky **6** cuckoo, insane, screwy, weirdo **7** bonkers, cracked, foolish, lunatic, meshuga, touched **8** bughouse, demented **9** senseless **10** addlepated, squirrelly **11** harebrained **12** crackbrained

nuzzle 3 pat, pet **4** buss, kiss **5** smack **6** caress, coddle, cosset, cuddle, fondle, nestle **7** embrace, snuggle

Nyasaland *see* **6** Malawi

nyctophobia
  fear of: 8 darkness **14** the dark of night

nyet
  Russian: 2 no

nymph 5 belle, dryad, houri, naiad, nixie, oread, sylph **6** beauty, daphne, kelpie, maenad, nereid, ondine, sprite, undine **7** charmer, galatea **8** Eurydice **9** hamadryad

Nymphaea
  epithet of: 9 Aphrodite
  means: 6 bridal

Nyx, Nox
  form: 7 goddess
  personifies: 5 night
  originated from: 5 Chaos
  children: 3 Ker **4** Eris **5** Fates, Geras, Momus, Moros, Oizys **6** Aether, Hemera, Hypnos, Somnus **7** Nemesis, Oneiroi **8** Thanatos

oaf 3 sap **4** boob, boor, clod, dolt, dope, fool, jerk, lout **5** booby, dummy, dunce, idiot, klutz, moron, ninny **6** lummox, nitwit **7** dullard, half-wit **8** bonehead, imbecile, numskull **9** blockhead, ignoramus, numbskull, simpleton **10** dunderhead, nincompoop

oafish 4 rude **5** crude **6** coarse, gauche, vulgar **7** boorish, doltish, loutish, uncouth **9** unrefined **10** unpolished

oak 7 Quercus
  varieties: 3 bur, cow, pin, red, she **4** bear, blue, cork, deer, Holm, jack, live, maul, post, silk **5** black, Emory, holly, scrub, ubame, water, white **6** basket, Belote, canyon, Ceylon, Daimyo, gambel, gander, Havard, Indian, island, Kermes, Konara, laurel, Oregon, poison, possum, Turkey, Turner, valley, willow, yellow **7** Ballota, Bartram, Belloot, Catesby, Durmast, English, Georgia, Italian, Kellogg, leather, Lebanon, overcup, scarlet, shingle, Spanish, tanbark, truffle, western **8** Arkansas, bluejack, chestnut, McDonald, mossy-cup, shinnery, Texas red **9** blackjack, Engelmann, flowering, Jerusalem, Mongolian, pubescent, swamp post **10** Chinquapin, Darlington, ring-cupped, Spanish red, swamp white **11** huckleberry, Japanese red, northern pin, northern red, Shumard's red **12** interior live, laurel-leaved, rock chestnut, southern live, yellow-barked **13** dwarf chestnut, oriental white, swamp chestnut **14** Austrian turkey, California live, yellow chestnut **15** California black, California field, California scrub, California white **16** high- ground willow **17** Japanese evergreen **18** Rocky Mountain scrub
  venerated by: 6 Druids

Oak, Gabriel
  character in: 22 Far From the Madding Crowd
  author: 5 Hardy

Oakie, Jack
  real name: 19 Lewis Delaney Offield
  born: 9 Sedalia (Sadalia) MO
  roles: 16 The Great Dictator **17** Alice in Wonderland

Oakland

baseball team: 2 A's **9** Athletics
football team: 8 Invaders

oar 3 row **4** pole **5** blade, rower, scull **6** paddle, propel **9** propeller
  blade: 4 palm, peel
  fulcrum: 5 thole **7** oarlock, rowlock
  part: 4 loom **5** shaft **6** collar

oarsman 5 pilot, rower **6** bowman **7** mariner, sculler **8** helmsman **9** gondolier, propeller

oasis 5 haven **6** asylum, harbor, refuge **7** retreat, sanctum, shelter **9** green spot, sanctuary, water hole **11** fertile area **13** watering place

oast 4 kiln, oven

oat, oats 5 Avena **11** Avena sativa
  varieties: 3 sea **4** wild **6** potato **8** animated **9** Tartarian **11** slender wild

Oates, Joyce Carol
  author of: 4 Them **9** Childwold **10** Bellefleur, Wonderland **11** Unholy Loves, Wheel of Love **15** Son of the Morning **18** A Bloodsmoor Romance **19** Do With Me What You Will

oath 3 vow **5** curse **6** avowal, pledge **8** cuss word, swearing **9** affidavit, blasphemy, expletive, obscenity, profanity **10** adjuration, deposition **11** affirmation, attestation, declaration, imprecation, malediction

oaths
  god of: 6 Horcus, Sancus **10** Dius Fidius, Semo Sancus

oatmeal 6 cereal **7** pottage **8** drammock, porridge

Obadiah 4 Obad **7** prophet **12** minor prophet
  father: 4 Azel **6** Jehiel **8** Izrahiah, Shemaiah
  son: 8 Ishmaiah
  predicted fall of: 4 Edom

Obata, Gyo
  architect of: 20 Dallas--Ft Worth Airport **25** National Air and Space Museum (Smithsonian Institution)

obdurate 5 cruel, harsh **6** mulish **7** adamant, callous, unmoved, willful **8** hardened, pitiless, stubborn, uncaring **9** immovable, merciless, obstinate, pigheaded, unfeeling, unpitying, unsparing, untouched **10** bullheaded, headstrong, inflexible, unmerciful, unyielding **11** cold-blooded, hardhearted, intractable **12** ungovernable, unman-

ageable **13** unsympathetic **14** uncontrollable **15** uncompassionate

obeah 5 charm, magic **6** fetish, voodoo **7** sorcery **10** witchcraft
  practiced in: 6 Guiana **10** West Indies

obedience 8 docility, yielding **9** deference, ductility, obeisance **10** accordance, allegiance, compliance, subjection, submission **11** conformance, dutifulness, willingness **12** acquiescence, subservience, tractability **14** conformability, submissiveness

obedient 5 loyal **6** docile **7** devoted, dutiful **8** amenable, faithful, obeisant, yielding **9** compliant, tractable **10** governable, law-abiding, respectful, submissive **11** acquiescent, deferential, subservient

obeisance 3 bow **5** honor **6** curtsy, esteem, fealty, homage, regard **7** loyalty, respect **8** courtesy, fidelity, humility, kneeling **9** deference, obedience, reverence **10** allegiance, humbleness, subjection, submission, veneration **11** prostration **12** genuflection **13** self-abasement

obelisk 5 pylon, shaft, tower **6** column, dagger, needle, pillar **8** memorial, monolith, monument

Oberon
  character in: 21 A Midsummer Night's Dream
  author: 11 Shakespeare
  consort: 7 Titania

Oberon
  opera by: 5 Weber
  character: 5 Reiza
  setting: 18 court of Charlemagne **21** court of Haroun al Rashid

Oberon, Merle
  real name: 26 Estelle Merle O'Brien Thompson
  husband: 14 Alexander Korda
  born: 8 Tasmania
  roles: 5 Hotel **7** Desiree **15** A Song to Remember **16** Wuthering Heights **19** The Scarlet Pimpernel **25** The Private Life of Henry VIII **30** The Private Life of Henry the Eighth

obese 3 fat **5** gross, heavy, plump, porky, pudgy, stout, tubby **6** chubby, fleshy, portly, rotund **7** paunchy **9** corpulent **10** overweight, potbellied

obesity 3 fat **7** fatness, liposis **8** adiposis, enormity **9** heaviness, plumpness, stoutness **10** corpulence, overweight

obey 4 heed, mind **5** bow to, serve **6** assent, concur **7** abide by, observe, respect, yield to **8** accede to, submit to **9** acquiesce, conform to, succumb to **10** comply with, toe the line **12** follow orders

obfuscate 4 blur **5** befog **6** garble, mess up, muddle **7** becloud, confuse, distort, fluster, obscure, stupefy **8** confound, scramble **10** complicate

obfuscation 8 flummery **9** confusion **10** doubletalk, mumbo jumbo

obi 4 sash **5** obeah **6** girdle

obiit 6 he died **7** she died

obiter dictum 9 diversion **10** digression, divagation, side remark

object 3 aim, end, use **4** body, butt, dupe, form, gist, goal, pith, prey **5** abhor, basis, cause, knock, point, sense, thing **6** balk at, carp at, design, device, dingus, gadget, intent, loathe, motive, oppose, quarry, reason, target, victim **7** article, cavil at, condemn, dislike, essence, frown on, meaning, mission, protest, purpose, subject **8** be averse, cynosure, denounce **9** abominate, criticize, doohickey, incentive, intention, objective, principle, recipient, substance **10** inducement, phenomenon **11** contrivance, explanation, thingamabob, thingamajig **12** be at odds with, disapprove of, significance **13** find fault with, take exception **18** remonstrate against

objection 4 beef, kick **5** cavil **7** protest **8** demurral, rebuttal **9** challenge, complaint, criticism, exception **10** dissension, opposition **11** disapproval, reservation **12** disagreement **13** contradiction **14** disapprobation, opposing reason **15** counter argument

objectionable 4 foul, vile **5** nasty **6** odious **8** unseemly **9** abhorrent, loathsome, obnoxious, offensive, revolting **10** abominable, despicable, disgusting, unbearable, unpleasant **11** displeasing, distasteful, intolerable, unendurable **12** disagreeable, unacceptable **13** inappropriate

objective 3 aim, end **4** fair, goal, just, mark, real **6** actual, design, intent, target **7** mission, purpose **8** detached, unbiased, unswayed **9** impartial, intention, uncolored **10** impersonal, open-minded **11** destination **12** uninfluenced, unprejudiced **13** disinterested, dispassionate

objectivity 8 fairness **10** detachment, neutrality **12** impartiality

object to 7 condemn, dislike **9** frown upon **12** disapprove of **14** discountenance **15** take exception to **16** find unacceptable

objet d'art 5 bijou, curio **7** bibelot, trinket **9** art object

oblation 4 gift **8** offering **9** offertory **10** collection

obligated 5 bound **6** forced, liable **7** pledged **8** beholden, indebted **9** committed **11** constrained

obligation 4 bond, care, debt, duty, oath, onus, word **6** charge, pledge **7** compact, promise **8** contract, guaranty, warranty **9** agreement, guarantee, liability **10** a favor owed, commitment, constraint **12** indebtedness **13** answerability, understanding **14** accountability, responsibility

obligatory 7 binding **8** coercive, enforced, required **9** mandatory, necessary, requisite **10** compulsory, imperative, peremptory **11** unavoidable

oblige 3 aid **4** bind, help, make **5** favor, force, impel, serve **6** assist, coerce, compel **7** require, support **8** obligate **9** constrain **11** accommodate, do a favor for, necessitate **13** do a service for, to be duty bound

obliged 5 bound **7** favored, pleased **8** assisted, beholden, indebted, required, thankful **9** compelled **12** accommodated

obliging 4 kind **6** polite **7** amiable, helpful **8** cheerful, friendly, gracious **9** agreeable, courteous **10** solicitous **11** complaisant, considerate, cooperative, good-natured, sympathetic **12** well-disposed **13** accommodating

oblique 3 sly **4** awry **5** askew **6** aslant, covert, hinted, masked, tilted, veiled **7** cloaked, devious, furtive, implied, slanted, sloping **8** allusive, diagonal, inclined, indirect, slanting, sneaking **9** suggested, underhand

obliterate 4 raze **5** erase, level **6** cancel, delete, efface, remove, rub out **7** abolish, blot out, destroy, expunge, wipe out **9** eradicate, write over **10** annihilate, strike over

obliteration 8 deletion **9** abolition, expunging, wiping out **11** blotting out, destruction, eradication **12** annihilation

oblivion 5 limbo **7** the void **9** blankness, disregard, obscurity, unconcern **11** blotting out, nothingness **12** nonexistence **13** forgetfulness, insensibility, obliviousness **14** insignificance **15** unconsciousness

oblivious 8 careless **9** forgetful, unaware of, unmindful **10** heedless of, insensible **11** inattentive, unconcerned, unobservant **12** disregardful, undiscerning **13** unconscious of

Oblonsky, Prince Stepan
    character in: 12 Anna Karenina
    author: 7 Tolstoy

obloquy 5 abuse, odium, shame **6** infamy, rebuke **7** calumny, censure, railing **8** contempt, disfavor, disgrace, ignominy, reviling **9** discredit, invective **10** defamation, opprobrium, scurrility **11** degradation, humiliation, verbal abuse **12** billingsgate,

condemnation, denunciation, dressing-down, vilification

obnoxious 4 foul, vile **5** nasty **6** odious **7** hateful **8** unseemly **9** abhorrent, loathsome, offensive, repellent, repugnant, revolting **10** abominable, despicable, detestable, disgusting, nauseating, unbearable, unpleasant **11** displeasing, intolerable, unendurable **12** disagreeable, insufferable **13** inappropriate, objectionable

oboe family
    instruments: 5 shawm **6** curtal, pommer, racket **7** bassoon, bombard, curtall, hautboy **8** crumhorn, schalmey, tenoroon **10** Cor Anglais, oboe d'Amore **11** English horn, heckelphone, sarusophone **12** oboe da caccia, sarrusophone **13** contra bassoon, double bassoon

O'Brian, Hugh
    real name: 11 Hugh J Krampe
    born: 11 Rochester NY
    roles: 9 Wyatt Earp **27** The Life and Legend of Wyatt Earp

O'Brien, Edna
    author of: 5 Night **11** A Pagan Place **13** The Lonely Girl **14** The Country Girl **20** August Is a Wicked Month **24** Girls in Their Married Bliss

O'Brien, Margaret
    real name: 18 Angela Maxine O'Brien
    born: 12 Los Angeles CA
    roles: 8 Jane Eyre **11** Little Women **15** Meet Me in St Louis **24** Our Vines Have Tender Grapes

O'Brien, Pat
    real name: 26 William Joseph Patrick O'Brien
    born: 11 Milwaukee WI
    roles: 12 Hildy Johnson, The Front Page **13** Some Like It Hot, The Last Hurrah **20** Angels with Dirty Faces **22** Knute Rockne All American
    autobiography: 12 Wind on My Back

obscene 4 blue, foul, lewd **5** bawdy, dirty **6** filthy, smutty, vulgar, x-rated **8** indecent, prurient **9** salacious **10** lascivious, lubricious **12** pornographic, scatological **16** morally offensive

obscenity 8 cuss word, lewdness **9** dirtiness, indecency, profanity, prurience, swear word, taboo word, vulgarity **10** filthiness, smuttiness **11** pornography **13** salaciousness **14** four-letter word, lasciviousness

obscuration 7 eclipse, masking, veiling **8** cloaking, clouding, covering **9** darkening, shadowing **10** concealing **11** concealment

obscure 3 dim, fog **4** blur, dark, hide, mask, veil **5** bedim, befog, block, cloak, cloud, cover, dingy, dusky, faint, murky, vague **6** cloudy, darken, hidden, muddle, screen, shadow, shroud, somber, unsung **7** becloud, conceal, confuse, cryptic, curtain, eclipse, shadowy, unclear, unknown, unnoted **8** befuddle, confused, disguise, nameless, puzzling **9** confusing, enigmatic, forgotten, lightless, obfuscate, uncertain, unheard of, unlighted **10** indefinite, indistinct, overshadow, perplexing, unrenowned **11** indefinable, inscrutable, little known, out-of-the-way, unimportant **12** unfathomable **13** inconspicuous, insignificant, unilluminated **15** inconsequential

obscurity 3 fog **4** mist **5** cloud, shade **6** shadow **7** dimness, mystery, opacity, privacy **8** darkness **9** ambiguity, seclusion, vagueness **10** cloudiness

obsequies 5 rites **6** burial **7** funeral **15** memorial service

obsequious 6 menial **7** fawning, servile, slavish **8** cowering, cringing, toadying **9** kowtowing, truckling **11** bootlicking, deferential, subservient, sycophantic **12** ingratiating, mealy-mouthed **14** apple-polishing

observance 4 rite **6** custom, regard, ritual **7** heeding, keeping, obeying **8** ceremony, practice **9** adherence, attending, attention, following, formality, solemnity **10** ceremonial, compliance **11** celebration, observation **13** commemoration **15** memorialization

observant 5 alert, awake, aware **7** careful, heedful, mindful **8** vigilant, watchful **9** attentive, conscious, regardful, wide-awake **10** perceptive **12** on the lookout

observation 4 heed, idea, view **5** probe **6** eyeing, notice, remark, search, seeing, survey, theory **7** comment, finding, opinion, viewing **8** interest, judgment, scrutiny, spotting, watching **9** assertion, attention, beholding, detection, diagnosis, discovery, glimpsing, observing, statement **10** cognizance, commentary, inspection, reflection **11** description, examination, heedfulness **12** surveillance, watchfulness **13** pronouncement **20** firsthand information

observatory 5 tower **7** lookout **9** satellite **11** planetarium
name: **4** Hale, Lick **6** Yerkes **7** Palomar, Whipple **8** Kitt Peak, Mt Wilson **11** Las Campanas, Mount Wilson **12** Big Bear Solar **14** Royal Greenwich

observe 3 eye, say, see **4** espy, heed, keep, mark, note, obey, ogle, spot, view **5** honor, opine, state, watch **6** assert, behold, detect, follow, notice, peer at, regard, remark, size up, survey **7** abide by, comment, declare, defer to, execute, fulfill, glimpse, inspect, make out, mention, perform, reflect, respect, stare at **8** adhere to, announce, carry out, discover, perceive, sanctify, theorize **9** celebrate, recognize, solemnize **10** be guided by,

comply with, consecrate **11** acknowledge, acquiesce to, commemorate, take stock of **12** catch sight of **14** pay attention to

observer 6 viewer **7** watcher **8** onlooker **12** investigator

obsessed 5 beset **7** haunted **8** hung up on, maniacal **9** dominated, possessed **10** controlled **15** having a fixation

obsession 5 craze, mania, quirk **6** phobia **8** fixation **9** fixed idea, monomania **11** infatuation **13** preoccupation **16** overwhelming fear **18** neurotic conviction

obsolescent 8 dying out **9** declining **11** on the way out **12** disappearing **16** becoming obsolete **17** becoming out-of-date

obsolete 3 out **5** dated, passe **6** bygone **7** antique, archaic, extinct **8** outdated, out of use, outmoded **9** out-of-date **10** antiquated **12** old-fashioned, out of fashion

obstacle 3 bar **4** curb, snag **5** block, catch, check **6** hurdle **7** barrier, problem **8** blockade, stoppage **9** barricade, hindrance, roadblock **10** difficulty, impediment, limitation **11** obstruction, restriction **12** interference **14** stumbling block

obstetrician
French: **10** accoucheur

obstinacy 8 rigidity **10** mulishness, resistance **11** willfulness **12** stubbornness **13** inflexibility, intransigence, pigheadedness

obstinate 6 dogged, mulish **7** staunch, willful **8** obdurate, resolute, stubborn **9** pigheaded, steadfast, tenacious, unbending **10** headstrong, inflexible, refractory, self-willed, unyielding **11** intractable **12** recalcitrant, ungovernable, unmanageable **14** uncontrollable **20** unreasonably stubborn

obstreperous 4 loud **5** noisy **6** unruly **8** perverse **9** clamorous, rampaging **10** boisterous, disorderly, refractory, roistering, uproarious, vociferous **11** disobedient **12** uncontrolled, ungovernable, unmanageable, unrestrained **14** uncontrollable

obstruct 3 bar **4** curb, halt, hide, mask, stop **5** block, check, cloak, close, cover, dam up, debar, delay, limit, stall **6** arrest, hinder, hobble, impede, plug up, retard, shroud, stifle, thwart **7** eclipse, inhibit, shut off **8** blockade, choke off, close off, restrict, suppress, throttle **9** barricade, frustrate **18** bring to a standstill

obstruction 3 bar **4** curb, snag, stop **5** block, check, hitch **6** hurdle **7** barrier **8** blockage, obstacle, stoppage **9** barricade, hindrance **10** bottleneck, impediment **11** encumbrance

obtain 3 get **4** earn, gain, hold, take

5 exist, glean, stand **6** attain, come by, gather, pick up, secure **7** achieve, acquire, prevail, procure, receive **9** get hold of **14** get one's hands on **16** gain possession of

obtainment 11 achievement, acquirement, acquisition, procurement

obtrude 5 eject, expel, force **6** butt in, impose, meddle, thrust **7** presume, project **9** interfere

obtrusive 4 nosy **5** brash **6** prying, snoopy **7** bulging, forward, salient **8** familiar, meddling **9** intruding, intrusive, prominent **10** aggressive, jutting out, meddlesome, projecting, protruding **11** conspicuous, impertinent, interfering, outstanding, protuberant, sticking out, trespassing **12** interrupting, presumptuous

obtuse 4 dull, slow **5** blunt, dense, thick **6** simple, stupid **7** blunted **8** ignorant, not sharp **9** unpointed **10** insensible, not pointed, slow-witted **11** insensitive, unsharpened **12** imperceptive, thick-skinned **15** uncomprehending

obtuseness 8 dullness **9** denseness, ignorance, stupidity **13** insensitivity **14** slow-wittedness **15** thick-headedness **16** lack of perception, simplemindedness **19** lack of comprehension

obverse 4 face **5** front **10** complement **11** counterpart
of coin: **4** head

obviate 5 avert, avoid, parry **6** divert, remove **7** fend off, prevent, ward off **8** preclude, stave off **9** forestall, sidetrack, turn aside **10** circumvent, do away with **11** nip in the bud

obvious 5 clear, plain **6** patent **7** evident, glaring, visible **8** apparent, distinct, man- ifest, palpable, striking, unhidden, unmasked, unveiled **10** undeniable **11** conspicuous, discernible, perceptible, self-evident, unconcealed, undisguised **12** in plain sight, unmistakable **24** plain as the nose on your face

ocarina 11 sweet potato **14** wind instrument

O'Casey, Sean
author of: **10** Purple Dust **12** The Green Crow **17** Juno and the Paycock **18** The Shadow of a Gunman **20** The Plough and the Stars

occasion 4 base, time **5** basis, cause, event **6** advent, affair, chance, elicit, ground, lead to, motive, prompt, reason **7** episode, grounds, inspire, opening, provoke, venture **8** incident, instance **9** adventure, happening, rationale, situation **10** bring about, experience, motivation, occurrence **11** celebration, explanation, opportunity, provocation **12** circumstance, special event, suitable time **13** justification,

opportune time
14 convenient time, important event, particular time

occasional 4 rare **6** fitful, random **8** sporadic, uncommon **9** irregular, recurring, scattered, spasmodic, uncertain **10** incidental, infrequent, now and then, unreliable **12** intermittent

occasionally 6 rarely, seldom **7** at times **8** fitfully **9** sometimes **10** now and then **11** irregularly **12** infrequently, once in a while, periodically, sporadically **14** from time to time, intermittently **15** every now and then, once in a blue moon

occidental 7 Western **8** American, European **9** Hesperian, Westerner

occlude 4 clog, plug **5** block, choke, close **6** shut up, stop up **7** congest, shut off, stopper **8** choke off, obstruct **9** barricade, constrict **11** strangulate

occult 4 dark **5** magic **6** arcane, hidden, mystic, secret, veiled **7** obscure, private **8** esoteric, mystical, shrouded **9** concealed **10** cabalistic, mysterious, unrevealed **11** undisclosed **12** supernatural

occupancy 3 use **6** tenure **7** tenancy **8** lodgment **9** enjoyment, habitancy **10** engagement, habitation, occupation, possession **11** inhabitancy

occupant 5 owner **6** lessee, lodger, native, renter, roomer, tenant **7** dweller, settler **8** colonist, occupier, resident **9** addressee **10** inhabitant **11** householder

occupation 3 job **4** line, work **5** craft, forte, trade **6** career, living, metier, sphere **7** calling, control, pursuit, seizure **8** activity, business, capacity, conquest, lifework, vocation **9** specialty **10** employment, line of work, livelihood, possession, profession, subjection **11** foreign rule, subjugation **14** specialization **15** military control **18** military occupation

occupied 5 in use **6** amused, took up, used up **7** dwelt in, engaged, lived in, overran, overrun, taken up **8** absorbed, tenanted **9** concerned, conquered, inhabited, resided in **12** had control of, held in thrall **13** was situated in **16** took possession of

occupy 3 use **4** be in, be on, busy, fill, hold **5** amuse, sit in **6** absorb, employ, engage, fill up, room in, take up **7** concern, conquer, dwell in, engross, enslave, inhabit, lodge in, overrun, pervade, possess **8** permeate, reside in, saturate **9** entertain, subjugate **10** monopolize **11** have control **12** be situated in, hold in thrall **14** be the tenants of **16** take possession of

occur 3 hit **4** rise **5** arise, ensue **6** appear, befall, crop up, emerge, happen, result, strike, turn up **7** be found, come off, develop **8** spring up **9** come

about, eventuate, take place, transpire **10** come to pass **11** materialize **13** cross one's mind, enter one's mind

occurrence 5 event **6** affair **7** episode, venture **8** business, incident, instance, occasion **9** adventure, emergence, happening, situation, unfolding **10** appearance, experience, proceeding **11** development, transaction **12** circumstance **13** manifestation **15** materialization

ocean 3 sea **4** deep, main, pond **5** flood, water **7** big pond, high sea **9** briny deep
god of: 3 Nun **4** Nanu **7** Neptune, Oceanus **8** Poseidon

Oceania, Oceanica 9 Melanesia, Polynesia **10** Micronesia **11** Australia
ocean: 12 South Pacific
island: 4 Cook, Guam, Fiji, Maui, Niue, Wake **5** Aunuu, Bonin, Kauai, Lanai, Tonga **6** Bikini, Futuna, Hawaii, Marcus, Midway, Rurutu, Tahiti, Tubuai, Tuvalu, Wallis **7** Gambier, Gilbert, Iwo Jima, Leeward, Mariana, Molokai, Phoenix, Solomon, Tokelau, Tuamotu, Tutuila, Vanuatu, Volcano **8** Aitu taki, Bismarck, Bora-Bora, Johnston, Kiribati, Marshall, Pitcairn, Windward **9** Australia, Christmas, Marquesas, Trobriand **10** New Zealand **12** New Caledonia, Western Samoa **14** Papua New Guinea **15** French Polynesia

oceanic 6 marine **7** aquatic, pelagic **8** seagoing **9** thalassic

Oceanid
form: 5 nymph
location: 3 sea
father: 7 Oceanus
mother: 6 Tethys

Oceanus
member of: 6 Titans
father: 6 Uranus
mother: 4 Gaea
consort of: 6 Tethys
father of: 8 Oceanids **9** river gods
son: 7 Proteus
daughter: 5 Doris, Persa **7** Philyra
form: 6 stream

ocelot 3 cat **7** wildcat

ochlophobia
fear of: 6 crowds

Ochoa, Severo
born: 5 Spain
profession: 10 biochemist

Ockelman, Constance Frances Marie
real name of: 12 Veronica Lake

O'Connor, Carroll
born: 7 Bronx NY
roles: 12 Archie Bunker, Archie's Place **14** All in the Family
restaurant: 12 The Ginger Man

O'Connor, Donald
born: 9 Chicago IL
roles: 9 Beau Geste **15** Singin' in the

Rain **18** Tom Sawyer Detective **21** Francis the Talking Mule

O'Connor, Flannery
author of: 9 Wise Blood **15** The Habit of Being **17** Mystery and Manners **20** A Good Man Is Hard to Find, The Violent Bear It Away

Octavia
brother: 8 Augustus
husband: 4 Nero **10** Mark Antony
grandson: 8 Caligula

October
flower: 6 cosmos **9** calendula
French: 7 Octobre
gem: 4 opal **10** tourmaline
German: 7 Oktober
holiday: 9 Halloween (31) **11** Columbus Day (12) **16** United Nations Day (24)
Italian: 7 Ottobre
number of days: 9 thirty-one
origin of name: 4 octo (Latin meaning eight)
place in year:
　Gregorian: 5 tenth
　Roman: 6 eighth
Spanish: 7 Octubre
Zodiac sign: 5 Libra **7** Scorpio

October Light
author: 11 John Gardner

Octopus, The
author: 11 Frank Norris

odd 4 rare **5** extra, funny, queer, spare, weird **6** casual, far-out, quaint, single, sundry, unique **7** bizarre, curious, not even, strange, surplus, unusual, various **8** freakish, left over, peculiar, periodic, singular, sporadic, uncommon **9** irregular, remaining, spasmodic, unmatched **10** occasional, outlandish **13** miscellaneous **15** being one of a pair **16** out of the ordinary **17** not divisible by two

oddball 3 nut **4** kook **5** freak **6** weirdo **8** crackpot, original **9** character, eccentric, screwball **10** one-of-a-kind

Odd Couple, The
character: 3 Roy **5** Myrna, Roger, Speed **6** Miriam, Murray, Vinnie **10** Felix Unger **11** Gloria Unger **12** Cecily Pigeon, Oscar Madison **14** Blanche Madison **15** Gwendolyn Pigeon, (Dr) Nancy Cunningham
cast: 10 Al Molinaro, Archie Hahn **11** Brett Somers, Carol Shelly, Jack Klugman, Larry Gelman, Monica Evans, Tony Randall **12** Garry Walberg, Janice Hansen, Ryan McDonald **13** Elinor Donahue, Joan Hotchkiss, Penny Marshall
setting: 11 New York City
Felix's job: 12 photographer
Oscar's job: 12 sportswriter
based on play by: 9 Neil Simon

Odd Couple, The
director: 8 Gene Saks
based on play by: 9 Neil Simon

cast: **10** Jack Lemmon (Felix Unger) **11** Herb Edelman, John Fiedler **13** Walter Matthau (Oscar Madison)

oddity 5 freak, sight **6** marvel, rarity, wonder **9** curiosity, queerness **10** phenomenon, uniqueness **11** abnormality, bizarreness, peculiarity, singularity, strangeness, unusualness **12** eccentricity, freakishness **13** individuality, unnaturalness **14** outlandishness
Latin: **8** rara avis

oddly amusing 5 droll, kooky **9** laughable, whimsical **10** ridiculous

odd person 3 nut **4** kook **5** flake, freak **6** looney, weirdo **7** oddball **8** crackpot **9** character, eccentric, screwball

odds and ends 4 olio **6** scraps **8** remnants **9** leftovers **10** hodgepodge, miscellany **11** this and that **13** bits and pieces **18** miscellaneous items

ode 4 epic, hymn, poem **5** lyric, paean, psalm, verse **6** ballad **8** canticle
type: **8** Horatian, Pindaric

Ode on a Grecian Urn
author: **9** John Keats

Ode on Indolence
author: **9** John Keats

Ode on Melancholy
author: **9** John Keats

Ode to a Nightingale
author: **9** John Keats

Ode to Autumn
author: **9** John Keats

Ode to Duty
author: **17** William Wordsworth

Ode to Psyche
author: **9** John Keats

Ode to the West Wind
author: **18** Percy Bysshe Shelley

Odets, Clifford
author of: **9** Golden Boy **12** Awake and Sing **14** The Country Girl **15** Waiting for Lefty **17** The Flowering Peach

Odin
also: **5** Othin
brother: **2** Ve **4** Vili
children: **4** Hodr, Thor **5** Baldr **6** Balder, Baldur
counterpart: **5** Woden, Wotan
court: **8** Valhalla
father: **3** Bor
god of: **3** war **6** poetry, wisdom **9** knowledge
grandson: **7** Volsung
home: **9** Gladsheim
horse: **8** Sleipnir
magic ring: **8** Draupnir
Norse myth: **10** chief deity
origin: **12** Scandinavian
raven: **5** Hugin, Munin
remaining eye: **3** sun
ruler of: **5** Aexir
spear: **7** Gungnir
throne: **10** Hlidskjalf

wife: **3** Fri **5** Frigg, Frija **6** Frigga
wolf: **4** Geri **5** Freki

odious 4 evil, foul, vile **5** hated, nasty **6** rotten **7** hateful, heinous, hideous **8** infamous **9** invidious, loathsome, monstrous, obnoxious, offensive, repugnant, repulsive, revolting, sickening **10** abominable, despicable, detestable, disgusting, nauseating, unbearable **11** intolerable, unendurable **12** contemptible **13** objectionable

odium 5 shame **6** hatred, infamy **7** disgust **8** contempt, disfavor, disgrace, dishonor, ignominy **9** antipathy, discredit, disesteem, disrepute **10** abhorrence, disrespect, opprobrium, repugnance **11** detestation, disapproval **14** disapprobation

odonata
class: **8** hexapoda
phylum: **10** arthropoda
group: **9** damselfly, dragonfly

odor 4 aura **5** aroma, scent, smell, stink **6** flavor, stench **7** bouquet, essence, perfume **9** effluvium, fragrance **10** atmosphere

odoriferous 4 rank **5** acrid, fetid **6** putrid, smelly **7** noisome, odorous, pungent, reeking, scented **8** aromatic, fragrant, perfumed, stinking **10** malodorous

odorous 4 rank **5** acrid, fetid **6** smelly **7** noisome, pungent, reeking, scented **8** aromatic, fragrant, perfumed, stinking

Odysseus
also: **7** Ulysses
king of: **6** Ithaca
father: **7** Laertes
mother: **8** Anticlea
hero of: **5** Iliad **7** Odyssey
wife: **8** Penelope **9** Callidice
son: **9** Telegonus **10** Polypoetes, Telemachus **11** Polyporthis
seduced by: **5** Circe
killed by: **9** Telegonus
epithet: **10** Laertiades

Odyssey
author: **5** Homer
character: **4** Zeus **5** Arete, Circe, Helen **6** Athene, Nestor, Scylla, Sirens **7** Calypso, Cyclops **8** Alcinous, Menelaus, Nausicaa, Odysseus, Penelope, Poseidon, Tiresias **9** Charybdis **10** Telemachus **11** Lotus-eaters

Oedipus
king of: **6** Thebes
father: **5** Laius
mother: **7** Jocasta
foster father: **7** Polybus
foster mother: **6** Merope **8** Periboea
wife: **7** Jocasta
son: **8** Eteocles **9** Polynices
daughter: **5** Ismene **8** Antigone
killed: **5** Laius
defeated: **6** Sphinx

Oedipus at Colonus

author: **9** Sophocles
character: **5** Creon **6** Elders, Ismene **7** Theseus **8** Antigone **9** Polynices

Oedipus Rex (Oedipus Tyrannus)
author: **9** Sophocles
character: **5** Creon, Laius **7** Jocasta **8** Tiresias

oeil-de-boeuf 16 small round window
literally: **8** bull's eye

Oeneus
king of: **7** Calydon
wife: **7** Althaea
son: **8** Meleager

oenology
science of: **5** wines **10** winemaking

Oenone
form: **5** nymph
father: **6** Cebren
husband: **5** Paris

Oersted, Hans Christian
field: **7** physics
nationality: **6** Danish
founded: **16** electromagnetism
isolated: **16** metallic aluminum
named for him: **11** oersted unit

oeuvre 4 work **5** works **13** artist's output

O'Faolain, Sean
author of: **15** The Heat of the Sun **17** A Nest of Simple Folk **22** Midsummer Night's Madness

of a piece 5 alike, equal **7** matched, the same **8** all in one **9** analogous, identical **10** equivalent, homogenous, synonymous **13** evenly matched, one and the same

of bad character 5 shady **8** unsavory **11** of ill repute **12** disreputable, unprincipled

off 2 by **3** bad, far, ill, odd **4** afar, away, down, from, kill, poor, stop **5** amiss, apart, aside, crazy, wrong **6** absent, begone, lessen, remote **7** distant, further, in error, stopped, tainted **8** abnormal, canceled, inferior, mistaken **9** imperfect

offal 4 junk, slag **5** dregs, trash, waste **6** debris, refuse **7** carcass, carrion, garbage, grounds, remains, residue, rubbish **8** leavings

off base 5 amiss, wrong **8** improper, mistaken **10** out of order, unsuitable **13** inappropriate

offbeat 3 odd **7** strange **8** peculiar **9** different, eccentric **14** unconventional

off-center 6 askew **7** strange **9** eccentric **10** imbalanced, nonaligned, unbalanced **12** unreasonable **14** unconventional

off-color 4 blue, lewd, racy, sexy **5** bawdy, dirty, salty, spicy **6** earthy, risque, smutty, wicked **7** naughty, obscene, raunchy **8** improper, indecent, scabrous **9** offensive **10** indelicate, indiscreet, suggestive

off duty 8 inactive 9 at leisure 10 unoccupied 13 on one's own time

Offenbach, Jacques
born: 7 Cologne, Germany
composer of: 13 La Belle Helene 15 Tales of Hoffmann, La Vie Parisienne 22 Orpheus in the Underworld

offend 3 err, sin, vex 4 fret, gall, miff, rile 5 anger, annoy, chafe, lapse, pique, wound 6 insult, madden, nettle, rankle 7 affront, disgust, incense, inflame 8 irritate 9 aggravate, displease, misbehave 10 antagonize, disgruntle, exasperate, transgress 13 fall from grace

offender 5 crook, felon 6 sinner 7 culprit 8 criminal, violator 9 wrongdoer 10 malefactor, trespasser

offense 3 sin 4 gibe, harm, slap, slip, snub, twit 5 abuse, crime, lapse, taunt 6 attack, charge, felony, insult 7 affront, assault, misdeed, outrage, umbrage 8 atrocity, enormity, evil deed, rudeness 9 impudence, indignity, insolence, offensive, violation 10 aggression, disrespect, infraction, peccadillo, wickedness 11 delinquency, humiliation, malfeasance, misdemeanor, shortcoming 13 embarrassment, transgression 15 breach of conduct

offensive 4 foul, rank, rude, ugly 5 nasty, onset 6 attack, horrid 7 abusive, assault, hideous, offense, uncivil 8 charging, impudent, insolent, storming 9 abhorrent, assailing, attacking, insulting, loathsome, obnoxious, onslaught, repugnant, repulsive, revolting, sickening, ungallant 10 abominable, aggression, aggressive, assaulting, bombarding, detestable, disgusting, nauseating, unmannerly, unpleasant 11 belligerent, distasteful, intolerable 12 disagreeable, embarrassing, insufferable 13 disrespectful, objectionable

offensiveness 8 rudeness 9 impudence, insolence, nastiness 10 disrespect, horridness, incivility 13 repulsiveness 14 unpleasantness 15 distastefulness

offer 3 bid 5 put up 6 bestow, extend, render, submit, tender 7 advance, hold out, present, proffer, propose, suggest 8 bestow on, offering, overture, proposal, propound, put forth 9 be willing, volunteer 10 invitation, put forward, submission, suggestion 11 make a motion, proposition 12 bring forward 14 put on the market 19 place at one's disposal

offer hospitality 4 host 7 welcome 8 play host 9 entertain 10 give a party, have guests 13 keep open house

offering 3 bid 4 alms, gift 5 goods, wares 6 course 7 charity, present, tribute 8 anathema, bestowal, donation, oblation 9 sacrifice 11 benefi-

cence 12 contribution
to God: 6 corban 7 deodate
to household deities: 4 bali

offertory 4 gift 8 oblation, offering 10 collection

offhand, offhanded 5 ad-lib, hasty 6 casual, chance, random 7 relaxed 8 careless, cavalier, heedless 9 facetious, haphazard, impromptu, unplanned, unstudied 10 improvised, nonchalant, off-the-cuff, unprepared 11 spontaneous, thoughtless, unconcerned, unrehearsed 12 off-the-record 14 extemporaneous, unpremeditated

office 3 job 4 post, role 8 capacity, function, position 10 commission, occupation 11 appointment

officer 3 cop 4 head 7 manager 8 director, gendarme, governor 9 constable, detective, executive, patrolman, policeman, president, secretary, treasurer 10 bureaucrat 12 commissioner 13 administrator, vice-president

officers 8 managers 10 executives, management 14 administration

Officers and Gentlemen
author: 11 Evelyn Waugh

offices 4 duty, help, task 5 favor, trust 6 charge 7 service 8 function, province 10 assistance

office seeker 7 hopeful, nominee 8 aspirant 9 candidate

office worker 5 clerk, steno 6 typist 9 file clerk, secretary 10 bookkeeper, keypuncher 13 data processor 14 clerical worker

official 5 agent 6 formal, vested 7 manager, officer 8 approved, chairman, director, licensed 9 authentic, certified, dignitary, executive, warranted 10 accredited, authorized, sanctioned, supervisor 11 functionary 13 administrator, authoritative 14 administrative 18 administrative head

official communication 5 edict, order, ukase 6 report 7 release 8 bulletin 10 communique 12 proclamation

officialdom 10 government 11 authorities, bureaucracy 14 administration

official paper 4 writ 5 order 8 document 10 instrument

officiate 3 run 4 head, lead 5 chair, emcee 6 direct, handle, manage 7 oversee, preside 8 moderate, regulate 9 supervise 10 administer 11 superintend 12 be in charge of

officious 6 prying 7 pompous 8 meddling 9 intrusive, kibitzing, obtrusive 10 high-handed, meddlesome 11 domineering, interfering, overbearing, patronizing 13 high and mighty, self-assertive, self-important 16 poking one's nose in

Offield, Lewis Delaney
real name of: 9 Jack Oakie

offset 6 redeem 7 balance, nullify 8

equalize, knock out 9 cancel out, make up for 10 counteract, neutralize 11 countervail 13 compensate for, counterweight 14 counterbalance

offshoot 4 limb 5 scion, shoot 6 branch 7 adjunct 9 aftermath, byproduct, outgrowth 10 descendant

offspring 3 fry 4 heir, seed 5 brood, child, issue, scion, spawn, young 6 family, litter 7 progeny 8 children, increase 9 posterity 10 descendant, succession 11 descendants

off the mark 5 amiss 6 afield, astray 9 off target 16 off the right track

off-the-record 5 privy 6 secret 7 private 11 undisclosed 12 confidential 16 not to be disclosed 17 not for publication

off the top of one's head 5 ad-lib 7 offhand 9 extempore, impromptu 10 improvised, unprepared 11 extemporary, unrehearsed 14 extemporaneous, unpremeditated

of good quality 4 good 6 worthy 8 superior 9 excellent 10 creditable

of high rank 5 noble, regal, royal 6 lordly, titled 7 courtly 11 blue-blooded 12 aristocratic

Of Human Bondage
author: 16 W Somerset Maugham
director: 12 John Cromwell
character: 5 Weeks 8 Hayward 11 Louisa Carey, Philip Carey 12 Sally Athelny, William Carey 13 Mildred Rogers, Miss Wilkinson, Thorpe Athelny
cast: 10 Bette Davis, Frances Dee, Kay Johnson 12 Leslie Howard

of its own kind
Latin: 10 sui generis

Of Mice and Men
author: 13 John Steinbeck
director: 14 Lewis Milestone
character: 4 Slim 5 Candy 6 Crooks, Curley 11 Lennie Small 12 George Milton
cast: 10 Betty Field 11 Lon Chaney Jr (Lenny) 15 Burgess Meredith, Charles Bickford
score: 12 Aaron Copland

of one's own right
Latin: 8 sui juris

of poor quality 5 junky 6 flimsy, shoddy, sleazy, trashy 8 inferior 11 substandard

of secondary importance 8 nonvital 9 accessory, extrinsic 10 incidental 11 dispensable, unnecessary 12 nonessential

often 3 oft 4 much 7 usually 8 commonly, ofttimes 9 generally, regularly 10 constantly, frequently, habitually, oftentimes, repeatedly 11 continually, customarily, over and over, recurrently 12 periodically, time and again

of the dead say nothing but good
Latin: 21 de mortuis nil nisi bonum
of the faith
Latin: 6 de fide
of their own kind
Latin: 10 sui generis
of the old school 5 passe 8 outdated, outmoded 9 out-of-date 12 conservative, old-fashioned 18 establishmentarian
Of Time and the River
author: 11 Thomas Wolfe
character: 10 Eugene Gant
oft-repeated 5 trite 7 popular 8 constant, familiar, frequent, habitual, well-worn 9 continual, recurring, well-known 10 persistent 11 widely known
of what good
Latin: 7 cui bono
Ogdoad
also: 3 Heh
origin: 8 Egyptian
number of gods: 5 eight
ogle 3 eye 6 gape at, gawk at, goggle, leer at 7 stare at 8 goggle at 10 give the eye, scrutinize 15 give the once-over, stare at greedily 16 cast sheep's eyes at, gaze at with desire
Ogma
origin: 5 Irish
god of: 6 poetry 9 eloquence
inventor of: 12 Ogham letters
Ogmios
origin: 6 Gaelic
god of: 9 eloquence
corresponds to: 7 Mercury
ogre, ogress 5 brute, demon, fiend, ghoul, harpy 6 despot, tyrant 7 bugbear, monster 8 bogeyman, dictator, martinet 11 slave driver
Ogygia
island of: 7 Calypso
Ogygus
king of: 7 Boeotia
father: 8 Poseidon
O'Hara, John
author of: 7 Pal Joey 11 A Rage to Live 13 The Instrument 14 From the Terrace, The Hat on the Bed 16 Butterfield Eight 17 Ten North Frederick 19 The Horse Knows the Way 20 Appointment in Samarra
O'Hara, Maureen
real name: 18 Maureen Fitzsimmons
nickname: 18 Queen of Technicolor
born: 7 Ireland 8 Milltown
roles: 10 Lady Godiva 11 The Quiet Man 13 North to Alaska, The Parent Trap 16 The Foxes of Harrow 19 How Green Was My Valley 20 Hunchback of Notre Dame 27 Miracle on Thirty-fourth Street
O'Hara, Scarlett
character in: 15 Gone With the Wind

family: 6 Gerald 7 Carreen, Suellen
author: 8 Mitchell
O Henry
real name: 19 William Sidney Porter
author of: 11 The Last Leaf 16 Cabbages and Kings, The Gift of the Magi 18 The Cop and the Anthem 19 The Ransom of Red Chief
Ohio
abbreviation: 2 OH
nickname: 7 Buckeye
capital: 8 Columbus
largest city: 9 Cleveland
others: 3 Ada 4 Kent, Lima 5 Akron, Berea, Cadiz, Niles, Parma, Piqua, Xenia 6 Athens, Canton, Dayton, Elyria, Lorain, Marion, Newark, Tiffin, Toledo, Warren 7 Ashland, Findlay, Fremont, Norwood, Wooster 8 Alliance, Bluffton, Fostoria, Lakewood, Marietta, Sandusky 9 Ashtabula, Kettering, Lancaster, Massillon, Struthers, Vermilion, Willowick 10 Cincinnati, Huntington, Portsmouth, Rocky River, Willoughby, Youngstown, Zanesville 11 Painesville, Springfield 12 Steubenville
college: 4 Kent 5 Akron, Hiram, Miami 6 Dayton, Kenyon, Xavier 7 Antioch, Oberlin, Wooster 8 Defiance, Dennison, Marietta, Ursuline 10 Wittenberg 11 Case Western 12 Bowling Green, Ohio Wesleyan
feature:
  hall of fame: 11 Pro Football
  race: 12 Soap Box Derby
tribe: 4 Erie 7 Wyandot 13 Mound Builders
people: 7 buckeye, Cy Young 8 Zane Grey 10 Clark Gable, T Hart Crane 11 Annie Oakley, Lillian Gish 12 James Thurber, Lowell Thomas, Norman Thomas 13 Neil Armstrong, Orville Wright, Thomas A Edison 14 Barney Old field, Clarence Darrow 15 William T Sherman 16 Sherwood Anderson 18 Norman Vincent Peale
  explorer: 7 La Salle
lake: 4 Erie 5 Grand 6 Berlin, Dillon, Hoover, Indian 8 Delaware 13 Mosquito Creek
land rank: 35 thirty-fifth
mountain:
  highest point: 12 Campbell Hill
physical feature:
  caverns: 4 Ohio, Zane 6 Seneca
  spring: 8 Blue Hole
president: 13 Ulysses S Grant 14 James A Garfield, Warren G Harding 15 William McKinley 16 Rutherford B Hayes 17 William Howard Taft 20 William Henry Harrison
river: 5 Grand, Miami 6 Maumee, Scioto, Wabash 7 Hocking 8 Cuyahoga, Sandusky 9 Muskingum, Tennessee 10 Cumberland 11 Monongahela
state admission: 11 seventeenth
state bird: 8 cardinal

state flower: 16 scarlet carnation
state motto: 27 With God All Things Are Possible
state song: 13 Beautiful Ohio
state tree: 7 buckeye
Ohm, Georg Simon
field: 7 physics
nationality: 6 German
discovered: 20 electrical resistance
named for him: 7 ohm unit
oil 4 balm, lard 5 cream, salve 6 anoint, grease, pomade 7 unguent 8 liniment, ointment 9 lubricant, lubricate, melted fat, petroleum 12 melted grease
type: 4 corn, fuel, hair 5 crude, motor, olive, whale 6 canola 7 cooking, mineral 9 safflower, vegetable
oily 5 fatty, lardy, slick 6 greasy, smarmy 7 buttery, fawning, servile 8 slippery, slithery, toadying, unctuous 9 groveling, sebaceous 10 lubricious, oleaginous 11 bootlicking, subservient 12 ingratiating
ointment 4 balm 5 salve 6 lotion, pomade 7 pomatum, unguent 8 liniment 9 emollient, spikenard
Ojibwa, Ojibway see 8 Chippawa
OK 4 fine, good 7 approve, endorse 8 all right, approval 9 authorize 11 endorsement 13 authorization
French: 7 d'accord
O'Keeffe, Georgia
born: 12 Sun Prairie WI
artwork: 7 Stables 9 Black Iris 14 Patio with Cloud 15 Lake George Barns 22 Light Coming on the Plains 26 Black Flower and Blue Larkspur
husband: 15 Alfred Stieglitz
Oklahoma
abbreviation: 2 OK 4 Okla
nickname: 6 Boomer, Sooner
capital/largest city: 12 Oklahoma City
others: 3 Ada 4 Alva, Enid, Hugo 5 Altus, Miami, Ponca, Tulsa 6 Duncan, El Reno, Guymon, Idabel, Lawton 7 Ardmore, Guthrie, Sapulpa, Shawnee 8 Anadarko, Fort Sill, Muskogee 9 Blackwell, Claremore, McAlester 10 Stillwater 12 Bartlesville
college: 5 Tulsa 6 Norman 7 Cameron 8 Langston, Phillips 10 Stillwater 11 Oral Roberts 12 Oklahoma City 15 Bethany Nazarene 17 American Christian
feature:
  hall of fame: 14 American Indian
  national park: 6 Platte
tribe: 3 Kaw, Oto 4 Iowa, Loup, Otoe, Waco 5 Caddo, Kansa, Osage, Ponca 6 Apache, Ottawa, Pawnee, Quapaw 7 Shawnee, Wichita 8 Arapahoe, Tawakoni
  Five Civilized Tribes: 5 Creek 7 Choctaw 8 Cherokee, Seminole 9 Chickasaw

people: 4 Okie **6** Sooner **9** Jim Thorpe **10** Will Rogers **12** Mickey Mantle **14** Maria Tallchief
   explorer: 8 Coronado
lake: 5 Atoka, Grand, Hulah **6** Texoma, Wister **7** Eufaula, Heyburn, Oologah **8** Keystone **9** Pensacola, Tenkiller **10** Fort Gibson **11** Thunderbird **12** Markham Ferry **17** Lake O' The Cherokees
land rank: 10 eighteenth
mountain: 6 Ozarks **8** Ouachita
   highest point: 9 Black Mesa
physical feature: 9 Panhandle
   plains: 5 Great
river: 3 Red **5** Grand **6** Little, Neosho **7** Washita **8** Arkan sas, Canadian, Cimarron **9** Verdigris **15** Muddy Boggy Creek
state admission: 10 forty-sixth
state bird: 23 scissor-tailed flycatcher
state fish: 9 white bass
state flower: 9 mistletoe
state motto: 22 Labor Conquers All Things
state song: 8 Oklahoma
state tree: 6 redbud

Oklahoma!
   director: 13 Fred Zinnemann
   cast: 10 Rod Steiger **11** Eddie Albert **12** Gordon MacRae, Shirley Jones **13** Gloria Grahame, James Whitmore **18** Charlotte Greenwood
   score: 21 Rodgers and Hammerstein
   choreographer: 12 Agnes de Mille
   song: 23 People Will Say We're in Love **24** Surrey with the Fringe on Top

Olbers, Heinrich Wilhelm Matthaus
   field: 9 astronomy
   nationality: 6 German
   discovered: 5 Vesta **6** comets, Pellas **9** asteroids

old 4 aged, used **5** hoary, of age **6** beat-up, bygone, of yore **7** ancient, antique, archaic, elderly, outworn, rundown, vintage, wornout **8** battered, decrepit, familiar, grizzled, much-used, obsolete, outdated, timeworn **9** crumbling, hackneyed, out-of-date, venerable, weathered **10** antiquated, broken-down, gray-headed, ramshackle, tumbledown **11** dilapidated, from the past, gray with age, obsolescent, time-honored, traditional **12** deteriorated, old-fashioned, white with age **13** weather-beaten **14** of long standing **15** long established

Old Aches and Pains
   nickname of: 11 Luke Appling
old age 6 dotage **7** ripe age **8** maturity, senility **11** advanced age **15** second childhood
Old and the Young, The
   author: 15 Luigi Pirandello

Old Bay State
   nickname of: 13 Massachusetts
Old Bulgarian
   also: 15 Old Church Slavic
   language family: 12 Indo-European
   group: 11 Balto-Slavic
   status: 7 archaic
   used in: 14 Orthodox church
Old Chinook
   nickname of: 10 Washington
Old Colony State
   nickname of: 13 Massachusetts
Old Curiosity Shop, The
   author: 14 Charles Dickens
   character: 5 Quilp **9** Fred Trent, Mrs Jarley **10** Kit Nubbles, Sally Brass **11** Grandfather **12** Sampson Brass **13** Dick Swiveller **15** Little Nell Trent **18** The Single Gentleman
Old Dominion
   nickname of: 8 Virginia
olden 4 past **6** bygone, former, of yore **7** ancient, long-ago **8** departed
Oldest Man 10 Methuselah
old-fashioned 5 corny, dated, passe **7** antique, archaic **8** obsolete, outdated, outmoded **9** out-of-date **10** antiquated, out of style **11** obsolescent, traditional **12** long-standing, out of fashion **13** unfashionable **14** behind the times
Old-Fashioned Girl, An
   author: 15 Louisa May Alcott
Old Franklin State
   nickname of: 9 Tennessee
old hand 3 pro **6** expert, master **8** virtuoso **9** authority **12** professional
old hat 5 passe, stale **6** demode **7** archaic, outworn **8** obsolete, outdated, outmoded **9** out-of-date **10** antiquated, superseded **11** obsolescent **12** old-fashioned **13** unfashionable **14** behind the times
old-line 11 established, traditional **12** conservative
Old Line State
   nickname of: 8 Maryland
Old Love
   author: 19 Isaac Bashevis Singer
Old Maid, The
   author: 12 Edith Wharton
Old Man and the Sea, The
   author: 15 Ernest Hemingway
   character: 7 Manolin **8** Santiago
Old Mortality
   author: 14 Sir Walter Scott
   character: 5 Edith **11** Henry Morton **12** Basil Olifant, Lord Evandale **19** John Balfour of Burley **21** Lady Margaret Bellenden **27** Colonel Grahame of Claverhouse
Old Mortality
   author: 19 Katherine Anne Porter
Old North
   nickname of: 13 North Carolina

Old Patagonian Express, The
   author: 11 Paul Theroux
old saw 5 adage, maxim **6** cliche, saying, truism **7** bromide, proverb **9** old saying **10** expression **11** old chestnut
oldster 5 elder **6** codger, old man **7** ancient **8** old woman **13** senior citizen
Old Testament
   first five books: 10 Pentateuch
   first six books: 9 Hexateuch
   first seven books: 10 Heptateuch
   books of: 3 Job **4** Amos, Ezra, Joel, Ruth **5** Hosea, Jonah, Kings, Micah, Na- hum, Songs, Tobit **6** Baruch, Daniel, Esther, Exodus, Haggai, Isaiah, Joshua, Judges, Judith, Psalms, Samuel, Sirach, Wisdom **7** Ezekiel, Genesis, Malachi, Numbers, Obadiah **8** Habakkuk, Jeremiah, Macabees, Nehemiah, Proverbs **9** Leviticus, Zechariah, Zephaniah **10** Chronicles **11** Deuteronomy **12** Ecclesiastes **13** Song of Solomon **14** Ecclesiasticus
Oldtown Folks
   author: 19 Harriet Beecher Stowe
Old Wives' Tale, The
   author: 13 Arnold Bennett
old-world 6 formal **7** courtly, gallant, old-line **8** European, orthodox **10** ceremonial, chivalrous, prescribed **11** ceremonious, continental, established, traditional **12** conservative, conventional, old-fashioned
Ole
   character in: 16 Giants of the Earth
   author: 7 Rolvaag
Olenska, Ellen
   character in: 17 The Age of Innocence
   author: 7 Wharton
oleoresin 3 gum **5** anime, apiol, elemi **6** balsam **7** solvent **10** turpentine
olio 4 stew **6** jumble, medley **7** melange, mixture **8** mishmash **9** potpourri **10** assortment, collection, hodgepodge, hotchpotch, miscellany
olive 12 Olea europaea
   varieties: 3 tea **4** wild **5** black, false, holly, sweet **6** common, desert, spurge **7** Russian **8** American, fragrant **11** Californian
olive-drab 5 khaki **13** greenish-brown
Oliver
   character in: 11 As You Like It
   author: 11 Shakespeare
Oliver!
   director: 9 Carol Reed
   based on story by: 14 Charles Dickens (Oliver Twist)
   cast: 8 Jack Wild, Ron Moody (Fagin) **10** Mark Lester (Oliver), Oliver Reed **11** Shani Wallis
   Oscar for: 7 picture **8** director
   remake of: 11 Oliver Twist
   song: 16 Consider Yourself, Food Glo-

rious Food **17** As Long As He Needs
Me

Oliver Twist
author: 14 Charles Dickens
character: 5 Fagin, Monks (Edward
Leeford), Nancy **6** Bumble **9** Bill
Sikes, Mrs Maylie **10** Mr Brownlow,
Rose Maylie
director: 9 David Lean
cast: 8 Kay Walsh **12** Alec Guinness
(Fagin), Robert Newton **13** Anthony
Newley (Artful Dodger) **16** Francis L
Sullivan, John Howard Davies
remade as: 7 Oliver!

Olivia
character in: 12 Twelfth Night
author: 11 Shakespeare

Olivier, Sir Laurence
born: 7 Dorking, England
wife: 11 Vivien Leigh **13** Joan Plowright
roles: 6 Becket, Hamlet (Oscar),
Henry V, Sleuth **7** Rebecca **11** Marathon Man **16** Wuthering Heights **17**
Pride and Prejudice, The Boys from
Brazil, The Devil's Disciple **19** Shoes
of the Fisherman **23** The Prince and
the Showgirl

olivine
variety: 7 peridot

olla 3 jar, pot **10** earthen pot

Olmsted, Frederick Law
landscape architect of: 11 Central
Park (NYC, with Calvert Vaux) **12**
Prospect Park (Brooklyn NY) **13**
Fairmount Park (Philadelphia) **14**
Biltmore Estate (Asheville NC),
Mount Royal Park (Montreal)

Olsen, Merlin (Jay)
sport: 8 football
team: 14 Los Angeles Rams
TV roles: 12 Father Murphy **15** Highway to Heaven **23** Little House on
the Prairie

O Lucky Man
director: 15 Lindsay Anderson
cast: 9 Alan Price **13** Rachel Roberts
15 Malcolm McDowell, Ralph Richardson
score: 9 Alan Price

Olwen
origin: 5 Welsh
form: 8 princess
father: 16 Yspadaden Penkawr

Olympic Games
site:
1896: 6 Athens
1900: 5 Paris
1904: 7 St Louis
1906: 6 Athens
1908: 6 London
1912: 9 Stockholm
1920: 7 Antwerp
1924: 5 Paris **8** Chamonix
1928: 8 St Moritz **9** Amsterdam
1932: 10 Lake Placid, Los Angeles
1936: 6 Berlin **21** Garmisch-

Partenkirchen
1948: 6 London **8** St Moritz
1952: 4 Oslo **8** Helsinki
1956: 9 Melbourne **15** Cortina
d'Ampezzo
1960: 5 Tokyo **11** Squaw Valley
1968: 8 Grenoble **10** Mexico City
1972: 6 Munich **7** Sapporo
1976: 8 Montreal **9** Innsbruck
1980: 6 Moscow **10** Lake Placid
1984: 8 Sarajevo **10** Los Angeles
1988: 5 Seoul **7** Calgary
1992: 9 Barcelona **11** Albertville
1994: 11 Lillehammer
1996: 7 Atlanta
1998: 6 Nagano
2000: 6 Sydney

Omaha
language family: 6 Siouan **7** Dhegiha
location: 4 Iowa **8** Nebraska, Oklahoma

Oman
other name: 13 Muscat and Oman
capital: 6 Masqat, Muscat
largest city: 5 Matra **6** Matrah
others: 3 Sur **4** Fida **5** Dubai, Nazwa,
Nigwa, Sohar, Wazit **6** Khasab, Mar-
bat, Murbat, Suwaih, Tinouf **7** Kha-
bura, Salalah **8** Ashkhara
government: 9 Sultanate
head of state/government: 6 sultan
monetary unit: 3 gaj, gaz **4** rial **5**
baiza, ghazi **7** mahmudi
island: 6 Masera, Masira **7** Masirah
10 Kuria Muria
mountain: 4 Qara **5** Hafit, Harim,
Nakhl, Tayin **8** el-Akhdar **11** Jabal
Akhdar **13** Green Mountain
highest point: 6 al-Sham
sea: 6 Indian **7** Arabian
physical feature:
cape: 7 Madraka **9** Ras Al Hadd **13**
Ras Dharbat 'Ali
gulf: 4 Oman
peninsula: 7 Arabian **8** Musandam
plain: 6 Dhofar **7** Batinah
strait: 6 Hormuz
people: 4 Arab
ruler: 12 Qabus Bin Said **13** Said
Bin Taimur
language: 4 Urdu **5** Hindi **6** Arabic **7**
Baluchi
religion: 5 Islam
war: 4 Gulf **11** Desert Storm

omega 3 end **4** last **5** final **6** ending **8**
terminus
opposite: 5 alpha

omen 4 sign **5** token **6** augury, herald
7 auspice, portent, presage, warning **9**
foretaste, harbinger, precursor **10**
foreboding, indication

ominous 7 unlucky **8** menacing, mina-
tory, monitory, sinister **9** dismaying,
ill-omened **10** foreboding, ill-starred,
portentous

omission 3 gap **4** hole **7** neglect **9** exception, exclusion, oversight **10** leaving out, negligence **11** delinquency,

elimination **12** noninclusion **13** neglected item **16** something omitted

omit 3 cut **4** drop, fail, jump, miss,
shun, skip **5** avoid, elide **6** bypass,
delete, except, forget, ignore, slight **7**
excerpt, exclude, let slip, neglect **8**
leave out, overlook, pass over, preclude, set aside **11** forget about

omnia vincit amor 15 love conquers
all

Omnibus
host: 13 Alistair Cooke

omnipotent 6 mighty **7** supreme **8** almighty, powerful, puissant **11** all-
powerful

omniscient 7 all-wise, supreme **8** infinite **9** all-seeing **10** all-knowing, preeminent

omnium gatherum 23 miscellaneous
collection

omnivorous 7 hoggish **8** edacious,
ravenous **9** crapulous, rapacious, voracious **10** gluttonous, polyphagic,
predacious **12** pantophagous

Omoo
author: 14 Herman Melville
character: 10 Captain Bob **15** Doctor
Long Ghost

Omphale
queen of: 5 Lydia
father: 8 Iardanus
husband: 6 Tmolus
son: 5 Lamus
served by: 8 Hercules

Omri
father: 6 Becher **7** Michael
son: 4 Ahab
daughter-in-law: 7 Jezebel

on 2 at **4** atop, near, over, upon **5**
about, above, ahead, along, anent **7**
against, forward, planned **8** abutting,
adjacent, attached, intended, touching
9 occurring **10** concerning, juxtaposed

on-and-off 6 spotty **8** episodic **9** irregular, spasmodic, temporary **10** now-
and-then, occasional

On Beginning and Perishing
author: 9 Aristotle

once 7 ages ago, long ago, one time **8**
formerly, hitherto, years ago **9** at one
time **10** heretofore, previously **11** a
single time, for the nonce, in times
past, some time ago **12** in the old
days, some time back **13** once upon a
time, on one occasion

once-in-a-lifetime 6 unique **7** special
8 singular **11** one-time-only

once more 4 anew **5** again **9** once
again, over again **11** one more time

on cloud nine 6 elated, joyful, joyous
8 ecstatic, euphoric **9** exuberant, rapturous **15** in seventh heaven

oncoming 5 close **7** looming, nearing
8 imminent **9** advancing, impending,
onrushing **11** approaching, bearing
down

on course 8 on target **15** on the right track

Ondine
author: **13** Jean Giraudoux

one 2 an **3** you **4** a man, lone, only, sole **5** a body, a soul, whole **6** a thing, entire, single, unique **7** a person, someone **8** complete, singular, solitary, somebody **10** individual, unrepeated

One, Two, Three
director: **11** Billy Wilder
cast: **11** James Cagney **12** Pamela Tiffin **13** Arlene Francis, Horst Buchholz
setting: **10** West Berlin
score: **11** Andre Previn

O'Neal, Ryan
real name: **16** Patrick Ryan O'Neal
born: **12** Los Angeles CA
daughter: **10** Tatum O'Neal
roles: **9** Love Story, Paper Moon **10** What's Up Doc **11** Barry Lyndon, Peyton Place **16** Rodney Harrington

O'Neal, Tatum
born: **12** Los Angeles CA
father: **9** Ryan O'Neal
roles: **9** Paper Moon **12** Bad News Bears **14** Little Darlings **19** International Velvet
husband: **11** John McEnroe

one and the same 5 equal **7** matched **9** identical

one by one 6 singly **10** one at a time, separately, single file **12** individually

One Day at a Time
character: **9** Ann Romano **11** Julie Cooper **13** Barbara Cooper **15** Dwayne Schneider
cast: **14** Bonnie Franklin **15** Pat Harrington Jr **17** Mackenzie Phillips, Valerie Bertinelli

One Day in the Life of Ivan Denisovich
author: **23** Aleksandr Solzhenitsyn Jr

One Flew Over the Cuckoo's Nest
director: **11** Milos Forman
based on story by: **8** Ken Kesey
cast: **13** Jack Nicholson **14** Louise Fletcher, Michael Beryman **15** William Redfield
Oscar for: **5** actor (Nicholson) **7** actress (Fletcher), picture **8** director **10** screenplay

One Hour with You
director: **11** George Cukor **13** Ernst Lubitsch
cast: **14** Genevieve Tobin **16** Maurice Chevalier **17** Jeanette MacDonald
remake of: **17** The Marriage Circle
song: **14** What Would You Do

one-hundred percent 5 sheer, total, utter, whole **7** supreme **8** absolute, complete **10** consummate **17** through-and-through

O'Neill, Eugene
author of: **8** The Straw **11** The Hairy Ape **12** Ah Wilderness, Anna Christie **13** Marco Millions **14** Glencairn Cycle **15** The Emperor Jones, The Iceman Cometh **16** Beyond the Horizon, Strange Interlude, The Great God Brown **18** Desire Under the Elms **20** The Moon of the Caribbees **22** A Moon for the Misbegotten, All God's Chillun Got Wings, Mourning Becomes Electra **24** Long Day's Journey into Night
daughter: **4** Oona
son-in-law: **7** Chaplin

Oneiros
also: **6** Oniros
origin: **5** Greek
god of: **6** dreams

oneness 5 union, unity **7** concord, harmony **8** entirety, identity, sameness, totality **9** agreement, aloneness, integrity, wholeness **10** uniformity, uniqueness **11** singularity **12** completeness **13** individuality

one-of-a-kind 4 rare **6** unique **7** strange, unusual **8** original **9** eccentric

oneology
science of: **5** wines **10** winemaking

onerous 5 heavy **6** taxing **7** arduous, painful, weighty **8** crushing, grievous **9** demanding, wearisome **10** burdensome, exhausting, oppressive **11** distressing **12** hard to endure

one thing in return for another
Latin: **10** quid pro quo

one-time 3 old **4** past **5** early, prior **6** former, recent **7** earlier, quondam **8** previous **9** erstwhile
French: **8** ci-devant

one voice 4 solo **6** unison **7** concert

one who has a fixed income
French: **7** rentier

On First Looking Into Chapman's Homer
author: **9** John Keats

on foot
French: **5** a pied

ongoing 7 endless, lasting **8** enduring, unbroken, unending **10** continuing, proceeding **11** never-ending, unremitting **13** uninterrupted

On Golden Pond
director: **10** Mark Rydell
based on play by: **14** Ernest Thompson
cast: **9** Jane Fonda **10** Doug McKeon, Henry Fonda (Norman Thayer Jr) **16** Katharine Hepburn
setting: **5** Maine
Oscar for: **5** actor (Fonda) **7** actress (Hepburn)

on guard 4 wary **5** alert **7** careful, heedful **8** cautious, vigilant, watchful

on hand 5 handy, on tap **6** at hand **9** available **10** accessible, convenient **14** at one's disposal

on horseback
French: **7** a cheval

onion 6 Allium **10** Allium cepa
varieties: **3** red, sea, top **4** leek, tree, wild **5** green, gypsy, pearl, swamp, Welsh, white **6** German, potato, yellow **7** Bermuda, Danvers, nodding, prairie, shallot, Spanish **8** climbing, Egyptian, false sea, scallion, Valencia **9** Catawissa, ever-ready, flowering, two-bladed **10** multiplier, red-skinned **16** Japanese bunching
origin: **9** Asia Minor
called by Robert Louis Stevenson: **14** rose among roots

Onion Field, The
author: **14** Joseph Wambaugh

Oniros see **7** Oneiros

On Liberty
author: **14** John Stuart Mill

onlooker 5 gazer, ogler **6** viewer **7** watcher, witness **8** beholder, kibitzer, observer **9** bystander, spectator **10** eyewitness, rubberneck

only 4 just, lone, sole **5** alone **6** barely, merely, purely, simply, single, singly, solely, unique **7** at least **8** by itself, singular, solitary **9** by oneself, exclusive, unmatched **10** individual, no more than, nothing but, one and only, unrepeated **11** exclusively **12** individually, unparalleled

on one's uppers 5 broke **9** destitute **10** down and out

On Plants
author: **9** Aristotle

On Revolution
author: **12** Hannah Arendt

onrush 4 flow, flux, gush, tide, wave **5** flood, onset, storm, surge **6** attack, charge, deluge, spring, stream **7** assault, cascade, current, torrent **9** avalanche

onset 4 push, raid **5** birth, sally, start **6** attack, charge, onrush, outset, thrust **7** assault, genesis, infancy, offense **8** founding, invasion, outbreak, storming **9** beginning, inception, incursion, offensive, onslaught **10** incipience, initiation **12** commencement, inauguration

onslaught 4 coup, push, raid **5** blitz, foray, onset, sally **6** attack, charge, putsch, thrust **7** assault, offense **8** invasion **9** incursion, offensive **10** aggression, blitzkrieg

on tap 5 handy **6** at hand, on hand **9** available **10** accessible, convenient

Ontario
bay: **6** Hudson
canal: **5** Trent **6** Rideau
capital: **7** Toronto
city: **3** Emo **4** Galt **6** London, Ottawa **7** Windsor **8** Hamilton, Kingston **9** Kitchener
explored by: **5** French **6** British
industry: **6** mining **11** agriculture **13**

manufacturing
lake: 6 Simcoe
province of: 6 Canada
river: 6 Ottawa, Thames 7 Niagara 10 St Lawrence
settled by: 9 Loyalists
university: 4 York 5 Brock, Trent 8 McMaster

on the alert 4 wary 7 careful, mindful, on guard 8 cautious, watchful 9 wide awake 12 on the lookout

On the Beach
author: 10 Nevil Shute
director: 13 Stanley Kramer
cast: 10 Ava Gardner 11 Fred Astaire, Gregory Peck 13 Donna Anderson 14 Anthony Perkins

on the contrary
French: 11 au contraire

on the dot 7 exactly 8 promptly 9 on the nose, precisely 10 punctually

on the face
Latin: 7 ex facie

on the go 4 busy 6 active, mobile 8 in motion 9 energetic, on the move 13 indefatigable

On the Heavens
author: 9 Aristotle

On the Morning of Christ's Nativity
author: 10 John Milton

on the move 5 astir 6 active, mobile 7 on the go 8 in motion

on the nose 5 exact 7 exactly, precise 8 accurate, on target 9 precisely 10 accurately, on the money

on the outer edges
Latin: 10 in extremis

on the right track 8 on course, on target

On the Soul
author: 9 Aristotle

On the Town
director: 9 Gene Kelly 12 Stanley Donen
cast: 9 Ann Miller, Gene Kelly, Vera-Ellen 12 Betty Garrett, Frank Sinatra
setting: 11 New York City
score: 11 Adolph Green, Betty Comden 16 Leonard Bernstein
song: 14 New York New York

On the Waterfront
director: 9 Elia Kazan
cast: 8 Lee J Cobb 10 Karl Malden, Pat Henning, Rod Steiger 12 Leif Erickson, Marlon Brando 13 Eva Marie Saint
Oscar for: 5 actor (Brando) 7 picture 8 director 10 screenplay 17 supporting actress (Saint)

on the whole 9 in general 10 by and large 27 considering the circumstances

onto 4 atop, upon 5 aware, privy 6 aboard

onus 4 duty, load 5 cross 6 burden,

strain, weight 9 liability 10 obligation 11 encumbrance 13 burden of proof 14 responsibility

onus probandi 13 burden of proof

onward, onwards 5 ahead, along 7 forward, ongoing 9 advancing, frontward 11 moving ahead, progressive
French: 7 en avant, en route

On Wings of Eagles
author: 10 Ken Follett

oodles 4 gobs, lots, many 5 heaps, loads, scads 6 plenty

ooze 4 drip, leak, mire, muck, seep, silt 5 bleed, drain, exude, slime, sweat 6 filter, sludge 7 dribble, leakage, seepage, soft mud, trickle 8 alluvium 9 discharge, exudation, percolate, secretion, transpire

oozing 5 leaky, weepy 6 sweaty 7 exuding, seepage, seeping 8 bleeding, sweating

opal
color: 3 red 5 black, white 6 orange 11 transparent
source: 6 Mexico 9 Australia 14 Lightning Ridge
variety: 8 fire opal

opalescent 5 milky 6 pearly 8 irisated, luminous 10 iridescent

opaque 4 dark, dull, hazy 5 muddy, murky 7 clouded, muddied, obscure, unclear 8 abstruse 9 difficult 12 impenetrable, unfathomable 14 nontranslucent, nontransparent, unintelligible 16 incomprehensible

opaqueness 7 opacity 8 dullness 9 denseness, muddiness, murkiness, obscurity 10 cloudiness 11 unclearness 15 impenetrability 17 unintelligibility 19 incomprehensibility

open 4 ajar, fair, just, wide 5 agape, begin, clear, crack, found, frank, plain, unbar 6 candid, create, direct, expand, gaping, honest, launch, unfold, unlock, unseal, unshut 7 artless, exposed, lay open, natural, not shut, sincere, unblock, unclose, yawning 8 commence, extended, outgoing, unbiased, unclosed, unfasten, unfenced, unfolded, unlocked, unsealed 9 available, coverless, establish, expansive, impartial, institute, not closed, objective, originate, receptive, unbigoted, unbounded, uncovered, uncrowded, undertake, welcoming 10 accessible, forthright, impersonal, inaugurate, responsive, unenclosed, unfastened 11 extroverted, uncluttered, uninhabited 12 permit access, unobstructed, unprejudiced 13 disinterested, doing business 15 straightforward

open-air 7 outdoor, outside 10 unconfined
Italian: 8 al fresco

open and aboveboard 6 candid, honest 7 ethical 10 forthright 12 on the up and up 15 straightforward

Open Boat, The
author: 12 Stephen Crane

Open City
director: 17 Roberto Rossellini
cast: 11 Aldo Fabrizi, Anna Magnani 16 Marcello Pagliero
setting: 4 Rome

open-eyed 5 alert, awake, aware 7 heedful, mindful 8 vigilant, watchful, wide-eyed 9 attentive, wide-awake

open-handed 6 lavish 7 liberal 8 generous, prodigal 9 bounteous, bountiful 10 altruistic, beneficent, benevolent, ungrudging, unstinting 11 magnanimous

openhandedness 10 generosity, liberality 11 benevolence, generousity, munificence 12 extravagance

openhearted 7 artless, sincere 8 trusting 9 ingenuous

opening 3 gap, job 4 gash, hole, rent, rift, slit, slot, spot, tear, vent 5 break, chink, cleft, crack, place, space, start 6 breach, chance 7 fissure, kickoff, preface, prelude, send-off, vacancy 8 aperture, occasion, overture, position 9 be ginning, first part, launching, situation 10 initiation 11 opportunity, possibility 12 commencement, inauguration, installation, introduction

openly 6 freely 7 frankly 8 directly, honestly, publicly 9 obviously

open-minded 4 fair 7 liberal 8 amenable, flexible, tolerant, unbiased 9 adaptable, impartial, objective, receptive 10 responsive, undogmatic 11 broad-minded 12 unprejudiced 13 disinterested, nonjudgmental

openmouthed 4 agog, awed 5 agape 6 aghast, amazed 8 wide-eyed 9 awestruck, bewitched, marveling, staggered, stupefied, surprised 10 astonished, confounded 10 dumbstruck, enthralled, spellbound 11 dumbfounded 12 wonderstruck 13 flabbergasted, thunderstruck

openness 6 candor 7 honesty 8 daylight 9 frankness, sincerity 11 artlessness 13 guilelessness 14 forthrightness 19 straightforwardness

open sanction 8 free hand, free rein 13 full authority
French: 12 catre blanche

open the eyes of 8 disabuse 11 set straight

open to choice 8 elective, optional 9 voluntary

openwork 3 net 4 lace 6 eyelet 7 lattice, Madeira, tracery 8 filigree

opera 5 score 7 musical 8 libretto 11 composition
by Bellini: 5 Norma
by Bizet: 6 Carmen
by Delibes: 5 Lakme
by Donizetti: 10 La Favorita 11 Don

Pasquale **12** Maria Stuarda **13** L'Elisir d'Amore **17** Lucia di Lammermoor **19** La Figlia di Regimente
by Gounod: 5 Faust
by Leoncavallo: 10 I Pagliacci
by Mozart: 8 Idomeneo **10** Magic Flute **11** Don Giovanni **12** Cosi fan tutte **16** Marriage of Figaro
by Offenbach: 15 Tales of Hoffmann
by Ponchielli: 10 La Gioconda
by Puccini: 5 Tosca **8** La Boheme **12** Manon Lescaut **15** Madame Butterfly
by Rossini: 8 Tancredi **11** William Tell **15** The Barber of Seville
by Smetana: 13 The Bartered Bride
by Strauss: 6 Salome **7** Elektra **15** Ariadne auf Naxos **16** Der Rosenkavalier
by Tchaikovsky: 12 Eugene Onegin
by Verdi: 4 Aida **6** Otello **8** Falstaff **9** Rigoletto **10** La Traviata **11** Il Trovatore
by Wagner: 8 Parsifal **9** Lohengrin **10** Tannhauser **16** Tristan and Isolde **17** The Flying Dutchman **21** The Ring of the Nibelungs
comic: 5 buffa **7** comique
glass: 9 lorgnette
hat: 5 crush, gibus
house: 3 Met **6** Sydney **7** La Scala **12** Covent Garden, Metropolitan
singer: 4 bass, diva **5** basso, buffa, buffo, tenor **7** soprano **8** baritone **9** contralto **10** coloratura, prima donna **12** mezzo soprano
singular: 4 opus
solo: 4 aria
text: 8 libretto
operate 2 go **3** run **4** go in, work **6** behave, manage, open up **7** oversee, perform **8** function **11** superintend **14** perform surgery **18** perform an operation
operating 6 active **7** working **8** in motion **9** operative **10** responsive
operation 5 force **6** action, agency, effect **7** conduct, pursuit, running, surgery, working **8** activity, exertion **9** influence, procedure **10** management, overseeing **11** exploratory, performance, supervision **15** instrumentality, superintendence
operative 3 spy **4** dick **5** agent, in use **6** acting, active, shamus, worker **7** in force, working **8** in effect, in motion, workable **9** activated, detective, effective, effectual, operating **10** functional, private eye, responsive **11** efficacious, secret agent
operator 4 doer, user **5** agent, pilot **6** driver, worker **7** manager **9** performer
opere citato 14 in the work cited
abbreviation: 5 op cit
Ophelia
character in: 6 Hamlet
author: 11 Shakespeare

ophidiophobia
fear of: 6 snakes
Ophion
form: 7 serpent
created from: 9 north wind
created by: 8 Eurynome
Ophir
father: 6 Joktan
source of: 4 gold
opiate 4 dope **6** downer **7** anodyne **8** hypnotic, narcotic, nepenthe, sedative **9** analgesic, calmative, soporific, stupefier **10** depressant, painkiller, palliative **12** somnifacient, stupefacient, tranquilizer
opine 3 say **4** deem **5** allow, guess, offer, state, think **6** assume, reckon **7** believe, imagine, presume, suggest, surmise **8** conclude, consider, estimate **9** speculate, volunteer **10** conjecture, have a hunch
opinion 4 idea, view **6** belief, notion, theory **7** surmise **8** estimate, judgment, thinking **9** sentiment, suspicion **10** assessment, assumption, conception, conclusion, conjecture, conviction, estimation, evaluation, impression, persuasion **11** speculation
opinionated 8 dogmatic, obdurate, stubborn **9** obstinate, pigheaded, unbending **10** bullheaded, headstrong, inflexible, unyielding **12** closedminded **14** uncompromising
O Pioneers!
author: 11 Willa Cather
Opis
companion of: 7 Artemis
Opobalsammum 12 Biblical tree
Oppenheimer, Julius Robert
field: 7 physics
directed development of: 10 atomic bomb
location: 9 Los Alamos, New Mexico
chaired: 3 AEC **22** Atomic Energy Commission
Opper, Frederick
creator/artist of: 13 Happy Hooligan **17** Alphonse and Gaston, And Her Name Was Maud
opponent 3 foe **5** enemy, rival **8** resister **9** adversary, assailant, contender, disputant **10** antagonist, challenger, competitor, opposition
opportune 3 apt **5** happy, lucky **6** proper, timely **7** fitting **8** suitable **9** expedient, favorable, fortunate, welltimed **10** auspicious, convenient, felicitous, profitable, propitious, seasonable **11** appropriate **12** advantageous
opportunity 4 time, turn **5** means **6** chance, moment **7** opening **8** occasion **9** situation **10** good chance **11** contingency
oppose 4 buck, defy **5** fight **6** battle, combat, resist, thwart **7** contest **8** ob-

struct **9** withstand **12** be set against, speak against
opposed 3 con **4** anti **6** averse, pitted **7** adverse, against, counter, hostile **8** contrary, disputed, objected, resisted **9** contested, countered **10** confronted, contrasted, reciprocal **12** contradicted
opposer 5 rival **8** opponent **9** adversary **10** antagonist, competitor
opposite 5 other **6** facing **7** adverse, counter, reverse **8** contrary, converse, opposing **9** differing **11** conflicting **12** antagonistic, antithetical **13** contradictory, counteractive
opposite number 5 equal **8** parallel **10** equivalent **11** correlative, counterpart
opposition 3 foe **5** enemy, rival **6** enmity **8** aversion, defiance, opponent **9** adversary, contender, hostility, other side, rejection **10** antagonism, antagonist, competitor, negativism, resistance **11** contrariety, disapproval **12** disagreement
oppress 3 tax, try, vex **4** pain **5** abuse, worry **6** burden, deject, grieve, sadden, sorrow **7** depress, trouble **8** cast down, dispirit, maltreat **9** despotize, persecute, tyrannize, weigh down **10** discourage, dishearten
oppressed 7 crushed **9** exploited **10** tyrannized **11** downtrodden, subservient
oppressive 5 cruel, harsh **6** brutal, severe, trying, vexing **7** onerous, painful, wearing **8** despotic, grievous, pressing **9** worrisome **10** burdensome, depressing, repressive, tyrannical, unbearable **11** distressing, hardhearted, troublesome **12** discouraging **13** uncomfortable
oppressor 6 despot, tyrant **8** autocrat, dictator
opprobrious 4 base **6** wicked **7** abusive, corrupt, damning **8** infamous, reviling, shameful, shocking **9** malicious, maligning, nefarious, vilifying, vitriolic **10** censorious, deplorable, despicable, malevolent, outrageous, scandalous, scurrilous, unbecoming **11** acrimonious, disgraceful, fulminating **12** condemnatory, denunciatory, dishonorable, disreputable, faultfinding **13** hypercritical, objectionable, reprehensible
opprobrium 5 shame **6** infamy **8** disgrace, dishonor **9** disrepute **12** denunciation
Ops
origin: 5 Roman
goddess of: 6 plenty
husband: 6 Saturn
son: 7 Jupiter
called: 10 Magna Mater
corresponds to: 4 Rhea **6** Cybele **9** Dindymene **10** Berecyntia
opt for 4 pick, take **5** adopt **6** choose,

select, take up **7** embrace, espouse, fix upon, pick out **8** decide on, settle on

optimism 10 confidence **11** hopefulness **12** cheerfulness, sanguineness **13** bright outlook, encouragement

optimistic 6 bright **7** hopeful, roseate **8** buoyed up, cheerful, sanguine **9** confident, favorable, heartened, promising **10** auspicious, encouraged, heartening, propitious **11** encouraging, rose-colored **12** enthusiastic

Optimist's Daughter, The
author: 11 Eudora Welty

optimum 4 acme, A-one, best, peak **5** crest, ideal, prime **6** choice, height, select, zenith **7** capital, perfect, supreme **8** flawless **9** faultless, first-rate **10** perfection, unexcelled **11** superlative **12** quintessence

option 4 will **5** voice **6** choice, liking **8** decision, election, free will, pleasure **9** franchise, privilege, selection **10** discretion, partiality, preference **11** alternative **12** predilection

optional 4 open **8** elective, unforced **9** allowable, open- ended, voluntary **10** volitional **11** not required **12** discretional **13** discretionary, nonobligatory

opulence 6 bounty, plenty, riches, wealth **7** fortune **8** elegance, luxuries, richness **9** abundance, affluence, amplitude, profusion **10** cornucopia, lavishness, plentitude, prosperity **11** copiousness, great wealth **13** sumptuousness

opus 4 work **5** piece **6** effort **7** attempt, product **8** creation **9** handiwork, invention **10** brainchild, production **11** composition

oracle, Oracle 4 sage, seer **5** augur, sibyl **6** wizard **7** adviser, diviner, prophet **9** predictor, Scripture **10** forecaster, soothsayer **11** clairvoyant

oral 5 vocal **6** spoken, verbal, voiced **7** uttered **8** ingested **9** swallowed **10** of the mouth, verbalized **11** articulated, using speech
Latin: 8 viva voce

orange
varieties: 4 king, mock, sour, wild **5** blood, hardy, natal, navel, Osage, sweet **6** bitter, common, Panama, Temple **7** Florida, Mexican, Satsuma, Seville, Spanish **8** Bergamot, Mandarin, Otaheite, Valencia **9** Tachibana, vegetable **10** Chinese box, trifoliate **13** African cherry, Mediterranean **15** Jamaica mandarin **17** house-blooming mock
liqueur: 7 Curacao

orangutan, orang-outang 3 ape **4** mias **5** satyr **6** primate **10** anthropoid
characteristic: 8 arboreal **11** herbivorous
native land: 6 Borneo **7** Sumatra
species: 13 Pongo pygmaeus

ora pro nobis 9 pray for us

orate 6 recite, speak **7** declaim **11** make a speech

oration 4 talk **5** spiel **6** eulogy, sermon, speech **7** address, lecture, recital **9** discourse, monologue, panegyric **10** peroration **11** declamation **12** disquisition, formal speech

orator 6 talker **7** speaker **8** lecturer, preacher **9** declaimer **10** sermonizer **11** rhetorician, speechmaker, spellbinder **12** elocutionist **13** public speaker

oratory 6 speech **7** bombast **8** delivery, rhetoric **9** elocution, eloquence, preaching **11** declamation **12** speechifying, speechmaking **14** grandiloquence

orb 4 ball, moon **5** globe **6** sphere **7** globule **8** spheroid

orbit 3 way **4** path **5** cycle, route, track **6** circle, course **7** channel, circuit, pathway **10** trajectory **13** revolve around **14** circumnavigate

orchards
god of: 9 Vertumnus

orchestra 3 pit **4** band **6** stalls **7** parquet **8** ensemble, parterre **12** Philharmonic

orchestrate 5 adapt, score **7** arrange, compose

orchestration 5 score **10** adaptation **11** arrangement **12** organization

orchid
varieties: 3 bat, bee, fen, fly, nun, nut **4** baby, blue, dove, moth, nun's, rein, swan **5** black, chain, cigar, cobra, coral, giant, jewel, pansy, Salep, showy, snowy, spice, tiger, water, widow **6** bamboo, bottle, cradle, dollar, Easter, helmet, mirror, monkey, pigeon, ragged, sawfly, shower, spider, stream, virgin **7** Alaskan, cowhorn, fringed, hooker's, jumping, peacock, rainbow, rosebud, scarlet, soldier **8** bee-swarm, Cooktown, cranefly, fried-egg, gold-lace, greenfly, hyacinth, nun's-hood, poorman's, Savannah, scorpion, white nun, windmill, woodland **9** bluntleaf, butterfly, chocolate, Christmas, clam-shell, green rein, green swan, white rein **10** buttonhole, five-leaved, golden swan, hay-scented, late spider, leafy white, Sierra rein, slender bog **11** cockle-shell, crested rein, dancing-doll, dancing-lady, early spider, golden chain, green-winged, one-leaf rein, pink slipper, purple-spire, rattlesnake, round-leaved **12** green fringed, pink scorpion, purple-hooded, Southern rein, tall white bog, white fringed **13** crested yellow, golden fringed, green woodland, Northern green, ragged fringed, yellow fringed **14** crested fringed, large butterfly, little club-

spur, white butterfly **15** lesser butterfly, lily-of-the-valley **16** downy rattlesnake, Florida butterfly, Northern small bog, purple fringeless, small round-leaved, white-flowered bog **18** large purple fringed, leafy Northern green, small purple fringed, Southern small white **19** lesser purple fringed **20** greater purple fringed

Orcus
god of: 10 underworld
punishes: 7 perjury
corresponds to: 3 Dis **5** Hades, Pluto **8** Dis Pater

ordain 4 name, rule, will **5** elect, enact, frock **6** decree, invest **7** adjudge, appoint, command, dictate **8** delegate, deputize, instruct **9** determine, legislate, prescribe, pronounce **10** commission, consecrate

ordeal 4 care, pain **5** agony, grief, trial, worry **6** burden, misery, sorrow, strain, stress **7** anguish, concern, torment, tragedy, trouble **8** calamity, distress, pressure, vexation **9** heartache, nightmare, suffering **10** affliction, oppression **11** tribulation, unhappiness **12** wretchedness **16** trying experience

order 3 bid, law **4** body, book, calm, club, fiat, form, kind, rank, rule, sort, type **5** breed, caste, class, grade, group, guild, house, lodge, quiet, ukase **6** adjure, ask for, charge, decree, degree, demand, dictum, direct, engage, enjoin, family, status, stripe, system **7** agree to, bidding, caliber, call for, command, company, control, dictate, harmony, pattern, quality, request, reserve, silence, society, species, station **8** alliance, category, division, grouping, instruct, neatness, position, purchase, sorority, standing, tidiness **9** framework, structure, ultimatum **10** discipline, federation, fraternity, imperative, sisterhood, tabulation **11** arrangement, association, brotherhood, commandment, confederacy, designation, instruction, tranquility **12** codification, organization, peacefulness, tranquillity **13** pronouncement **14** categorization, classification

ordered 4 bade, neat, trim **7** regular, uniform **8** arranged **9** shipshape **10** systematic

orderliness 8 neatness, tidiness **10** discipline **12** organization

orderly 4 neat, tidy **5** civil, quiet **6** proper, spruce **8** peaceful **9** organized, peaceable, shipshape, tractable **10** classified, controlled, methodical, restrained, system atic **11** disciplined, uncluttered, well-behaved

ordinance 3 act, law **4** bull, fiat, rule, writ **5** canon, edict, order **6** decree, dictum, ruling **7** command, mandate, statute **9** enactment **10** regulation **11** commandment

ordinarily 7 as a rule, usually **8** commonly, normally **9** generally, regularly, routinely **10** habitually **11** customarily **12** on the average **14** conventionally

ordinary 4 dull, so-so **5** usual **6** common, normal **7** average, humdrum, routine, trivial, typical **8** everyday, familiar, habitual, mediocre, standard **9** customary **10** pedestrian, uninspired **11** commonplace, indifferent, stereotyped, traditional, unimportant **12** conventional, run-of-the-mill, unimpressive **13** insignificant, unexceptional, unimaginative, uninteresting **15** inconsequential, undistinguished

Ordinary People
   director: 13 Robert Redford
   author: 11 Judith Guest
   cast: 10 Judd Hirsch **13** Timothy Hutton **14** Mary Tyler Moore **16** Donald Sutherland
   Oscar for: 7 picture **8** director **12** screenwriter **15** supporting actor (Hutton)

ordinary wine
   French: 12 vin ordinaire

ordnance 4 arms **6** cannon **9** armaments, artillery, munitions

ordnance depot 6 armory **7** arsenal **18** military storehouse

ore 3 tin **4** gold, iron, lead, paco, rock, zinc **5** metal **6** bronze, copper, galena, sulfur **7** halvans, mineral **8** aluminum, cinnabar, hematite **9** melachite
   byproduct: 6 gangue
   deposit: 3 bed **4** lode, mine, vein **7** bonanza
   layer: 4 seam **5** stope
   trough: 6 strake
   worthless: 4 slag **5** dross, matte

Oread
   form: 5 nymph
   location: 8 mountain
   companion of: 7 Artemis

oregano
   name means: 16 joy of the mountain
   botanical name: 8 O vulgare, Origanum
   also: 6 organy, origan **8** marjoram **9** pizza herb **11** Mexican sage, winter sweet
   origin: 13 Mediterranean
   family: 4 mint
   cure for: 11 indigestion **14** loss of appetite
   first aid for: 12 spider stings **14** scorpion stings
   use: 5 pizza **6** broths **8** stuffing **12** tomato dishes **13** Italian dishes

Oregon
   abbreviation: 2 OR **4** Oreg
   nickname: 6 Beaver, Sunset **7** Webfoot **13** Sawdust Empire

capital: 5 Salem
largest city: 8 Portland
others: 5 Nyssa **6** Albany, Eugene **7** Ashland, Astoria, Medford **8** Portland, Roseburg **9** Corvallis, Pendleton **10** Grant's Pass, Willamette **12** Klamath Falls
college: 4 Reed **7** Pacific **8** Linfield, Portland **10** Willamette **13** Lewis and Clark
feature:
   fort: 5 Boise **6** Casper **7** Kearney, Laramie
   national park: 10 Crater Lake
tribe: 4 Coos **5** Alsea, Kusan, Modoc, Wasco, Yanan, Yunca **6** Cayuse, Chetco, Chinoo, Kuitsh, Molala, Siletz, Tenino, Umpqua **7** Bannock, Clatsop, Klamath, Sastean, Shastan, Takelma, Walpapi, Yaquina **8** Clackama, Klikitat, Nez Perce, Sahaptin, Umatilla **9** Kalapuyan, Tillamook **10** Kalapooian, Wallawalla
people: 10 Wayne Morse **12** Linus Pauling **15** Phyllis McGinley
   explorer: 13 Lewis and Clark
lake: 5 Abert, Waldo **6** Harney, McNary **7** John Day, Klamath, Malheur
   deepest in US: 6 Crater
land rank: 5 tenth
mountain: 6 Mazama, Tacoma, Walker, Wilson **7** Elkhorn, Grizzly, Jackass, Rainier, Tidbits, Wallowa **8** Cascades **9** Blue Coast, Marys Peak **10** Strawberry
   highest point: 4 Hood
physical feature:
   bay: 4 Coos
   caves: 11 Marble Halls
   wind: 7 Chinook
river: 5 Rogue, Snake **6** Imnaha, Owyhee, Powder, Umpqua **7** Blitzen, John Day, Klamath, Silvie's **8** Columbia **9** Deschutes **10** Willamette
state admission: 11 thirty-third
state bird: 17 western meadowlark
state fish: 13 Chinook salmon
state flower: 7 mahonia **11** Oregon grape
state motto: 8 The Union
state song: 14 Oregon My Oregon
state tree: 10 Douglas fir

Oregon Trail, The
   author: 14 Francis Parkman

Oresteia
   author: 9 Aeschylus
   trilogy includes: 9 Agamemnon, Eumenides **10** Choephoroe

Orestes
   author: 9 Euripides
   character: 5 Helen **6** Apollo, Furies **7** Electra, Pylades **8** Menelaus

Orestes
   father: 9 Agamemnon
   mother: 12 Clytemnestra
   sister: 7 Electra **9** Iphigenia
   wife: 8 Hermione

   son: 9 Tisamenus
   killed: 9 Aegisthus **12** Clytemnestra
   pursued by: 6 Furies

Orfeo, L'
   also: 17 The Story of Orpheus
   opera by: 10 Monteverdi

Orfeo ed Euridice
   also: 18 Orpheus and Eurydice
   opera by: 5 Gluck
   character: 4 Amor, Zeus **6** Furies

Orff, Carl
   born: 6 Munich **7** Germany
   composer of: 7 Der Mond, The Moon **8** Antigone, Die Kluge **9** Schulwerk **10** Prometheus **13** Carmina Burana, The Clever Girl **14** Catulli Carmina **16** Oedipus der Tyrann, Oedipus the Tyrant

organ 6 agency **7** journal, vehicle **9** harmonium **10** hurdy-gurdy, instrument **11** publication

organic 5 alive, quick **6** living **7** animate, natural, ordered, planned, unified **8** designed, physical **9** patterned **10** anatomical, harmonious, methodical, systematic **12** nonsynthetic **13** physiological **14** constitutional

organism 4 cell **5** plant, whole **6** animal, entity, sys tem **7** complex, network, society **8** creature **9** bacterium **10** federation **11** association, corporation, institution, living thing **13** microorganism

organization 4 club, firm, sect **5** corps, group, order, party, union **6** design, league, making, outfit **7** company, forming, harmony, pattern, society **8** alliance, assembly, business, grouping, ordering **9** arranging, formation **10** federation, fellowship, fraternity **11** arrangement, association, composition, corporation, formulation, structuring **12** constitution, coordination **13** establishment, incorporation

organizational 10 managerial **13** developmental **14** administrative

organize 4 file, form, tidy **5** found, group, index, order, set up **6** codify, create, neaten, tidy up **7** arrange, catalog, develop **8** classify, tabulate **9** establish, formulate, originate **10** categorize, coordinate **11** make orderly, systematize

organized 4 neat, tidy **7** logical, orderly **8** coherent **10** methodical, systematic

orgiastic 4 wild **6** wanton **7** drunken, riotous **9** abandoned, debauched, Dionysian, dissolute, libertine **10** dissipated, licentious **12** bacchanalian, unrestrained **13** overindulgent, undisciplined

orgy 7 debauch, wassail **8** carousal **9** bacchanal **10** saturnalia **11** bacchanalia

orient, the Orient 3 fix, set **4** Asia, find **6** locate, relate, square **7** situate

8 accustom **9** acclimate, reconcile **10** the Far East **11** Eastern Asia, familiarize

oriental 4 Arab, fine, Thai, Turk **5** Asian **6** bright, Indian, Korean **7** Asiatic, Chinese, Eastern, Iranian, shining **8** Japanese, lustrous, precious, superior **10** Vietnamese
  animal: 4 zebu **5** rasse
  building: 6 pagoda
  dish: 5 pilau, pilaw **6** pilaff
  drum: 6 tomtom
  food fish: 3 tai
  garment: 3 aba **6** sarong
  inn: 4 Khan **5** serai **6** imaret **11** caravansary
  laborer: 6 coolie
  market: 3 suk, sug **4** souk **6** bazaar
  nurse: 4 amah, ayah
  prince: 4 amir, haja
  sail: 6 lateen
  sash: 3 obi
  shrub: 3 tea **5** henna **8** oleander
  wagon: 5 araba
  weight: 2 mo **4** rotl, tael **5** catty, liang **6** cantar

orientation 8 location **9** alignment, direction, situation **10** adjustment **11** acclimation **15** acclimatization, familiarization

orifice 3 gap, pit **4** hole, slit, slot, vent **5** cleft, inlet, mouth **6** cavity, cranny, hollow, lacuna, pocket, socket **7** crevice, fissure, opening, passage **8** alveolus, aperture, entrance

origami
  Japanese art of: 12 paper folding

origin 4 base, line, race, rise, root **5** agent, basis, birth, breed, cause, house, stock **6** author, family, father, ground, growth, mother, reason, source, spring, strain **7** creator, descent, genesis, lineage, taproot **8** ancestry, nativity, producer **9** beginning, emergence, evolution, generator, inception, parentage, principle **10** derivation, extraction, foundation **12** commencement, fountainhead

Origin, The
  author: 11 Irving Stone

original 3 new **4** bold **5** basic, basis, first, fresh, novel **6** daring, primal, unique **7** example, initial, pattern, primary, seminal, strange, unusual **8** atypical, creative, ear- liest, germinal, primeval, singular, uncommon **9** different, essential, first copy, formative, inaugural, ingenious, inventive, prototype **10** aboriginal, newfangled, primordial, underlying, unfamiliar, unorthodox **11** fundamental, imaginative **12** introductory **13** extraordinary **14** unconventional

Original Amateur Hour, The
  host: 7 Ted Mack

originality 6 daring **7** newness, novelty **8** boldness **9** freshness, ingenuity **10** cleverness, creativity, uniqueness **11** imagination, singularity, unorthodoxy **13** individuality, inventiveness **17** unconventionality

originally 7 at first, by birth **8** uniquely **9** initially, unusually **10** creatively **11** differently, inventively **13** imaginatively

originate 4 come, flow, rise, stem **5** arise, begin, draft, found, issue, start **6** create, crop up, derive, design, devise, emerge, evolve, father, invent, sprout **7** develop, emanate, proceed **8** commence, conceive, envision, initiate, organize, spring up **9** establish, fabricate, formulate, germinate **10** inaugurate

origination 5 birth **7** genesis **9** inception, invention **10** conception, initiation **11** germination **12** commencement **13** establishment

Origin of Species, The
  author: 13 Charles Darwin

Origins of Totalitarianism, The
  author: 12 Hannah Arendt

Orion
  form: 5 giant
  vocation: 6 hunter
  pursued: 8 Pleiades
  killed by: 7 Artemis
  became: 13 constellation

Oriya
  language family: 12 Indo-European
  branch: 11 Indo-Iranian
  group: 5 Indic
  spoken in: 5 (northern) India

Orkney Islands
  county seat: 8 Kirkwall
  country: 8 Scotland
  firth: 8 Pentland
  island: 3 Hay **6** Rousay, Sanday **7** Westray **8** Stronsay **14** South Ronaldsay
  largest city: 6 Pomona

Orlando
  author: 13 Virginia Woolf
  character: 5 Sasha **14** Nicholas Greene **28** Archduchess Harriet of Roumania, Marmaduke Bonthrop Shelmerdine

Orlando
  character in: 11 As You Like It
  author: 11 Shakespeare

Orlando Furioso
  author: 7 Ariosto
  character: 6 Rogero **7** Rinaldo **8** Agramant, Angelica, Rodomont **9** Bradamant **11** Charlemagne

Ormazd 10 Ahura Mazda **12** supreme deity
  religion: 14 Zoroastrianism

ormolu 5 alloy, brass, paste **6** bronze **7** gilding **8** ornament
  imitation of: 4 gold
  used to decorate: 5 clock **9** furniture

ornament 4 deck, gild, trim **5** adorn **6** bedeck, enrich, finery, frills **7** festoon, furbish, garnish **8** beautify, decorate, furbelow, trick out, trimming **9** accessory, adornment, embellish **10** decoration, enrich ment **11** elaboration **13** embellishment **14** beautification

ornamental 4 gilt **5** fancy **6** chichi, rococo **10** decorative
  ball: 4 bead **6** pompom
  button: 4 stud
  grass: 4 neti
  loop: 5 picot
  metal: 5 niello

ornamentation 7 garnish **8** trimming **9** adornment **10** decoration **13** embellishment

ornate 5 fancy, showy **6** flashy, florid, lavish, rococo **7** adorned, baroque, flowery **9** decorated, elaborate, sumptuous **10** flamboyant **11** embellished, pretentious **12** ostentatious

ornery 4 curt, mean **5** surly, testy **6** crabby, grumpy, shirty **7** grouchy, peevish, waspish **8** snappish **9** dyspeptic, irascible, irritable **10** ill-natured **11** ill-tempered, quarrelsome **12** cantankerous

ornithophobia
  fear of: 5 birds

ornithopod
  type of: 8 dinosaur
  member: 9 Iguanodon **10** Edmontonia, Nodosaurus **11** Anatosaurus, Polacanthus, Saurolophus, Scolosaurus, Stegosaurus **12** Ankylosaurus, Camptosaurus, Lambeosaurus, Pisanosaurus **13** Acanthopolis, Corythosaurus, Hypsilophodon, Palaeoscincus **14** Thescelosaurus **15** Parasaurolophus, Procheneosaurus **17** Heterodontosaurus

orotund 4 full, rich **5** clear **6** strong **7** pompous, ringing, vibrant **8** resonant, sonorous **9** bombastic **10** resounding, rhetorical, stentorian
  Latin: 10 ore rotundo

oro y plata 13 gold and silver
  motto of: 7 Montana

Orozco, Jose Clemente
  born: 6 Mexico **7** Jalisco (Zapotlan) **12** Ciudad Guzman
  artwork: 5 Grief **9** Catharsis **11** Omniscience **12** House of Tears **16** National Allegory, Social Revolution **18** Hidalgo and Castillo

Orphans of the Storm
  director: 10 D W Griffith
  cast: 11 Dorothy Gish, Lillian Gish **17** Joseph Schildkraut

Orpheus
  vocation: 4 poet **8** musician
  mother: 8 Calliope
  wife: 8 Eurydice
  member of: 9 Argonauts
  went into: 5 Hades
  killed by: 7 Maenads

Orpheus in the Underworld

also: 15 Orphee aux Enfers
operetta by: 9 Offenbach
Orsino
  character in: 12 Twelfth Night
  author: 11 Shakespeare
ort 3 bit **5** crumb, dregs, scrap **6** morsel, refuse, trifle **7** remnant **8** leavings, leftover
orthodox 5 fixed, pious, usual **6** devout, narrow **7** limited, regular, routine **8** accepted, approved, official, ordinary, standard **9** customary, religious **11** commonplace, conformable, established, traditional **12** conventional **13** authoritative, circumscribed
orthoptera
  class: 8 hexapoda
  phylum: 10 arthropoda
  group: 4 leaf **5** stick **6** locust, mantid **7** cricket **9** cockroach **11** grasshopper
Orwell, George
  real name: 15 Eric Arthur Blair
  author of: 4 1984 **10** Animal Farm **18** Nineteen Eighty- Four **29** Politics and the English Language
oryx 5 beisa **6** pickax **7** gazelle, gemsbok **8** antelope, leucoryx
Osage (Wazhazhe)
  language family: 6 Siouan
  location: 6 Kansas **8** Arkansas, Missouri, Oklahoma
Oscan
  language family: 12 Indo-European
  branch: 6 Italic
Oschophoria
  origin: 8 Athenian
  event: 8 festival
  honoring: 7 vintage **8** Dionysus
oscillate 4 vary **5** pulse, swing, waver **6** change, seesaw **7** librate, pulsate, vibrate **8** hesitate **9** alternate, come and go, fluctuate, hem and haw, vacillate **10** ebb and flow, equivocate **12** shilly-shally **16** move back and forth
O'Shaughnessy, Brigid
  character in: 16 The Maltese Falcon
  author: 7 Hammett
osier 3 rod **4** wand **5** salix, withe **6** willow **7** dogwood, wilgers **9** twig-withy
  species: 14 Salix viminalis
  use: 6 wicker **8** basketry
Osiris
  origin: 8 Egyptian
  god of: 4 dead, Nile
  judge of: 4 dead
  king of: 4 dead
  wife: 4 Isis
  sister: 4 Isis
  son: 5 Horus
  brother: 3 Set **4** Seth **5** Horus
  killed by: 3 Set **4** Seth
Oskar Matzerath
  character in: 7 Tin Drum
  author: 5 Grass

Oslo
  capital of: 6 Norway
  former name: 11 Christiania
  landmark: 8 Storting (Parliament) **11** Royal Palace
  mountain: 12 Holmenkollen
  park: 7 Frogner
  peninsula: 8 Akershus
  street: 14 Karl Johansgate
Osmond, Gilbert
  character in: 18 The Portrait of a Lady
  author: 5 James
Ossian
  character in: 12 Gaelic poetry
ossify 6 harden **7** stiffen **9** fossilize
ossuary 8 boneyard **10** depository, receptacle
ostensible 6 avowed **7** alleged, assumed, feigned, implied, nominal, outward, seeming, surface, titular, visible **8** apparent, declared, illusory, manifest, specious **9** pretended, professed **10** presumable **11** perceivable
ostentation 4 airs, dash, fuss, pomp, ritz, show **5** glitz, gloss, swank **6** splash **7** display, glitter **8** flourish, pretense **9** pageantry, pomposity, showiness, spectacle
  French: 7 etalage
ostentatious 4 loud **5** gaudy, showy **6** flashy, florid, garish **7** pompous **8** affected, immodest, overdone **9** grandiose, obtrusive **10** flamboyant, showing off **11** conspicuous, exaggerated, pretentious **15** flaunting wealth
Osterreich *see* **7** Austria
ostracize 3 cut **4** oust, shun, snub **5** avoid, expel **6** banish, disown, reject **7** exclude, shutout **9** blackball, blacklist
Ostwald, Wilhelm
  field: 9 chemistry
  nationality: 6 German
  founded: 17 physical chemistry
O'Sullivan, Maureen
  born: 5 Boyle **7** Ireland **15** County Roscommon
  daughter: 9 Mia Farrow
  roles: 4 Jane (Tarzan movies) **16** David Copperfield **17** Pride and Prejudice **19** Hannah and Her Sisters
Otello
  also: 7 Othello
  opera by: 5 Verdi **7** Rossini
O tempora! O mores! 14 O times! O customs!
  said by: 6 Cicero
Othello
  director: 11 Stuart Burge
  author: 18 William Shakespeare
  character: 4 Iago **6** Cassio, Emilia **9** Desdemona
  cast: 11 Frank Finlay, Joyce Redman, Maggie Smith **15** Laurence Olivier
other 4 more **5** added, extra, spare **6**

unlike **7** further, reverse **8** contrary, opposite **9** alternate, auxiliary, different, remaining **10** additional, contrasted, dissimilar **11** contrasting **13** contradictory, supplementary **14** differentiated
Other Gods
  author: 9 Pearl Buck
Other Side of Midnight, The
  author: 13 Sidney Sheldon
other than 3 but **4** save **6** except, saving **7** barring, besides **9** excepting, excluding
otherwise 5 if not **6** or else **9** inversely **10** contrarily **11** differently **12** contrariwise
otherworldly 7 sublime **8** heavenly **9** celestial **14** transcendental
O times! O customs!
  Latin: 14 O tempora! O mores!
Otionia
  father: 10 Erechtheus
  sister: 10 Protogonia
  death by: 9 sacrifice
    for victory of: 9 Athenians
    over: 11 Eleusinians
otiose 4 idle, lazy **6** futile **7** laggard, resting, useless, worn-out **8** abortive, impotent, inactive, indolent, listless, slothful, sluggish **9** fruitless, lethargic, powerless, somnolent **10** unavailing **11** incompetent, ineffective, inoperative, unrewarding **12** unproductive
Otomi
  tribe: 7 Capotec
O'Toole, Peter
  born: 7 Ireland **9** Connemara
  roles: 6 Becket **7** Creator, Lord Jim **13** Man of La Mancha **14** Goodbye Mr Chips, My Favorite Year, The Last Emperor **16** Lawrence of Arabia, What's New Pussycat **18** How to Steal a Millon
O'Trigger, Sir Lucius
  character in: 9 The Rivals
  author: 8 Sheridan
Ott, Mel
  nickname: 9 Boy Wonder **12** Master Melvin
  sport: 8 baseball
  position: 8 outfield
  team: 13 New York Giants
Ottawa
  capital of: 6 Canada
  early name: 6 Bytown
  falls: 6 Rideau **9** Chaudiere
  landmark: 18 National Arts Centre **19** Dominion Observatory, Parliament Buildings
  river: 6 Ottawa, Rideau **8** Gatineau
  university: 8 Carleton
Ottawa
  language family: 9 Algonkian **10** Algonquian
  location: 4 Ohio **6** Canada, Kansas **7** Ontario **12** Lake Michigan
  leader: 7 Pontiac

Otter
origin: **12** Scandinavian
mentioned in: **8** Volsunga
form: **5** otter
father: **8** Hreidmar
killed by: **4** Loki

ottoman, Ottoman 4 seat, Turk **5** couch, divan, stool **7** sultane, Turkish **9** footstool
color: **3** red **9** vermilion
governor: **3** bey, dey **5** pasha
ruler: **5** Osman **8** Suleiman
standard: **4** ale

Ouagadougou
capital of: **10** Upper Volta **11** Burkina Faso

oui 3 yes

ounce
abbreviation of: **2** oz

ounce troy
abbreviation of: **3** oz t

Our Bill
creator: **14** Harry Haenigsen
character: **6** Walter

Our Crowd
author: **17** Stephen Birmingham

Our Miss Brooks
character: **8** Mrs Davis **12** Connie Brooks, Walter Denton **13** Osgood Conklin, Philip Boynton **14** Harriet Conklin
cast: **8** Eve Arden **10** Dick Crenna, Gale Gordon, Jane Morgan **14** Gloria McMillan, Robert Rockwell
Miss Brooks taught: **7** English
school: **11** Madison High

Our Mutual Friend
author: **14** Charles Dickens
character: **4** Wegg **5** Venus **6** Boffin **11** Bella Wilfer **17** Mortimer Lightwood, Young John Harmon (Handford, Rokesmith)

our sea
Latin: **11** mare nostrum
ancient Roman name for: **13** Mediterranean

Our Town
author: **14** Thornton Wilder
character: **12** Simon Stimson
Gibbs family: **2** Dr **3** Mrs **6** George **7** Rebecca
Webb family: **2** Mr **3** Mrs **5** Emily, Wally
director: **7** Sam Wood
cast: **10** Fay Bainter **11** Martha Scott **13** William Holden

oust 4 fire, sack **5** eject, evict, expel **6** banish, bounce, put out, remove, unseat **7** boot out, cashier, cast out, dismiss, kick out **8** throw out **9** discharge, give the ax **11** give the gate, send packing

ouster 6 firing **7** removal, sacking **8** bouncing, ejection, eviction **9** discharge, dismissal, expelling, expulsion, overthrow **10** banishment, cash-

iering **11** dislodgment, drumming out, throwing out **13** dispossession

out 2 ex **4** away **5** aloud, eject, forth, not in, passe **6** absent, begone, excuse, public **7** outside **8** exterior, external, revealed **9** in society, in the open, published **10** extinguish

out-and-out 4 pure, sure **5** sheer, total, utter **6** arrant **7** perfect **8** absolute, complete, hardened, outright, positive, thorough **9** confirmed, downright, unlimited **10** inveterate **11** straight out, unequivocal, unmitigated, unqualified **12** unregenerate, unrestricted **13** dyed-in-the-wool, thoroughgoing, unadulterated, unconditional **14** unquestionable

outbrazen 4 dare, defy, face **8** confront **9** challenge, stand up to

outbreak 5 burst **7** display **8** epidemic, eruption, invasion, outburst **9** explosion **10** outpouring **13** demonstration

outbuilding 4 barn, shed **5** privy **6** garage, stable **7** latrine **8** outhouse, woodshed

outburst 5 blast, burst **7** display, thunder **8** eruption, outbreak **9** explosion **10** outpouring **11** fulmination **13** demonstration

outcast 5 exile, rover **6** ousted, outlaw, pariah, roamer **7** refugee, runaway **8** banished, castaway, deportee, derelict, expelled, fugitive, rejected, vagabond **9** discarded **10** expatriate

Outcast of the Islands, The
author: **12** Joseph Conrad

Outcault, R F
creator/artist of: **11** Buster Brown **12** The Yellow Kid

outcome 3 end **5** fruit, issue **6** effect, payoff, result, upshot **9** aftermath, outgrowth **11** aftereffect, consequence

outcry 3 cry **4** howl, roar, yell, yelp, yowl **5** noise, shout, whoop **6** bellow, clamor, hubbub, scream, shriek, uproar **7** clangor, protest, screech **9** commotion, complaint, crying out, hue and cry, objection **10** cry of alarm, hullabaloo **12** caterwauling, remonstrance

outdated 5 passe **7** antique **8** outmoded **9** out-of-date **10** antiquated **12** old-fashioned

outdo 3 top **4** beat, best **5** excel, worst **6** better, defeat, exceed, outfox, outwit **7** eclipse, outplay, outrank, surpass **8** outclass, outshine, outstrip, overcome **9** transcend

outdoor festival
French: **13** fete champetre

outdoor market 5 agora **6** bazaar **10** flea market **11** marketplace

outer 6 distal, remote **7** extreme, farther, outside, outward, without **8** ex-

terior, external, outlying **9** outermost **10** farther out, peripheral

outer edge 3 lip, rim, tip **5** bound **6** margin **8** boundary **9** extremity

Outer Mongolia
also: **24** Mongolian People's Republic
border: **5** China **6** Russia **11** Soviet Union
capital: **4** Urga **5** Kulun **9** Ulan Bator
currency: **5** mongo **6** tugrik
desert: **4** Gobi **5** Shamo
language: **7** Khalka
mountain range: **5** Altai, Altay **7** Khangai

outermost 5 outer **6** utmost **7** extreme, outside, outward, surface **8** exterior, external **11** farthest out, most distant, superficial

outfit 3 fit, rig **4** gear **5** array, dress, equip, getup, habit, rig up **6** clothe, supply **7** appoint, costume, furnish **8** accouter, ensemble, wardrobe **9** equipment, provision, trappings **13** accoutrements, paraphernalia

outflow 5 issue **7** leakage, seepage **8** drainage **9** discharge

outgo 4 beat, cost, exit, pass **5** excel, issue, outdo **6** efflux, egress, outlay, outlet **7** outflow, surpass **8** outstrip **9** departure **11** expenditure

outgoing 4 warm **6** genial, social **7** amiable, cordial, exiting, leaving **8** friendly, going out, outbound, sociable **9** convivial, departing **10** gregarious **11** extroverted, sympathetic, warmhearted

outgoing person 9 extrovert **17** hail-fellow-well-met

outgrowth 3 end **4** knob, knot, node **5** bulge, fruit, issue, shoot **6** result, sequel, sprout, upshot **7** product **8** offshoot **9** aftermath **10** conclusion, projection **11** aftereffect, consequence, culmination, excrescence, outcropping **12** protuberance

outing 4 hike, ride, spin, tour, trip, walk **5** drive, jaunt, tramp **6** airing, junket, ramble **7** holiday **9** excursion **10** expedition

outlander 5 alien, exile **6** emigre **7** invader, settler **8** intruder, newcomer, stranger, wanderer **9** Auslander, barbarian, foreigner, immigrant **10** tramontane **12** ultramontane

outlandish 3 odd **5** kooky, queer, weird **6** far-out **7** bizarre, curious, strange, unusual **8** freakish, peculiar **9** eccentric, fantastic, grotesque, unheard-of **10** incredible, outrageous, ridiculous **12** preposterous, unbelievable, unimaginable, unparalleled **13** inconceivable **14** unconventional

outlast 6 endure, hold on, keep on, remain, stay on **7** carry on, hold out, outstay, outwear, perdure, persist, prevail, survive **8** continue

outlaw 3 ban, bar **4** deny, stop **5** felon

6 bandit, forbid, pariah **7** exclude, outcast **8** criminal, disallow, fugitive, prohibit, suppress **9** desperado, interdict, miscreant, proscribe **10** highwayman

outlay 3 fee **4** cost **5** outgo, price **6** charge **7** expense, payment **8** spending **11** amount spent, expenditure **12** disbursement

outlet 3 way **4** door, duct, exit, gate, path, vent **5** means **6** avenue, egress, escape, portal **7** channel, conduit, gateway, opening, passage

outline 4 plot **5** brief, trace **6** digest, limits, resume, review **7** contour, diagram, profile, summary, tracing **8** abstract, synopsis **9** blueprint, delineate, lineation, perimeter, periphery, sketch out **10** abridgment, silhouette **11** delineation **12** condensation
French: **6** apercu

outlook 4 view **5** scene, sight, vista **6** aspect, chance **7** picture, promise **8** attitude, forecast, panorama, prospect **9** spectacle, viewpoint **10** assumption **11** expectation, frame of mind, perspective, point of view, presumption, probability **12** anticipation

outlying 5 outer, rural **6** far-off, remote **7** distant, exurban **8** exterior, suburban **10** peripheral

outmoded 5 corny, dated, passe, tired **6** demode, old hat **7** antique, archaic, vintage **8** obsolete, old-timey, outdated **9** out-of-date **10** antiquated **12** old-fashioned, out-of-fashion **14** behind the times
French: **6** demode

Out of Africa
director: **13** Sydney Pollack
cast: **11** Meryl Streep (Baroness Karen Blixen, Isak Dinesen) **13** Robert Redford (Denys Finch Hatton) **19** Klaus Maria Brandauer (Baron Bror von Blixen)

out of bed 2 up **5** astir **9** up and at 'em **10** on one's feet, up and about **12** rise and shine

out-of-date 5 dated, passe **8** outmoded **10** antiquated **12** old-fashioned
French: **6** demode

out of doors 3 out **5** forth **6** abroad **7** outside **8** alfresco **12** in the open air

out-of-fashion 5 passe **8** obsolete, outmoded **9** out-of-date **12** old-fashioned
French: **6** demode

out of hand 4 wild **5** rowdy **6** unruly **10** disorderly **12** obstreperous, out of control, unmanageable, unrestrained **14** uncontrollable

out of keeping 8 atypical, peculiar, unseemly **9** anomalous, irregular **11** incongruous **12** inconsistent **13** inappropriate

out of kilter 4 awry **5** askew **6** uneven **7** crooked, oblique

out of line 6 unruly **9** excessive **10** exorbitant **12** presumptuous, unreasonable

out of many one
Latin: **13** e pluribus unum
motto of: **12** United States

out of one's head 3 mad **4** daft, nuts **5** crazy, nutty **6** insane **7** cracked, touched **8** demented, deranged, unhinged **10** unbalanced **12** mad as a hatter, off his rocker **15** mad as a March hare **17** nutty as a fruitcake

out of operation 4 dead, down **8** inactive **10** not working, out of order **11** inoperative

out of order 5 amiss **6** faulty **10** not working **11** inoperative, uncalled-for **13** inappropriate

out of place 3 odd **8** unseemly **10** unsuitable **11** incongruous, inconsonant **13** inappropriate

out of shape 4 bent **5** unfit **6** flabby, warped **7** crooked **8** deformed **9** distorted, untrained

out of sorts 5 cross, huffy, testy **6** crabby, cranky, touchy **7** bearish, grouchy, peevish **8** petulant, snappish **9** crotchety, irritable **10** ill-humored **11** ill-tempered **12** cantankerous **13** short-tempered

out of the books of
Latin: **8** ex libris

out of the fight
French: **12** hors de combat

out of the ordinary 4 rare **6** unique **7** notable, unusual **8** singular, uncommon **10** phenomenal, remarkable **11** exceptional **13** extraordinary

Out of the Past
director: **15** Jacques Tourneur
based on novel by: **13** Geoffrey Homes (Daniel Mainwaring) (Build My Gallows High)
cast: **9** Jane Greer **11** Kirk Douglas, Richard Webb **13** Rhonda Fleming, Robert Mitchum

out of touch 7 mixed-up **8** unstable **11** disoriented **12** out of contact **13** incommunicado

out-of-towner 7 tourist, visitor **9** sojourner, transient **11** nonresident

outpace 4 pass **5** outdo **6** exceed, outrun **8** outstrip

outpouring 6 deluge **7** barrage, gushing, outflow **8** effusion

output 4 crop, gain, take **5** yield **6** profit **7** harvest, produce, product, reaping, turnout **8** gleaning, proceeds **9** gathering **10** production **11** achievement **12** productivity **14** accomplishment

outrage 4 evil, gall, rile **5** anger, shock, wrong **6** arouse, enrage, insult, madden, offend, ruffle **7** affront, incense, provoke, steam up **8** atrocity, disquiet, enormity, iniquity **9** barbarity, indignity, infuriate **10** discompose, disrespect, exasperate, gross crime, scandalize **11** desecration, monstrosity, profanation **13** barbarousness, get one's back up, make one see red, slap in the face, transgression **17** make one's blood boil

outraged 3 mad **5** angry, irate, riled **6** fuming, raging **7** enraged, furious **8** incensed, inflamed, offended **9** affronted, indignant **10** displeased, infuriated

outrageous 4 base, foul, rank, rude, vile **5** gross **6** brutal, odious, wicked **7** abusive, extreme, galling, heinous, immense, inhuman **8** enormous, flagrant, inhumane, insolent, scornful, shocking **9** atrocious, barbarous, excessive, insulting, maddening, monstrous, nefarious, offensive, shameless **10** despicable, exorbitant, horrifying, immoderate, iniquitous, scandalous **11** disgraceful, infuriating, unspeakable, unwarranted **12** contemptible, contemptuous, exasperating, preposterous, unreasonable **13** disrespectful, reprehensible **14** unconscionable

outrageousness 8 enormity **9** immensity **10** wickedness **13** atrociousness, monstrousness, offensiveness **16** preposterousness

outre 8 improper

outreach 6 exceed **7** surpass

outright 4 full **5** sheer, total, utter **6** at once, entire, openly **7** utterly, visibly **8** absolute, complete, entirely, patently, promptly, thorough **9** downright, forthwith, instantly, on the spot, out-and-out **10** absolutely, altogether, completely, manifestly, thoroughly, unreserved **11** immediately, unmitigated, unqualified **12** demonstrably, undiminished **13** thoroughgoing, unconditional

outrival 3 dim **5** excel, outdo **6** exceed **7** eclipse, surpass **8** outshine **9** transcend **10** overshadow, tower above

outrush 4 gust **8** overflow

outset 4 dawn **5** birth, start **7** dawning **9** beginning, departure, threshold **12** commencement

outshine 3 dim **5** excel, outdo **6** exceed **7** eclipse, surpass **9** transcend **10** overshadow

outside 4 case, face, skin **5** alien, faint, outer **6** facade, remote, sheath, slight **7** coating, distant, foreign, obscure, outdoor, outward, strange, surface **8** covering, exterior, external, outdoors **9** nonnative, outer side, outermost **10** extraneous, out-of-doors, unfamiliar

outsider 5 alien **7** outcast **8** onlooker, stranger **9** bystander, foreigner, nonmember **14** nonparticipant

outskirts 3 rim 4 edge 6 limits, verges 7 borders, fringes, margins, suburbs 8 environs 9 periphery, precincts 10 perimeters 11 extremities

outspoken 5 blunt, frank 6 candid, direct, honest 7 artless 9 guileless, ingenuous, unsparing 10 forthright, unreserved 11 opinionated, plainspoken 13 undissembling 15 straightforward, undissimulating

outspread 5 broad 6 opened, spread 7 laid out 8 expanded, extended, unfolded, unfurled, unrolled 9 spread out, stretched 12 outstretched

outstanding 3 due 5 famed, great, owing 6 famous, unpaid 7 eminent, notable, payable 8 foremost, renowned, striking 9 best known, exemplary, in arrears, marvelous, memorable, prominent, unsettled 10 celebrated, noteworthy, phenomenal, remarkable 11 exceptional, magnificent, uncollected 13 distinguished, extraordinary, unforgettable

outstrip 4 pass 6 exceed, outrun 7 outpace, surpass 11 leave behind

outward 5 outer 7 evident, outside, surface, visible 8 apparent, exterior, external, manifest 10 observable, ostensible 11 perceivable, perceptible, superficial

outward appearance 4 mien 6 aspect, facade, manner 7 bearing 8 demeanor, exterior

Outward Bound
  author: 10 Sutton Vane

outwardly 7 clearly, visibly 9 evidently, seemingly 10 apparently, manifestly, ostensibly 13 on the face of it 16 to all appearances

outwards 3 out 4 away

outweigh 6 exceed 7 eclipse, surpass 8 override 9 rise above 10 overshadow 11 predominate, prevail over 13 be heavier than, weigh more than

outwit 4 dupe, foil, fool, trap 5 trick 6 baffle, outfox, take in, thwart 7 ensnare 8 outsmart 9 get around 10 circumvent 11 outmaneuver

outworn 5 dated, passe 6 bygone 7 defunct, disused, extinct 8 obsolete, rejected 9 abandoned, discarded, forgotten, out-of-date 10 antiquated, superseded 12 old-fashioned 13 unfashionable

ouzo
  type: 7 liqueur
  origin: 6 Greece
  flavor: 5 anise
  substitute for: 8 absinthe

oval 5 ovate, ovoid 6 curved, ovular 7 obovate, oviform, rounded 9 eggshaped 10 elliptical 11 ellipsoidal

ovation 6 cheers, homage, hurrah, hurray, huzzah 7 acclaim, fanfare, tribute 8 applause, cheering 9 adulation 11 acclamation

oven 3 umu 4 kiln, oast 5 baker, range, stove 6 hearth 7 broiler, chamber, kitchen, roaster
  clay: 7 tandoor
  fork: 7 fruggan, fruggin
  mop: 6 scovel

over 3 too 4 also, anew, done, else, gone, past 5 above, again, ended, extra, often 6 afresh, bygone, lapsed, no more, to boot 7 at an end, elapsed, expired, settled, surplus 8 finished, in excess, once more, too great 9 completed, concluded, excessive, remaining 10 additional, all through, in addition, passed away, repeatedly, terminated 11 a second time, superfluous

overabundance 4 glut 6 excess 7 surfeit, surplus 8 plethora 9 abundance, profusion 10 oversupply 11 superfluity 14 superabundance 15 supersaturation 21 embarrassment of riches
  French: 19 embarras de richesses

over again 4 anew 5 again 7 all over 8 once more 9 once again

overall 5 total 6 entire 7 general 8 complete, long-term, sweeping 9 extensive, long-range, panoramic 10 exhaustive, widespread 12 all-embracing, all-inclusive 13 comprehensive, thoroughgoing

over-and-above 5 added, extra 7 added on, besides 10 additional, in addition 13 supplementary

overawe 6 dazzle 9 overpower, overwhelm 10 intimidate

overbalance 5 upset 6 topple 8 outweigh

overbearing 5 cocky 6 lordly, snooty 7 haughty, high-hat, pompous, stuck-up 8 arrogant, despotic, egoistic 9 conceited, imperious, know-it-all 10 autocratic, disdainful, egotistical, high-handed, tyrannical 11 dictatorial, domineering, egotistical 13 high-and-mighty, self-assertive, self-important

overburden 3 tax 4 load, task, tire 5 whelm 7 exhaust, wear out 8 encumber, overwork, surcharge 9 overwhelm

overcast 4 dark, dull, gray, hazy 5 foggy, misty, murky 6 cloudy, dreary, gloomy, leaden 7 sunless 8 lowering 11 overclouded, threatening

overcharge 3 gyp, pad 4 rook, skin, soak 5 bleed, cheat, gouge, stick, sting, usury 6 extort, fleece 7 exploit 10 exaggerate

overcoat 3 mac 5 parka 6 duster, poncho, raglan, tabard, ulster 7 oilskin, paletot, topcoat 8 burberry, mackinaw 9 greatcoat, inverness, pea jacket 10 mackintosh, trenchcoat 12 chesterfield, Prince Albert

Overcoat, The
  author: 12 Nikolai Gogol
  character: 9 Petrovich 26 A Certain Important Personage 28 Akakii Akakiievich Bashmachkin

overcome 4 beat, best, lick 5 crush, quell 6 defeat, master, subdue 7 conquer, put down, survive, win over 8 suppress, surmount, vanquish 9 overpower, overthrow, overwhelm, transcend 11 prevail over, triumph over 14 get the better of

overconfident 5 brash 6 cheeky 8 arrogant, cocksure, egoistic, immodest, impudent 9 conceited 10 egoistical 11 egotistical, self-assured 12 presumptuous

overcrowd 3 jam 4 cram, fill, pack 5 stuff 7 congest

overcrowded 6 filled, jammed, packed 7 crammed, stuffed 9 congested, jampacked

overdecorated 5 gaudy, showy 6 flashy, garish 9 unsightly 12 ostentatious

overdelicacy 11 genteelness, prudishness 12 priggishness 14 overrefinement

overdo 4 gild 6 expand 7 amplify, ham it up, magnify, overact 8 overplay 9 embroider, overstate 10 do to excess, exaggerate 11 carry too far, hyperbolize 12 lay it on thick 13 stretch a point

overdue 4 late, slow 5 tardy 7 belated, delayed, past due 8 dilatory 10 behindhand, behind time, unpunctual 11 long delayed

overdue debt 7 arrears 10 balance due 18 balance outstanding

overflow 4 glut 5 flood 6 excess 7 run over, surplus 8 flow over, inundate, plethora, slop over 9 overspill, profusion 10 overspread, oversupply 11 copiousness, superfluity 13 overabundance 14 superabundance

overflowing 4 full 5 flush 7 replete, swamped 8 abundant, flooding 9 abounding, inundated 11 running over

overgarment 4 cape, coat, robe 5 cloak, habit, parka, shawl, smock 6 blazer, blouse, duster, jacket, kimono, mantle, poncho 7 sweater, topcoat, wrapper 8 cardigan, raincoat 9 gaberdine, housecoat

overgrown 4 rank 5 giant 7 blown-up 8 colossal, enlarged, forested, gigantic 9 luxuriant, oversized

overhang 3 jut 4 eave 5 bulge, drape, eaves, jetty 6 beetle, impend, sadden, shelve 7 project, suspend 8 protrude, threaten 9 projection

overhaul 4 beat, pass 5 catch 6 revamp 7 rebuild, remodel, restore, service 8 overtake, renovate 11 catch up with, recondition, reconstruct

overhead 3 nut 4 atop, roof 5 above, aloft, on top, upper 6 upward 7 ceiling, topmost, up above 8 superior 9 overlying, uppermost 11 overhanging

overindulge 4 baby 5 spoil, stuff 6 overdo, pamper, pig out 7 carouse, overeat 9 dissipate 11 mollycoddle

overjoyed 6 elated, joyous 8 ecstatic, euphoric, exultant, jubilant, thrilled 9 delighted, enchanted, exuberant, gratified 10 enraptured, enthralled 11 carried away, tickled pink, transported 12 happy as a lark

overlay 4 coat 5 cover, layer 6 carpet, veneer 7 blanket, coating 8 covering 11 superimpose

overload 3 tax 4 glut 5 flood, whelm 6 deluge, excess 7 burnout, surfeit 8 encumber 9 innundate, surcharge

overlook 4 miss, omit, skip 6 excuse, forget, give on, ignore, pass up, slight, survey, wink at 7 blink at, command, forgive, let ride, neglect 8 leave out, look over, pass over, shrug off 9 disregard, look out on 10 tower above 11 forget about, have a view of, leave undone

overlord 4 czar, tsar 7 emperor, monarch 8 autocrat 12 supreme ruler 13 absolute ruler

overly 3 too 4 very 6 highly, unduly 7 acutely, too much 8 overmuch, severely, to a fault, unfairly 9 extremely, intensely 10 needlessly 11 exceedingly, excessively 12 exorbitantly, immoderately, inordinately, unreasonably 18 disproportionately

overly trusting 5 naive 8 gullible 9 credulous 12 unsuspicious

overmodest 3 coy 4 prim 7 prudish 8 priggish 11 puritanical

overmuch 3 too 6 excess 7 surplus 8 plethora 9 profusion

overpass 4 span 6 bridge 9 crossover

overpower 4 beat, best, move, sway 5 crush, quell, worst 6 defeat, master, subdue 7 conquer 8 overcome, vanquish 9 influence, overwhelm

overpowering 6 mighty, strong 8 crushing 10 astounding 12 overwhelming

overpraise 4 line 7 blarney, fawning 8 flattery 11 fulsomeness

overpriced 6 costly 7 too high 9 expensive 10 exorbitant

overproud 4 vain 8 arrogant, egoistic 9 conceited 10 egoistical 11 egotistical, swell-headed 13 self-important

overrate 9 overprize, overvalue 10 overesteem, overpraise 12 overestimate 13 make too much of

overrefined 7 genteel, prudish 8 priggish 12 overdelicate

override 5 crush, quash 7 reverse 8 set aside 10 commission 11 countermand

overrule 4 deny, veto 5 annul, eject, repel, waive 6 cancel, refuse, reject, revoke 7 dismiss, nullify, outvote 8 disallow, outweigh, override, overturn, preclude, set aside, throw out 9 repudiate 10 invalidate 11 countermand

overrun 4 loot, raid, sack 5 choke 6 deluge, engulf, infest, invade 7 despoil, pillage, plunder, surplus 8 inundate, overgrow, pour in on, rove over 9 overwhelm, surge over, swarm over

overseas, oversea 5 alien 6 abroad, exotic 7 foreign 8 external 11 ultramarine 12 transoceanic 14 in foreign lands

oversee 3 run 4 boss, rule 5 guide, pilot, see to, steer, watch 6 direct, govern, handle, manage 7 carry on, command 8 attend to, overlook, regulate 9 supervise 10 administer 11 keep an eye on, preside over, superintend 12 have charge of

overseeing 7 bossing, guiding, running 8 guidance, handling, managing 10 leadership, management 11 attending to, supervising, supervision 13 administering 14 administrating, administration, superintending 15 superintendence

overseer 4 boss, head 5 chief 7 captain, foreman, manager 8 director, governor 10 supervisor, taskmaster 11 slave driver 13 administrator 14 superintendent

overshadow 3 fog 4 hide, mask, veil 5 cover, dwarf, shade 6 darken, screen, shroud 7 conceal, eclipse, obscure 8 outshine 9 tower over

overshadowing 7 eclipse, masking, shading, veiling 8 cloaking 9 darkening, eclipsing, obscuring 10 concealing, surpassing 11 concealment, obscuration 12 towering over

overshoe 3 gum 4 boot 5 arctic, gaiter, galosh, patten, rubber 7 galoshe

overshoot 4 pass 6 exceed, go over 8 go beyond

oversight 6 laxity, slight 7 blunder, mistake, neglect 8 omission 9 disregard 10 negligence 11 inattention 12 carelessness, heedlessness, inadvertence 13 careless error 14 neglectfulness 15 thoughtlessness

oversized 4 huge, vast 7 immense, mammoth 8 colossal, enormous, gigantic 10 monumental 14 Brobdingnagian

overspending 12 extravagance, throwing away

overspread 3 fog 4 coat, fill, pave 5 bathe, cloud, cover, paint, plate, smear 6 clothe, infest 7 blanket, diffuse, overlay, overrun, pervade, suffuse 8 disperse 9 whitewash

overstate 6 overdo, play up 7 enlarge, inflate, lay it on, magnify, stretch, touch up 8 increase, overdraw, oversell 9 embellish, embroider, enlarge on, overpaint 10 exaggerate, overstress 15 spread it on thick

overstep 6 exceed 7 violate 10 transgress

oversupply 4 glut 6 excess 7 surfeit, surplus, too much 8 plethora 11 undue amount 13 overabundance 14 superabundance

overt 4 open 5 plain 6 public 7 evident, obvious, visible 8 apparent, manifest, palpable, revealed 10 easily seen, noticeable, observable, ostensible 11 perceivable, perceptible, unconcealed, undisguised

overtake 4 go by, pass 5 catch, reach 6 befall, gain on 7 run down 8 approach, overhaul 11 catch up with

overtax 4 tire 5 abuse, hoist 6 burden, exceed, strain, stress 7 exhaust 8 overload, overwork 9 misemploy 10 overburden

over the hill 3 old 4 aged 5 aging 7 elderly 11 past the peak 13 past one's prime

overthrow 4 undo 5 crush 6 defeat, mutiny, topple 7 abolish, undoing 8 downfall, overcome, overturn, toppling 9 abolition, bring down, overpower, rebellion 10 do away with, revolution

overtire 3 fag 4 bush, do in, poop 5 drain 7 exhaust, fatigue, wear out 8 enervate

overtone 3 hue 4 hint 5 drift 8 coloring, innuendo 10 intimation, suggestion 11 connotation, implication, insinuation

overtrustful 8 gullible 9 credulous 12 unsuspecting, unsuspicious 13 unquestioning

overture 3 bid 6 motion, signal, tender 7 advance, gesture, preface, prelude 8 approach, foreword, offering, preamble, prologue, proposal 9 beginning 10 invitation, suggestion 11 opening move, proposition 12 introduction

overturn 4 beat, oust 5 crush, upend, upset 6 defeat, depose, thrash, topple 7 capsize, conquer, turn out 8 overcome, push over, vanquish 9 knock down, knock over, overpower, overthrow, overwhelm 14 turn topsy-turvy, turn upside down

overturning
French: 14 bouleversement

overweening 5 bossy, cocky, pushy 6 brassy 7 haughty, pompous 8 arrogant, egoistic 9 bigheaded, imperious 10 disdainful, egoistical, high-handed, immoderate 11 domineering, egotistical, overbearing, patronizing 12 presumptuous 13 high-and-mighty, overconfident, self-important

overweight 3 fat 5 dumpy, fatty, gross, hefty, obese, piggy, plump, pudgy, stout, tubby 6 chubby, chunky, fleshy, portly, rotund 7 fattish, well-fed 8 roly-poly 9 corpulent 10 potbellied, well-padded 11 beer-bellied, overstuffed 15 well-upholstered

overwhelm 4 beat, bury 5 crush, quash, quell, swamp 6 defeat, engulf 7 conquer, overrun, stagger 8 bowl over, confound, inundate, overcome, vanquish 9 devastate, overpower, overthrow, subjugate

overwhelming 8 crushing 10 staggering 11 astonishing, devastating 12 overpowering

overwork 3 tax 4 task, tire, toil 5 labor 6 burden, strain 7 exhaust, overtax, wear out 9 misemploy 10 overburden

overwrought 4 wild 5 riled 6 touchy, uneasy 7 excited, nervous, ruffled 8 agitated, frenzied, inflamed, wild-eyed, worked up 9 perturbed, wrought up 10 distracted, high-strung 11 carried away, overexcited

Ovid
   author of: 6 Amores 7 Tristia 8 Heroides 11 Ars Amatoria 12 The Art of Love 13 Metamorphoses

ovule 3 egg, nit 4 germ, ovum 6 embryo 7 seedlet

ovum 3 egg 4 cell, germ, seed 5 spore 6 gamete 8 oosphere

owe 8 be in debt 11 be obligated 12 be beholden to, be indebted to

owed 3 due 5 owing 6 unpaid 9 in arrears 11 outstanding

Owen Marshall, Counselor at Law
   character: 11 Jess Brandon 12 Frieda Krause 15 Melissa Marshall

cast: 9 Lee Majors 10 Arthur Hill 11 Joan Darling 17 Christine Matchett

owing 3 due 4 owed 6 unpaid 9 in arrears 11 outstanding

own 4 avow, have, hold, keep, tell 5 admit, allow, grant, yield 6 assent, concur, retain 7 concede, possess, private 8 disclose, maintain, personal 9 acquiesce, confess to, consent to, recognize 10 individual, particular 11 acknowledge

owner 6 holder, master 7 partner 8 landlady, landlord, mistress 9 co-partner, landowner, possessor 10 landholder, proprietor 11 householder, titleholder 12 proprietress

own up to 5 admit 6 accept 7 confess 8 blurt out 9 recognize 11 acknowledge 14 come clean about

ox 3 oaf 4 bull, clod, musk, urus, zebu 5 aiver, beast, bison, gayal, steer 6 auroch, banting, bovine 7 banteng, buffalo 10 clodhopper
   Cambodian: 7 Kouprey, Kouproh
   Celebesian: 3 goa, noa 4 anoa
   extinct: 4 urus 7 aurochs
   family: 7 bovidae
   genus: 3 bos
   horned: 4 reem
   hornless: 4 moil
   Indian: 4 gaur
   Paul Bunyan's: 4 Babe
      color: 4 blue
   stall: 4 crib
   team: 4 yoke
   Tibetan: 3 yak
   wild: 3 ure 4 anoa
   young: 4 stot 5 stirk

Ox-Bow Incident, The
   author: 21 Walter Van Tilburg Clark
   character: 5 Canby, Croft 6 Davies, Gerald, Martin, Tetley 9 Gil Carter
   director: 14 William Wellman
   cast: 10 Henry Fonda 11 Dana Andrews 12 Anthony Quinn 13 William Blythe 14 Mary Beth Hughes

oxen
   group of: 4 yoke

oxide 8 compound
   afterburn: 4 calx
   calcium: 4 calx, lime
   cobalt: 6 zaffer, zaffre
   element: 6 oxygen
   iron: 4 rust 8 hematite, limonite 9 colcothar, magnetite
   make by heat: 7 calcine
   sodium: 4 soda
   zinc: 6 cadmia

oxidize 4 burn, char, rust 7 corrode

Oxyderces
   epithet of: 6 Athena
   means: 10 bright-eyed

oxygen
   chemical symbol: 1 O

Oxylus
   origin: 8 Aetolian
   punishment: 5 exile
   chosen leader of: 10 Heraclidae
   led invasion of: 12 Peloponnesus

oyez 4 hear 6 attend
   cry used by: 10 court crier
   preceded: 12 proclamation

Oz *see Wizard of Oz*

Ozark Jubilee
   host: 8 Red Foley 10 Webb Pierce
   theme: 12 Sugarfoot Rag

Ozark State
   nickname of: 8 Missouri

Ozick, Cynthia
   author of: 10 Levitation 17 The Cannibal Galaxy 21 The Messiah of Stockholm

Ozzie and Harriet, The Adventures of
   cast: 11 David Nelson, Ozzie Nelson, Ricky (Eric) Nelson 13 Harriet Nelson

pa 3 dad, paw, pop **4** papa **5** daddy, pater **6** father
    mate: 2 ma

pace 4 clip, flow, gait, rate, step, walk **5** amble, speed, tread **6** motion, stride, stroll **7** saunter **8** momentum, slow gait, velocity

Pacelli, Eugenio Maria Giuseppe Giovanni 11 Pope Pius XII

pachyderm 5 hippo, rhino **8** elephant, ungulate **10** rhinoceros **12** hippopotamus
    characteristic: 4 tusk **5** ivory, trunk **12** thick-skinned
    prehistoric: 7 mammoth **8** mastodon

pachydermatous 4 hard **5** horny, tough **7** callous **8** callused, hardened, leathery **12** thick-skinned **13** elephant-hided

pacific 4 calm **5** quiet, still **6** gentle, placid, serene, smooth **7** halcyon, restful **8** dovelike, peaceful, tranquil **9** pacifying, peaceable, reposeful, unruffled **10** harmonious, untroubled **11** inoffensive, undisturbed **12** conciliatory

pacification 8 soothing **11** appeasement, peacemaking **12** conciliation, nonagression **14** reconciliation

Pacific island 3 Aru, Yap **4** Bali, Fiji, Guam, Maui, Oahu, Rapa, Truk, Wake **5** Mauru, Papua, Samoa **6** Hawaii, Kodiak, Midway, Ryukyu, Tahiti, Taiwan **7** Okinawa **8** Borabora, Eniwetok, Pitcairn, Tasmania **9** New Guinea **12** Bougainville

pacify 4 calm **5** allay, quiet **6** soothe **7** appease, assuage, compose, mollify, placate **9** reconcile **10** conciliate, propitiate

Pacino, Al
    real name: 13 Alberto Pacino
    born: 9 New York NY
    roles: 7 Serpico **8** Scarface **12** Author Author, Donnie Brasco, The Godfather **13** Scent of a Woman (Oscar) **15** Dog Day Afternoon **16** And Justice for All **17** Glengary Glen Ross **22** Does a Tiger wear a Necktie (Tony)

pack 3 box, jam, kit, lot, mob, set, tie **4** bevy, bind, cram, fill, heap, herd, load, mass **5** batch, bunch, clump, covey, crowd, drove, flock, group, horde, stuff, swarm, truss **6** bundle, gaggle, gather, packet, parcel, passel, throng **7** cluster, package **8** assemble **9** container, multitude **10** assortment, collection, miscellany **12** accumulation

package 3 box, kit **4** case, pack, wrap **6** bundle, carton, encase, packet, parcel, wrap up **9** container, wrappings

pack closely 4 cram, pack **5** press, stuff **7** compact **8** compress

packed 4 full **6** filled, jammed, loaded, massed, rammed, wedged **7** crammed, crowded, crushed, pressed, stuffed **8** overfull, squeezed **10** sandwiched **11** overcrowded

packet 3 bag, box **4** bale, pack, roll **5** pouch, sheaf **6** bundle, parcel, quiver **7** package

pact 4 bond **6** treaty **7** compact **8** alliance, contract, covenant **9** agreement, concordat **10** convention **11** concordance **13** understanding

pad 3 mat **4** fill **5** stuff **6** blow up, fatten, tablet **7** bolster, cushion, inflate, protect, puff out **8** mattress, notebook **9** upholster **10** cushioning, stretch out

padding 6 filler, lining **7** filling, packing, surfeit, surplus, wadding **8** stuffing, verbiage, wrapping **9** prolixity, verbosity, wordiness **10** redundancy **11** verboseness **12** extravagance **14** superabundance

Paderewski, Ignace (Ignacy Jan)
    born: 6 Poland **9** Kurilowka
    composer of: 5 Manru **9** Minuet in G

pad out 5 add to **6** expand, extend **7** amplify, augment, enlarge, stretch **8** elongate, increase, lengthen

padre 6 cleric, father, priest **8** chaplain **9** clergyman

paean 6 anthem, eulogy **7** hosanna **9** laudation, panegyric **10** hallelujah **11** acclamation **12** hymn of praise
    form: 4 hymn, song
    characteristic: 6 joyful **12** thanksgiving

Paeon
    form: 3 god
    position: 9 physician
    served gods of: 7 Olympia
    corresponds to: 6 Apollo

Paezan
    language family: 13 Macro-Chibchan
    group: 4 Paez **5** Choco **6** Warrau **8** Colorado

pagan 7 atheist, heathen, infidel **8** idolator **9** barbarian **10** heathenish, idolatrous, polytheist, unbeliever **11** nonbeliever **12** polytheistic

Paganini, Niccolo
    born: 5 Genoa, Italy
    played: 6 violin
    composer of: 19 The Carnival of Venice

page 3 boy, lad **4** beep, call, girl, leaf **5** folio, groom, sheet, youth **6** knight, number, summon **7** callboy, contact **8** announce **9** attendant, messenger **10** apprentice, manservant
    blank: 7 flyleaf
    left-hand: 5 verso
    right-hand: 5 recto

Page, Geraldine
    born: 12 Kirksville MO
    husband: 7 Rip Torn
    roles: 5 Hondo **9** Interiors **11** Pete-n-Tillie **14** Summer and Smoke **16** A Trip to Bountiful (Oscar), Sweet Bird of Youth

Page and Mistress Page
    characters in: 22 The Merry Wives of Windsor
    author: 11 Shakespeare

pageant 4 pomp, rite, show **6** parade, ritual **7** display **8** ceremony **9** spectacle **10** exhibition, procession **12** extravaganza

pageantry 4 pomp, rite, show **5** drama, flair **6** ritual, splash **7** display, glitter, pageant **8** ceremony, grandeur, splendor **9** showiness, spectacle, theatrics **10** flashiness **11** ostentation **12** extravagance, magnificence

Paget, James
    field: 7 surgery **8** medicine
    nationality: 7 British
    founder of: 9 pathology

Pagliacci, I
    also: 9 The Clowns
    opera by: 11 Leoncavallo
    character: 5 Canio, Nedda, Tonio **6** Silvio

Pagnol, Marcel
    author of: 5 Cesar, Fanny **6** Marius, Topaze

Pago Pago
    capital of: 13 American Samoa

Pahlavi *see Iran*

Paige, Leroy
    nickname: 7 Satchel
    sport: 8 baseball
    position: 7 pitcher

pain 3 vex, woe **4** ache, gall, hell, hurt, pang, rile **5** agony, annoy, chafe, grief, pinch, pique, smart, sting, throb, worry **6** aching, grieve, harass, misery, ordeal, sadden, sorrow, stitch, twinge **7** agonize, anguish, disturb, hurting, malaise, sadness, torment, torture, trouble **8** distress, smarting, soreness **9** displease, heartache, suffering **10** affliction, discomfort, exasperate, heartbreak **11** unhappiness **12** wretchedness

Paine, Thomas
  author of: **9** The Crisis **11** Common Sense **14** The Rights of Man

painful 3 sad **4** dire **5** sharp **6** aching, dismal, dreary, trying **7** arduous, hurtful, racking **8** grievous, grueling, pathetic, piercing, smarting, stinging, very sore **9** agonizing, difficult, sorrowful, throbbing, torturous **10** afflictive, disturbing, lamentable, unpleasant **11** disquieting, distasteful, distressful, distressing **12** disagreeable, excruciating

pain in the neck 4 bane **6** bother **7** torment **8** headache, nuisance **9** annoyance **10** affliction

painstaking 5 fussy **7** careful, earnest, finicky, precise **8** diligent, exacting, thorough **9** assiduous, energetic, strenuous **10** meticulous, scrupulous **11** industrious, persevering, punctilious **13** conscientious, thoroughgoing

paint 4 coat, daub, draw, limn, swab, tint **5** adorn, brush, color, cover, horse, rouge, shade, stain **6** depict, enamel, makeup, opaque, sketch **7** pigment, portray, stipple, touch up **8** cosmetic, decorate, describe, variegate **9** delineate, represent

Painted Bird, The
  author: **13** Jerzy Kosinski

painter 6 artist, drawer **8** sketcher **9** old master **10** delineator **11** illustrator, landscapist, miniaturist **13** watercolorist

Painter, Painter's Easel
  constellation of: **6** Pictor

painting 3 art, oil **5** draft, mural, piece **6** canvas, design, tablet **7** cartoon, daubing, drawing, graphic, picture, tableau **8** panorama, portrait, seascape **9** depiction, landscape, still life **10** cerography, watercolor **11** perspective **12** illustration
  colloidal: **7** tempera
  method: **9** encaustic
  on plaster: **5** secco **6** fresco
  one-color: **8** monotint **10** monochrome
  opaque: **7** gouache
  religious: **5** Pieta
  style: **5** genre
  tool: **5** brush, easel, knife **6** canvas, roller, sponge **7** palette **8** spraygun

pair 3 duo **4** dyad, mate, span, team, yoke **5** brace, match, unite **6** couple **7** combine, doublet, match up, pair off, twosome

pair off 10 go two by two **11** form couples

Paiute
  language family: **10** Shoshonean
  tribe: **12** Mono-Paviosto, Snake Indians **13** Digger Indians **14** Northern Paiute, Southern Paiute
  location: **4** Utah **5** Idaho **6** Nevada, Oregon **7** Arizona **10** California

Pakistan
  name means: **13** Land of the Holy, Land of the Pure
  capital: **9** Islamabad
  largest city: **7** Karachi
  others: **3** Dir, Sui **4** Mari, Sidi **5** Dacca, Qasim, Ralat **6** Chalna, Khulna, Lahore, Multan, Quetta **7** Larkana, Sialkot **8** Jamalpur, Lyallpur, Peshawar, Sargodha **9** Hyderabad **10** Gujranwala, Rawalpindi
  school: **9** U of Punjab **10** U of Karachi **12** U of Hyderabad **16** Allama Iqbal Open U **22** Pakistan U of Agriculture **39** Pakistan Institute of International Affairs
  division: **3** Dir **4** Sind, Swat **5** Hunza, Kalat **6** Bengal, Kharan, Punjab **7** Chitral **8** Khairpur, Peshawar **10** Bahawalpur, Waziristan **11** Baluchistan
  empire: **5** Gupta, Mogul **6** Kushan, Maurya **7** British, Magadha
  seceded state: **10** Bangladesh
  monetary unit: **4** anna, pice **5** paisa, rupee
  weight: **4** seer, tola **5** maund
  mountain: **3** Pab, Pub **4** Salt **6** Makran **7** Kirthar **8** Himalaya, Safed Koh, Sulaiman **9** Hindu Kush, Karakoram **11** Makran Coast **13** Central Makran **14** Takht-i-Sulaiman
  highest point: **9** Tirich Mir **12** Godwin Austin
  river: **3** Nal **4** Bado, Beas, Ravi, Swat, Zhob **5** Dasht, Indus, Kabul **6** Chenab, Ganges, Jamuna, Jhelum, Kundar, Porali, Sutlej **7** Jamunna
  sea: **7** Arabian
  physical feature:
    bay: **8** Soymiani
    canal: **4** Nara **5** Rohri
    cape: **5** Fasta, Jaddi **6** Jiwani
    delta: **6** Ganges **11** Char-Manpura
    desert: **4** Sind, Thal, Thar
    mountain pass: **5** Bolan **6** Khyber
    plateau: **11** Baluchistan
    valley: **5** Kohat
  people: **5** Sindi, Wazir **6** Afridi, Bengal, Mahsud, Pathan, Sindhi **7** Baluchi, Brahuis, Puktuns, Punjabi, Sherani **8** Khattack, Pushtuns, Shinwari, Yusefazi **11** Mohammedzai
    leader: **6** Jinnah **7** Aly Khan **8** Ayub Khan, Zia Ul-Haq **9** Ali Bhutto, Yahya Khan **13** Benazir Bhutto, Mujibur Rahman **15** Mah-

mud of Ghaznbi
    poet: **5** Iqbal, Iqbal
  language: **4** Urdu **6** Pushtu, Sindhi **7** Baluchi, Bengali, English, Punjabi
  religion: **5** Hindu, Islam **8** Buddhism **12** Christianity
  place:
    dam: **6** Mangla **7** Tarbela
    gardens: **8** Shalamar
    mosque: **8** Badshahi
    tomb: **15** Emperor Jahangir
  feature:
    clothing: **5** kurta, pugri, qamis **6** jinnah **7** dupatta, shalwar **8** sherwani **9** churidars
    food:
      bread: **8** chappati
      dish: **5** kebab, pilaf **6** qormas, salans, sautes **10** vermicelli
      yogurt: **4** dahi

Pakula, Alan
  director of: **13** Sophie's Choice **19** All the President's Men

pal 4 chum, mate, pard **5** buddy, crony **6** cohort, friend **7** comrade, partner **8** alter ego, intimate, sidekick **9** associate, colleague, companion, confidant **10** accomplice, bosom buddy **13** boon companion

palace 5 villa **6** castle **7** chateau, mansion **8** hacienda
  French: **6** palais
  Italian: **7** palazzo

palais 6 palace **17** municipal building **18** government building

Palamedes
  lieutenant of: **9** Agamemnon

pal around 7 consort, hang out **9** associate, be friends, run around **10** fraternize

palatable 5 tasty **6** savory **8** pleasant **9** agreeable, toothsome **10** appetizing

palatial 4 posh, rich **5** grand, noble, plush, regal, ritzy, showy **6** swanky **7** elegant, opulent, stately **8** imposing, splendid **9** grandiose, luxurious, sumptuous **10** monumental **11** magnificent

palaver 3 gab **4** chat, talk **5** prate **6** confer, gossip, parley **7** consult, discuss, prattle **8** chitchat, idle talk **10** chew the fat, chew the rag, conference, discussion

palazzo 6 palace

pale 3 pen, wan **4** fold, post **5** ashen, close, light, pasty, stake, white **6** anemic, blanch, paling, pallid, picket, sallow, whiten **7** closure, confine, deathly, ghastly, upright, whitish **8** bleached, palisade **9** bloodless, colorless, deathlike, enclosure, ghostlike **10** ash-colored, cadaverous, light-toned

Pale Horse, Pale Rider
  author: **19** Katherine Anne Porter

paleness 6 pallor **7** wanness **8** dullness **9** whiteness **13** colorlessness

paleontology

study of: 18 correlation of parts
founder: 13 Georges Cuvier

Palermo
 capital of: 6 Sicily

Palestine *see* **6** Israel

Palestrina, Giovanni Pierluigi da
 born: 5 Italy **10** Palestrina
 composer of: 11 Stabat Mater **18** Missa Papae Marcelli

Paley, Grace
 author of: 26 The Little Disturbances of Man **30** Enormous Changes at the Last Minute

Palici
 origin: 5 Roman
 form: 4 gods **5** twins
 gods of: 14 sulphur springs

paling 4 pale, rail **5** fence, stake **6** picket

Palinurus
 steersman of: 6 Aeneas

palisade 5 close, fence **7** bulwark, rampart **8** stockade **9** enclosure

palisades 4 crag **5** ledge **6** bluffs, cliffs **10** escarpment, promontory

pall 4 cloy, haze, sate **5** gloom, weary **6** shadow, sicken **7** dimness, satiate **8** darkness **10** become dull, be tiresome, depression, desolation, melancholy, moroseness, oppression

Palladio, Andrea
 real name: 26 Andrea di Pietro della Gondola
 architect of: 12 Villa Rotunda (Vicenza Italy) **14** Teatro Olimpico (Vicenza) **19** Church of Il Redentore (Venice) **26** Church of San Giorgio Maggiore (Venice)
 style: 9 Palladian

Pallas *see* **6** Athena

Pallas Athena *see* **6** Athena

pallet 3 bed, cot **4** bunk, tick **5** berth **8** mattress, platform

palliate 4 calm, curb, ease, hush, lull, tame **5** abate, allay, check, quiet, sooth, still **6** lessen, modify, reduce, soften, subdue, temper **7** assuage, comfort, cushion, lighten, relieve **8** decrease, diminish, minimize, mitigate, moderate **9** alleviate **10** ameliorate

palliative 4 balm **6** solace **7** anodyne, comfort **10** comforting

pallid 3 wan **4** ashy, blah, dull, pale **5** ashen, bland, pasty, vapid, waxen **6** boring, chalky, peaked, sallow **7** ghostly, humdrum, insipid, tedious **8** blanched, lifeless **9** bloodless, colorless **10** monotonous **13** anemic looking, unimaginative, uninteresting

pallor 7 wanness **8** paleness **9** pastiness, whiteness **10** ashen color, pallidness **11** ghostliness **13** bloodlessness, colorlessness

palm
 varieties: 3 Fan, Ita, Key, Nut, Oil, Wax **4** Cane, Date, Doom, Doub, Doum, Fern, Hair, Hemp, King, Lady, Nipa, Nypa, Rock, Sago, Step, Tala, Wine **5** Areca, Areng, As sai, Betel, Black, Bread, Broom, Curly, Grass, Honey, Inaga, Ivory, Jelly, Latan, Manac, Nikau, Peach, Queen, Royal, Snake, Spine, Sugar, Syrup, Toddy, Yatay, Zombi **6** Bamboo, Barbel, Barrel, Bottle, Cherry, Cohune, Coyoli, Gebang, Gomuti, Gru-gru, Hesper, Kentia, Licuri, Manila, Mazari, Needle, Nibung, Parlor, Pignut, Raffia, Rattan, Ruffle, Sagisi, Sentry, Silver, Thatch, Thread, Yellow **7** Arikury, Cabbage, Calappa, Coconut, Coquito, Feather, Fiji fan, Funeral, Jaggery, Leopard, Mexican, Moriche, Overtop, Palmyra, Prickly, Spindle, Talipot, Weddell **8** Betel nut, Carnauba, Cucurite, Dwarf fan, Fishtail, Good luck, Ivory-nut, Mangrove, Pandanus, Peaberry, Princess, Roebelin, Umbrella, Wild date, Windmill **9** Alexander, Alexandra, Butterfly, Christmas, Desert fan, Gippsland, Guadalupe, Hurricane, India date, Macarthur, Ouricouri, Panama-hat, Petticoat, Piccabeen, Porcupine, Pygmy date, Silver saw, Solitaire, Spiny-club, Traveler's **10** African oil, Black-fiber, Canary date, Chinese fan, Cuban belly, Cuban royal, Everglades, Franceschi, Saw cabbage, Sealing-wax, Thatch-leaf, Washington **11** American oil, Chilean wine, European fan, Gingerbread, Mexican blue, Morass royal, Senegal date, Slender lady, Woolly butia **12** Caribee royal, Egyptian doum, Florida royal, Miniature fan, Walking-stick **13** Australian fan, Australian ivy, Australian nut, Belmore sentry, Feather-duster, Florida silver, Florida thatch, Forster sentry, Golden feather, Miniature date, San Jose hesper **14** Common princess, East Indian wine, Puerto Rican hat, Tufted fish tail, Yellow princess **15** Burmese fishtail, Chinese fountain, Chinese windmill, Yellow butterfly **16** Hispaniolan royal, Northern bangalow, Puerto Rican royal **17** Australian cabbage, Clustered fishtail, Mexican Washington, Piccabeen bangalow **18** South American royal

Palm Beach Story, The
 director: 14 Preston Sturges
 cast: 9 Mary Astor **10** Joel McCrea, Rudy Vallee **15** William Demarest **16** Claudette Colbert

Palmer, Arnold
 sport: 4 golf
 noted for: 10 Arnie's Army

Palmer, Lilli
 real name: 17 Lillie Marie (Maria Lilli) Peiser
 born: 5 Posen **7** Germany
 husband: 11 Rex Harrison **14** Carlos Thompson
 roles: 11 Body and Soul
 autobiography: 22 Change Lobsters and Dance

Palmetto State
 nickname of: 13 South Carolina

Palm Sunday
 author: 12 Kurt Vonnegut

palmy 4 rosy **5** balmy, sunny **6** golden **7** booming, halcyon **8** blooming, pleasant, thriving **9** agreeable, bounteous, congenial **10** prosperous, successful **11** flourishing, pleasurable

Palmyra
 Biblical name: 6 Tadmor

palpable 5 clear, plain **7** evident, obvious, tactile, visible **8** apparent, definite, distinct, feelable, manifest, tangible **9** touchable **10** noticeable **11** discernible, perceivable, perceptible **12** recognizable, unmistakable

palpitate 4 beat **5** pound, shake, throb **6** quaver, quiver, shiver **7** flutter, tremble, vibrate **9** go pit-a-pat

palsied 7 quaking, shaking, spastic **9** trembling

palsy-walsy 5 close, palsy, thick **6** chummy **8** friendly, intimate **10** buddy-buddy **14** thick as thieves

paltriness 10 triviality **12** unimportance **14** insignificance **18** inconsequentiality

paltry 4 poor, puny **5** petty, sorry **6** measly, shabby **7** scrubby, trivial **8** inferior, picayune, piddling, trifling, wretched **11** unimportant **13** insignificant, of little value **14** inconsiderable **15** inconsequential

Pamela
 author: 16 Samuel Richardson
 character: 3 Mr B **9** Mrs Jervis, Mrs Jewkes **10** Lady Davers **13** Pamela Andrews

pamper 5 humor, spoil **6** coddle, cosset **7** cater to, indulge **8** give in to **11** mollycoddle

pampered 7 coddled, humored **8** indulged **9** catered to, cossetted

pamphlet 5 tract **6** folder **7** booklet, leaflet **8** brochure, bulletin, circular **9** monograph, throwaway

pan 3 boo, map, mug, pot **4** face, hiss **6** kisser **8** ridicule, saucepan **9** criticize

Pan
 also: 7 Sinoeis
 origin: 5 Greek
 form combined: 3 man **4** goat
 god of: 6 flocks **7** forests **8** pastures **9** shepherds
 father: 4 Zeus **6** Hermes
 loved: 4 Echo **5** Pitys **6** Syrinx
 invented: 5 pipes **6** syrinx
 corresponds to: 6 Faunus

panacea 6 elixir **7** cure-all, nostrum **13** universal cure

panache 4 dash, elan, tuft 5 flair, plume, style, verve 11 flamboyance

Panama
  capital/largest city: 10 Panama City
  others: 4 Daid 5 Ancon, Colon 6 Azuero, Balboa, Gamboa 8 Dos Bocas, Penonome, Santiago 9 Cristobal 10 Portobello
  division: 5 Cocle, Colon 6 Darien, Panama 7 Herrera 8 Chiriqui, Veraguas 9 Los Santos 12 Bocas del Toro
  measure: 7 celemin
  monetary unit: 4 cent 6 balboa 10 centesimos
  island: 5 Coiba, Pearl 6 Cebaco, Multas, Taboga 7 San Blas 10 Isla Del Rey 12 Bocas del Toro, Juan Gallegos 13 Barro Colorado
  lake: 5 Gatun
  mountain: 4 Baru, Maje 5 Chico, Gandi 6 Darien 7 Columan, San Blas, Veragua 8 Santiago, Tabasara 10 Costa Rican 14 Serrania de Sapo 15 Aspave Highlands 17 Cordillera Central
  highest point: 8 Chiriqui
  river: 5 Chepo, Sambu, Tuira 6 Bayano, Panugo 7 Chagres
  sea: 7 Pacific 9 Caribbean
  physical feature:
    bay: 5 Limon 6 Panama
    dam: 5 Gatun
    gulf: 6 Darien, Panama, Parita 7 Montijo, San Blas 8 Chiriqui 9 Mosquitos, San Miguel
    isthmus: 6 Darien, Panama 7 San Blas
    lagoon: 8 Chiriqui
    peninsula: 6 Azuero 8 Valjente
  people: 4 Cuna 5 Choco 6 Guaymi 7 mestizo
    canal builder: 7 Lesseps
    explorer: 6 Balboa 8 Bastidas, Columbus
    leader: 4 Royo 5 Arias 7 Noriega 8 Guerrero, Torrijos 9 Espriella 12 Simon Bolivar
    poet: 4 Miro 5 Korsi, Sinan
  language: 7 English, Spanish
  religion: 13 Roman Catholic
  place:
    church: 7 San Jose 15 Virgen del Carmen
    plaza: 13 Independencia
    ruins: 9 Old Panama
  feature:
    clothing: 7 montuno, pollera
    dance: 4 caja 7 pujador 9 tamborito
    tree: 4 yaya 5 maria, quira 6 alfaje, cativo
    US operation: 9 Just Cause
  food:
    meat: 6 tazajo
    soup: 8 sancocho

Panama City
  capital of: 6 Panama

pancake 4 blin 5 blini, crepe, kisra, latke, lefse 6 blintz, makeup 7 fritter, hotcake 8 flapjack, slapjack 11 griddlecake 12 silverdollar
  day: 13 Shrove Tuesday

Pancks
  character in: 12 Little Dorrit
  author: 7 Dickens

pancreas
  produces: 7 insulin

Pandareus
  father: 6 Lycaon, Merops
  daughter: 5 Aedon 6 Merope 9 Cleothera
  wounded: 8 Menelaus
  stole: 9 golden dog
  turned to: 5 stone
  killed by: 8 Diomedes

Pandarus
  character in: 18 Troilus and Cressida, Troilus and Criseyde
  author: 7 Chaucer 11 Shakespeare

Pandarus
  son: 7 Alcanor
  companion of: 6 Aeneas

pandemic 4 rife 7 rampant 8 epidemic 10 prevailing, widespread 21 dangerously contagious

pandemonium 3 din 5 chaos 6 bedlam, clamor, hubbub, racket, rumpus, tumult, uproar 7 turmoil 8 disorder 9 commotion 10 hullabaloo 11 disturbance

Pandemos
  epithet of: 9 Aphrodite

pander, panderer 4 mack, pimp 5 cadet 7 hustler 8 procurer 9 maquereau, souteneur 12 fleshpeddler

Pandion the Younger
  king of: 6 Athens
  later reigned in: 6 Megara

Pandora
  form: 10 first woman
  created by: 10 Hephaestus
  presented to: 10 Epimetheus
  daughter: 6 Pyrrha
  given by gods: 3 box
    box contained: 4 hope 5 evils

Pandrosos
  position: 9 priestess
  first priestess of: 6 Athena
  father: 7 Cecrops
  mother: 8 Agraulos

panegyric 6 eulogy, homage, praise 7 tribute 8 citation, encomium, good word 9 extolment, laudation 10 compliment 11 testimonial 12 commendation

panegyrize 4 laud 5 extol 6 praise 8 eulogize

panel 4 jury, pane 5 board, group, piece 6 insert 7 divider 8 bulkhead 9 committee, partition 10 round table 11 compartment, expert group, select group 13 advisory group

pang 4 ache, pain 5 agony, pinch, smart, stick, sting, throb 6 stitch, twinge 7 anguish 8 distress 9 suffering 10 discomfort

Pangloss
  character in: 7 Candide
  author: 8 Voltaire
  characteristic: 8 optimism

pang of conscience 5 demur, qualm 6 unease 7 remorse, scruple 9 misgiving 10 uneasiness 11 compunction

panhandle 3 beg, bum 5 cadge, mooch 6 hustle 7 solicit 9 importune

Panhandle State
  nickname of: 12 West Virginia

Panhellenius
  epithet of: 4 Zeus
  means: 14 god of all Greeks

panic 5 alarm, dread, go ape, scare 6 fright, horror, terror 7 anxiety 8 affright, hysteria 9 cold sweat, confusion, fall apart 10 go to pieces 11 nervousness, trepidation 12 apprehension, perturbation 13 consternation

panicky 6 scared 7 alarmed, anxious 9 terrified 10 frightened 13 panic-stricken, scared to death 14 terror-stricken

panic-stricken 6 afraid, scared 7 alarmed, anxious, fearful, panicky 9 terrified 13 scared to death 14 terror-stricken

Panjabi
  language family: 12 Indo-European
  branch: 11 Indo-Iranian
  group: 5 Indic
  spoken in: 5 (northern) India

Pankrits
  language family: 12 Indo-European
  branch: 11 Indo-Iranian
  form of: 5 Indic
  followed use of: 8 Sanskrit

pannier 3 bag 4 hoop 6 basket, dossel, pantry 7 corbeil, drapery 9 framework, overskirt
  literally: 11 breadbasket

Panoptes
  epithet of: 5 Argus
  means: 7 all eyes

panorama 5 scene, vista 6 survey 7 diorama, picture, scenery, tableau 8 long view, overview, prospect 10 scenic view 11 perspective 12 bird's-eye view

panoramic 3 ide 7 overall 8 bird's-eye, extended, sweeping 9 extensive 10 far-ranging 11 far-reaching 12 all-embracing, all-inclusive 15 all-encompassing

pansy 5 Viola
  varieties: 4 Wild 5 Field 6 Garden, Orchid 8 Japanese 9 Miniature 11 Monkey-faced 12 European wild

pant 4 blow, gasp, huff, puff 6 wheeze

pant after 4 seek 5 covet, crave 6 desire, pursue 7 hope for, long for, lust for, wish for **8** yearn for **9** hanker for, hunger for, lust after **11** thirst after, have a yen for **14** set one's heart on

Pantagruel *see* **22** Gargantua and Pantagruel

panther 3 cat **6** cougar **7** leopard

Pantomime Quiz
host: **10** Mike Stokey **15** Pat Harrington Jr

pantry 5 ambry, store **6** closet, galley, larder **7** butlery, buttery, pannier, spicery **8** cupboard, scullery

pants 5 jeans **6** denims, shorts, slacks **7** drawers, panties **8** breeches, britches, knickers, trousers **9** bluejeans, dungarees **10** underpants **11** undershorts **12** underdrawers

pantywaist 4 wimp **5** sissy, softy **7** crybaby, milksop **8** mama's boy, weakling **10** namby-pamby, sissypants, weak sister **11** Milquetoast, mollycoddle **13** sissy-britches

Panurge
character in: **22** Gargantua and Pantagruel
author: **8** Rabelais

Panza, Sancho
character in: **10** Don Quixote
author: **9** Cervantes

pap 3 rot **4** bosh, junk, mash, mush, pulp, tosh **5** gruel, paste **6** cereal, drivel, Pablum, trivia **7** rubbish, twaddle **8** soft food **10** balderdash, flapdoodle, triviality

papa 2 pa **3** dad, doc, paw, pop **5** daddy, poppy **6** father, priest **9** Hemingway
mate: **4** mama

Papa Bear
nickname of: **11** George Halas

Papago
language family: **5** Piman **10** Uto-Aztecan
location: **6** Mexico **7** Arizona
related to: **4** Pima

papal 9 apostolic, of the pope **10** pontifical

paper 4 bond, deed, news, opus, pulp, work **5** daily, draft, essay, stock, theme **6** record, report, tissue, weekly **7** article, gazette, journal, monthly, tabloid, writing **8** document, gift wrap **9** cardboard, chronicle, newspaper, newsprint, onionskin **10** instrument, manuscript, paperboard, periodical, stationery, typescript **11** certificate, com position, publication

Paper Chase, The
character: **10** James T Hart, Willis Bell **13** Asheley Brooks **14** Elizabeth Logan, Jonathan Brooks **15** Franklin Ford III **19** Thomas Craig Anderson **29** Professor Charles W Kingsfield Jr
cast: **10** James Keane **11** Robert Ginty **12** Deka Beaudine, John Houseman **13** James Stephens, Jonathan Segal

14 Francine Tacker, Tom Fitzsimmons
subject: **9** law school
Kingsfield's specialty: **11** contract law

paper measure 4 ream **5** quire

Paper Moon
director: **16** Peter Bogdanovich
cast: **9** Ryan O'Neal **10** Tatum O'Neal **12** Madeline Kahn (Trixie Delight) **13** John Hillerman
Oscar for: **17** supporting actress (O'Neal)

Papua New Guinea
formerly: **16** British New Guinea
capital: **11** Port Moresby
town: **3** Thu, Lae **4** Ioma **6** Kikori, Madang
province of: **9** Indonesia
province: **9** West Irian
monetary unit: **4** kina
island: **6** Misima **10** New Britain
archipelago: **8** Bismarck
lake: **6** Murray
river: **3** Fly **4** Ramu
sea: **5** Coral **7** Solomon
strait: **6** Torres
people: **4** Hula, Kate **5** Kiwai, Kwoma **6** Banaro **7** Arapesh **10** Melanesian
language: **7** English

papyrus 4 pith, reed **5** paper, sedge **6** scroll **7** bulrush **8** document **10** manuscript
accordion pleated: **6** orihon
genus: **7** Cyperus
origin: **5** Egypt **9** Nile delta **10** Nile valley
use: **3** mat **4** rope, shoe, sail **5** paper

par 5 level, usual **6** normal, parity **7** average, balance, the norm **8** equality, evenness, identity, sameness, standard **9** stability **11** equilibrium, equivalency **12** equal footing **13** identicalness

parable 4 myth, tale **5** fable, story **6** homily, legend **8** allegory, apologue, folk tale **9** folk story **12** morality tale

Paracelsus
author: **14** Robert Browning

parade 4 line, pomp, show **5** array, march, strut, train, vaunt **6** column, defile, flaunt, review, string **7** caravan, cortege, display, show off **8** vaunting **9** cavalcade, flaunting, march past, motorcade, pageantry, put on airs, spectacle **10** exposition, grandstand, procession **11** progression **13** demonstration

paradigm 5 ideal, model **6** matrix, sample **7** example, paragon, pattern **8** exemplar, original, standard **9** archetype, criterion, prototype, yardstick

paradise 3 joy **4** Eden **5** bliss **6** heaven, utopia **7** delight, ecstasy, nirvana, rapture **8** pleasure **9** enjoyment, happiness, Shangri-la, transport **11** happy valley **12** Garden of Eden, sat-

isfaction **13** gratification, seventh heaven **15** Land of Cockaigne

Paradise
also: **9** Paradisio
part three of: **12** Divine Comedy
author: **14** Dante Alighieri

Paradise Lost
author: **10** John Milton
character: **3** Eve, God **4** Adam **5** Satan **6** Christ **7** Lucifer

Paradise of the Pacific
nickname of: **6** Hawaii

Paradise Regained
author: **10** John Milton

paradisiacal 7 elysian, sublime **8** blissful, empyreal, empyrean, ethereal, heavenly **9** celestial, unearthly **12** otherworldly

paradox 5 poser **6** enigma, oddity, puzzle, riddle **7** anomaly **11** incongruity **13** inconsistency

paradoxical 9 ambiguous, enigmatic, equivocal **13** contradictory

paragon 4 norm **5** ideal, model **6** symbol **7** example, pattern **8** exemplar, paradigm, standard **9** archetype, criterion, prototype, yardstick **10** apotheosis

Paraguay
capital/largest city: **8** Asuncion
others: **3** Ita **4** Rica, Yuty **5** Belen, Luque, Pilar, Villa **7** Caacupe **8** Trinidad **9** Paraguari **10** Concepcion, Villarrica **11** Encarnacion **26** Puerto Presidente Stroessner
division: **6** Guaira, Itapua, Olimpo **7** Caazapa **8** Boqueron **9** Concepcion
measure: **3** pie **4** lino, lira, lire, vara **5** legua **6** cuadra, fanega
monetary unit: **4** peso **7** guarani, centimo
weight: **7** quintal
island:
floating island: **8** camalote
lake: **4** Vera, Ypoa **8** Ypacarai
river: **3** Apa **5** Guazu, Negro, Plata, Verde, Ypane **6** Acaray, Parana **7** Aguaray, Confuso **8** Paraguay **9** Aquidaban, Pilcomayo, Tebicuary, Tibiquare **10** Monte Lindo **14** Riacho Gonzales **15** Riacho Mosquitos
physical feature:
falls: **6** Guaira
plains: **5** Chaco
plateau: **6** Parana
people: **6** Abipon, Moskoi **7** Guarani, mestizo **8** Guayaqui
artist: **7** Bestard
author: **3** Pla **4** Baez **6** Alcala, Bastos, Correa, O'Leary **7** Cervera **8** Casaccia
composer: **8** Asuncion
leader: **5** Lopez **7** Francia **10** Stroessner **16** Antequera y Castro
sculptor: **8** Guggiari
language: **6** German **7** Guarani, Spanish

religion: 9 Mennonite **13** Roman Catholic
place:
  church: 10 Villarrica **11** Incarnation
  dam: 6 Itaipu
  memorial: 16 Pantheon of Heroes
  museum: 5 Godoi
  palace: 10 Government
feature:
  animal: 4 puma **5** tapir **6** iguana, jaguar **7** peccary
  bird: 6 toucan
  clothing: 5 fajas, typoi **6** poncho **7** rebozos **9** bombachas **10** alpargatas
  communes: 11 reducciones
  dance: 7 Sante Fe **15** Paraguayan polka
  fish: 7 piranha
  lace: 7 nanduti
  music: 8 quarania
  townspeople: 9 comuneros
  tree: 5 ceiba **7** lapacho **9** quebracho
food:
  bread: 5 chipa, mbeyu
  dish: 12 sopa paraguay
  tea: 9 yerba mate
  vegetable: 8 mandioca

parallel 4 akin, like, same, twin **5** alike, equal, match **6** follow **7** abreast, analogy, be alike, similar **8** analogue, likeness, relation **9** alongside, analogous, corollary, duplicate **10** collateral, comparable, comparison, concurrent, connection, equivalent, similarity **11** coextensive, coincidence, comparative, compare with, correlation, correlative, counterpart, equidistant, resemblance **12** correspond to **13** corresponding **14** correspondence

parallelism 8 affinity, likeness, sameness **9** agreement **10** comparison, similarity, similitude **11** resemblance **14** correspondence

parallelogram 5 rhomb **6** square **7** diamond, rhombus **8** rhomboid **9** rectangle **11** plane figure **13** quadrilateral

paralyze 4 stun **6** benumb, deaden, disarm, freeze, weaken **7** cripple, destroy, disable, petrify, stupefy, wipe out **8** demolish, enfeeble **10** debilitate, immobilize, neutralize **12** incapacitate

Paramaribo
  capital of: 8 Suriname

paramount 4 main **5** chief **6** utmost **7** capital, highest, leading, premier, supreme **8** cardinal, dominant, foremost, greatest, peerless, superior **9** essential, principal, unmatched **10** preeminent **11** outstanding, predominant **12** incomparable, preponderant, transcendent

paramour 3 man **4** doxy **5** lover, Romeo **6** gigolo **7** Don Juan **8** Casanova, fancy man, lothario, loverboy, mistress **9** boyfriend, concubine, courte-

san, inamorata, inamorato, kept woman **10** girlfriend, lady friend, sugar daddy

paranoid 4 wary **7** deluded **9** paranoiac **11** distrustful **14** oversuspicious

parapet 7 bulwark, rampart **8** abutment, palisade **9** barricade, earthwork **10** battlement, breastwork

paraphernalia 3 rig **4** gear **5** stuff **6** outfit, tackle, things **7** effects, harness, regalia **8** fittings, material, supplies, utensils **9** apparatus, equipment, trappings **10** belongings, implements, properties, provisions **11** accessories, furnishings **13** accoutrements

paraphrase 5 recap **6** rehash, reword **7** restate **9** rephrase **12** recapitulate

parasite 5 leech **6** beggar, cadger, loafer **7** moocher, shirker, slacker, sponger **8** deadbeat **9** goldbrick, scrounger **10** freeloader **11** bloodsucker
  inside host: 12 endoparasite
  outside host: 12 ectoparasite

parasol 5 shade **6** shadow **7** roundel **8** sunshade, umbrella
  mushroom: 7 lepiota

par avion 5 by air

parboil 4 boil **5** scald **6** blanch **7** precook

Parca
  origin: 5 Roman
  member of: 6 Parcae
  goddess of: 7 destiny **10** childbirth

Parcae *see* **5** Fates

parcel 3 lot **4** bale, pack, part, plot **5** allot, piece, tract **6** bundle, divide, packet **7** carve up, deal out, dole out, package, portion, section, segment, split up **8** allocate, dispense, disperse, division, fraction, fragment, property **9** allotment, allowance, apportion, partition **10** distribute **11** piece of land

parceling out 9 allotment, doling out, meting out **10** allocation, assignment, dealing out **12** distribution **13** apportionment

parcel out 5 allot **7** dole out, give out, mete out **8** allocate, dispense, divide up **9** apportion **10** distribute, portion out

parch 4 bake, burn, char, sear **5** dry up, singe **6** dry out, scorch, sun-dry, wither **7** blister, shrivel **9** dehydrate, dessicate, evaporate

parched 3 dry **4** arid **6** barren **8** withered **9** shriveled **10** dehydrated, desiccated

parchment 6 scroll, vellum **7** papyrus **8** goatskin **9** sheepskin

pardon 5 grace, mercy **6** excuse, wink at **7** absolve, amnesty, blink at, forbear, forgive, indulge, release, set free **8** overlook, reprieve, shrug off **9** discharge, disregard, exculpate, exoner-

ate, remission, vindicate **10** absolution, indulgence **11** deliverance, exculpation, forbearance, forgiveness **12** grant amnesty **16** forgive and forget

Pardoner
  character in: 18 The Canterbury Tales
  author: 7 Chaucer

pare 3 cut, lop **4** clip, crop, dock, hull, husk, peel, skin, trim **5** lower, prune, shave, shear, shell, shuck, slash, strip **6** lessen, reduce, shrink **7** curtail, cut back **8** decrease, diminish **11** decorticate

pare down 3 cut **4** trim **5** shave **6** reduce **7** abridge, curtail, cut down, shorten **8** condense, cut short, diminish **10** abbreviate

parent 3 dam **4** sire **5** model **6** father, mother **7** creator **8** ancestor, begetter, exemplar, original, producer **9** precursor, prototype **10** antecedent, forerunner, originator, procreator, progenitor **11** predecessor

parentage 5 birth, roots, stock **6** family, origin, strain **7** descent, lineage **8** ancestry, forbears, heredity, pedigree **9** ancestors, genealogy **10** background, derivation, extraction, family tree **11** antecedents

Parentalia
  origin: 5 Roman
  event: 8 festival

parenthetical 5 aside **6** braced, casual **8** inserted **9** bracketed **10** extraneous, immaterial, incidental, interposed, irrelevant **11** impertinent, intervening, superfluous

par excellence 8 superior **10** preeminent

parfait d'amour
  type: 7 liqueur
  flavor: 7 violets
  color: 6 purple

Paria
  form: 5 nymph
  loved by: 5 Minos
  children: 7 Chryses **9** Eurymedon, Nephalion, Philolaus

pariah 5 exile, rover, stray **6** outlaw, roamer **7** outcast **8** vagabond, wanderer **10** expatriate **11** undesirable, untouchable

paring 4 chip, snip **5** scrap, shred, slice **6** sliver **7** cutting, peeling, shaving **8** fragment

pari passu 6 fairly **7** equably **10** side by side **13** equal progress **17** without partiality

Paris
  airport: 4 Orly **9** Le Bourget **15** Charles de Gaulle
  area: 5 Passy **6** Clichy, Marais, Ternes, Wagram **7** Auteuil **8** Chaillot, Gobelins, Left Bank, St Honore **9** Les Halles, Right Bank, St Germain **10** Montmartre, Rive Droite, Rive

Gauche, Val de Grace **11** Ile de la Cite **12** Hotel de Ville, Latin Quarter, Montparnasse
capital of: 6 France
city planner: 9 Haussmann
island: 10 Ile St Louis **11** Ile de la Cite
landmark: 8 Pantheon **9** Notre Dame **10** Paris Opera, Sacre Coeur **11** Eiffel Tower, La Madeleine, Palais Royal **12** Elysee Palace, Hotel de Ville, Place Vendome **13** Arc de Triomphe, Palais Bourbon **14** Bois de Boulogne, Place de l'Etoile, Pompidou Center, Sainte Chapelle, Tomb of Napoleon **15** Bois de Vincennes **16** Luxembourg Palace **17** Hotel des Invalides, Place de la Bastille, Place de la Concorde **18** Jardin des Tuileries **20** Place Charles de Gaulle
nickname: 11 city of light
river: 5 Seine
street: 9 Haussmann, Invalides **10** Grand Armee **11** Saint Michel **12** Montparnasse, Saint Germain **13** Champs Elysees **15** Charles de Gaulle
subway: 5 Metro
university: 8 Sorbonne

Paris
character in: 14 Romeo and Juliet
author: 11 Shakespeare

Paris
position: 6 prince
father: 5 Priam
mother: 6 Hecuba
brother: 6 Hector **9** Polydorus
sister: 9 Cassandra
wife: 6 Oenone
abducted: 5 Helen
judgment of: 14 apple of discord
awarded apple to: 9 Aphrodite
killed by: 11 Philoctetes

parish 4 fold **5** flock, shire **6** canton, county **7** diocese, section **8** brethren, district, precinct, province **9** community, pastorate **10** department **11** archdiocese **12** congregation, neighborhood

parity 7 balance **8** equality, sameness **10** coequality, uniformity **11** equivalence, equivalency **14** correspondence

park 4 lawn **5** field, green, grove, woods **6** common, meadow, square **7** grounds, reserve **8** parkland, preserve, woodland **9** grassland, sanctuary **10** public park, quadrangle

Parker, Dorothy
author of: 6 Resume **9** Big Blonde **10** Enough Rope **13** Death and Taxes **18** After Such Pleasures **19** Laments for the Living

parkway 6 avenue **7** thruway **9** boulevard **12** thoroughfare

parlance 4 talk **5** idiom, lingo **6** speech **16** manner of speaking

Parlement of Fowles, The
author: 15 Geoffrey Chaucer

parley 4 talk **6** confab, powwow, summit **7** council, meeting, palaver **8** conclave **9** discourse, mediation, peace talk **10** conference, discussion **11** arbitration, negotiation **12** conversation

parliament 4 diet **5** court, house, junta **6** fan-tan, senate, sevens **7** cabinet, council **8** assembly, congress **9** high court **11** legislature **12** three estates
Communist: 6 Soviet **9** politburo, presidium
estate: 12 House of Lords **14** House of Commons
Germanic: 9 Bundesrat, Bundestag, Bolksraad **11** Volkshammer
Greek: 5 Boule
Icelandic: 7 Althing
Israeli: 7 Knesset **8** Knesseth
Scandinavian: 7 Lagting, Riksdag **8** Lagthing, Storting **9** Odelsting, Storthing
Spanish: 6 Cortes

parlor 5 salon **6** saloon **8** best room **9** front room **10** living room **11** drawing room, sitting room

Parnopius
epithet of: 6 Apollo
means: 9 locust god

parochial 5 local, petty, small **6** church, little, narrow, parish **7** insular, limited **8** regional **9** hidebound, illiberal, religious, sectional, small-town **10** provincial, restricted **11** countrified **12** narrow-minded

parodos
from Greek drama: 9 choral ode

parody 5 mimic **6** satire **7** lampoon, takeoff **8** satirize, travesty **9** burlesque, take off on **10** caricature

Parolles
character in: 20 All's Well That Ends Well
author: 11 Shakespeare

paroxysm 3 fit **5** spasm, spell **7** seizure **10** convulsion

parrot 3 ape **4** bird, echo, lory **5** macaw, mimer, mimic **6** chorus, monkey **7** copycat, imitate **8** cockatoo, imitator, parakeet **9** reiterate

parry 4 duck, shun **5** avert, avoid, dodge, elude, repel **7** beat off, fend off, repulse, ward off **8** sidestep, stave off **10** circumvent, fight shy of

Parsifal
opera by: 6 Wagner
character: 6 Kundry **8** Amfortas, Klingsor **9** Gurnemanz

Parsifal Mosaic, The
author: 12 Robert Ludlum

parsimonious 5 close, tight **6** frugal, saving, stingy **7** miserly, sparing, thrifty **9** niggardly, penurious **10** economical, ungenerous **11** closefisted,

tightfisted **13** money-grubbing, penny-pinching

parsimony 6 thrift **7** economy **8** meanness **10** stinginess **13** niggardliness **15** tightfistedness

parsley 19 Petroselinum crispum
varieties: 5 Horse **7** Chinese, Italian **12** Turnip-rooted
related herb: 4 dill **5** cumin **6** fennel
garland worn by: 8 Hercules
gives speed to: 6 horses
use in: 11 fines herbes **12** bouquet garni

parson 5 clerk, padre **6** cleric, divine, father, pastor, priest, rector **7** dominie **8** minister, preacher, reverend, shepherd, sky pilot **9** clergyman
French: 4 abbe, cure

parsonage 5 glebe, manse **7** deanery, rectory, Vatican **8** vicarage **9** pastorate

part 2 go **3** bit, job **4** care, chip, duty, hunk, item, open, rend, role, slit, task, tear, unit **5** break, chore, crumb, guise, leave, piece, place, scrap, sever, shard, share, sherd, shred, slice, split **6** branch, charge, cleave, depart, detach, detail, divide, go away, member, morsel, region, sector, set out, sliver, sunder **7** concern, cutting, disjoin, element, portion, push off, section, segment, snippet **8** breakoff, business, capacity, disguise, disunite, division, fraction, fragment, function, separate, set forth, start out **9** character, component, disengage, go one's way **10** assignment, break apart, department, disconnect, get up and go, ingredient, mosey along, say good-bye **11** be on one's way, call it quits, constituent, subdivision

partake 5 enjoy, savor, share **6** join in, sample **7** share in **8** engage in **11** participate

part from 5 leave **9** break with **12** separate from

Parthenia
epithet of: 6 Athena
means: 6 virgin

Parthenopaeus
father: 10 Hippomenes
mother: 8 Atalanta
member of: 18 Seven against Thebes

partial 6 biased, unfair, unjust **7** limited, slanted **8** one-sided, partisan **9** factional **10** fractional, incomplete, interested, prejudiced, subjective, unbalanced, unfinished **11** fragmentary, inequitable, predisposed, uncompleted **12** inconclusive, prepossessed

partiality 4 bent, bias, love, tilt **5** fancy, slant, taste **6** choice, liking **7** leaning **8** affinity, fondness, penchant, tendency, weakness **9** prejudice **10** attraction, favoritism, preference, proclivity, propensity **11** inclination **12**

one-sidedness, partisanship, predilection **14** predisposition

partially 6 in part, partly **7** partway **8** somewhat **9** piecemeal **12** fractionally, incompletely

participant 4 ally **5** party **6** cohort, fellow, helper, member, player, sharer, worker **7** partner **8** confrere, partaker **9** accessory, associate, colleague, performer **10** accomplice **11** contributor, shareholder **12** collaborator, participator

participate 5 share **6** join in **7** partake, perform **8** engage in, take part **9** play a part

particle 3 bit, jot **4** atom, iota, mite, snip, whit **5** crumb, grain, scrap, shred, speck, trace **6** morsel, tittle, trifle **7** granule, modicum, smidgen, snippet **9** scintilla

parti-colored 4 pied **5** plaid **6** motley **7** checked, dappled, mottled **8** colorful **9** checkered **10** variegated **11** many-colored **12** multicolored

particular 4 sole **5** exact, fixed, fussy, picky **6** single, strict **7** express, finicky, special **8** concrete, critical, definite, detailed, distinct, especial, exacting, explicit, itemized, personal, separate, specific **9** demanding **10** fastidious, individual, meticulous, scrupulous **11** painstaking, persnickety, punctilious, well-defined **12** hard to please

particularize 6 detail **7** itemize, specify **9** enumerate

particularly 6 mainly **7** notably **8** markedly **9** eminently, expressly, specially, supremely, unusually **10** definitely, distinctly, especially, explicitly, strikingly **11** principally, prominently **13** exceptionally **15** extraordinarily

particulars 5 facts, items **6** events **7** details **9** specifics **13** circumstances

parti pris 15 position decided **20** preconceived attitude

partisan 3 fan **4** ally **6** backer, biased, rooter, zealot **7** booster, devotee, partial, slanted **8** adherent, advocate, champion, follower, one-sided, upholder **9** guerrilla, insurgent, irregular, jayhawker, supporter **10** bushwacker, enthusiast, prejudiced, subjective, unbalanced **11** sympathizer

partition 4 wall **5** allot, fence, panel **6** assign, divide, screen **7** barrier, deal out, divider, mete out, parting, split up **8** allocate, bulkhead, dispense, disperse, dividing, division, separate **9** allotment, apportion, parcel out, separator, severance, splitting, subdivide **10** allocation, assignment, distribute, separation **11** demarcation, segregation **12** distribution, dividing wall **13** apportionment

partly 6 in part **7** part way **8** somewhat **9** not wholly, partially, to a de-

gree **10** relatively **12** fractionally, incompletely **13** after a fashion, comparatively

partly open 4 ajar **5** agape **6** gaping **7** cracked **8** half- open, unclosed **9** squinting **10** half-closed

partner 3 aid, pal **4** ally, chum, mate, wife **5** aider, buddy **6** fellow, friend, helper, sharer, spouse **7** comrade, co-owner, husband **8** confrere, helpmate, partaker, sidekick, teammate **9** accessory, assistant, associate, colleague, companion, co-partner **10** accomplice, better half, joint owner **11** confederate, participant **12** collaborator

Parton, Dolly
roles: **10** Nine to Five, Rhinestone **30** The Best Little Whorehouse in Texas

partridge
group of: **5** covey

Partridge
character in: **8** Tom Jones
author: **8** Fielding

Partridge Family, The
character: **13** Reuben Kinkaid **14** Danny Partridge, Keith Partridge, Tracy Partridge **15** Connie Partridge, Laurie Partridge **20** Christopher Partridge
cast: **8** Susan Dey **11** David Madden **12** Brian Forster, David Cassidy, Shirley Jones **13** Danny Bonaduce, Suzanne Crough **14** Jeremy Gelbwaks
song: **14** I Think I Love You

parturition 5 birth **8** delivery **10** childbirth **11** giving birth **12** childbearing

party 2 do **4** band, bash, body, crew, fete, gang, team, unit, wing **5** corps, force, group, squad **6** affair, at-home, league, soiree **7** accused, blow out, company, coterie, faction **8** alliance, claimant, conclave, litigant, wingding **9** appellant, coalition, defendant, festivity, gathering, plaintiff, reception **10** contestant, federation, petitioner, respondent **11** celebration, confederacy, get-together, participant, paticipator, perpetrator

party-pooper 4 drag **10** spoilsport, wet blanket

parvenu 4 snob **6** nobody **7** upstart **8** arrivist, mushroom **9** arriviste **12** nouveau riche

Pascal, Blaise
nationality: **6** French
invented: **7** syringe **13** adding machine **14** hydraulic press
author of: **7** Pensees **19** Lettres provinciales **20** Essay pour les coniques

Pascin, Julius
real name: **6** Pincas
born: **5** Vidin **8** Bulgaria
artwork: **6** Femmes **12** Les Deux Amies **17** Ginette et Mireille

Pasiphae

father: **6** Helios
mother: **7** Perseis
husband: **5** Minos
daughter: **7** Ariadne, Phaedra **9** Acacallis
became enamored of: **10** Cretan bull
mother of: **8** Minotaur

Pasithea
member of: **6** Graces

pass 2 go **3** cap, die, end, gap, hit, top, use, way **4** best, busy, fill, flow, give, go by, go on, hand, kick, lane, meet, toss **5** canal, exact, excel, gorge, gulch, leave, outdo, route, spend, throw, trail **6** accept, affirm, avenue, be over, canyon, convey, course, decree, depart, devote, elapse, employ, engage, exceed, expend, expire, finish, go away, go past, occupy, ordain, permit, pickle, plight, ratify, ravine, slip by, strait, take up, vanish **7** achieve, advance, approve, channel, confirm, consume, deliver, die away, eclipse, freebie, glide by, go ahead, let have, narrows, pathway, present, proceed, qualify, satisfy, slide by, surpass **8** blow over, dissolve, exigency, fade away, furlough, go beyond, go onward, hand over, juncture, legalize, melt away, outshine, outstrip, passaway, peter out, progress, quandary, sanction, transfer, transmit, turn over **9** authorize, disappear, evaporate, extremity, hand along, legislate, situation, terminate **10** accomplish, difficulty, free ticket, get through, move onward, over shadow, passageway **11** predicament, proposition **12** complication, run its course, solicitation, stand the test **13** authorization **15** amorous overture
French: **13** laissez passer

passable 4 fair, open, so-so **5** clear **6** not bad **8** adequate, fordable, mediocre, middling **9** allowable, crossable, navigable, tolerable **10** acceptable, admissible, pretty good **11** presentable, respectable, traversable **12** unobstructed

passage 3 way **4** hall, pass, path, road, tour, trek, trip **5** aisle, canal, piece, route, verse **6** access, clause, column, course, junket, tunnel, voyage **7** channel, chapter, hallway, journey, passing, portion, section, transit **8** approach, approval, corridor, movement, sanction, sentence **9** enact ment, excursion, paragraph, selection, ship's fare **10** acceptance, expedition, ordainment **11** affirmation, endorsement, legislation, progression **12** confirmation, legalization, ratification **13** authorization

passage out 4 exit **6** egress, outlet

Passages
author: **10** Gail Sheehy

Passage to India, A

author: 9 E M Forster
character: 6 Dr Aziz 8 Mrs Moore 12 Adela Quested 13 Cecil Fielding, Ronald Heaslop 16 Professor Godbole
setting: 11 Chandrapore 12 Marabar Caves
director: 9 David Lean
cast: 9 Judy Davis 12 Alec Guinness 13 Peggy Ashcroft 15 Victor Bannerjee
Oscar for: 17 supporting actress (Ashcroft)

passageway 4 exit, hall, lane, path, walk 5 aisle 6 access, arcade, tunnel 7 doorway, gangway, gateway, hallway, passage 8 corridor, entrance, entryway, sidewalk 12 companionway

pass away 3 die 6 depart, expire, pass on, perish 7 decease 8 pass over 13 go to one's glory 14 give up the ghost

pass by 4 go by, pass 5 lapse 6 elapse, roll by, slip by 7 glide by, slide by 8 slip away

passe 4 past 5 faded, hoary, stale 6 demode, lapsed, quaint 7 ancient, antique, archaic, disused, outworn, retired 8 obsolete, outdated, outmoded 9 out-of-date 10 antiquated 11 prehistoric 12 antediluvian, old-fashioned, out of fashion 13 superannuated

passenger 4 fare 5 rider 8 commuter, stowaway, traveler, wayfarer

Passepartout
character in: 26 Around the World in Eighty Days
author: 5 Verne

pas seul
ballet: 9 solo dance
literally: 8 solo step

passim 12 here and there, repeated item

passing 5 brief, death, dying 6 demise, fickle 7 decease, passage 8 adequate, fleeting 9 enactment, ephemeral, momentary, temporary, transient 10 evanescent, expiration, not failing, short-lived, transitory 11 impermanent, legislating

passing the bounds of propriety
French: 5 outre

passion 4 fire, idol, love, lust, rage, urge 5 ardor, craze, fancy, flame, gusto, heart, mania 6 desire, fervor, hunger, thirst, warmth 7 beloved, craving, ecstasy, emotion, feeling, rapture 8 loved one 9 carnality, eagerness, inamorata, intensity, obsession, sentiment, transport, vehemence 10 carnal love, enthusiasm 11 amorousness, earnestness, infatuation

passionate 3 hot 4 sexy 5 fiery 6 ardent, carnal, erotic, fervid, fierce, heated, loving, raging 7 amorous, earnest, excited, feeling, fervent, furious, intense, lustful 8 desirous, ecstatic, inflamed, sensuous, vehement 9 emo-

tional, heartfelt, wrought-up 11 tempestuous 12 enthusiastic, intoxicating

passionfruit
type: 7 liqueur
origin: 6 Hawaii
flavor: 5 peach

passionless 4 calm, cold 6 placid, serene 7 passive 8 tranquil 9 apathetic, unfeeling 10 spiritless 11 emotionless, indifferent, unemotional

Passion Play
author: 13 Jerzy Kosinski

passive 5 inert 6 docile 7 dormant, patient, pliable 8 enduring, inactive, lifeless, listless, resigned, yielding 9 apathetic, compliant, impassive, quiescent, tractable 10 spiritless, submissive 11 acquiescent, unassertive, unresisting 12 nonresistant

passiveness 6 apathy 7 inertia 8 docility 10 quiescence 11 resignation 12 acquiescence, lifelessness 14 submissiveness 16 unresponsiveness

passivity 6 apathy 7 inertia 8 docility, meekness 11 resignation 12 complaisance, lifelessness 13 nonresistance 14 submissiveness

pass muster 2 do 5 serve 6 answer 8 be enough 10 be adequate 12 be sufficient 14 be satisfactory

pass on 3 die 6 depart, expire 7 decease 8 pass away 13 go to one's glory 14 give up the ghost, leave this world 15 breathe one's last

pass over 6 ignore, slight 7 neglect 8 overlook 10 brush aside

pass up 4 miss 6 ignore, refuse

password 3 key 4 word 6 by word, slogan 7 keyword, tessera 9 catchword, watchword 10 open sesame, secret word, shibboleth 11 countersign, passe-parole

Password
host: 11 Allen Ludden

past 2 by 4 gone 5 ended, prior 6 beyond, bygone, former, gone by 7 ancient, earlier, elapsed, expired, history, long ago, through 8 departed, finished, previous 9 antiquity, days of old 10 days gone by, days of yore, historical, olden times, passed away, yesteryear 11 dead and gone, former times, times gone by 12 ancient times

pasta 4 orzo, ziti 6 elbows, shells 7 gnocchi, lasagna, pastina, ravioli, rotelli 8 ditalini, linguini, macaroni, rigatoni, tortelli 9 canelloni, cavatelli, fettucine, manicotti, spaghetti 10 tortellini, vermicelli
ingredient: 3 egg 5 flour

pasta sauce 4 ragu 5 pesto, salsa 6 tomato 7 alfredo 8 mushroom, pomodoro 9 bolognese, carbonara

past due 4 late 5 tardy 7 belated, overdue 9 in arrears 10 behindhand

paste 3 gum, hit 4 glue, seal, sock 5

affix, punch, stick 6 attach, cement 7 stickum 8 adhesive, mucilage

pastel 3 dim 4 pale, soft 5 chalk, faded, faint, light, muted 6 crayon 9 washed-out 13 coloring stick 14 coloring pencil

Pasternak, Boris
author of: 9 Dr Zhivago

Pasteur, Louis
field: 9 chemistry
nationality: 6 French
originated: 14 anti-rabies shot, pasteurization
founded: 12 microbiology
disproved: 21 spontaneous generation

pastime 3 fun 4 game, play 5 hobby, sport 9 amusement, avocation, diversion 10 relaxation 11 distraction 13 entertainment 14 divertissement

pastis
type: 7 liqueur
flavor: 8 licorice
substitute for: 8 absinthe

past one's prime 3 old 4 aged 5 aging 7 elderly 9 venerable 11 over the hill 12 in one's dotage

pastor 4 cure, dean 5 padre, vicar 6 cleric, father, parson, priest, rector 8 chaplain, minister, preacher 9 clergyman

pastoral 5 rural 6 rustic 7 bucolic, idyllic 8 arcadian, clerical, priestly 9 episcopal 10 sacerdotal 11 ministerial 14 ecclesiastical

Pastoral Symphony, The
author: 9 Andre Gide

pastorate 6 clergy 8 ministry, the cloth 10 priesthood

pastures
god of: 3 Pan 6 Dumuzi

pasty 3 wan 4 ashy, gray, pale 5 ashen, gluey, gooey, gummy, white 6 anemic, chalky, doughy, pallid, peaked, sallow, sticky 7 deathly, starchy 9 bloodless, colorless, ghostlike, glutinous, like paste 12 mucilaginous

pat 3 apt, dab, hit, pet, rap, tap 4 cake, daub, easy, glib, slap 5 exact, ideal, ready, slick, thump 6 caress, facile, fondle, simple, smooth, stroke, thwack 7 apropos, fitting, perfect, precise, reliant 8 flippant, suitable 9 contrived, pertinent, rehearsed

patch 3 fix, lot 4 area, darn, mend, plot, spot, zone 5 field, sew up, tract 6 garden, repair, stitch 7 expanse, stretch 8 clearing, insignia 9 reinforce 13 reinforcement

patchwork 4 hash, mess 6 jumble, medley, muddle, tangle 7 grab bag, melange, mixture 8 mishmash, mixed bag, pastiche, scramble 9 confusion, potpourri 10 hodgepodge, miscellany, salmagundi 11 gallimaufry 14 conglomeration, omnium-gatherum

pate 3 pie 4 brow, head 5 brain, crown, paste, pastry, patty, skull 6 noddle, noggin, noodle 9 meat paste

patella
bone of: 7 kneecap

patent 4 bald, bold, open, rank 5 clear, gross, overt, plain 6 permit 7 decided, evident, express, glaring, license, obvious 8 apparent, distinct, flagrant, manifest, palpable, registry, striking 9 copyright, downright, prominent 10 pronounced, unreserved 11 conspicuous, copyrighted, indubitable, self-evident, trademarked, transparent, unconcealed, undisguised 12 unmistakable 15 nonprescription

paterfamilias 6 father 17 father of the family, master of the family 20 master of the household

paternal 4 kind 6 tender 8 fatherly, parental, vigilant, watchful 9 concerned, indulgent 10 benevolent, fatherlike, interested, solicitous 11 patriarchal

Pater Patriae 18 father of his country

path 3 way 4 lane, plan, road, walk 5 byway, means, orbit, route, track, trail 6 access, by path, course 7 pathway, process, walkway 8 approach, footpath

pathetic 3 sad 6 moving, rueful, woeful 7 doleful, piteous, pitiful 8 dolorous, grievous, pitiable, poignant, touching, wretched 9 affecting, miserable, plaintive, sorrowful 10 deplorable, lamentable, to be pitied 11 distressing

Pathfinder, The
author: 19 James Fenimore Cooper
character: 9 Arrowhead, Dew-of-June 10 Charles Cap 11 Mabel Dunham, Natty Bumppo 12 Chingachgook 13 Jasper Western 14 Sergeant Dunham 18 Lieutenant Davy Muir

Pathfinders, The
author: 10 Gail Sheehy

pathogen 3 bug 4 germ 5 virus 7 microbe 8 bacillus 9 bacterium 13 microorganism

pathophobia
fear of: 7 disease

pathos 3 woe 5 agony 6 misery 7 anguish, feeling, sadness 8 distress 9 heartache, poignancy, sentiment 10 desolation 12 pitiableness 13 plaintiveness

Paths of Glory
director: 14 Stanley Kubrick
cast: 11 Kirk Douglas, Ralph Meeker 13 Adolphe Menjou

pathway 4 lane, path, road 5 alley, route, track 6 course 7 passage, walkway 8 footpath 10 passageway

patience 7 poise 7 stamina 8 industry, tenacity 9 composure, diligence, fortitude, restraint, tolerance 10 equanim-

ity, resolution, sufferance 11 application, forbearance, longanimity, persistence, self-control 12 perseverance, tirelessness

Patience 8 operetta
by: 7 Gilbert, Sullivan

patient 4 case 6 dogged, serene 8 composed, diligent, enduring, resolute, tireless 9 dauntless, tenacious, undaunted 10 determined, forbearing, persistent, sick person, unflagging, unswerving, unwavering 11 industrious, persevering, unfaltering, unperturbed 13 indefatigable, long-suffering, uncomplaining

patio 4 deck 5 lanai, porch 6 piazza 7 terrace, veranda

patois 5 argot, idiom, lingo 6 jargon 7 dialect 10 vernacular

Paton, Alan
author of: 19 Too Late the Phalarope 20 Cry the Beloved Country 24 Ah but Your Land Is Beautiful

pat on the back 6 praise 7 plaudit 10 compliment 12 commendation

patriarch 5 elder, ruler 6 father, leader, old man 8 male head 9 chieftain 13 paterfamilias

patrician 4 lord, peer 5 noble 6 lordly 7 genteel, stately 8 highborn, imposing, noble man, princely, well-bred 9 blueblood, dignified, gentle man 10 aristocrat, upper- class 12 aristocratic, silk-stocking

patrimony 3 lot 5 dower, share 6 devise, estate, legacy 7 portion 8 bestowal, heritage, jointure 9 endowment 10 bequeathal, birthright 11 inheritance 12 hereditament

patriotism
Latin: 11 amor patriae

Patroclus
father: 9 Menoetius
mother: 8 Periapis
friend: 8 Achilles
killed by: 6 Hector

patrol 5 guard, scout, watch 6 ranger, sentry, warden 7 protect 8 sentinel 9 safe guard, walk a beat, watch man, watch over 10 stand watch

patron 5 angel, buyer 6 backer, client, friend, helper 7 habitue, shopper, sponsor, visitor 8 advocate, attender, champion, customer, defender, financer, promoter, upholder 9 protector, spectator, supporter 10 benefactor, encourager, frequenter, wellwisher 11 sympathizer 12 benefactress 14 philanthropist

patronage 3 aid 4 help 5 favor, plums, trade 6 buying, custom, spoils 7 backing, charity, clients, dealing, support 8 advocacy, auspices, business, commerce 9 clientele, customers, fosterage 10 assistance, friendship, pork barrel, protection, purchasing 11 benefaction, sponsor-

ship 12 philanthropy 13 encouragement

patronize 5 humor 6 shop at 7 buy from 8 deal with, frequent 9 trade with 10 condescend

patsy 4 dupe, pawn, tool 7 cat's-paw, fall guy

patter 3 pad, pat, rap, tap 4 beat, drum 5 pound, thrum 6 tattoo 7 rat-a-tat, spatter, tapping 8 drumming, sprinkle

pattern 4 copy, form, mold, plan 5 draft, guide, ideal, mimic, model, motif, shape 6 design, follow, sample 7 emulate, example, fashion, imitate, paragon 8 exemplar, original, paradigm, parallel, simulate, specimen, standard 9 archetype, criterion, duplicate, prototype 10 apotheosis, stereotype 12 illustration

Patton
director: 17 Franklin Schaffner
cast: 10 Karl Malden (Omar Bradley) 12 George C Scott (George Patton), Stephen Young 13 Michael Strong
Oscar for: 5 actor (Scott), story 7 picture 8 director 9 screenplay (Francis Ford Coppola and Edmund H North)

Patton, George S
nickname: 15 Old Blood and Guts
served in: 3 WWI 4 WWII 11 World War One, World War Two
commander of: 9 Third Army
invasion of: 8 Normandy 11 North Africa
capture of: 6 Sicily
battle: 5 Bulge
wore: 21 ivory-handled revolvers
memoirs: 12 War As I Knew It

Patty Duke Show, The
character: 7 Richard 8 Ross Lane 9 Cathy Lane, Patty Lane 10 Martin Lane 14 Natalie Masters
cast: 9 Jean Byron, Patty Duke 10 Paul O'Keefe 14 Eddie Applegate 16 William Schallert

paucis verbis 10 by few words, in few words 12 with few words

paucity 4 lack 6 dearth 7 fewness, poverty 8 exiguity, poorness, puniness, scarcity, shortage, sparsity, thinness 10 deficiency, meagerness, scantiness, scarceness 13 insufficiency

Paul
former name: 4 Saul
birthplace: 6 Tarsus
teacher: 8 Gamaliel
companion: 5 Silas 7 Timothy 8 Barnabas, John Mark 9 Trophimus
cities visited: 4 Rome 5 Derbe, Perga, Troas 6 Lystra, Paphos 7 Antioch, Corinth, Ephesus, Iconium, Miletus, Salamis 8 Caesarea, Damascus, Neapolis, Philippi 9 Macedonia 12 Thessalonica
conversion place: 14 road to Damas-

cus
wrote: 8 epistles
Paul Bunyan
author: 12 James Stevens
character: 9 Shanty Boy 10 Hels Helson 11 King Bourbon 12 Sourdough Sam 13 Babe the Blue Ox 14 Hot Biscuit Slim 16 Johnny Inkslinger
Pauli, Wolfgang
field: 7 physics
researched: 13 quantum theory
established: 14 Pauli principle 18 exclusion principle
awarded: 10 Nobel Prize
Paulina
character in: 14 The Winter's Tale
author: 11 Shakespeare
Pauling, Linus Carl
field: 12 biochemistry
worked on: 8 proteins 18 molecular structure
advocated: 8 Vitamin C
awarded: 10 Nobel Prize
awarded for: 5 peace 9 chemistry
paunch 3 gut, pot 5 belly, tummy 7 abdomen, stomach 8 potbelly 9 bay window, beer belly, spare tire 10 midsection 11 breadbasket, corporation
pauper 6 beggar 7 almsman 8 bankrupt, indigent 9 insolvent, mendicant 10 poor person, starveling 11 charity case 12 down-and-outer
pause 3 gap 4 halt, rest, stop, wait 5 break, cease, delay, let up 6 hiatus 7 interim, time out 8 break off, hesitate, interval 9 cessation, interlude 10 deliberate, suspension 12 intermission, interruption
pave 3 tar 4 face 6 cement 7 asphalt, surface 8 black top 9 resurface 10 macadamize
pavement 4 slab 5 brick 6 cement, hearth, street, tarmac 7 asphalt, cobbles, macadam 8 concrete, driveway, flagging, sidewalk 9 flagstone
pavilion 4 tent, ward, wing 5 arbor, kiosk 6 gazebo 7 pergola 9 bandshell 11 summerhouse
Pavlov, Ivan Petrovich
nationality: 7 Russian
researched: 9 digestion
studied: 20 behavior conditioning 21 Pavlovian conditioning
awarded: 10 Nobel Prize
paw 2 pa 3 dad, pop, toe 4 feel, foot, grab, hand, maul, mitt, papa 5 daddy, flail, touch 6 caress, clutch, father, handle, scrape, strike 7 rough up 8 forefoot 9 mishandle
mate: 3 maw
pawn 4 bond, dupe, hock, tool 5 agent, patsy 6 flunky, lackey, pledge, puppet 7 cat's-paw 8 borrow on, creature, guaranty, henchman, hireling, security 9 assurance, guarantee, underling 10 instrument 12 raise money on 14 give as security

pawnbroker
French: 11 mont-de-piete
Pawnbroker, The
director: 11 Sidney Lumet
cast: 10 Rod Steiger (Sol Nazerman) 11 Brock Peters 12 Jaime Sanchez 19 Geraldine Fitzgerald
setting: 6 Harlem
Pawnee (Chahiksichhiks)
language family: 7 Caddoan
location: 5 Texas 8 Nebraska, Oklahoma 9 New Mexico
related to: 7 Arikara
god: 6 Tirawa
Pawtuxet
location: 13 Massachusetts
leader: 7 Squanto
Pax
origin: 5 Roman
goddess of: 5 peace
corresponds to: 5 Irene
pax vobiscum 14 peace be with you
pay 3 fee 4 foot, give, meet 5 grant, honor, remit, repay, serve, wages, yield 6 ante up, chip in, extend, income, profit, render, return, salary, settle 7 benefit, bring in, cough up, payment, present, proffer, stipend 8 be useful, earnings, paycheck, shell out 9 bear fruit, liquidate, reimburse 10 come across, compensate, make good on, recompense 12 compensation 13 reimbursement
payable 3 due 4 owed 5 owing 6 mature, unpaid 8 to be paid 9 in arrears, spendable 10 demandable, expendable, receivable 11 outstanding
pay attention 4 heed, note 6 attend, notice 7 observe
Payaya
language family: 12 Coahuiltecan
location: 5 Texas
pay back 5 repay 7 counter, get even 9 reimburse, retaliate 10 recompense, remunerate 15 make restitution
pay for 6 redeem 7 expiate 8 atone for 9 answer for, suffer for 10 compensate, recompense, remunerate 13 make amends for 17 make reparation for
pay heed 6 notice 8 consider 11 concentrate 12 pay attention 13 put one's mind to
pay homage 5 defer, honor 7 acclaim 10 pay tribute
paying back 9 repayment 11 getting even 12 making good on 13 reimbursement
paymaster 6 bursar, purser 7 cashier 10 cashkeeper
payment 3 fee, pay 4 debt 6 outlay, paying, salary 7 premium 8 defrayal, spending 9 allowance, discharge 10 recompense, remittance, settlement 11 expenditure, installment, liquidation 12 compensation, contribution, dis-

bursement, remuneration 13 reimbursement
pay no heed to 4 defy 6 ignore, slight 7 disobey, neglect, violate 8 overlook, pass over 9 disregard 10 brush aside, infringe on 14 shut one's eyes to 16 pay no attention to 17 transgress against
payoff 3 end 4 soap 5 bribe, graft 6 climax, crunch, finale, finish, grease, payola, result, upshot, windup 7 outcome 8 clincher 9 hush money 10 bottom line, conclusion, denouement, protection, resolution 11 culmination
pay off 5 bribe 6 buy off, suborn 13 grease the palm
payola 5 bribe, graft 6 grease, payoff
pay out 5 spend 6 expend, lay out 7 fork out 8 allocate, disburse, dispense, shell out 10 distribute
pay suit 3 woo 5 court 8 pay court
Payton, Walter
nickname: 9 Sweetness
sport: 8 football
position: 11 running back
team: 12 Chicago Bears
pay tribute to 4 laud, tout 5 boost, toast 6 praise, salute 7 applaud, commend 8 eulogize 10 compliment 16 sing the praises of
pea 5 Pisum 12 Pisum sativum
varieties: 4 Flat, Snow, Wild 5 Beach, Caley, Chick, Congo, Coral, Field, Glory, Green, Heart, Heath, Hoary, No-eye, Rough, Sugar, Sweet 6 Angola, Canada, Desert, Garden, Marble, Pigeon, Rosary, Scurfy, Winged, Winter 7 Catjang, Darling, English, Rabbit's, Seaside 8 Earthnut, Egyptian, Princess, Shamrock 9 Asparagus, Black-eyed, Butterfly, Chaparral, Jerusalem, Partridge, Perennial 10 Australian, Singletary, Wild winter 11 Everlasting, Sturt desert, Two-flowered, Winter sweet 12 Edible-podded 14 Austrian winter 15 Australian flame
peace 4 calm, ease 5 amity, truce 6 accord, repose 7 concord, content, entente, harmony 8 serenity 9 agreement, armistice, composure, placidity 12 pacification, tranquillity 14 reconciliation
god of: 4 Frey 5 Freyr
goddess of: 3 Pax 9 Concordia
Hebrew: 6 shalom
Russian: 3 mir
peace be with you
Latin: 11 pax vobiscum
peaceful 4 calm 5 quiet, still 6 placid, serene, silent 7 pacific, restful 8 amicable, friendly, tranquil 9 agreeable, peaceable, peacetime 10 harmonious, nonviolent, nonwarring, pacifistic, untroubled 11 undisturbed
peacefulness 4 calm 7 concord, har-

mony **8** calmness, serenity **9** placidity **11** tranquility

peacemaker 8 diplomat, mediator, placater **9** go-between **10** ambassador, arbitrator, negotiator **11** adjudicator, conciliator, pacificator, peacekeeper, peacemonger **12** intermediary

peacemaking 9 pacifying, placating, placatory **11** reconciling **12** conciliating, conciliatory, pacification

peace offering 6 amends **11** appeasement **12** conciliation

peace of mind 8 security, serenity **11** tranquility **16** freedom from worry

peace to you
  Hebrew: 14 shalom aleichem

peach 13 Prunus persica
  varieties: 4 Muir, Peak, Sims, Vine, Wild **5** Gaume, Hiley, Pavie **6** Carmen, Crosby, Desert, Foster, J H Hale, Lovell, Orejon, Paloro, Peen-to, Salwey **7** Dixigem, Dixired, Elberta, Persian, Quadong **8** Champion, Crawford, Isabella, Redhaven, Russelet **9** Alexander, Freestone, Halehaven, Rochester, Southland **10** Clingstone, Goldeneast, Heath Cling, Summer Snow **12** Chinese Cling, Iron Mountain, Mountain Rose, Oldmixon Free **13** Golden Jubilee, Old mixon Cling, Phillips Cling **14** Belle of Georgia
  peach-like: 7 apricot **9** nectarine

Peach State
  nickname of: 7 Georgia

Peachum, Polly
  character in: 12 Beggar's Opera
  author: 3 Gay

peachy 4 fine, keen **5** dandy, super, swell **9** excellent, marvelous, wonderful

peacock
  group of: 6 muster

Peacock
  constellation of: 4 Pavo

Peacock, Thomas Love
  author of: 12 Headlong Hall **14** Crotchet Castle, Nightmare Abbey

Peacock Spring, The
  author: 11 Rumer Godden

peak 3 tip, top **4** acme, apex **5** crest, crown, flood, prime **6** apogee, climax, summit, zenith **8** pinnacle **9** culminate **11** culmination

peaked 3 ill, wan **4** lean, pale, thin, weak **5** ashen, drawn, gaunt, spare, spiked, spiny, white **6** ailing, infirm, pallid, pointy, sallow, sickly, skinny, spiked **7** haggard, pinched, pointed, scrawny, tapered, wizened **9** emaciated, shriveled **11** debilitated

peal 3 din **4** boom, clap, ring, roar, roll, toll **5** blare, blast, clang, crack, crash, knell **6** rumble **7** clangor, resound, ringing **10** resounding **11** re-

verberate **13** reverberation **14** tintinnabulate **16** tintinnabulation

Peale, Charles Willson
  born: 17 Queen Anne County MD
  son: 9 Raphaelle, Rembrandt **12** Titian Ramsay
  artwork: 26 The Exhumation of the Mastodon
    portrait: 8 Franklin **9** Jefferson, John Adams **10** Washington

Peale, Raphaelle
  born: 13 Bucks County PA
  father: 14 Charles Willson
  brother: 9 Rembrandt **12** Titian Ramsay
  artwork: 12 After the Bath

Peale, Rembrandt
  born: 13 Bucks County PA
  father: 14 Charles Willson
  brother: 9 Raphaelle **12** Titian Ramsay
  artwork: 15 The Court of Death
    portrait: 9 Jefferson **10** Washington

peal of bells 7 clangor, ringing **16** tintinnabulation

peanut 3 pod, tot **4** puny, seed **5** petty, small **6** goober, legume, measly, paltry **8** earthpea **9** little one
  species: 15 Arachis hypogaea

Peanuts
  creator: 14 Charles Schultz
  character: 4 Lucy **5** Linus, Sally, Marcy **6** Pig Pen, Snoopy **9** Schroeder, Woodstock **11** Lucy Van Pelt **12** Linus Van Pelt, Charlie Brown **15** Peppermint Patty **19** Little Red Haired Girl
  Halloween figure: 12 Great Pumpkin
  Snoopy's plane: 12 Sopwith Camel
  Snoopy's foe: 8 Red Baron
  saying: 9 Good grief

pear 5 Pyrus **13** Pyrus communis
  varieties: 4 Bosc, Sand **5** Anjou, Asian, Blind, Melon, Smith **6** Balsam, Burrel, Butter, Comice, Common, Garber, Garlic, Orient, Seckel, Warden **7** Chinese, Kieffer, Prickly, Vinegar **8** Bartlett, Japanese, Oriental **9** Alligator, Evergreen, Muscadine **10** Beurre Bosc, Brandywine, Chaumontel **11** Birch-leaved, Bon Chretien, Paper-spined, Winter Nelis **12** Beurre d'Anjou, Easter Beurre, Sacred garlic, Willow-leaved **13** Flemish Beauty, Waite Bergamot **15** Doyenne du Comice **18** Duchesse d'Angouleme

pearl
  grows in: 6 oyster
  genus: 8 Pinctada
  source: 6 Red Sea **9** Caribbean **11** Persian Gulf **12** South Pacific **16** Gulf of California
  composed of: 5 nacre **9** aragonite **10** conchiolin **13** mother-of-pearl
  quality: 6 luster **11** iridescence
  color: 4 blue, rose **5** black, brown,

cream, green, white **6** yellow
  shape: 5 round **7** baroque
  type: 8 cultured, Oriental (saltwater) **9** simulated **10** freshwater

Pearl-Fishers, The
  also: 19 Les Pecheurs de Perles
  opera by: 5 Bizet
  setting: 6 Ceylon

Pearl of the Antilles *see* **4** Cuba

Pearly Gates 7 heaven
  mentioned in: 10 Revelation

peasant 4 boor, esne, peon, serf **5** churl, knave, yokel **6** farmer, rustic, worker **7** laborer, lowlife, villein **10** countryman, dirt farmer
  Arabic: 6 fellah
  Indian: 4 ryot **5** kisan **6** raiyat
  Irish: 4 kern
  Russian: 5 kulak **6** muzhik
  Scottish: 6 cotter

peasantlike 5 crude, rough **6** coarse, oafish, rustic, vulgar **7** boorish, loutish, uncouth **9** unrefined **10** unpolished

peccadillo 4 slip **5** lapse **6** boo-boo **7** blunder, faux pas, misdeed, misstep **8** petty sin, trespass **9** false move, wrong step **10** misconduct, wrongdoing **11** misdemeanor **13** transgression

peck 3 pat, rap, tap **4** buss, gobs, lots, mess **5** a slew, batch, bunch, heaps, scads, smack, snack, stack, thump **6** nibble, oodles, pick at, strike, stroke, worlds **8** light jab **9** abundance, light kiss **11** eight quarts
  abbreviation of: 2 pk

Peck, Gregory
  real name: 17 Eldred Gregory Peck
  born: 9 La Jolla CA
  roles: 8 Moby Dick **10** On the Beach, Spellbound **11** The Yearling **12** Duel in the Sun, Roman Holiday **15** The Paradine Case **16** Twelve O'Clock High **17** The Boys from Brazil, The Guns of Navarone **18** To Kill a Mockingbird (Oscar) **19** Gentleman's Agreement, The Keys of the Kingdom **21** The Snows of Kilimanjaro **26** The Man in the Gray Flannel Suit
  autobiography: 12 An Actor's Life

Peckinpah, Sam
  director of: 9 Straw Dogs **12** The Wild Bunch

Pecksniff
  character in: 16 Martin Chuzzlewit
  author: 7 Dickens

peculiar 3 odd **5** queer, weird **6** farout, quaint, unique **7** bizarre, curious, erratic, private, special, strange, typical, unusual **8** abnormal, distinct, freakish, personal, singular, specific **9** eccentric, exclusive, whimsical **10** capricious, individual, outlandish, particular **11** distinctive **13** idiosyncratic **14** characteristic, distinguishing, representative, unconventional

peculiarity 4 mark **5** badge, stamp,

trait **6** oddity **7** feature, quality **8** odd trait **9** attribute, queerness, weirdness **10** erraticism, uniqueness **11** abnormality, bizarreness, distinction, singularity, strangeness **12** eccentricity, freakishness, idiosyncrasy **13** particularity, unnaturalness **14** characteristic **21** distinguishing quality

pecuniary 6 fiscal **8** economic, monetary **9** budgetary, financial

pedagogic 7 bookish, donnish **8** academic, didactic, pedantic, tutorial **9** scholarly **11** educational **12** professorial **13** instructional

pedagogue, pedagog 5 tutor **7** teacher **8** academic, educator **9** professor **10** instructor, schoolmarm **12** educationist, schoolmaster **13** schoolteacher **14** schoolmistress

pedant 6 purist **8** bookworm **9** dogmatist **13** methodologist

pedantic 5 fussy **7** bookish, finicky, pompous, stilted **8** academic, didactic, dogmatic **10** nitpicking, scholastic **11** doctrinaire, punctilious **13** hairsplitting **14** overparticular

peddle 4 hawk, sell, vend **6** retail **7** deal out **8** dispense

Peder Victorious
    character in: 16 Giants of the Earth
    author: 7 Rolvaag

pedestal 4 base, foot **6** bottom, plinth **10** foundation

pedestrian 6 walker **7** mundane, prosaic, tedious, trekker **8** mediocre, ordinary, stroller **9** itinerant **10** ambulatory, for walking, unexciting **11** commonplace, peripatetic, unimportant **12** foot-traveler, run-of-the-mill **13** insignificant, perambulating, perambulatory, unimaginative **15** inconsequential

pedigree 4 line **6** family, strain **7** descent, lineage **8** ancestry **9** bloodline, parentage **10** derivation, extraction, family tree **13** line of descent

peek 3 pry **4** peep, peer **5** watch **6** glance **7** glimpse

peel 4 bark, hull, husk, pare, rind, skin, tear, zest **5** flake, scale, shuck, spade, strip **6** remove **7** undress **11** decorticate

peel off 6 remove **7** veer off **8** strip off

peep 4 peek, peer, skim, word **5** cheep, chirp, tweet **6** emerge, glance, murmur, mutter, squeak **7** chirrup, glimpse, peeping, peer out, twitter, whimper, whisper **9** come forth, quick look

peeper 3 eye **4** frog **6** voyeur **10** peeping Tom

peer 4 gape, gaze, look, lord, peek, peep **5** equal, noble, stare **6** appear, emerge, squint **7** compeer **8** noble-man **9** blue blood, gentleman, patrician **10** aristocrat

peerage 8 nobility **10** blue bloods, patricians **11** aristocracy

Peer Gynt
    author: 11 Henrik Ibsen
    character: 3 Ase **6** Anitra **7** Solveig **12** The Great Boyg **16** The Button Moulder
    suite composer: 5 Grieg

peerless 7 supreme **8** flawless **9** faultless, matchless, unequaled, unmatched, unrivaled **10** consummate, inimitable, preeminent, surpassing, unexcelled **11** superlative, unsurpassed **12** incomparable, transcendent

peeve 3 bug, eat, irk, vex **4** fret, gall, rile **5** annoy, chafe, eat at, frost, gripe **6** gnaw at, nettle **7** dislike, perturb, provoke **8** irritate, vexation **9** aggravate, annoyance, complaint, grievance **10** exasperate, irritation **11** aggravation, provocation **12** exasperation, give one a pain **13** pain in the neck **14** thorn in the side

peevish 4 mean **5** cross, huffy, sulky, surly, testy **6** crabby, cranky, grumpy **7** grouchy, pettish **8** churlish, petulant, snappish **9** fractious, irritable, querulous, splenetic **10** ill-humored, ill-natured **11** bad-tempered, ill-tempered, quarrelsome **12** cantankerous

peewee 4 tiny **5** dwarf, small, teeny **6** little, midget, minute **9** itsy-bitsy, itty-bitty, minuscule **10** diminutive, teeny-weeny **11** Lilliputian

Pee Wee
    nickname of: 11 Harold Reese

peg 3 pin **4** nail **5** cleat, dowel, spike, thole **6** skewer, toggle **8** fastener, tholepin

Pegasus
    form: 5 horse
    characteristic: 6 winged
    mother: 6 Medusa
    ridden by: 11 Bellerophon

Peggotty, Clara
    character in: 16 David Copperfield
    author: 7 Dickens

Pei, I M (Ieoh Ming)
    architect of: 12 East Building (National Gallery of Art), L'Enfant Plaza (Washington DC) **14** East-West Center (U of Hawaii), Mile High Center (Denver) **15** Place Ville Marie (Montreal) **16** John Hancock Tower (Boston) **18** Everson Museum of Art (Syracuse NY) **22** Kips Bay Plaza Apartments (NYC) **36** National Center for Atmospheric Research (Boulder CO)

peignoir 4 gown **6** kimono **8** negligee **9** nightgown **12** dressing gown

pejorative 7 mocking **8** debasing, negative, scornful **9** degrading, demeaning, slighting **10** belittling, derogatory,

detracting, disdainful, ridiculing, unpleasant **11** deprecatory, disparaging, downgrading **12** contemptuous, depreciatory, disapproving **15** uncomplimentary

Peking
    also: 7 Beijing
    means: 15 northern capital
    capital of: 5 China
    landmark: 9 Bell Tower, Drum Tower, Ming Tombs **10** Pei-hai Park **12** Palace Museum **13** Forbidden City **14** Hall of Classics, Temple of Heaven **15** Marco Polo Bridge **17** Temple of Confucius **18** Old Legation Quarter **19** Temple of Agriculture **20** Great Hall of the People, Hall of Supreme Harmony **21** Mausoleum of Mao Tse- tung **22** Palace of Heavenly Purity **26** Monument to the People's Heroes **32** Revolutionary and Historical Museum
    mountain: 7 Taihang
    river: 3 Hai **7** Ch'ao-pai **8** Yungting
    square: 9 T'ien-an Men
    university: 8 Tsinghua
    walled city: 5 Inner, Outer, Tatar **7** Chinese

pelagic 6 marine **7** aquatic, oceanic **9** thalassic **11** sea-dwelling

Pele
    real name: 24 Edson Arantes do Nascimento
    sport: 6 soccer
    team: 13 New York Cosmos
    nationality: 9 Brazilian

Peleus
    king of: 6 Phthia **9** Myrmidons
    father: 6 Aeacus
    mother: 6 Endeis
    brother: 7 Telamon
    half-brother: 6 Phocus
    wife: 6 Thetis **8** Antigone
    son: 8 Achilles
    daughter: 8 Polydora

pelf 4 gain **5** booty, lucre, money **6** mammon, riches, spoils

Pelican State
    nickname of: 9 Louisiana

pelisse 4 cape, coat **5** cloak **6** mantle

Pelleas (King Pelleas)
    character in: 16 Arthurian romance
    daughter: 6 Elaine

Pelleas and Melisande
    also: 18 Pelleas et Melisande
    opera by: 7 Debussy
    character: 6 Golaud, Yniold
    author: 18 Maurice Maeterlinck

pellet 3 pea **4** ball, bead, drop, pill **5** pearl, stone **6** marble, pebble, sphere **7** globule

pell-mell 6 rashly **7** hastily **8** slapdash **9** hurriedly, post haste **10** at half cock, carelessly, heedlessly, recklessly **11** hurry-scurry, impetuously, imprudently **12** incautiously **13** helter-skelter, precipitately, thoughtlessly

pellucid 5 clear, lucid **10** articulate **11** crystalline, translucent, transparent **12** intelligible **14** understandable

Pelops
  father: 8 Tantalus
  sister: 5 Niobe
  son: 6 Atreus, Sciron **7** Letreus **8** Pittheus, Thyestes **9** Alcathous **10** Chrysippus
  daughter: 7 Nicippe **8** Lysidice **9** Astydamia
  resurrected by: 6 Hermes

pelt 3 fur, hit, rap **4** belt, coat, hide, skin, sock **5** pound, punch, whack **6** batter, buffet, fleece, pepper, pummel, strike, thrash, thwack **7** clobber

pen 3 sty **4** cage, coop, crib, fold **5** draft, hutch, pound, quill, stall, write **6** corral, pencil, scrawl **7** compose, paddock **8** compound, scribble, stockade **9** ballpoint, enclosure

penal 7 of jails **8** punitive **9** punishing **10** corrective, penalizing **11** castigatory, retributive **12** disciplinary

penalty 4 fine **7** forfeit **8** handicap **9** suffering **10** assessment, forfeiture, infliction, punishment **11** retribution **12** disadvantage

penance 9 atonement, expiation, hair shirt, penitence **10** contrition, repentance **12** propitiation **13** mortification

penates
  protectors of: 4 home
  companions: 5 lares

penchant 4 bent, bias, gift, turn **5** fancy, flair, knack, taste **6** liking, relish **7** leaning **8** affinity, fondness, tendency **9** prejudice, proneness, readiness **10** attraction, partiality, preference, proclivity, propensity **11** disposition, inclination **12** predilection **14** predisposition

pendant 3 fob **5** charm **6** locket **15** hanging ornament

Pendennis
  author: 25 William Make peace Thackeray
  character: 9 Laura Bell **10** Henry Foker **12** Blanche Amory **13** Emily Costigan **14** Helen Pendennis, Major Pendennis **15** Arthur Pendennis

pendent, pendant 7 hanging, jutting, pensile **8** dangling, swinging **9** extending, pendulous, suspended **10** projecting, protruding **11** overhanging, protuberant

pendente lite 16 during litigation **19** with a lawsuit pending

pending 8 imminent **9** undecided, unsettled **10** in suspense, unfinished, unresolved, up in the air **11** in the offing **12** undetermined

pendulous 7 hanging, pendent, pensile, sagging **8** dangling, drooping, swinging **9** suspended

pendulum
  invented by: 7 Galileo

Penelope
  father: 7 Icarius
  mother: 8 Periboea
  husband: 8 Odysseus **9** Telegonus
  son: 6 Ifalus **10** Telemachus **11** Polyporthis
  fended off: 7 suitors

penetrate 3 get **4** bore **5** catch, enter, prick **6** decode, fathom, invade, pierce, seep in **7** cut into, discern, pervade, unravel **8** decipher, perceive, permeate, puncture, saturate, traverse **9** figure out, perforate **10** comprehend, cut through, impregnate, infiltrate, see through, understand **11** pass through

penetrating 4 keen **5** acrid, alert, alive, aware, harsh, heady, sharp, smart **6** astute, biting, clever, shrewd, strong **7** caustic, pungent, reeking **8** piercing, redolent, stinging **9** pervading, pervasive, trenchant **10** discerning, perceptive, percipient, permeating, saturating, thoughtful **11** intelligent, sharp-witted **13** perspicacious

penetration 5 foray, grasp **6** access, boring **7** insight, passage **8** infusion, invasion, keenness, piercing **9** intrusion, quickness, sharpness **10** astuteness, cleverness, perception, puncturing, shrewdness **11** discernment, perforation **12** intelligence, perspicacity

penguin 8 great auk

Penguin Island
  author: 13 Anatole France

peninsula 4 cape **5** point **8** headland **10** promontory

Peninsula State
  nickname of: 7 Florida

penitence 6 regret, sorrow **7** penance, remorse **9** atonement, attrition, expiation **10** contrition, repentance **11** compunction, humiliation

penitent 5 sorry **6** rueful **7** atoning, devotee, pilgrim **8** contrite **9** regretful, repentant **10** remorseful

penitentiary 3 can, pen **4** jail, stir **5** joint **6** prison **7** slammer **8** big house

Penn, Arthur
  director of: 12 Little Big Man **14** Bonnie and Clyde **16** The Miracle Worker

Penn, Sean
  wife: 7 Madonna **11** Robin Wright
  roles: 5 U-Turn **7** Bad Boys, The Game **11** Carlito's Way **12** She's So Lovely **14** Dead Man Walking **15** Shanghai Express **22** The Falcon and the Snowman **24** Fast Times at Ridgemont High

Pennacook (Merrimac)
  language family: 9 Algonkian **10** Algonquian
  location: 5 Maine **6** Quebec **7** New York, Vermont **10** New England **12** New Hampshire **13** Massachusetts
  leader: 11 Wannalancet **12** Passaconaway
  related to: 6 Abnaki

pen name
  French: 10 nom de plume

pennant 4 flag, jack **6** banner, burgee, colors, ensign, pennon **7** bunting **8** ensignia, standard, streamer **9** banderole, oriflamme

penniless 4 poor **5** broke, needy **6** busted, ruined **8** bankrupt, indigent, strapped, wiped out **9** destitute, flat broke, insolvent, moneyless **10** down-and-out, pauperized **12** impoverished **15** poverty-stricken

pennon 4 flag, jack **6** banner, colors, ensign **7** pennant **8** standard, streamer

Pennsylvania
  abbreviation: 2 PA **5** Penna
  nickname: 8 Keystone
  capital: 10 Harrisburg
  largest city: 12 Philadelphia
  others: 4 Erie, Etna, Plum, York **5** Avoca, Baden **6** Beaver, Bethel, Butler, Easton, Emmaus, Radnor, Ridley, Sharon **7** Altoona, Baldwin, Bristol, Chester, Ephrata, Hanover, Hershey, Lebanon, Reading **8** Abington, Braddock, Bradford, Bryn Mawr, Carlisle, Clairton, Harrison, Hazelton, Monessen, Scranton, Shamokin **9** Aliquippa, Allentown, Bethlehem, Charleroi, Haverford, Jeannette, Johnstown, Lancaster, Meadville, Mill Creek, Newcastle, Swissvale, Uniontown, Whitehall **10** Carbondale, Gettysburg, McKeesport, Norristown, Pittsburgh **11** Springfield, Wilkes Barre **12** State College, Williamsport
  college: 3 PSU **4** Penn, Pitt **5** Gratz, Thiel **6** Drexel, Lehigh, Temple **7** Juniata, LaSalle, Ursinus **8** Alliance, Bryn Mawr, Bucknell, Duquesne, Lycoming **9** Dickinson, Lafayette, Penn State, St Josephs, Villanova **10** Pittsburgh, Swarthmore **12** Carnegie Tech **17** Pennsylvania State
  feature:
    battle site: 10 Gettysburg
    bell: 7 Liberty
    hall: 12 Independence
    historical site: 11 Valley Forge
  tribe: 6 Seneca **7** Shawnee **8** Delaware **11** Lenni- Lanape **13** Susquehannock
  people: 5 Amish, Dutch **10** Stan Musial **11** Andrew Wyeth, Ethel Waters, Mary Cassatt, Stuart Davis **12** Andrew Mellon, Anthony Wayne, Margaret Mead, Martha Graham, Samuel Barber, Thomas Eakins **13** Clifford Odets, Gertrude Stein **14** George S Kaufman **15** Maxwell Anderson **19**

Stephen Vincent Benet
  explorer: 5 Brule 6 Hudson 11 Hendrickson
lake: 4 Erie 7 Harveys 8 Conneaut 10 Pymatuning 13 Wallenpaupack
land rank: 11 thirty-third
mountain: 5 South 6 Pocono 11 Alleghenies
  highest point: 5 Davis
physical feature:
  peninsula: 11 Presque Isle
  valley: 5 Great
president: 13 James Buchanan
river: 4 Ohio 6 Lehigh 7 Clarion, Genesee, Juniata, Licking, Towanda 8 Caldwell, Delaware, Schrader 9 Allegheny 10 Schuylkill 11 Monongahela, Susquehanna
state admission: 6 second
state bird: 12 ruffed grouse
state fish: 10 brook trout
state flower: 14 mountain laurel
state motto: 28 Virtue Liberty and Independence
state tree: 7 hemlock
penny 3 sum 4 cent 5 cheap, pence 6 copper, stiver 7 trivial
penny-pinching 5 close, tight 6 stingy 7 miserly 8 grudging 9 niggardly, penurious 10 ungenerous 11 tight-fisted 12 parsimonious
Penny Serenade
  director: 13 George Stevens
  cast: 9 Cary Grant 10 Irene Dunne 11 Beulah Bondi 13 Edgar Buchanan
pennyweight
  abbreviation of: 3 dwt
Penobscot
  language family: 9 Algonkian 10 Algonquian
  location: 5 Maine 13 Old Town Island
  members of: 17 Abnaki Confederacy
Penrod
  author: 15 Booth Tarkington
  sequel: 12 Penrod and Sam 13 Penrod Jashber
  character: 6 Herman, Verman 9 Sarah Crim 11 Rupe Collins 13 Marjorie Jones 15 Penrod Schofield
  dog: 4 Duke
pensee 7 thought 10 reflection
Pensees
  author: 12 Blaise Pascal
pension 5 grant 6 income, retire 7 annuity, stipend, subsidy 9 allowance 13 boardinghouse 17 retirement fund
pensive 3 sad 5 grave 6 dreamy, musing, solemn, somber 7 serious, wistful 8 dreaming 10 meditative, melancholy, reflective 11 day dreaming 13 contemplative, introspective 15 sadly thoughtful
Pentateuch 10 Law of Moses 28 first five books of Old Testament
  see also 7 books of 12 Old Testament
Penthesilea

queen of: 7 Amazons
father: 4 Ares
mother: 6 Otrere
sister: 9 Hippolyta
killed by: 8 Achilles
Pentheus
  king of: 6 Thebes
  father: 6 Echion
  mother: 5 Agave
  grandfather: 6 Cadmus
pent-up 7 boxed-up, checked, stifled 8 hedged-in, held back, penned-in, penned-up, reined in, stored-up 9 bottled-up, repressed 10 restrained, suppressed
penurious 5 close 6 frugal, stingy 7 miserly, sparing 8 stinting 9 niggardly 12 parsimonious 13 penny-pinching
penury 4 need, want 7 poverty 9 indigence, privation 10 bankruptcy, insolvency 11 destitution 14 impoverishment
peon 4 pawn, serf 5 slave 6 drudge, menial, worker 7 footman, laborer, orderly, peasant, servant
peony 7 Paeonia
  varieties: 4 Tree 7 Chinese, Tibetan 8 Majorcan 11 Chinese tree 12 Common garden
people 3 kin 5 folks 6 family, humans, the mob 7 kinfolk, mankind, mortals, the herd 8 citizens, humanity, populace, the crowd 9 ancestors, citizenry, commoners, human kind, relatives, the masses, the public, the rabble 10 population 11 Homo sapiens, human beings, individuals, inhabitants, John Q Public, men and women, the millions
People Are Funny
  host: 13 Art Linkletter
pep 3 vim, zip 4 dash, life, snap 5 gusto, verve, vigor 6 energy, ginger, spirit 8 vitality, vivacity 9 animation 10 enthusiasm, get-up-and-go, liveliness
Pepe Le Moko
  director: 14 Julien Duvivier
  cast: 9 Jean Gabin 13 Gabriel Gabrio, Mireille Balin
  remade as: 6 Casbah 7 Algiers
peperomia
  varieties: 3 Ivy 6 Prayer, Vining 7 Ivy-leaf, Leather, Red-edge 8 Coinleaf, Platinum 9 Flowering 10 Silveredge, Silver-leaf, Watermelon 11 Green-ripple 13 Emerald-ripple, Little fantasy
Pepin
  called: 8 the Short
  king of: 6 Franks
  son: 11 Charlemagne
Pepita
  character in: 21 The Bridge of San Luis Rey
  author: 6 Wilder
Peppard, George

born: 9 Detroit MI
wife: 15 Elizabeth Ashley
roles: 6 Tobruk 7 Banacek 8 The A-Team 16 The Carpetbaggers 19 Breakfast at Tiffany's
pepper 3 dot 6 shower, strafe 7 bombard 8 sprinkle 9 condiment, vegetable
pepper, peppercorn
  botanical name: 5 Piper 7 Pnigrum 8 Capsicum 10 Piperaceae 11 C frutescens
  color: 3 red 5 black, green, white
  origin: 5 India 6 Brazil, Ceylon 7 Malabar, Sarawak, Sumatra 8 Alleppey, Pandjang, Sri Lanka 11 Tellicherry
  varieties: 3 Red 4 Baby, Bell, Bird, Cone, Long, Wild 5 Betle, Black, Chili, Cubeb, Green, Japan, Sweet, White 6 Cherry 7 Cayenne, Celebes, Cluster, Tabasco 8 Capsicum 9 Mild water 10 Australian, Red cluster 12 Mountain long, Tabasco-sauce
  French: 6 poivre
  German: 7 pfeffer
  Italian: 4 pepe
  Latin: 5 piper
  Persian: 5 biber 6 pilpil
  Spanish: 8 pimienta
  Swedish: 6 peppar
  Sanskrit: 7 pippali
peppermint 6 Mentha
  varieties: 4 Gray 5 Black, River, White 6 Silver, Sydney 9 Blackbutt 10 Robert- son's 11 Broad-leaved 15 Mount Wellington 17 Narrow-leaved black 19 Nichol's willow-leaved
peppermint schnapps
  type: 7 liqueur
  flavor: 4 mint
peppery 3 hot 5 fiery, sharp, spicy 7 burning, piquant, pungent 14 highly seasoned
peppy 4 spry 5 brisk, perky 6 active, bouncy, frisky, lively, snappy 7 dynamic 8 animated, spirited, vigorous 9 energetic, full of pep, sparkling, sprightly, vivacious 12 enthusiastic
pep up 4 fire 6 excite, vivify, wake up 7 animate, enliven, quicken 8 vitalize
Pepys, Samuel
  author of: 10 Pepys' Diary
Pepys' Diary
  author: 11 Samuel Pepys
Pequot
  language family: 9 Algonkian 10 Algonquian
  location: 11 Connecticut, Rhode Island
perambulate 4 pace, tour, walk 5 amble, mosey 6 ramble, stroll 7 meander, saunter 9 promenade
perceivable 7 visible 8 apparent, distinct 10 detectable, noticeable, observable 11 discernible, perceptible 13 ascertainable

perceive 3 get, see **4** feel, hear, know, note **5** grasp, savvy, sense, smell, taste **6** deduce, detect, gather, notice **7** discern, make out, observe, realize **8** conclude, discover **9** apprehend, be aware of, recognize **10** comprehend, understand **11** distinguish

perceptible 5 clear, plain **7** evident, notable, obvious, visible **8** apparent, distinct, manifest, palpable, tangible, unhidden **9** prominent **10** detectable, noticeable, observable **11** conspicuous, discernible, perceivable, unconcealed, well-defined **12** discoverable, unmistakable **13** ascertainable

perception 5 grasp, sense **7** faculty **8** judgment **9** awareness, detection **10** cognizance, conception **11** discernment, recognition **12** apprehension **13** comprehension, consciousness, understanding **14** discrimination

perceptive 4 keen **5** acute, aware, quick, sharp **6** astute, shrewd **8** sensible **9** sensitive **10** discerning, insightful, responsive **11** intelligent, penetrating, quick-witted **13** understanding

perch 3 sit **4** land, rest, seat **5** eyrie, light, roost **6** alight, settle

Percival, Perceval
 character in: 16 Arthurian romance
 also see Parsifal

percolate 4 boil, brew **6** bubble, seethe

percussion instrument 4 gong **5** anvil, bells, tabor **6** chimes, rattle **7** celesta, cymbals, marimba, taboret, timpani **8** bass drum, side drum, triangle **9** castanets, dulcitone, snare drum, tenor drum, typophone, xylophone **10** kettledrum, tambourine **12** Glockenspiel, tubular bells

Percy, Walker
 author of: 8 Lancelot **12** The Moviegoer **14** Love in the Ruins **15** The Second Coming **16** The Last Gentleman

Perdita
 character in: 14 The Winter's Tale
 author: 11 Shakespeare

perdition 4 Hell, ruin **8** hellfire **9** damnation, ruination **11** destruction **12** condemnation

Perdix
 also: 9 Polycaste
 brother: 8 Daedalus
 son: 5 Talus
 changed into: 9 partridge

pere 6 father, senior

Pere Goriot
 author: 14 Honore de Balzac
 character: 15 Monsieur Vautrin **17** Eugene de Rastignac, Madame de Beauseant **18** Victorine Taillefer **26** Countess Anastasie de Restaud, Baroness Delphine de Nucingen

peregrination 4 trip **5** jaunt, sally **6** hiking, junket, roving, travel **7** journey, roaming **8** rambling, trekking **9** excursion, wandering **10** expedition

Peregrine Pickle
 author: 14 Tobias Smollett

Pereira, William
 architect of: 13 Cape Canaveral **20** Transamerica Building (San Francisco)

Perelman, S J
 author of: 10 Eastward Ha **15** One Touch of Venus (with Ogden Nash and Kurt Weill) **16** The Road to Miltown **18** Strictly from Hunger **24** Under the Spreading Atrophy

peremptory 5 final **6** biased, lordly **8** absolute, decisive, dogmatic **9** assertive, imperious **10** aggressive, highhanded, imperative, obligatory, undeniable **11** dictatorial, domineering, irrevocable, opinionated, overbearing, unavoidable, unequivocal **12** closedminded, irreversible **13** authoritative **14** unquestionable **16** incontrovertible

perennial 5 fixed **7** durable, lasting, undying **8** constant, enduring, timeless **9** ceaseless, continual, immutable, incessant, long-lived, permanent, perpetual, unceasing, unfailing **10** changeless, continuous, persistent, unchanging **11** everlasting, long-lasting, unremitting **12** imperishable **14** indestructible

Perez, Manuel Benitez
 nickname: 10 El Cordobes

perfect 4 pure, true **5** exact, ideal, whole **6** effect, entire, evolve, strict **7** achieve, develop, fulfill, precise, realize, sublime, supreme **8** absolute, accurate, complete, faithful, finished, flawless, peerless, thorough, unbroken, unerring **9** blameless, faultless, matchless, undamaged, unequaled, unrivaled, untainted **10** accomplish, consummate, immaculate, impeccable, scrupulous, unimpaired **11** superlative, unblemished, unmitigated, unqualified

perfection 6 purity **9** achieving, evolution, exactness, precision, sublimity **10** completion, excellence, ideal state **11** development, fulfillment, perfectness, realization, superiority **12** accurateness, consummation, flawlessness **13** faultlessness, impeccability **14** accomplishment

perfectly 5 fully, quite **6** purely, wholly **7** totally, utterly **8** entirely, superbly **9** downright, supremely **10** absolutely, altogether, completely, flawlessly, impeccably, infinitely, positively, thoroughly **11** faultlessly, wonderfully **12** consummately, preeminently, to perfection, without fault **13** without defect **14** to the nth degree, without blemish

perfidious 5 false, lying **6** shifty, sneaky **7** corrupt **8** cheating, disloyal, two-faced **9** deceitful, dishonest, faithless **10** traitorous, treasonous, unfaithful, untruthful **11** treacherous, treasonable **12** dishonorable, undependable, unscrupulous **13** double-dealing, untrustworthy

perfidy 6 deceit **7** treason **8** bad faith, betrayal **9** falseness, recreancy, treachery, two-timing **10** disloyalty, infidelity **11** double-cross, inconstancy **13** breach of faith, deceitfulness, double-dealing, faithlessness **14** unfaithfulness

perforate 4 bore, gash, hole, slit, stab **5** drill, prick, punch, slash, split, stick **6** pierce **8** puncture **9** lancinate, penetrate

perform 2 do **3** act **4** meet, play **5** enact **6** attain, depict, effect, finish, render, troupe **7** achieve, execute, fulfill, portray, present, pull off, realize **8** carry out, knock off **9** discharge, dispose of, polish off, represent **10** accomplish, bring about, consummate, perpetrate, take part in

performance 4 play, show **5** doing, opera **6** ballet **7** concert, conduct, recital **8** ceremony, dispatch, exercise **9** acquittal, discharge, execution, rendering, spectacle **10** attainment, completion, exhibition, performing, production **11** achievement, fulfillment, realization, transaction **12** consummation, effectuation, perpetration, presentation **13** entertainment **14** accomplishment

perfume 4 odor **5** aroma, scent, smell **7** bouquet, cologne, essence, extract, sweeten **9** aromatize, fragrance

perfumed 7 odorous, scented **8** aromatic, fragrant **11** odoriferous **12** sweet-scented **13** sweet-smelling

perfunctory 3 lax **5** hasty **6** casual **7** cursory, offhand, routine **8** careless, listless, lukewarm **9** apathetic, negligent **10** mechanical, spiritless, unthinking **11** halfhearted, inattentive, indifferent, passionless, superficial, unconcerned **13** disinterested

pergola 5 arbor, bower **6** ramada **7** balcony, trellis

Per Hanea
 character in: 16 Giants of the Earth
 author: 7 Rolvaag

perhaps 5 maybe **6** mayhap **8** peutetre, possibly **9** perchance **10** God willing, imaginably **11** conceivably **12** peradventure

Periboea
 father: 9 Alcathous, Hipponous
 husband: 6 Oeneus **7** Polybus
 son: 6 Tydeus **7** Olenias, Pelegon **14** Telamonian Ajax
 foster son: 7 Oedipus

Perichole, La
 character in: 21 The Bridge of San

Luis Rey
author: **6** Wilder

Pericles, Prince of Tyre
author: **18** William Shakespeare
character: **5** Cleon **6** Marina, Thaisa
7 Dionyza **9** Antiochus **10** Lysimachus

Periclymenus
father: **6** Neleus **8** Poseidon
grandfather: **8** Poseidon
gift: **13** shape-changing
killed by: **8** Hercules

periderm 4 bark **8** covering **9** sheathing

peridot
species: **7** olivine
source: **5** Burma, Mogok **8** Zebirget
color: **11** yellow-green

perigee 5 depth, nadir **8** low point

Perikeiromene (The Rape of the Ringlets)
author: **8** Menander

peril 4 risk **6** danger, hazard, menace, threat **7** pitfall **8** jeopardy, unsafety **10** insecurity **11** uncertainty **13** cause for alarm, vulnerability

perilous 5 risky, shaky **6** chancy, unsafe, unsure **7** ominous **8** insecure, slippery, ticklish **9** dangerous, hazardous, uncertain **10** precarious, vulnerable **11** threatening, venturesome

perimeter 4 edge **6** border, bounds, margin **8** confines **9** periphery **10** borderline **13** circumference

period 3 age, end, eon, era **4** halt, stop, term, time **5** close, epoch, limit **6** finale, finish, season **7** curtain **8** duration, interval **9** cessation, interlude
French: **6** siecle

periodic, periodical 6 cyclic **7** regular, routine **8** frequent, repeated, seasonal **9** recurrent, recurring **12** intermittent

periodical 5 daily, paper **6** annual, review, weekly **7** journal, monthly **8** bulletin, magazine **9** newspaper, quarterly **10** newsletter **11** publication **12** newsmagazine

periodically 5 often **9** regularly, routinely **10** frequently, repeatedly **12** occasionally

peripatetic 6 roving **7** migrant, nomadic, roaming, walking **8** rambling, tramping **9** itinerant, migratory, traveling, wandering **10** ambulating, ambulatory **12** Aristotelian, gallivanting **13** peregrinating

periphery 4 edge **5** bound **6** border **7** fringes **8** boundary **9** outskirts, perimeter **13** circumference

perish 3 die **5** decay **6** expire, vanish **7** crumble **8** pass away **9** disappear **10** come to ruin, wither away **11** be destroyed

perishable 8 fleeting, unstable **9**

ephemeral **10** evanescent, short-lived, transitory **12** decomposable

perished 4 dead, died **7** expired **8** lifeless **10** passed away

periwinkle 5 Vinca **12** Catharanthus
varieties: **4** Rose **6** Common, Lesser **7** Greater **10** Madagascar

perjury 13 false swearing **14** lying under oath **20** giving false testimony

Perker
character in: **14** Pickwick Papers
author: **7** Dickens

Perkins, Anthony
born: **9** New York NY
roles: **6** Psycho **11** Norman Bates **14** Catch Twenty-Two **17** Look Homeward Angel **18** Desire Under the Elms, Friendly Persuasion

perk up 4 lift **5** cheer, rally, renew **6** buoy up, lift up, revive **7** animate, enliven, gladden **8** brighten, vitalize **9** stimulate **10** rejuvenate

perky 3 gay **4** pert **5** alert, brisk, happy, saucy, sunny **6** jaunty, lively **7** smiling **8** animated, cheerful, spirited **9** sprightly, vivacious **11** free and easy **12** full of spirit, lighthearted

permanent 3 set **4** perm, wave **6** stable **7** abiding, durable, endless, eternal, lasting, undying **8** constant, enduring, immortal, infinite, unending, unfading **9** deathless, immutable, long-lived, perpetual, unfailing **10** changeless, unyielding **11** everlasting, long-lasting, never-ending, unalterable **12** imperishable

permeate 4 fill **5** imbue **6** infuse **7** pervade **8** saturate **9** penetrate **11** pass through, seep through, soak through

per mensem 10 by the month

permissible 5 legal, licit **6** lawful **7** allowed, granted **8** licensed **9** allowable, permitted, tolerated **10** admissible, authorized, legitimate, sanctioned **12** unprohibited

permission 5 grant, leave **6** assent, permit **7** consent, license **8** approval, sanction **9** agreement, allowance **10** compliance, concession, indulgence **11** approbation, endorsement **12** acquiescence, dispensation **13** authorization

permissive 3 lax **7** lenient **8** allowing, granting, tolerant **9** assenting, easygoing, indulgent **10** consenting, forbearing, permitting **11** acquiescent **13** unprohibitive **14** unproscriptive

permit 2 OK **3** let **5** allow **6** endure, suffer **7** agree to, approve, condone, endorse, let pass, license, warrant **8** bear with, sanction, tolerate **9** authority, authorize, consent to, put up with **11** give leave to **12** give assent to **13** authorization
French: **13** laissez passer

permit to leave 4 free **5** let go **6** excuse **7** dismiss, release, set free **8** liberate **9** allow to go, discharge, send forth

pernicious 5 fatal, toxic **6** deadly, lethal, mortal **7** baneful, harmful, noxious, serious **8** damaging, venomous **9** dangerous, injurious, malignant, poisonous **10** disastrous **11** deleterious, destructive, detrimental

pernod
type: **8** aperitif
flavor: **5** anise
substitute for: **8** absinthe
with gin: **7** Dubarry
with orange juice: **9** Tiger Tail
with rum: **8** Shanghai
with rye: **3** TNT

peroration 6 sermon, speech, tirade **7** address, lecture, oration **8** diatribe, harangue, jeremiad **9** discourse, philippic **10** filibuster **11** declamation, exhortation

perpendicular 4 sine **5** erect, plumb, sheer, steep **7** upright **8** vertical **10** right angle

perpetrate 2 do **5** enact **6** commit, pursue **7** execute, inflict, perform, pull off **8** carry out, transact

perpetration 5 doing **9** committal **10** commission, committing, performing **11** carrying out, performance

perpetrator 9 performer **11** participant

perpetual 7 abiding, endless, eternal, lasting **8** constant, enduring, repeated, unending **9** ceaseless, continual, incessant, permanent, sustained, unceasing **10** continuous **11** everlasting, never ending, unremitting **12** interminable **13** inexhaustible, uninterrupted

perpetuate 4 save **7** sustain **8** continue, maintain, make last, preserve **10** eternalize **11** immortalize, memorialize

perpetuity 7 all time, forever **8** eternity, infinity **9** end of time **10** permanence **11** endlessness **12** perpetuation, timelessness **13** perdurability, perennialness

perplex 5 mix up, stump **6** baffle, boggle, muddle, puzzle, rattle **7** confuse, mystify, nonplus **8** befuddle, bewilder, confound **9** dumbfound

perplexed 7 anxious, amazed, baffled, bemused, muddled, puzzled **8** confused, doubtful, involved **9** befuddled, intricate, mystified **10** astonished, bewildered, nonplussed

perplexing 4 hard, mazy **6** thorny **7** complex **10** mysterious
riddle: **9** conundrum

perplexity 9 confusion **10** bafflement, puzzlement **12** bewilderment **13** mystification

perquisite 3 due **4** gift, perk **5** right **6**

reward **7** benefit, present **9** advantage, emolument, privilege **10** honorarium, inducement, recompense **13** fringe benefit

Perrine, Valerie
born: **11** Galveston TX
roles: **5** Lenny **8** Superman **18** Slaughterhouse Five

Perry, Matthew Calbraith
served in: **10** Mexican War **19** War of Eighteen Twelve
rank: **9** commodore
helped establish: **7** Liberia
commander of: **17** US African Squadron
gained treaty with: **5** Japan

Perry, Oliver Hazard
nickname: **14** Hero of Lake Erie
served in: **13** Tripolitan War **19** War of Eighteen-Twelve
battle: **8** Lake Erie
commander of ship: **7** Niagara **8** Lawrence
defeated: **7** British
saying: **31** We have met the enemy and they are ours

Perry, William
nickname: **12** Refrigerator
sport: **8** football
team: **12** Chicago Bears

Perry Como Show, The
regulars: **8** Don Adams **9** Jack Duffy, Paul Lynde **10** Pierre Olaf **11** Kaye Ballard **12** Sandy Stewart **14** Fontane Sisters **17** Ray Charles Singers **18** Louis Da Pron Dancers **19** Peter Gennaro Dancers
announcer: **9** Dick Stark, Ed Herlihy **11** Frank Gallop, Martin Block **12** Durward Kirby
orchestra: **13** Mitchell Ayres
theme: **16** Dream Along with Me

Perry Mason
character: **6** Lt Drum **7** Lt Tragg **9** Paul Drake **10** Lt Anderson **11** Della Street **14** Hamilton Burger
cast: **9** Wesley Lau **10** Ray Collins **11** Barbara Hale, Raymond Burr **13** William Hopper, William Talman **15** Richard Anderson

persecute 3 vex **4** bait **5** abuse, annoy, bully, harry, hound **6** badger, harass, harrow, hector, plague **7** oppress, torment **8** maltreat **9** tyrannize, victimize

Persephone
also: **4** Cora, Kore **10** Perserpina, Proserpine
queen of: **5** Hades
father: **4** Zeus
mother: **7** Demeter
husband: **5** Hades
abducted by: **5** Pluto
ate seeds of: **11** pomegranate
epithet: **11** Carpophorus
corresponds to: **5** Brimo **6** Libera **8** Despoena

Persepolis
capital of: **13** Persian Empire
near modern-day: **10** Shiraz, Iran

Perseus
father: **4** Zeus
mother: **5** Danae
grandfather: **8** Acrisius
wife: **9** Andromeda
son: **6** Mestor, Perses **7** Alcaeus, Heleius **9** Electryon, Sthenelus
daughter: **10** Gorgophone
saved: **9** Andromeda
killed: **6** Gorgon, Medusa

perseverance 8 tenacity **10** doggedness, resolution **11** persistence **12** resoluteness **13** determination, steadfastness

persevere 6 hang on, keep on **7** persist **8** keep at it, plug away, work hard **9** not give up, stick to it **10** be resolute, be resolved, hammer away **11** be obstinate, be steadfast, hang in there

persevering 6 dogged **8** constant, diligent, resolute, sedulous **9** keeping on, steadfast, tenacious **10** determined, persistent, unflagging **11** hardworking, industrious, unremitting

Pershing, John J
nickname: **9** Black Jack
served in: **3** WWI **11** Philippines, World War One **18** Spanish-American War
commander of: **21** Mexican border campaign
trained: **27** American Expeditionary Forces
battle: **10** Kettle Hill **11** San Juan Hill
fought against: **5** Moros **11** Pancho Villa
rank: **16** brigadier general **18** general of the armies
memoirs: **26** My Experiences in the World War
won: **13** Pulitzer Prize (for history)

Persia *see* **4** Iran

Persian Gulf War
caused by: **4** Iraq **13** Saddam Hussein **14** Kuwait invasion
took place in: **4** Iraq **6** Kuwait **10** Middle East **11** Saudi Arabia
leaders:
  Allies: **11** Colin Powell **15** Khalid bin Sultan **18** H Norman Schwarzkopf
  Iraq: **13** Saddam Hussein
operations: **11** Desert Storm **12** Desert Shield
weapons: **4** Scud **5** AWACS **6** Abrams, Apache **7** Bradley, Patriot, Stealth **8** Tomahawk
battle: **6** Khafji **18** mother of all battles

Persian Mythology
god of light/truth: **7** Mithras

Persians, The
author: **9** Aeschylus

character: **6** Atossa, Xerxes **13** Ghost of Darius

persist 4 go on, last, stay **6** endure, hang on, hold on, remain **7** hold out, survive **8** continue, keep at it, not yield **9** not give up, persevere, stand fast, stick to it **10** be resolute **11** be obstinate, be tenacious, hang in there, never say die

persistence 8 tenacity **9** diligence **11** application **12** perseverance **13** determination

persistent 6 dogged **7** abiding, endless, eternal, lasting **8** constant, enduring, obdurate, resolute, stubborn **9** continual, incessant, obstinate, perpetual, steadfast, sustained, tenacious, unceasing, unfailing **10** continuous, determined, persisting, relentless, unshakable, unswerving **11** persevering, unrelenting, unremitting **12** interminable **13** inexhaustible

persnickety 5 fussy **6** choosy **7** finical, finicky **8** picayune **10** fastidious, fuddy-duddy, meticulous, nitpicking, particular, pernickety **11** overprecise, punctilious **13** overdemanding

person 4 body, soul **5** being, human **6** mortal **8** creature **9** earthling **10** human being, individual, living body, living soul

persona 5 being **6** facade **9** character

personable 4 warm **7** affable, amiable, cordial, likable, tactful **8** amicable, charming, friendly, outgoing, pleasant, sociable **9** agreeable **10** attractive, diplomatic **11** complaisant, sympathetic **12** well-disposed, well-mannered

Personae
author: **9** Ezra Pound

personage 3 VIP **5** nabob **6** bigwig **7** big name, big shot, notable **8** big wheel, luminary, somebody **9** celebrity, dignitary **11** heavyweight **12** leading light, public figure **13** high-muck-a-muck

persona grata 8 diplomat **16** acceptable person **34** acceptable diplomatic representative

personal 3 own **5** privy **6** bodily, inward, secret **7** private, special **8** intimate, physical **9** corporeal, exclusive **10** individual, particular, subjective **12** confidential

Personal Anthology, A
author: **15** Jorge Luis Borges

personality 3 ego **4** self **5** charm **6** makeup, nature **8** charisma, identity **9** magnetism **10** affability, amiability **11** disposition, temperament **12** friendliness **13** agreeableness, individuality **15** distinctiveness

persona non grata 15 unwelcome person **18** unacceptable person **33** unwelcome diplomatic representative

Personification of
aging: **4** Elli
air: **4** Amen, Amon **5** Ammon **6** Aether
astronomy: **6** Urania
breath: **4** Amen, Amon **5** Ammon
chaos: **4** Nunu
choral song: **11** Terpsichore
comedy: **6** Thalia
confusion: **5** Chaos
conscience: **5** Aidos
courage: **5** Arete **6** Virtus
dance: **8** Polymnia **10** Polyhymnia **11** Terpsichore
death: **4** Mors **6** Namtar **8** Thanatos
desert: **3** Set **4** Seth
desire: **6** Pothos
divine punishment: **3** Ate **7** Nemesis
east wind: **5** Eurus **9** Volturnus
echo: **4** Echo
emulation: **5** Zelos
familial affection: **6** Pietas
fate: **4** Norn **5** Moira, Moras
fear: **6** Deimos
femininity: **5** Neith
fire: **4** Logi
force: **3** Bia
good faith: **5** Fides
grain blight: **7** Robigus
heaven: **6** Uranus
hostile nature: **8** Fomorian
idyllic poetry: **6** Thalia
liberty: **8** Libertas
longing: **6** Pothos
lotus: **8** Nefertem
meditation: **6** Melete
memory: **5** Mneme, Munin
moon: **4** Luna
nature: **7** Erlking
night: **3** Nox
north wind: **6** Boreas
order: **7** Eunomia
pain: **5** Oizys
past: **3** Urd
peace: **5** Irene
prayer: **5** Litae
present: **8** Verdandi
punishment: **5** Poena, Poine
recklessness: **3** Ate
retribution: **7** Nemesis
revenge: **5** Poena, Poine
Roman nation: **8** Quirinus
sacred music: **8** Polymnia **10** Polyhymnia
sea: **3** Ler, Lir **5** Nammu **6** Pontus **8** Thalassa
sky: **6** Aether, Hathor
soul: **6** Psyche
southeast wind: **5** Eurus **9** Volturnus
south wind: **5** Notus **7** Ninurta
strength: **6** Cratus
sun: **3** Sol
thought: **5** Hugin
tragedy: **9** Melpomene
truth: **7** Alethia
unavailing effort: **5** Ocnus
victory: **4** Nike
wealth: **6** Plutus
west wind: **8** Favonius, Zephyrus
wind: **7** Ninurta
zeal: **5** Zelos

personify 6 embody **7** express **9** exemplify, incarnate, represent, symbolize **11** externalize, incorporate, personalize **12** characterize

personnel 4 crew **5** staff **7** members, workers **8** manpower **9** employees, work force **10** associates

Person to Person
host: **13** Edward R Murrow **18** Charles Collingwood

perspective 4 view **5** scape, scene, vista **7** outlook **8** overview, prospect **9** broad view, viewpoint **12** bird's-eye view

perspicacious 4 keen **5** acute, alert, awake, sharp **6** astute, shrewd **9** clear-eyed, sagacious **10** discerning, perceptive **11** clearheaded, keen-sighted, penetrating, sharp-witted **12** clear-sighted

perspicacity 6 acumen **8** keenness, sagacity **9** acuteness, alertness, sharpness **10** astuteness, perception, shrewdness **11** discernment **14** discrimination

persuadable 7 willing **8** amenable, obliging **9** malleable, tractable **10** open-minded **16** open to suggestion

persuade 3 get **4** coax, lure, move, sway **5** tempt **6** cajole, entice, induce, prompt **7** wheedle, win over **8** convince, inveigle, motivate, talk into **9** influence

Persuasion
author: **10** Jane Austen
character: **7** Mrs Clay **8** Mrs Croft **11** Lady Russell **12** Admiral Croft **25** Captain Frederick Wentworth
  Elliot family: **4** Anne **7** William **9** Elizabeth, Sir Walter
  Musgrove family: **4** Mary **6** Louisa **7** Charles **9** Henrietta

persuasive 6 cogent **7** coaxing, logical, winning **8** alluring, credible, forceful, inviting **9** effective, plausible, seductive **10** believable, compelling, convincing **11** influential

pert 4 flip, spry **5** alert, brash, brisk, fresh, nervy, perky, quick, saucy **6** brassy, brazen, cheeky, lively, nimble **7** chipper, flippant, impolite, impudent, insolent **9** audacious, energetic, insulting, sprightly, wide-awake **11** impertinent, smart-alecky **12** discourteous

pertain 2 be **5** apply, touch **6** befall, belong, relate **7** concern, connect

Perth *see* Australia

pertinacious 6 dogged **8** stubborn **9** obstinate, tenacious **10** persistent, unyielding **11** persevering

pertinacity 9 obstinacy **10** mulishness **11** persistence, willfulness **12** contrari-ness, obdurateness, perverseness, stubbornness **13** determination, inflexibility, intransigence, pigheadedness **14** bullheadedness, intractability

pertinence 9 relevance **11** germaneness **12** appositeness **13** applicability

pertinent 3 apt **4** meet **7** apropos, fitting, germane, related **8** apposite, material, relevant, suitable **9** befitting, concerned, congruent, connected **10** applicable, consistent, to the point
Latin: **5** ad rem

perturb 5 upset, worry **6** bother **7** disturb, fluster, trouble **8** disquiet, distress **10** discompose, disconcert

perturbation 5 alarm, upset, worry **6** dismay **7** anxiety, concern, turmoil **8** distress **9** agitation, commotion **10** excitement **11** disquietude, trepidation **12** apprehension, discomposure **13** consternation

perturbed 5 upset **7** annoyed, worried **8** agitated, troubled **9** disturbed **12** disconcerted

perturbing 6 vexing **7** irksome **8** annoying **9** vexatious **10** bothersome, irritating, unsettling **11** disquieting, distressing, troublesome **13** disconcerting

Peru
capital/largest city: **4** Lima
  Inca capital: **5** Cuzco
others: **3** Ica **4** Puno **5** Cuzco, Paita, Pisco, Tacna **6** Callao, Talara **7** Huanuco, Iquitos **8** Arequipa, Castilla, Chiclayo, Chimbote, Mollendo, Pucallpa, Trujillo **9** Cajamarca **10** Yurimaguas
school: **8** Trujillo **8** San Marcos
division: **3** Ica **4** Lima, Puno **5** Cusco, Cuzco, Junin, Piura, Tacna **6** Ancash, Loreto, Tumbes
  Inca empire: **13** Tahuantinsuyo
measure: **4** topo **5** galon **7** celemin
monetary unit: **3** sol **5** libra **6** dinero, reseta **7** centavo
weight: **5** libra **7** quintal
island: **6** Chinca **7** Chincha
lake: **8** Titicaca
mountain: **5** Andes **7** El Misti, Huamina **8** Coropuna
highest point: **9** Huascaran
river: **3** Ene, Ica, Ilo **4** Napo, Napu **5** Piura, Rimac **6** Amazon, Oroton, Pampas, Yaguas, Yavari **7** Curaray, Mantaro, Maranon, Pastaza, Tapiche, Ucayali **8** Apurimac, Huallaga, Urubamba **11** Madre de Dios, Paucartambo
sea: **7** Pacific
physical feature:
  current: **6** el nino
  desert: **5** Nazca **7** Atacama, Sechura
  drizzling rain: **8** ilovizna
  fog: **5** garua
  gulf: **9** Guayaquil
  plateau: **7** Tablazo

people: **4** Ande, Boro, Cana, Inca, Inka, Lama, Pano, Peba, Piro, Yutu **5** Campa, Carib, Chana, Colan, Colla, Jwaro, Moche, Nasca, Senci, Yagua, Yunca **6** Atalan, Aymara, Canchi, Chanca, Chanka, Chimer, Cholos, Cocama, Jibaro, Kechua, Omagua, Quiche, Quolla, Setibo, Sipibo **7** Changos, Chincha, Chuncho, Mestizo, Mochica **8** Amahuaca, Criollos, Mayoruma, Quechuia **9** Callawaya **10** Tiahuanaca, Tiatinagua **11** Chumpivilca
> **artist:** **4** Lazo **7** Montero, Sabogal, Szyszlo **8** Codesido
> **author:** **4** Vega **5** Palma, Prada **8** Caviedes **10** Mariategui
> **explorer:** **7** Pizarro
> **Inca leader:** **7** Huascar **9** Atahualpa **10** Manco Capac
> **leader:** **5** Balta, Pardo, Prado, Torre **7** Bolivar **8** Castilla, Fujimori **9** Santa Cruz **13** Belaunde Terry **15** Leguiay y Salcedo, Morales Bermudez

language: **6** Aymara **7** English, Quechua, Spanish
religion: **13** Roman Catholic
place:
> **bullring:** **11** Plaza de Acho
> **center of Lima:** **12** Plaza de Armas
> **church:** **10** La Compania
> **open market/street:** **9** Calle Real
> **ruins:** **5** Huaco **8** Chan-Chan **9** Cajamarca **11** Machu- Picchu **22** Fortress of Sacsayhuaman

feature:
> **animal:** **5** llama **6** alpaca, vicuna **7** guanaco
> **commune:** **6** ayllus
> **dance:** **5** cueca, kaswa **6** cachua
> **farmers:** **10** campesinos
> **priest:** **6** villac
> **slums:** **9** barriadas
> **tree:** **8** cinchona

food:
> **dish:** **3** aji, cuy **7** ceviche **10** anticuchos
> **drink:** **5** pisco **6** chicha **11** aguardiente

Perugino, Pietro
real name: **14** Pietro Vannucci
also called: **10** Il Perugino **14** Pier della Pieve
born: **5** Italy **15** Citta della Pieve
artwork: **24** The Crucifixion with Saints **26** Delivery of the Keys to St Peter **27** The Giving of the Keys to St Peter **32** Apparition of the Virgin to St Bernard, Christ Delivering the Keys to St Peter

perusal **5** study **6** review **7** reading **8** scanning, scrutiny **10** inspection, runthrough **11** examination, lookthrough **12** scrutinizing **13** contemplation

peruse **3** con **4** read, scan **5** study **6** search, survey **7** examine, inspect **10** scrutinize

pervade **4** fill **5** imbue **6** infuse **7** suffuse **8** permeate, saturate **9** penetrate **13** spread through **17** diffuse throughout

pervasive **4** rife **7** rampant **8** dominant **9** prevalent **10** ubiquitous **11** omnipresent, predominant

perverse **5** balky **6** dogged, mulish, ornery **7** wayward, willful **8** contrary, obdurate, stubborn **9** obstinate, pigheaded **10** hardheaded, headstrong, inflexible, rebellious **11** disobedient, intractable, wrongheaded

perversion **9** depravity **10** corruption, degeneracy, immorality **11** dissipation, dissolution

pervert **4** warp **5** abuse **6** debase, misuse **7** contort, corrupt, degrade, deprave, distort, falsify, subvert **8** misapply **9** desecrate **12** misrepresent

perverted **5** false **6** faulty, untrue, warped **7** corrupt, debased, deviant, twisted, unsound **8** aberrant, abnormal, degraded, depraved **9** contorted, distorted, erroneous, imperfect, unnatural **10** fallacious, unbalanced **12** misconceived, misconstrued **13** misunderstood

pesky **7** chafing, galling, irksome **8** annoying **9** maddening, obnoxious, offensive, vexatious **10** bothersome, disturbing, nettlesome **11** aggravating, distasteful, infuriating, pestiferous, troublesome **12** disagreeable, exasperating **13** objectionable

pessimism **5** gloom **7** despair **10** gloominess **12** hopelessness **13** gloomy outlook **14** discouragement **15** downheartedness

pessimist **7** kill-joy **8** sourpuss **9** Cassandra, defeatist, gloomy Gus **10** spoilsport, wet blanket **11** crepehanger **13** prophet of doom

pessimistic **6** gloomy **8** hopeless **10** despairing, dispirited **11** discouraged, downhearted

pest **4** bane **5** curse **6** blight, bother **7** scourge **8** nuisance, vexation **9** annoyance **10** irritation **13** pain in the neck

pester **3** irk, nag, vex **4** bait, fret **5** annoy, harry, taunt, worry **6** badger, bother, harass, hector, nettle, plague **7** disturb, provoke, torment, trouble **8** irritate

pesticide **3** DDT **7** biocide **8** fumigant **9** fungicide, germacide, vermicide **11** insecticide
> **user:** **12** exterminator

pestilence **6** blight, plague **7** disease **8** epidemic
> **god of:** **4** Irra

pesto sauce

ingredients: **5** basil **6** garlic **8** olive oil

pet **3** pat **4** baby, dear **6** caress, choice, fondle, stroke **7** beloved, darling, dearest, favored **8** favorite **9** cherished, preferred **10** sweetheart **14** apple of one's eye

pet activity **5** hobby **7** passion **8** interest **10** enthusiasm, hobbyhorse

Petain, Henri Philippe
rank: **7** general, premier
nationality: **6** French
leader of government at: **5** Vichy
convicted of: **7** treason

Peter **7** apostle
means: **4** rock
also called: **5** Simon **6** Cephas
father: **4** John **5** Jonas
brother: **6** Andrew
birthplace: **9** Bethsaida
hometown: **9** Capernaum
disciple of: **5** Jesus
companion: **4** John **5** James
rebuked: **7** Ananias **8** Sapphira
secretary: **8** Silvanus
pertaining to: **7** Petrine

Peter and the Wolf
composed by: **9** Prokofiev

Peter Grimes
opera by: **7** Britten
character: **11** Ellen Orford

Peter Heering, Cherry Heering
type: **6** brandy **7** liqueur
origin: **7** Denmark
flavor: **6** cherry
color: **3** red

Peter Ibbetson
author: **15** George Du Maurier

peter out **3** ebb **7** decline, dwindle, fall off, give out **8** diminish

Peter Pan
author: **11** James Barrie
character: **4** John, Smee **7** Michael **9** Nurse Nana, Tiger Lily **10** Tinker Bell **11** Captain Hook **12** Wendy Darling
locale: **14** Never-never Land

petiole **4** stem **5** spine, stalk, stipe **8** peduncle **9** leafstalk

petite **3** wee **4** tiny **5** small **6** little **9** miniature **10** diminutive

petition **3** ask, beg, sue **4** plea, pray, seek, suit, urge **5** press **6** appeal, invoke, orison, prayer **7** apply to, beseech, entreat **8** appeal to, call upon, entreaty, proposal **9** imploring, plead with, request of **10** invocation, supplicate **11** application, beseechment, requisition **12** solicitation, supplication

petitioner **6** suitor **8** claimant **9** solicitor, suppliant **10** supplicant

pet name **8** nickname **9** sobriquet **10** diminutive, endearment

pet phrase **5** maxim, motto **6** saying, slogan **9** catchword

Petre (Lord)

character in: 16 The Rape of the Lock
author: 4 Pope
petrified 4 hard **5** dense, solid, stony
6 frozen **8** hardened, rocklike **9** paralyzed **10** solidified **11** hard as a rock,
scared stiff **13** turned to stone
Petrified Forest, The
director: 10 Archie Mayo
based on play by: 14 Robert Sherwood
cast: 9 Dick Foran **10** Bette Davis **12**
Leslie Howard **14** Humphrey Bogart
(Duke Mantee)
setting: 7 Arizona
Petronius
author of: 9 Satyricon
Petruchio
character in: 19 The Taming of the
Shrew
author: 11 Shakespeare
Petticoat Junction
character: 10 Floyd Smoot, Sam
Drucker **11** Homer Bedloe, Kate
Bradley **12** Charlie Pratt, Dr Janet
Craig, Steve Elliott, Wendell Gibbs
14 Betty Jo Bradley, Uncle Joe Carson **15** Billie Jo Bradley, Bobbie Jo
Bradley
cast: 9 Frank Cady, Linda Kaye, Mike
Minor, Rufe Davis **10** Pat Woodell
11 Charles Lane **12** Bea Benaderet,
Byron Foulger, June Lockhart, Lori
Saunders **13** Edgar Buchanan,
Gunilla Hutton, Jeannine Riley **14**
Meredith MacRae, Smiley Burnette
setting: 11 Hooterville **14** Shady Rest
Hotel
train: 10 Cannonball
petto 5 chest **6** breast
petty 4 mean **5** minor, small **6** flimsy,
paltry, shabby, slight **7** ignoble, trivial
8 niggling, picayune, piddling, trifling
10 ungenerous **11** small-minded, unimportant **12** narrow-minded **13** insignificant **14** inconsiderable **15** inconsequential
petulance 9 poutiness, sulkiness **11**
fretfulness, peevishness **12** irritability
petulant 4 sour **5** cross, gruff, huffy,
sulky, surly, testy **6** grumpy, sullen,
tetchy, touchy **7** bearish, crabbed,
fretful, grouchy, peevish, pettish, uncivil **8** snappish **9** crotchety, fractious,
irascible, irritable **10** ill-natured, out
of sorts, ungracious **11** complaining,
contentious, ill-tempered, quarrelsome, thin-skinned **12** cantankerous,
faultfinding
Petulia
director: 13 Richard Lester
cast: 10 Arthur Hill, Pippa Scott **12**
George C Scott, Joseph Cotten **13** Julie Christie, Shirley Knight **18** Richard Chamberlain
setting: 12 San Francisco
petunia
varieties: 4 Wild **7** Mexican, Seaside

10 Large white **12** Common garden
14 Violet-flowered
peu a peu 14 little by little
peu de chose 14 trifling matter **17** unimportant matter
pew 4 seat **5** bench **6** settle
Peychaud Bitters
type: 8 aperitif
origin: 10 New Orleans
Peyton Place
author: 14 Grace Metalious
character: 9 Rita Jacks (Harrington)
10 Hannah Cord, Steven Cord **12**
Matthew Swain **13** Betty Anderson
(Harrington Cord Harrington), Elliott
Carson, Julie Anderson **14** Dr Michael Rossi, Dr Robert Morton,
George Anderson **16** Allison Mackenzie (Harrington), Leslie Harrington,
Norman Harrington, Rodney Harrington **18** Constance Mackenzie (Carson)
cast (television): 8 Ed Nelson **9** Kent
Smith, Mia Farrow, Ryan O'Neal **10**
Tim O'Connor **11** Kasey Rogers, Paul
Langton, Ruth Warrick **12** Henry
Beckman, James Douglas **13** Dorothy
Malone **14** Barbara Parkins, Patricia
Morrow, Warner Anderson **19** Christopher Connelly
director (movie): 10 Mark Robson
cast (movie): 9 Hope Lange **10** Lana
Turner, Lloyd Nolan **13** Arthur Kennedy
score: 11 Franz Waxman
Phaedo
author: 5 Plato
Phaedra
father: 5 Minos
mother: 8 Pasiphae
sister: 7 Ariadne
husband: 7 Theseus
son: 6 Acamas **8** Demophon
stepson: 10 Hippolytus
loved: 10 Hippolytus
death by: 7 hanging, suicide
Phaenna
origin: 5 Greek **7** Spartan
member of: 6 Graces
Phaethon
father: 6 Helios
mother: 7 Clymene
phalanx 6 column, parade **9** formation
13 ranks and files
Phallus
image of: 9 male organ
symbol of: 9 fertility
carried in: 6 comedy **9** festivals
associated with: 3 Pan **6** Hermes **7**
Demeter **8** Dionysus
phantasm 5 ghost, shade, spook **6** mirage, spirit, vision **7** fantasy, figment,
incubus, phantom, specter **8** delusion,
illusion, succubus **10** apparition
Phantasus
origin: 5 Greek
god of: 6 dreams

phantom 5 dream, ghost **6** mirage,
spirit, vision, wraith **7** chimera, specter **8** illusion, phantasm **10** apparition
13 hallucination
Phantom, The
creator: 7 Lee Falk **8** Ray Moore
nickname: 16 The Ghost Who Walks
mask: 5 black
costume: 6 purple
Phantom of the Opera, The
director:
1925 version: 12 Rupert Julian
1943 version: 11 Arthur Lubin
cast:
1925 version: 9 Lon Chaney **11**
Mary Philbin, Norman Kerry
1943 version: 10 Hume Cronyn,
Jane Farrar, Nelson Eddy **11**
Claude Rains **12** Edgar Barrier **13**
Susanna Foster
setting: 10 Paris Opera
Phaon
occupation: 7 boatman
location: 8 Mitylene
given: 5 youth **6** beauty
given by: 9 Aphrodite
pharos 5 light **6** beacon, signal **7** seamark **10** lighthouse, watchtower
phase 4 side, step, view **5** angle, facet,
guise, level, slant, stage **6** aspect, degree, period **7** feature **8** attitude, juncture **9** condition, viewpoint **10** appearance **11** development **12**
circumstance
pheasant
group of: 4 nest, nide
Phedre, Phaedra
author: 6 Racine
character: 6 Aricia **7** Theseus **10** Hippolytus
phenomenal 5 super **6** unique **7**
amazing, unusual **8** singular, superior,
uncommon **9** fantastic, marvelous,
unheard-of **10** incredible, miraculous,
prodigious, remarkable, stupendous,
surpassing **11** astonishing, exceptional, outstanding, sensational, spectacular **12** overwhelming, unparalleled
13 extraordinary, unprecedented
phenomenon 5 thing **6** marvel, rarity,
wonder **7** episode, miracle **8** incident,
occasion **9** actuality, curiosity, exception, happening, nonpareil, sensation
10 fact of life, occurrence, proceeding
11 contingency
phial 4 vial **6** bottle, vessel **9** container
Phidias
born: 6 Athens, Greece
artwork: 4 Zeus **6** Amazon **13** Lemnian Athene (Athena Lemnia) **15**
Apollo Parnopios, Athena Parthenos,
Athena Promachos
Philadelphia
baseball team: 8 Phillies
basketball team: 13 Seventy-Sixers
bay: 8 Delaware
football team: 5 Stars **6** Eagles

founded/planned by: 4 Penn
hockey team: 6 Flyers
landmark: 6 US Mint **8** City Hall **11** Liberty Bell **12** Christ Church, Congress Park **13** Franklin Field, Roosevelt Park **14** Betsy Ross House, Carpenter's Hall **15** Gloria Dei Church, Veterans Stadium **16** Independence Hall
means: 19 city of brotherly love
museum: 5 Rodin **15** Fels Planetarium **16** Barnes Foundation **17** Franklin Institute
river: 8 Delaware **10** Schuylkill
university: 4 Penn **6** Drexel, Temple **9** Jefferson, St Joseph's **22** Curtis Institute of Music

Philadelphia Story, The
director: 11 George Cukor
based on play by: 11 Philip Barry
cast: 9 Cary Grant **10** Ruth Hussey **12** James Stewart **16** Katharine Hepburn
Oscar for: 5 actor (Stewart)
remade as: 11 High Society

philanderer 3 rip **4** rake, wolf **5** flirt **6** lecher, tomcat, wanton **7** dallier, Don Juan, gallant, swinger, trifler **8** lothario, lover boy, rakehell **9** adulterer, libertine, womanizer **10** ladykiller **11** woman-chaser

philanthropic, philanthropical 7 liberal **8** generous **9** bounteous **10** almsgiving, beneficent, benevolent, charitable, munificent **11** magnanimous **12** eleemosynary, humanitarian

philanthropist 5 donor, giver **8** dogooder **9** almsgiver **11** contributor **12** humanitarian **13** Good Samaritan

philanthropy 6 bounty **7** charity **8** goodness **10** almsgiving, generosity, liberality **11** beneficence, benevolence, munificence **13** unselfishness **14** charitableness, openhandedness **15** humanitarianism **16** largeheartedness **18** public-spiritedness

Philaster
author: 30 Francis Beaumont and John Fletcher

Philemon
friend: 4 Paul
slave: 8 Onesimus
wife: 6 Baucis
entertained: 4 Hera, Zeus
became: 12 temple priest

Philip
hometown: 9 Bethsaida
disciple of: 5 Jesus

Philippines
named for: 15 Philip II of Spain
capital/largest city: 6 Manila
others: 3 Iba **4** Agoa, Bogo, Cebu, Debu, Naga, Palo **5** Albay, Davao, Gapan, Iriga, Lanao, Laoag, Pasay, Vigan **6** Aparri, Baguio, Cavite, Ilagan, Iloilo, Tarlac **7** Bacolod, Basilan, Calapan, Dagupan, Legaspi **8** Batangas, Caloocan, Cotabato, Taclo-

ban **9** Zamboanga **10** Cabanutuan, Dumaguette, Quezon City
school: 10 Santo Tomas **14** Ateneo de Manila
division: 4 Abra, Cebu **5** Aklan, Albay, Bohol, Capiz, Davao, Lanao, Leyte, Rizal, Samar **6** Agusan, Bataan, Cavite, Iloilo, Laguna, Quezon, Tarlac **7** Isabela, Lepanto, Surigao
measure: 4 loan **5** braza, catty, cavan, chupa, fardo, ganta, picul, punto **6** apatan, balita, lachsa, quinon **7** quilate **8** chinanta
monetary unit: 4 peso **6** conant, peseta **7** centavo
weight: 5 catty, picul **6** lachsa **7** quilate **8** chinanta
island: 4 Cebu, Cuyo, Jolo, Poro, Sulu **5** Batan, Bohol, Leyte, Luzon, Panay, Samar, Ticao **6** Culion, Lubang, Negros **7** Babuyan, Batanes, Bisayan, Masbate, Mindoro, Palawan, Paragua, Polillo, Visoyan **8** Mindanao **10** Corregidor, Marinduque
lake: 4 Taal **5** Lanao
mountain: 3 Iba **4** Mayo, Taal **5** Albay, Askja, Hibok, Mayon, Pulog **6** Pagsan **7** Banahao, Canlaon
highest point: 3 Apo
river: 4 Abra, Agno **5** Magat, Pasig **6** Agusan, Laoang **7** Cagayan **8** Mindanao, Pampanga
sea: 4 Sulu **5** Samar **7** Celebes, Pacific, Visayan **10** Philippine, South China
physical feature:
  bay: 6 Manila
  falls: 9 Pagsanjan **14** Maria Christina
  gulf: 4 Moro **5** Albay, Davao, Leyte, Ragay **8** Lingayen
  hot springs: 8 Los Banos
  national park: 12 Mayon Volcano
  ocean trench: 8 Mindanao
  peninsula: 6 Bataan
  storm: 6 bagyos **7** monsoon, typhoon
  volcano: 8 Pinatubo
people: 3 Ati, Eta, Ita, Tao **4** Aeta, Ifil, Moro, Sulu, Tino **5** Abaca, Aripa, Batak, Batan, Bicol, Bikol, Busao, Lutao, Mundo, Sinay, Tagal, Vicol, Yakan **6** Apayao, Baluga, Bilaan, Biscol, Bontoc, Bontok, Busaos, Ibanag, Ibilao, Ifugao, Igalot, Igorot, Illano, Isinai, Lutayo, Manabo, Manobo, Montes, Sambal, Tagala, Timaua, Timawa, Zambal **7** Bagoboo, Bisayan, Cagayan, Ilocano, Itanega, Malanoa, Mangyan, Naboloi, Negrito, Tagalog, Tirurai, Visayan **8** Arupaata, Babaylan, Bukidono, Filipino, Igorotte, Manguian, Pampanga **9** Arupaatta, Dulangane, Macajambo, Pampangan, Tinguiane **10** Magindanao, Pangasinan **11** Calalangane
  author: 5 Rizal
  explorer: 7 Legazpe **8** Magellan **10**

Villalobos
leader: 5 Ramos **6** Aquino, Marcos, Osmena, Quezon **9** Aguinaldo, Bonifacio, Macapagal, Magsaysay **11** Roxas y Acuna
language: 4 Moro **5** Bicol, Bikol **6** Ibanag **7** Cebuano, English, Ilocano, Spanish, Tagalog, Visayan **8** Filipino, Pilipino **9** Pampangan **10** Samar-Leyte **13** Bamboo-English
religion: 7 animism **9** Aglipayan **10** Protestant **13** Roman Catholic **15** Iglesia ni Kristo
place:
  church: 14 Saint Augustine
  esplanade: 6 Luneta
  fort: 4 Cota, Gota, Kota **5** Lotta **10** Corregidor
  president's palace: 10 Malacanang
  street: 7 Escolta
  US bases: 5 Clark **8** Subic Bay
  walled city: 10 Intramuros
feature:
  animal: 7 carabao, tamarau, tarsier **9** mouse deer
  bird: 7 creeper
  clothing: 4 saya **6** camisa **10** balintawak **12** mestiza terno **13** barong tagalog
  dance: 9 tinikling
  drama: 8 moro-moro
  guerrilla fighter: 3 huk
  musicians: 12 musikongbuho
  naval base: 6 Cavite
  song: 8 kundiman
  village: 8 barangay
food:
  dish: 3 poi **4** baha, sabu, taro **5** balut
  drink: 4 beno, vino **5** bubud **6** tampoy **7** pangasi

philistine 5 yahoo **6** savage **7** Babbitt, lowbrow, prosaic **8** ignorant **9** barbarian, bourgeois, unrefined, untutored **10** conformist, uncultured, uneducated, uninformed, unlettered **11** commonplace **12** conventional, uncultivated **13** unenlightened **15** conventionalist **16** anti-intellectual

Philistine city **4** Gath

Philius
epithet of: 4 Zeus
means: 8 friendly

Phillotson, Richard
character in: 14 Jude the Obscure
author: 5 Hardy

Philoctetes
author: 9 Sophocles
character: 8 Heracles, Odysseus **11** Neoptolemus
inherits arms of: 8 Hercules
father: 5 Poeas, Poias
killed: 5 Paris

philodendron
varieties: 5 Dubia, giant **6** common **7** cut-leaf, red-leaf **8** blushing **9** blackgold, heart-leaf, horsehead, spade-

leaf, split-leaf **10** fiddle-leaf, variegated, velvet-leaf **11** leather-leaf

Philomela
 position: 8 princess
 realm: 6 Athens
 father: 7 Pandion
 sister: 6 Procne
 brother-in-law: 6 Tereus
 raped by: 6 Tereus
 transformed into: 7 swallow **11**
 nightingale

Philomelides
 king of: 6 Lesbos
 defeated by: 8 Odysseus

philosopher/theologian 4 sage **6** sa-
 vant **7** thinker, wise man **8** logician,
 reasoner **9** theorizer **11** rationalist,
 truth seeker **12** dialectician **13** meta-
 physician
 Alsatian: 10 Schweitzer
 American: 4 Eddy **5** Dewey, James,
 Royce, Smith, Young **6** Mather,
 Peirce **7** Edwards, Niebuhr, Russell,
 Tillich **8** Williams **9** McPherson **14**
 Elijah Muhammad
 Austrian: 12 Wittgenstein
 British: 3 Fox **4** Hume, Inge, Knox,
 More, Owen **5** Bacon, Burke, Locke,
 Moore **6** Biddle, Cotton, Hobbes,
 Huxley, Newman, Wesley **7** Ben-
 tham, Bradley, Carlyle, Cranmer,
 Russell, Spencer **8** Berkeley, Wycliffe
 9 Whitehead **13** Thomas a Becket **14**
 William of Occam
 Chinese: 6 Lao-tzu **9** Confucius
 Christian: 6 Calvin, Luther, Origen, St
 Paul **7** Abelard **8** St Anselm **9** St Pat-
 rick **10** Duns Scotus, St Benedict **11**
 St Augustine **14** William of Occam
 15 St Thomas Aquinas **16** St Alber-
 tus Magnus
 Czech: 3 Hus
 Danish: 11 Kierkegaard
 Dutch: 7 Erasmus, Spinoza
 El Salvadorian: 9 Masferrer
 French: 5 Comte **6** Calvin, Pascal,
 Sartre **7** Abelard, Bergson, Diderot **8**
 Maritain, Rousseau, Voltaire **9** Des-
 cartes, Levy-Bruhl, Montaigne **11**
 Montesquieu
 German: 4 Kant, Marx **5** Buber, He-
 gel **6** Boehme, Fichte, Herder, Luther
 7 Husserl, Jaspers, Leibniz **9** Heideg-
 ger, Nietzsche, Schelling **10** Muhlen-
 berg **11** Melanchthon **12** Schopen-
 hauer **13** Thomas a Kempis **14**
 Schleiermacher
 Greek: 5 Plato **6** St Paul, Thales **8**
 Socrates **9** Aristotle **10** Anaxagoras,
 Anaximenes, Heraclitus, Parmenides,
 Pythagoras **11** Anaximander
 Indian: 6 Buddha **16** Siddharta Gau-
 tama
 Islamic: 7 al Kindi **8** al-Farabi, Aver-
 roes, Avicenna **9** al Ghazali **10** Ibn
 Khaldun
 Italian: 5 Bruno **7** Aquinas, Mazzini
 10 St Benedict, Zeno of Elea **17** St

Francis of Assisi
 Japanese: 6 Suzuki
 Jewish: 7 Spinoza **10** Maimonides
 Latin: 8 Plotinus **11** St Augustine
 Spanish: 8 Averroes **10** Maimonides
 13 Ortega y Gasset **16** Ignatius of
 Loyola
 Swedish: 10 Swedenborg
 Swiss: 7 Zwingli

Philosopher's Pupil, The
 author: 11 Iris Murdoch

philosophic, philosophical 4 calm **5**
 quiet, stoic **6** serene **7** erudite,
 learned, logical, patient, stoical **8** abstract, composed, rational, resigned,
 tranquil **9** impassive, judicious, sagacious, unexcited, unruffled **10** complacent, fatalistic, reasonable, theorizing,
 thoughtful **11** imperturbed, theoretical, unemotional **14** self-restrained

philosophy 4 calm, view **5** ideas, logic
 6 reason **7** beliefs, opinion, thought **8**
 doctrine, fatalism, patience, serenity,
 stoicism, thinking **9** basic idea, composure, esthetics, principle, reasoning,
 restraint, viewpoint **10** conception,
 theorizing **11** complacency, convictions, forbearance, impassivity, metaphysics, rationalism, resignation
 means: 12 love of wisdom
 branch: 6 ethics **8** ontology **10** aes-
 thetics **11** metaphysics **12** epistemol-
 ogy
 term: 8 noumenon **9** causality, dialec-
 tic, solipsism
 school of: 7 Sophism **8** idealism, Milesian, Stoicism **9** Epicurean, panthe-
 ism, Platonism **10** empiricism, prag-
 matism, Skepticism **11** rationalism
 12 Aristotelian, neoplatonism **13**
 Phenomenology, scholasticism **14** existentialism **17** logical positivism

Phil Silvers Show, The
 character: 6 Fender **7** Col Hall, Hen-
 shaw **8** Doberman **9** Sgt Ritzik **12**
 Sgt Joan Hogan **13** Rocco Barbella,
 Sgt Ernie Bilko
 cast: 8 Joe E Ross, Paul Ford **10** Alan
 Melvin, Herbie Faye **13** Harvey Lem-
 beck **15** Elisabeth Fraser, Maurice
 Gosfield
 setting: 6 Kansas **10** Fort Baxter

phlegmatic 4 calm, cool, dull **6** serene
 7 languid, passive, stoical **8** listless,
 sluggish, tranquil **9** apathetic, impassive, lethargic, unfeeling **10** nonchalant, spiritless **11** indifferent, insensitive, unconcerned, unemotional,
 unexcitable **12** unresponsive **13** imperturbable, unimpassioned **15** undemonstrative

phlox
 varieties: 4 blue, fall, moss, sand,
 star **6** annual, smooth **7** prickly **8**
 creeping, drummond, mountain,
 trailing **9** perennial, sword-leaf,
 thick-leaf **15** summer perennial

Phnom-Penh
 airport: 10 Pochentong
 also: 8 Pnom Penh
 capital of: 8 Cambodia **9** Kampuchea
 pagoda: 12 Preah Morokot
 river: 6 Mekong **8** Tonle Sap

phobia 5 dread **6** horror, terror **7** bugaboo, bugbear **8** aversion, loathing **12**
 apprehension **16** unreasonable fear **19**
 overwhelming anxiety
 fear of animals: 9 zoophobia
 fear of birds: 13 ornithophobia
 fear of blushing: 13 erythrophobia
 fear of bridges: 13 gephyrophobia
 fear of cats: 10 gatophobia **12** aelurophobia, ailurophobia
 fear of closed/confined spaces: 14
 claustrophobia
 fear of crowds: 11 ochlophobia
 fear of darkness/the dark of night:
 11 nyctophobia
 fear of death: 13 thanatophobia
 fear of death/dead bodies: 11 necrophobia
 fear of dirt: 10 mysophobia
 fear of disease: 11 pathophobia
 fear of fire: 10 pyrophobia
 fear of flowers: 11 anthophobia
 fear of flying: 10 aerophobia
 fear of germs: 11 mikrophobia
 fear of hair: 12 trichophobia
 fear of heights: 10 acrophobia
 fear of insanity: 13 dementophobia
 fear of lightning: 11 astraphobia
 fear of men: 11 androphobia
 fear of mice: 10 murophobia
 fear of numbers: 12 numerophobia
 fear of open spaces: 11 agoraphobia
 fear of pain: 10 algophobia
 fear of people: 12 anthrophobia
 fear of reptiles: 11 herpetophobia
 fear of snakes: 13 ophidiophobia
 fear of speaking aloud: 11 phonophobia
 fear of spiders: 13 arachnophobia
 fear of strangers: 10 xenophobia
 fear of thunder: 12 brontophobia
 fear of the number thirteen: 17 triskaidekaphobia
 fear of vehicles/driving: 11 amaxophobia
 fear of water: 10 aquaphobia **11** hydrophobia
 fear of women: 10 gynophobia

Phoebe
 member of: 6 Titans
 father: 6 Uranus
 mother: 4 Gaea
 sister: 6 Themis
 daughter: 4 Leto **7** Asteria
 identified with: 4 moon
 corresponds to: 5 Diana **7** Artemis

Phoebus see **6** Apollo

Phoenicia see **7** Lebanon

Phoenician Mythology
 god of agriculture/earth: 5 Dagon
 corresponds to Mesopotamian: 5
 Dagan

bird: 6 Phenix **7** Phoenix
goddess of fertility/reproduction: 7 Astarte

Phoenissae (The Phoenician Maidens)
  author: 9 Euripides
  character: 5 Creon **7** Jocasta, Oedipus **8** Adrastus, Antigone, Eteocles, Tiresias **9** Polynices **10** Menoikieus

Phoenix
  basketball team: 4 Suns **7** Mercury
  capital of: 7 Arizona
  event: 5 rodeo
  feature: 10 Papago Park **22** Desert Botanical Gardens
  football team: 9 Cardinals
  hockey team: 7 Coyotes
  river: 4 Salt

Phoenix
  also: 6 Phenix
  origin: 10 Phoenician
  form: 4 bird
  gift: 11 immortality
  king of: 9 Dolopians
  father: 7 Amyntor
  mother: 8 Cleobule
  brother: 6 Cadmus
  sister: 6 Europa
  foster son: 8 Achilles
  ancestor of: 11 Phoenicians

Pholus
  form: 7 centaur
  guarded: 4 wine
  wine a gift from: 8 Dionysus

phonograph 4 hi-fi **5** phono **6** stereo **8** Victrola **9** turntable **10** gramophone **12** record player

phonophobia
  fear of: 13 speaking aloud

phony, phoney 4 fake, hoax, mock, sham **5** bogus, false, fraud, trick **6** forged, pseudo, unreal, untrue **7** forgery **8** specious, spurious **9** deceptive, imitation, pretended, synthetic **10** artificial, fraudulent, not genuine **11** counterfeit, make-believe, unauthentic

Phorcys
  god of: 3 sea
  sister: 4 Ceto
  children: 5 Ladon **6** Graiae **7** Echidna, Gorgons **8** Phorcids
  harbor in: 6 Ithaca

phosphorus
  chemical symbol: 1 P

photograph 3 pic **4** film, snap **5** image, print, shoot, still **6** candid, glossy **7** mugshot, picture, tintype **8** likeness, portrait, snapshot **12** daguerrotype
  bath: 5 fixer, toner **7** reducer **9** developer
  book: 5 album

photographer
  American: 4 Haas, Hine, Penn, Riis, Rose, Tice **5** (Ansel) Adams, Annan, Arbus, Brady, Evans, Hawes, Lange, Lynes, Smith, White **6** Avedon, Coburn, Eakins, Man Ray, Strand, Turner, Weston **7** Burrows, Eastman, Gardner, Jackson, Watkins **8** Bogardus, Davidson, Steichen **9** Muybridge, O'Sullivan, Rothstein, Stieglitz **10** Cunningham, Southworth **11** Bourke-White, Eisenstaedt, Turberville **13** Watson-Schutze
  British: 5 Evans, Frith **6** Bailey, Beaton, Fenton, Mayall, Talbot **7** Cameron **8** Brewster, Robinson **9** Rejlander **10** MacPherson
  French: 5 Marey, Nadar **6** Baldus, DuCamp, Le Secq, Newton, Niepce **7** Lumiere **8** Daguerre **12** Sabatier-Blot **14** Cartier-Bresson
  German: 4 Hoch **5** Ernst **7** Hausman **8** Stelzner **13** Renger-Patzsch
  Hungarian: 7 Kertesz **10** Moholy-Nagy
  Japanese: 4 Ikko
  Scottish: 4 Hill **7** Adamson
  Spanish: 7 Picabia

photostat 4 copy **7** replica **9** duplicate, facsimile **12** reproduction

phrase 3 put, say **4** word **5** couch, idiom, maxim, state, utter, voice, words **6** cliche, dictum, impart, remark, saying, truism **7** declare, express, proverb **8** aphorism, banality, locution **9** enunciate, find words, platitude, utterance, verbalize, word group **10** articulate, expression **11** communicate

phraseology 5 style **7** diction, wording **13** choice of words **18** manner of expression

Phrixus
  father: 7 Athamas
  mother: 7 Nephele
  stepmother: 3 Ino
  sister: 5 Helle
  wife: 9 Chalciope
  son: 5 Argus, Melas **8** Phrontis **10** Cytissorus

physical 4 real **5** human, solid **6** actual, animal, bodily, carnal, living **7** fleshly, natural, sensual **8** apparent, concrete, corporal, existent, existing, external, material, palpable, tangible **9** corporeal, essential, of the body **11** substantive

physical checkup 4 exam **8** physical **11** examination **19** physical examination

physical condition 5 shape **7** fitness, stamina **12** constitution

physical disorder 6 malady **7** ailment, disease, illness **8** sickness **9** ill health, infirmity

physical training 3 gym **6** sports **8** exercise **9** athletics, shaping up **10** gymnastics, working out **12** conditioning

physician 2 GP, MD **3** doc **5** medic **6** doctor, medico **7** surgeon **8** sawbones **10** specialist **11** medicine man, pill peddler **13** medical doctor
  Alsatian: 10 Schweitzer
  American: 4 Long, Rush, Salk **5** Sabin **6** Dooley, Gorgas **7** Huggins, Whipple **8** Williams **9** Blackwell **11** Landsteiner
  British: 5 Paget **6** Adrian, Harvey, Jenner, Lister
  Canadian: 4 Best **7** Banting
  Dutch: 7 Eijkman
  French: 7 Charcot
  German: 6 Mesmer **7** Fechner, Virchow **10** Blumenbach
  Greek: 10 Herophilus **11** Hippocrates **12** Erasistratus
  Italian: 8 Malpighi
  Russian: 6 Pavlov
  Scottish: 4 Lind
  South African: 7 Barnard

Physician to Olympian gods 5 Paeon **6** Apollo

physicist
  American: 4 Hess, Rabi **5** Bethe, Gamow, Pauli, Yalow **6** Bekesy, Teller, Townes, Watson **7** Feynman, Richter, Seaborg **8** Einstein, Lawrence, Van Allen **9** Michelson **11** Chamberlain, Oppenheimer
  Austrian: 7 Doppler, Meitner
  British: 4 Born **5** Bragg, Hooke, Joule **6** Kelvin **7** Gilbert, Thomson **8** Chadwick, Rayleigh **9** Cockcroft **10** Rutherford
  Danish: 4 Bohr **7** Oersted
  Dutch: 6 Zeeman **7** Lorentz
  French: 6 Ampere **7** Broglie, Coulomb, Fresnel **8** Foucault **9** Becquerel **11** Joliot-Curie
  German: 3 Ohm **5** Hertz, Stark **6** Planck **7** Rontgen, Wegener **8** Humboldt, Roentgen **9** Kirchhoff, Mossbauer **10** Fahrenheit, Fraunhofer
  Indian: 5 Raman
  Irish: 7 Tyndall **10** Fitzgerald
  Italian: 5 Fermi
  Russian: 6 Landau **8** Cerenkov, Sakharov
  Scottish: 7 Rankine

Physics
  author: 9 Aristotle

physiognomy 4 face **5** shape **6** facade, visage **7** contour, outline, profile **8** features **10** silhouette **11** countenance

physiology
  founder: 13 William Harvey
  study of: 8 function
  study of nervous sytem: 15 neurophysiology

pianissimo
  music: 8 very soft
    abbreviation: 2 pp

pianist 4 Hess **5** Liszt, Watts **6** Busoni, Chopin, Gilels, Serkin **7** Cliburn, Hofmann, Richter **8** Backhaus, Horowitz, Schnabel, Schumann, Thalberg, von Bulow **9** Barenboim, Casadesus, Gieseking **10** Gottschalk, Rubinstein **12** Rachmaninoff

piano
  invented by: 10 Cristofori
  player piano: 9 Fourneaux
  forerunner: 6 spinet **10** clavichord **11** harpsichord
piano
  music: 4 soft
    abbreviation: 1 p
piazza 5 patio, porch **6** square **7** gallery, portico, veranda
Piazzi, Giuseppe
  field: 9 astronomy
  nationality: 7 Italian
  discovered: 5 Ceres
  catalogued: 5 stars
picaresque 6 daring **7** raffish, roguish, waggish **8** devilish, prankish, rascally, scampish **9** foolhardy **10** roistering **13** adventuresome **14** mischief-loving
Picasso, Pablo
  born: 5 Spain **6** Malaga
  artwork: 4 Dove **6** Guitar, Jester **7** Ma Jolie, Rooster, She-Goat **8** Guernica **9** Bull's Head, Notre Dame **11** Seated Woman, Woman Diving **12** Head of a Woman **13** Seated Bathers **14** Minotauromachy, Mother and Child, Women of Algiers **15** Ambroise Vollard, Man Holding a Lamb, The Charnel-House, The Large Profile, The Three Dancers **16** Nude in an Armchair **17** Girl Before a Mirror, The Glass of Absinth, The Three Musicians **20** Still Life with a Candle **22** Les Demoiselles d'Avignon **23** Portrait of Gertrude Stein
picayune, picayunish 5 dinky, petty, small **6** flimsy, little, measly, paltry, slight **7** trivial **8** niggling, nugatory, piddling, trifling **11** unimportant **13** insignificant **14** inconsiderable **15** inconsequential
Piccini, Nicola (Piccinni, Niccola)
  born: 4 Bari **5** Italy
  composer of: 5 Didon **6** Roland **11** The Good Girl **15** La buona figliola **18** Iphigenie en Tauride
pick 3 cut **4** crop **5** cream, elect, elite, pluck, prize **6** choice, choose, detach, flower, gather, opt for, select **7** collect, fix upon, harvest, pull off, pull out, the best **9** single out **10** decide upon, favored one, preference, settle upon
picket 4 pale, post **5** fence, go out, guard, hem in, pen in, stake, watch **6** corral, paling, patrol, sentry, shut in, strike, tether, wall in **7** boycott, enclose, hedge in, lookout, striker, upright, walk out **8** blockade, palisade, restrain, restrict, sentinel **9** blockader, boycotter, protester, restraint, stanchion
picketing 5 march **7** protest **8** marching, on strike, striking **10** protesting **12** protest march **13** demonstrating, demonstration

Pickett, George E
  served in: 8 Civil War **10** Mexican War
  side: 11 Confederate
  battle: 10 Gettysburg
  famous for: 6 charge
Pickford, Mary
  real name: 15 Gladys Mary Smith
  nickname: 18 America's Sweetheart
  born: 6 Canada **7** Toronto
  husband: 16 Douglas Fairbanks **18** Charles Buddy Rogers
  roles: 4 Rags **8** Coquette (Oscar) **9** Pollyanna **19** The Taming of the Shrew **21** The Poor Little Rich Girl **23** Rebecca of Sunnybrook Farm
  home: 8 Pickfair
  memoirs: 17 Sunshine and Shadow
  formed: 13 United Artists
    partners: 10 D W Griffith **14** Charlie Chaplin **16** Douglas Fairbanks
pickings 4 loot **5** booty **6** scraps, spoils **7** plunder, takings **9** leftovers
pickle 3 fix, jam **4** corn, dill, mess, sour **6** crisis, plight, scrape **7** dilemma, gherkin, mustard **8** cucumber, hot water, quandary **9** emergency, extremity, tight spot **10** difficulty, kosher dill, pretty pass **11** predicament **14** bread-and-butter
pickled 5 drunk **6** soused **8** powdered
pick on 5 annoy, bully **6** harass, jibe at **7** torment **8** browbeat
pick out 3 see **4** espy **6** choose, descry, detect, notice, select **7** discern, make out **8** perceive **12** catch sight of
pickup 4 rise **5** boost, truck **7** advance **9** impromptu **11** improvement **12** acceleration
pick up 3 buy, get **6** gather, lift up, look up, obtain, secure **7** acquire, develop, improve, procure **8** contract, retrieve **9** cultivate, get better
Pickwick Papers
  author: 14 Charles Dickens
  character: 6 Perker, Tupman, Wardle, Winkle **9** Sam Weller, Snodgrass **10** Mrs Bardell **11** Emily Wardle **12** Alfred Jingle, Rachel Wardle **13** Arabella Allen
picky 5 fussy **6** choosy **7** finicky **10** fastidious, particular **11** persnickety **14** discriminating
Picrochole
  character in: 22 Gargantua and Pantagruel
  author: 8 Rabelais
picture 3 see **4** copy, draw, film **5** fancy, flick, image, model, movie, paint, photo, study **6** cinema, depict, double, mirror, sketch **7** believe, drawing, essence, etching, feature, imagine, paragon, portray, tintype **8** envision, likeness, painting, snapshot **9** delineate, duplicate, facsimile, portrayal, represent **10** call to mind, carbon copy, conceive of, dead ringer,

embodiment, illustrate, photograph **11** delineation **12** illustration, see in the mind **13** daguerreotype, motion picture, moving picture, spitting image **14** representation **15** exemplification, personification
Picture of Dorian Gray, The
  author: 10 Oscar Wilde
  character: 9 James Vane, Sibyl Vane **13** Basil Hallward **15** Lord Henry Wotton
picturesque 6 exotic, quaint **7** unusual **8** artistic, charming, colorful, striking **9** beautiful, pictorial **10** attractive **11** distinctive, imaginative, interesting
Picus
  origin: 5 Roman **7** Italian
  god of: 11 agriculture
  father: 6 Saturn
  associated with: 10 woodpecker
  loved by: 5 Circe
  changed into: 10 woodpecker
  son: 6 Faunus
piddling 4 puny **5** petty, small **6** flimsy, little, measly, modest, paltry, skimpy, slight **7** trivial **8** picayune, trifling **9** niggardly **11** unimportant **13** insignificant **15** inconsequential
pie 4 tart **6** pastry, quiche **7** cobbler, dessert **8** turnover
  liner: 5 crust, shell
  top: 7 lattice **8** meringue
piebald 6 motley **7** dappled, flecked, mottled, spotted **8** many-hued, speckled **10** variegated **11** many-colored, varicolored **12** multicolored, particolored
piece 3 bit, cut, fix, pat **4** blob, case, hunk, item, lump, mend, part, play, unit, work **5** chunk, drama, essay, patch, scrap, shard, share, shred, slice, story, study, thing **6** amount, entity, length, member, paring, repair, review, sample, sketch, sliver, swatch **7** article, cutting, example, patch up, portion, restore, section, segment **8** creation, division, fraction, fragment, instance, quantity, specimen **9** component, selection **11** composition
piece de resistance 13 principal dish **14** principal event
piece goods 5 cloth, goods **6** fabric **8** dry goods, material **9** yard goods
piecemeal 9 gradually **10** fragmented, one at a time **14** little by little
piece of the action 3 cut, fee **5** piece **7** portion, rake-off **10** commission, percentage
pied 6 motley **7** checked, dappled, mottled, piebald **8** colorful **9** checkered **10** variegated **11** many-colored **12** parti-colored
pied-a-terre 17 temporary dwelling
  literally: 12 foot on ground
Pied Piper
  source: 6 German, legend

town: 7 Hamelin
plague: 4 rats
charmed by: 6 piping
led away: 4 rats 8 children

Pied Piper of Hamlin, The
  author: 14 Robert Browning

pier 4 anta, dock, mole, quay, slip 5 jetty, levee, wharf 6 pillar 7 landing, support 10 breakwater

pierce 3 cut 4 hurt, pain, stab 5 drill, lance, prick, spear, spike, stick, sting, wound 6 grieve, impale 7 affront 8 distress, puncture 9 penetrate, perforate 10 cut through, run through

Pierce, Franklin
  nickname: 29 Young Hickory of the Granite Hills
  presidential rank: 10 fourteenth
  party: 8 Democrat
  state represented: 2 NH
  defeated: 4 (John Parker) Hale 5 (Winfield) Scott
  vice president: 4 (William Rufus Devane) King (died in office)
  cabinet:
    state: 5 (William Learned) Marcy
    treasury: 7 (James) Guthrie
    war: 5 (Jefferson) Davis
    attorney general: 7 (Caleb) Cushing
    navy: 6 (James Cochran) Dobbin
    postmaster general: 8 (James) Campbell
    interior: 10 (Robert) McClelland
  born: 14 Hillsborough (Hillsboro) NH
  died/buried: 9 Concord NH
  education:
    academy: 7 Hancock 11 Francestown
    college: 7 Bowdoin
    studied: 3 law
  religion: 12 Episcopalian
  political career: 8 US Senate 16 state legislature 24 US House of Representatives
  civilian career: 6 lawyer
  military service: 6 US Army 10 Mexican War 16 brigadier general
  notable events of lifetime/term:
    Act: 6 Tariff (of 1857)
    bill: 14 Kansas-Nebraska
    civil war in: 6 Kansas
    first US: 10 World's Fair
    Manifesto: 6 Ostend
    Purchase: 7 Gadsden
    treaty of: 8 Kanagawa
  father: 8 Benjamin
  mother: 4 Anna (Kendrick)
  siblings: 5 Henry, Nancy 7 Charles, Harriet 9 Charlotte 12 John Sullivan 16 Benjamin Kendrick
    half sister: 9 Elizabeth
  wife: 4 Jane (Means Appleton)
  children: 8 Benjamin, Franklin 11 Frank Robert

piercing 3 raw 4 keen, loud 5 angry, cruel, sharp 6 biting, bitter, fierce, shrill 7 caustic, cutting, furious, grating, hurtful, intense, painful, probing 8 strident 9 agonizing, deafening, searching, shrieking, torturous 10 screeching 11 penetrating 12 earsplitting, excruciating 13 ear-shattering

Pierian
  pertains to: 5 Muses

Pierian Spring
  form: 8 fountain

Pierides *see* 5 Muses

Piero della Francesca (Piero dei Franceschi)
  born: 5 Italy 16 Borgo San Sepolcro
  artwork: 12 Duke of Urbino 15 The Resurrection 18 Federigo and His Wife 19 St John the Evangelist 20 Flagellation of Christ 23 The Compassionate Madonna, The Legend of the True Cross, The Old Age and Death of Adam 24 The History of the True Cross 45 The Madonna and Saints with Frederigo da Montefeltro

Piers Plowman
  author: 15 William Langland

Pietas
  personifies: 17 familial affection

piety 7 loyalty, respect 8 devotion, humility 9 godliness, piousness, reverence 10 devoutness 11 dutifulness, religiosity 13 religiousness

pig 3 hog 5 piggy, porky, swine 6 porker 7 glutton, guzzler 8 gourmand 9 chowhound 11 gormandizer
  male: 4 boar
  female: 3 sow
  young: 5 shoat 6 piglet 11 suckling pig

pigeon
  young: 5 squab 8 squeaker

pigeonhole 4 rank, rate, type 5 brand, cubby, group, label, niche 8 category, classify 9 cubbyhole 10 categorize 11 compartment

pigheaded 6 dogged, mulish 7 willful 8 contrary, obdurate, perverse, stubborn 9 insistent, obstinate, unbending 10 bullheaded, inflexible, refractory, unyielding 11 opinionated, wrongheaded

Piglet
  character in: 13 Winnie-the-Pooh
  author: 5 Milne

pigment 3 dye 4 tint 5 color 8 coloring, dyestuff 14 coloring matter

pigmentation 5 color 9 skin color 10 coloration

pigtail 5 braid, plait, queue 8 ponytail

pike 4 bill 5 lance, spear, spike 6 poleax 7 assegai, freeway, halberd, harpoon, highway, javelin, parkway, thruway 8 autobahn, hard road, speedway, toll road, turnpike 10 expressway, interstate, throughway 12 superhighway
  British: 12 King's Highway 13 Queen's highway
  German: 8 autobahn

piker 5 miser 7 niggard, trifler 8 tightwad 9 skinflint 10 cheapskate, pinchpenny 12 penny pincher

Pilar
  character in: 19 For Whom the Bell Tolls
  author: 9 Hemingway

pilaster 4 pier 6 column, pillar 7 support, upright 8 baluster

pile 3 nap 4 heap, mass, pier, post, shag, warp 5 amass, batch, fluff, grain, hoard, mound, plush, stack, store 6 fleece, gather, piling, pillar 7 collect, pyramid, support, surface, upright 8 assemble, quantity 9 abundance, amassment, profusion, stanchion 10 accumulate, assortment, collection, foundation 11 agglomerate, aggregation, fibrousness 12 accumulation

pile up 4 bank, heap 5 amass, hoard, mound, stack 7 collect 10 accumulate

pile-up 3 jam, mob 4 mass 5 snarl 6 crowding, gridlock 10 bottleneck, congestion 11 obstruction 12 overcrowding

pilfer 3 cop, rob 4 hook, lift 5 boost, filch, heist, pinch, steal, swipe 6 finger, pirate, snitch, thieve 7 purloin 8 shoplift 10 plagiarize

pilferer 5 thief 6 robber 7 burglar 10 shoplifter, sneak thief

pilgrim, Pilgrim 4 haji 5 exile, hadji 6 palmer 7 pioneer, Puritan, settler 8 newcomer, traveler, wanderer, wayfarer 9 foreigner
  father: 5 Alden
  founder: 10 Separatist
  interpreter: 7 Squanto
  leader: 8 Standish
  protector: 7 Templar
  ship: 9 Mayflower, Speedwell

Pilgrim, Billy
  character in: 18 Slaughterhouse Five
  author: 8 Vonnegut

pilgrimage 4 hadj, trek 6 ramble, roving, voyage 7 journey, roaming, sojourn 8 long trip 9 excursion, wandering 13 peregrination
  destination: 5 Mecca 10 Canterbury

Pilgrim's Progress, The
  author: 10 John Bunyan
  character: 7 Despair, Hopeful 8 Apollyon, Faithful 9 Christian, Ignorance 10 Evangelist 14 Worldly Wiseman

pill 3 rob 4 ball, pell 5 bolus 6 bullet, pellet, tablet, pilule 7 capsule 8 medicine 9 cigarette

pillage 3 rob 4 loot, raid, sack 5 booty, rifle, strip 6 fleece, maraud, piracy, ravage, spoils 7 despoil, looting, plunder, robbery 9 filchings 10 plundering

pillager 6 looter, vandal **7** brigand **9** despoiler, plunderer

pillar 3 VIP **4** pile, post, rock **5** shaft, wheel **6** column, piling **7** obelisk, support, upright **8** champion, mainstay, pilaster, somebody **9** colonnade, stanchion

Pillars of Society, The
   author: **11** Henrik Ibsen

pillow 3 pad **7** bolster, cushion **8** headrest

pilot 4 lead **5** flyer, guide, steer **6** airman, direct, escort, fly-boy, handle, leader, manage **7** aviator, birdman, conduct, control **8** aeronaut, coxswain, helmsman, navigate, wheelman **9** accompany, sky jockey, steersman

Pilot, The
   author: **19** James Fenimore Cooper

Pima (Aatam, Pima Alto)
   language family: **10** Uto-Aztekan
   location: **7** Arizona
   related to: **6** Papago
   descendants of: **7** Hohokam

Pima Alto see **4** Pima

pin 4 bind, clip, tine **5** affix, badge, clasp, dowel, medal, prong **6** brooch, fasten, pinion, secure, skewer **8** hold down, hold fast, restrain **10** decoration
   type: **3** hat **4** push **5** stick, thole **6** breast, common, diaper, safety **8** straight

pincer 4 claw **5** chela

pinch 3 bit, cop, jam, jot, nab, nip **4** bust, crib, grab, iota, lift, mite, pain, snip, spot **5** catch, cramp, crimp, crush, filch, run in, speck, steal, swipe, trace, trial, tweak **6** arrest, clutch, collar, crisis, misery, ordeal, pickle, plight, snatch, snitch, strait, tittle **7** capture, purloin, squeeze, tighten **8** compress, exigency, hardship **9** apprehend, emergency **10** affliction, difficulty, discomfort **11** predicament

Pinch, Tom
   character in: **16** Martin Chuzzlewit
   author: **7** Dickens

pinch hitter 5 proxy **7** stand-in **9** alternate **10** substitute

pinchpenny 5 miser **6** frugal, stingy **7** niggard, prudent, thrifty
   Dickensian: **7** Scrooge

Pindar
   author of: **4** Odes **8** Epinicea

pine 3 die, ebb **4** flag, long, sigh, wilt **5** covet, crave, droop, yearn **6** desire, expire, hanker, weaken, wither **7** decline, dwindle, pant for **8** languish **9** hunger for, waste away **11** have a yen for, thirst after **12** fail in health

pine 5 Pinus
   varieties: **3** air, nut, red **4** blue, chir, gray, hoop, Huon, Imou, Jack **5**

beach, cedar, Cuban, Emodi, giant, house, Kauri, pitch, Scots, screw, scrub, shore, slash, stone, sugar, white **6** Aleppo, Apache, Bhutan, Bishop, celery, Dammar, digger, ground, Jersey, Korean, limber, Mallee, Norway, Parana, Pinyon, Scotch, spruce, Torrey, Totara, yellow **7** Amboina, Benguet, big-cone, Chilean, Chinese, cluster, Cypress, Formosa, Georgia, Gerard's, hickory, jointed, long-tag, poverty, prickly, prince's, running, Soledad **8** Austrian, Buddhist, cow's-tail, knob-cone, lacebark, Loblolly, longleaf, mahogany, Monterey, mountain, Nepal nut, oldfield, princess, umbrella **9** Brazilian, Calabrian, Chilghoza, Jerusalem, lodgepole, Oyster Bay, shortleaf, white-bark **10** Australian, Bunyabunya, dwarf stone, Macedonian, Moreton Bay, red cypress, Swiss stone, Tenasserim **11** African fern, bristlecone, common screw, Japanese red, Parry pinyon, Port Jackson, thatch screw, twisted-leaf, Veitch screw **12** black cypress, Canary Island, Chinese water, eastern white, frankincense, Italian stone, Mexican stone, Mexican white, two-leaved nut, western white **13** dwarf Siberian, Japanese black, Japanese white, Mexican yellow, New Caledonian, Norfolk Island, Swiss mountain, table mountain **14** Himalayan white, Rottnest Island, southern yellow **15** Mueller's cypress **16** Japanese umbrella, single-leaf pinyon **18** Rough-barked Mexican **19** Rocky Mountain yellow

Pine Tree State
   nickname of: **5** Maine

pin hope on 6 bank on **7** count on, long for, wish for **8** aspire to, yearn for **10** anticipate

pink 8 Dianthus
   varieties: **3** Sea **4** fire, moss, pine, rose, wild **5** cameo, clove, dairy, grass, marsh, swamp **6** button, ground, indian, Kirtle, maiden **7** cheddar, cottage, cushion, Mullein, rainbow **8** Childing, Deptford, election **11** cluster-head **13** fringed indian, spottle kirtle **16** California indian

pinnacle 3 cap, top **4** acme, apex, peak **5** crest, crown, spire, tower **6** belfry, height, summit, tiptop, vertex, zenith **7** steeple **9** bell tower, campanile

pinochle
   also known as: **7** binocle, pinocle **8** penuchle
   derived from: **7** bezique
   points/game: **11** one thousand
   lowest card: **4** nine

pinpoint 3 dot, jot **4** iota, spot **5** speck

6 detail **8** home in on, localize, zero in on **12** characterize

pint
   abbreviation of: **2** pt

pinxit 11 he painted it **12** she painted it

pioneer 5 found, start **6** create, father, herald, invent, leader **7** develop, founder **8** colonist, discover, explorer **9** be a leader, developer, establish, harbinger, innovator, precursor **10** antecedent, forerunner, lead the way, pathfinder, show the way **11** establisher, predecessor, trailblazer **12** first settler, frontiersman **13** blaze the trail **14** early immigrant, founding father
   Hebrew: **6** halutz **7** chalutz

Pioneers, The
   author: **19** James Fenimore Cooper
   character: **10** Indian John **11** Judge Temple, Natty Bumppo **13** Oliver Edwards **14** Hiram Doolittle **15** Elizabeth Temple

pious 4 holy **5** godly **6** devout, divine **7** sainted, saintly **8** faithful, reverent, unctuous **9** dedicated, insincere, pietistic, religious, spiritual **10** worshipful **11** reverential **12** hypocritical **13** rationalizing, sanctimonious, self-righteous **14** holier-than-thou

Pip
   character in: **17** Great Expectations
   author: **7** Dickens

pipe 4 duct, main, peep, sing, tube **5** cheep, chirp, trill, tweet **6** warble **7** conduit, twitter, whistle **8** conveyor **9** conductor **10** play a flute **12** play a bagpipe

Pippa Passes
   author: **14** Robert Browning

piquant 3 hot **4** acid, racy **5** peppy, salty, sharp, spicy, tangy, zesty **6** biting, bitter, bright, clever, lively, savory **7** mordant, peppery, pungent, rousing **8** animated, incisive, piercing, spirited, stinging, vigorous **9** sparkling, trenchant **11** interesting, provacative, stimulating **13** scintillating **14** highly seasoned, strong-flavored

pique 3 ire, irk, vex **4** gall, goad, miff, snit, spur, stir **5** annoy, peeve, rouse, spite **6** arouse, excite, grudge, kindle, malice, nettle, offend **7** affront, incense, perturb, provoke, quicken, umbrage **8** disquiet, irritate, vexation **9** annoyance, displease, stimulate **10** discomfort, exasperate, irritation, resentment **11** displeasure, humiliation, ill feelings, indignation **12** exasperation, hurt feelings **13** embarrassment, mortification, put one's back up **14** vindictiveness

piqued 5 angry, riled, vexed **6** galled, miffed, peeved **7** annoyed, aroused, excited, kindled, nettled, stirred **9** affronted, irritated **10** displeased, stimulated

Pirandello, Luigi

author of: 17 The Old and the Young **18** Tonight We Improvise **19** The Late Mattia Pascal **31** Six Characters in Search of an Author

pirate 3 rob **5** steal **6** raider, robber, sea dog **7** brigand, corsair, plunder **8** marauder **9** buccaneer, privateer **10** freebooter
  flag: 9 blackjack **10** Jolly Roger
  name: 4 Kidd **6** Morgan **7** Lafitte **10** Blackbeard

Pirate Coast see **18** United Arab Emirates

Pirates of Penzance, The

author: 9 W S Gilbert
comic opera by: 18 Gilbert and Sullivan
character: 4 Kate, Ruth **5** Edith, Mabel **6** Isabel **8** Frederic, Sergeant **10** Pirate King **14** General Stanley

pis aller 10 last resort **12** last resource

Pisan Cantos

author: 9 Ezra Pound

Pisanio

character in: 9 Cymbeline
author: 11 Shakespeare

Pisces

symbol: 4 fish
planet: 7 Jupiter, Neptune
rules: 7 secrets
born: 13 February-March

Pisistratus

tyrant of: 6 Athens
father: 11 Hippocrates
son: 7 Hippias **10** Hipparchus

Pissarro, Camille

born: 8 St Thomas **16** Danish West Indies
artwork: 8 Red Roofs **15** Morning Sunlight **21** Lower Norwood Snow Scene **28** Peasant Woman with a Wheelbarrow

pistol (revolver) 3 gat, gun, rod **4** colt, iron **5** luger **6** heater, mauser **7** firearm, sidearm **9** automatic, derringer **20** Saturday night special

pit 3 dip, nut **4** dent, hole, nick, pock, scar, seed **5** gouge, gully, match, notch, stone **6** cavity, crater, dimple, furrow, hollow, indent, kernel, oppose, trough **7** scratch **8** contrast, pockmark **9** concavity, juxtapose **10** depression, set against **11** indentation

Pit, The

author: 11 Frank Norris

Pit and the Pendulum, The

author: 13 Edgar Allan Poe

pitch 3 bob, dip, fix, lob, set, shy, top **4** apex, cant, cast, fall, fire, hurl, jerk, jolt, peak, rock, tone, toss **5** angle, chuck, crown, erect, fling, grade, heave, level, lurch, place, plant, point, raise, set up, shake, slant, sling, slope, sound, throw **6** degree, height, let fly, locate, plunge, propel, settle, summit, topple, tumble, zenith **7** bob-

bing, incline, rocking, station **8** delivery, harmonic, lurching, pinnacle, undulate **9** declivity, establish, oscillate **10** undulation **11** oscillation **12** fall headlong

speed of: 9 vibration

pitcher 3 jar, jug **4** ewer **6** carafe **8** decanter **9** container **10** spitballer
  and catcher: 7 battery
  award: 7 Cy Young
  brother duo: 4 Dean **5** Perry **6** Niekro
  Hall of Famer: 4 Dean, Ford, Wynn **5** Young **6** Hunter, Koufax, Palmer, Willis **7** Carlton, Fingers **8** Drysdale **9** Newhouser
  left-hander: 8 southpaw
  relief staff: 7 bullpen
  reliever: 7 fireman

pitch in 5 begin **7** share in **8** take part **9** cooperate, get to work, join hands **10** act jointly, contribute, get started **11** collaborate, participate **12** make an effort, pull together, work together

pitch into 5 fly at **6** assail, have at **7** assault, set upon

piteous 3 sad **6** moving, woeful **7** pitiful **8** pathetic, pitiable, poignant, touching **9** affecting **10** deplorable **11** distressing **12** heart-rending **13** heartbreaking

pitfall 4 risk, trap **5** peril, snare **6** ambush, danger, hazard **7** springe **8** quagmire **9** booby trap, quicksand **14** stumbling block

pith 4 core, gist, meat **5** heart, point **7** essence, meaning **12** significance

pithy 5 terse **6** cogent **7** concise **8** forceful, succinct **9** effective, trenchant **10** expressive, meaningful, to the point **12** concentrated

pitiful 3 sad **4** poor **5** sorry **6** abject, measly, moving, paltry, shabby **7** doleful, forlorn, piteous **8** dreadful, god- awful, mournful, pathetic, pitiable, poignant, touching, wretched **9** miserable, plaintive, worthless **10** abominable, despicable, lamentable **11** distressing **12** arousing pity, contemptible, heartrending

pitiless 5 cruel **6** brutal **7** inhuman, unmoved **8** ruthless, uncaring **9** heartless, merciless, unpitying, unsparing, untouched **10** implacable, relentless, unmerciful **11** cold-blooded, hardhearted, indifferent, insensitive, unrelenting

pittance 4 mite **5** crumb **6** little, trifle **7** minimum, modicum, smidgen

Pittsburgh

baseball team: 7 Pirates
feature: 14 Fort Pitt Museum **15** Buhl Planetarium
football team: 8 Steelers
formerly: 8 Fort Pitt **12** Fort Duquesne
hockey team: 8 Penguins

noted for: 5 steel
river: 4 Ohio **9** Allegheny **11** Monongahela
university: 8 Duquesne **14** Carnegie-Mellon

Pittypat, Aunt

character in: 15 Gone With the Wind
author: 8 Mitchell

pituitary

located in: 5 brain
known as: 11 master gland

pity 5 mercy, shame **6** lament, lenity, regret **7** charity, feel for, weep for **8** bleed for, clemency, humanity, leniency, sad thing, sympathy **10** compassion, condolence, indulgence, kindliness, tenderness **11** crying shame, forbearance, magnanimity **12** feel sorry for **13** commiseration

piu

music: 4 more

pivot 4 axis, axle, hang, rely, spin, turn **5** focus, hinge, twirl, wheel, whirl **6** center, circle, depend, rotate, swivel **7** fulcrum, hinge on, revolve **9** pirouette

pivotal 5 vital **7** crucial **8** critical, decisive **9** climactic **11** determining

pivotal point 4 axis **12** turning point **13** crucial moment

pixie, pixy 3 elf **5** fairy **6** sprite **10** leprechaun

pizazz 5 flair, vigor, style **6** energy, spirit **8** vitality

pizzicato

music: 21 plucked instead of bowed
abbreviation: 4 pizz

placable 7 lenient **8** flexible, tolerant, yielding **9** indulgent, relenting **10** appeasable, forbearing **12** reconcilable

placard 4 bill, sign **6** notice, poster **8** bulletin **13** advertisement

placate 4 calm, lull **5** quiet **6** pacify, soothe **7** appease, assuage, mollify, win over **9** alleviate **10** conciliate, propitiate

placatory 9 appeasing, pacifying **10** mollifying **12** conciliatory **13** accommodative

place 3 fix, job, put, set **4** area, city, digs, duty, farm, firm, home, land, plot, post, rank, rest, shop, site, spot, town, zone **5** abode, affix, array, berth, house, lodge, niche, plant, point, ranch, space, stand, state, store, venue **6** assign, attach, county, harbor, invest, locale, locate, office, region, settle **7** appoint, borough, company, concern, country, deposit, install, quarter, shelter, situate, station, village **8** building, business, classify, district, domicile, dwelling, ensconce, find hire, function, identify, locality, location, lodgings, position, premises, property, province, quarters, remember, standing, township, vicinity **9** recognize, residence, situation, territory **10** commission, get a job for, habitation **11** appointment, find work for, whereabouts **12** neighborhood **13** establishment

Latin: 4 situ

Place in the Sun, A
   director: 13 George Stevens
   based on novel by: 15 Theodore Dreiser (An American Tragedy)
   cast: 14 Keefe Brasselle, Shelley Winters **15** Elizabeth Taylor, Montgomery Clift
   Oscar for: 5 score **9** direction **10** screenplay

placement 8 grouping, location **10** assignment, employment **11** arrangement, disposition, positioning

place of residence 4 home **5** abode, house **7** address, lodging **8** domicile, dwelling **9** residence **10** habitation **14** living quarters

place to stand on
   Greek: 6 pou sto

place upright 5 erect, raise **7** stand up

placid 4 calm, mild **5** quiet **6** gentle, poised, serene, smooth **7** pacific, restful **8** composed, peaceful, tranquil **9** collected, unexcited, unruffled **10** untroubled **11** undisturbed, unexcitable **13** imperturbable, self-possessed **15** undemonstrative

plague 3 irk, vex, woe **4** bane, evil, fret, gall, pain, pest **5** agony, chafe, curse, harry, haunt, peeve, worry **6** badger, blight, bother, burden, cancer, harass, misery, nettle **7** afflict, disturb, perturb, scourge, torment, trouble **8** aggrieve, calamity, disquiet, distress, hardship, pandemic **9** embarrass, persecute, suffering **10** affliction, Black Death, pestilence, visitation

French: 5 peste

Plague, The
   author: 11 Albert Camus
   character: 7 Rambert **10** Jean Tarrou **11** Joseph Grand **14** Father Paneloux, Raymond Cottard **15** Dr Bernard R Rieux

plain 4 bald, bare, open **5** blunt, clear, frank, naked, vivid **6** candid, common, direct, homely, honest, modest, simple **7** average, glaring, legible, obscure, obvious, plateau, prairie, sincere, visible **8** apparent, clear-cut, distinct, everyday, explicit, manifest, ordinary, palpable, specific, straight, striking, uncomely, unlovely **9** grassland, outspoken, prominent, tableland, unadorned, undiluted **10** forthright, pronounced, unaffected, unassuming, unhandsome, unreserved, well-marked **11** commonplace, conspicuous, discernible, not striking, open country, outstanding, plain-spoken, unambigu-

ous, undecorated, undisguised, unequivocal, ungarnished, unvarnished, well-defined **12** matter-of- fact, not beautiful, unattractive, unmistakable, unornamented **13** unembellished, unpretentious, without frills **14** comprehensible, understandable **15** straightforward, undistinguished

plainly 6 baldly, openly, simply **7** bluntly, clearly, frankly, visibly, vividly **8** candidly, directly, honestly, markedly, modestly **9** doubtless, obviously **10** apparently, definitely, distinctly, explicitly, manifestly, ordinarily, positively, strikingly, undeniably **11** beyond doubt, discernibly, prominently, undoubtedly **12** unaffectedly, unassumingly, unmistakably, without doubt **13** conspicuously, unambiguously, unequivocally **14** comprehensibly, unquestionably

plainness 10 homeliness, simplicity **12** ordinariness

plainspoken 4 open **5** bluff, blunt, frank, plain **6** candid, direct, honest **7** genuine, sincere **8** explicit, straight **9** open-faced, outspoken, unsparing **10** above board, forthright, point-blank **11** straight-out **15** straightforward

plaint 3 cry, sob **4** beef, moan, wail **5** gripe **6** charge, grouse, grudge, lament, regret, squawk **7** grumble, reproof **8** reproach **9** complaint, grievance, objection **10** accusation, resentment **12** remonstrance

plaintive 3 sad **6** rueful **7** doleful, moaning, piteous, pitiful, tearful **8** dolorous, grievous, mournful, pathetic, wretched **9** lamenting, sorrowful, woebegone **10** lugubrious, melancholy **12** heartrending

plait 5 braid, queue, twine, twist, weave **7** pigtail **10** intertwine

plan 3 aim, map, way **4** form, idea, plot **5** frame, shape **6** design, devise, intend, lay out, map out, method, scheme, sketch **7** diagram, outline, prepare, program, project, propose, purpose **8** block out, conceive, contrive, organize, proposal, strategy, think out **9** blueprint, fabricate, procedure, stratagem **10** conception, suggestion **11** proposition

French: 8 demarche

Planchet
   character in: 18 The Three Musketeers
   author: 5 Dumas (pere)

Planck, Max
   field: 7 physics
   nationality: 6 German
   developed: 13 quantum theory **15** Planck's constant
   awarded: 10 Nobel Prize

plane 3 jet **4** bird, flat **5** level, plumb **6** degree, status **7** regular, station **8** aircraft, airplane, position, standing **9**

condition, elevation

type: 4 jack **5** block

planet, planets 13 celestial body
   first: 7 Mercury
   second: 5 Venus
   third: 5 Earth
      satellite: 4 Moon
   fourth: 4 Mars
      satellite: 6 Deimos, Phobos
      nickname: 9 Red Planet
   fifth: 7 Jupiter
      satellite: 2 Io **6** Europa **8** Amalthea, Callisto, Ganymede
      characteristic: 7 red spot
   sixth: 6 Saturn
      satellite: 4 Rhea **5** Dione, Janus, Mimas, Titan **6** Phoebe, Tethys **7** Iapetus **8** Hyperion **9** Enceladus
      characteristic: 5 rings
   seventh: 6 Uranus
      satellite: 5 Ariel **6** Oberon **7** Miranda, Titania, Umbriel
      color: 9 blue-green
      characteristic: 5 rings
   eighth: 7 Neptune
      satellite: 6 Nereid, Triton
      color: 5 green
   ninth: 5 Pluto
      satellite: 6 Charon
   asteroid/minor planet/planetoid: 4 Eros, Juno **5** Ceres, Vesta **6** Chiron, Hermes, Icarus, Pallas **7** Astraea, Hidalgo

planetary 6 astral **7** earthly **9** celestial **11** terrestrial **12** astronomical

Planet of the Apes
   director: 18 Franklin J Schaffner
   based on novel by: 12 Pierre Boulle
   cast: 9 Kim Hunter **12** Maurice Evans **13** Roddy McDowall **14** Charlton Heston
   script: 10 Rod Serling

plank 4 deal, deck, slab **5** board, shole, stone **8** platform

planned 7 devised, schemed **8** designed, expected, foreseen, intended, prepared **9** mapped out, organized, projected, rehearsed **10** calculated, purposeful, thought out **11** intentional, prearranged, prepared for **12** premeditated

planner 6 author, framer **7** creator, deviser **8** arranger, designer **9** architect, organizer

plant 4 bush, herb, mill, moss, shop, slip, tree, vine, weed, wort, yard **5** algae, flora, fungi, grass, set in, shrub, works **6** flower, foster, infuse, set out **7** factory, foundry, herbage, implant, inspire, instill, scatter, sow seed **8** business, engender, seedling **9** broadcast, cultivate, establish, inculcate, propagate, vegetable **10** transplant, vegetation **13** establishment, sow the seeds of **14** put in the ground

plaster 4 coat, daub, sand **5** grout, smear **6** bedaub, gypsum, lather,

stucco **7** overlay, spackle
mixture of: 4 lime **5** water **6** gypsum

plastered 5 drunk **6** coated, daubed, soused **7** covered, crocked, smeared, swacked **8** mortared, polluted, stuccoed **10** inebriated **11** intoxicated

plastic 4 soft **6** pliant, supple **7** ductile, elastic, pliable **8** flexible, formable, moldable, shapable, yielding **9** malleable, tractable

plate 4 dish **6** saucer **7** helping, platter, portion, serving **10** platterful **11** serving dish

plateau 4 mesa **5** table **6** upland **8** highland **9** tableland

platform 4 dais, goal, plan **5** creed, plank, stage, stand **6** podium, policy, pulpit, tenets **7** program, rostrum

Plath, Sylvia
author of: 5 Ariel **10** The Bell Jar

platinum
chemical symbol: 2 Pt

platitude 3 saw **6** cliche, old saw, truism **7** bromide **8** banality, chestnut **11** commonplace

platitudinous 5 banal, corny, stale, tired, trite, vapid **6** jejune **8** bromidic, ordinary **9** hackneyed **10** pedestrian, unexciting, unoriginal **12** clicheridden, conventional **13** unimaginative

Plato
author of: 4 Laws **5** Crito **6** Phaedo **7** Apology, Gorgias, Sophist, Timaeus **8** Philebus, Republic **9** Symposium **10** Parmenides

platoon 4 band, body, crew, team, unit **5** corps, force, group **10** detachment

platter 4 dish, disk, lanx **6** salver **7** record **8** trencher **9** recording

plaudit, plaudits 4 rave **5** cheer, kudos **6** hurrah, huzzah, praise **7** acclaim, bouquet, ovation **8** applause, approval, cheering **10** compliment, hallelujah **11** approbation **12** commendation

plauditory 8 admiring, praising **9** extolling, laudatory, praiseful **12** commendatory **13** complimentary

plausible 5 sound, valid **6** likely **7** logical, tenable **8** credible, feasible, possible, probable, rational, sensible **10** acceptable, believable, convincing, persuasive, reasonable **11** conceivable, justifiable

Plautus
author of: 7 Stichus **8** Mercator **9** Amphitruo, Menaechmi, Pseudolus **10** Amphitryon **14** Miles Gloriosus

play 3 act, fun, toy **4** jest, lark, romp, room, show **5** antic, caper, drama, enact, farce, frisk, revel, space, sport, sweep, swing **6** act out, cavort, comedy, frolic, gambol, leeway, trifle **7** disport, have fun, pageant, perform, skylark, tragedy, vie with **8** pleasure,

take part **9** amusement, diversion, elbowroom, enjoyment, make merry, melodrama, perform on, personify, represent, spectacle **10** recreation **11** impersonate, merrymaking

playboy 4 rake, wolf **5** Romeo, sheik **6** lecher **7** Don Juan, swinger **8** Casanova, hedonist, Lothario, party boy **9** jet-setter, ladies' man, partygoer, womanizer **10** lady-killer, profligate **14** pleasure seeker **15** good-time Charlie

Playboy of the Western World, The
author: 19 John Millington Synge
character: 8 Old Mahon **9** Widow Quin **10** Shawn Keogh **16** Christopher Mahon, Margaret Flaherty (Pegeen)

play down 9 underplay **11** deemphasize

played out 4 beat **5** all in, spent, weary **6** bushed, done in, pooped **7** drained, wearied, worn out **8** depleted, dog tired, fatigued, tired out, unreeled **9** dead tired, exhausted

player 4 jock, mime **5** actor **6** mummer **7** actress, athlete, trouper **8** gamester, opponent, thespian **9** adversary, contender, performer **10** antagonist, competitor, contestant, team member **11** entertainer, participant

play false 4 dupe **5** trick **6** betray **7** deceive, two-time **10** be disloyal **12** be unfaithful **13** be treacherous

playfellow 3 pal **4** chum **5** buddy **6** friend **8** playmate

playful 6 frisky, impish, lively **7** amusing, coltish, jesting, waggish **8** humorous, mirthful, prankish, sportive **9** fun-loving, sprightly **10** capricious, frolicsome, rollicking **12** lighthearted
French: 8 espiegle

play host 4 host **9** entertain **10** give a party, have guests **13** keep open house

playing field 4 bowl **5** arena **7** diamond, stadium **8** gridiron **10** playground **12** amphitheater

playing piece 3 man **4** disk **5** piece **7** counter

play in water 3 dip **4** swim **6** dabble, paddle, splash

play Judas 6 betray **7** sell out, two-time **9** play false **11** double-cross

playmate 3 pal **4** chum **5** buddy **6** friend **10** playfellow

play of spirit
French: 10 jeu d'esprit

play on words
French: 3 pun **9** jeu de mots

plaything 3 toy **4** dupe **5** patsy, sport **6** bauble, trifle **9** diversion

play truant 3 cut **4** skip **8** be absent **9** play hooky

play with 5 bandy **7** torment, toy with **11** have fun with

playwright 6 author, writer **9** dramatist, scenarist **10** dramatizer, dramaturge, librettist, play doctor **12** dramatic poet, dramaturgist, scriptwriter **13** melodramatist

plea 4 suit **5** alibi **6** appeal, excuse, prayer **7** apology, begging, defense, pretext, request **8** argument, entreaty, petition **10** adjuration, beseeching **11** explanation, extenuation, vindication **12** solicitation, supplication **13** justification

plead 3 ask, beg **6** adjure, enjoin **7** beseech, entreat, implore, request, solicit **8** appeal to, petition **9** importune **10** supplicate

pleader 6 beggar **8** advocate, defender, implorer **9** apologist, beseecher **10** importuner, supplicant

plead with 3 beg **4** pray **6** adjure **7** beseech, implore **10** supplicate

Pleasance, Donald
born: 7 England, Worksop
roles: 12 The Caretaker **14** The Great Escape **16** You Only Live Twice **17** The Eagle Has Landed **24** The Greatest Story Ever Told

pleasant 4 fine, good, mild, nice, soft, warm **6** genial, gentle, lovely, polite **7** affable, amiable, cordial, likable, tactful **8** amicable, charming, cheerful, friendly, inviting, pleasing, sociable **9** agreeable, congenial, enjoyable **10** attractive, felicitous, gratifying, gregarious, satisfying **11** good-humored, good-natured, pleasurable **13** companionable

Pleasant Island see **5** Nauru

pleasantry 4 jape, jest, joke, quip **5** sally **6** bon mot **8** greeting **9** wisecrack, witticism **10** salutation

pleasant-tasting 4 mild **5** sweet, tasty **6** savory **8** luscious **9** delicious, palatable, succulent **10** appetizing, delectable **11** scrumptious **13** mouthwatering

please 3 opt **4** like, suit, want, will, wish **5** amuse, charm, elate, elect **6** choose, desire, divert, prefer, thrill, tickle **7** content, delight, gladden, gratify, satisfy **8** enthrall, entrance **9** enrapture, entertain, fascinate, make happy **10** be inclined **14** give pleasure to
French: 12 s'il vous plait
German: 5 bitte
Spanish: 8 por favor

pleased 4 glad **5** happy, proud **6** elated **8** thrilled **9** delighted, gratified

please reply
French: 4 rsvp **20** repondez s'il vous plait

pleasing 6 genial, polite **7** affable, amiable, amusing, likable, winning **8** charming, cheerful, friendly, inviting, mannerly **9** agreeable, congenial, diverting, enjoyable **10** attractive, delightful, gladdening, gratifying, satisfying **11** captivating, fascinating, good-humored, good- natured, pleasurable **12** entertaining, well-mannered

pleasing inactivity
Italian: **14** dolce far niente

pleasurable 8 pleasing **9** agreeable, enjoyable **10** delightful

pleasure 3 fun, joy **4** like, will, wish **5** bliss, cheer, mirth **6** choice, desire, gaiety, option **7** delight, elation, rapture **9** amusement, diversion, enjoyment, festivity, happiness, merriment, selection **10** exultation, jubilation, preference, recreation **11** high spirits, inclination **13** entertainment, gratification **15** beer and skittles **16** lightheartedness
goddess of: 8 Voluptas

pleasure-giving 7 amusing **8** pleasing **9** agreeable, enjoyable **10** delightful **11** pleasurable **12** entertaining

Pleasure of His Company, The
author: **19** Cornelia Otis Skinner

pleasure trip 4 tour **5** jaunt **6** outing **8** vacation **9** excursion

pleat 4 fold **5** crimp, frill **6** crease

pleated 6 fluted, folded **7** creased, crimped **10** corrugated

plebeian 3 low **4** base, mean **5** banal **6** coarse, common, vulgar **7** lowborn, lowbrow, popular **8** commoner, everyman, low-class, ordinary **9** bourgeois, common man, unrefined **10** average man, uncultured **11** bourgeoisie, commonplace, proletarian **12** uncultivated

plebs 5 demos **6** masses **7** commons **8** populace **9** commoners, hoi polloi, plebeians **11** bourgeoisie **12** common people

plecoptera
class: **8** hexapoda
phylum: **10** arthropoda
group: **8** stone fly

pledge 3 vow **4** bail, bond, oath, pact, pawn, word **5** swear, troth **6** assert, avowal, surety **7** compact, promise, warrant **8** contract, covenant, guaranty, security, warranty **9** agreement, assurance, guarantee **10** adjuration, collateral

Pleiades
father: **5** Atlas
mother: **7** Pleione
half-sisters: **6** Hyades
names: **4** Maia **6** Merope **7** Alcyone, Celaeno, Electra, Sterope, Taygete
number of daughters: **5** seven

plenary 4 full **6** entire **7** perfect **8** absolute, complete

plenitude 4 glut, heap, mass **5** flood **6** bounty, plenty, wealth **7** quality, surfeit, surplus **8** fullness, plethora, totality **9** abundance, amplitude, profu-

sion, repletion, wholeness **10** cornucopia, entireness, quantities **11** ample supply, copiousness, full measure, sufficiency **12** completeness **14** more than enough

plenteous 6 lavish **7** copious, profuse **8** abundant **9** bountiful, plentiful

plentiful 4 lush **5** ample, large **6** lavish **7** copious, liberal, profuse **8** abundant, generous, infinite, prolific **9** abounding, bounteous, bountiful, plenteous, unsparing, unstinted **11** overflowing **13** inexhaustible

plenty 4 gobs, lots, slew **5** scads **6** luxury, oceans, oodles, riches, wealth, worlds **8** opulence **9** abundance, affluence, good times, great deal, plenitude, profusion, well-being **10** prosperity **11** ample amount, good fortune, sufficiency **12** a full measure
goddess of: **3** Ops

plethora 4 glut **5** flood **6** excess, wealth **7** overage, surfeit, surplus **8** fullness **9** abundance, amplitude, plenitude, profusion **10** oversupply, redundancy, surplusage **11** superfluity **13** overabundance **14** more than enough, superabundance

pliable 5 lithe **6** limber, pliant, supple **7** elastic, plastic, springy, willing **8** flexible, yielding **9** adaptable, compliant, receptive, resilient, tractable **10** manageable, responsive, submissive **11** acquiescent **13** accommodating **14** easily bendable, impressionable

pliancy 8 docility, meekness, yielding **9** passivity **10** compliance, pliability, submission, suppleness **11** flexibility **12** complaisance

pliant 4 meek **6** supple **7** pliable **8** flexible, yielding **9** compliant **10** submissive **11** deferential

pliers
type: **10** fixed-joint **11** combination, needle-nosed, side- cutting **17** offset combination

plight 3 fix, jam **5** pinch, state, trial **6** crisis, muddle, pickle, scrape **7** dilemma, impasse, straits, trouble **8** distress, exigency **9** condition, emergency, extremity, situation **10** difficulty **11** predicament, tribulation, vicissitude **12** circumstance

Plisthenes
brother/half-brother: **8** Menelaus **9** Agamemnon
father: **6** Atreus
mother: **6** Cleola
sister/half-sister: **8** Anaxibia
sister-in-law: **12** Clytemnestra
uncle: **8** Thyestes

plod 4 drag, grub, moil, plug, slog, toil **5** grind, sweat, tramp **6** drudge, lumber, trudge, waddle **7** peg away, shuffle **8** struggle **9** persevere

plodding 4 dull **6** clumsy **8** trudging **9** laborious **10** pedestrian

plot 3 lot, map **4** area, draw, mark, plan, tale, yarn **5** chart, draft, field, patch, space, story, tract **6** action, design, scheme, sketch **7** collude, compute, diagram, outline, section **8** clearing, conspire, contrive, evil plan, intrigue, maneuver **9** blueprint, calculate, determine, incidents, narrative, story line, stratagem **10** conspiracy, secret plan **11** machination

plotting 4 wily **6** artful, crafty **7** cunning **8** scheming **9** conniving, designing **10** intriguing

Plough and the Stars, The
author: **10** Sean O'Casey

plover
group of: **4** wing **12** congregation

plow, plough 3 cut, dig **4** push, till, work **5** break, dig up, drive, forge, press, shove, spade **6** furrow, harrow, loosen, plunge, turn up **7** break up **8** bulldoze **9** cultivate
invented by:
cast iron: **7** Ransome
disc: **5** Hardy

plowable 6 arable **7** friable **8** farmable, tillable **10** cultivable

Plowright, Joan
born: **5** Brigg **7** England
husband: **15** Laurence Olivier
roles: **13** A Taste of Honey **14** The Entertainer

ploy 4 game, ruse, wile **5** trick **6** design, gambit, scheme, tactic **7** gimmick **8** artifice, maneuver, strategy **9** stratagem **10** subterfuge

pluck 4 draw, grab, grit, guts, jerk, pick, sand, yank **5** spunk, valor **6** daring, mettle, pull at, snatch, spirit, uproot **7** bravery, courage, pull off, pull out, resolve **8** boldness, temerity, tenacity **9** extirpate, fortitude **10** doggedness, resolution **11** persistence **12** perseverance **13** determination

pluck out 7 extract, pick out, pull out

plucky 4 bold, game **5** brave, gutsy **6** daring, spunky **7** doughty, valiant **8** fearless, intrepid, spirited, unafraid, valorous **9** audacious, dauntless, undaunted **10** courageous, mettlesome **11** lionhearted, unflinching **12** stouthearted

plug 4 bung, cork **5** close, stuff **6** fill up, stanch, stop up **7** shut off, stopper, stopple

plug up 3 dam **4** clog, plug **5** block, choke, dam up, stuff **6** stop up **7** congest **8** obstruct

plum
varieties: **3** hog **4** Coco, date, Duhr, gage, Java, sand, sloe, wild **5** beach, black, goose, Islay, Jaman, Lansa, Moxie, nanny, Natal, shore, Simon **6** August, Batoko, Canada, Cheney, cherry, common, Damson, ground, Indian, Jambul, Kaffir, Kelsey, Lomboy, Pigeon, Sapote, Sierra, Sisson **7**

apricot, Burbank, Cheston, Jambosa, Malabar, Orleans, Pacific, Spanish, Wickson **8** American, Assyrian, Burdekin, European, Hortulan, Jambolan, Japanese, Oklahoma, Prunello, Victoria **9** Allegheny, Chickasaw, Governor's, greengage, marmalade, Myrobalan, wild-goose **10** Madagascar **13** Queensland hog

plumb 4 lead, test, true **5** gauge, level, probe, sheer, sound **6** fathom **7** examine, measure, plummet **8** plumb bob, straight, vertical **9** penetrate

plume 3 pen **4** down **5** egret, pique, preen, pride, prize, quill **7** feather
military: **7** panache

Plumed Serpent, The
author: **10** D H Lawrence

Plummer, Christopher
real name: **28** Arthur Christopher Orme Plummer
born: **6** Canada **7** Toronto
wife: **11** Tammy Grimes **12** Elaine Taylor
roles: **14** Murder by Decree **15** The Sound of Music **18** Baron Georg von Trapp **20** The Man Who Would Be King **25** The Return of the Pink Panther

plummet 4 dive, fall **6** plunge, tumble **8** nosedive **12** fall headlong

plump 4 drop, firm, flop, plop, sink **5** blunt, buxom, obese, plunk, pudgy, solid, spill, stout **6** abrupt, chubby, direct, fleshy, portly, rotund, sprawl, stocky, tumble **7** rounded **8** collapse, outright **9** corpulent

plumpness
French: **10** embonpoint

plunder 3 rob **4** haul, loot, raid, sack, swag, take **5** booty, rifle, prize, strip **6** fleece, maraud, pilfer, ravage, spoils **7** despoil, pillage, ransack, takings **9** filchings **10** pilferings

plunderer 6 looter, vandal **7** brigand **8** pillager **9** despoiler

plunge 3 dip, fly, run **4** bolt, cast, dart, dash, dive, drop, duck, fall, jerk, roll, jump, leap, push, reel, rock, rush, sink, sway, tear, toss **5** douse, drive, heave, lunge, lurch, pitch, press, shoot, speed, surge, swarm, whisk **6** charge, hasten, hurtle, hustle, scurry, sprint, streak, thrust, tumble **7** descend, immerse, scuttle **8** scramble, submerge, submerse **12** fall headlong

plunk 4 pick, thud **5** pluck, plumb, strum, twang **6** dollar **7** exactly **8** squarely **9** precisely

plurality 4 bulk, most **8** majority **13** preponderance

plus 5 added, extra, other, spare **6** useful **7** helpful **9** auxiliary, desirable **10** additional, beneficial **12** advantageous, supplemental **13** supplementary

plush 4 lush, posh, rich **5** fancy, grand,

ritzy, swank, thick **6** classy, deluxe, lavish, snazzy, swanky **7** elegant, opulent **8** palatial **9** luxurious, sumptuous **11** extravagant

plushy 4 soft **5** cushy, swank **7** opulent, velvety **9** luxurious, sumptuous

Plutarch
author of: **13** Parallel Lives

Plutarch's Lives
author: **8** Plutarch

Pluto
also: **5** Hades
god of: **10** underworld
corresponds to: **3** Dis **5** Orcus **8** Dis Pater

Pluto
position: **5** ninth
satellite: **6** Charon

plutocrat 5 mogul **6** fat cat, tycoon **9** financier **10** capitalist

plutonic 7 abyssal, igneous **9** cimmerian, intrusive, vulcanian

plutonium
chemical symbol: **2** Pu

Plutus
author: **12** Aristophanes
character: **5** Cario **9** Chremylus **11** Blepsidemus
god of: **6** wealth

Plutus
personifies: **6** wealth
father: **6** Iasion
mother: **7** Demeter

Pluvius
epithet of: **7** Jupiter
realm: **4** rain

ply 3 fly, run **4** leaf, sail, work **5** layer, offer, plait, plate, press, sheet, slice, twist, wield **6** employ, follow, handle, lamina, pursue, sheath, strand, supply **7** besiege, carry on, labor at, operate, stratum, utilize **8** exercise, navigate, practice, put to use, urge upon **9** thickness **10** manipulate

poach 3 rob **4** cook **5** shirr, steal **6** plunge, simmer **7** trample **8** encroach, trespass

pocket 3 bag, get, pit **4** gain, lode, sack, vein **5** pouch, purse, pygmy, small, steal, strip, usurp **6** attain, bantam, cavity, come by, hollow, little, obtain, pilfer, strain, streak **7** chamber, compact, handbag, placket, receive **8** arrogate, envelope, portable **9** miniature **10** diminutive, receptacle **11** appropriate, compartment

Pocket, Herbert
character in: **17** Great Expectations
author: **7** Dickens

pocketbook 3 bag **5** pouch, purse **6** clutch, wallet **7** handbag, satchel **8** moneybag, notecase **9** coin purse **10** money purse **11** shoulder bag
French: **12** porte-monnaie

pocket flask 5 flask **6** bottle **7** canteen

pocket-sized 3 wee **4** tiny **5** dwarf, pygmy, small **6** bantam, little, midget, minute, petite **7** compact **9** miniature **10** diminutive, vest-pocket

poco
music: **6** little

Pocock, Mamie
character in: **14** The Ambassadors
author: **5** James

pod 4 case, hull, husk **5** shell **6** jacket, sheath **8** pericarp, seed case **10** seed vessel

Podgorica
capital of: **10** Montenegro
once called: Titograd

podium 4 dais, foot, wall **5** stipe **7** lectern **8** pedestal, platform **9** footstalk

Poe, Edgar Allan
author of: **6** Ligeia **7** Israfel, To Helen **8** The Bells, The Raven **10** Annabel Lee, The Gold Bug **18** The Purloined Letter **20** The Cask of Amontillado, The Pit and the Pendulum **22** The Masque of the Red Death **24** The Fall of the House of Usher, The Murders in the Rue Morgue **29** The Narrative of Arthur Gordon Pym

Poeas
also: **5** Poias
lit: **11** funeral pyre
pyre of: **8** Hercules
son: **11** Philoctetes

poem 3 lay, ode **4** epic, song **5** elegy, idyll, lyric, rhyme, verse **6** ballad, jingle, sonnet **8** doggerel, limerick, madrigal

Poema del Cid see **6** The Cid

Poems Chiefly in the Scottish Dialect
author: **11** Robert Burns

poet 4 bard **5** maker **6** lyrist, rhymer, singer **7** reciter **8** lyricist, minstrel, verseman **9** balladeer, balladist, poetaster, rhymester, sonneteer, versifier **10** improviser, librettist, songwriter

poetaster 4 bard, poet **6** rhymer, writer **8** poetizer, rimester **9** rhymester, versifier

poetic, poetical 5 lyric **7** lilting, lyrical, melodic, musical **8** metrical, rhythmic, songlike **9** melodious **11** imaginative

Poetics
author: **9** Aristotle

poetizer 4 bard, poet **6** rhymer, writer **8** rhymster **9** poetaster, versifier

poetry 5 poesy, rhyme, verse **13** versification
god of: **4** Odin, Ogma **5** Brage, Bragi, Othin **6** Apollo **7** Phoebus, Pythius **9** Musagetes

Pogo
creator: **9** Walt Kelly
character: **9** Porkypine, Wiley Catt **10** Boll Weevil **12** PT Bridgeport **13**

Deacon Mushrat, Mole MacCarony
alligator: 6 Albert
fox: 11 Seminole Sam
frog: 15 Moonshine Sonata
hound: 18 Beauregard Bugleboy
possum: 4 Pogo
skunk: 16 Ma'm'selle Hepzibah
snake: 7 Snavely
sorcerer: 10 Howland Owl
turtle/pirate captain: 14 Churchy La Femme
place: 15 Okefenokee Swamp

Pohjola
origin: 7 Finnish
identified with: 7 Lapland
location: 12 North Finland

poignant 3 sad **5** sharp **6** biting, moving, rueful, woeful **7** cutting, doleful, piquant, piteous, pitiful, pungent, tearful **8** grievous, pathetic, piercing, pitiable, touching **9** affecting, sorrowful, trenchant **10** lamentable **11** distressing, penetrating **12** heartrending

poilu
slang: 13 French soldier
in: 9 World War I

point 3 aim, end, hit, nib, run, tip, use **4** apex, bend, bode, core, game, gist, goal, item, mark, meat, pike, pith, spur, time, turn, unit **5** argue, cause, guide, heart, imply, level, limit, place, prong, prove, score, sense, slant, spike, stage, steer, tally, train, value **6** aspect, basket, degree, detail, direct, hint at, kernel, marrow, moment, number, object, reason **7** essence, feature, instant, portend, presage, purpose, quality, signify, suggest, testify **8** indicate, intimate, juncture, main idea, manifest, offshoot, position, sharp end **9** condition, extension, intention, objective, outgrowth **10** foreshadow, particular, projection, prominence, promontory **11** demonstrate **12** protuberance

point-blank 5 blunt **6** direct **10** forthright **11** plainspoken

Point Counter Point
author: 12 Aldous Huxley

point d'appui 4 prop, stay **24** point of battle line support

pointed 5 acute, blunt, sharp **6** biting, direct, peaked, pointy **7** cutting, fitting, hinting, telling **8** accurate, incisive, piercing **9** aciculate, acuminate, cuspidate, pertinent, trenchant **10** emphasized, forthright **11** appropriate, conspicuous, insinuating, penetrating

pointer 3 arm, tip **4** hand, hint **5** arrow, guide, stick **6** needle **7** caution, warning **9** indicator **10** admonition, advisement, suggestion **13** piece of advice **14** recommendation
dog breed: 16 German wirehaired **17** German shorthaired **25** wirehaired pointing griffon

pointless 4 dull **5** blunt **6** absurd, fu-

tile, obtuse, stupid **7** aimless, invalid, rounded, unedged, useless **8** bootless, worn down **9** fruitless, illogical, senseless, unpointed, worthless **10** irrational, irrelevant, ridiculous, unavailing **11** ineffectual, meaningless, purposeless, unsharpened **12** inapplicable, preposterous, unproductive, unprofitable, unreasonable

point of view 4 side **5** angle, slant **6** aspect **7** outlook **8** attitude **9** viewpoint **10** standpoint **11** frame of mind, perspective

point the way 5 guide, pilot, usher **6** direct **8** indicate, navigate **14** give directions

point to 5 argue, imply **6** denote **7** express **8** indicate

point up 6 stress **9** emphasize, underline **10** accentuate, underscore

Poirot, Hercule
detective created by: 14 Agatha Christie
nationality: 7 Belgian
famed for: 10 moustaches
phrase: 15 little grey cells
played by: 11 David Suchet (PBS Mystery) **12** Peter Sellers

poise 4 calm **5** raise **6** aplomb **7** balance, elevate **8** presence **9** assurance, composure, hold aloft, sangfroid **10** equanimity **11** savoir faire, self-command, self-control **13** self-assurance **14** presence of mind, self-confidence **15** be in equilibrium

poised 7 assured **8** composed **9** confident **10** controlled **11** self-assured **13** self-possessed

poison 4 bane, evil, harm **5** curse, taint, toxin, venom **6** cancer, canker, debase, defile, impair, infect, plague, weaken **7** corrode, corrupt, degrade, disease, outrage, pollute **8** enormity, make sick **9** malignity **10** adulterate, corruption, debilitate, malignancy, pestilence **11** abomination, contaminate

poisonous 5 fatal, toxic **6** deadly, lethal, mortal **7** baneful, noxious **8** venomous, virulent **10** pernicious **11** deleterious **12** pestilential

Poitier, Sidney
born: 7 Miami FL
wife: 13 Joanna Shimkus
roles: 11 Virgil Tibbs **12** A Patch of Blue, For Love of Ivy, Porgy and Bess **13** To Sir with Love **14** The Defiant Ones **15** A Raisin in the Sun **16** Lilies of the Field (Oscar) **17** They Call Me Mr Tibbs **19** In the Heat of the Night, The Blackboard Jungle, Uptown Saturday Night **23** Guess Who's Coming to Dinner?

Pokanoket *see* **10** Wampanoags

poke 3 dig, hit, jab **4** butt, drag, gore, idle, jolt, prod, push, stab **5** crawl, dally, delay, mosey, nudge, punch,

stick, thump **6** dawdle, fiddle, potter, thrust **7** meander, saunter, shamble, shuffle **8** hang back **10** dillydally **12** shilly-shally

poker
derived from: 5 as nas, gilet **6** brelan **7** primero **11** brouillotte
cards/hand: 4 five **5** seven
bets: 4 ante **5** chips
hand: 4 pair **5** flush **8** straight, two pairs **9** full house **10** royal flush **11** four of a kind **12** three of a kind **13** straight flush
term: 4 ante, call, fold **5** check, raise **6** ante up **7** reraise
variation: 4 draw, stud **5** jacks, Omaha **6** hold em, pai gow **8** jackpots **12** five-card draw **13** seven-card stud

poky, pokey 4 dull, jail, slow **5** dowdy, small **6** dreary, shabby, stodgy, stuffy **7** cramped **8** confined, dawdling, dilatory, frumpish **9** puttering **10** monotonous
creature: 5 sloth, snail **6** turtle **8** slowpoke, tortoise

Poland
other name: 6 Polska **17** the land of the plain
capital/largest city: 6 Warsaw
medieval capital: 6 Cracow, Krakow
others: 3 Lwo **4** Kodz, Kolo, Lida, Lodz, Lvov, Lyck, Nysa, Oels, Pila **5** Brest, Bytom, Chelm, Dukla, Narev, Opole, Posen, Radom, Sroda, Torun, Vilna **6** Danzig, Elblag, Gdansk, Gdynia, Gnesen, Grodno, Kalisz, Kielce, Kracow, Lublin, Poznan, Tarnow, Zabrze **7** Beuthen, Breslau, Chorzow, Garocin, Gliwice, Litousk, Litovsk, Lyublin, Oleztyn, Stettin, Wroclaw **8** Frombork, Gleiwitz, Katowice, Lidzbark, Liegnitz, Oswiecim, Przemysl, Szczecin, Tarnopol **9** Auschwitz, Bialogard, Bialystok, Bydgoszcz, Sosnowiec, Szcezecin, Walbrzych **11** Czestochowa
school: 6 Warsaw **12** Jagiellonian
division: 7 Galicia, Silesia **8** Podlesia, Volhynia **9** Lithuania, Pomerania
measure: 3 cal **4** mila, pret **5** morga, sazen, vloka, wloka **6** cwierc, cwierk, kwarta, lokiec **7** garniec **9** kwarterka
monetary unit: 4 abia **5** dalar, ducat, grosz, marka, zloty **6** fennig, groszy, gulden, halerz, ko rona **8** groschen
weight: 3 lut **4** funt **6** kamian **7** skrupul
island: 5 Wolin
lake: 5 Goplo, Mamry **8** Niegocin, Sniardwy **13** Stettin Lagoon
mountain: 5 Tatra **6** Beskid **7** Pieniny, Sudeten **9** Beshchady, High Tatra, Holy Cross **10** Carpathian
highest point: 4 Rysy
river: 3 Bug, San **4** Alle, Brda, Gwda,

Lyna, Nysa, Oder, Styr **5** Biala, Drana, Dwina, Narev, Narew, Notec, Podra, Seret, Warta, Wista **6** Neisse, Niemen, Nyeman, Pilica, Pripet, Prosna, Styrpa, Wieprz **7** Nemunas, Vistula, Wistoka **8** Dniester

sea: 6 Baltic

physical feature:
  forest: 10 Bialowieza
  gulf: 6 Danzig, Gdansk
  lagoon: 7 Stettin **12** Frischeshaff
  plain: 7 Silesia
  plateau: 6 Lublin

people: 4 Pole, Slav **5** Mazur **8** Silesian
  astronomer: 10 Copernicus
  author: 7 Reymont **8** Zeromski **10** Mickiewicz, Wyspianski **11** Sienkiewicz
  composer: 6 Chopin **10** Paderewski
  dynasty: 5 Piast **7** Jagello
  king: 7 Casimir **8** Augustus
  leader: 5 Kania **6** Gierek **7** Gomulka, Mieszko **8** Boleslaw **9** Pilsudski, Stanislaw **10** Jaruzel ski, Kosciuszko, Lech Walesa
  pope: 10 John Paul II **20** Cardinal Carol Wojtyla
  queen: 7 Jadwiga
  musician: 7 Kiepura **9** Landowska
  scientist: 5 Curie

language: 6 Kaszub, Polish **10** Pomeranian

religion: 13 Roman Catholic

title: 3 pan **4** pani

place:
  castle: 5 Wawel
  church: 6 St John **10** Panna Maria
  monastery: 9 Jasna Gora
  monument: 17 Heroes of the Ghetto
  national park: 5 Ojcow **10** Bialowieza
  palace: 7 Casimir

feature:
  folk dance: 5 polka **7** mazurka **9** krakowiak, polonaise
  union: 10 Solidarity

food:
  dish: 5 bigos **6** pirogi **7** borscht **7** kolduny
  drink: 5 vodka **7** Krupnik
  sausage: 8 kielbasa
  soup: 7 barszca

Polanski, Roman
  director of: 4 Tess **7** Macbeth **9** Chinatown **13** Rosemary's Baby

polar 3 icy **6** arctic, frigid, wintry **7** glacial, ice-cold **8** freezing **9** antarctic **11** nothernmost **12** southernmost

polaroid 6 camera
  invented by: 4 Land

pole 3 rod **4** mast, spar **5** shaft, staff, stick **6** tongue **9** pikestaff
  flax holder: 7 distaff
  pertaining to: 5 nodal
  sacred: 7 Asherah
  Scottish: 5 caber

tribal: 5 totem
vehicular: 4 neap

police, police officer 4 cops, dick, fuzz, tidy **5** clean, guard **6** neaten, patrol, tidy up **7** clean up, control, marshal, officer, protect, sheriff **8** blue coat, flatfoot, gendarme, regulate, spruce up, troopers **9** gendarmes, men in blue, patrolmen **10** traffic cop **11** arm of the law, keep in order **12** constabulary, cop on the beat
French: 8 gendarme
Italian: 11 carabiniere

Police Woman
  character: 9 (Det) Joe Styles, (Lt) Paul Marsh **11** (Det) Pete Royster, (Lt) Bill Crowley **12** (Sgt Suzanne) Pepper Martin
  cast: 9 Ed Bernard **11** Val Bisoglio **12** Earl Holliman **14** Angie Dickinson, Charles Dierkop

policy 3 way **4** plan, rule **5** habit, style **6** custom, design, method, scheme, system **7** program, routine, tactics **8** behavior, platform, practice, strategy **9** principle, procedure

polish 3 oil, wax **4** buff, sand **5** class, emend, glaze, gloss, grace, rouge, rub up, shine **6** pumice, refine, smooth **7** burnish, correct, culture, enhance, finesse, improve, perfect, sauvity, touch up, varnish **8** abrasive, courtesy, elegance, round out, urbanity **9** gentility, politesse, sandpaper **10** politeness, refinement **11** cultivation, good manners

polished 4 able, deft, fine, oily **5** oiled, suave, waxed **6** buffed, expert, glassy, glazed, glossy, polite, rubbed, sanded, shined, urbane **7** capable, elegant, genteel, refined, skilled **8** cultured, finished, mannerly, masterly, skillful, smoothed **9** brilliant, burnished, courteous, masterful, practiced, varnished **10** cultivated, profi- cient **11** experienced **12** accomplished

polish off 6 finish **8** complete, get rid of **9** dispose of

polite 4 high **5** civil, elite **6** proper **7** courtly, elegant, gallant, genteel, refined **8** cultured, mannerly, polished, well-bred **9** civilized, courteous, diffident, patrician **10** cultivated, respectful **11** ceremonious, fashionable, gentlemanly, well-behaved **12** well-mannered

politeness 7 decorum **8** courtesy **9** gentility, propriety **10** refinement **11** good manners

Polites
  character in: 7 Odyssey
  brother: 5 Paris **6** Hector
  companion: 8 Odysseus
  father: 5 Priam
  mother: 6 Hecuba
  sister: 9 Cassandra

transformed by: 5 Aeaea, Circe
transformed into: 3 hog, pig **5** swine

politic 4 wily, wise **5** chary, suave **6** artful, astute, shrewd, subtle **7** mindful, prudent, tactful **8** cautious, discreet, scheming **9** designing, expedient, judicious, opportune **10** contriving, diplomatic **11** calculating, circumspect, machinating **13** Machiavellian

political party 3 GOP **4** Tory, Whig **5** Labor **7** faction **9** Communist, Greenback, Socialist **10** Democratic, Republican **11** Know-Nothing

political refugee 2 DP **5** exile **6** emigre **10** expatriate **15** displaced person

politician 8 politico **9** incumbent, statesman **10** campaigner, legislator **12** officeholder, office seeker **13** public servant

politics 10 government, statecraft **11** party policy **13** statesmanship **14** affairs of state

Politics
  author: 9 Aristotle

Politic Would-Be, Lord and Lady
  characters in: 7 Volpone
  author: 6 Jonson

Polixenes
  character in: 14 The Winter's Tale
  author: 11 Shakespeare

Polk, James Knox
  presidential rank: 8 eleventh
  party: 8 Democrat
  state represented: 2 TN
  defeated: 4 (Henry) Clay **6** (James Gillespie) Birney
  vice president: 6 (George Mifflin) Dallas
  cabinet:
    state: 8 (James) Buchanan
    treasury: 6 (Robert John) Walker
    war: 5 (William Learned) Marcy
    attorney general: 5 (John Young) Mason **6** (Isaac) Toucey **8** (Nathan) Clifford
    navy: 5 (John Young) Mason **8** (George) Bancroft
    postmaster general: 7 (Cave) Johnson
  born: 2 NC **17** Mecklenburg County
  died/buried: 2 TN **9** Nashville
  education: 11 prep schools **16** tutored privately
    University: 13 North Carolina
  religion: 9 Methodist
  political career: 16 state legislature **17** Speaker of the House **24** US House of Representatives
    governor of: 9 Tennessee
  civilian career: 6 lawyer
  notable events of lifetime/term:
    boundary dispute: 9 Northwest
    discovery in California of: 4 gold
    Proviso: 6 Wilmot
    treaty of: 16 Guadalupe Hidalgo
    war: 7 Mexican

father: 6 Samuel
mother: 4 Jane
siblings: 7 John Lee **9** Jane Maria, Naomi Tate **10** Lydia Eliza **12** Marshall Tate, Samuel Wilson **14** William Hawkins **15** Franklin Ezekiel, Ophelia Clarissa
wife: 5 Sarah (Childress)
children: 4 none

polka 5 dance **10** round dance **13** Bohemian dance

poll 4 head, vote **5** count, tally **6** census, survey, voting **7** canvass, figures, returns **8** register, sampling **9** interview, nose count **10** count noses, voting list **11** voting place

Pollack, Sydney
director of: 11 Out of Africa (Oscar) **12** The Way We Were **15** Absence of Malice **23** They Shoot Horses Don't They?

Pollock, Jackson
born: 6 Cody WY
artwork: 5 Scent **9** Blue Poles **10** The She-Wolf **11** Convergence **12** Autumn Rhythm **13** Eyes in the Heat **17** Easter and the Totem **20** Guardians of the Secret

pollutant 5 fumes, smoke, waste **7** exhaust **8** emission, impurity

pollute 4 foul, soil **5** dirty, sully **6** befoul, debase, defile **7** deprave, profane **9** desecrate **10** adulterate, make filthy **11** contaminate

polluted 4 foul **5** dirty, drunk **6** impure, soiled **7** corrupt, profane, smashed, unclean **9** poisonous **12** contaminated

pollution 7 fouling, soiling **8** defiling, dirtying, foulness, impurity **9** befouling, pollutant **11** uncleanness **12** adulteration **13** contaminating, contamination

Pollux see **15** Castor and Pollux

Pollyanna
director: 10 David Swift
based on story by: 13 Eleanor Porter
cast: 9 Jane Wyman **10** Karl Malden **11** Hayley Mills, Richard Egan

polo
equipment: 6 mallet
period of play: 7 chukker
championship: 10 Camacho Cup **13** Coronation Cup **16** Cup of the Americas

Polonius
character in: 6 Hamlet
author: 11 Shakespeare

Polska see **6** Poland

poltergeist 5 ghost **6** spirit
literally: 10 noise-ghost
manifestation: 5 knock, noise, prank

Poltergeist
director: 10 Tobe Hooper
cast: 12 Craig T Nelson **14** Jobeth Williams **16** Beatrice Straight

co-writer/producer: 15 Steven Spielberg

poltroon 6 coward, craven **7** caitiff, chicken, dastard **11** yellow-belly

polygon 10 multiangle **11** plane figure
eight-sided: 7 octagon
equal angled: 6 isogon
five-sided: 8 pentagon
four-sided: 6 square **7** rhombus **8** tetragon **9** rectangle, trapezoid
nine-sided: 7 nonagon
seven-sided: 8 heptagon
six-sided: 7 hexagon
ten-sided: 7 decagon
three-sided: 8 triangle
twelve-sided: 9 dodecagon

Polyhymnia
also: 8 Polymnia
member of: 5 Muses
personifies: 5 dance **11** sacred music
mother: 9 Mnemosyne

polymer 5 dimer, nylon **6** hydrol **7** hexamer **8** oligomer

Polynesia
name means: 11 many islands
cities: 4 Apia **7** Papeete **8** Auckland, Pago Pago **9** Nukualofa
island: 4 Cook, Line **5** Samoa, Tonga **6** Easter, Ellice, Hawaii, Midway, Tahiti, Tubuai, Tuvalu **7** Austral, Maupiti, Phoenix, Society, Tokelau, Tuamotu **8** Pitcairn **9** Marquesas **10** New Zealand **15** French Polynesia
sea: 7 Pacific
people: 3 Ati **5** Maori **6** Kanaka, Nivean, Samoan, Tongan **9** Nesogaean **10** Polynesian
   explorer: 4 Cook **6** Tasman, Wallis **8** Magellan **9** Roggeveen **12** Bougainville
language: 4 Niue, Uvea **5** Maori **6** Samoan, Tongan **7** Austral, Tagalog, Tokelau **8** Hawaiian, Tahitian **9** Marquesan, Tuamatuan **10** Mangarevan
religion: 12 Christianity
place:
   legendary origin: 8 Hawaiiki
feature:
   chief: 5 matai
   clothing: 5 pareu **6** sarong **8** lava-lava
   dance: 4 hula, siva
   dwelling: 4 fale
   family social unit: 4 aiga
   priest: 7 kahunas
   supernatural power: 4 mana
food:
   dish: 3 kai, poi **4** taro **8** palusami
   drink: 3 ava **4** kava, kawa

Polynices
also: 10 Polyneices
father: 7 Oedipus
mother: 7 Jocasta
uncle: 5 Creon
brother: 7 Oedipus **8** Eteocles
sister: 6 Ismene **8** Antigone
killed by: 8 Eteocles

polyp 5 coral, hydra, tumor **6** growth, isopod **7** octopod **10** sea anemone

Polyphemus
form: 7 Cyclops **12** one-eyed giant
father: 6 Elatus **8** Poseidon
mother: 6 Thoosa
joined: 9 Argonauts
killed: 4 Acis
blinded by: 8 Odysseus
loved: 7 Galatea

Polyphides
king of: 6 Sicyon
vocation: 4 seer
protected: 8 Menelaus **9** Agamemnon

polyphony 7 organum **8** faburden **11** fauxbourdon **12** counterpoint

Polypoetes
king of: 10 Thesprotia
father: 6 Apollo **8** Odysseus **9** Pirithous
mother: 6 Phthia **9** Callidice **10** Hippodamia
leader of: 6 Greeks

polysaccharide 6 insulin, starch **7** dextrin **8** galactin, lichenin **9** cellulose **12** carbohydrate

Polyxena
father: 5 Priam
mother: 6 Hecuba
loved by: 8 Achilles

Pomaria see **7** Algeria

Pomerania
capital: 7 Stettin
city: 5 Thorn, Torun **6** Anklam
country: 6 Poland **7** Germany
island: 5 Rugen **6** Usedom
province: 7 Pomorze

pommel, pummel 4 beat, hilt, horn, knob, pake **6** finial, strike **9** saddlebow

Pomona
origin: 5 Roman
goddess of: 10 fruit trees

pomp 4 show **5** front, glory, style **7** display **8** ceremony, flourish, grandeur, splendor **9** pageantry, showiness, solemnity, spectacle **10** brilliance **11** affectation, grandiosity, ostentation, pompousness **12** magnificence **14** stately display **15** pretentiousness

pompous 4 vain **5** proud **6** lordly, uppish **7** haughty **8** affected, arrogant, mannered, overdone, puffed-up, snobbish **9** conceited, egotistic, grandiose, imperious **10** blustering, swaggering **11** overbearing, patronizing, pretentious **12** ostentatious, presumptuous, supercilious, vainglorious **13** condescending, high and mighty, self-important

Ponchielli, Amilcare
born: 5 Italy **7** Cremona
composer of: 10 La Gioconda **15** Dance of the Hours

poncho 4 cape **5** cloak, shawl **6** mantle, serape

pond 4 pool, tarn 5 basin 6 lagoon 9 small lake, water hole

ponder 4 muse 5 study 6 wonder 7 examine, reflect 8 cogitate, consider, mull over, ruminate 9 brood over, cerebrate, reflect on, speculate, think over 10 deliberate, meditate on, puzzle over 11 contemplate

ponderous 3 big 4 dull 5 bulky, heavy, hefty, large, wordy 6 boring, bovine, dreary 7 awkward, droning, hulking, labored, lumpish, massive, tedious, weighty 8 cumbrous, enormous, sluggish, unlively, unwieldy 9 corpulent, graceless, lumbering, wearisome 10 burdensome, cumbersome, long-winded, lusterless, monotonous, unexciting, ungraceful 11 heavy-handed

pontiff 4 pope 6 bishop, priest 8 pontifex

pontifical 7 pompous 8 churchly, clerical, dogmatic, priestly 9 apostolic, episcopal, imperious 11 opinionated, overbearing, patronizing, pretentious 13 authoritarian, condescending 14 ecclesiastical

Pontus
personifies: 3 sea
father: 2 Ge
son: 6 Nereus 7 Phorcys

pony 3 nag 4 crib, trot 5 glass, horse, pinto 7 mustang 9 racehorse
breed: 6 Exmoor 8 Shetland

Pooh *See* 13 Winnie-the-Pooh

pooh-pooh 5 knock 7 disdain, put down, run down, sneer at 8 belittle 9 disparage

Pooka *see* 4 Puca

pool 3 pot 4 ally, bank, lake, mere, pond, tarn 5 group, kitty, merge, share, union, unite 6 puddle, splash, stakes 7 combine 8 alliance, fishpond, millpool 9 coalition 10 amalgamate, collective 11 association, consolidate, cooperative 13 confederation

Poole, Grace
character in: 8 Jane Eyre
author: 6 Bronte

poop 3 fag 4 bush, deck, do in, tire 7 exhaust, fatigue, wear out 8 enervate

pooped 4 beat 5 all in, spent, tired, weary 6 bushed, done in 7 drained, wearied, worn out 8 fatigued, tired out 9 dead tired, exhausted, played out

poor 3 sad 4 bare, dead, vain, worn 5 broke, empty, needy, sorry 6 barren, fallow, faulty, futile, hard up, in need, in want, meager, paltry, wasted 7 forlorn, sterile, unhappy, unlucky, wanting 8 badly off, bankrupt, beggarly, depleted, desolate, devoid of, grieving, indigent, inferior, pathetic, pitiable, strapped, unworthy, wretched 9 defective, deficient, destitute, exhausted, fruitless, imperfect, infertile, insolvent, in straits, miserable, moneyless, penniless, unfertile, worthless 10 distressed, inadequate, pauperized 11 impecunious, unfortunate 12 impoverished, uncultivable, unproductive, unprofitable 15 poverty-stricken

Poor People
author: 16 Fyodor Dostoevsky

Poor Richard's Almanack
author: 16 Benjamin Franklin

Poor White
author: 16 Sherwood Anderson

pop 4 bang, boom, come, shot, snap, soda 5 arise, blast, burst, crack 6 appear, report 7 explode 8 detonate 9 discharge, explosion, soft drink 10 detonation

pope 3 Leo 4 John, Paul, Pius 5 Peter, Urban 6 Adrian, Eugene, Julius, Martin, Sixtus 7 Clement, Gregory 8 Benedict, Innocent, John Paul, Nicholas 9 Alexander, Callistus
also: 12 Bishop of Rome 13 Vicar of Christ 14 Primate of Italy, Supreme Pontiff 16 Archbishop of Rome 18 Metropolitan of Rome, Patriarch of the West 25 Servant of the Servants of God
office: 6 Papacy 7 Holy See 11 Seat of Peter
elected by: 18 College of Cardinals
elected in: 8 conclave
signal that election is concluded: 10 white smoke
resides: 4 Rome 10 the Vatican 11 Vatican City
former residence: 13 Lateran Palace
summer residence: 14 Castel Gondolfo
papal land holding: 9 patrimony 21 patrimony of Saint Peter
first pope: 10 Saint Peter
pope who crowned Charlemagne: 6 Leo III
pope who excommunicated Luther: 4 Leo X
pope who authorized Michelangelo to paint Sistine Chapel: 8 Julius II
"September Pope": 9 John Paul I
original name of pope:
Alexander VI: 15 Rodrigo de Borgia
Callistus III: 15 Alfonso de Borgia
Clement VII: 14 Giulio de' Medici
John XXIII: 22 Angelo Giuseppe Roncalli
John Paul I: 13 Albino Luciani
John Paul II: 12 Karol Wojtyla 18 Archbishop of Krakow
Leo X: 16 Giovanni de' Medici
Pius XI: 12 Achille Ratti
Pius XII: 35 Eugenio Maria Giuseppe Giovanni Pacelli
popes of Avignon papacy: 6 Urban V 8 Clement V, John XXII 9 Clement VI, Gregory XI, Nicholas V 10 Innocent VI 11 Benedict XII
popes during Great Western Schism:
Avignon: 10 Clement VII 12 Benedict XIII
Pisa: 9 John XXIII 10 Alexander V
Rome: 7 Urban VI 10 Boniface IX, Gregory XII 11 Innocent VII
papal bull/encyclical: 11 Unam sanctam 12 Humanae vitae, Rerum novarum, Vox in excelso 13 Pacem in terris 15 Mater et magistra 19 Populorum progressio 22 Sacerdotalis caelibatus

Pope, Alexander
author of: 10 The Dunciad 12 An Essay on Man 15 Eloisa to Abelard 16 The Rape of the Lock 18 An Essay on Criticism 20 Epistle to Dr Arbuthnot

Pope, John Russell
architect of: 17 Jefferson Memorial 20 National Gallery of Art 23 Temple of the Scottish Rite 24 National Archives Building

Popeye
character in: 9 Sanctuary
author: 8 Faulkner

Popeye
cartoonist: 10 Elzie Segar
character: 5 Bluto, Wimpy 7 Swee' Pea 8 Olive Oyl
food: 7 spinach

popinjay 3 fop 4 beau 5 dandy 7 coxcomb

poplar 7 Populus 22 Liriodendron tulipifera
varieties: 4 gray 5 black, downy, tulip, white 6 balsam, Eugene, yellow 8 Car- olina, Lombardy, necklace 10 Queensland 12 Chinese white, silver-leaved 13 Western balsam

poppy 7 Papaver
varieties: 3 sea 4 blue, bush, corn, snow, tree, wind, wood 5 field, opium, plume, satin, tulip, water, Welsh 6 arctic, desert, horned 7 Asiatic, flaming, Iceland, Mexican, prickly, Shirley, Western 8 Flanders, harebell, Matilija, oriental 9 Celandine 10 California, island tree 12 Mexican tulip 13 yellow Chinese 14 California tree
drug: 5 opium 6 heroin 8 morphine

poppycock 3 rot 4 bosh, bunk, jive, tosh 5 froth, fudge, hooey, stuff, trash 6 drivel, humbug 7 baloney, blabber, blather, eyewash, fustian, garbage, hogwash, inanity, prattle, rubbish, twaddle 8 falderal, flummery, nonsense, tommyrot, wish-wash 9 absurdity, gibberish, moonshine, rigmarole 10 applesauce, balderdash, flapdoodle, hocus-pocus, mumbo-jumbo, rigamarole 11 abracadabra, jabberwocky 12 fiddlefaddle, gobbledygook

poppy seed
botanical name: 7 Papaver 11 P somniferum (sleep- bearing poppy)
color: 4 blue 5 white

origin: 4 Asia **6** Europe
guards against: 9 creditors
use: 5 bread, cakes, rolls **6** sweets **10** vegetables **11** butter sauce

populace 4 folk **6** people, public **7** society **9** citizenry, community **10** population

popular 5 cheap, civic, civil, stock **6** famous, public, social **7** admired, current, general, in favor **8** accepted, approved, communal, familiar, favorite, in demand, national, orthodox **9** community, preferred, prevalent, well-known, well-liked **10** affordable, celebrated, democratic **11** established, fashionable, inexpensive, of the people, sought-after

popularity 4 fame, note **5** favor, glory, kudos, vogue **6** esteem, regard, renown, repute **7** acclaim, fashion **8** approval **9** celebrity, notoriety **10** acceptance, admiration, notability, reputation **11** acclamation

popular opinion
Latin: 9 vox populi

popular whim 3 fad **4** rage **5** craze, mania **7** passion **11** infatuation

populate 6 occupy, people, settle **7** inhabit

populated 5 urban **7** peopled, settled **8** citified, occupied **9** inhabited

population 4 folk **6** people, public **8** citizens, populace **9** citizenry, habitancy, residents **11** body politic, commonality, inhabitants

populous 5 dense **6** jammed **7** crowded, peopled, teeming **8** swarming, thronged

porcelain 5 china **11** ceramic ware

porch 4 stoa **5** lanai, stoop **7** balcony, narthex, portico, veranda **8** solarium, verandah **9** colonnade, vestibule

pore 4 hole, read, scan **5** probe, study **6** outlet, peruse, ponder, review, search, survey **7** dig into, examine, explore, inspect, orifice **8** aperture, consider **9** delve into

Porfiry
character in: 18 Crime and Punishment
author: 10 Dostoevsky

Porgy
author: 13 DuBose Heyward

Porgy and Bess
opera by: 14 George Gershwin
character: 4 Bess **5** Clara, Crown, Porgy **6** Serena **11** Sportin' Life
setting: 10 Catfish Row

pornographic 4 blue, lewd **5** bawdy, dirty, gross **6** coarse, filthy, smutty, vulgar **7** obscene **8** indecent, off-color, prurient **9** salacious **10** lascivious, licentious

porous 4 lacy **6** spongy **7** riddled **8** cellular, pervious **9** absorbent, perme-

able, sievelike **10** penetrable **11** honeycombed

porpoise 4 leap **5** whale **6** palach, puffer, seahog **7** cowfish, dolphin, surface **8** cetacean
genus: 8 Phocaena **9** Delphinus

porridge 4 pobs, samp **5** atole, brose, brout, gruel **6** cereal **7** crowdie, oatmeal, polenta **8** flummery

porringer 4 bowl, dish **6** vessel **9** container **10** receptacle

Porsena, Lars
nationality: 8 Etruscan
attacked: 4 Rome
to reinstate: 7 Tarquin

port 4 dock, pier, quay **5** haven, wharf **6** harbor, refuge **7** dry dock, landing, mooring, seaport, shelter **9** anchorage, harborage **11** destination

port
type: 4 wine **6** brandy
origin: 8 Portugal
variety: 4 ruby **5** tawny **7** vintage
with brandy: 9 Betsy Ross
with vermouth: 10 Broken Spur

portable 5 handy, light, small **6** bantam, pocket **7** compact, folding, movable **8** cartable, haulable, liftable **9** ready-to-go **10** convenient, conveyable, manageable, vest-pocket **11** pocket-sized

portal, portals 4 adit, arch, door, gate **5** entry **6** wicket **7** doorway, gateway, portico **8** approach, entrance **9** threshold, vestibule **10** portcullis **11** entranceway

Port-au-Prince
capital of: 5 Haiti

porte-monnaie 5 purse **10** pocketbook **12** money-carrier

portend 4 bode **5** augur **6** denote, herald, warn of **7** bespeak, betoken, point to, predict, presage, signify, suggest **8** forebode, forecast, foretell, forewarn, prophesy **9** foretoken, prefigure **10** foreshadow

portent 4 omen, sign **5** token **6** augury, boding, threat **7** presage, warning **9** harbinger **10** foreboding **11** forewarning

portentous 6 superb **7** amazing, fateful, ominous, pompous **8** alarming, menacing **9** bombastic, grandiose, prophetic **10** foreboding, incredible, prodigious, remarkable, stupendous, surprising **11** astonishing, exceptional, frightening, pretentious, significant, superlative, threatening **12** inauspicious, intimidating, unpropitious

porter 4 brew **5** stout **6** bearer, coolie, redcap, skycap **7** carrier **8** conveyer **9** conductor

Porter, Katherine Anne
author of: 11 Ship of Fools **12** Old Mortality **14** Flowering Judas **15** The

Leaning Tower **18** Pale Horse Pale Rider

Porter, William Sidney
real name of: 6 O Henry

portfolio 4 case, file **5** album **6** binder, folder **7** dossier **8** envelope **9** scrapbook **10** securities

Porthos
character in: 18 The Three Musketeers
author: 5 Dumas (pere)

Portia
character in: 12 Julius Caesar **19** The Merchant of Venice
author: 11 Shakespeare

portico 4 stoa **5** lanai **6** piazza **7** balcony, veranda, walkway

portion 3 cut, lot, sum **4** dole, doom, fate, luck, part **5** carve, cut up, moira, piece, sever, share, slice, split **6** amount, divide, kismet, parcel, ration, sector **7** break up, deal out, destiny, fortune, helping, measure, section, segment, serving **8** allocate, disperse, division, fraction, fragment, quantity, separate **9** allotment, allowance, demarcate, partition **10** allocation, distribute, percentage

portion out 5 allot **6** ration **7** dole out, mete out, prorate **8** allocate, dispense, divide up **9** apportion, parcel out **10** distribute, measure out

Portland
basketball team: 12 Trail Blazers
football team: 8 Breakers
river: 8 Columbia **10** Willamette
university: 4 Reed

Port Louis
capital of: 9 Mauritius

portly 3 big, fat **4** full **5** beefy, burly, heavy, large, obese, plump, pudgy, round, stout, tubby **6** brawny, chubby, fleshy, rotund, stocky **9** corpulent

Portman, John
architect of: 15 Peachtree Center (Atlanta)

portmanteau 3 bag **4** grip **5** cloak **6** mantle, valise **8** suitcase **9** gladstone

Port Moresby
capital of: 9 New Guinea

Portnoy's Complaint
author: 10 Philip Roth

Port of Spain
capital of: 17 Trinidad and Tobago

Porto-Novo
capital of: 5 Benin

portrait 5 cameo **6** sketch **7** drawing, picture **8** likeness, painting, vignette **9** depiction **10** impression, photograph **11** description

Portrait of a Lady, The
author: 10 Henry James
character: 11 Madame Merle, Pansy Osmond **12** Isabel Archer **13** Gilbert Osmond, Lord Warburton, Ralph

Touchett **14** Caspar Goodwood **18** Henrietta Stackpole

Portrait of the Artist as a Young Man
author: 10 James Joyce
character: 4 Emma **12** Simon Dedalus **14** Stephen Dedalus

portray 3 ape **4** draw, play **5** carve, enact, mimic, model, paint **6** depict, detail, figure, pose as, sketch **7** imitate, narrate, picture **8** describe, set forth, simulate **9** delineate, represent, sculpture **10** illustrate, photograph **11** impersonate **12** characterize

portrayal 7 picture **8** portrait **9** picturing **11** delineation, description **14** representation **16** characterization

ports
god of: 8 Portunus

Portugal
capital/largest city: 6 Lisbon
others: 4 Beja, Faro, Ovar **5** Braga, Evora, Olhao, Porto, Viseu **6** Aveiro, Guarda, Leiria, Oporto, Sintra **7** Algarve, Amadora, Bragama, Cascoes, Coimbra, Covilha, Estoril, Funchal, Granada, Setubal **8** Barreiro, Portimao **9** Lusitania **10** Portalegre **14** Vila Nova de Gaia
  Roman city: 10 Portus Cale
school: 5 Minho **6** Aveiro, Lisbon, Oporto **7** Coimbra
division: 3 Goa **4** Tejo, Tete **5** Beira, Evora, Macao, Minho, Timor **6** Azores, Loanda **7** Algarve, Madeira **8** Alemteho, Rebatejo **9** Cape Verde **10** Mozambique **11** Estremadura
  Roman district: 9 Lusitania
measure: 2 pe **4** bota, moio, vara **5** almud, fanga, geira, linha, milha **6** almude, covado **7** alquier, ferrado, selamin **8** alqueire
monetary unit: 3 avo, rei **4** peca, real **5** conto, crown, dobra, indio, justo, rupia **6** escudo, macuta, octave, pataca, testad, tostao, vintem **7** angalar, centavo, crusado, miereis, testone **8** equipaga, johannes
weight: 4 onca, once **5** libra, marco **6** arroba **7** arratel **9** excropulo
island: 6 Azores **7** Madeira **8** Terceira
mountain: 4 Acor, Lapa **5** Gerez, Marao, Mousa **6** Bornes, Peneda **7** Larouco **8** Caramulo **9** Caldeirao, Monchique **14** Serra da Estrela
highest point: 11 Pico da Serra
river: 3 Sor, Tua **4** Lima, Mino, Mira, Sado, Seda, Tago, Tajo, Tejo, Vara **5** Douro, Duero, Le goa, Micha, Minho, Sabar, Tagus, Vouga, Zatas **6** Cavado, Chanca, Quarto, Tamega, Zezere **7** Mondego, Selamin, Sorraia **8** Quadiana, Tonelada
ocean: 8 Atlantic
physical feature:
  bay: 7 Setubal
  cape: 4 Roca **7** Mondego **8** Espichel **9** St Vincent

peninsula: 7 Iberian
port: 4 Faro **6** Aveiro, Lisbon, Oporto **7** Leixoes
people: 4 Celt, Moor **7** Iberian **10** Portuguese
  artist: 7 Pereira **9** Goncalves **13** Soares dos Reis
  author: 5 Dinis **6** Camoes, Vieira **7** Garrett, Vicente **9** Deus-Ramos
  explorer: 3 Cam, Cao **4** Dias, Diaz **6** Cabral, Da Gama **7** Almeida **8** Magellan **11** Albuquerque **23** Prince Henry the Navigator
  king: 6 Manuel, Philip, Sancho **7** Alfonso **9** Ferdinand, Sebastian
  leader: 5 Eanes **6** Dombal, Soares **7** Caetano, Carmona, Salazar, Spinola
  queen: 5 Maria **9** Elizabeth
language: 10 Portuguese
religion: 13 Roman Catholic
place:
  church: 5 Jesus **6** Christ **11** Os Jeronimos, Sao Lourenco **12** Old Cathedral **13** Santa Engracia **16** Sao Vicente de Fora
  city square: 15 Praca do Comercio
  dam: 6 Belver, Idanha **13** Castelo do Bode
  fortress-church: 12 Leco do Bailio
  monastery: 8 Alcobaca **12** Hieronymites **20** Santa Maria da Victoria
  monument: 11 Discoveries
  museum: 13 Soares dos Reis
  palace: 6 Cintra
  shrine: 6 Fatima
  colony: 5 Macad, Macao
  former colony: 3 Goa **5** Timor **6** Angola **7** Sao Tome **8** Principe, St Thomas **9** Cape Verde **10** Mozambique **12** Guinea Bissau
feature:
  song: 4 fado
food:
  dish: 8 bacalhau, bucellas **10** calcavella **11** carcavellos
  sausage: 8 linguica
  wine: 4 port **7** madeira

Portuguese Guinea *see* **12** Guinea-Bissau

Portuguese West Africa *see* **6** Angola

Portunus
origin: 5 Roman
god of: 5 ports **7** harbors

posada 3 inn **12** halting place

pose 3 air, set **4** cast, mien **5** group, order, state, style **6** line up, stance, submit **7** advance, arrange, bearing, bring up, posture, present, propose, show off, suggest **8** attitude, carriage, position, propound, set forth, throw out **9** mannerism, postulate **10** put forward

Poseidon
also: 9 Asphalius
origin: 5 Greek
god of: 3 sea

caused: 11 earthquakes
father: 6 Cronos
mother: 4 Rhea
brother: 4 Zeus
wife: 10 Amphitrite
lover: 2 Ge **6** Aethra, Medusa, Thoosa **7** Demeter
child: 5 Arion **6** Triton **7** Antaeus, Pegasus, Theseus **8** Chrysaor **10** Polyphemus
symbol: 5 horse **7** trident
epithet: 11 Ennosigaeus, Hippocurius **12** Prosclystius
corresponds to: 7 Neptune

poser 5 facer **6** puzzle **7** problem **8** examiner, stickler

posh 4 chic **5** fancy, ritzy, smart, swell **6** chi-chi, classy, deluxe, lavish, swanky **7** elegant, opulent, refined, stylish **9** high-class, luxurious **11** extravagant

position 3 fix, job, put, set **4** duty, pose, post, role, site **5** array, caste, class, locus, lodge, order, place, stand, state **6** career, charge, ground, locate, office, plight, stance, status **7** arrange, deposit, opinion, outlook, posture, situate, station, vantage **8** attitude, capacity, eminence, function, locality, location, prestige, standing **9** condition, elevation, establish, placement, situation, viewpoint **10** assignment, commission, importance, notability, prominence **11** appointment, consequence, disposition, distinction, frame of mind, point of view

position decided upon
French: 9 parti pris

positive 4 firm, good, real, sure **5** total **6** narrow, useful **7** assured, certain, gainful, helpful **8** absolute, cocksure, complete, decisive, definite, dogmatic, explicit, obdurate, salutary **9** assertive, confident, convinced, effective, immovable, practical, satisfied, veritable **10** applicable, autocratic, beneficial, conclusive, definitive, optimistic, undisputed, undoubting **11** affirmative, cooperative, dead certain, dictatorial, irrefutable, opinionated, overbearing, practicable, progressive, self-assured, serviceable, unequivocal, unqualified **12** confirmatory, constructive, contributory, unchangeable **13** corroborative, thoroughgoing **16** incontrovertible

positively 9 assuredly, certainly, decidedly, literally **10** absolutely, definitely **11** confidently, indubitably **12** emphatically, indisputably, unmistakably, without doubt **13** affirmatively, categorically, unqualifiedly **14** beyond question, unhesitatingly, unquestionably

possess 3 own **4** grab, have, hold **5** boast, enjoy **6** absorb, fixate, obsess, occupy **7** acquire, bedevil, bewitch, command, conquer, consume, control, enchant, overrun 8 dominate, maintain, take over, vanquish 9 fascinate, hypnotize, influence, mesmerize

Possessed, The
author: 16 Fyodor Dostoevsky
character: 5 Marya, Pyotr 6 Shatov 7 Nikolay 16 Varvara Stavrogin 17 Stepan Verhovensky

possession 4 hold 5 asset, poise, title 6 effect, owning 7 command, control, control, custody, tenancy 8 calmness, coolness, dominion, province, resource 9 belonging, composure, occupancy, ownership, placidity, sangfroid, territory 10 equanimity, even temper, occupation, possessing 11 equilibrium, self-control 12 accoutrement, protectorate

possibility 4 hope, odds, risk 6 chance, gamble, hazard 7 promise 8 prospect 9 prospects 10 likelihood 11 contingency, eventuality, feasibility, probability, workability 12 potentiality 14 practicability

possible 8 credible, feasible, workable 9 potential, thinkable 10 achievable, admissible, attainable, cognizable, compatible, contingent, imaginable, manageable, obtainable, reasonable 11 conceivable, performable, practicable 12 hypothetical

possibly 5 at all, maybe 6 mayhap 7 could be, perhaps 8 in any way, normally 9 at the most, perchance 10 by any means, God willing 11 conceivably

post 2 PX 3 fix, job, put, set 4 base, beat, camp, pale, part, pile, pole, role, seat, send, spot, work 5 brace, house, lodge, place, put up, round, shaft, stake 6 advise, column, inform, locate, notify, office, picket, report, settle, splint, tack up 7 apprise, declare, install, mission, publish, quarter, routine, situate, station, support, upright 8 acquaint, announce, capacity, disclose, exchange, fasten up, function, instruct, mainstay, position, proclaim 9 advertise, broadcast, circulate, enlighten, establish, make known, situation 10 assignment, settlement

postdate 6 follow 7 succeed 9 come after

poster 4 bill, sign 6 notice 7 placard 8 bulletin 13 advertisement

posterior 3 bum, can 4 back, butt, prat, rear, rump, seat, tail, tush 5 fanny, stern, tushy 6 behind, bottom, caudal, dorsal, hinder 7 keister 8 backside, buttocks, derriere, hindmost, rearward 9 aftermost

posterity 5 heirs, issue, young 6 family 7 descent, history, lineage, progeny 8 children 9 offspring 10 succession, successors 11 descendants

post hoc, ergo propter hoc 29 after

this therefore because of it
describes: 14 logical fallacy

Posthumus, Leonatus
character in: 9 Cymbeline
author: 11 Shakespeare

Postman Always Rings Twice, The
director: 10 Tay Garnett
based on story by: 10 James M Cain
cast: 10 Hume Cronyn, Lana Turner 12 John Garfield 13 Cecil Kellaway

postpone 4 stay 5 defer, delay, table, waive 6 put off, remand, shelve 7 adjourn, lay over, reserve, suspend

postponement 4 stay 5 delay 6 recess 7 tabling 8 abeyance, deferral 9 deferment, extension 10 suspension

postscript 2 ps 5 rider 7 codicil 8 addendum 10 attachment

postulate 5 axiom, guess 6 assume, hazard, submit, theory 7 premise, presume, propose, surmise, theorem 8 put forth, theorize 9 speculate 10 assumption, conjecture, hypothesis, presuppose 11 hypothesize, presumption

posture 3 air, set 4 case, mien, mood, pose, post, tone 5 phase, place, shape, state, tenor 6 aspect, stance, status 7 bearing, contour, station 8 attitude, carriage, position, standing 9 condition, situation 11 predicament 12 circumstance

Postvorta
form: 5 nymph
member of: 7 Camenae
knowledge of: 4 past

posy 5 bloom, motto 6 flower, phrase 7 blossom, bouquet, corsage, garland, nosegay

pot 3 pan 4 ruin 5 crock, kitty 6 vessel 9 container, marijuana 11 rack and ruin
Spanish: 4 olla

potable 3 ale 5 clean, drink, water 6 liquor 8 beverage, quencher 9 drinkable

potage 4 soup 9 thick soup

potassium
chemical symbol: 1 K

potato 16 Solanum tuberosum
varieties: 3 air, yam 4 duck, swan, wild, Zulu 5 Idaho, Irish, Maine, rural, swamp, sweet, white 6 Russet 7 Burbank, epicure, prairie, Telinga
dish: 4 chip 5 baked, salad 6 mashed 8 au gratin 9 lyonnaise, scalloped 11 french fries 12 baked stuffed

Potawatomi
language family: 9 Algonkian 10 Algonquian
location: 4 Ohio 6 Kansas 7 Indiana 8 Illinois, Michigan, Oklahoma 9 Wisconsin
leader: 7 Pontiac
united with: 6 Ojibwa, Ottawa 7 Ojibway

Potemkin

director: 17 Sergei Eisenstein
cast: 14 Vladimir Barsky 16 Alexander Antonov 17 Grigori Alexandrov
famous segment: 11 Odessa Steps

potency 3 vis 5 force, power 6 energy 8 efficacy, strength, virility, vitality

potent 5 solid, tough 6 mighty, strong 7 dynamic 8 forceful, forcible, powerful, vigorous 9 effective, operative 10 compelling, convincing, formidable, impressive, persuasive 11 efficacious, influential 12 overpowering

potentate 4 lord 5 chief, mogul, ruler 6 prince, satrap, sultan 7 emperor, monarch 8 overlord, suzerain 9 chieftain, sovereign

potential 6 covert, hidden, latent 7 dormant, lurking, passive 8 implicit, possible 9 concealed, quiescent, unexerted 10 unapparent, unrealized 11 conceivable, undisclosed, unexpressed

potentiality 7 ability 10 capability 13 possibilities

potentially
Latin: 7 in posse

pother 3 ado 4 fuss, stir, to-do 6 bustle, flurry, hustle, tumult 8 activity 9 agitation, commotion

Pothos
companion of: 9 Aphrodite
personifies: 6 desire 7 longing

potion 4 brew, dram 5 draft, tonic 6 elixir 7 mixture, philter 8 libation, potation 10 concoction

Potlatch people see 8 Kwakiutl

Pot of Gold, The
author: 7 Plautus

Potok, Chaim
author of: 9 The Chosen 10 Wanderings 15 The Book of Lights

potpourri 4 hash, mess, olio, stew 6 jumble, medley, mosaic, motley 7 farrago, goulash, melange, mixture 8 mishmash, pastiche 9 patchwork 10 hodgepodge, miscellany, salmagundi 11 gallimaufry, olla podrida

pottage 4 soup, stew 6 brewis 8 porridge

Potter, Beatrix
author of: 11 (The Tale of) Peter Rabbit 21 The Tailor of Gloucester

Potter, Muff
character in: 9 Tom Sawyer
author: 5 Twain

potter's field 8 boneyard, cemetery 9 graveyard 12 burial ground 13 burying ground

pottery 5 china 8 clayware, crockery 11 ceramic ware, earthenware

pouch 3 bag, kit, sac 4 sack 5 purse 6 pocket, wallet 7 handbag, satchel 8 carryall, ditty bag, reticule, rucksack 9 container 10 pocketbook, receptacle

Poulenc, Francis
born: 5 Paris 6 France
member of: 6 Les Six, The Six

composer of: 9 Les Biches **13** The Carmelites **22** Dialogues des Carmelites

poultice 7 plaster **8** dressing **10** medicament

poultry 3 hen **4** cock, duck, fowl, swan **5** capon, geese, goose, quail **6** grouse, layers, pigeon, turkey **7** chicken, peacock, rooster **8** pheasant **9** partridge **10** guinea fowl
breed: 6 Ancona, Bantam **7** Cornish, Dorking, Leghorn **9** Wyandotte **12** Plymouth Rock **14** Rhode Island Red
disease: 3 pip **4** roup, tick
farm: 7 hennery
house: 4 coop

pounce 4 jump, leap **5** fly at, swoop **6** ambush, dash at, jump at, plunge, snatch, spring **8** downrush, fall upon, surprise

Pounce, Peter
character in: 13 Joseph Andrews
author: 8 Fielding

pound 4 bang, beat, drub, drum, maul **5** clomp, clout, crush, grind, march, paste, smack, stomp, throb, thump, tramp **6** batter, bruise, cudgel, hammer, pummel, strike, thrash, thwack, wallop **7** clobber, crumble, pulsate, thunder, trounce **8** lambaste **9** fustigate, palpitate, pulverize **13** sixteen ounces
abbreviation: 2 lb

Pound, Ezra
author of: 6 Cantos **8** Personae **11** Exultations, Pisan Cantos

pound troy
abbreviation: 3 lb t

pour 3 tap **4** drip, drop, flow, gush, ooze, rain, seep, slop **5** drain, flood, issue, spill, spout **6** decant, deluge, drench, effuse, squirt, stream **7** cascade, draw off, dribble, lade out **15** rain cats and dogs **16** come down in sheets **17** come down in buckets

pourboire 3 tip **8** gratuity
literally: 11 for drinking

pourparler 29 informal preliminary conference
literally: 10 for talking

Poussin, Nicholas
born: 6 France **10** Les Andelys
artwork: 10 The Seasons **14** Birth of Bacchus, St John on Patmos **17** Bacchanalian Revel **18** The Burial of Phocion **19** The Poet's Inspiration **20** The Arcadian Shepherds **23** Landscape with Polyphemus, The Holy Family on the Steps **27** The Adoration of the Golden Calf

pou sto 14 place to stand on, where I may stand **16** base of operations

pout 4 crab, fret, fume, mope, sulk **5** brood, frown, lower, scowl **6** glower
French: 5 moue

poverty 4 lack, need, want **6** dearth, penury **7** beggary, deficit, paucity **8** scarcity, shortage **9** indigence, neediness, pauperism, privation **10** bankruptcy, deficiency, insolvency, meagerness, mendicancy **11** destitution **13** insufficiency, pennilessness **14** impoverishment

poverty-stricken 4 poor **5** broke, needy **8** indigent **9** destitute, penniless **10** down and out

powder 4 dust, talc **5** emery **6** pollen, talcum **7** crumble **9** pulverize
antiseptic: 6 formin **7** aristol
applier: 4 puff
cookery: 4 soda
cosmetic: 5 blush, rouge **7** compact
poisonous: 5 robin

powder-blue 5 azure **6** pastel **7** sky-blue **8** pale-blue **9** light-blue, robin's egg

powdery 5 dusty, mealy **6** chalky, floury, grated, ground, milled **7** crushed, pestled **8** shredded **10** comminuted, pulverized, triturated

Powell, Dick
real name: 14 Richard E Powell
born: 14 Mountain View AR
wife: 11 June Allyson **12** Joan Blondell
costar: 10 Ruby Keeler
roles: 7 Mrs Mike **8** Cornered **12** Johnny O'Clock **13** Murder My Sweet **15** Footlight Parade **17** Forty-second Street **32** Gold Diggers of Nineteen Thirty-three

Powell, Jane
real name: 12 Suzanne Burce
born: 10 Portland OR
roles: 5 Irene **12** Royal Wedding **13** A Date with Judy **27** Seven Brides for Seven Brothers

Powell, John
nickname: 4 Boog
sport: 8 baseball
team: 16 Baltimore Orioles

Powell, Michael
codirector: 17 Emeric Pressburger
director of: 11 The Red Shoes **14** Black Narcissus **16** Stairway to Heaven

Powell, SR
creator/artist of: 22 Sheena Queen of the Jungle

Powell, William
born: 12 Pittsburgh PA
wife: 13 Carole Lombard
costar: 8 Myrna Loy
roles: 10 Philo Vance, The Thin Man **11** Nick Charles **12** My Man Godfrey **13** Mister Roberts **14** Life with Father **16** The Great Ziegfeld **22** How to Marry a Millionaire

power 4 gift, sway **5** brawn, force, might, right, ruler, skill, vigor **6** energy, genius, muscle, status, talent **7** faculty, license, operate, potency, quality **8** activate, aptitude, capacity, energize, iron grip, pressure, prestige, property, strength, vitality **9** attribute, authority, endowment, influence, puissance **10** capability, competence
Latin: 3 vis

Power, Tyrone
born: 12 Cincinnati OH
wife: 9 Annabella **14** Linda Christian
roles: 10 Jesse James **12** Blood and Sand **13** The Razor's Edge **14** Nightmare Alley, The Mark of Zorro **15** The Sun Also Rises **18** Captain from Castile

powerful 5 hardy, husky, stout **6** brawny, cogent, mighty, moving, potent, robust, sturdy **7** intense, rousing **8** athletic, emphatic, exciting, forceful, incisive, muscular, stalwart, vigorous **9** effective, energetic, herculean, strapping **10** able-bodied, commanding, invincible

powerhouse 9 strongman **10** power plant **15** generating plant

powerless 4 weak **6** feeble, infirm **7** unarmed **8** crippled, disabled, feckless, helpless, impotent **9** incapable, pregnable, prostrate **10** impuissant, vulnerable, weaponless **11** debilitated, defenseless, immobilized **13** incapacitated

powerlessness 8 debility, weakness **9** impotence, inability, infirmity **10** enervation, feebleness, inadequacy, incapacity **12** helplessness, incapability, inefficiency **13** vulnerability

Power Politics
author: 14 Margaret Atwood

powers that be 9 higher-ups **10** government **11** authorities **13** establishment **14** administration

Powhatan
language family: 9 Algonkian **10** Algonquian
tribe: 11 Confederacy
location: 8 Atlantic, Maryland, Virginia
leader: 8 Powhatan **11** Opechancano **13** Wahunsonacock
member: 10 Pocahontas

powwow 4 meet, talk **5** forum **6** caucus, confer, huddle, parley **7** consult, convene, council, discuss, meeting, palaver **8** assembly, colloquy, conclave, congress **9** discourse, interview **10** colloquium, conference, convention, discussion, round table **12** consultation

Poyser, Martin
character in: 8 Adam Bede
author: 5 Eliot

practicable 6 doable, viable **8** feasible, possible, workable **9** practical **10** achievable, attainable, functional

practical 4 able **5** solid, sound **6** expert, useful, versed **7** skilled, trained, veteran, working **8** seasoned, sensible, skillful **9** efficient, judicious, practiced, pragmatic, qualified, realistic **10**

functional, hardheaded, instructed, proficient, systematic, unromantic **11** down-to-earth, experienced, pragmatical, serviceable, utilitarian **12** accomplished, businesslike, matter-of-fact **13** unsentimental

practical joke 4 jape **5** caper, prank, stunt, trick

practically 6 all but, almost, nearly **8** actually, in effect **9** basically, in the main, just about, virtually **11** essentially **13** fundamentally, substantially

practice 2 do **3** use, way **4** deed, mode, play, rule, ruse, ways, wont **5** apply, dodge, drill, habit, train, trick, usage **6** action, custom, device, effect, follow, manner, method, pursue, ritual, work at **7** conduct, fashion, perform, process, qualify, routine, utilize **8** carry out, engage in, exercise, live up to, maneuver, rehearse, tendency, training **9** execution, operation, perform in, procedure, rehearsal, seasoning, set to work, turn to use **10** discipline, observance, prepare for, repetition **11** application, be engaged in, performance, preparation

practiced 4 able, fine **5** adept **6** adroit, expert **7** capable, drilled, pursued, skilled, trained **8** masterly, polished, seasoned, skillful, worked at **9** competent, engaged in, masterful, qualified, rehearsed **10** cultivated, proficient **11** experienced, prepared for **12** accomplished

practice sorcery 5 charm **7** bewitch, conjure, enchant **9** work magic **10** cast a spell

Practicing History
  author: **15** Barbara W Tuchman

practitioner 6 doctor **7** dentist **9** performer **12** professional

pragmatic 5 sober **8** sensible **9** hardnosed, practical, realistic **10** hardheaded, hard-boiled **11** down-to-earth, utilitarian **12** businesslike, matter-of-fact, unidealistic **13** materialistic, unsentimental

Praia
  capital of: **9** Cape Verde

prairie 3 bay **5** llano, pampa, plain **6** camass, meadow, steppe **7** quamash **9** grassland
  apple: **9** breadroot
  berry: **9** trampillo
  chicken: **6** grouse
  dog: **6** gopher, marmot
  schooner: **12** covered wagon
  state: **8** Illinois
  wolf: **6** coyote

Prairie, The
  author: **19** James Fenimore Cooper
  character: **4** Inez **9** Dr Battius, Ellen Wade, Hard-Heart, Paul Hover **10** Esther Bush **11** Abiram White, Ishmael Bush, Natty Bumppo **16** Captain Middleton

Prairie State
  nickname of: **8** Illinois

praise 4 laud, tout **5** cheer, exalt, extol, honor **6** esteem, eulogy, hurrah, regard, revere **7** acclaim, applaud, approve, build up, commend, glorify, plaudit, respect, root for, tribute, worship **8** accolade, applause, approval, encomium, eulogize, venerate **9** adoration, celebrate, good words, laudation, panegyric **10** admiration, compliment, panegyrize **11** approbation, compliments, testimonial **12** appreciation, commendation, congratulate **14** congratulation
  Hebrew: **6** hallel

praise be to God
  Latin: **7** laus Deo

praiseful 8 praising **9** extolling, laudatory **10** plauditory **12** commendatory **13** complimentary

praiseworthiness 5 merit **10** excellence **12** admirability, desirability **14** commendability

praiseworthy 4 fine **6** worthy **8** laudable **9** admirable, estimable, excellent, exemplary **11** commendable, meritorious

pram, praam, prahm 4 boat **5** buggy **6** vessel **7** rowboat **8** carriage, stroller **12** perambulator

prance 4 jump, leap, romp, skip **5** bound, caper, dance, frisk, strut, vault **6** bounce, cavort, frolic, gambol, spring **7** swagger

prank 4 joke, lark **5** antic, caper, spoof, stunt, trick **6** gambol **8** escapade, mischief **9** horseplay **10** shenanigan, tomfoolery

prate 3 gab, yak **4** blab, brag, chat, crow, talk **5** boast **6** babble, gabble, jabber **7** blabber, chatter, prattle, twaddle, twattle

Prathet Thai *see* **8** Thailand

prattle 3 gab, yak **4** blab **5** prate **6** babble, gabble, hot air, jabber **7** blather, chatter, twaddle **8** cackling, chitchat, gabbling **9** gibbering, jabbering

Pravda 15 Soviet newspaper
  literally: **5** truth

pray 3 beg, bid, sue **4** urge **5** cry to, plead **7** beseech, entreat, implore, request, solicit **8** call upon, invocate, petition **9** importune **10** supplicate

prayer 6 litany, orison, praise **7** worship **9** adoration **12** thanksgiving **13** glorification

prayerful 4 holy **5** godly, pious **6** devout, solemn **8** reverent **9** pietistic, religious, spiritual **10** worshipful **11** reverential

prayers 4 hope, plea, suit **5** dream **6** appeal **7** request **8** entreaty, petition **10** aspiration, invocation **11** beseechment **12** solicitation, supplication

prayer service 9 devotions **13** prayer meeting **14** worship service

pray for us
  Latin: **11** ora pro nobis

pray to 3 beg **5** plead **7** address, entreat, worship **8** call upon, petition, venerate **10** supplicate

preach 4 urge **6** advise, exhort **7** counsel, declare, expound, profess **8** admonish, advocate, homilize, proclaim, stand for **9** discourse, hold forth, preachify, prescribe, pronounce, propagate, sermonize **10** evangelize, promulgate

preacher 5 vicar **6** curate, parson, pastor **8** chaplain, homilist, minister, reverend, sky pilot **9** churchman, clergyman **10** evangelist, prebendary, sermonizer **12** ecclesiastic **13** man of the cloth

preachy 8 didactic, pedantic **10** moralistic, moralizing

prearranged 7 planned **10** calculated, deliberate, purposeful **11** intentional **12** premeditated

pre-Cambrian 5 Azoic **6** Eozoic **7** primary **10** Archeozoic **11** Proterozoic

precarious 5 risky, shaky **6** chancy, unsafe **7** dubious **8** alarming, critical, doubtful, insecure, perilous, sinister, ticklish, unstable, unsteady **9** hazardous, uncertain **10** touch-and-go, unreliable, vulnerable **12** questionable, uncontrolled, undependable **13** problematical

precaution 4 care **7** caution, defense **8** prudence, security, wariness **9** foresight, provision, safeguard **10** protection **11** carefulness, forethought, heedfulness **12** anticipation **14** circumspection

precede 8 antecede, antedate, go before **9** go ahead of **10** come before

precedence, precedency 8 priority **10** importance, preference, prevalence **11** antecedence, preeminence **12** predominance, preexistence

precedent 5 model **7** example, pattern **8** standard **9** criterion, guideline

preceding 5 prior **6** former **7** earlier **8** anterior, previous **9** aforesaid, foregoing **10** antecedent, first-named, precursory **11** preexistent, preliminary **14** abovementioned, aforementioned, first-mentioned

precept 3 law **4** bull, code, rule **5** axiom, canon, edict, maxim, motto, tenet, truth, ukase **6** byword, decree, dictum **7** dictate, mandate, statute **8** standard, teaching **9** ordinance, principle, yard stick **10** regulation **11** commandment, declaration

preceptor 5 coach, tutor **6** mentor **7** advisor, teacher **8** director **9** admonitor, counselor, principal **10** headmaster **12** headmistress

precincts 7 suburbs 8 environs 9 districts, outskirts 10 boundaries 12 subdivisions 15 surrounding area

precious 4 dear, rare 5 fussy, sweet 6 adored, choice, costly, dainty, prissy, prized, valued 7 beloved, darling, finical, finicky, lovable 8 adorable, affected, uncommon, valuable 9 cherished, expensive, exquisite, priceless, treasured 10 fastidious, high-priced, invaluable, meticulous, particular 11 beyond price, inestimable, overrefined, pretentious

precipice 4 crag 5 bluff, cliff, ledge 8 headland, palisade 9 cliff edge, declivity 10 escarpment

precipitate 4 cast, hurl, rash, spur 5 drive, fling, hasty, throw 6 abrupt, hasten, launch, let fly, propel, rushed, speedy, thrust 7 advance, bring on, hurried, quicken, speed up 8 catapult, expedite, headlong, reckless 9 discharge, foolhardy, impetuous, imprudent, impulsive 10 accelerate, incautious 11 thoughtless

precipitation 4 hail, rain, rush, snow 5 haste, sleet 8 rainfall, rashness 9 hastiness 11 impetuously

precipitous 5 hasty, sharp, sheer, steep 6 abrupt 9 impetuous

precis 5 brief 6 apercu, digest, resume, sketch 7 epitome, outline, rundown, summary 8 abstract, synopsis 10 abridgment, compendium 12 condensation 14 recapitulation

precise 4 true 5 exact, fussy, rigid 6 strict 7 careful, express, finicky, literal 8 accurate, clear-cut, definite, distinct, explicit, incisive, specific 9 unbending 10 fastidious, inflexible, meticulous, particular, to the point 11 painstaking, unequivocal

precision 5 rigor 8 accuracy, fidelity 9 attention, exactness 11 factualness, preciseness 12 authenticity, truthfulness 14 meticulousness

preclude 3 bar, dam 4 balk, curb, foil, stop 5 avert, avoid, block, check, debar, deter 6 arrest, hamper, hinder, thwart 7 head off, inhibit, prevent 8 stave off 9 forestall, frustrate 11 nip in the bud

preclusion 9 exclusion, restraint 10 prevention

precocious 3 apt 5 quick, smart 6 bright, clever, gifted, mature 8 advanced 9 brilliant

preconception 4 bias 6 notion 9 fixed idea, prejudice 11 prejudgment, presumption 14 predisposition

precursor 4 mark, omen, sign 5 token, usher 6 herald 7 portent, symptom, warning 8 vanguard 9 harbinger, messenger 10 antecedent, forerunner 11 predecessor

precursory 5 prior 8 anterior, previous

9 precedent 10 antecedent 11 preexistent

predaceous, predacious 9 predatory, rapacious 10 meat-eating 11 carnivorous, flesh-eating

predate 7 precede 8 antecede, antedate, go before

predatory 8 thievish 9 larcenous, marauding, pillaging, piratical, rapacious, raptorial, vulturine 10 plunderous, predacious

predecessor 7 forbear 8 ancestor, forebear, foregoer 10 antecedent, forefather, forerunner

predestination 4 fate 6 kismet 7 destiny, fortune 8 God's will 10 providence 13 inevitability, preordination 16 predetermination

predetermined 5 fated 7 decided, planned 8 destined 10 calculated, deliberate, preplanned 11 intentional, prearranged, predestined 12 foreordained, premeditated

predicament 3 fix, jam 4 bind, mess 5 pinch 6 corner, crisis, pickle, plight, scrape, strait 7 dilemma, trouble 8 hot water, quandary 9 imbroglio, sad plight 10 difficulty, perplexity

predicate 4 base, real, rest, true 5 found, imply 6 affirm, assert 7 commend, connote, declare 8 proclaim

predict 4 omen 5 augur 6 divine 7 betoken, foresee, presage 8 envision, forecast, foretell, prophesy 10 anticipate 13 prognosticate

prediction 6 augury 7 portent 8 forecast, prophecy 10 divination 11 declaration, foretelling, soothsaying 12 announcement, anticipation, proclamation 13 crystal gazing 15 prognostication

predilection 4 bent, bias, love 5 fancy, favor, taste 6 desire, hunger, liking, relish 7 leaning 8 appetite, fondness, penchant, tendency 9 prejudice, proneness 10 attraction, partiality, preference, proclivity, propensity 11 inclination 13 prepossession 14 predisposition

predispose 6 bias, lure, sway, urge 5 tempt 6 entice, induce, prompt, seduce 7 dispose, incline, win over 8 persuade 9 encourage, influence, prejudice

predisposed 3 apt 5 given, prone 8 inclined

predisposition 7 leaning 8 tendency 11 inclination

predominance 7 command, control 8 currency 9 dominance, supremacy 10 ascendancy, importance, prevalence 11 preeminence, superiority 12 universality

predominant 4 main 5 chief, major 6 potent, ruling, strong 7 leading, supreme 8 dominant, forceful, powerful,

reigning, vigorous 9 ascendant, important, paramount, sovereign 11 controlling, influential 13 authoritative

predominate 4 lead 7 prevail 8 dominate

predominating 5 chief 6 ruling 8 dominant, superior 9 principal 10 commanding, prevailing 11 controlling, predominant 13 authoritative

preeminence 9 greatness, supremacy 10 ascendancy, importance, leadership, notability, prominence 11 distinction, superiority 12 predominance

preeminent 4 best 5 famed 6 famous 7 eminent, honored, supreme 8 dominant, foremost, greatest, peerless, renowned, superior 9 matchless, paramount, unequaled, unrivaled 10 celebrated, consummate 11 illustrious, predominant, unsurpassed 12 incomparable, second to none, unparalleled 13 distinguished
French: 13 par excellence

preempt 4 take 5 seize, usurp 8 arrogate, take over 10 commandeer, confiscate 11 appropriate, expropriate

preen 3 pin 4 perk, trim 5 adorn, dress, groom, plume, pride, primp, prink 6 brooch, smooth
wings: 4 whet

preexistent 5 prior 8 anterior, previous 9 precedent 10 antecedent, precursory

preface 4 open 5 begin, proem, start 6 launch 7 prelude 8 commence, foreword, initiate, lead into, overture, preamble, prologue 9 introduce 12 introduction

prefer 3 opt 4 file 5 adopt, elect, exalt, fancy, favor, lodge, offer 6 select, take to, tender 7 dignify, elevate, ennoble, fix upon, pick out, present, proffer, promote 8 graduate, set forth 9 single out

preference 4 bent, bias, pick 5 fancy 6 liking, option 7 leaning 8 favoring, priority 9 advantage, prejudice, proneness, selection, supremacy 10 ascendancy, partiality, precedence, proclivity, propensity 11 first choice, inclination 12 predilection 13 predomination 14 predisposition
French: 4 gout

prefigure 4 hint, type 6 shadow, typify 7 foresee, imagine, presage, suggest 9 adumbrate 10 foreshadow

pregnant 4 full, rich 6 fecund, filled, gravid 7 copious, fertile, fraught, replete, seminal, teeming, weighty 8 forceful, fruitful, prolific 9 abounding, expecting, gestating, important, luxuriant, momentous, plenteous, potential, with child, with young 10 impressive, life-giving, meaningful, parturient, productive, suggestive 11 having a baby, proliferous, provocative, signifi-

cant **12** fructiferous, in a family way
French: 8 enceinte

prehistoric 3 old **7** ancient **10** immemorial
continent: 8 Atlantis
epoch: 6 Eocene **7** Miocene **8** Pliocene **9** Oligocene, Paleocene **11** Pleistocene
era: 8 Cenozoic, Mesozoic **9** Paleozoic **10** Archeozoic **11** Proterozoic
implement: 4 celt **6** eolith
period: 7 Neogene, Permian **8** Cambrian, Devonian, Jurassic, Silurian, Triassic **9** Paleogene **10** Cretaceous, Ordovician, Quaternary
reptile: 8 dinosaur

prehistoric era 6 Ice Age **8** Cenozoic, Jurassic, Mesozoic, Triassic **9** Paleozoic **10** Cenomanian, Cretaceous **11** Precambrian **15** Upper Cretaceous **16** Pleistocene Epoch

prehistoric man *see* **8** early man

prejudice 3 ill, mar **4** bias, harm, hurt, loss, sway **5** slant, spoil, taint **6** damage, impair, infect, injure, injury, poison **7** bigotry **8** jaundice **9** detriment **10** favoritism, impairment, partiality, predispose, unfairness **11** contaminate, intolerance, prejudgment **12** disadvantage, one-sidedness, predilection **13** preconception **14** discrimination, predisposition

prejudiced 6 biased, unfair, unjust **7** bigoted, slanted **9** arbitrary **10** intolerant **11** close-minded, opinionated **12** narrow-minded

prejudicial 3 bad **6** biased **7** harmful, hurtful **8** damaging, inimical, sinister **9** injurious **11** deleterious, detrimental

prelate 5 abbot **6** bishop, cleric **9** churchman, clergy man **12** ecclesiastic

preliminary 9 prelusive, prelusory **10** initiatory, precursory, prefactory **11** preparative, preparatory **12** introductory

prelude 7 opening, preface **8** overture, preamble, prologue **9** beginning **11** preliminary, preparation **12** introduction

premature 3 raw **5** green, hasty **6** callow, unripe **7** too soon, unready **8** abortive, ill-timed, immature, previous, too early, untimely **9** embryonic, overhasty, unfledged, unhatched, vestigial **10** incomplete, unprepared **11** inopportune, precipitate, rudimentary, undeveloped **12** unseasonable

premeditated 7 planned, plotted, studied, willful **8** intended **9** conscious, contrived, voluntary **10** calculated, considered, deliberate, predevised, purposeful **11** in cold blood, intentional, prearranged, predesigned **13** predetermined **22** with malice aforethought

premeditation 4 plan **6** design **7** pur-

pose **11** calculation, forethought, preplanning **12** deliberation

premier 3 bet **4** head **5** chief, first **6** oldest **7** leading, supreme **8** earliest, foremost **9** principal **13** prime minister

Preminger, Otto
director of: 5 Laura **11** Carmen Jones **16** Anatomy of a Murder

premise 6 theory **8** argument **9** postulate, principle **10** assumption, hypothesis **11** presumption, proposition, supposition **14** presupposition

premises 4 site **8** environs, property, vicinity **9** precincts

premium 4 gain, gift **5** award, bonus, prize **6** bounty, return, reward **7** benefit, payment **8** priority **9** high value, incentive **10** great stock, recompense, reparation **11** overpayment **12** appreciation, compensation, inflated rate, remuneration **13** consideration, encouragement

premonition 4 omen, sign **5** hunch, token **6** augury **7** auspice, feeling, inkling, portent, presage **9** foretoken **10** foreboding, indication, prediction **11** forewarning **12** presentiment

Prendergast, Maurice Brazil
born: 6 Canada **7** St John's **12** Newfoundland
artwork: 6 Dieppe **8** Seashore **11** Picnic Grove **12** The Promenade **16** Ponte della Paglia **17** Along the Boulevard, Four Girls in Meadow **24** Umbrellas in the Rain Venice

Prentice, John
creator/artist of: 8 Rip Kirby

preoccupation 9 immersion, obsession **10** absorption, detachment, dreaminess, employment **11** abstraction, involvement **16** absentmindedness

preoccupied 6 absent, dreamy **8** absorbed, immersed, involved, obsessed **9** engrossed, wrapped up **10** abstracted, distracted **12** absent-minded

preoccupy 6 absorb, arrest, obsess, take up, wrap up **7** engross, immerse **9** fascinate

preparation 8 prudence, readying **9** foresight, preparing, provision, safeguard **10** precaution **11** expectation, forethought **12** anticipation

preparations 5 plans **7** elixirs **8** guidance, measures, mixtures, training, tutelage **9** dressings, education, seasoning, tinctures **11** concoctions, confections **12** arrangements **13** preliminaries, prepared foods, prescriptions **14** qualifications

prepare 3 fix **5** adapt, prime, ready **7** arrange, be ready, provide **8** get ready **9** make ready, rearrange, take steps

prepared 4 done **5** fixed, ready **6** cooked, primed **7** planned **8** arranged,

finished **9** made ready, rehearsed **11** provided for

prepayment 6 credit **7** advance **9** allowance **11** downpayment

preponderance, preponderancy 4 bulk, glut, mass **6** excess **7** surfeit, surplus **8** majority, plethora **9** dominance, plurality, profusion **10** domination, lion's share, oversupply, prevalence, redundance **12** predominance **14** superabundance

preponderant 3 key **4** main **5** chief, first, major, prime **7** highest, leading, primary, supreme **8** dominant, foremost, greatest **9** paramount, principal, uppermost **10** prevailing **11** outstanding, predominant

prepossessing 4 nice **7** winsome **8** alluring, charming, engaging, inviting, pleasant, striking **9** beguiling **10** attractive, bewitching, enchanting, entrancing, personable **11** captivating, fascinating, tantalizing

preposterous 5 inane, outre, silly **6** absurd, stupid **7** asinine, bizarre, fatuous, foolish, idiotic **9** imbecilic, laughable, ludicrous **10** irrational, outrageous, ridiculous **11** nonsensical, unthinkable **12** unreasonable

prerequisite 4 need **6** demand **8** demanded, exigency, required **9** called for, condition, de rigueur, essential, mandatory, necessary, necessity, postulate, requisite **10** imperative, sine qua non **11** requirement, stipulation **13** indispensable, qualification

prerogative 3 due **5** claim, grant, right **6** choice, option **7** freedom, liberty, license, warrant **9** advantage, exemption, franchise, privilege **10** birthright

presage 4 bode, omen, osse, sign **5** augur, token **6** augury, herald **7** betoken, portend, portent, predict **8** forecast, foreshow, foretell, indicate **9** foresight **10** foreboding, foreshadow, indication, prediction, prescience, prognostic **11** premonition **12** presentiment

presbyter 5 elder **13** church officer

prescience 7 presage **9** foresight, prevision **13** foreknowledge

prescribe 3 fix, set **4** rule, urge **5** enact, order **6** assign, decree, demand, direct, enjoin, impose, ordain, settle **7** appoint, command, dictate, require, specify **8** advocate, proclaim **9** authorize, establish, institute, legislate, recommend, stipulate

prescribed 3 set **5** fixed **6** thetic **9** formulary

prescript 3 law **4** rule **5** order **7** precept, statute **10** regulation

prescriptive 7 binding **8** demanded, dictated, didactic, required **9** customary, mandatory, requisite **10** compulsory, imperative, obligatory

presence 3 air 4 life, look, mien 5 being, curse, favor, ghost, group, midst 6 aspect, entity, figure, manner, shadow, spirit, vision, wraith 7 bearing, company, eidolon, phantom, specter 8 carriage, charisma, demeanor, features, phantasm, revenant, vitality 9 character, existence 10 apparition, attendance, deportment, expression, lineaments 11 reification, subsistence 12 neighborhood 13 manifestation

presence of mind 6 aplomb 8 calmness, coolness 9 composure, sangfroid 10 equanimity, steadiness 14 self-possession 16 imperturbability

present 2 in 3 fee, now, tip 4 alms, aver, boon, cite, gift, give, here, near, nigh, read, show, tell 5 about, award, frame, grant, offer, state, today 6 accord, allege, assert, at hand, bestow, bounty, call up, chip in, coeval, confer, donate, hand in, impart, legacy, nearby, on hand, recite, relate, render, rooted, submit, summon, supply, tender, turn in 7 advance, bequest, bring on, current, declare, deliver, display, dole out, exhibit, expound, give out, instant, largess, mete out, not away, produce, profess, proffer, propose, provide, recount, vicinal 8 donation, embedded, existent, existing, give away, give over, gratuity, hand over, nowadays, oblation, offering, propound, put forth 9 apprise of, attending, draw forth, endowment, ensconced, hold forth, immediate, implanted, in the room, introduce, make known, not absent, on-the-spot, prevalent, pronounce, surrender, the moment, unremoved 10 asseverate, come up with, contribute, here and now, liberality, perquisite, put forward 11 benefaction, communicate 12 accounted for, bring forward, contemporary, in attendance

presentable 4 chic, so-so 6 decent, modish, not bad, proper 7 stylish 8 becoming, passable, suitable 9 tolerable 10 acceptable, good enough 11 appropriate, fashionable, fit to be seen, respectable

presentation 3 fee, tip 4 boon, gift, show 5 favor, grant, offer 6 bounty 7 advance, display, exhibit, largess, present, proffer 8 bestowal, exposure, gratuity, oblation, offering, overture, proposal 9 unfolding 10 appearance, compliment, disclosure, exhibition, exposition, liberality, production, proffering, submission, unfoldment 11 benefaction, performance, proposition 13 demonstration

Present at the Creation
author: 11 Dean Acheson

presentiment 7 feeling 10 foreboding 11 forewarning, premonition 12 apprehension

presently 3 now 4 anon, soon 7 shortly 8 directly, in a while, this week, this year 9 at present, currently, forth with 10 any time now, before long, pretty soon 11 after a while, at the moment 12 in a short time
French: 11 tout a l'heure

preservation 6 saving 7 defense 9 salvation 10 protection 11 maintenance, safekeeping 12 conservation, safeguarding

preservative 4 salt 5 brine, spice 8 marinade 12 formaldehyde

preserve, preserves 3 can, dry, jam 4 corn, cure, park, salt, save, seal 5 guard, haven, jelly, nurse, put up, smoke, sweet 6 comfit, defend, embalm, foster, freeze, pickle, refuge, season, secure, shield 7 care for, compote, mummify, protect, reserve, shelter 8 conserve, insulate, keep safe, maintain, marinate 9 dehydrate, keep sound, marmalade, safeguard, sanctuary, sweetmeat, watch over 10 confection, keep intact, perpetuate 11 refrigerate, reservation

preside 4 boss, host, rule 5 chair, watch 6 direct, govern, manage 7 command, conduct, control, hostess, oversee 8 chairman, overlook, regulate 9 keep order, supervise 10 administrate, take the chair

president, President 4 head 5 ruler 8 chairman 12 chief officer, chief of state, first citizen 14 chief executive 16 commander in chief, executive officer, head of government

President of the United States
first: 16 George Washington
second: 9 John Adams
third: 15 Thomas Jefferson
fourth: 12 James Madison
fifth: 11 James Monroe
sixth: 15 John Quincy Adams
seventh: 13 Andrew Jackson
eighth: 14 Martin Van Buren
ninth: 20 William Henry Harrison
tenth: 9 John Tyler
eleventh: 10 James K Polk
twelfth: 13 Zachary Taylor
thirteenth: 15 Millard Fillmore
fourteenth: 14 Franklin Pierce
fifteenth: 13 James Buchanan
sixteenth: 14 Abraham Lincoln
seventeenth: 13 Andrew Johnson
eighteenth: 13 Ulysses S Grant
nineteenth: 16 Rutherford B Hayes
twentieth: 14 James A Garfield
twenty-first: 17 Chester Alan Arthur
twenty-second: 15 Grover Cleveland
twenty-third: 16 Benjamin Harrison
twenty-fourth: 15 Grover Cleveland
twenty-fifth: 15 William McKinley
twenty-sixth: 17 Theodore Roosevelt
twenty-seventh: 17 William Howard Taft

twenty-eighth: 13 Woodrow Wilson
twenty-ninth: 14 Warren G Harding
thirtieth: 14 Calvin Coolidge
thirty-first: 13 Herbert Hoover
thirty-second: 18 Franklin D Roosevelt
thirty-third: 12 Harry S Truman
thirty-fourth: 17 Dwight D Eisenhower
thirty-fifth: 12 John F Kennedy
thirty-sixth: 14 Lyndon B Johnson
thirty-seventh: 13 Richard M Nixon
thirty-eighth: 11 Gerald R Ford
thirty-ninth: 11 (James E) Jimmy Carter (Jr)
fortieth: 12 Ronald Reagan
forty-first: 10 George Bush
forty-second: 11 (William Jefferson) Bill Clinton

President's Analyst, The
director: 16 Theodore J Flicker
cast: 8 Will Geer 11 James Coburn 12 Severn Darden 16 Godfrey Cambridge

preside over 5 chair, guide 6 direct, govern, manage 7 conduct 8 dominate 9 supervise 10 administer 11 superintend

Presley, Elvis Aron
nickname: 7 The King 14 Elvis the Pelvis 15 King of Rock n Roll
born: 6 Tupelo 11 Mississippi
wife: 9 Priscilla
daughter: 9 Lisa Marie
father: 6 Vernon
mother: 6 Gladys
twin brother: 11 Jessie Garon
manager: 16 Colonel Tom Parker
home: 9 Graceland
location: 7 Memphis 9 Tennessee
song: 8 Hound Dog 10 All Shook Up 11 Don't Be Cruel 12 Love Me Tender 13 Jailhouse Rock 14 Blue Suede Shoes 15 Heartbreak Hotel 17 That's All Right Mama
film: 7 G I Blues 9 Loving You 10 Blue Hawaii, King Creole 12 Love Me Tender, Viva Las Vegas 13 Jailhouse Rock

press 2 TV 3 beg, bug, dun, hit, hug, jam, mob, pet, tap, tax 4 army, body, cram, duty, heap, herd, host, iron, mash, mill, pack, prod, push, rush 5 beset, bunch, clasp, crowd, crush, drove, exact, flick, force, horde, hound, hurry, media, plead, radio, set on, steam, stuff, surge, swarm 6 appeal, bother, burden, caress, compel, duress, enjoin, exhort, extort, fondle, gather, huddle, legion, mangle, push in, reduce, smooth, strain, stress, throng 7 cluster, collect, depress, embrace, entreat, flatten, implore, newsmen, oppress, snuggle, squeeze, trouble 8 assemble, bear down, bear upon, calender, compress, condense, hot-press, insist on, pressure, printing, push down 9 annoyance, be hard put, constrain, constrict, final form, force down, force from, importune, multitude, reporters **10** compulsion, congregate, newspapers, obligation, supplicate, television, thrust down **11** journalists, periodicals, publication **12** bear down upon, broadcasting, come together, news services, newspapermen **14** Fourth Estate

press down 7 compact, depress **8** push down

press forward 5 drive **6** push on **7** advance **10** forge ahead

press home 6 stress **9** emphasize, underline **10** accentuate, underscore

pressing 5 vital **6** crying, needed, urgent **7** crucial, exigent, needful **8** critical **9** clamoring, demanding, essential, important, insistent, necessary **10** imperative **11** importunate **13** indispensable

pressing necessity 6 crisis **7** urgency **8** exigency **9** emergency

press on 9 move ahead, persevere **10** accelerate, forge ahead **11** move forward

pressure 4 bias, care, load, need, pull, sway, want **5** force, hurry, pinch, power, press, trial **6** burden, demand, strain, stress, weight **7** anxiety, density, gravity, potency, squeeze, straits, tension, trouble, urgency **8** coercion, distress, exigency, interest **9** adversity, grievance, heaviness, influence, necessity **10** affliction, compaction, compulsion, difficulty, oppression

pressure measurement 6 pascal **10** atmosphere

prestige 4 fame, mark, note **5** glory, honor **6** esteem, import, regard, renown, report, repute **7** account, respect **8** eminence **9** authority, celebrity **10** importance, notability, prominence, reputation **11** consequence, distinction, preeminence **12** significance

prestigious 5 famed **6** famous **7** eminent, honored, notable **8** esteemed, renowned **9** acclaimed, important, prominent, reputable, respected, wellknown **10** celebrated **11** illustrious, outstanding **13** distinguished

Preston, Robert
  real name: 21 Robert Preston Meservey
  born: 17 Newton Highlands MA
  roles: 4 Mame **9** Semi-Tough **11** The Music Man **12** Junior Bonner **14** Victor Victoria **16** How the West Was Won

presumable 6 likely **8** apparent, probable **10** ostensible

presumably 6 likely **8** probably **9** assumably, doubtless **10** apparently, ostensibly **13** presumptively **14** unquestionably **15** in all likelihood **16** in all probability

presume 4 dare **5** fancy, guess, posit **6** assume, deduce, gather, have it, impose, take it **7** believe, imagine, suppose, surmise, suspect, venture **8** be so bold, conceive, make bold, make free **9** postulate, take leave **11** hypothesize, rely too much, think likely **12** take a liberty

presumed 7 assumed, deduced, posited **8** believed, imagined, supposed, surmised **9** suspected **10** postulated **13** took advantage **15** taken for granted

presumption 3 lip **4** gall **5** brass, cheek, guess, nerve, pride **6** belief, daring **7** egotism, premise, surmise **8** audacity, boldness, chutzpah, rudeness **9** arrogance, flippancy, impudence, insolence, postulate **10** assumption, conjecture, effrontery **11** forwardness, haughtiness, prejudgment, speculation, supposition **12** impertinence **13** preconception **14** presupposition

presumptuous 4 bold **5** brash, cocky, fresh, lofty, nervy, proud **6** brassy, brazen, daring, lordly **7** forward, haughty, pompous **8** arrogant, assuming, snobbish **9** audacious, imperious, shameless **10** disdainful **11** dictatorial, domineering, overbearing, patronizing **12** contemptuous, overfamiliar **13** overconfident

presuppose 6 assume **7** presume, suppose **9** speculate **10** conjecture **11** hypothesize

presupposed 7 assumed **8** presumed, supposed **10** speculated **11** conjectured

presupposition 7 premise **10** assumption **11** postulation, presumption

pretend 4 fake, sham **5** claim, fancy, feign, mimic, put on **6** affect, assume **7** imagine, imitate, playact, purport, suppose **8** simulate **9** dissemble **10** masquerade **11** counterfeit, dissimulate, impersonate, make believe

pretended
  French: **9** soi-disant

pretender 5 faker, fraud, phony **8** claimant, imposter

pretense 4 airs, fake, hoax, mask, sham, show **5** cloak, cover, feint, guile, trick, vaunt **6** deceit **7** bluster, bombast, display, pretext **8** boasting, bragging, disguise, trickery **9** deception, false show, imposture, invention, pomposity **10** camouflage, pretension, showing off, subterfuge **11** affectation, counterfeit, fabrication, fanfaronade, make-believe, ostentation **12** affectedness

pretension 4 airs, pomp, show **5** claim, right, title **7** bombast, display **8** ambition, pretense, snobbery **9** hypocrisy, pomposity, showiness **10** aspiration, showing off **11** affectation, os-

tentation **13** grandioseness **14** self-importance **16** ostentatiousness

pretentious 4 airy, smug **5** gaudy, lofty, showy, stagy **6** flashy, florid, garish, ornate, tawdry **7** blown-up, fatuous, pompous, stuck-up **8** affected, assuming, boastful, inflated, overdone, pedantic, puffed-up, snobbish **9** bombastic, flaunting, insincere, presuming, unnatural **10** hoity-toity, theatrical **11** exaggerated, extravagant, overbearing **12** ostentatious, self-praising **13** high-and-mighty, self-important

pretentiousness 4 cant **6** humbug **9** hypocrisy **11** insincerity **17** sanctimoniousness

preternatural 5 eerie, weird **6** arcane, occult **7** bizarre, strange, uncanny **8** esoteric, mystical **9** unearthly, unworldly **10** miraculous, mysterious, superhuman **11** hypernormal, preterhuman, supernormal **12** extramundane, metaphysical, supernatural, supranatural **14** transcendental

pretext 5 basis, bluff, feint **6** excuse, ground **8** pretense **9** semblance **10** pretension, subterfuge **11** vindication

pretty 4 fair **5** bonny **6** comely, dainty, fairly, goodly, lovely, rather **7** shapely, sightly, well-set **8** alluring, charming, delicate, engaging, fetching, graceful, handsome, somewhat, wellmade **9** beauteous, beautiful **10** adequately, attractive, moderately, reasonably **11** captivating, good-looking, symmetrical, well-favored

pretty child 4 doll **5** cutie **10** living doll

prevail 3 win **4** rule **5** exist, reign **6** abound, obtain, win out **7** conquer, succeed, triumph **8** have sway, hold sway, overcome **9** be a winner, be current **11** be prevalent, be the victor, carry the day, gain the palm, predominate **12** be victorious, be widespread, preponderate

prevailing 3 set **4** main **5** fixed, usual **6** normal **7** current, general, in style, popular **8** definite, dominant **9** customary, prevalent, principal **10** accustomed, widespread **11** established, predominant **12** conventional, preponderant

prevail over 4 beat **5** outdo **6** defeat **7** eclipse, surpass **8** overcome

prevail upon 4 sway **8** convince, persuade **9** influence

prevalent 4 rife **5** usual **6** common, normal **7** general, popular, rampant **8** abundant, everyday, familiar, frequent, habitual, numerous **9** customary, extensive, pervasive, universal **10** prevailing, ubiquitous, widespread **11** commonplace **12** conventional

prevaricate 3 fib, lie **4** fake **6** palter **7** deceive, distort, falsify, mislead, perjure **8** hoodwink, misstate **9** be evasive, dissemble **10** equivocate, tell a story **11** counterfeit **12** be untruthful, misrepresent

prevarication 3 fib, lie **5** fable **7** fiction, untruth, whopper **9** fairy tale, falsehood, fish story, invention **11** fabrication **12** equivocation **16** cock-and-bull story **17** misrepresentation

prevent 3 bar, dam **4** balk, foil, halt, stop, veto **5** avert, avoid, block, deter **6** arrest, forbid, thwart **7** deflect, draw off, fend off, obviate, rule out, ward off **8** hold back, preclude, prohibit, stave off, turn away **9** forestall, frustrate, intercept, sidetrack, turn aside **10** anticipate, counteract **11** nip in the bud

prevention 6 defeat **8** stoppage **9** avoidance, hindrance, obviation, restraint, thwarting **10** deterrence, inhibition, preclusion **11** elimination, frustration **12** interception **13** forestallment

preview 5 sneak **6** sample, survey **8** futurama **9** foretaste **10** inspection

previous 5 early, prior **6** before, former **7** earlier **8** foregone **9** aforesaid, erstwhile, foregoing, preceding **10** antecedent **14** aforementioned

previously 4 once **6** before **7** earlier, long ago **8** back when, formerly **9** at one time, a while ago, earlier on **10** a while back, heretofore **11** in times past **12** sometime back

Prevost, Abbe
author of: 12 Manon Lescaut

prey 3 eat **4** dupe, food, game, gull, kill **5** patsy, prize, quest **6** devour, infest, pigeon, quarry, sucker, target, victim **7** cat's-paw, consume, fall guy, live off **8** feed upon **9** feast upon **10** fasten upon, fatten upon, parasitize

Priam
king of: 4 Troy
father: 8 Laomedon
brother: 8 Tithonus
wife: 6 Hecuba
son: 5 Paris **6** Hector **9** Polydorus
daughter: 8 Polyxena **9** Cassandra
number of sons: 5 fifty
number of daughters: 5 fifty
killed by: 11 Neoptolemus

Priamid
father: 5 Priam

Priapus
god of: 5 herds **7** gardens **9** fertility, male power **11** procreation
father: 8 Dionysus
mother: 9 Aphrodite
corresponds to: 7 Mutinus

price 3 fee **4** cost, fine, rate **5** value, worth **6** amount, assess, charge, outlay **7** expense, penalty **8** appraise, evaluate, par value **9** face value, list price **10** forfeiture, punishment

Price, Fanny

character in: 13 Mansfield Park
author: 6 Austen

Price, Vincent
born: 9 St Louis MO
wife: 11 Coral Browne **12** Edith Barrett
roles: 6 The Fly **8** The Raven **10** House of Wax **13** Tower of London **15** The House of Usher **20** The Pit and the Pendulum **22** The Masque of the Red Death
expert in: 3 art

Price Is Right, The
host: 9 Bob Barker **10** Bill Cullen

priceless 4 dear, rare **6** costly, prized, valued **8** peerless, precious, valuable **9** cherished, expensive, treasured **10** high-priced, invaluable **11** beyond price **12** incomparable, without price **13** irreplaceable **17** worth a king's ransom

prick 5 stick **6** pierce **8** puncture

prickle 4 barb, itch **5** point, quill, smart, sting, thorn **6** tingle **7** barbule, bristle, spicule

prickly 5 itchy **6** coarse, thorny **8** scratchy, stinging **9** vexatious

pride 3 joy **4** airs, pomp, show **5** honor **6** egoism, parade, vanity **7** comfort, conceit, delight, dignity, display, egotism, swagger **8** pleasure, self-love, smugness **9** arrogance, be proud of, enjoyment, happiness, immodesty, pomposity, vainglory **10** pretension, self-esteem **11** haughtiness, ostentation, self-respect **14** self-importance

Pride and Prejudice
author: 10 Jane Austen
character: 7 Mr Darcy **9** Mr Bingley, Mr Collins, Mr Wickham **14** Charlotte Lucas **15** Caroline Bingley **21** Lady Catherine de Bourgh
  Bennet daughters: 4 Jane, Mary **5** Kitty, Lydia **9** Elizabeth
director: 14 Robert Z Leonard
cast: 10 Mary Boland **11** Edmund Gwenn, Greer Garson, Karen Morley **13** Ann Rutherford, Edna May Oliver **15** Laurence Olivier **16** Maureen O'Sullivan

Pride of the Yankees, The
director: 7 Sam Wood
cast: 8 Babe Ruth **9** Dan Duryea **10** Gary Cooper (Lou Gehrig) **12** Teresa Wright **13** Walter Brennan

priest 5 padre **6** cleric, father **8** minister, preacher **9** churchman **13** man of the cloth

priesthood 5 cloth **6** clergy **8** ministry, the cloth **9** pastorage

Priestley, J B
author of: 9 Bright Day **11** Lost Empires **13** Angel Pavement **17** The Good Companions

Priestley, Joseph
field: 9 chemistry

nationality: 7 British
discovered: 6 oxygen **7** ammonia **13** nitrogen oxide
invented: 11 carbonation

priestly 8 churchly, clerical **10** sacerdotal **14** ecclesiastical

prig 5 bigot, prude **6** pedant **7** puritan **8** bluenose **9** formalist, hypocrite, nitpicker, pretender **10** fuddy-duddy **11** faultfinder **12** bluestocking, precisionist, stuffed shirt **14** attitudinarian

priggish 4 prim, smug **6** stuffy **7** prudish **9** blue-nosed **10** tight-laced **11** puritanical, straitlaced **13** self-righteous, self-satisfied

prim 4 smug, tidy **5** fussy **6** prissy, proper, strict, stuffy **7** haughty, prudish **8** priggish, starched **9** squeamish, unbending **10** fastidious, fuddy-duddy, inflexible, no-nonsense, particular **11** overprecise, puritanical, stiff-necked, straitlaced

prima donna 4 diva, lead, star **6** singer **9** principal
literally: 9 first lady

primarily 6 mainly, mostly **7** chiefly, largely **9** basically, generally, in the main **11** essentially, principally **13** fundamentally, predominantly **14** for the most part **16** first and foremost

primary 3 key **4** main, star **5** basal, basic, chief, first, prime, vital **6** innate, native, oldest, primal, ruling, utmost **7** highest, initial, leading, nascent, natural **8** cardinal, dominant, earliest, greatest, inherent, original, primeval **9** beginning, elemental, essential, important, necessary, primitive, principal, prominent **10** aboriginal, elementary, indigenous, primordial, rudimental **11** fundamental, predominant, preparatory, rudimentary **12** introductory

primary constituent 5 basic **9** basic need, essential, necessity, requisite **10** sine qua non

primate 3 ape, man **5** avahi, indri, lemur, loris, potto **6** aye-aye, baboon, bishop, galago, gibbon, mammal, monkey **7** gorilla, tamarin, tarsier **8** marmoset, simpoona **9** orangutan, tree shrew **10** archbishop, chimpanzee

prime 2 A1 **3** ace, fit **4** best, main, peak, pink **5** adapt, basal, basic, bloom, breed, brief, chief, coach, early, first, groom, guide, lucky, raise, ready, train, tutor, vital **6** adjust, choice, fill in, flower, Grade A, height, heyday, inform, innate, native, oldest, primal, prompt, ruling, school, seemly, select, timely, utmost, zenith **7** educate, fitting, highest, leading, maximal, natural, prepare, primary, quality, supreme, top-hole **8** best days, cardinal, crowning, earliest, get ready, greatest, inherent, instruct, maturity, original, peerless, suitable, superior **9** befitting, elemental, essential, expedient, important, intrinsic, make ready, matchless, necessary, opportune, paramount, preferred, principal, provident, top-drawer, top-flight, unmatched, well-timed **11** superlative, unsurpassed, without peer **12** unparalleled

prime example 5 model **7** classic **8** exemplar **9** archetype

prime mover 6 author **9** initiator, organizer
Latin: 12 primum mobile

Prime of Miss Jean Brodie, The
author: 11 Muriel Spark

primer 3 cap **4** book **5** paint **6** manual, reader **8** hornbook, textbook **9** undercoat

primeval 5 early **6** oldest, primal **7** ancient, archaic **8** earliest, original **9** ancestral, legendary, primitive **10** aboriginal, indigenous, primordial **11** fundamental, prehistoric **12** antediluvian, mythological

primitive 4 bare **5** crude, early, first **6** native, simple **7** antique, archaic, artless, ascetic, austere, primary, Spartan **8** backward, earliest, original **9** beginning, unlearned, unrefined, unskilled **10** aboriginal, elementary **11** rudimentary, uncivilized, undeveloped

primordial 5 first **6** primal **7** initial **8** original, primeval **9** beginning, primitive **10** elementary **11** fundamental, prehistoric

primp 5 groom, plume, preen **6** doll up, make up **7** gussy up **8** prettify, spruce up

primrose 7 Primula **15** Primula vulgaris
varieties: 4 baby, cape, star **5** fairy **6** German, poison **7** Chinese, English, evening **8** bird's-eye **9** buttercup **12** beach evening, white evening **13** desert evening **14** Mexican evening

primum mobile 10 prime mover **16** first moving thing

primus inter pares 16 first among equals

prince
Italian: 8 principe
Turkish: 3 beg, bey

Prince
original name: 18 Prince Rogers Nelson
alias: 9 The Artist **30** The Artist Formerly Known as Prince
nickname: 12 Royal Badness
born: 2 MN **11** Minneapolis
recording: 6 For You, Parade, Prince **9** Dirty Mind **10** Purple Rain **11** Controversy, Crystal Ball **20** Around the World in a Day
film: 10 Purple Rain **12** 3 Chains o' Gold **13** Sign o' the Times **14** Graffiti Bridge **18** Under the Cherry Moon

Prince, The
author: 18 Niccolo Machiavelli

Prince and the Pauper, The
author: 9 Mark Twain
character: 4 Hugo **8** Tom Canty **9** John Canty **10** Hugh Hendon **11** Miles Hendon **19** Edward Prince of Wales

Prince Edward Island
abbreviation: 3 PEI
bay: 5 Rollo **6** Egmont **7** Bedeque **8** Cardigan, Malpeque **9** Cascumpec **12** Hillsborough
capital: 13 Charlottetown
gulf: 10 St Lawrence
people: 4 Scot **5** Irish, Scots **6** French **7** English
discoverer: 7 Cartier
province of: 6 Canada
river: 4 Dunk **5** Eliot, Yorke **12** Hillsborough
strait: 14 Northumberland

Prince Igor
also: 9 Kniaz Igor
opera by: 7 Borodin
character: 11 Khan Konchak
contains: 17 Polovetsian dances

princely 3 big **5** noble, royal **8** generous **11** magnificent

prince of darkness 5 Satan **7** Lucifer **8** the Devil **9** Beelzebub

Prince of Peace 5 Jesus **6** Christ

Princess and the Pea, The
author: 21 Hans Christian Andersen

Princess Casamassima
author: 10 Henry James

Princess Daisy
author: 12 Judith Krantz

Princesse de Cleves, La
author: 14 Mme de LaFayette

Princess Flavia
character in: 15 Prisoner of Zenda
author: 4 Hope

Prince Valiant
creator: 12 Harold Foster
character: 5 Ilene **9** Prince Arn **10** King Arthur
wife: 5 Aleta
nickname: 3 Val

principal 4 dean, fund, main, star **5** basic, chief, first, money, prime **6** master **7** capital, leading, primary, supreme **8** cardinal, dominant, foremost, greatest, superior, ultimate **9** essential, paramount, preceptor, prominent **10** capital sum, headmaster, leading man, preeminent **11** fundamental, predominant **13** most important

principal constituent 4 base **12** chief feature **14** main ingredient

principal dish of a meal
French: 17 piece de resistance

principal event
French: 17 piece de resistance

principality 5 angel **9** princedom **14** celestial being, heavenly spirit

principally 6 mainly, mostly **7** chiefly, largely **8** above all **9** basically, primarily **10** especially **12** particularly **13** fundamentally, predominantly **14** for the most part **16** first and foremost

principe 6 prince

principle 3 law **4** code, fact, rule, view **5** axiom, basis, canon, credo, creed, dogma, honor, maxim, tenet, truth **6** belief, dictum, ethics, morals, theory, virtue **7** element, formula, honesty, precept, probity, scruple, theorem **8** attitude, doctrine, goodness, morality, position, rudiment, scruples, teaching **9** direction, integrity, rectitude, standards **10** assumption, regulation **11** fundamental, proposition, uprightness

principled 6 honest **7** upright **9** honorable **10** aboveboard, forthright

Pringle, John
real name of: 11 John Gilbert

prink 4 deck, fuss **5** adorn, preen, primp **6** spruce

print 3 die **4** copy, text, type **5** issue, plate, press, stamp, write **7** compose, edition, engrave, etching, gravure, impress, picture, publish, woodcut **10** lithograph, silkscreen **11** letterpress

printing press
invented by:
rotary: 3 Hoe
web: 7 Bullock

prior 6 former **7** earlier **8** anterior, previous **9** aforesaid, erstwhile, foregoing, prefatory **10** antecedent, precursory **11** going before, preexistent, preexisting, preparatory **14** aforementioned

Prioress
character in: 18 The Canterbury Tales
author: 7 Chaucer

priority 7 urgency **9** immediacy, seniority **10** ascendancy, precedence, precedency, preference **11** antecedence, preeminence, superiority

priory 5 abbey **6** friary **7** convent, nunnery **8** cloister **9** hermitage, monastery

Prism, Letitia
character in: 27 The Importance of Being Earnest
author: 5 Wilde

prison 3 can, jug, pen **4** brig, gaol, jail, stir, tank **5** clink, joint, pokey, tower **6** cooler **7** dungeon, slammer **8** bastille, big house **9** calaboose, jailhouse

Prisoner of Zenda
author: 11 Anthony Hope
character: 14 Princess Flavia **17** Lady Rose Burlesdon, Rudolph Rassendyll **18** Antoinette de Mauban, Fritz von Tarlenhein **21** Michael Duke of Strelsau **22** Rudolph King of Ruritania
director: 12 John Cromwell
cast: 9 Mary Astor **10** David Niven **12** C Aubrey Smith, Ronald Colman

(Rudolf Rassendyll) **16** Madeleine Carroll **18** Douglas Fairbanks Jr (Rupert of Hentzau)
setting: 9 Ruritania

prissy 4 prim **5** fussy **6** proper, stuffy **7** finicky, prudish **8** overnice **9** sissified **10** effeminate **11** strait-laced

Prissy
character in: 15 Gone With the Wind
author: 8 Mitchell

pristine 4 pure **8** unmarred, virginal **9** undefiled, unspoiled, unsullied, untouched **10** unpolluted **11** untarnished **14** uncontaminated

Pritchett, V S
author of: 11 Midnight Oil **16** Collected Stories, The Spanish Temper **19** On the Edge of the Cliff

privacy 6 secret **7** privity, retreat, secrecy **8** security, solitude **9** integrity, isolation, seclusion **10** retirement, withdrawal **11** privateness **12** dissociation, solitariness **13** sequestration

private 4 dark **5** fixed, privy **6** buried, closed, covert, hidden, lonely, remote, secret **7** cryptic, express, limited, obscure, special **8** confined, desolate, esoteric, hush-hush, isolated, lonesome, personal, secluded, solitary **9** concealed, exclusive, inviolate, invisible, nonpublic, not public, reclusive **10** classified, indistinct, mysterious, restricted, undercover, under wraps, unofficial, unrevealed **11** clandestine, nonofficial, sequestered, underground, undisclosed **12** confidential, off-the-record, unfrequented

privateer 6 pirate **7** brigand, corsair **9** buccaneer

private eye 4 dick **6** shamus **7** gumshoe **9** detective **12** investigator

Private Life of Henry VIII, The
director: 14 Alexander Korda
cast: 11 Merle Oberon, Robert Donat **12** Binnie Barnes **14** Elsa Lanchester (Anne of Cleves) **15** Charles Laughton (Henry VIII)

Private Life of the Master Race, The
author: 13 Bertold Brecht

Private Lives
author: 10 Noel Coward
character: 10 Elyot Chase, Sibyl Chase **12** Amanda Prynne, Victor Prynne

Private Lives of Elizabeth and Essex, The
director: 13 Michael Curtiz
cast: 10 Bette Davis (Elizabeth I), Errol Flynn (Essex) **11** Donald Crisp **12** Vincent Price **13** Nanette Fabray **17** Olivia de Havilland
also known as: 17 Elizabeth the Queen

privately 7 sub rosa **8** in secret, secretly **9** between us, entre nous, in private **12** in confidence **14** confiden-

tially **15** between you and me **16** between ourselves **17** behind closed doors

privation 4 lack, need, want **5** pinch **6** misery, penury **7** beggary, poverty, straits **8** distress, exigency, hardship **9** indigence, neediness, pauperism **10** bankruptcy, mendicancy **11** destitution **14** impoverishment **15** impecuniousness

privilege 3 due **4** boon **5** allow, favor, grant, honor, power, right, title **6** patent, permit **7** benefit, charter, empower, entitle, freedom, liberty, license **8** pleasure **9** advantage, authority, franchise **10** birthright **11** entitlement, prerogative **12** prerequisite

privileged 4 free **6** exempt, immune **7** allowed, excused, granted, limited, special **8** entitled, licensed **9** empowered, not liable, permitted, warranted **10** authorized, sanctioned **13** unaccountable

prize 3 cup, gem, pip **4** like, lulu **5** award, catch, crown, dandy, honey, honor, jewel, medal, peach, pearl, value **6** admire, esteem, honors, regard, reward, ribbon, trophy **7** cherish, diamond, guerdon, honored, laurels, premium, respect, winning **8** accolade, champion, citation, hold dear, look up to, pure gold, treasure **9** humdinger, medallion **10** appreciate, blue ribbon, decoration, set store by **11** crackerjack, masterpiece

prized 4 dear **8** esteemed, precious **9** cherished, treasured

prizefight 2 go **4** bout **5** match **6** boxing **7** contest **10** fisticuffs

prizefighter 3 pug **5** boxer **7** slugger **8** pugilist **9** flyweight **11** heavyweight, lightweight **12** bantamweight, middleweight, welterweight **13** featherweight **16** light heavyweight

pro 3 for **5** forth **6** before, expert, master **8** favoring **9** authority **11** affirmative
opposite: 3 con **7** amateur

probability 4 odds **6** chance **10** likelihood

probable 6 likely **7** logical, seeming, tenable **8** apparent, assuring, credible, expected, possible, presumed, supposed **9** plausible, promising, thinkable **10** believable, in the cards, ostensible, presumable, reasonable **11** conceivable, encouraging, presumptive

probably 6 likely **10** most likely, presumably, supposedly **11** as like as not **15** in all likelihood

probe 4 hunt, quiz, seek, test **5** query, study, trial **6** pursue, review, search, survey **7** examine, fish for, inquest, inquire, inquiry, inspect, pry into, rummage **8** analysis, look into, question, research **9** penetrate **10** inspec-

tion, scrutinize **11** examination, exploration, interrogate, investigate **13** investigation

probity 5 honor **6** virtue **7** decency, honesty **8** goodness, morality **9** character, integrity, principle **11** uprightness **12** straightness **13** righteousness **14** high-mindedness **15** trustworthiness **16** incorruptibility

problem 5 poser, query **6** puzzle, riddle, unruly **8** question, stubborn **9** conundrum, difficult **10** difficulty **11** intractable **12** disagreement, hard to manage, incorrigible, unmanageable

problematic 7 dubious, unknown **8** doubtful, puzzling **9** difficult, enigmatic, uncertain, unsettled, worrisome **10** perplexing **11** paradoxical, troublesome **12** questionable, undetermined

pro bono publico 16 for the public good

proboscis 4 beak, nose **5** snoot, snout, trunk **6** siphon, sucker, syphon **7** rostrum
monkey: 4 kaha **5** kahua

procedure 2 MO **3** way **4** mode **6** course, manner, method **7** process, routine **8** approach, strategy **9** technique **11** methodology **13** modus operandi

proceed 2 go **3** act **4** come, flow, go on, grow, move, stem, work **5** arise, begin, ensue, issue, start **6** derive, follow, move on, push on, result, set out, spring **7** advance, carry on, emanate, go ahead, operate, press on, succeed **8** be caused, commence, continue, function, progress, take rise **9** be derived, go forward, move ahead, originate, undertake

proceedings 4 case, suit **5** cause, trial **6** doings, events, report **7** account, actions, affairs, lawsuit, matters, minutes, records, returns **8** activity, archives, goings on **9** incidents, memoranda **10** happenings, litigation, operations **11** occurrences **12** transactions

proceeds 3 net **4** gain, gate, pelf, take **5** gross, lucre, money, yield **6** assets, income, profit, reward **7** returns, revenue **8** earnings, pickings, receipts, winnings **9** box office

process 3 can, dry **4** fill, flow, flux, mode, plan, ship, step, writ **5** alter, candy, smoke, treat, usage **6** change, course, freeze, handle, manner, method, motion, policy, scheme, system **7** convert, measure, passage, prepare, project, summons **8** deal with, function, movement, practice, preserve, progress, subpoena **9** dehydrate, dispose of, freeze-dry, procedure, transform, unfolding **10** court order, proceeding

procession 4 file, line, rank **5** array, march, train **6** column, course, parade

7 caravan, cortege, pageant, passage **8** progress, sequence **9** cavalcade, motorcade **10** succession **11** progression

Procheneosaurus
   type: **8** dinosaur **10** ornithopod
   location: **6** Canada
   period: **10** Cretaceous

proclaim 3 cry **4** tell **5** blare, state, voice **6** affirm, assert, blazon, herald, report, reveal **7** call out, declare, divulge, give out, profess, publish, release, sing out, trumpet **8** announce, disclose, set forth **9** advertise, broadcast, circulate, enunciate, hawk about, make known, publicize **10** make public, promulgate

proclamation 5 edict, ukase **6** decree **12** announcement **13** pronouncement

proclivity 3 yen **4** bent, bias **5** taste **6** desire, liking **7** impulse, leaning **8** affinity, appetite, penchant, soft spot, tendency **9** affection, prejudice, proneness **10** partiality, propensity **11** disposition, inclination **12** predilection **14** predisposition

procrastinate 3 lag **5** dally, defer, delay, stall, tarry **6** dawdle, linger, loiter **7** adjourn **8** hang back, hesitate, hold back, kill time, postpone, put on ice **9** temporize, waste time **10** be dilatory, dillydally **11** play for time **12** drag one's feet

procrastinating 4 slow **5** tardy **6** remiss **8** dilatory **9** reluctant **12** footdragging **13** dillydallying

procreate 3 get **4** bear, sire **5** beget, breed, spawn **6** create, father, mother **7** produce **8** conceive, engender, generate, multiply **9** propagate, reproduce **10** bring forth **11** give birth to, proliferate

procreation
   god of: **7** Priapus

procreator 4 sire **6** father **8** begetter

procrustean 7 drastic **8** ruthless **19** conforming at any cost

Procrustes
   also: **5** giant **8** Damastes **9** Polypemon
   seized: **9** travelers
   killed by: **7** Theseus
   tied them to: **3** bed
   made them fit by: **10** stretching **14** cutting off their feet

procure 3 buy, get, win **4** earn, gain, take **5** evoke, seize **6** attain, come by, effect, elicit, gather, incite, induce, obtain, pick up, secure **7** achieve, acquire, receive **8** contrive, purchase **10** accumulate, bring about, commandeer, lay hands on **11** appropriate

procurement 4 gain **7** seizure **8** purchase **10** attainment, purchasing **11** achievement, acquirement, acquisition **12** accumulation **13** appropriation

prod 3 jab, nag **4** flog, goad, lash, move, poke, push, spur, stir, urge,

whip **5** egg on, impel, prick, rouse, shove, speed **6** excite, exhort, incite, needle, prompt, propel, stir up **7** actuate, animate, provoke, quicken **8** motivate, pressure **9** encourage, instigate, stimulate

prodigal 4 lush **5** ample **6** lavish, myriad, wanton **7** copious, profuse, replete, spender, teeming, wastrel **8** abundant, generous, numerous, reckless, swarming, wasteful **9** abounding, bounteous, bountiful, countless, excessive, exuberant, impetuous, luxuriant, plentiful, unthrifty **10** exorbitant, gluttonous, immoderate, inordinate, numberless, profligate, squanderer, thriftless **11** dissipating, extravagant, improvident, innumerable, intemperate, overliberal, precipitate, spendthrift **13** multitudinous

prodigality 10 imprudence, lavishness **12** extravagance, improvidence, overspending, wastefulness

prodigious 3 big **4** huge, rare, vast **5** grand, great, large **6** mighty, unique **7** amazing, immense **8** colossal, enormous, gigantic, renowned, singular, striking, terrific, uncommon, unwonted, wondrous **9** marvelous, monstrous, startling, wonderful **10** astounding, impressive, miraculous, monumental, noteworthy, remarkable, stupendous, surprising, tremendous **11** astonishing, exceptional, farreaching, uncustomary, unthinkable **12** dumbfounding, overwhelming, unimaginable **13** extraordinary, inconceivable, unprecedented

prodigiously 10 enormously, incredibly, remarkably **12** inordinately, tremendously **13** astonishingly, exceptionally, extravagantly, outstandingly, spectacularly **14** overwhelmingly

prodigiousness 6 rarity **8** enormity, hugeness, vastness **9** uniqueness **11** singularity **12** extravagance

prodigy 4 whiz **6** expert, genius, marvel, master, rarity, wizard, wonder **7** stunner, whiz kid **8** rara avis **9** sensation **10** mastermind, phenomenon, wunderkind **11** wonder child

produce 4 bear, form, give, make, show **5** beget, bloom, cause, found, frame, hatch, set up, shape, yield **6** adduce, afford, create, devise, effect, evince, evolve, flower, fruits, greens, invent, reveal, sprout, supply, unmask, unveil **7** achieve, advance, bring in, compose, concoct, develop, display, divulge, exhibit, fashion, furnish, present, provide, staples, turn out, uncover **8** bring off, bring out, conceive, disclose, discover, generate, manifest, set forth **9** bear fruit, construct, fabricate, institute, make plain, originate, procreate, put on view, show forth **10** accomplish, bring

about, come up with, effectuate, foodstuffs, give life to, give rise to, put in force, vegetables **11** bring to pass, give birth to, manufacture, materialize **14** bring into being

Producers, The
   director: **9** Mel Brooks
   cast: **9** Dick Shawn **10** Gene Wilder, Zero Mostel **11** Kenneth Mars

production 4 film, play, show **5** drama, movie **6** cinema, circus, making **7** display, exhibit, musical, showing **8** building, carnival, creation **9** execution, formation, producing, stage show **10** appearance, disclosure, revelation **11** fabrication, fulfillment, manufacture, origination, performance **12** construction, effectuation, introduction, presentation **13** demonstration, entertainment, manifestation, manufacturing, motion picture **15** materialization

productive 4 busy, rich **6** active, fecund, paying, useful **7** causing, copious, dynamic, fertile, gainful, teeming **8** creating, creative, fruitful, prolific, valuable, vigorous, yielding **9** effectual, luxuriant, plenteous, plentiful, producing **10** invaluable, profitable, worthwhile **11** efficacious, moneymaking, proliferous **12** contributing, fructiferous, remunerative

profanation 9 sacrilege **10** defilement **11** desecration

profane 3 lay **4** evil, foul, lewd, mock, vile **5** abuse, bawdy, crude, nasty, scorn, waste **6** coarse, debase, filthy, ill-use, impure, misuse, offend, revile, ribald, sinful, unholy, vulgar, wicked **7** abusive, earthly, godless, impious, obscene, outrage, pervert, pollute, satanic, secular, ungodly, violate, worldly **8** agnostic, diabolic, off-color, temporal, unchaste, undevout, unseemly **9** atheistic, blaspheme, desecrate, hellbound, heretical, misemploy, shameless, unsaintly **10** irreverent, prostitute **11** blasphemous, contaminate, irreligious, terrestrial, unbelieving **12** nonreligious, sacrilegious

profanity 5 filth, oaths **7** cursing, cussing, impiety **8** swearing **9** blasphemy, obscenity, scatology **10** dirty words, execration, expletives, scurrility, swearwords **11** irreverence, obscenities, ungodliness **12** billingsgate **15** four-letter words

profess 3 act, own, say **4** aver, avow, fake, sham, tell **5** admit, claim, feign, offer, put on, state, vouch **6** affirm, allege, assert, assume, depose **7** advance, certify, confess, confirm, contend, declare, embrace, pretend, purport **8** announce, lay claim, maintain, practice, proclaim, propound, simulate **9** believe in, dissemble, enunciate, hold forth **10** asseverate, put forward **11** acknowledge, counterfeit, dissimulate

professed 6 avowed **7** alleged **8** admitted **9** confessed, purported **12** acknowledged, self-declared **14** self-proclaimed

profession 3 job, law, vow **4** line, post, word, work **5** claim, craft, field, trade, troth **6** avowal, career, metier, office, pledge, plight, sphere **7** calling, promise, pursuit, service **8** averment, business, endeavor, industry, medicine, position, practice, teaching, vocation **9** assertion, assurance, guarantee, situation, specialty, statement, testimony **10** allegation, confession, deposition, employment, line of work, occupation, walk of life **11** affirmation, attestation, declaration, undertaking, word of honor **12** announcement, confirmation **13** pronouncement **15** acknowledgement

professional 4 paid **5** adept **6** expert **9** authority, competent, practiced **10** specialist **11** experienced

professionalism 5 savvy, skill **7** know-how **9** expertise **10** expertness

professor 3 don **6** regent **7** adjoint, teacher **8** lecturer **10** instructor
retired: 8 emeritus

Professor, The
author: 15 Charlotte Bronte

professorial 6 teachy **7** bookish, donnish, preachy **8** academic, didactic, pedantic, teachery **11** pedagoguish **13** schoolmarmish **15** schoolmasterish **16** schoolteacherish

Professor's House, The
author: 11 Willa Cather

proffer 5 offer **6** extend, tender **7** advance, hold out, present

proficiency 5 knack, skill **6** acumen **7** ability, know-how **8** aptitude, capacity, deftness, facility **9** adeptness, dexterity, expertise, handiness **10** adroitness, capability, competence **13** qualification **14** accomplishment

proficient 3 apt **4** able, deft, good **5** adept, handy, quick, ready, sharp **6** adroit, clever, expert, gifted **7** capable, skilled, trained **8** masterly, polished, skillful, talented **9** competent, dexterous, effective, efficient, masterful, practiced, qualified, versatile **11** experienced **12** accomplished, professional

profile 4 form, side, tale **5** shape **6** figure, sketch **7** contour, drawing, outline, picture, skyline **8** half face, portrait, side view, vignette **9** biography **10** lineaments, silhouette **11** delineation **13** configuration

Profiles in Courage
author: 12 John F Kennedy

profit 3 pay, use **4** boon, earn, gain, good, help **5** avail, favor, money, serve, value **6** income, return **7** ac-

count, benefit, revenue, service, utility, utilize **8** earnings, interest, proceeds, receipts **9** advantage, make money **11** advancement

profitable 6 paying, useful **7** gainful **8** fruitful, salutary, valuable **9** favorable, lucrative, rewarding **10** beneficial, invaluable, productive, well-paying, worthwhile **11** moneymaking, serviceable **12** advantageous, remunerative

profitmaking 8 business **11** moneymaking **13** noncharitable

profits 4 gate, take **5** gains, yield **6** assets, income **7** returns, revenue **8** earnings, receipts

profligacy 10 lavishness **11** dissipation, dissolution, prodigality, unrestraint **12** extravagance, immoderation, improvidence, recklessness, wastefulness **13** excessiveness

profligate 4 evil, fast, rake, roue, wild **5** loose, satyr **6** erotic, lavish, sinful, sinner, wanton, wicked **7** corrupt, immoral, pervert, satyric, wastrel **8** degraded, depraved, prodigal, reckless, wasteful **9** abandoned, debauched, debauchee, dissolute, libertine, reprobate, sybaritic, unbridled, unthrifty, wrongdoer **10** degenerate, dissipated, dissipater, iniquitous, lascivious, licentious **11** extravagant, improvident, promiscuous, spendthrift **12** unprincipled, unrestrained

pro forma 15 according to form, as a matter of form

profound 4 deep, keen, sage, wise **5** acute, sober, utter **6** abject, hearty, moving, severe **7** decided, erudite, extreme, intense, knowing, learned, radical, serious, sincere **8** complete, educated, informed, piercing, positive, thorough **9** heartfelt, out-and-out, recondite, sagacious, scholarly **10** all-knowing, consummate, deep-seated, omniscient, pronounced, reflective, thoughtful **11** enlightened, far-reaching, penetrating **12** intellectual, soul-stirring **13** comprehensive, knowledgeable, philosophical, thoroughgoing

profundity 5 abyss, depth **6** wisdom **8** deepness, sagacity, sapience **9** erudition **11** learnedness, penetration **12** abstractness, abstruseness, profoundness **13** reconditeness, sagaciousness **16** impenetrableness

profuse 4 rich **5** ample, wordy **6** lavish, prolix **7** copious, diffuse, verbose **8** abundant, generous, prodigal, rambling, wasteful **9** bounteous, bountiful, excessive, garrulous, unthrifty **10** digressive, discursive, immoderate, inordinate, long-winded, loquacious, munificent **11** extravagant, improvident, intemperate, spendthrift

profuseness 9 abundance, diffusion, profusion, prolixity, verbosity, wordi-

ness **10** lavishness **11** copiousness, diffuseness

profusion 4 glut **5** waste **6** excess **7** surfeit, surplus **8** plethora **9** abundance, multitude **10** oversupply **11** superfluity **12** extravagance, multiplicity

progenitor 8 ancestor, forebear **10** forefather

progeny 3 kin, son **4** clan, heir, line, race, seed **5** blood, breed, child, heirs, issue, scion, stock, young **6** family **7** kindred, lineage **8** children, offshoot **9** offspring, posterity **10** descendant

prognosticate 7 predict, presage **8** forecast, foretell, prophesy **9** foretoken

prognostication 6 augury **8** forecast, prophecy **10** divination, prediction

prognosticator 4 seer **5** augur **7** prophet **9** predictor **10** forecaster

program 4 bill, book, card, list, plan, show **5** slate **6** agenda, design, docket, expect, intend, line up, notice, series, sketch **7** arrange, outline **8** bulletin, calendar, playbill, register, schedule, syllabus **9** timetable **10** curriculum, production, prospectus **12** presentation

progress 4 gain, grow, rise **5** climb, get on, mount, ripen **6** action, course, grow up, growth, mature, stride **7** advance, develop, headway, improve, proceed, process, success **8** get ahead, increase, movement **9** get better, go forward, move ahead, promotion, unfolding **10** betterment, enrichment, gain ground **11** achievement, advancement, development, enhancement, furtherance, improvement, make headway, make strides

progression 3 run **5** chain, climb, order **6** ascent, course, series, strain, string **7** advance **8** progress, sequence **10** succession **11** advancement, continuance, furtherance **12** continuation **14** continuousness **15** consecutiveness

progressive 7 dynamic, gradual, liberal, ongoing **8** activist, advanced, populist, up-to-date **9** advancing, enlarging, reformist, spreading, traveling **10** ameliorist **11** incremental **12** enterprising

prohibit 3 ban, bar **4** curb, deny, stay, stop, veto **5** block, check, delay, limit **6** enjoin, forbid, hamper, hinder, impede, negate **7** inhibit, obviate, prevent, repress **8** disallow, obstruct, preclude, restrain, restrict, suppress, withhold **9** proscribe

prohibited
German: 8 verboten

prohibition 3 ban **4** veto **5** edict **7** embargo, sanction **10** temperance **11** forbiddance **12** interdiction

prohibitive, prohibitory 9 enjoining, hindering **10** forbidding, inhibitive, injunction, preventative, repressive **11**

disallowing, obstructive, restraining, restrictive, suppressive **12** inadmissible, unacceptable **13** disqualifying **15** circumscriptive

project 3 aim, job **4** cast, emit, fire, goal, plan, send, task, work **5** draft, eject, expel, fling, frame, shoot, throw **6** beetle, design, devise, extend, hurtle, invent, jut out, launch, map out, propel, scheme **7** concoct, outline, propose **8** activity, ambition, bend over, contrive, forecast, overhang, protrude, stand out, stick out, throw out, transmit **9** calculate, discharge, ejaculate, intention, objective, plan ahead **10** assignment **11** extrapolate, undertaking **12** predetermine

projected 6 hurled **7** hurtled, planned **8** extended, forecast, launched, overhung, proposed, stood out, stuck out **9** mapped out, propelled, protruded **10** catapulted **11** conjectural

projectile 4 dart **5** arrow, spear **6** rocket **7** javelin, missile

projecting part 3 arm, ell, leg **4** eave, limb, tail **6** branch, feeler, member **7** antenna **8** tentacle **9** appendage

projection 4 brow, bump, eave **5** bulge, guess, jetty, jutty, ledge, ridge, shelf **8** estimate, forecast, overhang **9** extension, extrusion **10** estimation, prediction, prospectus, protrusion **11** guesstimate **12** protuberance **13** approximation, extrapolation

Prokofiev, Serge
born: **6** Russia **9** Sontsovka
composer of: **6** Lt Kije **10** Cinderella, The Gambler **11** War and Peace **13** Scythian Suite, The Fiery Angel **14** Lieutenant Kije, Romeo and Juliet, The Prodigal Son **15** Alexander Nevsky, Peter and the Wolf **17** Classical Symphony **22** The Love for Three Oranges **57** Cantata for the Twentieth Anniversary of the October Revolution

proletarian 6 worker **7** laborer **10** working man

proletariat 5 plebs **6** rabble, the mob **7** populus **8** canaille, laborers, populace **9** commonage, commoners, hoi polloi, the masses **10** commonalty **11** lower orders, rank and file, wage earners **12** lower classes, vulgus mobile, working class **15** the common people **16** the great unwashed

proliferate 4 teem **5** breed, hatch, spawn, swarm **8** increase, multiply **9** procreate, propagate, pullulate **10** regenerate **11** overproduce

prolific 4 lush **6** fecund **7** copious, fertile, profuse **8** abundant, breeding, creative, fruitful, yielding **9** luxuriant **11** germinative, multiplying, procreative, progenitive, proliferous, propagating **12** reproductive

prolix 5 wordy **7** verbose **10** long-winded

prolixity 9 verbosity, wordiness **11** profuseness **14** long- windedness

prologue 7 opening, preface, prelude **8** foreword, overture, preamble **9** beginning **12** introduction

prolong 5 delay **6** extend, retard **7** drag out, draw out, spin out, stretch, sustain **8** continue, elongate, lengthen, maintain, protract **9** attenuate **10** perpetuate

prolongation 5 delay **9** extending, extension **10** drawing out **11** attenuation, dragging out, lengthening, protraction, retardation **12** perpetuation **13** streching out

prolonged 7 lengthy **8** drawn-out, extended **9** continued, long-lived **10** continuing, lengthened, persistent, protracted **11** long-lasting

prom 3 hop **4** ball **5** dance **9** cotillion, promenade

promenade 3 hop **4** ball, prom, walk **5** dance **6** soiree, stroll **9** cotillion

Prometheus
member of: **6** Titans
father: **7** Iapetus
mother: **6** Themis **7** Clymene
brother: **5** Atlas **10** Epimetheus
son: **9** Deucalion
created mankind from: **4** clay
stole: **4** fire
punished by: **4** Zeus
chained to: **4** rock
released by: **8** Hercules

Prometheus Bound
author: **9** Aeschylus
character: **2** Io **3** Bia **6** Hermes, Kratos **7** Oceanus **10** Hephaestus

Prometheus Unbound
author: **18** Percy Bysshe Shelley
character: **4** Asia, Ione **5** Earth **7** Jupiter, Mercury, Panthea **8** Hercules **9** Demogoron

prominence 3 tor **4** bump, dune, fame, hill, hump, knob, lump, mark, mesa, name, node, peak, rise, spur **5** bluff, bulge, cliff, crest, honor, jetty, jutty, knoll, knurl, might, mound **6** credit, height, renown, rising, summit, weight **7** dignity, hillock, majesty, process **8** eminence, grandeur, mountain, nobility, outshoot, overhang, pinnacle, prestige, salience, splendor, swelling **9** celebrity, convexity, elevation, extension, extrusion, greatness, influence, notoriety, precipice **10** brilliance, importance, notability, popularity, projection, promontory, protrusion, reputation, tumescence **11** distinction, excrescence, excurvature, preeminence, superiority **12** protuberance, significance

prominent 6 convex, famous **7** bulging, eminent, evident, glaring, honored, jutting, leading, notable, ob-

vious, salient, staring, swollen **8** apparent, definite, excurved, extended, renowned, striking, swelling **9** arresting, important, respected, well-known **10** celebrated, easily seen, jutting out, noticeable, preeminent, projecting, pronounced, protruding, protrusive, remarkable **11** conspicuous, discernible, illustrious, outstanding, prestigious, protuberant **12** recognizable **13** distinguished

promiscuous 3 lax **4** fast, lewd, wild **5** loose, mixed **6** casual, impure, medley, motley, rakish, wanton **7** aimless, chaotic, diverse, immoral, jumbled, mingled, mixed-up, satyric **8** careless, confused, immodest, sweeping, unchaste **9** composite, desultory, dissolute, haphazard, perplexed, scrambled, wholesale **10** commingled, disordered, disorderly, dissipated, intermixed, lascivious, licentious, uncritical, undirected, unvirtuous, variegated **11** disarranged, incontinent, indifferent, intemperate, unselective **12** disorganized, of easy virtue, undiscerning **13** helter-skelter, heterogeneous, miscellaneous **14** indiscriminate

promise 3 vow **4** aver, avow, oath, word **5** agree, augur, imply, swear, troth, vouch **6** assure, avowal, hint of, parole, pledge, plight **7** be bound, betoken, suggest, warrant **8** covenant, indicate, warranty **9** agreement, assurance, guarantee, potential, undertake **11** declaration, stipulation, swear an oath, word of honor

Promised Land 6 Canaan
nickname of: **10** California **6** Israel

promising 4 rosy **5** happy, lucky **6** bright, rising **7** hopeful **8** assuring, cheerful, cheering **9** advancing, favorable, fortunate, looking up **10** auspicious, of good omen, optimistic, propitious, reassuring **11** encouraging, inspiriting, up-and-coming

promissory note 3 IOU **4** bond, chit **6** pledge **7** promise **9** agreement **10** obligation **11** certificate

promontory 4 cape, hill, ness, spur **5** bluff, cliff, jetty, jutty, point **6** height **8** headland, overhang **9** peninsula, precipice **10** embankment, projection

promote 3 aid **4** abet, ease, help, plug, push **5** raise **6** assist, foster, prefer, refine **7** advance, develop, elevate, enhance, forward, further, support, upgrade, work for **8** advocate, expedite, graduate **9** advertise, cultivate, encourage, publicize

promoter 6 backer **8** advocate, champion **9** proponent, supporter

promotion 4 hype **5** raise **7** advance, fanfare, puffery **8** ballyhoo, boosting, progress **9** elevation, publicity, upgrading **10** preferment **11** advancement, advertising, furtherance **12**

promulgation 13 advertisement, encouragement

promotive 7 helpful **9** conducive **10** beneficial **12** contributive, contributory, instrumental

prompt 3 cue **4** goad, keen, move, prod, push, spur, stir **5** alert, alive, cause, drive, eager, force, impel, press, quick, ready, sharp **6** active, assist, bright, excite, incite, induce, intent, lively, on time, propel, remind, thrust, timely **7** actuate, animate, dispose, help out, incline, inspire, instant, on guard, provoke, zealous **8** activate, inspirit, motivate, occasion, open-eyed, persuade, punctual, vigilant, watchful **9** attentive, determine, efficient, immediate, influence, instigate, observant, open- eared, stimulate, wide-awake **10** on one's toes **12** jog the memory, unhesitating **13** instantaneous

prompting 6 cueing, urging **7** goading **8** egging on **10** motivation **11** exhortation

promptly 3 pat **4** anon, soon, tite **6** pronto **7** quickly, swiftly **10** punctually **11** immediately

promptness 5 haste **8** alacrity, celerity, dispatch **9** quickness, readiness, swiftness **11** punctuality **15** expeditiousness

promulgate 6 foster **7** explain, expound, present, promote, sponsor **8** instruct, set forth **9** elucidate, enunciate, interpret **11** communicate

promulgation 9 fostering, promotion **11** circulation, instruction, sponsorship **12** distribution, presentation, transmission **13** communication **14** interpretation

prone 3 apt **4** flat **5** level **6** liable, likely **7** subject, tending **8** disposed, face-down, inclined **9** prostrate, reclining, recumbent **10** accustomed, habituated, horizontal **11** predisposed, susceptible

proneness 4 bent, bias, turn **7** leaning **8** penchant, tendency **9** prejudice **10** proclivity, propensity **11** inclination **12** predilection **14** predisposition

prong 4 barb, hook, horn, spur, tine **5** point, spike, tooth **6** branch **10** projection

pronoun 2 he, it, me, my, us, we, ye **3** all, any, few, her, his, one, she, thy, who, you **4** hers, mine, ours, some, thee, them, they, that, this, thou, what, whom **5** no one, their, these, thine, those, which, whose, yours **6** anyone, itself, myself, nobody **7** anybody, herself, himself, nothing, someone, whoever **8** somebody, whomever **9** everybody, something, whosoever **10** everything, themselves
French: 2 il, je, tu **3** ils, lui, mes, moi **4** elle, vous

German: 2 er, es, du **3** ich, mir, sie **4** dein, mein, mich, sich
Italian: 2 io, me, mi, ti, tu, vi **3** cio, lei, lui, mio, tei, voi **4** egli, ella, essa, esse, essi, loro
Spanish: 2 el, la, lo, me, mi, tu, yo **4** ella, ello, suyo, tuyo **5** usted

pronounce 3 say **4** emit, form, rule **5** frame, judge, orate, sound, speak, state, utter, voice **6** decree **7** declare, enounce **8** announce, proclaim, vocalize **9** enunciate **10** articulate

pronounced 4 bold **5** broad, clear, plain, vivid **6** patent **7** decided, evident, obvious, visible **8** apparent, clear-cut, definite, distinct, manifest, positive, unhidden **9** arresting **10** noticeable **11** conspicuous, outstanding, undisguised, well-defined **12** recognizable, unmistakable **14** unquestionable

pronouncement 6 decree **11** declaration **12** announcement, proclamation

pronto 3 now **4** asap, fast, stat **5** quick **7** quickly **8** promptly **11** immediately

Pronuba
epithet of: 4 Juno

pronunciamento 5 edict **12** proclamation **13** pronouncement

pronunciation 6 accent **10** inflection **11** enunciation **12** articulation **16** manner of speaking

proof 4 test **5** essay, proof, sheet, trial **6** galley, ordeal **8** scrutiny, weighing **9** probation **10** assessment **11** attestation, examination **12** confirmation, ratification, verification **13** certification, corroboration, documentation **14** substantiation

proofreader's mark 3 cap, rom **4** dele, ital, stet **5** caret, space

prop 3 set **4** lean, rest, stay **5** brace, stand **6** hold up, pillar **7** bolster, shore up, support **8** buttress, mainstay, shoulder, underpin **9** stanchion, supporter, sustainer **13** reinforcement
French: 11 point d'appui

propaganda 6 hoopla **8** ballyhoo **9** party line, promotion, publicity **10** persuasion **11** advertising

propagandist 6 zealot **8** activist, exponent **9** apologist, proponent, publicist **12** spokesperson

propagate 3 air, sow **4** bear, tell **5** beget, breed, hatch, issue, rumor, spawn, spray **6** blazon, herald, impart, notify, preach, purvey, repeat, report, spread **7** bestrew, give out, implant, instill, publish, scatter, trumpet **8** disperse, engender, generate, increase, multiply, proclaim, put forth **9** broadcast, circulate, enunciate, give birth, inculcate, make known, procreate, publicize, reproduce

propagation 6 laying, siring **7** bearing **8** breeding, hatching, issuance, spawning, yielding **9** begetting, diffu-

sion, gestation, pregnancy, spreading **10** dispersion, generation **11** circulation, engendering, giving birth, procreation, publication **12** distribution, reproduction, transmission **13** dissemination

pro patria 14 for one's country

propel 4 cast, goad, hurl, poke, prod, push, send, toss **5** drive, eject, force, heave, impel, pitch, shoot, shove, sling, start **6** launch, thrust **7** project **8** catapult **9** discharge **11** precipitate, set in motion

propeller, screw
invented by: 7 Stevens **8** Ericsson

propensity 4 bent, bias, turn **5** fancy, favor, taste **6** liking **7** leaning **8** affinity, penchant, pleasure, sympathy, tendency, weakness **9** prejudice **10** attraction, partiality, preference, proclivity **11** disposition, inclination **12** predilection **14** predisposition

proper 3 apt, fit, own **4** meet, nice, true **5** per se, right **6** decent, marked, modest, polite, seemly **7** apropos, correct, express, fitting, germane, precise, typical **8** assigned, becoming, decorous, orthodox, peculiar, relevant, specific, suitable **9** befitting, courteous, pertinent **10** acceptable, applicable, individual, particular, respective **11** appropriate, conformable, distinctive **12** conventional **14** characteristic, distinguishing, representative
French: 11 comme il faut

properly 5 aptly, right **7** exactly **8** decently, politely, suitably **9** correctly, perfectly, precisely **10** acceptably, accurately, decorously, tastefully **12** without error **13** appropriately **14** conventionally

property 4 hold, land, mark **5** acres, badge, funds, goods, means, point, stock, title, trait **6** aspect, assets, estate, moneys, realty, wealth **7** acreage, capital, earmark, effects, estates, feature, grounds, quality **8** chattels, holdings, treasure **9** attribute, ownership, resources, territory **10** belongings, real estate **11** investments, peculiarity, possessions, singularity **12** appointments, idiosyncrasy **13** individuality, particularity **14** characteristic, proprietorship

prophecy 6 augury **7** portent **8** forecast **10** divination, prediction, revelation **15** prognostication
god of: 6 Apollo **7** Phoebus, Pythius **9** Musagetes

prophesy 4 warn **5** augur **6** divine **7** forbode, foresee, portend, predict, presage **8** forecast, foretell, forewarn, soothsay **9** apprehend, premonish **13** prognosticate

prophet 4 seer **5** augur, guide, sibyl **6** oracle **7** diviner, palmist, seeress **8** preacher, sorcerer **9** Cassandra, divinator, geomancer, predictor, sorceress **10** evangelist, forecaster, foreteller, prophesier, prophetess, soothsayer **11** clairvoyant, intercessor, interpreter **12** crystal gazer **13** fortune-teller **14** prognosticator

Prophet, major 6 Baruch, Daniel, Elijah, Isaiah **7** Ezekiel **8** Jeremiah

Prophet, minor 3 Gad **4** Amos, Joel **5** Hosea, Jonah, Micah, Nahum **6** Haggai, Nathan **7** Malachi, Obadiah **8** Habakkuk **9** Zechariah, Zephaniah

Prophetess 4 Anna **6** Miriam **7** Deborah **9** Cassandra

prophetic, prophetical 5 vatic **6** mantic **7** fateful, ominous **8** oracular **10** portentous, predictive, presageful

Prophetic Books
    author: **12** William Blake

prophylactic 8 hygienic **10** preventive **13** contraceptive

propinquity 7 kinship **8** affinity, nearness, vicinity **9** closeness, proximity **10** similarity

propitiate 4 calm **5** allay **6** pacify, soothe **7** appease, assuage, mollify, placate **10** conciliate **11** accommodate

propitiation 8 soothing **11** appeasement **12** conciliation, pacification

propitious 3 fit **5** bonny, happy, lucky **6** benign, golden **8** suitable **9** agreeable, favorable, fortunate, opportune, promising, well-timed **10** auspicious, beneficial, felicitous **12** advantageous, providential

proponent 6 backer, friend, patron, votary **7** booster **8** advocate, champion, defender, endorser, espouser, exponent, partisan, upholder **9** apologist, spokesman, supporter **10** enthusiast, vindicator **14** representative

proportion 5 ratio **7** balance, harmony **8** evenness, symmetry **9** agreement **11** consistency, correlation, perspective **12** distribution, relationship **14** commensuration, correspondence

proportionate 5 equal **8** balanced **10** comparable, equivalent **12** commensurate **13** commensurable, corresponding

proportions 3 fit, lot **4** area, bulk, form, gear, mass, part, size, span **5** adapt, gauge, grade, match, order, poise, quota, range, ratio, scope, shape, share, width **6** amount, degree, equate, extent, spread, volume **7** balance, breadth, conform, correct, expanse, measure, portion, rectify, segment **8** capacity, division, equalize, fraction, graduate, modulate, regulate **9** amplitude, apportion, greatness, harmonize, magnitude **10** dimensions **12** measurements

proposal 3 bid **4** idea, plan, plot, suit **5** draft, offer **6** appeal, course, design, motion, scheme, sketch, theory **7** out-

line, proffer, program, project **8** overture, prospect **9** stratagem **10** conception, invitation, nomination, prospectus, resolution, suggestion **11** proposition **12** presentation **14** recommendation

propose 3 aim, woo **4** hope, mean, plan, plot **6** aspire, design, expect, intend, scheme, submit, tender **7** advance, present, proffer, purpose, suggest, venture **8** affiance, propound, put forth, set about, set forth **9** determine, have a mind, introduce, recommend, undertake **10** come up with, have in mind, have in view, put forward **11** contemplate **14** pop the question **21** offer for consideration

proposition 4 deal, pass, plan **5** issue, offer, point, topic **6** matter, scheme **7** advance, bargain, solicit, subject **8** contract, proposal, question **9** agreement, assurance, guarantee **10** resolution, suggestion **11** make a pass at, negotiation, stipulation, undertaking **14** recommendation

propound 4 pose **5** boost **6** assert **7** advance, profess, propose **8** put forth, set forth

proprieties 7 decorum, manners **8** protocol **9** amenities, etiquette **10** civilities **11** conventions

proprietor 5 owner **6** holder, master **7** manager **8** landlord **9** landowner, possessor **10** landholder **11** titleholder **12** proprietress

propriety 7 aptness, decorum, dignity, fitness **8** courtesy **9** etiquette, formality, rightness **10** seemliness **11** correctness, good manners, savoir faire **12** becomingness, decorousness, good behavior, suitableness **13** applicability **14** respectability **15** appropriateness

propulsion 6 launch, thrust **9** launching **10** propelling

prop up 5 brace **7** bolster, support **8** buttress

pro rata 12 in proportion

prorate 6 divide **9** apportion **10** distribute

prosaic 3 dry **4** blah, dull, flat **5** prosy, stale, trite, vapid, wordy **6** common, jejune **7** humdrum, tedious **8** ordinary, plebeian, tiresome **9** hackneyed **10** monotonous, pedestrian, spiritless, unpoetical **12** matter-of-fact **13** platitudinous, unimaginative, uninteresting

Prosclystius
    epithet of: **8** Poseidon
    means: **7** flooder

proscribe 3 ban **4** damn **5** curse, exile **6** banish, forbid, outlaw **7** boycott, censure, condemn **8** denounce, prohibit **9** interdict, repudiate **10** disapprove **12** anathematize **13** excommunicate

proscription 3 ban **7** barring, censure **8** anathema **9** interdict **11** forbid-

dance, prohibition **12** condemnation, denunciation, interdiction **15** excommunication

prose 3 dry **4** dull **5** novel **7** fiction, quality, tedious, writing **8** sequence **9** discourse **10** expression **11** commonplace **13** unimaginative

prosecute 3 sue, try **4** wage **6** direct, go with, handle, indict, manage, pursue **7** arraign, carry on, conduct, execute, go to law, perform, prolong, stick to, sustain **8** continue, deal with, follow up, maintain **9** discharge, persist in **10** administer, put on trial, see through **11** take to court **12** bring to trial **14** bring to justice

prosecution 4 suit **6** action **7** conduct, pursuit **11** performance **14** administration

Proserpina *see* **10** Persephone

prosit 11 may it do good
    used as: **5** toast

prospect, prospects 4 hope, plan, seek, view **5** scene, vista **6** aspect, design, search, vision **7** chances, explore, go after, look for, outlook, picture, promise, scenery **8** ambition, panorama, proposal **9** candidate, foretaste, intention, landscape, work a mine **10** expectancy, likelihood **11** expectation, possibility, probability **12** anticipation **13** contemplation

prospective 4 to be **6** coming, future, in view, likely, to come **7** looming **8** destined, eventual, expected, foreseen, hoped-for, intended, possible **9** about to be, impending, in the wind, looked-for, potential, promising **10** in prospect **11** approaching, forthcoming, threatening

prosper 4 gain **5** get on **6** flower, thrive **7** advance, succeed **8** fare well, flourish, fructify, get ahead, grow rich, increase, make good, progress **9** bear fruit **15** make one's fortune

prosperity 4 ease, gain **6** luxury, plenty, profit, wealth **7** advance, success, welfare **8** good luck, progress **9** abundance, advantage, affluence, blessings, golden age, good times, palmy days, run of luck, well-being **11** advancement, good fortune
    god of: **4** Frey **5** Freyr, Niord, Njord **12** Bonus Eventus
    goddess of: **5** Salus

Prospero
    character in: **10** The Tempest
    author: **11** Shakespeare

prosperous 4 fair, good, rich, rosy **5** happy, lucky, sunny **6** bright, golden, timely **7** hopeful, moneyed, opulent, smiling, wealthy, well-off **8** affluent, cheering, pleasing, thriving, well-to-do **9** favorable, fortunate, opportune, promising **10** auspicious, heartening, of good omen, propitious, reassuring, successful **11** comfortable, encouraging, flourishing **12** on easy street

Pross, Miss
character in: 16 A Tale of Two Cities
author: 7 Dickens

prostitute 4 bawd, jade, slut, tart **5** abuse, hussy, lower, spoil, whore **6** chippy, debase, defile, demean, floozy, harlot, hooker, misuse **7** cheapen, corrupt, debauch, degrade, hustler, pervert, profane, sell out, trollop **8** call girl, misapply, strumpet **9** courtesan, desecrate, misdirect, misemploy **12** streetwalker **14** lady of the night

prostrate 4 deck, flat **5** abase, floor, prone, spent **6** fagged, kowtow **7** bow down, flatten, laid out, worn out **8** bowed low, overcome **9** bone weary, crouching, dead tired, exhausted, kneel down, lying flat, overthrow, recumbent **10** beseeching, horizontal **11** on one's knees **12** on bended knee, stretched out, supplicating **13** lying face down **15** fall to one's knees

prostration 3 bow, woe **5** grief **6** misery, sorrow **7** anguish, despair **8** distress, kneeling, weakness **9** abasement, dejection, heartache, impotence, lowliness, paralysis, weariness **10** depression, desolation, enervation, exhaustion, subjection, submission **11** desperation, despondency **12** genuflection, helplessness, wretchedness **13** depth of misery

prosy 4 dull, flat **5** banal, inane **6** stupid **7** humdrum, prosaic, tedious **9** wearisome **11** commonplace **13** uninteresting

protagonist 4 diva, hero, lead, star **7** heroine **9** headliner, principal, superstar, title role **10** leading man, prima donna **11** leading lady **12** danseur noble, jeune premier **13** jeune premiere, main character **14** prima ballerina **16** central character

protect 4 hide, keep, save, tend, veil **5** cover, guard **6** defend, harbor, screen, secure, shield **7** care for, shelter, sustain **8** conserve, maintain, preserve **9** look after, safeguard, watch over **10** take care of

protected 4 safe **5** saved **6** immune, secure **7** guarded, secured **8** anchored, defended, shielded **9** sheltered **10** inviolable **12** invulnerable

protection 3 aid **4** care, keep, wall **5** cover, fence, guard, haven, shade **6** asylum, buffer, charge, harbor, refuge, safety, saving, screen, shield **7** barrier, custody, defense, shelter, support **8** guarding, immunity, preserve, security **9** preserver, safeguard, sanctuary **10** assistance **11** safekeeping **12** championship, conservation, guardianship, preservation

protective 7 careful, heedful **8** fatherly, guarding, maternal, motherly, paternal, sisterly, vigilant, watchful **9** avuncular, brotherly, defensive, shielding **10** preventive, sheltering, solicitous **11** safekeeping **12** big-brotherly, safeguarding

protective covering 4 coat, husk, mail **5** armor, shell **6** shield **7** coating, plating **8** carapace **10** coat of mail **11** suit of armor **12** armor plating

protectorate 6 colony **7** mandate **8** province, dominion **9** satellite, territory **10** dependency, possession, settlement

protege 4 ward **5** pupil **6** charge **7** student, trainee **9** dependent

pro tempore 9 temporary **11** temporarily **15** for the time being

protest 3 vow **4** aver, avow, beef, deny, kick **5** gripe, march, offer, sit-in, speak, state **6** affirm, allege, assert, assure, attest, avouch, cry out, insist, object, oppose, strike **7** boycott, contend, declare, dispute, dissent, hold out, profess, testify **8** announce, complain, demurral, disagree, maintain, propound, put forth, set forth **9** enunciate, objection, picketing, pronounce **10** asseverate, contradict, controvert, disapprove, disclaimer, dissidence, opposition, put forward, resistance **11** beg to differ, deprecation **12** disaffection, disagreement, remonstrance, renunciation **13** contradiction, demonstration, remonstration, take exception **14** discountenance

Protestant 5 Amish **6** Mormon, Quaker, Shaker **7** Baptist, Puritan **8** Anglican, Huguenot, Lutheran **9** Adventist, Calvinist, Methodist, Unitarian **12** Episcopalian, Presbyterian **17** Congregationalist **18** Christian Scientist

protest meeting 5 rally, sit-in **13** demonstration

Proteus
character in: 20 Two Gentlemen of Verona
author: 11 Shakespeare

Proteus
god of: 3 sea
king of: 5 Egypt
father: 7 Oceanus
mother: 6 Tethys
wife: 8 Psamathe
son: 13 Theoclymenus
daughter: 7 Theonoe
gift: 8 prophesy **12** form-changing **13** shape-changing

Prothoenor
leader of: 9 Boeotians

protocol 5 usage **7** customs, decorum, manners **8** good form **9** amenities, etiquette, formality, standards **11** conventions, proprieties **14** code of behavior, court etiquette, diplomatic code **17** dictates of society

prototypal 5 model **7** classic **9** exemplary **10** archetypal, definitive **12** prototypical

prototype 5 model **7** example **8** original **9** archetype

protozoan 4 cell **5** ameba, cilia **6** amoeba **7** euglena **8** flagella, protista **9** eukaryote, pseudopod **10** paramecium, plasmodium **11** microscopic, unicellular **17** nonphotosynthetic

protract 6 extend, keep up **7** drag out, draw out, prolong, spin out **8** lengthen **9** keep going **10** stretch out

protracted 4 long **7** lengthy **8** drawn-out, extended **9** continued, long-lived, prolonged **10** lengthened, persistent **11** long-lasting

protraction 4 stay **7** lasting **9** extension **10** continuing, drawing out **11** continuance, dragging out, persistence **12** perseverance, prolongation

protrude 5 belly, bulge, swell **6** jut out **7** project **8** stand out, stick out **11** push forward

protrusion 4 bump, hump **6** hernia **8** swelling **9** extension **10** projection **12** prolongation, protuberance

protuberance 3 bow **4** bump, hump, knob, knot, lump, node, weal, welt **5** bulge, gnarl, ridge **6** rising **8** swelling **9** convexity, elevation, roundness **10** projection, prominence **11** excrescence, excurvature

protura
class: 8 hexapoda
phylum: 10 arthropoda
characteristic: 5 small **6** minute **7** eyeless **8** wingless

proud 4 fine, smug, vain **5** aloof, cocky, grand, great, happy, lofty, noble **6** august, lordly, snooty, snotty, strict, uppish, uppity **7** bloated, exalted, haughty, high-hat, pleased, pompous, revered, stately, storied, stuck-up, swollen **8** affected, arrogant, assuming, boastful, braggart, bragging, elevated, euphoric, glorious, inflated, insolent, majestic, prideful, puffed up, reserved, snobbish **9** admirable, cherished, conceited, contented, delighted, dignified, flaunting, gratified, honorable, imperious, know-it-all, satisfied, venerable **10** complacent, disdainful, high-minded, intolerant, principled, scrupulous **11** egotistical, independent, magnificent, overbearing, patronizing, punctilious **12** contemptuous, self-praising, supercilious, vainglorious **13** condescending, distinguished, high-and-mighty, self-important, self-satisfied **14** self-respecting, self-sufficient

Proudie, Dr
character in: 16 Barchester Towers
author: 8 Trollope

Proust, Marcel
author of: 23 Remembrance of

Things Past **24** A la Recherche du Temps Perdu

prove 3 try **4** test **5** check, end up, probe **6** affirm, attest, result, try out, uphold, verify, wind up **7** analyze, bear out, certify, confirm, examine, justify, support, sustain, warrant, witness **8** document, evidence, look into, make good, manifest, result in, validate **9** ascertain, establish, eventuate, testify to **11** corroborate, demonstrate **12** authenticate, substantiate

proved 5 known **6** proven, upheld **8** affirmed, attested, borne out, verified **9** certified, confirmed, supported, sustained, warranted, witnessed **10** documented **11** established **12** corroborated, demonstrable **13** authenticated, substantiated

prove false 5 belie **6** refute, reject **7** explode **8** disprove **9** discredit **10** invalidate

proven 5 known **6** proved, upheld **8** accepted, affirmed, attested, borne out, verified **9** certified, confirmed, supported, sustained, warranted, witnessed **10** documented, verifiable **11** established **12** corroborated, demonstrable **13** authenticated, substantiated

provender 3 hay **4** chow, corn, eats, feed, food, grub, oats **5** grain **6** fodder, forage, ration, viands **7** nurture **10** provisions **11** subsistence

proverb 3 mot, saw **5** adage, axiom, maxim, moral, motto **6** byword, cliche, dictum, saying, truism **7** bromide, epigram, precept **8** aphorism, apothegm **9** platitude **11** commonplace **13** accepted truth, popular saying

prove wrong 5 belie **6** expose, refute **7** explode **8** disprove **9** discredit

provide 3 arm, fit, pay **4** give, plan **5** allow, award, cater, equip, grant, offer, state, yield **6** accord, afford, bestow, confer, donate, impart, outfit, render, save up, submit, supply, tender **7** arrange, deliver, furnish, prepare, present, produce, require, specify **8** dispense, get ready **9** make plans, postulate, stipulate **10** accumulate, contribute

provide for 7 care for **8** attend to, wait upon **9** look after **10** minister to, take care of

providence 8 prudence **9** foresight, husbandry, provision **11** forethought **14** circumspection, farsightedness, forehandedness

provident 4 wary **5** chary, ready **6** frugal, saving **7** careful, prudent, thrifty **8** cautious, discreet, equipped, vigilant **9** farseeing, judicious **10** discerning, economical, farsighted, forehanded, foreseeing, thoughtful **11** circumspect, foresighted, precautious **12** parsimonious, well-prepared

province 3 job **4** area, duty, part, role, zone **5** field, place, state **6** canton, charge, county, domain, office, region, sphere **7** section, station **8** business, capacity, function **9** authority, bailiwick, territory **10** assignment, department **11** subdivision **12** jurisdiction **13** scope of duties **14** arrondissement, responsibility

provincial 4 rude **5** crude, gawky, local, rough, rural **6** clumsy, gauche, homely, narrow, oafish, rustic **7** awkward, boorish, bucolic, country, hayseed, insular, loutish **8** cloddish, clownish, down-home, homespun, regional, yokelish **9** backwoods, parochial, small-town, unrefined **10** unpolished **11** clodhopping, countrified, territorial **15** unsophisticated

provision 6 giving **8** donation **9** endowment, providing, supplying **10** furnishing

provisional 6 acting, pro tem **7** interim **9** surrogate, temporary, tentative **10** substitute **11** conditional **12** probationary **15** for the time being

provisions 4 feed, food, term **6** clause, fodder, forage, stores, string, viands **7** article, commons, edibles, proviso **8** eatables, supplies, victuals **9** condition, groceries, provender, readiness, requisite **10** limitation, obligation, precaution, sustenance **11** arrangement, comestibles, forethought, preparation, requirement, reservation, restriction, stipulation, wherewithal **12** anticipation, modification **13** qualification **14** forehandedness, prearrangement

proviso 5 rider **6** clause, string **8** addition **9** amendment, condition **10** limitation **11** requirement, restriction, stipulation **12** modification **13** qualification

provocation 4 goad, spur **5** cause, pique **6** insult, slight **7** affront, offense **8** prodding, stimulus, vexation **9** actuation, annoyance **10** excitation, incitement, irritation, motivation **11** aggravation, fomentation, instigation, stimulation **12** perturbation

provocative 4 sexy **6** vexing **7** irksome **8** alluring, annoying, arousing, exciting, inviting, tempting **9** beguiling, provoking, ravishing, seductive, thrilling, vexatious **10** attractive, bewitching, enchanting, entrancing, intriguing, irritating **11** aggravating, captivating, fascinating, stimulating, tantalizing **12** intoxicating, irresistible

provoke 3 irk, vex **4** fire, gall, move, rile, stir **5** anger, annoy, cause, chafe, evoke, grate, impel, pique, rouse **6** arouse, awaken, compel, create, effect, elicit, enrage, excite, foment, incite, induce, kindle, madden, prompt, put out, stir up **7** actuate, agitate, animate, bring on, incense, inflame, inspire, outrage, produce, quicken **8** generate, get to one, irritate, motivate **9** aggravate, call forth, establish, galvanize, infuriate, instigate, stimulate **10** bring about, exasperate, give rise to **11** get one's goat, put in motion **15** try one's patience **16** get under one's skin

prow 3 bow **4** stem **5** front **10** forward end

prowess 4 grit, guts **5** knack, might, nerve, power, skill, spunk, valor, vigor **6** daring, genius, mettle, spirit, talent **7** ability, bravery, courage, faculty, heroism, know-how, stamina **8** aptitude, boldness, strength **9** adeptness, derring-do, endurance, fortitude, gallantry, hardihood **10** competence, expertness **11** intrepidity, proficiency **12** fearlessness, skillfulness **13** dauntlessness **14** accomplishment

prowl 4 hunt, lurk, roam **5** creep, range, skulk, slink, snack, stalk, steal **6** ramble **8** scavenge

prowler 7 burglar **10** peeping Tom **16** suspicious person

proximate 4 near **5** close **6** beside, nearby, next to **8** adjacent, imminent, next-door **11** forthcoming

proximity 7 presence **8** locality, nearness, vicinity **9** closeness **10** contiguity **11** propinquity **12** togetherness

proximo *see month*

proxy 3 sub **4** vote **5** agent **6** ballot, deputy **7** stand-in **9** alternate **10** substitute

prude 4 prig **6** modest **7** puritan **9** hypocrite **10** goody- goody **13** prim and proper

prudence 4 care, tact **6** thrift, wisdom **7** caution, economy **9** austerity, foresight, frugality, parsimony **10** discretion, precaution **11** calculation, thriftiness **14** thoughtfulness

prudent 4 sage, sane, wary, wise **5** chary **6** frugal, saving, shrewd **7** careful, guarded, heedful, politic, sapient, sparing, thrifty **8** cautious, discreet, prepared, rational, sensible, vigilant **9** expedient, judicious, provident, sagacious, wideawake **10** discerning, economical, farsighted, prudential, reflecting, thoughtful **11** circumspect, considerate, foresighted, levelheaded, precautious, well-advised **13** self-possessed

Prud'hon, Pierre-Paul
  born: 5 Cluny **6** France
  artwork: 14 Venus and Adonis **15** The Rape of Psyche **16** Empress Josephine **33** Crime Pursued by Vengeance and Justice **38** Justice and Divine Vengeance Pursuing Crime

prudish 3 shy **4** prim, smug **5** timid **6** demure, modest, prissy, queasy, stuffy **7** finical, mincing, precise, stilted **8** pedantic, priggish, skittish, starched **9**

squeamish, Victorian **10** fastidious, old-maidish, overmodest, particular **11** punctilious, puritanical, straitlaced **13** sanctimonious, self-righteous

prudishness 8 primness **10** prissiness, puritanism **11** overmodesty **12** overdelicacy, priggishness **14** overrefinement

prudish phrase 9 euphemism **10** bowdlerism

prune 3 cut, lop **4** clip, crop, pull, snip, thin, trim **5** shear **6** reduce **7** abridge, clarify, curtail, shorten, thin out **8** condense, simplify **10** abbreviate

prunelle
  type: 7 liqueur
  origin: 6 France
  flavor: 4 plum

pruning 6 digest **8** clipping, snipping, synopsis, trimming **10** shortening **11** abridgement, cutting back, cut-down form **12** abbreviation, condensation

prurient 4 lewd, sexy **6** carnal **7** fleshy, goatish, immoral, lustful, obscene, priapic, satyric **9** lecherous, salacious **10** hot-blooded, lascivious, libidinous, licentious, lubricious, passionate **12** concupiscent

pry 4 butt, nose, peek, peer, poke, tear, work, worm **5** break, crack, delve, force, jimmy, lever, mix in, prize, probe, smoke, sniff, snoop, wrest, wring **6** butt in, ferret, horn in, meddle, search, winkle, wrench **7** explore, extract, inquire, intrude, squeeze **9** interfere, intervene **15** stick one's nose in

prying 4 busy, nosy **7** peering, raising, seeking **8** levering, snooping **9** searching **10** intrusive, meddling **11** inquisitive

Prynne, Hester
  character in: 16 The Scarlet Letter
  author: 9 Hawthorne

Pryor, Richard
  born: 8 Peoria IL
  roles: 6 The Wiz **9** Stir Crazy **12** Silver Streak **17** Lady Sings the Blues **19** Uptown Saturday Night

psalm 3 ode **4** hymn, poem, song **5** canon, chant, verse **6** praise **7** cantata, glorify, introit **8** canticle

Psalter 12 Book of Psalms

Psamathe
  member of: 6 Nereid
  form: 8 princess
  husband: 7 Proteus
  son: 5 Linus **6** Phocus **12** Theoclymenus
  daughter: 7 Theonoe

pseudo 4 fake, mock, sham **5** bogus, false, phony **6** forged **7** feigned **8** spurious **9** pretended, simulated, soidisant **10** fictitious, fraudulent, selfstyled **11** counterfeit, make-believe **13** self-described

pseudonym 5 alias **6** anonym **7** pen name **8** cognomen, nickname **9** false name, sobriquet, stage name **11** assumed name **16** professional name
French: 10 nom de plume **11** nom de guerre **12** nom de theatre

pseudonymous 7 assumed **10** fictitious **11** pseudonymic

psocoptera
  class: 8 hexapoda
  phylum: 10 arthropoda
  group: 8 booklice

psyche 2 id **3** ego **4** mind, self, soul **5** anima **6** bowels, make up, spirit **8** superego **10** penetralia **11** personality, unconscious **12** subconscious

Psyche
  personifies: 4 soul
  loved by: 4 Eros **5** Cupid
  persecutor: 5 Venus
  immortalized by: 7 Jupiter
  daughter: 8 Voluptas

psychic 5 augur **6** medium, mental, mystic, occult, voyant **7** diviner, prophet, voyante **8** cerebral **9** paragnost, sensitive, spiritual **10** soothsayer, telepathic **11** clairvoyant, telekinetic, telepathist **12** extrasensory, intellectual, spiritualist, supernatural, supersensory **13** preternatural

Psycho
  director: 15 Alfred Hitchcock
  cast: 9 John Gavin, Vera Miles **10** Janet Leigh **12** Martin Balsam **14** Anthony Perkins
  score: 15 Bernard Herrmann
  feature: 10 Bates Motel **11** shower scene

psychoanalysis 7 therapy **8** analysis **14** physchotherapy

psychoanalyst 6 shrink **7** analyst **12** headshrinker

psychologist/psychiatrist
  American: 4 Hall, Hull **5** Dewey, James, Lewin **6** Harlow, Horney, Miller, Rogers, Terman, Tolman, Watson, Witmer **7** Cattell, Chomsky, Erikson, Goddard, Guthrie, Johnson, Masters, Skinner **8** Brothers, Wechsler **9** Thorndike **10** Westheimer
  Austrian: 5 Adler, Freud, Reich
  British: 5 Ellis **7** Eysenck **9** Titchener
  French: 5 Binet
  German: 5 Wundt **6** Koffka, Kohler **7** Fechner **9** Helmholtz, Kraepelin **10** Ebbinghaus, Wertheimer **11** Krafft-Ebing
  Russian: 6 Pavlov
  Swiss: 4 Jung **6** Piaget

psychology 4 head, mind **6** makeup **7** feeling **8** attitude **15** mental processes
  problem/illness: 6 phobia **7** obesity, smoking **8** hysteria, neuroses, paranoia, schizoid **9** drug abuse, obsession, psychoses **10** alcoholism, compulsion, depression **11** sociopathic **13** schizophrenia **14** sexual deviance

15 anxiety reaction **17** passive-aggressive
  term: 2 id **3** ego **6** libido **7** empathy **8** neuroses, superego **9** catatonic, cognition, psychoses **10** inhibition, repression **11** behaviorism, unconscious **12** conditioning, transference **13** actualization, Rorschach test **14** identification, Oedipus complex **19** operant conditioning **20** behavior modification
  type: 6 social **7** Gestalt **8** abnormal, clinical **9** cognitive **10** industrial **11** educational **12** experimental **13** developmental, physiological, psychometrics, psychophysics

psychopomp
  conductor of spirits to: 5 Hades **10** otherworld
  epithet: 12 psychopompus
  epithet of: 6 Charon, Hermes

psychosis 8 dementia, insanity, neurosis, paranoia **9** paranomia, unreality **10** pathomania **12** hallucinosis **13** schizophrenia **14** mental disorder

psychotherapy 7 therapy **8** analysis **14** psychoanalysis

psychotic 3 mad, nut **4** kook, loon **5** crazy, kooky, loony, nutty **6** insane, madman, maniac **7** lunatic **8** demented, deranged **9** disturbed **10** psychopath **12** insane person, psychopathic **15** non compos mentis

Ptah
  origin: 8 Egyptian
  deity of: 17 universal creation
  worshiped at: 7 Memphis

Ptolemy
  author of: 8 Almagest **9** Geography

pub 3 bar, inn **5** local **6** bistro, saloon, lounge, tavern **7** bar room, ginmill, rummery, rum shop, taproom **8** alehouse, grogshop, pothouse **9** road house, speakeasy **10** beer parlor **11** public house

pubescent 7 teenage **8** immature, juvenile **10** adolescent

public 3 mob **4** folk, open **5** civic, civil, frank, overt, plain, state, trade **6** buyers, common, in view, masses, nation, patent, people, shared, social **7** evident, exposed, general, in sight, obvious, outward, patrons, popular, society, visible **8** apparent, audience, communal, divulged, everyone, manifest, national, passable, populace, revealed, societal, unbarred, unfenced **9** available, citizenry, clientele, community, disclosed, followers, following, free to all, hoi polloi, multitude, notorious, political, statewide, unabashed, unashamed, unbounded, used by all **10** accessible, attendance, nationwide, not private, observable, population, purchasers, recognized, supporters, unenclosed **11** body politic, bourgeoisie, commonality, conspicuous, countrywide, discernible, perceivable, proletariat, rank and file, unconcealed, undisguised **12** acknowledged, constituency, unobstructed, unrestricted **14** community-owned

publication 4 book, news **5** issue, paper **6** digest, report **7** edition, gazette, journal, tabloid **8** bulletin, magazine, pamphlet **9** broadcast, newspaper **10** periodical **11** circulation, information **12** announcement, notification

public disturbance 4 riot **6** fracas, ruckus, uproar **7** turmoil **9** commotion

public house 3 bar, pub **5** local **6** saloon, tavern **7** gin mill, taproom **8** alehouse **9** roadhouse

publicity 4 hype, plug, puff **5** blurb, flack **7** build-up, puffery, write-up **8** ballyhoo, currency **9** attention, notoriety, promotion **10** propaganda, publicness **11** advertising, circulation, information **12** promulgation, public notice, salesmanship

publicize 4 hype, plug, puff, push, sell **6** herald **7** acclaim, promote **8** announce, ballyhoo, emblazon, proclaim **9** advertise, broadcast, make known, propagate **10** make public, promulgate **11** circularize **12** propagandize

publicly
    Latin: 11 coram populo

public matter
    Latin: 10 res publica

public notice 5 edict, ukase **6** decree **8** bulletin **9** manifesto **12** proclamation **13** pronouncement **14** pronunciamento
    French: 7 affiche

public speaking 7 oratory **9** lecturing **12** speechmaking

public-spirited 8 generous **10** altruistic, benevolent **12** humanitarian

publish 3 air **4** tell, vent **5** issue, print, utter **6** herald, impart, put out, spread **7** declare, diffuse, divulge, give out, placard, promote, release, trumpet **8** announce, bring out, disclose, proclaim **9** advertise, broadcast, circulate, make known, propagate, publicize **10** make public, promulgate, put to press **11** communicate, disseminate

Puca
    also: 5 Pooka
    origin: 5 Irish
    form: 6 spirit
    corresponds to: 4 Puck

Puccini, Giacomo
    born: 5 Italy, Lucca
    composer of: 5 Tosca **8** La Boheme, Turandot **12** Manon Lescaut **14** Gianni Schicchi, Madam Butterfly **15** Madama Butterfly **18** La Fanciulla del West **22** The Girl of the Golden West

puce 3 red **7** dark red **13** purplish-brown

Puck
    also: 15 Robin Goodfellow
    character in: 21 A Midsummer Night's Dream
    author: 11 Shakespeare
    form: 6 spirit
    characteristic: 11 mischievous
    corresponds to: 4 Puca **5** Pooka

pucker 4 fold, tuck **5** pinch, pleat, purse **6** crease, gather, ruffle, rumple, shrink **7** crinkle, crumble, squeeze, wrinkle **8** compress, contract **12** draw together

puckered 6 pursed, rucked, tucked **7** creased, crinkly, pinched, pleated **8** crinkled, gathered, wrinkled **10** compressed, corrugated

puckish 5 elfin **6** impish **7** playful **8** annoying **9** whimsical **11** mischievous

pudding 5 jello **6** junket **7** custard, dessert, tapioca **8** pandowdy **9** charlotte, yorkshire **14** floating island

pudgy, podgy 3 fat **5** buxom, dumpy, obese, plump, squat, stout, tubby **6** chubby, chunky, fleshy, rotund, stocky, stubby **7** paunchy **8** roly-poly, thickset

Pueblo (Cliff Dwellers)
    language family: 4 Tewa, Zuni **6** Queres, Tanoan **10** Shoshonean
    tribe: 4 Hopi, Tiwa, Towa, Tuei **5** Acoma, Kiowa **6** Isleta
    location: 4 Utah **7** Arizona **8** Colorado **9** New Mexico
    noted for: 5 adobe **12** architecture
    spirit: 7 Kachina **8** Katchina

puerile 3 raw **5** green, inane, petty, silly, vapid **6** callow, simple **7** babyish, foolish, trivial **8** childish, immature, juvenile, piddling **9** childlike, frivolous, infantile, senseless, worthless **10** irrational, ridiculous, sophomoric **11** harebrained, nonsensical

Puerto Rico
    name means: 8 rich port
    other name: 9 Borinquen **15** San Juan Bautista
    capital/largest city: 7 San Juan
    others: 5 Cayey, Coamo, Lares, Ponce **6** Caguas, Dorado, Manati, Utuado **7** Arecibo, Bayamon, Fajardo, Guanica, Guayama, Humacao **8** Adjuntas, Cabo Rojo, Mayaguez **9** Aquadilla **11** Santa Isabel
    government: 32 self-governing commonwealth of the U S
    measure: 6 cuerda **10** caballeria
    island: 4 Mona **7** Culebra, Vieques **13** Caja de Muertos **15** Greater Antilles
    lake: 5 Loiza **6** Carite **8** Dos Bocas **9** Caonillas, Guatajaca
    mountain: 4 Toro **5** Cayey **6** Yunque **8** Guilarte, Luquilla **10** Torrecilla **17** Cordillera Central
    highest point: 5 Punta
    river: 5 Camuy, Canas, Loiza, Yauco **6** Anasco, Manati, Tanama **7** Arecibo, Fajardo, La Plata **9** Caonillas
    sea: 8 Atlantic **9** Caribbean
    physical feature:
      bay: 5 Sucia **6** Rincon **8** Boqueron **9** Aquadilla **14** Phosphorescent
      sound: 7 Vieques
    people: 6 gibaro **10** borinqueno
      explorer: 8 Columbus **11** Ponce de Leon
      leader: 10 Munoz Marin
    language: 7 English, Spanish
    religion: 10 Protestant **13** Roman Catholic
    place:
      area of San Juan: 7 Hato Rey **10** Rio Piedras
      beach: 7 Condado
      cathedral: 15 San Juan Bautista
      fortress: 7 El Morro **11** San Jeronimo **12** San Cristobal
      governor's residence: 11 La Fortaleza
      museum: 14 El Museo de Ponce
      reservoir: 5 Loiza
      tomb: 11 Ponce de Leon
    feature:
      bird: 4 rola **7** yeguita
      festival: 6 Casals
      housing development: 14 urbanizaciones
      song: 9 aguinaldo
      strolling musicians: 9 parrandas
      tree: 4 mora **5** yafua, yaray **8** emajagua, guayrote **10** guaranguao
    food:
      dish: 4 sama, sisi **9** moreillas **11** lechon asado
      drink: 3 rum **10** anis-golila

puff 3 bow **4** blow, draw, emit, gasp, hump, node, pant, plug, suck, wisp **5** bloat, blurb, bulge, heave, smoke, swell, whiff **6** blow up, breath, dilate, exhale, expand, extend, flurry, inhale, rising, wheeze **7** bluster, bombast, distend, inflate, puffery, stretch **8** ballyhoo, be winded, dilation, encomium, flattery, flummery, swelling **9** convexity, discharge, elevation, euphemism, extension, inflation, panegyric, publicity, sales talk **10** be inflated, distention, exhalation, overpraise, protrusion, tuberosity **12** be distended, breathe hard, excrescence, excurvature **12** exaggeration, inflammation, protuberance, protuberancy **13** overlaudation **16** overcommendation **17** misrepresentation

puffed 5 baggy **7** bulbous, swollen **9** ballooned

puffed up 4 vain **5** proud, puffy **7** swollen **8** inflated **9** conceited **11** swell-headed **12** vainglorious **13** self-important

puffery 4 hype **7** big talk, bluster, bombast **9** hyperbole **11** braggadocio

puff out 5 bloat, bulge, swell **6** billow, expand **7** balloon, distend, enlarge, inflate

puffy 3 fat 5 round 6 fleshy 7 bloated, bulging, swollen 8 enlarged, expanded, inflamed, inflated, puffed up 9 corpulent, distended

pugilist 3 pug 5 boxer 7 battler, bruiser, fighter 12 prizefighter

pugnacious 7 defiant, hostile, warlike 8 menacing, militant 9 bellicose, combative, fractious 10 aggressive, unfriendly 11 belligerent, contentious, quarrelsome, threatening 12 antagonistic, disputatious 13 argumentative

pugnacity 9 hostility 10 antagonism 12 belligerence 13 combativeness 14 aggressiveness, fighting spirit 15 contentiousness

puissance 5 force, might, power 6 energy 7 potency, prowess 8 strength

pulchritude 6 beauty 8 fairness 9 bonniness, good looks 10 comeliness, loveliness, prettiness 12 gorgeousness, handsomeness 13 beauteousness, exquisiteness 14 attractiveness, personableness

pulchritudinous 4 fair, fine 5 bonny 6 comely, lovely, pretty 8 gorgeous, handsome 9 beauteous, beautiful, ravishing 10 attractive 11 good-looking

Pulitzer
  author: 10 W A Swanberg

Pulitzer Prize
  originator: 14 Joseph Pulitzer
  administered by: 18 Columbia University
  awarded for: 4 play 5 drama, music, novel 6 poetry 7 cartoon, feature, fiction, history, letters 9 biography, criticism, editorial, reporting 10 commentary, journalism, literature, nonfiction 11 photography 13 autobiography

pull 2 go 3 lug, rip, tow, tug 4 drag, draw, grab, haul, jerk, lure, move, rend, rive, tear, yank 5 drive, sever, shake, split, trawl, troll, twist, wrest, wring 6 allure, appeal, detach, dig out, entice, remove, sprain, strain, uproot, wrench 7 attract, draw out, extract, gravity, stretch, weed out 8 withdraw 9 extirpate, influence, magnetism, take in tow 10 allurement, attraction, enticement 11 fascination 14 attractiveness

pull apart 3 rip, tug 4 drag, rend, tear 6 detach, wrench 7 extract 8 separate 9 criticize, disengage 10 disconnect

pull away 5 wrest 7 remove 8 drawback, withdraw

pull back 7 back off, retreat 8 fall back, withdraw

Pullman, George Mortimer
  nationality: 8 American
  developed: 9 (railroad) dining car 11 (railroad) sleeping car

pull off 4 pull 6 commit, effect 7 execute, perform 8 carry out 10 perpetuate 13 participate in

pull on 3 don 5 put on 7 get into

pull one's leg 3 kid 4 fool, hoax 5 tease, trick 7 deceive 9 make fun of

pull out 5 leave 7 draw out, extract 8 withdraw

pull over, pullover 4 cite, stop 5 shirt 6 arrest, jersey, slip on, ticket, t-shirt 7 maillot, sweater 8 slip over

pull together 4 join 5 unite 7 pitch in, share in 8 take part 9 cooperate, join hands 10 act jointly, join forces 11 collaborate, participate

pull to pieces 5 shred 4 rend 6 tear up 7 destroy 9 tear apart

pull up 4 halt, rein, stop, weed 5 check, hoist 6 arrest, uplift, uproot 7 extract, reprove

pulp 4 curd, mash, mush, pith 5 crush, flesh, paste, puree, slush, smash 6 squash, tissue 7 journal 8 magazine 9 masticate

pulsate 4 beat, tick, wave 5 pound, pulse, shake, throb, thump, waver 6 quaver, quiver, shiver 7 flutter, shudder, tremble, vibrate 8 undulate 9 alternate, come and go, oscillate, palpitate 10 ebb and flow 11 reverberate

pulse 4 beat 5 throb, thump 6 quiver, rhythm, stroke 7 cadence, pulsate, shudder, tremble, vibrate 9 oscillate, palpitate, pulsation, vibration 10 recurrence, undulation 11 oscillation, palpitation

pulverize 4 mash, mill 5 crumb, crush, grind, mince, pound 6 powder 7 atomize, crumble 9 comminate, granulate, triturate 12 reduce to dust

pulverized 6 ground, milled 7 crumbed, crushed, pounded 8 atomized, crumbled, crunched, powdered 10 granulated 12 ground to dust

pummel 4 beat, maul 5 pound 6 batter, thrash 7 trounce

pump 4 quiz, shoe, well 5 grill 7 inflate, slipper 8 question 9 draw water

Pump
  constellation of: 6 Antlia

Pump House Gang, The
  author: 8 Tom Wolfe

pumpkin 5 fruit, gourd, melon 6 squash 9 vegetable 12 jack o'lantern

pun
  French: 9 jeu de mots

punch 3 box, hit, jab 4 beat, blow, chop, clip, conk, cuff, pelt, plug, poke, slam, sock, swat 5 baste, clout, knock, paste, pound, smite, thump, whack 6 pummel, strike, stroke, thrust, thwack, wallop 7 clobber 8 haymaker 10 roundhouse

punchy 3 fat 5 dazed 6 stubby 8 confused, forceful 9 befuddled

punctilious 5 exact, fussy, picky, rigid 6 proper, strict 7 correct, finicky, precise 8 exacting, rigorous 9 demanding 10 meticulous, particular, scrupulous 11 painstaking

punctual 5 early, quick, ready 6 on time, prompt, steady, timely 7 instant, not late, regular 8 constant, on the dot 9 immediate, well-timed 10 in good time, seasonable 11 expeditious 13 instantaneous

punctuate 4 lace 5 break 6 pepper 7 scatter 8 separate, sprinkle 9 interrupt 11 intersperse

punctuation mark 4 dash 5 colon, comma, pause, point, slash 6 accent, ending, hyphen, parens, period, quotes 7 bracket 8 ellipsis 9 semicolon 10 apostrophe 11 parenthesis 12 question mark 13 quotation mark 16 exclamation point

puncture 3 cut 4 bite, hole, nick, pink 5 break, prick, stick, sting, wound 6 pierce 7 deflate, let down, opening, rupture 9 knock down, shoot down 10 depreciate 11 perforation

pundit 4 guru, sage 5 guide 6 critic, expert, master, mentor, savant, wizard 7 thinker 9 authority 13 learned person

pungent 3 hot 4 acid, keen, racy, sour, tart 5 acrid, acute, nippy, salty, sharp, smart, spicy, tangy, witty 6 biting, bitter, clever, savory, snappy, strong 7 acetous, caustic, cutting, mordent, peppery, piquant, pointed 8 incisive, piercing, poignant, smarting, stinging, stirring, vinegary, wounding 9 brilliant, flavorful, invidious, palatable, sarcastic, sparkling, trenchant 10 astringent, flavorsome, keen-witted 11 acrimonious, penetrating, provocative, stimulating, tantalizing 12 sharp-tasting 13 scintillating, sharp-smelling 14 highly flavored, highly seasoned

punish 4 beat, fine, flog, whip 6 avenge, rebuke 7 chasten, correct, reprove 8 admonish, chastise, imprison, penalize, sentence 9 castigate, dress down, retaliate 10 discipline, take to task 11 get even with, take revenge 14 bring to account 15 take vengeance on

punishing 5 harsh, penal 6 brutal, severe 7 abusive 8 scolding 9 torturing 10 chastizing, tormenting 11 castigating

punishment 4 fine 5 price 7 damages, deserts, flaying, forfeit, hanging, payment, penalty, penance, redress 8 flogging, punition, spanking, whipping 10 chastening, correction, crucifying, discipline, reparation 11 castigation, retribution 12 chastisement, penalization

punk 4 hood, lout, poor 5 bully, lousy, rowdy, tough 6 crummy, rotten 7 hoodlum, ruffian 8 hooligan 9 barbarian, roughneck 10 delinquent

Punt see 7 Somalia

Puntarvolo
   character in: 22 Every Man Out of His Humour
   author: 6 Jonson

punt e mes
   type: 8 aperitif
   origin: 5 Italy
   flavor: 6 orange
   color: 12 reddish-brown

puny 4 poor, thin, tiny, weak **5** frail, light, petty, runty, small **6** bantam, feeble, flimsy, infirm, little, meager, measly, paltry, sickly, slight, weakly **7** fragile, shallow, tenuous, trivial **8** delicate, impotent, picayune, piddling, runtlike, sawed-off, trifling **9** emaciated, miniature, mite- sized, pint-sized, worthless **10** diminutive, inadequate, picayunish, under sized **11** unimportant **12** insufficient **13** insignificant **14** inconsiderable, underdeveloped

pupa 3 egg **5** larva, nymph **6** cocoon **7** wiggler **9** chrysalis **14** transformation

pupil 4 coed, tyro **5** tutee **6** novice **7** learner, scholar, student, trainee **8** beginner, disciple, initiate **9** schoolboy **10** apprentice, schoolgirl **11** probationer **13** undergraduate

puppet 3 toy **4** doll, dupe, pawn, tool **6** flunky, lackey **7** cat's-paw, manikin, servant **8** creature, henchman, hireling **9** jackstraw, lay figure, underling **10** figurehead, instrument, man of straw, marionette **11** subordinate

puppeteer 4 sarg **5** (Bil) Baird **8** Geppetto **9** Jim Henson **10** Shari Lewis

puppy 3 dog, pet, pup **6** canine

Purcell, Henry
   born: 6 London **7** England
   composer of: 9 Fantasias **10** Bell Anthem, Dioclesian, King Arthur (The British Worthy), The Tempest **12** Golden Sonata **13** Dido and Aeneas **14** The Indian Queen

purchase 3 buy **4** edge, hold **6** buying, pay for, pick up **7** footing, support, toehold **8** foothold, leverage **9** advantage, influence **11** acquirement, acquisition

pure 4 full, mere, neat, true **5** basic, clean, fresh, moral, sheer, stark, utter, whole **6** chaste, decent, entire, higher, virgin **7** angelic, ethical, perfect, sincere, sinless, sterile, unmixed, upright **8** absolute, abstract, complete, flawless, germfree, innocent, positive, purebred, sanitary, spotless, straight, thorough, unmarred, virginal, virtuous **9** blameless, downright, faultless, guileless, guiltless, healthful, inviolate, out-and-out, pedigreed, righteous, unalloyed, undefiled, unmingled, unspoiled, unsullied, untainted, wholesome **10** antiseptic, immaculate, inviolable, sterilized, uninfected, unmodified, unpolluted **11** conjectural,

disinfected, fundamental, pure- blooded, speculative, theoretical, unblemished, uncorrupted, unqualified, untarnished **12** full-strength, hypothetical, thoroughbred **13** unadulterated, unimpeachable **14** above suspicion, uncontaminated

puree 4 bisk, pulp, soup **5** paste **6** bisque

purely 4 only **5** fully **6** merely, simply, solely, wholly **7** cleanly, morally, piously, totally **8** chastely, devoutly, entirely, worthily **9** admirably **10** absolutely, completely, flawlessly, in all honor, innocently, virginally, virtuously **11** essentially, faultlessly **13** incorruptibly

Purgatory, Purgatorio
   part II of: 12 Divine Comedy
   author: 14 Dante Alighieri

purge 4 kill, oust **5** crush, expel **6** banish, emetic, pardon, physic, purify, remove, up- root **7** clean up, cleanse, cleanup, clyster, dismiss, expiate, purging, rout out, shake up **8** aperient, atone for, clean out, get rid of, laxative, sweep out, wash away **9** cathartic, discharge, eliminate, eradicate, liquidate, purgation, purgative **10** do away with **11** exterminate **12** obtain pardon (from), purification **15** obtain remission (from) **16** obtain absolution (from) **17** obtain forgiveness

purification 7 baptism **9** cleansing **13** sterilization

purify 4 boil **5** clear **6** filter **7** clarify, distill **8** make pure, sanitize **9** disinfect, sterilize **10** chlorinate, pasteurize **13** decontaminate

Purim 11 Feast of Lots
   celebrates: 11 deliverance
   heroine: 6 Esther
   villian: 5 Haman
   month: 4 Adar

Puritani, I
   also: 11 The Puritans
   opera by: 7 Bellini
   character: 14 Oliver Cromwell, Queen Henrietta **16** Lord Arthur Talbot

puritanical 4 prim **5** rigid, stiff **6** narrow, prissy, severe, strict, stuffy **7** ascetic, austere, bigoted, prudish, puritan, stilted **8** dogmatic, priggish **9** bluenosed, fanatical **11** stiff-necked, straitlaced **13** sanctimonious

Puritan State
   nickname of: 13 Massachusetts

purity 5 honor, piety **6** virtue **7** clarity, decency, honesty, modesty **8** chastity, fineness, holiness, lucidity, morality, pureness, sanctity **9** cleanness, clearness, innocence, integrity, limpidity, plainness, rectitude, virginity **10** brilliance, chasteness, directness, excellence, immaculacy, simplicity, temperance, uniformity **11** cleanliness, homogeneity, saintliness, uprightness

12 virtuousness **13** guilelessness, guiltlessness **14** immaculateness **15** clear conscience **16** incorruptibility

purlieu 4 area **5** haunt, limit **6** border, locale, region, resort **7** district, environ **8** out- skirt **11** surrounding **12** neighborhood

purloin 3 rob **5** steal **6** pilfer **11** appropriate, make off with

Purloined Letter, The
   author: 13 Edgar Allan Poe

purloiner 5 thief **6** robber **7** burglar **8** pilferer

purple 4 plum, puce, racy **5** color, grape, lilac, lurid, mauve, royal **6** florid, orchid, turgid, violet **7** crimson, flowery, furious, fuchsia, magenta **8** amethyst, burgundy, imperial, lavender **9** gastropod

Purple Land see **7** Uruguay

Purple Rose of Cairo, The
   director: 10 Woody Allen
   cast: 9 Mia Farrow **11** Danny Aiello, Jeff Daniels

purport 3 aim, end **4** gist **5** claim, drift, point, sense, tenor, trend **6** alege, burden, design, import, intent, object, reason **7** bearing, meaning, profess, purpose **9** intention, objective, rationale, substance **11** implication **12** significance **13** signification

purpose 3 aim **4** goal, hope, mean, plan, will, wish **5** elect, point, sense **6** aspire, choose, decide, design, desire, intend, intent, motive, object, reason, scheme, target **7** drive at, meaning, mission, persist, project, propose, resolve, think to **8** ambition, conclude, endeavor, function, proposal, set about **9** determine, intention, objective, persevere, rationale, undertake **10** aspiration, motivation, resolution **11** contemplate, disposition, expectation, fixed intent, have a mind to, raison d'etre **13** commit one self, determination

purposeful 7 decided, studied **8** resolute, resolved **9** committed, conscious **10** calculated, considered, deliberate, determined **11** intentional **12** premeditated, strong-willed

purposefulness 7 purpose, resolve **10** resolution **11** decidedness **12** decisiveness, resoluteness **13** determination

purposeless 6 random **7** aimless, useless **8** needless, plotless **9** desultory, driftless, haphazard, irregular, senseless, unplanned **11** meaningless **12** functionless, undetermined, unprofitable

purposely 8 by design **9** advisedly, expressly, knowingly, on purpose, willfully, wittingly **10** designedly, with intent **11** consciously, voluntarily **12** calculatedly, deliberately **13** intentionally

purse 3 bag **4** fold, fund, knit **5** award,

bunch, pinch, pleat, pouch, prize, stake **6** clutch, coffer, gather, pucker, wallet **7** handbag, sporran, wrinkle **8** contract, moneybag, proceeds, treasury, winnings **10** pocketbook **11** shoulder bag
French: **12** porte-monnaie

purser 6 bursar **7** cashier **9** paymaster **10** cashkeeper

pursue 4 seek **5** aim at, chase, track, trail **6** aim for, follow, try for **7** be after, carry on, go after, perform **8** aspire to, engage in, labor for, run after **9** race after, strive for **10** chase after, push toward

pursuer 5 pupil **6** seeker **7** devotee, student **8** disciple, follower, searcher **10** aficionado

pursuit 4 hunt **5** chase **6** search **7** pastime **8** activity **9** following **10** occupation

purvey 3 get **4** give, hand **5** cater, equip, yield **6** obtain, outfit, supply **7** deliver, furnish, procure, provide

purveyor 4 pimp **6** seller **8** procurer, provider, supplier

purview 3 ken **4** area **5** field, range, reach, realm, savvy, scope, sweep **6** domain, extent **7** compass, horizon, outlook **8** dominion, overview **9** territory, viewpoint **10** commission, experience **11** mental grasp **13** comprehension, understanding **14** responsibility

push 2 go **3** dun, ram **4** butt, goad, jolt, move, plug, prod, spur, sway, urge, work, worm **5** boost, drive, egg on, elbow, fight, foray, force, forge, harry, hound, impel, nudge, press, rouse, shove, stick, stuff, vigor, wedge **6** arouse, badger, coerce, compel, energy, exhort, harass, heckle, hustle, incite, induce, inroad, jostle, plunge, prompt, propel, thrust, wiggle **7** advance, animate, buffalo, inspire, promote, provoke, squeeze **8** ambition, browbeat, motivate, persuade, shoulder, struggle, vitality **9** advertise, constrain, encourage, importune, incursion, instigate, make known, publicize, stimulate, strong-arm **10** get-up-and-go **11** make one's way, prevail upon, vim and vigor **12** force one's way, propagandize **13** determination

pushcart 5 wagon **6** barrow **8** handcart **10** handbarrow **11** wheelbarrow

push forward 4 goad, prod, spur **5** drive, impel, press **9** urge along

Pushkin, Alexander (Aleksandr)
author of: **12** Boris Godunov, Eugene Onegin **16** The Queen of Spades **17** The Bronze Horseman **19** The Captain's Daughter

push through 6 hasten **7** advance, forward **8** dispatch, expedite **10** accelerate, facilitate

pushy 8 forceful **9** assertive, insistent **10** aggressive **11** domineering **12** strong-willed **13** self-assertive

pusillanimous 7 fearful **8** cowardly, timorous **10** spiritless **11** lily-livered **12** apprehensive, fainthearted, mean-spirited

pusillanimousness 8 timidity **9** cowardice **12** yellow streak **13** yellow feather **16** faint heartedness **18** chickenheartedness

puss 3 cat, mug, pan **4** face **5** kitty **6** feline, kisser, kitten

pussyfoot 5 dodge, evade, hedge, sneak **6** tiptoe, weasel **8** sidestep **13** evade the issue **14** beg the question **15** walk on eggshells **16** straddle the fence

put 3 fix, lay, set **4** cast, pose, rest, word **5** bring, drive, force, heave, offer, pitch, place, state, throw **6** assign, employ, impute, phrase, submit **7** ascribe, deposit, express, present, propose **8** position **9** attribute, enunciate **10** articulate

put a damper on 4 cool, dull **7** depress, squelch **10** discourage, dishearten

put an edge on 4 hone, whet **6** excite **7** sharpen **9** stimulate

put an end to 4 halt, stop **5** annul, quash **6** cancel, finish, repeal, revoke **7** abolish, blot out, rescind, squelch, wipe out **8** abrogate, demolish, dispatch, stamp out **9** eliminate, eradicate, finish off **10** discourage, do away with, put a stop to **12** write finis to

put aside 5 table **6** forget **7** discard, lay away **10** relinquish

put away 3 eat **4** down, stow **5** stash **6** commit **7** confine, consume **9** drink down

put back 4 rout **5** delay **6** defeat, demote, impair, reject, return **7** replace, restore **9** reinstate

put down 4 note, post **5** crush, enter, knock, quash, quell **6** dispel, enlist, record, subdue **7** deposit, disdain, sneer at, squelch **8** belittle, derogate, laugh off, pooh-pooh, suppress **9** denigrate, disparage, humiliate, write down **10** depreciate

put forth 5 offer **6** extend, put out **7** proffer, send out

put forward 4 pose **6** assert **7** advance, profess, propose **8** propound

put in irons 5 chain **6** fetter **7** manacle, shackle **8** handcuff

put in motion 4 move **5** begin, start **6** arouse, launch **8** activate, carry out, commence, initiate **9** instigate, undertake

put in order 5 array **6** neaten, tidy up **7** arrange **8** organize **10** straighten

put in plain sight 4 show **6** set out **7** display, exhibit

put in shackles 6 fetter, hobble **7** enchain, enslave, manacle **8** handcuff, imprison

put into circulation 4 move **5** issue, print **7** publish **10** pass around

put into effect 6 effect **7** achieve, enforce, execute, fulfill, realize **8** carry out, complete **10** accomplish, administer, consummate, effectuate, perpetrate **12** carry through

put into words 5 voice **7** express **8** describe **9** verbalize **10** articulate **11** communicate

Putnam, Abbie
character in: **18** Desire Under the Elms
author: **6** O'Neill

put off 5 delay, repel, stall **6** offend, rebuff, recess **7** adjourn, repulse, set sail, suspend **8** hold back, launched, offended, postpone, rebuffed, repelled, repulsed **9** interrupt **11** discontinue **13** procrastinate

put off guard 4 lull **6** disarm **10** make unwary

put on 3 don **5** affix **6** attach **7** dress in, get into, stick on **8** fasten to

put-on 4 hoax, joke **8** pretense **11** affectation

put on guard 4 warn **5** alert **6** advise, tip off **7** caution **8** forewarn **9** make ready **10** precaution

put out 3 irk **5** annoy, issue **6** quench, retire **7** produce, publish **8** irritate **9** strike out **10** extinguish **11** manufacture **13** leave the shore

put out of order 5 mix up, upset **6** jumble, mess up, muddle **7** confuse, scatter **8** disarray, disorder, displace, put askew, scramble **10** disarrange **11** disorganize

putrefaction 3 rot **5** decay **7** rotting **8** spoilage, spoiling **10** rottenness **12** decompostion

putrefy 3 rot **4** turn **5** decay, spoil, taint **6** molder **8** putresce, stagnate **9** decompose **10** biodegrade **11** deteriorate **12** disintegrate

putrescent 4 foul, rank **5** fetid **6** smelly **7** rotting **8** decaying, spoiling, stinking **9** offensive **10** malodorous, putrefying **11** decomposing

putrid 3 bad **4** foul, rank **5** fetid **6** rancid, rotten, spoiled **7** tainted **8** decaying, polluted, purulent, stinking **9** putrefied **10** putrescent **11** decomposing **12** contaminated, putrefactive

putridity 5 decay, filth, taint **8** foulness, impurity **9** dirtiness, pollution, purulence, rancidity **10** rottenness **11** putrescence, uncleanness **13** contamination, decomposition

putsch 6 revolt **8** uprising

putter 4 fool, idle, laze, loaf, loll **5**

dally, drift **6** dawdle, diddle, fiddle, loiter, lounge, piddle, potter, tinker **8** golf club, lallygag **10** dillydally

put to death 4 do in, hang, kill, slay **5** slain **6** done in, hanged, killed, murder, poison, rub out **7** bump off, butcher, execute **8** dispatch, executed, massacre, murdered, poisoned, strangle **9** bumped off, butchered, finish off, massacred, strangled, suffocate **11** assassinate, electrocute, exterminate **12** assassinated, electrocuted, exterminated

put to flight 4 rout, shoo **5** chase **6** dispel **7** cast out, scatter **8** drive off, send away **11** send packing

put together 4 join **5** unite **7** combine **8** assemble

put to shame 6 ashame **7** chagrin, mortify **9** discomfit, embarrass, humiliate

put to sleep 4 lull **5** quiet **6** sedate **8** knock out **9** narcotize **11** anesthetize

put to use 3 use **5** apply **6** employ, engage, occupy **7** exploit, utilize **9** make use of

put under a spell 5 charm **7** bewitch, enchant **8** entrance **9** fascinate, mesmerize, spellbind

put up 3 can **4** hang **5** erect, house, lodge, raise, store **6** billet **7** shelter **8** preserve **11** accommodate **14** furnish room for

put up with 4 bear, take **5** abide, brave, brook, stand **6** endure, suffer **7** stomach, sustain, undergo **8** stand for, submit to, tolerate **9** withstand **11** countenance

Puvis de Chavannes, Pierre Cecile
born: 5 Lyons **6** France
artwork: 6 Summer **13** Shepherd's Song **14** Ludus pro patria **16** The Poor Fisher- man **17** Life of St Genevieve, The Inspiring Muses **21** Science Arts and Letters

Puzo, Mario
author of: 12 The Godfather

puzzle 4 foil, mull **5** brood, stump **6** baffle, enigma, outwit, ponder, riddle, wonder **7** confuse, dilemma, mystery, mystify, nonplus, perplex, problem **8** bewilder, confound, hoodwink **9** conundrum **10** bafflement, difficulty, perplexity **12** bewilderment, complication **13** mystification

puzzled 6 amazed **7** baffled **8** befogged, confused, troubled **9** astounded, befuddled, mystified, perplexed **10** bewildered, confounded, nonplussed

puzzling 7 elusive **8** baffling **9** confusing, enigmatic **10** mysterious, mystifying, perplexing **11** bewildering, confounding, enigmatical **12** unfathomable **16** hard to understand, incomprehensible

Pyanepsia
origin: 5 Greek **8** Athenian
event: 8 festival
honoring: 6 Apollo **7** harvest

Pygmalion
author: 17 George Bernard Shaw
character: 12 Henry Higgins **14** Eliza Doolittle
basis for: 10 My Fair Lady
director: 14 Anthony Asquith
cast: 11 Wendy Hiller (Eliza Doolittle) **12** Leslie Howard (Professor Henry Higgins) **13** Wilfrid Lawson

Pygmalion
king of: 6 Cyprus
avocation: 8 sculptor
statue named: 7 Galatea
loved: 7 Galatea
statue changed to: 5 woman
wife: 7 Galatea
daughter: 6 Paphos **8** Metharme

pygmy 3 elf, toy, wee **4** mite, runt, tiny **5** dwarf, elfin, short, small **6** bantam, midget, peewee, shrimp **7** manikin **8** dwarfish, half-pint, Tom Thumb **9** miniature, pipsqueak **10** diminutive, homun culus, undersized **11** Lilliputian

Pyncheon family
character in: 24 The House of the Seven Gables
members: 6 Phoebe **8** Clifford, Hepzibah **12** Judge Jaffrey
author: 9 Hawthorne

Pynchon, Thomas
author of: 1 V **15** Gravity's Rainbow **23** The Crying of Lot Forty-Nine

Pyongyang
capital of: 10 North Korea

Pyramus
form: 5 youth
location: 7 Babylon
loved: 6 Thisbe
died at tomb of: 5 Ninus

pyre 8 woodpile
rite: 7 funeral
method: 7 burning

Pyrigenes
epithet of: 8 Dionysus
means: 10 born of fire

Pyriphlegethon *see* **10** Phlegethon

pyromaniac 7 firebug **8** arsonist **10** incendiary **11** firestarter

Pyronia
epithet of: 7 Artemis
means: 11 fire goddess

pyrope
species: 6 garnet
color: 3 red

pyrophobia
fear of: 4 fire

pyrotechnics 9 fireworks **16** brilliant display **19** dazzling performance

Pyrrhus
king of: 6 Epirus
triumphed over: 5 Romans
result: 11 heavy losses
phrase: 14 Pyrrhic victory

Pythagoras
born: 5 Samos
vocation: 11 philosopher **13** mathematician
created: 7 theorem
of: 13 right triangle

Pythia
priestess of: 6 Apollo
location: 6 Delphi
delivered: 7 oracles

Pythias
friend: 5 Damon

Pythius *see* **6** Apollo

Qatar
capital/largest city: 4 Doha **7** al-Dawha
others: 3 Juh **5** Wagra **6** Dukhan, Umm-Bab **7** al-Khawr, Musayid, Umm Said
government: 7 emirate
head of state/government: 4 emir
monetary unit: 5 riyal **6** dirham
highest point: 13 Aba al-Bawl Hill
physical feature:
  bay: 5 Salwa
  cape: 5 Rakan **6** Laffan **8** Ushayriq **9** al-Matbakh
  gulf: 7 Bahrain, Persian
people: 4 Arab **6** Pushtu, Yemeni **7** Baluchi, Iranian **9** Pakistani
  rulers: 12 Great Britain, Ottoman Turks
  sheik/sheikh: 18 Ahmad bin Ali al-Thani **22** Khalifa bin Hamad al-Thani
language: 6 Arabic
religion: 5 Islam
  sect: 7 Wahhabi
war: 4 Gulf **11** Desert Storm

QED 21 quod erat demonstrandum

quack 4 fake, sham **5** phony **6** pseudo **9** charlatan, pretender **10** fake doctor, fraudulent **11** counterfeit, quacksalver **15** medical impostor

quackery 5 bluff, guile **6** deceit **7** cunning **9** deception, duplicity **12** charlatanism

Quadrigesima 4 Lent **9** forty days

quaff 4 down, gulp, swig **5** drink, lap up, swill **6** guzzle, imbibe, tipple **7** swallow, toss off **8** belt down, chug-a-lug **9** knock back **11** drink deeply

quagmire 3 bog, fen, fix, jam **4** mess, mire, ooze, quag, sump **5** marsh, pinch, swamp **6** crisis, morass, muddle, pickle, plight, scrape, slough, sludge, strait **7** dilemma **8** hot water, quandary **9** imbroglio, intricacy, quicksand **10** difficulty, perplexity **11** Gordian knot, involvement, predicament **12** entanglement

quail 3 shy **5** cower, quake, shake **6** blanch, flinch, recoil, shrink **7** run away, shudder, tremble **8** fight shy, turn tail **9** lose heart **10** be cowardly, lose spirit, take fright **11** lose courage **12** have cold feet **16** shake in one's boots **17** shiver in one's shoes, show a yellow streak

quail
  group of: 4 bevy **5** covey

quaint 3 odd **4** rare **5** droll, queer **6** unique **7** antique, bizarre, curious, strange, unusual **8** charming, fanciful, old-timey, original, peculiar, singular, uncommon **9** eccentric, whimsical **10** antiquated, outlandish **11** out-of-the-way, picturesque **12** old-fashioned **13** extraordinary **14** unconventional

quake 4 wave **5** quail, shake, spasm, throb **6** blanch, quaver, quiver, ripple, shiver, thrill, tremor **7** shudder, tremble **9** trembling **10** earthquake **18** seismic disturbance

Quaker
  founder: 9 George Fox
  group: 7 friends
  pronoun: 4 thee, thou

qualification 4 gift **5** forte, skill **6** talent **7** ability, faculty, fitness, proviso **8** aptitude, bona fide, capacity, property, standard **9** attribute, condition, endowment, exception, exemption, objection, postulate, provision, requisite **10** capability, competency, credential, limitation **11** achievement, arrangement, eligibility, requirement, reservation, restriction, stipulation **12** escape clause, modification, prerequisite, suitableness **13** certification **14** accomplishment

qualified 3 fit **4** able, meet **5** adept, equal **6** expert, fitted, suited, versed **7** capable, guarded, hedging, knowing, limited, skilled, trained **8** eligible, equipped, licensed, reserved, skillful, talented **9** ambiguous, certified, competent, efficient, equivocal, practiced **10** authorized, indefinite, proficient, restricted **11** conditional, efficacious, experienced, provisional **12** accomplished

qualify 3 fit **4** ease **5** abate, adapt, alter, endow, equip, limit, ready, train **6** adjust, enable, ground, modify, narrow, permit, reduce, soften, temper **7** assuage, certify, empower, entitle, license, make fit, prepare **8** describe, diminish, mitigate, moderate, restrain, restrict, sanction **9** authorize, condition, give power, measure up **10** be accepted, be eligible, commission, legitimate **11** accommodate **12** characterize, circumscribe, make eligible

qualifying 9 tempering **10** mitigating **11** eligibility, extenuating, preparatory

quality 4 mark, rank **5** blood, class, grade, merit, trait, value, worth **6** aspect, family, nature **7** caliber, dignity, faculty, feature **8** capacity, eminence, position, property, standing **9** attribute, character **11** disposition, distinction, high station, temperament **12** constitution, social status **13** qualification **14** characteristic

Quality Street
  author: 12 James M Barrie

qualm 4 turn **6** nausea **7** scruple, vertigo **9** faintness, giddiness, misgiving **10** dizzy spell, hesitation, queasiness, reluctance, uneasiness **11** compunction, reservation, sick feeling **13** indisposition, unwillingness **14** disinclination **18** twinge of conscience

quandary 3 fix, jam **4** mire **5** pinch, crisis, morass, pickle, plight, scrape, strait **7** dilemma, impasse **8** hot water, quagmire **9** imbroglio **10** difficulty **11** involvement, predicament **12** entanglement, kettle of fish

quantities 4 lots, much **5** heaps, loads **7** amounts

quantity 3 sum **4** area, bulk, dose, mass, size **5** quota, share **6** amount, dosage, extent, length, number, volume **7** expanse, measure, portion **8** vastness **9** abundance, aggregate, allotment, amplitude, extension, greatness, magnitude, multitude **10** proportion **11** measurement **13** apportionment

quarantine 7 confine, isolate **9** isolation, segregate, sequester **13** sequestration **15** cordon sanitaire **18** medical segregation

Quare Fellow, The
  author: 12 Brendan Behan

quarrel 3 jar, nag, row **4** carp, feud, fuss, spat, tiff **5** argue, brawl, cavil, clash, fight, scrap **6** bicker, differ, strife **7** contend, discord, dispute, dissent, fall out, wrangle **8** argument, be at odds, conflict, squabble **9** altercate, bickering, complaint, find fault, have words, objection **10** contention, difference, dissension, dissidence, falling out **11** controversy **12** disagreement **13** breach of peace, contradiction, misunderstand **14** apple of discord

15 be at logger heads **16** bone of contention, misunderstanding

quarreling 6 strife **7** discord **8** clashing, conflict, disunity, friction **9** bickering, disputing, scrapping, wrangling **10** contention, dissension, dissidence, squabbling **11** discordance **12** disagreement

quarrelsome 7 peevish **8** captious, churlish, contrary, militant, petulant **9** bellicose, combative, fractious, irascible, querulous, truculent **10** pugnacious **11** belligerent, contentious **12** antagonistic, cantankerous, disagreeable, disputatious **13** argumentative

quarry 3 bed, dig, pit **4** game, lode, mine, prey **5** catch, stone **6** source, victim **8** excavate

quart
abbreviation: 2 qt

quarter, quarters 4 area, part, pity, post, side, spot, zone **5** board, house, lodge, mercy, place, put up, realm, rooms **6** billet, domain, fourth, locale, region, sphere **7** housing, install, lodging, shelter, station, terrain **8** clemency, district, humanity, leniency, locality, location, lodgings, position, precinct, province, sympathy **9** percent, direction, one-fourth, situation, territory **10** compassion, fourth part, indulgence, quadrisect **11** place to live, place to stay, three months **13** quarter dollar, specific place **14** accommodations **15** twenty-five cents

quarterstaff 4 pole **5** staff **6** cudgel

quartz
varieties: 4 sard **5** agate, topaz **8** amethyst **9** carnelian, tiger's-eye **11** rock crystal

quash 4 ruin, stop, undo, void **5** annul, crush, erase, quell, smash, wreck **6** cancel, delete, dispel, efface, quench, recall, revoke, squash, subdue, vacate **7** blot out, destroy, expunge, nullify, put down, repress, rescind, retract, reverse, squelch **8** abrogate, dissolve, override, overrule, overturn, set aside, suppress **9** devastate, eradicate, extirpate, overthrow, overwhelm, repudiate, strike out **10** annihilate, extinguish, invalidate, obliterate, put an end to **11** countermand, exterminate

quasi 4 near, part, semi **6** almost, ersatz **7** halfway, seeming, virtual **8** apparent, somewhat, so-called **9** imitation, synthetic **10** resembling

Quasimodo
character in: 23 The Hunchback of Notre Dame
author: 4 Hugo

Quatermain, Allan
character in: 17 King Solomon's Mines
author: 7 Haggard

quaver 4 beat, sway, wave **5** quake, shake, throb, trill, waver **6** falter, quiver, shiver, teeter, totter, tremor, wobble, writhe **7** pulsate, shudder, tremble, tremolo, vibrate, vibrato, wriggle **9** oscillate, trembling, vibration **14** tremulous shake

quay 4 dock, mole, pier **5** basin, jetty, levee, wharf **6** marina **7** landing **10** waterfront

queasy 5 giddy, upset **6** uneasy **7** bilious, sickish **8** nauseous, qualmish, troubled **9** nauseated, sickening, uncertain **10** nauseating **13** uncomfortable **16** sick to the stomach

Quebec
borders: 7 Ontario **8** Labrador **9** Hudson Bay **12** Newfoundland, United States **13** Atlantic Ocean **16** Gulf of St Lawrence
cape: 5 Gaspe
city: 6 Quebec **8** Montreal **10** Chicoutimi, Sherbrooke **13** Trois Rivieres
highest point: 18 Mont Jacques Cartier
hockey team: 9 Canadiens, Nordiques
island: 9 Anticosti
lake: 5 Gouin **9** Bienville, Eau Claire, Saint Jean **10** Mistassini **11** Manicouagan
mineral: 4 gold, zinc **6** copper **7** iron ore **8** asbestos **9** limestone
mountain: 5 Otish **10** Laurentian, Shickshock **11** Appalachian **12** Monteregians
province of: 6 Canada

Quechua
tribe: 4 Inca

queen 5 ranee **7** czarina, empress **8** princess **13** female monarch
French: 5 reine
German: 7 Konigin
Latin: 6 regina
Spanish: 5 reina

queen/empress/princess
of Egypt: 9 Cleopatra, Nefertari, Nefertiti **10** Hatshepsut, Hetepheres
of England: 3 Mab **4** Anne, Bess, Jane, Mary **7** Eleanor **8** Boadicea, Victoria **9** Catherine, Charlotte, Elizabeth, Guinevere **10** Bloody Mary, Elizabeth I **11** Elizabeth II, Jane Seymour
of France: 7 Eugenie **9** Josephine **11** Marie Louise **14** Marie de Medicis **15** Marie Antoinette
of Italy/Rome: 7 Poppaea **9** Agrippina, Messalina **13** Livia Drusilla
of Monaco: 8 Caroline **9** Stephanie **10** Grace Kelly
of the Netherlands: 7 Beatrix, Juliana **10** Wilhelmina
of Poland: 7 Jadwiga
of Portugal: 5 Maria **9** Elizabeth
of Russia: 9 Alexandra, Catherine **17** Catherine the Great
of Scotland: 4 Mary **13** Saint Margaret **16** Mary Queen of Scots

of Spain: 8 Isabella **16** Elizabeth Farnese
of Sweden: 9 Christina
of Syria: 7 Zenobia
in folklore: 3 Mab **7** Titania

Queen Christina
director: 15 Rouben Mamoulian
cast: 8 Ian Keith **10** Greta Garbo, Lewis Stone **11** John Gilbert **12** C Aubrey Smith

Queen Mab
author: 18 Percy Bysshe Shelley

Queen of Amazons 9 Hippolyta, Hippolyte

Queen of Hearts
character in: 28 Alice's Adventures in Wonderland
author: 7 Carroll

Queen of Heaven 4 Hera, Mary **6** Ishtar **7** Mylitta

Queen of Spades, The
also: 12 Pikovaya Dama
opera by: 11 Tchaikovsky
character: 4 Lisa **6** Herman **8** Countess

Queen of Spades, The
author: 16 Alexander Pushkin

Queen of the Surf
nickname of: 14 Esther Williams

Queen's Necklace, The
author: 14 Alexandre Dumas (pere)
character: 5 Oliva **13** Count de Charny **15** Cardinal de Rohan, Count Cagliostro, Marie Antoinette **16** Andree de Taverney **18** Philippe de Taverney **21** Jeanne de la Motte Valois

Queequeg
character in: 8 Moby Dick
author: 8 Melville

queer 3 gay, odd **4** daft, harm, hurt, rare, ruin **5** crazy, dizzy, droll, faint, fishy, funny, giddy, shady, spoil, weird, woozy, wreck **6** absurd, damage, exotic, impair, injure, quaint, qualmy, queasy, thwart, unique **7** bizarre, comical, curious, disrupt, erratic, reeling, strange, touched, unusual **8** abnormal, bohemian, doubtful, fanciful, freakish, original, peculiar, uncommon, unhinged **9** eccentric, fantastic, grotesque, homosexual, irregular, laughable, ludicrous, unnatural **10** capricious, compromise, farfetched, irrational, outlandish, remarkable, ridiculous, suspicious, unbalanced, unexampled, unorthodox **11** astonishing, exceptional, light-headed, out of the way, slightly ill, vertiginous **12** preposterous, questionable, unparalleled **13** extraordinary, nonconforming, unprecedented **14** unconventional
French: 5 outre

quell 4 calm, dull, ease, hush, lull, rout, ruin, stay, stem **5** abate, allay, blunt, crush, quash, quiet, still, worst, wreck **6** becalm, deaden, defeat, pacify, quench, reduce, soften, soothe, subdue **7** appease, assuage, compose, conquer, destroy, mollify, put down, scatter, silence, squelch **8** beat down, disperse, mitigate, overcome, palliate, stamp out, suppress, vanquish **9** alleviate, overpower, overthrow, overwhelm, subjugate **10** extinguish **11** tranquilize

quench 4 cool, sate **5** allay, crush, douse, quell, slake **6** dampen, put out, stifle **7** appease, blow out, put down, satiate, satisfy, smother **8** stamp out, suppress **10** annihilate, extinguish

Quentin Durward
author: 14 Sir Walter Scott
character: 8 Isabelle **9** Le Balafre **10** Jacqueline **11** King Louis XI **12** Lady Hameline **13** Ludovic Lesley **15** Countess of Croye **16** William de la Marck **18** Hayraddin Maugrabin **20** King Louis the Eleventh **21** Charles Duke of Burgundy **23** Count Philip de Crevecoeur

querulous 4 sour **5** cross, fussy, testy, whiny **6** cranky, touchy **7** crabbed, finical, finicky, fretful, grouchy, peevish, pettish, waspish, whining **8** captious, exacting, petulant, shrewish **9** difficult, grumbling, irascible, irritable, long-faced, obstinate, resentful, splenetic **10** nettlesome **11** complaining, quarrelsome **12** disagreeable, discontented, disputatious, dissatisfied, faultfinding

query 3 ask **4** quiz **5** doubt, issue, quest **6** demand, impugn, search **7** dispute, examine, impeach, inquest, inquiry, inspect, problem, request, suspect **8** distrust, look into, mistrust, question, sound out **9** catechize, challenge, inquire of **10** controvert **11** examination, inquisition, interrogate, investigate, make inquiry **13** interrogation, investigation

quest 4 hunt, seek **6** pursue, search, voyage **7** crusade, journey, mission, pursuit, seeking **9** adventure **10** enterprise, pilgrimage **11** exploration

Quested, Adela
character in: 15 A Passage to India
author: 7 Forster

Quest for Fire
director: 17 Jean-Jacques Annaud
cast: 10 Ron Perlman **12** Rae Dawn Chong **13** Everett McGill

question 3 ask, rub **4** pump, quiz, test **5** doubt, drill, grill, issue, query **6** impugn, matter, motion, oppose **7** dispute, dubiety, examine, problem, subject, suspect **8** distrust, look into, mistrust, proposal, sound out **9** catechize, challenge, inquire of, misgiving, moot point, objection **10** difficulty, disbelieve **11** controversy, interrogate,

investigate, proposition, uncertainty **12** cross- examine **13** consideration

questionable 4 moot **5** fishy, shady **6** unsure **7** dubious, in doubt, suspect **8** arguable, doubtful, puzzling, unproven **9** ambiguous, confusing, debatable, enigmatic, equivocal, in dispute, uncertain, undecided **10** apocryphal, disputable, indefinite, mysterious, mystifying, perplexing, suspicious **12** hypothetical **13** controversial, problematical

queue 3 row **4** file, line, rank **5** chain, train **6** column, string

quibble 3 nag **4** carp, spar **5** argue, cavil, dodge, fence, fudge, shift **6** bicker, haggle, hassle, nicety, niggle, waffle **7** evasion, nitpick, shuffle **8** artifice, pretense, squabble, subtlety, white lie **9** be evasive, duplicity **10** equivocate, pick a fight, subterfuge **11** distraction **12** equivocation **13** dodge the issue, prevarication

quick 3 apt **4** able, deft, fast, keen, spry **5** acute, adept, agile, alert, brief, brisk, eager, fiery, fleet, hasty, rapid, sharp, smart, swift, testy **6** abrupt, active, adroit, astute, brainy, bright, clever, expert, facile, flying, frisky, lively, nimble, prompt, shrewd, speedy, sudden, touchy, winged **7** hurried, peppery, waspish **8** animated, choleric, headlong, petulant, skillful, snappish, spirited, vigilant, vigorous **9** dexterous, energetic, excitable, impatient, impetuous, impulsive, irascible, irritable, sagacious, splenetic, sprightly, vivacious, whirlwind, wideawake **10** discerning, high-strung, hotblooded **11** accelerated, expeditious, hot-tempered, intelligent, light-footed, penetrating, precipitate **12** nimble-footed **13** perspicacious, temperamental

quicken 4 fire, goad, move, rush, spur, stir, urge **5** drive, egg on, hurry, impel, pique, press, rouse, speed **6** affect, arouse, excite, hasten, hustle, incite, kindle, propel, revive, vivify **7** actuate, advance, animate, enliven, further, hurry on, inspire, provoke, refresh, sharpen **8** activate, dispatch, energize, enkindle, expedite, inspirit, vitalize **9** galvanize, instigate, stimulate **10** accelerate, invigorate **11** precipitate

quick glance
French: 9 coup d'oeil

quickly 4 anon, fast, soon **6** keenly, presto, pronto **7** briefly, hastily, rapidly, swiftly **8** promptly, speedily **9** instantly **11** immediately **12** lickety-split

Quickly, Mistress
character in: 22 The Merry Wives of Windsor
author: 11 Shakespeare

quickness 5 haste, speed **6** acuity

8 alacrity, celerity, keenness, rapidity **9** acuteness, alertness, dexterity, sharpness **10** cleverness, nimbleness, promptness **15** expeditiousness

quick-tempered 5 cross, testy **6** cranky, shirty, touchy **7** grouchy, peevish, waspish **8** choleric, churlish, shrewish, snappish **9** emotional, excitable, irascible, irritable **10** ill-humored **11** bad-tempered, hot-tempered, quarrelsome **12** cantankerous **13** temperamental

quick-witted 4 keen **5** acute, alert, aware, quick, ready, sharp, smart, witty **6** astute, bright, clever, shrewd **8** incisive **9** brilliant, wide-awake **10** discerning, perceptive **11** clearheaded, intelligent, penetrating **13** perspicacious

quid pro quo 4 swap **5** trade **8** exchange **9** tit for tat **21** something for something

quien sabe? 8 who knows?

quiescence 7 latency **8** dormancy, inaction **10** inactivity

quiescent 6 latent **7** dormant **8** inactive **10** in abeyance

quiet 3 low, mum **4** calm, curb, dull, ease, hush, lull, meek, mild, mute, rest, soft, stay, stop **5** abate, allay, blunt, check, fixed, inert, peace, plain, quell, still **6** arrest, at rest, deaden, docile, dozing, gentle, humble, hushed, lessen, mellow, modest, muffle, pacify, placid, repose, sedate, serene, settle, silent, simple, soften, soothe, stable, steady, stifle, subdue, weaken **7** assuage, clement, comfort, compose, dormant, halcyon, mollify, not busy, pacific, passive, patient, relieve, restful, silence, smother, subdued, suspend, unmoved **8** becalmed, calmness, comatose, composed, decrease, immobile, inactive, mitigate, moderate, muteness, not rough, not showy, palliate, peaceful, quietude, reserved, reticent, retiring, serenity, sleeping, stagnant, taciturn, tranquil **9** alleviate, collected, contented, easygoing, immovable, lethargic, makequiet, noiseless, not bright, peaceable, placidity, quietness, set at ease, soundless, stillness, temperate, unruffled, voiceless **10** coolheaded, gentleness, motionless, phlegmatic, put a stop to, relaxation, slumbering, speechless, stationary, stock-still, unassuming, untroubled **11** discontinue, tranquility, tranquilize, undisturbed, unexcitable, unobtrusive, unperturbed **12** bring to an end, even-tempered, inarticulate, peacefulness, tranquillity **13** at a standstill, dispassionate, imperturbable, noiselessness, soundlessness, unimpassioned, unpretentious **14** unostentatious, unpresumptuous

15 uncommunicative, undemonstrative

quietly 5 coyly **6** calmly, humbly, meekly, mildly, mutely, softly, tamely **8** demurely, modestly, placidly, serenely, silently **9** bashfully, inaudibly, patiently **10** composedly, moderately, peacefully, tranquilly **11** collectedly, contentedly, diffidently, noiselessly, pacifically, soundlessly, temperately, unexcitedly **12** speechlessly, unassumingly, unboastfully **13** unobtrusively, unperturbedly **15** dispassionately, unpretentiously, without ceremony **16** unostentatiously **17** undemonstratively

Quiet Man, The
  director: 8 John Ford
  author: 13 Liam O'Flaherty
  cast: 9 John Wayne **12** Maureen O'Hara **14** Mildred Natwick, Victor McLaglen **15** Barry Fitzgerald
  setting: 7 Ireland
  score: 11 Victor Young
  Oscar for: 8 director

quietness 5 peace, quiet **7** silence **8** softness **9** stillness **12** peacefulness

quietude 4 calm, rest **6** repose **8** easiness **9** composure

quill 3 pen **4** fold, hair, pick, seta, stem, tube **5** pluck, plume, spike, spine, spool **6** bobbin, needle **7** bristle, feather, spindle **9** toothpick

Quilp
  character in: 19 The Old Curiosity Shop
  author: 7 Dickens

quilt 5 cover **6** spread **7** blanket **8** coverlet **9** bedspread, comforter

Quin, Widow
  character in: 24 Playboy of the Western World
  author: 5 Synge

Quincy, M. E.
  character: 3 Lee **5** Danny, (Sgt) Brill **11** Sam Fujiyama, (Dr) Robert Astin **12** (Lt) Frank Monahan
  cast: 9 Robert Ito **10** John S Ragin **11** Jack Klugman, Joseph Roman, Val Bisoglio **12** Garry Walberg **13** Lynette Mettey
  setting: 10 Los Angeles **11** Danny's Place

Quinn, Anthony
  born: 6 Mexico **9** Chihuahua
  wife: 16 Katherine DeMille
  roles: 8 La Strada **10** Viva Zapata **11** Lust for Life **13** Zorba the Greek **17** The Guns of Navarone **22** Requiem for a Heavyweight, The Shoes of the Fisherman
  autobiography: 14 The Original Sin

Quintana and Friends
  author: 16 John Gregory Dunne

quintessence 4 core, gist, pith, soul **5** heart **6** elixir, marrow, nature **7** essence **8** exemplar, quiddity, sum total **9** substance **10** embodiment **12** distillation **15** personification, sum and substance

quip 3 gag, pun **4** barb, gibe, jape, jeer, jest, joke **5** crack, sally, spoof, taunt **6** banter, retort **7** epigram, putdown, riposte, sarcasm **8** badinage, raillery, repartee, wordplay **9** wisecrack, witticism
  French: 6 bon mot **14** double entendre

Quirinus
  origin: 5 Roman
  god of: 3 war
  personifies: 11 Roman nation
  identified with: 7 Romulus

quirk 4 kink, turn, whim **6** fetish, foible, oddity, vagary, whimsy **7** caprice **8** crotchet, odd fancy **9** mannerism **10** aberration **11** abnormality, affectation, peculiarity, sudden twist **12** eccentricity, idiosyncrasy

quisling 6 puppet **7** traitor **12** collaborator **16** collaborationist

quit 3 end, rid **4** free, stop **5** cease, clear, forgo, leave, let go, waive, yield **6** depart, desist, disown, exempt, forego, give up, reject, resign, retire **7** abandon, disavow, drop out, forsake, take off **8** abdicate, absolved, forswear, renounce, withdraw **9** acquitted, foreswear, leave a job, surrender, terminate **10** discharged, exculpated, exonerated, relinquish **11** discontinue

quite 4 very **5** fully, truly **6** highly, hugely, indeed, in fact, in toto, really, surely, vastly, verily, wholly **7** exactly, in truth, totally, utterly **8** actually, entirely, outright **9** assuredly, certainly, extremely, in reality, out-and-out, perfectly, precisely, unusually, veritably **10** absolutely, altogether, completely, enormously, positively, remarkably, throughout **11** exceedingly, excessively **12** considerably **13** exceptionally

Quito
  capital of: 7 Ecuador

quiver 3 tic **4** jerk, jolt, jump, pant **5** quake, shake, spasm, throb **6** quaver, shiver, totter, tremor, twitch, wobble **7** flicker, flutter, pulsate, seizure, shudder, tremble, vibrate, wriggle **8** convulse **9** fluctuate, oscillate, palpitate, pulsation, quivering, twitching, vibration **10** convulsion **11** palpitation

Quiverful, Mr
  character in: 16 Barchester Towers
  author: 8 Trollope

quivering 7 shaking **9** agitating, quavering, shimmying, shivering, trembling, vibrating **10** flittering, fluttering, shuddering, twittering **11** palpitating

qui vive? 12 who goes there?

quixotic 4 wild **6** absurd, dreamy, madcap, poetic **7** utopian **8** fanciful, romantic **9** fantastic, impulsive, visionary, whimsical **10** chimerical, idealistic, ridiculous, starry-eyed **11** impractical, ineffective, sentimental, unrealistic **12** preposterous **13** inefficacious

quiz 3 ask, rib **4** exam, joke, mock, pump, test **5** prank, query, taunt, tease **6** banter **7** examine, inquest, inquiry **8** question, ridicule, sound out **9** catechism, eccentric, inquire of **11** examination, inquisition, interrogate, investigate, questioning **12** cross-examine **13** interrogation, investigation **16** cross-examination

Quiz Kids
  host: 8 Joe Kelly **14** Clifton Fadiman

quizzical 3 coy **4** arch **6** joking **7** baffled, curious, mocking, puzzled, teasing **8** derisive, impudent, insolent **9** bantering, inquiring, perplexed, searching **11** inquisitive, questioning

quoad hoc 12 as much as this, to this extent

quod erat demonstrandum 17 which was to be shown **24** which was to be demonstrated
  abbreviation: 3 QED

quod erat faciendum 16 which was to be done

quod vide 8 which see
  abbreviation: 2 qv

quo jure? 11 by what right?

quo modo 3 how **9** in what way **19** in the same manner that

quondam 4 erst, late, once, past **6** bygone, former **8** formerly, sometime **9** erstwhile

quota 4 part **5** share **6** ration **7** measure, minimum, portion **8** quantity **9** allotment **10** allocation, assignment, percentage, proportion **12** distribution **13** apportionment

quotation 5 quote **7** cutting, excerpt, extract, passage **8** citation, clipping **9** reference, selection **12** illustration

quote 4 cite, name **6** adduce, recall, repeat, retell **7** excerpt, extract, refer to **8** instance **9** exemplify, recollect, reproduce **10** paraphrase

quoted passage 7 excerpt, extract **9** quotation

quotidian 5 daily **6** common **8** everyday, ordinary **11** commonplace

Quo Vadis?
  author: 17 Henryk Sienkiewicz
  character: 4 Nero **5** Chilo, Lygia, Peter **8** Vinitius **9** Petronius, Tigellius
  director: 11 Mervyn LeRoy
  cast: 7 Leo Genn **11** Deborah Kerr **12** Peter Ustinov, Robert Taylor
  setting: 11 ancient Rome

Ra
  also: **2** Re
  origin: **5** Greek **10** Heliopolis
  god of: **3** sun
  also worshipped by: **9** Egyptians

Rabat, Rabbat
  capital of: **7** Morocco

rabbi 6 master, rabbin **7** scholar, teacher **9** clergyman **15** spiritual leader

rabbinical, rabbinic 8 clerical

rabbit 4 cony, hare, jack, lure **5** bunny, coney, lapin **6** novice, rodent **8** beginner **10** cottontail, pacesetter

Rabbit Is Rich
  author: **10** John Updike

Rabbit Redux
  author: **10** John Updike

rabble 3 mob **5** swarm **7** the herd **8** populace, riffraff **9** commoners, hoi polloi, the masses **11** proletariat, rank and file **12** lower classes **15** disorderly crowd **16** the great unwashed
  French: **8** canaille
  German: **17** Lumpenproletariat

Rabelais, Francois
  author of: **22** Gargantua and Pantagruel

rabid 4 wild **6** ardent, crazed, raging **7** berserk, fervent, frantic, violent, zealous **8** deranged, frenzied, maniacal, wild-eyed **9** fanatical **11** hydrophobic **17** foaming at the mouth

race 3 fly, run **4** dart, dash, heat, rush **5** hurry **6** hasten, hustle **7** contest, operate **8** campaign **11** competition

racecourse 4 turf **5** track **6** course **9** racetrack

Rachel
  father: **5** Laban
  husband: **5** Jacob
  sister: **4** Leah
  son: **6** Joseph **8** Benjamin
  slave: **6** Bilhah

Rachmaninov (Rachmaninoff, Rakhmaninov), Sergei
  born: **6** Russia **8** Novgorod
  composer of: **15** Symphonic Dances **16** The Isle of the Dead **19** Second Piano Concerto **26** Rhapsody on a Theme by (of) Paganini

Racine, Jean Baptiste
  author of: **6** Phedre **7** Athalie **8** Berenice **10** Andromache **11** Britannicus

racism 7 bigotry **8** color bar **9** color line **10** race hatred, racial bias **11** segregation **15** racial prejudice **20** racial discrimination

rack 4 buck, gait, hurt, neck, pace, pain, path **5** agony, cloud, exert, frame, raise, track, trail, worry, wreck, wring **6** canter, holder, strain **7** afflict, agonize, draw off, oppress, stretch, torment, torture **8** distress **9** suffering **10** destruction, excruciate, iron maiden

racked 4 torn **5** paced **6** framed, pained, traced, walked **7** annoyed, tracked, trotted, wronged, worried **8** cantered, suffered, tortured **9** afflicted, anguished, destroyed, oppressed, tormented **10** persecuted

racket 3 din **4** game, line, roar, stir **5** babel **6** clamor, hubbub, rumpus, tumult, uproar **7** clangor, clatter, turmoil **8** business, shouting **9** commotion, loud noise **10** hullabaloo, hurlyburly, occupation, turbulence **11** disturbance, pandemonium **12** caterwauling, vociferation

racketeer 4 hood **5** crook **6** bagman, bandit, extort **7** hoodlum, mafioso, mobster **8** criminal, gangster **12** extortionist

racking 7 painful **9** agonizing, torturous **10** tormenting, unbearable **11** intolerable, unendurable **12** excruciating, insufferable

raconteur 8 fabulist, narrator, romancer **10** anecdotist **11** storyteller **13** teller of tales **14** spinner of yarns

racy 4 keen **5** bawdy, crude, heady, lurid, zesty **6** erotic, lively, ribald, risque, smutty, vulgar **7** buoyant, glowing, obscene, zestful **8** animated, exciting, immodest, indecent, offcolor, prurient, spirited, vigorous **9** energetic, fast-paced, salacious, sparkling **10** suggestive **11** stimulating **12** exhilarating, pornographic

radar
  invented by: **4** Watt **6** Watson

Radcliffe, Mrs Ann
  author of: **10** The Italian **21** The Mysteries of Udolpho

raddle 3 rod **4** reed, scar, twig **5** fence, hedge, rouge, stick, weave **6** branch, ruddle **8** hematite, red ocher, red ochre **10** interweave

radiance, radiancy 3 joy **5** gleam, gleem, sheen **6** dazzle, luster **7** glitter, rapture, sparkle **8** lambency, splendor **9** animation, happiness **10** brightness, brilliance, brilliancy, effulgence, luminosity, refulgence **11** coruscation, iridescence **12** luminousness, resplendence **13** incandescence
  god of: **5** Baldr **6** Balder, Baldur

radiant 5 aglow, happy, sunny **6** bright, elated, joyous **7** beaming, glowing, pleased, shining **8** blissful, dazzling, ecstatic, flashing, gladsome, gleaming, luminous, lustrous **9** brilliant, delighted, effulgent, overjoyed, rapturous, refulgent, sparkling **10** glittering **12** incandescent **13** scintillating

radiate 4 beam, pour, shed **5** carry **6** spread **7** diffuse, diverge, give off, give out, scatter **8** disperse, emit heat, transmit **9** branch out, circulate, emit light, spread out **11** disseminate

radical 4 rash **5** basic, rebel **6** severe **7** drastic, extreme **8** left-wing, militant **9** extremist, firebrand **10** immoderate, inordinate **11** freethinker, fundamental, precipitate **13** revolutionary **22** antiestablishmentarian

radio
  invented by: **7** Donovan, Fleming, Marconi **8** De Forest, Nicolson **9** Armstrong, Fessenden **12** Alexanderson

radium
  chemical symbol: **2** Ra

radon
  chemical symbol: **2** Rn

raffish 3 low **4** fast, wild **5** cheap, rowdy, showy **6** common, flashy, rakish, tawdry, vulgar **7** boorish **8** rakehell **9** worthless **10** dissipated **12** devil-may-care, disreputable

raft 3 lot **4** mass **5** barge, float **6** plenty **7** carrier, pontoon **8** flatboat, platform, quantity **9** abundance, multitude

Raft, George
  real name: **11** George Ranft
  born: **9** New York NY
  roles: **8** Scarface **11** Johnny Angel **12** Guido Rinaldo **13** Some Like It Hot

rag 3 kid, rib **4** scap, song, tune, twit **5** cloth, taunt, taunt, tease **6** harass **7** torment **8** magazine **9** newspaper **11** ragtime tune **14** worn-out garment

ragamuffin 3 bum **4** hobo, waif

5 gamin, tramp **6** beggar, gamine, hoyden, sloven, urchin, wretch **7** vagrant **8** derelict, vagabond **9** itinerant, ragpicker **10** panhandler, street arab **11** guttersnipe **14** tatterdemalion

rage 3 fad, ire **4** boil, fume, fury, mode, rant, rave, roar **5** craze, furor, mania, pique, storm, vogue, wrath **6** blow up, choler, frenzy, seethe, spleen, temper **7** explode, fashion, ferment, flare up, madness, passion, rampage, umbrage **8** paroxysm, the thing **9** animosity, fulminate, raise cain, throw a fit, vehemence **10** bitterness, excitement, irritation, resentment, the "in" thing **11** displeasure, high dudgeon, indignation, the last word **12** current style, le dernier cri, perturbation, violent anger **13** temper tantrum **14** the latest thing **15** fly off the handle, froth at the mouth

ragged 4 rent, torn, worn **5** seedy, tacky **6** beat up, frayed, shabby, shaggy, shoddy **7** patched, run down, worn-out **8** battered, shredded, strained, tattered **9** overtaxed **10** aggravated, threadbare, worn to rags **11** exacerbated

ragging 5 chaff **6** banter **7** kidding, ribbing, teasing **8** chaffing, needling, raillery, taunting, twitting

raging 3 mad **4** wild **5** angry, livid, rabid, rough **6** fierce, raving, stormy **7** fervent, frantic, furious, rampant, violent **8** frenzied, incensed, storming **9** turbulent **10** blustering, ferocious, infuriated **11** tempestuous

Raging Bull
director: 14 Martin Scorsese
cast: 8 Joe Pesci **12** Frank Vincent, Robert De Niro (Jake La Motta) **13** Cathy Moriarty
Oscar for: 5 actor (De Niro)

Ragnarok
also: 15 Gotterdammerung **17** Twilight of the Gods
origin: 12 Scandinavian
event: 11 final battle
battlefield: 6 Vigrid

ragout 4 hash, stew **7** borscht, goulash **9** fricassee

Ragtime
author: 10 E L Doctorow

raid 4 bust **5** foray, onset, sally, storm **6** attack, inroad, invade, razzia, sortie **7** assault, round-up **8** invasion **10** pounce upon **14** surprise attack

Raiders of the Lost Ark
director: 15 Steven Spielberg
cast: 10 Karen Allen, Wolf Kahler **11** Paul Freeman **12** Harrison Ford
sequel: 29 Indiana Jones and the Last Crusade **30** Indiana Jones and the Temple of Doom

rail 3 bar **4** rage, rant **5** scold, fence, train **6** blow up, scream, take on **7** barrier, carry on, declaim, inveigh,

railing, railway, the cars **8** banister, railroad **9** fulminate **10** vituperate, vociferate **11** rant and rave **14** foam at the mouth

rail at 5 scold **6** berate **7** chew out **9** castigate **14** inveigh against

railing 3 bar **5** fence, grate, rails **6** fender **7** barrier, parapet, support **8** banister **9** enclosing **10** balustrade

raillery 5 chaff, sport **6** banter, japing, joking, satire **7** fooling, jesting, joshing, kidding, ragging, razzing, ribbing, teasing **8** badinage, chaffing, roasting, twitting **10** lampoonery, persiflage, pleasantry

railroad sleeping car
French: 8 wagon-lit

railroad station 5 depot **8** terminal, terminus

railway 4 tube **5** track, train **6** cogway, subway **7** cogroad, trolley **8** elevated, monorail, railroad **9** streetcar

raiment 4 duds, togs **5** dress **6** attire **7** apparel, clothes, costume, threads **8** clothing, garments **11** habiliments

rain, rains 4 down, drop, mist, pour **5** spate **6** deluge, lavish, shower, squall **7** drizzle, monsoon, torrent **8** downpour, drencher, plethora, rainfall, send down, sprinkle **9** hurricane, rainstorm **10** cloudburst **11** precipitation, thundershower **15** rain cats and dogs **16** come down in sheets **17** come down in buckets
god of: 4 Thor

Rainbow
goddess of: 4 Iris

Rainbow, The
author: 10 D H Lawrence
character: 10 Anna Lensky **11** Lydia Lensky, Tom Brangwen **12** Will Brangwen **14** Ursula Brangwen **15** Anton Skrebensky

Rainbow Bridge *see* **7** bifrost

raincoat 3 mac **4** mack **6** poncho, ulster **7** oilskin, slicker **8** burberry **9** tarpaulin **10** mackintosh, trenchcoat, waterproof

rainless 3 dry **4** arid, sere **10** desertlike

Rains, Claude
born: 6 London **7** England
wife: 11 Isabel Jeans
roles: 9 Notorious **10** Casablanca, Now Voyager **13** Mr Skeffington **14** Anthony Adverse **15** The Invisible Man **16** Lawrence of Arabia **17** Here Comes Mr Jordan **20** The Phantom of the Opera **23** Mr Smith Goes to Washington **24** The Adventures of Robin Hood

rain shower 6 shower **7** drizzle **8** sprinkle **12** thunderstorm

rainstorm 6 deluge, shower **8** downfall, downpour **10** cloudburst **12** thunderstorm

rainy 3 wet **4** damp **7** drizzly, showery **11** pouring rain **18** raining cats and dogs

raise 3 end **4** grow, hike, lift, rear, spur, urge **5** amass, boost, breed, build, erect, nurse, pique, put up, rouse, set up, spark **6** arouse, awaken, excite, foster, hike up, jack up, kindle, obtain, stir up **7** advance, bring in, bring up, canvass, collect, develop, elevate, inflame, inflate, inspire, nurture, procure, produce, sharpen, solicit **8** increase, summon up **9** construct, cultivate, elevation, promotion, stimulate, terminate **10** make higher, put forward **11** advancement

raise aloft 5 boost, hoist **6** lift up, uplift **7** elevate, upraise

raised 4 bred, grew **5** anted, built, grown **6** anteed, convex, jacked, lifted, reared, roused **7** aroused, erected, exalted, hoisted, honored, incited **8** elevated, embossed, leavened, mustered **9** brought up, collected **10** cultivated **11** resurrected

Raisin in the Sun, A
director: 12 Daniel Petrie
based on play by: 17 Lorraine Hansberry
cast: 7 Ruby Dee **9** Ivan Dixon **10** Diana Sands **13** Claudia McNeil, Sidney Poitier
setting: 7 Chicago

rake 4 comb, goat, roue **5** rogue, satyr, scour, sport **6** lecher, pepper, rascal **7** Don Juan, playboy, ransack, seducer, swinger **8** Casanova, Lothario, enfilade, prodigal, rakehell **9** debauchee, libertine, womanizer **10** immoralist, profligate, sensualist, voluptuary

rake-off 3 cut, fee **5** piece **10** percentage **16** piece of the action

Rake's Progress, The
etchings by: 7 Hogarth
opera by: 10 Stravinsky
character: 10 Ann Trulove, Nick Shadow **11** Baba the Turk, Mother Goose, Tom Rakewell

rakish 4 airy **6** breezy, dapper, jaunty, sporty **7** dashing, gallant, immoral, lustful **8** cavalier, debonair, depraved, sporting **9** bumptious, debauched, dissolute, lecherous, libertine **10** dissipated, lascivious, profligate, sauntering, swaggering

rally 4 meet, rush **5** score, unite **6** caucus, gather, muster, pick up, powwow, revive **7** catch up, collect, get well, improve, recruit, reunite, revival **8** assemble, assembly, recovery **9** come round, gathering, get better, reconvene **10** assemblage, convalesce, convention, reassemble, recuperate **11** convocation, improvement, mass meeting, pull through, restoration **12**

call together, congregation, recuperation **13** convalescence

ram 3 hit, jam **4** beat, bump, butt, dash, goat, slam **5** crash, drive, force, smash **6** batter, hammer, hurtle, strike, thrust **7** run into

Ram
constellation of: 5 Aries

ramble 3 gad **4** hike, roam, rove, wind **5** amble, drift, range, snake, twist **6** stroll, wander, zigzag **7** meander, saunter, traipse **8** gad about, idle walk **9** gallivant **11** perambulate, peregrinate

rambling 6 prolix, uneven **7** diffuse **10** circuitous, digressive, discursive, disjointed

rambunctious 4 wild **5** noisy, rowdy **6** active, unruly **7** raucous, untamed, violent **9** irascible **10** boisterous, pugnacious **11** quarrelsome **14** uncontrollable

Rameau, Jean-Philippe
born: 5 Dijon **6** France
composer of: 6 Platee **8** Dardanus **13** Les Fetes d'Hebe **14** Castor et Pollux **15** Castor and Pollux **16** Les Indes Galantes, The Indigo Suitors **17** Hippolyte et Aricie **20** La Princesse de Navarre

ramification 3 arm **4** part, spur **5** prong **6** branch **8** division, offshoot **9** branching, outgrowth **10** divergence, separation **11** consequence, subdivision

rampage 4 rage **5** storm **7** run amok, run riot

rampant 4 rife **5** erect **6** raging **8** epidemic, pandemic **9** prevalent, unchecked, universal **10** on hind legs, standing up, widespread **12** ungovernable, unrestrained **14** uncontrollable

rampart 4 barrier, bastion, bulwark, parapet **9** barricade, earthwork **10** breastwork **13** defensive wall, fortification **14** protective wall

Ramsay, William
field: 9 chemistry
nationality: 7 British
discovered: 4 neon **5** argon (in air) **6** helium **7** krypton
awarded: 10 Nobel Prize

ramshackle 5 shaky **6** flimsy, shabby **7** rickety, run-down **8** decrepit, unstable, unsteady **9** crumbling, tottering **10** tumbledown **11** dilapidated **13** deteriorating

Ramtil *see* **5** Niger

ranch 4 farm **5** range **6** grange, spread **7** acreage, station **8** hacienda **10** plantation

rancher 6 cowboy, farmer, gaucho **7** cowhand, cowpoke **8** herdsman, sheepman, stockman **9** cattleman **10** cowpuncher

rancid 3 old **4** foul, gamy, high, rank **6** putrid, strong **8** mephitic, stinking **10** malodorous

rancor 4 hate **5** spite **6** animus, enmity, hatred, malice, spleen **7** ill will **8** acrimony **9** animosity, antipathy, hostility **10** antagonism, bitterness, ill feeling, resentment **11** malevolence **12** spitefulness

rancorous 5 nasty **6** bitter **7** hostile **8** churlish, spiteful, vengeful, venomous **9** splenetic **10** ill-natured **11** acrimonious **12** antagonistic

Rand, Ayn
author of: 6 Anthem **13** Atlas Shrugged **15** The Fountainhead **17** Romantic Manifesto
philosophy: 11 objectivism

Randall, Tony
real name: 16 Leonard Rosenberg
born: 7 Tulsa OK
wife: 13 Heather Harlan
roles: 9 Mr Peepers **10** Felix Unger, Pillow Talk **12** Harvey Weskit, The Odd Couple **13** Fatal Instinct, The Mating Game **20** The Seven Faces of Dr Lao **22** Hitler's SS: Portrait in Evil

random 5 stray **6** casual, chance **7** aimless, offhand **9** haphazard, hit-or-miss, unplanned **10** accidental, fortuitous, occasional, undesigned, unexpected, unintended **12** adventitious **13** unintentional **14** unpremeditated

range 3 run **4** roam, rove **5** field, gamut, limit, orbit, reach, ridge, scope **6** bounds, domain, extend, massif, plains, radius, sierra, sphere, wander **7** explore, pasture, purview, stretch, variety **8** province **9** selection **11** grazing land **16** chain of mountains

Rangoon
capital of: 5 Burma **7** Myanmar
former name: 5 Dagon **6** Yangon
founder: 10 Alaungpaya
landmark: 10 Sule Pagoda **15** Shwe Dagon Pagoda
name means: 11 end of strife
river: 7 Rangoon
square: 12 Independence

rangy 4 tall **5** broad, lanky **9** expansive, extensive

rank 3 row **4** bald, file, foul, line, lush, rate, sort, tall, type, wild **5** class, crass, dense, grade, gross, level, nasty, order, sheer, stale, stand, total, utter **6** arrant, coarse, column, estate, filthy, jungly, lavish, rancid, status **7** come out, echelon, glaring, profuse, quality, rampant **8** absolute, complete, flagrant, position, standing, tropical **9** atrocious, be classed, come first, downright, have place, luxuriant, monstrous, overgrown **10** outrageous, scurrilous **11** highgrowing, ill smelling, unmitigated **12** over abundant **14** classification, social standing, strong smelling

rank and file 6 troops **17** enlisted personnel, general membership

Rankine, William John Macquorn
field: 7 physics
nationality: 8 Scottish
devised: 12 Rankine Cycle, Rankine Scale **26** Fahrenheit temperature scale
author of: 22 Manual of the Steam Engine

rankle 4 gall, rile **5** chafe, gripe, pique **6** fester **8** irritate **10** not sit well

ransack 3 gut **4** comb, loot, raid, rake, sack **5** rifle, scour, strip **6** ravage, search **7** despoil, pillage, plunder **8** lay waste **9** devastate, vandalize **14** rummage through, turn upside down

ransom 3 buy **4** free, save **5** atone, price **6** redeem, rescue **7** deliver, expiate, reclaim, recover, release **8** liberate, retrieve **10** liberation, redemption

Ransom, John Crowe
member of: 12 the Fugitives
author of: 14 I'll Take My Stand **16** Captain Carpenter **30** Bells for John Whiteside's Daughter

rant 4 fume, rage, rave, yell **5** orate, scold, spout, storm **6** bellow **7** bluster, bombast, bravado, explode **8** harangue **11** declamation **12** exaggeration

rap 3 jaw, pan, tap **4** bang, chat, drum, talk **5** blame, knock, roast, speak, thump **6** dump on **7** clobber **8** converse **9** criticize **10** come down on **11** communicate **14** responsibility, shoot the breeze

rapacious 6 greedy **7** looting, wolfish **8** covetous, grasping, ravenous, thievish **9** marauding, mercenary, pillaging, predatory, voracious **10** avaricious, insatiable, plundering, ransacking

rapacity 5 greed **7** avarice **10** greediness **12** covetousness, graspingness **13** mercenariness

Rape of Lucrece
author: 18 William Shakespeare
character: 7 Tarquin **9** Collatine

Rape of the Lock, The
author: 13 Alexander Pope
character: 5 Ariel **7** Belinda, Umbriel **9** Lord Petre **10** Thalestris

Raphael 9 archangel

Raphael
real name: 14 Raffaello Santi **15** Raffaello Sanzio
born: 5 Italy **6** Urbino
artwork: 7 Disputa **8** Julius II **10** Entombment **14** Sistine Madonna **17** The School of Athens, The Virgin and Child **18** Madonna di Casa Tempi, The Transfiguration **19** The Triumph of Galatea **21** Baldassare Castiglione **22** The Marriage of the Virgin **24** The Expulsion of Heliodorus **28** The Madonna and Child with St John (La Belle Jardiniere)

architect of: 11 Villa Madama (Rome) **16** Pandolfini Palace (Florence) **22** Vidoni-Caffarelli Palace (Rome)

rapid 4 fast **5** brisk, fleet, hasty, quick, swift **6** active, flying, prompt, speedy **7** express, hurried, instant, rushing **8** agitated, feverish **9** galloping, unchecked **11** accelerated, expeditious, precipitate

rapidity 5 haste, speed **8** celerity, velocity **9** fleetness, quickness, swiftness **10** promptness

rapidly 4 fast **5** apace **7** briskly, hastily, quickly, swiftly **8** pell-mell, speedily **9** hurriedly, like a shot, overnight **10** in high gear **11** at full speed **13** expeditiously, helter-skelter

rapids 5 chute **7** current **10** white water

rapport 3 tie **4** link **10** connection, fellowship **11** affiliation, camaraderie **12** relationship **13** understanding **17** interrelationship

rapprochement 6 accord **7** detente, entente **9** agreement **10** adjustment, compromise, settlement **11** appeasement, arrangement **12** conciliation, pacification **13** accommodation, harmonization, reconcilement, understanding **14** reconciliation **16** mutual concession

rapscallion 5 knave, rogue, scamp **6** rascal **7** low-life, villain **8** scalawag **9** scoundrel **10** blackguard, ne'er-do-well, rascallion **14** good-for-nothing

rapt 6 dreamy, enrapt, intent **7** bemused, charmed **8** absorbed, ecstatic **9** attentive, bewitched, delighted, enchanted, engrossed, entranced, rapturous **10** captivated, enraptured, enthralled, fascinated, interested, moonstruck, spellbound **11** transported

rapture 3 joy **5** bliss **6** thrill **7** delight, ecstasy, elation **8** euphoria, felicity **9** beatitude

rapturous 4 rapt **8** beatific, blissful, ecstatic **10** enraptured, enthralled

rare 3 few **6** scarce, unique **7** unusual **8** uncommon **10** hard to find, infrequent **11** exceptional, seldom found **16** few and far between

rarefied 4 thin **6** dilute, purify, rarify, reduce, refine, subtle **7** inflate **8** diminish **9** attenuate, extenuate

rarely 6 hardly, seldom **8** not often **10** hardly ever, uncommonly **12** infrequently, scarcely ever **15** once in a blue moon, on rare occasions **17** once in a great while

raring 4 agog, avid, keen **5** eager **8** desirous **9** impatient **12** enthusiastic

rarity 6 oddity **7** anomaly **8** scarcity **11** unusualness **12** uncommonness **14** remarkableness

rascal 3 cad, imp **4** rake **5** devil, knave, rogue, scamp **7** villain **8** rakehell, scalawag **9** prankster, reprobate, scoundrel, trickster **10** blackguard, delinquent **11** rapscallion

rash 5 brash, hasty **6** abrupt **7** foolish **8** careless, headlong, heedless, reckless **9** foolhardy, impetuous, imprudent, impulsive, premature, unadvised, unchecked **10** incautious, indiscreet, ungoverned, unthinking **11** adventurous, harebrained, injudicious, precipitate, thoughtless **12** devil-may-care, uncontrolled **13** irresponsible

rashness 8 audacity, boldness **9** riskiness **12** heedlessness, indiscretion, recklessness **13** foolhardiness, impulsiveness **15** precipitousness, thoughtlessness

Rashomon
   author: 18 Ryunosuke Akutagawa
   director: 13 Akira Kurosawa

Raskolnikov
   character in: 18 Crime and Punishment
   author: 10 Dostoevsky

rasp 3 irk, nag, rub, vex **4** file **5** chafe, grate, worry **6** abrade, scrape, wheeze **7** grating, scraper, scratch **8** abrasive, irritate **9** huskiness **10** hoarseness

raspberry 11 Rubus idaeus
   varieties: 3 red **4** hill **5** black, dwarf **6** Mysore, purple **8** European **9** flowering, Mauritius **11** American red **13** Rocky Mountain **15** Purple-flowering **22** Rocky Mountain flowering
   brandy: 9 Framboise

rasping 5 harsh, raspy, rough **6** hoarse **7** chafing, grating, nagging **8** abrading, scraping, worrying **9** offensive **10** irritating

Rasselas
   author: 13 Samuel Johnson
   character: 5 Imlac **6** Pekuah **7** Nekayah
   Rasselas's title: 17 Prince of Abyssinia

rat 3 cad, cur **4** fink, heel **5** churl, knave, louse **6** betray, rascal, rotter, squeal, vermin **7** bounder, villain **8** informer, inform on **9** scoundrel **10** blackguard **11** stool pigeon

rate 3 fee **4** cost, deem, dues, levy, pace, rank, toll **5** class, count, price, speed, tempo **6** charge, figure, look on, regard, tariff **7** expense, measure **8** classify **10** assessment

rate highly 5 prize, value **6** admire, esteem **7** cherish, respect **8** treasure

Rathbone, Basil
   real name: 25 Philip St John Basil Rathbone
   born: 11 South Africa **12** Johannesburg
   roles: 6 Tybalt **7** Karenin **10** Dawn Patrol **11** Mr Murdstone **12** Anna Karenina **14** Romeo and Juliet, Sher-

lock Holmes, The Mark of Zorro **16** A Tale of Two Cities, David Copperfield **20** The Last Days of Pompeii **24** The Adventures of Robin Hood **25** The Hound of the Baskervilles

rather 4 a bit, very **5** quite **6** fairly, kind of, pretty, sort of **8** slightly, somewhat **10** moderately, more or less, relatively **13** comparatively

rathskeller 6 saloon **8** beer hall
   vessel: 4 Toby **5** stein **6** seidel **7** tankard **8** pilsener, schooner

ratification 2 OK **4** okay **7** consent **8** approval, sanction **10** validation **11** affirmation, endorsement **12** confirmation **13** authorization, corroboration **14** seal of approval

ratify 2 OK **4** okay **6** affirm, uphold **7** agree to, approve, certify, confirm, endorse, support **8** accede to, make good, sanction, validate **9** authorize, consent to, make valid **11** acknowledge **12** authenticate

rating 4 mark, rank **5** class, grade, ratio, value **6** degree, rebuke, sailor, seaman **7** ranking **8** standing **9** appraisal **10** assessment, evaluation, percentage **14** classification

ratio 8 equation **10** proportion **11** arrangement **12** distribution **13** apportionment, fixed relation **15** proportionality **17** interrelationship **20** proportional relation

ration, rations 3 due **4** dole, food **5** allot **6** stores **7** measure, mete out **8** allocate **9** allotment, apportion, food share, provender, provision **10** provisions **13** apportionment

rational 4 sage, sane, wise **5** lucid, solid, sound **6** normal **7** logical **8** all there, balanced, credible, feasible **9** advisable, judicious, plausible, sagacious **10** reasonable **11** clearheaded, responsible **12** compos mentis **13** perspicacious **15** in one's right mind

rationale 5 basis, logic **6** excuse, reason **7** grounds **9** reasoning **10** key concept, philosophy **11** explanation, foundations **16** underlying reason

rationalize 6 excuse **7** explain, justify **8** palliate **9** whitewash **10** account for **11** explain away **13** put a gloss upon **14** make excuses for **16** make allowance for

ratite 3 em(e)u, moa **4** kiwi, rhea **7** ostrich **9** cassowary

rattan 4 cane, lash, palm, whip **5** thong **6** switch, wicker

Ratti, Achille 10 Pope Pius XI

rattle 3 gab, jar **4** faze **5** clang, clank, clink, prate, shake, throw, upset **6** bounce, flurry, jangle **7** agitate, blather, chatter, clatter, confuse, disturb, fluster, maunder, nonplus, perturb **8** bewilder, clacking, distract **9** discomfit **10** discompose, disconcert **11** roll loosely

rattlebrained 4 dumb 5 silly 6 stupid 7 asinine, doltish, foolish, idiotic, moronic, witless 9 brainless, imbecilic 10 fool-headed, half-witted 11 harebrained, lamebrained

rattled 5 fazed, upset 7 annoyed 9 disturbed, flustered, perturbed, thrown off 10 distracted 11 discomposed 12 disconcerted

rattle on 3 gab 4 blab 5 prate, run on 6 babble, gabble 7 blabber, chatter, prattle 16 run off at the mouth

ratty 4 poor, worn 5 angry, cross, nasty, testy 6 cranky, shabby, touchy 7 tangled, unkempt 8 wretched 9 irascible, motheaten 11 dilapidated

raucous 4 loud 5 harsh, raspy, rough 6 hoarse, shrill 7 blaring, grating, jarring 8 grinding, jangling, piercing, strident 9 dissonant 10 discordant, stertorous 11 cacophonous 12 earsplitting, inharmonious

raunchy 4 lewd 5 dirty, gross 6 coarse, smutty, vulgar 8 off-color

Rauschenberg, Robert
born: 12 Port Arthur TX
artwork: 3 Bed 5 Barge 7 Jammers 8 Monogram 11 Retroactive

ravage 3 gut 4 loot, raid, rape, raze, ruin, sack 5 strip, waste, wreck 6 maraud 7 despoil, destroy, overrun, pillage, plunder, ransack, shatter 8 demolish, desolate, lay waste, spoliate 9 devastate 10 lay in ruins

rave 4 wax 5 fume, go on, gush, rage, rant 5 be mad, kudos, storm 6 babble, bubble, ramble 7 be angry, bluster, carry on, explode, flare up, run amok, sputter, thunder 8 flattery 9 be furious, expatiate, go on and on, good press, laudatory 10 effervesce, high praise, rhapsodize 11 blow one's top, compliments

ravel 4 undo 6 unknit 7 unravel, untwine, untwist

Ravel, Maurice
born: 6 France 7 Ciboure
composer of: 6 Bolero 7 La Valse, Mirrors 8 Jeux d'eau 9 Fountains 11 Mother Goose, Sheherazade 14 Daphnis et Chloe 15 Gaspard de la Nuit, L'Heure Espagnole 17 Rapsodie Espagnole, The Tomb of Couperin 20 Pavane for a Dead Infant 21 Don Quichotte a Dulcinee 22 L'Enfant et les Sortileges, Pavane for a Dead Princess 27 Pavane pour une infante de funte, Valses nobles et sentimentales

raven 3 jet 4 crow, dark, inky, rook 5 black, ebony, sable 6 devour 9 coalblack

Raven, The
author: 13 Edgar Allan Poe
woman 6 Lenore
refrain: 9 nevermore

ravenous 6 greedy, hungry 7 piggish,

---

starved 8 covetous, famished, grasping, ravening, starving 9 insatiate, predatory, rapacious, voracious 10 avaricious, gluttonous, insatiable

ravine 3 gap 4 pass, rift, wadi 5 abyss, break, chasm, cleft, crack, gorge, gulch, gully, split 6 arroyo, breach, canyon, clough, divide, valley 7 fissure 8 crevasse

raving 3 mad 4 wild 6 insane 7 ranting 8 frenzied 9 delirious

ravish 4 rape 5 abuse, charm, cheer 6 defile, snatch, tickle 7 delight, enchant, gladden, outrage, overjoy, violate 8 deflower, enthrall, entrance, knock out 9 captivate, enrapture, fascinate, transport

ravishing 8 alluring, charming, gorgeous, smashing, splendid, striking 9 beautiful 10 bewitching, delightful, enchanting, entrancing 11 captivating, fascinating, sensational

raw 4 bare, cold, damp, rare 5 basic, bleak, crude, frank, fresh, green, harsh, plain, rough, young 6 biting, bitter, brutal, callow, chilly, rookie, unripe 7 cutting, natural, nipping, numbing, unbaked, untried 8 blustery, freezing, ignorant, immature, inexpert, piercing, pinching, uncooked, untaught, untested 9 inclement, underdone, undrilled, unfledged, unrefined, unskilled, untrained, windswept 10 amateurish, unprepared, unseasoned 11 not finished, undercooked, undeveloped, unexercised, uninitiated, unpracticed, unprocessed, unvarnished 13 inexperienced, undisciplined, unembellished 15 not manufactured

rawboned 4 lean 5 gaunt, lanky, spare 7 angular

Rawdon, Captain
character in: 10 Bleak House
author: 7 Dickens

Rawhide
character: 5 Mushy 8 Gil Favor, Ian Cabot, Wishbone 9 Jim Quince, Pete Nolan 10 Rowdy Yates 11 Joe Scarlett, Solomon King 13 Clay Forrester 14 Hey Soos Patines
cast: 10 Sheb Wooley 11 Charles Gray, David Watson, Eric Fleming, Robert Cabal, Rocky Shahan, Steve Raines 12 James Murdock, Paul Brinegar 13 Clint Eastwood 16 Raymond St Jacques

Rawlings, Marjorie Kinnan
author of: 11 The Yearling

rawness 3 nip 4 bite 5 chill 8 rudeness 9 crudeness, greenness, roughness, sharpness, vulgarity 10 chilliness 12 inexperience

ray 3 arm 4 beam, fish, line 5 gleam, light, manta, shaft, shine, skate, trace 6 branch, streak, stream, stripe 7 radi-

---

ate 8 particle, plowfish, radiance 9 emanation, radiation

Ray, Man
born: 14 Philadelphia PA
artwork: 4 Gift (Le Cadeau) 7 Manikin 9 The Lovers 13 Observing Time 45 The Rope Dancer Accompanies Herself with Her Shadows

Rayleigh, John William Strutt
field: 7 physics
nationality: 7 British
discovered: 5 argon
awarded: 10 Nobel Prize

rayon
invented by: 4 Swan

raze 4 fell, ruin 5 level, smash, wreck 6 reduce, remove, topple 7 destroy, flatten, wipe out 8 demolish, pull down, tear down 9 break down, dismantle, knock down 10 obliterate

razor
invented by: 6 Schick 8 Gillette

Razorback State
nickname of: 8 Arkansas

Re see 2 Ra

reach 3 get, hit 4 find, go to, grab, make, move 5 climb, enter, get to, grasp, seize, touch 6 attain, clutch, come to, extend, grab at, land at, secure, spread 7 contact, stretch 8 amount to, approach, arrive at 9 get hold of, set foot in 10 get as far as, outstretch, stretch out

reachable 6 at hand 8 possible 10 accessible, achievable, attainable, obtainable, procurable

reach the top 6 arrive 7 prosper, succeed 8 make good 13 hit the big time

react 4 work 6 answer, behave, resist, return 7 respond 11 reverberate

reaction 5 reply 6 answer, reflex 8 backlash, response 11 restoration 13 counteraction 14 chemical change 17 counterrevolution, right-wing comeback

reactionary 7 diehard 8 mossback, rightist 9 right-wing 10 regressive 11 right-winger 12 reversionary 17 ultraconservative 20 counterrevolutionary

react to 5 reply 6 answer 7 respond 11 acknowledge

read 2 go 3 say 4 note, scan, show 5 study, utter 6 adduce, peruse, recite 7 analyze, deliver, discern, explain, present 8 construe, decipher, indicate, perceive, pore over 9 apprehend, interpret, translate 10 comprehend, glance over, understand 11 extrapolate

Read, Piers Paul
author of: 5 Alive 9 Polonaise 10 Monk Dawson, The Junkers, The Upstart 18 Professor's Daughter

Reade, Charles
author of: 13 Peg Woffington 23 The Cloister and the Hearth

readily 6 at once, easily, freely, pronto **7** quickly **8** in no time, promptly, smoothly, speedily **9** expressly, hands down, instantly, willingly **10** graciously **11** immediately, straightway **12** effortlessly, ungrudgingly

readiness 8 alacrity, dispatch **9** alertness **10** promptness **12** preparedness

read the riot act 5 chide, scold **6** berate, rebuke **7** censure, chasten, correct, lecture, reprove **8** admonish **9** dress down, reprimand **10** take to task

ready 3 apt, fit, set **4** deft, keen, ripe, up to **5** acute, alert, eager, equip, handy, on tap, prone, sharp **6** adroit, all set, artful, astute, at hand, bright, clever, expert, facile, fit out, liable, mature, on hand, primed, prompt, shrewd, speedy **7** cunning, equal to, prepare, present, tending, willing **8** disposed, inclined, masterly, punctual, skillful **9** attentive, dexterous, fitted out, furnished, ingenious, in harness, versatile, wide-awake **10** accessible, discerning, perceptive, put in order **11** acquisitive, expeditious, predisposed, quick-witted, resourceful, serviceable

ready for use 5 handy, on tap **6** at hand, on hand **9** available **10** accessible, convenient **11** at one's elbow **14** at one's disposal

ready-made 10 off-the-rack **11** prêt-à-porter, ready-to-wear, store-bought

ready money 4 cash **8** currency **10** cash on hand

ready to go 5 peppy **9** full of pep **10** raring to go **17** full of vim and vigor **24** bright-eyed and bushy-tailed

Reagan, Ronald Wilson
  nickname: 5 Dutch **6** Ronnie
  presidential rank: 8 fortieth
  party:
    current: 10 Republican
    former: 10 Democratic
  state represented: 2 CA
  defeated: 6 (James Earl) Carter (Jr) **7** (Walter Frederick "Fritz") Mondale **8** (John Bayard) Anderson
  vice president: 4 (George Herbert Walker) Bush
  cabinet:
    state: 4 (Alexander M) Haig (Jr) **6** (George P) Shultz
    treasury: 5 (Donald T) Regan
    defense: 10 (Caspar W) Weinberger
    attorney general: 5 (William French) Smith
    interior: 5 (James) Watt **5** (William P) Clark
    agriculture: 5 (John R) Block
    commerce: 8 (Malcolm) Baldrige
    labor: 7 (Raymond J) Donovan
    health and human services: 7 (Margaret M) Heckler **9** (Richard S) Schweiker

  education: 4 (Terrel H) Bell
  HUD: 6 (Samuel R) Pierce (Jr)
  transportation: 4 (Elizabeth H) Dole **5** (Andrew L) Lewis (Jr)
  energy: 5 (Donald P) Hodel **7** (James B) Edwards
  born: 9 Tampico IL
  college: 6 Eureka
  religion: 17 Disciples of Christ
  interests: 2 TV **5** track **6** movies **8** football **9** chops wood **10** basketball, jelly beans **13** weightlifting **15** horseback riding
  vacation spot: 14 Rancho del Cielo (Santa Barbara CA)
  dog: 5 Lucky
  author: 18 Where Is the Rest of Me?
  political career:
    governor of: 10 California
  civilian career: 5 actor **17** radio sportscaster
    host: 15 Death Valley Days **22** General Electric Theater
    president of: 17 Screen Actors Guild
    roles: 8 King's Row **10** Brother Rat **13** John Loves Mary, The Hasty Heart **15** Bedtime for Bonzo **19** The Voice of the Turtle **20** Cattle Queen of Montana **21** The Girl from Jones Beach **22** Knute Rockne All American
  military service: 6 US Army **7** captain **10** World War II
  notable events of lifetime/term:
    approval of: 10 MX missiles
    assassination attempt on: 6 Reagan **14** Pope John Paul II
    attempted assassination on Reagan by: 15 John W Hinckley Jr
    bombing of: 5 Libya
    hostages freed in: 4 Iran
    invasion of: 7 Grenada
    marines sent to: 7 Lebanon
    nuclear disaster at: 9 Chernobyl
    Russians shot down: 14 Korean airliner
    scandal: 8 Irangate
  father: 10 John Edward
    nickname: 4 Jack
  mother: 5 Nelle (Wilson)
  siblings: 4 (John) Neil
  wife: 4 Jane (Wyman) **5** Nancy (Davis)
    Nancy Davis born: 18 Anne Frances Robbins
  children: 6 Ronald **7** Maureen, Michael (adopted) **8** Patricia
    Patricia also actress known as: 10 Patti Davis
  first lady:
    program: 9 Drug abuse, Just Say No **12** Alcohol abuse **18** Foster Grandparents

real 4 pure, true **5** solid, valid **6** actual, honest **7** certain, factual, genuine, sincere **8** absolute, bona fide, positive, rightful, tangible, truthful **9** authentic,

unalloyed, unfeigned, veracious, veritable **10** legitimate, unaffected **11** not affected, substantial, substantive, unvarnished **12** well-grounded **13** unadulterated **14** unquestionable

realistic 4 real **7** genuine, graphic, natural, precise **8** faithful, lifelike, truthful **9** authentic, depictive, objective, pragmatic **10** true-to-life **11** descriptive, down-to-earth **12** naturalistic **16** representational

reality 4 fact **5** truth **6** verity **9** actuality **11** materiality, tangibility **12** corporeality **14** substantiality **17** physical existence

realization 7 success **8** grasping **10** attainment, perception **11** achievement, culmination, fulfillment **12** appreciation, consummation **13** comprehension, understanding **14** accomplishment

realize 2 do **3** get, net **4** gain **5** clear, grasp **6** absorb, attain, fathom, gather, profit **7** achieve, acquire, cognize, discern, execute, fulfill, imagine, make out, perform, produce **8** carry out, complete, conceive, make good, perceive **9** actualize, apprehend, discharge, make money, penetrate, recognize **10** accomplish, appreciate, bring about, comprehend, consummate, effectuate, understand **11** bring to pass **12** carry through

realized 3 got **6** gained, netted, proved, proven **7** cleared, grasped, made out, saw into **8** absorbed, accepted, effected, executed, existing, fathomed, gathered, imagined, made good, profited **9** completed, conceived, discerned, fulfilled, perceived, performed **10** actualized, penetrated, recognized, understood **11** appreciated, apprehended, consummated, established **12** accomplished, comprehended

really 5 truly **6** indeed, in fact, surely, verily **8** actually **9** certainly, genuinely, literally, veritably **10** absolutely, positively, truthfully **13** categorically **14** unquestionably

realm 4 land **5** field, orbit, state **6** domain, empire, nation, region, sphere **7** country, demesne, kingdom **8** dominion, monarchy, province **11** royal domain

real McCoy, the 4 real **7** genuine **9** authentic **12** the real thing

Realpolitik 10 expediency **13** power politics

reap 3 get, win **4** earn, gain **5** glean, score **6** derive, gather, obtain, profit, secure, take in **7** acquire, bring in, harvest, procure, realize

rear 3 aft, end **4** back, heel **5** after, nurse, raise, stern, train **6** dorsal, foster **7** bring up, care for, cherish, develop, educate, nurture, postern, tail end **8** back part, hind part, hindmost **9** aftermost, after part, at the back, cultivate, in the back, posterior

Rear Window
director: **15** Alfred Hitchcock
based on story by: **15** Cornell Woolrich
cast: **10** Grace Kelly **11** Raymond Burr **12** James Stewart, Thelma Ritter, Wendell Corey

reason 3 wit **4** head **5** cause, logic, sense, solve **6** acumen, brains, figure, motive, sanity **7** grounds, insight **8** lucidity, occasion **9** awareness, faculties, intellect, normality, rationale, reasoning **10** perception **11** common sense, discernment, exhortation, explanation, penetration, rationality **12** apprehension, intelligence, perspicacity, think through **13** argumentation, comprehension, justification, mental balance, understanding **15** clearheadedness

reasonable 4 fair, just, sage, sane, wise **5** sound **6** likely, proper **7** fitting, knowing, lenient, logical, natural, patient, prudent **8** credible, moderate, possible, probable, rational, sensible, suitable, thinking **9** equitable, impartial, judicious, objective, plausible, temperate, tolerable **10** admissible, coolheaded, legitimate, not extreme, reflective, thoughtful **11** circumspect, intelligent, justifiable, levelheaded, not unlikely, of good sense, predictable, well-founded **12** not excessive, well-grounded **13** understanding **14** understandable **15** of sound judgment

reasonableness 5 logic **6** sanity, wisdom **8** fairness, prudence **9** good sense **10** moderation **11** credibility, objectivity, rationality **12** good judgment, impartiality, intelligence **13** judiciousness **14** circumspection, thoughtfulness **15** clearheadedness

reasonably 6 almost, fairly **8** passably, somewhat **10** moderately, more or less **13** approximately

reasoning 5 basis, logic **6** ground **7** thought **8** analysis, argument, thinking **9** deduction, inference, rationale **10** cogitation, reflection **11** penetration **13** ratiocination **14** interpretation

reason out 8 mull over **10** deliberate **12** think through

reassure 5 cheer **6** buoy up, uplift **7** bolster, comfort **8** inspirit **9** encourage **13** inspire hope in

reassured 6 buoyed **9** bolstered, comforted, heartened **10** emboldened, encouraged, inspirited

reassuring 7 hopeful **10** auspicious, comforting, heartening **11** encouraging

Reb 2 Mr **5** Rabbi **6** Mister

rebate 6 refund **8** discount **9** abatement

Rebecca
author: **15** Daphne du Maurier
character: **10** Jack Favell, Mrs Danvers (Danny) **12** Frank Crawley **13** Colonel Julyan, Maxim de Winter
house: **9** Manderley
director: **15** Alfred Hitchcock
cast: **10** Nigel Bruce **12** Joan Fontaine **13** George Sanders **14** Judith Anderson (Mrs Danvers) **15** Laurence Olivier (Maxim de Winter)
Oscar for: **7** picture

Rebecca
character in: **7** Ivanhoe
author: **5** Scott

Rebecca see **7** Rebekah

Rebecca of Sunnybrook Farm
author: **17** Kate Douglas Wiggin
character: **4** Cobb **8** Adam Ladd **11** Aunt Miranda **14** Rebecca Randall **15** Emma Jane Perkins

Rebekah
also: **7** Rebecca
father: **7** Bethuel
husband: **5** Isaac
brother: **5** Laban
son: **4** Esau **12** Isaac, Jacob

rebel 3 shy **4** riot **5** avoid, quail, react, wince **6** flinch, mutiny, recoil, revolt, rise up, shrink **7** seceder, traitor, upstart **8** deserter, maverick, resister, turncoat **9** anarchist, dissenter, insurgent **10** iconoclast, malcontent, separatist **12** secessionist **13** nonconformist, revolutionary, revolutionist **15** insurrectionist

rebellion 6 mutiny, putsch, revolt **8** defiance, sedition, upheaval, uprising **9** coup d'etat **10** insurgency, revolution **12** insurrection

rebellious 6 unruly **7** defiant **8** contrary, mutinous, up in arms **9** alienated, fractious, insurgent, seditious, truculent, turbulent **10** disorderly, pugnacious, refractory **11** disobedient, intractable, quarrelsome **12** contumacious, recalcitrant, ungovernable, unmanageable **13** insubordinate, revolutionary **14** uncontrollable **15** insurrectionary

rebelliousness 8 defiance **9** rebellion **12** disobedience

Rebel Without a Cause
director: **11** Nicholas Ray
cast: **8** Sal Mineo **9** James Dean, Jim Backus **11** Natalie Wood

Rebirth
god of: **4** Gwyn

rebound 3 bob **6** bounce, recoil, reecho **7** flounce **8** recovery, ricochet **10** spring back

rebounding 7 rubbery, springy **9** resilient **11** ricocheting **12** bouncing back

rebuff 4 deny, snub **5** check, repel, spurn **6** ignore, put off, refuse, reject, slight **7** decline, put-down, refusal, repulse **8** turn down **9** disregard, rejec-

tion **10** putting off **12** cold shoulder **13** slap in the face **15** keep at a distance

rebuke 5 blame, chide, scold, score **6** berate **7** censure, chew out, chiding, lecture, reproof, reprove, upbraid **8** admonish, berating, call down, reproach, reproval, scolding **9** dress down, reprimand **10** admonition, chewing out, take to task, upbraiding **11** castigation, disapproval **12** admonishment, dressing down, remonstrance, reprehension, take down a peg **13** find fault with, tongue-lashing **15** remonstrate with

rebuttal 5 reply **6** answer, denial, retort **7** defense, riposte **8** disproof, negation, response **9** disproval, rejoinder **10** refutation **11** confutation **12** counterreply, disagreement, surrejoinder **13** contradiction **15** counterargument

recalcitrant 5 balky **6** mulish, unruly **7** willful **8** contrary, stubborn **9** obstinate, pigheaded, unwilling **10** bullheaded, headstrong, refractory **11** disobedient, intractable **12** unsubmissive

recall 5 place **6** memory, revive **8** call back, remember **9** reanimate, recognize, recollect **10** reactivate, remobilize **11** reinstitute, remembrance **12** recollection **17** ability to remember

recant 4 deny **5** unsay **6** abjure, disown, recall, renege, repeal, revoke **7** disavow, rescind, retract **8** disclaim, forswear, renounce, take back, withdraw **9** foreswear, repudiate **10** apostatize **12** eat one's words **14** change one's mind

recantation 6 denial **9** disavowal **10** refutation, retraction, revocation **11** repudiation **12** renunciation

recapitulate 5 recap, sum up **6** relate, repeat, reword **7** recount, restate **8** rephrase **9** epitomize, reiterate, summarize **15** repeat in essence

recapture 6 retake **7** reprise **15** experience again

recede 3 ebb **5** abate **6** back up, go back, retire **7** regress, retreat, subside **10** retrogress

receipt 7 arrival, release, voucher **9** admission, discharge, receiving, reception **10** acceptance, admittance, possession, recipience **11** acquisition, transferral

receipts 3 pay **4** gain, gate, take **5** share, split, wages **6** income, recipe, return **7** formula, payment, profits, returns, revenue **8** earnings, proceeds **9** emolument **10** net profits **12** remuneration **13** reimbursement

receive 3 get **4** meet **5** admit, greet, put up **6** accept, come by, obtain, regard, secure, suffer, take in **7** acquire, adjudge, approve, be given, react to, sustain, undergo, welcome **8** meet with, submit to **9** encounter, entertain **10** experience **11** accommodate

receive willingly 6 accept **10** take gladly **16** accept with thanks **18** accept with open arms

receive with favor 6 praise **7** approve **10** appreciate

receive with open arms 6 invite **7** embrace, welcome **13** accept eagerly **19** roll out the red carpet

recent 3 new **4** late **5** fresh, novel **6** modern **8** up-to-date **9** latter-day **12** contemporary **13** up-to-the-minute

receptacle 3 bag, bin, box, can, jar **4** file, tray **6** basket, bottle, hamper, holder, hopper, vessel **7** carrier **8** receiver **9** container **10** depository, repository **11** compartment

reception 2 do **4** fete **5** party **6** affair, soiree **7** welcome **8** greeting **11** recognition **15** social gathering

receptive 8 amenable, friendly **10** accessible, hospitable, interested, open-minded, responsive **11** susceptible **12** approachable **17** favorably disposed

recess 3 bay, gap **4** bend, cell, cove, fold, gulf, lull, nook, pass, rest, slot **5** break, cleft, gorge, inlet, letup, niche, pause **6** alcove, corner, harbor, hiatus, hollow **7** holiday, interim, respite, time out **8** interval, vacation **9** interlude **10** pigeonhole **11** coffee break, indentation **12** intermission **14** breathing spell

recessed 4 sunk **6** paused, sunken **7** delayed **8** deferred, extended, indented **9** adjourned, dissolved, postponed, prolonged, withdrawn **10** terminated
church wall: **5** ambry
wall: **6** alcove

recesses 6 depths **10** inmost part, penetralia

recession 10 depression **11** recessional **16** economic downturn

recherche 4 rare **5** prize **6** choice, exotic, scarce, select, unique **7** special, unusual **8** original, superior, uncommon, valuable **9** different, priceless **10** one of a kind **11** exceptional

recipe 2 Rx **4** cure, rule **5** axiom **6** elixir, remedy **7** formula, receipt **12** instructions, prescription

recipient 4 heir **5** donee, taker **6** getter **7** legatee **8** accepter, acquirer, obtainer, receiver **9** presentee **11** beneficiary

reciprocal 6 common, linked, mutual, shared **8** returned **9** bilateral, exchanged, one for one **10** equivalent **11** give-and-take **12** interchanged, interrelated **13** complementary, corresponding, given in return **14** interdependent **15** interchangeable

reciprocate 4 feel **6** return **7** requite, respond **9** retaliate **10** make return **11**

act likewise, give and take, interchange **12** give in return **19** return the compliment

reciprocity 8 exchange **11** give and take, interchange

recital 4 talk **6** report **7** concert, telling **8** delivery, reciting **9** discourse, narration, narrative, rendition **10** recitation **11** description, particulars, performance **12** dissertation, oral exercise **13** public reading **14** graphic account, recapitulation

recite 4 tell **5** quote, speak **6** relate, repeat **7** declaim, deliver, narrate, perform, recount **10** say by heart **11** communicate

reckless 4 rash, wild **5** giddy, hasty **6** daring, fickle, madcap, unwary **7** flighty, foolish, unaware **8** careless, cavalier, heedless, mindless, unsteady, volatile **9** daredevil, desperate, foolhardy, imprudent, impulsive, negligent, oblivious, unheeding, unmindful **10** incautious, indiscreet, insensible, neglectful, regardless, unthinking, unwatchful **11** harebrained, inattentive, precipitate, thoughtless, unconcerned **12** devil-may-care, unsolicitous **13** inconsiderate, irresponsible, uncircumspect **14** scatterbrained

recklessly 4 fast **5** blind **6** rashly, wildly **7** hastily **8** headlong **9** headfirst **10** carelessly, heedlessly **11** audaciously, desperately, impetuously, impulsively **12** unmindfully **13** irresponsibly, unconcernedly

recklessness 7 abandon **8** rashness **9** disregard, unconcern **10** imprudence, profligacy **11** impetuosity **12** heedlessness, immoderation **13** foolhardiness **15** thoughtlessness **16** irresponsibility

reckon 3 add **4** bank, cope, deal, deem, plan, rank, rate **5** add up, class, count, fancy, guess, judge, tally, think, total, value **6** assess, decide, esteem, expect, figure, handle, regard **7** account, adjudge, balance, bargain, compute, imagine, presume, suppose, surmise **8** appraise, consider, estimate **9** calculate, determine, speculate

reckoning 3 tab **4** bill, doom **5** count, tally, total **6** adding, charge **7** account **8** estimate, judgment **9** appraisal, summation **10** estimation, evaluation **11** calculation, computation **13** final judgment **19** settling of an account

reclaim 6 reform, rescue **7** correct, recover, rectify, restore

reclame 9 notoriety, publicity

recline 4 lean, loll, rest **6** lounge, repose, sprawl **7** lie back, lie down **12** take one's ease

reclining 7 lolling, resting **8** lounging, reposing **9** lying down, recumbent

recluse 3 nun **4** monk **5** crank, loner **6** hermit, hidden, secret **7** ascetic, eremite, erratic, oddball **8** cenobite,

crackpot **9** eccentric **10** cloistered **11** sequestered **13** nonconformist

recognition 6 notice **9** discovery **10** acceptance, validation **13** comprehension, understanding **14** acknowledgment, identification **19** diplomatic relations

recognizable 5 clear, plain **8** distinct **10** detectable **11** discernable, perceivable, perceptible **12** identifiable, intelligible **13** ascertainable **14** comprehensible, understandable **15** distinguishable

recognizance 4 bond **6** pledge **10** obligation **11** recognition **15** acknowledgement

recognize 3 see **4** know, spot **5** admit, place, sight **7** discern, make out, pick out, realize, respect, yield to **8** identify, submit to **9** be aware of, concede to **10** appreciate, comprehend, understand **11** acknowledge **14** give the floor to

recognized 5 known **8** accepted, admitted, approved, familiar, realized **9** customary **10** accredited **11** traditional **12** acknowledged, conventional

recoil 4 fail, kick **5** blink, cower, demur, quail, shirk, start, wince **6** blench, cringe, falter, flinch, revolt **7** fly back, rebound, retreat **8** draw back, hang back, jump back **9** bound back **10** shrink back, spring back

recoil at 4 hate **5** abhor **6** detest, eschew, loathe **7** despise **9** abominate, shudder at **10** shrink from **12** be revolted by **14** view with horror **18** feel aversion toward

recoiling 7 wincing **9** flinching **10** rebounding **11** drawing back **13** shrinking back, springing back

recollect 5 place **6** recall **8** remember **10** call to mind

recollection 4 mind **6** memoir, memory, recall, record **11** remembrance **12** reminiscence **13** retrospection
French: **8** souvenir

recommend 4 urge **5** favor, order **6** advise **7** counsel, endorse, propose, suggest **8** advocate, vouch for **9** encourage, prescribe **10** put forward **11** speak well of

recommendable 9 advisable, favorable **10** worthwhile

recommendation 4 plug **6** behest, praise **8** approval, good word **9** reference **11** endorsement **12** commendation

recompense 3 pay **5** repay **6** return, reward **7** payment **9** reimburse, repayment **10** compensate, remunerate, reparation **12** compensation, remuneration **15** indemnification

reconcile 5 fix up **6** adjust, make up, resign, settle, square **7** correct, patch up, rectify, reunite, win over **8** persuade **9** harmonize **10** conciliate, propitiate **11** set straight

reconcile oneself 6 submit **9** acquiesce **13** resign oneself

reconciliation 8 fixing up, making up, settling, squaring **10** adjustment, correction, patching up, rectifying **11** resignation, winning over **12** conciliation **13** justification, rectification **15** setting straight

recondite 4 deep **6** arcane, hidden **7** obscure **8** abstruse, esoteric **9** concealed **10** mysterious **16** incomprehensible

reconnaissance 6 survey **7** viewing **8** scouting, scrutiny **10** inspection **11** exploration, observation **12** surveillance **13** investigation **14** reconnoitering

reconnoiter 4 look **5** probe, scout **6** patrol, picket, survey **7** examine **8** remember, traverse

reconsider 5 amend **6** modify, ponder, review, revise **7** correct, rethink, sleep on **8** mull over, reassess **9** reexamine, think over **10** reevaluate **13** think better of **15** think twice about

reconstitute 7 restore **9** recompose **10** add water to **11** reconstruct

reconstruct 7 rebuild **8** make over, recreate **10** reassemble **11** reestablish **12** reconstitute

record 3 log **4** copy, file, list, memo, note, post, show, tape **5** admit, enter **6** annals, career, docket, enroll, report **7** account, archive, catalog, conduct, history, jot down, jotting, journal **8** document, indicate, register, take down **9** chronicle, introduce, write down **10** adventures, background, memorandum, transcribe **11** experiences, make an entry, performance, proceedings **12** unbeaten mark **14** top performance

French: 11 compte rendu

record, phonograph 2 EP, LP **5** vinyl **7** platter

invented by: 4 Bell **6** Edison **7** Tainter **8** Berliner **10** Goldenmark

recount 4 tell **6** detail, recite, relate **7** explain, narrate **8** describe **9** count over

recoup 5 atone **6** redeem, regain **7** recover, replace **8** make good, retrieve **9** make up for, reacquire **13** make amends for

recourse 6 choice, option, resort **11** alternative, other choice

recover 4 heal, mend **5** rally **6** offset, pick up, recoup, redeem, regain, retake, revive **7** balance, get back, get well, improve, reclaim, restore, win back **8** make good, retrieve, revivify **9** make up for, reacquire, recapture, reconquer, repossess **10** come around, compensate, convalesce, recuperate, rejuvenate **11** pull through, resuscitate

recovery 4 cure **5** rally **6** recoup, rescue, upturn **7** revival, salvage **8** comeback **9** retrieval **10** betterment, regainment **11** improvement, reclamation, reformation, restoration **12** recuperation **13** business cycle, convalescence

recreancy 8 apostasy **9** cowardice, desertion **10** cravenness, disloyalty, infidelity **13** faithlessness, pusillanimity **14** unfaithfulness

recreant 6 coward, craven, yellow **8** apostate, cowardly, deserter, disloyal, renegade **9** undutiful **10** unfaithful **11** lily-livered **12** dishonorable **13** pusillanimous, yellow-bellied

recreation 4 play **5** hobby, sport **7** pastime **9** amusement, avocation, diversion **10** relaxation **13** entertainment **15** leisure activity

recrimination 5 blame **6** charge **10** accusation **13** countercharge

recruit 4 hire **5** raise, renew **6** employ, enlist, enroll, muster, novice, recoup, revive, rookie **7** draftee, provide, recover, restore **8** beginner, newcomer **9** conscript **10** recuperate

rectangle 3 box **6** oblong, square **7** polygon **10** quadrangle **13** parallelogram, quadrilateral

rectangular 4 long **6** square **7** boxlike **11** right-angled **12** quadrangular **13** quadrilateral

rectification 6 fixing, reform **7** redress **8** righting, squaring **9** remedying, repairing **10** adjustment, correction, regulation **12** setting right **15** putting straight, putting to rights **16** straightening out

rectify 3 fix **4** cure, mend **5** amend, emend, focus, right **6** adjust, attune, reform, remedy, repair, revise, square **7** correct, redress **8** put right, regulate, set right **9** make right **10** straighten

rectitude 5 honor **7** decency, probity **8** morality **9** integrity, principle **11** uprightness **12** virtuousness **13** righteousness **15** high-mindedness **16** incorruptibility **17** irreproachability

rector 6 cleric, parson, pastor, priest **8** minister, preacher **9** churchman, clergyman **12** ecclesiastic

recumbent 4 flat **5** prone **6** supine **7** leaning **8** couchant **9** lying down, prostrate, reclining **10** horizontal **12** stretched out

recuperate 4 heal, mend **7** get well, improve, recover **8** come back **9** get better **10** come around, convalesce **11** be on the mend, pull through **14** return to health **16** regain one's health

recuperation 8 recovery **11** restoration **13** convalescence

recuperative 11 restorative **15** health-restoring

recur 6 repeat, resume, return **7** persist **8** come back, continue, reappear **9** come again **10** occur again

recurrence 5 cycle, round **6** repeat, return **7** relapse, renewal, reprise, routine **8** iterance, rotation **10** continuity, repetition **11** periodicity **12** reappearance

recurrent 7 regular **8** frequent, periodic **9** recurring, repeating **10** repetitive **11** reappearing **12** intermittent **14** appearing again

red 4 pink, rose, rosy, ruby, wine **5** aglow, coral, flame, ruddy **6** auburn, cherry, florid, maroon **7** burning, crimson, flaming, flushed, glowing, scarlet **8** blooming, blushing, cardinal, inflamed, reddened, rubicund **9** rubescent, vermilion **12** blood-colored

Red and the Black, The (Le Rouge et le Noir)

author: 8 Stendhal

character: 6 Fouque **8** M de Renal **11** Julien Sorel **16** Mathilde de la Mole

Red Badge of Courage, The

author: 12 Stephen Crane

character: 6 Wilson **10** Jim Conklin **12** Henry Fleming

red-blooded 5 lusty, peppy, vital **6** ardent, robust, strong, sturdy **7** dynamic, intense **8** forceful, powerful, spirited, vigorous **9** energetic **10** hot-blooded, passionate

Red Branch

origin: 5 Irish

warriors of: 9 Conchobar

Redburn

author: 14 Herman Melville

red-cheeked 4 rosy **5** ruddy **6** robust **8** blushing **12** apple-cheeked

Red Cross Knight

character in: 15 The Faerie Queene

author: 7 Spenser

redden 4 burn, glow **5** blush, color, flame, flush **9** go crimson **12** become florid

reddish 4 rosy, ruby **5** ruddy, rufus **6** flushy, rufous **7** roseate **8** rubicund

reddish-brown 4 rust **5** henna **6** auburn, copper, russet, sienna **8** chestnut, cinnamon

Red Earth People see **3** Fox

redeem 4 keep, save **5** cover **6** defray, ransom, recoup, reform, regain, rescue, settle **7** buy back, convert, fulfill, reclaim, recover, satisfy **8** atone for, make good, retrieve **9** discharge, make up for, repossess **10** evangelize, repurchase

redeemed 5 saved **7** claimed, rescued **8** made good, ransomed, reformed **9** atoned for, delivered, fulfilled, recovered **10** carried out, regenerate **11** repossessed

redemption 6 excuse, pardon, ransom, reform, rescue 7 salvage 8 recovery 9 amendment, atonement, exemption, expiation, salvation 10 conversion 11 deliverance, reformation

Redford, Robert
real name: 20 Charles Robert Redford
born: 13 Santa Monica CA
roles: 8 The Sting 10 The Natural 11 Legal Eagles 12 The Candidate, The Way We Were 13 Downhill Racer 14 The Great Gatsby 15 Jeremiah Johnson 17 Barefoot in the Park 19 All the President's Men 20 Three Days of the Condor 29 Butch Cassidy and the Sundance Kid
director: 8 Quiz Show 14 Ordinary People (Oscar) 17 The Horse Whisperer 19 A River Runs Through It

Redgrave, Corin
born: 6 London 7 England
sisters: 4 Lynn 7 Vanessa
roles: 8 The Magus 17 A Man for All Seasons 20 In the Name of the Father 23 Four Weddings and a Funeral

Redgrave, Lynn
born: 6 London 7 England
father: 18 Sir Michael Redgrave
sister: 15 Vanessa Redgrave
roles: 10 Georgy Girl, Howard's End 13 The Bostonians 14 The Happy Hooker 26 Whatever Happened to Baby Jane
author of: 7 Vanessa 16 Pussies and Tigers

Redgrave, Sir Michael
born: 7 Bristol, England
daughter: 4 Lynn 7 Vanessa
roles: 11 Dan Peggotty 15 The Lady Vanishes 16 David Copperfield 22 Mourning Becomes Electra 27 The Importance of Being Earnest

Redgrave, Vanessa
born: 6 London 7 England
father: 18 Sir Michael Redgrave
sister: 12 Lynn Redgrave
husband: 14 Tony Richardson
roles: 5 Julia, Yanks 6 Agatha, Blow-Up, Morgan 7 Camelot, Isadora 9 Guinevere 16 Mary Queen of Scots 17 The Lady from the Sea

red-hot 5 aglow, fiery 6 heated, raging 7 blazing, burning, glowing, intense 12 all-consuming

red-letter 5 happy, lucky 6 banner 10 auspicious, felicitous

redness 4 glow 5 blush, flush 8 rosiness 9 ruddiness 10 floridness

redolence 5 aroma, savor 7 bouquet 9 fragrance, good smell 12 pleasant odor

redolent 5 balmy, spicy 6 savory, smelly 7 mindful, odorous, reeking, scented 8 aromatic, fragrant, perfumed, stinking 9 evocative, odiferous 10 expressive, indicative, suggestive 11 odoriferous, reminiscent 13 sweet-smelling

Redon, Odilon
born: 6 France 8 Bordeaux
artwork: 10 In the Dream, The Cyclops 11 Le Vieil Ange 13 Flowers of Evil 15 Violette Heymann

redouble 7 augment, magnify 8 heighten, multiply 9 intensify

redoubtable 7 awesome 8 alarming, imposing 10 formidable 11 illustrious 12 awe-inspiring

redound 4 lead, tend 5 cause, surge 6 abound 7 conduce, incline 8 overflow 10 contribute 11 reverberate

redress 4 ease 5 amend, right 6 amends, reform, relief, remedy 7 correct, payment, rectify, relieve 8 easement, set right 9 make up for 10 recompense, reparation 11 restitution 12 compensation, satisfaction 13 compensate for, rectification 15 indemnification 18 make retribution for

Red River
director: 11 Howard Hawks
cast: 9 Joanne Dru, John Wayne 11 John Ireland 13 Walter Brennan 15 Montgomery Clift

Reds
director: 12 Warren Beatty
cast: 11 Diane Keaton (Louise Bryant), Paul Sorvino 12 Warren Beatty (John Reed) 13 Jack Nicholson, Jerzy Kosinski 14 Edward Herrmann 16 Maureen Stapleton
Oscar for: 8 director 17 supporting actress (Stapleton)

Red Shoes, The
author: 21 Hans Christian Andersen
director: 13 Michael Powell 17 Emeric Pressburger
cast: 12 Marius Goring, Moira Shearer 13 Anton Walbrook 14 Robert Helpmann

Red Skelton Show, The
character: 8 Gertrude 10 Heathcliff 13 Mean Widdle Kid 14 San Fernando Red, Sheriff Deadeye, Willie Lump-Lump 16 Bolivar Shagnasty 17 Cauliflower McPugg 18 Clem Kadiddlehopper 20 Freddie the Freeloader
saying: 7 I dood it
closing line: 8 God bless

Red Sky at Morning
author: 15 Richard Bradford

reduce 3 cut 4 bust, curb, diet, dull, ease, thin 5 abate, blunt, break, check, force, lower, slash, water 6 damage, demote, dilute, lessen, retard, soften, temper, weaken 7 assuage, atrophy, cripple, cut down, leave in 8 diminish, discount, enfeeble, mark down, minimize, mitigate, moderate, modulate, slim down, slow down, tone down, trim down 9 bring down, checkmate, undermine 10 debilitate, devitalize, slenderize 11 lower in rank 12 incapacitate

reduced form 6 digest 7 summary 9 short form 11 abridgement, contraction 12 abbreviation, condensation

reduce speed 4 slow 5 brake 6 rein in 8 slow down 10 decelerate

reduce to nothing 5 erase 7 abolish, destroy, wipe out 8 lay waste 9 eradicate, liquidate 10 annihilate 11 exterminate

reductio ad absurdum 22 reduction to an absurdity

reduction 3 cut 5 break 8 decrease, discount 9 abatement, lessening 10 concession 11 abridgement, subtraction

reduction to an absurdity
Latin: 18 reductio ad absurdum

redundancy 6 excess 7 surplus 8 verbiage 9 tautology 10 repetition 11 diffuseness, superfluity 13 overabundance 14 circumlocution, repetitiveness

redundant 5 extra 6 excess 7 surplus 10 pleonastic 11 dispensable, inessential, overflowing, repetitious, superfluous, unnecessary 12 tautological 13 superabundant

redwood 19 Adenanthera pavonina, Sequoia sempervirens
varieties: 4 dawn 5 coast, giant 7 Madeira

reed
varieties: 3 bur 4 vine 5 Burma, giant 6 common 14 Mauritania vine

reed 9 six cubits

Reed, Sir Carol
director of: 6 Oliver (Oscar) 11 The Third Man

Reed, Walter S
field: 12 bacteriology
discovered cause of: 11 yellow fever

reef 3 bar 4 bank, flat, spit 5 shelf, shoal 7 sandbar, shallow

reek 4 fume 5 smell, smoke, steam, stink 6 stench 7 give off 9 effluvium, emanation

reel 4 rock, roll, spin, sway 5 lurch, pitch, swirl, waver, whirl 6 rotate, teeter, totter, wobble 7 revolve, stagger, stumble

reeling 5 dizzy, giddy, shaky 6 whirly 8 spinning, unsteady 10 staggering 11 vertiginous

Reese, Harold
nickname: 6 Pee Wee
sport: 8 baseball
position: 9 shortstop
team: 15 Brooklyn Dodgers

Reeve
character in: 18 The Canterbury Tales
author: 7 Chaucer

Reeve, Christopher
born: 9 New York NY
author of: 7 Still Me

roles: 8 Superman **9** Deathtrap **13** The Bostonians **15** Remains of the Day, Somewhere in Time **18** Village of the Damned

refer 2 go **4** cite, send, turn **6** advert, allude, direct, submit **7** consult, deliver, mention **8** hand over, transfer, transmit **9** pass along

referee 5 judge **6** decree, settle, umpire **7** arbiter, mediate **8** judgment, mediator, moderate **9** arbitrate, determine, intercede, intervene, moderator, pronounce **10** adjudicate, arbitrator **11** adjudicator, intercessor **12** intermediary

reference 4 hint **7** inkling, mention **8** allusion, good word, innuendo **10** deposition, intimation, suggestion **11** affirmation, credentials, endorsement, implication, testimonial **13** certification **14** recommendation

reference book 5 atlas, bible **6** manual **9** guidebook **10** dictionary **12** encyclopedia

refine 6 filter, purify, strain **7** cleanse, develop, improve, perfect, process **9** cultivate

refined 5 clean, suave **6** gentle, polite, urbane **7** courtly, elegant, genteel **8** cleansed, cultured, delicate, finished, graceful, ladylike, mannerly, polished, purified, well-bred **9** civilized, clarified, courteous **10** cultivated, fastidious **11** gentlemanly **14** discriminating

refinement 5 grace **6** finish, nicety, polish, step up **7** advance, culture, dignity, finesse, suavity **8** breeding, civility, cleaning, courtesy, delicacy, elegance, fineness, revision, urbanity **9** amendment, cleansing, gentility, propriety **10** betterment, filtration, gentleness, politeness **11** advancement, cultivation, development, discernment, enhancement, good manners, improvement, progression, savoir faire, step forward **12** amelioration, distillation, graciousness, purification, tastefulness **13** courteousness, rectification **14** discrimination, fastidiousness

refitting 8 adapting **10** adaptation, remodeling **11** reequipping, resupplying

reflect 4 cast, copy, muse, show, undo **5** image, study, think, throw **6** betray, evince, expose, mirror, ponder, reason, return, reveal **7** condemn, display, exhibit, express, imitate, present, rebound, uncover **8** cogitate, consider, disclose, give back, indicate, manifest, meditate, mull over, register, ruminate, send back, set forth **9** bring upon, cerebrate, dwell upon, represent, reproduce, speculate, throw back, undermine **10** deliberate **11** concentrate, contemplate, demonstrate

reflection 4 blot, idea, slur, view **5** image, study **6** insult, musing, notion **7** opinion, reproof, thought **8** reproach, thinking **9** attention, pondering, sentiment **10** cogitation, conviction, derogation, impression, imputation, meditation, rumination **11** cerebration, insinuation, mirror image, pensiveness **12** deliberation **13** concentration, consideration, disparagement

French: 6 pensee

reflective 7 pensive **8** thinking **9** judicious, pondering **10** meditative, ruminative, thoughtful **11** speculative **13** contemplative

reform 4 mend **5** amend, atone, emend **6** better, remedy, repair, repent, revise **7** convert, correct, improve, rebuild, rectify, remodel, restore **8** progress **9** amendment **10** correction **12** mend one's ways, rehabilitate **13** rectification **16** set straight again, turn over a new leaf

reformation 6 change, reform **9** amendment, reforming **10** alteration, conversion **11** improvement **12** modification **14** reorganization

refractory 5 balky **6** mulish, unruly **7** restive, wayward, willful **8** contrary, stubborn **9** fractious, obstinate, pigheaded **10** rebellious **11** disobedient, intractable **12** unmanageable

refrain 5 avoid, forgo **6** desist, eschew, forego, refuse, resist **7** abstain, forbear, hold off **8** leave off, renounce **11** curb oneself, keep oneself **12** stay one's hand **15** restrain oneself

refrain from 5 avoid, forgo **6** desist, eschew, forego **7** abstain, forbear **8** leave off, renounce

refresh 3 jog **4** prod **5** brace, renew, rouse **6** arouse, awaken, prompt, revive, stir up, vivify **7** cool off, freshen, quicken, recruit, restore **8** activate, energize, recreate **9** reanimate, stimulate **10** invigorate, rejuvenate, strengthen

refreshed 7 revived **8** animated, restored, vivified **9** enlivened, freshened **11** invigorated

refreshing 7 bracing **11** revivifying **12** invigorating **13** strengthening **15** thirst-quenching

refreshment 4 bite, eats **5** drink, snack **6** bracer **7** potable **8** beverage, cocktail, pick-me-up, potation **9** appetizer, drinkable, refresher **10** recreation, relaxation **11** hors d'oeuvre, nourishment, restoration, restorative **12** food and drink, invigoration, rejuvenation **14** reinvigoration, thirst quencher

refrigerate 4 cool **5** chill **6** freeze **7** congeal **8** keep cold, keep cool, put on ice **9** keep on ice

Refrigerator, The nickname of: 12 William Perry

refuge 4 home **5** haven **6** asylum, harbor, resort **7** hideout, retreat, shelter **8** safehold **9** anchorage, harborage, sanctuary **10** protection **12** port in a storm **14** help in distress, place of shelter

refugee 2 DP **5** exile **6** bolter, eloper, emigre **7** escapee, evacuee, runaway **8** emigrant, fugitive **9** absconder **10** expatriate **15** displaced person

refulgent 6 bright, lucent **7** glowing, lambent, radiant, shining **8** luminous, relucent **9** brilliant

refund 5 remit, repay **6** rebate, return **7** pay back **9** reimburse, repayment **10** recompense, remittance, remunerate **12** amount repaid **13** give back money, reimbursement **18** make restitution for **19** make compensation for

refurbish 4 mend, redo **5** clean, fix up, renew **6** repair, tidy up **7** freshen, improve, remodel, restore **8** overhaul, renovate, spruce up **11** recondition

refusal 2 no **3** nay **4** veto **6** denial **7** regrets **8** turndown **9** declining, rejection **10** nonconsent **11** declination, disapproval **13** nonacceptance, noncompliance, unwillingness

refuse 2 no **4** deny, junk, veto **5** spurn, trash, waste **6** forbid, litter, reject **7** decline, garbage, rubbish, say no to **8** disallow, prohibit, turn down, withhold

refuse pile 4 dump **6** midden **11** rubbish heap

refuse to submit 4 defy **5** rebel **6** resist **7** disobey, hold out, violate **10** transgress **12** fail to comply

refutation 4 veto **6** denial **7** counter **8** negation, rebuttal **9** disavowal **11** confutation, repudiation **12** invalidation **13** contradiction

refutatory 8 contrary, opposing **10** discrepant **11** conflicting, disagreeing **12** antithetical, inconsistent **13** contradictory **14** countervailing, irreconcilable

refute 4 deny **5** rebut **6** answer **7** confute, counter **8** disprove **9** challenge **10** contradict, invalidate **12** give the lie to

regain 6 recoup, redeem, retake **7** get back, reclaim, recover, win back **9** gain anew, get again, retrieve **9** recapture, repossess

regal 5 grand, noble, proud, royal **6** august, kingly, lordly **7** queenly, stately **8** imposing, kinglike, majestic, princely, splendid **9** queenlike **10** princelike **11** magnificent **13** splendiferous

regale 3 ply **4** fete **5** amuse, feast **6** divert, please **7** banquet, delight, lionize **8** enthrall **9** entertain **10** serve nobly **11** wine and dine **15** feed sumptuously

Regan

character in: **8** King Lear
author: **11** Shakespeare

regard 3 eye, see **4** care, heed, hold, mind, note, rate, scan, view **5** judge, point, think, value, watch **6** accept, admire, aspect, behold, detail, esteem, follow, gaze at, look at, matter, notice, reckon, survey, take in **7** account, believe, concern, put down, respect, set down, subject, thought **8** consider, estimate, listen to, look upon, look up to, note well, relation **9** attention, hearken to, reference **10** admiration, connection, estimation, meditation, reflection, scrutinize **11** contemplate, observation, think well of **12** appreciation **13** cast the eyes on, consideration, think highly of **14** pay attention to

regardful 5 civil **6** polite **7** mindful **8** reverent **9** courteous, observant **10** respectful **11** deferential, reverential

regard highly 6 admire, esteem **7** respect **10** appreciate

regarding 4 in re **5** about, anent **7** apropos **10** concerning, respecting

regardless 6 anyhow, anyway **10** for all that **11** nonetheless **12** nevertheless **15** notwithstanding **19** in spite of everything

regard with repugnance 4 hate **5** abhor **6** detest, loathe **7** despise **8** execrate **9** abominate, can't stand, shudder at **10** recoil from, shrink from **11** can't stomach **12** be revolted by **13** be nauseated by, find repulsive **18** feel aversion toward

regard with suspicion 5 doubt **7** suspect **8** distrust, mistrust, question

regenerate 5 renew **6** redeem, reform, revive, uplift **7** restore **8** inspirit, reawaken, retrieve, revivify **9** enlighten, resurrect **10** rejuvenate **11** resuscitate **12** generate anew **13** give new life to, make a new man of

regent 4 king **5** queen, ruler **8** governor **9** protecter, protector

regime 4 rule **5** power, reign **7** command, control, dynasty **8** dominion **9** direction **10** government, leadership, management **12** jurisdiction **14** administration

regimen 4 diet, rule **6** system **10** government

regimentation 5 order, rigor **6** method, system **7** control, regimen **9** orthodoxy **10** discipline, regulation, uniformity **12** rigorousness **13** methodization **19** doctrinaire approach

Regin
origin: **12** Scandinavian
mentioned in: **8** Volsunga
brother: **6** Fafnir
raised: **6** Sigurd

region 4 area, land, zone **5** field, range, realm, space, tract **6** domain, sphere **7** country, expanse **8** district, locality, province, vicinity **9** territory **12** neighborhood

regional 5 areal, local, zonal **7** dialect **10** locational, provincial **11** territorial **12** geographical

register 3 log **4** dial, mark, roll, show **5** diary, gauge, meter, range, scale **6** betray, enlist, enroll, heater, ledger, record, sign up **7** betoken, check in, compass, counter, daybook, exhibit, express, logbook, point to, portray, set down **8** disclose, heat duct, heat vent, indicate, manifest, note down, radiator, recorder, registry, take down **9** indicator, write down **10** calculator, heat outlet, hot-air vent, record book **12** put in writing

regnat populus 16 let the people rule
motto of: **8** Arkansas

regress 3 ebb **4** back, exit, fall **6** go back, recede, return, revert **7** relapse, retreat, reverse **8** fall back, pass back, withdraw **9** backslide **10** lose ground, retrogress **11** deteriorate **12** move backward

regressive 8 backward **9** declining, worsening **10** retrograde **13** retrogressive

regret 3 rue, woe **4** moan **5** grief, mourn, qualm **6** bemoan, bewail, lament, repent, sorrow, twinge **7** anguish, apology, deplore, eat crow, remorse, scruple **8** be rueful, grieve at, weep over **9** apologies, grievance, heartache, rue the day **10** be sorry for, contrition, repentance, ruefulness **11** be ashamed of, compunction, lamentation, reservation **12** be remorseful, eat humble pie, eat one's words, self-reproach **13** feel sorrow for, regretfulness, second thought **14** disappointment, feel remorse for, remorsefulness **15** dissatisfaction **16** feel distress over, pang of conscience, self-condemnation

regretful 6 rueful **8** contrite **9** sorrowful **10** apologetic, remorseful **15** selfreproachful

regrettable 6 woeful **7** unhappy **8** grievous, pitiable **10** calamitous, deplorable, lamentable **11** unfortunate

regular 3 set **4** even, fine, real **5** daily, fixed, plain, usual **6** common, normal, proper, smooth, steady, trusty **7** classic, correct, genuine, habitue, natural, typical, uniform **8** absolute, accepted, complete, constant, everyday, faithful, familiar, frequent, habitual, loyalist, ordinary, orthodox, periodic, stalwart, standard, thorough, true blue **9** customary, recurrent, recurring, unvarying **10** consistent, dependable, invariable, periodical, unchanging **11** commonplace, down-to-earth, established, old reliable, symmetrical, undeviating **12** well-balanced **16** wellproportioned

regulate 3 fix **5** guide **6** adjust, direct, govern, handle, manage **7** balance, control, monitor, oversee, rectify **8** moderate, modulate, organize **9** supervise **10** regularize **11** superintend

regulation 4 rule **5** edict, order **6** decree **7** command, control, dictate, statute **8** handling **9** adjusting, direction, ordinance **10** adjustment **11** commandment **13** standing order

regulator 5 guide **7** manager **8** director, governor, overseer **9** moderator, modulator **10** adjustment, supervisor **14** superintendent **15** adjusting device

regurgitate 4 barf **5** vomit **7** throw up **8** disgorge

rehabilitate 3 fix **4** save **6** redeem, remake **7** restore, salvage **8** make over, readjust, renovate **9** reeducate, refurbish, reinstate **11** recondition, reconstruct, resocialize, set straight **13** straighten out **16** restore to society

rehash 6 repeat, retell, reword **7** restate **8** rephrase **9** iteration, rechauffe

rehearsal 5 drill, recap **7** tryout **7** hearing, reading, test run **8** audition, exercise, practice, trial run **9** polishing **10** perfecting, repetition, run-through **11** preparation, reiteration, walkthrough **14** recapitulation

rehearse 5 drill, ready, train **6** go over, polish, recite, relate, repeat, retell **7** narrate, prepare, recount **8** practice **9** reiterate **10** run through **13** read one's lines **14** give a recital of, study one's lines

rehoboam 18 oversize wine bottle

Rehoboth
founder: **6** Nimrod

Reich, Charles
author of: **20** The Greening of America

Reichsfuhrer 11 Reich leader
chief of: **8** SS troops

reign 4 rule **6** govern, regime, regnum, tenure **7** command **8** dominion, hold sway, regnancy, tutelage **9** dominance, influence **10** government, incumbency **11** sovereignty, supervision **12** wear the crown **13** hold authority **14** have royal power, sit on the throne **15** occupy the throne **17** exercise authority **19** exercise sovereignty
Hindu: **3** raj

reign over 4 rule **6** govern **7** command, control **8** dominate

reimburse 5 pay up, remit, repay **6** rebate, refund **7** pay back **8** square up **9** indemnify **10** compensate, recompense, remunerate **15** make restitution

reimbursement 6 refund **9** indemnity, repayment **12** compensation, remuneration

rein, reins 4 curb, hold **5** check, limit, watch **6** bridle **7** control, harness **8**

hold back, restrict, suppress **9** restraint **11** keep an eye on

Reiner, Carl
born: **7** Bronx NY
son: **9** Rob Reiner
roles: **15** Your Show of Shows **21** It's a Mad Mad Mad Mad World
created: **15** Dick Van Dyke Show
director: **5** Oh God **7** The Jerk **8** The Comic **11** Where's Poppa?
novel: **13** Enter Laughing

Reiner, Rob
father: **10** Carl Reiner
roles: **8** Meathead **10** Mike Stivik **14** All in the Family
director of: **6** Misery **9** Stand By Me **11** A Few Good Men **15** This Is Spinal Tap **16** The Princess Bride **17** When Harry Met Sally

reinforce 4 prop **5** steel **7** bolster, brace up, fortify, support **8** buttress **10** strengthen **12** make stronger

reinforcement 4 stay **5** brace, strut **7** bracing, support **10** assistance **11** buttressing **13** strengthening

reinstate 5 renew **6** revive **7** readmit, restore **11** reestablish, reinstitute, reintroduce

reinstatement 7 renewal, revival **11** restoration **13** reinstitution **14** reintroduction **15** reestablishment

reiterate 5 resay **6** hammer, rehash, repeat, retell, reword, stress **7** iterate, reprise, restate **8** rephrase **11** pound away at **12** recapitulate **13** go over and over

reject 4 deny **5** repel, spurn **6** rebuff, refuse **7** castoff, decline, discard, disdain, dismiss, flotsam, repulse, say no to **8** castaway, disallow, shrug off, turn down, turn from **9** repudiate

rejected 6 denied, dumped, jilted **7** cast off, outcast, refused, spurned, unloved **8** disowned, forsaken, lovelorn **9** abandoned, discarded, disproved **10** unaccepted, repudiated **11** invalidated

rejection 6 rebuff **7** disdain, refusal **8** scorning, spurning **9** declining, dismissal, rebuffing, rejecting, ruling out

rejoice 5 exult, glory, revel **6** be glad **7** be happy, delight **8** be elated, jubilate **9** be pleased, celebrate, make merry **10** exhilarate, sing for joy **11** be delighted, be overjoyed **13** be transported

rejoice in 5 eat up, enjoy, savor **6** relish **7** revel in **9** delight in **13** be pleased with, get a kick out of **14** take pleasure in

rejoicing 5 mirth **6** gaiety **7** delight, ecstasy, elation, jollity, jubilee, revelry, triumph **8** cheering, gladness, pleasure, reveling **9** festivity, good cheer, happiness, jubilance, merriment **10** exultation, joyfulness, jubilation, liveliness **11** celebration, merrymaking

rejoin 6 answer, retort **7** respond

rejoinder 5 reply **6** answer, retort, return **7** riposte **8** backtalk, comeback, rebuttal, repartee, response **10** refutation **11** surrebuttal **12** counterblast, remonstrance, surrejoinder **13** countercharge **16** counterstatement

rejuvenate 6 revive **7** restore **8** revivify **9** reanimate **10** revitalize **12** reinvigorate **14** put new life into **17** make youthful again

relapse 4 fall **5** lapse **6** revert, worsen **7** decline, regress, reverse **8** fall back, sink back, slip back, turn back **9** backslide, reversion, worsening **10** degenerate, recurrence, regression, retrogress **11** backsliding, falling back **13** deterioration, retrogression **15** return to illness, turn for the worse

relate 3 say **4** link, tell **5** apply, refer, speak, state, utter **6** attach, belong, convey, detail, impart, recite, report, reveal **7** concern, connect, divulge, narrate, pertain, recount **8** describe, disclose **9** appertain, associate, feel close, make known **10** be relevant **11** communicate, have rapport **12** be responsive, interact well, recapitulate **13** be sympathetic, have reference, particularize **15** feel empathy with, give an account of

related 3 kin **4** akin, said, told **7** kindred, recited **8** narrated, reported **9** recounted **15** of the same family

related by blood 3 kin **4** akin **7** kindred **14** consanguineous, of the same stock **21** having a common ancestor

relation 3 kin, tie **4** bond, link **5** tie-in **6** regard, report **7** account, bearing, concern, kinsman, recital, telling, version **8** relative **9** narrating, narration, narrative, reference, relevance, retelling **10** connection, pertinence, recitation **11** affiliation, application, association, correlation, description **13** applicability, communication **17** interrelationship

relationship 3 kin **5** blood, union **6** affair **7** kindred, kinship, liaison, sibship, society **8** affinity, alliance **10** connection **11** affiliation, association, correlation **13** consanguinity

relative 3 kin **4** clan, kith **5** blood, folks, tribe **6** allied, cousin, family, people **7** cognate, germane, kinfolk, kinsman, related **8** relation, relevant **9** connected, dependent, kinswoman, pertinent, referable **10** affiliated, applicable, associated, comparable, connection, connective, correlated, kith and kin, pertaining, relational, respective **11** appropriate, comparative, correlative, not absolute **12** interrelated **13** flesh and blood **14** interconnected

relax 4 bend, calm, ease, idle, laze, loaf, rest **5** let up, slack **6** be idle, be lazy, ease up, loosen, soften, soothe, unbend, unwind **7** cool off, holiday,

make lax, slacken, take ten **8** decrease, loosen up, take five, vacation **9** lie around **10** take it easy **12** enjoy oneself **13** make less tense **14** make less severe, make less strict

relaxation 3 fun **5** games, hobby, sport **6** repose **7** bending, leisure, pastime **8** pleasure **9** abatement, amusement, avocation, diversion, enjoyment, loosening, remission **10** recreation, slackening **11** refreshment **12** rest from work **13** entertainment

relaxed 3 lax **4** calm, cool, easy, slow, soft **5** loose, slack **6** at ease, casual, gentle, remiss **7** flaccid, lenient **8** informal, laid back, unstrict **9** easygoing, leisurely, negligent, nerveless, unnervous **10** unstrained **11** free and easy, thoughtless
French: **6** degage

relaxed manner 4 ease **5** poise **6** aplomb **9** composure **10** confidence **11** naturalness **12** unconstraint **14** unaffectedness

relay 3 leg **4** race, tour **5** shift **6** length **8** transfer, transmit **9** conductor, regulator, satellite **10** retransmit
cylinder: **5** baton
part: **8** armature, receiver **11** transmitter **13** electromagnet
race: **6** medley **10** track event

release 4 free **5** let go, loose, untie **6** detach, let out, unbind **7** freeing, present, relieve, set free, unloose **8** liberate, set loose, unfasten **9** circulate, discharge, disengage, dismissal, extricate, letting go, releasing **10** distribute, liberating, liberation **11** circulation, communicate, extrication, publication, setting free **12** distribution, emancipation, set at liberty, setting loose

relegate 3 bar **5** eject, expel **6** assign, banish, charge, commit, demote, reject **7** cast out, consign, discard, dismiss, exclude, keep out, shut out **8** delegate

relent 4 bend, melt **5** let up, relax, yield **6** give in, soften, unbend, weaken **7** give way **8** have pity **10** be merciful, capitulate, come around **11** give quarter, grow lenient **12** become milder **14** grow less severe

relentless 4 hard **5** harsh, rigid, stern, stiff **6** severe **7** adamant **8** pitiless, rigorous, ruthless **9** merciless **10** implacable, inexorable, inflexible, unyielding **11** remorseless, undeviating, unrelenting **14** uncompromising

relevance 7 aptness, fitness, meaning **9** propriety **10** pertinence **11** materiality, relatedness, suitability **12** significance **13** applicability **15** appropriateness

relevant 3 apt, fit **6** allied, suited, tied in **7** apropos, bearing, cognate, fitting, germane, related **8** apposite, material, suitable **9** connected, intrinsic, pertinent, referring **10** applicable, associated, concerning, to the point **11** appropriate, significant **12** on the subject, to the purpose

reliable 4 true **5** solid, sound **6** trusty **8** faithful **9** unfailing **10** dependable **11** responsible, trustworthy **12** tried and true **13** conscientious

reliance 5 faith, trust **6** belief, credit **8** credence **9** assurance **10** confidence, dependence

relic 5 scrap, token, trace **7** antique, memento, records, remnant, vestige **8** artifact, fragment, heirloom, keepsake, reminder, souvenir **11** remembrance

relief 4 balm, cure, dole, rest **5** break, cheer **6** remedy **7** anodyne, elation, panacea, respite, welfare **8** antidote, easement, lenitive **9** abatement, reduction **10** mitigation, palliation, palliative **11** alleviation, assuagement, peace of mind **12** amelioration **13** encouragement **16** public assistance **17** welfare assistance
Italian: 7 rilievo

relieve 3 aid **4** calm, ease, free, help, mark **5** abate, allay, cheer, spell **6** assist, let out, pacify, remove, set off, solace, soothe, subdue, succor, temper **7** appease, assuage, break up, comfort, console, lighten, mollify, release, replace, support, take out **8** contrast, mitigate, palliate, reassure **9** alleviate, encourage, interrupt, punctuate **12** free from fear

relieved 5 freed **6** calmed, exempt **7** cheered, excused, solaced **8** consoled **9** comforted, reassured **10** encouraged

religion 4 cult, sect **5** canon, creed, dogma, faith, piety **6** belief, church, homage **7** worship **8** devotion, theology **9** adoration, godliness, reverence **10** devoutness, persuasion, veneration **11** affiliation, belief in God **12** belief in gods, denomination, spirituality **13** system of faith **15** system of worship

religionist 8 believer

religiosity 5 piety **8** devotion **10** fanaticism **15** religious fervor

religious 3 nun **4** holy, monk **5** exact, friar, godly, rigid **6** ardent, devout, divine, priest, sacred **7** devoted, staunch **8** constant, faithful, unerring **9** spiritual, steadfast **10** devotional, fastidious, God-fearing, meticulous, scrupulous, unswerving **11** punctilious, theological, undeviating **12** wholehearted **13** conscientious **14** denominational **15** spiritual-minded

religious belief 5 canon, credo, creed, dogma, tenet **8** doctrine

religious fervor 5 piety **7** ecstasy **8** holiness **9** godliness **10** devoutness **12** religiosity, spirituality

religious group 4 sect **12** denomination

religious orders
   Christian: 6 Jesuit **7** Cluniac, Templar **8** Capuchin, Theatine, Trappist, Ursuline **9** Carmelite, Dominican **10** Carthusian, Cistercian, Franciscan **11** Augustinian, Benedictine, Camaldolite **16** Sisters of Charity **20** Order of the Visitation
   non-Christian: 4 Sufi **7** Jainism **8** Dasanami

relinquish 4 cede, deny, drop, quit, shed **5** forgo, leave, let go, waive, yield **6** forego, give up, resign, vacate **7** abandon, cast off, discard, dismiss, forbear, forsake, release **8** abdicate, break off, disclaim, hand over, lay aside, put aside, renounce, sign away **9** deliver up, repudiate, surrender

relinquishable 9 forgoable **10** expendable, foregoable **11** dispensable **12** renounceable

relinquished 5 ceded, let go **6** gave up **7** forgone, given up, yielded **8** cast away, foregone, forsaken **9** abandoned, given away, renounced **10** left behind

relinquishment 7 cession **8** giving up, yielding **9** letting go, rejection, surrender **10** abnegation **11** repudiation **12** renunciation

relish 3 dig **4** like, love, tang, want, wish, zest **5** enjoy, fancy, gusto, savor, spice, taste **6** accent, desire, dote on, flavor, liking, palate **7** delight, longing, stomach **8** appetite, fondness, groove on, penchant, piquancy, pleasure **9** condiment, delight in, enjoyment, hankering, rejoice in **10** appreciate, ebullience, enthusiasm, exuberance, partiality, propensity **11** luxuriate in **12** appreciation, be crazy about, predilection, satisfaction **13** gratification
   type: 4 beef, corn **5** sweet **7** chutney **6** pickle, tomato **10** chili sauce, piccalilli **11** horseradish

reluctance 10 hesitation **13** unwillingness **14** disinclination

reluctant 3 shy **4** slow **5** loath **6** averse **7** laggard **8** hesitant **9** diffident, unwilling **10** indisposed **11** disinclined

rely 3 bet **4** bank, lean, rest **5** count, swear, trust **6** credit, depend, reckon **7** believe **10** feel sure of **11** be dependent **12** give credence

remain 4 go on, last, stay, wait **5** abide, stand **6** be left, endure, hang on, hold up, linger **7** not move, not stir, persist, prevail, stay put, subsist, survive **8** continue, stand pat **10** be left over, stay behind

remainder 4 rest **5** waste **6** excess, refuse **7** balance, overage, remains, remnant, residue, surplus, wastage **8** leavings, residual, residuum **9**

leftovers, scourings **10** surplusage **11** superfluity

remains 4 body **5** stiff **6** corpse, scraps **7** cadaver **8** dead body **9** leftovers

remark 3 say, see **4** espy, mark, mind, note, view, word **6** behold, look at, notice, regard, survey **7** comment, mention, observe, pay heed **8** perceive **9** attention **10** commentary, give heed to, make note of, reflection, take note of **11** contemplate, observation **12** fix the mind on, say in passing, take notice of **13** consideration **14** pay attention to

remarkable 6 signal **7** notable, unusual **8** singular, striking **9** memorable **10** impressive, noteworthy, phenomenal **11** conspicuous, exceptional, outstanding **13** distinguished, extraordinary, unforgettable

Remarque, Erich Maria
   author of: 25 All Quiet on the Western Front

Rembrandt (Harmensz) van Rijn
   born: 6 Leiden, Leyden **14** The Netherlands
   artwork: 6 Balaam **9** Bathsheba **13** The Night Watch (The Sortie of the Company of Captain Banning Cocq) **14** The Jewish Bride **15** Old Woman Reading, The Bridal Couple **19** The Blinding of Samson **20** Christ Healing the Sick **21** The Stoning of St Stephen **22** Man with the Golden Helmet, Self-Portrait with Saskia, The Descent from the Cross **24** The Anatomy Lesson of Dr Tulp, The Syndics of the Cloth Hall **36** Aristotle Contemplating the Bust of Homer

remedial 7 healing, helpful, mending **8** curative, salutary, sanative **10** beneficial, corrective **11** meliorative, reformative, restorative, therapeutic **12** advantageous, correctional, prophylactic

remedy 3 aid, fix **4** calm, cure, ease, heal, help, mend **5** amend, emend, right **6** relief, repair, soothe **7** assuage, correct, cure-all, improve, mollify, nostrum, panacea, rectify, redress, relieve, restore **8** make easy, medicine, mitigate, palliate, regulate, set right **9** alleviate, make sound, treatment **10** ameliorate, assistance, corrective, make better, medicament, medication, preventive **13** rectification **15** restore to health

remember 3 tip **6** recall, reward **9** not forget, recognize, recollect **10** appreciate, bear in mind, call to mind, have in mind, keep in mind, take care of, take note of **11** bring to mind **12** bear in memory

remember that thou must die
   Latin: 11 memento mori

remembrance 5 favor, relic, token **6** memory, recall **7** memento **8** keepsake, memorial, reminder, souvenir **9** nostalgia **11** recognition, remembering **12** recognizance, recollection, reminiscence **13** commemoration

Remembrance of Things Past
author: **12** Marcel Proust

Remembrance Rock
author: **12** Carl Sandburg

Remick, Lee
born: **8** Quincy MA
roles: **16** Anatomy of a Murder, The Long Hot Summer **18** Days of Wine and Roses

remind 9 put in mind, suggest to **11** bring back to, bring to mind, put in memory **16** awaken memories of

reminder of death
Latin: **11** memento mori

Remington, Frederic Sackrider
born: **8** Canton NY
artwork: **12** Bronco Buster **23** Roping Horses in the Corral **32** Cavalry Charge on the Southern Plains

reminisce 4 mull, muse **6** ponder **7** reflect **8** hark back, look back, remember **9** recollect, think back **12** tell old tales **16** exchange memories, swap remembrances

reminiscent 9 nostalgic, remindful, similar to **11** analogous to, remembering **12** recollecting **13** retrospective

remiss 3 lax **4** idle, lazy, slow **5** loose, slack **6** sloppy **7** laggard, loafing **8** careless, derelict, dilatory, inactive, indolent, slipshod, slothful, uncaring **9** do-nothing, forgetful, negligent, oblivious, shiftless, undutiful, unmindful **10** delinquent, neglectful, unthinking, unwatchful **11** inattentive, indifferent, thoughtless

remission 4 cure **5** lapse, pause **6** hiatus, pardon **7** respite, retreat **8** decrease **9** abatement, acquittal, cessation, reduction, shrinkage **10** absolution, diminution, hesitation, moderation, modulation, subsidence **11** exoneration, forgiveness, vindication

remit 3 pay **4** free, send, ship **5** clear, let go, relax, slack **6** excuse, let out, pardon, reduce **7** absolve, forgive, forward, release, set free, slacken **8** decrease, diminish, dispatch, liberate, make good, moderate, overlook, pass over, transmit **9** discharge, reimburse **10** compensate **11** put to rights **13** send in payment

remnant 3 bit **5** piece, relic, scrap, shred, token, trace **7** discard, remains, residue, vestige **8** fragment, leavings, leftover, monument, residuum, survival **9** remainder **11** odds and ends

remodel 4 redo **5** adapt, alter, fix up **6** change, modify **7** convert, reshape **8** overhaul, renovate **9** refashion, transform **11** recondition

remodeling 6 change **10** alteration,

conversion **12** modification **13** transmutation **14** transformation

remonstrance 6 rebuke **7** censure **8** reproach, scolding **9** criticism, reprimand **10** admonition

remonstrate 5 argue, chide, demur, scold **6** differ, object, rebuke **7** censure, chasten, contend, dispute, dissent, protest, reprove, upbraid **8** admonish, complain, reproach **9** criticize **10** take to task **11** expostulate **13** call to account

remorse 3 rue **4** pang **5** grief, guilt, qualm **6** regret, sorrow **7** anguish **9** penitence **10** contrition, repentance, ruefulness **11** compunction, lamentation, self-reproof **12** self-reproach **13** regretfulness **14** second thoughts

remorseful 8 contrite, penitent **9** chastened, regretful, repentant, sorrowful **10** apologetic **13** grief-stricken **18** conscience-stricken

remote 3 far **4** slim **5** alien, alone, aloof, faint, quiet **6** exotic, far-off, lonely, meager, slight **7** distant, dubious, faraway, foreign, removed, strange **8** detached, doubtful, isolated, secluded, separate, set apart, solitary, unlikely **9** withdrawn **10** far-removed, segregated **11** God-forsaken, implausible, out of the way, sequestered, standoffish

removal 6 moving, ouster **7** doffing **8** deletion, ejection **9** discharge, dismissal, expulsion, taking off, taking out **10** amputation, carting off, cutting away, dislodging, evacuation, lopping off **11** carrying off, chopping off, elimination, transferral **12** cancellation, displacement **14** transportation **15** transplantation

remove 4 doff, drop, fire, move, oust, quit **5** eject, erase, expel, leave, shift **6** cancel, change, cut off, delete, depart, go away, lop off, retire, unseat, vacate **7** blot out, boot out, cart off, chop off, cut away, dismiss, extract, kick out, retreat, take off, take out, wipe out **8** amputate, carry off, dislodge, displace, evacuate, get rid of, sweep out, take away, transfer, withdraw **9** discharge, eliminate, take leave, transport **10** make an exit, transplant

removed 3 off **4** away, took **5** alone, aloof, apart **6** remote **7** distant, faraway **8** abstract, detached, isolated, reticent, secluded **9** alienated, separate, unrelated, withdrawn **10** segregated, unsociable **11** interspaced, standoffish

remove from office 4 oust **6** depose, unseat **9** discharge

remunerate 3 pay **5** award, grant, repay **6** reward **7** requite, satisfy **9** indemnify, reimburse, vouchsafe **10**

compensate, recompense **15** make restitution

remuneration 7 payment **9** repayment **10** recompense, reparation **12** compensation **13** reimbursement **15** indemnification

Remus
father: **4** Mars
mother: **4** Ilia **9** Rea Silvia **10** Rhea Silvia
twin brother: **7** Romulus
raised by: **7** she-wolf

renaissance 7 rebirth, renewal, revival **10** rekindling, renascence, resurgence **11** reawakening, reemergence, restoration **12** regeneration, rejuvenation, resurrection, risorgimento **14** revitalization, revivification **15** reestablishment

rend 3 cut, rip **4** hurt, pain, rive, sear, tear **5** break, crack, sever, split, wound **6** cleave, divide, pierce, sunder **7** afflict, rupture, shatter **8** dissever, fracture, lacerate, polarize, splinter **12** disintegrate, fall to pieces **15** break into pieces

render 2 do **4** cede, give, make, play **5** allot, grant, remit, yield **6** accord, donate, give up, supply, tender **7** deal out, dole out, execute, hand out, pay back, perform, present, requite **8** construe, dispense, fork over, hand over, pay as due, shell out, turn over **9** cause to be, interpret, surrender, translate **10** relinquish **12** give in return, make requital **13** cause to become, make available, make payment of

render impotent 6 defuse, weaken **7** disable, unnerve **8** paralyze **9** undermine **10** devitalize, emasculate

render inoperable 6 damage, impair **7** cripple, disable **12** incapacitate

render null and void 4 void **5** annul **6** cancel, repeal, revoke **7** abolish, nullify, rescind, retract, reverse **8** abrogate, dissolve **10** invalidate

rendezvous 4 date **5** focus, haunt, mecca, tryst **6** gather, muster **7** retreat **8** assemble **9** encounter, tete-a-tete **10** engagement, focal point **11** appointment, assignation, get together **12** meeting place, watering hole **14** gathering place, stamping ground **15** agreement to meet **17** meet by appointment **18** prearranged meeting

rendition 7 edition, reading, version **9** depiction, portrayal, rendering **11** arrangement, performance, translation **14** interpretation

rend the air 3 cry **4** bawl, howl, wail **6** clamor, scream, shriek, squeal **7** screech **9** caterwaul

Renee Mauperin
author: **24** Edmond and Jules de Goncourt

renegade 5 rebel **6** outlaw **7** heretic,

runaway, slacker, traitor **8** apostate, betrayer, defector, deserter, forsaker, fugitive, mutineer, mutinous, quisling, recreant, turncoat **9** dissenter, insurgent **10** backslider, traitorous, treasonist, unfaithful

renege 7 back out, fink out, pull out **8** back down, fall back, withdraw **9** repudiate, weasel out **11** get cold feet **12** turn one's back **13** break a promise, break one's word **16** go back on one's word

renew 4 save **6** extend, pick up, redeem, resume, retain, revive **7** prolong, refresh, restore, salvage **8** continue, maintain **9** make sound, reinstate, sign again **10** begin again, offer again, regenerate, rejuvenate, revitalize **11** reestablish, take up again **12** reinvigorate **16** put back into shape

renewal 7 revival **9** extension **10** redemption **11** restoration **12** regeneration **13** reinstatement **14** revitalization

Renoir, Pierre-Auguste
born: 6 France **7** Limoges
artwork: 4 Lise **6** La Loge **10** The Bathers **12** Margot Berard, The Umbrellas **14** La Grenouillere **19** Le Moulin de la Galette **28** Mme Charpentier and Her Children, The Luncheon of the Boating Party

renounce 4 cede, deny, quit **5** forgo, waive **6** abjure, disown, eschew, forego, give up, recant, reject, resign **7** abandon, cast off, disavow, discard, dismiss **8** abdicate, abnegate, abrogate, disclaim, forswear, lay aside, part with, put aside, turn from, write off **9** cast aside, foreswear, repudiate **10** relinquish **13** give up claim to **15** wash one's hands of

renovate 3 fix **4** mend **6** remake, repair, revamp **7** improve, remodel, restore **8** make over **9** modernize, refurbish **10** redecorate

renown 4 fame, mark, note **6** repute, status **7** acclaim **8** eminence **9** celebrity, notoriety **10** popularity, prominence, reputation **11** distinction

renowned 5 famed, noted **6** famous **7** eminent, notable, popular **9** acclaimed, prominent, well-known **10** celebrated, noteworthy **11** outstanding **13** distinguished

rent 3 fee, gap, let, rip **4** dues, gash, hire, hole, rift, slit, tear **5** break, chasm, chink, cleft, crack, lease, split **6** breach, hiatus, rental, schism, tatter, wrench **7** charter, fissure, opening, payment, rent out, rupture **8** cleavage, crevasse, division, fracture **11** buy the use of **12** sell the use of

rente 6 income **7** revenue **12** annual income

rentier 21 one who has a fixed income

renunciation 6 denial **7** refusal **8** for-

going, spurning **9** disavowal, eschewing, foregoing, rejection, repulsion **10** abjuration, renouncing **11** abandonment, disclaiming, forswearing, repudiation **12** foreswearing **14** relinquishment

Renwick, James, Jr
architect of: 8 Main Hall (Vassar College) **11** Grace Church (NYC) **15** Corcoran Gallery (now Renwick Gallery, Washington, DC) **19** St Patrick's Cathedral (NYC) **22** Smithsonian Institution (Washington DC)
style: 13 Gothic Revival

reopen 7 restart **8** begin anew, reconvene, start anew **10** recommence, reinitiate **11** reestablish, reinstitute **12** reinaugurate

repair 2 go **3** fix **4** mend, move **5** amend, emend, patch, renew, shape, state **6** fixing, remedy, remove, retire **7** correct, mending, patch up, rebuild, rectify, redress, restore **8** make good, overhaul, patching, set right, withdraw **9** condition, make up for, refurbish, repairing **10** rebuilding **11** recondition **12** refurbishing **14** reconditioning

reparation 6 amends, return **7** damages, redress **8** requital **9** quittance **10** recompense **11** restitution **12** compensation, satisfaction **13** peace offering

repartee 6 banter, bon mot **7** riposte **8** badinage, chit chat, word play **10** persiflage, witty reply **11** witty retort **12** pleasantries **14** snappy comeback

repast 4 food, meal **5** board, feast, snack, table **6** spread **7** banquet **8** victuals **9** provision **11** nourishment, refreshment

repay 5 match **6** refund, return, reward **7** pay back, requite **9** get back at, indemnify, pay in kind, reimburse **10** recompense, remunerate **11** get even with, reciprocate **12** make requital **14** give in exchange, make a return for **15** make restitution, make retribution **19** return the compliment

repayment 10 paying back, recompense **12** compensation **13** reimbursement **17** making restitution

repeal 4 void **5** annul **6** cancel, revoke **7** abolish, nullify, rescind, voiding **8** abrogate, set aside **9** abolition, annulment **10** abrogation, invalidate, revocation **11** termination **12** cancellation, invalidation **13** nullification **18** declare null and void

repeat 4 echo, redo, tell **5** mimic, quote, rerun **6** pass on, recite, relate, retell **7** imitate, recount, restate, retread, say over **8** say again **9** duplicate, reiterate, reproduce **10** repetition **11** duplication, reiteration **12** perform again

repeated exercises 4 rote **5** drill **8** practice, training

repel 4 foil, rout **5** check **6** dispel, offend, oppose, put off, rebuff, resist, revolt, sicken **7** deflect, disgust, fend off, forfend, hold off, keep off, keep out, repulse, scatter, turn off, ward off **8** alienate, beat back, disperse, nauseate, push back, stave off, throw off **9** chase away, drive away, drive back, force back, frustrate, keep at bay, withstand

repellent 5 proof **9** abhorrent, loathsome, offensive, repelling, repugnant, repulsive, resisting, revolting, sickening **10** disgusting, nauseating **11** distasteful, impermeable

repent 3 rue **6** bemoan, bewail, lament, regret, repine **7** deplore **8** mea culpa, weep over **9** be ashamed **10** be contrite, be penitent **11** be regretful, feel remorse

repentance 5 grief, guilt **6** regret, sorrow **7** remorse **9** penitence **10** contrition **11** compunction **12** self-reproach **16** self-condemnation **17** pangs of conscience

repercussion 4 echo **6** effect, result **8** backlash, reaction **10** concussion, side effect **11** aftereffect, consequence **13** reverberation **15** boomerang effect

repetition 6 repeat **9** iteration, retelling **11** reiteration, restatement **14** recapitulation

repetitious 5 wordy **6** prolix **8** repeated **9** redundant **10** repetitive

Repin, Ilya Efimovich
born: 6 Russia **8** Chugeyev
artwork: 15 The Volga Boatmen **18** Zaporozhye Cossacks **19** They Did Not Expect Him **26** Ivan the Terrible Kills His Son

replace 5 spell **6** return **7** put back, restore, succeed **8** supplant **9** supersede

replaceable 10 disposable, expendable **11** dispensable

replenish 5 renew **6** refill, reload **7** refresh, reorder, replace, restock, restore

replenished 7 renewed **8** refilled, replaced, restored **9** restocked

replenishment 7 renewal **9** refilling **10** restocking **11** replacement, restoration

replete 4 full **5** sated **6** gorged, loaded **7** crammed, fraught, stuffed, teeming **8** brimming, satiated **9** abounding, jam-packed, surfeited **11** well-stocked

repletion 4 glut **6** excess **7** surfeit, surplus **9** abundance, plenitude, profusion, satiation **11** sufficiency

replica 4 copy **5** model **6** double **8** likeness **9** duplicate, facsimile, imitation **12** reproduction

reply 5 react **6** answer, rejoin, retort **7** counter, respond **8** reaction, response **9** rejoinder **14** acknowledgment

reply if you please
French: **4** rsvp **20** repondez s'il vous plait

reply to 6 answer **7** counter, react to **8** retort to **9** respond to **11** acknowledge

repondez s'il vous plait 11 please reply **16** reply if you please
abbreviation: **4** rsvp

report 4 bang, boom, note, talk, tell, word **5** crack, noise, rumor, sound, state, story **6** appear, detail, expose, gossip, recite, record, relate, reveal, show up, tell on **7** account, article, check in, divulge, hearsay, message, missive, recount, summary, version, write-up **8** announce, denounce, describe, disclose, dispatch, relation **9** discharge, narration **10** communique, detonation, memorandum **11** communicate, description, information
French: **11** compte rendu

reporter 7 newshen, newsman **8** newshawk **9** anchorman, announcer, columnist, newshound, newswoman **10** journalist, newscaster **11** commentator **12** newspaperman **13** correspondent **14** newspaperwoman

repose 3 lie **4** calm, ease, rest **5** quiet, relax **6** be calm, settle **7** leisure, recline, respite **8** quietude **10** inactivity, quiescence, relaxation **11** tranquility **12** peacefulness, tranquillity

repository 5 depot **8** magazine **9** warehouse **10** storehouse

reprehend 5 decry **7** censure, condemn, reprove **8** denounce, reproach **9** criticize **10** disapprove

reprehensible 3 bad **4** base, evil, foul, vile **6** guilty, wicked **7** heinous, ignoble **8** blamable, culpable, infamous, shameful, unworthy **9** nefarious **10** censurable, despicable, villainous **11** blameworthy, condemnable, disgraceful, inexcusable, opprobrious **12** unpardonable **13** objectionable, unjustifiable

reprehension 6 rebuke **7** censure, reproof **8** reproach **9** criticism **11** disapproval **12** condemnation, denunciation **14** disapprobation

represent 2 be **4** mean, show **5** enact, equal, state **6** denote, depict, pose as, sketch, typify **7** betoken, express, outline, picture, portray, present, serve as **8** appear as, describe, indicate, stand for **9** delineate, designate, symbolize **10** illustrate **11** emblematize, impersonate **12** characterize

representation 5 image **6** effigy, emblem, symbol **7** epitome, essence, picture **8** likeness **9** depiction, portrayal **10** embodiment **12** illustration **15** exemplification **16** characterization

representative 2 MP **3** rep **5** agent, envoy, proxy **6** deputy, varied **7** deputed, elected, proctor, typical **8** balanced, delegate, elective, emissary, symbolic **9** delegated, exemplary, spokesman, surrogate, typifying **10** delegatory, democratic, denotative, emblematic, legislator, mouthpiece, republican, substitute, symbolical **11** assemblyman, congressman, delineative, descriptive **12** exemplifying, illustrative **13** assemblywoman, congresswoman **14** characteristic, crosssectional

repress 4 curb, hide, mask, veil **5** box up, check, cloak, cover, crush, pen up, quash, quell **6** hold in, muffle, shut up, squash, stifle, subdue **7** conceal, control, inhibit, put down, silence, smother, squelch **8** bottle up, hold back, keep down, restrain, strangle, suppress

repression 8 muffling **9** holding in, restraint, retention **10** inhibition, throttling **11** concealment, holding back, suppression

reprieve 4 lull, stay **5** delay, pause **6** pardon, parole **7** amnesty, respite **8** breather **9** remission **10** moratorium, suspension **11** adjournment **12** postponement **14** breathing spell

reprimand 4 trim **5** chide, scold **6** berate, rail at, rebuff, rebuke, revile **7** censure, chew out, chiding, lecture, obloquy, tell off, upbraid **8** admonish, berating, chastise, denounce, reproach, reproval, scolding, take down, trimming **9** castigate, criticism, criticize, disparage, dispraise, dress down, reprehend, reprobate **10** admonition, chewing out, opprobrium, take to task, upbraiding **11** castigation **12** admonishment, denunciation, dressing down, remonstrance **13** disparagement **16** rap on the knuckles

reprisal 7 redress, revenge **8** requital **9** tit for tat, vengeance **11** counterblow, retaliation, retribution **13** counterattack **16** counteroffensive
Latin: **10** quid pro quo

reproach 4 blot, slur, spot **5** blame, chide, scold, shame, stain, taint **6** charge, insult, malign, rail at, rebuke, revile, stigma, tirade, vilify **7** asperse, blemish, censure, condemn, offense, reproof, reprove, scandal, tarnish, upbraid **8** admonish, denounce, diatribe, disgrace, dishonor, scolding **9** castigate, criticism, criticize, discredit, disparage, indignity, reprimand **10** stigmatize, take to task, tongue-lash, upbraiding **11** degradation, humiliation **12** remonstrance **13** call to account, embarrassment

reprobate 3 bad, low **4** base, evil, rake, roue, vile **5** scamp **6** pariah, rascal, rotter, sinner, wanton, wicked **7** corrupt, outcast **8** castaway, depraved, derelict, evildoer, prodigal, rakehell **9** abandoned, dissolute, miscreant, shameless, wrongdoer **10** black sheep, degenerate, immoralist, profligate, voluptuary **11** rapscallion, untouchable **12** incorrigible, transgressor, wicked person

reproduce 4 copy, redo, sire **5** beget, breed, match, spawn **6** mirror, repeat, re-echo **7** imitate, reflect **8** generate, multiply **9** duplicate, procreate, propagate, replicate, represent **11** counterfeit, proliferate

reproduction 4 copy **7** replica **8** breeding, likeness **9** duplicate, facsimile, imitation **10** carbon copy, generation, simulation **11** procreation, propagation **13** progeneration, proliferation **14** multiplication, representation
goddess of: **7** Astarte

reproductive system
component: **5** penis **6** testes, uterus, vagina **7** ovaries

reproof 5 blame **6** rebuke **7** censure, chiding **8** reproach, scolding **9** criticism, reprimand **10** admonition **12** condemnation, dressing-down, remonstrance

reprovable 7 at fault **8** blamable, culpable **10** censurable **11** blameworthy **12** reproachable

reprove 5 chide, scold **6** rebuke **7** censure, chasten **8** admonish, reproach **9** castigate, reprimand

reptile 3 asp, eft **4** newt, teju **5** agama, anole, gecko, skink, snake, viper **6** dragon, iguana, lizard, mugger, turtle **7** crawler, creeper, serpent, tuatara **8** basilisk, dinosaur, groveler, terrapin, tortoise **9** alligator, chameleon, crocodile, pterosaur **10** salamander, vertebrate **11** Gila monster, pterodactyl

republic 9 democracy
Latin: **10** res publica

Republic
author: **5** Plato

Republican Party
also called: **3** GOP **13** Grand Old Party
president belonging to: **4** Bush, Ford, Taft **5** Grant, Hayes, Nixon **6** Arthur, Hoover, Reagan **7** Harding, Lincoln, (Andrew) Johnson **8** Coolidge, Garfield, Harrison, McKinley **9** (Theodore) Roosevelt **10** Eisenhower
symbol: **8** elephant

Republic of China see **6** Taiwan

repudiate 4 deny, void **5** annul **6** cancel, desert, disown, reject, repeal, revoke **7** abandon, abolish, cast off, disavow, discard, forsake, nullify, protest, rescind, retract, reverse **8** abrogate, disclaim, dissolve, renounce

repudiation 6 denial **9** disavowal, rejection **10** abrogation, disclaimer, retraction

repugnance 4 hate **5** odium **6** hatred **7** disgust **8** aversion, loathing **9** antipathy, revulsion **10** abhorrence **11** abomination, detestation

repugnant 4 foul, vile 5 nasty 6 odious 7 adverse, counter, hateful, opposed 8 contrary, unsavory 9 abhorrent, loathsome, obnoxious, offensive, repellent, repulsive, revolting, sickening 10 abominable, detestable, disgusting, nauseating, unpleasant 11 distasteful, uncongenial, undesirable, unpalatable 12 antipathetic, disagreeable, insufferable, unacceptable, unappetizing 13 objectionable

repulse 4 shun 5 avoid, repel, spurn 6 ignore, rebuff, refuse, reject 7 refusal 8 shunning, spurning 9 rejection

repulsion 6 hatred 7 disgust, dislike 8 aversion, distaste, loathing 9 antipathy 10 abhorrence, repugnance 11 abomination, detestation 13 indisposition 14 disinclination

repulsive 4 vile 5 nasty 6 odious 7 hateful 9 abhorrent, loathsome, obnoxious, offensive, repellent, repugnant, revolting 10 abominable, detestable, disgusting, nauseating 11 distasteful 12 disagreeable 13 objectionable

repulsiveness 8 ugliness 13 loathsomeness, offensiveness 14 disgustingness, unpleasantness 16 disagreeableness

reputable 7 honored 8 esteemed, reliable 9 respected 10 creditable 11 respectable, trustworthy

reputation 4 name 7 stature 8 standing

repute 3 say 4 deem, fame, hold, view 5 judge, think 6 esteem, reckon, regard, renown 7 account, believe, suppose 8 consider, estimate, standing 9 celebrity, notoriety 10 prominence 14 respectability

request 3 ask 4 seek 6 ask for, bid for, desire, sue for 7 call for, entreat, solicit 8 petition 9 importune 11 application 12 solicitation

requiem 5 dirge 6 lament 8 threnody

requiescat in pace 11 rest in peace 16 may he rest in peace 17 may she rest in peace

require 3 bid 4 lack, miss, need, want 5 crave, imply, order 6 charge, compel, desire, direct, enjoin, entail, oblige 7 command, dictate 9 constrain 11 necessitate

required 6 forced, needed 7 obliged 9 compelled, essential, necessary 10 compulsory, imperative, obligatory

requirement 4 must 8 standard 9 criterion, essential, guideline, requisite 12 prerequisite 13 specification **Latin:** 10 sine qua non 11 desideratum

requisite 4 must, need 6 needed 8 required 9 essential, mandatory, necessary, necessity 10 compulsory, imperative, obligatory 11 requirement 12 prerequisite 13 indispensable

Latin: 10 sine qua non 11 desideratum

requisition 4 form 7 request 11 application

requital 7 redress 9 repayment 11 retaliation 12 compensation 15 indemnification

rescind 4 void 5 annul, quash 6 cancel, recall, repeal, revoke 7 abolish, discard, nullify, retract, reverse 8 abrogate, dissolve, override, overrule 10 invalidate 11 countermand 12 counterorder

rescinding 6 recall 7 voiding 8 recision 9 abolition 10 abrogation, retraction, revocation 11 abolishment, dissolution 12 cancellation, invalidation 13 nullification

rescue 4 save 6 ransom, saving 7 deliver, freeing, recover, release, salvage 8 liberate, recovery 9 extricate 10 liberation 11 deliverance, extrication

research 5 probe, study 7 delving, inquiry 8 analysis, scrutiny 10 inspection 11 examination, exploration, factfinding, investigate, scholarship 13 investigation

resemblance 7 analogy 8 affinity, likeness, parallel 10 congruence, similarity, similitude 14 correspondence

resemble 5 favor 6 be like 8 be akin to, look like, parallel 9 take after

resent 7 dislike

resentful 5 angry 6 bitter 7 annoyed 8 grudging, offended, provoked 10 displeased 12 dissatisfied

resentfulness 5 anger, spite 10 bitterness 15 dissatisfaction

resentment 3 ire 4 huff 5 anger, pique, spite 6 animus, malice, rancor 7 dudgeon, ill will, offense, umbrage 8 acerbity, acrimony, asperity, jealousy, soreness, sourness 9 animosity, crossness 10 bitterness, irritation 11 displeasure, indignation 12 irritability, vengefulness 14 vindictiveness

reservation 4 date 5 doubt 7 booking, proviso, scruple, strings 8 preserve 9 condition, hesitancy, provision 10 encampment, reluctance, settlement 11 appointment, compunction, stipulation, uncertainty 12 installation 13 accommodation, establishment, qualification 14 prearrangement

reserve 4 book, hold, keep, save 5 amass, delay, extra, hoard, lay up, spare, stock, table 6 backup, engage, retain, shelve, unused 7 husband, nest egg, savings 8 conserve, keep back, postpone, preserve, salt away, schedule, withhold 9 aloofness, reticence, stockpile 10 additional, prearrange

reserved 5 aloof, taken 6 booked, formal 7 distant, engaged 8 bespoken, retained, reticent, strained, unsocial 9 inhibited, spoken for 10 restrained, unsociable 11 ceremonious, constrained, standoffish 12 unresponsive 15 uncommunicative, undemonstrative

reservoir 4 fund, pool, tank, well 5 basin, fount, hoard, stock, store 6 supply 7 backlog, cistern 8 millpond 9 container, stockpile 10 depository, receptacle, repository 12 accumulation

res gestae 5 deeds 10 things done 15 accomplishments

reshape 4 redo 5 adapt, alter, block 6 change, modify, reform, remold, rework 7 convert, reframe, remodel 9 refashion, transform

reside 3 lie 4 live, rest, room 5 dwell, exist, lodge 6 belong, occupy 7 inhabit, sojourn 8 domicile

residence 3 pad 4 digs, flat, home, room, stay 5 abode, house, place 7 address, lodging, sojourn 8 domicile, dwelling, quarters 9 apartment, homestead, household 10 habitation **French:** 10 pied a terre

resident 5 local 6 lodger, tenant 7 citizen, denizen, dweller 8 occupant, townsman 9 sojourner 10 inhabitant 11 housekeeper

residual 5 extra 7 abiding, lasting, surplus 8 enduring, leftover 9 lingering, remaining 10 continuing 13 supplementary

residue 4 rest 5 dregs 6 scraps 7 balance, remains, remnant 8 leavings 9 remainder

resign 4 quit 5 leave 6 give up, submit 8 abdicate, disclaim, renounce 9 reconcile 10 relinquish

resignation 8 fatalism, patience, quitting, stoicism 9 departure 10 equanimity, retirement, submission, withdrawal 11 passiveness 12 acquiescence 13 nonresistance 14 submissiveness

resign oneself 5 yield 6 submit 9 acquiesce

resilience 6 recoil 7 rebound 8 buoyancy 10 elasticity 11 flexibility 12 adaptability 13 changeability, nonuniformity 16 lightheartedness

resilient 5 hardy 6 supple 7 buoyant, elastic, rubbery, springy 8 flexible 9 adaptable, expansive, resistant, tenacious 10 rebounding, responsive 13 irrepressible

resin 3 gum, lac, tar 5 amber, copal, elemi, epoxy, jalap, myrrh, pitch, rosin 6 balsam, guaiac, mastic 7 galipot, lacquer, shellac

resist 4 balk, foil, stem, stop 5 fight, repel 6 baffle, combat, oppose, refuse, reject, thwart 7 contest, counter, weather 8 beat back, turn down 9 frustrate, withstand 10 counteract

resistance 6 mutiny, rebuff 7 refusal 8

defiance, struggle **9** obstinacy, rebellion, rejection **10** contention, insurgency, opposition **11** obstruction **12** insurrection **13** intransigence, noncompliance, recalcitrance

resolute 5 stern **6** dogged, steady **7** earnest, staunch, zealous **8** decisive, diligent, intrepid, stubborn, untiring, vigorous **9** assiduous, obstinate, purposive, steadfast, tenacious, unbending **10** deliberate, determined, inflexible, persistent, relentless, unflagging, unswerving, unwavering, unyielding **11** industrious, persevering, undeviating, unfaltering, unflinching **12** pertinacious, strong-minded, strong-willed **13** indefatigable **14** uncompromising

resoluteness 7 purpose, resolve **8** decision, tenacity **11** decidedness, persistence **12** decisiveness, perseverance **13** determination, steadfastness **14** purposefulness

resolution 3 aim **4** goal, plan, zeal **6** design, energy, intent, mettle, motion, object, spirit **7** promise, purpose, resolve **8** ambition, proposal, solution, tenacity **9** constancy, intention, objective, resolving, stability **10** resilience, steadiness **11** earnestness, persistence **12** perseverance, resoluteness **13** determination, steadfastness **14** aggressiveness **16** indefatigability

resolve 4 plan **6** answer, decide, design, intend, set out, settle, vote on **7** adjudge, clear up, explain, purpose **8** decision **9** determine, elucidate **10** commitment, resolution **12** resoluteness **13** determination **14** make up one's mind

resonant 4 full, rich **7** booming, orotund, ringing, vibrant **8** sonorous **9** bellowing **10** resounding, stentorian, thunderous **11** reverberant

resort 3 use **4** hope **5** apply, avail **6** chance, employ, take up **7** utilize **8** exercise, recourse **9** expedient

resound 4 echo, peal, ring **5** clang **6** re-echo **7** vibrate **11** reverberate **14** tintinnabulate

resounding 7 echoing, ringing **9** re-echoing **10** thundering, thunderous **13** reverberating

resource 8 recourse **9** expedient **11** wherewithal

resourceful 4 able **5** ready, sharp, smart **6** adroit, artful, bright, shrewd **7** capable, cunning **8** creative, original, skillful, talented **9** competent, effectual, ingenious, inventive **10** innovative, proficient **11** imaginative **12** enterprising

resourcefulness 9 ingenuity **10** creativity, enterprise **13** inventiveness

resources 5 funds, means, money **6** assets, income **7** capital, effects, revenue **10** belongings, collateral **11** possessions, wherewithal

respect 5 honor, point, sense **6** detail, esteem, matter, notice, praise, regard **7** bearing, feature, viewing **8** approval, courtesy, relation **9** affection, attention, deference, laudation, reference, relevance, reverence **10** admiration, connection, particular, veneration **11** point of view, recognition **12** appreciation, circumstance **13** consideration

respectability 7 decency, decorum **9** gentility, propriety **11** correctness, genteelness

respectable 4 fair **5** ample, civil, noble **6** decent, honest, polite, proper, worthy **7** correct, courtly, passing, refined, upright **8** becoming, decorous, moderate, polished **9** admirable, dignified, estimable, honorable, reputable **10** aboveboard, admissible, sufficient **11** presentable **12** considerable, praiseworthy, satisfactory

respected 6 valued, worthy **7** admired, honored, revered **8** esteemed **9** admirable, venerated

respectful 5 civil **6** formal, genial, polite **7** amiable, winning **8** admiring, decorous, gracious, mannerly, obliging, reverent **9** attentive, courteous, regardful **10** personable, solicitous **11** ceremonious, deferential, reverential **13** accommodating

respects 4 heed, obey **5** honor, prize, value **6** admire, esteem, fealty, follow, regard, revere **7** abide by, cherish, defer to, observe, regards, tribute **8** adhere to, consider, venerate **9** greetings **10** appreciate, understand **11** acknowledge, compliments **12** remembrances **13** consideration

Respighi, Ottorino
born: 5 Italy **7** Bologna
composer of: 8 La Fiamma, The Birds **14** The Pines of Rome **18** The Fountains of Rome **19** La Boutique Fantasque, The Fantastic Toyshop **27** Ancient Airs and Dances for Lute

respiration 9 breathing

respiratory system
component: 4 lung, nose **6** larynx **7** pharynx, trachea **8** voice box, windpipe **9** bronchius, diaphragm
action: 9 breathing

respire 7 breathe

respite 4 lull **5** break, delay, letup, pause **6** recess **8** reprieve **9** extension **12** intermission

resplendence 6 dazzle, luster **7** glitter **8** lambency, radiance **10** brilliance, luminosity, refulgence **12** circumstance, magnificence

resplendent 6 bright **7** beaming, blazing, glowing, lambent, radiant **8** dazzling, gleaming, luminous, lustrous, splendid **9** brilliant, refulgent, sparkling **10** glittering **11** coruscating

respond 5 react, reply **6** answer, rejoin **7** speak up **9** recognize **11** acknowledge

respond to 6 answer **7** act upon, react to, reply to **8** thank for **11** acknowledge

response 5 reply **6** answer, retort, return **7** riposte **8** comeback, feedback, reaction, rebuttal **9** rejoinder **10** impression **13** countercharge **14** acknowledgment **16** counterstatement

responsibility 4 duty, task **5** blame, order, trust **6** burden, charge **8** function **9** liability **10** obligation **11** culpability, reliability **13** answerability, dependability **14** accountability **15** trustworthiness

responsible 5 adult, of age **6** guilty, liable, mature **7** at fault, capable **8** culpable, reliable **9** demanding, executive, important **10** answerable, creditable, dependable **11** accountable, challenging, trustworthy **13** conscientious **14** administrative

responsive 5 alive, awake, sharp **8** reactive **9** receptive, sensitive **11** retaliative, retaliatory, susceptible, sympathetic **13** compassionate, understanding **14** impressionable

responsiveness 6 action **7** concern **8** interest **9** attention, awareness **11** sensitivity **13** understanding

res publica 8 republic, the state **12** commonwealth, public matter

rest 2 be **3** end, lay, lie, nap, set **4** base, ease, halt, hang, keep, laze, lean, loaf, loll, lull, prop, rely, stay, stop **5** break, death, exist, hinge, let up, pause, peace, place, quiet, relax, sleep, stand **6** demise, depend, holder, lounge, others, recess, remain, repose, reside, scraps, siesta, snooze, trivet **7** balance, be based, be found, be quiet, decease, deposit, holiday, leisure, lie down, recline, remains, remnant, residue, respite, set down, slumber, support **8** breather, platform, vacation **9** cessation, departure, leftovers, remainder, stillness **10** complement, quiet spell, relaxation, standstill, suspension **11** hibernation, take time out **12** intermission, interruption **13** take a breather
Latin: 8 residuum

restaurant 5 diner **6** eatery **7** beanery, tearoom **9** cafeteria, chophouse, grillroom, hashhouse, lunchroom **11** coffeehouse **12** luncheonette
French: 4 cafe **6** bistro **9** brasserie
German: 11 rathskeller

restful 4 calm **5** quiet **6** placid, serene **7** pacific, relaxed **8** peaceful, soothing, tranquil **10** unagitated **11** comfortable, undisturbed

restfulness 4 ease **5** quiet **6** repose **8** serenity, softness **10** relaxation **11** tranquility **12** tranquillity

rest in peace
Latin: **16** requiescat in pace

restitution 6 amends **7** redress, replevy **8** replevin, requital, restoral **9** atonement, indemnity, repayment **10** recompense, reparation **11** restoration **12** compensation, remuneration, satisfaction **13** reimbursement, reinstatement **15** indemnification

restive 5 balky **6** mulish, ornery, unruly **7** fidgety, wayward, willful **8** contrary, stubborn **9** fractious, pigheaded **10** rebellious, refractory **11** disobedient, intractable **12** recalcitrant, unmanageable

restless 5 awake, jumpy **6** fitful, uneasy **7** anxious, fidgety, fretful, jittery, nervous, on the go, unquiet, wakeful, worried **8** agitated **9** excitable, impatient, incessant, insomniac, on the move, sleepless, transient, unsettled **10** disquieted, highstrung **11** hyperactive **13** uncomfortable

restoration 7 revival **8** recovery **12** recuperation **13** convalescence, reinstatement **14** rehabilitation, reintroduction, reinvigoration **15** reestablishment

restorative 5 tonic **6** elixir **7** bracing, healing **8** curative **10** beneficial, energizing, fortifying **11** revivifying **12** invigorating, revitalizing **13** strengthening

restore 3 fix **4** cure, dose, heal, mend **5** rally, renew, treat **6** do over, recoup, remedy, repair, rescue, return, revive **7** convert, get back, patch up, put back, rebuild, reclaim, recover, refresh, remodel, retouch, touch up **8** energize, give back, make over, make well, medicate, renovate, retrieve, revivify, recreate **9** reanimate, refurbish, reinstall, reinstate, stimulate **10** exhilarate, revitalize, strengthen **11** recondition, reconstruct, reestablish, reinstitute, resuscitate **12** rehabilitate, reinvigorate

restored 4 kept **5** saved **7** revived **8** replaced **9** conserved, pressured **11** replenished **13** rehabilitated

restrain 3 gag **4** bind, curb, hold, stop **5** check, leash, limit **6** arrest, bridle, fetter, muzzle, pinion, temper, tether **7** chasten, contain, curtail, harness, inhibit, prevent, shackle, trammel **8** handicap, hold back, restrict, suppress, withhold

restrained 4 cool **5** aloof **6** curbed **7** checked, distant **8** held back, reined in, reserved **10** controlled, unfriendly

restraint 4 curb **5** check **7** control **10** limitation

restrict 4 curb, hold **5** check, cramp, crimp, hem in, limit **6** hamper, impede, narrow, thwart **7** confine, inhibit, prevent, squelch **8** hold back,

obstruct, straiten, suppress **9** constrain, frustrate **12** circumscribe

restricted 7 cramped, limited **8** confined, hampered, held back **9** exclusive **10** suppressed **13** circumscribed

restriction 4 rule **7** control, curbing, proviso **9** condition, provision **10** limitation, regulation **11** requirement, reservation, stipulation **13** consideration, qualification

restrictive 8 limiting **9** confining, exclusive **12** constraining

result 4 stem **5** arise, end up, ensue, fruit, issue, owe to **6** derive, effect, happen, pan out, report, sequel, spring, upshot, wind up **7** finding, opinion, outcome, product, turn out, verdict **8** decision, judgment, reaction, solution **9** aftermath, culminate, eventuate, originate, outgrowth **10** resolution **11** aftereffect, consequence, development, eventuality **13** determination

resume 2 CV **3** bio **4** go on **5** brief **6** digest **7** epitome, proceed, summary **8** abstract, continue, reembark, synopsis **9** biography, summation **10** abridgment, recommence **11** reestablish **12** condensation
Latin: **15** curriculum vitae
French: **6** precis

resumption 11 recommenced, restoration **12** continuation

resurgam 15 I shall rise again

resurgence 6 return **7** rebirth, renewal, revival **10** renascence **11** reemergence, renaissance **12** rejuvenation **13** recrudescence

ret 4 soak **6** dampen

retailer 5 store **6** dealer, seller, trader **8** merchant, provider, supplier **9** tradesman **10** wholesaler **11** distributor, storekeeper, tradeswoman **12** merchandiser
French: **9** vivandier **10** vivandiere

retain 4 hold, keep **5** grasp **6** absorb, recall **7** possess **8** hang on to, hold on to, maintain, memorize, remember **9** recollect

retainer 7 servant **8** employee **9** attendant

retainership 4 hire **6** employ **7** service **10** employment

retaliate 5 repay **6** avenge, pay off, return **7** counter, pay back, requite, revenge **11** reciprocate

retaliation 6 talion **7** deserts, revenge **8** reprisal, requital **9** vengeance **10** recompense **11** comeuppance, eye for an eye, interchange, just deserts, lex talionis, retribution **12** compensation **13** reciprocation **14** tooth for a tooth

retard 4 clog, drag **5** block, brake, check, delay **6** arrest, baffle, detain, fetter, hamper, hinder, hold up, impede, slow up **7** draw out, inhibit,

prevent, prolong, slacken **8** hold back, obstruct, slow down **10** decelerate

retarded 4 dull, slow **6** simple **7** idiotic, moronic, unsound **8** backward, disabled **9** imbecilic, mongoloid, subnormal **10** slow-witted **11** handicapped **12** simpleminded

reticent 3 shy **5** quiet **6** closed, silent **7** subdued **8** reserved, retiring, taciturn **9** diffident, withdrawn **10** restrained **11** tight-lipped **12** closemouthed **15** uncommunicative

retinue 5 court, staff, suite, train **6** convoy **9** courtiers, employees, entourage, followers, following, personnel, retainers **10** associates, attendance, attendants

retire 6 depart, go away, remove, resign, resort, secede, turn in **7** drop out, retreat **8** abdicate, flake out, withdraw

retired
French: **8** ci-devant

retiring 3 shy **4** meek **5** quiet, timid **6** demure, humble, modest **7** bashful **8** reserved, reticent, sheepish, timorous, unsocial **9** diffident, shrinking, withdrawn **10** unassuming **11** unassertive **12** self-effacing **13** inconspicuous, unpretentious **15** uncommunicative

retort 3 say **4** quip **5** rebut, reply **6** answer, rejoin, return **7** counter, respond, riposte **8** fire back, rebuttal **9** rejoinder

retract 4 deny **6** abjure, disown, draw in, recall, recant, recede, recoil, reel in, repeal, revoke **7** disavow, rescind, retreat, reverse **8** abnegate, abrogate, disclaim, draw back, forswear, peel back, pull back, renounce, take back, withdraw **9** foreswear, repudiate

retraction 6 recall **8** recision **9** disavowal **10** disclaimer, refutation, withdrawal

retreat 2 go **3** den **4** bolt, flee, port **5** haunt, haven, leave **6** asylum, depart, escape, flight, harbor, recoil, refuge, resort, retire, shrink **7** abscond, getaway, privacy, sanctum, shelter, shy away **8** back away, draw back, fall back, hideaway, move back, solitude, turn tail, withdraw **9** departure, isolation, reclusion, sanctuary, seclusion **10** evacuation, immurement, retirement, withdrawal **11** hibernation, rustication

retrench 5 slash **6** reduce, scrape, scrimp **7** curtail, cut back, cut down **8** conserve, cut costs **9** economize **15** tighten one's belt

retribution 6 amends, return, reward **7** justice, nemesis, penalty, redress, revenge **8** reprisal, requital **9** vengeance **10** punishment, recompense, reparation **11** just deserts, restitution, retaliation, vindication **12** satisfaction **13** reciprocation, recrimination

retrieve 4 snag 5 fetch 6 ransom, recoup, redeem, regain, rescue 7 get back, reclaim, recover, salvage 9 recapture, repossess

retriever
dog breed: 5 Irish 6 golden, Gordon 7 English 8 Labrador 10 flat-coated 11 curly-coated 13 Chesapeake Bay

retrograde 5 worse 6 worsen 7 inverse, retreat, reverse 8 backward 10 regressive 13 retrogressive

retrogress 6 worsen 9 backslide

retrogression 7 decline, setback 9 worsening 11 backsliding

retrogressive 8 backward 9 declining, worsening 11 backsliding

retrospect 6 review 9 flashback, hindsight 11 remembrance 12 afterthought, reminiscence 15 reconsideration

return 3 net 4 earn, gain 5 gross, recur, repay, yield 6 advent, come to, go back, income, profit, render, reseat, reward 7 arrival, benefit, produce, provide, put back, requite, restore, revenue 8 announce, come back, earnings, give back, hand down, interest, proceeds, reappear, recovery, restoral, send back 9 advantage, reinstall, reinstate, retrieval, reversion 10 homecoming, recurrence 11 reciprocate, reestablish, restoration 12 compensation, reappearance 13 reinstatement 15 reestablishment

Return of the Native
author: 11 Thomas Hardy
character: 11 Diggory Venn, Eustacia Vye 12 Damon Wildeve 13 Clym Yeobright 17 Thomasin Yeobright

Reuben
father: 5 Jacob
mother: 4 Leah
brother: 3 Dan, Gad 4 Levi 5 Asher, Judah 6 Joseph, Simeon 7 Zebulun 8 Benjamin, Issachar, Naphtali
sister: 5 Dinah
descendant of: 9 Reubenite

Reuben sandwich
ingredient: 3 rye 8 dressing 10 corned beef, sauerkraut 11 Swiss cheese

reunite 5 rewed 7 remarry 9 reconcile

reveal 4 bare, show 6 betray, expose, impart, let out, unfold, unmask, unveil 7 display, divulge, exhibit, give out, lay bare, publish, uncover, unearth 8 disclose, evidence, manifest, point out

revealed 4 open 5 clear, known 7 evident, obvious 8 manifest

revel 4 romp 5 caper, enjoy 6 bask in, frolic, gambol, relish 7 carouse, delight, indulge, rejoice, roister, skylark 8 wallow in 9 celebrate

revelation 6 expose, vision 7 shocker 8 exposure, prophecy 9 admission, bombshell, discovery, eyeopener, unveiling 10 apocalypse, confession, disclosure, divulgence 11 divulgation, divulgement

revelatory 10 expressive 11 informative 13 communicative

reveler 6 barfly, ranter, player 7 drinker 8 bacchant, carouser, drunkard 9 roisterer, rollicker, skylarker 10 merrymaker

revelry 5 spree 7 jollity 8 carnival, carousal, festival, jamboree 9 high jinks, merriment, rejoicing 10 exultation, roistering 11 celebrating, celebration, merrymaking 12 conviviality 13 jollification 14 boisterousness
god of: 5 Comus

revenge 5 repay 7 pay back, requite 8 reprisal, requital 9 repayment, retaliate, vengeance, vindicate 10 recompense 11 eye for an eye, reciprocate, retaliation, retribution 12 satisfaction

revenue 3 pay 4 take 5 gains, wages, yield 6 income, profit, return, salary 7 annuity, pension, subsidy 8 earnings, interest, pickings, proceeds, receipts 9 allowance, emolument 12 compensation, remuneration

revenue, annual
French: 5 rente

reverberate 4 boom, echo, ring 5 carry 6 rumble 7 resound, thunder, vibrate

reverberation 4 boom, echo 6 rumble 7 ringing, thunder 8 rumbling 9 vibration 10 resounding, thundering

revere 5 honor 6 esteem 7 defer to, respect 8 venerate

revered 6 adored 7 admired, honored 9 estimable, respected, venerated, worshiped 10 worshipped

reverence 3 awe 4 fear 5 honor, piety 6 esteem, homage, regard 7 respect, worship 8 devotion 9 adoration, deference 10 admiration, devoutness, observance, veneration 11 prostration, religiosity 12 genuflection

reverent 4 pure 5 pious 6 devout, humble, solemn 7 adoring, awesome, devoted 8 faithful 9 religious, spiritual 10 respectful, worshipful

reverential 4 awed 10 respectful, worshipful 11 deferential

reverie 5 dream, fancy 6 musing 7 fantasy 8 daydream 9 dreamland, quixotism 10 brown study, meditation 12 extravagance 13 woolgathering 14 fantasticality

reverse 4 back, rear, tail, undo, void 5 annul, upend, upset 6 cancel, change, defeat, invert, mishap, negate, recall, recant, repeal, revoke, unmake, upturn 7 counter, failure, nullify, rescind, retract, setback, trouble 8 abrogate, backward, contrary, converse, hardship, inverted, opposite, override, overrule, set aside, turn over, withdraw 9 adversity, mischance, posterior, transpose 10 antithesis, invalidate, misfortune 11 countermand, counterpart, frustration 14 disappointment

revert 5 lapse 6 go back, repeat, return 7 regress, relapse 9 backslide 10 recidivate, retrogress

review 4 show 5 study, sum up 6 notice, parade, rehash, survey 7 analyze, journal, retrace, run over 8 critique, evaluate, hash over, magazine, reassess, report on, scrutiny 9 criticism, criticize, reexamine, reiterate, summarize 10 commentary, evaluation, exhibition, exposition, procession, reconsider, reevaluate, reflection, scrutinize 11 examination 12 presentation, reassessment, recapitulate, reevaluation 13 demonstration, retrospection 14 recapitulation 15 reconsideration
French: 11 compte rendu

revile 4 slur 5 abuse, curse, scold, scorn 6 berate, defame, deride, malign, rebuke, vilify 7 bawl out, chew out, slander, upbraid 8 belittle, denounce, execrate, reproach, sail into 9 blaspheme, castigate, denigrate, disparage 10 vituperate

reviler 6 critic, curser 8 vilifier 9 backbiter, slanderer 10 blasphemer

revise 4 edit, redo 5 alter, amend, emend, fix up 6 change, doctor, modify, recast, redact, revamp, review, update 7 correct, rectify, rewrite 8 emendate, overhaul

revision 6 change 7 edition 9 amendment, recension 10 alteration, correction, emendation 11 improvement 12 modification

revival 7 renewal 11 restoration 13 reinstatement, reinstitution, resuscitation

revive 5 dig up, renew 6 drag up, repeat 7 freshen, refresh, restage 8 reawaken 9 reanimate, reproduce, resurrect 11 resuscitate

revived 7 renewed 8 animated, repeated, restaged 9 enlivened, freshened, refreshed 10 reanimated, reawakened, reproduced 11 invigorated, resurrected 12 resuscitated

revocation 6 repeal 8 recision 9 abolition, annulment 10 abrogation, retraction 11 abolishment, elimination, repudiation 12 cancellation 13 nullification

revoke 4 void 5 annul, erase, quash 6 abjure, cancel, negate, recall, repeal, vacate 7 abolish, dismiss, expunge, nullify, rescind, retract, reverse 8 abrogate, call back, disallow, disclaim, override, overrule, renounce, set aside, take back, withdraw 9 repudiate 10 invalidate 11 countermand

revolt 4 coup, rise 5 rebel, repel,

shock **6** appall, mutiny, offend, rise up, sicken **7** disgust, dissent, horrify, repulse **8** disorder, distress, nauseate, sedition, uprising **9** rebellion **10** insurgency, opposition, **12** factiousness, insurrection
   German: 6 Putsch

revolting 4 foul, grim, vile **5** nasty **6** horrid, odious **7** hateful, noisome, noxious **8** dreadful, horrible, horrific, shocking, stinking **9** abhorrent, appalling, frightful, invidious, loathsome, obnoxious, offensive, repellent, repugnant, repulsive, sickening **10** abominable, disgusting, malodorous, nauseating **11** distasteful **12** disagreeable **13** objectionable

revolution 6 mutiny, revolt, rising **8** circling, gyration, rotation, uprising **9** rebellion **12** insurrection **14** circumrotation, circumvolution
   French: 4 coup **9** coup d'etat
   German: 6 Putsch

revolutionary 7 radical **8** mutinous **9** extremist, insurgent, seditious **10** dissenting, rebellious, subversive **13** superadvanced, unprecedented **15** insurrectionary

revolve 4 spin, turn **5** twist, wheel **6** circle, gyrate, rotate **12** circumrotate

revolver 3 gat, gun, rod **4** colt **6** pistol, weapon **7** firearm, handgun, rotator, sidearm **10** six-shooter **20** Saturday night special

revulsion 8 aversion, distaste, loathing **10** abhorrence, repugnance **11** detestation

reward 3 due **5** bonus, prize, repay, wages **6** bounty **7** deserts, guerdon, payment, premium, requite **9** reckoning **10** compensate, recompense, remunerate **12** compensation, remuneration **13** consideration
   Latin: 10 quid pro quo

rewarding 8 pleasant, valuable **9** enjoyable **10** delightful, gratifying, satisfying **11** pleasurable

rework 4 redo **5** adapt, alter **6** modify **7** remodel, reshape **9** refashion, transform

rex 4 king

Reykjavik
   capital of: 7 Iceland

Reynolds, Burt
   born: 10 Waycross GA
   wife: 9 Judy Carne **12** Loni Anderson
   roles: 4 Bean **6** Shamus **9** Dan August, Semi-Tough, The Player **10** Striptease **11** Cop-and-a-half, Deliverance **12** Boogie Nights **14** The Longest Yard **18** Smokey and the Bandit

Reynolds, Debbie
   real name: 19 Mary Frances Reynolds
   born: 8 El Paso TX
   husband: 11 Eddie Fisher
   roles: 13 The Singing Nun, The Tender Trap **15** Singin' in the Rain **19**

Tammy and the Bachelor **23** The Unsinkable Molly Brown

Reynolds, Sir Joshua
   born: 7 England **8** Plympton
   artwork: 14 Lord Heathfield, Miss Jane Bowles **15** Commodore Keppel **18** Mrs Francis Beckford **21** Mrs Abington as Miss Prue **25** Mrs Siddons as the Tragic Muse **38** Lady Sarah Bunbury Sacrificing to the Graces

Rhadamanthus, Rhadamanthys
   father: 4 Zeus
   mother: 6 Europa
   brother: 5 Minos **6** Aeacus **8** Sarpedon
   became a judge in: 5 Hades

rhapsodic 6 elated **7** beaming, excited **8** blissful, ecstatic, thrilled **9** delirious, overjoyed, rapturous **11** exhilarated, transported

Rhea
   member of: 6 Titans
   father: 6 Uranus
   mother: 4 Gaea
   brother: 6 Cronos, Cronus, Kronos
   husband: 6 Cronos, Cronus, Kronos
   son: 4 Zeus **5** Hades **8** Poseidon
   daughter: 4 Hera **6** Hestia **7** Demeter
   called: 10 Magna Mater
   corresponds to: 3 Ops **6** Cybele **9** Dindymene **10** Berecyntia
   epithet: 6 Antaea

Rhea Silvia
   form: 12 vestal virgin
   lover: 4 Mars
   son: 5 Remus **7** Romulus

Rheingold *see* **Ring des Nibelungen, Der**

Rhesus
   owned: 6 horses
   horses captured by: 8 Diomedes, Odysseus

rhetoric 4 bunk, wind **5** hokum, hooey **6** bunkum, hot air **7** fustian, oratory **8** euphuism **9** discourse, elocution, eloquence, hyperbole **10** hocus-pocus **11** flamboyance **13** magniloquence **14** grandiloquence

Rhetoric
   author: 9 Aristotle

rhetorical 5 showy, windy **6** florid, ornate, purple, verbal **7** aureate, flowery **8** eloquent, inflated **9** bombastic, grandiose, highflown, stylistic **10** decorative, discursive, euphuistic, expressive, flamboyant, linguistic, oratorical, ornamental **11** disputative, embellished, extravagant **12** disputatious, elocutionary, magniloquent **13** argumentative, grandiloquent

Rhoda
   character: 8 Gary Levy **9** Joe Gerard **12** Benny Goodwin **14** Ida Morgenstern, Sally Gallagher **17** Brenda Morgenstern, Martin Morgenstern **22** Rhoda Morgenstern Gerard
   cast: 9 Anne Meara, David Groh, Ron

Silver **11** Julie Kavner, Nancy Walker **12** Harold J Gould, Ray Buktenica **13** Valerie Harper

Rhode Island
   abbreviation: 2 RI
   nickname: 11 Little Rhody
   capital/largest city: 10 Providence
   others: 7 Bristol, Newport **8** Cranston, Kingston, Westerly **9** Pawtucket, Wakefield **10** Woonsocket
   college: 5 Brown **6** Bryant **8** Pembroke **10** Barrington, Providence **11** Salve Regina **13** Mount St Joseph, Roger Williams **15** Johnson and Wales, Naval War College
   feature: 7 Newport
   tribe: 7 Niantic **9** Wampanoag **12** Narragansett
   people: 8 Puritans **12** George M Cohan **13** Gilbert Stuart, Matthew C Perry, Roger Williams **15** Ambrose Burnside, Nathanael Greene **17** Oliver Hazard Perry
   island: 5 Block, Rhode **8** Prudence **9** Aquidneck, Conanicut
   lake: 8 Scituate
   pond: 7 Wordens **8** Stafford, Watchaug
   land rank: 8 fiftieth
   mountain: 10 Durfee Hill
      highest point: 12 Jerimoth Hill
   physical feature:
      bay: 12 Narragansett
      sea: 8 Atlantic
      sound: 11 Block Island
   river: 7 Seekonk **8** Pawtuxet **9** Pawcatuck, Pawtucket, Potowomut **10** Blackstone, Providence
   state admission: 10 thirteenth
   state bird: 14 Rhode Island Red
   state flower: 6 violet
   state motto: 4 Hope
   state song: 11 Rhode Island
   state tree: 8 red maple

Rhodesia *see* **8** Zimbabwe

rhodium
   chemical symbol: 2 Rh

rhododendron
   varieties: 4 tree **5** Bluet **6** Indian, Yunnan **7** catawba, fringed, Lapland, silvery, Smirnow **8** Carolina, Chapman's, Fortune's, Fujiyama, piedmont **9** Caucasian, honey-bell, West Coast **11** leather-leaf **12** willow-leaved

rhodolite
   species: 6 garnet

rhubarb 5 Rheum **16** Rheum rhabarbarum
   varieties: 4 wild **5** monk's **6** garden, Sikkim **7** spinach **8** mountain

rhyme 3 pun **4** poem, rune, song **5** chime, clink, meter, poesy, verse **6** jingle, poetry, rhythm **7** measure, poetize, versify **8** assonate, doggerel **10** consonance **12** alliteration
   game: 6 crambo

rhymer, rhymester 4 bard, poet **6** writer **8** minstrel, poetizer **9** poetaster, versifier **10** troubadour

Rhys, Jean
   author of: 7 Quartet **15** Voyage in the Dark, Wide Sargasso Sea

rhythm 4 beat, lilt, time **5** meter, pulse, swing, throb **6** accent, number, stress **7** cadence, measure **8** emphasis, movement **9** pulsation **10** recurrence **11** fluctuation, syncopation **12** accentuation

riant 3 gay **4** airy **5** jolly, merry **6** blithe, bright, jocund, jovial **7** smiling **8** cheer- ful, laughing, mirthful

rib 3 kid, rag **4** bait, bone, josh **5** chaff, costa, jolly, tease

ribald 4 lewd, racy, rude **5** bawdy, crude, gross **6** coarse, earthy, rakish, risque, vulgar, wanton **7** raffish, uncouth **8** improper, indecent, off-color, prurient, shocking **9** salacious, unrefined **10** lascivious, libidinous, licentious, suggestive

ribbon 3 bow, ray **4** band, sash **5** award, braid, prize, reins, strip **6** cordon, riband **7** binding, rosette **8** memorial, streamer **10** decoration

rice 5 Oryza **11** Oryza sativa
   varieties: 4 wild **6** Indian, pampas **7** basmati **8** mountain **9** Tennessee **10** annual wild
   dish: 5 grits, pilaf, pilau **7** pudding, risotto **8** porridge **9** jambalaya
   liquor: 4 sake

Rice, Anne
   lives: 10 New Orleans
   character: 6 Lestat **7** vampire
   author of: 11 Cry to Heaven **16** The Vampire Lestat **19** The Queen of the Damned **23** Interview with the Vampire

Rice, Elmer
   author of: 11 Street Scene **16** The Adding Machine

rich 4 dark, deep, fine, lush **5** flush, heavy, loamy, sweet, vivid **6** bright, costly, fecund, lavish, mellow **7** fertile, filling, intense, moneyed, opulent, wealthy, well-off **8** abundant, affluent, fruitful, in clover, precious, prodigal, resonant, sonorous, splendid, valuable, well-to-do **9** abounding, estimable, expensive, luxuriant, luxurious, priceless, sumptuous **10** euphonious, productive, propertied, prosperous **11** mellifluous **12** on easy street

Richard, Maurice
   nickname: 6 Rocket
   sport: 6 hockey
   position: 7 forward
   team: 17 Montreal Canadiens

Richard Cory
   author: 22 Edwin Arlington Robinson

Richard Diamond, Private Detective
   character: 3 Sam **6** Lt Kile **9** Lt Mc-

Gough **10** Karen Wells
   cast: 10 Russ Conway **11** Barbara Bain, Regis Toomey **12** David Janssen **13** Roxanne Brooks **14** Mary Tyler Moore
   viewers saw only Sam's: 4 legs

Richard I 11 Coeur de Lion, Lion-Hearted
   father: 7 Henry II
   mother: 7 Eleanor (of Aquitaine)
   brother: 4 John

Richard II
   author: 18 William Shakespeare
   character: 11 John of Gaunt **13** Edmund Langley, Thomas Mowbray **16** Henry Bolingbroke **20** Earl of Northumberland
   Duke of: 4 York **7** Aumerle, Norfolk **8** Hereford **9** Lancaster

Richard III
   author: 18 William Shakespeare
   character: 6 George **7** Richard **8** Edward IV, Lady Anne **10** Henry Tudor (Earl of Richmond) **11** Lord Stanley **12** Lord Hastings **13** Queen Margaret **14** Queen Elizabeth **15** Edward the Fourth **17** Sir William Catesby **19** Edward Prince of Wales
   Duke of: 4 York **8** Clarence **10** Buckingham, Gloucester

Richardson, Joely
   parents: 14 Tony Richardson **15** Vanessa Redgrave
   sister: 7 Natasha
   roles: 12 Event Horizon **13** 101 Dalmatians **14** Shining Through **17** Drowning By Numbers

Richardson, Henry Hobson
   architect of: 9 Sever Hall (Harvard) **11** Grace Church (West Medford MA) **13** Trinity Church (Boston) **23** State Asylum for the Insane (Buffalo NY) **27** Marshall Field Wholesale Store (Chicago)

Richardson, Natasha
   parents: 14 Tony Richardson **15** Vanessa Redgrave
   sister: 5 Joely
   roles: 11 Patty Hearst **12** The Handmaid's Tale **23** Every Picture Tells a Story

Richardson, Samuel
   author of: 6 Pamela (or Virtue Rewarded) **8** Clarissa (Harlowe) **19** Sir Charles Grandison

Richardson, Sir Ralph
   born: 7 England **10** Cheltenham
   roles: 6 Exodus **10** Oscar Wilde, Richard III, The Heiress **11** A Doll's House **12** Anna Karenina **13** Doctor Zhivago **15** Richard the Third **20** Little Lord Fauntleroy **24** Long Day's Journey into Night **26** Greystoke The Legend of Tarzan

Richardson, Tony
   wife: 15 Vanessa Redgrave
   daughter: 5 Joely **7** Natasha

   director of: 7 Blue Sky **8** Tom Jones (Oscar) **14** The Entertainer **15** Look Back in Anger **36** The Loneliness of the Long Distance Runner

riches 4 pelf **5** lucre, means **6** assets, mammon, wealth **7** fortune **8** opulence, treasure **9** resources **10** prosperity **11** possessions

richness 6 wealth **8** fullness, lushness, opulence **9** amplitude, intensity **10** lavishness, mellowness **12** completeness **13** luxuriousness

Richter, Charles Francis
   field: 10 geophysics, seismology
   developed: 12 Richter scale **24** measurement of earthquakes

rickety 4 weak **5** frail, shaky **6** feeble, flimsy, infirm, wasted, weakly, wobbly **7** fragile **8** decrepit, unsteady, withered **9** tottering **10** brokendown, tumbledown **11** debilitated, dilapidated, weakjointed **12** deteriorated

rid 4 free **5** clear, purge **6** remove **8** disabuse, liberate, unburden **9** disburden, eliminate **11** disencumber

Ridd, John
   character in: 10 Lorna Doone
   author: 9 Blackmore

riddance 6 ouster, relief **7** freeing, removal **8** ejection **9** clearance, expulsion **11** deliverance, dislodgment

riddle 5 poser, rebus **6** enigma, puzzle, secret **7** mystery, problem, puzzler, stumper **9** conundrum

ride 4 move **5** annoy, carry, drive, harry, hound **6** badger, handle, harass, hector, manage, needle, travel **7** control, journey, support **8** progress **9** transport

rider 5 affix **6** suffix **7** adjunct, codicil **8** addendum, addition, appendix **9** amendment, appendage **10** attachment, supplement

ridge 3 bar, rib, rim **4** bank, fret, hill, hump, rise, wale, weal, welt **5** bluff, crest, crimp, knoll, mound, spine **6** ripple **7** crinkle, hillock, wrinkle **10** promontory **11** corrugation

ridicule 3 guy, rib **4** gibe, jeer, josh, mock, razz, ride, twit **5** mimic, scorn, taunt, tease **6** deride, gibe at, parody **7** lampoon, laugh at, mockery, ribbing, sarcasm, scoff at, sneer at, snicker, teasing **8** belittle, derision, sneering, travesty **9** aspersion, burlesque, disparage, humiliate, make fun of, poke fun at **10** caricature, derogation, lampoonery **13** disparagement
   god of: 5 Momos, Momus

ridiculous 3 odd **5** crazy, droll, funny, inane, nutty, queer, silly **6** absurd, screwy **7** amusing, asinine, bizarre, comical, fatuous, foolish, idiotic **8** farcical **9** fantastic, frivolous, grotesque, laughable, ludicrous, screwball, senseless **10** hysterical, incredible, irrational, outlandish **11** astonishing, nonsensical **12** preposterous, unreasonable

Rienzi
   author: 18 Edward Bulwer-Lytton
   composer: 6 Wagner

Riesling, Paul
   character in: 7 Babbitt
   author: 5 Lewis

rife 5 close, dense, solid, thick **6** common, packed **7** crowded, general, studded, teeming **8** epidemic, pandemic, populous, swarming **9** chockfull, extensive, plumbfull, prevalent, universal **10** prevailing, widespread **11** predominant

riffraff 3 mob **4** herd, scum **5** crowd, dregs, trash **6** masses, proles, rabble, vermin **9** peasantry **10** commonalty **11** proletariat
   French: 8 canaille

rifle 3 rob **4** loot, sack **6** ravage **7** despoil, pillage, plunder, ransack **8** spoliate **10** burglarize

rifle, repeating
   invented by: 7 Spencer

Rifleman, The
   character: 10 Lou Mallory, Mark McCain **11** Lucas McCain **14** Miss Milly Scott **20** Marshal Micah Torrance
   cast: 7 Paul Fix **10** Joan Taylor **12** Chuck Connors **13** Patricia Blair **14** Johnny Crawford
   setting: 9 New Mexico, North Fork

rift 3 cut, gap **4** gash, gulf, rent, slit **5** abyss, break, chasm, chink, cleft, crack, fault, gorge, gulch, gully, split **6** breach, cranny, ravine **7** breakup, crevice, fissure, quarrel, rupture **8** aperture, crevasse, division, fracture **12** disagreement **16** misunderstanding

rig 4 gear **5** equip **6** fit out, outfit **8** carriage **9** apparatus, equipment, machinery

Riga *see* **Latvia**

Rigaud
   character in: 12 Little Dorrit
   author: 7 Dickens

Rigg, Diana
   born: 7 England **9** Doncaster
   title: 4 Dame
   roles: 6 Helena **8** Emma Peel **10** Bleak House **11** Lady Dedlock, The Avengers **12** Julius Caesar **21** A Midsummer Night's Dream **26** On Her Majesty's Secret Service

right 2 OK **3** due **4** deed, fair, good, just, meet, nice, real, sane, true, well **5** amend, emend, exact, grant, honor, ideal, legal, licit, moral, power, solve, sound, valid **6** actual, at once, decent, honest, lawful, morals, normal, proper, remedy, seemly, square, virtue **7** certain, correct, ethical, exactly, factual, fitting, freedom, genuine, liberty, license, perfect, precise, probity, redress, regular, standup, warrant **8** accurate, becoming, clear-cut, definite,

directly, goodness, morality, promptly, properly, rational, sanction, straight, suitable, suitably, truthful, virtuous **9** allowable, authentic, authority, correctly, desirable, equitable, exemplary, favorable, favorably, honorable, integrity, nobleness, opportune, ownership, perfectly, precisely, presently, privilege, propriety, rectitude, veracious, veridical, vindicate **10** aboveboard, accurately, admissible, completely, convenient, infallible, legitimate, permission, preferable, reasonable, recompense, scrupulous, undisputed, unmistaken **11** inheritance, immediately, irrefutable, prerogative, punctilious **12** advantageous, jurisdiction, satisfactory **13** appropriately, authorization, incontestable, justification, unimpeachable **14** proprietorship, satisfactorily, unquestionable
   Latin: 3 jus

right beside 6 next to **8** abutting, adjacent, touching

righteous 4 fair, good, holy, just **5** godly, moral, pious **6** chaste, devout, honest **7** ethical **8** elevated, innocent, reverent, virtuous **9** blameless, equitable, honorable, incorrupt, religious, spiritual, unsullied

righteousness
   goddess of: 4 Maat

righteous person
   Hebrew: 6 zaddik

rightful 3 due **4** just, true **5** legal, valid **6** lawful, proper **7** allowed, condign, correct, fitting, merited **8** deserved **9** deserving, equitable **10** authorized, designated, legitimate, prescribed, sanctioned **11** appropriate, inalienable **14** constitutional

right hand 4 aide, ally **6** helper **7** partner **8** adjutant **9** assistant
   French: 10 aide-de-camp

right of blood
   Latin: 12 jus sanguinis

right of soil/land
   Latin: 7 jus soli

Right People, The
   author: 17 Stephen Birmingham

right side up 7 upright **10** on one's feet

Right Stuff, The
   director: 13 Philip Kaufman
   author: 8 Tom Wolfe
   cast: 8 Ed Harris **10** Sam Shepard
   Oscar for: 5 score

right-wing 7 old-line **10** nonliberal **11** reactionary **12** conservative **14** nonprogressive

right-winger 8 rightist **11** reactionary **12** conservative

rigid 3 set **4** firm, hard, taut **5** fixed, harsh, sharp, stern, stiff, tense **6** formal, severe, strict, strong, wooden **7** austere **8** exacting, obdurate, rigorous, stubborn, unpliant **9** inelastic, strin-

gent, unbending **10** inflexible, unyielding **11** puritanical, unrelenting **14** uncompromising

Rigoletto
   opera by: 5 Verdi
   character: 5 Gilda **9** Maddalena **11** Sparafucile **12** Duke of Mantua **15** Countess Ceprano **16** Count of Monterone

rigorous 5 exact, harsh, stern, tough **6** severe, strict, trying **7** austere, correct, precise **8** accurate, exacting **9** demanding, stringent **10** meticulous, scrupulous **11** challenging, punctilious

rig out 4 garb **5** array, dress **6** attire, clothe

rile 3 irk, vex **4** gall, miff, roil **5** anger, annoy, chafe, gripe, peeve, pique **6** bother, enrage, nettle, offend, plague **7** incense, inflame, provoke **8** irritate **9** aggravate, infuriate

Riley, James Whitcomb
   called: 11 Hoosier poet
   author of: 18 Little Orphant Annie **25** When the Frost Is on the Punkin

rilievo 6 relief

Rilke, Rainer Maria
   author of: 11 Book of Hours **12** Duino Elegies, Life and Songs **13** Divine Elegies **16** Sonnets to Orpheus **19** Letters to a Young Poet

rill 5 brook, cleft, creek **6** furrow, groove, runnel, stream **7** channel, rivulet **9** streamlet

rim 3 lip **4** edge, side **5** brink, ledge, verge **6** border, margin **9** outer edge

Rimbaud, Arthur
   born: 6 France
   author of: 12 Le Bateau Ivre **13** A Season in Hell **14** The Drunken Boat **16** Les Illuminations **17** Sonnet of the Vowels

rime 3 ice **4** hoar **5** chink, cleft, crack, crust, frost **7** crevice, fissure **9** hoarfrost

Rime of the Ancient Mariner, The
   author: 21 Samuel Taylor Coleridge
   character: 6 Hermit **9** Albatross **12** Wedding Guest **14** Ancient Mariner

Rimsky-Korsakov, Nikolai (Nicholas)
   born: 6 Russia **8** Novgorod
   member of: 7 The Five
   composer of: 5 Mlada, Sadko **6** Kitezh **10** Night in May, Snow Maiden, Tzar Saltan **11** Sheherazade **12** Christmas Eve, Scheherazade **16** Spanish Capriccio **17** Capriccio Espagnol, The Golden Cockerel **21** Russian Easter Overture **29** Russian Easter Festival Overture

rind 4 bark, hull, husk, peel, skin **5** crust, shell **6** cortex, fringe **7** epicarp, surface **8** exterior
   pork: 9 crackling

ring 4 aura, band, bloc, buzz, call,

echo, gang, hoop, loop, peal, toll, tone **5** cabal, chime, clang, knell, party, sound **6** cartel, circle, cordon, herald, jangle, jingle, league, signal, strike, summon, tinkle **7** besiege, circuit, combine, enclose, quality, resound, seal off, vibrate **8** announce, blockade, encircle, proclaim, striking, surround **9** broadcast, encompass, perimeter, resonance, syndicate, ting-a-ling, vibration **10** federation **11** reverberate **12** circumscribe **13** circumference, reverberation **14** tintinnabulate **16** tintinnabulation

Ring and the Book, The
    author: **14** Robert Browning

Ring des Nibelungen, Der
    also: **12** The Ring Cycle **20** The Ring of the Nibelung(s)
    opera by: **6** Wagner
    part one: **12** Das Rheingold, The Rhine Gold
    part two: **10** Die Walkure **11** The Valkyrie
    part three: **9** Siegfried
    part four: **15** Gotterdammerung **17** Twilight of the Gods
    character: **4** Erda, Mime **5** Freia, Hagen, Wotan **6** Fafner, Fasolt **7** Gunther, Gutrune, Hunding **8** Alberich, Siegmund **9** Siegfried, Sieglinde, Valkyries **10** Brunnhilde

ringleader 5 chief **6** master **10** mastermind

ringlet 4 curl **6** circle

ring-shaped 5 round **8** circular

Rin Tin Tin, The Adventures of
    character: **5** Rusty, (Cpl) Boone **9** (Sgt) Biff O'Hara (Lt) Rip Masters
    cast: **8** Lee Aaker **9** Joe Sawyer **10** James Brown, Rand Brooks

Rio Bravo
    director: **11** Howard Hawks
    cast: **8** Ward Bond **9** John Wayne **10** Dean Martin **11** Ricky Nelson **13** Walter Brennan **14** Angie Dickinson

Rio de Janeiro
    airport: **6** Galeao
    architect: **5** Costa, Reidy **8** Niemeyer
    area: **4** Caju, Lapa **6** Catete, Gamboa, Gloria, Grajau, Tijuca **7** Catumbi, Ipanema **8** Botafogo **10** Copacabana, Vila Isabel **12** Sao Cristovao
    bay: **8** Botafogo, Jurujuba **9** Guanabara
    bridge: **11** Costa e Silva
    celebration: **8** Carnival **9** Mardi Gras
    discovered by: **6** Coelho
    former capital of: **6** Brazil
    island: **10** Governador
    lake: **16** Rodrigo de Freitas
    landmark: **10** Candelaria **14** Mount Corcovado **15** Maracana Stadium **17** Sugarloaf Mountain
        statue of: **17** Christ the Redeemer
    means: **14** river of January
    ocean: **8** Atlantic

    people: **8** Cariocas
    replaced as capital by: **8** Brasilia
    slums: **7** favelas
    suburb: **7** Niteroi

riot 4 rage **5** act up, arise, melee, rebel **6** fracas, mutiny, resist, revolt, rumpus, strife, tumult, uproar **7** rampage, run amok, trouble, turmoil **8** disorder, outburst, uprising, violence **9** commotion, confusion, rebellion **10** Donnybrook, turbulence **11** lawlessness, pandemonium **12** insurrection

rioting 6 tumult, uproar **7** turmoil **8** disorder, outbreak, violence **9** commotion **11** disturbance

riotous 4 loud, wild **5** arroar, noisy, randy **6** stormy, unruly, wanton **7** bacchic, rampant, violent **8** bacchian **9** debauched, dissolute, insurgent, plentiful, tumultuous, turbulent **10** boisterous, dissipated, licentious, rebellious **11** intemperate, overcopious **12** unrestrained **13** superabundant **15** insurrectionary
    party: **4** orgy

rip 3 cut, gap **4** rend, rent, rift, rive, slit, tear **5** burst, sever, shred, slash, split **6** cleave **7** fissure, rupture **8** cleavage, cut apart, fracture, incision, tear open **10** laceration

ripe 3 due, fit **4** come **5** ideal, ready **6** mature, mellow, primed, timely **7** perfect **8** complete, finished, seasoned **9** maturated **10** consummate **12** accomplished

ripen 3 age **4** grow **5** bloom, fruit **6** flower, mature, mellow **7** develop

Rip Kirby
    creator: **11** Alex Raymond **12** John Prentice

Ripley, Robert L
    author of: **14** Believe It or Not

Rip Van Winkle
    author: **16** Washington Irving

rise 4 bank, defy, dune, face, gain, go up, grow, hill, lift, meet, soar **5** climb, get up, knoll, march, mount, rebel, ridge, spire, stand, surge, swell, tower **6** ascend, growth, mutiny, resist, revolt, rocket, strike, thrive **7** advance, balloon, burgeon, disobey, elevate, headway, improve, prosper, stand up, succeed, upswing **8** addition, flourish, increase, progress **9** expansion, extension **10** embankment **11** advancement, enlargement

Rise and Fall of the Third Reich, The
    author: **14** William L Shirer

Rise of Silas Lapham, The
    author: **18** William Dean Howells
    character: **5** Irene **8** Mr Rogers, Penelope, Tom Corey **9** Mrs Lapham

risible 4 rich **5** comic, droll, funny, merry, silly, witty **6** absurd, jocose, jovial **7** amusing, comical, jocular **8** farcical, humorous, mirthful **9** face-

tious, laughable, ludicrous, whimsical **10** ridiculous **11** nonsensical

rising sun
    god of: **5** Janus

risk 4 dare **5** peril **6** chance, danger, gamble, hazard **7** imperil, venture **8** endanger, jeopardy **9** speculate **10** jeopardize **11** imperilment, speculation, uncertainty **12** endangerment

risky 6 chancy, daring, unsafe **8** insecure, perilous, ticklish **9** dangerous, daredevil, haphazard, hazardous, hit or miss, uncertain **10** precarious **11** adventurous, unprotected, venturesome

risque 4 blue, lewd, racy **5** bawdy, dirty, gross, spicy **6** coarse, daring, ribald, smutty, vulgar **7** immoral, obscene **8** immodest, improper, indecent, off-color **9** offensive, salacious **10** indecorous, indelicate, lascivious, licentious, suggestive **12** pornographic

rite 6 ritual **7** liturgy, service **8** ceremony **9** formality, solemnity **10** ceremonial, observance

rite of passage 6 ritual **7** baptism **8** ceremony, marriage **10** bar mitzvah, bat mitzvah, initiation **11** christening **12** confirmation

Rites of Passage
    author: **14** William Golding

Ritt, Martin
    director of: **3** Hud **7** Sounder **8** Norma Rae, The Front **26** The Spy Who Came in From the Cold

Ritter, John
    born: **9** Burbank CA
    father: **9** Tex Ritter
    roles: **9** Hooperman **11** Americathon, Jack Tripper **13** Three's Company **14** Captain Avenger

Ritter, Thelma
    born: **10** Brooklyn NY
    roles: **10** Pillow Talk, Rear Window, The Misfits **11** All About Eve **15** The Mating Season **17** Birdman of Alcatraz **18** With a Song in My Heart **19** A Letter to Three Wives, Pickup on South Street **21** The Proud and the Profane **27** Miracle on Thirty-Fourth Street

ritual 4 rite **7** service **8** ceremony **10** observance

ritual bathing place
    Jewish Orthodox: **6** mikvah

ritualistic 6 formal, solemn **10** ceremonial **11** ceremonious

ritualize 7 observe **9** celebrate, solemnize **13** ceremonialize

ritzy 4 chic, posh, tony **5** sharp, swank **6** classy, snazzy, spiffy **7** elegant, stylish **9** high-class, high-toned, luxurious, sumptuous

rival 3 foe **5** enemy, equal, excel, fight, match, outdo, touch **6** strive **7** eclipse, surpass **8** approach, opponent, opposing, outshine **9** adversary, competing, contender, disputant **10** antagonist, competitor, contending, contestant

Rivals, The
author: **23** Richard Brinsley Sheridan
character: **8** Bob Acres **9** Faulkland **11** Mrs Malaprop **13** Julia Melville, Lydia Languish **17** Sir Lucius O'Trigger **18** Sir Anthony Absolute **19** Captain Jack Absolute (Ensign Beverley)

rive 4 rend **5** crack, split **6** cleave, detach, divide, sunder **7** shatter **8** fracture

riven 4 rent, torn **5** split **7** cleaved, cracked **8** sundered **9** fractured, shattered

River, The
director: **10** Jean Renoir
based on novel by: **11** Rumer Godden
cast: **5** Radha **13** Adrienne Corri, Arthur Shields, Nora Swinburne **15** Patricia Walters
setting: **5** India **6** Bengal

Rivera, Diego
born: **6** Mexico **10** Guanajuato
artwork: **5** Sleep **8** Creation **11** Mother Earth **14** The Fecund Earth **15** Detroit Industry **18** Man at the Crossroads **21** Carnival of Mexican Life **23** Life in Pre-Hispanic Mexico

river mouth 5 delta, firth **7** estuary

rivers
god of: **6** Peneus, Simois **7** Inachus

Rivers, Reba
character in: **9** Sanctuary
author: **8** Faulkner

rivet 3 fix, pin **6** absorb, clinch, engage, fasten, occupy **7** engross **8** fastener **9** fascinate

Rivieres du Sud *see* **6** Guinea

rivulet 3 run **4** rill **5** brook, creek **6** stream **9** streamlet

Riyadh
capital of: **11** Saudi Arabia

Rizzuto, Phil
nickname: **7** Scooter
position: **9** shortstop
sport: **8** baseball
team: **14** New York Yankees

road 3 via, way **4** lane, path **5** byway, route, trail **6** avenue, street **7** freeway, highway, parkway **8** turnpike **9** boulevard **10** expressway, throughway **12** thoroughfare

Road Not Taken, The
author: **11** Robert Frost

roads
god of: **6** Hermes

road safety
god of: **6** Sancus **10** Semo Sancus

Road to Gandolfo, The
author: **12** Robert Ludlum

roam 3 gad **4** rove **5** drift, jaunt,

prowl, range, stray, tramp **6** ramble, stroll, travel, wander **7** meander, traipse **8** divagate **9** gallivant **11** peregrinate

roan 5 horse **7** grayish, reddish, tannish **8** blackish, brownish

Roan Stallion
author: **15** Robinson Jeffers

roar 3 bay, cry, din **4** bawl, boom, howl, roll, yell **5** blare, growl, grunt, noise, shout, snort **6** bellow, clamor, guffaw, outcry, racket, rumble, scream, shriek **7** bluster, resound, thunder **8** outburst **10** vociferate

roast 3 pan **4** bake **6** berate **7** scourge **8** barbecue **9** criticize

rob 4 bilk, lift, loot, raid, sack, skin **5** cheat, filch, heist, rifle, seize, steal **6** burgle, fleece, forage, hold up, pilfer, thieve **7** despoil, pillage, plunder, purloin, ransack, stick up, swindle **8** carry off, embezzle **9** bamboozle **10** burglarize **11** appropriate

Robards, Jason
born: **9** Chicago IL
wife: **12** Lauren Bacall
roles: **5** Julia **7** Isadora **9** Dick Diver **10** Ben Bradlee **11** Jamie Tyrone **12** Hour of the Gun **15** A Thousand Clowns, Dashiell Hammett, Melvin and Howard, The Disenchanted **16** Tender Is the Night **19** All the President's Men **24** Long Day's Journey into Night

Robbe-Grillet, Alain
author of: **8** Jealousy **9** The Voyeur **10** The Erasers **14** In the Labyrinth **19** Last Year at Marienbad

robber 4 yegg **5** crook, thief **6** bandit, con man, outlaw, pirate, raider **7** brigand, burglar, forager, rustler, sharper **8** Barabbas, marauder, swindler **9** buccaneer, despoiler, embezzler, larcenist, plunderer **10** highwayman, pickpocket

Robbins, Harold
author of: **8** The Betsy **13** The Inheritors **14** Dreams Die First, The Adventurers **16** The Carpetbaggers **17** The Dream Merchants **18** Never Love a Stranger **20** A Stone for Danny Fisher **21** Seventy-Nine Park Avenue

Robbins, Jerome
choreographer of: **8** Les Noces **9** Fancy Free, Interplay
director of: **13** West Side Story (with Robert Wise, Oscar)

robe 4 gown **5** dress, habit, smock **6** duster **7** costume, garment **8** bathrobe, vestment **9** housecoat
French: **8** negligee
Japanese: **6** kimono

Robe, The
author: **13** Lloyd C Douglas

robe-de-chambre 12 dressing-gown

Robert Kennedy and His Times
author: **20** Arthur M Schlesinger Jr

Roberts, Kenneth
author of: **16** Northwest Passage

Roberts, Rachel
born: **5** Wales **8** Llanelly
husband: **11** Rex Harrison
roles: **8** Foul Play **10** Oh Lucky Man **16** This Sporting Life **24** Murder on the Orient Express **29** Saturday Night and Sunday Morning

Robertson, Cliff
real name: **23** Clifford Parker Robertson
born: **9** La Jolla CA
wife: **11** Dina Merrill
roles: **5** PT-109 **6** Charly (Oscar) **9** Obsession **11** Falcon Crest

Robertson, Oscar
nickname: **7** The Big O
sport: **10** basketball
position: **5** guard
team: **14** Milwaukee Bucks **16** Cincinnati Royals

Robeson, Paul
born: **11** Princeton NJ
roles: **7** Othello **8** Show Boat **11** Brutus Jones **15** The Emperor Jones **17** King Solomon's Mines **22** All God's Chillun Got Wings

Robin Hood's Adventures
author: **7** unknown
character: **9** Friar Tuck **10** Little John **11** Will Scarlet **14** Band of Merry Men **18** Sir Richard of the Lea **19** Sheriff of Nottingham

robin's-egg-blue 4 aqua **5** azure **7** sky-blue **8** cerulean **9** light blue **10** aquamarine, powder-blue

Robinson, Edward G
real name: **18** Emmanuel Goldenberg
born: **7** Romania **9** Bucharest
roles: **8** Key Largo **12** Little Caesar, Rico Bandello **13** Scarlet Street **15** Double Indemnity, Flesh and Fantasy **16** House of Strangers **19** The Woman in the Window **20** A Dispatch from Reuters **21** Dr Ehrlich's Magic Bullet

Robinson, Edwin Arlington
author of: **6** Merlin **8** Amaranth, Tristram **10** King Jasper **11** Richard Cory **12** Captain Craig **13** Miniver Cheevy, Mr Flood's Party

Robinson, Jackie
sport: **8** baseball
team: **15** Brooklyn Dodgers
first black in: **12** major leagues

Robinson, Sugar Ray
real name: **19** Walker Smith Robinson
sport: **6** boxing
class: **12** middleweight, welterweight

Robinson Crusoe
author: **11** Daniel Defoe
character: **6** Friday

Rob Roy

author: 14 Sir Walter Scott
character: 11 Diana Vernon **18** Sir Frederick Vernon **23** Rob Roy Mac-Gregor Campbell
   Osbaldistone family: 5 Frank **7** William **9** Rashleigh **13** Sir Hildebrand
robust 3 fit **4** firm, hale, well, wiry **5** hardy, husky, lusty, sound, stout, tough **6** active, brawny, hearty, mighty, potent, rugged, sinewy, strong, sturdy, virile **7** healthy, staunch **8** athletic, forceful, muscular, powerful, stalwart, vigorous **9** energetic, healthful, strapping, wholesome **10** able-bodied **12** in fine fettle
French: 8 puissant
robustness 5 vigor **8** strength **10** good health, ruggedness, sturdiness **11** healthiness
Roche, Kevin
architect of: 13 Oakland Museum (CA) **14** Fine Arts Center (U of MA), Ford Foundation (NYC) **17** Knights of Columbus (New Haven CT) **21** One United Nations Plaza (NYC) **24** Union Carbide Headquarters (Danbury CT) **31** Power Center for the Performing Arts (U of Michigan)
Rochester
football team: 8 Panthers
Rochester, Edward
character in: 8 Jane Eyre
author: 6 Bronte
rock 3 bob, jar **4** crag, reef, roll, stun, sway, toss **5** cliff, flint, pitch, quake, shake, stone, swing, upset **6** gravel, marble, pebble, totter, wobble **7** agitate, bobbing, boulder, disturb, shaking **8** convulse, flounder, undulate, wobbling **9** limestone, oscillate, tottering **10** convulsion, undulation
rock & rye
type: 7 liqueur
flavor: 6 citrus
ingredient: 3 rye **9** rock candy
rock crystal
species: 6 quartz
color: 9 colorless
Rocket
nickname of: 14 Maurice Richard
rocket engine
invented by: 7 Goddard
Rockford Files, The
character: 10 John Cooper **11** Angel Martin, Jim Rockford **12** (Det) Dennis Becker **13** Beth Davenport, (Joseph) Rocky Rockford
cast: 9 Bo Hopkins, Joe Santos, Noah Beery **11** James Garner **14** Stuart Margolin **15** Gretchen Corbett
rock of Tarik see **9** Gibraltar
Rockwell, Norman
born: 9 New York NY
artwork:
   covers: 19 Saturday Evening Post
   mural: 15 Freedom of Speech

Rocky
director: 13 John G Avildsen
cast: 9 Burt Young **10** Talia Shire **11** Thayer David **12** Carl Weathers **15** Burgess Meredith **17** Sylvester Stallone (Rocky Balboa, the Italian Stallion)
setting: 12 Philadelphia
Oscar for: 7 editing, picture **8** director
sequel: 7 Rocky II, Rocky IV **8** Rocky III, Rocky Two **9** Rocky Four **10** Rocky Three
rod 4 cane, lash, mace, pale, pole, wand, whip **5** baton, birch, crook, staff, stake, stick **6** cudgel, rattan, switch **7** penalty, scepter, scourge **8** caduceus **9** stanchion **10** alpenstock, punishment **11** retribution **12** swagger stick
rod, Aaron's see **9** Aaron's rod
rodent 4 cavy, vole **5** coypu, gundi, hutia, mouse **6** agouti, beaver, cururo, gerbil, gopher, jerboa, nutria **7** blesmol, cane rat, hamster, lemming, mole-rat, rock rat **8** capybara, chipmunk, dormouse, pacarana, sewellel, spiny rat, squirrel, tucu-tuco, viscacha **9** chozchori, false paca, porcupine, woodchuck **10** chinchilla, prairie dog, springhare **11** kangaroo rat, pocket mouse, viscacha rat **13** kangaroo mouse **16** Speke's pectinator
Roderick Hudson
author: 10 Henry James
Roderick Random
author: 14 Tobias Smollett
character: 5 Strap **8** Narcissa **10** Tom Bowling **12** Miss Williams
Rodin, (Francois) Auguste Rene
born: 5 Paris **6** France
artwork: 7 The Kiss **10** Head of Iris, The Thinker, Victor Hugo, Walking Man **14** John the Baptist, The Age of Bronze, The Gates of Hell **16** Monument to Balzac **19** The Burghers of Calais **23** The Man with the Broken Nose
rodomontade 4 rant **5** boast **6** hot air **7** blather, bluster, bombast, fustian **8** bragging, folderol, nonsense, rhetoric **10** balderdash, doubletalk **11** braggadocio **12** boastfulness
roe 3 doe, elk, hen **4** buck, deer, eggs, fawn, fish, hart, hind, milt **5** spawn, sperm **6** caviar **8** fish eggs
of lobster: 5 coral
Roentgen, Rontgen, Wilhelm Konrad
field: 7 physics
nationality: 6 German
discovered: 5 X-rays
awarded: 10 Nobel Prize
Roethke, Theodore
author of: 9 Open House, The Waking **11** The Far Field **15** Straw for the Fire, Words for the Wind

Rogers, Ginger
real name: 23 Virginia Katherine McMath
born: 14 Independence MO
husband: 8 Lew Ayres **15** Jacques Bergerac, William Marshall
partner: 11 Fred Astaire
roles: 6 Top Hat **9** Stage Door **10** Hello Dolly, Kitty Foyle (Oscar) **12** Shall We Dance? **14** The Gay Divorcee **15** Flying Down to Rio, Tom Dick and Harry **17** Forty-Second Street **19** The Major and the Minor **21** The Barkleys of Broadway **30** The Story of Vernon and Irene Castle
Rogers, James Gamble
architect of: 22 Northwestern University (Chicago) **33** Columbia-Presbyterian Medical Center (NYC)
Rogers, Roy
real name: 11 Leonard Slye
born: 12 Cincinnati OH
wife: 9 Dale Evans
sidekick: 10 Gabby Hayes
singing group: 17 Sons of the Pioneers
horse: 7 Trigger
roles: 10 Apache Rose **11** Song of Texas **12** My Pal Trigger **13** Song of Arizona, Son of Paleface **17** Heart of the Rockies, Under Western Stars **18** Billy the Kid Returns **19** Tumbling Tumbleweeds **20** The Yellow Rose of Texas **22** Springtime in the Sierras
rogue 3 cur **5** devil, fraud, knave, scamp **6** bad man, rascal, rotter, varlet, wretch **7** bounder, hellion, villain **8** deceiver, evildoer, scalawag **9** miscreant, reprobate, scoundrel **10** blackguard, malefactor, mountebank, scapegrace **11** rapscallion **13** mischiefmaker **14** good-for-nothing **15** snake in the grass
Rogue Herries
author: 11 Hugh Walpole
roguish 3 sly **4** arch **5** saucy **8** devilish, rascally **11** mischievous
roil 3 irk, vex **4** mill, rile, stir **5** annoy, muddy **6** ruffle, seethe **7** agitate, disturb, perturb, provoke, turmoil **8** irritate **9** aggravate **10** exasperate
role 3 job **4** duty, part, pose, post, task, work **5** chore, guise **7** posture, service **8** capacity, function **9** character, portrayal **10** assignment **13** impersonation **14** representation **15** personification **16** characterization
Latin: 7 persona
roll 4 boom, coil, curl, echo, flip, flow, furl, knot, list, loop, reel, roar, rock, spin, sway, toss, tube, turn, wind **5** coast, crack, lurch, pitch, sound, spool, surge, swell, swing, swirl, throw, twirl, twist, wheel, whirl **6** billow, gyrate, muster, roster, rotate, rumble, scroll, tumble **7** booming, catalog, entwine, resound, revolve, rock-

ing, thunder, tossing, turning **8** cylinder, drumbeat, drumming, rumbling, schedule, tumbling, undulate **9** inventory **10** undulation **11** reverberate **13** reverberation **15** turn over and over

Rolland, Romain
   author of: 14 Jean-Christophe **16** The Soul Enchanted

rollicking 3 gay **5** happy, jolly, merry, sunny **6** bright, hearty, jocund, jovial, joyous, lively **7** gleeful, jocular, playful, romping **8** cheerful, mirthful, spirited **9** exuberant, gamboling, sparkling, sprightly **10** frolicking, frolicsome, hysterical, rip-roaring **12** lighthearted

Rolvaag, Ole Edvart
   author of: 15 Peder Victorious, Their Father's God **16** Giants in the Earth

roly-poly 3 fat **5** obese, plump, pudgy, round **6** chubby, rotund **9** corpulent

roman 5 novel **17** metrical narrative

Roman Catholic church
   council/synod: 4 Pisa **5** Basel, Trent **6** Nicaea, Vienne, Whitby **7** Ephesus, Pistoia, Sardica **9** Chalcedon, Constance **12** First Vatican **13** Fourth Lateran, Second Vatican **14** Constantinople **15** Ferrara-Florence
   official Vatican yearbook: 18 Annuario Pontificio
   first Christian emperor: 11 Constantine
   gifts of territory/sovereignty to papacy: 15 Donation of Pepin **21** Donation of Constantine

romance 4 bosh, call, pull **5** amour, idyll, novel **6** affair, allure **7** fantasy, fiction **8** illusion **9** courtship, exoticism, fairy tale, fish story, invention, love story, melodrama, moonshine, tall story **10** attachment, concoction, flirtation, love affair **11** fabrication, fascination, imagination **12** exaggeration, relationship, self-delusion **13** flight of fancy, tender passion **16** affair of the heart

Romance language see **5** Latin

Romances sans paroles
   author: 12 Paul Verlaine

Romancing the Stone
   director: 14 Robert Zemeckis
   cast: 11 Danny De Vito **14** Kathleen Turner, Michael Douglas
   sequel: 17 The Jewel of the Nile

Roman Holiday
   director: 12 William Wyler
   cast: 11 Eddie Albert, Gregory Peck **13** Audrey Hepburn
   Oscar for: 7 actress (Hepburn)

Romania
   other name: 7 Rumania
   capital/largest city: 9 Bucharest
   others: 4 Aiud, Arad, Cluj, Deva, Iasi **5** Bacau, Balta, Cerna, Jassy, Neamt, Sibiu, Turnu, Yassy **6** Braila, Brasov, Brasso, Eforie, Galatz, Galeti, Lupeni,

Mamaia, Oradea, Sighet **7** Bendery, Craiova, Focsani, Giurgiu, Ploesti, Severin **8** Bloiesti, Cernavti, Chisinau, Irongate, Kishenef, Satu-Mare, Temesvar **9** Constanta, Kolozsvar, Timisoara **10** Czernowitz **11** Klausenburg
   school: 4 Cuza
   division: 4 Alba, Iasi **5** Banat, Bihor, Jassy **6** Ardeal **7** Dobruja **8** Bucovina, Bukovina, Dobrogea, Moldavia, Walachia **9** Maramures **10** Bessarabia **12** Transylvania
      Roman province: 5 Dacia
   measure: 7 faltche
   monetary unit: 3 ban, lei, leu, lev, ley **4** bani **5** uncia **6** triens
   lake: 5 Sinoe **6** Snagov
   mountain: 5 Banat, Bihor **6** Codrul, Rodnei **7** Apuseni, Balkans, Caliman, Fagaras **8** Pietrosu **9** Moldavian **10** Carpathian, Moldoveanu **17** Transylvanian Alps
   highest point: 11 Moldoveanul
   river: 3 Alt, Jui, Olt **4** Prut **5** Aluta, Arges, Buzdu, Moros, Mures, Oltul, Schyl, Siret, Somes, Timis, Vedea **6** Crasna, Danube **7** Argesul **8** Bistrita, Ialomita, Iniester **9** Dimbovita, Jiul Mures
   sea: 5 Black
   physical feature:
      canal: 4 Bega
      forest: 6 Snagov **7** Baneasa
      gorge: 8 Iron Gate
      peninsula: 6 Balkan
      plain: 5 Banat **6** Moldavian, Walachian **13** Prahova Valley
      plateau: 7 Dobruja
      wind: 6 crivat
   people: 6 Dacian **8** Romanian, Rumanian
      artist: 8 Brancusi
      author: 7 Ionesco
      composer: 6 Enesco
      leader: 6 Carol I **7** Michael, Iliescu **8** Ioan Cuza **9** Ceausescu **12** Gheorghiu-Dej, Ion Antonescu
   language: 6 French, Magyar **7** Russian **8** Romanian, Rumanian **9** Hungarian
   religion: 7 Judaism **8** Lutheran **9** Calvinism, Unitarian **10** Protestant **13** Roman Catholic **16** Romanian Orthodox
   place:
      castle: 4 Bran **7** Huniady
      church: 5 Golia **9** Mihaivoda **10** Cretulescu, Patriarchy **11** Curtea Veche, Stavropdeos, Trei Ierarhi
      monastery: 5 Humor **6** Arbore **7** Voronet **8** Sucerita **9** Moldovita
      museum: 11 Peles Castle
      palace: 9 mogosoaia
      park: 7 Baneasa
      resort: 5 Venus **6** Eforie, Mamaia, Neptun **7** Jupiter **10** Costinesti
   feature:

      community gathering: 9 sezatoare
      game: 4 oina
   food:
      dish: 6 ciorba **7** mititei, sarmala **8** mamaliga **11** imam bayildi
      plum brandy: 5 tuica
Roman measure 2 as **5** cubit, libra **6** pondus **7** stadium

Roman Mythology
   collective name for gods: 6 Superi
   goddess of anguish: 8 Angerona
   goddess of agriculture: 5 Ceres **6** Dea Dia, Vacuna **13** Acca Laurentia
      Ceres corresponds to Greek: 7 Demeter
   goddess of the arts: 7 Minerva
      corresponds to Greek: 6 Athena
   goddess of baking: 6 Fornax
   goddess of chastity: 5 Fauna **7** Bona Dea
   goddess of childbirth: 5 Parca **6** Lucina, Matuta, Parcae **11** Mater Matuta
   goddess of the dawn: 6 Aurora, Matuta **11** Mater Matuta
      Aurora corresponds to Greek: 3 Eos
   goddess of destiny: 5 Parca **6** Parcae
   goddess of discord: 9 Discordia
   goddess of door hinges: 6 Cardea
   goddess of the earth: 6 Tellus
      corresponds to Greek: 4 Gaea
   goddess of the family: 6 Cardea
   goddess of fertility: 5 Fauna **6** Libera, Tellus **7** Bona Dea
      Libera corresponds to Greek: 10 Persephone
      Tellus corresponds to Greek: 4 Gaea
   goddess of flowers: 5 Flora
   goddess of fortune: 7 Fortuna
      corresponds to Greek: 5 Tyche
   goddess of fruit trees: 6 Pomona
   goddess of gardens: 5 Venus
      corresponds to Greek: 9 Aphrodite
   goddess of grain/protectress against grain blight: 6 Robigo
   goddess of harbors: 6 Matuta **11** Mater Matuta
   goddess of harmony: 9 Concordia
   goddess of the hearth: 4 Caca **5** Salus, Vesta
      Salus corresponds to Greek: 6 Hygeia
   goddess of heaven: 4 Juno
      corresponds to Greek: 4 Hera
   goddess of hunting: 5 Diana
      corresponds to Greek: 6 Phoebe **7** Artemis
   goddess of longevity: 11 Anna Perenna
   goddess of love: 5 Venus
      corresponds to Greek: 9 Aphrodite
   goddess of marriage: 4 Juno **6** Tellus
      corresponds to Greek: 4 Gaea, Hera
   goddess of marshes: 6 Marica **9** Dea

Marica
goddess of the moon: 5 Diana
  corresponds to Greek: 6 Phoebe **7** Artemis
goddess of peace: 3 Pax **9** Concordia
  Pax corresponds to Greek: 5 Irene
goddess of pleasure: 8 Voluptas
goddess of plenty: 3 Ops **10** Magna Mater
goddess of prosperity: 5 Salus
  corresponds to Greek: 6 Hygeia
goddess of the sea: 6 Matuta **11** Mater Matuta
goddess of sleeping infants: 6 Cunina
goddess of the spring: 5 Venus
  corresponds to Greek: 9 Aphrodite
goddess of storms: 11 Tempestates
goddess of victory: 8 Victoria
  corresponds to Greek: 4 Nike
goddess of vineyards: 6 Libera
  corresponds to Greek: 10 Persephone
goddess of war: 7 Bellona
  corresponds to Greek: 5 Enyon
goddess of wine: 6 Libera
  corresponds to Greek: 10 Persephone
goddess of wisdom: 7 Minerva
  corresponds to Greek: 6 Athena
god of agriculture: 5 Picus **6** Saturn **7** Eventus **12** Bonus Eventus
  corresponds to Greek: 6 Cronos, Cronus, Kronos
god of beginnings: 5 Janus
god of boundaries: 8 Terminus
god of commerce: 7 Mercury
  corresponds to Greek: 6 Hermes
god of the dead: 7 Veiovis
god of doorways: 5 Janus
god of drinking/revelry: 5 Comus
god of eloquence: 7 Mercury
  corresponds to Greek: 6 Hermes
god of farm boundaries: 8 Silvanus, Sylvanus
god of fertility: 7 Mutinus, Priapus **8** Lupercus, Picumnus
god of fire/metalworking: 6 Vulcan
  corresponds to Greek: 10 Hephaestus, Hephaistos
god of forest: 7 Virbius
god of gardens: 9 Vertumnus
god of good counsel: 3 Ops **6** Consus
god of grain/protector against grain blight: 7 Robigus
god of healing: 11 Aesculapius
  corresponds to Greek: 9 Asclepius
god of heavens: 4 Jove **7** Jupiter
  corresponds to Greek: 4 Zeus
god of herds: 8 Silvanus, Sylvanus
god of horse racing: 3 Ops **6** Consus
god of hospitality: 6 Sancus **10** Dius Fidius, Semo Sancus
god of the house: 8 Silvanus, Sylvanus
god of hunting: 7 Virbius
god of international affairs: 6

Sancus **10** Dius Fidius, Semo Sancus
god of landmarks: 8 Terminus
god of light: 6 Apollo
god of love: 4 Amor **5** Cupid
  corresponds to Greek: 4 Eros
god of luck: 7 Eventus **12** Bonus Eventus
god of medicine: 11 Aesculapius
  corresponds to Greek: 9 Asclepius
god of music: 6 Apollo
god of oaths: 6 Sancus **10** Dius Fidius, Semo Sancus
god of orchards: 9 Vertumnus
god of ports/harbors: 8 Portunus
god of prosperity: 7 Eventus **12** Bonus Eventus
god of the rising sun: 5 Janus
god of science: 7 Mercury
  corresponds to Greek: 6 Hermes
god of sea: 7 Neptune
  corresponds to Greek: 8 Poseidon
god of seasons: 9 Vertumnus
god of the setting sun: 5 Janus
god of sleep: 6 Somnus
  corresponds to Greek: 6 Hypnos, Hypnus
god of springs: 4 Fons
gods of sulphur springs (twins): 6 Palici
god of the sun: 3 Sol
  corresponds to Greek: 6 Helios **8** Hyperion
god of thievery: 7 Mercury
  corresponds to Greek: 6 Hermes
god of thunder: 7 Taranis
god of thunderstorms: 8 Summanus
god of the Tiber: 9 Tiberinus
god of uncultivated land: 8 Silvanus, Sylvanus
god of underworld: 3 Dis **5** Orcus **8** Dis Pater
  corresponds to Greek: 5 Pluto
god of war: 4 Mars **6** Mamers, Mavors **8** Quirinus
  corresponds to Greek: 4 Ares
god of weather: 4 Jove **7** Jupiter
god of weddings: 8 Talassio
  corresponds to Greek: 5 Hymen **9** Hymenaeus
god of the woods: 6 Faunus **8** Silvanus, Sylvanus
household gods: 5 lares **7** penates
nymphs/deities with gift of prophecy: 7 Camenae
  names: 6 Egeria **8** Carmenta **9** Antevorta, Postvorta
  correspond to Greek: 5 Muses
protectress of childbirth: 8 Carmenta
protectress of cows/oxen: 6 Bubona
protector of flocks/shepherds: 5 Pales
protectress of military age men: 8 Juventas
  corresponds to Greek: 4 Hebe
protectress of women: 5 Diana
  corresponds to Greek: 6 Phoebe **7** Artemis
protectress of women/marriage: 4

Juno
  queen of heaven: 4 Juno
    corresponds to Greek: 4 Hera, Here
  staff of Mercury: 8 Caduceus
  troublesome ghosts: 7 lemures
romantic 4 fond **5** mushy, soppy **6** ardent, dreamy, loving, tender, unreal **7** amorous, devoted, fervent, flighty, idyllic, utopian **8** enamored, fanciful, quixotic **9** fantastic, idealized, imaginary, sensitive, visionary, whimsical **10** idealistic, improbable, passionate **11** extravagant, impassioned, impractical, rhapsodical, sentimental, unrealistic, warmhearted **12** melodramatic, preposterous
Romantic Comedians, The
  author: 12 Ellen Glasgow
romanticize 8 idealize **9** embroider
Romantic Manifesto
  author: 7 Ayn Rand
Romany Rye, The
  author: 17 George Henry Borrow
Rome, ancient
  emperor: 4 Nero, Otho **5** Galba, Nerva, Titus **6** Trajan **7** Hadrian **8** Augustus, Caligula, Claudius, Commodus, Domitian, Tiberius **9** Caracalla, Vespasian, Vitellius **10** Diocletian **11** Constantine, Lucius Verus **13** Antoninus Pius **14** Marcus Aurelius
  emperor's bodyguard: 15 Praetorian Guard
  first citizen title: 8 princeps
  first triumvirate: 6 Caesar, Pompey **7** Crassus
  foe: 4 Gaul **5** Spain **6** Cimbri **7** Perseus, Philip V, Pyrrhus, Teutons **8** Carthage, Hannibal, Iberians, Jugurtha, Samnites, Tarentum, Umbrians **9** Etruscans, Macedonia, Seleucids **11** Latin League **12** Antiochus III **13** Achaean League, Hamilcar Barca
  general: 5 Sulla **6** Brutus, Marius, Pompey **7** Crassus **8** Octavian **10** Flaminius, Mark Antony **12** Julius Caesar **14** Caesar Augustus **20** Quintus Fabius Maximus, Scipio Africanus Major, Scipio Africanus Minor
  king: 12 Ancus Marcius **13** Numa Pompilius **16** Sextus Tarquinius **17** Tarquinius Priscus (Tarquin the Elder) **18** Tarquinius Superbus (Tarquin the Proud)
  reformer: 8 Gracchus
  republican ruler: 6 consul **7** senator, tribune **8** plebeian **9** optimates, patrician, populares **10** magistrate
  Roman peace: 9 Pax Romana
  second triumvirate: 6 Antony **7** Lepidus **8** Octavian (Caesar Augustus)
Rome, Roma
  airport: 8 Ciampino **15** Leonardo da Vinci
  area: 9 Cinecitta (Cinema City) **10** Trastevere **11** Vatican City

capital of: 5 Italy **6** Latium **11** Papal States, Roman Empire
church: 8 St Peter's **11** San Giovanni **18** Santa Maria Maggiore **19** San Paolo Fuori le Mura
Italian: 4 Roma
landmark: 5 Forum **7** Capitol **8** Pantheon **9** catacombs, Colosseum **12** Palazzo Doria **13** Circus Maximus, Lateran Palace, Sistine Chapel, Vatican Palace, Villa Borghese **14** Palazzo Corsini, Villa Farnesina **16** Baths of Caracalla, Castel Sant'Angelo, Palazzo Barberini **17** Arch of Constantine **19** Saint Peter's Basilica
legendary founders: 5 Remus **6** Aeneas **7** Romulus
nickname: 11 Eternal City
mountain: 8 Apennine
museum: 5 Doria **7** Colonna, Corsini, Vatican **8** Borghese, National **10** Capitoline
river: 5 Tiber
school: 33 Conservatorio di Musica Santa Cecilia
sea: 10 Tyrrhenian
seven hills: 7 Caelian, Viminal **8** Aventine, Palatine, Quirinal **9** Esquiline **10** Capitoline
square/piazza: 6 Popolo, Spagna **7** Colonna, Venezia **9** Quirinale **11** Campidoglio
state within: 11 Vatican City
street: 9 Appian Way, Emmanuele **11** Via del Corso **13** Corso Vittorio
subway: 13 Metropolitana
Romeo 4 beau **5** lover, sheik, swain, wooer **7** Don Juan, gallant **8** Casanova, cavalier, Lothario **9** boyfriend, Lochinvar
French: 8 paramour
Latin: 9 inamorato
Romeo and Juliet
author: 18 William Shakespeare
character: 5 Nurse, Paris **6** Tybalt **8** Benvolio, Mercutio **13** Friar Laurence
family: 7 Capulet **8** Montague
setting: 6 Verona
Romeo and Juliet
director:
  1936 version: 11 George Cukor
  1968 version: 16 Franco Zeffirelli
based on play by: 18 William Shakespeare
cast:
  1936 version: 12 Leslie Howard, Norma Shearer **13** Basil Rathbone, Edna May Oliver, John Barrymore
  1968 version: 9 Milo O'Shea **11** John McEnery, Michael York **12** Olivia Hussey **14** Leonard Whiting
score: 8 Nino Rota
Romeo and Juliet
symphony by: 7 Berlioz
opera by: 6 Gounod
orchestral piece by: 11 Tchaikovsky
ballet by: 9 Prokofiev

Romney, George
born: 7 England **15** Dalton-in-Furness
artwork: 5 Circe **9** Joan of Arc **11** Mrs Robinson, Sensibility **12** Mrs Davenport, Saint Cecilia **19** Mrs Carwardine and Son **22** The Death of General Wolfe **24** The Levenson-Gower Children **26** Sir Christopher and Lady Sykes
Romola
author: 11 George Eliot
character: 5 Bardo, Tessa **10** Tito Melema **15** Baldasarre Calvo
romp 3 hop **4** skip **5** caper, cut up, frisk, sport **6** frolic, gambol **7** disport, rollick
Romulus
father: 4 Mars
mother: 4 Ilia **9** Rea Silvia **10** Rhea Silvia
twin brother: 5 Remus
raised by: 7 she-wolf **9** Faustulus **12** Acca Larentia
first king of: 4 Rome
founder of: 4 Rome
Romus
father: 6 Aeneas **8** Ascanius
possible founder of: 4 Rome
Roncalli, Angelo Giuseppe 13 Pope John XXIII **22** Pope John the Twenty-Third
Ronsard, Pierre de
author of: 17 Sonnets pour Helene
member of: 7 Pleiade
roofing 4 tile, turf **5** slate, terne **6** thatch **7** asphalt, ceiling, pantile, shingle **8** housetop
Roof of the World *see* **5** Tibet
rook 3 gyp **4** bilk, crow, dupe, gull **5** cheat, cozen, raven, trick **6** castle, fleece **7** deceive, defraud, swindle **8** chessman **9** bamboozle, victimize
rookie 4 tyro **6** novice **8** beginner **9** fledgling, greenhorn **10** apprentice, tenderfoot
Rookies, The
character: 9 Jill Danko, (Officer) Mike Danko **10** (Lt) Eddie Ryker, (Officer) Chris Owens **12** (Officer) Terry Webster, (Officer) Willie Gillis
cast: 11 Kate Jackson, Sam Melville **14** Bruce Fairbairn, Michael Ontkean **16** Gerald S O'Loughlin **18** Georg Stanford Brown
room 4 area **5** range, scope, space **6** chance, extent, leeway, margin, volume **7** chamber, cubicle, expanse, lodging **9** allowance, provision, territory **11** compartment
French: 5 salle
Spanish: 4 sala
Room at the Top
director: 11 Jack Clayton
based on novel by: 10 John Braine
cast: 12 Heather Sears **14** Laurence Harvey, Simone Signoret **16** Hermione Baddeley

Oscar for: 7 actress (Signoret)
sequel: 11 Man at the Top **12** Life at the Top
Room 222
character: 6 Bernie **9** Pete Dixon **11** Liz McIntyre **12** Alice Johnson **14** Seymour Kaufman
cast: 11 Lloyd Haynes **13** David Jolliffe **14** Denise Nicholas, Karen Valentine **18** Michael Constantine
school: 15 Walt Whitman High
roomy 3 big **4** huge, long, vast, wide **5** ample, broad, large **7** immense, lengthy, sizable **8** generous, spacious **9** boundless, capacious, expansive, extensive, unlimited **10** commodious
Rooney, Mickey
real name: 9 Joe Yule Jr
born: 10 Brooklyn NY
wife: 10 Ava Gardner **13** Martha Vickers
co-star: 11 Judy Garland
roles: 4 Puck **8** Boys' Town **9** Andy Hardy **11** Sugar Babies **13** Mickey McGuire **14** Baby Face Nelson, National Velvet, The Human Comedy **21** A Midsummer Night's Dream **30** The Adventures of Huckleberry Finn
Roosevelt, Franklin Delano
presidential rank: 12 thirty-second
party: 10 Democratic
state represented: 2 NY
defeated: 5 (Jacob Sechler) Coxey, (John W) Aiken, (Thomas Edmund) Dewey, (William) Lemke **6** (Alfred Mossman) Landon, (Claude A) Watson, (David Leigh) Colvin, (Herbert Clark) Hoover, (Norman) Thomas, (Roger Ward) Babson, (William David) Upshaw, (William Hope) Harvey, (William Zebulon) Foster **7** (Earl Russell) Browder, (Wendell Lewis) Willkie **8** (Edward A) Teichert, (Verne L) Reynolds
vice president: 6 (Harry S) Truman, (John Nance) Garner **7** (Henry Agard) Wallace
cabinet:
  state: 4 (Cordell) Hull **10** (Edward Reilly) Stettinius (Jr)
  treasury: 6 (William Hartman) Woodin **10** (Henry) Morgenthau (Jr)
  war: 4 (George Henry) Dern **7** (Henry Lewis) Stimson **8** (Harry Hines) Woodring
  attorney general: 6 (Francis) Biddle, (Frank) Murphy **7** (Robert Houghwout) Jackson **8** (Homer Stille) Cummings
  navy: 4 (Frank) Knox **6** (Charles) Edison **7** (Claude Augustus) Swanson **9** (James Vincent) Forrestal
  postmaster general: 6 (Frank Comerford) Walker, (James Aloysius) Farley
  interior: 5 (Harold LeClaire) Ickes
  agriculture: 7 (Claude Raymond)

Wickard, (Henry Agard) Wallace
commerce: 5 (Daniel Calhoun) Roper, (Jesse Holman) Jones **7** (Henry Agard) Wallace, (Henry Lloyd) Hopkins
labor: 7 (Frances) Perkins (Wilson)
born: 10 Hyde Park NY
died: 13 Warm Springs GA **16** Little White House
buried: 10 Hyde Park NY
education:
  prep school: 6 Groton
  university: 7 Harvard
  law school: 8 Columbia
religion: 12 Episcopalian
interests: 3 art **4** polo **6** tennis, travel **7** fishing, hunting **8** shooting
vacation spot: 13 Warm Springs GA **16** Campobello Island (Canada)
dog: 4 Fala
author: 27 The Happy Warrior: Alfred E Smith
political career: 12 state senator
  assistant secretary of: 4 Navy
  governor of: 7 New York
civilian career: 6 lawyer **11** bank officer
notable events of lifetime/term: 4 D-Day, WWII **7** New Deal **10** atomic bomb, Depression, World War II **11** World War Two **13** United Nations **15** Atlantic Charter
  act: 9 Lend-Lease
  attack on: 11 Pearl Harbor
  conference: 5 Cairo, Yalta **7** Arcadia, Crimean, Teheran
  scandal: 11 Tammany Hall
quote: 24 A day that will live in infamy **31** Meet every day's troubles as they come **36** The only thing we have to fear is fear itself **50** This generation of Americans has a rendezvous with destiny **53** I pledge you I pledge myself to a new deal for the American people
father: 5 James
mother: 4 Sara (Delano)
siblings:
  half-brother: 5 James
wife: 7 (Anna) Eleanor (Roosevelt)
children: 5 James **7** Elliott **11** Anna Eleanor **13** John Aspinwell **14** Franklin Delano
first lady:
  author: 7 On My Own **13** This I Remember, This Is My Story **34** The Autobiography of Eleanor Roosevelt
  chairwoman: 25 UN Commission on Human Rights
  codirector: 23 Office of Civilian Defense
  member: 35 Democratic National Campaign Committee
  newspaper column: 5 My Day
  US delegate to: 2 UN

Roosevelt, Theodore
nickname: 5 Teddy

presidential rank: 11 twenty-sixth
party: 10 Republican
state represented: 2 NY
succeeded: 8 McKinley
defeated (second term): 4 (Eugene Victor) Debs **6** (Alton Brooks) Parker, (Thomas Edward) Watson **7** (Austin) Holcomb, (Silas Comfort) Swallow **8** (Charles Hunter) Corregan
vice president: 4 none (1st term) **9** (Charles Warren) Fairbanks
cabinet:
  state: 3 (John Milton) Hay **4** (Elihu) Root **5** (Robert) Bacon
  treasury: 4 (Leslie Mortier) Shaw, (Lyman Judson) Gage **9** (George Bruce) Cortelyou
  war: 4 (Elihu) Root, (William Howard) Taft **6** (Luke Edward) Wright
  attorney general: 4 (Philander Chase) Knox **5** (William Henry) Moody **9** (Charles Joseph) Bonaparte
  navy: 4 (John Davis) Long **5** (William Henry) Moody **6** (Paul) Morton **7** (Victor Howard) Metcalf **8** (Truman Handy) Newberry **9** (Charles Joseph) Bonaparte
  postmaster general: 5 (Charles Emory) Smith, (George von Lengerke) Meyer, (Henry Clay) Payne, (Robert John) Wynne **9** (George Bruce) Cortelyou
  interior: 8 (James Rudolph) Garfield **9** (Ethan Allen) Hitchcock
  agriculture: 6 (James) Wilson
  commerce and labor: 6 (Oscar Solomon) Straus **7** (Victor Howard) Metcalf **9** (George Bruce) Cortelyou
born: 13 New York City NY
died/buried: 2 NY **9** Oyster Bay **10** Long Island
education:
  university: 7 Harvard
  law school: 8 Columbia (did not graduate)
religion: 13 Dutch Reformed
interests: 7 hunting (African game), writing **9** exploring (South America) **14** natural history
author: 11 Rough Riders **14** Oliver Cromwell **16** Gouverneur Morris, Thomas Hart Benton **17** African Game Trails, The New Nationalism **19** The Winning of the West **20** Letters to His Children **21** America and the World War **24** The Foes of Our Own Household **25** Fear God and Take Your Own Part **27** A Booklover's Holiday in the Open, Ranch Life and the Hunting Trail, The Naval War of Eighteen-Twelve **28** Hero Tales from American History **29** Through the Brazilian Wilderness **33** Life Histories of African Game Animals

political career: 13 Vice President **15** NY State Assembly **24** US Civil Service Commission
  assistant secretary: 4 Navy
  governor of: 7 New York
  organized party: 9 Bull Moose **11** Progressive
civilian career: 6 author **7** rancher **14** public lecturer
military service: 15 NY National Guard **18** Spanish-American War
  organized cavalry regiment: 11 Rough Riders
  led charge up: 11 San Juan Hill
notable events of lifetime/term: 5 Panic (of 1907) **10** Square Deal **15** Nobel Peace Prize **22** San Francisco earthquake
  Act: 11 Reclamation **14** Meat Inspection **15** Hepburn Railroad, Pure Food and Drug
  bureau of: 12 Corporations **28** Immigration and Naturalization
  first flight by: 14 Wright Brothers
  revolution: 6 Panama
  treaty: 13 Hay-Pauncefote **15** Hay-Bunau-Varilla
quotes: 25 Hasten forward quickly there **28** Speak softly and carry a big stick
father: 8 Theodore
mother: 6 Martha (Bulloch)
siblings: 4 Anna **7** Corinne, Elliott
wife: 5 Alice (Hathaway Lee), Edith (Kermit Carow)
children: 6 Kermit **7** Quentin **8** Alice Lee, Theodore **10** Ethel Carow **16** Archibald Bulloch

rooster
young: 8 cockerel

root
3 fix, set **4** back, base, bind, bulb, clap, hail, nail, rise, stem **5** basis, boost, cheer, fount, radix, start, stick, tubes **6** bottom, fasten, ground, motive, origin, reason, second, source, spring **7** acclaim, applaud, bolster, cheer on, pull for, radicle, support **8** fountain, occasion, shout for **9** beginning, encourage, establish, inception, rationale **10** derivation, foundation, mainspring **11** fundamental **12** commencement, fountainhead

Root, John Wellborn
partner: 14 Daniel H Burnham
architect of: 10 The Rookery **12** Hotel Statler (Washington DC), Montauk Block **13** Hotel Tamanaco (Caracas) **17** Monadnock Building, Palmolive Building (Chicago) **19** Rand-McNally Building

root for
5 boost **6** urge on **7** cheer on, pull for

root out
5 dig up **6** remove **7** extract, pull out, uncover, unearth **8** discover **9** extirpate, ferret out **12** bring to light

Roots
author: 9 Alex Haley
character: 3 Tom **4** Ames, Bell, Noah

5 Binta, Fanta, Grill, Irene, Kizzy, Lewis, Mingo, Omoro 6 Justin, Martha, Ordell 7 Fiddler, Gardner, Nyo Boto 8 Kintango, Mathilda, Mrs Moore, Tom Moore 9 Evan Brent, Missy Anne 10 Brima Cesay, Capt Davies, Carrington, Jemmy Brent, Kadi Touray, Kunta Kinte, Sam Bennett, Sister Sara 11 Mrs Reynolds, Squire James 12 John Reynolds 13 Chicken George 14 Sir Eric Russell, Stephen Bennett 15 Ol' George Johnson, Third Mate Slater 17 Dr William Reynolds

cast: 8 Burl Ives, John Amos, Ren Woods 9 Ben Vereen, Brad Davis, Moses Gunn, O J Simpson, Vic Morrow 10 Billy Hicks, Ian McShane, John Schuck, Lynne Moody, Olivia Cole, Paul Shenar, Ralph Waite, Robert Reed 11 Beverly Todd, Cicely Tyson, Doug McClure, Edward Asner, Gary Collins, Harry Rhodes, Lane Binkley, LeVar Burton, Lorne Greene, Maya Angelou, Sandy Duncan 12 Carolyn Jones, Chuck Connors, Leslie Uggams, Lloyd Bridges 13 Louis Gosset Jr, Madge Sinclair, William Watson 14 George Hamilton, Lynda Day George, Macdonald Carey 15 Lillian Randolph, Scatman Crothers, Thalmus Rasulala 16 Raymond St Jacques, Richard Roundtree 18 Georg Stanford Brown 20 Lawrence Hilton-Jacobs

rope 3 gad, guy, tie, tow 4 bind, cord, fast, guss, hemp, line, lure, snag, trap, wire, yarn 5 cable, catch, chord, lasso, noose, riata, shank, strap, twine 6 corral, entice, hawser, lariat, seduce, string, tether 7 bobstay, cordage, halyard, lanyard, lashing, painter 8 dragline, restrain
fiber: 5 sisal

Rosaline
character in: 16 Love's Labour's Lost
author: 11 Shakespeare

rose 4 Rosa
varieties: 3 bog, dog, sun, tea, wax 4 baby, gold, moss, musk, rock, rush, sand, wood 5 briar, brier, China, fairy, field, malva, Ophir, pygmy, swamp 6 Alpine, Burnet, copper, cotton, damask, desert, French, ground, Karroo, Lenten, mallow, Nootka, Scotch, velvet 7 baby sun, Banksia, Bourbon, cabbage, cluster, Guelder, Manetti, pasture, prairie, rambler 8 Burgundy, Champney, Cherokee, chestnut, cinnamon, climbing, Japanese, Memorial, mountain, Noisette 9 Christmas, evergreen, hybrid tea, McCartney, Polyantha, Remontant, Turkestan 10 California, Chinquapin, shaggy-rock, underwater 11 confederate, giant velvet, hairy alpine 12 green Mexican, Hawaiian wood, Seven-sisters,

white Mexican 13 Himalayan musk, Hybrid Bourbon, Persian yellow, Stuart's desert 15 hybrid perpetual 16 York-and-Lancaster

Rose, Pete (Peter Edward)
nickname: 13 Charlie Hustle
sport: 8 baseball
position: 7 baseman 8 outfield
team: 14 Cincinnati Reds 20 Philadelphia Phillies
scandal: 8 gambling

Roseanne
former name: 4 Barr 6 Arnold
husband: 3 Tom 6 Thomas
television:
   show: 8 Roseanne
   husband: 3 Dan
   children: 2 DJ 5 Becky 7 Darlene
   sister: Jackie
   town: Lanford

Rosedale, Mr
character in: 15 The House of Mirth
author: 7 Wharton

Rosemary's Baby
director: 13 Roman Polanski
based on novel by: 8 Ira Levin
cast: 9 Mia Farrow 10 Ruth Gordon 14 John Cassavetes, Sidney Blackmer
Oscar for: 17 supporting actress (Gordon)

Rosenberg, Stuart
director of: 12 Cool Hand Luke

Rosenbloom, Maxie
nickname: 12 Slapsie Maxie
sport: 6 boxing
class: 16 light heavyweight

Rosencrantz
character in: 6 Hamlet
author: 11 Shakespeare

Rosenkavalier, Der
also: 18 The Knight of the Rose
opera by: 7 (Richard) Strauss
character: 6 Sophie 8 Octavian 9 Baron Ochs 11 Marschallin (Princess von Werderberg)

Rose of Sharon
character in: 16 The Grapes of Wrath
author: 9 Steinbeck

Rose Tattoo, The
director: 10 Daniel Mann
based on play by: 17 Tennessee Williams
cast: 11 Anna Magnani 13 Burt Lancaster
Oscar for: 7 actress (Magnani)

rosiness 5 bloom, blush, flush 7 redness 8 pinkness

Ross, Barney
real name: 14 Barnet Rosofsky
sport: 6 boxing
class: 12 welterweight

Ross, Herbert
director of: 14 The Goodbye Girl 15 The Turning Point

Ross, Katharine
born: 12 Los Angeles CA
aunt: 16 Katharine Hepburn

roles: 9 The Colbys 11 The Graduate 13 Stepford Wives 29 Butch Cassidy and the Sundance Kid

Rossellini, Roberto
director of: 6 Paisan 8 Open City 9 Stromboli 10 The Miracle 15 Germany Year Zero
wife: 13 Ingrid Bergman
daughter: 8 Isabella

Rossen, Robert
director of: 11 Body and Soul 14 All the King's Men

Rossetti, Dante Gabriel
author of: 17 The Blessed Damozel
born: 6 London 7 England
group: 14 Pre-Raphaelites
artwork: 12 Beata Beatrix 15 The Annunciation 17 Ecce Ancilla Domini

Rossini, Gioacchino Antonio
born: 5 Italy 6 Pesaro
composer of: 5 Moise 6 Otello 8 Tancredi 10 Le Comte Ory, Semiramide 11 William Tell 12 Mose in Egitto 13 Guillaume Tell, La Cenerentola 15 Barber of Seville 20 Il Barbiere di Siviglia 22 La Cambiale di Matrimonio

Rossner, Judith
author of: 11 Attachments 14 Ordinary People 19 Looking for Mr Goodbar

Rostand, Edmond
author of: 7 L'Aiglon 10 Chantecler 12 The Romancers 16 Cyrano de Bergerac

roster 4 list, roll 5 cadre, panel, slate 6 agenda, docket, muster, record 7 catalog, listing, posting 8 register, schedule 9 catalogue, directory

rostrum 4 dais 5 stage, stand, stump 6 podium, pulpit 7 lectern, soapbox 8 platform

rosy 4 pink 5 ruddy 6 bright, florid 7 flushed, glowing, hopeful, reddish 8 blooming, blushing, cheerful, cheering, flushing, inflamed, rubicund 9 confident, favorable, promising, reddening, rubescent 10 auspicious, felicitous, optimistic, propitious, reassuring 11 encouraging, high-colored, inspiriting 13 full of promise

Roszak, Theodore
born: 6 Poland, Poznan
artwork: 5 Raven, Surge 7 Anguish 9 Chrysalis, Scavenger, Sea Quarry 11 Sea Sentinel 12 Amorphic Form, Thorn Blossom 18 Specter of Kitty Hawk 20 The Whaler of Nantucket 27 Recollections of the Southwest

rot 3 mar 4 bosh, bull, bunk, harm, hurt, warp 5 decay, go bad, spoil, stain, taint, trash 6 damage, debase, defile, drivel, impair, infect, injure, jabber, molder, poison 7 blather, corrupt, crumble, deprave, inanity, pervert, pollute, putrefy, rubbish, twaddle 8 flummery, folderol, nonsense, putresce **9** absurdity, decompose, gibberish, moonshine, poppycock, purulence, putridity **10** balderdash, corruption, degenerate, flapdoodle **11** contaminate, deteriorate, putrescence **12** disintegrate, fiddle-faddle, gobbledygook, putrefaction **13** contamination, decomposition, deterioration **14** disintegration **16** stuff and nonsense

rotate 4 eddy, reel, roll, spin, turn **5** pivot, swirl, twirl, twist, wheel, whirl **6** change, circle, gyrate, swivel **7** revolve **9** alternate, circulate, pirouette **11** interchange

Roth, Philip
 author of: 8 The Facts **15** Goodbye Columbus **16** The Anatomy Lesson, Zuckerman Unbound **17** Portnoy's Complaint

Rothko, Mark
 born: 6 Dvinsk, Latvia, Russia **16** Daugavpils Latvia
 artwork: 5 Light **12** Central Green, Earth and Blue **14** Four Darks in Red

rotten 3 bad **4** base, foul, rank **5** dirty, fetid, nasty, reeky, venal **6** filthy, putrid, rancid, scurvy **7** corrupt, crooked, decayed, devious, immoral, tainted, very bad, vicious **8** criminal, decaying, indecent, purulent, two-faced **9** deceitful, dishonest, dissolute, faithless, insincere, mercenary, moldering, putrefied, worm-eaten **10** decomposed, iniquitous, putrescent, scurrilous, unpleasant, villainous **11** decomposing, disgraceful, treacherous **12** contemptible, dishonorable, unforgivable, unscrupulous **13** double-dealing, untrustworthy

rotter 3 cad, cur, rat **4** heel **5** knave, louse, rogue **6** no-good, rascal **7** bounder, caitiff, villain **9** scoundrel

rotund 3 fat **5** obese, ovate, ovoid, plump, pudgy, round, stout, tubby **6** chubby, curved, fleshy, portly **7** bulbous, lumpish, rounded **8** circular, globular **9** corpulent, egg-shaped, spherical **10** potbellied **11** full-fleshed

Rouault, Georges
 born: 5 Paris **6** France
 artwork: 3 Mr X **5** Clown **8** Le Chahut, Miserere, Twilight **9** The Mirror **10** The Old King **11** Fleurs du mal, The Holy Face **12** Head of a Clown **13** Little Olympia **14** The Three Judges **19** Small Family of Clowns **22** Christ Mocked by Soldiers **26** Les Reincarnations du Pere Ubu **28** The Child Jesus among the Doctors

roue 3 cad, rip **4** rake, wolf **6** lecher, wanton **7** bounder, dallier, Don Juan, playboy, seducer, trifler **8** Casanova, debauche, Lothario, rakehell **9** libertine, womanizer **10** profligate **11** philanderer, skirt-chaser

Rouget de Lisle 17 French army officer

composer of: 14 La Marseillaise

rough 3 raw **4** beat, hard, rude, wild **5** bluff, blunt, bumpy, crude, cruel, draft, green, gruff, harsh, hasty, husky, quick, raspy, rocky, scaly, sharp, surly, tough, vague **6** abrupt, beat on, broken, brutal, callow, choppy, clumsy, coarse, craggy, crusty, gauche, hoarse, jagged, knotty, ragged, raging, roiled, rugged, savage, severe, stormy, thrash, turbid, uneven, vulgar **7** austere, awkward, bearish, boorish, brusque, chapped, coarsen, drastic, extreme, general, gnarled, grating, ill-bred, inexact, jarring, loutish, outline, rasping, raucous, scraggy, sketchy, stubbly, uncouth, unlevel, untamed, violent **8** agitated, churlish, rigorous, scabrous, scratchy, strident, ungentle, unsmooth **9** brutalize, difficult, ferocious, imperfect, imprecise, inelegant, irregular, manhandle, sketch out, stringent, turbulent, uncourtly, unfeeling, ungenteel, unmusical, unrefined **10** discordant, incomplete, indelicate, push around, tumultuous, unfinished, ungracious, unmannerly, unpleasant, unpolished **11** approximate, cacophonous, ill-mannered, preliminary, rudimentary, tempestuous, unluxurious **12** inharmonious **13** inconsiderate, uncomfortable, ungentlemanly

rough going 8 struggle **10** difficulty **11** arduousness **13** laboriousness

Roughing It
 author: 9 Mark Twain
 character: 12 Brigham Young, Hank Erickson **16** Slade the Terrible

rough it 4 camp **7** camp out

roughneck 4 hood, lout, punk **5** bully, rowdy, tough **6** vandal **7** hoodlum, ruffian **8** hooligan **9** barbarian **10** delinquent

roughness 7 crudity **8** acrimony, aviation, pungency, violence **9** gruffness, harshness, vulgarity **10** coarseness, inelegance, unevenness, unkindness **11** raucousness **12** irregularity, unsmoothness, unrefinement **13** undevelopment

Rough Riders see Roosevelt, Theodore

rough sketch 5 draft **7** cartoon, outline

rough-textured 5 harsh **6** coarse, nubbly, shaggy, tweedy **7** bristly, prickly **8** scratchy **9** bristling **10** sandpapery

round 3 fat **4** full, oval **5** cycle, obese, orbed, ovate, ovoid, plump, pudgy, stout, total, tubby, whole **6** chubby, circle, curved, entire, fluent, intact, portly, rotund, series, smooth **7** flowing, globoid, perfect, rounded **8** circular, complete, globular, resonant, sonorous, spheroid, thorough, unbroken

9 corpulent, egg-shaped, spherical, undivided **10** ball-shaped, elliptical, harmonious, pear-shaped, procession, succession **11** cylindrical, full-fleshed, mellifluent, progression

roundabout 5 wordy **6** random, zigzag **7** devious, erratic, oblique, sinuous, winding **8** indirect, rambling, tortuous, twisting **9** desultory **10** circuitous, discursive, meandering, serpentine **12** labyrinthine **14** circumlocutory

roundaboutness 9 wandering **10** digression, meandering **11** indirection **14** circuitousness, circumlocution

rounded 6 convex **7** curving **11** protuberant

rounding out 10 developing **12** augmentation **13** amplification

rounding-out 10 complement, completion, perfecting **12** consummation

rounds 4 beat **5** route, skirt, watch **7** circuit

roundup 6 muster, resume **7** meeting, summary **8** assembly **9** gathering **11** convocation

round up 6 gather, muster, summon **7** collect, convene, convoke, marshal **8** assemble **10** accumulate **12** call together

rouse 4 call, goad, move, prod, spur, stir, wake **5** arise, awake, get up, pique, rally, waken **6** awaken, excite, foment, kindle, incite, stir up, summon, turn on, wake up **7** animate, inflame, inspire, provoke, shake up **8** activate **9** galvanize, instigate, stimulate

roused 2 up **5** astir, awake **7** excited, incited, kindled, rallied, shook up **8** awakened, inflamed, inspired, out of bed, shaken up **9** stirred up **10** up and about

rousing 5 brisk, peppy **6** active, lively **8** animated, exciting, stirring, vigorous **9** awakening, inspiring **10** energizing, refreshing, remarkable **11** provocative, stimulating **12** exhilarating, intoxicating **13** extraordinary

Rousseau, Henri Julien Felix
 nickname: 10 Le Douanier
 born: 5 Laval **6** France
 artwork: 3 War **8** The Dream **12** Child on Rocks, The Waterfall **13** The Hungry Lion **15** Carnival Evening, The Snake Charmer **16** Bouquet of Flowers, The Sleeping Gypsy **17** The Poet and his Muse

Rousseau, Jean Jacques
 author of: 5 Emile **11** Confessions **17** La Nouvelle Heloise, The Social Contract

Rousseau, (Pierre Etienne) Theodore
 born: 5 Paris **6** France
 artwork: 7 Evening **12** After the Rain **15** Edge of the Forest, Under the

Birches **18** Descent of the Cattle, Oak Trees at Apremont **19** The Marsh in the Landes **20** The Valley of Tiffauges **21** Meadow Bordered by Trees

roust 4 bust **5** rouse **6** arrest, hassle **7** capture, seizure **12** apprehension

rout 4 beat, drub, lick, ruin, trim **5** chaos, cream, crush, panic, quell, repel, worst **6** defeat, subdue, thrash **7** beating, clobber, conquer, licking, repulse, scatter **8** drive off, drubbing, lambaste, overcome, vanquish **9** chase away, drive away, overpower, overthrow **11** put to flight **15** disorganization **18** throw into confusion

route 3 run **4** beat, pass, path, road, ship, tack **5** remit, round, track **6** artery, course, detour, direct **7** circuit, highway, parkway, passage, roadway **8** dispatch, transmit, turnpike **9** boulevard, itinerary **10** throughway **12** thoroughfare

Route 66
character: 8 Linc Case **9** Tod Stiles **10** Buz Murdock
cast: 12 Glenn Corbett, Martin Milner **13** George Maharis
car: 8 Corvette

routine 4 dull **5** order, usual **6** boring, custom, method, normal, system **7** formula, regular, tedious, typical **8** habitual, ordinary, periodic, practice **9** customary, operation, technique **11** arrangement, predictable **12** conventional, run-of-the-mill **13** unexceptional

rove 4 roam **5** drift, prowl, range **6** ramble, stroll, travel, wander **7** meander, traipse **9** gallivant

roving 6 errant **7** aimless, gadding, migrant, nomadic, roaming, vagrant **8** errantry, rambling, restless **9** desultory, itinerant, traveling, uncertain, wandering **10** changeable, discursive, meandering, inconstant **11** peripatetic **14** discursiveness

row 4 file, line, rank, spat, tier, tiff **5** brawl, chain, melee, queue, range, scrap, set-to, train, words **6** column, fracas, scrape, series, string **7** echelon, quarrel, wrangle **8** argument, disorder, sequence, squabble **9** imbroglio, wrangling **10** difference, succession **11** altercation, contretemps

rowboat 3 gig **4** bark, dory **5** barge, canoe, dingy, scull, shell, skiff **6** barque, caique, dinghy, wherry
seat: 4 taft

rowdy 6 unruly **7** lawless, raffish **9** roughneck **10** boisterous, disorderly **11** mischievous **12** obstreperous

Rowena, Lady
character in: 7 Ivanhoe
author: 5 Scott

rowing
athlete: 10 James Dietz **14** Anthony Johnson

Rowlands, Gena
real name: 23 Virginia Cathryn Rowlands
born: 9 Cambria WI
husband: 14 John Cassavetes
roles: 5 Faces **12** Opening Night **23** A Woman Under the Influence

Roxana
subtitle: 20 The Fortunate Mistress
author: 11 Daniel Defoe

Roxane see Cyrano de Bergerac

royal 5 grand, regal **6** august, lavish, superb **7** stately **8** imposing, majestic, splendid **9** monarchal, sovereign **10** munificent **11** fit for a king, magnificent, resplendent

royalty 4 sway **7** command, majesty **8** dominion, hegemony, kingship, regality **9** queenship, supremacy **11** divine right, sovereignty

Royaume de Belgique see **7** Belgium

Roy Rogers Show, The
regular: 8 Pat Brady **9** Dale Evans
theme: 16 Happy Trails to You
horse: 7 Trigger
dog: 6 Bullet
jeep: 10 Nellybelle
ranch: 10 Double R Bar

Ruanda see **6** Rwanda

rub 4 buff, swab, wipe **5** annoy, braze, catch, chafe, clean, hitch, knead, pinch, scour, scrub, smear, thing, touch, trick **6** abrade, finger, handle, polish, secret, smooth, spread, strait, stroke **7** burnish, dilemma, massage, problem, rubdown, setback, slather, trouble **8** handling, hardship, kneading, obstacle, stroking **10** difficulty, impediment, manipulate **12** manipulation

Rubaiyat of Omar Khayyam, The
author: 11 Omar Khayyam
translator: 16 Edward FitzGerald

rubber, vulcanized
invented by: 8 Goodyear

rubber plant 13 Ficus elastica
varieties: 4 baby **5** dwarf **7** Chinese **8** American, creeping, Japanese **9** mistletoe **11** small-leaved **16** broadleaved India

rubberstamp 6 affirm **7** approve, endorse

rubber tree 10 Schefflera
varieties: 4 Para **5** India **8** Castilla **11** West African

rubbery 5 tough **6** supple **7** elastic **8** flexible **9** resilient **11** stretchable

rubbing 7 chafing **8** abrading, scraping **12** manipulation

rubbish 3 rot **4** bosh, junk **5** dross, offal, trash, waste **6** babble, debris, drivel, idiocy, jetsam, litter, refuse, rubble **7** blather, garbage, inanity, twaddle **8** folderol, nonsense **9** gibberish, rigmarole, silliness **10** balderdash, flapdoodle, rigamarole

rubbish heap 4 dump **6** midden **10** refuse pile

rubble 4 junk, rock **5** brash, chalk, stent, stone, talus, trash **6** debris, refuse **7** rubbish **8** nonsense **9** fragments **11** foolishness

rube 3 oaf **4** boor, clod, hick **5** yokel **6** rustic **7** bumpkin, hayseed, peasant **10** clodhopper

Rube Goldberg 10 cartoonist
known for: 23 complicated contraptions

rub elbows 3 mix **4** club **6** hobnob, mingle **7** consort, hang out **9** associate **10** fraternize

Rubens, Peter Paul
born: 6 Siegen **10** Westphalia
artwork: 8 Lion Hunt **10** The Rainbow **15** The Garden of Love **17** Laocoon and his Sons **18** Battle of the Amazons **20** The Raising of the Cross **21** Landscape with Het Steen **22** The Descent from the Cross **23** Altarpiece of St Aldefonso **26** The Adoration of the Shepherds **27** Marchesa Brigida Spinola-Doria, Mystic Marriage of St Catherine **29** Rape of the Daughters of Leucippus **34** Helene Fourment with Two of her Children

rubicund 3 red **4** rosy **5** ruddy **6** florid **7** flushed, reddish

rubidium
chemical symbol: 2 Rb

rub out 4 do in, kill, slay **5** erase **6** efface, murder **7** bump off, destroy, execute, expunge **8** massacre **10** obliterate, put to death **11** assassinate, exterminate

ruby
species: 8 corundum
source: 5 Burma, India, Mogok **7** Bangkok, Kashmir **8** Sri Lanka, Thailand
kind: 4 star
color: 3 red

ruckus 3 row **4** fray, to-do **5** brawl, broil, clash, fight, melee **6** battle, fracas, rumpus, uproar **7** scuffle **9** imbroglio **10** donnybrook, free-for-all **11** embroilment

ruddy 3 red **4** rosy **6** florid **7** flushed, reddish, roseate, scarlet **8** blushing, rubicund, sanguine **11** rosy-cheeked

rude 3 raw **4** wild **5** blunt, crude, fresh, green, gross, gruff, rough, saucy, sulky, surly **6** abrupt, callow, clumsy, coarse, crusty, gauche, homely, rugged, rustic, sullen, uneven, vulgar **7** abusive, artless, awkward, boorish, brusque, brutish, illbred, loutish, profane, scraggy, uncivil, uncouth **8** churlish, homebred, ignorant, impolite, impudent, indecent, insolent, slapdash, untaught **9** inelegant, insulting, makeshift, primitive, roughhewn, uncourtly, ungallant, unlearned, unrefined, untrained, untutored **10** illiterate, indecorous, indelicate, peremptory, provincial, uncultured, uneducated, ungraceful, ungracious, unladylike, unmannerly, unpolished **11** bad-mannered, countrified, impertinent, uncivilized, uncourteous, undignified **12** discourteous, roughly built **13** disrespectful, inconsiderate, ungentlemanly

rudeness 9 bluntness, impudence, insolence, sauciness **10** bad manners, coarseness, disrespect, incivility **11** boorishness, discourtesy **12** impertinence, impoliteness **14** ungraciousness **17** inconsiderateness

rudimentary 5 basic **6** simple **7** initial, primary **8** immature **9** elemental, formative, imperfect, premature, primitive, vestigial **10** elementary, incomplete, prototypal **11** undeveloped

rudiments 6 basics **7** essence **8** elements **9** beginning **10** principles **12** fundamentals

Rudkus, Jurgis and Antanas
    characters in: 9 The Jungle
    author: 8 Sinclair

Rudolph, Paul
    architect of: 16 Jewett Arts Center (Wellesley College) **24** Government Services Center (Boston) **28** School of Architecture Building (Yale)

rue 4 Ruta
    varieties: 4 bush, lady, wall **5** goat's **6** common, meadow **10** tall meadow **11** early meadow **12** Alpine meadow

rue 5 mourn **6** bemoan, lament, regret, repent, repine **7** deplore

rueful 3 sad **5** sorry **6** woeful **7** doleful **8** contrite, mournful, dolorous, penitent, repining **9** depressed, plaintive, regretful, sorrowful, sorrowing **10** deplorable, lamentable, melancholy, remorseful, unpleasant

ruff 9 sandpiper
    female: 3 ree

ruffian 4 hood, thug **5** brute, bully, crook, knave, rogue, rough, rowdy, tough **6** mugger **7** hoodlum, villain **8** gangster, hooligan **9** cutthroat, roisterer, roughneck, scoundrel **10** blackguard

ruffle 4 fold, muss, wave **5** frill, plait, pleat, ruche, upset **6** edging, excite, muss up, pucker, rimple, ripple, rumple **7** agitate, confuse, crinkle, disturb, flounce, perturb, roughen, trouble, wrinkle **8** dishevel, disorder, disquiet, furbelow, unsettle **9** aggravate, agitation, commotion, corrugate **10** disarrange, discompose, disconcert **11** disturbance

ruffled 5 upset, vexed **7** annoyed, frilled, nettled, pleated **8** agitated, flounced, troubled **9** nonplused, unsettled **10** nonplussed

ruffle one's feathers 3 vex **5** anger,

annoy, pique **6** enrage, madden, nettle **7** incense, outrage, provoke **9** displease, infuriate

Rugg
    character in: 12 Little Dorrit
    author: 7 Dickens

rugged 4 hale, hard, rude, wiry, worn **5** bumpy, hardy, harsh, husky, lined, rocky, rough, stern, tough **6** brawny, coarse, craggy, jagged, ridged, robust, severe, sinewy, sturdy, taxing, trying, uneven, virile **7** arduous, cragged, onerous, scraggy, uncouth **8** athletic, furrowed, muscular, stalwart, vigorous, wrinkled **9** difficult, graceless, irregular, laborious, masculine, roughhewn, strenuous, unrefined, weathered **12** uncultivated **13** weather-beaten

Ruggles of Red Gap
    director: 10 Leo McCarey
    cast: 9 ZaSu Pitts **10** Mary Boland **14** Charlie Ruggles **15** Charles Laughton
    remade as: 10 Fancy Pants

ruin, ruins 3 gut, pot **4** doom, fall, fell, harm, raze, seed **5** break, crush, decay, level, quash, quell, shell, spoil, upset, wreck **6** beggar, defeat, ravage, squash **7** destroy, failure, remains, shatter, undoing **8** bankrupt, demolish, downfall, lay waste, make poor, overturn, remnants, wreckage **9** breakdown, devastate, disrepair, overthrow, pauperize **10** impoverish **11** destruction, devastation, dissolution **14** disintegration

ruination 4 ruin **5** wreck **6** fiasco **7** trouble **8** disaster **9** adversity, cataclysm **11** destruction, devastation **12** misadventure

ruinous 4 dire **5** fatal **6** deadly **7** adverse, baneful **8** damaging, ravaging **10** calamitous, disastrous, pernicious **11** cataclysmic, deleterious, destructive, devastating **12** catastrophic

Ruisdael, Jacob (Jakob) van
    born: 7 Haarlem **14** The Netherlands
    uncle: 18 Salomon van Ruysdael
    artwork: 5 Dunes **12** The Waterfall **13** View of Haarlem **14** Bentheim Castle **15** Winter Landscape **17** The Jewish Cemetery **28** View on the Amstel near Amsterdam

rule 3 law, run **4** find, form, head, lead, sway **5** adage, axiom, canon, guide, judge, maxim, model, order, reign **6** custom, decide, decree, direct, empire, govern, manage, method, policy, regime, settle, system **7** adjudge, command, control, declare, formula, precept, prevail, resolve, routine **8** conclude, doctrine, dominate, domineer, dominion, pass upon, practice, regnancy, regulate, standard **9** authority, criterion, determine, direction, establish, guideline, influence, ordinance, precedent, principle,

pronounce, supremacy **10** adjudicate, administer, convention, domination, government, leadership, regulation, suzerainty **11** predominate, preside over, sovereignty **12** jurisdiction, prescription **14** administration
    type: 5 bench **7** folding **9** steel tape
    constellation of: 5 Norma

rule out 4 omit **6** delete, except **7** exclude **9** eliminate

ruler 4 boss, czar, emir, head, khan, king, lord, shah, tsar, tzar **5** chief, judge, queen, rajah, sheik **6** dynast, leader, prince, satrap, shogun, sultan **7** arbiter, emperor, manager, measure, monarch, pharaoh, referee, viceroy **8** chairman, director, governor, suzerain **9** chieftain, commander, potentate, president, sovereign, yardstick **10** controller, supervisor **11** coordinator, crowned head, head of state, tape measure **12** straightedge **13** administrator

rules of conduct 6 ethics **9** moral code **10** principles **12** code of ethics

Rules of the Game
    director: 10 Jean Renoir
    cast: 10 Jean Renoir, Mila Parely, Nora Gregor **11** Marcel Dalio

ruling 6 decree **7** regnant **8** decision, dominant, reigning **9** enactment, governing, prescript **10** commanding, widespread **11** controlling, predominant **13** authoritative, predominating

ruling class 11 aristocracy **13** Establishment

Ruling Class, The
    director: 10 Peter Medak
    cast: 10 Arthur Lowe **11** Alastair Sim, Peter O'Toole **12** Harry Andrews

rum
    drink: 4 Bolo, Grog **6** Mojito **7** Gauguin **8** Daiquiri, Navy Grog, Pina Fria **9** Borinquen, Hurricane **10** Pina Colada **12** Boston Cooler **13** Planter's Punch **14** Fish House Punch **15** Bacardi Cocktail **18** Barbados Rum Swizzle
    ingredient: 8 molasses **9** sugar cane
    origin: 10 West Indies
    type: 4 dark **5** light
    with apple brandy: 6 Bolero **8** Apple Pie
    with apricot brandy: 11 Apricot Lady
    with black coffee: 9 Black Rose
    with bouillon: 6 Creole
    with bourbon: 14 Artillery Punch
    with brandy: 15 Quaker's Cocktail
    with Cointreau: 7 Acapulco **8** Casa Blanca **11** Beachcomber **12** Blue Hawaiian
    with cola: 9 Cuba Libre
    with creme de cacao: 6 Panama
    with curacao: 6 Mai-Tai **8** Blue Lady **12** Blue Hawaiian
    with Dubonnet: 3 BVD **10** Bushranger

with Galliano: 9 Bossa Nova
with gin: 3 BVD
with guava: 8 Ocho Rios
with kahlua: 10 Black Maria
with milk: 6 Rum Cow **11** Tom-and-Jerry
with Pernod: 8 Shanghai
with sloe gin: 11 Shark's Tooth
with Tia Maria: 10 Black Maria
with vermouth: 6 Bolero **8** Apple Pie **10** Black Devil **11** Shark's Tooth

rumble 4 bang, boom, clap, roar, roll **7** booming, resound, thunder **8** drumming **9** resonance **11** reverberate **13** reverberation

Rumford, Benjamin Thomson
invented: 10 photometer **11** calorimeter

Rumina
protectress of: 14 nursing mothers

ruminant 3 cow, elk, yak **4** deer, oxen **5** bison, camel, llama, moose, sheep **6** alpaca, cattle, vicuna **7** buffalo, giraffe, pensive **8** antelope **10** chevrotain, meditative, thoughtful **13** contemplative

ruminate 4 mull, muse **5** brood, study, think, weigh **6** ponder **7** reflect **8** cogitate, consider, meditate, mull over **9** speculate, think over **10** deliberate, think about **11** contemplate

ruminating 6 musing **7** pensive **8** thinking **10** meditating, meditative, reflecting, reflective, thoughtful **11** chewing over, mulling over, speculative **13** contemplating, contemplative, introspective

rumination 5 study **6** musing **7** mulling, reverie, thought **8** brooding, thinking **9** pondering **10** cogitation, meditation, reflection **11** speculation **12** deliberation **13** consideration, contemplation **15** reconsideration

rummage 4 root **5** probe **7** examine, explore, ransack **10** disarrange, poke around **11** look through

rummy 3 sot **4** lush, soak **5** drunk, souse, toper **6** barfly, boozer **7** tippler **8** card game, drunkard **9** alcoholic **11** dipsomaniac
also known as: 3 gin, rum **4** rhum **5** romme **8** gin rummy
derived from: 8 conquien

rumor 4 talk **5** story **6** babble, gossip, report **7** hearsay, whisper **8** innuendo, intimate **9** circulate, insinuate **11** insinuation, scuttlebutt, supposition

rump 4 rear, seat **5** croup, stern **6** behind, bottom, breech, dorsum **7** rear end **8** backside, buttocks, derriere, haunches **9** posterior **12** hindquarters

Rumpelstiltskin
origin: 8 Germanic
form: 5 dwarf
spun: 4 flax
made: 4 gold

rumple 4 fold, muss **5** crimp, crush **6** crease, pucker, rimple, ruffle, tousle **7** crinkle, crumple, wrinkle **8** dishevel, disorder **9** corrugate **10** disarrange

rumpus 3 ado, row **4** fray, fuss, stir, to-do **5** brawl, melee, noise **6** affray, fracas, hubbub, pother, racket, ruckus, tumult, uproar **7** rhubarb, scuffle, tempest **8** brouhaha, upheaval **9** agitation, commotion, confusion, imbroglio **10** hullabaloo **11** disturbance, embroilment

run 2 be, go **3** fly, get, hie, jog, pen, ply **4** bolt, boss, cost, dart, dash, defy, flee, flow, go by, head, kind, last, meet, melt, pass, pour, push, race, roll, rush, sort, tear, tour, trip, trot, type, vary **5** bleed, bound, class, court, drift, drive, genre, glide, hurry, impel, incur, issue, leave, pilot, print, speed, spell, split, stand, surge, total, while **6** become, canter, course, decamp, direct, elapse, endure, escape, extend, gallop, hasten, hustle, invite, ladder, manage, motion, move on, outing, period, pierce, propel, scurry, series, sprint, streak, stream, thrust, vanish, voyage, wander **7** abscond, add up to, advance, bring on, compete, current, display, freedom, get past, journey, liquefy, meander, operate, oversee, passage, proceed, publish, running, scamper, stretch, take off, vamoose **8** amount to, campaign, continue, dissolve, duration, evanesce, maneuver, meet with, navigate, progress, scramble, separate, tendency **9** direction, disappear, enclosure, encounter, excursion, go quickly, lose color, penetrate, skedaddle, supervise **10** coordinate, pilgrimage **11** continuance **12** beat a retreat, continuation, perpetuation
baseball: 5 point, score, tally **17** circuit of the bases

run aground 7 founder **8** collapse

runaround 4 slip **5** dodge **6** bypass **7** evasion **8** shunning, sidestep **9** avoidance **11** elusiveness, evasiveness **12** equivocation

run around 7 consort, hang out **9** associate, pal around **10** fraternize

runaway 4 pure **6** bolter **7** escapee, perfect, refugee **8** absolute, complete, deserter, fugitive **9** out-and-out, unalloyed **10** skedaddler **11** unmitigated, unqualified

run away 3 fly **4** flee **5** elope **6** decamp, escape, run off **7** abscond, make off **8** sneak off **10** fly the coop, make a break, take flight **12** make a getaway

rundown 5 brief **6** digest, precis, resume, review, sketch **7** outline, summary **8** abstract, synopsis **12** capitulation, condensation

run-down 5 frail, seedy, tacky, tired, weary **6** ailing, beat-up, feeble, shabby, sickly **7** rickety, worn out **8** fatigued, tattered **9** crumbling, exhausted **10** broken- down, tumble-down **11** dilapidated **12** deteriorated

run down 4 scan **5** knock **6** slight **7** detract, put down, run over **8** belittle, derogate, ridicule **9** denigrate, deprecate, discredit, disparage, downgrade, enumerate, underrate **10** depreciate, undervalue

run-in 5 brush, set-to **6** battle, fracas **7** scuffle **8** skirmish **9** encounter **10** engagement

run into 4 meet **8** flow into **9** encounter **10** chance upon, meet up with **11** collide with

run off 3 fly **4** flee **5** elope **6** escape **7** abscond, make off, runaway **9** steal away **10** take flight **15** head for the hills

run off at the mouth 3 gab **5** prate **6** babble, gabble **8** rattle on **11** talk too much

run off with 5 seize **6** abduct, kidnap **7** bear off **8** carry off **9** elope with **11** abscond with, make off with

run-of-the-mill 4 dull, so-so **5** banal, stock, usual **6** common, modest **7** average, humdrum, mundane, routine, typical **8** everyday, mediocre, middling, ordinary, passable, standard **10** second-rate **11** commonplace, indifferent, nondescript **12** unimpressive **13** unimaginative **15** undistinguished

runt 3 elf **4** chit **5** dwarf, pygmy **6** midget, peewee, shrimp **8** half-pint, Tom Thumb **11** Lilliputian
Latin: 10 homunculus

run through 5 spend, waste **6** expend, pierce **7** deplete, exhaust **8** rehearse, squander

runty 5 short **6** bantam **7** dwarfed, squatty, stunted **9** pint-sized

Runyon, Damon
author of: 12 Guys and Dolls **16** Blue Plate Special

rupture 3 pop **4** part, rent, rift, snap **5** break, burst, clash, cleft, crack, split **6** breach, divide, schism, sunder **7** discord, disrupt, fissure **8** breaking, bursting, cleavage, dissever, disunion, disunite, fracture, friction, puncture **9** severance **10** dissension, falling out, separation **12** disagreement

R U R
author: 10 Karel Capek **22** Rossum's Universal Robots

rural 4 hick **6** rustic **7** bucolic, country **8** pastoral **10** provincial **11** countrified

rural area 6 sticks **7** boonies, country **8** farmland **9** backwater, backwoods, boondocks **10** hinterland **11** countryside

ruse 4 hoax **5** blind, dodge, feint, shift, trick **6** deceit, device, scheme **8** artifice, maneuver **9** deception, stratagem

10 subterfuge **11** contrivance, machination

rush 3 hie, run **4** dart, dash, goad, leap, push, race, spur, tear, urge, whip **5** drive, haste, hurry, press, speed, storm **6** charge, hasten, hustle, plunge, scurry, sprint, urgent **7** scamper, urgency **8** dispatch, expedite, pressure, scramble **9** emergency **10** accelerate **11** top priority

rush 6 Juncus

varieties: 3 bog **4** salt, soft, wood **5** spike **6** grassy **8** scouring **9** field wood, flowering **10** common wood, least spike **11** chair-maker's, greater wood, Japanese-mat **12** slender spike **13** dwarf scouring **14** common scouring **18** variegated scouring

Rush, Benjamin
field: 8 medicine
established first: 21 free medical dispensary
signer of: 25 Declaration of Independence

rush light 3 dip **5** torch **6** candle, tallow

Rushworth
character in: 13 Mansfield Park
author: 6 Austen

Ruskin, John
author of: 13 Fors Clavigera **14** Modern Painters **17** The Stones of Venice **27** The Seven Lamps of Architecture

Russell, Bertrand
author of: 19 Why I Am Not a Christian **20** Principia Mathematica (with Alfred North)

Russell, Jane
real name: 29 Ernestine Jane Geraldine Russell
born: 9 Bemidji MN
discovered by: 12 Howard Hughes
roles: 4 Waco **9** The Outlaw **13** The French Line **22** Gentlemen Prefer Blondes, The Revolt of Mamie Stover

Russell, Rosalind
born: 11 Waterbury CT
roles: 5 Gypsy **6** Picnic **8** The Women **9** Hired Wife **10** Auntie Mame **11** Sister Kenny **13** His Girl Friday **14** My Sister Eileen **22** Mourning Becomes Electra

russet 5 apple, umber **6** auburn, copper **10** terra-cotta **11** rust-colored **12** reddish-brown

Russia (includes constituent republics of the former USSR)
other name: 17 Russian Federation
former name: 4 USSR **11** Soviet Union **31** Union of Soviet Socialist Republics
member of: 3 CIS **31** Commonwealth of Independent States
capital/largest city: 6 Moscow
others: 4 Baku, Eisk, Kiev, Okha, Omsk, Poti, Riga **5** Anapa, Batum, Gorki, Gorky, Memel, Minsk, Sochi,
Vilna, Yeisk **6** Batumi, Erevan, Frunze, Odessa, Rostov, Samara, Tiflis **7** Alma-Ata, Derbent, Donetsk, Kharkov, Liepaja, Petsamo, Pivonia, Saratov, Tallinn, Tbilisi, Yerevan **8** Dushanbe, Kishinev, Murmansk, Pechenga, Taganrog, Tashkent **9** Ashkhabad, Astrakhan, Balaklava, Kronstadt, Kuibyshev, Leningrad, Nikolayev, Petrograd, Ulyanovsk, Volgograd, Yaroslavl **10** Kronshtadt, Sevastopol, Stalingrad, Sverdlovsk **11** Chelyabinsk, Kaliningrad, Makhachkala, Novorossisk, Novosibirsk, Vladivostok **12** St Petersburg, Vladisvostok **14** Dnepropetrovsk

division/country: 6 Latvia **7** Armenia, Belarus, Estonia, Georgia, Moldova, Siberia, Ukraine **8** Moldavia **9** Kirghizia, Lithuania, Turkmenia **10** Azerbaijan, Belorussia, Kazakhstan, Kyrgyzstan, Tajikistan, Uzbekistan **12** Tadzhikistan, Turkmenistan
former: 4 Kiev **8** Novgorod

government:
legislature: 4 Duma, Rada **7** Zemstvo **8** Congress

measure: 3 fut, lof **4** duim, fass, loof, pood, quar, stof **5** duime, foute, korec, korek, ligne, osmin, pajak, stoff, stoof, vedro, verst **6** charka, liniya, osmina, paletz, sagene, stekar, tchast, tsarki, versta, verste **7** archine, arsheen, botchka, chkalik, garnetz, verchoc, verchok **8** boutylka, chetvert, krouchka, kroushka **9** chetverik **10** dessiatine **11** polugarnetz

monetary unit: 5 altin, bisti, copec, denga, grosh, kopek, ruble, shaur **6** abassi, copeck, grivna, kopeck, piatak, rouble **7** poltina, valiuta **8** auksinas, deneshka, imperial, polushka **9** poltinnik **10** altininink, chervonets

weight: 3 lof, lot **4** dola, funt, lana, last, loof, loth, once, pood, poud **5** dolia

island: 5 Kuril **7** Hiiumaa, Karagin, Shantar, Vaygach, Wrangel **8** Kolguyev, Saaremaa, Sakhalin **9** Andreanof **12** Novaya Zemlya **13** Komandorskiye **14** Franz Josef Land, Novosibirskiye **15** Severnaya Zemlya

lake: 3 Seg **4** Aral, Azov, Kola, Sego, Topo, Vigo **5** Chany, Elton, Erara, Ilmen, Lacha, Onega, Pskov, Vozhe **6** Baikal, Byeloe, Ladoga, Peipus, Selety, Taymyr, Tengiz, Zaysan **8** Balkhash **10** Caspian Sea

mountain: 5 Altai, Lenin, Sayan, Urals **6** Anadyr, Elbrus, Koryak, Pamirs, Pobedy **7** Belukha, Crimean, Khibiny, Stanovi, Zhiguli **8** Caucasus, Dzhughur, Stanavoi, Tien Shan **9** Kopet Dagh, Narodnaya, Pamir-Alai, Yablonovy **10** Carpathian **11** Sikhote-Alin, Verkhoyansk

highest point: 9 Communism

river: 3 Don, Ili **4** Amur, Lena, Neva, Ural **5** Dvina, Kuban, Neman, Volga **6** Kolyma, Moskva **7** Dnieper, Pechora, Yenisei **8** Amu Darya, Dniester, Ob-Irtysh, Syr Darya **9** Indigirka

sea: 4 Aral, Azov, Kara **5** Black, Japan, White **6** Arctic, Baltic, Bering, Laptev **7** Barents, Caspian, Chukchi, Okhotsk, Pacific

physical feature:
gulf: 4 Azov **5** Mezen **9** Kara-Bogaz, Shelikhov
peninsula: 4 Kola **5** Yamal **6** Crimea, Taymyr **7** Chukchi, Karelia **9** Kamchatka **10** Mangyshlak
strait: 5 Tatar **6** Bering **8** Bosporus **11** Dardanelles

people: 3 Jew **4** Slav **5** Ersar, Kulak, Tatar, Uzbec **6** Kazakh, Soviet, Velika **7** Chukchi, Cossack, Kirghiz, Latvian, Russian, Tadzhik, Turkmen **8** Armenian, Estonian, Georgian, Siberian **9** Moldavian, Ukrainian **10** Lithuanian **11** Azerbaijani, Belorussian

actor: 12 Stanislavsky
author: 5 Gogol **7** Nabokov, Pushkin, Tolstoy **8** Turgenev **9** Ehrenburg, Pasternak, Sholokhov **10** Dostoevsky **12** Solzhenitsyn
composer: 6 Glinka **7** Borodin **9** Prokofiev **10** Mussorgsky, Stravinsky **11** Tchaikovsky **12** Rachmaninoff, Shostakovich **14** Rimsky-Korsakov
cosmonaut: 11 Yuri Gagarin
czar/tsar/tzar: 4 Ivan, Paul **5** Peter **6** Alexis **7** Michael **8** Nicholas **9** Alexander **12** Boris Godunov
dancer: 7 Nureyev, Pavlova **8** Danilova, Nijinsky **11** Baryshnikov
dynasty: 7 Romanov
early people: 3 Hun **4** Goth **5** Tatar **6** Khazar, Mongol, Tartar **8** Norsemen, Scythian **9** Cimmerian, Sarmatian, Varangian
empress: 9 Alexandra, Catherine
hereditary noble: 5 boyar
leader: 5 Beria, Lenin **6** Stalin, Suslov **7** Gromyko, Kosygin, Molotov, Trotsky, Yeltsin **8** Andropov, Brezhnev, Bukharin, Bulganin, Kerensky, Malenkov, Podgorny **9** Chernenko, Gorbachev **10** Khrushchev
monk: 8 Rasputin
prince: 4 Oleg **5** Rurik **8** Vladimir
revolutionary: 9 bolshevik **10** Decembrist
ruler: 5 Tatar **6** Mongol **8** Batu Khan
scientist: 6 Pavlov **9** Mendeleev **11** Tsiolkovsky
language: 5 Evenk, Tatar, Uzbek **6** Buriat, Kalmyk, Kazakh **7** Finnish, Kirghiz, Latvian, Russian, Tadzhik, Turkmen **8** Armenian, Estonian, Georgian, Ossetian **9** Moldavian,

Ukrainian **10** Lithuanian **11** Belorussian
  alphabet: 8 cyrillic
religion: 5 Islam **7** Judaism **8** Buddhism, Lutheran **10** Protestant **13** Roman Catholic **15** Russian Orthodox **16** Armenian Orthodox, Georgian Orthodox
place: 7 Kremlin **9** Red Square
  art gallery: 9 Tretyakov
  castle: 8 Starosty
  cathedral: 5 Sobor **7** Zagorsk **8** St Basils
  cemetery: 11 Piskarevsky
  museum: 9 Hermitage **12** Petrodvorets **18** Cathedral of St Isaac
  palace: 6 Winter
  park: 5 Gorky
  ruins: 7 Bukhara **10** Echmiadzin **15** Gediminas Castle
  prison: 8 Lubyanka
  street: 11 Kreshchatik **14** Nevski Prospekt
  theater: 7 Bolshoi
feature:
  collective farm: 7 kolkhoz
  country house: 5 dacha
  dance: 4 kolo **5** gopac, hopak, saber **6** cossac, trepak **7** cosaque, ziganka **8** kozachok **9** tzazatski
  dance company: 5 Kirov **7** Bolshoi
  labor camp: 5 gulag
  musical instrument: 9 balalaika
  secret police: 3 KGB, MGB **4** NKVD, OGPU **5** Cheka
  state farm: 7 sovkhoz
food:
  caviar: 13 ikra zernistia
  cereal: 5 kasha
  sour cream: 7 smetana
  dessert: 8 vareniki
  dish: 4 plov **5** pirau **6** pelemo **8** osetrina, shashlyk **16** kotleta po kievski
  drink: 4 kvas **5** kvass, vodka **6** chacha, kumiss
  filled pastries: 8 piroshki, pirozhki
  soup: 5 shchi **6** borshch **7** borscht, borsch
Russian village commune 3 mir
rust 3 rot **5** decay, stain **6** auburn, blight, russet **7** corrode, crumble, decline, oxidize **9** corrosion, oxidation **11** deteriorate **12** reddish-brown **13** reddish-yellow
rust-colored 5 henna **6** auburn, russet **8** cinnamon **12** reddish-brown
rustic 4 rube, rude **5** crude, plain, rough, rural, yokel **6** coarse, gauche, simple **7** awkward, boorish, bucolic, bumpkin, country, hayseed, loutish, peasant, uncouth **8** agrarian, churlish, cloddish, pastoral **9** inelegant, unrefined **10** clodhopper, countryman, provincial, uncultured, unpolished **11**

countrified **13** country person **15** unsophisticated
rustle 3 rub **4** hiss, stir **5** swish, whish **6** riffle
rustler 5 thief **6** bandit, outlaw **7** brigand **9** desperado
rusty 5 moldy, stiff **6** rotten, rusted **7** reddish, tainted **8** corroded, sluggish **11** rust-colored **13** out of practice
rut 3 cut **4** mark **5** ditch, habit, score, tread **6** furrow, groove, gutter, hollow, trench, trough **7** channel, depress, dig into, pattern **8** monotony **9** deep track **10** depression **11** dull routine
Ruth
  husband: 4 Boaz **6** Mahlon
  son: 4 Obed
  father-in-law: 9 Elimelech
  mother-in-law: 5 Naomi
  brother-in-law: 7 Chilion
Ruth, George Herman
  nickname: 4 Babe **12** Sultan of Swat
  sport: 8 baseball
  position: 8 outfield
  team: 14 New York Yankees
Rutherford, Dame Margaret
  born: 6 London **7** England
  roles: 7 The VIPs **10** Jane Marple **12** Blithe Spirit **27** The Importance of Being Earnest
Rutherford, Ernest
  field: 7 physics
  nationality: 7 British
  discovered: 6 proton **13** atomic nucleus, beta radiation **14** alpha radiation, gamma radiation
  awarded: 10 Nobel Prize
ruthless 5 cruel, harsh **6** brutal, deadly, savage **7** bestial, brutish, callous, inhuman, vicious **8** pitiless **9** barbarous, ferocious, heartless, merciless, murderous, unfeeling, unpitying, unsparing **10** relentless, sanguinary, unmerciful **11** cold-blooded, hardhearted, remorseless, unforgiving, unrelenting **12** bloodthirsty
ruthlessness 7 cruelty **9** barbarity, brutality, harshness **10** inhumanity, savageness **11** viciousness
Ruysdael, Salomon van
  born: 7 Naarden **14** The Netherlands
  nephew: 16 Jacob van Ruisdael
  artwork: 9 River Bank **10** River Scene **14** River Landscape **18** River with Ferry Boat
Rwanda
  other name: 6 Ruanda
  capital/largest city: 6 Kigali
  others: 6 Biumba, Butare, Kibuye, Nyanza **7** Astrida, Gisenyi, Kibungu **8** Cyangugu **9** Ruhengeri
  division:
    colonial: 12 Ruanda-Urundi

  monetary unit: 5 franc **7** centime
  lake: 4 Kivu **5** Ihema **6** Bufera, Bulera, Mohasi **7** Rugwero, Ruhnodo **8** Mugesera, Tshohoha
  mountain: 7 Mitumba, Virunga **8** Muhavura
  highest point: 9 Karisimbi
  river: 6 Kagera, Ruzizi **7** Akagera **8** Akanyaru **9** Luvironza **10** Nyawarongo
  physical feature:
    forest: 7 Nyungwe
    valley: 11 Western Rift
  people: 3 Twa **4** Hutu **5** Batwa, Pygmy, Tutsi **6** Bahutu, Watusi **7** Batutsi
    explorer: 5 Speke **6** Gotzen
    leader: 9 Kayibanda **11** Habyarimana
  language: 6 French **7** Swahili **11** Kinyarwanda
  religion: 7 animism **13** Roman Catholic
  place:
    game reserve: 6 Gabiro
    park: 6 Albert, Kagera **16** Virunga Volcanoes
  feature:
    clothing: 5 pagne
    king: 5 mwami
Ryan, Cornelius
  author of: 13 A Bridge Too Far, The Last Battle, The Longest Day
Ryan, Robert
  born: 9 Chicago IL
  roles: 6 Caught **8** The Set-Up **9** Billy Budd, Crossfire **12** Clash by Night, The Wild Bunch **13** Act of Violence, The Longest Day **14** About Mrs Leslie, God's Little Acre **17** Bad Day at Black Rock **18** The Woman on the Beach
Ryder, Albert Pinkham
  born: 12 New Bedford MA
  artwork: 12 The Race Track (Death on a Pale Horse) **15** Toilers of the Sea **27** Siegfried and the Rhine Maidens
rye 6 Secale
  varieties: 4 wild **5** giant **6** common **8** Aral wild, blue wild **9** Altai wild, giant wild, Volga wild **10** Canada wild **11** Chinese wild, Russian wild **12** Siberian wild, Virginia wild
  type: 6 liquor **7** whiskey
  origin: 7 Ireland **8** Scotland
  ingredient: 10 mash grains
  drink: 9 Cablegram **11** John Collins, Whiskey Sour
  with Cointreau: 10 Temptation
  with Pernod: 3 TNT
  with vermouth: 8 Brooklyn **9** Algonquin

Saarinen, Eero
  father: 5 Eliel
  architect of: 11 St Louis Arch **20** Gateway to the West Arch (St Louis) **26** Trans World Airlines Terminal (NYC) **28** General Motors Technical Center (Warren MI) **39** Columbia Broadcasting Company Headquarters (NYC)
  style: 13 International

Saarinen, Eliel
  son: 4 Eero
  architect of: 16 Cranbrook Academy (Bloomfield Hills MI) **18** Kleinhaus Music Hall (Buffalo) **19** Tanglewood Music Shed (MA) **20** Christ Lutheran Church (Minneapolis MN), First Christian Church (Columbus IN)

Saba *see* **5** Sheba

Sabbath 8 Lord's Day **9** day of rest

Sabbatical: A Romance
  author: 9 John Barth

saber, sabre 3 cut **4** kill, stab **5** blade, sword, wound **6** cutlas, rapier, strike **7** cutlass, soldier **8** scimitar **10** broadsword

Sabin, Albert Bruce
  field: 8 medicine
  developed: 16 oral polio vaccine

sable 3 fur, jet **4** dark, inky **5** black, ebony, raven

sabotage 3 sap **6** retard **7** cripple, destroy, disable, disrupt, subvert **8** paralyze **9** undermine, vandalize **10** subversion **12** incapacitate

sabra 11 Israeli-born **14** native of Israel

Sabra
  type: 7 liqueur
  origin: 6 Israel
  flavor: 6 orange **9** chocolate

Sac *see* **4** Sauk

saccharine 5 gooey, mushy, soppy, sweet **6** sugary, syrupy **7** candied, cloying, honeyed, maudlin, mawkish, sugared **9** offensive, oversweet, revolting, sickening **10** disgusting, nauseating **11** sentimental

sacerdotal 5 papal **8** clerical, pastoral, priestly **9** apostolic, canonical, episcopal **10** pontifical **11** ministerial **12** hierarchical **14** ecclesiastical

Sachs, Hans 13 Meistersinger

sack 3 bag, rob **4** loot, pack, raid **5** pouch, spoil, store, waste **6** duffel, maraud, rapine, ravage, tear up **7** de-spoil, pillage, plunder, ransack **8** spoliate **9** depredate, duffel bag, gunnysack, haversack, marauding **10** plundering, ravishment **11** depredation, devastation **12** despoliation

sackbut 18 medieval instrument
  resembles: 8 trombone

sacrament 3 vow **4** rite **5** troth **6** pledge, plight, ritual **7** liturgy, promise, service **8** ceremony, contract, covenant **9** solemnity **10** ceremonial, obligation, observance **11** affirmation **12** ministration

sacramental 4 holy **6** ritual **7** blessed **10** ceremonial, liturgical

Sacraments, Seven 7 Baptism, Penance **9** Eucharist, Last Rites, Matrimony **10** Holy Orders **12** Confirmation **13** Holy Communion **14** Extreme Unction, Reconciliation **18** Anointing of the Sick

sacred 4 holy **6** church **7** blessed, revered **8** Biblical, hallowed, hieratic **9** religious, venerable **10** sanctified, scriptural **11** consecrated **14** ecclesiastical

Sacred and Profane Love Machine, The
  author: 11 Iris Murdoch

Sacred writings 5 Bible **11** Bibliotheca

sacrifice 4 cede, loss **5** forgo, waive **6** forego, give up, homage **7** cession, forfeit, offer up **8** immolate, oblation, offering, renounce **9** surrender **10** concession, immolation, lustration, relinquish **12** renunciation **14** relinquishment

sacrilege 3 sin **7** impiety, mockery, outrage **8** iniquity **9** blasphemy, profanity, violation **10** irreligion, sinfulness, wickedness **11** desecration, impiousness, irreverence, profanation, profaneness

sacrilegious 7 impious, profane **10** irreverent **11** blasphemous, irreligious

sacrosanct 4 holy **5** godly **6** divine, solemn **8** hallowed, heavenly **9** celestial, inviolate, religious, spiritual **10** inviolable, unexamined **11** consecrated **12** unquestioned

sacrum
  bone of: 11 base of spine

sad 3 low **4** blue, grim, hard, hurt **5** grave **6** dismal, solemn, taxing, tragic, trying, woeful **7** adverse, crushed, doleful, forlorn, grieved, joyless, maudlin, pitiful, serious, unhappy **8** dejected, desolate, downcast, grievous, mournful, pathetic, touching, troubled, wretched **9** cheerless, depressed, difficult, miserable, sorrowful **10** calamitous, chapfallen, despairing, despondent, dispirited, distressed, lachrymose, lamentable, melancholy **11** crestfallen, distressing, pessimistic, troublesome, unfortunate **12** disconsolate, heartrending, heavyhearted, inconsolable **13** brokenhearted, griefstricken, heartbreaking **14** down in the dumps, down in the mouth
  French: 6 triste

Sadat, Anwar el-
  president of: 5 Egypt
  awarded: 15 Nobel Peace Prize
  author of: 18 In Search of Identity

sadden 4 damp, dash **5** crush **6** burden, deject, grieve, sorrow, subdue **7** depress **8** aggrieve, dispirit **10** discourage, dishearten

saddle with 9 stick with **10** burden with **12** encumber with **18** make responsible for

Sade, Marquis de
  author of: 7 Justine **8** Juliette **14** 120 Days of Sodom **26** The Philosopher in the Bedroom

sadistic 6 brutal **7** vicious **8** fiendish, perverse **9** perverted **12** bloodthirsty

sadness
  French: 9 tristesse

sad poem 5 elegy **6** lament

Sad Sack
  creator: 11 George Baker

Saehrimnir
  origin: 12 Scandinavian
  form: 4 boar
  served in: 8 Valhalla
  feat: 12 regeneration

safe 4 firm, sure, wary **5** sound, vault, whole **6** intact, modest, secure, stable, steady, unhurt **7** certain, guarded, prudent **8** cautious, defended, discreet, harmless, reliable, unbroken, unharmed **9** innocuous, protected, undamaged, unexposed, unscathed **10** dependable, protecting **11** circumspect, impregnable, out of danger, trustworthy, unscratched **12** conservative, invulnerable, noncommittal

safeguard 4 ward 5 armor, charm 6 amulet, buffer, defend, harbor, screen, secure, shield 7 bulwark, defense, fortify, protect, shelter 8 conserve, garrison, preserve, security, talisman 10 precaution, protection

safekeeping 4 care 6 charge 7 custody 8 security 9 husbandry 10 protection 12 conservation, guardianship, preservation

Safety Net, The
   author: 12 Heinrich Boll

saffron
   botanical name: 13 Crocus sativus
   also called: 6 Krokus
   Moorish: 6 Zafran
   of all spices most: 6 costly
   color: 6 orange, yellow 12 yellow-orange
   used as: 8 coloring, cosmetic, medicine 9 fabric dye
   origin: 5 Egypt, Syria 8 Holy Land 9 Palestine
   use: 4 rice 5 bread, rolls

sag 3 bow, dip 4 drop, fail, flag, flap, flop, keel, lean, list, sink, sway, tilt, tire 5 droop, pitch, slump, weary 6 billow, plunge, settle, weaken 7 decline, descend, give way 8 diminish

saga 4 epic, myth, tale, yarn 6 legend 7 history, romance 9 adventure, chronicle, narrative
   French: 11 roman-fleuve

sagacious 4 foxy, wise 5 acute, canny, sharp, smart, sound 6 astute, brainy, clever, shrewd 7 cunning, knowing, prudent, sapient, tactful 8 discreet, rational, sensible 9 judicious, practical 10 diplomatic, discerning, perceptive 11 calculating, intelligent 13 perspicacious 14 discriminating

sagacity 6 acumen, brains, smarts, wisdom 8 sapience 9 canniness, smartness 10 astuteness, braininess, cleverness, shrewdness 11 discernment 12 intelligence, perspicacity 13 judiciousness 14 discrimination

Sagan, Carl
   author of: 6 Cosmos 7 Contact 16 The Dragons of Eden

Sagan, Francoise
   real name: 16 Francoise Quoirez
   author of: 13 A Certain Smile 15 Aimez-vous Brahms 16 Bonjour Tristesse

sage 4 guru, wise 5 sound 6 astute, pundit, savant, shrewd 7 egghead, knowing, prudent, sapient, scholar, wise man 8 mandarin, sensible 11 intelligent, philosopher
   French: 6 savant
   Latin: 5 magus, solon

sage 6 Salvia 12 S officinalis
   varieties: 3 bog 4 baby, blue, gray, rose, sand, wood 5 black, lilac, Texas, white 6 autumn, common, desert, garden, purple, silver, yellow

---

7 bladder, gentian, scarlet, Spanish, thistle, Vervain 8 creeping, gray ball, mealy-cup, rose-leaf 9 Bethlehem, Jerusalem 11 Mexican bush 16 pineapple-scented

   means: 6 to heal, to save
   strengthens: 6 memory, wisdom 8 prudence
   makes men: 8 immortal
   origin: 7 Albania 10 Yugoslavia 13 Mediterranean
   use: 4 pork 6 breads, cheese 7 chicken, poultry, seafood 8 stuffing

Sage of Concord
   nickname of: 17 Ralph Waldo Emerson

Sagittarius
   symbol: 6 archer 7 centaur
   planet: 7 Jupiter
   rules: 10 philosophy 15 higher education
   born: 8 November, December

Sagittary
   form: 7 centaur
   carried: 3 bow

said 5 above, quoth 6 quoted, spoken, stated 7 related, uttered 8 repeated

Saigon
   capital of: 7 Vietnam
   now: 13 Ho Chi Minh City

sail 3 fly 4 boat, scud, skim, soar 5 drift, float, glide, steam 6 course, cruise, voyage 8 navigate 9 excursion

sailboat 4 saic, yawl 5 craft, ketch, sloop, yacht 6 vessel 7 sunfish 8 schooner 9 catamaran
   part: 4 boom, mast 6 canvas 7 rigging 9 mainsheet

sailcloth 4 duck 6 canvas

Sailing to Byzantium
   author: 7 W B Yeats

sailor 3 gob, tar 4 salt 6 sea dog, seaman 7 mariner, voyager 8 deckhand, seafarer 9 navigator, yachtsman
   terms: 3 yaw 4 ahoy, alee, conn, draw, fast, furl, heel, list, luff, moor, scud, tack, trim, wake 5 avast, belay, heave, hoist, lie to, pilot, pitch, weigh 6 aweigh 8 aweather, put about

sailors
   patron saint: 4 Elmo

Sails (of Argo)
   constellation of: 4 Vela

saint 6 martyr
   Buddhist: 5 arhat 11 bodhisattva
   Chinese: 8 immortal
   Islamic: 3 pir
   lives of the saints: 8 menology 9 hagiology 11 hagiography 13 acta sanctorum
   process of becoming: 12 canonization
   relic box: 6 chasse
   remains: 5 relic
   symbol: 4 halo

Saint, Eva Marie

---

   born: 8 Newark NJ
   roles: 6 Exodus 15 On the Waterfront 16 North by Northwest

saint, patron
   acolytes: 13 John Berchmans
   actors: 8 Genesius
   artists: 4 Luke
   astronomers: 7 Dominic
   athletes: 9 Sebastian
   authors: 14 Francis de Sales
   aviators: 15 Our Lady of Loreto 16 Therese of Lisieux 17 Joseph of Cupertino
   bakers: 8 Nicholas 18 Elizabeth of Hungary
   bankers: 7 Matthew
   barbers: 5 Louis 6 Cosmas, Damian
   barren women: 9 Felicitas 14 Anthony of Padua
   beggars/cripples: 5 Giles
   blind: 6 Odilia 7 Raphael
   bodily ills: 16 Our Lady of Lourdes
   boy scouts: 6 George
   brides: 14 Nicholas of Myra
   builders: 13 Vincent Ferrer
   butchers: 4 Luke 7 Hadrian 14 Anthony of Egypt
   carpenters: 6 Joseph
   cancer patients: 9 Peregrine
   children: 10 Santa Claus 14 Nicholas of Myra
   comedians: 5 Vitus
   cooks: 6 Martha 8 Lawrence
   deaf: 14 Francis de Sales
   dying: 6 Joseph 7 Barbara
   emigrants: 14 Frances Cabrini
   England: 6 George
   eye sufferers: 4 Lucy
   falsely accused: 15 Raymond Nonnatus
   farmers: 6 George 7 Isidore
   fishermen: 5 Peter 6 Andrew
   foreign missions: 13 Francis Xavier 16 Therese of Lisieux
   foundlings: 13 Holy Innocents
   France: 5 Denis
   gardeners: 6 Fiacre, Phocas 7 Adelard, Dorothy, Tryphon
   heart patients: 9 John of God
   hospitals: 9 John of God 12 Jude Thaddeus 16 Camillus de Lellis
   housewives: 4 Anne
   hunters: 6 Hubert 10 Eustachius
   invalids: 4 Roch
   Ireland: 7 Patrick
   Italy: 7 Anthony
   laborers: 5 James 7 Isidore 9 John Bosco
   lawyers: 3 Ivo 4 Ives 8 Genesius 10 Thomas More
   librarians: 6 Jerome
   lovers: 9 Valentine
   mariners: 4 Elmo 7 Michael 19 Nicholas of Tolentino
   mentally ill: 6 Dympna
   merchants: 14 Nicholas of Myra 15 Francis of Assisi
   metalworkers: 7 Eligius

miners: **7** Barbara
mothers: **6** Monica
musicians: **7** Cecilia, Dunstan **15** Gregory the Great
Norway: **4** Olaf, Olav
nurses: **6** Agatha **7** Alexius, Raphael **9** John of God **16** Camillus de Lellis
painters: **4** Luke
philosophers: **6** Justin **21** Catherine of Alexandria
physicians: **4** Luke **6** Cosmas, Damian **7** Raphael **9** Pantaleon
pilgrims: **5** James **7** Alexius
poets: **5** David **7** Cecilia
policemen: **7** Michael
poor souls: **19** Nicholas of Tolentino
postal workers: **7** Gabriel
priests: **19** Jean-Baptiste Vianney
printers: **8** Genesius **9** John of God **16** Augustine of Hippo
prisoners: **6** Dismas **7** Barbara **13** Joseph Cafasso
rheumatism: **15** James the Greater
sailors: **4** Elmo **7** Brendan, Erasmus, Eulalia **8** Cuthbert, Nicholas **11** Christopher **13** Peter Gonzales
scholars: **6** Brigid
scientists: **6** Albert
Scotland: **6** Andrew
sculptors: **6** Claude
seamen: **4** Elmo **14** Francis of Paolo
sick: **7** Michael **9** John of God **16** Camillus de Lellis
singers: **7** Cecilia, Gregory
skiers: **7** Bernard
shoemakers: **7** Crispin
soldiers: **6** George **7** Hadrian **8** Ignatius **9** Joan of Arc, Sebastian **13** Martin of Tours
Spain: **5** James **8** Santiago
students: **13** Thomas Aquinas **21** Catherine of Alexandria
surgeons: **6** Cosmas, Damian
tailors: **9** Homobonus
tax collectors: **7** Matthew
teachers: **15** Gregory the Great **21** Catherine of Alexandria, Jean Baptiste de la Salle
theologians: **9** Augustine **16** Alphonsus Liguori
throat sufferers: **6** Blaise
travelers: **7** Raphael **11** Christopher **14** Anthony of Padua, Nicholas of Myra
Wales: **5** David
winegrowers: **7** Vincent
workingmen: **6** Joseph
writers: **14** Francis de Sales
youth: **13** John Berchmans **15** Aloysius Gonzaga, Gabriel Possenti
Saint, The
author: **15** Leslie Charteris
character: **12** Simon Templar **26** Inspector Claude Eustace Teal
cast: **10** Roger Moore
Saint Anthony's fire 6 herpes **8** ergotism, shingles **10** erysipelas
Saint Elmo's fire 5 flame, hermo **6** castor, corona, furole, helena **9** corposant **12** luminescence
Saint Esprit 9 Holy Ghost **10** Holy Spirit
Saint-Exupery, Antoine de
author of: **11** Night Flight **12** Southern Mail **15** The Little Prince **16** Wind Sand and Stars
Saint Francis
born: **6** Assisi
called: **9** Poverello
Saint-Gaudens, Augustus
born: **6** Dublin **7** Ireland
artwork: **7** Puritan **13** Mrs Henry Adams (Grief) **14** General Sherman **15** Admiral Farragut **16** President Lincoln
Saint Jack
author: **11** Paul Theroux
Saint Joan
author: **17** George Bernard Shaw
Saint John's bread 5 carob
Saint John's wort 5 amber **6** tutsan **7** ascyrum, cammock **9** androseme, hypericum, rosin-rose **10** broombrush **11** Aaron's-beard
saintliness 6 purity **8** goodness, holiness **9** beatitude, godliness **11** blessedness **12** spirituality
Saint Lucia, St Lucia
capital: **8** Castries
highest point: **5** Gimie
island group: **8** Windward **14** Lesser Antilles
language: **6** patois
location: **9** Caribbean
saintly 4 good, holy **5** godly, moral, pious **6** devout **7** angelic, blessed, exalted, sinless, upright **8** beatific, faithful, reverent, virtuous **9** believing, religious, righteous, spiritual **10** benevolent
Saint Paul
born: **6** Tarsus
companion: **4** Luke
epistle: **5** Titus **6** Romans **7** Hebrews, Timothy **8** Philemon **9** Ephesians, Galatians **10** Colossians **11** Corinthians, Philippians **13** Thessalonians
Saint Paul's Cathedral (London)
architect: **4** Wren
Saint Peter
called: **4** Rock **5** Simon **6** Cephas
brother: **6** Andrew
Saint-Saens, (Charles) Camille
born: **5** Paris **6** France
composer of: **12** Danse Macabre **14** Samson et Dalila **16** Samson and Delilah **18** La Jeunesse d'Hercule **20** Carnival of the Animals
Saints' lives
writer of: **12** hagiographer
Saint Vincent, St Vincent
capital: **9** Kingstown
highest point: **9** Soufriere
Indian: **5** Carib **6** Arawak
island group: **8** Windward **14** Lesser Antilles
islands: **10** Grenadines
language: **6** patois
location: **9** Caribbean
volcano: **9** Soufriere
Saint Vitus' dance 6 chorea
sake 3 end **4** care, gain, good **5** cause **6** behalf, object, profit, regard **7** account, benefit, concern, purpose, respect, welfare **8** interest **9** advantage **11** enhancement **13** consideration
sake
type: **4** wine **6** spirit
origin: **5** Japan
ingredient: **4** rice
Sakharov, Andrei Dimitrievich
field: **7** physics
nationality: **7** Russian
researched: **14** nuclear fission
defended: **12** civil liberty
exiled to: **5** Gorky
awarded: **10** Nobel Prize
Saki
real name: **7** H H Munro
author of: **8** Reginald **20** Beasts and Super-Beasts **21** The Chronicles of Clovis **23** The Unbearable Bassington
salaam 3 bow **6** homage **9** obeisance
Salacia
partner of: **7** Neptune
salacious 4 lewd, sexy **7** lustful, obscene **8** indecent **9** lecherous **10** lascivious, libidinous **12** pornographic
salad days 5 prime, youth **6** heyday **9** flowering
salamander 3 eft **4** newt **5** giant, siren, tiger **6** lizard, red eft **7** axolotl, urodela **8** congo eel, mudpuppy **9** amphibian, fire-eater, proteidae **10** hellbender, necturidae **14** red-spotted newt
Salamis
father: **6** Asopus
mother: **6** Metope
son: **8** Cychreus
Salammbo
author: **15** Gustave Flaubert
character: **5** Matho **8** Hamilcar, Spendius **9** Narr Havas
setting: **8** Carthage
salary 3 pay **5** wages **6** income **7** stipend **8** earnings **9** allowance, emolument **10** recompense **12** remuneration
sale 3 cut **7** auction, bargain, selling, special **8** discount, exchange, markdown, transfer **9** reduction
Salem
suburb of: **6** Boston
old site of: **11** witch trials
salesperson 5 agent, clerk **6** vendor **8** huckster
salient 6 arrant, marked **7** glaring, notable, obvious **8** flagrant, manifest, palpable, striking **9** egregious, important, prominent **10** noteworthy, no-

ticeable, pronounced, protruding, re-markable **11** conspicuous, outstanding, substantial **12** consider-able

Salii
also: **6** Salian
form: **7** priests
priests of: **4** Mars
guarded: **7** ancilia **13** sacred shields

saline 4 salt **5** briny, salty **8** brackish

Salinger, J D 7 recluse
author of: **11** Nine Stories **14** Franny and Zooey **18** The Catcher in the Rye
character: **4** Esme

Salisbury
capital of: **8** Zimbabwe

Salisbury, Harrison E
author of: **16** American in Russia **19** A Journey for Our Times, Black Night White Snow

Salish (Flatheads)
language family: **8** Salishan
location: **5** Idaho **6** Oregon **7** Montana **10** Washington **15** British Columbia

Salk, Jonas Edward
field: **8** medicine
developed: **12** (inactivated) polio vaccine

salle a manger 10 dining room
literally: **13** hall for eating

sallow 3 wan **4** gray, pale **5** ashen, livid **6** anemic, pallid, sickly, yellow **7** bilious **9** jaundiced, washed-out, yellowish

sallowness 6 pallor **7** wanness **8** paleness **10** sickliness **11** biliousness **13** colorlessness, yellowishness

Sallust
author of: **9** Histories **13** War of Jugurtha **20** Conspiracy of Catiline

sally 3 mot **4** flow, pour, quip, raid, trip **5** erupt, foray, surge **6** attack, banter, charge, outing, retort, sortie, spring, thrust **7** debouch, journey **8** badinage, repartee **9** excursion, wisecrack, witticism **10** expedition **13** counterattack

Salmacis
form: **5** nymph
loved: **14** Hermaphroditus
joined with: **14** Hermaphroditus
became: **13** hermaphrodite **14** bisexual person

Salmagundi
author: **16** Washington Irving

salmon 4 fish, king **5** cohoe **6** silver **7** chinook, Pacific, quinnat, sockeye, spawner **8** Atlantic, humpback
enclosure: **4** yair
female: **4** raun **6** baggit
genus: **12** Oncorhynchus
hatchling: **4** pink **6** alevin
male: **3** gib **4** buck, cock
post-spawning: **4** kelt **7** shedder

pre-spawning: **7** gilling, girling
young: **4** parr **7** essling

Salome
father: **11** Herod Philip
mother: **8** Herodias
husband: **7** Zebedee
opera by: **7** (Richard) Strauss
character: **5** Herod (the Tetrarch) **8** Herodias, Jokanaan (John the Baptist) **9** Narraboth

salon 4 hall **7** gallery **11** drawing room **13** establishment

saloon 3 bar, inn, pub **6** bistro, tavern **7** barroom, ginmill, taproom **8** alehouse **9** roadhouse, speakeasy

salt 3 wit **4** best, corn, cure, pick, save **5** brine, briny, cream, elect, humor, savor, smack, souse, spice **6** choice, flavor, pickle, saline, season, select **8** brackish, marinate, piquancy, pungency **9** seasoning **12** quintessence

Salten, Felix
author of: **5** Bambi

saltwater 3 sea **5** brine, ocean

salty 4 racy **5** briny, funny, spicy, terse, witty **6** corned, ribald, risque, saline **7** pungent, zestful **8** brackish, improper

salubrious 7 bracing, healthy **9** healthful, wholesome **10** beneficial, lifegiving **11** therapeutic **12** invigorating

salubriousness 11 healthiness **13** healthfulness, wholesomeness

Salus
origin: **5** Roman
goddess of: **6** health **10** prosperity
corresponds to: **6** Hygeia

salutary 4 good **5** tonic **6** useful **7** healing, healthy **8** curative, sanitary **9** healthful, wholesome **10** beneficial, profitable **12** advantageous

salutation 3 bow **5** hello, howdy, toast **6** curtsy **7** address, welcome **8** greeting **9** reception
Hawaiian: **5** aloha
Italian: **4** ciao
Latin: **3** ave

salute 3 ave **4** hail, kiss **5** bow to, cheer, greet, honor, nod to, salvo **6** accost, homage, praise, wave to **7** address, applaud, respect, welcome **8** accolade, applause, greeting **9** laudation, reverence **11** acclamation, recognition **12** congratulate

Salvador
author: **10** Joan Didion

salvage 4 junk, save **5** scrap **6** debris, rescue **7** recover, remains, restore **8** recovery, retrieve **9** retrieval **11** reclamation **12** rehabilitate

salvation 4 rock **5** grace **6** rescue, saving **8** election, lifeline, mainstay, recovery, survival **9** retrieval **10** protection, redemption **11** deliverance, reclamation **12** preservation

salve 4 aloe, balm, calm, ease, hail **5**

hello **6** lessen, lotion, pacify, reduce, soothe, temper **7** anodyne, assuage, mollify, relieve, unguent **8** dressing, liniment, mitigate, moderate, ointment **9** alleviate, emollient, greetings **11** alleviative

salver 4 bowl, dish, tray **6** waiter **7** coaster

salvia 4 herb, mint, sage **5** shrub **8** mejorana **9** artemisia

salvo 5 burst **6** volley **7** barrage, battery **8** shelling **9** cannonade, fusillade **11** bombardment

sambuca
type: **7** liqueur
origin: **5** Italy
flavor: **5** anise **10** elderberry

same 4 like, twin, very **5** alike, equal **6** on a par **7** similar, uniform **8** parallel **9** identical, unchanged **10** consistent, equivalent, invariable **13** corresponding

same as previously given
Latin: **4** idem

sameness 6 parity **8** equality, evenness, likeness, monotony **10** similarity, uniformity **11** homogeneity **14** homogenousness

Samoa
capital:
American Samoa: **8** Pago Pago
Western Samoa: **4** Apia
studied by: **13** Margaret Mead
cities: **6** Utulei **7** Palauli **8** Fagatogo
division: **12** Western Samoa **13** American Samoa
monetary unit: **4** tala
island: **3** Ofu, Tau **4** Rose **5** Aunuu, Manua, Namua, Upolu **6** Manono, Nuulua, Savaii, Swains **7** Apolima, Nuutele, Olosega, Tutuila **8** Nuusafee
mountain: **4** Vaea **5** Alava **6** Savaii **7** Matafao **9** Rainmaker
highest point: **4** Fito **8** Silisili
sea: **12** South Pacific
physical feature:
bay: **5** Afono, Leone **6** Fagasa, Falefa, Safata **7** Lafanga, Masefau, Matautu **8** Massacre, Salealua **9** Saluofata
people: **6** Samoan **10** Polynesian
explorer: **9** Roggeveen **12** Bougainville
language: **6** Samoan **7** English
religion: **6** Mormon **9** Methodist **13** Roman Catholic **15** Latter Day Saints **19** Seventh-Day Adventist **26** Congregational Christianity
feature:
bird: **3** iao **4** lulu, lupe **6** manuao, manuma, maomao **7** manuali **8** manusina, manutagi
chief: **5** matai
chief's daughter: **5** taupo
cloth: **4** para, tapa
clothing: **5** pareu **8** lavalava, puletasi

dance: 4 siva
dwelling: 4 fale
food:
    drink: 3 ava

Samoyed
language family: 6 Uralic
spoken in: 7 Siberia

sample 3 try **4** test **5** model, taste **7** dip into, examine, example, pattern, portion, segment **8** instance, paradigm, specimen **10** experience **12** cross section, illustration **14** representative **15** exemplification

Samson 11 Hebrew judge
father: 6 Manoah
feature: 4 hair **8** strength
weapon: 7 jawbone
mistress/betrayer: 7 Delilah
hometown: 5 Zorah
fate: 7 blinded
brought down: 4 Gaza

Samson Agonistes
author: 10 John Milton

Samuel 11 Hebrew judge
father: 7 Elkanah
mother: 6 Hannah
hometown: 5 Ramah
anointed: 4 Saul **5** David

Sana, Sanaa
capital of: 10 North Yemen

San Antonio
basketball team: 5 Spurs
football team: 11 Gunslingers
landmark: 8 The Alamo **9** River Walk

sanctification 8 blessing **9** hallowing **12** consecration
Hebrew: 7 Kiddush

sanctified 4 holy **6** sacred **7** blessed **8** hallowed **11** consecrated

sanctify 5 bless, exalt **6** anoint, hallow, purify, uphold **7** absolve, beatify, cleanse **8** dedicate, enshrine, make holy **10** consecrate, legitimate, legitimize **12** legitimatize

sanctimonious 6 solemn **7** canting, pompous, preachy **8** unctuous **9** overblown, pietistic **11** pharisaical, pretentious **14** holier-than-thou

sanctimoniousness 4 cant, sham **6** humbug **9** hypocrisy **11** insincerity **15** pretentiousness

sanction 5 allow, favor, leave **6** accept, assent, permit, ratify **7** agree to, approve, consent, endorse, liberty, license, penalty, support **8** approval, coercion, pressure **9** authority, authorize **10** legitimate, permission **11** countenance, endorsement **12** commendation, confirmation, ratification **13** authorization

sanctuary 4 park **5** cover, haven **6** asylum, chapel, church, refuge, safety, shrine, temple **7** reserve, retreat, shelter **8** preserve **10** protection

Sanctuary
author: 15 William Faulkner

character: 5 Tommy **6** Popeye **9** Ruby Lamar **10** Lee Goodwin, Reba Rivers **11** Temple Drake **12** Gowan Stevens, Horace Benbow

sanctum sanctorum 12 holy of holies

sanctus 4 holy

Sancus
also: 10 Semo Sancus
origin: 5 Roman
god of: 5 oaths **10** road safety **11** hospitality **20** international affairs
corresponds to: 8 Hercules **10** Dius Fidius

sand 4 grit, guts **5** pluck, spunk **6** mettle **7** bravery, courage, resolve **8** backbone **9** fortitude **10** resolution **12** resoluteness

Sand, George
real name: 14 Aurore Dudevant
protege: 6 Chopin
author of: 5 Lelia **7** Indiana **8** Consuelo **9** Valentine **13** Story of My Life **14** The Country Waif, The Haunted Pool **17** Fanchon the Cricket **18** Les Maitres Sonneurs **23** The Countess of Rudolstadt

sandal 4 clog, flat, shoe, zori **5** scuff, thong **6** loafer **7** slipper **8** flipflop, huarache, moccasin, overshoe **10** espadrille

sandalwood 5 Algum, Almug

sandbank 4 dune, reef **5** shelf, shoal **7** shallow

sandbar 4 bank, flat, reef, spit **5** shelf, shoal **7** shallow

Sandbox, The
author: 11 Edward Albee

Sandburg, Carl
author of: 3 Fog **7** Chicago **12** Harvest Poems **13** Smoke and Steel **14** Abraham Lincoln, The Cornhuskers **15** Remembrance Rock

Sanders, George
born: 6 Russia **12** St Petersburg
wife: 10 Benita Hume, Magda Gabor **11** Zsa Zsa Gabor
roles: 6 The Fan **7** Ivanhoe, Rebecca **8** The Saint **9** The Falcon **11** All About Eve **12** Forever Amber, The Gay Falcon **18** The Moon and Sixpence **20** Foreign Correspondent **22** The Picture of Dorian Gray **24** The House of the Seven Gables
autobiography: 25 Memoirs of a Professional Cad

San Diego
airport: 14 Lindbergh Field
area: 7 La Jolla, Old Town **8** Coronado **9** Point Loma **10** Balboa Park, Mission Bay **13** Mission Valley **14** Gaslamp Quarter
baseball team: 6 Padres
football team: 8 Chargers
founder: 13 Junipero Serra
landmark: 11 San Diego Zoo **14** Wild Animal Park **30** Scripps Institute of Oceanography

sandpiper 3 ree **4** bird, ruff **5** reeve, stint, wader **6** common, oxbird, plover **7** fiddler, haybird, spotted, tipbird **8** graybird, sandpeep, shadbird **10** beachrobin

Sands of Iwo Jima
director: 9 Allan Dwan
cast: 8 John Agar **9** Adele Mara, John Wayne **13** Forrest Tucker

sandwich 3 BLT, sub **4** club, deli, hero **5** hogie **6** burger, hoagie, insert **7** grinder, western **8** laminate **9** interpose, submarine **10** lamination **11** combination

sane 5 lucid, sober **7** logical **8** all there, balanced, credible, rational, sensible **9** judicious, plausible, sagacious **10** farsighted, reasonable **11** clearheaded, responsible
Latin: 12 compos mentis

Sanford and Son
character: 5 Bubba **6** Melvin **10** Aunt Esther **11** Donna Harris, Fred Sanford, Grady Wilson, Rollo Larson **12** Julio Fuentes, Officer Smith (Smitty) **13** Lamont Sanford
cast: 8 Redd Foxx **9** Don Bexley **11** Hal Williams, LaWanda Page, Slappy White, Whitman Mayo **12** Demond Wilson, Lynn Hamilton **13** Gregory Sierra **15** Nathaniel Taylor

San Francisco
baseball team: 6 Giants
bay: 12 San Francisco
county: 5 Marin **8** San Mateo **12** San Francisco
football team: 11 Forty-Niners
known as: 12 City by the Bay **19** City by the Golden Gate
landmark: 8 Alcatraz **16** Golden Gate Bridge
noted for: 8 cable car **9** earthquake (1906) **26** crookedest street in the world
street/section: 6 Market **7** Lombard, Nob Hill **8** Presidio **9** Chinatown **10** Montgomery **11** Embarcadero, Russian Hill

sangaree, sangria
flavor: 5 fruit, spice

sangfroid 5 poise **6** aplomb **7** balance **8** coolness **9** composure **10** confidence, equanimity **11** tranquility **12** tranquillity **16** imperturbability

sanguine 3 red **4** rosy **5** happy, ruddy, sunny **6** bright, elated, florid **7** buoyant, crimson, flushed, glowing, hopeful, reddish, scarlet **8** blooming, cheerful, inflamed, rubicund **9** confident **10** optimistic **12** lighthearted

Sanhedrin 7 council

sanitarium, sanitorium 8 hospital **11** institution
French: 13 maison de sante

sanitary 5 clean **7** aseptic, healthy, sterile **8** germ-free, hygienic **9** healthful, wholesome **10** salubrious, sterilized, uninfected, unpolluted **11** disinfected **12** prophylactic

sanitorium *see* **10** sanitarium

sanity 5 sense **6** reason **8** lucidity, saneness **9** coherence, normality **11** rationality **12** sensibleness **14** reasonableness **15** clearheadedness

San Jose
  capital of: **9** Costa Rica

San Juan
  capital of: **10** Puerto Rico

San Juan Bautista *see* **10** Puerto Rico

San Marino
  capital/largest city: **9** San Marino
  enclave in: **5** Italy
  others: **10** Serravalle **13** Borgo Maggiore
  division: **8** Castelli
  government:
    legislature: **22** Great and General Council
  monetary unit: **4** lira, lire **9** centesimi
  mountain: **9** Apennines
  highest point: **6** Titano
  people: **7** Italian **11** San Marinese
    founder: **7** Marinus
  language: **7** Italian
  religion: **13** Roman Catholic
  place: **13** Valloni Palace **17** Palazzo del Governo **19** Basilica of San Marino
  church: **5** Pieve **9** St Francis

San Salvador
  capital of: **10** El Salvador

sans doute 12 without doubt

Sansovino, Andrea
  real name: **14** Andrea Contucci
  born: **5** Italy **14** Monte San Savino
  artwork: **15** Baptism of Christ **20** Virgin Child and St Anne

Sansovino, Il
  real name: **11** Jacopo Tatti
  born: **5** Italy **7** Caprese
  artwork: **4** Mars **7** Bacchus, Logetta, Neptune **10** Old Library **15** Madonna del Parto **16** St John the Baptist

sans pareil 12 without equal

sans peur et sans reproche 29 without fear and without reproach

sans souci 8 carefree **11** without care

Santa Cruz de Tenerife
  capital of: **13** Canary Islands

Santayana, George
  author of: **14** The Last Puritan **16** The Realms of Being, The Sense of Beauty **24** Skepticism and Animal Faith

Santiago
  capital of: **5** Chile

Santiago
  character in: **18** The Old Man and the Sea
  author: **9** Hemingway

Santo Domingo
  capital of: **17** Dominican Republic

Santo Domingo *see* **5** Haiti

Sao Tome
  capital of: **18** Sao Tome and Principe

Sao Tome and Principe
  capital/largest city: **7** Sao Tome
  others: **8** Trindade **11** Porto Alegre **12** Santo Antonio
  monetary unit: **5** dobra **6** escudo **7** centavo
  highest point: **7** Sao Tome
  sea: **8** Atlantic
  physical feature:
    bay: **11** Ana de Chaves
    gulf: **6** Guinea
  people: **7** African **10** Portuguese **11** Cape Verdean
    explorer: **7** Escobar **8** Santarem
  language: **10** Portuguese
  religion: **7** animism **13** Roman Catholic **19** Seventh Day Adventist **21** Evangelical Protestant

sap 3 rob, tax **4** ruin, wear **5** bleed, drain **6** impair, reduce, weaken **7** afflict, cripple, deplete, destroy, disable, exhaust, subvert **8** enervate, enfeeble **9** devastate, undermine **10** debilitate, devitalize

sapient 4 wise **7** knowing **8** profound **9** sagacious **10** discerning, perceptive **11** intelligent **12** knowledgeable

sap one's energy 3 fag **4** bush, poop, tire **5** drain, weary **6** tucker, weaken **7** deplete, exhaust, fatigue, wash out **8** enervate, enfeeble **10** debilitate, devitalize

Sapphira
  husband: **7** Ananias
  lied to: **5** Peter

sapphire 3 gem **4** blue **5** azure, jewel **6** indigo
  species: **8** corundum
  source: **5** Burma, Mogok **6** Ceylon **7** Kashmir **8** Sri Lanka, Thailand **9** Australia
  kind: **4** star

Sappho
  author: **14** Alphonse Daudet

Sarah, Sarai
  father: **5** Asher
  former name: **5** Sarai
  husband: **7** Abraham
  son: **5** Isaac
  slave: **5** Hagar
  burial place: **9** Machpelah

sarcasm 3 rub **4** gibe, jeer, jest **5** irony, scorn, sneer, taunt **7** mockery **8** contempt, derision, ridicule, scoffing **13** disparagement

sarcastic 5 acerb **6** biting, bitter, ironic **7** caustic, cutting, mocking, mordant **8** derisive, piercing, sardonic, scornful, sneering, stinging, taunting **11** disparaging **12** contemptuous

sarcoma 5 tumor **6** cancer, growth **8** neoplasm **10** malignancy

sarcophagus 4 pall **6** coffin

sard
  species: **6** quartz

sardine 4 bang, cram, fish, lile, lour, pack **5** crowd **7** alewife, anchovy, herring **8** pilchard

Sardinia
  other name: **8** Sardegna
  capital: **8** Cagliari
  cities: **4** Bono, Bosa **5** Nuoro, Olbia **7** Alghero, Bonorva, Sassari, Thatari **8** Iglesias, Oristano **11** Porto Torres
  division: **5** Nuoro **7** Arborea, Gallura, Sassari **8** Cagliari, Logudoro
  government: **13** region of Italy
  monetary unit: **7** carline
  island: **7** Caprera **8** Tavolara **9** Maddalena
  lake: **6** Omodeo
  mountain: **4** Rasu **5** Ferry, Linas **7** Gallura, Limbara **8** Marghine, Serpeddi, Vittoria **11** Gennargentu
  river: **5** Mannu, Tirso **6** Lascia **8** Coghinas **10** Flumendosa
  sea: **13** Mediterranean
  physical feature:
    gulf: **6** Orosei, Palmas **7** Asinara **8** Cagliari, Oristano
    plain: **7** Sassari **9** Campidano
    strait: **9** Bonifacio
  people:
    king: **12** Charles Felix **13** Charles Albert **14** Victor Emmanuel
    leader: **6** Cavour
    ruler: **4** Pisa **5** Genoa, Spain **7** Austria, Vandals **9** Byzantium, Phoenicia **12** House of Savoy
  language: **7** Italian
  religion: **13** Roman Catholic
  feature:
    towers: **7** nuraghi
  food:
    cheese: **6** romano **8** pecorino

Sardius 8 gemstone

sardonic 6 biting **7** caustic, cynical, jeering, mocking, mordant, satiric **8** derisive, scornful, sneering, taunting **9** sarcastic **11** disparaging **12** contemptuous

sardonyx 8 gemstone

Sargent, John Singer
  born: **5** Italy **8** Florence
  artwork: **6** Madam X (Madame Gautreau) **7** El Jaleo **17** The Wyndham Sisters **20** Robert Louis Stevenson **21** Carnation Lily Lily Rose **22** Daughters of Edward D Boit **24** Oyster Gatherers of Cancale

Sargon
  captured: **5** Accad
  successor: **11** Sennacherib

Saroyan, William
  author of: **12** My Name Is Aram **14** The Human Comedy **17** The Time of Your Life **22** My Heart's in the Highlands

Sarton, May
  author of: **5** Anger **11** Kinds of Love

17 Plant Dreaming Deep **20** Faithful Are the Wounds **33** Mrs Stevens Hears the Mermaids Singing

Sartor Resartus
author: **13** Thomas Carlyle

Sartre, Jean-Paul
author of: **6** Nausea, No Exit **8** The Words **17** The Roads to Freedom **19** Being and Nothingness
philosophy: **14** Existentialism
quote: **17** Hell is other people

sash **3** tie **4** band, belt **5** frame, scarf, strip **6** casing, corset, girdle, ribbon, window **7** baldric **8** casement **9** doorframe, waistband **10** cummerbund **11** windowframe
Japanese: **3** obi
pulley weight: **5** mouse
window: **5** chess

sashay **4** move, skip **5** glide, mince **6** chasse, travel

sashimi **7** raw fish **12** Japanese dish

Saskatchewan **5** river **8** province
boundary: **7** Alberta, Montana **8** Manitoba **11** North Dakota **12** Old Northwest **20** Northwest Territories
capital: **6** Regina
city: **8** Moose Jaw **9** Saskatoon **12** Prince Albert, Swift Current
country: **6** Canada
Indian: **4** Cree **9** Chipewyan **10** Assiniboin
lake: **8** Reindeer **9** Athabasca, Wollaston
mountain: **7** Cypress, Pasquia **9** Porcupine **14** Missouri Coteau
river: **9** Churchill, Frenchman
river mouth: **12** Lake Winnipeg

Sassoon, Siegfried
author of: **26** The Memoirs of a Fox-Hunting Man **26** The Memoirs of George Sherston **29** The Memoirs of an Infantry Officer

sassy **4** bark, bold, flip, rude, tree **5** brash, fresh, saucy **6** mouthy, snippy **7** forward **8** impolite, impudent, insolent **12** discourteous **13** disrespectful

Satan **6** Belial, Moloch **7** Lucifer, Old Nick **8** Apollyon, the Devil **9** Beelzebub **10** Old Scratch, the Evil One, the Tempter **11** fallen angel **12** the Foul Fiend **13** the Old Serpent **14** Mephistopheles **19** the Prince of Darkness

satanic **3** bad **4** evil, vile **5** cruel **6** wicked **7** demonic, heinous, hellish, inhuman, vicious **8** devilish, fiendish, infamous, infernal, sadistic **9** malicious, malignant **10** demoniacal, diabolical, malevolent

satchel, Satchel **3** bag **4** case, grip, sack **5** purse **6** valise **7** handbag **8** reticule, suitcase **9** carpetbag, Gladstone, schoolbag
pitcher, Hall of Famer: **5** Paige

sate **4** cloy, fill, glut **5** gorge, stuff **7** surfeit

satellite **4** moon **5** crony, toady **6** me-

nial, puppet, vassal **7** servant **8** disciple, follower, hanger-on, parasite, retainer **9** assistant, attendant, companion, sycophant, tributary, underling

satellite state **6** colony **8** dominion **10** possession **12** protectorate

satiate **4** bore, cloy, fill, glut, jade **5** slake, stuff, weary **6** overdo, quench, sicken **7** content, disgust, gratify, suffice, surfeit **8** nauseate, overfill, saturate

Satie, Erik
born: **6** France **8** Honfleur
composer of: **6** Parade **13** Pieces froides **16** The Three Gymnasts **19** Limp Preludes for a Dog **20** Pieces en forme de poire **23** Pieces in the Shape of a Pear

satiny **4** fine **5** shiny, silky **6** smooth

satire **5** irony **6** banter, parody, send up **7** lampoon, mockery, sarcasm, takeoff **8** acrimony, derision, raillery, ridicule, travesty **9** burlesque **10** caricature, persiflage

satirical **5** comic **6** biting, bitter **7** caustic, mocking, mordant **8** derisive, humorous, ironical, sardonic, scornful, sneering **9** malicious, sarcastic

satirize **4** mock **6** parody **7** lampoon **9** burlesque **10** caricature

satisfaction **5** pride **6** amends **7** comfort, content, damages, deserts, justice, payment, redress **8** pleasure, requital **9** answering, atonement, happiness, quittance, reckoning, repayment **10** correction, recompense, remittance, settlement **11** contentment, fulfillment, restitution **12** compensation, remuneration **13** gratification, rectification, reimbursement

satisfactory **2** OK **4** okay **8** adequate, all right, passable, suitable **9** competent **10** acceptable, sufficient

satisfied **5** happy **7** content, pleased **9** gratified **10** complacent **11** comfortable

satisfy **3** pay **4** fill, meet **5** annul, clear, remit, repay, serve, slake **6** answer, assure, pacify, pay off, please, quench, remove, settle **7** appease, content, delight, fulfill, gratify, mollify, requite, suffice **8** convince, persuade, reassure **9** discharge, reimburse **10** compensate, recompense

satisfying **8** pleasant, pleasing **9** agreeable, enjoyable, rewarding **10** delightful, fulfilling, gratifying **11** pleasurable

satori
term in: **3** Zen
means: **13** enlightenment

saturate **4** fill **5** cover, douse, imbue, souse **6** drench, infuse **7** immerse, pervade, suffuse **8** permeate, submerge **10** impregnate, infiltrate

saturated **3** wet **4** full **5** drunk, soggy, soppy **6** soaked, sodden **8** bursting

Saturday
day of: **15** Biblical Sabbath
French: **6** samedi
from: **8** Saturnus
German: **7** samstag
heavenly body: **6** Saturn
Italian: **6** sabato
observance: **13** Jewish Sabbath **20** Seventh Day Adventists
Spanish: **6** sabado

Saturday Night Fever
director: **10** John Badham
cast: **11** Barry Miller **12** John Travolta **15** Karen Lynn Gorney
setting: **8** Brooklyn
score: **7** Bee Gees
sequel: **12** Staying Alive

Saturday Night Live, NBC's
regular: **9** Mike Myers **10** Bill Murray, Chevy Chase, Dana Carvey, Dan Aykroyd, Jane Curtin **11** Eddie Murphy, Gilda Radner, John Belushi **13** Garrett Morris, Laraine Newman
group: **27** Not Ready For Prime Time Players
bits: **4** Bees **7** Samurai **9** Coneheads **10** Church Lady **13** Blues Brothers, Weekend Update **16** Pathological Liar **18** Rosanne Rosanna-Dana

Saturn
origin: **5** Roman
god of: **11** agriculture
consort of: **3** Ops
son: **5** Picus
corresponds to: **6** Cronos, Cronus, Kronos

Saturn
position: **5** sixth
satellite: **4** Rhea **5** Dione, Janus, Mimas, Titan **6** Phoebe, Tethys **7** Iapetus **8** Hyperion **9** Enceladus
characteristic: **5** rings

saturnalia, Saturnalia **4** orgy **5** revel, spree **7** carouse, debauch, revelry **8** carousal **9** bacchanal **10** debauchery
origin: **5** Roman
event: **8** festival
honoring: **6** Saturn **13** sowing of crops

saturnine **4** dour, glum, grim **5** grave, staid, stern, sulky **6** gloomy, moping, morose, solemn, somber, sullen **7** austere, serious **8** dejected, downcast, reserved, sardonic, taciturn **9** apathetic, cheerless, withdrawn **11** downhearted **15** uncommunicative

satyr
form: **4** faun **5** deity
location: **8** woodland
part: **3** man **4** goat
attendant of: **7** Bacchus
known for: **7** lechery

Satyricon
author: **9** Petronius

character: 4 Gito **8** Ascyltus, Eumolpus **9** Encolpius **10** Trimalchio

sauce 3 dip **4** sass **5** booze, gravy, salsa **6** fillip, flavor **7** alcohol **8** dressing, pertness **9** condiment, flippancy **12** impertinence

basil: 5 pesto

fish: 4 alec

hot: 7 Tabasco

Indian: 5 curry

salty: 3 soy

saucy 4 bold, pert, rude, trim **5** brash, cocky, fresh, natty, smart **6** brazen, cheeky, jaunty, lively, spruce **7** forward **8** flippant, impolite, impudent, insolent **9** audacious, barefaced, unabashed **11** impertinent, smart-alecky **12** discourteous **13** disrespectful

Saudi Arabia

capital/largest city: 6 Riyadh

others: 4 Abha, Hail, Taif **5** Hofuf, Hufuf, Jedda, Jidda, Yanbu, Yenbo **6** Anaiza, Dammam, Jiddah, Jubail **7** Alhofuf, Buraido, Dhahran **9** Ras Tanura

holy city: 5 Mecca **6** Medina

school: 5 Islam **13** King Abd al-Aziz **19** Imam Muhammad bin Saud **20** Petroleum and Minerals

division: 4 Asir, Nejd **5** Hejaz **6** El Hasa

government: 8 monarchy

head of state/government: 4 king

monetary unit: 5 girsh, gursh, pound, riyal

weight: 3 oke

mountain: 6 Tuwayq

highlands: 4 Asir **5** Hejaz

highest point: 5 Razih **10** Jebal Sawda

sea: 3 Red

physical feature:

desert: 3 Red **5** Dahna, Nafud, Nefud, Nufud **6** al-Dahy, Dahana **10** Rub al Khali

gulf: 5 Aqaba **7** Persian

peninsula: 7 Arabian

plain: 6 Tihama

plateau: 4 Nejd

people: 4 Arab **7** Bedouin

king: 4 Fahd, Saud **6** Faisal, Khalid **7** Ibn Saud **9** Abdul Aziz

religious leader: 8 Mohammed, Muhammad

language: 6 Arabic

religion: 5 Islam

sect: 5 Sunni **6** Shiite **7** Wahhabi

place:

shrine: 5 Kaaba **10** Black Stone

feature:

annual pilgrimage: 4 hadj, hajj

clothing: 3 aba **4** agal **5** thobe **6** ghutra

kingdom: 5 Hejaz **7** Minaean, Ottoman, Sabaean **9** Himyarite

laws of Islam: 6 sharia

village school: 6 kuttab

war: 4 Gulf **11** Desert Storm **12** Desert Shield

Sauguet, Henri

born: 6 France **8** Bordeaux

composer of: 6 La Nuit **10** Les Forains, Les Mirages

Sauk, Sac

family: 9 Algonkian **10** Algonquian

tribe: 3 Fox, Sac **8** Kickapoo

location: 4 Iowa, Ohio **6** Kansas **7** Indiana **8** Illinois, Michigan, Oklahoma **9** Wisconsin

leader: 9 Blackhawk

related to: 8 Kickapoo **9** Mesquakie **11** Potawatomie

involved in: 12 Black Hawk War

Saul

king of: 4 Edom **6** Israel

father: 4 Kish

daughter: 5 Merab **6** Michal

son: 7 Abinoam **8** Jonathan **10** Ishbosheth

anointed by: 6 Samuel

hometown: 6 Gibeah **8** Rehoboth

successor: 5 David

Saunders, Allen

creator/artist of: 9 Mary Worth

saunter 4 roam **5** amble, mosey, stray **6** loiter, ramble, stroll, wander **7** meander, traipse **8** straggle **9** promenade

sausage 5 frank, gigot, wurst **6** hotdog, salami, weenie, wiener **7** baloney, bologna **8** kielbasa **9** bratwurst, pepperoni **10** liverwurst **11** frankfurter

British: 6 banger

sauve qui peut 4 rout **8** stampede **18** every man for himself **23** let him save himself who can

savage 4 boor, wild **5** brute, cruel, feral, fiend, harsh, rough, yahoo **6** animal, bloody, brutal, fierce, maniac, native, rugged, unkind **7** brutish, hoodlum, ruffian, untamed, violent **8** barbaric, hooligan, pitiless, ruthless, sadistic **9** aborigine, barbarian, barbarous, ferocious, merciless, murderous, primitive **10** aboriginal, heathenish, relentless, uncultured, unmerciful **11** uncivilized **12** uncultivated **14** undomesticated

savagery 7 cruelty **8** ferocity **9** barbarism, barbarity, brutality **10** fierceness, inhumanity **12** pitilessness, ruthlessness

savanna, savannah 5 campo, plain **9** grassland

savant 6 genius **7** scholar **13** learned person

save 3 but **4** bank, free, help, hold, keep **5** amass, guard, hoard, lay by, lay up, put by, spare, stock, store **6** defend, except, garner, heap up, redeem, rescue, shield **7** deliver, deposit, husband, protect, put away, recover, reserve, salvage **8** conserve,

preserve, retrench, withhold **9** economize, safeguard **10** accumulate

save up 5 amass, hoard **7** collect, put away **8** salt away, sock away **10** accumulate **12** squirrel away

saving 5 close, tight **6** frugal, stingy **7** careful, miserly, prudent, sparing, thrifty **8** markdown, stinting **9** illiberal, niggardly, provident, redeeming, restoring **10** economical, reclaiming, redemptory, reparative **12** compensating, conservative

savings 3 IRA **5** hoard **7** nest egg, reserve

savior 5 freer **7** rescuer **8** champion, defender, guardian, redeemer **9** deliverer, liberator, preserver, protecter, protector, salvation **11** emancipator

Savior 5 Jesus **6** Christ **8** Redeemer **10** the Messiah **11** Jesus Christ, the Son of God **13** Prince of Peace

Savior anointed 5 Jesus

savoir-faire 4 tact **5** poise **6** aplomb, polish **7** finesse, know-how, suavity **8** presence, urbanity **9** assurance, composure **10** adroitness, discretion, smoothness **11** worldliness **12** complaisance, graciousness **14** self-possession

savoir-vivre 16 knowing how to live **19** knowledge of the world

savor 3 try **4** aura, gist, like, odor, soul, tang, zest **5** aroma, enjoy, scent, smack, smell, spice, taste, trait **6** flavor, nature, relish, sample, season, spirit **7** essence, quality **8** piquancy, property, pungency **9** character, fragrance, substance **10** appreciate, experience **11** peculiarity **13** particularity **14** characteristic

savory 5 tangy, tasty, yummy **6** honest **7** odorous, piquant, pungent **8** alluring, aromatic, charming, edifying, fragrant, luscious, tasteful **9** delicious, flavorous, palatable, reputable, toothsome **10** appetizing, attractive, delectable **11** inoffensive, respectable, scrumptious **13** mouth-watering

savory

botanical name: 8 Satureia, S montana **10** S hortensis

origin: 13 Mediterranean

varieties: 6 summer, winter

use: 4 eggs, meat **5** beans, salad **6** sauces **8** dressing **11** chicken soup

savvy 5 catch, get it **7** know-how **10** comprehend, understand **13** understanding

saw 3 cut **4** tool **5** adage, maxim, slash **6** saying **7** proverb **8** aphorism

type: 3 jig, rip **4** back, band, hack **5** miter **6** coping **7** keyhole **8** circular, crosscut

sawfly

varieties: 4 stem, wood **5** cedar **6** pergid **7** conifer **8** horntail **11** web spinning

saxophone
   type: **4** alto **5** tenor

say 2 do **4** hint, hold, read, tell, vote, word **5** bruit, claim, guess, imply, judge, mouth, rumor, speak, state, utter, voice **6** allege, assert, assume, chance, convey, phrase, reason, recite, remark, render, repeat, report, reveal, spread **7** comment, contend, declare, deliver, divulge, express, imagine, mention, perform, suggest, suppose, surmise **8** announce, disclose, intimate, maintain, rehearse, vocalize **9** circulate, franchise, insinuate, pronounce, verbalize **10** articulate, conjecture **11** communicate

Sayers, Dorothy L
   author of: **9** Whose Body **12** Strong Poison **14** Have His Carcase, The Nine Tailors, Unnatural Death **15** Clouds of Witness, Five Red Herrings **16** Busman's Honeymoon **19** Murder Must Advertise **30** Unpleasantness at the Bellona Club
   character: **6** Bunter **11** Harriet Vane **15** Lord Peter Wimsey

Say Hey Kid
   nickname of: **10** Willie Mays

saying 3 saw **5** adage, maxim, moral, motto **6** byword, dictum, truism **7** epigram, precept, proverb **8** aphorism, apothegm **10** expression

Sayonara
   director: **11** Joshua Logan
   author: **13** James Michener
   cast: **9** Miiko Taka **10** Red Buttons **11** James Garner, Martha Scott **12** Marlon Brando, Miyoshi Umeki **16** Ricardo Montalban
   score: **12** Irving Berlin
   Oscar for: **15** supporting actor (Buttons) **17** supporting actress (Umeki)

scabrous 5 dirty, rough, scaly **7** immoral, leprous **8** indecent, off-color **9** salacious **10** suggestive **12** pornographic

scalding 3 hot **5** harsh **7** boiling, caustic **8** seething, steaming **9** sarcastic

scale, scales 3 key, set **4** chip, film, husk, peel, rise, rule, skin **5** crust, flake, layer, mount, order, plate, range, ratio, scour, shave, shell, weigh **6** adjust, ascend, goupen, ladder, lamina, octave, rub off, scrape, series, spread **7** balance, chip off, clamber, climb up, coating, lamella, measure **8** escalade, membrane, register, regulate, spectrum, surmount **9** continuum, gradation, solfeggio **10** delaminate, graduation, proportion **11** calibration, progression **14** classification

scale down 4 trim **6** reduce **7** abridge, curtail, shorten **8** compress, condense, decrease, diminish, downsize, moderate **10** abbreviate

scale insects

varieties: 3 lac, pit, wax **5** giant **6** ensign **7** armored **8** mealybug, tortoise **12** ground pearls

scale note 2 do, fa, la, mi, re, so, ti **3** sol
   Guido's: **3** ela

scamp 3 imp, rip **5** cut-up, knave, rogue, tease **6** rascal, rotter **7** bounder, villain **8** blighter, scalawag **9** miscreant, prankster, scoundrel **10** scapegrace **11** rapscallion **13** mischiefmaker

scamper 3 fly, run, zip **4** dart, dash, flit, race, romp, rush, scud **5** frisk, hurry, scoot **6** frolic, gambol, hasten, scurry, sprint **7** scuttle **9** skedaddle **21** running about playfully

scan 4 skim **5** check, probe, scour, study, sweep **6** peruse, search, size up, survey **7** analyze, examine, explore, inspect **10** scrutinize

scandal 4 blot **5** abuse, libel, odium, shame, stain **6** expose, smirch, stigma **7** calumny, obloquy, outrage, slander **8** disgrace, dishonor, ignominy **9** aspersion, discredit, disesteem, sensation **10** debasement, detraction, opprobrium, revilement **12** vituperation **13** disparagement, embarrassment

scandalize 5 shock **6** appall, defame, insult, offend **7** horrify, outrage **10** calumniate

scandalmonger 6 gossip **8** busybody **10** talebearer, tattletale

scandalous 8 libelous, shameful, shocking **9** gossiping, offensive **10** defamatory, outrageous, scurrilous, slanderous **11** disgraceful **12** disreputable **13** reprehensible

Scandinavia 6 Norway, Sweden **7** Denmark, Faeroes, Iceland

Scandinavian (Norse)
   language family: **12** Indo-European
   branch: **8** Germanic
   group: **15** Western Germanic
   language: **6** Danish **7** Faroese, Swedish **9** Icelandic, Norwegian

scant 3 cut **4** bare **5** limit, short, small, stint **6** in need, meager, paltry, reduce, sparse **7** limited **8** exiguous, hold back **9** deficient **10** inadequate, incomplete **12** insufficient

scantiness 10 deficiency, inadequacy, meagerness, skimpiness **13** insufficiency

scanty 4 thin **5** short, small **6** meager, modest, paltry, skimpy, sparse **7** slender, stunted **9** deficient **10** inadequate, undersized **12** insufficient

scapegoat, Scapegoat 4 butt, dupe, gull **5** patsy **6** Azazel, victim **7** fall guy **11** whipping boy **13** laughingstock

scapolite
   source: **5** Burma, Mogok

scapula
   bone of: **13** shoulder blade

scar 3 cut, pit **4** dent, flaw, gash, hurt, mark, pock, seam **5** brand, wound **6** affect, bruise, damage, deface, defect, impair, mangle **7** blemish, scratch **8** cicatrix, lacerate, mutilate **9** disfigure, influence

Scaramouch(e) 6 coward, rascal **8** braggart, poltroon

scarce 4 rare **6** scanty, sparse **7** unusual, wanting **8** uncommon **9** deficient

scarcely 4 just **6** at most, barely, hardly **7** but just, faintly **8** slightly

scarcity 4 lack, want **5** stint **6** dearth, rarity **7** fewness, paucity **8** rareness, shortage, sparsity, thinness **10** deficiency, scantiness, sparseness **12** uncommonness **13** insufficiency

scare 4 turn **5** alarm, daunt, panic, shake, shock, start **6** harrow, shiver **7** horrify, jitters, startle, terrify **8** disquiet, frighten **9** terrorize **10** disconcert, dishearten, intimidate **11** nervousness, palpitation **13** consternation

scarecrow 6 effigy **8** straw man

Scarecrow
   character in: **13** The Wizard of Oz
   author: **4** Baum

scared 5 shaky, timid, upset **6** afraid **7** alarmed, fearful, nervous, spooked **8** startled, timorous **9** diffident, terrified, tremulous **10** frightened **12** apprehensive, fainthearted **13** panic-stricken

scarf 3 boa **4** sash, veil, wrap **5** ascot, shawl, stole **6** choker, cravat, tippet **7** foulard, muffler, overlay **8** babushka, bandanna, mantilla **11** neckerchief

Scarface
   director: **11** Howard Hawks
   cast: **8** Paul Muni **9** Ann Dvorak **10** George Raft **12** Boris Karloff

scarify 3 cut **6** incise, loosen **7** break up, scratch **8** lacerate **9** cultivate

Scarlatti, Alessandro
   born: **6** Sicily **7** Palermo
   composer of: **11** Stabat Mater **17** Mitridate Eupatore, The Triumph of Honor **18** Il Trionfo dell Onore **23** Gli equivoci nel sembiante

Scarlatti, Domenico
   born: **5** Italy **6** Naples
   composer of: **7** Sonatas **9** Cat's Fugue, Essercizi **18** Le Donne di Buon Umore **20** The Good-Humored Ladies **23** Ottavia risituita al trono

scarlet 3 red **6** cherry, claret **7** carmine **8** cardinal

Scarlet Letter, The
   author: **18** Nathaniel Hawthorne
   character: **5** Pearl **12** Hester Prynne **16** Arthur Dimmesdale **18** Roger Chillingworth

Scarlett *see* Gone With the Wind

scary 3 bad **5** awful, hairy **6** creepy **7**

fearful 8 alarming, menacing, shocking 9 difficult 10 disturbing, terrifying 11 frightening, goosepimply, hairraising, threatening 12 discomfiting

scat 3 off, out 4 away, shoo 5 be off, leave, scram 6 beat it, be gone, depart, get out, go away 7 get lost, vamoose

scathing 4 keen, tart 5 sharp 6 biting, brutal, savage 7 caustic, cutting, hostile, mordant, pointed, searing 8 incisive, stinging, virulent 9 ferocious, rancorous, scorching, trenchant, vitriolic, withering 10 lacerating 11 acrimonious, excoriating

scatter 3 sow 4 cast, flee, rout 5 strew, throw 6 dispel 8 disperse, sprinkle 9 broadcast, circulate, dissipate 10 distribute 11 disseminate

scatterbrained 4 rash, wild, zany 5 crazy, dizzy, giddy, nutty, silly 6 madcap, stupid 7 flighty, foolish 8 careless, heedless, reckless, unstable, unsteady 9 foolhardy, forgetful, frivolous, imprudent 11 birdbrained, empty-headed, harebrained 12 absentminded, muddleheaded 13 irresponsible

scattered 6 random, spotty 7 diffuse 9 irregular 10 infrequent, occasional

scattering 6 sowing 7 casting 8 strewing 9 dispersal 10 dispersing, sprinkling 12 broadcasting, distribution 13 dissemination

scavenger 5 hyena 6 magpie 7 vulture 8 salvager 9 collector

scenario 4 book, idea, plan 6 scheme 7 concept, outline, summary 8 abstract, game plan, synopsis, teleplay 10 conception, manuscript, screenplay French: 6 precis

scene 3 act 4 fuss, part, show, site, spot, to-do, view 5 place, sight, vista 6 locale, region, survey, vision 7 display, episode, picture, scenery, setting 8 backdrop, division, locality, location, panorama, position, prospect, sequence 9 commotion, spectacle 10 background 11 whereabouts

scenery 4 sets, view 5 vista 7 terrain 9 backdrops, landscape, spectacle 11 backgrounds

Scenes from a Marriage
director: 13 Ingmar Bergman
cast: 10 Liv Ullmann 13 Bibi Andersson 15 Erland Josephson

scent 4 odor, path, wake, wind 5 aroma, smell, sniff, spoor, trace, track, trail 6 course, detect, inhale 7 bouquet, breathe, discern, essence, perfume, pursuit, suspect 9 aromatize, fragrance, get wind of, recognize 11 distinguish

scented 5 spicy 7 odorous, piquant, pungent 8 aromatic, fragrant, perfumed 9 odiferous 13 sweet-smelling

Schaffner, Franklin
director of: 6 Patton (Oscar) 15 Planet of the Apes

schedule 3 fix 4 book, list, plan, roll 5 fit in, slate, table 6 agenda 7 appoint, program, put down, set down 8 calendar 9 inventory, timetable

Scheele, Karl Wilhelm
field: 9 chemistry
nationality: 7 Swedish
discovered: 6 oxygen 8 chlorine 9 glycerine

Scheider, Roy
born: 8 Orange NJ
roles: 4 Jaws 11 All That Jazz, Blue Thunder, The Seven-Ups 14 Fifty-two Pickup 19 The French Connection

Schell, Maria
real name: 15 Margarete Schell
born: 6 Vienna 7 Austria
brother: 16 Maximilian Schell
roles: 8 Cimarron, Gervaise 11 End of Desire, White Nights 13 The Last Bridge 20 The Brothers Karamazov

Schell, Maximilian
born: 6 Vienna 7 Austria
sister: 11 Maria Schell
roles: 5 Julia 13 The Young Lions 19 Judgment at Nuremberg (Oscar) 21 The Man in the Glass Booth

scheme 3 map, way 4 plan, plot, ruse 5 cabal, chart, frame, means, shift, study 6 course, design, device, devise, layout, method, policy, sketch, system 7 complot, concoct, connive, drawing, network, outline, program, project, tactics 8 conspire, contrive, grouping, intrigue, maneuver, organize, strategy 9 machinate, procedure, stratagem 10 connivance, conspiracy 11 arrangement, contrivance, delineation, disposition, machination 12 organization

scheming 3 sly 4 arch, wily 6 artful, crafty, shrewd, tricky 7 cunning 8 slippery 9 conniving, designing, insidious 10 contriving, intriguing 11 calculating 13 Machiavellian

Schiller, (Johann) Friedrich von
author of: 8 Ode to Joy 9 Don Carlos 11 Maria Stuart, William Tell 17 The Bride of Messina 18 The Maiden of Orleans

schism 5 break, split 8 division 10 separation 14 disassociation

Schlegel family
characters in: 10 Howards End
members: 5 Helen 8 Margaret, Theobald
author: 7 Forster

schlepp 3 lug 4 cart, haul, tote 5 carry 6 convey 9 transport

Schlesinger, Arthur M, Jr
author of: 13 A Thousand Days 15 The Age of Jackson 21 The Imperial Presidency 24 Robert Kennedy and His Times

Schlesinger, John
director of: 7 Darling 14 Midnight Cowboy (Oscar) 22 The Falcon and the Snowman

Schlesinger, Leon
creator/artist of: 9 Bugs Bunny

schmaltz 4 corn 14 sentimentalism, sentimentality

Schmeling, Max (Maxmillian Adolph Otto Siegfried)
nickname: 10 Black Uhlan
sport: 6 boxing
class: 11 heavyweight

Schneider, Romy
real name: 20 Rosemarie Albach-Retty
born: 6 Vienna 7 Austria
roles: 8 The Trial 11 The Cardinal 16 Boccaccio Seventy

Schoenberg, Arnold
born: 6 Vienna 7 Austria
composer of: 9 Erwartung 11 De Profundis, Expectation, Gurrelieder 12 The Lucky Hand 13 Moses and Aaron, Ode to Napoleon 14 Verklarte Nacht 16 Die Glucklich Hand, Resplendent Night 17 Transfigured Night 19 A Survivor from Warsaw, Pelleas and Melisande 26 The Book of the Hanging Gardens

Schoenius
father: 7 Athamas
mother: 8 Themisto
wife: 7 Clymene
daughter: 8 Atalanta

scholar 4 coed, sage 5 brain, grind, pupil 6 pundit, savant 7 egghead, learner, student, studier, wise man 8 bookworm, humanist, mandarin 9 collegian, schoolboy 10 schoolgirl 11 matriculant 12 intellectual 13 undergraduate

scholarly 6 humane 7 erudite, learned, liberal 8 academic, educated, informed, lettered, literate, well-read 12 intellectual

scholarship 5 grant 7 stipend 8 learning 9 education, endowment, erudition 12 intelligence, thoroughness 13 enlightenment

scholastic 8 academic, pedantic 9 pedagogic 11 educational 12 professorial 13 instructional

school 3 ism 4 view 5 bunch, crowd, faith, order, style, teach, train 6 belief, lyceum, method, system, theory 7 academy, college, educate, faction, thought 8 doctrine, instruct, seminary 9 institute 10 persuasion, university 12 denomination, kindergarten

schoolbook 3 abc 4 text 5 atlas 6 manual, primer, reader 7 grammar, lessons, speller

School for Scandal, The
author: 23 Richard Brinsley Sheridan
character: 5 Maria 6 Rowley 10 Lady Teazle 13 Joseph Surface, Lady

Sneerwell **14** Charles Surface, Sir Peter Teazle **16** Sir Oliver Surface

School for Wives, The
author: 7 Moliere
character: 5 Agnes **6** Horace, Oronte **7** Enrique **8** Arnolphe **9** Chrysalde

schooling 5 drill **8** drilling, training **9** education **11** instruction, preparation **14** indoctrination

schoolmaster 4 head **5** tutor **7** dominie, pedagog, scholar, teacher **9** pedagogue, principal, professor **10** headmaster, instructor **12** disciplinarian
fish: 7 snapper
genus: 8 Lutianus
species: 6 apodus

Schubert, Franz Peter
born: 6 Vienna **7** Austria
composer of: 6 Little (symphony), Tragic (symphony No 4) **8** Sad Waltz **9** Rosamunde **11** Winterreise **12** Trout Quintet **13** Mourning Waltz **17** Die Schone Mullerin **18** Unfinished Symphony (No 8) **24** Death and the Maiden Quartet, Symphony of Heavenly Length

Schulz, Charles
creator/artist of: 7 Peanuts

Schuman, William
born: 9 New York NY
composer of: 8 Undertow **9** Credendum **14** The Mighty Casey **16** American Festival **18** New England Triptych

Schumann, Robert Alexander
born: 7 Germany, Zwickau
composer of: 6 Myrten, Spring (symphony No 1) **7** Rhenish (symphony No 3) **8** Arabeske, Carnival **9** Papillons **10** Novelettes **11** Blumenstuck, Butterflies, Nachtstucke, Nightpieces, Novelletten **12** Bunte Blatter, Dichterliebe, Flower Pieces, Kinderscenen, Kreisleriana, Motley Leaves **14** Fantasiestucke **16** David's Band Dances, Symphonic Studies **18** Davidsbundlertanze **19** Frauenliebe und Leben

Schwann, Theodor
field: 7 biology
nationality: 6 German
established: 10 cell theory

Schwarzenegger, Arnold
roles: 5 Twins **7** Red Heat **8** Commando, Predator, Red Sonja, True Lies **11** Total Recall **13** The Terminator **15** Kindergarten Cop **17** Conan the Barbarian, Conan the Destroyer
wife: 12 Maria Shriver

Schweitzer, Albert
field: 8 medicine
worked in: 5 Gabon **6** Africa
founded: 17 Lambarene Hospital
awarded: 15 Nobel Peace Prize

Schwitters, Kurt
born: 7 Germany **8** Hannover

artwork: 7 Merzbau
collages called: 10 Merzbilden

science 3 art **5** skill **6** method **7** finesse **8** aptitude, facility **9** technique **10** discipline **11** acquirement
god of: 7 Mercury

scintilla 3 dot, jot **4** atom, iota **5** shred, spark, speck, trace **7** glimmer **10** smithereen

scintillate 4 joke, snap **5** amuse, charm, flash, gleam, glint, shine, spark **7** glimmer, glisten, glitter, shimmer, sparkle, twinkle **9** coruscate **10** effervesce

scintillating 5 witty **6** bright, lively **8** animated, charming, dazzling **9** brilliant, ebullient, exuberant, sparkling **10** glittering **11** stimulating **12** effervescent

scion 3 son **4** heir, seed **5** child, issue **7** heiress, progeny **8** daughter, offshoot **9** offspring, posterity, successor **10** descendant **11** progeniture

scissors 5 snips **6** blades, cutter, shears **7** clipper, snipper, trimmer
French: 8 secateur

scoff 4 jeer, mock, razz **5** flout, knock, taunt **6** deride, rail at, revile **7** condemn, laugh at, put down, run down **8** belittle, ridicule

Scofield, Paul
real name: 13 David Scofield
born: 7 England **14** Hurstpierpoint
roles: 8 King Lear **13** Sir Thomas More **17** A Man for All Seasons (Oscar)

scold 3 nag **5** chide, shrew **6** berate, carp at, nagger, rail at, rebuke, virago **7** censure, reprove, upbraid **9** castigate, criticize, dress down, reprehend, reprimand, termagant **10** complainer
Yiddish: 6 kvetch

scolding 7 chiding, reproof **8** berating, rebuking **9** reprimand, talking-to **10** admonition, upbraiding **11** castigation **12** admonishment **13** tongue-lashing

sconce 7 bracket **11** candlestick **12** candleholder

scoop 4 bail, beat **5** clean, clear, gouge, ladle, spoon **6** burrow, dig out, dipper, hollow, shovel, trowel **7** dish out, lade out, lift out **8** excavate

scoop out 3 dig **5** gouge **8** excavate

scoot 3 run **4** dash, rush **6** scurry, sprint

Scooter
nickname of: 11 Phil Rizzuto

scope 3 aim **4** area, goal, rein, room, span, vent **5** field, force, grasp, range, reach **6** bounds, effect, margin, motive, spread, vision **7** bearing, compass, freedom, liberty, purpose, stretch **8** ambition, confines, latitude **9** extension, influence, intention **10** competence **11** application, destination **13** determination

scorch 3 dry **4** char, sear **5** parch, singe **6** dry out, scathe, wither **7** blacken **8** discolor **9** dehydrate

score, scores 3 cut, mar, run, tab, win **4** bill, debt, gain, gash, goal, lots, make, mark, nick, slit **5** amass, count, facts, grade, hosts, judge, notch, point, slash, tally, truth **6** basket, charge, damage, deface, droves, groove, grudge, masses, pile up, strike, swarms, twenty **7** account, achieve, arrange, legions, reality, scratch, throngs **8** evaluate, incision, register **9** grievance **10** amount owed, difference, multitudes, obligation **11** orchestrate

scoria 4 slag **5** dross **6** cinder, refuse

scorn 5 spurn **6** ignore, rebuff, refuse, reject, slight **7** condemn, despise, disdain, mockery, repulse, sarcasm **8** contempt, derision, ridicule, scoffing, spit upon **9** arrogance, contumely, disregard, ostracize **10** look down on, opprobrium **11** haughtiness

scorned 7 derided, refused **8** despised, rebuffed, rejected, repulsed **9** disdained **10** deprecated, disparaged

scornful 6 lordly **7** cynical **8** arrogant, derisive, insolent, sardonic, scoffing, sneering **9** sarcastic **10** disdainful, ridiculing **11** disparaging **12** contemptuous, supercilious

Scorpio, Scorpius
symbol: 8 scorpion
planet: 4 Mars **5** Pluto
rules: 5 death **7** passion
born: 7 October **8** November

Scorpion 4 whip **7** scourge
constellation of: 8 Scorpius

Scorsese, Martin
director of: 6 Casino, Kundun **8** Cape Fear **9** Good Fellas **10** After Hours, Raging Bull, Taxi Driver **11** Mean Streets **12** The Last Waltz **14** Mad Dog and Glory **25** The Last Temptation of Christ

scotch 4 foil, kill, stop **5** crush, quash **6** thwart **7** destroy **8** confound, obstruct, sabotage, suppress **9** undermine **11** nip in the bud

scotch
type: 6 whisky **7** whiskey **10** single-malt
origin: 8 Scotland
ingredient: 12 cereal grains
drink: 10 Scotch Mist **14** Highland Cooler
with amaretto: 9 Godfather
with cherry brandy: 12 Blood and Sand
with Drambuie: 9 Rusty Nail
with gin: 12 Barbary Coast
with vermouth: 6 Rob Roy **8** Affinity **10** Bobby Burns
brands: 5 J and B **7** Dewars **10** White Horse **11** Chivas Regal, Wild Grouse **12** Johnny Walker

Scotia
poetic: **8** Scotland
Scotland
Roman name: **9** Caledonia
capital: **9** Edinburgh
symbol: **7** thistle
poetic: **6** Scotia
largest city: **7** Glasgow
others: **3** Ayr **4** Duns, Oban **5** Alloa, Banff, Brora, Burgh, Cupar, Ellon, Leith, Perth, Salen, Troon **6** Dundee, Girvan, Hawick **7** Airdrie, Alloway, Dunkeld, Falkirk, Frunock, Mallaig, Paisley, Renfrew **8** Aberdeen, Dumfries, Greenock, Hamilton, Kirkwall, Rothesay, Stirling **9** Clydebank, Dumbarton, Greenlock, Inverness, Kirkcaldy, Peter head, St Andrews **10** Coatbridge, Kilmarnock, Motherwell **11** Dunfermline, Grangemouth
school: **7** Glasgow **8** Aberdeen **9** Edinburgh **12** Saint Andrew's
division: **3** Ayr **4** Bute, Fife, Ross **5** Angus, Banff, Moray, Nairn, Perth **6** Argyll, Lanark, Orkney **7** Berwick, Kinross, Lothian, Peebles, Renfrew, Selkirk, Wigtown **8** Aberdeen, Ayrshire, Cromarty, Dumfries, Roxburgh, Shetland, Stirling **9** Buteshire, Caithness, Dumbarton **10** Kincardine, Midlothian, Sutherland **11** Clackmannan, Kincudbight **12** Renfrewshire **13** Stirlingshire
kingdom: **8** Dalriada **11** Northumbria, Strathclyde
government: **13** United Kingdom
measure: **3** cop **4** boll, cran, fall, mile, peck, pint, rood, rope, span **5** crane, lippy **6** audlet, davach, firlot, lippie, noggin **7** chalder, choppin **8** mutchkin, stimpart, stimpert **9** particate, shaftment, shathmont
monetary unit: **3** ecu **4** demy, doit, lion, mark, rial, ryal **5** bodle, broad, groat, plack, rider, turne **6** bawbee, folles **7** unicorn **8** atchison, hardhead **9** halfpenny **11** bonnetpiece
weight: **4** boll, drop **6** trone **6** bushel
island: **3** Rum **4** Aran, Bute, Eigg, Fair, Inch, Iona, Jura, Lona, Muck, Mull, Rhum, Skye **5** Arran, Barra, Islay, Lewis **6** Harris, Orkney, Staffa **7** St Kilda **8** Berneray, Cumbraes, Hebrides, Shetland **9** North Uist, South Uist
lake/loch: **3** Awe, Dee, Lin, Tay **4** Earn, Fyne, Gair, Gare, Linn, Ness, Oich, Ryan, Sloy **5** Duich, Leven, Lochy, Lough, Morar, Maree, Nevis **6** Laggan, Linnhe, Lomond **7** Katrine, Rannoch, St Mary's
mountain: **4** Hope **5** Attow, Dearg, Nevis, Tinto, Wyvis **7** Cheviot, Macdhui, Merrick **8** Grampian **9** Ben Lomond, Cairngorm, Highlands, Trossachs
hills: **5** Ochil **6** Calton, Sidlaw **7**

Cheviot
highest point: **8** Ben Nevis
river: **3** Ayr, Dee, Don, Esk, Tay **4** Doon, Glen, Nith, Norn, Spey **5** Afton, Annan, Clyde, Forth, Garry, North, Tweed, Ythan **6** Affric, Teviot, Tummel **7** Deveron **8** Findhorn
sea: **5** Irish, North **8** Atlantic, Hebrides
physical feature:
bay: **5** Scapa
canal: **10** Caledonian
channel: **5** Minch, North
firth: **3** Tay **4** Kyle, Lorn **5** Clyde, Forth, Lorne, Moray **6** Linnhe, Solway **7** Comarty, Dornoch **8** Pentland
glen: **8** Glen More **9** Great Glen
hillside: **4** brae
moor: **7** Rannoch
valley: **8** Trossach
people: **4** Gael, Pict, Scot **5** Norse
artist: **7** Raeburn
author: **5** Burns, Scott **6** Barrie, Cronin, Dunbar **7** Barbour, Douglas **8** Henryson **9** Stevenson **10** Conan-Doyle, MacDiarmid, Macpherson
economist: **5** Smith
historian: **7** Carlyle
inventor: **4** Bell
king: **5** David, James **6** Duncan **7** Kenneth, Macbeth, Malcolm, Stuarts, William **9** Alexander **14** Robert the Bruce
landowner: **5** laird
philosopher: **4** Hume
prime minister: **9** Macdonald, MacMillan **11** Douglas-Home
prince: **19** Bonnie Prince Charlie
queen: **4** Mary **13** Saint Margaret
religious leader: **8** John Knox
scientist: **7** Fleming
patronymic: **3** Mac
patron saint: **6** Andrew
language: **4** Erse **6** Celtic, Gaelic, Keltic, Lallan **7** English, Lalland
religion: **12** Episcopalian, Presbyterian **13** Roman Catholic
place:
abbey: **5** Kelso **7** Melrose **8** Dryburgh, Jedburgh
castle: **8** Stirling **9** Edinburgh **11** Eilean Donan
church/kirk: **7** St Giles **11** St Cuthbert's
coronation site: **12** Stone of Scone
royal residence: **8** Balmoral
Scott's home: **10** Abbotsford
street: **7** Prince's **9** Royal Mile **11** Sauchiehall
feature:
bird: **3** bae, cae **4** hern, muir, smeu **6** grouse, smeuth, snabby **7** jackdaw **8** throstle **9** swinepipe
clothing: **3** tam **4** kilt **6** tartan **7** filibeg **12** Harris tweeds **13**

Shetland knits **15** Fair Isle sweater
dance: **3** bob **4** reel **7** walloch **9** ecossaise **10** petronella **11** strathsprey **12** gilliecallum **13** Highland fling
game: **4** golf **12** caber tossing
holiday: **8** Hogmanay
monster: **6** Nessie **8** Loch Ness
musical instrument: **7** bagpipe
symbol: **7** thistle
food:
bread: **5** scone
cheese: **7** crowdie
dish: **6** haggis **12** finnan haddie **15** kippered herring
drink: **12** Scotch whisky
soup: **11** cock-a-leekie
football team: **6** Oilers
Scott, George C
born: **6** Wise VA
wife: **14** Trish Van Devere **15** Colleen Dewhurst
roles: **4** Rage **6** Patton (Oscar, refused) **8** Jane Eyre **16** The New Centurions **18** The Day of the Dolphin
Scott, Sir Walter
author of: **6** Rob Roy **7** Ivanhoe, Marmion **8** The Abbot, Waverley **10** Kenilworth **11** The Talisman **12** Guy Mannering, Old Mortality, The Antiquary **14** Quentin Durward **16** The Lady of the Lake **20** The Bride of Lammermoor, The Heart of Midlothian **23** The Lay of the Last Minstrel
Scottish Mythology
spirit/horse: **6** kelpie
scoundrel 3 cad, cur **5** crook, knave, rogue, scamp, thief **6** rascal, rotter, varlet, weasel **7** bounder, ruffian, sharper, varmint, villain **8** scalawag, swindler, turncoat **9** miscreant, trickster **10** blackguard, copperhead, mountebank, ne'er-do-well **11** fourflusher, rapscallion **12** carpetbagger
scoundrelly 3 low **4** mean **7** debased **8** rascally **10** degenerate, despicable, villainous **12** contemptible, disreputable **13** reprehensible
Scoundrel Time
author: **14** Lillian Hellman
scour 4 buff, comb, rake, scan **5** scrub, shine **6** abrade, polish, scrape **7** burnish, cleanse, ransack, rummage **8** brighten, traverse
scourge 3 rod **4** bane, beat, cane, flog, lash, whip **5** birch, blast, curse, flail, strap **6** punish, switch, terror, thrash **7** censure, chasten **8** chastise, scorpion, vexation **9** castigate, excoriate **10** affliction, discipline, flagellate **11** troublement **12** cat-o'-nine-tails
scout 3 spy **4** case **5** guide, pilot **6** escort, spy out, survey **7** lookout, observe **8** outrider, point man, vanguard **9** recruiter **11** reconnoiter **13** reconnoiterer

scowl 4 pout 5 frown, glare, lower 6 glower 7 grimace

scrabble 3 paw 4 claw, rake 5 climb 6 drudge, jostle, scrape, scrawl 7 clamber, grapple, scratch 8 struggle

scram 3 out 4 scat, shoo 5 be off, leave 6 beat it, begone, depart, get out, go away 7 get lost, vamoose 10 make tracks

scramble 3 run, vie 4 race, rush 5 clash, fight, mix up, scrap, upset 6 battle, combat, engage, garble, jostle, jumble, mess up, scurry, strive, tussle 7 collide, confuse, disturb, scatter, scuffle, shuffle 8 disorder, struggle, unsettle 9 scrimmage 10 disarrange, free-for-all 11 competition, disorganize

scramble up 5 climb, mount, scale 7 clamber

scrap 3 bit, dab, jot, row 4 atom, drop, iota, junk, spat 5 brawl, crumb, fight, grain, melee, speck, trace, trash 6 fracas, morsel, refuse, ruckus, sliver 7 abandon, glimmer, minimum, modicum, quarrel, snippet 8 brouhaha, fraction, fragment, jettison, molecule, particle, squabble 10 free-for-all, smattering, sprinkling

scrapbook 5 album 9 portfolio 11 memorabilia, miscellanea

scrape 3 dig 4 buff, gash, mark, rasp, save, skin 5 amass, clean, fight, glean, gouge, grate, graze, grind, plane, run-in, score, scour, scuff, stint 6 abrade, bruise, forage, gather, groove, obtain, pick up, plight, scrimp, secure, smooth, tussle 7 acquire, burnish, dilemma, procure, rub hard, scratch, scuffle, straits 8 abrasion 9 economize, tight spot 10 difficulty 11 predicament 13 confrontation

scratch 3 cut, mar, rub 4 claw, etch, gash, nick, omit, rasp 5 dig at, erase, grate, graze, grind, score 6 cancel, delete, incise, remove, rub out, scrape, scrawl, streak, strike 7 blemish, blot out, exclude, expunge, rule out 8 abrasion, cross out, lacerate, scribble, withdraw 9 eliminate 10 laceration

scratchy 5 rough 6 coarse 7 bristly, prickly 9 irritated 10 irritating

scrawl 4 draw 5 write 6 doodle 7 scratch, writing 8 scrabble, scribble, squiggle 10 penmanship 11 handwriting

scrawniness 8 lankness, leanness, slimness, thinness 10 skinniness, slightness 11 slenderness

scrawny 4 bony, lank, lean, puny 5 drawn, gaunt, lanky, runty, spare 6 sinewy, skinny, wasted 7 angular, scraggy, spindly, stunted 8 rawboned, skeletal 9 emaciated, fleshless 10 attenuated, undersized 11 underweight

screak 4 rasp 5 grate, grind 6 shriek, squeak 7 screech

scream 4 howl, loud, roar, wail, yell, yelp, yowl 5 shout, whine 6 bellow, cry out, holler, outcry, shriek, squawk, squeal 7 screech 11 lamentation

screech 3 cry 4 howl, rasp 6 screak, scream, shriek 9 caterwaul

screen 3 see, web 4 cull, mask, mesh, rate, show, sift, sort, veil, view 5 class, cloak, cover, eject, films, grade, grate, group, guard, order, shade, sieve 6 buffer, cinema, defend, filter, mantle, movies, secure, shield, shroud, sifter, size up, strain, winnow 7 arrange, conceal, curtain, defense, discard, lattice, present, preview, project, protect, secrete, shelter, shutter, weed out 8 colander, coverage, evaluate, jalousie, separate, strainer, withhold 9 eliminate, partition, safeguard 10 protection 11 concealment

screw 4 bolt, join, knot, turn, warp 5 clamp, exact, force, gnarl, rivet, twist, wrest, wring 6 adjust, attach, deform, driver, extort, fasten, garble, wrench 7 contort, distort, pervert, squeeze, tighten 8 fastener, misshape 9 propeller

screwball 3 nut 4 kook 5 flake, freak 6 looney 7 lunatic 8 crackpot 9 character, eccentric

screwdriver
  type: 6 rachet 11 spiral-drive 12 Phillips-head

screwy 3 odd 4 daft 5 batty, dotty, flaky, funny, kinky, kooky, nutty, queer, wacky, weird 6 weirdo 7 oddball 8 peculiar 9 eccentric 10 unbalanced

Scriabin, Aleksandr (Scriabine, Skryabin)
  born: 6 Moscow, Russia
  composer of: 7 Mystery 10 Prometheus 12 Vers la flamme 13 Poem of Ecstasy, The Divine Poem, The Poem of Fire

scribble 4 tear 5 squib 6 doodle, scrawl 7 scratch 8 squiggle 9 pull apart
  fiber: 4 wool
  procedure: 7 carding

scribe, Scribe 3 cut 4 mark, tool 5 clerk, score 6 author, copier, penman, writer 7 copyist, teacher 8 recorder 9 archivist, scrivener, secretary 10 amanuensis, translator 12 newspaperman, stenographer 13 calligraphist
  Biblical: 4 Ezra 6 Esdras
  French dramatist: 8 Augustin
  Palestinian: 5 sofer 6 sopher

scribe of gods 5 Thoth

scrimp 4 save 5 hoard, pinch, skimp, stint 8 begrudge 9 besparing 12 pinch pennies

scrimping 6 frugal 7 sparing 10 economical 11 economizing 12 cheeseparing 15 pinching pennies

scrip 5 paper 8 document 11 certificate

scripsit 7 he wrote 8 she wrote

script 4 book, hand 5 lines, score 6 dialog 7 cursive 8 dialogue, libretto, longhand, scenario 10 manuscript, penmanship 11 calligraphy, chirography, handwriting

Scriptures, the 5 Bible 6 the Law, oracle 8 holy writ, the Bible, the Torah 10 the Gospels 11 The Good Book 12 New Testament, Old Testament, the Word of God 13 the Pentateuch, the Septuagint 14 sacred writings *see also* 5 Bible

scroll of the Torah
  Hebrew: 11 Sepher Torah

Scrooge, Ebenezer
  character in: 15 A Christmas Carol
  author: 7 Dickens

scrub 4 swab 5 brush, scour 8 scouring 9 brushwood, scrubbing

scrubby 4 base 6 brushy 7 stunted 8 inferior 10 undersized

scrumptious 5 juicy, tasty 6 savory, tender 8 luscious, pleasant, pleasing 9 agreeable, delicious, enjoyable, flavorful, succulent, toothsome 10 appetizing, delectable, delightful, flavorsome 13 mouth-watering

scruple 3 shy 4 balk, care, halt 5 demur, pause, qualm, waver 6 blench, ethics, falter 7 anxiety, concern, refrain 8 hesitate 9 fluctuate, misgiving, principle 10 conscience, hesitation 11 compunction, fearfulness, uncertainty 12 apprehension, doubtfulness, protestation 13 squeamishness 17 conscientiousness

Scruples
  author: 12 Judith Krantz

scrupulous 5 exact 6 honest 7 careful, dutiful, precise, upright 8 cautious, exacting, sedulous 9 honorable 10 deliberate, fastidious, meticulous, principled 11 painstaking, punctilious 13 conscientious

scrupulousness 4 care 5 pains 9 exactness 14 meticulousness 17 conscientiousness

scrutinize 4 scan 5 probe, study 6 peruse, search, survey 7 explore, inspect, observe 11 investigate

scrutiny 5 study, watch 7 inquiry, perusal 9 attention 10 inspection 11 examination 12 surveillance 13 investigation

scuffle 3 row 4 spar 5 brawl, clash, fight, melee, scrap 6 fracas, jostle, rumpus, tussle 8 squabble, struggle 9 commotion, imbroglio 10 donnybrook, free-for-all

sculpsit 10 he carved it 11 she carved it 12 he engraved it 13 she engraved it 14 he sculptured it 15 she sculptured it

sculptor 6 artist, carver, caster, imager, molder 7 marbler, modeler 8

chiseler, engraver
constellation: 19 Apparatus Sculptoris
French: 5 Rodin
Greek: 7 Phidias **10** Praxiteles
Irish-American: 12 Saint-Gaudens
Italian: 7 Cellini **12** Michelangelo
tool: 6 chisel, graver **7** spatula **9** ebauchoir

sculpture 3 cut **4** bust, cast, head, work **5** cameo, carve, erode, model, mould **6** chisel, relief, statue **7** carving, erosion, faience **8** intaglio, statuary **9** cloissone, medallion, statuette
medium: 4 clay **5** china, stone **6** bronze, enamel, marble **7** ceramic **9** porcelain **10** terra cotta **11** earthenware

scum 4 film, slag **5** crust, dregs, dross, trash **6** rabble, refuse **7** deposit, rubbish, surface **8** riffraff

scurrility 5 abuse **8** rudeness **9** indecency, obscenity, profanity **13** offensiveness, salaciousness

scurrilous 3 low **5** gross **6** coarse, vulgar **7** obscene **8** churlish, derisive, indecent, reviling **9** insulting, offensive, shameless **10** derogatory, detracting, indelicate, slanderous **11** disparaging, foulmouthed **12** contemptuous

scurry 3 hie **4** race, rush, skim **5** haste, hurry, scoot, speed **6** bustle, hasten, hustle, spring **7** rushing, scamper, scuttle **8** hurrying, scooting, scramble **9** confusion, dispersal **10** scattering

scurvy 3 low **4** base, mean, vile **6** shabby **7** ignoble **9** worthless **10** despicable **12** contemptible, dishonorable

scuttle 4 sink **5** abort, hurry, scrap, speed, wreck **6** hasten, scurry **7** destroy, discard, scamper **8** dispatch, scramble

scuttlebutt 4 talk **5** rumor **6** gossip **7** hearsay, prattle, scandal **8** chitchat

Scylaceus
origin: 6 Lycian
ally of: 7 Trojans
death by: 7 stoning

Scylla
form: 5 nymph **7** monster
location: 3 sea **16** Straits of Messina **20** Whirlpool of Charybdis
father: 7 Phorcys
mother: 6 Hecate
loved by: 8 Poseidon
rival: 10 Amphitrite

Scyphius
first: 5 horse
created by: 8 Poseidon

sea 3 bay, ton **4** deep, gulf, host, lake, leap, lots, main, mass, slew, wave **5** bight, flock, flood, ocean, scads, spate, surge, swarm, swell, waves **6** legion, roller, scores, waters **7** breaker **9** abundance, multitude, profusion
French: 3 mer
god of: 5 Aegir, Memir **6** Nereus, Tri-

ton **7** Glaucus, Neptune, Phorcys, Proteus **8** Poseidon **9** Asphalius
goddess of: 3 Ino, Ran **6** Graeae, Graiae, Matuta **8** Dictynna, Menannan **9** Leucothea **10** Amphitrite

Sea, the Sea, The
author: 11 Iris Murdoch
Sea Around Us, The
author: 13 Rachel L Carson
seaboard 5 coast **9** shoreline
Seaborg, Glen Theodore
field: 7 physics
worked with: 14 actinide series **19** transuranic elements
headed: 3 AEC **22** Atomic Energy Commission
awarded: 10 Nobel Prize
seacoast 5 beach, coast, shore **7** seaside **8** littoral **9** coastland, coastline, shoreline, waterside
French: 4 cote
Italian: 4 lido **7** riviera
seafarers 4 tars **5** salts **7** sailors, seadogs **8** mariners
Seagull, The
author: 12 Anton Chekhov
character: 5 Masha **6** Polina **10** Pyotr Sorin **11** Yevgeny Dorn **12** Ilya Shamraev, Irina Arkadin **13** Boris Trigorin, Nina Zaretchyn **16** Semyon Medvedenko **17** Konstantin Treplev
Seah 15 Biblical measure
Sea Hawk, The
director: 13 Michael Curtiz
cast: 10 Errol Flynn **11** Claude Rains, Donald Crisp **14** Brenda Marshall
score: 21 Erich Wolfgang Korngold
seal 2 OK **3** dam, fix **4** cork, lock, mark, plug, shut, stop **5** brand, close, stamp **6** accept, affirm, emblem, fasten, figure, ratify, secure, settle, shut up, signet, stop up, symbol, verify **7** approve, certify, confirm, endorse, imprint **8** colophon, conclude, fastener, hallmark, insignia, sanction, validate **9** determine, establish, trademark **10** impression **12** authenticate
Latin: 10 imprimatur

seal
young: 3 pup
group of: 3 pod

sea lion
young: 3 pup

seam 3 gap **4** line, lode, mark, scar, vein **5** break, chink, cleft, crack, joint, layer, notch **6** breach, furrow, incise, suture **7** crevice, fissure, joining, opening, rupture, stratum, wrinkle **8** junction, juncture **9** interface

seaman 3 gob, tar **4** hand, mate, salt **5** bosun, middy **6** lubber, merman, sailor, sea dog **7** mariner **9** boatswain **10** bluejacket, midshipman

seamark 5 light **6** beacon, pharos, signal **10** lighthouse, watchtower

sea monster 6 dragon **9** Leviathan

seamstress 10 dressmaker
French: 9 midinette **10** couturiere

seamy 3 raw **4** dark **5** dirty, nasty, rough **6** coarse, sordid **7** squalid, unclean **10** unpleasant **11** unwholesome **12** disagreeable

Sea of Grass, The
author: 13 Conrad Richter

sear 4 burn, char, scar **5** blast, singe, steel **6** harden, scorch **7** blister **9** cauterize **10** caseharden

search 4 comb, drag, fish, hunt, look, seek, sift **5** check, frisk, probe, quest, rifle, scour, snoop, study **6** survey, tracer **7** dragnet, examine, explore, inquiry, inspect, pry into, pursuit, ransack, rummage **8** overhaul, scrutiny **10** inspection, scrutinize **11** examination, exploration **13** investigation

Search, The
director: 13 Fred Zinnemann
cast: 9 Ivan Jandl **13** Aline MacMahon **14** Jarmila Novotna **15** Montgomery Clift
setting: 6 Berlin

Searchers, The
director: 8 John Ford
cast: 8 Ward Bond **9** John Wayne, Vera Miles **11** Natalie Wood **13** Jeffrey Hunter

searching 4 dour, keen, nosy **5** sharp **6** prying, shrewd, snoopy **7** curious, groping **8** exacting, piercing, rigorous, thorough **9** observant, quizzical, unsparing **11** inquisitive, penetrating **13** investigative

Seascape
author: 11 Edward Albee

seashore 5 beach, coast

seasick 3 ill **5** barfy, dizzy, faint, giddy, woozy **6** queasy **8** qualmish, vomitous **9** nauseated, squeamish **11** vertiginous

seasickness
French: 8 mal de mer

seaside 5 beach, coast, shore **9** shoreline

season 3 age, dry **4** fall, lace, tame, term **5** adapt, color, drill, inure, prime, ripen, shape, spell, spice, stage, train **6** accent, autumn, finish, flavor, inform, leaven, mature, mellow, period, refine, soften, spring, summer, temper, winter **7** enhance, enliven, prepare, quarter, stretch **8** accustom, duration, heighten, interval, ornament, practice **9** condition, cultivate, embellish **10** discipline

seasoned 6 herbed, inured, salted, spiced **7** veteran **8** flavored, hardened, peppered **9** competent, qualified **10** acclimated, accustomed, habituated **11** experienced **12** familiarized

seasoning 4 dill, herb, mace, sage, salt, zest **5** aging, basil, clove, gusto, onion, spice, thyme **6** drying, garlic, ginger, nutmeg, pepper, relish **7** oregano, paprika, parsley **8** allspice, cinnamon, marjoram, practice, ripening, rosemary, training **9** condiment, flavoring **10** maturation **11** orientation, preparation **15** familiarization

seasons
  god of: 9 Vertumnus
  goddess of: 5 Horae, Hours

seat 3 box, hub **4** axis, core, home, rump, site, sofa **5** abode, bench, chair, couch, croup, divan, fanny, heart, house, locus, place **6** behind, bottom, center, locale, settle **7** address, capital, cushion, habitat, housing, nucleus, rear end, situate **8** backside, buttocks, derriere, domicile, dwelling, haunches, location, quarters **9** posterior, residence **10** incumbency, membership **12** hindquarters

seat of justice 5 bench, court **8** tribunal **9** judiciary **10** courthouse

Seattle
  baseball team: 8 Mariners
  basketball team: 11 Supersonics
  bay: 7 Elliott
  football team: 8 Seahawks
  lake: 10 Washington
  landmark: 11 Space Needle
  site of: 10 World's Fair
  sound: 5 Puget

Sea Wolf, The
  author: 10 Jack London

Sebastian
  character in: 12 Twelfth Night
  author: 10 Shakespeare

Seberg, Jean
  born: 14 Marshalltown IA
  husband: 10 Romain Gary
  roles: 6 Lilith **7** Airport **9** Saint Joan **10** Breathless **16** Bonjour Tristesse

Secchi, Angelo
  field: 9 astronomy
  nationality: 7 Italian
  classified: 5 stars

secede 4 quit **5** leave **6** resign, retire **7** forsake **8** withdraw **12** disaffiliate

secession 10 separation, withdrawal **14** disaffiliation

seclude 4 hide **6** retire **7** isolate **8** separate **9** sequester **10** dissociate

secluded 6 covert, cut off, lonely, remote, shut in **7** private **8** closeted, confined, isolated, shut away, solitary **9** reclusive, sheltered, unvisited, withdrawn **10** cloistered **11** out-of-the-way, sequestered **12** unfrequented

seclusion 5 exile **6** asylum, hiding **7** retreat **8** cloister, hideaway, solitude **9** hermitage, isolation, reclusion, sanctuary **10** quarantine, retirement, withdrawal **11** concealment **13** sequestration

second 3 aid **4** abet, back, help, wink **5** agent, favor, flash, jiffy, other, proxy, trice **6** assist, back up, deputy, fill-in, helper, minute, moment, uphold **7** advance, another, endorse, further, instant, one more, outdone, promote, stand by, stand-in, support **8** advocate, delegate, exceeded, inferior **9** alternate, assistant, attendant, encourage, surpassed, twinkling **10** additional, lieutenant, substitute, understudy **11** alternating, subordinate **14** representative
  abbreviation: 1 s **3** sec

secondary 5 lower, minor, other **6** backup, lesser **7** smaller **8** inferior, mediocre, middling **9** alternate, ancillary, auxiliary, following, resultant **10** consequent, subsequent, subsidiary **11** subordinate

second childhood 6 dotage **8** senility

secondhand 4 used **8** indirect **10** derivative, hand me down

second-in-command 6 deputy **8** adjutant **9** assistant **10** lieutenant **13** vice president

second-rate 3 bad **4** poor, so-so **5** cheap, tacky **6** shabby **7** average **8** everyday, inferior, mediocre, middling **9** imperfect **10** inadequate, outclassed, pedestrian **11** commonplace, substandard **15** undistinguished

Second Sex, The
  author: 16 Simone de Beauvoir

second-story man 5 thief **6** robber **7** burglar **9** cracksman **10** cat burglar

second string 4 subs **5** bench **11** substitutes

second team 5 bench **11** substitutes

secrecy 6 hiding **7** mystery, privacy, private, silence, stealth **8** muteness, solitude **9** closeness, seclusion **10** covertness **11** concealment, furtiveness **13** sequestration **15** clandestineness, confidentiality, underhandedness **17** surreptitiousness **19** uncommunicativeness

secret 3 key, mum **4** dark **6** arcane, covert, enigma, hidden, mystic, occult, puzzle, recipe, unseen **7** formula, furtive, mystery, private, unknown **8** discreet, esoteric, hush-hush, secluded, stealthy **9** concealed, disguised, invisible, secretive **10** confidence, mysterious, undercover, unrevealed **11** camouflaged, clandestine, undisclosed, unpublished **12** confidential, unrevealable **13** surreptitious

Secret Agent
  character: 9 John Drake
  cast: 15 Patrick McGoohan
  theme: 14 Secret Agent Man

secretary 4 aide, desk **5** clerk **6** scribe **7** officer **8** recorder **10** amanuensis **12** stenographer
  French: 10 escritoire

secret council 8 conclave

secrete 4 hide, veil **5** cache, cloak, cover, stash **6** screen, shroud **7** conceal, curtain **8** disguise

secretive 3 mum, sly **4** mute **6** covert, silent **7** cryptic, evasive, furtive, laconic, private **8** discreet, reserved, reticent, stealthy, taciturn **9** enigmatic, withdrawn **10** mysterious **11** tight-lipped, underhanded, unrevealing **13** surreptitious **15** uncommunicative

secretiveness 7 mystery, stealth **9** reticence **11** furtiveness **14** inscrutability, mysteriousness **19** uncommunicativeness

Secret Life of Walter Mitty, The
  author: 12 James Thurber
  cast: 10 Danny Kaye

sect 4 camp, cult **7** faction **8** division **10** persuasion **11** affiliation **12** denomination

sectarian 6 narrow **7** limited **8** clannish **9** exclusive, parochial **10** provincial, restricted

section 4 area, part, side, unit, ward, zone **5** piece, range, share, slice **6** region, sample, sphere **7** chapter, cutting, measure, passage, portion, segment, terrain **8** district, division, province, specimen, vicinity **9** allotment, increment, territory **10** department, proportion **11** installment **12** neighborhood

sector 4 area, zone **7** theater **8** district

secular 3 lay **4** laic **6** carnal **7** earthly, fleshly, mundane, profane, sensual, worldly **8** material, temporal **9** nonsacred **11** nonclerical **12** nonreligious, nonspiritual **17** nonecclesiastical

secundum 11 according to

secure 3 get, set **4** bind, easy, safe, sure **5** fixed, tight **6** at ease, defend, ensure, fasten, immune, insure, obtain **7** acquire, assured, certain, protect, shelter, tie down **8** absolute, carefree, composed, defended, definite, in the bag, positive, surefire **9** confident, guarantee, protected, reassured, safeguard, sheltered **10** guaranteed **11** impregnable **12** invulnerable, unassailable, unattackable, unthreatened

securities 5 bonds, title **6** stocks **12** certificates

security 4 bond, care, hope, keep **5** faith, trust **6** guards, pledge, police, safety, surety, troops **7** defense, deposit, promise, support **8** reliance, sureness, warranty **9** assurance, certainty, guarantee **10** collateral, confidence, conviction, protection, safeguards **11** maintenance, safekeeping **12** absoluteness, decisiveness, definiteness, positiveness, preservation

sedate 4 calm, cool **5** grave, quiet, sober, staid, still **6** poised, serene, solemn, steady **7** serious, subdued **8** composed, decorous, reserved **9** collected, dignified, impassive, unexcited, unruffled **10** cool-headed **11** level-headed **13** imperturbable **15** undemonstrative

sedateness 7 decorum, dignity, gravity, reserve **8** calmness **9** composure, soberness, solemnity **11** impassivity, seriousness

sedative 6 easing, opiate **7** anodyne, calming **8** allaying, lenitive, narcotic, relaxing, soothing **9** analgesic, assuasive, calmative, composing, mitigator, soporific **10** comforting, palliative **11** alleviative **12** tranquilizer **13** tranquilizing

sedentary 5 fixed, inert, still **6** seated **7** resting, sitting **8** inactive, unmoving **9** quiescent **10** stationary, unstirring

sedge 4 reed **5** grass **10** marsh grass

sediment 4 lees, scum, slag **5** dregs, dross, waste **6** debris, sludge **7** grounds, remains, residue **8** leavings **9** settlings

sedition 6 mutiny, revolt **7** treason **8** defiance, uprising **9** rebellion **10** disloyalty, insurgency, subversion, unruliness **11** lawlessness **12** disobedience, insurrection **14** rebelliousness, subversiveness

Sedley, Amelia and Joseph
  characters in: 10 Vanity Fair
  author: 9 Thackeray

seduce 4 lure, ruin **5** abuse, charm, tempt **6** allure, defile, entice, ravish **7** attract, conquer, corrupt, debauch, deprave, pervert, violate, win over **8** deflower, disgrace, dishonor, persuade **9** captivate

seducer 3 cad **4** wolf **5** letch, Romeo **7** defiler, Don Juan, playboy **8** Casanova, Lothario, lover-boy, ravisher, violater **9** corrupter, debaucher, womanizer **10** deflowerer **11** philanderer **12** heartbreaker
  French: 4 roue

seductive 4 sexy **8** alluring, charming, enticing, tempting **9** beguiling, disarming **10** attractive, bewitching, come-hither, enchanting, voluptuous **11** captivating, provocative

seductress 4 vamp **5** siren **7** charmer, Jezebel, Lorelei, mantrap **9** temptress **11** adventuress, enchantress
  French: 7 cocotte **11** femme fatale

sedulous 6 dogged **8** diligent, thorough **9** assiduous, steadfast **10** determined, persistent **11** industrious, painstaking, persevering **13** conscientious, indefatigable

sedulousness 4 zeal **8** industry, tenacity **9** assiduity, diligence **11** persistence **12** perseverance

see 3 dig, eye, spy, woo **4** date, espy, know, meet, mind, spot, view **5** court, grasp, sight, visit, watch **6** attend, behold, descry, escort, fathom, notice, regard, survey **7** consult, discern, glimpse, observe, picture, realize, receive, undergo, witness **8** conceive, consider, discover, envision, meditate, perceive, register, ruminate **9** accom-

pany, apprehend, ascertain, determine, encounter, entertain, interview, recognize, visualize **10** appreciate, comprehend, experience, understand **11** contemplate, distinguish
  Latin: 4 vide

see above
  Latin: 9 vide supra

see after
  Latin: 8 vide post

see before
  Latin: 8 vide ante

see below
  Latin: 9 vide infra

seed 3 pit, sow **4** germ **5** basis, grain, heirs, issue, ovule, plant, stone **6** embryo, origin, source **7** progeny **8** children **9** beginning, offspring, posterity **11** descendants

seedy 4 worn **5** dingy, faded, lousy, mangy, ratty, spent, tacky **6** scuffy, shabby **7** haggard, sickish, squalid **8** slovenly **10** threadbare **11** debilitated

see fit 5 deign **6** choose, please

seek 3 try **4** hunt **5** court, essay, trace **6** demand, invite, pursue **7** attempt, examine, explore, inspect, request, solicit, venture **8** endeavor **9** undertake **10** scrutinize **11** investigate

seek out 4 find **6** pursue **7** embrace, look for, solicit

seem 4 look **6** appear

seeming 7 evident, obvious, surface **8** apparent, presumed, putative, supposed **10** ostensible **11** superficial

seemly 3 due **5** right **6** decent, polite, proper **7** correct, fitting, prudent, refined **8** becoming, decorous, suitable, tasteful, well-bred **9** befitting, courteous **10** acceptable, felicitous **11** appropriate **12** conventional
  French: 11 comme il faut

seep 4 drip, leak, ooze, soak **7** diffuse, dribble, suffuse, trickle **8** permeate **9** penetrate

seepage 4 ooze **5** flour, issue **7** leakage, outflow **9** discharge, dribbling, secretion, trickling

seer 4 sage **5** augur **6** medium, oracle **7** diviner, prophet, psychic **8** conjurer, sorcerer **9** stargazer **10** astrologer, soothsayer **11** clairvoyant, necromancer **13** fortuneteller **14** prognosticator

seesaw 5 waver **6** teeter **9** alternate, fluctuate, up-and-down, vacillate **12** teeter-totter

seethe 4 boil, brew, cook, fume, rage, rant, rave, roil, stew **5** churn, storm **6** blow up, bubble, simmer **7** bluster, smolder

seething 3 mad **7** boiling **8** agitated, bubbling, frenzied **10** distraught

see through 3 get **6** detect, effect, finish **7** achieve, execute, perform **8** carry out, complete, conclude **9** catch

onto, figure out, penetrate **10** comprehend, understand

Segal, Erich
  author of: 9 Love Story **12** Oliver's Story **16** Man Woman and Child

Segal, George
  born: 9 New York NY
  roles: 11 Blume in Love, Where's Poppa? **13** A Touch of Class **18** Fun with Dick and Jane **25** Who's Afraid of Virginia Woolf?

segment 3 leg **4** part **5** cut up, piece, stage **6** cleave **7** disjoin, portion, section, split up **8** disunite, division, separate **9** increment **11** installment

segmented 5 cut up **7** split up **9** sectioned, separated

segregate 6 cut off, detach, divide **7** divorce, isolate, seclude, sort out **8** disunite, insulate, separate **9** sequester **10** disconnect, quarantine

seine 3 net **4** drag, fish **5** trawl **7** dragnet

Seinfeld
  Network: 3 NBC
  cast: 11 Wayne Knight (Newman) **13** Jerry Seinfeld (Jerry) **14** Jason Alexander (George) **15** Michael Richards (Kramer) **17** Julia Louis-Dreyfus (Elaine)
  characters: 6 Newman **11** Elaine Benes, Cosmo Kramer **13** Jerry Seinfeld **14** George Costanza
  episodes/themes: 8 Man Hands, Soup Nazi **9** Marble Rye **10** The Contest **11** Junior Mints **12** masturbation, yada-yada-yada **16** Master of My Domain

seism 5 quake, shock **6** tremor **8** temblor, upheaval **10** earthquake

seize 3 bag, nab **4** grab, read **5** catch, glean, grasp, pinch, pluck, usurp **6** arrest, clutch, collar, gather, snatch **7** capture, embrace, impound, possess, utilize **8** arrogate **9** apprehend, overpower, overwhelm **10** commandeer, comprehend, confiscate, understand **11** appropriate

seize the day
  Latin: 9 carpe diem

seizure 3 fit **5** onset, spell, throe **6** access, arrest, attack, crisis, stroke, taking **7** capture, episode **8** grasping, paroxysm **9** abduction, snatching **10** convulsion, kidnapping, possession, usurpation, visitation **11** impressment **12** apprehension, confiscation **13** appropriation, commandeering

Sekhmet
  origin: 8 Egyptian
  goddess of: 4 evil

seldom 6 rarely **8** scarcely **10** uncommonly **12** infrequently, occasionally, sporadically

select 3 tap **4** A-one, pick, posh **5** elect, elite, fancy **6** choice, choose, chosen, opt for, picked, prefer **8** four-star, superior, top-notch **9** exclusive, first-rate, preferred **10** first-class, privileged

selection 4 pick **5** range **6** choice, medley, option **7** program, variety **8** choosing, decision **9** potpourri **10** collection, miscellany, preference

selective 5 fussy, picky **6** choosy **7** careful, finicky **8** cautious **10** discerning, fastidious, meticulous, particular **14** discriminating

Selene
goddess of: **4** moon
father: **8** Hyperion
mother: **5** Theia
brother: **6** Helios
sister: **3** Eos
loved: **8** Endymion
daughter: **5** Herse **6** Pandia
corresponds to: **5** Diana **7** Artemis

self 3 ego **6** person, psyche **8** identity **10** individual **11** homogeneity, personality
inner: **5** anima **6** animus
Universal: **5** Atman

self-abnegation 7 modesty **8** humility **10** diffidence **11** bashfulness

self-absorbed 4 vain **8** egoistic **9** egotistic **10** egocentric **11** egotistical **12** narcissistic

self-absorption 6 egoism, vanity **7** conceit **11** egocentrism, selfishness **16** self-centeredness

self-admiration 6 vanity **7** conceit, egotism **8** smugness **9** immodesty, vainglory

self-assertive 4 bold **7** dynamic **8** forceful **9** ambitious, confident **10** aggressive

self-assuming 4 vain **8** arrogant, egoistic **9** conceited **10** egoistical **11** egotistical

self-assurance 6 aplomb **9** brashness **12** cocksureness
French: **9** sangfroid

self-assured 5 brash, cocky **8** cocksure **9** confident

self-centered 4 vain **8** egoistic, immodest **9** conceited, egotistic **10** egocentric **11** egotistical, swellheaded **12** narcissistic

self-centeredness 6 egoism, vanity **7** conceit **10** narcissism **11** egocentrism

self-composure 5 poise **6** aplomb **8** calmness **10** equanimity

self-confidence 5 nerve, pluck **6** mettle, spirit **8** boldness, gameness **9** cockiness **10** resolution **12** cocksureness

self-conscious 7 awkward **8** affected **9** chagrined, ill at ease, unnatural **11** discomposed, embarrassed **12** disconcerted

self-consciousness 7 modesty, reserve, shyness **8** timidity **9** abashment, hesitancy, reticence **10** con-

straint, demureness, diffidence **11** bashfulness, fearfulness **12** apprehension, sheepishness

self-control 5 poise **6** aplomb **8** firmness, patience, sobriety **9** composure, soberness, soundness, stability, willpower **10** temperance **11** forbearance **14** cool-headedness, unexcitability **15** levelheadedness **16** imperturbability
French: **9** sangfroid **11** savoir faire

self-critical 6 humble, modest **9** diffident **13** perfectionist

self-criticism 7 modesty **8** humility **10** diffidence **13** perfectionism

self-deception 7 fantasy **8** delusion, illusion **13** hallucination

self-declared 5 sworn **6** avowed **8** admitted **9** confessed, professed **12** acknowledged

self-denial 8 eschewal **10** abnegation, abstention, abstinence, continence **11** forbearance **12** renunciation **14** abstemiousness

self-deprecation
also: **16** self-depreciation **7** modesty **8** humility, meekness **10** humbleness

self-doubt 11 uncertainty

self-effacement 7 modesty, shyness **8** humility, meekness **10** diffidence **11** bashfulness

self-esteem 5 pride **10** confidence

self-evident 5 plain **6** patent **7** glaring, obvious **8** apparent, distinct, explicit, manifest, palpable **10** unarguable, undeniable **11** unambiguous, unequivocal **12** unmistakable **16** incontrovertible

self-explanatory 5 clear, lucid, plain **7** obvious **8** manifest **12** intelligible **15** straightforward

self-governing 4 free **9** sovereign **10** autonomous **11** independent

self-government 8 autonomy, home rule **11** sovereignty **12** independence

self-gratifying 11 intemperate

self-importance 6 egoism, vanity **8** smugness **9** arrogance, immodesty, pomposity, vainglory **11** egocentrism

self-important 4 smug, vain **7** pompous **8** egoistic, immodest **10** egocentric **11** egotistical **12** vainglorious

self-indulgence 12 extravagance, incontinence, intemperance

self-indulgent 9 libertine, sybaritic **10** hedonistic, voluptuous **11** extravagant, incontinent, intemperate

selfish 4 mean **5** tight, venal **6** greedy, stingy **7** miserly **8** covetous, egoistic, grasping, grudging **9** egotistic, illiberal, mercenary, rapacious **10** avaricious, egocentric, ungenerous **11** egotistical **12** parsimonious, uncharitable

self-love 6 egoism, vanity **7** conceit, egotism **9** vainglory **10** narcissism **11** complacency, egocentrism, haughtiness **13** conceitedness **15** swellhead-

edness
French: **11** amour propre

self-possessed 4 calm, cool **6** poised **7** assured, courtly, refined **8** balanced, composed, polished, resolute **9** collected, confident **12** aristocratic **13** distinguished

self-possession 5 poise **6** aplomb **7** dignity **8** calmness, coolness **9** composure **10** confidence, equanimity, steadiness **16** imperturbability
French: **9** sangfroid

self-praise 6 vanity **7** conceit, egotism **8** bragging, smugness **9** arrogance, immodesty, vainglory **12** boastfulness
Italian: **11** braggadocio

self-propelling 9 automatic

self-questioning 10 uneasiness **13** soul-searching

self-reliance 8 sureness **9** assurance **12** independence

Self-Reliance
author: **17** Ralph Waldo Emerson

self-reliant 5 hardy **6** plucky **7** assured **8** resolute, spirited **10** mettlesome **11** independent **12** enterprising

self-reproachful 8 contrite **9** regretful **10** apologetic, remorseful

self-respecting 5 proud **7** upright **8** decorous **9** dignified, honorable **10** upstanding **11** circumspect **13** distinguished

self-restraint 9 willpower **10** continence **11** forbearance

self-righteous 4 smug **5** pious **7** pompous **9** insincere, pietistic **10** complacent, moralizing **11** pharisaical, pretentious **12** hypocritical, mealy-mouthed **13** sanctimonious **14** holier-than-thou

self-sacrificing 6 heroic **7** gallant **9** unselfish **10** altruistic, martyrlike

self-satisfaction 5 pride **6** vanity **8** smugness **11** complacency

self-satisfied 4 smug, vain **8** cocksure, priggish **9** overproud **10** complacent **11** egotistical **12** narcissistic, vainglorious **13** overconfident

self-secure 4 smug **7** content **9** contented **10** complacent

self-seeking 6 greedy **8** covetous

self-styled
French: **9** soi-disant

self-willed 8 obdurate, stubborn **9** obstinate, pigheaded **10** headstrong, refractory **11** intractable **12** ungovernable, unmanageable

sell 4 dump, hawk, vend **6** barter, betray, deal in, enlist, handle, market, peddle, unload **7** deceive, trade in, win over **8** convince, dispense

Selleck, Tom
roles: **8** Lassiter, Magnum PI **12** Thomas Magnum **15** High Road to China **16** Three Men and A Baby

seller 6 dealer, jobber, monger, trader, vendor **7** peddler **8** merchant, retailer, salesman **9** middleman, salesgirl, saleslady, tradesman **10** saleswoman, shopkeeper, wholesaler **11** salesperson, storekeeper

Sellers, Peter
real name: 19 Richard Henry Sellers
born: 7 England **8** Southsea
wife: 11 Britt Ekland
roles: 10 Being There **12** Casino Royale **13** Dr Strangelove, Murder by Death **14** A Shot in the Dark, The Pink Panther **16** What's New Pussycat? **17** Inspector Clouseau **18** The Mouse that Roared **21** The World of Henry Orient

Selli
priests of: 4 Zeus

sell out 6 betray **11** double-cross

semblance 3 air **4** cast, copy, look, show **5** image **6** aspect **7** bearing, replica **8** likeness, pretense **9** duplicate, facsimile **10** simulacrum **11** counterpart **12** reproduction **14** representation
French: 4 mien

Semele
also: 6 Thyone
father: 6 Cadmus
mother: 8 Harmonia
loved by: 4 Zeus
son: 6 Dionysus
sister: 3 Ino **5** Agave **7** Autonoe

seminal 7 primary **8** creative, fruitful, germinal, original **9** formative **10** generative, productive **11** germinative, originating

Seminole
language family: 9 Muskogean
tribe: 8 Cow Creek, Mikasaki
location: 6 Mexico **7** Florida, Georgia **10** Everglades
leader: 7 Osceola, Wild Cat **10** Coacoochie

Semiramis
queen of: 7 Assyria
husband: 5 Ninus
founder of: 7 Babylon

Semitic
language family: 11 Afro-Asiatic **13** Hamito-Semitic
eastern branch: 8 Akkadian, Assyrian **10** Babylonian
western branch: 4 Geez **5** Tigre **6** Arabic, Gurage, Harari, Hebrew, Minean, Sabean, Syriac **7** Amharic, Aramaic, Argobba, Moabite **8** Ethiopic, Tigrinya, Ugaritic **9** Canaanite **10** Himyaritic, Phoenician, Qatabanian
southwest branch: 6 Minean, Sabean **7** Amharic **10** Himyaritic, Qatabanian **11** North Arabic **19** South Arabic-Ethiopic

Semo Sancus *see* **6** Sancus

senatus consultum 17 Roman senate decree

send 4 cast, emit, head, hurl, lead, show, toss **5** drive, fling, guide, refer, relay, shoot, throw **6** convey, direct, launch, propel **7** conduct, deliver, forward, give off, project **8** dispatch, transmit **9** broadcast, cause to go, discharge **11** disseminate

send away 4 oust, rout, shoo **5** chase, evict

send forth 4 emit, gush **5** erupt, expel, issue, let go **7** dismiss, release **8** disgorge, dispatch **9** discharge

send off 4 post **7** forward **8** dispatch, disperse, transmit

send out 4 beam, emit **8** dispatch, transmit **9** discharge

send packing 3 axe, can **4** fire, oust, rout, sack, shoo **5** evict **6** bounce **7** cast out, dismiss

send to Coventry 3 cut **5** eject, expel **6** banish, ignore **7** cast out, exclude **9** ostracize

Seneca
language family: 9 Iroquoian
location: 7 New York **15** Canandaigua Lake
leader: 9 John Abeel, John O'Bail **11** Cornplanter
member: 19 League of the Iroquois

Senegal
capital/largest city: 5 Dakar
others: 5 Bakel, Matam, Thies **7** Bignona, Kaolack, Kaollak **8** Diourbel, Kedougou, Linguere, Rufisque **10** Saint-Louis, Ziguinchor **11** Richard-Toll, Tambacounda
division: 7 Sudanic **8** Sahelian **9** Casamance
    empire: 4 Mali **5** Jolof **6** Tekrur
monetary unit: 5 franc **7** centime
island: 5 Goree
lake: 6 Guiers
mountain: 6 Gounou
highest point: 12 Fouta Djallon
river: 4 Sine **6** Faleme, Gambia, Saloum **7** Senegal **9** Casamance
sea: 8 Atlantic
physical feature:
    desert: 5 Ferlo
    peninsula: 9 Cape Verde
people: 4 Lebu, Peul, Soce **5** Diola, Dyola, Foula, Laobe, Peulh, Serer, Wolof **6** Fulani, Serere **7** Bambara, Malinke, Tukuler, Tukulor **8** Mandingo
    leader: 7 Senghor
language: 5 Wolof **6** French
religion: 5 Islam **7** animism **13** Roman Catholic
feature:
    musical instrument: 4 kora
    tree: 6 acacia, baobab **7** juniper, oil palm **10** raffia palm

Senhor, Senhora 2 sr **3** man, sra **5** madam (Portuguese)

senile 6 doting, infirm **7** foolish **8** decrepit **9** doddering, senescent **13** superannuated

senior, Senior 4 head, over **5** above, chief, doyen, elder, older **6** better **7** veteran **8** superior

seniority 6 tenure **9** longevity **10** precedence
French: 4 pere

senor 2 Mr **3** don **5** title **6** mister **8** Spaniard

senora 3 Mrs, sra **4** lady, wife **5** madam, woman **8** mistress

senorita 4 lass, miss
abbreviation: 4 srta

senorita 6 wrasse
genus: 8 Oxyjulis
species: 11 californica

sensation 3 hit **4** stir, to-do **6** thrill, uproar **7** feeling, scandal **9** agitation, awareness, commotion, detection **10** impression, perception

sensational 5 cheap, lurid **6** superb **8** dramatic, exciting, galvanic, shocking, striking **9** emotional, excellent, thrilling **10** electrical, scandalous **11** exaggerated, exceptional, extravagant, outstanding, spectacular **12** meretricious **13** extraordinary **14** heartthrobbing

sensationalism 7 scandal **9** luridness, melodrama **13** grandstanding **15** blood and thunder **16** yellow journalism

sense 3 see, use **4** aura, espy, feel, good, mind, note **5** grasp, guess, point, sight, smell, taste, touch, value, worth **6** descry, detect, divine, reason, regard, take in, wisdom **7** benefit, discern, faculty, feeling, hearing, meaning, purpose, realize, suspect **8** efficacy, function, judgment, perceive, sagacity **9** apprehend, awareness, intuition, recognize **10** atmosphere, comprehend, definition, denotation, impression, understand **11** connotation, premonition, realization, recognition **12** appreciation, intelligence, perspicacity, practicality, presentiment **13** consciousness, signification, understanding **14** reasonableness

Sense and Sensibility
author: 10 Jane Austen
character: 10 Lucy Steele **13** Edward Ferrars, Robert Ferrars **14** Colonel Brandon, John Willoughby **16** Sir John Middleton
    Dashwood family: 4 John **5** Fanny **6** Elinor **8** Marianne

senseless 4 dumb, idle, numb **5** crazy, inane, nutty, silly **6** stupid, unwise **7** aimless, foolish, stunned, useless, witless **8** comatose, deadened **9** brainless, foolhardy, illogical, insensate, pointless **10** groundless, ill-advised, insensible, irrational, ridiculous **11** harebrained, meaningless, purposeless, unconscious **12** unreasonable **13** irresponsible

sense of duty 15 moral obligation **21** sense of responsibility

sensibilities 8 feelings, sore spot, thin skin **12** Achilles' heel **14** susceptibility

sensibility 7 feeling **10** perception **11** temperament **14** responsiveness

sensible 4 just, sage, sane, wise **5** aware, plain, sound **7** evident, knowing, logical, obvious, prudent, visible **8** apparent, apprised, credible, discreet, informed, palpable, possible, rational, tangible **9** cognitive, cognizant, conscious, judicious, plausible, sagacious **10** detectable, discerning, farsighted, noticeable, perceiving, perceptive, reasonable, responsive, thoughtful **11** discernible, enlightened, intelligent, perceptible, susceptible **13** perspicacious **14** discriminating

sensitive 4 fine, keen, sore **5** acute, exact **6** tender, touchy **7** painful, precise **8** accurate, delicate, faithful, sentient **10** perceptive, responsive **11** susceptible, thin-skinned **14** impressionable

sensitiveness 8 delicacy **10** touchiness

sensual 4 lewd, sexy **6** carnal, earthy, erotic **7** fleshly, lustful **9** lecherous **10** hedonistic, licentious, voluptuous

sensualist 8 hedonist, sybarite **9** libertine **10** voluptuary

sensuous 9 delicious, exquisite **10** delightful

sententious 7 orotund, pompous, preachy, stilted **8** didactic, pedantic **9** grandiose, high-flown, pietistic **10** judgmental, moralistic **13** sanctimonious

sentient 5 aware **7** alert to, alive to, awake to, mindful **8** sensible **9** conscious

sentiment, sentiments 4 idea **5** heart **6** notion **7** emotion, feeling, opinion, romance, thought **8** attitude **9** nostalgia, viewpoint **10** tenderness **11** romanticism **12** emotionalism **15** softheartedness

sentimental 5 mushy, weepy **7** maudlin, mawkish, tearful **8** pathetic, romantic **9** emotional, nostalgic **10** lachrymose **12** melodramatic, romanticized

Sentimental Education, A
author: **15** Gustave Flaubert
character: **6** Arnoux **9** Dambreuse, Rosanette **11** Des Lauriers, Louise Roque **14** Frederic Moreau

sentimentalism 4 corn, mush **5** slush **6** bathos, pathos **8** schmaltz **9** mushiness, soppiness **10** maudlinism, slushiness **11** mawkishness

sentimentality 4 mush **5** heart **6** bathos, pathos **10** sloppiness **11** mawk-

ishness, temperament **12** emotionalism
Yiddish: **6** kitsch

Sentimental Journey, A
author: **14** Laurence Sterne
character: **5** Maria **6** Yorick **7** La Fleur

sentinel 4 ward **5** guard, scout, watch **6** patrol, picket, ranger **7** lookout **8** guardian, watchman **9** guardsman

sentry 5 guard, watch **7** lookout, vedette, vidette **8** sentinel, watchman
greeting: **4** halt

Seoul
capital of: **10** South Korea

separate 3 cut **4** cull, fork, part, sift **5** break, crack, sever, split **6** bisect, detach, divide, ramify, remove, single, spread, sunder **7** crumble, disjoin, diverge, diverse, divorce, isolate, radiate **8** detached, discrete, distinct, disunite **9** bifurcate, break away, come apart, different, disunited, partition, segregate, subdivide **10** autonomous, disconnect, dissimilar, divaricate, individual **11** distinguish, independent

separated 6 cut off **7** severed **8** detached **10** disengaged **12** disconnected, disentangled

separate from 5 apart, leave

separately 5 apart **6** singly **7** asunder **9** severally **12** individually

Separate Tables
director: **11** Delbert Mann
based on play by: **15** Terence Rattigan
cast: **10** David Niven **11** Deborah Kerr, Wendy Hiller **12** Rita Hayworth **13** Burt Lancaster
Oscar for: **5** actor (Niven) **17** supporting actress (Hiller)

separation 3 gap **4** fork **5** break, space, split **6** breach, divide, schism **7** divider, divorce, good-bye, opening, parting, removal, sorting **8** boundary, distance, disunion, division, farewell, interval **9** branching, isolation, partition, severance **10** detachment, divergence **11** bifurcation, disjunction, segregation **12** estrangement **13** disconnection, disengagement **14** disassociation

Sepharvite god 10 Anammelech **11** Adrammelech

Sepher Torah 16 scroll of the Torah
literally: **9** book of law

September
characteristic: **11** harvest moon
event: **14** aurora borealis, Northern lights **15** autumnal equinox
flower: **5** aster **12** morning glory
French: **9** Septembre
gem: **8** sapphire **12** star sapphire
German: **9** September
holiday: **8** Labor Day (1st Monday) **10** Michaelmas (29) **15** Grandparents' Day

Italian: **9** Settembre
number of days: **6** thirty
origin of name: **6** septum (Latin meaning seven)
place in year:
　Gregorian: **5** ninth
　Roman: **7** seventh
Spanish: **10** Septiembre
Zodiac sign: **5** Libra, Virgo

septentrional 6 arctic **8** northern **11** hyperborean

Septuagint
abbreviation: **3** LXX
author: **10** the Seventy

sepulcher 4 tomb **5** crypt, grave, vault **7** ossuary **8** cenotaph **9** mausoleum, reliquary **10** necropolis

sepulchral 6 hollow **7** charnel **8** funereal, mournful, tomblike **10** lugubrious

sequel 3 end **6** finish, result, upshot **7** outcome, product **8** addendum, epilogue, follow-up, offshoot **9** aftermath, corollary, outgrowth **10** conclusion, postscript **11** consequence, culmination **12** continuation
French: **10** denouement

sequence 3 run **4** flow **5** chain, cycle, order, round, train **6** course, parade, series, string **7** routine **8** schedule **9** cavalcade **10** procession, succession **11** arrangement, progression **14** successiveness **15** consecutiveness

sequester 6 banish, lock up, retire **7** confine, isolate, seclude **8** separate, withdraw **9** segregate **10** quarantine

sequestered 8 closeted, confined, isolated, secluded **9** insulated, sheltered, withdrawn **10** cloistered **11** dissociated

sequin 4 coin, disk **5** ducat **7** spangle **8** ornament
French: **9** paillette

seraglio 3 oda **5** harem, serai **6** zenana **9** gynaeceum

serape 4 cape **5** shawl **6** mantle, poncho

seraph 5 angel

seraphic 7 angelic **8** beatific, ethereal, heavenly **9** celestial

Seraphim 6 angels

Serapis
origin: **5** Greek **8** Egyptian
form: **5** deity
combination of: **4** Apis, Hapi **6** Osiris

Serbia see **10** Yugoslavia

sere 3 dry **4** arid **6** barren **7** parched, wizened **8** droughty, scorched, withered **9** shriveled, unwatered, waterless **10** dehydrated, desiccated **12** dehumidified, moistureless

serene 4 calm, cool, fair **5** clear, quiet, still **6** bright, limpid, placid, poised, sedate, smooth **7** halcyon **8** composed, peaceful, pellucid, tranquil **9** dignified, unruffled **10** nonchalant, unobscured, untroubled **11** undisturbed, unexcitable, unperturbed **13** unimpassioned

serenity 7 dignity **8** calmness, coolness, quietude **9** composure, placidity **10** equanimity, quiescence **11** complacence, nonchalance, tranquility **12** peacefulness, tranquillity **13** collectedness
  French: 9 sangfroid

serf 6 cotter, thrall, vassal **7** bondman, peasant, villein

serfdom 4 yoke **6** thrall **7** bondage, slavery **9** servitude, thralldom, vassalage **11** enslavement, subjugation

Sergeant York
  director: 11 Howard Hawks
  cast: 10 Gary Cooper, Joan Leslie **12** George Tobias **13** Walter Brennan
  Oscar for: 5 actor (Cooper)

Sergestus
  origin: 6 Trojan
  companion to: 6 Aeneas

serial 7 regular **9** continued, piecemeal, recurring **10** continuous, sequential, successive **11** consecutive, incremental

series 3 set **5** chain, cycle, group, order **6** course, number, parade, string **8** sequence **10** procession, succession **11** progression

serious 3 bad, sad **4** grim **5** grave, heavy, sober, staid **6** rueful, sedate, severe, solemn, somber **7** crucial, decided, earnest, fateful, harmful, pensive, sincere, weighty **8** alarming, critical, dejected, downcast, frowning, perilous, resolute, resolved **9** crippling, dangerous, important, momentous, saturnine **10** determined, portentous, purposeful, thoughtful **13** consequential **14** incapacitating

seriousness 7 gravity **8** severity **9** sincerity, soberness, solemnity **10** importance **11** earnestness

sermon 6 homily, rebuke, tirade **7** lecture, reproof **8** diatribe, harangue **9** preaching **10** admonition, preachment **11** exhortation

serpent, Serpent 3 asp **5** cheat, devil, rogue, Satan, snake, viper **7** reptile, traitor **8** deceiver **9** trickster
  constellation of: 7 Serpens

Serpent Holder
  constellation of: 9 Ophiuchus

serpentine 4 mazy **6** spiral, zigzag **7** coiling, crooked, devious, sinuous, snaking, winding **8** flexuous, tortuous, twisting **10** circuitous, convoluted, meandering, round about, undulating **12** labyrinthine

Serpico
  director: 11 Sidney Lumet
  based on story by: 9 Peter Maas
  cast: 8 Al Pacino **9** Jack Kehoe **12** John Randolph
  setting: 11 New York City

serrate 5 notch **6** jagged, pinked, ridged **7** dentate, grooved, notched, toothed **10** sawtoothed

serration 5 notch, ridge, teeth, tooth **8** notching, sawtooth

servant 3 man **4** cook, girl, help, maid **5** valet **6** butler, flunky, helper, lackey, menial, minion, slavey **7** footman **8** domestic, employee, factotum, henchman, hired man, retainer, scullion **9** attendant, chauffeur, hired girl, hired help, man Friday, underling **10** girl Friday **11** housekeeper

serve 2 do **3** act, aid **4** help, pass, suit, tend, work **5** avail, spend, treat **6** assist, attend, be used, do duty, oblige, supply, wait on **7** content, deliver, further, perform, present, promote, satisfy, suffice, work for **8** carry out, complete, function, hand over, minister **9** officiate **11** fill the bill

service, services 3 aid, use **4** help, mend, rite **5** avail, labor **6** adjust, agency, bureau, effort, employ, profit, repair, ritual, system **7** benefit, support, utility, waiting **8** ceremony, facility, maintain, military **9** advantage, provision, treatment **10** assistance, attendance, ceremonial, department, employment, observance, usefulness **11** celebration, convenience, maintenance **12** ministration **13** accommodation

serviceable 5 tough **6** rugged, strong, sturdy, usable, useful **7** durable, lasting **8** workable **9** effective, operative, practical **10** functional **11** utilitarian

serviceman 6 marine, sailor **7** soldier **9** repairman

servile 4 oily **6** abject, humble, menial **7** fawning, in bonds, slavish **8** cringing, scraping, toadying, unctuous **9** groveling, truckling **10** obsequious, submissive **11** bootlicking, subservient, sycophantic

serving 6 acting **7** dishful, helping, portion, waiting **8** plateful **9** assisting, attending, sufficing **11** ministering

serving counter 3 bar **6** buffet **9** sideboard

servitude 5 bonds **6** chains **7** bondage, fetters, serfdom, slavery **8** shackles **9** thralldom, vassalage **10** oppression **11** enslavement, subjugation **12** enthrallment, imprisonment

Servius Tullius
  also: 7 Tullius
  king of: 4 Rome
  daughter: 6 Tullia
  son-in-law: 7 Tarquin
  killed by: 6 Tullia **7** Tarquin

sesame
  also called: 10 benne seeds
  botanical name: 14 Sesamum indicum
  fairy tale: 10 "open sesame" **25** Ali Baba and the Forty Thieves

  high in: 7 protein
  former/mythical use: 3 oil **8** medicine **10** opens locks **11** lighting oil **16** discovers secrets **21** discovers secret places
  use: 5 bread **6** salads **10** casseroles
  use like: 8 nutmeats **11** chopped nuts

Sesame Street
  character: 4 Bert, Elmo **5** Ernie, Herry, Oscar **6** Snuffy **7** Barkley, Big Bird, Muppets **8** the Count **12** Telly Monster **13** Cookie Monster **15** Mr Snuffleupagus

Sesostris
  king of: 5 Egypt

session 4 bout, term **5** round, synod **6** course, period **7** meeting, quarter, sitting **8** assembly, conclave, semester **10** conference, convention

set 3 cut, fit, fix, gel, kit, lay, put, sic **4** club, drop, firm, line, make, plop, post, rate, sink, stud, suit **5** adapt, align, array, banal, bunch, crowd, embed, fixed, group, imbed, order, place, plunk, ready, rigid, scene, stale, stiff, stock, style, trite, usual **6** adjust, assess, assign, attach, common, confer, create, decree, frozen, harden, line up, locale, locate, ordain, outfit, studio **7** arrange, bearing, complex, congeal, decided, faction, install, jellify, machine, prepare, profile, regular, release, routine, scenery, service, setting, situate, station, thicken, unleash **8** arranged, assembly, backdrop, carriage, definite, estimate, everyday, familiar, firmness, habitual, hardened, location, ornament, position, prepared, regulate, rigidity, solidify, stubborn **9** apparatus, calibrate, customary, determine, establish, hackneyed, immovable, obstinate, prescribe, represent, steadfast **10** accustomed, assortment, collection, inflexible **11** anticipated, commonplace, consolidate, established, prearranged **12** conventional
  French: 6 clique **7** coterie

Set
  also: 4 Seth
  origin: 8 Egyptian
  form: 6 animal
  personifies: 6 desert
  brother: 6 Osiris
  killed: 6 Osiris

set about 5 begin **6** assume **9** undertake **10** surrounded

set against 8 alienate, estrange

set apart 5 allot **6** detach, divide **7** earmark, isolate **8** allocate, separate **9** apportion, segregate **11** appropriate

set aside 4 kill **5** allot, annul **6** abjure, cancel, repeal, revoke **7** abandon, abolish, call off, destroy, discard, earmark, nullify, put away, rescind, retract, reverse **8** abrogate, allocate, override, overturn **9** designate, repudiate **10** invalidate **11** discontinue

set at ease 5 cheer **6** please **7** appease, comfort, content, gratify

set at liberty 4 free **5** let go **6** parole **7** manumit, release, unchain **8** liberate, unfetter **9** unshackle **10** emancipate

setback 4 flop, loss, snag **5** hitch, slump **6** defeat, mishap, rebuff **7** failure, relapse, reverse, undoing **8** reversal **9** adversity, mischance, worsening **10** misfortune, regression **13** retrogression **14** disappointment

set down 6 record **7** deposit

set forth 2 go **5** be off, leave **6** assert, avouch, depart **7** advance **8** advocate, propound **10** sally forth

set free 5 let go, loose, untie **6** acquit, loosen, pardon, parole, unbind, uncage, unlock **7** deliver, release **8** liberate, unfetter **9** discharge, disengage, extricate **10** emancipate

Seth *see* **3** Set

Seth
   means: 12 compensation
   father: 4 Adam
   mother: 3 Eve
   son: 4 Enos

set in 5 arise, ensue, occur **6** arrive

set in motion 5 begin, start **6** launch **8** initiate **9** instigate, originate **10** inaugurate

set in order 4 rank, sort **5** align **6** line up **7** arrange, marshal **8** classify, organize **9** methodize **11** systematize

set of beliefs 5 credo, creed, dogma, ethos **6** ethnic, tenets **8** doctrine **10** philosophy, principles **11** convictions

set off 6 depart **7** explode, go forth **8** detonate, start out **10** sally forth

set on fire 4 burn **5** light **6** ignite, kindle

set out 4 pose **5** array, begin, be off, place, range **6** deploy, embark, intend **7** arrange, display **9** undertake

set right 7 correct **8** disabuse

set store by 5 prize, value **6** esteem **7** respect **8** treasure

set straight 5 edify **6** advise, inform **7** educate **8** disabuse **9** enlighten

settee 4 seat, sofa **5** bench

setting 5 scene **6** fixing, locale **7** jelling **8** aligning, ambiance, locating, location, mounting **9** adjusting, arranging, decreeing, hardening, ordaining **10** congealing, regulating, thickening **11** arrangement, determining, environment, prescribing, solidifying **12** establishing, surroundings
   French: 6 milieu **11** mise-en-scene

setting sun
   god of: 5 Janus

settle 3 fix, pay, sag **4** calm, drop, land, sink **5** agree, allay, clear, droop,

light, lodge, perch, quiet **6** alight, choose, decide, locate, move to, pacify, people, soothe **7** arrange, clarify, clear up, compose, inhabit, rectify, resolve, satisfy, sit down, situate **8** colonize, make good, populate, take root **9** determine, discharge, establish, reconcile **11** precipitate

settled 4 sure **7** certain, decided

settlement 3 sum **4** camp, post **6** amount, colony, hamlet **7** bequest, outpost, payment, village **8** clearing, peopling **9** clearance, discharge **10** adjustment, colonizing, encampment, resolution **11** acquittance, arrangement, liquidation **12** amortization, colonization, compensation, satisfaction **14** reconciliation

settler 7 pioneer **8** colonist, squatter **9** colonizer, immigrant **11** homesteader **12** frontiersman

settle upon 6 bestow **7** consign **8** bequeath

settlings 4 lees **5** dregs **7** deposit, grounds, remains, residue **8** leavings

set-to 4 spat **5** brush, clash, run-in **6** battle, fracas **7** dispute, quarrel, scuffle **8** argument, skirmish, squabble **10** engagement, falling out **12** disagreement **13** confrontation
   French: 11 contretemps

setup 4 plan **6** scheme, system **8** practice **9** apparatus **11** arrangement **12** organization

set up 3 rig **5** erect, found **7** arrange, install **9** construct, establish, institute **10** inaugurate, prearrange

set upon 3 mug **5** beset, fly at **6** assail, attack **7** besiege, lunge at **9** pitch into

Seurat, Georges Pierre
   born: 5 Paris **6** France
   artwork: 9 The Chahut, The Circus, The Models, The Parade, The Uproar **10** The Bathers **12** Le Grand Jatte, The Yoked Cart **19** Une Baignade Asnieres **23** A Bathing Scene at Asnieres, The Bec du Hoc at Grand champ **40** Sunday Afternoon on the Island of La Grand Jatte

Seuss, Dr
   real name: 19 Theodore Seuss Geisel
   author of: 12 If I Ran the Zoo **14** The Cat in the Hat **15** Green Eggs and Ham, Horton Hears a Who, If I Ran the Circus **19** Horton Hatches the Egg **23** Mister Brown Can Moo Can You? **26** Thidwick The Big-Hearted Moose, How the Grinch Stole Christmas

Seve
   nickname of: 20 Severiano Ballesteros

Seven Against Thebes
   author: 9 Aeschylus
   character: 6 Ismene **8** Antigone, Eteocles **9** Polynices **11** Theban Women

   seven heroes: 6 Tydeus **8** Adrastus, Capaneus **9** Polynices **10** Amphiaraus, Hippomedon **13** Parthenopaeus

Seven Beauties
   director: 14 Lina Wertmuller
   cast: 11 Fernando Rey **13** Shirley Stoler **17** Giancarlo Giannini

Seven Brides for Seven Brothers
   director: 12 Stanley Donen
   cast: 9 Tammy Rall **10** Howard Keel, Jane Powell **11** Julie Newmar (Newmeyer), Russ Tamblyn **12** Jeff Richards **14** Virginia Gibson
   score: 11 Saul Chaplin **12** Johnny Mercer
   choreography: 11 Michael Kidd

Seven Pillars of Wisdom
   author: 10 T E Lawrence

Seven Samurai
   director: 13 Akira Kurosawa
   cast: 11 Yoshio Inaba **13** Toshiro Mifune **14** Takashi Shimura
   remade as: 19 The Magnificent Seven

seven seas 6 Arctic, Indian **9** Antarctic **12** North Pacific, South Pacific **13** North Atlantic, South Atlantic

Seven Sisters colleges 5 Smith **6** Vassar **7** Barnard **8** Bryn Mawr **9** Radcliffe, Wellesley **12** Mount Holyoke

Seventeen
   author: 15 Booth Tarkington
   character: 7 Genesis **9** Miss Pratt, Mrs Baxter **10** Jane Baxter, May Parcher **21** William Sylvanus Baxter

Seventh Seal, The
   director: 13 Ingmar Bergman
   cast: 9 Nils Poppe **11** Max von Sydow **13** Bibi Andersson **17** Gunnar Bjornstrand

Seventy-seven Sunset Strip
   character: 6 J R Hale, Kookie (Gerald Lloyd Kookson III), Roscoe **7** Suzanne **11** Jeff Spencer, Rex Randolph **12** Stuart Bailey
   cast: 9 Edd Byrnes **10** Louis Quinn, Roger Smith **11** Richard Long, Robert Logan **14** Jacqueline Beer **16** Efrem Zimbalist Jr
   Kookie's sayings: 10 a dark seven **12** the ginchiest **13** piling up the Z's **14** lend me your comb **15** play like a pigeon **17** headache grapplers **22** keep the eyeballs rolling

seven wonders of the ancient world 8 pyramids (Egypt) **12** Olympian Zeus (sculpted by Phidias) **15** Temple of Artemis (at Ephesus) **16** Colossus of Rhodes **22** Lighthouse (Pharos) at Alexandria **23** hanging gardens of Babylon (of Semiramis) **24** Mausoleum at Halicarnassus

Seven Year Itch, The
   director: 11 Billy Wilder
   cast: 8 Tom Ewell **10** Sonny Tufts **11** Evelyn Keyes, Victor Moore **13** Mari-

lyn Monroe
setting: 11 New York City

sever 3 saw **4** part, rend, rive, tear **5** slice, split **6** bisect, cleave, cut off, lop off **7** disjoin, rupture, split up **8** amputate, break off, cut in two, dissolve, disunite, separate, truncate **9** dismember, terminate **10** disconnect **11** discontinue

several 3 own **4** a few, some **6** divers, single, sundry **7** certain, diverse, express, private, special **8** assorted, distinct, peculiar, personal, separate, specific **9** different, exclusive **10** individual, particular, respective **11** distinctive, independent

severe 4 cold, dour, grim, wild **5** cruel, grave, harsh, plain, rough, sober, stern, stiff **6** biting, bitter, brutal, chaste, fierce, fuming, raging, savage, sedate, simple, somber, strict, taxing **7** austere, cutting, drastic, extreme, furious, intense, painful, serious, uniform, violent **8** piercing, rigorous, ruthless, stinging, vigorous **9** dangerous, demanding, difficult, draconian, merciless, saturnine, turbulent, unadorned, unsparing **10** forbidding, restrained, tumultuous **11** distressing, undecorated, unrelenting **12** conservative

severed 6 cut off **8** detached **9** uncoupled, unhitched **10** unfastened **11** unconnected **12** disconnected

Severini, Gino
born: 5 Italy **7** Cortona
artwork: 9 Harlequin **15** The Armored Train **25** Dancer Sea and Vase of Flowers **32** Dynamic Hieroglyph of the Bal Tabarin

severity 5 rigor **7** cruelty **8** acrimony, violence **9** austerity, gruffness, harshness, sternness **10** asceticism, difficulty, strictness, stringency **11** seriousness **12** grievousness

Seville
former name: 8 Hispalis
landmark: 7 Alcazar, Giralda
plain: 9 Andalusia
river: 12 Guadalquivir
ruler: 5 Moors **6** Romans **7** Vandals **8** Abbasids, Almohads, Iberians **9** Visigoths **10** Almoravids
Spanish: 7 Sevilla

sew 3 hem **4** mend, seam, tack **5** unite **6** fasten, ground, stitch, suture **10** run aground
loosely: 5 baste

sewage 5 waste **6** efflux, refuse **8** effluent **9** effluence

Seward, Dr
character in: 7 Dracula
author: 6 Stoker

sewing machine
invented by: 4 Howe

sex 4 Eros, love **6** coitus, gender, libido **7** coition **8** maleness **10** copulation,

femaleness, femininity, generation, lovemaking **11** masculinity, procreation **12** reproduction

Sexton, Anne
author of: 15 All My Pretty Ones **22** To Bedlam and Part Way Back **23** The Awful Rowing Toward God

sexual 6 coital, erotic **7** amatory, genital, marital, sensual **8** conjugal, intimate, venereal **10** copulatory, generative, libidinous **11** procreative **12** reproductive

sexually stimulating 3 hot **4** sexy **6** erotic, risque **9** salacious **10** suggestive **12** pornographic

sexy 4 lewd **5** bawdy **6** erotic **8** prurient **9** seductive **10** come-hither, coquettish, suggestive, voluptuous **11** flirtatious, provocative

Seychelles
capital/largest city: 8 Victoria
monetary unit: 4 cent **5** rupee
island: 4 Mahe **7** Aldabra, La Digue, Praslin **8** Farquhar **9** Desroches **10** Silhouette
highest point: 16 Morne Seychellois
sea: 6 Indian
people: 5 Asian **6** Creole, French, Indian **7** African, Chinese
  leader: 4 Rene **7** Mancham
language: 6 Creole, French **7** English
religion: 8 Anglican **13** Roman Catholic

sforzando
music: 12 sudden accent

Shabbas 7 Sabbath

shabby 3 low **4** mean, poor, torn, worn **5** cheap, dirty, mangy, raggy, ratty, seedy, sorry, tatty, tight **6** frayed, meager, ragged, sordid, unfair **7** ignoble, rundown, scruffy **8** beggarly, decaying, inferior, slovenly, unworthy, wretched **9** illiberal, miserable, neglected **10** ramshackle, threadbare, tumbledown, ungenerous **11** dilapidated **12** contemptible, deteriorated, dishonorable, impoverished

shabby bar 4 dive **5** joint **7** gin mill **9** honky-tonk

shack 3 hut **5** cabin **6** lean-to, shanty

shackle 3 bar, tie **4** balk, bind, cuff, curb, foil, rein **5** block, bonds, chain, check, cramp, cuffs, deter, irons, limit, stall **6** chains, fetter, hamper, hinder, hobble, hogtie, impede, pinion, retard, secure, tether, thwart **7** inhibit, manacle, prevent **8** encumber, handcuff, restrict **9** forestall, frustrate, hamstring, handcuffs **12** circumscribe

shackled 7 chained, in irons **8** in chains, manacled **10** handcuffed

shadchan, schatchen 10 matchmaker **14** marriage broker

Shaddai 3 God

shade 3 bit, dim, hue, jot **4** atom, cast, hint, hood, iota, tint, tone, veil, whit

5 blind, color, drape, tinge, touch, trace **6** awning, canopy, darken, screen, shadow, shield **7** curtain, modicum, shadows, shutter **8** darkness, particle, semidark **9** scintilla **10** suggestion
French: 7 soupcon
form: 6 spirit
location: 5 Hades

shadow, shadows 3 bit, dog **4** blot, hint, tail **5** cloud, ghost, hound, shade, smear, stain, stalk, taint, tinge, touch, trace, track, trail **6** blight, follow, pursue, smirch, smudge, threat **7** blemish, specter, whisper **8** penumbra **10** reflection, silhouette, suggestion

Shadow of a Doubt
director: 15 Alfred Hitchcock
cast: 10 Hume Cronyn **12** Joseph Cotten, Teresa Wright **14** Macdonald Carey **16** Patricia Collinge
remade as: 16 Step Down to Terror

Shadows on the Rock
author: 11 Willa Cather

shadowy 3 dim **5** shady **6** gloomy, unreal **7** obscure **8** illusory **9** tenebrous **10** indistinct **13** insubstantial

Shadrach
former name: 8 Hananiah
friend: 6 Daniel
companion: 7 Meshach **8** Abednego

shady 5 fishy **7** crooked, devious, dubious, shadowy **8** dishonest, unethical **10** suspicious **11** underhanded **12** disreputable, questionable **13** untrustworthy

shady dealings 5 fraud, graft **7** bribery **10** corruption, dishonesty

shaft 3 cut, pit, ray **4** barb, beam, dart, duct, flue, gibe, hilt, stem, vent, well **5** abyss, arrow, chasm, gleam, lance, patch, pylon, quill, shank, spear, spire, stalk, tower, trunk **6** cavity, column, funnel, handle, insult, pillar, streak, stream **7** affront, chimney, conduit, minaret, obelisk, spindle, steeple **8** brickbat, monolith, pilaster **9** aspersion **10** excavation

shaggy 5 bushy, downy, fuzzy, hairy, nappy, piled, wooly **6** tufted, woolly **7** bearded, hirsute, shagged, unshorn **9** whiskered **11** bewhiskered

shah 4 king **5** ruler **7** emperor, monarch **8** autocrat **9** sovereign

Shahaptian
tribe: 6 Numipu **8** Nez Perce

Shahn, Ben
born: 6 Kaunas **9** Lithuania
artwork: 5 Epoch **8** Handball **12** Seurat's Lunch, The Physicist **16** Pacific Land scape **18** Willis Avenue Bridge **28** The Passion of Sacco and Vanzetti

shake 3 jar, jog, mix **4** jerk, jolt, move, stir, stun, sway, wave **5** elude, quake, swing, touch **6** affect, bounce, jiggle, joggle, jostle, jounce, quaver, quiver, rattle, ruffle, shimmy, shiver, slough, totter, twitch, wobble **7** agitate, disturb, flicker, flutter, perturb, quaking, shudder, stagger, startle, tremble, unnerve, vibrate **8** brandish, disquiet, distress, flourish, frighten, throw off, unsettle, unstring **9** quivering, shivering, trembling **10** discompose, flickering, fluttering

shakedown 6 extort, payoff, search, tryout **7** testing **8** thorough **9** blackmail, extortion, hush money

Shakespeare, William
also: 10 bard of Avon **12** immortal bard
author of: 6 Hamlet, Henry V **7** Henry IV, Henry VI, Macbeth, Othello, Sonnets **8** King John, King Lear, Pericles (Prince of Tyre) **9** Cymbeline, Henry VIII, Richard II **10** Coriolanus, Richard III, The Tempest **11** As You Like It **12** Julius Caesar, Twelfth Night **13** Rape of Lucrece, Timon of Athens **14** Romeo and Juliet, The Winter's Tale, Venus and Adonis **15** Titus Andronicus **16** Love's Labour's Lost **17** Measure for Measure, The Comedy of Errors **18** Antony and Cleopatra, Troilus and Cressida **19** Much Ado About Nothing, The Merchant of Venice, The Taming of the Shrew **20** All's Well That Ends Well **21** A Midsummer Night's Dream **22** The Merry Wives of Windsor **23** The Two Gentlemen of Verona
birthplace: 15 Stratford-on-Avon
theater: 4 Swan **5** Globe
wife: 12 Anne Hathaway

shakeup 5 purge **7** cleanup **8** turnover **10** clean sweep **11** realignment **13** rearrangement, redisposition, restructuring **14** redistribution, reorganization

shake up 3 mix **4** stir **5** churn **7** agitate, disturb

shakiness 6 tremor **10** insecurity **11** instability, uncertainty **12** unsteadiness

shaky 4 weak **5** frail, jumpy **6** flimsy, unsafe, unsure, wobbly **7** dubious, fidgety, fragile, halting, jittery, nervous, teetery **8** hesitant, insecure, unstable, unsteady, wavering **9** faltering, hazardous, quivering, teetering, tottering, trembling, tremulous, uncertain, undecided **10** inconstant, irresolute, precarious, unreliable, unresolved **11** vacillating **12** undependable

shallow 5 shoal **6** frothy, slight **7** surface, trivial **8** knee-deep, skin-deep, trifling **9** frivolous **11** meaningless, superficial, unimportant **13** insubstantial **15** inconsequential

shalom 5 hello, peace **7** goodbye

shalom aleichem 10 peace to you

sham 3 act **4** copy, fake **5** bogus, false, feign, fraud, phony, put on, trick **6** af-

fect, assume, forged **7** feigned, forgery, imitate, pretend **8** pretense, simulate, spurious **9** imitation, pretended, simulated, synthetic **10** artificial, fraudulent **11** counterfeit, make-believe

Shamash
origin: 8 Akkadian
god of: 3 sun

shamble, shambles 4 limp **5** hitch, lurch, stall **6** hobble **7** shuffle **8** butchery **14** slaughterhouse

shame 5 guilt, odium **6** humble, stigma **7** chagrin, mortify, remorse, scandal **8** contempt, disgrace, dishonor, ignominy **9** disrepute, embarrass, humiliate **10** debasement, disrespect **11** degradation, humiliation, self-disgust **12** unworthiness **13** embarrassment, mortification **14** disappointment

shamed be the one who thinks evil of it
Latin: 20 honi soit qui mal y pense

shamefaced 5 sorry **7** abashed, crushed, humbled, put-down **8** blushing, sheepish **9** chagrined, disgraced, mortified **10** humiliated, remorseful **11** embarrassed

shameful 3 low **4** base, mean, vile **6** odious **7** heinous, ignoble **8** shocking, unworthy **9** dastardly, degrading **10** deplorable, despicable, inglorious, iniquitous, outrageous, villainous **11** disgraceful, ignominious, opprobrious **12** contemptible, dishonorable **13** reprehensible

shameless 4 pert **5** brash, saucy **6** brazen, wanton **7** forward, immoral **8** degraded, flagrant, immodest, impudent, indecent **9** abandoned, audacious, barefaced, boldfaced, dissolute, unabashed **10** indecorous, unblushing, unreserved **11** disgraceful **12** dishonorable

shamelessness 4 gall **5** brass, cheek **8** audacity **10** brazenness, effrontery **11** forwardness, presumption

shamus 3 tec **7** gumshoe **9** detective **10** private eye **12** investigator

Shane
director: 13 George Stevens
cast: 8 Alan Ladd **9** Van Heflin **10** Jean Arthur **11** Jack Palance **12** Elisha Cook Jr **13** Edgar Buchanan **14** Brandon de Wilde

Shanghai
area: 23 International Settlement
landmark: 13 Long Hua Temple **17** People's Opera House **28** Shanghai Industrial Exhibition
river: 6 Wusung **7** Huang-P'u, Yangtze

Shangri-La see **5** Nepal

shanty 3 hut **5** cabin, hovel, shack **6** lean-to

shape 4 form, make, mold, trim **5** ar-

ray, build, frame, guide, model, order **6** create, fettle, figure, health **7** contour, develop, fashion, outline, profile **8** physique **9** condition, construct, determine **10** silhouette **12** conformation **13** configuration

shapeless 5 baggy **8** formless **9** amorphous, irregular

shapely 3 fit **4** neat, trim **6** comely, gainly **11** symmetrical

shaper 9 architect, innovator **10** instigator, prime mover

Shapley, Howard
field: 9 astronomy
studied: 6 galaxy

Shardik
author: 12 Richard Adams

share 3 cut **4** dole, part **5** allot, cut up, quota, split **6** ration **7** deal out, divvy up, mete out, percent, portion **8** allocate **9** allotment, allowance, apportion **10** percentage **13** apportionment

shared 5 joint **6** common, public **7** general **8** communal **10** collective

share one's sorrow 7 condole **10** sympathize **11** commiserate

Sharif, Omar
real name: 15 Michael Shalhoub
born: 5 Egypt **10** Alexandria
roles: 3 Che **9** Dr Zhivago, Funny Girl, Funny Lady **11** Genghis Khan **12** Nick Arnstein **16** Lawrence of Arabia
expert on: 6 bridge

shark 3 ace **4** fish **5** cheat **6** expert, usurer, wizard **8** predator **9** trickster **12** extortionist

sharp 3 sly **4** acid, curt, fine, foxy, high, keen, sour, tart, wily **5** acrid, acute, alert, angry, awake, blunt, clear, cruel, edged, gruff, harsh, nippy, piked, quick, rapid, salty, sheer, spiny, steep **6** abrupt, artful, astute, barbed, biting, bitter, clever, crafty, crusty, fierce, keenly, marked, pointy, severe, shrewd, shrill, strong, sudden, thorny, tricky, unkind **7** acutely, alertly, angular, bearish, bristly, brusque, caustic, closely, crabbed, cunning, cutting, drastic, exactly, extreme, galling, intense, nipping, piquant, pointed, prickly, quickly, raucous, toothed, violent **8** abruptly, distinct, on the dot, piercing, promptly, scathing, serrated, spiteful, stinging, strident, suddenly, venomous, vertical, vigilant, vinegary **9** conniving, deceptive, excessive, on the nose, precisely, rancorous, unethical, vitriolic **10** contriving, discerning, immoderate, inordinate, perceptive, punctually **11** attentively, calculating, on the button, penetrating, precipitous **12** unprincipled, unscrupulous **13** precipitously
French: 5 juste
Spanish: 7 en punto

Sharp, Becky
character in: **10** Vanity Fair
author: **9** Thackeray

sharp-cornered 6 jagged **7** angular

sharp dresser 3 fop **4** dude **5** dandy
12 Beau Brummell, clotheshorse, fashion plate

sharpen 4 edge, hone, whet **5** grind, strop

sharply pointed 4 keen **5** acute **6** spiked **7** tapered **8** piercing **10** rapierlike **11** needle-nosed

sharpness 3 nip, wit **4** edge, tang **6** acuity, acumen **7** acidity, insight **8** acerbity, acridity, acrimony, keenness, pungency, saliency, tartness **9** acuteness, alertness, quickness **10** causticity, craftiness **12** perspicacity

sharp pain 4 pang, stab **5** cramp **6** twinge

sharpshooter
French: **10** tirailleur

sharp-sighted 5 acute **6** shrewd **8** piercing **9** far-seeing **10** discerning, perceptive **11** penetrating **13** perspicacious

sharp-witted 4 keen **5** acute, alert, canny, quick, smart **6** astute, brainy, clever

Shatner, William
born: **6** Canada **8** Montreal
roles: **8** Star Trek, T J Hooker **17** Captain James T Kirk

shatter 4 rive, ruin **5** break, burst, crack, crash, crush, quash, smash, split, spoil, upset, wreck **6** squash, sunder, topple **7** crumble, destroy, explode, scuttle **8** demolish, fracture, overturn, splinter **9** devastate, pulverize

shattered 6 broken, dashed **7** crushed, smashed **8** crumbled, decrepit **9** flustered **10** demolished, fragmented, splintered, tumbledown **11** crestfallen, demoralized **13** disillusioned, disintegrated

shave 3 cut, lop, mow **4** clip, crop, dock, pare, skin, snip, trim **5** brush, graze, prune, shear **6** barber, cut off, fleece, glance, scrape **7** scissor

Shaw, George Bernard
author of: **7** Candida **8** Pygmalion, Saint Joan **12** Major Barbara **13** Arms and the Man **14** Man and Superman **15** Heartbreak House **16** Back to Methuselah **17** The Devil's Disciple, The Doctor's Dilemma **18** Caesar and Cleopatra **19** Androcles and the Lion **20** Mrs Warren's Profession
member of: **13** Fabian Society

Shaw, Irwin
author of: **12** Top of the Hill **13** The Young Lions **14** Beggarman Thief, Rich Man Poor Man

Shaw, Robert

born: **7** England **12** Westhoughton
wife: **7** Mary Ure
roles: **4** Jaws **7** The Deep **8** The Sting **12** Swashbuckler **13** The Caretakers **17** A Man for All Seasons **20** Force Ten from Navarone **28** The Taking of Pelham One-Two-Three
author of: **14** The Hiding Place **21** The Man in the Glass Booth

Shawabti
origin: **8** Egyptian
form: **8** figurine
where used: **6** burial

shawl 4 wrap **5** scarf **6** mantle **7** paisley **10** fascinator
Mexican: **6** serape
Spanish: **8** mantilla

Shawnee
language family: **9** Algonkian **10** Algonquian
location: **4** Ohio **6** Kansas **8** Missouri, Oklahoma **9** Tennessee **12** Pennsylvania **13** South Carolina
leader: **8** Tecumseh **11** Tenskwatawa
related to: **8** Delaware

She
author: **13** H Rider Haggard
character: **6** Ayesha

shear 3 cut, lop **4** clip, crop, snip, trim **5** prune, shave **6** fleece, remove **7** deprive, relieve, scissor

Shearer, Norma
born: **6** Canada **8** Montreal
husband: **14** Irving Thalberg
roles: **8** The Women **9** A Free Soul **11** The Divorcee (Oscar) **14** Romeo and Juliet, Their Own Desire **15** Marie Antoinette **26** The Barretts of Wimpole Street

shears 5 clips, trims **6** prunes **7** pruners **8** clippers, scissors, trimmers

sheath 3 pod **4** case, coat, skin **6** casing, jacket **7** capsule, coating, wrapper **8** covering, envelope, membrane, scabbard, slipcase, wrapping **9** container **10** receptacle

sheathing 6 casing, siding **8** covering

Sheba
also: **4** Saba
visited: **7** Solomon
father: **6** Bichri, Joktan, Raamah **7** Jokshan
grandfather: **4** Cush **7** Keturah
people of: **7** Sabeans

Shebat 19 eleventh Hebrew month

she carved it
Latin: **8** sculpsit

shed 3 hut **4** cast, doff, drop, emit, molt **5** exude, hovel, shack, spill, strew, throw **6** lean-to, shanty, shower, slough, spread **7** cast off, discard, let fall, let flow, radiate, scatter **8** disperse, lose hair, toolshed **9** broadcast, discharge, tool house **10** distribute **11** disseminate, outbuilding

she died
Latin: **5** obiit

shed light on 7 clarify, explain **9** elucidate, explicate, make clear, make plain **10** illuminate

She Done Him Wrong
director: **13** Lowell Sherman
cast: **7** Mae West (Diamond Lil) **9** Cary Grant, Noah Beery **13** Gilbert Roland

shed tears 3 cry, sob **4** bawl, weep **6** boohoo **7** blubber

Sheehy, Gail
author of: **8** Passages **14** The Pathfinders

Sheeler, Charles
born: **14** Philadelphia PA
artwork: **9** Landscape, Upper Deck **11** Incantation **12** City Interior, Rolling Power **15** Bucks County Barn, River Rouge Plant **31** American Landscape Nineteen Thirty

sheen 4 glow **5** glaze, gleam, glint, gloss, shine **6** luster, patina, polish **7** burnish, glister, glitter, shimmer **8** radiance **9** shininess **10** brightness, brilliance, effulgence, glossiness, luminosity, refulgence **12** luminousness, resplendence

Sheen, Martin
real name: **12** Ramon Estevez
born: **8** Dayton OH
son: **12** Charlie Sheen **13** Emilio Estevez
roles: **5** Spawn **8** Badlands **12** The Believers **13** Apocalypse Now **14** Catch Twenty-two **18** The Subject Was Roses **20** The American President **27** The Execution of Private Slovik

Sheena, Queen of the Jungle
creator: **8** SR Powell **13** W Morgan Thomas
character: **3** Bob **4** Chim

she engraved it
Latin: **8** sculpsit

sheep
breed: **5** Iraqi **6** Hirrik, Merino, Panama, Romney, Somali **7** Cheviot, Karakul, Lincoln, Suffolk, Targhee **8** Columbia, Cotswold, Tatarian **9** Montadale, Romeldale, Southdown **10** Corriedale, Dorset Down, Dorset Horn, Shropshire, Sikkim Bera **11** Rambouillet **13** Hampshire Down **15** Border Leicester
female: **3** ewe
family: **7** Bovidae
genus: **4** Ovis
group of: **5** drove, flock **6** cosset
meat: **4** lamb **6** mutton
oil from: **7** lanolin
wild: **5** urial **6** argali **7** bighorn, mouflon
young: **4** lamb **7** lambkin **8** yearling

sheepish 3 shy **4** meek **5** timid **6** docile, guilty, humble **7** abashed, ashamed, bashful, fearful, hangdog, passive, servile **8** blushing, obedient, obeisant, timorous, yielding **9** chagrined, chastened, diffident, mortified, shrinking, tractable **10** shamefaced, submissive **11** embarrassed, subservient, unassertive, unresisting

sheepishness 7 chagrin **8** docility, meekness **10** diffidence **11** bashfulness **12** tractability **13** embarrassment **14** submissiveness **15** unassertiveness

Sheep Well, The
  also: 13 Fuente Ovejuna
  author: 10 Lope de Vega

sheer 4 fine, pure, thin **5** bluff, filmy, gauzy, plumb, sharp, steep, total, utter **6** abrupt **7** perfect, unmixed **8** absolute, complete, gossamer, vertical **9** out and out, unalloyed, unbounded, unlimited **10** consummate, diaphanous **11** precipitous, transparent, unmitigated, unqualified **12** unrestrained **13** perpendicular, unadulterated, unconditional

sheet 3 top **4** coat, film, leaf, pane, slab **5** layer, panel, piece, plate **6** sheath, square **7** blanket, coating, overlay **8** bed sheet, covering, membrane **9** rectangle

shegetz 12 non-Jewish boy, non-Jewish man

Sheldon, Sidney
  author of: 9 Bloodline **12** Rage of Angels, The Naked Face **15** If Tomorrow Comes **20** A Stranger in the Mirror **22** The Other Side of Midnight

shelf 4 bank, prop, reef, slab **5** ledge, shoal **6** mantel, mantle **7** bedrock, bracket, stratum **9** supporter **11** mantelpiece, mantlepiece

shell 3 pod **4** bomb, case, hulk, hull, husk, shot **5** pound, round, shuck **6** bullet, fire on, pepper, rocket **7** barrage, bombard, grenade, missile **8** carapace, skeleton **9** cartridge, framework **10** projectile

shellac 4 beat, drub, lick, whip **7** clobber, lacquer, trounce, varnish

Shelley, Mary Wollstonecraft
  father: 13 William Godwin
  husband: 18 Percy Bysshe Shelley
  author of: 12 Frankenstein

Shelley, Percy Bysshe
  author of: 7 Adonais, Alastor **8** Queen Mab, The Cenci **10** To a Skylark **16** A Defence of Poetry, Ode to the West Wind **17** Prometheus Unbound

shellfish 4 clam, crab **5** prawn **6** cockle, mussel, oyster, shrimp **7** abalone, lobster, mollusk, scallop **8** barnacle, crawfish, crayfish **9** trunkfish **10** crustacean **13** softshell crab
  spawn: 4 spat

shell out 3 pay **6** expend **8** allocate, disburse, dispense **10** contribute

shelter 5 cover, guard, haven, house, lodge **6** asylum, defend, harbor, refuge, safety, shield, take in **7** care for, housing, lodging, protect **8** quarters, security **9** safeguard, sanctuary **10** protection

Sheltered Life
  author: 12 Ellen Glasgow

shelve 5 defer, table **6** put off **7** suspend **8** lay aside, postpone, put aside, put on ice, set aside **10** pigeonhole

Shem
  father: 4 Noah
  brother: 3 Ham **7** Japheth
  son: 8 Arphazed
  descendant of: 6 Semite

shenanigans 5 sport **6** antics, capers, hijinx, pranks, stunts, tricks **8** deviltry, mischief, nonsense **9** highjinks, horseplay, silliness **10** buffoonery, tomfoolery **11** roguishness **12** monkeyshines, sportiveness **14** monkey business **15** mischievousness

she painted it
  Latin: 6 pinxit

shepherd 4 herd, lead, show, tend **5** guard, guide, pilot **6** direct, escort, herder, keeper, patron, shield **7** protect, shelter **8** champion, defender, guardian, herdsman, provider **9** custodian, protector, safeguard **10** benefactor

Shepherdess and the Sweep, The
  author: 21 Hans Christian Andersen

shepherds
  god of: 3 Pan **6** Tammuz

sherbet 3 ade, ice **6** sorbet **7** dessert

Shere Khan
  character in: 14 The Jungle Books
  author: 7 Kipling

Sheridan, Ann
  real name: 16 Clara Lou Sheridan
  nickname: 9 Oomph Girl
  born: 8 Denton TX
  husband: 10 Scott McKay **11** George Brent **12** Edward Norris
  roles: 8 King's Row **11** Silver River **12** Nora Prentiss **16** Wings for the Eagle **20** Angels with Dirty Faces

Sheridan, Philip H
  served in: 8 Civil War **10** Indian Wars
  side: 5 Union
  commander of: 19 Army of the Shenandoah
  rank: 22 general in chief of US army
  battle: 9 Five Forks **10** Cedar Creek, Winchester **11** Chattanooga, Chickamauga, Fisher's Hill **12** Sayler's Creek **18** Wilderness Campaign

Sheridan, Richard Brinsley
  author of: 9 The Critic, The Duenna, The Rivals **18** A Trip to Scarborough **19** The School for Scandal

sheriff 7 officer **9** constable
  men: 5 posse

Sheriff of Nottingham
  character in: 9 Robin Hood

Sherman, William Tecumseh
  nickname: 4 Cump
  served in: 8 Civil War **10** Mexican War
  side: 5 Union
  battle: 6 Shiloh **7** Atlanta, Bull Run **8** Savannah **9** Vicksburg **11** Chattanooga **15** Kenesaw Mountain
  fought against: 8 Johnston
  rank: 20 general in chief of army
  famous for: 13 march to the sea (Georgia)
  established: 29 Command and General Staff College
  saying: 9 War is hell

sherry
  type: 4 wine **6** brandy
  origin: 5 Jeres, Spain, Xerez
  varieties: 4 fino (dry) **5** cream **7** amoroso (sweet), oloroso (medium dry) **10** Manzanilla **11** Amontillado
  drink: 6 Adonis, Bamboo **9** Andalusia
  with gin: 11 Renaissance
  with vermouth: 6 Brazil

Sherwood, Robert E
  author of: 13 Idiot's Delight **15** Reunion in Vienna **18** The Petrified Forest **19** Roosevelt and Hopkins, There Shall Be No Night **20** Abe Lincoln in Illinois
  screenplay: 22 The Best Years of Our Lives

she sculptured it
  Latin: 8 sculpsit

she speaks
  Latin: 8 loquitur

She Stoops to Conquer
  author: 15 Oliver Goldsmith
  character: 6 Marlow **8** Hastings **10** Sir Charles **11** Tony Lumpkin **12** Mr Hardcastle **13** Mrs Hardcastle **14** Kate Hardcastle **16** Constance Neville

she wrote (it)
  Latin: 8 scripsit

shibah, shivah 14 mourning period
  literally: 9 seven days

shibboleth 6 byword, saying, slogan **8** apothegm **9** catchword

Shibboleth 17 Gileadite password

shield 4 keep, star **5** aegis, badge, cover, guard, house, shade **6** buffer, button, emblem, ensign, fender, harbor, screen, secure **7** buckler, defense, protect, shelter **8** insignia, keep safe, preserve **9** medallion, protecter, protector, safeguard **10** escutcheon, protection

Shield (of Sobieski)
  constellation of: 6 Scutum

shielded 6 hidden **7** guarded **9** concealed, protected, sheltered

Shields, Brooke
  real name: 20 Christa Brooke Shields
  born: 9 New York NY
  roles: 10 Pretty Baby **11** Endless Love **13** The Blue Lagoon, Suddenly Susan
  husband: 11 Andre Agassi

shift 2 go 4 move, slip, vary, veer 5 hitch, stint 6 change, swerve, switch 7 chemise, turning, veering 8 exchange, straight, transfer 9 deviation, transpose, variation 10 alteration, assignment, reposition 11 alternating, fluctuation, interchange 12 modification
French: 8 camisole

shiftless 3 lax 4 idle, lazy 8 careless, inactive, indolent, slothful 10 ne'er-do-well 13 lackadaisical 14 good-for-nothing 15 unconscientious

shifty 4 foxy, wily 6 crafty, sneaky, tricky 7 cunning, evasive 8 scheming, slippery 9 conniving, deceitful, dishonest 10 contriving, unreliable 11 maneuvering, treacherous 13 untrustworthy

Shikasta
author: 12 Doris Lessing

shiksa 14 non-Jewish woman

shillelagh 4 club 5 stick 6 cudgel 9 truncheon

shilly-shally 5 stall, waver 6 dawdle, dither, falter, seesaw 8 hesitate 9 fluctuate, hem and haw, oscillate, vacillate

shilly-shallying 8 dawdling, wavering 9 uncertain, undecided 10 indecision, indecisive, irresolute 11 vacillation

Shimazaki Toson
author of: 5 Hakai 20 The Broken Commandment

shimmer 4 beam, glow 5 blink, dance, flash, gleam, quake, shine, waver 6 quiver, shiver 7 flicker, flutter, glisten, sparkle, tremble, twinkle, vibrate 8 blinking 9 coruscate 11 scintillate 12 phosphoresce

shindig 3 hop 4 ball, bash, prom 5 dance, party 6 affair, shindy 7 blowout, revelry 9 barn dance, festivity, record hop 10 masked ball, the dansant
French: 4 fete, gala 6 soiree 9 bal masque 10 bal costume

shine 3 wax 4 beam, buff, glow 5 blink, flash, glare, gleam, glint, gloss, light, rub up, sheen 6 dazzle, luster, polish, waxing 7 buffing, burnish, flicker, glimmer, glisten, glister, glitter, radiate, shimmer, sparkle, twinkle 8 brighten, radiance 9 coruscate, irradiate, polishing 10 brightness, brilliance, burnishing, luminosity 11 scintillate 12 illumination, luminousness 13 incandescence

shininess 5 gleam, glint, gloss, sheen 6 luster, polish 7 shimmer

shining 5 aglow 6 glossy 7 glowing, radiant 8 gleaming, luminous, lustrous 9 brilliant, effulgent 11 illustrious 12 incandescent

Shining, The
author: 11 Stephen King

shiny 6 bright, glossy 7 glaring, glowing, radiant 8 gleaming, luminous, lustrous, polished 9 brilliant, burnished, effulgent, sparkling 10 glistening, glittering, shimmering 12 incandescent 13 scintillating

ship 4 crew, send 5 craft, liner, route, tramp, yacht 6 packet, tanker, vessel 7 carrier, cruiser, forward, steamer 8 dispatch 9 destroyer, freighter, steamship, transport 10 ocean liner

Ship of Fools
author: 19 Katherine Anne Porter
director: 13 Stanley Kramer
cast: 9 Jose Greco, Lee Marvin 10 Jose Ferrer 11 George Segal, Oscar Werner, Vivien Leigh 14 Simone Signoret 15 Elizabeth Ashley

shipshape 4 neat, snug, taut, tidy, trip, trim 5 tight 6 spruce 7 orderly

Shirer, William L
author of: 28 The Collapse of the Third Republic 29 The Rise and Fall of the Third Reich

shirk 4 duck, shun 5 avoid, dodge, elude, evade 6 escape, eschew, ignore 7 goof off, neglect 8 malinger, sidestep 9 goldbrick

shirker 5 piker 6 dodger, evader, loafer, rotter, truant 7 deserter, quitter, slacker 9 goldbrick 10 backslider, malingerer

Shirley Temple
ingredient: 9 ginger ale, grenadine
also called: 9 Roy Rogers

shirr 5 crimp, smock 6 gather, pucker 8 bake eggs

shirt 3 top 4 sark 5 frock, waist 6 blouse, bodice 10 underwaist

shirty 5 angry, irked, testy, vexed 7 annoyed 9 irritated 11 disgruntled

Shittimwood 12 Biblical tree

shiver 5 quake, shake 6 quaver, shimmy 7 shudder, tremble

shivers 3 bit 5 piece, shard 6 sliver 8 fragment

shivery 3 icy, raw 4 cold, cool 5 brisk, chill, crisp, nippy 6 arctic, biting, bitter, chilly, frigid, frosty, wintry 7 quaking, trembly 8 chilling 9 quivering 11 penetrating

shoal 3 bar 4 bank, flat 5 crowd, shelf 6 school 7 sand bar, shallow 8 sand bank

shock 3 jar, mat, mop 4 blow, bush, cock, crop, daze, jolt, mane, mass, pile, rick, rock, stun, turn 5 scare, shake, sheaf, stack, start, upset 6 appall, bundle, dismay, impact, offend, revolt, thatch, trauma 7 astound, disgust, disturb, horrify, outrage, perturb, stagger, startle, stupefy 8 astonish, bowl over, disquiet, distress, paralyze, surprise, unsettle 9 collision, overwhelm 10 concussion, discompose,

disconcert 11 disturbance 13 consternation

shocking 4 foul 5 awful 6 grisly, horrid, odious 7 ghastly, hideous, jarring, jolting 8 gruesome, horrible, indecent, terrible, wretched 9 abhorrent, appalling, frightful, monstrous, offensive, repellent, repugnant, revolting, startling, upsetting 10 abominable, astounding, detestable, disgusting, disturbing, horrifying, outrageous, perturbing, scandalous, staggering, stupefying, surprising, unsettling 11 astonishing, disgraceful, disquieting 12 insufferable, overwhelming 13 disconcerting, reprehensible

shoddy 3 low 4 base, mean, poor 5 dirty, nasty, tacky 6 shabby, sloppy, stingy 7 low-down, miserly 8 careless, inferior, slipshod 9 haphazard, negligent, niggardly 10 second-rate, ungenerous 11 inefficient 12 contemptible 13 inconsiderate, reprehensible

shoe
French: 9 chaussure

shoemaker 7 cobbler 9 bootmaker

Shoemaker's Holiday, The
author: 12 Thomas Dekker

Shoes of the Fisherman, The
author: 11 Morris L West

Shogun
author: 12 James Clavell

Sholokhov, Mikhail
author of: 19 And Quiet Flows the Don 21 The Virgin Soul Upturned

shoo 3 out 4 away, oust, rout, scat 5 be off, chase, leave, scram 6 beat it, be gone, depart, get out, go away 7 cast out, get lost, vamoose

shoot 3 bud, fly, hit 4 bolt, cast, dart, dash, drop, fell, fire, hurl, jump, kill, leap, nick, pelt, plug, race, rain, rush, stem, tear, toss, twig, wing 5 eject, fling, go off, hurry, shell, sling, speed, spray, sprig, spurt, sweep, throw, waste 6 charge, launch, let fly, pepper, propel, riddle, shower, spring, sprout 7 bombard, explode, pick off, tendril 8 catapult, detonate, open fire 9 discharge

Shootist, The
director: 9 Don Siegal
cast: 9 John Wayne, Ron Howard 10 Hugh O'Brien 11 Harry Morgan, Sheree North 12 James Stewart, Lauren Bacall, Richard Boone 13 John Carradine 15 Scatman Crothers

Shoot the Piano Player
director: 16 Francois Truffaut
cast: 11 Marie Dubois 12 Nicole Berger 14 Michele Mercier 15 Charles Aznavour
setting: 5 Paris

shop 3 buy 4 hunt, look, mart, mill 5 plant, store, works 6 browse, market, studio 7 factory 8 emporium, purchase, workshop 9 patronize 10 win-

dowshop **13** establishment
French: **7** atelier **8** boutique

shopkeeper 6 dealer, monger, trader, vendor **8** merchant, purveyor, retailer **9** tradesman

shopworn 5 banal, corny, faded, stale, tired, trite, vapid **6** jejune **10** threadbare

shore 4 bank, hold, land, prop **5** beach, brace, brink, coast **6** hold up, margin, strand **7** bolster, bulwark, seaside, support, sustain **8** buttress, mainstay, seaboard, seacoast, underpin **9** reinforce, riverbank, waterside **10** strengthen
Latin: **10** terra firma

shorebird 3 auk **4** rail, sora **5** snipe, stilt, wader **6** avocet, curlew, plover, puffin **7** lapwing **8** woodcock **9** guillemot, sandpiper **13** oyster catcher

shore up 4 prop **5** brace **6** prop up **7** bolster, support **8** buttress **9** reinforce

short 3 low **4** curt, lean, slim, thin **5** brief, cross, elfin, fleet, gruff, hasty, pygmy, quick, runty, scant, sharp, small, squat, terse, testy, tight **6** abrupt, bantam, little, meager, scanty, scarce, skimpy, slight, sparse, stubby **7** brusque, compact, concise, cursory, lacking, limited, not long, not tall, slender, stunted, summary, wanting **8** abridged, abruptly, dwarfish, fleeting, impolite, snappish, succinct, suddenly, unawares **9** condensed, curtailed, deficient, impatient, momentary, niggardly, pint-sized, truncated **10** by surprise, diminutive, short-lived **11** abbreviated, ill-tempered, Lilliputian, pocket-sized **12** insufficient **13** precipitously **14** without warning

shortage 4 lack, want **6** dearth **7** deficit **8** leanness, scarcity, sparsity **9** shortfall **10** deficiency, inadequacy, scantiness, sparseness **13** insufficiency

shortcoming 4 flaw **5** fault **6** defect, foible **7** blemish, failing, failure, frailty **8** drawback, handicap, weakness **10** deficiency, inadequacy **12** imperfection

shorten 3 cut **4** clip, pare, trim **5** prune, shave, shear **6** lessen, reduce **7** abridge, curtail, cut down **8** condense, contract, cut short, decrease, diminish **10** abbreviate

shortening 3 fat, oil **4** lard, oleo **6** butter, digest **7** cutting, summary **8** abstract, synopsis, trimming **9** hemming up, margarine, reduction **11** abridgement, compression, contraction, curtailment **12** abbreviation, condensation

short form 6 digest, precis **7** summary **8** abstract, synopsis **11** abridgement, contraction **12** abbreviation, condensation

Short Happy Life of Francis Ma-

comber, The
author: **15** Ernest Hemingway

short journey 5 jaunt **6** outing **7** day trip **9** excursion

short-lived 5 brief **7** passing **8** fleeting **9** ephemeral, momentary, temporary, transient **10** evanescent, transitory, unenduring **11** impermanent **24** here today and gone tomorrow

shortly 4 anon, soon **7** by and by **8** directly, in a trice, promptly **9** forthwith, presently **10** before long **11** immediately

short narrative 5 essay, story **6** sketch **8** anecdote **10** short story

shortsighted 4 rash **6** myopic **7** foolish **8** careless, heedless, purblind, reckless, weak-eyed **9** amblyopic, imprudent **10** ill-advised, incautious, unthinking **11** improvident, injudicious, nearsighted, thoughtless **12** undiscerning **13** uncircumspect

short-tempered 4 curt **5** cross, huffy, sharp, testy **6** abrupt, cranky, crusty, grumpy, shirty, touchy **7** bearish, grouchy, peevish, waspish **8** choleric, snappish **9** irascible, irritable, splenetic **10** ill-humored, out of sorts, short-fused **11** hot-tempered, ill-tempered **12** cantankerous

Shosha
author: **19** Isaac Bashevis Singer

Shoshone (Snake)
language family: **10** Shoshonean
location: **4** Utah **5** Idaho **6** Nevada **7** Wyoming
translator: **9** Sacagawea

Shoshonean
tribe: **4** Hopi, Moki **5** Snake **6** Hopitu, Paiute **7** Bannock **8** Comanche, Shoshoni

Shostakovich, Dmitri (Dimitri)
born: **6** Russia **12** St Petersburg
composer of: **7** The Nose **9** Leningrad (symphony No 7) **11** May the First **12** The Golden Age **17** Katerina Ismailova **19** Lady Macbeth of Mzensk

shot 2 go **3** hit, try **4** dose, move, play, toss **5** balls, blast, crack, drive, essay, guess, salvo, slugs, throw **6** beat-up, archer, bowman, chance, report, ruined, shabby, stroke, volley **7** attempt, bullets, gunfire, shooter, surmise, worn-out **8** decrepit, marksman, rifleman **9** discharge, explosion, fusillade, injection **10** ammunition, conjecture, detonation **11** dilapidated, projectiles **12** falling apart, sharpshooter

shot in the arm 4 lift **5** boost **6** uplift **8** stimulus **13** encouragement

shot in the dark 5 guess **6** notion, theory **9** guesswork, suspicion **10** assumption, conjecture, hypothesis

shoulder 3 rim **4** bank, bear, brow, bump, edge, push, side, take **5** brink, carry, crest, elbow, lunge, shove,

skirt, verge **6** assume, border, jostle, margin, take on, thrust, uphold **7** scapula, support, sustain **8** clavicle **9** undertake

shoulder blade 7 scapula **8** omoplate **9** bladebone

shout 3 cry **4** bawl, call, hoot, howl, roar, yell, yelp **5** burst, cheer, hollo, whoop **6** bellow, chorus, clamor, cry out, holler, hurrah, huzzah, outcry, scream, shriek **7** call out, exclaim, screech, thunder **8** outburst **9** hue and cry **10** hullabaloo

shout down 3 boo **4** hiss **6** hoot at, revile **7** catcall, condemn **8** denounce, drown out

shove 4 bump, butt, jolt, prod, push **5** boost, crowd, drive, elbow, force, impel, nudge **6** joggle, jostle, propel, thrust **8** shoulder

show 4 bare, bill, fair, give, lead, mark, play, pomp, pose, sham, sign **5** argue, coach, drama, endow, favor, front, grant, guide, movie, opera, prove, teach, token, tutor, usher **6** appear, attest, ballet, bestow, comedy, direct, effect, evince, expose, hint at, impart, inform, lavish, reveal, school, tender, unveil **7** bear out, bespeak, certify, conduct, confirm, display, exhibit, explain, lay bare, musical, picture, pretext, proffer, program, suggest, uncover **8** ceremony, delusion, disclose, dispense, evidence, illusion, indicate, instruct, intimate, manifest, operetta, point out, pretense, vaunting **9** establish, make clear, make known, represent, spectacle **10** appearance, disclosure, distribute, exhibition, exposition, expression, impression, indication, pretension, production, revelation **11** affectation, attestation, corroborate, counterfeit, demonstrate, performance, testimonial **12** bring to light, substantiate **13** demonstration, entertainment, manifestation, motion picture

Show Boat
author: **10** Edna Ferber

showcase 7 cabinet, counter, display, exhibit, vitrine

showdown 3 war **6** battle, climax, combat, crisis **7** face-off **8** clashing, conflict **9** collision, encounter **13** confrontation

shower 3 wet **4** fall, pour, rain, rush **5** flood, salvo, spray, surge **6** deluge, lavish, splash, stream, volley, wealth **7** barrage, bombard, drizzle, torrent **8** downpour, plethora, sprinkle **9** profusion **10** cloudburst, inundation **11** bombardment

showiness 5 eclat **7** glitter **8** splendor **9** jazziness **10** flashiness **11** ostentation **14** grandiloquence

Show-me State
nickname of: **8** Missouri

show-off 6 egoist **7** boaster, egotist, windbag **8** braggart, fanfaron, flaunter, strutter **9** extrovert, swaggerer **11** braggadocio **13** cock of the walk, exhibitionist **14** life of the party

showpiece 3 gem **5** jewel, pearl, pride, prize **6** rarity, wonder **7** classic, paragon **8** treasure **10** masterwork **11** chef d'oeuvre, masterpiece, prizewinner **17** piece of resistance

show up 4 come **5** outdo **6** appear, arrive, attend, crop up, expose, loom up, reveal, turn up **9** be present **11** come to light, make a fool of **12** come into view **13** become visible

showy 4 loud **5** gaudy, vivid **6** flashy, florid, garish, ornate **7** pompous **8** colorful, gorgeous, imposing, splendid, striking **9** brilliant **11** magnificent, pretentious **12** ostentatious

shred 3 bit, ion, jot, rag **4** atom, band, hair, iota, spot, whit **5** grain, piece, scrap, speck, strip, trace **6** morsel, ribbon, sliver, tatter **7** snippet **8** fragment, molecule, particle **9** scintilla

shrew 3 hag, nag **5** harpy, scold, vixen, yenta **6** kvetch, virago **7** she-wolf **8** battle-ax, fishwife, harridan, spitfire **9** termagant, Xanthippe

shrewd 3 sly **4** foxy, keen, wily, wise **5** acute, cagey, canny, quick, sharp, slick, smart **6** artful, astute, clever, crafty, shifty, smooth, tricky **7** careful, cunning, knowing, probing, prudent **8** cautious, piercing, scheming, sensible, slippery **9** designing, farseeing, sagacious **10** contriving, discerning, farsighted, perceptive **11** calculating, circumspect, intelligent, penetrating, quick-witted, self-serving, sharp-witted **12** disingenuous **13** Machiavellian, perspicacious

shrewdness 6 acumen **7** cunning, slyness **8** foxiness, keenness, wiliness **9** acuteness, cageyness, sharpness, slickness, smartness **10** artfulness, astuteness, cleverness, craftiness, smoothness, trickiness **11** carefulness, discernment **12** slipperiness **16** disingenuousness

shriek 3 cry **4** call, hoot, howl, peal, yell, yelp **5** shout, whoop **6** cry out, holler, out-cry, scream, squawk, squeak, squeal **7** screech

shrift 7 penance **9** atonement, expiation **10** confession

shrill 4 high, loud **6** piping **7** blaring, raucous **8** piercing, strident **9** clamorous **10** screeching **11** high-pitched, penetrating

shrimp 5 prawn **6** scampi **8** cocktail

shrine 5 altar **6** chapel, church, temple **7** sanctum **8** monument **9** sanctuary

shrink 3 ebb, shy **4** balk, duck, wane **5** cower, demur, dry up, quail, stick, wince **6** blench, bridle, cringe, flinch, lessen, pucker, recoil, reduce, refuse, retire **7** curtail, decline, deflate, dwindle, retreat, shorten, shrivel, shudder **8** compress, condense, contract, decrease, diminish, draw back, hang back, make less, withdraw **9** constrict **11** make smaller **12** draw together **13** become smaller

shrink from 4 hate, shun **5** abhor, evade **6** balk at, detest, eschew, loathe, resist **7** despise **8** recoil at **9** abominate, shudder at **12** be revolted by **13** find repulsive

shrinking 3 shy **5** timid **6** ebbing, waning **7** bashful **8** reticent, retiring, timorous **9** declining, dwindling **10** decreasing, shriveling **11** contraction, diminishing

shrive 6 pardon **7** absolve, forgive

shrivel 5 dry up, parch, wizen **6** pucker, scorch, shrink, wither **7** wrinkle

Shropshire Lad, A
author: 9 A E Housman

shroud 4 hide, pall, veil, wrap **5** cloak, cloud, cover, sheet **6** clothe, mantle, screen, swathe **7** blanket, conceal, envelop **8** covering **9** cerecloth, cerements **11** burial cloth **12** graveclothes, winding sheet

shrub 4 bush **5** brush **8** beverage **10** fruit drink

shrubbery 4 bush **5** brush **6** bushes, shrubs **9** brushwood **10** underbrush **11** undergrowth

shuck 4 husk, peel, shed **5** chaff, shell, strip

shudder 4 jerk, pang **5** quake, shake, spasm, throb **6** quaver, quiver, shimmy, shiver, tremor, twitch **7** flutter, tremble **8** paroxysm **9** pulsation, trembling **10** convulsion

shudder at 4 hate **5** abhor **6** detest, loathe **8** recoil at **9** abominate, can't stand **10** recoil from, shrink from

shuffle 3 mix **4** drag, gimp, limp, step **5** scuff, slide **6** clumsy, jumble, scrape **7** shamble **8** scramble **9** rearrange **10** disarrange **11** interchange

shul, schul 9 synagogue

shun 5 avoid, dodge, elude, evade, forgo **6** eschew, forego, ignore, refuse, reject **7** boycott, disdain **10** circumvent, fight shy of, shrink from **11** keep clear of, shy away from **12** have no part of, keep away from, steer clear of, turn away from

shut 3 box **4** cage, coop, draw, fold, lock, snap **5** clasp, close, drawn, latch **6** closed, closet, corral, draw to, fasten, intern, locked, lock in, secure **7** confine, drawn to, enclose, fence in, impound, latched, secured **8** cloister, closed up, fastened, imprison **9** barricade, constrain **11** incarcerate

shut down 4 halt, stop **5** cease **7** suspend **9** close down, interrupt **11** discontinue

Shute, Nevil
author of: 10 On the Beach

shut in 4 cage **5** caged, pen in **6** coop up, encage, lock up **7** confine, encaged, enclose **8** confined, cooped up, enclosed, locked up, restrain, restrict **10** restrained, restricted

shut one's eyes to 5 allow **6** ignore, wink at **8** overlook **9** connive in, disregard **11** pay no heed to **14** turn one's back on

shut out 3 bar **5** debar **6** defeat **7** exclude **8** obstruct, prohibit

shutter 5 blind, close, shade **6** screen **7** curtain

shut the door on 3 ban, bar **6** forbid, refuse, reject **7** exclude, keep out, shut out **8** prohibit

shut up 4 cage, coop, hush, lock, pent **5** close, pen in **6** immure **7** be quiet, confine, silence **8** imprison **11** incarcerate

shy 4 balk, meek, wary **5** chary, cower, dodge, leery, minus, scant, short, timid, under, wince **6** blench, demure, flinch, in need, modest, shrink, swerve **7** anxious, bashful, careful, fearful, lacking, needing, nervous, wanting **8** cautious, draw back, jump back, reserved, reticent, skittish, timorous **9** deficient, diffident, shrinking, tremulous **10** suspicious **11** distrustful **12** apprehensive **13** self-conscious

shy away from 4 duck, shun **5** avoid, dodge, spurn **6** balk at, refuse, reject **10** shrink from **12** steer clear of

Shylock
character in: 19 The Merchant of Venice
author: 11 Shakespeare

shyness 8 meekness, timidity **9** reticence **10** diffidence, insecurity **11** bashfulness **12** sheepishness, timorousness **14** self-effacement **15** unassertiveness

shyster 5 rogue **6** lawyer **8** attorney **10** mouthpiece **11** pettifogger **15** ambulance chaser

si 3 yes

Siam see **8** Thailand

Sibelius, Jean
born: 7 Finland **10** Tavastehus
composer of: 6 En Saga **7** Karelia, Legends, Tapiola, The Band **8** Kalevala **9** Finlandia **10** The Tempest **12** The Oceanides, Voces Intimae **14** Ride and Sunrise

Siberia 8 disfavor **10** punishment **14** undesirability
city: 4 Omsk **5** Chita, Tomsk **6** Kurgan **7** Irkutsk, Yakutsk
conqueror: 9 Timafeyev **11** Genghis Khan
continent: 4 Asia

gulf: 2 Ob
inhabitant: 4 Yaku **5** Sagai, Tatar **6** Tartar **7** Yukagir **8** prisoner **17** political prisoner
mountain range: 4 Ural **5** Altai, Altay
river: 2 Ob **3** Ket, Ili, Taz **4** Amga, Amur, Lena, Onon **5** Ishim, Tobol **6** Olekma
sea: 4 Kara **6** Laptev **7** Okhotsk

sibling 6 sister **7** brother
problem: 7 rivalry

sibyl 4 seer **5** augur **6** oracle **7** diviner **9** predictor, sorceress **10** forecaster, prophetess, soothsayer **13** fortune teller **14** prognosticator

Sibyls
form: 10 prophetess
inspired by: 5 deity **6** Apollo
names: 6 Libyan **7** Cumaean **10** Erythraean
prophecies: 14 Sibylline Books

sic 2 so **4** thus

Sicilian Vespers, The
also: 20 Les Vepres Siciliennes
opera by: 5 Verdi
character: 5 Elena **6** Arrigo **7** Procida **8** Monforte

Sicily
other name: 7 Sicilia **9** Trinacria, Triquetra
capital/largest city: 7 Palermo
others: 4 Aci **4** Enna, Noto **6** Ragusa **7** Augusta, Catania, Marsala, Messina, Trapani **8** Syracuse **10** Montelepre
division: 4 Enna **6** Ragusa **7** Catania, Messina, Palermo, Trapani **8** Siracusa, Syracuse **9** Agrigento **13** Caltanissetta
government: 13 region of Italy
measure: 5 salma **7** caffiso
monetary unit: 5 litra, oncia, uncia **6** carlin **7** carline, oncetta
island: 5 Egadi **6** Lipari, Ustica **7** Pelagie **11** Pantelleria
lake: 7 Pergusa **8** Camarina
mountain: 4 Erei, Moro, Sori **5** Atlas, Erici, Hybla, Iblei, Ibrei **7** Nebrodi, Vulcano **9** Apennines, Le Madonie, Stromboli **10** Peloritani
highest point: 4 Etna **5** Aetna
river: 4 Acis **5** Salso, Torto **6** Belice, Simeto **7** Mazzaro, Platani
sea: 6 Ionian **10** Tyrrhenian **13** Mediterranean
physical feature:
  cape: 4 Boeo, Faro **7** Lilibeo, Passaro, Passero, Pelorus
  gulf: 4 Noto **7** Catania
  strait: 7 Messina
  wind: 7 sirocco
people: 5 Elymi, Sican, Sicel **6** Sicani, Siculi
  author: 9 Lampedusa **10** Pirandello
  composer: 7 Bellini
  king: 4 Eryx **5** Bomba, Henry, Peter, Roger **7** Charles, Cocalus,

Leontes **9** Ferdinand, Frederick
ruler: 4 Rome **5** Arabs, Goths, Spain **6** Greeks **7** Germans, Normans, Vandals, Vikings **8** Carthage, Saracens **9** Aragonese, Byzantium, Egyptians, Phoenicia **15** Holy Roman Empire
language: 7 Italian
religion: 13 Roman Catholic
place:
  cathedral: 8 Monreale
  resort: 4 Enna **8** Taormina
  ruins: 14 Villa Imperiale **15** Temple of Concord **18** Valley of the Temples
feature:
  brigands: 5 Mafia
  evening stroll: 11 passeggiata

sick 3 ill **4** weak **5** frail, tired, weary **6** ailing, infirm, laid up, poorly, queasy, sickly, uneasy, unwell **7** crushed, grieved, invalid, unsound **8** delicate, stricken, troubled, wretched **9** afflicted, bored with, disturbed, miserable, nauseated, perturbed, suffering, unhealthy **10** disquieted, distressed, indisposed **11** discomposed, heartbroken **15** under the weather

sicken 5 repel, shock, upset **6** offend, revolt **7** disgust, horrify, make ill, repulse **8** nauseate **14** turn the stomach

sickening 4 foul, vile **5** nasty **7** noisome **8** horrible, unsavory **9** abhorrent, loathsome, offensive, repellent, repugnant, repulsive, revolting **10** disgusting, nauseating **11** distasteful

sickly 3 ill, wan **4** drab, flat, lame, pale, sick, weak **5** ashen, faint, frail, silly **6** ailing, feeble, flimsy, guilty, infirm, leaden, peaked, poorly, sneaky, torpid, unwell **7** insipid, invalid, unsound **8** delicate, smirking **9** afflicted, apathetic, bloodless, simpering, unhealthy **10** cadaverous, lackluster, namby-pamby, snickering, spiritless, uninspired, wishy-washy **11** ineffective **12** unconvincing **13** self-conscious

sickness 6 malady, nausea **7** ailment, disease, illness **8** debility, disorder, vomiting **9** complaint, frailness, ill health, infirmity **10** affliction, disability, invalidism, poor health, queasiness **11** unsoundness **12** qualmishness **13** indisposition

sic passim 12 so throughout

sic semper tyrannis 19 thus always to tyrants
motto of: 8 Virginia

sic transit gloria mundi 33 thus passes away the glory of this world

Siddhartha
author: 12 Hermann Hesse
story of: 6 Buddha

siddur 16 Jewish prayer book
literally: 5 order

side 3 hem, rim **4** area, body, brim,

edge, half, hand, part, sect, team, view **5** angle, bound, cause, facet, flank, group, house, light, limit, minor, party, phase, skirt, slant, stand, stock **6** allied, aspect, behalf, belief, border, circle, clique, fringe, lesser, margin, region, sector, strain **7** askance, coterie, faction, lateral, lineage, oblique, opinion, postern, quarter, related, section, segment, surface **8** alliance, attitude, boundary, division, indirect, marginal, position, skirting **9** accessory, bloodline, coalition, on one side, perimeter, periphery, secondary, territory, viewpoint **10** collateral, contingent, federation, incidental, standpoint, subsidiary **11** affiliation, association, unimportant **13** insignificant

Side
origin: 5 Irish
form: 7 fairies
owner: 14 Tuatha De Danann

sideboard 6 buffet **8** credenza

side by side 7 abreast **8** abutting, together **9** adjoining **11** cheek by jowl, in proximity
Latin: 9 pari passu

Side Effects
author: 10 Woody Allen

sidekick 3 pal **4** aide **5** buddy **6** deputy, friend **9** assistant **10** lieutenant

sideline 5 bench, hobby **8** boundary **9** avocation **14** put out of action

sidestep 4 duck **5** avert, avoid, dodge, elude, evade, skirt **6** bypass, escape **10** circumvent, fight shy of **12** steer clear of

sidestepping 7 dodging, ducking, eluding, evasion **8** skirting **9** avoidance **13** circumvention

sidewalk 4 curb **8** footpath, pavement **9** promenade

sideways, sideway 6 aslant **7** askance, lateral, oblique **8** crabwise, edgeways, edgewise, sidelong, sideward, sidewise **9** cross wise, laterally, obliquely, to the side **11** from one side

side with 5 agree **7** stand by, stick by, support **8** champion **12** take one's part

sidle 4 cant, edge, skew, veer **10** lateralize

Sidney, Sir Philip
author of: 7 Arcadia **15** Defence of Poesie, Defence of Poetry **18** Apologie for Poetrie, Astrophel and Stella

Sidney, Sylvia
real name: 11 Sophia Kosow
born: 7 Bronx NY
husband: 11 Luther Adler **12** Bennett A Cerf
roles: 4 Fury **7** Dead End **11** Street Scene **13** Les Miserables **15** Madame Butterfly **17** An American Tragedy **24** Summer Wishes Winter Dreams

Sidrophel
  character in: **8** Hudibras
  author: **6** Butler
siecle 3 age **6** period **7** century
Siegel, Jerry
  creator/artist of: **8** Superman
Siegfried
  origin: **8** Germanic
  mentioned in: **14** Nibelungenlied
  father: **7** Sigmund
  mother: **9** Sieglinde
  wife: **9** Kriemhild
  killed by: **5** Hagen
  same as: **6** Sigurd
  killed: **6** Fafnir
  won for Gunther: **10** Brunnhilde
  stole: **9** Tarnkappe
Sieg Heil 13 hail to victory
  salute used by: **5** Nazis
Sieglinde
  origin: **8** Germanic
  mentioned in: **14** Nibelungenlied
  husband: **7** Sigmund
  son: **9** Siegfried
Sienkiewicz, Henryk
  author of: **8** Quo Vadis?
Sierra Leone
  name means: **12** lion mountain
  other name: **9** Gold Coast **10** Grain
    Coast, Ivory Coast
  capital/largest city: **8** Freetown
  others: **2** Bo **5** Hepel, Kissi, Lungi,
    Pepel **6** Bonthe, Kenema, Makeni,
    Shenge, Sulima
  school: **6** Njaia U **9** Fourah Bay
  measure: **4** load **6** kettle
  monetary unit: **4** cent **5** leone
  island: **4** York **6** Banana, Turtle **7**
    Sherbro
  mountain: **4** Loma **10** Tingi Hills
  highest point: **9** Bintimani
  river: **3** Moa **4** Jong, Mano, Meli,
    Ribi, Sewa, Taia **5** Bagbe, Mongo,
    Morro, Rokel **6** Mabole, Rokkel,
    Scarcy, Waanje **13** Great Scarcies
    14 Little Scarcies
  sea: **8** Atlantic
  physical feature:
    bay: **5** Yawri **7** Sherbro
    cape: **8** Shilling **11** Sierra Leone
    peninsula: **7** Turners **11** Sierra
      Leone
    wind: **9** harmattan
  people: **3** Vai **4** Kono, Loko, Susu **5**
    Bulom, Kissi, Limba, Mende, Mendi,
    Temne **6** Creole, Fulani, Syrian **7**
    Gallina, Koranko, Kuranko, Sherbro,
    Yalunka **8** Lebanese, Mandingo
    explorer: **6** Cintra
    leader: **6** Margai **7** Stevens
  language: **4** Krio **5** Limba, Mende,
    Mendi, Temne **6** Creole **7** English
  religion: **5** Islam **7** animism **12** Christianity
  place:
    wharf: **10** King Jimmys
  feature:

cloth: **5** garra
  clothing: **5** lappa **6** caftan
  secret society: **4** poro
food:
  dish: **4** fufu **7** cassava
  sauce: **7** palaver
siesta 3 nap **4** rest **5** break, sleep **6** cat
  nap, snooze **10** forty winks
sieve 4 sift **6** filter, riddle, screen,
  sorter, strain **7** tattler **8** colander,
  strainer **9** separator **12** blabbermouth
sift 4 sort **5** drift, probe, study **6** filter,
  review, screen, search, winnow **7** analyze, inspect, scatter, sort out **8** separate **10** scrutinize **11** distinguish, investigate **12** discriminate
Siggeir
  origin: **12** Scandinavian
  king of: **5** Goths
  wife: **5** Signy
  causes death of: **7** Volsung
sigh 3 sob **4** hiss, long, moan, pine,
  weep **5** brood, groan, mourn, whine,
  yearn **6** grieve, lament, sorrow
sight 3 ken, see, spy **4** bead, espy,
  gaze, spot, view **5** image, scene, vista
  6 behold, seeing, survey, vision **7** display, exhibit, eyeshot, glimpse, observe, pageant, scenery, viewing **8**
  eyesight, perceive, prospect, scrutiny
  9 peepsight, sighthole, spectacle **10**
  appearance, visibility
sighted 3 saw **4** seen **6** seeing **8** not
  blind, observed
sightless 5 blind **8** unseeing **9** unsighted
sightly 4 fair **6** lovely, pretty **8** handsome, pleasing **9** appealing, beautiful
  10 attractive
Sigmund
  origin: **8** Germanic **12** Scandinavian
  mentioned in: **8** Volsunga **14** Nibelungenlied
  king of: **11** Netherlands
  father: **7** Volsung
  mother: **4** Liod, Ljod **5** Hliod
  wife: **7** Hiordis, Hjordis **8** Borghild **9**
    Sieglinde
  sister: **5** Signy
  lover: **5** Signy
  son: **6** Sigurd **9** Siegfried, Sinfiotli
sign 3 nod **4** clue, hint, mark, note,
  omen, wave **5** badge, brand, index,
  stamp, token, trait **6** emblem, ensign,
  figure, herald, motion, signal, symbol
  7 earmark, endorse, feature, gesture,
  go-ahead, placard, portent, presage,
  symptom, warning **8** evidence, forecast, inscribe, neon sign, road sign,
  signpost **9** autograph, billboard,
  guidepost, harbinger, indicator, nameplate, trademark **10** indication, intimation, prognostic, suggestion, underwrite **11** forewarning **13** manifestation
  14 characteristic *see also* **6** zodiac
signal 3 cue, nod **4** sign **6** beckon, famous, motion, unique **7** command,

eminent, gesture, guiding, honored,
notable, warning **8** high sign, password, pointing, renowned, singular,
striking **9** arresting, directing, direction, important, indicator, memorable,
momentous, prominent, watchword
10 commanding, impressive, indicating, indication, noteworthy, one of-a-kind, remarkable **11** conspicuous, distinctive, exceptional, illustrious, outstanding, significant **12** considerable
13 consequential, distinguished, extraordinary, unforgettable
significance 3 aim **4** note **5** drift,
  force, merit, sense, value, worth **6** import, intent, moment, object, virtue,
  weight **7** concern, gravity, meaning,
  portent, purpose **8** eminence, interest,
  priority **9** authority, direction, influence, intention, relevance **10** excellence, importance, notability, prominence **11** consequence, distinction,
  implication
significant 4 main **5** chief, grave,
  great, major, prime, vital **6** cogent,
  signal **7** eminent, knowing, notable,
  serious, telling, weighty **8** critical, distinct, eloquent, eventful, material,
  pregnant, symbolic **9** important, momentous, paramount, principal, prominent **10** emblematic, expressive, indicative, meaningful, noteworthy,
  portentous, remarkable, suggestive **11**
  exceptional, influential, outstanding,
  substantial, symptomatic **12** considerable **13** consequential, demonstrative
  14 representative
signify 4 mean, omen, show, tell **5** argue, augur, imply **6** convey, denote,
  evince, herald, hint at, import, reveal,
  typify **7** bespeak, betoken, connote,
  declare, exhibit, express, portend, predict, presage, promise, suggest **8** announce, disclose, evidence, forebode,
  foretell, indicate, intimate, manifest,
  proclaim, set forth, stand for **9** be a
  sign of, designate, represent, symbolize **10** foreshadow **11** communicate,
  demonstrate
signing up 7 joining **9** enlisting, enrolling **10** enlistment, enrollment **11** registering **12** registration **13** matriculating, matriculation
Sign of Four, The
  author: **19** Sir Arthur Conan Doyle
  character: **11** Mary Morstan **12** Dr
    John Watson **13** Jonathan Small **14**
    Sherlock Holmes, Thaddeus Sholto
Signoret, Simone
  real name: **32** Simone-Henriette-Charlotte Kaminker
  born: **7** Germany **9** Wiesbaden
  husband: **11** Yves Montand **12** Yves
    Allegret
  roles: **10** Madame Rosa **11** Ship of
    Fools **12** Room at the Top (Oscar)
    14 Is Paris Burning?

autobiography: 27 Nostalgia Isn't What It Used to Be

sign up 4 join **6** enlist, enroll, join up **8** register **9** volunteer **11** matriculate

Sigurd
origin: 12 Scandinavian
mentioned in: 8 Volsunga
father: 7 Sigmund
mother: 7 Hiordis, Hjordis
wife: 6 Gudrun, Kudrun **7** Guthrun
killed: 6 Fafnir
acquired treasure of: 8 Andavari
won for Gunnar: 8 Brynhild

Sigyn
origin: 12 Scandinavian
husband: 4 Loki

Sikes, Bill
character in: 11 Oliver Twist
author: 7 Dickens

Sikkim
capital/largest city: 7 Gangtok
others: 6 Dikchu, Lachen, Namchi, Rangpo, Rumtek **7** Lachung **9** Chungtang
government: 12 state of India
mountain: 7 Dongkya, Donkhya **9** Himalayas, Singalili **10** Darjeeling **12** Kanchenjunga
river: 5 Tista **6** Ranjit **9** Lachen Chu **10** Lachung Chu
physical feature:
mountain pass: 6 Natu La **7** Jelep La
storm: 7 monsoon
people: 4 Rong **5** Bhote **6** Bhotia, Bhutia, Indian, Lepcha **7** Tibetan **8** Nepalese **9** Mongoloid
king: 7 chogyal
religion: 5 Hindu **7** Lamaism **15** Tibetan Buddhism

Sikorsky, Igor
nationality: 7 Russian **8** American
invented: 10 helicopter

Silas Marner
author: 11 George Eliot
profession: 6 weaver
character: 5 Eppie **11** Dunstan Cass, Godfrey Cass **13** Aaron Winthrop, Nancy Lammeter

silence 3 gag **4** calm, curb, halt, hush, kill, rout, stop **5** allay, check, crush, peace, quash, quell, quiet, still **6** banish, deaden, defeat, muffle, muzzle, repose, squash, stifle, subdue **7** conquer, nullify, put down, quieten, repress, reserve, squelch **8** choke off, dumbness, muteness, overcome, serenity, suppress, vanquish **9** lay to rest, placidity, quietness, reticence, stillness, tongue-tie **10** extinguish, placidness, put an end to, strike dumb **11** taciturnity, tranquility **12** tranquillity **13** noiselessness, secretiveness, soundlessness **14** speechlessness **16** closemouthedness **19** uncommunicativeness

silent 3 mum **4** calm, dumb, idle, mute **5** inert, muted, quiet, still, tacit **6** covert, hidden, hushed, placid, serene, unsaid **7** dormant, implied, muffled **8** discreet, implicit, inactive, inferred, lifeless, peaceful, reserved, reticent, taciturn, tranquil, unspoken, wordless **9** concealed, intimated, noiseless, quiescent, secretive, soundless, suggested, unsounded, unwritten **10** insinuated, mysterious, speechless, tongue-tied, undeclared, understood, unrevealed, unstirring, untalked-of **11** close-lipped, tight-lipped, unexpressed, unmentioned, unpublished, untalkative, unvocalized **12** closemouthed, unpronounced **15** uncommunicative

Silent Spring
author: 13 Rachel L Carson

Silenus
god of: 6 forest
oldest: 5 satyr
father: 3 Pan **6** Hermes
foster father of: 8 Dionysus
teacher of: 8 Dionysus
companion of: 8 Dionysus
sons: 6 Sileni

silicon
chemical symbol: 2 Si

silk
fabric: 4 crin **5** crepe, ninon, satin, surah, tulle **6** faille, pongee, sendal, tussah **7** chiffon, foulard, organza, raw silk, taffeta **8** organzie, paduasoy **10** peau de soie **12** crepe de chine
lining: 7 sarsnet **8** sarcenet
measure: 6 denier
raw silk: 5 grege **6** greige **8** marabout
source: 6 cocoon **9** silkworms
waste: 4 noil **5** floss
watered: 5 moire
yarn/thread: 4 tram **5** floss

silk-stocking 6 uptown **8** highborn, highbred, wellborn **9** patrician **10** upper-class **11** blue-blooded **12** aristocratic

Silk Stockings
director: 15 Rouben Mamoulian
cast: 10 Janis Paige, Peter Lorre **11** Cyd Charisse, Fred Astaire
setting: 5 Paris
score: 10 Cole Porter
remake of: 9 Ninotchka

silky 4 fine, soft **6** satiny, smooth **11** fine-grained

silliness 5 folly **6** drivel, idiocy **7** inanity **9** absurdity, asininity, frivolity **10** buffoonery, tomfoolery **11** foolishness **13** pointlessness **14** playing the fool, ridiculousness

Sillitoe, Alan
author of: 10 Her Victory **29** Saturday Night and Sunday Morning **36** The Loneliness of the Long-Distance Runner

silly 3 mad **4** dumb **5** crazy, giddy, inane **6** absurd, frothy, insane, stupid, unwary, unwise **7** aimless, asinine, fatuous, foolish, idiotic, shallow, witless **8** childish, farcical **9** brainless, foolhardy, frivolous, laughable, ludicrous, pointless, senseless **10** ill-advised, irrational, ridiculous **11** empty-headed, harebrained, meaningless, nonsensical, purposeless **12** muddleheaded, preposterous, simpleminded, unreasonable **13** inappropriate, irresponsible, muddlebrained, rattlebrained **14** featherbrained **15** inconsequential

Silmarillion, The
author: 10 J R R Tolkien

silo 3 pit **5** tower
storage of: 6 fodder **7** missile

Silone, Ignazio
real name: 17 Secondo Tranquilli
author of: 9 Fontamara **12** Bread and Wine **26** The Story of a Humble Christian

Silvanus
also: 8 Sylvanus
god of: 5 herds, house, woods **12** farm boundary **16** uncultivated land

silver 5 coins, plate **6** argent, change **7** jewelry **8** argentum, platinum **9** argentine **10** silverware
chemical symbol: 2 Ag

Silver
horse of: 10 Lone Ranger

Silver, Long John
character in: 14 Treasure Island
author: 9 Stevenson

Silver, Mattie
character in: 10 Ethan Frome
author: 7 Wharton

Silvers, Phil
real name: 17 Philip Silversmith
born: 10 Brooklyn NY
roles: 9 Top Banana **13** Sergeant Bilko **15** High Button Shoes **22** A Guide for the Married Man **37** A Funny Thing Happened on the Way to the Forum
autobiography: 14 The Laugh Is on Me

s'il vous plaît 6 please **11** if you please

Simenon, Georges
author of: 8 The Train **12** Act of Passion **14** The Little Saint **15** Maigret's Memoirs **28** The Strange Case of Peter the Lett
character: 21 Inspector Jules Maigret

Simeon
father: 5 Jacob
mother: 4 Leah
brother: 3 Dan, Gad **4** Levi **5** Asher, Judah **6** Joseph, Reuben **7** Zebulun **8** Benjamin, Issachar, Naphtali
sister: 5 Dinah
canticle: 12 nunc dimittis
descendant of: 9 Simeonite

similar 4 akin, like, twin **5** close **6** allied **7** cognate, kindred **8** agreeing, matching, parallel **9** analogous, duplicate **10** comparable, equivalent, resembling **11** approximate, correlative, much the same, nearly alike **13** correspondent, corresponding

similarity 7 harmony, kinship, oneness **8** affinity, likeness, nearness, sameness **9** agreement, closeness, congruity, semblance **10** congruence, similitude **11** concordance, conformance, equivalence, parallelism, reciprocity, resemblance **13** comparability **14** conformability, correspondence

similarly 4 thus **5** alike **7** equally **8** likewise **11** furthermore, identically **15** correspondingly

similitude 7 analogy **8** likeness, sameness **10** similarity **11** parallelism, resemblance

simmer 4 boil, burn, foam, fume, stew **5** chafe, smart **6** bubble, burble, gurgle, seethe, sizzle

simmer down 7 cool off **8** calm down **14** collect oneself, compose oneself

Simmons, Jean
  born: 6 London **7** England
  husband: 13 Richard Brooks **14** Stewart Granger
  roles: 4 Trio **6** Hamlet **7** Desiree, Ophelia, The Robe **9** Spartacus, Young Bess **11** Elmer Gantry **12** Guys and Dolls **14** The Happy Ending **17** Great Expectations **19** Androcles and the Lion

Simon
  also known as: 5 Peter
  son: 13 Judas Iscariot
  disciple of: 5 Jesus

Simon, Neil
  author of: 10 Chapter Two, Plaza Suite **11** Biloxi Blues **12** The Odd Couple **15** The Sunshine Boys **16** Come Blow Your Horn **17** Barefoot in the Park **21** Last of the Red Hot Lovers **25** The Prisoner of Second Avenue

Simon & Simon
  character: 7 AJ Simon **9** Rick Simon **12** Cecilia Simon **13** Downtown Brown
  cast: 7 Tim Reid **10** Mary Carver **13** Gerald McRaney, Jameson Parker
  setting: 8 San Diego

Simon Boccanegra
  opera by: 5 Verdi
  setting: 5 Genoa
  character: 5 Maria, Paolo **6** Andrea, Fiesco, Pietro **14** Amelia Grimaldi, Gabriele Adorno

Simon Legree 8 overseer **11** slavedriver
  in: 14 Uncle Tom's Cabin

Simonov, Konstantin
  author of: 13 Days and Nights

Simon Templar *see* Saint, The

simpatico 7 likable **9** agreeable, congenial, gemutlich

simper 5 smirk **6** giggle, tee-hee, titter **7** snicker, snigger

simple 4 bare, dull, dumb, easy, open, slow, soft, true **5** basic, blunt, dense, frank, green, homey, naive, naked, plain, quiet, sheer, stark, thick **6** callow, candid, common, direct, honest, modest, obtuse, rustic, stupid **7** artless, foolish, natural, sincere **8** absolute, innocent, not fancy, ordinary, peaceful, straight, workaday **9** downright, elemental, guileless, ingenuous, out-and-out, unadorned, unfeigned, untrimmed, unworldly **10** elementary, manageable, not complex, unaffected, uninvolved **11** commonplace, fundamental, plain-spoken, rudimentary, thick-witted, undecorated, unvarnished **12** not difficult, not elaborate, uncompounded, unembellished, unpretentious **15** straightforward, unsophisticated

simple house 3 cot, hut **5** shack **6** chalet **7** cottage **8** bungalow

simpleminded 4 dull, dumb, slow **5** dense, silly, thick **6** stupid **7** asinine, fatuous, foolish, idiotic, moronic, witless **8** retarded **9** brainless, dim-witted, imbecilic **10** dull-witted, half-witted **11** empty-headed, harebrained, lamebrained **12** feeble-minded

simpleton 3 ass, oaf **4** dolt, dope, fool, hick, jerk, rube **5** booby, dummy, dunce, goose, idiot, ninny, stupe **6** donkey, rustic **7** dullard, jackass **8** dumbbell, imbecile, numskull **9** blockhead, greenhorn, ignoramus, numbskull **10** nincompoop

simplicity 6 candor, purity **7** clarity, honesty, naivete **8** easiness, openness, serenity **9** austerity, clearness, innocence, plainness, restraint, sincerity **10** directness **11** artlessness, cleanliness, naturalness, obviousness **12** truthfulness **13** guilelessness, unworldliness **19** straightforwardness

simply 7 clearly, lucidly, plainly, starkly **8** directly, modestly **9** naturally **10** explicitly **11** ingenuously **12** intelligibly, unaffectedly **15** uncomplicatedly, unpretentiously **17** straightforwardly

Simpson, O J (Orenthal James)
  nickname: 5 Juice
  sport: 8 football
  position: 11 running back
  team: 10 USC Trojans **12** Buffalo Bills **23** San Francisco Forty-Niners
  film: 11 The Naked Gun

Simpsons, The
  creator: 12 Matt Groening
  roles: 3 Apu, Moe **4** Bart, Lisa, Otto **5** Homer, Marge **6** Barney **7** Mr Burns **8** Smithers **11** Chief Wiggum **12** Mrs. Karbappel

simulate 3 act, ape **4** copy, fake, play,

pose, sham **5** feign, mimic, put on **6** affect, assume, invent **7** imitate, play-act, pretend **9** dissemble, fabricate **11** counterfeit, make believe

simulated 4 fake, sham **5** phony **6** forged **7** manmade, pretend **9** imitation, synthetic **10** artificial, fabricated **11** counterfeit, make-believe

simultaneous 6 coeval **10** coexistent, coexisting, coincident, concurrent, synchronal, synchronic **11** concomitant, synchronous **12** accompanying, contemporary **15** contemporaneous

sin 3 err **4** evil, fall, slip, vice **5** crime, error, lapse, shame, stray, wrong **6** breach, do evil, offend **7** do wrong, misdeed, offense, scandal **8** disgrace, evil deed, iniquity, trespass, villainy **9** violation **10** infraction, transgress, wrongdoing **13** transgression

Sin
  origin: 8 Akkadian
  god of: 4 moon

Sinatra, Frank
  real name: 20 Francis Albert Sinatra
  nickname: 8 The Voice **11** Old Blue Eyes **18** Chairman of the Board
  born: 9 Hoboken NJ
  wife: 9 Mia Farrow **10** Ava Gardner
  daughter: 12 Nancy Sinatra
  son: 14 Frank Sinatra Jr
  leader of: 7 Rat Pack
  roles: 8 Tony Rome **12** Angelo Maggio, Guys and Dolls, The Detective **14** The Joker Is Wild **17** The First Deadly Sin **18** From Here to Eternity **22** The Man with the Golden Arm

Sinbad the Sailor
  character in: 27 Arabian Nights' Entertainments

since 2 as **3** ago, for, yet **4** ergo, from **5** after, hence, later **6** thence, whence **7** because, whereas **8** in as much **9** therefore **10** afterwards **11** accordingly, considering **12** subsequently
  archaic: 4 sith
  prefix: 3 cis
  Scottish: 4 syne

sincere 4 real **5** frank **6** candid, honest **7** artless, earnest, genuine, natural, serious **8** truthful **9** authentic, guileless, heartfelt, ingenuous, unfeigned **10** forthright, unaffected **11** in good faith, undeceitful **12** wholehearted **15** straightforward

sincerely 5 truly **6** really **8** honestly **9** earnestly, genuinely, seriously **10** truthfully **14** wholeheartedly

sincerity 6 candor **7** honesty, probity **8** openness **9** frankness, good faith **11** artlessness, earnestness, genuineness, seriousness **12** truthfulness **13** guilelessness, ingenuousness **14** forthrightness, unaffectedness **16** wholeheartedness **19** straightforwardness

Sinclair, Upton
  author of: 9 The Jungle, World's End

12 Dragon's Teeth
character: 9 Lanny Budd

Sindhi
language family: 12 Indo-European
branch: 11 Indo-Iranian
group: 5 Indic
spoken in: 13 Northern India

sine die 17 without fixing a day (for future action or a future meeting)
literally: 13 without the day

sine prole 14 without progeny **16** without offspring

sine qua non 15 without which not **18** something essential **22** indispensable condition

sinew, sinews 4 grit, thew **5** fiber, nerve, power, vigor **6** muscle, tendon **7** stamina **8** ligament, strength, virility, vitality **10** resilience, strengthen

sinewy 4 wiry **5** beefy, nervy, thewy, tough **6** brawny, robust, strong **7** fibrose, stringy **8** muscular, powerful, vigorous

sinful 3 bad **4** evil, vile **5** wrong **6** errant, unholy, wicked **7** corrupt, heinous, immoral, impious, ungodly, wayward **8** criminal, depraved, shameful **9** miscreant **10** degenerate, despicable, iniquitous, profligate, villainous **11** disgraceful, irreligious, unrighteous

sing 3 hum **4** lilt, pipe **5** carol, chant, chirp, croon, trill, tweet **6** intone, warble **7** chir rup, whistle **8** melodize

Sing Along with Mitch
regulars: 10 Diana Trask **11** Mitch Miller **12** Leslie Uggams, Louise O'Brien, Sandy Stewart **13** Gloria Lambert, Sing Along Gang, Sing Along Kids

Singapore
other name: 8 Singa Pur
name means: 13 city of the lion
capital/largest city: 9 Singapore
others: 4 Tuas **6** Changi, Jurong **7** Nee Soon **9** Paya Lebar, Woodlands **10** Bukit Timah, Queenstown **12** Bukit Panjang **15** Toa Payoh New Town
   medieval town: 7 Temasek
school: 7 Nanyang **8** National **9** Singapore
monetary unit: 4 cent **6** dollar
island: 4 Ubin **5** Brani, Bukum, Pesek **7** Semakau **8** Merlimau, Southern **10** Ayer Chawan, Ayer Merbau **11** Blakang Mati, Tekong Besar **12** Tekong Kechil
mountain: 6 Mandai **7** Panjang
highest point: 10 Bukit Timah
river: 6 Jurong, Sungei **7** Kallang, Seletar **9** Singapore
sea: 6 Indian **10** South China
physical feature:
   harbor: 6 Keppel **9** Serangoon
   strait: 6 Johore, Pandan **8** Sembilan **9** Singapore

people: 5 Malay **6** Indian **7** Chinese **9** Malaysian, Pakistani, Sri Lankan
   founder: 7 Raffles
   leader: 10 Lee Kwan Yew
language: 5 Malay, Tamil **7** Chinese, English **8** Mandarin
religion: 4 Sikh **5** Hindu, Islam **6** Taoism **8** Buddhism **12** Christianity, Confucianism
place:
   amusement park: 8 New World **10** Great World, Happy World
   aquarium: 8 Van Kleef
   cathedral: 9 St Andrews
   gardens: 7 Botanic
   hall: 16 Victoria Memorial
   industrial park: 6 Jurong
   mosque: 6 Sultan
   park: 6 Farber **7** Merlion **12** Raffles Place
   street: 16 Raffles Boulevard
   temple: 17 One Thousand Lights
feature:
   boat: 4 junk **6** sampan
   clothing: 4 sari

singe 4 burn, char, sear **5** brand **6** scorch

singer 4 alto, bard, bass, diva, lark **5** tenor **6** canary **7** crooner, soprano **8** baritone, minstrel, songbird, songster, vocalist **9** chanteuse, chantress, contralto **8** cantatrice, songstress, troubadour **11** nightingale **12** countertenor, mezzo-soprano

Singer, Isaac Bashevis
author of: 6 Shosha **7** Old Love **8** The Manor **9** The Estate **13** Gimpel the Fool **15** The Family Moskat **16** In My Father's Court **24** The Spinoza of Market Street

singing group 4 trio **5** choir, nonet, octet **6** chorus, sextet **7** quartet, quintet **8** glee club **13** choral society **17** barbershop quartet

Singin' in the Rain
director: 9 Gene Kelly **12** Stanley Donen
cast: 9 Gene Kelly, Jean Hagen **11** Cyd Charisse **13** Donald O'Connor **14** Debbie Reynolds
song: 11 Make 'em Laugh

single 3 one **4** lone, sole **5** unwed **6** maiden **7** only one **8** bachelor, singular, solitary, spinster, wifeless **9** unmarried **10** individual, spouseless **11** husbandless

single file 8 one by one **10** Indian file, one at a time **13** in a single line **16** one behind another

single-handedly 5 alone **7** unaided **9** by oneself, on one's own **10** unassisted **11** without help

single-minded 4 firm **6** dogged **7** devoted, intense, staunch, zealous **8** resolved, tireless, untiring **9** dedicated, steadfast, tenacious **10** determined, inflexible, persistent, relentless, un-

swerving, unwavering **11** persevering, unflinching

singleness 12 bachelorhood, spinsterhood **14** unmarried state **17** single blessedness

single out 4 pick, take **6** choose, opt for, select **7** call out, extract, fix upon, pick out **8** decide on, set apart, settle on **11** distinguish

sing the praises of 4 hail, laud, tout **5** boost, cheer, exalt, extol, honor **6** praise **7** acclaim, applaud, approve, commend **8** eulogize **9** celebrate **10** compliment

singular 3 odd **4** rare **5** queer **6** choice, quaint, select, unique **7** bizarre, curious, strange, unusual **8** aberrant, abnormal, atypical, freakish, peculiar, peerless, superior, uncommon, unwonted **9** anomalous, different, eccentric, fantastic, marvelous, matchless, unequaled, unnatural, wonderful **10** noteworthy, outlandish, prodigious, remarkable, surpassing, unfamiliar **11** exceptional, uncustomary **12** unparalleled **13** extraordinary, unaccountable, unprecedented **14** unconventional **16** out-of-the-ordinary

Sinhalese
language family: 12 Indo-European
branch: 11 Indo-Iranian
group: 5 Indic
spoken in: 6 Ceylon **8** Sri Lanka

sinister 4 dark, dire, evil, foul, rank, vile **5** black **6** cursed, malign, wicked **7** adverse, fearful, hellish, ominous, unlucky **8** accursed, alarming, damnable, devilish, infernal, menacing, rascally **9** dismaying, insidious, malignant **10** despicable, detestable, diabolical, disturbing, malevolent, perfidious, villainous **11** disquieting, frightening, threatening, treacherous, unfavorable, unpromising **12** blackhearted, inauspicious, unpropitious **13** Machiavellian, reprehensible

sink 3 dig, dip, ebb, lay, sag, set **4** bore, bowl, bury, drop, fall, seep, slip, soak, tilt, wane **5** basin, drill, drive, droop, drown, gouge, lower, slant, slope, slump, stoop, yield **6** engulf, go down, lessen, plunge, reduce, shrink, worsen **7** decline, descend, give way, go to pot, go under, put down, regress, subside, succumb **8** diminish, excavate, languish, lavatory, scoop out, submerge, submerse, washbowl **9** hollow out, wash basin **10** degenerate, depreciate, go downhill, retrogress **11** deteriorate, go to the dogs

sinless 4 good, holy, pure **6** chaste **7** upright **8** innocent, spotless, virtuous **9** reputable, righteous

sinner 8 apostate, evildoer, offender **9** miscreant, misfeasor, reprobate, wrongdoer **10** backslider, malefactor, malfeasant, recidivist, trespasser **12** transgressor

Sinon
pretended to be: **13** Greek deserter
told Trojans of: **11** Trojan Horse

Sino-Tibetan
language branch: **7** Sinitic **12** Tibeto-Burman
includes: **4** Naga **5** Karen **7** Burmese, Chinese **8** Kuki-Chin, Mandarin

Sins, Seven 4 envy, lust **5** anger, pride, sloth **8** gluttony **12** covetousness

sinuosity 10 slinkiness **11** convolution, sinuousness **12** tortuousness

sinuous 6 curved, folded, volute, zigzag **7** bending, coiling, curving, twisted, winding **8** indirect, mazelike, rambling, tortuous, twisting **9** wandering **10** circuitous, convoluted, meandering, roundabout, serpentine, undulating **12** labyrinthine

sinuousness 9 sinuosity **10** slinkiness **11** convolution **12** tortuousness

Siouan
tribe: **4** Crow, Iowa **5** Ioway, Omaha, Osage, Sioux **6** Dakota, Mandan **7** Hidatsa **8** Minitari, Wazhazhe **10** Assiniboin, Gros Ventre **11** Assiniboine

Sioux *see* **6** Dakota

Sioux State
nickname of: **11** North Dakota

sip 3 lap, nip, sup **4** dram, drop **5** drink, savor, taste **6** sample **7** soupcon, swallow **10** thimbleful

siphon 4 tube **5** drain **7** draw off

siphonaptera
class: **8** hexapoda
phylum: **10** arthropoda
group: **4** flea

Sippar residents 11 Sepharvites

Siqueiros, David Alfaro
born: **6** Mexico **9** Chihuahua
artwork: **12** New Democracy **13** Echo of a Scream **14** Trial of Fascism **15** Ascent of Culture, Burial of a Worker **16** Towards the Cosmos **17** Death to the Invader **18** Polyforum Siqueiros **22** March of Humanity on Earth **24** Cuauhtemoc Against the Myth

sir *see* **6** mister

sire 4 king, lord **5** beget, breed **6** create, father **7** creator **9** originate **10** originator, progenitor

siren, Siren 4 horn, vamp **5** alarm, nymph, witch **6** sexpot **7** charmer, whistle **8** deceiver, sea nymph **9** temptress **10** seductress **11** enchantress **13** warning signal **15** bewitching woman
French: **11** femme fatale
form: **5** nymph
location: **3** sea
lured sailors by: **7** singing

Sir Gawain and the Green Knight
author: **7** unknown

character: **10** King Arthur **22** Sir Bernlak de Hautdesert
horse: **9** Gringalet

Sirian Experiments, The
author: **12** Doris Lessing

sissified 6 prissy **7** unmanly **8** womanish **10** effeminate

sissy 6 coward **8** weakling **9** fraidy-cat **10** scaredy-cat

sister 3 nun, kin, sib **5** nurse **6** female **7** sibling **8** feminist, relation, relative
nautically: **6** secure **10** strengthen
society: **8** sorority

Sister Carrie
author: **15** Theodore Dreiser
character: **11** G W Hurstwood **12** Carrie Meeber **13** Charles Drouet

Sister Woman
character in: **16** Cat on a Hot Tin Roof
author: **8** Williams

Sisyphean 4 hard **5** tough **6** uphill **7** arduous, onerous **8** toilsome **9** demanding, difficult, strenuous, wearisome **10** exhausting

Sisyphus
king of: **7** Corinth
father: **6** Aeolus
mother: **7** Enarete
brother: **9** Salmoneus
wife: **6** Merope
son: **5** Almus **7** Glaucus **8** Ornytion **10** Thersander
founded: **6** Ephyra **7** Corinth
rolled: **11** stone uphill

sit 3 lie **4** loll, meet, mind, rest, rule, stay **5** abide, chair, nurse, perch, reign, roost, squat, stand, teach, watch **6** attend, endure, gather, govern, linger, remain, reside, settle, sprawl **7** baby-sit, care for, convene, preside **8** assemble, be placed, be seated, chaperon **9** have a seat, officiate **10** deliberate **11** be in session

site 4 area, post, spot, zone **5** field, locus, place, point, scene **6** ground, locale, region, sector **7** section, setting, station **8** district, locality, location, position, province **9** territory **11** whereabouts

sit in judgment 5 judge **6** decide, settle **7** adjudge, mediate **9** arbitrate, reconcile **10** adjudicate **12** bring to terms

situ 5 place

situate 3 put, set **4** post **5** build, house, lodge, place, plant, stand **6** billet, locate, settle **7** install, station **8** ensconce, position **9** construct, establish

situation 3 fix, job **4** case, duty, post, role, seat, site, spot, work **5** berth, place, state **6** locale, office, plight, status **7** dilemma, posture, station **8** capacity, function, locality, location, position, quandary **9** condition **10** assignment, livelihood **11** predicament **13** circumstances **14** state of affairs

sit upon 5 brood, cover, hatch **8** incubate

Sivan 16 third Hebrew month

Six Characters in Search of an Author
author: **15** Luigi Pirandello

six cubits 4 reed

Six Million Dollar Man
character: **11** Dr Rudy Wells, (Col) Steve Austin **12** Oscar Goldman
cast: **9** Lee Majors **13** Martin E Brooks **15** Alan Oppenheimer, Richard Anderson
spinoff: **11** Bionic Woman

Sixty Minutes
correspondent: **9** Dan Rather, Ed Bradley **10** Andy Rooney, Steve Kroft **11** Diane Sawyer, Leslie Stahl, Mike Wallace, Morley Safer **13** Harry Reasoner

sizable 5 ample, broad, large, roomy **7** immense **8** spacious **9** capacious, good-sized

size 4 sum **4** area, bulk, mass, sort **5** array, grade, group, scope, total **6** amount, extent, spread, volume **7** arrange, bigness, content, expanse, stretch **8** capacity, classify, quantity, totality **9** aggregate, amplitude, greatness, largeness, magnitude **10** dimensions **11** measurement, proportions

sizzle 3 fry **4** hiss, spit **7** crackle, frizzle, hissing, sputter **8** splutter **10** sputtering

skate 3 nag, ray **4** skid, skim, slip **5** blade, coast, glide, horse, slide **6** rotter
female: **4** maid
genus: **4** Raja
mark: **4** cusp

skein 4 coil, hank, reel, yarn **5** twist **6** tangle, thread **9** filaments, twistings
members: **4** fowl **5** ducks, flock, geese **6** flyers

skeletal 4 bony, thin **5** gaunt **6** wasted **9** emaciated **10** cadaverous

skeleton 4 hulk **5** bones, frame, shell **9** framework
purpose: **7** support **8** protects **9** framework

Skelton, Red
real name: **21** Richard Bernard Skelton
born: **11** Vincennes IN
roles: **7** I Dood It **8** Ship Ahoy **12** Panama Hattie **16** Neptune's Daughter **17** The Fuller Brush Man **18** Clem Kadiddlehopper, Whistling in the Dark **20** Freddie the Freeloader

skeptic, sceptic 7 atheist, doubter, scoffer **8** agnostic **10** questioner, unbeliever **14** doubting Thomas

skeptical, sceptical 6 unsure **7** cynical, dubious **8** doubtful, doubting, scoffing **9** uncertain **11** incredulous, questioning, unbelieving, unconvinced **12** disbelieving **13** hypercritical

skepticism 5 doubt **7** dubiety **8** distrust, mistrust, unbelief **9** disbelief, suspicion **11** agnosticism, incredulity **12** doubtfulness **13** faithlessness

sketch 3 map **4** draw, plot, skit **5** chart, draft, graph, scene **6** depict, digest, precis, satire **7** drawing, lampoon, mark out, outline, picture, portray, summary, takeoff **8** abstract, rough out, synopsis, vignette **9** blueprint, burlesque, delineate, short play, summarize **11** preliminary **16** characterization

Sketch Book, The
author: **16** Washington Irving

sketchy 4 bare, hazy **5** brief, crude, light, rough, short, vague **6** meager, skimpy, slight **7** cursory, outline, shallow, slender **9** essential, rough-hewn, unrefined **10** incomplete, undetailed, unfinished, unpolished **11** preliminary, preparatory, provisional, superficial

skewed 5 slued **6** veered, warped **7** oblique, sheered, slanted, swerved, twisted **9** distorted

skewer 3 pin, rod **4** spit, stab **5** truss **6** pierce, skiver **7** impale **9** brochette **10** run through

skid 3 ski **4** drag, dray, skim, skip, sled, slip **5** coast, glide, skate, slide **6** runner, sledge **7** skitter **8** glissade, platform, sideslip

Skidbladnir
origin: **12** Scandinavian
ship of: **4** Frey **5** Freyr
feature: **11** collapsible

Skidmore, Owings, and Merrill
partners: **13** John Merrill Sr, Louis Skidmore **15** Nathaniel Owings
architects of: **10** Lever House (NYC) **11** AEC town site (Oak Ridge TN) **13** Banque Lambert (Brussels) **16** John Hancock Tower (Chicago) **17** Terrace Plaza Hotel (Cincinnati), US Air Force Academy (CO) **18** Mauna Kea Beach Hotel (Kamuela HI) **19** Istanbul Hilton Hotel (Turkey) **23** Beinecke Rare Book Library (Yale) **26** Chase Manhattan Bank Building (NYC) **33** American Republic Insurance Building (Des Moines IA)
world's tallest building: **10** Sears Tower (Chicago)

skiff 4 boat **6** dinghy **7** rowboat

skiing
athlete: **9** Phil Mahre **11** Bill Johnson, Cindy Nelson **13** Gustavo Thoeni, Robert Cochran **14** Marilyn Cochran, Martha Rockwell **15** Debbie Armstrong, Ingemar Stenmark, Jean Claude Killy **16** Michael Gallagher **17** Barbara Ann Cochran **20** Annemarie Proell Moser

skill 4 gift **5** craft, knack **6** acumen, tal-

ent **7** ability, cunning, faculty, knowhow, mastery, prowess **8** artistry, capacity, deftness, facility **9** adeptness, dexterity, expertise, handiness, ingenuity **10** adroitness, cleverness, competence, experience, expertness **11** proficiency **12** skillfulness **13** inventiveness

skilled 6 adroit, expert **7** trained **8** skillful **9** competent, masterful, practiced **10** proficient **12** accomplished

skilled worker 7 artisan **9** craftsman **10** technician **15** master craftsman

skillful 3 apt **4** able, deft, keen **5** adept, handy, sharp, slick **6** adroit, clever, expert, facile, gifted **7** capable, cunning, skilled, trained, veteran **8** masterly, talented **9** competent, dexterous, ingenious, masterful, practiced, qualified **10** proficient, well-versed **11** experienced **12** accomplished, professional

skim 3 fly **4** flip, ream, sail, scan, scud, skid, skip **5** coast, float, glide, skate, sweep **6** bounce, scrape **7** dip into **8** glissade **10** glance over **11** leaf through, move lightly **12** thumb through

skimp 5 pinch, stint **6** scrimp, slight **8** be frugal, be stingy, hold back, withhold **9** economize **11** cut expenses, scrape along

Skimpole, Harold
character in: **10** Bleak House
author: **7** Dickens

skimpy 5 close, scant, small, spare, tight **6** frugal, meager, modest, scanty, slight, sparse, stingy **7** miserly, scrimpy, sparing, wanting **8** exiguous, grudging, smallish, stinting **9** illiberal, niggardly, penurious, scrimping **10** inadequate, incomplete, too thrifty **11** close fisted, tightfisted **12** insufficient, parsimonious **13** pennypinching **14** inconsiderable

skin 3 fur, pod **4** bark, case, coat, flay, hide, hull, husk, peel, pelt, rind **5** shell **6** abrade, casing, fleece, jacket, scrape, sheath **7** lay bare **9** epidermis **10** complexion, integument **12** body covering, outer coating
outer layer: **9** epidermis
contains: **3** fat **4** hair, pore, root **5** nerve **6** vessel **8** oil gland **10** sweat gland
body's largest: **5** organ
sense of: **4** cold, heat, pain **5** touch **8** pressure, tickling

skinflint 5 miser **7** hoarder, niggard, scrooge **8** tightwad **10** pinchpenny **12** penny pincher

Skinner, Cornelia Otis
author of: **23** The Pleasure of His Company (with Samuel Taylor) **24** Our Hearts Were Young and Gay (with Emily Kimbrough)

skinny 4 lank, lean, thin, wiry **5** gaunt,

gawky, lanky, spare **6** slight **7** angular, scraggy, scrawny, slender, spindly **8** gangling, rawboned, shrunken, skeletal **9** emaciated

Skin of Our Teeth, The
author: **14** Thornton Wilder

skip 3 bob, cut, hop **4** flee, flit, jump, leap, miss, omit, romp, shun, trip **5** bound, caper, dodge, elude, evade **6** bounce, escape, eschew, gambol, ignore, prance, spring **7** abscond, make off, neglect **8** leap over, leave out, overlook, pass over **9** disappear, disregard, do without, play hooky, skedaddle **10** fly the coop **12** be absent from

skirmish 4 fray, tilt **5** brush, clash, joust, run-in, scrap, set-to **6** action, affray, battle, fracas, tussle **7** scuffle **8** struggle **9** encounter, firefight, scrimmage **10** engagement

skirt 3 hem, rim **4** edge, gird, kilt, maxi, mini, ring, shun **5** avoid, evade, flank, hem in, verge **6** border, bounds, circle, dirndl, fringe, girdle, margin **7** enclose, envelop **8** boundary, encircle, go around, lie along **9** crinoline, outer area, perimeter, periphery **10** circumvent, fight shy of **12** circumscribe, detour around

skittish 3 shy **4** wary **5** chary, jumpy, leery, shaky, timid **6** fitful, unsure **7** bashful, fearful, fidgety, flighty, guarded, jittery, nervous, restive **8** cautious, restless, unstable, unsteady, volatile **9** demurring, excitable, impulsive, mercurial, reluctant **10** suspicious **11** distrustful

skittles
equipment: **4** pins **6** cheese
also called: **5** closh **6** cloddy **8** rolypoly **10** Dutch bowls
tabletop version: **15** Enfield skittles

Skrymir
also: **10** Utgardloki
origin: **12** Scandinavian
form: **5** giant
took to Jotunheim: **4** Loki, Thor **7** Thialfi

Skuld 4 Norn
origin: **12** Scandinavian
form: **5** dwarf
personifies: **6** future
developed from: **5** Urdar
companions: **3** Urd **8** Verdandi

skulduggery, skullduggery 7 knavery **8** trickery **9** chicanery, deception **10** dirty trick **12** pettifoggery

skulk 4 hide, lurk **5** cower, creep, prowl, slink, sneak **9** pussyfoot

skull
contains: **5** brain

Skull place 7 Calvary **8** Golgotha

sky 5 space **9** firmament **10** atmosphere, outer space, the heavens **12** arch of heaven

goddess of: 3 Fri, Nut **5** Frigg, Frija **6** Frigga

sky blue 5 azure **8** cerulean, pale blue **9** clear blue, light blue

Sky King
character: 5 Penny **7** Clipper
cast: 10 Kirby Grant **11** Ron Haggerty **13** Gloria Winters
ranch: 11 Flying Crown
plane: 8 Songbird

skylarking 5 sport **6** antics **7** hijinks, romping **10** frolicking

skypilot 5 padre, rabbi **6** cleric, parson, priest **8** chaplain, minister **9** clergyman

skyward 2 up **6** upward **8** to the sky **10** heavenward **12** to the heavens

slab 3 wad **4** hunk, slat **5** block, board, chunk, plank, slice, wedge **10** thick slice

slack 3 lax **4** dull, easy, free, lazy, limp, slow, soft **5** baggy, loose, quiet, relax **6** easily, flabby, freely, limply, loosen, pliant, remiss, slowly, untied **7** flaccid, let up on, loosely, not busy, not firm, not taut, offhand, relaxed, slacken **8** careless, dilatory, flexible, heedless, inactive, indolent, listless, not tight, slapdash, slipshod, slothful, sluggish **9** leisurely, lethargic, negligent, slow-paced, unmindful, untighten **10** neglectful, nonchalant, permissive, slow-moving, sluggishly, unexacting, unfastened, unthinking **11** inattentive, indifferent, thoughtless, unconcerned, undemanding

slacken 4 curb, ease, flag, free, slow **5** abate, check, let go, let up, limit, loose, relax, slack **6** arrest, go limp, lessen, loosen, reduce, retard, soften, temper, weaken **7** dwindle, inhibit, release **8** decrease, diminish, keep back, mitigate, moderate, restrain, slow down, taper off **9** untighten

slacker 5 idler **6** dodger, loafer, truant **7** dallier, dawdler, goof-off, laggard, quitter, shirker **9** do-nothing, goldbrick **10** malingerer **14** good-fornothing, procrastinator

slag 5 dross **6** cinder, scoria **8** clinkers

slake 4 calm, cool, curb, ease, hush, sate **5** allay, quell, quiet, still **6** modify, quench, soothe, subdue, temper **7** appease, assuage, compose, gratify, mollify, relieve, satiate, satisfy **8** decrease, mitigate, moderate **9** alleviate **11** tranquilize **14** take the edge off

slake off 4 wane **5** abate **6** lessen, reduce, weaken **7** decline, subside **8** diminish, fade away, slack off

slam 3 hit **4** bang, bump, slap **5** crash, smack, smash, throw

slammer 3 jug, pen **4** jail, stir **5** clink **6** cooler, lockup, prison **8** big house, hoosegow **9** calaboose, jailhouse **12** penitentiary

Slammin' Sammy
nickname of: 8 Sam Snead

slander 4 soil **5** libel, smear, sully **6** defame, malign, revile, vilify **7** calumny **8** besmirch **9** falsehood **10** defamation, distortion **12** vilification **14** false statement **17** misrepresentation

Slaney, Mary *see* **10** Mary Decker

slang 4 cant, jive **5** argot, idiom, lingo **6** jargon **7** dialect

slant 4 bias, lean, list, rake, tilt, view **5** angle, color, pitch, slope **7** distort, incline, leaning **8** attitude **9** prejudice, viewpoint

slanted 4 awry **6** biased, tilted **7** colored, crooked, leaning, pitched, sloping **8** inclined **9** on an angle, on the bias **10** prejudiced

slanting 4 bias **5** alean, atilt **7** oblique, sloping **8** diagonal, glancing, inclined **10** distorting

slap 3 cut, hit **4** blow, clap, cuff, snub, swat **5** smack, whack **6** insult, rebuff, strike, wallop **9** rejection

slapdash 6 casual, sloppy **8** careless, slipshod, slovenly **9** haphazard

Slapsie Maxie
nickname of: 15 Maxie Rosenbloom

slash 3 cut, rip **4** drop, gash, mark, pare, rend, rent, slit, tear **5** lower, slice **6** reduce, stroke **8** decrease, lacerate, lowering **9** reduction **10** laceration

slate 4 list **6** ballot, tablet, ticket **10** blackboard, chalkboard

slattern 4 drab, slob, slut **5** bitch, frump **6** harlot, sloven **7** trollop

slatternly 6 frowsy, frumpy, sloppy, untidy **7** unkempt **8** slipshod, slovenly

slaughter 4 kill, slay **6** pogrom **7** butcher, destroy, killing, wipe out **8** decimate, massacre **9** bloodbath **10** annihilate, butchering, mass murder **11** exterminate

Slaughterhouse Five
author: 12 Kurt Vonnegut
character: 12 Billy Pilgrim
setting: 7 Dresden

Slav 4 Pole, Serb, Sorb, Wend **5** Croat, Czech **6** Bulgar, Slovak **7** Russian, Serbian, Slovene, Sorbian **8** Bohemian, Croatian, Moravian **9** Bulgarian, Ruthenian, Slavonian, Slovadian, Ukrainian

slave 4 prey, serf, toil **6** addict, drudge, menial, thrall, toiler, vassal, victim **7** chattel, plodder **8** bondsman **9** workhorse **11** bond servant

slaver 5 drool **6** drivel **7** slobber

slavery 4 toil **5** grind, labor, sweat **6** strain **7** bondage, serfdom, travail **8** drudgery, struggle **9** captivity, treadmill, vassalage **11** enslavement, impressment, subjugation **12** enthrallment

Slavic
language family: 12 Indo-European
group: 11 Balto-Slavic
subgroup: 12 Old Bulgarian **13** Eastern Slavic, Western Slavic **14** Southern Slavic **15** Old Church Slavic

slavish 5 exact **6** strict **7** literal, servile **9** imitative, slavelike **10** derivative, obsequious, submissive, unoriginal **11** subservient **13** unimaginative

slay 4 do in, kill **6** murder **7** destroy, execute **8** massacre **9** slaughter **10** annihilate

slayer 6 hit man, killer **7** butcher **8** assassin, murderer **11** executioner **12** exterminator

slaying 6 murder **7** killing **8** homicide **9** execution

sleazy 5 cheap, tacky **6** flimsy, shabby, shoddy, trashy, vulgar **7** schlock **13** insubstantial

sleek 4 oily **5** shiny, silky, slick, suave **6** glossy, satiny, smooth **7** fawning, velvety **8** lustrous, unctuous **12** ingratiating

sleep 3 nap **4** doze, rest **5** death, peace **6** repose, snooze **7** slumber
god of: 6 Hypnos, Hypnus, Somnus

sleeping 6 asleep, dozing **7** dormant, napping, resting **8** snoozing **9** quiescent, somnolent **11** hibernating **19** in the arms of Morpheus

Sleeping Beauty, The
composer: 11 Tchaikovsky

sleeping car (railroad)
invented by: 7 Pullman

sleeping infants
goddess of: 6 Cunina

sleeping place 3 bed, cot **4** bunk **5** berth **6** pallet **7** bedroom **9** dormitory **10** bedchamber

sleepless 5 alert **7** wakeful **8** restless, watchful **9** insomniac, wide awake **11** industrious

sleeplessness 8 insomnia **9** alertness, attention **11** wakefulness **12** restlessness

sleep lightly 3 nap, nod **4** doze **6** catnap, snooze **15** catch forty winks

sleepy 4 dull **5** quiet, tired, weary **6** drowsy **8** fatigued, inactive **9** exhausted

sleigh 4 dray, sled **6** cutter, sledge, troika **8** transport

Sleipnir
origin: 12 Scandinavian
horse of: 4 Odin **5** Othin
legs: 5 eight

slender 4 lean, poor, slim, thin, weak **5** faint, scant, small, spare **6** feeble, little, meager, narrow, remote, skinny, slight **7** willowy **8** delicate

Slender
character in: 22 The Merry Wives of Windsor
author: 11 Shakespeare

Sleuth
director: 17 Joseph L Mankiewicz
based on play by: 14 Anthony Shaffer
cast: 12 Michael Caine 15 Laurence Olivier

slew 3 lot, ton 4 gang, heap, load, lots, peck, pile, raft 5 batch, did in 6 killed 8 murdered 12 assassinated

Slezak, Walter
born: 6 Vienna 7 Austria
father: 9 Leo Slezak
roles: 5 Fanny 8 Lifeboat 11 Dr Coppelius

slice 3 cut 4 pare 5 carve, piece, sever, shave 6 cut off, divide 7 portion, section, segment, whittle 8 separate 9 dismember

slick 3 sly 4 coat, film, foxy, oily, scum, waxy, wily 5 sharp, shiny, sleek 6 clever, glassy, glossy, greasy, satiny, smooth, tricky 7 coating, cunning 8 slippery 10 make glossy 11 fast-talking 13 smooth-talking

slicker 8 raincoat 9 sou'wester 10 mackintosh, waterproof

slide 4 fall, pass, ramp, skid, slip, veer 5 chute, coast, glide, lapse, slope 7 slither 8 sideslip 11 diapositive 12 transparency

slide by 4 go by 5 lapse 6 elapse, roll by, slip by 7 glide by 8 slip away

slight 3 cut 4 lean, slap, slim, snub, thin, tiny 5 frail, small, spare 6 insult, little, modest, rebuff 7 fragile, limited, slender 8 moderate 10 incivility, negligible, restricted 11 unimportant 13 imperceptible, inappreciable, infinitesimal

slight amount 3 bit 4 dash, drop 5 pinch, touch, trace 6 little 7 smidgen, smidgin, soupcon 8 smidgeon 9 little bit 10 smattering

slightly 6 feebly, rarely 8 meagerly, scantily, scarcely, somewhat 10 negligibly 13 superficially 15 insignificantly

slim 4 lean, thin 5 faint, small 6 meager, remote, skinny, slight, svelte 7 distant, slender, thready, willowy 10 negligible

slime 3 mud 4 mire, muck, ooze 6 sludge

slimy 4 foul, vile 5 gummy, mucky, nasty 6 creepy, putrid, sticky 7 viscous 9 glutinous, loathsome, obnoxious, offensive, repulsive

sling 3 net 4 cast 5 fling, throw 9 slingshot 10 arm support

Slingin' Sammy
nickname of: 10 Sammy Baugh

slingshot 5 sling 8 catapult

slink 4 slip 5 creep, prowl, skulk, sneak, steal 6 tiptoe

slip 3 put 4 dock, drop, fail, fall, leak, pass, sink, skid 5 berth, error, glide, lapse, scrap, shoot, shred, slide, sneak, sprig, steal, strip 6 escape, sprout, ticket, worsen 7 blunder, chemise, cutting, decline, faux pas, receipt, sapling, voucher 9 petticoat, stripling, youngling, youngster 10 be revealed, get clear of, imprudence, underdress 12 indiscretion

slip away 4 go by 5 lapse 6 elapse, escape 7 run away, slide by 8 creep off 9 tiptoe off

slip by 4 go by, pass 5 lapse 6 elapse, pass by, roll by 7 glide by, slide by

slip of the tongue, a
Latin: 13 lapsus linguae

slipper 4 mule, shoe 5 scuff 6 sandal

slippery 4 foxy, oily, waxy, wily 5 slick, soapy 6 crafty, glassy, greasy, shifty, smooth, sneaky, tricky 7 devious 9 deceitful 10 contriving, unreliable 11 treacherous 13 untrustworthy

slipshod 3 lax 5 loose, messy 6 casual, sloppy, untidy 7 offhand 8 careless, slovenly 11 thoughtless

slip-up 4 flub, goof 5 botch, error, gaffe, lapse 6 boo-boo, bungle, foul-up, mess-up, miscue 7 blooper, blunder, clinker, faux pas, mistake, screw-up 9 oversight

slit 3 cut 4 gash 5 crack, slash 7 crevice, fissure 8 incision

slither 5 glide, slide 25 move with a side-to-side motion

sliver 5 crumb, shred, slice, snick 6 morsel 8 splinter

slivovitz
type: 6 brandy 7 liqueur
origin: 10 Yugoslavia
flavor: 4 plum

Sloan, John F
born: 11 Lock Haven PA
artwork: 12 McSorley's Bar 14 Wake of the Ferry 18 Hairdresser's Window 25 Backyards Greenwich Village

slob 6 sloven 8 slattern

slobber 4 slop 5 drool 6 drivel, slaver 7 dribble, sputter 8 salivate, splutter

sloe gin
type: 7 liqueur
flavor: 9 sloe berry 15 blackthorn berry
drink: 11 Sloe Gin Fizz
with bourbon: 9 Black Hawk
with rum: 11 Shark's Tooth
with vermouth: 10 Blackthorn

slogan 5 motto 6 byword 9 battle cry, catchword, watchword

sloop 4 boat, brig, ship 5 smack 8 sailboat, schooner

slop 3 mud 4 mire, muck, ooze 5 filth, slosh, slush, spill, swash, swill, waste 6 refuse, sludge, splash 7 garbage, spatter 8 splatter

Slop, Dr
character in: 14 Tristram Shandy
author: 6 Sterne

slope 3 tip 4 bank, bend, lean, tilt 5 angle, pitch, slant 7 descent, incline 9 downgrade 11 inclination

sloping 5 alean, steep 6 aslant 7 leaning, oblique, tilting 8 diagonal, inclined, on a slant, slanting 9 slantways 11 declivitous

sloppiness 5 chaos, mix-up, upset 6 jumble 7 clutter 8 disarray, disorder, shambles 9 messiness 10 disharmony, untidiness 12 dishevelment 14 disarrangement 15 disorganization

sloppy 3 wet 5 dirty, messy, muddy 6 marshy, sloshy, slushy, sodden, soiled, swampy, untidy, watery 7 unclean 10 disorderly

sloppy person 4 slob 6 sloven

slosh 3 lap 4 drop, mire, stir 5 slush, spill, swash 6 splash 8 flounder

slot 3 gap 4 slit 5 crack, niche, notch
machine: 14 one-armed bandit

sloth 6 phlegm, torpor 7 languor 8 idleness, laziness, lethargy 9 indolence, lassitude, torpidity 12 listlessness, sluggishness 13 do-nothingness, shiftlessness

slothful 3 lax 4 idle, lazy 5 inert 6 drowsy, otiose, supine, torpid 8 indolent, listless, sluggish 9 do-nothing, lethargic, negligent, shiftless 10 sluggardly 11 unambitious

slouch 4 bend 5 droop, hunch, idler, slump, stoop 6 loafer 7 laggard, shirker, slacker 8 sluggard 9 goldbrick, lazybones

Slovakia
formerly part of: 14 Czechoslovakia
capital/largest city: 10 Bratislava
others: 6 Kosice
head of state: 9 president
government: 8 republic
monetary unit: 5 crown 6 koruna
mountain: 7 Sudetes 8 Low Tatra 9 High Tatra, Slovak Ore 10 Carpathian, Nizke Tatry 11 Visoke Tatry 15 White Carpathian
river: 2 Uh 3 Vah 4 Hron 5 Nitra, Slana 6 Danube, Hornad, Ondava, Poprad 7 Laborec 8 Latorica
people: 5 Czech 6 Slavik, Slovak 7 Hungarian
language: 6 Slavik, Slovak
religion: 9 Christian 13 Roman Catholic

Slovenia
capital/largest city: 9 Ljubljana
others: 5 Celje, Koper, Kranj 7 Maribor
head of state: 9 president
government: 8 republic
monetary unit: 5 tolar
river: 4 Sava 5 Drava
sea: 8 Adriatic
people: 8 Slovenes
language: 7 Slovene
religion: 13 Roman Catholic

slovenly 5 dirty, dowdy, messy 6

frowzy, sloppy, untidy **7** unclean, unkempt **8** careless, slapdash, slipshod **10** disorderly, slatternly **11** indifferent, unconcerned

slow 3 dim, off **4** curb, dull, dumb, flag, late, long **5** brake, check, dense, heavy, loath, quiet **6** averse, boring, falter, hinder, hold up, impede, obtuse, retard, stupid, torpid **7** belated, delayed, laggard, lumpish, not busy, overdue, tedious, unhasty **8** backward, cautious, dawdling, dilatory, dragging, drawn out, extended, hesitant, inactive, obstruct, sluggish, tarrying **9** dim-witted, leisurely, lingering, ponderous, prolonged, reluctant, snaillike, unhurried **10** behind time, decelerate, deliberate, dull-witted, indisposed, protracted, unexciting, unpunctual

slowdown 4 curb, flag **5** brake, delay, letup, slump **6** ease-up, falter, hinder, impede, lessen, retard, slow-up **7** decline, fall off, letdown, setback, slowing, subside **8** diminish, downturn, flagging **9** grind down **10** decelerate, slackening, stagnation **11** reduce speed, retardation **12** deceleration

slow-moving 4 poky **5** pokey **6** idling **8** crawling, creeping, dawdling, sluggish **9** leisurely, snaillike **10** turtlelike **12** tortoiselike
  creature: 4 slug **5** loris, sloth, snail **6** turtle **8** tortoise

slowness 6 tedium **8** dullness **9** torpidity **10** snail's pace **12** backwardness, sluggishness

slow-paced 4 easy **7** gradual, laggard **8** sluggish **9** leisurely, lethargic, unhurried **10** deliberate

slowpoke 4 slug **5** idler, snail **7** dallier, dawdler, laggard, lie-abed, plodder **8** lingerer, slugabed, tortoise **9** saunterer, straggler **11** foot-dragger

slow to learn 4 dull **5** dense, inapt **7** stupid **8** retarded **10** slow-witted

slow up 4 stem **5** delay **6** detain, hinder, impede, retard **8** slow down

slow-witted 4 dull **5** dense **7** doltish, idiotic, moronic **8** backward, retarded **9** imbecilic

sludge 3 mud **4** mire, muck, ooze, slop **5** dregs, slime, slush **8** sediment

slug 3 bat, hit **4** bash, belt, sock **5** baste, clout, pound, punch, smite, thump, whack, whale **6** batter, strike, wallop **7** clobber **8** lambaste

sluggard 4 lazy **5** drone, idler, sloth, snail **6** loafer, truant, turtle **7** dawdler, laggard **8** loiterer, slothful, slowpoke, tortoise **9** do-nothing, lazybones **11** couch potato **12** lounge lizard **13** stick-in-the-mud

sluggish 4 lazy, slow **5** inert **6** torpid **7** languid **8** inactive, indolent, lifeless, listless, slothful **9** leisurely, lethargic,

soporific, unhurried **10** phlegmatic, protracted, spiritless

sluggishness 6 torpor **7** inertia **8** lethargy, slowness **9** lassitude **10** inactivity **12** listlessness

slum
  Portuguese: 6 favela

slumber 3 nap **4** doze **5** sleep **6** snooze **8** vegetate **9** hibernate **10** be inactive, lie dormant

slump 3 dip, sag **4** drop, fall, slip **5** droop, lapse **6** plunge, slouch, tumble **7** decline, give way, reverse, setback **8** collapse

slur 3 cut, dig **4** mark, skip, spot **5** smear, stain, sully, taint **6** defame, ignore, insult, malign, mumble, mutter, slight **7** affront, blacken, blemish, let pass **8** mumbling, overlook, pass over **9** disregard, gloss over, muttering **11** run together

slush 4 slop **6** bathos **9** soppiness **11** mawkishness, melting snow **14** sentimentalism, sentimentality

slushiness 5 slush **10** sponginess **11** mawkishness **14** sentimentalism, sentimentality

slut 4 doxy, jade **5** bimbo, frump, hussy, tramp, wench, whore **6** floozy, harlot, sloven, wanton **7** jezebel, trollop **8** slattern, strumpet **10** prostitute

sly 4 foxy, wily **6** artful, covert, crafty, secret, shrewd, sneaky, tricky **7** cunning, furtive, playful, private **8** stealthy **9** conniving **11** dissembling, mischievous **12** confidential

Slye, Leonard
  real name of: 9 Roy Rogers

slyness 5 craft **7** cunning, stealth **8** archness, foxiness, subtlety, wiliness **10** artfulness, craftiness, shrewdness, trickiness **11** furtiveness **15** underhandedness

smack 3 bit, hit, rap **4** blow, buss, clap, cuff, dash, hint, kiss, slap **5** savor, smell, smite, spank, taste, tinge, touch, trace, whack **6** buffet, flavor **7** suggest

small 4 mean, tiny, weak **5** faint, minor, petty, scant **6** feeble, lesser, little, meager, modest, narrow, petite, slight **7** bigoted, fragile, ignoble, trivial **8** not great, trifling **10** diminutive, provincial, undersized **11** of no account, opinionated, superficial, unimportant **13** insignificant **15** inconsequential

Small, Lennie
  character in: 12 Of Mice and Men
  author: 9 Steinbeck

small details
  Latin: 8 minutiae

smaller 4 less **5** lower **6** lesser, tinier **7** dinkier, littler, pettier, reduced, shorter **8** inferior

smallest 5 least **6** lowest **7** tiniest **8** dinkiest, pettiest, shortest **9** slightest

Small House at Allington, The
  author: 15 Anthony Trollope

small intestine
  part of: 15 digestive system
  lined with: 5 villi

small-minded 4 mean **5** petty **6** narrow **7** bigoted **9** parochial **10** prejudiced **12** mean-spirited

smallness 8 meanness, tininess **9** pettiness **10** meagerness, triviality **12** dwarfishness **14** insignificance **18** inconsequentiality

small piece 3 bit, dab **4** chip, drop, snip **5** crumb, grain, piece, pinch, scrap, shred, speck **6** dollop, morsel **7** granule, smidgen, smidgin **8** fragment, particle, smidgeon

small quantity 3 bit, dab, few **5** touch **7** smidgen, smidgin, soupcon **8** smidgeon **9** little bit

small round window
  French: 11 oeil-de-boeuf

small spot 3 dab, dot **5** fleck, speck

small talk 6 banter, gossip **7** chatter, prattle **8** chitchat, idle talk, repartee **9** bavardage, prattling **12** tittle-tattle

smart 4 ache, burn, chic, hurt, keen, neat, trim **5** brash, brisk, quick, sassy, sharp, sting, wince, witty **6** astute, blench, brainy, bright, clever, flinch, modish, shrewd, suffer **7** elegant, stylish **8** feel pain, vigorous **9** be painful, energetic **10** smart-aleck **11** fashionable, intelligent

smart aleck 6 smarty **7** show-off, windbag, wiseass, wise guy **8** blowhard, braggart, saucebox, wiseacre **9** know-it-all **11** smarty-pants **12** grand stander **13** exhibitionist

smarten up 7 dress up, improve **8** beautify, spruce up

smartness 6 acumen, wisdom **8** keenness, sagacity **9** acuteness **10** astuteness, cleverness, perception, shrewdness **12** intelligence, perspicacity

smash 3 hit **4** bang, bash, beat, blow **5** break, clout, crack, crash, crush **6** batter, strike, winner **7** clobber, crack-up, destroy, shatter, success, triumph **8** accident, demolish, splinter **9** collision, sensation **12** disintegrate

smash against 4 beat, lash **5** crash, pound, smite **6** batter, buffet **7** break on

smashed 5 drunk **6** soused, wasted, zapped, zonked **7** crashed, crushed **8** squashed **9** plastered, shattered **10** inebriated **11** intoxicated **12** under the influence **20** three sheets to the wind

smashing 5 great, super **6** superb **8** fabulous, terrific **9** fantastic, marvelous, wonderful **10** stupendous **11** magnificent, sensational **13** extraordinary

smashup 5 crash, wreck **7** crackup **8** accident **9** collision **12** fender bender

smattering 3 bit, dab 4 dash, drop 5 scrap 7 smidgen, smidgin, snippet 8 smidgeon 10 sprinkling

smear 3 mar, rub 4 blur, coat, daub, soil 5 cover, lay on, libel, stain 6 blotch, injure, malign, smirch, smudge, spread, streak 7 blacken, blemish, degrade, slander, splotch, tarnish 8 besmirch, besmudge 9 denigrate 10 accusation, obliterate

smell 4 feel, nose, odor, reek 5 aroma, fetor, scent, sense, sniff, stink 6 detect, stench 7 bouquet, perfume, suspect 8 perceive 9 emanation, fragrance, get wind of

smelly 4 rank 5 fetid 6 putrid 7 noisome, odorous, reeking 8 stinking 10 malodorous

Smerdyakov
  character in: 20 The Brothers Karamazov
  author: 10 Dostoevsky

Smetana, Bedrich
  born: 7 Bohemia 8 Litomysl 11 Leitomischl 14 Czechoslovakia
  composer of: 7 Ma Vlast 9 My Country 10 From My Life 11 Czech Dances 12 The Two Widows 16 The Bartered Bride

smidgen, smidgin, smidgeon 3 bit, dab 4 mite, snip 5 crumb, pinch, scrap, shred, speck, trace 6 dollop, morsel

Smike
  character in: 16 Nicholas Nickleby
  author: 7 Dickens

smile 4 beam, grin 5 favor, shine, smirk 6 simper

Smiles of a Summer Night
  director: 13 Ingmar Bergman
  cast: 11 Eva Dahlbeck 13 Ulla Jacobsson 15 Margit Carlquist 16 Harriet Andersson
  remade as: 17 A Little Night Music

Smiley's People
  author: 11 John Le Carre

Smintheus
  epithet of: 6 Apollo

smirch 4 blot, mark, soil, spot 5 dirty, smear, stain, sully, taint 6 blotch, damage, smudge, stigma 7 begrime, blacken, blemish, slander, tarnish 8 besmirch, besmudge, dishonor 9 discredit

smirk 4 grin, leer 5 sneer 6 simper 7 grimace

Smirke, Sir Robert
  architect of: 12 King's College (U of London) 13 British Museum (London) 19 Covent Garden Theater (London)
  style: 12 Greek Revival

smite 3 hit 4 swat 5 knock, smack, whack 6 enamor, strike, wallop 7 clobber

Smith, Adam
  author of: 18 The Wealth of Nations

Smith, Al
  creator/artist of: 11 Mutt and Jeff

Smith, Betty
  author of: 20 A Tree Grows in Brooklyn

Smith, Charles Aaron
  nickname: 5 Bubba
  sport: 8 football
  team: 14 Baltimore Colts

Smith, David
  born: 8 Decatur IN
  artwork: 3 Zig 4 Cubi 6 Oculus 8 Agricola, Main View, Sentinel, Star Cage 9 Australia, Royal Bird, Tank Totem 10 The Banquet 12 Detroit Queen 15 Lectern Sentinel 17 Medals for Dishonor 20 Hudson River Landscape 23 Song of an Irish Blacksmith

Smith, Harriet
  character in: 4 Emma
  author: 6 Austen

Smith, Lillian
  author: 12 Strange Fruit

Smith, Maggie
  born: 6 Ilford 7 England
  husband: 14 Robert Stephens
  roles: 7 Othello 15 California Suite, The Pumpkin Eater 17 Travels with My Aunt 24 The Prime of Miss Jean Brodie (Oscar)

Smith, Winston
  character in: 18 Nineteen Eighty-Four
  author: 6 Orwell

smithereen 3 bit 4 atom 5 crumb, shard 8 fragment, particle 9 scintilla

Smithson, James
  field: 9 chemistry
  nationality: 7 British
  discovered: 11 smithsonite 13 zinc carbonite
  funded: 22 Smithsonian Institution

smitten 8 enamored 9 bewitched 10 enraptured, infatuated

smoke 4 draw, fume, pipe, puff, reek, suck 5 cigar, fumes 6 billow, inhale 7 light up, smolder 9 cigarette, have a drag

Smoke
  author: 12 Ivan Turgenev
  character: 5 Irina 7 Potugin 13 Tanya Shestoff 16 General Ratmiroff, Grigory Litvinoff 18 Kapitolina Shestoff

smoke screen 4 ruse 5 cover, dodge, front 6 screen 9 deception 10 camouflage, subterfuge

smoky 5 dingy, grimy, sooty 6 fuming, smudgy 7 reeking 10 smoldering

smolder 4 burn, fume, rage 5 smoke 6 seethe

Smollett, Tobias George
  author of: 14 (The Expedition of) Humphry Clinker, Roderick Random 15 Peregrine Pickle

smooch 3 pet 4 buss, kiss, neck 5 smack, spoon 7 make out

smooth 4 calm, ease, easy, even, flat, glib, help, mild, open, pave 5 allay, level, silky, sleek, suave 6 facile, mellow, placid, polish, refine, serene, soften, soothe, steady 7 appease, assuage, flatten, mollify, orderly, perfect, prepare, velvety 8 civilize, composed, make even, mitigate, peaceful, pleasant 9 collected, cultivate, easygoing, make level 10 facilitate, flattering, harmonious, methodical, uneventful 11 well-ordered 12 ingratiating 13 self-possessed, well-regulated

smoothness 8 evenness, fineness, flatness 9 silkiness, sleekness

smooth the feathers 4 calm 6 pacify, soothe 7 appease, assuage, mollify, placate 10 conciliate

smooth-tongued 4 glib 5 suave 6 fluent 8 unctuous 10 flattering 11 fast-talking 12 hypocritical, ingratiating

smother 4 hide, mask, wrap 5 choke, quash, snuff 6 deaden, quench, shower 7 conceal 8 keep down, strangle, suppress, surround 9 choke back, envelop in, suffocate 10 asphyxiate, extinguish

Smothers Brothers Comedy Hour, The
  regulars: 10 Don Novello, Pat Paulsen 11 Bob Einstein, Leigh French, Steve Martin, Tom Smothers 12 Betty Aberlin, Dick Smothers, John Hartford, Nino Senporty, Spencer Quinn 13 Mason Williams 14 Jennifer Warren, Sally Struthers 16 Anita Kerr Singers 17 Jimmy Joyce Singers 18 Louis DaPron Dancers 19 Marty Paich Orchestra 20 Denny Vaughn Orchestra, Ron Poindexter Dancers 21 Nelson Riddle Orchestra

smudge 4 blot, mark, soil, spot 5 dirty, smear, stain 6 smutch

smudgy 5 dirty, messy 6 filthy, grubby, smeary 7 sullied 8 befouled, unwashed 9 besmeared

smug 8 superior, virtuous 10 complacent 13 self-righteous, self-satisfied

smuggle 5 sneak 15 export illegally, import illegally

smuggled goods 10 contraband 14 illegal exports, illegal imports 18 prohibited articles

smuggler 6 runner 9 gunrunner, rumrunner 10 bootlegger 13 contrabandist

smugness 7 egotism 9 immodesty 11 superiority 12 virtuousness 16 self-satisfaction 17 self-righteousness

smut 4 dirt, porn, soot 5 filth, grime 6 smudge 9 obscenity, scatology 11 pornography

smutty 4 lewd 5 dirty, grimy, sooty 6

filthy, soiled, vulgar **7** obscene **8** indecent **12** pornographic

Smyrna *see* **6** Myrrha

Smythe, Reginald
  creator/artist of: 8 Andy Capp

snack 3 eat, tea **4** bite, nosh **5** munch **6** nibble, tidbit **7** take tea **8** lap lunch, munchies, nibblies, pick-me-up, snackies **9** collation, crunchies, elevenses **10** finger food, light lunch **11** casse-croute, coffee break, light repast, refreshment

snag 3 bar, rip **4** grab, stub, tear **5** block, catch, hitch, stump **7** barrier **8** obstacle **9** hindrance **10** difficulty, impediment, projection, protrusion **11** encumbrance, obstruction **14** stumbling block

snail
  French: 8 escargot

snake 5 sneak, viper **7** reptile, serpent, traitor **8** ophidian **9** reptilian
  combining form: 4 ophi **5** ophio, ophis **6** herpes **7** herpeto
  expert: 13 herpetologist
  fear of: 13 herpetophobia
  genus: 7 Ophidia
  kind: 3 asp, boa, sea **4** file, habu, wart, whip **5** aboma, adder, cobra, coral, krait, mamba, tiger, viper **6** bongar, elapid, garter, gopher, python, taipan **7** rattler, sunbeam **8** anaconda, cerastes, moccasin, pit viper, ringhals **9** boomslang, colubrina, mole viper, puff adder **10** black mamba, bushmaster, copperhead, fer-de-lance, sidewinder **11** cottonmouth, diamond back, Gaboon viper, rattlesnake **12** slender blind **13** elephant-trunk, water moccasin **14** boa constrictor
  shedding: 7 ecdysis **8** moulting
  skin: 6 exuvia
  snake killer: 8 mongoose

Snake *see* **8** Shoshone

Snake, the
  nickname of: 10 Ken Stabler

Snake Pit, The
  author: 12 Mary Jane Ward, Sigrid Undset

snap 3 nip, pop **4** bark, bite, grab, lock, yelp **5** break, catch, cinch, clasp, click, close, crack, growl, hasty, latch, quick, snarl, spell **6** breeze, period, secure, snatch, sudden **8** careless, fastener, fracture **9** impulsive **11** thoughtless

snapdragon 11 Antirrhinum
  varieties: 4 wild **5** dwarf **6** common, garden, lesser **7** spurred **8** withered

snappish 4 edgy **5** cross, huffy, surly, testy **6** crabby, cranky, shirty, touchy **7** grouchy, huffish, peevish, waspish **8** captious, petulant **9** irascible, irritable, querulous **10** ill-humored, ill-natured, out of sorts **11** hot-tempered

12 cantankerous **13** quick-tempered, short-tempered

snappy 4 fast, tony **5** hasty, quick, rapid, ritzy, sharp, smart, swank, swift, swish **6** classy, dapper, jaunty, speedy, spiffy **7** stylish **12** lickety-split

snare 3 net **4** bait, hook, lure, ruse, trap **5** catch, decoy, noose, seize, trick **6** entrap **7** capture, ensnare, pitfall **9** deception **12** entanglement

snarl 3 mat **4** bark, clog, kink, knot, mess, snap **5** chaos, growl, ravel, twist **6** hinder, impede, jumble, muddle, tangle **7** confuse, lash out **8** disorder, entangle **9** confusion

snatch 3 bit, nab **4** grab, part, pull, take **5** catch, grasp, piece, pluck, seize, wrest **7** snippet **8** fragment

Snead, Sam
  nickname: 12 Slammin' Sammy
  sport: 4 golf
  won: 7 Masters

sneak 3 sly **4** slip **5** creep, knave, rogue, scamp, steal **6** lurker, rascal, secret, spirit **7** bounder, furtive, skulker, slinker, smuggle **8** scalawag, surprise **9** miscreant, scoundrel, secretive, underhand **11** rapscallion **13** surreptitious

sneak attack 4 raid **6** ambush **7** assault **9** ambuscade, incursion

sneakers
  brands: 4 Avia, Fila, Keds, Nike, Puma **5** Asics **6** Adidas, Reebok **7** Saucony **10** New Balance

sneak off 5 elope **6** decamp **7** abscond **9** steal away

sneaky 3 sly **4** mean **7** devious, furtive, vicious **9** malicious, secretive, underhand **10** traitorous **11** treacherous

sneer 4 jeer, leer, mock **5** scoff, scorn, smirk **6** deride, rebuff **7** disdain **8** belittle, ridicule

sneer at 5 knock, scorn **6** deride, malign **7** disdain, put down, run down **8** pooh-pooh **16** cast aspersions on

Sneerwell, Lady
  character in: 19 The School for Scandal
  author: 8 Sheridan

snicker 5 snort **6** cackle, giggle, simper, titter **7** snigger

snide 5 nasty **7** mocking **8** scoffing **9** malicious, sarcastic **11** insinuating **12** contemptuous

Snider, Edwin
  nickname: 4 Duke
  sport: 8 baseball
  position: 7 fielder
  team: 15 Brooklyn Dodgers

sniff 4 jeer, mock, odor **5** aroma, scoff, smell, snort, snuff, whiff **6** snivel **7** disdain, sniffle, snuffle **9** disparage

snip 3 bit, bob, cut, lop **4** brat, clip, crop, punk, snap, trim **5** clack, click,

piece, prune, scrap, shear, twerp **6** sample, shrimp, swatch **7** cutting **8** fragment

snippy 4 curt, rude **5** sassy, saucy, short **6** cheeky, snotty **7** brusque **8** flippant, impudent, insolent, snippety **11** ill-mannered, impertinent, smart-alecky

snivel 3 cry **5** sniff, whine **6** boohoo **7** sniffle **8** complain

sniveler 6 coward, whiner **7** crybaby **10** complainer

snob 7 elitist **13** social climber

snobbish 4 vain **6** snooty, snotty **7** haughty, high-hat, stuck-up **8** arrogant, superior **10** disdainful **11** overbearing, patronizing, pretentious **13** condescending

Snodgrass
  character in: 14 Pickwick Papers
  author: 7 Dickens

snoop 3 pry **7** meddler, Paul Pry **8** busybody **10** Nosy Parker **12** eavesdropper

Snoopy 6 beagle
  brother: 5 Spike
  creator: 6 Schulz
  friend: 9 Woodstock
  master: 12 Charlie Brown

snooze 3 nap **4** doze **5** sleep **6** catnap, drowse, siesta **7** slumber **10** forty winks

Snopes family
  characters in: 9 The Hamlet
  members: 2 Ab **4** Flem, Mink **5** Isaac
  author: 8 Faulkner

snort 4 blow, gasp, huff, jeer, pant, puff, rage **5** blast, grunt, scoff, sneer, storm

snout 3 neb **4** beak, bill, nose **5** snoot, spout **6** muzzle, nozzle **9** proboscis

Snow, C P (Charles Percy Snow, Lord Snow)
  author of: 9 The New Men **10** Last Things, The Masters **14** A Coat of Varnish **16** Corridors of Power **20** Strangers and Brothers

snowfall 4 firn, neve **6** flurry **8** blizzard
  Scottish: 6 onding

Snow Leopard, The
  author: 16 Peter Matthiessen

Snow Queen, The
  author: 21 Hans Christian Andersen

Snows of Kilimanjaro, The
  author: 15 Ernest Hemingway

snow-white 4 pure **5** snowy **9** lily-white, pure white **11** white as snow

Snow White and the Seven Dwarfs
  character: 3 Doc **5** Dopey, Happy, Queen **6** Grumpy, Sleepy, Sneezy, mirror **7** Bashful **14** Prince Charming

snowy 4 pure **5** white **7** nievous **8** pristine, spotless **9** blizzardy

snub 3 cut **5** blunt, check, scorn, short

dain **9** retrousse **11** repudiation **12** cold shoulder **16** turn up one's nose at **19** give the cold shoulder

snuff 5 scent, smell, sniff, whiff **7** sniffle, snuffle

snuff out 5 crush **8** suppress **10** extinguish, put an end to

snug 4 cozy, neat, safe **5** close, tight **6** secure **7** compact **8** tranquil **9** sheltered, skin-tight **11** comfortable **12** close-fitting, tight-fitting **13** well-organized

snuggle 3 hug **4** nest **6** cuddle, curl up, enfold, nestle, nuzzle

so
Latin: **3** sic

soak 3 wet **4** seep **5** bathe, enter, steep **6** absorb, drench, sink in, take in, take up **7** immerse, pervade **8** permeate, saturate **9** penetrate

soaked 5 soggy **6** sodden, soused **7** sopping **8** drenched **9** saturated **11** waterlogged, wringing wet

soak up 4 blot **6** absorb, take up **8** sponge up

soak up warmth 4 bask **11** warm oneself **12** toast oneself

Soames Forsyte
character in: **14** The Forsyte Saga
author: **10** Galsworthy

Soap
character: **5** Major **6** Benson **9** Billy Tate **10** Eunice Tate **11** Chester Tate, Corrine Tate, Danny Dallas, Jessica Tate, Jodie Dallas **12** Burt Campbell **18** Mary Dallas Campbell
cast: **7** Ted Wass **9** Jimmy Baio **11** Diana Canova **12** Billy Crystal, Cathryn Damon, Jennifer Salt, Robert Mandan **14** Arthur Peterson **15** Richard Mulligan, Robert Guillaume **16** Katherine Helmond

soar 3 fly **4** rise, wing **5** climb, float, glide, mount, tower **8** take wing

soave
music: **6** gentle

sob 3 cry **4** howl, wail, weep **6** lament, plaint, snivel **7** blubber, whimper

so be it 4 amen **7** let it be **9** let it be so

sober 3 dry, sad **4** cool, drab, dull, grim, sane **5** grave, sound, staid **6** dreary, sedate, solemn, somber, steady **7** joyless, prudent, serious, subdued **8** moderate, not drunk, rational **9** judicious, realistic, sorrowful, temperate **10** abstemious **11** level-headed **13** dispassionate

So Big
author: **10** Edna Ferber

sobriety 10 abstention, abstinence, continence, temperance **13** nonindulgence **14** abstemiousness

sobriquet 7 epithet, pet name **8** nickname **11** appellation

so-called
French: **9** soi-disant

soccer
athlete: **4** Pele **11** Johan Cruyff
players/team: **6** eleven
position: **6** goalie **7** forward **8** fullback, halfback **10** goalkeeper
championship: **8** World Cup **11** European Cup, National Cup **13** Cup Winner's Cup
violation: **5** hands **7** hacking, offside **11** obstructing
gaining control of ball: **4** trap

sociable 6 social **7** affable, cordial **8** friendly, gracious, outgoing **9** agreeable, congenial, convivial **10** gregarious, neighborly **11** extroverted **13** companionable

social 2 in **5** smart **7** stylish **8** friendly, pleasant, sociable **9** agreeable **10** gregarious, neighborly **11** cooperative, fashionable **14** interdependent

Social Contract, The
author: **19** Jean-Jacques Rousseau

social order
goddess of: **4** Hour **5** Horae

society 4 body, club **5** elite, group **6** circle, gentry, league **7** mankind **8** alliance, humanity, nobility **9** community, humankind **10** blue bloods **11** aristocracy, association, high society, social order **12** organization **14** the four hundred **16** the general public

sociologist
American: **4** Mead, Park, Ward **5** Coser, Gerth, Mills, Small, Wirth **6** Bendix, Cooley, Merton, Speier, Sumner, Thomas **7** Parsons, Sorokin **8** Eberhard **10** Lazarsfeld
British: **4** Webb **8** Hobhouse, Mannheim **12** Carr-Saunders
Danish: **6** Geiger
French: **4** Aron **5** Comte **8** Durkheim, Gurvitch **9** Friedmann
German: **5** Konig, Weber, Wiese **6** Simmel **8** Habermas, Luckmann **10** Dahrendorf, Horkheimer
Hungarian: **6** Lukacs **8** Mannheim
Israeli: **5** Buber **10** Eisenstadt
Norwegian: **6** Aubert **7** Galtung
Swedish: **8** Carlsson

sociopathic 9 alienated **10** antisocial, rebellious

sock 3 box, hit, sox **4** belt, blow, slap **5** punch, smack, smash **6** strike, wallop **7** clobber **8** knee sock **9** ankle sock **13** short stocking

Socrates
born: **6** Athens
taught using: **5** irony **6** method
disciple: **5** Plato **8** Xenophon
wife: **9** Xanthippe
death potion: **7** hemlock

sod 4 soil, turf **5** divot, earth, grass, sward **10** greensward

soda 3 pop **4** base, cola **5** tonic **6** bicarb, sodium **7** barilla, seltzer **8** bev-

erage, root beer **9** ginger ale, soft drink **11** bicarbonate **12** sarsaparilla
ash: **6** alkali
in faro: **9** first card
maker: **4** jerk

sodden 4 dull **5** heavy, lumpy, mushy, pasty, soggy, soppy **6** doughy, soaked **7** sopping **8** besotted, drenched, dripping, listless **9** saturated **10** wet through **14** expressionless

Soddy, Frederick
field: **9** chemistry
nationality: **7** British
discovered: **8** isotopes
worked with: **13** William Ramsay **16** Ernest Rutherford
awarded: **10** Nobel Prize

sodium
chemical symbol: **2** Na

Sodom
destroyed with: **5** Admah **6** Zeboim **8** Gomorrah

sofa 5 couch, divan **6** canape, lounge, settee **8** love seat **9** davenport **12** chesterfield

Sofia
Roman name: **12** Ulpia Serdica
Byzantine name: **9** Triaditsa
capital of: **8** Bulgaria
landmark: **13** Buyuk Dzhamiya **16** Saint Sofia Church **17** Saint George Church **24** Alexander Nevsky Cathedral **32** Cyril and Methodius National Library

soft 4 easy, kind, mild, pale, weak **5** downy, faint, furry, muted, quiet, silky, sleek **6** feeble, gentle, hushed, pliant, satiny, shaded, silken, smooth, supple, tender **7** lenient, not hard, pitying, pliable, restful, subdued, velvety **8** delicate, not sharp, shadowed, tolerant, tranquil, twilight **9** malleable, not strong **10** harmonious **11** sentimental, sympathetic **12** easily molded, low intensity **13** compassionate, pleasantly low **16** easily penetrated **19** having a breathy sound **21** requiring little effort **25** incapable of great endurance

soften 5 lower **6** lessen, subdue, temper **7** cushion, mollify **8** make soft, mitigate, moderate, palliate, tone down, turn down **10** ameliorate, make softer

softhearted 4 kind, soft, warm **6** benign, gentle, humane, kindly, tender **8** generous **9** forgiving, indulgent **10** benevolent **11** considerate, kindhearted, sympathetic, warmhearted **13** compassionate, tenderhearted

softly 6 easily, gently, mildly, weakly **7** quietly

softness 8 mildness **9** downiness, silkiness **10** fluffiness, gentleness, smoothness, tenderness **11** tranquility **12** tranquillity

soft soap 7 blarney **8** cajolery, flattery **10** persuasion

sogginess 7 wetness **8** dampness **9** mushiness **10** soddenness

soggy 5 heavy, mushy, pasty, soppy **6** doughy, soaked, sodden **7** sopping **8** drenched, dripping **9** saturated

Sogliardo
character in: **22** Every Man out of His Humour
author: **6** Jonson

Soglow, Otto
creator/artist of: **13** The Little King

soi-disant 8 so-called **9** pretended **10** self-styled **18** calling oneself thus

soigne, soignee 4 chic, neat, tidy **5** sleek, smart **6** classy, modish **7** elegant **11** well-groomed

soil 4 dirt, foul, land, loam, ruin, soot, spot **5** dirty, earth, grime, humus, muddy, smear, stain, sully **6** debase, defile, ground, region, smudge **7** blacken, country, tarnish **8** disgrace

soiled 5 dirty, grimy, messy **6** filthy, grubby, smudgy **7** muddied, sullied, unclean **8** begrimed, unwashed **9** besmeared

soiree 4 ball, prom **5** dance, party **9** cotillion, promenade

sojourn 4 stay **5** abide, pause, visit **6** stay at **7** holiday, layover **8** stay over, stopover, vacation

sojourner 6 lodger, tenant **7** pilgrim, tourist, visitor **8** traveler **9** transient, weekender **10** daytripper, vacationer

Sol
origin: **5** Roman
form: **3** god
personifies: **3** sun
corresponds to: **6** Helios **7** Mithras **8** Hyperion

sola, solus 5 alone **9** by oneself

solace 4 calm **5** cheer **6** soothe **7** assuage, comfort, console **8** reassure **10** help in need **11** consolation, reassurance **18** relief in affliction

solder 4 fuse, join, weld **5** braze, stick

soldier 2 GI **3** PFC **5** GI Joe, major **6** worker, zealot **7** captain, colonel, dogface, general, private, servant, trooper, veteran, warrior **8** corporal, follower, partisan, sergeant **10** lieutenant, serviceman, specialist **11** enlisted man, military man **14** militant leader **16** brigadier general

Soldier of Orange
director: **13** Paul Verhoeven
based on novel by: **13** Erik Hazelhoff
cast: **10** Peter Faber **11** Derek De Lint, Eddy Habbema, Rutger Hauer **12** Jeroen Krabbe **15** Susan Penhaligon
setting: **14** The Netherlands

Soldier's Embrace, A
author: **14** Nadine Gordimer

soldiery 5 army **6** legion, troops **7** legions, militia **8** military, soldiers **11** fighting men

sole 4 lone, only **6** single **8** solitary **9** exclusive

solely 5 alone **6** merely, purely, singly **8** uniquely **11** exclusively **14** single-handedly

solemn 4 dark, drab, grim, holy **5** grave, sober, staid **6** formal, gloomy, sacred, sedate, somber **7** earnest, serious, sincere **8** absolute **9** dignified, religious, spiritual, steadfast **10** ceremonial, depressing, determined **11** ceremonious **12** awe-inspiring

solemnity 3 awe **7** dignity **8** ceremony **9** formality, reverence **11** seriousness **12** circumstance

solemnize 4 mark **5** honor **6** hallow **7** observe **9** celebrate **10** consecrate **11** commemorate

solicit 3 ask **4** seek **5** plead **7** entreat, request **9** appeal for, importune

solicitation 6 appeal **7** request **8** entreaty **11** importuning

solicitor 6 beggar, lawyer **7** counsel **8** salesman **10** supplicant

solicitous 4 avid, keen **5** eager **6** ardent, intent **7** anxious, intense, longing, mindful, zealous **8** desirous **9** attentive, concerned, regardful **10** thoughtful **12** enthusiastic

solicitude 4 care, zeal **5** worry **7** anxiety, avidity, concern **9** attention **10** enthusiasm, inquietude, uneasiness **11** disquietude, fearfulness, overconcern **12** apprehension

solid 4 firm, hard, pure, real **5** dense, massy, sober, sound, tough **6** rugged, stable, steady, strong, sturdy **7** durable, genuine, lasting, unmixed **8** complete, concrete, constant, rational, reliable, sensible, tangible, thorough, unbroken **9** not hollow, unalloyed, unanimous, undivided, well-built **10** continuous, dependable, solidified **11** impermeable, levelheaded, substantial, trustworthy **12** impenetrable **13** uninterrupted **15** well- constructed

solidarity 5 union, unity **7** harmony **9** closeness **11** cooperation, unification

solidify 3 fix, gel, set **4** cake, jell **6** cement, harden **7** congeal, stiffen, thicken **9** coagulate **11** crystallize **12** agglomerate

soliloquy 9 monologue **10** solo speech

Solinus
character in: **17** The Comedy of Errors
author: **11** Shakespeare

solitariness 8 solitude **9** aloneness, seclusion **13** reclusiveness

solitary 4 lone **6** hidden, lonely, remote, single **8** desolate, isolated, lonesome, secluded **9** concealed **10** cloistered **11** out-of-the-way, uninhabited **13** companionless

solitude 9 aloneness, isolation, seclu-

sion, wasteland **10** desolation, loneliness, remoteness, wilderness

solo 5 alone **8** solitary **9** by oneself **10** unattended **12** singlehanded **13** unaccompanied
operatic: **4** aria

solo dance
ballet: **7** pas seul

Solomon
father: **5** David
mother: **9** Bathsheba
wife: **6** Naamah
son: **8** Rehoboam
brother: **5** Amnon **7** Absalom, Chileab **8** Adonijah
sister: **5** Tamar
visitor: **5** Sheba
wrote: **8** Proverbs **12** Ecclesiastes **13** Song of Solomon
built: **6** temple

Solomon Islands
capital/largest city: **7** Honiara
others: **4** Auki, Bina, Gizo, Luti **5** Kieta, Munda **6** Tulagi **7** Yandina **8** Kira Kira **9** Tangarare **10** Sasamungga
head of state: **14** British monarch **15** governor-general
member of: **14** Spearhead Group
monetary unit: **4** cent **6** dollar
island: **4** Buka, Gizo, Savo **5** Ndeni, Ulawa **6** Tulagi **7** Malaita, Rennell, Solomon, Vangunu **8** Choiseul, Sikaiana, Vanikoro **9** Santa Cruz **10** New Georgia, Ontong Java **11** Guadalcanal, Santa Isabel **12** Bougainville, San Cristobal
mountain: **5** Balbi
highest point: **11** Popomanasiu
ocean: **7** Pacific
physical feature:
  gulf: **4** Huon, Kula
  sound: **10** New Georgia
  strait: **13** Indispensable
people: **7** Chinese **8** European **10** Melanesian, Polynesian
  explorer: **14** Mendana de Neyra
  leader: **8** Mamaloni **9** Kenilorea
language: **7** English **13** Pidgin English **16** Melanesian pidgin
religion: **8** Anglican **13** Roman Catholic

so long
Spanish: **12** hasta la vista

solution 3 key **5** blend **6** answer, cipher **7** mixture, solving **8** emulsion **9** resolving **10** resolution, suspension, unraveling **11** explanation

solve 7 resolve, unravel, work out **8** decipher, unriddle, untangle **9** figure out **10** find the key **13** find the answer

solvent 7 diluent, soluble **9** dilutable **10** dissoluble, dissolvent **11** dissolvable **16** financially sound

Solymi

origin: 9 Asia Minor
occupation: 8 warriors

Solzhenitsyn, Aleksandr
author of: 13 The Cancer Ward **14** The First Circle **19** The Gulag Archipelago **22** August Nineteen-Fourteen **31** One Day in the Life of Ivan Denisovich

Somalia
other name: 4 Punt **10** Somaliland **12** Horn of Africa
capital/largest city: 9 Mogadishu **10** Mogadiscio
others: 5 Burao, Merca **6** Mereka **7** Berbera, Galkayu, Kismayu **8** Belet Uen, Hargeisa **9** Chisimaio
division: 6 Hawiya **9** Mijirtein **10** Midjertein
  colonial: 17 British Somaliland, Italian Somaliland
measure: 3 top **4** caba **5** chela, darat, tabla **6** cubito **8** parsalah
monetary unit: 4 besa **6** somalo **8** shilling **9** centesimi
weight: 8 parsalah
mountain: 5 Guban **11** Migiurtinia, Ogo Highland
highest point: 7 Surud Ad
river: 4 Juba **5** Daror, Nogal **9** Nugaaleed **11** Webi Shebeli **13** Webi Shabeelle
sea: 6 Indian
physical feature:
  bay: 5 Negro
  cape: 9 Guardafui
  desert: 4 Aror
  gulf: 4 Aden
  plateau: 3 Ogo **4** Haud
people: 3 Sab **4** Asha **5** Galla **6** Hawiya, Isbaak, Somali **7** Danakil, Hamitic, Marehan, Samaale, Shuhali **8** Rahanwin
  leader: 9 Siad Barre **12** Ali Shermarke
language: 6 Arabic, Somali **7** English, Italian
religion: 5 Islam
feature:
  boat: 4 dhow
  cloth: 7 banadir
  clothing: 4 futa, toga **6** sarong
  tree: 6 acacia, baobab **7** incense

Somaliland *see* **7** Somalia

somber 4 dark, drab, gray, grim **5** grave, sober **6** dreary, gloomy, solemn **7** serious **8** funereal, mournful, toneless **9** cheerless **10** depressing, melancholy

Some Like It Hot
director: 11 Billy Wilder
cast: 9 Joe E Brown, Pat O'Brien **10** George Raft, Jack Lemmon, Tony Curtis **13** Marilyn Monroe

Somers Islands *see* **7** Bermuda

something essential
Latin: 10 sine qua non

something for something
Latin: 10 quid pro quo

Something Happened
author: 12 Joseph Heller

sometime 4 late, once **5** later **6** former **7** quondam **8** formerly, previous **9** erstwhile **10** occasional

sometimes 7 at times **10** now and then, on occasion **12** occasionally, once in a while

somewhat 6 fairly, kind of, partly, sort of **8** passably **9** tolerably **10** moderately, more or less, reasonably **13** approximately

somnolent 4 dozy, dull **5** dopey **6** drowsy, groggy, sleepy, torpid **7** languid, nodding, out of it, yawning **8** hypnotic, sluggish **9** half-awake, lethargic, sopoforic **10** half-asleep, slumberous **11** heavy-lidded **13** semiconscious

Somnus
origin: 5 Roman
god of: 5 sleep
mother: 3 Nyx
brother: 4 Mors
corresponds to: 6 Hypnos, Hypnus

son
French: 4 fils

sone
unit of: 8 loudness

song 4 call, poem, tune **5** ditty, lyric, verse **6** ballad, melody, number, piping
French: 7 chanson

songbird 4 chat, lark, wren **5** robin, veery, vireo **6** canary, singer, thrush **7** warbler **9** nightingale

Song of Bernadette, The
author: 11 Franz Werfel
character: 13 Dean Peyramale **18** Sister Marie Therese **19** Bernadette Soubirous
director: 9 Henry King
cast: 8 Lee J Cobb **12** Vincent Price, William Eythe **13** Jennifer Jones **15** Charles Bickford
Oscar for: 7 actress (Jones)

Song of Hiawatha *see* **8** Hiawatha

Song of Roland, The *see* **15** Chanson de Roland

Song of Solomon
author: 12 Toni Morrison

Song of Solomon
bride: 9 Shulamite

Song of Songs, The
author: 16 Hermann Sudermann

Song of the Lark, The
author: 11 Willa Cather

Songs of Experience
author: 12 William Blake

Songs of Innocence
author: 12 William Blake

Sonnets from the Portuguese
author: 24 Elizabeth Barrett Browning

Sonnets to Orpheus
author: 16 Rainer Maria Rilke

Sonny
nickname of: 13 Charles Liston

Son of the Morning
author: 15 Joyce Carol Oates

sonorous 4 deep, rich **6** florid **7** ringing, vibrant **8** eloquent, resonant **9** full-toned, grandiose **10** flamboyant, impressive, resounding **13** reverberating

Sons and Lovers
author: 10 D H Lawrence
character: 10 Clara Dawes **11** Baxter Dawes **13** Miriam Leivers
  Morel family: 4 Paul **5** Annie **6** Arthur, Walter **7** William **8** Gertrude

Sons of thunder 4 John **5** James
also: 9 Boanerges

Soo
canals at: 13 Sault Ste. Marie

soon 4 anon **6** pronto **7** betimes, by and by, early on, ere long, quickly, shortly **8** directly **9** any minute, forthwith, instantly, presently, right away **10** before long **12** without delay **14** in a little while

sooner 6 before, in time **7** earlier **9** before now, in advance **10** beforehand **11** ahead of time

sooner or later 6 one day **7** finally, someday **8** in the end, sometime **10** eventually, ultimately **17** in the course of time, sometime or another

Sooner State
nickname of: 8 Oklahoma

soot 4 dirt, smut **5** crock, grime **6** carbon, smudge, smutch **7** residue **9** lampblack

soothe 4 calm, ease **6** lessen, pacify **7** appease, comfort, console, mollify, placate, relieve **8** mitigate, moderate **9** alleviate **11** tranquilize

soothing 4 mild **7** calming, healing, salving **9** appeasing, consoling, emollient, pacifying, placating **10** comforting, mitigating **13** tranquilizing

soothsayer 4 seer **5** sibyl **7** diviner, prophet **10** forecaster **13** fortune-teller

soothsaying 6 augury **8** divining, prophecy **10** divination, predicting, prediction **11** foretelling, prophesying

sooty 4 inky **5** black, dingy, dirty, grimy **6** smudgy, smutty **9** coal-black

sop 3 dip, tip, wet **4** dunk, soak **5** bribe **6** absorb, drench, payoff, payola, take up **8** gratuity, saturate **9** baksheesh, become wet, hush money

Sophie's Choice
author: 13 William Styron

Sophisms
author: 9 Aristotle

sophisticate 8 civilize **11** cosmopolite, disillusion, make worldly **12** cosmopolitan

sophisticated 6 subtle **7** complex,

studied, worldly **8** advanced, cultured, highbrow, mannered, precious, seasoned **9** difficult **10** artificial, cultivated **11** complicated, experienced, worldly-wise **12** cosmopolitan, intellectual

sophistry 6 deceit **7** fallacy **8** subtlety **9** casuistry, chicanery, deception **10** distortion **12** speciousness

Sophocles
author of: 4 Ajax **7** Electra, Oedipus **8** Antigone **10** Oedipus Rex, Trachiniae **11** Philoctetes **16** Oedipus at Colonus **18** The Trachinian Women

sophomoric 6 callow **7** foolish, puerile **8** childish, immature, juvenile **9** infantile **10** adolescent **12** schoolboyish

soporific 4 lazy **5** balmy, heavy **6** drowsy, sleepy **8** hypnotic, sedative, sluggish **9** lethargic, somnolent **10** slumberous **11** somniferous **12** sleep-inducer **13** sleep-inducing

soppiness 4 corn, mush **5** slush **6** bathos **7** wetness **9** mushiness **10** slushiness **11** mawkishness **14** sentimentalism, sentimentality

sopping 3 wet **5** soggy, soppy **6** soaked, sodden **8** drenched, dripping **9** saturated **10** bedraggled, soaking wet

sorcerer 5 witch **6** shaman, wizard **7** warlock **8** magician **11** medicine man

sorceress 5 siren, witch **11** enchantress

sorcery 8 witchery, wizardry **9** shamanism **10** black magic, necromancy, witchcraft **11** enchantment

Sordello
author: 14 Robert Browning

sordid 3 low **4** base, rank, vile **5** dirty, gross **6** filthy, putrid, rotten, vulgar, wicked **7** corrupt, ignoble, squalid, unclean **8** degraded, depraved **9** debauched **12** disreputable

Sordido
character in: 22 Every Man out of His Humour
author: 6 Jonson

sordino, con
music: 11 with the mute

sore 4 hurt **5** acute, angry, great, harsh, irked, sharp, upset, wound **6** aching, pained, severe, tender **7** bruised, extreme, grieved, hurting, painful **8** agonized, critical, grievous, smarting, sorespot, wounding **9** agonizing, desperate, indignant, irritated, sensitive **10** distressed, unbearable **11** distressing **12** inflammation

So Red the Rose
author: 10 Stark Young

Sorel, Julien
character in: 17 The Red and the Black
author: 8 Stendhal

sorely 5 badly **7** greatly **8** severely **9** extremely **10** critically **11** desperately

soreness 4 ache, pain **10** discomfort, irritation, tenderness

sorrel 3 bay **4** herb, roan, weed **5** brown, plant, Rumex **8** chestnut **12** reddish-brown
varieties: 3 red **4** dock, tree, wood **5** lady's, sheep **6** common, French, garden, Indian **7** redwood **8** Jamaican, mountain **10** violet wood **12** European wood

Sorrel, Hetty
character in: 8 Adam Bede
author: 5 Eliot

sorrow 3 woe **4** loss, weep **5** be sad, mourn, trial **6** grieve, lament **7** despair, sadness, travail, trouble **8** disaster, hardship **10** affliction, bad fortune, misfortune **11** catastrophe, unhappiness
French: 9 tristesse

sorrowful 3 sad **6** woeful **7** unhappy **8** affected, grieving, mournful **9** lamenting

Sorrows of Young Werther, The
author: 6 Goethe
character: 6 Albert **9** Charlotte (Lotte)

sorry 3 sad **6** woeful **7** grieved, pitiful, unhappy **8** contrite, pathetic, pitiable, wretched **9** miserable, regretful, repentant, sorrowful **10** deplorable, melancholy, remorseful, ridiculous **11** crestfallen **13** brokenhearted

sort 4 kind, list, make, sift, type **5** brand, class, grade, group, index, order **6** divide, person **7** arrange, catalog, species, variety **8** classify, organize, separate, take from **9** segregate **10** categorize, individual **11** systematize **14** classification

sortie 4 rush **5** onset **6** attack, charge **7** assault **8** storming **9** onslaught

sortilege 6 augury **7** auspice, sorcery **10** divination, witchcraft

sorting 8 dividing, grouping **9** arranging **10** organizing **11** classifying **12** categorizing

so-so 4 blah, fair **5** ho-hum **6** casual, modest **7** average, humdrum **8** adequate, bearable, mediocre, middling, ordinary, passable **9** tolerable **10** second-rate **11** commonplace, indifferent **12** run-of-the-mill **13** unexceptional **15** undistinguished

sot 4 lush, soak **5** drunk, rummy, souse, toper **8** drunkard, rumhound **9** alcoholic, inebriate **11** dipsomaniac

Soter
epithet of: 4 Zeus
means: 6 savior

Sothern, Ann
real name: 13 Harriette Lake
born: 12 Valley City ND
husband: 10 Roger Pryor **14** Robert Sterling

roles: 6 Maisie **8** Cry Havoc **10** Lady Be Good **16** Private Secretary **19** A Letter to Three Wives

so throughout
Latin: 9 sic passim

sotto voce
music: 11 in a low voice **13** in an undertone, under the voice

sought 6 hunted **7** pursued, quested **9** attempted, looked for **10** endeavored

soul 5 being, force **6** person, spirit **7** essence **8** creature, vitality **9** inner core **10** embodiment, individual, vital force **11** inspiration **12** quintessence

soul-searching 10 discontent, insecurity, uneasiness **15** dissatisfaction, self-questioning

soul-stirring 7 rousing **8** electric, exciting, stirring **9** inspiring, thrilling **11** galvanizing

sound 3 fit **4** deep, firm, good, seem, tone, wise **5** drift, hardy, noise, range, sober, solid, tenor, utter, voice **6** intact, robust, severe, signal, stable, strong, sturdy **7** durable, earshot, healthy, lasting, perfect, solvent **8** announce, rational, reliable, sensible, thorough, unmarred **9** come off as, competent, enunciate, pronounce, undamaged, well-built **10** articulate, dependable, make a noise, reasonable, suggestion, untroubled **11** implication, penetrating, responsible, substantial **13** thoroughgoing **15** hearing distance, well-constructed

Sound and the Fury, The
author: 15 William Faulkner
character: 6 Dilsey **17** Sydney Herbert Head
Compson family: 5 Jason **7** Candace (Caddy), Quentin **8** Benjamin (Benjy)

Sounder
director: 10 Martin Ritt
cast: 8 Taj Mahal **10** Kevin Hooks **11** Cicely Tyson **12** Paul Winfield **13** Carmen Mathews
sequel: 13 Sounder Part II

sound measure 7 decibel

sound mind in a sound body
Latin: 21 mens sana in cor pore sano

soundness of mind 6 reason, sanity **9** normality **12** mental health

Sound of Music, The
director: 10 Robert Wise
cast: 9 Peggy Wood **12** Julie Andrews (Maria Von Trapp) **13** Eleanor Parker **18** Christopher Plummer
setting: 7 Austria
score: 21 Rodgers and Hammerstein
Oscar for: 7 picture **8** director
song: 5 Maria **6** Do-Re-Mi **9** Edelweiss **16** My Favorite Things

sound out 3 ask **8** approach **15** make a proposal to, make overtures to, put out feelers to

soup
clear: 5 broth **8** bouillon, consomme
server: 6 tureen
spoon: 5 ladle
thick: 5 cream, gumbo **6** bisque, potage **7** chowder **10** minestrone

soupcon 3 bit, dab, jot, tad **4** clue, dash, drop, hint **5** pinch, shade, taint, taste, tinge, touch, trace, whiff **6** little, trifle **7** smidgen, smidgin, vestige **8** smidgeon **9** little bit, suspicion **10** smattering, sprinkling, suggestion **12** slight amount

Soupy Sales
character: 9 White Fang **10** Black Tooth **13** Herman the Flea, Hippy the Hippo, Pookie the Lion, Willie the Worm **14** Marilyn Monwolf

sour 3 bad **4** acid, dour, keen, tart, turn **5** nasty, sharp, spoil, surly, tangy, testy **6** crabby, cranky, curdle, rancid, sullen, turned **7** acerbic, bilious, crabbed, curdled, ferment, grouchy, peevish, spoiled, turn off, uncivil, waspish **8** alienate, choleric, embitter, jaundice, petulant, unsavory, vinegary **9** acidulous, clabbered, fermented, irritable, jaundiced, offensive, prejudice, repugnant **10** astringent, illdispose, ill-humored, unpleasant **11** bad-tempered, distasteful, ill-tempered **12** disagreeable

sourball 4 crab **5** crank, grump **6** grouch **9** hard candy **10** curmudgeon

source 4 font, head, root **5** basis, cause, fount **6** author, father, origin, rising, spring **8** begetter, fountain **9** authority, beginning, headwater **10** antecedent, derivation, foundation, prime mover, wellspring

source and origin
Latin: 11 fons et origo

Sourdough State
nickname of: 6 Alaska

sourness 7 acidity, vinegar **8** acerbity, acrimony, ill humor, pungency, tartness **9** acridness, greenness **10** bitterness

sourpuss 4 bear, crab **5** crank, grump **6** griper, grouch **7** grouser, killjoy **8** grumbler, sorehead **10** bellyacher, complainer, crosspatch, curmudgeon, spoilsport

Sousa, John Philip
born: 12 Washington DC
composer of: 9 El Capitan **14** Washington Post **25** The Stars and Stripes Forever

souse 3 dip, sot **4** duck, dunk, lush, soak **5** douse, drunk, rummy, steep, toper **6** barfly, boozer, drench, pickle **7** immerse, tippler **8** drunkard, inundate, marinate, saturate, submerge **9** alcoholic, inebriate **11** dipsomaniac

soused 5 drunk **6** dunked, potted, zapped, zonked **7** pickled, sloshed, smashed **8** immersed **9** plastered **10**

inebriated **11** intoxicated **17** under the influence **20** three sheets to the wind

South Africa
capital: 8 Cape Town, Pretoria **12** Bloemfontein
largest city: 12 Johannesburg
others: 3 Aus **4** Mara, Stad **6** Benoni, Bononi, Braker, Durban, Garies, Severn, Soweto, Umtata, Untata **7** Brakpan, Kokstad **8** Kaapstad, Mafeking, Modjadji **9** Germiston, Kimberley **10** East London, Oudtshoorn **11** Krugersdorp, Vereeniging **13** Port Elizabeth **16** Pietermaritzburg
school: 5 Natal **8** Capetown **13** Witwatersrand **15** Orange Free State
division: 5 Natal **8** Backveld **9** Transvaal **10** Basutoland **12** Cape Province **14** Cape of Good Hope **15** Orange Free State
independent homelands: 5 Venda **6** Ciskei **8** Transkei **10** bantustans **14** Bophuthatswana
goverment:
legislature: 4 Raad
measure: 4 vara
monetary unit: 4 cent, pond, rand **5** pound **6** florin **7** daalder **9** krugerrand
mountain: 3 Aux, Kop **5** Table **7** Kathkin **9** Stormberg **10** Devil's Peak, Sneeuwberg **11** Drakensberg **12** Giant's Castle **13** Witwatersrand **14** Mont-aux-Sources **15** Great Escarpment
highest point: 8 Injasuti
river: 3 Hex **4** Vaal **5** Nosob **6** Modder, Molopo, Orange, Tugela **7** Caledon, Kurumam, Limpopo **8** Olifants **9** Crocodile, Great Fish
ocean: 6 Indian **8** Atlantic
physical feature:
bay: 5 Algoa, False, Table **6** Mossel, Walvis **7** Walfish **8** Richard's, Saldanha **11** Saint Helena
cape: 7 Agulhas **8** Good Hope
current: 8 Benguela
desert: 5 Namib **8** Kalahari
plateau: 6 Karroo
region: 8 Highveld, Zululand **9** Kaffraria **11** Great Karroo **12** Little Karroo
people: 3 San **4** Boer, Yosa, Zulu **5** Asian, Bantu, Namas, Nguni, Pondo, Sotho, Swazi, Tembu, Venda, Xhosa **6** Damara, Kaffir **7** African, British, Bushmen, English, Swahili **8** Bechuana, Khoikhoi **9** Afrikaner, Hottentot
author: 5 Paton **7** Luthuli **8** Gordimer
civil rights advocate: 6 Gandhi
explorer: 8 Riebeeck
leader: 4 Biko, Tutu **5** Botha, Malan, Smuts, Tomba **6** Kruger, Rhodes **7** de Klerk, Hertzog, Mandela, Vorster **8** Verwoerd **9** Buthelezi, Pretorius
language: 4 Taal, Zulu **5** Bantu,

Hindi, Nguni, Sotho, Swazi, Tamil, Venda, Xhosa **6** Telegu, Thonga **7** English, Khoisan, Ndebele, Sesotho **8** Bujarati, Fanakalo **9** Afrikaans
religion: 5 Hindu, Islam **7** animism, Judaism **8** Anglican **9** Methodist **12** Episcopalian, Presbyterian **13** Dutch Reformed, Roman Catholic
place:
Cecil Rhodes' estate: 11 Groote Shuur
game reserve: 5 Mkuze **6** Kruger **8** Hluhluwe
monument: 11 Voortrekker
feature:
bird: 4 taha
bride price: 6 lobolo
flower: 5 coral **6** clivia, protea **7** cowslip, fuchsia **9** phygelius **10** lachenalia
oganization: 3 ANC **7** Inkatha **23** African National Congress
segregation: 9 apartheid
tree: 7 assagai **9** jacaranda
food:
corn: 6 mealie
drink: 9 sundowner
meat: 7 biltong **8** sosaties **9** boerewors

South America
bird: 5 macaw **7** seriema, tinamou **8** caracara
cape: 4 Horn
country: 4 Peru **5** Chile **6** Brazil, Guyana **7** Bolivia, Ecuador, Surinam, Uruguay **8** Colombia, Paraguay **9** Argentina, Venezuela **12** French Guiana
desert: 7 Atacama
explorer: 16 Francisco Pizarro **18** Pedro Alvares Cabral
hero: 12 Simon Bolivar **15** Jose de San Martin **16** Bernardo O'Higgins **18** Antonio Jose de Sucre
highest mountain: 9 Aconcagua
islands: 8 Falkland **9** Galapagos
lake: 8 Titicaca **9** Maracaibo
mountain range: 5 Andes
native: 2 Ge **3** Ona **4** Inca **5** Carib, Mayan **7** Quechua **10** Araucanian
plain: 5 llano, pampa
region: 9 Patagonia
river: 3 Apa **5** Plata **6** Amazon **7** Orinoco

South Carolina
abbreviation: 2 SC
nickname: 7 Calinky **8** Palmetto
capital/largest city: 8 Columbia
others: 5 Aiken, Greer, Union **6** Belton, Camden, Cheraw, Conway, Dillon, Seneca, Sumter **7** Bamberg, Laurens, Manning **8** Beaufort, Florence, Newberry, Rock Hill, Walhalla **9** Greenwood **10** Charleston, Greenville, Orangeburg **11** Spartanburg
college: 5 Allen, Coker **6** Furman, Lander **7** Claffin, Clemson, Erskine, Wofford **8** Benedict, Bob Jones, Co-

lumbia, Winthrop **13** Francis Marion **15** Citadel Military

explorer: 6 Ayllon, Ribaut

feature:
  beach: 6 Myrtle
  dam: 6 Saluda
  fort: 6 Sumter
  gardens: 7 Cypress

tribe: 5 Pedee, Sewee **6** Cusabo, Santee, Waxhaw, Yamasi **7** Catawba, Shawnee, Sugeree, Wateree **8** Congaree

people: 11 James Byrnes **12** Althea Gibson, John C Calhoun **13** Bernard Baruch, Francis Marion **14** Dizzy Gillespie

island: 3 Sea **6** Parris **10** Hilton Head

lake: 6 Marion, Murray **7** Catawba, Wateree **8** Hartwell, Moultrie **9** Clark Hill

land rank: 8 fortieth

mountain: 5 Kings **6** Little **9** Blue Ridge, Sassafras

physical feature:
  bay: 8 Carolina
  plateau: 8 Piedmont

president: 13 Andrew Jackson

river: 5 Broad **6** Edisto, Pee Dee, Saluda, Santee **7** Ashepoo **8** Savannah

state admission: 6 eighth

state bird: 12 Carolina wren

state flower: 13 yellow jasmine **17** Carolina jessamine

state motto: 18 While I Breathe I Hope **26** Prepared in Mind and Resources

state song: 8 Carolina

state tree: 8 palmetto

South Dakota
abbreviation: 2 SD **4** S Dak
nickname: 6 Coyote **8** Blizzard, Sunshine
capital: 6 Pierre
largest city: 10 Sioux Falls
others: 4 Lead, Leap **5** Huron **6** Custer, Eureka, Lemmon, Miller, Winner **7** Sturgis, Webster, Yankton **8** Aberdeen, Deadwood, Sisseton **9** Brookings, Rapid City **10** Vermillion
college: 5 Huron **7** Yankton **9** Augustana **10** Mount Marty, Sioux Falls **14** Dakota Wesleyan
explorer: 8 Varennes **13** Lewis and Clark
feature: 8 Deadwood
  battlefield: 11 Wounded Knee
  dam: 4 Oahe
  mine: 9 Homestake
  monument: 13 Mount Rushmore
  national park: 8 Badlands, Wind Cave
tribe: 5 Brule, Sioux **6** Dakota, Sutaio **8** Cheyenne
people: 10 Crazy Horse **11** Sitting Bull **12** George McGovern, Hubert Humphrey
lake: 4 Oahe **5** Sharp **8** Big Stone,

Traverse **11** Francis Case **13** Lewis and Clark

land rank: 9 sixteenth

mountain: 4 Bear **5** Sheep, Table **6** Crook's, Moreau
  highest point: 6 Harney
  hills: 5 Black **7** Prairie

physical feature:
  butte: 7 Thunder **9** Deer's Ears **10** Castle Rock
  cave: 5 Jewel

river: 3 Bad **5** Grand, James, White **6** Moreau **8** Big Sioux, Cheyenne, Missouri **10** Vermillion

state admission: 8 fortieth **11** thirty-ninth (with North Dakota)

state bird: 18 ring-necked pheasant

state flower: 12 pasqueflower

state animal: 6 coyote

state motto: 21 Under God the People Rule

state song: 15 Hail South Dakota

state tree: 11 white spruce **16** Black Hills spruce

southeast wind
associated with: 5 Eurus **9** Volturnus

Southern Comfort
type: 7 liqueur
origin: 10 New Orleans
flavor: 5 peach
base: 7 bourbon
drink: 13 Scarlett O'Hara **15** Plantation Punch
with bourbon: 14 Blended Comfort

Southern Cross
constellation of: 4 Crux

Southern Crown
constellation of: 15 Corona Australis

Southerner, The
director: 10 Jean Renoir
cast: 10 Betty Field **11** Beulah Bondi **12** Zachary Scott **13** Bunny Sunshine

Southern Fish
constellation of: 15 Piscis Austrinus

Southern Fly
constellation of: 5 Musca

Southern Rhodesia *see* **8** Zimbabwe

Southern Slavic
language family: 12 Indo-European
group: 11 Balto-Slavic
branch: 6 Slavic
language: 7 Slovene **9** Bulgarian **10** Macedonian **13** Serbo-Croatian

Southern Triangle
constellation of: 18 Triangulum Australe

South Korea *see* **5** Korea

South Vietnam *see* **7** Vietnam

South West Africa *see* **7** Namibia

south wind
associated with: 5 Notus

South Wind
author: 13 Norman Douglas

South Yemen *see* **5** Yemen

souvenir 4 scar **5** relic, token **6** em-

blem, memory, trophy **7** memento **8** keepsake, reminder **11** remembrance

sovereign 4 czar, free, king, lord, main, tsar **5** chief, major, prime, queen, regal, royal **6** kingly, potent, prince, ruling, utmost **7** emperor, highest, leading, monarch, queenly, supreme **8** absolute, autocrat, dominant, foremost, imperial, overlord, powerful, princely, reigning **9** chieftain, governing, paramount, potentate, prepotent, principal, uppermost **10** autonomous, self-ruling **11** all-powerful, crowned head, independent, monarchical **12** supreme ruler **13** self-directing, self-governing

sovereignty 4 sway **5** crown, power **6** throne **7** command, control, freedom, primacy, scepter **8** autonomy, dominion, home rule, kingship, lordship, self-rule **9** authority, supremacy **10** ascendancy **11** paramountcy **12** independence, jurisdiction, predominance **14** self-government **17** self-determination

Soviet Union *see* **6** Russia

sow 4 cast, seed **5** lodge, plant, set in, strew **6** inject, spread **7** implant, instill, scatter **8** disperse, sprinkle **9** broadcast, establish, introduce **11** disseminate

space 3 gap, sky **4** area, part, rank, room, seat, span, spot, term, time **5** berth, blank, break, chasm, ether, field, order, place, range, reach, scope, sweep, swing, width **6** hiatus, lacuna, line up, margin, period, set out, spread **7** arrange, breadth, compass, expanse, mark out, the void **8** distance, duration, infinity, interval, latitude, omission, organize, schedule, separate **9** amplitude, emptiness, keep apart, territory **10** distribute, interspace, interstice, outer space, separation, the heavens **11** nothingness, reservation, the universe **12** interruption, the firmament **13** accommodation

Space
author: 13 James Michener

spacecraft 4 ship **6** rocket **7** orbiter, shuttle **9** satellite **10** rocketship

space flight
US mission: 6 Apollo, Gemini, Skylab **7** Mercury
US rocket: 5 Atlas, Titan **6** Saturn **8** Redstone
US space shuttle: 8 Columbia **9** Discovery **10** Challenger
Soviet mission: 5 Soyuz **6** Salyut, Vostok **7** Voskhod
Soviet astronaut:
  first man in space: 11 Yuri Gagarin
  first woman in space: 19 Valentina Tereshkova
  first space walk by: 13 Aleksei Leonov

American astronaut: 9 John Glenn, John Young **11** Alan Shepard, Edward White, Edwin Aldrin, Frank Borman, James Lovell **12** Roger Chaffee, Wally (Walter) Schirra **13** Charles Conrad, L Gordon Cooper, Virgil (Gus) Grissom **14** Scott Carpenter, Thomas Stafford

  first man on moon: 13 Neil Armstrong

  Challenger seven: 12 Michael Smith, Ronald McNair **13** Francis Scobee, Gregory Jarvis, Judith Resnick **14** Ellison Onizuka **16** Christa McAuliffe

Spacek, Sissy
  real name: 19 Mary Elizabeth Spacek
  born: 9 Quitman TX
  roles: 6 Carrie **7** Missing **8** Badlands, The River **10** Raggedy Man **16** Crimes of the Heart **18** Coal Miner's Daughter (Oscar)

spacious 4 vast, wide **5** ample, broad, large, roomy **7** immense, sizable **8** enormous **9** capacious, expansive, extensive, uncrowded **10** commodious

spaciousness 9 amplitude, largeness, roominess **13** capaciousness **14** commodiousness

Spade, Sam
  character in: 16 The Maltese Falcon
  author: 7 Hammett

Spain
  other name: 6 Iberia **8** Hispania
  capital/largest city: 6 Madrid
  others: 4 Adra, Aspe, Baza, Elda, Horo, Irun, Jaen, Leon, Noya, Olot, Reus, Rota, Sama, Vigo **5** Baena, Bejar, Cadiz, Cieza, Cueta, Ecija, Eibar, Elche, Gades, Gadir, Gijon, Ibiza, Jerez, Jodar, Liego, Lorca, Oliva, Palma, Palos, Ronda, Siero, Ubeda, Xeres, Yecla, Zafra **6** Abdera, Aviles, Azuaga, Bilbao, Burgos, Coruna, Duenca, Gandia, Gerona, Getafe, Guadix, Hellin, Huelva, Huesca, Jativa, Lerida, Lucena, Malaga, Mataro, Merida, Murcia, Orense, Oviedo, Termel, Toledo, Utrera, Zamora **7** Almeria, Badajos, Cordoba, Daimiel, Granada, Jumilla, Linares, Logrono, Manresa, Segovia, Sevilla, Seville, Tarrasa, Vitoria **8** Alicante, Badalona, Figueras, Pamplona, Sabadell, Santiago, Torrente, Valencia, Zaragoza **9** Barcelona, Las Palmas, Saragossa
  school: 6 Ciudad, Madrid
  division: 4 Jaen, Leon, Lugo **5** Alava, Avila, Cadiz, Soria **6** Basque, Burgos, Coruna, Cuenca, Gerona, Huelva, Huesca, Lerida, Madrid, Malaga, Murcia, Orense, Oviedo, Teruel, Toledo, Zamora **7** Almeria, Caceres, Cordoba, Granada, Logrono, Navarra, Segovia, Sevilla, Vizcaya, Zadajoz **8** Albacete, Alicante, Baleares, Palencia, Valencia, Zaragoza **9** Cata-

lonia
  kingdom: 4 Leon **6** Aragon **7** Castile, Galicia, Granada, Navarre **8** Asturias **9** al-Andalus, Catalonia **12** Spanish March
  government: 8 monarchy
  legislature: 6 Cortes
  head of state: 4 king
  measure: 3 pie **4** codo, dedo, paso, vara **5** braza, cahiz, carga, legua, medio, palmo, sesma **6** cordel, cuarta, fanega, racion, yugada **7** azumbre, celemin, estadel, pulgada **8** fanegada
  monetary unit: 3 cob **4** duro **5** dobla **6** cuarto, dinero, escudo, peseta **7** alfonso, centimo, pistole **8** doubloon
  weight: 4 onza **5** frail, libra, marco, tomin **6** arroba, dinero, dracma **7** arienzo, quilate, quintal **8** tonelada
  island: 5 Ceuta, Ibiza, Iviza, Palma **6** Canary, Gomera, Hierro **7** Alboran, Majorca, Melilla, Minorca **8** Balearic, Mallorca, Tagomago, Tenerife **9** Lanzarote **13** Fuerteventura
  lake: 4 lago **8** Albufera
  mountain: 4 Gata **5** Aneto, Rouch **6** Cuenca, Estats, Europa, Gredos, Magina, Morena, Nethou, Nevada, Teleno, Toledo **7** Alcaraz, Banuelo, Catalan, Cerredo, Demanda, Iberian, La Sagra, Moncayo, Perdido **8** Almanzor, Asturias, Galician, Maladeta, Monegros, Montseny, Penalara, Pyrenees **10** Albarracin, Cantabrian, Guadarrama, Torrecilla
  highest point: 5 Teide **8** Mulhacen
  river: 3 Sil, Ter **4** Cega, Ebro, Esla, Lima, Mino, Muga, Tajo, Ulla **5** Adaja, Cinca, Douro, Duero, Genil, Jalon, Jucar, Navia, Odiel, Riaza, Segie, Tagus, Tinto, Turia **6** Alagon, Aragon, Eresma, Huerva, Jarama, Orbigo, Segura, Torote **7** Almeria, Almonte, Arlanza, Barbate, Cabriel, Gallego, Henares, Mijares, Perales **8** Duration, Guadiana **12** Guadalquivir
  sea: 8 Atlantic, Balearic **13** Mediterranean
  physical feature:
    bay: 5 Bahia **6** Biscay
    cape: 9 Trafalgar
    gulf: 5 Cadiz **8** San Jorge, Valencia
    peninsula: 7 Iberian
    plateau: 6 meseta
    strait: 9 Gibraltar
  people: 5 Diego, Gente, Latin **6** Basque, Espana **7** Catalan, Espanol, Iberian **8** Galician, Gallegos, Maragato
    architect: 5 Gaudi
    artist: 4 Dali, Goya, Gris, Miro **6** Ribera **7** El Greco, Murillo, Picasso **8** Zurbaran **9** Velazquez
    author: 4 Cela, Vega **5** Barea, Cueva, Rojas **6** Aleman, Alonso, Azorin, Baroja, Castro, Encina, Felipe, Ibanez, Miguel **7** Alarcon,

Becquer, Cernuda, Ercilla, Gongora, Guillen, Jimenez, Machado, Unamuno **8** Montalvo, Zorrilla **9** Benavente, Cervantes, Goytisola **10** Aleixandre, Espronceda, Lope de Vega, Pardo Bazan **11** Garcia Lorca **12** Lopez de Ayala **13** Tirso de Molina **17** Calderon de la Barca
    cellist: 6 Casals
    composer: 7 Albeniz **8** Granados, Victoria **13** Manuel de Falla
    converted Moslem: 7 morisco
    dynasty: 7 Almohad, Umayyad **9** Almoravid
    explorer: 6 Balboa, Cortes **7** Pizarro **8** Columbus
    Jesuit founder: 14 Ignatius Loyola
    king: 6 Pelayo, Philip, Ramiro, Sancho, Witiza **7** Alfonso, dracma **8** al-Mansur, Reccared, Roderick **9** Ferdinand, Leovigild **10** Juan Carlos **11** Abd al-Rahman, Reccosvinth
    leader: 4 Prim **5** Godoy **6** Franco **7** Canovas **11** Calvo Sotelo **13** Primo de Rivera **14** Suarez-Gonzalez
    queen: 8 Isabella **16** Elizabeth Farnese
    ruler: 4 Rome **5** Celts, Moors **6** Greece **7** Almeria, Vandals **8** Carthage **9** Phoenicia, Visigoths
    scholar: 8 Averroes
    singer: 7 Domingo **8** Iglesias
    warrior: 14 El Cid Campeador
  language: 6 Basque **7** Catalan, Spanish **8** Balearic, Galician **9** Castilian, Valencian
  expressions: 5 adios **10** buenos dias **11** que sera sera **12** hasta la vista
  religion: 7 Judaism **10** Protestant **13** Roman Catholic
  place:
    aqueduct: 7 Segovia
    bridge: 7 Cordoba
    castle: 7 Alcazar **12** Santa Barbara
    cathedral bell tower: 7 Giralda
    center of Madrid: 12 Puerto del Sol
    church/cathedral: 4 Leon **6** Burgos, Gerona, Toledo **7** Seville **9** Barcelona, San Isidro **10** Santa Maria **14** Sagrada Familia
    fountain: 6 Cibele
    library: 8 Columbus
    minaret: 7 Seville
    mosque: 11 Great Mosque **19** Santo Cristo de la Cruz
    museum: 5 Prado **15** Museo de Pinturas
    palace: 7 Granada, Naranco **8** Alhambra, Escorial **9** Real Mayor
    park: 6 Retiro
    resort: 8 Marbella **10** Costa Brava **12** Torremolinos
    shrine: 32 Saint James at Santiago de Compostela
    street: 7 Ramblas **13** Paseo del Prado **16** Plaza de la Cibeles **19**

Paseo de la Castellana
synagogue: 10 El Transito
theater: 6 Merida
wall paintings/caves: 8 Altamira
possession: 5 Ceuta **6** Melill
feature:
   bar: 6 tascas
   dance: 5 tango **8** fandango, flamenco
   estate: 10 latifundia
   matador's suit: 12 traje de luces
   political party: 7 Falange
food:
   dish: 6 cocido, paella **8** zarzuela
   soup: 8 gazpacho
span 4 arch, area, last, term, wing **5**
cover, cross, range, reach, scope,
spell, sweep, vault **6** bridge, endure,
extent, length, period **7** archway,
breadth, measure, stretch, survive,
trestle **8** distance, duration, interval **9**
extension, reach over, territory **10**
bridge over, dimensions **11**
proportions, reach across, stretch over
12 extend across
spangle 4 star **5** bedew **6** sequin **7**
glisten, glitter, shimmer, twinkle **9** bugle bead, coruscate, paillette
spaniel
   dog breed: 5 field **6** cocker, Sussex **7**
   clumber, Tibetan **8** Brittany **10** Irish
   water **13** American water, English
   cocker, Welsh springer **15** English
   springer **19** Cavalier King Charles
Spanish (language, person) 7 espanol
Spanish Guinea see **16** Equatorial
Guinea
Spanish Sahara see **13** Western Sahara
Spanish Tragedy, The
   author: 9 Thomas Kyd
   character: 7 Horatio, Lorenzo, Villupo
   9 Alexandro, Balthazar, Hieronimo
   10 Bel-Imperia **16** Ghost of Don Andrea
spank 3 hit, tan **4** beat, belt, blow,
cane, flog, hide, lick, slap, whip,
whop **5** birch, strap, whale **6** paddle,
strike, switch, thrash, wallop **8** paddling **10** flagellate
spanking 4 very **5** brisk, fresh **7** beating **8** paddling, whipping **9** extremely,
thrashing **10** punishment **12** chastisement
spanking new 5 fresh **6** unused **8**
brand new **9** untouched
spar 4 boom, mast, pole **5** argue, fight,
sprit **6** bicker **7** dispute, quarrel,
wrangle **8** crossbar **10** crosspiece
spare 3 odd **4** bony, cede, free, give,
keep, lank, lean, save, thin **5** amass,
extra, forgo, gaunt, grant, guard,
hoard, lanky, lay up, limit, pinch,
rangy, scant, stint, weedy **6** acquit, afford, defend, donate, excess, exempt,
forego, let off, meager, not use, par-

don, scanty, shield, skimpy, skinny,
slight, unused **7** forgive, haggard, husband, let go of, protect, release, relieve, reserve, scraggy, scrawny, shelter, skimp on, slender, surplus **8**
conserve, hold back, leftover, liberate,
part with, reprieve, set aside, skeletal,
withhold **9** auxiliary, emaciated, exonerate, fleshless, safeguard, show
mercy **10** additional, extraneous, relinquish, substitute, unconsumed **11**
economize on, have mercy on, superfluous, unnecessary, use frugally **12**
be merciful to, dispense with, supplemental **13** supernumerary, supplementary
spared 5 freed **6** exempt, immune **7**
excused **8** absolved, excepted, relieved
sparing 4 near **5** close, scant **6** frugal,
meager, saving, scanty, stingy **7** careful, miserly, thrifty **8** grudging, stinting **9** niggardly, penurious **10** economical, ungenerous **11** closefisted,
tightfisted **12** parsimonious
spark 3 bit, jot **4** atom, beam, fire,
iota, life **5** brand, ember, flash, gleam,
pique, trace **6** arouse, excite, incite,
spirit **7** flicker, glimmer, glitter, inspire, provoke, sparkle **8** vitality **9** animation, instigate, stimulate **10** get-up-
and-go
Spark, Muriel
   author of: 11 Memento Mori **14** The
   Driver's Seat, The Only Problem **17**
   The Mandelbaum Gate, Territorial
   Rights **19** Loitering with Intent **21** A
   Far Cry from Kensington **24** The
   Prime of Miss Jean Brodie
sparkle 3 pep, pop, vim **4** dash, elan,
fizz, foam, glow, life **5** be gay, brand,
cheer, ember, flash, froth, gleam,
glint, light, shine, verve **6** bubble,
dazzle, fizzle, gaiety, spirit **7** be witty,
flicker, glimmer, glisten, glitter, jollity,
rejoice, shimmer, twinkle **8** radiance,
vitality, vivacity **9** alertness, animation, briskness, coruscate, quickness
10 be cheerful, brilliance, ebullience,
effervesce, effulgence, exuberance,
liveliness, luminosity **11** be vivacious,
scintillate **12** cheerfulness, exhilaration, luminousness **13** effervescence,
scintillation
sparkling 5 fizzy **6** bubbly **7** fizzing,
twinkly **8** bubbling, dazzling, glittery
9 twinkling **10** glistening, glittering **11**
coruscating **12** effervescent **13** scintillating
Sparky Lyle
   nickname of: 16 Albert Walter Lyle
sparse 3 few **4** thin **5** scant, spare **6**
meager, scanty, scarce, skimpy,
spotty, strewn **7** diffuse **8** exiguous,
sporadic **9** dispersed, scattered,
spaced-out, uncrowded **10** infrequent
16 few and far between

sparseness 7 paucity **8** sparsity, thinness **10** meagerness, scantiness
Sparsit, Mrs
   character in: 9 Hard Times
   author: 7 Dickens
Spartacus
   director: 14 Stanley Kubrick
   cast: 8 Nina Foch **9** John Gavin **10**
   Tony Curtis **11** Jean Simmons, Kirk
   Douglas **12** Peter Ustinov **15** Charles
   Laughton, Laurence Olivier
   setting: 4 Rome
   score: 9 Alex North
spartan 4 hard **5** plain, stark, stern,
stiff **6** frugal, severe, simple, strict **7**
ascetic, austere **8** exacting, rigorous **9**
stringent **10** abstemious, inexorable,
inflexible, restrained, restricted **11** disciplined, self-denying **15** self-
disciplined
Sparti
   occupation: 8 warriors
spasm 3 fit, tic **4** grip, jerk, pang **5**
burst, cramp, crick, flash, onset, spell,
spurt, start, storm, throe **6** access, attack, frenzy, twitch **7** seizure, shudder, tempest **8** eruption, paroxysm **9**
explosion **10** convulsion
spasmodic 6 fitful **7** erratic, flighty **8**
fleeting, periodic, sporadic **9** desultory, irregular, mercurial, transient **10**
capricious, inconstant, occasional **12**
intermittent **13** discontinuous
spat 4 tiff **5** argue, fight, scrap, set-to **6**
bicker, differ **7** contend, dispute, dissent, quarrel, wrangle **8** disagree,
squabble **10** difference **11** altercation
12 disagreement **16** misunderstanding
spatter 4 slop, soil, spot **5** fleck, plash,
spray, spurt, stain, swash **6** mottle,
shower, splash **7** speckle, stipple **8**
splatter, sprinkle
spawn 4 eggs, seed, teem **5** beget,
breed, brood, fruit, yield **7** lay eggs,
produce, product **8** engender, generate, multiply **9** offspring, propagate,
reproduce **10** bring forth, give rise to
11 deposit eggs, give birth to, proliferate
speak 3 air, say **4** call, chat, deal, talk,
tell **5** imply, orate, refer, shout,
sound, state, treat, voice **6** advise,
confer, convey, cry out, dilate, impart,
mumble, murmur, mutter, preach, recite, relate, remark, report, reveal **7**
bespeak, comment, consult, declaim,
declare, discuss, divulge, expound, express, lecture, mention, suggest, whisper **8** announce, converse, disclose,
harangue, indicate, proclaim, vocalize
9 discourse, enunciate, expatiate, hold
forth, make known, pronounce, sermonize **10** articulate **11** communicate,
give a speech
speakeasy 3 bar **6** saloon, tavern **7**
gin mill **14** cocktail lounge
speaker 5 voice **6** orator, reader, talker

7 reciter 8 advocate, lecturer, preacher 9 declaimer, spokesman 10 discourser, monologist, mouthpiece, sermonizer 11 rhetorician, speechmaker, spokeswoman 13 valedictorian

speak highly of 4 laud 5 exalt, extol 6 praise 7 commend 8 eulogize 10 compliment 16 sing the praises of

speak ill of 4 slur 5 curse, knock, libel 6 defame, insult, malign, vilify 7 slander 8 bad-mouth 9 criticize, denigrate, discredit, disparage 13 find fault with 14 inveigh against

speak loudly 3 cry 4 bawl, call, hail, roar, yell 5 shout 6 bellow, clamor, cry out, halloo, holler 7 call out, speak up

speak of 7 mention, refer to 8 allude to 9 talk about, touch upon

speak to 6 talk to 7 address, lecture

speak together 3 gab, jaw, rap 4 chat, chin, talk 6 confer 7 chatter, palaver 8 chitchat, converse 10 chew the fat, chew the rag 11 communicate, confabulate

speak well of 4 laud 5 boost, extol 6 praise 7 acclaim, approve, commend, flatter, root for 8 eulogize 9 sweet talk 10 compliment, stick up for 13 speak highly of 16 sing the praises of 17 put in a good word for

spear 4 bolt, dart, gaff, gore, pike, spit, stab 5 lance, prick, shaft, spike, stick 6 impale, pierce 7 harpoon, javelin 8 puncture, transfix 9 penetrate 10 run through

spearhead 4 iron, lead 5 begin, found, start 6 launch, leader 7 creator, develop, founder, pioneer 8 begetter, conceive, initiate 9 establish, initiator, institute, originate, spokesman 10 inaugurate, instituter, prime mover 11 establisher, inaugurator, spokeswoman 12 avant-gardist

special 4 fast, good, rare 5 close, great, novel 6 ardent, proper, select, signal, unique 7 bargain, certain, devoted, endemic, feature, staunch, typical, unusual 8 distinct, especial, intimate, peculiar, personal, sale item, singular, specific, uncommon 9 headliner, high point, highlight, important, momentous, specialty, steadfast 10 attraction, individual, noteworthy, particular, remarkable 11 distinctive, exceptional, outstanding, specialized 12 extravaganza 13 distinguished, extraordinary 14 representative, unconventional 16 out of the ordinary 17 piece de resistance

specialist 4 buff 5 adept, maven 6 expert, master 9 authority 10 past master 11 connoisseur

specialization 5 focus, forte, major 6 metier 8 province 10 speciality 13 concentration

specialize 5 adapt, focus, major 6 pursue 10 narrow down 11 concentrate

specialty 4 bent, mark, turn 5 badge, focus, forte, hobby, major, stamp 6 genius, talent 7 earmark, faculty, feature, pursuit, special 8 aptitude 9 endowment, trademark 10 competence, profession 11 claim to fame, distinction

species 4 form, kind, make, sort, type 5 breed, class, genre, group, order 6 kidney, nature, stripe 7 variety 8 category, division 11 designation, subdivision 14 classification

specific 5 exact, fixed 6 minute, stated, unique 7 bounded, certain, endemic, limited, pointed, precise, special, typical 8 clear-cut, concrete, confined, definite, detailed, especial, peculiar, personal, relevant, singular, tied-down 9 intrinsic, pertinent, specified 10 individual, particular, pinned-down, restricted 11 categorical, determinate, distinctive, unequivocal 13 circumscribed 14 characteristic

specification 6 detail 7 clarity 9 condition, precision, substance 11 enumeration, itemization, requirement, stipulation 12 concreteness 13 particularity, qualification 17 particularization

specifics 4 cure, fact, item 5 datum 6 detail, physic 10 medication, particular 12 circumstance

specify 4 cite, name 5 order 6 adduce, define, denote, detail 7 call for, focus on, itemize 8 describe, indicate, set forth 9 designate, enumerate, stipulate 13 particularize

specimen 4 case, type 5 model 6 sample 7 example 8 exemplar, instance 9 prototype 14 representative 15 exemplification

specious 5 false 6 faulty, tricky, untrue 7 dubious, in valid, unsound 8 slippery, spurious 9 casuistic, deceptive, illogical, incorrect, unfounded 10 fallacious, inaccurate, misleading 11 sophistical 12 questionable 15 unsubstantiated

speck 3 bit, dot, jot, pin 4 drop, hair, iota, mark, mite, mote, spot, whit 5 fleck, grain, pinch, trace 6 shadow, trifle 7 glimmer, modicum, speckle 8 farthing, flyspeck, particle 9 scintilla

speckled 4 pied 6 dotted 7 flecked, spotted, studded 8 freckled, peppered 9 sprinkled

spectacle 5 scene, sight 6 marvel, parade, rarity, wonder 7 display, exhibit, pageant 9 curiosity, rare sight 10 exhibition, exposition, phenomenon, production 12 extravaganza, presentation 13 demonstration

spectacles 6 lenses, shades 7 glasses 8 bifocals, pince-nez 10 eyeglasses

spectacular 4 gala, rich 5 grand,

showy 6 daring 7 jeweled, opulent, stately 8 dramatic, fabulous, glorious, gorgeous, splendid, striking 9 daredevil, elaborate, marvelous, spectacle, sumptuous, thrilling 10 astounding, bespangled, eye-filling, impressive, theatrical 11 ceremonious, hairraising, magnificent, sensational 12 extravaganza, overwhelming 16 ostentatious show 19 elaborate production

spectator 3 fan 5 house 6 viewer 7 gallery, witness 8 audience, beholder, kibitzer, observer, onlooker 9 bystander, sightseer 10 aficionado, eyewitness 11 afficionado, theatergoer 12 rubbernecker

Spectator, The
author: 13 Joseph Addison, Richard Steele

specter 5 demon, ghost, ghoul, shade, spook 6 spirit, sprite, vision, wraith 7 banshee, fantasy, phantom 8 phantasm, presence, revenant 9 hobgoblin 10 apparition

spectral 4 airy 5 eerie, weird 6 creepy, spooky, unreal 7 ghastly, ghostly, phantom, shadowy, uncanny 8 ethereal, gossamer, vaporous 9 unearthly 10 chimerical, phantasmal, wraithlike 11 incorporeal 12 otherworldly, supernatural 13 insubstantial

speculate 4 muse 5 brood, dream, fancy, guess, study, think, wager 6 chance, gamble, hazard, ponder, reason, wonder 7 imagine, reflect, suppose, surmise, venture 8 cogitate, consider, meditate, ruminate, theorize 10 conjecture, deliberate, excogitate, play a hunch 11 contemplate, hypothesize, take a chance 13 play the market

speculation 4 risk 7 venture 8 gambling 9 guesswork 10 conjecture, estimation 11 supposition

speculative 4 iffy 5 dicey, risky 6 chancy 8 academic 11 conjectural, theoretical 12 experimental, hypothetical 13 suppositional

speculator 7 gambler, plunger 8 investor, operator, theorist 10 adventurer, arbitrager 11 arbitrageur

speech 4 talk 5 idiom, lingo, slang, voice 6 appeal, gossip, homily, jargon, sermon, tirade, tongue 7 address, chatter, comment, dialect, diction, lecture, oration, palaver, prattle, remarks, talking 8 chitchat, colloquy, converse, dialogue, diatribe, harangue, language, parlance, rhetoric, speaking 9 discourse, elocution, monologue, soliloquy, statement, utterance 10 discussion, expression, recitation, salutation 11 declamation, declaration, enunciation, exhortation, observation, valedictory 12 articulation, conversation, dissertation, vocalization 13 col-

loquialism, confabulation, pronouncement, pronunciation, verbalization

speechless 3 mum **4** dumb, mute **6** silent **7** aphonic **8** wordless **9** stupefied
10 tongue-tied

speed 3 aid, hie, run, zip **4** dart, dash,
help, race, rate, rush, tear, zoom **5**
boost, favor, gun it, haste, hurry, impel, speed, tempo **6** assist, barrel, gallop, hasten, hurtle, hustle, pick up,
plunge, propel, scurry, step up **7** advance, further, hurry up, promote,
quicken, tear off **8** alacrity, celerity,
dispatch, expedite, high tail, make
time, momentum, rapidity, step on it,
velocity **9** bowl along, briskness, fleetness, give a lift, hastiness, make
haste, move along, quickness, rapid-
ness, swiftness **10** accelerate, expedition, get a move on, go hell-bent, lose
no time, promptness, spurt ahead
11 push forward **12** acceleration **13**
burn up the road

speedily 4 fast **5** apace, quick **6**
pronto **7** hastily, rapidly, swiftly **8** in
no time, promptly **9** post haste, right
away, summarily **11** on the double **12**
lickety-split

speed up 4 rush **5** hurry **6** hasten,
step up **7** hop to it, quicken **8** expedite, multiply, step on it **9** encourage,
intensify **10** accelerate, facilitate, get a
move on **12** step on the gas

speedy 4 fast **5** brisk, early, fleet,
hasty, quick, rapid, ready, swift **6** abrupt, lively, sudden **7** express, hurried, running, summary **8** headlong **9**
quick-fire, rapid-fire **10** not delayed
11 precipitate

Spelaites
epithet of: 6 Hermes
means: 9 of the cave

spell 2 go **3** bit, hex **4** bout, free, lull,
mean, omen, snap, term, time, tour,
turn, wave **5** augur, break, charm,
hitch, imply, magic, pause, round,
stint, trick, while **6** allure, course, denote, herald, hoodoo, make up, period, recess, tenure, typify, voodoo **7**
bespeak, betoken, connote, glamour,
portend, presage, promise, purport,
rapture, release, relieve, respite, signify, sorcery, stretch, suggest **8**
amount to, cover for, duration, forebode, forecast, foretell, indicate, interval, stand for, witchery **9** form a
word, influence, interlude, represent,
symbolize **10** assignment, invocation,
mumbo jumbo, open-sesame **11** abracadabra, bewitchment, enchantment,
fascination, incantation, pinch-hit for,
take over for **12** magic formula

spellbind 5 charm **7** bewitch, enchant
8 enthrall, entrance, intrigue, transfix
9 enrapture, fascinate, hypnotize,
mesmerize, transport

spellbound 4 rapt **5** agape **7** charmed

8 wordless **9** awestruck, bewitched,
enchanted, entranced, possessed **10**
breathless, dumbstruck, enraptured,
enthralled, fascinated, hypnotized,
mesmerized, speechless, tongue-tied,
transfixed **11** openmouthed, transported

Spellbound
director: 15 Alfred Hitchcock
cast: 9 John Emery **11** Gregory Peck,
Leo G Carroll **13** Ingrid Bergman **14**
Michael Chekhov
score: 11 Miklos Rosza
Oscar for: 5 score
dream sequences by: 12 Salvador
Dali

spell out 6 define, detail **7** clarify,
clear up, explain, expound, specify **8**
describe **9** delineate, designate, elucidate, explicate, interpret, make plain
10 illustrate

Spemann, Hans
field: 7 zoology
nationality: 6 German
worked in: 20 embryonic development
awarded: 10 Nobel Prize

Spencer, Sir Stanley
born: 7 Cookham, England **9** Berkshire
artwork: 22 Resurrection of Soldiers,
The Resurrection Cookham **31** Christ
Preaching at Cookham Regatta **43**
Double Nude Portrait the Artist and
his Second Wife

spend 3 pay, use **4** dole, fill, give, pass
5 drain, empty, use up, waste **6** devote, employ, expend, invest, occupy,
outlay, pay out, take up **7** burn out,
consume, deplete, destroy, exhaust,
fork out, scatter, wear out **8** allocate,
disburse, dispense, shell out, squander
9 dissipate, while away **10** impoverish

spendable 9 available **10** expendable
13 discretionary

spend foolishly 5 waste **8** misspend,
squander **9** dissipate, throw away **11**
fritter away

spendthrift 6 lavish, waster **7** wastrel
8 prodigal, spend-all, wasteful **10** big
spender, profligate, squanderer **11** extravagant, improvident **12** overgenerous

Spengler, Oswald
author of: 19 The Decline of the
West

Spenlow, Dora
character in: 16 David Copperfield
author: 7 Dickens

Spenser, Edmund
author of: 8 Amoretti **12** Epithalamion **15** The Faerie Queene **22** The
Shepherde's Calendar

spent 4 beat, done, weak **5** faint,
weary **6** bushed, done in, used up **7**
laid low, wearied, worn out **8** drooping, fatigued, tired out **9** enfeebled,

exhausted, fagged out, played out,
powerless, prostrate **11** debilitated,
ready to drop **12** strengthless **14** on
one's last legs

Sperry, Elmer Ambrose
invented: 11 gyrocompass **22** airplane automatic pilot

spew 5 eject, expel, heave, vomit **6**
cast up **7** spit out **8** disgorge, throw
out **11** regurgitate

spew up 4 spew **5** eject, expel, spout,
vomit **6** cast up **7** cough up, throw up
8 disgorge **11** regurgitate

sphere 3 orb **4** area, ball, beat, pale **5**
globe, orbit, range, realm, scope **6** domain **7** compass, globule **8** province,
spheroid **9** bailiwick, round body, territory **10** experience

spherical 5 orbic, round **6** global, rotund **7** globate, globose, orbical **8**
globular **9** orbicular **11** globe-shaped
nearly: 8 obrotund

spheroid 3 orb **4** ball **5** globe **6** sphere
7 globule

spherule 4 ball, bead, drop **6** pellet **7**
droplet, globule

Sphinx
form: 7 monster
bust of: 5 woman
body of: 4 lion
father: 6 Typhon **7** Orthrus
mother: 7 Echidna **8** Chimaera
proposed: 7 riddles
location: 4 Giza **6** Thebes
answered by: 7 Oedipus

spice 3 zip **4** herb, kick, snap, tang,
zest **5** savor **6** accent, flavor, relish,
stacte **7** pizzazz **8** piquancy, pungency **9** condiment, flavoring, seasoning **10** excitement

spicule 4 barb **5** point, spine **7** prickle

spicy 3 hot **4** keen, racy **5** acute,
bawdy, fiery, nippy, pithy, salty,
sharp, tangy, witty, zippy **6** clever,
ribald, risque, snappy, strong **7** gingery, peppery, piquant, pungent **8** aromatic, improper, incisive, indecent,
off-color, piercing, redolent, spirited **9**
sparkling, trenchant **10** indelicate,
scandalous, suggestive **11** provocative
12 questionable **13** scintillating

spider
black widow marking: 9 hourglass
class: 9 Arachnida
combining form: 6 arachn **7** arachno
family: 7 Attidae **9** Drassidae **10** Citi-
gradae, Pisauridae
famous: 9 Charlotte
fear of: 13 arachnophobia
kind: 4 crab, wolf **5** taint **7** jumping
8 trap-door **9** orb weaver, solpugida,
tarantula **10** black widow **13** daddy
longlegs
mythology: 7 Arachne
nest: 5 nidus
order: 7 Araneae
part: 4 claw, coxa **5** femur, tibia **6**

tarsus **7** abdomen, mammula, patella, pedicel, scopula **9** chelicera, protaris, spinneret **10** pedipalpus, trochanter **11** calamistrum **13** cephalothorax
study of: **10** araneology **11** arachnology
young: **11** spiderlings

Spielberg, Steven
wife: **11** Kate Capshaw
former wife: **9** Amy Irving
company: **13** Dreamworks SKG
director of: **4** Jaws **7** Amistad **11** Poltergeist **12** Jurassic Park, The Lost World **14** Schindler's List (Oscar), The Color Purple **19** Raiders of the Lost Ark **21** ET The Extra Terrestrial **29** Close Encounters of the Third Kind, Indiana Jones and the Last Crusade **30** Indiana Jones and the Temple of Doom

spike 3 peg, pin **4** barb, nail, spur, tine **5** briar, point, prong, rivet, spine, stake, thorn **6** needle, skewer **7** bramble, bristle, hobnail **8** spikelet

spill 3 run **4** blab, drip, drop, dump, fall, flow, shed, slop, tell, toss **5** slosh, throw, waste **6** reveal, splash **7** let flow, pour out **8** disclose, overflow, overturn

Spillane, Mickey
real name: **13** Frank Morrison
author of: **8** I the Jury **12** Kiss Me Deadly **14** The Girl Hunters **15** The Death Dealers
character: **10** Mike Hammer

spin 4 roll, tell, turn **5** swirl, twirl, wheel, whirl **6** gyrate, invent, relate, render, rotate, unfold **7** concoct, narrate, recount, revolve **8** rotation, spinning **9** fabricate, pirouette

spinach 3 rot **4** bull, bunk **5** hokum, hooey, stuff **6** bunkum, hot air, humbug **7** baloney, blather, hogwash, potherb **8** claptrap, nonsense, tommyrot **9** poppycock, vegetable **10** applesauce **11** foolishness **16** stuff and nonsense

spinach 16 Spinacia oleracea
varieties: **4** wild **5** Cuban **6** Indian **7** Malabar **8** mountain **10** New Zealand **11** round-seeded **13** pricklyseeded

spinal column 4 back **5** spine **8** backbone

spindly 4 puny **5** frail, leggy **6** skinny **7** scraggy **8** skeletal

spine 4 barb, horn, spur **5** briar, point, prong, quill, spike, thorn **6** needle **7** bramble, bristle, prickle **8** backbone **9** vertebrae **12** spinal column

spinel
source: **5** Burma, Mogok
color: **3** red **5** mauve

spineless 4 weak **5** timid **7** fearful **8** cowardly, cowering, cringing, timorous, wavering **10** indecisive, irresolute, spiritless, weak-willed **11** lily-livered, vacillating **12** fainthearted **13** pusillanimous **14** chickenhearted

spinelessness 8 timidity, weakness **9** cowardice **10** indecision **11** fearfulness **12** cowardliness, irresolution **13** pusillanimity

spine-tingling 7 rousing **8** exciting **9** thrilling **11** hair-raising, sensational **12** breathtaking, electrifying

spinning jenny
invented by: **10** Hargreaves

spinoff 5 issue **6** result **7** ad junct, outcome **8** offshoot **9** byproduct, outgrowth **10** descendant, side effect, supplement **11** aftereffect, consequence

spin out 4 skid **7** draw out **8** lengthen **9** attenuate

spinster 6 virgin **7** old maid **14** unmarried woman

spinsterhood 8 celibacy **9** virginity **11** old maidhood

spiral 4 coil, curl, gyre **5** helix, screw, whirl, whorl **6** coiled, curled **7** helical, ringlet, spiroid, whorled, winding **8** curlicue, twisting **9** corkscrew **11** screw-shaped

Spiral Staircase, The
director: **13** Robert Siodmak
based on story by: **14** Ethel Lina White (Some Must Watch)
cast: **9** Kent Smith **11** George Brent **13** Rhonda Fleming **14** Dorothy McGuire, Ethel Barrymore

spire 3 cap, tip **4** apex, cone, peak **5** crest, point, shaft, tower **6** belfry, summit, turret, vertex **7** minaret, obelisk, steeple **8** pinnacle **9** bell tower, campanile

spirit 3 elf **4** mind, soul, urge, will **5** fairy, ghost, ghoul, heart, shade, spook **6** animus, dybbuk, goblin, psyche, sprite, wraith **7** banshee, bugaboo, bugbear, impulse, phantom, resolve, specter **8** phantasm, presence **9** hobgoblin, intellect **10** apparition, motivation, resolution
German: **5** Geist

spirited 4 bold **5** fiery, nervy **6** frisky, lively, plucky **8** fearless, intrepid **10** courageous, mettlesome

spiritless 4 dull, limp, tame **6** abject **8** cowardly, lifeless, listless **9** apathetic, spineless **10** unanimated, world-weary **11** passionless

spirit of the time
German: **9** Zeitgeist

spirits 3 aim, vim **4** bond, elan, fire, gist, glow, grit, guts, mood, sand, tone, vein, zeal, zest **5** ardor, drive, humor, pluck, sense, spunk, tenor, valor, verve, vigor **6** daring, effect, elixir, energy, fervor, intent, liquor, mettle, morale, stripe, temper, warmth **7** alcohol, avidity, bravery, courage, essence, extract, feeling, loyalty,

meaning, purport, purpose, sparkle **8** attitude, audacity, backbone, boldness, devotion, emotions, feelings, tincture, vitality, vivacity **9** animation, eagerness, fortitude, intention, sentiment, stoutness, substance **10** allegiance, attachment, enterprise, enthusiasm, liveliness **11** disposition, doughtiness, staunchness **12** fearlessness, significance **13** dauntlessness, sprightliness **16** stoutheartedness **17** alcoholic solution

spiritual 4 holy **5** godly, inner, moral, pious **6** divine, mental **7** blessed, churchy, ghostly, phantom, psychic **8** cerebral, hallowed, heavenly, platonic, priestly, spectral, supernal **9** celestial, Christian, innermost, of the soul, religious, unearthly, unfleshly, unworldly **10** devotional, immaterial, intangible, sacrosanct, sanctified **11** consecrated, incorporeal **12** metaphysical, otherworldly, supernatural **13** insubstantial, psychological **14** ecclesiastical

spirituality 5 piety **8** devotion, holiness **9** godliness, reverence **10** devoutness

spirituous 4 hard **6** strong **9** alcoholic, distilled **12** intoxicating

spit 3 bar, pop, rod **4** foam, hiss, reef, spew **5** atoll, drool, eject, fling, froth, shoal, throw **6** saliva, shower, shriek, skewer, slaver, sputum **7** dribble, scatter, slobber, spatter, spittle, sputter **8** headland, sandbank, turnspit **9** brochette, peninsula **10** promontory **11** expectorate

spite 3 irk, vex **4** gall, hate, hurt, pain **5** annoy, odium, sting, venom, wound **6** animus, enmity, grudge, harass, hatred, injure, malice, misuse, nettle, put out, rancor **7** ill will, mortify, provoke **8** bad blood, ill-treat, irritate, loathing, meanness **9** animosity, antipathy, hostility, humiliate, malignity, nastiness, vengeance **10** bitterness, resentment **11** detestation, malevolence **12** vengefulness **13** maliciousness, slap in the face **14** revengefulness, vindictiveness

spiteful 4 evil **5** nasty **6** bitter, malign, wicked **7** caustic, envious, hateful, hostile, vicious **8** grudging, vengeful, venomous **9** malicious, merciless, rancorous, resentful, sarcastic, splenetic **10** ill-natured, malevolent, vindictive **11** acrimonious, unforgiving **12** antagonistic

spitting image (spit and image) 4 copy, mate, twin **6** double **9** duplicate **15** perfect likeness

splash 3 ado, hit **4** cast, dash, daub, soil, stir, toss, wash **5** bathe, break, fling, plash, slosh, smack, smear, stain, strew, surge, swash **6** batter, blazon, buffet, effect, impact, paddle, plunge, shower, spread, streak, strike, uproar, wallow, welter **7** bestrew, scatter, spatter, splotch **8** besmirch, discolor, disperse, splatter, sprinkle **9** bespatter, broadcast, commotion, sensation **10** spattering **11** splattering

splashy 5 jazzy, showy **6** flashy **10** glittering **11** spectacular **12** ostentatious

splatter 4 dash **6** splash **7** spatter

splay 4 awry **5** askew, broad **6** aslant, clumsy, extend, tilted, warped **7** awkward, crooked, fanlike, slanted, sloping, turn out **8** inclined, slanting **9** distorted, fan-shaped, irregular, outspread, spread out **10** stretch out

spleen 4 bile, gall **5** anger, spite, venom **6** animus, enmity, hatred, malice, rancor **7** ill will **8** acrimony, ill humor, vexation **9** animosity, bad temper, hostility **10** bitterness, resentment **11** malevolence, peevishness **12** irritability, spitefulness

splendid 4 fine, high, rare, rich **5** grand, lofty, noble, regal, royal **6** august, costly, ornate, superb **7** elegant, eminent, exalted, stately **8** dazzling, elevated, flashing, gleaming, glorious, gorgeous, imposing, majestic, palatial, peerless, terrific **9** admirable, beautiful, brilliant, effulgent, estimable, excellent, marvelous, sumptuous, wonderful **10** glittering, preeminent, remarkable, surpassing **11** exceptional, illustrious, magnificent, outstanding, resplendent, splendorous **12** transcendent **13** distinguished, splendiferous

Splendid Splinter
  nickname of: 11 Ted Williams

splendor 4 fire, pomp **5** gleam, glory, light, sheen, shine **6** beauty, dazzle, luster, renown **7** burnish, glitter **8** grandeur, nobility, opulence, radiance **9** intensity, sublimity **10** augustness, brilliance, effulgence, irradiance, luminosity **11** preeminence, stateliness **12** gorgeousness, luminousness, magnificence, resplendence **13** incandescence

Splendor in the Grass
  director: 9 Elia Kazan
  based on story by: 11 William Inge
  cast: 9 Pat Hingle **11** Natalie Wood **12** Sean Garrison, Warren Beatty **14** Audrey Christie

splenetic 5 cross, nasty, surly, testy **6** cranky, malign **7** bilious, hostile, peevish **8** choleric, spiteful, venomous **9** irascible, rancorous **11** acrimonious, ill-tempered **12** cantankerous, disagreeable

splice 3 wed **4** join, knit **5** graft, merge, plait, unite **7** connect **8** dovetail **9** interlace **10** intertwine, interweave **12** interconnect

splinter 4 chip **5** smash, split **6** needle, shiver, sliver **7** break up, crumble, explode, shatter **8** fly apart, frac-

ture, fragment **9** pulverize **12** disintegrate

split 3 hew **4** deal, dole, dual, mete, part, rent, rift, rive, snap, tear, torn **5** allot, break, burst, cleft, crack, halve, mixed, riven, sever, share **6** bisect, breach, broken, cleave, differ, divide, ripped, schism, shiver, sunder, varied **7** be riven, cracked, diverge, divided, divorce, divvy up, fissure, give way, opening, portion, quarrel, rupture, severed, twofold **8** alienate, allocate, cleavage, disagree, dispense, disperse, dissever, disunion, disunite, division, fracture, ruptured, splinter **9** apportion, fractured, parcel out, partition, segmented, segregate, separated, set at odds, subdivide, undecided **10** alienation, ambivalent, break apart, difference, dissension, dissevered, distribute, divergence, falling out, separation, splintered **11** come between, part company, tear asunder **12** disagreement, estrangement

split off 7 deviate, diverge **8** separate **9** draw apart

split the difference 5 agree **6** settle **9** make a deal **10** compromise **11** come to terms, meet halfway **14** strike a bargain

splitting off 9 diverging **10** separating **12** drawing apart

splitting up 8 dividing **9** divorcing **10** breaking up, separating **11** subdividing **12** partitioning

splotch 4 blot, daub, mark, spot **5** smear, stain **6** blotch, smudge **13** discoloration

splurge 5 binge, spree **6** bender **8** live it up **10** indulgence, showing off **12** showy display **13** be extravagant, shoot the works **14** indulge oneself, self-indulgence **22** throw caution to the winds

splutter 4 hiss, spew, spit **5** burst, spray **6** gibber, jabber, mumble, seethe **7** bluster, slobber, spatter, sputter, stammer, stumble, stutter **9** hem and haw **11** expectorate

spoil 3 mar, rot **4** baby, flaw, harm, mold, ruin, sour, turn **5** addle, botch, decay, go bad, humor, taint **6** blight, bungle, coddle, damage, deface, foul up, impair, injure, mess up, mildew, muddle, pamper **7** blemish, destroy, disrupt, putrefy **8** mutilate **9** decompose, disfigure **11** deteriorate, mollycoddle, overgratify, overindulge

spoiled 3 bad, off **6** putrid, rotten, ruined **7** coddled, corrupt, decayed, gone bad, went bad **8** indulged, overripe, pampered **9** putrefied **10** decomposed, frustrated **12** deteriorated **15** rotten to the core

spoiler 6 vandal **8** underdog **9** deflector

spoils 4 haul, loot, swag, take **5** booty

6 bounty, prizes, quarry **7** plunder, profits **8** benefits, comforts, pickings **9** amenities, patronage **11** perquisites **12** acquisitions

spoilsport 4 drag **10** wet blanket **11** party-pooper

spoken 4 oral, said **5** parol **6** verbal, voiced **7** uttered **8** expressed **10** pronounced **11** articulated

spokesman 5 agent, PR man, proxy **6** backer, deputy **7** speaker **8** delegate, promoter **9** middleman, proponent, supporter, surrogate **10** mouthpiece, negotiator, press agent **11** protagonist

sponge 3 bum, dry, mop, rub **4** blot, swab, wash **5** cadge, clean, leech, mooch, towel **6** borrow, live on **7** cleanse, moisten **8** freeload, impose on, scrounge **9** panhandle

sponger 5 leech **6** cadger, sponge **7** moocher **8** barnacle, borrower, deadbeat **9** scrounger **10** freeloader **11** bloodsucker

sponsor 4 back **5** angel, set up **6** backer, patron, uphold **7** finance, promote, support **8** advocate, champion, defender, financer, guardian, partisan, promoter, start out, upholder, vouch for, warranty **9** guarantee, financier, guarantor, proponent, protecter, protector, supporter **10** advertiser, stand up for, underwrite

sponsorship 5 aegis **7** support **8** advocacy, auspices **9** patronage **12** championship

spontaneity 7 freedom **11** impetuosity, naturalness **12** unconstraint **13** impulsiveness, offhandedness **18** extemporaneousness

spontaneous 4 free **5** ad lib **7** natural, offhand, willing **8** unbidden **9** automatic, extempore, impetuous, impromptu, impulsive, ingenuous, unplanned, unstudied, voluntary **10** gratuitous, improvised, off the cuff, unprompted **11** independent, instinctive, uncontrived **12** unhesitating **13** unconstrained **14** extemporaneous, unpremeditated

spoof 3 kid **4** joke, josh, twit **6** parody, satire, sendup **7** joshing, kidding, lampoon, mockery, ribbing, takeoff **8** satirize, travesty **9** burlesque, take off on **10** caricature

spook 5 alarm, bogey, ghost, haunt, scare, shade **6** goblin, shadow, spirit **7** disturb, phantom, specter, startle, terrify, unnerve **8** disquiet, frighten, unsettle **9** hobgoblin, terrorize **10** apparition, intimidate

spooky 5 eerie, jumpy, scary, weird **6** creepy **7** ghostly, nervous **8** skittish **10** mysterious

sporadic 3 few **4** rare, thin **6** fitful, meager, random, scarce, sparse, spotty **8** isolated, periodic, uncommon **9** haphazard, irregular, scattered, spasmodic **10** infrequent, now and then, occasional **11** fragmentary **12** intermittent, widely spaced **13** discontinuous **16** few and far between

sport 3 fun, toy **4** bear, butt, game, goat, jest, joke, lark, play, romp, trip **5** abuse, caper, carry, chaff, dally, frisk, hobby, mirth, revel **6** antics, cavort, frolic, gaiety, gambol, misuse, monkey, take in, trifle **7** buffoon, contest, display, disport, exhibit, gambler, jesting, jollity, kidding, mockery, rollick, show off, skylark **8** badinage, derision, fair game, flourish, hilarity, illtreat, raillery, ridicule, scoffing, trifling **9** amusement, athletics, daredevil, diversion, festivity, joviality, make merry, play games, scapegoat **10** persiflage, pleasantry, recreation, relaxation, skylarking **11** competition, distraction, merrymaking **12** depreciation **13** entertainment, laughingstock **14** divertissement

sporting house 4 stew **5** house **6** bagnio, bordel **7** brothel **8** bordello, cathouse **10** bawdy house, fancy house, whorehouse **14** house of ill fame **16** house of ill repute **19** house of prostitution

sportive 6 blithe, frisky **7** playful **8** animated **10** frolicsome

sportsman 6 hunter **9** fisherman

Sportsman's Notebook, A
  author: **12** Ivan Turgenev

sporty 6 casual, flashy, jaunty **8** informal

spot 3 dot, fix, see, spy **4** area, bind, blot, daub, espy, flaw, mark, part, seat, site, slur, soil **5** brand, fleck, grime, locus, patch, place, point, smear, space, speck, stain, sully, taint, tract **6** blotch, defect, detect, locale, locate, plight, region, sector, smirch, smudge, splash, stigma **7** blemish, dilemma, discern, light on, pick out, quarter, section, spatter, speckle, splotch, station **8** discolor, discover, disgrace, district, flyspeck, locality, location, position, premises, reproach, sprinkle **9** aspersion, discredit, recognize, situation, territory **10** difficulty, imputation **11** predicament **12** bad situation, neighborhood **13** discoloration

spotless 4 pure **5** clean, snowy **7** perfect, shining **8** flawless, gleaming, pristine, unflawed, unmarred, unsoiled **9** faultless, stainless, unspotted, unstained, unsullied, untainted **10** immaculate, impeccable **11** unblemished, untarnished **14** irreproachable **15** unexceptionable

spotted 3 saw **6** dotted, espied, soiled **7** dappled, located, mottled, stained **8** detected, speckled **9** blemished, discerned, spattered **10** discovered **13** caught sight of

spotty 6 fitful, pimply, random, uneven **7** blotchy, dappled, erratic, flecked, mottled, spotted **8** episodic, freckled, splotchy, sporadic, unsteady, variable, wavering **9** broken out, desultory, irregular, spasmodic, uncertain **10** capricious, inconstant, unreliable, variegated **11** full of spots **12** disorganized, intermittent, undependable, unmethodical, unsystematic

spouse 4 mate, wife **7** consort, husband, partner **8** helpmate **10** better half

spout 3 jet, lip **4** beak, flow, go on, gush, nose, pipe, rant, spew, tube, vent, well **5** eject, erupt, expel, exude, issue, mouth, shoot, snout, spray, spurt, surge, vomit **6** nozzle, outlet, sluice, squirt, stream, trough **7** bluster, carry on, channel, conduit, pour out **8** disgorge, fountain, harangue **9** discharge, hold forth **10** waterspout **11** pontificate **12** emit forcibly **14** speak pompously

sprawl 4 flop, lean, loll, wind **5** slump **6** branch, extend, lounge, slouch **7** gush out, meander, recline **8** languish, reach out, straggle **9** spread out **10** stretch out **11** spread-eagle

spray 4 coat, mist, posy, twig **5** bough, burst, shoot, sprig, treat, vapor **6** dampen, nozzle, shower, splash, switch, volley **7** atomize, barrage, blossom, bouquet, drizzle, moisten, nosegay, scatter, spatter, sprayer, syringe **8** atomizer, disperse, droplets, moisture, sprinkle **9** discharge, fusillade, sprinkler, vaporizer

spread 3 air, lay **4** area, cast, coat, open, pave, shed, span, vent **5** apply, bruit, cloak, cover, feast, field, issue, range, reach, scope, smear, spray, story, strew, sweep, table, tract, width **6** bedaub, beshed, blazon, extend, extent, herald, length, notice, repeat, report, unfold, unfurl, unroll **7** account, advance, article, banquet, besmear, bestrew, breadth, circuit, compass, declare, diffuse, divulge, expanse, overlay, overrun, pervade, plaster, publish, radiate, scatter, spatter, stretch, suffuse, trumpet, untwine, write-up **8** announce, coverage, disperse, distance, increase, permeate, proclaim, sprinkle **9** broadcast, circulate, diffusion, expansion, extension, make known, penetrate, pervasion, propagate, publicize, radiation, spreading, suffusion, ventilate **10** dispersion, distribute, make public, permeation, promulgate, stretch out **11** communicate, disseminate, noise abroad, proliferate **13** amplification, dissemination, proliferation

spread out 5 broad, widen **6** expand, extend **7** broaden, diffuse, enlarge, radiate, stretch **8** expanded, extended, open wide **9** dispersed, outspread, scattered **10** distribute, unhampered

11 unconfirmed **12** unrestricted **14** unconcentrated

spree 4 bout, orgy, toot **5** binge, drunk, fling, revel **6** bender **7** carouse, debauch, revelry, splurge, wassail **8** carousal **9** bacchanal **10** saturnalia

sprightliness 8 buoyancy, spryness, vivacity **9** animation, briskness **10** breeziness, liveliness **16** lightheartedness

sprightly 3 gay **4** keen, spry **5** agile, alive, brisk, jolly, merry **6** active, blithe, breezy, cheery, jaunty, jovial, lively, nimble **7** buoyant, chipper, dashing, dynamic, playful **8** animated, cheerful, spirited, sportive **9** energetic, vivacious **10** blithesome, frolicsome **12** lighthearted

spring 3 hop, jet, pop, spa **4** come, dart, flow, gush, jump, kick, leap, loom, pool, pour, rise, rush, stem, well **5** arise, baths, begin, bound, caper, ensue, fount, issue, lunge, shoot, spout, spurt, start, surge, vault **6** appear, bounce, derive, gambol, recoil, reflex, result, sprout, stream **7** burgeon, crop out, descend, emanate, proceed, release, shoot up, start up, stretch, trigger **8** buoyancy, commence, fountain, mushroom **9** come forth, entrechat, germinate, originate, saltation, waterhole **10** break forth, burst forth, elasticity, resiliency **11** flexibility
  goddess of: **4** Hebe **5** Venus

spring back 6 bounce, recoil **7** rebound **8** ricochet

spring flowers
  goddess of: **6** Thallo

springlike 4 mild, soft, warm **5** balmy

springs
  god of: **4** Fons **6** Palici
  goddess of: **4** Idun **5** Idura, Ithun **6** Ithunn

spring up 4 grow, rise **5** arise, occur, pop up **6** crop up, emerge, happen, sprout **9** originate **10** burst forth

springy 6 bouncy, spongy, supple **7** elastic **9** resilient **10** rebounding

sprinkle 4 dash, dust, rain **5** spray, strew, water **6** powder, shower, splash, spread, squirt **7** bestrew, diffuse, drizzle, moisten, scatter, spatter **8** splatter

sprinkling 4 dash, drop, hint **5** pinch, touch **7** droplet, minimum, modicum, soupcon **8** sprinkle **10** smattering

sprint 3 run **4** dart, dash, kick, race, rush, tear, whiz **5** burst, shoot, spurt, whisk **7** scamper

sprit 3 bar **4** spar **8** crossbar **10** crosspiece

sprite 3 elf **5** fairy, pixie **10** leprechaun

sprout 3 bud, wax **4** grow **5** bloom, shoot, sprig **6** come up, flower, spread, thrive **7** blossom, burgeon **8** multiply, offshoot, put forth, spring up **9** germinate, outgrowth

spruce 4 chic, neat, tidy, trim **5** kempt, natty, sharp, smart **6** dapper **7** conifer, elegant **9** evergreen, shipshape **11** well-groomed **12** spick-and-span
French: 6 soigne

spruce 5 Picea
   varieties: 3 bog, cat, red **4** blue **5** black, Hondo, Sitka, snake, white, Yeddo **6** double, Norway **7** Alberta, big-cone, Finnish, hemlock **8** Colorado, Sakhalin, Siberian **9** Himalayan, tiger-tail **10** Black Hills **12** Colorado blue, Japanese bush

spry 4 deft, hale **5** agile, brisk, quick **6** active, frisky, hearty, jaunty, lively, nimble, supple **7** buoyant, chipper, playful **8** animated, spirited, sportive, vigorous **9** energetic, sprightly, vivacious **11** lightfooted

spunk 4 fire, grit, guts, salt, sand **5** heart, nerve, pluck **6** daring, ginger, mettle, pepper, spirit **7** bravery, courage **8** backbone, boldness, gumption **10** feistiness

spur 3 arm, leg **4** fork, goad, prod, whet, whip, wing **5** prick **6** branch, feeder, fillip, hasten, motive, siding **7** impetus, impulse **8** excitant, stimulus **9** boot spike, encourage, incentive, stimulant, stimulate, tributary **10** incitement, inducement **11** instigation, provocation, stimulation **13** encouragement

spurge 9 Euphorbia **11** Pachysandra
   varieties: 5 caper, leafy, melon **6** ipecac, myrtle, tramp's **7** cypress, mottled, seaside, slipper **8** fiddler's, Japanese **9** Allegheny, flowering **10** Indian tree

spurious 4 fake, mock, sham **5** bogus, false, phony **6** faulty, forged, hollow **7** feigned, unsound **8** specious **9** imitation, simulated **10** fallacious, fraudulent, not genuine **11** counterfeit, make-believe, unauthentic **12** illegitimate

spurn 4 mock, snub **5** flout, repel, scorn **6** rebuff, refuse, reject, slight **7** condemn, decline, disdain, dismiss, repulse, scoff at, sneer at **8** turn down **9** cast aside, disparage, repudiate **12** coldshoulder, look down upon **16** turn up one's nose at

spur-of-the-moment 5 ad-lib **7** offhand **9** extempore, impromptu **10** improvised, unprepared **11** extemporary, spontaneous, unrehearsed **14** extemporaneous, unpremeditated

spurt 3 jet **4** dart, dash, emit, flow, gush, gust, rush, tear, whiz **5** burst, flash, issue, lunge, scoot, shoot, speed, spout, spray, surge **6** access, spring, sprint, squirt, stream **7** pour out **8** disgorge, ejection, eruption,

fountain, outbreak, outburst **9** discharge, explosion, spring out **10** outpouring

spy 3 pry, see **4** find, peep, spot, view **5** scout, sight, snoop **6** behold, descry, detect, notice, shadow **7** discern, glimpse, make out, observe **8** discover, informer, Mata Hari, perceive, saboteur **9** keep watch, operative, recognize **11** reconnoiter, secret agent **12** catch sight of **13** undercover man, watch secretly **14** espionage agent, fifth columnist **16** agent provocateur **17** intelligence agent
   famous: 4 Abel, Hale **5** Andre, Caleb, Pitts **6** Arnold, Dulles, Philby, Powers, Smiley **8** Mata Hari **9** James Bond, Nicholson, Philbrick, Pinkerton, Rosenberg

Spy, The
   author: 19 James Fenimore Cooper

Spy Who Came In from the Cold, The
   director: 10 Martin Ritt
   based on novel by: 11 John LeCarre
   cast: 11 Claire Bloom, Oskar Werner **12** Peter Van Eyck **13** Richard Burton

Spy Who Loved Me, The
   author: 10 Ian Fleming
   director: 12 Lewis Gilbert
   cast: 10 Bernard Lee (M), Roger Moore (James Bond) **11** Barbara Bach, Curt Jurgens (Stromberg), Richard Kiel (Jaws)

squabble 3 row, war **4** spat, tiff **5** argue, brawl, clash, fight, run-in, scrap, set-to, words **6** battle, bicker, differ **7** contend, contest, dispute, quarrel, wrangle **8** argument **9** have words, lock horns **10** bandy words, contention, difference, dissension **11** altercation, controversy **12** disagreement

squadron 5 fleet **6** armada **8** flotilla **9** naval unit **10** escadrille **11** cavalry unit **12** military unit

squalid 4 foul, mean **5** dirty, nasty **6** abject, filthy, horrid, rotten, shabby, sloppy, sordid **7** decayed, reeking, run-down, unclean **8** battered, degraded, slovenly, wretched **9** miserable **10** broken-down, disheveled, ramshackle, slatternly, tumbledown **11** dilapidated **12** deteriorated

squalor 4 dirt **5** filth **6** misery **7** neglect, poverty **8** foulness, meanness, ugliness **9** dinginess, dirtiness, nastiness, seediness **10** abjectness, grubbiness, sordidness **11** squalidness, uncleanness **12** wretchedness **13** uncleanliness

squander 4 blow **5** spend, waste **6** lavish, misuse **7** consume, deplete, exhaust **8** misspend **9** dissipate, throw away **10** run through **11** fritter away **14** spend like water

squanderer 6 waster **7** wastrel **8**

prodigal **10** dissipater, profligate **11** spendthrift

squandering 7 wasting **8** prodigal, wasteful **9** imprudent **10** profligate **11** dissipating, extravagant, improvident, spendthrift **12** overspending, throwing away **14** frittering away **17** spending like water

square 3 box, fit **4** even, fogy, heal, hick, jerk, jibe, just, mend, park, prig **5** agree, align, blend, block, close, equal, green, match, place, plane, plaza, prude, tally **6** accord, adjust, candid, circus, cohere, common, concur, even up, fall in, honest, pay off, settle, smooth **7** arrange, balance, clear up, compose, conform, even out, flatten, mediate, patch up, rectify, resolve **8** block out, cornball, make even, quadrate, set right, settle up, truthful **9** arbitrate, discharge, equitable, harmonize, liquidate, make level, reconcile **10** clodhopper, correspond, quadrangle, straighten **11** marketplace **12** apple knocker, conservative **13** quadrilateral, stick-in-the- mud **15** straightforward
   type: 1 T **3** try **11** combination

Square
   character in: 8 Tom Jones
   author: 8 Fielding

Square
   constellation of: 5 Norma

square centimeter
   abbreviation: 4 sq cm

square decimeter
   abbreviation: 4 sq dm

square dekameter
   abbreviation: 5 sq dam

square foot
   abbreviation: 4 sq ft

square hectometer
   abbreviation: 4 sq hm

square inch
   abbreviation: 4 sq in

square kilometer
   abbreviation: 4 sq km

square meter
   abbreviation: 3 sq m

square mile
   abbreviation: 4 sq mi

square millimeter
   abbreviation: 4 sq mm

square rod
   abbreviation: 4 sq rd

square yard
   abbreviation: 4 sq yd

squash 3 jam **4** cram, mash, pulp **5** crowd, crush, level, quash, quell, smash, upset **6** dispel, squish **7** compact, destroy, flatten, put down, ram down, repress, squeeze, squelch, trample **8** compress, suppress **9** dissipate, overthrow, prostrate, undermine **10** annihilate, obliterate **11** concentrate

squash 9 Cucurbita
 varieties: 4 bush 5 acorn 6 autumn, banana, summer, turban, winter 7 Hubbard, scallop 8 pattypan, zucchini 9 cocozelle, crookneck 12 Boston marrow 13 sweet dumpling 15 Canada crookneck, summer crookneck, winter crookneck

squat 5 cower, dumpy, dwell, kneel, pudgy 6 chunky, cringe, crouch, encamp, hunker, lie low, locate, move in, shrink, square, stocky, stubby, stumpy 8 thickset

squawk 5 blare, croak, gripe 6 scream, squall 7 grumble, protest, screech 8 complain

squeak 3 cry 4 peep, yelp 5 cheep, chirp, creak, grate 6 shriek, shrill, squeal 7 screech

squeal 3 cry 4 bawl, blab, fink, peep, sing, wail, yell, yelp 5 cheep, whine 6 inform, scream, shriek, shrill, squeak 7 screech

squealer 3 pig, rat 4 fink 6 canary, piglet, snitch 7 stoolie, tattler, traitor 8 informer 10 tattletale 11 stool pigeon 12 blabbermouth

squeamish 3 coy 4 prim, sick 5 fussy 6 demure, modest, proper, queasy 7 finical, finicky, mincing, prudish, sickish 8 delicate, nauseous, priggish, qualmish 9 finicking 10 fastidious 11 puritanical, straitlaced 13 sanctimonious

Squeers, Wackford
 character in: 16 Nicholas Nickleby
 author: 7 Dickens

squeeze 3 hug, jam, pry, ram 4 butt, cram, edge, grip, hold, pack, push 5 clasp, cramp, crowd, drive, elbow, grasp, press, shove, stuff, wedge, wrest, wring 6 clutch, coerce, compel, defile, elicit, extort, jostle, thrust, wrench 7 compact, draw out, embrace, extract, passage, pull out, tear out 8 compress, crowding, crushing, force out, pinching, press out, pressure, shoulder, withdraw 9 extricate, narrowing, stricture 10 bottleneck 11 compression, concentrate, consolidate 12 constriction

squelch 4 hush 5 abort, crush, quash, quell, quiet, smash 6 retort, squash 7 put down, riposte, silence 8 silencer, suppress

squire 4 date, take 5 court 6 attend, escort 7 consort, gallant, planter 8 cavalier, chaperon 9 accompany, attendant, boyfriend, chauffeur, companion, landowner 14 lord of the manor 16 country gentleman

Squire
 character in: 18 The Canterbury Tales
 author: 7 Chaucer

squirm 4 bend, jerk, toss, turn 5 pitch, shift, smart, sweat, twist, wince 6 blench, fidget, flinch, shrink, twitch,

wiggle, writhe 7 agonize, contort, wriggle 8 flounder

squirt 3 jet 4 dash, gush, punk, runt 5 piker, shoot, spout, spray, spurt 6 shower, splash, stream 7 spatter 8 sprinkle 9 discharge, pipsqueak 10 besprinkle

Sri Lanka
 other name: 6 Ceylon 8 Serendib 9 Taprobane
 capital/largest city: 7 Colombo
  ancient capital: 11 Polonnaruwa 12 Anuradhapura
 others: 3 Uva 5 Galle, Kandy 6 Jaffna, Mannar, Matale, Matara 7 Badulla, Kegalle, Negombo 8 Kalutara, Mankulem, Moratuwa, Puttalam 9 Ratnapura 10 Batticaloa, Mullaitivu 11 Ambalangoda, Trincomalee
 division: 8 Dambulla, Sri Lanka 9 Taprobane
 measure: 4 para, seer 5 parah 6 amunam, parrah
 monetary unit: 4 cent 5 rupee
 island: 5 Delft 6 Mannar 8 Sri Lanka
 mountain: 5 Pedro 7 Sri Pada 9 Adam's Peak
 highest point: 14 Pidurutalagala
 river: 4 Kala 6 Deduru, Gal Ova 8 Aruvi Aru 9 Deburu Ova 11 Kelani Ganga 13 Mahaweli Ganga
 sea: 6 Indian
 physical feature:
  bay: 6 Bengal 8 Koddiyar
  falls: 8 Lazapana
  gulf: 6 Mannar
  peninsula: 6 Jaffna
  plateau: 6 Hatton
  strait: 4 Palk
 people: 5 Malay, Tamil, Vedda 6 Veddah, Weddah 7 Burgher, Mahinda, Malabar 8 Eurasian 9 Cingalese, Dravidian, Sinhalese 10 Singhalese
  leader: 11 Jayawardene 12 Bandaranaike
  ruler: 5 Dutch 7 British, Chinese 10 Portuguese
 language: 4 Pali 5 Tamil 7 English 9 Sinhalese
 religion: 5 Hindu, Islam 8 Buddhism
 place:
  fortress: 8 Sigiriya
  gardens: 8 Hakgalle 10 Peradiniya
  national park: 6 Ruhuna 8 Wilpattu
  temple: 5 Tooth 6 Gal Oya 7 Kelanya 8 Runaweli 9 Ruanvelli 10 Dankahlaka 12 Asokharamaya
 feature:
  animal: 5 loris 12 wild elephant
  clothing: 4 sari 5 camba 6 sarong 7 cambaya 8 sherwani
  dancer: 7 Kandyan
  drama: 5 kolam 7 nadagam
  festival: 8 Perahera
  shrine: 6 dagoba
  tree: 4 doon, hora, palu, tala 5

domba, ebony 7 talipot 8 halmilla, ironwood 9 satinwood 11 allaeanthus 12 shimohabodhi

SS-GB
 author: 11 Len Deighton

SS troops, chief of 12 Reichsfuhrer

stab 2 go 3 cut, jab, try 4 ache, bite, gash, gore, hurt, pain, pang, pass, shot, spit 5 essay, gouge, knife, lance, lunge, prick, qualm, slash, spear, spike, stick, sting, trial, wound 6 cleave, dagger, effort, impale, pierce, shiver, stroke, thrill, thrust, twinge 7 attempt, bayonet 8 endeavor, lacerate, transfix 10 laceration, run through

stability 5 poise 6 aplomb, fixity 7 balance 8 evenness, firmness, security, solidity 9 constancy, fixedness, solidness, soundness 10 continuity, durability, permanence, stableness, steadiness, sturdiness 11 abidingness, equilibrium, reliability 13 steadfastness 14 changelessness 16 unchangeableness

stabilize 7 balance 8 hold firm, make firm 10 hold steady, make steady

stabilizer 7 balance, ballast 8 additive 9 equipoise, gyroscope 10 ballasting 12 airplane part 14 counterbalance

stable 4 barn, byre, even, firm, mews, safe, true 5 fixed, loyal, solid, sound 6 moored, secure, steady, sturdy 7 abiding, durable, staunch, uniform 8 anchored, constant, cowhouse, cowshed, enduring, faithful, reliable, resolute, stalwart 9 immovable, steadfast 10 dependable, persisting, stationary, unchanging, unwavering 11 established, unfaltering 12 indissoluble, unchangeable

Stabler, Ken
 nickname: 8 the Snake
 sport: 8 football
 position: 11 quarterback
 team: 13 Houston Oilers 14 Oakland Raiders

staccato
 music: 12 disconnected 16 each note separate

stack 4 bank, flue, heap, load, lump, mass, pile, rick 5 amass, batch, bunch, clump, hoard, mound, sheaf 6 bundle, funnel, gather 7 chimney 8 assemble, mountain 9 amassment 10 accumulate 11 aggregation 12 accumulation

Stack, Robert
 born: 12 Los Angeles CA
 roles: 9 Eliot Ness 13 Name of the Game 15 The Untouchables 16 Written on the Wind 19 The High and the Mighty 24 The Bullfighter and the Lady

Stackpole, Henrietta
 character in: 18 The Portrait of a Lady
 author: 5 James

Stacte 5 spice

stadium 4 bowl, park **5** arena, field, stade **6** circus **8** ballpark, coliseum **9** palaestra **10** hippodrome **12** amphitheater

Stael, Madame de
author of: **7** Corinne **8** Delphine **9** On Germany **35** The Influence of Literature upon Society

staff 3 bat, man, rod **4** cane, crew, help, pole, team, tend, wand, work **5** cadre, force, group, stave, stick **6** crutch, cudgel, manage **7** retinue, scepter, service, support **8** advisors, bludgeon, flagpole **9** billy club, employees, flagstaff, personnel **10** alpenstock, assistants, shillelagh **12** walking stick

staff member 4 aide **6** worker **8** employee

stage 3 act **4** dais, play, spot, step **5** arena, drama, grade, level, phase, put on, sight, stump **6** acting, locale, period, podium, pulpit **7** perform, present, produce, rostrum, setting, show biz, soapbox, theater **8** bearings, locality, location, position, scaffold **9** dramatize, the boards

Stagecoach
director: **8** John Ford
cast: **9** John Wayne **10** Andy Devine **11** Louise Platt **12** Claire Trevor **13** John Carradine **14** George Bancroft, Thomas Mitchell
Oscar for: **15** supporting actor (Mitchell)

stagecraft 5 drama **7** theater **9** theatrics **10** dramaturgy **11** thespianism **12** dramatic arts

Stage Door
author: **10** Edna Ferber **14** George S Kaufman
director: **13** Gregory La Cava
cast: **11** Andrea Leeds, Gail Patrick **12** Ginger Rogers **13** Adolphe Menjou **16** Katharine Hepburn

stage setting
French: **11** mise en scene

stagger 3 jar **4** jolt, reel, stun, sway **5** amaze, lurch, shake, shock, waver **6** hobble, totter, wobble **7** astound, blunder, nonplus, overlap, shamble, startle, stumble, stupefy **8** astonish, bewilder, bowl over, confound, flounder, unsettle **9** alternate, dumbfound, give a turn, overwhelm, spread out **10** disconcert, knock silly, strike dumb **11** cause to reel, cause to sway, consternate, flabbergast, take in turns **12** make unsteady **15** throw off balance

staggering 7 amazing **8** shocking, stunning **9** startling **10** astounding **11** astonishing **12** breathtaking

stagnant 4 dead, dull, foul, lazy, slow **5** close, inert, quiet, slimy, stale, still **6** filthy, leaden, putrid, static, supine, torpid **7** dormant, dronish, languid,

tainted **8** inactive, lifeless, listless, polluted, sluggish, standing **9** lethargic, ponderous, putrefied, quiescent **10** monotonous, motionless, not flowing, not running, stationary, unstirring, vegetative **13** uncirculating

stagnate 7 go to pot, lie idle, putrefy **8** go to seed, lie still, vegetate **10** stand still **11** cease to flow, deteriorate, stop growing **14** become inactive, become polluted, become sluggish

stagy 5 phony **8** affected, mannered **9** unnatural **10** artificial, factitious, theatrical

staid 5 grave, quiet, sober, stiff **6** decent, demure, proper, sedate, seemly, solemn, somber **7** earnest, prudish, serious, settled, subdued **8** decorous, priggish, reserved **9** dignified **10** complacent **15** undemonstrative

stain 3 dye, mar **4** blot, daub, flaw, foul, mark, ruin, slur, soil, spot, tint **5** brand, color, dirty, grime, libel, patch, shame, smear, speck, spoil, sully, taint **6** befoul, blotch, debase, defile, impair, malign, smirch, smudge, stigma, vilify **7** blacken, blemish, pigment, slander, splotch, subvert, tarnish **8** besmirch, coloring, discolor, disgrace, dishonor, dyestuff, tincture **9** denigrate, discredit, disparage, undermine **10** imputation, stigmatize **13** discoloration

stainless 5 clean, moral **6** chaste, decent **8** spotless, unsoiled **9** exemplary, unspotted, unsullied, untainted **11** unblemished

Stairway to Heaven
director: **13** Michael Powell **17** Emeric Pressburger
cast: **9** Kim Hunter **10** David Niven **12** Roger Livesey **13** Raymond Massey
original title: **21** A Matter of Life and Death

stake 3 bar, bet, peg, pot, rod **4** ante, back, grab, haul, lash, loot, moor, pale, pawn, pile, play, pole, post, prop, risk, stay, take **5** booty, brace, hitch, kitty, prize, purse, share, spike, stand, stick, treat, wager **6** chance, column, define, fasten, fetter, hazard, hold up, marker, picket, pillar, reward, secure, spoils, tether **7** delimit, finance, jackpot, mark off, mark out, outline, peg down, returns, sponsor, support, trammel, venture **8** interest, make fast, pickings, standard, winnings **9** delineate, demarcate, speculate, subsidize **10** investment, jeopardize, underwrite **11** involvement, speculation

Stalag 17
director: **11** Billy Wilder
cast: **9** Don Taylor **11** Peter Graves **12** Neville Brand **13** Harvey Lem-

beck, Otto Preminger, Richard Erdman, Robert Strauss, William Holden
Oscar for: **5** actor (Holden)

stale 4 dull, flat **5** banal, close, fusty, musty, trite, vapid **6** common **7** humdrum, insipid, prosaic, tedious, wornout **8** mediocre, not fresh, ordinary, stagnant, unvaried **9** hackneyed, savorless, tasteless **10** monotonous, pedestrian, threadbare **11** commonplace **13** unimaginative, uninteresting

stalemate 3 tie **4** draw, halt **7** dead end, impasse **8** blockage, cul-de-sac, dead heat, deadlock, standoff **10** standstill

stalk 4 hunt, lurk, stem **5** haunt, march, prowl, shaft, spire, stamp, steal, stomp, strut, track, tramp, trunk **6** column, menace, stride **7** pedicel, pervade, swagger **8** hang over, threaten **9** creep up on, go through, sneak up on

stall 3 box, pen **4** cell, coop, halt, shed, shop, stop **5** block, booth, check, delay, kiosk, stand **6** arcade, arrest, hobble, impede, pull up, put off **7** bed down, confine, cubicle, disable, trammel **8** obstruct, paralyze, postpone **9** be evasive, interrupt, stop short, temporize **10** equivocate **11** compartment, play for time, stop running **12** incapacitate **13** orchestra seat

Stallone, Sylvester
born: **9** New York NY
nickname: **3** Sly
roles: **4** FIST **5** Rambo, Rocky (Oscar) **7** Copland **10** First Blood, Judge Dredd, Rhinestone **11** Cliffhanger **18** The Lords of Flatbush

stalwart 4 bold, firm, hale **5** beefy, brave, hardy, hefty, husky, manly, sound **6** brawny, gritty, heroic, mighty, plucky, robust, rugged, spunky, stable, strong, sturdy **7** gallant, staunch, valiant **8** constant, intrepid, muscular, powerful, resolute, valorous, vigorous **9** steadfast, strapping, unbending, undaunted **10** ablebodied, courageous, persistent, unflagging, unshakable, unswerving, unwavering, unyielding **11** indomitable, lionhearted, undeviating, unfaltering, unflinching, unshrinking **12** intransigent, stouthearted, strong-willed **14** uncompromising

stamina 4 pith **5** vigor **6** energy **8** vitality **9** endurance, hardiness, stoutness **10** ruggedness, sturdiness **12** perseverance, staying power

stammer 6 falter, fumble, mumble **7** sputter, stumble, stutter **8** splutter **9** hem and haw

stamp
block: **4** pane
collecting: **9** philately
first: **10** Penny Black
issued by: **12** Great Britain

inscribed with: 8 One Penny
picture of: 13 Queen Victoria
first-day hand stamper: 6 cachet
hole measurer: 16 perforation gauge
mounting paper: 5 hinge
not perforated: 11 imperforate
paper design: 9 watermark
rolls: 4 coil
tear holes: 12 perforations
tear slit: 8 roulette
unseparated group: 5 block
used mark: 8 postmark **12** cancellation
value suspended: 11 demonetized

stamp, stamp out 2 OK **3** die, tag **4** cast, kind, make, mark, mint, mold, seal, sort, type **5** brand, breed, clump, crush, erase, genre, label, march, order, print, pound, punch, quash, smash, stalk, stomp, strut, thump, tramp **6** banish, betray, emblem, expose, matrix, nature, put out, reveal, rub out, signet, step on, strain, stride, trudge **7** abolish, blot out, display, engrave, exhibit, impress, imprint, put down, squelch, trample, variety, voucher **8** get rid of, hallmark, identify, inscribe, intaglio, manifest, suppress, typecast **9** character, eliminate, engraving, eradicate, personify, signature, trademark **10** annihilate, do away with, extinguish, imprimatur, stigmatize, validation **11** attestation, certificate, demonstrate, distinguish, endorsement, exterminate, **12** characterize, official mark, ratification **13** certification **14** authentication, characteristic, identification

stampede 4 bolt, dash, flee, race, rout, rush **5** chaos, flood, panic **6** engulf **7** overrun, retreat, scatter **8** inundate **10** take flight **11** crowd around, pandemonium **12** beat a retreat
French: 12 sauve qui peut

stanchion 4 post, prop, stay **5** brace, strut **7** support, upright

stand 2 be **3** put, set **4** draw, face, hold, last, move, rank, rear, rest, rise, stay, step, take, tent **5** abide, argue, booth, brook, erect, exist, get up, hoist, honor, kiosk, mount, place, put up, raise, shift, stall, treat **6** bear up, effort, endure, obtain, pay for, policy, remain, remove, stance, suffer, uphold **7** carry on, commend, counter, defense, endorse, finance, hold out, opinion, persist, posture, prevail, provide, stick up, stomach, support, survive, sustain, undergo, weather **8** advocate, be placed, champion, continue, pavilion, position, sanction, submit to, tolerate **9** be located, be present, be upright, persevere, put up with, sentiment, undertake, viewpoint **10** resistance, set upright **11** be permanent, countenance, disposition, point of view **13** remain in force, take a position

Stand, The
author: 11 Stephen King
standard 3 leg **4** base, flag, foot, jack, post **5** basic, canon, guide, ideal, stock, usual **6** banner, column, common, ensign, normal, pillar **7** measure, pennant, regular, support, typical, upright **8** accepted, ordinary, streamer **9** criterion, customary, guideline, principle, prototype, stanchion, universal, yardstick **10** foundation, touchstone **11** requirement **13** specification
stand behind 4 back **7** endorse, support **8** champion, vouch for **9** recommend
standby 6 backup **9** alternate, available **10** substitute, understudy **11** old reliable **12** tried-and-true
stand by 4 keep **5** cling **6** adhere, be true, defend, hold to, keep to **7** be loyal, stick by **8** cleave to, maintain **10** be constant, be faithful, stick up for
stand fast 4 hold **6** resist **8** stand pat
stand for 4 bear **5** abide, favor, stand **6** embody **7** signify **8** advocate, submit to, tolerate **9** personify, put up with, represent, symbolize
stand-in 3 sub **5** agent, proxy **6** backup, deputy, double, fill-in, second **9** alternate, assistant, surrogate **10** substitute, understudy **11** pinch hitter, replacement
standing 3 age **4** life, rank, term, time **5** erect, fixed, grade, inert, order, place, still **6** at rest, static, status, tenure **7** dormant, footing, lasting, station, upended, upright **8** duration, inactive, position, stagnant, vertical **9** immovable, permanent, perpetual, quiescent, renewable **10** continuing, importance, motionless, reputation, stationary, unstirring **11** continuance **13** perpendicular
standoff 7 impasse **8** deadlock
standoffish 4 cool **5** aloof **6** formal, remote **7** distant, haughty **8** detached, reserved, solitary, taciturn **9** reclusive, withdrawn **10** antisocial, restrained, unfriendly, unsociable **12** inaccessible, misanthropic, unresponsive **14** unapproachable **15** uncommunicative, uncompanionable
standpoint 4 side **5** angle, slant **6** aspect **9** viewpoint **11** point of view
standstill 3 end **4** halt, stop **5** pause **6** hiatus **7** dead end, impasse **8** abeyance, deadlock, dead stop, full stop **9** breakdown, cessation, stalemate **10** suspension **11** termination **14** discontinuance
stand up for 4 back **5** boost **6** defend **7** further, promote, support **8** advocate, champion
stand up to 4 defy, face **5** brave **6** resist **8** confront **9** challenge

Stant, Charlotte
character in: 13 The Golden Bowl
author: 5 James
Stan the Man
nickname of: 10 Stan Musial
Stanton, Adam
character in: 14 All the King's Men
author: 6 Warren
Stanwyck, Barbara
real name: 11 Ruby Stevens
born: 10 Brooklyn NY
husband: 8 Frank Fay **12** Robert Taylor
roles: 9 Big Valley, The Colbys **10** Ball of Fire, The Lady Eve **11** Meet John Doe **12** Stella Dallas **15** Double Indemnity **16** Sorry Wrong Number **20** Cattle Queen of Montana **22** Christmas in Connecticut
staple 3 key **4** main **5** basic, chief, major, prime, vital **6** leader **7** feature, primary, product **8** resource, vendible **9** commodity, essential, necessary **11** fundamental, raw material **13** indispensable
Stapleton, Jean
real name: 12 Jeanne Murray
born: 9 New York NY
roles: 7 Dingbat **11** Edith Bunker **14** All in the Family
Stapleton, Maureen
born: 6 Troy NY
roles: 7 Airport **9** Interiors **12** Lonelyhearts **13** The Rose Tattoo **18** A View from the Bridge
star, stars 3 god, sun, VIP **4** diva, fate, hero, idol, lead, lion, name **5** comet, excel, giant, great, omens, shine **6** big wig, do well, galaxy, meteor, nebula, planet **7** destiny, feature, fortune, goddess, heroine, notable, soloist, starlet, succeed, top draw **8** asteroid, cynosure, eminence, immortal, luminary, mainstay, Milky Way, portents, showcase, stand out, virtuoso **9** celebrity, headliner, meteoroid, principal, satellite, top banana **10** prima donna **11** All-American, drawing card, play the lead, protagonist **12** famous person, gain approval, heavenly body **13** celestial body, constellation **14** main attraction, predestination, prima ballerina
brightest: 6 Sirius
brightness measure: 9 magnitude **10** luminosity
color: 3 red **4** blue **5** black, white **6** orange, yellow
distance measure: 6 parsec **9** light year
double star: 6 binary
exploding star: 4 nova **9** supernova
French: 6 etoile
name: 4 Mira, Ross, Vega, Wolf **5** Cygni, Deneb, Rigel, Spica **6** Altair, Luyten, Pollux **7** Antares, Canopus, Capella, Lalande, Polaris, Procyon,

Regulus, Tau Ceti **8** Achernar, Arcturus, Barnard's, Lacaille, Pleiades **9** Aldebaran, Fomalhaut **10** Beta Crucis, Betelgeuse **11** Delta Cephei, Epsilon Indi, Groombridge **12** Beta Centauri **14** Epsilon Eridani
nearest: 13 Alpha Centauri
position/motion: 7 azimuth **8** parallax **11** declination
type: 5 dwarf, giant **6** pulsar **7** cluster, neutron **8** variable **9** black hole, collapsed

Starbuck
character in: 8 Moby Dick
author: 8 Melville

starch 5 vigor **6** sizing **8** backbone, gumption **10** stiffening

starched 5 crisp, sized, stiff **7** starchy **9** stiffened

starchy 5 rigid, stiff **6** formal, proper **7** correct **10** meticulous

stare 3 eye **4** gape, gawk, gaze, ogle, peep, peer **5** glare, lower, watch **6** gaping, glower, goggle, ogling, regard **7** staring **8** once-over, scrutiny **9** fixed look **10** inspection, rubberneck

stare at 3 eye **4** ogle **5** watch **6** behold, gaze at, look at, regard **7** inspect, observe **10** scrutinize **11** contemplate

Star Is Born, A
director:
1937 version: 14 William Wellman
1954 version: 11 George Cukor
1976 version: 12 Frank Pierson
cast:
1937 version: 11 Janet Gaynor **13** Adolphe Menjou, Frederic March
1954 version: 10 Jack Carson, James Mason **11** Judy Garland **15** Charles Bickford
1976 version: 9 Gary Busey **11** Oliver Clark **15** Barbra Streisand **17** Kris Kristofferson
Oscar for:
1937 version: 5 story
song:
1954 version: 17 The Man That Got Away

stark 4 bare, bold, cold, grim, pure **5** bleak, blunt, clean, empty, fully, gross, harsh, naked, plain, plumb, quite, sheer, total, utter **6** arrant, barren, chaste, patent, severe, simple, vacant, wholly **7** austere, evident, forlorn, glaring, obvious, staring, utterly **8** absolute, complete, deserted, desolate, entirely, flagrant, forsaken, outright, palpable **9** abandoned, downright, out-and-out, unadorned, unalloyed, veritable **10** absolutely, altogether, completely, consummate **11** conspicuous, unmitigated **12** unmistakable

Stark, Johannes
field: 7 physics
nationality: 6 German

described: 11 Stark Effect **14** dispersed light
awarded: 10 Nobel Prize

Stark, Willie
character in: 14 All the King's Men
author: 6 Warren

starlet 7 actress, ingenue **9** bit player, pinup girl

Starsky and Hutch
character: 5 Hutch (Ken Hutchinson) **7** (Dave) Starsky **9** Huggy Bear **11** (Capt) Harold Dobey
cast: 9 David Soul **13** Antonio Fargas **14** Bernie Hamilton **17** Paul Michael Glaser
car: 10 Ford Torino

start 3 aid, shy **4** dawn, drop, edge, form, gush, jerk, jolt, jump, lead, leap, odds, rush, turn **5** beget, begin, birth, blink, bound, eject, erupt, evict, flush, forge, found, issue, leave, leg up, onset, rouse, set up, shoot, spasm, spurt, wince **6** blench, broach, chance, create, depart, embark, emerge, fall to, father, flinch, ignite, kindle, launch, origin, outset, pop out, propel, recoil, set off, set out, spring, take up, twitch **7** advance, backing, disturb, genesis, make off, opening, push off, scatter, set sail, support, take off, turn out, usher in **8** advocacy, commence, creation, dis place, embark on, engender, generate, get going, initiate, organize, priority, set about, set going, touch off **9** advantage, beginning, establish, fabricate, first step, inception, institute, introduce, originate, propagate, undertake, venture on **10** assistance, break forth, bring about, buckle down, burst forth, give rise to, inaugurate, initiation, plunge into, sally forth, venture out **11** break ground, put in motion, set in action **12** commencement, inauguration, introduction **14** set in operation

starting point 5 onset, start **8** zero hour **9** beginning
Latin: 12 terminus a quo

startle 3 jar **4** faze **5** alarm, scare, shake, shock, upset **7** perturb, unnerve **8** disquiet, frighten, surprise, unsettle **9** give a turn **10** discompose, disconcert, intimidate

Star Trek
character: 4 Sulu **5** Uhura **6** Scotty (Engineer Montgomery Scott), (Ensign Pavel) Chekov **7** Mr Spock **10** (Captain) James T Kirk, (Yeoman) Janice Rand **12** (Dr) Leonard McCoy **15** (Nurse) Christine Chapel
cast: 11 George Takei, James Doohan **12** Leonard Nimoy, Majel Barrett, Walter Koenig **13** DeForest Kelly **14** William Shatner **15** Grace Lee Whitney, Nichelle Nichols
ship: 10 (USS) Enterprise
aliens: 8 Klingons, Romulans

Spock's planet: 6 Vulcan
pet: 7 tribble

starve 3 yen **4** burn, deny, fast, gasp, long, lust, pine **5** crave, raven, yearn **6** aspire, cut off, famish, hunger, refuse, thirst **7** deprive **8** be hungry, go hungry, languish

Star Wars
director: 11 George Lucas
cast: 10 Kenny Baker, Mark Hamill (Luke Skywalker) **12** Alec Guinness, Carrie Fisher (Princess Leia), Harrison Ford (Han Solo), Peter Cushing **14** Anthony Daniels
voice of Darth Vader: 14 James Earl Jones
score: 12 John Williams
Oscar for: 5 score
sequel: 15 Return of the Jedi **20** The Empire Strikes Back

stasimon 9 choral ode
literally: 8 standing

state 3 put **4** form, land, mind, mode, mood, pass, pomp **5** guise, offer, phase, realm, shape, stage **6** aspect, luxury, morale, nation, people, plight, recite, relate, report, ritual, status **7** comfort, country, declare, explain, expound, express, kingdom, narrate, posture, present, recount, spirits **8** attitude, ceremony, describe, dominion, monarchy, official, position, propound, republic, set forth **9** condition, elucidate, formality, full dress, high style, situation, structure **10** ceremonial, government **11** body politic, frame of mind, predicament, state of mind **12** commonwealth, constitution, governmental, principality **13** circumstances

state abbreviations
Alabama: 2 AL **3** Ala
Alaska: 2 AK **4** Alas
Arizona: 2 AZ **4** Ariz
Arkansas: 2 AR **3** Ark
California: 2 CA **3** Cal **5** Calif
Colorado: 2 CO **4** Colo
Connecticut: 2 CT **4** Conn
Delaware: 2 DE **3** Del
Florida: 2 FL **3** Fla
Georgia: 2 GA
Hawaii: 2 HI
Idaho: 2 ID **3** Ida
Illinois: 2 IL **3** Ill
Indiana: 2 IN **3** Ind
Iowa: 2 IA
Kansas: 2 KS **4** Kans
Kentucky: 2 KY
Louisiana: 2 LA
Maine: 2 ME
Maryland: 2 MD
Massachusetts: 2 MA **4** Mass
Michigan: 2 MI **4** Mich
Minnesota: 2 MN **4** Minn
Mississippi: 2 MS **4** Miss
Missouri: 2 MO
Montana: 2 MT
Nebraska: 2 NE **4** Nebr

Nevada: **2** NV **3** Nev
New Hampshire: **2** NH
New Jersey: **2** NJ
New Mexico: **2** NM **4** N Mex
New York: **2** NY
North Carolina: **2** NC **4** N Car
North Dakota: **2** ND **4** N Dak
Ohio: **2** OH
Oklahoma: **2** OK **4** Okla
Oregon: **2** OR **4** Oreg
Pennsylvania: **2** PA **4** Penn **5** Penna
Rhode Island: **2** RI
South Carolina: **2** SC
South Dakota: **2** SD **4** S Dak
Tennessee: **2** TN **4** Tenn
Texas: **2** TX **3** Tex
Utah: **2** UT
Vermont: **2** VT
Virginia: **2** VA
Washington: **2** WA **4** Wash
West Virginia: **2** WV **3** W Va
Wisconsin: **2** WI **3** Wis
Wyoming: **2** WY **3** Wyo

state admittance
first: **8** Delaware
second: **12** Pennsylvania
third: **9** New Jersey
fourth: **7** Georgia
fifth: **11** Connecticut
sixth: **13** Massachusetts
seventh: **8** Maryland
eighth: **13** South Carolina
ninth: **12** New Hampshire
tenth: **8** Virginia
eleventh: **7** New York
twelfth: **13** North Carolina
thirteenth: **11** Rhode Island
fourteenth: **7** Vermont
fifteenth: **8** Kentucky
sixteenth: **9** Tennessee
seventeenth: **4** Ohio
eighteenth: **9** Louisiana
nineteenth: **7** Indiana
twentieth: **11** Mississippi
twenty-first: **8** Illinois
twenty-second: **7** Alabama
twenty-third: **5** Maine
twenty-fourth: **8** Missouri
twenty-fifth: **8** Arkansas
twenty-sixth: **8** Michigan
twenty-seventh: **7** Florida
twenty-eighth: **5** Texas
twenty-ninth: **4** Iowa
thirtieth: **9** Wisconsin
thirty-first: **10** California
thirty-second: **9** Minnesota
thirty-third: **6** Oregon
thirty-fourth: **6** Kansas
thirty-fifth: **12** West Virginia
thirty-sixth: **6** Nevada
thirty-seventh: **8** Nebraska
thirty-eighth: **8** Colorado
thirty-ninth/fortieth: **11** North
  Dakota, South Dakota
forty-first: **7** Montana
forty-second: **10** Washington
forty-third: **5** Idaho
forty-fourth: **7** Wyoming

forty-fifth: **4** Utah
forty-sixth: **8** Oklahoma
forty-seventh: **9** New Mexico
forty-eighth: **7** Arizona
forty-ninth: **6** Alaska
fiftieth: **6** Hawaii

state capitals
Alabama: **10** Montgomery
Alaska: **6** Juneau
Arizona: **7** Phoenix
Arkansas: **10** Little Rock
California: **10** Sacramento
Colorado: **6** Denver
Connecticut: **8** Hartford
Delaware: **5** Dover
Florida: **11** Tallahassee
Georgia: **7** Atlanta
Hawaii: **8** Honolulu
Idaho: **5** Boise
Illinois: **11** Springfield
Indiana: **12** Indianapolis
Iowa: **9** Des Moines
Kansas: **6** Topeka
Kentucky: **9** Frankfort
Louisiana: **10** Baton Rouge
Maine: **7** Augusta
Maryland: **9** Annapolis
Massachusetts: **6** Boston
Michigan: **7** Lansing
Minnesota: **6** St Paul
Mississippi: **7** Jackson
Missouri: **13** Jefferson City
Montana: **6** Helena
Nebraska: **7** Lincoln
Nevada: **10** Carson City
New Hampshire: **7** Concord
New Jersey: **7** Trenton
New Mexico: **7** Santa Fe
New York: **6** Albany
North Carolina: **7** Raleigh
North Dakota: **8** Bismarck
Ohio: **8** Columbus
Oklahoma: **12** Oklahoma City
Oregon: **5** Salem
Pennsylvania: **10** Harrisburg
Rhode Island: **10** Providence
South Carolina: **8** Columbia
South Dakota: **6** Pierre
Tennessee: **9** Nashville
Texas: **6** Austin
Utah: **12** Salt Lake City
Vermont: **10** Montpelier
Virginia: **8** Richmond
Washington: **7** Olympia
West Virginia: **10** Charleston
Wisconsin: **7** Madison
Wyoming: **8** Cheyenne

State Fair
author: **9** Phil Stong
movie composers: **7** Rodgers **11**
  Hammerstein

state in detail 7 explain, expound **8**
describe, spell out **9** explicate **16** give
a full account

stateliness 7 dignity, majesty **10** augustness

stately 5 grand, lofty, noble, proud, regal, royal **6** august, formal, lordly **7**

awesome, elegant, eminent **8** glorious,
imperial, imposing, majestic **9** dignified, grandiose **10** ceremonial, impressive **11** magnificent

statement 3 tab **4** bill **5** check, claim,
count, tally **6** avowal, charge, record,
remark, report, speech **7** account,
comment, invoice, mention, recital **8**
relation, sentence **9** assertion, manifesto, reckoning, testimony, utterance,
valuation **10** accounting, allegation,
communique, exposition, profession,
recitation **11** declaration, delineation,
explanation, observation **12** announcement, balance sheet **13** pronouncement, specification

state of affairs 5 state **6** status **9**
condition, situation **13** circumstances

State of the Union
director: **10** Frank Capra
cast: **10** Van Johnson **12** Spencer
  Tracy **13** Adolphe Menjou **14** Angela
  Lansbury **16** Katharine Hepburn

stateroom 5 cabin **8** quarters **11** compartment

statesman 8 diplomat **15** political
leader

statesmanship 9 diplomacy **19** political leadership

static 5 fixed, inert, still **8** immobile,
inactive, stagnant, unmoving **9** crackling, suspended **10** changeless, motionless, stationary, unchanging **12** interference

station 4 post, rank, site, spot, stop **5**
caste, class, depot, grade, level, place
6 assign, degree, locate, sphere, status
7 footing, install **8** ensconce, facility,
location, position, prestige, terminal,
terminus **9** condition, firehouse, place
ment **10** dispensary, guardhouse, importance **11** emplacement, whistle-
stop **12** headquarters

stationary 4 even, firm **5** fixed, inert
6 intact, moored, stable, steady **7** riveted, uniform **8** constant, immobile,
standing **9** dead-still, immovable, immutable, unchanged, unvarying **10**
motionless, stock-still, transfixed **11**
not changing, undeviating **12** unchangeable **13** standing still

Statius
author of: **6** Silvae **10** The Thebaid
  12 The Achilleid

statue 8 monument **9** sculpture **14**
representation

statuesque 5 regal **7** stately **8** majestic **9** dignified

stature 4 rank, size **5** place **6** height,
regard **8** eminence, position, prestige,
standing, tallness **9** elevation **10** importance, prominence, reputation **11**
distinction

status 4 rank **5** caste, class, grade,
place, state **6** degree **7** caliber, footing, station **8** eminence, position,

prestige, standing **9** condition, situation **10** estimation **11** distinction

statute 3 law **7** precept **9** prescript

statute law
Latin: **10** lex scripta

staunch, stanch 3 dam **4** firm, stem, true **5** check, loyal, solid, sound, stout **6** impede, rugged, steady, strong, sturdy **7** contain, zealous **8** constant, faithful, hold back, obstruct, resolute, stalwart **9** steadfast, well-built **10** watertight **11** substantial

stave off 7 beat off, fend off, keep off, ward off **9** keep at bay

stay 3 aim, guy, rib, rod **4** bunk, curb, foil, halt, live, pole, prop, rest, room, stem, stop **5** abide, block, brace, check, delay, dwell, lodge, quell, shore, stick, tarry, visit **6** endure, keep in, linger, rein in, remain, reside, splint, stifle, thwart **7** carry on, hold out, holiday, last out, persist, sojourn, support, ward off **8** abeyance, buttress, continue, hold back, mainstay, postpone, reprieve, restrain, standard, stopover, suppress, vacation, withhold **9** deferment, frustrate, persevere, staunchion **10** hang around, see through, suspension **12** postponement, reinforcement

stay put 4 stay **6** remain **8** stand pat

St Clare, Eva
character in: **14** Uncle Tom's Cabin
author: **5** Stowe

steadfast 4 keen, rapt **5** fixed **6** direct, intent, steady **8** resolute **9** attentive, obstinate, tenacious, undaunted **10** deep-rooted, deep-seated, inflexible, unchanging, unflagging, unwavering, unyielding **11** indomitable, persevering, unalterable, undeviating, unfaltering, unflinching **12** intransigent, single-minded, unchangeable, undistracted **14** uncompromising

steadfastness 8 tenacity **10** resolution **11** persistence **12** perseverance, resoluteness **13** determination

Steadfast Tin Soldier, The
author: **21** Hans Christian Andersen

steadiness 4 care **5** poise **6** aplomb **8** calmness, coolness, evenness, firmness **9** composure, sangfroid, stability **10** equanimity, resolution **11** carefulness, persistence, self-control, tranquility **12** resoluteness, tranquillity **13** dependability, steadfastness **14** presence of mind, self-possession **16** imperturbability

steady 4 even, firm, sure **5** sober **6** secure, stable **7** balance, careful, devoted, regular, serious, staunch **8** constant, faithful, frequent, habitual, hold fast, reliable, resolute, unending, untiring **9** ceaseless, confirmed, dedicated, immovable, incessant, stabilize, steadfast, tenacious, unceasing **10** continuing, continuous, coolheaded, deliberate, dependable, methodical, persistent, unflagging, unwavering **11** levelheaded, persevering, substantial, undeviating, unfaltering, unremitting **12** single-minded **13** conscientious

steal 3 buy, cop **4** copy, crib, flit, flow, lift, slip, take **5** creep, drift, filch, glide, pinch, skulk, slide, slink, sneak, swipe, usurp **6** borrow, elapse, escape, extort, filter, pilfer, pocket, rip off, snatch, snitch, thieve **7** bargain, defraud, diffuse, good buy, imitate, purloin, swindle **8** abstract, embezzle, good deal, liberate **10** burglarize, plagiarize **11** abscond with, appropriate, make off with **14** misappropriate

steal away 3 fly **4** bolt, flee, skip **5** elope **6** escape **7** get away, make off, slip out **8** creep off, slip away, sneak off **9** break free, tiptoe out **10** break loose, fly the coop **12** make a getaway

stealth 7 secrecy, slyness **10** covertness, sneakiness, subterfuge **11** furtiveness **12** stealthiness **13** secretiveness **15** unobtrusiveness **17** surreptitiousness

stealthy 3 sly **5** shady **6** covert, shifty, sneaky **7** devious, furtive **8** slippery, sneaking **9** secretive, underhand **11** clandestine, underhanded **12** huggermugger **13** surreptitious

steamboat
invented by: **6** Fulton **9** Symington

steamed up 5 angry, het up, irate **6** raging **7** enraged, furious, riled up **8** heated up, inflamed **10** infuriated **12** mad as a wet hen **14** hot and bothered **17** hot under the collar

steamer 4 boat, clam, ship **5** liner, trunk **10** paddleboat **11** side-wheeler **12** stern-wheeler **13** paddle-wheeler

steel 4 dirk, foil, gird **5** blade, brace, knife, nerve, saber, sword **6** dagger, rapier **7** bayonet, cutlass, fortify, machete **8** falchion, scimitar **10** broadsword
process invented by: **8** Bessemer

Steele, Sir Richard
pseudonym: **16** Isaac Bickerstaff
author of: **9** The Tatler (with Joseph Addison) **10** The Funeral **12** The Spectator (with Joseph Addison) **13** The Lying Lover **16** The Tender Husband **18** The Conscious Lovers

steely 4 hard **5** stony **6** flinty **9** heartless, unfeeling **10** forbidding **11** coldhearted

Steen, Jan
born: **6** Leiden, Leyden **14** The Netherlands
artwork: **7** Cabaret **11** The Egg Dance **12** Merry Company **14** Garden of the Inn **15** The Doctor's Visit, The Rhetoricians **16** The Morning Toilet **17** The Skittle Players **18** The World

Topsy-Turvy, Young Woman Dressing

Steenburgen, Mary
roles: **10** Cross Creek **12** Dead of Winter **13** Time After Time **22** Attic: Hiding of Anne Frank

steep 4 brew, bury, fill, soak **5** imbue, sharp, sheer, souse **6** abrupt, drench, engulf, infuse, plunge **7** immerse, pervade, suffuse **8** marinate, saturate, submerge **10** impregnate **11** precipitous

steeple 5 spire, tower **6** belfry **9** campanile

steer 3 aim, lay, run **4** bear, head, lead, make, sail **5** coach, guide, pilot **6** direct, govern, manage **7** conduct, proceed **8** navigate **9** supervise

steer clear of 4 shun **5** avert, avoid, dodge, evade, forgo, skirt **6** escape, eschew, forego **8** sidestep **9** keep shy of **11** abstain from, refrain from **16** give a wide berth to

Steerforth
character in: **16** David Copperfield
author: **7** Dickens

Steffens, Lincoln
author of: **19** The Shame of the Cities

Steiger, Rod
real name: **20** Rodney Stephen Steiger
born: **13** Westhampton NY
wife: **11** Claire Bloom
roles: **8** Waterloo **13** The Longest Day, The Pawnbroker, W C Fields and Me **15** On the Waterfront **19** In the Heat of the Night (Oscar)

Stein, Clarence S
architect of: **13** Temple Emanu-El (NYC)

Stein, Gertrude
author of: **10** Three Lives **13** Tender Buttons **20** The Making of Americans **27** Autobiography of Alice B Toklas
coined phrase: **14** lost generation

Steinbeck, John
author of: **8** The Pearl **10** Cannery Row, East of Eden, The Red Pony **12** Of Mice and Men, Tortilla Flat **15** In Dubious Battle **16** The Grapes of Wrath **18** Travels with Charley **24** The Winter of Our Discontent

Steinmetz, Charles P
field: **11** engineering
developed: **2** AC **18** alternating current

Stella, Frank
born: **8** Malden MA
artwork: **4** Jill **5** Itata **14** Jasper's Dilemma **15** Guadalupe Island

Stella, Joseph
born: **5** Italy **6** Naples
artwork: **8** Full Moon (Barbados) **9** Sunflower, The Bridge **14** Brooklyn Bridge **16** Pittsburgh Winter **18** New

York Interpreted **28** Battle of the Lights Coney Island

Stella Dallas
director: **9** King Vidor
cast: **9** John Boles **11** Anne Shirley **12** Barbara O'Neil **15** Barbara Stanwyck

stellar 6 astral, starry **7** leading **8** starring **9** brilliant, celestial, principal **11** outstanding

stem 3 dam **4** buck, cane, come, curb, grow, halt, rise, stay, stop **5** arise, block, check, deter, ensue, issue, quell, shank, shoot, speak, spire, stalk, stall, stock, trunk **6** arrest, derive, hinder, impede, oppose, resist, result, retard, spring, stanch, thwart **7** counter, pedicel, petiole, prevent, proceed, tendril **8** hold back, obstruct, peduncle, restrain, surmount **9** leafstalk, originate, withstand

stem from 5 arise, begin, start **6** derive **9** originate

stench 4 odor, reek **5** fetor, stink **8** bad smell **9** fetidness

Stendhal (Henri Marie Beyle)
author of: **17** The Red and the Black **18** Memoirs of an Egotist **22** The Charterhouse of Parma

Stengel, Charles Dillon
nickname: **5** Casey
sport: **8** baseball
position: **7** manager
team: **11** New York Mets **14** New York Yankees **15** Brooklyn Dodgers

Stentor
vocation: **6** herald
characteristic: **10** loud-voiced
voice as loud as: **8** fifty men

step 3 act **4** clip, gait, move, pace, rank, rung, span, walk **5** notch, phase, point, riser, stage, stair, strut, track, tramp, tread **6** action, degree, hobble, period, remove, stride **7** footing, measure, process, shamble, shuffle, swagger, trample **8** footfall, foothold, maneuver, purchase **9** footprint, gradation, procedure **10** proceeding

step down 4 quit **5** leave **6** resign, retire

Stephens, James
author of: **7** Deirdre **14** The Crock of Gold **21** The Charwoman's Daughter

Stephenson, George and Robert
nationality: **7** English
developed: **15** steam locomotive

Steppenwolf
author: **12** Hermann Hesse
character: **5** Maria, Pablo **7** Hermine **11** Harry Haller

Steps
author: **13** Jerzy Kosinski

step up 4 spur **6** come up **7** quicken, speed up **8** ap proach, escalate, expedite, increase **9** intensify **10** accelerate

stereotype 4 type **6** cliche **7** formula

8 typecast **10** categorize, pigeonhole **13** preconception

stereotyped 5 stale, trite **9** hackneyed **11** commonplace **13** unimaginative

sterile 4 bare, pure, vain **5** empty **6** barren, fallow, futile **7** aseptic, useless **8** abortive, bootless, impotent, infecund, sanitary **9** childless, fruitless, infertile, worthless **10** antiseptic, profitless, sterilized, unavailing, unfruitful, uninfected **11** disinfected, ineffective, ineffectual, unrewarding **12** unproductive, unprofitable **13** free from germs **14** uncontaminated

sterilize 6 purify **9** autoclave, disinfect **13** decontaminate

sterling 4 pure, true **5** noble **6** silver, superb, worthy **7** genuine, perfect **8** flawless, superior **9** admirable, estimable, first-rate, honorable **10** invaluable **11** meritorious, superlative

stern 4 cold, grim, hard **5** cruel, grave, harsh, rigid, sharp, stiff **6** brutal, gloomy, severe, somber, strict, unkind **7** austere, serious **8** coercive, despotic, frowning, pitiless, rigorous, ruthless, ungentle **9** reproving, stringent, unfeeling **10** forbidding, implacable, ironfisted, ironhanded, tyrannical, unmerciful **11** admonishing, coldblooded, reproachful **12** unreasonable **13** unsympathetic **14** unapproachable

Sterne, Laurence
author of: **14** Tristram Shandy **19** A Sentimental Journey
character: **9** Uncle Toby **12** Parson Yorick, Walter Shandy

sternum
bone of: **6** breast

Steve Canyon
creator: **12** Milton Caniff
character: **7** Cheetah **9** Madam Lynx **10** Doe Redwood, Miss Mizzou **11** Savannah Gay **13** Copper Calhoun **14** Herself Muldoon **17** Princess Sun Flower
wife: **6** Summer
ward/cousin: **12** Poteet Canyon
Summer's son: **13** Leigh ton Olson

Stevens, George
director of: **5** Giant (Oscar), Shane **8** Gunga Din **9** Swing Time **13** I Remember Mama, Penny Serenade **14** A Place in the Sun (Oscar), Woman of the Year **16** The Talk of the Town **19** The Diary of Anne Frank

Stevens, Gowan
character in: **9** Sanctuary
author: **8** Faulkner

Stevens, James
author of: **10** Paul Bunyan

Stevens, Wallace
author of: **7** The Rock **9** Harmonium **13** Sunday Morning **17** Transport to Summer **23** Peter Quince at the Clavier, The Idea of Order at Key West, The Man with the Blue Guitar

Stevenson, Robert
director of: **8** Jane Eyre **10** Back Street **11** Mary Poppins

Stevenson, Robert Louis
author of: **9** Kidnapped **13** The Black Arrow **14** Treasure Island **18** Travels with a Donkey **21** A Child's Garden of Verses, Doctor Jekyll and Mr Hyde, The Master of Ballantrae

St Evremond, Marquis
character in: **16** A Tale of Two Cities
author: **7** Dickens

stew 4 fret, fume, fuss **5** chafe, gripe, steep, tizzy, worry **6** grouse, ragout, seethe, simmer **7** agonize, fluster, flutter, grumble, mixture **10** miscellany

steward 5 agent, proxy **6** deputy, factor, waiter **7** bailiff, manager, trustee **8** executor, overseer **10** controller, supervisor **11** comptroller **13** administrator **14** representative, ship's attendant **15** flight attendant

Stewart, James
born: **9** Indiana PA
roles: **4** Rope **6** Harvey **7** Vertigo **10** Rear Window, Shenandoah **11** Elwood P Dowd **14** Cheyenne Autumn **16** Anatomy of a Murder, Destry Rides Again, The Stratton Story **17** Bell Book and Candle, It's a Wonderful Life **18** It's a Wonderful World, The Spirit of St Louis **19** The Glenn Miller Story **20** The Philadelphia Story (Oscar), You Can't Take It with You **22** The Greatest Show on Earth **23** Mr Smith Goes to Washington

Stewart, Mary
real name: **22** Florence Rainbow Stewart
author of: **11** Crystal Cave **14** The Hollow Hills **15** The Moon-Spinners **16** My Brother Michael, The Gabriel Hounds **18** Airs Above the Ground, The Last Enchantment

St George's
capital of: **7** Grenada

stick 3 bar, bat, cue, dig, fix, jab, pin, put, rod, set **4** balk, bind, cane, club, curb, fuse, glue, hold, join, last, mire, nail, pink, poke, pole, seal, snag, stab, stop, tack, twig, wand, weld **5** abide, affix, baton, billy, block, catch, check, fagot, leave, lodge, paste, place, plant, prick, punch, shift, snarl, spear, spike, staff, stall, stake, stand, stave, stump **6** adhere, attach, boggle, branch, burden, cement, cudgel, detain, endure, fasten, hamper, hinder, hog-tie, impede, insert, pierce, puzzle, scotch, skewer, stymie, switch, thrust, thwart **7** confuse, crosier, inhibit, perplex, shackle, trammel **8** bewilder, bludgeon, caduceus, continue, obstruct, puncture **9** checkmate, constrain, perforate, truncheon, victimize **10** immobilize, shillelagh

stick fast 4 hold **5** cling, stick **6** adhere, cleave

stickler 3 bug, nut **5** crank, poser **6** enigma, purist, puzzle, riddle, zealot **7** devotee, dilemma, fanatic, mystery, stumper **8** martinet **10** enthusiast, monomaniac

sticks 4 skis **5** bonds, glues, twigs **6** pastes, Podunk **7** adheres, boonies, catches, cements, country **8** kindling **9** backwoods, boondocks, golf clubs, provinces **10** hicksville, hinterland **11** countryside, hinterlands

stick together 4 bind, fuse, glue, hold, join **5** cling, stick, unite **6** cement, cohere

stick-to-itiveness 8 tenacity **9** endurance **10** resolution **11** persistence **12** perseverance, resoluteness **13** determination, tenaciousness

stickum 3 gum **4** glue **5** paste **6** cement **8** adhesive, mucilage **12** rubber cement

stick up for 5 boost **6** defend **7** root for **11** speak well of **17** put in a good word for

stick with 4 stay **5** abide **6** keep at **7** stand by **9** accompany, persevere

sticky 3 wet **4** damp, dank **5** gluey, gooey, gummy, humid, moist, muggy, pasty, tacky **6** clammy, clingy, steamy, sultry, viscid **7** viscous **8** adherent, adhesive, clinging, cohesive, sticking **9** glutinous, tenacious **10** gelatinous **12** mucilaginous

stiff 4 body, cold, cool, firm, grim, hard, high, iron, keen, prim, sore, taut **5** aloof, awful, brave, brisk, crisp, cruel, dense, fixed, gusty, harsh, heavy, rigid, sharp, smart, solid, steep, stern, tense, thick, tight, tough, undue **6** bitter, brutal, chilly, clumsy, corpse, dogged, forced, formal, raging, severe, staid, steely, strong, uneasy, viscid, wooden **7** austere, awkward, cadaver, clotted, decided, distant, drastic, extreme, fearful, intense, jellied, labored, precise, remains, settled, starchy, stately, staunch, steeled, stilted, uptight, valiant, violent, viscous **8** affected, constant, dead body, exacting, forceful, grievous, mannered, pitiless, pounding, powerful, resolute, resolved, rigorous, ruthless, spanking, stubborn, ungainly, unlimber, unshaken, vigorous **9** difficult, draconian, excessive, graceless, inelastic, inelegant, laborious, merciless, obstinate, resistant, steadfast, stringent, tenacious, unnatural **10** artificial, courageous, determined, exorbitant, formidable, gelatinous, immoderate, inflexible, inordinate, persistent, solidified, unswerving, unyielding **11** ceremonious, constrained, extravagant, indomitable, straitlaced, unfaltering, unflinching, unwarranted **12**

strong-willed, unreasonable **14** uncompromising

stiff-necked 6 mulish **7** will ful **8** contrary, obdurate, stubborn **9** obstinate, pigheaded, unbending **10** bullheaded, refractory, self-willed, unshakable, unyielding **11** intractable **12** intransigent, pertinacious

stiffness 7 tension **8** firmness, rigidity **9** aloofness, formality, tenseness, tightness **10** constraint **11** starchiness

stifle 3 gag **4** curb **5** check, choke **6** muffle, subdue **7** garrote, inhibit, repress, smother, squelch, swelter **8** keep back, restrain, strangle, suppress, throttle **9** suffocate **10** asphyxiate

stifling 3 hot **6** stuffy **7** airless **10** overheated

stigma 4 blot, flaw, mark, scar **5** brand, odium, shame, stain, taint **6** smirch, smudge **7** blemish, tarnish **8** disgrace, dishonor **11** mark of shame **12** besmirchment

stigmatize 5 brand, smear **6** debase, defame, smirch **7** villify **9** discredit, disparage

still 4 calm, hush **5** inert, quiet **6** at rest, hushed, pacify, settle, silent **7** appease, as suage, gratify, put down, repress, silence, turn off **8** immobile, overcome, restrain, suppress, unmoving **9** noiseless, soundless **10** motionless, put an end to, stationary, unstirring

stillness 4 calm, hush **5** quiet **6** repose **7** silence **8** calmness, inaction, quietude **9** composure **10** immobility, inactivity, quiescence **11** tranquility **12** tranquillity

Stillness at Appomattox, A
 author: 11 Bruce Catton

stilted 4 cold, prim **5** rigid, stiff **6** forced, formal, stuffy, wooden **7** awkward, labored, pompous, starchy, studied, uptight **8** mannered, priggish, starched **9** graceless, unnatural **10** artificial **11** ceremonious, constrained

Stilwell, Joseph W
 nickname: 10 Vinegar Joe
 served in: 3 WWI **4** WWII
 chief of staff for: 13 Chiang Kai-shek
 driven out of: 5 Burma

stimulant 5 tonic, upper **6** bracer **8** excitant **9** energizer

stimulate 3 fan **4** spur, stir, wake **5** alert, rouse **6** arouse, awaken, excite, incite, prompt, vivify **7** actuate, animate, inflame, inspire, quicken, sharpen **8** activate, enkindle, initiate, inspirit

stimulating 5 tonic **7** piquing **8** arousing, exciting, spurring, stirring, whetting **9** animating, provoking **10** energizing, refreshing **11** interesting, provocative

stimulus 4 goad, spur, whet **5** tonic **6** bracer, fillip, motive **7** impetus **8** excitant **9** activator, energizer, incentive, quickener, stimulant **10** incitement, inducement **11** provocation **13** encouragement

sting 3 cut, nip, rub, vex **4** ache, barb, bite, blow, burn, fire, gall, gnaw, goad, grip, hurt, itch, lash, move, pain, prod, rack, rasp, rile, sore, spur, stab, whip **5** anger, chafe, cross, egg on, grate, impel, pinch, pique, prick, shake, shock, smart, venom, wince, wound **6** arouse, awaken, excite, harrow, incite, insult, kindle, madden, nettle, offend, pierce, prompt, propel, stir up, tingle, twinge **7** actuate, agonize, disturb, incense, inflame, prickle, provoke, quicken, scourge, stinger, torment, torture **8** irritate, motivate, vexation **9** infuriate, instigate, penetrate **10** affliction, irritation

Sting, The
 director: 13 George Roy Hill
 cast: 10 Paul Newman, Ray Walston, Robert Shaw **13** Eileen Brennan, Robert Redford **14** Charles Durning
 score: 11 Scott Joplin
 Oscar for: 7 picture **8** director

stinginess 6 penury **9** parsimony **11** miserliness **13** niggardliness, penny-pinching **15** tight-fistedness

stinging 4 acid **5** harsh, sharp **6** biting, bitter **7** burning, caustic, cutting, pungent **8** piercing **9** sarcastic, satirical **10** astringent

stingy 4 lean, mean, thin **5** close, scant, small, tight **6** frugal, meager, modest, paltry, scanty, skimpy, sparse **7** miserly, scrimpy, slender, sparing **8** piddling, stinting **9** illiberal, niggardly, penurious **10** inadequate, ungenerous **11** closefisted, tightfisted **12** cheeseparing, insufficient, parsimonious **13** penny-pinching

stink 4 odor, reek **5** fetor **6** stench **8** bad smell **17** smell to high heaven

stint 3 job **4** curb, duty, part, save, task, term, turn **5** check, chore, limit, quota, shift **6** reduce, scrimp **8** hold back, restrain, restrict, withhold **9** constrain, cut down on, economize **10** assignment, engagement **12** circumscribe, pinch pennies

stipend 5 grant, wages **6** income, salary **7** pension **8** fixed pay **9** allowance, emolument **10** honorarium, recompense **11** scholarship **12** compensation, remuneration

stipulate 4 cite, name **5** agree, allow, grant, state **6** assure, insure, pledge **7** promise, provide, specify, warrant **8** indicate, set forth **9** designate, guarantee

stipulation 4 term **7** proviso **9** condition **10** limitation **11** requirement, restriction

stipulative 7 limited 9 qualified, tentative 10 contingent, restricted 11 conditional, provisional 16 with reservations

stir 3 act, mix 4 beat, fire, goad, jolt, move, prod, rush, spur, to-do, whip 5 blend, rouse, shake, sough, start 6 arouse, awaken, bustle, commix, excite, flurry, hasten, hustle, kindle, mingle, mixing, moving, pother, quiver, rustle, shiver, tumult, twitch, uproar, vivify, work up 7 agitate, animate, enflame, flutter, inspire, provoke, quicken, scamper 8 energize, inspirit, intermix, mingling, movement, prodding, rustling, scramble, stirring 9 agitation, commingle, commotion, electrify, stimulate 10 get a move on, step lively 11 set in motion 12 exert oneself, make an effort

stirred up 5 riled, upset 7 aroused, excited, kindled, ruffled 8 agitated, inflamed 9 disturbed 10 stimulated

stirring 5 astir, awake 6 moving 7 rousing 8 electric, exalting, exciting, in motion, spirited 9 inspiring, thrilling 10 up and about 11 galvanizing, stimulating 12 electrifying

stir up 5 upset 6 arouse, awaken, excite, kindle, ruffle 7 agitate, disturb 9 call forth, stimulate 10 antagonize

stir vigorously 3 mix 4 beat, whip 7 agitate

stitch 3 bit, jot, sew 4 ache, iota, kink, mend, pain, pang, seam, tack 5 baste, cramp, crick, piece, scrap, shoot, shred 6 suture, tingle, twinge, twitch 7 article, garment 8 particle 9 embroider 12 charley horse

St John's
  capital of: 17 Antigua and Barbuda

St Louis
  baseball team: 9 Cardinals
  football team: 9 Cardinals
  founded by: 13 Pierre Laclede
  hockey team: 5 Blues
  landmark: 11 Gateway Arch
  newspaper: 12 Post-Dispatch
  river: 11 Mississippi
  site of: 10 Exposition (1904)
  university: 10 Washington

stock 4 butt, clan, form, fund, haft, herd, hold, kind, line, pull, race, root, type 5 array, basic, birth, blood, breed, broth, cache, caste, equip, goods, grasp, hoard, house, offer, shaft, store, tribe, wares 6 cattle, family, fit out, formal, handle, origin, people, shares, source, staple, strain, supply 7 appoint, capital, descent, dynasty, furnish, lineage, provide, regular, reserve, routine 8 accoutre, ancestry, bouillon, heredity, pedigree, pro forma, quantity, standard 9 forebears, genealogy, inventory, livestock, ownership, parentage, provision, reservoir, selection 10 assortment, background,

extraction, family tree, investment 11 merchandise, nationality, progeniture 12 accumulation 13 capital shares

Stockhausen, Karlheinz
  born: 7 Germany, Modrath
  composer of: 5 Cycle, Tempi 6 Groups, Hymnen, Mantra, Zyklus 7 Anthems, Gruppen, Momente 8 Attuning, Gold Dust, Kontakte, Stimmung 9 Goldstaub, Zeitmasze 10 Procession, Prozession 12 Kontrapunkte 13 Klavierstucke 16 From the Seven Days 17 Aus den Sieben Tagen

Stockholm
  nickname: 16 Venice of the North
  capital of: 6 Sweden
  sea: 6 Baltic
  lake: 7 Malaren
  section: 8 Norrmalm 9 Sodermalm 11 Gamla Staden
  landmark: 7 Skansen 8 City Hall 11 Great Church
  site of: 10 Nobel Prize

stockpile 5 cache, hoard, stock, store 10 accumulate

stocky 5 dumpy, husky, pudgy, solid, squat, stout 6 blocky, chunky, stubby, stumpy, sturdy 8 thickset

stodgy 4 dull, flat 5 dated, heavy, lumpy, passe, staid, thick 6 boring, clumsy, dreary, narrow, prolix, stuffy 7 humdrum, pompous, prosaic, serious, starchy, tedious 8 lifeless, pedantic, tiresome 9 laborious, lumbering, wearisome 10 antiquated, inflexible, monotonous 12 indigestible, old-fashioned 13 uninteresting

stoic 4 calm 8 detached, fatalist, quietist, tranquil 9 impassive, unruffled 11 philosophic 13 dispassionate, imperturbable, unimpassioned

stoicism 8 fatalism 9 fortitude 11 impassivity, tranquility 12 tranquillity 16 imperturbability

Stoker, Bram
  author of: 7 Dracula

stole 3 fur 4 cape, robe, took, wrap 5 crept, orary, scarf 6 swiped 7 filched, pinched, sneaked, tiptoed 8 mantilla, pilfered, snatched, vestment 9 embezzled, purloined

stolen 3 hot 5 taken 6 swiped 7 filched, pinched 8 pilfered, snatched 9 embezzled, ill-gotten, purloined

stolid 4 dull 5 dense 6 bovine, obtuse 7 lumpish 8 sluggish 9 apathetic, impassive, lethargic 10 phlegmatic 11 insensitive, unemotional

stolidity 6 apathy 8 lethargy 9 inertness 11 impassivity 12 sluggishness

stomach 3 maw, pot 4 bear, bent, bias, craw, crop, guts, mind, take 5 abide, belly, brook, fancy, humor, stand, taste, tummy 6 desire, endure, hunger, liking, middle, paunch, relish, retain, suffer, temper, thirst 7 abdo-

men, gizzard, leaning, midriff, swallow 8 affinity, appetite, bear with, keenness, overlook, pass over, pleasure, potbelly, sympathy, tolerate 9 put up with 10 attraction, midsection, partiality, proclivity, propensity 11 breadbasket, countenance, disposition, inclination 12 predilection

stone 3 gem, nut, pip, pit 4 rock, seed 5 bijou, jewel 6 kernel, pebble 9 brilliant 10 throw rocks

Stone, Edward Durell
  architect of: 9 US Embassy 17 Museum of Modern Art 33 Kennedy Center for the Performing Arts

Stone, Irving
  author of: 9 The Origin 11 Lust for Life 12 Those Who Love 17 Sailor on Horseback, The President's Lady 19 Adversary in the House 21 The Agony and the Ecstasy

Stone, Oliver
  born: 9 New York NY
  profession: 6 writer 8 director
  films: 3 JFK 5 Nixon, U-Turn 7 Platoon (Oscar) 10 Wall Street 12 Patriot Games 14 Heaven and Earth 15 Midnight Express 18 Natural Born Killers 21 Born on the Fourth of July

stonefly
  varieties: 5 giant, green 6 spring, winter 8 perlodid 9 roachlike 11 green-winged 12 rolled-winged

Stone of Scone
  location: 8 Scotland
  purpose: 12 crowning king
  moved to: 16 Westminster Abbey

stoneware 5 china 7 ceramic, pottery 8 crockery

stony 3 icy 4 cold 5 blank, bumpy, chill, rocky, rough, stern 6 coarse, craggy, flinty, frigid, jagged, marble, pebbly, rugged, severe, steely, stolid, uneven 7 austere, callous, granite, lithoid, stoical 8 concrete, deadened, gravelly, hardened, indurate, obdurate, ossified, pitiless, rocklike, soulless, uncaring 9 bloodless, heartless, merciless, petrified, unfeeling, untouched 10 ada mantine, forbidding, fossilized, hard-boiled, inexorable, insensible, unaffected, unyielding

stool 5 bench 7 cricket, has sock, ottoman

stool pigeon 3 rat, spy 4 fink 5 decoy, patsy 6 snitch 7 peacher, stoolie, tattler 8 informer, squealer 10 talebearer, tattletale

stoop 3 bow, sag 4 bend, fall, sink 5 deign, droop, porch, slump, steps, yield 6 resort, slouch, submit 7 concede, descend, succumb 8 doorstep 9 acquiesce 10 condescend 11 entranceway 19 round-shoulderedness

stooped 4 bent 5 bowed 7 deigned, hunched 9 contorted 12 condescended

stop 3 ban, bar, end **4** curb, fill, halt, hold, idle, plug, quit, rest, seal, stay, stem, wait **5** abide, block, brake, break, caulk, cease, check, close, depot, deter, dwell, lapse, lodge, pause, put up, spell, stall, stand, tarry, visit **6** alight, arrest, cut off, desist, draw up, expire, falter, finish, hamper, hiatus, hinder, pull up, recess, rein in, repose, run out, stanch, stop up, thwart **7** close up, halting, layover, occlude, prevent, respite, sojourn, station, suspend **8** abeyance, break off, conclude, cut short, hold back, intermit, interval, leave off, obstruct, pass away, peter out, postpone, preclude, restrain, suppress, surcease, terminal, terminus, wind down **9** cessation, frustrate, interlude, stand fast, terminate **10** desistance, drop anchor, put an end to, standstill, suspension **11** come to a halt, come to an end, destination, discontinue, prohibition, termination **12** intermission, interruption **17** come to a standstill **18** bring to a standstill

stopgap 7 stand-by **9** contrived, emergency, expedient, impromptu, makeshift, temporary, tentative **10** improvised, substitute **11** provisional
Latin: 5 ad hoc **6** pro tem

stop in 4 call **5** visit **6** drop in, look in

stop off 4 call **5** visit **6** drop in, look in, stop by

stoppage 4 halt **5** check, tieup **6** arrest **7** barrier, embargo, staying **8** blockage, checking, clogging, gridlock, obstacle **9** checkmate, hindrance, restraint, stricture **10** disruption, impediment **11** curtailment, obstruction **12** interruption

Stoppard, Tom
author of: 10 Travesties **33** Rosencrantz and Guildenstern Are Dead

stopper 3 lid **4** bung, cock, cork, plug **5** spile

Stopping by Woods on a Snowy Evening
author: 11 Robert Frost

Stop the Music
host: 9 Bert Parks
orchestra: 9 Harry Salter
vocalist: 9 June Valli **11** Jaye P Morgan, Jimmy Blaine **12** Marion Morgan **13** Betty Ann Grove, Estelle Loring

stop up 3 jam **4** clog **5** block, choke **8** obstruct

store 3 lot **4** fund, hold, host, keep, mart, pack, pile, save, shop **5** amass, array, cache, faith, hoard, lay by, lay in, lay up, stash, stock, trust, value, wares **6** credit, esteem, gather, heap up, legion, market, plenty, regard, riches, scores, supply, volume, wealth **7** deposit, effects, husband, put away, reserve, satiety **8** emporium, lay aside, overflow, plethora, quantity, reliance, richness, salt away, sock away, stow away **9** abundance, inventory, multitude, profusion, provision, reservoir, stockpile **10** accumulate, confidence, cornucopia, dependence, estimation, exuberance, luxuriance **11** copiousness, full measure, prodigality, supermarket **12** accumulation **13** establishment

storehouse 4 bank, silo **5** depot, vault **7** arsenal, granary **8** elevator, magazine, treasury **9** stockroom, warehouse **10** depository, repository

storied 4 epic **6** fabled **8** fabulous **9** legendary

Stories and Texts for Nothing
author: 13 Samuel Beckett

storm 3 ado, row **4** blow, fume, fuss, gale, rage, rant, rave, roar, rush, stir, tear, to-do **5** burst, furor, snarl, stalk, stamp, stomp, tramp **6** assail, attack, charge, clamor, deluge, flurry, hubbub, pother, ruckus, squall, strike, tumult, uproar **7** assault, besiege, bluster, carry on, cyclone, rampage, tempest, tornado, torrent, turmoil, twister, typhoon **8** blizzard, brouhaha, downpour, eruption, fall upon, outbreak, outburst, upheaval **9** agitation, commotion, explosion, fulminate, hurricane, raise hell **10** cloudburst, hullabaloo **11** blow one's top, disturbance **12** blow one's cool, vent one's rage

storm and stress
German: 13 Sturm und Drang
name of 18th century: 16 literary movement

storm troopers
German: 14 Sturmabteilung

stormy 4 foul, wild **5** rainy, rough, snowy, windy **6** raging, rugged **7** howling, roaring, squally, violent **8** blustery **9** inclement, turbulent **10** blustering **11** tempestuous

story 3 fib, lie **4** news, plot, tale, word, yarn **5** alibi, fable, piece **6** excuse, legend, report, sketch **7** account, article, parable, romance, tidings, version **8** allegory, anecdote, argument, dispatch, news item, white lie **9** falsehood, narrative, statement, testimony **10** allegation **11** fabrication, information **13** prevarication

Story of a Bad Boy, The
author: 19 Thomas Bailey Aldrich

Story of G I Joe, The
director: 14 William Wellman
cast: 13 Freddie Steele, Robert Mitchum **15** Burgess Meredith (Ernie Pyle)

Story of Louis Pasteur, The
director: 15 William Dieterle
cast: 8 Paul Muni (Pasteur) **11** Anita Louise **19** Josephine Hutchinson
Oscar for: 5 actor (Muni)

stout 3 big, fat, fit **4** able, bold, firm, true **5** brave, bulky, burly, hardy, heavy, hefty, husky, large, obese, plump, pudgy, round, solid, tough, tubby **6** brawny, chubby, daring, fleshy, heroic, mighty, plucky, portly, robust, rotund, rugged, spunky, steady, stocky, strong, sturdy **7** doughty, gallant, staunch, valiant **8** athletic, constant, enduring, faithful, fearless, intrepid, leathery, muscular, resolute, resolved, stalwart, thickset, untiring, valorous, vigorous **9** confident, corpulent, dauntless, steadfast, strapping **10** able-bodied, courageous, determined, inflexible, unshakable, unswerving, unwavering **11** indomitable, lionhearted, unfaltering, unflinching, unshrinking

Stout, Rex
author of: 10 Fer-de-Lance **12** Too Many Cooks **16** If Death Ever Slept
character: 5 Fritz **9** Nero Wolfe **13** Archie Goodwin

stouthearted 4 bold **5** brave, gutsy, hardy **6** heroic, plucky, spunky **7** valiant **8** fearless, intrepid, resolute, spirited, stalwart, unafraid, valorous **9** dauntless, undaunted **10** courageous **11** indomitable, lionhearted, unblenching, unflinching

stoutheartedness 4 grit, guts, sand **5** nerve, pluck, spunk, valor **6** daring, mettle **7** bravery, courage **8** boldness **12** fearlessness **13** dauntlessness

stoutness
French: 10 embonpoint

stow 3 jam, put, set **4** cram, load, pack, tuck **5** cache, crowd, place, stash, store, stuff, wedge **7** deposit, squeeze **8** ensconce, salt away

Stowe, Harriet Beecher
author of: 4 Dred **12** Oldtown Folks **14** Uncle Tom's Cabin

Strachey, Lytton
author of: 13 Queen Victoria **17** Elizabeth and Essex, Eminent Victorians
member of: 15 Bloomsbury Group

strafe 7 bombard **8** fire upon **10** machine-gun

straggle 4 rove **5** drift, stray **6** sprawl, wander **7** deviate, meander **8** divagate

straight 4 even, neat, tidy, true **5** clear, frank, right, solid, sound **9** candid, direct, evenly, honest, square, unbent **7** aligned, erectly, in order, orderly, upright **8** accurate, adjusted, arranged, directly, on a level, reliable, squarely, truthful, unbroken **9** ceaseless, forthwith, incessant, instantly, not curved, shipshape, sorted out, sustained, veracious **10** aboveboard, continuous, forthright, four-square, methodical, persistent, straightly, successive, unrelieved, unswerving, unwavering **11** consecutive, coordinated, immediately, trustworthy, undeviating **13** uninterrupted

straighten 4 tidy **5** align **6** adjust, neaten, unbend **7** even out **8** level out, square up **9** put in line **10** put in order, stand erect

straightening 7 tidying **9** adjusting, alignment, evening up, unbending **10** evening out **11** leveling out **13** putting in line **14** putting in order

straighten out 6 unbend **7** realign **8** redirect **10** discipline

straighten up 4 tidy **5** align, clean, order **6** neaten, tidy up **7** arrange, stand up **8** organize

straightforward 4 open **5** blunt, frank **6** candid, direct, honest, square **7** ethical, upright **8** straight **9** guileless, honorable **10** aboveboard, creditable, forthright, scrupulous **11** plainspoken, trustworthy

straightforwardness 6 candor **7** honesty **12** truthfulness **14** forthrightness

straight from the shoulder 4 open **5** frank **6** candid, direct, openly **7** bluntly, frankly, sincere **8** candidly, directly **9** downright

straightness 7 honesty **8** evenness **10** directness **11** uprightness

strain 3 air, tax, tug **4** kind, line, pull, sift, song, sort, toil, tune, type, vein **5** blood, breed, drain, force, grain, grind, group, heave, labor, people, press, sieve, streak, stock, trait, twist **6** burden, drudge, effort, extend, family, filter, genius, injure, injury, melody, overdo, purify, refine, screen, sprain, stress, weaken, winnow, wrench **7** descent, distend, exhaust, fatigue, lineage, overtax, species, stretch, tension, tighten, try hard, variety, wear out **8** ancestry, bear down, elongate, exertion, hardship, heredity, make taut, overwork, pressure, protract, struggle, tendency **9** draw tight, make tense, overexert, parentage **10** buckle down, derivation, extraction, overburden **11** disposition, huff and puff, inclination **12** do double duty, drive oneself, exert oneself **14** predisposition, work like a horse, work like a slave

strained 5 tense **6** touchy **8** volatile **9** explosive **10** precarious

strait 7 channel, narrows, passage

straitened 5 broke, needy **6** hard-up **7** pinched **8** bank rupt, indigent, strapped, wiped-out **9** destitute, penniless, penurious **10** distressed, pauperized, restricted **11** embarrassed **12** impoverished **15** poverty-stricken

Strait Is the Gate
    author: **9** Andre Gide

straitlaced 4 prim **5** rigid, stiff **6** formal, narrow, proper, severe, strict **7** austere, prudish, uptight **8** reserved **9** inhibited **11** puritanical **14** overscrupulous **15** undemonstrative

straits 3 fix **4** hole **6** pickle, plight **8** distress **9** extremity **10** difficulty **11** predicament **13** embarrassment

strand 4 bank, cord, lock, rope **5** beach, braid, coast, fiber, leave, shore, tress, twist **6** desert, ground, maroon, string, thread **8** filament, necklace, seacoast, seashore **9** component, go aground, riverside, shipwreck **10** ingredient, run aground **15** leave high and dry, leave in the lurch

stranded 5 stuck **6** ashore **7** aground, beached **8** grounded **9** foundered **11** shipwrecked **14** left high and dry, left in the lurch

strange 3 new, odd **4** lost **5** alien, queer **6** uneasy, unused **7** awkward, bizarre, curious, erratic, foreign, unknown, unusual **8** aberrant, abnormal, freakish, peculiar, singular, uncommon **9** alienated, anomalous, eccentric, estranged, fantastic, ill at ease, irregular, unnatural **10** bewildered, farfetched, out of place, outlandish, unexplored, unfamiliar **11** discomposed, disoriented, out-of-the-way **12** unaccustomed, undiscovered, unhabituated **13** extraordinary, unaccountable, uncomfortable **14** unconventional

Strange Fruit
    author: **12** Lillian Smith

Strange Interlude
    author: **12** Eugene O'Neill

strangeness 7 anomaly, oddness **9** queerness **10** aberration **11** abnormality, peculiarity **12** eccentricity, idiosyncrasy, irregularity, unconformity **13** nonconformity

stranger 5 alien **8** newcomer, outsider **9** auslander, foreigner, immigrant, outlander

Stranger, The
    author: **11** Albert Camus

Strangers on a Train
    director: **15** Alfred Hitchcock
    cast: **9** Ruth Roman **11** Leo G Carroll, Marion Lorne **12** Robert Walker **13** Farley Granger **17** Patricia Hitchcock
    remade as: **20** Once You Kiss a Stranger

strange to say
    Latin: **13** mirabile dictu

strangle 3 gag **4** stop **5** burke, check, choke, crush, quell **6** muzzle, stifle **7** garrote, put down, repress, smother, squelch **8** choke off, snuff out, suppress, throttle **9** suffocate **10** asphyxiate, extinguish

strangulate 8 choke off, compress, strangle **9** constrict

strap 3 tie **4** band, beat, belt, bind, cord, flog, lash, whip **5** flail, leash, thong, truss **6** tether, thrash **7** scourge

strapped 8 bankrupt, wiped out **9** insolvent, penniless **12** impoverished, without funds

strapping 5 burly, hardy, husky, stout **6** brawny, robust, strong, sturdy **8** muscular, powerful, stalwart

stratagem 4 game, plan, plot, ploy, ruse, wile **5** blind, dodge, feint, trick **6** deceit, device, scheme, tactic **8** artifice, intrigue, maneuver, trickery **9** deception **10** subterfuge **11** contrivance, machination

strategic 3 key **4** wary **5** vital **6** clever **7** careful, crucial, cunning, guarded, planned, politic, prudent, turning **8** cautious, critical, decisive, military, tactical, vigilant **9** important, momentous, principal **10** calculated, deliberate, diplomatic **11** significant **13** consequential, precautionary

strategy 4 game **5** craft, wiles **6** policy, scheme **7** cunning, devices, tactics **8** artifice, art of war, game plan, plotting **9** war policy **10** artfulness, craftiness **11** grand design, machination, maneuvering **12** military plan **15** military science

stratosphere 3 sky **5** ozone **7** heavens **8** upper air **12** high altitude **14** wild blue yonder

stratum 4 band, belt, seam, zone **5** layer

Strauss, Johann (the Elder)
    composer of: **13** Radetzky March

Strauss, Johann (the Younger)
    composer of: **6** The Bat **13** Die Fledermaus, The Gipsy Baron **16** Der Zigeunerbaron
        waltz: **12** Emperor Waltz **13** The Blue Danube **23** Tales from the Vienna Woods

Strauss, Joseph
    composer of: **17** Music of the Spheres **27** The Village Swallows in Austria

Strauss, Levi
    make of: **5** jeans **9** dungarees

Strauss, Richard
    born: **6** Munich **7** Germany
    composer of: **6** Salome **7** Don Juan, Elektra **8** Arabella **9** Capriccio **10** Don Quixote **14** Ein Heldenleben **15** Ariadne auf Naxos **16** Der Rosenkavalier, Domestic Symphony, Till Eulenspiegel **19** Die Frau ohne Schatten **20** Die Aegyptische Helena, Thus Spake Zarathustra **21** Also Sprach Zarathustra **23** Death and Transfiguration

Stravinsky, Igor Feodorovich
    born: **6** Russia **11** Oranienbaum
    composer of: **4** Agon **6** Threni **7** Orpheus **8** The Flood **9** Card Party, Fireworks **10** Oedipus Rex, Petrouchka, Petruschka, Pulcinella **11** Jeu de Cartes, The Firebird **13** Dumbarton Oaks, Psalm Symphony **14** The Nightingale **15** Abraham and Isaac, The Rite of Spring **16** Requiem

Canticles, The Rake's Progress **18** Le Sacre du Printemps

straw 3 hay **4** tube **5** chaff **7** pipette

strawberry 8 Fragaria
varieties: 4 mock **5** beach **6** barren, Dunlap, garden, Indian **7** sow-teat **8** Klondike, Rosacean, Virginia, woodland
liqueur: 13 creme de fraise

Straw Dogs
director: 12 Sam Peckinpah
cast: 9 T P McKenna **11** Susan George **12** Peter Vaughan **13** Dustin Hoffman

straw man 6 effigy **9** scapegoat, scarecrow

stray 4 lost, roam, rove, waif **5** drift **6** random, wander **7** digress, drifter **8** go astray, sepa rate, set apart, straggle, straying, vagabond, wanderer **9** itinerant, misplaced, scat tered, straggler **10** lost animal, lost person **11** lose one's way

straying 5 lapse **8** drifting, rambling **9** departure, deviation, wandering **10** abberation, digression, divergence

streak 3 bar, bed, fly **4** band, blot, blur, cast, dart, dash, daub, line, lode, race, rush, seam, tear, vein, whiz, zoom **5** layer, level, plane, smear, speed, strip, touch **6** blotch, hurtle, smirch, smudge, strain, stripe **7** portion, splotch, stratum

stream 3 jet, run **4** blow, file, flow, flux, gush, pour, race, rill, rush, teem, tide, waft, wave **5** brook, burst, creek, float, flood, issue, river, shoot, spate, spill, spout, spurt, surge **6** abound, branch, course, deluge, extend, feeder, onrush, sluice **7** current, flutter, freshet, rivulet, torrent **8** effusion, fountain, overflow **9** profusion, tributary **11** watercourse

streamer 4 flag **6** banner, burgee **7** pennant

streamlet 3 run **4** rill **5** brook, creek **7** rivulet

streamlined 4 racy **5** clean, sleek **7** compact **8** up-to-date **9** organized **10** futuristic, modernized, simplified **11** aerodynamic

stream of abuse 6 tirade **8** diatribe, harangue **9** contumely, invective **12** vituperation

Streep, Meryl
real name: 16 Mary Louise Streep
born: 14 Basking Ridge NJ
roles: 8 Ironweed, Silkwood **11** Out of Africa **13** Falling in Love, Sophie's Choice (Oscar), The Deer Hunter **14** Before and After, Kramer vs Kramer **20** Postcards from the Edge, The House of the Spirits **25** The Bridges of Madison County, The French Lieutenant's Woman

street 3 way **4** lane, mews, road **5** alley, block, route **6** avenue **7** highway,

roadway, terrace, thruway **8** turnpike **9** boulevard **10** expressway **12** thoroughfare

Streetcar Named Desire, A
author: 17 Tennessee Williams
director: 9 Elia Kazan
cast: 9 Kim Hunter (Stella Dubois Kowalski) **10** Karl Malden **11** Vivien Leigh (Blanche Dubois) **12** Marlon Brando (Stanley Kowalski)
setting: 10 New Orleans
score: 9 Alex North
Oscar for: 7 actress (Leigh) **15** supporting actor (Malden) **17** supporting actress (Hunter)

Streets of San Francisco, The
character: 9 (Det Lt) Mike Stone **10** (Inspector) Dan Robbins **11** (Inspector) Steve Keller
cast: 10 Karl Malden **12** Richard Hatch **14** Michael Douglas

strega
type: 7 liqueur
origin: 5 Italy
flavor: 6 spices **10** orange peel
with brandy: 10 Strega Flip

Streisand, Barbra
real name: 20 Barbara Joan Streisand
born: 10 Brooklyn NY
husband: 11 Elliot Gould
roles: 5 Yentl **9** Funny Girl (Oscar), Funny Lady **10** Fanny Brice, Hello Dolly, What's Up Doc? **11** A Star Is Born **12** The Main Event, The Way We Were **13** The Prince of Tides **20** The Mirror Has Two Faces
recordings: 10 The Concert **11** A Star Is Born **23** The Barbra Streisand Album

strength 4 beef, grit, kick, pith, sand, size **5** brawn, force, forte, might, pluck, power, sinew, spice, vigor **6** anchor, mettle, number, purity, spirit, succor, virtue **7** bravery, muscles, potency, stamina, support **8** backbone, buttress, efficacy, firmness, mainstay, security, solidity, tenacity, vitality **9** endurance, fortitude, hardiness, intensity, lustiness, puissance, stoutness, toughness, viability **10** robustness, sturdiness, sustenance **13** concentration, effectiveness **16** stoutheartedness
Latin: 3 vis

strengthen 4 prop **5** brace, renew, steel **6** harden **7** build up, enhance, fortify, improve, restore, shore up, support, sustain **8** buttress **9** reinforce

strength of character 4 grit, guts **5** pluck, spunk **6** mettle **7** resolve **8** backbone **9** fortitude **10** resolution **12** resoluteness **13** steadfastness

strenuous 4 hard **5** eager **6** active, ardent, dogged, taxing, uphill **7** arduous, dynamic, earnest, intense, zealous **8** animated, diligent, sedulous, spirited, untiring, vigorous **9** assiduous, difficult, energetic, laborious,

punishing **10** exhausting, on one's toes **11** hardworking, industrious, painstaking **12** enterprising **13** indefatigable

stress 4 beat, mark **5** force, value, worth **6** accent, affirm, assert, burden, moment, repeat, strain, weight **7** anxiety, concern, feature, gravity, meaning, sawdust, tension, urgency **8** emphasis, pressure **9** emphasize, necessity, underline **10** accentuate, importance, insist upon, oppression, prominence, underscore **11** consequence, seriousness **12** accentuation, significance **13** consideration

stretch 4 span, term, tire **5** cover, reach, spell, stint, tract, while, widen **6** burden, deepen, expand, extend, period, sprawl, spread, spring, strain **7** distend, draw out, expanse, fatigue, lie over, over tax, pull out **8** distance, draw taut, duration, elongate, interval, lengthen, overtask, over work, protract, put forth, reach out, tautness, traverse **9** be elastic, draw tight, make tense, make tight, overexert **10** elasticity, exaggerate, overburden, overcharge, overstrain, push too far, resiliency **11** carry too far **12** be expandable, be extendable **14** push to the limit

stretchable 7 elastic, rubbery **8** flexible **9** resilient

stretching 9 extending, extension **10** drawing out, elongation **11** attenuation, enlargement, lengthening, protraction **12** prolongation **13** amplification

stretching out 8 outreach **9** expansion, extending, extension **10** elongation **11** attenuation, lengthening **12** prolongation

stretch out 6 expand, extend **7** amplify, augment, draw out **8** elongate, lengthen, protract

Strether
character in: 14 The Ambassadors
author: 10 Henry James

strew 3 sow **6** litter **7** scatter **8** disperse **9** broadcast **11** disseminate

stricken 3 ill **4** hurt, sick **7** injured, smitten, wounded **8** blighted, diseased **9** afflicted, taken sick **13** incapacitated

strict 4 nice **5** exact, rigid, stern **6** severe **7** austere, perfect **8** absolute, complete, exacting, rigorous, unerring **9** stringent **10** fastidious, inflexible, meticulous, scrupulous, unyielding **13** authoritarian, conscientious **14** uncompromising

strictly required
French: 9 de rigueur

stride 4 gait, lope, pace, step **5** march, stalk **7** advance, headway **8** long step, progress **11** advancement, improvement **13** take long steps

strident 5 harsh **6** shrill **7** grating, jarring, rasping, raucous **8** clashing, grinding, jangling, piercing, twanging **9** dissonant **10** discordant, screeching **11** cacophonous, high-pitched

Striebel, John H
creator/artist of: 10 Dixie Dugan

strife 6 unrest **7** discord, trouble, turmoil, warfare **8** conflict, disquiet, fighting, struggle, upheaval, violence **10** contention, convulsion, disharmony, dissension **11** altercation, disturbance

Strife
author: 14 John Galsworthy

strike 3 bat, box, hit, run, tap **4** bang, beat, belt, bump, clap, clip, club, come, cuff, drub, find, flog, lash, make, meet, pelt, ring, slam, slap, slug, sock, toll, whip, wipe **5** chime, clout, erase, flail, knell, knock, light, pound, punch, reach, smash, smite, sound, thump, tie-up, whack, whale **6** affect, arrive, assail, attack, batter, buffet, cancel, chance, charge, cudgel, delete, effect, fold up, hammer, pommel, remove, seem to, thrash, wallop **7** achieve, arrange, assault, boycott, impress, occur to, protest, put away, ram into, run into, scourge, scratch, stumble, unearth, walk out **8** appear to, bump into, come upon, cross out, dawn upon, discover, fall upon, lambaste, pull down, take down **9** burst upon, devastate, eliminate, encounter, eradicate, knock into, take apart **10** come across, flagellate, meet head-on **11** beat against, collide with, dash against **12** labor dispute, work stoppage

strike a bargain 5 agree **6** settle **9** make a deal **10** compromise **11** come to terms, meet halfway **18** split the difference **20** reach an understanding

strike back 7 counter, get even, hit back, pay back, riposte **9** fight back, retaliate **13** counterattack

strike dumb 4 daze, stun **5** amaze, shock **7** astound, stagger, stupefy **8** astonish, dumfound **9** dumbfound, electrify **11** flabbergast

strike noisily 4 bang, beat, clap, slam **5** thump

strike out 6 delete, fan out, set off, set out **7** take out **10** sally forth

strike sharply 3 rap **4** slap **5** crack

striking 6 marked **7** notable **9** prominent **10** astounding, impressive, noteworthy, noticeable, remarkable, surprising **11** conspicuous, outstanding **13** extraordinary

Strindberg, August
author of: 9 Miss Julie, The Father **10** A Dream Play **12** The Creditors **14** The Ghost Sonata **15** The Dance of Death

string 3 row **4** cord, file, line, rope **5** chain, queue, train, twine **6** column,

extend, parade, series, spread, strand, thread **7** binding, stretch **8** necklace, sequence **10** procession, succession

stringent 5 close, harsh, spare, stern, stiff, tight **6** cogent, frugal, severe, strict **7** sparing **8** exacting, forceful, rigorous **9** demanding, effectual, unbending **10** inflexible, unyielding **14** uncompromising

strip 3 rob **4** band, flay, loot, peel, raid, sack, skin, slip, tear **5** field, flake, rifle, shave **6** denude, divest, length, ravage, remove, ribbon, stripe, unwrap **7** deprive, despoil, disrobe, draw off, lay bare, measure, plunder, pull off, ransack, uncover, undrape, undress **8** airstrip, desolate, lay waste, spoliate, unclothe **9** steal from **11** disencumber

stripe 3 bar **4** band, line, tape **5** braid, strip, swath **6** ribbon, streak **7** chevron **8** insignia **9** striation

stripling 3 boy, lad **5** minor, youth **8** teenager, young man **9** schoolboy, youngster **10** adolescent

stripped 4 bare, nude **5** naked **6** peeled, unclad **7** denuded, exposed, unrobed **8** disrobed, divested **9** unclothed, uncovered, undressed

strive 3 vie **4** push **5** essay, fight, labor **6** battle, strain **7** contend, try hard **8** endeavor, struggle **9** take pains, undertake **10** do one's best **12** apply oneself, do one's utmost, exert oneself, spare no pains **15** work like a Trojan **18** move heaven and earth **20** leave no stone unturned

striving 4 toil **5** exert, labor **6** effort, strain **7** toiling, travail **8** exertion, struggle **9** straining **10** struggling

stroke 3 bat, hit, pat, pet, tap **4** blow, chop, coup, deed, feat, poke, slap, sock, swat **5** brush, chime, fluke, punch, whack **6** caress, chance, wallop **7** massage, ringing, seizure, tolling **8** accident, apoplexy, flourish, movement, sounding, striking **11** achievement, coincidence, piece of luck, transaction **15** brain hemorrhage

stroll 4 tour, turn, walk **5** amble, mosey **6** ramble, wander **7** meander, saunter **9** poke along, promenade **14** constitutional

stroller 4 pram **5** buggy **6** ambler, walker **7** rambler **8** carriage **9** itinerant, pushchair, saunterer **10** promenader **12** perambulator

strong 3 hot **4** able, bold, deep, keen, tart **5** burly, clear, close, fiery, hardy, nippy, sharp, solid, sound, stout, tangy, tough, vivid **6** ardent, biting, brawny, bright, cogent, fervid, fierce, gritty, hearty, mighty, moving, plucky, potent, robust, savory, severe, sinewy, sturdy **7** buoyant, capable, devoted, earnest, fervent, healthy, intense, piquant, pungent, skilled, violent, zeal-

ous **8** animated, athletic, definite, diligent, distinct, emphatic, faithful, forceful, muscular, powerful, puissant, sedulous, spirited, stalwart, tireless, vehement, vigorous **9** assiduous, competent, confirmed, effective, energetic, herculean, resilient, tenacious, undiluted **10** compelling, convincing, courageous, deep-seated, persistent, proficient **11** impassioned, persevering, resourceful **12** advantageous, concentrated, highly spiced, high-spirited, unmistakable **13** indefatigable, well-qualified **14** highly flavored, highly seasoned
Spanish: 5 macho

Strong
character in: 7 Erewhon
author: 6 Butler

strong-arm 3 cow **5** bully, force **6** coerce, compel **8** browbeat, threaten **10** intimidate

strong feeling 4 fear, hate, heat, love, zeal **5** anger, ardor **6** fervor, sorrow, warmth **7** despair, emotion, passion, sadness **8** jealousy **9** happiness, vehemence **12** satisfaction

stronghold 4 fort, hold, home, keep **6** bunker, center, locale, refuge **7** bastion, bulwark, citadel, rampart, redoubt **8** fastness, fortress, safehold, stockade **10** battlement, blockhouse **13** fortification

strongly committed 4 true **5** loyal **6** ardent **7** devoted, staunch, zealous **8** adhering, faithful **9** dedicated, steadfast **10** passionate, unwavering

strong point 5 forte **6** anchor **8** mainstay, strength

strong-willed 5 pushy **8** forceful, positive **9** assertive **10** aggressive **11** domineering, self-assured **13** self-assertive

structural support 3 bar **4** beam, prop, stud **5** brace, joist **6** girder, rafter, timber **7** trestle **12** underpinning

structure 4 form, plan **6** design, makeup **7** arrange, edifice, pattern **8** assemble, building, conceive, organize **9** construct, formation **11** arrangement, composition, put together **12** conformation, construction, organization **13** configuration

struggle 3 vie, war **4** duel, feud, pull, push, spar, tilt **5** argue, brawl, brush, clash, fight, grind, joust, labor, match, scrap, trial **6** action, battle, combat, differ, effort, engage, jostle, oppose, resist, strain, stress, strife, strive, tussle **7** compete, contend, contest, grapple, quarrel, scuffle **8** conflict, endeavor, exertion, long haul, skirmish, work hard **9** encounter, lock horns, take pains **10** engagement **11** altercation, cross swords **15** work like a Trojan **18** move heaven and earth **20** leave no stone unturned

strut 4 sail **6** parade, sashay **7** peacock, swagger **9** promenade

Struthiomimus
type: 8 dinosaur, theropod
known as: 15 ostrich dinosaur
period: 10 Cretaceous
characteristic: 9 toothless

Stryver
character in: 16 A Tale of Two Cities
author: 7 Dickens

Stuart, Gilbert
born: 15 North Kingston RI
artwork: 16 George Washington

Stuart, J E B
served in: 8 Civil War
side: 11 Confederate
commander of: 7 cavalry
battle: 7 Bull Run **8** Antietam **10** Gettysburg **14** Fredericksburg **16** Chancellorsville **18** Peninsular campaign

Stuart Little
author: 7 E B White

stub 3 end **4** bump, butt, dock, tail **5** crush, knock, snuff, stump **6** fag end, scrape **7** receipt, remains, tamp out, voucher **10** extinguish, torn ticket **11** counterfoil

stubble 5 beard **6** stumps **8** bristles, whiskers **9** cut stalks **16** five-o'clock shadow

stubborn 6 dogged, mulish, strong, sturdy **7** willful **8** forceful, obdurate, perverse, resolute **9** concerted, immovable, obstinate, pigheaded, resistant, tenacious, unbending, unmovable **10** bullheaded, headstrong, inflexible, persistent, purposeful, refractory, self-willed, unshakable, unyielding **11** indomitable, intractable, opinionated, uncompliant **12** hard to handle, recalcitrant, ungovernable, wholehearted

stubbornness 10 mulishness, obstinancy, resistance **11** willfulness **13** intransigence, pigheadedness

stubby 5 dumpy, pudgy, squab, squat, tubby **6** chubby, chunky, stocky, stodgy, stumpy **7** squatty **8** thickset

Stubtoe State
nickname of: 7 Montana

stuck 3 dug, put **4** held **5** bound, fixed, fused, glued, mired, poked **6** balked, curbed, jabbed, joined, nailed, pasted, pinned, placed, sealed, spiked, tacked, thrust, welded **7** adhered, affixed, boggled, impeded, planted, pricked, punched, saddled, snarled, speared, stabbed, stalled, stumped, stymied **8** attached, burdened, cemented, fastened, inserted **9** punctured **10** obstructed, perforated **11** immobilized

stuck-up 4 vain **5** cocky, snooty, uppish, uppity **7** haughty, high-hat **8** arrogant, snobbish **9** bigheaded, conceited **10** disdainful, egocentric, hoity-toity **11** overbearing, swellheaded **13** self-important, self-satisfied

stud 3 dot **4** beam, buck, dude, sire **5** board, rivet **6** button **7** upright **8** fastener, macho man, nailhead

student 4 coed **5** pupil **6** reader **7** analyst, learner, scholar, watcher **8** disciple, examiner, follower, observer, reviewer **9** collegian, schoolboy, spectator **10** schoolgirl **11** commentator, interpreter, matriculant **13** undergraduate

studied 8 measured **10** calculated, deliberate, purposeful **11** intentional **12** premeditated

studious 6 brainy, intent **7** bookish, earnest, erudite **8** academic, cerebral, diligent, literate, well-read **9** laborious, scholarly **10** determined, purposeful, scholastic **11** painstaking **12** intellectual

Studs Lonigan
series includes: 11 Judgment Day **12** Young Lonigan **29** The Young Manhood of Studs Lonigan
author: 13 James T Farrell

study 3 den **4** cram, read **5** grind, probe **6** office, peruse, review, search, studio, survey **7** examine, explore, inquiry, library, observe, reading **8** analysis, consider, learning, pore over, read up on, research, scrutiny **9** delve into, education **10** glance over, inspection, scrutinize **11** examination, exploration, hit the books, inquire into, instruction, investigate, read closely, reading room, scholarship **13** consideration, investigation, school oneself, search through

Study in Scarlet, A
author: 19 Sir Arthur Conan Doyle
character: 12 Dr John Watson **13** Jefferson Hope, Tobias Gregson **14** Sherlock Holmes **17** Inspector Lestrade

Study of History, A
author: 14 Arnold J Toynbee

stuff 3 act, bit, jam, pad, wad **4** best, bosh, bunk, cram, fill, gear, heap, load, pack, pile, sate, stow **5** cache, crowd, gorge, hokum, hooey, stash, store, thing, trash, wedge **6** burden, fill up, humbug, matter, staple, tackle, things, thrust, tricks, utmost **7** effects, essence, hogwash, overeat, rubbish, satiate, spinach, twaddle **8** darndest, falderal, material, nonsense **9** component, empty talk, substance **10** balderdash, belongings, gluttonize, ingredient, make a pig of **11** constituent, foolishness, overindulge, performance, possessions, raw material **12** quintessence **13** paraphernalia

stuff-and-nonsense 3 rot **4** bosh, bull, bunk, fill **5** hokum, hooey, trash **6** bunkum, drivel, humbug **7** baloney, hogwash, spinach, twaddle **8** buncombe, claptrap, nonsense, tommyrot **9** poppycock **10** applesauce, balder-

dash, tomfoolery **11** foolishness **12** fiddlesticks **13** horsefeathers

stuffed 4 full **6** filled, jammed, loaded, packed, rammed, wadded **7** crammed, crushed, replete **8** overfull, satiated, squeezed **10** sandwiched

stuff in 4 cram, pack **6** devour **8** bolt down, compress, gobble up, wolf down

stuffing 5 farce **7** filling, pack ing, padding, wadding **8** dressing **9** forcemeat

stuffy 4 cold, smug **5** close, fusty, heavy, muggy, musty, staid **6** stodgy, sultry **7** airless, pompous **8** reserved, stagnant, stifling **9** clogged-up, congested, high-flown, stopped-up, stuffed-up **10** old-fogyish, oppressive, sweltering **11** pretentious, straitlaced, suffocating **12** supercilious, unventilated **13** ill-ventilated, self-satisfied, stale-smelling

stultify 4 balk **6** hinder, impair, impede, thwart **7** cripple, inhibit, nullify, vitiate **8** suppress **9** frustrate, hamstring **11** make useless

stumble 3 hit **4** fall, reel, roll, sway, trip **5** botch, lurch, pitch, spill **6** bungle, falter, happen, hash up, hobble, mess up, slip up, sprawl, topple, totter **7** blunder, misstep, shamble, stagger **8** flounder **10** take a spill **12** come by chance, make mistakes, pitch forward

stumble upon 4 find **7** learn of **8** come upon, discover **10** chance upon, happen upon **14** find by accident

stumbling block 3 bar, rub **4** snag **5** block, catch, hitch **6** hamper, hurdle **7** barrier, problem **8** drawback, obstacle **9** detriment, hindrance **10** difficulty, impediment **11** obstruction **12** complication, interference

stump 3 end **4** butt, foil, stub, thud **5** befog, clomp, clonk, clump, clunk, stamp, stomp, tramp **6** baffle, nubbin, stymie **7** confuse, mystify, nonplus, perplex **8** bewilder, confound, dumfound, footfall, stomping, tramping **9** bamboozle, dumbfound

stun 4 daze, numb **5** amaze, shock **7** astound, stagger, startle, stupefy **8** astonish, dumfound **9** dumbfound **11** flabbergast

stunner 4 doll **5** beaut, Venus **6** beauty, eyeful **8** knockout **9** dreamboat **10** good-looker

stunning 6 dazing, lovely **7** amazing, numbing **8** shocking, striking **9** beautiful, exquisite, startling **10** astounding, staggering, stupefying **11** astonishing, dumfounding **12** dumbfounding, electrifying **14** flabbergasting

stunt 3 act **4** curb, feat **5** abort, check, cramp, dwarf, limit, stint, trick **6** impede, number, stifle **7** curtail, delimit **8** restrain, restrict, suppress

stunted 5 dumpy, runty **6** bantam **7** dwarfed, squatty, wizened **9** pint-sized **13** foreshortened

Stunt Man, The
director: **11** Richard Rush
cast: **9** Alex Rocco **11** Peter O'Toole (Eli Cross) **13** Allen Goorwitz, Sharon Farrell **14** Barbara Hershey, Steve Railsback

stupefaction 5 shock **8** numbness, surprise **9** amazement **12** astonishment

stupefied 5 dazed **6** amazed **7** shocked, stunned **8** benumbed **10** dumbstruck, dumfounded **11** dumbfounded **13** flabbergasted, thunderstruck

stupefy 4 daze, stun **5** amaze, shock **7** astound, nonplus, stagger **8** astonish, confound, dumfound, surprise **9** dumbfound, overwhelm **11** flabbergast

stupefying 8 shocking, stunning **11** dumfounding **12** dumbfounding, electrifying, overwhelming **14** flabbergasting

stupendous 3 big **4** huge, vast **5** giant, great, jumbo **6** mighty **7** amazing, immense, mammoth, massive, titanic, unusual **8** colossal, enormous, fabulous, gigantic, imposing, stunning, terrific **9** cyclopean, herculean, marvelous, monstrous, very great, very large, wonderful **10** astounding, gargantuan, incredible, monumental, phenomenal, prodigious, remarkable, surprising, tremendous, unexpected **11** astonishing, elephantine **13** extraordinary

stupid 4 dull, dumb **5** dense, inane, inept, silly **6** absurd, oafish, obtuse, simple, unwise **7** aimless, asinine, boorish, doltish, fatuous, foolish, idiotic, moronic, witless **8** backward, childish, heedless, mistaken, reckless, tactless **9** brainless, cretinous, dimwitted, duncelike, foolhardy, ill-judged, imbecilic, imprudent, pointless, senseless **10** half-witted, ill-advised, indiscreet, irrelevant, weak-minded **11** empty-headed, meaningless, nonsensical, purposeless, thoughtless **12** absentminded, muddleheaded, preposterous, simpleminded, slow-learning, unreasonable **13** ill-considered, inappropriate, irresponsible, rattlebrained, unintelligent

stupor 4 daze **5** faint **6** apathy, torpor **7** inertia **8** blackout, lethargy, numbness **9** inertness **10** somnolence **12** stupefaction **13** insensibility

sturdy 4 able, firm **5** brave, burly, gutsy, hardy, heavy, solid, sound, stout, tough **6** daring, dogged, gritty, heroic, mighty, plucky, robust, rug-

ged, secure, sinewy, spunky, strong **7** defiant, doughty, durable, gallant, lasting, valiant **8** enduring, fearless, forceful, intrepid, muscular, powerful, resolute, spirited, stalwart, stubborn, vigorous, well-made **9** dauntless, strapping, unabashed, undaunted, well-built **10** courageous, determined, invincible **11** indomitable, substantial, unshrinking **12** high-spirited, stouthearted **15** well-constructed

Sturges, John
director of: **14** The Great Escape **19** The Magnificent Seven

Sturges, Preston
director of: **10** The Lady Eve **16** Sullivan's Travels **17** The Palm Beach Story, Unfaithfully Yours **21** Hail the Conquering Hero **24** The Miracle of Morgan's Creek

Sturmabteilung 13 storm troopers

Sturm und Drang 22 German literary movement (18th century)
literally: **14** storm and stress

stygian 3 dim **4** dark **5** black, murky **6** dreary, gloomy, somber **7** hellish **8** funereal, infernal, starless **9** tenebrous, unlighted

style 3 fad **4** call, elan, kind, mode, name, pomp, rage, sort, type **5** charm, class, craze, favor, flair, grace, model, taste, trend, vogue **6** design, luxury, manner, polish **7** arrange, comfort, fashion, pattern **8** currency, elegance **9** affluence, designate **10** smoothness **11** savoir faire
French: **4** gout

stylish 3 hip, new **4** chic **5** natty, smart, swank **6** dapper, latest, modern, modish, with-it **7** a la mode, elegant, in vogue, voguish **8** up-to-date **9** in fashion **11** fashionable **13** sophisticated, up-to-the-minute

stymie 4 balk **5** block, check, stump **6** baffle, hinder, puzzle, thwart **7** confuse, mystify **8** confound, obstruct **9** frustrate

Styracosaurus
type: **8** dinosaur **10** ceratopsid
location: **12** North America
period: **10** Cretaceous
characteristic: **6** horned

Styron, William
author of: **12** The Long March **13** Sophie's Choice **15** Darkness Visible **17** Lie Down in Darkness **18** Set This House on Fire **25** The Confessions of Nat Turner

Styx
form: **5** river
location: **5** Hades **10** underworld
father: **7** Oceanus
ferryman: **6** Charon

suave 6 silken, smooth, urbane **7** affable, elegant, politic **8** charming, gracious, mannerly, polished, unctuous **9**

civilized **10** diplomatic, flattering **12** ingratiating **13** smooth-tongued

sub 5 below, proxy, under **6** backup, deputy, second **7** beneath, standby, stand-in **9** alternate, submarine, surrogate **10** substitute, understudy **11** pinch-hitter

subaltern 4 aide **6** helper **9** assistant **10** lieutenant **11** subordinate

subconscious 3 dim **7** dawning **9** intuitive **10** subliminal **11** instinctive

subdivide 6 divide **7** split up **8** separate **9** partition

subdivision 3 arm **4** wing **6** branch **7** chapter, section **8** offshoot **11** development **12** neighborhood

subdue 3 bow **4** calm, curb, down, drub, ease, foil, mute, rout, trim, whip **5** allay, break, check, crush, floor, quell, salve, smash, still **6** deaden, defeat, master, mellow, muffle, reduce, soften, soothe, temper, thrash **7** appease, assuage, conquer, mollify, oppress, overrun, put down, relieve, slacken, subject, trample **8** mitigate, moderate, overcome, palliate, surmount, tone down, vanquish **9** meliorate, overpower, overwhelm, quiet down, soft-pedal, subjugate **10** ameliorate **11** triumph over **12** tranquillize

subdued 4 dull **5** cowed, muted, quiet **7** abashed, crushed, humbled, muffled, quelled **8** deadened, overcame **10** humiliated, indistinct, lackluster **11** intimidated, overpowered

subduer 6 victor, winner **9** conqueror, overcomer **10** subjugator, vanquisher **11** intimidator

subject 4 bare, case, gist, open, pith, text **5** field, issue, liege, motif, prone, study, theme, topic **6** affair, expose, liable, matter, submit, thesis, vassal **7** bound by, citizen, concern, exposed, lay open **8** business, disposed, follower, obedient, question **9** dependent, subjected, substance **10** answerable, discipline, in danger of, make liable, put through, vulnerable **11** stipulatory, subordinate, subservient, susceptible

subjection 11 subjugation **12** subservience **13** regimentation, subordination

subjective 5 inner **6** biased **7** partial **8** partisan, personal **9** emotional **10** individual, prejudiced **12** nonobjective

subjoin 5 add on, affix, annex **6** append, attach, tack on

subjugate 4 tame **5** crush, quell **6** subdue **7** conquer, put down **8** dominate, suppress, vanquish **10** over master

subjugation 6 chains, thrall **7** bondage, slavery **9** dominance, mastering, servitude, thralldom **10** conquering, domination **11** enslavement, vanquishing

subjugator 6 master, victor 7 subduer 9 conqueror, dominator 10 vanquisher 11 slavemaster

sublimate 4 turn 5 exalt, shift 6 divert, purify 7 channel, convert, elevate, ennoble 8 redirect, transfer 9 transform, transmute 12 spiritualize

sublime 4 high 5 grand, great, lofty, noble 6 superb 7 exalted, stately 8 elevated, imposing, majestic, splendid, terrific, very good 9 estimable, excellent, marvelous, wonderful 12 awe-inspiring, praiseworthy

submarine
　　invented by: 7 Holland
　　even keel: 4 Lake
　　torpedo: 8 Bushnell

submerge 4 dive, sink 5 douse, drown, flood, souse 6 deluge, engulf, go down, plunge 7 go under, immerse 8 inundate, pour over, submerse

submerse 5 drown 6 engulf 7 immerse 8 inundate, submerge

submersion 7 sinking 8 drowning 9 immersion 10 inundation 11 submergence

submission 8 giving in, meekness, tameness, yielding 9 handing in, obedience, passivity, surrender, tendering 10 compliance, remittance, submitting 11 passiveness 12 acquiescence, capitulation, presentation, subservience, tractability 13 nonresistance 14 submissiveness

submissive 4 meek, mild 6 docile, humble, pliant 7 dutiful, fawning, passive, servile, slavish 8 crawling, obedient, toadying, yielding 9 compliant, malleable, tractable, truckling 10 obsequious 11 acquiescent, bootlicking, complaisant, deferential, subservient, unassertive 12 capitulating, ingratiating, nonresisting 13 accommodating

submissiveness 8 docility, meekness 9 passivity 10 compliance 11 resignation 12 complaisance, tractability

submit 3 bow 4 bend, cede 5 agree, argue, claim, defer, kneel, offer, stoop, yield 6 accede, assert, commit, comply, give in, give up, resort, tender 7 contend, hold out, present, proffer, propose, succumb, suggest 8 back down, put forth 9 acquiesce, surrender, volunteer 10 capitulate, put forward 12 knuckle under

submit an offer 3 bid 6 tender 7 proffer, propose

submit to 4 bear, take 5 abide, brave, brook, stand 6 endure, suffer 7 stomach, undergo 8 stand for, tolerate 9 put up with

subnormal 3 bad, low 5 seedy, sorry 6 crummy, dismal, shabby, sleazy, subpar 7 abysmal 8 below par, inferior, mediocre, wretched 9 defective, deficient 10 inadequate, second-rate

11 below normal, substandard 12 insufficient

subordinate 4 help 5 lower 6 junior, lackey, lesser, menial, worker 7 servant, subject 8 hireling, inferior 9 ancillary, assistant, attendant, auxiliary, dependent, of low rank, outranked, secondary, subaltern, underling 10 subsidiary 11 subservient

subordination 10 subjection 11 inferiority, subjugation 12 subservience 13 regimentation

suborn 5 bribe 6 buy off, pay off

sub rosa 8 covertly, in secret, on the sly, secretly 9 in private, privately 12 off-the-record 14 confidentially 15 behind-the-scenes 17 behind closed doors

subscribe 4 help, sign 6 assent, chip in, donate 7 consent, endorse, support 8 hold with 9 undersign 10 contribute

subsequent 4 next 7 ensuing 9 following, proximate 10 consequent, succeeding, successive

subsequently 2 so 5 after, later, since 9 afterward, following 10 succeeding 12 consequently

subservient 6 docile, menial 7 fawning, servile, slavish, subject 8 cringing, toadying 9 accessory, ancillary, auxiliary, prostrate, truckling 10 obsequious, subsidiary 11 bootlicking, subordinate, sycophantic 12 contributory, ingratiating

subside 3 ebb, sag 4 calm, drop, ease, sink, wane 5 abate, let up 6 cave in, lessen, recede, settle, shrink 7 descend, dwindle 8 decrease, diminish, level off, melt away, moderate

subsidence 5 letup 6 easing, ebbing, waning 7 calming 9 abatement, dwindling, lessening, recession, shrinking 10 decreasing, inactivity, moderation 12 diminishment

subsidiary 5 extra, lower, minor 6 branch, junior, lesser 7 adjunct 8 addition, division, inferior 9 accessory, affiliate, auxiliary, secondary 10 additional, supplement 11 subordinate 12 supplemental 13 supplementary

subsidy 3 aid 4 gift 5 award, grant 7 backing, support 9 allotment, provision 10 fellowship, grant-in-aid, honorarium, subvention 11 scholarship, sponsorship 13 appropriation, assistantship

subsist 4 live 5 exist 7 survive 9 stay alive 11 feed oneself, support life 12 make ends meet 23 keep body and soul together

subsistence 6 living, upkeep 7 support 8 survival 10 livelihood, sustenance 11 maintenance, nourishment

substance 4 body, core, germ, gist, pith, soul 5 force, heart, means, money, sense, stuff 6 burden, import,

intent, marrow, matter, riches, thrust, wealth 7 element, essence, keynote, purport, reality 8 backbone, material, property, solidity 9 actuality, affluence, basic idea, main point 10 ingredient 11 connotation, constituent, corporality 12 corporeality, quintessence 13 corporealness

substandard 3 bad 4 poor 5 awful, lousy 6 crummy, shoddy 8 below par, inferior, terrible 9 imperfect 10 second-rate 11 second-class 12 below average

substantial 3 big 4 firm, full 5 ample, bulky, large, massy, solid, sound 7 massive, sizable 8 abundant 9 plenteous, plentiful 10 monumental 12 considerable

substantiate 5 prove 6 verify 7 confirm, support, sustain 11 corroborate, demonstrate 12 authenticate

substantiated 6 proved, proven 7 factual 8 verified 9 supported 11 well-founded 12 corroborated, demonstrated, well-grounded 13 authenticated

substantiation 5 proof 8 evidence 11 affirmation 12 verification 13 corroboration, demonstration, documentation 14 authentication

substitute 3 act 6 backup, change, ersatz, fill in, switch 7 standby, stand in, stopgap 8 deputize, exchange, pinch-hit, take over 9 alternate, makeshift, surrogate, temporary 10 understudy 11 alternative, pinch hitter, replacement

substitution 5 shift 6 change, switch 8 exchange, swapping 9 variation 10 alteration 11 replacement

substructure 4 base 6 ground 10 foundation, groundwork 12 underpinning

subsume 5 cover 6 assume, deduce 7 explain, include, involve 8 consider 13 subcategorize

subterfuge 4 ruse, sham, wile 5 blind, dodge, guile, shift, trick 6 scheme 7 evasion 8 artifice, intrigue, pretense, scheming 9 casuistry, chicanery, deception, duplicity, imposture, sophistry, stratagem 10 camouflage, sneakiness 11 deviousness, evasiveness, game-playing, machination, make-believe, smoke screen

subtle, subtile 3 sly 4 cagy, deft, fine, foxy, keen, wily 5 light, quick, sharp, slick 6 artful, astute, clever, crafty, expert, shifty, shrewd, tricky 7 cunning, devious, elusive, refined 8 delicate, indirect, masterly, skillful 9 deceptive, designing, ingenious, underhand 10 discerning 11 understated 13 perspicacious, sophisticated 14 discriminating

Subtle

character in: 12 The Alchemist
author: 6 Jonson

subtleties 7 nuances **10** fine points **11** refinements **12** distinctions

subtract 6 deduct, detach, lessen, reduce, remove **8** decrease, diminish, take away, withdraw

subtraction 7 removal **8** decrease **9** deduction, lessening, reduction **10** diminution, taking away, withdrawal **11** diminishing

suburbs 8 environs, vicinity **9** outskirts, periphery, precincts

sub verbo 12 under the word **15** under the heading

subversion 4 fall, ruin **6** defeat, mutiny **8** disorder, sabotage **9** overthrow, rebellion **10** corruption, disruption **11** destruction

subversive 7 traitor **8** quisling **9** insurgent, seditious **10** incendiary, traitorous, treasonous **11** seditionary **12** collaborator **13** revolutionary **14** fifth columnist **15** insurrectionary **16** collaborationist

subvert 3 mar **4** ruin, undo **5** smash, spoil, upset, wreck **6** defile, poison, ravage **7** despoil, destroy, disrupt, shatter **8** demolish, overturn **9** devastate, overthrow, undermine **11** contaminate

sub voce 21 under the specified word
literally: 13 under the voice

subway 2 El **4** tube **5** metro, train **11** underground
New York City line: 3 BMT, IND, IRT
San Francisco: 4 BART

succeed 3 hit, win **5** avail, catch, click **6** accede, do well, follow, move up **7** inherit, prevail, prosper, replace, triumph **8** make a hit, make good, supplant, take over **9** bear fruit, strike oil

succeed at 2 do **6** attain **7** execute, fulfill, perform, realize **8** carry out **9** make a go of **10** accomplish

succeeding 5 later **6** coming, future **7** ensuing **8** oncoming **9** following, impending, posterior **10** consequent, subsequent, successive

succeed to 6 follow **7** inherit **15** ascend the throne

succes d'estime 15 critical success

success 3 hit **4** fame **5** smash **7** triumph, victory **8** conquest **9** affluence **10** ascendancy, attainment, prosperity **11** achievement, advancement, fulfillment, good fortune

successful 4 rich **6** proven **7** perfect, wealthy, well-off **8** achieved, affluent, complete, fruitful, thriving **9** effective **10** prosperous, triumphant **11** efficacious, flourishing **12** accomplished, acknowledged

successful completion 7 success, victory, winning **9** execution **10** making good **11** achievement, culmina-

tion, fulfillment, realization **12** consummation **14** accomplishment

succession 3 run **5** chain, cycle, round, train **6** course, series **8** sequence **9** accession **10** assumption, procession, stepping-up, taking over **11** inheritance, progression

successive 7 ensuing **10** continuous, succeeding **11** consecutive

successor 4 heir **5** donee **7** devisee, heiress, heritor, legatee **8** follower, parcener **9** heritress, joint heir **10** coparcener, substitute **11** beneficiary, replacement, reversioner **12** heir apparent

succinct 4 neat **5** brief, crisp, pithy, short, terse, tight **6** direct, gnomic **7** clipped, compact, concise, summary **9** condensed **10** aphoristic, to the point **12** epigrammatic

succinctness 7 brevity **9** crispness, terseness **11** compactness, conciseness **12** condensation

succor 3 aid **4** help **5** nurse **6** assist, back up, relief, shield, wait on **7** comfort, nurture, protect, relieve, support, sustain **8** befriend **10** assistance, minister to, sustenance, take care of **11** helping hand, lend a hand to, maintenance **13** accommodation

succulent 5 juicy **6** fleshy **9** toothsome **10** appetizing

succumb 3 die **5** yield **6** accede, expire, give in, submit **7** defer to, give way, go under **8** pass away **9** surrender **10** capitulate, comply with **12** fall victim to

such as
Latin: 2 eg **13** exempli gratia

such is life
French: 9 c'est la vie

sucker 3 sap **4** boob, butt, dupe, fool, goat, gull, jerk, mark **5** chump, patsy **6** pigeon, victim **7** cat's-paw, fall guy **8** easy mark, fair game, pushover **9** schlemiel, soft touch **11** sitting duck

Sucker State
nickname of: 8 Illinois

suck up 6 absorb, soak up **7** drink in **8** sponge up **9** swallow up

Sucre
legal capital of: 7 Bolivia

Sudan
capital/largest city: 8 Khartoum
others: 3 Waw, Yei **4** Juba **5** Kosti, Meroe, Nyala, Obeid, Opari, Segon **6** Atbara, Suakin **7** Aluboyd, Elobeid, Geneina, Kassala, Malakal **8** Elfasher, Omdurman **9** al-Ubayyid, Elgeneina, Port Sudan, Wad Medani
division: 7 Jonglei **9** Upper Nile **12** Bahr el Ghazal **16** Eastern Equatoria, Western Equatoria
ancient kingdom: 4 Alwa, Funj, Kush **7** Maqurra
measure: 2 ud

monetary unit: 5 pound **8** piastres
weight: 5 habba
lake: 2 No **4** Chad, Toad **6** Nasser
mountain: 4 Nuba **7** Imatong **9** Dongotona **10** Jabal Marra, Jebel Marra **18** Ethiopian Highlands
highest point: 7 Kinyeti
river: 4 Nile **5** Sobat **6** Atbara **8** Blue Nile **9** White Nile **10** Bahr el-Arab **11** Bahr el-Jebel **12** Bahr el-Ghazal
sea: 3 Red
physical feature:
  desert: 6 Libyan, Nubian
  gum forest: 8 Kordofan
  plain: 6 Gezira
  sandstorm: 6 haboob
  plateau: 8 Kordufan
  swamp: 4 Sudd
people: 3 Bor, Dor, Fur **4** Arab, Bari, Beri, Bobo, Daza, Egba, Fula, Golo, Nuba, Nuer, Poul, Sere **5** Anuak, Bongo, Dinka, Fulah, Hausa, Joluo, Junje, Mosgu, Mossi, Negro, Tibbu, Volta **6** Acholi, Azande, Gurusi, Hamite, Lotuho, Makari, Nilote, Nubian, Senufo, Surhai, Tuareg **7** Balante, Baqqara, Gubayna, Jaaliin, Nilotes, Shilluk, Songhai, Songhay, Songhoi, Sourhai **8** Kababish, Mandingo, Menkiera **9** Sarakille **10** Gurmantshi, Shaiquiyya
  leader: 5 Mahdi **9** al-Nimeiry **10** Mehemet Ali **22** Jaafar Mohammed al-Nemery
language: 2 Ga **3** Efe, Ewe, Ibo, Kru, Vak, Vei **4** Efik, Mole, Tshi **6** Arabic, Nubian, Yoruba **7** English **8** Mandango, Mandingo **9** Ta Bedawie
religion: 5 Islam **7** animism **12** Christianity
place:
  canal: 7 Jonglei
  dam: 6 Sennar **8** Roseires **10** Jebel Aulia
  temple: 4 Lion
  tomb: 5 Mahdi
feature:
  boat: 6 murkab
food: 4 dura **5** dukhn, kisra

Sudanese Republic see **4** Mali

sudden 4 rash **5** hasty, quick, rapid **6** abrupt, speedy **7** instant **9** immediate, impetuous **10** surprising, unexpected, unforeseen **11** precipitate, unlooked-for **13** instantaneous, unanticipated, unforeseeable

suddenly 7 quickly **8** abruptly, in no time **9** all at once, instantly, on the spot **11** in an instant **12** all of a sudden, unexpectedly **13** at short notice **14** without warning **21** in the twinkling of an eye

sudden movement 4 dart, jolt **5** flash, spurt

sudden noise 3 pop **4** bang, clap, slam **5** burst, crash **6** report **9** explosion

Sudermann, Hermann

author of: 5 Honor **8** Dame Care **14** The Song of Songs

suds 3 ale **4** beer, brew, foam **5** draft, froth, lager **10** malt liquor

sue 3 beg **4** pray **5** plead **6** appeal **7** beseech, entreat, implore **8** petition **9** importune **10** supplicate

Sue, Eugene (Marie-Joseph)
author of: 15 The Wandering Jew **19** The Mysteries of Paris

suffer 4 ache, bear, hurt, pine **5** stand **6** endure, grieve, lament **7** agonize, despair, drop off, fall off, stomach, sustain, undergo **8** bear with, feel pain, tolerate **9** go through, put up with, withstand **10** be impaired **11** deteriorate

suffer for 6 pay for **8** atone for **9** answer for

suffering 3 woe **4** ache, care, hurt, pain, pang **5** agony, dolor, grief, throe, trial **6** misery, sorrow, twinge **7** anguish, anxiety, torment, torture, travail **8** distress, soreness **9** heartache **10** affliction, discomfort, heavy heart, irritation **11** tribulation

suffice 2 do **4** last, meet, pass **5** avail, get by, serve **6** answer, make do **7** fulfill, qualify, satisfy

sufficiency 6 enough, plenty **7** surfeit **8** adequacy **9** abundance, ampleness, profusion

sufficient 5 ample **6** enough, plenty **7** copious, minimal **8** abundant, adequate **9** plenteous, plentiful **11** up to the mark **12** satisfactory

suffocate 3 gag **5** choke **6** quench, stifle **7** garrote, smother **8** snuff out, strangle, throttle **10** asphyxiate, extinguish

suffuse 4 fill, soak **5** cover, steep **6** infuse **7** diffuse, overrun, pervade **8** overflow, permeate, saturate **9** transfuse **10** impregnate, infiltrate, overspread

Sugar State
nickname of: 9 Louisiana

sugary 5 mushy, sweet **6** syrupy **7** cloying, fulsome, gushing, honeyed, mawkish **8** cajoling, unctuous **10** flattering, saccharine

suggest 3 bid **4** move, urge **5** imply, posit **6** advise, hint at, submit **7** advance, counsel, propose **8** advocate, indicate, intimate, propound **9** give a clue, recommend **16** lead one to believe

suggested 6 hinted **7** implied, oblique **8** implicit, indirect, possible, proposed

suggestion 3 dab, tip **4** dash, hint, tint **5** grain, shade, taste, tinge, touch, trace **6** advice, urging **7** counsel, feeling, pointer, soupcon **9** prompting, suspicion **10** intimation, sprinkling **11** exhortation **14** recommendation

suggestive 4 lewd, racy **5** bawdy,

loose **6** risque, sexual, wanton **8** allusive, improper, indecent, off-color, prurient, unseemly **9** evocative, remindful, seductive, shameless **10** expressive, indelicate, licentious **11** provocative, reminiscent, stimulating

sui generis 6 unique **10** one of a kind

sui juris 14 of one's own right

suit 3 fit **4** duds, garb, plea, togs **5** befit, court, getup, habit, match **6** appeal, attire, become, beseem, follow, livery, oblige, outfit, please, prayer, wooing **7** apparel, begging, clothes, content, costume, delight, gladden, gratify, raiment, satisfy, uniform **8** clothing, entreaty, jell with, make glad, petition **9** addresses, agree with, conform to, courtship, do one good, overtures, tally with, trappings **10** accord with, attentions, comply with, fall in with, habiliment, lovemaking, square with **11** accommodate, go along with **12** be becoming to, blandishment, correspond to, dovetail with, solicitation, supplication **13** accoutrements, be agreeable to, harmonize with **14** be acceptable to, be convenient to **15** be appropriate to **16** be appropriate for

suitable 3 apt, fit **4** meet **5** right **6** proper, seemly, worthy **7** apropos, fitting, germane **8** adequate, becoming, relevant **9** befitting, congruous, cut out for, pertinent, qualified **10** applicable, seasonable **11** appropriate **12** commensurate

suitcase 3 bag **4** grip **6** valise **7** satchel **8** knapsack, rucksack **9** duffel bag, gladstone, two-suiter **11** portmanteau **12** overnight bag, traveling bag

suite 3 set **4** flat **5** chain, court, group, rooms, round **6** convoy, series **7** company, cortege, retinue **8** servants **9** apartment, followers, following **10** attendants **11** progression

suited 3 fit **7** adapted, attired, clothed, dressed, good for, matched **8** adjusted, agreeing, becoming **9** agreeable **11** appropriate, harmonizing

suit of armor 4 mail **5** armor **9** chain mail **10** coat of mail

suitor 4 beau, love **5** flame, lover, swain, wooer **6** fellow **7** admirer, gallant **8** young man **9** boyfriend **10** sweetheart

sulfur
chemical symbol: 1 S

sulk 4 crab, fret, fume, mope, pout **5** brood, chafe, frown, grump, scowl **6** glower, grouch **7** grumble **8** be in a pet, be miffed, be put out, be sullen, look glum **9** be in a huff **11** be resentful **12** be out of humor

sulky 6 morose, sullen **7** pouting **8** petulant

sullen 4 blue, dark, glum, grim, sore,

sour **5** cross, heavy, moody, sulky, surly **6** crabby, dismal, dreary, gloomy, grumpy, morose, somber, touchy **7** crabbed, doleful, forlorn, grouchy, peevish **8** brooding, desolate, dolorous, funereal, mournful, petulant, scowling **9** cheerless, glowering, resentful, saturnine, splenetic, unamiable **10** depressing, foreboding, ill-humored, ill-natured, melancholy, out of humor, out of sorts, unsociable **11** ill-tempered **13** temperamental
French: 8 farouche

sullied 5 dirty **6** impure, soiled **7** defiled, stained, unclean **9** tarnished

Sullivan, John L (Lawrence)
nickname: 15 Boston Strong Boy
sport: 6 boxing
class: 11 heavyweight
fought: 12 bareknuckled

Sullivan, Louis H
architect of: 16 Guaranty (now Prudential) Building (Buffalo NY) **18** Auditorium Building (Chicago), Wainwright Building (St Louis MO) **21** Carson Pirie Scott Store (Chicago), Stock Exchange Building (Chicago), Merchants' National Bank (Grinnell, IA), National Farmers' Bank (Owatonna, MN)
principle: 21 "form follows function"
student: 16 Frank Lloyd Wright

Sullivan, Pat
creator/artist of: 11 Felix the Cat

Sullivan's Travels
director: 14 Preston Sturges
cast: 10 Joel McCrea **12** Veronica Lake **13** Robert Warwick **15** William Demarest

sully 4 ruin, soil, spot **5** dirty, spoil, stain **6** befoul, defame, defile, smudge **7** begrime, besmear, blemish, corrupt, pollute, tarnish **8** disgrace, dishonor **10** adulterate **11** contaminate

Sully, Thomas
born: 7 England **10** Horncastle
artwork: 13 Queen Victoria **23** The Passage of the Delaware **28** Colonel Thomas Handasyd Perkins **29** Washington Crossing the Delaware

sultan 4 king **5** ruler **7** emperor, monarch **9** sovereign

sultana 5 grape **6** raisin **7** empress **11** sultan's wife

sultry 3 hot **4** sexy **5** close, humid, muggy **6** erotic, stuffy, sweaty **7** sensual **8** stifling **10** oppressive, sweltering, voluptuous **11** provocative, suffocating

sum 4 cash, coin, jack **5** bread, bucks, dough, funds, score, tally, whole **6** amount, moolah **7** lettuce, measure **8** currency, entirety, quantity, sum total, totality **9** aggregate, summation

sumac 4 Rhus
varieties: 5 dwarf, lemon, scrub, sugar, swamp **6** desert, laurel, poi-

son, smooth, velvet **7** scarlet, shining, tanner's, tobacco, wing-rib **8** fragrant, lemonade, Sicilian, staghorn, Venetian **9** elm-leaved, evergreen, Virginian **11** small-leaved **12** sweet-scented

sum and substance 4 core, crux, gist, guts, meat **5** heart **7** essence **10** brass tacks **11** nitty-gritty

Sumatra
  chevrotain: 4 napu
  city: 5 Medan **6** Padang **9** Palembang
  country: 9 Indonesia
  crop: 3 tea **6** coffee, rubber
  currency: 6 rupiah
  empire: 9 Srivijaya
  highest point: 10 Mt Kerintji
  inhabitant: 5 Batak, Malay **11** Minangkabau
  mountain range: 7 Barisan
  river: 4 Musi, Siak **6** Asahan
  squirrel shrew: 4 tana
  strait: 5 Sunda **7** Malacca

Sumerian Mythology *see* **19** Babylonian Mythology

summa cum laude 17 with highest praise

summarily 6 at once **7** quickly **8** directly, promptly, speedily **9** forthwith, on the spot **11** arbitrarily, immediately, straightway **12** straightaway, with dispatch, without delay **13** at short notice, precipitately

summarize 5 sum up **6** digest **7** abridge, outline **8** abstract, compress, condense **9** capsulize, epitomize, synopsize **10** abbreviate **11** concentrate **12** recapitulate

summary 4 curt **5** brief, hasty, rapid, short, terse, token **6** apercu, digest, precis, resume, sketch, sudden, survey **7** concise, cursory, epitome, hurried, rundown **8** abridged, abstract, analysis, succinct, syllabus, synopsis **9** breakdown, condensed **10** abridgment, peremptory **11** perfunctory **12** abbreviation, condensation, short version **13** instantaneous

Summa Theologiae
  author: 13 Thomas Aquinas

summation 5 total **6** review **7** summary **8** addition **9** reckoning **19** concluding statement

Summer and Smoke
  author: 17 Tennessee Williams
  director: 14 Peter Glenville
  cast: 9 Una Merkel **10** Rita Moreno **12** Earl Holliman **13** Geraldine Page **14** Laurence Harvey

summerhouse 5 arbor, cabin, kiosk **6** cabana, gazebo, pagoda **7** cottage

Summerson, Esther
  character in: 10 Bleak House
  author: 7 Dickens

Summertime
  director: 9 David Lean
  based on story by: 14 Arthur Laurents (The Time of the Cuckoo)
  cast: 10 Isa Miranda **13** Darren McGavin, Rossano Brazzi **16** Katharine Hepburn
  setting: 6 Venice

summery 3 hot **4** warm **5** balmy, close, humid, muggy, sunny **6** stuffy, sultry, torrid, vernal **8** aestival, roasting, stifling, sunshiny **9** scorching, temperate **10** oppressive, summerlike

summit 3 tip, top **4** acme, apex, peak **5** crest, crown **6** apogee, climax, height, vertex, zenith **8** pinnacle **11** culmination **12** highest point **13** crowning point

summon 4 call **5** rouse **6** beckon, call on, draw on, gather, invoke, muster, strain **7** call for, call out, command, send for **8** activate, subpoena **9** call forth **12** call together

summons 4 call **8** citation, subpoena **12** notification

summon up 4 stir **5** evoke **6** arouse, excite **7** collect, marshal, provoke **8** assemble **9** call forth, stimulate

summum bonum 9 chief good **11** highest good

sumptuous 4 dear, posh, rich **5** grand, plush, regal **6** costly, deluxe, lavish, superb **7** elegant **8** splendid **9** elaborate, expensive, luxurious **10** exorbitant, munificent **11** extravagant, magnificent, spectacular

sumptuousness 4 luxe **6** luxury **8** elegance, grandeur, richness, splendor **12** magnificence **13** expensiveness, luxuriousness

sum total 6 amount **8** totality **9** aggregate **11** final result

sum up 3 add **5** tally, total, tot up **6** reckon **7** compute, count up **9** calculate, enumerate, summarize

sun
  god of: 2 Ra, Re **3** Sol, Utu **5** Horus **6** Apollo, Helios **7** Shamesh **8** Hyperion

Sun Also Rises, The
  author: 15 Ernest Hemingway
  character: 10 Bill Gorton, Jake Barnes, Robert Cohn **11** Pedro Romero **15** Lady Brett Ashley, Michael (Mike) Campbell

sunbathe 3 tan **4** bask **12** soak up the sun **13** catch some rays

Sunday
  means: 11 day of the sun
  heavenly body: 3 sun
  day of: 4 rest **7** worship **8** blue laws
  observance: 16 Christian Sabbath
  French: 8 dimanche
  Italian: 8 domenica
  Spanish: 7 domingo
  German: 7 sonntag

Sunday best 6 finery **8** glad rags **11** fine clothes **16** best bib and tucker

sunder 4 rend, rive **5** crack, sever **6** cleave, divide **8** separate **9** tear apart **10** break in two **11** break in half

sundown 4 dusk **6** sunset **7** evening **8** eventide, twilight **9** nightfall

Sundowners, The
  director: 13 Fred Zinnemann
  cast: 11 Deborah Kerr, Dina Merrill, Glynis Johns **12** Peter Ustinov **13** Robert Mitchum
  setting: 9 Australia

sundry 4 many **5** mixed **6** divers, motley, myriad, varied **7** diverse, several, various **8** assorted, manifold, numerous **9** different **12** multifarious **13** heterogeneous, miscellaneous

sun-filled 4 fair **5** clear, sunny **6** bright, cheery **8** cheerful **9** cloudless

sunfish 5 dwarf, perch, pigmy, sunny **6** redear **7** lepomis, longear, teleost **8** bluegill, sailboat **9** blackband **10** Sacramento **11** bluespotted, centrarchid, pumpkinseed, yellowbelly

sunflower 10 Helianthus **12** Balsamorhiza
  varieties: 4 ashy **5** giant, showy, stiff, swamp **6** common, desert, Oregon **7** dark-eye, Mexican **8** thin-leaf **10** Maximilian **12** cucumber-leaf

Sunflower State
  nickname of: 6 Kansas

sunless 4 dark, dull, gray, hazy **5** bleak, foggy, misty, murky, rainy **6** cloudy, dismal, dreary, gloomy, leaden, somber **8** overcast **9** cheerless **10** depressing

sunny 4 fair, fine **5** clear, happy, jolly, merry **6** blithe, breezy, bright, cheery, genial, jovial, joyful, joyous, sunlit **7** affable, amiable, buoyant, shining, smiling **8** cheerful, sunshiny **9** brilliant, cloudless, sparkling, unclouded **10** optimistic **12** lighthearted

sunrise 4 dawn **5** sunup **6** aurora **7** dawning **8** cockcrow, daybreak, daylight **10** break of day, crepuscule, newborn day **15** dawn's early light **16** rosy-fingered dawn

sunset 4 dusk **7** sundown **8** blue hour, eventide, gloaming, twilight **9** nightfall **10** close of day, crepuscule

Sunset Boulevard
  director: 11 Billy Wilder
  cast: 8 Jack Webb **9** Fred Clark **11** Hedda Hopper **12** Buster Keaton **13** Cecil B DeMille, Gloria Swanson (Norma Desmond), William Holden **16** Erich von Stroheim

Sunset State
  nickname of: 6 Oregon

sunshade 3 hat **5** visor **6** awning **7** parasol, roundel **8** sombrero, umbrella

Sunshine State
  nickname of: 7 Florida **9** New Mexico

sunstone
  species: 8 feldspar

suntan 3 tan **5** brown **6** bronze **7** sunburn

suo jure 14 in one's own right

suo loco 14 in one's own place **19** in one's rightful place

Suomen Tasavalta *see* **7** Finland

Suomi *see* **7** Finland

sup 3 eat, sip **4** dine, feed **5** drink, feast, supra **6** absorb, supper, supply **7** consume **8** superior **10** supplement **11** superlative **13** supplementary

super 4 A-one, fine **5** grand, great, prime, prize, swell **6** grade-A, superb, tip-top **7** capital **8** peerless, superior, terrific, top-notch **9** excellent, fantastic, first-rate, marvelous, matchless, non pareil, superfine, wonderful **10** first-class, tremendous, unexcelled, world-class **11** outstanding, superlative **12** incomparable **13** extraordinary

superabound 4 teem **5** swarm **6** thrive **7** burgeon **8** be rich in, flourish, overflow

superabundance 4 glut, riot **5** flood, spate **6** deluge, excess, plenty **7** surfeit, surplus **8** overdose, overflow, pleonasm, plethora **9** avalanche **10** inundation, oversupply, redundance **11** superfluity **12** extravagance **13** overabundance **14** more than enough **French: 19** embarras de richesses

superabundant 4 lush **6** lavish **7** copious, profuse, teeming **8** swarming, thriving **9** exuberant, luxuriant **10** burgeoning **11** flourishing, overflowing

superb 4 A-one, rare, rich **5** elect, grand, regal **6** choice, costly, deluxe, golden, lordly, select, tip-top **7** elegant, stately **8** gorgeous, imposing, laudable, majestic, peerless, precious, princely, splendid, top-notch, very fine **9** admirable, excellent, expensive, exquisite, first-rate, luxurious, marvelous, matchless, priceless, sumptuous, top-drawer **10** first-class **11** crackerjack, magnificent **12** breathtaking, praiseworthy **15** of the first water

Super Bowl
1967:
    winner: 15 Green Bay Packers
    loser: 16 Kansas City Chiefs
    site: 8 Coliseum **10** Los Angeles
1968:
    winner: 15 Green Bay Packers
    loser: 14 Oakland Raiders
    site: 5 Miami **10** Orange Bowl
1969:
    winner: 11 New York Jets
    loser: 14 Baltimore Colts
    site: 5 Miami **10** Orange Bowl
1970:
    winner: 16 Kansas City Chiefs
    loser: 16 Minnesota Vikings
    site: 10 New Orleans **13** Tulane Stadium
1971:

winner: 14 Baltimore Colts
loser: 13 Dallas Cowboys
site: 5 Miami **10** Orange Bowl
1972:
    winner: 13 Dallas Cowboys
    loser: 13 Miami Dolphins
    site: 10 New Orleans **13** Tulane Stadium
1973:
    winner: 13 Miami Dolphins
    loser: 18 Washington Redskins
    site: 8 Coliseum **10** Los Angeles
1974:
    winner: 13 Miami Dolphins
    loser: 16 Minnesota Vikings
    site: 7 Houston **11** Rice Stadium
1975:
    winner: 18 Pittsburgh Steelers
    loser: 16 Minnesota Vikings
    site: 10 New Orleans **13** Tulane Stadium
1976:
    winner: 18 Pittsburgh Steelers
    loser: 13 Dallas Cowboys
    site: 5 Miami **10** Orange Bowl
1977:
    winner: 14 Oakland Raiders
    loser: 16 Minnesota Vikings
    site: 8 Pasadena, Rose Bowl
1978:
    winner: 13 Dallas Cowboys
    loser: 13 Denver Broncos
    site: 9 Superdome **10** New Orleans
1979:
    winner: 18 Pittsburgh Steelers
    loser: 13 Dallas Cowboys
    site: 5 Miami **10** Orange Bowl
1980:
    winner: 18 Pittsburgh Steelers
    loser: 14 Los Angeles Rams
    site: 8 Pasadena, Rose Bowl
1981:
    winner: 14 Oakland Raiders
    loser: 18 Philadelphia Eagles
    site: 9 Superdome **10** New Orleans
1982:
    winner: 23 San Francisco Forty-Niners
    loser: 17 Cincinnati Bengals
    site: 7 Pontiac **10** Silverdome
1983:
    winner: 18 Washington Redskins
    loser: 13 Miami Dolphins
    site: 8 Pasadena, Rose Bowl
1984:
    winner: 17 Los Angeles Raiders
    loser: 18 Washington Redskins
    site: 12 Tampa Stadium
1985:
    winner: 23 San Francisco Forty-Niners
    loser: 13 Miami Dolphins
    site: 8 Palo Alto **15** Stanford Stadium
1986:
    winner: 12 Chicago Bears
    loser: 18 New England Patriots
    site: 9 Superdome **10** New Orleans

1987:
    winner: 13 New York Giants
    loser: 13 Denver Broncos
    site: 8 Pasadena, Rose Bowl
1988:
    winner: 18 Washington Redskins
    loser: 13 Denver Broncos
    site: 8 San Diego **17** Jack Murphy Stadium
1989:
    winner: 23 San Francisco Forty-Niners
    loser: 17 Cincinnati Bengals
    site: 5 Miami **16** Joe Robbie Stadium
1990:
    winner: 23 San Francisco Forty-Niners
    loser: 13 Denver Broncos
    site: 9 Superdome **10** New Orleans
1991:
    winner: 13 New York Giants
    loser: 12 Buffalo Bills
    site: 5 Tampa **12** Tampa Stadium
1992:
    winner: 18 Washington Redskins
    loser: 12 Buffalo Bills
    site: 9 Metrodome **11** Minneapolis
1993:
    winner: 13 Dallas Cowboys
    loser: 12 Buffalo Bills
    site: 8 Pasadena, Rose Bowl
1994:
    winner: 13 Dallas Cowboys
    loser: 12 Buffalo Bills
    site: 7 Atlanta **11** Georgia Dome
1995:
    winner: 23 San Francisco Forty-Niners
    loser: 16 San Diego Chargers
    site: 5 Miami **9** Joe Robbie
1996:
    winner: 13 Dallas Cowboys
    loser: 18 Pittsburgh Steelers
    site: 5 Tempe **8** Sun Devil
1997:
    winner: 15 Green Bay Packers
    loser: 18 New England Patriots
    site: 9 Superdome **10** New Orleans
1998:
    winner: 13 Denver Broncos
    loser: 15 Green Bay Packers
    site: 8 San Diego
1999:
    winner: 13 Denver Broncos
    loser: 14 Atlanta Falcons
    site: 5 Miami **9** Pro Player

supercilious 5 proud **6** lordly, snooty, uppity **7** haughty, pompous, stuck-up **8** arrogant, prideful, snobbish **10** disdainful **11** egotistical, magisterial, overbearing, patronizing **12** vainglorious **13** condescending, high-and-mighty, self-important

superciliousness 4 airs **7** hauteur **8** snobbery **9** arrogance, pomposity **10** lordliness, snootiness **11** haughtiness **12** snobbishness **14** disdainfulness

superficial 4 slim **5** faint, outer, silly, trite **6** flimsy, hollow, myopic, slight **7** cursory, minimal, nodding, partial, passing, shallow, summary, surface **8** exterior, mindless, skin-deep **9** desultory, frivolous **10** incomplete **11** empty-headed, perfunctory **12** lacking depth, narrow-minded, on the surface

superficiality 6 myopia **9** frivolity **11** cursoriness, shallowness **13** desultoriness **16** narrow-mindedness, shortsightedness

superfine 4 A-one **6** choice, grade-A, superb, tip-top **8** superior, top-notch **9** excellent, extra fine, first-rate **10** first-class **11** outstanding, overrefined, superlative **13** extraordinary

superfluity 3 fat **5** extra, frill **6** excess, luxury **7** greater, surfeit, surplus **8** overflow, overmuch, plethora **11** gingerbread **12** extravagance **13** embellishment **14** superabundance

superfluous 5 extra, spare **6** excess **7** surplus **8** needless **9** excessive, redundant **10** extraneous, gratuitous, pleonastic **11** inessential, unnecessary **12** nonessential, overgenerous **13** superabundant, supernumerary **14** supererogatory

superhuman 4 epic **5** great **6** divine, heroic **7** godlike, supreme **8** superior **9** herculean, unearthly **10** miraculous, omnipotent **12** otherworldly, supermundane, supernatural, supranatural, transcendent **13** preternatural

superintend 3 run **4** boss **6** direct, govern, manage **7** oversee **9** supervise, watch over **10** administer **12** administrate, have charge of

superintendence 6 charge **7** bossing, running **9** direction, governing **10** leadership, management, overseeing **12** jurisdiction **14** administration

superintendent 4 boss, head **5** chief **6** warden **7** foreman, headman, manager, proctor, steward **8** director, guardian, overseer **9** custodian **10** supervisor

superior 4 boss, fine **5** chief **6** better, choice, deluxe, leader, lordly, senior **7** greater, haughty, notable **8** arrogant, foremost, higher-up, peerless, snobbish **9** commander, excellent, first-rate, imperious, matchless, nonpareil, unrivaled **10** inimitable, noteworthy, preeminent, supervisor **11** exceptional, illustrious, patronizing **12** incomparable, more advanced, vainglorious **13** condescending, distinguished, high-and-mighty
French: 13 par excellence

superlative 4 best **5** crack, prime **6** expert **7** supreme **8** foremost, greatest, peerless, superior **9** exquisite, first-rate, matchless, nonpareil, paramount, unequaled, unmatched, unrivaled **10** consummate, preeminent,

surpassing **11** magnificent, unsurpassed **12** incomparable, transcendent, unparalleled **15** of the first water **17** of the highest order

superman
German: 10 Ubermensch

Superman
artist: 11 Jerry Siegel
creator: 10 Joe Shuster
character: 4 Lara **5** Jor-el, Kal-el **8** Eben Kent, Lois Lane, Sy Horton **9** Clark Kent **10** Jimmy Olsen, Martha Kent, Perry White **22** Inspector Bill Henderson **23** Professor JJ Pepperwinkle
place: 7 Krypton **10** Metropolis, Smallville **14** telephone booth
nickname: 10 Man of Steel
director: 13 Richard Donner
cast: 9 Glenn Ford, Ned Beatty **11** Gene Hackman **12** Jackie Cooper, Margot Kidder (Lois Lane), Marlon Brando **14** Valerie Perrine **16** Christopher Reeve

supernatural 6 mystic, occult **7** psychic **9** spiritual, unearthly **10** miraculous, paranormal **12** otherworldly, supranatural **13** preternatural, superphysical **14** transcendental

superpatriotism 8 jingoism **10** chauvinism **11** nationalism

supersede 7 discard, replace, succeed **8** displace, set aside, supplant

supervise 4 boss, head **5** guide **6** direct, govern, handle, manage, survey **7** conduct, control, oversee **8** regulate **9** look after, watch over **10** administer **11** preside over, superintend **12** have charge of

supervision 6 orders **7** control **8** guidance **9** direction **10** governance, government, management, regulation **12** surveillance **15** superintendence

supervisor 4 boss, head **5** chief **7** foreman, manager, steward **8** director, overseer **9** commander **13** administrator **14** superintendent

supper club 4 cafe **6** bistro **7** cabaret **9** nightclub, night spot

supplant 6 depose **7** replace **8** displace **9** supersede **14** take the place of

supple 5 lithe **6** limber, pliant **7** elastic, lissome, plastic, pliable **8** amenable, bendable, flexible, graceful, yielding **9** adaptable, compliant, malleable, tractable **10** submissive **11** acquiescent, complaisant, coordinated

supplement 5 add to, annex, extra, rider **6** extend, insert **7** adjunct, augment, codicil, section **8** addendum, addition, appendix, increase **9** added part, corollary, extension **10** attachment, complement, postscript **12** augmentation

supplementary 5 added, extra **6** backup **7** added on, reserve **8** appended, attached, expanded, extended

9 ancillary, auxiliary, enlarging, secondary **10** additional, amplifying, augmenting **11** subordinate **13** complementary

suppliant 5 asker **6** beggar, cadger, seeker, suitor **7** almsman **8** claimant **9** almswoman, appellant, beseecher, entreater, mendicant **10** petitioner, supplicant **11** supplicator

Suppliants, The
author: 9 Aeschylus
character: 6 Danaus **8** Pelasgus **19** Fifty Sons of Aegyptus **20** Fifty Maiden Daughters
Suppliants, The
author: 9 Euripides
character: 6 Aethra, Evadne **7** Theseus **8** Adrastus

supplicate 3 ask, beg **4** pray **5** plead **6** ask for **7** entreat **8** appeal to, call upon, petition

supplication 3 cry **4** plea, suit **6** appeal, orison, prayer **7** bumming, cadging, request **8** entreaty, mooching, petition **10** invocation **11** application, beseechment, imploration, imprecation, panhandling **12** solicitation

supplies 4 gear **5** goods, items **8** material **9** equipment, foodstuff, trappings **10** provisions **13** accoutrements

supply 4 fund, give **5** cache, equip, grant, quota, stock, store, yield **6** bestow, outfit, render **7** deal out, deliver, furnish, present, provide, reserve **9** providing, provision, reservoir **10** allocation, come up with, contribute, furnishing **12** provisioning

support 3 aid **4** base, bear, help, hold, keep, lift, pile, post, prop, stay **5** abide, boost, brace, brook, carry, favor, means, shore, stand **6** assist, back up, bear up, clinch, column, defend, endure, foster, hold up, pay for, pillar, ratify, second, succor, suffer, uphold, upkeep, verify **7** backing, bear out, bolster, comfort, confirm, defense, endorse, espouse, finance, further, keeping, nurture, shore up, sustain, warrant **8** abutment, accredit, advocacy, advocate, buttress, champion, espousal, maintain, pedestal, pilaster, sanction, strength, tolerate, vouch for **9** establish, guarantee, patronage, patronize, promotion, put up with, reinforce, stanchion, subsidize **10** assistance, livelihood, provide for, stand up for, stick up for, strengthen, sustenance, underwrite **11** buttressing, consolation, corroborate, countenance, furtherance, go along with, involvement, maintenance, subsistence **12** substantiate, underpinning **13** encouragement

supportable 9 endurable **10** defensible, verifiable **11** sustainable **12** demonstrable, maintainable

supporter 4 ally **6** backer, helper, patron **8** adherent, advocate, champion, defender, disciple, follower, partisan, upholder **10** benefactor, well-wisher **11** sympathizer

supposable 8 credible **9** thinkable **10** believable, imaginable **11** conceivable, perceivable

suppose 5 fancy, guess, judge, posit **6** assume, divine, gather, reckon **7** believe, imagine, presume, surmise, suspect **8** conceive, consider **9** predicate **11** hypothesize **14** take for granted

supposed 5 given **7** alleged, assumed **8** probable, putative **9** imaginary **11** conjectural, speculative, theoretical **12** hypothetical

supposition 4 idea, view **5** given, guess **6** belief, notion, theory, thesis **7** opinion, surmise **9** guesswork, postulate, suspicion **10** assumption, conjecture, hypothesis **11** predication, presumption, proposition, speculation

suppress 4 bury, curb, hide **5** check, crush, quash, quell, still **6** keep in, muffle, quench, squash, stifle, subdue **7** conceal, control, cover up, inhibit, put down, repress, silence, smother, squelch **8** hold back, keep back, overcome, restrain, restrict, snuff out, withhold **9** overpower **10** extinguish, keep secret, put an end to **11** hold in leash, keep private **12** put a damper on **13** put under wraps

suppressant 4 curb **5** brake **7** control **9** restraint

suppressed feelings 7 reserve **9** restraint **10** constraint, diffidence

supremacy 5 power **7** mastery, primacy **10** ascendancy, domination, precedence **11** omnipotence, paramountcy, preeminence, sovereignty, superiority **13** transcendency

supreme 4 tops **5** chief, first, prime **6** ruling **7** extreme, highest, leading, perfect, topmost **8** absolute, dominant, foremost, peerless **9** matchless, nonpareil, paramount, principal, sovereign, unequaled, unlimited, unmatched, unrivaled, uppermost **10** commanding, consummate, unexcelled **11** all-powerful, superlative, unqualified, unsurpassed **12** front-ranking, immeasurable, incomparable, second to none, unparalleled

Supreme Court
 Chief Justices: 3 Jay (John) **4** Taft (William Howard) **5** Chase (Salmon), Stone (Harlan Fiske), Taney (Roger Brooke), Waite (Morrison), White (Edward) **6** Burger (Warren), Fuller (Melville), Hughes (Charles Evans), Vinson (Frederick), Warren (Earl) **8** Marshall (John), Rutledge (John) **9** Ellsworth (Oliver), Rehnquist (William)
 Associate Justices: 5 Black (Hugo), Story (Joseph), White (Byron) **6**

Breyer (Stephen), Fortas (Abe), Holmes (Oliver Wendell), Powell (Lewis), Scalia (Antonin), Souter (David), Thomas (Clarence) **7** Brennan (William), Cardozo (Benjamin), Douglas (William O), Kennedy (Anthony), O'Connor (Sandra Day), Stevens (John), Stewart (Potter) **8** Blackmun (Harry), Brandeis (Louis), Ginsburg (Ruth Bader), Goldberg (Arthur), Marshall (Thurgood) **11** Frankfurter (Felix)
 Cases: 15 Marbury v Madison **17** Gideon v Wainwright **18** McCulloch v Maryland **20** Griswold v Connecticut
  abortion: 8 Roe v Wade
  antitrust: 8 E C Knight **11** Standard Oil **15** Swift and Company **22** American Tobacco Company
  civil rights: 9 Bakke Case **15** Plessy v Ferguson **30** Brown v Board of Education of Topeka
  Japanese internment: 22 Korematsu v United States **24** Hirabayashi v United States
  rights of accused: 15 Miranda v Arizona **17** Escobedo v Illinois
  slavery: 13 Dred Scott Case **14** Scott v Sandford

surcease 4 quit, rest, stop **5** abate, cease, pause **7** die away, respite **8** conclude, leave off **11** come to an end, discontinue **17** come to a standstill

surcharge 3 tax **4** levy **6** excise, impost

surcingle 4 band, belt **5** girth **6** girdle **8** cincture

sure 4 fast, firm, true **5** solid, sound **6** stable, steady **7** assured, certain **8** accurate, fail-safe, faithful, flawless, positive, reliable, surefire, unerring **9** confident, convinced, unfailing **10** dependable, infallible, undoubting **11** trustworthy **12** never-failing

sure bet 4 fact **5** cinch **7** reality **9** actuality, certainty, sure thing **13** inevitability **14** inescapability

surely 7 no doubt **8** of course, to be sure **9** assuredly, certainly, doubtless **10** by all means, definitely, for certain, infallibly, positively **11** come what may, indubitably, undoubtedly, without fail **12** emphatically, without doubt **14** unquestionably

sureness 6 surety **9** assurance, certainty, certitude **10** confidence **11** assuredness **12** positiveness **13** self-assurance **14** conclusiveness, self-confidence, self-possession

sure thing 4 fact **5** cinch **7** reality, sure bet **9** actuality, certainty **13** inevitability **14** inescapability

surety 4 bail, bond **8** sureness **9** certainty, certitude, guarantee **10** confidence **12** positiveness

surface 3 top **4** coat, face, skin **5**

crust, shell **6** facade, finish, veneer **7** coating, outside **8** covering, exterior **11** superficies

Surface family
 characters in: 19 The School for Scandal
 member: 6 Joseph **7** Charles **9** Sir Oliver
 author: 8 Sheridan

surfeit 4 cloy, glut, sate **5** gorge, stuff **6** excess **7** satiate, satisfy, surplus **8** overmuch, plethora **9** plenitude, profusion, repletion, satiation **10** oversupply, surplusage **11** exorbitance, overindulge, prodigality, superfluity **12** extravagance **13** overabundance **14** more than enough, superabundance **15** supersaturation

surfeited 4 full **5** sated **6** gorged **7** glutted, replete, stuffed **8** overfull, satiated **9** satisfied

surge 4 rush, wave **5** flood, swell **7** torrent

Suriname
 other name: 7 Surinam **11** Dutch Guiana
 capital/largest city: 10 Paramaribo
 others: 6 Albina **7** Totness **9** Groningen **10** Brokopondo, Onverwacht **13** Nieuw Nickerie **14** Nieuw Amsterdam
 measure: 7 ketting
 monetary unit: 4 cent **7** guilder
 lake: 14 Van Blommestein
 mountain: 4 Emma **6** Kayser, Oranje **10** Tumuc-Humac, Wilhelmina **13** Eilerts Il Haan, Van Ach Van Wyck **15** Guiana Highlands
 highest point: 10 Julianatop
 river: 7 Maroni **8** Nickerie, Suriname **9** Coppename **10** Courantijn, Courantyne, Tapanahoni
 ocean: 8 Atlantic
 physical feature:
  falls: 7 Kaieteur
  people: 4 Boni, Bush, Trio **5** Djuka, Dutch **6** Creole, Wayana **7** African, Chinese **10** Amerindian, Boschneger, West Indian **11** Asian Indian
  settler: 22 Lord Willoughby of Parham
 language: 5 Carib, Dutch, Hindi **6** Arawak **7** English **8** Javanese, Taki-Taki **10** Hindustani **11** Sranan Tongo **12** Sranang Tongo
 religion: 5 Hindu, Islam **10** Protestant **13** Roman Catholic
 feature:
  canoe: 6 corial
  clothing: 4 sari **5** dhoti **6** kamisa, sarong **10** kotomissie
  hat: 3 fez
  hut: 5 benab
  scarf: 9 selendong
  tree: 4 dali, lana, mora **5** dalli, genip, icica **7** acuyari, quassia **9** bethabara

food:
drink: 7 paiwari

surliness 8 ill humor, rudeness **9** bad temper **11** discourtesy, grouchiness **12** irascibility

surly 4 rude, sour **5** cross, gruff, harsh, testy **6** abrupt, crusty, grumpy, sullen, touchy **7** bearish, crabbed, grouchy, hostile, peevish, uncivil, waspish **8** choleric, churlish, insolent, petulant, snappish, snarling **9** irascible, splenetic, unamiable **10** ill-humored, ill-natured, unfriendly **11** bad-tempered **12** discourteous

surmise 4 deem, idea **5** guess, infer, judge, opine, posit, think **6** belief, notion **7** believe, imagine, opinion, presume, suppose, suspect, thought **8** conclude, consider, theorize **9** suspicion **10** assumption, conjecture, hypothesis, presuppose **11** hypothesize, presumption, speculation, supposition **13** shot in the dark

surmount 3 top **4** best **5** clear, climb, scale, worst **6** defeat, master **7** conquer, get over **8** overcome, vanquish **11** prevail over, triumph over **14** get the better of

surpass 3 top **4** beat, best **5** excel, outdo **6** exceed, outrun **7** eclipse **8** go beyond, outclass, outshine, outstrip, override **9** rise above, transcend **10** overshadow **11** go one better, leave behind, outdistance, triumph over **12** be better than, be superior to **13** have it all over

surplus 4 glut **5** extra **6** excess **7** overage, surfeit **8** leftover, overflow, plethora, residual **10** oversupply, surplusage **11** superfluity, superfluous **14** overproduction

surprise 4 stun **5** amaze, shock **6** ambush, wonder **7** astound, nonplus, set upon, stagger, startle, stupefy **8** astonish, confound, discover, dumfound, fall upon **9** amazement, bombshell, burst in on, dumbfound, take aback **10** defy belief, pounce upon, revelation, wonderment **11** flabbergast, incredulity **12** astonishment, take unawares **13** boggle the mind

surprise attack
French: 10 coup de main

surrender 4 cede **5** forgo, let go, waive, yield **6** accede, forego, give up, render, submit, vacate **7** abandon, concede, forsake **8** delivery, forgoing, give over, giving up, hand over, part with, renounce, turn over, yielding **9** deliver up, foregoing **10** capitulate, relinquish, submission **11** lay down arms **12** capitulation, renunciation **14** relinquishment **15** throw in the towel **16** show the white flag

surreptitious 6 covert, hidden, secret, veiled **7** furtive **8** hush-hush, stealthy **9** concealed, secretive **10** undercover

surrogate 6 acting, deputy **7** interim, stand-in **9** temporary **10** substitute **11** provisional

surround 4 belt, ring **5** hedge, hem in **6** circle, enfold, engird, girdle, shut in **7** close in, compass, enclose, envelop, fence in, hedge in **8** encircle **9** encompass **12** circumscribe

surrounding area 7 suburbs **8** environs, vicinity **9** outskirts, precincts

surroundings 5 scene **6** milieu **7** habitat, setting **8** ambience, environs **10** atmosphere, conditions **11** environment **13** circumstances
French: 11 mise en scene

surveillance 5 vigil, watch **8** scrutiny, trailing **11** observation **13** eavesdropping

survey 4 plot, poll, scan **5** gauge, graph, plumb, probe, scout, study **6** fathom, review **7** canvass, delimit, examine, inspect, measure, observe **8** analysis, block out, consider, look over, overview **10** scrutinize **11** contemplate, reconnoiter **12** pass in review **13** investigation

survival 5 relic **6** living **7** atavism, vestige **8** hangover **9** carry-over, throwback **11** subsistence **12** continuation, keeping alive

survive 4 last **5** abide, exist **6** endure, hang on, live on **7** hold out, outlast, outlive, persist, prevail, subsist **8** be extant, continue **9** keep alive **11** live through

surviving 6 extant **7** abiding, lasting **8** enduring, existent, existing, living on **9** hanging on, outliving, to be found **10** continuing, holding out, outlasting, persistent, persisting, subsisting **11** in existence **13** living through

Susann, Jacqueline
author of: 14 The Love Machine **15** Once Is Not Enough **16** Valley of the Dolls

Susanna
husband: 6 Joakim
accused of: 8 adultery
saved by: 6 Daniel

susceptible 4 open **5** prone **7** alive to, subject **8** liable to, sensible **9** sensitive **10** disposed to, responsive, vulnerable **11** conducive to, receptive to, sensitive to, sympathetic

suspect 5 doubt, fancy, guess, judge, opine, posit, think **7** believe, imagine, presume, suppose, surmise **8** distrust, misdoubt, mistrust, question, theorize **9** speculate **10** conjecture **11** hypothesize, wonder about **14** alleged culprit, be suspicious of **19** have one's doubts about

suspend 4 halt, hang, quit, stay, stop **5** cease, check, defer, delay, sling, swing, table **6** append, arrest, dangle, put off, shelve **7** reserve **8** break off, cut short, leave off, postpone, with-

hold **9** interrupt, stop short **10** put an end to **11** discontinue **12** bring to a stop **18** bring to a standstill

suspenders 6 braces, straps **7** gallows, garters, hangers **8** elastics, galluses **10** supporters

suspense 7 anxiety, tension **8** edginess **9** curiosity **10** indecision **11** expectation, incertitude, uncertainty **12** anticipation **15** indetermination

suspenseful 7 anxious **8** dramatic, exciting **9** climactic, uncertain

suspension 4 stay **5** pause **6** hiatus, recess **7** tabling **8** abeyance, deferral **12** postponement **14** discontinuance

suspicion 4 idea **5** guess, hunch **6** notion **7** feeling, surmise **8** distrust, mistrust **10** conjecture, hypothesis **11** supposition

Suspicion
director: 15 Alfred Hitchcock
cast: 9 Cary Grant **10** Nigel Bruce **12** Joan Fontaine **13** Dame May Whitty **15** Cedric Hardwicke
Oscar for: 7 actress (Fontaine)

suspicious 4 wary **5** shady **7** dubious, suspect **8** doubtful, doubting, slippery **9** ambiguous **10** untrusting **11** distrustful, incredulous, mistrustful, open to doubt **12** disbelieving, questionable **13** untrustworthy

sustain 4 bear, feed, prop **5** abide, brave, brook, stand **6** bear up, endure, hold up, keep up, suffer, uphold **7** nourish, nurture, prolong, support, underpin **8** maintain, protract, tolerate, underpin **9** keep alive, withstand **10** experience **12** carry on under **14** hold out against

sustenance 4 food, gear **5** bread, means **6** living **7** aliment, support **9** provender **10** provisions **11** maintenance, nourishment, subsistence
heaven-sent: 5 manna

sustineo alas 16 I sustain the wings
motto of: 10 US Air Force

Sutherland, Donald
born: 6 Canada, St John **12** New Brunswick
roles: 4 MASH **5** Klute **13** Hawkeye Pierce **14** Eye of the Needle, Ordinary People **16** Fellini's Casanova **17** The Eagle Has Landed **26** Invasion of the Body Snatchers

Sutpen, Colonel Thomas
character in: 14 Absalom Absalom
author: 8 Faulkner

Suva
capital of: 4 Fiji

Suzanne
character in: 19 The Marriage of Figaro
author: 12 Beaumarchais

svelte 4 fine, lean, neat, slim, thin, trim **5** lithe, spare **7** elegant, lissome, shapely, slender, willowy **8** graceful **9** sylphlike

Svengali
   character in: 6 Trilby
   author: 9 Du Maurier

Sverige *see* **6** Sweden

swab 3 dab, mop **4** daub, lout, wipe **5** clean, cloth, patch, scrub **6** cotton, sponge **7** cleanse **8** specimen
   brand name: 4 Q-tip

swagger 5 strut, sweep **6** parade, sashay, stride **7** saunter **11** swashbuckle

swaggerer 6 gascon **7** boaster, bragger **8** blowhard, braggart, strutter **11** braggadocio

swain 4 beau **6** fellow, suitor **7** admirer, gallant **8** cavalier, young man **9** boyfriend **10** sweetheart

swallow 3 bit, nip, sip **4** down, gulp, swig **5** drink, quaff, swill, taste **6** credit, devour, gobble, guzzle, hold in, imbibe, ingest, tipple **7** believe, fall for, repress **8** gulp down, hold back, keep back, mouthful, suppress, withhold

swallow up 5 drown, eat up, swamp **6** absorb, engulf **7** consume, envelop **8** inundate **9** overwhelm **10** assimilate

swallow words 6 mumble, mutter

swamp 3 bog, fen **4** fill, mire, moor, ooze, quag, sink, slew, slue **5** bayou, beset, flood, marsh, swale **6** deluge, engulf, morass, slough **7** besiege, bottoms, envelop **8** inundate, quagmire, submerge, wash over **9** everglade, marshland, overwhelm, snow under, swallow up

swamped 7 deluged, flooded, glutted, overrun **9** inundated **11** overwhelmed

Swan
   constellation of: 6 Cygnus

swan
   young: 6 cygnet
   group of: 4 bevy

swank 4 airs **5** ritzy **6** la-di-da, snooty, swanky **9** high-class, top-drawer **11** pretensions, pretentious **12** affectations, ostentatious **15** pretentiousness **16** superciliousness

swanky 4 chic, posh, rich **5** fancy, grand, jazzy, plush, ritzy, sharp, showy, smart, swank **6** flashy, snazzy, spiffy, sporty **7** dashing, elegant, splashy, stylish **9** sumptuous **11** fashionable

Swan Lake
   composer: 11 Tchaikovsky

Swanson, Gloria
   real name: 25 Gloria Josephine Mae Swenson
   born: 9 Chicago IL
   husband: 12 Wallace Beery
   roles: 13 Sadie Thompson, The Trespasser **15** Sunset Boulevard

swap 5 trade **6** barter, dicker, switch **7** bargain **8** exchange **11** give and take

sward 3 sod **4** lawn, rind, skin, turf **5** grass

swarm 4 herd, host, mass, rush, teem **5** cloud, crowd, drove, flock, horde, press, surge **6** abound, legion, myriad, stream, throng **7** cluster, overrun **8** stampede **9** multitude

swarthy 4 dark **5** dusky, swart, tawny **6** brunet **8** brunette **11** dark-skinned **12** brown-colored, brown-skinned, olive-skinned **14** dark-complected **16** dark-complexioned

swashbuckler 9 buccaneer, daredevil **10** adventurer

swashbuckling 4 bold **7** dashing **8** boasting **9** audacious, daredevil

swat 3 hit, tap **4** bash, belt, slam, slap, slug, sock **5** clout, knock, smack, smite, whack **6** buffet, strike, thwack, wallop **7** clobber

swathe 4 bind, wrap **5** cloak, cover **6** encase, enfold, enwrap **7** envelop, sheathe, swaddle

sway 4 bend, grip, hold, lead, list, move, reel, rock, roll, rule, spur, vary, wave **5** alter, clout, impel, power, reign, rouse, shift, swing, waver **6** change, domain, incite, induce, prompt, swerve, totter, waving, wobble **7** command, control, dispose, mastery, stagger, swaying **8** hesitate, iron hand, motivate, persuade, swinging, to-and-fro, undulate **9** authority, direction, encourage, fluctuate, influence, oscillate, pendulate, pulsation, stimulate, vacillate **10** domination, government, predispose, suzerainty, undulation **11** fluctuation, oscillation **12** back and forth, dictatorship, jurisdiction, manipulation

Swaziland
   capital/largest city: 7 Mbabane
   others: 5 Bunya, Hluti, Mpaka, Nsoko, Stegi **6** Gollel, Mhlume **7** Big Bend, Lobamba, Manzini **8** Havelock, Malkerns **9** Geodgegun, Hlatikulu, Mankaiana, Mankayana, Nhlangano, Pigg's Peak, Rocklands
   government: 22 constitutional monarchy
   head of state: 4 king
   monetary unit: 4 rand **9** lilangeni
   mountain: 8 Highveld **11** Drakensberg
   highest point: 7 Emlembe
   river: 5 Usutu **6** Komati, Lomati **8** Mhlatuze, Ngwavuma, Umbeluzi, Umbuluzi
   physical feature:
      forest: 5 Usutu
      plateau: 7 Lebombo, Lubombo
   people: 5 Asian, Bantu, Swazi **11** Eurafricans
      king: 3 Kbe **5** Nyama **6** Mswati **7** Sobhuza
      prince: 6 Sozisa
   language: 5 Ngumi **7** English, Siswati

9 Afrikaans **10** Portuguese
   religion: 7 animism **10** Protestant **13** Roman Catholic
   feature:
      bride payment: 6 lobolo
      god: 14 Mkhulumngcandi
      ritual dance: 7 Incwala

swear 3 vow **4** aver, avow, cuss **5** curse, vouch **6** adjure, assert, attest, pledge **7** certify, promise, warrant **9** blaspheme **10** take an oath, utter oaths **11** bear witness

swear by 7 believe, count on **9** believe in **10** put faith in

sweat 4 ooze, toil **5** exude, worry **6** effort **7** agonize **8** drudgery, hard work, perspire **9** exudation **12** perspiration

sweaty 3 wet **6** clammy, sticky **10** perspiring

Sweden
   other name: 7 Sverige
   capital/largest city: 9 Stockholm
   others: 4 Lund, Umea **5** Boden, Boras, Edane, Falun, Gavle, Lulea, Malmo, Pitea, Visby **6** Arvika, Kiruna, Orebro **7** Uppsala **8** Goteborg, Jokkmokk, Vasteras **9** Jonkoping, Linkoping, Sundsvall **10** Eskilstuna, Gottenburg, Norrkoping, Skelleftea **11** Halsingborg
   school: 4 Lund **7** Uppsala **8** Goteborg **9** Stockholm
   division: 3 Lan **4** Laen **5** Skane **6** Kalmar, Orebro **7** Dalarna, Gotland, Lapland **8** Alvsborg, Blekinge, Elfsborg, Gotaland, Jamtland, Malmohus, Norrland, Svealand
   government: 22 constitutional monarchy
      legislature: 7 Riksdag
   head of state: 4 king
   measure: 3 aln, fot, ref **4** alar, amar, famn, kapp, last, stop **5** carat, foder, kanna, linje, nymil, spann **6** fathom, jumfru **7** oxhuvud, tunland **8** fjarding, koltunna, tunnland
   monetary unit: 3 ore **5** krona, krone **7** carolin **8** skilling **9** rigsdaler
   weight: 3 ass, lod **4** last, mark, sten **5** carat **6** nylast **7** centner, lispund **8** skalpund, skeppund **9** shippound
   island: 5 Oland **7** Gotland
   lake: 4 Ster **5** Asnen, Malar, Silja, Vaner **6** Vanern, Vetter, Wenner **7** Hielmar, Malaren, Vattern **8** Dalalven **9** Hjalmaren
   mountain: 4 Sarv **5** Ammar **6** Helags, Kjolen, Ovniks, Sarjek **7** Kjollen
   highest point: 5 Kebne **10** Kebnekaise
   river: 3 Dal **4** Gota, Klar, Lule, Pite, Umea **5** Indal, Kalix, Lulea, Pitea, Ranea, Torne **6** Lainio, Muonio **7** Ljusnan **8** Angerman
   sea: 6 Baltic **8** Atlantic
   physical feature:
      canal: 4 Gota
      gulf: 7 Bothnia

sound: 6 Kalmar
strait: 7 Oresund 8 Kattegat 9 Skagerrak
people: 4 Lapp 5 Norse, Swede 6 Viking
  actress: 9 Liv Ullman 10 Greta Garbo 13 Ingrid Bergman
  astronomer: 7 Celsius 8 Angstrom
  author: 8 Lagerlof 10 Lagerkvist, Strindberg
  diplomat: 12 Hammarskjold
  director: 13 Ingmar Bergman 14 Arne Sucksdorff
  inventor: 5 Nobel
  king: 4 Vosa, Wasa 5 Oscar 6 Gustav 8 Gustavus 10 Carl Gustav 12 Gustav Adolph 13 Charles Gustav 22 Jean Baptiste Bernadotte
  philosopher/scientist: 10 Swedenborg
  queen: 9 Christina
  scientist: 8 Linnaeus
language: 4 Lapp 7 Swedish
religion: 19 Evangelical Lutheran
place:
  castle: 9 Gripsholm
  center of Stockholm: 11 Gamla Staden
  park: 7 Skansen 12 Millesgarden
  theater: 18 Drottningholm Court
  walled city: 5 Visby
food: 11 smorgasbord
  cheese: 7 fontina 8 jarlberg 9 jarlsberg
  dish: 10 kottbullar
  drink: 5 glogg 7 aquavit

Swedish Punch
type: 7 liqueur
origin: 6 Sweden
base: 3 rum
with gin: 5 Biffy
with vermouth: 9 Grand Slam

Sweeney Among the Nightingales
author: 7 T S Eliot

sweep 3 arc, fly 4 dart, dash, race, rush, scud, tear, zoom 5 hurry, spell, swing, swish, swoop, whisk 6 charge, gather, scurry, stroke 7 stretch 8 distance

sweeping 5 broad 7 blanket, radical 9 extensive, out-and-out, wholesale 10 exhaustive, large-scale, widespread 11 far-reaching, wide-ranging 12 all-inclusive 13 comprehensive, thoroughgoing

sweepings 4 dirt, dust 6 refuse

sweep off one's feet 7 enchant 8 bedazzle 9 captivate, overpower, overwhelm

sweet 4 dear, kind, nice 5 candy, fresh 6 dulcet, mellow, smooth, sugary 7 amiable, cloying, darling, dessert, lovable, nonsalt, not salt, tuneful 8 fragrant, pleasant, pleasing 9 agreeable, melodious, sweetmeat, wholesome 10 attractive, confection, euphonious, saccharine 11 good-natured, melliflu-

ous, silver-toned, sympathetic 12 non-fermented

Sweet Bird of Youth
director: 13 Richard Brooks
based on play by: 17 Tennessee Williams
cast: 8 Ed Begley 10 Paul Newman 13 Geraldine Page, Shirley Knight 17 Madeleine Sherwood
Oscar for: 15 supporting actor (Begley)

sweetheart 4 beau, dear, love 5 flame, honey, lover, swain 6 fiance, old man, steady, suitor 7 beloved, darling, fiancee, old lady 8 ladylove, mistress, true love 9 boyfriend, inamorata, valentine 10 girlfriend, lady friend 15 gentleman friend
French: 6 cherie

sweet life
Italian: 9 dolce vita

Sweet Mama Stringbean
nickname of: 11 Ethel Waters

sweetmeats 5 candy 6 sweets 7 bonbons 10 sugar candy 11 confections 13 confectionery

sweet-natured 5 sweet 6 benign, gentle, kindly 7 likable, lovable 8 pleasant 13 compassionate

sweetness
French: 7 douceur

sweet roll 3 bun 6 Danish 7 cruller 8 doughnut 10 coffee cake 11 cinnamon bun

sweets 5 candy 7 goodies 8 desserts 10 sugar candy, sweetmeats 11 confections 13 confectionery

sweet-scented 8 aromatic, fragrant, perfumed, redolent

sweet-smelling 5 spicy 7 scented 8 aromatic, fragrant, perfumed, redolent 9 odiferous

sweet talk 6 cajole, praise 7 blarney, flatter 8 cajolery, flattery, soft soap 10 compliment 11 endearments, loving words 13 blandishments 14 fond utterances

Sweetwater
nickname of: 16 Nathaniel Clifton

sweet words 7 blarney 8 flattery, soft soap 9 sweet talk 12 honeyed words

swell 3 fop, wax 4 A-one, fine, good, grow, okay, puff, rise, wave 5 bloat, bulge, dandy, great, heave, mount, super, surge, throb, widen 6 billow, blow up, comber, expand, extend, fatten, puff up 7 amplify, breaker, burgeon, distend, inflate, stretch, thicken 8 fabulous, heighten, increase, lengthen, splendid, terrific 9 excellent, first-rate, intensify, marvelous, spread out 10 delightful, first-class, tremendous, undulation 11 pleasurable 12 clotheshorse, fashion plate, smart dresser

swell-headed 8 egoistic, puffed up 9

conceited 10 egoistical 11 egotistical 12 vainglorious 13 self-important

swelling 4 bump, lump 5 bulge, swell 8 dilation 9 puffiness 10 distension 11 enlargement 12 protuberance

swell out 5 bloat, bulge 6 billow, expand 7 distend, inflate, puff out

swelter 3 fry 4 boil, cook 5 be hot, broil, sweat 8 languish, perspire

sweltering 3 hot 5 humid, muggy 6 sultry, torrid 7 burning 8 sweating 10 oppressive, perspiring

sweltry 3 hot 4 dank 5 humid, muggy 6 baking, clammy, steamy, sticky, sultry, torrid 7 boiling 8 broiling, roasting, sizzling, stifling 9 scorching 10 blistering 11 suffocating

Swept Away
subtitle: 38 by an unusual destiny in the blue sea of August
director: 14 Lina Wertmuller
cast: 16 Mariangela Melato 17 Giancarlo Giannini

swerve 3 shy, yaw 4 tack, turn, veer 5 avert, dodge, sheer, shift, stray 6 careen, change 7 deviate, digress, diverge 9 turn aside

swift 4 fast 5 brisk, fleet, hasty, quick, rapid 6 abrupt, flying, prompt, speedy 8 headlong 9 immediate 11 expeditious, precipitate

Swift, Jonathan
author of: 11 A Tale of a Tub 15 A Modest Proposal 16 Battle of the Books, Gulliver's Travels
fictional places: 6 Laputa 8 Lilliput 11 Brobdingnag
character: 6 Yahoos 10 Houyhnhnms 14 Lemuel Gulliver

swiftness 5 haste, speed 8 alacrity, celerity, dispatch, rapidity 9 quickness

swill 4 mash, slop, swig 5 quaff, waste 6 guzzle, refuse, scraps, soak up, tipple 7 garbage 8 chugalug, gulp down

swimming
athlete: 9 Diana Nyad, John Naber, Mark Spitz 10 Dawn Fraser, Kim Linehan, Linda Jezek 11 Claudia Kolb, Debbie Meyer, John Hencken 12 Brian Goodell, Bruce Furniss, Greg Louganis, John Kinsella 13 Jim Montgomery, Kornelia Ender, Michael Burton, Tracy Caulkens 14 Charles Hickcox, Duke Kahanamoku, Esther Williams, Gertrude Ederle 15 Cynthia Woodhead 16 Shirley Babashoff 17 Johnny Weissmuller

Swinburne, Algernon Charles
author of: 16 Hymn to Perserpine 17 Atalanta in Calydon 18 Songs Before Sunrise

swindle 2 do 3 con, gyp 4 bilk, dupe, gull, hoax, rook 5 cheat, cozen, fraud, mulct, steal, trick 6 delude, fleece, racket, rip-off 7 con game, deceive, defraud 8 embezzle, hoodwink 9 bamboozle, defalcate **12** embezzlement **14** confidence game

swindler 3 gyp **5** cheat, crook, faker, fraud **6** con man **7** sharper **8** chiseler, deceiver **9** charlatan, embezzler **10** mountebank **12** rip-off artist

swine 3 cad, cur, rat **4** pigs **5** beast, brute **6** animal
  group of: 5 drift **7** sounder

Swineherd, The
  author: 21 Hans Christian Andersen

swing 4 drop, hang, loop, move, rein, rock, sway, turn **5** pivot, rally, scope, sweep, whirl **6** dangle, decide, handle, manage, rotate, seesaw, stroke, wangle **7** compass, extract, freedom, inveigh, liberty, license, listing, pull off, rocking, rolling, suspend, swaying **8** maneuver, pitching, undulate **9** determine, influence, oscillate **10** accomplish, manipulate **11** be suspended, oscillation

Swing Time
  director: 13 George Stevens
  cast: 9 Eric Blore **11** Fred Astaire, Victor Moore **12** Betty Furness, Ginger Rogers **14** Helen Broderick
  score: 10 Jerome Kern **13** Dorothy Fields
  Oscar for: 4 song
  song: 12 A Fine Romance **14** Pick Yourself Up **20** The Way You Look Tonight

swirl 4 bowl, eddy, reel, roll, spin, swim, turn **5** churn, twirl, twist, wheel, whirl **6** gyrate, rotate **7** revolve

Swiss Family Robinson
  director: 10 Ken Annakin
  cast: 9 John Mills **10** Janet Munro **14** Dorothy McGuire, James MacArthur, Sessue Hayakawa
  author: 16 Johann Rudolf Wyss
  character: 13 Emily Montrose
    Robinson family: 4 Jack **5** Fritz **6** Ernest **7** Francis

switch 3 box, rod, tan **4** cane, jerk, lash, move, whip **5** birch, lever, shift, shunt, stick, swing, trade, whisk **6** button, change, handle **8** exchange **9** sidetrack **11** alternation

Switzerland
  also: 6 Suisse (French) **7** Schweiz (German) **8** Helvetia (Latin)
  capital: 4 Bern(e)
  largest city: 6 Zurich
  others: 3 Zug **4** Bale, Bern, Biel, Brig, Chur, Nyon, Sion, Thun **5** Basel, Basle, Berne, Coire, Surat, Vevey **6** Geneva, Geneve, Glarus, Lugano, Sarnen, Schwyz **7** Altdorf, Fyzabad, Herisau, Locarno, Lucerne, Luzerne, Zermatt **8** Lausanne, Montreux, St Moritz **9** Neuchatel, Solothurn **10** Bellinzona, Interlaken, Winterthur **12** Schaffhausen
  school: 4 Bern **5** Basel **8** Catholic,

Lausanne **28** Federal Institute of Technology
  division: 3 Uri, Zug **4** Bern, Chur, Nyon, Vaud **5** Aarau, Basel, Basle, Berne, Sankt, Waadt **6** Aargau, canton, Gallen, Geneva, Geneve, Glaris, Glarus, Luzern, Obwald, Schwyz, St Gall, Tessin, Ticino, Valais, Wallis, Zurich **7** Atldorf, Grisons, Lucerne, Nidwald, Thurgau **8** Fribourg, Obwalden, St Gallen **9** Appenzell, Neuchatel, Neuenberg, Solothurn **10** Graubunden **11** Unterwalden **12** Schaffhausen
  measure: 3 imi, pot **4** aune, fuss, muid, pied, zoll **5** lieue, linie, maass, pouce, staab, toise **6** perche, strich **7** klafter, viertel **9** quarteron **10** holzlafter **11** holzklafter
  monetary unit: 5 franc, rappe **6** hallar, rappen **7** centime, duplone **8** baetzner
  weight: 4 fund **5** pfund **7** centner, quintal **12** zugthierlast
  lake: 3 Uri, Zug **4** Biel, Thon, Thun **5** Ageri, Leman, Morat **6** Bienne, Brienz, Geneva, Lugano, Sarnen, Wallen, Zurich **7** Hallwil, Lucerne, Lungern **8** Maggiore, Viervald **9** Bielersee, Constance, Neuchatel, Sarnersee, Thunersee
  mountain: 3 Dom **4** Alps, Jura, Rigi, Rosa, Todi **5** Adula, Blanc, Cenis, Eiger, Genis, Karpf, Righi **6** Linard, Pizela, Sentis **7** Bernina, Beverin, Grimsel, Pilatus, Rotondo **8** Balmhorn, Jungfrau **9** Weisshorn **10** Diablerets, Matterhorn, St Gotthard, Wetterhorn **11** Burgenstock **12** Dufourspitze **13** Rheinwaldhorn **14** Finsteraarhorn
    mountain pass: 5 Cenis, Furka, Gemmi **6** Albula, Kinzig, Maloja, Usteri **7** Bernina, Brenner, Grimsel, Simplon, Splugen **8** Lotschen **10** St Gotthard
  highest point: 12 Dufourspitze
  river: 2 Po **3** Aar, Inn **4** Aare, Arve, Thur, Toss **5** Broye, Doubs, Linth, Reuss, Rhine, Rhone, Saane **6** Limmat, Maggia, Safane, Sarine, Ticino **8** Engadine, Pratigau
  physical feature:
    glacier: 5 Rhone
    plateau: 5 Swiss
  people: 5 Swiss
    artist: 4 Klee
    author: 5 Hesse, Spyri **6** Keller **8** Gotthelf, Rousseau **10** Durrenmatt
    educational reformer: 10 Pestalozzi
    hero: 4 Tell
    psychologist: 4 Jung **6** Piaget
    religious leader: 6 Calvin **7** Zwingli
    scientist: 9 Bernoulli
  language: 5 Ladin **6** French, German **7** Italian **8** Romansch **14**

Switzerdeutsch
  religion: 9 Calvinism **10** Protestant **13** Roman Catholic
  place:
    castle: 7 Chillon
    fountain: 7 Jet d'Eau
    playhouse: 6 Zurich
    resort: 5 Arosa, Davos **6** Gstaad **7** Zermatt **8** St Moritz **9** Schwagalp **10** Interlaken
    street: 14 Bahnhofstrasse
    tower: 5 Clock
  feature:
    animal: 4 ibex **7** chamois
    flower: 9 edelweiss
    pageant: 9 Alpenfest
  food:
    cheese: 6 bagnes, sbrinz **7** Gruyere **10** Emmentaler **11** Appenzeller
    dish: 5 rosti **6** fondue **8** raclette **11** grisons beef **14** bundnerfleisch
    drink: 11 cheri-suisse **14** marmotchocolat

Swiveller, Dick
  character in: 19 The Old Curiosity Shop
  author: 7 Dickens

swollen 5 puffy **7** bloated, bulging, swelled **8** inflated, puffed-up **9** distended

swoon 5 faint **8** collapse, keel over **13** fall prostrate **17** become unconscious

swoop 4 dive, drop, rush **5** pitch, sweep **6** plunge, pounce, spring **7** descend, plummet **8** nose-dive, swooping **9** sweep down **12** rush headlong

sword 4 epee, foil **5** blade, saber, steel **6** rapier **7** cutlass **8** scimitar **10** broadsword

sybarite 8 hedonist **10** sensualist, voluptuary

sybaritic 4 rich **6** lavish **7** sensual **9** dissolute, epicurean, luxurious **10** dissipated, hedonistic, voluptuous **12** luxury-loving, pleasure-bent **13** self-indulgent **14** pleasure-loving **15** pleasure-seeking

sycamore 8 Platanus **18** Acer pseudoplatanus
  varieties: 7 eastern **8** Egyptian

sycophant 4 tool **5** slave, toady **6** fawner, flunky, jackal, lackey, puppet, stooge, yes-man **7** cat's-paw **8** hanger-on, parasite, truckler **9** brown-nose, flatterer **10** bootlicker **11** lickspittle, rubber stamp **13** apple-polisher

Sydney
  bay: 5 Walsh **11** Rushcutter's **13** Woolloomooloo
  capital of: 13 New South Wales
  cove: 4 Farm
  founder: 7 Phillip
  harbor: 7 Darling **11** Port Jackson
  island: 4 Goat **6** Garden
  landmark: 10 Opera House **11** Wynyard Park **13** Harbour Bridge **14** Fitzroy Gardens **15** Mitchell Library

16 Australian Museum, Hyde Park Barracks, Saint James Church **18** Rushcutter's Bay Park **21** Royal Botanical Gardens
river: 10 Parramatta
university: 9 Macquarie **13** New South Wales

sylvan 5 bushy, leafy, woody **6** wooded, woodsy **8** arcadian, forested, timbered, woodland **9** luxuriant, overgrown **10** forestlike

Sylvanus *see* **8** Silvanus

Sylvia
character in: 20 Two Gentlemen of Verona
author: 11 Shakespeare

symbol 4 mark, sign **5** badge, token **6** emblem, figure, signal **10** indication **14** representation **15** exemplification

symbolize 4 mean **5** imply **6** denote, embody, symbol **7** betoken, connote, express, signify **8** stand for **9** emblemize, exemplify, personify, represent, signalize **10** allegorize **11** emblematize

symmetrical 7 orderly, regular **8** balanced **9** congruent **12** well-balanced **16** well-proportioned

symmetry 4 form **5** order **7** balance, harmony **8** congruity **10** conformity, regularity **11** equilibrium, orderliness, parallelism, shapeliness **15** proportionality

sympathetic 6 benign, humane, kindly **7** feeling, pitying **8** friendly, merciful **9** agreeable, approving, benignant, sensitive **10** benevolent, comforting **11** soft-hearted, warmhearted **12** sympathizing, welldisposed **13** commiserative, compassionate, tenderhearted, understanding

sympathize 4 back, pity, side **5** agree, favor **7** approve, feel for, go along, support **8** sanction **9** empathize **10** appreciate, be in accord, be sorry for **11** condole with, have pity for, stand behind

sympathy 4 pity **5** amity, favor, grief **6** accord, regard, sorrow **7** concern, concert, concord, empathy, feeling, harmony, rapport, support **8** advocacy, affinity, approval, sanction **9** agreement, communion, patronage, unanimity **10** compassion, consonance, fellowship, friendship, tenderness **11** well-wishing **12** congeniality, partisanship **13** commiseration, fellow feeling, understanding

Symplegades
form: 5 rocks
location: 8 Bosporus **9** Euxine Sea
characteristic: 8 clashing, dark-blue

symposium 5 forum, synod **6** debate, parley, powwow **7** meeting **8** colloquy, congress **10** conference, discussion, round table **12** deliberation **15** panel discussion

Symposium
author: 5 Plato
character: 7 Agathon **8** Phaedrus, Socrates **9** Pausanias **10** Alcibiades **11** Aristodemus **12** Aristophanes

symptom 4 mark, sign **5** token **6** signal **7** earmark, warning **8** evidence, giveaway **10** indication **15** prognostication

synagogue
Yiddish: 4 shul **5** schul

synchronal 11 concomitant, synchronous **12** contemporary, simultaneous

synchronous 10 synchronal **11** concomitant **12** contemporary, simultaneous

syndicalist 5 rebel **9** anarchist, insurgent **13** revolutionary

syndicate 5 group, trust, union **6** cartel, league, merger **7** combine **8** alliance **9** coalition **10** consortium, federation **11** association

Synge, John Millington
author of: 14 Riders to the Sea **19** Deirdre of the Sorrows **20** In the Shadow of the Glen **27** The Playboy of the Western World

synod 4 diet **13** governing body **15** advisory council **21** ecclesiastical council

synonym 8 analogue **10** equivalent **11** another name

synonymous 4 like, same **5** alike, equal **7** coequal **10** equivalent

synopsis 5 brief **6** apercu, digest, precis, resume **7** epitome, outline, rundown, summary **8** abstract, argument **11** abridgement

synopsize 6 digest **7** abridge, outline **8** abstract, condense **9** summarize

Synoptist 12 Gospel writer

synthesize 3 mix **4** fuse **5** blend **7** combine **8** compound **10** amalgamate

synthetic 4 fake, sham **5** phony **6** ersatz **7** man-made **9** unnatural **10** artificial **11** counterfeit **12** manufactured

Syria
other name: 4 Aram
capital/largest city: 8 Damascus
others: 4 Hama, Homs, Nawa **5** Busra, Calno, Derra, Emesa, Halab, Hamah, Idlib, Jerud, Raqqa **6** Aleppo, Calneh, Dumeir, Fajami, Tadmor, Ugarit **7** Antioch, Latakia, Palmyra **8** Seleucia **9** Ghabaghib
school: 6 Aleppo, Syrian **11** Arab Academy
measure: 5 makuk **6** garava
monetary unit: 4 lira **5** pound **6** talent **7** piaster
weight: 4 cola **5** artal, ratel **6** talent
lake: 5 Merom **7** Djeboid **8** Tiberias
mountain: 6 Carmel **7** Alawite, Libanus **10** Nusairiyya **11** Anti-Lebanon
highest point: 6 Hermon
river: 3 Asi **6** Balikh, Barada, Jordan, Khabur, Yarmuk **7** Orontes **9** Asi Knabur, Euphrates
sea: 13 Mediterranean
physical feature:
desert: 5 Hamad **6** Hauran, Syrian
heights: 5 Golan
people: 4 Arab, Kurd, Turk **5** Alawi, Aptal, Druse, Druze **6** Afshar, Aissor, Aushar, Avshar, Awshar **7** Amorite, Ansarie, Bedouin, Nosaris, Saracen, Shemite **8** Ansarieh, Armenian **9** Ansariyah **10** Circassian **12** Khachaturian
king: 5 Rezin **6** Faisal, Hazael **8** Benhadad **9** Antiochus
leader: 10 T E Lawrence **12** Hafiz al-Assad **16** Lawrence of Arabia
queen: 7 Zenobia
ruler: 4 Rome **5** Arabs **6** France, Greeks, Persia **7** Mongols **8** Abbasids **9** Mamelukes, Phoenicia, Seleucids **11** Seljuk Turks **12** Ottoman Turks
language: 6 Arabic, French, Syriac **7** Aramaic, English, Kurdish, Turkish **8** Armenian
religion: 5 Druze, Islam **7** Alawite **12** Christianity **13** Greek Orthodox **23** Eastern Rite Christianity
place:
dam: 5 Tabqa **9** Euphrates
ruins: 7 Palmyra
square: 7 Martyrs'
feature:
animal: 9 dromedary
clothing: 3 aba **4** abah **7** abayyah **8** kafiyyah
marketplace: 4 souk
tent: 8 bayt shar
village common: 6 maidan

Syrinx
form: 5 nymph
location: 8 mountain
transformed into: 4 reed
transformed by: 3 Pan
made into: 7 panpipe
pipes called: 6 syrinx

system 4 body, unit **5** setup **6** method, scheme, theory **7** program, regimen, routine **8** organism **9** procedure, structure **10** hypothesis **11** arrangement **12** constitution, organization **13** modus operandi **15** mode of operation

systematic 4 neat, tidy **7** ordered, orderly, planned, precise, regular **8** constant **9** organized **10** methodical **12** businesslike, systematized **13** well-organized, well-regulated

systematization 5 order **8** ordering **9** gradation **10** organizing **11** arrangement **12** categorizing, codification, organization **13** methodization **14** categorization, classification

systematize 5 order **7** arrange **8** classify, organize **9** methodize

systematized 7 ordered **8** arranged, codified **9** organized **10** classified, methodized, systematic

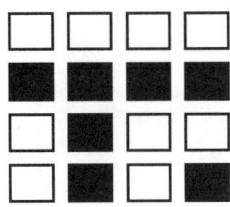

tab 3 lip **4** bill, cost, flap, loop **5** check, PC key, price, strip, tally **6** tongue **7** eyehole **10** projection

tabard 4 cape, coat **5** cloak, tunic

Tabard Inn
starting point in: 18 The Canterbury Tales

tabernacle 6 church, temple **14** house of worship

Tabeth 16 tenth Hebrew month

Tabitha
also called: 6 Dorcas
revived by: 5 Peter
hometown: 5 Joppa

table 4 fare, list, roll **5** board, chart, index **6** record, roster, shelve, spread **7** catalog **8** lay aside, postpone, put aside, register, schedule, syllabus, synopsis **9** inventory **10** tabulation

Table
constellation of: 5 Mensa

tableau 4 view **5** scene **7** pageant, picture, setting **8** grouping **9** depiction, spectacle, still life **11** arrangement, delineation **12** illustration **13** picturization

tableau vivant 13 living picture

tablespoon
abbreviation: 3 tbs **4** tbsp

tablet 3 pad **4** leaf **5** bolus, panel, sheet, wafer **6** pellet, plaque, troche **7** lozenge, memo pad, surface **8** flat cake, thin slab **9** tablature **10** pad of paper, writing pad

tableware 5 china **6** dishes, plates **7** cutlery **8** crockery, utensils **9** chinaware, glassware **10** dinnerware, silverware **14** cups and saucers

taboo, tabu 3 ban **4** no-no **6** banned **8** anathema, outlawed, verboten **9** forbidden, social ban **10** in bad taste, prohibited, proscribed **11** disapproved, prohibition, unthinkable **12** interdiction, proscription, religious ban, unacceptable **13** unmentionable

tabulate 4 file, list, rank, rate, sort **5** chart, grade, group, index, order, range **6** codify **7** arrange, catalog, compute, diagram, sort out **8** classify, organize **9** methodize **10** categorize, make a table **11** systematize

tace
music: 6 silent

tacit 7 assumed, implied **8** implicit, inferred, unspoken, unstated, wordless

10 undeclared, understood **11** unexpressed **15** taken for granted

taciturn 5 aloof, quiet **6** silent **7** laconic **8** reserved, reticent **9** secretive **11** tight-lipped **12** close-mouthed **15** uncommunicative

tack 3 add, peg, pin, way **4** clap, nail, slap, veer **5** affix, sheer, shift, spike, thole **6** append, attach, change, fasten, method, swerve, switch, zigzag **7** go about **8** approach, tholepin **9** short nail **12** change course **14** course of action

tackle 3 try **4** gear, lift **5** assay, begin, crane, hoist, jenny, throw, tools, winch **6** accept, assume, attack, take on, take up **7** attempt, capstan, derrick, embrace, go about, halyard, rigging **8** endeavor, engage in, material, set about, windlass **9** apparatus, enter upon, equipment, trappings, undertake **10** appliances, embark upon, implements **11** instruments **12** appointments **13** accoutrements, paraphernalia

tack on 3 add **5** annex **6** adjoin, append, attach **7** stick on, subjoin **8** fasten to

tacky 5 dowdy, gluey, gooey, gucky, gummy, messy, ratty, seedy, tatty **6** grubby, shabby, shoddy, sloppy, sticky, untidy, viscid **7** stringy, unkempt, viscous **8** adhesive, frazzled, slipshod, slovenly **10** disordered

tact 7 finesse, suavity **8** delicacy **9** diplomacy, suaveness **10** discretion **11** savoir faire, sensibility **13** consideration **14** circumspection
French: 11 savoir-faire

tactful 5 suave **6** polite, smooth, subtle **7** politic **8** decorous, delicate, discreet, mannerly **9** sensitive **10** diplomatic, thoughtful **11** considerate

tactic 3 way **4** line, plan, tack **6** method, policy, scheme **8** approach **9** stratagem **14** course of action

tactics 9 maneuvers **18** battle arrangements, military operations

tactless 4 curt, rude **5** blunt, brash, rough **6** abrupt, clumsy, gauche, stupid **7** boorish **8** impolite **9** hamhanded, impolitic, imprudent, untactful **10** blundering, indelicate, indiscreet **11** insensitive, thoughtless **12** undiplomatic **13** ill-considered,

inconsiderate
French: 6 gauche

tactlessness 8 curtness **9** bluntness, gaucherie **10** abruptness, clumsiness, indelicacy **13** insensitivity, tastelessness

taedium vitae 5 ennui **12** tedium of life **22** feeling life is wearisome

Taft, William Howard
presidential rank: 13 twenty-seventh
party: 10 Republican
state represented: 2 OH
defeated: 4 (Eugene Victor) Debs **5** (William Jennings) Bryan **6** (Daniel Braxton) Turney, (Eugene Wilder) Chafin, (Thomas Edward) Watson, (Thomas Louis) Hisgen **8** (August) Gillhaus
vice president: 7 (James Schoolcraft) Sherman
cabinet:
state: 4 (Philander Chase) Knox
treasury: 8 (Franklin) MacVeagh
war: 7 (Henry Lewis) Stimson **9** (Jacob McGavock) Dickinson
attorney general: 10 (George Woodward) Wickersham
navy: 5 (George von Lengerke) Meyer
postmaster general: 9 (Frank Harris) Hitchcock
interior: 6 (Walter Lowrie) Fisher **9** (Richard Achilles) Ballinger
agriculture: 6 (James) Wilson
commerce and labor: 5 (Charles) Nagel
born: 12 Cincinnati OH
died: 12 Washington DC
buried: 25 Arlington National Cemetery
education:
university: 4 Yale
law school: 10 Cincinnati
religion: 9 Unitarian
interests: 4 golf
author: 22 Four Aspects of Civic Duty **23** The United States and Peace **30** Our Chief Magistrate and His Powers **33** The Anti-Trust Act and the Supreme Court **65** The Presidency: Its Duties Its Powers Its Opportunities and Its Limitation
political career: 18 US Solicitor General
judge: 19 Federal Circuit Court
president of: 21 Philippines

Commission
civil governor of: 11 Philippines
secretary of: 3 War
US Supreme Court: 12 Chief Justice
civilian career:
  law professor: 4 Yale
  president: 22 American Bar Association
notable events of lifetime/term: 19 Postal Savings System
  Act: 10 Webb-Kenyon **11** Mann-Elkinst **12** Payne-Aldrich
  sinking of: 7 Titanic
father: 8 Alphonso
mother: 6 Louisa (Maria Torrey)
siblings: 5 Fanny **11** Henry Waters **12** Horace Dutton **15** Samuel Davenport
  half-brothers: 11 Peter Rawson **13** Charles Phelps
wife: 5 Helen (Herron)
  nickname: 6 Nellie
children: 11 Helen Herron **13** Charles Phelps **14** Robert Alphonso
first lady:
  author: 24 Recollections of Full Years

tag 3 add, dog, tab **4** card, heel, mark, name, slip, stub, tail, term **5** add on, affix, annex, hound, label, title, trail **6** append, attach, attend, fasten, follow, handle, join to, marker, shadow, tack on, ticket **7** earmark, moniker, pendant **8** cognomen, identify, nickname **9** accompany, appendage, sobriquet

Tahiti
artist: 7 Gauguin
author: 9 Stevenson
capital: 7 Papeete
formerly: 8 Otaheite
island group: 7 Society
isthmus: 7 Taravao
ocean: 7 Pacific
volcano: 5 Roniu **7** Orohena

tail 3 dog **4** butt, seat **5** fanny, stalk, track, trail **6** follow, shadow **7** back end, rear end **8** buttocks

tail end, tail-end 4 back, butt, rear, rump, tail **6** caudal **7** hind end, rear end **8** backside, buttocks, last part **9** posterior

tailor 3 fit, sew **4** make, redo **5** adapt, alter, build, shape **6** change, create, design, devise, modify **7** convert, fashion, produce **8** clothier, costumer **9** construct, couturier, fabricate, transform **10** dressmaker, seamstress

taint 3 mar, rot **4** blot, flaw, ruin, soil, spot, turn **5** dirty, fault, go bad, smear, spoil, stain, sully **6** damage, debase, defect, defile, smudge, stigma **7** blemish, putrefy, tarnish **8** besmirch **12** imperfection

tainted 5 dirty **6** impure, rotten **7** spoiled, stained, unclean **9** blemished, tarnished **10** besmirched

Taipei
capital of: 6 Taiwan

Taiwan
name means: 11 terraced bay
other name: 7 Formosa **11** Ilha Formosa **15** Republic of China
capital/largest city: 6 Taipei
others: 4 Suao **5** Shoka, Takao **6** Tainan **7** Chilung, Hualien, Keelong, Keelung, Taoyuan **8** Fengshan, Kaohiung, Taichung **9** Kaohsiung
school: 7 Soochow, Tunghai **14** National Taiwan
monetary unit: 4 yuan **6** dollar
island: 5 Matsu **6** Lan Hsu, Penghu, Quemoy, Taiwan **7** Hungtou, Huoshao **10** Pescadores
mountain: 5 Tatun **6** Tzukao **7** Taitung **15** Chungyang Shanmo
highest point: 5 Yu Shan **8** Morrison **10** Sinkao Shan **11** Hsin-Kao Shan
river: 5 Wuchi **7** Tachia **7** Choshui, Hualien, Tanshui
sea: 7 Pacific **9** East China **10** Philippine, South China
physical feature:
  cape: 7 Olwanpi
  channel: 5 Bashi
  gorge: 6 Taroko
  storm: 7 monsoon, typhoon
  strait: 6 Taiwan **7** Formosa
people: 4 Yami **5** Hakka, Hoklo **7** Chinese, Malayan **9** Fukienese, Taiwanese **10** Indonesian, Polynesian **12** Kwangtungese
  goddess: 5 Matsu
  leader: 7 Koxinga **9** Sun Yat-sen **10** Yen Chia-Kan **13** Chiang Kai-shek **14** Cheng Cheng-Kung, Chiang Ching-kuo
language: 4 Amon, Amoy **5** Hakka, Kuo Yu **6** Minnan **9** Taiwanese **15** Mandarin Chinese
religion: 6 Taoism **7** animism **8** Buddhism **12** Christianity, Confucianism
place:
  museum: 14 National Palace
  square: 12 Presidential
feature:
  festival: 5 Ghost
  political party: 10 Kuomintang
food:
  feast: 6 pai-pai

Tajikistan
other name: 12 Tadzhikistan
capital/largest city: 8 Dushanbe
head of state: 9 president
government: 8 republic
monetary unit: 5 ruble
mountain: 13 Communism Peak
people: 5 Tajik, Uzbek **7** Tadzhik
language: 7 Tadzhik
religion: 11 Sunni Muslim

Taj Mahal 4 tomb **9** mausoleum
location: 4 Agra **5** India
built by: 9 Shah, Jahan
for: 4 wife

take 3 buy, get, lug, nab, net, see, use

4 bear, bilk, deem, draw, feel, gain, grab, grip, haul, have, heed, hire, hold, know, lead, loot, mark, mind, move, need, obey, read, rent, sack, tote, work **5** bring, brook, carry, catch, cheat, claim, clasp, filch, grasp, gross, guide, infer, lease, seize, stand, steal, use up, usher, usurp **6** accept, assume, attain, clutch, convey, deduce, deduct, demand, derive, divest, employ, endure, escort, fleece, follow, look on, obtain, pilfer, pocket, profit, regard, remove, secure, snatch, suffer **7** acquire, agree to, believe, call for, capture, conduct, consume, deliver, make out, observe, pillage, plunder, purloin, receive, require, respect, stomach, succeed, suppose, undergo **8** accede to, assent to, conceive, conclude, consider, listen to, perceive, proceeds, purchase, shoulder, submit to, subtract, take away, tolerate, transfer **9** ascertain, be ruled by, consent to, deprive of, eliminate, get hold of, interpret, lay hold of, put up with, respond to, transport, undertake **10** commandeer, comply with, comprehend, confiscate, experience, lay hands on, take effect, understand **11** appropriate, begin to work, go along with, necessitate **13** help oneself to **14** avail oneself of, misappropriate

take aback 5 amaze **6** astound **8** astonish, surprise **9** overwhelm

take a crack at 3 try **5** essay **6** hazard, tackle, take on **7** attempt, venture **9** have a go at, undertake **11** make a stab at

take advantage of 3 use **5** avail **7** exploit, utilize **10** profit from

take after 4 copy, echo **6** follow, repeat **7** imitate **8** resemble, simulate **9** duplicate, reproduce

take apart 7 destroy **8** demolish **9** dismantle, knock down **11** disassemble

take a powder 4 blow, exit **5** go out, leave, scram, split **6** cut out, depart, escape **8** withdraw

take away 5 seize **6** lessen, reduce **7** abridge, bear off, curtail, detract **8** carry off, decrease, subtract **9** deprive of **11** make off with

take a whack at 3 try **5** essay **6** hazard, tackle **7** attempt, venture **8** give a try **9** have a go at **10** give a whirl **12** take a crack at

take back 6 abjure, recall, recant, renege **7** disavow, retract, reverse **8** forswear, withdraw

take captive 3 bag **4** snag, take, trap **5** catch, seize, snare **7** capture, ensnare **9** apprehend, lay hold of **12** take prisoner

take care 6 beware, be wary **9** be careful **10** be cautious **17** look before you leap

take care of 4 tend **6** assume **7** nurture **8** attend to, shoulder **10** minister to

take exception 5 demur **6** object, resent **11** look askance

take flight 3 fly **4** flee **6** escape, run off **7** abscond, fly away, run away, run free, take off **9** make a dash **10** fly the coop **12** make a getaway

take for granted 6 assume **10** undervalue

take heed 4 mind **6** beware **7** look out **8** take care, watch out **11** take warning

take hold 4 bite, grab, grip **5** grasp **6** clutch **7** catch on

take in stride 12 not skip a beat **13** be unperturbed

take into custody 3 bag, nab **4** book, bust, hold **5** catch, pinch, seize **6** arrest, collar, detain, secure **7** capture **9** apprehend **12** take prisoner

take into service 4 hire **6** employ, engage, retain, secure, take on

take issue 5 demur **6** differ **8** disagree **12** be at variance, stand opposed

take no notice of 6 ignore **9** disregard **11** pay no heed to **15** fail to recognize **16** pay no attention to **17** fail to acknowledge

take notice
    Latin: **8** nota bene

take notice of 3 see **4** heed, mark, note **6** call on, regard **7** observe **8** call upon **9** recognize **10** get a load of **11** acknowledge **14** pay attention to

take nourishment 3 eat **4** feed **10** break bread **14** take sustenance

takeoff 5 spoof **6** parody, satire **7** lampoon **9** burlesque **10** caricature

take off 4 doff, lift **5** leave **6** decamp, depart, detach, remove **7** lift off, peel off, run away **8** strip off **14** leave the ground

take off guard 5 catch **8** surprise **14** take by surprise

take on 4 bear, hire **6** accept, assume, engage **8** shoulder **9** undertake

take one's breath away 4 daze, stun **5** shock **7** stupefy **8** astonish, dumfound **9** dumbfound, electrify **11** flabbergast **15** make one's eyes pop

take out 4 date **5** court **6** delete, escort, remove **7** extract, isolate **8** abstract, separate, take home, withdraw **9** strike out

take over 4 take **5** seize **6** assume, take on, take up **8** shoulder **10** commandeer, confiscate **11** appropriate, expropriate, gain control

take pains 6 strive **7** attempt, try hard **8** endeavor, go all out **10** do one's best **11** give one's all **12** make an effort **15** knock oneself out **16** give one's best shot

take pleasure in 4 like, love **5** adore,

eat up, enjoy, fancy, savor **6** dote on, relish, relish **7** revel in **9** rejoice in **10** appreciate **13** be pleased with, get a kick out of

take possession of 5 claim **10** confiscate **11** appropriate, expropriate

take prisoner 3 bag, nab **4** book, bust **5** catch, pinch, seize **6** arrest, collar **7** capture **9** apprehend **11** take captive **15** take into custody

take sick 3 ail **6** sicken **8** collapse **9** become ill **10** be stricken

take stock of 5 audit, check **6** assess, review, survey **7** examine, inspect **8** look over **9** inventory

take sustenance 3 eat **4** feed **10** break bread **15** take nourishment

take the cake 5 excel **7** beat all, surpass **12** beat the devil, win hands down

take the edge off 6 lessen, pacify, soothe, temper **7** appease, assuage, lighten, mollify **8** tone down

take the first step 5 begin, start **6** launch, set out **8** commence, embark on, initiate **9** undertake **10** inaugurate

take the place of 7 replace **8** displace, supplant **9** supersede

take to be 4 deem, hold **5** count, judge, think **6** assume, regard, view as **7** account, believe **8** consider **10** look upon as

take to heart 4 heed, mind **6** attend **8** consider **9** hearken to **13** give thought to **14** pay attention to

take to one's heels 3 fly **4** flee **6** escape **7** get away, run away **10** fly the coop, make a break, take flight **12** make a getaway **15** head for the hills

take to task 5 chide, scold **6** accuse, berate, charge, rail at, rebuke **7** bawl out, censure, chasten, chew out, reprove, upbraid **8** admonish, chastise, reproach **9** castigate, criticize, dress down, reprimand **10** tongue-lash **11** remonstrate **13** call to account

take turns 5 share **6** rotate **9** alternate

take under one's wing 6 assist, defend **7** protect **8** befriend **9** look after

take unfair advantage of 5 abuse **6** misuse **7** exploit

take up 4 lift **6** absorb, accept, assume, occupy, pick up, resume, soak up, suck up **7** discuss, drink in **8** consider, continue, sponge up, talk over **9** cultivate, swallow up

taking a siesta 6 dozing **7** napping **8** snoozing **10** taking a nap **18** catching forty winks

takings 4 loot **5** booty **6** spoils **7** plunder **8** pickings

Talaria
    form: **7** sandals
    owner: **6** Hermes **7** Mercury
    characteristic: **6** winged

tale 3 fib, lie **4** epic, myth, saga, yarn

5 fable, novel, rumor, story **6** legend, report **7** account, fiction, hearsay, recital, romance, scandal, untruth **8** anecdote **9** falsehood, fish story, narration, narrative, tall story **10** short story **11** fabrication, scuttlebutt **12** tittle-tattle **13** falsification, piece of gossip **16** cock-and-bull story

talebearer 6 gossip **7** blabber, reciter, tattler **8** busybody, informer, reporter, telltale **10** newsmonger, tattletale **11** storyteller **12** blabbermouth **13** scandalmonger

talent 4 bent, gift, turn **5** flair, forte, knack, skill **6** genius **7** faculty **8** aptitude, capacity, facility, strength **9** endowment **10** capability **11** proficiency

Talent 14 Biblical weight

talented 4 able **5** adept **6** expert, gifted, born for, capable, endowed, skilled **8** artistic, polished **9** brilliant, competent **10** proficient **11** well-endowed **12** accomplished

Tale of a Tub, A
    author: **9** Ben Jonson **13** Jonathan Swift

Tale of Genji
    author: **19** Lady Murasaki Shikibu

Tale of Two Cities, A
    author: **14** Charles Dickens
    character: **7** Gaspard, Stryver **9** Dr Manette, Miss Pross **11** Jarvis Lorry, John Barstad **12** Lucie Manette, Sydney Carton **13** Charles Darnay, Jerry Cruncher, Madame Defarge **18** Marquis St Evremonde
    director: **10** Jack Conway
    cast: **12** Blanche Yurka, Isabel Jewell, Reginald Owen, Ronald Colman (Sydney Carton) **13** Basil Rathbone, Edna May Oliver **14** Elizabeth Allan
    setting: **16** French Revolution

Tales Before Midnight
    author: **19** Stephen Vincent Benet

Talese, Gay
    author of: **14** Honor Thy Father **16** Thy Neighbor's Wife

Tales of a Fourth Grade Nothing
    author: **9** Judy Blume

Tales of a Wayside Inn
    author: **24** Henry Wadsworth Longfellow

Tales of Hoffmann, The
    also: **18** Les Contes d'Hoffmann
    opera by: **9** Offenbach
    character: **6** Stella **7** Antonia, Olympia **9** Dr Miracle, Giulietta **11** E T A Hoffmann **14** mechanical doll

Tales of Manhattan
    author: **16** Louis Auchincloss

talisman 4 tiki **5** charm **6** amulet, fetish, grigri **10** lucky piece

Talisman, The
    author: **14** Sir Walter Scott
    character: **7** Conrade, El Hakim **10** Sir Kenneth **15** Queen Berengaria

19 Theodorick of Engaddi **20** Lady Edith Plantagenet **21** Richard the Lion-Hearted **31** Grand Master of the Knights Templars

talk 3 gab, jaw, rap, say **4** cant, chat, word **5** argot, idiom, lingo, noise, prate, rumor, slang, speak, state, utter **6** babble, bunkum, confab, confer, gossip, hot air, intone, jargon, parley, patois, powwow, preach, report, sermon, speech, take up, tirade **7** address, blarney, blather, chatter, consult, declare, deliver, dialect, discuss, express, hearsay, lecture, oration, palaver, prattle, twaddle **8** chitchat, colloquy, converse, dialogue, harangue, language, proclaim, rattle on, verbiage **9** discourse, enunciate, negotiate, pronounce, tete-a-tete, utterance **10** bandy words, conference, discussion, rap session, recitation, speak about **11** declamation, exhortation, pontificate, scuttlebutt **12** blatherskite, consultation, conversation, tittle-tattle **13** confabulation

talkative 5 gabby, talky, windy, wordy **6** babbly, chatty, prolix **7** gossipy, verbose, voluble **8** effusive **9** garrulous **10** long-winded, loquacious

talk big 4 brag, crow **5** boast, vaunt **13** puff oneself up **15** blow one's own horn **19** pat oneself on the back

talk down to 9 patronize **10** condescend

talker 6 gabber, gossip, magpie, orator **7** babbler, speaker, windbag **8** lecturer, prattler **9** chatterer, converser **10** chatterbox, mouthpiece **11** rumormonger, speechifier, speechmaker **12** blatherskite, spokesperson **13** scandalmonger **17** conversationalist

talk nonsense 6 babble, drivel, ramble

Talk of the Town, The
    director: **13** George Stevens
    cast: **9** Cary Grant **10** Jean Arthur **12** Ronald Colman **13** Edgar Buchanan, Glenda Farrell

talk out of 4 balk **6** thwart **8** dissuade **10** discourage

talk over 6 confer, review **7** consult, discuss, hash out

Talk-show hosts 5 Leeza **7** Jay Leno, Geraldo **8** Cristina **9** Ricki Lake **10** Jenny Jones **11** Phil Donahue, Conan O'Brian, Arsenio Hall, Maury Povich **12** Johnny Carson, Oprah Winfrey **13** Rosie O'Donnell, Jerry Springer **14** David Letterman, Montel Williams, Regis & Kathy Lee **17** Sally Jessy Raphael

talk to 7 address, lecture, speak to **12** converse with

talk together 4 talk **6** confer **7** discuss **8** converse **9** discourse

tall 3 big **4** high **5** lanky, lofty, rangy **6** absurd **7** soaring, stringy **8** elevated,

gangling, towering **10** incredible, long-limbed **11** embellished, exaggerated, implausible **12** preposterous, unbelievable **13** hard to believe, hard to swallow

tallow 3 fat, tip **5** taper **6** bougie, candle, cierge **9** rushlight

Tall State
    nickname of: **8** Illinois

tall story 3 fib, lie **4** yarn **5** fable **7** fiction, untruth, whopper **9** fairy tale, falsehood, fish story, invention **11** fabrication **16** cock-and-bull story

tally 3 add, sum **4** jibe, list, mark, poll, post **5** agree, count, match, score, sum up, total **6** accord, census, concur, muster, reckon, record, square **7** catalog, compute, conform **8** coincide, mark down, register, scorepad, tabulate **9** calculate, harmonize, reckoning, scorecard **10** correspond **11** enumeration

talon 4 claw, nail, spur

Talos
    form: **5** youth **7** monster
    calling: **8** inventor
    made of: **5** brass **6** bronze
    made by: **10** Hephaestus
    guarded: **5** Crete
    destroyed by: **5** Medea
    uncle: **8** Daedalus
    killed by: **8** Daedalus
    because of: **8** jealousy

talus
    bone of: **5** ankle
    connected to: **5** tibia **6** fibula

Tamar
    father: **5** David
    mother: **6** Maacah
    husband: **2** Er **4** Onan **5** Judah, Uriah
    brother: **5** Amnon **7** Absalom, Chileab, Solomon **8** Adonijah
    son: **5** Zarah **6** Pharez
    daughter: **8** Maachiah
    father-in-law: **5** Judah

Tamburlaine the Great
    author: **18** Christopher Marlowe
    character: **6** Cosroe **7** Mycetes, Orcanes **8** Bajazeth **9** Callepine, Techelles, Zenocrate **10** Theridamas, Usumcasane

tame 4 curb, damp, dull, flat, meek, mild, rein **5** break, check, quiet, timid, train **6** boring, bridle, broken, docile, gentle, govern, manage, master, placid, pliant, serene, subdue **7** conquer, control, pliable, prosaic, repress, subdued, tedious **8** amenable, domestic, dominate, lifeless, overcome, regulate, restrain, suppress, timorous, tranquil **9** tractable **10** make docile, submissive, unexciting **11** complaisant, domesticate, unresisting **12** domesticated **13** uninteresting

tameness 8 docility **9** placidity **10** gentleness, insipidity **12** complai-

sance, tractability **13** domestication **14** submissiveness

Taming of the Shrew, The
    author: **18** William Shakespeare
    character: **6** Bianca, Gremio, Tranio **8** Baptista, Lucentio **9** Hortensio, Katharina, Petruchio, Vincentio
    director: **16** Franco Zeffirelli
    cast: **11** Michael York, Natasha Pyne **13** Richard Burton (Petruchio) **14** Michael Hordern **15** Elizabeth Taylor (Katharina), Vernon Dobtcheff
    score: **8** Nino Rota

Tammuz
    origin: **8** Sumerian
    god of: **9** shepherds
    Hebrew month: **6** fourth

Tam O'Shanter
    author: **11** Robert Burns

Tampa Bay
    football team: **7** Bandits **10** Buccaneers
    baseball team: **9** Devil Rays

tamper 3 mix **4** muck **6** butt in, fiddle, horn in, meddle, tinker **7** intrude, obtrude **9** interfere, intervene **10** fool around, mess around **12** monkey around

tamper with 5 alter **6** change, doctor **7** falsify

tan 4 roan **5** beige, brown, khaki, sandy, tawny **6** bronze, sorrel, suntan **7** bronzed **8** brownish, cinnamon, sunburnt **9** sunburned, suntanned **10** light brown **11** yellow-brown

Tanah Airkita see **9** Indonesia

Tan, Amy
    author of: **14** The Joy Luck Club **18** The Kitchen God's Wife **22** The Hundred Secret Senses

Tananarive, Antananarivo
    capital of: **10** Madagascar

Tanaquil
    origin: **5** Roman
    form: **5** queen
    husband: **7** Tarquin **17** Tarquinius Priscus

Tandy, Jessica
    born: **6** London **7** England
    husband: **10** Hume Cronyn **11** Jack Hawkins
    roles: **8** The Birds **10** The Gin Game **12** Forever Amber **16** Driving Miss Daisy (Oscar) **21** A Streetcar Named Desire

tang 3 bit **4** bite, hint, odor, reek **5** aroma, punch, savor, scent, smack, smell, sting, tinge, touch, trace **6** flavor **8** acridity, piquancy, pungency, tartness **9** acridness, sharpness, spiciness **10** suggestion

Tange, Kenzo
    architect of: **11** Press Center (Kofu) **16** Shizuoka Building (Tokyo) **19** Olympic Sports Stadia (Tokyo) **24** Kagawa Prefectural Offices (Takama-

tsu) **30** Imabara Municipal Office Building

tangibility 11 materiality, palpability **12** touchability

tangible 4 real **5** solid **6** actual **7** obvious **8** clear-cut, concrete, manifest, material, palpable, physical, positive **9** corporeal, touchable **10** verifiable **11** indubitable, substantial

tangle 3 fix, net, web **4** knot, maze, mesh, muss **5** ravel, skein, snarl, twist **6** jumble, jungle, ruffle, rumple, tousle **7** impasse, network **8** dishevel, disorder **9** labyrinth **10** disarrange

tangled 6 knotty **7** chaotic, complex, jumbled, mixed-up, snarled **11** complicated, intertwined

Tanguy, Yves
 born: 5 Paris **6** France
 artwork: 4 Fear **17** Mama Papa is Wounded, Untitled Landscape **18** Rose of the Four Winds **20** Slowly Toward the North **22** Four O'Clock in Summer Hope, Indefinite Divisibility **23** Multiplication of the Arcs **25** Extinction of Useless Lights

tank 3 vat **6** boiler **7** cistern **8** aquarium, fish tank **9** container, reservoir **10** armored car, receptacle **11** storage tank

Tannhauser and the Tournament of Song at Wartburg
 opera by: 6 Wagner
 also: 41 Tannhauser und der Sangerkrieg auf dem Wartburg
 character: 5 Venus **7** Wolfram **9** Elizabeth

Tanoan
 tribe: 4 Tuei **5** Kiowa **6** Isleta

tantalize 4 bait **5** charm, taunt, tease, tempt **6** entice, lead on **7** bewitch, provoke, torment **8** intrigue **9** captivate, fascinate, titillate **15** whet the appetite **18** make one's mouth water

tantalizing 7 teasing **8** inviting, tempting **9** appealing, leading on **10** intriguing **11** fascinating

Tantalus
 king of: 4 Pisa **7** Phrygia
 father: 8 Thyestes
 wife: 12 Clytemnestra
 son: 6 Pelops
 daughter: 5 Niobe
 punishment in Hades: 6 hunger, thirst

tantamount 4 like **5** equal **9** analogous **10** comparable, equivalent, on a par with **12** commensurate **13** commensurable

tantrum 3 fit **5** storm **7** flare-up, rampage **8** outburst, paroxysm **9** explosion **12** fit of passion **13** burst of temper, conniption fit

Tanzania
 other name: 12 isle of cloves
 capital/largest city: 11 Dar es Salaam
 new capital: 6 Dodoma

others: 4 Wete, **5** Kilwa, Lindi, Moshi, Tanga, Ujiji **6** Arusha, Kigoma, Mwadui, Mwanza, Tabora **7** Korogwe, Mtwara **8** Morogoro, Zanzibar **12** Kwasemangube, Zanzibar Town
 division: 8 Zanzibar **17** union of Tanganyika
 monetary unit: 4 cent **8** shilling
 weight: 8 farsalah
 island: 5 Mafia, Pemba **6** Latham **8** Zanzibar
 lake: 5 Eyasi, Nyasa, Rukwa **6** Malawi, Natron, Nyassa **7** Manyara **8** Victoria **10** Tanganyika
 mountain: 4 Kibo, Mero **8** Usambara
 highest point: 11 Kilimanjaro
 river: 4 Lupa, Ruvu, Wami **5** Ruaha **6** Kagera, Luwegu, Mbaesa, Rufiji, Rungwa, Ruvuma **7** Nkululu, Pangani **8** Mbenkuru **11** Mbarangandu
 sea: 6 Indian
 physical feature:
  crater: 10 Ngorongoro
  gorge: 7 Olduvai
  national park: 9 Serengeti
  plains: 9 Serengeti
  steppe: 5 Masai **8** Iwembere
  valley: 9 Great Rift
 people: 2 Ha **4** Arab, Gogo, Goma, Haya, Hehe **5** Asian, Bantu, Masai **6** Arusha, Chagga, Sukuma, Wagogo, Wagoma **7** African, Makonde, Sambara, Sandawe, Shirazi, Swahili, Wabunga, Zongora **8** Nyakyusa, Nyamwezi
  early man: 13 zinjanthropus
  explorer: 6 Da Gama **7** Rebmann **11** Livingstone
  leader: 5 Sayid **6** Karume **7** Nyerere **16** Sultan of Zanzibar
  language: 5 Bantu **6** Arabic **7** English, Khoisan, Nilotic, Swahili **8** Cushitic, Gujarati
 religion: 5 Islam **7** animism **12** Christianity
 feature:
  animal: 6 dik-dik
  cattle barn: 4 byre
  clothing: 4 sari **6** bui bui
  fly: 6 tsetse
  holiday: 8 Saba Saba
  homestead: 8 manyatta
 food:
  dish: 5 ugali

Tao Te Ching
 author: 6 Lao-tzu

Taotieh
 origin: 7 Chinese
 form: 6 animal

tap 3 pat, rap, use **4** cock, drum, peck, thud **5** spout, touch, valve **6** broach, employ, faucet, hammer, spigot, stroke, uncork, unplug **7** draw off, exploit, utilize **8** draw upon, stopcock **9** put to work, unstopper

taper 3 dip, wax **4** wick **5** light **6** candle, cierge, narrow **8** decrease **9** nar-

rowing **10** diminution **12** come to a point

taper off 4 wane **5** abate **6** weaken **7** slacken, subside **8** decrease, diminish, fade away, slack off

tapestry 3 rug **5** arras, tapis **6** Bruges, fabric, mosaic **7** Gobelin, hanging, montage, weaving **8** Aubusson **12** wallcovering

Tapley, Mark
 character in: 16 Martin Chuzzlewit
 author: 7 Dickens

Tappertit, Simon
 character in: 12 Barnaby Rudge
 author: 7 Dickens

Taprobane see **8** Sri Lanka

taproom 3 bar, pub **6** lounge, saloon, tavern **8** alehouse **11** bar and grill, public house **14** cocktail lounge

Taras Bulba
 author: 12 Nikolai Gogol
 character: 5 Ostap **6** Andrii, Yankel **26** Daughter of the Polish Waiwode

Tarascans, Tarascos
 location: 6 Mexico **9** Michoacan **14** Central America
 leader: 8 Zincicha **9** Tangaxoan, Tariacuri

Tarawa
 capital of: 8 Kiribati

Tar Baby
 author: 12 Toni Morrison

Tarchetius
 king of: 9 Alba Longa

tardy 4 late, slow **5** slack **6** remiss **7** belated, languid, overdue **8** crawling, creeping, dilatory, slowpoke, sluggish **9** leisurely, not on time, reluctant, slow-paced, snail-like **10** behindhand, behind time, unpunctual **14** slow as molasses **15** procrastinating

tare 12 Biblical weed **15** weight deduction

target 3 aim, end **4** butt, dupe, goal, goat, gull, mark, plan, prey **5** design, intent, object, pigeon, victim **7** purpose **8** ambition **9** intention, objective **13** laughingstock

Targitaus
 father: 4 Zeus
 first inhabitant of: 7 Scythia

Tar Heel State
 nickname of: 13 North Carolina

tariff 3 fee **4** cost, duty, fare, levy, rate, rent **5** price **6** charge, excise, impost **7** expense **8** input tax **9** excise tax, export tax **10** assessment, commission, freightage

Tarkington, Booth
 author of: 6 Penrod **9** Seventeen **10** Alice Adams **13** Kate Fennigate **14** The Man from Home **17** Monsieur Beaucaire **19** The World Does Not Move **23** The Magnificent Ambersons

Tarleton, Stuart and Brent

characters in: 15 Gone With the Wind
author: 8 Mitchell

tarnish 3 dim **4** blot, dull, foul, soil, spot **5** dirty, erode, stain, sully, taint **6** befoul, darken, defame, defile, smirch, vilify **7** blacken, blemish, corrode, degrade, oxidize **8** besmirch, discolor, disgrace, dishonor **9** denigrate, discredit **10** lose luster, stigmatize **17** drag through the mud

tarnished 5 dirty **6** soiled **7** stained, sullied **8** oxidized **10** discolored

Tarnkappe
origin: 8 Germanic
mentioned in: 14 Nibelungenlied
form: 5 cloak
gives wearer: 8 strength **12** invisibility
stolen by: 9 Siegfried
stolen from: 8 Niblungs **9** Nibelungs

tarot
Italian: 6 naibes **7** attutti **8** tarocchi
German: 5 tarok
French: 5 tarau, tarot
cards/deck: 12 seventy-eight
division: 11 major arcana, minor arcana **12** lesser arcana **13** greater arcana
suit: 3 cup **4** coin, wand **5** baton, money, sword **6** cudgel **8** pentacle
face card: 4 king, page **5** knave, queen, valet **6** knight
major arcana: 4 Fool, Moon **5** Death **7** Justice **8** Judgment **9** Hanged Man **14** Wheel of Fortune

tarpaulin 4 tarp **6** canvas **9** dropcloth **15** waterproof cover

Tarpeia
form: 12 vestal virgin
father: 15 Spurius Tarpeius
betrayed: 4 Rome
betrayed to: 7 Sabines
killed by: 7 Sabines

Tarquin
king of: 4 Rome
origin: 8 Etruscan
also called: 17 Tarquinius Priscus **18** Tarquinius Superbus
wife: 8 Tanaquil

tarragon
botanical name: 20 Artemisia dracunculus
means: 6 dragon **12** little dragon
Arab: 7 tarkhum
French: 8 estragon
origin: 7 Siberia
used as: 8 purifier
flavor: 8 licorice
use: 4 fish **5** salad, sauce **10** mayonnaise **14** Bearnaise sauce

tarry 3 lag **4** bide, rest, stay, wait **5** abide, dally, delay, pause, stall **6** dawdle, linger, put off, remain **7** be tardy **8** hang back, postpone, stave off, take time **9** temporize **10** hang

around **13** cool one's heels, procrastinate

tarsal
bone of: 5 ankle

tart 3 pie **4** acid, sour **5** acerb, acrid, sharp, spicy, tangy **6** acetic, barbed, biting, bitter, crusty **7** caustic, cutting, piquant, pungent, sourish **8** vinegary **10** astringent **11** pastry shell

tartan
fabric: 6 woolen
pattern: 5 plaid
identifies: 4 clan
in: 8 Scotland **9** Highlands
skirt: 4 kilt
trousers: 5 trews

Tartarean *see* **8** infernal

Tartarin of Tarascon
author: 14 Alphonse Daudet

Tartarus
form: 5 abyss
below: 5 Hades
imprisoned: 6 Titans

tartness 7 acidity, sarcasm **8** acerbity **9** sharpness **11** astringency

Tartuffe
author: 7 Moliere
character: 5 Damis, Orgon **6** Dorine, Elmire, Valere **7** Cleante, Mariane **14** Madame Pernelle

Tarzan
author: 18 Edgar Rice Burroughs
character: 3 Boy **4** Jane **7** Cheetah
Tarzan also called: 15 Lord of Greystoke, Lord of the Jungle
comic strip creator: 9 Hal Foster **12** Burme Hogarth
played by: 6 Ron Ely **9** Lex Barker **11** Elmo Lincoln **12** Buster Crabbe **17** Johnny Weissmuller

task 3 job **4** duty, work **5** chore, labor, stint **6** charge, errand **7** mission **8** business **10** assignment **11** undertaking **14** responsibility

Task, The
author: 13 William Cowper

taskmaster 4 boss **6** despot, master, tyrant **7** foreman, headman, manager **8** director, martinet, overseer, stickler **10** supervisor **11** Simon Legree, slave driver **14** disciplinarian, superintendent

Tasmania
bay: 5 Storm **6** Oyster
capital: 6 Hobart
city: 10 Launceston
country: 9 Australia
formerly: 14 Van Diemen's Land
island: 4 Echo **6** Sorell
mountain: 4 Ossa **6** Cradle
river: 3 Esk
strait: 4 Bass
birthplace of: 10 Errol Flynn

Tasso, Torquato
author of: 6 Aminta **7** Rinaldo **18** Jerusalem Delivered

taste 3 bit, nip, sip, try, yen **4** bent, bite, feel, meet, tang, test, whim **5** crumb, enjoy, fancy, savor, smack **6** desire, flavor, hunger, liking, morsel, relish, sample, thirst **7** craving, decorum, discern, forkful, insight, leaning, longing, savor of, smack of, swallow, undergo **8** appetite, delicacy, fondness, judgment, mouthful, penchant, piquancy, spoonful, yearning **9** encounter, hankering, partake of, propriety **10** experience, partiality, propensity, take a sip of **11** correctness, discernment, disposition, inclination, take a bite of **12** eat a little of, predilection **14** discrimination, drink a little of
French: 4 gout

tasteful 7 elegant, refined **8** artistic, becoming, cultured, esthetic, handsome, suitable **9** beautiful, exquisite **10** attractive, well-chosen

tasteless 3 low **4** flat, mild, rude, weak **5** bland, cheap, crass, crude, gaudy, gross, tacky **6** coarse, common, flashy, garish, ribald, watery **7** insipid, uncouth **8** improper, indecent, unseemly **9** inelegant, offensive, unrefined **10** disgusting, flavorless, indecorous, indelicate, uncultured, unesthetic, unflavored, unsuitable **11** distasteful, insensitive

tastemakers 7 leaders **10** avant-garde, innovators **12** stylesetters, trendsetters

tasty 3 hot **5** spicy, tangy, yummy **6** savory **7** piquant, zestful **8** luscious **9** delicious, flavorful, palatable, toothsome **10** appetizing, delectable, flavorsome **11** good-tasting, scrumptious **12** full-flavored, well-seasoned

Tatar, Mr
character in: 22 The Mystery of Edwin Drood
author: 7 Dickens

Tatius
also: 5 Titus
co-ruler with: 7 Romulus

Tatler, The
author: 13 Joseph Addison, Richard Steele

tattered 4 torn **6** broken, ragged, ripped, shabby, shaggy **10** disheveled **11** dilapidated

tatters 4 rags **6** shreds **7** patches

tattle 3 rat **4** blab **5** prate **6** gabble, gossip, snitch, squeal, tell on **7** blather, chatter, hearsay, prattle, twaddle **8** inform on **9** loose talk **11** mudslinging **12** tittle-tattle **13** tonguewagging

tattletale 3 rat **4** fink **5** sneak **6** gossip, snitch **7** ratfink, stoolie, tattler **8** betrayer, busybody, informer, squealer, telltale **8** informer **10** newsmonger, talebearer **11** rumormonger, stool pigeon **12** blabbermouth, troublemaker **13** scandalmonger

Tatum, Edward Lawrie
 field: 8 genetics **12** biochemistry
 discovered: 19 gene characteristics
 awarded: 10 Nobel Prize
taunt 3 guy, rag **4** gibe, jeer, jive, mock, slur, twit **5** scoff, sneer, tease **6** deride, harass, insult, jeer at **7** provoke, ragging, sneer at, snigger, torment **8** chaffing, derision, ridicule **9** make fun of, poke fun at, snigger at **10** harassment, make game of, tormenting **11** provocation
Taura
 form: 3 cow
 attribute: 6 sacred
taurobolium
 rite of: 7 baptism
Taurog, Norman
 director of: 6 Skippy (Oscar) **8** Boys Town
Taurus
 symbol: 4 bull
 planet: 5 Venus
 rules: 5 money **9** resources
 born: 3 May **5** April
taut 4 neat, snug, tidy, trig, trim **5** rigid, smart, tense, tight **6** spruce **7** orderly **8** not loose, not slack **9** shipshape, unbending, unrelaxed **10** drawn tight, inflexible, no-nonsense **11** under strain **12** businesslike **13** well-regulated **15** well-disciplined
tavern 3 bar, pub **4** dive **6** bistro, saloon **7** barroom, gin mill, taproom **8** alehouse, drinkery, grogshop **9** beer joint, brasserie, honky-tonk, roadhouse **10** restaurant **11** public house **12** watering hole **14** cocktail lounge
 French: 7 auberge
 German: 8 Brauhaus
tawdry 4 loud **5** cheap, crass, gaudy, showy, tacky **6** flashy, garish, tinsel, vulgar **7** raffish **8** gimcrack **9** inelegant, obtrusive, tasteless **10** flamboyant **11** conspicuous, pretentious **12** meretricious, ostentatious
tawny 3 tan **4** fawn **5** beige, dusky, olive, sandy **6** bronze **7** swarthy **8** brownish **10** light brown **14** yellowish-brown
tax 3 sap, try **4** duty, lade, levy, load, tire, toll **5** drain, weigh **6** assess, burden, charge, custom, excise, impost, saddle, strain, tariff, weight **7** deplete, exhaust, stretch, wear out **8** exertion, overwork **10** assessment, obligation, overburden
 kind: 4 city **5** sales, state **6** county, excise, income, luxury **8** property **11** inheritance **12** excess profit
Taxi
 character: 9 John Burns, Tony Banta **10** Alex Rieger **11** Elaine Nardo, Latka Gravas **12** Bobby Wheeler, Louie De Palma
 cast: 9 Carol Kane, Tony Danza **10** Judd Hirsch **11** Andy Kaufman,

Danny DeVito, Jeff Conaway **12** Marilu Henner **13** Randall Carver
 company: 11 Sunshine Cab
taxicab 4 hack **6** jitney **7** droshky, hackney **8** hired car, rickshaw **10** automobile **11** jinrickshaw
Taxi Driver
 director: 14 Martin Scorsese
 cast: 10 Peter Boyle **11** Jodie Foster **12** Albert Brooks, Harvey Keitel, Robert De Niro **13** Leonard Harris **14** Cybill Shepherd
 setting: 11 New York City
 score: 15 Bernard Herrmann
 script: 12 Paul Schrader
taxon 5 class, genus, order **6** family, phylum **7** kingdom, species
taxonomy
 study of: 17 structure contrast **19** structure comparison
Taylor, Elizabeth
 born: 6 London **7** England
 husband: 8 Mike Todd **10** John Warner **11** Eddie Fisher, Nicky Hilton **13** Richard Burton **14** Michael Wilding
 roles: 5 Giant **7** Ivanhoe **9** Cleopatra **11** Little Women **12** The Sandpiper **14** A Place in the Sun, National Velvet, Raintree County **16** Butterfield Eight (Oscar), Cat on a Hot Tin Roof, Father of the Bride **18** Suddenly Last Summer **19** The Taming of the Shrew **25** Who's Afraid of Virginia Woolf (Oscar)
Taylor, Robert
 real name: 22 Spangler Arlington Brugh
 wife: 12 Ursula Thiess **15** Barbara Stanwyck
 roles: 7 Camille, Ivanhoe **8** Quo Vadis **11** Billy the Kid **14** Waterloo Bridge **20** Magnificent Obsession
Taylor, Zachary
 nickname: 16 Old Rough and Ready
 presidential rank: 7 twelfth
 party: 4 Whig
 state represented: 2 LA
 defeated: 4 (Lewis) Cass **8** (Martin) Van Buren
 vice president: 8 (Millard) Fillmore
 cabinet:
  state: 7 (John Middleton) Clayton
  treasury: 8 (William Morris) Meredith
  war: 8 (George Walker) Crawford
  attorney general: 7 (Reverdy) Johnson
  navy: 7 (William Ballard) Preston
  postmaster general: 8 (Jacob) Collamer
  interior: 5 (Thomas) Ewing
 born: 12 Montebello VA **12** Orange County
 died: 12 Washington DC
 buried: 12 Louisville KY
 education: 9 no college **16** privately

tutored
 religion: 12 Episcopalian
 political career: 21 none prior to presidency
 civilian career: 7 planter, soldier
 military service: 6 US Army **12** major general
  War: 7 Mexican **9** Black Hawk **19** War of Eighteen-Twelve **14** Second Seminole
 notable events of lifetime/ presidency:
  treaty: 13 Clayton-Bulwer
 father: 7 Richard
 mother: 5 Sarah (Dabney Strother)
 siblings: 6 George **7** Hancock **11** Sarah Bailey **12** Elizabeth Lee, Emily Richard **13** Joseph Pannill **21** William Dabney Strother
 wife: 8 Margaret (Mackall Smith)
 children: 7 Richard **9** Sarah Knox **10** Ann Mackall **13** Margaret Smith, Mary Elizabeth, Octavia Panill
Tchad *see* **4** Chad
Tchaikovsky, Peter (Piotr Ilyich Chaikovsky)
 born: 6 Russia **8** Votkinsk
 composer of: 7 Manfred, Mazeppa **8** Iolanthe, Pathetic (symphony No 6), Swan Lake **9** Joan of Arc **10** Nutcracker **12** Eugene Onegin, Winter Dreams **14** Italian Caprice, Romeo and Juliet, The Enchantress **16** The Queen of Spades **17** Francesca da Rimini, The Sleeping Beauty **22** Eighteen-Twelve Overture
tea 16 Camellia sinensis
 varieties: 4 chai **5** Assam, Bohea, China, green, pekoe **6** Ceylon, Oolong, Oswego, Tisane **7** African, Arabian, cambric, crystal, Lapsang, Mexican, redroot, Spanish **8** bergamot, camomile, Earl Grey, Labrador, mountain, Paraguay, Siberian, Souchong, Woodruff **9** gunpowder, lemon balm, New Jersey, sassafras **10** Darjeeling, Philippine **11** Appalachian, Orange Pekoe **14** Irish breakfast **16** English breakfast
teach 5 coach, drill, edify, prime, tutor **6** inform, school **7** educate, implant, prepare **8** exercise, instruct **9** enlighten, inculcate **10** discipline **12** indoctrinate
Teach
 character in: 21 The Master of Ballantrae
 author: 9 Stevenson
teacher 3 don **5** coach, tutor **6** master, mentor **7** maestro, trainer **8** educator **9** preceptor, professor **10** instructor, schoolmarm **12** schoolmaster **13** schoolteacher **14** schoolmistress
teaching 5 dogma, tenet **6** belief **7** nurture, precept **8** doctrine, pedagogy, training, tutelage, tutoring **9** education, principle, schooling **10** convic-

tion, philosophy **11** inculcation, instructing, instruction, preparation **14** indoctrination

tea dance
    French: **10** the dansant

teal
    group of: **5** ducks
    color: **4** blue **5** green

team 3 rig, set **4** ally, band, crew, five, gang, join, nine, pair, side, unit, yoke **5** force, group, merge, party, squad, staff, unify, unite **6** circle, clique, couple, eleven, league, tandem **7** combine, company, coterie, faction **8** alliance, federate **9** coalition, cooperate **10** amalgamate, federation, sports team, yoked group **11** association, consolidate, get together, incorporate **12** band together, join together **13** confederation

teammate 4 ally **7** partner **8** coplayer, coworker **9** associate, colleague, co-partner **11** confederate **12** collaborator

team spirit 10 group pride, solidarity **13** esprit de corps

team up 4 ally **5** unite **9** cooperate **10** join forces **11** collaborate

tear 3 fly, gap, hie, rip, run **4** bolt, dart, dash, grab, hole, mist, pull, race, rend, rent, rift, rive, rush, scud, slit, snag, swim, whiz, yank **5** abuse, break, crack, fault, pluck, scoot, seize, sever, shoot, shred, speed, split, spurt, sweep, whisk **6** breach, cleave, damage, divide, gallop, hasten, hustle, injury, plunge, ravage, scurry, snatch, sprint, sunder, wrench **7** disrupt, fissure, hard use, opening, rupture, scamper, scuttle **8** disunite, teardrop, scramble, splinter **9** come apart, hotfoot it, pull apart, skedaddle **10** impairment, make tracks **11** destruction **12** pull to pieces

tear down 4 raze **5** level, smash, wreck **7** destroy, flatten **8** demolish **9** dismantle, take apart

tearful 5 teary, weepy **6** crying **7** bawling, crushed, sobbing, wailing, weeping **8** mournful **9** lamenting, sniveling **10** blubbering, lachrymose, whimpering **11** heartbroken **12** inconsolable **13** brokenhearted

tear off 5 sever **6** detach, rip off **7** pull off **8** break off, separate **10** wrench away

Teasdale, Sara
    author of: **8** Love Song **11** Helen of Troy **13** Dark of the Moon **14** Flame and Shadow, Rivers to the Sea, Strange Victory

tease 3 guy, irk, nag, rag, vex **4** bait, gall, gibe, goad, haze, jeer, josh, mock, pest, rile, twit **5** annoy, chafe, harry, mimic, pique, scoff, sneer, taunt, worry **6** bad- ger, bother, harass, hazing, heckle, hector, mocker,

needle, pester, plague, teaser **7** bedevil, chafing, laugh at, needler, provoke, razzing, snigger, taunter, torment, worrier **8** derision, heckling, irritate, needling, ridicule **9** aggravate, make fun of, mimicking, persecute, tantalize, tormentor **10** harassment, tantalizer **11** persecution

teaspoon
    abbreviation: **3** tsp

Teazle, Sir Peter and Lady
    characters in: **19** The School for Scandal
    author: **8** Sheridan

technical 5 trade **10** mechanical, vocational **11** complicated, nonacademic **13** technological

technique 3 art, way **4** form **5** craft, knack, style **6** manner, method, system **7** formula, know-how **8** approach, facility **9** procedure **10** adroitness, expertness, technology **11** proficiency **12** skillfulness

tedious 3 dry **4** drab, dull, long, slow **5** vapid **6** boring, dismal, dreary, jejune, tiring **7** humdrum, insipid, irksome, onerous, prosaic **8** drawn-out, lifeless, tiresome, wearying **9** fatiguing, laborious, wearisome **10** burdensome, exhausting, monotonous, oppressive, unexciting **13** time-consuming, unimaginative, uninteresting

tediousness 5 ennui **7** boredom **8** dullness, monotony

tedium 3 rut **5** ennui **7** boredom **8** drabness, dullness, monotony, sameness **10** dreariness **11** routineness **12** tiresomeness

tedium of life
    Latin: **12** taedium vitae

teem 4 brim, gush **5** swarm **6** abound **8** be full of, overflow **9** be overrun **15** burst at the seams

teeming 4 full **7** crowded **8** swarming **9** abounding, bounteous **11** overflowing

teeny-weeny 3 wee **4** tiny **5** dwarf **6** little, minute, petite **9** miniature, minuscule **10** diminutive, pocket-size **11** lilliputian, microscopic, pocket-sized

teeter 4 reel, sway **5** lurch, waver **6** seesaw, totter, wobble **7** stagger **8** hesitate **9** vacillate

teetotaler 3 dry **9** abstainer **10** nondrinker **14** prohibitionist

Tegucigalpa
    capital of: **8** Honduras

Tegyrius
    king of: **6** Thrace

Tehani
    character in: **17** Mutiny on the Bounty
    authors: **4** Hall **8** Nordhoff

Tehran, Teheran
    capital of: **4** Iran

    landmark: **10** Melaat Park **12** Marble Palace, Marmar Palace **14** Azadai Monument, Gulestan Palace, Saadabad Palace **15** Freedom Monument, Hosseineh Mosque, Shahyad Monument **23** Center for Islamic Studies
    means: **9** warm place
    mountain: **6** Elburz **8** Demavend
    ruler: **8** Khomeini **23** Muhammad Reza Shah Pahlavi

Telamon
    king of: **7** Salamis
    member of: **9** Argonauts
    father: **6** Aeacus
    mother: **6** Endeis
    brother: **6** Peleus
    half-brother: **6** Phocus
    wife: **6** Glauce **7** Eriboea
    son: **4** Ajax **6** Teucer
    friend: **8** Hercules

Telegonus
    father: **7** Proteus **8** Odysseus
    mother: **5** Circe
    wife: **2** Io **8** Penelope
    killed: **8** Odysseus
    killed by: **8** Hercules

telegraph
    invented by: **5** Morse, Woods **6** Edison **7** Marconi

Telemachus
    father: **8** Odysseus
    mother: **8** Penelope
    son: **7** Latinus

Telemann, Georg Philipp
    born: **7** Germany **9** Magdeburg
    composer of: **9** Fantasias **10** Times of Day **12** Don Quichotte **14** Die Tageszeiten, Musique de Table

Telemus
    vocation: **4** seer
    father: **7** Eurymus
    warned: **10** Polyphemus

telepathy 3 ESP **10** sixth sense **11** second sight **12** clairvoyance **19** spirit communication, thought transference **22** extrasensory perception

telephone
    invented by: **4** Bell
    type: **3** cell, pay, TDD **6** mobile, rotary **8** cellular, portable, princess, wireless **9** extension, touch-tone **10** push-button

Telephone, The
    opera by: **7** Menotti

telescope
    invented by: **7** Galileo **10** Lippershey
    astronomical: **6** Kepler

telesterion
    form: **8** building
    purpose: **8** religion **11** celebration

television
    invented by: **5** Baird **8** Zworykin **10** Farnsworth

tell 3 ask, bid, own, say, see **4** blab **5** bruit, count, order, speak, spout, state, utter, weigh, write **6** advise, babble, betray, blazon, depict, detail, direct, figure, impart, inform, number, recite, reckon, relate, report, reveal, sketch, unfold **7** apprise, command, compute, confess, declare, discern, divulge, express, find out, mention, narrate, portray, predict, publish, recount, request **8** acquaint, count off, describe, disclose, estimate, forecast, foretell, identify, instruct, perceive, register, set forth **9** apprehend, ascertain, broadcast, calculate, chronicle, enumerate, enunciate, influence, make known, pronounce, recognize **10** take effect **11** communicate, distinguish **12** discriminate **17** breathe a word about

Teller, Edward
  field: **7** physics
  developed: **8** atom bomb **12** hydrogen bomb

telling 5 solid, valid **6** cogent, potent **7** decided, weighty **8** decisive, definite, forceful, material, positive, powerful, striking **9** effective, effectual, important, momentous, trenchant **10** conclusive, definitive, impressive **11** efficacious, influential, significant **13** consequential

telltale 6 gossip **7** tattler **8** busybody, giveaway, informer, squealer **9** affirming, betraying, divulging, revealing, verifying **10** confirming, disclosing, newsbearer, talebearer, tattletale **11** informative **12** blabbermouth, enlightening **13** scandalmonger

Tellus
  called: **10** Terra Mater
  origin: **5** Roman
  goddess of: **5** earth **8** marriage **9** fertility **11** agriculture
  corresponds to: **4** Gaea

temerity 4 gall **5** brass, cheek, nerve **8** audacity, boldness, chutzpah, rashness **9** brashness, freshness, impudence, insolence, pushiness, sauciness **10** brazenness, effrontery **11** forwardness **12** impertinence, indiscretion **13** foolhardiness, intrusiveness

Temin, Howard Martin
  field: **8** genetics, oncology
  discovered: **20** reverse transcriptase
  awarded: **10** Nobel Prize

temper 3 ire **4** bile, calm, fury, gall, mood, rage **5** allay, anger, humor, pique, quiet, still, wrath **6** animus, anneal, choler, dander, harden, pacify, soften, soothe, spleen **7** appease, balance, compose, dudgeon, emotion, ferment, passion, toughen, umbrage **8** acrimony, bad humor, calmness, mitigate, moderate, palliate, vexation **9** annoyance, composure, huffiness **10** irritation, strengthen **11** displeasure, disposition, equilibrium, frame of mind, indignation, peevishness, tranquilize **12** churlishness, irascibility, irritability

temperament 4 bent, cast, mood,

soul, tone **5** humor, tenor **6** makeup, nature, spirit, temper **7** leaning, quality **8** tendency **9** character **10** complexion **11** disposition, frame of mind, personality

temperamental 5 fiery, moody **6** fickle **7** erratic, peppery, willful **8** unstable, volatile **9** emotional, excitable, explosive, hotheaded, mercurial, sensitive, turbulent **10** capricious, headstrong, high-strung, hysterical, mettlesome, passionate, unreliable **11** tempestuous, thin-skinned **12** undependable **13** unpredictable

temperance 8 prudence, sobriety **9** restraint **10** abstention, abstinence, discretion, moderation, self-denial **11** forbearance, prohibition, self-control, teetotalism **14** abstemiousness, self-discipline

temperate 4 calm, cool, even, mild, sane, soft, warm **5** balmy, sober, sunny **6** gen- tle, mellow, sedate, steady **7** clement, patient, sparing **8** composed, moderate, pleasant, rational, tranquil **9** collected, easygoing, unruffled **10** coolheaded, reasonable **11** levelheaded **13** dispassionate, self-possessed, unextravagant, unimpassioned **14** self-controlled, self-restrained

temperature measurement 6 degree, Kelvin **7** Celsius **10** Fahrenheit

tempest 5 chaos, furor, storm **6** hubbub, tumult, uproar **8** brouhaha, outbreak, upheaval **9** agitation, cataclysm, commotion **10** hurly-burly, turbulence **11** disturbance

Tempest, The
  author: **18** William Shakespeare
  character: **5** Ariel **6** Alonso **7** Antonio, Caliban, Gonzalo, Miranda **8** Prospero **9** Ferdinand, Sebastian

Tempestates
  origin: **5** Roman
  goddesses of: **6** storms

tempestuous 3 hot **5** fiery **6** raging, stormy **7** excited, frantic, furious, violent **8** agitated, feverish, frenzied **9** emotional, explosive, turbulent, wrought-up **10** hysterical, passionate, tumultuous **11** impassioned, overwrought

Templar, Simon
  character in: **8** The Saint
  author: **9** Charteris

temple 4 fane, kirk **6** chapel, church, mosque, pagoda, priory, shrine **7** convent **8** basilica, pantheon **9** cathedral, joss house, monastery, sanctuary, synagogue **10** house of God, tabernacle **12** meeting house

Temple, Shirley
  married name: **18** Shirley Temple Black
  born: **13** Santa Monica CA
  roles: **5** Heidi **10** Bright Eyes **15** Wee

Willie Winkie **16** Little Miss Marker, The Little Colonel, The Littlest Rebel **18** Poor Little Rich Girl **21** Susannah of the Mounties **23** Rebecca of Sunnybrook Farm

tempo 4 clip, gait, pace, rate, time **5** meter, speed **6** pacing, stride, timing **8** momentum, velocity

tempo giusto
  music: **10** strict time

temporal 3 lay **5** civil **6** mortal **7** mundane, passing, profane, secular, worldly **8** day-to-day, fleeting, fugitive **9** ephemeral, temporary, transient **10** evanescent, noneternal **11** impermanent, nonclerical **12** nonspiritual **17** nonecclesiastical

temporary, temporarily 5 brief, fleet **7** interim, passing, stopgap **8** fleeting, fugitive **9** ephemeral, momentary, provisory, transient **10** evanescent, short-lived, transitory **11** impermanent, provisional **13** flash-in-the-pan
  Latin: **10** pro tempore

temporary dwelling
  French: **10** pied-a-terre

temporize 5 delay, hedge, stall, tarry, waver **8** hang back, maneuver **9** hem and haw, vacillate **10** equivocate **11** play for time **12** drag one's feet, tergiversate **13** procrastinate

tempt 3 try, woo **4** bait, draw, goad, lure, pull, risk **5** charm, decoy, prick, rouse **6** allure, arouse, entice, incite, invite, seduce **7** attract, bewitch, provoke **8** appeal to, intrigue, inveigle **9** captivate, tantalize **12** put to the test **13** take one's fancy **14** fly in the face of **15** whet the appetite

temptation 4 bait, draw, lure, pull, urge **5** charm, snare, spell **8** stimulus, tempting **9** incentive, seduction **10** allurement, attraction, enticement, incitement, inducement **11** captivation, fascination, provocation

tempter 5 Satan **7** enticer, seducer **8** the Devil

temptress 4 vamp **5** Circe, flirt, siren **7** charmer, Delilah, Jezebel, Lorelei, vampire **8** coquette **9** odalisque, sorceress **10** seductress **11** enchantress, femme fatale

tempus fugit 9 time flies

Ten (10)
  director: **12** Blake Edwards
  cast: **7** Bo Derek **11** Dudley Moore **12** Julie Andrews

tenable 6 viable **8** arguable, rational, sensible, workable **9** excusable **10** condonable, defendable, defensible, vindicable **11** justifiable, warrantable **12** maintainable

tenacious 3 set **4** fast, firm, hard, iron **6** dogged, mulish **7** adamant, staunch **8** clinging, constant, obdurate, resolute, stalwart, stubborn **9** immovable, obstinate, pigheaded, steadfast, unbending **10** determined, inexorable, inflexible, persistent, relentless, unswerving, unwavering, unyielding **11** persevering, undeviating, unfaltering, unremitting **12** intransigent, unchangeable **14** uncompromising

tenaciousness 8 tenacity **9** endurance **10** resolution **11** persistence **12** perseverance, resoluteness **13** determination **16** stick-to-itiveness

tenacity 8 strength **9** toughness **10** resolution **11** persistence **12** cohesiveness, perseverance, resoluteness **13** determination, tenaciousness **16** stick-to-itiveness

tenant 6 lessee, lodger, renter, roomer **7** boarder, denizen, dweller **8** occupant, resident **10** inhabitant **11** householder, leaseholder, paying guest

Tenant of Wildfell Hall, The
  author: 10 Anne Bronte

Tenants, The
  author: 14 Bernard Malamud

Ten Commandments
  also: 9 Decalogue
  given to: 5 Moses
  where given: 10 Mount Sinai
  inscribed on: 12 stone tablets
  first: 32 Thou shalt have no other Gods before me
  second: 37 Thou shalt not bow down before graven images
  third: 44 Thou shalt not take the name of the Lord thy God in vain
  fourth: 34 Remember the Sabbath Day and keep it holy
  fifth: 26 Honor thy father and thy mother
  sixth: 16 Thou shalt not kill
  seventh: 26 Thou shalt not commit adultery
  eighth: 17 Thou shalt not steal
  ninth: 46 Thou shalt not bear false witness against thy neighbor
  tenth: 17 Thou shalt not covet

Ten Commandments, The
  director: 13 Cecil B DeMille
  cast: 8 Nina Foch **9** John Derek **10** Anne Baxter, Debra Paget, Yul Brynner **11** Martha Scott **12** Vincent Price **13** John Carradine, Yvonne De Carlo **14** Charlton Heston (Moses), Judith Anderson **15** Cedric Hardwicke, Edward G Robinson

tend 3 aim **4** bear, head, lead, lean, mind, move **5** be apt, guide, nurse, point, watch **6** extend, foster, manage, wait on **7** care for, nurture **8** attend to, be liable, be likely **9** bid fair to, gravitate, look after, supervise, watch over **10** minister to, predispose, take care of **11** keep an eye on

tendency 3 aim, set **4** bent **5** drift, drive, habit, trend **6** course **7** heading, impulse, leaning, turning **8** penchant **9** direction, proneness, readi-

ness **10** proclivity, propensity **11** disposition, gravitation, inclination **14** predisposition

tender 3 raw **4** fond, give, good, kind, soft, sore, weak **5** frail, green, place, young **6** aching, benign, callow, caring, dainty, extend, feeble, gentle, hand in, loving, prefer, submit, weakly **7** advance, fragile, hold out, painful, present, proffer, propose, suggest, swollen **8** delicate, generous, immature, inflamed, juvenile, merciful, propound, underage, youthful **9** lay before, sensitive, volunteer **10** benevolent, put forward, thoughtful, vulnerable **11** considerate, sentimental, softhearted, sympathetic, warmhearted **12** affectionate **13** compassionate, inexperienced, understanding **14** impressionable **15** unsophisticated

tenderfoot 4 tyro **6** novice, rookie **8** beginner, neophyte **9** fledgling, greenhorn **10** apprentice

tenderhearted 4 mild **6** benign, gentle, humane **8** generous, merciful **10** altruistic, benevolent, responsive, thoughtful **11** considerate, kindhearted, softhearted, sympathetic, warmhearted **13** compassionate, understanding

tenderheartedness 4 pity **5** heart **7** empathy **8** sympathy **10** compassion

tendering 6 giving **8** offering **9** advancing, extending, proposing **10** holding out, preferring, proffering, submitting, suggesting **11** propounding **12** volunteering

Tender Is the Night
  author: 16 F Scott Fitzgerald
  character: 8 Abe North **9** Dick Diver **11** Nicole Diver, Tommy Barban **12** Rosemary Hoyt

tenderness 4 love **6** aching, warmth **7** rawness **8** delicacy, fondness, goodness, humanity, kindness, mildness, smarting, softness, soreness, sympathy **9** affection **10** compassion, gentleness, humaneness, kindliness, lovingness **11** beneficence, benevolence, painfulness, sensitivity **12** mercifulness **14** loving kindness

tendon 4 cord **5** sinew
  connects: 4 bone **6** muscle

tendril 4 coil, curl **5** crook, shoot, sprig, twist **6** winder **7** climber, ringlet

tenebrous 3 dim **4** dark **5** murky **6** gloomy **7** obscure, shadowy **8** darkened, obscured **13** unilluminated

tenet 4 rule, view **5** canon, credo, creed, dogma, maxim **6** belief, thesis **7** opinion **8** doctrine, ideology, position, teaching **9** principle **10** conviction, persuasion

Tennessee
  abbreviation: 2 TN **4** Tenn
  nickname: 7 Big Bend **9** Volunteer **11**

Old Franklin
  capital: 9 Nashville
  largest city: 7 Memphis
  others: 5 Alcoa, Paris **6** Camden, Sparta **7** Bristol, Dickson, Pulaski **8** Franklin, Gallatin, Oak Ridge **9** Cedar Hill, Cleveland, Inglewood, Kingsport, Knoxville, Lexington **10** Greenbrier, Morristown, Old Hickory **11** Chattanooga, Clarksville, Springfield **12** Fayetteville, Murfreesboro **14** Hendersonville
  college: 4 Fisk, Lane **5** Bryan, Siena **6** Bethel **7** Belmont, Lambuth, Lemoyne **8** Milligan, Tusculum **10** Vanderbilt **12** Southwestern **13** David Lipscomb **14** Meharry Medical **17** Tennessee Wesleyan
  feature: 12 The Hermitage
    dam: 6 Norris, Wilson **7** Douglas
    fort: 5 Henry **8** Donalson, Nashboro
    national park: 6 Shiloh **13** Cumberland Gap **19** Great Smoky Mountains (with North Carolina)
    national parkway: 12 Natchez Trace
  tribe: 7 Shawnee **8** Cherokee **9** Chickasaw
  people: 7 Sequoya **8** John Bell **9** James Agee **10** Grace Moore **11** Bessie Smith, Cordell Hull **12** Davy Crockett **18** Carey Estes Kefauver **23** Alvin Cullum "Sergeant" York **32** Ernest Jennings "Tennessee Ernie" Ford
    explorer: 6 Arthur, De Soto **7** Jolliet, La Salle, Needham **9** Marquette
  lake: 7 Douglas **8** Barkeley, Cherokee, Reelfoot, Watts Bar **10** Center Hill **11** Chickamauga
  land rank: 12 thirty-fourth
  mountain: 5 Guyot **7** Lookout, Smokies **9** Blue Ridge **10** Cumberland, Great Smoky
    highest point: 13 Clingman's Dome
  physical feature:
    basin: 9 Nashville
    highlands: 11 Appalachian
    plain: 7 Coastal
    plateau: 10 Cumberland
  president: 10 James K Polk **13** Andrew Jackson, Andrew Johnson
  river: 3 Elk **4** Duck **5** Caney, Obion, Stone **6** Clinch **7** Hatchie, Holston **8** Hiwassee **9** Tennessee **10** Cumberland **11** French Broad, Mississippi **15** Little Tennessee
  state admission: 9 sixteenth
  state bird: 11 mockingbird
  state flower: 4 flag, iris **6** maypop **13** passion flower
  state motto: 16 America at Its Best **22** Agriculture and Commerce
  state song: 11 My Tennessee **17** The Tennessee Waltz **19** My Homeland

Tennessee **26** When It's Iris Time in Tennessee

state tree: 11 tulip poplar **12** yellow poplar

tennis

athlete: 8 Don Budge, Jan Kodes, Rod Laver, Tom Okker **9** Bjorn Borg, Ivan Lendl, Stan Smith **10** Arthur Ashe, Bill Tilden, Jack Kramer, Maria Bueno, Pam Shriver, Roy Emerson, Steffi Graf **11** Alice Marble, Andre Agassi, Boris Becker, Edward Dibbs, Ilie Nastase, John McEnroe, Ken Rosewall, Monica Seles, Pete Sampras, Tracy Austin **12** Althea Gibson, Darren Cahill, Francois Durr, Jimmy Connors, John Newcombe, Mats Wilander, Roscoe Tanner, Virginia Wade **13** Dennis Ralston, Harold Solomon, Manuel Orantes, Manuel Santana, Martina Hingis, Martin Riessen, Wendy Turnbull **14** Brian Gottfried, Guillermo Vilas, Hana Mandlikova, Pancho Gonzalez, Rosemary Casals **15** Charles Pasarell, Chris Evert Lloyd, Maureen Connolly, Richard Stockton, Vitas Gerulaitis **17** Donald Schollander, Nancy Richey Gunter **18** Margaret Smith Court, Martina Navratilova **20** Helen Wills Moody Roark **21** Billie Jean Moffitt King, Evonne Goolagong Cawley

cup: 5 Davis

Tennyson, Alfred, Lord

author of: 4 Maud **7** Mariana, Ulysses **10** Enoch Arden, In Memoriam (A H H) **12** Locksley Hall, Morte d'Arthur **16** The Lady of Shalott **18** The Idylls of the King **26** The Charge of the Light Brigade

tenor 4 gist **5** drift, sense, trend **6** course, import, intent, nature, object **7** content, essence, meaning, purport, purpose **8** argument, tendency **9** direction, intention, substance **11** connotation, implication **12** significance

tense 4 taut **5** brace, drawn, rigid, shaky, stiff, tight **6** braced, draw up, on edge, uneasy **7** anxious, excited, fearful, fidgety, jittery, nervous, restive, stiffen, uptight **8** agitated, make taut, restless, strained, timorous **9** tighten up, tremulous, wrought-up **10** high-strung, inflexible, unyielding **12** apprehensive

tension 5 dread **6** spring, strain, stress **7** anxiety, pulling, tugging **8** bad vibes, exertion, pressure, rigidity, tautness, traction **9** hostility, misgiving, stiffness, straining, tightness **10** stretching **11** fearfulness, nervousness, restiveness, trepidation **12** apprehension, elastic force, perturbation **13** bad vibrations, combativeness

tent 3 pup **4** care, hard **5** gauze, probe, tepee **6** bigtop, canvas, search, teepee, wigwam **7** shelter **8** pavilion **10** tabernacle

tentacle 3 arm **6** feeler **9** appendage

tentative 4 iffy **5** trial **6** acting **8** not final, proposed **9** ad interim, temporary, undecided, unsettled **10** contingent, indefinite, not settled **11** conditional, probational, provisional, speculative, unconfirmed **12** experimental, probationary **15** subject to change **18** under consideration

tentative procedure 4 test **5** flier, trail **6** feeler, tryout **7** venture **10** experiment **12** trial balloon

tenuous 4 slim, thin, weak **5** frail, shaky **6** flimsy, paltry, slight **7** fragile, shallow, slender **8** delicate, gossamer **9** uncertain **10** indefinite **11** halfhearted, unsupported **12** unconvincing **13** unsubstantial

tenure 4 rule, term, time **5** reign **7** tenancy **9** occupancy, retention **10** incumbency, occupation, permanency, possession **11** entitlement, job security **14** administration

tepee, teepee 4 chum, tent **5** lodge **6** wigwam **7** wickiup

tepid 4 cool, mild **7** languid, warmish **8** lukewarm, moderate **9** apathetic, impassive, temperate **10** nonchalant, phlegmatic **11** halfhearted, indifferent, unemotional **13** lackadaisical **14** unenthusiastic

tequila

type: 6 spirit

origin: 6 Mexico

made from: 5 agave **6** maguey

used with: 4 lime, salt **5** lemon

drink: 7 Chapala **8** El Diablo

with creme de cacao: 8 Toreador

with kahlua: 9 Brave Bull

with orange juice: 7 Sunrise

with Tia Maria: 9 Brave Bull

with triple sec: 9 Margarita

Teraphim

origin: 6 Hebrew

form: 4 idol

Ter Borch, Gerard

born: 6 Zwolle **14** The Netherlands

artwork: 8 Flea Hunt **10** The Concert **14** Peace of Munster **21** The Parental Admonition

Terbrugghen, Hendrick

born: 8 Deventer **14** The Netherlands

artwork: 14 The Flute Player **19** Liberation of St Peter **21** The Calling of St Matthew

Tereshkova, Valentina

first: 12 woman in space

terete 7 tapered **11** cylindrical

tergal 4 back **6** dorsal

Terkel, Studs

author of: 4 Race **7** Working **9** Hard Times **10** "The Good War" **14** American Dreams

term, terms 3 age, dub, era, tag **4** call, cite, item, name, span, time, word **5** catch, cycle, epoch, idiom,

reign, spell, stage, state, style, while **6** clause, course, detail, period, phrase, status, string **7** dynasty, footing, proviso **8** duration, interval, position, standing **9** condition, designate, provision, relations, requisite **10** expression, span of time **11** appellation, designation, requirement, stipulation **12** characterize, circumstance, prerequisite **14** administration

termagant 3 nag **4** fury **5** scold, shrew, vixen **6** ogress, virago **7** hellcat, hellion, she-wolf, tigress **8** battle-ax, fishwife, harridan, spitfire **9** Xanthippe

Termagant

character in: 21 medieval morality plays

terminal 3 end **4** last **5** depot, fatal, final, stand **6** deadly, lethal, mortal **7** station **8** terminus **10** concluding

terminate 3 end **4** stop **5** cease, close, lapse **6** expire, finish, run out, wind up **8** complete, conclude **11** come to an end, discontinue **12** bring to an end

termination 3 end **4** halt **5** close, finis, lapse **6** ending, finale, finish, windup **7** closing **8** stoppage **9** cessation **10** completion, concluding, conclusion, expiration **15** discontinuation

terminus 3 end **4** stop **5** depot, limit **6** ending **7** extreme, station **8** boundary, last stop, terminal **9** extremity **10** conclusion

Terminus

origin: 5 Roman

god of: 9 landmarks **10** boundaries

terminus ad quem 10 end to which, final limit **11** ending point

terminus a quo 9 beginning **12** end from which **13** starting point

termite

variety: 6 desert **7** dry wood **8** damp wood **10** powderpost, rotten wood **11** soldierless **12** subterranean

Terms of Endearment

director: 12 James L Brooks

based on novel by: 13 Larry McMurtry

cast: 11 Debra Winger **13** Jack Nicholson **15** Shirley MacLaine

Oscar for: 7 actress (MacLaine), picture **8** director **15** supporting actor (Nicholson)

Terpsichore

member of: 5 Muses

personifies: 7 dancing **10** choral song

Terra

goddess of: 5 Earth

Greek: 4 Gaea

mother: 5 Chaos

offspring: 6 Pontus, Titans, Uranus **7** Erinyes, Oceanus **8** Cyclopes **9** mountains **13** Hecatonchires

terrace 4 roof **5** level, patio, plane, porch **6** street **7** balcony, plateau **9**

esplanade, promenade **10** embankment

Terraced Bay *see* **6** Taiwan

terra-cotta 4 clay **6** russet **8** brownish **12** reddish-brown **14** brownish-orange

terrain 4 area, zone **5** tract **6** ground, milieu, region **7** setting **8** district **9** territory **10** topography **11** countryside, environment **12** surroundings

terra incognita 11 unknown land **14** unexplored land, unknown subject **16** unknown territory

terrapin 3 box **4** emyd, emys **6** slider, turpin, turtle **8** tortoise **11** diamond back
  family: 8 Emydidae
  female: 6 heifer
  male: 4 bull

terrestrial 4 land **6** earth's, global, ground **7** earthly, mundane, worldly **8** riparian **10** earthbound

terrible 3 bad **4** dire, huge **5** awful, great, harsh, rough, scary **6** brutal, fierce, horrid, odious, severe, strong **7** beastly, extreme, fearful, ghastly, hateful, heinous, hideous, intense **8** alarming, dreadful, enormous, fearsome, horrible, shocking, terrific **9** appalling, excessive, harrowing, monstrous, obnoxious, offensive, repulsive, revolting, upsetting **10** disturbing, formidable, horrifying, immoderate, inordinate, terrifying, tremendous, unpleasant **11** distasteful, distressing, frightening, intolerable **12** insufferable **13** objectionable

terrier
  dog breed: 3 fox **4** bull, Skye **5** Cairn, Irish, Welsh **6** border, Boston **7** Norfolk, Tibetan, wire fox **8** Airedale, Lakeland, Scottish, Sealyham **9** Kerry Blue **10** Australian, Bedlington, Manchester **13** Dandie Dinmont **17** soft-coated wheaten, Staffordshire bull, West Highland white **18** miniature schnauzer **21** American Staffordshire

terrific 3 fab **4** fine, good, huge **5** awful, great, harsh, marvy, scary, super **6** bang-up, fierce, severe, superb **7** extreme, fearful, intense, sensash **8** alarming, dreadful, enormous, fabulous, fearsome, smashing, splendid, terrible **9** excellent, excessive, fantastic, harrowing, marvelous, monstrous, upsetting, wonderful **10** disturbing, horrifying, immoderate, inordinate, remarkable, stupendous, superduper, terrifying, tremendous **11** distressing, exceptional, frightening, sensational **13** extraordinary **14** out of this world

terrified 6 afraid, scared **7** alarmed, panicky **9** petrified **10** frightened **11** scared stiff **13** panic-stricken **14** terror-stricken **17** frightened to death

terrify 3 cow **5** abash, alarm, daunt, panic, scare, unman, upset **6** appall,

dismay **7** agitate, disturb, horrify, overawe, petrify **8** disquiet, frighten **10** intimidate **17** make one's skin crawl **20** make one's blood run cold **22** make one's hair stand on end

terrifying 5 awful, dread **7** fearful **8** alarming, dreadful **9** frightful **11** frightening, hair-raising

territory 4 area, land, pale, zone **5** clime, realm, state, tract **6** bounds, colony, domain, empire, limits, locale, nation, region, sector **7** acreage, kingdom, mandate, terrain **8** confines, district, dominion, province **9** bailiwick **10** dependency **11** countryside **12** commonwealth, principality, protectorate

terror 3 awe **4** fear **5** alarm, dread, panic **6** dismay, fright, horror **7** anxiety **8** affright, disquiet **9** agitation **11** disquietude, trepidation **12** apprehension, perturbation **13** consternation **16** fear and trembling

terrorize 3 cow **5** abash, force **6** menace **7** terrify **8** browbeat, bulldoze, threaten **10** intimidate

terror-stricken 6 afraid, scared **7** alarmed, panicky **9** horrified, petrified, terrified **11** scared green, scared stiff **13** panic-stricken, scared to death

Terry and the Pirates
  creator: 12 Milton Caniff
  character: 7 Pat Ryan **8** Terry Lee **10** Dragon Lady

terse 4 curt, neat **5** brief, clear, crisp, pithy, short **6** abrupt **7** clipped, compact, concise, laconic, pointed, summary **8** clearcut, incisive, succinct **9** axiomatic, condensed, trenchant **10** compressed **11** unambiguous **12** epigrammatic **18** brief and to the point

terseness 7 brevity **8** curtness **9** crispness **10** abruptness **11** compactness, conciseness **12** succinctness

Tesman family
  characters in: 11 Hedda Gabler
  members: 5 Hedda **6** George **7** Juliana
  author: 5 Ibsen

Tess (of the D'Urbervilles)
  author: 11 Thomas Hardy
  director: 13 Roman Polanski
  cast: 8 John Bett **10** Peter Firth, Tom Chadbon **14** Rosemary Martin **15** Nastassia Kinski (Tess)

test 4 exam, quiz **5** check, final, flyer, probe, proof, prove, trial **6** dry run, feeler, try out, verify **7** analyze, confirm, examine, midterm **8** analysis, validate **9** catechism **11** corroborate, examination, investigate, questioning **12** confirmation, substantiate, verification **13** comprehensive, corroboration, investigation, questionnaire

Testament 5 Bible **7** the Book **10** Scriptures **12** New Testament, Old Testament

testament 6 legacy **7** bequest **10** settlement

tester 6 canopy **8** examiner **10** questioner

testify 4 show **5** prove, swear **6** affirm, attest, evince **7** declare, signify **8** evidence, indicate, manifest **11** bear witness, demonstrate **12** give evidence

testimonial 5 medal **6** ribbon, trophy **7** tribute **8** citation, memorial, monument **9** affidavit, reference **10** deposition **11** certificate, endorsement **12** commendation **14** recommendation

testimony 5 proof **6** avowal **7** witness **8** averment, evidence **9** affidavit, statement **10** deposition, indication, profession **11** affirmation, attestation, endorsement **12** confirmation, verification **13** certification, corroboration, demonstration, documentation, manifestation **14** acknowledgment

testy 5 cross, moody **6** crabby, cranky, crusty, filthy, grumpy, snappy, sullen, touchy **7** fretful, peevish, waspish **8** captious, caviling, choleric, churlish, perverse, petulant, snappish, snarling **9** fractious, impatient, irascible, irritable, splenetic **10** ill-humored **11** acrimonious, contentious **12** cantankerous, faultfinding, sharp-tongued **13** quick-tempered, temperamental

tete-a-tete 4 chat, talk **6** parley **9** interview **12** conversation **13** confabulation

tether 3 tie **4** cord, rein, rope **5** chain, leash **6** fasten, halter, hobble, secure

Tethys
  member of: 6 Titans
  father: 6 Uranus
  mother: 4 Gaea
  husband: 7 Oceanus
  mother of: 8 Oceanids **9** river gods
  daughters: 13 three thousand
  foster child: 4 Hera

Tetragrammaton
  consonants in: 10 name for God **4** JHVH, IHVH, JHWH, YHVH, YHWH

Teutonic 5 Dutch **6** German, Gothic, Nordic **7** British, English **8** Germanic **12** Scandinavian
  alphabet character: 4 rune
  demon: 3 alp
  goddess of death: 3 Hel, Ran
  goddess of peace: 7 Nerthus
  god of peace: 6 Balder
  god of thunder: 4 Thor
  god of war: 3 Tiu, Tyr
  god of wisdom: 4 Odin

Teutonic Mythology *see* **17** Germanic Mythology

Texas
  abbreviation: 2 TX **3** Tex
  nickname: 8 Lone Star
  capital: 6 Austin
  largest city: 7 Houston
  others: 4 Gail, Rice, Vega, Waco **5** Bryan, Marfa, Ozona, Pampa, Tyler,

Wiley **6** Baylor, Borger, Dallas, Denton, El Paso, Kileen, Laredo, Odessa, Quanah, Sonora **7** Abilene, Denison, Lubbock **8** Amarillo, Beaumont, Floydada **9** Fort Worth, Galveston **10** San Antonio **13** Corpus Christi
college: **3** SMU, TCU **4** Rice **5** Lamar, Wiley **6** Austin, Baylor **7** St Mary's, Trinity **10** Texas A and M **12** Southwestern **14** Texas Christian **16** Abilene Christian **17** Southern Methodist
feature:
  fort: **5** Alamo
  national park: **7** Big Bend **18** Guadalupe Mountains
  national seashore: **11** Padre Island
  state park: **10** San Jacinto
tribe: **4** Adar, Waco **5** Caddo, Lipan **6** Apache, Biloxi, Jumano, Kichai, Shuman, Tejano **7** Alabama, Hasinai, Tonkawa **8** Comanche, Querecho **9** Coushatta, Karankawa
people: **10** James S Hogg **12** Edward M House, Thomas C Clark **13** John B Connally, Samuel Houston **14** Chester W Nimitz, Mirabeau B Lamar, Samuel T Rayburn, Stephen F Austin, William B Travis **15** John Nance Garner, Thomas T Connally **19** Katherine Anne Porter
explorer: **4** Vaca **7** La Salle
island: **5** Padre
lake: **6** Falcon, Sabine, Texoma **7** Amistad
river: **3** Red **5** Pecos **6** Brazos, Neches, Nueces, Sabine **7** Trinity **8** Colorado **9** Rio Grande **10** San Jacinto
land rank: **12** second
physical feature:
  bay: **13** Corpus Christi
  port: **7** Houston **9** Galveston **13** Corpus Christi
president: **14** Lyndon B Johnson **17** Dwight D Eisenhower
  Republic of Texas: **10** Sam Houston
state admission: **12** twenty-eighth
state bird: **11** mockingbird
state flower: **10** bluebonnet, yellow rose
state motto: **10** Friendship
state song: **13** Texas Our Texas
state tree: **5** pecan
baseball team: **7** Rangers
text 5 motif, theme, topic, verse, words **6** manual, primer, sermon, thesis **7** content, passage, subject, wording **8** argument, sentence, textbook, workbook **9** paragraph, quotation **10** schoolbook **13** subject matter
textile 4 yarn **5** cloth, fiber **6** fabric **8** filament, material **9** yard goods **10** piece goods
texture 3 nap **4** feel, look **5** grain, touch, weave **6** makeup **7** quality, surface **8** fineness **9** character, structure **10** coarseness **11** composition

Tey, Josephine

real name: **19** Elizabeth MacKintosh
author of: **10** Brat Farrar **15** Miss Pym Disposes, The Singing Sands **17** The Daughter of Time **19** A Shilling for Candles
character: **9** Alan Grant

Thackeray, William Makepeace
author of: **9** Pendennis **10** Vanity Fair **11** Barry Lyndon, Henry Esmond, The Newcomes **13** The Virginians

Thaddeus of Arimathea see **5** Judas

Thai-Austronesian
language branch: **9** Thai-Kadai **12** Austronesian
includes: **5** Batak, Malay **6** Fijian, Samoan **7** Tagalog **8** Hawaiian, Javanese **15** Bahasa Indonesia
spoken in: **4** Fiji, Java **5** China, Samoa **6** Hawaii, Taiwan **7** Sumatra **9** Indonesia, Polynesia **10** Madagascar **11** Philippines **12** Easter Island

Thailand
name means: **13** land of the free
other name: **4** Siam **11** Prathet Thai
capital/largest city: **6** Bankok **7** Bangkok
  old capital: **8** Thonburi **9** Ayutthaya
  others: **4** Ubon **5** Puket **6** Nakhon, Ranong **7** Ayudhya, Ayuthea, Lampang, Lamphur, Lopburi, Rahaeng, Singora, Songkla **8** Khonkaen, Kiangmai, Songkhla, Sukhotai, Thonburi **9** Ayutthaya, Chiangmai, Chiengmai **10** Ratchasima **11** Phitsanulok **14** Ubonratchthani
kingdom: **5** Funan **6** Khymer **8** Thonburi **9** Ayutthaya, Chiang Mai, Dvaravati, Sukhothai **12** Subarnabhumi
school: **9** Thammasat **13** Chulalongkorn
head of state: **4** king
measure: **2** wa **3** can, ken, niv, rai, sat, sok, wah **4** cohi, keup, niou, tang **5** kwien, leeng, sesti, vouah **6** kabiet, kanahn **7** chaimeu **8** changawn **9** anukabiet
monetary unit: **2** at **3** att **4** baht **5** cutty, fuang **6** pynung, salung **11** bullet money
weight: **3** bat, hap, pay, sen, sok **4** baht, haph, kati, klam **5** catty, chang, fuang, picul, pilul, tical **6** fluang, graini, salung, **7** tamlung
island: **2** Ko **3** Kut, Tao **4** Chan, Rawi **5** Chang, Lanta, Samui, Thalu **6** Libong, Phuket **7** Phangan, Terutao
lake: **9** Nong Lahan
mountain: **5** Dawna, Khieo **6** Phanom **8** Dang Raek, Kao Prawa, Maelamun **9** Khao Luang **11** Bilauktaung
highest point: **8** Inthanon **11** Doi Inthanon
river: **3** Chi, Mun, Nan, Yom **4** Ping **5** Menam **6** Mekong, Meping **7** Sal-

ween **10** Chaophraya
sea: **7** Andaman
physical feature:
  gulf: **4** Siam **8** Thailand
  isthmus: **3** Kra
  pass: **12** Three Pagodas
  peninsula: **5** Malay
  plateau: **5** Korat **6** Khorat
people: **3** Lao, Mon **4** Lawa, Shan, Thai **5** Malay **6** Indian, Khymer **7** Chinese, Siamese **9** Cambodian **10** Vietnamese
king: **4** Rama **7** Chakkri, Mongkut **10** Chao Phraya **12** Prahjadhipok **13** Chulalongkorn **17** Bhumibol Adulyadej
leader: **9** Phraruang **12** Kukrit-Pramoj
language: **3** Lao, Tai **4** Ahom, Shan, Thai **5** Kadai, Malay **7** Bangkok, Chinese, English **9** Krung Thep
religion: **5** Islam **8** Buddhism **12** Christianity, Confucianism **17** Theravada Buddhism
place:
  dam: **8** Bhumibol
  palace: **5** Grand
  ruins: **7** Ayuthia **9** Ayutthaya
  street: **7** Yawarai
  temple: **4** Dawn **7** Trimitr **10** Wat Phra Keo **11** Royal Chapel **13** Emerald Buddha
feature:
  canal: **5** klong
  clothing: **6** panung, sarong **12** saffron robes
  festival: **12** Surin Round Up
  houseboat: **6** sampan
  temple: **3** wat
  tree: **4** teak
food:
  fruit: **5** camut **6** durian, litchi, pomelo **8** rambutan **10** mangosteen

Thais
author: **13** Anatole France
character: **8** Athanael
composer: **8** Massenet

Thalassa
personifies: **3** sea

thalassic 6 marine **7** aquatic, deep-sea, neritic, oceanic, pelagic

Thales
field: **11** mathematics
nationality: **5** Greek
discovered: **18** geometry principles
predicted: **11** sun's eclipse

Thalestris
character in: **16** The Rape of the Lock
author: **4** Pope

Thalia
member of: **5** Muses **6** Graces
personifies: **6** comedy **13** idyllic poetry
lover: **4** Zeus
killed by: **5** Erato

Thallo

member of: 5 Horae
goddess of: 13 spring flowers

Thamyris
vocation: 4 poet 8 musician
father: 9 Philammon
mother: 7 Argiope
punished for: 9 arrogance
punished by: 5 Muses
punishment: 7 maiming 8 blinding

thanatophobia
fear of: 5 death

Thanatos
personifies: 5 death

thank 5 bless 12 be grateful to 13 be much obliged 18 express gratitude to

thankful 7 obliged 8 beholden, grateful 10 indebted to 12 appreciative, full of thanks 16 feeling gratitude 22 expressing appreciation

thankfulness 6 thanks 9 gratitude 12 appreciation, gratefulness

thankless 4 vain 7 ingrate, useless 8 bootless, caviling, critical, heedless 9 fruitless, unmindful, unwelcome 10 profitless, ungracious, ungrateful, uninviting, unpleasant, unrewarded, unthankful 11 distasteful, thoughtless, undesirable, unrewarding 12 disagreeable, faultfinding 13 inconsiderate, unappreciated 14 unacknowledged, unappreciative

thanks 5 grace 8 blessing 9 gratitude 11 benediction 12 appreciation, gratefulness

thanks be to God
Latin: 10 Deo gratias

thanksgiving 6 thanks 8 blessing

Thanksgiving
started by: 8 Bradford, Pilgrims
traditional food: 4 corn, yams 6 turkey 10 pumpkin pie 13 sweet potatoes 14 cranberry sauce
symbol: 9 ear of corn 12 horn of plenty

thank you
French: 5 merci
German: 5 danke
Spanish: 7 gracias
Italian: 6 grazie
Japanese: 4 domo

Thank You, Jeeves
author: 11 P G Wodehouse

thank you very much
French: 9 merci bien 13 merci beaucoup
German: 10 danke schon
Japanese: 11 domo arigato
Spanish: 13 muchas gracias

That Certain Feeling
author: 12 Kingsley Amis

Thatcher, Becky
character in: 9 Tom Sawyer
author: 5 Twain

Thatcher, Judge
character in: 15 (The Adventures of)

Huckleberry Finn
author: 5 Twain

That Girl
character: 8 Ann Marie, Lou Marie 10 Helen Marie, Ruth Bauman 11 Jerry Bauman 12 Don Hollinger, Judy Bessemer 14 Dr Leon Bessemer
cast: 9 Lew Parker 10 Ted Bessell 11 Alice Borden, Bonnie Scott, Marlo Thomas 12 Bernie Kopell 13 Dabney Coleman 14 Carolyn Daniels, Rosemary DeCamp

that is
Latin: 2 ie 5 id est

that is to say
Latin: 3 viz 9 videlicet

that's life
French: 9 c'est la vie

thaw 4 melt, warm 5 relax 6 soften, unbend, warm up 7 liquefy, melting, thawing 8 dissolve 11 break the ice

Thea
companion of: 7 Artemis
ravished by: 6 Aeolus
changed into: 4 mare
mare named: 6 Euippe

Theale, Milly
character in: 17 The Wings of the Dove
author: 5 James

theater 4 site 5 arena, drama, house, movie, odeum, place, scene, stage 6 cinema, lyceum 7 gallery, setting 8 assembly, audience, coliseum 9 colosseum, music hall, playhouse 10 assemblage, auditorium, movie house, spectators 11 histrionics, lecture hall, theatricals 12 amphitheater, show business

theatrical 4 film 5 hammy, movie, showy, stage, stagy 6 flashy 7 fustian, show-biz, stilted 8 affected, dramatic, mannered, thespian 9 grandiose, unnatural 10 artificial, histrionic 11 exaggerated, extravagant, pretentious, spectacular 12 magniloquent, ostentatious, show-business 13 entertainment, grandiloquent 14 larger-than-life

theatrical trick
French: 13 coup de theatre

Thebaid
author: 7 Statius
character: 4 Atys 5 Creon 6 Ismene, Tydeus 7 Jocasta, Theseus 8 Antigone, Capaneus, Eteocles, Opheltes, Tiresias 9 Menoeceus, Polynices 10 Amphiaraus, Hippomedon, Melanippus

the bottle 5 booze, drink, sauce 6 liquor 7 alcohol 8 demon rum

the dansant 8 tea dance

thee therefore
Latin: 8 te igitur

theft 5 fraud 7 larceny, looting, robbery 8 burglary, filching, rustling,

stealing, thievery 9 hijacking, pilfering, swindling 10 purloining 11 shoplifting 12 embezzlement
god of: 6 Hermes 7 Mercury

Theia
also: 4 Thia
member of: 6 Titans
father: 6 Uranus
mother: 4 Gaea
brother: 8 Hyperion
mother of: 8 Cercopes
son: 6 Helios
daughter: 3 Eos 6 Selene

the life of the land is maintained by righteousness
Hawaiian: 52 ua mau ke ea o ka aina i ka pono
motto of: 6 Hawaii

Them
author: 15 Joyce Carol Oates

theme 3 air 4 song, text, tune 5 essay, focus, motif, point, topic, tract 6 melody, report, review, strain, thesis 7 keynote, premise, subject 8 argument, critique, question, treatise 9 discourse, leitmotif, monograph 10 commentary 11 composition, proposition 12 dissertation

Then Again, Maybe I Won't
author: 9 Judy Blume

thence 6 whence 9 from there, therefore 11 accordingly, in due course 13 from that place

the next world 6 Heaven 8 eternity, paradise 12 the hereafter 14 the world to come

the norm 7 the mean, the rule 9 the median 10 the average 14 the common thing

the Occident 7 the West 20 the western hemisphere

theologian see 22 philosopher/ theologian

theological 4 holy 6 sacred 8 Biblical, dogmatic 9 apostolic, canonical, doctrinal, religious, spiritual 10 scriptural 14 ecclesiastical

theology 5 dogma 8 divinity, doctrine, religion

Theophane
bore: 3 ram
fleece of ram: 6 golden

theoretical 8 abstract, academic, putative 11 conjectural, postulatory, speculative 12 hypothetical, nonpractical 13 suppositional

theorize 5 infer, posit, think 6 assume 7 imagine, presume, propose, suppose, surmise 8 propound 9 formulate, postulate, predicate, speculate 10 conjecture 11 hypothecate, hypothesize

theory 3 law 4 idea, view 5 guess 6 belief, notion, thesis 7 concept, opinion, science, surmise, thought 8 doctrine, ideology, judgment 9 deduction, postulate, principle **10** conclusion, conjecture, hypothesis, persuasion, philosophy **11** presumption, speculation, supposition

therapeutic, therapeutical 7 healing **8** curative, remedial, salutary, sanative **11** restorative **12** ameliorative

therapy 7 healing **9** treatment **14** rehabilitation

thereafter 5 later **9** after that, afterward **10** afterwards, from then on **11** thenceforth **12** subsequently **14** from that time on

therefore 2 so **4** ergo, thus **5** hence **11** accordingly **12** consequently, on that ground **13** for that reason, in consequence, on that account **14** for which reason

there is no disputing about tastes
    Latin: **27** de gustibus non est disputandum

there it is
    French: **5** voila

Therese Raquin
    author: **9** Emile Zola
    character: **7** Camille, Laurent

There Shall Be No Night
    author: **15** Robert E Sherwood

thereupon 4 then **6** at once **7** thereon **8** directly, suddenly, upon that **9** forthwith, in a moment, upon which **11** immediately **12** straightaway, without delay

thermometer
    invented by: **7** Galileo, Reaumur
    mercury: **10** Fahrenheit

Thero
    nurse of: **4** Ares

theropod
    type of: **8** dinosaur
    member: **10** Allosaurus, Antrodemus **11** Coelophysis, Gorgosaurus **13** Albertosaurus, Compsognathus, Struthiomimus, Tyrannosaurus

Theroux, Paul
    author of: **9** Saint Jack **16** The Mosquito Coast **20** Riding the Iron Rooster **21** The Great Railway Bazaar **23** The Old Patagonian Express

Thersites
    mentioned in: **5** Iliad
    origin: **5** Greek
    characteristics: **4** ugly **8** deformed **11** quarrelsome
    accused Agamemnon of: **5** greed
    accused Achilles of: **9** cowardice
    fought in: **9** Trojan War
    killed by: **8** Achilles

the same as 4 like **7** equal to **9** a match for **12** comparable to, equivalent to, tantamount to **16** commensurate with

thesaurus 8 synonymy **10** word finder **11** synonymicon **12** word treasury **13** synonym finder **17** synonym dictionary **18** semantic dictionary

Thescelosaurus
    type: **8** dinosaur **10** ornithopod
    location: **6** Canada **12** United States
    period: **10** Cretaceous

These Three
    director: **12** William Wyler
    based on play by: **14** Lillian Hellman (The Children's Hour)
    cast: **10** Alma Kruger, Joel McCrea **11** Merle Oberon **13** Miriam Hopkins **15** Bonita Granville, Catherine Doucet

Theseus
    king of: **6** Athens
    father: **6** Aegeus **8** Poseidon
    mother: **6** Aethra
    wife: **7** Phaedra
    consort: **9** Hippolyta
    lover: **7** Ariadne
    son: **6** Acamas **8** Demophon **10** Hippolytus, Melanippus
    helmsman: **10** Nausithous
    killed: **5** Sinis **6** Sciron **8** Minotaur **10** Cretan bull, Procrustes

thesis 5 essay, paper, tract **6** notion, theory **7** article, concept, surmise **8** argument, critique, proposal, treatise **9** discourse, monograph, postulate, term paper **10** commentary, conjecture, hypothesis **11** composition, proposition, speculation, supposition **12** disquisition, dissertation

Thesmia
    epithet of: **7** Demeter
    means: **12** goddess of law

Thesmophorus
    epithet of: **7** Demeter
    means: **8** lawgiver

thespian 3 ham **4** star **5** actor, extra **6** co-star, player, walk-on **7** actress, ingenue, trouper **8** juvenile **9** bit-player, guest star, performer, tragedian **10** leading man **11** leading lady, stage player

Thespis 9 Greek poet
    originator of: **12** Greek tragedy

Thessalus
    king of: **8** Thessaly
    father: **5** Jason **8** Hercules
    mother: **5** Medea **9** Chalciope

the state
    Latin: **10** res publica

Thetis
    member of: **7** Nereids
    husband: **6** Peleus
    sister: **8** Eurynome
    son: **8** Achilles

the very words
    Latin: **14** ipsissima verba

the world over 10 every place, everywhere, far and wide, near and far **11** in all places

They Shoot Horses, Don't They?
    director: **13** Sydney Pollack
    cast: **8** Gig Young **9** Bruce Dern, Jane Fonda **10** Red Buttons **12** Susannah York **13** Bonnie Bedelia **15** Michael Sarrazin

Oscar for: **15** supporting actor (Young)

They Won't Forget
    director: **11** Mervyn LeRoy
    cast: **10** Lana Turner, Otto Kruger **11** Allyn Joslyn, Claude Rains **12** Elisha Cook Jr **13** Gloria Dickson

thiasus
    also: **7** thiasos
    group worshipping: **11** patron deity
    followers of: **8** Dionysus
        followers called: **6** satyrs **7** maenads

thick 3 big, fat **4** deep, dull, dumb, slow, wide **5** broad, bulky, close, dense, fuzzy, great, heavy, husky, piled, solid **6** chummy, heaped, hoarse, lavish, obtuse, packed, strong, stupid, viscid, wooden **7** blurred, clotted, compact, copious, crowded, decided, devoted, doltish, extreme, intense, liberal, muffled, profuse, teeming, throaty, viscous **8** abundant, familiar, friendly, generous, guttural, intimate, profound, sisterly, swarming **9** brotherly, condensed, fatheaded, glutinous, plenteous, unstinted **10** coagulated, dull-witted, gelatinous, indistinct, munificent, pronounced, slow-witted **11** inseparable, overflowing **12** concentrated, impenetrable, inarticulate

thicken 3 set **4** cake, clot, jell **5** muddy **6** darken, deepen, muddle **7** compact, congeal, jellify **8** condense **9** coagulate, intensify **10** gelatinize

thicket 4 bush, wood **5** brake, brush, copse, grove, scrub **6** bushes, covert, forest, shrubs **7** bracken **9** shrubbery **10** underbrush **11** undergrowth

thickheaded 4 dull, dumb, slow **5** blank, dense, dopey, thick **6** obtuse, stupid **8** ignorant **9** dim-witted, fatheaded **10** boneheaded, dull-witted, half-witted, slow-witted **11** blockheaded, thick-witted **12** dunderheaded, thick-skulled **13** chuckleheaded, knuckleheaded

thickset 5 bulky, close, dense, dumpy, husky, solid, squat, stout, tubby **6** chunky, packed, stocky, stubby, stumpy, sturdy **8** close-set, heavyset, roly-poly

thickskinned 4 hard **5** horny, tough **6** inured **7** callous **8** callused, hardened **9** unfeeling, unmovable **10** impervious, insensible **11** insensitive, unconcerned **13** imperturbable, unsusceptible **14** pachydermatous

thick-skulled 4 dull **5** dense **6** stupid **11** thickheaded **12** dunderheaded

thick-witted 4 dull, slow **5** dense **6** stupid **7** idiotic, moronic **9** dim-witted, imbecilic **11** thickheaded **12** dunderheaded, simple-minded

thief 5 crook **6** bandit, mugger, robber **7** burglar, filcher, rustler **8** hijacker, pilferer, swindler **9** defrauder, embezzler, holdup man, larcenist, purloiner, racketeer **10** highwayman, pickpocket, shoplifter **12** housebreaker, kleptomaniac **13** confidence man, pursesnatcher **14** second-story man

Thief of Bagdad, The
director: **9** Tim Whelan **12** Ludwig Berger **13** Michael Powell
cast: **4** Sabu **9** Rex Ingram **10** John Justin, June Duprez **11** Conrad Veidt

Thieves' Carnival
also: **15** Le Bal des Voleurs
author: **11** Jean Anouilh

thievish 3 sly **6** sneaky **7** furtive **8** stealthy, thieving **9** dishonest, larcenous, secretive, thieflike **13** lightfingered, surreptitious **14** stickyfingered

thigh 3 ham, leg **4** hock **5** femur, flank, ilium **6** gammon
pain: **8** meralgia

Thimbu, Thimphu
capital of: **6** Bhutan

thin 4 fine, lank, lean, slim, weak **5** faint, gaunt, lanky, prune, runny, scant, sheer, spare, water **6** dilute, feeble, narrow, not fat, reduce, skinny, slight, sparse, watery **7** curtail, diluted, fragile, scrawny, slender, spindly **8** delicate, diminish, finespun **9** emaciated, water down **10** inadequate, threadlike **11** transparent **12** insufficient **13** unsubstantial

thin-blooded 3 wan **4** pale, weak **6** anemic, sickly

thing, things 3 act **4** deed, feat, gear, item **5** event, gizmo, goods, point **6** action, affair, aspect, detail, dingus, entity, gadget, matter, object, person **7** article, clothes, concern, effects, feature, thought **8** business, clothing, creature, movables **9** doohickey, equipment, happening, statement **10** belongings, human being, occurrence, particular, proceeding **11** eventuality, living being, possessions, thingamabob, thingamajig, transaction **12** circumstance **13** paraphernalia

Thing
legislative body of: **11** Scandinavia

thing already done
French: **12** fait accompli

thingamajig 5 gizmo **6** doodad, gadget **11** contraption, contrivance, thingamabob **15** whatchamacallit

thing of no value
Latin: **5** nihil

things done
Latin: **9** res gestae

think 4 deem, mean, plan **5** brood, fancy, guess, judge **6** design, expect, intend, ponder, reason, recall, reckon **7** believe, dwell on, imagine, presume, propose, purpose, reflect, suppose, surmise **8** cogitate, conceive, conclude, contrive, meditate, mull

over, remember, ruminate **9** recollect, speculate **10** anticipate, deliberate, have in mind, keep in mind **11** contemplate, use one's mind, use one's wits **13** rack one's brain

thinkable 8 knowable **10** imaginable **11** conceivable, perceivable

think about 4 mull **6** debate, ponder **7** reflect **8** consider, mull over **10** deliberate

think alike 5 agree **11** be of one mind, see eye to eye

thinker 4 sage **6** savant, wizard **7** egghead, scholar **9** intellect **10** mastermind **11** mental giant, philosopher **13** metaphysician

Thinker, The
by: **5** Rodin

think fit 4 deem **5** deign, stoop **7** consent **10** condescend

think highly of 5 favor, honor, value **6** admire, esteem, revere **7** approve, respect **8** look up to, venerate **10** set store by

think ill of 4 hate **5** decry **6** detest **7** condemn, deplore, despise, dislike **8** object to **9** abominate, disparage, frown upon **10** disapprove **13** look askance at **14** discountenance **15** take exception to **16** find unacceptable, view with disfavor

thinking 4 view **5** smart, stand, study **6** belief, bright **7** concept, surmise, thought **8** cultured, educated, judgment, position, rational, studious **9** brainwork, deduction, inference, reasoning **10** conclusion, cultivated, impression, meditation, meditative, reflection, reflective, rumination, thoughtful **11** intelligent, speculation **12** deliberation **13** consideration, contemplation, contemplative, philosophical, sophisticated, using one's head **15** paying attention

Thinking Reed, The
author: **15** Dame Rebecca West

think over 5 study, weigh **8** cogitate, consider, mull over **11** reflect upon **12** deliberate on

think through 5 weigh **6** ponder **7** analyze **8** appraise, consider, evaluate

think up 5 frame, hatch **6** create, invent **7** concoct, dream up **8** conceive, contrive

think well of 4 like **6** admire **8** look up to **10** appreciate

Thin Man, The
author: **15** Dashiell Hammett
character: **4** Asta (pet terrier) **7** Morelli **11** Nick Charles, Nora Charles **13** Arthur Nunheim, Mimi Jorgensen **15** Herbert Macaulay **18** Christian Jorgensen
Wynant family: **5** Clyde **7** Dorothy, Gilbert
director: **11** W S Van Dyke II

cast: **4** Asta **8** Myrna Loy (Nora Charles) **13** William Powell (Nick Charles)
thin man is: **6** victim
sequel (film): **14** Another Thin Man **15** After the Thin Man **16** Song of the Thin Man **18** The Thin Man Goes Home

Thin Mountain Air, The
author: **10** Paul Horgan

thin out 5 prune **6** dilute, reduce, weaken **7** weed out **9** water down **10** adulterate

thinskinned 5 cross, huffy, sulky, testy **6** grumpy, sullen, touchy **7** crabbed, peevish **8** petulant, snappish **9** irascible, irritable, sensitive, squeamish **11** ill-tempered, quarrelsome, susceptible **12** cantankerous **13** oversensitive **14** hypersensitive

third estate
French: **9** tiers etat

Third Man, The
director: **9** Carol Reed
based on story by: **12** Graham Greene
cast: **10** Alida Valli **11** Orson Welles (Harry Lime) **12** Joseph Cotten, Trevor Howard **16** Wilfrid Hyde-White
setting: **6** Vienna

Third Wave, The
author: **12** Alvin Toffler

thirst 3 yen **4** itch, lust, pant **5** ardor, covet, crave, yearn **6** desire, fervor, hunger, relish **7** craving, passion, stomach **8** appetite, keenness, voracity, yearning **9** hanker for, hankering **11** thirstiness

thirsty 3 dry **4** avid **5** eager **7** parched **9** thirsting

Thirteen O'Clock
author: **19** Stephen Vincent Benet

Thirty-Nine Steps, The (The 39 Steps)
author: **10** John Buchan
director: **15** Alfred Hitchcock
cast: **11** Robert Donat **13** Godfrey Tearle, Lucie Mannheim, Peggy Ashcroft **16** Madeleine Carroll

This Above All
author: **10** Eric Knight

Thisbe
loved: **7** Pyramus
location: **7** Babylon
death by: **7** suicide
death at tomb of: **5** Ninus

this is
Latin: **6** hoc est

This Is Your Life
host: **12** Ralph Edwards
announcer: **9** Bob Warren

thistle 7 Cirsium
varieties: **3** Oat **4** Bull, Holy, Milk, Star **5** Glove, Plume, White **6** Canada, Cotton, Golden, Scotch, Silver

7 Blessed, St Mary's **8** Fishbone, Mountain, Plumless **9** Argentine, Thornless **10** Great globe, Small globe **11** Mountain sow **14** Acanthus-leaved
emblem of: 8 Scotland

Thomas 7 apostle
means: 4 twin
also called: 7 Didymus, Doubter **8** Doubting

Thomas, Ambroise
born: 4 Metz **6** France
composer of: 6 Mignon

Thomas, Danny
real name: 16 Amos Muzyad Jacobs
born: 11 Deerfield MI
daughter: 11 Marlo Thomas
roles: 13 The Jazz Singer **16** Make Room for Daddy **19** I'll See You in My Dreams

Thomas, Dylan
author of: 8 Fern Hill **13** Under Milk Wood **23** A Child's Christmas in Wales

Thomas, George H
nickname: 20 The Rock of Chickamauga
served in: 8 Civil War **10** Mexican War
side: 5 Union
commander of: 19 Army of the Cumberland
battle: 9 Nashville **11** Chattanooga, Chickamauga

Thomas, Marlo
real name: 14 Margaret Thomas
born: 9 Detroit MI
father: 11 Danny Thomas
husband: 11 Phil Donahue
roles: 8 That Girl

Thomas, W Morgan
creator/artist of: 22 Sheena Queen of the Jungle

Thomas a Kempis
author of: 20 The Imitation of Christ

Thomson, Joseph John
field: 7 physics
nationality: 7 British
discovered: 8 electron
awarded: 10 Nobel Prize

Thomson, Thomas John
born: 6 Canada **9** Claremont
artwork: 9 Spring Ice **11** The Jack Pine **12** Northern Lake **13** Northern River

Thomson, Virgil
born: 12 Kansas City MO
composer of: 9 Portraits **16** The Mother of Us All **21** Four Saints in Three Acts

thong 4 band **5** strap, strip **6** sandal **7** binding **8** swimsuit **9** underwear

Thor
origin: 12 Scandinavian
god of: 4 rain **7** farming, thunder
rode: 7 chariot
chariot pulled by: 5 goats

wielded: 6 hammer **7** Miolnir
father: 4 Odin **5** Othin

thorax 5 chest, trunk **6** breast, cavity **8** forebody

Thoreau, Henry David
author of: 6 Walden (Life in the Woods) **17** Civil Disobedience

thorium
chemical symbol: 2 Th

thorn 2 th **4** rune

thorn 3 woe **4** bane, barb, care, gall, spur **5** cross, curse, spike, spine, sting **6** plague **7** prickle, scourge, torment, trouble **8** nuisance, vexation **9** annoyance, sore point **10** affliction, bitter pill, infliction, irritation

thorn 9 Crataegus
varieties: 3 Box **4** Lily, Pear **5** Camel, Hedge, White **6** Christ, Karroo, Mysore, Sallow, Sickle, Winter **7** Thirsty **8** Cockspur, Egyptian, Kangaroo, Quick-set **9** Jerusalem, Paper-bark **10** Washington **11** Crucifixion **13** Yellow-fruited

Thornbirds, The
author: 17 Colleen McCullough

Thornburg, Betty June
real name of: 11 Betty Hutton

Thornfield
house in: 8 Jane Eyre
author: 6 Bronte

Thornhill, Squire
character in: 19 The Vicar of Wakefield
author: 9 Goldsmith

thorn in the side 4 bane **7** torment **9** annoyance **10** irritation

thorny 4 dire, hard **5** spiny, tough **6** barbed, spiked, sticky, trying **7** arduous, brambly, complex, crucial, irksome, prickly **8** annoying, critical, involved, ticklish **9** bristling, dangerous, difficult, vexatious **10** formidable, nettlesome, perplexing **11** complicated, troublesome

thorough 4 full, pure **5** sheer, total, utter **6** entire **7** careful, perfect, uniform **8** absolute, complete, of a piece **9** downright, out-and-out **10** consistent, definitive, exhaustive, meticulous **11** painstaking, unmitigated, unqualified **12** all-embracing, all-inclusive

thoroughbred 7 unmixed **8** purebred **9** blueblood, pedigreed, racehorse **10** aristocrat **11** full-blooded, pure-blooded **12** silkstocking

thoroughfare 4 road **6** avenue, street **7** freeway, highway, parkway, roadway, thruway **8** main road, turnpike **9** boulevard, concourse **10** expressway, interstate **12** superhighway **13** through street

thoroughgoing 5 utter **6** arrant **7** extreme **8** outright **9** confirmed, notorious, out-and-out **11** undisguised, unmitigated

thoroughly 5 fully **7** totally, utterly **8** entirely **9** carefully, downright, out-and-out, perfectly, uniformly **10** absolutely, completely, throughout **11** inclusively **12** consistently, exhaustively, meticulously **13** in all respects **15** from top to bottom **17** through and through **18** from beginning to end

Thorpe, Isabella
character in: 15 Northanger Abbey
author: 6 Austen

Thorpe, Jim (James Francis)
sport: 8 football **13** track and field
won: 8 Olympics
named: 11 All-American

Thorvaldsen, Albert Bertel
born: 7 Denmark **10** Copenhagen
artwork: 4 Hope **9** Lord Byron **14** Cupid and Psyche **16** The Lion of Lucerne **22** Cupid and the Three Graces **24** Jason with the Golden Fleece

Thoth
origin: 8 Egyptian
god of: 5 magic **6** wisdom **8** learning
scribe of: 4 gods
inventor of: 6 letter **7** numbers
corresponds to: 6 Hermes
head of: 3 dog **4** ibis

though 3 tho, yet **4** even, that **5** still **6** albeit, even if **7** granted **8** although, granting **9** admitting **12** nevertheless **15** notwithstanding

thought 3 aim, end **4** goal, idea, plan, view **5** credo, dogma, fancy, tenet **6** belief, caring, design, intent, musing, notion, object, regard, scheme **7** concept, concern, opinion, purpose, reverie, surmise **8** doctrine, judgment, kindness, thinking **9** attention, intention, objective, sentiment **10** brown study, cogitation, conception, conclusion, meditation, reflection, rumination **11** expectation, imagination, speculation, supposition **12** anticipation, deliberation **13** consideration, contemplation, introspection
French: 6 pensee

thoughtful 4 kind **6** caring, loving, musing **7** pensive, probing, serious, wistful **8** thinking **9** attentive **10** meditative, neighborly, reflective, solicitous **11** considerate, kindhearted **13** contemplative, introspective

thoughtfulness 7 probing, thought **8** kindness, thinking **10** meditation, reflection **11** questioning **13** attentiveness, consideration, contemplation **14** solicitousness **15** kindheartedness

thoughtless 4 dumb, rash, rude **5** silly **6** stupid, unkind **7** foolish **8** careless, heedless, impolite, reckless **9** imprudent **10** ill-advised, indiscreet, neglectful, unthinking **11** harebrained, improvident, inadvertent, inattentive, insensitive **12** absent-minded, unreflecting **13** ill-considered, inconsiderate, rattlebrained **14** scatterbrained

thoughtlessness 7 neglect **8** rashness, rudeness **9** oversight, unconcern **10** imprudence, negligence, unkindness **11** inattention **12** carelessness, heedlessness, impoliteness, recklessness **13** insensitivity **15** inattentiveness **16** absentmindedness

Thousand Clowns, A
director: **7** Fred Coe
based on play by: **11** Herb Gardner
cast: **11** Barry Gordon **12** Jason Robards, Martin Balsam **13** Barbara Harris
setting: **11** New York City
Oscar for: **15** supporting actor (Balsam)

Thousand Days, A
author: **20** Arthur M Schlesinger Jr

thou too
Latin: **8** tu quoque

thrall 4 serf **5** slave **6** chains **7** bondage, serfdom, servant, slavery **9** servitude **11** enslavement, subjugation

thralldom 6 chains **7** bondage, serfdom, slavery **9** servitude **11** enslavement, subjugation

thrash 4 beat, cane, drub, flog, jerk, lash, maul, toss, whip **5** birch, flail, heave, solve, spank, strap **6** jiggle, joggle, plunge, pommel, squirm, switch, thresh, tumble, wiggle, writhe **7** flounce, resolve, scourge, trounce **8** argue out, lambaste **9** thresh out **10** flagellate

threadbare 4 dull, worn **5** banal, stale, stock, tacky, trite **6** boring, frayed, jejune, ragged, shabby **7** cliched, humdrum, napless, prosaic, raveled, routine, worn-out **8** bromidic, everyday, pileworn **9** hackneyed, well-known **11** commonplace, stereotyped **12** conventional, overfamiliar **15** the worse for wear

threads 4 duds, togs **6** attire **7** apparel, clothes, strands, strings **8** clothing, garments **9** filaments

threat 4 omen, risk **5** peril **6** danger, hazard, menace **7** ill omen, portent, warning **8** jeopardy **10** foreboding **11** commination, premonition **12** intimidation

threaten 3 cow **4** warn **6** impend, menace **7** imperil **8** endanger, forewarn, hang over **9** terrorize **10** be imminent, intimidate, jeopardize

threatening 4 grim **7** baleful, ominous, warning **8** alarming, imminent, menacing, sinister **9** ill-omened, impending **10** forbidding, foreboding **11** approaching, forewarning, terrorizing **12** inauspicious, intimidating, unpropitious

three
French: **5** trois

Three-Cornered Hat, The
author: **21** Pedro Antonio de Alarcon

Three Faces of Eve, The
director: **15** Nunnally Johnson
cast: **8** Lee J Cobb **9** Nancy Kulp **10** David Wayne **12** Vince Edwards **14** Joanne Woodward
narration by: **13** Alistair Cooke
Oscar for: **7** actress (Woodward)

Three Lives
includes: **9** Melanctha **11** The Good Anna **13** The Gentle Lena
author: **13** Gertrude Stein

Three Men in a Boat
author: **13** Jerome K Jerome

Three Musketeers, The
author: **14** Alexandre Dumas (pere)
director: **13** Richard Lester
character: **5** Athos **6** Aramis **7** Porthos **8** Planchet **9** D'Artagnan **12** Lady de Winter **17** Cardinal Richelieu **18** Constance Bonacieux
cast: **10** Oliver Reed **11** Faye Dunaway (Milady), Michael York (D'Artagnan), Raquel Welch **12** Frank Findlay **14** Charlton Heston, Christopher Lee **16** Geraldine Chaplin **18** Richard Chamberlain
sequel: **17** The Four Musketeers

Threepenny Opera, The
author: **6** Brecht
composer: **5** Weill
based on: **15** The Beggar's Opera
by: **7** John Gay
song: **11** Mack the Knife

three R's 6 'riting **7** reading **9** 'rithmatic

Three's Company
character: **5** Larry **9** Janet Wood **10** Helen Roper **11** Chrissy Snow, Jack Tripper **12** Stanley Roper
cast: **10** John Ritter, Norman Fell **11** Joyce DeWitt **12** Audra Lindley, Richard Kline **13** Suzanne Somers

Three Sisters
director: **10** John Sichel **15** Laurence Olivier
author: **12** Anton Chekhov
character: **13** Fyodor Kuligin **14** Baron Tusenbach, Vassily Solyony **17** Alexandr Vershinin
Prozorov family: **4** Olga **5** Irina, Masha **6** Andrey **7** Natasha
cast: **9** Alan Bates **11** Derek Jacobi, Jeanne Watts **13** Joan Plowright, Louise Purnell **15** Laurence Olivier

Three Soldiers
author: **13** John Dos Passos

threnody 5 dirge, elegy **6** lament **7** requiem

threshold 4 dawn, door, edge, sill **5** brink, limen, onset, start, verge **6** portal **7** doorway, gateway, opening, prelude **8** doorsill, entrance **9** beginning, groundsel, inception **10** groundsill **11** entranceway **12** commencement **13** starting point

thrift 7 economy **8** prudence **9** frugality, husbandry, parsimony **10** moderation **11** springness, thriftiness **14** reasonableness **15** closefistedness **16** parsimoniousness

thriftiness 5 tight **6** thrift **7** economy **8** prudence **9** frugality, parsimony **13** penny-pinching **15** closefistedness, tightfistedness **16** parsimoniousness

thriftless 6 lavish **8** feckless, prodigal, wasteful **11** extravagant, improvident

thrifty 6 frugal, saving, stingy **7** sparing **9** niggardly, penny-wise **10** economical **11** closefisted, economizing, tightfisted **12** parsimonious **13** penny-pinching

thrill 4 fire, glow, kick, stir **5** flush, rouse, throb **6** arouse, excite, quiver, tickle, tingle, tremor **7** delight, impress, inspire, tremble **9** adventure, electrify, enrapture, galvanize, stimulate, transport **12** satisfaction

thrilled 4 agog **7** excited **9** delighted, overjoyed **11** transported

thrilling 7 awesome **8** engaging, exciting, riveting, stirring **9** absorbing, exquisite **10** delightful **11** fascinating, pleasurable, provocative, sensational, tantalizing, titillating **12** electrifying

thrip
variety: **6** banded **10** tube tailed **11** heterothrip, merothripid

thrive 3 wax **4** boom **5** bloom, get on **6** fatten **7** burgeon, prosper, succeed **8** flourish, get ahead, grow rich

thriving 4 busy, lush, rank, rich **7** wealthy, well-off **8** blooming, in clover, vigorous, well-to-do **9** flowering, luxuriant **10** blossoming, prospering, prosperous, succeeding, successful **11** flourishing

throat 3 maw **4** craw, gula, neck **5** gorge **6** gullet **7** chamber, jugulum, passage, pharynx
lozenge: **6** pastil
nautical: **3** jaw **4** jaws, nock
part: **6** fauces, larynx, tonsil **7** glottis, trachea
pertaining to: **5** gular
seizing: **4** knot **5** hitch **12** cuckold's knot
swelling: **6** goiter

throaty 3 dry, low **4** base, deep **5** gruff, husky, thick **6** hoarse **7** cracked, grating, rasping **8** croaking, guttural, resonant, sonorous **9** fulltoned

throb 4 beat, jerk, pant **5** heave, pulse, shake **6** quiver, tremor, twitch **7** beating, flutter, pulsate, shaking, tremble, vibrate **9** palpitate, pulsation, quivering, throbbing, trembling, vibration **10** fluttering **11** oscillation, palpitation **13** reverberation

throes 5 agony, chaos, pangs **6** ordeal, spasms, tumult **7** anguish, turmoil **8** disorder, paroxysm, upheaval **9** confusion, paroxysms **10** convulsion, disruption

thrombus 4 clot **9** blood clot **11** coagulation

throng 3 jam **4** army, cram, herd, host, mass, mill, pack, rush **5** bunch, crowd, crush, flock, flood, horde, press, surge, swarm **6** deluge, gather, huddle, stream **7** cluster, collect **8** assemble, converge **9** multitude **10** assemblage, congregate

thronged 4 full **6** jammed, mobbed, packed **7** crammed, crowded, flocked, swarmed, teeming **8** swarming **9** congested, jampacked **11** overflowing

throttle 3 gag, gas **4** stop **5** block, burke, check, choke **6** stifle **7** garrote, seal off, shut off, silence, smother **8** choke off, gas pedal, strangle **9** fuel lever, fuel valve **11** strangulate

through, thru 4 done, past **5** ended **6** direct **7** express **8** finished, from A to Z, to the end **9** all the way, completed, concluded **10** terminated **12** long-distance **15** from first to last **18** from beginning to end **20** from one end to the other

through and through 5 total **6** wholly **7** totally, utterly **8** complete **10** completely, thoroughly **15** from top to bottom **18** from beginning to end **20** from one end to the other

through my fault
Latin: **8** mea culpa

throughout 7 all over **10** all the time, everywhere **11** in every part **16** all the way through **18** from beginning to end

Through the Looking Glass
sequel to: **28** Alice's Adventures in Wonderland
author: **12** Lewis Carroll
character: **4** Gnat, Lion **5** Alice, Dinah **7** Red King, Unicorn **8** Red Queen **9** Red Knight, White King **10** Tweedledee, Tweedledum, White Queen **11** Black Kitten, White Kitten, White Knight **12** Humpty Dumpty

throw 3 lob, pit, put, shy **4** cast, hurl, shot, toss **5** chuck, fling, floor, heave, impel, pitch, place, put in, put on, sling **6** hurtle, launch, let fly, propel, unseat **7** project **8** delivery **9** knock down, put around

throw away 7 cast off, discard **8** get rid of

throw down 5 let go **8** drop hard, hurl down, toss down **9** fling down

throw into disorder 5 upset **7** agitate, disrupt **10** disarrange

throw off 4 emit, gush **5** exude **7** abandon, cast off, mislead **8** get rid of, shake off, shrug off **9** cast aside, discharge, give forth, pour forth

throw off the scent 7 confuse, mis-

lead **8** confound **19** throw out a red herring

throw out 4 beam, emit, oust **5** eject, evict, expel, exude **6** banish, bounce, remove **7** discard, dismiss, toss out **8** get rid of, jettison **9** cast aside, throw away

throw overboard 4 dump **7** cast off, discard **8** jettison, toss over

throw suspicion upon 11 cast doubt on **17** bring into question

throw up 4 barf, spew **5** eject, expel, spout, vomit **6** cast up, spew up **7** cough up **8** disgorge **9** discharge **11** regurgitate

thrust 3 jab, jam, ram **4** butt, pass, poke, prod, push, raid, stab **5** boost, drive, foray, force, impel, lunge, press, sally, shove, swipe **6** attack, charge, pierce, plunge, propel, sortie, strike, stroke **7** assault, impetus, impulse, riposte **8** momentum **9** incursion **10** aggression

thrust aside 4 dump **6** shelve **7** discard **8** get rid of, throw off, throw out **9** cast aside, dispose of, throw away

thrust at 6 assail, attack **7** lunge at **8** strike at

thrust out 4 spew, spit **5** eject, expel, vomit **6** extend, propel **7** protrude

Thucydides
author of: **28** History of the Peloponnesian War

thud 4 bang **5** clunk, knock, smack, thump

thug 4 hood **6** bandit, gunman, hit man, killer, mugger, robber **7** hoodlum, mobster, ruffian **8** assassin, gangster, murderer **9** cutthroat

thumb 5 hitch **6** finger, handle **9** hitchhike **10** catch a ride, hitch a ride **11** flip through, leaf through

Thumbelina
author: **21** Hans Christian Andersen

thumbnail 5 brief, short **7** compact, concise

thump 3 hit, jab, rap **4** bang, beat, clip, cuff, poke, slam, slap, swat, thud **5** clout, clunk, knock, pound, punch, smack, whack **6** batter, bounce, buffet, pommel, strike, thwack **8** collapse, lambaste

thunder 4 boom, clap, echo, peal, roar, roll **5** crack, crash **6** rumble **7** explode, resound **8** rumbling **9** discharge, explosion **11** reverberate, thunderbolt, thunderclap
god of: **4** Thor **5** Donar **7** Taranis

thunderbolt 4 dart **5** flash, shaft **6** stroke

Thunderstorms, god of 8 Summanus

thunderstruck 4 agog, awed **5** agape **6** aghast, amazed **8** confused, overcome **9** astounded, awestruck, perplexed, surprised **10** astonished, be-

wildered **11** dumbfounded **13** flabbergasted

Thunder-ten-Tronckh
character in: **7** Candide
author: **8** Voltaire

Thurber, James
author of: **12** The New Yorker **14** Is Sex Necessary (with E B White), The Catbird Seat **16** The Owl in the Attic **18** My Life and Hard Times, The Thurber Carnival **26** The Secret Life of Walter Mitty

Thurber Carnival, The
author: **12** James Thurber

Thurio
character in: **20** Two Gentlemen of Verona
author: **11** Shakespeare

Thursday
French: **5** jeudi
from: **4** Thor
German: **10** donnerstag
heavenly body: **4** Jove **7** Jupiter
Italian: **7** giovedi
Latin: **9** Dies Jovis
observance: **12** Holy Thursday, Thanksgiving **13** Corpus Christi **14** Maundy Thursday **17** Ascension Thursday
Scandinavian: **7** torsdag
Spanish: **6** jueves

thus 2 so **4** ergo **5** hence **6** like so **8** like this **9** as follows, in this way, therefore, wherefore **11** accordingly **12** consequently, in this manner **13** for this reason
Latin: **3** sic

thus always to tyrants
Latin: **17** sic semper tyrannis
motto of: **8** Virginia

thus passes away the glory of this world
Latin: **21** sic transit gloria mundi

Thus Spake Zarathustra
also: **21** Also Sprach Zarathustra
author: **18** Friedrich Nietzsche

thwack 3 box, hit, rap **4** bang, blow, slam, slap **5** baste, clout, knock, smack, thump, whack **6** buffet, paddle, strike, wallop

Thwackum
character in: **8** Tom Jones
author: **8** Fielding

thwart 3 bar **4** balk, foil, stop **5** check, cross **6** baffle, hinder, oppose **7** inhibit, prevent, ward off **8** obstruct, stave off **9** frustrate **10** contravene

Thyestean banquet
meal of: **10** human flesh

Thyestes
author: **6** Seneca

Thyestes
father: **6** Pelops
mother: **10** Hippodamia
brother: **6** Atreus
half-brother: **10** Chrysippus

sister-in-law: 6 Aerope
son: 9 Aegisthus
daughter: 7 Pelopia
Thyiad *see* **9** bacchante
Thymbraeus
father: 7 Laocoon
thyme
botanical name: 6 Thymus **9** T vulgaris
varieties: 4 Wild **5** Basil, Lemon, Water **6** Common, Garden, Golden **7** Caraway, Spanish
symbol of: 8 activity
attracts: 4 bees
conjures: 9 fairy folk
use: 4 fish **7** poultry **8** stuffing **10** Creole food **21** New England clam chowder
Thyrus
staff of: 8 Dionysus
tipped with: 8 pine cone
twined with: 3 ivy **5** vines
thysanoptera
class: 8 hexapoda
phylum: 10 arthropoda
group: 5 thrip
thysanura
class: 8 hexapoda
phylum: 10 arthropoda
group: 8 firebrat **10** silverfish **11** bristletail
Tia Maria
type: 6 brandy **7** liqueur
origin: 7 Jamaica
flavor: 6 coffee
with rum: 10 Black Maria
with tequila: 9 Brave Bull
with vodka: 12 Black Russian
tiara 4 band **5** crown, miter **6** diadem **7** coronet **8** frontlet, ornament **9** headdress
Tibet
other name: 3 Bod **4** Bhot **5** Tobet **8** Hsitsang **10** Land of Snow **14** Roof of the World
capital: 5 Lassa, Lhasa
city: 3 Noh **5** Karak **6** Chamdo, Gartok **7** Changtu, Totling **8** Gyangtse, Jihkatse, Shigatse **9** Chiangtzu
government: 23 autonomous region of China
monetary unit: 5 tanga
lake: 3 Aru, Bam, Bun, Nam **4** Mema, Tosu **5** Jagok, Tabia **6** Dagtse, Garhur, Kashun, Nam Iso, Seling, Tangra, Yamdok **7** Kyaring, Teriman, Tsaring, Zilling **8** Jiggitai **9** Tengrinor **11** Manasarowar
mountain: 5 Kamet, Sajum **6** Kailas, Kunlun **7** Bandala **8** Himalaya **9** Karakoram
highest point: 7 Everest
river: 3 Nak, Nau, Sak **4** Song **5** Hwang, Indus **6** Mekong, Sutlej, Yellow **7** Hwang Ho, Matsang, Melsang, Salween, Tsangpo, Yangtze **11** Brahmaputra

physical feature:
plain: 4 Kham **9** Chang Tang
valley: 7 Tsangpo
people: 5 Asian, Balti, Bodpa, Drupa **6** Bhotia, Champa, Drokpa, Khamba, Khambu, Panaka, Sherpa, Tangut **7** Bhotiya, Bhutani, Gyarung, Taghlik, Tibetan **9** Mongoloid
patron god: 14 Avalokitesvara
ruler: 4 Yuan **6** Mongol **9** dalai lama **13** Songtsan Gampo
language: 5 Balti **6** Ladkhi **7** Bhutani, Bodskad **8** Sanskrit **9** Bhutanese
religion: 5 Bonko **7** Lamaism
place:
Indian border: 11 McMahon Line
palace: 7 Potalaf
temple: 7 Jokhang **10** Tashi Lumpo **11** Tashi Lhunpo
feature:
animal: 3 dzo, yak **5** kiang **7** mastiff **8** musk deer **10** giant panda
clothing: 5 chuba
dance: 4 cham **9** achelhamo
dog: 9 lhasa apso
leader: 9 dalai lama
legend: 4 yeti **17** abominable snowman
monastery: 8 lamasery
monk: 4 lama
food:
dish: 6 tsamba, tsampa
drink: 5 chang
tibia
bone of: 4 shin
tic 5 spasm **6** twitch **12** facial twitch **13** tic douloureux **19** trigemi nal neuralgia
tick 3 dot, tap **4** beat, line, list, mark, nick, note **5** blaze, check, clack, click, enter, notch, swing, throb **6** record, slight, stroke **7** scratch, vibrate **8** mark down, register, ticktock **9** checkmark, chronicle, oscillate, pulsation, vibration
ticket 3 tag **4** card, mark, pass, slip, stub **5** label, slate **6** ballot, coupon, marker, roster **7** sticker, voucher **14** list of nominees, traffic summons
type: 4 trip **7** parking, traffic **9** admission
free: 11 Annie Oakley
tickle 4 itch **5** amuse, cheer, prick, sting, throb **6** divert, please, regale, stroke, thrill, tingle, twitch **7** delight, enchant, enliven, gladden, gratify, prickle, rejoice **8** enthrall, entrance **9** captivate, fascinate, titillate **12** scratchiness **15** do one's heart good
ticklish 4 hard **5** itchy, tough **6** knotty, thorny, tickly, touchy, tricky **7** awkward, prickly **8** critical, delicate, scratchy, tingling **9** difficult, intricate, sensitive, uncertain **11** complicated
tidal basin 3 bay **5** inlet, sound **6** lagoon **7** estuary **11** arm of the sea

tidbit 3 bit **4** item **5** treat **6** morsel **8** delicacy, mouthful **9** choice bit
tide 4 flow, neap, wave **5** drift, state **7** current **8** movement, tendency, undertow **9** direction **10** ebb and flow, wax and wane **11** rise and fall
tidings 4 news, word **6** advice, notice, report **8** good word **11** declaration, information **12** announcement, intelligence, notification
tidy 4 neat, trig, trim **5** ample, array, clean **6** goodly, neaten, tidy up **7** arrange, careful, clean up, orderly, precise, regular, sizable **8** neaten up, spotless, spruce up **9** organized, regulated, shipshape **10** immaculate, methodical, meticulous, put in order, straighten, systematic **11** substantial **12** businesslike, considerable, straighten up **15** in apple-pie order
tidy up 5 clean **6** neaten **9** freshen up **10** put in order, straighten
tie 3 rod **4** ally, band, beam, belt, bind, bond, cord, draw, duty, join, knot, lash, line, link, rope, sash, yoke **5** brace, ca- ble, cinch, limit, marry, match, truss, unite **6** attach, bow tie, clinch, couple, cravat, engage, fasten, girdle, hamper, hinder, ribbon, secure, string, tether **7** confine, connect, kinship, necktie, support **8** affinity, cincture, dead heat, make a bow, make fast, relation, restrain, restrict, tied vote **9** constrain, crossbeam, fastening **10** allegiance, connection, cummerbund, obligation **11** affiliation, come out even **12** relationship **13** connecting rod **15** divide the honors
Tiepolo, Giovanni Battista (Giambattista)
born: 5 Italy **6** Venice
artwork: 10 Kaisersaal (salon) **11** Treppenhaus (staircase) **14** The Crucifixion **16** Ronaldo and Armida **20** Madonna of Mount Carmel **21** The Communion of St Lucia, The Triumph of Aphrodite **24** St Thekla and the Pestilence **28** Apotheosis of Francesco Barbaro **28** The Worship of the Bronze Serpent
tier 3 row **4** bank, file, line, rank, step **5** layer, level, range, story **7** stratum **14** stratification
Tierney, Gene
born: 10 Brooklyn NY
husband: 11 Oleg Cassini
roles: 5 Laura **10** Belle Starr **11** Tobacco Road **13** A Bell for Adano **16** Leave Her to Heaven **18** The Ghost and Mrs Muir
tiers etat 11 third estate
in French politics: 7 commons
tie-up 3 jam **4** snag **5** block, hitch, snarl **6** slow-up **7** failure **8** blockage, gridlock, stop page **9** breakdown **10** bottleneck, disruption **11** malfunction **13** embouteillage

tie up 3 tie **4** bind, gird, lash, rope **5** hitch, snarl, strap, truss **6** engage, fasten, hinder, impede, occupy, secure, tangle **8** entangle

tiff 4 huff, miff, rage, snit, spat **5** clash, run-in, scrap, tizzy, words **6** hassle **7** dispute, quarrel, rhubarb, wrangle **8** argument, ill humor, squabble **10** difference **11** altercation **12** disagreement **16** misunderstanding

tiger 3 cat **6** cougar, jaguar **7** fighter, wildcat
    young: 5 whelp

Tiger Joy
    author: 19 Stephen Vincent Benet

tiger's-eye
    species: 6 quartz

Tigger
    character in: 13 Winnie-the-Pooh
    author: 5 Milne

tight 4 busy, firm, full, hard, high, snug, taut **5** blind, close, dense, drunk, exact, happy, harsh, lit up, rigid, scant, solid, stern, stiff, tense, tipsy, tough **6** firmly, frugal, gorged, hard-up, jammed, juiced, loaded, scarce, secure, severe, skimpy, sloppy, soused, stewed, stingy, stoned, strict, trying, zonked **7** austere, closely, com- pact, crammed, crowded, drunken, miserly, onerous, pickled, pie-eyed, smashed, solidly, sparing, stuffed **8** grudging, rigorous, securely, too small **9** deficient, difficult, illiberal, jam-packed, niggardly, penurious, plastered, skintight, stringent, worrisome **10** burdensome, compressed, glassy-eyed, impassable, inadequate, inebriated, inflexible, in one's cups, nip-and-tuck, nose-to-nose, tyrannical, ungenerous, unyielding **11** closefisted, constricted, dictatorial, impermeable, intoxicated, troublesome, well-matched **12** close-fitting, impenetrable, insufficient, parsimonious **13** closely fitted, feeling no pain **14** fitting closely, uncompromising **20** three sheets to the wind

tighten 5 pinch **6** anchor, fasten, narrow, secure **7** squeeze **8** contract, make fast, make taut **9** constrict **14** take up the slack

tighten one's belt 4 save **5** skimp, stint **6** scrimp **8** conserve, cut costs **9** economize **11** cut expenses **12** pinch pennies

tightfisted 5 cheap, mingy, tight **6** greedy, stingy **7** miserly **9** illiberal, niggardly, penurious **10** avaricious **11** closefisted **12** cheeseparing, parsimonious **13** penny-pinching

tightfistedness 6 penury **9** parsimony **10** stinginess **11** miserliness **13** niggardliness, penny-pinching

tight-fitting 4 snug **5** tight **8** too small **9** skintight **11** constricted **12** constricting **15** like a second skin

tight-laced 4 prim **6** prissy, stuffy **7** prudish **8** priggish **9** inhibited, repressed, Victorian **11** puritanical, standoffish, straitlaced **13** self-righteous

tight-lipped 3 mum **4** curt **5** brief, quiet, short, terse **8** discreet, reserved, reticent, taciturn **10** unsociable **11** untalkative **12** close-mouthed **15** uncommunicative

tightly packed 5 dense **6** jammed **7** compact, crammed, stuffed **10** compressed **12** concentrated

tightwad 5 miser, piker **7** niggard, Scrooge **9** lickpenny, skinflint **10** cheapskate, pinchpenny **12** money-grubber

Tiki
    Polynesian: 8 first man **6** amulet

till 3 sow **4** even, farm, plow, seed, tray, unto up to **6** before, coffer, drawer, harrow, plough **7** as far as, develop, prepare **8** moneybox, treasury **9** cultivate **12** cash register
    geological: 5 drift

tillable 6 arable **8** farmable, plowable **10** cultivable

tillage 7 farming, plowing **11** agriculture, cultivation

Till Eulenspiegel
    also: 16 Tyll Eulenspiegel
    origin: 8 Germanic
    means: 14 practical joker

Tillie the Toiler
    creator: 12 Russ Westover
    character: 3 Mac **7** Mr Chase

Tilney, Henry
    character in: 15 Northanger Abbey
    author: 6 Austen

tilt 3 row, tip **4** cant, lean, list, rake, spar, tiff **5** brawl, fence, fight, grade, joust, pitch, slant, slope **6** affray, battle, combat, oppose **7** contest, dispute, incline, quarrel **8** argument, skirmish, squabble **9** encounter **10** tournament **11** altercation

Timaeus
    author: 5 Plato

Timandra
    father: 9 Tyndareus
    mother: 4 Leda
    brother: 6 Castor, Pollux
    sister: 5 Helen **12** Clytemnestra
    husband: 7 Echemus, Phyleus
    son: 5 Meges
    cursed by: 9 Aphrodite

timber 4 bush, logs, wood **5** copse, trees, woods **6** boards, forest, lumber **7** thicket

timberland 5 woods **6** forest, sticks **8** woodland

timbre 4 tone **5** pitch **9** resonance

time, times 3 age, day, eon, era **4** beat, days, hour, term, week, year **5** clock, cycle, epoch, event, match, month, phase, spell, stage, tempo,

while, years **6** adjust, chance, decade, moment, period, rhythm, season **7** century, episode, freedom, instant, liberty, measure, stretch **8** duration, incident, interval, occasion **10** experience, generation **11** opportunity, synchronize

time flies
    Latin: 11 tempus fugit

time-honored 6 common, normal **7** regular, revered **8** accepted, standard **9** customary, respected, universal

timeless 7 abiding, durable, endless, eternal, lasting, undying **8** enduring, immortal, infinite, unending **9** boundless, ceaseless, deathless, immutable, incessant, permanent, perpetual **10** continuous, persistent **11** everlasting, never-ending **12** interminable, unchangeable **13** never-stopping **14** indestructible

timely 6 prompt **8** punctual **9** opportune, well-timed **10** convenient, felicitous, seasonable **12** providential

Time Machine, The
    author: 7 H G Wells
    character: 4 Eloi **5** Weena **8** Morlocks **12** Time Traveler

Time of Your Life, The
    author: 14 William Saroyan
    director: 8 H C Potter
    cast: 8 Ward Bond **11** James Cagney, Wayne Morris **12** Jeanne Cagney **13** William Bendix **17** Broderick Crawford

timepiece 5 clock, watch **8** horologe **11** chronometer

Time Remembered
    author: 11 Jean Anouilh

Timerman, Jacobo
    author of: 38 Prisoner Without a Name Cell Without a Number

timesaving 5 quick **6** speedy **9** efficient **11** expeditious

time without end 7 forever **8** eternity, infinity

timeworn 3 old **4** aged, worn **5** dated, hoary, passe, stale, trite **6** age-old, beat-up, old-hat, shabby **7** ancient, antique **8** battered, dog-eared, obsolete, overused **9** hackneyed, out of date, venerable, weathered **10** antiquated **12** antediluvian

timid 3 coy, shy **6** afraid, humble, modest, scared **7** bashful, fearful **8** cowardly, retiring, sheepish, timorous **9** diffident, shrinking, spineless, weak-kneed **10** unassuming **12** apprehensive, fainthearted **13** pusillanimous

timidity 7 modesty, shyness **8** cold feet, humility **9** cowardice, timidness **10** diffidence **11** bashfulness, fearfulness, trepidation **12** sheepishness, timorousness **13** spinelessness **16** faint-heartedness

timidness 7 shyness **8** meekness, timidity **10** diffidence, insecurity **11** bashfulness **12** timorousness **14** submissiveness **15** unassertiveness **16** faintheartedness

Timon of Athens
   author: 18 William Shakespeare
   character: 6 Lucius **7** Flavius **8** Lucullus **9** Apemantus, Ventidius **10** Alcibiades, Sempronius

Timor
   capital: 4 Dili
   country: 8 Portugal **9** Indonesia
   islands: 5 Sunda **11** Lesser Sunda
   strait: 5 Ombai

timorous 3 shy **4** meek **5** timid **6** afraid **7** anxious, bashful, fearful **8** retiring **9** shrinking **10** submissive **12** fainthearted

timorousness 7 shyness **8** cold feet, meekness, timidity **9** cowardice **11** fearfulness, trepidation **16** faintheartedness

Timothy
   mother: 6 Eunice
   grandmother: 4 Lois
   companion: 4 Paul **8** Silvanus

tin
   chemical symbol: 2 Sn

tincture 6 elixir **7** essence, extract, spirits **8** solution **11** concentrate

Tinder Box, The
   author: 21 Hans Christian Andersen

Tin Drum, The
   author: 11 Gunter Grass
   director: 17 Volker Schlondorff
   character: 14 Oskar Matzerath
   cast: 10 Mario Adorf **12** David Bennent (Oskar) **13** Angela Winkler **16** Daniel Olbrychski **17** Katharina Tahlbach
   Oscar for: 11 foreign film

tine 3 die, tip **4** barb, lose, tyne **5** point, prong, spike **6** bodkin, branch, perish, skewer **7** destroy, forfeit

tinge 3 dye **4** cast, dash, hint, lace, tint, tone, vein **5** color, imbue, shade, smack, stain, taste, touch, trace **6** flavor, infuse, nuance, season **7** instill, soupcon **9** suspicion

tingle 5 sting, throb **6** thrill, tickle, tremor **7** flutter, prickle **9** prickling, pulsation **11** palpitation

Tinker, Tailor, Soldier, Spy
   author: 11 John Le Carre

Tinker Bell
   character in: 8 Peter Pan
   author: 6 Barrie

tinkle 4 ding, peal, ping, ring **5** chime, chink, clank, clink, plink **6** jingle **9** ting-a-ling

tin lizzie 3 car **4** auto, heap **5** motor **6** jalopy, wheels **7** flivver, machine, vehicle **8** motorcar **10** automobile **12** motor vehicle

Tin Man, Tin Woodsman

character in: **13** The Wizard of Oz
   author: 4 Baum

tinsel 4 sham, show **5** gloss **6** sequin **7** glitter, spangle **8** pretense **9** gaudiness **10** camouflage, decoration, masquerade **11** affectation, false colors, make-believe, ostentation

tint 3 dye, hue **4** hint, tone, wash **5** color, frost, shade, stain, tinge, touch, trace **6** nuance **7** pigment **8** coloring, tincture **10** suggestion

Tintern Abbey
   author: 17 William Wordsworth

tintinnabulate 4 peal, ring, toll **5** chime, clang, knell, sound **6** jingle, tinkle

tintinnabulation 4 gong, peal, ring, toll **5** chime, knell **6** jingle **7** clangor, pealing, ringing **8** clanging, ding-dong, jingling, tinkling **11** peal of bells

Tintoretto, Jacopo
   real name: 13 Jacopo Robusti
   born: 5 Italy **6** Venice
   artwork: 8 Paradise **13** The Last Supper **14** The Crucifixion **16** The Road to Calvary **17** Bacchus and Ariadne **18** Apotheosis of St Roch, The Flight into Egypt **20** Susannah and the Elders **21** The Temptation of Christ **26** St Mark Frees a Christian Slave **27** The Finding of the Body of St Mark **32** The Miracle of St Mark Rescuing a Slave

tiny 3 wee **5** pygmy, runty, small, teeny **6** bantam, little, midget, minute, petite **8** dwarfish **9** itsy-bitsy, miniature, minuscule, pint-sized **10** diminutive, teeny-weeny, undersized **11** Lilliputian, microscopic, pocket-sized **12** teensy-weensy

Tiny Alice
   author: 11 Edward Albee

Tiny Tim
   character in: 15 A Christmas Carol
   author: 7 Dickens

tip 3 cap, pat, tap, top **4** acme, apex, barb, brow, cant, clue, head, hint, hook, lean, list, peak, rake, tilt **5** crest, crown, pitch, point, prong, slant, slope, spike, upend, upset **6** advice, reward, stroke, summit, tip-off, topple, upturn, vertex, zenith **7** capsize, incline, leaning, lowdown, pointer, sharpen, tilting, tipping, warning **8** gratuity, over turn, pinnacle, slanting **9** baksheesh, lagniappe **10** admonition, inside dope, perquisite, suggestion, turn turtle **11** forewarning **13** word to the wise
   French: 7 douceur

tipcart 4 cart **8** dumpcart, pushcart

Tiphys
   member of: 9 Argonauts
   occupation: 9 steersman

tip off 3 tip **4** warn **5** alert **6** caveat **7** caution, warning **8** forewarn **11** forewarning

tip over 5 upend, upset **7** capsize **8** flip over, keel over, overturn, turn over **10** turn turtle

Tippett, Michael Kemp
   born: 6 London **7** England
   composer of: 9 King Priam **13** The Knot Garden **15** A Child of Our Time **20** The Midsummer Marriage **22** The Vision of St Augustine **32** Concerto for Double String Orchestra

tipple 5 drink, quaff **6** guzzle, imbibe, liquor **8** beverage

tippler 3 sot **4** lush, soak, wino **5** drunk, rummy, souse, toper **6** bibber, boozer, sponge **7** guzzler, imbiber, swiller, tosspot **8** drunkard **9** alcoholic, inebriate **10** booze hound **11** dipsomaniac

tipsy 4 high **5** awash, blind, drunk, happy, lit-up, stiff, tight **6** juiced, loaded, sloppy, sodden, soused, stewed, stoned **7** drunken, pickled, pie-eyed, smashed **9** inebriate, plastered **10** glassy-eyed, inebriated, in one's cups **11** intoxicated **12** half seas over **13** feeling no pain **20** three sheets to the wind

tip-top 4 A-one **5** elite, super **7** supreme **8** very fine **10** consummate **11** exceptional, superlative **13** extraordinary

tirade 5 curse **6** screed **7** lecture **8** diatribe, harangue, jeremiad, scolding **9** invective, reprimand **11** castigation, fulmination **12** condemnation, denunciation, dressing-down, vilification, vituperation

tirailleur 10 skirmisher **12** sharpshooter

Tirane, Tirana
   capital of: 7 Albania

tire 3 fag, irk **4** bore **5** annoy, weary **6** bother, tucker **7** disgust, exhaust, fatigue, wear out **8** be sick of **10** make sleepy **11** be fed up with **12** lose interest, lose patience

tire
   invented by: 6 Dunlop **7** Thomson

tired 4 beat **5** all in, weary **6** bushed, drowsy, fagged, pooped, sleepy **7** wearied, worn out **8** dog-tired, fatigued, tuckered **9** enervated, exhausted, played out

tireless 6 steady **7** devoted, staunch **8** constant, faithful, resolute, untiring **9** steadfast, unceasing, unwearied **10** determined, unflagging, unswerving **11** hard-working, industrious, nevertiring, persevering, unfaltering, unremitting **13** indefatigable

Tiresias
   also: 9 Teiresias
   vocation: 4 seer **7** prophet
   father: 6 Everes
   mother: 8 Chariclo
   grandfather: 6 Udaeus
   home: 6 Thebes

struck: **5** blind
character in: **7** Odyssey **10** Oedipus Rex
characteristic: **9** blind seer

tiresome 4 drab, dull, hard **6** boring, deadly, dismal, tiring, trying, vexing **7** arduous, fagging, humdrum, irksome, tedious, wearing **8** annoying, wearying **9** difficult, fatiguing, laborious, wearisome **10** bothersome, exhausting, monotonous **13** uninteresting

Tishri 18 seventh Hebrew month

Tisiphone
member of: **6** Furies

'Tis Pity She's a Whore
author: **8** John Ford
character: **6** Donado, Florio, Putana **7** Soranzo, Vasques **8** Bergetto, Giovanni, Grimaldi **9** Annabella, Hippolita **11** Richardetto **16** Friar Bonaventura

tissue
kind: **4** bone, skin **5** nerve **6** muscle

titan 5 giant, great, mogul **7** magnate

Titan
race of: **4** gods
father: **6** Uranus
mother: **2** Ge **4** Gaea
names: **5** Coeus, Crius **6** Cronus **7** Iapetus, Oceanus **8** Hyperion
sisters: **8** Titaness
names of sisters: **4** Rhea **5** Theia **6** Phoebe, Tethys, Themis **9** Mnemosyne

Titan, The
sequel to: **12** The Financier
author: **15** Theodore Dreiser
character: **13** Peter Laughlin **15** Berenice Fleming, Stephanie Platow **16** Aileen Cowperwood **23** Frank Algernon Cowperwood

Titan, the see **6** Helios

Titaness see **5** Titan

Titania
character in: **21** A Midsummer Night's Dream
author: **11** Shakespeare

titanic 4 huge, vast **5** giant, great, stout **6** mighty, strong **7** immense, mammoth **8** colossal, enormous, gigantic, whopping **9** herculean, humongous, monstrous **10** gargantuan, monumental, prodigious, stupendous

titanium
chemical symbol: **2** Ti

tit for tat 8 exchange **10** quid pro quo **13** an eye for an eye

Titian
real name: **15** Tiziano Vecellio
born: **5** Italy **13** Pieve di Cadore
artwork: **5** Pieta **12** The Bacchanal, Tribute Money **13** Noli Me Tangere **15** Diana and Actaeon, The Rape of Europa **16** The Pesaro Madonna, The Venus of Urbino **17** Bacchus and Ariadne, The Death of Actaeon, The

Girl in a Fur Wrap, The Three Ages of Man **18** Charles V at Muhlberg, The Adrian Bacchanal, The Young Englishman **19** Francis I Roi de France **20** Sacred and Profane Love **21** Venus and the Lute Player **23** The Madonna of the Cherries **24** Pope Paul III and his Nephews, The Assumption of the Virgin

titillate 5 charm, rouse, tease, tempt **6** allure, arouse, excite, seduce, tickle, turn on **7** attract, provoke **8** entrance **9** captivate, fascinate, stimulate **15** whet the appetite

titillating 8 alluring, exciting, tempting **9** seductive **10** suggestive **11** provocative

title 3 dub **4** deed, name, rank, term **5** claim, crown, grade, label, place, right **6** status, tenure **7** entitle, epithet, station **8** christen, nobility, position **9** condition, designate, ownership **10** legal right, lordly rank, noble birth, possession **11** appellation, designation **12** championship

titled 5 named, noble, regal, royal **6** called, lordly **7** courtly **8** entitled **10** designated **11** blue-blooded **12** aristocratic

Titograd 9 Podgorica
capital of: **10** Montenegro

titter 5 chirp, smirk **6** cackle, giggle, simper, teehee **7** chuckle, snicker, snigger

tittle 3 bit, dot, jot **4** atom, iota, mite **5** speck **8** particle

Tittle, Y A (Yelberton Abraham)
sport: **8** football
position: **11** quarterback
team: **13** New York Giants **14** Baltimore Colts **23** San Francisco Forty-Niners

titular 7 known as, nominal **8** so-called **10** in name only, ostensible **11** in title only

Titus
surname: **6** Justus
hometown: **7** Corinth
companion: **4** Paul

Titus see **6** Tatius

Titus Andronicus
author: **18** William Shakespeare
character: **5** Aaron **6** Chiron, Marcus, Tamora **7** Alarbus, Lavinia **9** Bassianus, Demetrius **10** Saturninus

Tiu
Germanic god of: **3** sky, war
Norse: **3** Tyr
eponym of: **7** Tuesday

tizzy 4 snit **6** dither, swivet **7** dudgeon **8** tailspin
British: **8** sixpence

Tjaden
character in: **25** All Quiet on the Western Front
author: **8** Remarque

to 2 ad, on **3** for **4** into, near, unto, upon, with **5** about, until **6** at hand, closed, toward **7** against, forward **8** together **10** concerning, included in **11** contained in
prefix: **2** ac, ad
Scottish: **3** tae

toad
group of: **4** knot

toady 4 fawn **6** fawner, flunky, stooge, yes-man **8** hanger-on, kowtow to, parasite, truckler **9** flatterer, sycophant **10** bootlicker, curry favor **11** apple-polish, lickspittle **13** apple-polisher, backscratcher

To Althea, From Prison
author: **15** Richard Lovelace

to a man 3 all **8** every one **9** one and all **10** completely **12** to the last man

To a Skylark
author: **18** Percy Bysshe Shelley

toast 3 dry **4** heat, warm **5** brown, grill, honor **6** salute, warm up **9** celebrate **10** compliment **11** commemorate **12** browned bread, clink glasses **15** drink one's health

tobacco
varieties: **4** tree, wild **6** Indian **7** jasmine, Turkish **9** broadleaf, flowering, Nicotiana **12** long-flowered **16** Nicotiana rustica, Nicotiana tabacum

Tobacco Road
author: **15** Erskine Caldwell
character: **3** Ada **4** Dude **5** Pearl **6** Bessie **8** Ellie May **9** Lov Bensey **12** Jeeter Lester

To Be or Not To Be
director: **13** Ernst Lubitsch
cast: **9** Jack Benny **11** Robert Stack **12** Lionel Atwill **13** Carole Lombard, Felix Bressart
setting: **6** Poland

To Catch a Thief
director: **15** Alfred Hitchcock
cast: **9** Cary Grant **10** Grace Kelly **12** John Williams **17** Jessie Royce Landis
setting: **13** French Riviera

Tocqueville, Alexis de
author of: **18** Democracy in America

tocsin 4 bell **5** alarm **7** warning

today 3 now **7** this day, this era **8** nowadays, this time **9** in this era, on this day, this epoch **10** the present **11** in this epoch, modern times **13** in modern times, the present age, the present day **15** in this day and age

Todd, Richard
real name: **27** Richard Andrew Palethorpe-Todd
born: **6** Dublin **7** Ireland
roles: **13** The Hasty Heart, The Longest Day **14** The Virgin Queen **15** A Man Called Peter

toddle 6 waddle, wobble **14** take short steps, walk unsteadily

toddler 3 tot 4 babe, baby, tyke 5 child 6 infant 9 little one

to-do 3 ado 4 fuss, stir 5 furor, noise 6 bustle, flurry, hubbub, hustle, pother, racket, ruckus, rumpus, tumult, uproar 7 turmoil 8 activity 9 agitation, commotion 10 excitement, hullabaloo, hurly-burly 11 disturbance

Toe, The
nickname of: 8 Lou Groza

to err is human
Latin: 16 errare humanum est

toff 3 nob 4 beau 5 dandy, swell 10 young blood

Toffler, Alvin
author of: 11 Future Shock 12 The Third Wave

toga 3 aba 4 garb, gown, robe 6 trabea 7 garment 12 outergarment
virilis: 9 white robe 11 manhood robe

Togo
other name: 14 French Togoland
capital/largest city: 4 Lome
others: 5 Badon, Kpeme 6 Anecho, Ansoho, Blitta, Klonto, Nuatja, Palime, Sokode 7 Bassari, Dopango, Pagonda 8 Atakpame, Tabligbo 10 Niamtougou
school: 5 Benin 6 Mawull
monetary unit: 5 franc 7 centime
mountain: 4 Togo 7 Atakora, Koronga
highest point: 7 Baumann
river: 3 Oti 4 Anie, Haho, Mono, Ogou
sea: 8 Atlantic
physical feature:
  bight: 5 Benin
  gulf: 6 Guinea
  plain: 4 Mono
people: 3 Ana, Ewe, Twi 4 Mina 5 Hausa 6 Akposa, Kabrai 7 Bassari, Cabrais, Kabrais, Ouatchi 8 Konkomba, Kotokoli, Lotokoli
  leader: 7 Eyadema 15 Sylvanus Olympio 16 Nicolas Grunitzky
language: 3 Ana, Ewe, Twi 4 Mina 5 Hausa 6 French, Kabrai, Kabrie 7 Bassari, Dagomba, Ouatchi 8 Kotokoli, Lotocoli
religion: 5 Islam 7 animism 12 Christianity

togs 4 duds 6 attire, outfit 7 apparel, clothes, threads 8 clothing, garments

To Have and Have Not
director: 11 Howard Hawks
based on novel by: 15 Ernest Hemingway
cast: 12 Dolores Moran, Lauren Bacall 13 Walter Brennan 14 Humphrey Bogart 15 Hoagy Carmichael
remade as: 13 The Gunrunners 16 The Breaking Point

To His Coy Mistress
author: 13 Andrew Marvell

toil 4 grub, moil, work 5 grind, labor, pains, slave, sweat 6 drudge, effort 7

travail 8 drudgery, exertion, hardship, hard work, industry, struggle, work hard 11 application, elbow grease 12 apply oneself, exert oneself 14 work like a horse

toiler 4 peon, serf, swot 5 navvy, prole, slave 6 drudge, flunky, menial, slavey, worker 7 grubber, laborer, servant, slogger 9 workhorse 10 wage earner 11 galley slave

toilet 2 WC 3 can, loo 4 john 5 privy 7 commode, latrine 8 facility, lavatory, men's room, outhouse, rest room, washroom 10 ladies' room 11 convenience, water closet

toilet water 5 scent 7 cologne, essence, perfume 9 fragrance

toilsome 4 hard 5 tough 6 tiring, uphill 7 arduous, onerous, tedious 8 wearying 9 difficult, effortful, fatiguing, herculean, laborious, strenuous, wearisome 10 burdensome, exhausting 12 backbreaking

To Jerusalem and Back
author: 10 Saul Bellow

token 4 mark, sign 5 index, proof 6 jetton, symbol 7 for show, memento, minimal, nodding, nominal, passing 8 evidence, keepsake, reminder, souvenir, symbolic 9 vestigial 10 expression, indication 11 perfunctory, remembrance, superficial, testimonial 13 manifestation

To Kill a Mockingbird
director: 14 Robert Mulligan
based on novel by: 9 Harper Lee
cast: 9 John Megna 10 Mary Badham 11 Gregory Peck 12 Philip Alford
Oscar for: 5 actor (Peck)

Tokyo
airport: 6 Haneda
capital of: 5 Japan
district: 5 Ginza 6 Keihin 7 Chiyoda 8 Yokohama 10 Marunouchi 18 Tama New Town Project
former name: 3 Edo
island: 6 Honshu
landmark: 8 Ueno Park 11 Meiji Shrine 12 National Diet 14 Imperial Palace, Kitanomaru Park 19 Komazawa Olympic Park
means: 14 Eastern capital

tolerable 4 fair, so-so 7 allowed, average 8 abidable, accepted, adequate, bearable, mediocre, middling, ordinary, passable 9 allowable, endurable, innocuous, permitted 10 acceptable, admissible, fairly good, sufferable 11 commonplace, indifferent, permissible 12 run-of-the-mill 14 fair-to-middling

tolerance 7 charity 8 fairness, goodwill, patience, sympathy 9 endurance 10 compassion, sufferance 11 forbearance 13 brotherly love, fair treatment, fellow feeling, power to endure 15 lack of prejudice

tolerant 4 easy, fair, soft 7 lenient, liberal, patient, sparing 8 moderate 9 easygoing, forgiving, indulgent, unbigoted 10 charitable, forbearing, permissive 11 broad-minded, kindhearted, softhearted, sympathetic 12 unprejudiced 13 compassionate, uncomplaining, understanding

tolerate 3 let 4 bear, take 5 abide, admit, allow, brook, stand 6 endure, permit, suffer, wink at 7 indulge, stomach, undergo 8 be easy on, be soft on, sanction, submit to 9 consent to, put up with, recognize, vouchsafe

To Let
author: 14 John Galsworthy

to life
Hebrew: 7 lehayim 8 lechayim

Tolkien, J R R
author of: 9 The Hobbit 15 The Silmarillion 17 The Lord of the Rings
creature: 3 ent orc
fictional setting: 11 Middle Earth

toll 3 fee, tax 4 duty, levy, loss 6 charge, impost, tariff 7 payment, penalty, tribute, undoing 8 exaction 9 depletion, sacrifice 10 assessment, disruption, extinction 11 destruction 12 annihilation 13 extermination

Tolstoy, Leo
author of: 11 War and Peace 12 Anna Karenina, Resurrection 17 The Kreutzer Sonata 18 Death of Ivan Ilyitch

Toltec
city: 4 Tula
preceded: 5 Aztec
tribe: 4 Itza

To Lucasta, Going to the Wars
author: 15 Richard Lovelace

tom 3 cat 6 tomcat 10 male turkey

tomato 12 Lycopersicon 24 Lycopersicon lycopersicum
varieties: 4 Husk, Pear, Tree 6 Cherry 7 Currant 10 Gooseberry, Strawberry 11 Mexican husk
soup: 8 gazpacho
sauce: 6 catsup 7 ketchup

tomb 5 crypt, grave, vault 8 monument 9 mausoleum, sepulcher 11 burial place 12 resting place 13 burial chamber

tomboy 3 meg 4 girl, romp 5 rowdy 6 female, gamine, hoiden, hoyden, tomrig 8 strumpet

Tom Brown's School Days
author: 12 Thomas Hughes

tombs
god of: 6 Anubis

tomcat 3 cat, tom 9 womanizer

tomfoolery 4 play 6 antics 8 drollery, nonsense 9 high jinks, horseplay, silliness 10 goofing off, skylarking 11 foolishness 12 lollygagging, monkeyshines, prankishness 13 fooling around, messing around, playing around

Tom Jones
 also: **29** The History of Tom Jones Foundling
 author: **13** Henry Fielding
 character: **6** Square **7** Bridget, Western **8** Mrs Honor, Thwackum **9** Mrs Miller, Partridge **11** Black George, Nightingale **12** Master Blifil **13** Lady Bellaston, Sophia Western **15** Squire Allworthy
 director: **14** Tony Richardson
 cast: **11** Joyce Redman **12** Albert Finney, Diane Cilento, Hugh Griffith, Susannah York **14** Dame Edith Evans
 score: **11** John Addison
 Oscar for: **5** score **7** picture **9** direction **10** screenplay

Tomlin, Lily
 real name: **14** Mary Jean Tomlin
 born: **9** Detroit MI
 roles: **7** Laugh-In **8** Edith Ann **9** Ernestine, Nashville, The Player **11** The Late Show **14** Moment By Moment **20** Flirting with Disaster **27** The Incredible Shrinking Woman

tommyrot 3 rot **4** bosh, bull, bunk, crap, tosh **5** bilge, hokum, hooey, trash **6** bunkum, drivel, humbug **7** baloney, hogwash, spinach, rubbish, twaddle **8** buncombe, claptrap, folderol, malarkey, nonsense **9** poppycock **10** applesauce, balderdash, tomfoolery **11** foolishness **12** bullfeathers, fiddlefaddle **13** horsefeathers **16** stuff-and-nonsense

tomorrow 9 the future, the morrow **11** in the future **12** in days to come **16** the day after today **17** the next generation
 Spanish: **6** manana

Tom Sawyer
 author: **9** Mark Twain
 character: **8** Huck (Huckleberry) Finn, Injun Joe **9** Aunt Polly, Joe Harper **10** Muff Potter **13** Becky Thatcher

Tom Thumb the Great
 author: **13** Henry Fielding

ton
 abbreviation: **1** t

tone 3 hue **4** cast, lilt, mood, note, tint **5** color, pitch, shade, sound, style, tenor, tinge **6** accent, chroma, firm up, manner, soften, spirit, stress, subdue, temper **7** cadence, quality **8** attitude, harmonic, make firm, moderate, modulate, overtone, tonality **10** inflection, intonation, make supple, modulation

Tone, Franchot
 real name: **27** Stanislas Pascal Franchot Tone
 born: **14** Niagara Falls NY
 wife: **11** Jean Wallace **12** Joan Crawford **13** Barbara Payton **15** Dolores Dorn-Heft
 roles: **10** Uncle Vanya **11** Phantom

Lady **13** Three Comrades **16** Advise and Consent **17** Five Graves to Cairo, Mutiny on the Bounty **23** The Lives of a Bengal Lancer

tone up 7 make fit, shape up **9** condition **10** put in shape

Tonga
 other name: **15** Friendly Islands
 capital/largest city: **9** Nukualofa
 others: **3** Mua, Pea **6** Neiafu **7** Haakame, Kolonga, Kolovai **8** Fuaamotu
 division: **5** Vavau **6** Haapai **9** Tongatapu
 government: **8** monarchy
 head of state: **4** king
 monetary unit: **6** paanga, seniti
 island: **3** Eua, Kao, Ono **4** Kotu **5** Tofua, Vavau **6** Haapai, Lifuke, Nomuka **7** Otu Tolu **9** Tongatapu
 highest point: **3** Kao
 sea: **7** Pacific
 people: **10** Polynesian
  explorer: **4** Cook **5** Bligh **6** Tasman
  king: **11** George Tupou **14** Taufaahau Tupou
  missionary: **12** Shirley Baker
  queen: **6** Salote
 language: **6** Tongan **7** English
 religion: **9** Methodist **12** Christianity **25** Wesleyan Free Church of Tonga
 feature:
  fabric: **4** tapa
  spiritual king: **8** tui tonga

tongue 3 lap **4** flap, lick, spit **5** point, shaft **6** lingua, patois, speech **7** dialect, lingula **8** language **10** promontory, vernacular, vocabulary **13** organ of speech, power of speech, style of speech
 tastes: **4** salt, sour **5** sweet **6** bitter

tongue-lash 5 scold **6** berate, rail at, rebuke **7** bawl out, chew out, reprove, upbraid **8** reproach **9** castigate, reprimand **10** take to task

tongue-lashing 6 rebuke **7** censure, chiding, reproof **8** reproach, scolding **9** reprimand **10** bawling-out, chewing-out, upbraiding **11** castigation, reprobation **12** dressing-down, remonstrance

tonic 6 bracer, pickup **7** keynote **8** pick-me-up **9** analeptic, refresher, stimulant **10** invigorant **11** restorative

Tono-Bungay
 author: **7** H G Wells

tonsure 3 cut **4** trim **8** bald spot **11** shaven patch

too
 French: **4** trop

tool 4 dupe, pawn **5** agent, means **6** device, medium, puppet, stooge **7** cat's-paw, machine, utensil, vehicle **8** hireling **9** apparatus, appliance, implement, mechanism **10** instrument **11** contrivance, wherewithal **12** intermediary **15** instrumentality

carpenter's: 3 adz, awl, bit, peg, saw **4** adze, nail, rasp, vise **5** auger, brace, edger, gouge, knife, lathe, plane, ruler, screw **6** bodkin, chisel, gimlet, hammer, pliers, router, sander **7** bradawl, scraper **9** hand drill, try square **11** screwdriver
cutting/shaping: 2 ax **3** adz, axe, saw **4** adze, burr, file, froe, frow, rasp **5** burin, croze, gouge, knife, plane, razor, shave, wedge **6** chisel, sander, shears, trepan **7** hatchet, scraper **8** scissors
drilling/boring: 3 awl, bit, zax **4** pick **5** chuck, drill **6** gimlet, wimble **7** bradawl **11** countersink
farmer's: 2 ax **3** axe, hoe **4** plow, rake **5** spade **6** cradle, harrow, pickax, plough, scythe, seeder, shovel, sickle, tiller, trowel **7** hayfork **9** plowshare **10** cultivator
gripping/turning: 6 pliers, wrench **11** screwdriver
holding: 4 vise **5** clamp
measuring: 4 rule **5** gauge, level **6** square **7** caliper **8** dividers **10** micrometer
mechanic's: 3 awl, zax **4** burr, file, vise **5** bevel, lathe **6** bodkin, pliers **7** bradawl, crowbar **8** calipers **9** jackscrew **11** screwdriver **12** monkey wrench
pounding/striking: 4 maul **5** punch, wedge **6** hammer, mallet

too little 4 lack **6** dearth, scanty, scarce **7** paucity **8** scarcity, shortage **9** deficient, not enough, scantness **10** deficiency, inadequacy, inadequate **12** insufficient **13** insufficiency

too many
 French: **6** de trop

too much 4 glut **5** flood **6** excess **7** profuse, surfeit, surplus **8** fullness, overflow, plethora **9** avalanche, excessive, profusion, repletion **10** inundation, oversupply **12** overabundant **13** overabundance **14** superabundance
 French: **4** trop

Toonerville Folks
 creator: **11** Fontaine Fox
 character: **7** skipper **13** Aunt Eppie Hogg **15** Little Scorpions, Powerful Katrina, Suitcase Simpson **20** Mickey Himself McGuire **22** Terrible Tempered Mr Bang
 rode on: **7** trolley

to one side 4 over **5** aloof, apart, aside **6** aslant **14** on the sidelines

to one's liking 7 fitting **8** pleasant, pleasing, suitable **9** agreeable **10** acceptable, gratifying **11** appropriate, to one's taste **12** satisfactory

toot 4 blow, honk **5** binge, blare, blast, spree **6** bender **7** trumpet **8** wingding

tooth 3 cog, nib **4** barb, cusp, fang, spur, tang, tine, tusk **5** molar, point, spike, thorn **6** canine, cuspid **7**

grinder, incisor **8** bicuspid, sprocket **9** serration

toothed 6 fanged, tusked **7** dentate, notched, serrate, virgate

toothsome 6 savory **8** luscious **9** delicious, palatable **10** appetizing

Toots
  character in: 12 Dombey and Son
  author: 7 Dickens

top 3 cap, lid, van **4** acme, apex, best, brow, cork, fore, head, lead, peak **5** chief, cover, crest, crown, excel, front, noted, outdo, upper **6** better, exceed, famous, summit, tiptop, vertex, zenith **7** eclipse, eminent, highest, notable, put over, stopper, surpass, topmost **8** complete, fore most, greatest, outshine, outstrip, pinnacle, renowned **9** paramount, principal, put a top on, transcend, uppermost, upper part **10** celebrated, first place, overshadow, preeminent

topaz
  color: 4 blue **5** brown **6** yellow
  source: 5 Japan **6** Brazil, Mexico, Saxony **13** Ural Mountains **18** Cairngorm Mountains
  month: 8 November

Topaz
  director: 9 Hitchcock
  book by: 4 Uris

Topaze
  author: 12 Marcel Pagnol

topaz quartz
  species: 6 quartz
  color: 4 blue, pink **5** brown, green **6** sherry

toper 3 sot **4** lush, soak **5** drunk **6** boozer **7** tippler **8** drunkard **9** alcoholic **11** dispomaniac

Top Hat
  director: 12 Mark Sandrich
  cast: 9 Eric Blore **11** Fred Astaire **12** Ginger Rogers **14** Helen Broderick **19** Edward Everett Horton
  score: 12 Irving Berlin
  song: 12 Cheek to Cheek **22** Top Hat White Tie and Tails

topic 4 text **5** theme **6** thesis **7** keynote, subject

topical 5 local **6** timely **7** current, limited **9** localized, parochial **10** particular, restricted **12** contemporary

Topkapi
  director: 11 Jules Dassin
  cast: 12 Peter Ustinov, Robert Morley **14** Melina Mercouri **16** Maximilian Schell
  book by: 6 Ambler
  setting: 8 Istanbul
  Oscar for: 15 supporting actor (Ustinov)

topknot 4 comb, tuft **5** crest **9** cockscomb, headdress, headpiece

topmost 3 top **4** head **5** chief **7** highest, leading, supreme **8** foremost **9**

paramount, principal, uppermost **10** preeminent

topnotch 3 ace **4** best **5** prime **6** choice, finest, tip-top **7** supreme **8** superior, very fine **9** excellent, first-rate, nonpareil, unequaled, unrivaled **10** preeminent **11** outstanding, unsurpassed **12** incomparable, unparalleled

top of the head 4 dome, pate **5** crown **6** noggin, noodle

Topper
  director: 13 Norman Z McLeod
  based on novel by: 11 Thorne Smith
  cast: 9 Cary Grant **11** Alan Mowbray, Billie Burke, Hedda Hopper, Roland Young **16** Constance Bennett
  sequel: 13 Topper Returns **16** Topper Takes a Trip

topple 4 fall **5** crush, quash, quell, smash, upset **6** defeat, sprawl, tumble **7** abolish, shatter, tip over **8** fall over, over come, overturn, turn over, vanquish **9** bring down, overpower, overthrow **12** pitch forward

tops 4 aces, A-one, fine **5** great, prime, super, swell **6** choice, grade-A, superb, tip-top **7** capital **8** peerless, sterling, superior, terrific, top-notch **9** excellent, first-rate, marvelous, matchless, superfine, wonderful **10** first-class, inimitable, out-of-sight, tremendous **11** outstanding, superlative **12** incomparable **13** extraordinary

top-secret 5 privy **7** private **8** eyes-only, hush-hush **12** confidential

topsoil 4 dirt, loam **5** earth

Topsy
  character in: 14 Uncle Tom's Cabin
  author: 5 Stowe

topsy-turvy 5 messy **6** untidy **7** chaotic **8** confused, inverted, reversed **9** confusing, inside out **10** disorderly, upside down **11** disarranged, wrong side up **12** disorganized

Torah 10 law of Moses

torch 5 brand **7** cresset **8** arsonist, flambeau **9** firebrand **9** set fire to **10** flashlight

torment 3 nag, vex **4** bane, pain, rack **5** agony, annoy, curse, worry **6** harass, harrow, misery, pester, plague **7** afflict, agonize, anguish, despair, scourge, torture, trouble **8** distress, irritate **9** annoyance, persecute, suffering **10** irritation

tormenter 5 bully, tease **6** despot, tyrant **7** coercer **9** oppressor **10** browbeater **11** intimidator

tormenting 7 painful, racking **9** agonizing, torturous **10** unbearable **11** unendurable **12** excruciating, insufferable

torn 4 rent, slit **5** split **6** ragged, ripped **8** ruptured, shredded **9** unraveled

tornado 4 wind **5** storm **6** funnel, squall, vortex **7** cyclone, twister, ty-

phoon **8** outburst **9** hurricane, whirlwind, windstorm **10** waterspout **12** thunderstorm
  belt: 7 Midwest
  cloud: 4 tuba

torn apart 4 rent **6** ripped **7** asunder **8** in pieces, in shreds, shredded

toro 4 bull

Toronto
  baseball team: 8 Blue Jays
  bay: 6 Humber
  football team: 9 Argonauts
  former name: 4 York
  harbor: 5 Inner
  hockey team: 10 Maple Leafs
  lake: 7 Ontario
  landmark: 7 CN Tower **12** Ontario Place, O'Keefe Centre **13** Dufferin Grove **14** Dominion Centre **15** Roy Thompson Hall **16** Maple Leaf Stadium, St Lawrence Centre **17** Commerce Court West **18** Royal Ontario Museum **20** Nathan Phillips Square
  park: 7 Chorley, Stanley, Trinity **8** Winthrow **9** Cedarvale **12** Center Island **16** Winston Churchill
  street: 5 Yonge
  university: 4 York

torpedo 4 sink **5** wreck **7** destroy, missile, scuttle **9** explosive **10** projectile

torpedo (marine)
  invented by: 6 Fulton

torpid 4 dull, lazy **5** inert **6** drowsy, sleepy **7** dormant, languid, passive **8** inactive, indolent, listless, sluggish **9** apathetic, lethargic, somnolent **10** half asleep, languorous, slow-moving, spiritless **12** slow-thinking **13** lackadaisical

torpor, torpidity 6 apathy **7** inertia, languor **8** dullness, laziness, lethargy **9** indolence, lassitude **10** drowsiness, inactivity, sleepiness, somnolence **11** languidness, passiveness **12** listlessness, sluggishness

torrent 4 gush, rain, rush **5** burst, flood, salvo **6** deluge, rapids, stream, volley **7** barrage, cascade, Niagara **8** cataract, downpour, effusion, eruption, outburst **9** discharge, heavy rain, rapid flow, waterfall **10** cloudburst, outpouring, white water

Torrey, John
  field: 6 botany
  developed: 16 botanical library

Torricelli, Evangelista
  nationality: 7 Italian
  discovered concept leading to development of: 9 barometer

torrid 3 hot **4** sexy **5** fiery **6** ardent, erotic, fervid, heated, sexual, sultry **7** amorous, boiling, burning, excited, fervent, intense, lustful **8** broiling, desirous, parching, sizzling, spirited, tropical, vehement **9** hot and dry, scorching **10** passionate, sweltering **11** hot and heavy, impassioned

torte 4 cake **7** dessert **9** layer cake

tortilla 7 tostada **8** corncake **11** Mexican cake
  griddle: 5 comal

Tortilla Flat
  author: 13 John Steinbeck

tortuous 4 bent **5** snaky **6** spiral, zigzag **7** crooked, devious, sinuous, turning, winding, wriggly **8** indirect, involved, twisting, wrongful **9** ambiguous **10** circuitous, convoluted, meandering, roundabout, serpentine **11** complicated **12** full of curves, hard to follow, labyrinthine

tortuousness 9 sinuosity **11** indirection, sinuousness **12** convolutions **14** circuitousness

torture 4 pain, rack **5** abuse, agony, prick, smite, trial, wring **6** harrow, ordeal **7** anguish, cruelty, torment **8** distress, maltreat, mistreat **9** brutality, suffering **10** infliction, punishment **11** tribulation **12** put to the rack

torturous 5 cruel **7** galling, irksome, painful, racking **8** annoying **9** agonizing, anguished, harrowing, miserable, tormented, torturing **10** anguishing, distressed, tormenting, unpleasant **11** distressful, distressing **12** disagreeable, excruciating

tory 8 loyalist, royalist **12** conservative

Tosca
  opera by: 7 Puccini
  character: 7 Scarpia **9** Angelotti **11** Floria Tosca **16** Mario Cavaradossi

To Sir With Love
  director: 12 James Clavell
  cast: 4 Lulu **10** Judy Geeson **11** Suzy Kendall **13** Sidney Poitier **16** Christian Roberts
  setting: 6 London

toss 3 lob **4** cast, flip, hurl, jerk, rock, roll, sway **5** churn, fling, heave, pitch, shake, sling, throw **6** joggle, let fly, propel, tumble, wiggle, writhe **7** agitate, flounce, wriggle **8** flourish, undulate **9** oscillate

toss about 4 roil **5** bandy **6** jostle, jounce

toss back and forth 5 bandy **8** exchange

total 3 add, sum **4** full **5** add up, gross, sheer, solid, sum up, utter, whole **6** entire, figure, reckon, tote up **7** add up to, compute, perfect, total up **8** absolute, combined, complete, entirety, figure up, integral, outright, sum total, sweeping, thorough, totality **9** aggregate, calculate, down right, out-and-out, unlimited, wholesale **10** full amount, undisputed, unmodified **11** unqualified, whole amount **13** comprehensive, unconditional

totaling 8 addition, coming to **9** reckoning **10** adding up to

totalitarian 7 fascist **8** despotic **9** fascistic, tyrannous **10** autocratic, tyrannical **11** dictatorial **12** undemocratic **16** unrepresentative

totally 7 solidly, utterly **8** entirely **9** downright, out-and-out, perfectly **10** absolutely, completely, thoroughly, throughout **15** unconditionally **18** from beginning to end **20** without qualification

tote 3 lug **4** bear, cart, drag, haul, move, pack, pull **5** carry, fetch **6** convey **7** schlepp **9** transport

to the city and the world
  Latin: 10 urbi et orbi
  form of address used on: 10 papal bulls

to the four winds 7 all over **10** everywhere, far and wide **26** to the four corners of the world

to the letter 5 exact, right **7** correct, precise **8** accurate, explicit, specific **9** on the nose

To the Lighthouse
  author: 13 Virginia Woolf
  character: 4 Prue **5** James **7** Camilla **8** Mr Ramsey **9** Mr Tansley, Mrs Ramsey **11** Lily Briscoe **12** Mr Carmichael

to the point 6 direct **7** apropos, germane **8** explicit, relevant **9** pertinent **12** to the purpose

to the rear 3 aft **4** back **5** abaft **6** astern, behind **8** backward, rearward **9** backwards, sternward **10** to the stern **14** toward the stern

to the stern 6 astern, behind **8** rearward **9** sternward **10** to the stern

to the word
  Latin: 8 ad verbum

to this extent
  Latin: 8 quoad hoc

Toto
  dog in: 13 The Wizard of Oz
  author: 4 Baum

totter 4 reel, rock, sway **5** lurch, shake, waver **6** falter, teeter, waddle, wobble **7** shuffle, stagger, stumble **9** oscillate, vacillate

tottering 5 shaky **6** wobbly **7** rickety, shaking **8** insecure, topheavy, unstable, unsteady, wobbling **9** doddering, quivering, trembling **10** ramshackle, staggering

Toucan
  constellation of: 6 Tucana

touch 3 art, bit, paw, pet, rub, use **4** abut, cite, dash, feel, fire, form, gift, hand, hint, join, meet, melt, move, note, stir, sway, tint, work **5** equal, flair, match, pinch, rival, rouse, skill, smack, speck, style, taste, thumb, tinge, trace, unite **6** adjoin, affect, arouse, border, broach, caress, excite,

finger, finish, fondle, handle, hint at, manner, method, pawing, polish, sadden, soften, strike, stroke, thrill **7** concern, consume, contact, feeling, finesse, impress, inflame, inspire, mastery, mention, quality, refer to, soupcon, surface, texture, utilize **8** allude to, artistry, bear upon, come near, come up to, converge, deal with, deftness, fineness, fondling, handling, inspirit, resort to, thumbing **9** awareness, direction, electrify, fingering, influence, palpation, pertain to, suspicion, technique **10** adroitness, intimation, manipulate, perception, sprinkling, suggestion, virtuosity **11** be in contact, compare with, familiarity, guiding hand, realization **12** acquaintance, manipulation **13** communication, comprehension, understanding

touched 3 mad **4** daft, felt, nuts **5** crazy, moved, nutty **6** insane, joined **7** abutted, cracked, handled **8** demented, deranged, unhinged **10** unbalanced **12** mad as a hatter **13** off one's rocker, out of one's head **14** off one's trolley **15** mad as a March hare

Touchett, Ralph
  character in: 18 The Portrait of a Lady
  author: 5 James

touching 3 sad **6** moving, tender **7** pitiful **8** dramatic, pathetic, poignant, stirring **9** affecting, emotional, heartfelt, saddening, sorrowful **11** distressing, sentimental **12** heartrending **13** heartbreaking

touch me not
  Latin: 13 noli me tangere

Touch of Evil
  director: 11 Orson Welles
  cast: 10 Janet Leigh, Ray Collins **11** Joanna Moore, Orson Welles, Zsa Zsa Gabor **12** Akim Tamiroff, Dennis Weaver **13** Joseph Calleia **14** Charlton Heston
    cameo: 15 Marlene Dietrich **19** Mercedes McCambridge

touch off 5 shoot **6** set off **7** explode, fire off, trigger **8** activate, detonate **9** discharge

touch on 4 pose **6** broach, submit **7** advance, bring up, mention, propose, suggest **9** introduce

touchstone 4 norm, rule **5** basis, gauge, guide, model, proof **7** example, measure, pattern **8** standard **9** benchmark, criterion, guideline, precedent, principle, yardstick

Touchstone
  character in: 11 As You Like It
  author: 11 Shakespeare

touch upon 7 apply to, concern, mention, refer to **8** allude to, bear upon, relate to **9** appertain

touchy 5 cross, huffy, surly, testy **6**

bitter, crabby, grumpy **7** awkward, fragile, grouchy, peevish, waspish **8** captious, critical, delicate, petulant, snappish, ticklish **9** concerned, difficult, irascible, irritable, querulous, resentful, sensitive **10** precarious **11** thinskinned **12** cantankerous **13** quick-tempered

tough 4 cold, firm, hard, hood, lout, mean, punk, wily **5** bully, cagey, canny, cruel, hardy, rigid, rough, rowdy, solid, stern **6** brutal, crafty, dogged, knotty, mulish, rugged, savage, strict, strong, sturdy, thorny, trying **7** adamant, arduous, callous, complex, durable, hoodlum, inhuman, irksome, lasting, onerous, ruffian, vicious **8** baffling, barbaric, enduring, exacting, grievous, hooligan, involved, leathery, obdurate, perverse, pitiless, puzzling, ruthless, stubborn, ticklish, toilsome **9** barbarian, confusing, difficult, enigmatic, heartless, heavy-duty, intricate, laborious, obstinate, pigheaded, resistant, roughneck, strenuous, unbending, unfeeling **10** bullheaded, delinquent, exhausting, formidable, hardheaded, inflexible, perplexing, unyielding **11** bewildering, calculating, cold-blooded, complicated, hardhearted, hard-to-solve, infrangible, insensitive, troublesome **12** bloodthirsty, impenetrable **13** unsympathetic **14** uncompromising

toughen 4 firm **5** inure, steel **6** firm up, harden, season, temper **7** fortify, stiffen **8** accustom **9** acclimate, habituate **10** discipline, strengthen **11** acclimatize

Toulouse-Lautrec, Henri Marie Raymond de
born: **4** Albi **6** France **8** Albigois
artwork: **7** Friends **13** The Inspection **16** At the Moulin Rouge **24** Au Salon de la Rue des Moulins **27** Jane Avril at the Jardin de Paris **29** Cirque Fernando The Equestrienne **29** In the Parlor at the Rue des Moulins **29** The English Girl at Le Star Le Havre **30** La Goulue Entering the Moulin Rouge

toupee 3 rug, wig **6** carpet, peruke **7** periwig **9** hairpiece

tour 4 trek, trip **5** jaunt, visit **6** junket, safari, travel, voyage **7** inspect, journey **8** sightsee **9** excursion, itinerary

tourist 7 pilgrim, tripper, voyager **8** traveler, vagabond, wanderer, wayfarer **9** journeyer, sightseer **10** rubberneck **12** excursionist, globetrotter

tourmaline
color: **3** red **4** blue, pink **5** green

tournament 4 game **5** event, match **7** contest, rivalry, tourney **11** competition

tourney 4 game **5** event, joust, match **7** contest, rivalry **10** tournament **11** competition

tousled 5 messy **6** mussed, untidy **7** rumpled, tangled, unkempt **8** mussed-up, uncombed **10** disheveled, disordered

tout 4 plug, push **5** boost, exalt, extol, vaunt **6** praise, talk up **7** acclaim, commend, glorify, promote, tipster **8** ballyhoo, eulogize, give a tip **9** advertise, brag about, celebrate, publicize, recommend **10** aggrandize, noise about

tout a fait 8 entirely
literally: **12** wholly to fact

tout a l'heure 7 just now **8** very soon **9** presently **14** just a moment ago
literally: **15** wholly to the hour

tout de suite 6 at once **11** immediately
literally: **19** wholly consecutively

tout ensemble 11 all together

tout le monde 8 everyone **9** everybody **13** the whole world

tovarich 8 comrade

tow 3 lug **4** drag, draw, haul, lift, pull **5** hoist, trail

toward the end
Latin: **5** ad fin

toward the front 5 ahead **6** before **7** forward **9** to the fore **13** in the vanguard **14** in the forefront

toward the rear 4 back **6** astern **8** backward, rearward **9** sternward

toward the stern 6 astern **8** rearward **9** sternward **10** to the stern

tower 4 keep, loom, rock, soar **5** mount, outdo, spire, surge **6** ascend, belfry, castle, column, exceed, pillar, refuge, turret **7** bulwark, eclipse, minaret, obelisk, overtop, shoot up, steeple, surpass **8** mainstay, outclass, outshine, overhang, rise high **9** bell tower, rise above, transcend **10** foundation, overshadow, skyscraper, stronghold, wellspring **12** fountainhead

towering 4 high, tall **5** lofty **6** alpine **7** soaring, sublime, supreme **8** dominant, foremost, mounting, peerless, snowclad, superior **9** ascending, matchless, paramount, principal, unequaled, unmatched, unrivaled **10** cloud-swept, preeminent, surpassing, unexcelled **11** cloud-capped, overhanging **12** incomparable, second to none, transcendent, unparalleled **13** extraordinary

Tower of London, The
author: **24** William Harrison Ainsworth

tower over 5 dwarf **7** surpass **8** dominate **9** rise above

Townes, Charles Hard
field: **7** physics
invented: **5** maser
awarded: **10** Nobel Prize

town hall
German: **7** Rathaus

town house 8 row house **10** brownstone, pied-a-terre **13** city residence

township 4 town **7** village **11** subdivision **12** municipality

toxic 5 fatal **6** deadly, lethal, mortal **7** noxious **8** poisoned, venomous **9** poisonous, unhealthy **10** pernicious

toxin 4 bane **5** venom **6** poison **8** pathogen

toy 4 play, tiny, yoyo **5** dally, pygmy, sport **6** bantam, bauble, fiddle, gadget, gewgaw, little, midget, trifle **7** dwarfed, for play, stunted, trinket **8** gimcrack **9** miniature, plaything, small-size **10** diminutive, small-scale **11** Lilliputian

Toy Bulldog
nickname of: **12** Mickey Walker

Toynbee, Arnold
author of: **15** A Study of History

to your health
French: **11** a votre sante

toy with 8 play with **9** flirt with **10** trifle with **16** amuse oneself with

trace 3 bit, jot, map **4** draw, drop, find, hint, hunt, iota, mark, seek, sign **5** dig up, relic, shade, tinge, token, touch, track, trail **6** depict, flavor, trifle **7** diagram, hunt for, look for, mark out, nose out, outline, remains, uncover, unearth, vestige **8** describe, discover, draw over, evidence **9** delineate, ferret out, footprint, light upon, little bit, search for, suspicion, track down **10** come across, indication, suggestion **11** small amount

trace to 6 credit **7** ascribe **8** charge to **9** attribute

Trachiniae
author: **9** Sophocles
characters: **4** Iole **6** Hyllus, Nessus **8** Deianira, Heracles

track 3 way **4** mark, path, rail, sign, tack **5** dirty, route, scent, spoor, trace, trail **6** course, follow **9** footprint, guide rail

track and field
athlete: **7** Jim Ryun, Ray Ewry **8** Al Oerter, Lee Evans, Zola Budd **9** Ben Jonson, Bob Beamon, Carl Lewis, Henry Rono, Jim Thorpe **10** Bob Mathias, Bob Seagren, Edwin Moses, Grete Waitz, James Hines, Jesse Owens, John Carlos, Lasse Viren, Mac Wilkins, Paavo Nurmi, Peter Snell, Steve Ovett, Wyomia Tyus **11** Bill Rodgers, Bruce Jenner, Marty Liouri, David Wottle, Dick Fosbury, Doug Padilla, Emil Zatopek, Joni Huntley, Ralph Boston, Randy Matson, Tommie Smith **12** Dwight Stones, Frank Shorter, Harvey Glance, Jay Silvester,

Kathy Hammond, Maren Seidler, Rafer Johnson, Sebastian Coe, Willie B White, Wilma Rudolph **13** Allan Feurbach, Arnie Robinson, Janice Merrill, Kathy McMillan, Kipchoge Keino, Rodney Milburn, Ronny Ray Smith, Rosalyn Bryant, William Toomey **14** Alberto Salazar, Francie Larrieu, Roger Bannister **15** Martha Rae Watson, Renaldo Nehemiah, Willie Davenport **16** Madeleine Manning, Mary Decker Slaney, Richard Wohlhuter, Steve Prefontaine **17** Alberto Juantoreno **18** Jackie Joyner-Kersee, Stephanie Hightower **21** Babe Didrikson Zaharias **22** Florence Griffith-Joyner

tract 3 lot **4** area, plot, zone **5** essay **6** parcel, region **7** booklet, expanse, leaflet, quarter, stretch **8** brochure, district, pamphlet, treatise **9** monograph, territory **12** disquisition

tractable 4 tame **6** docile **8** amenable, obedient, yielding **9** compliant, teachable, trainable **10** governable, manageable, submissive **12** controllable, easy to manage **13** easy to control

tractate 8 treatise **9** discourse, monograph **12** disquisition, dissertation

Tracy, Spencer
 born: 11 Milwaukee WI
 costar: 16 Katharine Hepburn
 roles: 7 Desk Set **8** Adam's Rib, Boys Town (Oscar) **10** Pat and Mike **12** San Francisco, Tortilla Flat **13** The Last Hurrah **14** Cass Timberlane, Inherit the Wind, Woman of the Year **15** State of the Union **16** Father of the Bride, Keeper of the Flame **17** Bad Day at Black Rock **18** Captains Courageous (Oscar), The Old Man and the Sea **19** Judgment at Nuremberg **23** Guess Who's Coming to Dinner

Traddles
 character in: 16 David Copperfield
 author: 7 Dickens

trade 3 buy **4** deal, line, shop, swap **5** craft **6** barter, buyers **7** calling, patrons, pursuit **8** business, commerce, exchange, shoppers, vocation **9** clientele, customers, patronize **10** buy and sell, do business, employment, handicraft, line of work, occupation, profession **12** transactions **13** merchandising **16** business dealings, buying and selling

trade commodity 5 goods, wares

trademark 6 emblem **7** feature **8** property **9** specialty **11** peculiarity **14** characteristic

trade off 4 swap **5** trade **6** barter **8** exchange

trader 6 dealer, monger, seller **7** drummer **8** merchant, retailer **10** shopkeeper, trafficker, wholesaler **11** sales-

person, storekeeper **12** merchandiser, tradesperson **14** businessperson

tradesman 6 dealer, seller **8** merchant, retailer **9** craftsman **10** shopkeeper **11** storekeeper

tradition 4 lore, myth, saga, tale **5** habit, usage **6** custom, legend **8** folklore, practice **10** convention **12** superstition

traditional 3 old **5** fixed, usual **7** typical **8** habitual, historic **9** ancestral, customary **10** accustomed, inveterate **11** established **12** acknowledged, conventional

traduce 5 abuse, libel, smear, sully **6** defame, malign, vilify **7** run down, slander **8** backbite, bad-mouth, besmirch **9** deprecate, disparage **10** calumniate

traffic 4 cars, deal **5** buses, ships, trade **6** barter, doings, planes, riders, trains, trucks **7** bootleg, contact, freight, smuggle **8** business, commerce, dealings, exchange, tourists, voyagers **9** commuters, relations, smuggling, travelers **10** buy and sell, enterprise, passengers **11** bootlegging, intercourse, pedestrians, proceedings **12** transactions, vacationists **13** excursionists

tragedy 3 woe **4** blow **5** grief **6** misery, sorrow **7** anguish, setback **8** accident, calamity, disaster, reversal, sad thing **9** heartache **10** affliction, heartbreak **11** catastrophe

tragic 3 sad **4** dire **5** awful, fatal **6** deadly, dreary, woeful **7** piteous, pitiful, ruinous, serious, unhappy **8** dramatic, dreadful, grievous, horrible, mournful, pathetic, pitiable, shocking, terrible **9** appalling, frightful **10** calamitous, deplorable, disastrous, lamentable **11** destructive, devastating, unfortunate **12** catastrophic **13** heartbreaking

trail 3 dog, tow, way **4** drag, draw, fall, flow, hunt, mark, path, poke, sign, tail **5** float, hound, scent, spoor, trace, track **6** be down, course, dangle, dawdle, follow, lessen, shrink, stream **7** dwindle, pathway, subside **8** decrease, diminish, footpath, grow weak, hand down, peter out, taper off **9** drag along, grow faint, grow small, lag behind **10** bridle path, drag behind, footprints, move slowly **11** beaten track **14** bring up the rear

trailblazers 7 leaders **8** pioneers **10** avant-garde, innovators **11** forerunners, originators, tastemakers **12** trendsetters

train 2 el **3** aim, set **4** line **5** break, chain, drill, focus, level, point, queue, sight, teach, trail, tutor **6** column, direct, escort, school, series, subway **7** caravan, cortege, educate, prepare, retinue **8** elevated, exercise, instruct,

practice, rehearse, sequence **9** afterpart, appendage, entourage, followers **10** attendants, discipline, get in shape, procession, succession **11** bring to bear, domesticate, progression **12** continuation

Train, The
 director: 17 John Frankenheimer
 cast: 10 Albert Remy **11** Michel Simon **12** Jeanne Moreau, Paul Scofield **13** Burt Lancaster

trained 4 able **6** expert, master **7** capable, skilled **8** schooled, seasoned **9** competent, qualified **11** experienced **12** accomplished

trainee 4 boot **5** cadet **6** rookie **7** private, rookie, student **9** greenhorn **10** apprentice

trainer 5 coach, tutor **7** teacher **16** athletic director

training 5 drill **8** coaching, drilling, practice, teaching **9** education, schooling **10** discipline **11** preparation **14** apprenticeship, indoctrination

traipse 3 gad **4** roam, walk **5** range, tramp, tread **6** stroll, trapes, wander **7** meander, saunter **8** gadabout **9** gallivant

trait 4 mark **5** quirk **7** earmark, feature, quality **8** hallmark **9** attribute, mannerism **11** peculiarity **12** idiosyncracy **14** characteristic

traitor 3 rat **5** Judas, rebel **6** ratter **7** ratfink, serpent **8** apostate, betrayer, deceiver, deserter, mutineer, quisling, renegade, turncoat **9** hypocrite **11** false friend **12** double-dealer **13** double-crosser, revolutionary **14** fifth columnist **15** snake in the grass **20** wolf in sheep's clothing

traitorous 5 false **7** corrupt **8** disloyal, renegade **9** betraying, faithless **10** perfidious, treasonous, unfaithful **11** treacherous

tramp 3 bum **4** hike, hobo, roam, rove, slog, trek, walk **5** march, prowl, stamp, stomp **6** ramble, trudge, wander **7** floater, meander, traipse, trample, vagrant **8** derelict **9** gallivant, itinerant **10** panhandler **11** perambulate, peregrinate **15** knight-of-the-road

trample 5 crush, stamp, stomp **6** squash **7** flatten, run over **14** grind under foot **15** step heavily upon

trance 4 coma, daze **5** dream, spell **6** stupor, vision **7** reverie **8** daydream, hypnosis **9** pipe dream **10** absorption, brown study **11** abstraction **12** sleepwalking **13** concentration, preoccupation, woolgathering

tranquil 4 calm, cool, mild **5** quiet, still **6** gentle, placid, serene **7** halcyon, restful **8** composed, peaceful **9** unexcited, unruffled **11** undisturbed, unperturbed **13** self-possessed

tranquility 4 calm, hush **5** peace, quiet **6** repose **7** concord, harmony **8**

quietude, serenity **9** composure, placidity, stillness **11** restfulness **12** peacefulness

tranquilize 4 calm, drug, lull **5** allay, quiet, relax, still **6** becalm, pacify, sedate, settle, soothe **7** appease, assuage **9** alleviate

transact 2 do **5** exact **6** handle, manage, settle **7** achieve, carry on, conduct, execute, perform **8** carry out, exercise **9** discharge **10** accomplish, take care of **12** carry through

transaction 4 deal **6** affair **7** bargain, dealing, venture **8** exchange **9** operation **10** enterprise, settlement **11** negotiation **15** business dealing, piece of business

transcend 5 excel, outdo **6** exceed **7** eclipse, outrank, surpass **8** go beyond, outrival, outshine, outstrip, overleap, overstep, surmount **9** rise above **10** overshadow **11** outdistance

transcendence 5 merit **8** eminence **9** exceeding, greatness **10** exaltation, excellence, surpassing **11** distinction, preeminence, superiority

transcendental 5 great **6** mental **7** supreme, unusual **8** elevated, peerless, superior, uncommon **9** exceeding, intuitive, matchless, spiritual, unequaled, unrivaled **10** surpassing **11** unsurpassed **12** incomparable, metaphysical **13** extraordinary

transfer 4 cede, deed, move, send **5** bring, carry, shift **6** change, convey, moving, remove **7** consign, deeding, removal, sending **8** bringing, carrying, hand over, make over, relegate, relocate, shifting, shipment, transmit, turn over **9** conveying, transport **10** delivering, relegation, relocating, relocation **11** consignment, transmittal **12** transporting **14** transportation

transferable 8 catching **10** contagious, infectious **12** communicable **13** transmissible, transmittable

transferal 8 delivery, transfer **10** giving over **11** handing over, transmittal **12** transmission

transference 5 shift **6** change **7** passage, removal **9** transport **11** transmittal **12** dislodgement, displacement, transmission **13** transmittance

transfiguration 10 conversion **13** metamorphosis, transmutation **14** transformation

transfigure 6 change **9** transform **12** metamorphose

transfix 3 pin **4** hold, stab, stun **5** rivet, spear, spike, stick **6** absorb, impale, pierce, skewer **7** astound, bewitch, enchant, engross, fix fast, terrify **8** astonish, hold rapt, intrigue **9** captivate, fascinate, hypnotize, mesmerize, penetrate, spellbind **10** run through

transform 4 turn **5** alter **6** change, recast, remold **7** convert, remodel **8** make over **9** refurbish, transmute **11** reconstruct, transfigure **12** metamorphose, transmogrify

transformation 6 change **9** restyling **10** alteration, conversion, remodeling **13** metamorphosis, transmutation **15** transfiguration

transgress 3 err, sin **4** slip **5** break, cross, fault, lapse, wrong **6** exceed, impose, offend **7** digress, infract, violate **8** infringe, trespass

transgression 3 sin **5** crime, error, lapse, wrong **6** breach **7** misdeed, offense **8** evil deed, iniquity, trespass **9** violation **10** immorality, infraction, wrongdoing **11** lawbreaking **12** encroachment, infringement, overstepping **13** contravention

transgressor 5 felon **6** sinner **7** culprit **8** criminal, evildoer, offender, violator **9** miscreant, wrongdoer **10** lawbreaker, malefactor, trespasser

transience 7 brevity **11** evanescence **12** ephemerality, impermanence

transient 5 brief **7** passing **8** fleeting, soon past, temporal **9** ephemeral, momentary, short-term, temporary **10** evanescent, perishable, short-lived, transitory, unenduring **11** impermanent **14** passing through **24** here today and gone tomorrow

transistor
  invented by: 7 Bardeen **8** Brattain, Shockley

transition 4 jump, leap **6** change **7** passage, passing **8** shifting **9** gradation, variation **10** alteration, changeover, conversion, graduation **11** progression **13** transmutation **14** transformation

transitory 5 brief **7** passing **8** fleeting, fugitive **9** ephemeral, temporary, transient **10** evanescent, not lasting, short-lived, unenduring **11** impermanent **24** here today and gone tomorrow

translate 4 turn **5** alter, apply **6** change, decode, recast, render, reword **7** clarify, convert, explain **8** decipher, rephrase, simplify, spell out **9** elucidate, interpret, make clear, transform, transmute **10** paraphrase

translucence 7 clarity **8** lucidity **10** luminosity **12** transparency **16** semitransparency

translucent 8 pellucid **10** semiopaque, translucid **15** semitransparent

transmissible 8 catching **10** contagious, infectious **12** communicable, transferable **13** transmittable

transmission 4 note **7** message, passage, passing, sending **8** delivery, dispatch, transfer **9** broadcast **10** conveyance, forwarding, remittance **11** handing over, transmittal **12** transfer-ence, transferring **13** communication **14** transportation

transmit 4 send, ship **5** carry, issue, relay, remit **6** convey, pass on, spread **7** deliver, forward **8** dispatch, televise, transfer **9** broadcast **11** communicate, disseminate

transmittable 8 catching **10** contagious, infectious **12** communicable, transferable

transmittal 7 sending **8** delivery, transfer **10** giving over, transferal **11** handing over **12** transmission

transmutation 6 change **10** conversion **13** metamorphosis **14** transformation **15** transfiguration

transmute 5 alter **6** change **7** convert **9** transform **12** metamorphose

transparency 6 purity **7** clarity **8** lucidity **9** clearness, sheerness **11** obviousness **14** diaphanousness

transparent 4 thin **5** clear, gauzy, lucid, plain, sheer **6** glassy, limpid, patent **7** evident, obvious, visible **8** apparent, clear-cut, distinct, explicit, manifest, palpable, peekaboo, pellucid **10** diaphanous, see-through **11** perceptible, self-evident, translucent, unambiguous, unequivocal **12** crystalclear, unmistakable

transpire 5 arise, occur **6** appear, befall, chance, crop up, evolve, happen, turn up **7** come out, leak out **9** be met with, eventuate, take place **10** be revealed, come to pass, make public **11** become known, be disclosed, come to light, show its face

transplant 5 graft, repot, shift **7** replant, transfer **8** displace, relocate, resettle **9** transport, transpose

transport 3 bus, lug **4** bear, cart, lift, move, send, ship, take, tote **5** bring, carry, charm, fetch, train, truck **6** convey, moving, remove, thrill **7** bearing, bewitch, carting, delight, deliver, enchant, freight, removal, sending, vehicle **8** airplane, carrying, delivery, dispatch, enthrall, entrance, shipment, shipping, transfer, transmit, trucking **9** captivate, cargo ship, carry away, conveying, electrify, enrapture, freighter, overpower **10** cargo plane, conveyance **12** freight train

transportation 7 cartage, haulage, portage, removal, transit **8** delivery, dispatch, movement, shipment **9** transport **10** conveyance, transferal **12** transference, transmission **13** transmittance

transported 5 moved **6** lifted **7** charmed **8** ecstatic, thrilled, uplifted **9** bewitched, entranced **10** captivated, enthralled **11** carried away, electrified **13** beside oneself

transverse 5 cross **6** across **7** athwart, oblique, transom **8** crossbar, crossing, diagonal, traverse **9** crosswise **10** crosspiece, horizontal

transversely 9 crossways, crosswise, laterally

Transylvania
  region of: 7 Romania
  city: 4 Cluj
  fictional home of: 7 Dracula

trap 3 net, pit **4** lure, ploy, ruse, seal, stop, wile **5** catch, feint, snare, trick **6** ambush, device, enmesh, entrap, lock in **7** ensnare, pitfall, springe **8** artifice, entangle, hold back, hunt down, maneuver **9** booby trap, stratagem **11** machination **16** compartmentalize

trappings 4 garb, gear **5** array, dress **6** attire, outfit, things **7** apparel, clothes, costume, effects, raiment, vesture **8** adjuncts, clothing, fittings **9** ornaments, trimmings **10** adornments, habiliment, investment **11** decorations **13** accoutrements, paraphernalia **14** embellishments

trash 3 rot **4** bums, crap, junk, scum **5** dregs, dross, tripe, waste **6** debris, drivel, idlers, litter, refuse, rubble, tramps **7** garbage, hogwash, loafers, residue, rubbish, twaddle **8** castoffs, leavings, nonsense, riffraff **9** poppycock, sweepings **10** balderdash **11** foolishness, ne'er-do-wells, odds and ends **15** good-for-nothings, unsavory element

trashy 4 vile **5** cheap, inane, junky, tacky **6** flashy, flimsy **7** rubbish, trivial, useless **8** riff-raff, trumpery, wasteful **9** worthless **13** insignificant

trauma 4 hurt **5** shock, wound **6** injury, stress

travail 4 pain, toil **5** labor, worry **6** strain, stress **7** anguish **8** delivery, distress, drudgery, exertion, hard work, hardship **9** suffering **10** birth pains, childbirth, labor pains **11** parturition **12** accouchement

travel 2 go **4** be on, move, roam, rove, sail, tour, trek, wend **5** cross, drive, range, visit **6** cruise, junket, voyage, wander **7** journey, proceed **8** pass over, progress, sightsee, traverse **9** globetrot, hitchhike, take a trip **11** pass through, press onward

traveler 5 gypsy, nomad, rover **7** drummer, migrant, pilgrim, tourist, trekker, tripper, voyager **8** vagabond, wanderer, wayfarer **9** itinerant, journeyer, sightseer **10** vacationer **12** excursionist, globetrotter

Traveller Without Luggage
  author: 11 Jean Anouilh

Travels With a Donkey
  author: 20 Robert Louis Stevenson
  donkey: 9 Modestine

Travels With My Aunt
  author: 12 Graham Greene

travel through 2 do **5** cover, cross, visit **8** traverse **9** negotiate **11** pass through

traverse 4 span **5** cross **6** bridge, travel **8** go across, move over, overpass **9** cross over, cut across, intersect, move along, negotiate, reach over **10** extend over, run through, travel over **11** move through, pass through, reach across

travesty 4 sham **5** farce, spoof **6** parody, satire **7** lampoon, mockery, take-off **8** disgrace **9** burlesque **10** caricature, distortion, perversion **17** misrepresentation

Traviata, La
  also: 9 The Misled **23** The Woman Who Was Led Astray
  opera by: 5 Verdi
  based on a story by: 14 Alexandre Dumas (fils)
    called: 7 Camille **17** La Dame aux Camelias
  character: 8 Violetta **14** Alfredo Germont

Travolta, John
  born: 11 Englewood NJ
  roles: 6 Carrie, Grease **7** Face/Off, Mad City **9** Get Shorty **10** Tony Manero **11** Pulp Fiction, Urban Cowboy **12** She's So Lovely, Staying Alive **13** Primary Colors **14** Moment By Moment **15** Vinnie Barbarino **17** Welcome Back Kotter **18** Saturday Night Fever

trawl 3 net **4** drag, fish, haul, line **5** seine, troll **6** dredge **7** dragnet

Treacher, Arthur
  real name: 11 Arthur Veary
  born: 7 England **8** Brighton
  roles: 11 Mary Poppins **14** National Velvet, Thank You Jeeves **16** David Copperfield **20** Magnificent Obsession

treacherous 5 false, risky **6** tricky, unsafe, untrue **7** devious **8** disloyal, perilous, two-faced **9** dangerous, deceitful, deceptive, faithless, hazardous **10** misleading, perfidious, precarious, traitorous, treasonous, unfaithful **12** falsehearted **13** untrustworthy

treachery 5 guile **6** deceit **7** perfidy, treason **8** apostasy, betrayal, trickery **9** deception, duplicity, falseness **10** disloyalty, infidelity **11** double cross **13** breach of faith, deceitfulness, double-dealing, faithlessness **15** underhandedness **17** untrustworthiness

tread 4 gait, hike, pace, roam, rove, step, walk **5** prowl, range, stamp, stomp, tramp **6** step on, stride, stroll, trudge, walk on **7** trample **8** footfall, footstep

treason 6 mutiny, revolt **7** perfidy **8** apostasy, betrayal, sedition **9** duplicity, rebellion, treachery **10** conspiracy, disloyalty, insurgence, revolution, subversion **11** lese majesty **12** insurrection

treasonable 9 faithless, seditious **10** perfidious, subversive, traitorous **11** treacherous

treasure 3 gem **4** gold **5** hoard, jewel, prize, store, value **6** esteem, jewels, regard, revere, riches, silver **7** cherish, deposit, paragon **8** bank upon, dote upon, gold mine, hold dear **11** pride and joy **14** apple of one's eye **17** pearl of great price

treasure chest 3 box **4** case **5** chest, trunk **6** coffer

treasured 4 dear **5** loved **6** adored, valued **7** beloved **8** precious **9** cherished

Treasure Island
  author: 20 Robert Louis Stevenson
  character: 7 Ben Gunn **8** Smollett **9** Dr Livesey **10** Jim Hawkins **14** Long John Silver **15** Squire Trelawney
  director:
    1934 version: 13 Victor Fleming
    1950 version: 11 Byron Haskin
  based on novel by: 20 Robert Louis Stevenson
  cast:
    1934 version: 10 Lewis Stone **12** Jackie Cooper (Jim Hawkins), Wallace Beery (Long John Silver) **15** Lionel Barrymore
    1950 version: 11 Basil Sydney **12** Robert Newton (Long John Silver) **13** Bobby Driscoll (Jim Hawkins) **16** Walter Fitzgerald

Treasure of the Sierra Madre, The
  director: 10 John Huston
  cast: 7 Tim Holt **12** Bruce Bennett, Walter Huston **13** Alfonso Bedoya, Barton MacLane **14** Humphrey Bogart
  Oscar for: 8 director **10** screenplay **15** supporting actor (Huston)

treasurer 6 banker, bursar, purser, teller **7** auditor, cashier **9** financier **10** accountant, bookkeeper, cash-keeper, controller **16** financial officer **17** minister of finance **22** secretary of the treasury **24** Chancellor of the Exchequer

Treasure State
  nickname of: 7 Montana

treasury 4 bank, safe, till **5** funds, purse, vault **6** coffer **8** money box **9** anthology, exchequer, strongbox, thesaurus **10** collection, compendium, depository, repository, storehouse **11** bank account, compilation

treasury note 4 bill **8** bank note **9** greenback **12** currency note **17** silver certificate

treat 3 joy **4** blow, coat, give **5** apply, cover, favor, grant, imbue, stand **6** attend, divert, doctor, handle, manage, remedy, spring, thrill **7** comfort, delight, discuss, patch up, take out **8** consider, deal with, look upon, medicate, pleasure, relate to **9** act toward, small gift, try to cure, try to heal **10** impregnate, minister to, speak about, write about **12** prescribe for, satisfaction **13** gratification

treat as inferior 7 disdain **9** patronize **12** condescend to **18** look down one's nose at **19** discriminate against

treatise 4 text **5** essay, study, tract **6** manual, memoir, report, thesis **8** textbook, tractate **9** discourse, monograph **12** dissertation

treatment 3 way **4** cure **6** course, remedy **7** conduct, process, regimen, therapy **8** antidote, approach, handling, treating **9** doctoring, operation, procedure **10** management, medication **11** application, medical care **12** manipulation

treaty 4 deal, pact **6** accord **7** bargain, compact, entente **8** covenant **9** concordat **13** understanding **15** formal agreement **22** international agreement

tree 3 ash, elm, fir, oak **4** bush, palm, pine, wood **5** beech, birch, chase, maple, plane, plant, scrub, staff, stake, stick **6** corner, cudgel, redbud, spruce, timber, willow **7** gallows, lineage, live oak, sapling **8** ancestry, chestnut, hardwood, mahogany, pedigree, seedling **9** ailanthus, evergreen **10** cottonwood, eucalyptus

Tree Grows in Brooklyn, A
author: **10** Betty Smith
character:
  Nolan family: 5 Katie **6** Neeley **7** Francie, Johnnie
  director: **9** Elia Kazan
  cast: **9** James Dunn **10** Lloyd Nolan **12** Joan Blondell **14** Dorothy McGuire, Peggy Ann Garner
  Oscar for: **7** special (Garner) **15** supporting actor (Dunn)

treeless 4 bald, bare **6** barren **7** denuded **8** unwooded **10** unforested

Treeplanters State
nickname of: **8** Nebraska

tref 9 not kosher

trek 4 hike, plod, roam, rove, sail, slog, trip **5** jaunt, march, range, tramp **6** junket, outing, travel, trudge, voyage, wander **7** journey, odyssey, passage **8** traverse **9** excursion, migration **10** expedition, pilgrimage **11** peregrinate **13** peregrination

trellis 5 arbor, bower, cross, frame, grill, trail **6** gazebo, screen **7** lattice, network, pergola **8** espalier **10** interweave **11** summerhouse

tremble 5 quail, quake, shake, waver **6** quaver, quiver, shiver **7** flutter, pulsate, shudder **9** palpitate

trembling 5 shaky **7** quaking, shaking **8** unsteady **9** doddering, quavering,

quivering, shivering **10** shuddering **11** palpitating

tremblor 5 quake, seism, shock **6** tremor **8** upheaval **10** earthquake

tremendous 4 fine, huge, vast **5** giant, great, major **7** amazing, awesome, immense, mammoth, sizable, titanic, unusual **8** colossal, enormous, fabulous, gigantic, terrific, towering, uncommon **9** excellent, fantastic, first-rate, humongous, important, marvelous, monstrous, wonderful **10** formidable, gargantuan, incredible, noteworthy, stupendous **11** elephantine, exceptional **12** considerable **13** consequential, extraordinary

tremolo
  music: **9** trembling, vibrating **30** rapid reiteration of a single pitch

tremor 3 jar **4** jolt **5** quake, shake, shock, spasm, throb, waver **6** quiver, shiver **7** flutter, shaking, shudder, tremble **8** paroxysm **9** pulsation, quavering, quivering, shivering, trembling, vibration **10** convulsion **11** palpitation

tremulous 5 jumpy, shaky, timid **6** wobbly **7** aquiver, excited, fearful, jittery, keyed-up, nervous, panicky, quaking **8** aflutter, agitated, atremble, hesitant, restless, wavering, worked-up **9** faltering, impatient, quivering, trembling, uncertain **10** irresolute, stimulated **13** on tenterhooks, panic-stricken

trench 3 cut, rut **4** scar **5** canal, ditch, drain, fosse, slash, slice **6** dugout, furrow, gutter, trough **7** channel, wrinkle **8** aqueduct **9** earthwork **10** depression

trenchant 4 acid, keen, tart **5** crisp **6** bitter **7** acerbic, caustic, concise, mordant, probing **8** clear-cut, distinct, incisive, scathing **9** sarcastic, scorching **10** razor-sharp **11** acrimonious, penetrating, well-defined

trend 4 bent, flow, mode **5** drift, style **7** fashion, impulse, leaning **8** movement, tendency **9** direction **10** proclivity, propensity **11** inclination

trendsetters 7 leaders **8** trendies, vanguard **10** avant-garde, innovators **11** pacesetters, tastemakers **12** advance guard, stylesetters, trailblazers

trendy 2 in **4** chic, tony **5** swank **6** modern, modish, with-it **7** current, faddish, popular, stylish, voguish **8** up-to-date **10** all the rage **11** fashionable **13** up-to-the-minute

Trenor, Gus and Judy
characters in: **15** The House of Mirth
author: **7** Wharton

Trent, Little Nell
character in: **19** The Old Curiosity Shop
author: **7** Dickens

trepidation 4 fear **5** alarm, dread,

panic, worry **7** anxiety, jitters **8** cold feet, disquiet **10** uneasiness **11** butterflies, disquietude, jitteriness, nervousness **12** apprehension **13** consternation

trespass 3 sin **5** error, wrong **6** invade **7** impinge, intrude, misdeed, offense **8** encroach, infringe, iniquity, invasion **9** evildoing, intrusion, violation **10** immorality, infraction, misconduct, wrongdoing **11** delinquency, misbehavior **12** encroachment, infringement, overstepping **13** transgression, unlawful entry, wrongful entry

tress 4 curl, hair, lock, mane **5** braid, plait **6** strand **7** ringlet, wimpler **8** spitcurl

trestle 4 beam **5** board, brace, frame, table **6** timber **9** framework

trial 2 go **3** try, woe **4** care, pain, shot, test **5** agony, essay, flyer, whirl, worry **6** burden, effort, misery, ordeal, trying, tryout **7** anguish, attempt, bad luck, hearing, testing, test run, torment, trouble, venture **8** accident, distress, endeavor, hardship, vexation **9** adversity, court case, heartache, suffering **10** affliction, litigation, misfortune **11** cross to bear **12** misadventure, wretchedness

Trial, The
author: **10** Franz Kafka
character: **4** Leni **7** Joseph K **9** Titorelli **11** The Advocate

trial and error 10 experiment **13** investigation **15** experimentation **20** process of elimination

tribe see **11** ethnic group

Tribes of Israel see **6** Israel

tribulation 3 woe **4** care, pain **5** agony, grief, trial, worry **6** misery, ordeal, sorrow **7** anguish, bad luck, torment, trouble **8** distress, hardship, vexation **9** adversity, heartache, suffering **10** affliction, ill fortune, misfortune **11** unhappiness **12** wretchedness

Tribulation Wholesome
character in: **12** The Alchemist
author: **6** Jonson

tribunal 3 bar **5** bench, court, forum **6** judges **9** authority, judiciary **10** ruling body **11** judge's bench, judge's chair **14** seat of judgment

tributary 6 branch, feeder, source, stream **7** helping, subject **8** affluent **9** ancillary, auxiliary, confluent, secondary **10** subjugated, subsidiary **11** subordinate **12** contributing, contributory

tribute 3 tax **4** duty, levy, toll **5** bribe, honor, kudos **6** esteem, eulogy, excise, impost, payoff, praise, ransom **7** payment, respect **8** accolade, encomium, memorial **9** extolling, gratitude, laudation, panegyric **10** assessment, blood money, compliment, settlement **11** recognition, testimonial **12** commendation, pound of flesh **13**

consideration, peace offering **14** acknowledgment

trice 3 sec **4** jiff, wink **5** blink, flash, jiffy, shake **6** minute, moment, second **7** instant **9** coup d'oeil, twinkling **11** split second

trichophobia
  fear of: 4 hair

trichoptera
  class: 8 hexapoda
  phylum: 10 arthropoda
  group: 3 fly **6** caddis

trick 3 art, gag **4** bait, dupe, feat, gift, gull, have, hoax, joke, ploy, ruse, trap, wile **5** antic, blind, bluff, caper, cheat, dodge, feint, fraud, knack, prank, put-on, skill, stunt **6** deceit, device, number, outfox, outwit, resort, secret, take in **7** deceive, gimmick, know-how, mislead, swindle **8** artifice, deftness, flimflam, hoodwink, maneuver **9** bamboozle, chicanery, deception, dexterity, imposture, sophistry, stratagem, technique **10** adroitness, hocus-pocus, manipulate, subterfuge **11** contrivance, machination, outmaneuver **13** practical joke, sleight of hand **16** prestidigitation

trickery 5 guile **6** bunkum, deceit **8** artifice, flimflam, pretense, quackery, wiliness **9** chicanery, deception, duplicity, imposture, rascality, stratagem **10** artfulness, craftiness, hocus-pocus, shiftiness **11** crookedness, deviousness **12** charlatanism, skullduggery, slipperiness **13** deceitfulness

trickiness 6 deceit **7** cunning, slyness **8** trickery **9** duplicity **10** craftiness **15** underhandedness

trickle 4 drip, leak, ooze, seep **5** exude **7** dribble, seepage **9** percolate

trickster 5 cheat, joker **6** dodger, rascal **8** deceiver, impostor, sleeveen **9** prankster

tricky 3 sly **4** foxy, wily **5** risky **6** artful, crafty, shifty, unsafe **7** cunning, devious **8** rascally, slippery, unstable **9** dangerous, deceptive, difficult, hazardous **10** touch-and-go, unreliable **11** complicated, underhanded **12** hard to handle, undependable **13** temperamental, unpredictable

trident
  form: 5 spear
  number of prongs: 5 three
  scepter of: 7 Neptune **8** Poseidon

trifle 3 bit, dab, jot, nip, toy **4** dash, drop, idle, iota, mite, play **5** crumb, dally, pinch, scrap, speck, tinge, touch, trace **6** bauble, dawdle, gewgaw, linger, little, morsel, sliver **7** modicum, nothing, trinket **8** fragment, gimcrack, kill time **9** bagatelle, plaything, waste time **10** dillydally, knickknack, sprinkling, triviality **11** deal lightly, small matter **12** amuse oneself, treat lightly **13** small quantity

trifler 5 flirt, idler **6** coquet **7** dabbler, dallier **8** coquette **10** dilettante

trifling 4 puny **5** petty, small, sorry, token **6** paltry, slight **7** nominal, trivial **8** beggarly, niggling, nugatory, picayune, piddling **9** worthless **10** negligible **11** unimportant **13** beneath notice, inappreciable, insignificant **14** inconsiderable **15** inconsequential

trifling circumstances
  Latin: 8 minutiae

trifling matter
  French: 10 peu de chose

trigger 5 shoot **6** set off **7** fire off **8** activate, detonate, touch off **9** discharge

trikerion 11 candelabrum, candlestick **12** candleholder

Trilby
  author: 15 George du Maurier
  character: 5 Gecko, Sandy, Taffy **8** Svengali **12** Little Billee **14** Trilby O'Ferrall

trill
  music: 7 shaking, tremolo **9** quavering

trim 3 cut, fit, lop **4** clip, crop, deck, form, lean, pare, slim, thin **5** adorn, array, lithe, prune, shape, shave, shear, shift, sleek, state **6** adjust, bedeck, border, change, fettle, kilter, limber, paring, piping, supple, svelte **7** arrange, balance, bedizen, compact, cutting, fitness, furbish, garnish, lissome, pruning, shapely, slender, willowy **8** athletic, beautify, clipping, cropping, decorate, equalize, ornament, shearing, trick out, trimming **9** adornment, condition, embellish, embroider, shipshape **10** decoration, distribute **11** streamlined **13** embellishment, ornamentation

Trim, Corporal
  character in: 14 Tristram Shandy
  author: 6 Sterne

trimming 4 trim **5** frill **7** cutting, pruning, slicing **8** clipping **9** adornment **10** decoration, shortening, truncation **11** abridgement, contraction, curtailment **12** abbreviation **13** embellishment

Trinacria see **6** Sicily

Trinidad and Tobago
  capital/largest city: 11 Port of Spain
  others: 4 Debe, Toco **5** Arima **6** Canaan, Coryal, Labrea **7** San Juan, Siparia **8** Rio Claro, Tunapuna **10** Roxborough **11** San Fernando, Scarborough **12** Princess Town, Sangre Grande **14** Charlotteville
  school: 6 Fatima **8** St Mary's **11** Queen's Royal
  head of state: 14 British monarch **15** governor general
  monetary unit: 4 cent **6** dollar
  island: 12 Chacachacare, Little Tobago **14** Bird of Paradise

lake: 5 Pitch
mountain:
  hills: 7 Trinity **10** Montserrat **12** Three Sisters
  highest point: 5 Aripo
  river: 6 Caroni **7** Ortoire **8** Oropuche, Trinidad
  sea: 8 Atlantic **9** Caribbean
  physical feature:
    bay: 5 Cocos, Guapo **6** Matura, Mayaro
    channel: 12 Dragon's Mouth **13** Serpent's Mouth
    gulf: 5 Paria
    point: 5 Radix **6** Arenal, Galera **7** Chupara, Galeota **8** Columbus
  people: 5 Irish **6** French, Syrian **7** African, Chinese, English, Spanish **8** European, Lebanese **10** East Indian, Portuguese, Venezuelan **11** Asian Indian **13** Latin American
    explorer: 8 Columbus
    leader: 8 Williams
  language: 6 French **7** Chinese, English, Spanish **10** Portuguese **12** French Patois
  religion: 5 Hindu, Islam **8** Anglican **10** Protestant **12** Christianity **13** Roman Catholic
  place:
    asphalt lake: 9 Pitch Lake
    mansions: 16 Magnificent Seven
    park: 18 Queen's Park Savannah
  feature:
    bird: 7 oilbird **8** cocorico
    clothing: 4 sari **5** dhoti
    dance: 6 Dragon, Shango
    festival: 6 Hosein, Lights
    fish: 5 guppy
    music: 7 calypso, goombay
    tree: 4 mora
  food:
    drink: 16 Angostura Bitters

Trinity
  author: 8 Leon Uris

trinket 3 toy **5** bijou, charm, jewel **6** bauble, gewgaw, notion, trifle **8** gimcrack, ornament **9** bagatelle, plaything **10** knickknack

trip 3 bob, err **4** flip, flub, fool, muff, pull, skip, slip, tour, trek, undo **5** caper, catch, dance, fluff, foray, jaunt, outdo, throw, upset **6** bungle, cruise, frolic, gambol, junket, outfox, outing, prance, safari, set off, slip up, voyage **7** blunder, commute, confuse, flounce, journey, misstep, release, scamper, stumble **8** activate, fall over, flounder, hoodwink, throw off **9** excursion **10** disconcert, expedition, pilgrimage **11** step lightly

Triple Crown 7 Belmont **9** Preakness **13** Kentucky Derby
  winner: 5 Omaha **7** Assault **8** Affirmed, Citation **9** Sir Barton, Whirlaway **10** Count Fleet, Gallant Fox, War Admiral **11** Seattle Slew, Secretariat

Triple Sec *see* 9 Cointreau

Tripoli
   capital of: 5 Libya

Triptolemos, Triptolemus
   favorite of: 7 Demeter
   inventor of: 4 plow 5 wheel
   patron of: 11 agriculture

Triquetra *see* 6 Sicily

triskaidekaphobia
   fear of: 14 number thirteen

Trismegistus *see* 5 Thoth

Tristan and Isolde
   also: 16 Tristan und Isolde
   opera by: 6 Wagner
   character: 5 Melot 8 Brangane, Kurwenal 18 King Mark of Cornwall

triste 3 sad 10 melancholy

tristesse 6 sorrow 7 sadness 10 melancholy

Tristram
   author: 22 Edwin Arlington Robinson
   character in: 16 Arthurian romance

Tristram Shandy
   author: 14 Laurence Sterne
   character: 6 Dr Slop 8 Mr Yorick 10 Toby Shandy 11 Widow Wadman 12 Corporal Trim, Walter Shandy

trite 5 banal, silly, stale 6 common 7 cliched, humdrum, routine, shallow, worn-out 8 bromidic, everyday, ordinary, overdone, shopworn 9 frivolous, hackneyed 10 pedestrian, threadbare 11 commonplace, oft-repeated, stereotyped, unimportant 12 run-of-the-mill 13 platitudinous

Tritogeneia *see* 6 Athena

Triton
   god of: 3 sea
   father: 8 Poseidon
   mother: 10 Amphitrite
   shape: 6 merman
   trumpet: 10 conch-shell

triumph 3 hit, win 4 best, coup 5 smash 6 subdue 7 conquer, mastery, prevail, succeed, success, surpass, victory 8 conquest, overcome, smash hit, vanquish 9 overwhelm 10 ascendancy, attainment, gain the day 11 achievement, superiority 12 come out on top, take the prize 14 accomplishment, get the better of

triumphal 5 proud 6 joyous 8 exultant 9 ascendant, rewarding 10 fulfilling, gratifying, successful, triumphant, victorious 11 spectacular

triumphant 6 elated, joyful 7 winning 8 exultant, jubilant 9 rejoicing 10 conquering, first-place, successful, victorious 11 celebrating 12 prizewinning

Triumph of Death, The
   author: 17 Gabriele D'Annunzio

trivia
   Latin: 8 minutiae

trivial 4 idle, puny, slim 5 banal, petty, small, trite 6 common, flimsy, little,
meager, paltry, slight, two-bit 7 foolish 8 beggarly, everyday, niggling, nugatory, ordinary, picayune, piddling, trifling 9 rinky-dink, worthless 10 incidental, pedestrian 11 commonplace, meaningless, unessential, unimportant 13 inappreciable, insignificant, of little value 14 inconsiderable 15 inconsequential

triviality 5 frill 6 trifle 9 frivolity 10 paltriness 12 nonessential, unimportance 14 insignificance 18 inconsequentiality

troglodyte 5 brute 6 hermit 9 barbarian 11 cave dweller

Troilus
   father: 5 Priam
   mother: 6 Hecuba

Troilus and Cressida
   author: 18 William Shakespeare
   character: 4 Ajax 5 Priam 6 Hector 7 Ulysses 8 Achilles, Diomedes, Pandarus 9 Agamemnon

Troilus and Criseyde
   author: 15 Geoffrey Chaucer
   character: 8 Diomedes, Pandarus

trois 5 three

Trojan Horse
   made of: 4 wood
   made by: 7 Epeiosk
   contained: 8 Odysseus, warriors

Trojans, The
   also: 10 Les Troyens
   opera by: 7 Berlioz
   part one: 14 La Prise de Troie 16 The Capture of Troy
   part two: 19 Les Troyens a Carthage 20 The Trojans in Carthage
   character: 4 Dido 6 Aeneas, Hector

Trojan War
   length: 8 ten years
   combatants: 6 Greeks 7 Trojans
   cause: 5 Helen, Paris 14 Apple of Discord

Trojan Women, The
   author: 9 Euripides
   character: 5 Helen 6 Hecuba 8 Astyanax, Menelaus, Odysseus, Polyxena 9 Agamemnon, Cassandra 10 Andromache, Talthybius 11 Neoptolemus

troll 3 imp 4 ogre 5 dwarf, gnome 6 goblin
   origin: 12 Scandinavian
   form: 12 supernatural
   inhabits: 10 subterrain

trollop 4 doxy, slut 5 bitch, doxie, frump, hussy, trull, whore 6 floozy, harlot, wanton 7 baggage 8 slattern, strumpet 10 prostitute

Trollope, Anthony
   author of: 9 Orley Farm, The Warden 15 The Way We Live Now 16 Barchester Towers, Framley Parsonage
   character: 11 Phineas Finn

troop, troops 4 army, band, file, gang, herd, step, unit 5 bunch,
crowd, crush, drove, flock, horde, march, press, swarm, tramp 6 parade, stride, throng, trudge 7 cavalry, company, militia 8 infantry, soldiers, soldiery, troopers 9 aggregate, gathering 10 armed force, assemblage 11 cavalry unit, fighting men, police force 12 congregation 13 military force

trop 3 too 7 too many, too much

Trophonius
   vocation: 7 builder
   father: 7 Erginus
   brother: 8 Agamedes
   god of: 5 earth
   killed: 8 Agamedes
   became: 6 oracle
      oracle called: 14 Zeus Trophonius

trophy 4 palm 5 award, booty, honor, kudos, medal, prize, relic, spoil 6 wreath 7 laurels, memento 8 citation, souvenir 9 loving cup 10 blue ribbon 11 testimonial

tropical 5 muggy 6 sultry, torrid 8 stifling 10 sweltering 11 hot and humid

troppo, non
   music: 10 not too much

Tros
   king of: 4 Troy
   father: 12 Erichthonius
   mother: 8 Astyoche
   wife: 10 Callirrhoe
   son: 4 Ilus 8 Ganymede 9 Assaracus

trot 3 jog 9 go briskly 11 step quickly, walk smartly

troth 8 fidelity 9 betrothal 10 affiancing, engagement 12 faithfulness

Trotwood, Betsey
   character in: 16 David Copperfield
   author: 7 Dickens

trouble 3 fix, row, vex, woe 4 blow, care, fuss, heed, mess, pain, pass, snag, work 5 agony, annoy, grief, harry, labor, pains, pinch, think, trial, upset, worry 6 affect, attend, badger, bother, burden, crisis, defect, dismay, effort, grieve, harass, misery, ordeal, pester, pickle, plague, pother, put out, scrape, sorrow, strain, strait, stress, strife, unrest 7 afflict, agitate, ailment, attempt, concern, depress, dilemma, discord, disturb, ferment, ill wind, oppress, perturb, reverse, setback, torment 8 disaster, disorder, disquiet, distress, disunity, exertion, hardship, hot water, quandary, rainy day, struggle, take time, unsettle, vexation 9 adversity, agitation, annoyance, attention, breakdown, challenge, commotion, deep water, hard times, suffering 10 affliction, convulsion, difficulty, disability, discommode, discompose, disconcert, discontent, dissension, irritation, make uneasy, misfortune, opposition 11 competition, disturbance, embroilment, instability, malfunction, predicament, tribulation 12 entanglement, exert oneself

13 inconvenience, make the effort **14** discontentment **15** dissatisfaction

troubled 5 upset **7** worried **8** bothered, careworn **9** disturbed, perturbed **10** distressed **12** heavyhearted

troublemaker 6 gossip **7** inciter **8** agitator, fomenter, provoker **9** miscreant **10** incendiary, instigator **11** rumormonger, scaremonger **12** rabble-rouser **13** mischief-maker, scandalmonger **16** agent provocateur

troublesome 4 hard **5** heavy, pesky, tough **6** cursed, knotty, taxing, thorny, tiring, trying, vexing **7** arduous, irksome, onerous, tedious **8** annoying, tiresome, unwieldy **9** demanding, difficult, fatiguing, harassing, herculean, laborious, wearisome, worrisome **10** bothersome, burdensome, cumbersome, disturbing, irritating, oppressive, tormenting, unpleasant **11** disobedient, distressing **12** disagreeable, exasperating, inconvenient, uncontrolled **13** undisciplined

troublesomeness 5 trial **10** difficulty **11** arduousness **13** inconvenience, laboriousness, vexatiousness, worrisomeness **14** bothersomeness

Trouble with Harry, The
  director: **15** Alfred Hitchcock
  cast: **11** Edmund Gwenn **12** John Forsythe **14** Mildred Dunnock, Mildred Natwick **15** Shirley MacLaine

troubling 6 vexing **8** worrying **9** worrisome **10** bothersome, disturbing, unsettling

trough 4 duct, moat, race, tray **5** canal, ditch, flume, gorge, gully **6** furrow, hollow, ravine, trench **7** channel **8** aqueduct **10** depression

trounce 4 beat, drub, lick, trim, whip **5** cream, skunk **6** humble **7** clobber **8** vanquish **9** overpower, overwhelm **10** take care of **11** carry the day **14** get the better of

troupe 4 band, cast **5** group, troop **6** actors **7** company, players **10** performers **11** road company

trouper 5 actor **7** actress **8** thespian **9** performer **13** touring player **15** repertory player

trousers 5 jeans, pants **6** chinos, slacks **7** drawers **8** breeches, britches, jodhpurs, knickers, overalls **9** dungarees **10** pantaloons **11** bellbottoms **12** pedal pushers **14** knickerbockers

Trovatore, Il
  also: **13** The Troubadour
  opera by: **5** Verdi
  character: **7** Azucena, Leonora, Manrico **11** Count di Luna

Troy
  abducted queen: **5** Helen
  archaeologist: **6** Blegen **8** Dorpfeld **10** Schliemann
  defender: **5** Eneas **6** Aeneas

  Greek name: **5** Ilion
  hero: **6** Hector
  king: **5** Priam
  Latin name: **5** Ilium
  modern name: **9** Hissarlik
  mountain: **3** Ida
  neighboring city in NY: **6** Albany **10** Watervliet
  river: **6** Hudson
  city in: **7** Alabama, New York **8** Michigan
  story: **5** Iliad **7** Odyssey
  surrounding region: **5** Troad, Troas

Troy, Sergeant
  character in: **22** Far From the Madding Crowd
  author: **5** Hardy

truancy 3 cut **7** absence **11** absenteeism, nonpresence **12** playing hooky **13** nonappearance, nonattendance **14** cutting classes, skipping school

truant 4 gone **5** idler **6** absent, dodger, evader, loafer, no show **7** drifter, goof-off, missing, not here, shirker, slacker, vagrant **8** absentee, deserter, layabout **9** goldbrick **10** delinquent, malingerer, nonpresent, not present **11** boondoggler, hooky-player **12** nonattendant, playing hooky

truce 4 halt, lull, rest, stay, stop **5** break, pause **7** respite **9** armistice, cease-fire **12** interruption **14** breathing spell, discontinuance **23** suspension of hostilities

Trucial Oman, Trucial States *see* **18** United Arab Emirates

truck 3 rig, van **5** lorry **15** eighteen-wheeler
  type: **5** panel **6** pickup **7** trailer **8** delivery

truckle 3 bow **4** fawn **5** court, defer, yield **6** grovel, pander, submit **7** flatter **8** bootlick, butter up, suck up to **9** shine up to **10** curry favor, take orders **11** apple-polish, fall all over **12** knuckle under **17** ingratiate oneself

truculence 8 defiance, ill humor **9** hostility, ill temper, pugnacity, surliness **10** fierceness **11** bellicosity **12** belligerence, churlishness **14** aggressiveness

truculent 4 rude, sour **5** cross, nasty, sulky, surly **6** fierce, touchy **7** defiant, hostile, peevish **8** churlish, insolent, petulant, snappish, snarling **9** bellicose **10** aggressive, ill-humored, ill-natured, pugnacious, ungracious **11** bad-tempered, belligerent, ill-tempered

Trudeau, Garry
  creator/artist of: **10** Doonesbury

Trudeau Pierre
  home: **6** Canada
  office: **13** prime minister

trudge 4 drag, limp, plod **5** clump, march, tramp **6** hobble, lumber **7** shamble

true 4 even, firm, full, just, pure, real **5**

exact, legal, loyal, right, usual, valid **6** actual, lawful, normal, proper, steady, strict, trusty **7** correct, devoted, factual, genuine, literal, precise, regular, staunch, typical **8** absolute, accurate, bona fide, constant, faithful, official, positive, reliable, rightful, true-blue, truthful **9** authentic, simon-pure, steadfast **10** dependable, legitimate, unswerving, unwavering **11** trustworthy **14** unquestionable

true being 4 core, soul **6** nature, psyche, spirit **7** essence

True Grit
  director: **13** Henry Hathaway
  based on novel by: **13** Charles Portis
  cast: **8** Kim Darby **9** John Wayne **11** Jeremy Slate **12** Glen Campbell, Robert Duvall **14** Strother Martin
  Oscar for: **5** actor (Wayne)

Truffaut, Francois
  director of: **11** Day for Night, Jules and Jim **19** Shoot the Piano Player, The Four Hundred Blows

truism 3 saw **5** adage, axiom **6** cliche, dictum, saying **9** platitude

truly 6 indeed, in fact, really, surely, verily **7** exactly, in truth, no doubt **8** actually, honestly, to be sure **9** assuredly, certainly, correctly, factually, genuinely, literally, precisely, sincerely **10** absolutely, accurately, definitely, faithfully, positively, truthfully, upon my word **11** beyond doubt, in actuality, indubitably, so help me God **12** indisputably **13** incontestably, unequivocally **14** beyond question, unquestionably **15** all kidding aside, without question

Truman, Harry S
  nickname: **15** Give Em Hell Harry
  presidential rank: **11** thirty-third
  party: **10** Democratic
  state represented: **8** Missouri
  succeeded upon death of: **9** Roosevelt
  defeated: **5** (Farrell) Dobbs, (Thomas Edmund) Dewey **6** (Claude A) Watson, (Norman) Thomas **7** (Henry Agard) Wallace **8** (Edward A) Teichert, (James Strom) Thurmond
  vice president: **7** (Alben William) Barkley
  cabinet:
    state: **6** (James Francis) Byrnes **7** (Dean Gooderham) Acheson **8** (George Catlett) Marshall **10** (Edward Reilly) Stettinius (Jr)
    treasury: **6** (Frederick Moore) Vinson, (John Wesley) Snyder **10** (Henry) Morgenthau (Jr)
    war: **6** (Kenneth Claiborne) Royall **7** (Henry Lewis) Stimson **9** (Robert Porter) Patterson
    defense: **6** (Robert Abercrombie) Lovett **7** (Louis Arthur) Johnson **8** (George Catlett) Marshall **9** (James Vincent) Forrestal

attorney general: 5 (Thomas Campbell) Clark **6** (Francis) Biddle **7** (James Howard) McGrath **9** (James Patrick) McGranery
navy: 9 (James Vincent) Forrestal
postmaster general: 6 (Frank Comerford) Walker **8** (Robert Emmet) Hannegan **9** (Jesse Monroe) Donaldson
interior: 4 (Julius Albert) Krug **5** (Harold LeClaire) Ickes **7** (Oscar Littleton) Chapman
agriculture: 7 (Charles Franklin) Brannan, (Claude Raymond) Wickard **8** (Clinton Presba) Anderson
commerce: 6 (Charles) Sawyer **7** (Henry Agard) Wallace **8** (William Averell) Harriman
labor: 5 (Maurice Joseph) Tobin **7** (Frances), Perkins (Wilson) **13** (Lewis Baxter) Schwellenbach
born: 2 MO **5** Lamar **8** Missouri
died: 2 MO **8** Missouri **10** Kansas City
buried: 2 MO **8** Missouri **12** Independence
education:
　law school: 21 Kansas City School of Law (did not graduate)
religion: 7 Baptist
interests: 5 piano **7** history
vacation spot: 2 FL **7** Florida, Key West
author: 14 Year of Decision **19** Years of Trial and Hope
political career: 8 US Senate **13** Vice President
　presiding judge of: 13 Jackson County
civilian career: 6 farmer
　owned: 9 men's store **12** haberdashery
military service: 5 major **9** World War I **15** MO National Guard **18** Army Reserve colonel
notable events of lifetime/term: 4 NATO **5** V-E Day **8** Fair Deal **9** Korean War **17** iron-curtain speech **20** assassination attempt **31** North Atlantic Treaty Organization
　act: 11 Taft-Hartley **12** Bretton-Woods
　airlift to: 6 Berlin
　conference: 7 Potsdam
　dropping of first: 5 A-bomb **8** atom bomb
　plan: 8 Marshall **9** Point Four
　signing of: 9 UN charter
　Treaty of: 12 Rio de Janeiro
　trial of: 9 Alger Hiss
father: 12 John Anderson
mother: 6 Martha (Ellen Young)
siblings: 8 Mary Jane **10** John Vivian
wife: 9 Elizabeth (Virginia Wallace)
　nickname: 4 Bess
children: 12 Mary Margaret
Trumbull, John
　born: 9 Lebanon CT

artwork: 21 The Battle of Bunker Hill **26** The Resignation of Washington **28** The Declaration of Independence **29** The Surrender of General Burgoyne **32** The Capture of the Hessians at Trenton **38** The Surrender of Lord Cornwallis at Yorktown **46** The Death of General Montgomery in the Attack of Quebec, The Death of General Warren at the Battle of Bunker Hill
trumpery 5 showy, trash **6** deceit, trashy, trivia **7** rubbish, twaddle, useless **8** frippery, nonsense, trifling **9** deception, worthless **11** nonsensical
trumpet 4 honk, horn **5** blare, bugle **6** cornet **7** clarion **8** proclaim **10** hearing aid
Trumpet of the Swan, The
　author: 7 E B White
trump up 4 fake **6** invent, make up **7** concoct, falsify **9** fabricate
truncate 3 bob, lop, nip **4** clip, crop, dock, snub, trim **5** prune **7** abridge, curtail, shorten **8** amputate, condense, cut short **10** abbreviate
truncheon 3 bat **4** club **5** baton, billy, stick **6** cudgel **8** bludgeon **9** billyclub
trunker 3 box, die **4** body, bole, dado, line, main **5** chief, pants, shaft, snout, stock, torso **6** coffer, engine, locker, shut up, thorax **7** baggage, close in
truss 3 tie **4** beam, bind, prop, stay **5** brace, hitch, shore, strap, tie up **6** bind up, fasten, girder, pinion, secure **7** confine, support **8** make fast **9** constrict, framework, stanchion **12** underpinning
trust 4 care, duty, hope **5** faith, hands **6** accept, assume, belief, charge, credit, expect, look to, rely on **7** believe, count on, custody, keeping, presume, swear by **8** credence, feel sure, reliance, sureness **9** certainty, certitude, count upon **10** anticipate, confidence, conviction, depend upon, obligation, protection **11** assuredness, contemplate, have faith in, safekeeping, subscribe to, take on faith, take stock in **12** guardianship **14** give credence to, responsibility, take for granted
trusted 6 trusty **8** reliable **9** unfailing **10** dependable **11** trustworthy
trustee 8 guardian **9** caretaker, custodian, protector
trusteeship 4 care **6** charge **7** custody **10** protection **11** safekeeping **12** guardianship
trusting 8 gullible, trustful **9** believing, credulous **12** unsuspicious
trustworthy 4 true **5** loyal **6** honest **7** ethical, trusted, upright **8** faithful, reliable, true-blue **9** honorable, steadfast **10** aboveboard, dependable, scrupulous **11** responsible **12** tried and true

13 incorruptible, unimpeachable **14** high-principled
trusty 7 trusted **8** reliable **9** unfailing **10** dependable **11** trustworthy
trusty companion 3 pal **5** buddy, crony **6** friend **8** intimate, sidekick **9** confidant **10** bosom buddy, confidante
truth 3 law **4** fact **5** facts **6** verity **7** reality **8** accuracy, fidelity, trueness, veracity **9** actuality, exactness, integrity **11** reliability **12** authenticity, faithfulness, truthfulness **15** proven principle, trustworthiness
　Russian: 6 Pravda
　also name of: 9 newspaper
　god of: 7 Mithras
truth conquers all things
　Latin: 18 vincit omnia veritas
truthful 4 open, true **5** exact, frank **6** candid, honest **7** artless, correct, factual, precise, sincere **8** accurate, faithful, reliable **9** authentic, guileless, veracious **10** aboveboard, meticulous, scrupulous **11** trustworthy, undeceitful, unvarnished **13** unadulterated **15** straightforward
truthfulness 6 candor **7** honesty **8** veracity
Truth or Consequences
　host: 10 Jack Bailey, Steve Dunne **12** Ralph Edwards
try 2 go **3** aim, use **4** risk, seek, shot, test, turn **5** crack, essay, fling, prove, trial, whack **6** effort, sample, strain, strive, tackle **7** adjudge, attempt, venture **8** endeavor **9** have a go at, partake of, undertake **10** adjudicate, deliberate, put to a test **11** opportunity **12** have a fling at, make an effort, take a crack at
trying 4 hard **5** pesky, tough **6** taxing, vexing **7** arduous, irksome, onerous, tedious **8** tiresome **9** difficult, fatiguing, harrowing, wearisome **10** bothersome, burdensome, exhausting, irritating **11** aggravating, distressing, troublesome **12** exasperating
tryout 4 test **5** trial **7** hearing **8** audition **10** experiment
try out 3 fry **6** render **7** compete **8** audition **9** give a test **11** performance
tryst 4 date **7** meeting, vis-a-vis **9** tete-a-tete **10** engagement, rendezvous **11** appointment, assignation
try the patience of 5 annoy **7** provoke **8** irritate **10** exasperate
try to equal 5 rival **7** compete, emulate
Tuatha De Danann 4 gods
　origin: 5 Irish
　mother: 4 Danu
tub 3 keg, kit, pot, tun, vat **4** bath, boat, butt, cask, ship, tank, tram, wash **5** barge, bathe, fatso, fatty, keeve, tramp **6** barrel, bucket, firkin, ore car, vessel **7** cistern, tankard **8**

cauldron, slow boat **9** container, freighter

tube 4 duct, hose, pipe **7** conduit **8** cylinder

tuber 3 anu, yam **4** beet, bulb, corm, eddo, root, taro **5** jalop, shoot **6** potato, turnip **8** rutabaga, swelling **11** enlargement

Tuchman, Barbara W
author of: 14 A Distant Mirror, The First Salute **15** The Guns of August, The March of Folly **17** Practicing History

tuck 3 put **4** cram **5** pleat, shove, stick, stuff **6** enwrap, gather, insert, pucker, roll up, ruffle, shroud, swathe, thrust **7** crinkle, swaddle

tucker 3 fag **4** bush, poop, tire **5** weary **7** exhaust, fatigue

tuckered out 5 all in, tired, weary **6** bushed, done in, pooped **8** fatigued **9** exhausted, fagged out

Tudor
dynasty of: 7 England
rulers: 8 Henry VII **9** Henry VIII **8** Edward VI **5** Mary I **10** Elizabeth I

Tudor, Antony
choreographer of: 11 Lilac Garden **12** Pillar of Fire

tuebor 11 I will defend

Tuei *see* **6** Isleta

Tuesday
from: 3 Tiw
heavenly body: 4 Mars
French: 5 mardi
Italian: 7 martedi
Spanish: 6 martes
German: 8 dienstag

tuft 4 wisp **5** batch, brush, bunch, clump, crest, plume, sheaf **6** bundle, tassel **7** cluster, topknot

tug 3 lug, tow **4** drag, draw, haul, jerk, pull, yank **6** wrench **7** wrestle

tulip 6 Tulipa
varieties: 4 lady, star **5** globe **7** Turkish **9** butterfly, guinea-hen, waterlily **10** Sierra star **11** golden globe, purple globe **16** common late garden **17** common early garden

Tulkinghorn
character in: 10 Bleak House
author: 7 Dickens

Tullia
father: 14 Servius Tullius
husband: 7 Tarquin

Tullius *see* **14** Servius Tullius

Tulsa
football team: 7 Outlaws

tumble 3 mix **4** dive, drop, fall, flip, roll, toss **5** whirl **6** bounce, jumble, plunge, stir up, topple **7** descend, shuffle, stumble **9** cartwheel **10** somersault

tumbledown 5 shaky **7** rickety, rundown **8** decaying, decrepit, unstable **9** crumbling, tottering **10** broken-down,

jerry-built, ramshackle **11** dilapidated, falling-down **14** disintegrating

tumbler 3 cog, dog **5** drier, glass, lever **6** goblet, vessel **7** acrobat, athlete, gymnast, juggler **12** somersaulter

tumbrel 4 cart **5** wagon **7** tipcart **8** dumpcart

tumbril
French: 7 fourgon

tumid 5 puffy **6** turgid **7** bloated, bulging, dilated, pompous, swollen **8** enlarged, expanded, inflated **9** bombastic, distended, edematous, tumescent **11** protuberant **12** magniloquent **13** grandiloquent

tummy 3 gut **5** belly **6** paunch, tumtum **7** abdomen, midriff, stomach **9** bay window **11** breadbasket

tumor 3 wen **4** cyst, lump, wart **5** pride **6** cancer, growth **7** bombast, sarcoma **8** hematoma, neoplasm, swelling, tubercle **9** carcinoma, papilloma, pomposity **11** tumefaction

tumult 3 ado, din **6** bedlam, bustle, clamor, hubbub, racket, uproar **7** turmoil **8** disorder, upheaval **9** agitation, commotion, confusion **10** excitement, hullabaloo **11** disturbance, pandemonium

tumultuous 4 loud **5** noisy, rough, rowdy **6** stormy, unruly **7** chaotic, furious, lawless, raucous, riotous, violent **8** agitated, confused **9** clamorous, disturbed, turbulent **10** boisterous, disorderly, uproarious **11** tempestuous

tun 3 keg, tub, vat **4** butt, cast, drum **6** barrel **8** hogshead

tune 3 air **4** aria, line, song, step **5** adjust, ditty, motif, pitch, theme **6** accord, adjust, melody, number, strain, unison **7** concert, concord, harmony **9** agreement **10** conformity

tuneful 6 catchy, dulcet **7** lyrical, musical **9** melodious

tungsten
chemical symbol: 1 W

tunic 4 robe **5** cloak **6** jacket, mantle, poncho, tabard **7** garment, surcoat

Tunica
tribe: 10 Chitimacha

Tunis
capital of: 7 Tunisia

Tunisia
other name: 8 Carthage **9** Ifriqiyah
capital/largest city: 5 Tunis
others: 4 Beja, Sfax, Susa **5** Gabes, Gofsa **6** Djerba, Mateur, Nabeul, Remada, Sousse, Tozeur **7** Bizerte, Kairwan **8** Carthage, Jendouba, Kairouan, Monastir, Tebourba, Zaghouan **9** Grombalia **10** Ferryville
empire: 8 Carthage **13** Barbary States
school: 5 Tunis **16** Pasteur Institute
measure: 5 saa **4** saah **5** cafiz **6** mettar **8** milerole
monetary unit: 5 dinar **6** dollar **7**

millime
weight: 3 saa **4** rotl **5** artal, ratel, uckia
island: 6 Djerba, Galite
lake: 6 Achkel, Djerid **7** Bizerte
mountain: 5 Atlas **6** Mrhila **7** Tebessa **8** High Tell, Zaghouan **12** Northern Tell **17** Dorsale Tunisienne
highest point: 6 Chambi
river: 8 Medjerda, Mellegue
sea: 13 Mediterranean
physical feature:
cape: 3 Bon **5** Blanc **8** Rasaddar
desert: 6 Sahara
gulf: 5 Gabes, Tunis **8** Hammamet
oasis: 5 Gabes, Gafsa, Nefta **6** Djerba, Tozeur **9** El Oudiane **13** El Hamma Djerid
plains: 5 Sahel
salt lake: 11 Chott Djerid, Shatt Djerid
valley: 8 Medjerda
wind: 5 chile **6** chilli **7** sirocco
people: 3 Jew **4** Arab **6** Berber
artist: 5 Gorgi, Turki
dynasty: 6 Hafsid **7** Fatimid **8** Aghlabid, Almohade **10** Husseinite
leader: 6 Ben Ali **9** Bourguiba
language: 6 Arabic, Berber, French
religion: 5 Islam **7** Judaism **12** Christianity
place:
center of Tunis: 13 Place d'Afrique
mosque: 5 Great **7** Zitouna
museum: 5 Bardo, Kouba **6** Sousse
palace: 14 Dar Ben Abdallah
ruins: 8 Carthage
street: 14 Habib Bourguiba
feature:
cap: 7 chechia
clothing: 5 jebba **7** safasri **9** babbouche
market: 4 souk
food:
dish: 7 mesfouf **8** couscous
drink: 4 iban **5** legmi
fruit: 12 deglet en nour

Tunney, Gene
real name: 17 James Joseph Tunney
nickname: 14 Fighting Marine
sport: 6 boxing
class: 11 heavyweight

Tuonela
also: 6 Manala
origin: 7 Finnish
name of: 10 afterworld
form: 6 island
lacked: 3 sun **4** moon

Tupman
character in: 14 Pickwick Papers
author: 7 Dickens

tu quoque 7 thou too

Turandot
opera by: 7 Puccini
character: 3 Liu **4** Pang, Ping, Pong **5** Calaf, Timur **8** Turandot (Princess of China)

turbid 5 muddy, murky **6** cloudy,

opaque, roiled **7** clouded, unclear **8** agitated **9** disturbed, stirred up, unsettled

turbulence 4 fury **6** frenzy, hubbub, tumult, unrest, uproar **7** ferment, rioting, torrent, turmoil **8** disorder, violence **9** agitation, commotion **10** excitement, unruliness **11** disturbance

turbulent 5 rowdy **6** fierce, raging, stormy, unruly **7** chaotic, furious, riotous, violent **8** agitated, restless **9** clamorous, disturbed **10** blustering, boisterous, disorderly, tumultuous, uproarious **11** tempestuous

tureen 4 bowl, dish **9** casserole, container **10** receptacle

turf 3 sod **4** area, peat, plot, soil **5** divot, grass, haunt, sward, track **7** verdure **9** racetrack, territory **10** greensward

Turgenev, Ivan
  author of: 5 Smoke **9** First Love **10** Virgin Soil **14** Fathers and Sons **18** A Month in the Country **19** A Sportsman's Notebook, A Sportsman's Sketches, The Torrents of Spring

turgid 5 puffy, showy **6** florid, ornate **7** flowery, pompous, swollen **8** inflated, puffed up **9** bombastic, grandiose, overblown **10** hyperbolic

Turkey
  capital: 6 Angora, Ankara
  largest city: 8 Istanbul
  others: 4 Enos, Troy, Urfa **5** Adana, Bursa, Izmir, Konya, Maras, Siirt, Sivas **6** Aintab, Edessa, Edirne, Elaziz, Marash, Samsun, Smyrna **7** Antakya, Antioch, Erzurum, Kayseri, MMersin, Scutari, Trabzon, Uskudar **8** Stamboul **9** Byzantium, Eskisehir, Gaziantep **10** Adrianople **14** Constantinople
  school: 6 Aegean, Ankara **8** Istanbul
  division: 4 Pera, Sert **5** Siirt, Troad **6** Angora, Eyalet, Thrace **7** Anadolu, Beyoglu, Cilicia **8** Anatolia **9** Asia Minor, Kurdistan
  measure: 3 dra, oka, pik **4** draa, khat, kile, zira **5** berri, kileh, zirai **6** arshin, chinik, fortin, halebi **7** nocktat
  monetary unit: 4 lira, para **5** akcha, asper, kurus, pound, rebia **6** akcheh, zequin **7** aetilik, beshlik, piaster **8** medjidie
  weight: 3 oka, oke **4** aqui, dram, rotl **5** artal, cheke, kerat, obolu, ratel **6** batman, dirhem, kantar, maunch, miskal **7** drachma, quintal, yusdrum
  island: 6 Cyprus, Kibris
  lake: 3 Tuz, Van **7** Egridir **8** Beysehir
  mountain: 2 Ak **3** Ala **4** Alai, Dagh, Kara **5** Hasan, Hinis, Honaz, Murat, Murit **6** Ala Dag, Bingol, Bolgar, Pontic, Suphan, Taurus **7** Aladagh, Erciyas **8** Karacali **10** Kackar Dagi
  highest point: 6 Ararat
  river: 4 Aras, Kura **5** Araks, Dicle,

Firat, Gediz, Goksu, Halys, Irmak, Kizil, Mesta, Murat, Sarus **6** Araxes, Ceyhan, Seihun, Seyhan, Seylan, Tigris **7** Kurucay, Muradsu, Orontes, Sakarya **8** Granicus, Macestus, Maeander, Menderes **9** Euphrates **13** Buyukmenderes
  sea: 4 Aral **5** Black **6** Aegean **7** Marmara **13** Mediterranean
  physical feature:
    cape: 4 Baba, Ince **5** Bafra **6** Anamur, Helles, Hinzir **7** Karatas, Kerempe
    gulf: 3 Cos **5** Izmir **7** Antalya
    inlet: 10 Golden Horn
    peninsula: 9 Anatolian, Gallipoli
    plateau: 9 Anatolian
    strait: 8 Bosporus **9** Bosphorus **11** Dardanelles
  people: 4 Arab, Kurd, Turk **6** Seljuk
    king: 8 Mausolus
    leader: 5 Inonu, Osman **6** Ecevit **7** Demirel **8** Menderes, Suleiman **12** Kemal Ataturk
    poet: 5 Homer
  language: 6 Arabic **7** Kurdish, Turkish
  religion: 5 Islam **7** Judaism **12** Christianity **13** Greek Orthodox, Roman Catholic
  place:
    bridge: 6 Galata
    dam: 9 Gokcekaya
    mosque: 4 Blue, Yeni **8** Selimiye **11** Hagia Sophia, Sultan Ahmed
    museum: 7 Topkapi
    ruins: 4 Troy **7** Ephesus **8** Pergamum
    tomb: 12 Kemal Ataturk
  feature:
    cap: 3 fez **6** calpac **7** calpack
    clothing: 6 caftan, dolman, jelick **7** yashrak **8** charshaf, maharmah, shakseer
    goat hair: 6 mohair
    grill: 6 mangal
    harem: 5 serai **8** seraglio
    musical instrument: 5 canum, kanum **6** canoon, johnie, kussir, zither **8** crescent, jingling
    pipe: 10 meerschaum
  food:
    dish: 5 halva, pilaw **10** doner kebab, shish kebab
    drink: 4 boza, raki **5** airan, pasha, rakee **6** mastic
    pastry: 7 baklava
    turkey: 4 hind

Turkic
  language family: 6 Altaic
  group: 5 Kazak, Nogai, Uigur, Uzbek, Yakut **7** Chuvash, Kirghiz **8** Turkoman **10** Karakalpak **11** Azerbaijani **14** Osmanli Turkish

Turkmenistan
  capital/largest city: 9 Ashkhabad
  head of state: 9 president
  government: 8 republic

  monetary unit: 5 ruble
  river: 8 Amu Darya
  sea: 7 Caspian
  physical feature: 13 Kara Kum Desert
  people: 7 Turkmen **10** Turkmenian
  language: 6 Turkic **10** West Turkic
  religion: 11 Sunni Muslim
  feature: 9 Altyn Depe

turmeric
  botanical name: 12 Curcuma longa
  also called: 7 tumeric **13** Crocus indicus, Indian saffron
  family: 6 ginger
  color: 6 yellow
  used as: 3 dye **6** amulet **8** cosmetic, medicine
  origin: 4 Asia **9** Caribbean, East India
  charm against: 5 ghost **10** tree spirit

turmoil 4 mess **5** chaos **6** tumult, uproar **7** ferment **8** disorder **9** agitation, commotion, confusion **10** convulsion **11** disturbance, pandemonium
  French: 14 bouleversement

turn 2 do, go **3** act, arc, lie, put **4** bend, coil, come, deed, flex, hang, look, loop, make, rest, ride, roll, send, shot, sour, spin, time, veer, walk, wing **5** alter, apply, crack, curve, drive, eject, fling, hinge, pivot, round, scare, shift, shock, spell, spoil, start, stint, swing, throw, twist, whack, wheel, whirl **6** action, become, chance, change, curdle, depend, direct, effort, fright, gyrate, invert, period, reside, rotate, sprain, stroll, swerve, swivel, wrench, zigzag **7** acidify, attempt, convert, deliver, execute, ferment, perform, reverse, revolve, service, winding **8** gyration, overturn, roll over, rotation, surprise **9** cause to go, deviation, discharge, transform **10** accomplish, alteration, revolution

turn a deaf ear to 6 ignore, slight **9** disregard

turn aside 5 avert **6** divert **7** deflect, deviate **8** turn away

turn away 5 avert **6** give up **8** alienate, estrange, send away **9** turn aside **12** turn one's back

turnback 4 fold, quit, tack **5** repel **6** defect, desert, return, revert **7** forsake, regress, relapse, repulse, retrace, retreat, reverse **9** backslide

turncoat 5 Judas **6** bolter **7** traitor **8** apostate, betrayer, defector, deserter, quisling, renegade **12** double-dealer

turn down 5 spurn **6** refuse, reject **14** lower the volume, refuse to accept

Turner, Joseph Mallord William
  born: 6 London **7** England
  artwork: 12 The Shipwreck, The Slave Ship, Tintern Abbey **17** Dawn After the Wreck **20** Dido Building Carthage **22** Venice S Giorgio Maggiore **24** The Sun of Venice Going to Sea **25** The Thames near Walton

Bridge, Ulysses Deriding Polyphemus **30** Burning of the Houses of Parliament **32** Snowstorm Hannibal Crossing the Alps **32** The Falls of the Rhine at Schaffhausen **34** The Bay of Baiae with Apollo and the Sibyl **37** Fighting Temeraire Tugged to her Last Berth **47** The Parting of Hero and Leander from the Greek of Musaeus **50** The Shipwreck Fishing Boats Endeavoring to Rescue the Crew

Turner, Kathleen
roles: 8 Body Heat **9** Serial Mom **12** Prizzi's Honor **13** The Real Blonde, War of the Roses **17** Romancing the Stone, The Jewel of the Nile **18** Peggy Sue Got Married

Turner, Lana
real name: 29 Julia Jean Mildred Frances Turner
nickname: 11 Sweater Girl
born: 9 Wallace ID
discovered at: 16 Schwab's Drugstore
husband: 9 Artie Shaw, Lex Barker **10** Bob Topping **12** Stephen Crane
roles: 7 Madame X **11** Peyton Place **15** By Love Possessed, Imitation of Life **26** The Postman Always Rings Twice

turning 4 bend **5** curve **7** bending, curving, winding **8** pivoting, rotating, spinning, twisting, whirling **9** revolving, swiveling

turnip 12 Brassica rapa
group: 8 Rapifera
varieties: 6 Indian **7** Italian, Swedish **8** rutabaga, seven-top

turn off 4 bore, exit **5** douse, leave, repel **6** revolt, sicken **7** disgust, repulse **8** alienate, turn away **9** switch off **10** deactivate

turn of phrase 5 idiom **8** locution, phrasing **10** expression **11** phraseology

Turn of the Screw, The
author: 10 Henry James
character: 5 Flora, Miles **7** Mr Quint **8** Mrs Grose **10** Miss Jessel **12** The Governess

turn on 5 start, tempt **6** allure, attack, entice, excite **7** actuate, attract **8** activate, energize, interest, switch on

turn one's stomach 6 revolt, sicken **7** disgust **8** nauseate

turnout 5 crowd **6** output, throng **8** assembly, audience **9** gathering **10** assemblage, production

turn out 4 garb, oust **5** array, dress, eject, end up, evict, exile, expel **6** appear, attend, attire, banish, clothe, evolve, fit out, invest, rig out, show up, unfold **7** cast out, come out, costume, develop, kick out **8** drive out, send away **9** switch off **11** come to light

turn over 4 flip **5** upset **6** bestow, ro-

tate **7** deliver **8** flipflop, give over, hand over, overturn **9** surrender **10** relinquish, somersault

turn pale 4 fade **6** blanch, whiten **7** lighten

turn tail 4 flee **7** retreat, run away **8** back away **12** beat a retreat

turn to account 7 exploit, utilize **8** profit by, put to use **9** make use of **12** capitalize on

turn topsy turvy 5 upset **7** capsize, confuse, tip over **8** flip-flop, overturn, put askew **10** disarrange, turn turtle **11** disorganize

turn turtle 5 upset **7** capsize, tip over **8** flip over, keel over, overturn, turn over **14** turn upside down

turn up 4 come **6** appear, arrive, crop up, drop in, emerge, loom up, show up **7** develop, surface **11** come to light

Turpentine State
nickname of: 13 North Carolina

turpitude 4 evil, vice **8** baseness, lewdness, vileness **9** depravity **10** corruption, debauchery, defilement, degeneracy, immorality, perversion, sinfulness, wickedness, wrongdoing **13** dissoluteness **14** licentiousness

turquoise 4 aqua **5** stone **7** mineral, sky-blue **10** aquamarine **12** greenish-blue, Prussian-blue
source: 12 United States

turret 5 tower **6** belfry, cupola, garret, gazebo, louver, terret **7** minaret, rotator, steeple **8** gunhouse, gunmount **9** belvedere, pepperbox **10** watchtower
tool: 5 lathe

turtle 3 box **4** musk, wood **6** slider **7** painted, reptile, snapper, spotted **8** slowpoke, terrapin, tortoise **10** turtle-dove **11** leatherback
dorsal shell: 8 carapace
nautical: 5 upset **6** pocket **7** capsize **8** overturn
order: 8 Chelonia
ventral shell: 8 plastron
young: 7 turtlet

Turveydrop
character in: 10 Bleak House
author: 7 Dickens

tussle 4 fray **5** brawl, fight, melee, scrap, set-to **6** battle, fracas **7** grapple, scuffle, wrestle **8** conflict, struggle **10** donnybrook, free-for-all **11** altercation

tussock 4 hair, tuft **5** brush, bunch, clump, grass, sedge **7** bulrush, cluster, thicket **8** feathers

tutelage 8 coaching, guidance, teaching, training, tutoring **9** direction, education, schooling **10** discipline **11** inculcation, instruction, supervision, trusteeship **12** guardianship **14** indoctrination

tutor 4 guru **5** coach, drill, teach **6** master, mentor, school **7** prepare,

teacher **8** instruct **10** instructor **11** give lessons

tutorial 5 class **8** didactic, edifying **11** educational, instructive **12** prescriptive

tutti
music: 3 all **18** all players together, all singers together

Tuvalu
other name: 13 Ellice Islands, Lagoon Islands
capital: 8 Funafuti
head of state: 14 British monarch **15** governor general
monetary unit: 4 cent **6** dollar
island: 3 Nui **6** Niutao **7** Nanumea, Vaitupu **8** Funafuti **9** Nanumanga, Niulakita, Nukufetau **10** Nukulaelae
highest point: 5 Nuwak
sea: 7 Pacific
people: 6 Samoan **10** Polynesian
leader: 5 Lauti
language: 6 Samoan **7** English **8** Tuvaluan **10** Polynesian
religion: 10 Protestant **12** Tuvalu Church

twaddle 3 rot **4** bosh, bunk **5** trash, tripe **6** babble, drivel, gabble, jabber, piffle **7** chatter, prattle, rubbish **8** claptrap, idle talk, nonsense, tommy-rot **9** jabbering, silly talk **10** balderdash **16** stuff-and-nonsense

Twain, Mark
real name: 13 Samuel Clemens
author of: 9 Tom Sawyer **10** Roughing It **12** A Tramp Abroad, The Gilded Age **15** (Adventures of) Huckleberry Finn **18** The Innocents Abroad **20** Life on the Mississippi **21** The Mysterious Stranger, The Prince and the Pauper **29** The Man That Corrupted Hadleyburg **36** A Connecticut Yankee in King Arthur's Court **41** The Celebrated Jumping Frog of Calaveras County

twang 9 resonance, vibration **10** nasal sound **13** reverberation

Tweedledee
character in: 22 Through the Looking Glass
author: 7 Carroll

Tweedledum
character in: 22 Through the Looking Glass
author: 7 Carroll

tweet 4 peep **5** cheep, chirp **7** chirrup, chitter, twitter

Twelfth Night
author: 18 William Shakespeare
character: 5 Feste, Maria, Viola (Cesario) **6** Olivia, Orsino **7** Antonio **8** Malvolio **9** Sebastian **12** Sir Toby Belch **18** Sir Andrew Aguecheek

Twelve Angry Men
director: 11 Sidney Lumet
cast: 8 Ed Begley, Lee J Cobb **10** E G Marshall, Henry Fonda, Jack Warden

11 Jack Klugman, John Fiedler **12** Martin Balsam

Twelve O'Clock High
director: **9** Henry King
cast: **10** Dean Jagger **11** Gary Merrill, Gregory Peck, Hugh Marlowe **15** Millard Mitchell
Oscar for: **15** supporting actor (Jagger)

Twentieth Century
director: **11** Howard Hawks
based on play by: **8** Ben Hecht **16** Charles MacArthur
cast: **11** Roscoe Karns **13** Carole Lombard, John Barrymore **14** Walter Connolly

Twentieth Century, The
narrator: **14** Walter Cronkite

twenty-one see **9** blackjack

Twenty Questions
host: **10** Bill Slater, Jay Jackson
panelist: **11** Herb Polesie **12** Bobby McGuire **13** Johnnie McPhee **14** Dickie Harrison, Florence Rinard **15** Fred Van De Venter

Twenty Thousand Leagues Under the Sea
author: **10** Jules Verne
character: **7** Conseil, Ned Land **11** Captain Nemo **22** Professor Pierre Aronnax
submarine: **8** Nautilus

Twenty Years After
author: **14** Alexandre Dumas (pere)

Twice-Told Tales
author: **18** Nathaniel Hawthorne

Twightwee see **5** Miami

twilight **3** ebb, eve **4** dusk **6** sunset **7** decline, evening, sundown **8** eventide, gloaming, moonrise **9** half-light, last phase, nightfall **14** edge of darkness

Twilight of the Gods **8** Ragnarok
German: **15** Gotterdammerung

Twilight Zone, The
host: **10** Rod Serling

twin **4** dual, like **5** alike **6** double, paired **7** matched, twofold **9** duplicate, identical

Twin **6** Thomas

twine **4** coil, cord, rope, wind **5** braid, cable, plait, twist, weave **6** string, thread **7** binding, entwine **9** interlace **10** intertwine

twinge **4** pain, pang, stab **5** cramp, spasm, throb **6** stitch, tingle, twitch

twinkle **4** glow **5** blaze, flare, flash, gleam, shine **7** flicker, glimmer, glisten, shimmer, sparkle **11** scintillate

Twinkleton, Miss
character in: **22** The Mystery of Edwin Drood
author: **7** Dickens

Twins
constellation of: **6** Gemini

twirl **4** spin **5** pivot, twine, wheel, whirl **6** gyrate, rotate **7** revolve **9** pirouette

twist **3** arc, way **4** bend, coil, curl, idea, kink, knot, pull, roll, spin, turn, veer, wind, wrap, yank **5** curve, pivot, ravel, slant, snake, swing, twine, whirl, wrest **6** change, method, notion, rotate, spiral, sprain, swerve, swivel, system, tangle, wrench, zigzag **7** contort, distort, entwine, meander **8** approach, rotation, surprise **9** corkscrew, interlace, treatment **10** intertwine, involution **11** convolution, development

twisted **4** bent **6** warped **7** crooked, gnarled **8** deformed **9** contorted, distorted, misshapen

twisting **7** crooked, curving, turning **9** contorted, revolving, spiraling, swiveling

twist out of shape **4** warp **6** deform **7** contort, distort

twitch **3** tic **4** jerk **5** shake, spasm, throb **6** quaver, quiver, squirm, tremor, wiggle, writhe **7** tremble **8** paroxysm **10** convulsion

twitter **4** fuss, peep, stew **5** cheep, chirp, tizzy, tweet, whirl **6** bustle, flurry, pother, uproar, warble **7** chatter, chirrup, ferment, fluster, flutter **8** chirping **10** turbulence **11** chirrupping

two-faced **5** false **7** devious **8** slippery **9** deceitful, deceptive, dishonest, insincere **10** perfidious **11** dissembling, double-faced, duplicitous, forktongued, treacherous, underhanded **12** dishonorable, disingenuous, falsehearted, hypocritical **13** doubledealing, untrustworthy

twofold **4** dual **6** double **7** two-part

Two Gentlemen of Verona, The
author: **18** William Shakespeare
character: **5** Julia **6** Silvia, Thurio **7** Proteus **9** Valentine **11** Duke of Milan

Two Lands, The see **5** Egypt

two of a kind **4** pair **5** twins **6** couple **7** doublet

two-part **4** dual, twin **6** double, paired **9** bipartite

twosome **3** duo **4** pair **5** brace **6** couple

2001: A Space Odyssey
author: **13** Arthur C Clarke
director: **14** Stanley Kubrick
character: **4** Dave **5** Steve
computer: **3** HAL
cast: **3** HAL **10** Keir Dullea **12** Gary Lockwood **16** William Sylvester
song: **20** Thus Spake Zarathustra (Richard Strauss)
sequel: **24** Two Thousand Ten: Odyssey Two

two-time **6** betray **10** be disloyal **11** double-cross **12** be unfaithful **13** be treacherous, play false with **14** break faith with

two-timing **5** false **6** tricky **7** perfidy **8** bad faith, betrayal, disloyal, trickery **9** deceiving, deception, duplicity, falseness, treachery **10** disloyalty, perfidious **11** double-cross, duplicitous, treacherous **13** breach of faith, double-dealing, faithlessness **14** double-crossing

two-wheeler **4** bike **5** cycle **7** bicycle

Two Years Before the Mast
author: **18** Richard Henry Dana Jr

Tybalt
character in: **14** Romeo and Juliet
author: **11** Shakespeare

Tyche
origin: **5** Greek
goddess of: **7** fortune
corresponds to: **7** Fortuna

tycoon **4** boss **5** mogul, nabob **6** big gun, bigwig **7** big shot, magnate **8** big wheel **9** potentate **12** entrepreneur **13** industrialist **17** captain of industry

tyke **3** kid, tad, tot **5** child **6** shaver, squirt, wee one **9** little one

Tyler, John
presidential rank: **5** tenth
party: **4** Whig **20** Democratic-Republican
state represented: **2** VA **8** Virginia
defeated: **5** no-one
succeeded upon death of: **8** Harrison
vice president: **4** none
cabinet:
state: **6** (Abel Parker) Upshur **7** (Daniel) Webster, (John C) Calhoun
treasury: **4** (George Mortimer) Bibb **5** (Thomas) Ewing **7** (John Canfield) Spencer, (Walter) Forward
war: **4** (John) Bell **7** (John Canfield) Spencer, (William) Wilkins
attorney general: **6** (Hugh Swinton) Legare, (John) Nelson **10** (John Jordan) Crittenden
navy: **5** (John Young) Mason **6** (Abel Parker) Upshur, (George Edmund) Badger, (Thomas Walker) Gilmer
postmaster general: **7** (Francis) Granger **9** (Charles Anderson) Wickliffe
born: **2** VA **8** Greenway, Virginia **17** Charles City County
died/buried: **2** VA **8** Richmond, Virginia
education: **14** William and Mary
religion: **12** Episcopalian
vacation spot: **2** VA **7** Hampton **8** Virginia
political career: **8** US Senate **12** State Council **13** vice president **24** US House of Representatives
delegate to: **13** State Assembly
governor of: **8** Virginia

civilian career: 6 farmer, lawyer

military service: 19 War of Eighteen Twelve

notable events of lifetime/term:
  act: 6 Tariff (of 1842)
  annexation of: 5 Texas
  treaty: 16 Webster-Ashburton

father: 4 John

mother: 4 Mary (Marott Armistead)

siblings: 7 William **8** Wat Henry **10** Maria Henry **12** Anne Contesse **14** Christina Booth **15** Martha Jefferson **18** Elizabeth Armistead

wife: 5 Julia (Gardiner) **7** Letitia (Christian)

children: 4 John, Mary **5** Alice, Julia, Pearl **6** Robert **7** Lachlan, Letitia **8** Tazewell **9** Elizabeth **12** Anne Contesse, Lyon Gardiner **13** David Gardiner, John Alexander **16** Robert FitzWalter

Tyll Eulenspiegel *see* **16** Till Eulenspiegel

Tyndall, John
  field: 7 physics
  nationality: 5 Irish
  studied diffusion of: 5 light

Tyndareus
  wife: 4 Leda
  daughter: 6 Phoebe **8** Philonoe, Timandra **12** Clytemnestra

Tyndaridae *see* **15** Castor and Pollux

type 4 font, kind, race, sort **5** brand, class, genus, group, model, order, print **6** design, family, phylum, sample **7** pattern, species, variety **8** category, division, specimen, typeface **9** archetype, prototype **10** typography

type, movable
  invented by: 9 Gutenberg

Typee
  author: 14 Herman Melville
  character: 3 Tom (Melville) **4** Toby **6** Marnoo, Mehevi **7** Fayaway **8** Kory-Kory

typewriter

invented by: 5 Soule **6** Sholes **7** Glidden

Typhoeus
  form: 7 monster
  father: 8 Tartarus
  mother: 2 Ge
  number of heads: 10 one hundred

typhoon 4 gale, gust, wind **5** storm **7** cyclone, tempest, tornado, twister **9** hurricane, whirlwind

Typhoon
  author: 12 Joseph Conrad

typical 5 model, stock, usual **6** normal **7** average, regular **8** ordinary, orthodox, standard **9** exemplary, in keeping **10** individual, prototypal, true to type **11** distinctive, in character **12** conventional, to be expected **14** characteristic, representative

typify 5 sum up **6** embody **7** betoken, connote, pass for **8** instance, stand for **9** epitomize, exemplify, incarnate, personify, represent **10** illustrate **12** characterize

typography measure 2 em, en **4** pica **5** point

Tyr
  origin: 12 Scandinavian
  god of: 7 victory
  father: 4 Odin **5** Othin
  mother: 3 Fri **5** Frigg, Frija **6** Frigga
  killed by: 4 Garm

tyrannical 7 fascist **8** despotic **9** imperious **10** oppressive **11** dictatorial, domineering **13** authoritarian

tyrannize 7 oppress **8** domineer, overlord **10** slave drive

tyrannized 9 exploited, oppressed **11** downtrodden, subservient **12** harshly ruled

Tyrannosaurus
  type: 8 dinosaur, theropod
  location: 7 Montana **12** North America
  period: 10 Cretaceous

tyrannous 8 despotic **9** imperious **10**

iron-handed, oppressive, repressive, tyrannical

tyranny 7 cruelty, fascism **8** coercion, iron fist, iron hand, iron rule, severity **9** despotism, harshness **10** domination, oppression, repression **11** persecution **12** dictatorship **13** reign of terror **15** totalitarianism

tyrant 5 bully **6** despot **8** dictator, martinet **10** persecutor, taskmaster **11** cruel master, slave driver

Tyre
  king of: 5 Hiram

tyro 6 intern, novice, rookie **7** learner, recruit, trainee **8** beginner, initiate, neophyte, newcomer **9** greenhorn **10** apprentice, tenderfoot

Tyro
  father: 9 Salmoneus
  loved by: 8 Cretheus, Poseidon
  son: 5 Aeson **6** Neleus, Pelias
  grandson: 5 Jason **6** Nestor

Tyrrheus
  occupation: 8 shepherd

Tyson, Cicely
  born: 9 New York NY
  roles: 5 Roots **7** Sounder **33** The Autobiography of Miss Jane Pittman

Tyson, Mike
  original name: 7 Michael
  nickname: 8 Iron Mike
  born: 2 NY **8** Brooklyn **17** Bedford-Stuyvesant
  wife: 11 Robin Givens
  manager: 9 Cus D'Amato **10** Bill Cayton **11** Jimmy Jacobs
  trainer: 12 Angelo Dundee
  promoter: 7 Don King
  boxing title: 3 IBF, WBA, WBC **11** heavyweight
  defeated: 6 Holmes, Spinks, Thomas, Tillis, Tucker **7** Berbick
  defeated by: 7 Douglas (Buster)
  convicted of: 4 rape

tzimmes 4 fuss **6** uproar **10** hullabaloo
  literally: 4 stew **9** mixed dish

Ubangi-Shari *see* **22** Central African Republic

Ubermensch **8** superman

ubiquitous **7** allover **9** pervading, pervasive, prevalent, universal, worldwide **10** everywhere, widespread **11** everpresent, omnipresent **12** all-pervading

ubiquitously **10** everywhere **11** extensively

ubi supra **19** where mentioned above

Ucalegon
   counselor to: **5** Priam

Uccello, Paolo
   real name: **11** Paolo di Dono
   born: **5** Italy **8** Florence
   artwork: **8** The Flood **12** The Night Hunt **15** Sir John Hawkwood **18** The Rout (Battle) of San Romano **20** St George and the Dragon

Udall, Nicholas
   author of: **19** Ralph Roister Doister

Uganda
   capital/largest city: **7** Kampala
   others: **4** Arua, Gulu, Lira **5** Atiak, Jinja, Mbale, Mengo **6** Kasese, Kiboga, Kitgum, Masaka, Moroto, Pajule, Soroti, Tororo **7** Entebbe, Kachung, Kilembe, Mbarara, Mombasa **8** Kyenjojo **11** Port Masindi
   school: **8** Makerere
   division: **4** Toro **6** Ankole, Busoga **7** Buganda, Bunyoro
   monetary unit: **4** cent **8** shilling
   island: **4** Sese
   lake: **5** Kioga, Kyoga **6** Albert, Edward, George **8** Victoria
   mountain: **4** Oboa **5** Elgon **7** Virunga **9** Mufumbiro, Ruwenzori **18** Mountains of the Moon
   highest point: **10** Margherita
   river: **4** Aswa, Kafu **5** Pager **7** Katonga **9** White Nile **10** Albert Nile **12** Victoria Nile
   physical feature:
      falls: **5** Owens **8** Kabalega **9** Murchison
      plateau: **6** Ankole **11** East African
      valley: **9** Great Rift
   people: **4** Alur, Gisu, Soga, Teso **5** Ateso, Bantu, Chiga, Ganda, Langi, Lango, Nkole, Pygmy **6** Acholi, Ankole, Bagisu, Bakega, Basiga, Batoro **7** Baganda, Banyoro, Bunyoro, Hamitic, Lugbara, Nilotic, Sudanic **9** Nyoro-Toro **10** Banyankole,

Karamojong
   explorer: **5** Baker, Speke **7** Stanley
   king: **6** Mutesa, Mwanga **8** Kabarega
   leader: **5** Obote **6** Mutesa **7** Omukama **11** Idi Amin Dada
   language: **5** Ateso, Ganda **7** English, Luganda, Swahili
   religion: **5** Islam **7** animism **8** Anglican **10** Protestant **13** Roman Catholic
   place:
      airport: **7** Entebbe
      dam: **10** Owens Falls
      national park: **6** Kidepo **14** Murchison Falls, Queen Elizabeth
   feature:
      clothing: **7** busuuti
      council of chiefs: **6** lukiko
      dance group: **17** Heart Beat of Africa
      king: **6** kabaka
   food:
      drink: **6** waragi

ugliness **8** ill-favor **9** grossness **10** homeliness **11** hideousness, monstrosity **12** unseemliness **13** frightfulness, grotesqueness, monstrousness, repulsiveness, unsightliness **14** unpleasantness **16** unattractiveness

ugly **4** foul, mean, vile **5** nasty **6** homely, horrid, odious **7** hideous, hostile, ominous **8** dreadful, horrible, menacing, unseemly **9** abhorrent, dangerous, difficult, frightful, grotesque, monstrous, obnoxious, offensive, repellent, repugnant, repulsive, sickening, unsightly **10** abominable, disgusting

ugly as sin **7** hideous **9** frightful, grotesque, monstrous, repulsive

Ugly Duckling, The
   author: **21** Hans Christian Andersen

ukase **4** fiat **5** edict, order **6** decree, dictum, ruling **7** command, mandate, statute **9** directive, manifesto, ordinance **10** injunction **12** proclamation **13** pronouncement

Ukraine
   capital/largest city: **4** Kiev
   others: **4** Lviv (Lvov), **6** Odessa **7** Donetsk, Kharkov, Lugansk (Voroshilovgrad) **8** Mariupol (Zhdanov) **9** Krivoi Rog, Zaporozhe **14** Dnepropetrovsk
   head of state: **9** president
   government: **8** republic

   monetary unit: **6** grivna **10** karbovanet
   mountain: **7** Crimean **10** Carpathian
   river: **3** Bug **6** Donets **7** Dnieper
   sea: **5** Black
   people: **7** Russian **9** Ukrainian
   language: **9** Ukrainian
   religion: **17** Ukrainian Catholic, Ukrainian Orthodox
   feature: **25** Askaniya Nova Nature Reserve

Ulan Bator
   capital of: **8** Mongolia

ulcer **4** sore **6** canker

Uller
   also: **4** Ullr
   origin: **8** Teutonic
   god of: **12** winter sports
   stepfather: **4** Thor

Ullmann, Liv
   born: **5** Japan, Tokyo
   nationality: **9** Norwegian
   roles: **7** Persona **10** Face to Face **11** Forty Carats, Lost Horizon **12** The Emigrants **16** Cries and Whispers **19** Scenes from a Marriage

ulna
   bone of: **8** lower arm
   neighbor: **6** radius

ulterior **6** covert, hidden, secret **7** selfish **9** concealed, undivulged, unrevealed **11** self-serving, undisclosed, unexpressed **13** opportunistic

ultimate **3** end **4** acme, apex, last, peak **5** final **6** height, utmost **7** extreme, maximum, supreme **8** crowning, eventual, greatest, terminal **9** at the peak, high point, last straw, long-range, resulting **10** conclusive, definitive
   French: **7** dernier

Ultima Thule **12** far-off region **15** uttermost degree

Ultor
   epithet of: **7** Jupiter
   means: **7** avenger

ultra **7** extreme **9** excessive, extremist

ultramodern **8** advanced, brand-new **10** avant-garde, newfangled **13** in the vanguard, up-to-the-minute

ulu **5** knife
   used by: **11** Eskimo women

ululate **4** hoot, howl, wail **6** lament

Ulysses
   author: **10** James Joyce

character: 10 Molly Bloom **12** Blazes Boylan, Buck Mulligan, Leopold Bloom **14** Stephen Dedalus

Ulysses *see* **8** Odysseus

umber 5 brown **7** pigment **9** dark-brown **14** yellowish-brown

umbilicus 5 navel **11** belly button

umbrage 5 pique, shade **6** leaves, shadow **7** foliage, offense, outrage **10** resentment

umbrella 6 brolly **7** parasol **11** bumbershoot

Umbrellas of Cherbourg, The
director: **11** Jacques Demy
cast: **10** Anne Vernon **15** Nino Castelnuovo **16** Catharine Deneuve
score: **13** Michel Legrand

Umbrian
language family: **12** Indo-European
branch: **6** Italic

umpire 5 judge **7** arbiter, mediate, referee **8** mediator, moderate **9** arbitrate, go-between, moderator **10** adjudicate, arbitrator, negotiator **11** adjudicator, intercessor

umpteen 4 many, slew **5** loads (of)

Una
character in: **15** The Faerie Queene
author: **7** Spenser

unabbreviated 5 uncut **8** complete, undocked, unpruned **9** uncropped, unreduced, unsnipped, untrimmed **10** full-length, unabridged **11** uncondensed, uncurtailed, unshortened **12** uncompressed, unexpurgated

unable 5 unfit **6** cannot **8** helpless, impotent **9** incapable **10** inadequate, unequipped **11** incompetent, unqualified
to tell pitch: **8** tone deaf

unabridged 5 uncut **6** entire, intact **8** complete **10** full-length **11** uncondensed

unacceptable 8 below par, improper, unseemly, unworthy **9** deficient, out of line, unwelcome **10** disallowed, inadequate, unsuitable **11** displeasing, intolerable **12** inadmissible, not allowable, not up to snuff **13** insupportable **14** unsatisfactory **15** not up to standard

unacceptableness 8 disfavor, disgrace, ignominy **18** unsatisfactoriness

unaccommodating 4 rude **8** churlish **9** difficult, unhelpful **10** inflexible, intolerant, unyielding **11** disobliging **13** inconsiderate

unaccompanied 4 lone, solo **5** alone, apart **6** single, singly **8** isolated, lonesome, separate, solitary **9** a cappella, by oneself **10** unattended, unescorted **12** all by oneself **13** companionless

unaccountable 3 odd **4** free **5** clear, queer, weird **6** exempt, immune **7** bizarre, curious, excused, strange, unusual **8** baffling, innocent, peculiar **9** blameless, not liable, unheard-of

10 inculpable, intriguing, mysterious, surprising **11** astonishing, unexplained **12** inexplicable, unfathomable **13** extraordinary, not answerable **14** not responsible **16** incomprehensible

unaccustomed 3 new, odd **4** rare, wild **5** green, new to, novel, queer **6** quaint, unique, unused **7** amazing, bizarre, curious, foreign, not used, strange, ungiven, untried, unusual **8** original, peculiar, singular, uncommon **9** fantastic, startling, unheard-of **10** remarkable, surprising, unfamiliar, unversed in **11** astonishing, out-of-the-way, unpracticed **12** unacquainted, unhabituated, unimaginable **13** extraordinary, inexperienced **14** unfamiliar with **16** out of the ordinary

unacknowledged 9 anonymous **10** unanswered **11** disregarded **12** unidentified, unrecognized

unadorned 4 bald, bare **5** naked, plain, stark **6** simple **7** austere **11** undecorated **12** unornamented **13** unembellished **15** straightforward

unadulterated 4 pure, true **5** clear, uncut **7** genuine **9** unalloyed, untainted **14** untampered-with

unadventurous 5 chary, timid **7** careful **8** cautious, hesitant **11** circumspect

unadvisable 5 silly **6** stupid, unwise **8** unseemly **9** imprudent **11** inadvisable, inexpedient, injudicious, undesirable **15** disadvantageous

unaesthetic 9 tasteless **10** inartistic **11** insensitive **16** undiscriminating

unaffected 4 open **5** frank, naive, plain **6** candid, direct, honest, simple **7** genuine, natural, sincere, unmoved **8** innocent **9** childlike, guileless, ingenuous, unfeeling, unstirred, untouched, unworldly, wholesome **10** impervious, unbothered, unreserved **11** indifferent, insensitive, openhearted, plain-spoken, unconcerned, undesigning, undisturbed **12** unresponsive **13** unsympathetic **15** straightforward, unsophisticated

unaffectedness 4 ease **11** naturalness **12** unconstraint

unafraid 4 bold **5** brave **6** daring, heroic, plucky **7** valiant **8** fearless, intrepid, stalwart, valorous **9** audacious, daredevil, dauntless **10** courageous **11** indomitable, lionhearted, venturesome **12** stouthearted **13** adventuresome

unaggressive 3 shy **4** meek **5** timid **7** passive **8** peaceful, timorous **9** peaceable, shrinking **11** unambitious **14** unenterprising

unagitated 4 calm **6** gentle, placid, serene **8** composed, tranquil **9** collected, unexcited, unruffled **10** untroubled **11** undisturbed, unperturbed **13** self-possessed

unalloyed 4 pure **7** unmixed **11** unqualified **13** unadulterated

unalterable 5 fixed, rigid **6** stable **8** constant **9** immutable, indelible, obstinate, permanent, perennial **10** inflexible, persistent **11** irrevocable **12** indissoluble, unchangeable **13** irretrievable

unambitious 4 easy, lazy **6** humble, modest, simple **8** slothful **10** unaspiring **12** unaggressive **14** unenterprising

unamiable 4 sour **5** cross, surly, testy **6** sullen **7** grouchy, hostile, peevish **8** churlish **9** irascible **10** ill-humored, unfriendly, unpleasant, unsociable **11** bad-tempered, uncongenial **12** disagreeable

unamorous 4 cold, cool **6** frigid **8** unloving **11** passionless

unanimated 4 dull, flat, limp **5** inert, vapid **7** insipid **8** lifeless **10** insentient **11** unconscious

unanimity 6 accord **7** concord, harmony **9** agreement, consensus **11** concordance, concurrence **17** meeting of the minds

unanimous 6 allied, united **9** accordant, consonant, of one mind **10** harmonious, like-minded

unannounced 6 secret, sudden **8** surprise, withheld **10** suppressed, unheralded **11** undisclosed, unlooked for, unpublished **12** unadvertised **13** unanticipated

unanticipated 6 sudden **8** surprise **10** unexpected, unforeseen, unheralded **11** unannounced, unlooked-for, unpredicted

unappealing 10 disgusting, uninviting, unpleasant **11** displeasing **12** disagreeable, unappetizing, unattractive

unappetizing 6 horrid **7** insipid **10** bad-tasting, disgusting, uninviting **11** unpalatable **12** disagreeable

unapproachable 4 cold, cool **5** aloof **6** remote, unique **7** austere, awesome, distant, supreme **8** foremost, peerless, superior **9** matchless, nonpareil, unequaled, unrivaled **10** forbidding, inimitable, preeminent **11** beyond reach, stand-offish, unreachable **12** inaccessible, incomparable, intimidating, second to none, unattainable, unparalleled **13** beyond compare

unasked 6 wanton **8** unbidden, unsought, unwanted **9** uninvited, unwelcome **10** gratuitous **11** uncalled-for, undesirable, unrequested, unsolicited

unassertive 3 shy **5** timid **6** humble, modest **7** bashful **8** sheepish **9** diffident, shrinking

unassertiveness 7 modesty, shyness **8** docility, timidity **9** timidness **10** diffidence, humbleness **11** bashfulness **12** sheepishness

unassuming 5 muted, plain **6** homely, modest, simple **7** natural **9** easygoing

11 unassertive, unobtrusive **13** unpretentious **14** unostentatious

unattached 5 apart, split **6** single **8** detached, separate **9** separated **11** unconnected **12** disconnected

unattractive 4 dull, ugly **5** plain **6** homely **8** frumpish **11** unappealing, undesirable **12** unappetizing

unauthentic 4 fake, mock, sham **5** bogus, false, phony **6** untrue **7** dubious **8** doubtful **9** imitation, synthetic **10** fraudulent **11** counterfeit **12** questionable

unauthenticated 8 disputed **10** apocryphal, unverified **15** unsubstantiated

unauthorized 6 banned, covert **7** furtive **8** outlawed, unlawful **9** concealed, unallowed, underhand **10** prohibited, unapproved, unofficial **11** clandestine, uncertified, unpermitted, unwarranted **12** unaccredited, unsanctioned **13** under-the-table

unavailable 5 taken **6** scarce **7** lacking, married **9** not at hand **10** nonpresent **11** nonexistent

unavailing 4 idle, vain, weak **5** empty, inept **6** futile, no good **7** invalid, useless **8** bootless, impotent **9** fruitless, worthless **11** ineffective, ineffectual **12** unproductive, unsuccessful

unavoidable 4 sure **5** fated, fixed **7** certain **9** necessary, requisite **10** compulsory, imperative, inevitable, obligatory **11** inescapable **13** unpreventable **14** uncontrollable

unaware 8 heedless, ignorant, unwarned **9** in the dark, unalerted, unknowing, unmindful **10** unapprised **11** incognizant, unconscious **12** off one's guard, unacquainted, unsuspecting **13** unenlightened

unawares 8 abruptly, by chance, suddenly **9** by mistake **10** by accident, by surprise, mistakenly **11** unknowingly, unwittingly **12** accidentally, out of nowhere, unexpectedly, unthinkingly **13** inadvertently, involuntarily, unconsciously **14** without warning **15** unintentionally **16** like a thunderbolt **20** like a bolt from the blue, like a thief in the night

unbalanced 3 mad **4** daft, loco **5** batty, nutty, wacky **6** crazed, uneven, warped **7** bonkers, cracked, leaning, unequal, unglued, unsound **8** demented, deranged, lopsided, unhinged, unpoised, unstable, unsteady **9** disturbed, illogical, psychotic, unsettled **10** irrational, unadjusted **11** not all there **12** psychopathic

unbearable 11 intolerable, unendurable, unthinkable **12** inadmissible, insufferable, unacceptable **13** insupportable

unbecoming 4 ugly **6** homely, vulgar **8** improper, unfitted, unseemly,

unsuited **9** offensive, tasteless, unsightly **10** indecorous, unsuitable **11** unappealing, unbefitting **12** unattractive **13** inappropriate

unbelief 5 doubt **7** dubiety **9** disbelief **10** skepticism **11** incredulity **12** doubtfulness

unbelievable 5 false **6** absurd, insane **7** amazing, asinine, idiotic **10** astounding, farfetched, incredible, irrational, remarkable, ridiculous **11** astonishing **12** preposterous, unimaginable, unreasonable **13** hard to swallow

unbeliever 7 atheist, heathen infidel, skeptic **8** apostate **10** godless one **11** disbeliever, nonbeliever

unbelieving 7 dubious **8** doubting **9** quizzical, skeptical **10** suspicious **11** distrustful, incredulous, questioning, unconvinced **12** disbelieving, nonbelieving

unbend 5 relax **6** relent, unflex **10** straighten **12** straighten up **13** straighten out

unbending 4 firm **5** rigid, stiff, tough **6** severe, strict **8** stubborn **9** obstinate **10** inflexible, stone-faced, unyielding **11** hard as nails **14** uncompromising

unbent 5 erect **7** relaxed, unbowed, upright, yielded **8** relented, straight, uncurved, unflexed **9** unstooped **12** straightened

unbiased 4 fair, just **7** liberal, neutral **8** detached, tolerant **9** impartial, unbigoted **10** fair-minded, open-minded, undogmatic **11** broad-minded **12** uninfluenced, unprejudiced **13** disinterested, dispassionate

unbigoted 8 tolerant, unbiased **10** open-minded **11** broad-minded **12** unprejudiced

unbind 4 free, undo **5** loose, untie **6** detach, loosen, ungird **7** deliver, release, undress **8** let loose, unfasten

unblamable 5 clear **8** innocent **9** blameless, guiltless, not guilty **10** inculpable, not at fault **14** not responsible

unblemished 4 pure **7** perfect **8** flawless, spotless, unmarred, unsoiled **9** unsullied **10** immaculate, unvitiated **11** white as snow **13** unadulterated **14** uncontaminated **15** clean as a whistle

unblock 4 free, open **5** unbar, unjam **6** unclog, unstop

unborn 5 fetal, later **6** coming, future, to come **7** in utero **9** embryonic **10** subsequent, succeeding **11** prospective

unbosom oneself 7 confess, confide, lay bare **15** unburden oneself

unbound 4 free **5** freed, loose **6** loosed, untied **8** detached, let loose,

loosened, released **10** unconfined, unfastened **12** unrestrained

unbounded 8 absolute **9** boundless, unbridled, unlimited **12** uncontrolled, unrestrained, unrestricted **13** unconditional, unconstrained

unbreakable 5 tough **6** strong

unbroken 5 whole **6** entire, intact **7** endless **8** complete **9** ceaseless, continual, incessant, uncracked, undivided, unsmashed **10** continuous, sequential, successive, unruptured **11** consecutive, progressive, unremitting, unshattered **12** undiminished **13** uninterrupted

unbuckle 4 undo **6** loosen **7** release, unhitch, unstrap **8** uncouple, unfasten

unburden 4 free **6** reveal **7** confess, confide, relieve, unbosom **8** disclose **9** disburden **10** unencumber **11** disencumber **15** get off one's chest **18** get out of one's system

unbusinesslike 6 casual, sloppy **8** informal **11** impractical, inefficient

uncalculated 9 unplanned **10** accidental, unintended **11** inadvertent **14** unpremeditated

uncalled-for 6 wanton **7** unasked **8** needless, unneeded, unsought, unwanted **9** redundant, uninvited **10** gratuitous, unprompted **11** unjustified, unnecessary, unsolicited **12** nonessential **14** supererogatory

uncanny 5 eerie, weird **6** spooky **7** curious, strange **8** inspired **9** fantastic, intuitive, marvelous, unearthly, unheard-of, unnatural **10** incredible, mysterious, prodigious, remarkable, unexampled **11** astonishing, exceptional **12** unbelievable, unimaginable **13** extraordinary, uncomfortable

uncanonical 12 unauthorized, unscriptural

Uncas
  character in: **20** The Last of the Mohicans
  author: **6** Cooper

unceasing 7 endless, eternal **8** constant **9** continual, incessant, perpetual, sustained **10** continuous, persistent, without end

uncelebrated 6 unsung **7** obscure, unknown **9** anonymous **14** uncommemorated

unceremonious 4 curt, rude **5** hasty, rough **6** abrupt **7** brusque **8** informal **11** precipitate

uncertain 4 hazy **6** fitful, unsure **7** dubious, erratic, not sure, obscure, unclear **8** doubtful, hesitant, nebulous, not fixed, variable, wavering **9** debatable, undecided, unsettled **10** disputable, indefinite, indistinct, in question, irresolute, unresolved, up in the air **11** conjectural, fluctuating, not definite, speculative, unconfirmed, vacillating

12 not confident, questionable, undetermined **13** indeterminate, unpredictable

uncertainty 4 odds, risk **5** doubt **6** chance, gamble **8** quandary **9** ambiguity, confusion, hesitancy, vagueness **10** hesitation, indecision, perplexity, unsureness **11** ambivalence, vacillation **12** equivocation, irresolution, shilly-shally **14** indefiniteness

unchain 4 free **7** release, set free **8** liberate, unfetter **9** unshackle

unchangeable 5 rigid **6** stable **7** uniform **8** stubborn **9** immutable, obstinate, permanent **10** inflexible, invariable **11** unalterable **12** intransigent

unchanging 4 fast, firm **5** fixed **6** stable, static **7** abiding, durable, lasting **8** constant **9** immutable, permanent, steadfast **10** monotonous **11** everlasting **12** indissoluble

unchaperoned 10 unattended, unescorted **12** unsupervised **13** unaccompanied

uncharacteristic 8 atypical **12** out of keeping **16** unrepresentative

uncharitable 5 tight **6** stingy, unkind **7** miserly **9** illiberal, niggardly, unfeeling **10** unfriendly, ungenerous, ungracious **11** closefisted, insensitive, tightfisted **12** parsimonious **13** unsympathetic **15** uncompassionate

unchaste 4 lewd **5** loose **6** erotic, impure **7** corrupt, immoral **8** immodest **9** abandoned, debauched **10** dishonored

unchecked 4 free **5** loose **6** unruly **7** liberal, rampant **8** reinless, unreined **9** out of hand, unbridled, unmuzzled **10** unhindered **12** out of control, unrestrained, unsuppressed

uncial 6 script
form: 5 large, round
used in: 5 Greek, Latin

unciform 10 hook-shaped

uncivil 4 curt, rude **5** blunt, surly **6** abrupt, gauche **7** boorish, brusque **8** impolite **10** ungracious **11** illmannered **12** disagreeable, discourteous

uncivilized 4 rude **6** savage, vulgar **7** boorish, brutish, ill-bred, uncouth, untamed **8** barbaric, churlish **9** barbarous, obnoxious, ungenteel **10** uncultured, unpolished **12** uncultivated

unclad 4 bare, nude **5** naked **7** exposed, unrobed **8** disrobed, in the raw, starkers, stripped **9** in the nude, unclothed, uncovered, undressed **10** stark-naked **15** in the altogether

unclean 4 evil, foul, tref, vile **5** dirty, dusty, grimy, messy, muddy, sooty **6** filthy, impure, soiled **7** defiled, immoral, obscene, smutted, stained **8** polluted, unchaste **9** blemished **10** besmirched

unclear 3 dim **4** hazy **5** blear, faint, foggy, fuzzy, misty, vague **6** bleary, cloudy, vapory **7** clouded, obscure, shadowy **8** shrouded, vaporous **9** ambiguous, uncertain **10** indefinite, indistinct

Uncle Remus
author: 18 Joel Chandler Harris

Uncle Sam
personification of: 7 America

Uncle Tom's Cabin
author: 19 Harriet Beecher Stowe
character: 5 Eliza, Topsy **10** Eva St Clare **11** Simon Legree

Uncle Vanya
author: 12 Anton Chekhov
character: 6 Marina **12** Mihail Astrov **13** Ivan Voynitsky (Uncle Vanya) **14** Marya Voynitsky **15** Sonya Andreyevna **16** Yelena Andreyevna **19** Alexandr Serebryakov

unclose 4 open **6** reveal, unclog, unfold, unshut, unstop, unwrap **7** unblock
poetic: 3 ope

unclothed 4 bare, nude **5** naked **6** unclad **7** exposed, unrobed **8** stripped **9** in the nude, uncovered, undressed

unclouded 5 clear, light, sunny **6** bright, serene **10** unobscured

uncollected 4 owed **5** owing, upset **6** shaken **8** agitated, troubled **9** disturbed, perturbed **11** discomposed, outstanding

uncolored 4 bald, bare, true **5** plain, stark **6** simple **9** unadorned **11** unvarnished **12** unelaborated **13** unembellished **15** straightforward

uncombed 5 messy **6** blowsy, frowzy, matted, mussed, untidy **7** ruffled, rumpled, snarled, tangled, tousled, unkempt **11** disarranged

uncomfortable 4 edgy **5** tense, upset **6** on edge, uneasy **7** awkward, keyed up, nervous, painful **8** confused, strained, troubled **9** ill at ease **10** bothersome, disquieted, irritating, out of place **11** discomfited, discomposed, distressful **13** on tenterhooks

uncommitted 9 unpledged **11** undedicated

uncommon 4 rare **5** novel **6** scarce, unique **7** bizarre, curious, notable, supreme, unusual **8** peculiar, peerless, superior **9** matchless, unmatched **10** infrequent, remarkable, unexcelled, unfamiliar **11** exceptional, outstanding, superlative **12** incomparable, unparalleled **13** extraordinary **14** unconventional **15** once in a lifetime **16** few and far between

uncommunicative 3 mum, shy **4** dumb, mute **5** quiet **6** silent **8** reserved, reticent, retiring, taciturn **9** secretive, withdrawn **10** speechless, tongue-tied, unsociable **11** untalkative **12** close-mouthed, inexpressive

uncomplicated 4 easy **5** clear, plain **6** simple **10** uninvolved

uncomplimentary 8 critical, derisive, negative **9** insulting **10** unadmiring **11** disparaging **12** disapproving, unflattering

uncompromising 4 firm **5** rigid, stiff **6** strict **8** exacting, hardline, obdurate **9** immovable, unbending, unvarying **10** inexorable, inflexible, scrupulous, unyielding **11** unrelenting

unconcealed 4 bald, bare, open **5** overt **6** in view **7** exposed, in sight, obvious, visible **8** apparent, manifest, revealed **9** uncovered **11** discernible, perceivable, perceptible **12** in plain sight, out in the open

unconcentrated 4 weak **7** diffuse, diluted, thinned **9** dispersed, scattered, spread out **11** watered down

unconcern 10 dispassion **11** insouciance, nonchalance **12** indifference

unconcerned 4 cold **5** aloof **6** serene **7** distant, unaware, unmoved **8** composed, uncaring **9** apathetic, oblivious, unfeeling, unmindful **10** impervious, nonchalant, uninvolved, untroubled **11** indifferent, insensitive, passionless, unperturbed **12** unresponsive **13** unsympathetic

unconditional 5 utter **6** entire **8** absolute, complete, outright **9** downright, unlimited **10** conclusive **11** categorical, unqualified **12** unrestricted **13** thoroughgoing

unconfident 3 shy **5** timid **7** bashful **8** reticent, retiring, timorous **9** diffident, shrinking, uncertain

unconfirmed 7 dubious **8** unproved **10** unapproved, unverified **11** unvalidated **12** questionable **14** uncorroborated **15** unsubstantiated

unconformity 7 anomaly **9** deviation **10** aberration, divergence **11** abnormality, peculiarity **12** eccentricity, idiosyncrasy, irregularity **13** nonconformity

uncongenial 9 ill-suited, unamiable **10** dissimilar, unfriendly, unpleasant **12** disagreeable, incompatible **13** unsympathetic

unconnected 7 severed **8** detached, discrete, separate **9** uncoupled, unhitched, unrelated **12** disconnected

unconquerable 6 innate **9** ingrained **10** inveterate, invincible, unbeatable **12** impenetrable, invulnerable, undefeatable **14** insurmountable, unvanquishable

unconscionable 7 extreme **9** excessive **10** immoderate, inordinate, outrageous **11** inexcusable, unjustified, unwarranted **12** indefensible, preposterous, unforgivable, unpardonable, unreasonable **13** unjustifiable

unconscious 3 out **6** latent **7** in a

coma, out cold 8 comatose, **in a faint 9** insensate, senseless, unknowing, unmindful **10** suppressed, unrealized **11** incognizant **12** unsuspecting **14** dead to the world

unconstitutional 7 illegal **8** unlawful **12** unauthorized

unconstrained 4 bold, easy **7** natural, relaxed **8** unforced **9** abandoned **10** unaffected **11** spontaneous, uninhibited

French: 6 degage

unconstraint 4 ease **7** abandon **8** boldness, free will, openness **9** frankness **11** naturalness, spontaneity

uncontrollable 6 unruly **7** wayward **12** ungovernable, unmanageable

uncontrolled 4 free, wild **8** absolute **9** abandoned, unlimited **10** ungoverned **12** unrestrained

unconventional 3 odd **4** rare **5** crazy, kinky, nutty, queer, wacky, weird **6** far-out, quaint, unique **7** bizarre, curious, offbeat, strange, unusual **8** aberrant, atypical, bohemian, freakish, original, peculiar, singular, uncommon **9** different, eccentric, fantastic, irregular **10** newfangled, outlandish, unorthodox **11** exceptional **12** unaccustomed **13** extraordinary, idiosyncratic, nonconforming, nonconformist **15** individualistic

unconvinced 7 dubious **8** doubtful **9** skeptical, uncertain, unsettled

unconvincing 5 false, fishy **7** dubious, suspect **10** suspicious **11** implausible **12** questionable, unbelievable

uncooked

French: 9 au naturel

uncooperative 6 ornery **7** selfish **8** perverse, stubborn **9** difficult, unhelpful, unwilling **11** intractable **12** intransigent

uncoordinated 6 clumsy **7** awkward **8** ungainly **9** graceless

uncouple 4 undo **6** detach, loosen, unhook **7** release, unhitch **8** unbuckle

uncoupled 8 detached, loosened **9** separated, unhitched **10** disengaged **11** unconnected **12** disconnected

uncourageous 5 timid **8** cowardly, timorous **9** dastardly, shrinking **13** pusillanimous

uncourtly 7 ill-bred, uncivil, uncouth **9** ungallant **10** ill- behaved, ungracious, unmannerly **11** uncourteous **12** discourteous **13** ungentlemanly

uncouth 4 rude **5** crass, crude, gross, rough **6** callow, coarse **7** boorish, brutish, ill-bred, loutish, uncivil **8** barbaric, churlish, impolite **9** unrefined **10** indelicate, uncultured, unmannerly **11** ill-mannered, uncivilized **12** uncultivated

uncover 4 bare, undo **5** dig up, strip **6** denude, dig out, expose, reveal,

unmask, unveil, unwrap **7** disrobe, lay bare, uncloak, undrape, undress, unearth **8** disclose, unclothe **9** make known, unsheathe **11** make visible **12** bring to light

uncovered 4 bare **5** bared, dug up, naked **7** exposed, noticed **8** detected, revealed **9** disclosed, made known **10** discovered **13** brought to view **14** brought to light

uncovering 8 exposure **9** divulging, unmasking **10** disclosure, divulgence, laying open, revelation **15** bringing to light **20** bringing out in the open

uncritical 4 dull, dumb **6** casual, obtuse, stupid **7** inexact, offhand, shallow **8** careless, ignorant, slipshod **9** imprecise, untutored **10** inaccurate, uneducated, unschooled, unthinking **11** perfunctory, superficial **12** unreflecting **16** undiscriminating

unctuous 4 oily, smug **6** smarmy **7** fawning, honeyed, servile **8** slippery, too suave **9** pietistic, too smooth **10** flattering, obsequious **11** sycophantic **12** honey- tongued, ingratiating **13** sanctimonious, self-righteous

uncultivated 3 raw **4** wild **7** uncouth **8** unfarmed, unplowed, untilled **9** unrefined **10** unimproved **11** undeveloped

uncultivated land

god of: 8 Silvanus, Sylvanus

uncultured 5 crass **6** coarse, common, vulgar **7** low-bred **9** inelegant, unrefined **10** unpolished **12** uncultivated

uncustomary 4 rare **6** unique **7** amazing, unusual **8** singular, uncommon, unwonted **9** unheard-of **10** incredible, unexpected **11** astonishing, exceptional **12** unaccustomed, unbelievable **13** extraordinary, unanticipated

undaunted 5 brave **6** gritty, heroic, plucky **7** unfazed, valiant **8** fearless, intrepid, resolute, stalwart, valorous **9** not put off **10** courageous, undismayed **11** indomitable, unflinching, unperturbed, unshrinking **12** stouthearted **13** undiscouraged

undeceive 8 disabuse **10** disenchant **11** disenthrall, disillusion **12** open one's eyes **13** break the spell **15** burst one's bubble **19** bring one down to earth **20** shatter one's illusions

undecided 4 open **5** vague **6** unsure **7** dubious, pending **8** not final, wavering **9** tentative, uncertain, unsettled **10** indecisive, indefinite, in abeyance, in a dilemma, irresolute, of two minds, open-minded, unresolved, up in the air **11** fluctuating, vacillating **12** undetermined, unformulated **16** hemming and hawing **17** blowing hot and cold **20** going around in circles

undecorated 4 bare **5** blank, plain, stark **6** simple **7** austere **9** unadorned **13** unembellished

undedicated 11 indifferent, uncommitted

undefiled 4 pure **5** clean **6** chaste, intact, virgin **7** natural **8** innocent, spotless **9** stainless, unsullied **10** unpolluted

undemanding 4 easy **6** low-key, simple **7** patient, relaxed **9** easygoing **10** submissive **12** easy to please, laissez-faire **14** live-and-let-live

undemonstrative 3 shy **4** cold **5** aloof **7** distant, stoical **8** reserved **9** impassive **11** unemotional **12** inexpressive, unresponsive **14** self-controlled

undeniable 4 sure **6** patent, proven **7** certain, obvious **8** decisive, manifest **10** conclusive **11** established, indubitable, irrefutable **12** beyond a doubt, demonstrable, indisputable **13** incontestable **14** unquestionable **16** incontrovertible

undeniably 6 surely **9** certainly **10** decisively, definitely **11** irrefutably **12** conclusively, demonstrably, indisputably **13** incontestably **14** beyond question, unquestionably **16** incontrovertibly

undependable 6 fickle **7** erratic, flighty **8** unstable, variable, wavering **10** capricious, changeable, inconstant, unreliable **13** irresponsible, unpredictable, untrustworthy

under 3 sub **5** below, lower, neath, short **7** beneath, sedated **8** inferior, less than **9** because of **11** subordinate, unconscious

undercover 3 sly **6** covert, hidden, secret **7** furtive, sub rosa **8** hush-hush, stealthy **9** concealed, disguised, incognito **10** unrevealed **11** clandestine, undisclosed **12** confidential **13** surreptitious

French: 8 a couvert

undercurrent 4 aura, hint, mood **5** sense, tinge, vibes **7** quality, riptide **8** undertow **9** undertone **10** atmosphere, intimation, suggestion, vibrations **12** crosscurrent

undercut 9 discredit, undermine, undersell **10** compromise

underestimate 7 dismiss, put down **8** belittle, minimize, misjudge **9** deprecate, discredit, disparage, disregard, sell short, underrate, undersell **10** depreciate, undervalue **11** detract from **12** miscalculate

undergarment 3 bra **4** BVDs, slip **5** pants, shift, teddy, thong **6** boxers, corset, girdle, shorts **7** chemise, panties **8** bloomers, camisole, knickers, lingerie, skivvies **9** brassiere, petticoat, union suit **12** jockey shorts

undergo 5 brave, stand **6** endure, suffer **7** sustain, weather **8** submit to **9** encounter, go through, withstand **10** experience

undergraduate 4 coed, soph **5** frosh, plebe **6** junior, senior **7** scholar, student **8** freshman **9** sophomore, undegreed **10** degreeless, nondegreed **13** underclassman, upperclassman

underground 6 buried, covert, secret **7** sub-rosa **10** undercover **11** belowground, clandestine **12** subterranean **13** surreptitious **15** below the surface

underground chamber 4 tomb **5** crypt, vault **6** cellar **8** catacomb **9** sepulcher

underhand, underhanded 6 covert, crafty, sneaky, tricky **7** corrupt, crooked, cunning, devious, evasive, furtive, illegal **8** sneaking, stealthy **9** conniving, dishonest, unethical **10** fraudulent **12** unprincipled, unscrupulous **13** surreptitious

underhandedness 5 guile **6** deceit **7** slyness **8** trickery **9** chicanery, deception, duplicity **10** sneakiness, trickiness **13** secretiveness

underline 6 accent, stress **7** dwell on, point up **9** emphasize, press home **10** accentuate, underscore **15** bring into relief

underling 4 serf **6** flunky, lackey, menial, minion, thrall, vassal **7** servant, subject **8** employee, hireling, inferior **9** attendant, hired hand **11** subordinate

underlying 5 basic **6** covert **7** beneath, radical **8** implicit **9** elemental, essential **10** subtending **11** fundamental

undermine 4 foil, ruin **5** erode **6** injure, riddle, scotch, thwart, weaken **7** cripple, destroy, subvert, torpedo **8** sabotage **9** eat away at, frustrate, hamstring **10** neutralize **11** burrow under, tunnel under

underneath 5 below, lower **6** bottom, hidden **9** disguised, subject to **14** misrepresented

undernourished 8 starving, underfed **12** malnourished

under obligation 5 bound **6** liable **7** obliged **8** beholden, indebted **9** obligated **10** answerable, in one's debt **11** accountable, responsible

underpart 4 sole **5** belly, tails **6** bottom **9** lower side, underside

underpin 4 bear **7** bolster, support **10** strengthen **12** substantiate

underpinning 4 base **5** basic **6** ground **7** support **9** essential **10** foundation, groundwork **11** fundamental **12** substructure

underplay 8 play down **11** deemphasize

underprivileged 4 poor **5** needy **6** in need **7** hapless, unlucky **8** badly-off, deprived, ill-fated, indigent **9** destitute, penniless, penurious **10** illstarred, pauperized **11** handicapped,

unfortunate **12** impoverished **13** disadvantaged **22** in adverse circumstances

underrate 6 slight **8** belittle, derogate, minimize **9** denigrate, deprecate, disparage **10** depreciate, undervalue **13** underestimate

underscore 4 mark **6** accent, deepen, play up, stress **7** feature, point up **8** heighten **9** emphasize, intensify, press home, underline **10** accentuate **15** draw attention to

underscoring 6 stress **8** emphasis **11** underlining

underside 4 back, sole **5** belly, tails **6** bottom **7** reverse **9** lower side, underpart

undersized 4 tiny **5** elfin, short, small **6** little, petite, slight **7** stunted **8** dwarfish **10** diminutive **11** lilliputian

underskirt 4 slip **7** pannier **9** crinoline, hoopskirt, petticoat

understand 3 dig, get, see **4** hear, know, read, take **5** grasp, learn **6** absorb, accept, assume, can see, fathom, gather, take it **7** be aware, discern, make out, presume, realize **8** conclude, perceive **9** apprehend, interpret, recognize **10** appreciate, comprehend, take to mean **14** sympathize with, take for granted

understandable 8 apparent **12** recognizable, unmistakable **14** comprehensible

understanding 4 pact **5** grasp **7** empathy, insight, knowing **8** sympathy, tolerant **9** agreement, awareness, intuition, knowledge, sensitive **10** cognizance, compassion, compromise, discerning, perception, perceptive, responsive **11** concordance, sensitivity, sympathetic **12** appreciation, appreciative, apprehension **13** compassionate, comprehension **17** meeting of the minds

understate 8 minimize **11** deemphasize

understated 9 minimized **10** restrained **12** conservative, deemphasized

understatement 7 litotes **10** minimizing **20** conservative estimate

understudy 3 sub **6** backup, double, fill-in, relief **7** stand-by, stand-in **9** alternate, surrogate **10** substitute **11** pinch hitter, replacement

undertake 3 try **5** begin, essay, start **6** assume, strive, tackle, take on **7** attempt **8** commence, embark on, endeavor, set about, shoulder **9** agree to do, enter upon **11** promise to do **13** get involved in

undertaking 3 job **4** task **6** effort **7** concern, project, pursuit, venture **8** endeavor **10** commitment, enterprise

Under the Greenwood Tree
  author: 11 Thomas Hardy

under the influence 5 drunk **6** sodden, soused, wasted, zapped, zonked **7** smashed **8** besotted **9** plastered **10** inebriated **11** intoxicated **20** three sheets to the wind

under the weather 3 bad, ill **4** sick **6** ailing, sickly, unwell **9** unhealthy **10** indisposed

undertone 4 aura, hint, mood **5** scent, sense, tinge, trace **6** flavor, mumble, murmur, nuance **7** feeling, inkling, low tone, quality, whisper **8** coloring **10** atmosphere, intimation, suggestion **11** connotation, implication **12** subdued voice, undercurrent

undervalue 6 slight **8** belittle, derogate **9** discredit, disparage, underrate **10** depreciate **13** underestimate

underwear 3 bra **4** BVDs, slip **5** pants, teddy, thong **6** boxers, briefs, corset, girdle, shorts **7** chemise, panties **8** bloomers, camisole, knickers, lingerie, skivvies **9** brassiere, petticoat, union suit **12** jockey shorts, smallclothes **14** unmentionables

underweight 4 bony, lank **5** gaunt, lanky **6** skinny **7** scrawny, spindly **8** skeletal, underfed **9** emaciated **12** skin-and-bones **13** hollow-cheeked **14** spindle- shanked, undernourished

underworld 4 Hell **5** Hades, limbo **6** the mob **8** mobsters, the Mafia **9** criminals, gangsters, purgatory **10** Cosa Nostra **11** shades below **12** the syndicate **13** bottomless pit, nether regions **14** organized crime **15** criminal element, infernal regions **16** abode of the damned
  god of: 3 Dis **5** Hades, Orcus, Pluto **8** Dis Pater

under wraps 6 hidden, secret **9** concealed **10** suppressed, under cover

underwrite 3 aid **4** back **7** approve, endorse, finance, sponsor, support, warrant **8** invest in, sanction, validate **9** guarantee, subsidize **11** countersign

underwriter 5 angel **6** backer, patron **7** sponsor **8** investor **9** financier, guarantor

undeserving 3 bad **8** inferior, unworthy

undesirable 5 unfit **8** disliked, improper, unbidden, unsavory, unseemly, unwanted, unworthy **9** offensive, unpopular **10** unbecoming, uninviting, unsuitable, unwelcomed **11** distasteful, unbefitting, unwishedfor **12** disagreeable, inadmissible, unacceptable, unattractive **13** inappropriate, objectionable **14** unsatisfactory

undetectable 12 unnoticeable, unobservable **13** imperceptible, unsubstantial

undetermined 6 chance **7** unfixed, unknown **8** unproved, unproven

9 uncertain, undecided 10 indefinite, irresolute 13 indeterminate, unascertained

undeveloped 3 raw 5 crude, green 6 callow, unripe 8 immature, inchoate, unformed 9 embryonic, half-baked 10 unfinished 11 rudimentary, unexploited 12 uncultivated

undignified 3 low 7 boorish 8 improper, shameful, unseemly, unworthy 9 degrading, inelegant, tasteless, unrefined 10 beneath one, indecorous, indelicate, in bad taste, unbecoming, unladylike, unsuitable 11 unbefitting 13 discreditable, inappropriate, ungentlemanly 18 beneath one's dignity **Latin:** 8 infra dig 15 infra dignitatem

undiluted 4 neat, pure 5 sheer 7 unmixed 8 straight 11 unfortified 12 full-strength 13 unadulterated

Undine
form: 6 spirit
location: 5 water
sex: 6 female

undiscerning 11 insensitive 12 unperceptive 14 indiscriminate

undisciplined 4 wild 6 fickle, fitful 7 erratic, wayward, willful 8 unsteady, untaught 9 mercurial, untrained, untutored 10 capricious, changeable, inconstant, uneducated, unfinished, unreliable, unschooled 11 unpracticed 12 obstreperous, uncontrolled, undependable, unrestrained 13 unpredictable

undisclosed 6 hidden, secret 7 private 9 concealed 10 unrevealed 12 confidential

undisguised 4 open 5 clear, utter 7 evident, obvious 8 complete, distinct, manifest, unhidden 9 out-and-out 10 plain as day, pronounced, unreserved 11 unconcealed 12 unmistakable, wholehearted 13 thoroughgoing 24 plain as the nose on one's face

undismayed 7 uncowed 8 unafraid, unscared 9 confident, unabashed, unalarmed, undaunted 12 unfrightened 13 undiscouraged, unintimidated

undisputed 4 sure 7 certain, granted 8 accepted 9 undoubted 10 conclusive, undeniable 11 beyond doubt, indubitable, irrefutable, past dispute, uncontested 12 acknowledged, indisputable, unchallenged, unquestioned 13 a matter of fact, incontestable 14 beyond question, freely admitted, unquestionable 15 without question 16 incontrovertible

undistinguished 5 plain, usual 6 common 7 prosaic 8 everyday, mediocre, ordinary 10 pedestrian, unexciting 11 commonplace 12 run-of-the-mill, unremarkable 13 unexceptional 18 nothing to rave about

undistracted 4 calm 6 serene, stolid

7 unfazed 9 impassive, unruffled 10 untroubled 11 undisturbed

undisturbed 4 calm, cool 5 quiet 6 placid, serene, steady 7 equable, unmoved 8 composed, peaceful, tranquil 9 collected, inviolate, unexcited, unruffled, untouched 10 of solitude, unagitated, unbothered, untroubled 11 left in order, unperturbed 13 imperturbable, self-possessed, uninterrupted

undivided 5 solid, whole 6 entire, united 7 unified, unsplit 8 complete 9 of one mind, unanimous 10 not divided, unstinting 12 wholehearted

undo 3 end 4 free, open, ruin, void 5 annul, erase, loose, quash, untie 6 cancel, defeat, loosen, offset, repair, unbind, unfold, unhook, unknot, unlace, unlock, unwrap 7 destroy, nullify, rectify, reverse, subvert, unchain, unravel, wipe out 8 demolish, overturn, unbutton, unfasten 9 disengage, eliminate, make up for, undermine 10 counteract, invalidate, neutralize 11 disentangle 13 compensate for 14 counterbalance

undogmatic 7 liberal 8 flexible, tolerant 10 open-minded 11 broad-minded

undoing 4 doom, jinx, ruin 5 upset 6 defeat 7 erasure, nemesis 8 collapse, downfall, negation, reversal, weakness 9 annulment, breakdown, overthrow, ruination, thwarting, wiping out 11 cause of ruin, destruction 12 Achilles' heel, cancellation, invalidation 13 counteraction, nullification 14 neutralization

undomesticated 4 wild 5 feral 6 ferine, savage 7 untamed 8 barbaric 9 barbarous 11 uncivilized

undone 6 ruined 9 come apart, destroyed 10 incomplete, unfastened 12 not completed

undoubted 4 sure 5 utter 7 certain 8 absolute, complete, definite, positive 11 indubitable, unequivocal 12 indisputable 13 unimpeachable 14 unquestionable

undoubtedly 6 surely 7 no doubt 9 assuredly, certainly, decidedly, doubtless 10 absolutely, definitely, positively, undeniably 11 indubitably 12 beyond a doubt, unmistakably, without doubt 13 unequivocally 14 beyond question, unquestionably 15 without question

undress 5 strip 6 nudity 7 disrobe, uncover, undrape 8 disarray, unclothe 9 nakedness 10 dishabille 18 take off one's clothes

undressed 4 bare, nude 5 naked 6 unclad 7 denuded, exposed, unrobed 8 disrobed, stripped, undraped 9 unclothed, uncovered

Undset, Sigrid
author of: 6 The Axe 20 Kristin Lavransdatter, The Master of Hestviken

undue 6 unmeet 8 impolite, improper, needless, overmuch, too great, unseemly, unworthy 9 excessive, tasteless 10 ill-advised, indiscreet, in bad taste, inordinate, not fitting, unbecoming, unsuitable 11 superfluous, uncalled-for, unjustified, unnecessary, unwarranted 13 inappropriate, objectionable

undulate 4 coil 5 slink, weave 9 fluctuate 11 rise and fall

undulating 4 wavy 5 bumpy 6 uneven

undulation 7 coiling 8 slinking, twisting 10 contortion 11 convolution 16 rising and falling

undutiful 6 remiss 8 disloyal 11 disobedient

undying 6 steady 7 abiding, endless, eternal, lasting 8 constant, enduring, immortal, unending, unfading, untiring 9 continual, deathless, incessant, perennial, permanent, perpetual, unceasing 10 continuing 11 everlasting, never-ending, unfaltering, unrelenting, unremitting 12 imperishable, neverfailing, undiminished 13 uninterrupted 14 indestructible

unearth 4 find, show 5 dig up 6 dig out, exhume, expose, reveal 7 display, divulge, exhibit, root out, uncover 8 disclose, discover, disinter, dredge up, excavate 9 disentomb, ferret out 10 come across, come up with 12 bring to light

unearthly 5 awful, eerie, weird 6 absurd 7 extreme, ghostly, phantom, strange, uncanny, ungodly, unusual 8 abnormal, ethereal, spectral, terrible 10 horrendous, unpleasant 11 disembodied, incorporeal, unspeakable 12 disagreeable, extramundane, supernatural 13 extraordinary, preternatural

unease 5 worry 7 tension 8 disquiet 9 misgiving 10 discomfort, uneasiness 11 disquietude 12 apprehension

uneasiness 5 dread 6 dismay 7 anxiety 9 agitation, misgiving 10 discomfort, foreboding 11 disquietude, distraction, nervousness 12 apprehension, discomfiture, discomposure, perturbation 16 apprehensiveness

uneasy 4 edgy 5 nervy, tense, upset 6 on edge, queasy, unsure 7 awkward, irksome, nervous, uptight, worried 8 strained, troubled, worrying 9 disturbed, ill at ease, perturbed, upsetting 10 bothersome, disquieted, disturbing, unpleasant 11 constrained, disquieting 12 apprehensive 13 uncomfortable

uneatable 8 inedible 11 not fit to eat

uneconomical 4 dear 6 costly 8 wasteful 9 expensive 10 exorbitant, high-priced, immoderate, overpriced 11 extravagant 12 unreasonable

uneducated 8 ignorant, untaught 9 unlearned, untrained, untutored 10 illiterate, uncultured, unlettered, unschooled 12 uncultivated, uninstructed 13 unenlightened

unelaborated 4 bald, bare 5 plain, stark 6 simple 9 essential, unadorned, uncolored 11 fundamental, unvarnished 13 unembellished 15 straightforward

unembellished 4 bald, bare 5 naked, plain, stark 7 austere 9 unadorned 11 undecorated 12 unornamented

unemotional 4 cold, cool 6 formal, remote 7 distant 8 lukewarm, reserved 9 apathetic, impassive, unfeeling 11 indifferent, passionless, unconcerned 12 unresponsive 15 undemonstrative

unemployed 4 axed, idle 5 fired 6 canned, sacked, unused 7 bounced, jobless, laid-off 8 workless 9 at leisure, at liberty, booted-out, dismissed, on the dole, on welfare, out of a job, out of work 10 discharged, unoccupied 11 pink-slipped

unencumbered 4 free 6 vacant 7 unladen 8 expedite 10 unburdened, unhindered 13 unhandicapped

unending 6 steady 7 endless, eternal, lasting 8 constant, enduring 9 continual, incessant, perennial, permanent, perpetual, unceasing 10 continuous, unwavering 11 everlasting, neverending, unremitting 12 undiminished 13 uninterrupted

unendurable 7 racking 9 agonizing, torturous 10 tormenting, unbearable 11 intolerable 12 excruciating, insufferable

unenlightened 8 ignorant 9 in the dark, unlearned 10 uneducated, uninformed 11 uninitiated 12 uninstructed

unenterprising 4 lazy 11 unambitious 12 unaggressive

unenthusiastic 8 lukewarm 10 unspirited 11 halfhearted, indifferent 13 unimpassioned

unequal 6 biased, uneven, unfair, unjust, unlike 7 bigoted, partial 9 different, disparate, unmatched 10 dissimilar, not uniform, prejudiced 11 inequitable

unequaled 7 supreme 8 peerless 9 matchless, paramount, unmatched, unrivaled 10 consummate, unexcelled 11 ne plus ultra, unsurpassed 12 incomparable, second to none, unapproached, unparalleled 13 beyond compare 16 beyond comparison

unequivocable 4 bald 5 utter 8 outright 9 out-and-out 11 categorical, unqualified

unequivocal 5 clear, final 7 certain 8 absolute, clear-cut, decisive, definite, emphatic 11 unambiguous 12 indis-

putable 13 incontestable 16 incontrovertible

unequivocally 7 clearly 9 certainly, downright 10 completely, decisively, definitely, thoroughly 12 emphatically, indisputably, unmistakably 13 incontestably 14 unquestionably, wholeheartedly 16 incontrovertibly

unerring 4 sure 7 certain, precise 8 constant, faithful, reliable 9 faultless, unfailing 10 infallible, unchanging

unessential 8 nonvital 9 accessory, extrinsic 10 disposable, expendable 11 dispensable, superfluous, unimportant, unnecessary 12 nonessential

unethical 5 dirty, shady, wrong 6 shoddy, unfair 7 devious 8 unworthy 9 dishonest, underhand 10 unladylike 12 dishonorable, disreputable, questionable, unprincipled 13 ungentlemanly 14 unconscionable

uneven 4 awry, bent 5 bumpy, lumpy, rough 6 angled, coarse, craggy, curved, jagged, tilted, unfair, unjust, unlike 7 crooked, not flat, slanted, sloping, unequal 8 lopsided, not level, not plumb, one-sided, unsmooth 9 different, disparate 10 dissimilar, illmatched, unbalanced

unevenness 7 oddness 9 bumpiness, lumpiness, roughness 10 jaggedness, ruggedness 11 crookedness 12 irregularity 14 changeableness

uneventful 4 dull 5 quiet, usual 6 boring 7 average, humdrum, prosaic, routine, tedious 8 ordinary, standard, tiresome 10 monotonous 11 commonplace 12 conventional 13 insignificant, unexceptional, uninteresting

unexcelled 7 supreme 8 flawless, peerless, superior, unbeaten 9 faultless, matchless, unequaled, unmatched, unrivaled 10 consummate 11 unsurpassed 12 incomparable, second to none, transcendent, unapproached, unparalleled 13 beyond compare

unexceptional 5 usual 6 normal 7 mundane, typical 8 ordinary, standard 9 customary 12 conventional, run of the mill

unexcited 4 calm, cool 6 placid, serene 7 unmoved 8 composed, detached 9 collected, unruffled 11 undisturbed, unemotional 13 dispassionate, unimpassioned

unexciting 4 dull, flat 5 vapid 6 boring 7 insipid 10 lackluster

unexpected 6 sudden 9 startling, unplanned 10 accidental, surprising, undesigned, unforeseen, unintended 11 astonishing, unlooked-for, unpredicted 12 out of the blue 13 unanticipated, unintentional

unextinguished 5 alive 10 unquenched 12 still burning

unfaded 5 fresh 6 bright 8 undimmed 10 unwithered

unfailing 4 true 5 loyal 6 steady 7 endless 8 constant, enduring, faithful, reliable 9 continual 10 continuous, dependable, infallible, unchanging, unwavering 12 never-failing 13 inexhaustible

unfair 4 foul 5 dirty 6 biased, unjust 7 corrupt, crooked, partial, unequal 8 not right, onesided, partisan 9 dishonest, underhand, unethical 10 not cricket, prejudiced 11 inequitable 12 dishonorable, unprincipled, unreasonable, unscrupulous 14 unconscionable

unfaithful 5 false 6 faulty, untrue 7 inexact 8 disloyal, unchaste 9 deceitful, distorted, erroneous, faithless, imperfect 10 adulterous, inaccurate, inconstant, perfidious 11 not accurate, treacherous 12 falsehearted 13 untrustworthy

Unfaithfully Yours
director: 14 Preston Sturges
cast: 10 Rudy Vallee 11 Rex Harrison 12 Edgar Kennedy, Linda Darnell 15 Barbara Lawrence

unfaithfulness 7 falsity, perfidy 9 falseness, treachery 10 disloyalty, fickleness, infidelity 11 inconstancy 13 faithlessness 14 perfidiousness

unfaltering 4 firm, sure 6 steady 8 enduring, resolute 9 obstinate, steadfast, unfailing 10 dependable, persistent, unflagging, unswerving, unwavering 11 persevering, undeviating 12 never-failing, wholehearted

unfamiliar 3 new 5 novel 6 exotic, unique 7 curious, foreign, strange, unknown, unusual 9 different 10 ignorant of, unversed in 11 a stranger to, little known, out-of-the-way, unexposed to, uninitiated, unskilled in 12 not well-known, unacquainted, unconversant 13 not acquainted, unpracticed in 14 unaccustomed to 15 inexperienced in, uninformed about 18 unenlightened about

unfamiliarity 9 ignorance 11 strangeness 12 inexperience 15 lack of knowledge

unfashionable 5 dated, dowdy, passe 6 frumpy, old-hat 8 outmoded 9 out-of-date, unstylish 12 old-fashioned

unfasten 4 undo 5 unpin, untie 6 detach, unbind, unbolt, unhook, unlace, unlash, unlink, unlock 7 unclose, unhitch, unlatch, unstick 8 unbutton, uncouple

unfastened 5 apart, undid 6 undone, untied 7 severed, unlaced, unstuck 8 detached, unhooked 9 unbuckled, uncoupled, unhitched 11 unconnected 12 disconnected

unfathomable 4 deep, vast 6 arcane, remote, subtle 7 complex, extreme, obscure 8 abstract, abstruse, esoteric, profound, puzzling **9** enigmatic **10** bottomless, perplexing **16** hard to understand, incomprehensible

unfavorable 3 bad **4** poor **7** adverse, unhappy **8** unsuited, untimely **9** illsuited **10** ill-favored, regretable **11** inopportune, regrettable, unfortunate, unpromising **12** inauspicious, inconvenient, infelicitous, unpropitious, unseasonable **15** disadvantageous

unfeasible 10 impossible, infeasible, unsuitable, unworkable **11** impractical **12** unachievable **13** impracticable

unfeeling 4 cold **5** cruel **9** heartless **11** hardhearted, insensitive **13** unsympathetic

unfeigned 4 real, true **7** genuine, sincere **10** unaffected

unfetter 4 free **7** release, set free, unchain **8** liberate **9** unshackle

unfilled 4 open **5** blank, empty **6** hollow, vacant **7** drained **9** available **10** unoccupied

unfinished 5 crude, rough **6** undone **7** lacking, sketchy, wanting **8** immature **9** deficient, imperfect, unnatural, unpainted, unrefined, unstained **10** incomplete, unexecuted, unpolished **11** uncompleted, unfulfilled, unlacquered, unvarnished

unfit 4 sick, weak **5** frail **6** infirm, not fit, sickly **7** not up to, unequal, unready, unsound, useless **8** delicate, disabled, unsuited **9** incapable, not suited, unhealthy, unskilled, untrained **10** inadequate, ineligible, not equal to, unequipped, unprepared, unsuitable **11** debilitated, ill-equipped, incompetent, ineffective, inefficient, not designed, unqualified **12** ill-contrived, not cut out for **13** inappropriate, incapacitated

unflagging 4 firm **5** fixed **6** steady **7** staunch **8** constant, enduring, resolute, tireless, unshaken, untiring **9** steadfast, tenacious, undaunted **10** determined, persistent, relentless, undrooping, unswerving, unwavering, unyielding **11** indomitable, persevering, undeviating, unfaltering, unremitting **13** indefatigable **14** uncompromising

unflappable 4 calm, cool **6** placid, serene **8** composed **9** collected **10** coolheaded **11** unexcitable **13** imperturbable, self-possessed

unflinching 4 firm, game **6** gritty, plucky, steady, strong **7** staunch **8** fearless, resolute, stalwart, unshaken **9** steadfast, tenacious, unabashed, undaunted **10** persistent, unswerving, unwavering, unyielding **11** indomitable, unfaltering, unshrinking **12** unhesitating

unfold 4 bare, show, tell **6** open up, reveal, unfurl, unroll, unveil, unwrap **7** divulge, explain, expound, lay open,

open out, present, recount, uncover **8** describe, disclose, set forth **9** elucidate, explicate, make known, spread out **10** stretch out

unfolding 4 rise **5** birth, start **9** beginning, evolution, inception, unfurling **10** revelation **11** development

unforced 4 easy **5** frank **6** candid, casual **7** natural, relaxed **8** informal **9** easygoing **10** unaffected **13** unconstrained

unforeseen 6 abrupt, sudden **8** surprise **9** unplanned **10** accidental, surprising, unexpected, unintended **11** unlooked-for, unpredicted **12** out of the blue **13** unanticipated

unforeseen danger 7 pitfall **8** exigency **9** emergency **11** contingency

unforgettable 7 notable **8** eventful, exciting **9** important, memorable, thrilling **10** noteworthy **11** significant

unfortunate 5 sorry **6** cursed, jinxed, woeful **7** hapless, unblest, unhappy, unlucky **8** ill-fated, ill-timed, luckless, untimely, wretched **10** disastrous, illadvised, ill-starred **11** inopportune, regrettable, unfavorable **12** inauspicious, infelicitous, unpropitious, unprosperous, unsuccessful

unfounded 4 idle **5** false **6** untrue **8** baseless, spurious **9** erroneous **10** fabricated, groundless

unfrequented 5 empty **6** lonely **7** remote, uncouth **8** isolated, solitary **9** unvisited **11** out-of-the-way **16** off the beaten path

unfriendly 4 cold **5** aloof **6** at odds, chilly **7** distant, haughty, hostile, warlike **8** inimical, snobbish **9** on the outs, reclusive, withdrawn **10** ungracious, unsociable **11** belligerent, contentious, quarrelsome, uncongenial **12** antagonistic, disagreeable, disputatious, inhospitable **13** at loggerheads, at sword's point, unsympathetic

unfruitful 4 vain **6** barren, fallow, futile **7** useless, worn-out **8** infecund **9** fruitless **10** unavailing **11** purposeless, unrewarding **12** impoverished, unproductive, unprofitable **14** unremunerative

unfulfilled 8 thwarted **10** frustrated, unrealized **11** unsatisfied
French: 6 manque

unfurl 4 open **6** expand, spread, unfold, unroll **7** develop, roll out **8** shake out **9** spread out

ungainly 5 stiff **6** clumsy, klutzy **7** awkward **9** lumbering, maladroit **10** ungraceful **13** uncoordinated

ungallant 4 rude **7** boorish, uncivil, uncouth **8** impolite **9** uncourtly **10** illbehaved, ungracious, unmannerly **11** ill-mannered, uncourteous **12** discourteous **13** ungentlemanly

ungenerous 4 mean, near **5** close,

cruel, petty, small, venal **6** greedy, shabby, sordid, stingy **7** miserly, selfish, sparing **8** churlish, covetous, cowardly, grudging **9** illiberal, mercenary, niggardly, penurious, rapacious **10** avaricious **11** small-minded **12** narrow-minded, parsimonious, uncharitable

ungifted 8 mediocre **9** unskilled **10** amateurish, unskillful, untalented **14** unaccomplished

unglue 6 unseal **7** peel off, unstick **9** pull apart

ungodly 4 base, vile **5** awful **6** rotten, sinful, wicked **7** corrupt, ghastly, godless, heinous, immoral, impious **8** depraved, dreadful, terrible **9** dissolute **10** degenerate, horrendous, iniquitous, outrageous, villainous **11** blasphemous **12** dishonorable, unreasonable

ungovernable 6 unruly **7** defiant, froward, naughty, wayward **8** contrary, mutinous, perverse, stubborn **9** fractious, obstinate **10** disorderly, rebellious, refractory **11** disobedient, intractable **12** noncompliant, recalcitrant, unmanageable, unsubmissive

ungraceful 5 inept **6** clumsy **7** awkward **9** inelegant

ungracious 4 rude **5** bluff, blunt, gruff, harsh, short **6** abrupt, coarse, crusty, vulgar **7** boorish, brusque, loutish, uncivil, uncouth **8** churlish, grudging, impolite **9** uncourtly, ungallant **10** ill-behaved, unladylike, unmannerly **11** bad-mannered, illmannered, impertinent, uncourteous **12** disagreeable, discourteous, inhospitable **13** disrespectful, ungentlemanly

unguarded 6 unwary **8** careless, tactless, too frank **9** imprudent, unmindful, unwatched **10** incautious, indiscreet, undefended **11** defenseless, unpatrolled, unprotected **12** undiplomatic, unrestrained **13** ill-considered, uncircumspect

unguent 4 balm **5** cream, salve **6** lotion **8** ointment **9** emollient

ungula 4 hoof, nail

ungulate 2 ox **3** cow, gnu, hog, pig, yak **4** boar, calf, deer, goat, ibex **5** camel, daman, horse, llama, tapir **6** hoofed, vicuna **7** buffalo, caribou, giraffe, peccary **8** antelope, elephant, hooflike, ruminant **9** dromedary **10** hartebeest, rhinoceros, wildebeest **12** hippopotamus

unhampered 4 free **8** expedite **9** unimpeded **10** unconfined **12** unencumbered, unrestrained, unrestricted

unhandy 5 inept **6** clumsy, gauche, klutzy **7** awkward **8** bumbling, fumbling, inexpert, unwieldy **9** all thumbs, ham-handed, maladroit, unskilled **10** cumbersome, unskillful

11 inefficient 12 inconvenient, unmanageable 14 butterfingered

unhappiness 3 woe 5 grief 6 misery, sorrow 7 anguish, sadness 8 distress 9 heartache

unhappy 3 bad, sad 4 blue, poor 5 inapt, sorry 6 gloomy, somber, unwise 7 adverse, awkward, doleful, foolish, forlorn, hapless, joyless, unlucky 8 dejected, downcast, luckless, unseemly 9 depressed, imprudent, longfaced, sorrowful, woebegone 10 despondent, dispirited, ill-advised, melancholy, unbecoming, unsuitable 11 crestfallen, injudicious, regrettable, unbefitting, unfortunate 12 heavyhearted, infelicitous, unsuccessful 13 inappropriate 14 down in the mouth

unharmed 5 whole 6 unhurt 9 uninjured, unscathed, untouched 10 in one piece, unaffected 14 with a whole skin

unhealthy 3 bad 4 sick, weak 6 ailing, feeble, infirm, morbid, poorly, sickly, unwell 7 harmful, hurtful, invalid, not well, noxious, unsound 8 depraved, diseased, negative, perilous 9 dangerous, degrading, hazardous 10 corrupting, indisposed, morally bad 11 destructive, detrimental, undesirable, unhealthful, unwholesome 12 demoralizing, in poor health, insalubrious 13 contaminating

unheard-of 3 odd 4 rare 6 unique 7 amazing, curious, unknown, unusual 8 freakish, original, singular, uncommon 9 irregular, matchless 10 incredible, outlandish, outrageous, phenomenal, unexpected 11 exceptional 12 incomparable, preposterous, unbelievable, unparalleled, unreasonable 13 extraordinary, inconceivable, unprecedented

unheated 3 icy 4 cold 6 chilly, drafty, frosty 7 ice-cold 8 unwarmed

unheeding 7 ignored 8 mindless 12 disregarding

unhelpful 7 of no use, useless 8 in the way 9 hindering 11 disobliging 13 inconsiderate, uncooperative

unheralded 6 unsung 10 unexpected, unforeseen 11 unacclaimed, unannounced, unlooked-for 12 unproclaimed, unpublicized, unrecognized 13 unanticipated

unhesitating 5 eager, quick, ready 6 direct, prompt 9 immediate 10 unreserved 11 unflinching 12 wholehearted, without delay 13 instantaneous 18 without reservation

unhinge 6 detach 7 disrupt 8 separate, unsettle 9 disengage, dislocate, disorient, unbalance 10 disconnect 13 disarticulate

unhitch 6 detach 8 separate, uncouple, unfasten 9 disengage 10 disconnect

unhitched 8 detached 9 uncoupled 10 unfastened 12 disconnected

unholy 4 base, evil, vile 5 awful 6 rotten, sinful, wicked 7 corrupt, heinous, immoral, ungodly 8 depraved, dreadful, shocking 9 dishonest 10 horrendous, iniquitous, outrageous, villainous 12 dishonorable, unreasonable

Unholy Loves
author: 15 Joyce Carol Oates

unhurried 4 easy, slow 7 gradual 9 leisurely 10 deliberate, slow-moving

unicorn
form: 5 horse
feature: 4 horn
symbolizes: 6 purity 8 chastity
constellation of: 9 Monoceros

unidentified 5 vague 7 unknown, unnamed 8 nameless 9 anonymous, unlabeled 11 unspecified 12 undesignated, unrecognized

unification 5 union, unity 6 fusion, merger 7 uniting 8 alliance, junction 9 coalition, combining 11 coalescence, combination, confederacy 12 amalgamation 13 confederation, consolidating, consolidation, incorporation

uniform 4 even, garb 5 alike, array, at one, dress, equal, habit 6 attire, in line, in step, livery 7 apparel, costume, regalia, regular, similar, the same 8 agreeing, constant, in accord, of a piece, unvaried, vestment 9 consonant, identical, of one mind, unaltered, unvarying 10 conforming, consistent, harmonious, unchanging 11 regimentals, undeviating

uniformity 8 equality, monotony, sameness 10 consonance 11 consistency, equivalency, homogeneity 15 standardization

unify 3 wed 4 ally, fuse, join 5 blend, merge, unite 6 couple, link up 7 combine 8 coalesce, federate 10 amalgamate 11 confederate, consolidate, form into one, incorporate 12 lump together 13 bring together

unilluminated 3 dim 4 dark 5 murky, unlit 6 gloomy 7 obscure 8 darkened 9 lightless, unlighted

unimaginable 10 incredible 12 unbelievable 13 inconceivable 16 incomprehensible

unimaginative 4 dull 5 stale, stock, trite, usual, vapid 6 dreary 7 cliched, humdrum, prosaic, routine, tedious 8 everyday, mediocre, ordinary 9 hackneyed 10 pedestrian, uncreative, unexciting, uninspired, unoriginal, unromantic 11 commonplace, predictable 12 run-of-the-mill, unremarkable 13 uninteresting

unimpaired 4 good 5 clear, sound 6 intact, unhurt 8 unbroken, unharmed 9 uninjured, unscathed, unspoiled 10 undeformed

unimpassioned 4 calm, cool 6 placid,

serene, stolid 7 unmoved 8 detached, unloving 9 apathetic, impassive, objective, unexcited 11 indifferent, unemotional 13 dispassionate

unimpeachable 4 pure 5 clean, solid 7 perfect 8 reliable, spotless, unmarred 9 blameless, faultless, inviolate, stainless, undefiled, untainted 10 immaculate, impeccable, inculpable, infallible 11 trustworthy, unblemished 12 unassailable 13 above reproach, totally honest 14 beyond question, irreproachable, unquestionable 15 beyond criticism, unchallengeable

unimportant 5 minor 6 lesser, meager, paltry, slight 7 trivial 8 inferior, mediocre, not vital, nugatory, piddling, trifling 10 immaterial, irrelevant, low-ranking, negligible, of no moment, second-rate 11 subordinate 12 nonessential, not important 13 insignificant 14 inconsiderable 15 inconsequential, of no consequence

uninformed 6 unread 7 unaware 8 ignorant 9 in the dark, not with it, unadvised, unknowing, unlearned 10 uneducated, unschooled 12 unconversant, uninstructed 13 unenlightened

uninhabited 5 empty 6 vacant 8 deserted, forsaken 9 abandoned, unlived in, unpeopled, unsettled 10 unoccupied, untenanted 11 unpopulated

uninhibited 4 fast, free, open, rash 5 frank 6 candid, daring, madcap, not shy, unwary 8 careless, heedless, immodest, reckless, uncurbed, unreined 9 abandoned, impetuous, impulsive, outspoken, unbridled, unchecked, unguarded, unimpeded, unstopped 10 capricious, flamboyant, forthright, headstrong, incautious, indiscreet, unhampered, unhindered, unreserved 11 instinctive, plainspoken, spontaneous 12 free-spirited, uncontrolled, unobstructed, unrestrained, unrestricted 13 unconstrained 15 straightforward, unself-conscious

uninjured 5 whole 6 intact, unhurt 8 unharmed 9 unscathed, untouched 10 in one piece 14 with a whole skin

uninspired 4 dull 5 stale, stock, trite, vapid 7 cliched, humdrum, prosaic, unmoved 8 ordinary 9 hackneyed, unexcited, unstirred, untouched 10 pedestrian, unaffected, unexciting, unoriginal 11 commonplace, indifferent, predictable, unemotional, unimpressed 12 run-of-the-mill, uninfluenced, unstimulated 13 unimaginative, uninteresting

uninspiring 4 dull 5 bland, stale 6 boring 7 insipid, prosaic 10 lackluster 13 uninteresting

uninstructive 6 barren 9 unhelpful 10 unedifying 12 unproductive 13 uninformative

unintelligent 4 dull, dumb, slow

5 blank, dense, dopey, thick 6 obtuse, stupid 7 asinine, doltish, idiotic, moronic 8 retarded 9 cretinous, dimwitted, imbecilic 10 dull- witted, halfwitted, slow-witted 11 blockheaded, thickheaded 12 simpleminded

unintelligible 8 baffling, puzzling 9 confusing, illegible, insoluble 10 incoherent, perplexing 11 meaningless 12 impenetrable, inarticulate, unfathomable 14 undecipherable 16 incomprehensible

unintentional 9 unplanned, unwitting 10 accidental, fortuitous, undesigned, unintended, unthinking 11 inadvertent, involuntary, unconscious 14 unpremeditated

uninterested 5 aloof, blase 6 remote 8 heedless, listless, uncaring 9 apathetic, incurious, unmindful 10 above it all, uninvolved 11 indifferent, unconcerned 13 unimpressive

uninteresting 3 dry 4 drab, dull 5 trite, vapid 6 boring, dreary, jejune 7 humdrum, insipid, prosaic, tedious 8 lifeless, ordinary, tiresome, unmoving 9 colorless, wearisome 10 monotonous, pedestrian, uneventful 11 uninspiring 12 unsatisfying 13 insignificant

uninterrupted 8 unbroken 9 ceaseless, continual, incessant 10 continuous 11 unremitting

uninviting 8 annoying 9 offensive 10 unalluring, unpleasant, untempting 11 displeasing, distasteful, unappealing, undesirable, unwelcoming 12 disagreeable, unappetizing, unattractive

uninvolved 4 easy 5 clear 6 simple 7 neutral, obvious, outside 8 detached 9 impartial 10 unaffected 13 disinterested, dispassionate, uncomplicated

union 5 blend, guild, unity 6 fusion, league, merger 7 amalgam, joining, mixture, oneness, uniting, wedding 8 alliance, marriage, unifying 9 synthesis 10 federation, fraternity 11 affiliation, association, combination, corporation, partnership, unification 12 amalgamation 13 confederation, consolidation
  type: 5 craft, labor, trade

Union of Soviet Socialist Republics
  abbr: 4 CCCP, USSR
  see **Russia**

unique 8 by itself, peerless, singular 9 matchless, nonpareil, unequaled, unmatched, unrivaled 10 inimitable, one of a kind, surpassing, unexampled, unexcelled 11 distinctive, unsurpassed 12 incomparable, unapproached, unparalleled

unit 4 part 5 group, whole 6 entity, member 7 element, measure, package, section, segment 8 category, division, quantity 9 component 10 detachment

11 constituent, measurement 12 denomination

Unitas, Johnny
  nickname: 7 Johnny U
  sport: 8 football
  position: 11 quarterback
  team: 14 Baltimore Colts

unite 4 ally, fuse, join, pool 5 blend, merge, unify 6 couple 7 combine 8 coalesce, federate, lock arms, organize 10 amalgamate, homogenize, join forces 11 confederate, consolidate, incorporate 12 join together, lump together 13 stand together

united 3 one 5 fused 6 allied, joined, merged, pooled 7 blended, coupled, leagued, unified 8 combined 9 federated, of one mind, unanimous 10 collective 11 amalgamated, in agreement 12 consolidated, incorporated 14 joined together, lumped together

United Arab Emirates
  other name: 11 Pirate Coast, Trucial Oman 13 Trucial States
  capital/largest city: 8 Abu Dhabi
  others: 5 Ajman, Dubai, Kalba, Tarif 6 Sharja 7 Fujaira 11 Ras al Khaima 12 Umm al Qaiwain
  division: 5 Ajman, Dibai, Dubai 6 Sharja 7 Fujaira, Sharjah 8 Abu Dhabi, Fujairah 11 Ras al Khaima, Umm al Qaiwan 12 Ral al Khaimah, Umm al-Qaiwain
  monetary unit: 3 fil 6 dirham
  highest point: 5 Hafit
  physical feature:
    desert: 10 Rub al Khali
    gulf: 4 Oman 7 Persian
    oasis: 7 Buraimi 9 Al Buraymi
    peninsula: 7 Arabian
  people: 4 Arab 6 Indian 7 African, Iranian 9 Pakistani 10 South Asian
    leader: 22 Zaid Bin Sultan al-Nahayan
  language: 5 Farsi 6 Arabic 7 English, Persian
  religion: 5 Islam
  war: 4 Gulf 11 Desert Storm

United Arab Republic 3 UAR
  onetime union of: 5 Egypt, Syria

United Kingdom
  union of: 12 Great Britain 15 Northern Ireland

United States
  capital: 12 Washington DC
  largest city: 11 New York City
  others: 4 Nome 5 Miami 6 Boston, Dallas, El Paso 7 Chicago, Detroit, Houston, Memphis, Phoenix, San Jose, Seattle 8 Columbus, Honolulu, San Diego 9 Anchorage, Baltimore, Cleveland, Milwaukee 10 Los Angeles, New Orleans, San Antonio 12 Indianapolis, Jacksonville, Philadelphia, Salt Lake City, San Francisco
  school: 3 MIT 4 Penn, Yale 5 Brown 6 Baylor, Drexel, Vassar 7 Amherst,

Colgate, Cornell, Fordham, Harvard, Oberlin 8 Bryn Mawr, Columbia, Stanford, Wesleyan 9 Dartmouth, Princeton, Radcliffe 10 Bennington 12 Johns Hopkins, Mount Holyoke
  division: 4 Iowa, Ohio, Utah 5 Idaho, Maine, Texas 6 Alaska, Hawaii, Kansas, Nevada, Oregon 7 Alabama, Arizona, Florida, Georgia, Indiana, Montana, New York, Vermont, Wyoming 8 Arkansas, Colorado, Delaware, Illinois, Kentucky, Maryland, Michigan, Missouri, Nebraska, Oklahoma, Virginia 9 Louisiana, Minnesota, New Jersey, New Mexico, Tennessee, Wisconsin 10 California, Puerto Rico, Washington 11 Connecticut, Mississippi, North Dakota, Rhode Island, South Dakota 12 New Hampshire, Pennsylvania, West Virginia 13 Massachusetts, North Carolina, South Carolina 18 District of Columbia
  island: 4 Guam, Long, Maui, Oahu 5 Block, Ellis, Kauai, Lanai, Umnak 6 Hawaii, Kodiak, Niihau, Unimak, Virgin 7 Baranof, Key West, Long Key, Molokai, Nunivak, Sanibel 8 Aleutian, Hawaiian, Key Largo, Shumagin, Unalaska 9 Atka Amlia, Canal Zone, Chichagof, Kahoolawe, Nantucket, Snipe Keys 10 Islamorada, Oyster Keys, Puerto Rico, St. Lawrence 11 Longboat Key 12 Santa Barbara 13 American Samoa, Marquesas Keys, Prince of Wales, Santa Catalina, Summerland Key 15 Martha's Vineyard 16 Cantout Enderbury 26 Trust Territory of the Pacific
  lake: 4 Erie, Mead 5 Huron, Tahoe 6 Cayuga, Finger, George, Itasca, Oneida, Seneca 7 Iliamma, Ontario 8 Michigan, Superior 9 Champlain, Great Salt, Salton Sea, Teshekpuk, Winnebago 10 Okeechobee 11 Yellowstone 13 Pontchartrain, Wallenpaupack, Winnipesaukee 14 Lake of the Woods
  mountain: 4 Hood 5 Coast, Green, Kenai, Ozark, Rocky, White 6 Alaska, Brooks, DeLong, Elbert, Helena, Mesabi, Pocono, Shasta 7 Cascade, Chugach, Foraker, Harvard, Kilauea, Massive, Olympic, Olympus, Rainier, St Elias, Whitney 8 Catskill, Davidson, Endicott, Katahdin, Mauna Loa, Mitchell, Ouachita, St Helens, Wrangell 9 Allegheny, Blue Ridge, Kuskokwim, North Peak, Pikes Peak 10 Black Hills, Blanca Peak, Grand Teton, Washington, Williamson 11 Appalachian, Santa Monica 12 Sierra Nevada 14 Berkshire Hills
  highest point: 6 Denali 8 McKinley
  river: 3 New, Red 4 Gila, Iowa, Milk, Ohio, Rock 5 Black, Cedar, Coosa, Flint, Grand, Green, James, Neuse, Osage, Pearl, Pecos, Snake, White, Yukon 6 Brazos, Hudson, Neches,

Neosho, Nueces, Owybee, Pee Dee, Platte, Powder, Sabine, Salmon, Wabash **7** Alabama, Big Horn, John Day, Klamath, Potomac, Roanoke, San Juan, St Johns, Trinity **8** Arkansas, Big Black, Canadian, Cheyenne, Cimarron, Colorado, Columbia, Delaware, Humboldt, Illinois, Kentucky, Kootenay, Missouri, Niabrana, Ouachita, Savannah **9** Allegheny, Deschutes, Des Moines, Minnesota, Rio Grande, Smoky Hill, St Francis, Tennessee, Tombigbee, Wisconsin **10** Cumberland, Republican, Sacramento, San Joaquin, St Lawrence, Tallapoosa **11** Connecticut, Mississippi, North Platte, South Platte, Susquehanna, Yellowstone **12** Tallahatchie **14** Little Colorado, Little Missouri

sea: 6 Arctic, Bering **7** Pacific **8** Atlantic, Beaufort

physical feature:

bay: 5 Tampa **7** Bristol, Prudhoe **8** Biscayne, Monterey **9** Apalachee **10** Chesapeake **12** San Francisco

desert: 4 Gila **5** Mojave **7** Painted **8** Colorado, Vizcaino **9** Black Rock **11** Death Valley

falls: 7 Niagara

gulf: 6 Alaska, Mexico **10** California

plain: 5 Great

plateau: 8 Colorado, Piedmont **10** Cumberland **11** Appalachian

strait: 6 Bering **7** Florida

people:

architect: 4 Root **5** Davis **6** Upjohn, Wright **7** Burnham, Downing, Furness, Gilbert, Gropius, Latrobe **8** Bogardus, Holabird, Sullivan **9** Bullfinch, Jefferson **10** Richardson **14** Mies van der Rohe

artist: 5 Henri, Homer, Leutz, Moses, Peale, Wyeth **6** Copley, Durand, Millet, Rothko, Stuart **7** Audubon, Cassatt, O'Keeffe, Pollock, Sargent **8** Whistler

author: 3 Poe **4** Grey, Inge, Loos, Luce, West, Wouk **5** Aiken, Albee, Beach, Benet, Crane, Eliot, Frost, Guest, Harte, Hecht, James, Lewis, Oates, Odets, O'Hara, Paine, Pound, Stowe, Twain, Vidal, Welty, Wolfe, Wylie **6** Bellow, Bierce, Bryant, Cabell, Capote, Cather, Cooper, Cullen, Ferber, Holmes, Hughes, Irving, Kilmer, Lanier, London, Lowell, Mather, Millay, Miller, Norris, O'Neill, Porter, Styron, Updike, Wilder **7** Angelou, Baldwin, Clemens, Costain, Dreiser, Emerson, Gallico, Hammett, Hellman, Howells, Jeffers, Kerouac, Lardner, Malamud, Nabokov, Roethke, Stevens, Thoreau, Webster, Wharton, Whitman **8** Anderson, Bradbury, Caldwell,

Cummings, Faulkner, Macleish, McCarthy, Melville, Michener, Mitchell, Morrison, Rawlings, Robinson, Sandburg, Schwartz, Sherwood, Sinclair, Teasdale, Whittier, Williams **9** Burroughs, Dickinson, Dos Passos, Hawthorne, Hemingway, McCullers, Steinbeck **10** Fitzgerald, Longfellow, Tarkington

composer: 4 Ives, Kern **5** Cohan, Loewe, Sousa **6** Berlin, Foster, Joplin, Lerner, Porter **7** Copland, Gilbert, Rodgers **8** Gershwin, Sullivan **9** Bernstein **11** Hammerstein

explorer: 4 Byrd, Pike **5** Boone, Cabot, Clark, Lewis, Perry **6** Hudson, Joliet **7** Jolliet **8** Columbus **9** Marquette **10** Eric the Red

leader: 3 Jay **4** Clay, King, Penn **5** Bryan, Davis, Henry, Paine **6** Revere, Sumner **7** Stevens, Webster **8** Franklin, Humphrey **9** Goldwater

military leader: 3 Lee **4** Pike **5** Clark, Gates, Grant, Meade, Tyler **6** Austin, Custer, Marion, Patton **7** Bradley, Houston, Jackson, Sherman **8** Marshall, Pershing **9** MacArthur, Roosevelt, Stillwell **10** Eisenhower, Vandenburg, Washington **11** Schwarzkopf

president: 4 Bush, Ford, Polk, Taft **5** Adams, Grant, Hayes, Nixon, Tyler **6** Arthur, Carter, Hoover, Monroe, Pierce, Reagan, Taylor, Truman, Wilson **7** Clinton, Harding, Jackson, Johnson, Kennedy, Lincoln, Madison **8** Buchanan, Coolidge, Fillmore, Garfield, Hamilton, Harrison, McKinley, Van Buren **9** Cleveland, Jefferson, Roosevelt **10** Eisenhower, Washington

sculptor: 4 Rush **6** Calder, French, Rogers **7** Borglum **8** Greenough, Remington **12** Saint-Gaudens

language: 7 English, Spanish

religion: 5 Amish **6** Mormon **7** Baptist, Judaism, Shakers **8** Lutheran **9** Methodist **10** Protestant **11** Pentacostal **12** Episcopalian, Presbyterian **13** Roman Catholic **14** Church of Christ, Congregational **15** Eastern Orthodox, Latter Day Saints **19** Seventh Day Adventist

place:

national park: 4 Zion **5** Platt **6** Acadia **7** Big Bend, Glacier, Olympic, Redwood, Sequoia **8** Wind Cave, Yosemite **9** Haleakala, Mesa Verde, Multnomah **10** Crater Lake, Everglades, Grand Teton, Hot Springs, Isle Royale, Shenandoah **11** Bryce Canyon, Canyonlands, Grand Canyon, Kings Canyon, Mammoth Cave, Yellowstone **12** Mount Rainier **13** Mount McKinley, Virgin Islands **14** Lassen Volcanic, Rocky Mountains **15** Carls-

bad Caverns, Petrified Forest **19** Great Smoky Mountains

possession: 4 Guam **10** Puerto Rico **13** American Samoa, Virgin Islands **14** Mariana Islands **15** Caroline Islands, Marshall Islands

feature:

colony: 7 Roanoke **8** Plymouth **9** Jamestown **11** Rhode Island **12** New Amsterdam, New Hampshire **14** New Netherlands **16** Massachusetts Bay

festival: 9 Mardi Gras

national symbol: 9 bald eagle

tree: 7 redwood, sequoia

unity 5 peace, union **6** accord, entity, fusion, league, merger **7** concord, harmony, joining, oneness, rapport **8** alliance, goodwill **9** synthesis, unanimity, wholeness **10** federation, fellowship, friendship **11** affiliation, association, cooperation, partnership, unification **12** amalgamation, amicableness **13** compatibility, confederation, consolidation, understanding **14** likemindedness

universal 7 general **9** worldwide **10** ubiquitous, widespread **11** omnipresent **12** affecting all, all-embracing, all-inclusive **13** international

Universal creator

Egyptian: 4 Ptah

universality 8 currency **10** prevalence **12** predominance **17** comprehensiveness

universe

god of: 6 Amen Ra, Amon Ra

university 6 campus, school **7** academy, college **11** institution

English: 6 Oxford **9** Cambridge

Cambridge: 7 Harvard

former: 9 alma mater

French: 8 Sorbonne

Hanover: 9 Dartmouth

lecturer: 9 prelector

New Haven: 4 Yale

New Jersey: 9 Princeton

New York: 8 Columbia

Providence: 5 Brown

session: 4 term **7** seminar **8** semester

Wit: 4 Lyly, Nash **5** Peele **6** Greene

unjust 6 biased, unfair, warped **7** partial **8** one-sided, partisan, wrongful **9** unmerited **10** prejudiced, unbalanced, undeserved **11** inequitable, unjustified, unwarranted

unjustifiable 11 inexcusable **12** indefensible

unjustly 7 falsely, wrongly **8** unfairly **10** wrongfully **11** dishonestly, faithlessly, inequitably **12** undeservedly

unkempt 5 messy **6** sloppy, untidy **7** rumpled, tousled **8** mussed-up, slovenly, uncombed **9** ungroomed **10** disheveled, disordered **11** disarranged

unkind 4 mean **5** nasty **7** abusive **8** uncaring **9** malicious, unfeeling

10 unfriendly, ungenerous, ungracious 11 insensitive, thoughtless 12 inhospitable, uncharitable 13 inconsiderate, unsympathetic

unknot 5 untie 7 unsnarl 8 untangle 11 disentangle

unknowable 12 inaccessible 13 inconceivable

unknown 7 obscure, unnamed 8 nameless 9 anonymous, unheard-of 10 unrenowned 12 uncelebrated, undesignated, undetermined, undiscovered, unidentified

unknown authors
abbr.: 4 anon
author of: 4 Edda (elder) 7 Beowulf 8 Everyman, King Horn, Stasimon 10 Cinderella 11 Poema del Cid 12 Panchatantra, Vercelli Book, Volsunga Saga 14 Gesta Romanorum, Sibylline Books 15 Chanson de Roland, The Forty Thieves, The Song of Roland 16 Grettir the Strong 17 The Nibelungenlied 20 Aucassin and Nicolette, Robin Hood's Adventures 23 The Dream of the Red Chamber, The Thousand and One Nights 26 Sir Gawain and the Green Knight 29 Collection of Ten Thousand Leaves 29 The Arabian Nights' Entertainment

unladylike 4 rude 6 coarse, common, vulgar 7 ill-bred, uncouth 8 impolite 10 unmannerly 12 discourteous

unlawful 7 illegal, illegit, illicit, lawless 8 criminal 9 forbidden 10 prohibited, unlicensed, unofficial 12 unauthorized 13 against the law 16 unconstitutional

unlawful act 5 crime 6 felony 10 wrongdoing 11 lawbreaking, malfeasance, misdemeanor

unleash 4 free 5 let go 7 release, set free 8 let loose, liberate 12 give free rein

unlettered 8 ignorant, untaught 9 unlearned, untutored 10 illiterate, uneducated, unschooled 11 unscholarly

unlighted 3 dim 4 dark 5 murky, unlit 6 gloomy 7 stygian, sunless 8 moonless 9 lightless 13 unilluminated

unlikable, unlikeable 7 hateful 9 offensive, unlovable 10 hard to like, unloveable, unpleasant 11 displeasing, unappealing 12 disagreeable

unlike 7 diverse, unalike, unequal 9 different, disparate 10 dissimilar

unlikelihood 12 doubtfulness, unlikeliness 13 improbability

unlikely 8 hopeless 10 improbable 11 unpromising 12 questionable, unbelievable, unpropitious 19 scarcely conceivable

unlikeness 8 contrast, variance 9 disparity, variation 10 difference, divergence 13 dissimilarity, dissimilitude

unlimited 4 huge, vast 5 total 7 endless, immense 8 absolute, complete, infinite 9 boundless, limitless, unbounded, unchecked 11 unqualified 12 immeasurable, totalitarian, uncontrolled, unrestrained, unrestricted 13 comprehensive, inexhaustible, unconstrained 15 all- encompassing

unload 4 dump 7 off-load 8 get rid of, unburden 9 dispose of 10 unencumber

unlooked for 6 sudden 7 unasked 8 surprise 10 unexpected, unforeseen, unheralded 11 unannounced, uncalled for, unpredicted, unsolicited 13 serendipitous, unanticipated

unlovable, unloveable 7 hateful 9 unlikable 10 hard to like, unlikeable, unpleasant 11 displeasing, unappealing 12 disagreeable

unloving 4 cold, cool 6 frigid 11 indifferent, passionless 13 unimpassioned

unlucky 6 cursed, jinxed 7 hapless, unhappy 8 ill-fated, luckless, untoward 9 ill-omened 10 ill-starred 11 star- crossed, unfortunate 12 inauspicious, misfortunate

unman 7 unnerve 8 castrate 10 discourage, emasculate

unmanageable 5 balky, bulky 6 mulish, unruly 7 awkward, unhandy, wayward, willful 8 ungainly, unwieldy 9 fractious, pigheaded 10 cumbersome, rebellious, refractory 11 disobedient, intractable, troublesome 12 incorrigible 14 uncontrollable

unmanly 5 timid 6 yellow 8 cowardly, sissyish, womanish 9 sissified, weak-kneed 10 effeminate 11 lily-livered, unmasculine, weakhearted 12 fainthearted 13 pusillanimous 14 chickenhearted

unmannerly 5 crude, gross, surly 6 coarse 7 boorish, ill- bred, loutish, uncivil, uncouth 8 impolite 10 ungracious, unladylike 11 ill-mannered 12 badly behaved, discourteous 13 ungentlemanly

unmarked 5 clean, clear 9 undamaged, undefaced, unnoticed 10 unobserved 11 unblemished 15 undistinguished

unmarried 4 free 5 unwed 6 maiden, single 7 old maid, widowed 8 bachelor, divorced, spinster, unwedded, virginal, wifeless 9 available, fancy free 10 spouseless, unattached 11 husbandless 21 footloose and fancy-free

unmarried girl
French: 10 jeune fille
German: 8 fraulein
Spanish: 8 senorita

Unmarried Woman, An
director: 12 Paul Mazursky
cast: 9 Alan Bates 11 Cliff Gorman 13 Jill Clayburgh, Michael Murphy

unmask 4 bare, show 6 betray, expose, reveal, unveil 7 lay open, uncover 8 disclose, discover 12 bring to light

unmasking 6 baring 8 betrayal, exposure 9 discovery, unveiling 10 disclosure, laying open, revelation, uncovering 15 bringing to light

unmatched 6 unlike 7 diverse, supreme, unequal 8 peerless, variable 9 differing, disparate, matchless, unequaled 10 dissimilar 12 second to none, unparalleled 13 beyond compare

unmerciful 4 cold, evil 5 cruel, harsh 6 brutal, severe, unkind 7 brutish, extreme, inhuman 8 inhumane, pitiless, ruthless 9 excessive, heartless, inclement, merciless, unfeeling, unpitying, unsparing 10 malevolent, relentless 11 hardhearted 14 unconscionable

unmindful 3 lax 6 remiss 7 unaware 8 careless, derelict, heedless 9 forgetful, negligent, oblivious, unheeding 11 thoughtless, unconscious

unmistakable 5 clear, plain 6 patent 7 evident, glaring, obvious 8 apparent, distinct, manifest, palpable 9 prominent 10 pronounced, undeniable 11 conspicuous, unequivocal 12 indisputable 14 unquestionable

unmistakably 7 clearly, plainly 8 palpably, patently 9 certainly, decidedly, downright, evidently, glaringly, obviously 10 definitely, distinctly, manifestly, positively, thoroughly, undeniably 11 prominently 12 indisputably 13 conspicuously, unequivocally 14 unquestionably 17 beyond all question

unmitigated 6 arrant 8 absolute, unabated, unbroken 9 downright, out-and-out 10 persistent, unrelieved 11 unqualified 12 unalleviated 13 uninterrupted

unmixed 4 neat, pure 5 sheer 6 simple 8 straight 9 unalloyed, unblended, undiluted, unmingled 13 unadulterated

unmoved 4 calm, cold, firm 5 aloof 6 dogged 7 devoted, staunch 8 resolute, resolved, uncaring, unshaken 9 dedicated, obstinate, steadfast, unfeeling, unpitying, unstirred, untouched 10 determined, inflexible, not shifted, persistent, relentless, unaffected, unswerving, unwavering 11 indifferent, unconcerned, undeviating, undisturbed, unfaltering 12 stonyhearted, uninterested, unresponsive 14 uncompromising

unmoving 4 dead, dull 5 fixed, inert, still 6 boring, serene 8 immobile 9 powerless 10 motionless, stationary 11 emotionless 13 at a standstill

unnamed 8 nameless, unsigned 9 anonymous, incognito 10 innominate, uncredited, unreported, unrevealed 11 undisclosed, unspecified 12 pseudonymous, undesignated, undiscovered, unidentified **14** unacknowledged

unnatural 4 fake **5** phony, put-on **6** forced **7** assumed, stilted, studied, unusual **8** aberrant, abnormal, affected, freakish, mannered, peculiar **9** anomalous, contrived **10** artificial, theatrical **13** self-conscious

unnecessary 5 extra **6** excess **7** surplus **8** needless, overmuch **9** auxiliary, excessive **10** expendable, gratuitous, unrequired **11** dispensable, superfluous, uncalled- for, unessential **13** supplementary

unnerve 5 daunt, scare, upset **7** agitate, unhinge **8** frighten, unsettle **10** intimidate

unnerving 5 scary **8** daunting **9** upsetting **10** enervating, unsettling **11** frightening

unnoticeable 3 dim **5** faint **6** hidden **7** obscure **9** concealed **10** indistinct, unassuming, unemphatic, unobserved **11** unobtrusive **12** undetectable **13** imperceptible, inconspicuous, insignificant, undiscernible **14** unostentatious

unnoticed 6 unfelt, unseen **7** unheard, unnoted **8** unheeded, untasted **10** not smelled, overlooked, unobserved **11** disregarded, unperceived **12** undiscovered

unobservant 4 dull **5** blind **8** unseeing **9** unmindful **11** incognizant

unobstructed 4 fair, free, open **5** clear **8** apparent **9** unimpeded **10** unhampered, unhindered **11** unprevented

unobtainable 9 hard to get **10** impossible, out of reach, out of touch **11** unavailable, unreachable **12** improcurable, inaccessible

unobtrusive 3 shy **6** humble, modest **7** bashful **8** reserved, reticent, retiring **9** diffident **10** unassuming **11** unassertive **13** inconspicuous, unpretentious **14** unostentatious

unoccupied 4 idle **5** empty **6** vacant **8** unfilled **9** abandoned, unengaged **10** untenanted **11** uninhabited

unofficial 8 informal **12** unauthorized

unorganized 5 loose **6** casual, random **7** aimless, chaotic **8** confused **9** haphazard, orderless, unordered **10** disjointed, unarranged, undirected **11** harum-scarum **12** unclassified, unsystematic **13** helter-skelter **14** unsystematized

unornamented 4 bald, bare **5** blank, naked, plain, stark **6** simple **7** austere **9** unadorned **11** undecorated **13** unembellished

unorthodox 7 erratic **9** eccentric, irregular **14** unconventional

unostentatious 3 shy **5** plain, quiet **6** humble, modest, simple **9** unadorned, unaffected **10** unassuming **11** con-

strained **13** inconspicuous, unpretentious **14** unpresumptuous

unpaid 3 due **4** owed **5** owing **9** in arrears **11** outstanding

unpaid debt 5 debit **7** arrears **9** liability **10** balance due, obligation **12** indebtedness

unpalatable 5 nasty **8** inedible, unsavory **9** repellent, repulsive **10** badtasting, unpleasant **11** displeasing, distasteful **12** disagreeable, unappetizing **13** hard to swallow

unparalleled 4 best, rare **5** alone, crack, elect **6** unique **8** gilt-edge, peerless, singular **9** matchless, superfine, unequaled, unmatched, unrivaled **10** crackajack, inimitable, unimitated **11** unsurpassed **12** unapproached **13** unprecedented **15** of the first water

unperceptive 5 blind **9** unfeeling **11** insensitive, unobservant **12** imperceptive, impercipient **13** unsympathetic

unperturbed 4 calm, cool **6** poised **8** composed, tranquil **9** collected, unexcited, unruffled **10** coolheaded, nonchalant, unagitated, undismayed, untroubled **11** levelheaded, undisturbed **13** unimpassioned

unplanned 9 impromptu **10** accidental, fortuitous, improvised, unexpected, unforeseen **11** spontaneous **12** uncalculated **13** unintentional **14** extemporaneous, unpremeditated **15** spur-of-the-moment

unpleasant 5 nasty, pesky **7** irksome, noisome **8** annoying, churlish **9** obnoxious, offensive, repugnant, repulsive, unlikable, vexatious **10** illhumored, ill-natured **11** displeasing, distasteful **12** disagreeable, unattractive **13** objectionable

unpleasantness 8 ugliness **9** ill nature, nastiness **12** churlishness **13** obnoxiousness, offensiveness, repulsiveness **15** distastefulness **16** disagreeableness, unattractiveness

unpointed 4 dull **5** blunt **6** dulled **11** unsharpened

unpolished 3 raw **5** gawky, inept, rough **6** cloudy, clumsy **7** amateur, awkward, unwaxed **8** inexpert, unbuffed, unglazed, unshined **9** inelegant, unrefined, unskilled **10** uncultured, unfinished, unskillful **11** unburnished, unpracticed **12** uncultivated **13** inexperienced **14** unaccomplished **15** unsophisticated

unpopular 7 snubbed **8** disliked, rebuffed, rejected, slighted, unwanted **9** disdained, neglected, unwelcome **10** unaccepted **11** disapproved, undesirable **12** looked down on, unacceptable

unpopulated 5 rural **9** backwoods, unpeopled, unsettled

unprecedented 5 novel **6** unique **9** unheard-of **10** unexampled **11** excep-

tional **12** unparalleled **13** extraordinary **15** hitherto unknown

unpredictable 6 fitful **7** erratic **8** fanciful, unstable, variable **9** arbitrary, eccentric, impulsive, mercurial, uncertain, whimsical **10** capricious, changeable, inconstant

unprejudiced 4 fair, just **8** unbiased, unswayed **9** impartial, objective, unbigoted **10** even-handed, fair-minded, open-minded, undogmatic **11** broadminded **12** uninfluenced **13** disinterested

unpremeditated 5 ad-lib **9** impetuous, impromptu, impulsive, unplanned **10** accidental, improvised, unintended **11** involuntary, spontaneous **12** uncalculated, unthought-out **13** unintentional **14** extemporaneous **15** spur-of-the-moment

unprepared 5 ad-lib **7** offhand, unready **8** off guard **9** extempore, impromptu **10** flat-footed, improvised **11** spontaneous, unrehearsed **14** extemporaneous **15** spur-of-the-moment

unprepossessing 4 grim **5** seedy **10** ill-favored, ill- looking **12** unattractive

unpressed 5 baggy **6** mussed, sloppy **7** creased, rumpled **8** unironed, wrinkled **9** shapeless, uncreased

unpretentious 5 plain **6** homely, humble, modest, simple **10** unassuming, unimposing **11** unelaborate, unobtrusive **14** unostentatious

unprincipled 6 amoral **12** unscrupulous **14** conscienceless, unconscionable

unproductive 4 poor **6** barren **7** sterile, useless **8** bootless **9** infertile **10** unfruitful, unyielding **11** ineffective, ineffectual, inefficient **12** unprofitable

unprofessional 6 shoddy, sloppy **7** amateur **8** bungling, careless **9** negligent, unethical **10** amateurish **11** incompetent, inefficient, unpracticed **12** unprincipled **13** inexperienced, undisciplined, unworkmanlike **14** unbusinesslike

unprofitable 4 vain **7** useless **8** bootless **11** ineffective, ineffectual

unprogressive 7 diehard **8** backward, standpat, stubborn **9** benighted, rightwing **11** reactionary, reactionist **12** conservative **17** ultraconservative

unprolific 6 barren **7** sterile **9** infertile, unfertile **10** nonbearing **12** unproductive

unpromising 5 bleak **9** ill-omened **10** forbidding **11** unfavorable **12** inauspicious, unpropitious

unpropitious 7 adverse **8** contrary **9** unfitting **10** unsuitable **11** unfavorable **12** antagonistic, inauspicious, infelicitous

unprotected 4 open **5** naked **6** unsafe **7** exposed, unarmed **8** helpless, insecure, perilous **9** dangerous, hazardous, unguarded **10** undefended, vulnerable **11** defenseless

unproven 7 in doubt **8** arguable, doubtful **10** indefinite, in question, up in the air **11** open to doubt, unconfirmed **12** experimental, inconclusive, questionable **13** unestablished **14** open to question

unpunctual 4 late **5** tardy **7** belated **10** behindhand, behindtime

unqualified 5 total, unfit, utter **8** absolute, complete, inexpert, positive, thorough, unsuited **9** downright, out-and-out, unskilled, untrained **10** consummate, undisputed, uneducated, unprepared, unschooled **11** ill-equipped, incompetent **13** inexperienced, unconditional

unquenched 8 unslaked **11** unsatisfied **14** unextinguished

unquestionable 4 sure **5** clear, plain **6** proven **7** certain, evident, obvious, perfect **8** definite, flawless **9** blameless, errorless, faultless **10** impeccable, undeniable **11** beyond doubt, irrefutable, self-evident, unequivocal **12** indisputable, uncensurable **13** uncontestable, unimpeachable **14** irreproachable

unquestionably 6 surely **7** totally **9** certainly, doubtless **10** absolutely, completely, definitely, positively, unarguably **12** conclusively, indisputably, without doubt **13** unequivocally

unravel 4 undo **5** feaze, solve **6** unfold, unfurl, unknit **7** clear up, resolve **8** decipher, separate, untangle **9** pull apart **10** disinvolve **11** disentangle

unreachable 10 impossible, out of touch **11** out of the way, unavailable, unrealistic **12** inaccessible, unobtainable **14** unapproachable

unreal 4 airy **5** dream **6** dreamy **7** ghostly, not real, phantom, shadowy **8** ethereal, illusive, illusory, imagined, spectral **9** dreamlike, fantastic, imaginary, legendary **10** chimerical, fictitious, idealistic, intangible **11** nonexistent **13** insubstantial **16** phantasmagorical

unrealistic 4 wild **5** crazy, silly **6** absurd **7** asinine, foolish **8** crackpot, delusory, fanciful **9** illogical **10** idealistic, improbable, infeasible, starry-eyed **11** impractical **12** unreasonable

unrealized 8 thwarted **10** frustrated, incomplete **11** nonexistent, unfulfilled, unsatisfied **14** unaccomplished

unreasonable 5 undue **6** absurd, biased, mulish, unfair **7** bigoted **8** obdurate, stubborn, too great **9** excessive, fanatical, illogical, obstinate, pigheaded, senseless, unbending **10** bullheaded, exorbitant, far-fetched, headstrong, immoderate, inflexible, inordinate, irrational, prejudiced, un-

yielding **11** extravagant, intractable, nonsensical, opinionated, uncalled-for, unwarranted **12** closed-minded, preposterous, ungovernable, unmanageable **13** unjustifiable

unreasoning 8 careless, heedless **9** impulsive **10** irrational, unthinking **11** thoughtless **13** unintelligent

unrecognizable 9 disguised, incognito **10** in disguise **11** camouflaged **14** unidentifiable

unrecognized 6 unsung **7** cryptic, unknown **9** incognito, unnoticed

unrefined 3 raw **5** crude, rough **6** coarse, vulgar **7** boorish, low-bred **9** inelegant

unrehearsed 7 offhand **8** informal **9** extempore, impromptu, impulsive, unplanned, unstudied **10** improvised, off-the-cuff, unprepared **11** extemporary, spontaneous **14** extemporaneous, unpremeditated **15** improvisational, spur-of-the-moment **19** off the top of one's head

unrelated 6 not kin, unlike **7** foreign **8** unallied **10** dissimilar, extraneous, irrelevant, non-germane **11** unconnected **12** inapplicable, incompatible, unassociated **13** inappropriate

unrelenting 5 rigid **6** steady **7** adamant, endless **8** constant, unabated, unbroken **9** ceaseless, incessant, tenacious, unbending **10** implacable, inexorable, inflexible, relentless, unrelieved, unswerving, unwavering, unyielding **11** undeviating, unremitting **14** uncompromising

unreliable 4 fake **5** false, phony **6** fickle **8** fallible, mistaken, unstable **9** deceitful, erroneous, uncertain **10** capricious, changeable, inaccurate, inconstant **12** questionable, undependable **13** irresponsible, untrustworthy

unremarkable 5 usual **6** common **7** average **8** everyday, mediocre, ordinary **11** commonplace **12** unimpressive, unsurprising **13** insignificant, unexceptional **15** undistinguished

unremitting 6 dogged **8** constant, tireless, untiring **9** ceaseless, continual, incessant, unceasing **10** continuous, persistent **11** persevering

unrepentant 7 callous **8** hardened, obdurate, unatoned **9** unashamed **10** uncontrite, unexpiated **11** remorseless **12** incorrigible, unregenerate

unrepressed 4 free, open **7** liberal **8** effusive, outgoing **9** expansive, exuberant **11** extroverted, uninhibited **12** unrestrained

unreserved 4 full, open **5** frank **6** entire **11** unqualified **12** wholehearted

unresolved 4 moot **5** vague **7** pending **8** doubtful, unsolved **9** tentative, uncertain, undecided, unsettled **10** disputable, unanswered **11** contestable, speculative **12** questionable, undeter-

mined **13** problematical, unascertained

unresponsive 4 cold, cool, dull, limp **5** inert **6** frigid **7** passive **8** lifeless **9** apathetic, unfeeling **11** cold-blooded, inattentive, indifferent, unemotional **13** dispassionate, unsympathetic

unresponsiveness 6 apathy **7** inertia **9** lassitude, passivity **11** inattention, passiveness **12** indifference

unrest 5 chaos **6** tumult **7** anarchy, discord, ferment, protest, turmoil **8** disorder, disquiet, upheaval **9** agitation, rebellion **10** discontent, turbulence **12** restlessness **15** dissatisfaction

unrestrained 8 uncurbed **9** abandoned, boundless, excessive, unbridled, unchecked, unlimited **10** immoderate, inordinate, unfettered, ungoverned, unhampered, unhindered, unreserved **11** extravagant, intemperate, uninhibited, unrepressed **12** uncontrolled, unrestricted, unsuppressed **13** irrepressible

unrestraint 6 excess **7** abandon **9** uncontrol **10** unruliness **12** extravagance, immoderation, recklessness **13** excessiveness, impulsiveness

unrestricted 8 absolute, complete **9** out-and-out, unbounded, unlimited **11** unqualified **12** unrestrained **13** unconditional

unrigid 3 lax **4** easy, limp, soft **5** loose **6** giving, limber, mobile, pliant, supple **7** elastic, lenient, plastic, pliable **8** flexible, informal, merciful, tolerant, yielding **9** indulgent, malleable **11** conformable

unrigorous 4 easy **5** loose, slack **6** casual, sloppy **7** inexact **8** careless, slapdash **9** imprecise

unripe 5 green **8** immature **10** unseasoned **11** undeveloped **14** underdeveloped

unrivaled 8 superior, topnotch **9** unequaled **10** undisputed **11** unsurpassed

unroll 6 reveal, uncoil, unfold, unfurl, unwind **7** display, lay open, play out **9** spread out

unruffled 4 calm, cool, even, mild **5** quiet, still **6** placid, serene, smooth **8** composed, tranquil **9** collected **10** coolheaded, nonchalant, unagitated, untroubled **11** undisturbed, unperturbed **13** self-possessed

unruly 4 wild **5** rowdy **7** restive, wayward, willful **8** contrary, perverse **9** fractious, unbridled **10** boisterous, disorderly, headstrong, refractory **11** disobedient, intractable **12** obstreperous, ungovernable, unmanageable **13** undisciplined **14** uncontrollable

unsafe 5 risky **7** exposed **8** insecure, perilous **9** dangerous, hazardous, unguarded **10** undefended, unreliable, vulnerable **11** defenseless, treacherous, unprotected **13** untrustworthy

unsatisfactory 4 poor **5** inept, unfit **8** below par, inferior, unworthy **9** deficient **10** inadequate, ineligible, unsuitable **12** inadmissible, unacceptable **13** inappropriate

unsavory 3 bad **4** flat, foul **5** nasty **7** insipid, tainted **9** tasteless **10** bad-tasting, nauseating, unpleasant **11** distasteful, unpalatable **12** disagreeable, unappetizing

unscathed 5 sound, whole **6** entire, intact, unhurt **7** perfect **8** unharmed **9** uninjured, untouched **10** unimpaired **11** unscratched **13** all in one piece

unscholarly 8 ignorant **9** unlearned **10** illiterate, uneducated, uninformed **11** ill-informed **13** unintelligent

unschooled 3 raw **5** green **6** callow **8** ignorant, untaught **9** unlearned **10** illiterate, uneducated, uninformed, unlettered, unseasoned **11** uninitiated **13** inexperienced

unscrupulous 5 sharp **6** amoral **7** crooked, devious, immoral **9** unethical **12** dishonorable, unprincipled

unseasonable 6 too hot **7** too cold, too warm **8** abnormal, untimely

unseasoned 3 raw **5** bland, green, plain **6** callow **7** untried **8** immature **13** inexperienced

unseeing 5 blind **7** unaware **9** oblivious, sightless **11** unobservant

unseemly 4 rude **5** crude, gross **6** coarse, vulgar **7** boorish, loutish **8** churlish, improper, indecent, unworthy **9** incorrect, offensive, tasteless **10** indecorous, indelicate, out of place, unbecoming, unladylike, unsuitable **11** distasteful, ill-mannered, unbefitting, undignified **12** discourteous, disreputable **13** discreditable, inappropriate, reprehensible, ungentlemanly

unselfconscious 7 artless **10** unaffected **13** unpretentious

unselfish 7 liberal **8** generous, handsome, princely, selfless **10** altruistic, benevolent, big-hearted, charitable, open-handed **11** considerate, magnanimous, magnificent **12** humanitarian **13** philanthropic **15** self-sacrificing

unserviceable 7 useless **8** unusable

unsettle 5 upset **6** bother, rattle, ruffle **7** agitate, confuse, disturb, fluster, perturb, trouble, unhinge **8** bewilder, confound, disorder **9** unbalance **10** disconcert **13** throw off guard

unsettled 5 fazed **7** anxious, nervous, ruffled **8** agitated, confused, doubtful **9** disturbed, nonplused, perturbed, undecided **10** disquieted, distracted, nonplussed, up in the air **11** discomfited **12** disconcerted **16** at sixes and sevens

unshackle 4 free **7** release, set free, unchain **8** liberate, unfetter

unshakable 4 fast **6** stable **7** abiding, staunch **8** constant, enduring **9** dauntless, permanent, steadfast, unruffled **10** changeless, inflexible, unsinkable, unwavering **11** levelheaded, unflappable **13** imperturbable

unshaken 4 calm, cool **6** poised, serene, stable **7** staunch, unmoved **8** composed, constant, resolved **9** steadfast, tenacious, undaunted, unexcited, unruffled **10** controlled, determined, inflexible, relentless, unaffected, unswerving, untroubled, unwavering **11** levelheaded, undeviating, undisturbed, unemotional, unfaltering, unflinching, unperturbed **13** self-possessed **14** uncompromising

unshapely 5 baggy **9** amorphous, shapeless

unshaven 5 hairy **7** bearded, bristly, hirsute, stubbly, unkempt **9** whiskered **11** bewhiskered

unsheathe 4 bare **6** expose **7** pull out **8** withdraw

unsightly 4 ugly **6** horrid, odious **7** hideous u **9** obnoxious, offensive, repellent, repulsive, revolting, sickening **11** distasteful **12** unattractive

unsigned 9 anonymous **13** bearing no name

unskilled 5 green, inept **7** untried **9** untrained **10** amateurish, apprentice **11** incompetent, unqualified **13** inexperienced

unskillful 5 inept **6** clumsy, unable **7** awkward **8** inexpert **9** incapable, maladroit, untrained **10** amateurish **11** incompetent, ineffective, unpracticed **13** inexperienced

unsmiling 3 sad **4** glum, grim **5** grave **6** dismal **7** austere, joyless, serious **9** cheerless, grim-faced

unsociable 7 haughty **9** withdrawn **10** antisocial, unfriendly, ungracious **11** introverted **14** unapproachable

unsoiled 4 pure **5** clean, fresh, white **6** chaste **8** innocent, pristine, spotless **9** unstained, unsullied **10** immaculate **11** unblemished, untarnished

unsolicited 4 free **8** unforced, unsought, unwanted **9** undesired, uninvited, unwelcome, voluntary **10** gratuitous, unasked for **11** spontaneous, unnecessary, unrequested, unwished for, volunteered

unsophisticated 4 open **5** green, naive **6** candid **7** artless, natural **8** homespun, innocent, trusting **9** ingenuous, unstudied, unworldly **10** unaffected, unassuming **11** uncontrived **13** undissembling, unpretentious **15** straightforward

unsound 3 mad, off **4** weak **5** risky, shaky, unfit, wrong **6** absurd, ailing,

faulty, feeble, flawed, infirm, insane, marred, sickly, unsafe **7** foolish, invalid, rickety, tottery **8** confused, crippled, decrepit, deranged, diseased, drooping, impaired, insecure, not solid, not valid, perilous, specious, spurious, unhinged, unstable, unsteady **9** blemished, dangerous, defective, erroneous, hazardous, illogical, imperfect, incorrect, senseless, uncertain, unfounded, unhealthy, unsettled, untenable **10** disordered, fallacious, groundless, irrational, precarious, unbalanced, unreliable **11** languishing, mentally ill **12** in poor health **13** off one's rocker, unsubstantial

unsoundness 7 frailty **8** delicacy, weakness **9** fragility, frailness, shakiness **11** decrepitude, derangement, instability **12** unsteadiness

unsparing 4 full **6** giving, lavish **7** copious, liberal, profuse **8** abundant, generous **9** bountiful, plenteous, plentiful, unlimited **10** big-hearted, munificent, ungrudging, unstinting **11** extravagant, magnanimous, unqualified **13** unconditional

unspeakable 4 huge, vast **5** awful, great **6** odious **7** fearful, immense **8** enormous, shocking **9** abhorrent, frightful, loathsome, monstrous, repellent, repulsive, revolting, sickening, unheard-of **10** abominable, disgusting, incredible, nauseating, prodigious **11** astonishing, unutterable **12** overwhelming, unimaginable **13** extraordinary, inconceivable, inexpressible, undescribable

unspecified 5 vague **7** general, unnamed **9** undefined, unsettled **10** indefinite **11** unannounced, unindicated, unmentioned **12** undesignated, undetermined, unpublicized, unstipulated

unspoiled 4 open **7** artless, natural, perfect **8** pristine, spotless, trusting, unharmed, unmarred **9** preserved, undamaged, unscarred, unspotted, unstudied, unworldly **10** unaffected, unassuming, unimpaired, unpampered **11** unblemished, uncorrupted **13** unpretentious **15** unself-conscious, unsophisticated

unspoken 5 tacit **6** silent **7** implied **8** implicit **9** ineffable, not voiced, unuttered **10** understood **11** unexpressed

unspotted 5 clean **8** spotless, unsoiled **9** undefiled, unstained, unsullied **11** unblemished

unstable 4 weak **5** frail, shaky, tippy **6** fickle, fitful, flimsy, wobbly **7** erratic, fragile, rickety **8** changing, insecure, shifting, unsteady, volatile **9** emotional, mercurial, tottering **10** capricious, changeable, fly-by-night, irrational **11** fluctuating, vacillating **12** inconsistent **13** irresponsible, unpredictable, unsubstantial

unstained 5 clean 8 spotless 9 unspotted, unsullied, untainted 11 unblemished, uncorrupted

unsteady 6 fickle, wobbly 7 rickety 8 doubtful, unstable 10 unreliable 12 questionable, undependable 13 untrustworthy

unstinting 11 unqualified 12 enthusiastic, unrestrained, wholehearted

unstooped 5 erect 6 unbent 7 upright 8 straight, vertical

unstudied 4 glib 6 casual 7 artless, natural 8 informal, unforced, unversed 9 guileless, unuttered 10 unaffected 11 spontaneous 12 uncalculated

unsubmissive 6 unruly 7 defiant, froward, naughty, wayward 8 contrary, mutinous, perverse, stubborn 9 fractious, insurgent, obstinate, seditious, undutiful 10 disorderly, rebellious, refractory, unyielding 11 disobedient, intractable 12 noncompliant, recalcitrant, ungovernable, unmanageable 13 insubordinate

unsubstantial 4 airy, weak 5 filmy 6 feeble, flimsy 7 unsound 8 ethereal, fanciful, illusory 9 idealized, imaginary 10 jerrybuilt 11 lightweight 12 undetectable 13 imperceptible 17 indistinguishable

unsubstantiated 8 disputed 10 unverified 15 unauthenticated

unsuccessful 4 poor, vain 6 foiled, futile, hard up 7 baffled, hapless, unlucky, useless 8 abortive, badly off, luckless, strapped, thwarted 9 fruitless, moneyless, penniless 10 ill-starred, profitless, unavailing, unfruitful 11 ineffectual, unfortunate 12 unproductive, unprofitable, unprosperous 14 unremunerative

unsuitability 9 unfitness, wrongness 11 impropriety, uselessness 12 unseemliness 13 inconsistency 15 incompatibility, unacceptability 17 inappropriateness

unsuitable 5 inapt, unfit 7 unhappy, useless 8 improper, unseemly 9 unfitting, worthless 10 inadequate, indecorous, out of place, unbecoming, unsuitable 11 incongruous, unbefitting 12 inadmissible, incompatible, inconsistent, infelicitous, out of keeping, unacceptable 13 inappropriate

unsuited 5 inapt, wrong 9 unfitting 10 out of place 13 inappropriate

unsullied 5 clean 8 spotless, unsoiled 9 undefiled, uninjured, untainted 10 unpolluted 11 unblackened, unblemished, uncorrupted, untarnished 14 uncontaminated

unsupportable 6 faulty 9 unfounded, untenable 12 indefensible

unsure 3 shy 5 timid 7 bashful 8 hesitant, insecure, reserved 9 unassured, uncertain, undecided 11 in a quandary, unconfi- dent, unconvinced 12 self-doubting 15 self-distrustful

unsurpassed 4 best 7 highest, supreme 8 greatest, peerless, superior 9 matchless, nonpareil, paramount, unequaled, unmatched, unrivaled 10 consummate, unexcelled 11 exceptional 12 incomparable, transcendent, unparalleled

unsuspecting 5 naive 6 unwary 7 unaware 8 gullible, off guard, trusting 9 believing, credulous 12 overtrustful, unsuspicious 13 overcredulous

unsuspicious 5 naive 8 gullible, trustful, trusting 9 credulous 12 unsuspecting 13 unquestioning

unswerving 4 firm 6 steady, strong 7 devoted, staunch 8 faithful, resolute, resolved, unshaken, untiring 9 dedicated, steadfast, undaunted 10 determined, inflexible, unflagging, unwavering, unyielding 11 undeviating, unfaltering, unflinching, unremitting 12 single-minded 14 uncompromising

unsympathetic 7 callous 8 pitiless, uncaring 9 heartless, repellent, repugnant, unfeeling, unlikable 10 hardboiled, unlikeable, unmerciful, unpleasant 11 coldhearted, displeasing, hardhearted, indifferent, uncongenial 12 antipathetic, unattractive 15 uncompassionate

unsystematic 6 sloppy 7 chaotic, jumbled, muddled 8 confused 9 haphazard, unplanned 10 disordered, disorderly 12 disorganized, unmethodical

untainted 4 pure 5 clear 9 unsullied 11 uncorrupted 13 unadulterated

untalented 5 inept 8 mediocre, ungifted 9 unskilled 10 amateurish, unskillful 14 unaccomplished

untamed 4 wild 5 feral 6 savage 9 unsubdued 11 uncivilized 12 uncultivated

untangle 5 solve 7 clear up, unravel, unsnarl, untwist 9 extricate 11 disentangle 13 straighten out

untarnished 6 bright 7 perfect, shining 8 flawless, polished, spotless, unsoiled 9 faultless, undefiled, unstained, unsullied, untainted 10 immaculate, impeccable, undisputed, unoxidized 11 unblackened, unblemished 12 unbesmirched 13 unimpeachable

untaught 6 unread 7 natural 8 ignorant 9 untutored 10 illiterate, uneducated, unlettered, unschooled 11 spontaneous 12 uninstructed

untenable 4 weak 6 faulty, flawed 7 invalid, unsound 8 baseless, specious, spurious 9 debatable, erroneous, illogical 10 fallacious, groundless, unreliable 11 contestable 12 indefensible, questionable 13 insupportable, unjustifiable, unsustainable 14 unmaintainable

unthinkable 11 unwarranted 12 unimaginable 13 inconceivable, insupportable, unjustifiable 16 incomprehensible, out of the question

unthinking 7 witless 8 careless, heedless, mindless, tactless 9 imprudent, negligent, senseless 11 inadvertent, insensitive, thoughtless 12 undiplomatic 13 inconsiderate, uncircumspect

untidiness 5 chaos, mix-up, upset 6 jumble 7 clutter 8 disarray, disorder, scramble, shambles 9 confusion, messiness 10 sloppiness 12 dishevelment 14 disarrangement 15 disorganization

untidy 5 dowdy, messy 6 frowsy, mussed, sloppy 7 chaotic, rumpled, tousled, unkempt 8 careless, confused, littered, mussed up, slipshod, slovenly 9 cluttered 10 bedraggled, disarrayed, disheveled, disorderly, slatternly, topsy-turvy 12 unmethodical 13 helter-skelter

untie 4 free, undo 5 loose 6 loosen, unbind, unlace 7 unchain, unstrap 8 make free, unfasten 11 disentangle

untilled 6 fallow 8 unplowed 12 uncultivated

until we meet again
French: 5 adieu 8 au revoir
German: 14 auf Wiedersehen
Hawaiian: 5 aloha
Italian: 4 ciao 5 addio 11 arrivederci
Japanese: 8 sayonara
Spanish: 5 adios

untimely 5 inapt 7 unhappy 8 ill-timed, mistimed, unseemly 9 imprudent, premature, unfitting 10 ill-advised, malapropos, out of place, unbecoming, unexpected, unsuitable 11 inopportune, unbefitting, unfortunate 12 inconvenient, infelicitous 13 inappropriate

untiring 5 fresh 6 steady 7 devoted, earnest, patient, staunch, zealous 8 constant, diligent, resolute, sedulous, tireless 9 assiduous, dedicated, steadfast, tenacious, unceasing, unwearied 10 determined, persistent, relentless, unflagging 11 never tiring, persevering, unfaltering, unremitting 12 wholehearted 13 indefatigable

untold 6 myriad, secret, unsaid 7 endless, private, unknown 8 hushed up, infinite, numerous, unspoken, withheld 9 concealed, countless, limitless, unbounded, uncounted, unrelated 10 numberless, suppressed, unnumbered, unreported, unrevealed 11 innumerable, undisclosed, unexpressed, unpublished 12 immeasurable, incalculable, undetermined

Untouchables, The
character: 7 Rossman 9 Eliot Ness, Lee Hobson 10 Cam Allison, Frank Nitti 11 Enrico Rossi 14 Martin Flaherty 18 William Youngfellow

cast: 10 Jerry Paris **11** Bruce Gordon, Paul Picerni, Robert Stack, Steve London **13** Abel Fernandez, Anthony George, Nick Georgiade
narrator: 14 Walter Winchell

untouched 3 new **4** pure **5** alone **6** intact, virgin **8** pristine, unharmed **9** uninjured **10** unaffected, unmolested

untoward 5 amiss **6** unruly **7** adverse **8** contrary **9** difficult **11** unfavorable **12** inauspicious, unpropitious

untrainable 6 unruly **11** intractable, unteachable **12** ungovernable

untrained 3 raw **5** green **7** untried **9** unskilled **11** unqualified **13** inexperienced

untried 3 raw **5** green **6** callow **8** immature, untested **10** unseasoned **13** inexperienced

untroubled 4 calm **6** placid, serene **7** halcyon, relaxed **8** carefree, careless, peaceful, tranquil **9** easygoing, unworried **10** unbothered **11** free-and-easy, undisturbed, unperturbed **12** happy-go-lucky, lighthearted

untrue 4 fake, sham **5** false **6** made up **7** not true **8** disloyal, spurious, unchaste **9** dishonest, erroneous, faithless, falsified, incorrect, unfounded **10** adulterous, fallacious, fictitious, fraudulent, groundless, inaccurate, inconstant, perfidious, unfaithful, untruthful **11** promiscuous, treacherous **12** meretricious **13** double-dealing

untrustworthy 5 false **6** fickle, shifty, untrue **7** corrupt, crooked, devious **8** disloyal, fallible, slippery, two-faced **9** corrupted, deceitful, dishonest, faithless, insincere, uncertain, unethical **10** capricious, inconstant, perfidious, unfaithful, unreliable, untruthful **11** treacherous **12** dishonorable, disreputable, questionable, undependable, unprincipled, unscrupulous **13** irresponsible **15** unauthenticated

untruth 3 fib, lie **4** hoax, tale, yarn **5** fable, story **6** canard, humbug **8** flimflam **9** deception, falsehood, fish story, invention **11** fabrication **12** equivocation **13** falsification, prevarication **16** cock-and-bull story **17** misrepresentation

untruthful 5 false, lying **8** specious, spurious **9** deceptive, dishonest **10** fraudulent, mendacious

untutored 5 naive **6** native, unread **8** ignorant, untaught **10** illiterate, uneducated, unlettered, unschooled **12** uninstructed **15** unsophisticated

untypical 3 odd **4** rare **5** alien **7** bizarre, deviant, strange, unusual **8** aberrant, abnormal, atypical, uncommon **9** anomalous, irregular, unnatural **10** unfamiliar **16** unrepresentative

unused 3 new **7** strange, untried **8** left over, not given, pristine, unopened **9**

remaining, untouched **10** unemployed **12** unaccustomed, unacquainted, unhabituated

unusual 4 rare **5** novel **6** unique **7** curious, offbeat, strange **8** atypical, peculiar, singular, uncommon **9** unequaled, unheard-of, unmatched, untypical **10** noteworthy, one of a kind, phenomenal, remarkable, surprising, unfamiliar **11** exceptional **12** incomparable, unparalleled **13** extraordinary, unprecedented **16** out of the ordinary

unvaried 4 even **5** fixed **6** steady **7** regular, uniform **8** all alike, constant **9** identical, unchanged **10** all the same, invariable, monotonous, unchanging **11** homogeneous, unalterable, undeviating

unvarnished 3 raw **4** bald, bare **5** blunt, crude, frank, naked, plain, stark **6** candid, direct, honest, simple **7** sincere **8** straight **9** unadorned, uncolored **10** unfinished **11** fundamental, undisguised **13** unembellished **15** straightforward **23** straight-from-the-shoulder

unvarying 4 even **6** steady **7** regular, uniform **8** constant **10** unwavering

unveil 4 bare **6** reveal **7** divulge, publish, uncloak, uncover **8** announce, disclose **9** broadcast, make known, unsheathe **12** bring to light

unveiled 5 bared **8** divulged, laid bare, revealed **9** announced, broadcast, disclosed, made known, published, uncovered **14** brought to light

unveiling 4 show **5** array **7** display, exhibit, showing **10** exhibition, exposition **13** demonstration

unverified 7 alleged, rumored **8** disputed **15** unauthenticated, unsubstantiated

unwarranted 7 illegal **8** culpable, unlawful **9** arbitrary, unfounded **10** censurable, groundless, unapproved **11** inexcusable, uncalled-for, unjustified **12** indefensible, unauthorized, unreasonable, unsanctioned

unwary 4 rash **5** hasty **7** unalert **8** careless, headlong, heedless, reckless **9** imprudent, unguarded **10** incautious, indiscreet, unwatchful **11** precipitate **12** disregardful **13** uncircumspect

unwashed 4 foul **5** dirty, grimy, muddy **6** filthy, grubby, smudgy, soiled **7** unclean **8** begrimed

unwasteful 6 frugal **7** thrifty **9** effective, effectual, efficient **10** productive

unwavering 4 firm **6** steady, strong **7** staunch **8** faithful, resolute, unshaken, untiring **9** dedicated, steadfast, tenacious **10** determined, persistent, unflagging, unswerving **11** persevering, undeviating, unfaltering, unflinching,

unremitting **12** single-minded **14** uncompromising

unwelcome 7 outcast **8** excluded, rejected, unwanted **9** thankless, uninvited, unpopular **10** uncared for, unpleasant, unrequired **11** displeasing, distasteful, undesirable, unessential, unnecessary, unwished for **12** disagreeable, unacceptable

unwell 3 ill, low **4** sick **5** frail **6** ailing, infirm, laid up, poorly, queasy, sickly **7** run-down **8** delicate, qualmish **10** indisposed **11** off one's feed **15** under the weather

unwholesome 3 bad **4** evil, foul **5** toxic **6** deadly, filthy, sinful, wicked **7** baneful, harmful, hurtful, immoral, noxious, ruinous **8** depraved, venomous **9** corrupted, dangerous, degrading, poisonous, polluting, unhealthy **10** corrupting, pernicious **11** deleterious, detrimental, undesirable, unhealthful **12** demoralizing, dishonorable, insalubrious, unnourishing **13** contaminating

unwieldy 5 bulky, heavy **6** clumsy **7** awkward, weighty **8** not handy **10** burdensome, cumbersome **12** hard to handle, incommodious, inconvenient **13** uncomfortable

unwilled 6 reflex **9** automatic **11** involuntary, unconscious **12** uncontrolled **13** nonvolitional

unwilling 5 loath **6** averse **7** against, opposed **9** demurring, reluctant, resistant **10** dissenting, indisposed, undesirous **11** disinclined **12** not in the mood, recalcitrant **14** unenthusiastic

unwillingness 8 aversion **10** opposition, reluctance, resistance **13** indisposition **14** disinclination

unwise 4 dumb **5** crazy, silly **6** stupid **7** foolish, unsound **8** reckless **9** foolhardy, imprudent, senseless **10** ill-advised **11** improvident, inadvisable, injudicious **12** shortsighted, unreasonable **13** irresponsible, unintelligent

unwitting 7 unaware, unmeant **9** unknowing, unplanned **10** accidental, undesigned, unexpected, unthinking **11** inadvertent, involuntary **12** unconsenting **13** unintentional **14** unpremeditated

unwonted 4 rare **7** unusual **8** atypical, uncommon **10** infrequent, remarkable, unexpected, unfamiliar **11** exceptional **12** unaccustomed **13** extraordinary

unworkmanlike 6 clumsy, sloppy **11** inefficient

unworldly 4 holy, pure **5** godly, green, moral, naive, pious **6** callow, devout, divine, sacred, solemn **7** ethical **8** ethereal, heavenly, innocent, trusting **9** aesthetic, celestial, religious, spiritual, unearthly **10** idealistic, immaterial, provincial **12** intellectual, metaphysical, overtrusting **13** inexperienced, philosophical **14** transcendental **15** unsophisticated

unworried 4 calm **6** serene **7** relaxed **8** carefree, composed, peaceful, tranquil **9** easygoing, unruffled **10** untroubled

unworthy 5 unfit **7** ignoble **8** improper, shameful, unseemly **9** degrading, unethical **10** unbecoming, unsuitable **11** unbefitting **12** dishonorable, disreputable, unacceptable **13** discreditable, inappropriate, objectionable

unwrap 4 open **6** loosen, unbind **7** uncover

unwrinkled 4 even, flat **6** ironed, smooth **7** unlined **8** smoothed **9** uncreased, unrumpled

unwritten 4 oral **5** tacit, vocal **7** assumed, implied **8** implicit, inferred, unstated **9** customary **10** spoken only, understood, unrecorded **11** traditional, unexpressed **12** unformulated, unregistered **13** by word of mouth

unwritten law
Latin: **13** lex non scripta

unyielding 4 firm, hard **5** rigid, stiff, stony, tough **6** wooden **8** resolute, rocklike, stubborn **9** obstinate, steadfast, unbending, unpliable **10** determined, inexorable, inflexible, persistent, unswerving, unwavering **11** undeviating **15** uncompromising

up 4 atop, lift, over, rear **5** about, above, aloft, along, aside, astir, at bat, built, close, equal, erect, raise **6** apiece, ascend, higher, lifted **7** abreast, batting, forward, promote, skyward, through **8** advanced, cheerful, increase, out of bed, overhead, standing, together, windward **9** northward **10** optimistic **11** constructed

up and about 5 afoot, astir **6** active, mobile, roused **7** walking **8** out of bed **10** ambulatory, on one's feet

up-and-down 6 fitful, seesaw, uneven **7** bobbing **8** jouncing, wavering **11** alternating, fluctuating, vacillating

upbraid 5 scold **6** berate, rebuke, revile **7** bawl out, censure, chew out, reprove **8** admonish, chastise, denounce, reproach **9** castigate, dress down, reprimand **10** tongue-lash

upbringing 7 rearing **8** breeding, training **10** background

upcoming 6 coming, nearby **7** looming, nearing, pending **8** imminent **9** impending, momentary **11** approaching, drawing nigh, forthcoming, in the offing, prospective

update 5 amend, emend, renew **6** recast, revamp, revise, rework **7** restore, touch up, upgrade **8** overhaul, renovate **9** refurbish **10** rejuvenate, reorganize, streamline

up for grabs 4 open **9** available

upgrade 5 raise, slope **6** ascent, better **7** advance, dignify, elevate, incline, inflate, promote **8** gradient

upheaval 5 flood, quake **6** blowup, tumult **7** turmoil **8** disorder, upthrust **9** cataclysm, explosion, tidal wave **10** disruption, earthquake, revolution **11** catastrophe, disturbance

uphill 4 hard **5** tough **6** rising, taxing, tiring, upward **7** arduous, onerous **8** toilsome, wearying **9** ascending, difficult, fatiguing, strenuous, wearisome **10** burdensome, enervating, exhausting **12** backbreaking

uphill work 8 struggle, tough job **10** difficulty, rough going **11** arduousness **12** hard sledding **13** laboriousness

uphold 4 bear, prop **5** brace, carry, raise, shore **6** defend, hold up, prop up **7** approve, bolster, confirm, elevate, endorse, protect, shore up, support, sustain **8** advocate, buttress, champion, maintain, preserve, underpin **9** encourage **10** stand up for, underbrace **11** acknowledge, corroborate

upholder 7 devotee **8** adherent, advocate, defender, partisan **9** supporter

up in the clouds 6 elated, joyful, joyous **8** ecstatic, euphoric **9** exuberant, rapturous **11** on cloud nine **15** in seventh heaven

Upis
goddess of: **10** childbirth

Upjohn, Richard
architect of: **13** Trinity Church (NYC)
style: **13** Gothic Revival

upkeep 4 keep **6** living **7** support **8** expenses, overhead **10** management, sustenance **11** maintenance, subsistence **12** conservation, preservation

upland 4 high, rise **5** ridge **6** height **7** plateau **8** eminence, highland **9** elevation, high place, high point **10** prominence

uplift 5 edify, raise **6** better, refine **7** advance, bracing, elevate, improve, inspire, lifting, shoring, support, upgrade **8** civilize, propping **9** cultivate, elevation **10** betterment, bolstering, enrichment, refinement **11** advancement, buttressing, cultivation, edification, enhancement, improvement **12** underpinning

uplifting 9 elevating, elevation, improving, inspiring **11** improvement **12** enlightening **13** enlightenment, inspirational

upon 2 at, on **4** atop **5** about **6** toward **7** against, thereon **9** by means of, thereupon **10** after which, thereafter

upper 3 top **4** high **5** major **6** higher, inland **7** eminent, greater, topmost **8** elevated, northern, superior **9** important

upper-case letter 7 capital **9** majuscule **13** capital letter

upper class 5 elite **6** gentry, uptown **7** (high) society **8** highborn, highbred, wellborn **9** beau monde, haut monde, high-class, patrician, top drawer **10** upper crust **11** aristocracy, blue-blooded **12** aristocratic, silk-stocking **14** creme de la creme, to the manor born **15** to the manner born

upper crust 5 elite **6** gentry **7** (high) society **9** beau monde, haut monde, top drawer **10** upper class **11** aristocracy **14** creme de la creme

upper hand 4 edge, sway **5** power **7** command, control, mastery **8** whip hand **9** advantage, authority, supremacy **10** domination **12** predominance

upper house 6 Senate **12** House of Lords

uppermost, upmost 3 top **4** main **5** chief, first, major, prime **7** highest, leading, primary, supreme, topmost **8** crowning, dominant, foremost, greatest, loftiest **9** essential, paramount, principal **10** preeminent **11** predominant **12** transcendent **13** most important

Upper Volta
other name **11** Burkina Faso (Fasso)
capital/largest city: **11** Ouagadougou
others: **4** Kaya **7** Banfora **9** Koudougou **10** Ouahigouya
division: **7** Yatenga **9** Tenkodogo **11** Fada Ngourma
monetary unit: **5** franc **7** centime
mountain: **4** Tema
highest point: **8** Nakourou **10** Tenakourou, Tenekourou
river: **5** Komoe **6** Mekrou, Sourou **8** Pendjari, Red Volta **10** Black Volta, White Volta
physical feature:
  plateau: **5** Sahel **7** Sikasso, Voltaic
  wind: **9** harmattan
people: **4** Bobo, Lobi, Samo **5** Bella, Bissa, Dyula, Fulbe, Hausa, Mande, Marka, Mossi, Puehl **6** Fulani, Senufo, Tuareg **7** Grunshi, Voltaic, Yatenga **8** Mandingo **9** Gourounsi **15** Bunsansi Gambaga
  French governor: **7** Hesling
  god: **4** Wuro **5** Tenga
  king: **4** Naba **5** Mogho
  leader: **5** Oubri, Zerbo **7** Yameogo **8** Lamizana **9** Mogho Naba
language: **4** Bobo, Lobi, More, Samo **5** Dyula, Mande, Mossi **6** French
religion: **5** Islam **7** animism **12** Christianity
place:
  game reserve: **11** Arlyand Pama
feature:
  animal: **5** hyena **6** duiker, jackal **7** gazelle, warthog **10** hartebeest
  tree: **4** shea **6** acacia, baobab, karite, locust

upright 3 rib **4** fair, good, just, pale, pier, pile, pole, post, prop **5** erect, moral, shaft, stake, strut **6** column, honest, picket, pillar **7** ethical, support, upended **8** reliable, standard, vertical **9** honorable, righteous, stanchion **10** aboveboard, high-minded, principled, standing-up, upstanding **11** trustworthy **12** on the up-and-up **13** perpendicular

uprightness 5 honor **7** dignity, honesty **8** morality **9** integrity **13** righteousness **15** trustworthiness

uprising 4 riot **6** mutiny, revolt **8** outbreak **9** rebellion **10** insurgence, revolution **12** insurrection

uproar 3 ado **4** stir, to-do **5** furor **6** clamor, tumult **7** turmoil **9** agitation, commotion **11** disturbance, pandemonium **16** state of confusion

uproarious 4 loud, wild **5** noisy **6** raging, stormy **7** furious, intense, riotous **9** clamorous, hilarious, turbulent, very funny **10** boisterous, disorderly, hysterical, tumultuous **11** tempestuous **13** sidesplitting

uproot 6 banish **7** abolish, cast out, destroy, root out, wipe out **8** dislodge, displace, force out **9** eliminate, extirpate **10** annihilate, do away with **11** exterminate

upset 3 ire, irk, mad, vex **4** beat **5** anger, annoy, crush, irked, messy, mix up, pique, quash, smash, upend, vexed, worry **6** bother, cancel, change, defeat, enrage, grieve, invert, jumble, muddle, mussed, rattle, thrash, untidy **7** agitate, angered, annoyed, capsize, chaotic, confuse, conquer, disturb, enraged, fluster, furious, grieved, incense, jumbled, mixed-up, perturb, reverse, tip over, trouble, trounce, unnerve, upended, worried **8** agitated, bothered, capsized, confused, demolish, disorder, distress, incensed, inverted, overcome, overturn, slovenly, troubled, turn over, unnerved, upturned, vanquish **9** discomfit, disturbed, infuriate, overpower, overthrow, overwhelm, perturbed **10** discompose, disconcert, disheveled, disordered, disorderly, disquieted, distressed, hysterical, overturned, tipped over, topple over, topsy-turvy, turned over, upside-down **11** disarranged, disorganize, overwrought, wrong side up **12** disorganized **13** make miserable **14** turn topsy-turvy

upsetting
  French: 14 bouleversement

upshot 3 end **6** effect, payoff, result, sequel **7** outcome **8** offshoot **9** aftermath, outgrowth **10** conclusion **11** aftereffect, consequence, culmination, eventuality **16** final development

upside down 7 chaotic **8** reversed **10** disorderly **11** topsy turvey **12** bottomside up **16** at sixes and sevens

upstairs 2 up **11** above stairs, second floor

upstanding 4 good, tall, true **5** erect, moral, on end **6** honest **7** ethical, upright **8** straight, truthful, vertical, virtuous **9** honorable, righteous **11** trustworthy **13** incorruptible, perpendicular

upstart 4 snip, snob, snub **6** nobody **7** bounder, parvenu **8** mushroom **9** conceited, newly-rich **10** adventurer **12** nouveau riche **13** self-assertive

upsurge 4 gain, push, rise **5** spurt **6** pickup, thrust, upturn **7** advance, upswing **8** increase **11** improvement

upswing 4 rise **6** pickup **7** upsurge **11** improvement, upward trend

uptight 5 tense **7** anxious, fearful, nervous, worried, wound up **8** insecure, neurotic, troubled **9** unbending **10** unyielding **12** apprehensive

up-to-date 2 in **3** new **5** today **6** modern, modish, timely, trendy, with-it **7** current, stylish **9** in fashion **12** contemporary **13** up-to-the-minute
  French: 9 au courant

upturn 4 gain, push **6** thrust **7** advance, upsurge **8** increase **9** expansion **11** improvement

upward 4 high, more **5** above, aloft **7** skyward **9** ascending, uppermost

upward movement 4 rise **5** climb **6** ascent, rising, upturn **7** scaling, take-off **8** climbing, mounting **9** ascension

upward trend 4 rise **5** boost **6** pickup **7** advance, upsurge, upswing **8** increase **11** improvement

uraeus
  figure of: 3 asp **5** cobra
  on: 9 headdress
  of: 7 pharoah

Uralic
  language branch: 7 Samoyed **10** Finno-Ugric

Urania
  member of: 5 Muses
  personifies: 9 astronomy

uranium
  chemical symbol: 1 U

Uranus
  mother: 4 Gaea
  wife: 4 Gaea
  father of: 6 Giants, Titans **8** Cyclopes **10** Titanesses **13** Hecatonchires
  castrated by: 6 Cronos, Cronus Kronos

Uranus
  position: 7 seventh
  satellite: 5 Ariel **6** Oberon **7** Miranda, Titania, Umbriel
  color: 9 blue-green
  characteristic: 5 rings

Urartu *see* **7** Armenia

urban 4 city, town **5** civic **8** citified **9** municipal **11** worldly- wise **12** cosmopolitan, metropolitan **13** sophisticated

urban area 3 urb **4** city **9** inner city **10** metropolis **11** megalopolis **16** metropolitan area

urbane 5 civil, suave **6** polite, smooth **7** courtly, elegant, gallant, genteel, politic, refined, tactful **8** debonair, gracious, mannerly, polished, well-bred **9** civilized, courteous **10** chivalrous, cultivated, diplomatic **11** gentlemanly **12** cosmopolitan, well-mannered **13** sophisticated

urchin 3 boy, imp, lad **4** brat, waif **5** gamin, stray, whelp, youth **6** gamine, laddie **8** young pup **9** stripling, young punk, youngster **10** young rogue, young tough **11** guttersnipe

Urd 4 Norn
  origin: 12 Scandinavian
  form: 8 giantess
  personifies: 4 past
  developed from: 5 Urdar
  companion: 5 Skuld **8** Verdandi

Urey, Harold Clayton
  field: 9 chemistry
  isolated: 9 deuterium
  awarded: 10 Nobel prize

urge 3 yen **4** back, coax, goad, itch, poke, prod, push, spur, sway, wish **5** drive, egg on, fancy, force, press, prick, speed **6** advise, desire, exhort, hasten, hunger, motive, reason, thirst **7** beseech, counsel, craving, dictate, entreat, implore, impulse, longing, passion, push for, quicken, request, solicit, suggest **8** advocate, appeal to, argue for, champion, convince, persuade, petition, pressure, stimulus, yearning **9** hankering, importune, incentive, plead with, prescribe, prompting, recommend **10** accelerate, inducement, motivation, supplicate **11** prevail upon, provocation

urgency 4 need, urge, want **5** press **6** stress **8** exigency, pressure **9** necessity **10** importance, insistence **11** persistence **14** imperativeness **15** importunateness

urgent 5 grave **6** ardent **7** crucial, earnest, fervent, intense, serious, weighty, zealous **8** critical, pleading, pressing, required, spirited **9** demanding, essential, heartfelt, important, insistent, momentous, necessary **10** beseeching, compelling, compulsory, imperative, obligatory, passionate **12** wholehearted **13** indispensable

urge on 4 push **5** boost **7** cheer on, pull for, root for

urging 7 bidding, counsel, goading **8** egging on **9** prompting **11** exhortation

Uri 6 canton
  in: 11 Switzerland
  home of: 11 William Tell

Uriah
  father: 7 Shemiah

wife: 9 Bathsheba
served: 5 David
urinary system
  component: 6 kidney, ureter **7** bladder, urethra
  rids body of: 5 salts, waste, water **8** minerals
Uris, Leon
  author of: 5 Topaz **6** Exodus **7** Trinity **9** Battle Cry **10** Armageddon
urn 3 jar, pig **4** ewer, kist, tomb, vase **5** grave, steen **6** teapot **7** samovar **9** coffeepot
  botanical: 7 capsule **11** spore-bearer
  in keno: 5 goose
Ursa Major 9 Great Bear
  contains: 9 Big Dipper
Ursa Minor 10 Little Bear
  contains: 7 Polaris **12** Little Dipper
Uruguay
  other name: 10 Purple Land
  capital/largest city: 10 Montevideo
  others: 4 Fray, Melo **5** Minas, Rocha, Salto **6** Bentos, Rivera **7** Artigas, Colonia, Dolores, Durazno, Florida, San Jose **8** Mercedes, Paysandu, Trinidad **9** Maldonado **10** Las Piedras, Santa Lucia, Tacuarembo **12** Treinta y Tres **13** San Jose de Mayo
  measure: 4 vara **6** cuadra, suerte
  monetary unit: 4 peso **9** centesimo, centisimo
  weight: 7 quintal
  island: 5 Lobos
  lake: 5 Merin, Mirim **18** Embalse del Rio Negro
  mountain: 6 Animas **10** Grand Hills **14** Cuchilla Grande
  highest point: 15 Mirador Nacional
  river: 4 Malo **5** Mirim, Negro, Plata **6** Parana, Ulimar **7** Cuareim, Queguay, Uruguay **8** Yaguaron **9** Cebollati **10** Tacuarembo
  sea: 8 Atlantic
  physical feature:
    estuary: 5 Plata
  people: 4 Yaro **5** Swiss **6** Indian **7** Italian, mestizo, Russian, Spanish **8** Charruas
    artist: 6 Figari
    author: 4 Rodo **5** Reyes **6** Onetti **7** Sanchez **9** San Martin **10** Ibarbourou
    leader: 5 Oribe **6** Rivera **7** Artigas **9** Lavelleja **10** Bordaberry **14** Batlle y Ordonez
  language: 7 Italian, Spanish
  religion: 13 Roman Catholic
  place:
    resort: 12 Punta del Este
    square: 13 Independencia
  feature:
    animal: 4 puma **6** jaguar **8** capybara **9** armadillo
    bird: 4 rhea **5** nandu **7** hornero, ostrich
    cattle ranch: 8 estancia
    cowboy: 6 gaucho

dance: 5 tango **7** milonga
festival: 8 Carnival **13** Semana Criolla
lasso: 10 boleadoras
metal straw: 8 bombilla
music: 9 candomble
musical drama: 7 tablado
ruling class: 10 Patriciado
food:
  barbecue: 5 asado
  dish: 7 puchero **9** churrasco **13** asado con cuero
  drink: 4 mate
U S A
  author: 13 John Dos Passos
  character: 10 Ben Compton, Mary French **11** Joe Williams **12** Margo Dowling **13** Fainy McCreary (Mac), Janey Williams **14** J Ward Morehouse **15** Charley Anderson, Eleanor Stoddard, Eveline Hutchins **18** Anne Elizabeth Trent **22** Richard Ellsworth Savage
usable 5 handy **6** useful **9** adaptable **10** functional **11** serviceable
usage 3 use **4** care, mode **5** habit **6** custom, manner, method, system **7** control **8** good form, habitude, handling, practice **9** etiquette, operation, tradition, treatment **10** convention, employment, management **12** manipulation
use 3 aid, ply, sap **4** good, help, work **5** apply, avail, drain, exert, spend, treat, usage, value, waste, wield, worth **6** devour, employ, expend, handle, profit **7** benefit, consume, deplete, exhaust, exploit, operate, service, utilize **8** deal with, exercise, function, handling, profit by, put to use, resort to, squander **9** act toward, advantage, dissipate, enjoyment, make use of, operation, swallow up, throw away **10** employment, manipulate, run through, usefulness **11** application, convenience, fritter away, utilization **12** behave toward, capitalize on **13** make the most of **14** serviceability
used 3 old **5** eaten, spent **7** applied, treated **8** actuated, consumed, depleted, employed, occupied, operated, utilized **9** customary, exercised, exhausted, exploited, practiced **10** accustomed, habituated, secondhand **11** implemented, manipulated
used up 4 beat, shot **5** all in, spent **6** wasted **7** worn out **8** depleted, tired out **9** exhausted
useful 5 handy, utile **7** helpful **8** valuable **9** effective, practical, rewarding **10** beneficial, convenient, functional, profitable, time-saving, worthwhile **11** serviceable, utilitarian **12** advantageous
usefulness 5 avail, value, worth **6** profit **7** benefit, purpose, utility **9** advantage **11** convenience, helpfulness,

suitability **12** adaptability, practicality **13** effectiveness **14** serviceability
useless 4 vain **6** futile **7** of no use **8** bootless, unusable **9** fruitless, unhelpful, worthless **10** inadequate, profitless, unavailing **11** incompetent, ineffectual, inefficient **12** unproductive **13** impracticable, inefficacious, nonfunctional, unserviceable
uselessness 6 vanity **8** futility, idleness **9** inutility **10** inefficacy **13** fruitlessness, worthlessness
Uses of Enchantment, The
  author: 15 Bruno Bettelheim
use sparingly 4 save **5** hoard, stint **6** scrimp **7** cut back, dole out **8** conserve, not waste, preserve
use to advantage 7 exploit **8** profit by **12** capitalize on **13** turn to account
use up 5 drain, spend **6** expend, finish **7** consume, deplete, exhaust **9** dissipate **10** run through
Ushant
  author: 11 Conrad Aiken
usher 4 lead, show **5** guide, steer **6** attend, convoy, direct, escort, herald, launch, leader, porter, ring in, squire **7** conduct, precede, preface **8** announce, director, proclaim **9** conductor, introduce **10** doorkeeper, gatekeeper, inaugurate
Usnech *see* **6** Usnach
USSR *see* **6** Russia
Ustinov, Peter
  born: 6 London **7** England
  roles: 7 Topkapi **8** Quo Vadis? **9** Billy Budd, Spartacus **12** We're No Angels
usual 4 stock, trite **6** common, normal, wonted **7** popular, regular, routine, typical **8** expected, familiar, habitual, ordinary, orthodox, standard **9** customary, hackneyed **10** accustomed, prescribed, threadbare **11** commonplace, established, oft-repeated, traditional **12** conventional, run-of-the-mill **15** well-established
usurer 9 loan shark **11** money lender
usurp 4 grab **5** steal **7** preempt **8** arrogate **10** commandeer **11** appropriate **12** encroach upon, infringe upon
usurpation 6 taking **7** seizure **8** grabbing, stealing **10** arrogation, preemption **13** appropriation
Utah
  abbreviation: 2 UT
  nickname: 6 Mormon **7** Beehive
  capital/largest city: 12 Salt Lake City
  others: 3 Roy **4** Moab, Orem **5** Delta, Heber, Kanab, Logan, Magna, Manti, Nepli, Ogden, Price, Provo **6** Beaver, Eureka, Kearns, Layton, Murray, Tooele, Vernal **7** Bingham **8** American **9** Bountiful **11** Brigham City
  college: 5 Weber **11** Westminster **12** Brigham Young

feature:
bridge: 7 Rainbow
dam: 6 Hoover **10** Glen Canyon
gorge: 7 Flaming
national historic site: 11 Golden Spike
national monument: 8 Dinosaur **14** Natural Bridges
national park: 4 Zion **6** Arches **11** Bryce Canyon, Canyonlands, Capital Reef
reef: 7 Capital
tribe: 3 Ute **5** Piute, Uinta(h), Yampa **6** Navajo, Paiute **7** Gosiute **8** Paviotso, Shoshoni
people: 7 Mormons **10** Maude Adams **11** Karl G Maeser **12** Brigham Young **13** John M Browning **15** Latter-Day Saints **16** George Sutherland **19** Daniel Cowan Jackling
explorer: 9 Dominguez, Escalante
lake: 4 Mead, Swan, Utah **6** Powell, Sevier **9** Great Salt
land rank: 8 eleventh
mountain: 4 Lena, Lion, Waas **5** Cedar, Henry, Hogup, Peale, Rocky, Trail, Uinta **6** Frisco, Navajo, Swasey, Wahwah **7** Granite, Griffin, Hawkins, Pennell, Terrace, Wasatch **8** Linnaeus **9** Confusion
highest point: 9 Kings Peak
physical feature:
basin: 5 Great
canyon: 4 Echo
desert: 6 Sevier
plateau: 7 Wasatch **8** Colorado, Tavaputs
river: 4 Bear **5** Grand, Green, Weber **6** Jordan, Sevier, Virgin **7** San Juan **8** Colorado
basketball team: 4 Jazz **6** Starzz
state admission: 10 forty-fifth
state bird: 7 seagull
state flower: 8 sego lily
state motto: 8 Industry
state song: 14 Utah We Love Thee
state tree: 10 blue spruce
utensils 4 gear **5** tools **6** outfit, silver,

tackle **8** flatware **9** apparatus **10** implements, silverware **11** instruments **13** paraphernalia

utilitarian 5 handy **6** usable, useful **8** sensible, valuable, workable **9** effective, efficient, practical, pragmatic **10** beneficial, convenient, functional, profitable **11** serviceable **12** advantageous

utility 3 aid, gas, use **4** help **5** avail, extra **6** backup **7** benefit, reserve, service **8** function **9** accessory, advantage, alternate, auxiliary, secondary, surrogate, telephone **10** additional, substitute, usefulness **11** convenience, electricity **12** availability, supplemental **13** public service **14** serviceability

utilization 3 use **10** employment **11** application **12** exploitation

utilize 3 use **6** employ **7** exploit **8** profit by, put to use, resort to **9** make use of **12** capitalize on **13** bring into play, make the most of, turn to account **14** avail oneself of, have recourse to, put into service **15** take advantage of

utmost, uttermost 4 acme, best, main, peak, tops **5** chief, first, major, prime **6** tiptop, zenith **7** capital, highest, leading, maximum, primary, supreme, the most **8** cardinal, foremost, greatest, last word, ultimate **9** paramount, principal, sovereign **10** preeminent **11** predominant

Uto-Aztecan (Nahuatl)
tribe: 4 Pima **5** Aatam, Aztec, Nahua **6** Mexica, Papago **8** Pima Alto

utopia 4 Eden **6** heaven **7** Erewhon **8** paradise **9** ideal life, Shangri-la **12** perfect bliss, perfect place **13** seventh heaven

utopian 9 visionary **10** idealistic, unfeasible, unworkable **11** unrealistic **12** otherworldly, unattainable, unrealizable **13** impracticable, insubstantial, unfulfillable

Utrillo, Maurice

born: 5 Paris **6** France
mother: 14 Suzanne Valadon
artwork: 16 The Church at Deuil, The Church of Blevy **17** Church at St Hilaire **19** La Petite Communiante **22** Sacre Coeur de Montmartre

ut supra 7 as above

utter 3 say **4** emit, pure, talk, tell, yell **5** sheer, shout, speak, state, total, voice **6** entire, mutter, reveal **7** declare, deliver, divulge, exclaim, express, perfect, whisper **8** absolute, complete, disclose, outright, proclaim, thorough, vocalize **9** downright, enunciate, out-and-out, pronounce, unchecked **10** articulate, unmodified, unrelieved **11** categorical, unequivocal, unmitigated, unqualified

utterance 4 talk, word **6** answer, remark, speech **7** opinion **9** discourse, statement **10** expression **11** declaration, exclamation **12** articulation, proclamation, vocalization **13** pronouncement, verbalization

utterly 4 just **5** fully **6** wholly **7** totally **8** entirely, outright **9** downright, extremely, perfectly **10** absolutely, completely, thoroughly **14** to the nth degree

uttermost 6 utmost **7** extreme, maximum, supreme **9** outermost, sovereign **12** extreme limit

uxorious
doting on: 8 one's wife
from Latin: 4 uxor, wife

Uzbekistan
capital/largest city: 8 Tashkent
others: 9 Samarkand
head of state: 9 president
government: 8 republic
monetary unit: 5 ruble
river: 8 Amu Darya, Syr Darya
sea: 4 Aral
people: 5 Uzbek
language: 5 Uzbek
religion: 5 Islam **11** Sunni Muslim

Uzi 10 Israeli gun, machine gun

vacancy 3 gap **4** hole, void **5** abode, place **6** breach, cavity, hollow **7** crevice, fissure, housing, lodging, opening **9** emptiness, situation **10** empty space, vacantness **11** room for rent **12** house for rent

vacant 4 dull, free, idle, open **5** aloof, blank, blase, clear, empty, vapid **6** unused, wooden **7** deadpan, for rent, leisure, vacuous **8** deserted, detached, for lease, forsaken, not in use, unfilled **9** abandoned, apathetic, incurious, oblivious, poker-face, unengaged **10** tenantless, unemployed, unoccupied, untenanted **11** indifferent, unconcerned, unfurnished, uninhabited **12** unencumbered **14** expressionless **15** uncomprehending

vacate 4 quit **5** empty, leave **6** give up, resign **8** abdicate, evacuate, hand over **9** surrender **10** depart from, relinquish

vacate the throne 4 cede, flee, quit **5** yield **6** give up, resign, retire **7** abandon **8** abdicate **10** relinquish

vacation 4 rest **5** leave, R and R **6** recess **7** holiday **8** furlough, holidays **10** sabbatical **12** intermission **13** take a vacation **14** leave of absence **17** rest-and-recreation
French: 8 vacances

vaccine 5 serum **8** antitoxin
inventor: 4 Salk **5** Sabin **6** Jenner **7** Pasteur

vacillate 4 reel, rock, roll, sway, toss **5** pitch, shift, waver **6** falter, teeter, totter, wobble **7** flutter, vibrate **8** hesitate **9** fluctuate, hem and haw, oscillate **12** shilly-shally **14** blow hot and cold

vacillating 7 swaying **8** wavering **9** diffident, uncertain, vibrating **10** hesitating, irresolute, on the fence **11** fluctuating, uncertainty **12** irresolution **15** shilly-shallying

vacillation 7 swaying **8** wavering **9** faltering, vibration **10** indecision **11** fluctuation, uncertainty **12** irresolution **15** shilly-shallying

Vacuna
origin: 6 Sabine
goddess of: 11 agriculture

vacuous 4 dull, idle, void **5** blank, empty, inane, silly **6** stupid, vacant **7** fatuous, foolish **8** indolent, unfilled

9 senseless **11** empty-headed, purposeless

Vaduz
capital of: 13 Liechtenstein
vae victis 18 woe to the vanquished
vagabond 4 hobo **5** gypsy, nomad, rover, tramp **6** roamer, roving **7** drifter, floater, migrant, nomadic, rambler, roaming, vagrant **8** bohemian, carefree, homeless, rambling, wanderer, wayfarer **9** footloose, itinerant, transient, traveling, wandering, wayfaring **10** journeying **11** beachcomber

Vagabond Lover
nickname of: 10 Rudy Vallee
vagary 4 kink, whim **5** fancy, humor, quirk **6** notion, oddity, whimsy **7** caprice, fantasy, impulse **8** crotchet, daydream **10** brainstorm, erraticism **11** peculiarity **12** eccentricity, idiosyncrasy, passing fancy

vagrant 3 bum **4** hobo **5** nomad, rover, tramp **6** beggar, loafer, roamer, roving **7** floater, migrant, nomadic, roaming **8** homeless, rambling, vagabond, wanderer **9** itinerant, transient, wandering **10** panhandler **11** peripatetic **15** knight-of-the-road

vague 4 hazy **5** fuzzy, loose **6** casual, random, unsure **7** general, unclear **8** confused, nebulous **9** imprecise, uncertain, unsettled **10** ill-defined, indefinite, inexplicit, undetailed, unspecific **11** not definite, unspecified **12** undetermined

vaguely 5 dimly **6** hazily **7** loosely **8** dreamily, slightly, vacantly **9** obscurely, sketchily **11** nebulously **12** ambiguously **12** indistinctly

vagueness 8 haziness **9** ambiguity, confusion, fuzziness **11** uncertainty **13** lack of clarity **14** indefiniteness

vain 4 idle **5** cocky, proud, silly **6** futile **7** foolish, pompous, stuck-up, useless **8** arrogant, boastful, bootless, dandyish, egoistic, nugatory, puffed-up, trifling **9** conceited, egotistic, fruitless, pointless, worthless **10** disdainful, profitless, swaggering, unavailing **11** egotistical, ineffective, ineffectual, superficial, time- wasting **12** self-admiring, superciliouos, unprofitable, unsuccessful, vainglorious **13** self-important, self-satisfied

Vainamoinen
origin: 7 Finnish
hero of: 8 Kalevala
form: 8 magician
opposes: 5 Louhi **11** Joukahainen

vainglorious 5 cocky **7** haughty, pompous, stuck-up **8** affected, arrogant, boastful, bragging, insolent **9** conceited **10** egoistical, pretentious, swaggering **11** egotistical, swell-headed **12** narcissistic, supercilious **13** full of oneself, self-important

vainglory 6 vanity **7** conceit, swagger **9** cockiness **10** pretension **11** braggadocio **14** self-importance **16** overbearing pride

vale 6 good-by **8** farewell
valedictory 4 last **5** final **7** parting **8** farewell, terminal, ultimate **9** departing **10** conclusive **11** leavetaking **14** farewell speech **19** commencement address

Valentine
character in: 20 Two Gentlemen of Verona
author: 11 Shakespeare

Valentino, Rudolph
real name: 16 Rodolfo (Alfonzo Raffaele Pierre Philibert) Guglielmi
born: 5 Italy **12** Castellaneta
wife: 9 Jean Acker **14** Natasha Rambova
roles: 8 The Sheik **12** Blood and Sand **16** The Son of the Sheik **17** Monsieur Beaucaire **30** The Four Horsemen of the Apocalypse

valerian 9 Valeriana
varieties: 3 red **5** Greek **6** common **7** African **8** American **11** long-spurred

Valery, Paul
author of: 7 Cahiers, Charmes **12** The Young Fate **13** Le Jeune Parque **16** Sketch of a Serpent **20** The Graveyard by the Sea

Valhalla
origin: 8 Teutonic
hall of: 4 Odin **5** Othin

valiant 4 bold **5** brave, noble **6** daring, heroic **7** gallant **8** fearless, intrepid, knightly, resolute, stalwart, unafraid, valorous **9** audacious, dauntless, undaunted **10** chivalrous, courageous **11** lionhearted, unflinching **12** bold-spirited, great-hearted, stouthearted

valid 4 good **5** legal, licit, sound

6 lawful, proper, strong **7** fitting, genuine, logical, weighty **8** accurate, decisive, forceful, official, powerful, suitable, truthful **9** authentic, effective, legalized, realistic **10** acceptable, applicable, compelling, convincing, legitimate **11** substantial, well- founded **12** well-grounded **13** authoritative, being in effect **14** constitutional, legally binding

validate 5 enact, prove, stamp **6** ratify, verify **7** certify, confirm, sustain, warrant, witness **8** legalize, sanction **9** authorize, make legal, make valid **10** make lawful **11** corroborate, countersign **12** authenticate, make official, substantiate

validation 8 sanction **12** confirmation, legalization, ratification **13** authorization, certification

validity 5 force, logic, power, right **6** weight **7** grounds, potency **8** accuracy, legality, strength **9** authority, soundness, substance **10** legal force, legitimacy, properness **11** suitability **12** authenticity, truthfulness **13** acceptability, applicability, effectiveness **14** conclusiveness, convincingness

valise 3 bag **4** grip **7** handbag, luggage, satchel **8** suitcase **9** briefcase, Gladstone **11** portmanteau

Valjean, Jean
  character in: 13 Les Miserables
  author: 4 Hugo

Valkyrie
  origin: 8 Teutonic
  home: 8 Valhalla
  attendant of: 4 Odin **5** Othin
  queen: 8 Brunhild, Brynhild **10** Brunnhilde

Vallee, Rudy
  real name: 17 Hubert Prior Vallee
  nickname: 16 The Vagabond Lover
  born: 13 Island Point VT
  played: 9 saxophone
  wife: 9 Jane Greer
  roles: 16 The Vagabond Lover **17** The Palm Beach Story, Unfaithfully Yours **41** How to Succeed in Business Without Really Trying

Valletta
  capital of: 5 Malta

valley 3 cut, dip, gap **4** dale, dell, glen, vale **5** basin, chasm, glade, gorge, gulch, gully **6** bottom, canyon, divide, hollow, ravine **8** water gap

Valley Forge
  author: 15 Maxwell Anderson

Valley of Horses, The
  author: 9 Jean M Auel

Valley of the Dolls
  author: 16 Jacqueline Susann

valor 4 grit, guts **5** nerve, pluck, spunk **6** daring, mettle **7** bravery, courage, heroism **8** boldness, chivalry **9** fortitude, gallantry **11** intrepidity **12** fearlessness **13** dauntlessness

valorous 4 bold **5** brave, gutsy **6** heroic, plucky **7** valiant **8** fearless, intrepid, stalwart, unafraid **9** dauntless **10** courageous **11** indomitable, lionhearted **12** stouthearted

valse 5 waltz

valuable 4 dear, good **6** costly, prized, useful, valued **7** admired, helpful **8** esteemed, fruitful, precious **9** expensive, important, priceless, respected, treasured **10** beneficial, high-priced, invaluable, profitable, worthwhile **11** serviceable, significant, utilitarian **12** advantageous

valuation 9 appraisal **10** assessment, evaluation **14** estimated value

value, values 3 use **4** cost, help, rate **5** assay, count, judge, merit, price, prize, rules, weigh, worth **6** admire, amount, assess, charge, esteem, ideals, profit, reckon, revere, size up **7** beliefs, benefit, cherish, compute, customs, respect, service, utility **8** appraise, evaluate, prestige, treasure **9** advantage, appraisal, greatness, moral code, practices, standards **10** admiration, appreciate, assessment, estimation, excellence, importance, set store by, usefulness **11** conventions, market price, superiority **12** code of ethics, institutions, significance

valued 6 prized **7** revered **8** esteemed **9** cherished, respected, treasured **11** appreciated **14** highly regarded

valueless 7 trivial, useless **9** worthless **11** of no account, unimportant **13** insignificant **14** good for nothing **15** inconsequential

vamoose 3 out **4** away, scat, shoo **5** be off, leave, scram **6** beat it, begone, depart, get out, go away **7** get lost

vamp 5 siren **9** temptress **10** seductress **11** enchantress, femme fatale **12** introduction

Vamp
  nickname of: 9 Theda Bara

vampire 3 bat **7** Dracula **11** bloodsucker

van 4 cart, dray, head **5** lorry, scout, truck, wagon **6** camper, picket **7** trailer **8** sentinel, vanguard **9** first line, forefront, front rank **10** avant-garde, large truck **12** advance guard, covered truck **13** front of an army **16** foremost division
  french: 7 fourgon

Van, Bobby
  real name: 10 Robert King
  born: 9 New York NY
  roles: 10 Kiss Me Kate, On Your Toes **11** No No Nanette **12** It's Only Money, The Ladies' Man **13** Small Town Girl **23** The Affairs of Dobie Gillis

van Alen, William
  architect of: 16 Chrysler Building (NYC)

Van Allen, James Alfred
  field: 7 physics
  invented: 18 radio proximity fuse
  discovered: 22 Van Allen radiation belts

Van Buren, Martin
  nicknames: 9 The Red Fox **17** The Little Magician **18** The Careful Dutchman
  presidential rank: 6 eighth
  party: 8 Democrat
  state represented: 7 New York
  defeated: 5 (Hugh Lawson) White **6** (William Person) Mangum **7** (Daniel) Webster **8** (William Henry) Harrison
  vice president: 7 (Richard Mentor) Johnson
  cabinet:
    state: 7 (John) Forsyth
    treasury: 8 (Levi) Woodbury
    war: 8 (Joel Roberts) Poinsett
    attorney general: 6 (Benjamin Franklin) Butler, (Felix) Grundy, (Henry Dilworth) Gilpin
    navy: 8 (James Kirke) Paulding **9** (Mahlon) Dickerson
    postmaster general: 5 (John Milton) Niles **7** (Amos) Kendall
  born/died/buried: 12 Kinderhook NY
  education:
    Academy: 10 Kinderhook
    college: 4 none
    studied: 3 law
  religion: 13 Dutch Reformed
  vacation:
    toured: 6 Europe (1853-1855)
  author: 64 Inquiry into the Origin and Course of Political Parties in the United States
  political career: 8 US Senate **11** state Senate **13** vice presi dent **20** state Attorney General
    governor of: 7 New York
    secretary of: 5 State
    minister: 12 Great Britain
  civilian career: lawyer
  notable events of lifetime/term: 5 Panic (of 1837)
    treaty: 16 Webster-Ashburton
    war: 9 Aroostook
  father: 7 Abraham
  mother: 5 Maria (Hoes Van Alen)
  siblings: 6 Derike, Hannah **7** Abraham **8** Lawrence
  wife: 6 Hannah (Hoes)
  children: 4 John **6** Martin **7** Abraham **13** Smith Thompson

Vance, Vivian
  real name: 11 Vivian Jones
  born: 12 Cherryvale KS
  roles: 9 I Love Lucy **10** Ethel Mertz

Vancouver
  hockey team: 7 Canucks

vandal 6 looter, raider **7** ravager, wrecker **8** marauder, pillager, saboteur **9** barbarian, despoiler, destroyer, plunderer **10** demolisher

vandalism 6 damage **10** de facement **11** destruction **17** malicious mischief

vandalize 3 mar **5** trash, wreck **6** damage, deface **7** despoil, destroy

Vanderlyn, John
born: **10** Kingston NY
artwork: **14** Ariadne on Naxos **20** The Death of Jane McCrea **28** Marius Amid the Ruins of Carthage **31** Ariadne Asleep on the Island of Naxos

Van Dyck, Sir Anthony
born: **7** Antwerp **8** Flanders
artwork: **8** Charles I (in Hunting Dress) **11** Iconography **18** Madonna of the Rosary **19** Blessed Herman Joseph, Cardinal Bentiroglio **20** Ecstasy of St Augustine **21** Marchesa Elena Grimaldi

Van Dyke, Dick
born: **12** West Plains MO
roles: **11** Mary Poppins **12** Bye Bye Birdie **15** Diagnosis Murder, Dick Van Dyke Show
brother: **5** Jerry
son: **5** Barry

Vane, Sutton
author of: **12** Outward Bound

Vanessa
author: **11** Hugh Walpole

Van Gogh, Vincent
born: **12** GrootZundert **14** The Netherlands
artwork: **10** Pere Tanguy **11** Cafe at Night, L'Arle sienne **13** The Olive Grove **14** The Starry Night **15** The Potato Eaters **16** The Bridge at Arles **18** Portrait of Dr Gachet, The Chair and the Pipe **22** Cornfield with Cypresses

vanguard 3 van **7** leaders **8** forerank **9** first line, forefront, front line, front rank, spearhead **10** avant-garde, in novators, leadership, modernists **11** pacesetters, tastemakers **12** advance guard, trailblazers, trendsetters

Van Helsing, Dr
character in: **7** Dracula
author: **6** Stoker

vanish 3 die, end **5** cease **6** die out, expire, perish **7** die away **8** dissolve, fade away, melt away, pass away **9** disappear, evaporate, terminate **13** dematerialize **15** become invisible

vanished 4 dead, gone, lost **7** defunct, died out, extinct **11** disappeared

vanishing 8 dying out **10** ex tinction, fading away **11** passing away **12** disappearing **13** disappearance **15** dematerializing

vanitas vanitatum 16 vanity of vanities

vanity 4 sham **5** folly, pride **6** mirage **7** compact, conceit, egotism, falsity, inanity **8** de lusion, futility, idleness, self- love **9** emptiness, powder box, vainglory, vanity bag **10** hollowness, narcissism, self-praise, vanity case **11** makeup table, mirror table, self-conceit, uselessness **13** dressing table, fruitlessness, worthlessness **14** self-admiration, superficiality

Vanity Fair
author: **25** William Makepeace Thackeray
character: **10** Becky Sharp **11** Miss Crawley **12** Amelia Sedley, Joseph (Jos) Sedley **13** George Osborne, Rawdon Crawley **14** Sir Pitt Crawley **20** Captain William Dobbin

vanity of vanities
Latin: **16** vanitas vanitatum

vanquish 4 beat, best, drub, lick, rout **5** crush **6** defeat, master, subdue, thrash **7** conquer **8** overcome **9** overpower, overthrow, overwhelm, subjugate **11** triumph over

vanquisher 6 master, victor, winner **7** subduer **8** champion **9** conqueror **10** subjugator

vanquishment 6 defeat **7** mastery, triumph, victory, winning **8** conquest **10** conquering, overcoming

Van Slyke, Helen
author of: **10** No Love Lost **15** A Necessary Woman, The Heart Listens **18** Always Is Not Forever

Van Tassel, Katrina
character in: **23** The Legend of Sleepy Hollow
author: **6** Irving

Vanuatu
other name: **11** New Hebrides
capital/largest city: **4** Vila
others: **5** Santo **6** Forari **10** Luganville
school: **7** Malapoa
monetary unit: **5** franc **7** centime
island: **3** Api, Epi **4** Aoba, Gaua, Malo, Tana, Vate **5** Banks, Efate, Maewo, Santo, Tanna **6** Ambrym, Mabrim, Torres **8** Anei tyum, Malekula **9** Erromanga, Pentecost, Vanua Lava **13** Espiritu Santo
mountain: **6** Lopevi
highest point: **11** Tabwemasana
sea: **7** Pacific
people: **8** European **10** Melanesian, Polynesian **11** Micronesian
  explorer: **4** Cook **7** Queiros
  leader: **4** Lini
language: **6** French **7** Bislama, English **16** Melanesian Pidgin
religion: **7** animism **8** Anglican, John Frum **10** Protestant **12** Presbyterian **13** Roman Catholic
feature:
  cult: **5** cargo

vapid 4 dull, flat, lame, tame **5** bland, empty, stale **7** insipid **8** lifeless **9** colorless, pointless **10** flavorless, wishy-washy **11** meaningless, uninspiring **12** unsatisfying **13** characterless

vapor 3 dew, fog **4** haze, mist, smog **5** fumes, smoke, steam **6** miasma **8** moisture

vaporize 5 dry up **7** distill **8** condense, melt away **9** dissipate, evaporate

Varden, Gabriel/Dolly
character in: **12** Barnaby Rudge
author: **7** Dickens

Vargas Llosa, Mario
author of: **13** The Green House **16** The Time of the Hero **26** Conversation in the Cathedral **27** Aunt Julia and the Scriptwriter **34** Captain Pantoja and the Special Service

variable 6 fickle, fitful, uneven, unlike **7** diverse, mutable **8** changing, shifting, unstable, wavering **9** alterable, different, spasmodic, unsettled **10** capricious, changeable, inconstant, indefinite **11** fluctuating

variance 4 odds **6** change **7** dispute, quarrel **9** deviation, disparity **10** contention, difference, dissension, divergence, unlikeness **11** discrepancy, incongruity **12** disagreement, modification **13** dissimilarity, inconsistency

variant 7 altered, derived, take off **8** modified **9** departure, different, divergent, variation **10** alteration **11** transformed **12** modification **14** transformation

variation 6 change **7** variant, variety **8** mutation, variance **9** departure, deviation, diversity **10** aberration, alteration, difference, divergency, innovation **11** discrepancy **12** disagreement, modification **13** metamorphosis **14** transformation

varicolored 6 calico, motley, tartan **7** dappled, flecked, marbled, mottled, piebald **9** multi-hued **10** iridescent, opalescent, variegated **11** rainbowlike, technicolor **12** multicolored, particolored **13** polychromatic

varied 5 mixed **6** motley, sundry **7** diverse, various **8** assorted **9** different **10** variegated **11** diversified **13** heterogeneous, miscellaneous

variegated 4 pied **6** motley **7** checked, dappled, mottled, piebald **9** checkered **12** parti-colored

variety 4 hash, kind, race, sort, type **5** brand, breed, class, genre, genus, group, stock, tribe **6** change, family, jumble, medley, motley, strain **7** melange, mixture, species **8** category, division, pastiche **9** diversity, patchwork, variation **10** assortment, collection, difference, hodgepodge, innovation, miscellany, subspecies **11** subdivision **12** denomination, multiplicity, unconformity **13** dissimilarity, heterogeneity, nonuniformity **14** classification, omnium-gatherum **15** diversification

various 3 few **4** many, some **5** other **6** divers, myriad, sundry, varied

7 diverse, several **8** assorted, manifold, numerous **9** countless, different **10** dissimilar **11** innumerable **12** multifarious **13** miscellaneous, multitudinous

varlet 3 cur **6** rascal, wretch **7** villain **9** scoundrel **10** blackguard

Varner, Will
character in: **9** The Hamlet
author: **8** Faulkner

varnish 4 gilt **5** adorn, cover, gloss, stain **6** excuse, soften **7** conceal, lacquer **8** disguise, mitigate **9** embellish, gloss over **10** smooth over

vary 4 veer **5** alter, shift **6** change, depart, differ, modify **7** deviate, dissent, diverge **8** be unlike, contrast, disagree **9** alternate, disaccord, diversify, fluctuate

vase 3 jar, jug, pot, urn **5** crock, diota **8** canister **9** container **10** jardiniere

Vashti
husband: **9** Ahasuerus
replaced by: **6** Esther

vassal 4 serf **5** helot, liege, slave **6** tenant, thrall **7** bondman, servant, subject, villein **8** retainer **9** bondslave, bondwoman, dependent **11** subordinate

vassalage 4 yoke **7** bondage, serfdom, slavery **9** servitude **11** enslavement

vast 4 huge, wide **5** great, jumbo **7** endless, immense, titanic, very big **8** colossal, enormous, far-flung, gigantic, infinite, spacious **9** boundless, capacious, extensive, limitless, monstrous, unbounded, unlimited, very large **10** monumental, prodigious, stupendous, tremendous, voluminous, widespread **11** far-reaching, measureless, significant, substantial **12** immeasurable, interminable

vastness 7 bigness **8** enormity, hugeness **9** immensity, largeness **12** enormousness

Vatican City 10 papal state
enclave in: **4** Rome
includes: **7** Vatican **13** Sistine Chapel **16** St. Peter's Basilica
retreat: **14** Castel Gandolfo
statue: **7** Laocoon

Vaughan Williams, Ralph
born: **7** Britain **10** Down Ampney
composer of: **3** Job **8** The Wasps **9** Flos Campi **10** Antarctica (symphony No 7), **11** Old King Cole **12** A Sea Symphony **13** Hugh the Drover, On Wenlock Edge, Sir John in Love, Songs of Travel **14** Riders to the Sea, The House of Life, The Sons of Light **15** A London Symphony, The Poisoned Kiss **16** The Lark Ascending **17** A Pastoral Symphony **18** Five Tudor Portraits, Sinfonia Antartica **19** The Pilgrim's Progress **22** Toward the Unknown Region

Vaughn, Robert

born: **9** New York NY
roles: **7** Bullitt **12** Napoleon Solo **15** The Man from UNCLE **19** The Magnificent Seven **22** The Young Philadelphians

vault 4 arch, dome, jump, leap, safe, tomb **5** bound, clear, crypt **6** arcade, cupola, hurdle, spring **7** ossuary **8** catacomb, jump over, leapfrog, leap over, wall safe **9** mausoleum, polevault, sepulcher, strongbox **10** arched roof, spring over, strongroom **13** arched ceiling, burial chamber

vaunt 5 strut **6** brag of, flaunt **7** exult in, show off, swagger **9** crow about, gasconade, gloat over **10** boast about

vaunted 7 exalted, praised **11** gloated over, overpraised **12** boasted about

veer 3 yaw **4** jibe, tack, turn **5** curve, dodge, drift, shift, wheel **6** swerve, zigzag **7** go about **9** come round, turn aside **15** change direction

Vegas
character: **5** Angie **6** Binzer **8** Beatrice, Dan Tanna **10** Bernie Roth **11** (Sgt) Bella Archer
cast: **10** Tony Curtis **11** Judy Landers, Robert Urich **12** Naomi Stevens, Phyllis Davis **13** Bart Braverman

vegetable 3 pea **4** bean, beet, corn **6** carrot, greens, legume, squash, turnip **7** cabbage, lettuce, parsnip, produce, spinach **8** broccoli, eggplant, lima bean, rutabaga, zucchini **10** string bean **11** cauliflower

vegetarian 5 vegan **8** meatless **9** herbivore **11** herbivorous

vegetation 5 flora, grass, sloth, weeds **6** leaves, plants, torpor **7** foliage, herbage, languor, loafing, verdure **8** dormancy, idleness, lethargy **9** flowerage, indolence, plant life, shrubbery **10** inactivity **11** hibernation, languidness, rustication **12** sluggishness
god of: **6** Dumuzi

vehemence 4 heat, zeal **5** ardor **6** fervor, warmth **7** passion **9** intensity

vehement 3 hot **4** wild **5** eager, fiery, rabid **6** ardent, fervid, fierce, heated, stormy **7** earnest, excited, fanatic, fervent, furious, intense, violent, zealous **8** agitated, forceful, frenzied, vigorous **9** emotional, fanatical, hotheaded **10** passionate **11** impassioned, tempestuous **12** enthusiastic

vehemently 5 hotly **6** wildly **7** eagerly **8** ardently, fiercely, strongly **9** earnestly, excitedly, fervently, furiously, intensely, violently, zealously **10** vigorously **11** emotionally, fanatically **12** passionately **13** tempestuously **16** enthusiastically

vehicle 3 bus, car **4** tool **5** agent, means, organ, plane, train, truck **6** agency, device, medium **7** bicycle **9** mechanism **10** automobile, conveyance, instrument, motorcycle, rocket

ship **12** intermediary **14** transportation

veil 3 dim **4** hide, mask **5** cloak, cloud, cover **6** enwrap, mantle, screen, shroud **7** blanket, conceal, curtain, envelop, obscure **8** covering **10** camouflage

veiled 3 dim **5** murky **6** draped, hidden **7** muffled **8** obscured, shrouded **9** concealed, covered up, disguised, enveloped, enwrapped **11** camouflaged

veiling 3 net **4** mesh **8** cloaking, covering **9** obscurity **10** concealing

vein 3 rib, web **4** bent, hint, line, lode, mark, mood, seam, tone **5** fleck, layer, stria, style, touch **6** furrow, manner, marble, nature, strain, streak, stripe, temper, thread **7** stratum **8** tendency **9** capillary, character **10** complexion, propensity **11** blood vessel, disposition, inclination, temperament **12** predilection **14** predisposition

Velazquez (Velasquez), Diego Rodriguez de Silvay
born: **5** Spain **7** Seville
artwork: **8** Philip IV **10** Las Meninas **13** Luis de Gongora, Pope Innocent X, Venus and Cupid **14** Cardinal Borgia **17** Don Gaspar de Guzman, Isabella of Bourbon **18** Adoration of the Magi, The Tapestry Weavers **19** The Infanta Margarita, The Surrender of Breda **20** Infanta Maria Theresia **21** An Old Woman Cooking Eggs **22** Portrait of a Court Jester, Portrait of Juan de Pareja **23** The Immaculate Conception **30** Prince Balthasar Carlos at the Hunt

veloce
music: **4** fast

velocity 4 pace **5** haste, speed **8** alacrity, celerity, rapidity **9** fleetness, quickness, swiftness **10** expedition, speediness

venal 5 shady **6** greedy **7** corrupt, crooked, selfish **8** bribable, covetous, grasping **9** dishonest, mercenary, rapacious **10** avaricious **11** corruptible **12** unprincipled, unscrupulous **13** money-grubbing

venality 7 avarice **10** corruption **11** bribe-taking **13** mercenariness, money-grubbing

vend 4 hawk, sell **5** trade **6** barter, deal in, market, peddle, retail **7** auction, trade in **8** huckster **11** merchandise

Vendetta, La
author: **14** Honore de Balzac

vendor, vender 6 dealer, hawker, monger, seller, trader **7** peddler **8** huckster, merchant, purveyor, retailer, salesman, supplier **9** tradesman **10** wholesaler **12** merchandiser **13** street peddler

veneer 4 coat, mask, show **5** front, layer **6** casing, facade, facing, jacket, sheath **7** coating, overlay, wrapper **8** covering, envelope, pretense **10** outer layer

venerable 3 old **4** aged **5** hoary **6** august **7** admired, ancient, elderly, honored, revered **8** esteemed **9** respected, venerated **11** patriarchal, white-haired

venerate 5 adore, extol, honor **6** admire, esteem, hallow, revere **7** cherish, glorify, idolize, respect, worship **8** look up to **9** reverence **11** pay homage to

venerated 4 holy **5** loved **6** adored, sacred **7** honored, revered **8** hallowed **9** respected **10** reverenced, worshipped **12** paid homage to

veneration 3 awe **5** honor **6** esteem, homage, wonder **7** respect, worship **8** devotion **9** adoration, adulation, reverence **10** admiration, exaltation **11** idolization **13** glorification

venereal 6 carnal, sexual **7** genital

Venezuela
  name means: 12 little Venice
  capital/largest city: 7 Caracas
  others: 4 Aroa, Coro **6** Atures, Cumana, Merida **7** Barinas, Barines, Cabello, Guaware, Maracay, Maturin **8** Asuncion, Carupano, La Guaira, La Gyayra, Tacupita, Valencia **9** Barcelona, Maracaibo, Tacarigua **12** Barquisimeto, Puerto La Cruz, San Cristobal **13** Ciudad Bolivar, Puerto Cabello **18** Santo Tome de Guayana
  division: 4 Lara **5** Apure, Sucre, Zulia **6** Aragua, Falcon, Merida **7** Barinas, Bolivar, Cojedes, Guarico, Monagas, Tachira, Yaracuy **8** Carabobo, Trujillo
  measure: 5 galon **6** fanega **7** estadel
  monetary unit: 4 peso **5** medio **6** fuerte **7** bolivar, centimo **8** morocota **10** venezolano
  weight: 3 bag **5** libra
  island: 4 Aves **7** Cubagua, Tortuga **9** La Orchila, Los Roques, Margarita **11** Los Hermanos **12** La Blanquilla
  lake: 9 Maracaibo, Tacarigua
  mountain: 3 Pao **4** Pava, Yair **5** Andes, Duida, Icutu **6** Concha, Cuneva, Merida, Parima, Sierra, Yumari **7** Imutaca, Masaiti, Roraima **8** Gurupira **9** Pacaraima **10** Auyan-Tepui **11** Turimiquire **18** Cordillera del Norte
  highest point: 7 Bolivar
  river: 3 Oro, Pao **4** Meta **5** Apure, Caura, Negro, Suata, Tigre, Unare, Zulia **6** Amazon, Arauca, Caroni, Cuyuni **7** Guanare, Guanipa, Guarico, Orinoco, Oritueo, Paragua, Suapure, Vichada, Yuruari **8** Guaviare, Manapire, Ventuari **9** Cuchivero **10** Casiquiare, Portuguesa
  sea: 8 Atlantic **9** Caribbean
  physical feature:

  falls: 5 Angel
  gulf: 5 Paria **6** Triste **9** Venezuela
  highlands: 6 Guiana **7** Guayana, Segovia
  plains: 6 Llanos
  people: 4 Bare, Pume **5** Bello, Carib, pardo, zambo **6** Arawak, Creole, Timote **7** Charoya, Guahibo, Kaliana, mestizo, mulatto, Otomaca, Timotex **8** Caquetio, Guarauno, Matilone **11** Maquiritare
    artist: 7 Marisol
    author: 5 Bello **8** Gallegos **13** Diaz-Rodriguez
    explorer: 8 Columbus
    god: 5 Tsuma
    leader: 4 Paez **5** Gomez, Leoni **6** Castro **7** Bolivar, Miranda **10** Betancourt **12** Guzman Blanco **14** Herrera Campins
  language: 4 Pume **7** Spanish
  religion: 5 Islam **7** Judaism **10** Protestant **13** Roman Catholic
  feature:
    animal: 4 puma **5** sloth **6** jaguar, ocelot **7** manatee, peccary **8** anteater, capybara **9** armadillo
    cowboy: 7 llanero
    dance: 6 joropo **16** diablos danzantes
    folk entertainment: 10 burriquita
    musical instrument: 6 cuatro **7** maracas
    street performance: 8 parranda
  food:
    black beans: 8 caraotas
    bread: 5 arepa
    dish: 7 hallaca **8** cachapos, pabellon
    soup/stew: 8 sancocho
vengeance 7 revenge **8** avenging, reprisal, requital **11** malevolence, retaliation, retribution **12** ruthlessness **13** an eye for an eye, implacability **14** revengefulness, vindictiveness **15** a tooth for a tooth
veni, vidi, vici 19 I came I saw I conquered
  author: 12 Julius Caesar
venial 5 minor **6** slight **7** trivial **9** allowable, excusable **10** defensible, forgivable, not serious, pardonable **11** justifiable, unimportant, warrantable
Venice
  art exhibition: 8 Biennale
  artist: 7 Bellini, Codussi **8** Fabriano, Longhena, Mantegna, Palladio, Scamozzi, Veronese **9** Canaletto, Carpaccio, Giorgione, Sansovino **10** Tintoretto
  capital of: 6 Veneto **15** Venezia province
  church: 18 San Giorgio Maggiore, Santa Maria dei Frari **19** Santi Giovanni e Paolo
  Italian: 7 Venezia
  landmark: 6 Ca' d'Oro **9** Campanile **10** Grand Canal **11** Doge's Palace

  13 Bridge of Sighs **15** Libreria Vecchia **16** Palazzo Rezzonico, Saint Mark's Church **20** Accademia di Belle Arti **21** Palazzo dei Procuratori **22** Scuola Grande di San Rocco **23** Palazzo Vendramin-Calergi
  port: 8 Marghera
  resort: 9 Lido Beach
  sea: 8 Adriatic
  small canal: 3 rii
  tomb: 5 Titan
  traveler: 9 Marco Polo
Venn, Diggory
  character in: 17 Return of the Native
  author: 5 Hardy
venom 3 ire **4** gall, hate **5** anger, spite, toxin, virus **6** choler, enmity, grudge, hatred, malice, poison, rancor, spleen **7** ill will **8** acrimony, savagery **9** animosity, barbarity, brutality, hostility **10** bitterness, resentment **11** malevolence **12** spitefulness **13** maliciousness, rancorousness
venomous 5 cruel, fatal, toxic **6** bitter, brutal, deadly, lethal, malign, savage **7** abusive, caustic, hostile, noxious, vicious **8** spiteful, virulent **9** malicious, malignant, poisonous, rancorous, resentful **10** malevolent **11** ill-disposed **12** bloodthirsty
vent 3 air, tap **4** bare, drip, emit, flue, gush, hole, ooze, pipe **5** exude, spout, utter, voice **6** effuse, escape, faucet, let out, outlet, reveal, spigot **7** air hole, chimney, debouch, declare, divulge, express, opening, orifice, release **8** aperture, disclose, exposure, venthole **9** discharge, let escape, pour forth, utterance **10** disclosure, expression, revelation, smoke stack, ventilator **11** communicate, declaration
ventilate 3 air, sow **5** voice **6** aerate, air out, report, review, spread **7** analyze, declare, discuss, dissent, divulge, examine, express **9** broadcast, circulate, comment on, criticize, oxygenate, publicize, talk about **10** bandy about **11** disseminate, noise abroad
ventilator 3 fan **4** flue **7** aera tor **10** exhaust fan, smoke stack **14** air conditioner
venture 2 go **3** bet, try **4** dare, risk **5** flyer, offer, wager **6** chance, gamble, hazard, plunge, submit, tender, travel **7** advance, attempt, hold out, presume, proffer, project **8** endeavor, make bold **9** adventure, risk going, strive for, undertake, volunteer **10** enterprise, put forward, take a flyer **11** speculation, uncertainty, undertaking
venturesome, adventuresome 4 bold, rash **5** risky **6** daring, tricky, unsafe, unsure **7** dubious **8** doubtful, insecure, perilous, reckless, ticklish **9** ambitious, audacious, dangerous, daredevil, energetic, foolhardy, hazardous, impetuous, impulsive,

uncertain **10** aggressive, precarious **11** adventurous, speculative **12** enterprising, questionable

venturesomeness 6 daring **8** audacity, boldness **9** derring-do **11** impetuosity **12** recklessness

Venus
origin: **5** Roman **7** Italian
goddess of: **4** love **6** beauty, spring **7** gardens
son: **6** Aeneas
grandson: **5** Iulus
epithet: **7** Erycina **8** Gene trix **10** Erticordia
also see Aphrodite

Venus and Adonis
author: **18** William Shakespeare

veracious 4 true **6** honest **7** sincere **8** accurate, faithful, truthful **10** scrupulous **11** punctilious

veracity 5 truth **6** candor, verity **7** honesty, probity **8** accu racy, openness **9** exactness, frankness, integrity, sincerity **10** exactitude **11** correctness **12** truthfulness **13** guileless ness, ingenuousness **14** verisimilitude

Vera-Ellen
real name: **13** Vera-Ellen Rohe
born: **12** Cincinnati OH
roles: **9** On the Town **14** White Christmas

veranda
Hawaiian: **5** lanai

verbal 4 oral, said **5** vocal **6** spoken, voiced **7** in words, of verbs, of words, uttered **9** expressed, unwritten

verbal exchange 6 dialog **8** dialogue **10** discussion **12** conversation

verbalize 5 speak, utter, voice **7** express **10** articulate **12** put into words

verbal thrust 4 dig **4** gibe, jeer **5** taunt **12** cutting remark

verbatim 5 exact **7** exactly, literal, precise **8** accurate, faith ful **9** literally, literatim, precisely **10** accurately, faithfully **11** to the letter, word for word **15** chapter and verse, letter for letter
Latin: **14** ipsissima verba

verbatim et literatim 21 in exactly the same words **29** word for word and letter for letter

verbena
varieties: **4** moss, rose, sand **5** clump, lemon, shrub **7** red sand **8** pink sand **9** beach sand **10** desert sand, Mojave sand, yellow sand **12** common garden

verbiage 9 logorrhea, loquacity, prolixity, verbosity, wordiness **10** volubility **11** verboseness **12** effusiveness **14** circumlocution, grandiloquence, longwindedness

verbose 5 gabby, wordy **6** prolix **7** voluble **8** effusive **9** garrulous, talka-

tive **10** longwinded, loquacious **13** grandiloquent **14** circumlocutory

verbosity 9 diffusion, prolixity, talkiness, wordiness **11** diffuseness **13** talkativeness **14** long-windedness

verboten 9 forbidden **10** prohibited

Verdandi 4 Norn
origin: **12** Scandinavian
form: **3** elf
personifies: **7** present
developed from: **5** Urdar
companions: **3** Urd **5** Skuld

verdant 4 lush **5** green, leafy, shady, turfy **6** grassy **7** meadowy **8** blooming, thriving **9** luxuriant **10** burgeoning, springlike **11** flourishing

Verdi, Giuseppe
born: **5** Italy **7** Busseto
composer of: **4** Aida **6** Otello **7** Macbeth, Nabucco, Othello **8** Falstaff **9** Don Carlos, Il Corsaro, Rigoletto, The Misled **10** La Traviata **11** Il Trovatore **13** The Troubadour **14** Manzoni Requiem **15** Simon Boccanegra

verdict 6 answer, decree, ruling **7** finding, opinion **8** decision, judgment, sentence **9** valuation **10** assessment, estimation **11** arbitrament, arbitration **12** adjudication **13** determination

Vere, Captain
character in: **9** Billy Budd
author: **8** Melville

Vereen, Ben
born: **7** Miami FL
roles: **5** Roots **6** Pippin **13** Chicken George **20** Jesus Christ Superstar

verge 3 end, hem, lip, rim **4** brim, edge **5** bound, brink, ledge, limit, skirt **6** be near, border, flange, fringe, margin **7** confine, extreme **8** approach, boundary, frontier, terminus **9** threshold **11** approximate **12** be on the brink

verge upon 4 abut **5** flank **6** adjoin, border **8** be next to **10** neighbor on

Vergil, Virgil
author of: **6** Aeneid **8** Bucolics, Eclogues, Georgics

verification 5 proof **7** support **9** guarantee **10** validation **12** confirmation **13** accreditation, certification, corroboration, documentation **14** authentication, substantiation

verify 5 prove **7** certify, confirm, support, sustain, witness **8** accredit, attest to, document, validate, vouch for **9** establish, guarantee, testify to **11** corroborate **12** authenticate, substantiate

verily 4 amen **5** truly **6** really **9** certainly, yes indeed **10** positively

veritable 4 real, true **5** utter, valid **6** actual **7** genuine, literal **8** absolute, bona fide, complete, positive, true-blue **9** authentic **13** incontestable, unimpeachable **14** unquestioned **17** through-and-through

Verlaine, Paul
author of: **6** Wisdom **7** Sagesse **8** Langueur **17** Songs Without Words **19** Romances sans Paroles

Vermeer, Jan
born: **5** Delft **7** Holland
artwork: **11** View of Delft **12** The Lace Maker, The Procuress **13** Drinking Scene **14** A Street in Delft, The Head of a Girl **15** Alle gory of Faith, Girl with a Red Hat **16** The Artist's Studio **18** Girl Reading a Letter, Girl with a Wine-glass **19** A Girl Asleep at a Table, A Painter in his Studio **20** A Woman Weighing Pearls **22** Maidservant Pouring Milk **23** Young Woman with a Water Jug **24** A Soldier and a Laughing Girl **31** Christ in the House of Mary and Martha

vermilion 3 red **7** scarlet **8** cinnabar **9** bright red **15** mercuric sulfide

vermin 4 ants, lice, mice, owls, rats **5** crows, fleas, foxes, pests **6** snakes, wolves **7** bed bugs, coyotes, roaches, spiders, weasels **8** termites, varmints **9** water bugs **10** centipedes, silverfish **11** birds of prey **18** pestiferous insects

Vermont
abbreviation: **2** VT
nickname: **13** Green Mountain **20** Four-Season Recreation
capital: **10** Montpelier
largest city: **10** Burlington
others: **5** Barre, Stowe **7** Grafton, Newfane, Newport, Rutland **8** St Albans, Winooski **9** Bountiful, Vergennes **10** Bennington **11** Brattleboro
college: **7** Goddard, Norwich, Trinity, Windham **8** Marlboro **10** Bennington, Middlebury, St Michaels
feature:
  covered bridge: **5** Scott
  house: **15** Old Constitution
  monument: **6** Battle
people: **9** John Deere, John Dewey **10** Ethan Allen **12** Brigham Young **13** Warren R Austin **15** Stephen A Douglas
lake: **7** Caspian, Dunmore, Seymour **8** Bomoseen **9** Champlain **10** Willoughby **12** Memphremagog
land rank: **10** forty-third
mountain: **5** Green, White **7** Bromley, Hogback, Taconic **8** Prospect, Stratton
  highest point: **9** Mansfield
physical feature:
  uplands: **10** New England
  valley: **9** Champlain
president: **14** Calvin Coolidge, Chester A Arthur
river: **4** West **5** Otter, White **7** Saxtons **8** Lamoille, Nulhegan, Winooski **10** Missisquoi **11** Connecticut
state admission: **10** fourteenth
state bird: **12** hermit thrush
state animal: **11** Morgan horse
state flower: **9** red clover

state motto: 15 Freedom and Unity
state song: 11 Hail Vermont
state tree: 10 sugar maple

vermouth
type: 4 wine **6** brandy **8** aperitif
origin: 5 Italy **6** France
varieties: 3 dry **5** sweet
drink: 9 Boomerang **11** Bittersweet
with bourbon: 9 Allegheny
with brandy: 3 BVD
with Dubonnet: 3 BVD
gin: 5 Bijou, Bronx, Tango **6** Caruso **7** Bermuda, Caberet, Martini **10** Bloodhound
with rum: 6 Bolero **8** Apple Pie **10** Black Devil **11** Shark's Tooth
with rye: 8 Brooklyn **9** Algonquin
with scotch: 8 Affinity **10** Bobby Burns
with sherry: 6 Bamboo, Brazil
with sloe gin: 10 Blackthorn
with vodka: 8 Kangaroo **9** Corkscrew
with whiskey: 9 Manhattan

vernacular 4 cant **5** idiom, lingo, slang **6** jargon, patois **7** dialect **8** parlance, shoptalk **9** the vulgar **12** common speech, native tongue **13** natural speech **14** informal speech, native language

vernal 3 new **5** fresh, green **6** spring **8** youthful **10** springlike

Verne, Jules
author of: 19 Five Weeks in a Balloon **21** From the Earth to the Moon **26** Around the World in Eighty Days **32** Twenty Thousand Leagues Under the Sea
character: 11 Captain Nemo, Phineas Fogg **12** Passepartout

Veronese, Paolo (Cagliari)
born: 5 Italy **6** Verona
artwork: 12 Book of Esther **13** The Last Supper **14** Supper at Emmaus **15** The Rape of Europa, Triumph of Venice **17** Mary with the Saints, The Finding of Moses, The Marriage at Cana, Wisdom and Strength **19** Martyrdom of St George, The Choice of Hercules **21** Esther before Ahasuerus **22** Feast at the House of Simon **24** Mars and Venus United in Love, The Feast in the House of Levi, The Temptation of St Anthony **31** Jesus and the Centurion of Capernaum **32** The Family of Darius before Alexander

Verrocchio, Andrea del
real name: 31 Andrea di Michele di Francesco Cione
born: 5 Italy **8** Florence
artwork: 5 David **15** Boy with a Dolphin **17** Christ and St Thomas **18** The Baptism of Christ **19** Bartolommeo Colleoni **23** Christ and Doubting Thomas **25** Beheading of John the Baptist

versatile 3 apt **4** able **5** handy

6 adroit, clever, expert, gifted **7** protean **8** talented **9** adaptable, all-around, ingenious, many-sided **10** proficient **11** many-skilled, resourceful **12** accomplished, multifaceted

verse 4 poem **5** meter, rhyme, stave **6** jingle, poetry, stanza **7** measure, strophe

versed 4 able **5** adept **6** expert, taught **7** erudite, learned, skilled, tutored **8** lettered, schooled, skillful, well-read **9** competent, practiced, scholarly **10** at home with, instructed, proficient **11** enlightened, experienced **12** accomplished, familiar with, well-informed **14** acquainted with, conversant with

versifier 4 bard **6** rhymer, writer **8** minstrel, poetizer, poetling, rhymster **9** poetaster, rhymester **10** rhymesmith, troubadour, versemaker, versesmith **11** versemonger **12** balladmonger

version 4 side **5** story **6** report **7** account **9** depiction, rendering **10** adaptation, paraphrase, re-creation **11** description, re statement, translation **14** interpretation

vers libre 9 free verse

vertebral column
bone of: 5 spine **8** backbone

vertex 3 cap, tip **4** apex, peak **5** crown **6** summit, zenith **8** pinnacle **12** highest point **13** crowning point

vertical 5 plumb, sheer **7** up right **12** ninety-degree **13** perpendicular

vertiginous 5 dizzy, giddy, shaky **6** whirly **7** reeling **11** lightheaded

vertigo 7 reeling **8** fainting **9** dizziness, giddiness **12** unsteadiness **15** lightheadedness

Vertigo
director: 15 Alfred Hitchcock
cast: 8 Kim Novak **12** James Stewart **16** Barbara Bel Geddes
setting: 12 San Francisco
score: 15 Bernard Herrmann

verve 3 vim, zip **4** dash, elan, fire, zeal **5** ardor, drive, force, gusto, punch, vigor **6** energy, fervor, relish, spirit, warmth **7** abandon, feeling, passion, rapture, sparkle **8** vitality, vivacity **9** animation, eagerness, vehemence **10** enthusiasm, liveliness

Verver, Maggie
character in: 13 The Golden Bowl
author: 5 James

very 4 bare, mere, most, much, pure **5** exact, extra, plain, quite, sheer, truly **6** deeply, highly, hugely, mighty, really, simple, vastly **7** awfully, exactly, fitting, greatly, notably, perfect, precise, totally **8** actually, entirely, markedly, specific, suitable, terribly **9** assuredly, certainly, decidedly, eminently, essential, extremely, immensely, intensely, necessary, obviously, perfectly, precisely, unusually,

veritably **10** abnormally, absolutely, abundantly, completely, defi nitely, especially, particular, profoundly, remarkably, strikingly, thoroughly, uncommonly, undeniably **11** appropriate, exceedingly, excessively **12** emphatically, surpassingly, tremendously **13** exceptionally, significantly **14** unquestionably

very best
French: 14 creme de la creme

Very Easy Death, A
author: 16 Simone de Beauvoir

very great 4 huge **6** severe **7** extreme, intense, mammoth, titanic **8** colossal, enormous, gigantic **9** excessive, monstrous **10** gargantuan, immoderate, inordinate, prodigious **11** magnificent, spectacular **14** Brobdingnagian

very nearly 6 almost **7** close to **9** just about **10** more or less, not far from **13** approximately

very old 4 aged **6** primal **7** ancient, antique, archaic **8** primeval **10** antiquated, primordial **11** prehistoric **12** antediluvian

very soon
French: 11 tout a l'heure

vessel 3 cup, jar, jug, keg, mug, pot, tub, vat **4** boat, bowl, butt, cask, dish, duct, scow, ship, tube, vase, vein **5** barge, craft, crock, flask, glass, liner, plate, yacht **6** artery, barrel, beaker, carafe, flagon, goblet, packet, tanker, whaler **7** caldron, collier, cruiser, platter, tankard, trawler, tugboat, tumbler, utensil **8** decanter, paquebot, sailboat **9** capillary, container, ferry boat, freighter, houseboat, steamboat, steamship **10** ocean liner, receptacle

vest 3 rig **4** garb, robe **5** array, drape, dress **6** attire, clothe, enwrap, fit out, jacket, jerkin **7** apparel, deck out, doublet, envelop **8** accouter **9** waistcoat

Vesta
origin: 5 Roman
goddess of: 6 hearth
festival: 8 Vestalia
corresponds to: 4 Caca **6** Hestia

vestal 4 pure **6** chaste, maiden, simple, virgin **8** maidenly, virginal, virtuous **9** pure woman, undefiled, unmarried, unworldly **10** immaculate **15** unsophisticated

vested 5 fixed **7** settled **8** absolute, complete **9** permanent **10** guaranteed **11** established, inalienable **12** indisputable **14** unquestionable

vestibule 4 hall **5** entry, foyer, lobby **6** lounge **7** hallway, passage **8** anteroom, corridor **10** passageway **11** antecham ber, entrance way, waiting room **12** entrance hall

vestige 4 sign **5** relic, token, trace

6 record **7** memento, remnant **8** evidence, souvenir

vestment 3 alb **4** garb, gear **5** amice, dress **6** livery, outfit **7** apparel, clothes, costume, raiment, regalia, uniform **8** clothing **9** trappings **13** accoutrements

vesture 4 robe **5** robes **7** apparel, clothes, garment, raiment **8** clothing, garments **9** vestments

vetch 5 Vicia

varieties: 3 cow **4** bard, bird, milk **5** crown, hairy, Sitka **6** bitter, common, kidney, purple, smooth, spring, tufted, winter **8** Narbonne **9** horse-shoe, Hungarian, woolly-pod **12** large Russian

veteran 3 vet **6** expert, master **7** old hand **8** old-timer, seasoned **9** ex-soldier **10** campaigner, old soldier, war veteran **11** experienced **12** ex-serviceman **13** long- practiced

veto 4 deny, void **6** denial, enjoin, forbid, negate, reject **7** nullify, prevent, refusal **8** disallow, prohibit, turn down **9** rejection **10** prevention **11** disallowing, prohibition **12** disallowance **16** turn thumbs down on

vex 3 bug, irk **4** fret, gall, miff, pain, rile **5** anger, annoy, chafe, harry, pique, upset, worry **6** badger, bother, grieve, harass, hassle, nettle, pester, plague, ruffle **7** chagrin, disturb, provoke, torment, trouble **8** distress, irritate **9** displease **10** exasperate **18** ruffle one's feathers

vexation 5 pique, trial **6** hassle **7** torment **8** headache, nuisance **9** annoyance **10** affliction, harassment, irritation **11** aggravation **13** pain in the neck

vexatious 5 pesky **6** thorny, vexing **8** annoying, nettling **9** badgering, harassing, hectoring, provoking, troubling, worrisome **10** bothersome, irritating **11** disquieting, pestiferous, troublesome

vexed 5 irked, riled, testy **6** galled, miffed, piqued **7** annoyed, nettled, peevish **8** provoked **9** irritated **11** disgruntled, exasperated

viable 6 usable **8** feasible, workable **9** adaptable, practical **10** applicable **11** practicable

viaduct 4 ramp, span **8** overpass

vial 5 ampul, flask, phial **7** ampoule

via media 10 a middle way

viands 4 cate, diet, eats, fare, food **7** cuisine, edibles, vittles **8** victuals **9** provender **10** foodstuffs, provisions

vibrancy 4 fire **5** ardor **7** elation **8** vitality, vivacity **9** animation **10** enthusiasm **11** high spirits

vibrant 4 deep, loud **5** alive, eager, vital, vivid **6** ardent, bright, florid, lively **7** fervent, glowing, intense,

orotund, pealing, pulsing, radiant, ringing **8** animated, bell-like, colorful, forceful, luminous, lustrous, resonant, sonorous, spirited, vehement **9** brilliant, deep-toned, energetic, quivering, thrilling, throbbing, vibrating, vivacious **10** fluttering, glittering, resounding, shimmering **11** full of vigor, resplendent, reverber ant **12** electrifying, enthusiastic

vibrate 4 beat, sway **5** quake, swing, throb, waver **6** quaver, quiver, ripple, wobble **7** flut ter, pulsate, tremble **8** undulate **9** oscillate, palpitate, pendulate **11** reverberate

vibration 5 quake **6** quiver, tremor **7** quaking **9** quivering, throbbing, trembling

vicar 6 cleric, parson, pastor **8** preacher **9** churchman, clergyman **12** ecclesiastic

vicarious 6 mental **7** by proxy **8** imagined, indirect **9** imaginary, surrogate **10** empathetic, fantasized, secondhand **11** at one remove, sympathetic

Vicar of Wakefield, The
author: 15 Oliver Goldsmith
character: 6 George, Olivia, Sophia **7** Deborah **10** Dr Primrose, Mr Burchill **14** Arabella Wilmot **15** Squire Thornhill **19** Sir William Thornhill

vice 4 flaw **5** fault **6** defect **7** blemish, failing, frailty **8** iniquity, weakness **9** depravity, weak point **10** corruption, debauchery, degeneracy, profligacy, wantonness, wickedness **11** shortcoming **12** imperfection **14** licentiousness

vice president
resigned: 10 Spiro Agnew **12** John C Calhoun
accused of treason: 9 Aaron Burr **17** John C Breckinridge
youngest elected: 17 John C Breckinridge
elected by Senate: 14 Richard Johnson
elected but did not serve: 11 William King
rejected nomination: 11 Frank Lowden, Silas Wright
lived longest: 15 John Nance Garner
succeeded to presidency: 9 John Tyler **10** Gerald Ford **12** Harry S Truman **13** Andrew Johnson **14** Calvin Coolidge, Chester A Arthur, Lyndon B Johnson **15** Millard Fillmore **17** Theodore Roosevelt

vice versa 9 in reverse **10** conversely **12** contrariwise **16** the other way round **18** in the opposite order

vicinity 4 area **6** region **8** environs, locality, vicinage **9** adjoining, precincts, proximity **11** environment, propinquity **12** neighborhood, surroundings

vicious 3 bad **4** base, evil, foul, mean, vile, wild **5** awful, cruel, gross, nasty, surly **6** brutal, fierce, horrid, savage,

sullen, wicked **7** hateful, heinous, hellish, immoral, inhuman, untamed, violent **8** churlish, depraved, fiendish, libelous, shocking, spiteful, terrible, venomous **9** abhorrent, atrocious, barbarous, dangerous, ferocious, invidious, malicious, monstrous, nefarious, offensive, predatory, rancorous **10** abominable, defamatory, diabolical, ill-humored, ill-natured, malevolent, pernicious, slanderous, villainous, vindictive **11** acrimonious, ill-tempered, treacherous **12** bloodthirsty

viciousness 4 evil **6** malice **7** cruelty **8** ferocity, savagery, villainy, violence **9** barbarity, brutality, ill nature **10** fierceness, wickedness **11** heinousness

vicissitude 6 change **8** mutation **9** variation **10** difficulty, mutability, succession **11** fluctuation

Vicomte of Bragelonne, The
author: 14 Alexandre Dumas (pere)

victim 4 butt, dead, dupe, gull, mark, pawn, prey, tool **5** patsy **6** pigeon, quarry, sucker, target **7** injured, wounded **8** casualty, fatality, innocent **9** scapegoat

victimize 3 con **4** dupe, gull, hoax **5** bully, cheat, cozen **6** betray, delude **7** deceive, defraud **8** hoodwink **9** bamboozle

victor 6 winner **8** champion, medalist **9** conqueror **10** vanquisher **11** prizewinner

Victoria, Queen
realm: 13 British Empire
House of: 7 Hanover
Prince Consort: 6 Albert
son; successor: 9 Edward VII

Victoria
capital of: 8 Hong Kong **10** Seychelles

Victoria
origin: 5 Roman
goddess of: 7 victory
corresponds to: 4 Nike

Victorian 4 prim, smug **6** narrow, proper, stuffy **7** insular, prudish **8** priggish **9** pietistic **10** tight-laced **11** puritanical, straitlaced **12** conventional, hypocritical **13** sanctimonious

victorious 7 winning **8** champion **10** conquering, successful, triumphant **11** vanquishing **12** championship, prize-winning

Victor Victoria
director: 12 Blake Edwards
cast: 10 Alex Karras **11** James Garner **12** Julie Andrews **13** Robert Preston **14** John Rhys-Davies **15** Lesley Ann Warren
setting: 5 Paris

victory 7 laurels, success, the palm, triumph **8** conquest, the prize **9** supremacy, ascendancy **11** superiority
god of: 3 Tyr
goddess of: 4 Nike **8** Victoria

Victory
author: **12** Joseph Conrad
character: **4** Lena, Wang **5** Jonas, Pedro **8** Davidson **9** Axel Heyst, Schomberg **13** Martin Ricardo

victuals 4 chow, diet, eats, fare, feed, food, grub, meat **5** meals **6** fodder, forage, repast, stores, viands **7** cooking, cuisine, edibles, rations, vittles **8** supplies **9** groceries, provender **10** foodstuffs, provisions **11** comestibles, nourishment, refreshment

Vidal, Gore
author of: **4** Burr **5** Kalki **6** Julian **8** Creation **16** Myra Breckinridge **18** Eighteen Seventy-Six, The Judgment of Paris **19** Visit to a Small Planet

Vidar
origin: **12** Scandinavian
father: **4** Odin **5** Othin
killed: **6** Fenrir, Fenris

vide 3 see
vide ante 9 see before
vide infra 8 see below
videlicet 6 namely **11** that is to say
abbreviation: **3** viz
vide post 8 see after **10** see further
vide supra 8 see above
vide ut supra 10 see as above **16** see as stated above

Vidor, King
director of: **8** The Crowd **12** Stella Dallas, The Big Parade **16** Northwest Passage

vie 4 life **5** fight **6** strive **7** compete, contend, contest **8** be a rival, struggle, tilt with **9** challenge

Vienna
airport: **9** Schwechat
area: **11** Innere Stadt
capital of: **7** Austria
early name: **4** Wena **9** Vindobono
German: **4** Wien
landmark: **6** Prater **7** Hofburg **10** Stadtsoper **13** Saint Stephen's **15** Albertina Museum, Belvedere Palace **16** Historical Museum, Schonbrunn Palace
river: **6** Danube
ruler: **8** Hapsburg
street: **11** Ringstrasse

Vientiane, Viengchan
capital of: **4** Laos

vi et armis 20 with force and with arms

Vietnam
other name: **5** Annam **15** French Indochina
capital: **5** Hanoi **6** Saigon
largest city: **6** Saigon **13** Ho Chi Minh City
others: **3** Hue, Ron **4** Ngai, Vinh **5** Dalat, Hoa Da, Hoian **6** Annhon, Cholon, Danang, Hongay **7** Bacninh, Cam Ranh, Caobang, Donghoi, Hoabinh, Namdinh, Quinhon, Songoan, Tayninh, Viettri, Vinhloi **8** Binhdinh, Haiphong, Nhatrang, Panthiet, Phan Rang, Quangtri, Quangyen, Thanhhoa, Vinhlong **9** Haiphoang, Longxuyen **11** Dienbienphu
school: **3** Hue **5** Hanoi **9** Ho Chi Minh
division: **5** Annam, North, South **6** Tonkin **11** Cochin China
measure: **4** gang, phan, thon
monetary unit: **2** xu **4** dong **7** piaster
weight: **3** can, yet **4** uyen
mountain: **6** Badinh, Badink **7** Nindhoa, Ninhhoa **8** Fansipan, Knontran, Ngoklinh, Ngoolink, Tchepone, Tclepore **18** Annamese Cordillera
highest point: **8** Fan Si Pan
river: **2** Bo, Ca, Da, Lo, Ma **3** Chu, Gam, Koi, Red **4** Chay **5** Nhiha **6** Mekong **7** Dongnai
sea: **10** South China
physical feature:
   delta: **6** Mekong **8** Red River
   gulf: **4** Siam **6** Tonkin **7** Tonking **8** Thailand
   peninsula: **11** Indochinese
people: **3** Hoa, Man, Meo, Tai, Tay **4** Cham, Kinh, Nung, Thai **5** Khmer, Malay, Muong **7** Chinese **8** Annamese, Annamite **9** Cambodian **10** montagnard, Vietnamese
   leader: **5** Le Loi **8** Le Duc Tho **9** Ho Chi Minh **11** Ngo Dinh Diem, Pham Van Doug **14** Nguyen Van Thieu
language: **3** Yue **4** Cham **5** Khmer, Rhade **7** French **7** Chinese, English **9** Cantonese **10** Vietnamese
religion: **6** Cao Dai, Hoa Hao, Taoism **7** animism **8** Buddhism **12** Christianity, Confucianism **13** Roman Catholic
place:
   ruins: **10** Nguyen tomb
feature:
   army: **4** ARVN **5** COSVN **8** Communsi, Viet Cong, Viet Minh
   clothing: **5** ao dai
   new year: **3** Tet
view 3 eye, ken, see **4** gaze, look, note, peek, peep, scan **5** judge, scene, sight, study, vista, watch **6** behold, belief, gaze at, glance, look at, notion, regard, survey, take in, theory, vision **7** diorama, examine, explore, feeling, glimpse, inspect, observe, opinion, outlook, picture, scenery, thought, witness **8** attitude, consider, glance at, judgment, panorama, perceive, pore over, prospect **9** landscape, sentiment, spectacle **10** conception, conviction, scrutinize, think about **11** contemplate, perspective
view as 4 deem, hold **5** count, judge, think **6** regard **7** account, believe **8** consider, take to be **10** look upon as
viewpoint 4 bias, side **5** angle, slant **6** aspect, belief **7** feeling, opinion **8** attitude, position **9** sentiment **10** conviction, standpoint **11** orientation, perspective **12** vantage point **16** frame of reference

view with disfavor 7 condemn, dislike **8** object to **9** frown upon **10** disapprove, think ill of **13** look askance at, regard as wrong **14** discountenance **15** take exception to

view with horror 5 abhor **6** eschew **8** sicken at **9** abominate, shudder at **10** recoil from, shrink from

vif
music: **6** lively

vigilance 4 care, heed **7** caution, concern **8** prudence **9** alertness, attention **10** precaution **11** carefulness, forethought, guardedness, heedfulness **12** cautiousness, watchfulness **14** circumspection

vigilant 4 wary **5** alert, chary **7** careful, guarded, heedful, on guard, prudent **8** cautious, watchful **9** attentive, observant, wide-awake **10** on one's toes, on the alert **11** circumspect, on one's guard **12** on the lookout, on the qui vive

vigor 3 pep, vim, zip **4** dash, elan, fire, zeal **5** ardor, drive, force, might, power, verve **6** energy, fervor, spirit **7** passion, stamina **8** haleness, strength, vitality, vivacity **9** animation, hardiness, intensity, vehemence **10** enthusiasm, liveliness, robustness **11** earnestness **12** forcefulness

vigorous 4 bold, hale **5** hardy, lusty, vital **6** active, ardent, brawny, lively, mighty, robust, strong, sturdy, virile **7** dynamic, intense, vibrant **8** forceful, muscular, powerful, spirited **9** assertive, energetic **10** aggressive

vigorously 4 hard **7** briskly, lustily **8** actively, cogently, forcibly, robustly, strongly, sturdily **9** with force **10** forcefully, powerfully **11** strenuously **13** energetically

Vigrid
origin: **12** Scandinavian
final battlefield of: **4** gods

Viking, viking 4 Dane **6** pirate **7** mariner **8** Norseman, Northman, searover **9** plunderer **12** Scandinavian
boat: **8** long ship
burial: **9** ship grave
chieftain: **4** jarl
exploration: **5** Italy, Spain **6** France, Russia **7** England, Germany, Iceland, Ireland, Vinland **9** Greenland
famous: **4** Eric **8** Eirikson, Ericsson **10** Eric the Red **11** Leif Ericson
governing council: **4** Ting **5** Thing **8** Folkmoot
legend: **4** Edda, saga
origin: **6** Norway, Sweden **7** Denmark, Finland
warrior: **7** beserk **9** berserker
writing: **4** rune

Vila
capital of: 7 Vanuatu

vile 3 bad, low **4** base, evil, foul, lewd, mean, ugly **5** aw ful, gross, nasty **6** coarse, filthy, odious, sinful, smutty, sordid, vulgar, wicked **7** beastly, hateful, heinous, ignoble, immoral, obscene, vicious **8** depraved, shameful, shocking, wretched **9** abhorrent, degrading, execrable, invidious, loathsome, nefarious, obnoxious, offensive, perverted, repellent, repugnant, repulsive, revolting, salacious **10** abominable, degenerate, despicable, detestable, disgusting, iniquitous, unpleasant, villainous **11** disgraceful, foul mouthed, humiliating **12** contemptible **13** objectionable

Vile Bodies
author: 11 Evelyn Waugh

vileness 4 evil **8** foulness, iniquity, villainy **9** depravity, nastiness **10** immorality, odiousness **11** degradation, heinousness, viciousness **12** wretchedness **13** offensiveness

Vili
origin: 12 Scandinavian
brother: 4 Odin **5** Othin

vilification 5 libel **7** calumny, slander **10** defamation **13** disparagement

vilifier 5 scold **6** carper, critic **7** reviler **9** backbiter

vilify 5 abuse **6** defame, revile **7** slander **8** bad-mouth, dis honor **9** criticize, disparage **14** inveigh against

vilifying 7 abusive **8** libelous **9** malignant **10** calumnious, defamatory, slanderous

villa, Villa 5 aldea, dacha **6** castle, Pancho **7** chateau, mansion **9** residence **13** coun try estate

village 4 burg **6** hamlet, suburb **8** hick town **9** smalltown **11** whistlestop **12** municipality

Village, A
author: 10 Sholem Asch

villain 3 cad, cur, rat **5** knave, louse, rogue **6** rascal, rotter, varlet **7** caitiff, stinker **8** evil doer, scalawag **9** miscreant, scoundrel **10** blackguard, malefactor **11** rapscallion **12** transgressor, wicked person **15** snake in the grass

villainous 4 base, evil, foul, vile **6** wicked **7** caddish, heinous **8** horrible, infamous **9** monstrous, nefarious **10** abominable, despicable, detestable, maleficent **12** blackguardly **13** reprehensible

villainy 4 evil **8** vileness **9** depravity, rascality **10** wickedness **11** viciousness, maleficence

Villa-Lobos, Heitor
born: 6 Brazil **12** Rio de Janeiro
composer of: 6 Choros **20** Bachianas Brasileiras

Villefort

character in: 21 The Count of Monte Cristo
author: 5 Dumas (pere)

villein 4 carl, esne, serf **5** ceorl, churl, slave **6** drudge **7** bondman, peasant **9** bondwoman

Villette
author: 15 Charlotte Bronte

Villon, Francois
author of: 9 The Legacy **16** Le grand testament, Le petit testament
quote: 25 Mais ou sont les neiges d'antan **31** But where are the snows of yesteryear

Villuppo
character in: 17 The Spanish Tragedy
author: 3 Kyd

vim 2 go **3** pep, zip **4** dash, fire, snap, zeal **5** ardor, drive, force, might, power, punch, verve, vigor **6** energy, fervor, spirit **7** passion, potency **8** strength, vitality, vivacity **9** animation, intensity, vehemence **10** enthusiasm, liveliness

vin, vino 4 wine

Vincentio
character in: 17 Measure for Measure
author: 11 Shakespeare

vincit omnia veritas 16 truth conquers all **22** truth conquers all things

vindicate 4 free **5** clear **6** acquit, assert, defend, excuse, uphold **7** absolve, bear out, bolster, justify, support **8** advocate, champion, maintain **9** discharge, exculpate, exonerate **11** corroborate **12** substantiate

vindication 6 excuse **7** apology, defense **11** explanation **13** justification

vindictive 6 bitter, malign **8** avenging, punitive, spiteful, vengeful **9** malicious **10** malevolent, revengeful **11** retaliative, retaliatory, unforgiving

vinegarish 4 acid, sour, tart **5** harsh **6** acidic, biting **7** acerbic, pungent **9** acidulous **10** astringent

vin ordinaire 12 ordinary wine **20** inexpensive table wine

vintage 3 era, old **4** aged, date, fine, rare **5** epoch, great, prime, prize **6** choice, period **7** ancient, antique **8** sterling, superior **9** excellent, out-of-date, wonderful **11** outstanding **12** old-fashioned

Viola (Cesario)
character in: 12 Twelfth Night
author: 11 Shakespeare

violate 4 rape **5** abuse, break **6** defile, invade, ravish **7** disobey, outrage, profane **8** dishonor, infringe, trespass **9** blaspheme, desecrate, disregard, trample on **10** contravene, transgress **12** encroach upon

violation 5 abuse **6** breach **8** trespass **9** sacrilege **10** defilement, infraction **11** desecration, dishonoring **12** en-

croachment, infringement **13** contravention, nonobservance, transgression

violence 4 fury, rage **5** force, might, power **6** impact **7** out rage **8** ferocity, savagery, severity **9** brutality, intensity, onslaught **10** bestiality, fierceness **11** desecration, profanation **13** ferociousness, physical force **16** bloodthirstiness

violent 3 hot **4** wild **5** cruel, fiery **6** brutal, fierce, insane, raging, savage, severe, strong, unruly **7** berserk, furious, intense, rampant **8** maniacal, vehement **9** explosive, ferocious, hotheaded, murderous, unbridled **10** passionate **11** full of force, intractable, tempestuous **12** ungovernable **14** uncontrollable

Violent Bear It Away, The
author: 15 Flannery O'Connor

Violent Land, The
author: 10 Jorge Amado

violet 5 Viola
varieties: 3 dog, red **4** bush, pale, pine, rock, tree, wood **5** coast, cream, dame's, false, flame, green, marsh, pansy, sweet, water **6** Alaska, alpine, Canada, garden, German, horned, plains, stream **7** African, English, Mexican, Olympic, Persian, redwood, scarlet, striped, two-eyed **8** bird-foot, crowfoot, dog-tooth, florist's, hook-spur, Labrador, larkspur, Missouri, trailing **9** early blue, evergreen, ivy-leaved, marsh blue, sage brush, tall white **10** Australian, great basin, Philippine, sweet white, western dog, woolly blue, yellow wood **11** Alpine marsh, American dog, arrow-leaved, Confederate, downy yellow, early yellow, lance-leaved, long-spurred, northern bog, strap-leaved **12** eastern water, great-spurred, kidney-leaved, northern blue, smooth yellow **13** common African, Halberd-leaved, northern downy, northern white, purple prairie, southern coast, white dog-tooth, yellow prairie **14** primrose-leaved, triangle-leaved **16** California golden, large-leaved white **17** round-leaved yellow, western sweet white **18** western round-leaved

violin family
instruments: 3 kit **5** cello, rebec, viola **7** baryton **8** bass viol, lyra viol, violetta **10** hurdy-gurdy **11** viola d'a more, violoncello **12** tromba marina, viola pomposa **13** lira da braccio **14** violino piccolo **15** hardanger fiddle

viper 3 asp, boa **5** adder, krait **9** puff adder **10** copperhead, fer-de-lance **11** rattlesnake
group of: 4 nest

Viper's Tangle, The
author: 15 Francois Mauriac

virago 3 nag **4** fury **5** harpy, scold,

shrew, vixen **6** dragon, gorgon **7** she-wolf **8** battle-ax, fishwife, harridan **9** termagant, Xanthippe

Virbius
origin: **5** Roman
god of: **6** forest **7** hunting

Virchow, Rudolf
field: **8** medicine **9** pathology
nationality: **6** German
completed formulation of: **10** cell theory

Virgil *see* **8** Vergil

virgin 4 girl, lass, maid, Mary, pure **6** chaste, damsel, maiden, unused **7** unmixed **8** pristine **9** unalloyed, undefiled, unsullied, untouched **10** unpolluted **13** unadulterated **14** uncontaminated
constellation of: **5** Virgo

Virgin *see* **4** Mary

Virginia
abbreviation: **2** VA
nickname: **11** Old Dominion
capital: **8** Richmond
largest city: **7** Norfolk
others: **5** Galax, Luray, Salem **6** Marion **7** Bedford, Bristol, Emporia, Fairfax, Pulaski, Roanoke **8** Danville, Hopewell, Manassas, Staunton, St Albans, Tazewell, Yorktown **9** Arlington, Lexington, Lynchburg **10** Alexandria, Appomattox, Petersburg, Portsmouth, Waynesboro, Winchester **11** Newport News **12** Hampton Roads, Martinsville, Williamsburg **13** Virginia Beach **14** Fredericksburg **15** Charlottesville
college: **3** Lee **7** Hampton, Madison, Radford **8** Longwood, Richmond **10** Washington **11** Mary Baldwin, Old Dominion **13** Randolph Macon **14** Averett Hollins, Mary Washington, William and Mary
feature:
  battle site: **7** Bull Run **8** Fair Oaks, Manassas, Richmond, Yorktown **10** Petersburg, Seven Pines, Wilderness **12** Spotsylvania **14** Fredericksburg **16** Chancellorsville
  dam: **4** Kerr
  historical site: **10** Monticello **11** Mount Vernon **12** Williamsburg **13** Stratford Hall
  national monument: **26** George Washington Birthplace
  national park: **10** Shenandoah **26** Colonial National Historical
tribe: **6** Saponi, Tutelo **7** Monacan **8** Manahoac, Meherrin, Nottaway, Pamunkey, Powhatan **9** Matchotic **10** Appomuttoc
people: **9** Henry Clay, John Rolfe, John Smith **10** Robert E Lee, Walter Reed **11** George Mason **12** John Marshall, Patrick Henry **13** Samuel Houston **14** Cyrus McCormick **15** Meriwether Lewis **17** Booker T Washington, Richard Evelyn Bird

18 Light-Horse Harry (Henry) Lee
lake: **4** Kerr **5** Smith
land rank: **11** thirty-sixth
mountain: **5** Cedar **6** Clinch, Elliot **8** Baldknob **9** Allegheny, Blueridge
  highest point: **6** Rogers
physical feature:
  bay: **10** Chesapeake
  bridge: **7** Natural
  caverns: **5** Luray
  port: **7** Norfolk **8** Richmond **10** Portsmouth **11** Newport News
  tunnel: **7** Natural
  valley: **9** Shenandoah
president: **9** John Tyler **11** James Monroe **12** James Madison **13** Woodrow Wilson, Zachary Taylor **15** Thomas Jefferson **16** George Washington **20** William Henry Harrison
river: **3** Dan **4** York **5** James **7** Potomac, Rapidan, Roanoke **10** Appomattox, Shenandoah **12** Rappahannock
state admission: **5** tenth
state bird: **8** cardinal
state flower: **16** flowering dogwood
state motto: **17** Thus Ever To Tyrants
state song: **24** Carry Me Back to Old Virginia
state tree: **7** dogwood

Virginian, The
author: **10** Owen Wister
character: **5** Betsy, Randy, Steve **6** Shorty **7** Trampas **9** Molly Wood **10** Judge (Henry) Garth
cast: **8** Lee J Cobb **10** Gary Clarke, James Drury, Pippa Scott, Randy Boone **11** Doug McClure **12** Roberta Shore
setting: **11** Shiloh Ranch **16** Wyoming Territory

Virginians, The
author: **25** William Makepeace Thackeray

Virgin Mary
ingredient: **11** tomato juice

Virgin Soil
author: **12** Ivan Turgenev

Virgo
symbol: **6** virgin
planet: **7** Mercury
rules: **7** service
zodiac: **5** sixth
born: **6** August **9** September

virile 4 bold **5** brave, hardy, husky, lusty, macho, manly **6** brawny, heroic, manful, mighty, potent, robust, strong **7** valiant **8** fearless, forceful, muscular, powerful, resolute, stalwart, vigorous **9** audacious, masculine, masterful, strapping, undaunted **10** courageous **12** stouthearted

virtual 5 tacit **7** implied **8** implicit, indirect **9** essential, practical **11** substantial

virtually 8 in effect **9** in essence **11** essentially, in substance, practically

13 substantially **14** for the most part **23** for all practical purposes, to all intents and purposes

virtue 5 honor, value **6** purity, reward **7** benefit, decency, honesty, modesty, probity **8** chastity, goodness, morality, strength **9** advantage, good point, innocence, integrity, principle, rectitude, virginity **11** strong point, uprightness

virtuosity 7 mastery **8** artistry, wizardry **14** accomplishment

virtuoso 4 whiz **6** expert, genius, master, wizard **7** artiste, prodigy **10** master hand

virtuous 4 good, just, pure **5** moral **6** chaste, decent, modest **7** ethical, upright **8** innocent, laudable, virginal **9** continent, exemplary, honorable, righteous, unsullied **11** commendable, meritorious **12** praiseworthy **14** high-principled

virtuous person
Hebrew: **6** zaddik

Virtus
personifies: **7** courage

virtute et armis 15 by virtue and arms
motto of: **11** Mississippi

virulent 5 toxic **6** bitter, deadly, lethal, malign **7** harmful, hostile, hurtful, noxious, vicious **8** spiteful, venomous **9** injurious, malicious, poisonous, rancorous, resentful, unhealthy **10** malevolent, pernicious **11** acrimonious, deleterious

virus 3 bug **4** germ **7** microbe **11** computer bug **13** microorganism

vis 5 force, power **8** strength

visage 3 air **4** face, look, mien **5** image **6** aspect **7** profile **8** demeanor, features **9** semblance **10** appearance **11** countenance, physiognomy

vis-a-vis 8 eye to eye, together **9** in company, privately, tete-a-tete **10** face-to-face, side by side **11** as opposed to **12** in contrast to **14** as compared with, confidentially **19** as distinguished from

viscera 4 guts **6** bowels **7** innards, insides **8** entrails **10** intestines

visceral 3 gut **5** crude **6** earthy **11** instinctive

viscous 5 gluey, gooey, gummy, slimy, tacky, thick **6** sticky, syrupy, viscid **9** glutinous

Vishnu
in trinity of: **4** Siva **5** Shiva **6** Brahma
religion: **8** Hinduism
called: **9** Preserver
avatar: **7** Krishna

visibility 7 ceiling, clarity, horizon **10** definition, prominence **11** range of view **12** distinctness **14** perceptibility **15** conspicuousness, discernibleness

visible 4 open **5** clear, plain **6** in view,

marked, patent **7** blatant, evident, glaring, in focus, in sight, obvious, pointed, salient, seeable **8** apparent, distinct, manifest, palpable, revealed **9** prominent **10** noticeable, observable, pronounced **11** conspicuous, discernible, inescapable, perceivable, perceptible, well-defined **12** unmistakable

vision 4 idea **5** dream, fancy, ghost, sight **6** notion **7** concept, fantasy, phantom, specter **8** daydream, eyesight, illusion **9** foresight **10** apparition, conception, perception, revelation **11** discernment, imagination **15** materialization

visionary 4 seer **6** dreamy, unreal, zealot **7** dreamer, fanatic, fancied, utopian **8** delusive, fanciful, idealist, illusory, romantic, theorist **9** imaginary, unfounded **10** chimerical, daydreamer, idealistic, starry-eyed **11** imaginative, impractical **13** insubstantial

Vision of Judgement, The
    author: **9** Lord Byron

visit 4 call, stay **5** haunt, smite **6** affect, assail, attack, befall, call on, punish **7** afflict, assault, go to see, sojourn **8** drop in on, frequent, happen to, look in on, stay with **9** sojourn at **10** be a guest of

Visit, The
    author: **19** Friedrich Durrenmatt

visitant 5 alien **7** arrival, visitor

visitor 5 guest **6** caller **7** company, tourist, tripper, voyager **8** traveler **9** journeyer, sightseer, sojourner, transient **10** houseguest, vacationer

vista 4 view **5** scene **6** vision **7** outlook, picture, scenery **8** panorama, prospect **9** landscape **11** perspective

visual 5 optic **6** ocular **7** optical, seeable, visible **9** for the eye **10** noticeable, observable, ophthalmic **11** perceptible

visualize 5 fancy, image **7** dream of, foresee, imagine, picture **8** envision **10** conceive of, daydream of **16** see in the mind's eye

vita 3 bio **6** resume **9** biography **13** autobiography **15** curriculum vitae

vital 4 life, live **5** alive, basic, chief, quick **6** lively, living, urgent, viable **7** animate, crucial, dynamic, primary, serious, vibrant **8** animated, cardinal, critical, existing, forceful, foremost, material, pressing, spirited, vigorous **9** breathing, energetic, essential, important, necessary, paramount, requisite, vivifying **11** fundamental, significant **13** indispensable

vitality 3 pep, vim, zip **4** zeal, zest **5** verve, vigor **6** energy **8** dynamism, strength, vivacity **9** animation, life force **10** ebullience, enthusiasm, exuberance, liveliness **13** animal spirits

vitalize 6 excite, vivify **7** animate, quicken **8** activate, energize **9** stimu-

late **10** invigorate, strengthen **11** bring to life

vital part 9 essential, necessity, requisite **10** key element, sine qua non **11** requirement

Vital Parts
    author: **12** Thomas Berger

vital principle 5 blood **6** source **9** lifeblood **10** sine qua non

vitals 5 belly **6** bowels **10** intestines **11** vital organs **14** liver and lights

Vita Nuova
    author: **14** Dante Alighieri

vitiate 3 mar **4** thin, undo, void **5** spoil, taint **6** blight, cancel, debase, defile, dilute, impair, infect, injure, poison, weaken **7** abolish, corrupt, pervert, pollute **8** sabotage **9** discredit, undermine **10** adulterate, depreciate, invalidate, make faulty, obliterate **11** contaminate

vitriolic 4 acid **5** acerb, nasty, sharp **6** biting **7** abusive, acerbic, caustic, cutting **8** sardonic, scathing **9** sarcastic, satirical, withering **11** acrimonious **13** hypercritical

vituperate 5 abuse **6** carp at, defame, malign, rail at, rebuke, revile, vilify **7** censure **9** castigate **10** speak ill of **14** inveigh against

vituperation 5 abuse, blame, scorn **6** insult, rebuke, tirade **7** censure, obloquy, slander **8** acrimony, scolding **9** invective **10** defamation, revilement, scurrility **11** castigation, deprecation **12** calumniation, denunciation, faultfinding, vilification **13** tongue-lashing

vituperative 5 harsh **7** abusive **8** scornful **9** insulting, maligning, vilifying **10** censorious, defamatory, scurrilous, slanderous **11** acrimonious, deprecatory

vivace
    music: **5** quick **9** vivacious

vivacious 3 gay **5** jolly, merry, sunny, vital **6** active, bright, bubbly, cheery, genial, lively **7** buoyant **8** animated, bubbling, cheerful, spirited **9** convivial, ebullient, sparkling, sprightly **10** frolicsome, full of life **12** effervescent, lighthearted

vivacity 3 zip **4** dash, elan **5** gaity, verve, vigor **6** energy, spirit **8** buoyancy, vitality **9** animation **10** ebullience, liveliness **13** effervescence

Vivaldi, Antonio
    born: **5** Italy **6** Venice
    composer of: **10** Gloria Mass **14** L'Estro Armonico, The Four Seasons **16** Judith Triumphant **17** Juditha Triumphans, Le Quattro Stagioni **19** Harmonic Inspiration

viva voce 5 aloud **6** orally

Viva Zapata!
    director: **9** Elia Kazan
    cast: **10** Jean Peters **12** Anthony

    Quinn, Marlon Brando
    Oscar for: **15** supporting actor (Quinn)
    script: **13** John Steinbeck

vive 8 long live (whomever)
    opposite: **4** a bas

vive valeque 15 live and keep well

Vivian
    also: **16** The Lady of the Lake
    character in: **16** Arthurian romance
    lover: **6** Merlin

Vivian Grey
    author: **16** Benjamin Disraeli

vivid 3 gay **4** deep, loud, rich **5** clear, shiny, showy **6** bright, florid, garish, lively, moving, strong **7** glowing, graphic, in tense, radiant, shining **8** colorful, definite, distinct, dramatic, emphatic, forceful, lifelike, luminous, lustrous, powerful, stirring, striking, true-life, vigorous **9** brilliant, effulgent, energetic, marvelous, memorable, pictorial, realistic **10** astounding, expressive, impressive, remarkable **11** astonishing, conspicuous, descriptive, inescapable, luminescent, picturesque, resplendent **12** unmistakable **13** extraordinary

vividness 9 intensity **10** brightness, brilliance

vivified 7 revived **8** animated, awakened **9** enlivened, quickened, vitalized **11** invigorated

vivify 6 revive, wake up **7** animate, enliven, quicken **8** vitalize **10** invigorate

vixen 4 fury **5** scold, shrew, witch **6** virago **8** fishwife, harridan, spitfire **9** female fox, termagant

Vladimir
    character in: **15** Waiting for Godot
    author: **7** Beckett

Vlaminck, Maurice de
    born: **5** Paris **6** France
    artwork: **8** Red Trees, The Storm **15** Hamlet in the Snow, Winter Landscape **17** The Bridge at Chatou **18** Picnic in the Country, Street at Marly-le-Roi **21** Landscape with Red Trees

vocabulary 4 cant **5** argot, idiom, lingo, slang, style **6** jargon, patois, speech, tongue **7** dialect, lexicon **8** language, glossary, phrasing **9** word stock **10** vernacular **11** phraseology, terminology

vocal 4 open, oral, sung **5** blunt, frank, lyric **6** candid, choral, direct, spoken, voiced **7** uttered, voluble **8** operatic, viva-voce **9** outspoken, vocalized **10** forthright, of the voice **11** articulated, plainspoken

vocalize 3 air, say **4** sing, vent **5** speak, utter **7** express **9** ventilate **10** articulate **12** put into words

vocation 3 job **4** line, post, role, task

5 berth, field, stint, trade **6** career, estate, metier **7** calling, pursuit, station **8** business, lifework **9** situation **10** assignment, employment, line of work, occupation, profession

vocational 3 job **5** trade **6** career **9** technical **11** specialized **12** occupational

vociferate 4 howl, yell, yelp **5** shout, shout **6** bellow, clamor, cry out, holler, shriek, squeal **7** bluster, call out, exclaim, screech **9** ejaculate **11** make a racket **12** raise a rumpus

vociferation 3 cry **4** howl, yell, yelp **5** noise, shout **6** bellow, clamor, outcry, shriek, squeal, uproar **7** screech **11** ejaculation, exclamation

vociferous 4 loud **5** noisy, vocal **6** shrill **7** blatant **8** piercing, shouting, strident, vehement **9** clamorous, outspoken **10** boisterous, loud-voiced, uproarious **11** importunate

vodka
origin: **6** Poland, Russia
drink: **10** Moscow Mule **12** Cosmopolitan
with amaretto: **9** Godmother
with bouillon: **8** Bullshot
with cider: **15** Brewster Special
with Cognac: **7** Cossack
with cranberry juice: **10** Cape Codder
with creme de cacao: **7** Barbara **9** Ninotchka **11** Russian Bear **12** Velvet Hammer, White Russian
with curacao: **8** Aqueduct
with Galliano: **16** Harvey Wallbanger
with gin: **15** Russian Cocktail
with kahlua or Tia Maria: **12** Black Russian
with kirsch: **12** Volga Boatman
with orange juice: **11** screwdriver
with tomato juice: **10** Bloody Mary
with vermouth: **8** Kangaroo **9** Corkscrew

vogue 3 fad **4** mode, rage **5** craze, style, trend **6** custom **7** fashion **8** currency, practice, the thing **10** acceptance, popularity **11** the last word **12** popular favor **14** the latest thing **15** prevailing taste

voguish 4 chic **5** smart **6** modish **7** faddish, stylish **11** fashionable

voice 3 air, say **4** alto, bass, part, role, tone, vent, vote, will, wish **5** speak, state, tenor, utter **6** choice, desire, option, reveal, singer, speech **7** declare, divulge, express, opinion, singers, soprano **8** announce, baritone, delivery, disclose, proclaim, vocalize **9** contralto, enunciate, pronounce, ventilate **10** articulate, intonation, modulation, prefer ence, vocal sound **11** communicate **12** articulation, mezzo-soprano **13** participation, power of speech

voiceless 3 mum **4** deaf, mute, surd **6** silent **7** anaudia, aphonic, spirate

voice of the people
Latin: **9** vox populi

void 4 bare, emit, free, null, pass **5** annul, blank, clear, drain, eject, empty, purge **6** barren, cancel, devoid, recant, repeal, revoke, vacant, vacuum **7** abolish, drained, emptied, exhaust, invalid, lacking, nullify, pour out, rescind, reverse, vacuity, wanting **8** depleted, evacuate, nugatory, renounce, throw out **9** destitute, discharge, emptiness, exhausted, repudiate **10** empty space, invalidate, not in force **11** countermand, inoperative

voidance 7 voiding **8** ejection, emission **9** discharge, expulsion

Voight, Jon
born: **9** Yonkers NY
roles: **7** Joe Buck **8** The Champ **10** Coming Home (Oscar) **11** Deliverance **13** The Odessa File **14** Catch Twenty-Two, Midnight Cowboy

voila 3 see **4** look **9** there it is

volatile 4 rash, wild **5** brash, giddy, moody **6** fickle, fitful **7** erratic, flighty, gaseous **8** eruptive, reckless, unstable, unsteady, vaporous, variable **9** explosive, frivolous, mercurial, spasmodic, unsettled **10** capricious, changeable, evaporable, inconstant, irresolute, vaporizing **12** undependable **13** temperamental, unpredictable

volition 4 will **6** choice, option **8** choosing, decision, free will **10** discretion, resolution **13** determination

volley 5 burst, salvo **6** shower **7** barrage **8** outbreak, outburst **9** broadside, discharge, fusillade **10** outpouring

Volpone (The Fox)
author: **9** Ben Jonson
character: **5** Celia, Mosca **7** Bonario, Corvino, Voltore **9** Corbaccio, Peregrine **18** Lady Politic Would-Be, Lord Politic Would-Be

Volsung
origin: **12** Scandinavian
mentioned in: **8** Volsunga
grandfather: **4** Odin **5** Othin
son: **7** Sigmund
daughter: **5** Signy

Volsunga
origin: **9** Icelandic **12** Scandinavian
form: **4** saga
time: **17** thirteenth century
subject: **8** Volsungs

Volta, Alessandro, Count
nationality: **7** Italian
invented: **15** electric battery
discovered: **10** methane gas

Voltaic
also: **3** Gur
language family: **16** Niger-Kordofanian
group: **10** Niger-Congo
includes: **5** Mossi

Voltaire, Francois
real name: **19** Francois Marie Arouet

author of: **5** Zadig, Zaire **6** Alzire, Merope **7** Candide, L'Ingenu, Mahomet **11** The Henriade **16** The Maid of Orleans **23** Philosophical Dictionary
member of: **11** Philosophes

Volturnus
origin: **5** Roman
personifies: **4** wind **8** east wind **13** southeast wind

voluble 4 glib **5** wordy **6** chatty, fluent **7** twining **8** effusive, flippant, rotating, twisting **9** garrulous, talkative **10** loquacious

volume 4 book, bulk, heap, mass, size, tome **5** folio, sound, tract **6** amount, extent, quarto **7** measure **8** capacity, loudness, quantity, treatise, vastness **9** abundance, aggregate, magnitude, monograph **10** dimensions

voluminous 5 ample, large **7** copious, massive, sizable **8** abundant **9** extensive

Volund see **7** Wayland

voluntary 6 willed **8** free-will, intended, optional, unforced **10** deliberate **11** intentional, volunteered **13** discretionary, noncompulsory

volunteer 5 offer **6** extend, tender, unpaid **7** advance, present, proffer, recruit **8** enlistee **9** voluntary **10** put forward **11** step forward **12** unpaid worker **13** charityworker

Volunteer State
nickname of: **9** Tennessee

Voluptas
origin: **5** Roman
goddess of: **8** pleasure

voluptuary 4 rake, roue **7** epicure, gourmet, seducer **8** gourmand, hedonist, sybarite **9** bon vivant, debauchee, high liver, libertine, womanizer **10** gastronome, sensualist **14** pleasure seeker

voluptuous 4 soft **6** carnal, erotic, sexual, smooth, wanton **7** fleshly, lustful, sensual **8** sensuous **9** debauched, dissolute, luxurious, sybaritic **10** dissipated, hedonistic, lascivious, licentious, profligate **13** self-indulgent **14** pleasure-loving **15** pleasure-seeking

vomit 4 barf, emit, puke **5** eject, expel, heave, retch **7** bring up, throw up, upchuck **8** disgorge **9** discharge, spew forth **10** belch forth **11** regurgitate **15** toss one's cookies

Vonnegut, Kurt, Jr
author of: **8** Jailbird **9** Slapstick **10** Cat's Cradle, Palm Sunday **11** Player Piano **18** Slaughterhouse Five **20** Breakfast of Champions **22** Happy Birthday Wanda June

Von Sternberg, Josef
director of: **12** The Blue Angel

Von Sydow, Max

real name: 18 Carl Adolph von Sydow

born: 4 Lund **6** Sweden

roles: 12 The Emigrants **14** The Seventh Seal **15** The Virgin Spring **16** Wild Strawberries **24** The Greatest Story Ever Told

voracious 6 greedy **7** hoggish **8** edacious, ravenous **10** gluttonous, insatiable, omnivorous

vortex 4 eddy **7** cyclone, twister **9** maelstrom, whirlpool, whirlwind

votary 3 fan **4** buff **6** zealot **7** admirer, devotee, fanatic, habitue **8** adherent, champion, disciple, follower, partisan **10** aficionado, enthusiast **11** afficionado

vote 3 say **4** poll **5** voice **6** ballot, choice, option, ticket **8** approval, decision, election, judgment, suffrage **9** franchise, selection **10** plebiscite, preference, referendum **11** cast a ballot **13** determination

vouch 4 back **6** affirm, attest, back up, uphold, verify **7** certify, confirm, endorse, support, sustain, swear to, warrant, witness **8** attest to, maintain **9** guarantee **11** corroborate **12** authenticate

voucher 4 chip, chit **5** check, proof **6** surety, ticket **7** receipt, warrant **8** warranty **9** affidavit, debenture **10** credential **11** certificate **12** verification **14** authentication

vouchsafe 4 give **5** allow, deign,

favor, grant **6** bestow, convey, tender **7** concede **10** condescend

vow 4 oath, word **5** swear, troth, vouch **6** affirm, assert, assure, parole, pledge, plight, stress **7** declare, promise, resolve **8** contract **9** emphasize **11** word of honor **13** solemn promise

vox populi 14 popular opinion **16** voice of the people

voyage 4 sail **6** cruise **7** passage **8** crossing, navigate **9** ocean trip **10** sea journey

Voyage of the Beagle, The
    author: 13 Charles Darwin

voyager 5 rover **7** cruiser, pilgrim, rambler, tourist **8** traveler, wayfarer **9** jet-setter, journeyer, sightseer **10** adventurer **12** excursionist, globe-trotter, peregrinator **13** world traveler

Voyage to the Bottom of the Sea
    character: 6 Doctor **8** Kowalsky, Stu Riley, (Cdr/Capt) Lee Crane **9** Patterson **10** (Lt Cdr) Chip Morton **11** (Chief Petty Officer) Curley Jones **12** Chief Sharkey **14** (Adm) Harriman Nelson
    cast: 9 Allan Hunt, Del Monroe **10** Henry Kulky, Paul Trinka **11** Richard Bull, Terry Becker **12** David Hedison **13** Robert Dowdell **15** Richard Basehart
    submarine: 7 Seaview
    explorer: 7 Sea Crab
    mini-sub: 10 Flying Fish

Vronsky, Count Alexei

character in: **12** Anna Karenina
    author: 7 Tolstoy

Vulcan
    origin: 5 Roman
    god of: 4 fire **12** metalworking
    epithet: 8 Mulciber
    corresponds to: 10 Hephaestus, Hephaistos

vulgar 3 low **4** base, rude **5** crude, dirty, gross, rough **6** coarse, common, filthy, ribald, risque, smutty **7** boorish, ill-bred, lowbrow, obscene, uncouth **8** impolite, indecent, off-color, ordinary, plebeian **9** offensive, tasteless, unrefined **10** suggestive **11** ill-mannered, proletarian **12** pornographic, uncultivated

vulgarian 3 oaf **4** boor, lout **5** brute, yahoo **7** Babbitt **9** ignoramus **10** philistine **16** anti-intellectual

vulgarity 8 bad taste, rudeness **9** crudeness, grossness, indecency, indecorum, obscenity **10** coarseness, ill manners, indelicacy, smuttiness **11** boorishness, pornography **12** impoliteness **13** tastelessness

vulnerable 4 weak **7** exposed **8** helpless, insecure **9** sensitive, unguarded **10** easily hurt, undefended **11** defenseless, susceptible, thin-skinned, unprotected

Vye, Eustacia
    character in: 17 Return of the Native
    author: 5 Hardy

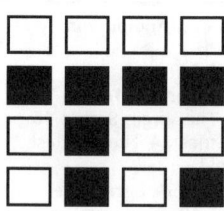

wacky, whacky 3 odd **4** nuts **5** crazy, kooky **6** cuckoo, insane, kookie **7** cracked, foolish, touched **9** eccentric, senseless **10** irrational **12** crackbrained

wad 3 bat, pad **4** cram, head, heap, lump, mass, tuft **5** money, stuff **6** bundle, riches, stop up **7** fortune **8** bankroll, plumbago

waddle 3 wag **4** sway **6** hobble, toddle, totter, wobble

wade 4 ford, plod, plow, toil, trek **5** labor **6** drudge, trudge **9** walk in mud **11** walk in water

wafer 4 chip **5** candy, flake **6** cookie **7** cracker **15** unleavened bread

waft 4 blow, puff **5** drift, float

wag 3 bob, wit **4** card, move, stir, wave **5** clown, droll, flick, joker, shake **6** jester, jiggle, switch, twitch, waggle, wiggle, wigwag **7** buffoon, farceur, flicker, flutter **8** comedian, humorist, jokester **9** oscillate **11** wisecracker **14** life of the party

wage 3 fee, pay **6** income, salary **7** carry on, conduct, payment, revenue, stipend **8** earnings, engage in, maintain, practice **9** emolument, undertake **10** recompense **12** compensation, remuneration

wage earner 6 worker **8** employee **9** job holder **12** hourly worker

wager 3 bet, pot **4** ante, pool, risk **5** fancy, guess, stake **6** assume, gamble, hazard **7** imagine, jackpot, presume, suppose, surmise, venture **8** make a bet, theorize **9** speculate **10** conjecture, take a flyer **11** speculation, try one's luck **12** tempt fortune **15** hazard an opinion

wages 3 bet, fee, pay **4** gage, hire **6** fights, reward, return, salary **7** engages, payment, stipend **8** conducts, earnings **9** emolument **10** prosecutes, recompense **12** remuneration

wage war 5 fight **6** combat **7** contend, make war **8** do battle **12** march against

waggery 5 chaff **6** banter, riding **7** joshing, kidding, ragging, ribbing **8** chaffing, drollery, raillery, twitting **French: 8** badinage

waggish 5 droll, funny **7** comical, puckish **8** humorous

waggle 4 wave **5** wield **8** brandish

Wagner, Honus
　real name: 15 John Peter Wagner
　nickname: 14 Flying Dutchman
　sport: 8 baseball
　position: 9 shortstop
　team: 17 Pittsburgh Pirates

Wagner, Richard
　born: 7 Germany, Leipzig
　composer of: 5 Faust **6** Rienzi **7** Die Feen **8** Parsifal **9** Lohengrin **10** Tannhauser, The Fairies **14** Siegfried Idyll **16** The Mastersingers, Tristan and Isolde, Wesendonck Lieder **17** The Flying Dutchman **20** Der Ring des Nibelungen, The Ring of the Nibelungs **27** Die Meistersinger von Nurnberg
　　the Ring Cycle Part 1: 12 Das Rheingold, The Rhine Gold
　　the Ring Cycle Part 2: 10 Die Walkure **11** The Valkyrie
　　the Ring Cycle Part 3: 9 Siegfried
　　the Ring Cycle Part 4: 15 Gotterdammerung **17** Twilight of the Gods

Wagner, Robert
　born: 9 Detroit MI
　wife: 11 Natalie Wood
　roles: 6 Switch **10** Hart to Hart **13** It Takes a Thief, Prince Valiant, The Longest Day **24** All the Fine Young Cannibals

wagon 3 car, van **4** cart, dray, tram, wain **5** coach, lorry, tonga, truck **7** caisson **10** automobile, battleship
　covered: 15 prairie schooner
　maker: 10 wainwright
　police: 10 Black Maria
　Russian: 6 telega
　sideless: 6 rolley
　track: 3 rut

Wagon Train
　character: 9 Bill Hawks **11** Barnaby West, Cooper Smith, Duke Shannon **14** Charlie Wooster, Major Seth Adams **15** Christopher Hale, Flint McCullough
　cast: 8 Ward Bond **11** Scott Miller, Terry Wilson **12** Frank McGrath, John McIntire, Michael Burns, Robert Fuller, Robert Horton

waif 5 gamin, stray **6** gamine, urchin **7** mudlark **9** foundling **10** ragamuffin, street arab **11** guttersnipe **13** homeless child **14** tatterdemalion

wail 3 cry **4** bawl, howl, keen, moan, roar, weep, yell **5** groan, shout, whine **6** bellow, bemoan, bewail, cry out, lament, outcry, plaint **7** keening, moaning, wailing **9** caterwaul **10** rend the air **11** lamentation

waist 3 top **5** shirt **6** blouse, bodice, middle **7** midriff **9** mid-region, waistband, waistline **10** middle part, midsection, shirtwaist

waistband 4 belt, sash **5** cinch **6** girdle

waistcoat 4 vest **5** benjy **6** jacket, jerkin, veskit, vestee, weskit **7** singlet **French: 5** gilet

wait 4 halt, stay, stop **5** dally, delay, pause, tarry **6** linger, put off **7** suspend **8** postpone, stopover **9** deferment **10** suspension **11** continuance **12** postponement

wait for 6 expect **10** anticipate

Waiting for Godot
　author: 13 Samuel Beckett
　character: 8 Estragon, Vladimir

wait on 5 serve **6** assist, attend

waive 4 stay **5** defer, forgo, let go, table, yield **6** give up, not use, put off, shelve **7** forbear, lay over **8** disclaim, forswear, postpone, renounce **9** surrender

waiver 9 dismissal **10** abdication, disclaimer **11** abandonment **12** renunciation **14** relinquishment

wake 4 fire, path, stir, wash **5** rally, rouse, trail, train, vigil **6** arouse, course, excite, kindle, revive **7** enliven, provoke, quicken **8** backwash **9** galvanize, stimulate **11** resuscitate

wakeful 4 wary **5** alert, astir **7** careful, heedful **8** cautious, restless, vigilant, watchful **9** insomniac, observant, sleepless **10** unsleeping **11** circumspect

wake up 4 rise **5** arise **6** vivify **7** animate, enliven **8** vitalize **9** stimulate

Walcott, Joe
　real name: 18 Arnold Raymond Cream
　nickname: 9 Jersey Joe
　sport: 6 boxing
　class: 11 heavyweight

Walden, or Life in the Woods
　author: 17 Henry David Thoreau

Wales
　other name: 5 Cymru **7** Cambria
　part of: 13 United Kingdom

title of British heir apparent: 13
Prince of Wales
capital: 7 Cardiff
cities: 4 Rhyl, Ross **5** Flint, Towyn **6**
Amlwch, Bangor, Brecon, Sidney **7**
Cwmbran, Herford, Newport, Rhon-
dda, Swansea **8** Aberdare, Caerleon,
Holyhead, Pembroke **9** Fishguard,
Glamorgan **10** Caernarvon, Caerphilly, Carmarthen **11** Aberystwyth
12 Milford Haven **13** Kidderminster,
Merthyr-Tydfil
division: 5 Clwyd, Dyfed, Flint,
Gwent, Powys **6** Radnor **7** Denbigh,
Gwynedd **8** Anglesey, Cardigan,
Monmouth, Pembroke **9** Brecknoch,
Glamorgan, Merioneth **10** Caernarvon, Carmarthen, Montgomery
emblem: 4 leek
government: 29 constituent part of
Great Britain
measure: 5 cover **7** cantred, crannoc,
listred
island: 4 Mona **5** Caldy **8** Anglesey,
Holyhead
lake: 4 Bala **6** Vyrnwy
mountain: 6 Berwyn **8** Cambrian **9**
Prescelly **13** Brecon Beacons
highest point: 7 Snowdon
river: 3 Dee, Usk, Wye **4** Alun, Taff,
Tawe, Teme, Towy **5** Clwyd, Conwy,
Dovey, Neath, Teifi **6** Conway, Severn, Vyrnwy
sea: 5 Irish **8** Atlantic
physical feature:
　bay: 7 Swansea **8** Cardigan, Trema-
　doc, Tremadog
　channel: 7 Bristol **9** St George's
　hills: 7 Malvern
　peninsula: 5 Lleyn
　strait: 5 Menai
　valley: 7 Rhondda
people: 4 Celt, Kelt **5** Cymry, Kymry,
Welsh **7** Brython, Silures, Taffies **8**
Awabokal, Cambrian **9** Siluridan
　actor: 6 Burton **8** Williams **13**
　Richard Burton, Emlyn Williams
　artist: 4 John
　author: 3 Map **5** Jones, Lewis,
　Mapes, Parry **6** Machan, Thrale **9**
　Llewellyn **11** Dylan Thomas **14**
　Dafydd ap Gwylym
　god: 3 Deu, Dew **4** Bran, Gwyn **5**
　Dylan **7** Gwydion
　leader: 5 Bevan **6** Rhodri **8** Hywel
　Dwa **11** Cadwallader **12** Bishop
　Morgan **13** Owen Glendower **16**
　David Lloyd George **18** Llewelyn
　ap Gruffydd
language: 5 Welsh **6** Celtic, Cymric,
Keltic, Kymric **7** Cymraeg, English
religion: 8 Anglican **9** Methodist **10**
Protestant **12** Presbyterian
place:
　bridge: 6 Severn
　castle: 6 Conway **7** Harlech **9**
　Beaumaris **10** Caernarvon, Caer-
　philly **11** Aberystwyth

feature:
　festival: 10 Eisteddfod
　stories: 10 Mabinogion
food:
　dish: 8 flummery
Walesa, Lech
　born: 6 Poland
　leader of: 10 Solidarity
　voted: 7 premier
wander aimlessly 5 amble, stray **7**
ramble, stroll **7** meander, saunter
wandering 5 lapse **8** rambling, straying **9** deviation **10** aberration, digressive, discursive, maundering, meandering, roundabout **11** abnormality **12**
idiosyncrasy **13** nonconformity **14** circumlocutory
Wandering Jew, The
　author: 9 Eugene Sue
Wanderings
　author: 10 Chaim Potok
wane 3 ebb **4** fade, sink **5** abate,
droop, waste **6** ebbing, fading, lessen,
weaken, wither **7** abating, decline,
dwindle, subside **8** decrease, diminish, fade away **9** dwindling, lessening,
recession, subsiding, weakening, withering
wangle 4 worm **5** trick **6** jockey,
scheme **7** finagle, wheedle **8** engineer,
intrigue, maneuver **9** machinate **10**
manipulate
wanness 6 pallor **8** grayness, paleness
9 ashenness **10** sallowness, sickliness
13 colorlessness
want 4 hunt, lack, need, seek, wish **5**
covet, crave, fancy **6** dearth, demand,
desire, hunger, penury **7** be needy,
craving, hope for, long for, paucity,
pine for, poverty, require, wish for **8**
scarcity, shortage, yearn for, yearning
9 indigence, necessity, pauperism, privation, requisite **10** deficiency, insolvency **11** destitution, requirement **13**
impecuniosity, insufficiency, pennilessness **14** impoverishment
Wanted: Dead or Alive
　character: 11 Josh Randall
　cast: 12 Steve McQueen
　job: 12 bounty hunter
　gun: 8 Mare's Leg
wanting 5 short **6** absent **7** lacking,
missing **9** defective, deficient, imperfect **10** inadequate **11** substandard **12**
insufficient
wanton 4 bawd, fast, jade, lewd, rake,
roue, slut, tart **5** gross, hussy, loose,
satyr, whore **6** chippy, harlot, lecher
7 bestial, immoral, lustful, obscene,
seducer, trollop, willful **8** careless,
heedless, mindless, needless, strumpet, sybarite, unchaste **9** abandoned,
adulterer, concubine, debauched, debauchee, dissolute, lecherous, libertine,
malicious, senseless, womanizer **10**
deliberate, fornicator, groundless, licentious, malevolent, profligate,

prostitute, sensualist, unprovoked, voluptuary **11** fornicatrix, promiscuous,
unjustified, whoremaster **13** inconsiderate, irresponsible
wapiti 3 elk **4** deer **11** American elk
　female: 3 cow
　literally: 9 white rump
　male: 4 bull
　species: 16 Cervus canadensis
Wapshot Chronicle
　author: 11 John Cheever
war 5 clash, fight **6** attack, battle, combat, invade **7** contend **8** conflict,
fighting, struggle **10** opposition **11**
hostilities
　god of: 4 Ares, Odin **5** Othin **8** Quiri-
　nus
　goddess of: 4 Enyo **6** Athena,
　Athene, Inanna, Ishtar, Pallas, Saitis
　7 Bellona, Mylitta **11** Tritogeneia **12**
　Pallas Athena **18** Alalcomenean
　Athena
War and Peace
　author: 10 Leo Tolstoy
　character: 7 Kutuzov **8** Napoleon **13**
　Natasha Rostov, Nikolay Rostov, Pi-
　erre Bezuhov **14** Anatole Kuragin **15**
　Andrey Bolkonsky **19** Ellen Kuragin
　Bezuhov **22** Princess Marya Bolkon-
　sky
War and Remembrance
　author: 10 Herman Wouk
warble 4 lump, purl, sing **5** carol,
larva, trill, tumor, yodel **6** growth,
quaver, ripple **7** twitter, vibrate, whistle
war cry 6 slogan **8** Geronimo
ward 4 zone **5** avert, block, repel **6**
charge, thwart **7** beat off, fend off,
prevent, quarter **8** pavilion, precinct,
stave off, turn away **9** dependent,
forestall
　French: 7 protege
warden 5 guard **6** keeper, ranger, sentry **7** curator, manager **8** guardian,
watchman **9** protector **14** superintendent
Warden, The
　author: 15 Anthony Trollope
ward off 5 avert **7** prevent
wardrobe 4 togs **5** chest **6** attire,
closet, outfit **7** apparel, clothes **8**
clothing, garments **10** cedar chest **12**
clothespress
　French: 6 bureau **7** armoire, com-
　mode **10** chiffonier **11** habillement
wares 4 line **5** stock **7** staples **8** supplies **9** inventory **11** commodities,
merchandise
warfare 5 fight **6** battle, combat **8**
conflict, fighting **11** hostilities
Warhol, Andy
　born: 14 Philadelphia PA
　artwork: 9 Brillo Box, Liz Taylor **13**
　Marilyn Monroe **16** Campbell's Soup

Can **20** Green Coca-Cola Bottles
protegee: **12** Edie Sedgwick

wariness **7** caution **9** alertness, suspicion, vigilance **11** carefulness, guardedness, heedfulness **12** watchfulness **14** circumspection

warlike **7** hostile, martial, valiant **8** inimical, militant, military **9** bellicose, combative **10** unfriendly **11** belligerent, contentious, threatening
Indian: **8** Arapahoe

warlike attitude **9** hostility, pugnacity **11** bellicosity **12** belligerence, belligerency **13** combativeness **14** aggressiveness

warm **3** hot **4** cook, heat, kind, melt, thaw **5** cheer, happy, sunny, tepid, vivid **6** bright, heated, heat up, joyful, joyous, kindly, lively, loving, simmer, tender **7** affable, cordial, earnest, fervent, glowing, intense **8** animated, cheerful, friendly, gracious, outgoing, pleasant, spirited, vehement, vigorous **9** brilliant **10** passionate **11** kindhearted, sympathetic **12** affectionate, enthusiastic **13** compassionate, tenderhearted

warmhearted **4** kind **6** genial, kindly, loving **7** cordial **10** solicitous **11** sympathetic **12** affectionate **13** compassionate

warm-hued **3** red **4** rosy **5** ruddy, vivid **6** golden, orange, yellow **7** crimson, roseate, scarlet **8** blushing

warmish **5** tepid **7** cooling

warm oneself **4** bask **12** soak up warmth, toast oneself

warmth **3** joy **4** fire, heat, zeal **5** ardor, cheer, verve, vigor **6** fervor, spirit **7** hotness, passion **8** kindness, sympathy **9** animation, happiness, intensity, vehemence **10** affability, compassion, cordiality, enthusiasm, excitement, joyfulness, kindliness, liveliness, lovingness, tenderness **11** earnestness **12** cheerfulness, friendliness, graciousness **15** kindheartedness **17** tenderheartedness

warn **5** alert **6** advise, inform, notify, signal **7** apprise, caution, counsel **8** admonish

warning **4** hint, omen, sign **5** alarm, token **6** advice, notice, signal **7** portent, presage **8** appraisal **9** foretoken **10** intimation **12** notification

War of the Worlds, The
author: **7** H G Wells
invasion by: **8** Martians

war of words **7** dispute, quarrel **8** argument **11** altercation, controversy **12** disagreement

warp **4** bend, bent, bias **5** quirk, twist **6** debase, deform, infect **7** contort, corrupt, distort, leaning, mislead, pervert **8** misguide, misshape, tendency **9** prejudice, proneness **10** contortion, distortion, partiality, proclivity,

propensity **11** deformation, disposition, inclination **14** predisposition

warrant **3** vow **4** aver, avow **5** swear **6** affirm, assert, assure, attest, permit, pledge **7** certify, declare, justify, license, promise **9** authorize, guarantee **10** asseverate, permission **13** authorization

warranty **6** pledge **9** agreement **11** certificate

Warren, Robert Penn
author of: **5** Flood **7** Audubon **8** Promises **10** Now and Then **12** Incarnations **14** All the King's Men **18** World Enough and Time
member of: **12** the Fugitives

warring **7** hostile **8** battling, clashing, fighting, opposing **9** combatant **10** contending **11** belligerent, conflicting, contentious

warrior **7** fighter, soldier, veteran **9** combatant, man-at-arms **10** campaigner **11** legionnaire

Warsaw
area: **11** Stare Miasto
capital of: **6** Poland
landmark: **14** Kazimierzowski **25** Palace of Culture and Science
Polish: **8** Warszawa
river: **7** Vistula
square: **5** Rynek

warship **5** Maine, U-boat **6** corvet **7** Alabama, cruiser, frigate, gunboat, Monitor **8** Bismarck, corvette, Graf Spee, ironclad, man-of-war **9** destroyer, ironsides, Merrimack, submarine **11** dreadnought, torpedo boat **12** Constitution, Old Ironsides **13** Constellation **15** aircraft carrier **16** superdreadnought
fleet: **6** armada
part: **6** turret
plating: **5** armor

War Within and Without
author: **19** Anne Morrow Lindbergh

wary **5** alert **7** careful, guarded, heedful, mindful, prudent, wakeful **8** cautious, discreet, vigilant, watchful **9** suspicious **11** circumspect

wash **3** mop, rub, wet **4** bath, lave, soak, swab, wipe **5** bathe, clean, float, flood, rinse, scour, scrub **6** drench, shower, sponge **7** cleanse, immerse, launder, laundry, moisten, mopping, shampoo **8** ablution, cleaning, inundate, irrigate, lavation, scouring **9** cleansing **10** laundering

washbasin **3** tub **4** bowl **5** laver **6** lavabo **8** lavatory

washed out **4** drab, dull, pale **5** dingy, faded, white **6** dreary, grayed **8** bleached **9** colorless

washed up, washed-up **4** lost, shot **6** bathed, broken, ruined, undone **7** done for, preened, through **8** bankrupt, done with, fatigued, finished **9** played out, showered

washing **6** laving **7** bathing, laundry, purging, rinsing, soaking **8** cleaning, scouring **9** ablutions, drenching, scrubbing, showering **10** laundering, shampooing

Washington
abbreviation: **2** WA **4** Wash
nickname: **7** Chinook **9** Evergreen
capital: **7** Olympia
largest city: **7** Seattle
others: **4** Omak **5** Pasco **6** Renton, Tacoma, Yakima **7** Ephrata, Everett, Hoquiam, Othello, Pullman, Spokane **8** Aberdeen, Bellevue, Longview, Puyallup, Richland **9** Anacortes, Bremerton, Kennewick, Vancouver, Wenatchee **10** Bellingham, Burlington, Walla Walla **11** Port Angeles
college: **7** Gonzaga, Seattle, Whitman **9** Evergreen, Whitworth **10** Puget Sound **14** Seattle Pacific **15** Pacific Lutheran
feature:
  dam: **10** Bonneville, **11** Grand Coulee
  fort: **5** Lewis
  national park: **7** Olympic **12** Mount Rainier **13** North Cascades
tribe: **3** Hoh **5** Lummi, Makah, Twana **6** Cayuse, Samish, Skagit, Yakima **7** Chinook, Clallam, Clatsop, Cowlitz, Dwamish, Nooksak, Palouse, Quaitso, Sanpoil, Spokane, Squaxon, Tulalip **8** Chehalis, Chimakum, Colville, Nespelim, Nez Perce, Okanagon, Pishquow, Puyallup, Quileute, Quinault, Sahaptin, Salishan, Sinkiuse **9** Nisqually, Quinaielt, Semiahmoo, Skokomish, Swinomish **10** Senijextee, Shoalwater **11** Shahaptaine
people: **7** Seattle **10** Bing Crosby **11** Hank Ketcham **12** Elisha P Ferry **13** Marcus Whitman **15** William O Douglas **19** Isaac Ingalls Stevens
  explorer: **4** Cook, Gray **6** Heceta **9** Vancouver **13** Lewis and Clark
lake: **4** Soap **5** Moses, Union **6** Chelan, Ozette **7** Cle Elum, Cushman, Kachess **8** Crescent, Quinault **9** Keechelus, Wenatchee **10** Washington
land rank: **9** twentieth
mountain: **4** Blue, Jack, Tunk **5** Adams, Baker, Lemei, Logan, Moses, Sloan **6** Kettle, Quartz, Simcoe, Stuart **7** Shuksan **8** Cascades, Olympics, St Helens **11** Kettle River
  highest point: **7** Rainier
physical feature:
  falls: **10** Snoqualmie
  port: **6** Tacoma **7** Everett, Seattle **10** Bellingham
  sound: **5** Puget **7** Rosario
river: **5** Snake, White **6** Yakima **7** Spokane **8** Columbia, Quinault **9** Snohomish **10** Snoqualmie **11** Pend Oreille
state admission: **11** forty-second

state bird: 15 willow goldfinch
state fish: 14 steelhead trout
state flower: 17 coast rhododendron **19** western rhododendron
state motto: 7 By and By (Alki)
state song: 16 Washington My Home
state tree: 14 western hemlock

Washington, George
nickname: 18 Father of His Country
presidential rank: 5 first
party: 10 Federalist
state represented: 2 VA
elected: 11 unanimously
vice president: 5 (John) Adams
cabinet:
  state: 9 (Thomas) Jefferson
  treasury: 8 (Alexander) Hamilton
  war: 4 (Henry) Knox **7** (James) McHenry **9** (Timothy) Pickering
  attorney general: 3 (Charles) Lee **8** (Edmund Jennings) Randolph, (William) Bradford
born: 2 VA **9** Wakefield **18** Westmoreland County
died/buried: 11 Mount Vernon
religion: 12 Episcopalian
interests: 7 fishing, hunting, theater **17** scientific farming
vacation: 11 Mount Vernon
author: 33 The Journal of Major George Washington
political character: 9 president **16** House of Burgesses **24** First Continental Congress **25** Second Continental Congress
  signed: 12 Constitution
civilian career: 6 farmer **8** surveyor
military career:
  war: 13 Revolutionary **15** French and Indian
notable events of lifetime/term: 18 American Revolution
  crossed: 13 Delaware River
  rebellion: 7 Whiskey
  winter at: 11 Valley Forge
father: 9 Augustine
mother: 4 Mary (Ball)
siblings: 5 Betty **6** Samuel **7** Charles, Mildred **13** John Augustine
  half-brother: 6 Butler **8** Lawrence **9** Augustine
  half-sister: 4 Jane
wife: 6 Martha (Dandridge Custis)
children:
  stepchildren: 15 John Parke Custis **17** Martha Parke Custis

Washington DC
airport: 6 Dulles **8** National
basketball team: 7 Mystics, Wizards
capital of: 12 United States
designed by: 7 L'Enfant
football team: 8 Redskins
hockey team: 8 Capitals
landmark: 4 Mall **7** Capitol, Ellipse **8** Pentagon **10** White House **11** National Zoo **12** Ford's Theatre, Franklin Park, Supreme Court **13** Lafayette Park, Rock Creek Park **14** Farragut

Square, Reflecting Pool, Watergate Hotel **15** Lincoln Memorial, McPherson Square **16** National Archives **17** Jefferson Memorial, Library of Congress, National Arboretum **18** Washington Monument **21** Frederick Douglass Home, Robert F Kennedy Stadium **22** Smithsonian Institution **23** National Sculpture Garden **25** Arlington National Cemetery **33** Kennedy Center for the Performing Arts
museum: 5 Freer **7** Renwick **8** Corcoran **9** Hirshhorn **10** African Art **11** Smithsonian **13** Dumbarton Oaks **15** National Gallery **17** Folger Shakespeare **18** Phillips Collection **23** National Portrait Gallery
river: 7 Potomac **9** Rock Creek
street/avenue: 4 Ohio **7** New York, Potomac **12** Constitution, Independence, Pennsylvania **13** Massachusetts
university: 6 Howard **8** American, Catholic **10** Georgetown **11** George Mason **16** George Washington

Washington Square
author: 10 Henry James

wash one's hands of 4 deny, quit **6** give up **7** abandon, decline, disavow, forsake **8** abnegate, cast away, disclaim, forswear, renounce **9** repudiate **10** relinquish

washout 6 fiasco, fizzle **7** failure, letdown **8** disaster **14** disappointment

wash out 4 fade, fail **6** bleach **7** deplete, fatigue **8** enervate, enfeeble **10** debilitate, devitalize

wasp 5 vespa **6** vespid
  variety: 5 paper **6** cuckoo, ensign, hornet, potter, spider **12** yellow jacket

waspish 5 huffy, testy **6** crabby, cranky, ornery, shirty **7** bearish, fretful, peevish, pettish **8** petulant, snappish **9** crotchety, fractious, irascible, irritable, querulous **12** cantankerous

Wasps, The
author: 12 Aristophanes
character: 10 Bdelycleon, Philocleon
  dog: 5 Labes

wassail 5 drink, punch, revel, toast **6** liquor, tipple **7** carouse, revelry **8** beverage, carousal

waste 3 die, ebb, rob **4** fade, loot, melt, raze, raze, ruin, sack, sink, void, wane **5** abate, crush, decay, drain, dregs, droop, empty, offal, smash, spoil, strip, trash, wreck **6** barren, burn up, debris, devour, litter, misuse, ravage, razing, refuse, scraps, steppe, tundra, weaken, wither **7** crumble, decline, deplete, despoil, destroy, dwindle, exhaust, garbage, looting, pillage, plunder, rubbish, shatter, subside **8** badlands, decrease, demolish, diminish, leavings, misapply, misspend, needless, prey upon, remnants, squander, wrecking **9** devastate, dis-

appear, dissipate, emptiness, evaporate, excrement, leftovers, misemploy, ruination, sweepings **10** demolition, plundering, remainders, wilderness **11** destruction, devastation, dissipation, expenditure, fritter away, prodigality, squandering **12** despoliation, extravagance **14** misapplication

waste away 4 fail, rust **7** corrode, decline, eat into

wasted 5 spent **6** used-up **7** ravaged **9** emaciated, exhausted **12** unproductive

wasteful 8 prodigal **9** unthrifty **10** thriftless **11** extravagant, improvident, spendthrift, squandering **12** uneconomical

wastefulness 10 imprudence, lavishness **11** prodigality, squandering **12** extravagance, improvidence

wasteland 6 desert

Waste Land, The
author: 7 T S Eliot
editor: 9 Ezra Pound

waste time 5 dally **6** dawdle, loiter **10** dillydally

watch 3 eye, see **4** heed, look, mark, mind, note, ogle, save, tend **5** alert, guard, scout, stare **6** attend, be wary, gaze at, guards, look at, look on, notice, patrol, peep at, peer at, picket, regard, sentry, survey, tend to **7** be chary, care for, examine, lookout, observe, oversee, protect, stare at **8** pore over, preserve, sentinel, sentries, take heed **9** attention, patrolman, vigilance **10** observance, scrutinize **11** contemplate, observation, superintend, supervision **15** superintendence

watch fire 6 beacon
  kinds: 4 bale **6** signal

watchful 4 wary **5** alert, aware, canny, chary **6** shrewd **7** careful, guarded, heedful, mindful, prudent **8** cautious, open-eyed, vigilant **9** attentive, observant **11** circumspect

watchfulness 4 care, heed **9** attention, diligence, vigilance **13** attentiveness

watchman 5 guard, scout **6** patrol, picket, sentry **7** lookout **8** sentinel **9** patrolman

Watch on the Rhine
director: 13 Herman Shumlin
based on play by: 14 Lillian Hellman
cast: 9 Paul Lukas **10** Bette Davis **19** Geraldine Fitzgerald
Oscar for: 5 actor (Lukas)

watch over 5 guard **6** attend **7** oversee, protect **11** superintend

watchtower 6 beacon, pharos, signal **7** seamark **8** landmark **10** lighthouse

watchword 5 motto **6** byword, slogan

water 3 cut, dip, sea, wet **4** damp, lake, pond, pool, soak, tear, thin **5** douse, flood, H two O, ocean, river, souse **6** dampen, deluge, dilute,

drench, lagoon, splash, stream **7** immerse, moisten **8** inundate, irrigate, sprinkle, submerge **10** adulterate
goddess of: 4 Enki

Water Carrier (Water Bearer)
constellation of: 8 Aquarius

watercolor
French: **9** aquarelle

watercourse 5 canal, river **6** strait **7** channel, conduit, narrows, passage **8** aqueduct

water down 3 cut **6** censor, dilute, weaken **7** thin out **9** expurgate **10** adulterate

watered down 4 weak **6** dilute **7** diluted **8** weakened **11** adulterated

waterfall 7 cascade, Niagara **8** cataract

waterfront 4 dock, mole, pier, quay **5** basin, jetty, levee, wharf **6** marina **7** landing

waterless 3 dry **4** arid, sere **6** barren **7** parched, thirsty **10** desertlike

Waterloo Bridge
director: 11 Mervyn LeRoy
cast: 11 Vivien Leigh **12** Lucile Watson, Robert Taylor **13** Virginia Field
remade as: 4 Gaby

Water Monster (Sea Serpent)
constellation of: 5 Hydra

water of life
Latin: **9** aqua vitae

Waters, Ethel
nickname: 19 Sweet Mama Stringbean
born: 9 Chester PA
roles: 5 Pinky **6** Beulah **21** The Member of the Wedding

Watership Down
author: 12 Richard Adams

Water Snake
constellation of: 6 Hydrus

watertight 9 nonporous **10** impervious **11** impermeable

waterway 5 canal, inlet, river, route **6** gutter, strait, strake, stream **7** channel

Water Wonderland
nickname of: 8 Michigan

watery 3 wet **4** damp, thin, weak **5** fluid, moist, teary **6** liquid, rheumy **7** aqueous, diluted, tearful, tearing **11** adulterated

Watling, Belle
character in: 15 Gone With the Wind
author: 8 Mitchell

Watt, James
nationality: 8 Scottish
developed: 11 steam engine **12** piston engine

Watteau, Jean Antoine
born: 6 France **12** Valenciennes
artwork: 6 Gilles **8** Mezzetin **9** La Finette **10** La Toilette **12** Joys of Living, L'indifferent **13** La Gamme d'Amour **16** Company in the Park, La Lecon de Musique **18** Enseigne de

Gersaint, Gersaint's Signboard, La Comedie Francaise, La Concert de Famille **20** Le Dejeuner en plein air, L'assemblee dans un parc **21** Harlequin and Columbine **23** Embarquement pour Cythere, Italian and French Theater, Jupiter Surprises Antiope, Les Amusements Champetres **24** Conversation in the Open Air, The Embarkation for Cythera

wattle 6 Acacia
varieties: 5 black, broom, cedar, glory, green, hairy, oven's, Sally, swamp **6** frosty, golden, mudgee, orange, silver, sticky **7** bramble, buffalo, coastal, prickly, weeping, Wyalong **8** blue-leaf, cinna- mon, graceful, screw-pod, sunshine **9** red-leaved **10** golden-rain, needle-bush **11** Cootamundra, Mount Morgan, Wallangarra **12** Sydney golden **14** Peppermint-tree **16** Queensland silver

Watts, Sir George Frederic
born: 6 London **7** England
artwork: 4 Hope **14** Physical Energy **17** Paolo and Francesca **19** Anastasio degl'Onesti **45** Caractacus Led in Triumph Through the Streets of Rome **54** Alfred Inciting his Subjects to Prevent the Landing of the Danes

Waugh, Evelyn
author of: 9 Men at Arms **10** Vile Bodies **11** The Loved One **13** Black Mischief, Edmund Campion **14** A Handful of Dust, Decline and Fall **15** A Little Learning **19** Brideshead Revisited **20** Officers and Gentlemen **22** Unconditional Surrender

wave 4 coil, curl, file, flap, line, rank, rise, roll, rush, sway, tier **5** curve, flood, pulse, shake, surge, swell, swing, train, twirl, wield **6** billow, column, comber, deluge, motion, quiver, ripple, roller, signal, spiral, string **7** breaker, flutter, gesture, pulsate, tremble, vibrate, winding **8** brandish, flourish, increase, undulate, whitecap **9** advancing, oscillate, pulsation, vibration **10** salutation, undulation **11** gesticulate, heightening **13** gesticulation

wave at 4 hail **6** signal **7** gesture

wave on 6 beckon, signal **7** gesture **11** gesticulate

waver 4 flap, reel, sway, vary **5** pause, shake, swing, weave **6** careen, change, falter, quiver, totter, wobble **7** flutter, stagger, tremble **8** hesitate, undulate **9** fluctuate, vacillate **10** dillydally **12** shilly-shally

wavering 8 hesitant, waffling **9** undecided **10** hesitating, indecisive, irresolute **11** vacillating

Waverley
author: 14 Sir Walter Scott
character: 12 Flora MacIvor **14** Don-

ald Bean Lean, Edward Waverley **15** Rose Bradwardine **16** Baron Bradwardine **17** Evan Dhu MacCombich **24** Fergus MacIvor Vich Ian Vohr **25** Prince Charles Edward Stuart

wavy 4 onde, unde **5** curly **6** coiled, curved **7** rolling, sinuous, winding **8** mazelike, rippling, tortuous **10** meandering, serpentine, undulating **11** curvilinear **12** labyrinthine

wax 4 grow **5** swell, widen **6** become, blow up, dilate, expand, extend, thrive **7** balloon, develop, enlarge, fill out, inflate, puff out **8** increase

way 3 far, off **4** area, form, lane, pass, path, road, room, wont **5** habit, means, route, space, trail, usage **6** course, custom, far off, manner, method, nature, region, system **7** conduct, passage, pathway, process **8** behavior, distance, practice, remotely, vicinity **9** direction, procedure, technique **12** neighborhood

wayfarer 8 traveler, wanderer **9** sojourner

Wayfaring Stranger
nickname of: 8 Burl Ives

way in 4 door, gate **5** entry **6** access, portal **7** doorway, gateway, ingress **8** approach, entrance

Wayland
also: 6 Volund **7** Wieland
origin: 8 European
king of: 5 elves

waylay 4 lure **5** decoy **6** ambush, assail, attack, entrap **7** assault, ensnare, set upon **8** inveigle

Wayne, Anthony
nickname: 10 Mad Anthony
served in: 10 Indian Wars **16** Revolutionary War
captured: 10 Stony Point
battle: 10 Brandywine, Germantown **13** Fallen Timbers

Wayne, David
real name: 13 Wayne McMeekan
born: 14 Traverse City MI
roles: 5 Sakini **6** Adam's Rib **12** The Front Page **13** Mister Roberts, Tonight We Sing **15** Huckleberry Finn **16** Portrait of Jennie **26** The Teahouse of the August Moon

Wayne, John
real name: 21 Marion Michael Morrison
nickname: 4 Duke
born: 11 Winterset IA
roles: 5 Hondo **6** Chisum **8** Ringo Kid, Rio Bravo, The Alamo, True Grit (Oscar) **9** McLintock, Rio Grande **10** Stagecoach **11** The Quiet Man, The Shootist **12** The Searchers **14** Rooster Cogburn, The Green Berets **16** How the West Was Won **17** The Sands of Iwo Jima **27** The Man Who Shot Liberty Valance

Way of All Flesh, The

author: 12 Samuel Butler
character: 9 Mr Overton
 Pontifex family: 5 Ellen **6** Althea, Ernest, George **8** Theobald **9** Christina

Way of the World, The
 author: 15 William Congreve
 character: 6 Foible **7** Fainall, Witwoud **8** Mirabell, Waitwell **10** Mrs Fainall, Mrs Marwood **12** Lady Wishfort, Mrs Millamant **17** Sir Wilfull Witwoud

way of thinking 7 beliefs **9** principle **10** conviction **11** persuasions

way out 4 exit **6** egress, escape, outlet

Ways of Escape
 author: 12 Graham Greene

wayward 5 balky **6** fickle, fitful, mulish, unruly **7** erratic, restive, willful **8** contrary, perverse, stubborn, variable **9** mercurial, obstinate, whimsical **10** capricious, changeable, headstrong, inconstant, rebellious, refractory, self-willed **11** disobedient, fluctuating, intractable, troublesome **12** inconsistent, incorrigible, recalcitrant, undependable, ungovernable, unmanageable **13** insubordinate

Wazhazhe *see* **5** Osage

weak 4 lame, poor, puny, soft, thin **5** faint, frail, shaky, spent **6** feeble, flimsy, unsafe, wasted, watery **7** brittle, diluted, exposed, fragile, insipid, lacking, unmanly **8** cowardly, delicate, helpless, timorous, unsteady, wide open **9** breakable, enervated, exhausted, frangible, powerless, spineless, tasteless, unguarded, untenable **10** assailable, effeminate, irresolute, namby-pamby, vulnerable, wishy-washy **11** adulterated, debilitated, defenseless, ineffective, ineffectual, inefficient, unprotected, unsupported **12** unconvincing **13** inefficacious, unsubstantial, untrustworthy **14** unsatisfactory

weaken 3 sap **4** fade, fail, flag, thin, wane **5** abate, droop, lower, unman, waste **6** dilute, expose, impair, lessen, soften **7** cripple, dwindle, exhaust, thin out **8** diminish, enervate, mitigate, moderate **9** undermine **10** devitalize, emasculate

weakened 5 frail **6** dilute, faulty, flawed, watery **7** diluted **8** delicate, disabled **9** enfeebled **10** undermined **11** adulterated, debilitated, watered down

weakling 4 twit, wimp **5** mouse, sissy **6** coward **7** chicken, milksop **9** cream puff, jellyfish **10** namby-pamby, pantywaist **11** milquetoast, mollycoddle

weak-minded 4 daft, dull **7** foolish **8** backward, mindless **10** irresolute **11** addleheaded, vacillating **12** feebleminded, muddleheaded, thick-skulled

weakness 4 bent, bias **5** fault **6** defect, hunger, thirst **7** failing, frailty, leaning, passion **8** appetite, debility, fondness, lameness, penchant, tendency **9** prejudice, proneness, shakiness **10** deficiency, feebleness, flimsiness, proclivity, propensity **11** inclination **12** debilitation, imperfection, unsteadiness **13** vulnerability **14** susceptibility **15** ineffectiveness **16** unconvincingness, unsubstantiality **17** untrustworthiness

weak point 4 flaw **5** break, crack, fault **6** defect **10** deficiency **11** shortcoming **12** Achilles heel

weak position 8 handicap **12** disadvantage

weak-willed 8 hesitant, wavering **10** hesitating, indecisive, irresolute

wealth 4 fund, mine **5** goods, means, money, store **6** assets, bounty, estate, luxury, mammon, riches **7** capital, fortune **8** chattels, fullness, opulence, property, richness **9** abundance, affluence, amplitude, plenitude, profusion, resources **10** easy street, prosperity **11** copiousness **12** independence **13** luxuriousness

wealthy 4 rich **5** flush **6** loaded **7** moneyed, well-off **8** affluent, well-to-do **9** well-fixed **10** prosperous, well- heeled

weapon 3 arm **5** guard, means **6** attack, resort **7** bulwark, defense, measure, offense **8** armament, resource, security **9** offensive, safeguard **10** protection **14** countermeasure

weaponry 4 arms, guns **8** armament, materiel, ordnance

wear 3 don, tax, use **4** duds, fray, last, tire, togs, wrap **5** drain, erode, put on, shred, weary **6** abrade, attire, damage, endure, injury, shroud, slip on, swathe **7** apparel, clothes, corrode, dress in, eat away, exhaust, fatigue, frazzle, rub away, service, swaddle, utility **8** clothing, costumes, garments, overwork, wash away **9** disrepair **10** employment, overburden **11** application, consumption, utilization **12** dilapidation **13** deterioration **14** disintegration

wear away 4 rust **5** erase, erode **7** corrode, eat into

weariness
 French: 5 ennui

wearing apparel 4 duds, garb, rags, togs, wear **5** dress **6** attire, finery **7** clothes, costume, raiment, regalia, threads **8** clothing, ensemble, garments, wardrobe
 French: 11 habillement

wearing away 7 erosion **8** abrasion, friction, grinding, scraping **9** corrosion

wearing down 6 tiring **7** eroding, erosion **8** abrasion, friction, grinding, scraping **10** overcoming

wearisome 4 dull **6** boring, dreary,

tiring, trying **7** arduous, irksome, tedious **8** annoying, tiresome, toilsome **9** fatiguing, laborious, vexatious **10** bothersome, burdensome, exhausting, irritating, monotonous, oppressive

wear out 4 tire **7** exhaust, fatigue **8** enervate, enfeeble **10** debilitate

weary 3 fag **4** beat, dull, tire **5** all in, blase, bored, fed up, jaded, spent, tired **6** boring, bushed, done in, drowsy, pooped, sleepy, tiring, tucker **7** annoyed, drained, exhaust, fatigue, humdrum, overtax, play out, routine, tedious, tire out, worn-out **8** dog tired, fatigued, overwork, tiresome **9** disgusted, exhausted, fatiguing, impatient, soporific, wearisome **10** dispirited, exhausting, monotonous, overburden **11** somniferous **12** discontented, dissatisfied

weather 3 dry, tan **4** face, rust **5** brave, clime, stand **6** bleach, season **7** climate, oxidize, toughen **8** confront, windward **9** withstand **11** temperature
 god of: 4 Jove **7** Jupiter

weather line 6 isobar

weave 4 fuse, join, knit, lace, link, loom, meld, wind **5** blend, braid, curve, plait, snake, twist, unify, unite **6** mingle, writhe, zigzag **7** combine, entwine, meander, texture **9** interlace **10** crisscross, intertwine **11** incorporate

Weaver, Earl
 nickname: 15 Earl of Baltimore
 sport: 8 baseball
 position: 7 manager
 team: 16 Baltimore Orioles

Weaver, Dennis
 born: 8 Joplin MO
 roles: 7 Chester, McCloud **8** Gunsmoke **9** Gentle Ben **13** Kentucky Jones

Weaver, Sigourney
 born: 12 Los Angeles CA
 roles: 5 Alien **6** Aliens **10** Eyewitness **12** Ghostbusters **17** Gorillas in the Mist **26** The Year of Living Dangerously

web 3 net **4** maze, mesh, trap **5** snare **6** screen, tangle, tissue **7** complex, netting, network **8** gossamer **9** labyrinth, screening

Web and the Rock, The
 author: 11 Thomas Wolfe
 character: 10 Esther Jack **12** George Webber

Webb, Jack
 born: 13 Santa Monica CA
 wife: 11 Julie London
 roles: 6 The Men **7** Dragnet **9** Joe Friday **15** Sunset Boulevard

Webber, George
 character in: 16 The Web and the Rock **18** You Can't Go Home Again
 author: 5 Wolfe

Webb family

characters in: 7 Our Town
member: 5 Emily, Wally
author: 6 Wilder

Weber, Karl Maria Friedrich Ernst von
born: 6 Lubeck **7** Germany
composer of: 6 Oberon **9** Euryanthe **13** Der Freischutz **20** Invitation to the Dance

Weber, Max
born: 6 Russia **9** Bialystok
artwork: 11 The Geranium **17** Chinese Restaurant **18** Adoration of the Moon

Webfoot State
nickname of: 6 Oregon

Webster
character: 6 George **7** Webster **9** Katherine
cast: 10 Alex Karras, Susan Clark **13** Emmanuel Lewis

Webster, John
author of: 13 The White Devil **17** The Duchess of Malfi

we cannot
Latin: 11 non possumus

we command
Latin: 8 mandamus

wed 3 tie **4** bind, fuse, link, mate, meld **5** blend, hitch, marry, merge, unify, unite, weave **6** attach, commit, couple, devote, pledge, splice **7** combine, espouse, make one, win over **8** dedicate **11** incorporate

wedded 4 tied **5** bound, fused **6** joined, linked, melded, merged, united **7** blended, devoted, marital, married, pledged, unified **9** committed, connected **12** incorporated

wedding 8 marriage, nuptials

wedding anniversaries
first: 5 clock, paper
second: 5 china **6** cotton
third: 5 glass **7** crystal, leather
fourth: 4 silk **5** linen **20** electrical appliances
fifth: 4 wood **10** silverware
sixth: 4 iron, wood
seventh: 4 wool **6** copper **8** desk sets **16** pen and pencil sets
eighth: 4 lace **6** bronze, linens
ninth: 5 china **7** leather, pottery
tenth: 3 tin **8** aluminum **14** diamond jewelry
eleventh: 5 steel **11** accessories **14** fashion jewelry
twelfth: 4 silk **6** pearls **11** colored gems
thirteenth: 4 furs, lace **8** textiles
fourteenth: 5 ivory **11** gold jewelry
fifteenth: 7 crystal, watches
twentieth: 5 china **8** platinum
twenty-fifth: 6 silver **21** sterling silver jubilee
thirtieth: 5 pearl **7** diamond
thirty-fifth: 4 jade **5** coral
fortieth: 4 ruby

forty-fifth: 8 sapphire
fiftieth: 4 gold **13** golden jubilee
fifty-fifth: 7 emerald
sixtieth: 7 diamond

weddings
god of: 8 Talassio

wedge 3 jam, ram **4** cram, pack, rend, rive **5** chock, chunk, crowd, force, press, split, stuff **6** cleave **7** squeeze

wedlock 8 marriage **9** matrimony

Wednesday
Dutch: 8 woensdag
French: 8 mercredi
German: 8 mittwoch
heavenly body: 7 Mercury
Italian: 9 mercoledi
name comes from: 4 Odin **5** Woden
observance: 12 Ash Wednesday
Spanish: 9 miercoles
Swedish: 6 onsdag

wee 4 tiny **5** dwarf, scant, teeny **6** little, minute, petite, scanty **9** itty-bitty, miniature, minuscule **10** diminutive, teeny-weeny, undersized **11** Lilliputian, microscopic

weed 3 bur, hoe, nag, pot **4** burr, butt, cull, dock, hemp, rake **5** cigar, joint, vetch **6** darnel, harrow, pull up, root up, uproot **7** tobacco **8** nuisance, plantain, purslane, toadflax **9** cigarette, crabgrass, cultivate, dandelion, eliminate, extirpate, marijuana **12** mourning band

weed out 6 banish **7** abolish, discard **8** get rid of, throw out **9** eliminate

Weena
character in: 14 The Time Machine
author: 5 Wells

weeny 3 wee **4** tiny **5** frank, small, teeny **6** hotdog, little, teensy, wiener **11** frankfurter

weep 3 cry, orp, sob **4** bawl, bend, drip, leak, lerm, ooze, shed, tear, wail **5** exude, mourn **6** bewail, boohoo, lament, shower **7** blubber, lapwing, whimper **8** sweating **9** exudation
genus: 8 Vanellus

weep over 5 mourn **6** bemoan, bewail, lament

weevil
variety: 4 boll, rice

Wegener, Alfred L
field: 10 geophysics **11** meteorology
nationality: 6 German
theory of: 16 continental drift

Wegg
character in: 15 Our Mutual Friend
author: 7 Dickens

weigh 4 lift **5** count, hoist, raise, scale **6** burden, charge, ponder, regard **7** balance, compare, measure **8** consider, encumber, evaluate, ruminate **11** contemplate **12** counterbalance

weigh anchor 4 sail **7** cast off, set sail, ship out

weigh down 4 load **6** anchor, burden

7 oppress **8** encumber, obligate, overload

weight 3 tax **4** heft, load, mass **5** value **6** burden, import, saddle, strain, stress **7** ballast, concern, oppress, tonnage, urgency **8** emphasis, encumber, poundage, pressure **9** heaviness, influence, magnitude **10** importance **11** consequence **12** significance **13** consideration, ponderousness

weight, unit of
of Afghanistan: 3 pau, paw, ser, sir
of Algeria: 4 rotl
of Argentina: 4 last **5** grano, libra **7** quintal **8** tonelada
of Austria: 4 marc, saum, unze **5** denat, karch, pfund, stein **7** centner, pfennig **8** vierling **9** quantchen
of Belgium: 4 last **5** carat, livre, pound **6** charge **7** chariot **9** esterling
of Bolivia: 5 libra, marco
of Borneo: 4 para **6** chapah
of Brazil: 3 bag **4** onca, onza **5** libra **6** arroba, oitava **7** arratel, quilate, quintal **8** tonelada
of Bulgaria: 3 oka, oke **5** tovar
of Cambodia: 4 mace, tael
of Chile: 5 grano, libra **7** quintal
of China: 3 fan, fen, hao, kin, ssu, tan, yin **4** chee, chin, dong, shih, tael, tsin **5** catty, chien, picul, tchin, tsien **6** kungli **7** haikwan, kungfen, kungssu, kungtun **8** kungchin **9** candareen **10** kupingtael
of Colombia: 3 bag **4** saco **5** carga, libra **7** quilate, quintal
of Costa Rica: 3 bag **4** caja **5** libra
of Cuba: 5 libra **6** tercio
of Ecuador: 5 libra
of Egypt: 3 kat, ket, oka, oke **4** dera, heml, khar, okia, rotl **5** artal, artel, deben, kerat, minae, minas, okieh, pound, ratel, uckia **6** hamlah, kantar **7** drachma, quintal
of El Salvador: 3 bag **4** caja **5** libra
of England: 3 bag, kip, tod, ton **4** keel, last, mast, maun **5** barge, fagot, grain, maund, pound, score, stand, stone, truss **6** bushel, cental, fangot, firkin, fother, fotmal, pocket **7** quarter, quintal, sarpler
of Estonia: 4 lood, nael, puud
of Ethiopia: 3 pek **4** kasm, natr, oket, rotl **5** alada, artal, mocha, neter, ratel, wakea **6** wogiet **8** farasula **9** mutagalla
of France: 3 sol **4** gros, kilo, marc, once **5** carat, livre, pound, tonne, uckia **6** gramme, passir **7** tonneau **8** esterlin **9** esterling
of Greece: 3 mna, oka, oke **4** mina, obol **5** litra, livre, maneh, pound **6** diobol, dramme, kantar, obolos, obolus, stater, talent **7** chalcon, chalque, drachma **8** diobolon, talanton
of Guatemala: 4 caja **5** libra
of Guinea: 4 akey, piso, uzan **5** benda, seron **6** quinto **8** aguirage

of Hungary: 7 vamfont **8** vammazsa
of Iceland: 4 pund **5** pound, tunna **6** smjors
of India: 3 mod, pai, ser, vis **4** dhan, drum, hoen, kona, myat, pala, pank, pice, raik, ruay, tael, tali, tank, tola, wang, yava **5** adpad, bahar, hubba, masha, maund, tical **6** abucco, karsha **8** mangelin
of Indonesia: 5 catty, ounce, thail **6** soekoe
of Iran: 3 ser **4** dram, dung, rotl, sang, seer **5** abbas, artel, maund, pinar, ratel **6** dirhem, gandum, karwar, miscal, nakhod, nimman **7** abbassi **8** tcheirek
of Italy: 5 carat, libra, oncia, pound **6** carato, denaro, libbra, ottava
of Japan: 2 mo **3** fun, kin, kon, rin, shi **4** kati, kwan, niyo **5** carat, catty, momme, picul **6** kwamme **8** hiyakkin
of Java: 4 amat, pond, tali **5** pound **6** soekel
of Korea: 3 won
of Latvia: 9 liespfund
of Libya: 3 pik, saa **4** kele **5** teman, uckia **6** gorraf, misura **7** mattaro, termino **8** kharouba
of Malaysia: 4 chee, mace, tael, wang **7** tampang
of Mexico: 3 bag **4** onza **5** carga, libra, marco **6** adarme, arroba, ochava, tercio **7** quintal
of Mongolia: 3 lan
of Morocco: 4 rotl **5** artal, artel, gerbe, ratel **6** dirhem, kintar **7** quintal
of Myanmar: 2 ta **3** can, mat, moo, pai, vis **4** binh, dong, kyat, ruay, viss **5** bahar, behar, candy, tical, ticul **6** abucco **7** peiktha
of the Netherlands: 3 ons **4** last, lood, pond **5** bahar, grein **6** korrel **7** wichtje **8** esterlin
of Nicaragua: 3 bag **4** caha, caja **8** tonelada
of Norway: 3 lod **4** mark, pund **9** skaalpund **10** bismerpund
of Pakistan: 4 seer, tola **5** maund
of Paraguay: 7 quintal
of Peru: 5 libra **7** quintal
of the Philippines: 5 catty, fardo, picul, punto **6** lachsa **7** quilate **8** chinanta
of Poland: 3 lut **4** funt **5** uncya **6** kamian **7** centner, skrupul
of Portugal: 4 grao, onca, once **5** libra, marco **6** arroba, oitava **7** arratel, quintal **9** excropulo
of Russia: 3 lof, lot **4** dola, funt, lana, last, loof, loth, once, pood, poud **5** dolia
of Saudi Arabia: 3 oke
of Scotland: 4 boll, drop **5** trone **6** bushel
of Somalia: 8 parsalah
of Spain: 4 onza **5** frail, grano, libra,

marco, tomin **6** adarme, arroba, dinero, dracma, ochava **7** arienzo, quilate, quintal **8** caracter, tonelada
of Sudan: 5 habba
of Sweden: 3 ass, lod, ort **4** last, mark, sten **5** carat **6** nylast **7** centner, lispund **8** skalpund, skeppund **9** shippound
of Switzerland: 4 fund **5** pfund **7** centner, quintal **12** zugthierlast
of Syria: 4 cola, rotl **5** artal, artel, ratel **6** talent
of Tanzania: 8 farsalah
of Thailand: 3 bat, hap, pai, pay, sen, sok **4** baht, haph, kati, klam, klom **5** catty, chang, coyan, fuang, picul, pilul, tical **6** fluang, graini, salung, sompay **7** tamlung
of Tunisia: 3 saa **4** rotl **5** artal, artel, ratel, uckia **6** kantar
of Turkey: 3 oka, oke **4** aqui, dram, kile, rotl **5** artal, artel, cheke, kerat, obolu, ratel **6** batman, dirhem, kantar, maunch, miskal **7** drachma, quintal, yusdrum
of Uruguay: 7 quintal
of Venezuela: 3 bag **5** libra
of Vietnam: 3 can, yet **4** uyen
of Yugoslavia: 3 oka **5** dramm, tovar, wagon **7** satlijk
weightlessness 8 buoyancy **9** lightness **11** zero gravity
weighty 5 grave, heavy, hefty, vital **6** solemn, taxing, trying, urgent **7** arduous, crucial, earnest, massive, onerous, serious **8** critical, crushing, cumbrous, pressing **9** difficult, essential, important, ponderous **10** burdensome, cumbersome, oppressive **11** significant, substantial, troublesome **12** considerable **13** consequential

Weill, Kurt
 born: 6 Dessau **7** Germany
 composer of: 8 Happy End **13** Lady in the Dark **15** Down in the Valley **18** The Lindbergh Flight, The Threepenny Opera **19** Die Dreigroschenoper **31** Rise and Fall of the City of Mahagonny **32** Aufstieg und Fall der Stadt Mahagonny

Weir, Peter
 director of: 7 Witness **9** Gallipoli **11** The Last Wave **26** The Year of Living Dangerously

weird 3 odd **4** wild **5** crazy, eerie, kooky, nutty, queer **6** far-out, mystic, spooky **7** bizarre, curious, ghostly, magical, strange, unusual **8** abnormal, freakish, peculiar **9** eccentric, grotesque, irregular, unearthly, unnatural **10** mysterious, outlandish, phantasmal, unorthodox **12** supernatural **14** unconventional
weirdo 3 nut **4** kook **5** flake, freak **6** looney **7** lunatic, oddball **8** crackpot, original **9** character, eccentric, screwball **10** one-of-a-kind

Weird sisters 5 Fates, Norns
Weisenfreund, Muni
 real name of: 8 Paul Muni
Weismuller, Johnny
 real name: 20 Peter John Weissmuller
 born: 9 Windbar PA
 Olympic sport: 8 swimming
 Olympic gold medals: 4 five
 wife: 9 Lupe Velez
 roles: 6 Tarzan **9** Jungle Jim
Weiss, Peter
 author of: 10 Marat/Sade **14** Vanishing Point
welcome 4 meet **5** admit, greet **6** at home, salute, wanted **7** embrace, receive, usher in, winning **8** accepted, admitted, charming, engaging, enticing, greeting, inviting, pleasant, pleasing **9** agreeable, entertain, reception **10** delightful, gratifying, salutation **11** comfortable

Weld, Tuesday
 real name: 12 Susan Ker Weld
 born: 9 New York NY
 husband: 11 Dudley Moore
 roles: 12 I Walk the Line **14** Play It as It Lays **16** The Cincinnati Kid, Wild in the Country **19** Looking for Mr Goodbar

welfare 4 good **6** health, profit, relief **7** benefit, success, the dole **9** advantage, happiness
well 3 jet, run **4** flow, fund, good, gush, hale, mine, ooze, pool, pour, rise **5** amply, fount, fully, issue, lucky, right, shaft, sound, spout, spurt, store, surge **6** easily, fairly, hearty, justly, kindly, nicely, proper, robust, source, spring, stream, strong, warmly **7** chipper, fitting, healthy, readily, rightly **8** famously, fountain, laudably, properly, suitably, very much, vigorous **9** agreeably, capitally, carefully, correctly, favorable, favorably, fortunate, promising, quite well **10** abundantly, acceptably, adequately, auspicious, completely, familiarly, felicitous, intimately, personally, prosperous, splendidly, successful, thoroughly **11** approvingly, commendably **12** advantageous, auspiciously, considerably, propitiously, satisfactory, successfully, sufficiently **13** substantially **14** advantageously, satisfactorily **15** sympathetically **16** enthusiastically
 hole drilled in ground for: 3 gas, oil **5** water
well-adjusted 6 normal, secure **8** sensible
Welland, May
 character in: 17 The Age of Innocence
 author: 7 Wharton
well-behaved 6 polite, sedate **8** decorous

well-being 4 ease, good, luck, weal **6** health, profit **7** benefit, comfort, fortune, success, welfare **8** felicity, good luck **9** advantage, affluence, happiness **10** prosperity

wellborn 8 highbred **9** patrician **10** upper-class **12** aristocratic, silk-stocking

Wellbred
    character in: 19 Every Man in His Humour
    author: 6 Jonson

well-bred 5 civil, suave **6** polite, urbane **7** elegant, gallant, genteel, refined **8** cultured, ladylike, mannerly, polished **9** civilized, courteous **10** cultivated **11** gentlemanly **13** sophisticated

well-chosen 3 apt **4** fine **5** prize **6** choice, seemly, select **7** apropos, correct, fitting, special **8** superior **9** excellent **11** appropriate

well-considered 7 careful, prudent **8** cautious **10** thoughtful **11** circumspect

well-coordinated 6 smooth **8** graceful **9** dexterous **10** effortless

well-defined 5 clear, plain **8** clear-cut, definite, distinct, palpable **10** pronounced

well-dressed 4 chic **5** natty, smart **6** dapper **11** fashionable

well-educated 7 erudite, learned **8** cultured, literate **9** scholarly **10** cultivated **13** knowledgeable

Weller, Sam
    character in: 14 Pickwick Papers
    author: 7 Dickens

Welles, Orson
    real name: 17 George Orson Welles
    born: 9 Kenosha WI
    wife: 9 Paola Mori **12** Rita Hayworth
    formed: 14 Mercury Theatre
    radio show: 14 War of the Worlds
    roles: 8 Jane Eyre **11** Citizen Kane, The Third Man, Touch of Evil
    director of: 7 Macbeth, Othello **8** Falstaff **11** Citizen Kane, The Stranger, Touch of Evil **23** The Magnificent Ambersons

well-favored 4 fair **5** bonny **6** comely, pretty **7** sightly, winsome **8** fetching, handsome **9** beautiful **10** attractive **11** good looking

well-fed 5 hefty, plump, stout **6** portly, rotund **9** corpulent

well-fixed 4 rich **7** moneyed, wealthy **8** affluent **10** prosperous

well-founded 7 factual **9** supported **12** corroborated **13** substantiated

well-groomed 4 neat, tidy **5** natty **6** spruce **10** impeccable

well-grounded 5 valid **7** factual **8** reliable **9** supported **10** undeniable, undisputed, unshakable **11** irrefutable **12** corroborated, indisputable **13** in-

contestable, substantiated **16** incontrovertible

well-heeled 4 rich **7** moneyed, wealthy **8** affluent **10** in the chips, in the money, prosperous

Wellington
    capital of: 10 New Zealand

Wellington, Duke of
    also: 15 Arthur Wellesley
    nickname: 6 Hookey **12** The Great Duke
    nationality: 7 British
    served in: 5 India **14** Napoleonic Wars
    battle: 6 Assaye **7** Vitoria **8** Talavera, Waterloo **9** Salamanca
    served as: 13 prime minister
    memoirs: 20 Wellington Dispatches

well-kept 4 heat, neat, tidy **7** orderly **9** organized **10** systematic **11** disciplined, uncluttered

well-known 4 open **5** famed, noted **6** common, famous **7** big-time, eminent, evident, leading, obvious, popular **8** familiar, infamous, renowned **9** important, notorious, prominent **10** celebrated, scandalous, understood **11** established, illustrious, outstanding

well-lighted 5 lit up **6** ablaze, bright **11** illuminated

well-made 4 fine **7** perfect **8** executed, flawless **9** faultless **11** beautifully

Wellman, William
    director of: 5 Wings **9** Beau Geste **11** A Star Is Born **13** Nothing Sacred **15** The Story of GI Joe **16** The Ox-Bow Incident

well-mannered 6 polite **7** genteel, refined **8** cultured, decorous, ladylike, polished **9** courteous, dignified **10** cultivated **11** gentlemanly

well-matched 5 close **10** nip-and-tuck

well-off 4 rich **5** flush **6** loaded **7** moneyed, wealthy **8** affluent **10** prosperous **11** comfortable

well-padded 5 plump, stout **6** chubby, fleshy, portly, rotund **9** corpulent

well-proportioned 7 classic, elegant, shapely **8** graceful **11** symmetrical

well-read 7 erudite, learned **8** cultured, literate **9** scholarly **10** cultivated

well-reasoned 4 wise **10** perceptive, thoughtful **11** intelligent

well-rehearsed 6 smooth **7** planned **8** prepared **9** practiced

Wells, H G (Herbert George)
    author of: 5 Kipps **10** Tono-Bungay **11** Ann Veronica **14** The Time Machine **15** The Invisible Man **16** Outline of History **17** Love and Mr Lewisham, The War of the Worlds **19** The History of Mr Polly **22** The Shape of Things to Come **23** Mr Britling Sees It Through

wellspring 4 font **6** origin, source **9** beginning **10** birthplace **12** fountainhead

well-stocked 4 full **11** overflowing

well-suited 6 proper **7** correct, fitting **8** suitable **9** congenial, congruous **10** compatible, harmonious **11** appropriate

well-to-do 4 rich **7** moneyed, wealthy **8** affluent **10** in the chips, in the money, prosperous

well up 4 boil, rise **6** bubble **7** surface

well-ventilated 4 airy **5** windy **6** breezy, drafty

well-versed 7 knowing **9** qualified **10** conversant **11** experienced **13** knowledgeable
    French: 9 au courant

well-wisher 6 friend **8** advocate, champion **9** supported

Welsh Mythology
    goddess: 3 Don
    goddess of fire/fertility/agriculture/household/wisdom: 6 Brigit
    king: 4 Bran, Llud, Ludd, Nudd
    magician: 5 Lloyd
    paradise: 5 Annwn **6** Annfwn
    prince: 5 Pwyll **7** Kilwich
    princess: 5 Olwen
    romantic tales: 10 Mabinogian

welt 4 bump, lump, mark, wale, weal **6** bruise, streak, stripe **8** swelling **9** contusion

Weltanschauung 25 manner of looking at the world

Weltansicht 9 world view

Weltschmerz 6 sorrow **9** world pain **10** melancholy **20** sentimental pessimism

Welty, Eudora
    author of: 12 Delta Wedding, Golden Apples **13** Losing Battles **14** The Ponder Heart **15** A Sweet Devouring **19** The Robber Bridegroom **20** The Optimist's Daughter

wench 4 doxy, girl, lass, maid, slut **5** whore **6** damsel, lassie, maiden **8** strumpet **10** prostitute

Wend 4 Slav, Sorb
    in: 7 Germany

wend 4 make **5** hie to

went 3 ran **4** flew, left **5** faded, got on **6** flew by, lapsed, passed **7** elapsed, sallied **8** departed, filed off, passed by, took wing, vanished **9** proceeded, took leave **10** shuffled on, took flight **11** disappeared, forged ahead **12** sallied forth **13** pressed onward

Wentworth, Captain Frederick
    character in: 10 Persuasion
    author: 6 Austen

Werfel, Franz
    author of: 9 Mirror Man **19** Forty Days of Musa Dagh, The Song of Bernadette

Werle, Gregers

character in: 11 The Wild Duck
author: 5 Ibsen

Werner, Oskar
real name: 24 Oskar Josef Bschliess-mayer
born: 6 Vienna **7** Austria
roles: 11 Jules and Jim, Ship of Fools **17** Voyage of the Damned **22** Fahrenheit Four Fifty One, The Shoes of the Fisherman **26** The Spy Who Came in from the Cold

Wertmuller, Lina
director of: 9 Swept Away (by an unusual destiny in the blue sea of August) **13** Seven Beauties

Wescott, Glenway
author of: 14 The Grandmother, The Pilgrim Hawk **16** The Apple of the Eye **17** Apartment in Athens

Wessex
fictional place created by: 5 Hardy

West, Benjamin
born: 13 Springfield PA
artwork: 17 Death on a Pale Horse **19** Death of General Wolfe **22** Saul and the Witch of Endor

West, Dame Rebecca
real name: 28 Cicily Isabel Fairfield Andrews
author of: 8 The Judge **11** Harriet Hume **13** Birds Fall Down **15** The Thinking Reed **19** The Strange Necessity **20** The Fountain Overflows **21** The Return of the Soldier **22** Black Lamb and Grey Falcon

West, Jessamyn
author of: 11 Leafy Rivers **13** A Matter of Time **18** Except for Me and Thee **21** The Friendly Persuasion **22** The Massacre at Fall Creek

West, Mae
born: 10 Brooklyn NY
roles: 3 Sex **8** Sextette **9** I'm No Angel **10** Diamond Lil **13** Klondike Annie **14** Go West Young Man **15** Night After Night, She Done Him Wrong **16** Myra Breckinridge **17** My Little Chickadee
autobiography: 28 Goodness Had Nothing To Do With It
quote: 6 Beulah peel me a grape **22** Come up and see me sometime

West, Morris L
author of: 7 Proteus **9** Harlequin **13** The Salamander **14** The Clowns of God **15** The Tower of Babel **17** The Devil's Advocate **22** The Shoes of the Fisherman

West, Nathanael
author of: 12 A Cool Million **16** Miss Lonelyhearts **17** The Day of the Locust

Westcott, Edward Noyes
author of: 10 David Harum

Westenra, Lucy
character in: 7 Dracula
author: 6 Stoker

Western, Sophia
character in: 8 Tom Jones
author: 8 Fielding

Western Sahara
other name: 13 Spanish Sahara
capital: 6 Al Aiun **7** El Aaiun
city: 3 Zug **5** Daora, Smara **6** Aargub, Dakhla, Tichla **9** Asqueimat, Bir Gandus **10** Bir Enzaran **12** Guelta Zemmur
government: 33 disputed territory claimed by Morocco
river: 7 Uad Atui **8** Uad Assag **13** Saguia el Hamra
sea: 8 Atlantic
physical feature:
  cape: 6 Barbas **7** Bojador
  desert: 6 Sahara
  wind: 5 leste **6** gibleh
people: 4 Arab **6** Berber
language: 16 Hassaniyya Arabic
religion: 5 Islam
feature:
  political group: 14 Polisario Front

Western Samoa
other name: 17 Navigator's Islands
capital/largest city: 4 Apia
others: 6 Safotu, Sataua **7** Faleolo, Palauli, Poutasi, Tuasivi **8** Fagamalo, Falelima, Lufilufi **9** Falealupo, Mulifanua **10** Samalaeulu, Satupaitea
monetary unit: 4 sene, tala
island: 5 Upolu **6** Manono, Savaii **7** Apolima
mountain: 4 Fito, Vaea
highest point: 13 Mauga Silisili
sea: 7 Pacific
physical feature:
  bay: 4 Asau, Salu **6** Safata **7** Lafanga, Matautu **8** Fangaloa, Salealua **9** Saluofata
  strait: 7 Apolima
people: 6 Samoan **10** Melanesian, Polynesian
  author: 20 Robert Louis Stevenson (Tusitala, Teller of Tales)
  explorer: 6 Wilkes **9** Roggeveen **12** Bougainville
language: 6 Samoan **7** English
religion: 9 Methodist **10** Protestant **13** Roman Catholic **14** Congregational
place:
  observatory: 4 Apia
  tomb: 9 Stevenson
feature:
  chief: 5 matai
  clothing: 5 pareu **8** lavalava, puletasi
  dance: 4 siva
  daughter of chief: 5 taupo
  house: 4 fale
food:
  dish: 8 palusami
  drink: 3 ava

Western Star
author: 19 Stephen Vincent Benet

Westhus, Haie

character in: 25 All Quiet on the Western Front
author: 8 Remarque

West Indies 11 archipelago
Associated States: 7 Antigua, Grenada, St Lucia **9** Anguilla, Dominica **12** St Kitts-Nevis
bird: 4 tody **6** mucaro
channel: 7 Jamaica **9** Old Bahama
component: 4 Cuba **5** Haiti **6** Tobago **7** Bahamas, Jamaica **8** Barbados, Trinidad **10** Hispaniola, Puerto Rico **13** Virgin Islands **14** Leeward Islands, Lesser Antilles **15** Greater Antilles, Windward Islands **17** Dominican Republic
crop: 6 coffee **9** sugarcane
fish: 4 pega **5** pelon
formerly: 10 federation
fruit: 5 papaw **6** pawpaw **7** genipap
islands: 5 Turks **6** Caicos, Cayman, Virgin **7** Bahamas, Leeward **8** Windward
kale: 7 malanga
lizard: 6 arbalo
music: 7 calypso
passage: 4 Mona **8** Windward
rodent: 5 hutia
sea: 9 Caribbean
shark: 4 gata
sorcery: 3 obi **5** obeah
tree: 5 genip **6** aralie
tribesman: 5 Carib **6** Arawak **7** Ciboney
vessel: 6 droger, drogher
volcano: 5 Pelee

Westinghouse, George
nationality: 8 American
invented: 8 air brake **12** railroad frog **20** railroad signal system

Westlake, Donald E
author of: 8 Bank Shot **10** The Hot Rock **13** Dancing Aztecs **15** Brothers Keepers
  as Richard Stark: 9 The Hunter **10** The Seventh
  as Tucker Coe: 19 Murder Among Children

Westover, Russ
creator/artist of: 15 Tillie the Toiler

West Side Story
director: 10 Robert Wise **13** Jerome Robbins
cast: 10 Rita Moreno **11** Natalie Wood, Russ Tamblyn **13** Richard Beymer **14** George Chakiris
score: 15 Stephen Sondheim **16** Leonard Bernstein
Oscar for: 7 picture **8** director **15** supporting actor (Chakiris) **17** supporting actress (Moreno)

West Virginia
abbreviation: 2 WV **3** W Va
nickname: 8 Mountain **9** Panhandle
capital: 10 Charleston
largest city: 10 Huntington
others: 5 Logan **6** Elkins, Keyser, Ripley, Vienna, Weston **7** Beckley,

Grafton, Spencer, Weirton **8** Fairmont, Wheeling **10** Clarksburg **11** Moundsville, Parkersburg
college: 5 Salem **7** Bethany, Concord **8** Marshall, Wheeling **9** Bluefield **10** Charleston **14** Davis and Elkins **16** Alderson Broaddus **20** West Virginia Wesleyan
feature:
   historical site: 12 Harper's Ferry
   national road: 10 Cumberland
tribe: 7 Moneton
people: 9 Pearl Buck **14** Arthur I Boreman **19** Walter Philip Reuther **24** Thomas "Stonewall" Jackson
   explorer: 12 Morgan Morgan
island: 14 Blennerhassett
lake: 4 Lynn
land rank: 10 forty-first
mountain:
   highest point: 10 Spruce Knob
physical feature:
   cavern: 6 Seneca
   plateau: 9 Allegheny
   rock: 6 Seneca
   spring: 8 Berkeley **12** White Sulphur
river: 3 Elk **4** Ohio **6** Gauley **7** Kanawha, Potomac, Tug Fork **8** Big Sandy, Guyandot **11** Monongahela
state admission: 11 Thirty-fifth
state bird: 8 cardinal
state fish: 10 brook trout
state flower: 11 great laurel **15** big rhododendron **17** great rhododendron
state motto: 25 Mountaineers Are Always Free
state song: 17 West Virginia Hills **20** This Is My West Virginia **27** West Virginia My Home Sweet Home
state tree: 10 sugar maple

Westward Ho!
author: 15 Charles Kingsley

west wind
associated with: 8 Favonius, Zephyrus

wet 3 dip **4** damp, dank, rain, soak **5** humid, moist, rainy, soggy, steep, storm, water **6** clammy, dampen, drench, liquid, shower, soaked, sodden, splash, stormy, watery **7** immerse, moisten, showery, soaking, sopping, squishy, wetness **8** dampened, dampness, dankness, drenched, dripping, inundate, irrigate, moisture, sprinkle, submerge **9** exudation, liquified, moistness, rainstorm **10** clamminess **11** waterlogged **12** condensation **13** precipitation

wet blanket 4 drag **6** damper **10** spoilsport **11** party-pooper

wet down 5 spray **6** dampen **7** moisten **8** sprinkle

wettish 4 damp **5** moist **6** clammy

we who are about to die salute thee

Latin: 19 morituri te salutamus
said by: 15 Roman gladiators
said to: 13 Roman emperors

whack 2 go **3** box, hit, rap, try **4** bang, belt, blow, cuff, slam, slap, slug, sock, stab, turn **5** baste, clout, crack, knock, pound, punch, smack, smite, thump, trial **6** strike, wallop **7** attempt, venture **8** endeavor

whale 4 beat, cane, drub, flog, orca, whip **6** baleen, thrash **9** bastinado
constellation of: 5 Cetus
group of: 3 gam, pod
swallowed: 5 Jonah
Melville: 8 Moby Dick

whammy 3 hex **4** jinx **5** curse **7** evil eye **9** evil spell

wharf 3 key **4** dock, pier, quai, quay, slip **5** jetty **6** marina **7** landing **10** breakwater

Wharton, Edith
author of: 10 Ethan Frome, The Old Maid **15** The House of Mirth **17** The Age of Innocence **21** The Custom of the Country

Whatever Happened to Baby Jane?
director: 13 Robert Aldrich
cast: 10 Bette Davis **11** Victor Buono **12** Joan Crawford **15** Marjorie Bennett

What Every Woman Knows
author: 12 James M Barrie
character: 9 John Shand **15** Charles Venables **18** Comtesse de la Briere, Lady Sybil Tenterden
   Wylie family: 5 Alick, David, James **6** Maggie

what it takes 5 knack, skill **7** ability, know-how, mastery **9** expertise **10** capability, competence, expertness **11** proficiency **13** the right stuff

What Mrs McGillicuddy Saw!
author: 14 Agatha Christie

What Price Glory?
author: 15 Maxwell Anderson

What's Happening!!
character: 5 Rerun **6** Dwayne **7** Shirley **9** Dee Thomas, (Mama) Mrs Thomas **11** Roger (Raj) Thomas
cast: 9 Fred Berry, Mabel King **12** Ernest Thomas **13** Haywood Nelson **15** Danielle Spencer, Shirley Hemphill

What's My Line?
host: 8 John Daly
panelist: 8 Hal Block **9** Fred Allen **10** Steve Allen **11** Bennett Cerf **13** Arlene Francis **15** Louis Untermeyer **16** Dorothy Kilgallen

wheat 8 Triticum
varieties: 4 club, rice **5** durum, dwarf, India, river **6** Alaska, common, German, Polish, starch **7** English, poulard **8** hedgehog **10** one-grained, two-grained **13** Mediterranean

product: 4 bran **5** bread, flour, pasta **6** cereal **8** macaroni **9** spaghetti

Wheat State
nickname of: 6 Kansas

wheedle 4 coax, lure **5** charm **6** cajole, entice, induce **7** beguile, flatter **8** butter up, inveigle, persuade, soft soap

wheel 4 disk, drum, hoop, ring, roll, spin **5** pivot, round, swirl, twirl, whirl **6** caster, circle, gilgal, gyrate, roller, rotate, swivel **7** revolve **9** pirouette

Wheel of Fortune
host: 8 Pat Sajak
assistant: 10 Vanna White

wheels 3 car **4** auto, heap **5** motor **6** jalopy **7** flivver, vehicle **8** motorcar **9** tin lizzie **10** automobile

wheeze 4 gasp, hiss, pant, puff **7** panting, whistle

whelp 3 boy, cub, kid, lad, pup **4** brat **5** child, puppy, youth **6** urchin **9** stripling, youngster **14** whippersnapper

whence 9 from where **10** antecedent **14** from what source

Where Eagles Dare
director: 12 Brian G Hutton
based on novel by: 15 Alistair MacLean
cast: 7 Mary Ure **12** Robert Beatty **13** Clint Eastwood, Patrick Wymark, Richard Burton **14** Michael Hordern

wherefore 2 so **3** why **7** because **13** for what reason

where I may stand
Greek: 6 pou sto

where mentioned above
Latin: 8 ubi supra

whereupon 8 upon what **10** after which **14** upon which point

wherewithal 4 cash **5** funds, means **6** assets **7** capital **9** financing, resources

whet 4 edge, hone, stir **5** grind, pique, strop, tempt **6** allure, arouse, awaken, entice, excite, induce, kindle **7** animate, provoke, quicken, sharpen **9** stimulate **11** put an edge on

whether willing or not
Latin: 12 nolens volens

which see
Latin: 2 qv **8** quod vide

which was to be demonstrated
Latin: 3 QED **21** quod erat demonstrandum

which was to be done
Latin: 17 quod erat faciendum

which was to be shown
Latin: 3 QED **21** quod erat demonstrandum

whiff 4 hint, odor, puff **5** aroma, draft, scent, smell, sniff, trace **6** breath, breeze, zephyr **7** bouquet
French: 7 soupcon

Whig Party

president belonging to: 5 Tyler **6** Taylor **8** Fillmore, Harrison

while 2 as **3** yet **4** idle, till, time, when **5** until **6** during, effort, whilst **7** filling, interim, trouble, whereas **8** although, occasion

whim 4 urge **5** fancy, quirk **6** notion, vagary **7** caprice, conceit, impulse **8** crotchet **11** inspiration **12** eccentricity

whimper 3 sob **4** pule **5** whine **6** snivel **7** blubber, sniffle, sobbing **9** cry softly, sniveling **11** sob brokenly **16** whine plaintively

whimsical 5 droll **6** fickle, fitful, quaint **7** amusing, erratic, waggish **8** fanciful, notional, quixotic **9** eccentric **10** capricious, changeable, chimerical **12** inconsistent

whimsy, whimsey 4 bent, wish **5** fancy, humor, prank, quirk **6** notion, vagary **7** caprice, fantasy **8** escapade, drollery **11** make-believe

whine 3 cry, sob **4** fret, mewl, moan, wail **6** grouse, murmur, mutter, snivel **7** grumble, whimper **8** complain **9** complaint **11** gripe meekly **12** plaintive cry **14** cry plaintively

whip 3 rod **4** beat, cane, drub, flap, flog, jerk, jolt, lash, lick, maul, rout **5** birch, flick, spank, strap, thong, whisk **6** rattan, snatch, switch **7** cowhide, rawhide, scourge, trounce **8** birch rod, vanquish **9** horsewhip, toss about **10** blacksnake, flagellate **13** cat-o'-nine-tails, defeat soundly, move violently **14** beat decisively, beat into a froth

Whip 8 scorpion

whip hand 4 sway **5** power **7** control, mastery **9** advantage, authority, dominance, supremacy, upper hand **10** ascendancy, domination

whipped 5 caned, waled **6** beaten, darted, flayed, frothy, lashed, roused **7** flogged, frothed, incited, revived, spanked, subdued, swished, whisked **8** defeated, overlaid, punished, scourged, switched **9** chastised **10** vanquished

whir 3 hum **4** buzz, purr **5** drone **7** whisper

whirl 2 go **3** try **4** reel, spin, stab, turn **5** crack, fling, pivot, swirl, trial, twirl, whack, wheel **6** circle, dither, flurry, gyrate, rotate **7** attempt, revolve, turning **8** circling, gyration, pivoting, rotation, spinning, swirling, twirling, wheeling **9** feel dizzy, feel giddy, pirouette, revolving, turn round **10** dizzy round, rapid round, revolution **12** merry-go-round **17** state of excitement **18** dizzying succession

whirlpool 4 eddy **5** swirl, whirl **6** vortex **9** maelstrom **15** whirling current

whirlwind 4 rash **5** hasty, quick, rapid, short, swift **7** cyclone, tornado, twister **8** headlong **9** breakneck, impetuous, impulsive **10** waterspout

whirly 5 dizzy, giddy, shaky **7** reeling **8** spinning **11** vertiginous

whisk 3 fly, zip **4** beat, bolt, dart, dash, race, rush, tear, whip, whiz **5** bound, brush, flick, hurry, scoot, shoot, speed, spurt, sweep **6** hasten, scurry, spring, sprint
type: 4 wire **6** French **8** omelette

whiskbroom 5 brush

whiskered 5 bushy, hairy **6** shaggy **7** bearded, bristly, hirsute **8** unshaven **11** bewhiskered, mustachioed

whiskers 3 awn **5** beard **7** stubble **8** bristles

whiskey, whisky 3 gin, rum, rye **4** corn, shot **5** booze, hooch, Irish, juice, vodka **6** liquor, red eye, rotgut, Scotch **7** alcohol, aquavit, blended, bourbon, spirits **8** eau-de-vie **9** aquavitae, firewater, moonshine, unblended **10** sneaky pete, usquebaugh **11** mountain dew **14** John Barleycorn, white lightning
type: 3 rye **6** Scotch **7** bourbon
drink: 8 hot toddy **14** Klondike Cooler
with beer: 11 Boilermaker
with Benedictine: 10 Frisco Sour
with Cointreau: 16 Canadian Cocktail
with vermouth: 9 Manhattan

whisper 3 hum **4** blab, buzz, hint, purr, sigh, tell **5** blurt, bruit, drone, rumor **6** gossip, murmur, mutter, reveal, rustle **7** breathe, confide, divulge, inkling **8** disclose, innuendo, intimate **9** undertone **10** suggestion **11** insinuation

**whist
derived from: 8** triomphe
descendant: 6 bridge
number of players: 4 four
six tricks: 4 book

**Whistle
author: 10** James Jones

**Whistler, James Abbott McNeill
born: 8** Lowell MA
artwork: 6 Etudes **9** Harmonies, Nocturnes **10** Rosa Corder **12** Arrangements, The White Girl **13** Thomas Carlyle **15** Cicely Alexander, Wapping-on-Thames **24** Venetian Palaces Nocturnes **28** Arrangement in Grey and Black No 1 (The Artist's Mother) **29** Chelsea Nocturne in Blue and Green **31** Princess of the Land of the Porcelain **35** Falling Rocket Nocturne in Black and Gold **37** Cremorne Lights Nocturne in Blue and Silver

whistle-stop 5 stump **8** campaign **11** electioneer

whit 3 dab, dot, jot **4** chip, dash, drop, iota, mite, snip **5** crumb, grain, pinch, speck **6** morsel, tittle, trifle **7** modicum, smidgen **8** fragment, particle, splinter **9** scintilla

white 3 wan **4** ashy, fair, gray, pale, pure **5** ashen, blond, clean, filmy, hoary, ivory, milky, pasty, pearl, smoky, snowy **6** benign, chalky, chaste, cloudy, frosty, leaden, pallid, pearly, sallow, silver **7** ghostly, silvery **8** blanched, bleached, grizzled, harmless, innocent, spotless, virtuous **9** alabaster, bloodless, Caucasian, colorless, stainless, undefiled, unspotted, unstained, unsullied **10** cadaverous, immaculate **11** translucent, unblemished, unmalicious

**White, E B (Elwyn Brooks)
author of: 11** One Man's Meat **12** Stuart Little **13** Charlotte's Web **14** Is Sex Necessary? (with James Thurber) **19** The Trumpet of the Swan
column: 13 Talk of the Town

White, Stanford see **17** Mead McKim and White

**White, T H (Terence Hanbury)
author of: 15** The Book of Merlyn **16** The Ill-Made Knight **17** The Witch in the Wood **18** The Candle in the Wind, The Sword in the Stone **20** The Once and Future King

**White Album
author: 10** Joan Didion

**White Company, The
author: 19** Sir Arthur Conan Doyle

**White Heat
director: 10** Raoul Walsh
cast: 11 James Cagney **12** Edmond O'Brien, Virginia Mayo **16** Margaret Wycherly

**White-Jacket
author: 14** Herman Melville

whiten 4 pale **5** clean, frost **6** blanch, bleach, silver **7** lighten

whiteness 6 pallor **7** wanness **8** paleness **9** snowiness **10** sallowness **13** colorlessness

**White Nights
director: 14** Taylor Hackford
cast: 12 Gregory Hines **18** Mikhail Baryshnikov
choreographer: 10 Twyla Tharp

**White Rabbit
character in: 28** Alice's Adventures in Wonderland
author: 7 Carroll

whitewash 6 excuse **7** absolve, cover up, justify **8** downplay, minimize, play down **9** calcimine, exonerate, vindicate
paint made by mixing: 12 lime and water

**Whitewater
author: 10** Paul Horgan

whitish 4 buff, pale **6** chalky, creamy **7** grayish

**Whitman, Bert
creator/artist of: 14** The Green Hornet

**Whitman, Walt
author of: 12** Song of Myself **13** Leaves of Grass **18** Oh Captain My

Captain **33** When Lilacs Last in the Dooryard Bloom'd

Whitmore, James
born: **13** White Plains NY
roles: **4** Them **5** Bully **8** Oklahoma **9** Battlecry **10** Will Rogers **11** Black Like Me **12** Battleground, Harry S Truman, Tora Tora Tora **15** Command Decision, Give 'em Hell Harry **19** The Next Voice You Hear

Whitney, Eli
nationality: **8** American
invented: **9** cotton gin
pioneered use of: **14** mass production

Whittier, John Greenleaf
author of: **9** Snow-Bound **10** Maud Muller **14** The Barefoot Boy **16** Barbara Frietchie

whittle 3 cut **4** clip, pare **5** carve, shave, slash **7** curtail, shorten **8** decrease

whiz 3 fly, hum, zip **4** bolt, buzz, dart, dash, hiss, race, rush, scud, tear, whir, zoom **5** adept, drone, scoot, shark, shoot, speed, spurt, sweep, swish, whine, whisk **6** expert, genius, hasten, master, scurry, sizzle, sprint, wizard **7** prodigy, scuttle, whistle **11** crackerjack

who goes there?
French: **7** qui vive

who knows?
Spanish: **9** quien sabe

whole 4 body, bulk, full, hale, unit, well **5** sound, total, uncut **6** entire, intact, robust, system **7** essence, healthy, perfect **8** complete, ensemble, entirety, totality, unbroken, unharmed, vigorous **9** aggregate, undivided, uninjured **10** assemblage, unabridged **12** completeness, quintessence, undiminished

wholehearted 4 true **7** earnest, serious, sincere, zealous **8** complete, emphatic **9** unfeigned **10** unreserved, unstinting **12** enthusiastic

wholesome 4 hale, nice, pure, well **5** clean, fresh, hardy, moral, sound **6** decent, honest, worthy **7** chipper, dutiful, ethical, healthy, upright **8** blooming, hygienic, innocent, sanitary, vigorous, virtuous **9** exemplary, healthful, honorable, uplifting **10** nourishing, nutritious, principled **11** meritorious, responsible **12** invigorating **13** strengthening

whole world, the
French: **11** tout le monde

wholly 5 fully, quite **7** totally, utterly **8** as a whole, entirely **9** perfectly **10** altogether, completely, thoroughly
Latin: **6** in toto

whoop 3 cry **4** hoot, howl, roar, yell **5** cheer, hollo, shout **6** bellow, cry out, holler, hurrah, outcry, scream, shriek **7** screech **9** hue and cry

whopper 3 fib, lie **6** big one **7** fiction **9** falsehood, fish story, tall story **16** cock-and-bull story

whopping 4 huge **5** giant, large **8** thumping, whacking, whapping **10** incredible **13** extraordinary

whore 4 pro **4** bawd, doxy, jade, slut, tart **5** hussy, tramp **6** chippy, harlot, hooker, prosty, wanton **7** demirep, hustler, trollop **8** call girl, mistress, strumpet **9** concubine **10** prostitute **12** streetwalker
French: **9** courtesan **12** demimondaine

whorl 4 coil, curl, roll **5** helix **6** circle, spiral **9** corkscrew **11** convolution

Who's Afraid of Virginia Woolf?
author: **11** Edward Albee
director: **11** Mike Nichols
cast: **11** George Segal, Sandy Dennis **13** Richard Burton **15** Elizabeth Taylor
Oscar for: **7** actress (Taylor) **17** supporting actress (Dennis)

Who Said That?
host: **8** John Daly **11** Robert Trout **13** Walter Kiernan
panelist: **9** Bill Henry **12** Bob Considine, H V Kaltenborn, June Lockhart **14** John Mason Brown, Morey Amsterdam **17** John Cameron Swayze

Who's on First?
comedy routine by: **6** Abbott **8** Costello
first base: **3** who
second base: **4** what
third base: **9** I don't know
shortstop: **9** I don't care
catcher: **5** today
pitcher: **8** tomorrow
left field: **3** why
center field: **7** because

Who's on First?
author: **17** William F Buckley Jr

wicked 3 bad, low **4** base, evil, foul, vile **5** acute, awful, gross, rowdy **6** cursed, fierce, impish, raging, severe, sinful **7** corrupt, extreme, fearful, galling, heinous, hellish, immoral, intense, knavish, naughty, painful, rampant, Satanic, serious, vicious **8** depraved, devilish, dreadful, fiendish, infamous, rascally, shameful **9** atrocious, malicious, monstrous, nefarious **10** abominable, bothersome, degenerate, iniquitous, malevolent, scandalous, villainous **11** disgraceful, mischievous, troublesome **12** blackhearted, dishonorable, incorrigible **13** reprehensible

wickedness 4 evil **6** infamy **8** baseness, foulness, iniquity, vileness **9** depravity, malignity **10** immorality, sinfulness **11** malevolence **13** maliciousness, nefariousness

Wicked Witch of the West

character in: **13** The Wizard of Oz
author: **4** Baum

Wickfield, Agnes
character in: **16** David Copperfield
author: **7** Dickens

Wickford Point
author: **13** John P Marquand

Wickham, Mr
character in: **17** Pride and Prejudice
author: **6** Austen

wide 4 vast **5** ample, broad, fully, great, large, roomy **7** dilated, immense **8** expanded, extended, spacious **9** boundless, capacious, distended, extensive, outspread **10** commodious, completely

wide-awake 2 up **5** alert, aware, quick **8** vigilant, watchful **9** attentive, insomniac, observant, sleepless

widely 3 far **5** broad **6** abroad **7** broadly, greatly, largely **10** by and large, far and near **11** extensively

widely known 5 famed, noted **6** common **7** popular **8** familiar **9** universal, worldwide

widen 6 expand, extend, spread **7** broaden, enlarge, stretch

widened 7 swelled, swollen **8** enlarged, expanded, extended **9** broadened, distended, stretched

wide open 4 ajar, vast **5** agape **6** gaping **7** exposed, yawning **8** extended, unfenced **9** cavernous, expansive, outspread, unbounded **12** outstretched, unobstructed

wide open spaces 7 boonies, country **9** boondocks **11** countryside, hinterlands

wide-ranging 5 broad **7** immense **8** sweeping **9** extensive, universal, unlimited **10** exhaustive **11** diversified, far-reaching **12** encyclopedic **13** comprehensive

Wide Sargasso Sea
author: **8** Jean Rhys

widespread 5 broad **9** extensive, outspread, pervasive, worldwide **10** nationwide **11** far-reaching

Widmark, Richard
born: **9** Sunrise MN
roles: **4** Coma **7** Madigan **8** The Alamo **11** Kiss of Death **12** The Long Ships **16** Halls of Montezuma, How the West Was Won **19** Judgment at Nuremberg

Widow Douglas
character in: **15** (The Adventures of) Huckleberry Finn
author: **5** Twain

wie geht's 9 how are you?

wield 3 ply, use **4** wave **5** apply, exert, swing **6** employ, handle, manage **7** display, utilize **8** brandish, exercise, flourish **10** manipulate

wife 3 rib **4** mate **5** bride, squaw, woman **6** missus, spouse **7** consort,

old lady 8 helpmate, helpmeet 9 companion
French: 5 femme
German: 4 frau

Wife of Bath
character in: 18 The Canterbury Tales
author: 7 Chaucer

Wifey
author: 9 Judy Blume

wig 3 rug 4 fall 6 carpet, peruke, switch, topper, toupee, wiglet 7 periwig 9 hairpiece

Wiggin, Kate Douglas
author of: 23 Rebecca of Sunnybrook Farm

wiggle 3 wag 4 jerk 5 shake, twist 6 quiver, squirm, twitch, writhe 7 flutter 8 writhing 9 squirming

wigwam, Wigwam 3 hut 4 tent, tipi 5 hogan, lodge, tepee 6 teepee 7 weekwam, wickiup 11 Tammany Hall

Wilcox family
characters in: 10 Howard's End
members: 4 Paul, Ruth 5 Henry 7 Charles
author: 7 Forster

wild, wilds, the wild 3 mad 4 bush, rash 5 bleak, feral, giddy, madly, nutty, rabid, rough, waste 6 choppy, crazed, fierce, insane, madcap, raging, raving, rugged, savage, unruly, wooded 7 berserk, bizarre, flighty, frantic, furious, howling, lawless, natural, untamed, violent 8 barbaric, blustery, demented, desolate, fanciful, forested, frenzied, insanely, maniacal, reckless, unbroken, unhinged 9 abandoned, fanatical, fantastic, ferocious, furiously, illogical, lawlessly, naturally, overgrown, primitive, rampantly, screwball, turbulent, violently, wasteland 10 disorderly, maniacally, uninformed 11 harebrained, impractical, tempestuous, uncivilized, uninhabited 12 uncultivated, ungovernable, unrestrained 13 rattlebrained, undisciplined 14 undomesticated

wild animal 5 beast, brute

Wild Ass's Skin
author: 14 Honore de Balzac

Wild Bunch, The
director: 12 Sam Peckinpah
cast: 10 Ben Johnson, Robert Ryan 11 Warren Oates 12 Edmond O'Brien 13 William Holden 14 Ernest Borgnine

wildcat 3 cat 4 lynx 6 ocelot

Wild Duck, The
author: 11 Henrik Ibsen
character: 5 Werle 8 Old Ekdal 9 Gina Ekdal 12 Gregers Werle, Hjalmar Ekdal 13 Hedvig Relling

Wilde, Cornel
real name: 19 Cornelius Louis Wilde
born: 9 New York NY
wife: 11 Jean Wallace
roles: 9 Maracaibo 11 Omar Khayyam

12 Forever Amber, The Naked Prey 15 A Song to Remember 21 A Thousand and One Nights 22 The Greatest Show on Earth

Wilde, Oscar
author of: 6 Salome 17 The Critic as Artist 18 Lady Windermere's Fan 22 The Ballad of Reading Gaol, The Picture of Dorian Gray 27 The Importance of Being Earnest

Wilder, Billy
director of: 11 One Two Three 12 The Apartment (Oscar) 13 Some Like It Hot 14 The Lost Weekend (Oscar) 15 Double Indemnity, Stalag Seventeen, Sunset Boulevard 16 The Seven Year Itch 18 Love in the Afternoon 24 Witness for the Prosecution

Wilder, Gene
real name: 14 Jerry Silberman
born: 11 Milwaukee WI
roles: 12 Silver Streak, The Producers 14 Blazing Saddles, Bonnie and Clyde 17 Young Frankenstein 22 The World's Greatest Lover 27 Start the Revolution Without Me 43 The Adventures of Sherlock Holmes' Smarter Brother

Wilder, Laura Ingalls
author of: 26 The Little House on the Prairie

Wilder, Thornton
author of: 7 Our Town 9 The Cabala 13 The Matchmaker 14 The Ides of March 16 The Woman of Andros 17 The Skin of Our Teeth 20 Heaven's My Destination 21 The Bridge of San Luis Rey

wilderness 4 bush 5 waste 6 barren, desert, forest, plains, tundra 7 barrens 8 badlands, wasteland 9 mountains

Wildeve, Damon
character in: 17 Return of the Native
author: 5 Hardy

Wild Is the River
author: 14 Louis Bromfield

Wild Kingdom
host/narrator: 9 Jim Fowler, Stan Brock 13 Marlin Perkins

Wild One, The
director: 12 Laslo Benedek
cast: 9 Lee Marvin 10 Mary Murphy 12 Marlon Brando

Wild Strawberries
director: 13 Ingmar Bergman
cast: 12 Ingrid Thulin 13 Bibi Andersson 14 Victor Sjostrom 17 Gunnar Bjornstrand

Wild Wild West
character: 10 James T West 13 Artemus Gordon
cast: 10 Ross Martin 12 Robert Conrad
traveled by: 5 train

wile, wiles 4 coax, lure, ploy, ruse, trap 5 charm, guile 6 cajole, entice, gambit, seduce 7 cunning 8 artifice,

maneuver, persuade, subtlety, trickery 9 chicanery, expedient, stratagem 10 artfulness, craftiness, subterfuge 11 contrivance, machination

Wilfer, Bella
character in: 15 Our Mutual Friend
author: 7 Dickens

Wilhelm, Kate
author of: 10 City of Cain, Fault Lines 11 The Planners 14 The Infinity Box 16 The Clewiston Test 19 More Bitter than Death 26 Where Late the Sweet Birds Sang

Wilhelm Meister
author: 6 Goethe

Wilhelm Tell
also: 11 William Tell
author: 17 Johann von Schiller

wiliness 5 guile 7 cunning, slyness 8 artifice, foxiness, scheming, trickery 10 artfulness, craftiness 11 machination

Wilkes family
characters in: 15 Gone With the Wind
members: 4 John 5 Honey, India 6 Ashley 15 Melanie Hamilton
author: 8 Mitchell

will 4 want, wish 5 endow 6 bestow, confer, desire 7 craving, feeling, longing, resolve, wish for 8 attitude, bequeath, pleasure, yearning 9 hankering, testament 10 conviction, preference, resolution 11 disposition, inclination 12 resoluteness 13 determination

Willard, Frank
creator/artist of: 11 Moon Mullins

Willet, John
character in: 12 Barnaby Rudge
author: 7 Dickens

willful 6 mulish, unruly 7 planned, studied 8 designed, intended, obdurate, perverse, stubborn 9 obstinate, pigheaded 10 bullheaded, deliberate, determined, headstrong, inflexible, persistent, purposeful, unyielding 11 intentional, intractable 12 contemplated, premeditated, ungovernable 13 undisciplined 14 uncompromising

Williams, Esther
nickname: 13 Mermaid Tycoon 14 Queen of the Surf 17 Hollywood's Mermaid
born: 12 Los Angeles CA
husband: 13 Fernando Lamas
roles: 13 Bathing Beauty 15 Jupiter's Darling, Ziegfeld Follies 16 Dangerous When Wet, Neptune's Daughter 20 Million Dollar Mermaid

Williams, Janey
character in: 3 USA
author: 9 Dos Passos

Williams, Robin
born: 9 Chicago IL
roles: 6 Popeye 12 Mork and Mindy 15 Good Will Hunting (Oscar)

18 Good Morning Vietnam **23** The World According to Garp

Williams, Ted
nickname: **6** the Kid **16** Splendid Splinter
sport: **8** baseball
position: **8** outfield
team: **12** Boston Red Sox

Williams, Tennessee
author of: **10** Camino Real **13** The Rose Tattoo **14** Summer and Smoke **16** Cat on a Hot Tin Roof, Night of the Iguana, Sweet Bird of Youth **17** Orpheus Descending, The Glass Menagerie **18** Small Craft Warnings, Suddenly Last Summer **21** A Streetcar Named Desire **24** The Roman Spring of Mrs Stone

Williams, William Carlos
author of: **7** Tempers **8** Paterson **9** White Mule **11** Al Que Quiere **20** Pictures from Brueghel

William Tell
also: **13** Guillaume Tell
opera by: **7** Rossini
character: **6** Arnold **7** Gessler

William the Conqueror
also: **17** William of Normandy **21** William I King of England
fought against: **8** Harold II
battle: **8** Hastings
succeeded by: **6** Henry I **9** William II

Willie and Joe
creator: **11** Bill Mauldin

willing 4 game **5** ready **7** content **8** amenable **9** agreeable, compliant, not averse **10** responsive

willingly 4 gain, lief, soon **6** freely, gladly, liefly **7** eagerly, happily, readily **8** by choice **10** cheerfully, graciously **11** voluntarily **12** with pleasure

willingness 4 zeal **8** alacrity **9** eagerness, readiness **10** enthusiasm **11** inclination

Willoughby, John
character in: **19** Sense and Sensibility
author: **6** Austen

willow 5 Salix
varieties: **3** bay, red **4** bush, goat, gray, seep **5** black, crack, false, Niobe, Pekin, pussy, silky, water, white **6** Arctic, arroyo, basket, desert, golden, laurel, puzzle, woolly, yellow **7** brittle, prairie, sandbar, scouler, shining, weeping **8** creeping, florist's, polished, Virginia **9** bayleaved, bearberry, flowering, sprouting **10** cricket- bat, dragon-claw, large pussy, small pussy **11** greenscaled, heart-leaved, peach-leaved, Port Jackson **13** halberd-leaved **16** Wisconsin weeping

willowy 5 lithe **6** limber, pliant, supple, svelte **7** lissome **8** flexible **9** sylphlike

Wills, Chill

born: **12** Seagoville TX
group: **26** Chill Wills and the Avalon Boys
voice of: **21** Francis the Talking Mule
roles: **5** Giant **8** The Alamo **10** Way Out West **11** The Yearling **15** Meet Me in St Louis

Wills, Garry
author of: **14** Nixon Agonistes, Reagan's America **16** Inventing America

Will Scarlet
character in: **9** Robin Hood

willy-nilly 8 perforce **10** helplessly, inevitably **11** inescapably, unavoidably **12** compulsively, irresistibly **14** uncontrollably
Latin: **12** nolens volens

Wilmer
character in: **16** The Maltese Falcon
author: **7** Hammett

Wilson, Edmund
author of: **11** Axel's Castle **19** To the Finland Station

Wilson, Myrtle
character in: **14** The Great Gatsby
author: **10** Fitzgerald

Wilson, Sloan
author of: **26** The Man in the Gray Flannel Suit

Wilson, Woodrow
name at birth: **19** Thomas Woodrow Wilson
nickname: **5** Tommy
presidential rank: **12** twenty-eighth
party: **10** Democratic
state represented: **2** NJ
defeated: **4** (Eugene Victor) Debs, (William Howard) Taft **5** (James Franklin) Hanly **6** (Allen Louis) Benson, (Arthur Edward) Reimer, (Charles Evans) Hughes, (Eugene Wilder) Chafin **9** (Theodore) Roosevelt
vice president: **8** (Thomas Riley) Marshall
cabinet:
  state: **5** (Bainbridge) Colby, (William Jennings) Bryan **7** (Robert) Lansing
  treasury: **5** (Carter) Glass **6** (William Gibbs) McAdoo **7** (David Franklin) Houston
  war: **5** (Newton Diehl) Baker **8** (Lindley Miller) Garrison
  attorney general: **6** (Alexander Mitchell) Palmer **7** (Thomas Watt) Gregory **10** (James Clark) McReynolds
  navy: **7** (Josephus) Daniels
  postmaster general: **8** (Albert Sidney) Burleson
  interior: **4** (Franklin Knight) Lane **5** (John Barton) Payne
  agriculture: **7** (David Franklin) Houston **8** (Edwin Thomas) Meredith
  commerce: **8** (William Cox) Red-

field **9** (Joshua Willis) Alexander
  labor: **6** (William Bauchop) Wilson
born: **2** VA **8** Staunton
died/buried: **2** DC **10** Washington
education:
  college: **8** Davidson **18** College of New Jersey (later known as Princeton U)
  law School: **20** University of Virginia
  university: **12** Johns Hopkins
religion: **12** Presbyterian
author: **8** The State **16** George Washington **18** Division and Reunion **27** A History of the American People **28** More Literature and Other Essays **34** An Old Master and Other Political Essays **41** President Wilson's Case for the League of Nations **47** Congressional Government: A Study in American Politics
political career:
  governor of: **9** New Jersey
civilian career: **6** lawyer
  professor of history: **15** Bryn Mawr College **18** Wesleyan University
  professor of jurisprudence: **9** Princeton
  president of: **9** Princeton
notable events of lifetime/term: **14** Fourteen Points **15** League of Nations
  Act: **7** Adamson **8** Sedition **9** Espionage **10** Child Labor **11** Liberty Loan, Panama Canal **14** Federal Reserve **15** Federal Farm Loan **16** Clayton Antitrust, Selective Service **22** Federal Trade Commission
  conference: **3** ABC **10** Paris Peace
  18th Amendment: **11** Prohibition
  program: **10** New Freedom
  sinking of: **9** Lusitania
  Treaty: **10** Versailles
  won: **15** Nobel Peace Prize
quote: **34** The world must be made safe for democracy
father: **13** Joseph Ruggles
mother: **5** Janet (Woodrow)
siblings: **13** Joseph Ruggles **14** Annie Josephson **16** Marion Williamson
wife: **5** Edith (Bolling Galt), Ellen (Louise Axson)
children: **13** Jessie Woodrow **15** Eleanor Randolph, Margaret Woodrow

wilt 3 die, ebb, sag **4** fade, flag, sink, wane **5** droop **6** recede, weaken, wither **7** decline, dwindle, shrivel, subside **8** decrease, diminish, languish **10** degenerate **11** deteriorate

Wilt the Stilt
nickname of: **15** Wilt Chamberlain

wily 3 sly **4** foxy **5** alert, sharp **6** artful, crafty, shifty, shrewd, tricky **7** crooked, cunning, devious **8** guileful, scheming **9** deceitful, deceptive, designing, underhand **10** intriguing **11** calculating, treacherous

Wimbledon
suburb of: 6 London
site of: 16 tennis tournament
court surface: 5 grass

win 3 bag, get, net 4 earn, gain, sway
6 attain, induce, master, obtain, pick
up, secure 7 achieve, acquire, collect,
conquer, convert, prevail, procure,
realize, receive, success, triumph, victory 8 conquest, convince, overcome,
persuade, vanquish 9 influence
10 accomplish

win acceptance 9 establish 10 ingratiate

wince 5 cower, quail 6 cringe, flinch,
recoil, shrink 7 grimace, shudder 8
cowering, cringing, draw back, quail-
ing 9 shrinking

wind 3 air, lap 4 bend, blow, clue,
coil, curl, fold, gale, gust, hint, loop,
news, puff, roll 5 blast, bluff, curve,
draft, scent, smell, snake, twine, twirl,
twist, whiff 6 breath, breeze, hot air,
ramble, report, wander, zephyr, zigzag 7 bluster, bombast, cyclone, entwine, inkling, meander, sinuate, tempest, tidings, tornado, twaddle,
twister, typhoon, whisper 8 boasting,
idle talk 9 aerophone, hurricane,
knowledge, whirlwind 10 intimation,
suggestion 11 braggadocio, fanfaronade, information 12 intelligence
god of: 5 Eurus, Niord, Njord, Notus
6 Aquilo, Auster, Boreas 8 Favonius,
Zephyrus
father: 8 Astraeus
mother: 3 Eos

windfall 7 bonanza

Windhoek
capital of: 7 Namibia

Wind in the Willows, The
author: 14 Kenneth Grahame
character: 4 Mole, Toad 6 Badger 8
Water Rat

windless 4 calm 5 still 8 stifling

window 3 bay 5 oriel 6 dormer 7
opening, orifice, transom 8 aperture,
casement, porthole, skylight

Winds of War, The
author: 10 Herman Wouk

windstorm 4 gale 6 squall 7 cyclone,
tempest, tornado, twister, typhoon 9
hurricane, whirlwind

windswept 4 bare 5 bleak 6 barren 8
desolate 13 weatherbeaten

windup 3 end 5 close 6 ending, finish
10 completion, conclusion, expiration
11 termination

wind up 3 end 4 halt, stop 5 cease,
close 6 finish, settle 8 complete, conclude 9 terminate

windy 5 blowy, empty, gabby, gusty,
wordy 6 breezy 7 verbose 8 blustery,
rambling 9 bombastic, garrulous, talkative 10 loquacious, meandering,
rhetorical 13 grandiloquent

wine
French: 3 vin
Italian: 4 vino
god of: 7 Bacchus
goddess of: 6 Libera

wine-colored 6 claret 8 burgundy,
cardinal

winemaking
god of: 9 Aristaeus

Winesburg, Ohio
author: 16 Sherwood Anderson

Winfrey, Oprah
born: 12 Kosciusko MS
host of: 19 The Oprah Winfrey Show
author of: 17 Make the Connection
20 Oprah An Autobiography 21 In
the Kitchen with Rosie
Roles: 7 Beloved 14 The Color Purple
23 The Women of Brewster Place

wing 3 ala, fly, set 4 band, clip, flap,
knot, nick, soar, zoom 5 annex,
graze, group 6 circle, clique, pennon,
pinion 7 adjunct, aileron, coterie, faction, section, segment 8 addition, cou-
lisse 9 appendage, extension
10 fraternity

Winged Horse
constellation of: 7 Pegasus

Winger, Debra
husband: 13 Timothy Hutton
roles: 10 Black Widow, Cannery Row
11 Urban Cowboy 17 Terms of
Endearment 22 An Officer and a
Gentleman

Wingert, Dick
creator/artist of: 6 Hubert

Wingfield family
characters in: 17 The Glass Menagerie
member: 3 Tom 5 Laura 6 Amanda
author: 8 Williams

Wings
director: 15 William A Wellman
cast: 8 Clara Bow 10 Gary Cooper 12
Richard Arlen 18 Charles Buddy
Rogers
Oscar for: 7 picture

Wings of the Dove, The
author: 10 Henry James
character: 8 Kate Croy, Lord Mark 9
Mrs Lowder 11 Milly Theale 12 Mrs
Stringham 13 Merton Densher, Sir
Luke Strett

wink at 6 ignore 7 condone, let pass 8
overlook 9 disregard

Winkle
character in: 14 Pickwick Papers
author: 7 Dickens

winner 5 champ 6 master, victor 8
champion 9 conqueror 10 vanquisher

Winnie-the-Pooh
author: 7 A A Milne
character: 3 Owl 5 Kanga 6 Eeyore,
Piglet, Rabbit, Tigger 7 Baby Roo 16
Christopher Robin

winning 7 amiable 8 charming, engag-

ing, pleasing 9 appealing, beguiling,
disarming 10 attractive, bewitching,
entrancing 11 captivating 12 ingratiating, irresistible

Winnipeg
hockey team: 3 Jets

win over 4 beat, best 5 charm 6 defeat, seduce 7 convert 8 overcome,
vanquish 9 captivate, overpower

winsome 5 sweet 6 comely 7 amiable,
likable, lovable 8 charming, cheerful,
engaging, pleasing 9 agreeable, appealing, endearing 10 attractive,
bewitching, delightful

Winter, Lady de
character in: 18 The Three
Musketeers
author: 5 Dumas (pere)

Winter, Maxim de
character in: 7 Rebecca
author: 9 Du Maurier

Winterbourne
character in: 11 Daisy Miller
author: 5 James

Winter of Our Discontent, The
author: 13 John Steinbeck

Winters, Shelley
real name: 14 Shirley Schrift
born: 9 St Louis IL
husband: 13 Tony Franciosa
15 Vittorio Gassman
roles: 11 A Double Life 12 A Patch of
Blue 14 A Place in the Sun 16 A
House Is Not a Home 19 The Diary
of Anne Frank 20 The Poseidon
Adventure

Winterset
author: 15 Maxwell Anderson

winter sports
god of: 4 Ullr 5 Uller

Winter's Tale, The
author: 18 William Shakespeare
character: 7 Camillo, Leontes,
Paulina, Perdita 8 Florizel, Hermione
9 Autolycus, Polixenes

Winter Wonderland
nickname of: 8 Michigan

wintry 3 icy, raw 4 cold 5 bleak,
chilly, harsh, polar, snowy, stark 6
arctic, chilly, dreary, frigid, frosty,
frozen, gloomy, stormy 7 glacial 8 Siberian 9 cheerless

wipe 3 dry, mop, rub 4 swab 5 apply,
brush, clean, erase, rub on, scour,
scrub, swipe, towel 6 banish, remove,
rub off, sponge, stroke

wiped out 5 broke 6 failed, ruined 8
bankrupt, indigent, strapped 9 destitute, insolvent, penniless 12 impoverished

wipe out 4 ruin 5 erase 7 abolish, destroy, eclipse 8 bankrupt 9 devastate,
eliminate, eradicate, extirpate, liquidate 10 annihilate, obliterate 11 exterminate

wiping out 7 erasing 9 eclipsing, expunging **10** abolishing, destroying **11** eliminating, eradicating **12** annihilating, obliterating

wire 5 cable **8** filament, telegram **9** cablegram, telegraph

wiry 4 lean **5** agile, kinky, lanky, spare, stiff **6** limber, pliant, sinewy **7** brittle

Wisconsin
    abbreviation: 2 WI **3** Wis
    nickname: 6 Badger
    capital: 7 Madison
    largest city: 9 Milwaukee
    others: 5 Ripon **6** Antigo, Beloit, Cudahy, Neenag, Racine, Wausau **7** Ashland, Baraboo, Bloomer, Kenosha, Menasha, Oshkosh, Portage, Shawano **8** Appleton, Boscobel, Green Bay, Lacrosse, Superior, Waukesha **9** Eau Claire, Fond du Lac, Sheboygan, Shorewood, Wauwatosa, West Allis **10** Brookfield, Janesville **12** Steven's Point
    college: 5 Ripon **6** Beloit **7** Alverno, Carroll, Viterbo **8** Carthage, Lawrence **9** Marquette, Northland
    feature:
        fort: 6 Howard **8** Crawford **9** Winnebago
        national lakeshore: 14 Apostle Islands
    tribe: 3 Fox, Sac **4** Sauk **5** Huron **6** Oneida, Ottawa **8** Chippewa, Kickapoo **9** Winnebago **10** Potawatomi
    people: 11 Orson Welles **12** Fredric March, Harry Houdini, Spencer Tracy **13** Hamlin Garland **14** Joseph McCarthy, Georgia O'Keeffe, Thornton Wilder **16** Frank Lloyd Wright **17** Robert M LaFollette
    explorer: 6 Joliet **7** Allouez, Nicolet **8** Radisson **9** Marquette **12** Groseilliers
    island: 8 Madeline
    lake: 6 Geneva, Poygan **7** Kenosha, Mendota, Wissota **8** Michigan, Superior **9** Winnebago
    land rank: 11 twenty-sixth
    mountain: 7 Baraboo **9** Sugarbush **10** Blue Mounds
        highest point: 9 Timm's Hill
    physical feature:
        glacial hills: 13 Kettle Moraine
        rock formations: 8 The Dells
    river: 3 Fox **4** Wolf **7** St Croix **8** Chippewa **9** Black Rock, Wisconsin **11** Mississippi
    state admission: 9 thirtieth
    state bird: 5 robin
    state fish: 11 muskellunge
    state flower: 5 pansy **6** violet **10** wood violet
    state motto: 7 Forward
    state song: 11 On Wisconsin
    state tree: 10 sugar maple
wisdom 6 brains **8** sagacity **9** teachings **10** philosophy, principles, profundity **11** discernment, penetra-

tion **12** apperception, intelligence **13** comprehension, judiciousness, understanding
    god of: 2 Ea **4** Enki, Odin **5** Othin, Thoth
    goddess of: 6 Athena, Athene, Brigit, Pallas, Saitis **7** Minerva **11** Tritogeneia **12** Pallas Athena **18** Alalcomenean Athena

wise 3 way **4** sage **6** manner **7** knowing, respect, sapient **8** profound **9** judicious, sagacious **10** discerning, perceptive **11** intelligent **13** knowledgeable, perspicacious, understanding

Wise, Robert
    director of: 11 I Want to Live **13** West Side Story (with Jerome Robbins, Oscar) **15** The Sound of Music (Oscar)

wiseacre 4 fool, sage **5** idiot **7** tomfool **9** know-it-all, simpleton **10** smart aleck

Wise Blood
    author: 15 Flannery O'Connor

wisecrack 4 jest, joke, quip **5** flash, sally **8** cut jokes **9** witticism **11** smart saying

Wise men see **4** Magi

wise up 5 edify **6** advise, in form **7** apprise **9** enlighten, make aware

wish 3 yen **4** hope, long, love, pine, want, whim, will **5** crave, yearn **6** aspire, desire, hunger, thirst **7** command, craving, leaning, longing, request **8** ambition, appetite, fondness, penchant, yearning **10** aspiration, partiality **11** inclination **12** predilection

wishes 11 compliments **13** felicitations **15** congratulations

wish for 4 want **5** covet, crave **6** desire

Wishfort, Lady
    character in: 16 The Way of the World
    author: 8 Congreve

wishful 4 avid **5** eager **6** keen on, pining **7** anxious, craving, hopeful, longing, wanting, wistful **8** aspiring, bent upon, desirous, fanciful, yearning **9** ambitious, expectant

wish well 10 felicitate **12** congratulate

wishy-washy 4 blah, dull, weak **5** inane, vapid, wimpy **6** jejune **7** insipid **8** wavering **10** indecisive, irresolute **11** ineffective, ineffectual, vacillating **12** equivocating, noncommittal **14** tergiversating **15** shilly-shallying

wisp 4 lock, tuft **5** bunch, shred, torch, twist **6** bundle, rumple **8** fragment **10** whisk broom **11** ignis fatuus **13** friar's lantern

wispy 4 thin **5** frail **6** slight **8** fleeting, nebulous

wistaria, wisteria

    varieties: 4 pink, wild **5** silky, water **7** Chinese **8** Japanese **9** Rhodesian

Wister, Owen
    author of: 12 The Virginian

wistful 3 sad **6** musing, pining **7** craving, doleful, forlorn, longing, pensive **8** desirous, mournful, yearning **9** hankering, sorrowful, woebegone **10** meditative, melancholy, reflective **12** disconsolate **13** contemplative, introspective

wit 3 wag **4** gags **5** comic, humor, joker, jokes, quips, sense **6** acumen, banter, brains, jester, joking, levity, wisdom **7** cunning, funster, gagster, insight, punster, sparkle, waggery **8** comedian, drollery, humorist, jokester, judgment, raillery, sagacity, satirist, vivacity **9** funniness, intellect **10** astuteness, brightness, cleverness, jocularity, perception, shrewdness, witticisms **11** discernment, penetration, wisecracker **12** intelligence, perspicacity **13** comprehension, epigrammatist, sagaciousness, understanding
    French: 8 badinage **9** bel-esprit **10** persiflage

witch 3 hag **4** fury **5** crone, scold, shrew, vixen **6** beldam, ogress, virago **7** seeress **8** battle-ax, harridan **9** sorceress, temptress, termagant **10** prophetess **11** enchantress

witchcraft 5 obeah **6** hoodoo, voodoo **7** sorcery **8** black art, witchery, wizardry **9** diabolism, fetishism, voodooism **10** black magic, divination, necromancy **11** conjuration, enchantment

with
    French: 4 avec, chez

with a grain of salt
    Latin: 13 cum grano salis

with a lawsuit pending
    Latin: 12 pendente lite

with authority
    Latin: 10 ex cathedra

withdraw 2 go **5** leave, split **6** depart, go away, recall, recant, remove, retire **7** extract, rescind, retract, retreat, take off, vamoose **9** disappear, unsheathe

withdrawal 4 exit **6** egress **7** leaving, retreat **9** departure **10** retirement, retraction **14** discontinuance

withdrawn 3 shy **5** quiet **8** reserved, retiring, unsocial **9** reclusive **10** unfriendly **11** introverted **15** uncommunicative

wither 4 fade, wilt **5** abash, blast, droop, dry up, shame **7** cut down, mortify, shrivel **9** dehydrate, desiccate, humiliate

withered 3 dry **4** arid, sere **5** dried, faded **6** shrunk, wilted **7** decayed, dried up, drooped, stunned, wizened **9** petrified, shriveled **10** languished

withering 6 biting **7** caustic **8** scathing **9** shrinkage, shrinking, wrinkling

10 shriveling **11** contracting, contraction, devastating

with few words
Latin: **12** paucis verbis

with force and with arms
Latin: **9** vi et armis

with great praise
Latin: **13** magna cum laude

withheld 4 kept **7** checked, forbore, refused, starved **8** kept back **9** boycotted, refrained

with highest praise
Latin: **13** summa cum laude

withhold 4 hide, keep **6** hush up, retain **7** conceal, cover up **8** suppress

withhold from 4 deny **6** refuse

within 2 on **4** into **5** inner **6** during, inside **7** indoors **8** inwardly
combining form: **3** eso **4** endo
prefix: **5** intra

within an inch of 4 near **6** all but, almost, nearly

with-it 7 current **8** up-to-date
French: **9** au courant

with one's own two hands 7 oneself, unaided **10** unassisted

without 4 save **5** minus **6** beyond, except, unless **7** lacking, nowhere, outside, wanting **8** exterior, external, free from, outdoors **9** excepting **10** externally
appointment: **7** sine die
care: **8** sine cure
charge: **4** free **6** gratis **8** sine cure
combining form: **4** ecto
doubt: **9** sine dubio
feet: **4** apod **6** apodal
French: **4** sans
horns: **7** acerous
Latin: **4** sine
law: **8** anarchic
light: **7** aphotic
life: **5** amort **9** inanimate
luster: **3** mat **5** matte
offspring: **9** sine prole
prefix: **2** in
roads: **7** invious
saddles: **8** asellate, bareback
subcalyx leaves: **9** bractless
teeth: **5** morne **8** edentate
this: **7** sine hoc
tongue, teeth, or claws: **5** morne
which not: **10** sine qua non
wings: **7** apteral **8** apterous

without a doubt 6 surely **8** of course **9** certainly **10** absolutely, positively **11** indubitably **12** indisputably **14** unquestionably

without basis 7 unsound **9** unfounded **10** groundless, ungrounded **11** unjustified, unsupported **15** unsubstantiated

without care
French: **9** sans souci

without charge 4 free **10** gratuitous,

on the house **13** complimentary
Latin: **6** gratis

without doubt
French: **9** sans doute

without end 7 endless, eternal, forever **8** immortal, infinite, timeless, unending **9** ceaseless, continual, endlessly, eternally, perpetual **10** immortally, infinitely, timelessly, unendingly **11** ceaselessly, continually, everlasting, never-ending **13** everlastingly **14** lasting forever

without equal
French: **10** sans pareil

without error 4 true **5** exact, right **7** correct, perfect, precise, sinless **8** accurate, truthful, unerring **9** faultless **10** infallible

without exception 5 never **6** always, wholly **8** entirely **10** absolutely, completely, invariably, positively

without fear and without reproach
French: **22** sans peur et sans reproche

Without Feathers
author: **10** Woody Allen

without funds 5 broke **6** ruined **8** bankrupt, indigent, strapped, wiped out **9** destitute, flat broke, insolvent, penniless **10** stone broke **12** impoverished

without light 3 dim **4** dark **5** black, dusky, murky, shady **6** opaque **7** obscure, shadowy, stygian, sunless

without limit
Latin: **11** ad infinitum

without limitation 6 wholly **7** totally, utterly **8** entirely **9** endlessly **10** absolutely, completely, definitely, positively, thoroughly **11** boundlessly **13** unequivocally **15** unconditionally
French: **12** carte blanche

without notice 5 ad-lib **9** impromptu **10** improvised **11** extempory **14** extemporaneous
Latin: **9** extempore

without offspring, without progeny
Latin: **9** sine prole

without the day
Latin: **7** sine die

without which not
Latin: **10** sine qua non

with praise
Latin: **8** cum laude

withstand 4 bear, defy **5** brave **6** endure, resist, suffer **7** weather **8** confront, cope with, tolerate

witless 3 mad **5** crazy **6** insane, stupid **7** fatuous, foolish, unaware **9** slaphappy

witness 3 see **4** mark, note, sign, view **5** proof **6** attend, behold, look on, notice, verify **7** bear out, certify, confirm, endorse, initial, observe **8** attester, attest to, beholder, deponent,

document, evidence, looker-on, observer, onlooker, perceive, validate, vouch for **9** establish, spectator, testifier, testimony **10** validation **11** corroborate, countersign **12** authenticate, confirmation, substantiate, verification **13** corroboration, documentation **14** authentication, substantiation

Witness for the Prosecution
director: **11** Billy Wilder
based on play by: **14** Agatha Christie
cast: **11** Tyrone Power **14** Elsa Lanchester **15** Charles Laughton, Marlene Dietrich

wits 4 mind **6** sanity **9** composure **14** coolheadedness

witticism 4 jest, joke, quip **5** sally **7** epigram
French: **6** bon mot **10** jeu d'esprit

witty 5 comic, droll, funny **6** bright, clever, jocose **7** amusing, jocular, waggish **8** humorous, mirthful **9** brilliant, sparkling, whimsical **11** quickwitted **13** scintillating

witty saying 4 jest, quip **6** bon mot **7** epigram **9** witticism **13** clever comment

Witwoud, Sir Wilfull
character in: **16** The Way of the World
author: **8** Congreve

wizard 4 sage, seer, whiz **5** adept, shark **6** expert, genius, oracle **7** diviner, prodigy, wise man **8** conjurer, magician, sorcerer, virtuoso **9** enchanter **10** soothsayer **11** clairvoyant, necromancer

Wizard of Id, The
creator: **10** Johnny Hart **11** Brant Parker
character: **4** King **5** Spook **6** jester, Rodney, Tyrant

Wizard of Oz, The
director: **13** Victor Fleming
author: **10** L Frank Baum
cast: **4** Toto **8** Bert Lahr (Zeke, Cowardly Lion) **9** Jack Haley (Hickory, Tin Woodsman), Ray Bolger (Hunk, Scarecrow) **11** Billie Burke (Good Witch of the North), Frank Morgan (wizard), Judy Garland (Dorothy Gale) **13** Clara Blandick **15** Charley Grapewin **16** Margaret Hamilton (Almira Gulch, Wicked Witch of the West), The Singer Midgets (Munchkins)
other roles: **6** Aunt Em **10** Uncle Henry
score: **9** E Y Harburg **11** Harold Arlen
remade as: **6** The Wiz
place: **6** Kansas **8** Land of Oz **11** Emerald City
Dorothy wore: **8** red shoes

wizened 3 dry **5** dried **7** dried up **8** shrunken, withered, wrinkled **9** shriveled

WKRP in Cincinnati

character: 10 Andy Travis, Herb Tarlek, Les Nessman **12** Venus Flytrap **13** Arthur Carlson, Dr Johnny Fever **14** Bailey Quarters **15** Jennifer Marlowe

cast: 7 Tim Reid **9** Gary Sandy **10** Gordon Jump **11** Frank Bonner, Jan Smithers **12** Loni Anderson **14** Howard Hesseman, Richard Sanders

wobble 4 reel, sway **5** quake, shake, waver **6** shimmy, teeter, totter **7** quaking, shaking, stagger, swaying **8** wavering **9** shimmying, teetering, tottering **12** unsteadiness

wobbly, Wobbly 5 loose, shaky **7** doubtful **8** hesitant, insecure, unstable, unsteady, wavering **9** quavering, trembling **11** vacillating
union: 17 Industrial Workers

Wodehouse, P G (Pelham Grenville)
author of: 8 Full Moon **14** Thank You Jeeves **15** The Mating Season
character: 6 Jeeves, Psmith **13** Bertie Wooster

Woden
origin: 10 Anglo-Saxon
chief of: 4 gods

woe 5 agony, gloom, grief, trial, worry **6** misery, sorrow **7** anguish, anxiety, despair, torment, torture, trouble **8** calamity, distress **9** adversity, dejection, heartache, suffering **10** affliction, depression, melancholy, misfortune **11** tribulation **12** wretchedness

woebegone 3 sad **4** glum **6** gloomy **7** doleful, forlorn **8** dejected, funereal, mournful, tortured, troubled, wretched **9** agonizing, anguished, miserable, sorrowful, suffering **10** distressed

woeful 3 bad, sad **5** awful, cruel **6** tragic **7** doleful, painful, unhappy **8** crushing, dreadful, grievous, hopeless, horrible, terrible, unlikely, wretched **9** agonizing, appalling, miserable, sorrowful **10** calamitous, deplorable, depressing, disastrous, lamentable **11** distressing, unpromising **12** catastrophic, heartrending **13** disheartening, heartbreaking

woe to the vanquished
Latin: 9 vae victis

Wofford, Chloe Anthony
real name of: 12 Toni Morrison

Wojtyla, Karol
real name of: 14 Pope John Paul II **18** Archbishop of Krakow

wolf 4 bolt, gulp **5** scarf **6** devour, gobble **7** consume
constellation of: 5 Lupus
group of: 4 pack

Wolf, The
author: 11 Frank Norris

Wolfe, Nero *see Stout, Rex*

Wolfe, Thomas
author of: 14 The Hills Beyond **16** The Web and the Rock **17** Look Homeward Angel, Of Time and the River **18** You Can't Go Home Again
character: 10 Eugene Gant **12** George Webber

Wolfe, Tom
author of: 11 Radical Chic **13** The Right Stuff **14** The Painted Word **16** The Pump House Gang **21** From Bauhaus to Our House **23** The Bonfire of the Vanities **24** Mau-mauing the Flak Catchers **26** The Electric Kool-Aid Acid Test **43** The Kandy Kolored Tangerine Flake Streamline Baby

Wollstonecraft, Mary
husband: 13 William Godwin
daughter: 25 Mary Wollstonecraft Shelley
author of: 30 A Vindication of the Rights of Women

Wolverine State
nickname of: 8 Michigan

woman 4 girl, lady, maid, wife **5** flame, lover **6** damsel, maiden, matron **7** beloved, darling, dowager, females, fiancee, sweetie **8** ladylove, mistress **9** charwoman, concubine **10** girlfriend, hand maiden, sweetheart, sweetie pie **11** chambermaid, housekeeper, maidservant
French: 5 femme **8** paramour
Latin: 9 inamorata

Woman, first 3 Eve **5** Embla **7** Pandora

Woman in White, A
author: 13 Wilkie Collins

womanish 7 unmanly **8** feminine, ladylike **9** sissified **10** effeminate

womanlike 8 feminine **10** effeminate

womanly 8 feminine, matronly

Woman of Substance, A
author: 21 Barbara Taylor Bradford

Woman of the Year
director: 13 George Stevens
cast: 10 Fay Bainter **12** Reginald Owen, Spencer Tracy **16** Katharine Hepburn

Woman's Life, A
author: 15 Guy de Maupassant

Women, The
director: 11 George Cukor
based on play by: 15 Clare Boothe Luce
cast: 11 Hedda Hopper **12** Joan Crawford, Joan Fontaine, Marjorie Main, Norma Shearer **15** Paulette Goddard, Rosalind Russell
remade as: 14 The Opposite Sex

Women in Love
director: 10 Ken Russell
based on novel by: 10 DH Lawrence
character: 11 Gerald Crich **12** Rupert Birkin **14** Gudrun Brangwen, Ursula Brangwen
cast: 9 Alan Bates **10** Oliver Reed **11** Eleanor Bron **12** Jennie Linden **13** Glenda Jackson
Oscar for: 7 actress (Jackson)

wonder 3 awe **4** gape **5** sight, stare **6** marvel, ponder, rarity **7** miracle **8** cogitate, meditate, question **9** amazement, spectacle, speculate **10** conjecture, phenomenon **11** fascination **12** astonishment, stupefaction

wonder child
German: 10 wunderkind

wonderful 4 fine, good **5** great, super **6** divine, superb, tiptop, unique **7** amazing, capital **8** fabulous, singular, smashing, striking, terrific **9** admirable, excellent, fantastic, marvelous **10** astounding, incredible, miraculous, phenomenal, staggering, surprising **11** astonishing, crackerjack, fascinating, magnificent, sensational, spectacular **13** extraordinary

Wonderland State
nickname of: 5 Maine

wonderstruck 4 agog **6** amazed **8** thrilled **9** astounded, stupefied **10** astonished, enthralled, spellbound **11** dumbfounded **13** flabbergasted

Wonder Woman
character: 9 (Corp) Etta Candy **11** Diana Prince, Joe Atkinson, (Maj) Steve Trevor **13** Gen Blankenship
cast: 11 Lynda Carter **12** Lyle Waggoner **13** Beatrice Colen, Normann Burton **14** Richard Eastham

wont 3 apt, use **4** used, vain **5** habit, haunt, usage **6** custom, desire **8** accustom, inclined, practice **10** accustomed

wonted 3 apt **5** prone **6** likely **7** given to **10** accustomed, habituated

woo 3 sue **5** chase, court **6** cajole, pursue **7** address, entreat, solicit **8** petition **9** importune

wood 3 log **4** bush **5** brake, brush, copse, grove **6** boards, forest, lumber, planks, siding, timber **7** thicket **8** firewood, kindling **9** clapboard, wallboard **10** timberland

Wood, Grant
born: 9 Anamosa IA
artwork: 12 Spring in Town **13** Stone City Iowa **14** American Gothic **15** Woman with Plants **16** Parson Weems' Fable **18** Dinner for Threshers, John B Turner Pioneer **21** Daughters of Revolution

Wood, John, Sr
architect of: 6 Circus (Bath)

Wood, Natalie
real name: 13 Natasha Gurdin
born: 14 San Francisco CA
husband: 12 Robert Wagner
roles: 5 Gypsy **10** Brainstorm **12** The Great Race, The Searchers **13** West Side Story **17** Inside Daisy Clover **18** Rebel Without a Cause, Splendor in the Grass **19** Sex and the Single Girl **23** This Property Is Condemned **25**

Love with the Proper Stranger **27** Miracle on Thirty- fourth Street

wooded 5 treed **8** forested

wooden 4 dull **5** frame, rigid, stiff **6** clumsy, vacant **7** awkward, deadpan **8** lifeless, ungainly **9** impassive, unbending **10** inflexible, ungraceful **11** unemotional **14** expressionless

Woodhouse, Emma
character in: 4 Emma
author: 6 Austen

woodland 5 copse, grove, treed **6** forest **7** coppice, thicket **8** forested

wood of life
Latin: 11 lignum vitae

woods
god of: 8 Silvanus, Sylvanus

Woods, Sara
real name: 13 Sara Bowen-Judd
author of: 11 Done to Death **12** My Life Is Done **13** Yet She Must Die **15** A Show of Violence, Knives Have Edges **16** And Shame the Devil **17** The Third Encounter, Trusted Like the Fox **18** Bloody Instructions
character: 15 Anthony Maitland

Woodstock
also called: 11 The Cavalier
author: 14 Sir Walter Scott

Woodstock
director: 15 Michael Wadleigh
cast: 6 The Who **7** Santana **8** Joan Baez **9** Joe Cocker **12** Richie Havens **13** John Sebastian, Ten Years After **17** Jefferson Airplane **19** Crosby Stills and Nash **20** Country Joe and the Fish, Sly and the Family Stone
Oscar for: 11 documentary

Woodward, Bob
author of: 4 Veil **19** All the President's Men (with Carl Bernstein)

Woodward, Joanne
born: 13 Thomasville GA
husband: 10 Paul Newman
roles: 12 A Fine Madness, Rachel Rachel **15** Three Faces of Eve (Oscar) **16** The Long Hot Summer **43** The Effect of Gamma Rays on Man-in-the-Moon Marigolds

woodwind instrument 4 oboe **5** flute **7** bassoon, piccolo **8** clarinet **9** bass flute **10** cor anglais **12** bass clarinet **13** double bassoon

wooer 4 beau, love **5** flame, lover, swain **6** adorer, suitor **7** admirer, courter **8** para mour **10** sweetheart

wool
fabric: 4 felt **5** crepe, llama, serge, tweed, twill **6** alpaca, angora, boucle, covert, faille, melton, vicuna, woolen **7** challis, doeskin, Donegal, worsted **8** cashmere, homespun, shetland **9** Astrakhan, camelhair, gabardine, sharkskin **10** hopsacking **11** Harris tweed, herringbone

Woolf, Virginia

author of: 7 Orlando **8** The Waves, The Years **10** Jacob's Room **11** Mrs Dalloway **14** A Room of One's Own **15** To the Lighthouse
member of: 15 Bloomsbury Group

wool-gather 8 daydream, muse idly

woolly, wooly 5 downy, furry, fuzzy, hairy, sheep, vague **6** fleecy, lanate, lanose **7** blurred, muddled, unclear **8** confused, floccose, peronate **10** flocculent, indistinct **12** disorganized

woozy 4 hazy **5** dizzy, faint, foggy, fuzzy, giddy, shaky **6** punchy **7** muddled **9** befuddled **11** light-headed

word, words 3 vow **4** chat, dirt, news, poop, term **5** edict, order, rumor, set-to, voice **6** advice, avowal, decree, gossip, letter, notice, phrase, pledge, remark, report, ruling, signal **7** command, comment, dictate, dispute, explain, express, hearsay, lowdown, mandate, message, promise, quarrel, summons, tidings **8** argument, audience, bulletin, chitchat, colloquy, decision, describe, dialogue, dispatch, locution, telegram **9** assertion, assurance, bickering, direction, discourse, interview, sobriquet, ultimatum, utterance, wrangling **10** articulate, communique, conference, contention, discussion, expression **11** altercation, appellation, declaration, designation, information, scuttlebutt **12** consultation, intelligence, tittletattle **13** communication, pronouncement
French: 9 tete-a-tete

word for word and letter for letter
Latin: 19 verbatim et literatim

wordiness 9 diffusion, prolixity, verbosity **11** diffuseness, profuseness

wording 8 language, phrasing **11** phraseology

wordless 4 dumb, mute **5** tacit **6** silent **8** implicit, taciturn **10** speechless **11** unexpressed

word of honor 3 vow **4** oath **6** pledge **9** assurance

word play 6 banter **7** jesting, kidding
French: 8 badinage, repartee

Words, The
author: 14 Jean-Paul Sartre

Wordsworth, William
author of: 7 Michael **9** Ode to Duty **10** The Prelude **12** Tintern Abbey **14** Lyrical Ballads (with Coleridge) **16** The Ruined Cottage **24** Intimations of Immortality **25** Resolution and Independence
home: 11 Dove Cottage

wordy 5 windy **6** prolix, turgid **7** fustian, gushing, verbose **8** effusive, mumbling **9** bombastic, garrulous, redundant, talkative **10** discursive, loquacious, rhetorical, roundabout **12** tautological **13** grandiloquent

work, works 2 do, go **3** act, job, run, win **4** book, deed, duty, feat, form, gain, line, make, mill, mold, move, shop, song, task, toil, yard **5** beget, cause, chore, craft, enact, labor, opera, piece, plant, shape, slave, solve, sweat, trade **6** drudge, effect, effort, office, output **7** achieve, calling, drawing, execute, exploit, factory, fashion, foundry, innards, insides, operate, perform, produce, product, pursuit, succeed, trouble **8** building, business, concerto, contents, creation, drudgery, endeavor, engender, exertion, function, industry, maneuver, painting, progress, symphony, transmit, vocation **9** originate, sculpture, structure **10** assignment, employment, enterprise, manipulate, occupation, production, profession **11** achievement, composition, performance, transaction
Latin: 4 opus **5** opera
French: 6 metier

work, artistic or literary
French: 6 oeuvre

workaday 5 plain **6** common **7** humdrum, prosaic, routine **8** ordinary **10** unexciting **11** commonplace

work at 3 try **5** essay **6** tackle **7** attempt **8** endeavor

workbench 5 board, table **7** counter

work conquers all
Latin: 16 labor omnia vincit
motto of: 8 Oklahoma

worker 4 doer, hand **5** grind **6** drudge, toiler **7** artisan, hustler, laborer, plodder **8** achiever, employee, producer **9** craftsman, performer **11** breadwinner, eager beaver, proletarian

work for 6 assist **7** support **8** champion

working 3 job **4** duty, toil **5** labor, tasks **6** action, chores, fluent, usable, useful **8** business, drudgery, employed, exertion, industry, laboring **9** effective, operation, operative, practical **10** employment, occupation, profession **11** assignments, functioning, performance

Working
author: 11 Studs Terkel

working-class 5 labor **8** plebian **10** blue-collar **11** proletarian

working class 4 Non-U **9** commoners, common man **10** lower class **11** blue collars, proletariat
Greek: 9 hoi polloi

workmanlike 5 adept **8** skillful **9** efficient **10** productive

workmanship 5 skill **9** handcraft, handiwork, technique **10** handicraft **11** manufacture **12** construction

work out 5 solve, train **6** figure, reckon **7** compute, resolve **8** exercise, practice **9** ascertain, calculate, determine

Works and Days
author: **6** Hesiod

work saver 9 appliance **11** convenience

work-saving 4 easy **6** simple **9** efficient

worktable 4 desk **5** bench, board, table **7** counter

work together 5 unite **7** pitch in, share in **8** take part **9** cooperate **11** collaborate, participate

work toward 3 try **4** seek **6** aim for **7** attempt **8** aspire to, endeavor, reach for

work up 4 goad, urge **5** upset **6** excite **7** agitate, ferment, provoke

work with 5 coach, drill, teach, train **6** assist **8** exercise, instruct **9** cooperate **11** collaborate

world 3 age, era, orb **4** gobs, lots, star **5** class, Earth, epoch, globe, group, heaps, realm, times **6** domain, nature, oodles, people, period, planet, sphere, system **7** mankind, society **8** creation, division, duration, everyone, humanity, industry, universe **9** everybody, humankind, macrocosm **10** profession
Latin: **6** cosmos
Russian: **3** mir

World According to Garp, The
author: **10** John Irving
director: **13** George Roy Hill
cast: **10** Glenn Close, Hume Cronyn **11** John Lithgow **12** Jessica Tandy, Mary Beth Hurt **13** Robin Williams

World Enough and Time
author: **16** Robert Penn Warren

worldly 5 blase **6** astute, shrewd, urbane **7** callous, earthly, fleshly, knowing, mundane, profane, secular **8** material, physical, temporal **9** corporeal, mercenary **11** experienced, terrestrial **12** cosmopolitan **13** sophisticated

world pain
German: **11** Weltschmerz

world view
German: **11** Weltansicht

world-weary 5 blase, bored, jaded **9** unexcited

worldwide 4 rife **6** global **8** catholic, ecumenic, globular, planetal, sweeping **9** universal

worm 4 edge, inch **5** crawl, creep, steal **6** writhe **7** wriggle **9** penetrate **10** infiltrate
kinds: **4** inch, tape **5** angle, earth

worn 4 weak **5** dingy, drawn, faded, seedy, spent, tired, weary **6** frayed, shabby, wasted **7** abraded, haggard, pinched, rickety, wearied **8** battered, decrepit, dog-tired, drooping, fatigued **9** enfeebled, exhausted **10** threadbare, tumbledown **11** debilitated, dilapidated

worn-out 4 dead, shot **5** spent, tired **6** beat-up, effete, shabby, used-up **7**

run-down **9** exhausted **10** threadbare **11** dilapidated **12** deteriorated

worn thin 9 motheaten **10** threadbare **11** dilapidated

worried 6 afraid, scared **7** anxious, fearful **9** concerned **10** distressed **12** apprehensive

worrisome 5 fussy, pesty **6** trying, uneasy, vexing **7** anxious, fretful, irksome **8** annoying **10** bothersome, despairing, disturbing, irritating, tormenting **11** aggravating, troublesome **12** apprehensive

worry 3 vex, woe **4** care, fret, stew **5** agony, beset, dread, grief, harry, upset **6** badger, bother, dismay, harass, hector, misery, pester, plague **7** agitate, agonize, anguish, anxiety, bugaboo, concern, despair, disturb, perturb, problem, torment, trouble **8** distress, vexation **9** misgiving, persecute **10** difficulty, uneasiness **12** apprehension **13** consternation

worsen 4 fail, slip **5** erode, lapse, slide **7** decline **10** degenerate, retrogress **11** deteriorate **12** disintegrate

worsening 7 setback **9** inflaming **10** increasing, regressing, regression **11** aggravating, heightening **12** exacerbating, intensifying **13** retrogressing, retrogression

worship 5 adore, exalt, extol **6** admire, esteem, praise, pray to, revere **7** adulate, glorify, idolize, lionize **8** dote upon, venerate **9** adoration, reverence **10** exaltation, veneration **11** devotionals

worshipful 5 pious **6** devout **8** reverent

worshiping 7 adoring **8** exalting **9** adoration, adulation, adulating, idolizing, reverence **10** exaltation, glorifying, magnifying, venerating, veneration **11** idolization **13** glorification, magnification

worst 3 bad **4** beat, best, rout **5** floor, outdo **6** defeat, lowest, outwit **7** conquer, poorest, triumph **8** inferior, overcome, vanquish **9** discomfit **10** overmaster, unpleasant

worth 3 use **4** cost, good **5** merit, price, value **6** assets, estate, wealth **7** benefit, effects, utility **8** holdings **9** appraisal, resources, valuation **10** importance, usefulness **11** consequence, possessions

worth having 8 valuable **9** desirable

Worthing, Jack
character in: **27** The Importance of Being Earnest
author: **5** Wilde

worthless 6 futile, paltry **7** trivial, useless **8** bootless, piddling, unusable **9** fruitless, meritless, pointless **10** unavailing **11** ineffectual, undeserving, unimportant **12** meretricious, unpro-

ductive **13** insignificant **14** good-for-nothing

worthless objects 4 junk **5** trash **7** garbage, rubbish **8** discards **11** odds and ends

worthwhile 4 good **6** usable, useful **8** valuable **9** rewarding **10** beneficial, profitable

worthy 3 fit, VIP **4** good, name **5** moral, noble **6** bigwig, decent, honest, leader, proper **7** big shot, ethical, fitting, notable, upright **8** big wheel, great man, immortal, laudable, luminary, official, reliable, suitable, virtuous **9** admirable, befitting, deserving, dignitary, estimable, excellent, honorable, personage, reputable **10** creditable **11** appropriate, commendable, meritorious, respectable

worthy of imitation 5 model **9** emulative, exemplary

Wotan
origin: **8** Germanic
chief of: **4** gods
corresponds to: **4** Odin **5** Othin

Wouk, Herman
author of: **13** The Winds of War **14** The Caine Mutiny **17** War and Remembrance **19** Marjorie Morningstar
character: **12** Captain Queeg

wound 3 cut **4** gash, harm, hurt, pain, slit, tear **5** slash, sting **6** bruise, damage, grieve, injure, injury, lesion, offend, pierce, trauma **7** anguish, mortify, torment **8** distress, lacerate, vexation **9** contusion **10** affliction, irritation, laceration **11** provocation

wounded 3 cut **4** hurt **6** mauled **7** damaged, injured, pierced, stabbed **8** impaired, ruptured, stricken **11** traumatized

wrack 4 kelp, ruin **5** ruins, trash **6** clouds, refuse **7** destroy, seaweed, torment **8** downfall, eelgrass, wreckage **9** cloud rack **11** destruction, storm clouds

wraith 5 ghost, shade, spook **6** spirit **7** phantom, specter **8** phantasm **10** apparition **15** materialization
Irish: **7** banshee
German: **12** doppelganger
French: **8** revenant

wrangle 4 tiff **5** argue, brawl **6** bicker **7** dispute, quarrel **8** squabble

wrangling 6 strife **7** arguing, discord **8** clashing, friction **9** bickering **10** contention **11** quarrelling

wrap 4 bind, cape, coat, fold, gird, hide, mask, veil, wind **5** cloak, cover, scarf, shawl, stole **6** bundle, clothe, encase, enfold, girdle, jacket, mantle, shroud, swathe **7** conceal, enclose, envelop, sweater **8** surround

wrapper, wrapping paper 4 case **6** casing, jacket, sheath **8** covering, envelope, slipcase **9** container

wrapping 6 caping, hiding **7** veiling **8** cerement, bundling, swathing **9** embracing, packaging, shrouding **10** engrossing, enswathing, enveloping **11** enshrouding, surrounding

wrap up 3 end **4** pack **6** finish, wind up **7** engross, envelop, involve, package **8** bundle up, complete, conclude **9** polish off **11** dress warmly

wrath 3 ire **4** bile, fury, gall, rage **5** anger **6** animus, choler, rancor, spleen **8** vexation **9** animosity, hostility **10** irritation, resentment **11** displeasure, indignation **13** irritableness

wrathful 3 mad **5** angry, irate **6** bitter, raging **7** furious **8** incensed, virulent

wreak 4 vent, work **5** visit **7** execute, indulge, inflict, unleash

wreak vengeance 6 avenge **7** get even, revenge **9** retaliate

wreath 5 crown **6** diadem, laurel **7** chaplet, coronet, festoon, garland
Hawaiian: 3 lei

wreathe 4 bend, coil, wind **5** curve, twist **7** entwine, envelop **8** encircle **10** intertwine, interweave

wreck 3 end **4** mess, raze, ruin **5** break, crash, death, level, ruins, smash, total, up set **6** finish, ravage, wretch **7** breakup, crack-up, destroy, shatter, undoing **8** demolish, derelict **9** devastate, over throw **10** disruption **11** destruction, devastation, dissolution **12** annihilation

wreckage 4 ruin **5** ruins **6** jet sam **7** flotsam, remains **8** shambles **11** destruction

Wren, P C
author of: 9 Beau Geste

wrench 3 rip **4** jerk, pull, tear, warp **5** force, twist, wrest, wring **6** sprain, strain **7** distort, pervert **12** misrepresent
type: 6 monkey, socket **7** spanner

wrest 3 get, rip **4** earn, gain, grab, jerk, make, pull, take, tear **5** force, glean, twist, wring **6** attain, obtain, secure, wrench **7** achieve, extract, squeeze

wrestle 4 toil **5** labor **6** battle, strive, tussle **7** contend, grapple, scuffle **8** struggle **10** struggling

wrestling
athlete: 8 Dan Gable

wretch 3 cur, pig, rat **4** hobo, waif, worm **5** knave, louse, rogue, swine, tramp **6** misfit, rascal, rotter, varlet **7** castoff, outcast, stinker, villain **8** derelict, scalawag, sufferer, vagabond **9** scoundrel **10** blackguard **11** unfortunate

wretched 3 low **4** base, mean, vile **5** awful, lousy, sorry **6** abject, gloomy, rotten, shabby, sleazy **7** crushed, doleful, forlorn, hapless, pitiful, scruffy, unhappy, worried **8** dejected, downcast, dreadful, hopeless, inferior, pathetic, pitiable, terrible **9** cheerless, depressed, miserable, nig gardly, sorrowful, woebegone, worthless **10** abominable, despairing, despicable, despondent, melancholy **11** crestfallen, unfortunate **12** contemptible, disconsolate, disheartened, inconsolable **13** brokenhearted

wretchedness 4 pain **6** misery, sorrow **7** despair, torment, trouble **8** distress, hardship **9** adversity **10** affliction, melancholy, misfortune **11** un happiness **12** hopelessness

wriggle 5 twist **6** squirm, wangle, writhe **7** meander

Wright, Frank Lloyd
architect of: 8 Taliesin (Spring Green WI) **10** Robie House (Chicago) **11** Martin House (Buffalo NY), Unity Church (Oak Park IL) **12** Fallingwater (Kaufmann House Bear Run PA), Taliesin West (near Phoenix AZ) **13** Imperial Hotel (To kyo) **16** Guggenheim Museum (NYC) **22** Marin County Civic Center (CA) **35** Larkin Company Administration Building (Buffalo NY) **45** S C Johnson and Son Wax Company Administration Center (Racine WI)
style: 6 Modern **7** Organic, Prairie

Wright, Orville and Wilbur
invented: 8 airplane
first plane: 6 Flyer I **9** Kitty Hawk

Wright, Richard
author of: 8 Black Boy **9** Native Son **17** Uncle Tom's Children

wring 4 hurt, pain, rend, stab **5** choke, force, press, twist, wrest **6** coerce, grieve, pierce, sadden, wrench **7** agonize, extract, squeeze, torture **8** compress, distress

wrinkle 4 fold, idea **5** crimp, fancy, pleat, slant, trick **6** crease, device, furrow, gather, notion, pucker, rimple, rumple **7** crumple, gimmick **9** crow's-feet, viewpoint **11** corrugation

wrinkled 3 old **4** aged **5** lined **6** folded, ridged, rucked, rugate, rugose, rugous, seamed **7** creased, crimped, rimpled, rippled, ruckled, rumpled **8** crimpled, furrowed, puckered **9** shriveled

writ 10 court order **11** sealed order **14** mandatory order

write 3 pen **4** copy, show **5** draft **6** author, draw up, record, scrawl **7** compose, dash off, jot down, make out, produce, set down, turn out **8** inscribe, scribble **10** transcribe

write down 3 jot **4** note, post **5** enter **6** record

write in full 5 add to **6** expand, extend, pad out **7** amplify, augment, stretch **9** expatiate

write out 6 expand, extend **7** amplify, enlarge, stretch **8** lengthen

writer 4 hack, poet **6** author, critic, penman, scribe **7** copyist **8** essayist, novelist, reporter, reviewer, scrawler **9** columnist, dramatist, scribbler **10** journalist, librettist, playwright, songwriter **11** penny-a-liner **12** calligrapher, newspaperman **13** correspondent **14** newspaperwoman
French: 11 litterateur

write to 7 address **8** send word **9** drop a line, send a card, send a note **10** correspond **11** send a letter

write-up 4 item **5** piece, story **7** article

write up 5 cover **6** report

writhe 4 jerk **5** flail **6** squirm, thrash, thresh, wiggle **7** contort, wriggle

writing 4 book, play, poem, tome, work **5** diary, essay, novel, print, story **6** column, letter, report, script, volume **7** article, copying, journal, penning **8** critique, document, drafting, libretto, longhand **9** authoring, composing, editorial, recording **10** inscribing, manuscript, penmanship **11** calligraphy, composition, publication **12** transcribing
Latin: 4 opus

writings
Hebrew: 7 Ketubim

written agreement 6 treaty **7** compact **8** contract

written law
Latin: 10 lex scripta

written-out form 9 extension **12** augmentation **13** amplification

wrong 3 bad, sin **4** awry, bilk, evil, harm, hurt, ruin, vice **5** abuse, amiss, cheat, crime, false, inapt, kaput, unfit **6** faulty, fleece, injure, injury, ruined, sinful, unfair, unjust, untrue, wicked **7** crooked, defraud, illegal, illicit, immoral, inexact, inverse, misdeed, offense, reverse, swindle, unhappy, unsound **8** criminal, dishonor, evil deed, ill-treat, immodest, improper, iniquity, maltreat, mistaken, mistreat, opposite, trespass, unlawful, unseemly, villain **9** dishonest, erroneous, felonious, illogical, incorrect, injustice, unethical, unfitting **10** dishonesty, fallacious, illegality, immorality, inaccurate, indecorous, indelicate, iniquitous, malapropos, mistakenly, sinfulness, unbecoming, unfairness, unsuitable, wickedness, wrongdoing **11** blameworthy, erroneously, incongruous, incorrectly, inexcusable, unbefitting, undesirable, unwarranted **12** dishonorable, inaccurately, infelicitous, unlawfulness **13** inappropriate, reprehensible, transgression, unjustifiable **15** unrighteousness

wrongdoer 5 crook, felon, knave, rogue **6** rascal, sinner **7** culprit, misdoer, villain **8** evildoer, offender **9** miscreant, scoundrel **10** blackguard, delinquent, lawbreaker, malefactor, trespasser **11** perpetrator **12** transgressor

wrongdoing 3 sin **4** evil, vice **5** crime **8** misdeeds **10** misconduct **11** delinquency, malfeasance, misbehavior

wrongful 3 bad **6** unfair, unjust **7** illegal **8** criminal, unlawful **10** iniquitous, inequitable **12** illegitimate
act: 4 tort
dispossession: 6 ouster

wrongheaded 3 wry **8** perverse, stubborn **9** misguided

wrong side out 9 backwards **10** topsy-turvy

wrought 4 made **6** beaten, formed, worked **7** crafted **8** hammered **9** fashioned **11** constructed, handcrafted

wrought-up 7 excited **8** agitated **9** emotional **10** hysterical

wry 3 dry **5** askew, droll **6** bitter, ironic, warped **7** amusing, caustic, crooked, cynical, satiric, twisted **8** perverse, sardonic **9** contorted, distorted, sarcastic

Wunderkind 11 wonder child **12** child prodigy

Wurster, William
architect of: 13 Cowell College (UC Berkeley) **17** Ghirardelli Square (San Francisco CA)

Wuthering Heights
character: 9 Ellen Dean **10** Heathcliff, Mr Lockwood **11** Edgar Linton **14** Isabella Linton **15** Catherine Linton, Frances Earnshaw, Hareton Earnshaw, Hindley Earnshaw **16** Linton Heathcliff **17** Catherine Earnshaw
director: 12 William Wyler
author: 11 Emily Bronte
cast: 10 David Niven **11** Donald Crisp, Flora Robson, Leo G Carroll, Merle Oberon (Cathy) **15** Laurence Olivier (Heathcliff) **19** Geraldine Fitzgerald

Wyatt, James
architect of: 8 Pantheon (London) **9** Lee Priory (Kent) **10** Stoke Poges (Buckinghamshire) **13** Fonthill Abbey (Wiltshire) **14** Dodington House Gloucestershire) **15** Heveningham Hall (Suffolk) **16** Sandleford Priory (Berkshire)
style: 13 Gothic Revival

Wyatt, Jane
born: 9 Campgaw NJ

roles: 9 Boomerang **11** Lost Horizon **15** Father Knows Best **17** Great Expectations **19** Gentleman's Agreement **21** None But the Lonely Heart

Wyatt Earp, The Life and Legend of
character: 10 Morgan Earp, Virgil Earp **11** Ben Thompson, Doc Holliday **12** Bat Masterson, Bill Thompson **13** Old Man Clanton
cast: 9 Hal Baylor **10** Denver Pyle, Dirk London, Hugh O'Brien **12** John Anderson **13** Douglas Fowley **14** Trevor Bardette **20** Mason Alan Dinehart III
setting: 8 OK Corral **9** Dodge City, Ellsworth, Tombstone
Wyatt's pistols: 15 Buntline Special

Wyeth, Andrew Newell
born: 2 PA **10** Chadds Ford
father: 7 N C Wyeth
artwork: 9 Grape Wine, River Cove **12** Nick and Jamie **14** Christina Olson, Distant Thunder **15** Christina's World **22** Winter Nineteen Forty-six

Wyler, William
director of: 6 Ben Hur (Oscar) **7** Jezebel **9** Dodsworth, Funny Girl, The Letter **10** Mrs Miniver (Oscar), The Heiress, These Three **12** Roman Holiday **14** The Little Foxes **15** Counsellor-at-Law **16** Wuthering Heights **18** Friendly Persuasion **22** The Best Years of Our Lives (Oscar)

Wylie, Philip
author of: 13 Opus Twenty-one **19** A Generation of Vipers

Wyman, Jane
real name: 14 Sarah Jane Fulks
born: 10 St Joseph MO
husband: 12 Ronald Reagan
daughter: 13 Maureen Reagan
son: 13 Michael Reagan
roles: 5 So Big **9** Pollyanna **11** Falcon Crest, The Blue Veil, The Yearling **13** Johnny Belinda (Oscar) **14** Angela Channing, The Lost Weekend **17** The Glass Menagerie **20** Magnificent Obsession

Wyndham, John
real name: 16 John Beynon Harris
author of: 14 The Kraken Wakes **15** Consider Her Ways **17** The Midwich Cuckoos, Trouble with Lichen **19** The Day of the Triffids

Wyoming

abbreviation: 2 WY **3** Wyo
nickname: 8 Equality
capital: 8 Cheyenne
largest city: 6 Casper
others: 4 Cody, Lusk **7** Bighorn, Buffalo, Laramie, Rawlins, Worland **8** Gillette, Greybull, Kemmerer, Riverton, Sheridan, Sundance **11** Rock Springs
feature:
  center: 11 Buffalo Bill
  dam: 8 Shoshone
  fort: 7 Laramie
  historical preserve: 11 Fort Bridger
  national grassland: 11 Tunder Basin
  national monument: 11 Devil's Tower, Fossil Butte
  national park: 10 Grand Teton **11** Yellowstone
  reservoir: 12 Flaming Gorge
tribe: 4 Crow **5** Kiowa, Sioux **7** Arapaho, Bannock **8** Cheyenne
people: 11 Buffalo Bill **14** Jackson Pollock **16** Nellie Tayloe Ross **18** Francis Emroy Warren
  explorer: 4 Colter, Stuart **7** Bridger **10** Bonneville
lake: 7 Jackson **11** Yellowstone
land rank: 5 ninth
mountain: 3 Elk **5** Cloud, Moran **6** Absaro, Hoback, Tetons **7** Bighorn, Fremont, Laramie, Rockies **8** Atlantic, Sheridan **9** Wind River **10** Black Hills **11** Rattlesnake
  highest point: 11 Gannett Peak
physical feature: 11 Jackson Hole
  basin: 7 Wyoming
  cave: 8 Shoshone
  hot springs: 11 Thermopolis
  plains: 5 Great
river: 4 Bear, Wind **5** Green, Snake **6** Platte, Powder, Tongue **7** Bighorn **8** Cheyenne, Shoshone **10** Sweetwater **11** Yellowstone **12** Belle Fourche
state admission: 11 forty-fourth
state bird: 17 western meadowlark
state flower: 10 painted cup **16** Indian paintbrush
state motto: 11 Equal Rights
state song: 7 Wyoming
state tree: 10 cottonwood

Wyss, Johann Rudolf
author of: 22 The Swiss Family Robinson
  inspired by: 14 Robinson Crusoe

X Y Z

Xanthippe, Xantippe 3 hag **4** fury **5** scold, shrew, vixen **6** dragon, virago **7** scolder **8** spitfire **9** termagant
husband: 8 Socrates
Xanthus and Balius
horses of: 8 Achilles
trait: 8 immortal
Xenia
epithet of: 6 Athena
means: 10 hospitable
xeno- 6 prefix **7** foreign, strange
Xenoclea
form: 9 priestess
xenon
chemical symbol: 2 Xe
xenophobia
fear of: 9 strangers
xerox 4 copy
Xerxes *see* **9** Ahasuerus
X-Files
Creator: 11 Chris Carter
director: 11 Chris Carter
characters: 3 Mr. X (Steven Williams) **9** Fox Mulder (David Duchovny) **10** Alex Krycek (Nick Lea), Dana Scully (Gillian Anderson), Deep Throat (Jerry Hardin) **13** Walter Skinner (Mitch Pileggi) **19** Cigarette-Smoking Man (William B. Davis)
x-ray 9 radiogram **10** radiograph **13** roentgenogram **14** roentgenograph
X-ray tube
invented by: 8 Coolidge
yacht 4 boat, race, sail, ship, yawl **5** ketch, sloop **6** cruise, cutter **7** catboat **8** schooner
race: 11 America's Cup
yachting
athlete: 9 Ted Turner **11** Lowell North
yahoo 4 lout **5** brute, yokel **7** lowbrow **9** barbarian, ignoramus, vulgarian
Yahoos
fictional people in: 16 Gulliver's Travels
author: 5 Swift
Yahweh 3 God **4** Lord **5** Jahve, Jahwe, Yahve, I Am, I am I am, Jahveh **7** Creator, Eternal, Jehovah **8** Absolute, Almighty, Infinite
component: 2 he **3** yod, vav
pronunciation: 6 Adonai, Elohim **9** forbidden
transliteration: 4 YHVH
Yale, Linus, Jr

invented: 12 cylinder lock **27** dial-operated combination lock
Yalta
in: 7 Ukraine
conference participant: 6 Stalin **9** Churchill, Roosevelt
yam 9 Dioscorea **14** Ipomoea batatas
varieties: 4 wild **5** Negro, water, white **6** Attoto, potato, yellow **7** Chinese **11** sweet potato
Yamasaki, Minoru
architect of: 14 St Louis Airport (MO) **16** World Trade Center (NYC) **21** Woodrow Wilson Building (Princeton NJ)
yammer 3 cry **4** carp, harp, howl, wail, yell **5** whine **7** grumble, whimper **8** complain
yank 3 tug **4** jerk, pull **5** pluck, wrest **6** snatch, wrench **7** draw out, extract, pull out
Yankee, Yank 2 GI **5** teddy **6** gringo **8** American, doughboy **10** Northerner
Spanish: 6 yanqui
Yankee Doodle Dandy
director: 13 Michael Curtiz
cast: 10 Joan Leslie **11** James Cagney (George M Cohan) **12** Irene Manning, Walter Huston
Oscar for: 5 actor (Cagney)
yanqui 6 Yankee **9** US citizen
Yaounde
capital of: 8 Cameroon
yap 3 yip **4** blab, gush, rave, talk, yawp, yelp **5** scold **6** babble, gabble, gossip, jabber, rave on, tattle **7** blather, chatter, lecture, palaver, prattle **8** complain, converse
Yaqui
language family: 6 Cahita
location: 6 Mexico, Sonora **7** Arizona
yard 4 lawn **5** close, court **6** garden **7** confine, grounds, pasture **8** compound **9** enclosure, three feet
abbreviation: 2 yd
yardbird 3 con **5** felon **7** convict **8** prisoner
yard goods 5 cloth **6** fabric **8** material, textiles
Yard of Sun
author: 14 Christopher Fry
yardstick 4 rule **7** measure **8** standard **9** criterion
Yaren District
capital of: 5 Nauru

yarn 4 tale **5** story **7** account **8** anecdote **9** adventure, narrative **10** experience
Yastrzemski, Carl
nickname: 3 Yaz
sport: 8 baseball
team: 12 Boston Red Sox
Yates, Peter
director of: 7 Bullitt **12** Breaking Away
yawn 3 gap **4** bore, gape **5** chasm **8** open wide, oscitate
yawp 4 roar, yelp **5** noise **6** clamor, squawk, yammer
Yaz
nickname of: 15 Carl Yastrzemski
Yazoo
author: 12 Willie Morris
year, years 3 age, era **4** time **5** cycle, epoch **6** period
abbreviation: 2 yr
Yearling, The
director: 13 Clarence Brown
author: 22 Marjorie Kinnan Rawlings
cast: 9 Jane Wyman **10** Chill Wills **11** Gregory Peck **14** Claude Jarman Jr
character: 9 Ora Baxter **10** Jody Baxter **11** Oliver Hutto, Penny Baxter **12** Grandma Hutto **14** Twink Weatherby **19** Fodder-Wing Forrester
yearn 4 ache, long, pine, sigh, want, wish **5** crave **6** hanker, hunger, thirst **8** languish
yearning 3 yen **4** ache, want, wish **5** fancy **6** desire, hunger, thirst **7** craving, longing, passion **9** hankering **10** aspiration **11** inclination
Year of Living Dangerously, The
director: 9 Peter Weir
cast: 9 Linda Hunt (Billy Kwan), Mel Gibson **15** Sigourney Weaver
setting: 7 Jakarta
Oscar for: 17 supporting actress (Hunt)
year of wonders
Latin: 14 annus mirabilis
Yeats, William Butler
author of: 7 A Vision **8** The Tower **9** Last Poems **14** Leda and the Swan **15** The Winding Stair **18** Sailing to Byzantium **19** Among School Children, The Wild Swans at Coole **21** Easter Nineteen Sixteen **22** The Lake Isle of Innisfree **29** An Irish Airman Foresees His Death

yegg 6 bomber 9 cracksman 11 safe-cracker

yell 3 boo, cry 4 bawl, hoot, howl, roar, yowl 5 cheer, hollo, shout, whoop 6 bellow, clamor, cry out, holler, hurrah, huzzah, outcry, scream, shriek, squall, squeal 7 screech

yellow 4 gold 5 blond, lemon, ocher 6 afraid, canary, craven, flaxen 7 chicken, fearful, saffron 8 cowardly, timorous 10 frightened 12 apprehensive, fainthearted 13 pusillanimous 14 chickenhearted

yellow-belly 6 coward 7 caitiff, chicken, dastard 8 poltroon

Yellowhammer State
  nickname of: 7 Alabama

yellowish 4 buff 5 blond, cream 6 blonde, creamy, flaxen

Yellow Kid, The
  creator: 10 R F Outcault
  trademark: 10 nightshirt
  place: 5 slums 11 Hogan's Alley
  coined term: 16 yellow journalism
  first: 10 comic strip

yelp 3 yap, yip 4 bark, howl 5 shout 6 clamor, holler, scream, shriek, squeal 7 screech

Yemen, North
  other name: 4 Sana
  capital/largest city: 4 Sana 5 Sanaa
  others: 4 Moka, Taiz 5 Dahhi, Damar, Jibla, Mocha, Mukha, Taizz, Umram 7 Hodeida, Hudayda
  monetary unit: 4 fils, rial 5 riyal
  island: 5 Zugar 6 Hanish
  highest point: 6 Shuayb
  river: 5 Abrad, Zabid 6 al-Jawf, Surdud
  sea: 3 Red
  physical feature:
    desert: 10 Rub al Khali
    gulf: 4 Aden
    lowlands: 6 Tihama
    peninsula: 7 Arabian
    strait: 11 Bab el Mandeb
  people: 4 Arab 5 Zaidi 6 Shafai, Yemeni 8 Yemenite
    leader: 16 Ali Abdallah Saleh 19 Abd al-Aziz Abd al-Ghani
  language: 6 Arabic
  religion: 5 Islam
  place:
    ruins: 5 Marib
  feature:
    dagger: 7 jambiya
    king: 4 imam
    kingdom: 4 Saba 5 Sheba 11 Arabia Felix
    tree: 3 fig 5 carob, mango, myrrh
  food:
    coffee: 5 mocha

Yemen, South
  capital: 4 Aden 14 Madinat al-Shaab
  largest city: 4 Aden
  others: 5 Ahwar, Shihr, Tarim 6 Balhaf, Damqut, Seiyun, Shabwa, Shibam, Zamakh 7 Mukalla
  monetary unit: 4 fils 5 dinar
  island: 5 Perim 7 Kamaran, Socotra
  mountain: 7 Djehaff
  highest point: 6 Thamir
  river: 4 Bana 6 Tibban 7 Masilah 9 Hadramaut
  sea: 6 Indian 7 Arabian
  physical feature:
    desert: 10 Rub al Khali 12 Empty Quarter
    gulf: 4 Aden
    peninsula: 7 Arabian
    valley: 9 Hadramawt
  people: 4 Arab
  language: 6 Arabic
  religion: 5 Islam
  feature:
    animal: 4 ibex, oryx
    clothing: 4 futa

yen 4 ache, long, pine, sigh, want, wish 5 crave, fancy, yearn 6 aching, desire, hanker, hunger, relish, thirst 7 craving, longing, passion 8 appetite, languish, yearning 9 hankering 10 aspiration 11 inclination

yenta 3 hen 6 gossip 8 busybody 12 blabbermouth

Yentl
  director: 15 Barbra Streisand
  based on story by: 19 Isaac Bashevis Singer
  cast: 13 Mandy Patinkin 15 Barbra Streisand

Yeobright, Thomasin and Clym
  characters in: 17 Return of the Native
  author: 5 Hardy

yeoman 4 chap, exon 5 churl, clerk, swain 6 farmer, fellow 7 granger, plowman, servant 8 graycoat, retainer 9 beefeater 10 freeholder 12 petty officer

Yerby, Frank
  author of: 8 Fair Oaks 10 Health Card 11 Griffin's Way 12 Pride's Castle 16 The Foxes of Harrow 21 Hail the Conquering Hero

yes 3 aye, yea 4 amen, okay, true 5 truly 6 assent, indeed, it is so, just so, really, so be it, surely, verily 7 consent, exactly, granted, no doubt 8 approval, of course, to be sure 9 agreement, assuredly, certainly, doubtless, precisely 10 acceptance, positively 11 affirmation, undoubtedly 12 acquiescence, emphatically 13 affirmatively, authorization
  French: 3 oui
  German: 2 ja
  Spanish: 2 si

yesterday 7 the past 10 bygone days, days of yore, olden times, time gone by 11 former times 13 the recent past 14 the good old days 17 the day before today 22 on the day preceding today

yet 3 but 4 also, even, then, up to 5 again, still, while, until 6 no less, though 7 besides, earlier, even now, further, however, thus far 8 although, hitherto, moreover 9 presently 10 eventually, ultimately 12 nevertheless 15 notwithstanding

yew 5 Taxus
  varieties: 4 plum 5 Irish 6 golden 7 Chinese, English, Florida, Western 8 American, Japanese, Southern 11 Chinese plum, Plum-fruited 12 Japanese plum, Prince Albert 14 Harrington plum

Yggdrasil
  also: 9 Iggdrasil
  origin: 12 Scandinavian
  kind of tree: 12 evergreen ash
  roots: 5 three
  binds: 6 Asgard 7 Midgard 8 Niflheim 10 Mithgarthr

yield 3 pay, sag 4 bear, crop, earn, gain, give 5 beget, break, burst, defer, droop, forgo, grant, spawn, split, waive 6 accede, cave in, give in, give up, kowtow, ren- der, return, submit, supply 7 bow down, concede, forbear, furnish, give way, harvest, pay ment, premium, produce, product, provide, revenue, succumb, truckle 8 collapse, cry uncle, earnings, generate, interest, proceeds, renounce 9 acquiesce, gleanings, procreate, surrender 10 capitulate, relinquish

yielding 3 lax 4 soft 6 ceding, spongy 7 sagging 8 flexible, obedient 9 compliant 11 complaisant 13 accommodating

Yigdal 22 Jewish liturgical prayer
  literally: 12 becomes great

Yizkor 33 Jewish service to commemorate the dead
  literally: 9 be mindful

Ymir
  origin: 12 Scandinavian
  progenitor of: 6 giants
  earth made from: 5 flesh
  water made from: 5 blood
  heavens made from: 5 skull

yoga, yogi 5 Hindu 6 mystic 7 ascetic

Yogi Bear
  creator: 12 Hanna-Barbera
  character: 6 BooBoo
  setting: 14 Jellystone Park

yoke 3 tax 4 bond, join, link, load, pair, span, team 5 brace, clasp, hitch, trial, unite 6 at tach, burden, collar, couple, fasten, strain, weight 7 bondage, coupler, harness, serfdom, slavery 8 distress, pressure, troubles 9 servitude, thralldom, vassalage 10 oppression 11 enslavement, tribulation

yokel 4 clod, hick, rube 7 bumpkin, hayseed, peasant, plowboy 10 clodhopper, provincial

yolk 6 yellow

yonder 3 yon 5 there 6 far-off 7 faraway, farther, thither

Yorick
  skull in: 6 Hamlet
  author: 11 Shakespeare
Yorick, Mr
  character in: 14 Tristram Shandy
  author: 6 Sterne
York, Michael
  born: 6 Fulmer **7** England
  roles: 6 Tybalt **7** Cabaret **11** Lost Horizon **14** Four Musketeers, Romeo and Juliet, The Forsyte Saga **15** Three Musketeers **19** The Island of Dr Moreau **24** The Last Remake of Beau Geste
York, Susannah
  real name: 23 Susannah Yolande Fletcher
  born: 6 London **7** England
  roles: 5 Freud **6** Images **8** Jane Eyre, Tom Jones **12** The Awakening
  author of: 18 In Search of Unicorns
Yossarian
  character in: 14 Catch Twenty-two
  author: 6 Heller
You Asked for It
  host: 8 Art Baker **9** Jack Smith
You Bet Your Life
  host: 11 Groucho Marx
  announcer: 14 George Fenneman
You Can't Go Home Again
  author: 11 Thomas Wolfe
  character: 10 Esther Jack **11** Lloyd McHarg **12** George Webber **13** Else von Kohler **14** Foxhall Edwards
You Can't Take It With You
  author: 8 Moss Hart **14** George S Kaufman
  director: 10 Frank Capra
  cast: 10 Jean Arthur, Mischa Auer **12** Edward Arnold, James Stewart **15** Lionel Barrymore
  Oscar for: 7 picture **8** director
young 3 cub, pup **4** baby, kids **5** child, issue, minor, whelp **6** boyish, callow, junior, kitten, youths **7** budding, girlish, growing, progeny, puerile, teenage **8** childish, children, immature, juvenile, underage, youthful **9** beardless, infantile, juveniles, offspring, teenagers **10** adolescent, descendant, sophomoric, youngsters **11** adolescents, undeveloped **13** inexperienced
  god of: 7 Angus Og
  goddess of: 4 Hebe
Young, Chic
  creator/artist of: 7 Blondie
Young, Denton True
  nickname: 2 Cy **7** Cyclone
  sport: 8 baseball
  position: 7 pitcher
  team: 12 Boston Braves, Boston Red Sox **16** Cleveland Indians, St Louis Cardinals
Young, Loretta
  real name: 13 Gretchen Young
  husband: 12 Grant Withers
  roles: 13 Cause for Alarm **14** The

Bishop's Wife **15** Come to the Stable **18** The Farmer's Daughter (Oscar) **20** Rachel and the Stranger
Young, Robert
  born: 9 Chicago IL
  roles: 10 Relentless **11** H M Pulham Esq **13** Marcus Welby M D **15** Father Knows Best **16** Strange Interlude
Young Adventure
  author: 19 Stephen Vincent Benet
Young Frankenstein
  director: 9 Mel Brooks
  cast: 8 Teri Garr **10** Gene Wilder, Peter Boyle **11** Gene Hackman **12** Madeline Kahn, Marty Feldman **14** Cloris Leachman
  score: 10 John Morris
young girl
  French: 10 jeune fille
young lady
  German: 8 fraulein
Young Lonigan
  author: 13 James T Farrell
Young Manhood of Studs Lonigan
  author: 13 James T Farrell
youngster 3 boy, kid, tot **4** baby, girl **5** child, minor, youth **7** progeny **8** juvenile, teenager **9** fledgling, offspring **10** adolescent
young Turks 6 rebels **8** radicals, upstarts **9** activists **10** insurgents **15** revolutionaries
young woman
  French: 10 demoiselle
you're welcome
  German: 5 bitte
Your Show of Shows
  regular: 9 Bill Hayes, Jerry Ross, Sid Caesar **10** Carl Reiner **11** Imogene Coca **12** Howard Morris, Nellie Fisher **13** James Starbuck, Robert Merrill **16** Marguerite Piazza
youth 3 boy, kid, lad **4** kids **5** bloom, child, minor, prime, teens **6** heyday **7** boyhood **8** children, girlhood, juvenile, minority, teenager **9** childhood, fledgling, juveniles, schoolboy, stripling, teenagers, youngster **10** adolescent, pubescence, youngsters **11** adolescence, adolescents
youthful 5 fresh, young **6** boyish, callow **7** girlish, puerile, teenage **8** childish, immature, juvenile **10** adolescent, sophomoric **12** enthusiastic, light hearted **13** inexperienced
yowl 3 bay, cry **4** bawl, roar, wail, yelp **5** shout, whine **6** bellow, holler, scream, shriek, squeal **7** screech **9** caterwaul
Ypres
  in: 7 Belgium
  WWI: 10 battle site
yuan
  currency of: 5 China
yucca 5 agave

varieties: 4 blue **6** banana **9** San Angelo, spineless **11** twisted-leaf
Yugoslavia
  other name: 8 Dalmatia **34** Kingdom of the Serbs Croats and Slovenes
  capital/largest city: 7 Beograd **8** Belgrade
  others: 3 Nis **4** Pola, Pula, Savo, Zara **5** Agram, Bosna, Budva, Fiume, Kotor, Pirot, Rieka, Rtanj, Senta, Split, Tuzla, Uskub, Zadar **6** Bitola, Bitolj, Ca Haro, Maglaj, Morava, Mostar, Osijek, Prilep, Ragusa, Rijeka, Skopje, Trogir, Visoko, Zagreb **7** Cetinje, Laibach, Maribor, Novisad, Skoplje, Spalato **8** Monastir, Pristina, Sarajevo, Subotica, Titograd **9** Banja Luka, Dubrovnik, Ljubljana, Podgorica, Smederevo
  divisioin/former division: 6 Bosnia, Serbia **7** Croatia **8** Crna Gora, Slovenia **9** Macedonia, Vojvodina, Voyvodina **10** Montenegro **11** Hercegovina, Herzegovina **14** Kosovo-Metohija
  measure: 3 oka, rif **4** akov, ralo **5** donum, khvat, lanaz, plaze, stopa **6** motyka, ralico **9** danoranja
  monetary unit: 4 para **5** dinar
  weight: 3 oka **5** dramm, tovar, wagon **7** satlijk
  island: 3 Rab **4** Arbe, Brac, Cres, Hvar, Pago **5** Mljet, Solta, Susac, Susak **7** Korcula
  lake: 4 Bled **5** Ohrid **6** Prespa **7** Ochrida, Scutari
  mountain: 5 Karst **6** Balkan **7** Rhodope **8** Crna Gora, Durmitor **9** Sar-Pindus **10** Karawanken
    Alps: 6 Carnic, Julian **7** Dinaric **9** Slovenian **16** Northern Albanian
  highest point: 7 Triglav
  river: 3 Una **4** Drim, Drin, Ibar, Krka, Kupa, Sava, Tisa **5** Anube, Bosna, Cazma, Drava, Drina, Raska, Tamis, Timok, Tisza, Vrbas **6** Danube, Morava, Vardar, Velika **7** Neretva **9** Vojvodina
  sea: 8 Adriatic
  physical feature:
    bay: 5 Kotor
    cave: 8 Postojna
    channel: 7 Narento
    gulf: 5 Kotor **7** Kvarner, Trieste
    hot springs: 16 Krapinske Toplice
    peninsula: 6 Balkan **7** Istrian
  people: 4 Serb, Slav **5** Croat **7** Slovene **8** Albanian **10** Macedonian **11** Montenegrin
    author: 6 Andric, Djilas, Krleza **7** Dedijer
    leader: 4 Tito **5** Dusan, Pasic **6** Djilas **7** Nemanja **9** Milosevic, Obrenovic **13** Mikhailovitch
    ruler: 5 Peter **9** Hapsburgs **12** Ottoman Turks
    sculptor: 9 Mestrovic
  language: 7 Bosnian, Slovene **8** Alba-

nian, Croatian **9** Hungarian, Slovenian **10** Macedonian **11** Montenegrin **13** Herzegovinian, Serbo-Croatian
  alphabet: 5 Latin **8** Cyrillic
  religion: 5 Islam **13** Roman Catholic **15** Eastern Orthodox, Serbian Orthodox
  place:
    amphitheater: 4 Pula
    bridge: 9 Stari Most
    fortress: 10 Kalemedgan
    monastery: 8 Sopocani
    mosque: 6 Begova **15** Bajrakli Dzamija
    ruins: 14 Hadrian's Palace
    square: 8 Republic
  feature:
    coffee house: 7 kafanas
    fields: 5 polje
    military governor: 7 vojvodi
    musical instrument: 5 gusla
    poems: 5 pesme
    slippers: 6 opanki
  food:
    dessert: 4 pita
    drink: 5 rakia **6** rakija **7** maraska **9** slivovitz **10** sljivovice **13** Turkish coffee
    meat: 7 shaslik **9** cevapcici **10** culbastija
    soup: 6 corbas
Yuit *see* **6** Eskimo
Yukon Territory
  border: 6 Alaska **15** British Columbia, Selwyn Mountains **18** Mackenzie Mountains
  capital: 10 Whitehorse
  country: 6 Canada
  event: 8 gold rush (1897)
  Indian: 4 Dene **6** Eskimo **7** Kutchin **8** Loucheux **9** Athabasca
  lake: 6 Kluane **9** Great Bear
  mineral: 4 gold **6** silver
  mountain: 3 Joy **5** Logan **6** Harper **7** Kennedy **8** Campbell
  region: 8 Klondike
  river: 5 Pelly **9** Porcupine
  sea: 8 Beaufort
  town: 4 Elsa, Faro, Mayo, Snag **5** Rocky **6** Dawson **8** Franklin, Wernecke **9** Mackenzie
yule 4 Noel **9** Christmas
Yule, Joe, Jr
  real name of: 12 Mickey Rooney
Yuman
  tribe: 6 Mohave, Mojave **8** Hualapai
Zachariah
  father: 4 Babi, Elam **9** Barachias
  wife: 9 Elizabeth
  son: 3 Abi **14** John the Baptist
  succeeded: 8 Jeroboam
  visitor: 7 Gabriel
zaddik 14 virtuous person **15** righteous person
Zadkine, Ossip
  born: 6 Russia **8** Smolensk
  artwork: 4 Stag **6** Christ **7** Orpheus

9 Musicians **10** The Prophet **13** Woman with a Fan **14** Mother and Child **16** The Destroyed City
Zadok
  father: 5 Baana, Immer **6** Ahitub
  son: 7 Shallum
  daughter: 7 Jerusha
  served: 5 David
zaftig 5 buxom, plump **6** bosomy
Zagreus
  form: 5 child, deity
  father: 4 Zeus
  mother: 6 Semele **10** Persephone
Zaire
  other name: 5 Congo **12** Belgian Congo **13** Congo-Kinshasa **17** Congo-Leopoldville
  capital/largest city: 8 Kinshasa
  others: 4 Baya, Boma, Lebo **5** Aketi, Ilebo **6** Banana, Kamina, Kasaji, Kikwit, Matadi, Sandoa **7** Butembo, Kananga, Kolwezi **8** Bakwanga, Yangambi **9** Kisangani **10** Lubumbashi, Luluabourg, Mutshatsha **12** Port-Francqui, Stanleyville **14** Elisabethville
  school: 5 Zaire **8** Lovanium
  division: 4 Kivu **5** Kasai, Shaba **7** Equator, Katanga **8** Oriental
  monetary unit: 5 zaire **6** makuta
  lake: 4 Kivu **5** Mweru, Tumba **6** Albert, Edward, Upemba **9** Mai-Ndombe **10** Tanganyika
  mountain: 7 Crystal, Mitumba, Virunga **9** Ruwenzori **10** Nyaragongo **18** Mountains of the Moon
  highest point: 10 Margherita
  river: 4 Ruki, Uele **5** Congo, Dengu, Ibina, Kasai, Lindi, Zaire **6** Likati, Lomami, Lukuga, Ubangi **7** Aruwimi, Lualaba, Lulonga
  sea: 8 Atlantic
  physical feature:
    falls: 4 Kivu **6** Tshopo **7** Stanley
    forest: 5 Ituri
    valley: 9 Great Rift
  people: 4 Kuba, Luba, Yaka **5** Bantu, Bashi, Bemba, Kongo, Lulue, Lunda, Mongo, Pygmy **6** Azande, Baluba, Watusi **7** Bakongo, Nilotes, Tshokwe **8** European, Mangbetu, Sudanese
    explorer: 3 Cao **7** Stanley
    leader: 6 Mobutu (Sese Seko) **7** Lumumba, Tshombe **8** Kasavubu
    ruler: 7 Belgium, Leopold
  language: 5 Bantu **6** French **7** Chiluba, Kikongo, Lingala, Swahili **8** Sudanese, Tshiluba
  religion: 5 Islam **7** animism, Kimbang **10** Protestant **13** Roman Catholic
  place:
    dam: 4 Inga **9** Le Marinee **10** Del Commune
    national park: 6 Albert, Upemba **7** Garamba
  feature:
    animal: 5 hyena, okapi **7** giraffe,

gorilla **10** rhinoceros
  fish: 11 electric eel
Zambia
  other name: 16 Northern Rhodesia
  capital/largest city: 6 Lusaka
  others: 4 Kafu **5** Choma, Isoka, Kabwe, Kitwe, Mansa, Mbala, Mongu, Mpika, Mumba, Ndola **6** Mwenda **7** Chipata, Luapula, Mankoya **8** Balovale, Chingola, Luanshya, Mazabuka, Mufulira, Mulobezi **11** Livingstone
  division: 7 Puapula **10** Copperbelt **11** Barotseland
  monetary unit: 5 ngwee **6** kwacha
  lake: 5 Mweru **6** Kariba **9** Bangweulu **10** Tanganyika
  mountain: 8 Muchinga
  highest point: 12 Mafinga Hills
  river: 5 Congo, Kafue **7** Luangwa, Luapula, Zambezi **8** Chambezi **9** Chambeshi
  physical feature:
    cave: 5 Nsalu **14** Chifabwa Stream
    falls: 7 Kalambo **8** Victoria
    gorge: 6 Kariba
    plateau: 7 Zambian
    swamp: 7 Lukanga **9** Bangweulu **12** Mweru Wantipa
    valley: 8 Chambezi **9** Great Rift
  people: 4 Lozi **5** Bantu, Bemba, Ngoni, Tonga
    developer: 6 Rhodes
    explorer: 11 Livingstone
    hero: 11 Chitimukulu
    leader: 6 Kaunda
  language: 4 Lozi **5** Bemba, Lunda, Tonga **6** Luvale, Nyanja **7** English **9** Afrikaans
  religion: 5 Hindu, Islam **7** animism **10** Protestant **13** Roman Catholic
  place:
    botanical garden: 10 Munda Wanga
    dam: 5 Kafue **6** Kariba
    game reserve: 6 Valley
    library: 20 Hammerskjold Memorial
    museum: 11 Livingstone
    national park: 5 Kafue, Sumbu **12** South Luangwa
  feature:
    canoe: 10 nalikwanda
    king: 7 litunga
    king's aide: 5 sungu, twite **8** inabanza
    taxi: 6 zamcab
zany 3 nut **4** wild **5** balmy, batty, booby, buffo, clown, comic, crazy, cutup, daffy, dizzy, goofy, inane, nutty, silly, wacky **6** jester, nitwit, screwy, weirdo **7** buffoon, half-wit, lunatic **8** bonehead, clownish, imbecile, lunkhead, numskull **9** blockhead, eccentric, harlequin, ludicrous, pantaloon, simpleton, slapstick **10** nincompoop, noodlehead, outlandish **11** nonsensical person
French: 7 farceur

Zapotec
  language family: 5 Otomi 6 mixtec
  location: 6 Mexico, Oaxaca
zapped 5 drunk 6 killed, soused,
  wasted, zonked 7 smashed 9 destroyed, plastered 10 inebriated 11
  annihilated, intoxicated
zeal 4 fire, zest 5 ardor, gusto, verve,
  vigor 6 fervor, relish 7 passion 8 devotion, industry 9 animation, eagerness, intensity, vehemence 10 enthusiasm, fanaticism, fierceness,
  intentness 11 earnestness
zealot 3 fan, nut 4 buff 5 bigot, crank
  6 pusher 7 devotee, fanatic, hustler 8
  believer, champion, crackpot, go- getter, livewire, partisan 9 extremist 10
  enthusiast
zealous 5 eager, rabid 6 ardent, fervid,
  fierce, gung ho, raging, raving 7 devoted, earnest, fanatic, fervent, intense 8 animated, vehement, vigorous
  10 passionate 11 impassioned, industrious 12 enthusiastic
Zebedee
  wife: 6 Salome
  son: 4 John 5 James
Zeboim
  destroyed with: 5 Admah, Sodom 8
  Gomorrah
Zebulun
  father: 5 Jacob
  mother: 4 Leah
  brother: 3 Dan, Gad 4 Levi 5 Asher,
  Judah 6 Joseph, Reuben, Simeon 8
  Benjamin, Issachar, Naphtali
  sister: 5 Dinah
  descendant of: 10 Zebulunite
Zechariah
  father: 5 Bebai, Hosah 6 Jehiel,
  Pashur 7 Isshiah 8 Jehoiada, Jonathan 9 Berechiah 11 Jeberechiah,
  Meshelemiah
  grandfather: 4 Iddo
  mother: 6 Merari
  son: 8 Jahaziel
  daughter: 6 Abijah
Zeffirelli, Franco
  director of: 14 Romeo and Juliet 19
  The Taming of the Shrew 20 Brother
  Sun Sister Moon
Zeitgeist 18 the spirit of the time
Zelos
  origin: 5 Greek
  personifies: 4 zeal 9 emulation
  father: 11 Titan Palles
  mother: 4 Styx
  brother: 3 Bia 6 Cratus
  sister: 4 Nike
Zemeckis, Robert
  director of: 15 Back to the Future 17
  Romancing the Stone
zenith 4 acme, apex, best, peak 6 apogee, climax, summit, vertex 7 maximum 8 pinnacle 11 culmination
Zenobia (Zeena)

character in: 10 Ethan Frome
  author: 7 Wharton
zephyr 8 west wind 9 puff of air 10
  gentle wind 11 breath of air, light
  breeze
Zephyrus
  personifies: 8 west wind
  father: 8 Astraeus
  mother: 3 Eos
  loved: 10 Hyacinthus
  son: 6 Balius 7 Xanthus
Zeppelin, Ferdinand Graf von
  nationality: 6 German
  invented: 9 dirigible 21 rigid dirigible
  airship
  famous ship: 10 Hindenberg
zero 2 no 3 nil, zip 5 aught, nadir,
  zilch 6 cipher, naught 7 nothing 8
  goose egg 11 nonexistent, nothingness
zero hour 5 onset, start 7 liftoff 9 beginning 12 commencement
zest 3 joy, zip 4 salt, tang, zeal, zing 5
  gusto, savor, spice, taste, verve 6 flavor, relish, thrill 7 delight, passion 8
  appetite, piquancy, pleasure 9 eagerness, flavoring, seasoning 10 enthusiasm, excitement 12 exhilaration, satisfaction
zestful 6 active, lively 7 dynamic, vibrant 8 animated, spirited, vigorous 9
  vivacious 12 invigorating
zesty 5 spicy, tangy 7 piquant
Zeus
  also: 7 Cenaean 9 Atabyriam, Ithoma-
  tas 10 Anchesmius 11 Panomphaeus
  12 Cithaeronian
  birthplace: 5 Crete
  brother: 5 Hades 8 Poseidon
  corresponds to: 4 Amen, Amon, Jove
  5 Ammon 6 Amen Ra, Amon Ra 7
  Jupiter
  daughter: 4 Hebe 6 Athene 10
  Eileithyia, Persephone
  epithet: 5 Areus, Arius, Sotor 6
  Aqueus, Nemean, Philus 7 Alastor,
  Apemius, Ctesius, Lycaeus, Polieus,
  Stenius 8 Agoraeus, Aphesius, Apomyius, Catharius, Chthonius, Coccygius, Hecaleius, Lecheates, Mechaneus 10 Cataebates, Coryphaeus,
  Homagyrius, Laphystius, Meilichius
  11 Eleutherius 12 Panhellenius
  father: 6 Cronus
  form: 5 deity
  god of: 7 heavens
  lover: 4 Leto 7 Demeter
  mother: 4 Rhea
  position: 7 supreme
  sister: 4 Hera 6 Hestia 7 Demeter
  son: 4 Ares 6 Apollo, Hermes
  wife: 4 Hera 5 Metis
zigzag 4 awry, tack 6 angles, forked,
  jagged 7 chevron, crankle, crooked,
  notched, sinuous, stagger 8 crotched,
  serrated, sideling, traverse 9 bifurcate
  10 circuitous, deflection
Zilpah

slave of: 4 Leah
  concubine of: 5 Jacob
  son: 3 Gad 5 Asher
Zimbabwe
  other name: 8 Rhodesia 16 Southern
  Rhodesia
  capital/largest city: 6 Harare 9 Salisbury
  others: 5 Gwelo, Gweru 6 Kariba,
  KweKwe, Mutare, QueQue, Umtali 7
  Gatooma, Rusambo, Selukwe, Sha-
  bani 8 Bulawayo, Zimbabwe 10 Beit-
  bridge
  monetary unit: 4 cent 6 dollar
  lake: 4 Kyle 6 Kariba
  mountain: 5 Vumba 6 Manica 7 Inyanga 11 Chimanimani, Matopo Hills
  highest point: 9 Inyangani
  river: 4 Sabi, Save 5 Lundi 6 Shashi
  7 Limpopo, Umniati, Zambezi
  physical feature:
    falls: 8 Victoria
    grassland: 4 veld
    plateau: 8 Highveld 11 Mashona-
    land
  people: 3 Ila 4 Sena 5 Asian, Bantu,
  Bemba, Sotho, Tongo, White 6 Indian 7 Barotse, Chinese, English,
  Mashoma, Mashona, Ndebele 8 Coloured, Japanese, Matabele 9 Afrikaner 10 Balokwakwa
    developer: 6 Rhodes
    explorer: 11 Livingstone
    king: 9 Lobengula, Mzilikaze
    leader: 5 Nkomo 6 Mugabe 7
    Sithole 8 Muzorewa 9 Ian D Smith
  language: 3 Ila 5 Bantu, Shona 7
  English, Ndebele
  religion: 7 animism 8 Anglican 12
  Christianity, Presbyterian 13 Dutch
  Reformed, Roman Catholic
  place:
    dam: 6 Kariba
    national park: 6 Hwange, Wankie
    7 Matopos 9 Inyan gani
    13 Victoria Falls
    ruins: 5 Khami 6 Temple 8 Zim-
    babwe 9 Acropolis 13 Valley of
    Ruins
  feature:
    cattle pen: 5 kraal
    game: 5 tsoro 7 mandani
    hut: 4 kaia
    kingdom: 5 Rozwi 10 Monomotapa
    tree: 4 teak 6 baobab, mopani
Zimbalist, Efrem, Jr
  born: 9 New York NY
  father: 14 Efrem Zimbalist
  mother: 9 Alma Gluck
  daughter: 18 Stephanie Zimbalist
  roles: 3 FBI 13 Wait Until Dark 15 By
  Love Possessed 16 The Chapman Report 23 Seventy-seven Sunset Strip
zinc
  chemical symbol: 2 Zn
zing 3 pep, vim, zap, zip 4 dash, snap,
  tang, whiz, zest 5 gusto, speed, vigor,
  whine 6 energy, spirit 7 liven up

8 satirize, vitality **9** animation, criticize **10** enthusiasm, liveliness

zingara, zingaro 5 gypsy

Zinnemann, Fred
 director of: 5 Julia **8** High Noon, Oklahoma **9** The Search **12** The Nun's Story **13** The Sundowners **17** A Man for All Seasons (Oscar) **18** From Here to Eternity (Oscar)

Zion 6 utopia **9** city of God **11** City of David **13** ancient Israel
 hill in: 9 Jerusalem
 built on the hill: 6 Temple

zip 3 fly, nil, pep, run, vim **4** buzz, dart, dash, hiss, life, nada, rush, zero, zest **5** aught, close, drive, force, gusto, hurry, power, punch, speed, verve, vigor, whine, zilch **6** cipher, energy, impact, naught, spirit, streak **7** nothing, whistle **8** goose egg, strength, vitality, vivacity **9** animation, intensity **10** enthusiasm, exuberance, liveliness **13** effervescence

zipper
 invented by: 6 Judson

Zipporah
 father: 5 Reuel **6** Jethro
 husband: 5 Moses
 son: 7 Eliezer, Gershom

zircon
 source: 5 Burma **6** Ceylon **8** Cambodia, Sri Lanka **9** Kampuchea

zirconium
 chemical symbol: 2 Zr

zloty
 currency of: 6 Poland

zodiac 4 belt, zone **5** stars **7** circuit
 fire sign: 3 Leo **5** Aries **11** Sagittarius
 earth sign: 5 Virgo **6** Taurus **9** Capricorn
 air sign: 5 Libra **6** Gemini **8** Aquarius
 water: 6 Cancer, Pisces **7** Scorpio
 division: 4 sign **5** decan **6** trigon
 number of houses: 6 twelve
 falling between two signs: 4 cusp

Zola, Emile
 author of: 4 Nana **7** The Soil **8** Germinal **10** L'Assommoir **11** The Downfall, The Dram Shop **13** Therese Raquin **14** The Human Animal **20** The Experimental Novel

zone 4 area, belt, ward **5** tract **6** region, sector **7** quarter, section, terrain **8** district, locality, location, precinct **9** territory

zonked 5 drunk **6** soused, wasted, zapped **7** smashed **9** plastered **10** inebriated **11** intoxicated

zoo 8 vivarium **9** menagerie

zoom 3 fly, zip **4** buzz, race, rise, soar **5** climb, flash, shoot, speed **6** ascend, rocket, streak **7** advance, take off **9** skyrocket

zoophobia
 fear of: 7 animals

Zophar
 friend: 3 Job **5** Elihu **6** Bildad **7** Eliphaz

Zorba the Greek
 director: 17 Michael Cacoyannis
 based on the story by: 11 Kazantzakis
 cast: 9 Alan Bates **11** Irene Pappas, Lila Kedrova **12** Anthony Quinn
 score: 16 Mikis Theodorakis
 Oscar for: 17 supporting actress (Kedrova)

zori 14 Japanese sandal

zucchini 5 gourd **6** squash **12** summer squash

Zuckerman Unbound
 author: 10 Philip Roth

Zurich
 festival: 12 Sechselanten
 landmark: 8 Rietberg **9** Kunsthaus **15** CG Jung Institute **17** Centre Le Corbusier, Fraumunster Kirche **21** Grossmunster Cathedral
 religious figure: 7 Zwingli **9** Bullinger
 river: 6 Limmat
 Roman name: 7 Turicum

Zweig, Arnold
 author of: 7 Claudia **24** The Case of Sergeant Grischa